4th Edition

Importers
Manual
USA

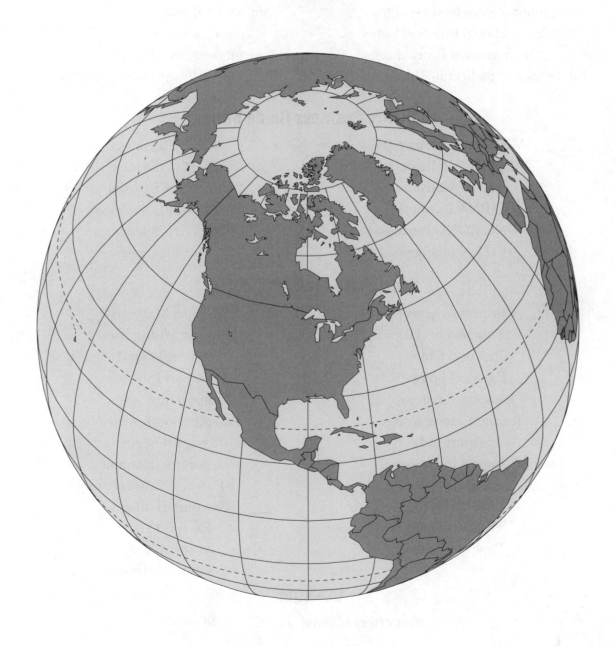

World Trade Press
Publications

General References

Importers Manual USA

Dictionary of International Trade

Global Connect!

Global Road Warrior

A Basic Guide to Exporting

Services: The Export of the 21st Century

The Short Course in International Trade Series

International Contracts

International Business Culture

International Business Ethics

International Business Plans

International Economics

International Intellectual Property Rights

International Joint Ventures

International Marketing

International Marketing Blunders

International Negotiating

International Payments

International Trade Documentation

Country Business Guide Series

ARGENTINA Business

AUSTRALIA Business

CANADA Business

CHINA Business

HONG KONG Business

JAPAN Business

KOREA Business

MEXICO Business

PHILIPPINES Business

SINGAPORE Business

TAIWAN Business

USA Business

Passport to the World Series

Passport Argentina

Passport Brazil

Passport China

Passport France

Passport Germany

Passport Hong Kong

Passport India

Passport Indonesia

Passport Israel

Passport Italy

Passport Japan

Passport Korea

Passport Malaysia

Passport Philippines

Passport Poland

Passport Russia

Passport Singapore

Passport South Africa

Passport Spain

Passport Switzerland

Passport Taiwan

Passport Thailand

Passport UK

Passport USA

Passport Vietnam

CD-ROM

Importers Manual USA CD-ROM

Global Connect! CD-ROM

Global Road Warrior CD-ROM

4th Edition

Importers
Manual
USA

**The Single Source
Reference Encyclopedia
for Importing
to the United States**

Edward G. Hinkelman

Myron Manley

James L. Nolan, Ph.D.   Karla C. Shippey, J.D.

Wendy Bidwell   Alexandra Woznick

United States Customs Service
George R. Tuttle, Sr., Esq.
Dale O. Torrence, Esq.
Swiss Bank Corporation
Hapag Lloyd Shipping Lines
Insurance Company of North America
American Association of Exporters and Importers
United States Department of Agriculture, APHIS

WORLD TRADE PRESS®
Books, E-Content & Maps for International Trade

IMPORTERS MANUAL USA

4th Edition

PUBLISHER

World Trade Press
1450 Grant Avenue, Suite 204
Novato, CA 94945 USA
Tel: (415) 898-1124; Fax: (415) 898-1080; Toll-Free in USA: (800) 833-8586
Email: sales@worldtradepress.com
www.WorldTradePress.com
www.WorldTradeREF.com
www.GlobalRoadWarrior.com
www.HowToConnect.com

CREDITS

Illustrations and maps: Rachel Zuniga, David Baker, and Robert Wolchock. Cover design: Brad Greene

DISCLAIMER

Material for this publication has been obtained from information supplied by U.S. government agencies, foreign government embassies, consulates and agencies, industry and trade organizations, from personal interview and by telephone and correspondence. We have diligently tried to ensure the accuracy of all of the information in this publication and to present as comprehensive a reference work as space would permit. The fluidity and fast pace of today's business world makes the task of keeping data current and accurate an extremely difficult one. Our purpose is to give you information so that you can become aware of importing issues and can discover resources most useful for your particular business. As you contact the resources within this book, you will no doubt learn of new and exciting business opportunities and of additional trading requirements that have arisen even within the short time since we published this edition. If we find errors, we will strive to correct them in preparing future editions. The publishers take no responsibility for inaccurate or incomplete information that may have been submitted to them in the course of research for this publication. The facts published indicate the result of those inquiries and no warranty as to their accuracy is given.

Cataloging-in-Publication Data

Hinkelman, Edward G., 1947-
      Importers Manual USA : the single source reference encyclopedia
  for importing to the United States / Edward G. Hinkelman. . . . [et al.] -- Fourth ed.
     p. cm.
     Includes bibliographical references and index.
     ISBN 1-885073-93-3

ACKNOWLEDGEMENTS

Reference books are rarely the product of one individual. *Importers Manual USA* is the combined effort of literally hundreds of people in the United States and overseas. I owe a great debt of gratitude to those in the U.S. Customs Service, other U.S. governmental agencies, the U.S. foreign service, the foreign service of our trading partners, banks, law firms, shipping firms, and the insurance industry whose knowledge, expertise and support made this book possible.

First Incarnation

Special thanks to those who contributed to the first incarnation of this book: Carolyn McMahon, Bonnie Beijen, Hugh Grigsby, William Whittaker, and Bob Gandenberger for the germ of the idea for a reference book.

The 1993 Edition

Ed Zaccaro, Insurance Company of North America; C. von der Decken, Hapag Lloyd; Rachelle Bijou, ICC Publishing Corporation; Bonnie Sweeny, Swiss Bank Corporation; Dave Semling at Mill Valley Services; Carol at the Presentation Works; the folks at Desktop Publishing of Larkspur California; Jerry Fletcher for his understanding; Teddy Olwyler for her suggestions; Kelle Olwyler for her encouragement; David Garfinkel for his coaching; Lyn Lawton and Heidi Longo for their early work on the Country Index; Barry Schiller, California State Automobile Association, San Francisco; and Francis G. McFaul, U.S. Department of Commerce, International Trade Administration.

The 1995 Edition

U.S. Customs Service, San Francisco office; Annie Sutton, Public Affairs Specialist, and the veterinarian, agricultural, and legal consultants of U.S. Department of Agriculture's Animal and Plant Health Inspection Service (APHIS); Greg A. Pitkoff, Director of Communications, National Customs Brokers & Forwarders Association of America, Inc., New York, NY; Nick Orsini of the Foreign Trade Division, Bureau of the Census, at the U.S. Department of Commerce, Washington, DC.

Libraries

The San Francisco Public Library; the Marin County Civic Center Library; the Marin County Law Library; the San Rafael Public Library; the Sonoma Country Library, Main Branch; the U.S. Department of Commerce Library in San Francisco; and the Mill Valley Public Library.

The Third and Fourth Editions

Seattle Customs Commodity Specialists: Steve Bailey, Helene Mikes, Roberta Choy, Don Schreiber, Bob Phillips, Connie Chancey, Georgann Falotico, Pat Hughes, Scott Johnson; San Francisco Customs Commodity Specialists: Dick Peltier, Jeff Nii, Carlton Roe, Doug Johnstone, Steve Goldberg, John Merillat; Don Kerlin, U.S. Coast Guard, Chief, Recreational Boating, Product Assurance Branch; Jim Summers, U.S. Food and Drug Administration, Center for Food Safety; Pete Pearson, American Presidents Line; Carmen L. Alston, Chief, U.S. Bureau of Alcohol, Tobacco and Firearms, Firearms and Explosives Imports Branch; Virginia Alford, U.S. Bureau of Alcohol, Tobacco and Firearms; William Marmura, U.S. Department of Energy, Office of Fossil Energy; Rick Foley, Federal Energy Regulatory Commission; Dr. Murphy, Animal and Plant Health Inspection Service; Dr. Garcia, Animal and Plant Health Inspection Service; Barbara Roth, Office of Solid Waste, U.S. Environmental Protection Agency; Henry P. Lau, Chief, Chemical Inventory Section, U.S. Environmental Protection Agency; Sheri Thomas, Federal Trade Commission; Nicole Collins, U.S. Department of Commerce Textile Unit; Naomi Goldberg, U.S. Department of Commerce Textile Unit; Michael Yanchulis, Office of Pesticide Programs, U.S. Environmental Protection Agency; Clive R. Van Orden, U.S. Department of Transportation, National Highway Traffic Safety Administration, Office of Vehicle Compliance; Bob Griffin, formerly of U.S. Department of Agriculture, Animal and Plant Health Inspection Service, Plant Protection and Quarantine (plants); Victor Harabin, U.S. Department of Agriculture, Animal and Plant Health Inspection Service, Plant Protection and Quarantine (plants); Deborah Knott, U.S. Department of Agriculture, Animal and Plant Health Inspection Service, Plant Protection and Quarantine (insects); James (Bud) Pedimarsh, U.S. Department of Agriculture, Animal and Plant Health Inspection Service, Plant Protection and Quarantine (plants); Polly Lehtonen, U.S. Department of Agriculture, Animal and Plant Health Inspection Service, Plant Protection and Quarantine (seed examination facility); Linda Wisniowski, U.S. Food and Drug Administration, Import Operations; Frank Krivda, U.S. Consumer Product Safety Commission, Compliance: bikes, toys; Patrician Fairall, U.S. Consumer Product Safety Commission, Compliance: FFA; Tims Jones, U.S. Consumer Product Safety Commission; John Lee, U.S. Department of Transportation, National Highway Traffic Safety Administration, Domestic Compliance; George Shifflett, U.S. Department of Transportation, National Highway Traffic Safety Administration, Import Compliance; Elizabeth Levy, U.S. Department of Commerce; Nancy Lee, Center for Disease Control; S. Marti-Volkoff, Federal Communications Commission; U.S. Customs; U.S. Department of Agriculture; U.S. Food and Drug Administration; U.S. Consumer Product Safety Commission; U.S. Department of Transportation, National Highway Traffic Safety Administration; U.S. Department of Commerce; Federal Trade Commission; U.S. Environmental Protection Agency; U.S. Fish and Wildlife Service; U.S. Bureau of Alcohol, Tobacco and Firearms; World Wildlife Fund: Allison Rogers and Ginette Hemley.

Edward G. Hinkelman
Novato, California
November 2003

Contents

Tab 3: International Banking

Tab 4: U.S. Customs Entry and Clearance

Tab 5: Entry Procedures and Documentation

Tab 6
Packing, Shipping, Insurance

CONTAINER PACKING

Tab 7: Commodity Index

Introduction

World Trade and The Global Economy

International trade is not new to the world, but the current scope of it is. International trade and commerce has historically led to great power and wealth for both the individuals and nations that see beyond their local shores to the opportunities that lie beyond the horizon.

Ancient Phoenician, and later Venetian, traders boldly sailed small ships to ports of call throughout the Mediterranean, selling their products and buying what were to them exotic goods of foreign cultures. In the process, they established trade routes that are still in use today.

In the late 15th century and early 16th century, European demand for foreign products, especially spices, led to the great voyages of discovery of Christopher Columbus, Vasco da Gama, and Ferdinand Magellan.

Today, businessmen and women fly in jumbo jets to every corner of the world, selling their own products, buying raw materials to supply their factories, and buying finished goods for consumers who are as enamored of the exotic products of foreign cultures as were the Venetians of the 15th century.

In the last three decades, the world has truly become a global marketplace. Worldwide imports and exports have soared as most governments have come to realize that liberal trade policies are good for domestic consumers, workers, and businesses alike.

In those last two decades, combined U.S. imports and exports have risen from $84 billion in 1970 to $471 billion in 1980, to $889 billion in 1990, and to $2,507 billion in 2000! While imports have outpaced exports, U.S. exports have been surging in the past five years as world markets have opened, U.S. export restrictions have lessened, and U.S. exporters have become more aggressive.

Importing to the United States

Importing to the U.S. is the process of bringing goods from a foreign economy into the domestic U.S. economy. Rapid changes in the fast-paced global economy, as well as new rules—such as those found in the General Agreement on Tariffs and Trade (GATT), the North American Free Trade Agreement (NAFTA), and the 1993 Customs Modification Act (Mod Act), all of which are covered in the second edition of *Importers Manual USA*—can make this first step a daunting one for old hands and newcomers alike. Nevertheless, importing concerns are limited to the part of the operation aimed at clearing goods through U.S. Customs. Once goods are cleared, the importing process ends and the considerations of running a particular type of business begin.

Importing to the U.S. ranges from the small-time operator carrying a briefcase of costume jewelry or suitcase of leather jackets back from an overseas vacation trip to the large-scale corporate importers, with transactions measured in hundreds of millions of dollars.

Importing provides many benefits to the U.S. economy and U.S. consumers. Imported products offer the consumer a wider selection of products; competition between foreign producers and U.S. producers helps keep domestic prices more competitive; and, as we have seen in the automobile industry, competition has led to the design and production of better quality domestic products.

Furthermore, opening our domestic markets to friendly countries has generally led to the vitalization of their economies, resulting in greater demand for U.S. products. U.S. exports that have benefited significantly include pharmaceuticals; machine tools; aerospace, high-technology, and biotechnology products; entertainment items—films, video, and music; and a wide range of consumer products.

Why Import?

The first question an individual or business considering importing should ask is simply "Why import?" The process of importing is often complex and introduces a whole range of variables that do not exist when conducting business domestically.

When establishing your personal and corporate purposes, you will need to determine whether you are importing to satisfy a market demand for a product or, if you have a source for an item, to establish the market for the product in the U.S. On the other hand, you may want to travel the world specifically to find a product that inspires you to establish a new business in the U.S.

What are your strengths? Do you have experience as a buyer or purchasing agent? Do you have experience as a manufacturer of an item? Do you have experience in sales or marketing? Do you have general business expertise? The prospective importer needs to answer these questions to assess capabilities and establish his or her best position in the market chain running from the source to the ultimate consumer.

Before deciding to import, you should be able to identify distinct advantages to importing a foreign product over purchasing a domestic one. If you don't make this determination ahead of time, you could find yourself returning home from an expensive buying trip only to find that the goods you so laboriously sought out, purchased, and imported can be obtained in the U.S. from a wholesaler for less money than you paid for them overseas. In addition, not only must you, as an importer, handle the demands of your domestic business, you must also be able to do business in other countries. In effect, you will be dealing with the bureaucracies of two and possibly more countries. It is therefore of utmost importance to have good reasons to import a product.

For more information and ideas, refer to "18 Reasons to Go into Importing" on page 16 and "18 Reasons Not to Go into Importing" on page 16.

Elements of the Import Process

While the level at which you import will determine the depth of understanding required for success in each of the subject areas, the general requirements for importing a product are the same whether you are a small- or large-scale importer. The following is an overview of the main steps involved in the import process.

Legal Considerations of International Trade

The greatest source of problems for U.S. businesspeople doing business internationally is the erroneous assumption that they can operate abroad according to the same rules that apply in the U.S. When you do business internationally, you are subject not only to U.S. law, but to the laws of any country involved in your business transaction. This may be the case even if you do not physically visit the other country.

The more complex your transactions, the more you travel abroad, the more you deal in product liability or in politically sensitive products, the more you obtain and extend credit, the more you trust others to follow through on their end of the bargain, the greater will be your chances of experiencing legal difficulties while conducting business internationally.

For a complete discussion of these issues refer to the "International Law" section, beginning on page 6.

Finding Suppliers

If you are planning to establish an ongoing importing business, it is advisable that you choose your foreign suppliers with even greater care than you would a domestic supplier. Your need to rely on individuals who are in a country 6,000 miles away, and who may be speaking another language, will be greater than when dealing with a domestic supplier who is only 500 miles away, who speaks your language, and who can easily be contacted by telephone.

There are numerous InfoLists beginning that detail the process of securing suppliers. For example: "Finding Sources" on page 27, "26 Sources of Information" on page 28, "Buying from the Source" on page 27, "Letters and E-mails of Request" on page 32, and "10 Tips About Suppliers" on page 33.

Also refer to the Commodity Index, beginning on page 423 for lists of the principal exporting countries for specific commodities.

Negotiating

Once you have secured an appropriate supplier, you will need to establish the terms and conditions of the sale. This is likely to involve communicating and negotiating with individuals of different nationalities, races, and cultural backgrounds. Be aware that you will be on their turf and that your established methods of communicating and dealing may not work at all. You may have to research and make special preparations to ensure successful negotiations.

Refer to the "10 Tips for Negotiating" on page 35 and "10 Tips for Negotiating in a Long-Term Relationship" on page 36.

Contracts for Purchase

You will need to know when a purchase contract is necessary and how it must be structured. When dealing with both U.S. and foreign laws, you will find it imperative to understand how they will affect you.

You and your supplier may agree to use the legal structure of either the U.S. or the supplier's country to govern your contract, or you may chose to settle conflicts through arbitration or mediation. In any case, all parties to the transaction should have well-defined responsibilities, and all terms of the purchase should be stated in the contract.

Refer to "Drafting the International Sales Contract" on page 110, and "Solving Contract Disputes" on page 118.

International Banking Letters of Credit

Your supplier will prefer that you prepay for your merchandise, while you will strive to establish 30-, 60-, 90-, or even 180-day, credit terms. The laws of some countries, however, require payment for goods before or as they are exported.

The political stability of the exporting country, the quality of its trade relationship with the U.S., and your relationship with your supplier will determine your ability to secure better payment terms for your purchases.

In many international transactions, the buyer and seller will agree to use a documentary letter of credit as the method of payment. You will need to know the different types of documentary credits and how they work.

You will also need to understand at least a minimum about foreign exchange dealings. Otherwise you risk getting caught in currency fluctuations, which have the potential for destroying your profit margin.

Refer to "International Banking" on page 135, "Documentary Credits (Letters of Credit) on page 148, and "An Introduction to Foreign Exchange" on page 144.

Packing and Labeling

You should specify packing and labeling requirements for your goods in your purchase contract. First, specify how the merchandise is to be labeled to satisfy U.S. Customs and other government agency requirements. Second, specify how the merchandise is to be packed to withstand ocean or air shipment to the U.S. Third, consider specifying packaging in the country of origin, which will make the item ready for immediate retail stocking and sale in the U.S.

Refer to "Country of Origin Marking" on page 251, "Packing of Goods and Commingling" on page 208, and the commodity specific "Marking and Labeling Requirements" subhead for your commodity in the Commodity Index section.

International Freight Transportation

The terms of your sale will determine whether you or your supplier is responsible for making shipping arrangements. Regardless of who is responsible, you will want to select an appropriate mode of transport as well as the best carrier, routing, container, and scheduling for your shipment. Consolidation, containerization, and intermodal transport may or may not save money. Cost-benefit analyses will help to establish the most desirable method.

Refer to Tab 5—"Packing, Shipping, Insurance" on page 355. Also, for explanation of terms of sale that include freight, insurance, etc., refer to "Drafting the International Sales Contract" on page 110.

Insurance

Your merchandise will have to be insured by you or the shipper. It is important to insure the full value of the shipment, which can include packing, shipping, cartage, storage, duties, and taxes. You can do this on an individual-policy basis through the freight forwarder or carrier, or on a term-policy basis with a broker or an insurance company, preferably in the U.S. Be certain that you are insured whenever you have an "insurable interest."

Refer to "Marine Insurance" on page 395.

Customs Entry and Clearance

Your first responsibility as an importer in dealing with U.S. Customs will be to know—*before* your purchase abroad—how your product is regulated by U.S. Customs and other U.S. government agencies. We cannot overestimate the advantages of understanding and knowing these requirements before negotiating contracts overseas.

Most importers employ the services of a customs broker to handle the Customs entry and clearance process. Customs brokers are licensed professionals who handle the clearance of goods through Customs on a day-to-day basis and are therefore experienced with documentation requirements.

Your knowledge, in concert with the efforts of a competent customs broker, will help to keep this very important part of your import operation running smoothly.

Your second responsibility will be to secure and present proper documentation, to your customs broker or to U.S. Customs. Each document required by U.S. Customs, except for those produced domestically in the U.S., should be specifically required of your foreign supplier in a contract. Your receipt of specified documentation should be established as a prerequisite for payment.

For information about entering goods through U.S. Customs, refer to Tab 4—U.S. Customs Entry and Clearance. For information about customs brokers, refer to "Selecting and Working with a Customs Broker" on page 73 and "Customs Brokers, Freight Forwarders, and Professional Associations" on page 72.

For specific regulatory information for your product, refer to Tab 6—Commodity Index.

Marketing

Once your goods have arrived in the U.S., it will be your job to get them to market. If you have an established wholesale or retail distribution system, this may be a predetermined matter. If you are seeking to establish a market, you will have many choices to make with regard to your merchandising. For most businesses, this step is where "the rubber meets the road" because no business becomes viable until it produces cash flow.

Basis of Success

Whether your import business is a success will depend on the range of your knowledge of each part of the process and your ability to absorb that knowledge and put it into practice.

The four major areas of knowledge and expertise that will be factors in your success are:

1. Knowledge of your product;
2. Knowledge of the import process itself;
3. Expertise in marketing your goods domestically; and
4. Expertise in the management of your business:

Importers Manual USA is primarily concerned with item #2, knowledge of the import process.

Importers Manual USA

Importers Manual USA is a desktop reference encyclopedia and source book for the process of importing into the United States. This reference is unique in that it addresses in one volume the specific how-to information you need to know:

- International legal issues
- International banking and letters of credit
- U.S. Customs entry and clearance
- Packing
- Shipping
- Insurance

In addition, the Commodity Index contains detailed articles on importing all commodity group, organized according to the Harmonized Tariff Schedule of the United States (HTSUS). The HTSUSA is the document Customs uses to classify and calculate duties on entries.

Importers Manual USA has been designed as an easy-to-use reference, the main purpose of which is to educate and, even more importantly, to save both the professional and small-time importer immense amounts of time, energy, money, and frustration.

Notes:

InfoLists
Contents

#1: 18 Reasons to Go into Importing 16
#2: 18 Reasons Not to Go into Importing 16
#3: Key Elements of a Successful Import Operation 17
#4: 13 Ways Import Businesses Fail 17
#5: 30 Easy-to-Import Products 18
#6: 17 Difficult-to-Import Products 19
#7: Top 50 Imports to the U.S. 20
#8: Top 50 Suppliers of U.S. Imports 21
#9: Costs Associated with Importing a Product 22
#10: Starting an Import Business with Little Capital 22
#11: Product Requirements 23
#12: Know Your Product 23
#13: Know Your Market 24
#14: Know Your Competition 26
#15: Buying from the Source 27
#16: Finding Sources 27
#17: 26 Sources of Information 28
#18: How to Use Sources 28
#19: Letters and E-mails of Request 32
#20: Sample Letter of Request for Sources 32
#21: Sample Letter of Request to Potential Suppliers 33
#22: 10 Tips About Suppliers 33
#23: Supplier Checklist 35
#24: 10 Tips for Negotiating 35
#25: 10 Tips for Negotiating in a Long-Term Relationship 36
#26: Business Meeting Pointers 36
#27: Tips for Attending Trade Fairs 37
#28: Overseas Buying Trips 39
#29: U.S. Passports 39
#30: Visas 43
#31: State Department Travel Information 43
#32: Health Regulations for International Travel 44
#33: U.S. Currency Declaration Regulations 44
#34: The Female Traveler 45
#35: Pre-Trip Product Planning 46
#36: Conducting Country Research 47
#37: Travel Phone Numbers and Web sites 49
#38: What Time Is It in . . .? 50
#39: Personal Travel 52
#40: Accommodations 54
#41: 13 Ways to Cut Travel Costs 55
#42: Managing Your Absence 55
#43: Packing for Personal Travel 55
#44: Documentation for Medications 56
#45: U.S. Customs Pre-Registration 56
#46: Handling Money Overseas 56
#47: As You Travel 57
#48: 22 Health Suggestions 57
#49: 13 Tips for Travel Safety 58
#50: What to Do in Case of 58
#51: Help from U.S. Consuls Abroad 59
#52: Coming Home 61
#53: U.S. Customs Hints 61
#54: Suggestions for Working with U.S. Customs 64

#55: U.S. Import Requirements 64
#56: 10 Suggestions for Faster Customs Clearance 65
#57: Key Changes From the Mod Act 65
#58: Reasonable Care Checklists 71
#59: Customs Brokers, Freight Forwarders, and
         Professional Associations 72
#60: Selecting and Working with a Customs Broker 73
#61: Role of the Customs Attorney 74
#62: The American Association of Exporters and Importers 75
#63: 13 Ways to Sell Imports 76
#64: Import Goods Duty-Free! 77
#65: Update on the WTO and GATT 78
#66: Update on NAFTA 79
#67: 23 Advantages and Uses of Foreign Trade Zones .. 80
#68: U.S. Customs and Border Protection Offices 81
#69: U.S. Government Agencies 84
#70: U.S. Government Bookstores 87
#71: Top Web sites for the Importer 87
#72: Customs and Border Protection Information Sources . 88
#73: Top Publications for the U.S. Importer 89

InfoList #1

18 Reasons to Go into Importing

1. To obtain raw materials not available in the U.S.
2. To obtain products not manufactured in the U.S.
3. To obtain products and commodities directly from the source of supply, when that source is in a foreign country.
4. To obtain products and commodities at lower cost than in the U.S.
5. To add foreign products to your product line in an established retail, wholesale, mail-order, or other business in the U.S.
6. To take advantage of specific connections in a foreign country.
7. To exercise greater control over the supply of foreign-made products you have been purchasing in the U.S.
8. To arrange for contract manufacture of products overseas at a lower total cost.
9. To arrange for overseas contract manufacture of products requiring specialized labor not available in the U.S.
10. To take advantage of foreign government subsidies provided to those setting up manufacturing facilities designed to produce goods for export.
11. To take advantage of special financing deals provided by the exporting country or banks in the exporting country.
12. To earn a living while travelling and seeing the world.
13. You are an experienced designer of products you seek to have manufactured to your specifications at a specialized facility, or you simply wish to take advantage of lower materials or labor costs.
14. You are an experienced manufacturer who seeks to have products produced to your specifications at a specialized facility, or you simply wish to take advantage of lower materials or labor costs.
15. You have sales experience with imported products and seek to find your own overseas suppliers and start your own business.
16. You have a desire to operate internationally and are sophisticated enough to handle the complexities inherent in international trade and the import process.
17. You have knowledge of the price structure for the goods you seek to import and are confident that there is sufficient margin for the venture to be profitable.
18. You are an experienced businessperson who simply wants to expand your operations globally.

InfoList #2

18 Reasons Not to Go into Importing

1. You are not precise or detail-oriented enough to be able to handle the complexities of an import operation.
2. You lack business experience and/or have no business sense for buying and selling products.
3. You have no established or researched potential market for the goods you plan to import.
4. You have found no reliable source of supply even after conducting extensive research in all the likely countries of origin.
5. You are not emotionally prepared for the hassle of dealing overseas, with U.S. Customs, etc.
6. You are wildly undercapitalized for the venture you have in mind.
7. You are unfamiliar with the merchandise you are thinking of importing.
8. You are unfamiliar with the market for the goods you are interested in importing.
9. You are unfamiliar with the pricing structure for the goods you are interested in importing.
10. The margin differential between buying the goods in the U.S. versus the total landed cost of the goods from the country of origin does not justify establishing an import operation.
11. There may be better opportunities, with greater certainty, in the U.S.
12. Your views of the world and its people are narrow and you would find it difficult to by flexible and to operate outside your present frame of reference.
13. You are incapable of dealing with the differences of language and custom between yourself and foreign suppliers.
14. Your likely overseas source of supply is so undependable that you risk losing business to domestic competitors with more dependable domestic suppliers.
15. Shipping goods to the U.S. may take too long. You perhaps need a supplier closer to home.
16. You are unable to obtain the quality of product that your market or manufacturing process requires.
17. It may be impossible to personally manage production or to inspect the quality of products adequately from afar, or too expensive to hire someone else to do it for you.
18. Civil unrest and/or political instability in the exporting country make long-term business prospects uncertain.

InfoList #3

Key Elements of a Successful Import Operation

1. **General business knowledge and experience**
   The experience and/or ability to operate a business effectively.

2. **Knowledge of the import process**
   Experience with, or knowledge of the entire import process from finding suppliers to U.S. Customs entry and clearance.

3. **Knowledge of product**
   Thorough knowledge of the products you plan to import, based on experience or knowledge gained form being a broker, designer, manufacturer, retailer, wholesaler, or other experience related to the product.

4. **Knowledge of costs**
   Knowledge of all costs of obtaining and bringing the product to market.

5. **Access to low cost supply**
   Ability to obtain products or commodities at the source for the best (lowest) possible price.

6. **Relationship with supplier(s)**
   Ability to establish and maintain a good working relationship with your supplier.

7. **Ability to establish a market**
   Ability to successfully find or develop a market for the goods you import.

8. **Knowledge of price structure**
   Knowledge of the pricing structure for the imported goods which enables you to know how much to pay and how much to charge.

9. **Knowledge of market**
   Specialized knowledge of the wholesale, retail, mail-order, or other market for the product, based on actual experience or special knowledge.

10. **Ability to sell to a specific market efficiently**
    Past experience or special knowledge that enables you to sell your product or commodity for the best (highest) possible price once you have imported it.

11. **Working capital**
    An appropriate amount of working capital for the size and type of import operation you envision.

12. **Working relationship with "professional partners"**
    Your ability to establish and maintain good working relationships with your professional partners:
    - Customs broker
    - Freight forwarder
    - Banker
    - Attorney
    - Customs lawyer
    - Accountant

InfoList #4

13 Ways Import Businesses Fail

1. Individual does not have the required business knowledge or expertise to make a success of what is, first and foremost, a business.

2. Individual or company refuses to take the process of importing seriously. Thinks that importing from Africa or Asia is the same as ordering goods from the state next door. Never commits to acquiring the knowledge and expertise required to succeed in the new, specialized venture.

3. Importer is not familiar enough with the product to be able to discern differences in quality, specifications, or price that are meaningful to the intended market. Imports goods the domestic consumer market will simply not accept.

4. Failure to factor in all the costs of importing and bringing the product to market.

5. Inability to spot or guard against foreign exchange fluctuations which wipe out potential profit.

6. Inability to assess political changes occurring in the country of origin which might affect the relationship with a foreign supplier.

7. Inability to maintain a good working relationship with supplier.

8. Lack of understanding of the domestic market. Inability to sell goods cost-effectively in the U.S.

9. Inadequate working capital for the size and scope of the import operation.

10. Inability to establish and maintain good working relationships with the importer's "professional partners:"
    - Customs broker
    - Freight forwarder
    - Banker
    - Attorney
    - Customs lawyer
    - Accountant

11. Failure to meet strict U.S. Customs regulations for:
    - Marking and labeling
    - Quotas
    - Other requirements

12. Failure of goods to meet other U.S. governmental regulatory agency requirements for:
    - Product safety
    - Quality standards
    - Other standards

13. Goods arrive too late for seasonal sale.

InfoList #5

30 Easy-to-Import Products

The following products are relatively simple to import in that they are not subject to significant restrictions, prohibitions, permits, licenses, or documentation other than basic Customs requirements. Refer to the Commodity Index listing for each item for specific information.

1. **Appliances, Household**. Other than those producing radiation. Refer to Commodity Index Chapter 84: Large Mechanical Appliances and Machines, beginning on page 848; and Chapter 85: Electronics and Components, beginning on page 857.

2. **Art**. Specifically original works of art. Refer to Commodity Index Chapter 97: Works of Art, Collector's Pieces, and Antiques, beginning on page 915.

3. **Brushes**. Refer to Commodity Index Chapter 96: Miscellaneous Manufactured Articles, beginning on page 911.

4. **Cork**. Refer to Commodity Index Chapter 45: Cork and Articles of Cork, beginning on page 653.

5. **Cutlery**. Refer to Commodity Index Chapter 82: Metal Tools and Implements, beginning on page 842.

6. **Flowers, Artificial**. Refer to Commodity Index Chapter 67: Feathers, Down, Artificial Flowers, and Wigs, beginning on page 783.

7. **Fur, Artificial**. Refer to Commodity Index Chapter 43: Fur and Fur Products, beginning on page 642.

8. **Gems and Gemstones**. Refer to Commodity Index Chapter 71: Gems, Jewelry, and Related Products, beginning on page 803.

9. **Glass and Glass Products**. Refer to Commodity Index Chapter 70: Glass and Glassware, beginning on page 799.

10. **Jewelry**. Refer to Commodity Index Chapter 71: Gems, Jewelry, and Related Products, beginning on page 803.

11. **Leather Goods**. Other than those derived from endangered species. Refer to Commodity Index Chapter 42: Leather Articles, beginning on page 635.

12. **Leather Hides**. Other than those derived from endangered species. Refer to Commodity Index Chapter 41: Raw Hides, Skins, and Leather, beginning on page 629.

13. **Lighting Fixtures**. Refer to Commodity Index Chapter 94: Furnishings, beginning on page 898.

14. **Luggage**. Refer to Commodity Index Chapter 42: Leather Articles, beginning on page 635; and Chapter 46: Baskets and Wickerware, beginning on page 655.

15. **Machine Tools**. Refer to Commodity Index Chapter 84: Large Mechanical Appliances and Machines, beginning on page 848.

16. **Base Metals**. Refer to Commodity Index Chapters 72 through 81 starting on page 808.

17. **Musical Instruments**. Refer to Commodity Index Chapter 92: Musical Instruments, beginning on page 891.

18. **Optics, Optical Goods**. Refer to Commodity Index Chapter 90: Optical, Medical, and Precision Instruments, beginning on page 880.

19. **Paper and Paper Products**. Refer to Commodity Index Chapter 47: Wood Pulp and Paper Waste, beginning on page 660; Chapter 48: Paper and Paperboard, beginning on page 662; and Chapter 49: Printed Materials, beginning on page 665.

20. **Pearls**. Refer to Commodity Index Chapter 71: Gems, Jewelry, and Related Products, beginning on page 803.

21. **Plastics and Plastic Products**. Refer to Commodity Index Chapter 39: Plastics and Articles Thereof, beginning on page 618.

22. **Rubber and Rubber Products**. Refer to Commodity Index Chapter 40: Rubber and Articles Thereof, beginning on page 623.

23. **Saddlery**. Refer to Commodity Index Chapter 42: Leather Articles, beginning on page 635.

24. **Sporting Goods**. Refer to Commodity Index Chapter 95: Toys, Games, and Sports Equipment, beginning on page 903.

25. **Stone and Stone Products**. Refer to Commodity Index Chapter 68: Articles of Stone and Related Products, beginning on page 792.

26. **Tile, Ceramic**. Refer to Commodity Index Chapter 69: Ceramic Products, beginning on page 795.

27. **Tools, Hand**. Refer to Commodity Index Chapter 82: Metal Tools and Implements, beginning on page 842 and Chapter 85: Electronics and Components, beginning on page 857.

28. **Umbrellas**. Refer to Commodity Index Chapter 66: Umbrellas and Related Items, beginning on page 781.

29. **Utensils**. Refer to Commodity Index Chapter 82: Metal Tools and Implements, beginning on page 842.

30. **Wallpaper**. Refer to Commodity Index Chapter 48: Paper and Paperboard, beginning on page 662.

InfoList #6
17 Difficult-to-Import Products

The following products are "difficult" to import because of stringent regulatory requirements by one or more U.S. governmental agency. With a very few exceptions, however, it is possible to import all the products listed below. Refer first to the Commodity Index listing for the product to get an overview of the regulations, then speak with a customs broker who has experience with the product. In some cases all that is required is an additional form which your broker presents with your Customs entry.

1. **Drugs**. Highly regulated by U.S. Food and Drug Administration (FDA); extensive requirements for drug quality and drug-producing establishments. FDA entry documentation required. Refer to Commodity Index Chapter 30: Pharmaceutical Products, beginning on page 569.

2. **Radioactive Materials**. Highly regulated by the Nuclear Regulatory Commission (NRC). NRC import authorization and licensing required. Refer to Commodity Index Chapter 84: Large Mechanical Appliances and Machines, beginning on page 848.

3. **Arms and Armaments**. Highly regulated by the Bureau of Alcohol, Tobacco, and Firearms (BATF). BATF import licensing and import permits required; stringent restrictions on the types of arms permissible. Refer to Commodity Index Chapter 93: Arms and Ammunition, beginning on page 894.

4. **Alcoholic Beverages**. Highly regulated by the Bureau of Alcohol, Tobacco, and Firearms (BATF). BATF import permit required; extensive labeling requirements, compliance with product standards of fill and identity, other federal, state, and municipal alcohol regulations, federal excise tax payable at entry. Refer to Commodity Index Chapter 22: Beverages, Spirits, and Vinegar, beginning on page 533.

5. **Dairy Products**. Highly regulated by the U.S. Food and Drug Administration (FDA) and the U.S. Department of Agriculture (USDA). Quotas, licensing, permits, quarantine restrictions, and entry and notification procedures apply depending upon the specific product and its point of origination. Refer to Commodity Index Chapter 4: Dairy Products, beginning on page 449.

6. **Poultry, Poultry Products, and Eggs**. Highly regulated by the U.S. Department of Agriculture (USDA). Import restrictions, port inspections, product certification, plant certification, and import permits apply. Refer to Commodity Index Chapter 2: Meat, beginning on page 437; and Chapter 4: Dairy Products, beginning on page 449.

7. **Meat and Meat Products**. Highly regulated by the U.S. Department of Agriculture (USDA). Import restrictions, port inspections, product certification, plant certification, and import permits apply. Refer to Commodity Index Chapter 2: Meat, beginning on page 437.

8. **Toys**. Highly regulated by the U.S. Consumer Product Safety Commission (CPSC): stringent safety standards apply, defect reporting requirements, recordkeeping for electrical toys or articles, extensive marking and labeling requirements. Refer to Commodity Index Chapter 95: Toys, Games, and Sports Equipment, beginning on page 903.

9. **Live Animals**. Highly regulated by the U.S. Fish and Wildlife Service (FWS), U.S. Public Health Service Centers for Disease Control (CDC), U.S. Department of Agriculture (USDA), and U.S. Food and Drug Administration (FDA), depending upon species. Restricted port of entry, quarantine, prior notification, license, import/export documentation, recordkeeping, etc. apply depending upon species. Refer to Commodity Index Chapter 1: Live Animals, beginning on page 429.

10. **Textiles and Textile Products**. Subject to complex quota restrictions, U.S. Customs country-of-origin declarations, labeling requirements, and flammability standards. Refer to Commodity Index Chapters 50 through 63 starting on page 670.

11. **Motor Vehicles**. Stringent U.S. Department of Transportation (DOT) safety standards and U.S. Environmental Protection Agency (EPA) emission-control standards. Refer to Commodity Index Chapter 87: Vehicles, beginning on page 867.

12. **Aircraft and Aerospace Products**. Stringent Federal Aviation Administration (FAA) and National Aeronautics and Space Administration (NASA) standards. Refer to Commodity Index Chapter 88: Aircraft and Parts, beginning on page 873.

13. **Prepared Foods**. Subject to regulations of the U.S. Food and Drug Administration (FDA). Entry notification, certification, extensive labeling requirements, compliance with product standards, fill and identity standards, and entry notification. Refer to Commodity Index Chapters 16, 19, 20, and 21, beginning on pages 504, 521, 525, and 530, respectively.

14. **Radiation-Producing Goods and Radio Frequency Devices.** Subject to regulation and restrictions of the U.S Food and Drug Administration (FDA) and the U.S. Federal Communications Administration (FCC). Entries must comply with standards and entry notifications. Refer to Commodity Index Chapters 84, 85, 90, and 92 beginning on pages 848, 857, 880, and 891, respectively.

15. **Fertilizers.** Subject to compliance with U.S. Department of Agriculture (USDA) requirements for fertilizers of organic origin, U.S. Federal Trade Commission (FTC) and Consumer Products Safety Commission (CPSC) standards for products marketed to consumers, U.S. Environmental Protection Agency (EPA) regulation for products containing toxic or hazardous substances, and U.S. Department of Transportation (DOT) regulations on transport. Refer to Commodity Index Chapter 31: Fertilizers, beginning on page 580.

16. **Paints and Related Products.** Subject to U.S. Federal Trade Commission (FTC) and Consumer Product Safety Commission (CPSC) standards for consumer products, U.S. Environmental Protection Agency (EPA) requirements for toxic or hazardous substances, and compliance with U.S. Department of Transportation (DOT) regulations on transportation of hazardous and toxic substances. Refer to Commodity Index Chapter 32: Paints and Related Products, beginning on page 584.

17. **Explosives, Fireworks, and Other Combustibles.** Subject to compliance with U.S. Federal TRade Commission (FTC) and Consumer Product Safety Commission (CPSC) standards and U.S. Bureau of Alcohol, Tobacco, and Firearms (BATF) regulations and permit requirements, among others. Refer to Commodity Index Chapter 36: Explosives, Fireworks, and Other Combustibles, beginning on page 604.

InfoList #7

Top 50 Imports to the U.S.

Leading items in U.S. general imports (U.S. Customs value) worldwide in millions of U.S. dollars

HTSUSA 2-Digit Commodity	1998	1999	2000	2001	2002	% Change 2001–2002
78—Road vehicles	119,726	146,202	161,682	157,409	168,173	6.8
77—Electrical machinery, apparatus & appliances	79,365	88,592	108,813	84,710	81,225	-4.1
29—Crude Oil	37,252	50,662	89,786	74,427	79,368	6.6
75—ADP equipment; office machines	76,755	84,443	92,165	75,861	76,970	1.5
76—Television, VCR, etc.	42,449	50,959	70,487	62,821	66,268	5.5
84—Clothing	53,742	56,413	64,296	63,862	63,810	0
74—General industrial machinery & equipment	28,811	31,447	34,709	33,258	35,201	5.8
51—Organic chemicals	18,327	21,860	28,563	29,626	30,213	2
54—Medicinal chemicals	10,908	13,542	14,694	18,624	24,719	32.8
89—Toys, games, sporting goods	18,695	18,991	20,017	20,909	22,059	5.5
82—Furniture and parts; bedding, mattresses, etc.	13,339	16,178	18,927	18,612	21,572	16
87—Professional scientific and control instruments	15,500	17,641	22,014	21,399	20,909	-2.3
33—Petroleum Preparations	10,947	14,160	25,657	24,604	20,702	-15.9
72—Specialized machinery	22,986	21,632	22,733	19,552	18,443	-5.7
69—Manufactures of metals	13,506	14,406	16,228	15,540	16,690	7.4
65—Textile yarn, fabrics, made-up articles	12,896	13,575	15,175	14,613	16,099	10.2
85—Footwear	13,881	14,068	14,854	15,235	15,386	1
64—Paper, paperboard and articles thereof	12,793	13,407	15,184	14,819	14,434	-2.6
67—Iron and steel	17,159	13,369	15,808	12,449	14,211	-14.2
79—Airplanes	7,052	8,775	12,393	14,705	12,672	-13.8
34—Natural Gas	5,273	6,304	10,966	16,303	12,220	25
27—Gem Diamonds	8,497	9,902	12,060	10,625	12,088	13.8
57—Plastics in primary forms	8,565	9,276	10,643	10,379	10,761	3.7
05—Vegetables and fruit	8,365	9,261	9,283	9,522	10,196	7.1
03—Fish, crustaceans, etc.	8,104	8,902	9,906	9,750	10,005	2.6
58—Plastics in nonprimary forms	6,137	7,010	8,034	8,263	9,139	10.6
24—Cork and wood	7,616	8,925	8,235	7,969	7,874	-1.2
63—Wood manufactures other than furniture	5,647	7,094	7,222	7,000	7,853	12.2
89—Jewelry	5,270	5,692	6,459	6,265	7,109	13.5
68—Aluminum	5,970	6,288	6,955	6,404	6,758	5.5
89—Basketware	3,834	4,396	4,842	5,590	6,564	17.4
59—Chemicals n.e.s.	4,833	5,072	5,731	5,927	6,174	4.2
81—Lighting, plumbing	3,393	4,327	5,106	4,895	5,566	13.7
88—Photographic equipment	6,114	5,661	6,915	5,577	5,328	-4.5
89—Records / magnetic media	4,383	4,696	5,166	4,886	5,280	8.1
89—Artwork / antiques	3,976	4,913	5,876	5,460	5,192	-4.9
73—Metalworking machinery	7,926	6,787	7,731	6,589	5,082	-22.9
62—Rubber tires and tubes	4,095	4,636	4,782	4,213	4,763	13.1
83—Travel goods, handbags and similar containers	3,946	4,148	4,432	4,301	4,392	2.1
01—Meat and meat preparations	2,848	3,258	3,840	4,254	4,269	.4
55—Chemicals - cosmetics	2,895	3,151	3,541	3,753	4,195	11.8
89—Printed materials	3,075	3,336	3,698	3,723	3,960	6.4
68—Copper	3,046	3,435	4,393	4,106	3,518	-14.3
11—Alcoholic beverages, distilled	2,296	2,617	2,946	3,060	3,275	7
88—Watches, clocks, and parts	3,210	3,257	3,485	3,048	3,204	5.1
28—Metalliferous ores and metal scrap	4,099	3,657	3,829	3,237	3,091	-4.5
88—Optical goods	2,727	3,075	4,021	3,453	2,840	-17.8
68—Platinum	3,051	3,498	5,688	5,229	2,826	-46

* % change from 2001 to 2002. Compiled from official statistics of the U.S. Department of Commerce. Sorted by general imports, customs value in 2002.

InfoList #8

Top 50 Suppliers of U.S. Imports

General imports, U.S. Customs, millions of U.S. dollars

Country/Region	1998	1999	2000	2001	2002	% Change 2001-2002
Canada	174,843.8	198,324.0	229,209.1	216,968.8	210,589.6	-2.9
Mexico	94,708.7	109,706.5	135,910.5	131,433.0	134,732.2	2.5
China	71,155.9	81,785.9	100,063.0	102,280.5	125,167.9	22.4
Japan	121,981.6	131,403.6	146,576.6	126,601.7	121,494.2	-4
Germany	49,823.9	55,093.5	58,736.6	59,151.3	62,480.4	5.6
United Kingdom	34,792.5	39,190.8	43,458.9	41,396.9	40,869.7	-1.3
South Korea	23,936.5	31,262.0	40,300.3	35,184.7	35,575.2	1.1
Taiwan	33,122.9	35,198.5	40,514.2	33,391.3	32,199.3	-3.6
France	24,077.3	25,909.6	29,782.4	30,295.5	28,408.0	-6.2
Italy	21,012.8	22,438.0	25,049.8	23,823.8	24,290.3	2
Malaysia	19,001.4	21,428.6	25,568.3	22,336.4	24,009.8	7.5
Ireland	8,384.9	11,002.4	16,409.8	18,539.5	22,387.9	20.8
Brazil	10,122.5	11,313.8	13,855.0	14,462.4	15,812.1	9.3
Venezuela	9,282.4	11,269.2	18,648.5	15,236.0	15,108.5	-.8
Thailand	13,434.3	14,323.8	16,389.1	14,728.6	14,799.3	.5
Singapore	18,357.4	18,187.7	19,186.5	14,979.2	14,792.6	-1.2
Saudi Arabia	6,338.9	8,237.3	14,219.1	13,333.5	13,142.8	-1.4
Israel (Incl. Gaza Strip & West Bank)	8,628.0	9,869.8	12,974.6	11,970.9	12,442.2	3.9
India	8,224.6	9,083.3	10,686.5	9,737.6	11,818.0	21.4
Philippines	11,948.9	12,379.7	13,936.8	11,330.6	10,985.3	-3
Netherlands	7,591.0	8,472.7	9,703.6	9,500.3	9,863.8	3.8
Belgium & Luxembourg	8,421.9	9,208.3	9,930.8	10,129.1	9,834.9	-2.9
Indonesia	9,337.6	9,514.0	10,385.5	10,104.8	9,643.7	-4.6
Switzerland	8,675.9	9,596.3	10,173.9	9,574.4	9,382.4	-2
Hong Kong	10,538.4	10,531.4	11,452.2	9,649.7	9,328.4	-3.3
Sweden	7,836.7	8110.7	9,603.0	8,850.8	9,287.2	4.9
Russia	5,733.7	5,805.0	7,796.4	6,261.3	6,824.9	9
Australia	5,381.9	5,290.4	6,438.6	6,479.0	6,478.2	0
Nigeria	4,194.6	4,361.1	10,548.5	8,786.3	5,964.2	-32
Norway	2,873.6	4,051.3	5,710.5	5,207.4	5,830.5	12
Spain	4,784.3	5,055.3	5,731.0	5,191.9	5,677.7	9.4
Colombia	4,651.5	6,275.8	6,968.6	5,696.4	5,606.3	-1.6
Dominican Republic	4,443.1	4,282.0	4,384.0	4,182.9	4,168.6	-.3
South Africa	3,055.5	3,195.1	4,204.2	4,428.3	4,027.1	-9.1
Austria	2,558.0	2,910.3	3,232.5	3,990.4	3,817.4	-4.3
Chile	2,452.9	2,935.9	3,227.9	3,554.6	3,781.2	6.4
Iraq	1,199.4	4,193.2	6,111.1	5,800.6	3,592.8	-38.1
Turkey	2,545.6	2,627.4	3,042.0	3,054.4	3,514.8	15.1
Finland	2,594.8	2,909.7	3,249.7	3,394.3	3,444.3	1.5
Honduras	2,544.9	2,713.1	3,090.0	3,126.5	3,264.0	4.4
Denmark	2,381.7	2,824.9	2,974.4	3,400.4	3,236.1	-4.8
Argentina	2,252.1	2,598.5	3,102.2	3,015.9	3,185.4	5.6
Costa Rica	2,745.5	3,958.5	3,547.2	2,886.9	3,141.7	8.8
Angola	2,251.5	2,424.8	3,557.0	3,099.6	3,114.5	.5
Guatemala	2,072.0	2,265.7	2,605.1	2,589.4	2,799.8	8.1
Hungary	1,567.4	1,891.9	2,715.6	2,964.6	2,638.8	-11
Trinidad and Tobago	970.9	1,293.6	2,228.4	2,380.9	2,437.3	2.4
Vietnam	553.4	609.0	821.7	1,052.6	2,394.7	127.5
Algeria	1,631.3	1,830.7	2,724.3	2,694.4	2,364.7	-12.2
Pakistan	1,691.4	1,740.4	2,167.4	2,249.4	2,304.6	2.5

* % change from 2001 to 2002. Compiled from official statistics of the U.S. Department of Commerce. Sorted by general imports, customs value in 2002.

InfoList #9

Costs Associated with Importing a Product

The total costs of importing a product will generally be far greater than the selling price quoted by the foreign supplier at his or her place of business. When you think of cost you must think in terms of "total landed cost." Total landed cost is the total of *all* the costs of purchasing the product and getting it to the U.S.

The following list is intended to give you an idea of the types of costs associated with importing a product. Some items may not be relevant to your particular operation.

1. Product design costs
2. Model or sample costs
3. Dies, molds, patterns (note that in certain cases U.S. Customs duty must be paid on these items, even if these dies, etc. were produced and remain in the country of origin)
4. Manufacturing set-up costs (labor and materials)
5. Cost of goods manufactured (labor, materials, overhead, profit)
6. Buyer's agent fees
7. Facilitation payments
8. Export documentation fees
9. Export taxes or fees
10. Labeling of merchandise (for U.S. Customs)
11. Product packaging for retail or wholesale sale in the U.S.
12. Packing/crating for international shipment
13. Transportation to dock
14. Short-term warehousing at the dock
15. Ocean, rail, trucking, or air freight charges
16. Insurance
17. U.S. import duty
18. Customs broker fees
19. Import documentation fees
20. Costs associated with satisfying any additional U.S. regulatory agency requirements
21. International payment fees (letter of credit, etc.)
22. Foreign exchange fees
23. Transport to warehouse
24. Domestic short-term warehousing
25. Inspection fees
26. Transfer from port to your warehouse
27. Overseas travel and entertainment
28. Other overhead costs (attorney, interpreters, translators, international telephone, telex, fax, delivery services, etc.)

InfoList #10

Starting an Import Business with Little Capital

Almost any business can be started with a small amount of initial capitalization. However, importing presents problems for small-time operators because of the added costs of travel and transportation as well as the problems associated with governmental regulation of certain products. Nevertheless, many established importers started as small-time operators. Here are a number of tips for those who seek to start an import operation with restricted working capital:

1. **Start close to home.** Start your business by importing goods from Mexico, Canada, Central America, or from anywhere you can get to inexpensively. In general, the closer the supplier, the more control you can exercise and the less expensive it will be to do business.

2. **Pre-sell merchandise.** If you know what you're after, or know how to find what others want to buy, you might be able to pre-sell the merchandise. Consider whether it is more advantageous to quote a fixed price or a percentage commission on top of the total landed cost.

3. **Get prepayment for goods.** If you are paid for the merchandise before you leave on your buying trip, you effectively increase your working capital. You may not even have to use your own money for anything beyond travel expenses.

4. **Import small amounts.** You can gain valuable experience while limiting your risks by importing small amounts of easy-to-import products. Concentrate on those products which are least regulated by U.S. government agencies.

5. **Import products for an established market.** It is best to start importing products for which you have an established market. For example, if you have a retail store, import goods which would sell there.

6. **Act as a buyer's agent.** Many importers get their start by acting as an agent for a more established company. Many companies prefer to have someone act as their agent to avoid the costs of sending their own people overseas. You will be a good candidate for this if you have special qualifications, such as knowledge of the merchandise and/or knowledge of the country.

7. **Import as you travel on other business.** Get your start by importing small quantities while overseas on vacation or on other business.

8. **Don't quit your "day job".** Start importing as a sideline while keeping your regular job to fund the import business.

9. **Use flight coupons to pay for travel.** Many people who have jobs that require travel save their bonus flight coupons to pay for travel to the country of origin of the products they want to import.

InfoList #11
Product Requirements

The business of importing demands a stronger knowledge of the product than do most domestic merchandising businesses. The greater your overall knowledge of the product (and market), the greater will be your chances of success. Prior experience in the design, manufacturing, or marketing of the product is the ideal foundation for success in an import business. You need a high degree of knowledge at every stage of the process:

1. **Point of purchase**
   In order to get what you really want from your supplier, you must be clear about your product requirements and be able to communicate them. Otherwise you may find yourself getting what you ask for, which is not really what you want.

2. **Export requirements**
   You will need to know enough about your product to satisfy all applicable country-of-origin export requirements that may exist.

3. **Transport requirements**
   Many products need special handling in transport. You should know these requirements in order to effectively specify them to the shipper. In some cases, knowledge of the most cost-effective transport method for your merchandise makes the difference between profit and loss.

4. **U.S. Customs and other agency requirements**
   U.S. Customs and other agency requirements regarding entry, classification, valuation, marking and labeling, and requirements of other agencies can result in significant problems if you do not know exactly how they affect your product.

5. **Sales requirements**
   Reduced to its simplest terms, importing is basically the transfer of goods from one country's economy to that of another country. You will need to know the market for your product domestically. To successfully establish a marketing program, you will need to know your merchandise well.

6. **Seasonality of the product**
   Christmas products have to arrive in time for the complete holiday selling season. Some products sell in cold months, others only in warm months. You need to know both the seasonal aspect of your products and the lead time it takes to get them from the country of origin to your market on time.

InfoList #12
Know Your Product

The following list of questions is designed to get both prospective and established importers to think clearly about what they might need to learn about the products they seek to import. Some items on this list may not relate directly to your product. Often, the overall knowledge a person possesses about a product is what makes him or her successful.

General Information

1. What names does the product goes by, including its generic and trade names in the language of the exporting country?

2. What is the product's history of development?

3. What aspects of culture and/or folklore are associated with the product?

4. What nationalities and social/economic classes traditionally make, broker, or sell the product?

Specifications

5. What are the units of measure in which the product is bought and sold, including the foreign names of those units? Be aware that many products sold in the U.S. must adhere to specific standards of weight, fill, and size for that product.

6. What product models or variations are available? The product may have numerous models or variations for different markets. It may be that certain models of the product which are excellent sellers in the exporting country would be terrible sellers in the U.S. in general, or in specific regions of the U.S.

7. What design types are produced regionally?

8. What are the size variations? What are the sizes in which the product is normally available/manufactured? For example, an importer of garments or footwear must take into consideration that different nationalities have different body proportions. Be sure that you import your product in a size that is appropriate for the U.S. market. Garments and footwear are only obvious examples of size considerations. Other products may need to be specially sized for your market in the U.S.

9. What are the electrical or other technological requirements for U.S. usage? Certain products may be manufactured to operate only on 220v current in the country of origin and will need to be modified to operate on 110v in the United States.

Source

10. What is the product's traditional country of origin?

11. What are the emerging countries of origin for the product?

12. What are the product centers for the product or commodity within the country of origin?

Production

13. What are the product's component materials?

14. What countries export these component materials?

15. How are the component materials obtained by the local manufacturers?

16. What is the cost structure of the product's component materials?

17. What are the incremental mark-ups on the component materials from the original source to the manufacturer by percentage and actual cost?

18. What are the conditions of the manufacture of the product in the exporting country? Are they made in modern factories, small workshops, or by cottage or craft industry?

19. What types of individuals work in these factories and workshops? Are they unskilled, semi-skilled, or highly skilled workers, and how easily can the necessary skills be acquired?

20. What are workers' labor rates? Are they paid hourly, daily, monthly, or by the piece? What will these rates buy in essential commodities in the country of origin?

21. Does manufacture involve any unusual techniques?

22. How does workmanship vary from country to country, locale to locale, and factory to factory? "Quality" is a subjective valuation and varies from individual to individual and from culture to culture. The seller's idea of quality may not be yours. Be sure to buy the quality your market demands.

23. What is the capitalization required to establish a manufacturing facility for that product in the country of origin versus the United States?

Regulation of Product

24. What, if any, exporting country regulations and documentation affect the exportability of your product?

25. What transport regulations affect the product? Air or sea transport of certain hazardous products may be regulated or prohibited.

26. What special requirements of U.S. Customs and other U.S. governmental regulating agencies affect the importation, classification, valuation, or duty status of the product?

27. Are there any imminent export or import restrictions affecting the product?

Other

28. Are any pending technological changes expected to affect the product?

InfoList #13

Know Your Market

Knowledge of the merchandise is important, but by no means is it sufficient to establish a successful import operation. In order to succeed you must also know the buying and the selling market for your products.

1. Buying and Selling Experience

Nothing takes the place of active buying and selling experience. The most successful importers are constantly in touch with the market for their products and commodities. For example, department store buyers are required to spend a minimum amount of time working "the floor" as salespeople to get a feel for what people are buying and what they are asking for.

Learning the hard way. A small group of newly certified graduate gemologists from the Gemological Institute of America (GIA), one of the most prestigious gemological schools in the world, found out the hard way. Six months of intensive study had made these individuals quite knowledgeable about colored gem stones. They raised more than $30,000 (1975 dollars) from relatives and friends to finance a gem-purchasing trip to South America. After purchasing and importing high quality gemstones to the U.S. they discovered that they had paid altogether too much for gemstones for which they had no established market. Their error was not in knowledge of their product, but rather in knowledge of the price structure and market for that product. They were forced to liquidate their stock at a loss and start over.

2. Volatility of the Market

Changes in the market for goods can easily spell disaster to established ventures as well as to new ones. Many variables impact the market for merchandise and even experts can be caught off guard. Your job as an importer and a business person is to know as much about your market as possible. Be in tune with its variations: know when, how and why it changes.

In a fast-paced world, if you are only aware of the fluctuations in your regional market, you may be caught off guard by events, competition, or changes in foreign markets. For example, in an international situation where the price of a commodity is going up, the importer who buys last is at a disadvantage; whereas when the price is decreasing, the importer who buys last gains an edge.

3. Your Market's Quality Requirements

The buyer defines quality. Most markets for merchandise have exceedingly narrow ranges of acceptable quality.

Each market has its own minimum standards of acceptability and maximum price, no matter what the quality.

Before purchasing an item, you should know the tolerance for quality in your own market. Incremental quality increases of 10% can end up costing your customers 50% or more. Many consumers may not be able to discern the higher quality for which they are asked to pay substantially more. Your job is to know and assess the quality range your customers can discern, can afford, and will want.

Once you have established the quality and price range your market requires, make sure your suppliers understand that they have to come through with what you need. It is not enough to indicate that you want "quality." You must define quality, which is a very subjective matter. In actuality, you do not require an item of quality, you require an item that is produced according to your set of specifications. To get this you need to define and communicate your standards of quality in a technical way that does not leave room for interpretation.

4. Seasonality of Merchandise

Did you hear the one about the importer of Christmas ornaments whose merchandise arrived on December 26th? It isn't funny. As importer you must get your merchandise to market at the appropriate time to sell.

A great deal of merchandise such as wearing apparel, Christmas goods, and certain sporting goods are sold seasonally. Since orders of imported goods often require substantially more lead time than domestic orders, you need to know the seasonality of your merchandise. This becomes even more important if you supply component products to manufacturers of seasonal merchandise.

If you know when your clients need an item, you should schedule backwards from that date. For example, if you have an item to sell retail at Christmas, the retailer should have it in stock by the mid-November, Thanksgiving at the very latest.

The following movements of merchandise may each take from several days to several weeks to accomplish. You will have to allow for each in your planning.

- Retailer's warehouse to retail store shelves
- Importer's warehouse to retailer's warehouse
- Clearance through U.S. Customs
- Transport from overseas port to U.S. port of entry
- Transport from point of manufacture in exporting country to port of export
- Manufacturing time
- Preliminary research, planning, and design

The total process could take from several weeks to more than a year!

5. Conducting Market Research

You must constantly conduct some form of market research. It can range from highly structured research conducted by an outside consulting firm to a "seat-of-the-pants" approach, with you asking the right people the right questions.

Market research, whether called that, market assessment on a seasonal- or new-product basis, or something else is an integral part of good business planning. It should be conducted by every company on an ongoing basis. It is your means of setting goals for your business.

The importance of research cannot be overemphasized for any business, but it is especially crucial for importers. The greater the distance between product source and market, the greater the time and costs of getting it to the ultimate consumer. Domestic suppliers may be in a better position

than importers to serve their customers on a timely basis. Therefore, importers need to be in tune with market trends, and stay ahead of the market.

Market research is a huge subject and beyond the scope of this publication. A number of excellent books on the subject are available in business libraries and bookstores. However, the best way to start a market research program is to establish a format for your research which takes into account the variables affecting your product, market and business.

6. Who is Your Market?

What type of individual and what type of business constitutes the natural target audience for the product you seek to import and sell?

1. Is the individual of a particular age, social, or economic group?
2. Is the individual more interested in fashion or more interested in quality and durability?
3. Is the individual interested in the snob appeal of your item?
4. Is the person interested in a bargain?
5. Is the person interested in the "story" that goes along with the item?
6. Is the person already buying the product or do you have to educate them to buy either a new product or your product specifically?
7. What needs are you filling with the product?

7. Where is Your Market?

Define the geographic location of your potential market. This can mean a neighborhood, a city, a metropolitan area, a country, a state, a region, or an entire country. A clear definition of your market area will keep your marketing efforts focused.

1. Who needs your product and why?
2. What makes your product different and desirable?
3. Where do you find the people who need your product?
4. What other criteria product lead to acceptance or rejection?
5. List prospective market areas which could support a sales program for your product.
6. Test the various prospective markets to determine where your marketing efforts will be most productive.

You may find it prohibitively expensive to reach a large market area in the beginning. The cost of making each sale often increases dramatically in proportion to the distance of the sale from your base of operation. You may find it more appropriate to deal in a small, local geographic area and achieve greater coverage. Alternatively, you may benefit from wider distribution and the economics of scale that result. Be aware of the point of diminishing return when expanding.

Also remember that certain parts of the country are more advanced stylistically than others.

8. Contact Potential Buyers/Customers

If you are established in a business, the best place to start your research is with your clients. You should be enough in tune with them to know their current product requirements as well as their future needs, and have enough rapport to be able to find out what you don't already know. If you know your market and your clients or customers well enough, you will always be in a position to offer them what they need rather than what you've got. It is always easier to supply demand than to create it.

If you are not yet in business, or want to change the scope of an established business, your question should be, "How do I know which import items will sell?" To find out, you need to know how to ask questions and listen to the responses.

You need to believe in your product. Nevertheless it is easier to import, or to bring to market, goods that the customers want to buy. If the goods you like are not what other people want, keep looking until you find a large enough market for the merchandise you prefer to deal in. Ultimately, however, you should be in business to serve your clients.

Seek out likely customers, develop good rapport, and ask them:

1. What do you need?
2. What are your customers asking for?
3. What is selling well?
4. What is hard or difficult to find?
5. What is costing you more than it really should?
6. What would you place an order for right now?
7. How much would you pay?
8. Would you pay C.O.D.?
9. What terms would you require?
10. Would you prepay for those goods?
11. I'm going to XYZ countries. What goods from those countries are in demand?
12. What stores and businesses are interested in goods from those countries?

Note: Don't be fooled by what is on display in either wholesale or retail businesses. Sometimes, what is on display is what's left because it didn't sell!

InfoList #14
Know Your Competition

Here are a number of questions you or your company might ask concerning your competition.

1. What products are competitive with ours?
2. Who and where are our competitors?
3. How are their products marketed?
4. How and why does their marketing work or fail to work?
5. What are the weak points in their marketing organization?
6. What are their short- and long-range plans?
7. What business problems are they facing?
8. Do they have any unusual advantages?
9. Are they efficient?
10. What is the extent and quality of their research and development effort?
11. What new products are they developing?
12. Who and where are their suppliers?
13. What are they paying for merchandise?
14. What supply problems do they have?
15. If they have labor problems, why?
16. What is the manufacturing cost of their goods?
17. How do our products compare with theirs?
18. How many middlemen handle their product before it reaches the consumer?
19. What are their sales terms, credit requirements, and commissions? What compensation terms are extended to distributors, to sales people, and to retailers of their goods?
20. How are their goods advertised?
    a. Promotion techniques?
    b. Media?
    c. Ad expenditures?
21. How does the marketplace view our products compared to theirs?
21. How good is their after-sales service?
23. How does their pricing compare to ours?
24. How are the above factors likely to change?
25. How much does the competition know about you?

InfoList #15
Buying from the Source

As an importer you need to purchase as close to the product source as possible. You also need to bring the goods as close to the ultimate consumer as is economically feasible. The more you know about the market and price structure for your product, the better able you will be to insert yourself into the most profitable position in the market chain.

1. Middlemen

All economies worldwide rely on a series of middlemen to bring goods to market. Each middleman moves the merchandise one step further toward the ultimate consumer, adding both value and cost.

2. Flow Chart from Source to Ultimate Consumer

As an exercise, create a flow chart of the movement of your product from the source of the raw materials and component parts, through its processing and/or manufacture as a the final product, to its sale to the ultimate consumer.

In your analysis, describe the service or function each middleman provides, what makes this stop a necessary part of the structure, location where it occurs, how much the service costs, the provider's margin of profit, and your assessment of the strengths and weaknesses at every stage within the market.

Be aware that the price for which an item is on display in either a wholesale or retail situation may be either an inflated or deflated price. An item offered for sale at retail for $45 may have cost as little as $5 or as much as $40. Be careful when making assumptions about costs.

3. Where Are You Located in the Flow?

- What is your current position in the flow?
- What place in the market chain has the greatest strategic advantage?
- What are the most profitable positions to be in?
- Where would you like to be?

You may be in a position to cut out one of the intermediate suppliers and get closer to the source, or to cut out one of the middlemen at the other end and get closer to the ultimate consumer. Be careful: if it is easy to bump someone else out of the market flow, it may be equally easy for someone to bump you out next time. In any case, it may be unwarranted, or unprofitable to attempt to get closer to the source or to do the retail or wholesale distribution yourself. It just may be more profitable to leave that job to others.

InfoList #16
Finding Sources

One of the most treasured and protected secrets of any import operation is its list of suppliers. Importers will go to almost any length to maintain the confidentiality of their sources of supply of vital materials or products. Many importers see that the greater the shroud of mystery surrounding the business, and the more difficult it appears to those on the outside, the better. It is in the interests of these importers to not to cooperate with you, their potential competitor. The higher the entry barriers, the more secure their position.

There are many ways to find sources of supply. These depend upon product, country of origin, and the ability of the importer to research, plan ahead, and be patient.

You can either find overseas sources of supply while at home, or while on an overseas trip. Research done in the United States is the most cost-effective. Although some suppliers will be difficult to locate from the U.S., there will always be some preliminary research that is better done at home. For example, if you seek items available only from nomadic merchants in India whose shops are tents, you will not be able to locate them from the U.S. But you can ascertain the probable locations in India where such items are traditionally found before leaving the U.S.

Pre-planning allows you to set up a series of appointments with prospective suppliers before leaving the U.S. If these sources of supply turn out to be unacceptable, you will have at least gained some experience and a basis for comparison.

In all but the most primitive countries, research time costs three to 10 times as much as time spent conducting research from the U.S. Do your homework and save time and money.

InfoList #17
26 Sources of Information

1. The Internet—Many of the organizations, agencies, and sources listed below have Web sites, and a growing number of Web sites are solely devoted to international trade.

2. Foreign government embassies and consulates in the United States

3. Foreign chambers of commerce in the U.S. and in the exporting country

4. Domestic U.S. banks with international operations

5. Foreign bank branches in the U.S.

6. Banks in the exporting country

7. Foreign trade development organizations with offices in the U.S. and/or in the foreign country

8. International consultants and lawyers

9. United Nations agencies and other major international and regional organizations, such as the WTO, the EU, ASEAN, and the OECD

10. U.S. Department of Commerce libraries in major U.S. cities

11. U.S. Department of Commerce country desks, Washington DC

12. Other importers

13. U.S. exporters with experience and connections in the exporting country

14. Domestic U.S.- and foreign-trade publications

15. National airlines of the country of origin

16. Shipping companies

17. Customs brokers

18. Freight forwarders

19. Export trade associations of the exporting country

20. Yellow Pages in the exporting country

21. Trade shows, fairs, and exhibitions

22. Travel agents

23. Church groups and missions

24. Travel guides

25. Ads placed in overseas publications

26. Foreign students in the U.S.

InfoList #18
How to Use Sources

1. Online Sources

An ever-increasing fund of information is available on the Internet, and it can be particularly useful for locating international data. Many of the items in this InfoList contain reference to Web sites; you should also refer to "Top Web sites for the Importer" on page 87. For example, you can use the Internet to gather information on the country or region you wish to do business in or a company you are considering as a supplier, to make travel arrangements, to gather regulatory information on importing into the U.S., and to find prospective suppliers.

Much of the information on the Internet is available for free or at a minimal cost. However, there are other online information services that provide access to proprietary information for a fee; sometimes it is accessed through the Internet, other times, via their own system. Some examples include Knight-Ridder Information Services, Lexis/Nexis, Dow Jones New Service, and Individual. These companies can often provide access to foreign newspapers and business publications that are difficult to find elsewhere.

2. Foreign Government Offices in the U.S.

The most efficient way to start a search for suppliers is to write a letter of request to the nearest consulate, embassy, or commercial attaché of the exporting country of the products you seek. Check your local telephone directory or call directory assistance to find out if there is a listing for a consulate of the country in which you are interested in your area. If not, call the embassy of the country in Washington, DC for a referral to the consulate serving your area. You may also want to check The Electronic Embassy on the Internet at http://www.embassy.org/. This Web site has contact information for all embassies in Washington, DC as well as web links to more than 50 embassies with their own Web sites.

Unless you are proposing a large and significant transaction, we recommend that you write a letter to the local consulate requesting information before writing to the commercial attaché at the embassy in Washington. Such letters are usually forwarded to the local consulate anyway.

Consular offices are usually established to promote the commercial interests of and protect the rights of their citizens in the host country. They also issue travel and business visas to citizens of the host country. Consular officers are generally eager to assist with requests for sources of supply in their country. It is their job to promote home-country exports. Consular offices often have export directories for the home country that can refer you to sources. Some have the information on their embassy's Web site or can refer you to other government and trade sources on the Internet. Note that developing nations will not have the information as readily accessible, and often respond to such requests only if they have time. They are also far less likely to have extensive online information available.

It is possible to call these consular offices directly, but we recommend that you first write a formal letter of request for information. The written request is a clear communication, and it creates a positive record of the request. Make an initial call to obtain the name of the commercial officer or attaché so that your letter is properly addressed. In many cases, the consulate or embassy will not respond to any request until they have received it in writing. A fax is usually acceptable. Make a call to the consulate after you think your letter has arrived, to verify its arrival and to indicate your sincere interest in doing business. Be sure to note the name of the individual you speak to.

In all likelihood the consulate will send you a response letter within several weeks, with a list of names and addresses of businesses who are suppliers of items similar to the ones you requested. You should send letters immediately to each lead, giving more detailed information concerning the products you seek. Always mention the U.S.-based consulate and individual who referred the supplier to you. And while it can be safely assumed that every businessperson wants to respond quickly to a request for information on their products, these suppliers will take such a request even more seriously when names with titles (commercial attaché, etc.) are mentioned.

Although most industrialized countries have consular and trade offices throughout the U.S., some foreign countries do not. Consulates are most likely to be located in cities where the foreign country has a significant business or cultural interest. If there is no consulate near you, write directly to the embassy in Washington DC, addressing the inquiry to the commercial attaché.

3. Chambers of Commerce

The various foreign chambers of commerce in the United States are excellent sources of information on overseas suppliers. Names and addresses of U.S.-based country-of-origin chambers of commerce for countries that export to the U.S. can be found by calling directory assistance in Washington DC, New York, and other major U.S. cities. The nearest consulate or embassy for a country can likely refer you to an appropriate chamber of commerce. If you have Internet access, check the World Index of Chambers of Commerce & Industry, which lists more than 800 organizations at http://www1.usa1.com/~ibnet/chamshp.html.

Chambers of commerce are essentially special-interest associations established to further the interests of their members. They assist U.S. importers in finding suppliers that among the members of their chamber. Some have been known to forward requests to other chambers and associations. In rare instances, they may refer you to suppliers who are not members. However, remember that they were not established with that purpose in mind.

The general exception to this rule is the *national* chamber of commerce of a country. Most chambers of commerce are private organizations, but many countries have national chambers which are actually government or quasi-governmental agencies. In some countries, all businesses must register with their national chamber of commerce as a prerequisite for being in business. This is a form of government control on their licensing and activities.

Chambers of commerce can be categorized in three groups. The first is the national or government chamber of commerce, which is an agency of the government. For example, in Great Britain it is the British Overseas Trade Board. An example of the second type of chamber of commerce is the British American Chamber of Commerce. This association is designed to promote British companies, i.e. exports from Britain to the United States. The American British Chamber of Commerce is an example of the third type. It is designed to promote U.S. companies, i.e. exports from the U.S. to the U.K.

Although each of these groups was established with different and often contradictory purposes and goals, useful commercial information can be obtained from all three types. All chambers of commerce have membership directories. Usually they have international divisions with specialized listings of exporters and importers. Their primary purpose will be to refer you to companies that are members of their organization. If they have a newsletter or a Web site, they may be willing to publish your request in an import/export opportunities section.

Members of chambers of commerce are generally more established businesses. For certain products the more established company may not be your best opportunity. Old and established may mean that their products and styles are more rigid and/or dated, and may indicate a larger internal bureaucracy with more paperwork and more overhead. Nevertheless, they can also represent stability, something the importer looks for in an overseas source of supply.

4. Governmental Export Trade Ministries

These are the official governmental trade promotion agencies of countries. They often work closely with consulates in the host country. Some are extremely well organized, helpful, and efficient, and others are hopelessly uncoordinated and unresponsive. The purpose of these organizations is to promote their country's mercantile trade. The U.S. equivalent is the U.S. Department of Commerce. These agencies have export trade directories and sometimes computer or other data banks of information on products and suppliers. They often have bilingual staff to assist overseas businesspeople with requests. English is the most common second language for business. These agencies often have trade publications on how to do business in their country. Many are available free, while others are sold at a nominal cost. The names and addresses of many of these agencies are available from the U.S.-based consulates.

Many of these trade promotion agencies and ministries now have information available on the Internet. You may find links through the Web site maintained by the U.S. embassy of the country you are importing from (try http://www.embassy.org), or check the Global Trade Point Network, maintained by the United Nations Trade Point Development Centre at http://www.unicc.org/untpdc/index1.html. The latter site provides links to the major government offices in each country which are involved in trade promotion.

5. Product-Specific Export Associations

An excellent source of names and addresses of potential suppliers is the product-specific export trade association for your desired product in the exporting country. You will find that virtually every product group has its own trade association ready to do what it can to assist those who wish to do business with their members.

Start your search for these associations by contacting the consulate or embassy of the exporting country for the name and address of the associations which relate to your products. You may also want to check with the nearest business library, either within a large city's library system, or within a college or university library, and ask for assistance in identifying appropriate trade organizations through the various directories they have available.

6. Banks

International bankers are perhaps the best internationally connected individuals in the commercial realm. Since the vast majority of international trade goes through banks, bankers are in a good position to know what is going on. Many banks have special economic information services which can potentially assist the importer in finding suppliers. If unable to help in finding suppliers, they may be able to help by running credit checks on potential suppliers whose names are obtained from other sources. They may also have publications which relate to economic and business conditions in the country in question. Some information produced by the bank may be available on their Web site. One resource for finding an international bank's Web site is BankWeb at http://www.bankweb.com/; it lists international banks by region and country.

When dealing with a bank, be sure to speak with someone who has international experience. Your personal/corporate bankers can often give an introduction to someone in the international department. It is a wise person indeed who cultivates banking relationships.

One sure way to get assistance here in the United States is to deal directly with a U.S. branch of a major overseas bank headquartered in the country of origin of the products you seek to import. For instance, when doing business in Switzerland, deal with the Swiss Bank Corporation; when doing business in Japan, deal with the Sumitomo Bank. These banks have far greater expertise, knowledge, and sources for their home country than would a U.S. bank with a branch in that country.

The largest number of foreign bank branches in the U.S. are located in New York, with Los Angeles a close second. Other major U.S. cities, particularly San Francisco, have many foreign banks as well.

7. International Consultants and Lawyers

Major international consultants now have offices in over 100 countries worldwide, and many law offices have an increasing number of foreign offices as well. Their services may be quite expensive, but for some types of commodities, it is worthwhile to inquire, particularly if you have concerns about legal or tax issues. However, even the smallest importer can benefit from the wisdom of these companies through their many publications, both printed and online.

Some companies, like Ernst & Young and Price Waterhouse, have books on doing business in certain countries available for free. While intended primarily for their cus-

tomers, they are often willing to give out small numbers to prospective customers as well. Many libraries keep an entire collection of the "Doing Business" guides from Price Waterhouse. All of these companies now have extensive Web sites, and the Web sites of the offices in the country you are interested in may have a whole guide available online. For example, the main Ernst & Young Web site (http://www.ey.com/) has a tax guide with brief information on almost every country in the world. However, the Canadian office of Ernst & Young has an entire guide to doing business in Canada mounted on their Web site.

8. National Airlines

Most national airline companies of potential source countries, such as Japan Air Lines, Air France, Varig (Brazil), or Aerolineas Argentinas, have promotional departments that produce brochures and books extolling the virtues of visiting and doing business in their country. Some of these publications are excellent resources on the cultural aspects of doing business in the country and often contain valuable addresses.

Most airlines also conduct economic research for purposes of determining their market for freight services and might be willing to make some of this information available. While they may not give be able to give you actual names of sources of supply, they may tell you where to find the information. Start with a telephone call to the customer service or public relations department of the airline's local business office.

Another source of information within a given airline is the cargo or freight services headquarters. Since the air cargo section of the airline has a vested interest in boosting import/export trade, they might be willing to assist you in finding sources of supply.

In order to get this information, you will need to contact the main business office in the United States of the airline in question. Many are in New York, but there is no one city which houses most of the airline offices. Check an OAG guide at your local library, or call a reservations agent for the airline (usually a toll-free call) and ask him or her. Virtually all the major airlines now have Web sites; while much of the information is concerned with flight routes and reservations, some have business information, links to other important sites in the country, or contact information for their business offices. Refer to "Travel Phone Numbers and Web sites" on page 49, or go to Airlines of the Web at http://w0.itn.net/airlines/ for links to most passenger and cargo airlines.

9. Export Trade Directories

Export trade directories for specific countries are excellent sources of supplier information. These reference books are often hundreds of pages in length, often with small print and advertising. They are usually organized so that you can obtain supplier information by company name alphabetically, by product or commodity, and by geographic location within the country of origin.

Export directories are found in the reference sections of larger libraries, especially business libraries or business sections of larger public libraries. Other sources for these directories are embassies and consulates of the country foreign chambers of commerce and trade missions in the U.S., and U.S. Department of Commerce libraries in major U.S. cities. One of the largest publisher of country-specific trade directories is Kompass International S.A., Saint Laurent, 73800 Cruet, France; Tel: [33] 4-79-65-25-08; FAX [33] 4-79-84-13-95; Web site: http://www.kompass-int.com/.

10. Yellow Pages in the Exporting Country

One of the most overlooked sources of product information is the yellow pages. Yes, they do have yellow pages in Hong Kong, Bangkok, Paris, Rome, and just about everywhere else. In some countries, particularly in Asia, they publish English-language yellow pages directories in addition to directories in the language of the country.

To obtain a copy of the yellow pages directory of a major foreign city, first try contacting the consulate, or chamber of commerce of that country. The next line of inquiry involves calling your local telephone company office here in the U.S. and asking where you might find the specific directory. One source is NYNEX Information Resources, which may be contacted at (800) 719-5656. If you plan to do business over a period of time in a city overseas, get a directory during your visit there. Almost every hotel will have a copy, and most hotel managers will help you obtain one. A third source is the Internet. An increasing number of countries are posting both white pages and yellow pages listings in searchable directories on the World Wide Web. Go to World Directories at http://www.global-yp.com/world.htm for a listing with hyperlinks.

While a great majority of business introductions are prearranged, once you are in the exporting country, don't hesitate to call a potential supplier directly. Identify yourself, your company, and your purpose. Once you are there, many suppliers may even arrange your transportation to their production facilities and showrooms.

11. Trade Journals

Most countries have trade journals for specific commodity groups. These may be independently published or be ancillary to a trade association. If you intend to concentrate on a particular commodity group, you should identify the journals that pertain to those commodities and obtain copies. Many will contain supplier advertisements that may be of help to you. You may also wish to place an advertisement yourself. A number of these journals have special sections listing import/export trade opportunities, often as a free service. Some of these publications come in the form of a book of products and producers consisting of paid advertisements. Product specific trade journals are also an excellent source for entrepreneurial importers looking for new ideas.

Contact the commercial section of the country's consulate, chamber of commerce, or export trade associations for information on such resources.

12. International and Regional Organizations

Some of the most prolific publishers in the world are the United Nations agencies and other international and regional organizations. While most of them cannot provide specific assistance to individual importers, they have a vast store of economic, demographic, and legal information available for sale, and the prices are often quite reasonable. Other than the United Nations, and its agencies, other important publishers in this category are the World Trade Organization (WTO), the World Bank, the International Monetary Fund (IMF), the Organization for Economic Cooperation and Development (OECD), and the European Community (EU). In the U.S., one major source for publications from all of these sources and others is Bernan Associates, Tel: (800) 274-4447, (301) 459-7666); Web site: http://www.bernan.com/. You may also want to check the Internet for these organizations, since most have some information mounted on their Web sites.

13. Business Libraries

Most major cities in the United States have public, university business, and commercial libraries. A number of these purchase export directories and subscribe to various trade and business publications of other countries. Business libraries are a much underutilized source of information in the U.S. Access to university libraries may be restricted, so it is always best to call in advance.

14. International Trade Shows, Fairs, and Exhibitions

Every major country in the world has trade fairs and exhibitions of its products. One type is the "national exposition" of general merchandise produced in that country. Another is the commodity specific trade show exhibiting one type of merchandise, such as jewelry, computers, or footwear.

Consulates and commercial attachés will almost always have trade fair and exhibition dates and information for their country. These events are excellent opportunities to view competitive merchandise from a large number of suppliers.

15. Religious Organizations in Emerging Countries

In a number of developing countries, religious organizations play a key role in the development of local businesses, such as handicraft cooperatives. These groups provide assistance to local people by establishing the organizational structure for cottage industries. Although they may be difficult to contact, and may require sleuthing even in the country of origin, these cooperatives sometimes produce very marketable merchandise, especially for the gift trade. Try contacting consulates, international religious organizations, such as the World Council of Churches, relief organizations, and the Peace Corps for leads.

InfoList #19
Letters and E-mails of Request

Businesspeople in the U.S. (receptive to informality and immediacy) are accustomed to conducting business by telephone, letters, and e-mail. The most accepted form of business contact in foreign countries is through a letter of request via an e-mail, the post, fax, telex, or cable.

You will need at least two types of letters of request in seeking suppliers. Either use your company letterhead or give complete contact information in your e-mail. To obtain leads about potential suppliers, write a general letter of request for suppliers' names, sending one to each relevant consulate, chamber of commerce, and other third-party group whose purpose is to assist U.S. importers. Responses to these letters should give you a good beginning list of leads. Once you have the leads, you should write a letter of request, with more details, to each supplier.

Your general letter of request should contain the following elements:

1. The nature of your business.
2. A statement to the effect that you are seeking suppliers of a particular type of merchandise. Be sure to describe the product in enough detail so that they can steer you in the right direction. However, avoid being overly technical. If the product you seek is unusual, you might include a photo or a sketch.
3. An estimate of the number of units per month or per year you are interested in purchasing.
4. The date you hope to have shipments begin. Including a date can motivate your source to expedite a response to your request.
5. A request for the names, complete addresses, and, if possible, telephone numbers of potential suppliers of the product in that country.
6. A request for the names of regions and geographic areas which produce the products you desire. Because many industries are grouped geographically, knowing the region may be half the battle.
7. The names and addresses of relevant product-specific export trade associations.
8. A request for printed information, brochures, pamphlets, etc. concerning the products in question, or on doing business in their country.
9. Thanks in advance for all the help they are sure to give you.
10. A bank reference; for example: Banker: Bank of America, 315 Montgomery Street, San Francisco, CA.

Letters of request made directly to potential suppliers should contain more detailed information and specifications of the product(s) you seek. Your ability to describe your product in technical terms will determine the adequacy of the supplier's response. Companies unable to supply your product may refer you to other possible suppliers.

InfoList #20
Sample Letter of Request for Sources

AB Leather Goods Company
123 Grant Avenue
San Francisco, California 94XXX
USA

Consulate General, Republic of Colombia
870 Market Street
San Francisco, California 94102

Dear Sirs:

We are wholesalers of fine leather goods. We have been in business for eight years and are interested in expanding our product line of imported wallets for men and women.

Would you please help us by providing the names and addresses of any trade organizations in Colombia that represent producers of leather goods, and any printed materials you have about doing business in Colombia, and about the Colombian leather industry in particular? Also, are there any specific geographic areas where leather goods are manufactured in Colombia?

We expect to be purchasing 1,000 wallets per month within six months. If you know of any producers in Colombia who have an existing product line, or who would be able to manufacture to our specification, please include their names, full addresses, and phone and fax numbers.

We look forward to a mutually beneficial business relationship with producers in Colombia. Thank you in advance for your gracious help in assisting us to locate suppliers.

Sincerely yours,

Bank reference: Bank of America, 315 Montgomery Street, San Francisco, California

InfoList #21
Sample Letter of Request to Potential Suppliers

AB Leather Goods Company
123 Grant Avenue
San Francisco, California 94XXX
USA

Manufacturas en Cuero de Medellin
Calle XX, No. XX-XX
Medellin, Colombia

Dear Sirs:

Your company name has been given to us by the Consulate General of Colombia in San Francisco, California, USA.

We are wholesalers of fine leather goods. We have been in business for eight years and are interested in expanding our product line of imported wallets for men and women.

We are looking for a producer of leather goods in Colombia that can manufacture a product line of fine wallets in calf skin on a contract basis to our exacting specifications.

We expect to purchase 1,000 wallets per month within five months. If your company is interested in supplying us, please forward a letter in response including any brochures or photographs of your existing product line and perhaps a sample of a small leather accessory in calf skin.

Our president, Mr. Edward Baker, will be in Colombia the first two weeks of March to interview potential suppliers. It would be helpful for us to have a response by the third week of February.

We thank you in advance for your assistance.

Sincerely yours,

Banker reference: Bank of America, 315 Montgomery Street, San Francisco, California

InfoList #22
10 Tips About Suppliers

1. Go to the Ultimate Source
As a buyer, one of your major goals is to purchase goods for the least cost possible. Generally, this means that you will want to purchase from the original producer of the product. A company that wants to supply your needs may seek a secondary supplier and become a middleman in the transaction. There are advantages and disadvantages to this. The advantage is that you get your product, sometimes for less trouble than if you went to the original source. The disadvantages include increased cost, longer lead time, and less control.

2. Export Trading Companies
The import/export regulations of some countries are so stringent that only specialized import/export trading houses are knowledgeable and connected enough to handle such transactions. For example, in Japan large conglomerate trading houses have a virtual monopoly on trade. Centrally planned socialist/communist countries, such as the People's Republic of China (PRC), set up a limited number of specialized corporations to serve as the sole importers and exporters. (In the case of the PRC more autonomy has been given to smaller trading houses and some individual firms during recent years.)

These trading houses often provide a worthwhile service, especially in countries whose import/export documentation and licensing is difficult. Also, they act as a go-between for smaller producers who may have difficulty communicating in English, or who may not have fax or telex equipment for easy international communication. Some of these organizations go so far as to finance and guarantee the export transaction.

3. Developing a Supplier Relationship
Ongoing overseas business relationships require the same considerations that guide domestic relationships. Contrary to popular belief, all overseas suppliers are not ready to drop what they are doing just to get an importer's product ready by the next morning. The dollar is no longer that almighty.

If you seek product quality and supplier reliability, pay particular attention to the manner in which you cultivate your business relationships. Every country has its own standards of business communication. To be effective you will need to learn them and be willing to go the extra mile to do so.

4. Established versus New Businesses
Be aware that there may be trade-offs between doing business with established businesses and new businesses. Established businesses may offer the best service, but may cost more. The younger, smaller companies often have less overhead and are able to supply a product for very competitive prices. However, they may be less able to offer you the type of service you need. A small company may be adequate if you do not require a high degree of after-sale service, or if you are personally making the overseas buying trips and making all arrangements yourself.

5. Keep in Touch

Call, write, visit, and/or fax your suppliers on a regular basis. Out of sight should not translate to out of mind. Keeping your suppliers advised of your business requirements on a regular basis will help them to serve you better.

6. Make It Easy for Your Supplier to Succeed

Become an expert at developing product specifications that your supplier can understand, and cannot help but succeed in fulfilling. Don't use U.S. slang—it does not translate.

7. Create the Desired Impression

1. Dress according to the requirements of your business and purpose.

2. Always be punctual, even if others are not.

3. Learn at least 10 phrases in the local language, especially the customary greetings.

4. Communicate your knowledge and appreciation of their country and customs.

5. Accommodate the values of your suppliers without disregarding your own.

6. Always follow through on your agreements.

8. Useful Attitudes toward Negotiations

1. Don't approach a seller with overt suspicion.

2. The seller needs to make a profit to survive to serve you the next time.

3. Learn the local business customs beforehand. Example: In much of North Africa, it is expected that you shout during negotiations, whereas in Thailand shouting is seen as a sign of weakness. Also, raising your hands above your head is considered an act of aggression in Thailand. Buy a copies of Do's and Taboos Around the World and Gestures, both by Roger E. Axtell, John Wiley & Sons publisher.

4. Don't be in too much of a rush. Business is usually conducted at a slower pace overseas.

5. Remember that the best route to a given end result may not be the shortest or most direct.

6. Allow yourself the opportunity to work within the framework of another person's or country's business style.

7. Remember that you are on their turf now and have to play by their rules.

9. Understand the Seller's Attitudes and Position

1. How well established is the seller in the local marketplace?

2. Is the seller the new business with the right single product at the right time, or the established supplier with many products and services to offer?

3. What are the seller's attitudes toward foreigners (that means YOU!)?

4. Is the seller in need of cash?

5. Does the timing of the sale affect the seller? (Prices are often cheaper when buying from traditional Chinese as the Chinese New Year approaches. Reason? It is good luck to have all your bills paid going into the new year!)

6. Does the seller start with a high price or does he have a best-offer-take-it-or-leave-it attitude?

7. Is entertainment part of the negotiation package?

10. Questions to Ask Before Committing to a Supplier

1. Is this a one-shot deal?

2. Is this going to be part of an ongoing relationship?

3. Is this supplier concerned about my well being or just about getting the most out of this transaction?

4. Am I getting the best possible price?

5. What do I have to do to get better terms?

6. Is the supplier saying "Yes" to everything just to please me, or is he or she going to follow through?

7. Am I really getting the goods I require?

8. Am I getting the quality my customers require?

9. If this transaction were to go bad, how would it go bad?

10. Have I asked for an impossible delivery date which the supplier cannot possibly adhere to?

11. Is there any leeway I can give the supplier either now or later to make it easier for him or her to follow through?

12. Am I getting all the documentation I need for export formalities, and for U.S. import formalities?

InfoList #23
Supplier Checklist

Use this checklist to determine if you are working with the right supplier. If you answer "No" to very many of the questions below, it would be wise to continue your search for another supplier.

1. Has this supplier been in business long enough to know the business and be stable?

2. Have I received references concerning reliability and ethics?

3. Have I checked the references and found them to be good?

4. Does this person / company understand what I need?

5. Does the supplier understand my concept of quality?

6. Has the supplier been accommodating to our needs, and realistic in his or her promises?

7. Do I trust this person to follow through on the transaction as we have discussed it, and as it is in the contract?

8. Will the supplier make enough of a profit to service the account properly and want to do business with us in the future?

9. Is the supplier's plant properly equipped for production of the merchandise we are ordering?

10. Will this supplier be able to handle increases in production if the demand for the product increases?

11. Will this supplier let me know if there is a problem, or will he or she try and gloss over it until it becomes a disaster for me?

12. Is there someone at this place of business who is capable of properly handling the export and U.S. import documentation required?

13. Will this supplier be willing to work toward a solution when difficulties arise?

14. Am I dealing with this supplier because he or she is the right one for me, or because I cannot find any other?

15. Do I have a gut feeling that this is the right supplier for me?

InfoList #24
10 Tips for Negotiating

1. Don't let yourself get tied to having to do business with one supplier. Your attachment to a single deal will drive the price up, or keep it from coming down. Create the option for alternative opportunities even if you don't plan to use them.

2. Be prepared by knowing about the country-of-origin price structure as well as the U.S. price structure. Know how much you can afford to pay and still make an adequate margin of profit.

3. Price sheets usually serve as guidelines only. The quantity of an order, terms of payment, as well as personalities, will ultimately determine price.

4. Learn what the product costs your supplier. Although this may be impossible to find out precisely, you should be able to estimate it by knowing something about the material or component costs.

5. Does the supplier need money? It's hard to think of asking "Are you short of cash? If so, I'd like to make a ridiculously low offer for these goods!" This is something that you'll just have to sense from the seller's body language, the tone of the negotiations, the state and condition of the business and by asking the right questions.

6. Don't rush to fill conversational voids. If you make an offer that is low, just sit there. Don't squirm—let the others squirm. Many people give themselves away by making an offer, experiencing some silence, and then filling it by saying, "Well perhaps we could do better."

7. Get the seller to invest so much time in you that he or she would prefer to sell to you at a small profit than lose the sale to you and make no profit at all.

8. What might be considered unethical in our culture may be established business practice in others. Learn as much as you can about how business is conducted in the country you do business in and establish how you are going to respond to local practice.

9. Find two suppliers of the same goods. Remember that pricing is a matter of supply and demand. Let the suppliers know that you have alternatives. However, if you play one against the other be prepared to find that they are bosom buddies or for one to say "Fine! Buy it from the other supplier! I own that shop as well!"

10. Be prepared to walk away from a transaction if you cannot get what you need. This is perhaps the most difficult thing for some people to do. It is helpful to realize that very few opportunities are really the opportunity of a lifetime.

InfoList #25

10 Tips for Negotiating in a Long-Term Relationship

1. Look at the long-term consequences of any action you take with your supplier. Correct any errors that go against you, but also correct errors you find that go against your supplier.

2. Consider that if you make a tough deal today, taking advantage of your supplier's temporary weakness, it may come back to haunt you in the future, when your supplier may have the chance to get even.

3. Ask your supplier what he or she needs from you—besides money—to make the relationship run smoothly. Listen carefully and take careful note of the issues that come up. Many a supplier increases prices in subtle ways to compensate for problematic clients.

4. Establish what it is that you need in order to be successful. Differentiate between the window-dressing and your real issues. Let your supplier know what is important to you.

5. Negotiate a contract that gives you what you need in product and service and gives your supplier a fair price for supplying it. Consider the savings of not having to make as many trips to resolve problems, fewer defects, fewer missed shipment dates, etc.

6. Become friendly with your supplier. Be considerate of his or her family as well. In some cultures small gifts are appropriate. Although some prefer to keep everything on a business-only basis, you may find that having a personal relationship with your supplier will serve to cement the business relationship as well.

7. Consider negotiating for an exclusive supplier relationship, or perhaps an exclusive distributorship in your geographic area.

8. Actively look for ways in which you can support each other. Are there business opportunities you can share? Is there information you have that will help your supplier? Are you familiar with new equipment or manufacturing processes that will help your supplier? Do you have information about competitors that you can share?

9. Is it feasible or worthwhile for you to have an ownership position in the supplier company? Can you help by becoming a partner? Will such a relationship work over a period of time?

10. Keep lines of communication open with your supplier. Don't just communicate when you have an order and when you have a problem. Nearly every business has a fax machine. Send letters or short notes keeping them advised of your plans and progress. Think of your suppliers as partners in your business, who need to be kept current on what is going on.

InfoList #26

Business Meeting Pointers

1. Create a vision of what you want to accomplish as a result of the meeting.

2. Identify all the key components of what has to happen for the vision to become a reality.

3. Identify ahead of time all the objections, barriers, and problems the other side might have to your proposal or ideas.

4. Create a response to each possible objection.

5. Create a solution to each problem the other side might have with your proposal.

6. Learn enough about your counterpart on the other side of the bargaining table to be confident that you know how to reach him or her.

7. Put yourself in a positive mental state appropriate for the session.

8. Determine early on who has ultimate authority to set terms.

9. Don't be intimidated or overwhelmed by the seller's opening bravado. He or she is probably just as concerned about the outcome as you are.

10. Expect negative responses. Work around them by finding alternative solutions.

11. Learn how to operate in a context of no agreement.

12. Try not to put yourself in a position in which you have greater need to buy the commodity than the seller to sell it. The price you pay, given that position, will be higher. Establish alternative suppliers/deals.

13. Know what concessions you can and cannot make before the session starts.

14. Notice the seller's body language. Remember that body language means different things in different cultures.

15. Understand the seller's problems without taking them on as your own.

16. Be wary when your counterpart plays dumb.

17. Don't back the seller into a corner unless you really know what you are doing.

18. Don't brag. In most cultures bragging is a sign of weakness.

19. Be careful of the seller's pride. In some cultures, losing face is worse than losing money. Find a way to get a better price and terms without causing the seller to lose face.

20. Don't criticize the seller's merchandise if it doesn't meet your approval. Instead, explain that it is not right for your clients, that your clients will not buy it, or that your clientele cannot afford to pay the price, etc.

21. Speak clearly and don't use slang to communicate.

22. Don't become overly involved emotionally or agitated, unless it works for you.

23. Be prepared to walk away from any session if you can't get what you need.

24. Be prepared to back up your bluffs! If you don't mean it, don't say it.

25. Don't drink excessively.

26. Don't make phony promises.

27. Don't be belligerent.

28. Don't oppose the seller's belligerence. Just get out of the way of it, let it go by you.

29. Learn the seller's complete position.

30. Isolate problems when appropriate, group problems when appropriate.

31. Don't be impulsive. Impulsive decisions usually mean losing money.

32. Look for a variety of ways to give the seller what he wants without giving up what you need.

33. Be sure your tough questions are being answered, not side-stepped.

34. Verify statements that involve concessions.

35. Clarify all points made during the meeting by repeating the statement back to the others.

36. You can't insist on a delivery schedule based on a rate of production your supplier can't meet and expect no problems.

37. "No" does not always mean no.

38. "Yes" does not always mean yes.

39. It is always easier to get someone to say "Yes" than it is to get them to do what they said "Yes" to!

40. A contract is only as good as those who sign it.

InfoList #27
Tips for Attending Trade Fairs

Overseas trade fairs can be extremely effective for making face-to-face contacts and purchases, identifying suppliers, checking out competitors, and finding out how business really works in the host country. However, the cost of attending such fairs can be high. To maximize the return on your investment of time, money, and energy, you should be very clear about your goals for the trip and give yourself plenty of time for advance research and preparation.

You should also be aware of the limitations of trade fairs. The products on display probably do not represent the full range of goods available on the market. And while trade fairs give you an opportunity to make face-to-face contacts with many people, both exhibitors and buyers are rushed, which may make meaningful discussions and negotiations difficult.

Do Your Homework

Allow several months for preparation—more if you first need to identify the fair that you will attend. Even under ideal circumstances, you should begin laying the groundwork a year in advance. Don't forget that exhibiting at or attending a fair in a foreign country means more complex logistics: numerous faxes and phone calls involving you, the show operator, and local support people, plus customs and transportation delays.

Participating in international trade fairs should be considered a long-term investment. At domestic fairs, you may exhibit on a regular basis with short-term sales and marketing goals. But at foreign fairs, it is often best to participate to establish your company, make contacts for the future, and learn more about a market, its consumers, and products. New exporters may not generate high sales, but they often come away with information that assists them with future marketing and product development.

Selecting an Appropriate Trade Fair

Once you have identified some fairs, contact the organizers for literature and a show prospectus, attendee list, and exhibitor list. Ask lots of questions! Be sure not to neglect trade organizations in the host country, independent show-auditing firms, and attendees. Find out whether there are "must attend" fairs for your product group. Fairs that concentrate on other related, commodities might also be worthwhile. Be aware that there may be preferred seasons for trade in some products.

Your research needs to cover a number of points:

1. **Audience**
   Who is the intended audience? Is the fair open to the public or to trade professionals only? Are the exhibitors primarily foreigners looking for local buyers or locals looking for foreign buyers? (Many trade fairs are heavily weighted to one or the other.) Decide whether you are looking for an exposition of general merchandise produced in one region, a commodity-specific trade show, or both.

2. **Statistics**

    How many people attended the fair the last time it was held? What were the demographics? What volume of business was done? How many exhibitors were there? How big is the exhibition space? What was the ratio of foreign to domestic attendees and exhibitors?

3. **Specifics**

    Who are the major exhibitors? Are any particular publications or organizations associated with the fair? On what types of products does the fair focus? Does the fair have a theme that changes each time? How long has the fair been in existence? How often is it held? Is it always in the same location, or does it move around? How much does it cost to attend? Are there any separate or special programs connected with the event, and do they require additional fees? What does it cost to rent space?

Before You Go

1. If you have not already spoken with someone who has attended the fair, be sure to find someone who will give you advice, tips, and general information.

2. Make your reservations and travel arrangements well in advance, and figure out how you are going to get around once you get there. Even if the fair takes place in a large city, do not assume that getting around will be easy during a major trade fair. If the site is in a small city or a less-developed area, the transportation and accommodation systems are likely to become overburdened sooner than in metropolitan areas.

3. Will you need an interpreter for face-to-face negotiations? A translator to handle documents? Try to line up providers well in advance of your need for their services.

4. For printed materials, pay attention to language barriers and make preparations that will help you overcome them. Assess any literature and decide what should be available in translation or in bilingual editions. Have all translation work done by a true professional, particularly if technical terms are used. Consider having a bilingual business card, and add the country and international dialing code information to the address and telephone number. Find out from the show organizers which countries will be represented, and prepare information in the languages of those countries as well, if necessary.

5. Do you need hospitality suites and/or conference rooms? Reserve them as soon as you can.

6. Contact people you would like to meet before you go. Organize your appointments around the fair.

7. Familiarize yourself with the show's hours, locations (if exhibits and events are staged at multiple venues), and the schedule of events. Then prioritize.

While You Are There

1. Wear businesslike clothes that are comfortable. Find out what the norm is for the area and the season.

2. Immediately after each contact, write down as much information as you can. Do not depend on remem-

bering it. Several companies now make inexpensive portable business card scanners with optical character recognition (OCR) software to read the information into a contact management program.

3. Be sensitive to the selling styles of the country you are in. Are hard-sell approaches taboo? Are you dealing with the right person? Status within one's company is often very important; someone may want to be clear about your position, and you will want to be sure your aren't causing offense by going to the wrong level.

4. Consider arriving a day early to get fully oriented, confirm appointments, and rest up.

5. It's common sense: make sure you take breaks, even if you have to schedule them. You'll end up having far more energy and being more effective.

After the Fair

1. Within a week after the fair, write letters to new contacts and follow up on requests for literature. If you have press releases and questionnaires, send them out quickly.

2. Write a report evaluating your experiences while they are still fresh in your mind. Even if you don't have to prepare a formal report, spend some time organizing your thoughts on paper for future reference. Aim to quantify the results. Did you meet your goals? Why or why not? What would you do differently? What unforeseen costs or problems arose?

3. With your new contacts and your experiences in mind, start preparing for your next trade fair.

As a Buyer You Should . . .

1. Familiarize yourself with customs regulations on the products that you seek to purchase and import into your own country or elsewhere. Be sure to get such information on any and all products that you might be interested in.

2. Set specific goals for supplier leads and for gathering industry information. For example, target the numbers of contacts made, leads converted to purchases, seminars and presentations attended, and booths visited. Other goals might be cost-to-return benefit ratio, amount of competitor information gathered, and percentage of projected purchases actually made.

3. List all the products that you seek to purchase, their specifications, and the number of units you plan to purchase of each.

4. Know the retail and wholesale market prices for the goods in your home country and in the country where you will be buying. List the highest price you can afford to pay for each item and still get a worthwhile return.

5. List the established and probable suppliers for each of the products or product lines that you plan to import. Include addresses and telephone numbers and note your source for the information. Before you go, contact suppliers to confirm who will attend and to make appointments.

InfoList #28
Overseas Buying Trips

Why Go?

If you are an importer considering an overseas buying trip, the first question you should ask is "Why go at all?" Much overseas travel is unnecessary. It takes time away from business and personal pursuits at home, may be filled with uncertainty, and can cost thousands of dollars.

Consider doing international business by mail, by fax, or by telephone as an alternative to travel. Also, a number of countries have export promotion groups which are set up to help facilitate and even guarantee trade transactions.

Consider hiring an agent in the exporting country. You may be able to establish a relationship with a buyer's agent who will be able to find the products you need.

Tip: Be careful how you legally structure an agency relationship: you may be setting yourself up for liability you never expected. Refer to "Agency" on page 100.

Consider sending a subordinate who has manufacturing or marketing knowledge of the product. Such a person may be in a better position to know what to buy anyway.

The benefits of the trip should outweigh the costs by a substantial margin.

Establish Clear Objectives Before You Go

Establishing clear objectives for your trip abroad should be your top priority. Plan each trip so that a number of diverse purposes can be served at the same time. Establish primary and secondary goals before you go.

Some Objectives for Business Travel

1. To locate a source of supply impossible to find from the U.S.
2. To establish a personal rapport with suppliers and/or buying and shipping agents.
3. To solve problems with suppliers, agents, and/or foreign government officials in person.
4. To render technical expertise in person or on site.
5. To supervise or train overseas personnel in specialized manufacturing procedures or techniques.
6. To personally supervise the selection of merchandise.
7. To seek new suppliers of products.
8. To view new product lines first-hand.
9. To view competitive merchandise from a number of suppliers at trade fairs.
10. To obtain legal counsel in the country of origin, or to be present during a legal proceeding.
11. To negotiate contracts in person.
12. To research the folklore and culture surrounding imported products.
13. To research and become more familiar with the marketing system.
14. To mix business with personal travel or to mix personal travel with business.

InfoList #29
U.S. Passports

When Required

A U.S. citizen needs a passport to depart or enter the U.S. and to enter and depart most foreign countries. Exceptions include short-term travel between the U.S. and Mexico, Canada, and some countries in the Caribbean. Your travel agent, airline, or the nearest embassy or consulate of the country you are traveling to can tell you if you need a passport. Even if you are not required to have a passport to visit a country, U.S. Immigration requires you to prove your U.S. citizenship and identity when you reenter the U.S. Make certain that you take with you adequate documentation to pass through U.S. Immigration upon your return. A U.S. passport is the best proof of U.S. citizenship. Other documents to prove U.S. citizenship include an expired U.S. passport, a certified copy of your birth certificate, a Certificate of Naturalization, a Certificate of Citizenship, or a Report of Birth Abroad of a Citizen of the United States. To prove your identity, either a valid driver's license or a government identification card that includes a photo or a physical description is adequate.

Remember that if you need a visa, you must first obtain a passport, since visas cannot be processed without them. For more information, see "Visas" on page 43.

Beware of a passport that is about to expire. Some countries will not permit you to enter and will not place a visa in your passport if the remaining validity is less than six months. If you return to the U.S. with an expired passport, you are subject to a passport waiver fee of $100, payable to U.S. Immigration at the port of entry.

All persons must have their own passport. Since January 1981, family members are not permitted to be included in each other's passports.

The Secretary of State has the statutory authority to invalidate U.S. passports for travel to countries with which the United States is at war, where armed hostilities are in progress, or where there is imminent danger to the public health and physical safety of U.S. travelers. If you have any questions about these restrictions, contact the Department of State Office of Passport Policy and Advisory Services, 2401 E Street NW, Washington DC, 20522-0907. Tel: (202) 663-2662 and Fax: (202) 663-2654.

How to Apply

It takes anywhere from two to several weeks to obtain a passport. However, it is best to apply two months in advance. Applications are processed according to the departure date indicated on the application form. If you give no departure date, the passport agency will assume you are not planning any immediate travel. Your passport will be returned to you by mail at the address you provided on your application.

It is best to apply through one of the 5,000 Clerks of Court or Post Offices which accepts passport applications. Passport Agencies tend to have extremely long lines during the busiest months which results in longer waiting times for people applying in person at a passport agency. You can search (by state, state / city, or zip code) to find the location nearest you at http://iafdb.travel.state.gov.

For your first passport, you must appear in person with a completed form DSP-11, *Passport Application*, at one of the U.S. passport agencies (listed on page 42) or at one of the several thousand federal or state courts or U.S. post offices authorized to accept passport applications.

If you have had a previous passport and wish to obtain another, you may be eligible to apply by mail. See below for information on applying by mail.

What to Bring When You Apply

1. A properly completed, but unsigned, passport application (DSP-11). Do not sign it!

   This form is available online at http://www.travel.state.gov/passport_obtain.html, from passport agencies by mail, or may be picked up and completed in person at the agency as you apply. **Note:** Although a Social Security number is not required for issuance of a passport, Section 603E of the Internal Revenue Code of 1986 requires passport applicants to provide this information. Passport Services will provide this information to the Internal Revenue Service (IRS) routinely. Any applicant who fails to provide the information is subject to a $500 penalty enforced by the IRS. All questions on this matter should be referred to the nearest IRS office.

2. Proof of U.S. citizenship (a, b, or c):

   a. Use your previously issued passport. If you are applying for a first passport, or cannot submit a previous passport, you must submit other evidence of citizenship.

   b. If you were born in the U.S., you should produce a certified copy of your birth certificate (a certified copy will have a registrar's raised, embossed, impressed, or multicolored seal and the date the certificate was filed with the registrar's office). If you cannot obtain a birth certificate, submit a notice from a state registrar stating that no birth record exists, accompanied by the best secondary evidence possible. This may include a baptismal certificate, a hospital birth record, notarized affidavits of older relatives having personal knowledge of the facts of your birth, or other documentary evidence such as early census, school records, family Bible records, and newspaper files.

   c. If you were born abroad, you can use:
   - A Certificate of Naturalization
   - A Certificate of Citizenship
   - A Report of Birth Abroad of a Citizen of the United States of America (Form FS-240)
   - A Certification of Birth (Form FS-545 or DS-1350)

   If you do not have any of these documents and are a U.S. citizen, you should take all available proof of citizenship to the nearest U.S. passport agency and request assistance in proving your citizenship.

3. Proof of identity

   You must also establish your identity to the satisfaction of the person accepting your application. The following items are generally acceptable documents of identity if they contain your signature and if they readily identify you by physical description or photograph:
   - A previous U.S. passport
   - A certificate of naturalization or citizenship
   - A valid driver's license
   - A government or military identification card

   The following are not acceptable: social security card, learner's or temporary driver's license, credit card, temporary or expired identity card or document, any document that has been altered or changed in any manner

4. Two Photographs

   The photos must be recent (taken within the past six months), identical, 2x2 inches, and in either color or black and white. They must show a front view, full face, on a plain, light (white or off-white) background. (Vending machine photographs are not acceptable.)

5. The correct fee

   The fee for an adult's (18 years of age and older) first-time, 10 year passport is $65.00. This includes the $55.00 passport fee and the $10.00 execution fee. (The application fee for a passport by mail for adults is $55.00.) Check the link, http://www.travel.state.gov/passport_obtain.html for information about the methods of payment accepted.

Applying for a Passport by Mail

You may apply for your passport by mail if you already have a passport and it is undamaged, you still have the same name as in the passport (or you can legally document the change), it was issued within the past 15 years, and you were over 16 years old at the time it was issued. Note: If the passport has been mutilated, altered, or damaged in any manner, you cannot apply by mail. You must apply in person and use Form DSP-11, present evidence of U.S. citizenship, and acceptable identification.

Download a DSP-82 *Application For Passport By Mail* from the Department of State's Web site at the following link: http://www.travel.state.gov/passport_renewal.html. Fill it out, sign it, and date it. Attach to it:

a) Your most recent passport;

b) Two identical passport photographs (see previous section on passport photographs); and

c) A $55 fee. Make your check or money order payable to Passport Services. (The $10 execution fee is waived for those eligible to apply by mail.)

If your name has been changed, enclose the Court Order, Adoption Decree, Marriage Certificate, or Divorce Decree specifying another name for you to use. (Photocopies will not be accepted.) If your name has changed by any other means, you must apply in person.

Mail the completed DSP-82 application and attachments to the National Passport Center, P.O. Box 371971, Pittsburgh, PA 15250-7971. Your previous passport will be returned to you with your new passport.

If you need faster service, you can use an overnight delivery service. Go to the following link for more information: http://www.travel.state.gov/passport_expedite.html.

Obtaining a Passport Quickly

Passport agencies will expedite issuance of passports for an additional fee. A surcharge of $60 per passport (plus overnight delivery costs) is assessed for expedited service. The fee applies to expedited processing for all passport services, including issuance, amendment, extension of validity, and adding visa pages. Expedited passports will be processed within three business days of receipt by a Passport Agency, except when a passport must be denied or delayed. If the three-day processing deadline cannot be met, the expedite fee will be refunded. If desired, payment for overnight return of the issued passport should also be sent with the application.

Expedited processing is available only for travelers who are leaving in less than 10 days and can document their departure with plane tickets or confirmed reservations. Travelers who need to obtain foreign visas to depart within two to three weeks may also request expedited service. Expedited service is not available to travelers who cannot document their travel.

Travelers with very short deadlines may wish to apply directly at a Passport Agency. The New York Passport Agency handles *only* expedited applications on a scheduled appointment basis. However, many requests for expedited service can be handled by one of the 5,000 clerks of court and post offices which accept passport applications and forward them to Passport Services for issuance. If this option is selected, prepaid overnight delivery for each application is recommended both to and from the Passport Agency.

Expedited passport renewals by mail must include applicable passport fees, proof of imminent departure, $60 per passport, and overnight delivery costs. Mail applications to Passport Services - Lockbox, Attn: Passport Supervisor 371971, 500 Ross Street, Rm. 154-0670, Pittsburgh, PA 15262-0001; clearly mark the envelope "EXPEDITE." Mailed applications will be processed within three days of receipt at the National Passport Center.

If you are leaving on an emergency trip within five working days, apply in person at the nearest passport agency and present your tickets or travel itinerary from an airline, as well as the other required items. Or, apply at a court or post office and have the application sent to the passport agency through an overnight delivery service of your choice (you should include a self-addressed, prepaid envelope for the return of the passport). Be sure to include your dates of departure and travel plans on your application.

Additional Visa Pages

If you require additional visa pages before your passport expires, submit your passport to one of the passport agencies listed at the end of this section. If you travel frequently to countries that require visas, you may request a 48-page passport at the time you apply.

Change of Name

If you have changed your name, you will need to have your passport amended. Fill out Form DS-19, *Passport Amendment/Validation Application*, which is available online at http://www.travel.state.gov/name_change.html or any office that is authorized to accept passport applications. Submit the DS-19 along with proof of the name change (Court Order, Adoption Decree, Marriage Certificate, or Divorce Decree) to the nearest passport agency. There is no fee for this service. If your name has changed by any other means, you must apply in person.

You may send Form DS-19, the proof of the name change, and your current valid passport to the following address:
Charleston Passport Center
Attention: Amendments
1269 Holland Street
Charleston, South Carolina 29405

Altered or Mutilated Passport

If you mutilate or alter your U.S. passport in any way (other than changing the personal notification data), you may render it invalid, cause yourself much inconvenience, and expose yourself to possible prosecution under the law (22 US C 1543).

A passport that has been mutilated, altered, or damaged in any manner cannot be used for renewal by mail. You must apply in person and use Form DSP-11, present evidence of U.S. citizenship, and acceptable identification.

Loss or Theft of a U.S. Passport

Passport Services regards the loss of a passport as a serious matter. Lost or stolen passports can be, and are, used for fraudulent purposes. If your passport is lost or stolen in the U.S., report the loss or theft. Download Form DS-64 (http://www.travel.state.gov/report_ppt.html) and provide detailed answers to the questions. Sign and submit it to US Department of State, Passport Services, Consular Lost / Stolen Passport Section, 1111 19th Street, NW, Suite 500, Washington, DC 20036, or to the nearest passport agency. If you are abroad, report the loss immediately to local police authorities and contact the nearest U.S. embassy or consulate.

If you wish to obtain another passport, you must download Form DS-11 (http://www.travel.state.gov/report_ppt.html) and submit a detailed statement explaining the circumstances surrounding the loss or theft of the passport and stating what efforts have been made to recover it. Brief notations such as "lost," "stolen," or "burned" are not sufficient. You must fill out a Form DS-64, *Statement Regarding Lost or Stolen Passport*, or a statement containing the information requested on the DS-64. You will be required to complete a Form DS-11 in the prescribed manner, present acceptable identification, and submit two new photographs and the required fees. You should submit other acceptable evidence of citizenship in order to avoid delay in issuance of the replacement passport.

New York Passport Agency Telephone Appointment System

The New York Passport Agency only provides services by appointment for those traveling within 14 calendar days. Walk-in appointments are not available; instead, an automated telephone appointment system permits customers to schedule appointments for passports from their homes,

24 hours a day, seven days a week up to 10:00 a.m. on the day of departure.

For those customers eligible to use the appointment system, it can be reached from a touchtone telephone by dialing (212) 399-5290. Applicants will be prompted to provide the required information, including their social security number which they should have handy at the time of the call. Those without social security numbers will be instructed by the system on how to make an appointment.

Only those scheduled for appointments should come to the Passport Agency. Applications from customers without acceptable documentation cannot be processed; these customers will be required to reschedule their appointments by telephone. The appointment telephone line provides additional information for passport applicants.

National Passport Information Center

In 1996, the State Department awarded a contract to AT&T to establish the National Passport Information Center (NPIC) in Dover, New Hampshire. The NPIC was created because the U.S. passport agencies have been unable to keep up with public telephone inquiries, leaving a large number of customers dissatisfied. This is *not* a free service; callers are informed at the outset of their call as to the charge per minute. Both voice response units and live operators will be available for caller inquiries. The voice response units are available 24 hours a day, seven days a week and a live operator is available during business hours from Monday through Friday. The NPIC will answer inquiries in English, Spanish and via TDD.

To reach the National Passport Information Center, call (900) 225-5674. The hearing impaired may reach the NPIC via a TDD line at (900) 225-7778. The charge is 55¢ per minute for recorded information and $1.50 per minute for operator service. The charge will appear on your telephone bill. If you are calling from a telephone that blocks calls to 900 numbers, you may also reach the NPIC via a toll-free number and pay for the service with a credit card. The number for this is (888) 362-8668 (for the TDD, call (888) 498-3648). Callers will be charged a flat fee of $5.50 per call and must pay with a major credit card.

Passport Agencies

There are passport agencies in the following cities.

Boston Passport Agency
Thomas P. O'Neill Federal Bldg., Rm. 247
10 Causeway Street, Suite 247
Boston, MA 02222-1094
Tel: (617) 878-0900

Chicago Passport Agency
Kluczynski Federal Office Bldg.
230 South Dearborn Street, 18th Floor
Chicago, IL 60604-1564
Tel: (312) 341-6020

Connecticut Passport Agency
50 Washington Street
Norwalk, CT 06854
Tel: (203) 299-5443

Honolulu Passport Agency
Prince Kuhio Federal Building
300 Ala Moana Blvd.
Suite 1-330
Honolulu, HI 96850
Tel: (808) 522-8283

Houston Passport Agency
Mickey Leland Federal Bldg.
1919 Smith Street
Suite 1400
Houston, TX 77002-8049
Tel: (713) 751-0294

Los Angeles Passport Agency
Federal Building
11000 Wilshire Blvd.
Suite 1000
Los Angeles, CA 90024-3615
Tel: (310) 575-5700

Miami Passport Agency
Claude Pepper Federal Office Bldg., 3rd Floor
51 Southwest First Avenue
Miami, FL 33130-1680
Tel: (305) 539-3600

New Orleans Passport Agency
One Canal Place (corner of Canal and North Peters Streets)
365 Canal Street, Suite 1300
New Orleans, LA 70130-6508
Tel: (504) 412-2600

New York Passport Agency
376 Hudson Street
New York, NY 10014
Tel: (212) 206-3500

Philadelphia Passport Agency
U.S. Custom House
200 Chestnut St., Room 103
Philadelphia, PA 19106-2970
Tel: (215) 418-5937

San Francisco Passport Agency
95 Hawthorne Street
5th Floor
San Francisco, CA 94105-3901
Tel: (415) 538-2700

Seattle Passport Agency
Henry Jackson Federal Office Bldg.
915 Second Avenue
Suite 992
Seattle, WA 98174-1091
Tel: (206) 808-5700

Washington Passport Agency
1111 19th Street NW
Washington, DC 20524
Tel: (202) 647-0518

InfoList #30
Visas

A visa is an endorsement or stamp placed in your passport by a foreign government that permits you to visit that country for a specified purpose and a limited time—for example, a three-month tourist visa. In most case you must obtain visas before you leave the U.S.; you may not be able to obtain visas for some countries once you have departed. Apply directly to the embassy or nearest consulate of each country you plan to visit, or consult a travel agent. U.S. passport agencies cannot help you obtain visas. Refer to "Visas and Work Permits" on page 92 for more information.

Foreign Entry Requirements

The U.S. Department of State Bureau of Consular Affairs publishes *Foreign Entry Requirements* annually (Department of State Publication 10331), which details visa-related information for travelers going to different countries. It is available from the Consumer Information Center, Pueblo, CO 81009, or it may be accessed through the Internet on the Consular Affair's Web site (http://travel.state.gov). However, it is advisable to verify the latest visa requirements with the embassy or consulate of each country you plan to visit.

Because a visa is stamped directly onto a blank page in your passport, you will need to give your passport to an official of each foreign embassy or consulate. You will also need to fill out a form, and you may need one or more photographs. Many visas require a fee. The process may take several weeks for each visa, so apply well in advance of your trip, especially if you need to apply for visas to visit several different countries.

Tourist Card

If the country you plan to visit only requires a tourist card, you can obtain one from the country's embassy or consulate. In some cases you may be able to obtain one from the airline serving the country or from your travel agent. Be sure to confirm the procedure before you show up at the airport.

However, a tourist card or tourist visa will not give you the right to conduct business in the country. Consult with the embassy or consulate for requirements for conducting business.

Proof of Citizenship

Check with the embassy or consulate of each country you plan to visit to learn what proof of citizenship is required of visitors. Even if a country does not require a visitor to have a passport, it will require some proof of citizenship and identity. Also remember that no matter what proof of citizenship a foreign country requires, U.S. Immigration has strict requirements for your reentry to the U.S.

InfoList #31
State Department Travel Information

The U. S. Department of State issues Consular Information Sheets, Travel Warnings, and Public Announcements to inform travelers of conditions abroad. Consular Information Sheets are available for every country of the world. They include such information as locations of the U.S. Embassy and any Consulates in the subject country, unusual immigration practices, health conditions, minor political disturbances, unusual currency or entry regulations, crime and security information, and drug penalties. Consular Information Sheets present information in a factual manner so the traveler can make his or her own decisions concerning travel to a particular country.

Countries where avoidance of travel is recommended will have Travel Warnings as well as Consular Information Sheets. Public Announcements are issued as a means to disseminate information quickly about terrorist threats and other relatively short-term conditions overseas which pose significant risks to the security of American travelers.

Consular Information Sheets, Travel Warnings, and Public Announcements are available on the U.S. Department of State's Web site, http://travel.state.gov.

How to Access Consular Information Sheets and Travel Warnings

By Telephone or Fax.   Consular Information Sheets and Travel Warnings may be heard anytime by calling Overseas Citizens Services at (202) 647-5225 or 888-407-4747 (toll free) from a touchtone phone. The recording is updated as new information becomes available. They are also available via Consular Affairs' automated fax system at (202) 647-3000.

By Internet.   Consular Affairs provides Consular Information Sheets, Travel Warnings, and Public Announcements on the Internet. Go directly to the link, http://travel.state.gov/travel_warnings.html. Select the first letter of the country for which you are looking for the information; select the name of the country from the list.

The same information is also available on the Consular Affairs Bulletin Board (CABB). Dial (301) 946-4400 on your modem. The login is travel and the password is info. Other popular online services such as CompuServe, Dialog, and Dow Jones may also provide access.

In U.S. Government Offices.   Consular Information Sheets and Travel Warnings are available at any of the regional passport agencies, field offices of the U.S. Department of Commerce, and U.S. embassies and consulates abroad, or by writing and sending a self-addressed, stamped envelope to the Overseas Citizens Cervices, Bureau of Consular Affairs, Room 4811, N.W., U.S. Department of State, Washington DC, 20520-4818.

Through Your Travel Agent.   The reservations systems used by travel agents provide access to State Department travel information.

InfoList #32
Health Regulations for International Travel

Immunization

Under international health regulations adopted by the World Health Organization, a country may require international certificates of vaccination against yellow fever and cholera as a condition of entry. Typhoid vaccinations are not required for international travel, but are recommended for areas where there is risk of exposure. Smallpox vaccinations are no longer given. Check your healthcare records to insure that your measles, mumps, rubella, polio, diphtheria, tetanus, and pertusis immunizations are up-to-date. Medication to deter malaria and other preventative measures are advisable for certain areas. No immunizations are needed to return to the United States.

Information on immunization requirements, U.S. Public Health Service recommendations, and other health hints are included in the annual publication *Health Information for International Travel* (stock #017-023-00192-2), available for $6.50 from the Superintendent of Documents, U.S. Government Printing Office, Washington DC, 20402-9325, order line (202) 783-3238. You may also obtain such information from local and state health departments or physicians. This information is also available on the 24-hour International Travelers Hotline at the Centers for Disease Control: (404) 332-4559 or through the CDC's Web site on the Internet at http://www.cdc.gov/.

It is not necessary to be vaccinated against a disease you will not be exposed to and few countries will refuse to admit you if you arrive without the necessary vaccinations. Officials will either vaccinate you, give you a medical follow-up card, or, in rare circumstances, put you in isolation for the incubation period of the disease you were not vaccinated against. Check requirements before you depart.

If vaccinations are required, they must be recorded on approved forms, such as those in the booklet PHS-731, *International Certificate of Vaccination.* If your doctor or public health office does not have this booklet, it can be obtained from the Superintendent of Documents, U.S. Government Printing Office, Washington DC, 20402-9325, order line (202) 783-3238 or from any Government Printing Office bookstore. It must be signed by a licensed physician or by a person designated to sign the certificate. Keep it with your passport.

HIV Testing Requirements

Some countries require visitors to produce certification that they are free of the human immunodeficiency virus (HIV). Most often these regulations apply to applicants for residence or work permits, but they may apply to any visitors, or for some categories of temporary visitors. Many countries accept U.S. tests, but you may be required to be tested on arrival. Check with the embassy or consulate of the countries you will visit for the latest information, as these requirements have been changing rapidly.

InfoList #33
U.S. Currency Declaration Regulations

It is not illegal to transport monetary instruments across the U.S. border, and there is no limit to the amount you may bring into or take out of the country. However, if you transport, attempt to transport, or cause to be transported (including by mail or other means) more than $10,000 in monetary instruments on any occasion into or out of the United States, you must file a report (Customs Form 4790) with Customs.

Monetary instruments include U.S. or foreign coin in current circulation, currency, traveler's checks, money orders, and negotiable instruments, or investments securities in bearer form.

Reporting is required under the Currency and Foreign Transactions Reporting Act (Public Law 97-258, 31 USC 1101 et seq.), as amended. Failure to comply can result in civil and criminal penalties and may lead to forfeiture of the monetary instruments.

If you have questions, contact a Customs Management Center or U.S. Customs and Border Protection, 1300 Pennsylvania Avenue NW, Washington DC, 20229, www.customs.treas.gov.

InfoList #34
The Female Traveler

Business Strategies

1. Prepare in advance what to expect, not only in terms of business, but attitude of the local culture towards women.

2. Behave and dress conservatively; it is your first and basic step toward gaining respect.

3. Anticipate equality issues as they will likely surface.

4. Maintain a sense of humor. A foreign country has many oddities, your presence possibly being one of them. Relieve some of the stress with a humorous outlook.

5. Brush off sexual innuendos and comments about appearance and carry on with the business at hand. Keep a cultural outlook on such remarks. If a member of the other delegation becomes a problem or nuisance, take him aside and inform him that it makes you uncomfortable, or tell another member of his delegation to put a stop to it.

6. Exhibit tolerance and understanding for the other culture. Questions about your marital status and family may prove ubiquitous as it interests people how things work for you.

7. If you are a team leader, prepare your delegation in advance to treat you in a matter-of-fact, supportive fashion. A reaction from a delegation unaccustomed to working with females in authority may be derailed a bit if they observe your role is nothing but routine.

8. Generational attitude differences may exist towards women. Prepare to adjust to them.

9. Professional behavior, a respect for local traditions, and an in-demand service or product will assist you as a businesswoman.

Health Issues

Traveling involves extra stress and health concerns to consider. Change of diet, time zone, and living conditions will take up an enormous amount of physical reserve. Women should consider taking extra vitamin, mineral, and food supplements to ensure optimum physical health. Since many travelers avoid meat in developing countries, supplements are further encouraged. Other points to consider:

1. Expect to experience irregular menstrual cycles or none at all due to jet lag, stress, and new and irregular eating and sleeping habits.

2. Bring any female hygiene products that you use at home, i.e.: tampons, pads, medication, prescriptions, etc. as they may not be readily available at your destination.

3. Birth control pills may not work properly if you experience stomach upset or diarrhea. If you vomit within three hours of digesting a pill, take another to ensure proper protection.

4. Yeast infections become more problematic in hot, humid climates. Stick to cotton undergarments and clothing that is loose fitting to allow maximum air flow to your body. Nylons and tight pants may also induce yeast infections. Come prepared with medication.

5. Carry the telephone number or e-mail of your gynecologist at home in case you have urgent questions. Try and steer clear of gynecological examinations in developing countries due to hygienic conditions.

Helpful Resources

1. **Advancing Women**
   Web: www.advancingwomen.com

2. **Canasian Businesswomen's Network**
   Email: cabninfo@apfc.apfnet.org

3. **The International Alliance (TIA)**
   Email: info@t-i-a.com

4. **Organization of Women in International Trade (OWIT)**
   Web: www.owit.org

5. **Women in Technology International (WITI)**
   Web: www.witi.org/Center/Offices/About
   Email: info@witi.org

6. **Women's Institute of Management (WIMNET)**
   Web: www.jaring.my/wimnet

7. **Working Woman**
   Web: www.workingwoman.com

General Safety Tips

1. Prearrange transportation for your arrival. In many countries, hagglers and touts will approach you at the airport offering transportation options. If you have none, decline and find the transportation booth in the airport; or, if possible, befriend someone on your flight with whom you might share a cab.

2. If you are being dropped off in an unlit area, ask your driver to wait until you are safely inside. Women should avoid traveling alone at night.

3. Find out from your hotel staff where it is safe to go alone and what areas merit avoiding.

4. If you plan on meeting with a stranger, do it in a busy place outside of your hotel.

5. If you encounter someone gesturing or honking for you to stop, do not stop until you have found a busy public place with plenty of lighting before determining the problem.

6. If you find yourself on a crowded bus, subway, or train with a male pressing up against you in an obviously sexual way, try embarrassing him by shouting in English. Public shame or humiliation will often keep further advances at bay.

7. Try and look for other women to sit near on public transport. If you feel uncomfortable in any situation, get out of it.

Hotel Safety Tips

1. Ask for a room on the second floor or higher and near the center of the hallway corridor away from fire exits where would-be assaulter can lurk and escape with more ease.

2. Don't feel shy about asking to see your room before deciding to take it.

3. Do not let anyone except the front desk clerk see or overhear the number of your room.

4. Do not show your room key in public, and keep it under tight security.

5. Avoid stairwells, an easy place for assaulters to hide, and don't travel in elevators alone with male strangers about whom your instincts send you a warning bell. If a stranger is wandering the halls when you plan to enter or exit your room, wait until he leaves. If he doesn't, report him to the front desk.

6. Do not open the door for anyone who knocks whom you do not expect. Use the peephole. Call the front desk if necessary to verify the presence of any hotel staff wishing to enter.

7. When leaving the room, put out the "do not disturb" sign, and leave the TV on if you wish to deter possible thieves.

8. Pack a flashlight should the lights suddenly go out.

9. Take the business card of your hotel before going out in case you get lost. Do not give out the name of your hotel unless absolutely necessary, and do not share with anyone that you are alone. Use your creativity and make up a story if you must.

10. Always lock the door when you are inside the room. A portable extra door-locking device may prove a prudent pre-trip purchase. A rubber door stopper is also an easy item to pack

InfoList #35

Pre-Trip Product Planning

Planning your overseas buying trip (especially the first time around) can be more difficult and time-consuming than the trip itself. In a sense, it should be. Thorough pre-departure planning should make the trip itself a matter of simply following through on well-made plans.

The following lists and comments are designed to assist in the planning of an overseas venture. Remember that time spent here in the U.S. is cheaper than time spent overseas. Calculate overseas time as three to 10 times more expensive. Thorough pre-planning makes good sense.

Product and Market

1. List all the products you seek to purchase.

2. List your established and highly probable customers for each product or product line you plan to import.

3. Establish and list, in detail, the product specifications for each item you seek to purchase. If the specifications are more subjective than objective, create some method of conveying the subjective quality to your product sheet.

4. List the quantities of each item you plan to purchase, with the number presold in parentheses and the number prepaid in double brackets. Example: bamboo living room sets 150 (64) ((15)), i.e. you want to purchase 150 sets of furniture, 64 have been ordered or presold, of which 15 have been prepaid.

5. List the "no later than" delivery dates for presold or ordered merchandise. For example, 100 units, November 15th. If you have standing orders, note the quantity requirements over time. For example, 65 units per month for six months.

6. Know and list the seasonality of each product you seek to purchase. Research and list customer seasonality requirements for each product. Research shipping time from point of origin to your customer. List latest dates for shipment from the country of origin.

7. Calculate the approximate shipping weight and volume required per unit of merchandise. This will enable you to know your shipping requirements for the merchandise.

8. Calculate (through use of a shipping agent or overseas freight forwarder) the shipping charges for various quantities of your commodity.

9. Know about U.S. Customs and Border Protection prohibitions or restrictions on the commodities you seek to purchase and import, including quotas. (Refer to the U.S. Customs section, beginning on page 193, for general information and to the Commodity Index section, beginning on page 423, for specific information on the commodity you seek to import; also contact a customs broker.)

10. List U.S. Customs and Border Protection packing, shipping, and labeling requirements, if any, for your commodity. (Refer to "Country of Origin Marking" on page 251, "Special Marking Requirements" on

page 253, and "Packing of Goods and Commingling" on page 208 for more information.)

11. Know and list required U.S. Customs documentation for the importation of your product or commodities. (Refer to "Entry Procedures and Documentation" on page 293 and the Commodity Index section of this manual relevant to your product for specific documents required. Also speak to a customs broker about required documentation.)

12. Know about the U.S. Customs classification procedure for your product or commodity. There may be several potential classifications for your commodity, each of which may be subject to substantially different rates of duty. There may also be classifications with lower duty rates which can be satisfied with only minor alterations of your imported product. (Refer to "Classification—Liquidation" on page 244.)

13. Know the duties and tariffs which apply to your commodities. (Refer to a customs broker, U.S. Customs and Border Protection, the Commodity Index of this manual for "Sample Duty Rates," or the Harmonized Tariff Schedules of the United States (HTSUS), available at most major city libraries, or from the U.S. Government Printing Office in Washington, DC)

14. Know the retail/wholesale market prices for the goods in the U.S.

15. Know and list the maximum prices you can afford to pay and still get a worthwhile rate of return on your time and investment.

16. Analyze as thoroughly as possible the likelihood of being able to successfully import the commodity.

Potential Suppliers

1. For each potential supplier, list the name, address, telephone, fax, telex number, and products.

2. List the source of the recommendation for each potential supplier.

3. Write letters to suppliers telling them that you plan to be in their country on certain dates.

   Refer to "Letters and E-mails of Request" on page 32 to learn how to structure a letter of request.

4. Follow up on any references that the potential supplier has provided.

5. Get financial statements and references if possible. (Your banker may be able to help.)

6. Obtain and take notes on samples/specifications/catalog photos.

7. Collect price sheets.

8. Outline the sales and delivery terms of each supplier.

9. Note any guarantees or warranties on the products.

10. Sketch out an itinerary of which potential suppliers you plan to visit and in what sequence.

InfoList #36
Conducting Country Research

The scope of your analysis of the country in which you plan to travel will be determined by:

- The type of products you seek to purchase;
- The length of time to be spent in the country;
- The purpose and importance of the visit;
- The services you are likely to require; and
- The degree of your involvement.

Use the following list as a guideline for your country research. Information can be obtained from your public library, travel books, travel agents, airlines, international banks, chambers of commerce, consulates, embassies, the export trade ministries of exporting countries, the U.S. Department of Commerce, and many sources.

1. General Information
a. Business holidays
b. Business hours
c. Local time zones
d. Weather conditions
e. Clothing required
f. Electrical requirements for travel appliances
g. Weights and measures
h. Credit cards honored
i. Postal system
   1) Services available
   2) Reliability
   3) Rates
   4) Special cautions
j. Telephone system
   1) Availability
   2) Quality of service/reliability
      • Domestic
      • International
   3) How to get the best rates
   4) Procedure of use
      • Signals
      • Coins required
   5) Availability of "White & Yellow" Pages
   6) Fax machines
      • Availability
      • Use protocols
k. Telex
   1) Availability
   2) Nature of service/reliability
      • Domestic
      • International
   3) Rates
   4) Procedure of use
   5) Cautions
   6) Credit facilities
l. Banking facilities
   1) Local banks
   2) Your U.S. bank correspondent branch

2. Demographic and Economic Factors

a. Population of country
b. Major cities
c. Population of major cities
d. Median age of population
e. Percentage of population in work force
f. Salary of different types of workers
g. Standard of living
h. Major commercial centers
i. Major banking/financial centers
j. Major manufacturing/product centers
k. Major agricultural regions
l. Major ports
m. Major airports
n. Natural resources
o. Imports
p. Exports
q. Balance of payments
r. Gross national product/gross domestic product
s. Per capita income

3. Monetary Issues

a. Name of currency
b. Units of currency
c. Present exchange rate
d. History of exchange rate
e. Expected fluctuations (see your banker)
f. Recent devaluations
g. Exchange rate government fixed versus free floating
h. Discrepancies between "official" and free market exchange rates
i. History of inflation

4. Travel Requirements

a. Visa requirements (ask consulate or travel agent)
b. Immunization requirements (ask travel agent)
c. Onward ticket requirements (ask travel agent)
d. Minimum financial requirements to enter country (ask consulate or travel agent)
e. Police report required (some countries require proof of your good character—ask at consulate)

5. Business Practices, Services, and Facilities

a. Local business attitudes, etiquette, and practices
b. Degree of business formality
c. Acceptable dress (for your type of business)
d. Attitudes towards U.S. citizens
e. Procedure for appointing an agent
f. Special buying/selling seasons
g. Methods of business communication
h. Usual firmness of price/delivery quotations

i. Usual method of payment
j. Usual credit terms
k. Methods of debt collection
l. Patent and trademark protection
m. Banking services available
n. Local negotiation practices
o. Use of contracts
p. Contract enforcement
q. Settling of contract disputes
r. Use of arbitration
s. Local business services available
   1) Secretarial services
   2) Copy services
   3) Translation services
   4) Interpreter services
t. Importance of appointments; required timing: weeks, days, or hours ahead
u. Importance of letters of introduction and from whom
v. Business cards in local language
w. Strength of local trade organizations
x. Political sensitivity of your commodities
y. Duty free ports
z. Free trade zones
aa. Packing facilities
bb. Warehouse facilities
cc. Processing facilities
dd. Port facilities

6. Country-of-Origin Export Controls for Your Commodity

a. Restrictions and prohibitions
b. Documentation
c. Inspection
d. Licensing
e. Export quotas/visas (especially textiles)

7. Language

a. Language of the people
b. Language of business
c. Learn at least 10 phrases in local language
d. Availability of interpreters
e. Availability of translators

InfoList #37
Travel Phone Numbers and Web sites

International Airlines

Airlines of the Web
  http://w0.itn.net/airlines

4Airlines.com
  http://www.4airlines.com

AerLingus (Ireland) ....(800) 474-7424
  http://www.aerlingus.ie

Aeroflot (Russia)...........................(888) 340-6400
  http://www.aeroflot.com

Aerolineas Argentinas ....(800) 333-0276
  http://www.aerolineas.com.ar

Aeromexico ....(800) 237-6639
  http://www.aeromexico.com

Air Afrique ....(900) 659-7000
  http://www.airafrique-airlines.com

Air Canada ....(800) 247-2262
  http://www.aircanada.ca

Air France.......................................(800) 237-2747
  http://www.airfrance.com

Air India...(800) 223-2250
  http://www.airindia.com

Air Jamaica ....(800) 523-5585
  http://www.airjamaica.com

Air New Zealand...........................(800) 262-1234
  http://www.airnz.com

Alaska Airlines..............................(800)252-7522
  http://www.alaska-air.com

Alitalia (Italy)................................(800) 223-5730
  http://www.alitalia.it

All Nippon Airways (Japan)........(800) 235-9262
  http://www.ana.co.jp

American Airlines ....(800) 433-7300
  http://www.aa.com/

Asiana Airlines (South Korea)...................(800) 227-4262
  http://flyasiana.com/index.htm

Austrian Airlines ....(800) 843-0002
  http://www.aua.at/aua

Avianca Airlines (Colombia)......................(800) 284-2622

Bahamas Air ....(800) 222-4262
  http://www.bahamasair.com

British Airways..............................(800) 247-9297
  http://www.british-airways.com

Cathay Pacific Airways (Hong Kong).......(800) 233-2742
  http://www.cathay-usa.com

China Airlines (Taiwan) ....(800) 227-5118
  http://www.china-airlines.com

Continental Airlines......................(800) 525-0280
  http://www.continental.com

Czech Airlines................................(800) 223-2365
  http://www.csa.cz

Delta Airlines ....(800) 221-1212
  http://www.delta-air.com

Egyptair ....(800) 334-6787
  http://www.egyptair.com

El Al Israel Airlines ....(800) 223-6700
  http://www.elal.co.il

Ethiopian Airlines (Eastern USA) ....(800) 445-2733
  http://www.ethiopianairlines.com

EVA Airways (Taiwan)..................(800) 695-1188

Finnair ....(800) 950-5000
  http://www.finnair.fi

Garuda Indonesia ....(800) 342-7832

Gulf Air (Bahrain).........................(800) 553-2824

Hawaiian Airlines..........................(800) 367-5320

Iberia Airlines (Spain)...................(800) 772-4642
  http://www.iberia.com

Icelandair ....(800) 223-5500
  http://www.icelandair.com

Japan Airlines.................................(800) 525-3663
  http://www.jal.co.jp

KLM Royal Dutch Airlines...........(800) 374-7747
  http://www.klm.nl

Korean Air ....(800) 438-5000
  http://www.koreanair.com

Lan Chile Airlines..........................(800) 735-5526
  http://www.lanchile.com/index2.html

LOT Polish Airlines.......................(800) 223-0593
  http://www.lot.com

Lufthansa (Germany).....................(800) 645-3880
  http://www.lufthansa.com

Mexicana Airlines ....(800) 531-7921
  http://www.mexicana.com/

Northwest Airlines ....(800) 225-2525
  http://www.nwa.com

Philippine Airlines.........................(800) 435-9725
  http://www.philippineair.com

Qantas Airlines (Australia) ....(800) 227-4500
  http://www.qantas.com

Royal Air Maroc.............................(800) 292-0081

SAS Scandinavian Airline Systems............(800) 221-2350
  http://www.sas.se

Saudia Arabian Airlines...............(800) 472-8342

Singapore Airlines ....(800) 742-3333
  http://www.singaporeair.com/

South African Airways...................(800) 722-9675
  http://www.saa.co.za

Taca International Airlines (Mexico)..........(800) 535-8780
  www.grupotaca.com/ing/index.html

TAP Air Portugal ....(800) 221-7370
  http://www.tap.pt

Thai Airways ....(800) 426-5204
  http://www.thaiair.com

United Airlines...............................(800) 241-6522
  http://www.ual.com

USAir..(800) 428-4322
  http://www.usair.com

VARIG Brazilian Airways.............(800) 468-2744
  http://www.varig.com.br/english

International Car Rental Reservations

Alamo...(800) 327-9633

Avis International ....(800) 331-1084
  http://www.avis.com

Budget ....(800) 527-0700

Dollar...(800) 800-4000

Dollar Rent a Car ....(800) 800-6000

Hertz International.........................(800) 654-3001
  http://www.hertz.com

National..(800) 227-3876
   http://www.nationalcar.com
Payless...(800) 237-2804
   http://www.paylesscar.com
Thrifty..(800) 367-2277
   http://www.thrifty.com

International Hotel Reservations

Choice...................................(800) 4-CHOICE (424-6423)
   http://www.hotelchoice.com
Forte..(800) 225-5843
   http://www.forte-hotels.com
Four Seasons..(800) 332-3442
Hilton International...............(800) HILTONS (445-8667)
   http://www.hilton.com
Holiday Inn..(800) 465-4329
   http://www.holiday-inn.com
Hyatt...(800) 233-1234
   http://www.hyatt.com
Inter-Continental...(800) 327-0200
   http://www.intercontinental.com
Kempinski..(800) 426-3135
Leading Hotels of the World.....................(800) 223-6800
Marriott..(800) 228-9290
   http://www.marriott.com
Nikko..(800) 645-5687
Novotel...(800) 221-4542
   http://www.novotel.com
Omni.....................................(800) THE-OMNI (843-6664)
Preferred Hotels & Resorts........................(800) 323-7500
Regent International....................................(800) 545-4000
Renaissance...(800) 228-9898
Sheraton...(800) 325-3535
   http://www.sheraton.com
Westin Hotels...(800) 228-3000
   http://www.westin.com

InfoList #38
What Time Is It in . . .?

Use the chart below to determine what time it is in any of the listed countries. Use Column 1 as your reference if you live in the Eastern Time Zone (such as New York or Miami), or Column 2 as your reference if you live in the Pacific Time Zone (such as San Francisco or Los Angeles). Add or subtract the number of hours shown from your own time to find the time elsewhere.

Example: If you live in New York and want to find the time in France, note that Column 1 for France says +6, which means it is 6 hours later. When it is noon in New York, it is 6:00 PM in Paris. If you live in Los Angeles and want to find the time in Hong Kong, note that Column 2 for Hong Kong says +16, which means it is 16 hours later. When it is noon in Los Angeles, it is 4:00 AM the next day in Hong Kong.

The time differences shown are based on Standard Time, and may require adjustment if either you or the country you are looking up are following Daylight Savings Time (DST). Most of the United States is in DST from the first Sunday in April until the last Sunday in October. Many, but not all, countries north of the Tropic of Cancer also use daylight time during a similar period. Daylight time is not used in most tropical areas. Countries in the southern hemisphere that follow a daylight savings time (for example, Chile and parts of Australia) use it during their summertime, often from mid-October through mid-March. The dates vary considerably from country to country and even from year to year. If you are in daylight savings and the county you are calling is not, *subtract* one more hour.

A double dagger (††) following the name of a country indicates that its territory falls into more than one time zone. If most the major cities fall into one zone, only that information is given. If major cities fall into more than one zone, several representative cities or regions are given.

	Column 1 N.Y. (EST)	Column 2 L.A. (PST)
Afghanistan	+ 9-1/2	+12-1/2
Albania	+6	+9
Algeria	+6	+9
American Samoa	-6	-3
Angola	+6	+9
Antigua & Barbuda	+1	+4
Argentina††	+2	+5
Armenia	+9	+12
Aruba	+1	+4
Australia††		
Aust. Capital Territory	+15	+18
South Australia	+14-1/2	+18-1/2
New South Wales	+15	+18
Northern Territory	+14-1/2	+18-1/2
Queensland	+15	+18
Victoria	+15	+18
Western Australia	+13	+16
Austria	+6	+9
Azerbaijan	+9	+12
Bahamas	0	+3
Bahrain	+8	+11

	Column 1 N.Y. (EST)	Column 2 L.A. (PST)		Column 1 N.Y. (EST)	Column 2 L.A. (PST)
Bangladesh	+11	+14	Guatemala	-1	+2
Barbados	+1	+4	Guinea	+5	+8
Belarus	+7	+10	Guyana	+1	+4
Belgium	+6	+9	Haiti	0	+3
Belize	-1	+2	Honduras	-1	+2
Benin	+6	+9	Hong Kong	+13	+16
Bermuda	+1	+4	Hungary	+6	+9
Bolivia	+1	+4	Iceland	+5	+8
Bosnia–Herzegovina	+6	+9	India	+10-1/2	+13-1/2
Botswana	+7	+10	Indonesia††	+12	+15
Brazil††			Iran	+8-1/2	+11-1/2
Eastern Brazil	+2	+5	Iraq	+8	+11
Western Brazil	+1	+4	Ireland	+5	+8
Brunei	+13	+16	Israel	+7	+10
Bulgaria	+7	+10	Italy	+6	+9
Burundi	+7	+10	Ivory Coast	+5	+8
Cameroon	+6	+9	Jamaica	0	+3
Canada††			Japan	+14	+17
Newfoundland	+1-1/2	+4-1/2	Jordan	+7	+10
Atlantic Zone	+1	+4	Kampuchea (Cambodia)	+12	+15
Eastern Zone (incl. Montreal,			Kazakhstan	+11	+14
Ottawa, Toronto)	0	+3	Kenya	+8	+11
Central (incl. Winnipeg)	-1	+2	Korea	+14	+17
Mountain (incl. Calgary)	-2	+1	Kuwait	+8	+11
Pacific (incl. Vancouver)	-3	0	Kyrgyz Republic	+10	+13
Cape Verde Islands	+4	+7	Laos	+12	+15
Cayman Islands	0	+3	Latvia	+7	+10
Central African Rep.	+6	+9	Lebanon	+7	+10
Chad	+6	+9	Lesotho	+7	+10
Chile	+1	+4	Liberia	+5	+8
China	+13	+16	Libya	+7	+10
Colombia	0	+3	Liechtenstein	+6	+9
Congo	+6	+9	Lithuania	+7	+10
Costa Rica	-1	+2	Luxembourg	+6	+9
Croatia	+6	+9	Macau	+13	+16
Cuba	0	+3	Macedonia	+6	+9
Cyprus	+7	+10	Madagascar	+8	+11
Czech Republic	+6	+9	Malawi	+7	+10
Denmark	+6	+9	Malaysia	+13	+16
Djibouti	+8	+11	Maldives	+10	+13
Dominica	+1	+4	Malta	+6	+9
Dominican Republic	+1	+4	Mauritania	+5	+8
Ecuador	0	+3	Mauritius	+9	+12
Egypt	+7	+10	Mexico††		
El Salvador	-1	+2	Most of Mexico, incl. Mexico City, Guadalajara,		
Equatorial Guinea	+6	+9	and Monterrey	-1	+2
Estonia	+7	+10	BCN, incl. Tijuana	-3	0
Ethiopia	+8	+11	Nayarit, Sinaloa, Sonora	-2	+1
Fiji	+17	+20	Moldova	+7	+10
Finland	+7	+10	Monaco	+6	+9
France	+6	+9	Mongolia	+13	+16
Gabon	+6	+9	Morocco	+5	+8
Gambia	+5	+8	Mozambique	+7	+10
Georgia	+8	+11	Myanmar (Burma)	+11-1/2	+14-1/2
Germany	+6	+9	Namibia	+7	+10
Ghana	+5	+8	Nepal	+10-3/4	+13-3/4
Greece	+7	+10	Netherlands	+6	+9
Greenland††	+2	+5	Netherlands Antilles	+1	+4
Grenada	+1	+4	New Zealand	+17	+20
Guam	+15	+18	Nicaragua	-1	+2

	Column 1 N.Y. (EST)	Column 2 L.A. (PST)
Niger Republic	+6	+9
Nigeria	+6	+9
Norway	+6	+9
Oman	+9	+12
Pakistan	+10	+13
Panama	0	+3
Papua New Guinea	+15	+18
Paraguay	+1	+4
Peru	0	+3
Philippines	+13	+16
Poland	+7	+10
Portugal	+5	+8
Puerto Rico	+1	+4
Qatar	+8	+11
Romania	+7	+10
Russia†† (*Note:* Russia covers 11 time zones.)		
Moscow	+8	+11
Novosibirsk	+12	+15
St. Petersburg	+8	+11
Rwanda	+7	+10
St. Kitts	+1	+4
St. Lucia	+1	+4
Saudi Arabia	+8	+11
Senegal	+5	+8
Serbia & Montenegro	+6	+9
Sierra Leone	+5	+8
Singapore	+13	+16
Slovakia	+6	+9
Slovenia	+6	+9
South Africa	+7	+10
Spain	+6	+9
Sri Lanka	+10-1/2	+13-1/2
Suriname	+2	+5
Swaziland	+7	+10
Sweden	+6	+9
Switzerland	+6	+9
Syria	+8	+11
Taiwan	+13	+16
Tajikistan	+10	+13
Tanzania	+8	+11
Thailand	+12	+15
Togo	+5	+8
Trinidad & Tobago	+1	+4
Tunisia	+6	+9
Turkey	+7	+10
Turkmenistan	+10	+13
Turks & Caicos Islands	0	+3
Uganda	+8	+11
Ukraine	+7	+10
United Arab Emirates	+9	+12
United Kingdom	+5	+8
Uzbekistan	+10	+13
Virgin Islands	+1	+4
Uruguay	+2	+5
Venezuela	+1	+4
Vietnam	+12	+15
Western Samoa	-6	-3
Yemen	+8	+11
Zaire††	+6	+9
Zimbabwe	+7	+10

InfoList #39
Personal Travel

Travel Agents

If you plan to do a lot of international travel, you may want to establish an ongoing relationship with a good travel agent. Avoid agents who specialize in pleasure travel because they will be less attuned to your needs than will an experienced business travel agent.

Travel agents receive a commission paid by airlines and hotels. Usually there will be no added cost to you for using their services. Agents can:

1. Research and book transportation and accommodations;

2. Advise on visas, immunizations, etc.;

3. Answer many varied questions related to overseas travel;

4. Assist in locating sources of information; and

5. Modify your itinerary as required.

Travel Plans Online

The best place to research an upcoming trip is the internet. Air fares, lodging and hotel information, car rentals, and specials are advertised online. Here are a few Web sites you may want to investigate:
www.expedia.com
www.orbitz.com
www.travelocity.com
www.priceline.com
www.travel.com

Air Transport from the U.S.

Air transport is the fastest and usually the least expensive means of international travel. In one day or less you can travel to almost any major capital of the world.

For many years the U.S. and other governments regulated the airline industry to insure passenger safety and often the financial stability of airlines. The association which acts for the international airline industry is "IATA" (International Air Transport Association). In conjunction with various governments, the airline industry has fixed prices on most routes. Prices used to be the same, no matter what airline you used. The only option for a reduced price was with charter companies.

Charters

The best deals on airfares are with charters offering special fares without restrictions on a first-come basis. Travel agents often do not suggest charters because of their relative unreliability and lower commission structure.

Charter flights leave from major U.S. cities and go almost everywhere. Sometimes the best opportunity is a charter to a major regional city such as Frankfurt or Hong Kong where you can get connections to other cities.

Some airline companies sponsor their own package charters. Look carefully at the package offered. A low air fare may be a loss leader offset by high cost ground packages for hotel, etc.

Charters almost always have specific departure and return dates, so be sure you can conduct your business in the time allotted. Some include hotel accommodations and can offer very attractive deals. Others include stays in several foreign capitals, such as Hong Kong, Taipei, Seoul, and Manila. Be sure to research the options and choose what is most appropriate for you.

To find an inexpensive charter:

1. Ask your travel agent;

2. Research other agents by telephone and the Internet;

3. Read the Sunday travel supplement of a major city paper (especially in a port city);

4. Find a travel agent in a neighborhood which has a large ethnic population of the country you plan to visit. There is a high likelihood that such agents will know of special charters to accommodate their local clientele;

5. Fly local "bush" airlines in foreign countries which have less expensive fares, but may require a more "adventuresome" individual who is willing to put up with some discomforts along the way. Be aware that some such operations have deplorable safety records.

Inter-European airfares are universally more expensive per kilometer than those for the same distance in the U.S. Sometimes they are cheaper if you purchase a ticket with a European company such as Air France or British Airways while they are offering a special. Check the internet for cheap flights and specials.

Warning

There have been occasions when airlines or companies that sell charter flights or tour packages have gone out of business with little warning, stranding passengers overseas. If you know from the media or from your travel agent that an airline is in financial difficulty, ask your travel agent or airline what recourse you would have if the airline ceased to operate. Some airlines may honor the tickets of a defunct airline, but they usually do so with restrictions.

Before you purchase a charter flight or tour package, read the contract carefully. Unless it guarantees they will deliver services promised or give a full refund, consider purchasing trip insurance. If you are unsure of the reputation of a charter company or tour operator, consult your local Better Business Bureau, or the American Society of Travel Agents at 1101 King Street, Suite 200, Alexandria, VA 22314, Tel (703) 739-2782, to learn if the company has a complaint record.

Ocean Transport

In the fast-paced world of international business, ocean transport as a means of getting to your destination has become less and less viable. It takes longer and costs more, unless you work your way across as a crewmember (which has also become more difficult in recent years).

The attractions of traveling by ocean liner are simple: time to plan strategy, recuperate, and rest. Ocean travel is also best for those who do not like to fly. Travel by ship may also be the most reasonable way to return to the U.S. with an automobile purchased overseas. Consider the extra time spent on the way over as buying-strategy planning

time and the way back as selling-strategy planning time, away from intense pressures. You will also not be subject to the jet lag of air transport.

Travel by Train

Rail transport overseas (especially in Europe) is more highly developed and relied upon than it is in the U.S. Fewer people overseas have access to automobiles and gasoline prices are significantly higher so governments have made great efforts to develop this efficient form of public inter-city transportation.

For short distances, air travel is often more trouble than it is worth—a false economy in time and expenditure. If the distances are not great, it may even take more time to get to an airport, wait, fly, and get from the airport to the destination than it does to take the train the whole distance. Furthermore, taking the train from city to city will give you time to relax and absorb what you have learned from your trip. Travel by train gives you the opportunity to see the countryside and is an infinitely better environment for meeting people than is traveling by air.

Some rail networks have unlimited 15-30-60-180 day use passes (e.g. Eurail Pass) which can be helpful if you plan a heavy schedule of travel in a short period of time. While they were actually designed for the student and tourist, business people can make use of them as well.

Tip: Be sure to research local train travel rules for each country. In Spain, for example, you must present a boarding card to enter the train, even if you have a Eurail Pass. Consult your travel agent for information and advice.

Buses

Buses are rarely a pleasant means of transport while overseas. More often than not they are extremely crowded, dirty, run on erratic schedules, and are difficult for someone unfamiliar with language to get around on. Do not expect to find many local equivalents of Greyhound in foreign countries (Europe excepted).

Taxis

Taxi services are usually well developed in most countries and provide excellent door-to-door service within a city. Some tips:

1. Be sure the meter is on and working, or settle on a price before you start out.

2. Ask at your hotel about appropriate tips if any.

3. Ask your travel agent beforehand about distances between airport and city, and best means of transport.

4. Have someone at the hotel write the name and address of your destination in the local language for you to show the taxi driver.

Automobile Travel

Driving or renting an automobile can be an excellent alternative to public transportation in a number of instances.

Advantages of Renting an Automobile

1. Freedom to come and go as you wish.

2. You will always have a place to lock things up (get an auto with locking trunk).

3. Useful for getting to out-of-the way places.

4. Useful for transporting small amounts of goods.

Notes About Renting an Automobile

1. Rentals require valid international or state drivers license (consult with travel agent or AAA) and often a valid major credit card or substantial cash deposits.

2. Additional fees may be required for mandatory insurance.

3. In some countries the safe driving condition of the rental car is your responsibility.

4. Rental cars are available in most countries, but for a wide range of prices.

Driver's License

If you intend to drive overseas, check with the embassy or consulate of the countries you will visit to learn their driver's license, road permit, and auto insurance requirements. If possible, obtain road maps before you go.

Many countries do not recognize a U.S. driver's license. Most, however, accept an international driver's permit. Before departure, obtain one at a local office of an automobile association. You must be at least age 18, and you will need two passport-size photographs and your valid U.S. license. Certain countries require road permits instead of tolls to use their divided highways and will fine drivers without a permit.

Auto Insurance

Car rental agencies overseas usually provide auto insurance, but in some countries, the required coverage is minimal. A good rule of thumb when renting a car overseas is to purchase insurance coverage that is at least equivalent to that which you carry at home.

In general, your U.S. auto insurance does not cover you abroad. However, your policy may apply when you drive to countries that border the United States. Check with your insurer to see if your policy covers you in Canada, Mexico, or countries south of Mexico. Even if your policy is valid in one of these countries, it may not meet its minimum requirements. If you are under-insured for a country, auto insurance can usually be purchased on either side of the border.

InfoList #40
Accommodations

1. Many travelers wait until they reach their destination before making hotel reservations. However, you may be tired and unfamiliar with your surroundings on arrival and could have difficulty locating a hotel to meet your needs. Therefore, no matter what type of hotel you stay in, try to make confirmed reservations beforehand.

2. Be sure to research and know the busy or peak seasons in the cities you will be visiting. You may find it impossible to find hotel space for those seasons unless you book accommodations far in advance.

3. Ask your travel agent, consult a travel guide, or look in *The Global Road Warrior, 5th Edition* about customary tipping for each country you visit.

4. Be sure to know when the latest check-in time is—don't lose your reservation because of a delay.

5. Confirm reservations for lodging as you progress along on your trip from city to city.

6. Some train stations and airports have travel desks to assist you in finding lodging.

7. It is always best to have a hotel reservation for at least the first night you arrive in a foreign city.

8. Stay in a hotel appropriate for your type of business or mission overseas.

9. Try to arrange for commercial rates (business discounts of 5-40%) before you leave the U.S. A simple e-mail or letter of request to the hotel management, stating that your company plans to use their hotel over a period of time may be sufficient.

10. Ask for commercial rates at the registration desk. You will be surprised how many times they will give it to you.

11. Most hotels have safe deposit boxes you can use for your valuables. Be careful, though. There have been reports of abuses involving hotel staff with access to both keys to the safe deposit box.

12. In a high rise hotel, always check the fire escape route.

13. If you are concerned about the hazard of fire in a high rise hotel, ask for a room on the first five stories of the hotel.

14. Do not leave valuables in plain sight in your hotel room. If the hotel does not have a safe and if you cannot take things with you, lock them into your suitcase. This will not prevent theft of your entire suitcase, but will keep housekeepers from pilfering what is openly available.

InfoList #41
13 Ways to Cut Travel Costs

1. Fly charter planes in coach class.
2. Find a package tour that fits your needs, even if it was designed for tourists.
3. Travel off-season to save on transportation and lodging costs.
4. Stay at small hotels or pensions outside of the commercial districts of cities. Do not stay at the international hotels.
5. When registering at hotels show business card and request commercial rate (after asking what the regular rate is).
6. Eat where the locals eat. Don't eat American-style meals, especially breakfast. Eat only when hungry.
7. Pay for your travel using credit cards that give you bonus miles toward free flights.
8. Take public transportation whenever possible.
9. Eat and drink nonimported food and liquor.
10. Smoke local cigarettes. Better yet, don't smoke at all.
11. Don't over-tip or double-tip. Many restaurants include a service charge in the bill.
12. Seek out discounts and bonuses offered to tourists, especially package deals.
13. For an extended stay, rent a house or an apartment.

InfoList #42
Managing Your Absence

1. If appropriate, give power of attorney to your attorney, accountant, business associate, or family member before you leave. Refer to "Power of Attorney" on page 100.
2. Pay existing bills and prepay bills that will come due during your absence, especially telephone, utilities, and payable-upon-presentation bills such as American Express and Diners Club.
3. Notify police, post office, and newspaper delivery services of your absence. Have all deliveries stopped.
4. Leave your itinerary with several people in your organization and/or family.
5. Leave a list of credit cards, travelers checks, passport information, and suitcase combination lock numbers with someone accessible by telephone in the U.S.
6. Make sure employees have enough work to keep busy during your absence.
7. Notify all those individuals who rely upon you or who should know of your whereabouts at all times.
8. Put valuables in a safe deposit box.

InfoList #43
Packing for Personal Travel

1. Travel light.
2. Quality molded suitcases will last longer and are worth the money, especially if you plan to travel frequently.
3. Leave enough room for articles purchased overseas and brought back with you. Consider packing a foldable canvas bag in your other baggage to handle the overflow on the way home.
4. If your suitcases use keys, be sure to keep one set on your person and another in your briefcase.
5. Pack any sharp items such as tweezers or scissors in luggage to be checked in, not in your carry-on luggage.
5. Pack clothing that is appropriate for the climate and your business.
6. Pack leisure clothing appropriate for the trip.
7. Be sure your medical kit is appropriate for the destination:
    a. Prescriptions to be filled while travelling
    b. Vitamins
    c. Prescription drugs
    d. Anti-diarrhea pills
    e. Anti-malarial pills
    f. Extra eyeglasses
    g. Extra pair of contact lenses plus accessories
    h. Water purification tablets
    i. Medical bracelet if appropriate
8. Documents:
    a. Passport
    b. International health certificate
    c. Visas
    d. Driver's license/international driver's license
    e. Travelers checks and personal checks
    f. Credit cards
    g. Extra passport photos
    h. Refund locations for travelers checks
    i. Travelers check numbers
    j. Birth certificate (if necessary)
    k. Address book (leave photo copy at home!)
    l. Letters of introductions from bank, businesses, local police, government official, etc.
    m. Tickets and vouchers
    n. Business cards
    o. Business brochures (if applicable)

InfoList #44

Documentation for Medications

Carry Your Prescription With You

If you have any preexisting medical problems and travel abroad, be sure to carry a letter from your doctor describing your condition and information on any prescription medicines you must take. You should also have the generic names of the drugs. Leave medicines in their original, labeled containers which should make Customs processing easier. A doctor's certificate may not suffice as authorization to bring all prescription drugs into all foreign countries. Travelers have been arrested for drug violations when carrying items not considered to be narcotics in the United States. To ensure you do not violate the drug laws of the countries you visit, consult the embassy or consulate of those countries for precise information before leaving the United States if you have any doubts regarding the status of your medication.

Medical Alert Bracelets

If you have allergies, reactions to certain medicines, or other unique medical problems, consider wearing a medical alert bracelet or carrying a similar warning.

Several private organizations provide listings of physicians to international travelers. Membership in these organizations is generally free, although a donation may he requested. Membership entitles the traveler to a number of traveler's medical aids, including a directory of physicians with their overseas locations, telephone numbers and doctors' fee schedules. The physicians are generally English-speaking and provide medical assistance 24 hours a day. The addresses of these medical organizations are in travel magazines or may be available from your travel agent.

InfoList #45

U.S. Customs Pre-Registration

Foreign-made personal articles taken abroad are subject to duty and tax on your return unless you have proof of prior possession such as a receipt, bill of sale, an insurance policy, or a jeweler's appraisal. If you do not have proof of prior possession, items such as foreign-made watches, cameras, or tape recorders that can be identified by serial number or permanent markings may be taken to the Customs office nearest you or at the port of departure for registration before departing the United States. The certificate of registration provided can expedite free entry of these items when you return.

InfoList #46

Handling Money Overseas

1. Before you leave the U.S. purchase US $50 to $200 worth of the local currency from your bank or a local foreign exchange-service such as Thomas Cook.

2. Purchase internationally recognized traveler's checks in a number of different denominations before you leave. Many banks will waive the 1% service charge for established customers. AAA (auto club) also waives traveler's checks fees for its members.

3. Be sure to keep the traveler's check purchase receipt (with check serial numbers) separate from the checks. Leave a copy of the receipt at your office in the U.S. as well.

4. Purchase traveler's checks in foreign currency denominations if you think the dollar is about to go down — or if you don't want to be at the mercy of the money changers overseas.

5. Be sure your credit cards are valid. Keep a copy of all your credit card numbers in another part of your luggage and with an associate, relative, or friend in the U.S. in case you need to report lost or stolen cards. American Express, Visa, and MasterCard are accepted almost everywhere in the world.

6. Banks in many countries now have automated teller machines (ATMs). Be sure to bring a credit or bank card that has a wide range of use.

7. There is little reason to carry large amounts of cash anymore. Travelers checks, access to cash machines, payment by credit card, etc. have made it possible to travel with relatively small amounts of cash.

8. Bring U.S. cash in larger denominations if you know you can get a better exchange rate or a better purchase price for cash in the country of destination. However, this is not recommended for the faint of heart. The risks are great. Other than the obvious risk of theft, currency exchange controls of the country may prohibit such a transaction. Also note #10 below.

9. Be sure to comply with U.S. Currency Export reporting rules for amounts of U.S. $10,000 or more in any monetary instrument. Contact Customs for details.

10. Money belts are good, but thieves are so familiar with them that they may ask for your belt after asking for your wallet and watch! The new way to hide your money is in a money pouch that secures to your ankle or around your waist inside your clothes. Check out different models of both at a good luggage store.

11. Note that a great deal of counterfeit U.S. currency in $100s, $50s, and $20s is being passed overseas. The advent of the color copier and more sophisticated off-set lithography techniques has made this possible. Look carefully at any stack of bills that you are given. It is very easy to miss seeing a counterfeit $100 in a stack of twenty bills.

InfoList #47
As You Travel

Leaving the U.S.

1. Register personal items of foreign origin, such as camera, watch, etc., with U.S. Customs to avoid paying duty upon your return. It is best to carry U.S. receipts for these items with you just in case you need to prove that you bought them in the U.S.
2. Forward currency declaration forms to U.S. Customs if required.
3. Know where you will be staying.
4. Confirm flight and accommodations.
5. Know your arrival time.
6. Pre-plan transfer from airport to hotel.
7. Notify your potential suppliers of your arrival ahead of time. They may arrange to pick you up at the airport.
8. Have appointments already set up for the first few days after your arrival.

Managing Your Arrival

1. Plan on delays for health control, passport control, and customs clearance.
2. Be sure you are not carrying amounts of cigarettes, liquor, currency, or other items in excess of the specified travel allowance for the country in question.
3. Remember that certain countries ban items they find objectionable, such as obscene or seditious literature, or, in Islamic countries, alcohol.
4. Call your hotel to confirm reservations immediately after clearing customs, especially if your flight is late.
5. Complete a police registration card in countries that require one.
6. Register with the U.S. Embassy or Consulate if you expect to be in the country for some time or in countries where there is civil unrest.
7. After notifying any important parties of your arrival, sleep—or at least rest—to overcome effects of jet lag.
8. Immediately obtain a local map.
9. Immediately obtain local guide books to the country.

Expense Accounting and Receipts

1. Keep receipts of purchases so you can document your Customs declaration when you return to the U.S.
2. Account for all monies spent in the course of your business activities to make the job of expense accounting easier once you get back home.
3. Make sure your receipts indicate the type of currency.

InfoList #48
22 Health Suggestions

1. Don't eat food from street vendors.
2. Don't eat any raw foods except for fruit and vegetables you peel yourself.
3. Don't eat seafood away from the ocean.
4. Don't eat shellfish.
5. Eat in international hotel restaurants.
6. Don't eat unwashed food.
7. Eat only freshly cooked food.
8. Inspect the kitchen first, if possible. Draw your own conclusions!
9. Yogurt, cheeses, and fully cooked eggs are usually OK.
10. Don't drink tap water.
11. Drink bottled waters, soft drinks, hot tea, coffee, boiled milk, or bottled beer or wine; avoid hard liquor.
12. If you need to drink tap water, first let visible junk settle, skim off the top, boil for 10 minutes. Or, use chlorine or tincture of iodine. Aerate for taste.
13. Be careful of ice cubes—they are rarely made from purified water.
14. Drinking out of the bottle with a straw is usually better than drinking out of a glass that may have been rinsed in bad water.
15. Wear medical alert bracelets or other identification if you have a medical condition.
16. Always carry a supply of any needed prescription drug to last longer than your expected stay overseas.
17. Do not try to save money by avoiding medical attention.
18. All but the worst hotels will be able to refer you to a doctor.
19. Most large hotels will have a nurse or nurse practitioner on staff.
20. Do not undergo surgery overseas unless it is absolutely necessary.
21. Carry basic nausea as well as "turista" (diarrhea) medicine.
22. To find a competent doctor, consult
    a. International hotel
    b. U.S. Embassy
    c. U.S. consulates
    d. U.S. military base
    e. Recommendations from resident U.S. expatriates.

InfoList #49
13 Tips for Travel Safety

1. Before leaving the U.S., obtain a U.S. Department of State Consular Information Sheet for each country you plan to visit, and any Travel Warnings which may have been issued. Consular Information Sheets and Travel Warnings may be heard anytime by calling Overseas Citizens Services at (202) 647-5225 from a touchtone phone. Refer to "State Department Travel Information" on page 43 for information on other means of accessing the information.

2. Call the U.S. embassy or consular office upon arrival in a foreign country and ask if there are any special public safety or health hazards in the country you are visiting. Are U.S. citizens disliked or resented locally?

3. Be conservative in your dress and manners. Consider that you may be wearing watches, jewelry, and clothing worth 10 years' earnings to a local laborer. Don't flaunt your wealth. You could lose it, along with your life.

4. Leave your expensive and flashy jewelry at home. If you must take it with you, cover it up in public and display it only at appropriate social events. Leave it in the hotel safe when it is not in use.

5. Ask at the hotel about safety issues. Is it safe to walk certain streets by day? Safe by night? What are the safe areas? What are the dangerous areas?

6. Don't carry large amounts of cash on your person. Modern banking, credit cards, travelers checks, and other payment mechanisms make carrying substantial amounts of cash obsolete and risky.

7. Remember that when you are in a foreign country you are subject to local laws, not U.S. laws. It may be illegal to do things which are not illegal at home. By world standards the U.S. is a permissive society. Foreign laws are much tougher in many areas.

8. Know where you are going. Those who appear confused and indecisive are prime targets for con artists and muggers. The best protection against getting mugged is often an upright and purposeful posture.

9. Don't let your possessions out of your sight.

10. Use a money belt or money pouch which attaches to your ankle.

11. Beware of pickpockets in crowd situations.

12. It you use a shoulder bag, keep it on the side away from the street and hold it with your hand. Robbers on motorbikes grab bags as they speed by.

13. Travel with a small combination padlock in underdeveloped countries. It will come in handy.

InfoList #50
What to Do in Case of . . .

Loss of Passport
Your passport is your most important travel document. Keep it with you, or better yet leave it in the hotel safe and carry a photocopy of the relevant pages. If it is lost or stolen, report the loss immediately to the nearest U.S. Embassy or Consulate. You will need to apply for a new passport or travel document in person. You will need evidence of U.S. citizenship, two passport-sized photos, the application fee, a police report of the theft (if available), and an explanation of how it was lost or stolen. If you have no evidence of U.S. citizenship, the application process will be more complicated, but personnel will still be able to help you. A photocopy of the stolen passport is extremely helpful in these circumstances.

Loss of Credit Cards
Immediately call each of the issuing card companies and report the loss. Keep a list of the credit cards you carry and the emergency telephone numbers for reporting losses, separate from your credit cards. Register all your credit cards with an agency that notifies all credit card issuers in the case of a loss. Contact your issuing credit card company for details.

Major credit card issuers, especially American Express and large U.S. banks such as Bank of America, Citibank, etc. will be able to issue you a new card and a cash advance within a day or two.

Loss of All Funds
If your loss of funds does not include loss of your credit cards, go to a bank and ask for a cash advance.

If you don't have credit cards, or have lost them as well, call a relative or friend in the U.S. and ask that they send a bank wire transfer to you at a local bank.

If you have no credit cards, no checks, and no friends in the U.S. who can send money, and if you can't work something out with one of your suppliers in the country, go to the U.S. embassy or consulate. They are not authorized to advance funds to you, but they will help you with options.

Loss of Tickets
Loss of airline tickets is very problematic. Depending upon the type of ticket you have (had) you may not be able to get a replacement ticket at all. Start by immediately contacting the airline or other carrier. Don't wait until departure time to report the loss. You may be given a replacement, but don't count on it. You will probably have to buy a replacement ticket and file a lost ticket claim upon your return to the U.S. If you have a good relationship with your travel agent in the U.S., try calling them for help in getting things sorted out.

If the airline cannot or will not help you and if you have lost everything else as well (money, credit cards, etc.), go to the U.S. embassy or consulate. They may be able to supply you with a ticket home. (You do have to reimburse them!)

Illness

Don't wait until you are really sick. Call the U.S. Embassy or Consulate, or go to the reception desk of a good hotel, even if you are not registered there. Ask for the name of a doctor that speaks English, or simply a doctor they recommend that can help with the particular problem you have.

Political Unrest

Do your best to stay out of civil unrest in the countries you visit. Participating in demonstrations is asking for trouble. Your participation is about as welcome as would be a third party intervention in a dispute you are having with your spouse back home!

In the case of serious political unrest, it is best to know how to get out quickly. Americans have been used as pawns in political disputes they have nothing to do with. What happened to U.S. citizens in Iraq just as the Gulf War was breaking out provides a case in point.

Getting Arrested

Through any means possible, get word to the U.S. Embassy or Consulate that you have been arrested. Don't sign anything. U.S. federal law forbids a consular officer from acting as your legal representative. However, such officials can help get word to friends or relatives in the U.S. who can help.

Beyond notifying U.S. authorities there are two mutually exclusive strategies you could employ: Remain calm. Do not get huffy, telling your captors that they can't do this to you because you are a U.S. citizen. (The fact is, they can, and they have!) On the other hand, it may be tactically advantageous to get extremely huffy, express your outrage, argue with the arresting authorities, tell them you are a U.S. citizen and they will be in big trouble for having arrested you (however, NEVER physically touch a captor). You will have to decide based on your situation.

Auto Accident

When renting an automobile, make sure that you have complete insurance coverage. It is possible that your U.S. policy will cover some part of the insurance on a rental car in a foreign country. It is unlikely that it will cover everything, and it may not be in force at all outside the U.S. (For example, you will need separate coverage to drive in Mexico.)

Be sure to keep a copy of your insurance documents with you. You may need to present them to authorities before they will release you from the scene of an accident.

1. Check for injuries and call for medical assistance.
2. Ask for proof of driver's name and owner's name of the other vehicle.
3. Note the driver's license number and registration number of the other vehicle.
4. Note the number of people in the other vehicle, their approximate ages and genders.
5. Sketch the accident scene, take photos if possible.
6. Get the names of witnesses if possible.
7. Call the insurance carrier to report the accident.
8. Don't sign any document that might admit fault.
9. If the accident is serious, it is best to call the closest U.S. consulate or embassy.

InfoList #51
Help from U.S. Consuls Abroad

The Overseas Citizens Services

Overseas Citizens Services (OCS) in the State Department's Bureau of Consular Affairs is responsible for the welfare and whereabouts of U.S. citizens traveling and residing abroad. OCS has three offices: American Citizens Services and Crisis Management, the Office of Children's Issues and the Office of Policy Review and Interagency Liaison.

American Citizens Services and Crisis Management corresponds organizationally to American Citizens Services offices set up at U.S. embassies and consulates throughout the world. ACS has six geographical divisions with case officers who assist in all matters involving protective services for Americans abroad, including arrests, death cases, financial or medical emergencies, and welfare and whereabouts inquiries. The office also issues Travel Warnings and Consular Information Sheets and provides guidance on nationality and citizenship determination, document issuance, judicial and notarial services, estates and property claims, third-country representation, and disaster assistance.

The Office of Children's Issues (CI) formulates, develops and coordinates policies and programs, and provides direction to foreign service posts on international parental child abduction and international adoptions. It also fulfills U.S. treaty obligations relating to the abduction of children.

The Office of Policy Review and Interagency Liaison (PRI) provides guidance concerning the administration and enforcement of laws on U.S. citizenship, and on the documentation of Americans traveling and residing abroad. The Office also provides advice on matters involving treaties and agreements, legislative matters, including implementation of new laws, conducts reconsiderations of acquisition and loss of U.S. citizenship in complex cases abroad, and administers the overseas federal benefits program.

OCS is open Monday-Friday, 8:15 a.m. to 5:00 p.m. Eastern time. The OCS toll-free hotline at 1-888-407-4747 is available from 8:00 a.m. to 8:00 p.m. Eastern time, Monday-Friday, except U.S. federal holidays. Callers who are unable to use toll-free numbers, such as those calling from overseas, may obtain information and assistance during these hours by calling 317-472-2328. For after-hour emergencies, call (202) 647-5226. The Office of Children's Issues can be reached by calling (202) 736-7000. Visit the State Department's Web site, www.travel.state.gov, for more information.

When to Register with the U.S. Embassy

When you are traveling abroad, register at the Consular Section of the nearest U.S. embassy or consulate if:

- You find yourself in a country or area that is experiencing civil unrest, has an unstable political climate, or is undergoing a natural disaster, such as an earthquake or hurricane.

- You plan to go to a country where there are no U.S. officials. In such cases, register in an adjacent country, leave an itinerary, and ask about conditions in the country you will visit and what third country may represent U.S. interests there.

- You plan to stay in a country for longer than one month.

Registration makes your presence and whereabouts known in case it is necessary for a consular employee to contact you in an emergency. During a disaster overseas, U.S. consular officers offer assistance to U.S. nationals and can even assist in evacuation should that becomes necessary. However, they cannot help you if they can't find you. Registration also makes it easier to apply for a replacement passport if yours is lost or stolen.

If you are traveling with an escorted tour to areas experiencing political uncertainty or other problems, find out if registration is being taken care of by your tour operator. If it is not, or if you are traveling on your own, leave a copy of your itinerary at the nearest U.S. embassy or consulate soon after arrival.

What U.S. Consuls Can Do

U.S. consular officers are located at U.S. embassies and consulates in most countries overseas. They are available to advise and help you if you are in any serious trouble.

Arrests Abroad. The rights an American enjoys in this country do not travel abroad. Each country is sovereign and its laws apply to everyone who enters regardless of nationality. The U.S. government cannot get Americans released from foreign jails. However, a U.S. consul will insist on prompt access to an arrested American, provide a list of attorneys, and provide information on the host country's legal system, offer to contact the arrested Americans family or friends, visit on a regular basis, protest mistreatment, monitor jail conditions, provide dietary supplements, if needed, and keep the State Department informed. ACS is the point of contact in the U.S. for family members and others who are concerned about a U.S. citizen arrested abroad.

Destitution. If destitute, Americans can turn to a U.S. consular officer abroad for help. ACS will help by contacting the destitute person's family, friends, or business associates to raise private funds. It will help transmit these funds to destitute Americans. ACS transfers approximately 3 million dollars a year in private emergency funds. It can approve small government loans to destitute Americans abroad until private funds arrive. ACS also approves repatriation loans to pay for destitute Americans' direct return to the U.S. Each year over $500,000 are loaned to destitute Americans.

If Ill or Injured. Should you become ill while abroad, contact the nearest U.S. embassy or consulate for a list of local doctors, dentists, medical specialists, clinics, and hospitals. If your illness or injury is serious, the consul can help you find medical assistance from that list and, at your request, will inform your family or friends of your condition. If necessary, a consul can assist in the transfer of funds from the United States. Payment of hospital and other expenses is your responsibility. Neither can consular officers supply you with medications.

In an emergency when you are unable to communicate, the consul will check your passport for the name and address of any relative, friend, or legal representative whom you wish to have notified. Because the U.S. Government cannot pay for medical evacuations, it is advisable to have private medical insurance to cover this.

Birth Abroad. A child born abroad to a U.S. citizen parent or parents generally acquires U.S. citizenship at birth. The U.S. parent or parents should contact the nearest U.S. embassy or consulate to have a Report of Birth Abroad of a Citizen of the United States of America prepared. This document serves as proof of acquisition of U.S. citizenship and is acceptable evidence for obtaining a U.S. passport and for most other purposes where one must show a birth certificate or proof of citizenship.

Death Abroad. When a U.S. citizen dies abroad, the consular officer reports the death to the next of kin or legal representative and arranges to obtain from them the necessary private funds for local burial or return of the body to the United States. Before you begin your trip, complete the address page in the front of your passport. Provide the name, address, and telephone number of someone to be contacted in an emergency. Do not give the names of your traveling companions in case the entire party is involved in the same accident.

Because the U.S. Government cannot pay for local burial or shipment of remains to the United States, it is worthwhile to have insurance to cover this. Following a death, a Report of the Death of an American Citizen (Optional Form 180) is prepared by the consular officer to provide the facts concerning the death and the custody of the personal estate of the deceased. Under certain circumstances, a consular officer becomes the provisional conservator of a deceased U.S. citizen's estate and arranges for the disposition of those effects.

Nonemergency Services. Consular officers provide non emergency services as well. These include information on Selective Service registration, travel advisories, absentee voting, and the acquisition or loss of U.S. citizenship. They arrange for the transfer of Social Security and other federal benefits to beneficiaries residing abroad, provide U.S. tax forms, and notarize documents. Consuls can also provide information on how to obtain foreign public documents.

What U.S. Consuls Cannot Do

Consular officers will do their best to assist U.S nationals abroad. However, they must devote priority time and energies to those who find themselves in the most serious legal, medical, or financial difficulties.

Because of limited resources, consuls cannot provide routine or commercial-type services. They cannot act as travel agents, information bureaus, banks, or law enforcement officers. U.S. federal law forbids a consular officer from acting as your legal representative. Consular officers cannot: find you employment; get you visas, residence permits or driving permits; act as interpreters; search for missing luggage; call your credit card company or bank; replace stolen travelers checks; or settle disputes with hotel managers. However, they can advise you on how to get assistance in these and other matters.

InfoList #52
Coming Home

1. Reconfirm your return reservation at least 72 hours before departure. Whenever possible, obtain a written confirmation. If you do it by phone, record the time, day, and the agent's name who took the call.

2. Take some time to put all the brochures and slips of paper you collected on your trip into some sort of order. Throw out what you don't need to lug home.

3. Arrange sales slips for all personal purchases in a file. This will make it easier to make personal declarations when you go through U.S. Customs.

4. Make sure you have all U.S. Customs-required documentation for your commercial purchases, especially for hand-carried items you will clear through Customs on your way home.

5. If necessary, buy another suitcase for miscellaneous personal purchases, brochures, samples, and commercial goods you have purchased.

6. Pack all the goods you will need to declare at U.S. Customs in one suitcase. This will make your passage through Customs easier.

7. Learn in advance how long it takes to get to the airport and how much it costs.

8. Arrange for transport to the airport one to two days in advance.

9. Before going to the airport, call your airline and ask about baggage weight restrictions.

10. If you have excess baggage, it may be less expensive to ship via air freight. Airline's excess baggage charges are often disproportionately high.

11. If you are visiting a country that is suffering a period of social or political unrest, find out how you would be able to leave the country in a hurry.

12. Leave plenty of time to arrive at the airport and deal with immigration and security formalities. In some countries, if you do not arrive a full hour before flight time, you will be denied entry and boarding.

13. Go to the front desk of your hotel and ask to see your bill well before departure time. If the bill is inaccurate, it is likely to be in the hotel's favor. You may overlook incorrect charges if you are in a rush to get to the airport.

14. Some countries levy an airport departure tax on travelers that can be as high as $50 per person. Ask the airline or a travel agent about such departure taxes.

15. Few "duty free" shops at airports have really good prices on merchandise. Also, all merchandise that you bring back to the U.S. is subject to Customs regulations. Refer to "U.S. Customs Hints" on page 61 for information about personal exemptions for returning U.S. residents.

16. Always make a full and complete declaration to Customs upon your return to the U.S. Nondeclaration and undervaluing of merchandise is unprofessional, unethical, and illegal. U.S. Customs has vast powers of search and seizure. The consequences of getting caught are not worth the possible savings.

InfoList #53
U.S. Customs Hints

Basic information for returning U.S. residents about their *personal* Customs exemptions.

Duty-Free Exemptions

Articles valued at $600, $800, or $1,200 (fair retail value in the country of acquisition) may be entered duty free provided:

- Articles are for personal use or gifts.

- Articles accompany you.

- You have been out of the country at least 48 hours. (Mexico and the U.S. Virgin Islands are exempt from the 48-hour limitation).

- You have not claimed the exemption within the preceding 30 days.

- You declare it to customs. If you do not declare it you risk losing it.

- The items are allowed in the country. Review the Prohibited and Restricted Items Section.

You may include in this duty-free exemption:

- 100 cigars and 200 cigarettes. Products of Cuban tobacco may be brought in only if acquired in Cuba.

- 1 liter (33.8 fl. oz.) wine, beer, or liquor, if 21 years of age or over. (Most states have restrictions on the amount of liquor or tobacco you can bring in).

If you are returning from a country (except American Samoa, Guam, or the U.S. Virgin Islands) your exemption is $800 if they are with your luggage.

Your exemption is $1,200 if you are returning from American Samoa, Guam, or the U.S. Virgin Islands. You may bring in 1,000 cigarettes as part of this amount. Of your $1,200 exemption, at least $600 worth of articles must have been purchased in the islands, and of the 1,000 cigarettes, $800 worth of cigarettes must have been purchased in the islands. Articles acquired in these islands need not accompany you but may be sent to the U.S. and claimed under your duty-free personal exemption if properly declared. Remember that shipping alcoholic beverages by mail is prohibited by U.S. postal laws.

If you are returning from any of the following 24 beneficiary countries, your customs exemption is $600: Antigua and Barbuda, Aruba, Bahamas, Barbados, Belize, Costa Rica, Dominica, Dominican Republic, El Salvador, Grenada, Guatemala, Honduras, Jamaica Montserrat, Netherlands Antilles, Nicaragua, Panama, Saint Christopher / Kitts and Nevis, Saint Lucia, Saint Vincent and the Grenadines, Trinidad and Tobago, British Virgin Islands. If one of two liters of alcoholic beverage is made in one of these countries you may bring two liters into the U.S. as a part of the $600 exemption.

Your exemption is $200 (retail value) if you cannot claim the $600, $800, or $1,200 exemption because of the 30-day or 48-hour minimum limitations. You may not make a joint or family exemption that is larger, and if the total is more than $200, duty is payable on the entire amount. For example, you may not deduct the $200 from a $500 item and only pay duty on $300. But you may include 50 cigarettes, 10 cigars, 150 milliliters (4 fl. oz.) of alcoholic beverages, **or** 150 ml. of perfume containing alcohol.

A gift you bring back with you from another country must be declared, and you may include it in your personal exemption.

Gift packages may be sent to friends and relatives and received free of duty if the value does not exceed $100 (retail) or $200 if sent from the U.S. Virgin Islands, American Samoa, or Guam.

Gifts for more than one person may be shipped in the same package, called a consolidated gift package, if they are individually wrapped and labeled with each recipient's name. Here's how to wrap and label a consolidated gift package:

Be sure to mark the outermost wrapper with:

• the words "UNSOLICITED GIFT" and the words "CONSOLIDATED GIFT PACKAGE";

• the total value of the consolidated package;

• the recipients' names; and

• the nature and value of the gifts inside (for example, tennis shoes, $50; shirt, $45; toy car, $15).

Packages marked in this way will clear Customs much more easily. If any item in the consolidated gift parcel is subject to duty and tax or worth more than the $100 gift allowance, the entire package will be dutiable.

Other articles purchased abroad and sent to the U.S. are dutiable when received in this country. Duty cannot be prepaid. Do not list these items on your declaration when you return, except as indicated for the U.S. insular possessions.

Articles imported in excess of your exemptions will be subject to duty as indicated below unless an item is entitled to free entry.

Example: You acquire goods valued at $2,500 from:

	U. S. insular possessions	Other countries or locations
Personal exemption (free of duty)	$1,200	$400
Flat duty rate	$1,000 at 1.5%	$1,000 at 3%
Various rates of duty	$300	$1,100

Certain items made in designated developing countries and territories are admitted duty free under the Generalized System of Preferences and the Caribbean Basin Recovery Act, but must nevertheless be declared to Customs. NAFTA makes free or reduced duty rates possible on some products grown, manufactured, or produced in Mexico and Canada.

You must declare, at the price paid, everything acquired abroad that you bring home, including gifts given to you and articles worn or used. If you fail to declare or understate the value, penalties can be substantial.

If you take out of or bring into the U.S. more than $10,000 in currency or negotiable instruments, you must file a report (Customs Form 4790) with U.S. Customs.

It is wise to register foreign-made, serially-numbered articles (e.g. cameras, watches) with Customs before you leave, or take with you proof of prior possession (e.g. sales slip). All firearms should be registered with Customs, whether made in the U.S. or abroad.

Articles purchased in "duty-free" shops in foreign countries are subject to U.S. Customs duty and restrictions but may be included in your personal exemption. Articles purchased in U.S. "duty-free" shops are subject to U.S. Customs duty and I.R.S. tax if reentered into the U.S.

Caution: A "good buy" overseas on a brand-name product may be due to its being counterfeit and thus subject to seizure.

Payment of Duty

Payment of duty is required at the time of your arrival on articles accompanying you and may be made by any of the following ways:

• U.S. currency (foreign currency is not acceptable)

• Personal check in the exact amount of duty, drawn on a national or state bank or trust company of the United States, made payable to the "U.S. Customs and Border Protection."

• Government check, money orders, or traveler's checks are acceptable if they do not exceed the duty amount by more than $50. (Second endorsements are not acceptable, identification must be presented)

• In some locations you may pay duty with a major credit card, either MasterCard or VISA.

Foreign-Made Personal Belongings

These articles are dutiable each time they are brought into the U.S. unless you have acceptable proof of prior possession. Documents that fully describe the article, such as bill of sale, insurance policy, jeweler's appraisal, or receipt of purchase, may be considered reasonable proof of prior possession.

Items that can be readily identified by serial number or other permanently affixed markings, may be taken to the Customs office nearest you and registered before your departure. The Certificate of Registration provided will expedite free entry of these items when you return. Keep the certificate as it is valid for any future trips as long as the information on it remains legible.

Registration cannot be accomplished by telephone nor can blank registration forms be given or mailed to you to be filled out at a later time.

Please Note

Goods from countries that are under economic sanctions by the United States are generally prohibited. The list of countries and goods changes periodically, but has recently included Afghanistan, Angola, Cuba, Iran, Iraq, Libya, North Korea, Serbia & Montenegro, and Sudan. There are severe restrictions on travel and transportation transactions with these countries and special licenses—hardly ever issued—are required to import commercial goods. Foreign visitors may be allowed to bring in some small articles for personal use on a temporary basis. For more information, contact the Office of Foreign Assets Control, Department of the Treasury, Washington DC, 20220, (202) 622-2520.

Restricted or Prohibited Articles

Some items must meet certain requirements, require a license or permit, or may be prohibited entry. Be particularly careful about bringing any of the following back from a trip: automobiles; biological materials; books, records, computer programs, and cassettes which may have been pirated; ceramic tableware with dangerous levels of lead.; cultural property, particularly pre-Columbia articles and various other archeological and ethnographic materials; drug paraphernalia; arms and ammunition; food products (bakery items and cured cheeses are admissible, but many other food products are not); fruits and vegetables; copies of gold coins; meats, poultry, livestock, and their by-products; narcotics and dangerous drugs; merchandise from countries subject to Foreign Assets Controls; pets; plants; textiles (which may be subject to quotas; trademarked articles; wildlife and fish; endangered species, and products of endangered species.

Your Customs Declaration

You will receive a Customs Declaration on board your plane or vessel as you return to the United States. Before you enter the U.S., you must fill out the identification portion. Families returning together may prepare a joint declaration, with children claiming the same exemption as adults (except for liquor). Children born abroad, who have never lived in the United States, are considered non-residents for Customs purposes.

Tip: Keep your receipts, sales slips, invoices, or other record of your purchases should there be a question concerning valuations. If you do not have specific supporting data, Customs will use standard price listings of goods from the country of acquisition to value the items in question.

In conformance with the simplified Customs Declaration form:

- You must complete a written declaration and include item #11 the total value of all goods acquired that are accompanying you if you arrive in the United States by aircraft or ocean vessel.

- If you exceed $1,400 per person ($400 tax-free exemption plus $1,000 dutiable at a flat 10% duty rate), you must list in writing all the articles acquired outside the United States and the price paid for each in U.S. currency or its equivalent in the country of acquisition. Repairs or alterations to articles taken abroad and returned must be declared, whether paid for or provided free of charge. State the fair retail value of acquisitions not purchased, such as gifts to you.

You must also list in writing your acquisitions when:

- You have exceeded the personal liquor or tobacco exemptions explained under "Duty-Free Exemptions."

(Note that excess amounts of alcoholic beverages are subject to federal excise taxes in addition to import duties.)

- You bring in items for business purposes or for someone else.

- You send home items acquired in the U.S. Virgin Island, American Samoa, or Guam.

- You are asked to do so by the Customs Inspector.

You may make an oral declaration if you arrive in the United States from Canada or Mexico—by car, bus, train, or on foot—and you have less than $400 worth of items to declare.

Play It Safe

Customs will be glad to furnish you with detailed pamphlets: Refer to "Customs and Border Protection Information Sources" on page 88. The brochure "Know Before You Go" (http://www.customs.ustreas.gov/xp/cgov/travel/vacation/know_brochure) is particularly helpful. Send a postcard to U.S. Customs and Border Protection, 1300 Pennsylvania Avenue NW, Washington DC, 20229.

InfoList #54
Suggestions for Working with U.S. Customs

1. Learn as much as you can about importing your product from this manual and other information sources before you call Customs with your questions. Use Customs for clarification of fine points, not for your complete education.

2. Don't call Customs with questions that can only be answered by other regulatory agencies of the U.S. government. Generally speaking, agency expertise does not overlap. For example, U.S. Customs will not be able to answer questions about Bureau of Alcohol, Tobacco and Firearms (ATF) requirements not enforced by Customs.

3. Find out about necessary import documentation and other agency requirements before you actually start importing.

4. Customs has enforcement responsibility for the regulations of a number of U.S. governmental agencies. Their responsibility to these agencies and to the U.S. public is significant and they take it seriously. Be prepared. Know what you're doing at all times. Don't expect Customs to overlook something "just this one time."

5. If you have a problem handling paperwork and other details, don't make your own Customs entries. Hire a customs broker who does this professionally and make life easier for yourself.

6. If you plan on importing a specific commodity over a period of time, establish a good relationship with a U.S. Customs commodity specialist. Help your commodity specialist help you: know everything about your commodity that you can. Respect his/her time pressures by keeping your questions limited to his/her area of expertise. Always be courteous—recognize that the Customs person has many other people clamoring for his/her attention, and is usually under a lot of pressure. Remember that this specialist probably knows more about Customs entry and clearance of that commodity than you will ever know.

7. Customs inspections of shipments is usual, so don't panic. Don't make life difficult for the inspector lest he/she return the favor.

8. You and Customs may disagree on the classification of an imported product. The disagreement will likely be that they see it in a higher duty-rate category, while you see it in a lower duty-rate category. "Presenting your case" for the lower rate category works better than "making an argument" for the lower rate category. Generally, your customs broker should be making your case for you. If you run up against a brick wall and are convinced that you have a good case, refer the matter to a customs lawyer who can work administratively for you with Customs.

InfoList #55
U.S. Import Requirements

1. An individual may make his own customs clearance of goods imported for personal use or business.

2. U.S. Customs and Border Protection does not require an importer to have a license or permit. However, other agencies may require a permit, license, or certification, depending on the commodity.

3. All merchandise coming into the United States must clear through Customs and is subject to a customs duty unless specifically exempted from this duty by law. Clearance involves a number of steps—entry, classification, liquidation.

4. Customs duties are, generally, an *ad valorem* rate (a percentage) which is applied to the dutiable value of the imported goods. Some articles, however, are dutiable at a *specific* rate of duty (so much per piece, liter, kilo, etc.); others at a compound rate of duty (a combination of both ad valorem and specific duties).

5. The dutiable value of merchandise is determined by Customs. Several appraisal methods are used to arrive at this value. Generally, the transaction value of the merchandise serves as the basis of appraisement. Transaction value is the price the buyer actually pays the seller in the transaction for the goods being imported.

6. The Harmonized Tariff Schedule of the United States (HTSUS), issued by the International Trade Commission, prescribes the rates of duty and classification of merchandise by type of product; e.g., animal and vegetable products, textile fibers and textile products.

7. The tariff schedule provides several rates of duty for each item: "general" rates for most-favored nations; "special" rates for special trade programs (free, or lower than the rates currently accorded most-favored nations); and "column 2" rates for imports not eligible for either general or special rates.

8. Processing fees may apply.

InfoList #56
10 Suggestions for Faster Customs Clearance

1. Include all information required on your customs invoices. Prepare your invoices carefully. Type them clearly. Allow sufficient space between lines. Keep the data within each column.

2. Make sure that your invoices contain the information that would be shown on a well-prepared packing list.

3. Mark and number each package so that it can be identified with the corresponding marks and numbers appearing on your invoice.

4. Show on your invoice a detailed description of each item of goods contained in each individual package.

5. Mark your goods legibly and conspicuously with the name of the country of origin, unless they are specifically exempted from the country of origin marking requirements, and with such other marking as required by the marking laws of the U.S.

6. Comply with the provisions of any special laws of the U.S. that may apply to your goods, such as the laws relating to foods, drugs, cosmetics, alcoholic beverages, and radioactive materials.

7. Observe closely the instructions with respect to invoicing, packaging, marking, labeling, etc., sent to you by your customer in the U.S. The customer has probably made a careful check of the requirements that will have to be met when your goods arrive.

8. Work with U.S. Customs in developing packing standards for your commodities.

9. Establishing sound security procedures at your facility and while transporting your goods for shipment. Do not allow narcotic smugglers the opportunity to introduce narcotics into your shipment. The 1993 Customs Modernization Act has set $500 as the minimum penalty for importation of undeclared controlled substances found in your shipment.

10. Consider shipping on a carrier participating in the Automated Manifest System or otherwise transmitting your entry documentation and declarations electronically through the National Customs Automation Program (NCAP), as it becomes available.

InfoList #57
Key Changes From the Mod Act

What is the Mod Act?
The Customs Modernization Act, passed in December 1993, amends the Tariff Act of 1930 (19 USC 1202 et seq.). This Mod Act, as it is known, is designed to streamline and automate the commercial operations of U.S. Customs. Subsidiary goals include improving compliance and enforcement and providing standards to ensure uniformity and due process in Customs procedures. The Act (Title VI) contains four main subtitles which revise existing statutes to accommodate electronic processing; establish the National Customs Automation program (NCAP); amend administrative procedures; and enact various miscellaneous conforming amendments. Most of the provisions either codify existing practice or implement anticipated technological changes.

Importers felt little immediate effect from most of the specific changes in the Act; however, over time it will radically change the way they conduct business. Many specific procedures ordered under the Mod Act have taken a couple of years to be formally implemented in the Customs Regulations. U.S. Customs and Border Protection is streamlined and automated in a way designed to speed up customs procedures. U.S. Customs and Border Protection has been continually evolving since 1994, which has resulted in the removal or complete reorganization of many middle-management layers.

Since 1996, a fundamental shift in philosophy within U.S. Customs and Border Protection has made itself more evident. Some of the major concepts behind these changes, as well as some of the specifics of the most important procedural changes, are discussed below.

Shared Responsibility
Shared responsibility means that importers and Customs have a mutual responsibility to ensure compliance with trade and Customs laws. At a minimum, this requires the trade to obtain and apply to its import transactions the information Customs makes available through its Basic Information Program. In addition, the trade is expected to:

- Apply information that Customs makes available under its "Targeted Information Program" to address specific industry and trade segment issues;

- Establish internal controls over its Customs operations;

- Ensure personnel involved in Customs activities are properly trained;

- Work in partnership with Customs to develop informed compliance programs; and

- Seek clarification when Customs requirements are not understood.

Finally, when it is discovered that importers have compliance problems, they will be expected to respond to Customs consultation, develop performance improvement plans and implement them.

In response to import community requests for guidance with respect to the importer's obligation to use reasonable care, Customs develops and solicits informal public comment on "draft" regulations, position statements, examples and checklists. Based on comments received from the trade and within the government, Customs may elect to modify and adopt all or any combination of its "draft" regulations, position statements, examples and checklists.

The checklists can assist in ensuring that the trade community understands the types of actions Customs could consider in determining whether reasonable care was exercised in a particular case. Similarly, these checklists could serve as an additional Customs tool in arriving at the appropriate course of informed compliance or enforcement action.

Informed Compliance

Customs defines "informed compliance" as "a shared responsibility wherein Customs effectively communicates its requirements to the trade, and the people and businesses subject to those requirements conduct their regulated activities in conformance with U.S. laws and regulations."Many importers, customs brokers, and others in the trade community, however, feel that the government's concept of shared responsibility puts a much greater onus on them than in the past.

The idea of informed compliance grew out of several factors:

1. **Trade Complexity.** NAFTA and the Uruguay Round of GATT have introduced change and increased complexity to international trade practices.

2. **Workload Challenge.** Customs expects to handle an increasing workload with a static work-force in the coming years.

3. **The Mod Act.** The Act assigns Customs the responsibility for clearly defining and communicating the responsibilities of the trade community and requires that the trade community act with reasonable care in meeting those responsibilities.

4. **Customs Organizational Structure.** Customs reorganization has created an environment that is designed to promote trade compliance. Customs new structure streamlines communication between headquarters and the field, provides a mechanism to prioritize trade issues, creates a direct line of authority for addressing trade matters that are national in scope, and promotes the initiative and empowerment of field managers on trade compliance concerns directly related to a local environment.

5. **Composition of Trade Community.** During 1994, the Customs Service cleared shipments for more than 318,000 commercial importers, 350 of whom accounted for more than half of all import value. Equally significant is the fact that 61 percent of all import value was attributable to the top 1,000 importers. Since most import activity is clearly attributable to a relatively small group of importers, a strategic approach to informed compliance that takes that demographic into account should produce the greatest benefits for the Customs Service and those it serves.

6. **Current Compliance.** Based on the results of Customs Fiscal Year (FY) 1995 baseline compliance measurement, 81 percent of all import transactions are currently in compliance with U.S. trade laws. Customs is committed to using compliance measurement data as the foundation upon which operational programs will be built to maximize trade compliance, particularly in areas that are of a strategic concern. While Customs is dedicated to raising the overall trade compliance rate, the FY-95 measurement indicates that some of the most critical trade issues are currently highly compliant. For example, only a trace of imports suspected of being manufactured by forced prison labor exists, and while there was some detection of intellectual property rights violations, the occurrences were not widespread. Likewise, there were instances of importations of restricted merchandise and imports with health and safety concerns, but statistically, they are occurring in a minuscule percentage of importations. Similarly, the FY-95 measurement shows that more than 99% of all revenue due the government is being collected.

In practical terms, informed compliance means that the importer and his agent must make an efffort to learn about all Customs procedures and regulations which might apply to his situation, he must apply them correctly, and in the event of an investigation or audit, he must be able to demonstrate that he has taken all proper steps to ensure compliance.

Reasonable Care

Certain accountabilities which were assigned to Customs have shifted to the importer and are identified under the concepts of "reasonable care."In meeting the reasonable care standard, a company must establish evidence of proper compliance with import regulations. The stated purpose of the informed compliance strategy is "To communicate to Customs officers and the trade, the strategy and processes involved in maximizing trade compliance through an informed compliance program that supports and promotes *the use of reasonable care* by all who do business with Customs."

Enforcement actions, such as seizure, investigation, and penalties will be reserved for those instances when an account has failed to live up to its obligation of using reasonable care or where necessary to prevent or penalize the introduction of restricted or prohibited goods into commerce. Therefore, it is crucial not only to use reasonable care, but also to document reasonable care procedures.

The "Reasonable Care Checklists" on page 71 may provide importers with a tool to assist them in the development of reasonable care programs designed to avoid compliance problems. Similarly, these checklists could serve as an additional Customs tool in arriving at the appropriate course of informed compliance or enforcement action.

Information Programs

Basic Information Program. Under this program, the Customs Service:

- Issues binding rulings within 30 days of request (120 days if the issue must be referred to a Customs attorney);

- Develops "draft" regulatory documents and gives the trade an opportunity to comment by posting these documents on the Customs Electronic Bulletin Board (CEBB);

- Establishes an outreach program to educate the trade in Mod Act responsibilities;

- Establishes a Customs Web Server for disseminating Customs information via the Internet; and

- Conducts internal seminars designed to increase Customs employee knowledge and to promote uniformity.

In addition, Customs is investigating the possibility of making CD-ROM discs available to the public at a nominal fee. The documents currently available through the Web site and on the CEBB would be considered for inclusion.

Targeted Information Program. This program provides information and assistance over and above that described above. It is used to address industries and trade segments which may require special efforts to close compliance gaps or to correct patterns of non-compliance. The targeted information program may also be used when complex new operational procedures are put into place.

The targeted information program utilizes a variety of tools and outlets, such as industry and commodity specific publications; video conferences; satellite broadcasts; videotapes; seminars; industry association-sponsored meetings; importer visits; and pre-importation reviews.

The Trade Enforcement Plan

Customs issues a Trade Enforcement Plan (TEP) annually, developed by the newly-created Office of Strategic Trade, together with the Offices of Field Operations and Investigations. The plan assesses the principal impediments to importer compliance with trade laws, develops a coordinated approach to improve compliance, and defines intra-agency responsibilities and time lines for accomplishing goals.

The five components of Customs annual TEP are: (1) compliance measurement, which produces baseline compliance level for each of the four-digit Harmonized Tariff numbers; (2) compliance assessment, which is the first phase of a Customs audit; (3) trade interventions, which applies targeting and analysis methodologies to emerging trade issues; (4) sustained customer interactions; and (5) investigations into critical areas of concern.

One intention of the TEP is to inform the international trade community of its responsibilities in complying with key trade laws, particularly those in "primary focus" industries.

Account-Based Compliance Efforts

To facilitate its informed compliance efforts, Customs made a fundamental shift in its approach from that of a transaction-based organization to account-based processing. Accounts are defined as every person or firm with whom Customs does business, or in whom Customs has an interest related to trade compliance. This includes all relevant business entities such as importers, carriers, brokers, manufacturers, warehouse proprietors, and sureties.

In support of this change in focus, the National Commodity Specialist Division while continuing to issue transaction-based rulings, now develops general informed compliance publications for distribution in a variety of media, both printed and online. The Customs Service coordinates educational training for accounts through activities such as pre-importation reviews, importer premises visits, local seminars, and other informational initiatives. Customs attorneys work with Customs account servicing personnel to address uniformity issues and to identify when rulings are needed to promote the informed compliance process. Perhaps most significant for major importers, Customs national account managers are assigned to work with certain "high volume" accounts to identify areas of non-compliance within a company's operation, and to develop strategies to establish and maintain high levels of trade compliance by the account.

Whether assigned an account manager or not, however, an importer's activities are consistently analyzed at industry, account, and transaction levels to identify trends, patterns, and anomalies which represent potential problems. While suspected areas of non-compliance are targeted for compliance reviews, standardized verification procedures, which are designed to promote the uniform and expeditious treatment of cargo, with minimal intrusion by Customs to validate compliance, detect trade violations, and interdict contraband.

Non-enforcement actions, such as increased outreach, education, and counseling of the account are employed by Customs to address instances of non-compliance when an account has not demonstrated a failure to apply reasonable care. Enforcement actions, such as seizure, investigation, and penalties are to be reserved for instances when an account has failed to use reasonable care or where necessary to prevent or penalize the introduction of restricted or prohibited goods into commerce.

Account Stratification

The Customs Service identifies each account by one of three levels of import activity: high-, medium-, and low-volume.

High Volume Accounts. Relatively few importers account for a majority of all import transactions; Customs therefore devotes a significant portion of its informed compliance resources to work with the high-volume accounts.

As part of this account-based approach, Customs may assign National Account Managers to work with those importers who are in the top tier of companies, by import value. Among these high volume companies, those that are heavily involved in "primary focus" industries are receiving first attention. The primary responsibility of the account manager is to ensure that the assigned account is fully aware of its reasonable care responsibilities, and to the extent possible, works with the account to ensure maximum compliance in a cost effective manner. Not all high volume accounts receive the immediate assignment of a Customs account manager. Nonetheless, by virtue of their considerable involvement in the import process, all high volume accounts are expected to develop the capabilities needed to adhere to the legal and regulatory requirements of importing.

Mid-Level Accounts. Whenever necessary, mid-level accounts are targeted by Trade Compliance Process Owners at the port level. The effort is coordinated by Customs headquarters to ensure an integrated, national approach to the compliance issues involving mid-level companies. The Offices of Strategic Trade and Field Operations provide local field personnel with the information and tools necessary to address informed compliance issues associated with each "mid-level" account. As part of that effort, port process owners receive automated data reports to enable them to coordinate their informed compliance efforts with other key ports through which each "mid-level" account imports. In addition, port process owners must rely on their own staff of operational analysis specialists, commodity and entry specialist teams, and inspection personnel to conduct informed compliance initiatives with mid-level accounts, focussing on trade compliance matters unique to their port.

Low Volume Accounts. Because they account for such a small percentage of all imports, Customs interacts with these accounts primarily on a transaction-by-transaction basis, relying on its Basic Information Program and technical assistance, when necessary, to promote a high level of compliance.

Compliance Measurement

Accounts are assessed by the Customs Service in two categories for compliance measurement:

- The first category is the compliance measurement bucket as a result of a compliance assessment. Every company or account is fit into one of the following three buckets: High Compliance found through the Compliance Assessment (CA), Low Compliance found through the CA, or Unknown Compliance (no CA completed).

- The second category for compliance measurement largely corresponds to the trade priority issues.

The majority of the current audit plan focuses on compliance assessments of the Top 1,000 firms, which enter the majority of U.S. imports (these firms are only 0.3% of the 350,000 importers, but they account for 61% of the total import value, or $400 billion, of all imported merchandise.) The specific company selections were made with consideration from several sources; a similar approach is used when reviewing firms that export from Canada and Mexico under the NAFTA rules of origin.

Primary Focus Industries and Trade Priority Issues

Trade compliance is a major goal regardless of commodity, but not all imported merchandise is equally significant at any given time, so the Customs Service identifies several "primary focus" industries within its annual Trade Enforcement Plans. Customs dedicates a large portion of its

informed compliance resources to work with those companies that import commodities related to these industries. There are three key factors that contribute to a commodity's prominence in Customs' trade enforcement plan: (1) the commodity's strategic impact on the nation's security or economic well-being; (2) its current compliance rate; and (3) its import volume.

The eight "primary focus" industries has remained stable since it was first published in 1994 and includes:

- Textiles
- Steel
- Autos and auto parts
- Critical components (e.g., fasteners and bearings)
- Advanced displays (e.g., CRTs and flat panels - computer monitor screens)
- Telecommunications
- Production equipment
- Agriculture

On the watch list (i.e., not critical, but being carefully monitored) are:

- Chemicals
- Petrochemicals

Anyone importing any of these categories of goods may be subject to a higher level of scrutiny; by the same token, the Customs Service has taken steps to provide more information to the trade on how to comply with the regulations related to imports in these industries.

Because not all important trade issues confronting Customs can be identified by industry sectors, additional specific and cross-cutting trade priorities have been identified in the annual Trade Enforcement Plans. For 1997, the twelve priority issues are:

- Anti-dumping and countervailing duties
- Classification
- Trade statistics
- Country of origin marking
- Embargoes and sanctions
- Intellectual property rights
- Trade agreements
- Public health and safety
- Transshipment
- Quota evasion
- Revenue
- Valuation

Many of these issues cut across a range of products or source countries while others may be closely linked with certain priority industries—textiles with quotas and transshipment, for instance. A few issues such as embargoes and convict labor are country-specific.

Interventions

The concept of interventions, Customs actions designed to deal with the root causes of trade non-compliance, is central to the Trade Enforcement Plan. Interventions are any actions designed to confront, resolve, or reduce the impact of major trade issues. These actions may cover a range from targeted informed compliance assistance for importers to integrated Compliance Measurement, Audit and Investigative activities in the fullest sense of enforced compliance.

This is mainly designed to raise the level of compliance in the primary focus industries, and on situations described in the list of trade priorities, especially NAFTA and NAFTA agricultural issues. The issue identification process as well as some interventions is also used to identify problems with other Customs processes, and thereby expedite suitable procedural remedies.

Customs Reorganization

Customs reorganization promotes both a "top-down" (headquarters communicating to the field) and a "bottom-up" (field offices to headquarters) approach to informed compliance. By removing two levels from the organizational structure (its district and regional offices), Customs can theoretically streamline communication between headquarters and the field, provide a mechanism to prioritize trade issues, create a direct line of authority for addressing trade concerns that are national in scope, and promote the initiative and empowerment of field managers on trade compliance matters directly related to a local environment.

For more information on the current structure of U.S. Customs and Border Protection and the areas of responsiblity for different offices, refer to "Organization and Responsibilities" on page 194, in the U.S. Customs Entry section. For contact information, refer to "U.S. Customs and Border Protection Offices" on page 81.

Recordkeeping and the (a)(1)(A) List

In one of the areas that directly affects importers, Subtitle A of the Mod Act specifically authorizes Customs to make reasonable audits of records required for the entry of goods and increases the recordkeeping responsibilities for those involved in importing. The procedures adopted are designed to reduce the paperwork required of importers at the time of entry by encouraging Customs to waive production of records at the time of entry while retaining the right to demand their production at a later date. Records may now be demanded from any owner, importer, consignee, importer of record, entry filer, or other interested party involved in importing goods into the U.S., or one who files a drawback claim, transports or stores merchandise carried or stored under bond, or knowingly causes importation or transportation or storage of merchandise under bond. Records may also be demanded from any agent of these parties or other person whose activities require filing a declaration, entry, or both. Many of the records one must maintain are in addition to documents required for entry.

If you are involved in any of these activities, the law requires you to maintain certain records for a specified period of time, generally five years (drawback records must be retained for three years after the date of the payment of a drawback claim). Records that must be kept include, but are not limited to, commercial invoices, packing lists, cer-

tificates of origin, declarations of foreign manufacturers, and any additional documents required for the particular entry, either in paper form or as electrically-generated or machine readable material. All such documents consist of those usually kept in the ordinary course of business: there is no requirement to prepare separate, additional documents to comply with the law.

Customs has promulgated the so-called "(a)(1)(A) list," describing documents which importers and others must retain for five years. (An exception is made for records of drawback claims, which must be kept until the third anniversary of the date the claim was paid.) The "interim" (a)(1)(A) list was published on January 3, 1996; it is effective as a final rule to the extent that importers may be subject to penalties for failure to retain or retrieve the indicated documents and records. A final rule with minor changes is expected in 1997. The (a)(1)(A) list is comprehensive and includes such items as bills of lading, invoices with corrections, foreign assemblers declarations, ATF permits, GSP declarations, and automotive products certificates. Some documents are specifically identified, but others may simply be identified by reference to the governing regulation. Even conscientious importers can face confusion in determining their obligations, but under the "informed compliance" concept of the Mod Act, the increased responsibility for record retention lies squarely with the importer.

A voluntary recordkeeping compliance certification program for qualified importers is to be established, pursuant to the Mod Act. Under this program, Customs will issue a warning letter for unintentional first time recordkeeping discrepancies in lieu of monetary penalties or other sanctions. At press time, information was not yet available on this program.

For more information on recordkeeping obligations, refer to 19 CFR 162 Subpart A, "Recordkeeping, Inspection, Examination, and Search," and to the (a)(1)(A) List."

Penalties

Anyone who fails to produce documents covered by the recordkeeping obligations of the Mod Act when demanded is subject to a monetary fine. Willful failure to maintain or produce documents can subject the party to a fine of the lesser of $100,000 or 75% of the value of the goods in the transaction in question, while negligence can result in a fine of the lesser of $10,000 or 40% of the value of the goods in question. Rates of duty on the goods may also be increased. Penalties are discretionary, not mandatory, and may be avoided in cases in which the party cannot produce the materials because of factors beyond its control or if Customs already has the materials. Penalties may also be assessed for submission of fraudulent information and for fraudulent drawback claims.

The Mod Act imposes additional criminal and civil penalties for presenting forged or altered documents at entry or for otherwise violating arrival, entry, clearance, or manifest requirements. These penalties also apply to electronic transmission of false or altered data or manifests to Customs (19 USC 1436). The Act also establishes monetary penalties for fraudulent submission of a false drawback claim, the amounts of which increase with repeated violations. (Refer to 19 CFR 191.9, "Falsification of drawback claims.") These penalties became effective on implementation of the nationwide automated drawback selectivity program (19 USC 1593A).

Classification and Liquidation

Before the Mod Act, importers were required to supply Customs with complete and accurate information so that Customs could assign classification and valuation; under the new "informed compliance" regulations, the responsibility for correctly classifying merchandise falls to the importer or his agent, often a customs broker. Moreover, these parties must be able to demonstrate that they used "reasonable care" in doing so. This ultimately places a much greater legal burden on the importer.

The Mod Act takes a novel approach to liquidation by allowing reconciliation to occur after entry. An importer who wishes to submit reconciliation for a particular entry can specify the intent to provide relevant data when it becomes available at a later time. The Mod Act permits Customs to liquidate an entry before the unknown information has been transmitted to Customs. The Act further imposes a responsibility on importers to use reasonable care in making entry so that Customs can rely on the accuracy of information and can streamline the entry and liquidation procedures. If an importer fails to use reasonable care in classifying and valuing merchandise and presenting entry data, Customs may impose a penalty in an amount commensurate to the level of culpability (see 19 USC 1592).

Detentions

Subtitle A also provides that Customs must make a decision on the admissibility of a shipment within five working days. Any goods not released within that period are considered to have been detained. After no more than five days, the authorities must issue a formal notice of detention to the importer or other interested party, complete with specifics as to what is required to rectify the situation. If Customs fails to make a determination within 30 days after presentation, the shipment is presumed to have been excluded. This 30 day period may be waived or extended based on specific administrative action or in compliance with the governing rules of other interested agencies.

Testing and Other Procedures

The Act provides for Customs to establish sampling and testing procedures and license accredited private testing laboratories. Customs must publish any precedent-setting decisions within 90 days. Provisions also enumerate merchandise subject to seizure and under what conditions.

Drawback Procedures

The Mod Act permits an importer to claim drawback within three years after the articles are exported or destroyed. A claim is considered filed when the drawback entry and all documents necessary to complete the claim are submitted or requested by application to Customs. An exception is made for landing certificates, which must be filed in accordance with the time limits prescribed by specific regula-

tion. The importer may accomplish a drawback filing electronically with permission of Customs. No extension of the time limit is allowed unless Customs is responsible for an untimely filing. Drawback claimants should file Customs Form 331 with the appropriate drawback office.

National Customs Automation Program

Subtitle B establishes the National Customs Automation Program (NCAP) for remote location electronic filing of customs documents. The subtitle also extends definitions on drawback rules and periods of eligibility and recapture and sets new manifest and invoice requirements designed to facilitate electronic filing. This subtitle also provides for electronic batch filing and periodic reconciliation of accounts. The new system will eventually allow importers to electronically file documentation for numerous entries as a group, as well as pay duties and fees on a periodic basis rather than filing and paying separately for each entry as it occurs.

There are currently a number of computerized and automated procedures available through the Automated Comnmercial System (ACS). They will be more fully integrated with other Customs needs in the Automated Commercial Environment (ACE), which should replace ACS by 1998. Some modules of these programs are available only to Customs Service employees, while others are available to the trade.

Other Provisions

Subtitle C of the Act consists of various administrative amendments aimed primarily at internal Customs procedures, such as allowing the waiver of fees on nonmaterial amounts, and technicalities affecting shippers. However, Section C also changes the rules under which goods may be seized and sold by Customs. Under the Act, the time that unclaimed merchandise must be held before it can be auctioned off is reduced from 12 to six months. Customs also has the option of appropriating the merchandise for its own use after giving the importer 30 days notice. And Customs may also dispose of merchandise immediately if it is unclaimed and officials deem that the cost of storing it is "disproportionate" to its value.

These procedures—designed to speed up operations in a computerized environment—become more important given that revamped liquidation procedures mandated elsewhere in the Act allow Customs more leeway to classify merchandise as unclaimed. These rules include entries submitted with incomplete paperwork as unclaimed along with truly unclaimed shipments lacking any paperwork.

Subtitle D consists of miscellaneous technical corrections designed to update and upgrade Customs authorization.

InfoList #58
Reasonable Care Checklists

Some Major Reasonable Care Questions

1. Have you taken measures or developed reliable procedures to ensure that your merchandise complies with other agency requirements (e.g., FDA, EPA/DOT, CPSC, FTC, Agriculture, etc.) prior to or upon entry, including the procurement of any necessary licenses or permits?

2. Have you taken measures or developed reliable procedures to check to see if your goods are subject to a Commerce Department dumping or countervailing duty investigation or determination, and if so, have you complied or developed reliable procedures to ensure compliance with Customs reporting requirements upon entry (e.g., 19 CFR 141.61)?

3. Is your merchandise subject to quota/visa requirements, and if so, have you provided or developed a reliable procedure to provide a correct visa for the goods upon entry?

4. Have you taken reliable measures to ensure and verify that you are filing the correct type of Customs entry (e.g., TIB, T&E, consumption entry, mail entry, etc.), as well as ensure that you have the right to make entry under the Customs Regulations?

Merchandise Description & Tariff Classification

1. Did you properly describe your merchandise to Customs in accordance with 19 USC 1481?

2. Did you properly classify your merchandise in accordance with 19 USC 1484?

3. Has Customs issued a ruling regarding the description of the merchandise or its tariff classification, and if so, has the ruling been followed?

4. If you can not find merchandise descriptions or tariff classification information, have you established a procedure for finding the information, and is it being followed?

5. Have you been involved in a Customs pre-classification of your merchandise relating to proper merchandise description and classification?

6. Have you consulted the tariff schedules, court cases and Customs rulings to assist you in describing and classifying the merchandise?

7. Have you consulted with a Customs expert (e.g., a Customs broker or Customs lawyer) to assist in the description and/or classification of the merchandise?

8. If you are claiming a conditionally free or special tariff classification/provision for your merchandise, how have you verified that the merchandise qualifies for such status? Have you developed procedures to get required documentation to support the claim? Do you have a NAFTA certificate of origin in your possession (if you are making a NAFTA preference claim)?

9. Is the nature of your merchandise such that a laboratory analysis is suggested to assist in proper description and classification?

10. Do you have a program in place to maintain and produce required Customs entry documentation and supporting information?

Valuation

1. Did you provide Customs with a proper declared value for your merchandise in accordance with 19 USC 1484 and 19 USC.1401a?

2. Has Customs issued a ruling regarding the valuation of the merchandise, and if so, has the ruling been followed?

3. Have you consulted the Customs valuation laws, *Customs Valuation Encyclopedia*, court cases and Customs rulings to assist you in valuing merchandise?

4. Have you consulted with a Customs expert to assist in the valuation of the merchandise?

5. If you purchased the merchandise from a "related" seller, have you reported that fact upon entry and taken measures to ensure that value reported to Customs is a correct "related party" value for the goods?

6. Have you taken measures to ensure that all of the legally required costs or payments associated with the imported merchandise have been reported to Customs (e.g., assists, commissions, indirect payments or rebates, royalties, etc.)?

7. If you are declaring a value based on a transaction where you were not the buyer, did you claim the transaction as a bona fide sale at arm's length and that the merchandise was destined to the United States at the time of the sale?

8. If you are claiming a conditionally free or special tariff classification/provision for your merchandise, have you established a program to ensure that you reported the required value information and obtained any required or necessary documentation to support the claim?

9. Have you established a program to produce any required entry documentation and supporting information?

Country of Origin/Marking/Quota

1. Have you established reliable procedures to ensure that you report the correct country of origin on Customs entry documents?

2. Have you established reliable procedures to verify or ensure that the merchandise is properly marked upon entry with the correct country of origin (if required) in accordance with 19 U.S.C. 1304 and any other applicable special marking requirement (watches, gold, textile labeling, etc)?

3. Have you obtained a Customs "ruling" regarding the proper marking and country of origin of the merchandise (See 19 CFR Part 177), and if so, have you established reliable procedures to ensure that you followed the ruling and brought it to Customs attention?

4. Have you consulted with a Customs "expert" regarding the correct country of origin / proper marking of your merchandise?

5. Have you taken reliable and adequate measures to communicate Customs country of origin marking requirements to your foreign supplier prior to importation of your merchandise?

6. If you are claiming a change in the origin of the merchandise or claiming that the goods are of U.S. origin, have you taken required measures to substantiate your claim?

7. If you are importing textiles or apparel, have you developed reliable procedures to ensure that you have ascertained the correct country of origin in accordance with 19 U.S.C. 3592 (Section 334, Pub. Law 103-465) and assured yourself that no illegal transshipment or false or fraudulent practices were involved?

8. Do you know how your goods are made from raw materials to finished goods, by whom and where?

9. Have you checked with Customs and developed a reliable procedure or system to ensure that the quota category is correct?

10. Have you developed reliable procedures to check the Status Report on Current Import Quotas (Restraint Levels) issued by Customs to determine if your goods are subject to a quota category which has "part" categories?

11. Have you taken reliable measures to ensure that you have obtained the correct visas for your goods if they are subject to visa categories?

12. In the case of textile articles, have you prepared or developed a reliable program to prepare the proper country declaration for each entry, i.e., a single country declaration (if wholly obtained / produced) or a multi-country declaration (if raw materials from one country were produced into goods in a second)?

13. Have you established a reliable maintenance program to ensure you can produce any required entry documentation and supporting information, including any required certificates of origin?

Intellectual Property Rights

1. If you are importing goods or packaging bearing a trademark registered in the U.S., have you checked or established a reliable procedure to ensure that it is genuine and not restricted from importation under the "gray-market" or parallel import requirements of U.S. law (see 19 CFR 133.21), or that you have permission from the trademark holder to import such merchandise?

2. If you are importing goods or packaging which consist of, or contain registered copyrighted material, have you checked or established a reliable procedure to ensure that it is authorized and genuine? If you are importing sound recordings of live performances, were the recordings authorized?

3. Have you checked or developed a reliable procedure to see if your merchandise is subject to an International Trade Commission or court ordered exclusion order?

4. Have you established a reliable procedure to ensure that you maintain and can produce any required entry documentation and supporting information?

InfoList #59
Customs Brokers, Freight Forwarders, and Professional Associations

Customs brokers are licensed by the U.S. Department of the Treasury and must demonstrate their knowledge of Customs regulations, procedures, tariffs, laws, and administrative rulings. The broker's task includes responsibility for assessing tariff classification, quota compliance, and anticipation of difficulties in the entry of the client's products. Brokers also often provide advice regarding shipping, including carriers, routes, and modes of transportation. Besides dealing with U.S. Customs, the customs broker must also keep current on the regulations of as many as 40 U.S. government agencies in order to represent clients before them.

Ocean freight forwarders are licensed by the Federal Maritime Commission (FMC), and international air cargo agents are licensed by the International Air Transportation Association (IATA). These forwarders advise clients on rates, routings, and modes of transport, assembling a customized package to cover the needs of the particular client, schedule, and commodity. Forwarders not only juggle the movements of specific shipments, but also must keep current on regulations such as those governing documentation, shipping, packaging, labeling, handling, licensing, and restrictions for both the U.S. and numerous foreign countries. Forwarders arrange for storage, disbursement, consolidation, bulk transit, and inland as well as international transport for door to door service. Forwarders can also help in preparing quotes, pro forma invoices, and other documents required for international payments.

The National Customs Brokers & Forwarders Association of America, Inc. (NCBFAA) represents customs brokers, international freight forwarders, and international air cargo agents in the U.S. Membership in this professional trade association includes 33 affiliated local and regional associations nationwide. Founded in 1897, the NBFAA represents the industry before Congress and regulatory agencies, maintaining national committees on policy and areas of industry concern. The national association operates educational programs and communications services for its members and the public aimed at disseminating information regarding current issues, as well as updates on rulings, decisions, and new and pending legislation.

You can find a customs broker or freight forwarder by referring to the Yellow Pages of a port city under the listing "Customs Brokers," "Freight Consolidating" or "Freight Forwarding." All customs brokers must be licensed by U.S. Customs and Border Protection. If you wish to work with a customs broker who is also a member of a professional association, you can get references through the national office of the NCBFAA.

The National Customs Brokers & Forwarders Association of America, Inc. (NCBFAA)

1200 18th Street, NW, #901
Washington DC 20036
(202) 466-0222, FAX (202) 466-0226
WEB: www.ncbfaa.org

InfoList #60
Selecting and Working with a Customs Broker

Customs brokers are licensed by the Department of Treasury, U.S. Customs and Border Protection to conduct business with U.S. Customs on behalf of individual and corporate importers. For a fee, the customs broker will expedite your Customs entries.

Note: Don't go into a relationship with a Customs broker thinking that his or her job is to handle everything without your input. The most effective combination is that of an informed importer working in harmony with a knowledgeable and competent Customs broker.

1. Find a customs broker who has a large enough business to adequately handle the types of services you require. If you have a small operation importing non-regulated items, with no cargo forwarding, a small outfit will probably be just fine. If you are a larger-scale importer with offices in a number of locations making many, frequent entries, and/or importing heavily-regulated products, a larger, more established firm with multiple offices may be indicated.

2. What is the reputation of the brokerage? How many years has it been in business? Don't be afraid to ask for references. Actually follow up on them.

3. How many licensed brokers on are staff? In multi-office customs brokerage firms Customs only requires one licensed broker per district. Therefore, it is possible to have a local office that works off the license of someone far away. For example, the licensed broker for the district of Dallas may work out of the Dallas office, but be the central licensee for offices in northern Texas, and areas of Oklahoma and Kansas.

4. What is the financial stability of the brokerage? Customs regulations state that "The liability for duties, both regular and additional, attaching on importation, constitutes a personal debt due from the importer to the U.S." and "Payment to a broker covering duties does not relieve the importer of liability if the duties are not paid by the broker."

   Ask for a financial statement, financial references and/or their bank and bank officer's name. Follow up with your research until you feel comfortable in your choice of broker.

5. Does the broker have the technical expertise and knowledge of your specific product(s)? Does the broker specialize in your product(s)? This becomes more of an issue with highly-regulated items such as textiles and other quota products.

6. Do you get along well with the broker? Do you feel that you have good enough communication with the broker that you can work together as "partners?"

7. What are the fees for handling your types of Customs entries? Be sure to ask up front how much it will cost to handle your business. Note that charges can add up for each additional form that your broker completes for you. Always ask for all fees, not simply the basic entry fee.

8. Be prepared to submit a financial statement if you plan to ask for credit terms. Note that brokers are just like any other business in handling their accounts. The problem with credit terms is that Customs duties may amount to $3,000 on an entry the broker charges $320 for processing. Brokers are not at all thrilled about extending soft credit terms to their clients. Net 10 days with immediate cut-off of credit terms if you are slow to pay is common.

9. Be prepared to provide your broker with a power of attorney. This is a legal document that empowers your broker to act as an agent on your behalf with Customs. It authorizes them to sign your name to documents. Refer to "Power of Attorney" on page 206.

10. You will be required to purchase either a surety bond for each importation or a continuous bond to cover a series of ongoing importations.

11. Note that you can make checks for Customs duties payable to your customs broker or to Customs. If you have any unresolved concerns about your broker, make the check payable directly to Customs, forwarding it to your broker along with a separate check to cover their fees.

12. Your customs broker should be a major player on your team of "professional partners." You can almost always get insights on such additional questions as how you can save on international transportation, Customs duties, warehousing, cartage, etc. Ask to be kept informed of any changes in Customs regulations which affect your products.

13. Your customs broker does much more than clear goods through Customs. These professionals can also provide door-to-door delivery of freight to one or to many locations across the U.S. They can help advise you on issues and opportunities such as Foreign Trade Zones, Temporary Importation under Bond, warehousing, cartage, pre-clearance of cargo, marking and labeling, other agency requirements, etc.

14. You can find a customs broker by referring to the "Yellow Pages" of a port city under the listing "Customs Brokers."

   To locate a customs broker who is a member of a trade association for brokers, Refer to "Customs Brokers, Freight Forwarders, and Professional Associations" on page 72, which provides the names, addresses, and telephone numbers of customs brokers associations throughout the U.S.

The National Customs Brokers & Forwarders Association of America, Inc. (NCBFAA)

1200 18th Street, NW, #901
Washington DC 20036
(202) 466-0222, FAX (202) 466-0226
Web: www.ncbfaa.org

InfoList #61

Role of the Customs Attorney

The Customs attorney advises and provides a varied group of services to his or her client. These include advising the client in connection with ongoing transactions to ensure that the correct rate of duty is being assessed, as well as providing advice and representation in various matters before the Customs Service or in litigation before the Court of International Trade.

The Customs attorney is active in counseling and representing importers on administrative matters before the United States Customs Service, at the local, regional and national levels. Areas of representation typically include advising importers on how to structure transactions to take full advantage of lower or free duty rates provided by the classification and valuation laws of the United States; representing importers who have had merchandise detained or seized, or against whom penalties or claims for liquidated damages have been asserted; representing importers involved in U.S. trademark, patent, or copyright issues; and representing importers in issues involving laws or quota restrictions for textiles and apparel. The Customs attorney also conducts compliance reviews for importers, and actively represents and assists importers in preparation for, during, or subsequent to, audits by the Customs Service. Other areas of emphasis include utilizing foreign trade zones for duty exemptions, drawbacks, the Generalized System of Preferences, U.S. goods returned exemptions, and marking requirements.

Activities before the administrative agency include settlement of disputes relating to possible classification and valuation of imported products as well as potential penalty assessments. Specific activities which a Customs attorney should consider in his or her review of import transactions include the following:

1. Correct classification of imported products under Headquarters rulings or pertinent court decisions.

2. Review of the status of pending issues or legislation regarding classification which could be of significance to the client.

3. Examination of the buyer/seller relationships, assists, the price paid or payable, and related and accounting procedures to verify that the proper import values are being reported to the Customs Service, and the appropriate duties paid thereon.

4. Review of the correctness of the marking of imported products and other agency laws which might affect the imported products.

5. Verification that there are no potential antidumping duties or countervailing duties applicable to the imported products or other relevant actions before the International Trade Commission or Office of the Special Trade Representative.

6. Verification that potential drawback is being properly captured and that the appropriate types of claims are being filed with the Customs Service.

7   Verification that the client has in effect appropriate recordkeeping procedures in compliance with the Customs laws and regulations and that the company will maintain these records over a five-year period of time.

These record requirements relate to all documents concerning the company's import transactions. (Under the Modernization Act, the importer may be assessed penalties if appropriate records are not maintained.)

A Customs attorney provides advice, consultation, and representation to Customs brokers, bonded warehouse owners, foreign trade zone operators, freight forwarders, and other law firms in such diverse, specialized areas as electronics, textiles, steel, general merchandise, automotive, and food products.

The Customs attorney must have a substantial litigation background with the skills and support staff necessary to fully pursue clients' rights in what is one of the most complex and least understood areas of the law. The Customs attorney must be admitted to practice before the United States Court of International Trade and the Court of Appeals for the Federal Circuit, as well as various other federal and state courts.

A Customs attorney's litigation practice encompasses a broad spectrum of customs cases, including classification and value, special duty exemption, seized or prohibited merchandise, and penalty actions.

The Customs attorney often has expertise in the related field of international trade practice, which may include antidumping and Section 301 law concerning unfair trade practices. Additionally, the Customs attorney may assist clients in the area of export licensing by offering consultation and representation to chemical, electronic, and high-technology clients in penalty proceedings for violation of the Export Administration Regulations or the International Traffic and Arms Regulations, and before the Department of Commerce and the Department of State with regard to export licensing issues. Representation may include establishing corporate procedures for controlling exports; determining controlled commodities; obtaining emergency export licenses, and special licenses, such as distribution and protect licenses; and assisting exporters prepare for systems reviews by the Office of Export Licensing.

Courtesy of:

The Law Offices of George R. Tuttle, Customs Lawyers

Three Embarcadero Center, Suite 1160
San Francisco, California 94111
(415) 986-8780

InfoList #62

The American Association of Exporters and Importers

The American Association of Exporters and Importers (AAEI) is a professional trade association representing U.S. businesses engaged in foreign trade. Founded in 1921, the AAEI promotes fair and open trade among nations. Its staff has developed strong expertise in numerous areas of trade and represents the foreign trade constituency before official bodies in Washington and around the country.

This voluntary association has more than 1,200 member firms covering a wide range of specific industries. The AAEI also includes members representing others involved in international trade, such as customs brokers, freight forwarders, trading companies, financial institutions, and attorneys, adding the perspective and support of even more parties with immediate interests in international trade. This broad base gives the association added heft as a voice for the concerns of its membership. This breadth has enabled the AAEI to deliver its pro-trade message without becoming bogged down in the particular problems of individual industries.

Services

The AAEI serves as a contact point with the executive and legislative branches and with government regulatory agencies. Its Weekly Trade Alert covers recent developments affecting international business and reports on deliberations and actions of various government bodies, including the Department of Commerce, the U.S. Trade Representative, the Department of the Treasury, U.S. Customs and Border Protection, the Food and Drug Administration, the Federal Trade Commission, and the Consumer Product Safety Commission, among others. Regular features cover Customs decisions, judicial rulings relevant to trade, reports on export trading firms, countertrade, a Pacific Rim trade report, and product standards developments. It also has a section for opportunities and a countertrade clearing house. A digest of special information is offered through the association's weekly ALERT-FAX.

The AAEI publishes a series of topical special reports, the Special Information Bulletins and Reference Manuals, which have covered such issues as the Harmonized Tariff Schedule, U.S. export controls, the Generalized System of Preferences, the Caribbean Basin Initiative, countertrade, the Foreign Sales Corporation Act, the U.S.-Israel Free Trade Agreement, the U.S.-Canada Free Trade Agreement, East-West trade, and related issues.

The Weekly Textile Quota Alert is a computer-based service available to members that allows them to keep abreast of the latest developments in the areas of textile quotas, embargoes, visas, and bilateral agreements. The GSP Subscription Service covers changes in eligibility, petitions to add and delete products in specific countries, legislative and executive activity, and publishes key documents. The Export Controls Progress Reports reports on changes in export controls policy and specific rulings; legislative, executive, and regulatory actions and initiatives; judicial decisions; and current news from the field. The association's International Trade Quarterly offers in-depth features on current issues in international trade, a Washington round-up, and sections on trade briefs and trade opportunities.

Programs

The AAEI actively monitors legislation and regulatory deliberations. It testifies before government bodies and intervenes in regulatory and legal proceedings in support of trade interests. Its staff offers advice, research capabilities, and support to members with specific trade concerns. Its One-Stop Hotline information and referral service can help with procedures and directions to the appropriate agencies, and it maintains a reference center for the use of members.

The association operates a network of active regional and national committees dealing with issues of interest to its members to share expertise and help set policy. Special committees are convened as needed to deal with specific areas of interest, such as automation, the Harmonized Tariff Schedule conversion, NAFTA, environmental and consumer issues, countervailing duties and antidumping issues, international finance, insurance, customs policy and enforcement, transportation, and trade legislation. Standing committees deal with general trade policy and regulation, formulating proactive policy positions to attempt to convey the opinions of international traders to government. The AAEI also helps organize industry-based associations to pool the expertise of members in a particular field for action on critical issues. For example, the association's Textile and Apparel Group has become the largest such interest group in the nation and is highly influential in lobbying for freer trade in these areas.

The AAEI sponsors an annual meeting held during World Trade Week in May which regularly attracts cabinet-level speakers for a series of briefing sessions to which all members are invited. AAEI conferences and seminars cover such topics as foreign exchange, international codes, transportation cost management, and trade legislation.

The AAEI maintains an exchange program with U.S. Customs and Border Protection through which members and Customs personnel can meet to discuss operational and policy issues. These briefings are scheduled at major ports nationwide and are available to members.

For more information, contact:

American Association of Exporters and Importers
P.O. Box 7813
Washington DC 20044-7813
Tel (202) 661-2181, FAX (202) 661-2185

InfoList #63
13 Ways to Sell Imports

1. Sell Wholesale to Retail Outlets

Almost any consumer product imaginable can be sold directly to retail outlets by an individual importer/sales person or a large-scale import/sales organization. One consideration is that the cost of traveling and making sales presentations makes selling a single product inefficient unless the product is in great demand or has a substantial margin of profit. Generally, you will be more effective if you have a whole product line of related goods to sell.

2. Sell to Distributors

An alternative to selling wholesale to retailers is to sell in bulk to distributors who have an established client base within a given geographic area and/or a specific industry group. They can often get wide coverage in a short time. Consider that they will need an even larger discount than retailers.

3. Sell Wholesale to Manufacturers

Most small- and medium-sized manufacturers don't have the time or inclination to travel the world, seeking raw materials and component parts for their manufacturing operations. They will often prefer to purchase from a reliable local supplier.

4. Wholesale Direct Mail

Some products may lend themselves to wholesale direct-mail marketing. One advantage of this marketing is that you can get large-scale distribution in a short time and avoid the discounts a distributor demands.

5. Retail Direct Mail

Some importers have cut out the middleman entirely by going direct to the consumer via direct mail sales. Beware: some products lend themselves to direct mail more than others. You will need a well-defined market niche, a high margin of profit, a superbly targeted mail campaign, and a highly effective—well-designed and written—marketing piece.

6. Catalog Sales

Some importers deal in items that they can sell to catalog houses while others seek to develop their own catalog company. The former opportunity generally means a lower margin of profit, lower risk, and lower required capitalization, while the latter generally offers the promise of a higher margin, greater risk, and the need for more capital. One of the key factors in a catalog business is the development of a mailing list of people or companies who will buy a particular type or style of product over and over again.

7. Retail

If you have an established retail business you are in an excellent position to gauge the market for products for your existing clientele. You will also have familiarity with wholesale and retail pricing structures and, if you buy right, the opportunity to take an ad-ditional slice of the profits by importing products yourself. Start by importing goods you are familiar with before branching out into new products.

Starting your own retail store at the same time you start your import business is much riskier. You likely will not have the necessary feel for the market for products you are importing, and you will be juggling too many responsibilities to handles all of them well.

8. The Web

Significant cost savings and conveniences are available by selling products online. The store window is a Web site homepage so the high overhead costs is non-existent. You may be the wholesaler who sells to retailers. Or you may sell products on auction sites (such as e-bay) or your own Web site.

9. Television Shopping Shows

Television shopping programs are an interesting and nontraditional means of selling imported products. However, they have an interest in the unusual and are always looking for new, offbeat merchandise. Consider that the pricing has to be just right and that there has to be an immediately available supply.

10. Contract Manufacturing

Submit proposals to existing wholesalers, distributors, or retailers of products similar to yours to manufacture products to their specification on a contract basis. Be prepared to be able to satisfy them that you are capable of following through on your proposal.

11. Act as an Agent

If you have good contacts with overseas sources of supply, and with U.S. distributors, wholesalers, or manufacturers who need those products, consider acting as an agent for the U.S. buyers and/or for the overseas sellers. This is a good route to follow if your contacts and expertise are better than your ability to finance a transaction.

Refer to "The Transferable Letter of Credit" in the Banking section for information on how to structure payment for such deals.

12. The "Show and Tell and Sell" Party

Many importers get their start by importing small quantities of a wide range of products that they know will be of interest to their friends and relatives. Upon their return from the buying trip they invite them over for a "show and tell and sell" party.

Some enterprising importers expanded on the theme by giving 10% commission to friends to host a theme import party (e.g. "Bali Imports Party").

13. "Flea" Markets

A big business has developed selling product lines of imported merchandise at large-scale flea markets across the country. Some importers have established distributorships in multi-state regions supplying quantities of merchandise to sellers who are paid a percentage of the profits. This method generally requires excellent direct-to-the-consumer pricing.

InfoList #64
Import Goods Duty-Free!

Preferential Trade Status

Through special trade agreements, the U.S. has established favorable—and in some cases, extremely favorable—trade conditions with specific countries and associations of countries. In a number of cases you can enter goods duty free as long as you satisfy the conditions of the specific program, usually having to do with origination of the products in the signatory country. Importers who take advantage of these programs are often able to undercut the competition by offering lower prices based on the more favorable duty rates they obtain on the products they import through these programs. Here is a review of trade categories and programs:

Generalized System of Preferences (GSP)

This is a program providing for duty-free entry of eligible merchandise into the United States from 117 countries, 26 nonindependent countries and territories, three associations of countries (the Cartagena Group in South America, ASEAN in Southeast Asia and the Pacific, and CARICOM in the Caribbean), and 36 least-developed countries which receive additional special preferential treatment. Refer to "Generalized System of Preferences (GSP)" on page 229.

Caribbean Basin Initiative (CBI)

Established by the Caribbean Basin Economic Recovery Act (CBERA), this is another program providing for duty-free entry of eligible merchandise into the United States from 24 developing countries of the Caribbean Basin. Refer to "Caribbean Basin Initiative (CBI)" on page 231.

North American Free Trade Agreement (NAFTA)

At the end of 1993 the United States, Canada, and Mexico signed a broad agreement to eliminate restrictions on the flow of goods, services, and investment among the three countries. This includes the phasing out of tariffs over a period of years, elimination of non-tariff barriers and full protection of intellectual property rights. The agreement also includes special treatment for the partners with regard to quotas and establishes a trilateral commission to adjudicate trade disputes. NAFTA supersedes the existing U.S.-Canada Free Trade Agreement, although the provisions governing trade with Canada remain essentially the same as under the earlier agreement and are incorporated into the new document. Refer to "The North American Free Trade Agreement (NAFTA)" on page 226 and to "Update on NAFTA" on page 79.

U.S.-Israel Free Trade Area Agreement

Israel is the beneficiary of a program providing for free or reduced rates of duty for eligible merchandise imported from Israel into the United States. "U.S.- Israel Free Trade Area Agreement" on page 234 for a fuller discussion of this program.

Compact of the Freely Associated States

The Compact of the Associated States provides for duty-free entry of eligible products manufactured in the Marshall Islands and the Federated States of Micronesia. Refer to General Note 9 of the Harmonized Tariff Schedule of the United States (HTSUS) and to "Compact of the Freely Associated States" on page 237.

Product Specific Preferences

The Automotive Products Trade Act provides for duty-free import of automotive parts to registered U.S. manufacturers. Refer to General Note 5 of the Harmonized Tariff Schedule of the United States (HTSUS).

The Articles for Duty-Free Treatment to the Agreement on Trade in Civil Aircraft provides for duty-free import of approved aircraft components for the manufacture of civil aircraft by U.S. firms. Refer to General Note 6 of the HTSUS.

Temporary Free Importation

An ATA carnet is an international customs document which may be used for the temporary duty-free importation of certain goods into a country (U.S.) in lieu of the usual customs documents required. Refer to "Temporary Free Importations" on page 220.

The Andean Trade Preference Act (ATPA)

Under the Andean Trade Preference Act (ATPA), eligible products from Bolivia, Colombia, Ecuador, and Peru may be imported duty free. Refer to Commodity Index Andean Trade Preference Act (ATPA), beginning on page 233 and to General Note 11 of the Harmonized Trade Schedule of the United States (HTSUS).

U.S. Foreign Trade Zones

U.S. Foreign Trade Zones are places in the U.S. which, for Customs purposes, are considered outside the Customs Territory of the U.S. There are many operations you can perform on goods to enable you to import them duty-free, or at reduced duty rates. Refer to "Foreign Trade Zones" on page 242.

Duty-Free Products and Commodities

There are thousands of products and commodities which are already duty-free. Refer to the Commodity Index, Sample Duty Rates subhead in this manual for examples of products which may be imported duty-free.

Jordan-USA Agreement

Jordan and the US signed an agreement on October 24th, 2000 to remove the commercial barriers and duties on goods and services originating in and traded between Jordan and the US. The agreement seeks to protect the environment, workers rights, and electronic trade. As far as e-trade is concerned, the two nations are working to alleviate tariff restrictions on the transfer of information. Jordan is the first Arab state to sign an agreement with the US which will remove customs barriers in the industrial, agricultural, and service arenas.

InfoList #65
Update on the WTO and GATT

What are the WTO and GATT?
The World Trade Organization (WTO), established January 1, 1995, is the legal and institutional foundation of the multilateral trading system. It is the embodiment of the results of the Uruguay Round trade negotiations and the successor to the General Agreement on Tariffs and Trade (GATT), providing the principal contractual obligations determining how governments frame and implement domestic trade legislation and regulations.

GATT began in 1947 as a response to predatory and protectionist trade in the 1930s. Since its beginning, GATT has lowered average global tariffs from an average of roughly 40% to the current 5%. The 1993 Uruguay Round agreement created an international body, the WTO, to administer the new provisions, the majority of which are designed to reduce tariff and nontariff barriers to international trade.Under the Uruguay Round agreements, overall tariffs are expected to fall to about 3.75%. There are currently 124 signatories to the Marrakesh Agreement Establishing the World Trade Organization, and more than 30 countries have requested to join the WTO. The U.S. ratified the agreement in December of 1994, and the European industrialized countries and Japan followed suit shortly thereafter. The agreement went into effect on January 1, 1995.

Key Provisions of the Uruguay Round
- **Import tariffs:** Eventual overall reduction of 33% in tariffs worldwide, with elimination by the U.S., European, and other industrial nations of all tariffs on pharmaceuticals, construction equipment, agricultural equipment, medical equipment, paper, steel, furniture, and some liquors. Substantial cuts will also be made for chemicals, wood, aluminum, scientific instruments, and toys. Most tariff reductions are being phased in over a five-year period.
- **Textiles:** A 10-year phase-out of all quotas under the Multi-Fiber Arrangement that protects industrialized countries from cheaper overseas imports. U.S. tariffs on textile imports are scheduled to fall by about 25%.
- **Agriculture:** Phased in cut of 36% on agricultural tariffs and crop export subsidies by industrialized nations and 24% by developing countries.
- **Intellectual property:** Strengthens enforcement for copyright, patent, and trademark infringement.
- **Procurement:** Federal, state, and local preferential "Buy America" rules will be outlawed, opening more markets to imported goods.
- **Dumping:** Tougher restrictions on the export of goods at below-cost and below home market prices.
- **Limits on local content rules:** The agreement would bar excessive local content requirements as well as requirements for net export of production.

How Does the Uruguay Round Agreement Affect U.S. Importers?
The primary benefits will accrue to exporters as tariffs fall on U.S. products sold abroad. Because the U.S. already has one of the lowest tariff structures in the world, import-

ers are not expected to realize many immediate benefits. Nevertheless, increased world trade activity—economists estimate a $200 billion annual gain in world trade by 2005—should promote imports as well as facilitate exports. The creation of an estimated 2 million new jobs in the U.S. should also serve to increase domestic demand for many imported products.

The planned phaseout of textile quotas should be a boon to importers of textiles and apparel as it opens U.S. markets to lower priced foreign goods that had been kept out by restrictive quotas. More stringent rules on dumping could hurt imports of steel, automotive products, and ships. Agricultural products should become easier to import, although producers operating with large government subsidies are expected to find their goods less competitive as they lose this support. In particular, import quotas on such tightly controlled commodities as sugar, cotton, peanuts, and dairy products will be phased out and tariffs eventually lowered on these products. The U.S. retains the right to initiate antidumping actions against foreign manufacturers of semiconductors, which could prevent any windfalls in growth of imports of electronic components.

WTO Functions and Structure
The essential functions of the WTO are:
- Administering and implementing the trade agreements which together make up the WTO;
- Acting as a forum for multilateral trade negotiations;
- Seeking to resolve trade disputes;
- Overseeing national trade policies; and
- Cooperating with other policy-making institutions involved in global economic decisions.

The Ministerial Conference is the highest WTO authority, meeting every two years. Several subsidiary bodies, including the General Council, which also convenes as the Dispute Settlement Body and as the Trade Policy Review Body, take care of the day-to-day work of the WTO. Other major bodies are the Councils for Trade in Goods, Trade in Services, and Trade-Related Aspects of Intellectual Property Rights; and the Committees on Trade and Development, Balance of Payments, and Budget, Finance and Administration. The General Council also established, in early 1995, a Committee on Trade and Environment. In addition, each of the plurilateral agreements of the WTO —those on civil aircraft, government procurement, dairy products and bovine meat—have their own management bodies which report to the General Council.

The WTO has many publications, both on its own activities and on international trade and economic policy in general. For more information, contact:

World Trade Organization (WTO)
Centre William Rappard 154
Rue de Lausanne
CH-1211 Geneva, Switzerland
[41] (22) 7395111; FAX [41] (22) 7395458
Web. www.wto.org/

InfoList #66
Update on NAFTA

What Is NAFTA?

The North American Free Trade Agreement (NAFTA) creates a preferred trade zone consisting of the U.S., Canada, and Mexico. Tariffs, quotas, and other trade barriers—such as licensing, local content, investment, and customs fee restrictions—are scheduled to be reduced or eliminated on transactions among the three countries. Some of the agreement's provisions became effective January 1, 1994, while others are scheduled to become operative over five or ten years. Restrictions on a few sensitive products will take as long as 15 years to be phased out.

The U.S. and Canada were already participants in a free trade agreement that allowed a great deal of the trade between the two countries to be conducted on a streamlined basis with reduced or no tariffs on the products involved. NAFTA extends and reorganizes these preferences to include similar provisions for Mexico, while Mexico in turn has agreed to open its markets to U.S. and Canadian products. Other countries in the Americas may eventually join NAFTA.

Key Provisions of NAFTA

Import Tariffs. At the time of signing, import tariffs averaged roughly 10% on goods entered into Mexico and 3% on those entered into the U.S. Many of these tariffs were eliminated or lowered on January 1, 1994, while most others are to be gradually reduced and eventually eliminated.

Local Content and Rules of Origin. Specific national local content requirements have been removed. However, NAFTA imposed rules of origin designed to restrict the agreement's benefits to products actually produced in the member countries. Compliance rules are complex and stringent. For more information, refer to "Rules of Origin" on page 226.

Certificates of Origin. Canada, Mexico and the U.S. established a uniform Certificate of Origin to certify that goods imported into their territories qualify for the preferential tariff treatment accorded by the NAFTA. Only importers who possess a valid Certificate of Origin may claim preferential tariff treatment for originating goods.

Quotas. Under NAFTA, quotas have been liberalized and eventually will be eliminated on imports from its members. During this transition, goods imported under quota from Mexico will not count against the total entry threshold amounts established for these products, so that absolute quotas are effectively raised for affected items imported from Mexico. The implementing regulations specify a schedule for specific products, including milk, cheese, and other dairy products; tomatoes and other fruit and vegetable products; sugars, syrups, and products containing them; orange juice; and some textile products.

Textiles and Apparel. Under NAFTA, the U.S. will immediately remove quotas on textiles and apparel wholly Mexican in origin. Quotas on other textile products imported from Mexico but failing to meet NAFTA origin rules will be phased out over 10 years. The U.S. will phase out tariffs on apparel imported from its NAFTA partners over 10 years and on textiles over eight. The rules of origin for textiles imported under NAFTA are particularly complex.

Agricultural Products. All U.S. and Mexican nontariff barriers are being converted into either tariff-rate quotas—allowing in unlimited quantities but charging higher rates once a threshold of imports has been reached—or ordinary tariffs with a set rate regardless of the amount of the product entered. These changes will be phased in over 10 years for most products.

Automotive Industry. As with textiles, the rules of origin specific to automotive products under NAFTA are particularly complex; they are based on a tariff change alone or a tariff change and a regional value-content requirement, which must be calculated using the net cost method. Relaxed Mexican tariff and nontariff barriers to foreign imports will allow greater and more economical flows of outside components into Mexico, which will in turn upgrade and increase the export production of the country's plants.

Electronic Products. The rules of origin for a significant number of electronic products are based strictly on a tariff change. This tariff change is structured to require that key subassemblies of the product be produced in North America. In another significant features of NAFTA, the three countries are harmonizing, in a series of staged reductions, their respective MFN tariff rates on computers, computer parts and certain computer peripherals. Once this has been accomplished, duties on goods will be payable only once upon entering the NAFTA territory. Once within the NAFTA territory, these articles are considered originating and may move among Canada, Mexico and the U.S. without payment of duty. In addition, on January 1, 1994, the three countries changed their MFN tariff rates to free on virtually all semi-conductors and all local area network apparatus.

Trilateral Trade Commission: NAFTA provided for the creation of a trilateral commission to adjudicate disputes under the agreement. This body is organized in an attempt to avoid national bias and is required to act on complaints within eight months. It will deal with antidumping and subsidy issues, as well as the implementation of the provisions of the agreement.

Temporary Admissions. NAFTA requires Canada, Mexico and the U.S. to grant duty-free temporary admission to certain classes of goods imported from another NAFTA country. Duty-free entry cannot be conditioned on whether or not directly competitive or substitutable goods are available in the importing country. In addition, the goods do not have to originate in a NAFTA country.

For More Information on NAFTA

The U.S. Customs NAFTA Center, located in Dallas, Texas provides more than 400 documents through an automated fax system. To retrieve these documents, dial NAFTA FAX at (972) 574-1582 from a touchtone phone. Trade Specialists are also available to answer specific questions and field requests for printed information. Call (972) 574-4061 during business hours. Also refer to "The North American Free Trade Agreement (NAFTA)" on page 226.

InfoList #67

23 Advantages and Uses of Foreign Trade Zones

U.S. Foreign Trade Zones (FTZs) are areas that are considered for Customs purposes to be outside U.S. Customs territory. FTZs therefore offer outstanding advantages to the importer (and exporter): merchandise can be landed and stored (and more) in a zone without being subject to U.S. Customs entry and clearance requirements.

1. Goods may remain in an FTZ for an unlimited amount of time. Thus, you can release your goods according to market demand, waiting for a favorable time and then make immediate deliveries, while avoiding possible cancellations of orders due to shipping delays. You can even wait for a favorable change in duty rates. However, you should realize that storage charges can eat into or offset these advantages.

2. You can save on transport costs by shipping goods to the FTZ in bulk and repacking them. Also, unassembled or disassembled goods, such as furniture or machinery, can be shipped for assembly it the zone.

3. Goods shipped in bulk can be dried in an FTZ to save duty which would have to be paid on the pre-evaporation or shrinkage amount; cleaned to save duty on dirt or culls; inspected and sorted to save duty on goods damaged by breakage, leaking, or seepage, or impure goods, on missing articles, and on waste, which can be destroyed or entered with duty being paid at a lower rate as recoverable waste.

4. Substandard goods may be processed and upgraded to meet requirements of federal regulatory agencies.

5. You may mark or label goods to meet U.S. Customs-enforced requirements, thus avoiding the fines that are assessed on improperly marked goods.

6. You can save on insurance by insuring goods only for cost plus transportation, rather than cost plus transportation plus duty and taxes.

7. FTZs do not require bonds for storage, manipulation, or manufacture. Nor are bonds are required for missing licenses, permits, or other documents; you may keep your merchandise in the zone until documents or copies are obtained. No bonding is required for exhibition within the FTZ.

8. Goods in excess of quotas may be held in the zone until the next quota period. The date of entry of the merchandise into Customs territory is the effective date applied for quota purposes, regardless of its status is, and whether or not it has been changed in form by manipulation or manufacture.

9. Goods subject to a quota may, under certain circumstances, be changed or manufactured into an item not subject to a quota, and entered into Customs territory. Proposed operations involving quota merchandise in such zones must obtain specific clearance from the FTZ's Executive Secretary. Basically, the Board will not approve operations which have the effect of directly circumventing a quota.

10. You can save money in duties by converting a product into an article which has a lower duty rate.

11. A sample of your product can be withdrawn from the zone and forwarded to Customs for a classification ruling, thus avoiding possible disputes over the classification of the product.

12. You can borrow on the goods stored in the zone using negotiable warehouse receipts as collateral.

13. Goods under $250.00 in value may be removed from a zone as an informal entry with duties paid to the Customs collector at the zone without affecting the status of the remaining goods.

14. Goods may be sold or auctioned in the zone, transferring duty and excise tax liability to the purchaser.

15. You may exhibit goods for an unlimiterd period without bond. Thus, you can display them where they are stored, establish showrooms of your own, or join with other importers in displaying merchandise in a permanent exhibit in the zone. You are not limited to a display of samples, but may sell from your stock in wholesale quantities.

16. Your goods are under federal protection—it is a federal offense to steal from a FTZ.

17. All foreign and domestic merchandise may be brought into the zone, so that you may combine them, use one to process the other, save by using domestic materials for packaging, etc., gaining a price advantage over wholly foreign or wholly domestic produced items, and avoiding sending domestic materials abroad for processing.

18. You can avoid hiring a special employee to receive, store, and then release your merchandise to your forwarding agent or broker.

19. Ship stores, aircraft supplies, and ground maintenance and repair equipment may be stockpiled at and withdrawn from a zone tax- and duty-free.

20. Goods in an FTZ may be exported without your having ever paid duty on them, and thus without having money tied up until drawback. Domestic goods are considered exported upon entering the zone for rebates of duty and Internal Revenue Service excise taxes. Thus an importer does not have to wait until he or she finds a foreign buyer, or to actually export the goods, to benefit by using the FTZ.

21. You do not have to complete your invoices until your goods are sold, so that you do not have to show the sale in your books until it is actually made. Thus, you may be able to postpone taxes to another period that is more to your advantage.

22. Merchandise may be withdrawn from a zone for exhibition at a trade fair without payment of duty or taxes. It must, however, be entered for consumption, exported, abandoned to the government, or destroyed within three months of the closing of the fair. Return of the goods to the FTZ for export satisfies this requirement.

23. You may transfer merchandise in Customs bonded warehouses to a zone for exportation or destruction before the term expires, cancelling the bond and removing a time limit for reexportation. This also applies to internal revenue bonded warehouses, with taxes paid recoverable by drawback once the goods are in a zone.

InfoList #68

U.S. Customs and Border Protection Offices

In late 1994, U.S. Customs and Border Protection began a major reorganization. Twenty Customs Management Centers (CMC) have been established to oversee the internal management functions of the Customs Service. Five Strategic Trade Centers (STC) have also been created to enhance Customs capacity to address major international trade issues, such as textile fraud, anti-dumping, and protection of U.S. intellectual property rights.

Customs and Border Protection

U.S. Customs and Border Protection (CBP)
1300 Pennsylvania Avenue NW
Washington, DC 20229
Web: www.customs.treas.gov

Office of the Trade Relations
(202) 927-1440; FAX (202) 927-1969

Office of Field Operations
(202) 927-0100; FAX (202) 927-0837
Trade Compliance Division
(202) 927-0390, 927-0300; FAX (202) 927-1096

Commercial Enforcement Branch
(202) 927-0005

Visa Requirements Branch

(202) 927-1959

Quota Branch
(202) 927-5850

Office of Information and Technology
(202) 927-0680; FAX (202) 927-2080
Laboratories & Scientific Services Division
(202) 927-0632; FAX (202) 927-2060

Office of International Affairs
(202) 927-0400; FAX (202) 927-2064

Office of Investigations
(202) 927-1600; FAX (202) 927-1948

Office of Regulations & Rulings
(202) 572-8700; FAX (202) 572-8844
International Trade Compliance Division
(202) 572-8733; FAX (202) 572-8844

Entry & Carrier Rulings Branch, (202) 572-8730
Intellectual Property Rights Branch, (202) 572-8710
Penalties Branch, (202) 572-8750
Regulations Branch, (202) 572-8760
Value Branch, (202) 572-8740

Tariff Classification Appeals Division
No main phone number.

General Classifications Branch, (202) 572-8780
Special Classification & Marking Br., (202) 572-8810
Textile Branch, (202) 572-8790

National Commodity Specialist Division
(646) 733-3000
1 Penn Plaza 11th Floor
New York, NY 10119

Special Products Branch, (646) 733-3060
Metal and Machinery Branch, (646) 733-3050
Textiles and Apparel Branch, (646) 743-3070

Office of Strategic Trade
(202) 927-0570; FAX (202) 927-2110

Customs and Border Protection NAFTA Center
Goods going to Canada: 1-800-661-6121
Goods going to Mexico: (202) 728-1600

Harbor Maintenance Fee Hotline
(317) 298-1250

Customs Service and Area Ports

S—Service Port (Both Internal And Trade Purposes)
E—Service Port (External Trade Purposes Only)
A—Area Port

Alabama
Mobile (S)
150 N. Royal St.
Mobile, AL 36602
Tel: (251) 441-5106

Alaska
Anchorage (SA)
605 W. Fourth Ave.
Anchorage, AK 99501
Tel: (907) 271-2675

Arizona
Douglas (A)
First St. & Pan American Ave
Douglas, AZ 85607
Tel: (520) 364-8486

Nogales (SA)
9 N. Grand Ave.
Nogales, AZ 85621
Tel: (520) 287-1410 Ext. 210

Phoenix (A)
3002 East Old Tower Road, Suite 400
Phoenix, AZ 85034
Tel: (602) 914-1400

San Luis (A)
Highway 95 and Border
San Luis, AZ 85349
Tel: (928) 627-8854

Tucson (E)
7150 S. Tucson Blvd.
Tucson, AZ 85706
Tel: (520) 670-6461

California
Calexico (E)
1699 East Carr Road
Calexico, CA 92231
Tel: (760) 768-2330

Los Angeles/Airport Area (A)
11099 S. La Cienega Blvd.
Los Angeles, CA 90045
Tel: (310) 215-2618

Los Angeles/Long Beach Seaport Area (A)
301 East Ocean Boulevard
Long Beach, CA 90802
Tel: (562) 366-5555

Otay Mesa (S)
9777 Via De La Amistad
San Diego, CA 92154
Tel: (619) 671-8000

San Ysidro (A)
720 E. San Ysidro Blvd.
San Ysidro, CA 92173
Tel: (619) 690-8800

Colorado
Denver (SA)
24735 East 75th Avenue
Denver, CO 80249
Tel: (303) 342-8400 Ext. 0

Connecticut
Hartford (A)
135 High St
Hartford, CT 06103
Tel: (860) 240-4306

Florida
Jacksonville (A)
2831 Talleyrand Ave.
Jacksonville, FL 32206
Tel: (904) 360-5020

Miami Airport (S)
6601 W. 25th St.
Miami, FL 33152
Tel: (305) 869-2800

Tampa (SA)
1624 E. 7th Ave., Suite 101
Tampa, FL 33605
Tel: (813) 228-2385

Georgia
Savannah (S)
1 East Bay Street
Savannah, GA 31401
Tel: (912) 447-9400

Illinois
Chicago (SA)
610 S. Canal St
Chicago, IL 60607
Tel: (312) 983-1100

Louisiana
Baton Rouge (A)
5353 Essen Lane
Baton Rouge, LA 70809
Tel: (225) 389-0261

New Orleans (S)
423 Canal St.
New Orleans, LA 70130
Tel: (504) 670-2391

Maine
Calais (A)
3 Customs Street
Calais, ME 04619
Tel: (207) 454-3621

Houlton (A)
Route 95 at the Border
Houlton, ME 04730
Tel: (207) 532-2131

Portland, ME (A)
312 Fore St.
Portland, ME 04101
Tel: (207) 771-3600

Maryland
Baltimore (S)
40 South Gay Street
Baltimore, MD 21202
Tel: (410) 962-2666

Massachusetts
Boston (SA)
10 Causeway St.
Boston, MA 02222
Tel: (617) 565-6149

Michigan
Detroit (S)
477 Michigan Ave.
Detroit, MI 48226
Tel: (313) 442-0368

Grand Rapids (A)
6450 Air Cargo Drive SE
Grand Rapids, MI 49512
Tel: (616) 942-5245

Port Huron (A)
526 Water St.
Port Huron, MI 48060-5471
Tel: (810) 985-7125

Sault Ste Marie (A)
International Bridge Plaza
Sault Ste Marie, MI 49783-1492
Tel: (906) 632-2631

Minnesota
Minneapolis (S)
330 2nd Avenue South
Minneapolis, MN 55401
Tel: (612) 348-1690

Missouri
Kansas City (E)
4100 North Mulberry Drive
Kansas City, MO 64116
Tel: (816) 584-1994

St. Louis(SA)
4477 Woodson Rd
St. Louis, MO 63134
Tel: (314) 428-2662

Montana
Great Falls (SA)
21 Third Street North
Great Falls, MT 59401
Tel: (406) 453-7631

New Jersey
New York/Newark Area (S)
1210 Corbin Street
Elizabeth, NJ 07201
Tel: (201) 443-0110

New York
Buffalo (SA)
111 W. Huron St.
Buffalo, NY 14202
Tel: (716) 646-3400

Champlain (SA)
198 West Service Rd.
Champlain, NY 12919
Tel: (518) 298-8346

New York/JFK Area (S)
Bldg #77
Jamaica, NY 11430
Tel: (718) 553-1750

Ogdensburg (A)
Ogdensburg Bridge Plaza
Ogdensburg, NY 13669
Tel: (315) 393-1390

Syracuse (A)
4034 South Service Road
North Syracuse, NY 13212
Tel: (315) 455-8446

North Carolina
Charlotte (S)
1901 Cross Beam Drive
Charlotte, NC 28217
Tel: (704) 329-6100

Raleigh/Durham (A)
120 Southcenter Ct
Morrisville, NC 27560
Tel: (919) 467-3552

Wilmington, NC (A)
721 Medical Center Drive
Wilmington, NC 28401
Tel: (910) 772-5900

North Dakota
Pembina (SA)
10980 Hwy 29
Pembina, ND 58271
Tel: (701) 825-6201

Ohio
Cleveland (SA)
6747 Engle Rd
Middleburg Heights, OH 44130
Tel: (440) 891-3800

Oregon
Portland (SA)
8337 NE Alderwood Road
Portland, OR 97220
Tel: (503) 326-2865

Pennsylvania
Harrisburg (A)
Harrisburg International Airport
517 Airport Drive
Middletown, PA 17057
Tel: (717) 782-4510

Philadelphia (S)
Second & Chestnut Sts
Philadelphia, PA 19106
Tel: (215) 597-4606

Rhode Island
Providence (SA)
49 Pavilion Ave.
Providence, RI 02905
Tel: (401) 941-6326

South Carolina
Charleston (S)
200 E. Bay St.
Charleston, SC 29401
Tel: (843) 579-6500

Greenville /Spartanburg (A)
150-A West Phillips Road
Greer, SC 29650
Tel: (864) 877-8006

Tennessee
Nashville (A)
322 Knapp Boulevard
Nashville, TN 37217
Tel: (615) 736-5861

Texas
Dallas/Ft.Worth (SA)
1205 Royal Lane
DFW Airport, TX 75261
Tel: (972) 574-2170

El Paso (S)
3600 East Paisano
El Paso, TX 79905
Tel: (915) 872-3444

Houston/Galveston (SA)
2350 N. Sam Houston Pkwy. East #1000
Houston, TX 77032-3100
Tel: (281) 985-6700

Laredo/Colombia (S)
Lincoln / Juarez Bridge, Administrative Bldg. #2
Laredo, TX 78040
Tel: (956) 523-7300

San Antonio (A)
9800 Airport Blvd.
San Antonio, TX 78216
Tel: (210) 821-6965

Virginia
Norfolk (S)
101 East Main Street
Norfolk, VA 23510
Tel: (757) 533-4200

Richmond (A)
4501 Williamsburg Road, Suite G
Republic Plaza
Richmond, VA 23231
Tel: (804) 226-9675

Vermont

Derby Line (A)
Interstate 91
Derby Line, VT 05830
Tel: (802) 873-3489

Highgate Springs (A)
Interstate 89 at the Border
Highstate Springs, VT 05460
Tel: (802) 868-2778

St. Albans (S)
505 Main Street
St. Albans, VT 05478
Tel: (802) 524-7352

Washington

Blaine (SA)
9901 Pacific Highway
Blaine, WA 98230
Tel: (360) 332-5771

Oroville (A)
33643 Highway 97
Oroville, WA 98844
Tel: (509) 476-2955

Seattle (SA)
1000 Second Ave., Suite 2100
Seattle, WA 98104
Tel: (206) 553-0770

Tacoma (SA)
2202 Port Of Tacoma Rd
Tacoma, WA 98421
Tel: (253) 593-6336

Wisconsin

Milwaukee (SA)
6269 Ace Industrial Drive
Cudahy, WI 53110
Tel: (414) 571-2860

Puerto Rico

San Juan (SA)
#1 La Puntilla Street
San Juan, PR 00901
Tel: (787) 729-6850

Virgin Islands (U.S.)

Charlotte/Amalie (SA)
5500 Veterans Drive
St. Thomas, VI 00801
Tel: (340) 774-2510 Ext. 221

InfoList #69

U.S. Government Agencies

These are some of the most important U.S. government contacts for the importer, including many of the main regulatory agencies and agencies which provide important data, such as the CIA or the Bureau of the Census.

Consumer Product Safety Commission (CPSC)

Office of Compliance
Washington DC 20207
Tel: 800-638-2772 or (301) 504-7912
Fax: (301) 504-0359
Web: www.cpsc.gov

Department of Agriculture (USDA)

Web: www.usda.gov

Animal and Plant Health Inspection Service (APHIS)
Legislative and Public Affairs
4700 River Rd., Unit 51
Riverdale, MD 20737
(301) 734-7799

Animal and Plant Health Inspection Service (APHIS)
Plant Protection and Quarantine (PPQ)
Director's Office
4700 River Rd., Unit 131
Riverdale, MD 20737
(301) 734-8261
(301) 734-8758 (PPQ permits)
Web: www.aphis.usda.gov/ppq

Animal and Plant Health Inspection Service (APHIS)
Veterinary Services (VS)
National Center for Import and Export
4700 River Rd., Unit 40
Riverdale, MD 20737
(301) 734-3277; FAX (301) 734-8226

Food Safety and Inspection Service (FSIS)
International Programs
Import Inspection Division
1400 Independence Avenue SW

Rm. 2137, South Building
Washington DC 20250
(202) 720-6400; FAX (202) 720-7990

Foreign Agricultural Service
U.S. Department of Agriculture
Public Affairs Division
Ag Stop 1004
FAF-USDA
1400 Independence Avenue SW
Washington DC 20250-1004
(202) 720-7115; FAX (202) 720-1727
Web: www.fas.usda.gov
    Import License Information System
    (202) 720-1342 (recordings), 720-1344 (assistance)

    International Trade Policy

    (202) 720-6887
    Import Policy Programs, Dairy Group
    (202) 720-2916

Department of Commerce (DOC)

1401 Constitution Ave. NW
Washington DC 20230
Web: www.doc.gov

Bureau of the Census
U.S. Census Bureau
Washington DC 20233
(301) 763-4636
Web: www.census.gov

International Trade Administration
Import Administration
Franklin Court Building, Suite 4100W
1099 14th Street NW

Washington DC 20005
(202) 482-1780

    Foreign Trade Zones Board, (202) 482-2862
    Statutory Import Programs, (202) 482-1660
    Antidumping/Countervailing Duties Enforcement
    Group, (202) 482-3793

International Trade Administration
Office of Textiles, International Agreements Division
(202) 482-4212, 482-3715 (Recorded information on
embargoed categories and known opening dates)

U.S. Patent and Trademark Office
Crystal Park 2 Building
2121 Crystal Drive, Suite 0100

Arlington, VA 22202
(703) 308-4357; FAX (703) 305-8664
Web: www.uspto.gov

U.S. Copyright Office
101 Independence Avenue SE
Washington DC 20559-6000
(202) 707-3000
Web: http://lcweb.loc.gov/copyright

National Institute of Standards & Technology (NIST)
Office of Information Services
Administration Building
Gaithersburg, MD 20899
(301) 975-3052 (Reference Desk)
Web: www.nist.gov

National Marine Fisheries Service (NMFS)
1315 East West Highway
SSMC3
Silver Spring, MD 20910
(301) 713-2239
Office of Protected Resources: (301) 713-2332
Inspection Services Division: (301) 713-2355
Web: www.nmfs.noaa.gov

Department of Health & Human Services

Centers for Disease Control (CDC)
1600 Clifton Rd.
Atlanta, GA 30333
Inquiries: (404) 639-3534
(404) 639-3311
Quarantine Division: (404) 498-1670
Web: www.cdc.gov

Food and Drug Administration (FDA)
5600 Fishers Lane
Rockville, MD 20857-0001
1-888-463-6332
Web: www.fda.gov

FDA Center for Biologics Evaluation and Research
Office of Compliance
Food and Drug Administration
1401 Rockville Pike
Rockville, MD 20852-1448
(301) 827-1800
Web: www.fda.gov/cber/cberftp.html

FDA Center for Drug Evaluation and Research
Office of Compliance
Food and Drug Administration
7500 Standish Place
Rockville, MD 20855-2773
(301) 827-8910
Web: www.fda.gov/cder

FDA Center for Devices and Radiological Health
Consumer Questions
1350 Piccard Drive
Rockville, MD 20850
(301) 827-3990
Web: www.fda.gov/cdrh/index.html

FDA Center for Devices and Radiological Health
Division of Small Manufacturers Assistance
1350 Piccard Drive
Rockville, MD 20850
(800) 638-2041; FAX (301) 443-8818

FDA Center for Food Safety and Applied Nutrition
5100 Paint Branch Parkway
College Park, MD 20740-3835
888-723-3366
Web: vm.cfsan.fda.gov/list.html

FDA Center for Veterinary Medicine
Adverse Reaction Reporting
7500 Standish Place
Rockville, MD 20855-2773
1-800-FDA-VETS
Web: www.fda.gov/cvm/default.html

Department of the Interior

Fish and Wildlife Service (FWS)
Office of Management Authority
4401 N. Fairfax Drive
Arlington, VA 22203-0700
(703) 358-2104
Web: www.fws.gov

Department of State

2201 C St. NW
Washington DC 20520
(202) 647-4000
Web: www.state.gov

Office of Defense Trade Controls
(703) 663-2700

Department of Transportation (DOT)

400 Seventh St. SW
Washington DC 20590
(202) 366-4000
Web: www.dot.gov

Research and Special Programs Administration
Hazardous Materials Information Center
400 Seventh St. SW
Washington DC 20590
(202) 366-4488

National Highway Traffic Safety Administration
Office of Vehicle Safety Compliance
Equipment & Import Division
400 Seventh St. SW
Washington DC 20590
(202) 366-0123 (hotline)
Web: www.nhtsa.dot.gov/cars/rules/import

Federal Aviation Administration
Environment and Energy Section
800 Independence Avenue SW
Washington DC 20591
(202) 267-3576
Web: www.faa.gov

Federal Railroad Administration (FRA)
1120 Vermont Avenue, NW
Washington DC 20590
(202) 493-6000
Web: www.fra.dot.gov/site

Department of the Treasury

Web: www.ustreas.gov

Office of Foreign Assets Control
1500 Pennsylvania Ave. NW
Washington DC 20220
Tel: (202) 622-2500, 622-2490 (Compliance)
Fax-on-demand: (202) 622-0077
Web: www.treas.gov/ofac

Bureau of Alcohol, Tobacco and Firearms (ATF)
650 Massachusetts Ave.

Room 5200
Washington DC 20001
Alcohol Import/Export Branch: (202) 927-8110
Tobacco Specialist: (202) 927-8210
Firearms & Explosives Import Branch: (202) 927-8320

Environmental Protection Agency (EPA)

Ariel Rios Building
1200 Pennsylvania Avenue, N.W.
Mail Code 3213A
Washington DC 20460
(202) 260-2090
Web: www.epa.gov

Office of Pollution Prevention and Toxics
TSCA System Information
(202) 554-1404 (TSCA Information Hotline)
Email: TSCA-Hotline@eepa.gov
Web: www.epa.gov/opptintr/index.html

Office of Pesticide Programs
(703) 305-7090

Office of Mobile Sources (OMS)
(202) 564-1682
Web: www.epa.gov/OMSWWW

Federal Insecticide, Fungicide, Rodenticide Act
(703) 305-5805

Federal Communications Commission (FCC)

Consumer and Governmental Affairs Bureau
445 12th Street SW
Washington DC 20554
(202) 418-1400
Web: www.fcc.gov

Federal Trade Commission (FTC)

Bureau of Consumer Protection
600 Pennsylvania Ave. NW
Washington DC 20580
Web: www.ftc.gov
   Division of Enforcement
   (202) 326-2996
   (202) 326-2841 (Textile and wool products labeling)
   Division of Advertising Practices
   (202) 326-3076

International Trade Commission

500 E Street SW
Washington DC 20436
(202) 205-2000
Web: www.usitc.gov
   Office of Tariff Affairs and Trade Agreements
   (202) 205-2592

   Office of Unfair Import Investigations
   (202) 205-2560

Office of U.S. Trade Representative

Public Affairs
600 17th St. NW
Washington DC 20508
(202) 395-3230
Web: www.ustr.gov

InfoList #70

U.S. Government Bookstores

The Government Printing Office (GPO) operates a number of U.S. Government bookstores around the country which carry many of the most popular GPO titles. You can also order any of the 12,000 GPO titles by mail order by calling (202) 512-1800.

A wide range of U.S. government publications are now available online through GPO Access. You may also browse the catalog, submit orders, or get other information through the Government Printing Office's Web site on the Internet at http://www.access.gpo.gov.

Following is a list (alphabetical by state) of the locations and telephone numbers of GPO Bookstores.

Los Angeles, CA	(213) 239-9844
Denver, CO	(303) 844-3964
Pueblo, CO	(719) 544-3142
Washington DC	(202) 512-0132
Jacksonville, FL	(904) 353-0569
Atlanta, GA	(404) 347-1900
Laurel, MD	(301) 953-7974
Detroit, MI	(313) 226-7816
Kansas City, MO	(816) 765-2256
New York, NY	(212) 264-3825
Portland, OR	(503) 221-6217
Pittsburgh, PA	(412) 395-5021
Houston, TX	(713) 228-1187
Seattle, WA	(206) 553-4270
Milwaukee, WI	(414) 297-1304

InfoList #71

Top Web sites for the Importer

U.S. Government Sites

There are many more U.S. government sites with important information for the importer. Refer to "U.S. Government Agencies" on page 84 for Internet addresses of other government agencies.

- **Customs and Border Protection - U.S. Department of Homeland Security**
  http://www.cbp.gov/xp/cgov/toolbox/publications
  This site was put up in the summer of 1996 and is still evolving. It may eventually replace the Customs Electronic Bulletin Board (CEBB), but in the meantime, the two sources have some differences in the information they offer.

- **GPO Access**
  http://www.access.gpo.gov
  This site provides access to the following databases: GPO Access, GPO Style Manual, and the U.S. Government Online Bookstore. It also gives valuable information in GPOListserv and Library Services.

General Reference for Trade

- **World Trade REF**
  www.worldtraderef.com
  Contains 42 essential data sets for international trade and logistics. Subscription.

General Resources for Importers

- **Business Network International**
  http://http://www.bni.com

- **I-TRADE: The International Trade Resource and Data Exchange**
  http://www.i-trade.com

- **NAFTA Customs Website**
  http://www.nafta-customs.org
  For importers trading with NAFTA countries.

International Organizations

- **EUROPA: Information on the EU**
  http://europa.eu.int/index.htm

- **International Monetary Fund (IMF)**
  http://www.imf.org

- **Organization for Economic Cooperation and Development (OECD)**
  http://www.oecd.org

- **The World Bank**
  http://www.worldbank.org

- **World Trade Organization (WTO)**
  http://www.wto.org

- **United Nations**
  http://www.un.org

Foreign Government Offices and Trade Organizations

- **The Electronic Embassy**
  http://www.embassy.org
- **World Index of Chambers of Commerce and Industry**
  http://www.worldchambers.com
- **World Trade Centers Association**
  http://www.wtca.org
- **Yahoo Government Sites**
  http://www.yahoo.com/Government/Countries
- **Yahoo International Trade Associations**
  http://www.yahoo.com/Business_and_Economy/International_Economy/Organizations/Trade_Associations

International Banks

- **Central Banking Resource Center**
  http://patriot.net/~bernkopf
- **Yahoo Bank List**
  http:/http://dir.yahoo.com/Business_and_Economy/Shopping_and_Services/Financial_Services/Banking/Banks

Airlines

- **4Airlines.Com**
  http://www.4airlines.com
- **Expedia**
  http://www.expedia.com
- **Orbitz**
  www.orbitz.com

International Business Information Sources

- **Dow Jones**
  http://www.dowjones.com
- **Knight Ridder Information**
  http://www.kri.com
- **Lexis-Nexis**
  http://www.lexis-nexis.com

Telephone and Fax Directories

- **International Telephone Directory**
  http://www.infobel.com/world/default.asp
- **International White and Yellow Pages**
  http://www.wayp.com/
- **World Directories**
  http://www.globalyp.com/world.htm

InfoList #72

Customs and Border Protection Information Sources

Important Publications

The following periodicals, books, brochures, and loose-leaf services are available from the GPO, unless otherwise noted. Refer to "U.S. Government Bookstores" on page 87 for purchasing and ordering information. They will also be available at many U.S. government depository libraries and some are available through the online sources described below.

Customs and Border Protection has many brochures and forms; some are available through the Web site or the CEBB. Some brochures are free, while others may cost a nominal amount. Similarly, some Customs forms are "salable" and cannot be given away. Contact U.S. Customs and Border Protection, National Distribution Center, 1300 Pennsylvania Avenue, NW, Washington DC 20229.

Customs Bulletin

Customs Regulations of the United States (Title 19 of the CFR)

Customs Valuation Encyclopedia (with updates) is comprised of relevant statutory provisions, Customs Regulations implementing the statute, portions of the Customs Valuation Code, judicial precedent, and administrative rulings involving application of valuation law.

Customs Valuation Under the Trade Agreements Act of 1979. Available from U.S. Customs and Border Protection, Office of Regulations and Rulings, Value Branch, 1300 Pennsylvania Avenue NW, Washington DC 20229.

Informed Compliance publications. U.S. Customs and Border Protection publishes an online series on important issues and commodities. At press time, the following topics were available: Textiles, General Classification, Special Classification, Value, International Agreements, Penalties, Entry, Duty and Refund Determination, and Intellectual Property Rights. These are available on the U.S. Customs and Border Protection Web site. Go directly to the *Informed Compliance* Publications link, www.cbp.gov/xp/cgov/toolbox/legal/informed_compliance_pubs.

NAFTA: The North American Free Trade Agreement, A Guide to Customs Procedures. 1994. Provides an overview of the benefits and requirements of the North American Free Trade Agreement. S/N 048-002-00122-2. $4.00

North American Free Trade Agreement: Certificate of Origin, Customs Form 434. FORM. 1993. Includes form and instructions. 2 p. Sold in Packages of 100 only. S/N 048-002-00120-6; $13.00.

United States Customs Foreign-Trade Zones Manual. 2003 book. S/N 048-002-00111-7; $13.00.

Online Information Sources

U.S. Customs and Border Protection Website. U.S. Customs and Border Protection mounted its Web site in August of 1996, and information is being added to the site on a regular basis. The most important information for the importer is in the Import/Export areas.

Complete versions of important regulatory information is available, including:

- The Harmonized Tariff Schedule of the US
- Title 19 of the Code of Federal Regulations
- Ruling letters

In addition, U.S. Customs and Border Protection has provided a number of publications relating to the following topics:

- Informed compliance
- U.S. Customs and Border Protection office locations
- Automated systems
- Intellectual property rights
- Quotas
- Marking regulations
- NAFTA

Customs Electronic Bulletin Board. CEBB is a free online source of customs information available for the trade community. The CEBB was the precursor to the U.S. Customs and Border Protection Web site; the available documents include:

- Excerpts from *Global Trade Talk*
- Customs news releases
- From the Commissioner
- Federal records and notices
- Proposed and final rulings
- Ruling Modification/Revocation
- Quota threshold status
- Currency conversion rates
- Customs directives
- Trade operations instructions
- *Customs Valuation Encyclopedia*
- ADD/CVD instructions and archive data
- Currency and quota archive data
- Customs extra
- NAFTA information
- Intellectual property rights information
- Mod Act information
- Canadian Customs Information
- Textiles - Quota

To access CEBB online, go to http://www.cebb.customs.treas.gov/public/default.htm.

InfoList #73
Top Publications for the U.S. Importer

World Trade Press Publications

Dictionary of International Trade, 5th Edition

Global Connect!, 4th Edition

Global Road Warrior, 4th Edition

Importers Manual USA

World Trade Almanac

Passport to the World business culture series (25 titles)

Country Business Guide series (12 titles)

Short Course in International Trade series (12 titles)

World Trade Press
1450 Grant Avenue, Suite 204
Novato, CA 94945
(415) 898-1124
FAX (415) 898-1080
E-mail: sales@worldtradepress.com

www.WorldTradePress.com

www.WorldTradeREF.com

www.HowToConnect.com

www.GlobalRoadWarrior.com

Books, Guides, and Reference Manuals

Container Specification

Hapag-Lloyd
699 Hoes Lane
Piscataway, NJ 08854
(732) 562-1800; FAX (732) 885-6132

Customs Law and Administration
Textile Quota Report

American Association of Exporters and Importers
P.O. Box 7813

Washington DC 20044-7813

(202) 661-2181; FAX (202) 661-2185

Do's and Taboos Around the World
Do's and Taboos of Hosting International Visitors
Do's and Taboos of International Trade

By Roger E. Axtell
John Wiley & Sons, Inc.
111 River Street
Hoboken, NJ 07030
(201) 748-6000, (201) 748-6088

Documentary Credits: UP 500 and 400 Compared
Funds Transfer in International Banking
Incoterms 1990 and *Guide to Incoterms 1990*
Key Words in International Trade (3rd edition)
ICC Guide to Documentary Credit Operations

ICC Publishing, Inc.
156 Fifth Ave. Suite 417
New York, NY 10010
(212) 206-1150; FAX (212) 633-6025
Web: www.iccbooksusa.com

Documentary Credits, A Practical Guide
Foreign Exchange and Money Market Operations
UBS (originally Swiss Bank Corporation)
Swiss Bank Tower
10 East 50th Street
New York, NY 10022
(212) 882-5000

Import Reference Manual (part of *International Trade Reporter*)
Bureau of National Affairs, Inc.
1231 25th Street NW
Washington DC 20037
(800) 372-1033; FAX (800) 253-0332

International Business Transactions
By Ralph H. Folsom and Michael Gordon
West Publishing Company
610 Opperman Drive
Eagan, MN 55123
(800) 328-9352; FAX (800) 741-1414

OAG Air Cargo Guide
Official Airline Guides Worldwide, Inc.
75 Remittance Drive, Suite 1570
Chicago, IL 60675-1570
(800) 323-3537; FAX (630) 515-3933

Trade Shows Worldwide
Manufacturing Worldwide
Gale Research Inc.
27500 Drake Road
Farmington Hills, MI 48331
(800) 877-GALE
Web: www.gale.com/gale.htm

The U.S. Custom House Guide
The Official Export Guide
400 Windsor Corporate Center
50 Millstone Road, Suite 200
East Windsor, NJ 08520-1415
(800) 221-5488

Periodicals

Journal of Commerce
Handbook for International Trade (part of the Journal of Commerce subscription)
Journal of Commerce
400 Windsor Corporate Center
50 Millstone Road, Suite 200
East Windsor, NJ 08520-1415
(888) 215-6084; FAX (609) 371-7883

World Trade
23211 South Pointe Drive, Suite 101
Laguna Hills, CA 92653
(949) 830-1340; FAX (949) 830-1328

Directories

Directory of United States Importers
Journal of Commerce
400 Windsor Corporate Center
50 Millstone Road, Suite 200
East Windsor, NJ 08520-1415
(888) 215-6084; FAX (609) 371-7883

Maritime Guide
Lloyd's Register of Shipping
71 Fenchurch Street
London EC3M 4BS, UK
[44] (20) 7709-9166; FAX [44] (20) 7488-4796

Country-Specific Information Series

Europa World Yearbook
Gale Research Inc.
27500 Drake Road
Farmington Hills, MI 48331
(800) 877-GALE
Web: www.gale.com/gale.htm

Martindale-Hubbell International Law Digest
Martindale-Hubbell
121 Chanlon Road
New Providence, NJ 07974
(800) 526-4902; FAX (908) 771-8704

Business Profile Series
Hong Kong Bank Group
452 5th Avenue
New York, NY 10018
(212) 525-8093

Doing Business in...
Price Waterhouse Coopers
1177 Avenue of the Americas
New York, NY 10036
(888) 609-7117

Web: www.pwcglobal.com. Click on the publications icon and do a search.

Doing Business in...
Ernst and Young International
Becket House
1 Lambeth Palace Road

London SE1 7EU
(800) 726-7339

U.S. Government Publications

A number of publications of the Customs Service is listed under "Customs and Border Protection Information Sources" on page 88. Some others of interest follow. These may be obtained from the USGPO at the number listed below; many are also available at the GPO bookstores located around the country, which are listed in the following InfoList.

19 CFR, Parts 1 to 199, Code of Federal Regulations (Customs Duties)
Background Notes (State Dept.)
U.S. Government Printing Office
P.O. Box 371954

Pittsburg, PA 15250
(866) 512-1800

National Trade Data Bank (NTDB)

(www.stat-usa.gov, published online)
Stat-USA

U.S. Department of Commerce
HCHB Room 4885
Washington DC, 20230
(202) 482-1986

International Law

Contents

Introduction

The greatest source of problems for U.S. residents doing business abroad is the erroneous assumption that they can operate according to U.S. laws and practices. When you trade internationally, you are subject not only to U.S. laws, but also to the laws of every country where you do business, even if you do not physically enter the other country.

The more complex your transactions, the more you travel overseas, the more you deal in high-risk or politically sensitive products, the more you obtain and extend credit, the more you trust others to perform their end of the bargain, the greater chance you will have of encountering legal difficulties in your international transactions.

This section reviews potential legal problems that you should keep in mind while traveling and doing business internationally. It addresses issues related to international travel, trading relationships, contracts, and world legal systems. The information is interrelated, and each section is equally important. Even if part of it does not seem relevant at the moment, you should review all of it so that, when legal issues arise (and they will), you can recognize them and can assert your legal rights.

Travel

The international travel issues covered include requirements for passports, visas, and work permits; registration with U.S. embassies overseas; ramifications of dual nationality; special customs considerations when traveling with commercial samples, protected items, negotiable instruments, and personal articles; compliance with foreign laws; and concerns related to driving abroad.

Trading Relationships

The international trading sections discuss the anti-bribery provisions of the Foreign Corrupt Practices Act, ramifications of agency and employment relationships abroad, types of relationships commonly formed with foreign suppliers, the role of domestic and foreign legal counsel, the need for insurance, the use of powers of attorney and notaries public, and import and export laws.

Contracts and Conflict Resolution

This part of the chapter concentrates on issues that arise when drafting and performing an international sales or purchase contract, including conflict resolution. Although you will most likely rely on the services of an attorney to draft and enforce the contract, you will need this knowledge to work in partnership with your attorney to your best advantage.

World Legal Systems

This section gives an overview of the world's major legal systems and the different requirements imposed on domestic and foreign business relationships.

Additional Resources

Other sources on commercial law include Martindale-Hubbell's *International Law Digest,* available at major public libraries and *International Business Practices,* available from the U.S. Government Printing Office.

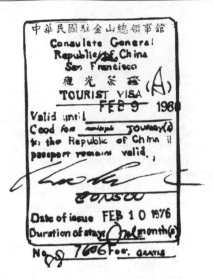

Passports

Your U.S. passport is your most important travel document. It identifies you as an individual and as a U.S. citizen. International travel without a passport can be impossible. As you travel you will need your passport to:

- board international flights
- cross national borders
- register at foreign hotels
- cash traveler's checks
- pay by credit card

For complete Passport information go to: http://travel.state.gov/passport_services.html.

Loss or Theft of a US Passport

Safeguard your passport. Its loss could cause you unnecessary travel complications as well as significant expense.

If your passport is lost or stolen in the U.S., report the loss or theft immediately to US Department of State; Passport Services; 1111 19th Street, NW, Suite 500; Washington, DC 20036; Tel: 202) 955-0430 (24 hours), or to the nearest passport agency. Should your passport be lost or stolen abroad, report the loss immediately to the local police and to the nearest U.S. embassy or consulate.

As a contingency, carry several duplicate passport photos and a photocopy of your passport in a separate and safe place while traveling. For full information on passports refer to "U.S. Passports" on page 39.

Warning! Even if you are not required to have a passport to visit a country, U.S. Immigration requires you to prove your U.S. citizenship and identity when you reenter the U.S. Make certain that you take with you adequate documentation (original birth certificate and photo ID) to pass through U.S. Immigration on your return.

Tip: Although not required by law, hotels in some countries may insist that you leave your passport with hotel management to be checked by local police, or as a guarantee that you will pay your hotel bill. Always ask either your travel agent or the local U.S. embassy or consulate before you give your passport to a hotel.

Visas and Work Permits

A visa is a certificate or stamp placed in your passport by a foreign government's embassy, consular office, or other representative. It permits you to either visit (tourist visa), conduct business (business visa), work (work permit or visa), or immigrate (residency visa or immigration visa) to the issuing country for a specified time. Most countries require foreigners working in their country to have a valid work permit in addition to a visa. Work permits are more difficult to obtain than business visas.

Before leaving the U.S., you should learn the entry requirements of each country you will visit and obtain all necessary visas. Each country has its own requirements: some insist that you obtain a visa in advance, some grant a visa at the border, some allow entry without a visa for particular purposes—such as tourism. Visa fees vary from country to country and for different types of visas. Passport photographs are often required. It can take from ten minutes to several weeks to obtain a visa. You should check with the embassy or consulate of the countries you plan to visit well in advance of your expected departure date.

Tip: In many countries, if you travel on a tourist visa, and once there decide to turn your pleasure trip into a buying trip, you won't have a problem. However you should be aware that business transactions are authorized under a business visa, and lack of a business visa could put you in a difficult position. For example, a foreign company with whom you make a contract could break the agreement on the grounds that you were doing business on a tourist and not a business visa. Though the argument might not hold up in a court of law, foreign countries tend to give preferential treatment to their own nationals, not to foreign nationals. By adhering carefully to visa requirements, you protect your own interests. To avoid problems, you can apply for a change of entry status and a new visa at a local immigration office while in the country. These offices also handle visa extensions, should you decide to stay after your visa expires.

Dual Nationality

Dual nationality means that an individual is a citizen of more than one country. It can result from being born in one country and then becoming a naturalized citizen of another, or from being the child of foreign nationals born in a country other than the parents' country of citizenship.

Are You a Dual National?

If any of the following conditions apply to you, dual nationality might be an issue:

- You were born in a foreign country and have since become a naturalized U.S. citizen;
- You were once a citizen of a foreign country, but have since become a naturalized U.S. citizen;
- Either of your parents is a citizen of a country other than your country of citizenship;
- You are married to a citizen of a country other than your country of citizenship.

Advantages and Disadvantages of Dual Nationality

Dual nationality has both advantages and disadvantages. Citizenship in a country may provide you with certain rights and business opportunities, such as tax or export credits, unavailable to foreigners. However a country claiming you as a citizen could detain you, could conscript you into its military, or could jail you and treat you under its own laws, without regard to the protections of your other country of nationality.

Research Dual Nationality Issues Before Foreign Travel

If you are in any of the categories listed above, *before* you depart the U.S., check your status (including military obligations) with the embassy or consulate of the country that might claim you as a citizen.

Tip: Countries with totalitarian regimes, torn by civil strife, or at war are more likely to regard you as one of their citizens. In some cases of dual nationality, foreign countries have refused to recognize the U.S. citizenship of persons arrested and have not allowed U.S. officials access to arrested U.S. citizens.

Registration with the U.S. Embassy or Consulate

The U.S. State Department recommends that in each country you visit you inform the U.S. Embassy of your travel plans. Although less of a consideration if you travel in Western Europe and stay in first class hotels, registration is highly recommended if you intend to travel the back roads of less developed and unstable countries.

When to Register

Register with the U.S. embassy or consulate if you are:

- Traveling to a country or area with civil unrest or an unstable political climate.
- Going to a country where there are no U.S. official offices (Lebanon, Iran, or Macedonia, for example). Register in an adjacent country, leave an itinerary, ask about conditions in the country you plan to visit, and find out which third country may represent U.S. interests.
- Going to a country or area that heavily restricts foreign travel. If you are on an escorted tour, make sure registration is made for you. If it is not, or if you are traveling on your own, leave a copy of your itinerary at the nearest U.S. embassy or consulate soon after arrival. Registration allows consular employees to help you more easily should you encounter difficulties.
- Planning to stay in another country for more than one month. Registration will facilitate replacement of a passport, and consular officials will be able to locate you should you need assistance or evacuation in an emergency.

U.S. consular officers can tell you about local conditions, customs and health issues. Refer to "Health Regulations for International Travel" on page 44 for discussion of vaccination certificates.

Tip: Though this safeguard may seem trivial to a U.S. citizen accustomed to unrestricted travel, it is not. U.S. citizens are often portrayed negatively. If you enter a region uninformed, you could become a pawn in a conflict you know nothing about. You also need to be aware of areas where there are significant health hazards. Refer to "Help from U.S. Consuls Abroad" on page 59 for additional information on consular assistance.

Traveling with Commercial Samples

Samples, advertising material, or equipment can often be temporarily brought into a country duty-free. Many countries issue and recognize a bond or document, such as an ATA Carnet, for the temporary entry of these articles without payment of customs duties. Some permit duty-free entry without documentation, provided specific restrictions are met. In some cases, you may have to request an exemption, a slow process of several months if the application is made to a central government agency.

ATA Carnets

ATA stands for "Admission Temporaire-Temporary Admission." An ATA carnet is an international customs document issued and recognized by member countries to the Customs Convention on the ATA Carnet. It authorizes the temporary duty-free importation of certain goods into a country. The carnet serves as both a customs entry document and as a guarantee against the payment of customs duties in the event that the items are in fact not reexported. Certain types of merchandise, such as textiles, are subject to quotas even when imported under an ATA carnet. The U.S. currently allows ATA carnets for temporary admission of professional equipment, commercial samples, and advertising material. Most ATA member countries also allow the use of carnets for temporary admission of these goods. ATA carnets can also be used for transit (in-bond movement of goods) in the U.S. under the applicable regulations, 19 CFR Part 114.

An ATA carnet is valid for one year. During that year the carnet holder may make as many trips as desired, provided the carnet has sufficient pages for each stop.

Local Chambers of Commerce, as affiliates of the Paris based International Chamber of Commerce, issue carnets to their residents. These associations guarantee the payment of duties to local customs for goods not reexported. In the U.S., contact the United States Council for International Business, 1212 Avenue of the Americas, New York, NY 10036, Tel (212) 354-4480, Web: uscib.org/index/asp. Refer to "Temporary Free Importations" on page 220 for more information.

Traveling with Expensive Personal Possessions

Unless it is your business to wear your wealth, don't do so while you are abroad. People in other countries tend to be more conservative with demonstrations of wealth than those in the U.S. To prevent the loss or theft of valuables such as jewelry, family photographs, or objects of sentimental value, you should leave them home when you travel. If jewelry is brought, it should be worn discreetly to prevent grab-and-run theft.

U.S. Customs Pre-Registration

Foreign-made products that have already been imported to the U.S. are subject to duty when reimported unless you can prove you owned them before you left.

You can avoid repaying this import duty by carrying a copy of the U.S. sales invoice with your travel documents to present to Customs when you reenter the U.S.

You can also register foreign-made products—especially items identified with serial numbers, such as watches, cameras, camcorders, and binoculars—with U.S. Customs before you leave the U.S. Carry the registration with you and present it to Customs when you reenter the U.S.

Hotel Safe-Deposit Boxes

Most hotels have safe-deposit boxes you can use for your valuables. Be careful, though: there have been reports of abuses involving hotel staff with access to both keys to the safe-deposit box.

Endangered Species Laws

Do not take products of endangered species (such as leopard furs or elephant ivory jewelry) through signatory countries to the international Convention on Trade in Endangered Species of Wild Fauna and Flora (CITES). Incidentally, the U.S. is a signatory to CITES, so theoretically you should not own, let alone import, any products made from these species in the first place.

Traveling with Negotiables

Both U.S. and foreign laws regulate the transfer of personal and corporate assets. Assets may include cash, checks, stocks, bonds, or any negotiable instrument, as well as equipment, products, and other tangible property.

U.S. Regulations

The U.S. does not limit the amount of funds or assets imported or exported. Also, negotiable instruments, in current circulation in any country and imported into the U.S. for monetary purposes, are admitted duty free and without formal Customs entry.

All imports of currency, coin, and negotiable instruments are subject to the Currency and Foreign Transactions Reporting Act (CFTR), 31 USC 5311 et seq. Pursuant to CFTR, you must file a transaction report, Customs **Form 4790**, with U.S. Customs when you transport more than $10,000 in monetary instruments, by any means, on any occasion, into or out of the U. S. Monetary instruments include U.S. or foreign coin, currency, traveler's checks, money orders, and negotiable instruments or investment securities in bearer form. Bank checks, traveler's checks or money orders made payable to the order of a named person, but bearing a restrictive endorsement or not endorsed at all, are not considered monetary instruments.

Foreign Country Requirements

Foreign governments usually do not limit the amount of cash you bring into the country, but they often strictly limit how much you take out. These limits may apply both to local currency and any U.S. currency the U.S. citizen brought into the country. Before you take large sums of currency or assets into a country, research any restrictions with their consulate or embassy in the U.S., or a banker.

Tip: If you import assets of any kind that result from a profit-making enterprise overseas, interest on invested monies, or any other form of income, you must declare the sums to the U.S. Internal Revenue Service (IRS) as income.

Refer also to "Foreign Assets Control Restrictions" on page 263 and "Monetary Instruments" on page 261.

Both U.S. and foreign laws regulate the transfer of personal and corporate assets. Assets may include cash, checks, stocks, bonds, or any negotiable instrument.

Local Registration

In many foreign countries individuals are required to register with the police on arrival in a city or town. Typical police registration cards ask for your name, passport number, local address, home address, destination, place from which you last came, place where you are going next, and your reason for traveling.

If you register at a hotel, the hotel will ask that you fill out the police registration card or will handle the formality for you. If you are staying with friends, or in an apartment, you will probably need to go to a police station to register in person.

To determine registration requirements for a particular country, you should call the U.S. Embassy in that country.

Obey Foreign Laws

When you are in a foreign country, you are subject to its laws. This means that not only must you comply with the laws of that country, but those laws will be applied to you in the same manner as to any citizen of that country. Foreign laws tend to be more stringent than U.S. laws. If you get into trouble, you will not be able to invoke the protection of U.S. laws.

Use common sense. Avoid areas of unrest and disturbance. Deal only with authorized outlets when you exchange money or buy airline tickets and traveler's checks. Do not deliver packages for anyone unless you are certain they do not contain drugs or other contraband. Do not carry concealed defensive canisters—pepper sprays, mace, etc.—even with a license, because in some countries mere possession is illegal and cause for arrest. Become familiar with local regulations before you sell personal effects, such as clothing, cameras, and jewelry. Strictly adhere to local laws. The penalties you risk can be severe.

Some countries—particularly those with totalitarian regimes, rampant civil strife, or warring factions—are sensitive about photographs. In such countries, you should refrain from photographing police and military installations and personnel; industrial structures including harbor, rail, and airport facilities; border areas; and scenes of civil disorder or other public disturbances, should you witness them during your stay. For taking such photographs, you may be detained and fined and your camera and all films may be confiscated.

For more information about prohibited and restricted activities, U.S. citizens should check with the U.S. embassy or consulate in the country concerned or with the Citizens Emergency Center before departing.

Drug Arrests

Despite repeated warnings, drug arrests and convictions of U.S. citizens abroad are still common. If you are caught with any drugs overseas, you are subject to local—not U.S.—laws. A number of countries impose stiffer penalties for drug violations and enforce existing drug laws more strictly. If you are arrested, you will find that:

- Few countries provide a jury trial.
- Most countries do not accept bail.
- Pretrial detention, often in solitary confinement, may last months.

- Prisons may lack even minimal comforts—bed, toilet, wash basin.
- Officials may not speak English.
- Physical abuse, confiscation of personal property, degrading or inhumane treatment, and extortion are possible.

If you are convicted, you face a sentence of:

- From 2 to 10 years in most countries.
- A minimum of 6 years' hard labor and a stiff fine in some countries.
- The death penalty in some countries.

Do not get involved with illegal drugs overseas. It can ruin more than your trip. It can ruin your life!

Tip: Some pharmaceutical products that are restricted or contraband in the U.S. are sold over the counter in foreign countries, where their use is perfectly legal. If you transport those products into the U.S., however, you will be breaking U.S. drug laws.

Legal Aid

Remember, you are subject to local laws. If you encounter difficulties with foreign authorities, U.S. consular officials can provide little assistance. Their ability to help is limited by both foreign and U.S. laws. The U.S. Government has no funds for your legal fees or related expenses.

If you find yourself in a dispute that could lead to legal or police action, consult a consular officer. Although U.S. consular officers cannot serve as attorneys or give legal advice, they can provide lists of local attorneys and can help you find adequate legal representation. These lists of attorneys, although carefully prepared, are compiled from local bar association lists and responses to questionnaires. Neither the Department of State nor U.S. embassies or consulates can assume responsibility for the professional caliber, competence, or integrity of the attorneys listed. Consular officers will attempt to protect your legitimate interests and to ensure that you are not discriminated against under local law. But they cannot get you out of jail. If you are arrested, ask the authorities to notify the consular officer at the nearest U.S. embassy or consulate. Under international agreement and practice, you have the right to talk to the U.S. consul. If you are denied this right, be persistent and try to have someone get in touch for you.

When alerted, U.S. officials will visit you, advise you of your rights according to local laws, and contact your family and friends if you so desire. Consuls can transfer money, food, and clothing to the prison authorities from your family or friends. If you are held under inhumane or unhealthful conditions or treated less favorably than others in the same situation, they will try to get you some relief.

Tip: When you are in a foreign country, you should be aware of the country's law. You will be held to the same standards. Until you are sure you know the rules, be circumspect in your personal and business dealings. Contact the U.S. Embassy in each country you visit. Tell them what you plan to do and where you plan to go in the country, and ask about unusual or strict laws that might affect you while visiting there.

Driving

Driver's License

If you intend to drive overseas, check with the embassy or consulate of the countries you will visit to learn their driver's license, road permit, and insurance requirements.

Some countries will recognize your U.S. state driver's license while others will not. Most, however, will accept an international driver's permit. Your local auto association will be able to issue an international driver's permit. You must be at least age 18, and you will need two passport size photographs and your valid U.S. license. Certain restrictions apply to international licenses. They are issued for specified periods of time, are not necessarily valid in every country, and must be presented with a valid U.S. state driver's license.

Auto Insurance

Many foreign countries require valid auto insurance and are far stricter than the U.S. in enforcing their requirements. Even a country that does not require insurance of its own citizens may require it of foreign drivers.

Car rental agencies overseas usually provide auto insurance, but in some countries, the required coverage is minimal. A good rule of thumb when renting a car overseas is to purchase insurance coverage that is at least equivalent to that which you carry at home.

Tip: Never assume that your U.S. auto insurance policy covers your driving abroad!

Accidents

Avoid accidents while driving abroad. Unfamiliarity with driving conditions and habits abroad leads many U.S. citizens into traffic accidents. Drive carefully, courteously and defensively. If you are involved in a driving accident in some countries, you will be considered guilty until proven innocent! For example, the police in Mexico usually detain all parties to a traffic accident until they determine who is at fault. You may be personally liable for any damage you cause while driving. The penalties can be devastating, such as providing financial support for a family whose breadwinner dies in the accident. Or you could be detained in a country until "things are straightened out," which could become a lengthy period.

Refer also to "What to Do in Case of . . ." on page 58.

Foreign Corrupt Practices Act

General Provisions

U.S. business owners are subject to the Foreign Corrupt Practices Act (FCPA). The FCPA makes it unlawful for any U.S. citizen or firm (or any person who acts on behalf of a U.S. citizen or firm) to use a means of U.S. interstate commerce—examples: mail, telephone, telegram, or electronic mail—to offer, pay, transfer, promise to pay or transfer, or authorize a payment, transfer, or promise of money or anything of value to any foreign appointed or elected official, foreign political party, or candidate for a foreign political office for a corrupt purpose (that is, to influence a discretionary act or decision of the official) for the purpose of obtaining or retaining business.

It is also unlawful for a U.S. business owner to make such an offer, promise, payment, or transfer to any person if the U.S. business owner knows, or has reason to know, that the person will give, offer, or promise directly or indirectly all or part of the payment to a foreign government official, political party, or candidate. For purposes of the FCPA, the term "knowledge" means both "actual knowledge"—the business owner in fact knew that the offer, payment, or transfer was included in the transaction—and "implied knowledge"—the business owner should have known from the facts and circumstances of a transaction that the agent paid a bribe, but failed to carry out a reasonable investigation into the transaction.

Tip: A business owner should make a reasonable investigation into the transaction if, for example, the sales representative requests a higher commission on a particular deal for no apparent reason, the buyer is a foreign government, the product has a military use, or the buyer's country is one where bribes are considered customary in business relationships.

The FCPA also contains provisions applicable to U.S. publicly held companies concerning financial recordkeeping and internal accounting controls.

Legal Payments

The provisions of the FCPA do not prohibit payments made to facilitate routine government action; a "facilitating payment" is one made in connection with an action that a foreign official must perform as part of the job. In comparison, a corrupt payment is made to influence an official's discretionary decision.

A person charged with violating FCPA provisions may assert as a defense that the payment was lawful under the written laws and regulations of the foreign country and therefore was not for a corrupt purpose. Alternatively, a person may contend that the payment was associated with demonstrating a product or performing a previously existing contractual obligation and therefore was not for obtaining or retaining business.

Tip: Corrupt payments are distinct from grease or "facilitating" payments made to an agent or official of a foreign government to expedite an action that the official would have taken anyway. For example, payments would not generally be considered corrupt if made to cover an official's overtime required to process export documentation for a legal shipment of merchandise or to cover the expense of additional crew to handle a shipment. Be careful, though. The distinction between a corrupt and a facilitating payment is not always obvious.

Enforcing Agencies; Criminal Penalties

The U.S. Department of Justice prosecutes criminal proceedings for FCPA violations. Firms are subject to a fine of up to US$2 million. Officers, directors, employees, agents, and stockholders are subject to fines of up to US$100,000, imprisonment for up to five years, or both.

A U.S. business owner may also be charged under other federal criminal laws. On conviction, the owner may be liable for one of the following: (1) a fine of up to US$250,000; or (2) if the owner derived pecuniary gain from the offense or caused a pecuniary loss to another person, a fine of up to twice the amount of the gross gain or loss.

Enforcing Agencies; Civil Penalties

Two agencies are responsible for enforcing civil provisions of the FCPA: the Department of Justice handles actions against domestic concerns, and the Securities and Exchange Commission (SEC) files actions against issuers. Civil fines of up to US$100,000 (but only up to US$10,000 in SEC actions) may be imposed on a firm, or on any officer, director, employee, agent, or stockholder acting for a firm. In addition, the appropriate government agency may seek an injunction against a person or firm that has violated or is about to violate FCPA provisions.

Conduct that constitutes a violation of FCPA provisions may also give rise to a cause of action under the federal Racketeer-Influenced and Corrupt Organizations Act (RICO), as well as under similar state statutes if such exist in a state with jurisdiction over the U.S. business.

Administrative Penalties

A person or firm held to have violated any FCPA provisions may be barred from doing business with the U.S. government. Indictment alone may result in suspension of the right to do business with the government.

Department of Justice Opinion Procedure

An issuer or domestic business concern may submit a written request to the Department of Justice to issue a written statement of opinion on whether specific proposed business conduct would be considered a violation of the FCPA. The person requesting the opinion must be a party to the transaction that is the subject of the request. The opinion procedure is detailed in 28 CFR Part 80. If the Department of Justice issues an opinion stating that certain conduct conforms with current enforcement policy, conduct in accordance with that opinion is presumed to comply with FCPA provisions.

Dilemmas Posed by the FCPA

The examples that follow illustrate two ways in which the Foreign Corrupt Practices Act poses dilemmas for U.S. citizens engaged in international business.

Example 1. If you have a partnership with foreign nationals, you may become liable under U.S. law for actions your foreign partners take that cause them no problems under their local law. For instance, if you own 49% of a foreign corporation with 51% local (foreign) ownership, and the local owners decide to bribe a local official, you may be liable under U.S. law if you benefit from the transaction. Even if bribery is illegal in both countries, U.S. penalties may be more stringent.

Example 2. You could become liable for a corrupt payment made by your foreign employee. For example, if you use a local purchasing agent who, in keeping with local custom, makes payments to government officials for export permits or preferential pricing from governmental entities, under FCPA the payments could be considered corrupt payments. You, the U.S. citizen, are subject to the FCPA. Your foreign employee is not. You will be the one to suffer the legal penalties.

Tip: The law requires that you monitor and evaluate the amount of money you pay your overseas agent or supplier. Always ask "Are we paying too much? Is this percentage too high? Who is getting that extra money?" If your agent is making corrupt payments, you may be subject to criminal liability.

Because of your liability under FCPA, you should insist that your written agreements with a foreign employee or agent expressly cover FCPA situations. To prevent problems, whenever you establish a relationship with someone in a foreign country to act as your purchasing or other business agent, insert a provision in the contract stating that any corrupt payment is cause for termination of the contract. As an employer, you must take a strong stand on this issue for your own protection. Unfortunately, protecting yourself can sometimes mean losing business.

Foreign Labor, Employment, and "Nationalist" Laws

Foreign Labor and Employment Laws

Both the U.S. and foreign governments have laws that, to varying degrees, regulate employment, including employee hiring, firing, benefits, workplace safety, etc. Foreign labor and employment laws, especially in socialist countries, are often stricter and more preferential to the employee than are U.S. laws. When you hire a national in a foreign country where you intend to do business, you must comply with that country's employment standards. Those standards are rarely if ever the same as those of the U.S.

Tip: The fact that you do not establish a manufacturing facility or set up an office in a foreign country where you have business dealings does not exempt you from its labor laws. In fact, you may find that, under the foreign country's labor laws, when you contract with a buyer's agent, you are entering into an employment relationship in which your responsibilities far surpass those you might have for a U.S. employee. In some countries, you may be able to structure your agreement as one for an independent contractor, and thus avoid some of the labor and employment law requirements. Such agreements must be carefully drafted and government approval may be necessary.

Responsibility of the Employer

In foreign countries, hiring an employee can be equivalent to adopting a child into a family. Your responsibility to your foreign employee may last years beyond his or her usefulness to your operation. Your company and you may be subject to significant requirements regarding insurance, vacations, working conditions, ability to fire, and severance pay. Employers in many European countries are required to give their employees a minimum of one month paid vacation each year and they have no authority to dictate when the vacation may be taken. Foreign employees get many more paid days off than those in the U.S.: in some countries as many as 12 legal holidays.

Employee Severance

Employee severance comes as perhaps the greatest shock to U.S. employers of foreign personnel. Termination benefits range from nothing to several or more years of salary paid over time or in a lump sum. In some instances, it may actually be more cost-effective to keep an unproductive employee on the payroll through the end of the contract than it would be to terminate. Some countries have dealer protective laws under which a person who employs a marketing agent is allowed to terminate the contract only for just cause, on payment of a substantial amount of termination compensation, and after lengthy advance notice of termination. Your contract with a dealer should include protective provisions, including clauses that define just cause for termination, specify the period required for advance notice, and provide for a finite employment term, such as one year, with an option to renew.

Tip: Your involvement in a corporate entity in some countries will incur a legal obligation to share a percentage of your profits with employees. Unless you are careful, this may also be read to mean that X percent of all your corporate profits must be shared with all your employees. So be careful about how you set up an overseas corporation to serve as a purchasing agent.

Nationalist Laws

Nationalist laws give special benefits to local employees of foreign-owned business organizations. They are designed to protect the domestic work force. For example, in some countries termination, even for cause, of an employee who works exclusively for you, can obligate you for as much as seven years severance pay, based on a formula that includes the last four years of his or her highest salary. You should fully research nationalist laws of any foreign country where you plan to establish employment or agency agreements with nationals.

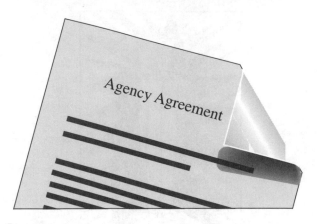

Power of Attorney

A power of attorney is a legal document authorizing one person to act on behalf of another: to enter into contracts, to sign documents, to sign checks and spend money, etc. If you intend to travel overseas a great deal, you should consider giving a power of attorney, or a limited power of attorney, to someone in the U.S. to handle specific business and personal transactions for you. You will also need to give a power of attorney to any customs broker whose services you use in order for them to handle your customs transactions. This is true whether you are out of the country or not. You may also need to give a power of attorney to someone overseas who can then conduct business transactions in your absence.

Tip: When you set up a power of attorney, make it broad enough in its language to cover the types of situations likely to arise while you are away. It should not be so broad, however, that it gives more power to that individual than you intend. Powers of attorney fall under "agency" laws, which vary from country to country. Before giving someone power of attorney in a foreign country, be sure you understand the legal ramifications.

For U.S. Bureau of Customs and Border Protection related issues refer also to "Power of Attorney" on page 206.

Notary

In the U.S., a notary provides legal verification of an individual's signature in business and legal transactions. In foreign countries, a notary does the same, but often has broader powers. Many countries require notaries to be trained in law, some require notaries to be lawyers also, and some have different types of notaries whose authority to certify certain documents depends on their training. For example, a foreign notary might prepare legal documents, do a title search, certify title, translate documents, certify translations, and file and register documents with government authorities. Foreign notarial fees are commonly higher than those in the U.S. because of the extended services provided.

Agency

The widely misunderstood term "agent" means a representative who normally has authority, perhaps even power of attorney, to make commitments on behalf of the firm he or she represents. Firms in the U.S. and other developed countries have stopped using the term and instead rely on the term "representative," since "agent" can imply more than intended. Any contract should state whether the representative or agent does or does not have legal authority to obligate the firm. You will generally be subject to employment and labor laws in countries in which you employ an agent.

Legal Questions to Consider

In the drafting of an agreement that establishes an agency relationship, you should pay special attention to safeguarding your interests in the event that the agent proves less than satisfactory. An escape clause is vital; it will allow you to end the relationship safely and cleanly if the agent does not work out. Some contracts specify that either party may terminate the agreement with written notice 30, 60, or 90 days in advance. The contract may also spell out exactly what constitutes just cause for ending the agreement. Other contracts specify a certain term for the agreement (usually one year) but arrange for annual renewal options unless either party gives advance written notice of its intention not to renew.

In all cases, the laws of the country where the agent is located may limit the contents of escape clauses and other provisions. For this reason, a U.S. firm should learn as much as it can about the legal requirements of the agent's country and should obtain qualified legal counsel in preparing the contract. Some of the legal questions to consider include:

- How far in advance must the agent be notified of the importer's intention to terminate the agreement? Three months satisfies the requirements of most countries, but a verifiable means of conveyance (e.g., registered mail) may be advisable to establish when the notice was sent and received.
- What is just cause for terminating a relationship? A written contract clause that specifies the reasons for termination usually strengthens the importer's position.

- Which country's laws (or which international convention) govern a contract dispute? Laws in the agent's country may forbid the agent to waive that nation's legal jurisdiction.
- What compensation is due the agent on dismissal? Depending on the length of the relationship and whether termination is for just cause as defined by the foreign country, the U.S. importer may be required to compensate the agent for losses.
- What must the agent give up if dismissed? The contract should specify the return of patents, trademarks, name registrations, customer records, and other such property.
- Should the agent be referred to as an "agent?" In some countries, the word "agent" implies power of attorney. The contract may need to specify that the agreement does not confer power of attorney.
- In what language should the contract be drafted? An English-language text should be the official language of the contract in most cases.

Tip: The agency or representative relationship is defined in each country according to that country's domestic law. If you are considering a working relationship with someone in a foreign country, be sure you understand the local agency laws and their ramifications for your agreement. You may clearly intend that you are engaging someone's services as an "independent contractor" (thereby avoiding employer-employee responsibility), but the foreign government may have a different interpretation of your agreement.

Research Agency Laws

A good place to begin gathering information about the employment and agency laws of the country in which you plan to do business is Martindale-Hubbell's *International Law Digest* available in the reference section of most larger public or law libraries. You could also contact an international law firm specializing in employment law, or a major international accounting firm. The following major international accounting firms have offices in nearly every country of the world:

- PriceWaterhouseCoopers
- Deloitte Touche
- Ernst & Young
- KPMG
- Grant Thornton
- BDO Seidman
- BKD

Banks, chambers of commerce, commercial consulates, and economic development organizations in the foreign country may also be of help.

Relationship with Foreign Supplier

At some point you will have to establish what kind of business relationship you want to have with your foreign supplier. Here are some options:

- Simple buyer/seller
- Exclusive buyer/seller
- Regional/country/industry distributorship
- Joint venture

Simple Buyer/Seller

The most common relationship is that of simple buyer and seller. The seller manufactures or represents one or more products and has a number of buyers. You become one of these buyers and are not given any special or out-of-the-ordinary terms. The seller sells on a first-come first-serve basis. At the beginning of the relationship, you will be expected either to prepay, or to pay with a Documentary Letter of Credit or Documents Against Payment. (Refer to "Methods of International Payment" on page 138 for explanation of these banking terms.) As the relationship matures you may be offered, or negotiate for, credit terms of 30, 60, or 90 days or more. As the buyer in a simple buyer-seller relationship, you will have no special or exclusive rights to merchandise or to territory. Sales agreements in these relationships can range from simple invoices to full-blown sales contracts. Refer to "Drafting the International Sales Contract" on page 110 and "International Sales Contract Checklist" on page 115 for more information.

Exclusive Buyer/Seller

In this relationship, the buyer successfully negotiates for exclusive rights to a manufacturer's product, product line, or entire production. Exclusive right can apply to an existing product, or, through a contract provision, to the custom manufacture of a buyer-designed product. The seller will generally negotiate for certain minimum purchases per unit time by the buyer. For example, 100 units per month at $X per unit for two years.

Regional/Country/Industry Distributorships

A distributorship agreement is essentially just a sophisticated sales agreement. It leaves certain terms open and assumes an ongoing relationship. In this relationship, the buyer negotiates and obtains rights for exclusive distribution of a product or product line within a specified geographic area or industry. Industry distributorships might be established for automotive, banking and financial services, chemicals, textiles and clothing, etc. Geographic distributorships can cover a metropolitan area, state, group of states, or an entire country. For example, if you want to import a product, and you already have an existing distribution network in the eleven western states of the U.S., you could negotiate for an exclusive distributorship for those states.

Tip: If the manufacturer or supplier already has distributors in the states for which you seek exclusive rights, don't give up. If you can demonstrate the advantages of working with you, the supplier can allow the other distributorship agreements to lapse or can buy them out to do business with you.

Joint Ventures

Joint ventures are often established between two or more entities having products, resources, or expertise that, when combined, will produce greater benefits for all parties. A joint venture usually involves the joining of parties either for a particular project or for an ongoing relationship with growth potential. For example, you may have a distribution network in the U.S. for a product manufactured and distributed only in Europe. The manufacturer is convinced that your organization is the best to distribute it but recognizes that you do not have the capital to do so. The foreign manufacturer/supplier might either invest money in your distributorship and obtain interest on the investment, purchase stock in your corporation, or even extend excellent credit terms to help you get started. You may also set up a separate agreement for this transaction alone, agreeing to a percentage split of profits from the venture.

Tip: Before becoming involved in joint ventures with foreign suppliers you should consider potential tax ramifications. Complex rules affect U.S. citizens, nonresident aliens, and aliens in these situations. Before engaging in a venture with a nonresident alien, consult an attorney or skilled international accounting firm with applicable expertise. Some joint ventures have sought to circumvent full payment of customs duties by artificially reducing the sale price of the imported product, then transferring back to the overseas supplier amounts that are actually product cost disguised as profit. If you remit such monies to your foreign supplier, you may be liable for additional duties to U.S. Customs.

Legal Counsel

The role of the attorney in business dealings varies from legal system to legal system. Attorneys are used more in the U.S. than in many foreign countries. In very complex agreements, they structure and negotiate the deal for the client, and they commonly take an active role in enforcing contracts from the time problems first arise. In other countries, attorneys usually draft the contract after the parties have negotiated the terms on their own, and their services are sought as a last resort in contract disputes.

Fees

Lawyers work either on a job, time, or retainer basis. For a single task, such as the drafting of a contract, your attorney will probably charge a fixed fee or an hourly rate. If you have a larger volume of business, you hire a lawyer on retainer, meaning the attorney will charge a set fee per month to handle most or all of your legal requirements. The tasks performed on a retainer basis are often limited by the retainer agreement. You should ask your attorney to clarify in advance which tasks are covered.

Tip: Always discuss fees with your lawyer in advance. In many jurisdictions, your lawyer is required to discuss fees with you before accepting your case. Nobody likes end-of-the-month billing surprises. If you address fees at the beginning, you will avoid misunderstandings.

Domestic Counsel

The best way to select counsel in the U.S. is through existing relationships. Ask other importers or your banker to recommend an attorney helpful in international transactions. When getting referrals, probe for specifics: What is the specific expertise of the attorney? Has the attorney done a good job for the recommender? Does the attorney give personal attention, or are problems delegated to someone in the firm less familiar with the client's needs?

Tip: A U.S. attorney with international business law expertise, along with a customs broker, freight forwarder, and banker, is an important member of your planning team. Personal rapport with your attorney is essential. You must feel at ease with your lawyer and be able to communicate openly. Your lawyer should be available on short notice to discuss problems that arise. In the course of a long-term association, you will most likely need to consult your attorney about questionable, embarrassing, and even illegal actions. The attorney you share them with should be someone competent and someone you like and trust.

When to Consult an Attorney

Call in counsel before you agree to any agreement that is out of the ordinary for you, such as your first international contract. If you have any intimation, even just a hunch, that something about a transaction is questionable, call your attorney. Get legal advice on any transaction involving substantial sums of money relative to your operations generally. For some transactions, do a cost-benefit analysis before deciding whether to call in counsel. Spending $500 to have your attorney review a file and draft a contract could save thousands of dollars in mistakes.

Tip: Be prepared when you call your lawyer. Always have the file, documents, or other pertinent information, and a list of specific questions, in front of you before you call. Preliminary planning will reduce wasted time, keep hourly fee charges to a minimum, and maximize the quality of services your attorney can provide.

Overseas Local Counsel

International business dealings will sometimes require that you have not only a U.S. attorney, but also competent foreign counsel at the overseas business site.

Tip: Be sure that any foreign attorney you select is fluent in English. This requirement is essential. Your ability to say hello, order food, and get directions in a foreign language is not sufficient fluency to negotiate contracts. You hire a foreign lawyer to do that for you. Make sure that lawyer is fluent in both languages. Many people engaging in international business overlook the language barrier. It hurts their business. Don't be one of them.

Though locating a reliable attorney overseas can be difficult if you are unfamiliar with the local area, there are many sources of help. Your international bank is a good place to begin inquiries. Ask your banker to give you some names of trustworthy, effective attorneys situated near your foreign business site. Major international accounting firms such as Ernst & Young, Touche Ross, and Coopers and Lybrand may have offices in the country and may be able to refer reliable attorneys. A number of U.S. legal firms have overseas offices or joint ventures with foreign firms and will provide referrals to local counsel. Although the commercial attaché of the U.S. embassy or consulate in the foreign country is not be permitted, for diplomatic reasons, to recommend a specific attorney, he or she may give you a short list of attorneys in the area.

Tip: If you plan to do business in the Middle East, you are strongly advised to have local legal counsel. Be especially careful about your local referral sources. Middle Eastern countries do not have the equivalent of U.S. conflict of law considerations. A government employee's recommendation of a local attorney may in fact be based on family ties or obligations, not on any special talent or proven reliability on the attorney's part. Find someone whom you can trust to be disinterested when seeking referrals to local counsel particularly in the Middle East.

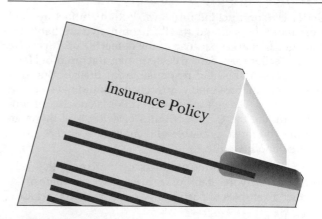

Insurance

General Business Insurance

General insurance on yourself, your business, and your products, including product liability insurance, is an absolute necessity. Your insurance broker will be able to advise you regarding how much insurance to carry. If your operation is large, you should talk to a lawyer and to a broker, both of whom are familiar with product liability. Assess the risks involved in your business. High-risk situations require greater coverage. One million dollars is the absolute minimum coverage for even a small, one-person import business. Overseas purchasing involves particular insurance problems. When your purchasing and reselling is limited to the continental U.S., your supplier will generally have insurance. This may not be the case with your foreign supplier. You need to carry enough insurance to cover any settlements, including those that reach into the millions of dollars.

Tip: If you have an ongoing relationship with an overseas supplier, you should consider including an indemnification provision in your contract. The provision should require your supplier to tender the defense in the event of a lawsuit, and to reimburse any losses you incur by selling his or her products.

Insurance Clause in Purchase Contracts

You should also consider including a provision about insurance in your purchase contracts. If your contract requires your supplier to have insurance as part of the business agreement, include a provision requiring the insured to provide proof, within 10 days of execution of the contract, that the insurance has been paid for. Require that your supplier's insurance company send you a letter verifying the supplier's insurance coverage, and stating that you will be notified directly if there is any lapse in the policy. Refer to "International Sales Contract Checklist" on page 115 for further information.

Tip: Reliance on your supplier's insurance coverage can be a mistake. You should request advice from legal counsel, freight forwarders, and insurers on whether to obtain your own coverage. You should also consider such factors as the nature and length of your relationship with your supplier in deciding whether to trust your supplier to obtain adequate coverage.

Product Liability Insurance

Under U.S. product liability laws, both manufacturer and merchant who sell and resell in commerce are liable for damages that arise because of the defect. Thus, if you are the U.S. seller for a defective item manufactured in Hong Kong, you can be held responsible for distributing that defective item, provided you knew or should have known of the defect. Though the foreign seller is equally responsible, you are the U.S. distributor or seller, and therefore you are the most available and most likely target for a product liability suit.

For a U.S. supplier, some products are more risky than others and may involve liability far in excess of the value of the product. Examples of particularly risky products include:

- Food
- Drugs
- Cosmetics
- Toys
- Machinery
- Flammable fabrics

If you sell products with high risk factors, carry product liability insurance in an amount adequate to the risk involved. This type of insurance guards against loss if you are sued for selling someone else's defective product, especially if it causes bodily harm. The insurance company agrees to indemnify (reimburse) you for any resulting financial loss up to the policy's limit, and provides your legal defense. Legal defense coverage includes court costs and attorney's fees.

Export Restrictions

The export of the following essential commodities has been banned. Exceptions to this ban are also noted: 1) Live animals - exceptions include breeding buffaloes, cows, goats, camels, some horses, fillies/mares, poultry, fish, shrimps, lobsters, crab and frogs; 2) Beef and mutton except cooked and canned beef and meat and 50% of the total production of commercial feed lot units, livestock farms and bilateral joint ventures; 3) Animal fat; 4) Milk and milk products except infant formula foods, weaning foods and food for invalids; 5) Vegetables all sorts including dehydrated vegetables and potato seeds - exceptions include (a) Dried methi leaves packed in small airtight containers or packets, onions, potatoes, garlic, zira, large chillies, asparagus, beans, artichokes, celery, broccoli and brussel sprouts; (b) Turmeric, tomatoes, lady fingers, turnips, carrots, radish, cauliflower, pumpkins, karela, green chillies, tinda, tori, karripatta, chichinda, arvi, petha, corriander leaves, spinach; 6) Grains, all sorts with the exception of maize and barley (subject to quota); 7) Pepper; 8) Pulses and beans, all sorts; 9) Blood meals, meat meals, corn gluten meals, corn gluton feed and sesame oil cakes; 10) Bran and fodder, all sorts except oil cakes, rice bran, wheat bran (subject to quota and special procedure); 11) Sann hemp and arte-misia seeds; 12) Edible oils, all sorts, including butter oil and vegetable ghee and oilseeds except castor seeds, poppy seeds, kapok seeds and sesame seeds; 13) Gur Khandsari and jaggery powder; 14) Intoxicants and intoxicating liquors as defined in the Prohibition (Enforcement of Hadd) Order, 1979; 15) Hides and skins, all sorts except lamb skins (grades I to V); 16) Wet blue leather made from cow hides and cow calf-hides; 17) Wild animal skins and garments

---

Export Laws

Every country in the world has laws governing which goods may be exported, and under what circumstances. Many U.S. business people put themselves in embarrassing and tough legal situations by unknowingly breaking local export laws. Countries generally monitor and restrict exports in the following categories:

- National security
- National treasures/artifacts
- Export tax
- Raw materials

If your products fall into any of these categories, call the U.S. based consulate or embassy of the exporting country.

National Security

Most countries restrict the export of raw materials or products that could have an adverse effect on national and international security. Some examples are: strategic materials such as radioactive materials; arms and armaments; and computers or computer chips that could be used in weapons.

National Treasures/Artifacts

Most countries have laws which restrict or ban the export of what are considered "national treasures," or "cultural property." These may include items of artistic, zoological, botanical, mineralogical, anatomical, historical, archaeological, paleontological, ethnographic, or numismatic interest. Items considered to be part of the "national treasure," are sometimes listed. For example, there is a privately owned firearms collection in Spain that cannot be exported. For more information refer to "Cultural Property" on pages 916 and 917.

Export Tax

Most countries are so export promotion oriented that they do not impose taxes on exported merchandise. A few, however, do charge taxes (usually small) on exports.

Export of Raw Materials

Some countries ban the export of unfinished raw materials to promote the development of local manufacturing operations using those materials. For instance, Thailand restricts the export of raw teak logs, resulting in increased employment of Thai nationals in sawmills and in the wood products industry.

U.S. Import Laws, U.S. Customs

The U.S. government monitors, regulates, and collects import duties on merchandise entering the country. The agency with primary responsibility for this effort is the U.S. Bureau of Customs and Border Protection which is part of the U.S. Department of the Treasury.

U.S. Bureau of Customs and Border Protection

The major responsibility of the U.S. Bureau of Customs and Border Protection is to administer the Tariff Act of 1930, as amended. Primary functions include the assessment and collection of all duties, taxes, and fees on imported merchandise; the enforcement of customs and related laws; and the administration of certain navigation laws and treaties. As a major enforcement organization, Customs combats smuggling and revenue fraud and enforces the regulations of numerous other federal agencies at ports of entry and along the land and sea borders of the U.S.

Restricted and Prohibited Merchandise

While many products are straightforward to import, requiring only simple paperwork, many others are heavily regulated and require significant knowledge of the process. Compliance with Customs and other governmental regulations is vital for a successful import operation. Refer to "17 Difficult-to-Import Products" on page 19 for a summary of products that are subject to heavy import regulations.

If you plan to import restricted products, refer to the listing(s) in the Commodity Index in this manual for information on those specific products. Then obtain the advice of a customs broker and a U.S. Customs "commodity specialist" at the proposed port of entry. Also speak with administrators at the agencies that regulate your products. Getting information from several sources is prudent.

Liability for Duties

There is no provision under which U.S. duties or taxes may be prepaid in a foreign country before exportation to the U.S. This is true even in the case of gifts sent through the mail.

In the usual case, liability for the payment of duty becomes fixed at the time an entry for consumption or for warehouse is filed with Customs. The obligation for payment is on the person or firm in whose name the entry is filed. If goods are entered for warehouse, the liability for the payment of duties may be transferred to any person who purchases the goods and desires to withdraw them in his or her own name.

Payment to a Customs broker will not relieve an importer of record of liability for Customs charges (duties, taxes, and other debts owed Customs) if the charges are not paid by the broker. Therefore, if the importer pays by check, Customs charges may be paid with a separate check payable to "U.S. Bureau of Customs and Border Protection," which will be delivered to Customs by the broker.

If an entry is made in the name of a Customs broker, the broker may obtain relief from statutory liability for the payment of increased or additional duties found due if (1) the actual owner of goods is named, and (2) within 90 days of the date of entry, the broker files with the district director a bond secured by the owner and a declaration by the owner agreeing to pay any additional amount.

Frequent Errors in Invoicing

If difficulties, delays, and possible penal sanctions affecting the importer are to be avoided, care must be exercised by foreign sellers and shippers in the preparation of invoices and other documents to be used in the entry of goods into the commerce of the U.S. Each document must contain all information required by law or regulations, and every statement of fact contained in the documents must be true and accurate.

Any inaccurate or misleading statement of fact in a document presented to a Customs officer in connection with an entry, or the omission from the document of required information, may result in delays in merchandise release, the detention of the goods, or a claim against the importer for forfeiture value. Even if the inaccuracy or omission is unintentional, the importer may have to establish that he or she exercised due diligence and was not negligent in order to avoid sanctions, with consequent delay in obtaining possession of goods and closing the transaction.

In particular, all statements relating to the merchandise description, price, or value—plus the amounts of discounts, charges, and commissions—must be accurately set forth. Equally important, for purchased goods, the invoice must designate the true names of the seller and purchaser. For goods shipped other than for purchase, the invoice must state the true names of the consignor and consignee. The invoice must reflect the real nature of the transaction pursuant to which the goods were shipped to the U.S.

The fundamental rule is that the shipper and importer must furnish Customs with all pertinent information for each import transaction to assist the Custom officers in determining the tariff status of the goods. Examples of omissions and inaccuracies to be avoided are:

- The shipper assumes that a commission, royalty, or other charge against the goods is a so-called "nondutiable" item and omits it from the invoice.

- A foreign shipper who purchases goods and sells them to a U.S. importer at a delivered price shows on the invoice the cost of the goods to the shipper instead of the delivered price.

- A foreign shipper manufactures goods partly with the use of materials supplied by the U.S. importer, but invoices the goods at the actual cost to the manufacturer, without including the value of the materials supplied by the importer.

- The foreign manufacturer ships replacement goods to a U.S. customer and invoices the goods at the net price without stating the full price less the allowance for defective goods previously shipped and returned.

- A foreign shipper who sells goods at list price less a discount invoices them at the net price and fails to show the discount.

- A foreign shipper sells goods at a delivered price but invoices them at a price f.o.b. the place of shipment and omits the subsequent charges.

- A foreign shipper indicates in the invoice that the importer is the purchaser, but in fact the person listed is either an agent who is receiving a commission for selling the goods or a party who will receive part of the proceeds of the sale of the goods sold for the joint account of the shipper and consignee.

- The foreign shipper identifies the goods by vague invoice descriptions, such as by listing part numbers or truncated or coded descriptions only, or by lumping various distinct items together as one article.

Antidumping and Countervailing Duties

Antidumping duties (ADs) are assessed on imported merchandise of a class or kind that is sold to purchasers in the U.S. at a price less than the fair market value. Fair market value of merchandise is the price at which it is normally sold in the manufacturer's home market.

Countervailing duties (CVDs) are assessed to counter the effects of subsidies provided by foreign governments, to merchandise that is exported to the U.S. These subsidies cause the price of such merchandise to be artificially low, which causes economic "injury" to U.S. manufacturers.

Investigation and Enforcement. The Department of Commerce (DOC), the International Trade Commission (ITC), and U.S. Customs all play a part in enforcing antidumping and countervailing duty laws. The DOC is responsible for the overall administration of AD and CVD laws and for investigating allegations of dumping or foreign subsidization of imports. If warranted by the investigation, the DOC also establishes the duty to be imposed on the merchandise. The ITC determines whether injury to industry has occurred or is likely to occur and whether an industry may be hampered in its start-up efforts because of alleged dumping or subsidies. Customs assesses ADs and CVDs once the rates have been established and the ITC has made the necessary determinations.

Both types of duties are established and assessed through the following process:

Investigation. AD or CVD investigations are typically initiated when a domestic industry files a petition with the DOC or when another interested party—an industry association, for example—alleges unfair competition by foreign manufacturers. On receipt of the petition, the DOC investigates the merits of the allegations to determine whether dumping or unfair subsidization has indeed occurred. The ITC, meanwhile, investigates whether there is reasonable indication that U.S. industries are, or are likely to be, harmed by the alleged dumping or subsidies. Results of these investigations are published in the Federal Register.

The DOC then calculates the difference between prices at which the merchandise in question is being sold in the U.S. and its fair market value. On the basis of this calculation, Commerce directs the Customs Service to: (1) assess cash deposits or require bonds on imports of the merchandise to cover possible AD or CVD duty liability, and (2) suspend liquidation of the entries until the DOC has determined whether dumping or subsidization has occurred and has calculated the proper dumping or countervailing margins.

Completion of Investigation. When the DOC and, if applicable, the ITC have completed their investigations and determined that dumping or subsidization has occurred, the DOC will publish an Antidumping or Countervailing Duty Order, which will be announced in the Federal Register. At this point, DOC will generally direct Customs to collect only cash deposits, bonding being no longer permitted.

Administrative Review/Final Settlement. Each year, on the anniversary of the final determination of dumping or subsidization, the DOC must, by law, perform an administrative review of the AD or CVD case if requested by interested parties to determine whether duty rates in effect for that first-year period are correct. The DOC publishes the results of this review in the Federal Register. At the one-year anniversary or completion of the administrative review, the DOC will direct Customs to liquidate the entries for the affected period. Customs will then review the entries and, if called for, make refunds to the importer or assess whatever additional duties may be owed.

Marking: False Impression or Origin

Section 42 of the Trademark Act of 1946 (15 USC 1124) prohibits the importation into the U.S. of any article of foreign origin that bears a name or mark that (1) copies or simulates the name of a manufacturer or trader afforded protection under U.S. law—including foreigners protected through treaty, convention, or U.S. law; or (2) is calculated to induce the public to believe that the article was manufactured in the U.S., or in any foreign country or locality other than the country or locality of actual manufacture.

An imported article bearing a name or mark prohibited by Section 42 of the Trademark Act is subject to seizure and forfeiture. However, on the filing of a petition by the importer before final disposition of the article, Customs may release it on condition that the prohibited marking is removed or obliterated or that the article and containers are properly marked. Alternatively, Customs may permit the article to be exported or destroyed under Customs supervision and without expense to the Government.

Section 43 of the Trademark Act of 1946 (15 USC 1125) prohibits the entry of goods marked or labeled with a false designation of origin or with any false description or representation, including words or other symbols tending to falsely describe or represent the same.

In many cases, the words "United States," the letters "U.S.A.," or the name of any city or locality in the U.S. appearing on an imported article of foreign origin, or on its container, are considered to be calculated to induce the public to believe that the article was manufactured in the U.S., unless the name showing the country of origin appears in close proximity to the name that suggests a domestic origin.

Deliberate removal, obliteration, covering, or altering of required country of origin markings after release from Customs is a crime punishable by fines and imprisonment (19 USC 1304(h)).

Civil and Criminal Fraud Laws

Section 592 of the 1930 Tariff Act, as amended (19 USC 1592), imposes a monetary penalty on any person who by fraud, gross negligence, or negligence enters or introduces, tries to enter or introduce, or aids or abets another person to enter or introduce merchandise into U.S. commerce by means of any material and false written or oral statement, document, or act, or any material omission. In some situations, the imported merchandise may be seized to secure payment of the penalty and forfeited for failure to pay. This civil fraud statute has been applied by the Customs Service to individuals and companies in the U.S. and abroad that have negligently or intentionally provided false information about importations into the U.S.

Another criminal fraud statute sanctions persons who present false information to Customs officers (18 USC 542), and yet another penalizes those who obtain the entry of products by giving less than the true weight or measure of the imported articles, by stating a false classification as to quality or value, or by paying less than the duty due (18 USC 541). These statutes provide for imprisonment, a hefty fine, or both, for each violation involving an importation or attempted importation.

Federal laws that prohibit money laundering and illegal drug transactions authorize the government to seize and cause the forfeit of property involved—or assets traceable to property involved—in violations of these laws. The Money Laundering Control Act expressly identifies importation fraud violations as unlawful activities. Penalties include imprisonment for up to 20 years for each offense and fines of up to $500,000. These statutes were enacted by Congress to discourage persons from evading the payment of lawful duties owed to the U.S., although these laws now apply regardless of whether the U.S. is deprived of lawful duties. They are enforced by special agents assigned to the Office of Enforcement who operate throughout the U.S. and in major trading centers worldwide. Suspected or known violations of any law involved with the importation of merchandise into the U.S. can be reported toll free and anonymously by calling 1-800 BE-ALERT (232-5378). Rewards are applicable in many instances associated with the reporting of fraud.

Laws Restricting Imports

Copyrights. The Copyright Act (17 USC 101 et seq.) restricts importation into the U.S. of any copies of a work that is protected by copyright and that is acquired outside of the U.S. Such works may be imported only with the copyright owner's authorization. To ensure that pirated versions of copyrighted materials do not enter the U.S., Customs' Intellectual Property Rights Branch enforces this law. Articles imported in violation of the Copyright Act are subject to seizure and forfeiture. Forfeited articles are destroyed or, if Customs is satisfied that the violation was unintentional, may be returned to the country of export. A test of substantial similarity is applied to determine if a work has been copied.

Copyright owners who seek import protection must register their claim to copyright protection with the U.S. Copyright Office and must record their registration with U.S. Customs. Procedures and regulations for recordation are found in 37 CFR 201.8 and 19 CFR 133.31 et seq. Articles imported by mail, marked for copyright, and addressed to the Copyright Office of the Library of Congress or to the Register of Copyrights, Washington, DC, pass Customs duty-free without issuing an entry. For questions about Customs enforcement of copyright requirements, contact the district or port director of Customs for your area or:

U.S. Customs Service
National Intellectual Property Rights
1300 Pennsylvania Avenue, NW, Room 3.5A
Washington, DC 20229
(202) 927-0810

Trademarks and Trade Names. U.S. Customs affords import protection for U.S. owners of registered trademarks and trade names that have been filed with the Commissioner of Customs and recorded pursuant to regulations in 19 CFR 133. Under this protection, articles of foreign or domestic manufacture that bear a mark or name copying or simulating a recorded trademark or trade name will be refused entry. It is also unlawful to import articles bearing genuine trademarks owned by a U.S. citizen or corporation without permission of the U.S. trademark owner. If the foreign and domestic trademark owners are parent and subsidiary companies or otherwise under common ownership and control, entry will be permitted.

The Customs Reform and Simplification Act of 1978 strengthened the protection afforded trademark owners against the importation of articles bearing a counterfeit mark. A "counterfeit trademark" is a spurious trademark identical with, or substantially indistinguishable from, a registered trademark. Articles bearing a counterfeit trademark seized by customs and forfeited to the government may be 1) given to any federal, state, or local government agency that has established a need for the article; 2) given to a charitable institution; or 3) sold at public auction if more than one year has passed since forfeiture and no eligible organization has established a need for the article. The counterfeit marks must be removed before the forfeited articles may be given away or sold. If removal of marking is not feasible, the articles are destroyed.

The law also provides an exemption from all restrictions on trademarked articles (limited to one of each type) that accompany a person arriving in the U.S., provided the articles are for personal use and not for sale.

Obscene, Immoral, or Seditious Materials. The import of articles considered obscene, immoral, or seditious are strictly prohibted under the Tariff Act (18 USC 552, 1462, 1465, 2251 et seq.). These laws specifically prohibit the importation of any book, writing, advertisement, circular, or picture containing any matter advocating or urging treason or insurrection against the U.S. or forcible resistance to any U.S. law. Any such materials that contain a threat to take the life of or inflict bodily harm on any person in the U.S. must be refused entry.

The law also prohibits importation of any obscene book, writing, advertisement, circular, picture, or other representation, figure, or image on or of paper or other material, or any instrument, or other obscene or immoral article. Shipments of material relating to sexual exploitation of minors are prohibited. Any drug or medicine for causing unlawful abortion is also prohibited under the Tariff Act. The mailing of pandering and sexually oriented advertisements that fail to comply strictly with legal requirements for such mailing is prohibited, and the U.S. Postal Service is authorized to order any sender to refrain from sending such materials.

Disobedience is punishable by contempt of court, which may involve imposition of fines and imprisonment. See 18 USC 3008, 3010.

Books. If you import a book that is seized by U.S. Customs as being obscene, and you decline to execute an assent to forfeiture on the grounds that the book is a classic, or is of recognized and established literary or scientific merit, you may file a petition for release of the book, addressed to the Secretary of the Treasury. You will have to supply evidence to support your claim, along with your petition. Unsupported statements or allegations will not be considered. If the ruling is favorable, your book will be released to the ultimate consignee.

Films. If you are importing films, you must certify on Customs **Form 3291** that your films contain no prohibited material as defined in Section 305 of the Tariff Act. If you claim your imported films as duty-free U.S. goods returned, you may instead make this certification on Customs **Form 3311**, in the space designated "Remarks".

A qualified Customs employee will preview films exposed abroad before release from Customs custody. Films imported as undeveloped negatives exposed abroad will be viewed after development in the U.S. Before developing and printing, such films must be weighed and an approximation of their length in feet must be given to Customs. Any objectional film will be detained pending instructions from U.S. Customs headquarters or a decision of the court as to its final disposition.

Detention Procedures. Customs seizes prohibited items at entry and sends notice of seizure to the consignee. If the articles are of small value and no criminal intent is apparent, Customs includes a blank assent to forfeiture, Customs

Form 4607, with the notice. If the articles are not needed for official use, they are destroyed when Customs receives the completed **Form 4607**. The case is then closed. However, for a repeat offender or for a situation in which the importation was deliberately made with intent to evade the law, Customs submits the facts and evidence (i.e. the prohibited article) to the U.S. attorney, who initiates prosecution.

Products of Convict or Forced Labor. The Tariff Act (18 USC 1761) prohibits the importation of merchandise produced, mined, or manufactured through convict, forced, or indentured-under-penal-sanctions labor. Customs enforces these provisions (19 CFR 12.45). Under Customs regulations (19 CFR 42), if a potential violation of this law is brought to the attention of U.S. Customs and is found to be reasonably substantiated by accompanying evidence, all such shipments will be temporarily detained. If, on investigation, the Commissioner of Customs determines that the products are the result of prohibited labor, the finding will be published in the Federal Register. All detained shipments will then be either reexported or destroyed.

If you import a shipment of merchandise detained as a product of prohibited forms of labor, you may petition the Commissioner of Customs for a redetermination of admissibility. To do so, you will have to submit a certificate of origin (19 CFR 43) signed by the foreign seller or owner of the article. The ultimate consignee must also provide a statement detailing every reasonable effort to ascertain the character of the labor used in producing the article and showing the results of the research. All relevant paperwork must be submitted to Customs within three months after the original importation. If Customs finds that the products are admissible, your shipment will be released, subject to normal entry requirements. If Customs decides your proof does not establish admissibility, you will be notified in writing that your merchandise is excluded from entry. After such notification, the merchandise will be destroyed within 60 days, unless you reexport it or file a further protest.

Unfair Competition or Business Practices. Section 337 of the Tariff Act of 1930 prohibits unfair methods of competition and unfair practices in the importation or sale of merchandise when the effect or tendency is 1) to destroy, injure substantially, or prevent the establishment of an efficiently and economically operated U.S. industry; or 2) to restrain or monopolize trade and commerce in the U.S. The International Trade Commission (ITC) conducts investigations of alleged Section 337 violations. If the ITC determines that a violation has occurred, or that there is reason to believe a violation has occurred, with respect to the importation of certain merchandise, it will issue an import exclusion order for all such merchandise. The order is published in the *Federal Register* and goes into effect on the date of its publication. The order becomes final after 60 days, unless revoked by the U.S. President. Customs refuses admission to all shipments of merchandise under import exclusion order. Until the order becomes final, however, the shipments may be provisionally imported under Customs bond (Customs **Form 301**). If the order is not revoked by presidential action, Customs recalls all provisional shipments when the order becomes final, provided the order requires a recall. If the President determines that entry of the merchandise is not in violation of Section

337, the bond is cancelled and the merchandise is not recalled.

Patent Protections. Section 337 of the Tariff Act of 1930 is most commonly invoked in the case of patent violations. The owner of a U.S.-registered patent who believes that merchandise being imported into the U.S. infringes the patent may apply for a Customs survey. The survey provides the patent owner with names and addresses of importers whose merchandise appears to infringe the registered patent. The application may be made by letter addressed to the Commissioner of Customs. It must give 1) the name and address of the patent owner; 2) if available, a description of the merchandise believed to infringe the registered patent; and 3) the country of manufacture. The patent owner must also submit a certified copy, plus three copies for Customs files, of the U.S. Patent and Trademark Office patent registration, and a check or money order to cover the fee for the survey. The applicant may request surveys for periods of 2, 4, or 6 months. If patent violation is confirmed, questionable merchandise is prohibited entry for the term of the patent. In some cases, a different term may be specified.

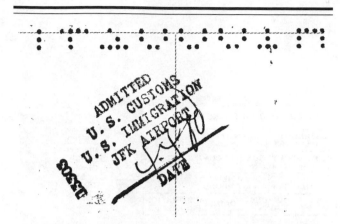

Reentry to the United States

All who reenter the U.S. from abroad must pass through immigration control. The U.S. Immigration and Naturalization Service (INS) works closely with U.S. Customs.

Nonresident Entry

If you are a U.S. resident alien and not a U.S. citizen, you will need a valid residency "green" card to gain entry to the U.S. A nonresident alien will require a U.S. visa or work permit to regain entry. U.S. Immigration may deny entry to foreign nationals for various reasons including:

- Those suspected of terrorist activities
- Those considered to be health risks
- Those convicted in a foreign court of law of certain felonies

Nonresident Customs Exemptions

The following articles may be brought in free of duty and internal revenue tax, provided they are for personal use, not for others, and not for sale.

- Personal effects (e.g., wearing apparel; articles of personal adornment; toilet articles; hunting, fishing, and photographic equipment; equipment for physically challenged persons)
- One U.S. quart (one liter) of alcoholic beverages (e.g., wine, beer, or liquor), if you are an adult nonresident
- 200 cigarettes, 50 cigars, or 4.5 pounds (2 kg) of smoking tobacco, or proportionate amounts of each
- Vehicles (e.g., automobiles, trailers, airplanes, motorcycles, boats), if imported in connection with your arrival

Gift Exemption. In addition to the above exemptions, articles of up to $100 in total value for use as bona fide gifts to other persons may be brought in free of duty and tax, as long as you will be in the U.S. for at least 72 hours and have not claimed this gift exemption in the past 6 months. You may include in this exemption up to 100 cigars, but not alcohol or cigarettes in any amount.

Note: Some states limit the amount of liquor that can be brought into the state. Customs cannot release alcoholic beverages in excess of restrictions of the state where you arrive.

Drafting the International Sales Contract

Nature of a Contract

Contracts are simply agreements, usually between a buyer and a seller. For example, when you say that you agree to purchase a quantity of product at a certain price from a supplier, you have entered into an oral contract. Whether you will be able to enforce your contract is another question. As you move from the domestic to the international setting, enforcement issues increase in complexity.

Importance of Having a Written Contract

Formalities of contract formation—such as whether a contract must be written, whether oral terms can modify written ones, and whether the parties must authenticate their signatures or certify to their authority—vary according to local practices. In general, keep in mind that a precisely drafted, written contract will help to eliminate misunderstandings between your supplier and you. It will also serve as proof of your agreement, should enforcement prove necessary.

The laws of some jurisdictions require certain contracts to be written in order to be enforceable. For example, the U.S. Uniform Commercial Code (UCC) provides that every contract for the sale of goods with an aggregate value exceeding $500 must be in writing to be enforceable. The foreign jurisdiction where you are doing business may or may not have a similar requirement. Some jurisdictions also require written contracts for the transfer of certain types of property, such as immovable property or lease-to-buy items. Observation of other formalities—such as notarization or signatures of witnesses—may be required. In some countries, an individual who works for a corporation may not be allowed to bind that company in a contract without a corporate resolution.

At the very least, you should have a written contract whenever you pay for, but do not take possession of, goods. If you are simply paying c.o.d. for goods, get a bill of sale or invoice for tax and customs purposes. Make sure that you have documentation of the sale, even if it is just a simple description of goods, quantity, and price. This is usually sufficient for general merchandise if you take physical delivery and ship the goods yourself, rather than having the seller handle packaging, shipping, and other transfer arrangements.

For a contract that will be performed over time—that is, a series of transactions—you should anticipate potential problems at the outset. Most people enter into an agreement to purchase and sell with the expectation that all will go smoothly and both parties will gain from the transaction. These positive expectations can be realized if your supplier and you provide for contingencies. Even with a simple sales contract, you must think about possible downstream problems. The first rule of successful international business is also the last rule: *decide how to resolve problems and disputes before they occur.*

Tip: The best time to agree on how downstream problems will be handled is when you have reached an initial agreement to do business together and all parties are feeling positive. If you can't agree to a means of dispute resolution when your contract is drafted, you are unlikely to reach agreement once a problem does arise. Remember: whenever title to goods is not transferred at the time you make the agreement, you should have at least a simple written contract. The complexity of your written contract should reflect the complexity of your transaction. All foreseeable problems should be addressed and resolved in express contractual terms.

Domestic and Foreign Contract Laws

International business transactions are complicated by the movement of goods and services between foreign jurisdictions with different legal systems. The drafting of a contract, performance or modification of contractual obligations, resolution of disputes, and enforcement of judgments or orders are relatively straightforward in domestic U.S. transactions, but they can be arduous tasks when you face international transactions subject to foreign laws and legal systems with which you are unfamiliar.

The U.S. System: Cross-State Recognition. The U.S. has 52 different legal systems: a federal one, one in each state, and one in the District of Columbia. The U.S. is a common law country. Its law is based on a division of powers between federal and state governments. On the federal level, various district and circuit courts interpret federal law in different regions of the country, with conflicts eventually resolved by the U.S. Supreme Court. All powers that are neither expressly delegated to the federal government nor specifically prohibited to the states are reserved to the states. Under this system, each state is free to enact its own laws, and its local courts are free to develop their own judicial interpretations of those laws. As a result, two states can have conflicting laws. Even if two states enact exactly the same statute, their courts may develop distinct—if not contrary—interpretations of that law.

Nevertheless, the U.S. Constitution requires local state courts to give "full faith and credit" to judgments and orders validly entered by a court in another state. For example, if your business is located in California and you have a supplier in Nevada who fails to deliver goods as required by your contract, you may sue for breach of contract in California and may get a judgment in your favor. You can then take your California judgment to Nevada, where the Nevada courts will most likely than not recognize and enforce it.

State courts also recognize the rights of parties to choose which state's laws will apply to a transaction, and the courts will usually uphold such an agreement. For example, a California buyer may agree to have Nevada law applied to a contract with a Nevada supplier. If suit for breach of the contract is brought in California, the court in California will interpret and apply Nevada laws.

Other Countries: Discretionary Recognition. Although in the U.S. your transactions can cross state lines with relative ease, this is not always the case in the international business setting. Courts in countries with common law systems—such as the U.S. and the United Kingdom—will usually recognize foreign country laws and judgments through a doctrine known as "comity." Many U.S. states and some foreign countries have laws for registration and recognition of foreign country judgments, although enforcement is usually still discretionary with the local court. In countries that are members of international trade conventions, such as the U.N. Convention on Contracts for the International Sale of Goods (CISG) or the Convention on the Recognition and Enforcement of Foreign Arbitral Awards, cross-border enforcement may be available, but the ease with which enforcement can be accomplished depends on the legal system of the member country and the extent to which it has developed methods of enforcement. Before you commit to an international sales contract, you must consider all ramifications of crossing international legal and cultural boundaries relevant to the particular transaction proposed. A contract that is impossible to enforce is worthless.

Uniform Contract Laws

The U.S.: Uniform Commercial Code (UCC). All of the states have adopted some form of the Uniform Commercial Code (UCC). The UCC was drafted by a national commission, primarily made up of lawyers, to serve as a model law on commercial sales. Each U.S. state has discretion to adopt the UCC intact or with modifications, and they may also amend it from time to time. Because it works well, the UCC has had a great impact both on domestic U.S. transactions and on international sales. U.S. commercial law is so well-developed that it has become a model for commercial law in many foreign countries.

Internationally: The United Nations Sales Convention. On January 1, 1988, the U.S. ratified the U.N. Convention on Contracts for the International Sale of Goods (CISG). This Convention establishes uniform legal rules to govern the formation of international sales contracts and the rights and obligations of the contracting parties. The CISG is designed to facilitate and stimulate international trade. When the U.S. became a signatory, it made a reservation to the effect that the CISG will apply only when the other party to the transaction also has its place of business in a country that applies the CISG.

The CISG applies automatically to all contracts for the sale of goods between traders from two different countries that have both ratified the Convention. To avoid application of the CISG, the contracting parties must expressly state that all or part of the CISG does not apply or must expressly stipulate to law other than the CISG. Parties can also expressly choose to apply the CISG to transactions not otherwise subject to this Convention.

The nations that have ratified the CISG include the following: Argentina, Australia, Austria, Bulgaria, Chile, China, Belarus, Denmark, Egypt, Finland, France, Germany, Guinea, Hungary, Iraq, Italy, Lesotho, Mexico, Netherlands, Norway, Spain, Sweden, Switzerland, Syria, Russia, U.S., and Zambia.

Convention Provisions. The provisions and scope of the CISG are similar to Article 2 of the Uniform Commercial Code (effective in the U.S.). The CISG comprises four parts:

- Part I, Sphere of Application and General Provisions (Arts. 1-13), provides that the CISG covers the international sale of most commercial goods.
- Part II, Formation of the Contract (Arts. 1-24), provides rules on offer and acceptance.
- Part III, Sale of Goods (Arts. 25-88), covers obligations and remedies of the seller and buyer and rules on the passing of risk and damages.
- Part IV, Final Provisions (Arts. 89-101), covers the right of a country to disclaim certain parts of the convention.

Applying (or Excluding) the CISG. U.S. businesses can avoid the difficulties of reaching agreement with foreign parties on choice-of-law issues through the use of the CISG, which may serve as a compromise in negotiating sale contract terms. Use of the CISG may decrease the time and legal costs otherwise involved in research of various unfamiliar foreign laws. Furthermore, the CISG may reduce problems of proof and recognition of foreign law in domestic and foreign courts. Application of the CISG may especially make sense for smaller firms—and for U.S. firms contracting with smaller companies—in countries where the legal systems are obscure, unfamiliar, undeveloped, or otherwise unsuited for international sales transactions.

Some larger, more experienced firms may prefer to continue their current practices, at least with regard to parties with whom they have been doing business regularly. A firm that chooses to exclude the CISG cannot do so by merely adding a choice of law clause—e.g., "the laws of XYZ shall apply"—to the contract, because the CISG may also be the law of the jurisdiction selected. Rather, the exclusion must be specific: "The provisions of the Uniform Commercial Code as adopted by the State of XYZ, and not the U.N. Convention on Contracts for the International Sale of Goods, shall govern this contract."

The CISG can be found in 15 USC app. To obtain an up-to-date listing of ratifying or acceding countries and their reservations call the U.N. Treaties Section at (212) 963-3918. For further information, contact the Office of the Assistant Legal Adviser for Private International Law, U.S. Department of State, at (202) 647-6575, or the Office of the Chief Counsel for International Commerce, U.S. Department of Commerce at (202) 482-0937.

Bilateral and Free Trade Agreements. The U.S., Canada, and Mexico have concluded the North American Free Trade Agreement (NAFTA). In addition to eliminating and reducing tariffs and similar trade barriers among these countries, this Agreement mandates the establishment of enforcement and dispute resolution systems for cross-border transactions that are covered under the Agreement. It also provides for substantial industrial and intellectual property right protection.

Bilateral trade agreements have been made between the U.S. and several Eastern European countries, Russia, and Mongolia. These congressionally approved agreements are required by the Trade Act of 1974 for these countries to receive Most Favored Nation (MFN) treatment. These agreements provide for reciprocal MFN status and contain guarantees on intellectual property rights and business facilitation—such as the right to establish commercial representation offices in a country through at most a simple registration process; the right to serve as, and to hire, agents; the right to deal directly with customers and end users of products and services; and the right to hire employees of a company's choice. The intellectual property right provisions include protection for computer software and trade secrets.

Important Contract Terms

When dealing internationally, you must consider the business practices and legal requirements of the country where the buyer or seller is located. Parties generally have the freedom to agree to any contract terms that they desire, but the laws of your country or the foreign country may require a written contract. In some transactions, the laws may even specify all or some of the contract terms. Whether a contract term is valid in a particular country is mainly of concern if you have to seek enforcement. Otherwise, you have fairly broad flexibility in negotiating contract provisions. However, you should always be certain to come to a definite understanding with the other party on four basic issues: the goods (quantity, type, and quality); the time of delivery; the price; and the time and means of payment.

Conflict of law problems occur when you leave terms out of your contract because the gaps will be filled in by application of the law. The result will vary depending on which law is chosen. If terms are vague and open to interpretation, or if any aspect is left to implication or custom, you will have to rely on the law to determine your rights and obligations should a dispute arise. Disputes will be resolved according to the laws of the country with jurisdiction (for example, the country designated in your contract or the country where both parties have the most significant contacts).

Accordingly, the best way to control the results of your contract is to clarify each party's responsibility in the agreement by paying close attention to each contract term. Always be specific. For instance, you may have an agreement that you will buy a certain quantity of a specific product, but how are you going to pick up the goods? Is someone going to box them? Do you want the entire order at once? When do you want them?

Tip: Even if you specify your choice of law and method of dispute resolution in the contract, you may find that you are doing business with a national of a country that does not recognize such stipulations. In that case, the foreign country may not enforce a U.S. judgment. Before concluding an agreement, do your homework: find out about the country's policy on choice of law and conflict resolution for international contracts. Martindale-Hubbell's *International Law Digest*, available at the reference desk of most larger public and law libraries, is a good place to start.

After you have determined whether the CISG or another law applies to a particular transaction, you should review the related documentation to ensure consistency with the CISG or other governing law. For agreements about to expire, companies should make sure renewals take into account the applicability (or nonapplicability) of the CISG.

Payment Term. In international business transactions, you will use different methods of payment, and possibly different currency, than you do in domestic transactions. You will have to become familiar with different currencies, currency restrictions, and exchange rates, and you will need to consider these issues each time you draft a contract. Contact your international banker for information about foreign exchange and currency restrictions.

Transport and Delivery Terms. In any sales agreement, definitions of transport and delivery terms are essential. The terms commonly used in international business transactions often sound similar to those used in domestic contracts, but they frequently have different meanings in global transactions. Confusion over these terms can result in a lost sale or a financial loss on a sale. For this reason, you must know the meaning of these terms before completing your agreement.

A full list of important terms and definitions is contained in *Incoterms 2000*, a book issued by ICC Publications, Inc., 156 Fifth Avenue, New York, NY 10010; Tel (212) 206-1150; FAX (212) 633-6025. *Guide to Incoterms*—also available from ICC—uses illustrations and commentary to explain how a buyer and seller divide risks and obligations, and therefore costs, in specific kinds of international transactions. The 2000 update of *Incoterms* resulted in several new terms and abbreviations; you should, therefore, take care to use the most recent edition of these terms to avoid confusion.

Incoterms 2000

1) EXW, Ex Works (...named place)

In Ex Works, the seller/exporter/manufacturer merely makes the goods available to the buyer at the seller's "named place" of business. This trade term places the greatest responsibility on the buyer and minimum obligations on the seller.

The seller does not clear the goods for export and does not load the goods onto a truck or other transport vehicle at the named place of departure.

The parties to the transaction, however, may stipulate that the seller be responsible for the costs and risks of loading the goods onto a transport vehicle. Such a stipulation must be made within the contract of sale.

If the buyer cannot handle export formalities the Ex Works term should not be used. In such a case Free Carrier (FCA) is recommended. The Ex Works term is often used when making an initial quotation for the sale of goods. It represents the cost of the goods without any other costs included. Normal payment terms for Ex Works transactions are generally cash in advance and open account.

2) FCA, Free Carrier (...named place)

In Free Carrier, the seller/exporter/manufacturer clears the goods for export and then delivers them to the carrier specified by the buyer at the named place.

If the named place is the seller's place of business, the seller is responsible for loading the goods onto the transport vehicle. If the named place is any other location, such as the loading dock of the carrier, the seller is not responsible for loading the goods onto the transport vehicle.

The Free Carrier term may be used for any mode of transport, including multimodal. The "named place" in Free Carrier and all "F" terms is domestic to the seller.

"Carrier" has a specific and somewhat expanded meaning. A carrier can be a shipping line, an airline, a trucking firm, or a railway. The carrier can also be an individual or firm who undertakes to procure carriage by any of the above methods of transport including multimodal. Therefore, a person, such as a freight forwarder, can act as a "carrier" under this term. In such a case, the buyer names the carrier or the individual who is to receive the goods.

The Free Carrier term is often used when making an initial quotation for the sale of goods. Normal payment terms for Free Carrier transactions are generally cash in advance and open account.

3) FAS, Free Alongside Ship (...named port of shipment)

In Free Alongside Ship, the seller/exporter/manufacturer clears the goods for export and then places them alongside the vessel at the "named port of shipment." [The seller's clearing the goods for export is new to Incoterms 2000.]

The parties to the transaction, however, may stipulate in their contract of sale that the buyer will clear the goods for export.

The Free Alongside Ship term is used only for ocean or inland waterway transport.

The "named place" in Free Alongside Ship and all "F" terms is domestic to the seller. The Free Alongside Ship term is commonly used in the sale of bulk commodity cargo such as oil, grains, and ore. Normal payment terms for Free Carrier transactions are generally cash in advance and open account, but letters of credit are also used.

4) FOB, Free On Board (...named port of shipment)

In Free On Board, the seller/exporter/manufacturer clears the goods for export and is responsible for the costs and risks of delivering the goods past the ship's rail at the named port of shipment. The Free On Board term is used only for ocean or inland waterway transport. The "named place" in Free On Board and all "F" terms is domestic to the seller. Normal payment terms for Free On Board transactions include cash in advance, open account, and letters of credit.

The Free On Board term is commonly used in the sale of bulk commodity cargo such as oil, grains, and ore where passing the ship's rail is important. However, it is also commonly used in shipping container loads of other goods.

The key document in FOB transactions is the "On Board Bill of Lading."

Sellers and buyers often confuse the Free On Board term with Free Carrier. Free On Board (FOB) does not mean loading the goods onto a truck at the seller's place of business. Free On Board is used only in reference to delivering the goods past a ship's rail in ocean or inland waterway transport. Free Carrier, on the other hand, is applicable to all modes of transport.

5) Cost and Freight (...named port of destination)

In Cost and Freight, the seller/exporter/manufacturer clears the goods for export and is responsible for delivering the goods past the ship's rail at the port of shipment (not destination).

The seller is also responsible for paying for the costs associated with transport of the goods to the named port of destination. However, once the goods pass the ship's rail at the port of shipment, the buyer assumes responsibility for risk of loss or damage as well as any additional transport costs.

The Cost and Freight term is used only for ocean or inland waterway transport.

The "named port of destination" in Cost and Freight and all "C" terms is domestic to the buyer. Normal payment terms for Cost and Freight transactions include cash in advance, open account, and letters of credit.

The Cost and Freight term is commonly used in the sale of oversize and overweight cargo that will not fit into an ocean freight container or exceeds weight limitations of such containers. The term is also used for LCL (less than container load) cargo and for the shipment of goods by rail in boxcars to the ocean carrier.

6) Cost, Insurance and Freight (...named port of destination)

In Cost, Insurance and Freight, the seller/exporter/manufacturer clears the goods for export and is responsible for delivering the goods past the ship's rail at the port of shipment (not destination).

The seller is responsible for paying for the costs associated with transport of the goods to the named port of destination. However, once the goods pass the ship's rail at the port of shipment, the buyer assumes responsibility for risk of loss or damage as well as any additional transport costs.

The seller is also responsible for procuring and paying for marine insurance in the buyer's name for the shipment. The Cost and Freight term is used only for ocean or inland waterway transport.

The "named port of destination" in Cost and Freight and all "C" terms is domestic to the buyer. Normal payment terms for Cost and Freight transactions include cash in advance, open account, and letters of credit.

7) Carriage Paid To (...named place of destination)

In Carriage Paid To, the seller/exporter/manufacturer clears the goods for export, delivers them to the carrier, and is responsible for paying for carriage to the named place of destination. However, once the seller delivers the goods to the carrier, the buyer becomes responsible for all additional costs.

In Incoterms 2000 the seller is also responsible for the costs of unloading, customs clearance, duties, and other costs if such costs are included in the cost of carriage such as in small package courier delivery. The seller is not responsible for procuring and paying for insurance cover. The CPT term is valid for any form of transport including multimodal The "named place of destination" in CPT and all "C" terms is domestic to the buyer, but is not necessarily the final delivery point.

The Carriage Paid To term is often used in sales where the shipment is by air freight, containerized ocean freight, courier shipments of small parcels, and in "ro-ro" (roll-on, roll-off) shipments of motor vehicles. A "carrier" can be a shipping line, airline, trucking firm, railway or also an individual or firm who undertakes to procure carriage by any of the above methods of transport including multimodal. Therefore, a person, such as a freight forwarder, can act as a "carrier" under this term. If subsequent carriers are used for the carriage to the agreed destination, the risk passes when the goods have been delivered to the first carrier.

8) Carriage and Insurance Paid To (...named place of destination)

In Carriage and Insurance Paid To, the seller/exporter clears the goods for export, delivers them to the carrier, and is responsible for paying for carriage and insurance to the named place of destination. However, once the goods are delivered to the carrier, the buyer is responsible for all additional costs.

In Incoterms 2000 the seller is also responsible for the costs of unloading, customs clearance, duties, and other costs if such costs are included in the cost of carriage such as in small package courier delivery. The seller is responsible for procuring and paying for insurance cover. The CIP term is valid for any form of transport including multimodal The "named place of destination" in CIP and all "C" terms is domestic to the buyer, but is not necessarily the final delivery point.

The Carriage and Insurance Paid To term is often used in sales where the shipment is by air freight, containerized ocean freight, courier shipments of small parcels, and in "ro-ro" (roll-on, roll-off) shipments of motor vehicles.

A "carrier" can be a shipping line, airline, trucking firm, railway or also an individual or firm who undertakes to procure carriage by any of the above methods of transport including multimodal. Therefore, a person, such as a freight forwarder, can act as a "carrier" under this term. If subsequent carriers are used for the carriage to the agreed destination, the risk passes when the goods have been delivered to the first carrier.

9) Delivered At Frontier (...named place)

In Delivered At Frontier, the seller/exporter/manufacturer clears the goods for export and is responsible for making them available to the buyer at the named point and place at the frontier, not unloaded, and not cleared for import.

In the DAF term, naming the precise point, place, and time of availability at the frontier is very important as the buyer must make arrangements to unload and secure the goods in a timely manner. Frontier can mean any frontier including the frontier of export. The DAF term is valid for any mode of shipment, so long as the final shipment to the named place at the frontier is by land. The seller is not responsible for procuring and paying for insurance cover.

10) Delivered Ex Ship (...named port of destination)

In Delivered Ex Ship, the seller/exporter/manufacturer clears the goods for export and is responsible for making them available to the buyer on board the ship at the named port of destination, not cleared for import.

The seller is thus responsible for all costs of getting the goods to the named port of destination prior to unloading.

The DES term is used only for shipments of goods by ocean or inland waterway or by multimodal transport where the final delivery is made on a vessel at the named port of destination. All forms of payment are used in DES transactions.

11) Delivered Ex Quay (...named port of destination)

In Delivered Ex Quay, the seller/exporter/manufacturer clears the goods for export and is responsible for making them available to the buyer on the quay (wharf) at the named port of destination, not cleared for import.

The buyer, therefore, assumes all responsibilities for import clearance, duties, and other costs upon import as well as transport to the final destination. This is new for Incoterms 2000. The DES term is used only for shipments of goods arriving at the port of destination by ocean or by inland waterway. All forms of payment are used in DEQ transactions.

12) Delivered Duty Unpaid (...named place of destination)

In Delivered Duty Unpaid, the seller/exporter/manufacturer clears the goods for export and is responsible for making them available to the buyer at the named place of destination, not cleared for import.

The seller, therefore, assumes all responsibilities for delivering the goods to the named place of destination, but the buyer assumes all responsibility for import clearance, duties, administrative costs, and any other costs upon import as well as transport to the final destination.

The DDU term can be used for any mode of transport. However, if the seller and buyer desire that delivery should take place on board a sea vessel or on a quay (wharf), the DES or DEQ terms are recommended. All forms of payment are used in DDU transactions. The DDU term is used when the named place of destination (point of delivery) is other than the seaport or airport.

13) Delivered Duty Paid (...named place of destination)

In Delivered Duty Paid, the seller/exporter/manufacturer clears the goods for export and is responsible for making them available to the buyer at the named place of destination, cleared for import, but not unloaded from the transport vehicle. The seller, therefore, assumes all responsibilities for delivering the goods to the named place of destination, including all responsibility for import clearance, duties, and other costs payable upon import.

The DDP term can be used for any mode of transport. All forms of payment are used in DDP transactions. The DDP term is used when the named place of destination (point of delivery) is other than the seaport or airport.

International Sales Contract Checklist

The following items are elements of a complete contract. While all items may not apply to every contract, referring to a checklist like this when considering a contract will help ensure that you have provided for as many contingencies as possible. Though you may not always be in a position to dictate the terms of your contract, you should be aware of key elements. You can be flexible regarding some contract terms, but there are terms that you should insist on to protect your interests.

1. Contract date
2. Identification of parties
3. Goods
   a. Description
   b. Quantity
   c. Price
4. Packaging arrangements
5. Transportation arrangements
   a. Carrier
   b. Storage
   c. Notice provisions
   d. Shipping time
6. Costs and charges
   a. Duties and taxes
   b. Insurance costs
   c. Handling and transport
   d. Terms defined
7. Insurance or risk of loss protection
8. Payment provisions
   a. Method of payment
   b. Medium of exchange
   c. Exchange rate
9. Import documentation
10. Inspection rights
11. Warranty provisions
12. Indemnity
13. Enforcement and Remedies
    a. Time is of the essence
    b. Modification
    c. Cancellation
    d. Contingencies
    e. Governing law
    f. Choice of forum
    g. Arbitration provisions
    h. Severability

Contract Provisions Explained

For a small, one-time sale, an invoice or a simple contract may be acceptable. For a more involved business transaction or an ongoing relationship, a formal written contract is preferable to define clearly the rights, responsibilities, and remedies of all parties. Contracts that involve capital goods, high credit risks, or industrial or intellectual property rights will require special protective clauses. In preparing such contracts, it is essential to obtain legal advice from a professional who is familiar with the laws and practices of both countries.

Tip: In drafting international contracts, it is extremely wise to have each party go through each contract provision and ask for express comprehension—such as: "Do you understand that you are assuming the responsibility for packing these goods according to our shipper's instructions?" You may also want to have the other party initial certain paragraphs if you are concerned that misunderstandings over performance are likely. Some multinational contracts have every paragraph initialed after the parties have spent weeks negotiating the contract through interpreters.

For a simple, one-time deal you need to consider at least the following clauses:

1. **Contract Date.** Specify the date when the contract is signed. This date is particularly important if payment or delivery times are fixed in reference to it for example, "shipment within 30 days of the contract date."

2. **Identification of Parties.** Name the parties, describe their relation to each other and designate the persons who are authorized to act for each party. The persons designated should also be the ones who sign the contract.
   Tip: If performance of the agreement extends beyond a single transaction, the person's authority to act for the foreign company should be established by a copy of a statement of capacity certified by a government official in that country. If the foreign company is a corporation or similar entity, authority to act should be established by a corporate resolution of the company's governing body, such as its board of directors. The foreign company may require similar certified proof of authority from you. Your contract should describe documents that will be considered satisfactory evidence of authority.

3. **Goods.** The provisions related to goods are essential to the contract. If these provisions are missing or are not sufficiently specific, enforcement of the contract may be impossible because the goods cannot be identified.
   a. **Description.** Describe the type and quality of the goods. You may simply indicate a model number or you may have to attach detailed lists, plans, drawings, or other specifications. This clause should be clear enough that both parties fully understand the specifications and have no discretion in interpreting them.
   Tip: For certain transactions, you may have to state performance specifications. For example: "Under conditions x, y, and z, the product will a, b, and c."
   b. **Quantity.** Specify the number of units, or other measure of quantity, of the goods. If the goods are measured by weight, you should specify net weight, dry weight, or drained weight.

Tip: If the goods are prepackaged and are subject to weight restrictions for sale in the U.S., you may want to ensure that the seller will provide goods packaged to comply with those restrictions.

c. **Price.** Indicate the price per unit or other measure, such as per pound or ton, and the extended price.

4. **Packaging Arrangements.** Set forth packaging specifications, especially for goods that can be damaged in transit. At a minimum, this provision should require the seller to package the goods in such a way as to withstand transportation. If special packaging requirements are necessary to meet consumer and product liability standards and expectations in the U.S., you should specify them also. Refer to "Country of Origin Marking" on page 251, "Country of Origin Marking" on page 251, and the marking and labeling portions of the Commodity Index chapters relevant to the specific products you intend to import.

5. **Transportation Arrangements.** This provision may simply state the name of the carrier you want to handle the freight shipment and who is to pay for transportation from point A to point B. However, if more than two or three carriers are involved or your goods require special treatment, you will have to add extra details to this provision.

Tip: Use very precise language. Also, look for the weak link in the handling of your shipment. Ask: "If something will go wrong, where will it go wrong?"

a. **Carrier.** Name a preferred carrier for transporting the goods. You should designate a particular carrier if, for example, a carrier offers you special pricing or is better able than others to transport the product.

b. **Storage.** Specify any particular requirements for storage of the goods before or during shipment, such as security arrangements, special climate demands, and weather protection needs.

c. **Notice Provisions.** Require the seller to notify you when the goods are ready for delivery or pickup, particularly if the goods are perishable or fluctuate in value. If your transaction is time-sensitive, you could even provide for several notices, which will allow you to track the goods and to take steps to minimize damages if delivery is delayed.

d. **Shipping Time.** State the exact date for shipping or provide for shipment within a reasonable time from the contract date. If this clause is included and the seller fails to ship on time, you may claim a right to cancel the contract, even if the goods have been shipped, provided that you do not accept delivery.

Tip: You may want to provide that you have the right to terminate the contract if the goods are not shipped by a specific date. An express statement of your termination right can avoid misunderstandings with the foreign supplier should you reject goods that are shipped later than the specified date, but still within a reasonable time from the contract date.

6. **Costs and Charges.** Specify which party is to pay any additional costs and charges related to the sale.

a. **Duties and Taxes.** Designate the party that will be responsible for import, export, and other fees and tax-

es and for obtaining all required licenses. For example, each party may be made responsible for paying the duties, taxes, and charges imposed by that party's own country, because a party is best situated to know the legal requirements of his or her own country.

Tip: You may request a "package deal," under which your supplier will be responsible for all costs of entry through U.S. Customs. If this proves impractical, you should at a minimum require your supplier to be responsible for export duties, taxes, or charges on your product or commodity, since your supplier is in the best position to know the requirements of his or her own country. Protect yourself with a provision that states: "Seller is responsible for paying all export duties and taxes and for obtaining any necessary export licenses."

b. **Insurance Costs.** Identify the party that will pay the costs of insuring the goods in transit. This is a critical provision because, if the goods are lost during transit, the party responsible bears the risk. A seller is typically responsible for insurance until title to the goods passes to the buyer, at which time the buyer becomes responsible for insurance or becomes the named beneficiary under the seller's insurance policy. It is crucial, then, to provide for the time at which the title of the goods will change hands. Refer to "Ownership Situations: Terms of Sale" on page 396 for an explanation of responsibilities under different trade terms.

c. **Handling and Transport.** Specify the party that will pay shipping, handling, packaging, security, and any other costs related to transportation, all of which should be specified.

d. **Terms Defined.** Contracts for the sale of goods most commonly use international trade terms—usually Incoterms as defined by the International Chamber of Commerce in Paris—to assign responsibility for the risks and cost of transport. Although international trade terms have been standardized, in practice their meanings can vary. Precise definitions of these terms are important to your contract because these terms can determine such items as the party responsible for insuring the goods at any one time, the time at which title to the goods will transfer from seller to buyer, and the party responsible for paying certain transportation costs. Refer to "Glossary of Technical Terms" on page 189 for explanations of the Incoterms. Refer to "Ownership Situations: Terms of Sale" on page 396 for a more complete discussion of trade terms.

Tip: If you use trade terms, be certain to establish your own definition or to specify the standard that you are using (e.g., FOB Incoterms 2000). For example, FOB (Free On Board) usually means that the risk of loss shifts to the purchaser once the goods have physically passed over the rail of the ship, regardless of whether they have been secured, or even set down, on the deck or in a cargo hold. If the goods are suspended from a crane mid-air on the deck side of the ship's rail, the risk of loss has passed to the buyer. However, in some trading circles, FOB also includes the costs of securing the shipment on board and means that title is transferred only after the goods are fastened for transport. By defining terms, you will avoid misunderstandings with suppliers whose trading practices are different than yours.

Tip: When establishing trade terms for your contract be sure to fully establish your own definition, or specify which standard you are using (e.g. FOB Incoterms 1990).

6. **Insurance or Risk of Loss Protection.** Specify the insurance required, the beneficiary of the policy, the party who will obtain the insurance and who will pay for it, and the date by which it must be obtained. You should also agree on which documents will be considered satisfactory evidence of insurance.

7. **Payment Provisions.** In a one-time transaction, the seller will typically seek the most secure form of payment before committing to shipment, while a buyer will want the goods cleared through customs and delivered in satisfactory condition before remitting payment. If payments cannot be made in advance, parties most often agree to use documentary credits. (Refer to the "International Banking" section, beginning on page 135 for an explanation of such payments.)

   a. **Method of Payment.** State the means by which payment will be tendered—for example, delivery of a documentary letter of credit or documents against payment; prepayment in cash or traveler's checks; or credit for a specified number of days. Refer to "Methods of International Payment" on page 138 for a complete discussion of payment methods.

   b. **Medium of Exchange.** Designate the currency to be used—for example, U.S. currency, currency of the country of origin, or currency of a third country.

   Tip: If you think the value of the U.S. dollar will decrease between the signing of the contract and the payment, specify U.S. dollars. If you believe that the currency of the country of origin will decrease relative to the U.S. dollar, specify that currency.

   c.**Exchange Rate.** Specify a fixed exchange rate for the price stated in the contract. You may use this clause to lock in a specific price and ensure against fluctuating currency values. Refer to "An Introduction to Foreign Exchange" on page 144 for a detailed discussion of exchange rates and foreign exchange.

8. **Import Documentation.** Designate the documents for exporting and importing that each party will be responsible for obtaining, completing, and presenting to customs. Shipment of the goods, and even the contract itself, may be made contingent on a party's having obtained in advance the proper licenses, inspection certificates, and other authorizations. For a discussion of general documentation requirements, read the U.S. Customs "Entry Process" on page 199 and consult the Commodity Index for documentation requirements specific to your product or commodity. For information specific to documentation in a banking/documentary credit context, refer to the "International Banking" section, beginning on page 135.

   Tip: Always make complete documentation—that is, documentation that is satisfactory for U.S. Customs entry—a requirement of any contract for the purchase of products or commodities.

9. **Inspection Rights.** Provide that you have a right to inspect goods before taking delivery to determine whether the goods meet the contract specifications. This clause should specify the person who will do the inspection—for example, you, your agent, a neutral third party, or a licensed in-spector; the location where the inspection will occur—for example, at the seller's plant, your warehouse, or a receiving dock; the time at which the inspection will occur; the presentation of a certified document of inspection, if needed; and any requirements related to the return of nonconforming goods, such as payment of return freight by the seller. You may not need this clause if you have an established relationship with your supplier.

   Tip: Your supplier may reject a provision that allows you to conduct your own inspection, particularly if the site of inspection is in the U.S. and the supplier is paying freight to the U.S. In this case, inspection by a third party may be justified, but for your protection, you should insist that the inspector certify his or her findings in writing: "Signed/certified by licensed inspector, finding 1, 2, and 3."

   Tip: A contract provision stating that the seller pays for return freight for any nonconforming goods will protect you in the event that you have to refuse a shipment.

10. **Warranty Provisions.** Limit or extend any implied warranties, and define any express warranties on property fitness and quality. The contract may, for example, state that the seller warrants that the goods are of merchantable quality, are fit for any purpose for which they would ordinarily be used, or are fit for a particular purpose requested by the buyer. The seller may also warrant that the goods will be of the same quality as any sample or model that the seller has furnished as representative of the goods. Finally, the seller may warrant that the goods will be packaged in a specific way or in a way that will adequately preserve and protect the goods.

11. **Indemnity.** Agree that one party will hold the other harmless from damages that arise from specific causes, such as a design flaw or manufacturing defect.

12. **Enforcement and Remedies**

   a. **Time Is of the Essence.** Stipulate that timely performance of the contract is essential. In the U.S., inclusion of this clause allows a party to claim breach merely because the other party fails to perform within the time prescribed in the contract. Although common in U.S. contracts, a clause of this type is considered less important in other countries, where contracting parties often waive or renegotiate terms, rather than sue for damages on breach of the contract.

   b. **Modification.** Require the parties to make all changes to the contract in advance and in a signed written modification.

   Tip: You should insist on this clause in contracts with foreign suppliers to avoid misunderstandings that can arise from oral modifications—when its your word against that of your supplier.

   c. **Cancellation.** State the reasons for which either party may cancel the contract and the advance notice required for cancellation.

   d. **Contingencies.** Specify any events that must occur before a party is obligated to perform the contract. For example, you may agree that the seller has no duty to ship goods until the buyer forwards documents that secure the payment for the goods.

   e. **Governing Law.** Choose the law of a specific jurisdiction to control any interpretation of the contract terms. The law that you choose will usually affect where you can sue or enforce a judgment and what laws, rules, and procedures will be applied. If you file suit in the U.S., where domestic counsel and commercial laws are familiar to you, your experience will be different than if you litigate in a foreign country, where you will be subject to unfamiliar laws, rules, and procedures and will have to rely on foreign counsel. Refer also to "Solving Contract Disputes" on page 118.

Tip: Dealing with the legal systems of foreign countries can be a lengthy, costly, and frustrating process. In some countries, bringing a lawsuit can ruin your business and personal reputation because such action is considered extremely offensive. For these reasons, you should consider alternative methods of dispute resolution—negotiation, mediation, or arbitration—for settling international commercial conflicts before resorting to the courts.

f. **Choice of Forum.** Identify the place where a dispute may be settled—for example, the country of origin of the goods, the country of destination, or a third country that is convenient to both parties. Refer also to "Solving Contract Disputes" on page 118.

g. **Arbitration Provisions.** Provide for arbitration as an alternative to litigation for resolving contract disputes. Arbitration is less formal procedurally than a court trial, but still allows the parties to present their claims before a neutral person or panel for an objective decision. This remedy is increasing in popularity in commercial disputes, largely because it is less adversarial, less costly, and faster than litigation. An arbitration clause should specify whether arbitration is binding or nonbinding on the parties; the country where arbitration will be conducted; the procedure for enforcement of an award; the rules governing the arbitration—such as the U.N. Commission on International Trade Law Model Rules; the institute that will administer the arbitration—such as the International Chamber of Commerce (Paris); the law that will govern procedural issues or the merits of the dispute; any limitations on the selection of arbitrators (for example, a national of a disputing party may be excluded from being an arbitrator); the qualifications or expertise of the arbitrators; the language in which the arbitration will be conducted; and the availability of translations and translators if needed. Refer also to "Solving Contract Disputes" on page 118.

Tip: You should agree to arbitrate only if you seriously intend to settle disputes in this way. If you agree to arbitrate but later file suit, the court is likely to uphold the arbitration clause and force you to settle your dispute as you agreed under the contract.

Tip: Arbitration is not used in all countries. For example, disputes in Mexico are rarely settled by arbitration. Moreover, some countries do not recognize arbitration awards from other jurisdictions. You should consult an attorney familiar with the law of the country of your supplier before assuming that you will be able to arbitrate potential contract disputes.

h. **Severability.** Provide that individual clauses can be removed from the contract without affecting the validity of the contract as a whole. This clause is important because it provides that, if one clause is declared invalid and unenforceable for any reason, the rest of the contract remains in force.

Solving Contract Disputes

Even the most honest, forthright and considerate business person will from time-to-time have a dispute with either a supplier or a customer. In the U.S., some business people immediately resort to legal measures to enforce a contract. In most countries, however, litigation is expensive, time consuming, frustrating and inappropriate. In some countries, a lawsuit is viewed as a personal affront and is an ineffective means of resolving a conflict. Even with a solid case, the chances of successfully enforcing your contract through legal action are unpredictable. Problems may arise in communicating and prosecuting your case. You may encounter differing legal notions regarding contractual rights. Your case could suffer because of local prejudices against foreign business operators.

Disputes

There are essentially two types of disputes that can arise between your supplier and you: those in which you have a claim against your supplier and those in which your supplier has a claim against you.

The circumstances in which you find that you have a claim against your supplier are many and varied. The goods may not be delivered, or delivery may be delayed. The wrong goods, or goods of a different quantity or quality may be delivered. Proper documentation might not accompany the goods. The goods might turn out to be defective after you have resold them. In all these cases, you will have a claim against the supplier in which you seek either performance or damages, or a combination of the two.

A supplier's claim against you will almost always be for nonpayment of all or part of the purchase price. For example, if you refuse to pay the supplier because the goods are not delivered, the quantity received is less than ordered, or the goods received are nonconforming, the supplier may seek a legal remedy.

Immediate and Temporary Relief

Communication with your supplier is essential to keeping the relationship smooth. For minor discrepancies, or even major calamities, your business relationships and reputation will benefit if you approach the problem with understanding and a view toward finding a resolution that will satisfy both your supplier and you. Negotiation, followed by a written confirmation of any modified contract terms, is the most effective means of resolution in terms of cost and time. A good rule to remember: create a working relationship with your suppliers, not an adversarial one.

If a dispute continues despite your informal attempts to resolve it, you should take steps to protect your rights. Your most imminent concern will probably be to recover your own property quickly or to find an immediate replacement supplier so that you can honor your own commitments to third parties. Your contract should expressly authorize either party to take steps to mitigate damages should the other party breach. For example, you can insist on a provision that allows you to take immediate possession or repossession of goods, provided you post a bond that will cover the amount of the other party's claim. You may also expressly reserve your right to pursue legal remedies available in your supplier's country, such as attachment or lien rights.

Arbitration

The parties to a commercial transaction may provide in their contract that any disputes over interpretation or performance of the agreement will be resolved through arbitration. In the domestic context, arbitration may be appealing for a variety of reasons. Frequently cited advantages over conventional courtroom litigation include potential savings in time and expense, confidentiality of the proceedings, and expertise of the arbitrators.

For transactions in which the parties to the agreement are from different countries, additional advantages are neutrality (international arbitration allows each party to avoid the domestic courts of the other) and ease of enforcement (foreign arbitral awards can be easier to enforce than foreign court decisions). In many international commercial transactions, arbitration makes good sense.

However, approach arbitration in an international setting with caution. In many countries, arbitration is unavailable or is just being developed. Although less adversarial than a court trial, arbitration is still viewed in many cultures with suspicion, if not abhorrence. A request for arbitration may be viewed as a personal insult to your supplier, and instead of being a means of dispute resolution, it may destroy the potential for settlement through private negotiation. Because of the complexity of the subject, legal advice should be obtained for specific transactions.

Advantages of Arbitration. The following are advantages of using arbitration as a means of dispute resolution:

1) An arbitration award may be more enforceable in a foreign country than a U.S. court judgment.

2) Other societies are not as litigious as the U.S. A foreigner who is sued is likely to be insulted. Arbitration may be a less offensive means of resolving a dispute.

3) You can choose arbitrators who are experts in your particular industry, which may be particularly important if your contracts cover technically advanced goods. Arbitrators with technical expertise can evaluate whether a shipment meets your specifications more knowledgeably than a court judge who does not have the same training.

4) Arbitration is usually an informal proceeding, less expensive and less time consuming than litigation.

5 Evidence given in arbitration and the arbitration decision itself are confidential, unless all of the parties agree to release all or some of this information.

Disadvantages of Arbitration. The following are reasons to avoid or be cautious in using arbitration for resolving disputes:

1) Arbitrators will not necessarily try to resolve the conflict based on clearly defined legal obligations and precedents. In court, if one party is guilty of a breach of contract, a judgment is entered in favor of the other party. In arbitration, even if evidence of breach is absolute, compromise is usually the end result. Thus, if your supplier has not fulfilled the contract and you choose to arbitrate the dispute, you could end up bearing part of the loss if the arbitrators believe that would be more equitable to all parties concerned, whereas if you had sued, the court might have awarded you full damages.

2) Even arbitration has an adversarial aspect. If you want to keep an ongoing relationship with your supplier, you will better serve your interests through immediate and diligent negotiation with your supplier than a lengthier and more costly process involving various third parties—attorneys, witnesses, arbitrators, investigators, etc.

3) Arbitration is more costly and will cause further delay. Although the delay will usually not be as long as the time required for litigation, the parties will need to choose arbitrators, set up the arbitration hearing, compile evidence and information for the arbitrator, prepare a presentation, and wait for a decision. These activities are more costly and time-consuming than simply negotiating a resolution.

International Arbitration Organizations. Many organizations around the world provide arbitration services. The most well-known U.S. organization is the American Arbitration Association (AAA). The International Chamber of Commerce (ICC) in Paris is the most prominent international organization. Other international arbitration organizations include the London Court of Arbitration, the Japan Commercial Arbitration Association, the U.N. Commission on International Trade Law (UNCITRAL), the U.N. Economic Commission for Europe, the U.N. Economic and Social Commission for Asia and the Pacific (formerly ACAPE), and the Inter-American Arbitration Commission. National and international trade associations often maintain arbitration panels and have their own rules that cover specific trades or industries—such as shipping and construction—or commodities—such as coffee, sugar, oils and fats, grains, cocoa, and cotton, wool, and other textiles.

Each arbitration association has its own rules of practice and procedure, but most are similar. For example, most arbitration rules provide that each party to a dispute may choose one arbitrator, and that the two appointed arbitrators will then elect a third "neutral" arbitrator.

Arbitration Terms. In an agreement to arbitrate (commonly inserted as a term in the contract for the transaction), the parties have broad power to agree on many significant aspects of the arbitration. The arbitration clause should contain at least these elements:

- An agreement to arbitrate.
- The name of an arbitration organization to administer the arbitration. The International Chamber of Commerce based in Paris, the American Arbitration Association in New York, and the Arbitration Institute of the Stockholm Chamber of Commerce in Sweden are three such prominent institutions.
- The rules that will govern the arbitration, usually incorporating a set of existing arbitration rules such as the U.N. Commission on International Trade Law (UNCITRAL) Model Rules. The location where the arbitration will be conducted, which may be a "neutral site." You should select a country that has adopted the U.N. Convention on Recognition and Enforcement of Foreign Arbitral Awards or another convention providing for the enforcement of arbitral awards.
- The law that will govern procedural issues or the merits of the dispute, for example, the law of the State of New York. Before you choose the governing law, you should find out whether it will be disadvantageous to your interests. Instead of specifying the law of a particular country or jurisdiction, you may take a neutral position. For example, you may stipulate that "the arbitrators shall apply equitable principles, without regard to the laws of any country. The arbitrators may tend toward application of this equitable approach even if you don't specifically request it. However, an express provision ensures that, if the laws of your supplier's country are especially unfavorable or undeveloped, they won't be applied. It is best to choose governing law with which you are reasonably familiar and comfortable.
- Any limitations you may prefer on the selection of arbitrators, for example, the exclusion of nationals from the countries of the disputing parties.
- Any particular qualifications or expertise that the arbitrators must have.
- The language in which the proceedings will be conducted.
- The effect of the arbitration decision—binding or nonbinding on the parties.

The typical arbitration clause looks like this:

"Any dispute between the parties that arises out of or in connection with this contract and that is not amicably settled shall be finally resolved by binding arbitration, conducted in the English language, in _____(location)_____ by ____(e.g., three)____ arbitrators in accordance with the _____(e.g., UN Commission on International Trade Law Model Rules)_____ of _____(e.g., the International Chamber of Commerce)_____ in effect at the time the dispute arises. Judgment on the award rendered may be entered in any court with jurisdiction."

Recognition and Enforcement of Award. For international arbitration to work effectively, the national courts in the countries of both parties to the dispute must recognize and support arbitration as a legitimate alternative means for resolving disputes. This support is particularly crucial at two stages of the arbitration process. First, if one party attempts to avoid arbitration after a dispute has arisen, the other party must be able to rely on the judicial system in either country to enforce the agreement to arbitrate by compelling arbitration. Second, the party that wins in the arbitration proceeding must be confident that the national courts will enforce the decision of the arbitrators. This will ensure that the arbitration process is not ultimately frustrated at the enforcement stage if the losing party refuses to pay or otherwise to satisfy the arbitral award.

The strong policy of U.S. federal law is to approve and support resolution of disputes by arbitration, a policy that is being adopted in many countries throughout the world. Most countries are now recognizing and enforcing arbitration awards made domestically, and many will allow cross-border enforcement of arbitration awards made in other countries. More than 80 countries, including the U.S., have ratified the U.N. Convention on the Recognition and Enforcement of Foreign Arbitral Awards (popularly known as the New York Convention). While several other arbitration treaties have been concluded, the New York Convention is by far the most important international agreement on commercial arbitration and may be credited for much of the explosive growth of arbitration of international disputes in recent decades.

Enforcement of arbitration awards is more common than enforcement of court judgments because arbitration is viewed as an outcome of an agreement between the parties. Most arbitration awards are not reviewed by foreign courts, unlike court judgments from other countries, which are usually carefully scrutinized. However, a foreign arbitral award that violates a country's laws or public policy is not likely to be recognized or enforced. For example, in Greece, where a summons and complaint must be served in person, an arbitral award resulting from a summons and complaint served by mail would not be honored. When you choose a procedure to follow in arbitrating, be aware of the rules governing such matters in both your and your supplier's countries.

Tip: If you are considering alternatives to litigation for resolving disputes, keep in mind the following.

1) It is always a nasty business to arbitrate or to battle it out in court. These should always be your very last resort. Try to negotiate disputes if at all possible. In many countries, especially in Asia and the Middle East, taking someone to court or to arbitration is regarded as an act of outright hostility. In China, for example, even the suggestion that disputes might not be amicably resolved raises eyebrows. If you initiate legal or arbitration proceedings, you can find that your relationship with the supplier has been irreparably damaged. The word can spread quickly that you do not do business as a "gentleman" and should be avoided. Protect yourself by provisions in the contract, but use that protection only as a last resort. Always try to negotiate an amicable settlement if

possible. A victory in court may be a Pyrrhic victory. Sometimes your business will be better served in the long run if you accept a breach of contract gracefully.

2)   You have many options regarding contractual provision for the settlement of contract disputes. We recommend that you put an arbitration clause in every contract. Failure to do so exposes you to lawsuits in foreign courts, which should be avoided. The type of arbitration you choose will depend on your unique circumstances. The International Chamber of Commerce is, in most cases, a fairly safe choice.

3)   Though the location for arbitration proceedings is negotiable, do not expect your foreign supplier to readily agree to arbitrate in the U.S. If the local country-of-origin Chamber of Commerce is sufficiently established in the supplier's locale, consider agreeing to arbitrate before it, unless your travel costs would be significant. Selecting a "neutral" country acceptable to both of you is a viable alternative.

4)   Always stipulate that arbitration be conducted in the English language.

5)   Before agreeing to arbitrate in a country other than that of the supplier, make sure that courts or another authority in the supplier's country will recognize and enforce an arbitration award rendered in the other country.

Litigation

If you have to resort to a lawsuit, the first hurdle you will face will be to find a court that can exercise its authority over your supplier and you. Even if you succeed in getting a favorable judgment, the biggest problem remains: collecting on it. Although the supplier will probably be able to get jurisdiction over you in the courts of the supplier's country, if you are neither present in that country nor have assets there, it will be difficult for your supplier to collect on a judgment against you. On the other hand, unless the supplier is present or has assets in the U.S., it is unlikely that you will be able to get jurisdiction in a U.S. court. You may have to seek legal recourse in the supplier's country.

To the extent possible, you would be wise to establish the best possible conditions for potential litigation when you first make your contract. The way to do this is to include clauses for choice of governing law and forum.

Forum. Forum refers to the place where any dispute will be settled. It is really a matter of convenience, and is usually negotiable. When it is infeasible for you to go to the supplier's country, or vice versa, to settle a dispute, you can jointly designate a third party country that would be more convenient.

Governing Law. The choice of law is critical. It determines not just where you can bring a suit or enforce a judgment, but what rules and procedures will govern the dispute settlement. Where and under what law you file suit will make a difference to you. If you file in the U.S., with domestic counsel familiar with commercial law and court procedures, your experience will be different than if you litigate your case in a foreign country, where you are subject to unfamiliar rules and must rely on foreign counsel.

Because of such complications, arbitration is a widely used means of settling international commercial disputes.

Measure of Damages in Breach of Contract Action. The measure of damages in a breach of contract action varies from country to country and among legal systems. In the U.S., damages are most commonly measured by the "lost benefit of the bargain rule." For example, if you contract to buy goods for $10 a unit when the market value of the goods is $12 a unit, and if your supplier fails to deliver, you are entitled to the $2 difference for the number of units you contracted to buy.

U.S. courts will also award consequential damages in certain circumstances. "Consequential damages" are losses that arise from a breach of contract and that, at the time you made the agreement, you made clear would result from breach. For example, you might tell a supplier that delivery at by a certain date is essential because you are reselling the product to someone who will incur substantial losses if you fail to perform timely. The supplier may then assure you that the goods will be delivered by that date. If the seller fails to deliver on time, causing you to incur damages for breach your resale contract, you can argue that your resulting financial losses are consequential damages. For this argument to hold up in court, you would have to show that your supplier knew or should have known at the time of contracting that you would become liable to a third party as a consequence of the seller's breach. To ensure that the seller has notice of the effect of a breach, you may describe in your written contract the consequential damages that can be expected to result in the event of breach.

Specific Performance. "Specific performance" is an alternative remedy to monetary damages. You can request a court to compel the breaching supplier to fulfill the contract agreement. If you have a contract to buy goods, you can demand those specific goods, and you may well get them. In civil law European countries, it is much easier to get specific performance than it is in the U.S. In the U.S., specific performance is usually not granted unless unique goods are involved. If you have a contract to purchase an item that cannot be duplicated—such as a Rembrandt—you may demand specific performance and get the actual painting. But if it is coal of #9 grade, which you can purchase elsewhere with relative ease, U.S. courts will probably grant you damages instead of specific performance.

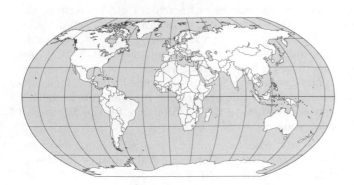

World Legal Systems

Introduction

Before you start trading in a foreign country, you should become familiar with its legal system, commercial laws, and export regulations. Gaining an overview of the law that will affect your relationship and transaction can be as important as running a background check on your supplier. You need to be aware of the major differences between the U.S. legal system and that of your supplier's country. These laws will influence your choices from the initial negotiation through enforcement of a contract. For example:

- You need to know which terms of your agreement are controlled by law and which are negotiable (if you negotiate a point already set by law, you've wasted your time, your negotiated term will be enforceable only to the extent allowed by the law, and by insisting on terms already fixed by law, you've given away your negotiating edge).
- You need to know whether the agreement you have in mind will be valid (if void, it will be unenforceable).
- You need to make an informed choice of which law will govern your agreement.
- You need to know to what extent the law will protect your interests beyond the terms of your agreement (you had better insist on protective contract terms if the law is inadequate or totally silent).
- You need to know what liabilities you might incur because of your supplier's actions or omissions—civil lawsuits, government-imposed fines, or other penalties—so that you can protect yourself by contract terms, such as for indemnity, proof of authority, or proof of compliance.
- You need to know the procedures that are available to enforce the contract or to recover for losses should your supplier breach and the extent to which these procedures will be an effective remedy.
- You need to know what your liability will be to your supplier just in case you cannot perform the contract.

Laws vary from country to country, even among countries with the same basic legal system. To get a brief overview of the law of the particular country where you intend to do business, we suggest that you consult the *Digest of Commercial Laws of the World* (Ocean Publications, published for National Association of Credit Management) or Martindale-Hubbell's *International Law Digest*. These sources are available in the reference section of most larger public and law libraries.

Essentially, there are four major types of legal systems in the world that provide for commercial law. These are common law, civil law, Islamic or Shari'ah law, and communist or socialist law. However, many countries have adopted various combinations of these in response to the influences of different cultures throughout their history. In Asia, Africa, and South America, the legal system of each country is usually that of its former colonial master. For instance, Hong Kong follows common law, and Brazil applies the civil law system. However, the laws of these countries have also been adapted in some areas to reflect their original heritage. Japan took most of its law from Germany and thus follows the civil law system, although the commercial code shows U.S. influence. The civil law system developed in Egypt combines Islamic principles with French codes, and some common law principles are also applied because of lingering British influence.

Common Law System

The U.S., the United Kingdom, and Canada are under the common law system, distinctive for its reliance on precedents established by judges in earlier cases. The courts in common law countries apply and interpret statutes by following the principles developed in earlier decisions or by extrapolating new principles from the old ones to apply when new situations arise. Trials are typically before one judge, and the parties may request a jury. Complex rules and procedures aimed at ensuring a fair trial have been developed. Evidence presented to the court can be in the form of oral testimony and documents. Each party has the right to cross-examine witnesses and each other.

Refer to the main entry "Common Law" on page 127 and to "Canadian Common Law" on page 127 for a specific example of common law.

Civil Law System

Except for the common law countries and those countries heavily influenced by them, most of the other countries of the free world have civil law systems. Civil law systems are characterized by comprehensive and systematic compilations of statutes, or codes of law, governing most aspects of human endeavor. The codes set forth legal principles on which judicial decisions are based. The civil law system uses non-jury trials (except in criminal cases), and civil law courts at trial and appellate levels are typically composed of a panel of judges. In contrast to the common law system, there are few well-defined rules of evidence and relatively little oral testimony or argument. Most evidence and arguments are presented to the court in writing. Legal decisions usually are not based on precedents set in prior cases, but rather on abstract legal interpretations of the codified laws. For these reasons, the result of any particular lawsuit is somewhat less predictable than it might be in a common law court, which tries to adhere to interpretations established by precedents.

Refer also to the main entry "Civil Law" on page 123, and to "French Civil Law" on page 124 for a specific example of civil law.

Islamic Law

In Moslem or Islamic countries, the Law of Islam as set forth in the Koran, is applied in cases involving crimes, family matters (e.g., divorce or inheritance), or personal injury. Commercial cases are usually handled in commercial law courts that apply civil law concepts. Most Middle Eastern countries follow the French (Napoleonic) commercial code. In some of these countries—such as Saudi Arabia—commercial cases are handled by administrative tribunals rather than by the courts.

Refer also to the main entry "Islamic (Shari'ah) Law" on page 130 and for an example of Islamic Law to "Saudi Arabian Islamic Law" on page 130.

Communist Commercial Law

Communist commercial law is the system used in China (PRC), Cuba, North Korea, and Vietnam. It is similar to the socialist law system that was in effect in the Soviet bloc until recent years. Under communist commercial law, foreign trade is primarily operated by the state.

Disputes with suppliers in communist countries should be settled by negotiation. These cultures take particular pride in honoring commitments. A communist enterprise is more than likely to follow contract terms scrupulously, unless a sudden shift in government policy affects the contract. In many of these countries, the initiation of an adversarial or adjudicative proceeding is considered a personal insult. Parties are expected to resolve their conflicts privately. Therefore, few avenues of effective legal recourse have developed. If you must resolve a conflict through a more formal process, insist on arbitration if possible. In most cases, communist countries will recognize and uphold arbitration awards. Keep in mind, though, that few cases ever reach arbitration.

Avoid seeking legal recourse in a communist court. Communist laws have a strong ideological content unsuitable for interpreting commercial relations. Your supplier, as defendant, will be an agency of the same government that operates the courts and will hold essentially similar ideological views. Communist court proceedings are open, direct, and heavily reliant on oral testimony and examination. There are few rules of evidence. Legal precedents are of little weight. The court will consider all the evidence, decide what facts it believes are of relative value or importance, and determine the issues based on general principles of law and the dictates of communist ideology.

Refer also to the main entry "Communist Law" on page 132 and for an example of communist law to "Chinese Communist Law" on page 133.

Civil Law

Civil law is a combination of the Roman and Germanic legal systems. It is rooted in the legal system of ancient Rome, eventually codified as the *Corpus Juris Civilis*. Roman law governed broad areas of personal, business, and government relationships. Germanic law developed from individual tribal customs among the nomadic peoples of Europe. It primarily fixed specific rules for the resolution of particular problems, rather than established broad moral precepts. Eventually, as various political forces unified the countries of Europe, an amalgamation of these two legal systems was developed, resulting in modern Civil Law.

Comparison with Common Law

If you are trading with a country that follows a civil law system, you will probably find a well-developed court system. However, you may find that the civil law of that country is less developed or less favorable to your interests than the U.S. common law. You will also discover a number of significant differences:

A court in a civil law country may be authorized by law to accept jurisdiction over any suit brought by a national of the country, regardless of whether the suit involves a foreigner or a transaction in that country. A court may take jurisdiction even if the foreigner is absent. Thus, even if your only contact with a supplier's country is a faxed order for goods, your supplier could still sue you overseas. Under U.S. common law, the concept of jurisdiction is more limited. U.S. courts generally require a closer connection, or nexus, between the place where suit is brought and the defendant.

- The civil law system did not originally establish specific rules for calculating damages in breach of contract cases, and many civil law countries have not yet clearly defined standards for this purpose. The amount of damages that a court may award can therefore be difficult to predict. As a result, plaintiffs in civil law countries commonly sue for actual or specific performance of the contract. This remedy requires the seller to deliver the goods and the buyer to remit payment as required by their contract. If the seller cannot deliver the goods, the buyer is awarded the greater of the contract price or the cost of replacement. Jurisdictions vary over whether replacement cost means actual or market cost of the goods.

- Commercial contracts—those between business persons or merchants—usually do not need to be in writing. However, oral contracts may be difficult to enforce in practice. Civil law courts typically accept written evidence, not oral testimony. The terms of an oral agreement are more difficult to prove than those of a written contract.

- Contract clauses stating "time is of the essence" are uncommon because of the preference in civil law countries to negotiate rather than litigate when a party cannot perform to the exact letter of the agreement. In common law countries, a breach of a contract containing such a clause will give rise to an immediate legal action for damages.

French and German Codes

Most modern civil law countries have modeled their laws on one of two civil law codifications: the French Code Civil (Napoleonic Code), or the German Code. Two separate Codes have arisen because of nationalistic and political influences.

French Code Civil. The French Code Civil was created during the French Revolutionary period and has survived since 1804, with modifications to reflect advances in society since that time. Its drafters attempted to set forth general rules in clear language that could be easily understood by every citizen. They created a concise, yet flexible Code in the form of a series of short articles that were not intended to limit judicial interpretation or application. If no single article applied to a situation, a court could combine articles and extrapolate a general rule consistent with the intent of the Code, although not specified in its text.

Property Law. The Code Civil classifies goods as either movable or immovable. Ownership of property is absolute, with a few restrictions related to public safety issues. A bona fide purchaser of movable property becomes its owner immediately. That is, title passes when the contract is made or at the time the goods being sold are specifically identified.

Contract Law. Parties governed by the Code Civil have freedom to contract, limited only by a few public policy considerations. If parties enter into an agreement lawfully, a court will uphold the terms of the contract.

German Code. The German Code, finalized in 1900, is more orderly and precise than the French Code Civil. It expresses more exacting principles for its use. The system consists of generally formulated rules that are meant to be applied to individual cases.

Property Law. Under the German Code, property ownership entails responsibilities to the community. Title to property passes on physical delivery of the goods or title documents to the buyer.

Contract Law. Parties are free to enter into contracts, within the limits set by good morals and statutory prohibitions intended to eliminate fraudulent practices by contracting parties. The Code emphasizes such ethical imperatives as good faith and fair dealings. Transactions involving transgressions of moral standards, abuses of the rights of others, or shady dealings do not have the protection of law.

French Civil Law

The French system of civil law is based on five original Napoleonic Codes and two more recently adopted codes. Of the Napoleonic, the Code Civil and the Code de Commerce are the most pertinent to commercial transactions. The Code Civil creates the fundamental legal framework for French society and includes general provisions on contracts, civil status, and property. The Code de Commerce covers commercial transactions and procedure, bills and notes, maritime law, bankruptcy, and jurisdiction of commercial courts. Other codes govern civil court organization, jurisdiction, and procedure; criminal law and procedure; and tax and labor law.

Governmental Structure. France is a democratic and social republic. The French Constitution provides for a president, who is elected for a seven-year term, and a Prime Minister. A National Assembly and a Senate comprise the French Parliament. Separate judicial and administrative court systems operate independently of each other.

Traders. Under French law, persons whose regular occupation is to be engaged in commercial transactions are considered "traders." They must register with the Register of Commerce and must fulfill a variety of record keeping and reporting requirements. Commercial courts, not civil courts, hear disputes between traders. Traders have the option to designate arbitration in contracts as the preferred means of dispute settlement.

Aliens. In general, the civil rights accorded a foreigner in France are the same as those given to French citizens, usually as agreed on under international treaty. Foreigners are permitted to own real property in France, but such property remains subject to French law. An obligation entered into between a foreigner and a French national is automatically under the jurisdiction of French courts, unless the French national chooses to waive this right. In most cases, foreigners may sue in French courts. Under the 1959 Franco-American Establishment Treaty, U.S. citizens in France have the same rights as French nationals as regards freedom of the press, legal aid, industrial property rights, commercial activity, access to French courts, and taxation.

A foreigner who intends to stay in France more than three months must obtain a residence permit. A foreigner who plans to start a business in France must also obtain a "trader's card" from local police. To obtain a trader's card, a foreigner must already have the proper long-term visa.

Exchange Control. Transfers of cash between France and foreign countries must be made through licensed intermediary credit or financial institutions. With some exceptions, annual reporting to the Bank of France is required for transfers of funds between France and abroad, or within France between residents and nonresidents. Reporting is also required for direct financial operations abroad and for trading of currency or interest. Individuals must make customs declarations when they make cross-border transfers of cash, stocks, or securities equal to or exceeding 50,000 francs. Customs declaration must also be made when individuals make cross-border transfers of cash, stocks, or securities by mail in excess of 10,000 francs.

Foreign Corporations. A number of legal formalities are required of foreign corporations before establishing a branch to do business in France. The corporation must first obtain Ministry of Finance authorization and must register with the French Register of Commerce. The company must designate an authorized representative in France, and the representative must obtain a trader's card, unless he or she is a citizen of an EEC nation. Various papers, including two certified copies of the corporation's charter and bylaws legalized by the French Consul, must be filed with the Registrar of Tribunal of Commerce. Complete French translations of all the required documents must be included. To receive authorization to do business, the corporate branch must be able to prove that it has an office address in France by presenting a commercial lease. Once these legal formalities have been fulfilled, French law treats the foreign corporation in the same manner as a French one.

Foreign Investments. No general prohibition is imposed against foreign ownership or control of businesses in France, but there are some limitations. For the most part, firms and individuals that plan to make a direct investment in France must first declare that intention to the French Ministry of Economy, which must approve the proposed investment. Unless allowed by international treaty, state-owned economic sectors—such as communications and electricity—are not open to foreign investment. Certain enterprises—such as transportation, petroleum extraction, banking, and insurance—are either entirely prohibited to foreign investment or are available only with special authorization. By treaty, U.S. citizens may acquire majority interests in existing companies and may control or manage enterprises in the fields of communications, air, or water transport, banking, natural resources, and electricity. U.S. citizens may also acquire and dispose of any interest in real or personal property, except ships. All foreign investments in France are subject to currency exchange and other regulation.

Import-Export Regulations. Importers and exporters must handle all import or export related financial transactions through agents authorized by the French Ministry of Economy and Finance or Post Office Departments. Although most French exports are unrestricted, there are exceptions. Occasionally certain export commodities will be prohibited, requiring export licensing. Others may be restricted as to final destination or country of origin.

Arbitration and Foreign Judgments. France has formal and informal bilateral agreements with many countries providing for enforcement of foreign judgments and arbitral decisions. In the absence of a treaty, the French government decides the enforceability of a foreign judgment based on a review of the documents in the case. To be enforceable in France, a judgment must issue from a court deemed by French law to have jurisdiction in the matter. The foreign judicial procedure and decision must also coincide with French international public policy and right to defense. When a French court grants enforcement of a foreign judgment, the foreign judgment becomes, in legal effect, a French judgment.

France recognizes arbitration for the settlement of commercial disputes only. Arbitral awards are not reviewed except for claims of procedural error, bias by the arbitrator, failure to observe due process, or conflict with French public or international policy.

Courts. France has two separate and independent tri-level court systems: judicial and administrative. A case is assigned to one of the five lower-level judicial courts depending on its nature and severity, whether it is criminal or civil, and the amount of money involved. Administrative courts hear cases involving the government in areas of contract, tort, and tax law, as well as appeals from administrative decisions.

Negotiable Instruments. France's formal requirements for bills of exchange differ from those of U.S. law only in that the words "Bill of Exchange" must appear on the document. Under French law, a bill of exchange can be rendered null by the absence of these words. It can also be nullified if the parties' names, the date and place of issuance and payment, or the order or amount to pay are missing. France is a signatory to the Geneva Agreements on promissory notes and bills of exchange. Parties to any bill of exchange fulfilling Geneva Agreement requirements come within the jurisdiction of commercial law regardless of whether they are traders and whether the bill had commercial purposes. For this reason, lawsuits pertaining to these bills of exchange are tried in commercial courts.

It is a criminal offense to write a check on insufficient funds, to withdraw the funds after having written a check, or to instruct the bank not to pay a check. The only lawful grounds for making a stop-payment order are bankruptcy and a lost or stolen check. France has strict time limits for presenting checks for payment. Checks written and payable in France must be presented for payment within eight days. Those written outside France for payment in France must be submitted within 20 or 70 days, depending on where the check was written.

Consumer Protection. In France, consumer protection is a matter of civil and criminal law and procedure, as well as of administrative and tax laws. French law protects the consumer in the use of goods, and in receipt of services intended to satisfy individual or family needs, including public services. Representative organizations of both private and public law handle consumer protection issues. Associations of Consumers are the most important private consumer protection organizations.

Contracts. Commercial and civil law in France are governed by separate codes. For this reason, French contract law has different rules for commercial and noncommercial contracts. A contract entered into by a trader for business purposes is commercial, regulated by the commercial code, and enforceable in commercial courts. Contracts between nontraders are civil, regulated under the civil code and enforceable in civil courts. The separation is so complete that a contract between a trader and a nontrader may be considered commercial inasmuch as it pertains to the trader but civil inasmuch as it pertains to the nontrader.

Civil contracts may be either oral or written. No special formality is required to render an oral contract valid. However, contracts with value of 5,000 francs or more must be in writing. An oral contract in this category cannot be validated simply by the presence of witnesses. Written contracts may be either privately or formally made. There must be as many originals of a private contract as there are parties to the agreement with differing interests, and that number must be specified on the document. Witnesses are not required. Civil contracts cannot stipulate that disputes be resolved by arbitration. The parties must file suit in court, but once a suit has been initiated, they can request arbitration.

To be valid, a commercial contract in France must have the consent of parties who are legally allowed to contract, a specific object not contrary to public policy, and some kind of consideration. Written evidence must be submitted to prove contracts between corporations, on maritime rights, for sale of businesses. Bills of exchange and promissory notes must also be shown by written evidence. A written contract can be established simply by exchange of correspondence. Some contracts, such as those pertaining to partnerships or corporations, must be registered with French fiscal authorities, at which time contract-registration taxes must be paid.

France is a party to the U.N. Convention on Contracts for the International Sale of Goods. Liability arising from such contracts is determined by the U.N. Convention, not French law. If choice of law is not specified in the contract, French courts determine the governing law by considering such factors as the character of parties, the place where the contract was offered and accepted, the location for performance, and its form and purpose. Unless the parties expressly stipulate otherwise, a contract should be in the form required by the law of the place where it is executed. Contracts executed in foreign countries are proved according to the law of that country.

Interest. The French government establishes the legal interest rate each year by Decree. An interest rate agreed on by contract must be in writing and can exceed the legal rate, if not usurious. If an interest rate is 33.33% higher than the ordinary rate that banks charged during the preceding quarter for a similar transaction, it is considered usurious. Charging a usurious interest rate is a crime.

Labor Relations. French employment and labor relation policies are extensive. The following discussion outlines only a few requirements as examples. Every employee must have a pre-employment medical examination, with annual physicals if hired. There are specific conditions and procedures for termination after an initial trial period, violations of which can result in fines to the employer and damages awarded to the employee. For most types of employment, the work week may not exceed 39 hours, with a maximum workday of 10 hours. Employers must provide an annual 30-workday paid vacation and leaves of absence for certain family events. France has a national minimum wage. Other wages are a matter of negotiation between employees or labor unions and the individual company. Employers must pay payroll tax and mandatory social benefits for each employee. Firms employing 50 or more persons are required to provide profit sharing and must have labor-management committees. Firms of more than 10 employees must have employee-elected personnel representatives,

who are accorded special employment protection under the law during their one-year term of service.

Notaries Public. A French notary is a high official appointed by the Minister of Justice. A notary must pass qualifying examinations and must possess at least a specified minimum professional experience. The number of notaries is limited, and all of them can practice anywhere in France. Notaries are exclusively authorized to prepare legal documents related to real estate, such as deeds of sale and mortgages, as well as deeds of gift and marriage contracts. Notaries verify and keep on file or record documents required by law to be notarized and any that parties want notarized. A notary can be sued for giving unsound advice on matters within his or her competence.

Principal and Agent. An agent can be authorized informally by a private writing—such as an agreement or letter—or formally by a notarized document. No form is prescribed for an agency agreement, but some situations require notarization. If the agency authorization is not in French, a legal translation must be presented before it can be used in any legal procedure. No matter what language it is in, the agreement should end with the words "bon pour pouvoir" (good for authority) in the principal's handwriting, appearing immediately before his or her signature. Although French law does not require a foreign agency authorization or power of attorney to be notarized and legalized by the French consulate, these legal precautions are advisable when initiating an agency relationship in France.

French law distinguishes between agencies that are general and specific, commercial and noncommercial. General agency gives management and administrative authority to handle all the principal's affairs except for the disposal of property, which must be specifically authorized in the agreement. Under specific agency, only limited functions are given to the agent, and those are expressly listed in the agreement. A commercial agent is a professional who buys and sells in the principal's name and must register as such with the Tribunal de Commerce. Foreign commercial agents are also required to register, but must first possess a valid trader's card. A written agreement is required to establish commercial agency. The legal requirements for commercial agents in France are stringent. They must scrupulously carry out the tasks for which they were engaged and are required to report regularly to the principal. A commercial agent is liable for his or her own mistakes, and those of any subagent, made while serving as an agent. The principal is absolved of this liability.

Records. All individuals or companies engaged in commercial activity in France must register their principal office in the Register of Commerce. Applications are made to the Tribunal of Commerce. This requirement applies to foreign or domestic commercial and noncommercial companies, whether doing business directly or indirectly through an agent, as well as to individuals. Traders must apply for registration within two weeks of beginning business activities, but companies are not subject to a time limit.

Sales. In a sales transaction, the seller's primary obligation is to deliver the goods, at his or her own expense unless the contract states otherwise, and to give certain warranties. Unless the contract otherwise stipulates, the buyer becomes the owner as soon as the parties agree on the goods and the price. Title changes regardless of whether delivery has occurred or money has changed hands. However, risk of loss for goods sold by weight, number, or measure passes to the buyer only after the goods have been weighed, counted, or measured. Sales contracts can be made as private agreements or by notarized deed, either of which will be satisfactory proof of the contract. Commercial contracts can also be proved by an accepted invoice, a signed broker's note or order, the parties' account books, correspondence, and even oral testimony.

Taxation. France levies a 42% tax on income from French sources on companies from foreign countries that have no international tax treaty with France. This tax applies equally to firms having permanent establishment in France, engaging in complete commercial cycle in France, or having an agent in France with authority to bind the company. The U.S. treaty limits the tax liability of U.S. firms to the taxes charged to companies with permanent establishment in France.

Common Law

Common law developed in England out of Norman customs and practices after the successful conquest of England in 1066. The conquerors established a court system to declare the common law for the entire country. As a result, the English court system was already strongly centralized, with a powerful interest group of law experts and practitioners, before any statutes were adopted in this country. By the time statutes were drafted, a massive body of unwritten common law was well-entrenched. The statutes served to codify, clarify, limit, and supplement the common law. English laws have changed significantly over the past two centuries, particularly in areas of labor, consumer protection, commercial, and property law. Statutory law has grown alongside common law, with judges free to interpret the statutes to accord with common law except when a statute contains an express limitation.

Comparison of US and Other Common Law Systems

If you are trading internationally with a supplier in a common law country, do not assume that country's laws are the same as those in the U.S. It is true that English com-

mon law has served as the foundation for legal systems in the U.S. and other countries and that these systems will have many similarities. However, they will also have major differences because of a characteristic unique to the common law: flexibility. They can be easily adapted to fill the needs of different cultures and changed to reflect advances within a single society. Thus, U.S. statutes and legal procedures are unique to the needs of U.S. citizens. Similarly, the common law system of Singapore has been modified to allow for that country's own cultural and societal demands.

Canadian Common Law

Governmental Structure. Canada was created by Royal Proclamation on May 22, 1867, as part of the Commonwealth of the United Kingdom. Its constitution is similar to that of England. Until the passage of the Canada Act in 1982, Canada was subject to laws enacted by the British Parliament, as well as those enacted by its own. The Canada Act achieved Canada's legislative independence from England, though the British Sovereign remains the Sovereign of Canada.

Canada has a Federal Parliament, which consists of the British Sovereign, Canadian Senate, and House of Commons. This Parliament has exclusive legislative jurisdiction over issues that affect the country as a whole. Each province also has a legislature with jurisdiction over subjects specifically affecting that province. Each category discussed below may be solely under federal jurisdiction, controlled by local laws only, or governed by both. As an example of provincial regulations, we have chosen some from Ontario because that province has a substantial commercial relationship with the U.S. Laws specific to that province are identified by the subhead "Ontario."

Court System. Canada's court system includes provincial and Dominion courts. The Supreme Court of Canada is the highest court and exercises appellate jurisdiction in civil and criminal cases. At the federal level, the Tax Court adjudicates tax, pension, and unemployment insurance issues. The Federal Court of Canada is the law, equity, and admiralty court for the entire country and has Appeal and Trial Divisions. The Trial Division handles such issues as actions involving the Crown or federal entities, conflicts between provinces or between the federal government and a provincial government, as well as suits pertaining to citizenship disputes, industrial property, estate tax issues, and any issues not under the jurisdiction of other courts. The Appeal Division hears appeals from the Trial and Tax Courts, and determines questions of law, jurisdiction, or practice, including review of federal decisions.

Aliens. Noncitizens in Canada are subject to all Canadian laws. As part of the British Commonwealth, Canada recognizes both Canadian and Commonwealth citizenship. Although citizens of other Commonwealth nations are not also Canadian citizens, they do have certain rights in Canada as Commonwealth citizens, most notably with regard to property ownership and succession. Canadian law restricts certain types of property ownership for noncitizens; for example, a noncitizen cannot own a Canadian ship.

With some regulatory exceptions, such as for persons who enter for short-term business purposes, all noncitizens seeking employment in Canada must obtain work visas validated by the Canadian Employment Commission. U.S. citizens entering Canada for business purposes have preferential treatment under the Canada/U.S. Free Trade Agreement.

Ontario. A noncitizens may own property in Ontario in keeping with Canadian law, but any holdings of agricultural land by noncitizens must be registered with the provincial government.

Arbitration and Judgment. Canada is a signatory to the U.N. Foreign Arbitral Awards Convention Act.

Ontario. Ontario honors written agreements specifying arbitration as the means of dispute settlement. If parties designate in writing that they prefer to resolve a dispute by arbitration, this method must be used, unless Ontario's Supreme Court rules otherwise. Ontario adopted an amended version of the Model Law on International Commercial Arbitration in 1988. Both Supreme and District Courts may recognize a foreign arbitral award, which is then enforceable as if it were a judgment or order of that court.

Ontario has statutory provisions for reciprocal recognition and enforcement of civil and commercial judgments of the U.S., individual U.S. states, the U.K., other Canadian provinces, and other countries. To be enforced, a judgment must be the result of a civil court proceeding or arbitration and must involve an award of money. Suit must be brought where Ontario law gives the foreign court jurisdiction over the matter in question, or in the Supreme Court of Ontario. There is a six-year time limit, beginning at the date of judgment, after which a foreign judgment is no longer enforceable in Ontario.

Negotiable Instruments. Bills of exchange, promissory notes, and checks are regulated under the Canadian Bills of Exchange Act and applicable English common law rules. The Canadian law resembles the negotiable instruments provisions of the U.S. Uniform Commercial Code. When the Canadian Act and the English common law rules diverge, the provisions of the Act are enforced. Specific regulations and practices govern nonpayment of financial obligations entered into between Canadians and foreigners. To enforce legal proceedings for the nonacceptance or dishonor of a foreign bill, certain notarial procedures must be followed.

Contracts. Unless otherwise stipulated by the parties to a contract, the uniform rules of Canada's International Sale of Goods Contract Convention Act govern sales contracts made between Canadian and foreign business entities. Agreement formation, breach of contract, buyers' and sellers' obligations, and third-party claims are some of the issues covered by the Convention.

Ontario. Ontario's Frustrated Contracts Act applies to nearly all types of contract under Ontario law. It allows for cancellation of payment owed when a contract cannot be fulfilled, as well as for recovery of any money already paid under the agreement. Under the Act, a contract that has been partially fulfilled can be upheld to that extent, with the unfulfilled segment being frustrated. Contracts for overseas transport of goods, insurance contracts, and contracts under which the goods to be sold have perished

before the contract is performed but without the seller's fault are not covered under the Act.

Foreign Corporations. As long as a foreign corporation intends to conduct business covered under the Canada Corporation Act, there are no federal licensing requirements. However some types of businesses are subject to other statutes that may require licensing, such as the Canadian and British Insurance Companies Act. In any case, all foreign companies conducting business in Canada must obtain a license in each Province where business will be conducted. Fees are charged for provincial business licenses.

Ontario. Ontario requires all foreign corporations wishing to conduct business in the Province to obtain a license first. The Ontario Minister of Consumer and Commercial Relations may impose restrictions, conditions, or other limitations on any license. Firms that neglect to obtain licenses, or that allow their agents or representatives to conduct business in the province before the license has been issued, risk fines of up to $25,000. Foreign companies doing business in Ontario must fulfill substantially the same reporting requirements and must pay substantially the same taxes on corporate income as domestic Ontario companies.

Exchange Controls. At present, no restrictions are imposed on currency entering or leaving Canada.

Foreign Investment in Canada. Canada welcomes beneficial foreign investments. Depending on the nature and dollar amount of the investment, governmental review to determine the benefit to Canada may be required. Whether an acquisition is subject to review depends on "acquisition thresholds" established by regulation. The review process is not required for investments falling below these regulatory thresholds, but all non-Canadians making Canadian investments must file notice with the Investment Canada Agency. The Agency determines the proposed investment's review status and informs the foreign investor. The Canadian federal government reviews proposed investments specifically related to Canada's cultural heritage or national identity on a case-by-case basis. Foreigners wishing to make a reviewable investment must apply to the Investment Canada Agency in advance.

Foreign Trade Regulations. Canada is a party to GATT. For U.S. importers, the most significant of Canada's many trade agreements is the North American Free Trade Agreement (NAFTA). Under this treaty, tariffs and other trade barriers between the U.S. and Canada have been progressively eliminated, and government procurement policies liberalized. U.S. acquisitions of Canadian businesses are currently reviewable at a higher dollar threshold than acquisitions by other nations, and U.S. business visitors to Canada enjoy simplified admission procedures and better access to financial services markets. In addition to many other general provisions regarding business relationships between the U.S. and Canada, the Agreement specifically provides for trade in automotive goods, alcoholic beverages, energy, and agricultural products.

Insurance Law. Canadian insurance law resembles that of both the U.K. and the U.S. Federal and provincial statutes regulate the insurance business, with Parliamentary jurisdiction based on its constitutional power to regulate trade and commerce.

Interest. Interest rates of 60% and above are prohibited by the Canadian Criminal Code. Any noncriminal rate of interest may be charged or contracted for, with the exception that Parliament reserves the right to restrict interest rates.

Environmental Protection. Canada has extensive federal and provincial environmental protection regulations. For example, interprovincial and transborder shipments of regulated dangerous goods, including hazardous waste, are subject to Transportation of Dangerous Goods Act requirements for labeling, shipping, registration, and notification. The Canadian Environmental Protection Act of 1988 regulates information disclosure, import and export, spill cleanup, nutrients, international air pollution, and ocean dumping issues pertaining to toxic substances. The Canada Labour Code requires worker information and training for handling hazardous materials.

Ontario. Ontario's environmental protection regulations are extensive and stringent, setting limits on discharge and covering all types of pollution. There are heavy penalties for violations. Common law doctrines of nuisance, negligence, strict liability, and riparian rights still apply. Ontario law interprets adverse environmental effect resulting from discharges and spills broadly. Individuals violating pollution-control regulations risk prison terms for actual pollution, and fines as high as $10,000 per day on first conviction. Corporate directors are required to exercise reasonable care to ensure that the corporation does not cause or permit damage to the environment, and the directors can be sued for damages for breach of that duty. Corporations face fines of up to $50,000 per day for violating environmental protection laws. For discharges resulting in actual pollution, corporate fines can go as high as $200,000 per day, absolute liability for the cost of spill clean-up and environmental restoration, and strict liability for other costs.

Employment. Enterprises that benefit more than one Province, such as banks, broadcasting, and the various types of transport industries are subject to federal jurisdiction. For these industries, Canadian law regulates industrial relations, standard hours of work, minimum and overtime wages, holidays and vacations, termination policies, employee safety, unemployment insurance, and equity in the workplace for minorities, women, disabled persons, and others. Employment policies in nonfederal enterprises are primarily a matter of provincial jurisdiction.

Ontario. Common law employment contract rules govern the employer-employee relationship in Ontario, along with extensive statutory regulation. The Ontario Labour Relations Board is instrumental in Ontario labor relations policy, its administrative decisions having spawned extensive case law on the subject. Under the Labour Relations Act, labor conflict resolution must be achieved by binding third-party arbitration rather than by strikes. In addition to stipulating a variety of minimum employment standards, Ontario statutes prohibit various types of discrimination in the workplace, promote protection of workers from workplace health and safety hazards, regulate the establishment of employee pension plans, man-

date workers' compensation, and establish an employer health tax.

Restricted Trade Practices. Canadian law prohibits trade practices by both Canadian and foreign firms that attempt to establish a monopoly in Canada. Bid-rigging, misleading advertising, refusal to deal, exclusive dealing and tied selling, consignment selling intended to control prices or discriminate against other dealers, market restrictions likely to substantially lessen competition, and setting resale prices by means of resale price maintenance agreements are some of the trade practices prohibited by Canadian law.

Ontario. The following sections are all provincial law specific to Ontario.

Licensing. Ontario requires licensing by the provincial government for the following kinds of business: collection agencies, itinerant sellers, dealers in livestock and livestock products, motor vehicle dealers, and sellers of liquor.

Notaries Public. Ontario notaries are authorized to perform all of the usual functions associated with that office. Ontario law distinguishes between notaries who are lawyers and those who are not. Notaries who are not also lawyers have three-year commissions, which may be renewed and which are sometimes subject to territorial limitations on their practice. Although it is customary in Ontario for a notary to affix a seal to an affidavit, oath, or declaration, absence of the seal does not invalidate a notarized document of that type.

Principal and Agent. In Ontario, common law rules apply to principal-agent relationships. The Powers of Attorney Amendment Act of 1983 governs powers of attorney.

Sales. Ontario's Sale of Goods Act, similar to the English Act, codifies the law pertaining to sales. Ontario statutes govern such issues as product liability, bills of sale, transfer of title, conditions and warranties, delivery and stoppage in transit, and remedies for breach of contract for buyer and seller. If a seller fails to deliver the goods, the buyer may sue for damages or specific performance. If the goods have changed hands, the seller may sue for the price. The seller may sue for nonacceptance if the buyer refuses the shipment. Damages are based on estimated loss. Product liability for defective goods is based on case law precedent.

Islamic (Shari'ah) Law

Shari'ah law was originally derived from the Koran, believed by Muslims to be the revelations of Allah to the Prophet Mohammed. The Prophet's supplemental teachings and actions were recorded and later gathered in documents called the "Sunna." The Koran and the Sunna are the two primary sources for Shari'ah law. They do not contain extensive detailed codes, but principles and precepts. Muslims believe that after Mohammed's death, the direct revelations of God ceased, and therefore the law can no longer be modified.

Traditional Legal System. The principles of Shari'ah law have been interpreted and applied in individual cases by judicial decisions. Conflicts were resolved in "quadi" courts by individual judges. To reach a judgment, a quadi resorted first to the Koran, then to the Sunna. If neither document provided a basis for judgment, the quadi had authority to employ certain principles of Islamic judicial reasoning, which involved analogy, fairness, and the public interest.

An individual quadi's judgment was final for the single case to which it applied, but was not considered an authoritative interpretation of Shari'ah law until and unless all qualified scholars of that time agreed unanimously with the interpretation. Once such an agreement was reached, a given interpretation was incorporated into the text of the law, and had the same immutable, irreversible, unchallengeable status as the Koran and Sunna texts. These judicial interpretations were gathered over the years into legal texts on which subsequent decisions were reached. Compilation of these texts ceased after the 10th century, and the body of traditional Shari'ah law has not changed since.

Modern Legal System. With the exception of Muslim countries on the Arabian peninsula, most Muslim countries no longer adhere to the strict traditional form of Shari'ah law. In all other Muslim countries and jurisdictions, Shari'ah law tends to be limited to family and succession law. Even these laws are now codified, so that reference to the traditional authoritative law texts is rarely made, except when existing statutes and codes are not relevant to a specific decision.

To accommodate the changes in modern societies, most Muslim countries have abandoned Shari'ah criminal, civil and commercial laws and have adopted modified codes based on European legal models. For example, Pakistan uses a case law system, with Shari'ah laws codified into statutes. Judicial decisions have replaced the traditional legal manuals as the ulti-

mate authority in these countries. The single-court system of quadis has been widely replaced with systems of appellate courts. Most countries that practice Shari'ah law in limited ways relegate issues such as family law to separate Shari'ah courts, handling all other legal conflicts in national courts. Some countries—such as Egypt and Tunisia—no longer have separate Shari'ah courts, but Shari'ah law is administered in a system of national courts. Many countries have abandoned the traditional Shari'ah procedures of evidence. Instead of accepting oaths as valid evidence, they have adopted Western procedures and philosophies. Many countries that still practice traditional Shari'ah law have found it necessary to institute significant procedural and other reforms to reflect the changing needs of their societies.

Comparison of Islamic Law to Common Law

Islamic law differs from Western legal systems in that it is religiously derived and constituted. Its precepts encompass not only civil, commercial, criminal, and family law, but also matters of religious observance and personal conscience. Islamic law is an ethical system, not a codified set of rules. Muslims consider it the direct revelation of the immutable, infallible will of God. It is therefore not open to question or modification. As can be imagined, this poses some problem in the changing and complex world of the 20th century. If you do business with a supplier in an Islamic country, be aware of the following:

- The terms of a contract are less likely to be enforceable if they modify standard legal precepts and practices, particularly those that are part of the religious tradition of Shari'ah law.
- If traditional Shari'ah law applies, parties cannot choose any other law to govern their agreement instead.
- Competency to contract *rashid* is a key concept in the law of transactions. A person who is not considered *rashid* is forbidden to conduct any kind of transaction. All of their business must be conducted by a guardian. This applies to persons who are minors, mentally incompetent, or immoral.
- There are four elements of Shari'ah transaction law: sale, hire, gift, and loan. Virtually all commercial transactions fall under one or a combination of these elements.
- Shari'ah law forbids usury and speculation, which normally means any transaction involving interest.
- Procedures before a quadi are determined by the single judge who is presiding. The judge decides which party has the burden of proof. Evidence is usually taken in the form of testamentary declaration by the party with the burden of proof or by witnesses. An oath by a party to the suit can be considered adequate evidence for a decision.

Saudi Arabian Islamic Law

An interesting example of a country that continues to practice Shari'ah law unadulterated by reform or westernization is Saudi Arabia. The following discussion outlines some basic areas of Shari'ah law, as practiced in Saudi Arabia, that pertain to international business. It should give you a sense of how Shari'ah law may affect your business prospects and procedures in nations that continue to adhere to the traditional law.

Governmental Structure. Saudi Arabia is a monarchy without a constitution. Governmental structure is determined according to royal decree. In Saudi Arabia, the word "law" means Shari'ah law. All regulations, secular or otherwise, are subordinate to and interpreted by principles set forth in the authoritative documents of Shari'ah law: the Koran, the Sunna, and the legal manuals comprising scholarly interpretations compiled through the 10th century.

Official Language. Saudi Arabia's official language is Arabic. All business records, transactions, and dealings must be in Arabic. Documents submitted to the Saudi government and courts must be either in Arabic or translated by a licensed translator. All judicial proceedings, including arbitration, must be in Arabic. Clauses in contracts stipulating to use of a foreign language, such as for legal proceedings or business paperwork, are unenforceable.

Aliens. Foreigners in Saudi Arabia are subject to the jurisdiction of Saudi courts and tribunals and have the same rights as Saudi nationals. Except for citizens of parties to the Gulf Co-Operation Council (GCC), foreigners are not allowed to own real estate, to engage in commercial trading activities (see Agency below), or to own publicly traded shares of Saudi joint stock companies. Non-GCC aliens must obtain entry visas, and if they wish to establish residence in Saudi Arabia, residence permits before arriving in Saudi Arabia. No visas or permits are issued to foreigners on arrival in Saudi Arabia, and no foreigners are permitted entry without properly approved documentation. Visa and permit requirements are burdensome, strictly observed by Saudi officials, and can change without notice.

Agency. In principle, persons not Saudi citizens are not permitted to conduct business in Saudi Arabia. In practical terms, this tends to apply to business transactions related to sales of foreign goods in Saudi Arabia. To accommodate this restriction, persons and firms with business dealings in Saudi Arabia contract with Saudi nationals in some form of agency relationship, such as power of attorney. Agency relationship can be terminated by either party without legal repercussion, but in practice most contractual arrangements are strictly enforced.

Courts. A variety of courts are available for adjudication, depending on the area of conflict. Civil actions, including those related to family, real estate, and leasing concerns, are generally handled in Shari'ah courts. Other matters— disputes with the public sector, private sector commercial disputes, enforcement of foreign judgments—are handled by Boards of Grievances. There are also separate judicial bodies that handle conflicts related to banking, negotiable instruments, and labor relations. Saudi court and tribunal rulings are not subject to any form of public disclosure. Judicial decisions are not based on precedent; prior decisions are not binding on subsequent cases of similar nature.

Law of Choice. Shari'ah law is considered immutable and divinely ordained, and therefore no other legal system is recognized. Even if a contract in Saudi Arabia stipulates that the law of a foreign country will be the deciding law in the case of dispute, no Saudi tribunal will uphold that contractual agreement. All disputes are settled according to the Saudi version of Shari'ah law. There are no exceptions.

Arbitration and Foreign Judgments. Arbitration is a viable option for most private-sector commercial disputes in Saudi Arabia. Both the arbitration agreement and the final award must pass through Saudi governmental approval processes in the court that would handle the suit if arbitration had not been preferred. No arbitration award not subjected to the ratification process or prior agreement approval can be enforced in Saudi Arabia. It is unlikely that judgments of foreign courts can be enforced in Saudi Arabia, though this is an area in transition. Historically, Saudi Arabia enforces foreign judgments only by explicit treaty with a foreign nation. At present, Saudi Arabia has such a treaty (the Arab League Treaty) with Lebanon, Jordan, Egypt, Iraq, Syria, and Yemen.

Contracts. Saudi contract law is not codified. It is a matter of adherence to Shari'ah law precepts, and within the limitations of Shari'ah law, it affords considerable freedom. Shari'ah law deems contracts with persons not *rashid* to be invalid. Contracts involving speculation and interest are entirely prohibited and unenforceable. Although written contracts are preferred, oral contracts supported by a witness or other proofs are enforceable. If contracts are breached, Saudi courts will award only proven direct damages. No damages will be awarded for lost opportunity or lost profit because these damages are speculative, and speculation is forbidden under Shari'ah law. Saudi courts will accept as a valid reason for a breach of contract events or effects beyond the breaching party's control or ability to anticipate (force majeure), undue hardship, and impossibility.

Sales Agreements. There is no comprehensive Saudi law pertaining to sales and sales contracts. Any contract for sale executed in Saudi Arabia or with a Saudi entity should explicitly spell out every single term. Even so, the foreigner doing business in Saudi Arabia should be aware that some terms enforceable in Western countries will not be enforceable under Shari'ah law. Examples: terms relating to title retention, repossession, remedies, disclaimers, and limitations on liability. Warranties are implicit in Shari'ah precepts; nevertheless each contract should spell out warranty terms specifically.

Interest. Interest is a gray area in Saudi Arabia: there is a discrepancy between business practice and official stance. Though Shari'ah law expressly forbids the charging and collecting of any form of interest, banks, and other commercial enterprises do regularly charge and collect interest with impunity. However, should a legal conflict arise involving such a transaction, no Saudi court will uphold a claim for payment of interest owed. Charging interest is commercially viable and is practiced in Saudi Arabia, but it is not enforceable in the courts.

Exchange Control. There are no restrictions on the transmittal of money or other means of exchange across Saudi borders. You can take money in and you can remove it without limitation. This applies both to foreign and Saudi currency.

Foreign Investment. A "foreign capital investment license" is required to invest in Saudi Arabia. By "foreign capital" the Saudis mean currency and other means of exchange, as well as such items as machinery and hardware, and intangibles such as trademarks or patents. The Saudi Ministry of Industry and Electricity determines whether a commercial venture is open for foreign investment and limits such opportunities to "economic development projects." Licenses are not granted simply because an application is made. To obtain a foreign capital investment license, a foreign firm must substantiate its expertise in the relevant area. Once granted, a license limits the licensee's area of involvement, including corporate objects, shareholders, and share capital. No modifications may be made to any covered area of corporate activity without prior approval of the Ministry of Industry and Electricity.

Foreign Corporations in Saudi Arabia. The activities of foreign corporations in Saudi Arabia are limited and tend to require foreign capital investment licenses. This applies to participation in joint ventures with national companies, as well as to the opening of branch offices by wholly foreign-owned companies. Special licenses are required for foreign companies engaging in technical and scientific services, market research, or product research. Companies so licensed are not permitted to engage in commercial transactions. Corporations entering into public-sector contracts, if not otherwise licensed, must register with the Ministry of Commerce. This is known as temporary commercial registry and applies to each contract, even if a company is involved in multiple concurrent contracts.

Commercial Registry. Saudi law requires every business entity of any form or nature to register with the Ministry of Commerce in each place where it conducts business. Parent and subsidiary companies, and main and branch offices must register separately. The Ministry of Commerce issues a registration number to each registrant, which must then be used without fail on all written correspondence. Firms requiring foreign capital investment licenses will have to provide evidence of license before they will be permitted to register.

Notaries Public. Notaries public are high public officials, on a par with judges, appointed and supervised by the Minister of Justice and the Supreme Judicial Council. They are experts in Shari'ah Law. There are extensive and burdensome requirements, which are subject to change without notice, pertaining to form and content of documents submitted to a notary in Saudi Arabia.

Employment. In Saudi Arabia, written and unwritten labor contracts are enforceable, with written contracts being the most common. There are stringent requirements for employers. These include such benefits as mandatory annual 15-day paid vacations for employees after the first year of employment, increasing to 21-day vacations after 10 continuous years. Terminated employees must be awarded "end-of-service" remuneration amounting to a half month's pay for each of the first five years of continuous service, and one month's pay for each subsequent year. This remuneration is calculated on the employee's most recent rate of pay, and is payable to employees terminated by the employer as well as those conscripted into military service, or leaving for circumstances beyond their control. Female employees leaving jobs for marriage or childbirth are also awarded end-of-service payment. If employment is terminated on the instigation of the employee and the employee observes the mandatory 30-day notice, he or she is due a modified version of the standard end-of-service payment. Employees and employers can terminate the employment relationship at will, and are expected to give 30 days' notice in the case of monthly employees and 15 days' notice for all others. When an employment relationship is contracted for a specified length of time and is terminated by the employer for no valid reason, the employee is entitled to damages, which tend to amount to between three and five months' salary.

Shipping. Maritime transport activities fall under the jurisdiction of the Ministry of Communications. Use of Sau-

di Arabian seaports is regulated under GCC Rules and Regulations. These are available in English translation.

Taxation. The central Saudi government levies taxes according to royal decree. At present there are no regional, local, or sales taxes. However, foreigners can be subject to income tax on investments in capital of Saudi businesses. Corporations are taxed on net income, with no distinction between types of businesses.

Communist Law

The originating text for communist law was the Communist Manifesto of Karl Marx and Friedrich Engels. The Manifesto did not provide a systematic code of laws, but a general, philosophical mandate from which codes were developed gradually after the successful Russian Bolshevik Revolution in 1917. By depriving the middle class of its ownership of the means of production, and thus its economic power, and by educating citizens to a way of life that would make the new social order attainable, the Communist Manifesto hoped to transform society into first a socialist and then a communist society. The laws were intended to implement that transformation and then cease to exist, once the new society was functioning smoothly without the need for rules and regulations.

Comparison with Common and Civil Law

There are many parallels between communist and civil law systems in the area of civil and criminal court procedures, but socialist law differs from common and civil law in that it is a state-centered, state-motivated system. Communism assumes that the good of the citizen inheres in the goals of the state, and therefore its mandate is to further the aims of the state, not to protect the rights of the individual citizen. The concept of checks and balances does not pertain.

In dealing with suppliers located in communist countries, you should keep in mind the following:

- Communist law does not distinguish between private law and public law. Changing policies of the state—such as for national economic planning—can expand or eliminate private, individual rights, even if already accrued.
- Contracts with communist government agencies are heavily influenced by state policy and by the need to implement a planned economy. For an

ample, escalation clauses are not used because of the need to know the exact price and its effect on the government's economic plan.

- Commercial contracts may only be entered into with government agencies. Negotiating these contracts can be extremely difficult. Government agencies are directed to purchase only at the lowest price existing in the world market for the particular product, and to sell at highly competitive world market prices.

- The Communist party plays a dominant role in the society.

- Generally, the foreigner must deal with agencies called "Foreign Trade Organizations" (FTO's) or state trading corporations. Each FTO or state trading corporation has jurisdiction over a particular commodity or type of commodity and each must follow explicit directives from higher governmental echelon. Each FTO is treated as a separate juridical entity, has its own budget, and can be sued individually.

Chinese Communist Law

Governmental Structure. China's constitution declares that Chinese Communist ideology controls in all matters. The highest government body with legislative powers is the National People's Congress. The Congress appoints the State Council, which exercises administrative powers. China's highest judicial body is the Supreme People's Court, which is responsible to the Congress. The Supreme People's Procuratorate, an independent body, enforces the constitution and laws.

Aliens. To enter, exit, transit, reside in, or travel about China, foreigners must have prior permission from the Ministry of Public Security and Foreign Affairs. Visas are required, and for residential stays, a foreigner must usually register with local public security agencies. Areas of China are classified into unrestricted, restricted, and non-open areas for foreigners who travel within the country.

Agency. Principals can generally be represented by agents in China. An agent will not be liable on a contract signed on behalf of the principal, provide the agent's capacity is clear. An agent can be appointed by a written power of attorney that specifies the matter, scope, and time for which the authority granted. If the principal is a foreigner not residing in China, the power of attorney must be notarized in the foreigner's country and attested by a local Chinese embassy or consulate.

Law of Choice. International contracts that designate a particular law to govern the transaction are enforceable, except when Chinese law mandates its application to a transaction. Unless otherwise expressly provided, Chinese law will apply.

Arbitration and Foreign Judgments. Arbitration is available before Chinese Arbitration Commissions. These are local arbitration boards established to handle economic contract disputes. Arbitration is initiated by petition. An arbitration panel is then chosen, usually consisting of one arbitrator chosen by each party and a third neutral arbitrator. The panel has authority to investigate, collect and hear evidence, and secure goods and proceeds until their final decision. Arbitration decisions may be appealed to the people's court. Parties may also agree to arbitrate un-

der internationally recognized arbitration rules. China has acceded to the U.N. Convention on the Recognition and Enforcement of Foreign Arbitral Awards.

Contracts. Economic contracts must be written and must comply with Chinese law, national policy, and plans. Parties have freedom to contract, but contracts are void if they violate law, national policy, national plans, or public interests. They are also void if executed by an agent without proper authority or if executed under fraud or coercion. For some contracts, specific provisions are mandated by law. Contract remedies for breach are provided by statute, including the right to keep an advance deposit, payment of consequential damages, return of property, and compensation for actual losses. Mitigation of damages is required when possible. Parties may cancel or modify their contracts by mutual written agreement for any reason, including force majeure.

Sales Agreements. No particular form is required for the purchase of personal property in China. Firms engaged in international sales usually use standard printed form agreements that follow international practices. China has ratified the U.N. Convention on Contracts for the International Sale of Goods, with the reservation that it will not agree to apply the Convention beyond the member states and it will not give effect to oral sales contracts. Prices for goods are often established pursuant to regulations adopted by the national or local governments. Some prices are not negotiable. Prices that are fixed and free typically fluctuate within a certain range.

Foreign Exchange. Strict controls are imposed on the allocation of foreign exchange. Profits must be remitted, imported components or raw materials must be purchased, and foreign personnel must be compensated in foreign currency, not China's domestic currency.

Foreign Investment. China's central government held a virtual monopoly over the country's foreign trade until the early 1980's. Little foreign investment was permitted, and then only for highly specialized purposes—acquiring new technology, assuring capital and raw material supplies, or promoting exports. However, foreign investment is being encouraged in oil drilling and refining, coal mining, property development, and labor-intensive manufacturing and assembly plants.

Import/Export Controls. All commodities exported from or imported to China must be channeled through licensed trading companies. Local and provincial governments often have their own regulations and restrictions on importing and exporting, as well. China is encouraging exports, and therefore has substantially reduced the number of commodities that require export licenses. However, licenses are still required to export corn, soybeans, tea, coal, and crude and refined oil.

Notaries Public. Notaries public have legal education or training. The signature of a notary evidences the legality of a document or act.

Taxation. Foreign investment enterprises and foreign enterprises with establishments in China are subject to an income tax at the rate of 33%. Some industries are subject to additional business taxes, and a 17% value-added tax (VAT) is levied.

Glossary of Common Legal Terms

acceptance An unconditional assent to an offer, or one conditioned on minor changes that do not affect material terms of the offer. *See* counteroffer, offer.

acknowledgment *See* authentication.

agency The relationship between an agent and a principal. The agent represents and acts on behalf of the principal, who instructs and authorizes the agent to so act. Refer to "Agency" on page 100.

after sight A term in a financial instrument making the instrument payable a specified number of days after presentation or demand. Example: a bill of exchange payable 30 days after sight matures and becomes payable 30 days after the person for whom the bill is drawn (the drawee) presents it to a bank (the payee).

at sight A term in a financial instrument under which the instrument is payable on presentation or demand. Example: a bill of exchange that is payable at sight is payable at the time the person for whom the bill is drawn (the drawee) presents it to a bank (the payee).

attachment The legal process for seizing property before a judgment to secure the payment of damages if awarded. Attachment may be sought before commencing a court action or during the action. This process is also referred to as sequestration. Example: a party who claims damages for breach of contract may request a court to issue an order freezing all transfers of specific property owned by the breaching party pending resolution of the dispute.

authentication The act of conferring legal authenticity on a written document, typically made by a notary public, who attests and certifies that the document is in proper legal form and that it is executed by a person identified as having authority to do so. Authentication is also referred to as acknowledgment.

bill of exchange A written instrument signed by a person (the drawer) and addressed to another person (the drawee), typically a bank, ordering the drawee to pay unconditionally a stated sum of money to yet another person (the payee) on demand or at a future time.

bona fide In or with good faith, honesty, and sincerity. Example: A bona fide purchaser is one who buys goods for value and without knowledge of fraud or unfair dealing in the transaction. Knowledge of fraud or unfair dealing may be implied if the facts are such that the purchaser should have reasonably known that the transaction involved deceit, such as when goods that are susceptible to piracy are provided without documentation of their origin.

counteroffer A reply to an offer that materially alters the terms of the offer. Example: a seller who accepts a buyer's offer on condition that the goods will be made of a different material has made a counteroffer. *See* acceptance, offer.

crossed check A check that bears on its face two parallel transverse lines, indicating that it cannot be presented for cash. A bank that accepts such a check will pay the proceeds only to another bank, which will credit the money to the account of the payee of the check.

execution The legal process for enforcing a judgment for damages, usually by seizure and sale of the debtor's personal property. Example: if a court awards damages in a breach of contract action and the breaching party fails to remit them, the party awarded damages may request the court to order seizure and sale of the breaching party's inventory to satisfy the award.

force majeure clause A contract clause that excuses a party who breaches the contract when performance is prevented by the occurrence of an event—such as a natural disaster, war, or labor strike—that is beyond the party's reasonable control.

juridical (juristic) act An action intended to have, and capable of having, a legal effect, such as the creation, termination, or modification of a legal right. Example: The signing of a power of attorney is a juridical act because it gives legal authority to an agent.

juridical (juristic) person An individual or entity recognized under law as having legal rights and obligations. Example: limited liability companies, corporations, and partnerships are entities recognized as juridical persons.

negotiable instrument A written document transferable merely by endorsement or delivery. Example: a check or bill of exchange is a negotiable instrument.

offer A proposal that is made to a specific individual or entity to enter into a contract. The proposal must contain definite terms and must indicate the offeror's intent to be bound by an acceptance. Example: a buyer's order to purchase designated goods on certain delivery and payment terms is an offer. *See* acceptance, counteroffer.

power of attorney A written document by which one individual or entity (the principal) authorizes another individual or entity (the agent) to perform stated acts on the principal's behalf. Example: a principal may execute a special power of attorney (authorizing an agent to sign a specific contract) or a general power of attorney (authorizing the agent to sign all contracts for the principal). *See* agency. Refer to "Power of Attorney" on page 100.

promoter of corporation The individual or entity that organizes a corporation.

rescind A contracting party's right to cancel the contract. Example: a contract may allow one party to rescind if the other party fails to perform within a reasonable time.

sequestration *See* attachment.

statute of frauds A law that requires designated documents to be in writing in order to be enforced by a court. Example: contracting parties may orally agree to transfer ownership of immovable property, but a court might not enforce that contract, and might not award damages for breach, unless the contract was written.

ultra vires An act performed without the authority to do so. Example: If a contract provision requires both parties to approve an assignment of the contract but one party agrees to an assignment without obtaining the other's consent, the assignment is ultra vires.

International Banking
Contents

International Banking Overview

Introduction

Major domestic, foreign, and international banks provide a wide range of services to their customers involved in import and export operations. These services fall into four main categories: connections and information, movement of funds and financing, other banking services, and foreign exchange operations.

This introduction to international banking is designed to provide an overview of these services. The following section—"Documentary Credits (Letters of Credit)," beginning on page 148—gives more detailed information concerning international payments.

If you are planning to operate in international trade, it is important to cultivate your banking relationships early and often. All business is ultimately conducted person to person, and nowhere is this more important than in the international arena. Begin by establishing a strong personal relationship with the bankers whose support you will need as your enterprise progresses. Importers who view a professional service provider—such as a banker, a customs broker, or an attorney—as a partner in their business tend to be significantly more successful than those who fail to utilize these resources to the fullest.

In many cases the quality of your ongoing relationship with your bank and banker will determine the availability of certain of the services listed below. Also, be aware that not all banks or bankers will be able to provide every service listed. This is especially true of limited local banking institutions with little exposure to the international field.

Types of Banking Organizations

As many as 13,000 state- and federally-chartered banking institutions operate in the U.S. These are extremely varied, ranging from small, special purpose local operations to giant international outfits. Of all these, about 50 can be classed as truly international in scope and operations. However, even the smallest local bank will have connections—known as correspondents—among larger institutions and can begin to set you on the road to hooking up with the expertise you need.

In addition, about 300 foreign banks maintain a presence in the U.S. Some of these maintain only a representative office, which cannot offer services, but which can provide information and direct you to the appropriate people in their home country. Other foreign banks run agencies in the U.S. These specially licensed offices can lend, handle trade bills, issue letters of credit, act as an intermediary for parent company business, and offer payment services, but may not accept deposits. Others have branches, which can offer any service that fully licensed domestic banks are allowed to offer. Still others are subsidiaries: locally incorporated, licensed banks owned by overseas parent firms. Any of these foreign owned operations may be a good place to start when looking for information about doing business in their home countries.

The U.S. also has offshore banks, known as Edge Act and Agreement banks. These are separately incorporated banks physically located in the U.S., but legally separate and designed to service international business for both U.S. residents and foreigners. These entities are restricted from offering certain domestic banking services, but are relieved of some regulatory and other requirements (for example, they are not required to maintain reserve deposits with the Federal Reserve system) to enable them to compete with foreign operations. Edge Act banks are federally chartered, while Agreement banks operate under state licenses.

Investment banks and venture capital firms may also be interested in helping larger growing internationally-oriented firms secure additional financing. If you are big enough to interest them, you already know about their services. If not, there's always the future.

Most of these same types of financial institutions exist in other countries, although the specifics vary widely depending on the local system. Consult the U.S. office of the main bank in the country you are interested in, or a U.S. bank with offices in that country.

Connections and Information

Connections

Through its branch and correspondent bank relationships throughout the world, your bank may be able to provide you with names and references for country-of-origin suppliers of the commodities or products you wish to import. At the very least your banker should be able to supply you with a letter of introduction to an officer of a local bank in the country of origin. Do not take these letters of introduction lightly. To successfully find a good source of supply you may need to follow up on a number of leads and this is a good one. Unless you represent an already well known, internationally renowned firm, such a reference from a bank could play a crucial role in establishing your credibility.

Tip: If you are certain of the country of origin of the product(s) you propose to import, make it a top priority to get in touch with the U.S. branch of the major foreign bank from that country as soon as possible. Call to establish who you should be speaking with. Then make the connection by phone and tell them exactly what type of contact you are looking for in their country. If they are in a position to help, make an appointment to see them in person.

Supplier Information

International banks are also in a position to assist in securing current information on the reputation, capabilities, and creditworthiness of firms and individuals with whom business may be contemplated. Because you have made your banker an unofficial "partner" in your operation, he or she has a stake in seeing that you do not end up doing business with unreliable firms. Ask your bankers if they can provide a financial or other report on the supplier firms in the country of origin.

Securing Overseas Credit

Two of the most underutilized sources of credit for importers are suppliers and export trade promotion services in the country of origin. In the U.S. most official and quasi-official trade facilitating organizations—such as the U.S. Department of Commerce (DOC), the Export-Import Bank of the United States (Eximbank) and the Private Export Funding Corporation (PEFCO)—are concerned almost exclusively with promoting and financing exports from the U.S. rather than two-way trade or imports into the country. The same is often true of the agencies abroad, but there it can work to your benefit because you are buying what they have to sell. With your approval, your bank can furnish your credit history and written references to these sources to assist you in obtaining credit and other services from such entities. An endorsement from your banker may also help in securing more favorable terms.

Tip: Don't be bashful about proposing imaginative financing alternatives to your supplier. One small-time importer making regular buying trips to the Orient was able to get favorable terms based on his presentation of himself as an ultra-reliable business partner. He paid cash, using traveler's checks, on the first trip; by personal check on the second trip; by post-dated personal check on the third trip; and was able to get 60-day credit terms on the fourth trip. Eventually several of his suppliers fronted large quantities of merchandise for him to establish a distribution network in the U.S.

without his having to finance the operation himself. It is okay to wheel and deal, but be sure you can deliver.

Domestic Market Information

Remember that importing merely involves getting the goods from one place (which happens to be overseas) to another (which happens to be in the U.S.), with an intermediate stop at U.S. Customs. This is a big task, but you aren't home free yet. You still have to know what you are doing in order to move the goods once you get them to their destination. Larger banks often conduct market studies and publish information on many types of commodities and domestic markets. This information can be a great help in marketing and distribution efforts. These reports are usually produced as studies organized by industry, commodity, or region.

Overseas Financial, Business, Economic, and Political Reports

Many of the larger banks produce reports on overseas financial, business, economic, and political conditions. These reports range from single page briefing sheets to thousand-page monsters with weekly updates. The smaller ones will often be provided free of charge, but the large-scale ones can be quite costly. Look to the major international banks for this sort of information.

Exchange Regulations

Many countries have complex and stringent currency regulations. Internationally-oriented banks deal with currency issues every day and are the obvious places to look for expertise on these matters. Although virtually any bank can hook you into the network, remember that there are no more than 50 institutions nationwide which can be considered players in international and foreign exchange business and choose accordingly.

Many importers get into trouble with country-of-origin currency regulations. Avoid this problem by asking your banker to check out any unusual potential problems in dealing with businesses in the country of origin.

Tip: If you are unsure of the expertise of your banker, ask for an officer in the foreign exchange department.

Country-of-Origin Export Regulations

While banks are not the prime source of this information, international banks can often assist U.S. importers in learning about country-of-origin export regulations for specific commodities.

Tip: Go to the U.S. office of an international bank headquartered or located in the country of origin for this information.

Joint Venture Partners

Your international banker may be in a position to introduce you to potential partners for a joint venture. In some instances banks have assisted in introducing an overseas manufacturer to a U.S. distributor. In other cases, the connection was made between overseas commodity suppliers and U.S. manufacturing companies which subsequently established plants both in the U.S. and the country of origin.

Tip: Even if you do not make the initial connection for your joint venture partner through your bank, try to arrange for a complete credit history of the potential partner through the bank. Also plan on using your bank as a reference to establish your *bona fides*.

Overseas Investment Information

You may wish to invest overseas to leverage your import operation. For example, some importers end up purchasing the company providing the goods they import into the U.S. in order to ensure a steady source of supply. Or you may wish to invest in the commodities from which your products are made, either by buying options on a commodities futures market in the country of origin, or by purchasing a share in an operation which produces these commodities. International banks often serve as the means of effecting such investments and thus may be able to assist you in finding and evaluating opportunities.

Letters of Introduction

Even if your business is well established, well regarded, and well recognized at home, it is unlikely that potential overseas suppliers will have any knowledge of you or any information on your creditworthiness or integrity. A well-written letter of introduction from your banker on bank letterhead may help break down some of these barriers. With an appropriate letter of introduction, overseas branches of your bank or its correspondent banks may be able to provide you with a wide range of excellent information on local suppliers and political and economic conditions.

Countertrade Connections

Trade with former Socialist countries and other nations lacking adequate hard currency reserves may require countertrade deals. In countertrade arrangements, a U.S. exporter trades U.S. goods for goods produced in another country and then sells those goods in the U.S. So why bring this up to importers? Because the U.S. exporter may have no real interest in marketing the products received and may be willing to cut a good deal on the very goods you need. A bank with good connections in the country of origin of the items you wish to import to the U.S. may be able to assist you in finding partners abroad for such countertrade deals.

Referrals to Local Professionals

International banks are often in an excellent position to recommend names of local attorneys, accountants, freight forwarders, and other professional people who can assist your overseas efforts.

High-Level Introductions. Larger banks can sometimes provide introductions to prominent local businesspeople, local bankers, potential investor groups, and government officials in foreign countries. Introductions to such movers and shakers can make all the difference in getting your deal going.

Movement of Funds and Financing

The following section serves as a review of the issues involved in and the primary methods used for making international trade payments.

A major factor determining the method of payment used is the degree of trust the seller/exporter has in the buyer/importer's ability and willingness to pay. In domestic situations, if the buyer has good credit, purchases are usually made on an open account (credit) basis. Open account terms may eventually be made available to you for purchases made abroad, but it is far more likely that another, more secure method of payment will be required. Foreign sellers always seek the most secure payment method from their perspective, while you, as the buyer, will seek the method of payment most advantageous to you.

Evaluation of Risks

International transactions pose risks for both seller and buyer. Exporters want to ensure timely and full payment for their goods, while importers want to be certain that they receive the goods they contract for as well as the documentation that is required for Customs clearance. One of the most important factors in reducing the risks is knowing what risks exist. For that reason, importers and exporters are both advised to consult with their professional partners (customs broker, banker, attorney) to determine an acceptable method of payment for each transaction.

In this discussion it is assumed that buyer and seller have agreed upon the substantive terms of a transaction, including:

- Merchandise, including quality, quantity, and specifications;

- Price to be paid per unit and total amount including the currency to be used in the transaction;

- Who will pay freight charges to the port of export as well as to the port of destination;

- Who will pay insurance during each leg of the journey;

- Shipment deadline(s);

- Required documentation and format; and

- Other special instructions or relevant matters affecting the transaction.

It is assumed that buyer and seller will draft and sign a formal commercial contract establishing these terms as conditions of the transaction. The next consideration is how the buyer will effect payment for the goods.

Methods of International Payment

Ranked from most secure for the exporter to the most desirable for the importer, the basic methods of payment are:

1. Prepayment (cash payment with order),
2. Documentary letter of credit,
3. Documentary collection or draft (documents against payment),
4. Open account or other credit terms.

In addition to these methods there are a number of less traditional methods including payment by personal or business check or credit card and the use of consignment sales. Each method of payment has its own set of advantages and disadvantages for both buyer and seller.

Prepayment or Cash with Order

Prepayment, or cash-in-advance, terms are the most favorable from the seller's point of view. For the seller, risk is substantially eliminated. Virtually all risk lies with the buyer who entrusts his money to the seller prior to the shipment of goods. Advance payment can create a cash flow problem for the importer and adds to the level of his or her risk.

Risks to the Importer/Buyer

Goods not shipped. The merchandise may not be shipped at all. The seller may, if unable or unwilling to ship the goods, retain the buyer's money and either refund it at a much later date, or not at all, in which case the importer usually has little recourse except to pursue a claim in the country of origin.

Goods shipped not goods ordered. The goods shipped may not be those contracted for, or the quality or quantity of goods shipped may be deficient.

Documents not forwarded. Documents necessary for exportation, shipment, and U.S. Customs entry and clearance may not be available when needed, or not available at all. These documents become more difficult to obtain as time goes on. Some documents may be virtually impossible to obtain after the fact.

Delay in shipment. Once the seller has possession of the funds, he or she may not be as concerned with moving the goods as when payment is tied to a shipping date. Prepayment, in many instances, removes the incentive on the part of the seller to deliver on time, whereas payment for goods on delivery invariably promotes a more expeditious availability of merchandise.

There is virtually no risk to the seller when orders are prepaid. Importers using this form of payment should know well and have boundless trust in their supplier. However, buyers should also remember that in many parts of the world, suppliers rely on prepayments or deposits to finance their production or acquisition of the goods to be sold and may be unable to conduct business without the implied credit from the buyer that such methods provide.

An alternative that is somewhat more palatable to the buyer is to pay with cash at the time of delivery. The buyer must be able to physically take possession of the goods and all necessary documentation at time of payment. This scenario gives the buyer some control, because he or she can reject the goods if they are not according to the terms agreed upon. However, this method still places the primary onus on the buyer who is operating away from home and may be confronted with a take-it-or-leave-it offer in a make-or-break situation.

Open Account or Credit Terms

At the other end of the spectrum, credit terms are most favorable to the importer/purchaser, with all risks accruing to the seller. The exporter/seller may consider open account transactions to be satisfactory, if not desirable, provided the buyer is well established, has demonstrated a long and favorable payment record, or has been thoroughly vetted for creditworthiness by an acceptably authoritative source. In open account arrangements, the exporter simply hands over the goods, billing the customer, who is expected to pay under agreed upon terms at a specified future date. Some of the largest firms abroad will make purchases only on an open account basis. Open account terms may also occur when the seller has excess inventory to move or when the seller has a very high profit margin built into the price structure to allow for potential losses.

Risks to the Exporter/Seller

By offering open credit terms to the buyer, the seller is exposing himself or herself to significant commercial risk. The seller passes title and physical control over the goods to the buyer prior to receiving payment. In most instances, full title passes to the buyer and the seller has no recourse to the goods, but only to the buyer for payment. The buyer may be unwilling or unable to pay the seller because of a lack of funds, a dispute over the goods delivered, or a basic unwillingness to pay.

In addition, the absence of external documents and the lack of direct involvement by banking intermediaries may make it difficult to pursue legal or other remedies. The exporter may be forced to pursue collection abroad, which can be difficult and costly. Also, receivables may be harder to finance, since drafts or other evidence of indebtedness are unavailable. On the other hand, the buyer may on occasion need to turn the goods over in order to finance the deal, although the importing business may not be the best place for someone who lives that close to the financial edge. It is little wonder that overseas suppliers are reluctant to deal on such terms.

Documentary Letters of Credit and Drafts

To protect the interests of both buyer and seller, documentary letters of credit or drafts are often used. Under both of these methods, outside intermediaries are involved and documents are required to be presented in order for payment to be made.

Both letters of credit and drafts may be paid immediately—that is, at sight—or at a later date. Drafts to be paid when presented are called sight drafts, while drafts that are to be paid at a later date—often well after the buyer receives the goods—are called time drafts or date drafts.

Since payment under these two methods is made on the basis of documents, all terms of sale need to be agreed to and clearly specified. For example, "net 30 days" should be specified as "net 30 days from acceptance" or "net 30 days from date of bill of lading," or some other similarly explicit event to avoid confusion and delay of payment. Likewise, the currency to be used in paying for the goods should be specified as "US$XXX" if payment is to be made in U.S. dollars or other currency or special arrangements. International bankers can explain local and bank requirements, as well as offer other helpful suggestions in how to structure such arrangements.

Banks charge fees—usually a (small) percentage of the amount of the payment—for handling letters of credit and generally lesser flat fees for handling drafts.

Documentary Collections

In a documentary collection the exporter forwards the goods to the importer, but forwards the documents (including all title and entry documents) necessary to take title and possession to his own bank for transmission to the buyer's bank. Under this arrangement—a form of international "cash on delivery"—the buyer's bank may not transfer the documents to the buyer until payment has been made or until the buyer's bank has guaranteed that payment will be made within a stated period of time.

Documentary collections function in the following manner:

1) Buyer and seller agree to the terms of the sale (as noted above);

2) Seller prepares goods and documentation for shipment;

3) Seller ships goods to buyer and then presents full documentation to his bank for transmission to the buyer's bank;

4) The buyer's bank receives the documents and notifies the buyer of their arrival;

5) Buyer inspects the documentation to ascertain its accuracy and completeness;

6) Buyer pays his bank for the documentation (including payment of the bank's fees);

7) In exchange for this payment, the bank turns the documentation over to the buyer;

8-9) Buyer then uses the documentation to take possession of and enter the goods;

8-9) Buyer's bank forwards payment to the seller's bank for the account of seller;

10) Seller's bank then credits the payment for the goods to the seller's account.

In this situation both the seller and the buyer experience only moderate risk.

Risks to the Seller

The buyer may not pay for the documents (and goods) which the seller has shipped. The buyer may not have actual funds or credit available when needed; the buyer may have lost the market for the goods; or simply have changed his or her mind about doing business with the seller.

In such cases, the seller may become liable for full freight charges, storage fees, cartage, legal and collection fees, spoilage, and other similar costs. The seller will have to ship the goods back to the port of origin, find a new buyer, or have the goods destroyed. In such a situation, the seller may be placed in a very compromising position.

However, there are several advantages to the buyer in this arrangement. First, the buyer has a period of time to secure financing (or sale) of the goods between the time the goods are ordered and the time he or she must actually pay for them. The buyer saves carrying charges during this time. In this type of arrangement, it is best for the seller to have a good association with the buyer.

Risks to the Buyer

Conversely, the buyer does not exercise any control over the date of shipment of the goods or the quality or quantity of goods shipped. The buyer may be desperately in need of the merchandise, whereas the seller might have changed the price, quantity, or the quality of the merchandise being forwarded. The buyer would then have the option to reject and not pay for the shipment. However, he might expose himself either to a greater loss or to a foregone profit by not accepting the shipment. In this case it is wise for the buyer to know the seller well enough to avoid these problems.

Import Letters of Credit

A letter of credit adds a bank's promise to pay the exporter to that of the importer once the exporter has complied with all the terms and conditions of the letter of credit. The importer applies for issuance of a letter of credit to the exporter and therefore is called the applicant; the exporter is referred to as the beneficiary.

Payment under a documentary letter of credit is based solely on the documents involved, not on the terms of sale or the condition of the goods sold. The documents essentially become the product, and the goods become largely irrelevant. Before payment, the bank responsible for making the payment verifies that all documents conform exactly to the terms in the letter of credit. If they do not match exactly, a discrepancy exists which must be resolved before payment can be made. Thus, the actual documents must comply with those specified in the letter of credit in every particular or detail.

A letter of credit issued by a U.S. bank is often confirmed by a foreign bank. This means that the foreign bank—the confirming bank—adds its promise to pay to that of the U.S.—or issuing—bank. An international banker can help importers determine what terms and level of bank involvement might be appropriate for a specific import transaction.

A letter of credit may be either irrevocable (that is, its terms cannot be altered unless both the importer and the exporter agree to the specific changes) or revocable (that is, either party may unilaterally make changes). A revocable letter of credit is inadvisable for the exporter, while it may offer some benefits to the importer. A letter of credit may be "at sight," requiring immediate payment upon presentation of the documents, or it may be a time or date letter of credit with payment to be made at a specified time in the future.

Any change made to a letter of credit after it has been issued is called an amendment. The fees charged by the banks involved in amending the letter of credit may be paid by either the exporter or the importer, but who is to pay which charges should be specified in the letter of credit in advance. Since changes can be time-consuming and expensive, every effort should be made to get the letter of credit right the first time.

The exporter is usually not paid until the advising or confirming bank receives the funds from the issuing bank, that is the advising bank does not advance funds before the transaction is fully completed. To expedite the receipt of funds, wire transfers may be used. However, individual bank practices vary, and the exporter may be able to obtain funds more rapidly by discounting the letter of credit at the bank. This does involve paying a service fee to the bank, as well as taking less than the face value.

A Typical Letter of Credit Transaction

Here is what typically happens when payment is made using an irrevocable letter of credit:

1. After the buyer and seller agree on the terms of a sale, the buyer arranges for his or her bank to open (issue) a letter of credit.

2. The buyer's bank prepares an irrevocable letter of credit, including all instructions to the seller concerning the shipment.

3. The buyer's bank sends the irrevocable letter of credit to a correspondent bank in the seller's country, requesting confirmation. The seller may request that a particular bank serve as the confirming bank. If not, the U.S. bank selects a foreign correspondent bank of its choice.

4. The foreign bank prepares a letter of confirmation to forward to the seller along with the irrevocable letter of credit.

5. The seller carefully reviews all conditions in the letter of credit. If the seller cannot comply with one or more of the conditions, the buyer is alerted, in which case the parties must negotiate an amendment to the letter of credit.

6. The seller arranges with his or her freight forwarder to deliver the goods to the appropriate port or airport.

7. When the goods are loaded, the forwarder completes the necessary documents.

8. The seller (or the forwarder) presents to the foreign correspondent bank all the specified documents indicating full compliance with the terms of the letter of credit.

9. The foreign correspondent bank reviews the documents. If they are in order, the documents are airmailed or sent by courier to the buyer's bank for review. If the documents are deemed satisfactory, the buyer's bank forwards the documents to the buyer.

10. The buyer (or agent) gets the documents needed to claim the goods.

11. A draft, which often accompanies the letter of credit, is paid by the seller's bank to the seller at the time specified; the draft may also be discounted at an earlier date.

Drafts

A draft, sometimes called a bill of exchange, is analogous to a foreign buyer's check. Like checks used in domestic commerce, drafts carry the risk that they may be dishonored.

Sight Drafts

A sight draft is used when the exporter/seller wishes to retain title to the shipment until it reaches its destination and is paid for. Before the cargo can be released, the original ocean bill of lading forwarded by the seller to the buyer through the agent banks must be properly endorsed by the importer/buyer and surrendered to the carrier, allowing the buyer to take title.

Air waybills of lading, on the other hand, need not be presented in order for the importer/buyer to claim the goods. Hence, there is an element of increased risk to the exporter/seller when a sight draft is used with an air shipment.

In actual practice, the bill of lading or air waybill is endorsed by the exporter/shipper and sent via the exporter's bank to the importer's bank or to another intermediary along with a sight draft, invoices, and other supporting documents specified by either the importer/buyer or the authorities in the buyer's country (for example, packing lists, consular invoices, or insurance certificates). The bank notifies the importer when it has received these documents. As soon as the draft is paid, the bank releases the bill of lading, enabling the buyer to obtain the shipment.

When a sight draft is being used to control the transfer of title of a shipment, some risk remains for the exporter because the importer's ability or willingness to pay may change between the time the goods are shipped and the time the drafts are presented for payment. If the buyer cannot or will not pay for and claim the goods, returning or disposing of them becomes the problem of the exporter.

Time Drafts and Date Drafts

If the exporter is willing to extend credit to the buyer, a time draft can be used to state that payment is due within a certain time after the buyer accepts the draft and receives the goods, for example, 30 days after acceptance. By signing and writing "accepted" on the draft, the buyer becomes formally obligated to pay within the stated time. Once this is done the draft is called a trade acceptance and can either be retained by the exporter until payable in full at maturity or sold to a bank at a discount for immediate payment.

A date draft differs slightly from a time draft in that it specifies a date on which payment is due, for example, December 1, 1995, rather than simply a number of days after the draft is accepted. When a sight draft or time draft is used, the importer/buyer can delay making payment by delaying acceptance of the draft. A date draft can prevent this delay in payment but still must be accepted by the importer.

When a bank accepts a draft, it becomes an obligation of the bank, creating a negotiable instrument known as a banker's acceptance. A banker's acceptance can also be sold to a bank at a discount for immediate payment or by the bank to a third party.

Other Payment Mechanisms

Credit Cards

The use of credit cards as a payment mechanism has increased dramatically in recent years. It is not at all uncommon for an individual to start an import (or other) business using $30,000 or more of credit card credit from a half dozen credit cards. In the past it was only importers of low dollar value products such as jewelry and handicrafts that did this. Now, even importers of industrial products, machinery and electronics use credit cards to facilitate a transaction and get an effective 15 to 40 days free financing.

In some instances the exporter/seller will want to add a surcharge or lessen the discount on the goods sold to offset the charges that banks assess to the seller on the credit card transaction. You should also realize that merchants are particularly resistant to accepting credit card payments in countries experiencing high inflation, which can heighten their risk between the time of the transaction and the time they actually get paid by the bank (regardless of when the buyer pays off the charges). The several percentage points that the seller demands may make it inadvisable to use your card unless you really need the credit, or know you can turn the goods over quickly at a good margin upon your return to the U.S.

Tip: Get one of the "mileage" affinity credit cards, such as the "Mileage Plus" card tied to United, or the "Advantage Card" tied to American Airlines and get credit for airline flight coupons when you charge items (including your overseas airline tickets) on the credit card. Some of these cards do have a maximum of $10,000 of purchases per month which can be credited to the mileage program. Get a gold card for each program to rack up miles as you spend.

Tip: Be aware that a charge in a foreign currency on your domestic U.S. credit card will often subject you to disadvantageous foreign exchange rates. One solution: agree on the amount of the charge in U.S. dollars and have the credit card slip made out in U.S. dollars. (This ploy may not work in countries that have strict exchange controls, but it is worth a try.)

Consignment Sales

In international consignment sales, the same basic procedure is followed as in the U.S. The goods are shipped to a U.S. distributor to be sold on behalf of the foreign exporter/supplier. The foreign exporter/seller retains title to the goods until they are sold by the distributor. After the goods are sold, payment is forwarded to the exporter. Under the terms of this method, the exporter has the greatest risk and least control over the goods and may have to wait for an extended period before getting paid.

The U.S. importer/distributor can promote this sort of transaction with the foreign supplier by proposing and perhaps paying for some form of risk insurance or offering a particularly good discount or terms.

Countertrade and Barter

International countertrade is a trade practice whereby a supplier commits contractually, as a condition of the sale, to undertake specified initiatives that compensate and benefit the other party. It implies a set of linked quid pro quo transactions. The resulting trade gets around existing difficulties, such as financial (usually a lack of foreign exchange), marketing, or public policy concerns, while fulfilling the objectives of the trading parties. Not all suppliers consider countertrade to be objectionable, although perhaps the majority of U.S. exporters grudgingly view countertrade as a necessary evil that barely enables them to do business in markets that would otherwise be closed to them.

Simple barter is the direct exchange of goods or services between two parties; no money changes hands, although the parties must still impute values to their products. Pure barter arrangements in international commerce are rare, because the parties' needs for the goods of the other seldom coincide and because arriving at a mutually agreeable valuation of the goods may pose problems.

The most common form of compensatory trade practiced today involves contractually linked, parallel trade transactions each of which involves a separate financial settlement. For example, a countertrade contract may provide that the U.S. exporter will be paid in a convertible currency as long as the U.S. exporter (or another entity designated by the exporter) agrees to import a related quantity of goods from the foreign country in return.

U.S. exporters can take advantage of countertrade opportunities by trading through an intermediary with countertrade expertise, such as an international broker, an international bank, or an export management company. Some export management companies offer specialized countertrade services. Exporters should bear in mind that countertrade often involves higher transaction costs and greater risks than more straightforward export transactions.

The U.S. Department of Commerce can advise and assist U.S. exporters faced with countertrade requirements. The Office of Countertrade and Finance monitors countertrade trends, disseminates information (including lists of potentially beneficial countertrade opportunities), and provides general assistance to enterprises seeking barter and countertrade opportunities. For information, contact the Office of Countertrade and Finance, U.S. Department of Commerce, 14th and Constitution N.W., Rm. 1104, Washington, DC 20230; tel. (202) 482-4434.

The International Trade Administration publishes *International Countertrade: A Guide for Managers and Executives* and *International Countertrade: Individual Country Practices*, which give more information on countertrade and its use worldwide. These publications are available from:

> U.S. Government Printing Office (USGPO)
> Superintendent of Documents
> 710 N. Capital Street, NW
> Washington, DC 20401
> (202) 512-0132 (Order line)
>
> www.access.gpo.gov

The USGPO accepts phone orders paid by credit card as well as mail orders paid by credit card, a check drawn on a U.S. bank, or an international money order.

General Banking Services

Home Country Services for Importers

Banks provide the primary source of funding, not only for smaller export-import operations, but for larger operations as well. Most extend short-term credit—due in less than one year—on the basis of a line of credit which allows the customer to draw down amounts as needed up to the maximum specified. U.S. banks usually offer two kinds of lines of credit: straight advances and acceptances. Advances supply loans of fixed maturities on demand. The borrower usually must pay down outstanding balances at a specified time (often semiannually). Under acceptance credit, the bank will accept (pay) drafts on behalf of the customer, such as for approved import transactions. The customers themselves do not receive the funds, which are only disbursed to third party payees to cover specific eligible expenses. Borrowers usually must pay down their outstanding balances within six months.

For longer term credit—usually for periods up to three years' duration—most banks offer a revolving credit facility. Similar to a line of credit, revolving credit allows the borrower to use as much as he or she desires up to an agreed upon ceiling, paying off the outstanding balance at will. Interest is charged only on the amounts used, although there may be an annual commitment fee on the unused portion of the loan.

Loans for a period longer than three years—often called term loans because they are for a set time period, or term—generally involve a set payment schedule. This may include features such as amortization, grace period, balloon payment, or any number of other repayment scenarios. Amortization requires that each periodic payment be apportioned between interest and principal, so that the loan is largely self-canceling during its life. A grace period waives repayment of principal (and sometimes of interest as well) for a specified length of time. A balloon payment requires full repayment of remaining principal at the end of the loan period with only interest or relatively small principal payments being required prior to the actual closeout. Such intermediate credit facilities are often rolled over at the expiration of the term.

U.S. banks usually charge interest rates based on the prime rate—the rate charged to "prime," or average, business customers. The rate paid fluctuates with the prime rate, and the base may be prime-plus or prime-less, depending on the bank, the relationship with the borrower, and the circumstances and risk assessment of the particular deal.

Local currency financing source. Your bank may also be able to assist you in locating financing for your import operation in local currency in the country of origin. Terms, conditions, and costs for such financing vary literally all over the map.

Deposit and Payment Services

Most banks usually accept deposits and offer payment services, such as checks. If you have regular—or even temporary—cash balances, you may be able to take advantage of a cash management or other type of account paying interest on these balances.

Your international banker should be able to assist you in moving funds overseas via bank wire transfer, drafts issued in U.S. dollars, drafts issued in foreign currencies, international money orders, and letters of credit.

Few businesspeople operating overseas will be able to use personal checks or even business checks drawn on a U.S. bank. However, anything may be possible. It also helps if your bank has a branch in the country in which you are doing business.

U.S. banks can also arrange to transfer funds and conduct other transactions, often using advanced computer systems. The Clearing House Interbank Payment System (CHIPS), which links 90 New York financial institutions, handles about 90% of foreign exchange transactions and essentially all Eurodollar transactions (*see* "An Introduction to Foreign Exchange" below). The Society for Worldwide Interbank Financial Telecommunications (SWIFT) links U.S. banks to an international network designed to transmit messages regarding foreign exchange, bank wire transfers, and other financial advisories.

Domestic Foreign Exchange

Banks can often provide you with a supply of major foreign currencies with which to pay expenses abroad. This domestic purchase of foreign currency will generally be limited to the small amounts required for incidentals upon arrival in a foreign country. More favorable exchange rates will be available in the country of destination, but it is nice to have some local currency available when you land.

Trust receipts

Trust receipts are used when you want goods released to you for purposes of inspection, assembly, or Customs clearance. This often occurs when goods arrive ahead of documentation. The bank guarantees your performance to the shipping company. Banks also call these "ship-side bonds."

Credit Cards

Your bank can probably issue MasterCard and Visa credit cards to assist you in dealing with your general travel expenses. You may even be able to use such instruments to make some overseas purchases of goods (*see* above). You may also be able to use your credit card to get a cash advance or travelers checks from a member bank overseas. Depending on the charges and exchange rates applied to such transactions by your home bank, the host country bank, and local regulations, this may not be a particularly cheap way to transfer or access funds abroad. However, it beats getting stuck overseas without funds, and for smaller transactions is often much simpler and quicker than trying to have funds transferred through the banking system.

Tip: American Express allows its cardholders to obtain traveler's checks (and in some instances cash) overseas from its offices on presentation of their card and a personal check. You can also arrange for cash advances on your card. There are daily limits based on whether you hold a green, gold, or platinum American Express card.

Traveler's Checks

Traveler's checks are generally safer than cash because they can be replaced. They are usually easy to cash and convert in all but the most difficult venues. You can obtain them in U.S. dollars as well as in most other major currencies, allowing you to keep your funds in a stable currency until you need to use them. Many banks will issue traveler's checks to their established customers at no extra charge.

An Introduction to Foreign Exchange

One of the added uncertainties of conducting trade on an international basis is the fluctuation in exchange rates among currencies. The relative value between the U.S. dollar and the seller's currency may change between the time the deal is made and the time payment is received. A devaluation or rise in the foreign currency against the dollar causes either a windfall or a loss to one party or the other involved in the transaction.

For example, if the buyer has agreed to pay ε 40,000 for a shipment and the Euro is valued at US$1.18 (its approximate value mid 2003), the buyer would expect to pay US$47,200. If the Euro later rose in value to US$1.22—an increase of just over 3.0%, a not unlikely occurrence in the volatile short-term foreign exchange market—payment at the new rate would require US$48,800, for an added cost of US$1,600 to the importer. On the other hand, if the foreign currency fell in value to US$1.14, the importer would have to pay only US$45,600, saving US$1,600.

Most exporters and importers prefer to avoid such risk and not speculate on fluctuations in foreign exchange markets. This is especially true where achieving a stated fixed landed cost of the goods is vital to the importer. For example, to satisfy an existing contract with a third party for raw materials or finished goods.

One of the simplest ways for a U.S. importer to avoid this type of risk is to have prices quoted and establish payment in U.S. dollars in sale and purchase contracts. Fortunately, the U.S. dollar is widely accepted as an international trading currency, and U.S. firms can often arrange to execute contracts and payments in dollars.

If the exporter/seller asks to receive payment in a foreign currency, the importer should consult an international banker before negotiating the purchase contract. Banks can offer advice on foreign exchange trends and risks. Many international banks can also help the importer hedge against such a risk if necessary.

Terms and Concepts

International trade and other transactions involving cross-border flows of funds require the participants to enter the world of foreign exchange. Foreign exchange is defined as claims payable in a foreign country in a foreign currency. (Foreign exchange is often referred to as forex or simply abbreviated as FX.) As a rule, businesses and individuals operate using their own national currencies— money recognized and legally acceptable for transactions (legal tender) within the particular currency zone (the territorial area in which a given currency is recognized, usually coinciding with national boundaries).

For example, the seller in Japan usually wants to be paid in his or her own currency—the yen (¥)—rather than in that of a U.S. importer, who in this case operates using U.S. dollars (US$). However, the seller may on occasion prefer to be paid, for example, in Euros (ε) in order to pay off obligations due in that currency to a German firm. And a French business traveler going to Montreal to negotiate a deal will need to pay expenses in Canadian dollars (Can$) rather than with Euros (E). A British investor may need to convert English pounds sterling (£) into Indian Rupees (Rs) to put funds into a venture in that country. All of these scenarios require the participants to convert a home currency into one or more foreign currencies or vice versa.

Currencies

A currency which can be readily exchanged for another is known as a convertible currency. If it can be fully, readily, and legally converted under virtually all circumstances, a currency is referred to as being unrestricted. Many countries maintain restricted convertibility on their currencies, often allowing full convertibility only for nonresidents while limiting the ability of residents to exchange domestic for foreign currencies. Other countries have inconvertible currencies, which cannot legally be taken out of the country or exchanged for foreign currencies at all. Yet other countries distinguish between foreign exchange involving current transactions (for goods and services) and those involving capital investments, with freedom of convertibility being restricted to some degree for one category or the other. This situation often results in what is known as a two-tier market, in which access to restricted currency is rationed and those who need it must obtain special authorization to acquire it. Such exchange controls ration the availability of foreign currency, which can block imports into the country. These limitations often result in a thriving illicit black market trade in currencies and commodities.

Hard currencies are those of large, strong economies which have few if any restrictions on the use and exchange of their currencies, while soft currencies are those for which there is little or no demand due to restrictions on free exchange (this is usually also a function of a limited or weak economy). International financial operations are usually transacted using key currencies, that is those which are relatively strong, broadly convertible, and generally accepted. Such currencies, sometimes referred to as reserve currencies, are used as a store of liquid wealth by other countries, which keep their international reserves in these hard currencies. The US dollar ($), Japanese Yen (¥), English pound (£), European Union Euro (E), Canadian dollar (Can$), and Swiss franc (SwF) are generally considered to be key or reserve currencies, and most international business is transacted using—or at least with reference to—these currencies.

Rates of Exchange

The exchange rate is simply the amount of a nation's currency that can be bought at a given time for a specified amount of the currency of another country. For example, as of mid 2003, $/¥=117.3, meaning that one U.S. dollar was equal to 117.3 Japanese yen. The exchange rate is given either as a direct quote—expressed as the number of units of one foreign currency against another, for example (.848E/$), or as an indirect quote, expressed as the number of US$ per unit of foreign currency (1.18$/E), which is the reciprocal of the first quote. Because the US$ is the most commonly traded currency, international foreign exchange transactions are usually quoted directly using the US$ as the reference point. (Note that the Euro is steadily gaining importance.) Thus an inquiry from a Swiss bank

to a German bank about their rates would be quoted not in SwF/E but in E/US$, even though both parties understand that the Swiss bank is interested in the rate of the E against the SwF, not the US$.

This necessitates the use of cross-rates, in which currencies are not compared directly with each other but in terms of a reference currency which serves as a common denominator. For example, in order to find the rate for the SwF/E, you must first have quotes on both currencies in US$ (1.2845SwF/US$ and .848E/US$), then use them to calculate the rate for SwF/E with reference to the common dollar rates of each (1.2845/.848=.1.514SwF/E).

Forex traders quote bid and ask price ranges, with the first figure always that at which they stand ready to buy currencies and the second (always higher) figure that at which they are willing to sell. This difference is conceptually similar to buying wholesale and selling retail, and constitutes the spread, or base profit margin for the institution. Professional traders deal not in full quotes but in a shorthand, referred to as pips or ticks. These are the last decimal places in a quote, usually 1/100th, or .01, of a percent (professionals are assumed to know the base rates and deal only in the marginal fluctuations).

The necessary series of conversions allows for the possibility of arbitrage, which involves taking advantage of temporal and spatial anomalies in pricing in the international currency markets. If, as in the example above, the German bank's price on SwF is less than the Swiss bank can get for them in Hong Kong, it will buy SwF from the German bank and immediately sell them to the Hong Kong bank to make a profit on the price differential. However, because virtually all international currency transactions are quoted against the US$ and because instant communications and 24-hour trading compensate for distance and time differences, the opportunities for such arbitrage are few. Professional traders now generally use the term to refer to trading for the institution's own account rather than for that of a client.

The actual amount received in a conversion, or the effective exchange rate, usually differs from the stated rate because it takes into account all taxes, commissions, and other costs that the public must pay to complete the transaction and actually receive the foreign funds.

Setting Exchange Rates

The relative value of one currency against another depends on a variety of economic and political factors, but ultimately it boils down to supply and demand. The main economic factor is the equilibrium rate, or purchasing power parity, at which goods would cost the same in each country. This ignores many important factors, such as quality, exportability, and long-term capital flow issues, but serves as a useful approximation of the relative strength of currencies against each other. If the same amount of currency in country A buys the same goods as an equivalent amount of currency in country B, the currencies are at parity. If the same amount of currency buys more goods in country A than in country B, then the currency of country A is undervalued and/or that of country B is overvalued.

A nation's current account balance (the sum of the value of goods and services it has exported during a given period netted against the value of those imported during the same period plus any transfer payments remitted abroad) can be used as a barometer of a country's economic strength. If the economy is consistently in a surplus position, that is it has received more than it has paid out, its currency can be expected to strengthen, or appreciate (rise in value) over time. Conversely, in a deficit position—one in which it spends more than it takes in—its currency will be expected to weaken, or depreciate (lose value) with respect to that of trading partners maintaining a surplus. Most countries keep foreign currency reserves to pay for current needs and serve as a cushion for fluctuations in the international income and outgo of funds.

Nations generally try to manage their currencies to maintain stable exchange rates against those of their trading partners. This can be done in a number of ways. The authorities may attempt to maintain a fixed exchange rate in which the value of their currency is linked to a commodity, such as gold, or to another strong currency, such as the US$. When a currency is linked directly to that of a stronger country (usually its main trading partner), it is said to be pegged to that of the stronger country whose lead it follows. The nations of the world have generally been unable to maintain such fixed rates in the volatile and increasingly integrated global economy of the 20th century, leading to the use of floating rates. Since the 1970s, most national currencies have floated, allowing their value to be determined through fluctuations against a variety of other currencies.

Floats can be clean, that is, determined solely by market forces without official interference (a situation that never really occurs in the real world), or dirty—managed to a greater or lesser extent by government authorities. Although some governments arbitrarily set exchange rates and policies to enforce them, such management usually involves intervention, or attempts to influence markets. This is accomplished primarily through open market operations in which the government buys or sells large quantities of its own or another country's currency or securities in an attempt to influence the relationship between the two by altering supply and demand factors. Because foreign exchange markets are so large and active, it has become virtually impossible for any government or international agency to effectively exercise control over exchange rates.

In practice, floating exchange systems rely on a variety of mechanisms to set actual prices. The main ones involve trade-weighted rates which hinge on the degree of importance of a given country's trade with the nation. A variation of this is to use a basket of currencies in which the exchange rate is figured in proportion to the value of the various currencies among the designated countries. This has been implemented by such schemes as the snake, a system in which northern European countries agreed to keep their currencies within a certain proportional relationship to each other (because adjustments occurred serially rather than simultaneously, the effect of such changes as they worked through the system was thought to resemble the undulations of a snake). The crawling peg—in which a country with a subsidiary currency commits to

adjust by incremental stages to maintain its agreed upon level with respect to the stronger currency that it tracks—represents a further variation on this theme. Often the pegged currency will have a daily or weekly limit on how much it can rise or fall to adapt to the target currency. The fixed band within which a currency is allowed to fluctuate is called the grid.

On occasion a currency cannot move either rapidly or far enough by using such mechanisms to reach an equilibrium point. The authorities must then realign, or change the official value of, the currency. Such realignments may require officials to devalue—officially reduce its value relative to that of the currency of another country—or revalue—officially raise its value relative to that of another country. In devaluation, the country's currency buys less, hurting imports (but also perhaps boosting sales of its now-cheaper exports). Upward revaluation allows the country to buy more abroad with its more valuable currency, but usually cuts into overseas sales of its now more expensive exports.

The Mechanics of Foreign Exchange Operations

Most foreign exchange trading stems from the need to acquire foreign currency for a specific transaction. If the conversion is for use in a current transaction, it occurs in the spot market at the current price, or spot rate, for immediate delivery (actually within two business days). If the foreign exchange is required for a future transaction, it occurs in the forward market for future delivery. The basic difference between the prices in the spot and forward markets is due to the relative levels of interest rates in the two countries. If a currency is actually held by the party, it can earn interest between now and when it is needed at prevailing money market rates. Or, conversely, it must be borrowed at a cost commensurate with the value of the interest earnings foregone by the lender. So the forward price will include the amount of interest which could be earned during the period, usually making forward rates higher than spot rates due to this premium.

However, there are instances in which other economic or political factors cause a currency to depreciate so that it can be bought more cheaply in the future than in the present. When such a discount or markdown exists, it is profitable to buy the currency forward rather than at spot prices.

Hedging Risks

The ability to buy forward foreign exchange allows businesses to hedge their risks by counterbalancing a current transaction through a similar future transaction to offset the effects of price changes during the interim. In currency trading this is often accomplished through a swap—the spot purchase (or sale) of foreign exchange and a simultaneous forward sale (or purchase) of the same currency. A spot purchase coupled with a future sale is known as an outward swap, while a spot sale linked to a forward purchase is an inward swap. A forward purchase or sale not covered by an offsetting spot transaction is known an outright transaction. Actual holdings of a currency are known as long positions, while those with uncovered future positions, that is with net indebtedness, are said to be short of exchange.

It is possible to buy forward (or futures) contracts for set amounts of major currency deliverable at a specified future date. These can vary from short-term spot/next swaps (in which the spot side is the current price and the offsetting closeout position is the price on the next business day) and tom/next swaps (in which the current price is that for the next business day and the offsetting position is valued at the price for the next business day after that) to positions as far out as one year.

Standard futures contracts are for two, three, six, and 12 months, but coverage can be achieved for intermediate periods through contracts that specify broken dates—those which fall between two standard contracts. In this case the rates are interpolated between those of the standard contracts. Most entities hedge long-term risks by rolling over a series of short-term contracts.

Options

While futures—contracts to buy or sell a specified quantity of foreign currency at a stated date in the future, the basis of forward transactions—are useful for hedging risks, options are largely speculative instruments. Options contracts allow foreign exchange traders the right to buy (call) or sell (put) specified quantities of currencies at a point in the future. If an option is in the money—that is the actual price is above the exercise price and therefore the option is profitable—it can be exercised. If it is out of the money (the exercise price being below the actual price and therefore unprofitable to exercise), it can be allowed to expire. Options traders seldom if ever take delivery of the actual currencies but simply close out the profitable contracts for the amount of the profit. Contracts known as American options can be exercised at any time during the life of the contract, while European options can only be exercised on the expiration date.

Markets

Despite the growth of trade and an increasingly interdependent global economy, most foreign exchange trading involves financial institutions trading for their own accounts rather than straight business transactions on behalf of clients. Such activity serves to add depth and liquidity to the forex market. Because of the high turnover in self- liquidating transactions—many of which are highly leveraged—the nominal dollar value of the volume of such trade far outstrips that of the underlying economic and monetary base that supports it. Major foreign exchange markets are run out of New York, London, Frankfurt, Amsterdam, Zurich, Singapore, Hong Kong, and Tokyo, but traders can operate anywhere thanks to modern communications links. Trading is most active during the business hours in these respective locations, but can occur 24-hours a day.

Euromarkets—consisting of informal markets to deal in transactions involving a currency outside of its country of origin—provide offshore international access to funds unencumbered by governmental regulation. London, Frankfurt, Zurich, and Amsterdam are the main centers of this

trade. The US$ accounts for about half of the Euromarket, with the Euro, Swiss Franc, and Japanese Yen collectively making up most of the remainder. The Asian dollar market, operating primarily out of Singapore, is also growing rapidly. Again the US$ is the primary currency, but use of the Japanese Yen is increasing. By some accounts, more US dollars are traded in such markets than in the domestic U.S. market. For example, the average daily turnover in the Singapore Asian dollar market was nearly US$150 billion in 2000.

Within the U.S., futures contracts are handled through the International Monetary Market of the Chicago Mercantile Exchange. Standard foreign exchange options are traded through the Philadelphia Stock Exchange and the Chicago Board Options Exchange. Many large, internationally-oriented banks will write specific nonstandard futures contracts to cover the needs of clients.

Documentary Credits (Letters of Credit)

General Section

The following material has been provided by Swiss Bank Corporation. World Trade Press gratefully acknowledges Swiss Bank Corporation for their contribution.

Growing economic interdependence and new transport possibilities have now made it feasible to do business with even the remotest corners of our planet. For many transactions, both prepayment and supply of the goods on a credit basis are out of the question. Besides, many countries have sunk deeply into debt in recent years. These trends have increased the desire for security on the part of both sellers and buyers.

If the purchase contract or similar agreement provides for payment against a documentary credit, it is up to the buyer to instruct his bank to open a documentary credit in favour of the seller.

The documentary credit is a

commitment on the bank's part to place an agreed sum at the seller's disposal on behalf of the buyer under precisely defined conditions.

When the seller receives such a documentary credit, he knows that a party independent of the buyer will make payment as soon as he has delivered the goods and the bank has handed over the prescribed documents and fulfilled the other conditions of the documentary credit. The buyer, on the other hand, is sure that the documentary credit amount will be released only against receipt of the documents he has specified.

So it is nothing more than a typical cash-on-delivery transaction requiring simultaneous performance. The documentary credit makes it possible to bridge both distance and time.

The Bank as Fiduciary

The bank assumes an extremely important fiduciary function between the parties. On the one hand, it must make certain on behalf of the issuing bank that the guaranteed sum is released only when the credit conditions have been complied with to the letter. On the other hand, the bank should do everything possible to safeguard the interests of the beneficiary (seller)—usually a customer of the advising, confirming bank—vis-à-vis the buyer should the documents fail to meet the credit conditions in any respect.

The "Uniform Customs and Practice for Documentary Credits"

In the course of time, a number of practices, expressions and terms have evolved between banks dealing with documentary credits. To ensure uniformity of interpretation in international trade, the International Chamber of Commerce in Paris has worked out the "Uniform Customs and Practice for Documentary Credits." These have been revised and brought up to date several times in the past. They are now applied by the banks in nearly all countries.

For the sake of simplicity, we shall refer to these rules in this publication with the abbreviation

UCPDC

(Uniform Customs and Practice for Documentary Credits).

The UCPDC states that it should be applied for all transactions where a bank is instructed by a customer to make a payment or to accept bills of exchange against receipt of certain documents.

The Term "Documentary Credit"

For the sake of simplicity, the expression "credit" will be used in this publication.

In actual practice, however, a number of different expressions have emerged for this type of business, all of which basically mean the same thing. People speak of "documentary letter of credit," "commercial letter of credit," "letter of credit" (L/C, elcee, LoC) or "Lettre de Crédit." In its forms, Swiss Bank Corporation uses the expression "documentary credit."

Different Terms

Some Important Principles

- Credits are separate transactions from the purchase contracts or other contracts on which they are based.

   Only the wording of the credit is binding on the bank.

   As far as customers are concerned, this means that the banks act only on the basis of the credit's text in carrying out the transaction, and cannot take into account any contract provisions that differ from the credit wording. The same applies to contracts modified at a later date without the credit text being changed accordingly. In this case, too, the bank will act exclusively in accordance with the valid credit wording when receiving and checking the documents.

- **Banks deal exclusively with the documents and not with goods (or services, etc.).**

   All the banks do is check, on the basis of documents presented to them, whether the conditions of the credit are fulfilled. They are not able to verify whether the goods supplied actually agree with those specified in the credit. The banks cannot be held liable for discrepancies between the goods invoiced and those actually delivered. It is up to the buyer and seller to settle questions of this nature between themselves.

   Buyers' complaints are settled directly between buyer and seller.

- **Banks assume no responsibility for the authenticity, form or validity of the documents.**

   The banks examine the documents they receive under a credit with due care. They check whether the documents appear on their face to comply with the specified terms and conditions.

- **Banks assume no responsibility for the acts of third parties taking any part in the credit transaction.**

   Banks assume no liability for

- delays, through no fault of their own, in the transmission of messages

- consequences of Acts of God

- acts of correspondent banks or other third parties whom they have instructed to carry out the transaction.

The Main Parties to a Documentary Credit Transaction

(Buyer's bank)

(Seller's bank)

How a Documentary Credit Functions

Acting in accordance with the agreements between seller and buyer, the buyer instructs his bank to open a credit.

Before the bank acts on the instructions, it checks whether the customer's balances or credit facilities will permit the payment to be made under the documentary credit.

If the bank is asked to open a documentary credit in favour of a foreign seller, it generally utilizes the services of a correspondent bank, if possible at the same location as the seller. This second bank is referred to as the advising bank. It forwards the credit of the issuing bank to the beneficiary.

Following receipt, the beneficiary checks whether he can meet the conditions mentioned in the credit and whether they agree with those stated in the purchase contract or other agreements.

If this is not the case, he asks the buyer directly to modify the credit conditions.

If the credit agrees with the purchase contract and the stipulated conditions can be met, the exporter will start manufacturing the goods or deliver them from stock. Following shipment, the beneficiary will assemble the required documents and present them to the advising bank.

The advising bank checks whether the documents received agree with the conditions of the credit in all respects. Afterwards it makes payment in the manner prescribed in the credit and transmits the documents to the issuing bank. The latter reimburses the advising bank the amount specified by the documents.

Issuance

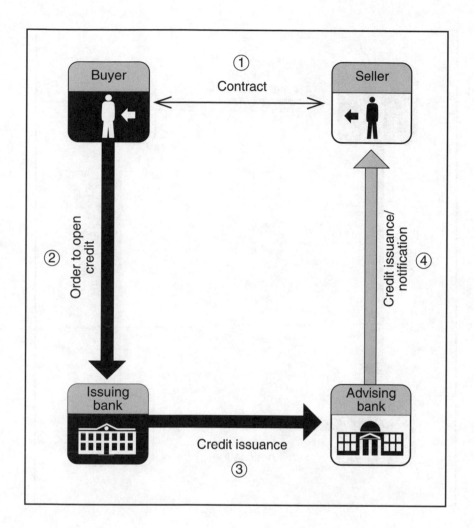

Issuance of a Letter of Credit

1. Buyer and seller agree on purchase contract.

2. Buyer applies for and opens a letter of credit with issuing ("buyer's") bank.

3. Issuing bank issues the letter of credit, forwarding it to advising ("seller's") bank.

4. Advising bank notifies seller of letter of credit.

Amendment

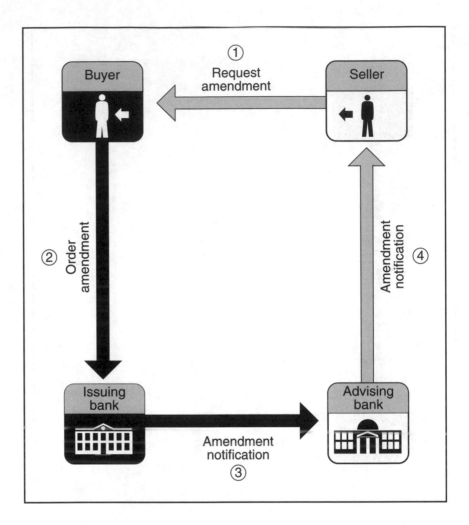

Amendment of a Letter of Credit

1. Seller requests (of the buyer) a modification (amendment) of the terms of the letter of credit. Once new terms are agreed upon:

2. Buyer issues order to issuing ("buyer's") bank to make an amendment to the terms of the letter of credit.

3. Issuing bank notifies advising ("seller's") bank of amendment.

4. Advising bank notifies seller of amendment.

Utilization

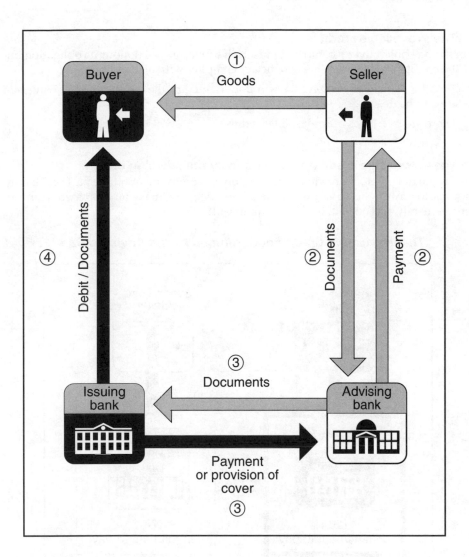

Utilization of a Letter of Credit

1. **Seller ships goods to buyer.**

2. **Seller forwards all documents (as stipulated in the letter of credit) to advising bank. Once documents are reviewed and accepted, advising bank pays seller for goods.**

3. **Advising bank forwards documents to issuing bank. Once documents are reviewed and accepted, issuing bank pays advising bank.**

4. **Issuing bank forwards documents to buyer. Seller's letter of credit, or account is debited.**

Forms of Documentary Credits

1. The revocable credit

The revocable credit can be modified or cancelled at any time. Because it offers little security, this form is hardly ever used.

2. The irrevocable credit

The issuing bank (buyer's bank) commits itself irrevocably to honour its obligation under the credit, provided that the beneficiary complies with all conditions.

Thus the beneficiary receives a firm undertaking of the issuing bank, giving him the security he desires.

There are two types of irrevocable credits:

a) The irrevocable credit not confirmed by the advising bank

Irrevocable documentary credits always involve a commitment on the part of the issuing bank to pay. In this case, the advising bank does not make any payment commitment. It merely acts on behalf of the issuing bank.

The Irrevocable Credit not Confirmed by the Advising Bank

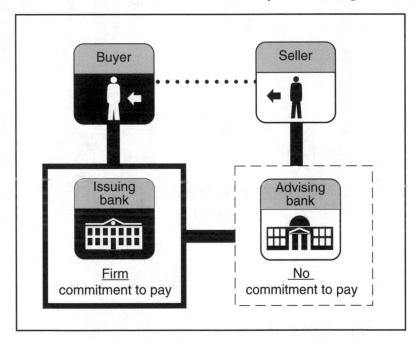

b) The irrevocable, confirmed credit

By confirming the credit, the advising bank enters into a commitment to pay that is independent of, and in addition to, the issuing bank's commitment. The confirming bank undertakes to honour its commitment regardless of whether or not the issuing bank is in a position to reimburse it.

The Irrevocable Confirmed Credit

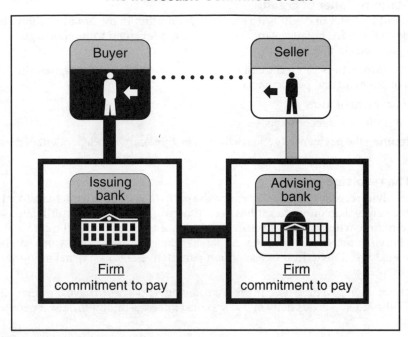

The documentary credit that affords an exporter the most security is one issued irrevocably by a foreign bank and confirmed by a domestic bank.

Availability

1. The sight credit

The amount is payable as soon as the prescribed documents have been presented and the bank has checked them. So the proceeds are normally at the immediate disposal of the beneficiary.

In some cases (e.g., foreign currencies) a few days may pass between presentation of the documents and actual transfer of the funds. As a rule it is the time required by the banks to remit the amount of the credit.

In the case of unconfirmed credits, situations can arise where the advising bank delays payment to the beneficiary until it has received the amount specified by the documents from the issuing bank.

2. The credit available against time drafts (usance credit)

In addition to presenting the documents, the beneficiary is required to draw a time draft on a specific bank (issuing, advising, or a third bank). After the documents have been found to be in order, the exporter receives the draft back after it has been accepted by the drawee bank, if he so wishes.

It is possible to discount this bank acceptance. So the draft can be cashed in immediately by the seller, while the buyer will be charged with the draft amount only upon maturity.

3. The deferred payment credit

The payment is not initiated immediately upon presentation of the documents, but only after a period of time specified in the credit.

A deferred payment credit allows the buyer a grace period, and ensures the seller that payment will be made on the due date.

Special Documentary Credits

1. Stand-by letter of credit

The stand-by letter of credit is a guarantee declaration in the broadest sense. It is used mainly in the USA, because American banks are prevented from giving guarantees by the regulations in that country.

Stand-by letters of credit can be used, for example, to guarantee the following types of payment and performance:

- repayment of loans
- fulfillment of subcontracts
- securing the payment of goods deliveries by third parties independent of the recipient

2. The revolving credit

The revolving credit is a commitment on the part of the issuing bank to restore the credit to the original amount after it has been utilized. The number of utilizations and the period of time within which these must take place are specified in the credit. It is either cumulative or non-cumulative. Cumulative means that unutilized sums can be added to the next instalment. In the case of non-cumulative credits, partial amounts not utilized in time expire.

The revolving credit is used in cases where a buyer wishes to have certain partial quantities of the ordered goods delivered at specified intervals (multiple delivery contract).

3. The transferable letter of credit

The beneficiary specified in the transferable letter of credit has the option of instructing his bank to transfer the credit fully or in part to another beneficiary.

4. The back-to-back credit

The "back-to-back" credit is a new credit opened on the basis of an already existing, *non-transferable* credit (original credit) in favour of another beneficiary (i.e., back-to-back).

The Documentary Credit and the Exporter

What benefits does the credit provide?

- The bank pays as specified in the credit independent of the buyer.
- The buyer cannot withhold the payment under any pretence.
- If the buyer wishes to complain about the goods, he must do this separately from the documentary credit, which gives the exporter a stronger negotiating position.
- The sort of delays that can occur in transmitting bank transfers are avoided to a large extent.
- Payments under documentary credits are generally made faster.

  The exporter enjoys these advantages only if he adheres precisely to the conditions of the credit.

  It should be noted that, in the case of credits in foreign currencies, the exchange risk can be eliminated by means of a forward sale of foreign exchange.

Which type of credit should the exporter demand?

Whether, for a particular transaction, it is better to open an irrevocable credit not confirmed by the advising bank or one confirmed by it depends on the circumstances of the particular case and the degree of security the exporter feels he needs.

- An irrevocable, unconfirmed credit:

  if the buyer's country has stable political conditions and an efficient banking system, and if the goods supplied are a product that could easily be sold to someone else if necessary.

- An irrevocable, confirmed credit:

  if any of the aforementioned points are not the case.

  The longer the delivery period, the more difficult it becomes to evaluate how the risk will develop with regard to the buyer's country and the banks there. If the goods to be delivered are the type that have very few potential customers or are made to order, substantial losses can be suffered if the documents are refused.

  The exporter can restrict these risks by requesting an irrevocable credit confirmed by the advising bank.

  The exporter should also prescribe that a credit be opened which requires the documents to be presented in his country and is also payable there. Otherwise, he would have to bear the possible consequences of loss of the documents in the mail or delayed transmission of them to the issuing bank. As a rule, it is impossible to confirm a credit payable in other countries.

What does the exporter do before the contract is closed?

- Makes enquiries about the creditworthiness and business practices of the buyer. The bank will generally be prepared to assist the exporter in obtaining this sort of information.
- Finds out which bank the buyer works with. The credit is normally issued by the bank with which the buyer maintains his account.
- Enquires about the regulations and experience of others in dealing with the buyer's country. Foreign currency restrictions and other rules in the buyer's country can delay the issuance of the credit. Chambers of commerce and the banks will be happy to provide the exporter with this information.
- If the exporter is prepared to supply the goods against an irrevocable credit not confirmed by the other bank, he enquires about the standing of the credit-issuing bank in the buyer's country.
- If he desires an irrevocable credit that is confirmed by his bank, he asks the bank whether it is ready and willing to confirm credits emanating from the buyer's country and the bank in question.

  The supply contract should be formulated in such a way that no difficulties arise later with regard to the credit's nature, conditions or procedure.

- For example, one should not readily accept contract provisions that specify credit documents such as acceptance reports, progress reports, etc., that have to be signed by the buyer.

  By refusing to sign such documents, the buyer can block the credit's availability.

  It is therefore advisable to demand a "no later than" clause as a credit condition, which provides for utilization of the credit without presentation of any papers counter-signed by the buyer. For instance:

  x% of the credit sum is payable against presentation of an acceptance report, signed by... (Buyer), but no later than... months after shipment, against the Seller's declaration that the contract conditions have been fulfilled and the object supplied is operating properly.

  In this case, it is not necessary to present the acceptance report.

What does the exporter do at contract closure?

The supply contract should contain the main data of the credit to be provided by the buyer, e.g.:

- Issuing bank
- Confirmation by the exporter's bank
- Time allowed for payment
- Validity period
- Bearer of the documentary credit expenses

Sample Supply Contract

> **Contract**
>
> XXX
> XX
> XXXXX
>
> XXX
> XXXXX
> XXXX
>
> XXXXX
> XX
>
> To secure payment, the buyer shall have bank x open an irrevocable credit (which is to be confirmed by bank y). The credit must remain valid for x months (corresponding to the delivery period) after issuance and be available at sight against presentation of the following documents:
>
> . . . .
> . . . .
> . . . .
>
> The cost of the credit shall be borne in full by the buyer.

The documents prescribed can vary considerably depending upon the import regulations in the buyer's country and the buyer's wishes.

The validity period of the credit should be set long enough to provide a reasonable amount of latitude and should include the time required for submission of the documents.

If the exporter is required by the contract to bear expenses arising in Switzerland, he should ask the bank for an estimate of the charges.

What does the exporter do when the credit arrives?

- Immediately upon receipt of the credit, the exporter checks whether its conditions agree with those of the supply contract and whether he is capable of complying with the clauses of the credit to the letter.

- If individual conditions of the credit have to be amended, which can be very time-consuming, the exporter should contact the buyer immediately so that the latter can instruct the issuing bank to make the required modifications.

- The modification becomes effective only when the exporter has received notification of the amendment from the advising/confirming bank.

- In the case of credits in foreign currency, the exporter decides whether to accept the concomitant risks himself or enter into a forward exchange transaction with the bank.

- Now the exporter should read the relevant Articles of the UCPDC and act in accordance with them.

  If the exporter fails to comply with even one of the credit's stipulations, the security afforded by the credit is lost, because it is possible to refuse acceptance of the documents in such cases.

Checklist (Upon Receipt of the Credit)

1. Are my name and address correct?	☐
2. Is the amount correct?	☐
3. Are the terms of delivery correct? (CIF, FOB, etc.)	☐
4. Is the validity period sufficiently long?	☐
5. Does the credit's availability form agree with the contract conditions?	☐
6. Can the goods be shipped by the prescribed transport route?	☐
7. Can the provisions relating to partial shipments and transhipment be met?	☐
8. Can I meet the shipping date?	☐
9. Certain goods are accepted by shipping companies for deck stowage only. If this is the case, is "on deck" stowage authorized?	☐
10. Can the insurance company provide the coverage specified?	☐
11. Are the goods correctly described?	☐
12. Is the credit confirmed?	☐
13. Can I present the documents with all of the clauses stipulated in the credit within the prescribed period?	☐
14. Does the forwarding agent have a copy of the credit?	☐

What does the exporter have to bear in mind when preparing the documents?

Documents that agree with the credit conditions in all respects make it possible for the credit to function without any snags.

The exporter should observe the following points when preparing the documents:

The invoice

- Is generally made out to the buyer specified in the credit.
- Is made out in the same currency as the credit amount.
- Contains exactly the same description of the goods as the credit.
- Value of the goods, individual prices and delivery terms agree with those specified in the credit.
- Any special notations, confirmations and attestations specified in the credit should be included on the invoice and—if required—signed.

The bill of exchange (draft)

- It should be drawn in the language of the credit. The bill of exchange form should carry any prescribed notations and clauses.

The insurance document

The insurance document specified in the credit must be submitted.

- It should be made out in the currency of the credit.
- In the absence of a stipulation to the contrary in the credit, it must be made out for the CIF value of the goods + 10%.

If the banks cannot determine the CIF value from the documents on their face, however, they will accept a minimum insurance amount that equals either the amount for which payment is requested under the credit or the amount of the commercial invoice, whichever is greater.

- The insurance document should list those risks for which the credit requires coverage.
- The insurance document must state expressly that the goods are insured starting no later than the shipping date.
- All insurance policies/certificates issued by the insurance company should be submitted to the bank and endorsed if necessary.

Sample Bill of Exchange

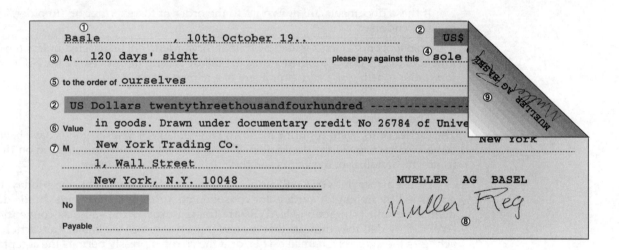

①	Place drawn and date
②	Bill of exchange currency and amount in numbers and words
③	Validity period
④	Number of originals (sole or first/second)
⑤	If issued to own order: endorsement required
⑥	Reference to credit
⑦	Drawee
⑧	Drawer (handwritten signature)
⑨	Endorsement

The transport documents

1. The ocean bill of lading

The banks will accept the following documents under this title:

- ocean bill of lading
- combined transport bill of lading
- short form bill of lading
- "received for shipment bill of lading," provided it carries the notation "on board."

Unless expressly permitted in the credit, the banks will reject the following bills of lading:

- charter party bills of lading
- bills of lading issued by a freight forwarder, if the forwarder does not act as carrier or as the agent of a named carrier.

2. Other marine transport documents

If the credit does not call specifically for an ocean bill of lading, the banks will accept a transport document that appears on its face to have been issued by a named carrier or his agent, and which indicates taking in charge of the goods, loading on board, or dispatch, and meets all other stipulations of the credit.

If the full set of transport documents consists of several identical originals, all of the originals should be submitted to the bank.

If these documents are drawn up to the order of the exporter or "to order," they must be endorsed.

Transport documents issued by freight forwarders will be rejected unless the document is the FIATA Combined Transport Bill of Lading (approved by the ICC) or the forwarder is acting as a carrier or agent of a named carrier.

3. The air waybill

The carrier or its agent confirms in the air waybill (AWB) that the goods have been received for carriage to the destination. This document contains information on the air route, the handling of the goods and their delivery to the consignee.

House air waybills (HAWB) are also common in the transport business today. They are issued by freight forwarders for consolidated air freight shipments. In the documentary credit transactions HAWBs are treated exactly the same as conventional AWBs, provided they indicate that the issuer itself assumes the liability as carrier or is acting as the agent of a named carrier, or if the credit expressly permits the acceptance of an HAWB.

4. Other transport documents

This heading includes, for instance:

- the postal receipt
- the rail waybill (duplicate)
- the forwarder's received bill of lading
- the road waybill

As a rule, none of these documents represents a negotiable instrument. They evidence the closure of the carriage contract between seller and carrier, and are documents in proof.

5. Additional documents

Any additional documents called for by the credit, such as certificates of origin, consular invoices, weight certificates, analysis certificates, etc., should be prepared by the parties prescribed in the credit.

In some cases, the certification and legalization of certain documents can take a considerable amount of time.

Sample Ocean Bill of Lading

```
BILL OF LADING FOR MULTIMODAL TRANSPORT OR PORT-TO-PORT SHIPMENT

1. SHIPPER
   SWISS EXPORT LTD              BOOKING No  55    B/L No  2
   INDUSTRIESTRASSE 200
   8050 ZUERICH - OERLIKON       REFERENCE No  ABC/22/66 bu

2. CONSIGNEE: ORDER OF
   TO ORDER

3. NOTIFY ADDRESS (carrier not responsible for failure to notify
                    see clause 21 hereof)          Shipping company
   TA PING CO. LTD                                 Schiffahrtsgesellschaft
   YACHT BUILDING                                  Société de transport maritime
   18-5, HARBOR STREET
   TAIPEI / TAIWAN

4. Pre-carriage by (*)        5. Place of receipt (*)
                                 ANTWERP   CFS
6. OCEAN VESSEL               7. PORT OF LOADING
   "HOLLANDIA"                   ROTTERDAM
8. PORT OF DISCHARGE          9. Place of delivery (**)
   KEELUNG                       KEELUNG  CFS
                              if goods to be transhipped by carrier at port of discharge.

10. Marks & Nos.    11. Number and kind of packages, description of goods   13. Gross weight kilos   14. Measurement m3

                    ON BOARD  -  FREIGHT PREPAID

ABC 1930-1934
VIA KEELUNG
TA PING          5 CASES CIF KEELUNG                    kos 1050
                   "HARMLESS CHEMICALS"

                 IRREVOCABLE CREDIT No 25AB/26008/01

                 IMPORT LICENSE No 75 DGL - 01111

Shipper's declaration of a value higher than the carrier's limit of liability - See clause 19:

Freight and charges          Freight: to be prepaid/to be collected
(particulars for calculation of freight only)

15. Freight payable at             16. Place and date of issue
    ANTWERP                            15.7.19
17. Number of original Bs/L        18 For the carrier
    3/3                                FORWARDING LTD

(*) Applicable only when document used for transhipment (see clause 2 b)
(**) Applicable only when document used for INTERMODAL transportation (see clause 2 c)    Page 2
```

Sample Forwarder's Received Bill of Lading

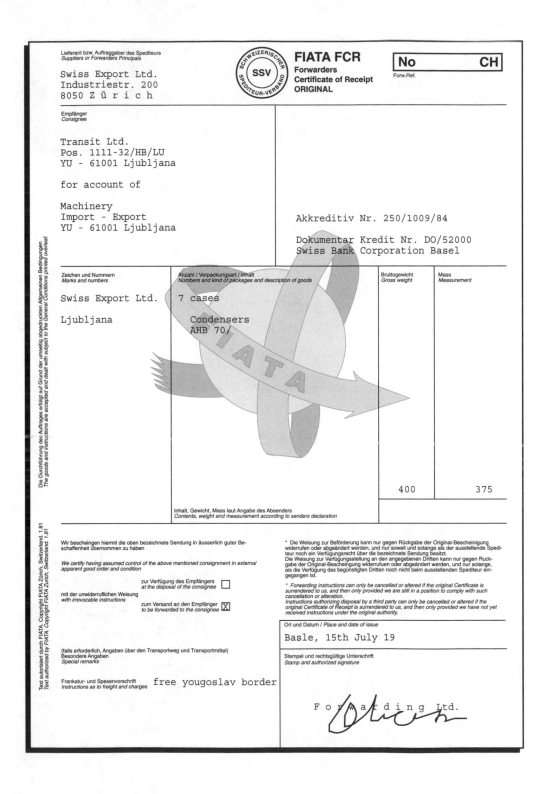

Sample Air Waybill

085 BSL | **7260 2751**   085-7260-2751

Shipper's Name and Address	Shipper's account Number	NOT NEGOTIABLE

SWISS EXPORT LTD
AIRFREIGHT DIVISION
ZUERICH

AIR WAYBILL
AIR CONSIGNMENT NOTE

swissair ✚

Issued by: Swiss Air Transport Co., Ltd., Zurich, Switzerland
Member of IATA (International Air Transport Association)

Copies 1, 2 and 3 of this Air Waybill are originals and have the same validity

Consignee's Name and Address | Consignee's account Number

IMPORT KONTOR
VIENNA

Phone: 633 7876

It is agreed that the goods described herein are accepted in apparent good order and condition (except as noted) for carriage SUBJECT TO THE CONDITIONS OF CONTRACT ON THE REVERSE HEREOF. THE SHIPPER'S ATTENTION IS DRAWN TO THE NOTICE CONCERNING CARRIERS' LIMITATION OF LIABILITY. Shipper may increase such limitation of liability by declaring a higher value for carriage and paying a supplemental charge if required.

Issuing Carrier's Agent Name and City

FORWARDING LTD
BASLE

Accounting information

Agent's IATA Code	Account No.
81-4 0000	

Airport of Departure (Addr. of the Carrier) and requested Routing
BSL-VIE

to	By first Carrier Routing and Destination	to	by	to	by	Currency	CHGS Code	WT/VAL PPD COLL	Other PPD COLL	Declared Value for Carriage	Declared Value for Customs
VIE	SWISSAIR					SFR		CQPP		NVD	

Airport of Destination	Flight/Date	For Carrier Use only Flight/Date	Amount of Insurance	INSURANCE - If carrier offers insurance and such insurance is requested in accordance with conditions on reverse hereof, indicate amount to be insured in figures in box marked amount of insurance.
VIENNA	SR436/8.7.			

Handling Information

No of Pieces RCP	Gross Weight	kg lb	Rate Class / Commodity item No.	Chargeable Weight	Rate / Charge	Total	Nature and Quantity of Goods (incl. Dimensions or Volume)
8	200,6	K	C 6750	201	1.90	381.90	CHEMICALS NOT RESTRICTED CONTRACT No 100-15-2
8	200,6						

Prepaid	Weight Charge	Collect	Other Charges
		381.90	AWA 15.00

Valuation Charge

Tax

Total other Charges Due Agent	
15.00	Shipper certifies that the particulars on the face hereof are correct and that insofar as any part of the consignment contains dangerous goods, such part is properly described by name and is in proper condition for carriage by air according to the applicable Dangerous Goods Regulations.

Total other Charges Due Carrier	
	SWISS EXPORT LTD / p.o. Forwarding LTD

Signature of Shipper or his Agent

Total Prepaid	Total Collect
15.00	381.90

Currency Conversion Rates	cc charges in Dest. Currency		
		07.07.	BASLE	Forwarding LTD

Executed on (Date) at (Place) | Signature of Issuing Carrier or its Agent

For Carrier's Use only at Destination	Charges at Destination	Total collect Charges

085-7260 2751

No. 3 - ORIGINAL for SHIPPER

Form 30.301
Printed in the Fed. Rep. Germany - Bartsch Verlag, Munich-Ottobrunn 600j (III)

Sample International Road Waybill

1 Absender (Name, Anschrift, Land) / Expéditeur (nom, adresse, pays) METALLWAREN AG CH-8904 AESCH	INTERNATIONALER FRACHTBRIEF / LETTRE DE VOITURE INTERNATIONAL Diese Beförderung unterliegt trotz einer gegenteiligen Abmachung den Bestimmungen des Übereinkommens über den Beförderungsvertrag im internat. Straßengüterverkehr (CMR) Ce transport est soumis, nonobstant toute clause contraire, à la Convention relative au contrat de transport international de marchandises par route (CMR)
2 Empfänger (Name, Anschrift, Land) / Destinataire (nom, adresse, pays) CIE PORTUGAISE D'ALUMINIUM P-PORTO	**16** Frachtführer (Name, Anschrift, pays) / Transporteur (nom, adresse, pays) TRANSPORT AG CH-4002 BASEL
3 Auslieferungsort des Gutes / Lieu prévu pour la livraison de la marchandise Ort/Lieu PORTO Land/Pays PORTUGAL	**17** Nachfolgende Frachtführer (Name Anschrift, Land) / Transporteurs successifs (nom, adresse, pays)
4 Ort und Tag der Übernahme des Gutes / Lieu et date de la prise en charge de la marchandise Ort/Lieu 8904 AESCH Land/Pays SCHWEIZ Datum/Date 18.8.19..	**18** Vorbehalte und Bemerkungen der Frachtführer / Réserves et observations des transporteurs
5 Beigefügte Dokumente / Documents annexés	

6 Kennzeichen u. Nr / Marques et numéros	**7** Anzahl d. Packstücke / Nombre des colis	**8** Art der Verpackung / Mode d'emballage	**9** Bezeichnung des Gutes* / Nature de la marchandise*	**10** Statistik-Nr. / No statistique	**11** Bruttogew. i. kg / Poids brut, kg	**12** Umfang in m³ / Cubage m³
95140/1-2	2	CAISSES	FITA DE ALPACA PARA O FABRICO DE COMPONENTES 0,6 x 350 x 700 (AS PER CONFIRMATION 1182 dd. 15.6.19..)		985.-	
Klasse / Classe	Ziffer / Chiffre	Buchstabe / Lettre (ADR)	(ADR)			

13 Anweisungen des Absenders (Zoll- und sonstige amtliche Behandlung) / Instructions de l'expéditeur (formalités douanières et autres) BANK REFERENZ CA 11-8804	**19** Zu zahlen vom / À payer par	Absender / L'expéditeur	Währung / Monnaie	Empfänger / Le Destinataire	
	Fracht / Prix de transport				
	Ermäßigungen / Réductions				
	Zwischensumme / Solde				
	Zuschläge / Suppléments				
	Nebengebühren / Frais accessoires				
	Sonstiges / Divers				
	Zu sahl. Gesamtsum. Total à payer				
14 Rückerstattung / Remboursement					
15 Frachtzahlungsanweisungen / Prescription d'affranchissement Frei / Franco FREIGHT PREPAID Unfrei / Non franco	**20** Besondere Vereinbarungen / Conventions particulières				

21 Ausgefertigt in / Etablie à BASEL am/le 18.8. 19..			**24** Gut empfangen / Réception des marchandises Datum / Date	
22 *TRANSPORT AG* (signature) Unterschrift und Stempel des Absenders / (Signature et timbre de l'expéditeur)	**23** Unterschrift und Stempel des Frachtführers / (Signature et timbre du transporteur)		am/le .... 19 .... Unterschrift und Stempel des Empfängers / (Signature et timbre du destinataire)	

25 Angaben zur Ermittlung der Tarifentfernung mit Grenzübergängen			**28** Berechnung des Beförderungsentgelts					
von	bis	km	frachtpfl. Gewicht in kg	Tarifstelle: Sonderabmachung	Güterarten	Währung	Frachtsatz	Beförderungsentgelt

26 Vertragspartner des Frachtführers ist - kein - Hilfsgewerbetreibender im Sinne des anzuwendenden Tarifs

27	Amtl. Kennzeichen	Nutzlast in kg		
Kfz				
Anhänger				Summe

Benutzte Gen. Nr ....   National, Bilateral, EG, CEMT

Ausfüllen unter der Verantwortung des Absenders / A remplir sous las responsabilité de l'expéditeur   **1 – 15** einschließlich / y compris et   **21 + 22** Die mit fett gedruckten Linien eingerahmten Rubriken müssen vom Frachtführer ausgefüllt werden. / Les parties encadrées de lignes grasses doivent être remplies par le transporteur.

Checklist (Prior to Submission of the Documents)

1. Do all documents refer to the same order and the same credit?	☐
2. Are all the documents present in the prescribed number and in complete sets?	☐
3. Do all of the dimensions, weights, number of packing units, and markings agree on all the documents?	☐
4. If necessary, have all documents been certified and/or legalized?	☐
5. Is the invoice addressed exactly as prescribed in the credit?	☐
6. Do the goods description, unit price and goods value in the invoice agree exactly with the text of the credit?	☐
7. Does the amount of the invoice not exceed the available credit sum?	☐
8. Is the bill of exchange legally signed?	☐
9. Does the bill of exchange have to be endorsed?	☐
10. Does the insurance document cover all of the risks specified?	☐
11. Is the insurance document endorsed?	☐
12. Has the delivery period been maintained?	☐
13. Does the freight notation on the transport document agree with the supply conditions?	☐
14. Is the consignee in the transport document or the order in the bill of lading correct?	☐
15. Is the bill of lading clean?	☐
16. Are "on deck" bills of lading allowed under the terms of the credit?	☐
17. Are charter party bills of lading allowed under the terms of the credit?	☐
18. Is the notify address in the bill of lading correct?	☐
19. Is the bill of lading endorsed?	☐
20. Are corrections on the transport and insurance documents initialled by the originator?	☐

What does the bank do upon receipt of the documents?

It checks whether the documents agree with the credit conditions and the UCPDC in all respects. Because this check must be carried out painstakingly, the bank requires a reasonable period of time for it.

If the documents are found to be in order, the bank proceeds as follows:

- **In the case of a confirmed credit**

Depending on the type of availability specified in the credit, it either pays the value of the documents, or it accepts a bill of exchange for that value and places it at the disposal of the beneficiary, or, in the case of a deferred payment credit, it issues the beneficiary an irrevocable promise to pay.

- **In the case of an unconfirmed credit**

The advising bank has no commitment to pay, to accept, or to issue a promise to pay. If adequate credit balances are available or special arrangements have been made, however, the bank will pay immediately or accept the prescribed draft. If this is not the case, the bank sends the documents to the issuing bank and demands respective cover.

If it wishes to do so, the advising bank can credit the beneficiary's account with the value of the documents even before the requested cover is received, but with the notation "under usual reserves" (u.u.r.).

The notation "u.u.r." means that the beneficiary is obliged to repay the credited amount plus interest, charges and exchange rate difference if the issuing bank fails to provide the cover for one reason or another.

Discrepancies in the Documents

If the documents are found to be *not* in order, the bank's commitment to pay is invalidated. Thus the exporter loses the surety he had obtained with the credit.

The bank and the exporter then work together to arrive at solutions to restore the credit's surety:

- If possible, the exporter can correct the documents or have them rectified in order to be able to present them within the periods specified in the credit.
- The advising bank can ask the issuing bank for authorization to accept the documents despite the discrepancies found.

If the exporter agrees, the advising bank can send the documents to the issuing bank for collection.

In the case of a sight credit, the advising/confirming bank has the prerogative of deciding whether it wishes to credit the exporter's account under proviso despite the discrepancies in the documents.

Provisional Payment

By making a provisional payment, the advising/confirming bank accommodates the exporter even though it has no commitment nor is authorized by the credit terms to do so. If the documents are not accepted by those ordering the credit or the issuing bank, the advising bank will demand repayment of the credited amount plus accrued interest, charges and exchange rate differences (if any).

The Documentary Credit and the Export Risk Guarantee (ERG)

- For the fulfilling of export orders involving special payment risks, it is often possible to apply for the Swiss government's Export Risk Guarantee. [For Swiss exporters.] Information on the detailed requirements and conditions can be obtained from the Export Risk Guarantee Office.[*]
- Under certain circumstances, the advising bank may be prepared to confirm a credit only if the exporter is granted the ERG and agrees to assign the ERG claims, together with the original claim, to the confirming bank. In this case the exporter mentions expressly in his application to the ERG that the bank is prepared to confirm the credit only if the ERG is granted for this transaction.

---

[*]Swiss Export Risk Guarantee Office (GERG), P.O. Box, 8032 Zurich

The Documentary Credit and the Importer

What benefits does the documentary credit provide?

- By opening a credit, the importer confirms his financial soundness and may be able to obtain more favourable payment terms.
- The goods will be delivered in accordance with the delivery conditions stated in the credit.
- The buyer receives the documents he has demanded reasonably quickly.
- The buyer can be certain that he only has to pay if the documents comply with the credit terms in all respects.

Incidentally it should be borne in mind that the exchange risk involved with import credits in foreign currencies can be eliminated by purchasing forward foreign exchange.

Which type of credit should the importer provide?

As a rule, the foreign seller will demand an irrevocable credit. In this case, the backing of a first-class Swiss bank should satisfy him. The issuing bank assumes the commitment to pay on behalf of the importer. This commitment should be covered by a credit agreement between the issuing bank and the importer. But if the foreign seller insists on having the credit confirmed additionally by his own bank, he should bear the additional cost of this.

If the importer and seller have agreed upon an extended payment period, it is necessary to open a deferred payment credit. This documentary credit form increases the importer's expenses because of the prolonged commitment on the part of the issuing bank.

The banks are pleased to supply their customers with free application forms for opening documentary credits.

All documentary credits opened by banks in Switzerland are subject to the UCP-DC. Consequently, these guidelines also apply to the instructions the importer gives his bank.

When filling out the individual items of the credit application form, observe the following points:

Sample Application Form for Opening Documentary Credit

Sender M ü l l e r Ltd. Tellstrasse 26 4053 Basle Our reference AB/02	**Instructions to open a Documentary Credit** Basle, 30th September 19.. Place / Date
Please open the following [X] irrevocable [ ] revocable documentary credit	**Swiss Bank Corporation** Documentary Credits P.O. Box 4002 Basle
Beneficiary ① Adilma Trading Corporation 27, Nihonbashi, Chiyoda-ku Tokyo 125 / Japan	Beneficiary's bank (if known) ④ Japanese Commercial Bank Ginza Branch Tokyo 37 / Japan
Amount ② US$ 70'200.--	Please advise this bank [ ] by letter [X] by letter, cabling main details in advance [ ] by telex / telegram with full text of credit
Date and place of expiry ③ 25th November 19.. in Basle	
Partial shipments [X] allowed [ ] not allowed Transhipment [ ] allowed [X] not allowed	Terms of shipment (FOB, C & F, CIF) CIF Rotterdam
Despatch from / Taking in charge at For transportation to Japan Rotterdam	Latest date of shipment Documents must be presented not later than 10th Nov. 19.. ③ 15 days after date of despatch
Beneficiary may dispose of the credit amount as follows [X] at sight upon presentation of documents ⑤ [ ] after ....days, calculated from date of	[ ] by a draft due .... drawn on [ ] you [ ] your correspondents which you / your correspondents will please accept
against surrender of the following documents ⑥ [X] invoice (....3......copies) Shipping document [X] sea: bill of lading, to order, endorsed in blank [ ] rail: dublicate waybill [ ] air: air consignment note [ ]	[X] insurance policy, certifcte (.......... copies) covering the following risks: "all risks" including war up to [ ] Additional documents final destination in Switzerland [X] Confirmation of the carrier that the ship is not more than 15 years old [X] packing list (3 copies)
Notify address in bill of lading / goods addressed to Müller AG, Tellstrasse 26,⑦ 4053 Basle	Goods insured by [ ] us [X] seller

Goods ⑧
 	
1'000 "Record players ANC 83 as per proforma invoice
     no. 74/1853 dd 10th September 19.."
 	
     at US$ 70.20 per item	

Your correspondents to advise beneficiary [ ] adding their confirmation [X] without adding their confirmation ⑨ Payments to be debited to our Swiss Francs.............account no 10-326'791.0	
NB. The applicable text is marked by [X]	
E 6801 N 1/2 3.81 5000	MÜLLER AG BASEL Signature _Müller Frey_ For mailing please see overleaf

Sidebar text (left margin): This credit is subject to the «Uniform customs and practice for documentary credits» fixed by the International Chamber of Commerce. It is understood that you do not assume any responsibility neither for the correctness, validity or genuineness of the documents which will be remitted to you nor for the description, quality, quantity and weight of the goods thereby represented.

1. **Beneficiary**

   The company name and address should be written completely and correctly. Incomplete or incorrect information results in delays and unnecessary additional cost.

2. **Amount**

   Is the figure a maximum amount or an approximate amount?

   If words like "circa," "ca.," "about," etc., are used in connection with the amount of the credit, it means that a difference as high as 10% upwards or downwards is permitted. In such a case, the same word should also be used in connection with the quantity.

3. **Validity period**

   The validity and period for presentation of the documents following shipment of the goods should be sufficiently long to allow the exporter time to prepare his documents and submit them to the bank.

   Under place of validity, state the domicile of either the advising or the issuing bank.

4. **Beneficiary's bank**

   If no bank is named, the issuing bank is free to select the correspondent bank.

5. **Type of availability**

   The various types of availability are discussed in the general section of this publication.

6. **Desired documents**

   Here the importer specifies precisely which documents he requires. To obtain effective protection against the supply of poor quality goods, for instance, he can demand the submission of analysis or quality certificates. These are generally issued by specialized inspection companies or laboratories.

7. **Notify address**

   Advice is given to the notify address of the imminent arrival of the ship at the port of destination or of the arrival of the goods at the airport. Notification is also given of damage during shipment, if any.

8. **Description of the goods**

   To avoid errors and misunderstandings, it is advisable to keep the goods description and quantity information brief and precise.

   If the credit amount carries the notation "ca.," the same notation should appear with the quantity.

9. **Confirmation order**

   It may happen that the foreign beneficiary insists on having the credit confirmed by the bank in his country.

Clear formulations speed up handling.

When checking compliance with the credit terms, banks are concerned exclusively with the documents presented and not with contract clauses. So it is very important to demand documents in the credit that clearly reflect the agreements reached between importer and exporter.

Instead of:	*Specify:*
The beneficiary must notify the buyer by cable when the goods are shipped.	Copy of the cable to the buyer with shipping information.
The ship may not be more than 15 years old.	Confirmation of the shipping company or its agent that the ship is not more than 15 years old.
The beneficiary must send duplicate documents to the buyer.	Confirmation of the seller that he has sent duplicates of the following documents to the buyer: ... ...
The certificate of origin must accompany the goods.	Confirmation of the carrier/forwarding agent that the goods are accompanied by a certificate of origin.

Amendment of the Credit Terms

An amendment of the credit terms ordered by the importer becomes effective only if all parties, i.e. the issuing bank, the exporter, and possibly also the foreign confirming bank, agree to the amendment.

Other Important Points for the Importer

Upon receiving the documents, the issuing bank checks whether they agree on their face with the wording of the credit and with the stipulations of the UCPDC, and charges the importer's account.

Documents in conformity with the credit cannot be rejected on grounds that the goods were not delivered as specified by the contract.

The question of liability and responsibility of the bank is spelled out in the UCPDC.

The Documentary Credit and the Intermediary

For the handling of documentary credit transactions in international transit trade, the banks offer the following possibilities:

The Transferable Letter of Credit

Allows the intermediary to have a credit opened in his favour transferred to his own supplier. The intermediary has to commit only a very limited amount of his own funds.

It must be clearly designated as "transferable."

A transfer of partial quantities to various sellers is possible only if the original credit permits partial deliveries.

Under the transferable credit, the documents should be demanded in such a way that they can also be utilized for the original credit.

Of course the intermediary has the right to replace the invoice from the transferred credit with his own.

The insurance amount should be established for the transfer in such a way that it at least covers the insurance amount prescribed in the original credit.

The credit can be transferred only under the terms stated in the original credit. However, the following exceptions are permitted:

- Unit prices and credit amount can be reduced.
- Delivery period and validity period can be shortened.

If the intermediary wishes that discretion be exercised regarding the identity of the ultimate buyer and the seller, he should make sure that the original credit only specifies documents that make no mention of the names of the ultimate buyer and the seller.

The intermediary should do everything in his power to see that the party ordering the original credit has it opened in the simplest possible form.

The fewer the documents specified and the simpler the terms stipulated in the original credit, the smoother the transaction can be handled.

Transferable credits call for exceptional care and knowledge. The bank will be pleased to place its long experience at the disposal of customers in the search for solutions to particular problems.

Transferable Credit

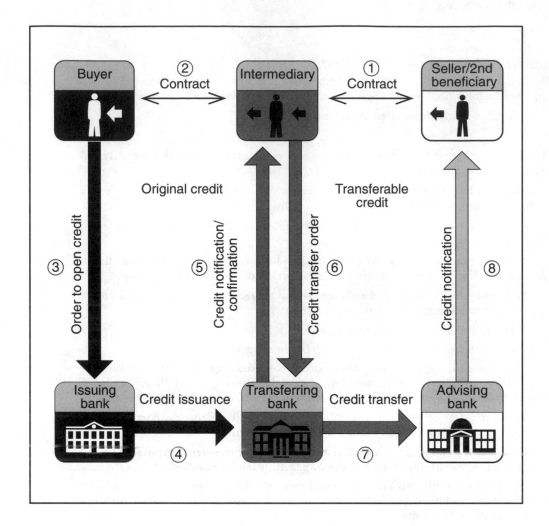

Transferable Credit

1. **Intermediary contracts with seller/2nd beneficiary to purchase goods.**

2. **Intermediary contracts to sell goods to buyer.**

3. **Buyer applies for and opens a letter of credit with issuing ("buyer's") bank.**

4. **Issuing bank issues the letter of credit, forwarding it to transferring bank.**

5. **Transferring bank notifies intermediary of letter of credit.**

6. **Intermediary orders transfer of letter of credit to seller/2nd beneficiary.**

7. **Transferring bank transfers credit in care of advising ("seller's") bank.**

8. **Advising bank notifies seller/2nd beneficiary of letter of credit.**

Sample Transferable, Confirmed Letter of Credit

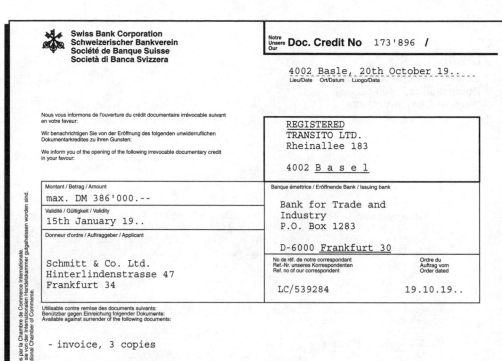

Swiss Bank Corporation
Schweizerischer Bankverein
Société de Banque Suisse
Società di Banca Svizzera

Notre Unsere Our **Doc. Credit No**   173'896   **/**

4002 Basle, 20th October 19..
Lieu/Date   Ort/Datum   Luogo/Data

Nous vous informons de l'ouverture du crédit documentaire irrévocable suivant en votre faveur:

Wir benachrichtigen Sie von der Eröffnung des folgenden unwiderruflichen Dokumentarkredites zu ihren Gunsten:

We inform you of the opening of the following irrevocable documentary credit in your favour:

REGISTERED
TRANSITO LTD.
Rheinallee 183

4002 B a s e l

Montant / Betrag / Amount	Banque émettrice / Eröffnende Bank / Issuing bank
max. DM 386'000.--	Bank for Trade and Industry P.O. Box 1283
Validité / Gültigkeit / Validity 15th January 19..	
Donneur d'ordre / Auftraggeber / Applicant	D-6000 Frankfurt 30

	No de réf. de notre correspondant Ref.-Nr. unseres Korrespondenten Ref. no of our correspondent	Ordre du Auftrag vom Order dated
Schmitt & Co. Ltd. Hinterlindenstrasse 47 Frankfurt 34	LC/539284	19.10.19..

Utilisable contre remise des documents suivants:
Benützbar gegen Einreichung folgender Dokumente:
Available against surrender of the following documents:

- invoice, 3 copies

- inspection certificate, evidencing that the goods are in accordance with the specifications mentioned below

- full set of clean shipped on board ocean bills of lading, made out to order and endorsed in blank

<u>covering</u>:   1'000 metric tons steel sheets DIN 456/243
               at DM 386.-- per mt, C & F Rotterdam

to be shipped from a Japanese seaport to Rotterdam
not later than 1st January 19..
Partial deliveries are permitted. Transhipment not allowed.
Documents to be presented not later than 15 days after date of shipment.

This documentary credit is transferable.

We confirm this documentary credit to you as irrevocably valid until 15th January 19..

            Yours faithfully

            Swiss Bank Corporation

*(vertical side text:)* Ce crédit est soumis aux « Règles et usances uniformes relatives aux crédits documentaires » approuvées par la Chambre de Commerce Internationale. Dieser Kredit unterliegt den « Einheitlichen Richtlinien und Gebräuchen für Dokumenten-Akkreditive » wie sie von der Internationalen Handelskammer gutgeheissen worden sind. This credit is subject to the « Uniform customs and practice for documentary credits » fixed by the International Chamber of Commerce.

F 6804N 1/8 2.82 10000

Sample Transferable Letter of Credit Order

TRANSITO AG
Import - Export - Kommission
Rheinallee 183, 4087 Basel
Telefon: (061) 251 87 87

Basle, 21st October 19..

Swiss Bank Corporation
Documentary Credits
P.O. Box

4002   B a s l e

Documentary credit no. 173896 - DM 386'000.--, opened
by Handels- und Industriebank, Frankfurt, by order of
Schmitt & Co. KG, Frankfurt, confirmed by yourselves

Dear Sirs,

Would you please transfer the above-mentioned documentary
credit as follows:

New beneficiaries :	Handels GmbH Sendlauerstrasse 28 Vienna 28
to be advised by :	Overseas Bank Ltd., Vienna
amount :	DM 350'000.--
validity :	5th January 19..,
price :	DM 350.-- per mt C & F Rotterdam

All other conditions remain unchanged. Please credit the
balance of funds in our favour to our DM account with
yourselves.

We appreciate your assistance in this matter and look forward
to receiving your advice of execution.

Yours faithfully

TRANSITO LTD.

Baumann

The Back-to-Back Credit

If a credit is not transferable for one reason or another, the bank may be prepared, under certain circumstances and assuming that the main risks can be covered satisfactorily, to open a credit on a back-to-back basis at the request of the intermediary. In this case, the bank's main surety is the original credit.

The more the specifications of the original and the back-to-back credit differ from each other, the more difficult it becomes to carry out the transaction.

Therefore it is advisable for the intermediary to contact his bank at an early stage. On the basis of its experience, the bank will help him look for solutions to his particular problem.

Assignment of the Credit Proceeds

If a relationship of sufficient trust exists between the intermediary and his supplier, the latter may sometimes be prepared to accept the assignment of a certain sum in place of a new documentary credit. In this case, the bank will consent to pay the supplier, on behalf of the credit beneficiary, the assigned sum from the amounts becoming available under the credit.

The security resulting from the assignment cannot be equated with that from a back-to-back or even a transferable credit, because the beneficiary from the assignment has no control over the presentation of documents in conformity with the credit by the intermediary (credit beneficiary).

When the supplier receives notification of the assignment, he has the assurance that the partial amounts cannot be used for any other purpose as they become available.

Sample Order of Assignment

MÜLLER AG

Postfach 10283, 4087 Basel
Telefon: (061) 247 86 86
Telex: 247 86 86 mulag ch

Basle, 20th October 19..

Swiss Bank Corporation
Documentary Credits
P.O. Box

4002 B a s l e

Documentary credit no. 204356 in our favour,
for SFr. 65'000.--, covering 200 tons of fertilizer

Dear Sirs,

In accordance with article 164 et seq. of the Swiss Law
of Contract we hereby assign from the above documentary
credit an amount of SFr. 300.-- per delivered ton of
fertilizer, total SFr. 60'000.--, to Dünger Ltd.,
Feldmeilenstrasse 21, 8002 Zurich.

Would you kindly inform Dünger Ltd., Zurich, that you
have taken note of this assignment and that the amount
due will be transferred to them once the credit has
been negotiated and the funds are freely available.

Yours faithfully

M ü l l e r Ltd.

Sample Forwarding of Assignment by the Bank

 **Swiss Bank Corporation
Schweizerischer Bankverein
Société de Banque Suisse
Società di Banca Svizzera**

Dünger Ltd.
Feldmeilenstrasse 21

8002 Z u r i c h

Your ref.	Our dept./ref. DOK/BU	Through dialing (061) 20 20 20	**4002 Basle,** 21st October 19..

Documentary credit no. 204356 in favour
Müller AG, Basel

Dear Sirs,

By order of Müller AG, Basle, we received the following
assignment:

In accordance with article 164 et seq. of the Swiss Law of
Contract we hereby assign from the above documentary credit
an amount of SFr. 300.-- per delivered ton of fertilizer, total SFr. 60'000.-- to Dünger Ltd., Feldmeilenstrasse 21, 8002 Zurich.

At the request of Müller AG, Basle, we confirm that we have
duly taken note of this assignment. We undertake to hold at
your disposal an amount up to SFr. 60'000.--. The amount due
will be transferred to you as soon as the credit has been
negotiated and the funds are freely available.

Yours faithfully,

Swiss Bank Corporation

Jenny Goy

E 90001 S

The Back-to-Back Credit

Procedure for assignment of credit proceeds (Stage 1 - Issuance)

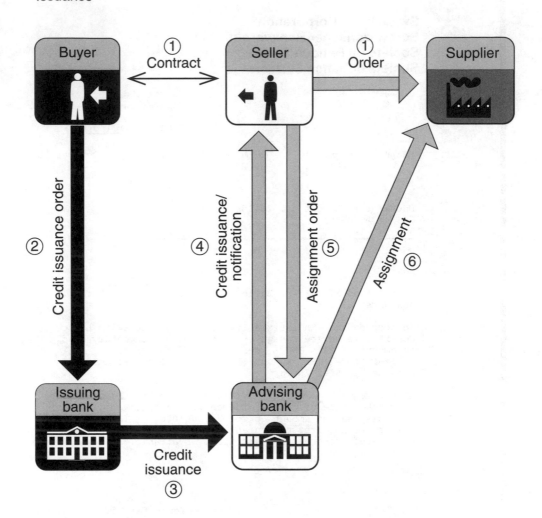

Stage 1
Issuance

1. **Buyer and seller negotiate a contract. Seller issues order to supplier.**

2. **Buyer applies for and opens a letter of credit with issuing ("buyer's") bank.**

3. **Issuing bank issues the letter of credit, forwarding it to advising ("seller's") bank.**

4. **Advising bank notifies seller of letter of credit.**

5. **Seller orders assignment of letter of credit to supplier.**

6. **Advising bank assigns letter of credit to supplier.**

The Back-to-Back Credit

Procedure for assignment of credit proceeds (Stage 2 - Utilization)

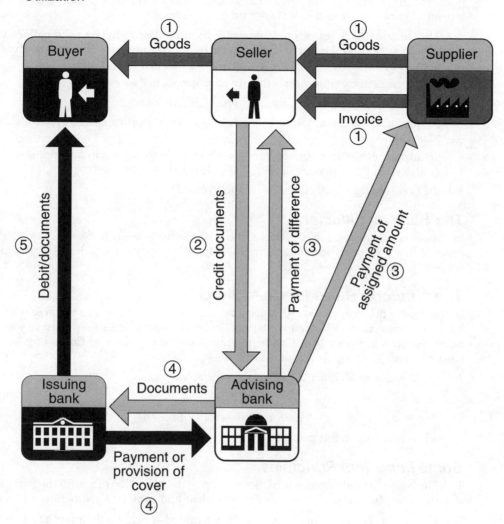

Stage 2
Utilization

1. Supplier ships goods and invoice to seller who in turn ships goods to buyer.

2. Seller forwards credit documents to advising ("seller's") bank.

3. Advising bank pays supplier amount assigned in seller's assignment order. Advising bank pays seller the difference between the letter of credit amount and the amount assigned to the supplier.

4. Advising bank forwards documents to issuing ("buyer's") bank. Issuing bank pays advising bank.

5. Issuing bank forwards documents to buyer and debits buyer's account.

DOCUMENTARY COLLECTIONS

General Section

Documentary collection is a practical way of handling trade transactions for which the parties to the contract are prepared to forgo the security offered by documentary credits, but still do not wish to make deliveries on open account.

The documentary collection is an order by the seller to his bank to collect a certain sum from the buyer against transfer of the shipping documents. Payment may be made by cash or by acceptance of a bill of exchange.

The documentary collection is mainly appropriate in cases where

- the buyer's ability and willingness to pay are not doubted

- the political, economic and legal conditions in the importing country are considered to be regular

- no import restrictions, such as foreign exchange controls, exist in the import country, or else all of the necessary licences have already been obtained

- the goods being supplied are not made to order

The Bank as Fiduciary

In the case of documentary collections, the banks agree to execute the seller's collection order. While doing everything in their power to collect the payment due, they do not assume any liability in this regard.

The "Uniform Rules for Collections"

In the course of time, various formulations, expressions and terms have arisen among banks in connection with documentary collection business. In order to ensure uniform interpretations in international trade, the International Chamber of Commerce in Paris has prepared "Uniform Rules for Collections."

For the sake of simplicity, we shall use the abbreviation

URC

(**U**niform **R**ules for **C**ollections)

when referring to this publication.

Some Important Principles

1.   The banks act only upon instructions given in the collection order. So the party issuing the order should be sure to give the bank clear and complete instructions.

2.   The banks check whether the documents received appear on their face to agree with the collection order. The bank is under no obligation to make any further check of the documents.

3.   The banks are not liable for the acts of third parties (such as forwarding agents, insurance companies, customs authorities, or even other banks) which are involved in the collection procedure. The banks assume no responsibility for

- delays through no fault of their own in the transmission of messages

- consequences of Acts of God

- acts or omissions by third parties

4.   Any discrepancies arising with respect to quality or quantity of the goods delivered are to be settled directly between the drawee and the principal.

Parties to the Documentary Collection Operation

The principal (remitter, seller, exporter)
- Usually the seller, who prepares the collection documents and submits them to the bank with the collection order.

The remitting bank
- Receives the documents from the remitter (seller) and forwards them to the collecting bank in accordance with the instructions received.

The buyer (drawee, importer)
- The collection papers are presented to him.

The collecting bank (presenting bank)
- Collects the cash payment or obtains the acceptance from the drawee in accordance with the instructions received from the remitting bank.

Documentary Collection Procedure

According to the arrangements between the buyer and the seller, the latter remits the agreed documents to the bank with instructions to present them to the buyer. As a rule, the remitting bank sends the documents to a correspondent bank (collecting or presenting bank), if possible at the same location as the buyer, with instructions to present them to the drawee.

On the basis of the collection order received, the collecting bank then notifies the buyer and informs him about the conditions under which he can take possession of the documents.

If the buyer draws the documents against payment, the collecting bank transfers the proceeds to the remitting bank for crediting to the remitter.

If the buyer draws the documents against acceptance of a bill of exchange, the collecting bank sends the acceptance back to the remitting bank or retains it on a fiduciary basis up to maturity. On maturity, the collecting bank collects the bill and transfers the proceeds to the remitting bank for crediting to the seller.

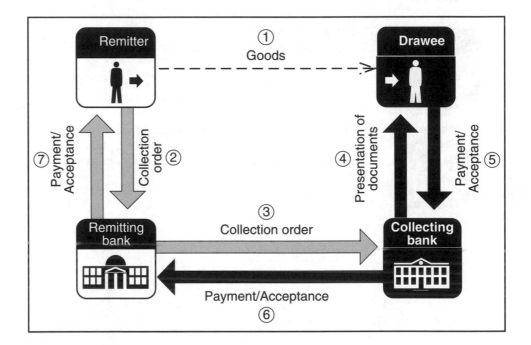

The Various Types of Collection

There are three types of collection:

1. Release of the documents against payment (D/P)

The collecting bank is allowed to release the documents to the buyer only against cash payment in the prescribed currency.

In this case, the URC prescribes that the documents may be released by the collecting bank only if the amount paid is freely available immediately, unless this is contrary to the provisions of local laws or regulations which cannot be avoided.

2. Release of the documents against acceptance (D/A)

The collecting bank is allowed to release the documents to the buyer only against acceptance of a bill of exchange. The seller must be aware that the bill of exchange represents his only security after the documents have been released. He will sell on this basis only if he is sure that the buyer will meet the bill at maturity.

Not all countries are familiar with Switzerland's strict Bills of Exchange Law.

3. Collection with acceptance—release of documents only against payment (Acceptance D/P)

The collecting bank presents a bill of exchange to the buyer for acceptance. The accepted bill remains at the collecting bank together with the documents up to maturity. Only then will the documents be released to the buyer.

The seller grants the buyer a certain payment term, but still wishes to be sure that the buyer can obtain the documents only after having made payment.

If the buyer refuses to accept the bill of exchange, the seller has early warning that he can expect trouble in completing the transaction. This gives him time to take appropriate precautions or possibly to look for another customer for the goods.

Although this type of collection is very seldom employed in actual practice, it is included here for the sake of completeness.

Special Services of the Bank

Shipment of the goods to the address of the collecting bank

If the goods are sent by rail, post, air freight or road to the buyer's address, the shipment will be surrendered to him without his first having to honour the collection documents presented to him by the bank.

If the seller wants to be sure that the buyer does not take possession of the goods before having paid, he can address them to the collecting bank or to a forwarding agent at the buyer's location with instructions to hold the consignment at the exclusive disposal of the bank. This should not be done, however, without first obtaining the consent of the collecting bank.

Monitoring

As far as possible, the banks monitor the proper processing of collection orders until the documents are redeemed. However, they cannot be held liable if the remitter receives no notification of delays for one reason or another and suffers inconvenience or damages as a result.

Without explicit instructions, the collecting bank takes no steps to store or insure the goods.

If a collection remains unpaid or a bill of exchange is not accepted and the presenting (collecting) bank receives no new instructions within 90 days, it is empowered to return the documents to the bank from which it received the collection order.

The Documentary Collection and the Exporter

What action does the exporter take?

The exporter carefully assembles the documents agreed between himself and the importer.

The exporter must bear in mind that regulations of the import countries often prescribe compulsory documents as well. The consulates of the import countries provide information on this.

The exporter makes certain that the documents are signed and endorsed where necessary.

In order to simplify collection transactions for the exporter, Swiss Bank Corporation is pleased to provide suitable forms and blank bill of exchange forms.

The remitting bank passes on the documents received from the exporter for collection without checking them.

In the case of documentary collection, the goods travel and are stored at the exporter's risk until payment/acceptance takes place. As a rule, the banks take no steps to protect the goods.

The banks cannot be held responsible if the goods are seized by customs in the consignee country and confiscated to cover the accrued storage costs.

1. The payment period agreed upon with the buyer.
2. Precise address of the buyer.
3. The buyer's bank (if known).
4. Instructions on what is to be done with the accepted bill of exchange.
5. The agreement with the buyer concerning charges.

   The supply contract should specify which party is to pay which charges. If the buyer refuses to honour his agreement to pay certain charges, they will be invoiced to the remitter.
6. Instructions regarding the lodging of a protest in the event of non-acceptance or non-payment.

   Protests cost money. So it is advisable to enquire about the consequences of protesting a bill in the buyer's country.
7. Address of the representative or agent in the buyer's country.

   Without express authorization, the collecting bank does not accept any instructions from the representative or agent.

Sample Collection Letter

Sender:	Documentary collection
M ü l l e r Ltd. Tellstrase 26 4053 <u>Basle</u>	Basle, 12th August 19.. Place / Date

Our Reference AK/83	Registered **Swiss Bank Corporation** **Schweizerischer Bankverein** Documentary collections P.O. Box 4002 B a s l e

We send you herewith the following documents for collection:

Amount	Maturity	Drawee ②
US$ 14'300.--	90 days sight ①	Maxwell Hammerton Inc. 12, Broadway New York, N.Y. 10014

Drawee's bank
Commercial Credit Bank ③
New York

Draft/ Receipt	Invoice com- mercial	Invoice cust.-/ consul.	Insur.- Cert.	Certif. of Orig.	Weight/ Packing List	Bill of Lading	Waybill	Postal-/ Forw.- Receipt	other documents	
1		4	2		2	3/3			2	analysis certificates

Goods: 100 barrels "Chemical products - harmless"

by: s/s CAP SAN GIORGIO   from: Le Havre   to: New York   on: 31.7.19..

Please follow the instructions marked «x»

Documents/goods to be delivered against		Draft ④		State the exact due-date	
payment ①	X acceptance	to be sent back after acceptance		to be collected on due-date	
X Your charges for drawee's account; if refused		X waive charges		do not deliver documents	
X Your correspondent's charges are for drawee's account; if refused		waive charges	x	do not deliver documents	
X Protest in case of	X non-payment / non-acceptance	X Do not protest in case of		non-payment	X non-acceptance
X Advise	X non-payment / non-acceptance	by airmail	X	by cable	X giving reasons

Please credit the proceeds as follows:

☒ to our   SFr   account Nr. 10-326'791.0

☐ remit to

Remarks:

In case of difficulties, the collecting bank is requested to inform our representatives: Messrs. Beach & Co. Inc., Broad Street 485, New York 34, who will be of assistance but who are not allowed to alter the above instructions.

Signature: _M ü l l e r Ltd_

Enclosures
E 6851 N 1/2 4.80 5000

The execution of this order is subject to the «Uniform rules for collections» issued by the International Chamber of Commerce

The Documentary Collection and the Importer

If the importer has purchased goods on a documentary collection basis, the collecting bank will notify him as soon as the documents are available for redemption.

The importer can inspect the documents at his bank. Once the importer has fulfilled the conditions required—acceptance or payment—the bank will release the documents and (if applicable) the goods.

What the Importer Should Know

- In the absence of authorization from the seller, the collecting bank is not empowered to allow the buyer to sample the goods or inspect their quality.
- The collecting bank may accept partial payments only if this is permitted by the collection order. In the absence of instructions to the contrary, it releases the documents only after having received full payment.
- As a special favour, the collecting bank can submit the collection documents to the importer in trust to allow him to inspect them at his leisure.

The decision whether to do so remains with the collecting bank, which bears responsibility for the documents vis-à-vis the remitting bank up to redemption and responsibility for their custody.

If the buyer is unable to honour the documents, he returns the complete set immediately to the collecting bank.

Closing Remarks

In the preceding sections we attempted to emphasize that, in the case of documentary credits, the seller receives the proceeds immediately upon presentation of his documents. In the case of documentary collection, on the other hand, the seller has to wait until the buyer has made payment or accepted a bill of exchange at the other end. In terms of security, the documentary credit is superior to collection, because the bank has committed itself to make payment upon presentation of proper documents. Sellers obtaining their proceeds by documentary collection must bear in mind that they are forced to rely on prompt redemption of the documents by the buyer.

The legal problems that can arise from disputes between the parties have been avoided deliberately, because different legal codes may apply depending on the circumstances.

We hope that this publication has helped to familiarize you with the rather complex subject of documentary operations. If some questions still remain unanswered, please have a talk with our specialists in the documentary operations departments of our branches. They will be pleased to work with you in solving your problems in this area.

UBS AG

(formerly Swiss Bank Corporation)

Glossary of Technical Terms

acceptance credit Refer to usance credit, page 155.

accepted draft Bill of exchange accepted by the drawee (acceptor) by putting his signature (acceptance) on its face. In doing so, he commits himself to pay the bill upon presentation at maturity.

all risks Extensive insurance cover, but usually excluding special risks (such as risks of war and strikes or perishing of the goods).

analysis certificate Confirmation concerning the chemical analysis of the goods, issued by a competent organization.

aval Joint and several guarantee on the draft of a person or firm, usually for the drawee, where the guarantor places his signature on the draft together with a notation indicating in whose favour his guarantee is given.

average Damage to vessel or cargo.

AWB Refer to air waybill, page 165.

back-to-back credit Refer to page 156.

bid bond Guarantee established in connection with international tenders. Guarantees fulfillment of the offer, i.e. that the contract will be signed if awarded.

bill of exchange Document issued in a legal form, precisely defined, of which the two following versions are most common: - draft, wherein the drawer instructs the drawee to pay a certain amount to a named person;   - promissory note, wherein the issuer promises to pay a certain amount.

bill of lading (B/L) Document giving title to the goods, signed by the captain or his deputy or by the shipping company or its agent, containing the declaration regarding receipt of the goods (cargo), the conditions on which transportation is made, and the engagement to deliver goods at the prescribed port of destination to the lawful holder of the bill of lading. Refer to page 162.

certificate of manufacture Confirmation of a producer that the goods have actually been produced by him in his factory.

c & f Abbreviation for "cost and freight," which means that the price of the goods includes all costs for the shipment and the freight up to the port of destination. It is up to the buyer to cover insurance from the port of shipment. (See Incoterms.)

charter party Contract according to which the owner leases the vessel to a charterer for a certain period or a certain voyage.

cif Abbreviation for "cost, insurance and freight," which means that price of the goods includes all costs for the shipment and freight and insurance up to the port of destination. (See Incoterms.)

cifci Abbreviation for "cost, insurance, freight, commission and interest." The same as "cif" plus commission and interest.

claused bill of lading Bill of lading containing additional clauses limiting the responsibility of the shipping company.

clean bill of lading Bill of lading which does not bear any superimposed clause or annotation expressly declaring the defective condition of the goods and/or the packaging.

clean letter of credit Letter of credit available without presentation of shipping documents. Refer also to "stand-by letter of credit," page 156.

CMR Abbreviation for "Convention relative au contrat de transport international de marchandises par route." See road waybill.

combined bill of lading Bill of lading covering several modes of transport.

combined transport Consignment sent by means of various modes of transport.

commercial letter of credit Documentary credit. Refer to page 148.

consular invoice Invoice with a certification of the consulate of the importing country usually issued on a special form. In use in only a few countries.

custody bill of lading Bill of lading issued by American warehouses.

customs invoice Invoice made out on a special form prescribed by the customs authorities of the importing country. Used only in a few countries.

D/A Abbreviation for "documents against acceptance." Refer to page 185.

D/A draft Documentary draft. Refer to page 185.

delivery order Order to deliver specified packages out of a combined consignment covered by one single bill of lading.

deferred payment Refer to page 155.

demurrage Extra charge to be paid if a vessel is not loaded or unloaded within the time allowed.

dock receipt Receipt issued by a warehouse supervisor or port officer certifying that goods have been received by the shipping company.

documentary draft Draft drawn by seller on buyer accompanied by shipping documents. Refer to page 178.

D/P Abbreviation for "documents against payment." Refer to page 185.

D/P draft Documentary draft. Refer to page 185.

draft Bill of exchange that has been drawn but not accepted.

endorsement Written declaration on a document made out to order, usually written on the back, with which the owner (endorser) assigns his rights to the person named in the endorsement (endorsee).

ex warehouse See "ex works."

ex works Price of the goods including packing. (See Incoterms.)

fas Abbreviation for "free alongside ship," which means the price of the goods covers transportation charges up to the port of shipment. Handling charges in the port of shipment, freight up to final destination and insurance are borne by the buyer. (See Incoterms.)

FCR Abbreviation for "forwarder's certificate of receipt."

fio Abbreviation for "free in and out." See "free in clause" and "free out clause."

foa Abbreviation for "free on board airport."

fob Abbreviation for "free on board," which means that the price of the goods covers transportation to the port of shipment and the usual loading charges. Freight and insurance from port of shipment are for the account of the buyer. (See Incoterms.)

for Abbreviation for "free on rail" used in connection with transportation by rail, indicating that the price covers the goods loaded on the railcar.

forwarder's bill of lading Bill of lading issued by a forwarding agent.

forwarding agent's bill of lading Bill of lading issued by a forwarding agent.

forwarding agent's receipt Receipt issued by a forwarding agent for goods received.

fot Abbreviation for "free on truck" used in connection with road haulage, meaning that the price covers the goods loaded on the truck. (See Incoterms.)

fpa See "free of particular average."

franco Free from duties, transportation charges and other levies. Used also as delivery condition, e.g. franco ... (named place of delivery), which means that the seller must bear all transportation charges and duties up to the named place.

free of particular average (fpa) Insurance cover that relates only to the consignment as a whole but does not cover the loss of single parcels or partial quantities.

free in clause Clause in the bill of lading indicating that the loading charges are for the account of the supplier.

free out clause Clause in the bill of lading indicating that unloading charges are for the account of the receiver.

full set All originals of the bill of lading, the insurance document, etc.

HAWB House air waybill. Refer to page 162.

house air waybill Refer to page 162.

Incoterms Publication of the International Chamber of Commerce regarding commercial trade and delivery terms. Refer to page 191.

inspection certificate Confirmation that the goods have been inspected prior to shipment, issued by a neutral organization.

institute strike clause Insurance clause internationally used regarding risks of strikes.

institute war clause Insurance clause internationally used regarding risks of war.

in trust (goods/documents) Refer to page 188.

letter of assignment Document with which the assignor assigns his rights to a third party.

letter of guarantee/letter of indemnity Declaration of indemnity on the part of a 3rd bank in the case of provisional negotiation. Refer to page 168.

mate's receipt Declaration issued by an officer of the vessel in the name of the shipping company stating that certain goods have been received on board his vessel.

measurement list List of the dimensions of the individual loaded cases.

merchant's credit Letter of credit issued by the buyer himself. Contains no commitment whatever on the part of the bank.

negotiation Action by which the advising bank buys the documents. Refer to page 168.

n.n. "Not negotiable." Copy of the ocean bill of lading.

notify address Address mentioned in a bill of lading or an air waybill, to which the carrier is to give notice when goods are due to arrive.

on board Notation on the bill of lading indicating that the goods have actually been loaded onto ship named.

on deck bill of lading Bill of lading containing the notation that goods have been shipped on deck.

option Right to take up an offer. Also the right to choose from several different possibilities, e.g., in the bill of lading, to designate one or several ports of discharge.

packing credit Advance granted by a bank in connection with shipments of storable goods guaranteed by the assignment of the payment expected later on under a documentary credit.

packing list List showing details of the goods contained in each case.

performance bond Guarantees proper fulfillment of the contract terms.

pro forma invoice Invoice established pro forma, the payment of which is not intended. Used   - as preliminary invoice together with a quotation   - for customs purposes in connection with shipments of samples, advertising material, etc.

progress report Declaration of the buyer in which he certifies the progress made by the seller up to a certain point of time. Refer to page 157.

promissory note See bill of exchange.

protest Legal procedure noting the refusal of the drawee to accept a bill of exchange (protest for non-acceptance) or to pay it (protest for non-payment). Essential in order to preserve the right of recourse on the endorser. Refer to page 160.

rail waybill Duplicate of the freight document drawn up in rail traffic, which is given to the shipper of the goods.

received for shipment bill of lading Bill of lading certifying only that goods have been received, but not evidencing that they have been loaded on board.

recourse Right of claim against the joint and several guarantors (e.g., endorsers, drawers) of a bill of exchange or cheque. See protest.

red clause Clause contained in a documentary credit authorizing the paying bank to make advances to the beneficiary on an unsecured basis even before the prescribed shipping documents have been presented.

reimbursing bank Bank from which the advising bank requests cover on payment during negotiation.

remittance (documentary) Forwarding of bills of exchange and/or documents.

restricted letter of credit Letter of credit, the negotiation of which is restricted to a bank specially mentioned.

revolving credit Documentary credit which, after utilization, is automatically reinstated for a further drawing. Refer to page 156.

road waybill Transport document issued for road haulage (CMR = Convention relative au contrat de transport international de marchandises par route).

shipped on deck Annotation in the bill of lading stating that the goods have been shipped on deck.

short form bill of lading Bill of lading on which the detailed conditions of transportation are not listed in full.

s.r. & c.c. Institute Strikes, Riots and Civil Commotions Clause. Internationally applied insurance clause regarding these risks.

straight bill of lading Bill of lading issued to the name of a certain party and which cannot be transferred by endorsement.

survey report Report of an expert, issued by an independent party. See inspection certificate.

through bill of lading, TBL Bill of lading covering goods being transhipped en route. It covers the whole voyage from port of shipment to final destination.

TPND Insurance clause covering theft, pilferage and non-delivery.

trust receipt Under British and American law: declaration issued by a client towards the bank that ownership of the goods remains with the bank even after release of the goods documents to the customer, and thus that the client has received the goods in trust only.

transferable Refer to page 156 and page 173.

T.T. Abbreviation for "telegraphic transfer," indicating that cover is remitted by cable.

under reserve Refer to page 168.

unrestricted letter of credit Letter of credit which may be negotiated through any bank at the beneficiary's choice.

usance credit Refer to page 155.

u.u.r. Abbreviation for "credit under usual reserves." Refer to page 168.

warehouse to warehouse clause Insurance clause indicating that the goods are insured from the warehouse of the seller up to the warehouse of the buyer.

warrant Collateral certificate used for lending on goods. Not common in Switzerland, because Swiss law (Art. 1153 OR) prevents Swiss warehouses from issuing documents of title.

weight list List of the weights of the individual parcels.

without recourse Purchase of a bill of exchange without recourse.

with particular average Insurance covering also the loss of single cases or partial quantities (as opposed to free from particular average, fpa).

Publications of the International Chamber of Commerce, Paris, France

The International Chamber of Commerce, as a world business organisation, has members in more than 80 countries. It acts to promote the greater freedom of world trade, to harmonize and facilitate business and trade practices, and to represent the business community at international levels.

Publications:

Uniform Customs and Practice for Documentary Credits

Rules unifying banking practice regarding documentary credits.

Uniform Rules for Collections

Codifies the main rules to be applied by the banks in connection with collection operations for drafts, their payment or non-payment, protest and for documentary collections.

The Problem of Clean Bills of Lading

An explanation of the problem arising out of the requirement for clean bills of lading together with a list of certain clauses often superimposed by carriers, for reference and optional use by parties to international sales contracts.

Incoterms 2000

International rules for the uniform interpretation of trade terms (FOB, CIF, etc.).

Uniform Rules for a Combined Transport Document

Uniform rules in connection with transport documents covering several modes of transport.

Guide to Documentary Credit Operations

Describes the basic steps required in financing an international credit transaction by means of a documentary credit operation.

These publications may be obtained from
ICC Publishing, Inc.
156 Fifth Ave.
New York, NY 10010 USA
Tel: (212) 206-1150
Fax: (212) 633-6025
Web: www.iccbooksusa.com

NOTES

U.S. Customs Entry and Clearance

Contents

The following section is adapted from the U.S. Department of the Treasury, U.S. Customs Service publication *Importing to the United States* (2003 edition). We have updated for current law—including revisions required by NAFTA, GSP, and the Customs Modernization Act, among others—and we have included the most current address and contact information available at publication.

Customs Service Organization

Mission

On March 1, 2003, the Bureau of Customs and Border Protection (CBP) came into being, a new agency within the Department of Homeland Security's Border and Transportation Security Directorate. CBP brings together all border agencies of the United States by uniting U.S. Customs, the Border Patrol, and the immigration and agriculture border inspection programs, formerly within the Immigration and Naturalization Service and the Department of Agriculture, respectively. The U.S. Customs Service was transferred from the jurisdition of the Treasury Department to the U.S. Department of Homeland Security and now shares as its' primary mission the goal to prevent terrorists and terrorist weapons from entering the United States. It continues to have a major responsibility to administer the Tariff Act of 1930, as it has been amended. And its' main duties still include the assessment and collection of all duties, taxes, and fees on imported merchandise; the enforcement of customs regulated laws; and the administration of certain navigation laws and treaties. As a major enforcement organization, the Bureau of Customs and Border Protection must combat smuggling and fraud and enforces the regulations of numerous other Federal agencies at ports of entry and along the land and sea borders of the United States.

Organization and Responsibilities

The customs territory of the U.S. consists of the 50 states, the District of Columbia, and Puerto Rico. The Bureau of Customs and Border Protection, an agency under the Department of Homeland Security, has its headquarters in Washington, DC, and is headed by a Commissioner of Customs.

The former Customs Service began a major reorganization in 1995 that is now largely in place. However, the adjustment period is sure to continue for the foreseeable future, especially as there has been a major shift in responsibility onto the port directors. Previously, there were seven Customs regions which were further divided into districts, and finally into ports. The reorganization has eliminated the two middle levels of management, the regions and districts. The intention is to place more resources at the port level, where there is the greatest interaction with the trade community, in the hope that it will improve efficiency and the level of service.

Under the reorganization, two new entities were created: Customs Management Centers (CMCs) and Strategic Management Centers (SMCs). The CMCs focus on internal administration and personnel issues; they are not intended to handle specific inquiries from the trade community. The five SMCs are designed as policy centers focusing on macro trade issues within specific geographic regions. The Chicago SMC focuses on Canada; the Dallas SMC on Mexico and Central America; the Long Beach SMC on the Pacific Rim; the Miami SMC on South America and the Caribbean; and the New York SMC on Europe,

Africa, and the Middle East. Service ports are Customs locations which provide a full range of cargo processing functions, including inspections, entry, collections, and verification.

The Office of Field Operations (OFO), headed by an Assistant Commissioner, oversees over 25, 000 employees with more than 19,000 dedicated and vigilant inspectors that protect U.S. borders. An annual operating budget of $1.1 billion provides for operations at 20 Field Operations offices; 317 ports of entry; 14 preclearance stations in Canada and the Caribbean; Immigration policy and programs; and Agricultural Quarantine Inspection (AQI) at all ports of entry in order to protect the health of U.S. plant and animal resources. OFO manages core Customs and Border Protection programs such as: Border Security and Facilitation, which handles Interdiction and Security, Passenger Operations, Targeting and Analysis and Canine Enforcement; Trade Compliance and Facilitation, under which falls Cargo Entry and Release, Summary Operations, Trade Risk Management, Enforcement, and Seizures and Penalties as well as expanding Trade operations to focus on anti-terrorism.

The Office of Information and Technology, headed by an Assistant Commissioner (AC), is responsible for implementation and support of information technology, research and development functions, and automation and technological strategies for meeting mission-related needs. Specifically, the Office is responsible for automated information systems, management of the research and development functions and all forensic and laboratory support of the agency. OIT personnel manage all computer and related resources including all operational aspects of the Computer Security Program; establish requirements for computer interfaces between Customs and Border Protection and various trade groups and government agencies; and manage matters related to automated import processing and systems development. OIT Personnel are responsible for managing all aspects of tactical communications, including the 24x7 operations of the National Law Enforcement Communications Center.

The Office of Investigations works in close coordination with other organizational elements involved in the U.S. Customs Service law enforcement mission to manage and control enforcement programs involving investigations, tactical interdiction, intelligence, and enforcement support service-wide. It formulates policies, plans, and programs relative to the Tactical Communications staff and the interdiction of smuggled merchandise and contraband, the detection of violations of Customs and related laws, and the protection and collection of the revenue. Specific responsibilities include the management of:

- Investigative functions which entail investigations of all violations of Customs and related laws and regulations;
- Interdiction functions which deter and detect

prohibited entry of contraband or other Customs or related violations through land, sea, or air operations; and

- Intelligence and communications functions which provide for the collection, analysis, and dissemination of strategic and tactical intelligence data for use by the operational elements of Customs, and tactical communications support for Customs enforcement operations management through the National Law Enforcement Communications Center.

The Office of Regulations and Rulings, headed by an Assistant Commissioner, is responsible for the development, implementation, and evaluation of Servicewide programs, policies, and procedures pertaining to regulations and rulings issued by and affecting Customs, and it has a major responsibility for providing informed compliance information to members of the trade community. It provides policy and technical support to Customs, the Department of the Treasury, the Congress, other government agencies, and the importing public concerning the application of Customs and other laws, regulations, and procedures administered by Customs. The Office monitors Customs legal decisions, programs, and procedures and issues decisions on matters related to claims (including claims for liquidated damages), fines, penalties, and forfeitures. It also issues rulings, legal determinations, and guidelines relating to classification and value of merchandise, carriers, drawback and bonds, entry, licensing, intellectual property rights, restricted merchandise, and disclosure law rulings.

The Office of Strategic Trade, headed by an Assistant Commissioner, is responsible for identifying and confronting major trade issues facing the United States by innovative research and analysis and by the creation of an array of coordinated interventions. The Office is also responsible for developing the strategies to assess the level of trade compliance, for publishing Customs compliance data to enable the trade to initiate their own efforts to achieve compliance, and for providing leadership for developing and implementing an integrated trade enforcement program. The Office exercises line authority over the Regulatory Audit function and the Strategic Trade Centers, and utilizes the analytical resources resident in the Strategic Trade Centers to address major trade issues, such as transshipment and intellectual property rights, which cannot be effectively addressed through transaction reviews at the ports. Finally, the Office has shared responsibility for developing effective methods of communication and cooperation with other U.S. agencies involved in trade and with U.S. businesses.

Offices of Field Operations

For contact information, refer to "U.S. Customs and Border Protection Offices" on page 81.

Arizona
Covers Arizona
Customs Management Center: Tucson, AZ
Bureau of Immigration and Customs Enforcement Office: Tucson, AZ
Service Ports: Nogales, AZ

East Texas
Covers Eastern Texas, the Texas Panhandle, Oklahoma
Customs Management Center: Houston, TX
Strategic Trade Center: Dallas, TX
Bureau of Immigration and Customs Enforcement Office : Dallas, TX; Houston, TX
Service Ports: DFW Airport, TX

East Great Lakes
Covers Upstate New York
Customs Management Center: Buffalo, NY
Office of Investigations: Buffalo, NY
Service Ports: Ogdensburg, NY

Gulf
Covers Alabama, Arkansas, Louisiana, Mississippi, and Tennessee
Customs Management Center: New Orleans, LA
Office of Investigations: New Orleans, LA
Service Ports: Mobile, AL

Mid America
Covers Ohio, Kentucky, Indiana, Illinois, Missouri, Kansas, Iowa, Nebraska, South Dakota, most of Wisconsin, and Southern Minnesota
Customs Management Center: Chicago, IL
Strategic Trade Center: Chicago, IL
Office of Investigations: Chicago, IL
Service Ports: Milwaukee, WI; Middelburg Heights, OH; Minneapolis, MN; St. Louis, MO; Chicago, IL
Laboratory: Chicago, IL

Mid Atlantic
Covers Pennsylvania, Delaware, Maryland, the District of Columbia, and Southern New Jersey
Customs Management Center: Baltimore, MD
Offices of Investigations: Baltimore, MD, Philadelphia, PA
Service Ports: Baltimore, MD; Philadelphia, PA; Washington, DC
Laboratory: Washington, DC

Mid Pacific
Covers Utah, most of Nevada, Northern California, Hawaii
Customs Management Center: San Francisco, CA
Office of Investigations: Honolulu, HI; San Francisco, CA
Laboratory: San Francisco, CA

New York
Covers the New York City area, Long Island, Northern New Jersey
Customs Management Center: New York, NY
Strategic Trade Center: New York, NY
Office of Investigations: Jamaica, NY; Newark, NJ; New York, NY
Laboratory: New York, NY

Northwest Great Plains
Covers North Dakota, Montana, Northern Iowa, Washington State.
Customs Management Center: Seattle, WA
Office of Investigations: Seattle, WA
Service Ports: Pembina, ND

North Atlantic
Covers Massachusetts, Maine, New Hampshire, Connecticut, Rhode Island, Vermont
Customs Management Center: Boston, MA
Office of Investigations: Boston, MA
Service Ports: Portland, ME; Providence, RI; St. Albans, VT

North Florida
Covers Northern Florida
Customs Management Center: Tampa, FL
Office of Investigations: Milton, FL; Tampa, FL
Service Ports: Tampa, FL

North Pacific
Covers Oregon, most of Idaho, Wyoming, Colorado, Alaska
Customs Management Center: Portland, OR
Office of Investigations: Englewood, CO
Service Ports: Anchorage, AK; Portland, OR

Puerto Rico & Virgin Islands
Covers Puerto Rico and the U.S. Virgin Islands
Customs Management Center: San Juan, PR
Office of Investigations: San Juan, PR
Laboratory: San Juan, PR

South Atlantic
Covers Virginia, West Virginia, North Carolina, South Carolina, Georgia
Customs Management Center: College Park, GA
Service Ports: Charleston, SC; Charlotte, NC; Savannah, GA; Norfolk, VA
Laboratory: Savannah, GA

South Florida
Covers Southern Florida
Strategic Trade Center: Miami, FL
Customs Management Center: Plantation, FL
Office of Investigations: Miami, FL

South Pacific
Covers most of Southern California (except Mexican border area, Southern Nevada
Customs Management Center: Long Beach, CA
Strategic Trade Center: Long Beach, CA
Office of Investigations: Los Angeles, CA; Torrance, CA; Las Vegas, NV
Service Ports: Los Angeles, CA
Laboratory: Terminal Island, CA

South Texas
Covers the most populated area of the Texas–Mexico border
Customs Management Center: Laredo, TX
Office of Investigations: San Antonio, TX

Southern California
Covers the California–Mexico border area
Customs Management Center: San Diego, CA
Office of Investigations: El Centro, CA, San Diego, CA

West Great Lakes
Covers Michigan
Customs Management Center: Detroit, MI
Service Ports: Detroit, MI

West Texas & New Mexico
Covers Western Texas and New Mexico
Customs Management Center: El Paso, TX
Office of Investigations: El Paso, TX

Ports of Entry and Customs Service Ports

Note: Customs service ports and ports of entry are listed at 19 CFR 101.3.

Key: Customs Service Ports in **boldface**
        + Drawback Unit/Office
        *Consolidated ports

ALABAMA

Birmingham	Huntsville	**Mobile**

ALASKA

Alcan	**Anchorage**	Dalton Cache
Fairbanks	Juneau	Ketchikan
Sitka	Skagway	St. Paul
Valdez	Wrangell	

ARIZONA

Douglas	Lukeville	Naco
Nogales	Phoenix	San Luis
Sasabe	Tucson	

ARKANSAS
Little Rock-North Little Rock

CALIFORNIA

Andrade	Calexico	Englewood
Eureka	Fresno	Palm Springs
L.A.-Long Beach +	Port Hueneme	Port San Luis
San Diego	**S.F.-Oakland +**	San Jose
San Ysidro	Tecate	

COLORADO

Broomfield	**Denver**

CONNECTICUT

Bridgeport	Hartford	New Haven
New London		

DELAWARE
Wilmington*

DISTRICT OF COLUMBIA
Washington

FLORIDA

Boca Grande	Daytona Beach	Fernandina Beach
Ft. Myers	Jacksonville	Key West
Miami +	Ocala	Orlando
Panama City	Pensacola	Port Canaveral
Port Everglades	Port Manatee	Ocala
Sanford	Sarasota	St. Petersburg
Tampa	West Palm Beach	

GEORGIA

Atlanta	Brunswick	**Savannah**

HAWAII

Hilo	**Honolulu**	Kahului
Nawiliwili/Port Allen		

IDAHO

Boise	Eastport	Porthill

ILLINOIS

Chicago +	Decatur	Dupage
Peoria	Rockford	
Rock Island/Moline/Davenport, IA		Waukegan
Wheeling		

INDIANA

Evansville/Owensboro, KY *		Ft. Wayne
Indianapolis	Lawrenceburg/Cincinnati, OH *	

IOWA
Davenport/Rock Island, IL/Moline, IL*   Des Moines

KANSAS
Wichita

KENTUCKY
Lexington   Louisville
Owensboro/Evansville, IN *

LOUISIANA
Baton Rouge   Gramercy   Lake Charles
Morgan City   **New Orleans +**
Shreveport/Bossier City

MAINE
Bangor   Bar Harbor   Bath
Belfast   Bridgewater   Calais
Eastport   Fort Fairfield   Fort Kent
Houlton   Jackman   Jonesport
Kittery   Limestone   Madawaska
Portland   Rockland   Van Buren
Vanceboro

MARYLAND
Annapolis   **Baltimore**   Cambridge/Cr-
isfield

MASSACHUSETTS
Boston +   Fall River   Gloucester
Lawrence   New Bedford   Plymouth
Salem   Springfield   Worcester

MICHIGAN
Battle Creek   **Detroit**   Grand Rapids
Muskegon   Port Huron
Saginaw/Bay City/Flint *   Sault Ste. Marie
Ypsilanti

MINNESOTA
Baudette   Crane Lake   **Duluth**/Superior,
WI
Ely   Grand Portage   Grand Marais
International Falls/Rainier   Isle Royal
Minneapolis/St. Paul   Noyes
Pinecreek   Rochester   Roseau
Warroad

MISSISSIPPI
Greenville   Gulfport   Pascagoula
Vicksburg

MISSOURI
Jackson   Kansas City   St. Joseph
St. Louis   Springfield

MONTANA
Butte   Del Bonita   **Great Falls**
Morgan   Opheim   Piegan
Raymond   Roosville   Scobey
Sweetgrass   Turner   Whitetail
Whitlash

NEBRASKA
Omaha

NEVADA
Las Vegas   Reno

NEW HAMPSHIRE
Lebanon   Portsmouth

NEW JERSEY
Atlantic City   Morristown
Perth Amboy (See N.Y./Newark)

NEW MEXICO
Albuquerque   Columbus   Santa Teresa

NEW YORK
Albany   Alexandria Bay   Binghamton
Buffalo/Niagara Cape Vincent
Champlain/Rouses Pt.   Clayton
Massena   **New York +**   Ogdensburg
Oswego   Rochester/Sodus   Sodus Point
Syracuse   Trout River *   Utica

NORTH CAROLINA
Beaufort/Morehead City   **Charlotte**
Durham   Raleigh/Durham   Wilmington
Winston-Salem

NORTH DAKOTA
Ambrose   Antler   Carbury
Dunseith   Fargo   Fortuna
Hannah   Hansboro   Maida
Neche   Noonan   Northgate
Pembina   Portal   Sarles
Sherwood   St. John   Walhalla
Westhope

OHIO
Ashtabula/Conneaut *Cincinnati/Lawrenceburg, IN *
Cleveland   Columbus   Dayton
Toledo/Sandusky*   Wilmington

OKLAHOMA
Oklahoma City   Tulsa

OREGON
Astoria   Coos Bay   Medford
Newport   **Portland**

PENNSYLVANIA
Erie   Harrisburg   Lehigh Valley
Philadelphia * Pittsburgh   Wilkes-Barre/Scran-
ton

PUERTO RICO
Aguadilla   Fajardo   Guanica
Humacao   Jobos   Mayaguez
Ponce   **San Juan**

RHODE ISLAND
Newport   **Providence**

SOUTH CAROLINA
Charleston   Columbia   Georgetown
Greenville/SpartanburgMyrtle Beach

SOUTH DAKOTA
Sioux Falls

TENNESSEE
Blountville   Chattanooga   Knoxville
Memphis   Nashville

TEXAS
Addison   Amarillo   Austin
Brownsville/Los Indios   Corpus   Christi
Dallas/Ft. Worth Del Rio
Del Rio/Amistad Dam   Eagle Pass
El Paso   Fabens   Freeport
Ft. Worth   Hidalgo/Pharr

		Laredo/Columbia
Houston/Galveston + *		
Lubbock	Midland	Port Arthur/Sabine*
Port Lavaca-Point Comfort		
Presidio	Progreso	Rio Grande City
Roma/Falcon Dam	San Antonio	

UTAH

Salt Lake City

VERMONT

Beecher Falls	Burlington	Derby Line
Highgate Springs	Norton	Richford
St. Albans		

VIRGIN ISLANDS

Charlotte Amalie	Christiansted	Coral Bay
Cruz Bay	Frederiksted	

VIRGINIA

Alexandria	Dublin	Dulles Airport
Front Royal	**Norfolk/Newport News***	
Richmond	Roanoke Airport	

WASHINGTON

Aberdeen	Anacortes*	Bellingham*
Blaine	Boundary	Danville
Everett*	Ferry	Friday Harbor*
Frontier	Laurier	Longview*
Lynden	Metaline Falls	Moses Lake
Neah Bay*	Nighthawk	Olympia*
Oroville	Point Roberts	Port Angeles*
Port Townsend*	**Seattle***	Spokane
Sumas	Tacoma*	

WEST VIRGINIA

Charleston

WISCONSIN

Ashland	Green Bay
Manitowoc (Milwaukee)	
Marinette (Milwaukee)	**Milwaukee**
Racine	Sheboygan (Milwaukee)

Consolidated Ports

Columbia River port includes:
Longview, WA and Astoria and Portland, OR.
Beaumont, Orange, Port Arthur, Sabine port of entry includes ports of the same name.
Port of Puget Sound includes:
Tacoma, Seattle, Port Angeles, Port Townsend, Neah Bay, Friday Habor, Everett, Bellingham, Anacortes and Olympia in the State of Washington.
Port of Rock Island includes:
Moline and Davenport, IA.
Port of Shreveport includes:
Bossier City, LA.

Designated User-fee Airports

User-fee airports are listed in 19 CFR 122.15 and described at 19 CFR 122.1 (m). At press time, the user-fee airports were in:
Addisson, TX; Blountville, TN; Broomfield, CO; Daytona Beach, FL; Decatur, IN; Dublin, VA; Edinburg, TX; Egg Harbor Township, NJ; Englewood, CO; Fargo, ND; Ft. Wayne, IN; Ft. Worth, TX; Johnson City, NY; Lexington, KY; Manchester, NH; Medford, OR; Melbourne, FL; Midland, TX; Morristown, NJ; Moses Lake, WA; Myrtle Beach, SC; Ocala, FL; Palm Springs, CA; Rochester, MN; San Bernadino, CA; Sarasota, FL; Scottsdale, AZ; Terre Haute, IN; Victorville, CA; Waterford, MI; Waukegan, IL; West Chicago, IL; West Trenton, NJ; Wheeling, IL; Wilmington, OH; Ypsilanti, MI.

Customs Preclearance Offices in Foreign Countries

These offices are listed in 19 CFR 101.5. At press time, the offices were in the following locations:
Aruba: Orangestad
The Bahamas: Freeport, Nasau
Bermuda: Kindley Field
Canada: Calgary, AB; Edmonton, AB; Montreal, PQ; Ottawa, ON; Toronto, ON; Vancouver, BC; Winnipeg, MB.

Entry of Goods

Entry Process

When a shipment reaches the U.S., the importer of record (i.e., the owner, purchaser, or licensed customs broker designated by the owner, purchaser, or consignee) will file entry documents for the goods with the port director at the port of entry. Imported goods are not legally entered until after the shipment has arrived within the port of entry, delivery of the merchandise has been authorized by Customs and estimated duties have been paid. It is the responsibility of the importer to arrange for examination and release of the goods. For more detailed regulatory information, refer to 19 CFR Part 142, "Entry Process."

Note: In addition to the U.S. Customs Service, importers should contact other agencies when questions regarding particular commodities arise. For example, questions about products regulated by the Food and Drug Administration should be forwarded to the nearest FDA district office (check local phone book under "U.S. Government" listings) or to the FDA Headquaters, Imports Division, 5600 Fishers Lane, Rockville, MD 20857, (301) 443-6553.

The same is true for alcohol, tobacco, firearms, wildlife products (furs, skins, shells), motor vehicles, and other products and merchandise regulated by the 60 federal agencies for which Customs enforces entry laws. Appropriate agencies are identified in this section and in the Commodity Index chapters covering specific products.

Goods may be entered for consumption, entered for warehouse at the port of arrival, or they may be transported inbond to another port of entry and entered there under the same conditions as at the port of arrival. Arrangements for transporting the merchandise to an interior port in-bond may be made by the consignee, by a customs broker, or by any other person having a sufficient interest in the goods for that purpose. *Unless your merchandise arrives directly at the port where you wish to enter it, you may be charged additional fees by the carriers for transportation to the port of entry from the port of arrival unless other arrangements have been made.* Under some circumstances, your goods may be released through your local Customs port even though they arrive at another port from a foreign country. Arrangements must be made prior to arrival at the Customs port where you intend to file your duties and documentation.

Goods to be placed in a foreign trade zone are not entered at the customhouse. Refer to "Foreign Trade Zones" on page 242 for further information.

24-Hour Advance Vessel Manifest Rule

Customs & Border Protection has recently implemented a 24-hour rule to facilitate the entry of goods into the U.S. and increase security at the nations ports. The aim of this rule is to allow Customs to pre-screen shipments entering the United States and target those that appear as high-risk. It also allows U.S. Customs officers to analyze the container content information and identify potential terrorist threats before the U.S.-bound container is loaded at the foreign seaport, not after it arrives in a U.S. port.

The 24-hour rule requires sea carriers and NVOCC's (Non-Vessel Operating Common Carriers) to provide U.S. Customs with detailed descriptions of the contents of sea containers bound for the United States 24 hours before a container is loaded on board a vessel. The effective date of implementation is December 2, 2002, however the enforcement date begins February 1, 2003. Carriers and/or NVOCC's will be required to submit a cargo declaration 24 hours before cargo is laden aboard the vessel at a foreign port. Customs will coordinate with other foreign governments to perform examinations of shipments deemed to be of high-risk.

Details of cargo manifest must be based on actual declaration of cargo by the shipper. The Required Data Elements in M/F are:

- The last foreign port before the vessel departs for US;
- The carrier's Standard Carrier Alpha Code SCAC code for each carrier (including each NVOCC);
- The carrier-assigned voyage number;
- The date the vessel is scheduled to arrive at the first US port in Customs territory;
- The numbers and quantities from the carrier's ocean bills of lading, either master or house;
- The first foreign port(place) where the carrier takes possession of the cargo destined to the United States;
- A precise cargo description(or the Harmonized Tariff Schedule (HTS) numbers to the 6-digit level which is received from shipper;
- The shipper's complete name and address from all bills of lading;
- The complete name and address of the consignee or the owner or owner's representative from all bills of lading;
- The vessel name, country of documentation and official vessel number assigned by International Marine Organization;
- The foreign port where the cargo is laden on board;
- Internationally recognized hazardous material code when such materials are being shipped;
- Container numbers(for containerized cargo); and
- The seal numbers for all seals affixed to containers.

The regulation requires a precise narrative description of the cargo or the 6-digit tariff number for those with the skill to provide it correctly. If there is doubt about the accuracy of a 6-digit tariff number, which can sometimes be difficult to ascertain, a precise narrative description should be used.

A precise narrative description is a description that is precise enough for Customs to be able to identify the shapes, physical characteristics, and likely packaging of the manifested cargo so that Customs can identify any anomalies in the cargo when a container is run through imaging equipment. The description must also be precise enough to identify any goods, which may emit radiation. How specific that information must be depends on the nature of the commodity. For example, "electronics" is not a precise description, but "CD players" or "computer monitors" would be.

Customs will continue to work with the trade industry to refine what descriptions are acceptable. Customs will not begin its enforcement actions with descriptions where the required level of precision is not clear; instead they will continue to notify the carriers when these more difficult commodities are not adequately described. However, cargo descriptions are one of the most important elements to assist Customs in precise targeting, and it is in the importer's best interest to become precise and compliant as quickly as possible. Not only will this avoid eventual enforcement action, but it may also avoid container "do not load" message and "holds" due to Customs not being comfortable that it knows what is in the container.

To be clear, IN NO CASE is a blank description, freight all kinds (FAK), said to contain (STC) with or without other description, general merchandise, "26 pallets", various retail merchandise, consolidated cargo or other similarly vague descriptions acceptable.

The following terms are meant to be used as a guide. They are illustrative, not exhaustive, examples of acceptable and unacceptable descriptions. Phrases or words in parenthesis are meant as examples.

NOT ACCEPTABLE	ACCEPTABLE
Apparel Wearing Apparel Ladies' Apparel Men's Apparel	Clothing Shoes Footwear Jewelry (may include watches)
Appliances	Kitchen AppliancesIndustrial AppliancesHeat Pump
Autoparts, Parts	New AutopartsUsed Autoparts
Caps	Baseball Caps Blasting Caps Bottle Caps Hub Caps
Chemicals, hazardous Chemicals, non-hazardous	Actual Chemical Name (not brand name) Or U.N. HAZMAT Code Identifier #
Electronic Goods Electronics	Computers Consumer Electronics, Telephones Electronic Toys (can include Gameboys, Game Cubes, Dancing Elmo Doll etc.) Personal/Household Electronics (i.e. PDA's, VCR's, TV's)
Equipment	Industrial Equipment, Oil Well Equipment Automotive Equipment, Poultry Equipment etc.
Flooring	Wood Flooring, Plastic Flooring, Carpet, Ceramic Tile, Marble Flooring
Foodstuffs	Oranges Fish Packaged Rice, Packaged Grain, Bulk Grain
Iron	Iron Pipes, Steel Pipes
Steel	Iron Building Material, Steel Building Material
Leather Articles	Saddles Leather Handbags Leather Jackets, Shoes
Machinery	Metal Working MachineryCigarette Making Machinery
Machines	Sewing Machines Printing Machines
Pipes	Plastic Pipes PVC Pipes Steel Pipes Copper Pipes
Plastic Goods	Plastic Kitchenware, Plastic Houseware, Industrial Plastics Toys, New/Used Auto Parts
Polyurethane	Polyurethane Threads Polyurethane Medical Gloves
	Personal Effects Household Goods

NOT ACCEPTABLE	ACCEPTABLE
Rubber Articles	Rubber Hoses Tires Toys Rubber Conveyor Belts
Rods	Welding Rods Rebar Aluminum Rods Reactor Rods
Scrap	Plastic Scrap Aluminum Scrap Iron Scrap
STC (Said to Contain)General CargoFAK (Freight of All Kinds)"No Description"	
Tiles	Ceramic Tiles Marble Tiles
Tools	Hand Tools Power Tools Industrial Tools
Wires	Electric WiresAuto HarnessCoiled Wire (Industrial)

The party that provides the cargo declaration information to Customs is responsible for ensuring that this information is accurate. Customs will initially use informed compliance with the carriers, but if repeated violations occur Customs may assess penalties or claims for liquidated damages.

The rule does not apply to cargo that is shipped to Canada or Mexico and into the U.S. by truck or rail. Customs has targeting personnel stationed at seaports in Canada and cooperation with Canadian authorities has been excellent. If the Customs administration of either country suspects that goods are being routed in an attempt to evade scrutiny, those goods would likely be treated as high risk. For vessels that are departing Canada or Mexico with cargo destined for the United States, the 24-hour rule does apply.

If a container is examined by Customs, either in the United States or at a foreign port, and the manifest description of the contents is, in Customs opinion, inaccurate, carriers can be held liable for penalties and NVOCC's can be held liable for liquidated damages. The rule indicates that in addition to penalties applicable under other provisions of law, carriers may be liable for civil penalties under 19 USC 1436 and NVOCC's may be liable for liquidated damages under 19 CFR 113.64(c).

Evidence of Right to Make Entry

Goods may be entered only by the owner, purchaser, or a licensed customs broker. When the goods are consigned "to order," the bill of lading properly endorsed by the consignor may serve as evidence of the right to make entry. An air waybill may be used for merchandise arriving by air.

In most instances, entry is made by a person or firm certified by the carrier bringing the goods to the port of entry and is considered the "owner" of the goods for customs purposes. The document issued by the carrier is known as a "Carrier's Certificate." An example of the format is shown in the appendix. In certain circumstances, entry may be made by means of a duplicate bill of lading or a shipping receipt. Refer to 19 CFR 141 Subpart B, "Right to Make Entry and Declarations on Entry" for more information.

Entry for Consumption

The entry of merchandise is a two-part process consisting of (1) filing the documents necessary to determine whether merchandise may be released from Customs custody and (2) filing the documents that contain information for duty assessment and statistical purposes. Both of these processes can be accomplished electronically via the Automated Broker Interface program of the National Customs Automation Program (NCAP), provided electronic filing is available. To become a participant in one of the programs available under NCAP, importers or brokers should request information from Customs.

Entry Documents

Within 15 calendar days of the date of arrival of a shipment at a U.S. port of entry, entry documents must be filed at a location specified by the port director, unless an extension is granted. These documents, as listed in 19 CFR 142.3 are:

a. Entry Manifest, Customs **Form 7533**; or Application and Special Permit for Immediate Delivery, Customs **Form 3461**, or other form of merchandise release required by the port director.

b. Evidence of right to make entry.

c. Commercial invoice or a pro forma invoice when the commercial invoice cannot be produced.

d. Packing lists if appropriate.

e. Other documents necessary to determine merchandise admissibility.

If the goods are to be released from Customs custody on entry documents, an entry summary for consumption must be filed and estimated duties deposited at the port of entry within 10 working days of the time the goods are entered and released.

Refer to 19 CFR Part 142 Subpart A, "Entry Documentation," for more information.

Surety

The entry must be accompanied by evidence that a bond is posted with Customs to cover any potential duties, taxes, and penalties that may accrue. Bonds may be secured through a resident U.S. surety company but may also be posted in the form of U.S. money or certain U.S. government obligations. They may also be posted electronically. In the event that a customhouse broker is employed for the purpose of making entry, the broker may permit the use of his bond to provide the required coverage. 19 CFR 142.4 lists bond requirements.

Entry Summary Documentation

Following presentation of the entry, the shipment may be examined by Customs or examination may be waived. The shipment is then released, provided no legal or regulatory violations have been noted. Entry summary documentation is filed and estimated duties are deposited within 10 working days of the release of the merchandise at a designated customhouse. Details are given in 19 CFR 142.16, "Entry Summary Documentation." Briefly, the documentation consists of:

a.   The entry package returned to the importer, broker, or his authorized agent after merchandise is permitted release.

b.   Entry summary (Customs **Form 7501**)

c.   Other invoices and documents necessary for the assessment of duties, collection of statistics, or the determination that all import requirements have been satisfied. This paper documentation can be reduced or eliminated when utilizing features of the Automated Broker Interface or the National Customs Automation Program (NCAP).

Electronic Entry

Customs & Border Protection continues to upgrade its capabilities to efficiently process goods entering into the United States. The current import system, the Automated Commercial System (ACS), was designed in 1984 and will not be able to meet the increasingly complex, long-term requirements impacted by the growth in trade, enforcement responsibilities, and legislation, therefore a new system, the Automated Commercial Environment (ACE), is set to replace and improve the ACS.

ACE will provide an integrated, fully automated information system to enable the efficient collection, processing, and analysis of commercial import and export data. It will simplify dealings between Customs and the trade community by automating time-consuming and labor-intensive transactions and moving goods through the ports and on to markets faster and at lower cost.

This new system will extend NCAP as well as continue to allow importers to file documentation and declarations, post bonds, and pay duties, fees, and taxes electronically. And also provide for electronic batch filing of multiple entries, periodic reconciliation of entries, and payment of duties, taxes, and fees on a monthly account basis.

ACE benefits include:

- Reduced data entry

- Reduced financial processing

- Reduced paper handling

- Increased access to data

ACE is a large-scale, complex project that will be the foundation of Customs-wide modernization.. In March 2002, Customs began building the foundational elements of ACE. In spring 2003, Customs began to provide support via the Internet to Customs trade account managers and 40 selected importers.

Customs is preparing for a planned and phased process for the transition from the old import system, ACS, to ACE. A transitional architecture will be in place to temporarily support dual operations and facilitate the transfer of data. Steadily over the period, official record systems and data will be migrated to ACE and dependence on the old system will diminish.

ACE Features Include:

Customs Web Portal

- Provides a single sign on for all system applications.

- Using a customized web page, the portal is a user-friendly starting point for all Customs Officers.

- Promotes communication, information sharing, and uniformity by permitting users to access information, and send and receive messages both within Customs and, externally, with the Trade and government agencies.

Account Management

- Aligns Customs with business practices used by the Trade, such as periodic payments, and maximizes trade compliance.

- Importers, brokers, and carriers will be organized by account. All related records and supporting transactions can be viewed and summarized in their account.

- All Customs transactions will be tracked and viewed by account. This provides integrated view of exports, imports, and in-bond movements. Results of routine, automated analyses will be displayed as ACE progresses.

Cargo Processing

- One standard data set for manifest for all modes of transportation.

- Gathers required information and provides data needed by Customs and government agencies to support import/export processes and fulfill Customs mission.

- Permits transfer of automated entry, entry summary, and manifest information from Importers, Brokers, and Carriers directly to Customs, as early as possible.

Border Security

- ACE promotes intelligence sharing and enforcement collaboration among government agencies.

- Cargo tracking and data mining will support CSI and C-TPAT, container X-Ray system, transponders, and other state-of-the-art security initiatives.

- ACE is not just a "Trade System." It allows Customs to capture advance data from the international supply chain and processes it.

Immediate Delivery

An alternate procedure that provides for immediate release of a shipment may be used in some cases by making application for a Special Permit for Immediate Delivery on Customs **Form 3461** prior to the arrival of the merchandise. Carriers participating in the Automated Manifest System can receive conditional release authorizations after leaving the foreign country, and up to five days before the landing in the U.S. If the application is approved, the shipment is released expeditiously following arrival. An entry summary must then be filed in proper form, either on paper or electronically, and estimated duties deposited within 10 working days of release. Release using **Form 3461** is limited to the following merchandise:

a.   Merchandise arriving from Canada or Mexico, if approved by the port director and an appropriate bond is on file.

b.   Fresh fruits and vegetables for human consumption arriving from Canada and Mexico and removed from the area immediately contiguous to the border to the importer's premises within the port of importation.

c.   Shipments consigned to or for the account of any agency or officer of the U.S. Government.

d.   Articles for a trade fair.

e.   Tariff-rate quota merchandise and under certain circumstances merchandise subject to an absolute quota. Absolute quota items require a formal entry at all times. In some cases the port director may allow perishable merchandise to be delivered to the importer's premises.

f.   In very limited circumstances, merchandise released to a warehouse followed within 10 working days by a warehouse withdrawal for consumption.

g.   Merchandise specifically authorized by Customs Headquarters to be entitled to release for immediate delivery.

More information on immediate delivery may be found at 19 CFR 142 Subpart C, "Special Permit for Immediate Delivery."

Entry for Warehouse

If it is desirable to postpone the release of the goods, they may be placed in a Customs bonded warehouse under a warehouse entry. The goods may remain in the bonded warehouse up to five years from the date of importation. At any time during that period, warehoused goods may be reexported without the payment of duty or they may be withdrawn for consumption upon the payment of duty at the rate of duty in effect on the date of withdrawal. If the goods are destroyed under Customs supervision, no duty is payable.

While the goods are in the bonded warehouse, they may, under Customs supervision, be manipulated by cleaning, sorting, repacking, or otherwise changing their condition by processes that do not amount to manufacturing. After manipulation and within the warehousing period, the goods may be exported without the payment of duty or they may be withdrawn for con-

sumption upon payment of duty at the rate applicable to the goods in their manipulated condition at the time of withdrawal. Perishable goods, explosive substances, or prohibited importations may not be placed in a bonded warehouse. Certain restricted articles, though not allowed release from custody, may be warehoused.

Information regarding bonded manufacturing warehouses is contained in section 311 of the Tariff Act. (19 USC 1311) and in 19 CFR 144, "Warehouse and Re-Warehouse Entries and Withdrawals."

Unentered Goods

The 1993 Customs Modernization Act (Mod Act) has substantially amended the provisions for unentered goods. These amendments are intended to facilitate the automation of Customs procedures, reduce the costs of storing and processing unclaimed or abandoned merchandise, and authorize the conversion of such merchandise to official use. The changes are noted throughout the following discussion.

Goods that remain unentered for more than 15 calendar days after arrival at the port of entry, or the port of destination for in-bond shipments, are subject to the provisions for unclaimed or abandoned merchandise. Such goods may be placed in a general-order warehouse at the importer's risk and expense. The Mod Act has expanded application of these provisions to cover not only merchandise for which no entry is made at all, but also for which a complete entry is not made within 15 days after arrival.

Under the Mod Act, carriers of unentered goods must notify a bonded warehouse that the merchandise is unentered. The warehouse will arrange with a bonded carrier or licensed cartage firm to transport the merchandise to the warehouse at the risk and expense of the consignee of the goods. If the goods are not entered within six months from the date of importation, Customs can dispose of them. Perishable goods, goods liable to depreciation, and explosive substances, however, may be sold sooner. Immediate sale is also permitted if the storage expense of the seized merchandise is deemed disproportionate to its value.

The Mod Act has also created several options for disposal of unentered goods. Customs may elect to sell them at public auction or to notify all known interested parties that clear title to the merchandise will vest in the U.S. 30 days after notice in the absence of an entry for consumption. If title vests in the U.S. under the second option, the government may sell the goods, retain them for official use, or transfer them to any federal, state, or local agency. The government recipient must pay all transfer and storage charges on retained or transferred merchandise. A party can apply to the Secretary of the Treasury for relief from the forfeiture of unclaimed or abandoned goods, which relief is discretionary and depends on whether the party can establish that no notice was received of the imminent transfer of title to the U.S.

If the unclaimed or abandoned goods are sold, storage charges, expenses of sale, duties, taxes, fees, and amounts for the satisfaction of liens will be paid from the sale proceeds. Any surplus remaining after these deductions is ordinarily payable to the holder of a duly endorsed bill of lading. This bill of lading must, however, cover those goods, and the claim must be made within 10 days of the sale. Carriers, not port directors, are required to notify a bonded warehouse of unentered merchandise. If the goods are subject to internal revenue taxes and will not bring enough on sale at public auction to pay the taxes, they are subject to retention by the U.S. government, destruction, or other disposition at the discretion of Customs.

For more information on the procedures for abandoned merchandise, refer to 19 CFR 127, "General Order, Unclaimed, and Abandoned Merchandise."

Mail Entries

Importers have found that in some cases it is to their advantage to use the mails to import merchandise into the U.S. Some benefits to be gained are:

a.   Ease in clearing shipments through Customs. The duties on parcels valued at the regulatory amount or less are collected by the letter carrier delivering the parcel to the addressee (see note below).

b.   Savings on shipping charges. Smaller, low-valued packages can often be sent less expensively through the mails.

c.   No entry required on duty-free merchandise not exceeding the regulatory amount in value (usually $2,000).

d.   No need to clear shipments personally if they are valued at less than the regulatory amount.

Note: The exact amount is set by regulation, but the statutory cap has been raised from $1,250 to $2,500 by the 1993 Customs Modernization Act.

Joint Customs and postal regulations provide that all parcel post packages must have a Customs declaration securely attached giving an accurate description and valuation of the contents. This declaration may be obtained from post offices. Commercial shipments must also be accompanied by a commercial invoice enclosed with the parcel bearing the declaration.

Each mail article containing an invoice or statement of value should be marked on the address side "Invoice enclosed." If the invoice or statement cannot conveniently be enclosed within the sealed article, it may be securely attached to the article. Failure to comply with any of these requirements will delay clearance of the shipment through Customs.

Packages other than parcel post, such as letter-class mail, commercial papers, printed matter, and samples of merchandise, must bear on the address side a label, **Form C1**, provided by the Universal Postal Union, or the endorsement "May be opened for customs purposes before delivery" or similar words definitely waiving the privacy of the seal and indicating that Customs officers may open the parcel without recourse to the addressee. Parcels not labeled or endorsed in this manner and found to contain prohibited merchandise or merchandise subject to duty or tax are subject to forfeiture.

Customs prepares the customs entry for mail importations not exceeding the regulatory amount in value, and the letter carrier at the destination delivers the parcel to the addressee upon payment of the duty. If the value of a mail importation exceeds the regulatory amount, the addressee is notified to prepare and file a formal Customs entry (consumption entry) for it at the Customs port nearest to him. A commercial invoice is required with the entry. The informal entry amount is set by regulation, but the statutory cap has been raised from $1,250 to $2,500 by the 1993 Customs Modernization Act.

A Customs processing fee of $5.00 will be assessed on each item of dutiable mail for which Customs prepares documentation. This nominal charge on all dutiable or taxable mail, in addition to the duty, is collected from the addressee. This is a postal fee (in addition to prepaid postage) authorized by international postal conventions and agreements as partial reimbursement to the Postal Service for its work in clearing packages through Customs and delivering them.

Note: The following exceptions are made with respect to the regulatory amount for informal entry:

- Articles classified in sub-chapters III and IV, HTSUS chapter 99 (temporary modifications of trade legislation and agricultural import restrictions)
- Billfolds and other flat goods
- Feathers and feather products
- Flowers and foliage, artificial or preserved
- Footwear
- Fur, articles of
- Gloves
- Handbags
- Headwear and hat braids
- Leather, articles of
- Luggage
- Millinery ornaments
- Pillows and cushions
- Plastics, miscellaneous articles of
- Rawhides and skins
- Rubber, miscellaneous articles of
- Textile fibers and products
- Toys, games, and sports equipment
- Trimmings

The limit for these articles is set at $250, except for textiles (fibers and products). However, almost all commercial shipments of textile fibers and products require formal entry regardless of value. Unaccompanied shipments of made-to-measure suits from Hong Kong require a formal entry regardless of value.

Shipment Detention

The 1993 Customs Modernization Act added new procedures for Customs to follow in detaining shipments. Pursuant to the Act, if Customs has authority to determine the admissibility of a shipment, that decision must be made within five working days (excluding weekends and holidays) following the date the merchandise is presented for customs examination. Any goods not released within that time are considered detained. No later than five days (excluding weekends and holidays) after deciding to detain the goods, Customs must issue a notice of detention to the importer or other party with an interest in the goods. The notice will include a description of what information would accelerate disposition if supplied to Customs by the importer.

If Customs fails to make a final determination on admissibility of detained merchandise within 30 days after it is presented for Customs examination, the merchandise is presumed to be excluded. The 30-day period may vary if specifically authorized by other laws.

Recordkeeping and the (a)(1)(A) List

Substantial recordkeeping is required for entries of imported merchandise, and Customs is authorized to make reasonable audits of records required for the entry of merchandise. Under the 1993 Customs Modernization Act (Mod Act), procedures have been amended to reduce paperwork demands on importers at the time of entry, but the recordkeeping requirements have been increased since compliance will largely be effected through audits after entry has taken place.

Customs has promulgated the "(a)(1)(A) list," describing documents which importers and others must retain for five years. (An exception is made for records of drawback claims, which must be kept until the third anniversary of the date the claim was paid.) The "interim" (a)(1)(A) list was published on January 3, 1996; it is effective as a final rule to the extent that importers may be subject to penalties for failure to retain or retrieve the indicated documents and records. The "(a)(1)(A)" list was republished and slightly amended in T.D. 98-56. The (a)(1)(A) list is comprehensive and includes such items as bills of lading, invoices with corrections, foreign assemblers declarations, ATF permits, GSP declarations, and automotive products certificates. Some documents are specifically identified, but others may simply be identified by reference to the governing regulation. Even conscientious importers can face confusion in determining their obligations, but under the "informed compliance" concept of the Mod Act, the increased responsibility for record retention lies squarely with the importer.

Customs may demand to examine the records of any of the following persons: owner of imported goods, importer, consignee, importer of record, entry filer, or other party who imports goods into U.S. customs territory, files a drawback claim, transports or stores merchandise carried or held under bond, or knowingly causes importation, transportation, or storage of merchandise under bond in U.S. customs territory. Records may also be demanded from agents acting for any of these parties, any person whose activities require filing a declaration, or both. To minimize potential exposure, importers should establish formal procedures for recordkeeping. Other parties involved in the import procedures may need to retain records for the first time.

A party who fails to comply with Custom's lawful demand for records is subject to monetary fine at an amount determined by Customs based on the particular situation. For willful failure to maintain, store, or retrieve demanded information, the fine for each release of goods may not exceed the lesser of $100,000 or 75% of the appraised value of the goods. For failure because of negligence, the penalty for each release may not exceed the lesser of $10,000 or 40% of the appraised value of the goods. Customs also has discretion to raise duty rates against such goods. These penalties are not mandatory, and Customs may remit or mitigate them on consideration of the circumstances. They may also be avoided on proof that the demanded information was lost because of a disaster or other event beyond the party's fault, that the party substantially complied with the demand, or that the information had been presented to and retained by Customs.

For more information on recordkeeping obligations, refer to 19 CFR 162 Subpart A, "Inspection, Examination, and Search," and to the (a)(1)(A) List."

Transportation of Merchandise in Bond

Not all merchandise imported into the United States and intended for domestic commerce is entered at the port where it arrives. The importer may prefer to enter the goods at a different location in the United States, in which case the merchandise will have to be further transported to that location. In order to protect United States revenue in these cases, the merchandise must travel in a bonded status from the port of arrival to the intended port of entry. This process is referred to as traveling under Immediate Transportation procedures and is accomplished by the execution of Customs Form 7512 (Transportation Entry and Manifest of Goods Subject to Customs Inspection and Permit). The merchandise is then placed with a carrier who accepts it under its bond for transportation to the intended destination, where the normal merchandise entry process will occur.

Right to Make Entry

Entry by Importer

Merchandise arriving in the U.S. by commercial carrier must be entered by the owner, purchaser, his authorized regular employee, or by the owner's licensed Customs broker designated by the owner, purchaser, or consignee. U.S. Customs officers and employees are not authorized to act as agents for importers or forwarders of imported merchandise, although they may give all reasonable advice and assistance to inexperienced importers.

The only persons who are authorized by the tariff laws of the U.S. to act as agents for importers in the transaction of their Customs business are Customs brokers who are private individuals or firms licensed by the Customs Service. Customs brokers will prepare and file the necessary Customs entries, arrange for the payment of the duties found due, take steps to effect the release of the goods in Customs custody, and otherwise represent their principals in customs matters. The fees charged for these services vary according to the Customs broker and the extent of services performed.

Every entry must be supported by one of the forms of evidence of the right to make entry outlined in this chapter. When entry is made by a Customs broker, a Customs power of attorney given by the person or firm for whom the Customs broker is acting as agent is made in the name of the Customs broker. Ordinarily, the authority of an employee to make entry for his employer is most satisfactorily established by a Customs power of attorney.

Entries Made by Others

Entry of goods may be made by a nonresident individual or partnership, or a foreign corporation through an agent or representative of the exporter in the U.S., a member of the partnership, or an officer of the corporation.

The surety firm guaranteeing any Customs bond required from a nonresident individual or organization must be incorporated in the U.S. In addition, a foreign corporation in whose name merchandise is entered must have a resident agent authorized to accept service of process on its behalf in the state where the port of entry is located.

A licensed Customs broker named in a Customs power of attorney may make entry on behalf of the exporter or the exporter's representative. The owner's declaration made by a nonresident individual or organization, which the Customs broker may request, must be supported by a surety bond providing for the payment of any increased or additional duties found due. Liability for duties is discussed in "Dutiable Status of Goods" on page 218. An owner's declaration executed in a foreign country is acceptable, but it must be executed before a notary public and must bear the notary's seal. Notaries public are found in all U.S. embassies around the world and in most of the larger consulates.

Power of Attorney

A nonresident individual, partnership, or foreign corporation may issue a power of attorney to a regular employee, Customs broker, partner, or corporation officer to act for the nonresident employer in the U.S. Any person named in a power of attorney must be a resident of the U.S. who has been authorized to accept service of process on behalf of the person or organization issuing the power of attorney. The power of attorney to accept service of process becomes irrevocable with respect to Customs transactions duly undertaken. Either Customs Form 5291 or a document using the same language as the form is acceptable. References to those acts that the issuer has not authorized his agent to perform may be deleted from the form or omitted from the document. Refer to 19 CFR 141.32, "Form for power of attorney" for more information.

A power of attorney from a foreign corporation must be supported by the following documents or their equivalent when foreign law or practice differs from that in the U.S.:

1. A certificate from the proper public officer of the country showing the legal existence of the corporation, unless the fact of incorporation is so generally known as to be a matter of common knowledge.

2. A copy of that part of the charter or articles of incorporation that shows the scope of business of the corporation and its governing body.

3. A copy of the document or part thereof by which the person signing the power of attorney derives his authority, such as a provision of the charter or articles of incorporation, a copy of the resolution, minutes of the meeting of the board of directors, or other document by which the governing body conferred the authority. In this case a copy of the bylaws or other document giving the governing board the authority to designate others to appoint agents or attorney is required.

A nonresident individual or partnership or a foreign corporation may issue a power of attorney to authorize the persons or firms named in the power of attorney to issue like powers of attorney to other qualified residents of the U.S. and to empower the residents to whom such powers of attorney are issued to accept service of process on behalf of the nonresident individual or organization.

A power of attorney issued by a partnership must be limited to a period not to exceed two years from the date of execution and shall state the names of all members of the partnership. One member of a partnership may execute a power of attorney for the transaction of the customs business of the partnership. When a new firm is formed by a change of membership, the power of attorney of the prior firm is no longer effective for any customs purpose. The new firm will be required to issue a power of attorney for the transaction of its custom business. All other powers of attorney may be granted for an unlimited period.

Customs **Form 5291** or a document using the same language as the form is also used to empower an agent other than an attorney-at-law or Customs broker to file protests on behalf of an importer under section 514 of the Tariff Act of 1930 as amended. (See 19 CFR 141.32.)

Foreign corporations may comply with Customs regulations by executing a power of attorney on the letterhead of the corporation. A nonresident individual or partner may use this same form.

Because the laws regarding incorporation, notion, and authentication of documents vary from country to country, the agent to be named in the power of attorney should consult the port director of Customs at the port of entry where proof of the document's existence may be required as to the proper form to be used and the formalities to be met.

More information on powers of attorney as they relate to the U.S. Customs Service may be found in 19 CFR 141 Subpart C, "Powers of Attorney."

Examination of Goods and Entry Documents

Prior to the release of the goods, the port director will designate representative quantities for examination by Customs officers under conditions properly safeguarding the goods. Some kinds of goods must be examined to determine whether they meet special requirements of the law. For example, food and beverages unfit for human consumption would not meet the requirements of the Food and Drug Administration.

Examination of goods and documents is necessary to determine, among other things:

a. The value of the goods for Customs purposes and their dutiable status.

b. Whether the goods must be marked with the country of their origin or require special marking or labeling. If so, whether they are marked in the manner required.

c. Whether the shipment contains prohibited articles.

d. Whether the goods are correctly invoiced.

e. Whether the goods are in excess of the invoiced quantities or a shortage exists.

f. Whether the shipment contains illegal narcotics.

One of the primary methods of smuggling narcotics into the U.S. is in cargo shipments. Drug smugglers will place narcotics into a legitimate cargo shipment or container to be retrieved upon arrival in the U.S. Because smugglers use any means possible to hide narcotics, all aspects of the shipment are examined, including: container, pallets, boxes, and product. Only through intensive inspection can narcotics be discovered. The 1993 Customs Modernization Act sets a minimum fine of $500 for importation of undeclared controlled substances. (Refer to 19 CFR 162 Subpart F, "Controlled Substances, Narcotics, and Marihuana" for more information.)

Textiles and textile products are considered trade-sensitive and as such may be subject to a higher percentage of examinations than other commodities.

Customs officers will ascertain the quantity of goods imported, making allowances for shortages under specified conditions and assessing duty on any excess. The invoice may state the quantities in the weights and measures of the country from which the goods are shipped or in the weights and measures of the U.S., but the entry must state the quantities in metric terms. Any information that Customs requires for the release of examined goods must be provided electronically or in paper form at the port of examination. A lack of information will not limit the authority of Customs to examine the goods.

Examination may be made in a Customs Service laboratory or at a private laboratory accredited by Customs. The 1993 Customs Modernization Act provides for the development of an accreditation program. Customs will authorize the release of a representative sample of imported goods for testing at an accredited laboratory. The test results from such a laboratory will be accepted in the absence of results from a Customs Service laboratory. Test results will be given to an importer on request, unless the results reveal information proprietary to the Customs Service or a copyright or patent holder. Testing at a private laboratory is at the importer's expense.

Excess Goods and Shortages

Careful documentation and packing—including full descriptions and counts by package and clear marking and numbering of all packages in the shipment with all this information being provided on the invoice—allows Customs to assess the true value of the entry. It also enables both Customs and the interested parties to determine if any part of the shipment is missing or if the shipment includes excess goods.

If any package that has been designated for examination is found by the Customs officer to contain any article not specified in the invoice or entry, and if Customs has reason to believe the article was omitted from the invoice or entry with fraudulent intent, Customs may impose a fine or even seize the entire package in which the article is found. In the absence of fraudulent intent, the value of the article will simply be added to the entry, and Customs will assess duties, fees, and taxes accordingly. *See e.g.,* 19 USC 1592 and 1595 a(c).

When a deficiency in quantity, weight, or measure is found by the Customs officer in the examination of any package that has been selected for examination, an allowance in duty will be made for the deficiency. Allowance in duty is made for deficiencies in packages not designated for examination, provided that before liquidation of the entry becomes final, the importer notifies the port director of Customs of the shortage and establishes to the satisfaction of the port director that the missing goods were not delivered to him.

Damage or Deterioration

Goods that are found by the Customs officer to be entirely without commercial value at the time of arrival in the U.S. because of damage or deterioration are treated as a "non-importation." No duties are assessed on these goods. When damage or deterioration is present with respect to part of the shipment only, allowance in duties is not made unless the importer segregates the damaged or deteriorated part from the remainder of the shipment under Customs supervision.

When the shipment consists of fruits, vegetables, or other perishable merchandise, allowance in duties cannot be made unless the importer files an application for an allowance with the port director within 96 hours after the unlading of the merchandise and before it has been removed from Customs custody.

On shipments consisting of any article partly or wholly manufactured of iron or steel, or any manufacture of iron or steel, allowance or reduction of duty for partial damage or loss as a result of discoloration or rust is precluded by law.

For more information, refer to 19 CFR 158 Subpart B, "Damaged or Defective Merchandise."

Tare and Draft

In ascertaining the quantity of goods dutiable on net weight, a deduction is made from the gross weight for just and reasonable tare, which is the allowance for a deficiency in the weight or quantity of the merchandise by reason of the weight of the box, cask, bag, or other receptacle that contains it and is weighed with it. The following schedule tares are provided for at 19 CFR 159.22:

Apple Boxes. 3.6 kilograms (8 lb.) per box. This schedule tare includes the paper wrappers, if any, on the apples.

China Clay in So-called Half-ton Casks. 32.6 kilograms (72 lb.) per cask.

Figs in Skeleton Cases. Actual tare for outer containers plus 13% of the gross weight of the inside wooden boxes and figs.

Fresh Tomatoes. 113 gm (4 oz.) per 100 paper wrappings.

Lemons and Oranges. 283 gm (10 oz.) per box and 142 gm (5 oz.) per half-box for paper wrappings, and actual tare for outer containers.

Ocher, Dry, in Casks. 8 % of the gross weight; in oil in casks, 12% of the gross weight.

Pimientos in Tins Imported from Spain.

Size can	Drained weights
3 kg	13.6 kg (30 lb.) —case of 6 tins
794 gm (28 oz.)	16.7 kg (36.7 lb.) —case of 24 tins
425 gm (15 oz.)	8.0 kg (17.72 lb.) —case of 24 tins
198 gm (7 oz.)	3.9 kg (8.62 lb.) —case of 24 tins
113 gm (4 oz.)	2.4 kg (5.33 lb.) —case of 24 tins

Tobacco, Leaf Not Stemmed. 59 kg (13 lb.) per bale; Sumatra: actual tare for outside coverings, plus 1.9 kg (4 lb.) for the inside matting and, if a certificate is attached to the invoice certifying that the bales contain paper wrappings and specifying whether light or heavy paper has been used, either 113 gm (4 oz.) or 227 gm (8 oz.) for the paper wrapping according to the thickness of paper used.

For other goods dutiable on the net weight an actual tare will be determined. An accurate tare stated on the invoice is acceptable for Customs purposes in certain circumstances. If the importer of record files a timely application with the port director of Customs, an allowance may be made in any case for excessive moisture and impurities not usually found in or upon the particular kind of goods.

Packing of Goods and Commingling

Packing

Information on how to pack goods for transport may be obtained from shipping manuals, carriers, forwarding agents, and other sources, such as the "Packing, Shipping, Insurance" section of this reference book. This chapter, therefore, deals with packing goods being exported in a way that will permit U.S. Customs officers to examine, weigh, measure, and release the goods promptly.

Orderly packing and proper invoicing go hand in hand. You will speed up the clearance of your goods through customs, if you:

- Invoice your goods in a systematic manner.
- Show the exact quantity of each item of goods in each box, bale, case, or other package.
- Put marks and numbers on each package.
- Show those marks or numbers on your invoice opposite the itemization of goods contained in the package that bears those marks and numbers.

When the packages contain goods of one kind only, or when the goods are imported in packages the contents and values of which are uniform, the designation of packages for examination and the examination for customs purposes

is greatly facilitated. If the contents and values differ from package to package, the possibility of delay and confusion is increased. Sometimes, because of the kinds of goods or because of the unsystematic manner in which they are packed, the entire shipment must be examined.

Pack and invoice your goods in a manner that makes a speedy examination possible. Always bear in mind that it may not be possible to ascertain the contents of your packages without full examination unless your invoice clearly shows the marks and numbers on each package (whether box, case, or bale) and specifies the exact quantity of each item of adequately described goods in each marked and numbered package.

Also, be aware that Customs examines cargo for narcotics that may be hidden in cargo, unbeknownst to the shipper or the importer. This can be time-consuming and expensive for both the importer and the Customs Service. Narcotics inspections may require completely stripping a container in order to physically examine a large portion of the cargo. This labor-intensive handling of cargo, whether by Customs, labor organizations, or private individuals, results in added costs, increased delays, and possible damage to the product. Importers can expedite this inspection process by working with Cus toms to develop packing standards that will permit effective Customs examinations with a minimum of delay, damage, and cost.

A critical aspect in facilitating inspections is how the cargo is loaded. "Palletizing" cargo—loading it onto pallets or other consolidated units—is an effective way to expedite such examinations. Palletization allows for quick cargo removal, or "devanning" of containers, in minutes using a forklift, compared to the hours it takes manually. Another example is leaving enough space at the top of a container and an aisle down the center to allow access by a narcotic-detector dog.

Your cooperation in these respects will help the Customs officers to decide which packages must be opened and examined; how much weighing, counting, or measuring must be done; and whether the goods are properly marked. It will simplify the calculation of tare and reduce the number of samples to be taken for laboratory analysis or for any other customs purpose. It will facilitate the verification of the contents of the packages as well as the reporting by Customs officers of missing or excess goods. And it will minimize the possibility that the importer may be asked to redeliver for examination packages that were released to him on the theory that the packages designated for examination were sufficient for that purpose.

Packing that amounts to a confusion of different kinds of goods makes it impracticable for Customs officers to determine the quantity of each kind of product in an importation and leads to various complications. No problem arises from the orderly packing of several kinds of properly invoiced goods in one package-it is indiscriminate packing that causes difficulty.

Commingling

Except as mentioned hereafter, whenever articles subject to different rates of duty are so packed together or mingled such that the quantity or value of each class of articles cannot be readily ascertained by Customs officers (without physical segregation of the shipment or the contents of any package thereof) the commingled articles shall be subject to the highest rate of duty applicable to any part of the commingled lot, unless the consignee or his agent segregates them under Customs supervision.

The three methods of ready ascertainment specified by General Note 17 of the HTSUS are (1) sampling, (2) verification of packing lists or other documents filed at the time of entry, or (3) evidence showing performance of commercial settlements tests generally accepted in the trade and filed in the time and manner as prescribed in the Customs Regulations.

The segregation is at the risk and expense of the consignee. It must be done within 30 days (unless a longer time is granted) after the date of personal delivery or the date of mailing of a notice to the consignee by the port director of Customs that the goods are commingled. The compensation and expenses of the Customs officers supervising the segregation must be paid for by the consignee.

Assessment of duty on the commingled lot at the highest applicable rate does not apply to any part of a shipment if the consignee or his agent furnishes satisfactory proof that (1) such part is commercially negligible, is not capable of segregation without excessive cost, and will not be segregated prior to its use in a manufacturing process or otherwise, and (2) the commingling was not intended to avoid the payment of lawful duties.

Any article for which such proof is furnished shall be considered for all Customs purposes as a part of the article, subject to the next lower rate of duty, with which it is commingled. In addition, the highest rate rule mentioned does not apply to any part of a shipment if there is furnished satisfactory proof that (1) the value of the commingled articles is less than the aggregate value would be if the shipment were segregated, (2) the shipment is not capable of segregation without excessive cost and will not be segregated prior to its use in a manufacturing process or otherwise, and (3) the commingling was not intended to avoid the payment of lawful duties.

Any merchandise for which such proof is furnished shall be considered for all Customs purposes to be dutiable at the rate applicable to the material present in greater quantity than any other material.

The above rules do not apply if the tariff schedules provide a particular tariff treatment for commingled articles. For more information on regulations regarding commingling, refer to 19 CFR 152.13 and General Note 17 of the HTSUS.

Suggestions for Exporters Sending Goods to the United States

For faster Customs clearance:

- Include all information required on your Customs invoices.
- Prepare your invoices carefully. Type them clearly. Allow sufficient space between lines. Keep the data within each column.
- Make sure that your invoices contain the information that would be shown on a wellprepared packing list.
- Mark and number each package so it can be identified with the corresponding marks and numbers appearing on your invoice.

- Show a detailed description on your invoice of each item of merchandise contained in each individual package.
- Mark your goods legibly and conspicuously with the country of origin unless they are specifically exempted from country-of-origin marking requirements, and with such other marking as is required by the marking laws of the United States. Exemptions and general marking requirements are detailed in Chapters 29 and 30.
- Comply with the provisions of any special laws of the United States that may apply to your

goods, such as laws relating to food, drugs, cosmetics, alcoholic beverages, radioactive materials, and others. (See Chapters 33, 34 and 35.)

- Observe the instructions closely with respect to invoicing, packaging, marking, labeling, etc., sent to you by your customer in the United States. He or she has probably made a careful check of the requirements that will have to be met when your merchandise arrives.

- Work with U.S. Customs to develop packing standards for your commodities.

- Establish sound security procedures at your facility and while transporting your goods for shipment. Do not give narcotics smugglers the opportunity to introduce narcotics into your shipment.

- Consider shipping on a carrier participating in the Automated Manifest System.

- If you use a licensed customs broker for your transaction, consider using a firm that participates in the Automated Broker Interface.

Informed Compliance

Definition

Informed compliance is a shared responsibility between Customs and the import community wherein Customs effectively communicates its requirements to the trade, and the people and businesses subject to those requirements conduct their regulated activities in accordance with U.S. laws and regulations. A key component of informed compliance is that the importer is expected to exercise reasonable care in his or her importing operations. Informed compliance benefits both parties: When voluntary compliance is achieved, Customs resources need not be expended on redundant examinations or entry reviews for the importer's cargo found to be dependably compliant. From the trade perspective, when voluntary compliance is attained, compliant importers are less likely to have their shipments examined or their entries reviewed. The Customs Service publishes a wealth of information to assist the import community in complying with Customs requirements. We issue rulings and informed compliance publications on a variety of technical subjects and processes. Most of these materials can be found on-line at **www.cbp.gov**. We urge importers to make sure they are using the latest versions of any printed materials.

Reasonable Care Checklists

Reasonable care is an explicit responsibility on the part of the importer. Despite its seemingly simple connotation, the term reasonable care defies easy explanation because the facts and circumstances surrounding every import transaction differ, from the experience of the importer to the nature of the imported articles. Consequently, neither the Customs Service nor the importing community can develop a reasonable care checklist capable of covering every import transaction. The Customs Service recommends that the import community examine the list of questions below. These questions may suggest methods that importers may find useful in avoiding compliance problems and in meeting the responsibilities of reasonable care. These questions are intended to promote compliance with Customs laws and regulations, but be aware that the list is advisory, not exhaustive. The checklist is intended as a guide and has no legal, binding or precedential effect on Customs or the importing community. The questions apply whether the importer of record conducts the transactions(s) him- or herself, or whether the importer hires others to do it

General Questions for All Transactions:

1. If you have not retained an expert (e.g., lawyer, customs broker, accountant, or customs consultant) to assist you in complying with Customs requirements, do you have access to the Customs Regulations (Title 19 of the Code of Federal Regulations), the Harmonized Tariff Schedule of the United States, and Customs Bulletin and Decisions? (All three are available from the Superintendent of Documents, Tel. 202.512.1800.) Do you have access to the Customs Web site at www.cbp.gov, Customs Electronic Bulletin Board (CEBB), or other research service that provides the information to help you establish reliable procedures and facilitate compliance with Customs law and regulations?

2. Has a responsible, knowledgeable individual within your organization reviewed your customs documentation to assure that it is full, complete and accurate? If the documentation was prepared outside your organization, do you have a reliable method to assure that you receive copies of the information submitted to Customs, that it is reviewed for accuracy, and that Customs is apprised of needed corrections in a timely fashion?

3. If you use an expert to help you comply with Customs requirements, have you discussed your importations in advance with that person, and have you provided him or her with complete, accurate information about the import transaction(s)?

4. Are identical transactions or merchandise handled differently at different ports or Customs offices within the same port? If so, have you brought this fact to Customs officials' attention?

Merchandise Description & Tariff Classification

Basic Question: Do you know what you ordered, where it was made, and what it is made of?

1. Have you provided a complete, accurate description of your merchandise to Customs in accordance with 19 U.S.C. 1481? (Also, see 19 CFR 141.87 and 19 CFR 141.89 for special merchandise description requirements.)

2. Have you provided Customs with the correct tariff classification of your merchandise in accordance with 19 U.S.C. 1484?

3. Have you obtained a Customs ruling regarding the description of your merchandise or its tariff classification (see 19 CFR Part 177)? If so, have you followed the ruling and apprised appropriate Customs officials of those facts (i.e., of the ruling and your compliance with it)?

4. Where merchandise description or tariff classification information is not immediately available, have you established a reliable procedure for obtaining it and providing it to Customs?

5. Have you participated in a Customs preclassification of your merchandise in order to get it properly described and classified?

6. Have you consulted the tariff schedules, Customs informed compliance publications, court cases or Customs rulings to help you properly describe and classify the merchandise?

7. Have you consulted with an expert (e.g., lawyer, customs broker, accountant, customs consultant) to assist in the description and/or classification of the merchandise?

8. If you are claiming a conditionally free or special tariff classification or provision for your merchandise (e.g., GSP, HTS Item 9802, NAFTA), how have you verified that the merchandise qualifies for such status? Do you have the documentation necessary to support the claim? If making a NAFTA preference claim, do you have a NAFTA certificate of origin in your possession?

9. Is the nature of your merchandise such that a laboratory analysis or other specialized procedure is advised for proper description and classification?

10. Have you developed reliable procedures to maintain and produce the required entry documentation and supporting information?

Valuation

Basic Questions: Do you know the "price actually paid or payable" for your merchandise? Do you know the terms of sale? Whether there will be rebates, tie-ins, indirect costs, additional payments? Whether "assists" were provided or commissions or royalties paid? Are amounts actual or estimated? Are you and the supplier "related parties"?

1. Have you provided Customs with a proper declared value for your merchandise in accordance with 19 U.S.C. 1484 and 19 U.S.C. 1401a?

2. Have you obtained a Customs ruling regarding valuation of the merchandise (see 19 CFR Part 177)? Can you establish that you followed the ruling reliably? Have you brought those facts to Customs attention?

3. Have you consulted the Customs valuation laws and regulations, Customs Valuation Encyclopedia, Customs informed compliance publications, court cases and Customs rulings to assist you in valuing merchandise?

4. If you purchased the merchandise from a "related" seller, have you reported that fact upon entry? Have you assured that the value reported to Customs meets one of the "related party" tests?

5. Have you assured that all legally required costs or payments associated with the imported merchandise (assists, commissions, indirect payments or rebates, royalties, etc.) have been reported to Customs?

6. If you are declaring a value based upon a transaction in which you were/are not the buyer, have you substantiated that the transaction is a bona fide "sale at arm's length" and that the merchandise was clearly destined to the United States at the time of sale?

7. If you are claiming a conditionally free or special tariff classification or provision for your merchandise (GSP, HTS Item 9802, NAFTA), have you reported the required value information and obtained the documentation necessary to support the claim?

8. Have you produced the required entry documentation and supporting information?

Country of Origin/Marking/Quota

Basic Question: Have you ascertained the correct country of origin for the imported merchandise?

1. Have you reported the correct country of origin on Customs entry documents?

2. Have you assured that the merchandise is properly marked upon entry with the correct country of origin (if required) in accordance with 19 U.S.C. 1304 and any other applicable special marking requirements (watches, gold, textile labeling, etc)?

3. Have you obtained a Customs ruling regarding the proper marking and country of origin of the merchandise (see 19 CFR Part 177)? If so, have you followed the ruling and brought that fact to Customs attention?

4. Have you consulted with a customs expert regarding the correct country of origin/proper marking of your merchandise?

5. Have you apprised your foreign supplier of Customs country-of-origin marking requirements prior to importation of your merchandise?

6. If you are claiming a change in the origin of the merchandise or claiming that the goods are of U.S. origin, have you taken required measures to substantiate your claim (e.g., do you have U.S. milling certificates or manufacturers' affidavits attesting to production in the United States)?

7. If importing textiles or apparel, have you ascertained the correct country of origin in accordance with 19 U.S.C. 3592 (Section 334, P.L. 103-465) and assured yourself that no illegal transshipment or false or fraudulent practices were involved?

8. Do you know how your goods are made, from raw materials to finished goods, by whom and where?

9. Have you ensured that the quota category is correct?

10. Have you checked the Status Report on Current Import Quotas (Restraint Levels), issued by Customs, to determine if your goods are subject to a quota category with "part" categories?

11. Have you obtained correct visas for those goods subject to visa categories?

12. For textile articles, have you prepared a proper country declaration for each entry, i.e., a single country declaration (if wholly obtained/produced) or a

multi-country declaration (if raw materials from one country were transformed into goods in a second)?

13. Can you produce all entry documentation and supporting information, including certificates of origin, if Customs requires you to do so?

Intellectual Property Rights

Basic Question: Have you determined whether your merchandise or its packaging use any trademarks or copyrighted material or are patented? If so, can you establish that you have a legal right to import those items into and/or use them in the United States?

1. If you are importing goods or packaging bearing a trademark registered in the United States, have you established that it is genuine and not restricted from importation under the "gray-market" or parallel-import requirements of United States law (see 198 CFR 133.21), or that you have permission from the trademark holder to import the merchandise?

2. If you are importing goods or packaging that contain registered copyrighted material, have you established that this material is authorized and genuine? If you are importing sound recordings of live performances, were the recordings authorized?

3. Is your merchandise subject to an International Trade Commission or court-ordered exclusion order?

4. Can you produce the required entry documentation and supporting information?

Miscellaneous

1. Have you assured that your merchandise complies with other agencies' requirements (e.g., FDA, EPA, DOT, CPSC, FTC, Agriculture, etc.) and obtained licenses or permits, if required, from them?

2. Are your goods subject to a Commerce Department dumping or countervailing-duty investigation or determination? If so, have you complied with Customs reporting requirements of this fact (e.g., 19 CFR 141.61)?

3. Is your merchandise subject to quota/visa requirements? If so, have you provided a correct visa for the goods upon entry?

4. Have you assured that you have the right to make entry under the Customs Regulations?

5. Have you filed the correct type of Customs entry (e.g., TIB, T&E, consumption entry, mail entry)?

Additional Questions for Textile and Apparel Importers

Section 333 of the Uruguay Round Implementation Act (19 U.S.C. 1592a) authorizes the Secretary of the Treasury to publish a list of foreign producers, manufacturers, suppliers, sellers, exporters, or other foreign persons found to have violated 19 U.S.C. 1592 by using false, fraudulent or counterfeit documentation, labeling, or prohibited transshipment practices in connection with textiles and apparel products. Section 1592a also requires any importer of record who enters or otherwise attempts to introduce into United States commerce textile or apparel products that were directly or indirectly produced, manufactured, supplied, sold, exported, or transported by such named person(s) to show, to the Secretary's satisfaction, that the importer has exercised reasonable care to ensure that the importations are accompanied by accurate documentation, packaging and labeling regarding the products' origin. Under section 1592a, reliance solely upon information from a person named on the list does not constitute the exercise of reasonable care. Textile and apparel importers who have a commercial relationship with any of the listed parties must exercise reasonable care in ensuring that the documentation covering the imported merchandise, its packaging and its labeling accurately identify the importation's country of origin. This demonstration of reasonable care must rely upon more information than that supplied by the named party.

In order to meet the reasonable care standard when importing textile or apparel products and when dealing with a party named on this list, an importer should consider the following questions to ensure that the documentation, packaging and labeling are accurate regarding country-of-origin considerations. This list is illustrative, not exhaustive:

1. Has the importer had a prior relationship with the named party?

2. Has the importer had any seizures or detentions of textile or apparel products that were directly or indirectly produced, supplied, or transported by the named party?

3. Has the importer visited the company's premises to ascertain that the company actually has the capacity to produce the merchandise?

4. Where a claim of an origin-conferring process is made in accordance with 19 CFR 102.21, has the importer ascertained that the named party actually performed that process?

5. Is the named party really operating from the country that he or she claims on the documentation, packaging or labeling?

6. Have quotas for the imported merchandise closed, or are they near closing, from the main producer countries for this commodity?

7. Does the country have a dubious or questionable history regarding this commodity?

8. Have you questioned your supplier about the product's origin?

9. If the importation is accompanied by a visa, permit or license, has the importer verified with the supplier or manufacturer that the document is of valid, legitimate origin? Has the importer examined that document for any irregularities that would call its authenticity into question?

Compliance Assessment/Compliance Measurement

Of primary interest to the trade community is the compliance assessment, which is the systematic evaluation of an importer's systems supporting his or her Customs-related operations. The assessment includes testing import and financial transactions, reviewing the adequacy of the importer's internal controls, and determining the importer's compliance levels in key areas. Compliance assessments are conducted in accordance with 19 U.S.C. 1509.

The assessment is conducted by an interdisciplinary team composed of a Customs auditor, import specialist, account manager, industry expert (highly knowledgeable of the electronics or auto parts or surgical equipment industries, for example), and possibly other Customs specialists (attorney, inspector, scientist). The compliance assessment utilizes professionally accepted statistical sampling and auditing techniques to review selected import transactions from the company's previous fiscal year.

Compliance assessments will evaluate the company's applicable customs operations such as:

- Record keeping
- Merchandise classification/trade statistics
- Merchandise quantities
- Antidumping/countervailing duty operations
- Quota conformity
- Merchandise value
- Warehouse or foreign trade zone operations
- Merchandise transshipment
- Special trade programs (GSP, CBI, others).

Companies found in compliance with Customs laws and regulations will get a report stating that fact. Companies whose systems are determined to be noncompliant will also get a report and will be asked to formulate, in cooperation with Customs advisors, a compliance improvement plan specifying corrective actions the company will take to increase compliance levels. Serious violations of law or regulation may result in Customs referring the company for a formal investigation or other enforcement actions.

By law, Customs is required to provide the importer with advance notice of an intended assessment and an estimate of its duration. Importers are entitled to an entry conference, during which the assessment's purpose will be explained and its duration provided. Using information from Customs data bases about the company or the importer's industry, the compliance assessment team may have prepared questionnaires seeking specific information about the importer's internal procedures; these questionnaires will also be distributed at the entry conference.

Upon completion of the assessment, Customs will schedule a closing conference, at which its preliminary findings will be explained. A closing conference may not be scheduled for companies found to have serious enforcement issues. If no enforcement action is taken, Customs will provide the company with a written report of the assessment's results.

The Importer Audit/Compliance Assessment Team Kit (also called the CAT Kit), which provides extensive details of the assessment procedure, can be found at Customs Web site, **www.cbp.gov**, or by calling the Customs Regulatory Audit Division office nearest you.

Compliance Measurement is the primary tool Customs uses to assess the accuracy of port-of-entry transactions and to determine the compliance rate for all commercial importations. By using statistical sampling methods, a valid compliance level for all commercial importations can be obtained. One of the Customs Service's goals is to assure that at least 99 percent of the import revenues legally owed the United States government are collected. Cargo is sampled for compliance with international trade laws at the port of entry, at the time of entry into the United States. Importers should be aware that misclassification of merchandise, among other violations, will be detected through the compliance measurement process.

A Notice to Small Business Importers

The Small Business Regulatory Enforcement Fairness Act was designed to create a more cooperative regulatory environment between federal agencies and small businesses.

Your comments are important. The Small Business and Regulatory Enforcement Ombudsman and 10 regional Fairness Boards were established to receive comments from small businesses about federal agency enforcement activities and to rate each agency's responsiveness to small business. If you wish to comment on the enforcement actions of the U.S. Customs Service, call 1.888.REG.FAIR (1.888.734.3247).

Invoices

Commercial Invoice

A commercial invoice, signed by the seller or shipper, or his agent, is acceptable for customs purposes if it is prepared in accordance with 19 CFR 141.86 through 141.89, and in the manner customary for a commercial transaction involving goods of the kind covered by the invoice. Importers and brokers participating in the National Customs Automation Program (NCAP) or the Automated Broker Interface (ABI) may elect to transmit invoice data via the Automated Invoice Interface or EDIFACT and eliminate the paper document.

The invoice must provide the following information, as required by the Tariff Act:

(1) The port of entry to which the merchandise is destined;

(2) The time when, the place where, and the person by whom and the person to whom the merchandise is sold or agreed to be sold, or if to be imported otherwise than in pursuance of a purchase, the place from which shipped, the time when and the person to whom and the person by whom it is shipped;

(3) A detailed description of the merchandise, including the name by which each item is known, the grade or quality, and the marks, numbers, and symbols under which sold by the seller or manufacturer to the trade in the country of exportation, together with the marks and numbers of the packages in which the merchandise is packed;

(4) The quantities in the weights and measures of the country or place from which the merchandise is shipped, or in the weights and measures of the United States;

(5) The purchase price of each item in the currency of the purchase, if the merchandise is shipped in pursuance of a purchase or an agreement to purchase;

(6) If the merchandise is shipped otherwise than in pursuance of a purchase or an agreement to purchase, the value for each item, in the currency in which the transactions are usually made, or, in the absence of such value, the price in such currency that the manufacturer, seller, shipper, or owner would have received, or was willing to receive, for such merchandise if sold in the ordinary course of trade and in the usual wholesale quantities in the country of exportation;

(7) The kind of currency, whether gold, silver, or paper;

(8) All charges upon the merchandise itemized by name and amount, including freight, insurance, commission, cases, containers, coverings, and cost of packing; and if not included above, all charges, costs, and expenses incurred in bringing the merchandise from alongside the carrier at the port of exportation in the country of exportation and placing it alongside the carrier at the first United States port of entry. The cost of packing, cases, containers, and inland freight to the port of exportation need not be itemized by amount if included in the invoice price, and so identified. Where the required information does not appear on the invoice as originally prepared, it shall be shown on an attachment to the invoice;

(9) All rebates, drawbacks, and bounties, separately itemized, allowed upon the exportation of the merchandise;

(10) The country of origin of the merchandise; and,

(11) All goods or services furnished for the production of the merchandise (e.g., assists such as dies, molds, tools, engineering work) not included in the invoice price. However, goods or services furnished in the United States are excluded. Annual reports for goods and services, when approved by the port director, will be accepted as proof that the goods or services were provided.

If the merchandise on the documents is sold while in transit, the original invoice reflecting this transaction and the resale invoice or a statement of sale showing the price paid for each item by the purchaser shall be filed as part of the entry, entry summary, or withdrawal documentation.

The invoice and all attachments must be in the English language, or shall be accompanied by an accurate English translation.

Each invoice shall state in adequate detail what merchandise is contained in each individual package.

If the invoice or entry does not disclose the weight, gage, or measure of the merchandise necessary to ascertain duties, the importer of record shall pay expenses incurred to obtain this information prior to the release of the merchandise from Customs custody.

Each invoice shall set forth in detail, for each class or kind of merchandise, every discount from list or other base price that has been or may be allowed in fixing each purchaser price or value.

When more than one invoice is included in the same entry, each invoice with its attachments shall be numbered consecutively by the importer on the bottom of the face of each page, beginning with number 1. If invoice is more than two pages, begin with number 1 for the first page of the first invoice and continue in a single series of numbers through all the invoices and attachments included in one entry. If an entry covers one invoice of one page and a second invoice of two pages, the numbering at the bottom of the page shall be as follows: Inv. 1, p.1; Inv. 2, p.2; Inv. 2, p.3.

Any information required on an invoice may be set forth either on the invoice or on the attachment.

Specific Requirements

1. **Separate Invoice Required for Each Shipment.** Not more than one distinct shipment from one consignor to one consignee by one commercial carrier shall be included on the same invoice.

2. **Assembled Shipments.** Merchandise assembled for shipment to the same consignee by one commercial carrier may be included in one invoice. The original bills or invoices covering the merchandise, or extracts therefrom, showing the actual price paid or agreed to be paid, should be attached to the invoice.

3. **Installment Shipments.** Installments of a shipment covered by a single order or contract and shipped from one consignor to one consignee may be included in one invoice if the installments arrive at the port of entry by any means of transportation within a period not to exceed 10 consecutive days.

    The invoice should be prepared in the same manner as are invoices covering single shipments and should include any additional information that may be required for the particular class of goods concerned. If it is practical to do so, the invoice should show the quantities, values, and other invoice data with respect to each installment, and the identification of the importing conveyance in which each installment was shipped.

4. **Production "Assist."** The invoice should indicate whether the production of merchandise involved costs for "assists" (i.e., dies, molds, tooling, printing plates, artwork, engineering work, design and development, financial assistance, etc.) that are not included in the invoice price. If assists were involved, state their value, if known, and by whom supplied. Were they supplied without cost, or on a rental basis, or were they invoiced separately? If the latter, attach a copy of the invoice.

    Whenever U.S. Customs requires information on the cost of production of goods for customs valuation, the importer will be notified by the port director.

Thereafter, invoices covering shipments of such goods must contain a statement on the cost of production by the manufacturer or producer.

5. **Additional Information Required.** Special information may be required on certain goods or classes of goods in addition to the information normally required on the invoice. Although the U.S. importer usually advises the exporter of these special situations, 19 CFR 141.89, which covers the requirements for these goods, has been reproduced in "Additional Information" on page 278. Also refer to 19 CFR 151.82 for information on invoices of cotton and 19 CFR 151.62 for invoices of wool or hair.

6. **Rates of Exchange.** In general, no rate(s) of exchange may be used to convert foreign currency for Customs purposes other than the rate(s) proclaimed or certified in 31 USC 372(a). For merchandise imported from a country having a currency for which two or more rates of exchange have been certified by the Federal Reserve Bank of New York (section 522 of the Tariff Act of 1930), the invoice will show the exchange rate or rates used in converting the U.S. dollars received for the merchandise into the foreign currency and the percentage of each rate if two or more rates are used. If a rate or combination of rates used in payment of costs, charges, or expenses is different from those used in payment for the merchandise, state that rate or combination of rates separately. Where dollars have not been converted at the time the invoice is prepared, that fact is stated on the invoice, in which case the invoice shall also state the rate or combination of rates at which the dollars will be converted or that it is not known what rate or rates will be used. Rates of exchange are not required for merchandise unconditionally free of duty or subject only to a specific rate of duty not depending on value. For more information, refer to 19 CFR 159 Subpart C, "Conversion of Foreign Currency."

Other Invoices

Pro Forma Invoice

If the required commercial invoice is not filed at the time the merchandise is entered, a statement in the form of an invoice (a pro forma invoice) must be filed by the importer at the time of entry. A bond is given for production of the required invoice not later than 120 days from the date of entry. If the invoice is needed for statistical purposes, it must generally be produced within 50 days from the date the entry summary is required to be filed. The U.S. importer will incur a liability under the bond for failure to file the invoice with the port director of Customs before the expiration of the 120-day period.

Although a pro forma invoice is not a document that is prepared by the exporter, it is of interest to exporters as it gives a general idea as to the kind of information needed for entry purposes and indicates what the importer may find necessary to furnish Customs officers at the time a

formal entry is filed for a commercial shipment if a properly prepared customs or commercial invoice is not available at the time the goods are entered. Some of the additional information specified for commodities under section 141.89 of the Customs Regulations may not be required when entry is made on a pro forma invoice. However, the pro forma invoice must contain sufficient data for examination, classification, and appraisal purposes. An example of the information to be included in a pro forma invoice is provided in 19 CFR 141.85.

Special Invoices

Special invoices are required for some merchandise. See a reproduction of 19 CFR 141.89 under "Additional Information" on page 278. Also refer to 19 CFR 151.82 for information on invoices of cotton and 19 CFR 151.62 for invoices of wool or hair.

Frequent Errors in Invoicing

If difficulties, delays, and possible penal sanctions affecting the importer are to be avoided, due care must be exercised by foreign sellers and shippers in the preparation of invoices and other documents to be used in the entry of goods into the commerce of the U.S. Each document must contain all information required by law or regulations, and every statement of fact contained in the documents must be true and accurate. Any inaccurate or misleading statement of fact in a document presented to Customs in connection with an entry, or the omission from the document of required information, may result in delays in merchandise release, the detention of the goods or a claim against the importer for domestic value. Even if the inaccuracy or omission was unintentional, the importer may be required to establish the exercise of due diligence and the absence of negligence to avoid sanctions with consequent delays in obtaining possession of goods and closing the transaction.

It is particularly important that all statements relating to merchandise description, price, or value and to amounts of discounts, charges, and commissions be truthfully and accurately set forth. It is also important that the invoices set forth the true name of the actual seller and purchaser of the goods, in the case of purchased goods, or the true name of the actual consignor and consignee, when the goods are shipped otherwise than to secure a purchase. It is important, too, that the invoice shall otherwise reflect the real nature of the transaction for which the goods were shipped to the U.S.

The fundamental rule is that the shipper and importer must furnish the Custom officers with all pertinent information with respect to each import transaction to assist the Custom officers in determining the tariff status of the goods. Examples of omissions and inaccuracies to be avoided are:

- The shipper assumes that a commission, royalty, or other charge against the goods is a so-called "nondutiable" item and omits it from the invoice.

- A foreign shipper who purchases goods and sells them to a U.S. importer at a delivered price shows on the invoice the cost of the goods instead of the delivered price.

- A foreign shipper manufactures goods partly with the use of materials supplied by the U.S. importer, but invoices the goods at the actual cost to the manufacturer without including the value of the materials supplied by the importer.

- The foreign manufacturer ships replacement goods to a customer in the U.S. and invoices the goods at the net price without showing the full price less the allowance for defective goods previously shipped and returned.

- A foreign shipper who sells goods at list price, less a discount, invoices them at the net price, and fails to show the discount.

- A foreign shipper sells goods at a delivered price but invoices them at a price FOB the place of shipment and omits the subsequent charges.

- A foreign shipper indicates in the invoice that the importer is the purchaser, when in fact the importer is either an agent who is receiving a commission for selling the goods or a party who will receive part of the proceeds of the sale of the goods sold for the joint account of the shipper and consignee.

- Invoice descriptions are vague if they list only part numbers, show truncated or coded descriptions, or lump various articles together as one when several distinct items are included.

Assignment of Duties, Fees, and Fines

Dutiable Status of Goods

Rates of Duty

All goods imported into the U.S. are subject to duty or duty-free entry in accordance with their classification under the applicable items in the Harmonized Tariff Schedule of the United States (HTSUS). An annotated, looseleaf edition of the tariff schedule may be purchased from the U.S. Government Printing Office, or it may be viewed online on the Customs & Border Protection Web site at www.cbp.gov/.

When goods are dutiable, ad valorem, specific, or compound rates may be assessed. An ad valorem rate, which is the type of rate most often applied, is a percentage of value of the merchandise, such as 5% ad valorem. A specific rate is a specified amount per unit of weight or other quantity, such as 5.9 cents per dozen. A compound rate is a combination of both an ad valorem rate and a specific rate, such as 0.7 cents per pound plus 10% ad valorem.

Before the Mod Act, importers were required to supply Customs with complete and accurate information so that Customs could assign classification and valuation; under the new "informed compliance" regulations, the responsibility for correctly classifying merchandise falls to the importer or his agent, often a customs broker. Moreover, these parties must be able to demonstrate that they used "reasonable care" in doing so. This is an important shift in philosophy that ultimately places a much greater legal burden on the importer.

Free of Duty or Dutiable

Rates of duty for imported merchandise may also vary depending upon the country of origin. Most merchandise is dutiable under the Most Favored Nation (MFN) - now referred to as normal trade relations (NTR) - rates in the General column under column 1 of the tariff schedule. Merchandise from countries to which the NTR rates have not been extended is dutiable at the full or "statutory" rates in column 2 of the tariff schedules.

Free rates are provided for many subheadings in columns 1 and 2 of the tariff schedule. Duty-free status is also available under various conditional exemptions that are reflected in the Special column under column 1 of the tariff schedule. It is the importer's burden to show eligibility for a conditional exemption from duty. One of the more frequently applied exemptions from duty occurs under the Generalized System of Preferences. GSP-eligible merchandise qualifies for duty-free entry when it is from a beneficiary developing country and meets other requirements as discussed on page 229. Other exemptions are found under subheadings in HTSUS Chapter 98. These subheadings include certain personal exemptions, exemptions for articles for scientific or other institutional purposes, and exemptions for returned U.S. goods. (Refer to the Commodity Index Chapter 98 on page 920.)

Rulings on Imports

The Customs Service makes its decision as to the dutiable status of merchandise when the entry is liquidated after the entry documents have been filed. When advance information is needed, do not depend on a small "trial" or "test" shipment since there is no guarantee that the next shipment will receive the same tariff treatment. Small importations may slip by, particularly if they are processed under informal procedures that apply to small shipments or in circumstances warranting application of a flat rate. An exporter, importer, or other interested party may get advance information on any matter affecting the dutiable status of merchandise by writing the Port Director where the merchandise will be entered or to the Office of Regulations and Rulings, Washington, DC 20229. Detailed information on the procedures applicable to decisions on prospective importations is given in 19 CFR part 177.

Importers may also obtain advance rulings from the Office of Regulations and Rulings regarding the application of NAFTA to prospective and ongoing transactions. Advance rulings must be requested in accordance with the procedures described in 19 CFR 181.93. Persons who request an advance ruling may obtain administrative review of that ruling in accordance 19 CFR 181.102. Appeals must be filed within 30 calendar days after issuance of the ruling and should contain:

- The name and address of the person seeking review (or of his or her agent);
- The Customs identification number or employer identification number in the case of a U.S. importer, the employer number or importer/ exporter number assigned by Revenue Canada in the case of a Canada exporter or producer, and the federal taxpayer registry number (RFC) in the case of a Mexican exporter or producer;
- The number and date of the advance ruling;
- The numbers and dates of any involved entries;
- The nature of, and justification for, the objection.

Ruling Requests

While you will find that, for many purposes, the ports are your best sources of information, informal information obtained on tariff classifications is not binding. Under 19 CFR part 177, the importing public may obtain a binding tariff classification ruling, which can be relied upon for placing or accepting orders or for making other business determinations, under Chapters 1 through 97 of the Harmonized Tariff Schedule (HTSUS) by writing to Director, National Commodity Specialist Division, Attn: Classification Rul ing Requests, U.S. Customs Service, 6 World Trade Center, Rm. 423, New York, NY 10048 or to any service port office of the Customs Service. The rulings will be binding at all ports of entry unless revoked by the Customs Service's Office of Regulations and Rulings.

The following information is required in ruling requests:

1. The names, addresses, and other identifying information of all interested parties (if known) and the manufacturer ID code (if known).

2. The name(s) of the port(s) in which the merchandise will be entered (if known).

3. A description of the transaction, for example, a prospective importation of (merchandise) from (country).

4. A statement that there are, to the importer's knowledge, no issues on the commodity pending before the Customs Service or any court.

5. A statement as to whether classification advice had previously been sought from a Customs officer, and if so, from whom, and what advice was rendered, if any.

A request for a tariff classification should include the following information:

1. A complete description of the goods. Send samples, if practical, and sketches, diagrams, or other illustrative material that will be useful in supplementing the written description.

2. Cost breakdowns of component materials and their respective quantities shown in percentages, if possible.

3. A description of the principal use of the goods, as a class or kind of merchandise, in the U.S.

4. Information as to commercial, scientific, or common designations as may be applicable.

5. Any other information that may be pertinent or required for the purpose of tariff classification.

6. Purchase price of article and approximate U.S. selling price.

Any of the first four requirements above may be disregarded if you are certain the information will not be of use for tariff classification purposes. However, to avoid delays, your request should be as complete as possible. If you send a sample, do not rely on that to tell the whole story. Also, please note that samples may be subjected to laboratory analysis, which is done free of charge. However, if a sample is destroyed during laboratory analysis, it cannot be returned.

Information submitted and incorporated in the response to a request for a Customs decision may be disclosed or withheld in accordance with the provisions of the Freedom of Information Act, as amended (15 USC 552; 19 CFR 177.8(a)(3)).

Protests

The importer may disagree with the dutiable status after the entry has been liquidated. A decision at this stage of the entry transaction is requested by filing a protest and application for further review on Customs **Form 19** within 90 days after liquidation. If the Customs Service denies a protest, dutiable status may then be determined through litigation against the Government. For more information on filing a protest, see 19 CFR 174.

NAFTA. There are special rules for consolidating multiple protests concerning a determination of origin for NAFTA preferential tariff treatment if one of the protests is filed by or on behalf of an exporter or producer. For more information, refer to 19 CFR 174.15, "Consolidation of protests filed by different parties."

Liability for Duties

No law or regulation provides for prepayment of U.S. duties or taxes in a foreign country before exportation to the U.S. This is true even for gifts sent through the mail.

Liability for the payment of duty usually becomes fixed at the time an entry for consumption or for warehouse is filed with Customs. The obligation for payment rests with the person or firm in whose name the entry is filed. When goods have been entered for warehouse, the liability for the payment of duties may be transferred to any person who purchases the goods and desires to withdraw them in his own name.

The 1993 Customs Modernization Act (Mod Act) authorizes periodic payment of duties. With advance permission from Customs, participants in the ABI may pay duties by filing a periodic import activity summary statement together with the payment. Interest is assessed against periodic payments from the first day of the month until the statement is filed. Refer to 19 CFR 24.25 for more information.

Payments made to a Customs broker do not relieve an importer of record of liability for Customs charges (duties, taxes, and other debts owed to Customs) in the event the charges are not paid by the broker. Therefore, if the importer pays by check, Customs charges may be paid by separate check, payable to "U.S. Customs Service", which will be delivered to Customs by the broker.

If the entry is made in the name of a Customs broker, the broker may obtain relief from statutory liability for the payment of increased or additional duties found due if (1) the actual owner of the goods is named, and (2) the owner's declaration, by which the owner agrees to pay the additional amount of duty, and the owner's bond are filed by the broker with the port director within 90 days of the date of entry.

The Mod Act has created a five-year statute of limitations for collection of unpaid duties. The U.S. government must initiate suit or action to collect unpaid duties within five years after the date of the alleged violation, or in the case of fraud, after the date the fraud is discovered. This period is interrupted for any time during which the person is absent from the U.S. or the property is absent or concealed. See 15 USC 1621.

User Fees

Customs user fees were established by the Consolidated Omnibus Budget Reconciliation Act of 1985. This legislation was expanded in 1986 to include a merchandise processing fee. Also in 1986, Congress enacted the Water Resources Development Act, which authorized the Customs Service to collect a harbor maintenance fee for the Army Corps of Engineers. Further legislation has extended the User Fee Program until 2003.

The merchandise processing fee (MPF) is 0.21 percent ad valorem on formally-entered imported merchandise (generally entries valued over $2,000), subject to a minimum fee of $25 per entry and a maximum fee of $485 per entry. On informal entries (those valued at less than $2,000), the MPFs are: $2 for automated entries, $6 for manual entries not prepared by Customs, and $9 for manual entries that are prepared by Customs.

The harbor maintenance fee is an ad valorem fee assessed on port use associated with imports, admissions into foreign trades zones, domestic shipments, and passenger transportation. The fee is assessed only at ports that benefit from the expenditure of funds by the Army Corps of Engineers for maintaining and improving the port trade zones. The fee is 0.125 percent of the value of the cargo and is paid quarterly, except for imports, which are paid at the time of entry. Customs deposits the harbor maintenance fee collections into the Harbor Maintenance Trust Fund. The funds are made available, subject to appropriation, to the Army Corps of Engineers for the improvement and maintenance of United States ports and harbors. There is a Harbor Maintenance Fee Hotline at Tel: (317) 298-1250.

Merchandise Processing Fees Under NAFTA

Goods originating in Canada that qualify to be marked as Canadian goods according to the Marking Rules, are exempt from the merchandise processing fee under NAFTA. For goods originating in Mexico that qualify to be marked as Mexican goods pursuant to Annex 311, the merchandise processing fee was eliminated on June 30, 1999. Other fees are unaffected and will be collected whether the goods originate in Canada or Mexico. These include harbor maintenance, cotton, beef, pork, honey, etc.

Containers or Holders

Lift vans, cargo vans, shipping tanks, pallets, and certain articles used in the shipment of goods in international traffic are designated as "instruments of international traffic" by the Customs Service, as defined at 19 CFR 10.41a. So long as this designation applies, they are not subject to entry or duty when they arrive, whether they are loaded or empty. Holders of merchandise of a different class may also be designated as instruments of international traffic upon application to the Commissioner of Customs. The applicant for release of duties under this provision must file a bond on Customs Form 301; the application must be filed at the port of arrival or a subsequent port. U.S.-made containers may also be entered duty-free under HTSUS classification 9801.00.10, "Products of the United States when returned after having been exported, without having been advanced in value or improved in condition by any process of manufacture or other means while abroad."

Special provisions are available for a wide variety of shipping devices arriving from NAFTA countries. Refer to new Customs regulations at 19 CFR 10.41b(b) for more information.

Any article designated as an instrument of international traffic must be entered and duty paid, if applicable, if it is diverted to a domestic use.

Containers specially shaped or fitted to contain a specific article or set of articles, suitable for long-term use and entered with the articles for which they are intended, are classifiable with the accompanying articles if they are of a kind normally sold therewith. Examples of such containers are: camera cases, musical instrument cases, gun cases, drawing instrument cases, and necklace cases. This rule does not apply to containers that give the importation as a whole its essential character.

Subject to the above rule, packing materials and packing containers entered with goods packed in them are classified with these goods if they are of a kind normally used for packing such goods. However, this does not apply to packing materials or containers that are clearly suitable for repetitive use.

Temporary Free Importations

Temporary Importation Under Bond (TIB)

Goods of the types enumerated below when not imported for sale or for sale on approval may be admitted into the U.S. under bond without the payment of duty for exportation within one year from the date of importation. Generally, the amount of the bond is double the estimated duties. The one-year period for exportation may, upon application to the port director, be extended for one or more further periods that, when added to the initial one year period, shall not exceed a total of three years. There is an exception in the case of articles covered in item 15, for which the period of the bond may not exceed six months.

and may not be extended. You will most often need to submit Customs Form 3461 or 7533 for TIB entries.

Merchandise entered under TIB must be exported before expiration of the bond period, or any extension, to avoid assessment of liquidated damages in the amount of the bond. Refer to 19 CFR 10.31–10.40 and HTSUS Chapter 98 for more information.

Classes of Goods Under HTSUS 9813

The following is a list of the classes of goods permitted duty-free entry under HTSUS 9813. The eight-digit classification code for each class of good is indicated below.

1. Merchandise to be repaired, altered, or processed (including processes that result in an article being manufactured or produced in the U.S. (HTSUS 9813.00.05)

    The following conditions must be met:

    a. The merchandise will not be processed into an article manufactured or produced in the U.S. if the article is: (1) alcohol, distilled spirits, wine, beer or any dilution or mixture of any or all of the foregoing; (2) perfume or other commodity containing ethyl alcohol whether denatured or not; or (3) a product of wheat.

    b. If merchandise is processed and results in an article being manufactured or produced in the U.S. other than those described above, (1) a complete accounting will be made to the Customs Service for all articles, wastes, and irrecoverable losses resulting from the processing, and (2) all articles will be exported or destroyed under Customs supervision within the bonded period. Valuable waste must also be exported or so destroyed unless duty, if applicable, is paid.

2. Models of women's wearing apparel imported by manufacturers for use solely as models in their own establishments. However, these items may require quota compliance. (HTSUS 9813.00.10)

3. Articles imported by illustrators and photographers for use solely as models in their own establishments to illustrate catalogs, pamphlets, or advertising matter. (HTSUS 9813.00.15)

4. Samples solely for use in taking orders for merchandise. These items may require quota compliance. (HTSUS 9813.00.20)

5. Articles solely for examination with a view to reproduction or for examination and reproduction (except photoengraved printing plates for examination and reproduction); and motion picture advertising films. (HTSUS 9813.00.25)

6. Articles intended solely for testing, experimental or review purposes, including specifications, photographs and similar articles for use in connection with experiments or for study. If articles under this category are destroyed in connection with the experiment or study, proof must be presented to satisfy the obligation under the bond to export the articles. (HTSUS 9813.00.30)

7. Automobiles, motorcycles, bicycles, airplanes, airships, balloons, boats, racing shells, and similar vehicles and craft, and the usual equipment of the foregoing, if brought temporarily into the U.S. by nonresidents for the purpose of taking part in races or other specific contests. Port directors may defer the exaction of a bond for a period not to exceed 90 days after the date of importation for vehicles and craft to take part in races or other specific contests for other than money purposes. If the vehicle or craft is not exported or the bond is not given within the period of such deferment, the vehicle or craft shall be subject to forfeiture. (HTSUS 9813.00.35)

8. Locomotives and other railroad equipment brought temporarily into the U.S. for use in clearing obstructions, fighting fires, or making emergency repairs on railroads within the U.S., for use in transportation otherwise than in international traffic when the Secretary of the Treasury finds that the temporary use of foreign railroad equipment is necessary to meet an emergency. (HTSUS 9813.00.40)

9. Containers for compressed gases, filled or empty, and containers or other articles in use for covering or holding merchandise (including personal or household effects) during transportation and suitable for reuse for that purpose. (HTSUS 9813.00.45)

10. Professional equipment, tools of trade, repair components for equipment or tools admitted under this item, and camping equipment imported by or for nonresidents sojourning temporarily in the U.S. for the nonresident's use, or by an organization represented by the nonresident that is a legally established business in a foreign country. (HTSUS 9813.00.50)

11. Articles of special design for temporary use exclusively in connection with the manufacture or production of articles for export. (HTSUS 9813.00.55)

12. Animals and poultry brought into the U.S. for the purpose of breeding, exhibition, or competition for prizes, and the usual equipment therefor. (HTSUS 9813.00.60)

13. Works of free fine arts, drawings, engravings, photographic pictures, and philosophical and scientific apparatus brought into the U.S. by professional artists, lecturers, or scientists arriving from abroad for use by them for exhibition and in illustration, promotion, and encouragement of art, science, or industry in the U.S. (HTSUS 9813.00.70)

14. Automobiles, automobile chassis, automobile bodies, cutaway portions of any of the foregoing, and parts for any of the foregoing, finished, unfinished, or cutaway, when intended solely for show purposes. These articles may be admitted only on condition that the Secretary of the Treasury has found that the foreign country from which the articles were imported allows or will allow substantially reciprocal privileges with respect to similar imports to that country from the U.S. If the Secretary finds that a foreign country has discontinued or will discontinue the allowance of such privileges, the privileges under this item shall not apply thereafter to imports from that country. (HTSUS 9813.00.75)

Temporary Entry and Commercial Samples under NAFTA

NAFTA provides for the duty-free importation of certain commercial samples and printed advertising materials. The commercial samples must be of negligible value, that is, their value cannot exceed one U.S. dollar (or the equivalent in the currency of Mexico or Canada) or they must be marked, torn, perforated or otherwise unsuitable for sale or use except as commercial samples. Only printed advertising materials classified in Chapter 49 of the HTSUS may be imported duty-free under this provision. The list includes brochures, pamphlets, leaflets, trade catalogues and year-books.

If an article imported into the United States under heading 9813.00.05 (See "Classes of Goods" item #1) is withdrawn for exportation to Canada or of Mexico, the duty assessed will be waived or reduced in an amount that does not exceed the lesser of the total amount of duty payable on the article that would have been payable on importation under chapters 1 through 97, inclusive, of the HTSUS or the total amount of customs duties paid to Canada or to Mexico on the exported article, unless such article is covered by section 203(a)(1) through 203(a)(8), inclusive, of the NAFTA Implementation Act. The amount of duties or refunds calculated on such articles pursuant to this note shall be adjusted to take into account any subsequent claim for preferential tariff treatment made to another NAFTA country. This applies to shipments to Canada on or after January 1, 1996, and to Mexico on or after January 1, 2001.

Relief from Liability

Relief from liability under bond may be obtained in any case in which the articles are destroyed under Customs supervision, in lieu of exportation, within the original bond period. However, in the case of articles entered under item 6, destruction need not be under Customs supervision where articles are destroyed during the course of experiments or tests during the bond period or any lawful extension, but satisfactory proof of destruction shall be furnished to the port director with whom the customs entry is filed.

ATA Carnet

ATA stands for the combined French and English words "Admission Temporaire-Temporary Admission." ATA carnet is an international customs document that may be used for the temporary duty-free importation of certain goods into a country in lieu of the usual customs documents required. The carnet serves as a guarantee against the payment of customs duties that may become due on goods temporarily imported and not re-exported. Quota compliance may be required on certain types of merchandise. ATA textile carnets are subject to quota and visa requirements.

A carnet is valid for one year. The traveler or businessperson, however, may make as many trips as desired during the period the carnet is valid provided the carnet has sufficient pages for each stop.

The U.S. currently allows ATA carnets to be used for the temporary admission of professional equipment, commercial samples, and advertising material. Most other countries allow the use of carnets for the temporary admission of these goods and, in some cases, other uses of the ATA carnet are permitted. ATA carnets can also be used for transit (in-bond movement of goods) in the U.S. under the applicable regulations, 19 CFR Part 114.

Local country carnet associations, as members of the International Bureau of the Paris-based International Chamber of Commerce, issue carnets to their residents. These associations guarantee the payment of duties to local customs authorities should goods imported under cover of a foreign-issued carnet not be re-exported. In the U.S., the U.S. Council of the International Chamber of Commerce, has been designated by U.S. Customs as the U.S. issuing and guaranteeing organization. A fee is charged by the Council for its service. Contact the U.S. Council for the ICC, 1212 Avenue of the Americas, New York, NY 10036; Tel: (212) 354-4480; Fax: (212) 575-0327. The Council also maintains an office in Washington, DC and offices around the country which can issue ATA Carnets. Further information on the ATA Carnet system can be found in *Carnet: Move Goods Duty-free Through Customs*, an informative free brochure published by the council.

The following countries currently participate in the ATA Carnet system: Algeria, Australia, Austria, Belgium, Bulgaria, Canada, Canary Islands, , China, Croatia, Cyprus, the Czech Republic, Denmark, Estonia, Finland, France, French Polynesia, French West Indies, Germany, Gibraltar, Greece, Hong Kong, Hungary, Iceland, India, Ireland, Israel, Italy, Ivory Coast, Japan, Lebanon, Luxembourg, Malaysia, Malta, Mauritius, Netherlands, New Zealand, Norway, Poland, Portugal, Romania, Senegal, Singapore, Slovakia, Slovenia, South Africa, South Korea, Spain, Sri Lanka, Sweden, Switzerland, Thailand, Turkey, the United Kingdom, and the United States. Many countries will issue carnets for some categories of merchandise and not others. Egypt and certain other countries have accepted the ATA convention but have not implemented the use of carnets.

Note on Taiwan. TECRO/AIT Carnets are used for temporary imports into Taiwan only, this is a bilateral arrangement between the Taipei Economic and Cultural Representative in the United States (TECRO) and the American Institute in Taiwan (AIT). The TECRO/AIT Carnet is acceptable for the following two categories of goods to be temporarily imported, unless importation is prohibited under the laws and regulations of the United States: (1) professional equipment; and (2) commercial samples and advertising material imported for the purpose of being shown or demonstrated with a view to soliciting orders. For more specifics, contact U.S. Customs Service, International Organizations and Agreements Division, Tel: (202) 927-1480; FAX (202) 927-6897.

Antidumping and Countervailing Duties

Antidumping and countervailing duties are types of additional duties used to offset the effects of two unfair trade practices that give imports an unfair advantage over competing U.S. goods.

Antidumping duties (ADs) are assessed on imported merchandise of a class or kind that is sold to purchasers in the U.S. at a price less than the fair market value. Fair market value of merchandise is the price at which it is normally sold in the manufacturer's home market.

Countervailing duties (CVDs) are assessed to counter the effects of subsidies provided by foreign governments to merchandise that is exported to the U.S. These subsidies cause the price of such merchandise to be artificially low, which causes economic "injury" to U.S. manufacturers.

The Department of Commerce, the International Trade Commission (ITC), and the U.S. Customs Service all play a part in enforcing antidumping (AD) and countervailing duty (CVD) laws. The Commerce Department is also responsible for their general administration; it determines whether the merchandise is sold at less than fair value or is subsidized. It also determines the amount of duties that must be assessed. The ITC makes the injury determinations. The Customs Service assesses the duties once Commerce and the ITC have made the necessary determinations. Establishing and assessing both kinds of duties occurs during the Investigation and Administration Review/Liquidation processes.

NAFTA Changes. Under NAFTA, Canada, Mexico and the United States retain the right to apply their antidumping and countervailing duty laws to goods imported from another NAFTA country. NAFTA also establishes a mechanism for independent binational panels to review final antidumping and countervailing duty determinations by administrative authorities in each country. Private parties wishing to contest an administrative decision respecting goods of a NAFTA country may request that a panel be established. In such cases, the panel process will substitute for domestic judicial review in the country where the administrative decision was made.

A binational panel will decide whether the antidumping or countervailing determination was made in accordance with the domestic law of the importing country. If a binational panel finds that an error was committed in the antidumping or countervailing determination, it may send the decision back to the appropriate government agency for correction. Decisions by a panel are binding and cannot be appealed to a domestic court. in addition, the Agreement establishes safeguard mechanisms designed to guarantee the integrity of the panel process.

GATT Changes. Interim rules implementing the amendments of the Uruguay Round Agreement Act to antidumping and countervailing duty regulations became effective May 11, 1995 and should be replaced by substantially similar final rules in 1997. These rules can be found at 19 CFR 353 (antidumping duties) and 19 CFR 355 (countervailing duties). Some of the changes include: determining that a petition has the requisite support of the domestic industry prior to initiating an investigation; new deadline requirements; a new procedure called "new shipper reviews," based on "normal administrative reviews;" and the end of a preference for calculating a single countrywide subsidy rate in countervailing duty proceedings.

Investigations

Although they may be initiated by the Commerce Department, AD and CVD investigations are usually initiated as the result of a petition from a domestic industry or other interested party such as a trade union or industry association. The party must simultaneously (that is, on the same day) file the petition with the Commerce Department and the ITC (the latter if an injury test is required). If the necessary elements are present in the petition, the Commerce Department and the ITC will initiate separate investigations. The investigations then continue with a series of preliminary and final determinations that, if appropriate, result in an "order" and the eventual assessment of AD and CVD duties. The following discussion is based upon the assumption that the injury test is required. If not, the outcome of the considerations is based solely upon the Commerce Department determinations.

The ITC makes the first preliminary determination concerning the likelihood of injury. If that determination is negative, the investigations are terminated. If it is affirmative, the Commerce Department then issues a preliminary determination with respect to the sales and/or subsidy issues. Later, based upon further review and comments received in the case, the Commerce Department issues a final determination. If either of these Commerce Department determinations is affirmative, Commerce will direct Customs to suspend liquidation of entries for merchandise subject to investigation and to require cash deposits or bonds equal to the amount of estimated dumping margin (the differential between the fair market value and the U.S. price) or the net subsidy.

Completing the Investigation

After a final affirmative determination by the Commerce Department, the ITC then follows with its final injury determination. If the ITC's final determination is also affirmative, the Commerce Department issues an AD or CVD order. At that time, Commerce directs Customs to require, with a very limited exception for new shippers, cash deposits of estimated duties. A negative final determination either by Commerce or the ITC would terminate the investigations. Both agencies announce their determinations, including orders and the results of the administration reviews described below, in the Federal Register.

Administrative Review/Final Settlement

Each year, in the anniversary month of the order, interested parties have the opportunity to request a review of the order with respect to individual producers or resellers covered by the order. The period of review is usually the 12 months preceding the anniversary month. However, the first review period also includes any term prior to the normal 12-month period for which the suspension of liquidation was directed. If no review is requested, Commerce will direct Customs to collect deposits and assess duties in the amount of the cash or bond rate in effect on the date of entry and to continue to require deposits at that rate for future entries. If a review is requested, Commerce carries out a review similar to its original investigation and issues revised rates for assessment and deposits. Upon receipt of instructions from the Commerce Department, Customs will collect duties and liquidate entries as directed.

Drawback—Refunds of Duties

Definition

Drawback is a refund of 99% of all ordinary Customs duties and internal revenue taxes. Drawback was initially authorized by the first tariff act of the U.S. in 1789. Since then it has been a part of the law, although from time to time the conditions under which it is payable have changed. For example, as a result of the Omnibus Trade & Competitiveness Act of 1988, antidumping and countervailing duties are not refundable on a drawback claim.

Purpose

The rationale for drawback has always been to encourage U.S. commerce or manufacturing, or both. It permits the U.S. manufacturer to compete in foreign markets without the handicap of including in his costs, and consequently in his sales price, the duty paid on imported merchandise. The types of drawback are authorized under 19 USC 1313, and implemented by 19 CFR Part 191.

Types of Drawback

Several kinds of drawback are described in 19 CFR 191.4. A brief review is given below.

Direct Identification Drawback. Direct identification drawback provides a refund of duties paid on imported merchandise that 1) is not used and is either exported or destroyed under Customs supervision; or 2) is partially or totally used in the manufacture of an exported article. Identification of the imported merchandise from import to export or destruction must be demonstrated through proper recordkeeping procedures. If the merchandise is not used in the U.S., drawback is available only if the articles are exported or destroyed within three years of the date of importation. If the imported merchandise is used in a manufacturing process, the articles must be exported within five years from the date of importation of the merchandise (19 USC 1313(a),(j)).

Substitution Drawback. Substitution drawback provides for a refund of duties paid on designated imported merchandise upon exportation or Customs-supervised destruction of articles manufactured or produced with the use of substituted domestic or imported merchandise that is of the same kind and quality as the designated imported merchandise. Same kind and quality means merchandise that is commercially interchangeable in a specific manufacturing process. Drawback is allowed if: 1) the imported materials are used in a manufacturing process within three years after receipt by the manufacturer; 2) the domestic materials, which are of the same kind and quality as the imported materials, are exported or destroyed before use in the U.S., or are used in a manufacturing process, within three years of receipt of the imported materials; and 3) if the materials are used in manufacturing, the articles are exported within five years of the date of importation of the designated material (19 USC 1313(b), (j)(2)).

Nonconforming Merchandise Drawback. Nonconforming merchandise drawback is a refund of duties on exportation or Custom-supervised destruction of merchandise rejected as nonconforming. This drawback is available for merchandise that does not conform to a sample or specifications, was shipped without the consignee's consent, or is determined to be defective as of the time of importation. Drawback may be claimed for such goods, provided that duties were paid, the goods were entered or withdrawn for consumption, and the goods are returned to Customs for exportation or destruction within three years after Customs released them (19 USC 1313(c)).

Other Types of Drawback. Several other types of drawback, less frequently claimed, are available. They pertain to imported salt for curing fish; exportation of meats cured with imported salt; material for construction and equipment of vessels and aircraft built for foreigners; foreign-built aircraft engines processed in the U.S.; direct identification same condition drawback; substitution same condition drawback; packaging materials; supplies for certain vessels and aircraft; merchandise exported from continuous Customs custody; merchandise transferred to a foreign trade zone from Customs territory; and refund of internal revenue taxes on imported distilled spirits, wines, or beer.

NAFTA Drawback

The NAFTA provisions on drawback and duty deferral apply to goods imported into Canada or the United States and subsequently exported to the other country (i.e., Canada or the United States) on or after January 1, 1996. The NAFTA provisions on drawback and duty deferral will apply to goods imported into Canada or the United States and subsequently exported to Mexico, or imported into Mexico and subsequently exported to Canada or the United States, on or after January 1, 2001. Thus, transactions involving either the importation of goods into Mexico or the exportation of goods to Mexico will not come under the drawback and duty deferral provisions of the NAFTA until January 1, 2001.

Under NAFTA, the amount of customs duties that will be refunded, reduced or waived is the lesser of the total amount of customs duties paid or owed on the goods or materials when imported into a NAFTA country and the total amount of customs duties paid or owed on the finished good in the NAFTA country to which it is exported.

No NAFTA country, on condition of export, will refund, reduce or waive the following: antidumping or countervailing duties, premiums offered or collected pursuant to any tendering system with respect to the administration of quantitative import restrictions, tariff rate quotas or trade preference levels, or a fee pursuant to Section 22 of the U.S. Agricultural Adjustment Act. Moreover, same condition substitution drawback was eliminated January 1, 1994.

NAFTA provides a new method for duty remission with respect to importations of goods under any of the following duty deferral programs that are subsequently exported to another NAFTA country. These duty deferral programs include foreign trade zones, temporary importations under bond, bonded warehouses, "maquiladoras," and inward processing programs. Upon exportation, the goods will be treated as if withdrawn for domestic consumption, thus subject to the applicable customs duties. The customs administration assessing such duties may waive or reduce them by an amount that does not exceed the total custom duties paid to the NAFTA country to which the goods are exported. Such reduction or waiver will be made when the claimant presents satisfactory evidence of the customs duties paid in the NAFTA country to which the article was exported. The claimant has 60 days to present this satisfactory evidence, otherwise the customs administration of the exporting country will collect the duties. Should a claimant subsequently obtain satisfactory evidence, the duties may be refunded to the extent allowed, upon timely presentation of the evidence according to the laws and regulations of each NAFTA country.

Procedure

The 1993 Customs Modernization Act permits an importer to claim drawback within three years after the articles are exported or destroyed. A claim is considered filed when the drawback entry and all documents necessary to complete the claim are submitted or requested by application to Customs. An exception is made for landing certificates, which must be filed in accordance with the time limits prescribed by specific regulation. The importer may accomplish a drawback filing electronically with permission of Customs. No extension of the time limit is allowed unless Customs is responsible for an untimely filing. Drawback claimants should file **Customs Form 331** with the appropriate drawback office.

Questions relating to legal aspects of drawback should be addressed to: Chief, Drawback Section, Office of Field Operations, U.S. Customs Service, 1300 Pennsylvania Avenue NW, Washington, DC 20229.

Civil and Criminal Fraud Laws

Section 592 of the Tariff Act of 1930, as amended (19 USC 1592), generally provides that any person who by fraud, gross negligence, or negligence, enters, introduces, or attempts to introduce, merchandise into the commerce of the U.S. by means of any material and false written document, oral statement, electronically transmitted data or information, or material act or omission will be subject to a monetary penalty. Penalties are usually not imposed for nonintentional repetitions of clerical errors through electronic systems. Under certain circumstances, the person's merchandise may be seized to ensure payment of the penalty and forfeited if the penalty is not paid.

Customs has applied the civil fraud statute in cases involving individuals and companies in the U. S. and abroad that have negligently or intentionally provided false information concerning imports into the U.S. In addition, a criminal fraud statute creates penalties against persons who present false information to Customs officers. A maximum of two years imprisonment, a $5,000 fine, or both, may be imposed for each violation involving an importation or attempted importation (18 USC 542). Additionally, the Money Laundering Control Act of 1986 and the Anti-Drug Abuse Act of 1988, created and amended Federal laws relating to criminal activities commonly known as "money laundering." The Acts created criminal and civil offenses that punishable by fines and imprisonment, enabling the government to prosecute and to seize and cause forfeiture of property involved in or traceable to property involved in Money Laundering or Bank Secrecy Act violations. Importation fraud violations are among the specified unlawful activities or predicate offenses within the Money Laundering Control Act. Penalties include imprisonment for up to 20 years for each offense and fines of up to $500,000.

Additionally, under Section 596 of the Tariff Act of 1930, as amended (19 U.S.C. 1595a(c)), the Customs Service is required to seize and forfeit all merchandise that is stolen or smuggled, as well as controlled substances, certain con-

traband articles, and plastic explosives that do not contain a detection agent. Merchandise may be seized and forfeited if: its importation is restricted or prohibited because of a law relating to health, safety or conservation; the merchandise is lacking a federal license required for its importation; the merchandise or packaging is in violation of copyright, trademark, trade name, or trade dress protections; the merchandise is intentionally or repetitively marked in violation of country of origin marking requirements; or the importation of the merchandise is subject to quantitative restrictions requiring a visa or similar document from a foreign government, and the document presented with the entry is counterfeit.

The fraud statutes were enacted by Congress to discourage persons from evading the payment of lawful duties owed to the U.S. However, these laws apply whether or not the U.S. is deprived of lawful duties. They are enforced by special agents assigned to the Office of Enforcement who operate throughout the U.S. and in major trading centers worldwide. Suspected or known violations of any law involved with the importation of merchandise into the U.S. can be reported toll free and anonymously by calling 1-800 BE-ALERT (232-5378). Rewards are applicable in many instances associated with the reporting of fraud.

The 1993 Customs Modernization Act imposes additional criminal and civil penalties for presenting forged or altered documents at entry or for otherwise violating arrival, entry, clearance, or manifest requirements. These penalties also apply to electronic transmission of false or altered data or manifests to Customs (19 USC 1436). The Act also establishes monetary penalties for fraudulent submission of a false drawback claim, the amounts of which increase with repeated violations. (Refer to 19 CFR 191.9, "Falsification of drawback claims.") These penalties became effective on implementation of the nationwide automated drawback selectivity program (19 USC 1593A).

Trade Agreements and Preferential Treatment Agreements

The North American Free Trade Agreement (NAFTA)

The North American Free Trade Agreement (NAFTA) was created on January 1, 1994, to form a preferred trade zone consisting of the U.S., Canada, and Mexico. Specifically, it was adopted according to the provisions of the North American Free Trade Agreement Implementation Act (107 Stat. 2057; this legislation also includes, as Title VI, the Customs Modernization Act, or Mod Act, referred to above). NAFTA supersedes the preexisting U.S.-Canada Free Trade Agreement (FTA), although the provisions of that earlier treaty remain essentially the same and are subsumed within the general framework of NAFTA. New provisions were negotiated to cover trade between the U.S. and Mexico, as well as between Mexico and Canada.

The agreement is divided into six titles dealing with general provisions, customs provisions, applications, dispute resolution, transitional provisions, and customs modifications. Parts of Title III further detail relief provisions and issues of agriculture, intellectual property, and standards. The parts of Title V cover transitional adjustment provisions, performance, customs user fees, internal revenue revisions, side agreements relating to labor and the environment, and the establishment of the North American Development Bank. Under the terms of NAFTA, tariffs, quotas, and nontariff barriers on most goods traded among the three countries are scheduled to be reduced, eased, or eliminated on transactions that are made among them. NAFTA provides for three classifications of goods affected by the agreement: products of Category A are allowed NAFTA benefits as of January 1, 1994; those of Category B, in 1998; and those of Category C, in 2003. The phase-out of restrictions on a few sensitive Category D products—such as textiles, automobiles, and certain food products—is scheduled to take as long as 15 years.

The U.S.-Canada FTA already allowed a great deal of the trade between these two countries to be conducted on a streamlined basis with reduced or no tariffs on the products involved and to a large degree mutual acceptance of the other's standards and procedures as equivalent. NAFTA extends and reorganizes these preferences to include many similar provisions for Mexico, while Mexico in turn has agreed to open its markets to U.S. and Canadian products. Goods eligible for special tariff treatment by the U.S. are denoted by a "CA" (Canadian) or an "MX" (Mexican) in the "Special Rates of Duty" column in the Harmonized Tariff Schedule of the United States (HTSUS).

Customs Regulations at 19 CFR Part 181, "North American Free Trade Agreement," implements the duty preference and related Customs provisions applicable to imported goods under NAFTA and the NAFTA Implementation Act. Other provisions implementing NAFTA and the Act are in 19 CFR Parts 10, 12, 24, 134, and 174.

Rules of Origin

In an effort to eliminate tariffs on eligible goods and to preclude outside countries from obtaining tariff benefits by merely passing their goods through one of the three signatory countries, "rules of origin" were devised. These rules determine origin for purposes of NAFTA eligibility, not for country of origin determination in other areas such as marking, quotas, dumping, and countervailing duty assessment. A lengthy appendix to 19 CFR Part 181 contains the NAFTA Rules of Origin Regulations. Refer also to 19 CFR 181 Subpart G, "Origin Verifications and Determinations."

There are four "origin criteria," which means that there are four ways in which goods generally meet the NAFTA rule of origin and quality for NAFTA tariff preference:

A. Goods "wholly produced or obtained" in the NAFTA region.

B. Goods containing non-originating inputs, but meeting the Annex 401 origin rules.

C. Goods produced in the NAFTA region wholly from originating materials, that is, produced from materials which may contain non-NAFTA materials, but which meet the NAFTA rule of origin.

D. Unassembled goods and goods classified in the same Harmonized System (HS) category as their parts, which do not meet the Annex 401 rule of origin, but contain sufficient North American regional value content. (Goods qualify in this category only under very limited circumstances.)

To qualify under preference criterion "A" on the NAFTA certificate of origin as goods "wholly obtained or produced" in one or more NAFTA countries, they must be one of the following:

- Mineral goods extracted in Canada, Mexico or the United States;

- Vegetable goods, as such goods are defined in the Harmonized System, harvested in Canada, Mexico or the United States;

- Live animals born and raised in Canada, Mexico or the United States; Meets Annex 401 Origin Criterion

- Goods obtained from hunting, trapping or fishing in Canada, Mexico or the United States;

- Goods (fish, shellfish and other marine life) taken from the sea by vessels registered or recorded with Canada, Mexico or the United States and flying its flag;

- Goods produced on board factory ships from the goods referred to in subparagraph (e) provided such factory ships are registered or recorded with that country and fly its flag;

- Goods taken by Canada, Mexico or the United States or a person of these countries from the seabed or beneath the seabed outside territorial waters, provided that Canada, Mexico or the United States has rights to exploit such seabed;

- Goods taken from outer space, provided they are obtained by Canada, Mexico or the United States or by a person of these countries and not processed in a non-NAFTA country;

- Waste and scrap derived from production in Canada, Mexico and/or the United States, or used goods collected in Canada, Mexico and/or the United States, provided such goods are fit only for the recovery of raw materials; and

- Goods produced in Canada, Mexico or the United States exclusively from goods referred to in subparagraphs (a) through (i), or from their derivatives, at any stage of production.

To qualify under preference criterion "B" on the NAFTA certificate of origin, goods must meet product-specific rules of origin set out in Annex 401. The Annex 401 rules of origin may be based on a change in tariff classification, a regional value-content requirement, or both. Tariff shift is the basis for most NAFTA rules of origin; it compares imported inputs and the finished good to be exported. You must know the harmonized system (HS) classification of both the good you are importing and any non-North American parts to apply the rule.

For goods to qualify under criterion "C" on the NAFTA certificate of origin, they must be produced entirely in NAFTA territories, although there may be some non-North American inputs. In general, the foreign materials must have been sufficiently transformed that new, originating parts have been created.

There are two limited circumstances under which a product may qualify for criterion "D1" or "D2" on the NAFTA certificate of origin. These are applicable when the good is produced entirely in the territory of one or more NAFTA countries, but one or more of the non-originating materials provided for as parts under the HS that are used in the production of the good does not undergo a change in tariff classification. Goods must have 50% or 60% North American value content (depending on the method used). These provisions never apply to products classified in HTSUS chapters 61–63 or other made-up textile items.

A commodity specific rule takes precedence over a general rule (there exist special exceptions for many products, mainly certain consumer products and agricultural goods). Also, under the de minimis rule, a product for which no more than 7% of the value (or weight, for some commodities) consists of nonregional inputs qualifies as an originating product under the definitions of NAFTA. Note that specific qualifying requirements are both complex and stringent. Refer to General Note 12 of the HTSUS for specifics.

Textiles and Apparel. The NAFTA provisions on trade in textiles and apparel are particularly detailed. The basic origin rule for textile and apparel articles is "yarn-forward." This means that the yarn used to form the fabric (which may later be used to produce wearing apparel or other

textile articles) must originate in a NAFTA country. Thus, a wool shirt made in Canada from fabric woven in Canada of wool yarn produced in Argentina would not be considered originating since the yarn does not originate within a NAFTA country. If, however, Argentine wool fiber was imported into Canada and spun into wool yarn, which was then used to produce the wool fabric, the shirt would be considered originating.

Less demanding rules of origin govern certain knitted underwear, brassieres, and shirts made from fabric in short supply in North America, and textile and apparel articles made from fabric not commonly produced in North America, such as silk or linen. On the other hand, stricter rules of origin exist for certain textile and apparel articles made of fibers that are produced in abundance in Canada, Mexico and the United States, such as cotton.

Automotive Products. The NAFTA rules of origin for automotive products are based on a tariff change alone or a tariff change and a regional value-content requirement. The Agreement requires that the regional value content for these products be calculated using the net cost method. The regional value-content requirement for autos and light vehicles, and their engines and transmissions, is now 50% under the net cost method; this percentage will be increased to 56% on January 1, 1998, and finally to 62.5% in 2002. The regional value-content requirement for other vehicles (e.g., tractors, vehicles for the transport of 16 or more persons, trucks), and their engines and transmissions, as well as other auto parts, is also currently 50% under the net cost method; this percentage will be increased to 55% as of January 1, 1998, and 60% in 2002.

Electronic Products. The rules of origin for a significant number of electronic products (e.g., computers, telecommunications equipment, televisions, machine tools, semiconductors) are based strictly on a tariff change. This tariff change is structured to require that key subassemblies of the product be produced in North America. Where necessary, the tariff schedules of Canada, Mexico and the United States were modified to accommodate these rules of origin. For example, television receivers with a picture tube of more than 14 inches in diameter may be considered originating only if the picture tube is produced or assembled in North America. Other electronic products may originate in one of two ways: by satisfying a tariff change or by meeting a less substantial tariff change and a regional value-content requirement. The first tariff change is generally stricter (requiring the non-originating materials to be classified in another chapter) and therefore has no regional value-content requirement. The alternative tariff change frequently involves a transformation of parts into a finished good. Since this alternate tariff change reflects a lesser degree of processing, the regional value-content requirement ensures significant North American content.

NAFTA Certificate of Origin

Canada, Mexico and the United States have established a uniform Certificate of Origin to certify that goods imported into their territories qualify for the preferential tariff treatment accorded by the NAFTA. Only importers who possess a valid Certificate of Origin may claim preferential tariff treatment for originating goods.

A Certificate of Origin may cover a single importation of goods or multiple importations of identical goods. Certificates that cover multiple shipments are called blanket certificates and may apply to goods imported within any twelve-month period specified on the Certificate. Although a Certificate of Origin may cover goods imported over not more than a twelve-month period, it remains valid for NAFTA preference claims made up to four years from the date upon which it was signed.

Importers claiming NAFTA preferential tariff treatment must make a declaration, based on a valid Certificate of Origin in their possession, on the import documentation. Where no claim for preferential tariff treatment is made at the time of importation, importers may request preferential tariff treatment no later than one year after the date on which the good was imported, provided a Certificate of Origin for the goods is obtained.

Importers must provide the Certificate to U.S. Customs on request, and must submit a corrected declaration and pay the corresponding duties whenever there is reason to believe that the Certificate contained inaccurate information. The Certificate of Origin must be completed and signed by the exporter of the goods. Where the exporter is not the producer, the exporter may complete the Certificate on the basis of:

- knowledge that the good originates;
- reasonable reliance on the producer's written representation that the good originates; or
- a completed and signed Certificate of Origin for the good voluntarily provided to the exporter by the producer.

NAFTA authorizes the importing country's customs administration to conduct verifications of the exporter or producer to determine whether goods qualify as originating as certified by the Certificate of Origin. Verifications are principally conducted by written questionnaires and verification visits. Additional verification can be done by telephone, facsimile or other means.

Key Provisions of NAFTA

Import Tariffs. At the time of signing, import tariffs averaged roughly 10% on goods entered into Mexico and 3% on those entered into the U.S. Many of these tariffs were eliminated or lowered on January 1, 1994, while most of the rest are to be gradually reduced and eventually eliminated over the scheduled life of the agreement.

Local Content and Origin Rules. Specific national local content requirements are to be removed. However, NAFTA imposes rules of origin designed to restrict the agreement's benefits to products actually produced in the member countries (see above).

Quotas. NAFTA calls for quotas to be liberalized and eventually eliminated on imports from its members. During this transition, the amount of goods imported under quota from Mexico and Canada will be expanded. These imports will not count against the total entry threshold amounts established for these products, so that absolute quotas are effectively raised for specific items imported from Mexico and Canada. The implementing regulations specify a schedule for specific products, including milk,

cheese, and other dairy products; tomatoes and other fruit and vegetable products; sugars, syrups, and products containing them; orange juice; and some textile products.

Textiles and Apparel. Under NAFTA, the U.S. will immediately remove quotas on textiles and apparel wholly Mexican in origin. Quotas on other textile products imported from Mexico but failing to meet NAFTA origin rules will be phased out over 10 years. The U.S. will phase out tariffs on apparel imported from its NAFTA partners over 10 years and on textiles over eight.

Agricultural Products. All U.S., Canadian, and Mexican nontariff barriers are to be converted into either tariff-rate quotas—allowing in unlimited quantities but charging higher rates once a threshold of level of imports has been reached— or ordinary tariffs with a set rate regardless of the amount of the product entered. These changes will be phased in over as long as 15 years for certain sensitive products.

Automotive Industry. Adjustments to the U.S. Corporate Fuel Economy rules will allow Mexican-produced parts and vehicles to be classified as domestic products, facilitating their import into the U.S. Relaxed Mexican tariff and nontariff barriers to foreign imports will allow greater and more economical flows of outside components into Mexico, which will in turn upgrade and increase the export production of the country's plants.

Drawback. NAFTA establishes new rules for drawbacks—refunds or waivers of duty on materials used in the production of products subsequently exported to a NAFTA partner. Existing drawback rules will expire for NAFTA parties in 2001. Upon expiration, changes will be implemented to avoid double taxation on such transactions. Under the new drawback arrangement, the amount of such waivers or refunds will be less than those on comparable nonoriginating materials.

Trilateral Trade Commission. NAFTA provides for the creation of a trilateral commission to adjudicate disputes under the agreement. This body is organized in an attempt to avoid national bias and is required to act on complaints within eight months. It will deal with antidumping and subsidy issues, as well as the implementation of the provisions of the agreement.

Entry Procedures

Formal Entries. As with other trade preference programs, the importer must make a claim under NAFTA to receive the tariff treatment. An importer can make a claim by:

1. Prefixing either "CA" or "MX" to the tariff classification number

2. Submitting Customs **Form 434, NAFTA Certificate of Origin; the Canadian Certificate of Origin (Canadian Form B-232), or the Mexican Certificate of Origin (Certificado de Origen)**

3. Submitting Customs **Form 7501, Entry Summary**

Informal Entries. Pursuant to 19 CFR 181.22(d) of the Agreement, the U.S. does not require a Certificate of Origin for entries valued at US $2,500 or less. For commercial shipments, however, the invoice accompanying the importation must include a statement certifying that the goods qualify as originating goods

Special Provisions for Sensitive Sectors

Nafta Annex 401, origin criteria for textiles and apparel products, ensures that most of the production relating to textiles and apparel occurs in North America. The basic origin rule for textiles and apparel is "yarn forward." This means that the yarn used to form the fabric must originate in a NAFTA country.

Sources of Additional Information

For additional information on NAFTA, there are a number of publications and help centers One important source for importer is The Harmonized Tariff Schedule of the U.S., General Note 12.

NAFTA: The North American Free Trade Agreement, A Guide to Customs Procedures, Customs Publication No. 571, provides an overview of the benefits and requirements of NAFTA. It is available from the U.S. Government Printing Office. For ordering information, call (202) 512-1800 or go to http://www.gpo.gov on the Internet. The GPO has other publications relating to NAFTA for sale, including the complete legal text of the agreement and the implementing laws. Other good electronic sources on NAFTA for U.S. importers includes the Customs Service web site (http://www.customs.treas.gov/) and the Customs Electronic Bulletin Board (CEEB). Refer to the Infolists for more on these electronic sources.

Generalized System of Preferences (GSP)

The Generalized System of Preferences is a program providing for free rates of duty for merchandise from beneficiary developing independent countries and dependent countries and territories to encourage their economic growth (see list on pages to follow).

This program was enacted by the U.S. in the Trade Act of 1974, became effective on January 1, 1976. The U.S. Congress allowed the GSP program to expire July 31, 1995, and it was not until mid-1996 that President Clinton signed legislation re-enacting the program effective October 1, 1996. Refunds, with interest, of duties paid on GSP-eligible imports during this period, are being made available. Importers should be aware that the GSP program expires once again on May 31, 1997, and it is quite possible that Congress will again allow it to lapse, either for several months or indefinitely.

Eligible Items

The GSP eligibility list contains a wide range of products classifiable under more than 4,000 different subheadings in the Harmonized Tariff Schedule of the United States. These items are identified either by an "A" or "A*" in the "Special" column under column 1 of the tariff schedule. Merchandise classifiable under a subheading designated in this manner may qualify for duty-free entry if imported into the U.S. directly from any of the designated countries and territories. Merchandise from one or more of these countries, however, may be excluded from the exemption if there is an "A*" in the "Special" column. The list of countries and exclusions, as well as the list of GSP-eligible articles, will change from time to time over the life of the program. You should consult the latest edition of the Harmonized Tariff Schedules of the United States for the most up-to-date information.

The following articles may not be designated as an eligible article for purposes of the GSP:

- Textile and apparel articles which are subject to textile agreements;

- Watches, except as determined by the President pursuant to section 503(c)(1)(B) of the Trade Act of 1974, as amended;

- Footwear, handbags, luggage, flat goods, work gloves and leather wearing apparel, the foregoing which were not eligible articles for purposes of the GSP on April 1, 1984;

- Any agricultural product of chapters 2 through 52, inclusive, that is subject to a tariff-rate quota, if entered in a quantity in excess of the in-quota quantity for such product; and

- Import-sensitive electronic articles, steel articles, semimanufactured and manufactured glass products;

- Any other articles which the President determines to be import-sensitive in the context of the GSP.

If advance tariff classification information is needed to ascertain whether or not your commodity is eligible under the GSP, you may obtain this information under the procedures previously discussed in "Dutiable Status of Goods" on page 218.

Claims

Formal Entries. For commercial shipments requiring a formal entry, a claim for duty-free status is made under GSP by showing on the entry summary that the country of origin is a designated beneficiary developing country and by showing an "A" with the appropriate GSP-eligible subheading. Eligible merchandise will be entitled to duty-free treatment provided the following conditions are met:

1. The merchandise must be destined for the U.S. without contingency for diversion at the time of exportation from the beneficiary developing country.

2. The merchandise must be imported directly from any beneficiary country into the customs territory of the United States.

3. The cost or value of materials produced in the beneficiary developing country and/or the direct cost of processing performed there must represent at least 35% of the appraised value of the goods.

The cost or value of materials imported into the beneficiary developing country may be included in calculating the 35% value-added requirement for an eligible article if the materials are first substantially transformed into new and different articles and are then used as constituent materials in the production of the eligible article. The phrase "direct costs of processing" includes costs directly incurred or reasonably allocated to the processing of the article,

Generalized System of Preferences (GSP) Independent Countries

Albania	Czech Republic	Lesotho	Sao Tome and Principe
Angola	Djibouti	Lithuania	Senegal
Antigua & Barbuda***	Dominica***	Macedonia (FYR)	Seychelles
Argentina	Dominican Republic	Mali	Sierra Leone
Armenia	Equatorial Guinea	Madagascar	Somalia
Bahrain	Ecuador*	Malawi	Slovakia
Bangladesh	Egypt	Malta	Slovenia
Barbados***	El Salvador	Mauritania	Solomon Islands
Belize***	Estonia	Mauritius	South Africa
Benin	Ethiopia	Moldova	Sri Lanka
Bhutan	Fiji	Mongolia	Suriname
Bolivia*	Gambia, The	Morocco	Swaziland
Bosnia & Herzegovina	Ghana	Mozambique	Tanzania
Botswana	Grenada***	Namibia	Thailand**
Brazil	Guatemala	Nepal	Togo
Bulgaria	Guinea	Niger	Tonga
Burkina Faso	Guinea Bissau	Nigeria	Trinidad and Tobago***
Burundi	Guyana***	Oman	Tunisia
Cambodia	Haiti	Pakistan	Turkey
Cameroon	Honduras	St Vincent / Grenadines***	Tuvalu
Cape Verde	Hungary	Panama	Uganda
Central African Republic	India	Papua New Guinea	Ukraine
Chad	Indonesia**	Paraguay	Uruguay
Chile	Jamaica***	Peru*	Uzbekistan
Colombia	Jordan	Philippines**	Vanuatu
Comoros	Kazakhstan	Poland	Venezuela*
Dem. Rep. Congo (Kinshasa)	Kenya	Romania	Western Samoa
Republic of Congo (Brazzaville)	Kiribati	Russia	Yemen Arab Republic
Costa Rica	Kyrgyz Rep.	Rwanda	Zambia
Cote d'Ivoire	Latvia	Saint Kitts and Nevis***	Zimbabwe
Croatia	Lebanon	Saint Lucia***	

* Member countries of the Cartagena Agreement—Andean Group (treated as one country).
** Association of South East Asian Nations—ASEAN (GSP-eligible countries only) treated as one country.
*** Member countries of the Caribbean Common Market—CARICOM (treated as one country).

GSP Non-Independent Countries and Territories

Anguilla	Falkland Islands	Netherlands Antilles	Turks and Caicos Islands
Aruba	French Polynesia	New Caledonia	Virgin Islands (British)
British Indian Ocean Terr.	Gibraltar	Niue	Wallis and Fortuna
Cayman Islands	Greenland	Norfolk Island	West Bank and Gaza Strip
Christmas Island	Heard & McDonald Islands	Pitcairn Islands	Western Sahara
Cocos (Keeling) Islands	Macao	Saint Helena	
Cook Islands	Montserrat ***	Tokelau	

such as the cost of all actual labor, dies, molds, tooling, depreciation on machinery, research and development, and inspection and testing. Business overhead, administrative expenses, salaries, and profit, as well as general business expenses such as administrative salaries, casualty and liability insurance, advertising and salesperson's salaries may not be considered as direct costs of processing.

Evidence of Country of Origin. If the merchandise is not wholly the product of a single beneficiary country, the exporter or other appropriate party should be prepared to submit a declaration to the port director, upon request, with detailed information concerning the production or manufacture of the merchandise. A sample GSP declaration form is given at 19 CFR 10.173(a)(1)(i). The information necessary for preparation of such a declaration must be retained for a five-year period. For merchandise which is wholly the product of a single beneficiary country, a statement to that effect must be included on the commercial invoice provided to Customs. Any evidence of country of origin submitted to Customs may be subject to verification; if the port director is prevented from obtaining verification, the entry may be treated as dutiable.

Informal Entries. The country of origin declaration described in the preceding paragraph is not required for informal entries, but the port director may ask for other evidence of country of origin. Importers planning to make informal GSP entries would be well-advised to have a GSP Declaration ready.

Sources of Additional Information

Customs rules and regulations on GSP are incorporated in 19 CFR 10.171–10.178. You should also refer to General Note 4 of the HTSUS. Address any question you may have as to the administrative or operational aspects of the GSP to the Executive Director, Trade Programs, Bureau of Border & Customs Protection, Washington, DC 20229, Tel: (202) 927-0390, 927-0300, FAX (202) 927-1096; or the International Organizations and Agreements Division, Bureau of Border & Customs Protection, Tel: (202) 927-1480, FAX (202) 927-6897. Requests for information concerning additions to, or deletions from, the list of eligible merchandise under GSP, or the list of beneficiary development countries, should be directed to the Chariman, Trade Policy Staff Subcommittee, Office of U.S. Trade Representative, 600 17th St., NW, Washington, DC 20506, Tel: (202) 395-6186.

Caribbean Basin Initiative (CBI)

The Caribbean Basin Initiative (CBI) is a program providing for the duty-free entry of merchandise from designated beneficiary countries or territories. This program was enacted by the U.S. as the Caribbean Basin Economic Recovery Act (CBERA), became effective on January 1, 1984, and has no expiration date.

Beneficiary Countries

The following countries and territories have been designated as beneficiary countries for purposes of the CBI:

Antigua and Barbuda	Haiti
Aruba	Honduras
Bahamas	Jamaica
Barbados	Montserrat
Belize	Netherlands Antilles
Costa Rica	Nicaragua
Dominica	Panama
Dominican Republic	Saint Kitts and Nevis
El Salvador	Saint Lucia
Grenada	Saint Vincent and the Grenadines
Guatemala	Trinidad and Tobago
Guyana	Virgin Islands, British

Eligible Items

The list of beneficiaries may change from time to time over the life of the program. Therefore, it is necessary to consult General Note 7(a) in the latest edition of the Harmonized Tariff Schedule of the United States (HTSUS), which will contain updated information.

Most products from designated beneficiaries are eligible for CBI duty-free treatment. These items are identified by either an "E" or "E*" in the Special column under column 1 of the HTSUS. The symbol "E" indicates that all articles provided for in the designated provision are eligible for preferential treatment except those noted below. The symbol "E*" indicates that some articles provided for in the designated provision are not eligible for preferential treatment. These goods include beef and veal, products; some sugars, syrups, and molasses products; and some textile products. The duty-free treatment provided under the CBI does not apply to watches and watch parts, various leather apparel goods, canned tuna, petroleum products, and a few other items. Refer to Note 7 of the HTSUS, 19 CFR 10.191(b)(2), and to 19 CFR 10.191–10.198 for more specifics.

Merchandise classifiable under a subheading designated by an "E" or "E*" may qualify for duty-free entry if imported into the U.S. directly from any of the designated countries and territories. Merchandise from one or more of these countries, however, may be excluded from time to time over the life of the program. Therefore, the latest edition of the HTSUS will contain the most up-to-date information.

Merchandise will be eligible for CBI duty-free treatment only if the following conditions are met:

1. For commercial shipments requiring a formal entry, a claim for preferential tariff treatment under CBI is made by showing that the country of origin is a designated beneficiary country and by inserting the letter "E" as a prefix to the applicable tariff schedule number on Customs Form 7501.

2. The merchandise must have been produced in a beneficiary country. This requirement is satisfied when

(1) the goods are wholly the growth, product, or manufacture of a beneficiary country, or (2) the goods have been substantially transformed into a new or different article of commerce in a beneficiary country.

3. The merchandise must be imported directly from any beneficiary country into the customs territory of the United States.

3. At least 35 percent of the appraised value of the article imported into the United States must consist of the cost or value of materials produced in one or more beneficiary countries and/or the direct costs of processing operations performed in one or more beneficiary countries. The Commonwealth of Puerto Rico and the U.S. Virgin Islands are defined as beneficiary countries for purposes of this requirement; therefore, value attributable to Puerto Rico or to the Virgin Islands may also be counted. In addition, the cost or value of materials produced in the customs territory of the United States (other than Puerto Rico) may be counted toward the 35 percent value-added requirement, but only to a maximum of 15 percent of the appraised value of the imported article.

The cost or value of materials imported into a beneficiary country from a non-beneficiary country may be included in calculating the 35 percent value-added requirement for an eligible article if the materials are first substantially transformed into new or different articles of commerce and are then used as constituent materials in the production of the eligible article. The phrase "direct costs of processing operations" includes costs directly incurred or reasonably allocated to the production of the article, such as the cost of actual labor, dies, molds, tooling, depreciation of machinery, research and development, inspection, and testing. Business overhead, administrative expenses and profit, as well as general business expenses, such as casualty and liability insurance, advertising, and salespeople's salaries, are not considered direct costs of processing operations..

Important Exceptions

Under Section 213(a)(5) of the CBERA, articles that are the growth product, or manufacture of Puerto Rico and that subsequently are processed in a CBI beneficiary country, may also receive duty-free treatment when entered, if the three following conditions are met:

1. They are imported directly from a beneficiary country into the customs territory of the U.S.

2. They are advanced in value or improved in condition by any means in a beneficiary country.

3. Any materials added to the article in a beneficiary country must be a product of a beneficiary country or the U.S.

Also, articles that are assembled or processed in whole from U.S. components or ingredients (other than water) in a beneficiary country may be entered free of duty. Duty-free treatment will apply if the components or ingredients are exported directly to the beneficiary country and the finished article is imported directly into the customs territory of the United States.

Commercial Compliance Division, U.S. Customs Service,

Although cutting of textile components no longer confers originating status under new textile rules of origin which became effective July 1, 1996, an important exception has been made for textile imports from CBI beneficiaries. Under 19 CFR 10.195(d), a textile component from foreign fabric may be cut to shape in the U.S. or Puerto Rico, exported to a beneficiary country for assembly into an article that is returned to the U.S. and entered or withdrawn for consumption.

If advance tariff classification information is needed to ascertain whether or not your merchandise would be eligible for CBI duty-free treatment, you may obtain this information under the procedures previously discussed in "Dutiable Status of Goods" on page 218.

Claim for Exemption Under CBI

Formal Entries. For commercial shipments requiring a formal entry, a claim for CBI duty-free treatment is made by showing on the entry summary that the country of origin is a designated beneficiary country and by adding the letter "E" as prefix to the applicable tariff schedule subheading. The port director may require evidence such as shipping papers, or invoices to demonstrate that the goods were "imported directly," in other words, that the shipment did not pass through any non-beneficiary countries, or if it did, that it was not sold or altered in any way. For a specific definition, refer to 19 CFR 10.193, "Imported directly."

The port director may also require evidence of the country of origin. If the merchandise is not wholly the product of a single beneficiary country, the exporter or other appropriate party should be prepared to submit a declaration to the port director, upon request, with detailed information concerning the production or manufacture of the merchandise. A sample CBI Declaration form is given at 19 CFR 10.198(a)(1)(i). The information necessary for preparation of such a declaration must be retained for a five-year period. For merchandise which is wholly the product of a single beneficiary country, a statement to that effect must be included on the commercial invoice provided to Customs. Any evidence of country of origin submitted to Customs may be subject to verification; if the port director is prevented from obtaining verification, the entry may be treated as dutiable.

If value is added to an article in a bonded warehouse or in a foreign trade zone in the U.S. or Puerto Rico after the final exportation from a beneficiary country, the importer or consignee must file the CBI Declaration with the entry summary.

Informal Entries. The country of origin declaration described in the preceding paragraph is not required for informal entries, but the port director may ask for other evidence of country of origin. Importers planning to make informal CBI entries would be well-advised to have a CBI Declaration ready.

Sources of Additional Information

Customs rules and regulations on the CBI are incorporated in 19 CFR 10.191–10.198 and in General Note 7 of the HTSUS. Address any questions to the port director of the port where the merchandise will be entered or to Director,

Washington, DC 20229..

Andean Trade Preference Act (ATPA)

The Andean Trade Preference Act (ATPA) is a program providing for the duty-free entry of merchandise from designated beneficiary countries. The ATPA was enacted into law by the U.S. on December 4, 1991 and is scheduled to expire on December 4, 2001.

Effective December 5, 2001, merchandise that is either entered or withdrawn from warehouse for consumption is not eligible for preferential tariff treatment under the ATPA unless Congress extends the act. Duties must be deposited for all merchandise entered on or after that date. Use of the "J" Special Program Indicator will result in rejection of the entry summary for all such merchandise. If Congress does renew the ATPA and makes it retroactive, a message will be issued to the trade community that describes how to request refunds. Please check Customs Web site for updates.

Beneficiary Countries

The following countries have been designated as beneficiary countries for purposes of the ATPA:

Bolivia   Ecuador
Columbia   Peru

Eligible Items

Most products from designated beneficiaries may be eligible for ATPA duty-free treatment. Products that are statutorily excluded include: textile and apparel articles that are subject to textile agreements; most footwear; preserved or prepared tuna in airtight containers; petroleum products; watches and watch parts from countries subject to Column 2 rates of duty; various sugar products; rum and tafia. Eligible items are identified by either a "J" or "J*" in the Special subcolumn under column 1 of the HTSUS. Merchandise classifiable under a subheading designated in the manner may qualify for duty-free entry if imported into the U.S. directly from any designated ATPA beneficiary country. Merchandise from one or more of these countries, however, may be excluded from duty-free treatment if there is a "J*" in the Special subcolumn. Some goods, while not eligible for duty-free status, may qualify for reduced duties. Refer to General Note 11 of the HTSUS for specifics.

Eligibility

Merchandise will be eligible for ATPA duty-free treatment only if the following conditions are met:

1. The merchandise must be imported directly from any beneficiary country into U.S. customs territory.
2. The merchandise must have been produced in a beneficiary country. This requirement is satisfied when: (1) the goods are wholly the growth, product, or manufacture of a beneficiary country, or (2) the goods have been substantially transformed into a new and different article of commerce in a beneficiary country.
3. At least 35% of the appraised value of the article must consist of the cost or value of materials produced in one or more ATPA or CBI beneficiary countries and/or the direct costs of processing operations performed in one or more ATPA or CBI beneficiary coun-

tries. The Commonwealth of Puerto Rico and the U.S. Virgin Islands are defined as beneficiary countries for purposes of this requirement; therefore, value attributable to Puerto Rico or the Virgin Islands may also be counted. In addition, the cost or value of materials produced in the customs territory of the U.S. (other than Puerto Rico) may be counted toward the 35% value-added requirement, but only to a maximum of 15% of the appraised value of the imported article.

The cost or value of materials imported into ATPA or CBI beneficiary countries from non-beneficiary countries may be included in calculating the 35% value-added requirement for an eligible article if the materials are first substantially transformed into new and different articles of commerce and are then used as constituent materials in the production of the eligible article. The phrase "direct costs of processing operations" includes costs directly incurred or reasonably allocated to the production of the article, such as the cost of actual labor, dies, molds, tooling, depreciation of machinery, research and development, inspection and testing. Business overhead, administrative expenses and profit, as well as general business expenses such as casualty and liability insurance, advertising and salespersons' salaries may not be considered as direct costs of processing operations.

If advance tariff classification information is needed to ascertain whether your merchandise would be eligible for ATPA duty-free treatment, you may obtain this information under the procedures previously discussed in "Dutiable Status of Goods" on page 218.

Claims For Exemption Under ATPA

Formal Entries. A claim for duty-free status is made under the ATPA by showing on the entry summary that the country of origin is a designated beneficiary developing country and by showing a "J" with the appropriate ATPA-eligible subheading.

Evidence of Country of Origin. If the merchandise is not wholly the product of a single beneficiary country, the exporter or other appropriate party should be prepared to submit a declaration to the port director, upon request, with detailed information concerning the production or manufacture of the merchandise. A sample declaration form is given at 19 CFR 10.173(a)(1)(i) for the GSP; ATPA claimants should simply substitute "ATPA" for "GSP." The information necessary for preparation of such a declaration must be retained for a five-year period. For merchandise which is wholly the product of a single beneficiary country, a statement to that effect must be included on the commercial invoice provided to Customs. Any evidence of country of origin submitted to Customs may be subject to verification; if the port director is prevented from obtaining verification, the entry may be treated as dutiable. The country of origin declaration described above is not required for informal entries, but the port director may ask for other evidence of country of origin. Importers planning to make informal ATPA entries would be well-advised to have a ATPA Declaration ready.

U.S.- Israel Free Trade Area Agreement

The U.S.-Israel Free Trade Area agreement is a program providing for free or reduced rates of duty for merchandise from Israel to stimulate trade between the two countries. This program was authorized by the U.S. in the Trade and Tariff Act of 1984 and implemented by the U.S.-Israel Free Trade Area Implementation Act of 1985 (99 Stat. 82) and Presidential Proclamation 5365 of August 30, 1985. The program became effective September 1, 1985, and has no termination date. As of January 1, 1995, all currently eligible reduced rate importations from Israel were accorded duty-free treatment.

The FTA Implementation Act was amended on October 2, 1996, authorizing the President to implement certain changes affecting the duty status of goods from the West Bank, Gaza Strip, and qualifying industrial zones (QIZs). By Presidential Proclamation 6955 of November 13, 1996, General Note 3(v) was created to implement the new program for these goods. Pursuant to General Note 3(v), duty-free treatment is allowed for products of the West Bank, Gaza Strip, or a QIZ, imported directly from the West Bank, Gaza Strip, a QIZ or Israel, provided certain requirements are met. Also as a result of Presidential Proclamation 6955, the eligibility requirements were modified for duty-free treatment of articles which are the product of Israel.

In the Harmonized Tariff Schedule of the United States, General Note 3(a)(v)(G), a QIZ is defined as any area that 1) encompasses portions of the territory of Israel and Jordan or Israel and Egypt; 2) has been designated by local authorities as an enclave where merchandise may enter without payment of duty or excise taxes; and 3) has been designated by the United States Trade Representative (USTR) in a notice published in the Federal Register as a local Customs ports for a current list of designated QIZs.

Eligible Items

The agreement relates to most tariff items listed in the Harmonized Tariff Schedule of the United States (HTSUS). These items are identified by "IL" in the "Special" column under column 1 of the Harmonized Tariff Schedule. Refer to General Note 8 of the HTSUS for more information.

An article imported into the Customs territory of the U.S. is eligible for treatment as a "Product of Israel" only if:

- That article is the growth, product, or manufacture of Israel, the West Bank, Gaza Strip, or a QIZ
- That article is imported directly from Israel, the West Bank, Gaza Strip, or a QIZ into the Customs territory of the U.S.;
- The sum of: (1) The cost or value of the materials produced in Israel, the West Bank, Gaza Strip, or a QIZ, plus (2) the direct costs of processing operations performed in Israel, the West Bank, Gaza Strip, or a QIZ is not less than 35% of the appraised value of such article at the time it is entered. If the cost or value of materials produced in the customs territory of the U.S. is included with respect to an eligible article, an amount not to exceed 15% of the appraised value of the article

at the time it is entered that is attributable to such U.S. cost or value may be applied toward determining the 35%.

- The cost or value of materials imported into Israel, the West Bank, Gaza Strip, or a QIZ from a third country may be included in calculating the 35% value-added requirement, provided they are first substantially transformed into new and different articles of commerce and are then used as constituent materials in the production of the eligible article.

No article may be considered to meet these requirements by virtue of having merely undergone:

- Simple combining or packaging operations; or
- Mere diluting with water or mere dilution with another substance that does not materially alter the characteristics of the article.

The phrase "direct costs of processing operations" includes, but is not limited to:

- All actual labor costs involved in the growth, production, manufacture, or assembly of the specific merchandise, including fringe benefits, on-the-job training, and the costs of engineering, supervisory, quality control, and similar personnel.
- Dies, molds, tooling, and depreciation on machinery and equipment that are allocable to the specific merchandise.

Direct costs of processing operations do not include costs that are not directly attributable to the merchandise concerned, or are not costs of manufacturing the product, such as (1) profit and (2) general expenses of doing business that are either not allocable to the specific merchandise or are not related to the growth, production, manufacture, or assembly of the merchandise, such as administrative salaries, casualty and liability insurance, advertising and sales staff's salaries, commissions, or expenses.

Claims for Exemption

Formal Entries. For commercial shipments requiring a formal entry, a claim for duty-free status is made under the U.S.–Israel Free Trade Agreement by showing on the entry summary that Israel is the country of origin and by showing an "IL" with the appropriate HTSUS subheading.

Evidence of Country of Origin. If the merchandise is not wholly the product of Israel, the exporter or other appropriate party should be prepared to submit a country of origin declaration to the port director, upon request, with detailed information concerning the production or manufacture of the merchandise. The information necessary for preparation of such a declaration must be retained for a five-year period. The United Nations Conference on Trade and Development (UNCTAD) Certificate of Origin Form A is used as documentary evidence to support duty-free and reduced-rate claims for Israeli articles covered by a formal entry. It does not have to be produced at the time of entry unless so requested by the Bureau of Customs & Border Protection. The form A may be presented on an entry by entry basis or may be used as a blanket declaration for a period of 12 months. The Form A can be obtained from the Israeli authorizing issuing authority or from UNCTAD, Two U.N. Plaza, Room 1120, New York, NY 10017, Tel. (212) 963-6895. For merchandise which is wholly the product of Israel, a statement to that effect must be included on the commercial invoice provided to Customs. Any evidence of country of origin submitted to Customs may be subject to verification; if the port director is prevented from obtaining verification, the entry may be treated as dutiable.

Informal Entries. The country of origin declaration described in the preceding paragraph is not required for informal entries, but the port director may ask for other evidence of country of origin. With regard to merchandise accompanying the traveler, it should be noted that in order to avoid delays to passengers, the inspecting Customs officer will extend Israeli duty-free treatment to all eligible articles when satisfied, from the facts available, that the merchandise concerned is a product of Israel.

Sources of Additional information

For more details, refer to General Note 8 of the HTSUS. Address any questions you may have about the administrative or operational aspects of the agreement to the Director, Commercial Compliance Division, U.S. Customs Service, Wahington, DC 20229; Tel: (202) 927-1480, FAX (202) 927-6897. Requests for information concerning policy issues related to the FTA Policy Staff Subcommittee, Office of U.S. Trade Representative, 600 17th St., NW, Washington, DC 20506; Tel: (202) 395-6186; Fax Retrieval System: (202) 395-4809.

U.S. - Jordan Free Trade Area Agreement

The United States-Jordan Free Trade Area (FTA) agreement, signed into law in September 2001, became effective December 17, 2001. It provides for the elimination of duties and commercial barriers in the trade of goods and services that originate in the United States and Jordan. Effective immediately, importers may file claims for preferential tariff treatment of designated articles that originate in Jordan.

Presidential Proclamation 7512 (December 7, 2001) created two new annexes that contain the modifications to the Harmonized Tariff Schedule of the United States (HTS) necessary to implement JFTA's provisions. This proclamation was published in the Federal Register on December 13, 2001 (66 FR 64497).

Proclamation 7512 amends the HTS by adding a new General Note 18 concerning the JFTA and a new Subchapter IX to Chapter 99 to provide for the JFTA's temporary tariff-rate quotas. Please refer to Quota Book Transmittals QBT-2001-595 and QBT-2001-596, dated December 11, 2001. Both can be found at Customs Web site, www.customs.gov under "Importing and Exporting." These QBTs provide additional information on import restraint limits and reporting instructions for tariff-rate quotas under the JFTA for the years 2001 and 2002. Annex II to Proclamation 7512 lists which HTS numbers have an immediate free rate of duty, which Chapter 1-97 HTS numbers are subject to tariff-rate quotas, and the schedule of staged tariff reductions for products of Jordan.

JFTA General Origin Rules

Section 102 of the JFTA (Public Law 107- 43, 115 Stat. 243; 19 U.S.C. 2112 Note) provides for the rules of origin to determine whether a good qualifies for preferential tariff treatment under the JFTA. Under the agreement, a good qualifies for preferential tariff treatment as a "Product of Jordan," only if:

(a) It is imported directly from Jordan into the U.S. and is wholly the growth, product, or manufacture of Jordan; or

(b) It is imported directly from Jordan into the U.S. and is a new or different article of commerce that has been grown, produced, or manufactured in Jordan; and

(c) The sum of: (1) the cost or value of the materials produced in Jordan, plus (2) the direct costs of processing operations performed in Jordan is not less than 35% of the appraised value of the article at the time it is entered into the territory of the U.S.

(d) If the cost or value of materials produced in the customs territory of the United States is included for purposes of determining whether an article meets the requirement of containing 35% domestic content, no more than 15 percent of that article's appraised value that is attributable to the United States cost or value at the time it is entered may be applied toward determining the 35%.

Simple combining or packaging operations or mere dilution with water or another substance is not sufficient to confer origin for purposes of this agreement.

There is no exception from paying the merchandise processing fees provided for in the agreement. These fees must be paid on entries of merchandise for which a preferentialtariff treatment claim is made under the JFTA.

The JFTA does not affect merchandise entered from a Qualifying Industrial Zone (QIZ). (See General Note 3[a][v], HTS, for a definition of QIZs.) Because duty reductions will be staged for certain products, it may be advantageous for importers to continue to enter merchandise manufactured in a Jordanian QIZ under General Note 3 (a)(v), rather than under the JFTA.

JFTA Textile and Apparel Articles Origin Rules

Pursuant to the provisions set forth under the JFTA Act, a textile or apparel article imported directly from Jordan into the customs territory of the United States will be eligible for preferential tariff treatment only if the following conditions are met:

1. The article is wholly obtained or produced in Jordan;

2. The article is a yarn, thread, twine, cordage, rope, cable or braiding, and a. the constituent staple fibers are spun in Jordan, or b. the continuous filament is extruded in Jordan;

3. The article is a fabric, including a fabric classified in chapter 59 of the HTS, and the constituent fibers, filaments or yarns are woven, knitted, needled, tufted, felted, entangled or transformed by any other fabric-making process in Jordan; or

4. The article is any other textile or apparel article that is wholly assembled in Jordan from its component pieces.

Textile and apparel articles not wholly obtained or produced in Jordan must comply with the above conditions and the value requirements described above under "General Origin Rules."

There are special rules for certain textile and apparel articles like knit-to-shape goods, linens, and certain fabrics and goods subjected to dyeing, printing, and two or more finishing operations (Please see General Note 18 HTS.)

An article is "wholly obtained or produced in Jordan" if it is wholly the growth, product, or manufacture of Jordan. For more details or clarification of this provision, please consult the General Origin Rules and the relevant HTS headings.

Elibible Items

Pursuant to Annex II of Presidential Proclamation 7512, a list of the HTS item numbers that are eligible for immediate duty-free treatment with respect to Jordanian goods that are either entered or withdrawn from warehouse for consumption, on or after December 17, 2001, may be found in the Federal Register (66 FR 64497-64734) dated December 13, 2001. This edition of the Federal Register may be found at the following Web site address:

www.access.gpo.gov/su_ docs/fedreg/a011213c.html

The Proclamation itself is included in the "Presidential Documents" section. The annex, including the staged rate reductions, can only be viewed by opening the .PDF files.

Importer Requirements

If preferential tariff treatment is claimed at the time of entry, a written claim shall be filed on the entry document by placing the symbol "JO" as a prefix to the HTS subheading for each article for which such treatment is claimed.

The importer shall be prepared to submit to Customs, upon request, a declaration setting forth all pertinent information concerning the article's production or manufacture. This information must be retained in the importer's files for five years.

The information on the declaration should contain at least the following:

1. A description of the article, quantity, numbers, and marks of packages, invoice number, and bills of lading;

2. A description of the operations performed in the article's production in Jordan and an identification of the direct costs of processing operations;

3. A description of any materials used in the article's production that are wholly the growth, product, or manufacture of Jordan, and a statement of the cost or value of these materials;

4. A description of the operations performed on, and a statement as to the origin and cost or value of, any foreign materials used in the article which are claimed to have been sufficiently processed in Jordan that they now qualify as materials produced in Jordan; and

5. A description of the origin and cost or value of any foreign materials used in the article that were not substantially transformed in Jordan.

The declaration shall be prepared, signed, and, upon request, submitted to the Customs officer concerned. Customs may request the importer's declaration when verifying a claim's validity for preferential tariff treatment under the JFTA. In this case, the importer should be prepared to supply any and all supporting documentation upon which the declaration was based. The importer's failure to provide the declaration and/or sufficient evidentiary documentation will result in the claim's denial.

Exclusions

A good shall not be considered to meet the requirements of being a "product of Jordan" if it:

- is imported into Jordan and, at the time of importation, would be classified under heading 0805 of the HTS; and

- is processed in Jordan into a good classified under any of subheadings 2009.11 through 2009.30 of the HTS.

There is no set expiration date for the JFTA. However, the provisions of and amendments made by the JFTAAct will cease to be effective upon the termination of the agreement by written notification from either the United States or Jordan. The FTA will expire six months after the date of such notification.

Until further notice from the Office of Trade Programs at Customs Headquarters, importers claiming preference under the JFTA must file their entries manually. Importers are urged to visit Customs Web site, www.customs.gov, for updates on the implementation status of the JFTA and on the automation status for filing entries under it.

Please address any questions you may have about the administrative or operational aspects of the JFTA to the port director where the merchandise will be entered or to the Executive Director, Office of Trade Programs, U.S. Customs Service, Washington, D.C. 20229

Compact of the Freely Associated States

The Compact of the Freely Associated States (FAS) is a program providing for the duty-free entry of merchandise from designated freely associated states of the U.S. This program was established by Presidential Proclamation 60 30 of September 28, 1989, Section 242, became effective on October 18, 1989, and has no termination date.

Beneficiary Countries

The following freely associated states have been designated as beneficiary countries for purposes of the FAS:

- Marshall Islands
- Federated States of Micronesia
- Republic of Palau

Note that the Republic of Palau is a recent addition to the FAS, having been removed from the GSP list.

Eligible Items and Claim for Exemption

The duty-free treatment is applied to most products from the designated beneficiaries. For commercial shipments requiring formal entry, a claim for duty-free status is made by placing the letter "Z" next to the eligible subheading. Refer to General Note 10 of the HSTUS for more information.

The following merchandise is excluded from the duty-free exemption:

1. Tunas and skipjack, prepared or preserved, not in oil, in airtight containers weighing with their contents not more than 7 kg each, "in excess" of the consumption quota quantity allowed duty-free entry.

2. Textile and apparel articles that are subject to textile agreements.

3. Footwear, handbags, luggage, flat goods, work gloves, and leather wearing apparel that were not eligible for GSP treatment, as discussed in Chapter 13, as of April 1, 1984.

4. Watches, clocks, and timing apparatus of Chapter 91 of the Harmonized Tariff Schedule (except such articles incorporating an optoelectronic display and no other type of display).

5. Buttons of subheading 9606.21.40 or 9606.29.20 of the Harmonized Tariff Schedule.

6. Any agricultural product of chapters 2 through 52, inclusive, that is subject to a tariff-rate quota, if entered in a quantity in excess of the in-quota quantity for such a product.

Duty-free treatment may be lost in a particular calendar year if the value of the quantity of articles exported to the U.S. by a freely associated state equals or exceeds certain amounts, as described in General Note 10(e) of the Harmonized Tariff Schedule of the United States (HTSUS). If in subsequent years exports to the U.S. from the country fall below the permissible limits, duty-free status may be reinstated.

Merchandise will be eligible for FAS duty-free treatment only if the following conditions are met:

1. It must be the growth, product, or manufacture of the freely associated state.

2. The merchandise must be imported directly from the freely associated state into U.S. customs territory.

3. At least 35% of the appraised value of the article imported into the U.S. must consist of the cost or value of materials produced in the beneficiary country and/or the direct costs of processing operations performed in the beneficiary country. In addition, the cost or value of materials produced in the customs territory of the U.S. may be counted toward the 35% value-added requirement, but only to a maximum of 15% of the appraised value of the imported article. The cost or value of the materials imported into the freely associated state from a non-beneficiary country may be included in calculating the 35% value-added requirement for an eligible article if the materials are first substantially transformed into new and different articles of commerce and are then used as constituent materials in the production of the eligible product.

Sources of Additional Information

Address any questions you may have about the administrative or operational aspects of the FAS to the director of the port where the merchandise will be entered or to the Director, Commercial Compliance Division, U.S. Customs Service, Washington, DC 20229, Tel: (202) (202) 927-0390, 927-0300, FAX (202) 927-1096..

African Growth and Opportunity Act (AGOA)

The African Growth and Opportunity Act (AGOA) provides duty-free treatment under the Generalized System of Preferences (GSP) to certain articles that would normally be excluded from GSP provisions. It also provides for the duty-free entry of specific textile and apparel articles and makes them free of any quantitative limits, provided strict conditions are met.

Enacted on May 18, 2000, as Title I of the Trade and Development Act of 2000 (Public Law 106-200, 114 Stat. 251),

AGOA became effective on October 1, 2000. The expanded GSP treatment remains effective through September 30, 2008. The preferential treatment of eligible textile and apparel articles is subject to certain limitations.

Beneficiary Countries

There are three types of beneficiary designations

under AGOA:

1. beneficiary sub-Saharan African countries;

2.   lesser developed beneficiary sub-Saharan African countries; and

3.   beneficiary sub-Saharan African countries eligible for textile/apparel benefits.

The President will monitor and review annually the current or potential eligibility of sub-Saharan African countries to be designated as beneficiary countries. Accordingly, the list of beneficiary countries may change over the life of the program. A current listing of designated countries is available on the Internet at: **www.agoa.gov.**

The following countries and territories have been designated as beneficiary sub-Saharan African countries for the purposes of the AGOA::

Benin	Mali
Botswana	Mauritania
Cape Verde	Mauritius
Cameroon	Mozambique
Central African Republic	Namibia
Chad	Niger
Republic of Congo (Brazzaville)	Nigeria
Djibouti	Rwanda
Eritrea	Sao Tome and Principe
Ethiopia	Senegal
Gabon	Seychelles
Ghana	Sierra Leone
Guinea	South Africa
Kenya	Tanzania
Lesotho	Uganda
Madagascar	Zambia
Malawi	

The following sub-Saharan African countries have been designated lesser developed beneficiary sub-Saharan African countries for the purposes of AGOA::

Benin	Madagascar
Cape Verde	Malawi
Cameroon	Mali
Central African Republic	Mauritania
Chad	Mozambique
Congo	Niger
Dfigouti	Nigeria
Eritrea	Rwanda
Ethiopia	Sao Tome and Principe
Ghana	Senegal
Guinea	Sierra Leone
Guinea-Bissau	Tanzania
Kenya	Uganda
Lesotho	Zambia

The following countries have established visa systems and can import textiles and apparel merchandise for purposes of the AGOA:

Kenya	Mauritius
Lesotho	South Africa
Madagascar	

In order for textile or apparel articles to be eligible for preferential treatment, the beneficiary sub-Saharan African country must be designated as eligible for textile/apparel benefits. This designation requires that the United States determine whether the country has satisfied the requirements of AGOA regarding that country's procedures to protect against unlawful transshipments (including an effective visa system) and the implementation of procedures and requirements similar in all material respects to the relevant procedures and requirements under Chapter 5 of the NAFTA. The United States Trade Representative will publish a Federal Register notice when it designates a country as eligible for preferential treatment. This information will be available on the Internet at **www.ustr.gov** and at **www.agoa.gov**.

Eligible Items

Expanded GSP Treatment

AGOA expands benefits available under the GSP program by offering duty-free treatment to a broader range of products. The President is permitted to extend duty-free treatment to imports of essentially all products except textiles and apparel as long as the products are the "growth, product or manufacture" of: (a) a beneficiary sub-Saharan African country; (b) are imported directly from a beneficiary sub-Saharan African country into the customs territory of the U.S.; (c) meet a value added requirement; and (d) the President determines that the products are not importsensitive in the context of imports from beneficiary sub-Saharan African countries. Sub-Saharan African beneficiary countries are also exempted from competitive-need limitations.

Approximately 1835 products have been designated as eligible for duty-free treatment under the GSP program for beneficiary sub-Saharan African countries. These articles will be designated by inserting the symbol "D" in the "Rates of Duty 1-Special" column of the Harmonized Tariff Schedule of the United

States for subheadings covering such articles. A list of products eligible for duty-free treatment under the AGOA has been published in the Federal Register and is available on the Internet at www.agoa.gov.

Preferential Treatment for Certain Textile and Apparel Articles

AGOA provides duty-free and quota-free benefits to imports of certain textile and apparel articles produced in eligible sub-

Saharan African countries. In most instances, these benefits are available regardless of the total volume of apparel exported from eligible countries to the United States. The six broad categories of textile and apparel articles that may receive preferential treatment are:

1.   Apparel articles assembled in beneficiary sub-Saharan African countries from fabric wholly formed and cut in the United States (from yarns wholly formed in the United States).

2.   Apparel articles cut in beneficiary sub-Saharan African countries from fabric wholly formed in the United States (from yarns wholly formed in the United

States), if those articles are assembled in one or more beneficiary countries with sewing thread formed in the United States.

3. Apparel assembled from regional and other fabric. This category generally covers apparel articles wholly assembled in one or more beneficiary sub-Saharan African countries from fabric wholly formed in one or more beneficiary sub-Saharan African countries from yarn originating either in the United States or one or more beneficiary sub-Saharan African countries. However, preferential treatment will be allowed through September 30, 2004, for apparel articles who lly assembled in one or more lesser developed beneficiary sub-Saharan African countries regardless of the country of origin of the fabric used to make such articles. Preferential treatment of apparel articles in this category is subject to a cap of 1.5 percent of overall U.S. apparel imports, growing to 3.5 percent of overall imports over an eight-year period. The cap is denominated in square meter equivalents (SMEs). The first year cap, applicable for the 12-month period beginning October 1, 2000, is 246,500,393 SMEs.

4. Sweaters, in chief weight of cashmere or containing 50 percent or more by weight of wool measuring 18.5 microns in diam-eter or finer, knit to shape in one or more beneficiary countries.

5. Apparel articles that are both cut (or knit to shape) and sewn or otherwise assembled in one or more beneficiary sub-Saharan African countries, from fabric or yarn not available in commercial quantities in the United States. This category covers:

   a) apparel assembled from fabrics or yarns that have been determined to be in short supply in the context of NAFTA, and

   b) articles assembled from additional fabrics or yarns that the President has proclaimed to be entitled to preferential treatment based on findings that the fabrics and yarns cannot be supplied by the domestic industry in commercial quantities in a timely manner.

6. Hand-loomed, handmade, and folklore articles. consultation with the beneficiary sub-Saharan African country or countries, the United States shall determine which, if any, particular textile and apparel goods shall be treated as handloomed, handmade, or folklore articles. After such determination, eligible articles must be certified by the competent authority of the beneficiary sub-Saharan African country (or countries) as being hand-loomed, handmade, or folklore articles.

With regard to these six broad categories, AGOA provides special rules that apply in order to determine eligibility for preferential treatment. The Customs regulations implementing AGOA reflect and clarify the statutory standards that must be complied with in order to receive the benefits available under the AGOA. These Customs regulations also include specific documentary, procedural, and other related requirements that must be met in order to obtain those benefits. A Certificate of Origin is required to certify that a textile or apparel article qualifies for pref-

erential treatment. Furthermore, in order to file a claim for preferential treatment, an importer must make a written declaration that the article qualifies for it. There are also visa requirements that must be met. The importer should consult both AGOA and the Customs Regulations prior to importation to ensure that all requirements are met.

Sources of Additional Information

The text of AGOA is available electronically at Internet site **www.agoa.gov**.

Customs rules and regulations about AGOA are incorporated in section 10.211-10.217 of the Customs Regulations. Additional regulations implementing the GSP provisions are incorporated in section 10.178 of the Customs Regulations. Customs regulations pertaining to the AGOA are also available at **www.agoa.gov**.

For answers to specific questions or to request a ruling, send inquiries to: Director, National Commodity Specialist Division, U.S. Customs Service, One Penn Plaza, 11th Floor, New York, NY 10119. Further information regarding importation procedures is available on the Customs Web site, www.cpb.gov. Customs has issued a new informed-compliance publication on AGOA, which can also be found at the Customs Web site.

The Office of the United States Trade Representative has prepared an African Growth and Opportunity Act Implementation Guide. The guide is available electronically from the AGOAWeb site, **www.agoa.gov**.

Questions about AGOA not covered in the guidebook may be directed to the Office of African Affairs at the Office of the United States Trade Representative, 600 17th Street, NW, Washington, DC 20508; tel. 202.395.9514, fax 202.395.4505, or to U.S. embassies or consulates abroad. Additional information on the GSP program is available at the USTR Web site, **www.ustr.gov/reports/gsp/contents.html**, or at **www.agoa.gov**, and from the GSP Information Center, Office of the U.S. Trade Representative, Room 518 Washington, DC 20508, Tel. 202.395.6971.

Additional information on the apparel cap, fabric and yarn not available in commercial quantities, and hand-loomed, handmade and folklore articles is available from the Department of Commerce Office of Textile and Apparel, **http://otexa.ita.doc.gov**.

United States - Caribbean Basin Trade Partnership Act (CBTPA)

The United States-Caribbean Basin Trade Partnership Act expands the trade benefits currently available to Caribbean and Central American countries under the Caribbean Basin Economic Recovery Act. (The Recovery Act is more commonly known as the Caribbean Basin Initiative, or CBI.)

The CBTPA allows specific textile and apparel articles to enter the United States free of duty or restrictions on quantity, provided certain conditions are met. It also extends NAFTA standards of duty to non-textile articles that were previously excluded from duty-free treatment under the CBI program.

The trade benefits provided by the CBTPA apply during the transition period that began October 1, 2000, and end on the earlier of September 30, 2008, or the date on which a freetrade agreement enters into force between the United States and the CBTPA beneficiary countries. (See Title II of the Trade and Development Act of 2000, enacted May 18, 2000 [Public Law 106-200, 114 Stat. 251] for details.)

Beneficiary Countries

The following countries have been designated as CBPTA beneficiary countries for the purposes of the CBPTA:

Antigua and Barbuda	Haiti
Aruba	Honduras
Bahamas	Jamaica
Barbados	Montserrat
Belize	Netherlands Antilles
Costa Rica	Nicaragua
Dominica	Panama
Dominican Republic	Saint Kitts and Nevis
El Salvador	Saint Lucia
Grenada	Saint Vincent and the Grenadines
Guatemala	Trinidad and Tobago
Guyana	British Virgin Islands
Haiti	

CBTPA's enhanced trade benefits are available to countries designated as CBTPA beneficiary countries. To receive these benefits, CBTPA countries must have satisfied the trade pact's requirements that the eligible country has implemented procedures and requirements that are similar in all material respects to the relevant procedures and requirements under

Chapter Five of NAFTA.

To date, the following countries have been designated by USTR as eligible for preferential treatment under the CBTPA because they have met the procedures established for qualifying for CBTPA. Importers are advised to contact their local port for a more recent list:

Belize Costa Rica	Dominican Republic
El Salvador	Guatemala Guyana
Haiti Honduras	Jamaica Nicaragua
Panama	Trinidad and Tobago

The USTR publishes in the *Federal Register* the names of CBPTA beneficiary countries and when they became eligible for preferential treatment. (These notices modify General Note 17 of the HTS by listing the countries that satisfy the requirements.)

Eligible Items

Preferential Treatment for Certain Textile and Apparel Articles

Certain textile and apparel articles may enter the United States free of duty and quantitative restrictions. The textile and apparel articles eligible for preferential treatment are:

1. Apparel articles assembled in one or more CBTPA beneficiary countries from fabrics wholly formed and cut in the United States, from yarns wholly formed in the United States.

2. Apparel articles cut in one or more CBTPA beneficiary countries from fabric wholly formed in the United States, from yarns wholly formed in the United States, if those articles are assembled in one or more CBTPA beneficiary countries with sewing thread formed in the United States.

3. Certain apparel articles knit to shape in a CBTPA beneficiary country from yarns wholly formed in the United States, and certain knitted or crocheted apparel articles cut and wholly assembled in one or more CBTPA beneficiary countries from fabrics formed in one or more CBTPA beneficiary countries or in one or more CBTPA beneficiary countries and the United States from yarns wholly formed in the United States. Apparel in this category is subject to annual quantitative limits expressed in square meter equivalents (SMEs). For the one-year period beginning October 1, 2000, the quantitative limit is 250,000,000 SMEs. In each succeeding one-year period through September 30, 2004, the quantitative limit will be increased by 16 percent, compounded annually. In each one-year period thereafter through September 30, 2008, the quantitative limit will be the amount in effect for the one-year period that ended September 30, 2004, unless another amount is provided by law.

4. Certain non-underwear T-shirts made in one or more CBTPA beneficiary countries from fabric formed in one or more CBTPA beneficiary countries from yarns wholly formed in the United States. Apparel in this category is subject to annual quantitative limits, which are expressed in dozens. For the one-year period beginning October 1, 2000, the quantitative limit is 4,200,000 dozen. In each succeeding one-year period through September 30, 2004, the quantitative limit will be increased by 16 percent, compounded annually. In each one-year period thereafter through September 30, 2008, the quantitative limit will be the amount in effect for the oneyear period that ended September 30, 2004, unless another amount is provided by law.

5. Brassieres cut and sewn or otherwise assembled in the United States, or one or more beneficiary CBTPA countries, or both. Underwear in this category is subject to the following requirement: In each of seven one-year periods starting October 1, 2001, at least 75 percent of the total declared customs value of the fabric contained in the articles entered the preceding year must be attributed to the aggregate cost of the fabric components formed in the United States.

6. Apparel articles that are both cut (or knit to shape) and sewn or otherwise assembled in one or more CBTPA beneficiary countries from fabric or yarn not available in commercial quantities in the United States. This category of apparel covers: a) apparel assembled from fabrics or yarns determined to be in short supply in the context of NAFTA, and b) articles assembled from other fabrics or yarns that the President has proclaimed to be entitled to preferential treatment, based on findings that the fabrics and yarns cannot be supplied by the domestic industry in commercial quantities in a timely manner.

7. Hand-loomed, handmade, and folklore articles. After consulting with CBTPA beneficiary countries, the United States will identify particular textile and apparel goods that all parties agree are handloomed, handmade, or folklore articles. Articles so determined (i.e., as being hand-loomed, handmade, or folklore) must then be certified by the CBTPA beneficiary country's competent authority as being hand-loomed, handmade, or folklore.

8. Certain textile luggage. This category includes:

   (a) textile luggage assembled in a CBTPA beneficiary country from fabric wholly formed and cut in the United States, from yarns wholly formed in the United States, and

   (b) textile luggage assembled from fabric cut in a CBTPA beneficiary country from fabric wholly formed in the United States, from yarns wholly formed in the United States. The Customs regulations that implement the CBTPA include specific documentary, procedural, and other requirements that must be met in order to obtain CBTPA benefits. Both the CBTPA and the Customs regulations should be consulted before importing merchandise in order to assure that all requirements have been met.

NAFTA Parity

Except for textile and apparel articles, the CBTPA allows NAFTA tariff treatment for goods previously excluded from the CBI program. Thus, imported footwear, canned tuna, petroleum and petroleum products, watches and watch parts, handbags, luggage, flat goods, work gloves and leather wearing apparel, when these goods qualify as CBTPA originating goods, are eligible for a reduction in duty equal to the rate given to Mexican products under the staged duty-rate reductions set forth in NAFTA.

Articles that the President has designated as eligible for CBTPA treatment are those whose duty rate in the "Special" sub column is followed by the symbol "R" in chapters 1 through 97 of the tariff schedule. Whenever a rate of duty other than "Free" appears in this sub column for any heading or subheading followed by the symbol "E" or "E*," and a lower rate of duty followed by the symbol "R" also appears in the sub column, an eligible article will receive the lower rate of duty.

Certain Beverages Made With Caribbean Rum

The CBTPA provides duty-free treatment to certain liqueurs and spirituous beverages produced in the territory of Canada from rum that is the growth, product or manufacture of a CBTPA beneficiary country or of the Virgin Islands of the United States.

Sources for Additional Information

Customs rules and regulations on the CBTPA are incorporated in sections 10.221-10.228 and 10.231-10.237 of the Customs Regulations. Customs regulations pertaining to the CBTPA are available on the Internet at: **www.customs.gov/news/fed-reg/notices/cbicbtpa.pdf** and **www.customs.gov/news/fed-reg/notices/cbtpacor.pdf**. Customs has also issued a new informed-compliance publication on CBTPA, which can also be found at our web site.

For answers to specific questions or to request a ruling, send inquiries to: Director, National Commodity Specialist Division, U.S. Customs Service, One Penn Plaza, 11th Floor, New York, NY 10119.

The text of the Trade and Development Act of 2000 may be accessed at **http://thomas.loc.gov** (type "CBTPA" at the search prompt). Further information on the CBTPA may be obtained from the Office of the United States Trade Representative Office of the Western Hemisphere, 600 17th Street, NW, Washington, DC 20508, tel. 202.395.5190; fax 202.395.9675.

Additional information on quantitative limitations, fabric and yarn not available in commercial quantities, and hand-loomed, handmade, and folklore articles may be available at the Department of Commerce Office of Textile and Apparel Internet site, **http://otexa.ita.doc.gov**. The Department of Commerce also provides detailed information on the CBTPA at **www.mac.doc.gov/CBI/webmain/intro.htm**.

Foreign Trade Zones

Foreign or "free" trade zones are secured areas considered to be legally outside a nation's customs territory, although physically located within it. Their purpose is to attract and promote international trade and commerce. The Foreign trade Zones Board authorizes operations based upon showing that the intended operations are not detrimental to the public interest. Subzones are special-purpose facilities for companies unable to operate effectively at public zone sites. Foreign trade zones are usually located in or near Customs ports of entry, at industrial parks, or terminal warehouse facilities. Foreign trade zones must be within 60 miles or 90 minutes' driving time from the Customs supervising office, while subzones have no limit and are located in the zone user's private facility. A Foreign Trade Zones Board, created by the Foreign Trade Zones Act of 1934, reviews and approves applications to establish, operate, and maintain foreign trade zones. It is important to note that although foreign trade zones are legally outside the Customs territory of the U.S., other federal laws, such as the Federal Food, Drug, and Cosmetic Act, are applicable to products and establishments with such zones.

Foreign exporters planning to expand or open up new U.S. outlets may forward their goods to a foreign trade zone in the U.S. to be held for an unlimited period while awaiting a favorable market in the U.S. or nearby countries without being subject to customs entry, payment of duty or tax, or bond.

Treatment of Goods

Merchandise lawfully brought into these zones may be stored, sold, exhibited, broken up, repacked, assembled, distributed, sorted, graded, cleaned, mixed with foreign or domestic merchandise, or otherwise manipulated or manufactured. However, imported merchandise for use in the zone, such as construction material and production equipment, must be entered for consumption before it is taken into a zone. The Foreign Trade Zones Board may determine, that an operation is not in the public interest. The resulting merchandise may thereafter be either exported or transferred into customs territory.

When foreign goods, in their condition at time of entry into the zone or after processing there, are transferred into customs territory of the U.S., the goods must be entered at the customhouse. If entered for consumption, duties and taxes will be assessed on the entered articles, according to the condition of the foreign merchandise at the time of entry into the zone. This occurs whether it has been placed in privileged foreign status or nonprivileged foreign status, merchandise prior to manipulation or manufacture, or on the basis of its condition at the time of entry for consumption, for foreign merchandise placed under nonprivileged status at the time of entry into the zone. Merchandise may be considered exported, for Customs or other purposes, upon its admission to a zone in zone-restricted status. However, the merchandise taken into a zone under zone-restricted status may be for the sole purpose of exportation, destruction (except destruction of distilled spirits, wines, and fermented malt liquors) or storage.

An important feature of foreign trade zones for foreign merchants entering the American market is that the goods may be brought to the threshold of the market, making immediate delivery certain and avoiding possible cancellation of orders due to shipping delays after a favorable market has closed.

Production of articles in zones by the combined use of domestic and foreign materials makes unnecessary either the sending of the domestic materials abroad for manufacture or the duty-paid or bonded importation of the foreign materials. Duties on the foreign goods involved in such processing or manufacture are payable only on the actual quantity of such foreign goods incorporated in merchandise transferred from a zone for entry into the commerce of the U.S. If there is any unrecoverable waste resulting from manufacture or manipulation, allowances are made for it, thereby eliminating payment of duty except on the articles that are actually entered. If there is any recoverable waste, it is dutiable only in its condition as such and in the quantity entered.

Another feature under the zone act is the authority to exhibit merchandise within a zone. Zone facilities may be utilized for the full exhibition of foreign merchandise without bond, for an unlimited length of time, and with no requirement of exportation or duty payment. Thus, the owner of goods in a zone may display his goods where they are stored, establish showrooms of his own, or join with other importers in displaying his merchandise in a permanent exhibition established in the zone. Because an importer may also store and process merchandise in a zone, the importer is not limited to mere display of samples but may also sell from stock in wholesale quantities. Retail trade is prohibited in such zones.

The owner of foreign merchandise that has not been manipulated or manufactured in any way that would effect a change in its U.S. tariff classification had it been taken into customs territory when first imported may, upon request to the port director of Customs, have its dutiable status fixed and liquidated. This dutiable status will apply irrespective of when the merchandise is entered into customs territory and even though its condition or form may have been changed by processing in the zone, as indicated above.

Domestic merchandise may be taken into a zone and, providing its identity is maintained in accordance with regulations, may be returned to customs territory free of quotas, duty, or tax, even though while in the zone it may have been combined with or made part of other articles. However, domestic distilled spirits, wine, and beer, and a limited number of other kinds of merchandise generally may not be processed while in the zone.

Advantages

Savings may result from manipulations and manufacture in a zone. For example, many products, shipped to the zone in bulk, can be dried, sorted, graded, or cleaned and bagged or otherwise packed, permitting savings of duties and taxes on moisture taken from content or on dirt removed and culls thrown out. Damaged packages or broken bottles can be removed from incoming shipments of packaged or bottled goods if evaporation results during shipment or while goods are stored in the zone, contents of barrels or other containers can be regauged and savings obtained, as no duties are payable on the portions lost or removed. In other words, barrels or other containers can be gauged at the time of transfer to customs territory to insure that duties will not be charged on any portion of their contents that has been lost due to evaporation, leakage, breakage, or otherwise. These operations may also be conducted in bonded warehouses.

Savings in shipping charges, duties, and taxes may result from such operations as shipping unassembled or disassembled furniture, machinery, etc., to the zone and assembling or reassembling it there.

Merchandise may be remarked or relabeled in the zone (or in a bonded warehouse) to conform to requirements for entry into the commerce of the U.S. if otherwise up to standard. Remarking or relabeling that would be misleading is not permitted in the zone. Substandard foods and drugs may, in certain cases, be reconditioned to meet the requirements of the Food, Drug, and Cosmetics Act.

There is no time limit as to how long foreign merchandise may be stored in a zone, or when it must be entered into customs territory, reexported, or destroyed.

Transfer of Goods in Bonded Warehouses

Foreign merchandise in Customs bonded warehouses may be transferred to the zone at any time before the limitation on its retention in the bonded warehouse expires, but such a transfer to the zone may be made only for the purpose of eventual exportation, destruction, or permanent storage.

When foreign merchandise is transferred to the zone from Customs bonded warehouses, the bond is cancelled and all obligations in regard to duty payment, or as to the time when the merchandise is to be reexported, are terminated. Similarly, the owner of domestic merchandise stored in Internal Revenue bonded warehouses may transfer goods to a zone and obtain cancellation of bonds. In addition, domestic goods moved into a zone under zone restricted status are considered exported on entering the zone for purposes of excise and other internal revenue tax rebates. A manufacturer, operating in customs territory and using dutiable imported materials in products, may also obtain drawback of duties paid or cancellation of bond, upon transferring the product to the zone for export and complying with the appropriate regulations.

For More Information

Location of, and general information on U.S. Foreign Trade Zones may be obtained from the Department of Commerce, International Trade Administration, Foreign Trade Zones Board, Washington, DC 20230, Tel: (202) 482-2862. Questions relating to legal aspects of Customs Service responsibilities in regard to foreign trade zones should be addressed to the Chief Entry and Carrier Rulings Branch, U.S. Customs Service, Washington, DC 20229. Questions relating to operational aspects of such responsibilities should be addressed to the appropriate port director of Customs. Also refer to 19 CFR 146, "Foreign Trade Zones."

The United States Customs Foreign-Trade Zones Manual provides instructions, guidelines, and other information for existing and prospective foreign trade zone grantees, operators, users, and Customs Officers. It may be purchased from the Superintendent of Documents, U.S. Government Printing Office, Washington, DC 20402, on the Web: http://bookstore.gpo.gov. Use GPO Stock No. 048-002-00128-1, the cost is $34.50.

Classification and Value

Classification—Liquidation

Classification

Classification and, when ad valorem rates of duty are applicable, appraisement are the two most important factors affecting dutiable status. Classifications and valuations, whether or not they are pertinent because an ad valorem rate of duty applies, must be provided by commercial importers when an entry is filed. In addition, classifications under the statistical suffixes of the tariff schedules must also be furnished even if this information is not pertinent to dutiable status. Accordingly, classification is initially the responsibility of an importer, customs broker, or other person preparing the entry papers.

Familiarity with the organization of the Harmonized Tariff Schedule of the United States (HTSUS) facilitates the classification process. The tariff schedule is divided into various sections and chapters dealing separately with merchandise in broad product categories. These categories, for example, separately cover animal products, vegetable products, products of various basic materials such as wood, textiles, plastics, rubber, and steel and other metal products in various stages of manufacture. Other sections encompass chemicals, machinery and electrical equipment, and other specified or non-enumerated products. The last section, Section XXII, covers certain exceptions from duty and special statutory provisions.

In Sections I through XXI, products are classifiable (1) under items or descriptions that name them, known as an *eo nomine* provision; (2) under provisions of general description; (3) under provisions that identify them by component material; or (4) under provisions that encompass merchandise in accordance with its actual or principal use. When two or more provisions seem to cover the same merchandise, the prevailing provision is determined in accordance with the legal notes and the General Rules of Interpretation for the tariff schedule. Also applicable are tariff classification principles contained in administrative precedents or in the case law of the U.S. Court of International Trade or the U.S. Court of Appeals for the Federal Circuit.

The Mod Act puts a heavier onus on the importer or his agents for correctly assigning tariff classification. For more information, refer to 19 CFR 152, "Classification and Appraisement of Merchandise" and to the General Rules of Interpretation in the HTSUS. For product-specific information on HTSUS classifications, see the Commodity Index section of this publication, beginning on page 423. For assistance with classifications, contact the Bureau of the Census, Foreign Trade Division, Washington, DC 20233, Tel: (301) 763-3041.

Liquidation

Customs officers at the port of entry or other officials acting on behalf of the port director review the classifications and valuations, as well as other required import information, for correctness or as a proper basis for appraisement, as well as for agreement of the submitted data with the merchandise actually imported. The entry summary and documentation may be accepted as submitted without any changes. In this situation, the entry is liquidated as entered. Liquidation is the point at which the Customs Service's ascertainment of the rate of duty and amount of duty becomes final for most purposes.

Liquidation is accomplished by posting a notice on a public bulletin board at the customhouse. However, an importer may receive an advance notice on Customs **Form 4333A** "Courtesy Notice" stating when and in what amount duty will be liquidated. This form is not the liquidation, and protest rights do not accrue until the notice is posted. Time limits for protesting do not start to run until the date of posting, and a protest cannot be filed before liquidation is posted.

The Customs Service may determine that an entry cannot be liquidated as entered for one reason or another. For example, the tariff classification may not be correct or may not be acceptable because it is not consistent with an established and uniform classification practice. If the change required by this determination results in a rate of duty more favorable to an importer, the entry is liquidated accordingly and a refund of the applicable amount of the deposited estimated duties is authorized. On the other hand, a change may be necessary that imposes a higher rate of duty. For example, a claim for an exemption from duty under a free-rate provision or under a conditional exemption may be found to be insufficient for lack of the required supporting documentation. In this situation the importer may be given an advance notice of the proposed duty rate advancement and an opportunity to validate the claim for a free rate or more favorable rate of duty.

If the importer does not respond to the notice, or if the response is found to be without merit, duty is liquidated in accordance with the entry as corrected and the importer is billed for the additional duty. The port may find that the importer's response raises issues of such complexity that resolution by a Customs Headquarters decision through the internal advice procedure is warranted. Internal advice from Customs Headquarters may be requested by the local Customs officers on their own initiative or in response to a request by the importer.

The Mod Act takes a novel approach to liquidation by allowing reconciliation to occur after entry. An importer who wishes to submit reconciliation for a particular entry can specify the intent to provide relevant data when it becomes available at a later time. The Mod Act permits Customs to liquidate an entry before the unknown information has been transmitted to Customs. The Act further imposes a responsibility on importers to use reasonable care in making entry so that Customs can rely on the accuracy of information and can streamline the entry and liquidation procedures. If an importer fails to use reasonable care in classifying and valuing merchandise and presenting entry data, Customs may impose a penalty in an amount commensurate to the level of culpability (see 19 USC 1592).

For more information on liquidation, refer to 19 CFR 159, "Liquidation of Duties."

Protests

After liquidation an importer may still pursue, on Customs **Form 19**, any claims for an adjustment or refund by filing a protest within 90 days after liquidation. For protest, extension, and suspension purposes, the reconciliation of entries that have been liquidated is treated as if it were an entry summary. To apply for a Headquarters ruling, a request for further review must be filed with the protest. The same **Form 19** can be used for this purpose. If filed separately, application for further review must still be filed within 90 days of liquidation. Filing may be accomplished electronically.

If a ruling on the question has previously been issued in response to a request for a decision on a prospective transaction or a request for internal advice, further review will ordinarily be denied. If a protest is denied, an importer has the right to litigate the matter by filing a summons with the U.S. Court of International Trade within 180 days after denial of the protest. The rules of the court and other applicable statutes and precedents determine the course of customs litigation.

While the Customs ascertainment of dutiable status is final for most purposes at the time of liquidation, a liquidation is not final until any protest that has been filed against it has been decided. Similarly, the administrative decision issued on a protest is not final until any litigation filed against it has become final.

Entries must be liquidated within one year of the date of entry unless the liquidation needs to be extended for another one-year period (not to exceed a total of four years from the date of entry). The Customs Service will suspend liquidation of an entry when required by statute or court order. A suspension will remain in effect until the issue is resolved. When suspension is removed, the entry must be liquidated within six months from the date Customs is notified of the removal. Notifications of extensions and suspensions are given to importers, surety companies, and customs brokers who are parties to the transaction. For more information on protests, refer to 19 CFR 174, "Protests."

NAFTA. There are special rules for consolidating multiple protests concerning a determination of origin for NAFTA preferential tariff treatment if one of the protests is filed by or on behalf of an exporter or producer. For more information, refer to 19 CFR 174.15, "Consolidation of protests filed by different parties."

Conversion of Currency

The conversion of foreign currency for Customs purposes must be made in accordance with the provisions of 31 USC 5151. This section states that Customs is to use rates of exchange determined and certified by the Federal Reserve Bank of New York. These certified rates are based on the New York market buying rates for the foreign currencies involved.

In the case of widely used currencies, rates of exchange are certified each day. The rates certified on the first business day of each calendar quarter are used throughout the quarter except on days when fluctuations of 5% or more occur, in which case the actual certified rates for those days are used. For infrequently used currencies, the Federal Reserve Bank of New York certifies rates of exchange upon request by Customs. The rates certified are only for the currencies and dates requested.

For Customs purposes, the date of exportation of the goods is the date used to determine the applicable certified rate of exchange. This remains true even though a different rate may have been used in payment of the goods. Information as to the applicable rate of exchange in converting currency for customs purposes in the case of a given shipment may be obtained from a port director of Customs. For more information, refer to 19 CFR 159 Subpart C, "Conversion of Foreign Currency."

Transaction Value

All merchandise imported into the United States is subject to appraisement. The valuation provisions of the Tariff Act of 1930 are found in section 402, as amended by the Trade Agreements Act of 1979. Pertinent portions are reproduced in Appendix 3, "Customs Valuation" on page 284. More information on transaction values can also be found in 19 CFR 152.103.

Generally, the customs value of all merchandise exported to the U.S. will be the transaction value for the goods. If the transaction value cannot be used, then certain secondary bases are considered. The secondary bases of value, listed in order of precedence for use, are:

1. Transaction value of identical merchandise,
2. Transaction value of similar merchandise,
3. Deductive value, and
4. Computed value.

The order of precedence of the last two values can be reversed if the importer so requests.

Transaction Value

The transaction value of imported merchandise is the price actually paid or payable for the merchandise when sold for exportation to the U.S., plus amounts for the following items if not included in the price:

- The packing costs incurred by the buyer.
- Any selling commission incurred by the buyer.
- The value of any assist.
- Any royalty or license fee that the buyer is required to pay as a condition of the sale.
- The proceeds, accruing to the seller, of any subsequent resale, disposal, or use of the imported merchandise.

The amounts for these items are added only to the extent that each is not included in the price actually paid or payable and information is available to establish the accuracy of the specific amount. If sufficient information is not available, then the transaction value cannot be determined and the next basis of value, in order of precedence, must be considered for appraisement. A discussion of these added items follows:

Packing costs consist of the cost incurred by the buyer for all containers and coverings of whatever nature and for the labor and materials used in packing the imported merchandise to ready it for export.

Any selling commission incurred by the buyer with respect to the imported merchandise constitutes part of the transaction value. Buying commissions do not. A selling commission means any commission paid to the seller's agent, who is related to or controlled by, or works for or on behalf of, the manufacturer or the seller.

The apportioned value of any assist constitutes part of the transaction value of the imported merchandise. First the value of the assist is determined; then the value is prorated to the imported merchandise.

Assists. An assist is any of the items listed below that the buyer of imported merchandise provides directly or indirectly, free of charge or at a reduced cost, for use in the production or sale of merchandise for export to the U.S.

- Materials, components, parts, and similar items incorporated in the imported merchandise.
- Tools, dies, molds, and similar items used in producing the imported merchandise.
- Merchandise consumed in producing the imported merchandise.
- Engineering, development, artwork, design work, and plans and sketches that are undertaken outside the U.S. "Engineering...," will not be treated as an assist if the service or work is (1) performed by a person domiciled within the U.S., (2) performed while that person is acting as an employee or agent of the buyer of the imported merchandise, and (3) incidental to other engineering, development, artwork, design work, or plans or sketches undertaken within the U.S.

Value. In determining the value of an assist, the following rules apply:

- The value is either (a) the cost of acquiring the assist, if acquired by the importer from an unrelated seller, or (b) the cost of the assist, if produced by the importer or a person related to the importer.
- The value includes the cost of transporting the assist to the place of production.
- The value of assists used in producing the imported merchandise is adjusted to reflect use, repairs, modifications, or other factors affecting the value of the assists. Assists of this type include such items as tools, dies, and molds. For example, if the importer previously used the assist, regardless of whether he acquired or produced it, the original cost of acquisition or of production must be decreased to reflect the use. Alternatively, repairs and modifications may result in the value of the assist having to be adjusted upward.
- In the case of engineering, development, artwork, design work, and plans and sketches undertaken elsewhere than in the U.S., the value is (a) the cost of obtaining copies of the assist, if the assist is available in the public domain; (b) the cost of the purchase or lease, if the assist was bought or leased by the buyer from an unrelated person; (c) the value added outside the U.S., if the assist was produced in the U.S. and one or more foreign countries.

So far as possible, the buyer's commercial record system will be used to determine the value of an assist, especially such assists as engineering, development, artwork, design work, and plans and sketches undertaken elsewhere than in the U.S.

Apportionment. Having determined the value of an assist, the next step is to prorate that value to the imported merchandise. The apportionment is done reasonably and according to generally accepted accounting principles. By the latter is meant any generally recognized consensus or substantial authoritative support regarding the recording and measuring of assets and liabilities and changes, the disclosing of information, and the preparing of financial statements.

Royalty or license fees that a buyer must pay directly or indirectly, as a condition of the sale of the imported merchandise for exportation to the U.S. will be included in the transaction value. Ultimately, whether a royalty or license fee is dutiable will depend on whether the buyer had to pay it as a condition of the sale and to whom and under what circumstances it was paid. The dutiability status will have to be decided on a case-by-case basis.

Charges for the right to reproduce the imported goods in the U.S. are not dutiable. This right applies only to the following types of merchandise:

- Originals or copies of artistic or scientific works.
- Originals or copies of models and industrial drawings.

- Model machines and prototypes.
- Plant and animal species.

Any proceeds resulting from the subsequent resale, disposal, or use of the imported merchandise that accrue, directly or indirectly, to the seller are dutiable. These proceeds are added to the price actually paid or payable, if not otherwise included.

The price actually paid or payable for the imported merchandise is the total payment, excluding international freight, insurance, and other c.i.f. charges, that the buyer makes to the seller. This payment may be direct or indirect. Some examples of an indirect payment are when the buyer settles all or part of a debt owed by the seller, or when the seller reduces the price on a current importation to settle a debt he owes the buyer. Such indirect payments are part of the transaction value.

However, if a buyer performs an activity on his own account, other than those which may be included in the transaction value, then the activity is not considered an indirect payment to the seller and is not part of the transaction value. This applies even though the buyer's activity might be regarded as benefiting the seller—for example, advertising.

Exclusions

The amounts to be excluded from transaction value are as follows:

1. The cost, charges, or expenses incurred for transportation, insurance, and related services incident to the international shipment of the goods from the country of exportation to the place of importation in the U.S.

2. Any reasonable cost or charge incurred for:

    Constructing, erecting, assembling, maintaining, or providing technical assistance with respect to the goods after importation into the U.S., or

    Transporting the goods after importation.

3. The customs duties and other Federal taxes, including any Federal excise tax for which sellers in the U.S. are ordinarily liable.

Note: Foreign inland freight and related charges in item 1 (see part 152, Custom Regulations), as well as items 2 and 3 above, must be identified separately.

Limitations

The transaction value of imported merchandise is the appraised value of that merchandise, provided certain limitations do not exist. If any of these limitations are present, then transaction value cannot be used as the appraised value, and the next basis of value will be considered. The limitations can be divided into four groups:

1. Restrictions on the disposition or use of the merchandise.

2. Conditions for which a value cannot be determined.

3. Proceeds of any subsequent resale, disposal, or use of the merchandise, accruing to the seller, for which an appropriate adjustment to transaction value cannot be made.

4. Related-party transactions where the transaction value is not acceptable.

The term "acceptable" means that the relationship between the buyer and seller did not influence the price actually paid or payable. Examining the circumstances of the sale will help make this determination.

Alternatively, "acceptable" can also mean that the transaction value of the imported merchandise closely approximates one of the following test values, provided these values relate to merchandise exported to the U.S. at or about the same time as the imported merchandise:

1. The transaction value of identical merchandise or of similar merchandise in sales to unrelated buyers in the U.S.

2. The deductive value or computed value for identical merchandise or similar merchandise. The test values are used for comparison only; they do not form a substitute basis of valuation.

In determining if the transaction value is close to one of the foregoing test values, an adjustment is made if the sales involved differ in:

- Commercial levels,
- Quantity levels,
- The costs, commission, values, fees, and proceeds added to the transaction value (price paid) if not included in the price, and
- The costs incurred by the seller in sales in which he and the buyer are not related that are not incurred by the seller in sales in which he and the buyer are related.

As stated, the test values are alternatives to the relationship criterion. If one of the test values is met, it is not necessary to examine the question of whether the relationship influenced the price.

Transaction Value of Identical or Similar Merchandise

When the transaction value cannot be determined, then the customs value of the imported goods being appraised is the transaction value of identical merchandise. If merchandise identical to the imported goods cannot be found or an acceptable transaction value for such merchandise does not exist, then the customs value is the transaction value of similar merchandise. The above value would be previously accepted customs values.

Besides the data common to all three transaction values, certain factors specifically apply to the transaction value of identical merchandise or similar merchandise. These factors concern (1) the exportation date, (2) the level and quantity of sales, (3) the meaning, and (4) the order of precedence of identical merchandise and of similar merchandise.

For more specifics on transaction values for identical and similar merchandise, refer to 19 CFR 152.104.

Exportation Date. The identical (similar) merchandise for which a value is being determined must have been sold for export to the U.S. and exported at or about the same time as the merchandise being appraised.

Sales Level/Quantity. The transaction value of identical (similar) merchandise must be based on sales of identical (similar) merchandise at the same commercial level and in substantially the same quantity as the sale of the merchandise being appraised. If no such sale exists, then sales at either a different commercial level or in different quantities, or both, can be used but must be adjusted to take account of any such difference. Any adjustment must be based on sufficient information, that is, information establishing the reasonableness and accuracy of the adjustment.

Meanings. The term "identical merchandise" means merchandise that is:

- Identical in all respects to the merchandise being appraised.
- Produced in the same country as the merchandise being appraised.
- Produced by the same person as the merchandise being appraised.

If merchandise meeting all three criteria cannot be found, then identical merchandise is merchandise satisfying the first two criteria but produced by a different person than the producer of merchandise being appraised.

Merchandise can be identical to the merchandise being appraised and still show minor differences in appearance. However, identical merchandise does not include merchandise that incorporates or reflects engineering, development, artwork, design work, and plans and sketches provided free or at reduced cost by the buyer and undertaken in the U.S.

The term "similar merchandise" means merchandise that is:

- Produced in the same country and by the same person as the merchandise being appraised.
- Like merchandise being appraised in characteristics and component materials.
- Commercially interchangeable with the merchandise being appraised.

If merchandise meeting the foregoing criteria cannot be found, then similar merchandise is merchandise having the same country of production, like characteristics and component materials, and commercial interchangeability but produced by a different person.

In determining whether goods are similar, some of the factors to be considered are the quality of the goods, their reputation, and existence of a trademark. Similar merchandise does not include merchandise that incorporates or reflects engineering, development, artwork, design work, and plans and sketches provided free or at reduced cost to the buyer and undertaken in the U.S.

Order of Precedence. It is possible that two or more transaction values for identical (similar) merchandise will be determined. In such a case the lowest value will be used as the appraised value of the imported merchandise.

Other Bases: Deductive and Computed Value

Deductive Value

If the transaction value of imported merchandise, of identical merchandise, or of similar merchandise cannot be determined, then deductive value is calculated for the merchandise being appraised. Deductive value is the next basis of appraisement at the time the entry summary is filed, to be used unless the importer designates computed value as the preferred method of appraisement. If computed value was chosen and subsequently determined not to exist for customs valuation purposes, then the basis of appraisement reverts to deductive value.

If an assist is involved in a sale, that sale cannot be used in determining deductive value. So any sale to a person who supplies an assist for use in connection with the production or sale for export of the merchandise concerned is disregarded for purposes of determining deductive value.

Basically, deductive value is the resale price in the U.S. after importation of the goods, with deductions for certain items. In discussing deductive value, the term "merchandise concerned" is used. The term means the merchandise being appraised, identical merchandise, or similar merchandise. Generally, the deductive value is calculated by starting with a unit price and making certain additions to and deductions from that price.

Unit Price. One of three prices constitutes the unit price in deductive value. The price used depends on when and in what condition the merchandise concerned is sold in the United States:

1. Time and Condition: The merchandise is *sold in the condition* as imported *at or about the date of importation* of the merchandise being appraised.

   Price: The price used is the unit price at which the greatest aggregate quantity of the merchandise concerned is sold at or about date of importation.

2. Time and Condition: The merchandise concerned is *sold in the condition as imported but not sold at or about the date of importation* of the merchandise being appraised.

   Price: The price used is the unit price at which the greatest aggregate quantity of the merchandise concerned is sold after the date of importation of the merchandise being appraised but before the close of the 90th day after the date of importation.

3. Time and Condition: The merchandise concerned is *not sold in the condition* as imported and *not sold before the close of the 90th day* after the date of importation of the merchandise being appraised.

   Price: The price used is the unit price at which the greatest aggregate quantity of the merchandise being appraised, after further processing, is sold before the 180th day after the date of importation.

This third price is also known as the "further processing price" or "superdeductive."

Additions. Packing costs for the merchandise concerned are added to the price used for deductive value, provided these costs have not otherwise been included. These costs are added regardless of whether the importer or the buyer incurs the cost. Packing costs means the cost of:

1. All containers and coverings of whatever nature; and

2. Packing, whether for labor or materials, used in placing the merchandise in condition, packed ready for shipment to the U.S.

Deductions. Certain items are not part of deductive value and must be deducted from the unit price. These items are as follows:

1. Commissions or Profit and General Expenses. Any commission usually paid or agreed to be paid, or the addition usually made for profit and general expenses, applicable to sales in the U.S. of imported merchandise that is of the same class or kind as the merchandise concerned regardless of the country of exportation.

2. Transportation/Insurance Costs. The usual and associated costs of transporting and insuring the merchandise concerned from (a) the country of exportation to the place of importation in the U.S. and (b) the place of importation to the place of delivery in the U.S., provided these costs are not included as a general expense under the preceding item 1.

3. Customs Duties/Federal Taxes. The customs duties and other Federal taxes payable on the merchandise concerned because of its importation plus any Federal excise tax on, or measured by the value of, such merchandise for which sellers in the U.S. are ordinarily liable.

4. Value of Further Processing. The value added by the processing of the merchandise after importation, provided sufficient information exists concerning the cost of processing. The price determined for deductive value is reduced by the value of further processing only if the third unit price (the superdeductive) is used as deductive value.

Superdeductive. The importer has the option to ask that deductive value be based on the further- processing price. If the importer makes that choice, certain facts concerning valuing the further-processing method, termed "superdeductive," must be followed.

Under the superdeductive, the merchandise concerned is not sold in the condition as imported and not sold before the close of the 90th day after the date of importation, but is sold before the 180th day after the date of importation.

Under this method, an amount equal to the value of the further processing must be deducted from the unit price in determining deductive value. The amount so deducted must be based on objective and quantifiable data concerning the cost of such work as well as any spoilage, waste or scrap derived from that work. Items such as accepted industry formulas, methods of construction, and industry practices could be used as a basis for calculating the amount to be deducted.

Generally, the superdeductive method cannot be used if the further processing destroys the identity of the goods. Such situations will be decided on a case-by-case basis for the following reasons:

1. Sometimes, even though the identity of the goods is lost, the value added by the processing can be determined accurately without unreasonable difficulty for importers or for the Customs Service.

2. In some cases, the imported goods still keep their identity after processing but form only a minor part of the goods sold in the U.S. In such cases, using the superdeductive method to value the imported goods will not be justified.

The superdeductive method cannot be used if the merchandise concerned is sold in the condition as imported before the close of the 90th day after the date of importation of the merchandise being appraised.

Computed Value

The next basis of appraisement is computed value. If customs valuation cannot be based on any of the values previously discussed, then computed value is considered. This value is also the one the importer can select to precede deductive value as a basis of appraisement. For more information on computed value, refer to 19 CFR 152.106.

Computed value consists of the sum of the following:

1. Materials, fabrication, and other processing used in producing the imported merchandise.

2. Profit and general expenses.

3. Any assist, if not included in items 1 and 2.

4. Packing costs.

Materials, Fabrication, and Other Processing. The cost or value of the materials, fabrication, and other processing of any kind used in producing the imported merchandise is based on (a) information provided by or on behalf of the producer and (b) the commercial accounts of the producer if the accounts are consistent with generally accepted accounting principles applied in the country of production of the goods.

Note: If the country of exportation imposes an internal tax on the materials or their disposition and refunds the tax when merchandise produced from the materials is exported, then the amount of the internal tax is not included as part of the cost or value of the materials.

Profit and General Expenses. The producer's profit and general expenses are used, provided they are consistent with the usual profit and general expenses reflected by producers in the country of exportation in sales of merchandise of the same class or kind as the imported merchandise. Some facts concerning the amount for profit and general expenses should be mentioned:

1. The amount is determined by information supplied by the producer and is based on his commercial accounts, provided such accounts are consistent with generally accepted accounting principles in the country of production.

Note: As a point of contrast, for deductive value the generally accepted accounting principles used are those in the U.S., whereas in computed value the generally accepted accounting principles are those in the country of production.

2. The producer's profit and general expenses must be consistent with those usually reflected in sales of goods of the same class or kind as the imported merchandise that are made by producers in the country of exportation for export to the U.S. If they are not consistent, then the amount for profit and general expenses is based on the usual profit and general expenses of such producers.

3. The amount for profit and general expenses is taken as a whole. This is the same treatment as occurs in deductive value.

Basically, a producer's profit could be low and his general expenses high, so that the total amount is consistent with that usually reflected in sales of goods of the same class or kind. In such a situation, a producer's actual profit figures, even if low, will be used provided he has valid commercial reasons to justify them and his pricing policy reflects usual pricing policies in the industry concerned.

Assists. If the value of an assist used in producing the merchandise is not included as part of the producer's materials, fabrication, other processing, or general expenses, then the prorated value of the assist will be included in computed value. It is important that the value of the assist is not included elsewhere because no component of computed value should be counted more than once in determining computed value.

Note: The value of any engineering, development, artwork, design work, and plans and sketches undertaken in the U.S. is included in computed value only to the extent that such value has been charged to the producer.

Packing Costs. The cost of all containers and coverings of whatever nature, and of packing, whether for labor or material, used in placing merchandise in condition and packed ready for shipment to the U.S. is included in computed value.

Under computed value, "merchandise of the same class or kind" must be imported from the same country as the merchandise being appraised and must be within a group or range of goods produced by a particular industry or industry sector. Whether certain merchandise is of the same class or kind as other merchandise will be determined on a case-by-case basis.

In determining usual profit and general expenses, sales for export to the U.S. of the narrowest group or range of merchandise that includes the merchandise being appraised will be examined, providing the necessary information can be obtained.

Note: As a point of contrast, under deductive value, "merchandise of the same class or kind" includes merchandise imported from other countries besides the country from which the merchandise being appraised was imported. Under computed value, "Merchandise of the same class or kind" is limited to merchandise imported from the same country as the merchandise being appraised.

Value If Other Values Cannot Be Determined

If none of the previous five values can be used to appraise the imported merchandise, then the customs value must be based on a value derived from one of the five previous methods, reasonably adjusted as necessary. The value so determined should be based, to the greatest extent possible, on previously determined values. In order for Customs to consider an importer's argument regarding appraisement, the information upon which the argument is based must be made available to Customs, whether it was generated by a foreign or domestic source. More information is available in 19 CFR 152.107(c).

Some examples of how the other methods can be reasonably adjusted are:

1. Identical Merchandise (or Similar Merchandise):

    a. The requirement that the identical merchandise (or similar merchandise) should be exported at or about the same time as the merchandise being appraised could be flexibly interpreted.

    b. Identical imported merchandise (or similar imported merchandise) produced in a country other than the country of exportation of the merchandise being appraised could be the basis for customs valuation.

    c. Customs values of identical imported merchandise (or similar imported merchandise) already determined on the basis of deductive value and computed value could be used.

2. Deductive Method: The 90-day requirement may be administered flexibly.

Marking

Country of Origin Marking

The U.S. customs laws require each imported article produced abroad to be marked in a conspicuous place as legibly, indelibly, and permanently as the nature of the article permits, with the English name of the country of origin, to indicate to the ultimate purchaser in the U.S. the name of the country in which the article was manufactured or produced. Articles that are otherwise specifically exempted from individual marking are an exception to this rule. The exceptions are discussed below.

For Customs purposes, "country" means the political entity known as a nation. Colonies, possessions, or protectorates outside the boundary of the mother country are considered separate countries. The "country of origin" is, in simple terms, the country of manufacture, production, or growth of the article.

Ultimate Purchaser. It is not feasible to state who will be the "ultimate purchaser" in every circumstance. Broadly stated, an "ultimate purchaser" may be defined as the last person in the U.S. who will receive the article in the form in which it was imported. Generally, if an imported article will be used in the U.S. in manufacture, which results in an article having a name, character, or usage different from that of the imported article, the manufacturer is the ultimate purchaser. If an article is to be sold at retail in its imported form, the purchaser at retail is the ultimate purchaser. A person who subjects an imported article to a process that results in a substantial transformation of the article is the ultimate purchaser, but if the process is merely a minor one that leaves the identity of the imported article intact, the processor of the article will not be regarded as the ultimate purchaser.

If the article is a good of a NAFTA country, the ultimate purchaser is the last person in the United States who purchases the good in the form in which it was imported. If the imported article is distributed as a gift, the recipient of the gift is the ultimate purchaser, unless it is a good of a NAFTA country, in which case the *purchaser* of the gift is the ultimate purchaser.

Detailed regulations may be found at 19 CFR Part 134, "Country of Origin Marking."

Marking Required

If the article (or the container when the container and not the article must be marked) is not properly marked at the time of importation, a marking duty equal to 10% of the customs value of the article will be assessed unless the article is exported, destroyed, or properly marked under Customs supervision before the liquidation of the entry concerned.

When an article (or its container) is required to be marked to indicate the country of origin of the article, the marking must be sufficiently permanent to remain on the article (or its container) until it reaches the ultimate purchaser. The marking must be legible and it must be located in a fairly conspicuous place.

When an article is of a kind that is usually combined with another article subsequent to importation but before delivery to an ultimate purchaser, and the name indicating the country of origin of the article appears in a place on the article so that the name will be visible after such combining, the marking shall include, in addition to the name of the country of origin, words or symbols that clearly show that the origin indicated is that of the imported article only and not that of any other article with which the imported article may be combined after importation. For example, if marked bottles, drums, or other containers are imported empty, to be filled in the U.S., they shall be marked with such words as "Bottle (or drum or container) made in (name of country)." Labels and similar articles so marked that the name of the country of origin of the article is visible after it is affixed to another article in this country shall be marked with additional descriptive words such as "label made (or printed) in (name of country)" or words of similar import.

In any case in which the words "United States," or "American" or the letters "U.S.A.," any variation of such words or letters, or the name of any city or locality in the U.S., or the name of any foreign country or locality in which the article was manufactured or produced, appear on an imported article or container, there shall appear, legibly and permanently, in close proximity to such words, letters or name, the name of the country of origin preceded by "Made in," "Product of," or other words of similar meaning. The marking may not need to include phrases such as "made in" or "product of" unless the name of any other country or locality appears on the article or its container.

If marked articles are to be repacked in the U.S. after release from Customs custody, importers must certify on entry that they will not obscure the marking on properly marked articles if the article is repacked or that they will mark the repacked container. If the importers do not repack, but resell to repackers, importers must notify the repackers of the marking requirements. Failure to comply with the certification requirements may subject importers to penalties and/or additional duties.

Marking Not Required—The "J" List

The following articles and classes or kinds of articles are not required to be marked to indicate the country of their origin, i.e., the country in which they were grown, manufactured, or produced. However, the outermost containers in which these articles ordinarily reach the ultimate purchaser in the U.S. must be marked to indicate the English name of the country of origin of the articles. This is sometimes called the "J-list," and may be found at 19 CFR 134.33.

Art, works of.

Articles classified subheads 9810.00.15, 9810.00.25, 9810.00.40, and 9810.00.45 of the HTSUS.

Articles entered in good faith as antiques and rejected as unauthentic.

Bagging, waste.

Bags, jute.

Bands, steel.

Beads, unstrung.

Bearings, ball, 5/8 inch or less in diameter.

Blanks, metal, to be plated.

Bodies, harvest hat.

Bolts, nuts, and washers.

Briarwood, in blocks.

Briquettes, coal or coke.

Buckles, 1 inch or less in greatest dimension.

Burlap.

Buttons.

Cards, playing.

Cellophane and celluloid in sheets, bands, or strips.

Chemicals, drugs, medicinal, and similar substances, when imported in capsules, pills, tablets, lozenges, or troches.

Cigars and cigarettes.

Covers, straw bottle.

Dies, diamond wire, unmounted.

Dowels, wooden.

Effects, theatrical.

Eggs.

Feathers.

Firewood.

Flooring, not further manufactured than planed, tongued and grooved.

Flowers, artificial, except bunches.

Flowers, cut.

Glass, cut to shape and size for use in clocks, hand pocket and purse mirrors, and other glass of similar shapes and sizes, not including lenses or watch crystals.

Glides, furniture, except glides with prongs.

Hairnets.

Hides, raw.

Hooks, fish (except snelled fish hooks).

Hoops (wood), barrel.

Laths.

Livestock.

Lumber, except finished.

Lumber, sawed.

Metal bars except concrete reinforcement bars; billets, blocks, blooms; ingots; pigs; plates; sheets, except galvanized sheets; shafting; slabs, and metal in similar forms.

Mica not further manufactured than cut or stamped to dimensions, shape, or form.

Monuments.

Nails, spikes, and staples.

Natural products, such as vegetables, fruit, nuts, berries, and live or dead animals, fish, and birds; all the foregoing that are in their natural state or not advanced in any manner further than is necessary for their safe transportation.

Nets, bottle wire.

Paper, newsprint.

Paper, stencil.

Paper, stock.

Parchment and vellum.

Parts for machines imported from same country as parts.

Pickets (wood).

Pins, tuning.

Plants, shrubs, and other nursery stock.

Plugs, tie.

Poles, bamboo.

Posts (wood), fence.

Pulpwood.

Rags (including wiping rags).

Rails, joint bars, and tie plates covered by subheadings 7302.10.10 through 7302.90.00 of the HTSUS.

Ribbon.

Rivets.

Rope, including wire rope, cordage, cords, twines, threads, and yarns.

Scrap and waste.

Screws.

Shims, track.

Shingles (wood), bundles of (except bundles of red-cedar shingles).

Skins, fur, dressed or dyed.

Skins, raw fur.

Sponges.

Springs, watch.

Stamps, postage and revenue, and government-stamped envelopes and postal cards bearing no printing other than official imprint thereon.

Staves (wood), barrel.

Steel, hoop.

Sugar, maple.

Ties (wood), railroad.

Tiles, not over 1 inch in greatest dimension.

Timbers, sawed.

Tips, penholder.

Trees, Christmas.

Weights, analytical and precision, in sets.

Wicking, candle.

Wire, except barbed.

Unless an article being shipped to the U.S. is specifically named in the foregoing list, it would be advisable for an exporter to obtain advice from U.S. Customs before concluding that it is exempted from marking.

If articles on the foregoing list are repackaged in the U.S., the new packages must be labeled to indicate the country of origin of the articles contained therein. Importers must certify on entry that, if they repackage, they will properly mark the repackaged containers; if they do not repackage, but resell to repackagers, notification of the marking requirements will be given to such repackagers. Failure to comply with the certification requirements may subject importers to penalties and marking duties.

Other Exceptions

The following classes of articles are excepted from the country of origin marking requirements under Section 304 of the Tariff Act, and are enumerated at 19 CFR 134.32. The usual container in which one of these articles is imported may also be excepted.

a. An article imported for use by the importer and not intended for sale in its imported or any other form.

b. An article that is to be processed in the U.S. by the importer or for his account otherwise than for the purpose of concealing the origin of the article and in such manner that any mark of origin would necessarily be obliterated, destroyed, or permanently concealed.

c. Articles for which the ultimate purchaser must necessarily know, or in the case of a good of a NAFTA country, must reasonably know, the country of origin by reason of the circumstances of their importation or by reason of the character of the articles even though they are not marked to indicate their country of origin.

The following classes of articles are also excepted from marking to indicate the country of their origin.

a. Articles that are incapable of being marked.

b. Articles that cannot be marked prior to shipment to the U.S. without injury.

c. Articles that cannot be marked prior to shipment to the U.S., except at an expense economically prohibitive of their importation.

d. Articles for which the marking of the containers will reasonably indicate the origin of the articles.

e. Crude substances.

f. Articles produced more than 20 years prior to their importation into the U.S.

g. Articles entered or withdrawn from warehouse for immediate exportation or for transportation and exportation.

h. Goods of a NAFTA country which are original works of art.

Although such articles are exempted from marking to indicate the country of their origin, the outermost containers in which the articles will ordinarily reach the ultimate purchaser in the U.S. must be marked to show the country of origin of such articles. Marking may not be required for containers from NAFTA countries; refer to 19 CFR 134.22(b)(2) for more information.

When the marking of the container of an article will reasonably indicate the country of origin of the article, the article itself may be exempt from such marking. This exemption applies only when the articles will reach the ultimate purchaser in an unopened container. For example, articles that reach the retail purchaser in sealed containers marked clearly to indicate the country of origin come within this exception. Materials to be used in building or manufacture by the builder or manufacturer who will receive the materials in unopened cases likewise come within the exemption. The following articles, as well as their containers, are excepted from marking to indicate the country of their origin.

a. Products of U.S. fisheries that are free of duty.

b. Products of possessions of the U.S.

c. Products of the U.S. exported and returned.

d. Articles valued at not more than $200 (or $100 for bona fide gifts) that are passed without entry.

Special Marking Requirements

The country of origin marking requirements are separate and apart from any special marking or labeling required on specific products by other agencies. It is recommended that the specific agency be contacted for any special marking or labeling requirements.

Metal tools and instruments. Certain articles are subject to special country of origin marking requirements under Section 304 of the Tariff Act, as listed in 19 CFR 134.43:

- Pipes and pipe fittings of iron, steel or stainless steel generally must be marked by means of die stamping, cast-in-mold lettering, etching, engraving, or continuous paint stenciling. If it is commercially or technically infeasible to mark by one of these methods, the marking may be done by an equally permanent method of marking, or, in the case of small-diameter pipe, tube and fittings, by tagging the bundles.

- Compressed gas cylinders designed for use for the transport and storage of compressed gases must be marked by means of die stamping, molding, etching, raised lettering, or an equally permanent method of marking.

- Manhole rings or frames, covers, and assemblies thereof must be marked on the top surface by means of die stamping, cast-in-mold lettering, etching, engraving, or an equally permanent method of marking.

The following articles, and parts thereof, must be marked legibly and conspicuously to indicate their origin by die-stamping, cast-in-the-mold lettering, etching (acid or electrolytic), engraving, or by means of metal plates that bear the prescribed marking and that are securely attached to the article in a conspicuous place by welding, screws, or rivets:

- Knives, forks, steels

- Cleavers, clippers, shears

- Scissors, safety razors, blades for safety razors

- Surgical instruments, dental instruments

- Scientific and laboratory instruments

- Pliers, pincers, nippers, and hinged hand tools for holding and splicing wire

- Vacuum containers and parts of the above articles

- Goods of a NAFTA country should be marked by any reasonable method which is legible, conspicuous, and permanent.

Watches and Clocks. Chapter 91, Additional U.S. Note 4 of the HTSUS sets forth special marking requirements applicable for watches and clocks.

Watch movements are required to be marked on one or more of the bridges or top plates to show:

1. The name of the country of manufacture
2. The name of the manufacturer or purchaser
3. In words, the number of jewels, if any, serving a mechanical purpose as frictional bearings

Clock movements must be marked on the most visible part of the front or back plate to show:

1. The name of the country of manufacture
2. The name of the manufacturer or purchaser
3. The number of jewels, if any

Watch cases shall be marked on the inside or outside of the back cover to show:

1. The name of the country of manufacture
2. The name of the manufacturer or purchaser

Clock cases and other cases provided for in Chapter 91, HTSUS, are required to be marked on the most visible part of the outside of the back to show the name of the country of manufacture.

The terms "watch movement" and "clock movement" refer to devices regulated by a balance wheel and hairspring, quartz crystal, or any other system capable of determining intervals of time, with a display or system to which a mechanical display can be incorporated. "Watch movements" include those devices that do not exceed 12 mm in thickness and 50 mm in width, length, or diameter; "clock movements" include those devices that do not meet the watch movement dimensional specifications. The term "cases" embraces inner and outer cases, containers, and housings for movements, together with parts or pieces, such as, but not limited to, rings, feet, posts, bases, and outer frames, and any auxiliary or incidental features, that (with appropriate movements) serve to complete the watches, clocks, time switches, and other apparatus provided for in Chapter 91, HTSUS.

Articles required to be marked in accordance with the special marking requirements in Chapter 91 must be conspicuously and indelibly marked by cutting, die-sinking, engraving, stamping, or mold-marking. Articles required to be so marked shall be denied entry unless marked in exact conformity with these requirements.

Movements with opto-electronic display only and cases designed for their use, whether entered as separate articles or as components of assembled watches or clocks, are not subject to the special marking requirements. These items need only to be marked with the marking requirements.

Watches and clocks are also subject to the normal country of origin marking requirements of 19 USC 1304, and under these requirements, the country of origin of the movement should appear conspicuously and legibly on the face of the dial or on the outside of the back. In addition, watch bands should be marked with the country of manufacture of the band, if it is made in a country different from the country of origin of the watch.

Native American-Style Goods. According to 19 CFR 134.43(c) and (d), Native American-style jewelry and arts and crafts must be indelibly marked with the country of origin by cutting, die-sinking, engraving, stamping, or some other permanent method. The indelible marking must appear legibly on the clasp or in some other conspicuous location, or alternatively, on a metal or plastic tag indelibly marked with the country of origin and permanently attached to the article. On textile articles, such as rugs, a sewn-in label is considered to be an equally permanent method.

By "Native American-style," Customs is referring to articles not actually made by Native Americans, but which incorporate traditional Native American design motifs, materials, and construction and could possibly be mistaken from genuine Native American crafts.

Exceptions to these marking regulations are made when it is technically or commercially infeasible to mark goods in the manner described above, or in the case of a good of a NAFTA country, the article may be marked by means of a string tag or adhesive label securely affixed, or some other similar method.

Title IV of the Tariff Suspension and Trade Act of 2000 (P.L. 106-476), also known as the Imported Cigarette Compliance Act of 2000, imposes special requirements on the importation of cigarettes and other tobacco products. Importers of cigarettes or other tobacco products are urged to contact the United States port of entry at which their merchandise will arrive for information about the new requirements.

Marking—False Impression

Section 42 of the Trademark Act of 1946 (15 USC 1124) provides, among other things, that no imported article of foreign origin that bears a name or mark calculated to induce the public to believe that it was manufactured in the U.S., or in any foreign country or locality other than the country or locality in which it was in fact manufactured, shall be admitted to entry at any customhouse in the U.S.

In many cases, the words "United States," the letters "U.S.A.," or the name of any city or locality in the U.S. appearing on an imported article of foreign origin, or on the containers thereof, are considered to be calculated to induce the public to believe that the article was manufactured in the U.S. unless the name to indicate the country of origin appears in close proximity to the name that indicates a domestic origin. Merchandise discovered after conditional release to have been missing a required country of origin marking may be ordered redelivered to Customs custody. If such delivery is not promptly made, liquidated damages may be assessed against the Customs bond. (See 19 CFR 141.113(a), cf.; 19 CFR Part 172; and Customs **Form 4647**.)

An imported article bearing a name or mark prohibited by Section 42 of the Trademark Act is subject to seizure and forfeiture. However, upon the filing of a petition by the importer prior to final disposition of the article, the port director of Customs may release it upon the condition that the prohibited marking be removed or obliterated or that the article and containers be properly marked; or the port director may permit the article to be exported or destroyed under Customs supervision and without expense to the Government.

Section 43 of the Trademark Act of 1946 (15 USC 1125) prohibits the entry of goods marked or labeled with a false designation of origin or with any false description or representation, including words or other symbols tending to falsely describe or represent the same. Deliberate removal, obliteration, covering, or altering of required country of origin markings after release from Customs custody is also a crime punishable by fines and imprisonment (19 USC 1304(1)).

Special Requirements

Prohibitions, Restrictions, and Other Agency Requirements

The importation of certain classes of merchandise may be prohibited or restricted to protect the economy and security of the U.S., to safeguard consumer health and well-being, and to preserve domestic plant and animal life. Some commodities are also subject to an import quota or a restraint under bilateral trade agreements and arrangements.

Many of these prohibitions and restrictions on importations are subject, in addition to Customs requirements, to the laws and regulations administered by other U.S. Government agencies with which Customs cooperates in enforcement. These laws and regulations may, for example, prohibit entry; limit entry to certain ports; restrict routing, storage, or use; or require treatment, labeling, or processing as a condition of release. Customs clearance is given only if these various additional requirements are met. This applies to all types of importations, including those made by mail and those placed in foreign trade zones.

The foreign exporter should make certain that the U.S. importer has provided proper information to (1) permit the submission of necessary information concerning packing, labeling, etc., and (2) that necessary arrangements have been made by the importer for entry of the merchandise into the U.S.

It may be impracticable to list all articles specifically; however, various classes of articles are discussed below. Foreign exporters and U.S. importers should consult the agency mentioned for detailed information and guidance, as well as for any changes to the laws and regulations under which the commodities are controlled.

Contents

Agricultural Commodities

Cheese, Milk, and Dairy Products

Cheese and cheese products are subject to requirements of the Food and Drug Administration and the Department of Agriculture. Most importations of cheese require an import license and are subject to quotas administered by the Foreign Agricultural Service of the Department of Agri-

culture. *See* "Import Quotas" on page 274, and also refer to 19 CFR 12.6, "Importation of Certain Cheeses."

The importation of milk and cream is subject to requirements of the Food, Drug, and Cosmetic Act and the Import Milk Act. These products may be imported only by holders of permits from the Department of Health and Human Services, Food and Drug Administration, Center for Food Safety and Applied Nutrition, Office of Food Labeling (HFS-156), 200 "C" Street NW, Washington, DC 20204; and the Department of Agriculture. Also refer to 19 CFR 12.7, "Milk and Cream."

Fruits, Vegetables, and Nuts

Certain agricultural commodities (including fresh tomatoes, avocados, mangoes, limes, oranges, grapefruit, green peppers, Irish potatoes, cucumbers, eggplants, dry onions, walnuts and filberts, processed dates, prunes, raisins, and olives in tins) must meet U.S. import requirements relating to grade, size, quality, and maturity (7 USC 608(e)). These commodities are inspected and an inspection certificate must be issued by the Food Safety and Inspection Service (FSIS) of the Department of Agriculture to indicate import compliance.

Inquiries on general requirements should be made to the Agricultural Marketing Service of the Department of Agriculture. Additional restrictions may be imposed by the Animal and Plant Health Inspection Service of that department, under the Plant Quarantine Act and by the Food and Drug Administration, Division of Import Operations and Policy (HFC-170), 5600 Fishers Lane, Rockville, MD 20857, under the Federal Food, Drug, and Cosmetic Act. Also refer to 19 CFR 12.10–12.15, "Plants and Plant Products."

Insects

Insects in a live state that are injurious to cultivated crops (including vegetables, field crops, bush fruit, and orchard, forest, or shade trees) and the eggs, pupae, or larvae of such insects are prohibited importation, except for scientific purposes under regulations prescribed by the Secretary of Agriculture.

All packages containing live insects or their eggs, pupae, or larvae, that are not injurious to crops or trees, are permitted entry into the U.S. only if covered by a permit issued by the Animal and Plant Health Inspection Service of the Department of Agriculture and are not prohibited by the U.S. Fish and Wildlife Service. Also refer to 19 CFR 12.31, "Plant Pests."

Livestock and Animals

Inspection and quarantine requirements of the Animal and Plant Health Inspection Service (APHIS) must be met for the importation of (1) all cloven-hoofed animals (ruminants), such as cattle, sheep, deer, antelope, camels, giraffes; (2) swine including the various varieties of wild hogs and the meat from such animals; (3) horses, asses, mules, and zebras; (4) all avian species including poultry and pet birds; (5) animal by-products, such as untanned hides, wool, hair, bones, bone meal, blood meal, animal casings, glands, organs, extracts or secretions of ruminants and swine; and (6) animal germ-plasm, including embryos and semen; and (7) hay and straw. A permit for importation must be obtained from APHIS before shipping from the country of origin.

In addition, all animal imports must be accompanied by a veterinary health certificate. Entry procedures for livestock and animals from Mexico and Canada are not as rigorous as those for animals from other countries. Entry of animals is restricted to certain ports that are designated as quarantine stations. For further information r efer to 19 CFR 12.24, "Domestic Animals, Animal Products, and Animal Feeding Materials."

Meat and Meat Products

All commercial shipments of meat and meat food products (derived from cattle, sheep, swine, goats, and horses) offered for entry into the U.S. are subject to the regulations of the Department of Agriculture and must be inspected by the Animal and Plant Health Inspection Service (APHIS) and the Food Safety and Inspection Service (FSIS) of that department prior to release by U.S. Customs. Meat products from other sources (including, but not limited to wild game) are subject to APHIS regulations and the provisions of the Federal Food, Drug, and Cosmetic Act, enforced by the Food and Drug Administration. Also refer to 19 CFR 12.8–12.9, "Meat and Meat-Food Products."

Plant and Plant Products

The importation of plants and plant products is subject to regulations of the Department of Agriculture and may be restricted or prohibited. Plants and plant products include fruits, vegetables, plants, nursery stock, bulbs, roots, seeds, certain fibers including cotton and broom- corn, cut flowers, sugarcane, certain cereals, and elm logs and elm lumber with bark attached. Import permits are required. Further information should be obtained from the Animal and Plant Health Inspection Service. Also certain endangered species of plants may be prohibited or require permits or certificates from the U.S. Fish and Wildlife Service (FWS), which enforces endangered species regulations. The Food and Drug Administration also regulates plant and plant products, particularly fruits and vegetables. Also refer to 19 CFR 12.10–12.15, "Plants and Plant Products."

Poultry and Poultry Products

Poultry—live, dressed, or canned; eggs, including eggs for hatching; and egg products are subject to the requirements and regulations of the Animal and Plant Health Inspection Service (APHIS) and the Food Safety and Inspection Service (FSIS) of the Department of Agriculture.

Except for live poultry and poultry products entering through land ports from Canada, permits are required, as well as special marking and labeling, and, in some cases, foreign inspection certification. The term "poultry" is defined as any live or slaughtered domesticated bird, e.g. chickens, turkeys, ducks, geese, swans, partridges, guinea fowl, pea fowl, non-migratory ducks, pigeons, and doves. Other birds (e.g., commercial, domestic, or pen-raised grouse, pheasants, quail, and migratory birds) as well as certain egg products are subject to APHIS regulations and to the provisions of the Federal Food, Drug, and Cosmetic Act, enforced by the Food and Drug Administration. Inquiry should also be made to the Fish and Wildlife Service about their requirements, restrictions, and prohibitions.

Seeds

The importation into the U.S. of agricultural and vegetable seeds and screenings is governed by the provisions of the Federal Seed Act of 1939 and regulations of the Agricultural Marketing Service within the Department of Agriculture. Shipments are detained pending the drawing and testing of samples. Also refer to 19 CFR 12.16, "Agricultural and Vegetable Seeds."

Wildlife and Pets

The importation of live wildlife (i.e., game animals, birds, plants) or any part or product made therefrom, and the eggs of wild or game birds, is subject to certain prohibitions, restrictions, and permit and quarantine requirements of several Government agencies. Importations of wildlife, parts, or their products must be entered at certain designated U.S. Fish and Wildlife Service (FWS) ports of entry unless an exception is granted by FWS, Department of the Interior. The Assistant Regional Director of Law Enforcement for the region in which the import will take place should be contacted for additional information or to request an exception to designated port permit.

On or after January 1, 1981, most firms (with some significant exceptions) importing or exporting wildlife must obtain a license from the Fish and Wildlife Service. Applications and further information may be obtained from the U.S. Fish and Wildlife Service, Assistant Regional Director for Law Enforcement, for the state in which the importer or exporter is located.

Endangered species of wildlife and certain species of animals and birds are generally prohibited entry into the U.S. and may be imported only under a permit granted by the U.S. Fish and Wildlife Service, Office of Management Authority, 4401 North Fairfax, Arlington, VA 22203, or by calling 1-800-358-2104.

Antique articles (at least 100 years old) that would otherwise be prohibited under the Endangered Species Act may be admitted provided certain conditions are met.

The taking and importation of marine mammals and their products are subject to the requirements of the Marine Mammal Protection Act of 1972 and cannot be imported without a permit from the National Marine Fisheries Service (NMFS) of the Department of Commerce or the U.S. Fish and Wildlife Service.

Regulations to implement the Convention on International Trade in Endangered Species of Wild Fauna and Flora became effective on May 23, 1977. Certain animals, mammals, birds, reptiles, amphibians, fish, snails, and clams, insects, crustaceans, mollusks, other invertebrates and plants may be prohibited or require permits or certification which may be obtained from the U.S. Fish and Wildlife Service. Other NMFS import requirements may also apply for certain species covered by the International Commission for the Conservation of Atlantic Tunas, e.g., Atlantic bluefin tuna.

Certain mammals, birds, reptiles, amphibians, fish, snails, clams, insects, crustaceans, mollusks, other invertebrates and plants may be prohibited entry without the prior issuance of a permit either from the foreign wildlife authority or from the Fish and Wildlife Service, Office of Management Authority.

The importation into the U.S. of any wild animal or bird is prohibited if the animal or bird was captured, taken, shipped, possessed, or exported contrary to the law of the foreign country or subdivision thereof. In addition, no wild animal or bird from any foreign country may be taken, purchased, sold, or possessed contrary to the laws of any State, territory, or possession of the U.S.

The importation of the feathers or skin of any wild bird, except for scientific and educational purposes, is prohibited, except for the species noted below. This prohibition does not apply to fully manufactured artificial flies used for fishing or to personally taken, noncommercial game birds. Feathers or skins of the following species are permitted entry: chicken, turkeys, guinea fowl, geese, ducks, pigeons, ostriches, rheas, English ring-necked pheasants, and pea fowl not taken from the wild.

On October 23, 1992, the Wild Bird Conservation Act became effective. This act focuses on live bird species listed in the Appendices to the Convention on International Trade in Endangered Species (CITES). Now, if you import live birds, you must meet the requirements of this law in addition to existing requirements of CITES, the Endangered Species Act, the Migratory Bird Treaty Act, or other applicable regulations. Import permits must be obtained from the Fish and Wildlife Service, Office of Management Authority.

Live birds, their parts and products that are protected under the Migratory Bird Treaty Act may be imported into the United States for scientific purposes or certain propagating purposes only under permits issued by the Fish and Wildlife Service, Office of Migratory Birds, located in the region where the importation will occur or where the importer resides.

Imports of birds (pets, migratory birds, falcons) are subject to the quarantine requirements of the USDA and Public Health Service. Quarantine space must be reserved in advance of import. Prior to export, health certificates must be obtained. Inquiries should be addressed to the appropriate agency.

Live birds protected under the Migratory Bird Treaty Act may be imported into the U.S. from foreign countries for scientific or propagating purposes only under permits issued by the U.S. Fish and Wildlife Service. These migratory birds and any game animals (e.g., antelope, mountain sheep, deer, bears, peccaries, squirrels, rabbits, and hares) imported from Mexico must be accompanied by Mexican export permits. Importations in this class are also subject to the quarantine requirements of the Department of Agriculture and the Centers for Disease Control. Appropriate inquiries in this respect should be directed to those agencies.

On June 9, 1989, the U.S. Fish and Wildlife Service announced a ban on the importation of most African elephant ivory and any products made from it. The ban covers all commercial and noncommercial shipments including household effects and personal baggage accompanying a tourist. There are limited exceptions for antiques, trophies, and personal household effects. For further information, contact the U.S. Fish and Wildlife Service, Office of Management Authority, 4401 N. Fairfax Drive, Arlington, VA 22203, Tel. 1-800-358-2104..

The importation of birds, cats, dogs, monkeys, and turtles is subject to the requirements of the Centers for Disease Control, Quarantine Division, and the Veterinary Services of the Animal and Plant Health Inspection Service, Department of Agriculture; and of the U.S. Fish and Wildlife Service.

The importation of turtles with a carapace length of less than four inches and of the viable eggs of turtles, tortoises and terrapins, is allowed by the U.S. Public Health Service only under strict requirements as to purpose and quantity. The U.S. Public Health Service does not allow the importation of live, non-human primates, including monkeys, as pets. For more information, also refer to 19 CFR 12.26–12.32, "Wild Animals, Birds, and Insects."

Arms, Ammunition, and Radioactive Materials

Arms, Ammunition, Explosives, and Implements of War

These items are prohibited importation except when a license is issued by the Bureau of Alcohol, Tobacco and Firearms of the Department of the Treasury, Tel:(202) 927-8320, or the importation is in compliance with the regulations of that department. The temporary importation, in-transit movement, and exportation of arms and ammunition is prohibited unless a license is issued by the Office of Defense Trade Control, Department of State, or unless a license exemption is available as set forth in 22 CFR 123.4 and other sections of 22 CFR. Importations of firearms, munitions of war, and related articles are subject to import permit requirements and restrictions set forth in 27 CFR parts 178 and 179.

Radioactive Materials and Nuclear Reactors

Many radioisotopes, all forms of uranium, thorium, and plutonium, and all nuclear reactors imported into the U.S. are subject to the regulations of the Nuclear Regulatory Commission (NRC), in addition to import regulations imposed by any other agency of the U.S. Authority to import these commodities or articles containing these commodities is granted by the NRC (10 CFR 110.)

Radioisotopes and radioactive sources intended for medical use are subject to the provisions of the Federal Food, Drug, and Cosmetic Act, enforced by the Food and Drug Administration.

In order to comply with the Nuclear Regulatory Commission requirements, the importer must be aware of the identity and amount of any NRC-controlled radioisotopes, or uranium, thorium, and plutonium, and of any nuclear reactor being imported into the U.S. To assure passage through Customs, the importer must demonstrate to U.S. Customs which NRC authority the controlled commodity is being imported under. The authority cited may be the number of a specific or general license, or the specific section of the NRC regulations that establishes a general license or grants an exemption to the regulations. The foreign exporter may save time for the prospective importer by furnishing him complete information concerning the presence of NRC-controlled commodities in U.S. importation.

Consumer Goods

Household Appliances

The Energy Policy and Conservation Act, as amended, calls for energy efficiency standards for household consumer appliances and for labeling them to indicate expected energy or secretions of consumption. The Department of Energy, Office of Codes and Standards, Washington, DC 20585, is responsible for test procedures and energy performance standards. The Federal Trade Commission, Division of Energy and Product Information, regulates the labeling of these appliances. The Act covers the following consumer products: (1) refrigerators and refrigerator-freezers and freezers; (2) room air-conditioners; (3) central air-conditioners and central air-conditioning heat pumps; (4) water heaters; (5) furnaces; (6) dishwashers; (7) clothes washers; (8) clothes dryers; (9) direct heating equipment; (10) kitchen ranges and ovens; (11) pool heaters; and (12) flourescent lamp ballasts.

Importations of these products must comply with the applicable Department of Energy and Federal Trade Commission requirements. Importers should contact these agencies for requirements that will be in effect at the time of anticipated shipment. It should be noted that not all appliances are covered by requirements of both agencies.

Note: Any consumer product offered for importation will be refused admission if the product fails to comply with an applicable consumer product safety rule, specified labeling or certification requirements, or is determined to be a hazardous product or contain a product defect that constitutes a substantial product hazard.

Flammable Fabrics

Any article of wearing apparel or interior furnishing, or any fabric or related material that is intended for use or which may be used in wearing apparel or interior furnishings cannot be imported into the U.S. if it fails to conform to an applicable flammability standard issued under section 4 of the Flammable Fabrics Act. This Act is administered by the U.S. Consumer Product Safety Commission, Washington, DC 20207. Certain products can be imported into the U.S. as provided in Section 11(c) of the Act for the purpose of finishing or processing to render such products not so highly flammable as to be dangerous when worn by individuals, provided that the exporter states on the invoice or other paper relating to the shipment that the shipment is being made for that purpose. The provisions of the Flammable Fabrics Act apply to products manufactured in the U.S., as well as to imported products.

Radiation Producing Products, Including Sonic Radiation

Television receivers, cold-cathode gas discharge tubes, microwave ovens, cabinet and diagnostic X-ray equipment and devices, laser products, ultrasound generating equipment, sunlamps, CD-ROMs, cellular and cordless telephones, and other electronic products for which there are radiation performance standards are subject to the Radiation Control for Health and Safety Act of 1968. An electronic product for which there is a radiation performance standard and that is imported for sale or use in the U.S. for which there is a radiation performance standard may be imported only if there is filed with each importation notice an electronic product declaration (**Form FD 2877**), which is issued by the Food and Drug Administration, National Center for Devices and Radiological Health. Also refer to 19 CFR 12.90–12.91, "Electronic Products."

The declaration must describe the compliance status of the product. The importer must affirm that the product meets one of the following (1) not subject to a standard (e.g., manufactured prior to the effective date of the applicable Federal standard); (2) complies with the standard and has a label affixed by the manufacturer certifying compliance; (3) does not comply with the standard but is being imported only for purposes of research, investigation, study, demonstration, or training; or (4) does not now comply with the standard but will be brought into compliance. The provisions of the Radiation Control for Health and Safety Act apply to electronic products manufactured in the U.S., as well as to imported products.

Radio Frequency Devices

Radios, tape recorders, stereos, televisions, citizen band radios or combinations thereof, and other radio frequency devices are subject to radio emission standards of the Federal Communications Commission under the Communications Act of 1934, as amended. Importations of such products may be accompanied by an FCC declaration (**FCC 740**) certifying that the imported model or device is in conformity with, will be brought into conformity, or is exempt from the Federal Communications Commission requirements.

Drugs, Cosmetics, and Processed Foods

According to 19 CFR 12.1(a), "The importation into the United States of food, drugs, devices, and cosmetics, as defined in section 201(f), (g), (h), and (i) of the Federal Food, Drug, and Cosmetic Act (21 USC 321 (f), (g), (h), and (i)) is governed by section 801 of the Act, as amended (21 USC 381) and regulations issued under authority of section 701(b) of the Act (21 USC 371(b)) by the Secretary of Health and Human Services and the Secretary of the Treasury (21 CFR 1.83–1.99)."

Foods and Cosmetics

The importation into the U.S. of food, beverages, drugs, devices, and cosmetics is governed by the provisions of the Federal Food, Drug, and Cosmetic Act, which is administered by the Food and Drug Administration of the Department of Health and Human Services. That Act prohibits the importation of articles that are adulterated or misbranded including products that are defective, unsafe, filthy, or produced under unsanitary conditions. The term "misbranded" includes statements, designs, or pictures in labeling that are false or misleading and failure to provide required information in labeling.

Imported products regulated by the Food and Drug Administration are subject to inspection at the time of entry. Shipments found not to comply with the laws and regulations are subject to detention. They must be brought into compliance, destroyed, or re-exported. At the discretion of the Food and Drug Administration, an importer may be permitted to bring a nonconforming importation into compliance if it is possible to do so. Any sorting, reprocessing, or relabeling must be supervised by the Food and Drug Administration at the expense of the importer.

Various imported foods such as confectionery, dairy products, poultry, eggs and egg products, meats, fruit, nuts, and vegetables are also subject to requirements of other agencies. Seafoods are also subject to the requirements of the National Marine Fisheries Service of the Department of Commerce.

Biological Drugs

The manufacture and importation of biological products for human consumption are regulated under the Public Health Service Act. Domestic and foreign manufacturers of such products must obtain a license for both the manufacturing establishment and the product intended to be produced or imported. Additional information may be obtained from the Food and Drug Administration, Center for Biologics Evaluation and Research. Also refer to 19 CFR 12.21–12.23, "Viruses, Serums, Toxins, Antitoxins, and Analogous Products for the Treatments of Man."

Biological drugs for animals are regulated under the Virus Serum Toxin Act administered by the Department of Agriculture. The importation of viruses, serums, toxins, and analogous products, and organisms and vectors for use in the treatment of domestic animals is prohibited unless the importer holds a permit from the Department of Agriculture covering the specific product. These importations are also subject to special labeling requirements. Also refer to 19 CFR 12.17–12.19, "Viruses, Serums, and Toxins for the Treatment of Domestic Animals."

Biological Materials and Vectors

The importation into the U.S. for sale, barter, or exchange of any virus, therapeutic serum, toxin, antitoxin, or analogous products, or arsphenamine or its derivatives (or any other trivalent organic arsenic compound), except materials to be used in research experiments, applicable to the prevention, treatment, or cure of diseases or injuries of man is prohibited unless these products have been propagated or prepared at any establishment holding an unsuspended and unrevoked license for such manufacturing issued by the Secretary, Department of Health and Human Services. Samples of the U.S.-licensed product must accompany each importation for forwarding by the port director of Customs at the port of entry to the Food and Drug Administration, Center for Biologics Evaluation and Research. Also refer to 19 CFR 12.21–12.23, "Viruses, Serums, Toxins, Antitoxins, and Analogous Products for the Treatments of Man," and 19 CFR 12.17–12.19, "Viruses, Serums, and Toxins for the Treatment of Domestic Animals."

A permit from the Centers for Disease Control is required for shipments of any etiological agent or insect, animal, or plant vector of human disease or any exotic living insect, animal, or plant capable of being a vector of human disease.

Narcotic Drugs and Derivatives

The importation of controlled substances including narcotics, marijuana, and other dangerous drugs is prohibited except when imported in compliance with regulations of the Drug Enforcement Administration of the Department of Justice. Examples of some of the prohibited controlled substances are amphetamines; barbiturates; coca leaves and derivatives such as cocaine; hallucinogenic substances such as LSD, mescaline, peyote, marijuana, and other forms of *cannabis*; opiates including methadone; opium including opium derivatives, such as morphine and heroin; and synthetic substitutes for narcotic drugs. For more information, refer to 19 CFR 162 Subpart F, "Controlled Substances, Narcotics, and Marihuana."

Drug Paraphernalia

Items of drug paraphernalia are prohibited from importation or exportation under 21 USC 863. The term "drug paraphernalia" means any equipment, product, or material of any kind that is primarily intended or designed for use in manufacturing, compounding, converting, concealing, producing, processing, preparing, injecting, ingesting, inhaling, or otherwise introducing into the human body a controlled substance, possession of which is unlawful under the Controlled Substances Act (Title II of Public Law 91-513). Items of drug paraphernalia include, but are not limited to the following items:

a. Metal, wooden, acrylic, glass, stone, plastic, or ceramic pipes with or without screens, permanent screens, hashish heads, or punctured metal bowls;

b. Water pipes;

c. Carburetion tubes and devices;

d. Smoking and carburetion masks;

e. Roach clips: meaning objects used to hold burning material, such as a marijuana cigarette, that has become too small or too short to be held in the hand;

f. Miniature spoons with level capacities of one-tenth cubic centimeter or less;

g. Chamber pipes;

h. Carburetor pipes;

i. Electric pipes;

j. Air-driven pipes;

k. Chillums;

l. Bongs;

m. Ice pipes or chillers;

n. Wired cigarette papers; or

o. Cocaine freebase kits.

The penalty for violation of this section is imprisonment of not more than three years and a fine under 18 USC.

Negotiable Instruments and Replicas

Gold and Silver

The provisions of the National Stamping Act, as amended (15 USC 291-300) are enforced in part by Customs & Border Protection and by the FBI. Articles made of gold or alloys thereof are prohibited importation into the U.S. if the gold content is one-half carat divergence below the indicated fineness. In the case of articles made of gold or gold alloys, including the solder and alloy of inferior fineness, a one-carat divergence below the indicated fineness is permitted. Articles marked "sterling" or "sterling silver" must assay at least 0.925 of pure silver with a 0.004 divergence allowed. Other articles of silver or silver alloys must assay not less than 0.004 part below the indicated fineness thereof. Articles marked "coin" or "coin silver" must contain at least 0.900 part pure silver with an allowable divergence therefrom of 0.004 part below.

A person placing articles of gold or silver bearing a fineness or quality mark such as 14K, sterling, etc., in the mail or in interstate commerce must place his name or registered trademark next to the fineness mark in letters the same size as the fineness mark. Because the trademark or name is not required at the time of importation, Customs has no direct responsibility for enforcement of the law. Persons making inquiry or seeking advice or interpretation of the law should consult the Department of Justice. For more information, refer to 19 CFR 11.13, "False designations of origin and false descriptions; false marking of articles of gold or silver."

Articles bearing the words "United States Assay" are prohibited importations. Articles made wholly or in part of inferior metal and plated or filled with gold or silver or alloys thereof and that are marked with the degree of fineness must also be marked to indicate the plated or filled content, and in such cases, the use of the words "sterling" or "coin" is prohibited.

All restrictions on the purchase, holding, selling, or otherwise dealing with gold were removed effective December 31, 1974, and gold may be imported subject to the usual Customs entry requirements. Under the Hobby Protection Act, any imitation numismatic item must be plainly and permanently marked "copy"; those that do not comply are subject to seizure and forfeiture. Unofficial gold coin restrikes must be marked with the country of origin. It is advisable to obtain a copy of the legal proclamation under which the coins are issued or an affidavit of government sanction of coins should be secured from a responsible banking official if the proclamation is unavailable.

Counterfeit Articles

Articles bearing facsimiles or replicas of coins or securities of the U.S. or of any foreign country are prohibited importation. Counterfeits of coins in circulation in the U.S.; counterfeited, forged, or altered obligations or other securities of the U.S. or of any foreign government; and plates, dies, or other apparatus that may be used in making any of the foregoing are prohibited importations. Refer to 19 CFR 12.48, "Counterfeit Coins, Obligations, and Other Securities; Illustrations or Reproductions of Coins or Stamps."

Monetary Instruments

Under the Currency and Foreign Transactions Reporting Act, 31 USC 5311 et seq., if a person knowingly transports, is about to transport, or has transported, more than $10,000 in monetary instruments at one time to, through, or from the U.S.; or if a person receives more than $10,000 at one time from or through a place outside the U.S., a report of the transportation (Customs **Form 4790**) must be filed with the U.S. Customs Service. Monetary instruments include U.S. or foreign coin, currency, traveler's checks in any form, personal and other checks, and money orders, either in bearer negotiable form or endorsed without restriction; and securities or stocks in bearer form. A bank check or money order made payable to a named person but not endorsed, or that bears a restrictive endorsement, is not considered to be a "monetary instrument." The Department of the Treasury regulations governing the report of monetary instruments are set forth at 31 CFR 103.

Postage Stamps

Facsimiles of U.S. postage stamps are prohibited except those for philatelic, educational, historical, or newsworthy purposes. Further information should be obtained from the U.S. Secret Service, Department of the Treasury. Also refer to 19 CFR 12.48, "Counterfeit Coins, Obligations, and Other Securities; Illustrations or Reproductions of Coins or Stamps."

Toxic and Hazardous Substances

According to 19 CFR 12.1(c), "the importation of hazardous substances, misbranded hazardous substances, or banned hazardous substances as defined in section 2 of the Federal Hazardous Substances Act, as amended (15 USC 1261), is governed under regulations issued under the authority of sections 10(b) and 14 of the Act, as amended (15 USC 1269, 1273), by the Consumer Product Safety Commission (16 CFR 1500.265–1500.272.)"

Pesticides

Section 17(c) of the Federal Insecticide, Fungicide, and Rodenticide Act (FIFRA) as amended, 1988, provides the statutory framework governing the importation of pesticides and devices into the U.S. Under this authority, the U.S. Customs Service regulations establish the requirements for importing pesticides and devices. Among the requirements, importers of pesticides and devices must submit a Notice of Arrival prior to importation. Pesticides must be registered in accordance with FIFRA Section 3 or they will be refused entry into the United States. Devices are not subject to product registration, but the labeling of both pesticides and devices must bear the producer establishment's number registered with the EPA. In addition, pesticides and devices may be refused entry, if they are: adulterated, misbranded, violate the provisions of FIFRA, or are injurious to health or the environment. For further information on importing pesticides or devices, you should contact the EPA Regional office serving the area where the pesticide or device will be imported. Also refer to 19 CFR 12.110–12.117, "Pesticides and Devices."

Toxic Substances

The Toxic Substances Control Act (TSCA), effective January 1, 1977, regulates the manufacturing, importation, processing, distribution in commerce, use, or disposal of any chemical substance or mixture that are broadly defined in Section 3 of TSCA. Section 3 specifies that certain substances are excluded from the definition of "chemical substance" based upon their use. These substances include, but are not limited to, foods, drugs, cosmetics, and active ingredients in pesticides. Importations will not be released from Customs custody unless proper certification that the import "complies with" or "is not subject to" the requirements of the Toxic Substances Control Act is presented to Customs, or if it is already identified as a food, drug, or active pesticide ingredient. For further information from EPA, call the TSCA Assistance Information Service (202) 554-1404, or refer to 19 CFR 12.118–12.127, "Chemical Substances in Bulk and as Part of Mixtures and Articles."

Hazardous Substances

The importation into the U.S. of dangerous caustic or corrosive substances in packages suitable for household use and of hazardous substances is regulated by the Hazardous Substance Act; the Caustic Poison Act; the Food, Drug, and Cosmetic Act; and the Consumer Product Safety Act. The marking, labeling, packaging, and transportation of hazardous materials, substances, wastes, and their containers is regulated by the Office of Hazardous Materials in the Department of Transportation. Hazardous waste is a special sub-category of hazardous substances and is regulated by the Resource Recovery and Conservation Act (RCRA), which requires a special EPA manifest for both imports and exports.

Intellectual and Industrial Property

Trademarks and Trade Names

Articles bearing counterfeit trademarks or marks that copy or simulate a registered trademark of a U.S. or foreign corporation are prohibited importation, provided a copy of the U.S. trademark registration is filed with the Commissioner of Customs and recorded in the manner provided by regulations. The U.S. Customs Service also affords similar protection against unauthorized shipments bearing trade names that are recorded with Customs pursuant to regulations. The importation of "parallel" or "gray market" goods is also restricted where the registered trade mark has been recorded with Customs and gray-market protection has been afforded. It is also unlawful to import articles bearing genuine trademarks owned by a U.S. citizen or corporation without permission of the U.S. trademark owner, if the foreign and domestic trademark owners are not parent and subsidiary companies or otherwise under common ownership and control, provided the trademark has been recorded with Customs. (15 USC 1124; 19 USC 1526). Refer to 19 CFR 133, "Trademarks, Trade Names, and Copyrights" for more information.

The Customs Reform and Simplification Act of 1978 strengthened the protection afforded trademark owners against the importation of articles bearing a counterfeit mark. A "counterfeit trademark" is defined as a spurious trademark that is identical with, or substantially indistinguishable from, a registered trademark. Articles bearing a counterfeit trademark that are seized by Customs and for

feited to the government may be (1) given to any Federal, state, or local government agency that has established a need for the article; (2) given to a charitable institution; or (3) sold at public auction if more than 90 days has passed since forfeiture and no eligible organization has established a need for the article. The counterfeit marks must be removed before the forfeited articles may be given away or sold. If this is not feasible, the articles are destroyed. The law also provides an exemption from all restrictions on trademarked articles (limited to one of each type) accompanying a person arriving in the U.S. when the articles are for personal use and not for sale. Only one infringing item of each type bearing a registered trademark is permitted. An individual may take advantage of this exemption only once within a 30-day period (19 U.S.C. 1526 (d); 19 CFR 148.55).

Copyrights

Section 602(a) of the Copyright Revision Act of 1976 (17 USC 602(a)) provides that the importation into the U.S. of copies of a work acquired outside the U.S. without authorization of the copyright owner is an infringement of the copyright. Articles imported in violation of the import prohibitions are subject to seizure and forfeiture. Forfeited articles shall be destroyed; however, the articles may be returned to the country of export whenever Customs is satisfied that there was no intentional violation. The substantial similarity test is employed to determine if a design has been copied. Copyright owners seeking import protection from the U.S. Customs Service must register their claim to copyright with the U.S. Copyright Office and record their registration with Customs in accordance with applicable regulations. For more information, refer to 19 CFR 133 Subpart D, "Recordation of Copyrights," and Subpart E, "Importations Violating Copyright Laws".

Obscene, Immoral, and Seditious Matter

Section 305, Tariff Act of 1930, as amended, prohibits the importation of any book, writing, advertisement, circular, or picture containing any matter advocating or urging treason or insurrection against the U.S., or forcible resistance to any law of the U.S., or containing any threat to take the life of or inflict bodily harm upon any person in the U.S., or any obscene book, writing, advertisement, circular, picture, or other representation, figure, or image on or of paper or other material, or any instrument, or other article that is obscene or immoral, or any drug or medicine for causing unlawful abortion unless otherwise authorized by law (e.g., FDA approved), or any lottery ticket (except if printed in Canada for use in a U.S. or, in some cases, other foreign lottery. Refer to 19 CFR 12.40–12.41, "Immoral Articles," and 19 CFR 145.51(a)(1), "Articles prohibited by section 305, Tariff Act of 1930."

Other Prohibitions and Restrictions

Petroleum and Petroleum Products

Importations of petroleum and petroleum products are subject to the requirements of the Department of Energy. An import license is no longer required. These importations may be subject to an oil import license fee collected and administered by the Department of Energy.

Products of Convict or Forced Labor

Merchandise produced, mined, or manufactured by means of the use of convict labor, forced labor, or indentured labor under penal sanctions is prohibited importation, provided a finding has been published in the *Federal Register* that certain classes of merchandise from a particular country, produced by convict, forced, or indentured labor, were either being, or are likely to be, imported into the U.S. in violation of section 307 of the Tariff Act of 1930, as amended (19 USC 1307). For more information, refer to 19 CFR 12.42–12.45, "Merchandise Produced by Convict, Forced, or Indentured Labor."

Products of Unfair Competition

Section 337 of the Tariff Act, as amended, prohibits the importation of merchandise if the President finds that unfair methods of competition or unfair acts exist. This section is most commonly invoked in the case of patent violations, although a patent need not be at issue. Prohibition of entries of the merchandise in question generally is for the term of the patent, although a different term may by specified.

Following a section 337 investigation, the International Trade Commission may find that unfair methods of competition or unfair acts exist with respect to the importation of certain merchandise. After the International Trade Commission has issued an order, the President is allowed 60 days to take action; should the 60 days expire without Presidential action, the order becomes final. During the 60-day period or until the President acts, importation of the merchandise is allowed under a special bond but it must be recalled by Customs if appropriate under the conditions of the order when it becomes final. If the President determines that entry of the merchandise is not in violation of section 337, the bond is canceled.

For more information, refer to 19 CFR 12.39–12.39a, "Unfair Competition."

Foreign Assets Control Restrictions

The Office of Foreign Assets Control (OFAC) in the Department of the Treasury administers regulations (31 CFR, Chapter V) that impose economic sanctions against a number of countries the U.S. government has judged to be hostile to U.S. foreign policy and national security objectives. Other regulatory agencies, including Export Enforcement at the Department of Commerce and Customs & Border Protection, cooperate with OFAC to ensure compliance.

Importation of merchandise or goods that contain components from the following countries, is prohibited: Taliban (Afghanistan), Cuba, Iran (see note below), Iraq, Libya, Serbia (see note below), and Sudan. These restrictions apply to the country of origin, regardless of where the item was acquired. These proscriptions do not apply to informational materials such as pamphlets, books, tapes, films, or recordings, except those from Iraq. There are also strong restrictions on the importation of rough diamonds from Sierra Leone, Angola, and Liberia. Contact your local port for more information on these so-called "conflict diamonds."

Note regarding Iran: The embargo on Iranian goods is being revised to allow the importation of carpets and foods for human consumption such as caviar and pistachios.

Please check with your local port to find out when the new regulations are scheduled to take effect. Until new regulations are published, the complete embargo is still in force.

Note regarding Serbia (Yugoslavia): The U.S. trade embargo against Serbia (Yugoslavia) has been partially lifted to permit the importation of Serbian merchandise. However, certain individuals or groups remain subject to the trade embargo. Refer to OFAC's website at www.treas.gov/ofac or contact the OFAC Licensing Division at (202) 622-2480 for a complete listing of prohibited parties.

Specific licenses are required to bring prohibited merchandise into the U.S., but they are rarely granted. Foreign visitors to the U.S., however, may be permitted to bring in small articles for personal use as accompanied baggage, depending on the goods and the country of origin.

Travelers should be aware of certain travel restrictions that may apply to these countries. Because of the strict enforcement of these prohibitions, those anticipating foreign travel to any of the countries listed above would do well to write in advance to the Office of Foreign Assets Control, Department of the Treasury, Washington, DC 20220, or to call (202) 622-2500. Also, for further information, refer to 19 CFR 12.150, "Merchandise Subject to Economic Sanctions.

Civil penalties imposed by OFAC are up to $10,000 for violations under the Emergency Economic Powers Act (50 USC 1701–1706), up to $50,000 for violations of the Trading With the Enemy Act (50 USC App. 1–44), and up to $275,000 for violations of the Iraqi Sanctions Act (104 Stat. 2047–2055). Other penalty caps vary. "

Other Products

Matches. The importation into the U.S. of white phosphorus matches is prohibited. Invoices covering matches must be accompanied by a certificate of official inspection, as described at 19 CFR 12.34.

Switchblade Knives. Many switchblade knives are prohibited or restricted under 15 USC 1241–1245. More details on Customs Service restrictions and procedures can be found at 19 CFR 12.95–12.103, "Switchblade Knives."

Lottery Matter. Under section 305 of the Tariff Act of 1930, as amended (19 USC 1305), lottery matter, except any lottery ticket, printed paper that may be used as a lottery ticket, or advertisement of any lottery, that is printed in Canada for use in connection with a lottery conducted in the United States, is prohibited. Also see 19 CFR 145.51.

Cultural Property and Pre-Columbian Artifacts. The 1970 UNESCO Convention on Means of Prohibiting and Preventing the Illicit Import, Export, and Transfer of Ownership of Cultural Property prohibits the importation into the U.S. of cultural property and certain archaeological and ethnological material. In addition, the U.S. government also prohibits the importation of pre-Columbian artifacts. For more information, refer to 19 CFR 12.104–12.104i, "Cultural Property," and to 19 CFR 12.105–12.109, "Pre-Columbian Monumental and Architectural Sculpture and Murals."

Also, importations of certain archeological and ethnographic material from El Salvador, Guatemala, Peru, Mali, and Canada are specifically restricted from entering the United States unless they are accompanied by an export certificate issued by the country of origin. The U.S. Customs Service has published import restrictions on objects and artifacts of this nature in the Federal Register; these restrictions may also be viewed at the U.S. Information Agency's Web site, **www.usia.gov/education/culprop.** These restrictions are aimed at deterring the pillage of other countries' cultural heritage and at fostering opportunities for access to cultural objects for legitimate scientific, cultural, and educational purposes.

Federal law also prohibits the importation of any article of cultural property stolen from museums or from religious or secular public monuments. Importers should be aware that a treaty exists between the United States and Mexico on cultural property recovery. Would-be buyers of such property should be aware that, unlike purchases of customary tourist merchandise, purchases of cultural objects do not confer ownership, should the object be found to be stolen. The U.S. National Stolen Property Act may be applicable in such cases, particularly if a country of origin declares by law that it owns all cultural objects, known or unknown, within its present-day political boundaries.

Purveyors of such merchandise have been known to offer fake export certificates. Prospective buyers should be aware that Customs inspectors are expert at spotting fraudulent export certificates that accompany cultural property. Customs inspectors will also examine declaration forms to determine whether any false information has been entered, since this also constitutes a violation.

For current information about countries for which the United States has issued specific import restrictions, contact the United States Information Agency, Washington, DC, Tel. (202) 619-6612, or visit the agency's Web site: http://exchanges.state.gov/education/culprop.

United States Trade Representative Actions

As authorized by the Trade Act of 1974, the United States Trade Representative (USTR) administers Section 301 complaints against foreign unfair trade practices that harm U.S. exporters. USTR actions that may directly affect U.S. importers include the suspension of concessions. For example, the USTR may suspend the normal-trade-relations rate of duty and substitute a substantially higher rate of duty on designated products from a foreign country that is found to be discriminating against U.S. products.

Importers and Internet shoppers should monitor the USTR web site (http://192.239.92.165/index.html) on a regular basis to determine whether their products may become subject to a substituted rate of duty. The USTR will normally propose a list of products and provide a comment period for businesses that may be affected by a higher duty rate.

The International Trade Administration at the Department of Commerce has set up a notification system that will advise importers of USTR actions that may affect imported products. Importers who wish to receive such notification should sign up at the following URL: http://www.ita.doc.gov/td/industry/otea/301-alert/form.html.

Importers should be advised that once the USTR has taken a Section 301 action, U.S. Customs is responsible for implementing the action as directed by USTR. Information on USTR actions that U.S. Customs is currently implementing is located at the following Internet address: http://www.customs.treas.gov/impoexpo/ustract.htm.

Textile and Apparel Products

The U.S. Customs Service administers a variety of import controls of certain cotton, wool, man-made fiber articles, silk blends and other vegetable fibers manufactured or produced in designated countries. Information concerning specific import controls in effect and visa requirements may be obtained from the Commissioner of Customs. Other information concerning the textile program may be obtained from the Department of Commerce, Office of Textiles, International Agreements Division. Refer to 19 CFR 12.130–12.132 for various Customs regulations on the entry of textiles and textile products.

Textile Visa Requirements

A textile visa is an endorsement in the form of a stamp on an invoice or export control license which is executed by a foreign government. It is used to control the exportation of textiles and textile products to the United States and to prohibit the unauthorized entry of the merchandise into this country.

The visa system is used to prevent illegal transshipments and quota fraud and to ensure that both the foreign government and the United States count merchandise and charge quotas in the same way so that overshipments, incorrect quota charges and embargoes can be avoided. If a visa has an incorrect category, quantity or other incorrect or missing data, or a shipment arrives without a visa, the entry is rejected and the merchandise is not released until the importer reports the discrepancy to the foreign government and receives a new visa or visa waiver from the government.

A visa does not guarantee entry of the merchandise into the U.S. If the quota closes between the time the visa is issued in the foreign country and the shipments arrival in the U.S. the shipment will not be released to the importer until the quota opens again. A visa may cover either quota or non-quota merchandise. Conversely, quota merchandise may or may not require a visa depending upon the country of origin.

Each visa agreement is different. Most are comprehensive agreements. This means that all commercial shipments of textiles or textile products of vegetable fibers, wool, man-made fibers, and silk blends covered by a category number from a country with which the U.S. has such an agreement must be accompanied by a visa in order to enter the U.S. However, other agreements cover only a specific, limited number of categories. A further difference can be found in agreements which require the visa to show the exact category and quantity in the shipment while others do not.

To administer these agreements, textile products are grouped under 3-digit category numbers. The category numbers were developed by the Committee for the Implementation of Textile Agreements (CITA), an interagency committee comprised of representatives from the Departments of State, Commerce, Labor, and the Treasury and the Office of the U.S. Trade Representative. These category designations cover several thousand 10-digit legal/statistical item numbers under which the merchandise is classified in the HTSUS.

When a shipment arrives at a port in the United States, the Customs import specialist reviews the visa documents for accuracy and completeness before releasing the merchandise. The review ensures that the category number, quantity, signature, date, and visa number are correct and match the shipment involved. Only after this action is completed and the merchandise is charged to the quota (if required) is the shipment released to the importer.

Electronic Visa Information System (ELVIS)

ELVIS is an electronic "visa" system for textiles. A visa works like a passport. It serves as an approval issued by a foreign country's government - or by its representative - and officially permits the exportation of textile products into the United States. It describes the shipment, certifies the country-of-origin, and authorizes the shipment to be charged against any applicable quota. Countries participating in the ELVIS can request a Visa Activity Report that will provide them with valuable textile quota information.

Countries participating in the ELVIS program: Bangladesh, Cambodia, China, Hong Kong, Indonesia, South Korea, Malaysia, Pakistan, Philippines, Singapore, Sri Lanka, Taiwan, and Thailand.

The big advantage to ELVIS is that it can protect a country's sensitive textile quota limits from visa misrepresentation and fraud against their quota restraints caused by illegal U.S. exportation. Exporters that illegally enter goods under another foreign country's quota limit can cost that country thousands of dollars in lost revenue by reducing the import allocation of the country reported by U.S. Customs.

With ELVIS, once the "electronic" visa information is received by Customs from a foreign country, it is held pending the transmission of entry and visa information by the actual importer, or his authorized representative, at entry. When documents are compared electronically by the system, and if the critical data elements sent by both the foreign country and the importer match, the shipment is released and the quota is reported. Without the matching criteria the shipment is detained or rejected thus protecting it from fraud.

All ELVIS participants are required to submit paper visas that support the electronic transmission, when starting the program. To participate countries must apply for ELVIS by submitting a written application/request to U.S. Customs that includes:

- name of the country's authorized service provider (asp). A signed agreement executed between the foreign government and its appointed ASP, or an indication that the foreign government is selecting an ASP.

- proof of technical capability. Supplied by the authorized service provider, the data ensure that the ASP can connect directly to a network that is pre-certified by Customs.

- contact(s) oversight. Person(s) responsible for ELVIS in the government of the foreign country.

For more information contact the Office of Field Operations at (202) 927-5399/5396, or visit the Customs Web site, Importing & Exporting, Textiles & Quotas.

Textile and Apparel Imports Under NAFTA

There are some additional requirements for textile and apparel goods imported under NAFTA. All commercial importations of textile and apparel goods must be accompanied by the appropriate declaration. A declaration made by each Canadian or Mexican manufacturer or producer of the goods must be furnished by the importer. If the port director cannot determine the country of origin because the information in the declaration is incomplete, the shipment is not entitled to preferential treatment under NAFTA. Some importers may need to submit a Certificate of Eligibility covering the goods. For more information, refer to 19 CFR 12.132, "Textile and apparel goods under the North American Free Trade Agreement."

Introduction to Country of Origin Rules

Section 334 of the Uruguay Round Agreements Act (Pub. L. 103-465, codified as 19 U.S.C. §3592) established rules of origin for textile and apparel products which are imported into the Customs Territory of the United States. Except as otherwise provided by statute, these rules apply for purposes of the Customs laws and the administration of quantitative restrictions (quotas). The law required the Secretary of the Treasury to promulgate implementing regulations, which appear as section 102.21 of the Customs Regulations (§102.21 CR, 19 CFR §102.21). Section 405 of the Trade and Development Act of 2000 (Pub. L. 106-200) amended Section 334 of the Uruguay Round Agreements Act to clarify the rules of origin for certain textile products. Please be advised that Customs is in the process of amending the regulations contained in 19 CFR §102.21 to reflect the changes mandated by Section 405.

The country of origin rules contained in 19 CFR §102.21 apply to textile and apparel products (see below for coverage) entered, or withdrawn from warehouse, for consumption on or after July 1, 1996. This date is set by law and does not provide for a grace period, shipments on the water, time entered into the port limits, entry rejects or any other exceptions except for certain pre-existing contracts entered into prior to July 20, 1994 which were required to be filed with the Commissioner of Customs. The country of origin rules, as amended by Section 405 of the Trade and Development Act of 2000, apply to goods entered or withdrawn from warehouse for consumption, on or after May 18, 2000.

Pre-Existing Contracts

All contracts to be considered for an 18-month grace period had to be submitted within 60 days after enactment of the Uruguay Round Agreements Act. Action has been completed on all contracts that were filed. All manufacturers who submitted such contracts were notified of the status of their contracts.

Coverage

The §334 country of origin rules for textile and apparel products apply to the textile items classified in Chapters 50 through 63 of the Harmonized Tariff Schedule (HTS) and to the following textile items in the HTS classifications listed below which have been defined by the World Trade Organization as textile and apparel products:

3005.90 Wadding, gauze, bandages and the like (nonadhesive)

3921.12 Woven, knitted or non-woven fabrics coated, covered or laminated with plastics

3921.13 Woven, knitted or non-woven fabrics coated, covered or laminated with plastics

3921.90 Woven, knitted or non-woven fabrics coated, covered or laminated with plastics

4202 Luggage, handbags, and flatgoods with an outer surface predominantly of textile materials

6405.20 Footwear with soles and uppers of wool felt

6406.10 Footwear uppers with 50% or more of the external surface area of textile materials

6406.99 Leg warmers and gaiters of textile material

6501- 6505 Headwear of textiles

6601 Umbrellas

7019 Yarns and woven fabrics of glass fibers

8708 Safety seat belts for motor vehicles

8804 Parachutes; their parts and accessories

9113.90 Watch straps, bands and bracelets of textile materials

9404.90 Comforters, quilts, pillows and cushions, and similar articles of textile materials

9502.91 Doll clothing

9612.10 Woven typewriter ribbons or similar ribbons, of man-made fibers More specific classifications for the above products, beyond the four digit headings or six digit subheadings provided above, can be found in the Federal Register, Vol. 60, No. 171, September 5, 1995, page 46198, and in §102.21 CR, (19 CFR §102.21).

General Rules for Country of Origin

In general, except as otherwise provided for by law, a textile or apparel product, for purposes of the Customs laws and the administration of quantitative restrictions, originates in a country, territory or insular possession according to the following rules:

Wholly Produced Goods

The country of origin is the country in which a product is wholly produced when a textile or apparel product is completely produced or manufactured (except for minor parts) in one country.

Yarn, Including Single and Multiple Yarns. The country of origin of yarn, thread, twine, cordage, rope, braiding, etc., is:

a. Staple yarn, etc.—The country in which yarn is spun

b. Filament yarn, etc.—The country in which filament is extruded

c. Plied, gimped and cabled yarns, etc.—The country in which the fibers or filaments used in the yarn are spun or extruded.

Fabric. The country of origin of a fabric is the country in which the fabric is woven, knitted, needled, tufted, felted, entangled or created by any other fabric-making process. (A fabric-making process is any manufacturing operation that begins with polymers, fibers, filaments, yarns, twine, cordage, rope, or fabric strips and results in a textile fabric.) Note that the country of origin of quilted fabrics is the country in which the fabrics are produced.

The country of origin of fabric classified under the Harmonized Tariff Schedule as of silk, cotton, man-made fiber, or vegetable fiber is the country in which the fabric is both dyed and printed when accompanied by two or more of the following finishing operations: bleaching, shrinking, fulling, napping, decating, permanent stiffening, weighting, permanent embossing or moireing.

All Other Textile Products. The country of origin of all other textile and apparel products is the country in which the components of a textile or apparel product are wholly assembled (except for minor attachments such as buttons, beads, spangles, embroidery, etc., or minor subassemblies such as collars, cuffs, pockets, plackets, etc.)

Note: The rules generally provide that processing operations or assembly (particularly for apparel), not cutting components, confer country of origin (however, this condition may vary under pre-existing contracts or with Israel and its insular possession).

Exceptions

a. The country of origin of knit-to-shape products is the country in which major parts are knitted or crocheted directly to the shape used in the finished product. Knit-to-shape means that the panels or parts (except minor parts) are knit to the shape used in the final assembly process, rather than knit into a tube or blanket of material that is cut to shape. Minor cutting, sewing or assembly does not affect whether components are knit to shape. Knit-to-shape applies when 50 percent or more of the exterior surface area (not including patch pockets, appliques, etc.) is knitted or crocheted. For hosiery, the addition of gussets or top elastics or the closing of toes does not affect the status of knit-to-shape.

b. The country of origin of articles made from yarn, strips, twine, cordage, rope or cables is the country in which the yarn, etc., is produced
HTSUS 5609—Articles produced from yarns

c. The country of origin of certain articles made from fabric in the following eighteen (18) Harmonized Tariff Schedule classifications is the country in which the fabric is both dyed and printed when accompanied by two or more of the following finishing operations: bleaching, shrinking, fulling, napping, decating, permanent stiffening, weighting, permanent embossing or moireing, excepting goods classified under such headings as of cotton or wool or consisting of fiber blends containing sixteen percent (16%) or more by weight of cotton (the HTS classifications are followed by general descriptions):

6117.10 knitted or crocheted shawls, scarves, mufflers, mantillas, veils and the like

6213 handkerchiefs, not knitted or crocheted

6214 shawls, scarves, mufflers, mantillas, veils and the like, not knitted or crocheted

6302.22 printed bed linen, not knitted or crocheted, of man-made fibers

6302.29 printed bed linen, not knitted or crocheted, of other textile materials

6302.52 table linen, not knitted or crocheted, of flax

6302.53 table linen, not knitted or crocheted, of man-made fibers

6302.59 table linen, not knitted or crocheted, of other textile materials

6302.92 toilet and kitchen linen of flax

6302.93 toilet and kitchen linen of man-made fibers

6302.99 toilet and kitchen linen of other textile materials

6303.92 curtains, including drapes, interior blinds and bed valances, not knitted or crocheted, of synthetic fibers

6303.99 curtains, including drapes, interior blinds and bed valances, not knitted or crocheted, of other textile materials

6304.19 bedspreads, not knitted or crocheted

6304.93 other furnishing articles, not knitted or crocheted, of synthetic fibers

6304.99 other furnishing articles, not knitted or crocheted, of other textile materials

9404.90.85 quilts, eiderdowns, comforters and similar articles

9404.90.95 other articles of bedding and similar furnishings

Multi-Country Rule

If the country of origin of a textile or apparel product cannot be determined by one of the above rules and the product is created as a result of processing in two or more countries, the country of origin is:

a. The country in which the most important assembly or most important manufacturing process occurs.

The most important processing operation must be determined on a case-bycase basis through binding rulings and court decisions. The resulting body of rulings and court decisions may serve as guidelines in the future. .

b. (A) If the most important assembly or manufacturing process cannot be determined, the country of origin is the last country in which an important assembly or manufacturing operation occurred.

For example: if the right half of a coat is assembled in one country and the left half is assembled in another country, and provided the processing steps in each country are equally balanced, then the country of origin is probably the country in which the two halves are sewn together (that is, the last country in which an important processing operation occurred because each half is equally impor-

tant. More realistically, if one yarn of a plied yarn is produced in one country and the other yarn is produced in a second country, and the yarns are twisted to form a plied yarn, then, assuming both yarns are equal in the final product, the country in which the yarns are twisted together is the country of origin because each yarn is equally important and you have to resort to the last country in which an important processing occurred.

Another example of when the last important processing rule would be used to determine origin is in the case of a tent in which the fabric for the roof and floor are produced in one country, the fabric for the walls is produced in another country, and all the fabrics are cut and assembled in a third country. As a tent is classified in heading 6306, according to the language of §334 its origin should be based on where the fabric for the tent is formed. But as the fabric is formed in different countries, and it is difficult to argue that fabric for roofs and floors is more important than fabric for walls, resort to the last important processing, i.e., where the fabrics are cut and sewn into the tent, renders the origin determination.

Multi-country processing of goods often leads to origin determinations based upon the place where the most important processing operation occurred or, if that cannot be ascertained, the last place where an important processing operation occurred. Such determinations can only be made on a case-by-case basis, conditioned upon the specific facts in each case. As such, binding rulings should be requested from:

> Office of Rulings and Regulations
> Commercial Rulings Division
> Customs & Border Protection
> 1300 Pennsylvania Ave., NW
> Washington, DC 20229

Although ruling requests may be sent to New York or Headquarters, as a general rule initial rulings are issued by the National Commodity Specialist Division in New York, while Customs Headquarters considers any appeals.

The requestor should be sure to specify that the ruling is requested pursuant to the textile and apparel rules of origin in §334, as amended. Complete information should be supplied as to manufacturing and processing and a sample (or drawings if a sample is not practical) showing exact subassemblies or processing steps should be submitted with the request for a ruling. Rulings requested from New York should be answered within 30 days if information provided by the requestor is complete.

Hierarchy of Rules

The above rules are arranged in a hierarchy to be applied in the following sequential order as specified in Customs Regulation §102.21 (c)(and pursuant to the amendments contained in Section 405 of the Trade and Development Act)(§102.21 is currently in the process of being amended to reflect the amendments to §334 set forth in Section 405):

1. Textile or apparel products wholly produced in one country.

2. Each foreign material undergoes requisite tariff shift (as provided in Customs Regulation 102.21).

All textile and apparel products are listed by 4-digit to 10-digit HTS classifications or groups of classifications in the tariff shift rules. The tariff shift rules simply explain the requirements to change the country of origin of textile and apparel products (as shown in the preceding section) by using tariff classifications rather than textile or apparel product descriptions. A tariff shift states that, for any given classification, to change the country of origin of a textile or apparel product there must be a shift from one Harmonized Tariff Schedule (HTS) classification to another as listed in the tariff shift rules and/or the processing which occurs must meet any other requirement that is specified in the tariff shift rules in Customs Regulation §102.21(e).

For example, one group of classifications in the tariff shift rules is 5208 through 5212, which contain the classifications for cotton woven fabrics. The tariff shift rule for classifications 5208-5212 states that:

- A change from greige fabric of heading 5208 through 5212 to finished fabric of heading 5208 through 5212 by both dyeing and printing when accompanied by two or more of the following finishing operations: bleaching, shrinking, fulling, napping, decating, permanent stiffening, weighting, permanent embossing, or moireing; or

- If the country of origin cannot be determined under the rule above, a change to heading 5208 through 5212 from any classification outside that group, provided that the change is the result of a fabric forming-making process.

To confer country of origin to a cotton woven fabric, a greige fabric must have been dyed and printed and accompanied by two or more specified finishing operations. For example, a greige fabric formed in China which is imported into Pakistan where it is dyed, printed, shrunk and permanently embossed will be country of origin Pakistan.

In the alternative, the creation of the fabric must be from some product other than another cotton woven fabric; for example, the fabric could be formed from cotton yarns, or from polyester and cotton yarns, from fibers or any other product except cotton woven fabric (e.g., joining two narrow fabrics). The second requirement of creating a fabric from a fabric forming process must also be met. This tariff shift rule merely restates the fabric rule (in the section above) using tariff classification terms or definitions.

The result is that the determination of the country of origin is defined in objective tariff classification shifts rather than subjective terms such as .substantial assembly. or .new commercial product.. By using HTS classifications, there is no doubt when a change in the country of origin occurs. If a shipper knows the classification of a textile product he is exporting, he merely has to locate the classification in the tariff shift rules to see if the required change of classifications occurred when the product was produced or manufactured. If the tariff shift has occurred and any other listed requirement is met, then the country of origin is changed by the processing.

For example, the tariff classification for 5204 through 5207 (cotton yarns) states that the tariff shift must be from any

other heading provided that the change or shift results from a spinning process. This defines the country of origin for spun yarns (see above). The tariff shifts for 5208 through 5212 require a shift from classifications for yarns, fibers or filaments that results from a fabric making process, or a change from greige fabric to finished fabric that is both dyed and printed when accompanied by two or more specified finishing operations. Similarly, shifts for 6302 require that the country of origin of certain linens must be from the fabric forming process, i.e., the country in which the fabric was woven and not the country in which the fabric for the linens were cut and sewn, while certain other linens may originate in the country where the fabric comprising the good was both dyed and printed when accompanied by two or more specified finishing operations.

3. Textile or apparel products for which the major components are knit-to-shape.

4. Textile or apparel products wholly assembled in one country except for the 16 specified exceptions.

When the product is produced in two or more countries and the country of origin cannot be determined by the four rules above, the country of origin is:

5. The country in which the most important processing occurs, and, if that cannot be determined,

6. The last country in which an important processing operation occurs.

Cutting does not confer country of origin. The above rules are based on assembly operations, not on cutting.

Special Considerations

Sets. If one or more components in a set are textile articles and there is no single country of origin for these components, the country of origin for each textile component of the set is determined separately. A composite good will continue to be considered as one combined good.

Products of Israel. Israel is an exception to the country of origin rules. The country of origin for textile and apparel products from Israel will continue to be determined by the rules in §12.130, CR (19 CFR §12.130), e.g., the origin of most garments is the country in which the components are cut to shape, although for tailored or complex garments, the origin is the country in which the garments are wholly assembled. In T.D. 96-58, published in the Federal Register on July 31, 1996, Customs explained how to determine the origin of textile and apparel products that are processed in Israel and another country. If Israel is determined not to be the country of origin under §12.130, CR (19 CFR §12.130), then the rules in §102.21 are applied to determine the origin. As Israel cannot be found to be the country of origin under §102.21, CR, the processing in Israel will be disregarded when applying the steps in §102.21.

Insular Possessions. The §102.21 country of origin rules apply to the insular possessions of the United States. The rules will be used to determine whether the goods qualify as a product of the insular possession under General Note 3(a)(iv) of the Harmonized Tariff Schedules of the United States.

However, Customs will continue to follow past rulings to determine whether foreign fabric has been subjected to a double substantial transformation, for purposes of the 50 percent foreign material content restriction under General Note 3(a)(iv). Cutting will continue to be used to maintain current status in achieving a double substantial transformation. The first portion of the substantial transformation test may occur when fabric is cut into components, while the second may occur when the components are assembled into wearing apparel. In determining whether the apparel meets the 50 percent foreign value limitation, components which undergo a double substantial transformation are (and will continue to be) treated as materials produced in the insular possession rather than as foreign materials.

This concept results in the fact that textile and apparel products produced in the insular possession, and which qualified for duty-free treatment in the past, continue to enter the U.S. commerce free of duties.

Components Cut in the U.S. from Foreign Fabric and Assembled Abroad (HTSUS 9802). The value of components cut to shape (but not to length, width or both) in the U.S. from foreign fabric and exported for assembly abroad into an article that is then returned is not included in the dutiable value of the finished article imported into the U.S. (See §10.25, CR).

a.   For textile and apparel products that do not have category numbers (e.g. umbrellas, parachutes), as well as all footwear and parts of footwear, assembled in a Caribbean Basin Initiative (CBI) country from components that were cut to shape (but not including pieces merely cut to length and/or width) in the U.S. from foreign fabric, the assembled textile articles are not subject to duty. (See, §10.26, CR).

This provision is necessary in the statute because under the country of origin rules cutting does not confer country of origin, and therefore components cut in the U.S. of foreign fabric are not considered to be U.S. products. The definition of textile and apparel products includes articles that were not considered as textile articles by the United States prior to implementation of the new World Trade Organization definitions. This provision continues the current duty free treatment under U.S. Note 2(b), Subchapter II, Chapter 98 of the Harmonized Tariff Schedule of the United States.

b.   The value of the components cut in the U.S. from foreign fabric, up to the 15 percent cap for U.S. origin materials, may be applied toward determining the minimum 35 percent requirement to qualify for the benefits of CBI.

NAFTA Overrides. Any NAFTA override rules currently in existence will continue to be applied if a NAFTA preference is claimed.

For example China is the country of origin of comforter shells and also the country of origin of down used to fill the shells. Both of these components are sent to Canada where the down is inserted into the shells. The country of origin of the finished comforter under the §334 rules of origin is China. However, NAFTA provides for an override rule that applies if a claim is made. Because the processing in Canada (a NAFTA country) satisfies the NAFTA duty preference rule, if a claim is made for duty preference at the time of entry (or within one year), the country of origin is Canada. The NAFTA preference rule continues to override the §334 country of origin rules in determining the country of origin for NAFTA products.

U.S. Goods Sent Abroad for Processing. For a U.S. produced textile good sent abroad for processing which results in an advancement in value or improvement in condition:

a.   For duty assessment purposes, the good will continue to be considered foreign under Note 2(a), Subchapter II, Chapter 98, HTS;

b.   For quota purposes, the good will continue to be considered foreign under §12.130(c), CR.

c.   For the purposes of the marking statute, 19 U.S.C. 1304, the origin of a textile or apparel good is determined by the rules under §102.21. Section 12.130 (c) no longer applies for marking purposes. See T.D. 00-41, 65 FR 42634 (July 11, 2000). Therefore, a U.S. good which is processed abroad (advanced in value or improved in condition) must be marked with the country of origin determined pursuant to §102.21.

For example, fabric woven in the United States is shipped to China where it is cut and sewn into tents. According to §102.21, the origin of the tents is the country where the fabric comprising the good was formed by a fabric-making process. Thus, the country of origin is the United States and the tents will not be required to be marked for purposes of the marking statute. However, the country of origin for duty assessment and quota purposes will be China. The goods are also still subject to the labeling rules of the Federal Trade Commission. If the U.S. fabric was cut to shape (as opposed to merely length and width) in the United States and assembled into tents in China, the tents could receive a partial duty exemption under subheading 9802.00.80, HTSUS.

Coverage

In addition to the textile items found in Chapters 50 through 63 of the HTSUS and any other classifications with category numbers, the following textile items in the classifications listed below also have been defined by the World Trade Organization as textile and apparel products and are subject to the U.S. country of origin rules for textile and apparel products: 3005—Nonadhesive wadding, gauze bandages; 3921—PVC and PU sheets, film, etc.; 4202—Luggage, handbags, etc.; 6605—Footwear of textiles; 6601—Umbrellas; 7019—Fiberglass yarns and fabrics; 8708—Automobile seat belts; 8804—Parachutes; 9113—Watch straps; 9404—Comforters, quilts, pillows; 9502—Doll clothing; 9612—Typewriter ribbons

The specific classifications of the above products up to 10 digits can be found in the Federal Register, Vol. 60, No. 171, September 5, 1995, page 46198, and in 19 CFR 102.21(e).

Marking and Labeling Requirements

Textile Fiber Products. All textile fiber products imported into the U.S. must be stamped, tagged, labeled, or otherwise marked with the following information as required by the Textile Fiber Products Identification Act, unless exempted from marking under section 12 of the Act:

a.   The generic names and percentages by weight of the constituent fibers present in the textile fiber product, exclusive of permissive ornamentation, in amounts of more than 5% in order of predominance by weight, with any percentage of fiber or fibers required to be designated as "other fiber" or "other fibers" appearing last. Fibers present in amounts of 5% or less must be designated as "other fibers."

b. The name of the manufacturer or the name or registered identification number issued by the Federal Trade Commission of one or more persons marketing or handling the textile fiber product. A word trademark, used as a house mark, registered in the U.S. Patent Office, may be on labels in lieu of the name otherwise required if the owner of such trademark furnishes a copy of the registration to the Federal Trade Commission prior to use.

c. The name of the country where processed or manufactured.

For the purpose of the enforcement of the Textile Fiber Products Identification Act, a commercial invoice covering a shipment of textile fiber products exceeding $500 in value and subject to the labeling requirements of the Act is required to show the information noted in Chapter 6, above, in addition to that ordinarily required on the invoices.

Regulations and pamphlets containing the text of the Textile Fiber Products Identification Act may be obtained from the Federal Trade Commission, Washington, DC 20580. For more information, also refer to 19 CFR 12.130–12.132, "Textiles and Textile Products" and the series of Customs Service "Informed Compliance" publications on textile imports.

Wool Products. Any product containing woolen fiber imported into the U.S.—with the exception of carpets, rugs, mats, upholsteries, and articles made more than 20 years prior to importation—shall be tagged, labeled, or otherwise clearly marked with the following information as required by the Wool Products Labeling Act of 1939:

a. The percentage of the total fiber weight of the wool product, exclusive of ornamentation not exceeding 5% of the total fiber weight of (1) wool, (2) recycled wool, (3) each fiber other than wool if the percent by weight of such fiber is 5% or more, and (4) the aggregate of all other fibers.

b. The maximum percent of the total weight of the wool product, of any nonfibrous loading, filling, or adulterating matter.

c. The name of the manufacturer or person introducing the product in commerce in the U.S.; i.e., the importer. If the importer has a registered identification number issued by the Federal Trade Commission, that number may be used instead of the individual's name.

For the purpose of the enforcement of the Wool Products Labeling Act, a commercial invoice covering a shipment of wool products exceeding $500 in value and subject to the labeling requirements of the act is required to show the information noted in "Commercial Invoice" on page 215.

The provisions of the Wool Products Labeling Act apply to products manufactured in the U.S. as well as to imported products. Pamphlets containing the text of the Wool Products Labeling Act and the regulations may be obtained from the Federal Trade Commission, Washington, DC

20580. Also refer to 19 CFR 11.12, "Labeling of wool products to indicate fiber content" and the Customs Service "Informed Compliance" publication on Fibers and Yarns.

Fur Products. Any article of wearing apparel imported into the U.S. and made in whole or in part of fur or used fur, with the exception of articles that are made of new fur of which the cost or manufacturer's selling price does not exceed $7, imported into the U.S. shall be tagged, labeled, or otherwise clearly marked to show the following information as required by the Fur Products Labeling Act:

a. The name of the manufacturer or person introducing the product in commerce in the U.S.; i.e., the importer. If the importer has a registered identification number, that number may be used instead of the individual's name.

b. The name or names of the animal or animals that produced the fur as set forth in the Fur Products Name Guide and as permitted under the rules and regulations.

c. That the fur product contains used or damaged fur when such is the fact.

d. That the fur product is bleached, dyed, or otherwise artificially colored when such is the fact.

e. That the fur product is composed in whole or in substantial part of paws, tails, bellies, or waste fur when such is the fact.

f. The name of the country of origin of any imported furs contained in a fur product.

For the purpose of enforcement of the Fur Products Labeling Act, a commercial invoice covering a shipment exceeding $500 in value of furs or fur products is required to show the information noted in "Commercial Invoice" on page 215.

The provisions of the Fur Products Labeling Act apply to fur and fur products in the U.S. as well as to imported furs and fur products. Regulations and pamphlets containing the text of the Fur Products Labeling Act may be obtained from the Federal Trade Commission, Washington, DC 20580. Also refer to 19 CFR 11.12a, "Labeling of fur products to indicate composition." In addition, there are special prohibitions on the importation of the skins of fur seals and sea otters listed at 19 CFR 12.60–12.63, as well as prohibitions on the importation of products of endangered species.

Dog or cat fur. The importation, exportation, transportation, distribution, or sale of any product that consists, or is composed in whole or in part, of any dog fur, cat fur, or both, is prohibited. Any such product that is imported exported, transported, distributed, or sold wil be seized and forfeited, and penalties may be imposed against any person who violates this law. In addition, anyone found to have violated this prohibition may be barred from importing or exporting any fur product. This prohibition does not apply to the importation, exportation, or transportation, for noncommercial purposes, of personal pets that are deceased, including a pet preserved through taxidermy.

The provisions of the Fur Products Labeling Act apply to fur and fur products in the United States as well as to imported furs and fur products. Regulations and pamphlets containing the text of the Fur Products Labeling Act may be obtained from the Federal Trade Commission, Washington, DC 20580.

Alcoholic Beverages

Any person or firm wishing to engage in the business of importing distilled spirits, wines, or malt beverages into the U.S. must first obtain an importer's basic permit from the Department of the Treasury, Bureau of Alcohol, Tobacco and Firearms (ATF), Alcohol Import/Export Branch, 650 Massachusetts Ave., Washington, DC 20226, Tel: (202) 927-8110.

That agency is responsible for administering the Federal Alcohol Administration Act. The basic permit requirements may not be applicable if the port director is satisfied that the liquor is for personal use or for experimental purposes in the making of analyses, tests, or comparisons.

Distilled spirits imported in bulk containers of a capacity of more than one gallon may be withdrawn from Customs custody only by persons to whom it is lawful to sell or otherwise dispose of distilled spirits in bulk. Bulk or bottled shipments of imported spirits or distilled or intoxicating liquors must at the time of importation be accompanied by a copy of a bill of lading or other documents, such as an invoice, showing the name of the consignee, the nature of its contents, and the quantity contained therein (18 USC 1263).

U.S. Customs will not release alcoholic beverages destined to any state for use in violation of its laws, and the importation of alcoholic beverages in the mails is prohibited (19 CFR 145.54).

The U.S. adopted the metric system of measure with the enactment of the Metric Conversion Act of 1975. In general, imported wine must conform with the metric standards of fill if bottled or packed on or after January 1, 1979. Imported distilled spirits, with some exceptions, must conform with the metric standards of fill if bottled or packed on or after January 1, 1980. Distilled spirits and wines bottled or packed prior to the respective dates must be accompanied by a statement to that effect signed by a duly authorized official of the appropriate foreign country. This statement may be a separate document or be shown on the invoice. Malt beverages including beer are not subject to metric standards of fill.

The blending or rectifying of wines or distilled spirits in class 6 manufacturing warehouses, or the bottling of imported distilled spirits in class 8 manipulation warehouses, is not permitted unless the proprietor has an appropriate permit from the ATF.

Marking Requirements

Imported wines in bottles and other containers are required to be packaged, marked, branded, and labeled in accordance with the regulations in 27 CFR Part 4. Imported malt beverages, including alcohol-free and nonalcoholic malt beverages, are also required to be labeled in conformance with the regulations in 27 CFR Part 7.

Each bottle, cask, or other immediate container of imported distilled spirits, wines, or malt beverages must be marked for customs purposes to indicate the country of origin of the alcoholic beverage contained therein, unless the shipment comes within legal exceptions.

Certificate of Label Approval

Labels affixed to bottles of imported distilled spirits and wine must be covered by certificates of label approval issued to the importer by the Bureau of Alcohol, Tobacco and Firearms. Certificates of label approval or photostatic copies must be filed with Customs before the goods may be released for sale in the U.S. Certificate of label approval requirements must also be met for fermented malt beverages if similar to the Federal requirements (27 CFR Parts 4, 5, and 7).

Foreign Documentation

Importers of wines and distilled spirits should consult the Bureau of Alcohol, Tobacco and Firearms about foreign documentation required; for example, certificates of origin, age, etc.

Requirements of Other Agencies

In addition, importation of alcoholic beverages is subject to the specific requirements of the Food and Drug Administration. Certain plant materials when used for bottle jackets for wine or other liquids are subject to special restrictions under plant quarantine regulations of the Animal and Plant Health Inspection Service. All bottle jackets made of dried or unmanufactured plant materials are subject to inspection upon arrival and are referred to the Department of Agriculture.

Wines or other distilled spirits from certain countries require original certificates of origin as a condition of entry: Bulgaria, Canada, Chile, France, Germany, Republic of Ireland, Jamaica, Mexico, Portugal, Romania, Spain, and United Kingdom.

Public Law 100-690, codified under 27 USC 213-219A, requires that a health warning appear on the labels of containers of alcoholic beverages bottled on or after November 18, 1989:

> **Government Warning:** (1) According to the Surgeon General, women should not drink alcoholic beverages during pregnancy because of the risks of birth defects. (2) Consumption of alcoholic beverages impairs your ability to drive a car or operate machinery and may cause health problems.

Motor Vehicles and Boats

Motor Vehicles

Imported motor vehicles are subject to safety standards under the Motor Vehicle Safety Act of 1966, revised under the Imported Vehicle Safety Compliance Act of 1988; to bumper standards under the Motor Vehicle Information and Cost Savings Act of 1972, which became effective in 1978; and to air pollution control standards under the Clean Air Act of 1968, as amended in 1977 and 1990. Most vehicles manufactured abroad that conform with U.S. safety, bumper, and emission standards are exported expressly for sale in the United States; therefore, it is unlikely that a vehicle obtained abroad meets all relevant standards. Be skeptical of claims by a foreign dealer or other seller that a vehicle meets these standards or can readily be brought into compliance. Nonconforming vehicles entering the United States must be brought into compliance, exported, or destroyed.

Vehicle Safety and Bumper Standards. As a general rule, all imported motor vehicles and items of motor vehicle equipment must comply with all applicable Federal Motor Vehicle Safety Standards in effect when these vehicles or items were manufactured. A Customs inspection at the time of entry will determine such compliance, which is verified by the original manufacturer's certification affixed to the vehicle or merchandise. A declaration, HS **Form 7**, must be filed when motor vehicles or items of motor vehicle equipment are entered. HS **Form 7** can be obtained from customs brokers or ports of entry.

If written approval is obtained from the U.S. Department of Transportation (DOT), certain temporary importations may be exempt from the requirements for certification and conformance, including vehicles brought in for research, investigation, studies, training, demonstrations, or competitive events. Also, vehicles imported for temporary use by certain nonresidents or members of foreign delegations or armed forces may not be required to comply. Vehicles and motor vehicle equipment imported solely with the intention of exportation and so labeled are also exempt from these requirements. Vehicles described in this paragraph may require EPA and DOT declarations (**form 3520-I** and HS **form 7**, respectively).

A DOT bond in the amount of 150% of the dutiable value must be posted at the port of entry when a noncertified or nonconforming vehicle is imported for permanent use. This bond is intended to assure conformance of the vehicle within 120 days after entry. The importer must also sign a contract with a DOT-registered importer, who will modify the vehicle to conform with all applicable safety and bumper standards, and who can certify the modification(s). A copy of this contract must be furnished to the Customs Service at the port of entry. Furthermore, the vehicle model and model year must, prior to entry, be determined to be eligible for importation. Federal regulations 49 CFR, parts 593 and 594 specify the petitioning process and fees required to obtain such a determination of eligibility.

For additional information or details on these requirements, contact the U.S. Department of Transportation,

National Highway Traffic Safety Administration, Director of the Office of Vehicle Safety Compliance, Equipment & Import Division, 400 Seventh St. SW, Washington, DC 20590, Tel: 1-800-424-9393, Web site: **www.nhtsa.dot.gov/cars/rules/import/**. Also refer to 19 CFR 12.80, "Motor Vehicles and Motor Vehicle Equipment Manufactured On or After January 1, 1968."

EPA Requirements. The Clean Air Act, as amended, prohibits the importation into the U.S. of any motor vehicle or motor vehicle engine not in conformity with emission standards prescribed by the U.S. Environmental Protection Agency (EPA). This restriction applies whether the motor vehicle or motor vehicle engine is new or used, and whether it was originally produced for sale and use in a foreign country, or originally produced (or late modified) to conform to EPA requirements for sale or use in the U.S. In addition to passenger cars, all trucks, multipurpose vehicles, (e.g., all-terrain vehicles, campers), motorcycles, etc. that are capable of being registered by a state for use on public roads or that the EPA has deemed capable of being safely driven on public roads, are subject to these requirements. The term "vehicle" is used below to indicate all EPA-regulated vehicles and engines. For more information, refer to 19 CFR 12.73–12.74, "Entry of Motor Vehicles and Motor Vehicle Engines Under the Clean Air Act, As Amended."

Certain imported automobiles may be subject to the gas-guzzler tax imposed by section 4064 of the Internal Revenue Code. The amount of the tax is based on a combined urban/highway fuel-economy (miles per gallon) rating assigned by the EPA for gas-guzzler tax purposes. This EPA rating may be different from fuel-economy ratings indicated by the manufacturer. If the EPA has not assigned a gas-guzzler fuel-economy rating for the model automobile you import, a rating must be independently determined. No tax is imposed on automobiles that have a combined fuel-economy rating of at least 22.5 miles per gallon.

The gas-guzzler tax is reported on **Form 720,** Quarterly Federal Excise Tax Return and **Form 6197,** Gas Guzzler Tax. Additional information may be obtained from your local district office of the Internal Revenue Service.

Nonroad Engine Imports. In accordance with the Clean Air Act and implementing regulations (40 CFR Parts 89, 90 and 91), the Environmental Protection Agency (EPA) began regulating certain nonroad diesel and gasoline engines, requiring that they meet federal emission standards beginning January 1, 1996.

"Nonroad," also referred to as "off-road" or "off-highway," is a term that covers a diverse group of engines and equipment. The nonroad category includes lawn and garden equipment, outdoor power equipment, recreational equipment, farm equipment, construction equipment, marine engines, and locomotives.

Prior to importation into the United States, regulated nonroad engines must be covered by an EPA-issued Certificate of Conformity. The certificate is issued by EPA to the engine manufacturer which declares that the engine family named on the certificate conforms with all applicable emissions standards and other requirements. It also permits the manufacturer to sell, offer for sale, introduce into commerce, or import into the United States, the named engine family. Certificates are issued for only one model year at a time. A label, confirming that the engine meets emission standards, must be affixed to the engine and be readily visible.

Upon request, an importer must provide an EPA **Form 3520-1** to Customs at the time of entry into the United States. This form must contain the following information about the engine: model, model number, serial number, horsepower, build date, and manufacturer. It must also include a description of the equipment/vehicle containing the engine, including the equipment manufacturer, equipment serial number, and the location of the EPA emissions label and engine serial number.

To obtain additional information and specific guidelines regarding the importation of nonroad engines subject to the EPA emissions standards, please refer to EPA's Web site at **www.epa.gov/oeca/ore/enfalert**, entitled Enforcement Alert. To obtain technical assistance, please contact the Office of Regulatory Enforcement, Air Enforcement Division, at Tel. (202) 564-8673 or (202) 564-1019.

U.S. Version Vehicles. Any person may import U.S.-version vehicles. All such 1971 and later models are required to have a label in a readily visible position in the engine compartment stating that the vehicle conforms to U.S. requirements. This label will read "Vehicle Emission Control Information" and will have a statement by the manufacturer that the vehicle meets U.S. EPA emission requirements at the time of manufacture. If this label is not present, the importer should obtain a letter of conformity from the manufacturer's U.S. representative—not from a dealership—prior to importation.

Non-U.S. Version Vehicles. Individuals are not permitted to import non-U.S. version vehicles (unless otherwise excluded or exempted). These vehicles must be imported (entered) by an Independent Commercial Importer (ICI) having a currently valid qualifying certificate of conformity for each vehicle being imported. The ICI will be responsible for performing all necessary modifications, testing, and labeling, as well as providing an emissions warranty identical to the emissions warranty required of new vehicles sold in the U.S. A list of approved ICIs is available from the EPA. Vehicles at least 21 years old are exempt from these provisions and may be imported without modification.

Excluded Vehicles. Vehicles manufactured before EPA requirements took effect (e.g., gasoline-fueled passenger vehicles manufactured prior to 1968 and motorcycles manufactured prior to 1978) are excluded from import restrictions and may be imported by any person without bond under the applicable declaration category on the EPA **Form 3520-1**.

- Not all conforming vehicles are eligible for importation, and ICIs are not required to accept vehicles for which they have qualifying certificates of conformity.

- EPA certification of ICIs does not guarantee the actions or work of the ICIs, nor does it regulate contractual agreements and working relationships with vehicle owners.

- EPA strongly recommends that prospective importers buy only U.S. version (labeled) vehicles, because of the expense and potential difficulties involved with importing a non-U.S. version vehicle.

- EPA strongly recommends that current owners of non-U.S. version vehicles sell or otherwise dispose of those vehicles overseas rather than ship and import them into the U.S., because of the expense and potential difficulties involved with importing a non-U.S. version vehicle.

- Before shipping a non-conforming vehicle for importation, EPA strongly recommends that the importer either make final arrangements with an ICI for modifications and testing, or obtain EPA approval in writing for importation. Storage fees at the ports are costly, and the vehicle may not be eligible for importation.

- The EPA policy that permitted importers a one-time exemption for vehicles at least five years old has been eliminated.

- EPA considers a U.S.-version vehicle that has had modifications to its drive train or emission control system to be a non-U.S.-version vehicle, even though it may be labeled a U.S.-version vehicle.

- For U.S.-version vehicles driven in Europe, a bond will not be required upon return to the U.S. if the vehicle participates in one of the EPA-approved catalyst control programs operating in Europe.

Other Requirements. To safeguard against importation of dangerous pests, the U.S. Department of Agriculture requires that the undercarriage of imported cars be free of foreign soil. Have cars steam-sprayed or cleaned thoroughly before shipment.

Nonresidents. Nonresidents may import an automobile or motorcycle and its usual equipment free of duty for a temporary stay to take part in races or other specific purposes. However, prior written approval from the EPA is required and such approval is granted only to those racing vehicles that EPA deems not capable of safe or practical use on streets and highways. If the contests are for other than money purposes, the vehicle may be admitted for 90 days without formal entry or bond if the Customs officer is satisfied as to the importer's identity and good faith. The vehicle becomes subject to forfeiture if it is not exported or if a bond is not given within 90 days of its importation. Prior authorization must be obtained from DOT if the vehicle does not conform to all applicable Federal motor vehicle safety standards.

Final Word of Caution. Modifications necessary to bring a nonconforming vehicle into conformity with the safety and bumper standards and/or emission standards may require extensive engineering, be impractical or even impossible, or the labor and materials may be unduly expensive. It is highly recommended that these modifications be investigated before a vehicle is purchased for importation. Moreover, under Federal Regulations 49 CFR parts 591 through 594, some vehicle models are prohibited from importation. It is highly recommended that these prohibitions and modifications be investigated before a vehicle is purchased for importation.

For Further Information. Environmental Protection Agency, Investigation/Imports Section (6405-J). Washington, DC 20460; Tel. (202) 564-9660; FAX (202) 565-2057..

Boats

Boat Safety Standards. Imported boats and associated equipment are subject to U.S. Coast Guard safety regulations or standards under the Federal Boat Safety Act of 1971. Products subject to standards must have a compliance certification label affixed to them. Certain hulls also require a hull identification number to be affixed. A U.S. Coast Guard import declaration is required to be filed with entries of nonconforming boats. Further information may be obtained from the Commandant, U.S. Coast

Guard, Washington, DC 20593. Also refer to 19 CFR 12.85, "Safety Standards for Boats and Associated Equipment."

Dutiability. Vessels that are brought into the U.S. for use in trade or commerce are not dutiable. Yachts or pleasure boats brought into the U.S. by nonresidents for their own use in pleasure cruising are also not dutiable. Yachts or pleasure boats owned by a resident or brought into the U.S. for sale or charter to a resident are dutiable. Further information may be found in U.S. Customs pamphlet "Pleasure Boats."

Restrictions on Use. Vessels that are foreign-built or of foreign registry may be used in U.S. waters for pleasure purposes and in the foreign trade of the U.S. However, Federal law prohibits the use of such vessels in the coastwise trade, i.e. the transportation of passengers or merchandise between points in the U.S., including carrying fishing parties for hire. Questions concerning the use of foreign- built or foreign-flag vessels should be addressed to the Chief, Entry and Carrier Rulings Branch, Office of Regulations and Rulings, U.S. Customs Service, 1300 Pennsylvania Avenue NW, Washington, DC 20229.

Import Quotas

An import quota is a quantity control on merchandise imported during a certain period of time. Quotas are established by legislation, by directives, and by proclamations issued under the authority contained in specific legislation; they are provided for in the HTSUS. The majority of import quotas are administered by the U.S. Customs Service. The Commissioner of Customs controls the importation of quota merchandise but has no authority to change or modify any quota. U.S. import quotas may be divided into two types: *absolute* and *tariff-rate*. Under NAFTA there are trade-preference levels, which are administered like tariff-rate quotas

The usual customs procedures generally applicable to other imports apply with respect to commodities subject to quota limitations. No import licenses are currently required for quota purposes for quotas administered by the Customs Service.

Merchandise is not regarded as presented for purposes of determining quota priority until an entry summary or withdrawal from warehouse for consumption has been submitted in proper form and the merchandise is located within the port limits.

Tariff-rate quotas provide for the entry of a specified quantity of the quota product at a reduced rate of duty during a given period. There is no limitation on the amount of the product that may be entered during the quota period, but quantities entered in excess of the quota for the period are subject to higher duty rates.

The quota status of a commodity subject to a tariff-rate quota cannot be determined in advance of its entry. The quota rates of duty are ordinarily assessed on such commodities entered from the beginning of the quota period until such time in the period as it is determined that imports are nearing the quota level. Port directors of Cus-

toms are then instructed to require the deposit of estimated duties at the over-quota duty rate and to report the time of official presentation of each entry. A final determination of the date and time when a quota is filled is made, and all port directors are advised accordingly. At that time, Customs officials are authorized to make the required adjustment in the duty rates on the portion of the merchandise entitled to quota preference.

Absolute quotas are quantitative; that is, no more than the amount specified may be permitted entry during a quota period. Some absolute quotas are global, while others are allocated to specified foreign countries. Imports in excess of a specified quota may be exported or warehoused for entry in a subsequent quota period, or it may be exported or destroyed under Customs supervision.

Some of the absolute quotas are invariably filled at or shortly after the opening of the quota period. Each of these quotas is therefore officially opened at noon Eastern Standard Time, or the equivalent in other time zones, on quanitty for these entries filed at the opening of the quota period exceeds the quota, the merchandise is released on a pro rata basis, the pro-rata being the ratio between the quota quantity and the total quantity offered for entry. This assures an equitable distribution of the quota. If not filled at the official opening of the quota period, the quota is thereafter administered on a first-come, first-served basis, in the order that each entry or entry summary is presented.

Quotas Administered by Customs

As provided in the Harmonized Tariff Schedule of the United States (HTSUS), the commodities listed below are subject to quota limitations in effect as of the date of publication. You may also want to refer to 19 CFR 132, "Quotas." Local Customs officers can be consulted about any changes. Information may also be obtained by contacting the Quota Staff, U.S. Customs Service, 1300 Pennsylvania Avenue NW, Washington, DC 20229, Tel. (202) 9270--5850.

Tariff-Rate Quotas.

- Anchovies
- Brooms
- Broom corn brooms
- Ethyl alcohol
- Lamb
- Line pipe
- Milk and cream
- Olives
- Sarsumas (mandarins)
- Tuna
- Upland cotton
- Wire rod

Tariff-Rate Quotas Under GATT. Presidential Proclamation 6763 implemented the GATT Uruguay Round Agreements for the following tariff-rate commodities. Quotas are listed by their HTSUS chapter number and the Additional U.S. Note (AUSN) number in that chapter.

Chapter 2, Additional U.S. Note 3 (2 AUSN 3)-Beef

4 AUSN 5-Milk and cream

4 AUSN 9-Dried milk and dried cream

4 AUSN 10-Dairy products

4 AUSN 11-Milk and cream (condensed or evaporated)

4 AUSN 12-Dried milk, dried cream, and dried whey (in excess of 224,981 kilograms)

4 AUSN 18-Canadian cheddar cheese

12 AUSN 2-Peanuts

17 AUSN 5-Sugar (including sugar cane)

17 AUSN 7-Articles containing more than 65 percent by dry weight of sugar described in 17 AUSN 2

17 AUSN 8-Articles containing more than 10 percent by dry weight of sugar described in 17 AUSN 3

17 AUSN 9-Blended syrups

18 AUSN 1-Cocoa powder

18 AUSN 2-Chocolate

18 AUSN 3-Chocolate and low-fat chocolate crumb

19 AUSN 2-Infant formula

19 AUSN 3-Mixes and doughs

20 AUSN 5-Peanut butter and paste

21 AUSN 4-Mixed condiments and mixed seasonings

21 AUSN 5-Ice cream

23 AUSN 2-Animal feed

24 ASUN 5-Tobacco

52 AUSN 5-Cotton

52 AUSN 6-Harsh or rough cotton

52 AUSN 7-Cotton

52 AUSN 8-Cotton

52 AUSN 9-Card strips made from cotton

52 AUSN 10-Fibers of cotton

Trade Preference Levels Under NAFTA. Presidential Proclamation 6411 implemented NAFTA and established trade preference levels on the following imported goods. The HTSUS chapter number followed by the U.S. Note (USN) number is indicated for each.

Goods Imported from Mexico:

Chapter 99, Subchapter VI, U.S. Note 4 (99 USN 4)-Milk and cream

99 USN 5-Dried milk and dried cream

99 USN 6-Dried milk and dried cream

99 USN 7-Milk and cream (condensed and evaporated)

99 USN 8-Cheese

99 USN 9-Tomatoes

99 USN 10-Tomatoes

99 USN 11-Onions and shallots

99 USN 12-Eggplants

99 USN 13-Chili peppers

99 USN 14-Squash

99 USN 15-Watermelons

99 USN 16-Peanuts

99 USN 18-Sugars derived from sugar cane or sugar beets

99 USN 19-Blended syrups

99 USN 20-Sugars derived from sugar cane or sugar beets

99 USN 21-Orange juice

99 USN 22-Orange juice

99 USN 25-Cotton

9906.96.01-Brooms

Section XI Additional U.S. Notes-cotton or man-made fiber apparel, wool apparel, cotton or man-made fiber fabrics and made-ups and cotton or man-made fibers yarns.

Goods Imported from Canada:

Section XI Additional U.S. Notes-cotton or man-made fiber apparel, wool apparel, cotton or man-made fiber fabrics and made-ups and cotton or man-made fibers yarns.

Tariff-Rate Quotas Under U.S.-Israel Agreement on Trade in Agricultural Products. Presidential Proclamation 6962 implemented the U.S.-Israel agreement for the following agricultural products:

Chapter 99, Subchapter VIII, U.S. Note 3-Butter, fresh or sour cream

Chapter 99, Subchapter VIII, U.S. Note 4-Dried milk

Chapter 99, Subchapter VIII, U.S. Note 5-Cheese and substitutes for cheese

Chapter 99, Subchapter VIII, U.S. Note 6-Peanuts

Chapter 99, Subchapter VIII, U.S. Note 7-Ice cream

Textile Articles. The U.S. Customs Service administers import controls of certain cotton, wool, man-made fiber articles, silk blends and other vegetable fibers manufactured or produced in designated countries. These controls are imposed on the basis of directives issued to the Commissioner of Customs by the Chairman of the Committee for the Implementation of Textile Agreements.

Customs administers the Caribbean Basin Initiative (CBI) Special Access Program on certain products which are made of U.S.-formed and cut fabric and accompanied by a certified form ITA-370P.

Information concerning specific import controls in effect and visa requirements may be obtained from the Commissioner of Customs. Other information concerning the textile program may be obtained from the Chairman, Committee for the Implementation of Textile Agreements, U.S. Department of Commerce, Washington, DC 20230. For more contact information on textile quotas, see "Textile and Apparel Imports Under NAFTA" on page 265, and for more information on textile visas, see "Textile Visa Requirements" on page 264.

Sugar Quotas. The major features of the Uruguay Round provisions for sugar and sugar-containing products include commitments to reduce subsidized exports by the European Union and South Africa, reductions in tariffs for sugar-containing products for a number of countries, and U.S. commitments to bind a current access level for sugar under the tariff-rate quota of 1,139,195 metric tons. In addition, the U.S. is replacing the current tariff-rate quota for sugar with a tariff equivalent of 17 cents per pound, to be reduced by 15 percent (to 14.45 cents per pound) by the end of the implementation period. The U.S. has also committed to replace the current Agricultural Amendment Act Section 22 quotas for sugar-containing products with tariff-rate quotas at the current levels of access. These tariffs will reduced by 15 percent over the implementation period. Modifications to the definitions of these quotas will be made to maintain the product coverage intended when they were first introduced.

Quota allocations for certain sugar-containing articles were also reduced and redistributed from their historical levels with the implementation of the NAFTA. U.S. and Mexican tariffs on sugar will be phased out in conjunction with the treatment of U.S. and Mexican border protection on sugar. At the end of year 15 of the agreement, there will be free trade in sugar between Mexico and the United States—this is the longest transition phase available under NAFTA. Although bilateral trade in sugar will be free of tariffs and non-tariff barriers at the end of 15 years, the shape of trade in sugar during this transition period is governed by the concept of "net production surplus" In essence, this is a means-tested approach to trade, with the decision parameter being the surplus of production over consumption. The level of duty free access to the market for sugar in the importing country is determined by calculating whether the exporting country is a "net surplus producer."

Beef Quotas. The Customs Service added 19 CFR 132.15, "Export certificate for beef subject to tariff-rate quota" in 1996. The new regulations require the importer to possess a valid export certificate at the time the beef is entered or

withdrawn for consumption. The export certificate number must be recorded on the entry summary or warehouse withdrawal form (CF 7501, column 34).

The regulations were created as a result of the Uruguay Round Agreements, which established a tariff-rate quota for imported beef. The specific imported beef, and the various countries eligible for the in-quota tariff rate can be found in Chapter 2 of the HTSUS, Additional U.S. Note 3.

Quotas or Licenses Administered by Other Government Agencies

Watches and Watch Movements. The Departments of Interior and Commerce administer import quotas on watches and watch movements from U.S. insular possessions admissible free of duty under General Note 3(a)(iv), U.S. Legal Note 5 to Chapter 91 of the HTSUS, on a licensing basis. Further information on the insular watch program may be obtained from the U.S. Department of Commerce, Import Administration, **Statutory Import Programs, Tel: (202) 482-1660.** Also refer to 19 CFR 10.181, "Watches and watch movements from U.S. Insular Possessions."

Dairy Products. Certain dairy products listed below are subject to annual import quotas assigned by the Department of Agriculture and may be imported at the in-quota rate only under import licenses issued by that department.

Detailed information on the licensing of these products, or the conditions under which limited quantities of the products may be imported without licenses, may be obtained from the Dairy Import Group, Foreign Agricultural Service, U.S. Department of Agriculture, Washington, DC 20250, Tel. 202.720.9439.

> Chapter 4, Additional U.S. Note 6 (4 AUSN 6)-Butter and fresh or sour cream
>
> 4 AUSN 7-Dried milk
>
> 4 AUSN 8-Dried milk or dried cream
>
> 4 AUSN 12-Dried milk, dried cream or dried whey (up to 224,981 kilograms)
>
> 4 AUSN 14-Butter substitutes
>
> 4 AUSN 16-Cheeses and substitutes for cheese
>
> 4 AUSN 17-Blue-molded cheese
>
> 4 AUSN 18-Cheddar cheese (except Canadian cheddar)
>
> 4 AUSN 19-American-type cheese
>
> 4 AUSN 20-Edam and Gouda cheese
>
> 4 AUSN 21-Italian-type cheese
>
> 4 AUSN 22-Swiss or Emmentaler cheese
>
> 4 AUSN 23-Cheese and substitutes for cheese
>
> 4 AUSN 25-Swiss or Emmentaler cheese The above products may be imported at the over-quota rate without an import license.

Appendix

Invoices

§ 141.83 Type of Invoice Required

(a) – (b) [Reserved]

(c) *Commercial invoice*

(1) A commercial invoice shall be filed for each shipment of merchandise not exempted by paragraph (d) of this section. The commercial invoice shall be prepared in the manner customary in the trade, contain the information required by §§141.86 through 141.89, and substantiate the statistical information required by §141.61(e) to be given on the entry, entry summary, or withdrawal documentation.

(2) The port director may accept a copy of a required commercial invoice in place of the original. A copy, other than a photostatic or photographic copy, shall contain a declaration by the foreign seller, the shipper, or the importer that it is a true copy.

(d) *Commercial invoice not required*

A commercial invoice shall not be required in connection with the filing of the entry, entry summary, or withdrawal documentation for merchandise listed in this paragraph. The importer, however, shall present any invoice, memorandum invoice, or bill pertaining to the merchandise which may be in his possession or available to him. If no invoice or bill is available, a pro forma (or substitute) invoice, as provided for in §141.85, shall be filed, and shall contain information adequate for the examination of merchandise and the determination of duties, and information and documentation which verify the information required for statistical purposes by §141.61(e). The merchandise subject to the foregoing requirements is as follows:

(1) Merchandise having an aggregate purchase price or value, as specified in paragraph (a) of this section, of $500 or less.

(2) Merchandise not intended for sale or any commercial use in its imported condition or any other form, and not brought in on commission for any person other than the importer.

(3) - (4) [Reserved]

(5) Merchandise returned to the United States after having been exported for repairs or alteration under subheadings 9802.00.40 and 9802.00.60, Harmonized Tariff Schedule of the United States (19 U.S.C. 1202).

(6) Merchandise shipped abroad, not delivered to the consignee, and returned to the United States.

(7) Merchandise exported from continuous Customs custody within 6 months after the date of entry.

(8) Merchandise consigned to, or entered in the name of, any agency of the U.S. Government.

(9) Merchandise for which an appraisement entry is accepted.

(10) Merchandise entered temporarily into the Customs territory of the United States under bond or for permanent exhibition under bond.

(11) Merchandise provided for in section 466, Tariff Act of 1930(19 U.S.C. 1466), which pertain to certain equipment, repair parts, and supplies for vessels.

(12) Merchandise imported as supplies, stores, and equipment of the importing carrier and subsequently made subject to entry pursuant to section 446, Tariff Act of 1930, as amended (19 U.S.C. 1446).

(13) Ballast (not including cargo used for ballast) landed from a vessel and delivered for consumption.

(14) Merchandise, whether privileged or nonprivileged, resulting from manipulation or manufacture in a foreign trade zone.

(15) Screenings contained in bulk importations of grain or seeds.

[T.D. 73 - 175, 38 FR 17447, July 2, 1973, as amended by T.D. 78 - 53, 43 FR 6069, Feb. 13, 1978; T.D. 79 - 221, 44 FR 46820, Aug. 9, 1979; T.D. 82 - 224, 47 FR 53728, Nov. 29, 1982; T.D. 84 - 213, 49 FR 41184, Oct. 19, 1984; T.D. 85 - 39, 50 FR 9612, Mar. 11, 1985; T.D. 89 - 1, 53 FR 51256, Dec. 21, 1988; T.D. 93 - 66, 58 FR 44130, Aug. 19, 1993; T.D. 94 - 24, 59 FR 13200, Mar. 21, 1994]

Note: *The requirement for a special Customs invoice was waived by the Customs Service on March 1, 1982. However, it may still be used. If a commercial invoice is used, it must be signed by the seller and shipper or their agents.*

Additional Information

§ 141.89 Additional information for certain classes of merchandise

Invoices for the following classes of merchandise, classifiable under the Harmonized Tariff Schedule of the United States (HTSUS), shall set forth the additional information specified: [75-42, 75-239, 78-53, 83-251, 84-149.]

Aluminum and alloys of aluminum classifiable under subheadings 7601.10.60, 7601.20.60, 7601.20.90, or 7602.00.00, HTSUS (T.D. 53092, 55977, 56143)—Statement of the percentages by weight of any metallic element contained in the article.

Articles manufactured of textile materials Coated or laminated with plastics or rubber, classifiable in Chapter(s) 39, 40, and 42—Include a description indicating whether the fabric is coated or laminated on both sides, on the exterior surface or on the interior surface.

Bags manufactured of plastic sheeting and not of a reinforced or laminated construction, classified in Chapter 39 or in heading 4202—Indicate the gauge of the plastic sheeting.

Ball or roller bearings classifiable under subheading 8482.10.50 through 8482.80.00, HTSUS (T.D. 68-306)—(1) Type of bearing (i.e. whether a ball or roller bearing); (2) If a roller bearing, whether a spherical, tapered, cylindrical, needled or other type; (3) Whether a combination bearing (i.e. a bearing containing both ball and roller bearings, etc.); and (4) If a ball bearing (not including ball bearing with integral shafts or parts of ball bearings), whether or not radial, the following: (a) outside diameter of each bearing; and (b) whether or not a radial bearing (the definition of radial bearing is, for Customs purposes, an antifriction bearing primarily designed to support a load perpendicular to shaft axis).

Beads (T.D. 50088, 55977)—(1) The length of the string, if strung; (2) The size of the beads expressed in millimeters; (3) The material of which the beads are composed, i.e. ivory, glass, imitation pearl, etc.

Bed linen and bedspreads Statement as to whether or not the article contains any embroidery, lace, braid, edging, trimming, piping or applique work.

Chemicals Furnish the use and Chemical Abstracts Service number of chemical compounds classified in Chapters 27, 28 and 29, HTSUS.

Colors, dyes, stains and related products provided for under heading 3204, HTSUS—The following information is required: (1) Invoice name of product; (2) Trade name of product; (3) Identity and percent by weight of each component; (4) Color Index number (if none, so state); (5) Color Index generic name (if none so state); (6) Chemical Abstracts Service number of the active ingredient; (7) Class of merchandise (state whether acid type dye, basic dye, disperse dye, fluorescent brightener, soluble dye, vat dye, toner or other (describe); (8) Material to which applied (name the material for which the color, dye, or toner is primarily designed).

Copper (T.D. 45878, 50158, 55977) articles classifiable under the provisions of Chapter 74, HTSUS—A statement of the weight of articles of copper, and a statement of percentage of copper content and all other elements—by weight—of articles classifiable according to copper content.

Copper ores and concentrates (T.D. 45878, 50158, 55977) classifiable in heading 2603, and subheadings 2620.19.60, 2620.20.00, 2620.30.00, and heading 7401—Statement of the percentage by weight of the copper content and any other metallic elements.

Cotton fabrics classifiable under the following HTSUS headings: 5208, 5209, 5210, 5211, and 5212—(1) Marks on shipping packages; (2) Numbers on shipping packages; (3) Customer's call number, if any; (4) Exact width of the merchandise; (5) Detailed description of the merchandise; trade name, if any; whether bleached, unbleached, printed, composed of yarns of different color, or dyed; if composed of cotton and other materials, state the percentage of each component material by weight; (6) Number of single threads per square centimeter (All ply yarns must be counted in accordance with the number of single threads contained in the yarn; to illustrate: a cloth containing 100 two-ply yarns in one square centimeter must be reported as 200 single threads); (7) Exact weight per square meter in grams; (8) Average yarn number use this formula:

$$\frac{100 \times (\text{Total Single Yarns Per Square Centimeter})}{(\text{Number of Grams Per Square Meter})}$$

(9) Yarn size or sizes in the warp; (10) Yarn size or sizes in the filling; (11) Specify whether the yarns are combed or carded; (12) Number of colors or kinds (different yarn sizes or materials) in the filling; (13) Specify whether the fabric is napped or not napped; and (14) Specify the type of weave, for example, plain, twill, sateen, oxford, etc., and (15) Specify the type of machine on which woven: if with Jacquard (Jacq), if with Swivel (Swiv), if with Lappet (Lpt.), if with Dobby (Dobby).

Cotton raw See §151.82 of this chapter for additional information required on invoices.

Cotton waste (T.D. 50044)—(1) The name by which the cotton waste is known, such as "cotton card strips"; "cotton comber waste"; "cotton lap waste"; "cotton silver waste"; "cotton roving waste"; "cotton fly waste"; etc.; (2) Whether the length of the cotton staple forming any cotton card strips covered by the invoice is less than 3.016 centimeters (1 3/16 inches) or is 3.016 centimeters (1 3/16 inches) or more.

Earthenware or crockeryware composed of a nonvitrified absorbent body (including white granite and semiporcelain earthenware and cream-colored ware, stoneware, and terra cotta, but not including common brown, gray, red, or yellow earthenware), embossed or plain; common salt-glazed stoneware; stoneware or earthenware crucibles; Rockingham earthenware; china, porcelain, or other vitrified wares, composed of a vitrified nonabsorbent body that, when broken, shows a vitrified, vitreous, semi-vitrified, or semivitreous fracture; and bisque or parian ware (T.D. 53236)—(1) If in sets, the kinds of articles in each set in the shipment and the quantity of each kind of article in each set in the shipment; (2) The exact maximum diameter, expressed in centimeters, of each size of all plates in the shipment; (3) The unit value for each style and size of plate, cup, saucer, or other separate piece in the shipment.

<u>Fish or fish livers</u> (T.D. 50724, 49640, 55977) imported in airtight containers classifiable under Chapter 3, HTSUS— (1) Statement whether the articles contain any oil, fat, or grease, (2) The name and quantity of any such oil, fat, or grease.

<u>Footwear</u>, classifiable in headings 6401 through 6405 of the HTSUS—

1. Manufacturer's style number.

2. Importer's style and/or stock number.

3. Percent by area of external surface area of upper (excluding reinforcements and accessories) that is:

    Leather a. _____%

    Composition leather b. _____%

    Rubber and/or plasticsc. _____%

    Textile materialsd. _____%

    Other (give separate

    percent for each type e. _____%

    of material)f. _____%

4. Percent by area of external surface area of outersole (excluding reinforcements and accessories) that is:

    Leather a. _____%

    Composition leather b. _____%

    Rubber and/or plastics c. _____%

    Textile materials d. _____%

           Other (give separate e. _____%

           percent for each f. _____%

           type of material)

You may skip this section if you choose to answer *all* questions A through Z below:

I. If 3(a) is larger than any other percent in 3 and if 4(a) is larger than any other percent in 4, answer questions F, G, L, M, O, Q, R, S, and X.

II. If 3(a) is larger than any other percent in 3 and if 4(c) is larger than any other percent in 4, answer questions F, G, L, M, N, O, Q, S and X.

III. If 3(a) plus 3(b) is larger than any single percent in 3 and 4(d), 4(e) or 4(f) is larger than any other percent in 4, stop.

IV. If 3(c) is larger than any other percent in 3 and if 4(a) or 4(b) is larger than any other percent in 4, stop.

V. If 3(c) is larger than any other percent in 3 and if 4(c) is larger than any other percent in 4, answer questions B, E, F, G, H, J, K, L, M, N, O, P, T and W.

VI. If 3(d) is larger than any other percent in 3 and if 4(a) plus 4(b) is greater than any single percent in 4, answer questions C and D.

VII. If 3(d) is larger than any other percent in 3 and if 4(c) is larger than any single percent in 4, answer questions A, C, J, K, M, N, P and T.

VIII. If 3(d) is larger than any other percent in 3 and if 4(d) is larger than any other percent in 4, answer questions U, Y and Z.

IX. If the article is made of paper, answer questions V and Z.

If the article does not meet any of the conditions I through IX above, answer all questions A through Z, below.

A. Percent of external surface area of upper (including leather reinforcements and accessories).

    Which is leather _____%

B. Percent by area of external surface area of upper (including all reinforcements and accessories).

    Which is rubber _____

    and/or plastics) _____%

C. Percent by weight of rubber and/or plastics is _____%

D. Percent by weight of textile materials plus rubber and/or plastics is _____%

E. Is it waterproof?

F. Does it have a protective metal toe cap?

G. Will it cover the wearer's ankle bone?

H. Will it cover the wearer's knee cap?

I. [Reserved.]

J. Is it designed to be a protection against water, oil, grease, or chemicals or cold or inclement weather?

K. Is it a slip-on?

L. Is it a downhill or cross-country ski boot?

M. Is it serious sports footwear other than ski boots? (Chapter 64 subheading note defines sports footwear.)

N. Is it a tennis, basketball, gym, or training shoe or the like?

O. Is it made on a base or platform of wood?

P. Does it have open toes or open heels?

Q. Is it made by the (lipped insole) welt construction?

R. Is it made by the turned construction?

S. Is it worn exclusively by men, boys or youths?

T. Is it made by an exclusively adhesive construction?

U. Are the fibers of the upper, by weight, predominately vegetable fibers?

V. Is it disposable, i.e., intended for one-time use?

W. Is it a "Zori"?

X. Is the leather in the upper pigskin?

Y. Are the sole and upper made of wool felt

Z. Is there a line of demarcation between the outer sole and upper?

The information requested above may be furnished on CF 5523 or other appropriate format by the exporter, manufacturer or shipper.

Also, the following information must be furnished by the importer or his authorized agent if classification is claimed under one of the subheadings below, as follows:

If subheading 6401.99.80, 6402.19.10, 6402.30.30, 6402.91.40, 6402.99.15, 6402.99.30, 6404.11.40, 6404.11.60, 6404.19.35, 6404.19.40, or 6404.19.60 is claimed:

Does the shoe have a foxing or foxing-like band? If so, state its material(s).

Does the sole overlap the upper other than just at the front of the toe and/or at the back of the heel?

<u>Definitions</u> for some of the terms used in Question A to Z above: For the purpose of this section, the following terms have the approximate definitions below. If either a more complete definition or a decision as to its application to a particular article is needed, the maker or importer of record (or the agent of either) should contact Customs prior to entry of the article.

a.   In an <u>exclusively adhesive construction</u>, all of the pieces of the bottom would separate from the upper or from each other if all adhesives, cements, and glues were dissolved. It includes shoes in which the pieces of the upper are stitched to each other, but not to any part of the bottom. Examples include:

1.   Vulcanized construction footwear;

2.   Simultaneous molded construction footwear;

3.   Molded footwear in which the upper and the bottom is one piece of molded rubber or plastic, and

4.   Footwear in which staples, rivets, stitching, or any of the methods above are either primary or even just extra or auxiliary, even though adhesive is a major part of the reason the bottom will not separate from the upper.

b.   <u>Composition leather</u> is made by binding together leather fibers or small pieces of natural leather. It does not include imitation leathers not based on natural leather.

c.   <u>Leather</u> is the tanned skin of any animal from which the fur or hair has been removed. Tanned skins coated or laminated with rubber and/or plastics are "leather" only if leather gives the material its essential character.

d.   A <u>Line of Demarcation</u> exists if one can indicate where the sole ends and the upper begins. For example, knit booties do not normally have a line of demarcation.

e.   <u>Men's, boy's and youth's</u> sizes cover footwear of American youths size 11 1/2 and larger for males, and does not include footwear commonly worn by both sexes. If more than 4% of the shoes sold in a given size will be worn by females, that size is "commonly worn by both sexes."

f.   Footwear is designed to *protect* against water, oil or cold or inclement weather only if it is sub-

stantially more of a protection against those items than the usual shoes of that type. For example, a leather oxford will clearly keep your feet warmer and drier than going barefoot, but they are not a protection in this sense. On the other hand, the snow-jogger is the protective version of the non-protective jogging shoe.

g.   <u>Rubber and/or plastics</u> includes any textile material visibly coated (or covered) externally with one or both of those materials.

h.   <u>Slip-on</u> includes:

1.   A boot that must be pulled on.

2.   Footwear with elastic cores that must be stretched to get it on, but not a separate piece of elasticized fabric that forms a full circle around the foot or ankle.

i.   <u>Sports footwear</u> includes only:

1.   Footwear that is designed for a sporting activity and has, or has provision for, the attachment of spikes, sprigs, cleats, stops, clips, bars or the like;

2.   Skating boots (without skates attached), ski boots and cross-country ski footwear, wrestling boots, boxing boots and cycling shoes.

j.   <u>Tennis shoes, basketball shoes, gym shoes, training shoes and the like</u> cover athletic footwear other than sports footwear, whether or not principally used for such athletic games or purposes.

k.   <u>Textile materials</u> are made from cotton, other vegetable fibers, wool, hair, silk or man-made fibers. Note: Cork, wood, cardboard and leather are not textile materials.

l.   In <u>turned</u> construction, the upper is stitched to the leather sole wrong side out and the shoe is then turned right side out.

m.   <u>Vegetable fibers</u> include cotton, flax and ramie, but does not include either rayon or plaiting materials such as rattan or wood strips.

n.   <u>Waterproof footwear</u> includes footwear designed to protect against penetration by water or other liquids, whether or not such footwear is primarily designed for such purposes.

o.   <u>Welt footwear</u> means footwear construction with a welt, that extends around the edge of the outer sole, and in which the welt and shoe upper are sewed to a lip on the surface of the insole, and the outer sole of which is sewed or cemented to the welt.

p.   A <u>zori</u> has an upper consisting only of straps or thongs of molded rubber or plastic. This upper is assembled to a formed rubber or plastic sole by means of plugs.

Fur products and furs (T.D. 53064)—(1) Name or names (as set forth in the Fur Products Name Guide (16 CFR 301.0) of the animal or animals that produced the fur, and such qualifying statements as may be required pursuant to § 7(c) of the Fur Products Labeling Act (15 USC 69e(c)); (2) A statement that the fur product contains or is composed of used fur, when such is the fact; (3) A statement that the fur product contains or is composed of bleached, dyed, or otherwise artificially colored fur, when such is the fact; (4) A statement that the fur product is composed in whole or in substantial part of paws, tails, bellies, or waste fur, when such is the fact; (5) Name and address of the manufacturer of the fur product; (6) Name of the country of origin of the furs or those contained in the fur product.

Glassware and other glass products (T.D. 53079, 55977)—Classifiable under Chapter 70, HTSUS—Statement of the separate value of each component article in the set.

Gloves—classifiable in subheadings 6116.10.20 and 6216.00.20—Statement as to whether or not the article has been covered with plastics on both sides.

Handkerchiefs—(1) State the exact dimensions (length and width) of the merchandise; (2) If of cotton indicate whether the handkerchief is hemmed and whether it contains lace or embroidery.

Hats or headgear—(1) If classifiable under subheading 6502.00.40 or 6502.00.60, HTSUS—Statement as to whether or not the article has been bleached or colored; (2) If classifiable under subheading 6502.00.20 through 6502.00.60 or 6504.00.30 through 6504.00.90, HTSUS—Statement as to whether or not the article is sewed or not sewed, exclusive of any ornamentation or trimming.

Hosiery—(1) Indicate whether a single yarn measures less than 67 decitex. (2) Indicate whether the hosiery is full length, knee length, or less than knee length. (3) Indicate whether it contains lace or net.

Iron or steel classifiable in Chapter 72 or headings 7301 to 7307, HTSUS (T.D. 53092, 55977)—Statement of the percentages by weight of carbon and any metallic elements contained in the articles, in the form of a mill analysis or mill test certificate.

Iron oxide (T.D. 49989, 50107)—For iron oxide to which a reduced rate of duty is applicable, a statement of the method of preparation of the oxide, together with the patent number, if any.

Machines, equipment and apparatus—Chapters 84 and 85, HTSUS—A statement as to the use or method of operation of each type of machine.

Machine parts (T.D. 51616)—Statement specifying the kind of machine for which the parts are intended, or if this is not known to the shipper, the kinds of machines for which the parts are suitable.

Machine tools: (1) Heading 8456 through 8462—machine tools covered by these headings equipped with a CNC (Computer Numerical Control) or the facings (electrical interface) for a CNC must state so; (2) heading 8458 through 8463—machine tools covered by these headings if used or rebuilt must state so; (3) subheading 8456.30. 10—EDM: (Electrical Discharge Machines) if a Traveling Wire (Wire Cut) type must state so. Wire EDM's use a copper or brass wire for the electrode; (4) subheading 8457.10.0010 through 8457.10.0050—Machining Centers. Must state whether or not they have an ATC (Automatic Tool Changer). Vertical spindle machine centers with an ATC must also indicate the Y-travel; (5) subheadings

8458.11.0030 through 8458.11.0090—horizontal lathes: numerically controlled. Must indicate the rated HP (or KW rating) of the main spindle motor. Use the continuous rather than 30-minute rating.

Madeira embroideries (T.D. 49988)—(1) With respect to the materials used, furnish: (a) country of production; (b) width of the material in the piece; (c) name of the manufacturer; (d) kind of material, indicating manufacturer's quality number; (e) landed cost of the material used in each item; (f) date of the order; (g) date of the invoice; (h) invoice unit value in the currency of the purchase; (i) discount from purchase price allowed, if any; (2) With respect to the finished embroidered articles, furnish: (a) manufacturers' name, design number, and quality number; (b) importer's design number, if any; (c) finished size; (d) number of embroidery points per unit of quantity; (e) total for overhead and profit added in arriving at the price or value of the merchandise covered by the invoice.

Motion picture films—(1) Statement of footage, title, and subject matter of each film; (2) Declaration of shipper, cameraman, or other person with knowledge of the facts identifying the films with the invoice and stating that the basic films were to the best of his knowledge and belief exposed abroad and returned for use as newsreel; (3) Declaration of importer that he believes the films entered by him are the ones covered by the preceding declaration and that the films are intended for use as newsreel.

Paper classifiable in Chapter 48—Invoices covering paper shall contain the following information, or will be accompanied by specification sheets containing such information:

(1) Weight of paper in grams per square meter; (2) Thickness, in micrometers (microns); (3) If imported in rectangular sheets, length and width sheets, in cm; (4) If imported in strips, or rolls, the width, in cm. In the case of rolls, the diameter of rolls in cm; (5) Whether the paper is coated or impregnated, and with what materials; (6) Weight of coating, in grams per square meter; (7) Percentage by weight of the total fiber content consisting of wood fibers contained by a mechanical process, chemical sulfate or soda process, chemical sulfite process, or semi-chemical process, as appropriate; (8) Commercial designation, as "Writing," "Cover," "Drawing," "Bristol," "Newsprint," etc.; (9) Ash content; (10) Color; (11) Glaze, or finish; (12) Mullen bursting strength, and Mullen index; (13) Stretch factor, in machine direction and in cross direction; (14) Tear and tensile readings; in machine direction, in cross direction, and in machine direction plus cross direction; (15) Identification of fibers as "hardwood" where appropriate; (16) Crush resistance; (17) Brightness; (18) Smoothness; (19) If bleached, whether bleached uniformly throughout the mass; (20) Whether embossed, perforated, creped or crinkled.

Plastic plates, sheets, film, foil, and strip of headings 3920 and 3921—(1) Statement as to whether the plastic is cellular or noncellular; (2) Specification of the type of plastic; (3) Indication of whether or not flexible and whether combined with textile or other material.

Printed matter classifiable in Chapter 49—Printed matter entered in the following headings shall have, on or with the invoices covering such matter, the following information: (1) Heading 4901—(a) Whether the books are: dictionaries, encyclopedias, textbooks, bound newspapers or journals or periodicals, directories, bibles or other prayer books, technical, scientific or professional books, art or pictorial books, or "other" books; (b) if "other" books, whether hardbound or paperbound; (c) if "other" books, paperbound, other than "rack size": number of pages (excluding covers). (2) *Heading 4902*—Whether the journal or periodical appears at least four times a week. If the journal or periodical appears other than at least four times a week, whether it is a newspaper supplement printed by a gravure process, is a newspaper, business or professional journal or periodical, or other than these; (3) *Heading 4904*—Whether the printed or manuscript music is sheet music, not bound (except by stapling or folding); (4) *Heading 4905*—(a) Whether globes, or not; (b) if not globes, whether in book form, or not; (c) in any case, whether or not in relief; (5) *Heading 4908*—Whether or not vitrifiable; (6) *Heading 4904*—Whether post cards, greeting cards, or other; (7) *Heading 4910*—(a) Whether or not printed on paper by a lithographic process; (b) if printed on paper by a lithographic process, the thickness of the paper, in mm; (8) *Subheading 4911.91*—(a) Whether or not printed over 20 years at time of importation; (b) if not printed over 20 years at time of importation, whether suitable for use in the production of articles of heading 4901; (c) if not printed over 20 years at time of importation, and

not suitable for use in the production of articles of heading 4901, whether the merchandise is lithographs on paper or paperboard; (d) if lithographs on paper or paperboard, under the terms of the immediately preceding description, thickness of the paper or paperboard, and whether or not posters; (e) in any case, whether or not posters; (f) in any case, whether or not photographic negatives or positives on transparent bases; (g) *Subheading 4911.99*—If not carnets, or parts thereof, in English or French, whether or not printed on paper in whole or in part by a lithographic process.

Pulp classifiable in Chapter 47—(1) Invoices covering chemical wood pulp, dissolving grades, in Heading 4702 shall state the insoluble fraction (as a percentage) after 1 hour in a caustic soda solution containing 18% sodium hydroxide (NaOH) at 20° C; (2) *Subheading 4702.00.0020*—Pulp entered under this subheading shall in addition contain on or with the invoice the ash content as a percentage by weight.

Refrigeration equipment (1) Refrigerator-freezers classifiable under subheading 8418.10.00 and (2) refrigerators classifiable under 8418.21.00—(a) statement as to whether they are compression or absorption type; (b) statement of their refrigerated volume in liters; (3) freezers classifiable under subheading 8418.30.00 and 8418.40.00—statement as to whether they are chest or upright type; (4) liquid chilling refrigerating units classifiable under subheading 8418.69.0045 through 8418.69.0060 statement as to whether they are centrifugal open-type, centrifugal hermetic-type, absorption-type or reciprocating-type.

Rolling mills—Subheading 8455.30.0005 through 8455.30.0085. Rolls for rolling mills: Indicate the composition of the roll—gray iron, cast steel or other—and the weight of each roll.

Rubber Products of Chapter 40—(1) Statement as to whether combined with textile or other material; (2) statement whether the rubber is cellular or noncellular, unvulcanized or vulcanized, and if vulcanized, whether hard rubber or other than hard rubber.

Screenings or scalpings of grains or seeds (T.D. 51096)—(1) Whether the commodity is the product of a screening process; (2) If so, whether any cultivated grains have been added to such commodity; (3) If any such grains have been added, the kind and percentage of each.

Textile fiber products (T.D. 55095)—(1) The constituent fiber or combination of fibers in the textile fiber product, designating with equal prominence each natural or manufactured fiber in the textile fiber product by its generic name in the order of predominance by the weight thereof if the weight of such fiber is 5 per centum or more of the total fiber weight of the product; (2) The percentage of each fiber present, by weight, in the total fiber content of the textile fiber product; (3) The name, or other identification issued and registered by the Federal Trade Commission, of the manufacturer of the product or one or more persons subject to § 3 of the Textile Fiber Products Identification Act (15 USC 70a) with respect to such product; (4) The name of the country where processed or manufactured. *See also* "Wearing Apparel" below.

Tires and tubes for tires of rubber or plastics—(1) Specify the kind of vehicle for which the tire is intended, i.e. airplane, bicycle, passenger car, on-the-highway light or heavy truck or bus, motorcycle; (2) If designed for tractors provided for in subheading 8701.90.10, or for agricultural or horticultural machinery or implements provided for in Chapter 84 or in subheading 8716.80.10, designate whether the tire is new, recapped, or used; pneumatic or solid; (3) Indicate whether the tube is designed for tires provided for in subheading 4011.91.10, 4011.99.10, 4012.10.20, or 4012.20.20.

Tobacco (including tobacco in its natural state) (T.D. 44854, 45871)—(1) Specify in detail the character of the tobacco in each bale by giving (a) country and province of origin, (b) year of production, (c) grade or grades in each bale, (d) number of carrots or pounds of each grade if more than one grade is packed in a bale, (e) the time when, place where, and person from whom purchased, (f) price paid or to be paid for each bale or package, or price for the vega or lot if purchased in bulk, or if obtained otherwise than by purchase, state the actual market value per bale; (2) If an invoice covers or includes bales of tobacco that are part of a vega or lot purchased in bulk, the invoice must contain or be accompanied by a full description of the vega or lot purchased; or if such description has been furnished with a previous importation, the date and identity of such shipment; (3) Packages or bales containing only filler leaf shall be invoiced as filler; when containing filler and wrapper but not more than 35 percent of wrapper, they shall be invoiced as mixed; and when containing more than 35 percent of wrapper, they shall be invoiced as wrapper.

Watches and watch movements classifiable under Chapter 91 of the HTSUS—For all commercial shipments of such articles, there shall be required to be shown on the invoice, or on a separate sheet attached to and constituting a part of the invoice, such information as will reflect with respect to each group, type, or model, the following;

(A) For watches, a thorough description of the composition of the watch cases, the bracelets, bands or straps, the commercial description (ebauche caliber number, ligne size and number of jewels) of the movements contained in the watches, and the type of battery (manufacturer's name and reference number), if the watch is battery-operated;

(B) For watch movements, the commercial description (ebauche caliber number, ligne size and number of jewels). If battery operated, the type of battery (manufacturer's name and reference number);

(C) The name of the manufacturer of the exported watch movements and the name of the country in which the movements were manufactured.

<u>Wearing apparel</u>—(1) All invoices for textile wearing apparel should indicate a component material breakdown in percentages by weight for all component fibers present in the entire garment, as well as separate breakdowns of the fibers in the (outer) shell (exclusive of linings, cuffs, waistbands, collars and other trimmings) and in the lining; (2) for garments that are constructed of more than one component or material (combination of knits and not knit fabric or combinations of knit and/or not knit fabric with leather, fur, plastic including vinyl. etc.), the invoice must show a fiber breakdown in percentages by weight for each separate textile material in the garment and a breakdown in percentages by weight for each nontextile material for the entire garment; (3) For woven garments—Indicate whether the fabric is yarn dyed and whether there are "two or more colors in the warp and/or filling"; (4) For all-white T-shirts and singlets—Indicate whether or not the garment contains pockets, trim, or embroidery; (5) For mufflers—State the exact dimensions (length and width) of the merchandise.

<u>Wood products</u>—(1) Wood sawed or chipped lengthwise, sliced or peeled, whether or not planed, sanded, or finger-jointed, of a thickness exceeding 6 mm (lumber), classifiable under Chapter 44, heading 4407, HTSUS, and wood continuously shaped along any of its edges or faces, whether or not planed, sanded or finger-jointed; coniferous: Subheading 4409.10.90 and Nonconiferous: Subheading 4409.20.90, HTSUS, and dutiable on the basis of cubic meters—

Quantity in cubic meters (m) before dressing; (2) Fiberboard of wood or other ligneous materials whether or not bonded with resins or other organic substances, under Chapter 44, Heading 4411, HTSUS, and classifiable according to its density—Density in grams per cubic centimeter (cm); (3) Plywood consisting solely of sheets of wood, classifiable under Chapter 44, Subheading 4412.11, 4412.12, and 4412.19, HTSUS, and classifiable according to the thickness of the wood sheets—Thickness of each ply in millimeter (mm);

<u>Wool and hair</u>—See § 151.62 of this chapter for additional information required on invoices.

<u>Wool products</u>, except carpets, rugs, mats, and upholsteries, and wool products made more than 20 years before importation (T.D. 50388, 51019)—(1) The percentage of the total fiber weight of the wool product, exclusive of orna-

mentation not exceeding 5 per centum of said total fiber weight, of (a) wool; (b) reprocessed wool; (c) reused wool; (d) each fiber other than wool if said percentage by weight of such fiber is 5 per centum or more; and (e) the aggregate of all other fibers; (2) the maximum percentage of the total weight of the wool product, of any nonfibrous loading, filling, or adulterating matter; and (3) the name of the manufacturer of the wool product, except when such product consists of mixed wastes, residues, and similar merchandise obtained from several suppliers or unknown sources.

<u>Woven fabric of man-made fibers</u> in headings 5407, 5408, 5512, 5513, 5514, 5515, 5516—

(1) State the exact width of the fabric.

(2) Provide a detailed description of the merchandise, (trade name, if any).

(3) Indicate whether bleached, unbleached, dyed, of yarns of different colors and/or printed.

(4) If composed of more than one material, list percentage by weight in each.

(5) Identify the man-made fibers as artificial or synthetic, filament or staple, and state whether the yarns are high tenacity. Specify the number of turns per meter in each yarn.

(6) Specify yarn sizes in warp and filling.

(7) Specify how the fabric is woven (plain weave, twill, sateen, dobby, jacquard, swivel, lappet, etc.).

(8) Indicate the number of single threads per square centimeter in both warp and filling.

(9) Supply the weight per square meter in grams.

(10) Provide the average yarn number using this formula:

$$\frac{100 \times \text{number of single threads per square centimeter}}{(\text{number of grams per square meter})}.$$

(11) For spun yarns, specify whether combed or carded.

(12) For filament yarns, specify whether textured or not textured.

<u>Yarns</u> —(1) All yarn invoices should show: (a) Fiber content by weight; (b) whether single or plied; (c) whether or not put up for retail sale (*See* Section XI, Note 4, HTSUS); (d) whether or not intended for use as sewing thread.

(2) If chief weight of silk—show whether spun or filament.

(3) If chief weight of cotton—show:

    (a) Whether combed or uncombed

    (b) Metric number (mn)

    (c) Whether bleached and/or mercerized.

(4) If chief weight of man-made fiber—show:

    (a) Whether filament, or spun, or a combination of filament and spun

    (b) If a combination of filament and spun—give percentage of filament and spun by weight.

(5) If chief weight of filament man-made fiber—show:

    (a) Whether high tenacity (See Section XI, note 6 HTSUS)

(b) Whether monofilament, multifilament or strip

(c) Whether texturized

(d) Yarn number in decitex

(e) Number of turns per meter

(f) For monofilaments—show cross-sectional dimension in millimeters

(g) For strips—show the width of the strip in millimeters (measure in folded or twisted condition if so imported).

Items or classes of goods may be added to or removed from the list from time to time.

Customs Valuation

Title 19—Customs Duties
Chapter 4—Tariff Act of 1930
Subtitle III—Administrative Provisions
Part I—Definitions and National Customs Automation Program
subpart a—definitions

Sec. 1401a. Value

(a) Generally

(1) Except as otherwise specifically provided for in this chapter, imported merchandise shall be appraised, for the purposes of this chapter, on the basis of the following

(A) The transaction value provided for under subsection (b) of this section.

(B) The transaction value of identical merchandise provided for under subsection (c) of this section, if the value referred to in subparagraph (A) cannot be determined, or can be determined but cannot be used by reason of subsection (b)(2) of this section.

(C) The transaction value of similar merchandise provided for under subsection (c) of this section, if the value referred to in subparagraph (B) cannot be determined.

(D) The deductive value provided for under subsection (d) of this section, if the value referred to in subparagraph (C) cannot be determined and if the importer does not request alternative valuation under paragraph (2).

(E) The computed value provided for under subsection (e) of this section, if the value referred to in subparagraph (D) cannot be determined.

(F) The value provided for under subsection (f) of this section, if the value referred to in subparagraph (E) cannot be determined.

(2) If the value referred to in paragraph (1)(C) cannot be determined with respect to imported merchandise, the merchandise shall be appraised on the basis of the computed value provided for under paragraph (1)(E), rather than the deductive value provided for under paragraph (1)(D), if the importer makes a request to that effect to the customs officer concerned within such time as the Secretary shall prescribe. If the computed value of the merchandise cannot subsequently be determined, the merchandise may not be appraised on the basis of the value referred to

in paragraph (1)(F) unless the deductive value of the merchandise cannot be determined under paragraph (1)(D).

(3) Upon written request therefor by the importer of merchandise, and subject to provisions of law regarding the disclosure of information, the customs officer concerned shall provide the importer with a written explanation of how the value of that merchandise was determined under this section.

(b) Transaction value of imported merchandise

(1) The transaction value of imported merchandise is the price actually paid or payable for the merchandise when sold for exportation to the United States, plus amounts equal to—

(A) the packing costs incurred by the buyer with respect to the imported merchandise;

(B) any selling commission incurred by the buyer with respect to the imported merchandise;

(C) the value, apportioned as appropriate, of any assist;

(D) any royalty or license fee related to the imported merchandise that the buyer is required to pay, directly or indirectly, as a condition of the sale of the imported merchandise for exportation to the United States; and

(E) the proceeds of any subsequent resale, disposal, or use of the imported merchandise that accrue, directly or indirectly, to the seller.

The price actually paid or payable for imported merchandise shall be increased by the amounts attributable to the items (and no others) described in subparagraphs (A) through (E) only to the extent that each such amount (i) is not otherwise included within the price actually paid or payable; and (ii) is based on sufficient information. If sufficient information is not available, for any reason, with respect to any amount referred to in the preceding sentence, the transaction value of the imported merchandise concerned shall be treated, for purposes of this section, as one that cannot be determined.

(2)(A) The transaction value of imported merchandise determined under paragraph (1) shall be the appraised value of that merchandise for the purposes of this chapter only if—

(i) there are no restrictions on the disposition or use of the imported merchandise by the buyer other than restrictions that —

(I) are imposed or required by law,

(II) limit the geographical area in which the merchandise may be resold, or

(III) do not substantially affect the value of the merchandise;

(ii) the sale of, or the price actually paid or payable for, the imported merchandise is not subject to any condition or consideration for which a value cannot be determined with respect to the imported merchandise;

(iii) no part of the proceeds of any subsequent resale, disposal, or use of the imported merchandise by the buyer will accrue directly or indirectly to the seller, unless an appropriate adjustment therefor can be made under paragraph (1)(E); and

(iv) the buyer and seller are not related, or the buyer and seller are related but the transaction value is acceptable, for purposes of this subsection, under subparagraph (B).

(B) The transaction value between a related buyer and seller is acceptable for the purposes of this subsection if an examination of the circumstances of the sale of the imported merchandise indicates that the relationship between such buyer and seller did not influence the price actually paid or payable; or if the transaction value of the imported merchandise closely approximates—

(i) the transaction value of identical merchandise, or of similar merchandise, in sales to unrelated buyers in the United States; or

(ii) the deductive value or computed value for identical merchandise or similar merchandise;

but only if each value referred to in clause (i) or (ii) that is used for comparison relates to merchandise that was exported to the United States at or about the same time as the imported merchandise.

(C) In applying the values used for comparison purposes under subparagraph (B), there shall be taken into account differences with respect to the sales involved (if such differences are based on sufficient information whether supplied by the buyer or otherwise available to the customs officer concerned) in—

(i) commercial levels;

(ii) quantity levels;

(iii) the costs, commissions, values, fees, and proceeds described in paragraph (1); and

(iv) the costs incurred by the seller in sales in which he and the buyer are not related that are not incurred by the seller in sales in which he and the buyer are related.

(3) The transaction value of imported merchandise does not include any of the following, if identified separately from the price actually paid or payable and from any cost or other item referred to in paragraph (1):

(A) Any reasonable cost or charge that is incurred for—

(i) the construction, erection, assembly, or maintenance of, or the technical assistance provided with respect to, the merchandise after its importation into the United States; or

(ii) the transportation of the merchandise after such importation.

(B) The customs duties and other Federal taxes currently payable on the imported merchandise by reason of its importation, and any Federal excise tax on, or measured by the value of, such merchandise for which vendors in the United States are ordinarily liable.

(4) For purposes of this subsection—

(A) The term "price actually paid or payable" means the total payment (whether direct or indirect, and exclusive of any costs, charges, or expenses incurred for transportation, insurance, and related services incident to the international shipment of the merchandise from the country of exportation to the place of importation in the United States) made, or to be made, for imported merchandise by the buyer to, or for the benefit of, the seller.

(B) Any rebate of, or other decrease in, the price actually paid or payable that is made or otherwise effected between the buyer and seller after the date of the importation of the merchandise into the United States shall be disregarded in determining the transaction value under paragraph (1).

(c) Transaction value of identical merchandise and similar merchandise

(1) The transaction value of identical merchandise, or of similar merchandise, is the transaction value (acceptable as the appraised value for purposes of this chapter under subsection (b) of this section but adjusted under paragraph (2) of this subsection) of imported merchandise that is—

(A) with respect to the merchandise being appraised, either identical merchandise or similar merchandise, as the case may be; and

(B) exported to the United States at or about the time that the merchandise being appraised is exported to the United States.

(2) Transaction values determined under this subsection shall be based on sales of identical merchandise or similar merchandise, as the case may be, at the same commercial level and in substantially the same quantity as the sales of the merchandise being appraised. If no such sale is found, sales of identical merchandise or similar merchandise at either a different commercial level or in different quantities, or both, shall be used, but adjusted to take account of any such difference. Any adjustment made under this paragraph shall be based on sufficient information. If in applying this paragraph with respect to any imported merchandise, two or more transaction values for identical merchandise, or for similar merchandise, are

determined, such imported merchandise shall be appraised on the basis of the lower or lowest of such values.

(d) Deductive value

(1) For purposes of this subsection, the term "merchandise concerned" means the merchandise being appraised, identical merchandise, or similar merchandise.

(2)(A) The deductive value of the merchandise being appraised is whichever of the following prices (as adjusted under paragraph (3)) is appropriate depending upon when and in what condition the merchandise concerned is sold in the United States:

(i) If the merchandise concerned is sold in the condition as imported at or about the date of importation of the merchandise being appraised, the price is the unit price at which the merchandise concerned is sold in the greatest aggregate quantity at or about such date.

(ii) If the merchandise concerned is sold in the condition as imported but not sold at or about the date of importation of the merchandise being appraised, the price is the unit price at which the merchandise concerned is sold in the greatest aggregate quantity after the date of importation of the merchandise being appraised but before the close of the 90th day after the date of such importation.

(iii) If the merchandise concerned was not sold in the condition as imported and not sold before the close of the 90th day after the date of importation of the merchandise being appraised, the price is the unit price at which the merchandise being appraised, after further processing, is sold in the greatest aggregate quantity before the 180th day after the date of such importation. This clause shall apply to appraisement of merchandise only if the importer so elects and notifies the customs officer concerned of that election within such time as shall be prescribed by the Secretary.

(B) For purposes of subparagraph (A), the unit price at which merchandise is sold in the greatest aggregate quantity is the unit price at which such merchandise is sold to unrelated persons, at the first commercial level after importation (in cases to which subparagraph (A)(i) or (ii) applies) or after further processing (in cases to which subparagraph (A)(iii) applies) at which such sales take place, in a total volume that is (i) greater than the total volume sold at any other unit price, and (ii) sufficient to establish the unit price.

(3)(A) the price determined under paragraph (2) shall be reduced by an amount equal to—

(i) any commission usually paid or agreed to be paid, or the addition usually made for profit and general expenses, in connection with sales in the United States of imported merchandise that is of the same class or kind, regardless of the country of exportation, as the merchandise concerned;

(ii) the actual costs and associated costs of transportation and insurance incurred with respect to international shipments of the merchandise concerned from the country of exportation to the United States;

(iii) the usual costs and associated costs of transportation and insurance incurred with respect to shipments of such merchandise from the place of importation to the place of delivery in the United States, if such costs are not included as a general expense under clause (i);

(iv) the customs duties and other Federal taxes currently payable on the merchandise concerned by reason of its importation, and any Federal excise tax on, or measured by the value of, such merchandise for which vendors in the United States are ordinarily liable; and

(v) (but only in the case of a price determined under paragraph (2)(A)(iii)) the value added by the processing of the merchandise after importation to the extent that the value is based on sufficient information relating to cost of such processing.

(B) For purposes of applying paragraph (A)—

(i) the deduction made for profits and general expenses shall be based upon the importer's profits and general expenses, unless such profits and general expenses are inconsistent with those reflected in sales in the United States of imported merchandise of the same class or kind, in which case the deduction shall be based on the usual profit and general expenses reflected in such sales, as determined from sufficient information; and

(ii) any State or local tax imposed on the importer with respect to the sale of imported merchandise shall be treated as a general expense.

(C) The price determined under paragraph (2) shall be increased (but only to the extent that such costs are not otherwise included) by an amount equal to the packing costs incurred by the importer or the buyer, as the case may be, with respect to the merchandise concerned.

(D) For purposes of determining the deductive value of imported merchandise, any sale to a person who supplies any assist for use in connection with the production or sale for export of the merchandise concerned shall be disregarded.

(e) Computed value

(1) The computed value of imported merchandise is the sum of—

(A) the cost or value of the materials and the fabrication and other processing of any kind employed in the production of the imported merchandise;

(B) an amount for profit and general expenses equal to that usually reflected in sales of merchandise of the same class or kind as the imported merchandise that are made by the producers in the country of exportation for export to the United States;

(C) any assist, if its value is not included under subparagraph (A) or (B); and (D) the packing costs.

(2) For purposes of paragraph (1)—

(A) the cost or value of materials under paragraph (1)(A) shall not include the amount of any internal tax imposed by the country of exportation that is directly applicable to the materials or their disposition if the tax is remitted or refunded upon the exportation of the merchandise in the production of which the materials were used; and

(B) the amount for profit and general expenses under paragraph (1)(B) shall be based upon the producer's profits and expenses, unless the producer's profits and expenses are inconsistent with those usually reflected in sales of merchandise of the same class or kind as the imported merchandise that are made by producers in the country of exportation for export to the United States, in which case the amount under paragraph (1)(B) shall be based on the usual profit and general expenses of such producers in such sales, as determined from sufficient information.

(f) Value if other values cannot be determined or used

(1) If the value of imported merchandise cannot be determined, or otherwise used for the purposes of this chapter, under subsections (b) through (e) of this section, the merchandise shall be appraised for the purposes of this chapter on the basis of a value that is derived from the methods set forth in such subsections, with such methods being reasonably adjusted to the extent necessary to arrive at a value.

(2) Imported merchandise may not be appraised, for the purposes of this chapter, on the basis of—

(A) the selling price in the United States of merchandise produced in the United States;

(B) a system that provides for the appraisement of imported merchandise at the higher of two alternative values;

(C) the price of merchandise in the domestic market of the country of exportation;

(D) a cost of production, other than a value determined under subsection (e) of this section for merchandise that is identical merchandise or similar merchandise to the merchandise being appraised;

(E) the price of merchandise for export to a country other than the United States;

(F) minimum values for appraisement; or

(G) arbitrary or fictitious values.

This paragraph shall not apply with respect to the ascertainment, determination, or estimation of foreign market value or United States price under subtitle IV of this chapter.

(g) Special rules

(1) For purposes of this section, the persons specified in any of the following subparagraphs shall be treated as persons who are related:

(A) Members of the same family, including brothers and sisters (whether by whole or half blood), spouse, ancestors, and lineal descendants.

(B) Any officer or director of an organization and such organization.

(C) An officer or director of an organization and an officer or director of another organization, if each such individual is also an officer or director in the other organization.

(D) Partners.

(E) Employer and employee.

(F) Any person directly or indirectly owning, controlling, or holding with power to vote, 5 percent or more of the outstanding voting stock or shares of any organization and such organization.

(G) Two or more persons directly or indirectly controlling, controlled by, or under common control with, any person.

(2) For purposes of this section, merchandise (including, but not limited to, identical merchandise and similar merchandise) shall be treated as being of the same class or kind as other merchandise if it is within a group or range of merchandise produced by a particular industry or industry sector.

(3) For purposes of this section, information that is submitted by an importer, buyer, or producer in regard to the appraisement of merchandise may not be rejected by the customs officer concerned on the basis of the accounting method by which that information was prepared, if the preparation was in accordance with generally accepted accounting principles. The term "generally accepted accounting principles" refers to any generally recognized consensus or substantial authoritative support regarding—

(A) which economic resources and obligations should be recorded as assets and liabilities;

(B) which changes in assets and liabilities should be recorded;

(C) how the assets and liabilities and changes in them should be measured;

(D) what information should be disclosed and how it should be disclosed; and

(E) which financial statements should be prepared.

The applicability of a particular set of generally accepted accounting principles will depend upon the basis on which the value of the merchandise is sought to be established.

(h) Definitions

As used in this section—

(1)(A) The term "assist" means any of the following if supplied directly or indirectly, and free of charge or at reduced cost, by the buyer of imported merchandise for use in connection with the production or the sale for export to the United States of the merchandise:

(i) Materials, components, parts, and similar items incorporated in the imported merchandise.

(ii) Tools, dies, molds, and similar items used in the production of the imported merchandise.

(iii) Merchandise consumed in the production of the imported merchandise.

(iv) Engineering, development, artwork, design work, and plans and sketches that are undertaken elsewhere than in the United States and are necessary for the production of the imported merchandise.

(B) No service or work to which subparagraph (A)(iv) applies shall be treated as an assist for purposes of this section if such service or work— (i) is performed by an individual who is domiciled within the United States; (ii) is performed by that individual while he is acting as an employee or agent of the buyer of the imported merchandise; and (iii) is incidental to other engineering, development, artwork, design work, or plans or sketches that are undertaken within the United States.

(C) For purposes of this section, the following apply in determining the value of assists described in subparagraph (A)(iv):

(i) The value of an assist that is available in the public domain is the cost of obtaining copies of the assist.

(ii) If the production of an assist occurred in the United States and one or more foreign countries, the value of the assist is the value thereof that is added outside the United States.

(2) The term "identical merchandise" means—

(A) merchandise that is identical in all respects to, and was produced in the same country and by the same person as, the merchandise being appraised; or

(B) if merchandise meeting the requirements under subparagraph (A) cannot be found (or for purposes of applying subsection (b)(2)(B)(i) of this section, regardless of whether merchandise meeting such requirements can be found), merchandise that is identical in all respects to, and was produced in the same country as, but not produced by the same person as, the merchandise being appraised.

Such term does not include merchandise that incorporates or reflects any engineering, development, artwork, design work, or plan or sketch that—

(I) was supplied free or at reduced cost by the buyer of the merchandise for use in connection with the production or the sale for export to the United States of the merchandise; and

(II) is not an assist because undertaken within the United States.

(3) The term "packing costs" means the cost of all containers and coverings of whatever nature and of packing, whether for labor or materials, used in placing merchandise in condition, packed ready for shipment to the United States.

(4) The term "similar merchandise" means— (A) merchandise that—

(i) was produced in the same country and by the same person as the merchandise being appraised,

(ii) is like the merchandise being appraised in characteristics and component material, and

(iii) is commercially interchangeable with the merchandise being appraised; or

(B) if merchandise meeting the requirements under subparagraph (A) cannot be found (or for purposes of applying subsection (b)(2)(B)(i) of this section, regardless of whether merchandise meeting such requirements can be found), merchandise that— (i) was produced in the same country as, but not produced by the same person as, the merchandise being appraised, and (ii) meets the requirement set forth in subparagraph (A)(ii) and (iii).

Such term does not include merchandise that incorporates or reflects any engineering, development, artwork, design work, or plan or sketch that—

(I) was supplied free or at reduced cost by the buyer of the merchandise for use in connection with the production or the sale for export to the United States of the merchandise; and

(II) is not an assist because undertaken within the United States.

(5) The term "sufficient information", when required under this section for determining—

(A) any amount—

(i) added under subsection (b)(1) of this section to the price actually paid or payable,

(ii) deducted under subsection (d)(3) of this section as profit or general expense or value from further processing, or (iii) added under subsection (e)(2) of this section as profit or general expense;

(B) any difference taken into account for purposes of subsection (b)(2)(C) of this section; or (C) any adjustment made under subsection (c)(2) of this section;

means information that establishes the accuracy of such amount, difference, or adjustment.

(June 17, 1930, ch. 497, title IV, Sec. 402, as added Aug. 2, 1956, ch. 887, Sec. 2(a), 70 Stat. 943; amended July 26, 1979, Pub. L. 96-39, title II, Sec. 201(a), 93 Stat. 194; Dec. 2, 1980, Pub. L. 96-490, Sec. 2, 94 Stat. 2556.)

Interim (a)(1)(A) List

Note: This is also known as the List of Records Required for the Entry of Merchandise. This interim list is dated December 21, 1995; it will be replaced by a substantially similar list in the future (possibly in 1997) which will become a final rule.

General Information

Section 508 of the Tariff Act of 1930, as amended (19 U.S.C. 1508), sets forth the general record keeping requirements for Customs-related activities. Section 509 of the Tariff Act of 1930, as amended (19 U.S.C. 1509) sets forth the procedures for the production and examination of those records (which includes, but is not limited to, any statement, declaration, document, or electronically generated or machine readable data).

Section 509(a)(1)(A) of the Tariff Act of 1930, as amended by title VI of Public Law 103- 182, commonly referred to as the Customs Modernization Act (19 U.S.C. 1509(a)(1)(A)), requires the production, within a reasonable time after demand by the Customs Service is made (taking into consideration the number, type and age of the item demanded) if "such record is required by law or regulation for the entry of the merchandise (whether or not the Customs Service required its presentation at the time of entry)". Section 509(e) of the Tariff Act of 1930, as amended by Public Law 103-182 (19 U.S.C. 1509(e)) requires the Customs Service to identify and publish a list of the records and entry information that is required to be maintained and produced under subsection (a)(1)(A) of section 509 (19 U.S.C. 1509 (a)(1)(A)). This list is commonly referred to as "the (a)(1)(A) list."

The Customs Service has tried to identify all the presently required entry information or records on the following list. However, as automated programs and new procedures are introduced, these may change. In addition, errors and omissions to the list may be discovered upon further review by Customs officials or the trade. Pursuant to section 509(g), the failure to produce listed records or information upon reasonable demand may result in penalty action or liquidation or reliquidation at a higher rate than entered. A record keeping penalty may not be assessed if the listed information or records are transmitted to and retained by Customs.

Other Recordkeeping Requirements. The importing community and Customs officials are reminded that the (a)(1)(A) list only pertains to records or information required for the entry of merchandise. An owner, importer, consignee, importer of record, entry filer, or other party who imports merchandise, files a drawback claim or transports or stores bonded merchandise, any agent of the foregoing, or any person whose activities require them to file a declaration or entry, is also required to make, keep and render for examination and inspection records (including, but not limited to, statements, declarations, documents and electronically generated or machine readable data) which pertain to any such activity or the information contained in the records required by the Tariff Act in connection with any such activity; and are normally kept in the ordinary course of business. While these records are not subject to administrative penalties, they are subject to examination and/or summons by Customs officers. Failure to comply could result in the imposition of significant judicially imposed penalties and denial of import privileges.

The following list does not replace entry requirements, but is merely provided for information and reference. In the case of the list conflicting with regulatory or statutory requirements, the latter will govern.

List of Records Required for the Entry of Merchandise

The following records (which includes, but is not limited to, any statement, declaration, document, or electronically generated or machine readable data) are required by law or regulation for the entry of merchandise and are required to be maintained and produced to Customs upon reasonable demand (whether or not Customs required its presentation at the time of entry). Information may be submitted to Customs at time of entry in a Customs authorized electronic or paper format. Not every entry of merchandise requires all of the following information. Only those records or information applicable to the entry requirements for the merchandise in question will be required/mandatory. The list may be amended as Customs reviews its requirements and continues to implement the Customs Modernization Act. When a record or information is filed with and retained by Customs, the record is not subject to record keeping penalties, although the underlying backup or supporting information from which it is obtained may also be subject to the general record retention regulations and examination or summons pursuant to 19 U.S.C. 1508 and 1509.

All references, unless otherwise indicated, are to title 19, Code of Federal Regulations, April 1, 1995 Edition, as amended by subsequent Federal Register notices.

I. General list or records required for most entries. Information shown with an asterisk (*) is usually on the appropriate form and filed with and retained by Customs:

141.11–.15	Evidence of right to make entry (airway bill/bill of lading or * carrier certificate, etc.) when goods are imported on a common carrier.
141.19	* Declaration of entry (usually contained on the entry summary or warehouse entry)
141.32	Power of attorney (when required by regulations)
141.54	Consolidated shipments authority to make entry (if this procedure is utilized)
142.3	Packing list (where appropriate)
142.4	Bond information (except if 10.101 or 142.4(c) applies)
Parts 4,18,122,123*	Vessel, Vehicle or Air Manifest (filed by the carrier)

II. The following records or information are required by 141.61 on Customs Form (CF) 3461 or CF 7533 or the regulations cited. Information shown with an asterisk (*) is contained on the appropriate form and/or otherwise filed with and retained by Customs:

142.3–3a	* Entry Number * Entry Type Code * Elected Entry Date * Port Code
142.4	* Bond information
141.61,142.3a	* Broker/Importer Filer Number
141.61,142.3	* Ultimate Consignee Name and Number/street address of premises to be delivered
141.61	* Importer of Record Number * Country of Origin
141.11	* IT/BL/AWB Number and Code * Arrival Date
141.61	* Carrier Code * Voyage/Flight/Trip * Vessel Code/Name * Manufacturer ID Number (for AD/CVD must be actual mfr.) * Location of Goods-Code(s)/Name(s) * U.S. Port of Unlading * General Order Number (only when required by the regulations)
142.6	* Description of Merchandise
142.6	* HTSUSA Number
142.6	* Manifest Quantity * Total Value * Signature of Applicant

III. In addition to the information listed above, the following records or items of information are required by law and regulation for the entry of merchandise and are presently required to be produced by the importer of record at the time the Customs Form 7501 is filed.

141.61	* Entry Summary Date
141.61	* Entry Date
142.3	* Bond Number, Bond Type Code and Surety code
142.3	* Ultimate Consignee Address
141.61	* Importer of Record Name and Address
141.61	* Exporting Country and Date Exported * I.T. (In-bond) Entry Date (IT Entries only) * Mode of Transportation (MOT Code)
141.61	* Importing Carrier Name
141.82	Conveyance Name/Number * Foreign Port of Lading * Import Date and Line Numbers * Reference Number * HTSUS Number

141.61	* Identification number for merchandise subject to Anti-dumping or Countervailing duty order (ADA/CVD Case Number)
141.61	* Gross Weight * Manifest Quantity
141.61	* Net Quantity in HTSUSA Units
141.61	* Entered Value, Charges, and Relationship
141.61	* Applicable HTSUSA Rate, ADA/CVD Rate, I.R.C. Rate, and/or Visa Number, Duty, I.R. Tax, and Fees (e.g. HMF, MPF, Cotton)
141.61	Non-Dutiable Charges
141.61	* Signature of Declarant, Title, and Date * Textile Category Number
141.83,.86	Invoice information which includes-e.g., date, number, merchandise (commercial product) description, quantities, values, unit price, trade terms, part, model, style, marks and numbers, name and address of foreign party responsible for invoicing, kind of currency Terms of Sale Shipping Quantities Shipping Units of Measurements Manifest Description of Goods Foreign Trade Zone Designation and Status Designation (if applicable) Indication of Eligibility for Special Access Program (9802/GSP/CBI) 141.89 CF 5523
141.89, et al	Corrected Commercial Invoice
141.86 (e)	Packing List
177.8	* Binding Ruling Identification Number (or a copy of the ruling)
10.102	Duty Free Entry Certificate (9808.00.30009)
10.108	Lease Statement

IV. Documents/records or information required for entry of special categories of merchandise (The listed documents or information is only required for merchandise entered (or required to be entered) in accordance with the provisions of the sections of 19 CFR (the Customs Regulations) listed). These are In addition to any documents/records or information required by other agencies in their regulations for the entry of merchandise:

4.14	CF 226 Information for vessel repairs, parts and equipment
7.8(a)	CF 3229 Origin certificate for insular possessions
7.8(b)	CF 3311 and Shipper's declaration for insular possessions

Documents required for entry of articles exported and returned

10.1-10.6	foreign shipper's declaration or master's certificate, declaration for free entry by owner, importer or consignee

10.7	certificate from foreign shipper for reusable containers
10.8	declaration of person performing alterations or repairs declaration for non-conforming merchandise
10.9	declaration of processing
10.24	declaration by assembler endorsement by importer
10.31,.35	Documents required for Temporary Importations Under Bond: Information required, Bond or Carnet
10.36	Lists for samples, professional equipment, theatrical effects

Documents required for Instruments of International Traffic:

10.41	Application, Bond or TIR carnet Note: additional 19 U.S.C. 1508 records: see 10.41b(e)
10.43	Documents required for exempt organizations
10.46	Request from head of agency for 9808.00.10 or 9808.00.20 HTSUS treatment

Documents required for works of art

10.48	declaration of artist, seller or shipper, curator, etc.
10.49,.52	declaration by institution
10.53	declaration by importer USFWS Form 3-177, if appropriate
10.59,.63	Documents/ CF 5125/ for withdrawal of ship supplies
10.66,.67	Declarations for articles exported and returned
10.68.,69	Documents for commercial samples, tools, theatrical effects
10.70,.71	Purebred breeding certificate
10.84	Automotive Products certificate
10.90	Master records and metal matrices: detailed statement of cost of production.
10.98	Declarations for copper fluxing material
10.99	Declaration of non-beverage ethyl alcohol, ATF permit
10.101-.102	Stipulation for government shipments and/or certification for government duty-free entries, etc.
10.107	Report for rescue and relief equipment
15 CFR 301	Requirements for entry of scientific and educational apparatus
10.121	Certificate from USIA for visual/auditory materials
10.134	Declaration of actual use (When classification involves actual use)
10.138	End Use Certificate

10.171	Documents, etc. required for entries of GSP merchandise
10.173,10.175	GSP Declaration (plus supporting documentation)
10.174	Evidence of direct shipment
10.179	Certificate of importer of crude petroleum
10.180	Certificate of fresh, chilled or frozen beef
10.183	Civil aircraft parts/simulator documentation and certifications
10.191-.198	Documents, etc. required for entries of CBI merchandise CBI declaration of origin (plus supporting information)
10.194	Evidence of direct shipment
[10.306	Evidence of direct shipment for CFTA]
[10.307	Documents, etc. required for entries under CFTA Certificate of origin of CF 353]

[Note: CFTA provisions are suspended while NAFTA remains in effect. See part 181]

12.6	European Community cheese affidavit
12.7	HHS permit for milk or cream importation
12.11	Notice of arrival for plant and plant products
12.17	APHIS Permit animal viruses, serums and toxins
12.21	HHS license for viruses, toxins, antitoxins, etc. for treatment of man
12.23	Notice of claimed investigational exemption for a new drug
12.26-.31	Necessary permits from APHIS, FWS & foreign government certificates when required by the applicable regulation
12.33	Chop list, proforma invoice and release permit from HHS
12.34	Certificate of match inspection and importer's declaration
12.43	Certificate of origin/declarations for goods made by forced labor, etc.
12.61	Shipper's declaration, official certificate for seal and otter skins
12.73 12.80	Motor vehicle declarations
12.85	Boat declarations (CG-5096) and USCG exemption
12.91	FDA form 2877 and required declarations for electronics products
12.99	Declarations for switchblade knives
12.104-.104i	Cultural property declarations, statements and certificates of origin Pre-Columbian monumental and
12.105-.109	architectural sculpture and murals certificate of legal exportation evidence of exemption

12.110	Pesticides, etc. notice of arrival
12.118-.127	Toxic substances: TSCA statements Textiles & textile products
12.130	Single country declaration Multiple country declaration VISA
12.132	NAFTA textile requirements
54.5	Declaration by importer of use of use of certain metal articles
54.6 (a)	Re-Melting Certificate
114	Carnets (serves as entry and bond document where applicable)
115	Container certificate of approval
128	Express consignments
128.21	* Manifests with required information (filed by carrier)
132.23	Acknowledgment of delivery for mailed items subject to quota Consent from trademark or trade name
133.21(b)(6)	Holder to import otherwise restricted goods
134.25,.36	Certificate of marking; notice to repacker
141.88	Computed value information
141.89	Additional invoice information required for certain classes of merchandise including, but not limited to: *Textile Entries:* Quota charge Statement, if applicable including Style Number, Article Number and Product *Steel Entries:* Ordering specifications, including but not limited to, all applicable industry standards and mill certificates, including but not limited to, chemical composition.
143.13	Documents required for appraisement entries bills, statements of costs of production value declaration
143.23	Informal entry: Commercial invoice plus declaration
144.12	Warehouse entry information
145.11	Customs Declaration for Mail, Invoice
145.12	Mail entry information (CF 3419 is completed by Customs but formal entry may be required.)
148	Supporting documents for personal importations
151 subpart B	Scale Weight
151 subpart B	Sugar imports sampling/lab information (Chemical Analysis)

151 subpart C	Petroleum imports sampling/lab information Out turn Report 24. to 25. - Reserved
151 subpart E	Wool and Hair invoice information, additional documents
151 subpart F	Cotton invoice information, additional documents
181.22	NAFTA Certificate of origin and supporting record
19 USC 1356k	Coffee Form O (currently suspended)

Entry Procedures and Documentation

Contents

Introduction

This chapter provides an overview of U.S. Customs and Border Protection (hereafter U.S. Customs) import procedures and documentation requirements. Most imports of non-regulated goods require minimal documentation and procedures. However, each complicating factor adds another document or step to the process. The chapter starts with the most basic import entry and then proceeds to more complicated entries with specialized requirements, procedures and documentation.

Import Requirements

- An individual may make his/her own Customs clearance of goods imported for personal or commercial use. All merchandise coming into the United States must clear Customs and is subject to Customs duty unless specifically exempted by law. Clearance involves a number of steps: entry, inspection, appraisement, classification and liquidation.

- U.S. Customs does not require an importer to have a license or permit. Other agencies may require a permit, license, or other certification, depending on what is being imported. Customs entry forms do ask for your importer number. This is either your Internal Revenue Service (IRS) business registration number, or if your business is not registered with the IRS or you do not have a business, your social security number.

- The importer must declare the dutiable value of merchandise. Final appraisement, however, is fixed by U.S. Customs. Several appraisement methods are used to arrive at this value. The transaction value serves as the primary basis of appraisement. Transaction value is the price actually paid or payable by the buyer to the seller for the goods imported. Other factors may also add to the dutiable value of merchandise, such as packing costs, selling commissions, royalty or licensing fees, etc. When the transaction value cannot be determined, then the value of the imported goods is the transaction value of identical merchandise. If merchandise identical to the imported goods cannot be found, then the value is the transaction value of similar merchandise. Similar merchandise means merchandise that is produced in the same country and by the same person as the merchandise being appraised. It must be commercially interchangeable with the merchandise being appraised and must have been exported to the United States at or about the same time the merchandise being appraised is exported to the United States.

- In an informal entry a U.S. Customs inspector determines the classification number of the imported goods. In a formal entry the importer or customs house broker is responsible. The Harmonized Tariff Schedule of the United States (HTSUS), prescribes the classification of merchandise by type of product; e.g., animal and vegetable products, textile fibers and textile products.

- The importer must pay estimated duties and processing fees if applicable. Customs makes the final determination of the correct rate of duty. The duty rate of an item is tied to its classification number. The HTSUS provides several rates of duty for each item. Customs duties are generally assessed at ad valorem rates (a percentage of the dutiable value of the imported goods). Some articles, however, are dutiable at a specific rate (so much per piece, liter, kilo, etc.); others at a compound rate of duty (i.e., combination of both ad valorem and specific rates).

- If formal entry is required the importer generally has to post a surety bond.

- It is the importer's responsibility to ensure that his or her goods being imported meet admissibility requirements—such as proper marking, safety standards, etc.—and that the proper permits, if required, have been obtained in advance of the goods arriving in the United States.

Arrival of Goods

Imported goods may not legally enter U.S. commerce until the shipment has arrived within the port of entry and Customs has authorized delivery of the merchandise. This is accomplished by filing the appropriate documents, either by the importer or by the importer's agent.

U.S. Customs does not notify the importer of the arrival of the shipment. The carrier of the goods usually makes notification of arrival. Arrangements should be made to ensure that the importer or their agent is informed immediately of arrival so that the entry can be filed and delays in obtaining the goods avoided.

U.S. Customs defines "entry" not merely as the arrival of goods at a port, but as the process of presenting documentation for clearing goods through Customs. Imported merchandise not entered through Customs in a timely manner (within 15 calendar days of arrival) is sent by Customs to a general order warehouse to be held as unclaimed. The importer is responsible for paying storage charges while unclaimed merchandise is held at the warehouse. If it remains unclaimed at the end of six months, the merchandise is sold at auction.

Some type of Customs entry must be made at the first port of arrival. Ordinarily entry is made there for consumption, for entry into a bonded warehouse, or for transportation in bond to another port where a consumption or warehouse entry will be made. If an importer does not wish to prepare and file the entry, commercial brokers, known as customs brokers and licensed by U.S. Customs, may act as an agent for the importer.

Customs house brokers must first secure a power of attorney from the importer to act as their agent. Brokers charge a fee for their services. A list of customs brokers may be obtained from the local Customs office or found in the yellow pages of the local telephone directory. See "Power of Attorney CF 5291" on page 336. See "Corporate Surety Power of Attorney CF 5297" on page 337.

In the case of a single noncommercial shipment, a relative or other individual may act as the importer's agent. This person must know the facts pertaining to the shipment and must be authorized in writing to act for the importer.

The law prohibits Customs employees from performing these tasks for the importing public. However, they will advise and give information to importers about Customs requirements.

Informal Entry

Definition

Informal entries cover personal or commercial shipments, including those by mail, of less than $2,000 value. However, textiles, certain types of footwear and other goods subject to quota/visa restrictions require a formal entry, as do personal shipments valued over $2000. Valuation in these cases is almost always the transaction value (sale price of the goods in the country of origin).

An informal entry does not require a customs bond and the final computation of duties (liquidation) is handled on the spot. In fact, the majority of informal entries do not require payment of import duties.

Finally, a port director may require a formal entry for any importation if he or she deems it necessary for the protection of the revenue of the U.S. or for admissibility or enforcement issues.

Procedure

In practical terms, there are five ways informal entries occur: 1) by mail, 2) by courier, 3) as accompanied baggage (goods) with a traveller, 4) as unaccompanied baggage (goods) shipped apart from a traveller, or 5) as a shipment by air, water, road or rail.

1) By Mail

Mail shipments of unregulated items are very straightforward. The overseas shipper fills out a simple form at a local post office and sends the package through the international postal system. If the goods are not regulated, and if there is no duty to be paid, the address in the U.S. gets the package delivered by the U.S. Postal Service.

Regulated items and other issues, however, can make a mail entry more complex. See "Mail Entry" on page 309.

2) By Courier

Courier shipments of unregulated items have become very straightforward. The overseas shipper fills out a simple form, typically on the courier's air waybill itself, and sends the package. If the goods are not regulated, and if there is no duty to be paid, the address in the U.S. simply gets the package delivered by the courier service. If duty is assessed on the shipment, the courier service can bill either the account of the shipper or addressee (consignee).

3) As Accompanied Baggage

Often, an international traveller will enter the United States with personal and business items acquired overseas that qualify for an informal entry. These are handled on the very straightforward Customs Declaration form CF 6059B that flight attendants and pursers hand out on airplanes and cruise ships prior to landing at a U.S. port or airport. This form simply asks for a listing of items purchased overseas, their value and their total value.

Be prepared for U.S. Customs inspection of the goods and requests for receipts for the goods purchased. Customs inspectors are trained to know the origin and value of many items, so, as always, honesty is the best policy.

If the goods are unregulated, do not infringe upon trademark laws and their value is less than $2,000, the traveller can clear Customs on the spot.

No duty is assessed if the dutiable value of the goods is less than $1,250. Duty is assessed if the dutiable value is greater than $1,250.

See "Customs Declaration CF 6059B" on page 330.

4) As Unaccompanied Baggage, or
5) As an Ocean or Air Shipment

When a shipment reaches the United States, the importer of record (i.e., the owner, purchaser, or licensed customs broker designated by the owner, purchaser, or consignee) will file entry documents for the goods with the port director at the port of entry. These documents typically include 1) Commercial Invoice, 2) Bill of Lading and 3) Declaration of Free Entry form CF 3299.

Imported goods are not legally entered until after the shipment has arrived within the port of entry, delivery of the merchandise has been authorized by Customs, and estimated duties have been paid. It is the responsibility of the importer of record to arrange for examination and release of the goods.

The importer gets an invoice from the merchant and an air waybill, bill of lading, or carrier's certificate from the shipping agent. The shipping agent or freight forwarder then submits a manifest to customs. The freight forwarder informs the importer when the goods have arrived and validates the bill of lading.

Finally, the importer contacts the storage / wharf company and pays wharfage and storage. The importer contacts U.S. Customs for the goods, U.S. Customs examines and assesses the goods; the importer pays duty and customs then releases the goods.

Goods admitted as informal entries do not require the posting of a bond and computation of duties (liquidation) is handled on the spot by the Customs inspector / agent.

When an informal entry is being made, the inspector, not the importer, is responsible for determining the classification number of the goods being imported. The inspector also completes the Customs forms used for informal entry.

See "Power of Attorney CF 5291" on page 336.

Basic Documents for Informal Entry

Document	Notes	Sample
Commercial Invoice	A	page 314
Bill of Lading/Air Waybill (B/L)	B	page 316
Customs Declaration CF 6059B	C	page 330
Declaration for Free Entry of Unaccompanied Articles (CF 3299)	D	page 332
Entry Summary (CF 7501) (can also be used for informal entry)	E	page 342

Notes:

A—COMMERCIAL INVOICE
(issued by the exporter / seller)
This is the key transaction or accounting document and shows the value and description of the merchandise.

B—BILL OF LADING
(issued by the shipping line or carrier of the goods)
This is the key transportation document. The bill of lading, airway bill, or carrier's certificate is used as evidence of the consignee's right to make entry.
Because goods may be entered only by the owner, purchaser, or by a licensed customs broker, evidence of the right to make entry is required. The bill of lading, air waybill and carrier's certificate serve this purpose. As long as the goods are consigned "to order," the bill of lading, properly endorsed by the consignor, may serve as evidence of the right to make entry. An air waybill may be used for merchandise arriving by air.
In most instances, entry is made by a person or firm certified by the carrier bringing the goods to the port of entry and is considered the "owner" of the goods for customs purposes. The document issued by the carrier is known as a "Carrier's Certificate." In certain circumstances, entry may be made by means of a duplicate bill of lading or a shipping receipt.

C—CUSTOMS DECLARATION (CF 6059B)
(filled out by the traveler / importer and handed directly to a Customs agent at the port and point of entry)
This is the well-known form that flight attendants and pursers hand out on airplanes and cruise ships prior to landing at a U.S. port or airport. This form simply asks for name and address of the importer, information about countries visited, whether fruits, vegetables or other foodstuffs are being imported, and a listing of items purchased overseas, their value and their total value.

D—DECLARATION FOR FREE ENTRY OF UNACCOMPANIED ARTICLES (CF 3299)
(issued by the importer or a customs broker working as agent for the importer)
This is the formal statement by the importer to the import authority identifying the seller, buyer, goods shipped, date of issuance, country of origin and country of final destination, quantity, description and cost of the goods, and shipping details. This is required by U.S. Customs to assess duties, and compile trade statistics. This form has different names in different countries. In the USA it is called the entry manifest.

E—ENTRY SUMMARY (CF 7501)
(issued by the importer or a customs broker acting as agent for the importer)
CF 7501 is the document used for formal entries, but may also be used for filing an informal entry.
The CF 7501 is the formal statement by the importer to U.S. Customs identifying the seller, buyer, goods shipped, date of issuance of the form, country of origin and country of final destination, quantity, description and cost of the goods, and shipping details. This form is required to assess duties and compile trade statistics.

Formal Entry

Definition

Formal entries cover commercial and personal shipments with a U.S. Customs valuation greater than $2,000 as well as shipments of certain commodities, such as textiles, some types of footwear and other goods subject to quota/visa restrictions, regardless of value. Formal entries require the filing of a Customs bond and may involve extensive paperwork.

Customs House Brokers

The importer may file his or her own formal entry. Because filing a formal entry can be complicated, however, U.S. Customs recommends that importers consider hiring a customs house broker to complete the transaction. A customs broker acts as the importer's agent in dealings with U.S. Customs. Lists of licensed customs brokers can be found on the port pages of the U.S. Customs web site at www.customs.ustreas.gov.

Brokers charge a fee for their services. A list of customs brokers may be obtained from the local Customs office or found in the yellow pages of the local telephone directory.

Customs house brokers must first secure a power of attorney from the importer to act as their agent. See "Power of Attorney CF 5291" on page 336. See "Corporate Surety Power of Attorney CF 5297" on page 337.

Evidence of Right to Make Entry

Goods may be entered only by the owner, purchaser, or a licensed customs broker. When the goods are consigned "to order," the bill of lading properly endorsed by the consignor may serve as evidence of the right to make entry. An air waybill may be used for merchandise arriving by air.

In most instances, entry is made by a person or firm certified by the carrier bringing the goods to the port of entry and is considered the "owner" of the goods for customs purposes. The document issued by the carrier is known as a "Carrier's Certificate." In certain circumstances, entry may be made by means of a duplicate bill of lading or a shipping receipt. Refer to 19 CFR 141 Subpart B, "Right to Make Entry and Declarations on Entry" for more information.

Entry for Consumption

The entry of merchandise is a two-part process consisting of (1) filing the documents necessary to determine whether merchandise may be released from Customs custody and (2) filing the documents that contain information for duty assessment and statistical purposes. Both of these processes can be accomplished electronically via the Automated Broker Interface program of the National Customs Automation Program (NCAP), provided electronic filing is available. To become a participant in one of the programs available under NCAP, importers or brokers should request information from Customs.

Entry Documents

Within 15 calendar days of the date of arrival of a shipment at a U.S. port of entry, entry documents must be filed at a location specified by the port director, unless an extension is granted. These documents, as listed in 19 CFR 142.3 are:

a.   Entry Manifest, Customs **Form 7533**; or Application and Special Permit for Immediate Delivery, Customs **Form 3461**, or other form of merchandise release required by the port director.

b.   Evidence of right to make entry.

c.   Commercial invoice or a pro forma invoice when the commercial invoice cannot be produced.

d.   Packing lists if appropriate.

e.   Other documents necessary to determine merchandise admissibility.

If the goods are to be released from Customs custody on entry documents, an entry summary for consumption must be filed and estimated duties deposited at the port of entry within 10 working days of the time the goods are entered and released.

Refer to 19 CFR Part 142 Subpart A, "Entry Documentation," for more information.

Surety (Customs Bond)

The entry must be accompanied by evidence that a bond is posted with Customs to cover any potential duties, taxes, and penalties that may accrue. A Customs bond is like an insurance policy that is payable to U.S. Customs in the event that the importer does not comply with import requirements. Bonds may be secured through a resident U.S. surety company but may also be posted in the form of U.S. money or certain U.S. government obligations. They may also be posted electronically. In the event that a customhouse broker is employed for the purpose of making entry, the broker may permit the use of his bond to provide the required coverage. 19 CFR 142.4 lists bond requirements.

Entry Summary Documentation

Following presentation of the entry, the shipment may be examined by Customs or examination may be waived. The shipment is then released, provided no legal or regulatory violations have been noted. Entry summary documentation is filed and estimated duties are deposited within 10 working days of the release of the merchandise at a designated customhouse. Details are given in 19 CFR 142.16, "Entry Summary Documentation." Briefly, the documentation consists of:

a.   The entry package returned to the importer, broker, or his authorized agent after merchandise is permitted release.

b.   Entry summary (Customs **Form 7501**)

c.   Other invoices and documents necessary for the assessment of duties, collection of statistics, or the determination that all import requirements have been satisfied. This paper documentation can be reduced or eliminated when utilizing features of the Automated Broker Interface or the National Customs Automation Program (NCAP).

Electronic Entry

Customs & Border Protection continues to upgrade its capabilities to efficiently process goods entering into the United States. The current import system, the Automated Commercial System (ACS), was designed in 1984 and will not be able to meet the increasingly complex, long-term requirements impacted by the growth in trade, enforcement responsibilities, and legislation, therefore a new system, the Automated Commercial Environment (ACE), is set to replace and improve the ACS.

ACE will provide an integrated, fully automated information system to enable the efficient collection, processing, and analysis of commercial import and export data. It will simplify dealings between Customs and the trade community by automating time-consuming and labor-intensive transactions and moving goods through the ports and on to markets faster and at lower cost.

This new system will extend NCAP as well as continue to allow importers to file documentation and declarations, post bonds, and pay duties, fees, and taxes electronically. And also provide for electronic batch filing of multiple entries, periodic reconciliation of entries, and payment of duties, taxes, and fees on a monthly account basis.

ACE benefits include:

- Reduced data entry
- Reduced financial processing
- Reduced paper handling
- Increased access to data

ACE is a large-scale, complex project that will be the foundation of Customs-wide modernization. In March 2002, Customs began building the foundational elements of ACE. In spring 2003, Customs began to provide support via the Internet to Customs trade account managers and 40 selected importers.

Customs is preparing for a planned and phased process for the transition from the old import system, ACS, to ACE. A transitional architecture will be in place to temporarily support dual operations and facilitate the transfer of data. Steadily over the period, official record systems and data will be migrated to ACE and dependence on the old system will diminish.

ACE Features Include:

Customs Web Portal

- Provides a single sign on for all system applications.
- Using a customized web page, the portal is a user-friendly starting point for all Customs Officers.
- Promotes communication, information sharing, and uniformity by permitting users to access information, and send and receive messages both within Customs and, externally, with the Trade and government agencies.
- Account Management
- Aligns Customs with business practices used by the Trade, such as periodic payments, and maximizes trade compliance.
- Importers, brokers, and carriers will be organized by account. All related records and supporting transactions can be viewed and summarized in their account.
- All Customs transactions will be tracked and viewed by

account. This provides integrated view of exports, imports, and in-bond movements. Results of routine, automated analyses will be displayed as ACE progresses.

Cargo Processing

- One standard data set for manifest for all modes of transportation.
- Gathers required information and provides data needed by Customs and government agencies to support import/export processes and fulfill Customs mission.
- Permits transfer of automated entry, entry summary, and manifest information from Importers, Brokers, and Carriers directly to Customs, as early as possible.

Border Security

- ACE promotes intelligence sharing and enforcement collaboration among government agencies.
- Cargo tracking and data mining will support CSI and C-TPAT, container X-Ray system, transponders, and other state-of-the-art security initiatives.
- ACE is not just a "Trade System." It allows Customs to capture advance data from the international supply chain and processes it.

Immediate Delivery

An alternate procedure that provides for immediate release of a shipment may be used in some cases by making application for a Special Permit for Immediate Delivery on Customs **Form 3461** prior to the arrival of the merchandise. Carriers participating in the Automated Manifest System can receive conditional release authorizations after leaving the foreign country, and up to five days before the landing in the U.S. If the application is approved, the shipment is released expeditiously following arrival. An entry summary must then be filed in proper form, either on paper or electronically, and estimated duties deposited within 10 working days of release. Release using **Form 3461** is limited to the following merchandise:

a. Merchandise arriving from Canada or Mexico, if approved by the port director and an appropriate bond is on file.

b. Fresh fruits and vegetables for human consumption arriving from Canada and Mexico and removed from the area immediately contiguous to the border to the importer's premises within the port of importation.

c. Shipments consigned to or for the account of any agency or officer of the U.S. Government.

d. Articles for a trade fair.

e. Tariff-rate quota merchandise and under certain circumstances merchandise subject to an absolute quota. Absolute quota items require a formal entry at all times. In some cases the port director may allow perishable merchandise to be delivered to the importer's premises.

f. In very limited circumstances, merchandise released to a warehouse followed within 10 working days by a warehouse withdrawal for consumption.

g. Merchandise specifically authorized by Customs Headquarters to be entitled to release for immediate delivery.

More information on immediate delivery may be found at 19 CFR 142 Subpart C, "Special Permit for Immediate Delivery."

Basic Documents for Formal Entry

Document	Notes	Sample
Commercial Invoice	A	page 314
Bill of Lading/Air Waybill (B/L)	B	page 316
Carrier's Certificate	C	page 331
Permit for Entry/ Immediate Delivery (CF 3461)	D	page 340
Entry Summary (CF 7501)	E	page 342
Customs Bond (CF 301)	F	page 334

Supplemental Basic Documents for Formal Entry (as required)

Document	Notes	Sample
Packing List	G	page 329
Certificate of Origin	H	page 338
Special Certificate of Origin (such as NAFTA Certificate of Origin)	H	page 339

Notes:

A—COMMERCIAL INVOICE
(issued by the exporter/seller)
This is the key transaction or accounting document and shows the value and description of the merchandise. Some commodities may require more detailed descriptions than others. (Refer to following sections on Textiles, Electronic Equipment and Foodstuffs).

B—BILL OF LADING
(issued by the shipping line or carrier of the goods)
This is the key transportation document. The bill of lading, airway bill, or carrier's certificate is used as evidence of the consignee's right to make entry.
As long as the goods are consigned "to order," the bill of lading, properly endorsed by the consignor, may serve as evidence of the right to make entry. An air waybill may be used for merchandise arriving by air.
In most instances, entry is made by a person or firm certified by the carrier bringing the goods to the port of entry and is considered the "owner" of the goods for customs purposes. The document issued by the carrier is known as a "Carrier's Certificate." In certain circumstances, entry may be made by means of a duplicate bill of lading or a shipping receipt.

C—CARRIER'S CERTIFICATE
(issued by the carrier)
This document informs U.S. Customs regarding the details of a shipment, including carrier, port of lading, date of arrival, consignee/owner of the goods, and description of the goods.

D—ENTRY/IMMEDIATE DELIVERY CF 3461
(issued by the importer or a customs broker working as agent for the importer)
Filing this form allows the importer or customs broker working as agent for the importer to gain possession of a shipment from a port of entry.
However, the goods are still considered to be in Customs's custody until the entry document package including the Entry Summary CF 7501 document has been presented to Customs.

E—ENTRY SUMMARY (CF 7501)
(issued by the importer or a customs broker working as agent for the importer)
The CF 7501 is the formal statement by the importer to U.S. Customs identifying the seller, buyer, goods shipped, date of issuance of the form, country of origin and country of final destination, quantity, description and cost of the goods, and shipping details. This form is required by U.S. Customs for formal entries to assess duties, and compile trade statistics.

F—SURETY OR CUSTOMS BOND CF 301
(generally issued by a third-party independent testing company or government authority)
A bond on Customs Form 301, containing the bond conditions, shall be filed out in the amount required by the port director to support the entry documentation.

G—PACKING LIST (OR BILL OF PARCELS)
(issued by the exporter/seller)
This identifies the contents of the shipment.

H—CERTIFICATE OF ORIGIN
(issued by the exporter/seller, local exporting country chamber of commerce or other authorizing agency).
This document declares the country of origin of the goods shipped. In the most straightforward transactions the exporter/seller makes a notation on the export declaration or at the bottom of the invoice: "Made in (country name)". A special Certificate of Origin form (such as a NAFTA Certificate of Origin) may be required to take advantage of preferential import duties.

Additional Documents - Textiles & Textile Products

The key factors in the importation of textile articles not knitted or crocheted are:

- Compliance with quota restraints and visa requirements

- Submission of U.S. Customs Country-of-Origin Declaration(s)

- Compliance with entry invoice requirements

- Compliance with labeling requirements under the Textile Fiber Products Identification Act (TFPIA) and/or the Wool Products Labeling Act (WPLA) and the Care Labeling Rule

- Compliance with flammability standards adopted and enforced by the Consumer Product Safety Commission (CPSC) under the Flammable Fabrics Act (FFA)

- Compliance with export licence requirements (if importing made-to-measure suits from Hong Kong)

- Compliance with Special Access or Regime entry requirements (if importing garments assembled and bleached, dyed, stone-washed, acid-washed, or perma-pressed abroad from components formed and cut in the US)

General Considerations

Textile Quotas. If you are interested in importing textile apparel articles or clothing accessories, the most important issue you need to be aware of is quotas. Under the Multi-Fiber Arrangement provisions of Section 204 of the Agricultural Adjustment Act, CITA (Committee for Implementation of Textile Agreements) initiates specific agreements with individual exporting countries. Section 204 of the Agricultural Adjustment Act covers textiles articles that: 1) are in chief value of cotton, wool, or man-made fibers, any textile fibers subject to the terms of any textile trade agreement, or any combination of such fibers; 2) contain 50% or more by weight of cotton or man-made fibers, or any textile fibers subject to the terms of any textile trade agreement; 3) contain 17% or more by weight of wool; or 4) if in chief value of textile fibers or textile materials, contain a blend of cotton, wool, or man-made fibers, any textile fibers subject to the terms of any textile trade agreement, or any combination of such fibers that, in total, amount to 50% or more by weight of all component fibers.

The U.S. has bilateral agreements with over 40 countries. Each agreement with each country is unique, and may specify quotas for a type of textile or a specific article. Visas or export licenses may be required. These agreements, however, often change. Therefore, if you are interested in importing any textile apparel articles or clothing accessories, you should contact the International Trade Administration's Office of Textile and Apparel or visit their Web: www.otexa.ita.doc.go.

Textile Country-of-Origin Declarations. U.S. Customs enforces CITA textile and textile product entry quotas). Requirements for entry include submission of Country-of-Origin Declarations with every shipment of woven textile apparel articles or clothing accessories, regardless of whether it is subject to a specific multi-fiber arrangement (19 CFR 12.130, 12.131). (CFR is the Code of Federal Regulations.)

Country of Origin. Quota restrictions are country-specific and therefore are applied based on the country of origin for the textiles shipped. The last country from which a textile shipment was exported to the U.S. is not necessarily its country of origin. A textile or textile product imported into the U.S. is considered a product of the particular foreign territory or country, or a U.S. insular possession, where it is wholly grown, produced, or manufactured. For the following discussion, "country" means a foreign territory or country, or a U.S. insular possession.

In 1996, U.S. Customs made major changes to country of origin rules for textile imports. The regulations at 19 CFR 102.21, "Textile and apparel products" were added to the 1996 Customs Regulations and became effective July 1, 1996. The newer rules do not provide for cutting components or cutting and hemming to confer country of origin as in the past. The basis of the new law is processing operations or assembly. Some of the most important changes for importers to be aware of are:

- Cutting does not determine the country of origin (previously cutting determined country of origin for 90 percent of wearing apparel imports). The new rules are based on processing or assembly operations.

- A subjective determination under the provisions of 19 CFR 12.130 is replaced by objective processing operations expressed in terms of tariff shifts. Dying, printing, and other finishing processes applied to fabrics no longer confer or change country of origin.

- Country of origin for textile and apparel products processed, assembled or manufactured in two or more countries is determined by where the most important processing occurs, and, if that cannot be ascertained, the last country in which an important processing operation occurs.

The country of origin is the country in which a product is wholly produced when a textile or apparel product is completely produced or manufactured (except for minor parts) in one country. For fabric, the country of origin is the country in which the fabric is woven, knitted, needled, tufted, felted, entangled or created by any other fabric-making process. The country of origin for staple yarn is the country in which yarn is spun; for filament yarn, the country in which filament is extruded; and for plied, gimped and cabled yarns, the country in which the fibers or filaments used in the yarn are spun or extruded. The country of origin of all other textile and apparel products is the country in which the components of a textile or apparel product are wholly assembled (except for minor attachments) except for knit-to-shape products. Knit-to-shape products are those composed of panels or parts, which are knitted or crocheted directly into the shape that will be used in construction of the final product. Minor cutting or sewing does not influence whether the product is considered knit-to-shape. The country of origin for knit-to-shape products is that country in which the major parts are knitted into the shape that will constitute the finished product. Once again, note that assembly, not cutting, now confers country of origin.

Declarations. All importations of textiles and textile products must be accompanied by one of the following three declarations. Goods subject to Section 204, Agricultural Act of 1956, as amended, must be accompanied by either a single-country or a multiple-country declaration. Goods not subject to Section 204 must be accompanied by a negative declaration.

Single-country declarations are used for entries of textiles or textile products which are wholly the growth, product, or manufacture of a single foreign country, territory, or U.S. insular possession. Information required includes: marks of identification and numbers; description of article and quantity; country of origin; and date of exportation.

Multiple-country declarations are used for entries of textiles or textile products which were subjected to manufacturing or processing operations in, and/or incorporate materials originating in more than one foreign country or territory. Information required includes: marks of identification and numbers; for articles, description, quantity, identification of manufacturing and/or processing operations, country, and date of exportation; for materials used to make articles, description of materials, country of production, and date of exportation.

Negative declarations must accompany all textile imports that are not subject to AAA Section 204 restrictions. Information required includes: marks of identification and numbers; descriptions of article and quantity; and country of origin.

The date of exportation to be indicated on the above declarations is the date on which the carrier leaves the last port in the country of origin, as determined by Customs. Diversion to another country during transit does not affect the export date.

Entry Invoices. You must provide certain additional information on the entry invoice for apparel which is neither knitted nor crocheted. The specific information varies depending on the nature of your product, as noted below.

TFPIA (Textile Fiber Products Identification Act) Requirements. All invoices for textile wearing apparel should indicate: 1) a component material breakdown in percentages by weight for all component fibers present in the entire garment, as well as separate breakdowns of the fibers in the (outer) shell (exclusive of linings, cuffs, waistbands, collars and other trimmings) and in the lining; 2) for garments that are constructed of more than one component or material (combination of knit and not-knit fabric or combinations of knit and/or not-knit fabric with leather, fur, plastic—including vinyl, etc.) the invoice must show a fiber breakdown in percentages by weight for each separate textile material in the garment and a breakdown in percentages by weight for each nontextile material of the entire garment; 3) for woven garments: indicate whether the fabric is yarn-dyed and whether there are "two or more colors in the warp and/or filling;" 4) for all-white T-shirts and singlets: indicate whether or not the garment contains pockets, trim, or embroidery; 5) for mufflers: state the exact dimensions, length, and width of the merchandise.

Wool Products Subject to WPLA Wool Products Labeling Act). When you offer for entry a wool product shipment valued at over $500 and subject to WPLA, you must include certain information intended to facilitate Customs monitoring and enforcement of that Act. This extra information is identical to that required by WPLA on labeling (see "Marking and Labeling Requirements" below), with the addition of the manufacturer's name. If your product consists of mixed waste, residues, and similar merchandise obtained from several suppliers or unknown sources, you may omit the manufacturer's name from the entry invoice.

Handkerchiefs. The entry invoice for a shipment of handkerchiefs must show: 1) the exact dimensions (length and width) of the merchandise, and 2) if made of cotton, whether hemmed and whether containing lace or embroidery.

Made-to-Measure Suits. Imports from Hong Kong of "made-to-measure" suits that do not accompany a returning traveler are subject to a special agreement. Suits made to the specific measurements of a particular person require a "made-to-measure" export license from the Hong Kong government. You must identify "made-to-measure" suits of Hong Kong origin on your entry summary by placing the symbol "G" as a prefix to the appropriate tariff number. The importer is responsible for the payment of any Customs duties at the time of importation, even if the suits are made to measure for an individual person. For more information, contact your nearest U.S. Customs port office.

Special Considerations for Wool Products

Wool Product Entry Requirements. Depending on the nature of your wool article imports, as many as three different types of special entry documents may be required. First, for all imported articles that contain textile fibers, yarns, and fabrics covered by the Agricultural Adjustment Act (AAA), including wool, you must file a U.S. Customs Textile Entry Declaration (see "Textile Country-of-Origin Declarations" below). Second, for all wool products subject to the WPLA, special information is required on the entry invoices (see "Wool Products Labeling Act" below). Finally, certain articles of apparel manufactured or produced in certain countries may be subject to quotas and other restraints under U.S. bilateral agreements. Such products require export licenses, certificates, or visas issued by the appropriate country of origin, in addition to other requisite entry paperwork.

Wool Products Labeling Act. The term "wool product" means any product or any portion of a product that contains, purports to contain, or in any way is represented as containing wool, reprocessed wool, or reused wool. All wool products imported into the U.S., except those made more than 20 years before importation, and except carpets, rugs, mats, and upholsteries, must have affixed a stamp, tag, label, or other means of identification as required by the WPLA. If you are importing wool products exempt from labeling under the WPLA, do not assume they are also exempt from labeling under the TFPIA. These are two distinct laws, with some overlapping requirements.

Regulatory Agencies

The Department of Commerce (DOC) Committee for Implementation of Textile Agreements (CITA) regulates certain textile imports under Section 204 of the Agricultural Adjustment Act. The Bureau of Customs & Border Protection enforces CITA textile and textile product entry quotas. Customs also enforces compliance with labeling and invoice requirements of the TFPIA and flammability standards under the FFA. The CPSC monitors imports and from time to time inspects textile shipments for compliance with FFA standards. If you are importing wool textiles, importation is subject to complex textile import regulations. The Federal Trade Commission (FTC) administers the WPLA requirements.

Textile Documents (in addition to Basic Documents)

Document	Notes	Sample
Textile Country-of-Origin Declaration(s)	I	—
Export Documentation and/or Visa for Textiles	J	—
Hong Kong Government Export License (if importing made-to-measure suits from Hong Kong)	K	—

I—TEXTILE COUNTRY-OF-ORIGIN DECLARATION
(issued by either the exporter or an authorizing agency in the country-of-origin; signed by the exporter or producer)

The textile country of origin declaration, which is currently required on all textile importations, continues to be a requirement for entry on textile imports from either Canada or Mexico. It must be filed with the entry package. For merchandise that is claimed as NAFTA originating, the textile declaration must be signed by the exporter or producer.

NAFTA Certificates of Origin (Customs Form 434). An importer of textiles for which NAFTA treatment is sought need not file a separate NAFTA Certificate of Origin in addition to the Customs Country-of-Origin Declaration. The declaration is sufficient. However, the importer must take care to submit a declaration from each U.S., Canadian, or Mexican producer or manufacturer. Thus, for multiple producers or manufacturers, a separate declaration must be filed for each. If a Customs port director cannot determine the country of origin because the declaration is absent or incomplete, the shipment is not entitled to preferential NAFTA tariff treatment or other NAFTA benefits. See 19 CFR 12.132

J—EXPORT DOCUMENTATION/VISA
A textile visa is an endorsement in the form of a stamp on an invoice or export control license which is executed by a foreign government. Visa numbers are required for all visas and export licenses. Most countries use the standard nine digit number system(e.g., 9IN123456). For shipments which require a textile visa or export license the visa number must be reported in column 34 on Customs Form 7501, Entry Summary.

K—HONG KONG GOVERNMENT EXPORT LICENSE/VISA
(issued by the exporter/seller)
For Hong Kong, made-to-measure suits of wool, man-made fiber, silk blend and vegetable fibers other than cotton, regardless of value, not accompanying the traveller, require visas.

Additional Documents - Computers & Electronics

The key factors in the importation of electronics and components are:

- Compliance with U.S. Food and Drug Administration (FDA) standards and entry notification for radiation-producing devices

- Compliance with U.S. Federal Communications Commission (FCC) standards and entry notification for radio frequency devices

- Compliance with U.S Department of Energy (DOE) performance standards

- Compliance with Consumer Product Safety Commission (CPSC) and Federal Trade Commission (FTC) requirements for consumer products

- Compliance with trademark, trade name, and copyright restrictions

General Considerations

Many electronic products and components may be imported without restrictions, permits, prior approval, special requirements, or additional paperwork. However, many others are subject to a variety of requirements enforced by a wide range of agencies, and it is necessary for importers to carefully check with the major agencies well in advance to be sure that they are in compliance with all relevant requirements for their specific electronics and component products.

Entry Invoices. You must provide certain information on the entry invoice for computers and electronics. The specific information varies depending on the nature of your product, as noted below. Though the following information is not meant to be exhaustive it serves the purpose of informing the importer as to key items that should be included on these entry invoices. Ensure that all general product descriptions detail the model number, item name, company's internal ID, and part number for each item.

Computer and Electronic Parts
Include what type of machine the part is for, the application or use of the machine, the function of the part, how the part performs this function and the use of the part.

Components
There are only two items for concern: what the standard industry designation is for the part and whether or not the component is assembled with anything else.

Systems
List a breakdown of what is included in the system or have a list of all the components of the system. There should be a designation that the items are part of a system and a listing of the use of the items and system.

Finished Goods
Include the standard industry designation for the included goods as well as an indication of the intended use. If the finished goods include a set or kit list, break out the included components (e.g. telephone set with battery and adapter).

Energy Efficiency Requirements. Both domestic and imported household consumer appliances must comply with applicable energy efficiency standards and labeling requirements under the Energy Policy and Conservation Act (EPCA) as amended. The DOE Consumer Products Efficiency Branch is responsible for test procedures and energy performance standards. The FTC Division of Energy and Product Information regulates household appliance labeling. You should contact these agencies (addresses below) to find out about any requirements that may be in effect at the time you anticipate making your shipment.

EPCA covers the following types of consumer products: 1) refrigerators and refrigerator-freezers; 2) freezers; 3) dishwashers; 4) clothes dryers; 5) water heaters; 6) room air conditioners; 7) home heating equipment other than furnaces; 8) television sets; 9) kitchen ranges and ovens; 10) clothes washers; 11) humidifiers and dehumidifiers; 12) central air conditioners; 13) furnaces; and 14) certain other types of household consumer appliances, as appropriate. Not all appliances are covered by requirements of both agencies.

Intellectual Property Provisions. Products such as microchips and recorded media (prerecorded tapes, records, computer software, and similar products) are subject to patent and trademark restrictions. The Intellectual Property Rights (IPR) branch of U.S. Customs enforces laws pertinent to entry of such products. Importers must be prepared to show valid authorization from trademark and copyright holders. Pirated products are subject to seizure.

CPSC and FTC Regulations. Some of the products found in this section are covered by the provisions of the Consumer Product Safety Act (CPSA), which establishes standards for the manufacturing and labeling of potentially hazardous consumer products. Imported consumer products for which such standards exist must comply with the full range of requirements prescribed for domestic products. In addition, the CPSA requires all manufacturers, distributors, retailers, and others involved in the commercial handling of such products to report immediately any potentially hazardous defects or failures to conform to established standards to the CPSC for investigation and potential action. Failure to submit such a Substantial Product Hazard Report can result in action by the CPSC. Contact the CPSC (see addresses at end of this chapter) with questions regarding specific products.

Regulatory Agencies

From a regulatory viewpoint, many electronic devices subject to regulation fall into two general categories: those that produce radio frequency energy, and those that produce radiation. Radiation-producing electronic devices are regulated by the FDA under the provisions of the Federal Food, Drug, and Cosmetic Act (FDCA) and the Radiation Control for Health and Safety Act of 1968 (RCHSA). Both imported and domestically produced electronic products must comply with all relevant FDA regulations. Whether you are importing a single product for personal use, or a commercial shipment for resale in the U.S., you must file an Electronic Product Declaration, **Form FD2877** for each product type for which official standards exist. You will not be permitted to enter a shipment unless you have filed these forms. You may obtain them from FDA, National Center for Devices and Radiological Health or from your customs broker.

Radio frequency (rf) devices are regulated by the FCC under the provisions of 47 CFR Parts 2 and 15. You must file a copy of FCC **Form 740** with each shipment of rf devices. If your shipment consists of more than one type of device, you must file a separate form for each type. The form certifies that the imported model or device is either in compliance with, or is exempt from, FCC requirements, and is so labeled. An FCC entry declaration form (FCC **Form 740**) is required for products covered under FCC regulations.

Some products, such as ultrasonic therapeutic devices and television receivers, fall under the jurisdiction of both the FCC and the FDA and must comply with both sets of regulations. Although for purposes of simplicity this section discusses the two categories as if they do not overlap, they do, and you should ascertain exactly which regulations your product is required to meet for which agency. Do not rely on one agency for information concerning the requirements of another agency. If you are in doubt as to the status of your commodity, contact both the FCC and the FDA.

Computers & Electronics Documents (in addition to Basic Documents)

Document	Notes	Sample
Electronic Product Declaration - Form FD2877	L	page 344
FCC Declaration Form FCC 740	M	page 346

L—ELECTRONIC PRODUCT DECLARATION FD2877)
The Form FDA 2877 must be completed for electronic products subject to Radiation Control Standards (21 CFR 1010 and 1020-1050) prior to entry into the United States. The local Food and Drug Administration (FDA) district office will review the declaration and notify the importer/agent if the products may be released into U.S. commerce or if they must be held under bond until exported, destroyed, or reconditioned. Until the shipment is released, it may be subject to redelivery for FDA examination

M—FCC DECLARATION FORM FCC 740
(issued by the exporter/seller)
This form must be completed for each radio frequency device, as defined in 47 U.S.C. 302 and 47 C.F.R. 2.801, which is imported into the Customs territory of the United States. The original shall be filed with U.S Customs on or before the date the shipment is delivered to a U.S. port of entry.

Additional Documents - Foodstuffs & Pharmaceuticals

The key factors in the importation of foodstuffs and pharmaceuticals are:

- Compliance with U.S. Food and Drug Administration (FDA) purity, identity, manufacturing, and other standards

- Compliance with FDA entry notification and other procedures

- Compliance with U.S. Department of Agriculture (USDA) Animal and Plant Health Inspection Services (APHIS) and the Food Safety and Inspection Service (FSIS) requirements; permits may be required

General Considerations

FDA Requirements. FDA regulations regarding importation of foods of any kind are extensive and stringent. Meat and fish products prepared from wild game and domesticated varieties of wild animals also fall within the FDA's purview. Prepared foods imported into the U.S. must comply with all requirements for those produced domestically.

FDA Inspections. Imported products regulated by the FDA are subject to port of entry inspection.

Detention of Shipment. If your shipment is found to be noncomplying, the FDA inspector may detain it at the port of entry. The FDA may allow you to bring the shipment into compliance before making a final decision regarding admittance. However, any sorting, reprocessing, or relabeling must be supervised by FDA personnel and is done at the importer's expense. Such conditional release to allow the importer to bring a shipment into compliance is a privilege, not a right. The FDA may consider subse-quent noncomplying shipments of the same type of product to constitute abuse of the privilege and require the importer to destroy or reexport the products. To ascertain what your legal responsibilities are, you should contact the FDA regarding the specific items to be imported.

USDA Requirements. APHIS and FSIS are the main USDA agencies responsible for enforcement of the regulations on the import of meat, poultry, fish, and seafood. You should check with these agencies to ascertain what your USDA responsibilities are with respect to imports.

Wildlife Products. If you are interested in importing products prepared from exotic animals, you should consult the U.S. Fish and Wildlife Service (FWS), which administers the provisions of the Endangered Species Act (ESA) and the Convention on International Trade in Endangered Species of Wild Fauna and Flora (CITES), to be sure that your intended import is not covered by these regulations. No animal products derived from animals on these lists may be imported. There are many restrictions on the importation and sale of any products derived from wild animals. However, products made from the meat of animals raised in captivity is unlikely to fall within the jurisdiction of endangered species legislation.

Regulatory Agencies

Importation of prepared meat and fish products falls primarily under the jurisdiction of the FDA, which enforces the requirements of the Federal Food, Drug, and Cosmetic Act (FDCA). The USDA controls imports of meat, poultry, fish, and seafood products to prevent contamination of U.S. food sources. The FWS regulates importation of products prepared from endangered species and wildlife.

Foodstuffs and Pharmaceutical Documents (in addition to Basic Documents)

Document	Notes	Sample
Establishment registration FDA 2541	N	page 347
Food Process Filing FDA 2541a & 2541c	O	page 348
Foreign veterinary certification when required		
FDA Import Permit where required		
APHIS Import Permit where required		
Certificate of Label Approval		
Certificate of Origin (for wines)		
Certificates of Age and Origin (for distilled spirits)		
Certificates of Non-Standard Fill (for non-standard fill items)		

N—ESTABLISHMENT REGISTRATION FDA 2541
  Foreign firms must register and file processing information before shipping any low-acid canned food or acidified low-acid canned food to the United States. This information must be provided to the FDA for each applicable product at the time of importation in order to assure compliance with registration and process filing acceptance.

O—FOOD PROCESS FILING FDA 2541A & 2541C
  (issued by the exporter/seller)
  These forms must be filed before shipping any low acid canned food or acidified low-acid canned food to the United States.

Other Documents

Document	Notes	Sample
Phytosanitary Certificate of Origin	P	
Foreign Veterinary Certificate	Q	

P—PHYTOSANITARY CERTIFICATE OF ORIGIN
(generally issued by a third-party independent testing company or government authority)
This document certifies that a shipment of imported plants or plant products (i.e., seeds, bulbs, flowers, fruits, vegetables, etc.) is free from pests or disease. This certificate requires on-site inspection(s) of the plants during the growing season and is usually provided by the agricultural ministry or department of the country of export.

Q—FOREIGN VETERINARY CERTIFICATE
(generally issued by a third-party independent testing company or government authority)
This document certifies that a shipment of live animals, fresh, chilled and frozen meats (and sometimes even canned meats) has been inspected for disease.

Warehouse Entry

Definition

Goods entered into the U.S. that are not intended for immediate release may be placed in a Customs bonded warehouse under a warehouse entry. The goods may remain in the bonded warehouse for up to five years from the date of importation. At any time during that period, warehoused goods may be re-exported without paying duty, or they may be withdrawn for consumption. The duty rate applied to the goods is the rate in effect on the date of withdrawal not the rate that was in effect when the goods were first entered into the warehouse. If the goods are destroyed under Customs supervision, no duty is payable.

Procedure

While the goods are in the bonded warehouse, they may, under Customs supervision, be manipulated by cleaning, sorting, repacking, or otherwise changing their condition by processes that do not amount to manufacturing. After manipulation, and within the warehousing period, the goods may be exported without the payment of duty, or they may be withdrawn for consumption upon payment of duty at the rate applicable to the goods in their manipulated condition at the time of withdrawal. Perishable goods, explosive substances, or prohibited importations may not be placed in a bonded warehouse. Certain restricted articles, though not allowed release from custody, may be warehoused. Information regarding bonded manufacturing warehouses is contained in section 311 of the Tariff Act (19 U.S.C. 1311).

Documents for Warehouse Entry

Document	Notes	Sample
Commercial Invoice	A	page 314
Bill of Lading/Air Waybill (B/L)	B	page 316
Special Permit for Immediate Delivery (CF 3461)	C	page 340
Entry Summary (CF 7501)	D	page 342
Customs Bond (CF 301)	E	page 334

A—COMMERCIAL INVOICE
(issued by the exporter/seller)
This is the key transaction or accounting document. This document shows the value and description of the merchandise. Some commodities may require more detailed descriptions than others. (refer to the following sections on Textiles, Electronic Equipment and Foodstuffs)

B—BILL OF LADING
(issued by the shipping line or carrier of the goods)
This is the key transportation document. The bill of lading, airway bill, or carrier's certificate is used as evidence of the consignee's right to make entry.

C—ENTRY MANIFEST OR IMPORT DECLARATION
(issued by the importer or a customs broker working as agent for the importer)
This is the formal statement by the importer to U.S. Customs identifying the seller, buyer, goods shipped, date of issuance, country of origin and country of final destination, quantity, description and cost of the goods, and shipping details. This is required to control imports, assess duties, and compile trade statistics.

D—ENTRY SUMMARY (CF 7501)
(issued by the importer or a customs broker working as agent for the importer)
The CF 7501 is the formal statement by the importer to U.S. Customs identifying the seller, buyer, goods

shipped, date of issuance of the form, country of origin and country of final destination, quantity, description and cost of the goods, and shipping details. This form is required by U.S. Customs for formal entries to assess duties, and compile trade statistics.

E—SURETY OR CUSTOMS BOND CF 301
(generally issued by a third-party independent testing company or government authority)
A bond on Customs Form 301, containing the bond conditions, shall be filed out in the amount required by the port director to support the entry documentation.

Foreign Trade Zone Entry

Definition

A Foreign Trade Zone Entry is the transfer of goods into a Foreign Trade Zone (FTZ).

A FTZ is a special commercial and industrial area in or near a United States port of entry where foreign and domestic merchandise, including raw materials and components, can be stored without becoming subject to payment of customs duties. Merchandise brought into these zones may be stored, sold, exhibited, repacked, assembled, sorted, graded, cleaned or otherwise manipulated prior to re-export or entry into the national customs territory.

Access to foreign trade zones is restricted and only authorized by the Foreign-Trade Zones Board, which is made up of the Secretary of Commerce and the Secretary of the Treasury. The Bureau of Customs & Border Protection handles their supervision. However, even though a foreign trade zone is considered part of the territory and jurisdiction of the United States, Customs entry procedures do not apply.

There are two types of foreign-trade zones: General Purpose Zones and Subzones. General purpose zones are usually located in an industrial park, on raw land or in port complexes whose facilities are available for use by the general public.

Subzones are sites sponsored by a general purpose zone grantee on behalf of an individual firm or firms. Subzones are single-purpose sites for operations that cannot be feasibly moved to, or accommodated in, a general purpose zone; e.g., oil refineries, automobile manufacturers.

Location of and general information on U.S. Foreign Trade Zones may be obtained from the Foreign Trade Zones Board; U.S. Department of Commerce; FCB-Suite 4100W; 1401 Constitution Ave., NW; Washington, DC 20230; Tel: [1] (202) 482-2862; Web: http://ia.ita.doc.gov/ftzpage.

Procedure

Foreign and domestic merchandise permitted in a zone may be stored, sold, exhibited, broken-up, repacked, assembled, distributed, sorted, graded, cleaned, mixed with foreign or domestic merchandise, otherwise manipulated, destroyed, or manufactured. On the other hand, machinery and equipment that is imported for use within a zone is not exempt from the payment of duty. Such equipment and supplies may include, but are not limited to: office furniture, machines, and equipment; construction machinery and materials; manufacturing machinery and equipment, tooling, and supplies; packaging machinery and equipment; food to be eaten in the zone and water and fuel that do not become part of a zone product.

In specific cases, the Foreign-Trade Zones Board may prohibit or restrict any activity in a zone in order to protect the public interest, health, or safety. All manufacturing is reviewed in terms of government policy and its net economic effect.

Many products subject to an internal revenue tax may not be manufactured in a zone. These products include alcoholic beverages, products containing alcoholic beverages (except domestic denatured distilled spirits), perfumes containing alcohol, tobacco products, firearms and sugar. In addition, the manufacture of clocks and watch movements is not permitted in a zone.

Retail trade is prohibited in zones, unless conducted under a permit issued by the zone grantee and approved by the Foreign-Trade Zones Board. Retail trade is then allowed only for the sale of domestic goods, or goods brought from the Customs territory following a regular Customs entry on which any applicable duties and/or taxes have been paid.

Merchandise may be admitted into a zone after application has been made on Customs Form 214, "Application for Foreign Trade-Zone Admission and/or Status Designation," or its electronic equivalent, and a permit is issued by the Port Director. The application for admission is submitted to the port director, including a statistical copy on Customs Form 214A to be transmitted to the Bureau of Census, unless the applicant has made arrangements for the direct transmittal of statistical information to that agency. The form will be signed by the zone operator, unless a separate individual or blanket approval has been given.

Application for admission may be made only by the person with the right to make entry. Right to make entry will be determined according to the provisions of Section 484(a) (19USC 1484(a)) Tariff Act, Customs Directive 099 3530-002, and other pertinent Service-wide instructions. However, a customhouse broker or foreign-trade zone operator may prepare and/or file the application on behalf of the person with the right to make entry, if a proper power of attorney is on file.

Merchandise does not achieve zone status until a permit is given by the port director for its admission (except in the case of domestic status merchandise for which no permit is required), and the zone operator signs for receipt of the merchandise into the zone.

The Customs Form 214 will be presented to the location designated by the port director within a port of entry. Customs will review the application and supporting documentation for completeness and to determine whether the application may be approved without a physical examination of the merchandise. Customs approves permits of admission for most low-risk shipments without examination.

Customs may examine merchandise to be admitted to a foreign-trade zone to:

- Determine if the goods are admissible to the zone.
- Determine the true liability of the zone operator for merchandise received in a zone under its bond.
- Reduce the need for further examination of the merchandise if it is later transferred to Customs territory, in the same condition, for consumption or warehouse.
- Ensure full compliance with all applicable laws and regulations.

The following documents must accompany the CF 214:

Commercial Invoice, Evidence of Right to Make Entry, Release Order, Application to Unlade, and Other Documentation.

After document review and physical examination, as appropriate under the above provisions, the port director shall issue a permit for the admission of merchandise to a zone.

Documents for Entry into a Foreign Trade Zone

Document	Notes	Sample
Commercial Invoice	A	page 314
Bill of Lading/Air Waybill (B/L) (Evidence of Right to Make Entry)	B	page 316
Application for Foreign Trade-Zone Admission CF 214	C	page 351
Application to Unlade CF 3171	D	page 352
Other Documentation	E	

A—COMMERCIAL INVOICE

The applicant shall submit two copies of an examination invoice meeting the requirements of Subpart F, Part 141 CR, for any merchandise, other than domestic status merchandise for which no permit is required, to be admitted into a zone. The notation on the invoice of tariff classification and value required by Section 141.90 CR need not be made, unless the merchandise is to be admitted in privileged foreign status.

B—BILL OF LADING OR OTHER EVIDENCE OF RIGHT TO MAKE ENTRY

The applicant for admission shall submit a document similar to that which would be required as evidence of the right to make entry for merchandise in Customs territory under Section 141.11 or 141.12 CR and CD 099 3530-002. This is generally the Bill of Lading.

C—RELEASE ORDER

Customs officers shall not authorize any merchandise for delivery to a zone until a release order has been executed by the carrier which brought the merchandise to the port, unless the merchandise is released back to that same carrier for delivery to the zone.

D—APPLICATION TO UNLADE

For merchandise unladen in the zone directly from the importing carrier, the application on Customs Form 214 shall be supported by an application to unlade on Custom Form 3171.

E—OTHER DOCUMENTATION

The port director may require additional information or documentation as needed to examine the merchandise under Customs selective processing criteria, or to determine whether the merchandise is admissible to the zone. This includes documentation such as export certificates for certain steel products and machine tools under voluntary restraint and information needed for selectivity processing such as importers' and manufacturers' numbers.

Mail Entry

Definition

A Mail Entry is the entry of goods to the Customs territory of the U.S. using another country's mail system to mail them to the United States.

Although many people use the terms shipping and mailing interchangeably, they are not the same, especially where U.S. Customs is concerned. Mailing is always via the international postal system, which is run jointly by international governments. Shipping, on the other hand, refers to private-sector carriers, those commercial delivery services that often promise to deliver packages in record time. Commercial delivery services usually use customs brokers or other agents to clear merchandise through Customs, which is a service you pay for in addition to the charge for shipping and any duty or processing fees owed to U.S. Customs.

Be aware that because different clearance procedures and regulations may apply to mailed vs. commercially shipped packages, this information applies only to goods entering the United States by way of the international mail system, and not to those shipped by commercial delivery services.

Warning. If you misrepresent the nature of the goods you are sending to the United States, whether by mail or commercial carrier, you may be liable for a penalty as well as any duty that might be owed on your merchandise. In addition, those goods could be subject to seizure.

Procedure

When you take your package to a foreign post office, the postal clerk will give you an international customs declaration. Be sure to fill it out with a full, accurate description of the goods inside and attach it to the parcel's exterior. By international treaty, all foreign post offices will have this form. In the very unlikely case that one isn't available, simply write the description and value on the outer wrapping of the package itself.

If the item is intended as a gift, write "unsolicited gift" on the outer wrapper. If the package contains your own used belongings, mark the package "personal goods returned." If the package contains new purchases you bought for your own use, mark it "personal purchases."

When a package first enters the United States, it arrives at a post office near the addressee. That Postal Service will route it to one of 13 Customs international mail facilities, where Customs inspectors will determine whether duty is owed. Customs then returns the package to the Postal Service for delivery (unless the value of the package is over $2000, in which case the package will be held by Customs until formal entry can be made). If duty is owed, the Postal Service will collect it from the recipient before delivering the package. If the package is a gift worth more than $100, the recipient will be charged duty. The sender can reimburse the recipient for whatever duty he or she has paid; however, by U.S. Customs regulation, duty cannot

be prepaid; in all cases, including gifts, the parcel's recipient bears responsibility for paying duty.

When you mail your goods through the Postal Service, the only fees you may have to pay are a postal service handling fee and, if duty is owned on your package, a Customs handling fee. You also have the option to protest a duty determination—before duty is paid, rather than after—as would be your situation if a courier service was handling your packages.

If the package does require payment of duty, Customs attaches a form called a mail entry (form CF-3419A), which shows how much duty is owed, and charges a $5 processing fee as well. When the post office delivers the package, it will also charge a handling fee.

Commercial goods Goods intended for resale, as well as any shipments exceeding $2,000 in value, may have special entry requirements. Such goods may require a formal entry in order to be admitted into the United States. If formal entry is required on a parcel, the parcel is held at the Customs International Mail Branch and notice is sent to the addressee of the package's arrival. The addressee can then go to the nearest Customs office to file the formal entry on the package. Once the Mail Branch has been notified that entry has been filed, the package will be released to the Postal Service and forwarded to its final destination.

Protest. If you believe you have been charged an incorrect amount of duty on a package mailed from abroad, you may file a protest with Customs. You can do this in one of two ways. You can accept the package, pay the duty, and write a letter explaining why you think the amount was incorrect. You should include with your letter the yellow copy of the mail entry (CF-3419A). Send the letter and the form to the Customs office that issued the mail entry, which you'll find on the lower left-hand corner of the form.

The other way to protest duty is to refuse delivery of the package and, within five days, send your protest letter to the post office where the package is being held. The post office will forward your letter to Customs and will hold your package until the protest is resolved.

Documents for Mail Entries

Mail Entries use documentation for either Formal or Informal Entries, depending upon the value of the package(s) being mailed and the type of goods they contain. Refer to the previous sections on Formal and Informal Entries.

Temporary Importation Under Bond (TIB)

Definition

Temporary Importation under Bond (TIB) is an entry whereby, under certain conditions, merchandise may be entered—for a limited time—into U.S. Custom's territory free of duty.

Instead of duty, the importer posts a bond for twice the amount of duty, taxes, etc. that would otherwise be owed on the importation. Under this procedure, the importer agrees to export or destroy the merchandise within a specified time or pay liquidated damages, which are twice the normal duty. Only certain items may be entered as a TIB.

Any article imported under the TIB provision must be exported within one year from the date of importation. However, upon application to the director of the port where the entry was filed, this one-year-period for exportation may be extended for further periods, which, when added to the initial one year, shall not exceed a total of three years. There are two exceptions to the above time limitations:

1. In the case of articles covered under Subheading 9813.00.75 (autos and parts for show purposes), the period of importation may not exceed six months and may not be extended;

2. Articles covered under Subheading 9813.00.50 (tools of trade), if seized for reasons other than by suit of private persons, have the requirement of exportation suspended during the period of seizure.

Procedure

In order to avoid paying liquidated damages, the importer must present proof to the Customs port where the entry occurred that the goods were reexported. If the item(s) being exported are being sent as unaccompanied cargo, the importer should take personal responsibility for sending a copy of the bill of lading (proof that the merchandise was actually loaded onto a ship or other conveyance) to the entry office of the port where the goods first entered the country. Accompanying the bill of lading should be a reference to the original entry number (line 1 of the CF 7501). The description of the item on the bill of lading should match the description of the item on the CF 7501 in all particulars, including serial numbers or other identifying factors. If the importer has used a customs broker to complete the transaction, Customs advises the importer to ask the broker for proof that export documentation was actually provided to the entry branch at the port of entry.

If the item(s) being re-exported are accompanying the importer as baggage, the item(s) should be taken to the entry office (if the importer is leaving from the same location where he/she arrived) for Customs to verify that the item is leaving the country. If the importer is leaving from a different location than the one where the TIB was issued, he/she should take the item to the International Arrivals area (if leaving from an airport), or Customs border port office (if leaving through a land border) and

request an inspector to fill out a CF 3495 Application for Exportation of Articles Under Special Bond. A copy of this CF form should then be sent by the importer to the original port of entry.

It is not enough to simply get proof of export from a Customs office. The importer must ensure that proof of exportation is submitted to the entry branch at the original port of entry in order to avoid liquidated damages.

In lieu of exportation, relief from liability may be obtained in any case in which the article is destroyed under Customs supervision within the original bond period.

Note: The importer should contact the original port of entry to determine exact requirements. Destruction may not have to happen in front of a Customs officer if the destroyed item is presented for inspection. (Please see section on Liability Issues.

However, in the case of articles under Subheading 9813.00.30, where articles are destroyed during the course of experiments or tests during the bond period, or any lawful extension, destruction need not be under Customs supervision but satisfactory proof of destruction shall be furnished to the port director with whom customs entry is filed.

Generally, destruction for purposes of satisfying the bond means destruction as an article of commerce. The article must have no commercial value whatsoever if it is to be considered destroyed.

Goods Eligible for TIB Entry

The only goods that qualify for TIB entry are those listed in subheadings 9813.00.05 through 9813.00.75 of the Harmonized Tariff Schedule of the U.S. (HTSUS). (See below.)

However, if the goods covered by these subheadings are being brought into the country for sale, or for sale-on-approval (i.e., a boat), they would not be eligible under the TIB provision. If the intent to sell is made after entry, then the importer's liability would be limited to the bond obligation.

Merchandise sold in the U.S. for exportation to a foreign purchaser is not considered "imported for sale or sale on approval" within the meaning of the law.

The following subheadings are listed as they appear in the fourteen HTSUS article descriptions.

Note: Theatrical props and scenery no longer require a TIB for duty free entry. "Theatrical scenery, properties, and apparel (9817.00.98) brought into the US by proprietors or managers of theatrical, ballet, opera or similar productions arriving from abroad for temporary use by them in such productions" are now DUTY FREE unless from a "Column 2" country. Since this is not a TIB provision, there is no one-year export (with extensions up to 3 years) requirement. In other words, these types of theatrical items can make a duty free entry.

The Fourteen TIB Subheadings

1. Articles to be repaired, altered or processed (including processes which result in an article's being manufactured or produced in the United States.) Subheading 9813.00.05.

2. Models of women's wearing apparel imported by manufacturers for use solely as models in their own establishments. Subheading 9813.00.10.

3. Articles imported by illustrators and photographers for use solely as models in their own establishments, in the illustrating of catalogues, pamphlets or advertising materials. Subheading 9813.00.15.

4. Samples solely for use in taking orders for merchandise. Subheading 9813.00.20.

5. Articles solely for examination with a view to reproduction, or for such examination and reproduction (except photoengraved printing plates for examination and reproduction) and motion picture advertising films. Subheading 9813.00.25.

6. Articles intended solely for testing, experimental or review purposes, including specification, photographs and similar articles for use in connection with experiments or for study. Subheading 9813.00.30.

7. Automobiles, motorcycles, bicycles, airplanes, airships, balloons, boats, racing shells, and similar vehicles and craft, and the usual equipment of the foregoing; all the foregoing which are brought temporarily into the United States by nonresidents for the purpose of taking part in races or other specific contests. Subheading 9813.00.35.

8. 8 Locomotives and other railroad equipment brought temporarily into the United States for use in clearing obstructions, fighting fires or making emergency repairs on railroads within the United States, or for use in transportation otherwise than in international traffic when the Secretary of the Treasury finds that the temporary use of foreign railroad equipment is necessary to meet an emergency. Subheading 9813.00.40.

9. Containers for compressed gasses, filled or empty, and containers or other articles in use for covering or holding merchandise (including personal or household effects) during transportation and suitable for reuse for that purpose. Subheading 9813.00.45.

10. Professional equipment, tools of trade, repair components for equipment or tools admitted under this heading, and camping equipment; all the foregoing imported by or for nonresidents sojourning temporarily in the United States and for the use of nonresidents. Subheading 9813.00.50.

11. Articles of special design for temporary use exclusively in connection with the manufacture or production of articles for export. Subheading 9813.00.55.

12. Animals and poultry brought into the United States for the purpose of breeding, exhibition, or competition for prizes and the usual equipment therefor. Subheading 9813.00.60.

13. Works of the free fine arts, engravings, photographic pictures and philosophical and scientific apparatus brought into the United States by professional artists, lecturers or scientists arriving from abroad for use by them for exhibition and in illustration, promotion and encouragement of art, science or industry in the United States. Subheading 9813.00.70.

14. Automobiles, automobile chassis, automobile bodies, cutaway portions of any of the foregoing, finished, unfinished or cutaway, when intended solely for show purposes. Subheading 9813.00.75

With respect to Subheading 9813.00.40, request for free admission of equipment for use in clearing obstructions, fighting fires or making emergency repairs as provided for in the first clause of subheading 9813.00.40, the Secretary of the Treasury has delegated approval authority to the applicable Port Director or other appropriate officer at the port. However, claims under the second clause (i.e., "for use in transportation otherwise than in international traffic") require approval of the Secretary of the Treasury, and every case in which claim is made under this clause should be forwarded to Customs Headquarters for approval.

Further Information

Customs port directors generally administer the TIB entry, bonding, and export provisions contained in section 10.31 to 10.40 of the Customs Regulation. Accordingly, for further information regarding TIB entry, bonding, and export particulars, a prospective importer should contact the port director where the intended importation will take place. The bond amount is based on the alternate classification. The alternate classification is the classification under which the merchandise would be entered as a regular consumption entry.

Entry Documents - Temporary Import Under Bond

Document	Notes	Sample
Commercial Invoice		page 314
Bill of Lading/Air Waybill (B/L)		page 316
Special Permit for Immediate Delivery (CF 3461)		page 340
Entry Summary (CF 7501)		page 342

ATA Carnet

Definition

The ATA Carnet is an international Customs document that a traveler may use to temporarily import certain goods into a country without having to engage in the Customs formalities usually required for the importation of goods, and without having to pay duty or value-added taxes on the goods.

The United States allows for the temporary importation of commercial samples, professional equipment and certain advertising materials by a nonresident individual.

Carnets are a security that participating countries accept as a guarantee against the payment of Customs duties that may become due on goods temporarily imported under a carnet and not exported as required. "ATA" stands for the combined French and English words "Admission Temporaire-Temporary Admission."

The ATA carnet simplifies the Customs formalities involved in temporarily importing goods into the U.S. and other countries. Without a carnet it would be necessary to go through the Customs procedures established in each country for the temporary admission of goods. The carnet allows the business traveler to use a single document for clearing certain categories of goods through Customs in several different countries. It may be used for unlimited exits from and entries into the U.S. and participating foreign countries during the one-year period of validity. They are accepted as the entry document and satisfy the importer's obligation to post a security in more than 87 countries.

Procedure

A carnet holder is obligated to present the goods and carnet to Customs to prove exportation. Failure to prove exportation on either a TIB or a carnet subjects the importer to liquidated damages equal to 110 percent of the duty and import tax. Goods imported under either a TIB or a carnet may not be offered for sale.

Domestic associations in participating countries that are members of the International Bureau of Chambers of Commerce issue carnets to residents to be used abroad. The United States Council for International Business http://www.uscib.org (USCIB) has been designated by U.S. Customs as the United States issuing and guaranteeing organization. A fee is charged by the Council for its service. The guaranteeing organization is held liable for the payment of liquidated damages if the carnet holder, such as the importer, fails to comply with Customs regulations.

An ATA carnet is valid for one year from the date of its issuance. Merchandise listed on an ATA carnet can be imported to and exported from any of the member countries as many times as needed during the one-year life of the carnet.

The following goods can be entered under an ATA Carnet:

- Commercial samples, professional equipment and advertising material imported into the United States by a nonresident.

- Ordinary goods such as computers, tools, cameras and video equipment, industrial machinery, automobiles, gems and jewelry, and wearing apparel.

- Extraordinary items, for example, Van Gogh's self-portrait, circus animals, jets, band instruments, satellites, human skulls, and the New York Philharmonic's equipment.

Merchandise not covered by the three above listed categories of goods are not eligible for importation into the U.S. by carnet. In addition, merchandise within those three categories intended for sale or sale on approval cannot be entered on a carnet—it must be entered as a regular Customs entry.

If the holder of an ATA carnet sells, donates or otherwise disposes of any of the goods listed on the carnet, the issuing organization will be required to pay liquidated damages equal to 100 percent of the import duties and taxes. That organization in turn will attempt to collect these moneys from the holder of the carnet who violated its terms. In some cases, the country where the violation occurred will hold both the organization that issued the carnet and the importer equally responsible. The importer is liable to his/her issuing association (and, in some cases, to the Customs authorities of the country where it was issued) for all duties and/or taxes and other sums which would normally be charged on the importation of such goods, as well as the amount charged as liquidated damages. If the U.S. Customs finds that there was fraud involved in the importation, additional penalties may be assessed.

If the expiring ATA carnet is a U.S.-issued carnet there will be no penalties or duties assessed by the United States, however, there may be penalties assessed by a foreign government if the carnet expired before the U.S. merchandise was exported from that country.

If the carnet is foreign-issued then liquidated damages will be assessed by U.S. Customs due to the carnet expiring before the merchandise could be exported out of the United States.

When processing a foreign-issued carnet, Customs must create a record of the transaction in order to protect the revenue and domestic commerce. Therefore, the U.S. Customs officer responsible for clearing the temporary importation must ensure that the port of importation, dates of Customs activities, and any departure from the original list of articles, are clearly shown in the appropriate fields.

When the merchandise leaves the U.S. the Customs officer must ensure that the required exportation dates are complied with, that the original list of articles agrees with what is being exported, and that the appropriate voucher is detached and forwarded to the port of importation.

The carnet document has a green cover page which provides the names of the carnet holder and issuing association, the carnet issue date, the carnet number, the countries in which the carnet may be used and a complete description of the goods covered. Two yellow sheets in the package are to be used upon exportation from and reimportation back into the issuing country. White sheets are used for the temporary importation into and reexportation from the second or additional countries. Blue sheets are used when transiting though countries.

Each sheet contains two parts - a counterfoil, which remains in the carnet and describes the actions taken by Customs officers each time goods enter or leave a country, and a detachable voucher, which contains a list of the goods covered by the carnet and serves as the required Customs document.

Basic Documents

Document	Notes	Sample
ATA Carnet	A	—

A—ATA CARNET
(issued by national chambers of commerce affiliated with the Paris-based International Chamber of Commerce (ICC))
An international customs document used for the temporary duty-free admission of certain goods into a country in lieu of the usual customs documents.

Commercial Invoice

Definition
The commercial invoice is the key accounting document describing a commercial transaction between a buyer and seller.

Issued By
The commercial invoice is issued by the exporter/seller.

Key Elements
The commercial invoice includes the following elements:

1. Name and address of seller
2. Name and address of buyer
3. Date of issuance
4. Invoice number
5. Order or contract number
6. Quantity and description of the goods
7. Unit price, total price, other agreed upon charges, and total invoice amount
8. Shipping details including: weight of the goods, number of packages, and shipping marks and numbers
9. Terms of delivery and payment
10. Any other information as required by the seller or buyer (e.g., country of origin)

Cautions and Notes
It is vitally important that the description of the goods and the terms listed in the commercial invoice correspond precisely with the description of goods in the contract of sale and with a documentary letter of credit (if that form of payment is used).

Sample Commercial Invoice

Indonesia Coffee Export Co.

Jalan Sudirman
Jakarta 10420, Indonesia

INVOICE

June 27, 2003
Invoice No. 98-123456

American Caffeine Import Company
125 Main Street
Seattle, Washington

Description of goods:
15 metric tons of 60-kilo bags of New Crop D.P. Sumatra Mandheling Arabica Grade 1 - Green Coffee -
As per buyer's purchase order No. 1234

TOTAL CIF Seattle, Washington, USA US$65,000.00

<u>Payment</u>:	By irrevocable documentary letter of credit No. 1234567 dated May 27, 1998 of The American Import Bank, Seattle, Washington USA
<u>Payment Terms</u>:	At 120 days' sight, draft drawn on San Francisco International Bank, San Francisco, California, USA
<u>Country of Origin</u>:	Indonesia
<u>Number of bags</u>:	250 bags
<u>Weights</u>:	Gross 15,000 kilo, Net 15,000 kilo
<u>Marks/No.</u>:	USA Made in Indonesia No. 12345.67
<u>Dispatch</u>:	Through ABC Freight Services, by sea from Jakarta via Sea Maritime Steamship Line to Seattle

Indonesia Coffee Export Co.

Indonesia Coffee Export Company

The Bill of Lading

Defined

A bill of lading is a document issued by a carrier to a shipper (exporter/seller/consignor), signed by the captain, agent, or owner of a vessel, furnishing written evidence regarding receipt of the goods (cargo), the conditions on which transportation is made (contract of carriage), and the engagement to deliver goods at the prescribed port of destination to the lawful holder of the bill of lading.

A bill of lading is, therefore, both a receipt for merchandise and a contract to deliver it as freight. There are a number of different types of bills of lading and a number of issues that relate to them as a group of documents.

Mini Glossary

NEGOTIABLE INSTRUMENT A written document (instrument) that can be transferred merely by endorsement (signing) or delivery. Checks, bills of exchange, bills of lading, and warehouse receipts (if marked negotiable), and promissory notes are examples of negotiable instruments and can be bought, sold or traded. Endorsement of such a document transfers the rights to money or goods as described in the negotiable instrument to the holder of the document.

Types of Bills of Lading Defined

STRAIGHT BILL OF LADING (non-negotiable)
A straight bill of lading indicates that the shipper will deliver the goods to the consignee. This is a non-negotiable document. The consignee need only present identification to claim the goods. A straight bill of lading is often used when payment for the goods has already been made in advance or when the goods are shipped on open account. A straight bill of lading, therefore, cannot be transferred by endorsement.

SHIPPER'S ORDER (NEGOTIABLE) BILL OF LADING
A shipper's order bill of lading is a title document to the goods (negotiable instrument), issued "to the order of" a party, usually the shipper, whose endorsement is required to effect its negotiation. Because it is negotiable, a shipper's order bill of lading can be bought, sold, or traded while goods are in transit. These are highly favored for documentary letter of credit transactions. The buyer usually needs the original or a signed copy as proof of ownership to take possession of the goods.

BLANK ENDORSED NEGOTIABLE BILL OF LADING
A blank endorsed negotiable bill of lading is one that has been endorsed without naming an endorsee. In simple terms, any person in possession of a blank endorsed negotiable bill of lading may claim possession of the goods. Possession of this document equals rights to possession of the shipment.

AIR WAYBILL
An air waybill is a form of bill of lading used for the air transport of goods and is not negotiable.

COURIER RECEIPT
A courier receipt is a document issued by a courier or delivery service evidencing receipt of goods for delivery to a named consignee and is not negotiable.

POST RECEIPT
A post receipt is a document issued by the postal service of a country evidencing receipt of goods for delivery to a named consignee.

MULTI-MODAL BILL OF LADING
A multi-modal bill of lading is a single bill of lading covering a single shipment by more than one mode of transport (for example by truck, then by rail and then by ship to its final destination).

CLEAN BILL OF LADING
A clean bill of lading is one where the carrier has noted that the merchandise has been received in apparent good condition (no apparent damage, loss, etc.) and that does not bear such notations as "Shipper's Load and Count," etc. Most forms of documentary payments require a "clean" bill of lading in order for the seller to obtain payment.

CLAUSED BILL OF LADING
Opposite of clean bill of lading, a claused bill of lading is one that contains notations that specify a shortfall in quantity or deficient condition of the goods and/or packaging. There are some circumstances in which transport documents with clauses are acceptable. For example, in the steel trade, such notations are the rule rather than the exception. If this is the case, the letter of credit should explicitly state which clause(s) will be deemed acceptable.

Issues and Notes Regarding Bills of Lading

Many issues concerning bills of lading come up with regard to satisfying the written instructions of the buyer for documentation in letter of credit transactions. These issues are not as relevant for U.S. Customs entry and clearance.

MULTIPLE MODES OF TRANSPORT
In documentary letter of credit transactions, if multiple modes of transport are permitted, or partial shipments allowed, and part of the goods will be shipped by one mode of transport and part by another, it is necessary to put "or" or "and/or" between the names of the required transport documents. For example, if the goods are to be shipped by both sea and air, the letter of credit might specify "marine bill of lading and/or air waybill."

ORIGINALS
In documentary credit transactions, the full set of original transport documents (one or more) must be presented. If the full set of transport documents consists of several originals, all of the originals should be submitted. The buyer can stipulate in the letter of credit the number of originals to be issued in a set, but many countries prefer or require that a set contain only one original of each document.

NAMED CARRIER

A transport document must appear on its face to have been issued by a named carrier or its agent. This does not mean that the buyer must name the carrier in the documentary credit application. It merely means that the transport document must indicate the name of the carrier. The applicant is free to stipulate a particular carrier, although this could cause delay in shipment.

ON DECK

An "on deck" notation on a transport document indicates that the goods have been placed above the deck level on the ship (subject to wind and weather). Such a notation will not be acceptable in letter of credit transactions unless specifically authorized. If the transport document shows that the goods are loaded on deck, any accompanying insurance document must show cover against "on deck" risks. Bear in mind, however, that dangerous or specialized cargo (including certain chemicals and live animals) often are or must be carried on deck.

ON BOARD

An "on board" notation on a bill of lading indicates that the goods have in fact been loaded on board or shipped on a named vessel. This notation is made by the carrier, the master of the ship, or the carrier's or master's agent. Unless expressly authorized, the transport document issued by the carrier must reflect that it is "on board" in order for the seller to obtain payment under a documentary credit.

Marine/Ocean/Port-to-Port Negotiable Bill of Lading

Definition

A marine bill of lading is a transport document covering port-to-port shipments of goods (for carriage of goods solely by sea).

Key Elements

The marine bill of lading contains the following elements:

1. Name of carrier with a signature identified as that of the carrier, or ship's master, or an agent of the carrier or ship's master

2. An indication or notation that the goods have been loaded "on board" or shipped on a named vessel. Also, the date of issuance or date of loading

3. An indication of the port of loading and the port of discharge

4. A sole original, or if issued in multiple originals, the full set of originals

5. The terms and conditions of carriage or a reference to the terms and conditions of carriage in another source or document

6. No indication that the document is subject to a charter party and no indication that the named vessel is propelled by sail only

7. Meets any other stipulations of a letter of credit (when applicable)

Cautions & Notes

Most notes relate to rules concerning bills of lading in transactions involving a letter of credit payment.

VESSEL NAME If the bill of lading includes the notation "intended vessel," it must also contain an "on board" notation of a named vessel along with the date of loading, even if the named vessel is the same as the intended vessel.

PORT OF LOADING If the document indicates a place where the goods were received by the carrier different from the port of loading, the document must also contain an "on-board" notation indicating the port of loading as named in the letter of credit and the named vessel, along with the date.

TRANSPORT DOCUMENTS If a documentary letter of credit calls for a port-to-port shipment but does not call specifically for a marine bill of lading, the banks will accept a transport document, however named, that contains the above information. Banks will normally accept the following documents under this title: ocean bill of lading, combined transport bill of lading, short form bill of lading, or received for shipment bill of lading, provided it carries the notation "on board."

ENDORSEMENT If the documents are drawn up "to the order of" the exporter or "to order," they must be endorsed.

TRANSSHIPMENT If the letter of credit prohibits transshipment, this document will be rejected if it specifically states that the goods will be transshipped.

TRANSFER IN TRANSIT Since this is a negotiable instrument, it may be endorsed and transferred to a third party while the goods are in transit.

Sample Marine/Ocean/Port-to-Port Bill of Lading

BILL OF LADING FOR MULTIMODAL TRANSPORT OR PORT-TO-PORT SHIPMENT

1. SHIPPER

SWISS EXPORT LTD
INDUSTRIESTRASSE 200

8050 ZUERICH – OERLIKON

BOOKING No   55   B/L No   2

REFERENCE No   ABC/22/66 bu

2. CONSIGNEE: ORDER OF

TO ORDER

3. NOTIFY ADDRESS (carrier not responsible for failure to notify see clause 21 hereof)

TA PING CO. LTD
YACHT BUILDING
18-5, HARBOR STREET
TAIPEI / TAIWAN

Shipping company
Schiffahrtsgesellschaft
Société de transport maritime

4. Pre-carriage by (*)	5. Place of receipt (*)
	ANTWERP CFS

6. OCEAN VESSEL	7. PORT OF LOADING
"HOLLANDIA"	ROTTERDAM

8. PORT OF DISCHARGE	9. Place of delivery (**)
KEELUNG	KEELUNG CFS

if goods to be transhipped by carrier at port of discharge.

10. Marks & Nos.	11. Number and kind of packages, description of goods	13. Gross weight kilos	14. Measurement m3
	ON BOARD – FREIGHT PREPAID		
ABC 1930-1934 VIA KEELUNG TA PING	5 CASES CIF KEELUNG "HARMLESS CHEMICALS"	kos 1050	
	IRREVOCABLE CREDIT No 25AB/26008/01		
	IMPORT LICENSE No 75 DGL - 01111		

Particulars furnished by shipper of the goods

Shipper's declaration of a value higher than the carrier's limit of liability - See clause 19:

Freight and charges
(particulars for calculation of freight only)

Freight: to be prepaid/to be collected

All agreements or freight engagements for the shipment of the goods are superseded by this Bill of Lading, except the conditions of the applicable tariff which are available from the carrier and which are deemed to be incorporated in this Bill of Lading. In case of inconsistency of any conditions of the applicable tariff with the terms stated on page 1 and 2 of this Bill of Lading the latter shall prevail unless otherwise expressly provided for herein. All the terms of this Bill of Lading, whether written, typed, stamped, or printed, are accepted and agreed by the merchant to be binding as fully as if signed by the merchant any local customs or privileges to the contrary notwithstanding. IN WITNESS WHEREOF the number of original Bills of Lading stated below all of this tenor and date has been signed, one of which being accomplished the others to stand void.

15. Freight payable at	16. Place and date of issue
ANTWERP	15.7.19

17. Number of original Bs/L	18 For the carrier
3/3	FORWARDING LTD

(*) Applicable only when document used for transhipment (see clause 2 b)
(**) Applicable only when document used for INTERMODAL transportation (see clause 2 c)

Page 2

Non-Negotiable Sea Waybill

Definition

A non-negotiable sea waybill is a transport document covering port-to-port shipments. It is not a title document, is not negotiable, and cannot be endorsed.

Key Elements

The non-negotiable sea waybill contains the following elements:

1. Name of carrier with a signature identified as that of the carrier, ship's master, or agent for the carrier or ship's master

2. An indication or notation that the goods have been loaded "on board" or shipped on a named vessel. Also, the date of issuance or date of loading

3. An indication of the port of loading and the port of discharge

4. A sole original, or if issued in multiple originals, the full set of originals

5. The terms and conditions of carriage or a reference to the terms and conditions of carriage in another source or document

6. No indication that the document is subject to a charter party and no indication that the named vessel is propelled by sail only (in letter of credit transactions)

7. Meets any other stipulations of a letter of credit (when applicable)

Cautions & Notes

Most notes relate to rules concerning bills of lading in transactions involving a letter of credit payment.

VESSEL NAME If the bill of lading includes the notation "intended vessel," it must also contain an "on board" notation of a named vessel along with the date of loading, even if the named vessel is the same as the intended vessel.

PORT OF LOADING If the document indicates a place where the goods were received by the carrier different from the port of loading, the document must also contain an "on-board" notation indicating the port of loading as named in the letter of credit and the named vessel, along with the date.

TRANSPORT DOCUMENTS If the letter of credit calls for a port-to-port shipment but does not call specifically for a marine bill of lading, the banks will accept a transport document, however named, that contains the above information. Banks will normally accept the following documents under this title: ocean bill of lading, combined transport bill of lading, short form bill of lading, or received for shipment bill of lading, provided it carries the notation "on board."

WAYBILLS Because they are not title documents, sea waybills eliminate many of the inconveniences of a bill of lading and offer advantages in situations where the rigid security of a bill of lading is not required. Waybills reduce the opportunity for fraud and they remove the problems of goods arriving ahead of documents.

Sea waybills are appropriate for shipments between associated companies, for shipments to an agent for sale at destination on an open account basis, and for shipments between companies that have established mutual trust.

Sample Non-Negotiable Sea Waybill

Carrier:
Hapag-Lloyd Container Linie GmbH, Hamburg

Express Cargo Bill
Multimodal Transport or Port to Port Shipment

PAGE 2

Hapag-Lloyd

Shipper:

ABC WINE COMPANY
1234 SPAIN STREET
SONOMA, CA 96476

Hapag-Lloyd Reference: 10347784

ECB-No.: HLCUOAK980300071

Export References:
USS-NL-000-008
C.H.R.NO: 5118
F.M.C.NO: 0087

Consignee:

DELAHAY WINE ENTERPRISES, LTD.
HAZELDONK 1408 - 1412
NL 4386 LH BREDA
THE NETHERLANDS

Forwarding Agent:
NALDUZAK ASSOCIATES, INC.
5088A DIAMOND HEIGHTS BLVD.
SAN FRANCISCO, CA 94131-1605

Consignee's Reference:

Notify Address (Carrier not responsible for failure to notify):

DELAHAY WINE ENTERPRISES, LTD.
HAZALDONK 1408 - 1412
NL 4386 LH BREDA
THE NETHERLANDS

Place of Receipt:

Pre-Carriage by:

Place of Receipt by Pre-Carrier:

Place of Delivery:

Ocean Vessel: 06E07
KOELN EXPRESS

Port of Loading:
OAKLAND, CA

Port of Discharge:
ROTTERDAM

Place of Delivery by On-Carrier:

Container Nos., Seal Nos.; Marks and Nos.	Number and Kind of Packages; Description of Goods	Gross Weight (kg)	Measurement (cbm)
HLCU 4073300 SEAL: 2902455 PO-DS: 3327-04G PO-C1: EL100093	1 X 40' CONTAINER SAID TO CONTAIN: 1246 CS CALIFORNIA WINES LESS THAN 14% ALCOHOL COMMODITY: 2204000000	19872 KGM	

SHIPPED ON BOARD DATE: MAR/06/1998
PORT OF LOADING: OAKLAND, CA
VESSEL NAME: KOELN EXPRESS

SHIPMENT PURSUANT TO SC NO. 98-500
SHIPPER'S LOAD, STOWAGE AND COUNT
FREIGHT COLLECT
PROTECT AGAINST EXTREME TEMPERATURES
THESE COMMODITIES LICENSED BY THE U.S. FOR ULTIMATE DESTINATION
THE NETHERLANDS.   DIVERSION CONTRARY TO U.S. LAW PROHIBITED.

Above Particulars as declared by Shipper. Without responsibility or warranty as to correctness by carrier.

RECEIPT

Total No. of Containers/Packages received by the Carrier:	Shipper's declared value (see clause 7(1) and 7(2) hereof):
1	

RECEIVED by the Carrier from the Shipper in apparent good order and condition (unless otherwise noted herein) the total number or quantity of Containers or other packages or units indicated in the box opposite entitled "Total No. of Containers/Packages received by the Carrier" for Carriage subject to all the terms and conditions hereof (INCLUDING THE TERMS AND CONDITIONS ON THE REVERSE HEREOF AND THE TERMS AND CONDITIONS OF THE CARRIER'S APPLICABLE TARIFF) from the Place of Receipt or the Port of Loading, whichever is applicable, to the Port of Discharge or the Place of Delivery, whichever is applicable. In accepting this Express Cargo Bill the Merchant expressly accepts and agrees to all its terms and conditions whether printed, stamped or written, or otherwise incorporated, notwithstanding the non-signing of this Express Cargo Bill by the Merchant.

Movement FCL/FCL   **Currency** USD

Charge	Rate	Basis	WT/MEA/VAL	Payment	Amount
THO	500.00	CTR	1	C	500.00
SEA	1701.00	CTR	1	C	1701.00
BAF	80.00	CTR	1	C	80.00
CAF	21.00	PCT	1701	C	357.21
THO	343.00	CTR	1	C	167.33

Place and Date of Issue:
CORTE MADERA, CA   MAR/05/1998

Freight Payable at:
BARKING, U.K.

For above named carrier
Hapag-Lloyd (America) Inc.
(as agent)

Total Freight Prepaid	Total Freight Collect	Total Freight
	2805.54	2805.54

90116743

Express Cargo Bill · Not Negotiable

Charter Party Bill of Lading

Definition

A charter party bill of lading is a transport document covering port-to-port shipments of goods issued by a party chartering a vessel (as opposed to a named carrier or shipping line).

Issued By

The charter party bill of lading is issued by the party chartering a vessel; specifically not a carrier.

Key Elements

The charter party bill of lading contains the following elements:

1. An indication that the bill of lading is subject to a charter party

2. A signature or authentication by the ship's master or owner, or an agent for the ship's master or owner

3. Does not name a carrier

4. An indication or notation that the goods have been loaded "on board" or shipped on a named vessel. Also, the date of issuance or date of loading

5. An indication of the port of loading and the port of discharge

6. A sole original, or if issued in multiple originals, the full set of originals

7. No indication that the named vessel is propelled by sail only

8. Meets any other stipulations of a letter of credit (when applicable)

Cautions & Notes

The charter party bill of lading may have preprinted wording indicating that the shipment has been loaded "on board" the "named vessel," but the document must still be signed as per number two above.

If preprinted wording is used, the date of issuance is deemed to be the date of loading on board. In all other cases the document must contain an "on board" "named vessel" notations along with the date the shipment was loaded on board.

Sample Charter Party Bill of Lading

CODE NAME: "CONGENBILL" . EDITION 1978

Shipper

Swiss Export Ltd.
Industriestrasse 200
CH-8050 Zürich-Oerlikon

Consignee

TO ORDER OF SHIPPER

Notify address

1st: ViaMAT (Far East)
1-10-7 Higashi Gotanda
Sinagawa-Ku, TOKYO 141
2nd: Suzuki K.K.
Saitama

Vessel	Port of loading
M/V TIGER	Cherbourg

Port of discharge
Yokohama

BILL OF LADING
TO BE USED WITH CHARTER-PARTIES

B/L No.
GGG/mzf 101

Reference No.
1150.01.23.

SHIPCRAFT TRANSPORT INC.

General Agents:

SHIPCRAFT A/S
(Hovedgaden 16)
P O Box 142
DK-2970 Hoersholm, Denmark
Phone: 4 2-571033
Telex: 37584 Shpcr Dk
Fax: 4 2-571044

Agent for Switzerland:

MAT TRANSPORT AG
Erlenstrasse 95
P.O. Box
CH-4002 Basel, Switzerland

Phone: 061 68 68 000
Fax: 061 68 68 001

Shipper's description of goods			Gross weight	
92HBFC0803T 1 - 240	240 packages ============	MACHINERY as per contract PQ 733 054 dated 12.10.19.. Letter of credit No. MC986CH34 dated 4.12.19..	452'500 kg ==========	1202 m3

ORIGINAL

(of which -0-(none) on deck at Shipper's risk; the Carrier not
being responsible for loss or damage howsoever arising)

Freight payable as per
CHARTER-PARTY dated   7. March 19..

FREIGHT ADVANCE.
Received on account of freight:

PREPAID AS AGREED

Time used for loading ....0.... days ....23.... hours.

S H I P P E D at the Port of Loading in apparent good order and
condition on board the Vessel for carriage to the
Port of Discharge or so near thereto as she may safely get the goods
specified above.

Weight, measure, quality, quantity, condition, contents and value unknown.

IN WITNESS whereof the Master or Agent of the said Vessel has signed
the number of Bills of Lading indicated below all of this tenor and date,
any one of which being accomplished the others shall be void.

FOR CONDITIONS OF CARRIAGE SEE OVERLEAF

Freight payable at	Place and date of issue
Basel/Switzerland	Basel, - 6. Mai 19..
Number of original Bs/L	Signature
3/3 (Three)	**MAT TRANSPORT AG** as agent of the owner i.e. Shipcraft Transport Inc.

Printed and sold
by Carl Svanberg Tryckeri AB, Box 91, 35103 Växjö,
by authority of The Baltic and International Maritime Conference,
Copenhagen.

Multimodal (Combined) Transport Document

Definition

A multimodal transport document is a bill of lading covering a shipment by two or more modes of transport, such as shipping by rail and by sea.

Issued By

The multimodal transport document is issued by a freight-forwarder, logistics firm, or carrier. In some instances the document may be filled out by the exporter/consignor, but then signed by an agent of the carrier.

Key Elements

The multimodal transport document contains the following elements:

1. Name of carrier or multimodal transport operator with a signature identified as that of the carrier, transport operator, ship's master, or agent of one of these

2. An indication that the shipment has been "dispatched," "taken in charge," or "loaded on board," along with a date

3. Indication of the place of receipt of the shipment, which may be different from the place of actual loading "on board" and the place of delivery of the shipment, which may be different from the place of discharge

4. A sole original, or if issued in multiple originals, the full set of originals

5. The terms and conditions of carriage or a reference to the terms and conditions of carriage in another source or document other than the multimodal transport document

6. No indication that the document is subject to a charter party and no indication that the named vessel is propelled by sail only

7. Meets any other stipulations of a letter of credit (when applicable)

Cautions & Notes

RECEIPT OF GOODS In multimodal situations the contract of carriage and liability is for a combined transport from the place of shipment to the place of delivery. Thus, the document evidences receipt of goods and not shipment on board.

DATE OF ISSUANCE The date of issuance of the document is deemed to be the date of dispatch unless there is a specific date of dispatch, taking in charge, or loading on board, in which case the latter date is deemed to be the date of dispatch.

TRANSPORT DOCUMENTS Even if a letter of credit prohibits transshipment, banks will accept a multimodal transport document that indicates that transshipment will or may take place, provided that the entire carriage is covered by one transport document.

A combined transport document issued by a freight forwarder is acceptable to banks in a letter of credit unless the credit stipulates otherwise or unless the credit specifically calls for a "marine bill of lading." The issuing freight forwarder accepts carrier responsibility for performance of the entire contract of carriage and liability for loss or damage wherever and however it occurs.

NEGOTIABILITY As a rule, multimodal transport documents are not negotiable.

Sample Multimodal (combined) Transport Document

BILL OF LADING FOR COMBINED TRANSPORT OR PORT TO PORT SHIPMENT

P&O Nedlloyd

North America Trade

NOT NEGOTIABLE UNLESS CONSIGNED "TO ORDER"

SHIPPER / EXPORTER	BOOKING NUMBER	BILL OF LADING NO	BROKERAGE

EXPORT REFERENCES

CONSIGNEE	FORWARDING AGENT - REFERENCES

POINT AND COUNTRY OF ORIGIN

NOTIFY PARTY   It is agreed that no responsibility shall attach to the Carrier or his Agents for failure to notify of the arrival of the goods see clause 20 on reverse

ALSO NOTIFY / ROUTING / INSTRUCTIONS

*PRECARRIAGE BY	*PLACE OF RECEIPT BY PRECARRIER	
EXPORTING CARRIER / VESSEL	PORT OF LOADING	LOADING PIER / TERMINAL
PORT OF DISCHARGE	*PLACE OF DELIVERY BY ONCARRIER	TYPE OF MOVEMENT

PARTICULARS FURNISHED BY SHIPPER (but not acknowledged by the Carrier (see clause 11)

MARKS AND NUMBERS	NO. OF PKGS.	H M	DESCRIPTION OF PACKAGES AND GOODS	GROSS WEIGHT	MEASUREMENT

EXCESS VALUATION: REFER TO CLAUSE 7 (3) ON REVERSE SIDE

FREIGHT CHARGES PAYABLE AT:	RV	ITEM NUMBER

**TOTAL NO OF CONTAINERS/PACKAGES RECEIVED BY THE CARRIER	FREIGHT AND CHARGES	PREPAID	COLLECT

Received by the Carrier from the Shipper in apparent good order and condition (unless otherwise noted herein) the total number or quantity of Containers or other packages or units indicated in the box above entitled ** "Total No of Containers/Packages received by the Carrier" for Carriage subject to all the terms and conditions hereof INCLUDING THE TERMS AND CONDITIONS ON THE REVERSE HEREOF AND THE TERMS OF THE CARRIER'S APPLICABLE TARIFF, from the Place of Receipt or the Port of Loading, whichever is applicable, to the Port of Discharge or the Place of Delivery, whichever is applicable. If the Carrier so requires, before he arranges delivery of the Goods one original Bill of Lading, duly endorsed, must be surrendered by the Merchant to the Carrier at the Port of Discharge or at some other location acceptable to the Carrier. In accepting this Bill of Lading Merchant expressly accepts and agrees to all its terms and conditions whether printed, stamped or written, or otherwise incorporated, notwithstanding the non-signing of this Bill of Lading by the Merchant.

IN WITNESS whereof .... original Bills of Lading (unless otherwise stated above) have been signed, one of which being accomplished, the others shall be void.

For P&O Nedlloyd Limited as Carrier:

AS AGENT(S) ONLY

*APPLICATION FOR COMBINED TRANSPORT ONLY			
B.L. NO	MO.	DAY	YEAR

EXCESS VALUE CHARGE (SEE CLAUSE 7 (3))		
RESP. CODE	**TOTAL CHARGES**	

Form 31 Rev. 2/97

Air Transport Document (Air Waybill)

Definition
An air waybill is a non-negotiable transport document covering transport of cargo by air from airport to airport.

Issued By
The air waybill is issued by the air carrier (or by a freight forwarder or logistics company). In some instances the document may be filled out by the exporter/seller/consignor, but then signed by an agent of the airline.

Key Elements
The air waybill contains the following elements:

1. Name of carrier with a signature identified as that of the carrier or its named agent

2. An indication that the goods have been accepted for carriage. Also, the date of issuance or date of loading

3. An indication of the actual date of dispatch (if required by a documentary credit), or, if the actual date of dispatch is not required by the letter of credit, the issuance date of the document is deemed to be the date of shipment

4. An indication of the airport of departure and airport of destination

5. Appears on its face to be the original

6. The terms and conditions of carriage or a reference to the terms and conditions of carriage in another source or document

7. Meets any other stipulations of a letter of credit (when applicable)

Cautions & Notes
FLIGHT DATA Information contained in the "for carrier use only" box concerning flight number and date are not considered to be the actual flight number and date. The air waybill should not be required to indicate an "actual flight date" since IATA regulations specify that reservations requested by the shipper shall not be inserted under "Flight/Date."

ORIGINALS Since air waybills are issued in three originals—one for the issuing carrier, one for the consignee (buyer), and one for the shipper/consignor (seller)—a documentary letter of credit should not require presentation of more than one original. Nor should it call for a "full set of original air waybills."

NEGOTIABILITY The air waybill is not a negotiable document. It indicates only acceptance of goods for carriage.

CONSIGNEE The air waybill must name a consignee (who can be the buyer). In a letter of credit payment situation the waybill should not be required to be issued "to order" and/or "to be endorsed" since it is not a negotiable instrument. Also, since it is not negotiable, and it does not evidence title to the goods, in order to maintain some control of goods not paid for by cash in advance, sellers often consign air shipments to their sales agents or freight forwarders' agents in the buyer's country.

Sample Air Waybill

085 BSL	7260 2751		085-7260-2751

Shipper's Name and Address | **Shipper's account Number**

SWISS EXPORT LTD
AIRFREIGHT DIVISION
ZUERICH

NOT NEGOTIABLE

AIR WAYBILL

AIR CONSIGNMENT NOTE

swissair ✚

Issued by: Swiss Air Transport Co., Ltd., Zurich, Switzerland
Member of IATA (International Air Transport Association)

Copies 1, 2 and 3 of this Air Waybill are originals and have the same validity

Consignee's Name and Address | **Consignee's account Number**

IMPORT KONTOR
VIENNA

Phone: 633 7876

It is agreed that the goods described herein are accepted in apparent good order and condition (except as noted) for carriage SUBJECT O THE CONDITIONS OF CONTRACT ON THE REVERSE HEREOF. THE SHIPPER'S ATTENTION IS DRAWN TO THE NOTICE CONCERNING CARRIERS' LIMITATION OF LIABILITY. Shipper may increase such limitation of liability by declaring a higher value for carriage and paying a supplemental charge if required.

Issuing Carrier's Agent Name and City

FORWARDING LTD
BASLE

Accounting information

Agent's IATA Code | **Account No.**
81-4 0000 | |

Airport of Departure (Addr. of the Carrier) and requested Routing

BSL-VIE

to	By first Carrier Routing and Destination	to	by	to	by	Currency	CHGS Code	WT/VAL PPD COLL	Other PPD COLL	Declared Value for Carriage	Declared Value for Customs
VIE	SWISSAIR					SFR	CCPP			NVD	

Airport of Destination	**Flight/Date**	For Carrier Use only Flight/Date	**Amount of Insurance**	**INSURANCE** - If carrier offers insurance and such insurance is requested in accordance with conditions on reverse hereof, indicate amount to be insured in figures in box marked amount of insurance.
VIENNA	SR436/8.7.			

Handling Information

No of Pieces RCP	Gross Weight	kg lb	Rate Class Commodity Item No.	Chargeable Weight	Rate / Charge	Total	Nature and Quantity of Goods (incl. Dimensions or Volume)
8	200,6	K	C 6750	201	1.90	381.90	CHEMICALS NOT RESTRICTED CONTRACT No 100-15-2
8	200,6						

Prepaid	Weight Charge	Collect	Other Charges
		381.90	AWA 15.00

Valuation Charge	

Tax	

Total other Charges Due Agent	
15.00	

Total other Charges Due Carrier	

Shipper certifies that the particulars on the face hereof are correct and that insofar as any part of the consignment contains dangerous goods, such part is properly described by name and is in proper condition for carriage by air according to the applicable Dangerous Goods Regulations.

SWISS EXPORT LTD / p.o. Forwarding LTD

....
Signature of Shipper or his Agent

Total Prepaid	Total Collect
15.00	381.90

Currency Conversion Rates	cc charges in Dest. Currency

07.07.   BASLE   Forwarding LTD
....
Executed on (Date)   at   (Place)   Signature of Issuing Carrier or its Agent

Charges at Destination	Total collect Charges

For Carrier's Use only at Destination	

085-7260 2751

No. 3 - ORIGINAL for SHIPPER

Form 30.301
Printed in the Fed. Rep. Germany - Bartsch Verlag, Munich-Ottobrunn 600j (III)

Road, Rail or Inland Waterway Transport Documents

Definition

Road, rail, or inland waterway bills of lading are transport documents covering transport of cargo from named points via truck, rail or barge transport.

Issued By

The road, rail or inland waterway transport document is issued by the carrier. In some cases, this document may be filled out by the consignor, but then signed by an agent of the carrier

Key Elements

The air waybill contains the following elements:

1. Name of carrier with a signature identified as that of the carrier or its named agent

2. An indication that the goods have been accepted for carriage. Also, the date of issuance or date of loading

3. An indication of the actual date of dispatch (if required by a documentary credit), or, if the actual date of dispatch is not required by the letter of credit, the issuance date of the document is deemed to be the date of shipment

4. An indication of the airport of departure and airport of destination

5. Appears on its face to be the original

6. The terms and conditions of carriage or a reference to the terms and conditions of carriage in another source or document

7. Meets any other stipulations of a letter of credit (when applicable)

Cautions & Notes

DATE OF SHIPMENT In road, rail, or inland waterway transport documents the date of issuance is considered the date of shipment unless there is a reception stamp, in which case that date is deemed to be the date of shipment.

TRANSPORT DOCUMENTS Unless otherwise stipulated in a documentary credit, banks will accept transport document(s) as presented as a "full set."

ORIGINALS Unless otherwise stipulated in a documentary credit, banks will accept road, rail, or inland waterway transport documents as originals whether marked as such or not.

Packing List/Bill of Parcels

Definition

A packing list is a document prepared by the shipper listing the kinds and quantities of merchandise in a particular shipment.

A copy of the packing list is often attached to the shipment itself and another copy sent directly to the consignee to assist in checking the shipment when received. It is also called a bill of parcels.

Issued By

The packing list is issued by the exporter/shipper/consignor.

Key Elements

The packing list contains the following elements:

1. Name and address of seller (consignor)
2. Name and address of buyer (consignee)
3. Date of issuance
4. Invoice number (reference to invoice that covers the particular shipment)
5. Order or contract number
6. Quantity and description of the goods
7. Weight of the goods
8. Number of packages
9. Shipping marks and numbers
10. Quantity and description of contents of each package, carton, crate or container
11. Any other information as required in the shipper's instructions (e.g., country of origin)

Cautions & Notes

The packing list is a more detailed version of the commercial invoice but without price information. The type of each container is identified, as well as its individual weight and measurements. The packing list is attached to the outside of its respective container in a waterproof envelope marked "Packing List Enclosed," and is immediately available to authorities in both the countries of export and import.

A packing list is not required in all transactions, but is a standard requirement by the export or import laws of certain countries and by some buyers. A packing list helps the consignee at the point of delivery and warehouse personnel to identify which contents may be found in which packages. Also, if custom authorities require an inspection, it allows them to easily identify the specific package they wish to open.

Customs Declaration CF 6059B

APHIS/FWS USE ONLY	**WELCOME TO THE UNITED STATES**	CUSTOMS USE ONLY

DEPARTMENT OF THE TREASURY
UNITED STATES CUSTOMS SERVICE

FORM APPROVED
OMB NO. 1515-0041

CUSTOMS DECLARATION

19 CFR 122.27, 148.12, 148.13, 148.110, 148.111

Each arriving traveler or responsible family member must provide the following information (only **ONE** written declaration per family is required):

1. Family Name

2. First (Given) Name   3. Middle Initial(s)   4. Birth Date *(day/mo/yr)*

5. Airline/Flight No. or Vessel Name or Vehicle License No.   6. Number of Family Members Traveling With You

7. (a) Country of Citizenship   7. (b) Country of Residence

8. (a) U.S. Address *(Street Number/Hotel/Mailing Address in U.S.)*

8. (b) U.S. Address *(City)*   8. (c) U.S Address *(State)*

9. Countries visited on this trip prior to U.S. arrival

a.   b.

c.   d.

10. The purpose of my (our) trip is or was: *(Check one or both boxes, if applicable)*   ☐ Business   ☐ Personal

11. I am (We are) bringing fruits, plants, meats, food, soil, birds, snails, other live animals, wildlife products, farm products; or, have been on a farm or ranch outside the U.S.:   ☐ Yes   ☐ No

12. I am (We are) carrying currency or monetary instruments over $10,000 U.S., or foreign equivalent: ☐ Yes   ☐ No

13. I have (We have) commercial merchandise, U.S. or foreign: *(Check one box only)*   ☐ Yes   ☐ No

14. The total value of all goods, including commercial merchandise, I/we purchased or acquired abroad and am/are bringing to the U.S. is: $ _____ *(U.S. Dollars)*

(See the instructions on the back of this form under "MERCHANDISE" and use the space provided there to list all the items you must declare. If you have nothing to declare, write "- 0 -" in the space provided above.)

SIGN BELOW AFTER YOU READ NOTICE ON REVERSE

I have read the notice on the reverse and have made a truthful declaration.

X _____
Signature   Date *(day/month/year)*

U.S. Customs use only -- Do not write below this line -- U.S. Customs use only

INSPECTOR'S BADGE NUMBER   STAMP AREA

TIME COMPLETED

Customs Form 6059B (012799)

NOTICE

ALL PERSONS ARE SUBJECT TO FURTHER QUESTIONING AND THEIR PERSONS, BELONGINGS, AND CONVEYANCE ARE SUBJECT TO SEARCH. (19 CFR 162.3 - 162.8)

The unlawful importation of controlled substances (narcotics, chemicals, prescription medicines if not accompanied by a prescription, etc.) regardless of amount is a violation of U.S. law.

AGRICULTURAL AND WILDLIFE PRODUCTS

To prevent the entry of dangerous agricultural pests and prohibited wildlife, the following are restricted: Fruits, vegetables, plants, plant products, soil, meats, meat products, birds, snails, and other live animals or animal products, wildlife and wildlife products. Failure to declare all such items to a Customs/Agricultural/Wildlife officer can result in penalties and the items may be subject to seizure.

CURRENCY AND MONETARY INSTRUMENTS

The transportation of currency or monetary instruments, REGARDLESS OF AMOUNT, IS LEGAL; however, if you take out of or bring into the United States more than $10,000 (U.S. or foreign equivalent, or a combination of the two) in coin, currency, traveler's checks or bearer instruments such as money orders, personal or cashier's checks, stocks or bonds, you are required BY LAW to FILE a report on Form 4790 with the U.S. Customs Service. If you have someone else carry the currency or instruments for you, you must also file the report. FAILURE TO FILE THE REQUIRED REPORT OR FAILURE TO REPORT THE TOTAL AMOUNT YOU ARE CARRYING MAY LEAD TO THE SEIZURE OF ALL THE CURRENCY OR INSTRUMENTS, AND MAY SUBJECT YOU TO CIVIL PENALTIES AND/OR CRIMINAL PROSECUTION.

MERCHANDISE

VISITORS (NON-RESIDENTS) must declare in item 14 the total value of all articles intended for others and all items intended to be sold or left in the U.S. This includes all gifts and commercial items or samples. (EXCEPTION: Your own personal effects, such as clothing, personal jewelry and camera equipment, luggage, etc., need not be declared.)

U.S. RESIDENTS must declare in item 14 the total value of ALL articles, including commercial goods and samples, they acquired abroad (whether new or used; dutiable or not; and whether obtained by purchase, received as a gift, or otherwise), including those articles purchased in DUTY FREE STORES IN THE U.S. OR ABROAD, which are in their possession at the time of arrival. Articles which you acquired on this trip mailed from abroad, (other than articles acquired in insular possessions and various Caribbean Basin countries) are dutiable upon their arrival in the U.S.

THE AMOUNT OF DUTY TO BE PAID will be determined by a Customs officer. U.S. residents are normally entitled to a duty free exemption of $400 on those items accompanying them; non-residents are normally entitled to an exemption of $100. Duty is normally a flat rate of 10% on the first $1000 above the exemption. If the value of goods declared in item 14 EXCEEDS $1400 PER PERSON, then list ALL articles below and show price paid in U.S. dollars or, for gifts, fair retail value. Please describe all articles by their common names and material. For example: MAN'S WOOL KNIT SWEATER; DIAMOND AND GOLD RING; etc. Also, please have all your receipts ready to present to the Customs officer, if requested. This will help to facilitate the inspection process.

COMMERCIAL MERCHANDISE can be defined as articles for sale, for soliciting orders, or other goods not considered personal effects of the traveler.

IF YOU HAVE ANY QUESTIONS ABOUT WHAT MUST BE REPORTED OR DECLARED, ASK A CUSTOMS OFFICER

DESCRIPTION OF ARTICLES *(List may be continued on another Form 6059B)*	VALUE	CUSTOMS USE
TOTAL ▷		

Paperwork Reduction Act Notice: The information collected on this form is needed to carry out the Customs, Agriculture, and Currency laws of the United States. We need it to insure that travelers are complying with these laws and to allow us to figure and collect the right amount of duty and taxes. Your response is mandatory. The estimated average burden associated with this collection of information is 3 minutes per respondent or recordkeeper depending on individual circumstances. Comments concerning the accuracy of this burden estimate and suggestions for reducing this burden should be directed to U.S. Customs Service, Information Services Group, Washington, D.C. 20229. DO NOT send completed form(s) to this office.

*U.S.G.P.O.:2000 —584-319   **Customs Form 6059B (012799)(Back)**

Carriers Certificate

carriers certificate

To the Port Director

_____   _____
(Port of entry)   (Date)

      The undersigned carrier, to whom or upon whose order the articles described below or in the attached document must be released,* hereby certifies that _____ of _____ is the owner or consignee of such articles within the purview of section 484(h), Tariff Act of 1930.

Marks and number of packages	Description and quantity of merchandise—Number and kind of packages	Gross weight in pounds	Foreign port of landing and date of sailing	Bill of lading number

Carrier _____   _____
                                                            (Name of carrier)

Voyage No. _____

Arrived _____   _____
                  (Date)   (Agent)

*Under the tariff laws of the United States Customs officers do not deliver the goods to the consignee. The goods are released from Customs custody to or upon the order of the carrier by whom the goods are brought to the port at which they are entered for consumption. When the goods are entered for warehouse, they are released from Customs custody to or upon the order of the proprietor of the warehouse.

Declaration for Free Entry, Unaccompanied Articles CF 3299 p. 1

DEPARTMENT OF THE TREASURY
United States Customs Service

DECLARATION FOR FREE ENTRY OF UNACCOMPANIED ARTICLES

19 CFR 148.6, 148.52, 148.53, 148.77

FORM APPROVED OMB NO. 1515-0053

Paperwork Reduction Act Notice: This request is in accordance with the Paperwork Reduction Act of 1995. We ask for the information in order to carry out the laws and regulations administered by the U.S. Customs Service. These regulations and forms apply to importers to ensure that they are complying with the law and to allow us to figure, collect, or refund the right amount of duty and tax. It is mandatory. The estimated average burden associated with this collection of information is 10 minutes per respondent depending on individual circumstances. Comments concerning the accuracy of this burden estimates and suggestions for reducing this burden should be directed to the U.S. Customs Service, Information Services Branch, Washington, DC 20229, and to the Office of Management and Budget, Paperwork Reduction Project (1515-0053), Washington, DC 20503.

PART I -- TO BE COMPLETED BY ALL PERSONS SEEKING FREE ENTRY OF ARTICLES (Please consult with the Customs official for additional information or assistance. REMEMBER--All of your statements are subject to verification. False declarations or failure to declare articles could result in penalties.)

1. IMPORTER'S NAME (Last, first and middle)

2. IMPORTER'S DATE OF BIRTH

3. IMPORTER'S DATE OF ARRIVAL

4. IMPORTER'S U.S. ADDRESS

5. IMPORTER'S PORT OF ARRIVAL

6. NAME OF ARRIVING VESSEL CARRIER AND FLIGHT/TRAIN

7. NAME(S) OF ACCOMPANYING HOUSEHOLD MEMBERS (wife, husband, minor children, etc.)

8. THE ARTICLES FOR WHICH FREE ENTRY IS CLAIMED BELONG TO ME AND/OR MY FAMILY AND WERE IMPORTED ➡

A. DATE

B. NAME OF VESSEL/CARRIER

C. FROM (Country)

D. B/L OR AWB OR I.T. NO.

E. NUMBER AND KINDS OF CONTAINERS

F. MARKS AND NUMBERS

PART II -- TO BE COMPLETED BY ALL PERSONS EXCEPT U.S. PERSONNEL AND EVACUEES

9. RESIDENCY ("X" appropriate box)

I declare that my place of residence abroad ☐ is ☐ was ➡

A. NAME OF COUNTRY

B. LENGTH OF TIME   Yr.   Mo.

C. RESIDENCY STATUS UPON MY/OUR ARRIVAL ("X" One)
☐ (1) Returning resident of the U.S.   (2) Nonresident: ☐ a. Emigrating to the U.S.   ☐ b. Visiting the U.S.

10. STATEMENT(S) OF ELIGIBILITY FOR FREE ENTRY OF ARTICLES
I the undersigned further declare that ("X" all applicable items and submit packing list):

A. Applicable to RESIDENT AND NONRESIDENT

☐ (1) All household effects acquired abroad for which free entry is sought were used abroad for at least one year by me or my family in a household of which I or my family was a resident member during such period of use, and are not intended for any other person or for sale. (9804.00.05, HTSUSA)

☐ (2) All instruments, Implements, or tools of trade, occupation or employment, and all professional books for which free entry is sought were taken abroad by me or for my account or I am an emigrant who owned and used them abroad. (9804.00.10, 9804.00.15, HTSUSA)

B. Applicable to RESIDENT ONLY

☐ All personal effects for which free entry is sought were taken abroad by me or for my account. (9804.00.45, HTSUSA)

C. Applicable to NONRESIDENT ONLY

☐ (1) All articles of apparel, personal adornment, toiletries and similar personal effects for which free entry is sought were actually owned by me and in the possession of myself, or those members of my family who accompanied me, at the time of departure to the United States and that they are appropriate and are intended for our personal use and not for any other person nor for sale. (9804.00.20 HTSUSA)

☐ (2) Any vehicles, trailers, bicycles or other means of conveyance being imported are for the transport of me and my family and such incidental carriage of articles as are appropriate to my personal use of the conveyance. (9804.00.35, HTSUSA)

PART III -- TO BE COMPLETED BY U.S. PERSONNEL AND EVACUEES ONLY

I, the undersigned, the owner, importer, or agent of the importer of the personal and household effects for which free entry is claimed, hereby certify that they were in direct personal possession of the importer, or of a member of the importer's family residing with the importer, while abroad, and that they were imported into the United States because of the termination of assignment to extended duty (as defined in section 148.74(d) of the Customs Regulations) at a post or station outside the United States and the Customs Territory of the United States, or because of Government orders or instructions evacuating the importer to the United States; and that they are not imported for sale or for the account of any other person and that they do not include any alcoholic beverages or cigars. Free entry for these effects is claimed under Subheading No. 9805.00.50, Harmonized Tariff Schedule of the United States.

1. DATE OF IMPORTER'S LAST DEPARTURE FROM THE U.S.

2. A COPY OF THE IMPORTER'S TRAVEL ORDERS IS ATTACHED AND THE ORDERS WERE ISSUED ON:

PART IV -- TO BE COMPLETED BY ALL PERSONS SEEKING FREE ENTRY OF ARTICLES (Certain articles may be subject to duty and/or other requirements and must be specifically declared herein. Please check all applicable items and list them separately in item D on the reverse.)

A. For U.S. Personnel, Evacuees, Residents and Non-Residents

☐ (1) Articles for the account of other persons.

☐ (2) Articles for sale or commercial use.

☐ (3) Firearms and/or ammunition.

☐ (4) Alcoholic articles of all types or tobacco products.

☐ (5) Fruits, plants, seeds, meats, or birds.

☐ (6) Fish, wildlife, animal products thereof.

B. For Residents and Non-Residents ONLY

☐ (7) Foreign household effects acquired abroad and used less than one year.

☐ (8) Foreign household effects acquired abroad and used more than one year.

C. For Resident ONLY

☐ (9) Personal effects acquired abroad.

☐ (10) Foreign made articles acquired in the United States and taken abroad on this trip or acquired abroad on another trip that was previously declared to U.S. Customs.

☐ (11) Articles taken abroad for which alterations or repairs were performed abroad.

Customs Form 3299 (100695)

Declaration for Free Entry, Unaccompanied Articles CF 3299 p. 2

D. LIST OF ARTICLES

(1) ITEM NUMBER CHECKED IN PART IV, A., B., C.	(2) DESCRIPTION OF MERCHANDISE	(3) VALUE OR COST OF REPAIRS	(4) FOREIGN MERCHANDISE TAKEN ABROAD THIS TRIP: *State where in the U.S. the foreign merchandise was acquired or when and where it was previously declared to U.S. Customs.*

PART V -- CARRIER'S CERTIFICATE AND RELEASE ORDER

The undersigned carrier, to whom of upon whose order the articles described in PART I, 8., must be released, hereby certifies that the person named in Part I, 1., is the owner or consignee of such articles within the purview of section 484(h), Tariff Act of 1930.

In accordance with the provisions of section 484(h), Tariff Act of 1930, authority is hereby given to release the articles to such consignee.

1. NAME OF CARRIER	2. SIGNATURE OF AGENT (Print and sign)	Date

PART VI -- CERTIFICATION TO BE COMPLETED BY ALL PERSONS SEEKING FREE ENTRY

I, the undersigned, certify that this declaration is correct and complete.

1. "X" One
☐ A. Authorized Agent* (From facts obtained from the importer) ☐ B. Importer

2. SIGNATURE	3. DATE

An Authorized Agent is defined as a person who has actual knowledge of the facts and who is specifically empowered under a power of attorney to execute this declaration (see 19 CFR 141.19, 141.32, 141.33).

PART VII -- CUSTOMS USE ONLY (Inspected and Released)	1. SIGNATURE OF CUSTOMS OFFICIAL	2. DATE

Customs Form 3299 (100695)(Back)

Customs Bond CF 301 (page 1)

United States Customs Service

CUSTOMS BOND

19 CFR Part 113

OMB No. 1515-0144

| CUSTOMS USE ONLY | BOND NUMBER 1 (Assigned by Customs) |
| | FILE REFERENCE |

In order to secure payment of any duty, tax or charge and compliance with law or regulation as a result of activity covered by any condition referenced below, we, the below named principal(s) and surety(ies), bind ourselves to the United States in the amount or amounts, as set forth below.

Execution Date

SECTION I--Select Single Transaction **OR** Continuous Bond (not both) and fill in the applicable blank spaces.

| ☐ SINGLE TRANSACTION BOND | Identification of transaction secured by this bond (e.g., entry no., seizure no., etc.) | Date of transaction | Port code |

| ☐ CONTINUOUS BOND | Effective date | This bond remains in force for one year beginning with the effective date and for each succeeding annual period, or until terminated. This bond constitutes a separate bond for each period in the amounts listed below for liabilities that accrue in each period. The intention to terminate this bond must be conveyed within the period and manner prescribed in the Customs Regulations. |

SECTION II-- This bond includes the following agreements. 2 (Check one box only, except that, 1a may be checked independently or with 1, and 3a may be checked independently or with 3. Line out all other parts of this section that are not used.

Activity Code	Activity Name and Customs Regulations in which conditions codified	Limit of Liability	Activity Code	Activity Name and Customs Regulations in which conditions codified	Limit of Liability
☐ 1	Importer or broker 113.62		☐ 5	Public Gauger. 113.67	
☐ 1a	Drawback Payments Refunds 113.65		☐ 6	Wool & Fur Products Labeling Acts Importation (Single Entry Only) 113.68	
☐ 2	Custodian of bonded merchandise. . . . . . . .113.63 (Includes bonded carriers, freight forwarders, cartmen and lightermen, all classes of warehouse, container station operators)		☐ 7	Bill of Lading (Single Entry Only) 113.69	
			☐ 8	Detention of Copyrighted Material (Single Entry Only). 113.70	
☐ 3	International Carrier. 113.64				
☐ 3a	Instruments of International Traffic 113.66		☐ 9	Neutrality (Single Entry Only) 113.71	
☐ 4	Foreign Trade Zone Operator. 113.73		☐ 10	Court Costs for Condemned Goods (Single Entry Only) 113.72	

SECTION III-- List below all tradenames or unincorporated divisions that will be permitted to obligate this bond in the principal's name including their Customs identification Number(s). 3 (If more space is needed, use Section III (Continuation) on back of form.)

Importer Number	Importer Name	Importer Number	Importer Name
		Total number of importer names listed in Section III:	

Principal and surely agree that any charge against the bond under any of the listed names is as though it was made by the principal(s).

Principal and surety agree that they are bound to the same extent as if they executed a separate bond covering each set of conditions incorporated by reference to the Customs Regulations into this bond.

If the surety fails to appoint an agent under Title 6, United States Code, Section 7, surety consents to service on the Clerk of any United States District Court or the U.S. Court of International Trade, where suit is brought on this bond. That clerk is to send notice of the service to the surety at:

Mailing Address Requested by the Surety

Name and Address	Importer No. 3	
	SIGNATURE 5	**SEAL**
Name and Address	Importer No. 3	
	SIGNATURE 5	**SEAL**
Name and Address 6	Surety No. 7	
	SIGNATURE 5	**SEAL**
Name and Address 6	Surety No. 7	
	SIGNATURE 5	**SEAL**

| SURETY AGENTS | Name 8 | Identification No. 9 | Name 8 | Identification No. 9 |

Customs Bond CF 301 (page 2)

Note: Turn carbons over before writing on back of form.

SECTION III (Continuation)

Importer Number	Importer Name	Importer Number	Importer Name

WITNESSES

Two witnesses are required to authenticate the signature of any person who signs as an individual or partner; however a witness may authenticate the signatures of both such non-corporate principals and sureties. No witness is needed to authenticate the signature of a corporate official or agent who signs for the corporation.

SIGNED, SEALED, and DELIVERED in the PRESENCE OF:	
Name and Address of Witness for the Principal	Name and Address of Witness for the Surety
SIGNATURE:	SIGNATURE:
Name and Address of Witness for the Principal	Name and Address of Witness for the Surety
SIGNATURE:	SIGNATURE:

EXPLANATIONS AND FOOTNOTES

1 The Customs Bond Number is a control number assigned by Customs to the bond contract when the bond is approved by an authorized Customs official.

2 For all bond coverage available and the language of the bond conditions refer to Part 113, subpart G, Customs Regulations.

3 The Importer Number is the Customs identification number filed pursuant to section 24.5, Customs Regulations. When the Internal Revenue Service employer identification number is used the two-digit suffix code must be shown.

4 If the principal or surety is a corporation, the name of the State in which incorporated must be shown.

5 See witness requirement above.

6 Surety Name, if a corporation, shall be the company's name as it is spelled in the Surety Companies Annual List published in the Federal Register by the Department of the Treasury (Treasury Department Circular 570).

7 Surety Number is the three digit identification code assigned by Customs to a surety company at the time the surety company initially gives notice to Customs that the company will be writing Customs bonds.

8 Surety Agent is the individual granted a Corporate Surety Power of Attorney, CF 5297, by the surety company executing the bond.

9 Agent Identification No. shall be the individual's Social Security number as shown on the Corporate Surety Power of Attorney, CF 5297, filed by the surety granting such power of attorney.

Customs Form 301 (050798)(Back)

Power of Attorney CF 5291

POWER OF ATTORNEY

Department of the Treasury
U.S. Customs Service
19 CFR 141.32

Check appropriate box:
☐ Individual
☐ Partnership
☐ Corporation
☐ Sole Proprietorship

KNOW ALL MEN BY THESE PRESENTS: That, _____

(Full Name of person, partnership, or corporation, sole proprietorship; Identify)

a corporation doing business under the laws of the State of _____ or a _____
doing business as _____ residing at _____
having an office and place of business at _____ , hereby constitutes and appoints each of
the following persons _____

(Give Full Name of each agent designated)

as a true and lawful agent and attorney of the grantor named above for and in the name, place, and stead of said grantor from this date and in Customs Port _____.
and in no other name, to make, endorse, sign, declare, or swear to any entry, withdrawal, declaration, certificate, bill of lading, or other document required by law or regulation in connection with the importation, transportation, or exportation of any merchandise shipped or consigned by or to said grantor; to perform any act or condition which may be required by law or regulation in connection with such merchandise; to receive any merchandise deliverable to said grantor;

To make endorsements on bills of lading conferring authority to make entry and collect drawback, and to make, sign, declare, or swear to any statement, supplemental statement, schedule, supplemental schedule, certificate of delivery, certificate of manufacture, certificate of manufacture and delivery, abstract of manufacture records, declaration of proprietor on drawback entry, declaration of exporter on drawback entry, or any other affidavit or document which may be required by law or regulation for drawback purposes, regardless of whether such bill of lading, sworn statement, schedule, certificate, abstract, declaration, or other affidavit or document is intended for filing in said port or in any other customs port;

To sign, seal and deliver for and as the act of said grantor any bond required by law or regulation in connection with the entry or withdrawal of imported merchandise or merchandise exported with or without benefit of drawback, or in connection with the entry, clearance, lading, unlading or

navigation of any vessel or other means of conveyance owned or operated by said grantor, and any and all bonds which may be voluntarily given and accepted under applicable laws and regulations, consignee's and owner's declarations provided for in a section 485, Tariff Act of 1930, as amended, or affidavits in connection with the entry of merchandise;

To sign and swear to any document and to perform any act that may be necessary or required by law or regulation in connection with the entering, clearing, lading, unlading, or operation of any vessel or other means of conveyance owned or operated by said grantor;

And generally to transact at the customhouses in said port any and all customs business, including making, signing, and filing of protests under section 514 of the Tariff Act of 1930, in which said grantor is or may be concerned or interested and which may properly be transacted or performed by an agent and attorney, giving to said agent and attorney full power and authority to do anything whatever requisite and necessary to be done in the premises as fully as said grantor could do if present and acting, hereby ratifying and confirming all that the said agent and attorney shall lawfully do by virtue of these presents; the foregoing power of attorney to remain in full force and effect until the _____ day of _____ 20____, or until notice of revocation in writing is duly given to and received by the Port Director of Customs of the port aforesaid. If the donor of this power of attorney is a partnership, the said power shall in no case have any force or effect after the expiration of 2 years from the date of its receipt in the office of the Port Director of Customs of the said port.

IN WITNESS WHEREOF, the said _____
has caused these presents to be sealed and signed: (Signature) _____
(Capacity) _____ (Date) _____
WITNESS: _____ _____

Customs Form 5291 (120195)   (Corporate seal)*(Optional)

Corporate Surety Power of Attorney CF 5297

The form (rotated 90°) contains the following text:

DEPARTMENT OF THE TREASURY
UNITED STATES CUSTOMS SERVICE

CORPORATE SURETY POWER OF ATTORNEY

Approved through 09/30/95; OMB No. 1515-0144

CUSTOMS USE ONLY

DATE RECEIVED

EFFECTIVE DATE

1. THIS FORM MUST BE TYPED.
2. DO NOT ALTER THIS FORM.
3. ORIGINAL TO BE SUBMITTED TO CUSTOMS. (See Option explained in Instruction no. 2.)

GRANT (Instruction No. 3a.)

CHANGE to Grant on file (Instruction No. 3b.)

☐ This is an address change

REVOCATION. The below-described powers previously granted are hereby revoked. (Instruction No. 3c.)

☐ This is a name change

GRANTEE:

NAME

SOCIAL SECURITY NO.

ADDRESS

GRANTOR:

Surety Company's Corporate Name

Surety No.

State Under Whose laws organized as a surety

District Code(s) for Customs district(s) in which authorized to do business and limit on any single obligation –OR– district(s) being added to the original grant:

District	Limit	District	Limit	District	Limit	District	Limit	District	Limit

Grantor appoints the above-named person (Grantee) as its attorney in fact to sign its name as surety to, and to execute, seal, and acknowledge any bond so as to bind the surety corporation to the same extent as if done by a regularly elected officer, limited only to the extent shown above as to Customs district and amount on any single bond obligation. This grant, or change to a grant on file, or revocation, as specified, shall become active on the effective date shown provided the Customs Form 5297 is received at a district office 5 days before the effective date shown; otherwise the specified action will become active at the close of business 5 working days after the date of receipt at the district office.

In witness whereof, the said Grantor, by virtue of authority conferred by its Board of Directors, has caused these presents to be sealed with its corporate seal and attested by any two principal officers.

Use a facsimile of corporate seal, and not impression seal.

Date Attested

Name and Title

SIGNATURE:

Name and Title

SIGNATURE:

Customs Form 5297 (100692)

Sample Certificate of Origin

Exporteur / Exportateur / Esportatore / Exporter	**Nr.** / **No.** 201884
MUELLER AG Birsstrasse 26 4132 Muttenz / Switzerland	**URSPRUNGSZEUGNIS** **CERTIFICAT D'ORIGINE** **CERTIFICATO D'ORIGINE** **CERTIFICATE OF ORIGIN**
Empfänger / Destinataire / Destinatario / Consignee	SCHWEIZERISCHE EIDGENOSSENSCHAFT CONFÉDÉRATION SUISSE CONFEDERAZIONE SVIZZERA SWISS CONFEDERATION
ADILMA TRADING CORPORATION 27, Nihonbashi, Chiyoda-Ku TOKYO 125 / Japan	**Ursprungsstaat** / Pays d'origine / Paese d'origine / Country of origin SWITZERLAND

Angaben über die Beförderung (Ausfüllung freigestellt)
Informations relatives au transport (mention facultative)
Informazioni riguardanti il trasporto (indicazione facoltativa)
Particulars of transport (optional declaration)

Bemerkungen / Observations / Osservazioni / Observations

LETTER OF CREDIT NR. 064204

Zeichen, Nummern, Anzahl und Art der Packstücke; Warenbezeichnung
Marques, numéros, nombre et nature des colis; désignation des marchandises
Marche, numeri, numero e natura dei colli; designazione delle merci
Marks, numbers, number and kind of packages; description of the goods

Nettogewicht / Poids net / Peso netto / Net weight kg, l, m³ etc./ecc.

ADILMA TRADING VIA TOKYO NR. 1-6 ORDER 0-535/1	6 cases	CYLINDER- PRESS COMPLETELY ASSEMBLED	12'140,0 kg

Bruttogewicht / Poids brut / Peso lordo / Gross weight

12'860,0 kg

Die unterzeichnete Handelskammer bescheinigt den Ursprung oben bezeichneter Ware
La Chambre de commerce soussignée certifie l'origine des marchandises désignées ci-dessus
La sottoscritta Camera di commercio certifica l'origine delle merci summenzionate
The undersigned Chamber of commerce certifies the origin of the above mentioned goods

Basel, 2 6. 04.

Basler Handelskammer
Chambre de Commerce de Bâle
Camera di Commercio di Basilea
Basle Chamber of Commerce

NAFTA Certificate of Origin

DEPARTMENT OF THE TREASURY
UNITED STATES CUSTOMS SERVICE

Aproved through 12/31/96
OMB No. 1515-0204
See back of form for Paper-
work Reduction Act Notice.

NORTH AMERICAN FREE TRADE AGREEMENT
CERTIFICATE OF ORIGIN

Please print or type

19 CFR 181.11, 181.22

1. EXPORTER NAME AND ADDRESS	2. BLANKET PERIOD (DD/MM/YY)
	FROM
	TO
TAX IDENTIFICATION NUMBER:	

3. PRODUCER NAME AND ADDRESS	4. IMPORTER NAME AND ADDRESS
TAX IDENTIFICATION NUMBER:	TAX IDENTIFICATION NUMBER:

5. DESCRIPTION OF GOOD(S)	6. HS TARIFF CLASSIFICATION NUMBER	7. PREFERENCE CRITERION	8. PRODUCER	9. NET COST	10. COUNTRY OF ORIGIN

I CERTIFY THAT:

• THE INFORMATION ON THIS DOCUMENT IS TRUE AND ACCURATE AND I ASSUME THE RESPONSIBILITY FOR PROVING SUCH REPRESENTATIONS. I UNDERSTAND THAT I AM LIABLE FOR ANY FALSE STATEMENTS OR MATERIAL OMISSIONS MADE ON OR IN CONNECTION WITH THIS DOCUMENT;

• I AGREE TO MAINTAIN, AND PRESENT UPON REQUEST, DOCUMENTATION NECESSARY TO SUPPORT THIS CERTIFICATE, AND TO INFORM, IN WRITING, ALL PERSONS TO WHOM THE CERTIFICATE WAS GIVEN OF ANY CHANGES THAT COULD AFFECT THE ACCURACY OR VALIDITY OF THIS CERTIFICATE;

• THE GOODS ORIGINATED IN THE TERRITORY OF ONE OR MORE OF THE PARTIES, AND COMPLY WITH THE ORIGIN REQUIREMENTS SPECIFIED FOR THOSE GOODS IN THE NORTH AMERICAN FREE TRADE AGREEMENT, AND UNLESS SPECIFICALLY EXEMPTED IN ARTICLE 411 OR ANNEX 401, THERE HAS BEEN NO FURTHER PRODUCTION OR ANY OTHER OPERATION OUTSIDE THE TERRITORIES OF THE PARTIES; AND

• THIS CERTIFICATE CONSISTS OF _____ PAGES, INCLUDING ALL ATTACHMENTS.

11.	11a. AUTHORIZED SIGNATURE	11b. COMPANY	
	11c. NAME (Print or Type)	11d. TITLE	
	11e. DATE (DD/MM/YY)	11f. TELEPHONE NUMBER ▷ (Voice)	(Facsimile)

Customs Form 434 (121793)

Import Declaration for Immediate Delivery CF 3461

How to Complete the CF 3461

The numbered steps correspond to the numbered boxes.

1. Date shipment arrived in USA.

2. Date you are filing documents with U.S. Customs.

3. Print 01 for a formal entry. If quota or visa restrictions apply, print 02.

4. Leave blank, will be assigned.

5. Print 2801 for air shipments. Print 2809 for ocean or mail (all surface) shipments.

6. Print an X if you are using a single entry bond only.

7. Print your social security number (or company federal tax ID number)

8. Print the number (social security number or company federal tax ID number) of the party receiving the shipment. Usually the same as the importer number.

9. Print your social security number (or company federal tax I.D. number)

10. If same as Block 11, print "same".

11. Print your (or your company's) name.

12. Leave blank.

13. See shipping documents.

14. Print the location where the merchandise is now. This will usually be shown on the arrival notice you received from the shipping company. For mail shipments, print OMF in large letters.

15. Name of Shipper (vessel name or air carrier or parcel post).

16. Print the port code for the port where your merchandise first arrived.

17. Leave blank.

18. Leave blank.

19. Print the total value of your shipment. Round off to the nearest whole dollar.

20. Print a brief description of the merchandise.

21. Leave blank.

22. Print the bill of lading or airway bill number. For mail shipments use the reference number on mail notice.

23. Print the total number of cartons (found on shipping documents).

24. List the tariff number for each line shown on the CF7501 (see Block 39 on the CF7501). If more room is needed, use a second CF3461 as a continuation sheet.

25. List the country code (for the country of origin) for each line shown on the CF7501 (see Block 15 on the CF7501).

26. List the Manufacturer's ID number for each line shown on the CF7501 (see Block 21 on the CF7501).

27. Complete as instructed on CF3461.

Import Declaration for Immediate Delivery CF 3461

United States Customs Service

Form Approved
OMB No. 1515-0069

ENTRY/IMMEDIATE DELIVERY

19 CFR 142.3, 142.16, 142.22, 142.24

1. ARRIVAL DATE	2. ELECTED ENTRY DATE	3. ENTRY TYPE CODE/NAME	4. ENTRY NUMBER
5. PORT	6. SINGLE TRANS. BOND	7. BROKER/IMPORTER FILE NUMBER	
	8. CONSIGNEE NUMBER		9. IMPORTER NUMBER

10. ULTIMATE CONSIGNEE NAME	11. IMPORTER OF RECORD NAME

12. CARRIER CODE	13. VOYAGE/FLIGHT/TRIP	14. LOCATION OF GOODS-CODE(S)/NAME(S)
15. VESSEL CODE/NAME		

16. U.S. PORT OF UNLADING	17. MANIFEST NUMBER	18. G. O. NUMBER	19. TOTAL VALUE

20. DESCRIPTION OF MERCHANDISE

21. IT/BL/ AWB CODE	22. IT/BL/AWB NO.	23. MANIFEST QUANTITY	24. H.S. NUMBER	25. COUNTRY OF ORIGIN	26. MANUFACTURER NO.

27. CERTIFICATION	28. CUSTOMS USE ONLY

27. CERTIFICATION

I hereby make application for entry/immediate delivery. I certify that the above information is accurate, the bond is sufficient, valid, and current, and that all requirements of 19 CFR Part 142 have been met.

SIGNATURE OF APPLICANT

X

PHONE NO.	DATE

29. BROKER OR OTHER GOVT. AGENCY USE

28. CUSTOMS USE ONLY

☐ OTHER AGENCY ACTION REQUIRED, NAMELY:

☐ CUSTOMS EXAMINATION REQUIRED.

☐ ENTRY REJECTED, BECAUSE:

DELIVERY AUTHORIZED:	SIGNATURE	DATE

Statement Required by 5 CFR 1320.21: The estimated average burden associated with this collection of information is 15 minutes per respondent or recordkeeper depending on individual circumstances. Comments concerning the accuracy of this burden estimate and suggestions for reducing this burden should be directed to U.S. Customs Service, Information Services Branch, Washington, DC 20229, and to the Office of Management and Budget, Paperwork Reduction Project (1515-0069) Washington, DC 20503.

Paperwork Reduction Act Notice: This information is needed to determine the admissibility of imports into the United States and to provide the necessary information for the examination of the cargo and to establish the liability for payment of duties and taxes. Your response is necessary.

Customs Form 3461 (010189)

Import Summary CF 7501

How to Fill Out CF 7501

The numbered steps correspond to the numbered boxes on the CF7501.

1. Leave blank. Entry number will be assigned to you.

2. Print 01 for a formal entry. If quota or visa restrictions apply, print 02.

3. Enter the date you submit the documents to the Customhouse.

4. Print the date you submit the entry to the Customs.

5. Print 2801 for air shipments. Print 2809 for ocean or mail (all surface) shipments.

6. Print 3-digit surety code (shown on bond).

7. Print "9" for a single-entry bond. (Print "8" for a continuous transaction bond.)

8. Leave blank.

9. Enter two-digit code for state.

10. Leave blank.

11. Print your (or your company's) name.

12. Print your social security number (or company federal tax I.D. number)

13. Print the two-letter country code.

14. Print the date that the shipment left the exporting country.

15. Print the two-letter country code.

16. Leave blank.

17. Leave blank unless your goods traveled to port of entry from another U.S. port of arrival.

18. Same as line 17.

19. Print the bill of lading or airway bill number. For mail shipments use the reference number on mail notice.

20. Print 10 for ship, 30 for truck, 40 for air, or 50 for mail.

21. Print Manufacturer's Identification Number.

22. Leave blank.

23. Print the name of the ship, or the name of the air carrier. For mail shipments print parcel post.

24. Leave blank for air shipments. For ocean shipments, enter port code.

25. Print the location where the merchandise is now. This will usually be shown on the arrival notice you received from the shipping company. For mail shipments, print OMF in large letters.

26. Print the port code for the port where your merchandise first arrived.

27. Print the date that the merchandise arrived in the U.S.

28. Print 001 (you will list a separate line for each tariff number you were given. The next line, if there is one, will be 002). Any additional lines should be placed on the CF7501 continuation sheet to allow room for the Block 39 Summary on the lower portion of the CF7501.

29. Print a brief description of the merchandise.

30. Print the tariff classification number.

31. Print the gross weight of the merchandise in kilograms.

32. Print the net quantity of the merchandise, measured in whole units of quantity.

33. Print the invoice value of the merchandise, measured in U.S. dollars. Round the dollar amount to the nearest whole dollar. Do not show cents. Do not show the dollar sign. Just below the value, print the letter C followed by the shipping and insurance costs. Just below the shipping/insurance costs, print the letter R if the importer of the goods is related to the manufacturer/exporter of the goods, or print the letter N if these two parties are not related (see below for definition of "related parties").

34. The terms on which you purchased your imported merchandise can affect the value you enter in block 33. Since the entered value is in most cases the basis on which the Customs Service calculates the duty owed, you should be aware that Customs does not charge duty on the cost of shipping and insuring the merchandise from the overseas port to the United States. In order for you not to overstate the entered value, and hence pay more duties and fees than necessary, you should ask a Customs Import Specialist to review your invoice to determine whether these costs were included in the price you paid for your imported merchandise. If so, they can be deducted from the amount you enter in block 33. Note that the cost of international freight and insurance must always be shown beneath the entered value on the CF7501, whether or not these costs were included in the purchase price.

35. Related Parties Defined: Related parties include: Members of the same family; officer or director of an organization and the organization itself; two persons with joint office/directorship positions over one or more organizations; partners; owner/holder of 5% or more of stock/share in and organization and that organization; two or more persons directly or indirectly controlling, controlled by, or under common control, with any person.

36. Print the rate of duty from the HTS.

37. Compute the amount of duty and print that amount in this box.

38. Place an X in the two appropriate boxes.

39. Print the total amount of duty you will be paying. If none, show 0.

40. Print the total amount of tax you will be paying. If none, leave blank.

41. Show the total amount of fees you will be paying. This value must match the amount in the Block 39 summary.

42. Print the total amount of duty, taxes and fees you will be paying.

43. Complete as instructed on the CF7501

TEV: Total entered value of all lines of merchandise must be shown on the CF7501 in Block 33, across from the Block 39 Summary. Round the dollar amount to the nearest whole dollar. Do not show cents. Do not show the dollar sign.

Import Summary CF 7501

DEPARTMENT OF THE TREASURY
UNITED STATES CUSTOMS SERVICE

ENTRY SUMMARY

Form Approved OMB No. 1515-0065

(1) Entry No.	(2) Entry Type Code	3. Entry Summary Date
4. Entry Date	(5) Port Code	
6. Bond No.	7. Bond Type Code	8. Broker/Importer File No.

9. Ultimate Consignee Name and Address

10. Consignee No.

(11) Importer of Record Name and Address

(12) Importer No.

(13) Exporting Country

14. Export Date

(15) Country of Origin

16. Missing Documents

State

(17) I.T. No.

(18) I.T. Date

(19) B/L or AWB No.

20. Mode of Transportation

21. Manufacturer I.D.

22. Reference No.

(23) Importing Carrier

24. Foreign Port of Lading

25. Location of Goods/G.O. No.

26. U.S. Port of Unlading

(27) Import Date

(28) Line No.	(29) Description of Merchandise			33. (A) Entered Value (B) CHGS (C) Relationship	34. (A) T.S.U.S.A. Rate (B) ADA/CVD Rate (C) I.R.C. Rate (D) Visa No.	(35) Duty and I.R. Tax	
	30. (A) T.S.U.S.A. No. (B) ADA/CVD Case No.	31. (A) Gross Weight (B) Manifest Qty.	(32) Net Quantity in T.S.U.S.A. Units			Dollars	Cents

SAMPLE

(36) Declaration of Importer of Record (Owner or Purchaser) or Authorized Agent

I declare that I am the

☐ Importer of record and that the actual owner, purchaser, or consignee for customs purposes is as shown above.

OR

☐ owner or purchaser or agent thereof.

I further declare that the merchandise

☐ was obtained pursuant to a purchase or agreement to purchase and that the prices set forth in the invoices are true.

OR

☐ was not obtained pursuant to a purchase or agreement to purchase and the statements in the invoices as to value or price are true to the best of my knowledge and belief.

I also declare that the statements in the documents herein filed fully disclose to the best of my knowledge and belief the true prices, values, quantities, rebates, drawbacks, fees, commissions, and royalties and are true and correct, and that all goods or services provided to the seller of the merchandise either free or at reduced cost are fully disclosed. I will immediately furnish to the appropriate customs officer any information showing a different state of facts.

Notice required by Paperwork Reduction Act of 1980: This information is needed to ensure that importers/exporters are complying with U.S. customs laws, to allow us to compute and collect the right amount of money, to enforce other agency requirements, and to collect accurate statistical information on imports. Your response is mandatory. (Continued on back of form.)

▼ U.S. CUSTOMS USE ▼		TOTALS
A. Liq. Code	B. Ascertained Duty	(37) Duty
	C. Ascertained Tax	(38) Tax
	D. Ascertained Other	(39) Other
	E. Ascertained Total	(40) Total

(41) Signature of Declarant, Title, and Date

Customs Form 7501 (112295)

Electronic Product Declaration Form FDA 2877 (page 1)

| **DEPARTMENT OF HEALTH AND HUMAN SERVICES**
PUBLIC HEALTH SERVICE
FOOD AND DRUG ADMINISTRATION

DECLARATION FOR IMPORTED ELECTRONIC PRODUCTS SUBJECT TO RADIATION CONTROL STANDARDS | Form Approved OMB No. 0910-0025
Expiration Date: 11/30/2003
INSTRUCTIONS
1. If submitting entries electronically through ACS/ABI, hold FDA-2877 in entry file. Do not submit to FDA unless requested.
2. If submitting paper entry documents, submit the following to FDA:
 a. 2 copies of Customs Entry Form (e.g. CF 3461, CF 3461 Alt, CF 7501, etc.)
 b. 1 copy of FDA 2877
 c. Commercial Invoice(s) in English. |

U.S. CUSTOMS PORT OF ENTRY	ENTRY NUMBER	DATE OF ENTRY

NAME & ADDRESS OF MANUFACTURING SITE; COUNTRY OF ORIGIN	NAME & ADDRESS OF IMPORTER & ULTIMATE CONSIGNEE *(if not importer)*

PRODUCT DESCRIPTION	QUANTITY *(Items/Containers)*	MODEL NUMBER(S) & BRAND NAME(S)

DECLARATION: I / WE DECLARE THAT THE PRODUCTS IDENTIFIED ABOVE: *(Mark X applicable statements, fill in blanks, & sign)*

☐ **A. ARE NOT SUBJECT TO RADIATION PERFORMANCE STANDARDS BECAUSE THEY:**

　☐ 1. Were manufactured prior to the effective date of any applicable standard; Date of Manufacture _____ .

　☐ 2. Are excluded by the applicability clause or definition in the standard or by FDA written guidance.
　　　Specify reason for exclusion _____.

　☐ 3. Are personal household goods of an individual entering the U.S. or being returned to a U.S. resident. (Limit: 3 of each product type).

　☐ 4. Are property of a party residing outside the U.S. and will be returned to the owner after repair or servicing.

　☐ 5. Are components or subassemblies to be used in manufacturing or as replacement parts (NOT APPLICABLE to diagnostic x-ray parts).

　☐ 6. Are prototypes intended for on going product development by the importing firm, are labeled "FOR TEST/EVALUATION ONLY," and will be exported, destroyed, or held for future testing (i.e., not distributed). (Quantities Limited - see reverse.)

　☐ 7. Are being reprocessed in accordance with P.L. 104-134 or other FDA guidance, are labeled "FOR EXPORT ONLY," and will not be sold, distributed, or transferred without FDA approval.

☐ **B. COMPLY WITH THE PERFORMANCE STANDARDS** WHICH ARE APPLICABLE AT DATE OF MANUFACTURE AND THAT A CERTIFICATION LABEL OR TAG TO THIS EFFECT IS AFFIXED TO EACH PRODUCT. COMPLIANCE DOCUMENTED IN:

　☐ 1. Last annual report or Product/Initial report

　　_____　　_____
　　ACCESSION NUMBER of Report　　Name of MANUFACTURER OF RECORD *(Filed report with FDA/CDRH)*

　☐ 2. Unknown manufacturer or report number; State reason: _____

☐ **C. DO NOT COMPLY WITH PERFORMANCE STANDARDS;** ARE BEING HELD UNDER A TEMPORARY IMPORT BOND; WILL NOT BE INTRODUCED INTO COMMERCE; WILL BE USED UNDER A RADIATION PROTECTION PLAN; AND WILL BE DESTROYED OR EXPORTED UNDER U.S. CUSTOMS SUPERVISION WHEN THE FOLLOWING MISSION IS COMPLETE:

　☐ 1. Research, Investigations/Studies, or Training (attach Form FDA 766)

　☐ 2. Trade Show/Demonstration; List dates & use restrictions _____

☐ **D. DO NOT COMPLY WITH PERFORMANCE STANDARDS;** ARE HELD AND WILL REMAIN UNDER BOND; AND WILL NOT BE INTRODUCED INTO COMMERCE UNTIL NOTIFICATION IS RECEIVED FROM FDA THAT PRODUCTS HAVE BEEN BROUGHT INTO COMPLIANCE IN ACCORDANCE WITH AN FDA APPROVED PETITION. *(See Form FDA 766.)*

　☐ 1. Approved Petition is attached.　　☐ 2. Petition Request is attached.　　☐ 3. Request will be submitted within 60 days.

WARNING: Any person who knowingly makes a false declaration may be fined not more than $10,000 or imprisoned not more than 5 years or both, pursuant to Title 18 U.S.C. 1001. Any person importing a non- compliant electronic product may also be subject to civil penalties of $1000 per violation, up to a maximum $300,000 for related violations pursuant to Title 21 U.S.C. 360pp.	SIGNATURE OF IMPORTER OF RECORD NAME AND TITLE OF RESPONSIBLE PERSON

Public reporting burden for this collection of information is estimated to average 0.2 hour per response, including the time for reviewing instructions, searching existing data sources, gathering and maintaining the data needed, and completing reviewing the collection of information. Send comments regarding this burden estimate or any other aspect of this collection of information, including suggestions for reducing this burden to:

　　　Food and Drug Administration
　　　CDRH (HFZ-342)
　　　2094 Gaither Road
　　　Rockville, MD 20850

An agency may not conduct or sponsor, and a person is not required to respond to, a collection of information unless it displays a currently valid OMB control number.

FORM FDA 2877 (12/00)　　　　PREVIOUS EDITION IS OBSOLETE.　　Created by: PSC Media Arts (301) 443-2454　　PAGE 1 OF 2 PAGES

Electronic Product Declaration Form FDA 2877 (page 2)l

INSTRUCTIONS TO IMPORTERS/BROKERS OF ELECTRONIC PRODUCTS

PURPOSE: The Form FDA 2877 must be completed for electronic products subject to Radiation Control Standards (21 CFR 1010 and 1020-1050) prior to entry into the United States. The local Food and Drug Administration (FDA) district office will review the declaration and notify the importer/agent if the products may be released into U.S. commerce or if they must be held under bond until exported, destroyed, or reconditioned. Until the shipment is released, it may be subject to redelivery for FDA examination.

PAPER OR ELECTRONIC SUBMISSION: Paper entries may be made by submitting the signed original FDA 2877 along with U.S. Customs forms to the local FDA district office; if electronic products are given a MAY PROCEED, a signed copy of CF 3461 will be returned, or if not given a MAY PROCEED, a FDA Notice of Action will be issued. For electronic entries, follow U.S. Customs Service ACS/ABI format and procedures, supported by a signed copy of this form or similar letter. Multiple entries of the same product and model families that are filed electronically may be supported by one form dated not more than 12 months previously.

DECLARATION: Select A, B, C, or D and then select the appropriate number; fill in requested information and sign. For electronic entries, AofC (affirmation of compliance) = RA#, RB#, RC#, or RD# (e.g., Radiation Declaration A5 = RA5). **Transmit model number using AofC code MDL and transmit brand name using FDA line level brand name field. If RA3 or RA6 is selected, you must transmit quantity (number of units) using the Quantity and Unit of Measure Pairs at the FDA line level.**

DECLARATION A: Importers should be prepared to demonstrate compliance to or non-applicability of FDA standards, regulations, or guidance. Components or sub-assemblies must be non-functioning. Products being reprocessed must be exported by the importer, without intermediate transfer of ownership. For RA3 the quantity limit is 3 and for RA6 the limit = 50 units TV products, microwave ovens, and Class 1 laser products limit = 200 units CD-ROM and DVD (digital versatile disc) laser products; see May 14, 1997, notice to industry issued by the Center for Devices and Radiological Health (CDRH).

DECLARATION B: If declaration RB1 is selected, provide the FDA Establishment Identifier (FEI) of the manufacturer who filed the radiation product/abbreviated report to FDA, CDRH, Rockville, Maryland. To transmit the accession number of that report use AofC code ACC. If the manufacturer cannot be determined or located, the importer must be able to provide evidence showing a certification (certifi.) label on each product and state reason: returned to orig exporter or certifi. label evidence. The new AofC codes (RB1, RB2) for this declaration will not be activated until a process is made available to determine the FEI of the responsible firm. Continue to use RAB in electronic transmission until the FEI query is available and industry is notified of its availability.

DECLARATION C: Noncompliant products may be imported only for research, investigations/studies, demonstration or training. They should be used only by trained personnel and under controlled conditions to avoid unnecessary radiation exposure. Product(s) will be detained by the local FDA district office. Since product(s) for which "C" Declarations are made will be under Temporary Import Bond (TIB) or equivalent, ultimate disposition is limited to export or destruction under U.S. Customs supervision when the purpose has been achieved or the length of time stated has expired. For purposes other than demonstration, the Form FDA 766, outlining protections, must be approved by FDA prior to use. The importer/broker must include with the FDA 766:

1.   A full description of the subject electronic product(s).
2.   The purpose for which the product(s) is being imported.
3.   How the product(s) will be used.
4.   Where the product(s) will be located.
5.   The approximate length of time and dates the product(s) will be in this country.

For product(s) being used for trade shows/demonstrations, list the dates and use restrictions (Form FDA 766 is not required). A sign stating that the product does not comply with FDA performance standards must be displayed and viewable at all times during the use of product(s). All medical products, cabinet x-ray, or Class IIIb and IV lasers may NOT operate (turn on product(s)) at trade shows.

DECLARATION D: Noncompliant products must be brought into compliance with standards under FDA supervision and following a plan approved by FDA. The plan, documented on the Form FDA 766, must address technical requirements, labeling, and reporting. Some plans may need approval by both the CDRH and the local FDA district office. Use of this declaration is limited to occasional shipments; ongoing reconditioning is considered manufacturing that is handled through other means. Product(s) will be detained by the local FDA district office. An FDA 766 must be filed indicating the procedure intended to bring the product into compliance. This procedure will include a satisfactory corrective action plan and/or a product report. The FDA 766 must include all of the information requested under Declaration C. The approximate length of time will be for the amount of time needed to bring product(s) into compliance. Declaration D is also made for failure to provide reports, failure to certify, etc.

If an importer/broker intends to import equipment into the United States for purposes of research, investigation, studies, demonstrations, or training but also wishes to retain the option of bringing the product into compliance with the performance standard, check Declarations C and D on the FDA 2877 and insert the word "or " between the Affirmations. Note: The U.S. Customs Service will treat this entry as a "D" Declaration for purposes of duty. Such requests must be made on the FDA 766; include Items 1, 2, and 3 under Declaration C, a statement of the need to use the option "C" or "D" Declaration, a statement of how the product(s) will be brought into compliance and the approximate length of time necessary to evaluate or demonstrate the product(s) and the time necessary to bring the product(s) into compliance (both actions must be accomplished within the period of time granted by FDA). For electronic entries select Declaration RD3.

Ultimately, product(s) must be brought into compliance with the applicable standard in accordance with a corrective action plan which has been approved by the FDA. If the product(s) are not brought into compliance within the allotted time frame of the approved application and an extension is not requested of, or granted by, the FDA, the local FDA district office shall refuse entry on the shipment and require the product(s) to be either exported or destroyed under U.S. Customs supervision.

If additional guidance is needed, please contact your local FDA district office or consult the following FDA web pages: www.fda.gov/cdrh, www.fda.gov/ora/hier/ora_field_names.txt, and www.fda.gov/ora/compliance_ref/rpm_new2/contens.html.

[Ref: 21 U.S.C. 360mm, 21 CFR 1005, 19 CFR 12.90-12.91.]   FDA: CP 7382.007/.007A

FORM FDA 2877 (12/00)   PREVIOUS EDITION IS OBSOLETE.   PAGE 2 OF 2 PAGES

FCC Declaration Form FCC 740

FEDERAL COMMUNICATIONS COMMISSION
Washington, DC 20554

Approved by OMB
3050-0059
Expires   08-31-2003

STATEMENT REGARDING THE IMPORTATION OF RADIO FREQUENCY DEVICES CAPABLE OF CAUSING HARMFUL INTERFERENCE

(Read instructions before completing form. Please type or print clearly in ink.)

PART I - All Blocks **MUST** Be Completed

Date of Entry	Entry Number	Port of Entry[1]	Harmonized Tariff Number[2]	Quantity of Item (not number of containers)[3]

Device Model/Type Name or #	Trade Name	FCC ID	Description of Equipment

Manufacturer's Name and Address	Consignee's Name and Address	Importer's Name and Address

Printed or Typed Name of Importer or Consignee	Signature of Importer or Consignee	Date (Month/Day/Year)

Warning: Any person who knowingly makes a false declaration may be fined not more than $250,000 or imprisoned not more than 5 years, or both, pursuant to 18 U.S.C. § 1001.

PART II - With Regard to the Importation of the Described Radio Frequency Device(s), **I DECLARE THAT:**
(Place an "X" in only one box)

	1. The FCC has issued a grant of equipment authorization for the FCC ID listed above.
	2. An FCC grant of equipment authorization and an FCC ID are not required, but the equipment complies with FCC technical requirements.
	3. The described equipment is being imported in limited quantitites for testing and evaluation for compliance with technical requirements or marketing suitability. The equipment will not be offered for sale or otherwise marketed. (See Instructions)
	4. The described equipment is being imported in limited quantities for demonstration at industry trade shows and will not be offered for sale or otherwise marketed. (See Instructions)
	5. The described equipment is being imported solely for export. It will not be offered for sale or otherwise marketed in the U.S.
	5(a). The described equipment is a non-U.S. standard cellular phone that can only function outside of the U.S. (See Instructions)
	6. The described equipment is being imported for use exclusively by the U.S. Government.
	7. Three or fewer radio receivers, computers, or other unintentional radiators as defined in Part 15 of the FCC Rules, are being imported for an individual's personal use and are not intended for sale.
	8. The described equipment is being imported for repair and will not be offered for sale or otherwise marketed.

1. Port of Entry Use Schedule D - Classification of U.S. Customs Districts and Ports for U.S. Foreign Trade Statistics - a four digit code i.e., New York City, NY 1001.
2. Harmonized Tariff Number - Harmonized Tariff Schedule of the United States
3. The quantity must be total number of items, not number of containers

FCC Form 740   August 2000

Establishment Registration FDA 2541

Public reporting burden for this collection of information is estimated to average .17 hours per response, including the time for reviewing instructions, searching existing data sources, gathering and maintaining the data needed, and completing and reviewing the collection of information. Send comments regarding this burden estimate or any other aspect of this collection of information, including suggestions for reducing this burden to: Food and Drug Administration, LACF Registration Coordinator (HFS-618), Center for Food Safety and Applied Nutrition, 200 C Street, S.W., Washington, DC 20204.

An agency may not conduct or sponsor, and a person is not required to respond to, a collection of information unless it displays a currently valid OMB control number.

FORM APPROVED: OMB No. 0910-0037
EXPIRATION DATE: 8-31-2005

FOR FDA USE ONLY

FCE No.	Date Received by FDA
OOB Code	Date	District
Reference		

DEPARTMENT OF HEALTH AND HUMAN SERVICES
Food and Drug Administration

FOOD CANNING ESTABLISHMENT REGISTRATION

TYPE OF SUBMISSION

☐ Initial Registration
☐ Relocation *(new registration required)*
☐ Change of Registration Information

Specify Type of Change _____

Enter Current FCE: *(If applicable)* _____

FOOD PROCESSING PLANT LOCATION

Establishment Name _____

Number and Street _____

City and State or Province _____

Zip (or other Postal Code) _____

Country (if other than U.S.) _____

Telephone No. (___) _____   Telefax No. (___) _____

PREFERRED MAILING ADDRESS   ☐ Same as Plant Location

Establishment Name _____

Number and Street _____

City and State or Province (or other Subdivision) _____

Zip (or other Postal Code) _____

Country (if other than U.S.) _____

Telephone No. (___) _____   Telefax No. (___) _____

LOW ACID AND/OR ACIDIFIED FOODS PROCESSED AT THIS LOCATION

Food Product name, form or Style, and packing Medium
(Do not list meat and poultry foods under the jurisdiction of the Food Safety and Inspection Service of the U.S. Department of Agriculture)

	(Check One)	
	Low-Acid	Acidified

PLEASE SEND THE FOLLOWING:

Number of Copies

_____ Process filing forms used for low-acid aseptic processes (FORM FDA-2541c).

_____ Process filing forms used for all processing methods except low-acid aseptic (FORM FDA-2541a).
NOTE: A separate form is required for each product-process combination.

_____ Registration and Process Filing Instructions

_____ LACF & Acidified Regulations (21 CFR 108, 113, 114)

See "Instructions for Establishment Registration and Process Filing for Acidified and Low-Acid Canned Foods" for guidance in completing this form. Forward all copies of completed form to:

**Food and Drug Administration
LACF Registration Coordinator (HFS-618)
Center for Food Safety & Applied Nutrition
5100 Paint Branch Parkway
College Park, Maryland 20797-4006**

AUTHORIZED COMPANY REPRESENTATIVE

Name, Address and Title of Authorized Representative: _____

Signature: _____   Date: _____

Phone Number: (___) _____   at   ☐ Plant Location   ☐ Mailing Address

NOTE: No commercial processor shall engage in the processing of low-acid or acidified foods unless completed Forms FDA 2541 and FDA 2541a or FDA 2541c have been filed with the Food and Drug Administration, 21 CFR 108.25(c)(1) and (2) and 108.35(c)(1) and (2).

FORM FDA 2541 (9/02)   PREVIOUS EDITION IS OBSOLETE

PSC Media Arts (301) 443-1090   EF

Food Process Filing FDA 2541a (page 1)

DEPARTMENT OF HEALTH AND HUMAN SERVICES ■ PUBLIC HEALTH SERVICE ■ FOOD AND DRUG ADMINISTRATION
FOOD PROCESS FILING FOR ALL METHODS EXCEPT LOW-ACID ASEPTIC

(Use FDA booklet titled: "Instructions for Establishment Registration and Process Filing for Acidified and Low-Acid Canned Foods" for completing Form FDA 2541a.)

FORM APPROVED: OMB NO. 0910-0037
EXPIRATION DATE: 8/31/05

See OMB Statement on back of page.

2 0 _ _ _ / _ _ / _ _
Y Y Y Y — M M D D S S S

FCE _ _ _ _ _ _ _   SID _ _ _ _ / _ _ _ / _ _ _

A. PRODUCT

Name, Form or Style, and Packing Medium:

pH: _ _ . _ _ . _ _ (Before Acidification)

Governing Regulation:
☐ low-acid (21 CFR 108.35/113)
☐ acidified (21 CFR 108.25/114)

Type of Submission:
☐ new
☐ replaces _ _ _ / _ _ _ / _ _ _
☐ cancels _ _ _ / _ _ _ / _ _ _

Process Use:
☐ scheduled
☐ alternate for
☐ emergency for

B. PROCESSING METHOD

NAME OF STERILIZER (MFR. & TYPE):

HEATING MEDIUM (e.g., Steam, water, immersion or spray, steam-air)

1. ☐ Still
   a. ☐ Horizontal   b. ☐ Vertical
      Divider Plates (complete for a. or b.)
      ☐ None   ☐ Perforated
   c. ☐ Crateless
      Bottom Surface (complete for c.)
      ☐ Solid   ☐ Perforated

2. ☐ Agitating
   a. ☐ End over End
      ☐ Axial
   b. ☐ Continuous
      ☐ Batch

3. ☐ Hydrostatic
   ☐ Inner Chain only
   ☐ Outer Chain only
   ☐ Both Inner and
      Outer Chain
   ☐ Single Chain
   ☐ Multiple Chain

4. ☐ Flame

5. ☐ Other (explain)

6. ☐ **Acidified**
   Maximum Equilibrium pH: _ _ . _
   Method of Acidification:
   Acidifying Agent:
   Pasteurization Method:
   Preservative Used:
   Concentration:

CONTAINER TYPE:

1. ☐ Tinplate/Steel Can
2. ☐ Aluminum Can
   ☐ 2-piece
   ☐ 3-piece
   ☐ Welded
   ☐ Cemented

3. ☐ Glass or Ceramic
4. ☐ Flexible Pouch (specify material):

5. ☐ Semirigid (specify material):
   Lid _____ Body _____
   Seal Method
6. ☐ Other (specify):

PROCESS ESTABLISHMENT SOURCE (Limit entry to 30 characters)

DATE LAST ESTABLISHED
_ _ _ _ _ _
Y Y Y Y M M

C. CRITICAL FACTORS: AS DELINEATED BY PROCESS AUTHORITY TO ASSURE COMMERCIAL STERILITY (Check or Describe)

None of the following . . . . NO ☐
Maximum Water Activity (a $_w$) . . . . . MW ☐ (. _ _ _)
Consistency / Viscosity . . . . CV ☐
   Value . . . . (_ _ _ _ . _ _ _)
   Units . . . .
   Method Name . . . .
   Temperature . . . . (_ _ _ . _ _)
Container Position in Retort . . . . . . CP ☐
Nesting of Containers . . . . NC ☐
Fill Method (check applicable method) . FM ☐
   Hand or Volumetric . . . .
   Vibrating or Tumble . . . .
   Other (specify) . . . .
% Solids . . . . SO ☐ (_ _ _ . _)
Solid to Liquid Ratio (wt. to wt.) . . . . SL ☐ (_ _ _ . _)
Drained wt./Net wt. Ratio . . . . DW ☐ . _ _ . _

PROCESS RECOMMENDATIONS ATTACHED?
☐ YES   ☐ NO

Arrangements of Pieces in Container . . . . . AP ☐
Formulation Changes . . . . FC ☐
Preparation Method . . . . PM ☐
Product Quality . . . . PQ ☐
Matting Tendency . . . . MT ☐
Layer Pack . . . . LP ☐
Max. Flexible Pouch/Semirigid Container Thickness in Retort . . . MP ☐ (_ . _ _)
Max. Residual Air (Flexible Pouch/Semigrid Container) . . . . . . MR ☐ (_ . _ _) c.c.
Particle Size . . . . PS ☐
Syrup Strength . . . . SS ☐ (_ . _ _)
Starch Added . . . . SA ☐ (_ _ . _ _)
   Max. % . . . .
   Type . . . .
Other Binder . . . . OB ☐
Min. % Moisture of Dry Ingredients . . . . . MM ☐ (_ _ . _ _)
Other (specify) . . . . OT ☐

NOTE: No commercial processor shall engage in the processing of low-acid or acidified foods unless completed Forms FDA 2541 and FDA 2541a have been filed with the Food and Drug Administration, 21 CFR 108.25(c)(1) and (2) and 108.35(c)(1) and (2).

PSC Media Arts (301) 443-1090   EF

Food Process Filing FDA 2541a (page 2)

D. SCHEDULED PROCESS (Do *not* write in shaded areas -- Check appropriate box and enter numerical values on dashed lines.)

FCE: _____ SID: _____

CONTAINER DIMENSIONS

- Cont. No.
- Diameter or Length
- Height or Width
- Height or Maximum Pouch or Semirigid Container Thickness

Inches & Sixteenths

CAPACITY UNITS
- ☐ Oz.
- ☐ Gal.
- ☐ ML
- ☐ Other _____

SCHEDULED PROCESS (Check Only One in Each Column)

- Step No.
- Temp (°F)
- Process Time (Minutes)
- Sterilization Temp (°F)

LACF
- ☐ Min. IT / ☐ Process Temp. / ☐ Process Time / ☐ Process Temp.

Acidified or a_w Controlled
- ☐ Min. IT / ☐ Process Time / ☐ Process Temp.
- ☐ Fill / ☐ Hold Time / ☐ Other
- ☐ Center / ☐ Other
- ☐ N/A / ☐ N/A / ☐ N/A

°F Minutes °F

Least Sterilizing Value of the Scheduled Process
- ☐ F_0
- ☐ Other F Value

Death Rate (z):
- Ref. Temp.(T): _____
- ☐ IS Value
- ☐ Other: _____

OTHER CRITICAL FACTORS TO ASSURE COMMERCIAL STERILITY PER SOURCE AUTHORITY

- Thruput — Containers per Minute — ☐ N/A
- Headspace — Inches — ☐ Net ☐ Gross — ☐ N/A

Speed
- Reel Speed — RPM
- Reel Diameter — Inches — ☐ N/A
- Steps Per Turn of Reel — Number
- Chain / Conveyer Speed — Inches — ☐ Feet ☐ Carriers ☐ Flights (per minute)

- Maximum Weight — Ounces — ☐ Drained ☐ Fill — ☐ N/A
- Minimum Net Weight — Ounces — ☐ N/A
- Minimum Free Liq. at Closing — Ounces — ☐ N/A
- Minimum Container Closing Machine Gauge Vacuum — In. Hg.
- Temp. (± 3° F) — ☐ N/A

OTHER (Specify)

FORM FDA 2541a (9/02) Page 2

FOR FDA USE ONLY

AUTHORIZED INDIVIDUAL

FULL NAME (Please Type or Print) TELEPHONE NUMBER

SIGNATURE DATE

COMMENTS:

PLANT NAME / ADDRESS

PREFERRED MAILING ADDRESS

Food Process Filing FDA 2541c)

DEPARTMENT OF HEALTH AND HUMAN SERVICES ■ Public Health Service ■ Food and Drug Administration

FOOD PROCESS FILING FOR LOW-ACID ASEPTIC SYSTEMS

(USE FDA BOOKLET TITLED "ASEPTIC PACKAGING SYSTEM SUPPLEMENT")

(TYPE OR PRINT ALL INFORMATION REQUESTED, IF AN ITEM DOES NOT APPLY ENTER "NA". FILE ACIDIFIED ASEPTIC (pH 4.6 or BELOW) ON FORM 2541a)

FORM APPROVED: OMB No. 01910-0037
EXPIRATION DATE: 9/30/02

FDA USE ONLY

DATE RECEIVED BY FDA

NOTE: No commercial processor shall engage in the processing of low-acid foods unless completed Forms FDA 2541 and FDA 2541c have been filed with the Food and Drug Administration, 21 CFR 108.35 (c)(1) and (2).

1. FCE _ _ _ _ _

2. ESTABLISHMENT NAME

   ADDRESS (No. and Street)

   CITY　　　　　　　　　STATE

   ZIP CODE　　　　　COUNTRY

3. SID 2 0 $\underline{Y\ Y\ Y\ Y}$ - $\underline{M\ M}$ / $\underline{D\ D}$ / $\underline{S\ S\ S}$

4. ☐ NEW　☐ CANCELS　☐ REPLACES $\underline{Y\ Y\ Y\ Y}$ - $\underline{M\ M}$ / $\underline{D\ D}$ / $\underline{S\ S\ S}$

5. ☐ SCHEDULED　☐ ALTERNATE FOR $\underline{Y\ Y\ Y\ Y}$ - $\underline{M\ M}$ / $\underline{D\ D}$ / $\underline{S\ S\ S}$

6. SUP SID 2 0 $\underline{Y\ Y\ Y\ Y}$ - $\underline{M\ M}$ / $\underline{D\ D}$ / $\underline{S\ S\ S}$

7. PRODUCT NAME, FORM OR STYLE, AND PACKING MEDIUM

8. NAMES OF STERILIZING SYSTEMS

   a. Product[1]

   b. Packaging

9. PROCESS ORIGIN

   No. Source for 8.a. and 8.b.

   a.

   b.

   Date (mm/yyyy)

10. CONTAINER TYPE (Check one)

    a. ☐ Tinplate or Steel Can　　b. ☐ Aluminum Can　　c. ☐ Glass　　d. ☐ Other (Specify below and in item 22 if necessary)

11. MAXIMUM WATER ACTIVITY[2]	12. pH		13. MAXIMUM CONSISTENCY OR VISCOSITY IN CENTIPOISES OR APPROPRIATE UNITS				
	Normal	Max.[3]	Value at 77±2°F	Value at Other Temp	Other Temp (°F)	Viscosity Characteristic	Method Name
0 .	.	.				N☐ P☐ D☐	

14. SPECIFIC GRAVITY AT 77±2°F	15. INSIDE DIAMETER OF HOLDING TUBE (Inches)	16. HOLDING TUBE LENGTH (Inches)

17. OTHER CRITICAL CONTROL FACTORS (Check all that apply)

- 61 ☐ Percent Solids
- 62 ☐ Ratio of Solids to Liquids
- 63 ☐ Syrup Strength
- 68 ☐ Method of Preparation
- 70 ☐ Formulation
- 71 ☐ Rehydration (specify method in 22)
- 72 ☐ Particulates (specify maximum size in 22)
- 73 ☐ Other (specify in 22)

18. CONTAINER DIMENSIONS (Inches and Sixteenths)			
No.	Diameter or Length	Height or Width	Height
1			
2			
3			
4			
5			
6			

19.				SCHEDULED PROCESS			20. MAXIMUM FOOD FLOW RATE (gal / min)	21. THRUPUT (containers / minute)
Minimum Initial[4] Temp (°F)	Temp (°F)	Time (sec)	Least Sterilizing Value (°F)[5]	Temp (°F)	Flow Correction Factor			
		.	.		.	.		
		.	.		.	.		
		.	.		.	.		
		.	.		.	.		

FOOTNOTES

1. For steam injection, enter volume increase and thermal expansion factors in 22.
2. If reduced water activity is used as an adjunct to the process, specify the maximum water activity.
3. Where acidification is followed for normally low-acid fruits, vegetables or vegetable products for the purpose of thermal processing, specify the maximum finished product equilibrium pH.
4. If a critical factor is in the process.
5. Or equivalent scientific basis of process adequacy.

AUTHORIZED COMPANY REPRESENTATIVE

NAME (Type or Print)　　　　　　　　TITLE

SIGNATURE　　　　　　　DATE　　　　　PHONE NO.

22. COMMENTS

FORM FDA 2541c (4/02)　　　PREVIOUS EDITION IS OBSOLETE.

Created by: PSC Media Arts (301) 443-2454

Application for Foreign Trade Zone CF 214

OMB No. 1515-0086.

CENSUS USE ONLY	DEPARTMENT OF THE TREASURY United States Customs Service **APPLICATION FOR FOREIGN-TRADE ZONE ADMISSION AND/OR STATUS DESIGNATION** 19 CFR 146.22, 146.32, 146.35-146.37, 146.39-146.41, 146.44, 146.53, 146.66	1. ZONE NO. AND LOCATION *(Address)* 2. PORT CODE

3. IMPORTING VESSEL (& FLAG)/OTHER CARRIER		4. EXPORT DATE	5. IMPORT DATE	6. ZONE ADMISSION NO.
7. U.S. PORT OF UNLADING	8. FOREIGN PORT OF LADING		9. BILL OF LADING/AWB NO.	10. INWARD M'FEST NO.
11. INBOND CARRIER	12. I.T. NO. AND DATE		13. I.T. FROM *(Port)*	

14. STATISTICAL INFORMATION FURNISHED DIRECTLY TO BUREAU OF CENSUS BY APPLICANT?   ☐ YES   ☐ NO

15. NO. OF PACKAGES AND COUNTRY OF ORIGIN CODE	16. DESCRIPTION OF MERCHANDISE	17. HTSUS NO.	18. QUANTITY (HTSUS)	19. GROSS WEIGHT	20. SEPARATE VALUE & AGGR CHGS.
		21. HARBOR MAINTENANCE FEE (19 CFR 24.24) ⟹			

22. I hereby apply for admission of the above merchandise into the Foreign-Trade Zone. I declare to the best of my knowledge and belief that the above merchandise is not prohibited entry into the Foreign-Trade Zone within the meaning of section 3 of the Foreign-Trade Zones Act of 1934, as amended, and section 146.31, Customs Regulations.

23. I hereby apply for the status designation indicated:

☐ NONPRIVILEGED FOREIGN (19 CFR 146.42)   ☐ PRIVILEGED FOREIGN (19 CFR 146.41)   ☐ ZONE RESTRICTED (19 CFR 146.44)   ☐ DOMESTIC (19 CFR 146.43)

24. APPLICANT FIRM NAME	25. BY *(Signature)*	26. TITLE	27. DATE
F.T.Z. AGREES TO RECEIVE MERCHANDISE INTO THE ZONE ⟹	28. FOR THE F.T.Z. OPERATOR *(Signature)*	29. TITLE	30. DATE
PERMIT — Permission is hereby granted to transfer the above merchandise into the Zone.	31. PORT DIRECTOR OF CUSTOMS: BY *(Signature)*	32. TITLE	33. DATE
PERMIT — The above merchandise has been granted the requested status.	34. PORT DIRECTOR OF CUSTOMS: BY *(Signature)*	35. TITLE	36. DATE

PERMIT TO TRANSFER	37. The goods described herein are authorized to be transferred: ☐ without exception ☐ except as noted below

	38. CUSTOMS OFFICER AT STATION *(Signature)*	39. TITLE	40. STATION	41. DATE
	42. RECEIVED FOR TRANSFER TO ZONE *(Driver's Signature)*	43. CARTMAN	44. CHL NO.	45. DATE

FTZ OPERATOR'S REPORT OF MERCHANDISE RECEIVED AT ZONE	46. To the Port Director of Customs: The above merchandise was received at the Zone on the date shown except as noted below:

	47. FOR THE FTZ OPERATOR *(Signature)*	48. TITLE	49. DATE

(See back of form for Paperwork Reduction Act Notice.)   **Customs Form 214 (022696)**

Application for Unlading CF 3171 (page 1)

Form Approved OMB No. 1515-0013

United States Customs Service

**APPLICATION-PERMIT-SPECIAL LICENSE
UNLADING-LADING-OVERTIME SERVICES**

19 CFR 4.10, 4.30, 4.37, 4.39, 4.91, 10.60, 24.16,
122.29, 122.38, 123.8, 146.32, 146.34

CUSTOMS USE ONLY

APPROVED

No.

Date/Time

Signature of Customs Officer

1. Name of Vessel, Vehicle or Aircraft	2. Port

3. Flag	4. Name and Nationality of Owner/Operator	5. Name/Phone No. of Agent

6. Arriving from (Port Name and Country)	7. Date/Time of Arrival	8. Locations (Dock/Terminal)*

Day Phone _____

Night Phone _____

9. Application is made for a permit for the operations indicated:

☐ (1) To unlade merchandise (intended to be unladen at this port, as shown by the manifest), baggage or passengers. To discharge ballast, and to land "in bond" merchandise. (Sec. 551, Tariff Act of 1930).

☐ (2) To land supplies, ship's stores, sea stores, or equipment not to be reladen, subject, however, to free or duty-paid entry (Sec. 446, Tariff Act of 1930).

☐ (3) To lade merchandise or baggage requiring Customs supervision.

☐ (4) To land and release for repair, adjustment, or refilling and to relade under Customs supervision articles of carrier's equipment. (Articles to be reverse side hereof showing date and hour of unlading and relading.) The undersigned certifies the articles listed on the reverse hereof for release under this term is to be landed only for the purpose mentioned in this item and will be reladen on this carrier.

☐ (5) Other _____

10. Itinerary of Vessel/Aircraft (show port country and departure dates for entire voyage including U.S. itinerary)*

11. TYPE OF CARGO: ☐ Container   ☐ Break Bulk   ☐ Bulk   ☐ Other (Specify) _____

12. List all carriers, including carriers sharing or chartering space onboard the vessel and check the box that describes how the carrier presented the cargo manifest.*

SCAC	AMS	CF 1302	Paperless	SCAC	AMS	CF 1302	Paperless
	☐	☐	☐		☐	☐	☐
	☐	☐	☐		☐	☐	☐
	☐	☐	☐		☐	☐	☐
	☐	☐	☐		☐	☐	☐
	☐	☐	☐		☐	☐	☐

13. Application is made for a special license for overtime services of Customs officers and employees for:

☐ Entrance, Clearance   ☐ Unlading, lading, etc.   ☐ Other: _____

☐ on _____ at _____ or   ☐ Per supplemental oral request
     (Date)   (Time)

14. Bond No.	15. Application is made for a Term Permit and Special License
	From: To:

16. Principal on Bond	17. Surety Company Code	18. Amount of Bond	19. Date of Bond

20. Importer Number (Party to be billed; show hyphens)	21. Address of Agent	
	22. Signature	23. Date

This PERMIT is not valid until properly lodged with a Customs officer at the point of discharge and all operations indicated therein are performed under Customs supervision.

*use back for additional space; (Instructions and Paperwork Reduction Act Notice on reverse)   **Customs Form 3171 (01/02)**

Application for Unlading CF 3171 (page 2)

CONTINUED FROM ITEM #9 (4): RECORD OF ARTICLES RELEASED AND RELADEN

UNLADEN AND RELEASED						RELADEN		
Date	Time	Description of Articles	Released to		Insp. Badge #	Date	Time	Insp. Badge #
			Signature	Company				

Continued from # 8 - additional Locations:

Continued from # 9 (5) - Other:

Continued from # 10 - additional Itinerary of Vessel:

Continued from # 12 - additional SCAC Codes:

SCAC	AMS	CF 1302	Paperless	SCAC	AMS	CF 1302	Paperless
	☐	☐	☐		☐	☐	☐
	☐	☐	☐		☐	☐	☐
	☐	☐	☐		☐	☐	☐
	☐	☐	☐		☐	☐	☐
	☐	☐	☐		☐	☐	☐

INSTRUCTIONS

Customs Form 3171 shall be filed in duplicate. (When a term permit is requested, additional copies may be required for local purposes). Items shall be completed as follows:

1. Name or number of vessel, vehicle, or aircraft (On term permit "Not Applicable.")

2. Port at which application is filed.

3. Flag of vessel.

4. Name of shipping company, airlines etc., which owns or operates the vessel, vehicle or aircraft and their nationality.

5. Name and day/night phone numbers of party filing application.

6. Name of port or place and country from which a vessel, vehicle, or aircraft is arriving. (On Term Permit show "Not applicable.")

7. Give the date of arrival or expected arrival when request covers a specific vessel, vehicle, or aircraft.

8. List all places of lading, unlading, etc. If request is for overtime services only state where services are to be performed.

9. Check appropriate items.

10. Show port, country and sailing dates for the itinerary of the vessel/aircraft, including U.S. itinerary.

11. Check the appropriate box/boxes.

12. List all carriers, including carriers sharing or chartering space onboard the vessel and check the box that describes how the carrier presented the cargo manifest.

13. Indicate purpose for which services are requested and date and time. (If date and time are not known, check "per supplemental oral request.")

14. Self-Explanatory.

15. When requesting a term permit, show dates or period to be covered.

16-21. Self-Explanatory.

22-23. Signature and date of party submitting request.

PAPER REDUCTION ACT NOTICE: The Paperwork Reduction Act of 1995 says we must tell you why we are collecting this information, how we will use it, an whether you have to give it to us. We ask for the information to carry out the Customs Service laws of the United States. This form is used by carriers to request specific Customs services relating to the lading or unlading of merchandise and by Customs to authorize requested activities. It is also used to permit and control various statutes. Another major use of this form is to request Customs services during other than regular hours of service. It is mandatory.

Statement Required by 5 CFR 1320.21: The estimated average burden associated with this collection of information is 6 minutes per respondent or recordkeeper depending on individual circumstances. Comments concerning the accuracy of this burden estimate and suggestions for reducing this burden should be directed to U.S. Customs Service Information Services Branch, Washington, DC 20229, and to the Office of Management and Budget, Paperwork Reduction Project (1515-0013), Washington, DC 20503.

Customs Form 3171 (Back)(01/02)

Packing, Shipping, Insurance
Contents

Benefits and Opportunities of Efficient Container Packing

Material for this section on container packaging has been provided by Hapag-Lloyd AG. World Trade Press gratefully acknowledges this contribution.

You will really gain from taking extra care when stowing your products into a container:

- By saving yourself worry and expense, since your goods will reach your customer in good condition.
- By cutting transport costs for land transport and on commodity box rates, for instance, which are charged irrespective of utilization.

- By saving time and stowage material thanks to properly prepared and expert measures for ensuring safety of your goods.
- By preserving your good reputation for reliable deliveries of goods in perfect condition.

Smoothly executed container operations will ensure that you enjoy a competitive edge over your competitors. One important essential here is "correct" stowing, on which we aim to assist you with this brief manual. The facts conveyed in the manual are based on the experience and knowledge of cargo superintendents and stowage advisors as well as analysis of cargo damages.

However, this manual will not be able to answer all your questions. Whenever you need advice or information for your shipments, your Hapag-Lloyd Sales Office or your Hapag-Lloyd Agent in Europe or overseas will put you into immediate contact with an experienced stowage advisor.

Preparation for Container Transports

General Rules for Packing Containers

Goods of the following nature are not to be packed together

- Dusty goods not together with dust sensitive goods.

- Odor emitting goods not together with odor sensitive goods.

- Goods/packaging giving off moisture not together with moisture sensitive goods/packaging.

- Heavy parcels not to be placed on light parcels.

- Goods with protruding parts, sharp edges or corners not together with goods in comparatively soft packaging (e.g. sacks or bales).

- Wet goods not together with dry goods.

- If joint packing cannot be avoided, put the wet goods below the dry ones and separate them by dunnage. Place additional dunnage or sawdust under the wet goods.

As a general rule

Separate different types of packaging effectively from each other (e.g. cardboard boxes and wooden crates).

Do not ship goods with damaged packaging, but repair the packaging carefully before packing.

For especially sensitive goods, line the container with paper or foil.

When packing goods sensitive to odor, the container must be odorless.

Should this not be the case, the container should be washed out. Any remaining odors can be neutralized by using an industrial deodorant.

When packing odorous cargo or cargo that might damage the container through leakage, you should line it with foil and add absorbent materials (such as peat moss, sawdust, silica gel). In this way you can avoid unnecessarily costly cleaning expenses.

Please inform us when shipping loose scrap metal or ore in containers. We will advise you about packing and unpacking methods that help you to avoid damage to the containers and thus save you trouble and expense.

Mixed stow of wet and dry commodities.

Weight Limits and Weight Distribution

The weight limits of the Hapag-Lloyd containers correspond to the norm ISO 668:

Permissible gross weights:

20' containers 24,000 kg (52,910 lbs)

40' containers 30,480 kg (67,200 lbs)

According to the 1985 change of the norm the permissible gross weight of most Hapag-Lloyd 20' containers is 30,480 kg (67,200 lbs).

The *technically maximum payload* results from the permissible gross weight minus tare of the container and can vary depending on the constructional series of the container. (You will find more precise details in our brochure "Container Specification.")

Apart from the constructionally defined load capacity of the container, the permissible weight limits of road and rail transport in the respective countries must be considered. Details about the possibilities of and restrictions on carrying out land transport overseas can be obtained from our Hapag-Lloyd Sales Offices and Hapag-Lloyd Agents.

If the permissible load is used to the full, all bottom cross member should be used for load support since the floors of containers are not suited for point loads. The bottom cross members are the load bearing elements taking the cargo pressure off the floor.

In order to avoid overloading when planning the packing of the container, the *line load* should be calculated by the following rule of thumb. The line load corresponds to the cargo weight in relation to the load transfer area of the cargo in longitudinal direction of the container. (Example: a load with a weight of 10 t with a load transfer length of 4 m (13'2") has a line load of 10 : 4 m (13'2") = 2.5 t/m (0.76 t/ft). The line load must not exceed the following limits:

for 20' containers: 4.5 t/m (1.37 t/ft)

for 40' containers: 3.0 t/m (0.91 t/ft).

Thus a relatively heavy piece of cargo or a cargo unit with a small load transfer area must be loaded in such a way that the load bearing area is increased in order to stay within the permissible floor loading limits. This may be done through dunnage (layered in alternate directions, the lowest layer lengthwise) or by using a "sled" the skids of which are orientated container lengthwise. When arranging the skids or the battens on the container floor, the following should be taken into account:

Timber dunnage used for load distribution must have a certain minimum width and lateral distance from the center-line of the container, because of the construction of a Standard Container's floors (above).

The load bearing area is increased with dunnage layered in alternate directions.

Type of container	20'	40'
A. width of timber-dunnage minimum	0.10 m (4")	0.15 m (6")
B. lateral distance of the timber-dunnage from the container center line minimum to each side	0.4 m (1'4")	0.4 m (1'4")

If a parcel exceeds this weight limit, please make use of our heavy duty Flats and Platforms; these are built with a special reinforced floor construction. (Platforms are in principle used only for ocean transport). Our stowage advisors are at your disposal at any time and can show you how to take advantage of container transport, even in borderline cases.

In order to enable containers to be packed by forklift truck, all Hapag-Lloyd containers meet the ISO-Recommendation 1496/1. This means that any forklift truck can drive into a container if the following limits are not exceeded:

Front axle load (payload + tare)	5,460 kg (12,000 lbs)
Contact area per wheel	142 cm^2 (22 sq. in)
Width of wheel	ca. 180 mm (7")
Width of track	ca. 760 mm (30")

Containers can be packed with forklift trucks, which do not exceed certain weights and are equipped with a suitable telescopic mast.

The cargo weight distribution within the container should be balanced, i.e. the cargo's centre of gravity should fall within the following limits:

Type of container	20'	40'
Longitudinal direction	maxim. + 0.60 m from the centre of the container	maxim + 0.90 m
Transverse direction	in the center of the container	
Height	at or below the center of gravity of the container	

All Hapag-Lloyd containers meet the test requirements laid down in the ISO Norm 1496/1 for the load strength of side walls, front walls, doors and roof:

Construction element	Test load
Side walls	0.6 times the weight of the max. payload
Front wall and doors	0.4 times the weight of the max. payload
Roof	300 kg (660 lbs) for a surface of 600 x 300 mm (24" x 12")*

* This corresponds approximately to the weight of two persons working on the roof.

Asymmetrical weight distribution in a container requires special measures during transport and handling.

Stowage Plan

There are three main reasons for producing a stowage plan prior to packing a container:

- To achieve optimal utilization of the container's capacity.

- To simplify and increase the speed of packing and unpacking.

- To plan for necessary cargo securing aids well in advance.

For the stowage planning you require precise details of

- exact weights and measurements of the cargo to be loaded and its packaging,

- exact inside dimensions and permissible load limits of the containers. (Please ask for the Hapag-Lloyd brochure "Container-Specification.")

Prior to producing the stowage plan, you should select the container type which is best suited to your shipment. Your Hapag-Lloyd Sales Office or your Hapag-Lloyd Agent will gladly provide you with information about the broad range of Hapag-Lloyd special containers, as will our brochure "Container Specification." (You will find details of our worldwide sales network in our monthly schedule as well as in our "List of Agents.")

When selecting the type of container and producing the stowage plan, you should take account of

- the load limits of the container

- the load limits for inland transport in both the shipper's and consignee's country

- the weight distribution within the container

- the facilities available to the consignee to unpack the container.

Our sales offices and agents will gladly assist you in all these matters.

For the production of a stowage plan use a drawing of the container from the top and from the side (on draft paper), drawn to scale. Draw the pieces to be packed to scale or alternatively cut them out of the paper (again to scale) and lay them on the plan.

If this procedure seems too troublesome, you can also pre-stow your cargo in a rectangle which has been drawn in chalk or paint corresponding in size to the container.

Two further important items

Please note that the inside dimensions of door (and roof) openings are normally smaller than the inside dimensions of the container. You achieve an optimal utilization of the available space if the parcel sizes are divisible of the internal container dimensions given, e.g. for an inner width of the container of 2.31 m (7'7"), it is advantageous to put four cartons of 0.56 m (1'10") next to each other; 4 x 0.56 m (1'10") = 2.24 m (7'4"), i.e. only 0.08 m (3") unused.

Cartons of 0.61 m (2') width are highly disadvantageous since a lot of space is wasted; 3 x 0.61 m (2') = 1.83 m (6'), i.e. 0.48m (1'7") unused.

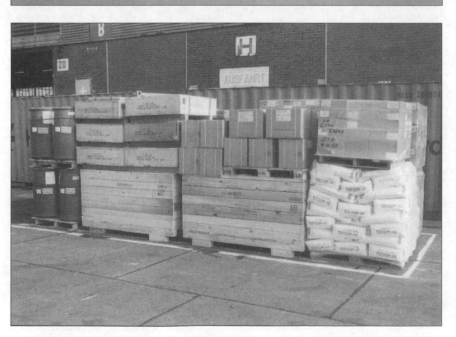

To prepare the packing of a container either a stowage plan can be drawn to scale...
(upper photo)

... or the goods can be pre-stowed on an area of container size (lower photo).

Container Check Prior to Packing

Every container used on international routes must bear a valid CSC Safety Approval plate, as provided for in the International Convention on Safe Containers of December 2, 1972. All Hapag-Lloyd Containers are fitted with the plate.

In order to ensure that you receive only containers in sound conditions, we check all containers arriving or leaving port terminals or inland depots.

However, in addition to this inspection, we recommend that you always carry out a careful check of the container to prevent possible later damage to cargo.

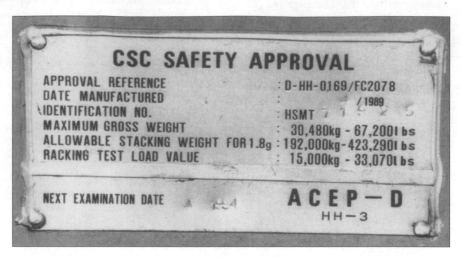

Checklist (external)

1. No hole or cracks in walls and roof.

2. Doors can be easily operated.

3. Locking roods and handles function properly.

4. No placards/labels, e.g. IMO-placards, remain from the previous cargo.

Special containers

5. For Flats:

   Stanchions (if ordered) are complete and inserted properly.

6. For Open Top Containers:

   Roof bows are completed and inserted properly.

7. For Open Top Containers:

   Tarpaulins are undamaged and the right size, tarpaulin rope ends are undamaged.

8. For Hard Top Containers:

   The roof is undamaged, the roof fastening fits properly and is accessible.

Checklist (internal)

9. Container is waterproof

   Test method: stand inside the container, close both doors tightly and examine for any light coming through cracks, holes, door gaskets, etc.

10. Container is absolutely dry inside.

    Should there be any sweat water or hoar-frost, wipe this away so as to prevent any corrosion damage to cargo.

11. Container is clean, free of dirt and cargo residue and odorless.

12. No nails or other protruding objects that might damage cargo are present.

Please inform your Hapag-Lloyd Sales Office or Hapag-Lloyd Agent immediately of any defects so that they can ensure that you are provided with a sound container.

You will find this label on the inside of container doors.

> **Attention!**
>
> Before loading the shipper must check the proper condition of the container. By accepting the container the shipper recognizes its suitability for the loading of the cargo to be carried
>
> Furthermore, attention is drawn to the fact that the consignee is obliged to return the container after discharging clean and suitable for the transport of every kind of cargo.
>
> This applies especially when poisonous, dangerous or obnoxious cargo has been transported.
>
> All labels referring to cargo shall be removed.
>
> In case of doubt please contact the next Hapag-Lloyd Representative.

Container Check After Packing

We recommend that after packing you verify, that the following checklist items have been fulfilled:

1. The container was loaded taking into account:

   - type of cargo
   - strains during transport
   - characteristics of the container.

2. A copy of the packing list is fixed at an easily visible position inside the container, for possible customs checks.

3. When shipping goods in wooden packaging to Australia or New Zealand:

   A copy of the certificate issued by the appropriate agricultural authority stating that the wood used has been treated according to the quarantine regulations must be displayed in a prominent position inside the container.

4. Doors and, in case of open top containers, hardtop or tarpaulin are carefully locked. (Strong steel wire, padlocks or High Security Seals offer protection against pilferage.)

5. The door handles are secured by seals to reduce the risk of pilferage (please note seal numbers!). Upon request we can supply you with Hapag-Lloyd seals.

6. For Open Top Containers:

   The tarpaulins and the tarpaulin ropes are correctly fixed (meeting customs requirements).

7. If cargo in special containers is covered with tarpaulins:

   Ensure the tarpaulins are securely fastened.

8. Old placards are removed.

9. For Reefer Containers with refrigeration unit and heatable Tank Containers ensure the correct temperature has been set. The temperature recorder of the Reefer Unit is running so that temperatures are constantly noted.

A properly sealed door reduces the risk of pilferage (above and below).

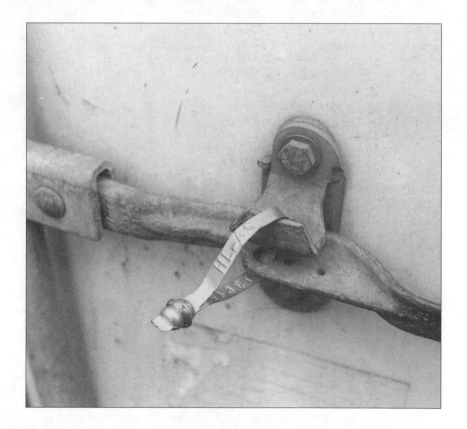

Strains Caused by Container Transports

Mechanical Strains

In order to enable you to judge which cargo securing measures are effective and will prevent possible damage, a summary of the mechanical strains to which your cargo may be exposed may be useful.

In door-to-door transport, the container is packed at the shipper's premises and is not unpacked until it arrives at the consignee's. In contrast to conventional break bulk transport, during the entire transport only the container itself is handled and not each package separately.

The cargo securing done by the shipper must withstand strains resulting from sea and land transport as well as from container handling. The sealed container rules out any visual inspection of the cargo within. No stowage corrections can be effected once packing has been done.

Basically, a distinction needs to be drawn between strains of two types:

Static strains are caused by storage and stacking. In the main, these arise from stacking pressure and the resultant bending and folding strains on the bottom layers of cargo. Stacking pressure depends on the dimensions and weights of the items stacked and the height of the stack.

Dynamic strains occur during loading of the container, during sea or land transport and during handling.

With dynamic strains, a distinction is made between jolts (accelerations) and vibrations.

Jolts (accelerations) occur during loading, when braking and on bends, when a container is set down, during shunting, during handling, and are also caused by the rolling, pitching, lurching and plunging of a ship at sea.

Vibrations occur in all forms of transport. These are caused by the engine, gearbox, transmission, suspension and road surface, etc.

So as to give you an outline of the strains involved in different means of transport, we have reprinted two tables from the brochure "Transport Chain 40" published by the Study Group for Combined Transport.

Type of transport	Vibrations up to max. Hz.	Normal vibration range Hz.	Max. Acceleration g.
Rail transport	800	16 – 350	1,0 *
Road transport	500		
– truck with conventional suspension		10 – 20	4,0
– trailer with conventional suspention		10 – 20	4,5
truck with pneumatic suspension		10 – 20	0,4
trailer with pneumatic suspension		10 – 20	1,5
saddle trailer with conventional suspension		10 – 20	1,5
Air transport	3000	60 – 400	0,6
Seaborne transport	700	0,1 – 10 **	1,3
Container handling	160	bis 5	0,4 ***

*   1,0 g with 16 Hz. filtering
** 0,05 – 0,1 Hz. during rolling and pitching

*** This rate declines with higher frequencies, so that at 160 Hz. it is no more than 0,05 g

Jolt strain on load surfaces:

```
-- -- -- --    rail wagon
..............  Boeing 707 F
—-—-—-—   truck, pneumatic suspension
- - - - -      trailer, ditto
· - · - · -    truck, conventional suspension
----------     trailer, ditto
               container handling
```

Jolt strains
(no reliable, generally applicable data are available in respect of shipping)

Since it is normally not possible to know in advance the accelerations likely to affect a container during a forthcoming voyage, one can only work by rule of thumb. In this context, please see the figures to the right (gravitational acceleration g = 9.81 m/s^2).

Potential jolting (acceleration) during truck transport.

Potential jolting (acceleration) during rail transport.

Potential jolting (acceleration) during sea transport.

Climatic Strains

Goods to be shipped are often subject to considerable climatic strains. These already commence during storage and continue during container packing. The strains are caused by being exposed to very disparate climatic zones during transport by truck, rail or barge; during loading, and most especially, during ocean transport. Extreme climatic strains are caused by shipment in winter at below-zero temperatures and transport into or through the tropics and also by transport from the latter into colder regions.

All closed containers protect the cargo from external climatic influences such as rain, snow, sea water, salt water spray, dust and sun radiation (heat and UV radiation).

Although the cargo is protected against external influences, condensation may occur inside the container. The containers are closed waterproof after packing. Thus the relative humidity inside the container is determined by the temperature and air humidity at the time of packing. Furthermore, it depends on the humidity of the cargo and its packaging. The relative humidity inside the container thus changes according to the changes in temperature.

Condensation may occur when a drop in temperature coincides with a source of humidity inside the container.

During a voyage to the Far East following results were obtained:

But even in port considerable differences between outside and inside temperature may occur!

The following differences to outside temperature are possible:

- in the temperate zone
  directly under the roof   20°C / 68°F
  inside the container   10°C / 50°F

- in the subtropical and
  tropical zone directly
  under the roof   30°C / 86°F

Temperature variations may not only result from changing outside temperatures, but also through spontaneous heating of the cargo.

Sources of humidity may be:

- cargo itself

- dunnage

- packaging

- air entrapped during packing.

In particular, moisture condensing on the container walls, roof and on the packages or dripping from the roof onto the cargo may cause the following damage:

- rust

- mould

- stains and discolorations

- caking together of wet cartons

- removal of labels

- collapse of the stow.

Measuring point	Temperature in °C		Relative humidity in %	
	Max.	Min.	Max.	Min.
Outside atmosphere	31.5 89°F	1.5 35°F	99	45
Container – on deck	42.0 108°F	4.5 40°F	82	51
– under deck	33.0 91°F	15.5 60°F	75	38

Securing Cargo

General Rules for Securing Cargo

The contents of a container must be secured against shifts towards all sides, and especially towards the door.

Gaps between packages and/or container sides must be filled. To secure the cargo, the possibilities for lashing offered by the longitudinal rails on the floor and roof should be used.

Whenever packing a container or securing a cargo, attention should be paid to the Guidelines for Packing and Securing Cargoes in Containers for Transport by Land or by Sea (Container Packing Guidelines) issued by the International Maritime Organization (IMO) and the International Labour Organisation (ILO) on March 27, 1987.

Securing of goods towards the door at the corner posts or in the corrugation of the side walls. For low profile corrugations the front ends of the square timbers must be adapted to the shape of the channels.

A crate is braced against the corner posts and with large bearing-surfaces against the side walls (either with dunnage—left side —or with air bags —right side).

Securing Facilities within the Container

You may use the following construction elements of a Hapag-Lloyd container for securing the cargo:

Construction element	Cargo securing
Lashing bars on corner posts, roof and floor longitudinal rails or bull rings in the floor	For the fastening of ropes, plastic ribbons, metal hoops, quick fasteners, etc.
Corrugated steel walls	For cargo securing in longitudinal direction transverse square timbers can be fitted into the recesses.
Corner posts	Suitable for the distribution of extreme point loads, e.g. by shoring.
Wooden container floor	Securing by timber connectors. Nailing.

Side and front walls as well as the doors can only take large surface loads, and are unsuited for point loads. For load limits of the walls see "Weight Limits and Weight Distribution" on page 358.

Cargo Securing Aids

Stowage aids	Bracing and load distribution	Securing cargo in sections	Filling out gaps	Loading in several layers	Separating different goods	Securing cargo at lashing points	Fixing pallets and sledges with wooden blocks	Increasing friction
Wooden beams & planks / Blocks / Dunnage / Stowage grids	■	■	■	■	■			
Empty pallets / Air bags	■		■		■			
Empty packages	■	■						■
Intermediate decks and walls	■	■		■	■			
Nets		■				■		
Timber connectors							■	
Plastic foam / Corrugated cardboard			■					
Used tires			■					■
Ropes / Wire / Bands / Steel straps / Plastic straps / Chains / Nylon straps / Hercules / Span sets						■		■
Plastic mats / Sisal mats / Sacks / Rough paper / Anti-slipping spray / Gum mat								■

The containers are equipped with lashing bars and/or bull rings depending on constructional series.

Climatic Protection

Packaging of Goods

Export packaging has five functions:

- to protect the goods
- to keep them storable
- to make them transportable
- to ensure that they can be handled and
- to provide information on the cargo and its handling.

These functions must also be fulfilled when goods are transported in containers. Whether and to what extent packaging (and hence packaging costs) can be saved by transport in containers depends among other things on the cargo and the transport:

When packing a container with cargo in different types of packaging, the strains on these are greater than would be the case with cargo in uniform packaging.

If the container contains several layers on top of each other, the lowest layer must be capable of supporting the upper ones. The required stacking strength depends on the packaging material, transport duration and humidity conditions.

Door-to-door transport offers the greatest savings in packaging costs since the parcels remain in the protective container during the entire transport. They are directly affected only during packing and unpacking of the container. Under certain circumstances door-to-door transport enables cargo to be shipped without casing (e.g. for some types of machines and vehicles).

If during certain stages of the transport the cargo is handled "conventionally," i.e. unprotected by a container, its packaging must be able to withstand the strains of conventional handling.

Some special containers act in part as packaging and hence reduce packaging requirements (e.g. Reefer and Bulk Containers).

Loading of an unpacked engine for door-to-door transport (right).

Seaworthy packaging of machinery parts (below).

Protection against Humidity

Hapag-Lloyd ships and containers assist in protecting your cargo against condensation:

The double hull of the container vessels reduce the influence of air and water temperature on the hold.

The climatic conditions of the hold can be influenced by an electric ventilation system.

Special containers (e.g. Ventilated Containers or Flats with stanchions and stowage grids) permit the exchange of air between cargo hold and the interior of the container.

Furthermore, you have a range of alternatives as a precaution against cargo damage:

Do not pack moisture sensitive packages together with moisture exuding goods. Should this unavoidable, packages to be well separated and protected.

Put packages and dunnage as dry as possible into the container, i.e. store these in dry premises beforehand. If packages and dunnage are stored in open or damp space, they will absorb moisture from the surroundings. Wood should be of a humidity not exceeding 12-14%, and corrugated cardboard have a maximum water content of 8% (corresponding to DIN 53102).

Select those cargo securing means which cannot cause damage to the cargo as a result of climatic influences (e.g. rust).

When packing, ensure that air is allowed to circulate.

This can be achieved by stowage in blocks, interspersed with ventilation channels or by using separating material (dunnage). A space of 100 mm to 120 mm (4" to 5") between cargo and container roof should be left free.

When transporting moisture exuding goods, put paper or other moisture absorbing material onto the cargo. Plastic sheets are unsuitable for this purpose.

Moisture absorbing materials, e.g. silica gel, can prevent condensation. They are, however, only effective when used in absolutely air tight space, e.g. for shrink wrapped cargo. For 1 m^3 enclosed air, approximately 500 g absorbent material is required (recipe: 1/2 ounce per cu./ft).

Despite the use of absorption material, sweat water damage may occur since under extreme conditions these materials may exude the previously absorbed moisture.

Climatic Protecting Aids

In order to protect the cargo from climatic influences additional aids are available. The following table gives you a summary of various aids and their effects:

Effect / Aids	Humidity absorption	Humidity repellent	Humidity exclusion	Insulation	Slowing down of natural Ripening process
Drying agents (sachets) Silica Gel Pillo Dri Air Dri Bag Brano Gel	■				
Drying aids (sheets) Dew Catcher Cargo Dry System Preapre - Sheet Non-Sweat Paper Moisture Grip	■				
Paper	■				
VCI inhibitors		■			
Plastic foil			■		
Fats, oils		■			
Insulating foil				■	
Gases					■

Moisture emitting goods are to be covered with paper to avoid damage through dropping condensation

Cargo in Temperature Controlled Containers

For cargo that requires temperatures maintained at a constant level, Hapag-Lloyd supplies Insulated and Reefer Containers with or without their own cooling device.

Insulated containers do not have their own cooling facility. During ocean transport they are connected with the central cooling plant of the ship. The temperature range lies between -25°C and +40°C, (-14°F to 104°F), depending on type of ship and trade route. Since these containers lack a cooling unit, their pre- and on-carriage must be executed in the shortest possible time to prevent damage to cargo.

Reefer Containers have their own electrically operated cooling unit. Many of them have a diesel generator to provide power supply and are thus independent of external electricity supply during pre- and on-carriage. The maintainable temperature ranges from -25°C to +25°C, (-13°F to +77°F).

These temperatures can be maintained if the difference to the outside temperature does not exceed the following limits:

- for heating maximum 42°C (76°F)
- for cooling maximum 60°C (108°F).

For the temperature ranges applicable to the different construction series, please refer to our brochure "Container Specification."

Thus it is easily possible to maintain a constant temperature of say -18°C (0°F) or +12°C (+54°F) during sea and land transport.

During storage at container terminals, the containers are exposed to severe conditional stresses (i.e. sun radiation). Thus storage should be kept as short as possible. When transporting Reefer Containers, which are run by diesel generators on land, ensure that they are equipped with sufficient fuel.

Please remember the Insulated and Reefer Containers are designed merely to maintain the temperature required by the particular cargo. They cannot cool down cargo to the required temperature. Consequently reefer cargo must be packed in a precooled state.

The temperature to be set will depend on the goods being shipped. When booking the cargo, please give us the appropriate cooling instructions.

There are certain types of cargo that "breathe," i.e. they not only give off heat, but due to a maturing process produce gas. In such cases it may be necessary to replace the air in the container by fresh air from the outside. All Hapag-Lloyd Reefer Containers have facilities for a controlled fresh-air supply. Please indicate such a requirement when booking.

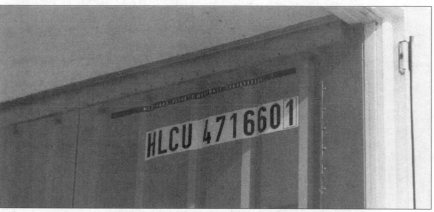

Temperature controlled cargo may only be packed up to the "load line" to enable circulation of the cooling air.

Hold of a container vessel with couplings for Insulated Containers.

Packing a Reefer Container directly out of a cold-storage depot through an airlock.

Stowage in the container and packing of the cargo are crucial for maintaining a set temperature:

1. The entire floor grating must be evenly loaded with cargo. Should this be impossible, then all free spaces must be spread with cardboard or similar material so as to prevent a draft. This also applies to any gaps that could occur between pelletized cargoes.

2. A void space of at least 12 cm must be left between the cargo and the roof. Markings on the side walls indicate the maximum permissible cargo height.

3. Stowage should on the one hand be sufficiently loose to allow an air current to pass upwards between the separate packages, and on the other sufficiently tight to prevent the occurrence of any drafts. This is often ensured by the shape (bulges) of the packages, which should nevertheless be stacked—and special attention needs to be paid to this point—precisely on top of each other.

4. The packing must be sufficiently strong to bear the stack load and at the same time to protect the contents.

5. The packing must conform to the properties of the product: e.g. cartons with ventilation apertures permitting air circulation to the interior should be used for goods needing fresh air.

Cross-section of a loaded Reefer Container.

Advice on Packing and Securing Various Goods

Cartons, Cases, and Crates

When shipping cartons in containers you should bear two things in mind:

- With increasing humidity the stability of cartons decreases. (Countermeasures see "Protection against Humidity" on page 370).

- Cartons that move within the container are subject to crushing. A compact stow, the filling out of gaps and the bracing of cargo prevent this.

With regard to packing the following procedure is recommended:

- Check whether the cargo fills the entire volume of the container. If the entire container volume is not required for the cargo, pack the cargo in such a way that the entire floor area is covered to the same height. You thus achieve an equal weight distribution. Furthermore you save cargo securing material and save labor through lower stacking heights. Start the packing process at the front of the container (opposite of the doors), from the sides to the middle.

- Make full use of available space and do not leave gaps.

- You can achieve a particularly solid stow if you pack the units interlocking like bricks.

The parcels can be linked with each other and with the floor by timber connectors. This prevents the cargo from shifting.

- If gaps are unavoidable, brace the cargo row for row as packing progresses (suitable securing aids for load support and distribution see "Cargo Securing Aids" on page 368).

- Large and heavy crates should be put into the centre of the container and be braced against the corner posts. When bracing against the side walls ensure a large bearing surface.

Properly stowed cartons.

A crate is braced against the corner posts and with large bearing-surfaces against the side walls (either with dunnage—left side—or with air bags—right side).

Pallets, Forklift Adapted Unit Loads

The attainable utilization of the container is determined by the dimensions of the pallets:

The optimal size of the pallet depends on the internal dimensions of the container, the form and weight of the packages.

Fourway pallets (i.e. those that can be lifted from all four sides by a forklift truck), usually make best use of the floor area of a container.

The recommended packing patterns for standard pallet sizes are shown in the chart to the right.

Type of Container	20'			40'		
Pallet size mm in	Recommended packing pattern	max. no.	Floor utilization %	Recommended packing pattern	max. no.	Floor utilization %
1000 x 800 40" x 32"	1	14	83,2	1	28	81,2
1100 x 800 44" x 32"	1	14	91,4	1	28	89,3
1100 x 900 44" x 35 1/2"	1	12	88,1	1	26	93,3
1100 x 1100 44" x 44"	1	10	99,7	1	20	87,7
1100 x 1400 44" x 55"	1	8	91,3	1	16	89,3
1200 x 800 48" x 32"	2/3	11	78,4	2/3	23	80,1
1200 x 1000 48" x 40"	3	10	89	2/3	20	87,0

Packing pattern "1" for pallets.

Packing pattern "2" for pallets.

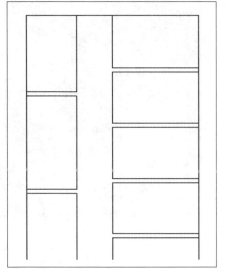

Packing pattern "3" for 4-way pallets only.

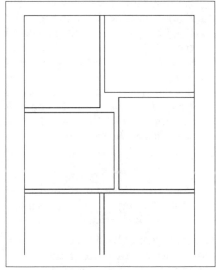

For the transport of pallets in containers it is important that cargo is well secured on the pallets, and that the pallets are well secured inside the container:

Fix the cargo by lashing, gluing or shrink wrapping it on to the pallet.

To secure the pallets (for single layered stowage) 2 to 4 timber connectors under each pallet should suffice.

If only one row of pallets fits into the container, place it in the middle.

Should the container be wide enough for two or more pallets, place the rows close to the container sides.

If gaps cannot be avoided, leave these in the centre of the container. This ensures an equal distribution of the load and requires less use of securing facilities.

The second layer of pallets is secured by stepwise packing.

Drums, Barrels, and Plastic Cans

For the packing of drums, barrels and plastic cans the following procedure is recommended:

- Ensure that no leakage exists prior to packing; do not load leaking units.

- Place units with liquids on longitudinal wood dunnage. This prevents damage should leakage occur.

- Always stow drums and barrels with the drainage holes upwards.

- Drums are best stowed standing upright next to each other. The optimum arrangement of the units on the container floor can be determined by dividing the width of the container by the unit diameter:

Staggered packing of drums and securing towards the door.

If no remainder results: packing pattern "Full."

If a remainder of more than 73.2% of the unit diameter results, packing pattern "A."

Should the remainder amount to 50 – 73.2% of the unit diameter: packing pattern "B."

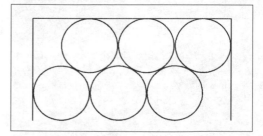

The number of units which you can place in a container is shown in the table at right.

Barrel diameter inch	cm	Packing pattern	Number per 20' Container	Number per 40' Container
10	25.4	Full	207	423
11	27.9	B	168	344
12	30.5	B	154	315
13	33.0	A	119	252
14	35.5	B	102	216
15	38.1	Full	90	186
16	40.6	B	80	165
17	43.2	B	65	140
18	45.7	Full	60	130
19	48.2	A	59	120
20	50.8	B	52	108
21	53.3	B	44	88
22	55.8	Full	40	84
22.5	57.1	Full	40	83
23	58.4	A	39	80
23.5	59.7	A	36	79
24	61.0	A	36	76
24.5	62.2	B	30	66
25	63.5	B	30	63
26	66.0	B	27	57
27	68.6	B	24	53
28	71.1	B	24	51
29	73.7	Full	23	48
30	76.2	Full	21	45
31	78.7	A	21	45
32	81.3	A	20	42
33	83.8	A	20	41
34	86.4	B	14	30
35	88.9	B	14	28
36	91.4	B	14	28
37	94.0	B	12	26
38	96.5	B	12	24
39	99.1	B	12	24
40	101.6	B	11	23

If you want to calculate the number of rows (from the front to the doors) please use the following formulae:

For "Full" and "A":
$$\frac{\text{Inner length of container}}{\text{Drum diameter}}$$

For "B":
$$1 + \frac{\text{Inner length of container less drum diameter}}{0.866 \times \text{drum diameter}}$$

Drums and barrels must be secured at the door end. For this several alternatives can be used:

- Bracing with wood.
- Securing with steel straps, preferably in "Olympic rings linkage."
- Staggered stowage (resulting from differing unit heights or using empty pallets) supports the top layer.

Wooden barrels are not built to withstand pressure around the middle. When packed horizontally, the following precautions should be taken:

Support the barrels at the ends with battens so the middle does not touch the container floor; prevent rolling by means of wedges.

When loading plastic cans in a container, two things should be observed:

- Check plastic cans for leakages, since one leaking unit endangers the stability of the entire stowage.
- Cover all layers with stowage gratings or dunnage to ensure stability of the stow. Jolts from below or vibration can otherwise easily cause a layer to "bulge" (bulging effect) and may dislodge individual cans.

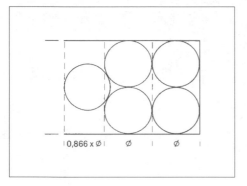

Number of rows for packing patterns "Full" and "A."

Number of rows for packing pattern "B."

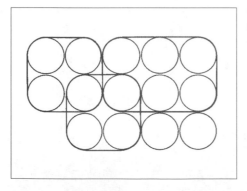

Drums are secured by means of steel straps in "Olympic-Rings" linkage.

Wooden barrels are supported at the ends and secured against rolling by means of wedges.

Interim layer of dunnage timber or plywood sheets (above left and right).

Bagged Goods

Inexpert packing of bags in containers may cause the following damage:

When opening the doors of the container the bags slide out.

Denting of the container walls by excessive pressure may cause the container to get jammed in its slot and lead to damage during discharge.

To prevent damage you should pack the bags in such a way that they cannot shift as the ship rolls. For this you have two alternatives:

- *Stowage in alternate directions* so that each tier binds the tier above and below it (this, however, does not prevent plastic bags from shifting).

- *The palletizing of bags.* Under certain conditions the use of oneway pallets may even be more economical than the relatively time consuming packing (and unpacking) of the container with bagged cargo.

    The optimum size of a pallet is determined by the internal dimensions of the container, the shape of the bags and the weight put on each pallet.

    The bagged cargo is secured on the pallets through plastic straps or shrink wrapping (merely non-organic goods).

Bags shrinkwrapped on a pallet.

Bales

Most baled cargo is comparatively insensitive to mechanical transport strains, but can be easily damaged when packing or unpacking. Thus the following procedure is recommended:

- During packing, take care that the external covering of the bales is not damaged.

- To facilitate unpacking by forklift, place wooden planks lengthwise on the floor of the container and between each layer of bales while packing.

- If the bales are not flush with the doors, braces against the corner posts are usually sufficient for securing the cargo.

Bales can be stowed on their flat sides or in an upright position.

Rolls and Coils

Rolls and coils may be placed in the container upright (i.e. vertically, "eye to sky"), or on their side (i.e. horizontally). Different rules apply to the packing of paper and steel rolls.

Horizontal packing

Paper rolls may be packed on top of each other. Secure the bottom layer by wedges. Place suitable padding between layers to avoid movement. Fill out gaps at the sides. To avoid chafing place cardboard strips between side walls and paper rolls.

Heavy steel coils should be packed on heavy duty wooden cradles and have an underpinning of blocks or skids to increase the bearing surface. Use strong steel wire lashing with tensioning screws to secure each roll individually to the cradle and to each other. Lash these rolls to the container through their centre holes. Reinforce the front end of the container with cross bars positioned at the height of the centre of the rolls. Fill out empty spaces with wood.

Upright packing

Place paper rolls close to each other and fill out gaps. Secure at the door ends with nets or planks.

Steel coils should also be placed close to each other. For securing, link them with steel straps or brace them with wood.

Heavy steel coils which are shipped on skids or pallets should be securely fastened down.

For an optimum arrangement of the rolls please see "Drums, Barrels, and Plastic Cans" on page 375.

When packing more than one layer, stepwise stowage (different package heights, empty pallets) will secure the top layer (see chart in the section "Pallets, Forklift Adapted Unit Loads" on page 374).

Securing of paper reels stowed in the roll.

Securing of heavy steel coils.

Securing of coils stowed "eye to sky."

Machinery, Heavy Lifts, and Oversized Items

These goods also can be transported by containers. This is especially advantageous in door-to-door transport as cargo needs to be secured only once.

The transport of heavy and oversized cargo requires particularly careful measures for cargo securing. Here are some rules which must be adhered to at all times:

- Check the regulations concerning weights and measures for inland transport both in the supplier's and the consignee's country.

- When packing the container, take into consideration whether the consignee has the mechanical and other facilities required for unpacking.

- All transport arrangements should be worked out well in advance. Our stowage advisors are at your disposal at all times; please contact your Hapag-Lloyd Sales Office or your Hapag-Lloyd Agent.

Machinery and heavy goods

Machines and heavy goods are often loaded into the container from the top. For this, Hapag-Lloyd will provide you with Open Top Containers, either with tarpaulin or hardtop, or Flats.

Heavy goods are usually transported on Flats or Platforms because of the higher load bearing capacity of the floor. Flats may be used for door-to-door transports, whereas Platforms are in principle only used for ocean transport. You will find detailed information about load limits in the Hapag-Lloyd brochure "Container Specification" or you can contact our stowage advisors.

For cargo securing we recommend the following procedure:

If only one item is loaded into the container, it should be placed in the middle of the container so that the centre of gravity of the cargo is as close as possible to the container's own centre of gravity, or better still below.

Heavy single items require load distribution supports since the point load of these items is too heavy for the container floor. Limits for the floor loading of Standard and Open Top Containers are

- 4.5 t/m (1.37 t/ft) inner length of a 20' container, and

- 3.0 t/m (0.91 t/ft) inner length of a 40' container.

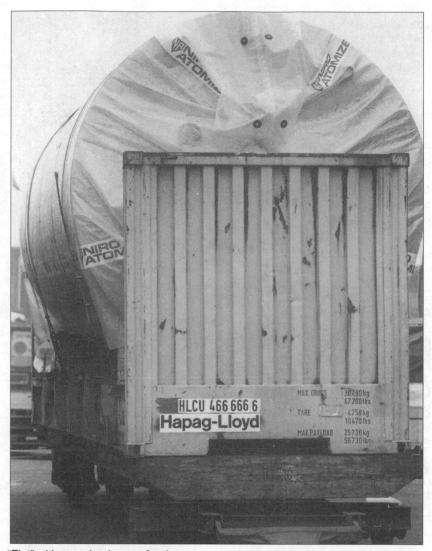

"Flat" with oversized cargo for the door-to-door transport (above).

Sub-chassis and fastening for a single heavy lift (below).

If only two battens are used, they must be placed lengthwise and be at least 80 cm (2'8") from each other (see first chart in section "Weight Limits and Weight Distribution" on page 358).

Goods shipped on a wooden sled should be firmly bolted to it. The sled should be braced against the corner posts as well as against the bottom longitudinal rails and cross members; preferably not only on the floor but also at the height of the centre of gravity of the cargo against the corner posts. It is particularly important to brace top heavy goods at the level of their centre of gravity.

When using side walls for bracing ensure a large bearing surface.

Properly secured machinery.

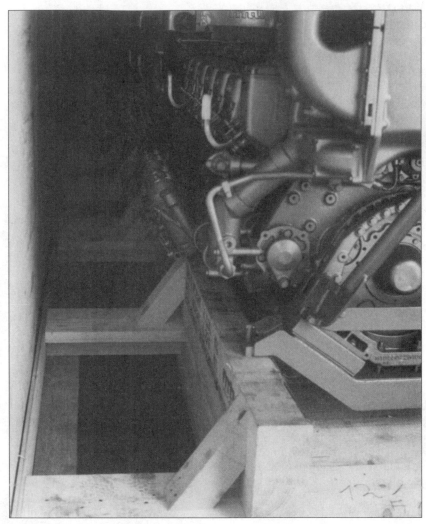

The cargo is firmly bolted to the bedding and chocked against the side walls with a large bearing surface area (above).

Top-heavy goods are secured at the level of their center of gravity (below).

Oversized goods

For oversized goods, Open Top Containers, Flats or Platforms are suitable, depending on the direction in which the item exceeds the inner dimensions of the container. (Platforms are in principle used only for ocean transport.)

We will gladly advise you on the choice of the most suitable container. In our brochure "Container Specification" you will find information about the dimensions and load limits.

Even slightly overwidth goods can be stowed under deck if ample space is left for the cell guides. In these cases you can possibly save on premium freight by careful stowage on the container. Detailed information is available from our Sales Offices and Hapag-Lloyd Agents. In general, the same rules apply for securing of oversized cargo as for heavy goods. In case of doubt, please contact our experienced stowage advisors, who will gladly assist you.

If the goods are covered with special tarpaulins, stow the original tarpaulins and roof beams securely in the container.

Even overwidth goods can be stowed under deck, if ample space is left for the cell guides (above and below).

Uncontainerizable cargo can be transported by Hapag-Lloyd container vessels. If notified well in advance, large areas below deck as well as large free deck areas can be made available for transports of these items.

For this unit a complete bay under deck was made available.

Exceptionally bulky pieces can be stowed on large free deck areas.

Vehicles

All types of vehicles, ranging from motor cars to road building machinery, may be transported by container vessels.

In a few countries vehicles may be classified as dangerous goods and in some other countries there may be official recommendations regarding the carriage of vehicles by sea.

Please ensure vehicles are prepared in accordance with such instructions.

We recommend that batteries should be disconnected and fuel drained prior to loading the container.

Motor cars and small trucks

These vehicles can normally be wheeled into Standard Containers without difficulty (if necessary by us-ing a small drive-on ramp). Load these vehicles absolutely dry. Leave a gap open in windows to facilitate air circulation.

Special span sets are available for lashing motor cars and small trucks.

Trucks, road construction, and farm machinery

These can be shipped in Open Top Containers with tarpaulin or hardtop, on Flats and Platforms (Platforms are in principle used only for ocean transport).

Use steel wire with tensioning screws to secure cargo.

Place additional wedges in front of and behind all wheels (the wedges should have a height of at least one sixth of the wheel diameter).

Securing of a tractor by means of wedges and steel wire with turnbuckles.

Cars can be driven into Standard Containers across a small drive-on ramp.

Glass Sheets

Due to its dimensions and weight, glass is best loaded into the container from the top. For this Hapag-Lloyd will provide you with Open Top Containers with a tarpaulin and hardtop.

Sheet glass in open top container.

In addition to careful packaging of sheets of glass in boxes, crates or A-frames, further cargo securing measures may be taken:

- Place the sheets, if possible, lengthwise in the container.

- When shipping several A-frames in a container, provide buffer zones between them.

- Provide additional covering for the glass as it is extremely moisture sensitive.

Bulk Liquids

Bulk liquids can be transported in our special Tank Containers. Please observe the following:

Tank Containers must be filled to at least 80% to avoid dangerous surge movements during transport.

Tank Containers must generally not be filled to more than 95% to allow for a possible heat expansion of the contents.

Please observe the working limits affixed to the Tank Containers.

You can find more information about Hapag-Lloyd Tank Containers in our brochure "Container Specification." Furthermore, our experienced stowage advisors are at your disposal at any time.

Non-hazardous liquids like wine, latex or ink can also be transported in "liquid bulk bags" in Standard, Open Top or Bulk Containers. We can advise you about purchasing opportunities. Lashing points to suspend these inlets in the aforementioned container types are available.

Bulk Solids

Loose bulk solids can be transported in our 20' Bulk Containers, and similarly in our Standard and Open Top Containers by using an inlet.

Bulk, Standard and Open Top Containers are all equipped with rings for suspension of the inlet.

The inlets currently in use are designed to match our more recent 20' Standard Containers.

Cargo has to be secured by a barrier on the door side, and indeed this is a strictly enforced mandatory requirement in many countries.

Apart from the four steel struts, our door barrier forms part of the inlet, is simple, and can be fitted rapidly and securely.

Further information may be found in our brochure Standard Containers with Inlets.

Suspending the inlet in a Bulk Container...   ... and in an Open Top Container.

An inlet fitted in a Bulk/Open Top Container.

Suspension points and intervals for a standard container (below).

Securing the inlet.

Interior view of an inlet after installation.

Door barrier.

Lengthy Goods

Due to their dimensions and weight, lengthy goods are best loaded into the container from the side or from the top. Hapag-Lloyd will provide you with flats or Open Top Containers with tarpaulin or hardtop.

Securing of lengthy goods in an Open Top Container...

For cargo securing we recommend the following procedure:

Strap the entire container load together with strong steel straps, which have been put into the container prior to packing.

This relieves pressure on the side walls. In case of using Flats place in the stanchions and tie them together above the load to keep them from splaying.

...and on a Flat.

Material increasing friction should be placed between the individual layers of lengthy goods, since these goods have a tendency to slide lengthwise subjecting the end walls to stress.

Insert a vertical wooden bulkhead between cargo and front walls to distribute pressure caused by a possible shifting of the cargo on the corner posts and to avoid point loads.

Livestock

Transport boxes for animals can be loaded on flats on deck for easy access at any time.

Personnel looking after the animals may travel on the ships.

Containers containing fodder can be stowed near the animals on deck.

Familiarize yourself with the quarantine regulations of the country of destination and of the transit ports.

Even livestock can be transported. Fodder can be stowed nearby. Keepers may travel on the ship.

Standard Specifications for Containers

Overall dimensions (see table) and corner castings are standardized for all types of containers (ISO 668, ISO 1161).

Standard Specification ISO 668	Length		Width		Height		
Overall Dimensions	20' 6 058 mm	40' 12 192 mm	8' 2 438 mm	8' 2 438 mm	8'6" 2 591 mm	9'6" 2 896 mm	
Internal Dimensions Standard C.	5 867 mm 19'3"	11 998 mm 39'4 3/8"	2 330 mm 7'7 3/4"	2 197 mm 7'2 1/2"	2 350 mm 7'8 1/2"	2 655 mm 8'8 1/2"	
Door Opening Standard Container	–	–	2 286 mm 7'6"	2 134 mm 7'	2 261 mm 7'5"	2 566 mm 8'5"	

Minimum requirements are laid down for internal dimensions (see table), gross weight and the capacity of a container floor to carry a fork-lift truck during cargo handling.

According to ISO 668 containers may be utilized up to the following gross weights:

20' containers:
24 000 kg (52 910 lbs) according to the latest issue of ISO 668, valid for most Hapag-Lloyd 20' containers;

30 480 kg (67 200 lbs) valid for all new Hapag-Lloyd 20' containers; exceeds ISO minimum standards;

20 320 kg (44 800 lbs) only valid for some containers.

40' containers:
30 480 kg (67 200 lbs).

A container floor is capable of carrying a fork-lift truck with a maximum axle load of 5 460 kg (12 040 lbs), if the contact area per wheel is at least 142 cm² (22 sq.ft) (ISO 1496/I).

Minimum Requirements for Hapag-Lloyd Containers

● All containers comply with the standards for overall dimensions and corner castings.

● All containers exceed the minimum requirements for internal dimensions.

● Exposed timber is treated according to Australian requirements (exceptions: 40' flats and platforms).

● Container inside dimensions mentioned in the following pages are nominal figures. Because of production tolerances a difference in measurements is possible:

Tolerances	Length	Width	Height
Maximum Difference	10 mm 3/8"	10 mm 3/8"	10 mm 3/8"

Standard Container   40' / 20'

- Suitable for any general cargo.
- 20' containers may be equipped with liner bags suitable for bulk cargo, e.g. malt.
- Fork-lift pockets on a number of the 20' containers (see footnote 1).

- All 40' containers suitable for Gooseneck chassis.
- Various lashing devices on the top and bottom longitudinal rails and the corner posts (both 20' + 40') Lashing devices have a permissible load of 1 000 kg (2 205 lbs) each.

- **Note permissible weight limits for road and rail transport.**

High Cube Standard Container   40'

9'6"
2.9 m

- Especially for light, voluminous cargo and overheight cargo up to max. 2,70 m (8' 10¹/₄") (see table).
- All containers suitable for Gooseneck chassis.

- Numerous lashing devices on the top and bottom longitudinal rails and the corner posts.
- Lashing devices have a permissible load of 1 000 kg (2 205 lbs) each.

- **Consider overheight for inland transportation.**
- **Note permissible weight limits for road and rail transport.**

Hardtop Container   40′

- This container type has been designed and developed by Hapag-Lloyd.
- The 40′ hardtop container has particularly been constructed for:
  - long loads which cannot be transported in the 20′ hardtop container
  - heavy loads
  - high and excessively high loads
  - loading, e. g. by crane, through roof opening and door side.
- The roof can be removed by using a forklift. The weight of the steel roof is approx. 450 kg (990 lbs) each section.
- With the roof removed and the door-header swung out, it is much easier to load cargo using a crane via the door side.
- In case your cargo has overheight the roof sections can be lashed to a sidewall inside the container using only some 13 cm (5 ¹/₈″) of space.
- If required, we can provide disposable tarpaulins for the transport which can be fastened to the walls on the outside using lashing devices.
- The capacity of the container floor exceeds the ISO 1496/1 standard by 33 %, so that a forklift whose front axle weight does not exceed 7,280 kg (16,000 lbs) can be used inside.
- The hardtop container provides many lashing devices to fasten your goods.

The lashing devices on the corner posts and on the longitudinal rails of the roof and floor are capable of bearing loads of up to 2,000 kg (4,410 lbs) each, and those in the middle of the side walls up to 500 kg (1,100 lbs) each. Lashing to the side walls can only be done after the roof has been closed.

- The roof can easily be raised by about 70 mm (2 ³/₄″), using the roof locking devices so that the door-header can be swung out without removing the roof.

- This container type has been designed for heavy loads. Whilst considering the technical data (including the permissible spreaded load limitations) please bear in mind the prevalent weight restrictions for land transport.
- For further information please see page 13 and our brochure "The 40′ Hardtop".

- **Note permissible weight limits for road and rail transport.**

Hardtop Container   20′

- This container type has been designed and developed by Hapag-Lloyd.
- It has especially been constructed for
  - heavy loads
  - high, and excessively high loads
  - loading, e.g. by crane, through roof opening and door side.
- The steel roof of some series (please see footnote) is fitted with forklift rings so that it can be removed by using a forklift. The weight of the steel roof is approx. 450 kg (990 lbs).
- With the roof removed and the door-header swung out, it is much easier to load cargo using a crane via the door side.

  In case your cargo has overheight the roof sections can be lashed to a sidewall inside the container using only some 13 cm (5 1/8″) of space.

- If required, we can provide disposable tarpaulins for the transport which can be fastened to the walls on the outside using lashing devices.
- The capacity of the container floor exceeds the ISO 1496/1 standard by 33 %, so that a forklift whose front axle weight does not exceed 7,280 kg (16,000 lbs) can be used inside.
- The hardtop container provides many lashing devices to fasten your goods.

The lashing devices on the corner posts and on the longitudinal rails of the roof and floor are capable of bearing loads of up to 2,000 kg (4,410 lbs) each, and those in the middle of the side walls up to 500 kg (1,100 lbs) each. Lashing to the side walls can only be done after the roof has been closed.

- This container type has been designed for heavy loads. Whilst considering the technical data (including the permissible spreaded load limitations) please bear in mind the prevalent weight restrictions for land transport.

- **Note permissible weight limits for road and rail transport.**

Open Top Container   40′

- Especially for
  - overheight cargo
  - loading from top side, e.g. by crane
  - loading from door side, e.g. with cargo hanging from overhead tackle.

- Door header can be swung out on all open top containers.

- If required, we can provide disposable tarpaulins. For fastening tarpaulins, lashing bars are available on the outside of the walls. Using one way tarpaulins requires the corner castings to be accessible.

- The capacity of the floor for use of forklift trucks exceeds the ISO standard by 33 % on all 40′ open top containers.

- Numerous lashing devices on the top and bottom longitudinal rails and the corner posts.

Lashing devices have a permissible load of 1 000 kg (2 205 lbs) each.

- **Note permissible weight limits for road and rail transport.**

Open Top Container   20′

- Especially for
  - overheight cargo
  - loading from top side, e.g. by crane
  - loading from door side, e.g. with cargo hanging from overhead tackle.

- Door header can be swung out on all open top containers.

- If required, we can provide disposable tarpaulins. For fastening tarpaulins,

lashing bars are available on the outside of the walls. Using one way tarpaulins requires the corner castings to be accessible.

- Forklift pockets on a number of containers (please see footnote 1).

- The capacity of the floor for use of forklift trucks exceeds the ISO standard by 33% on all 20′ open top containers.

- Numerous lashing devices on the top and bottom longitudinal rails and the corner posts. Lashing devices have a permissible load of 1 000 kg (2 205 lbs) each.

- **Note permissible weight limits for road and rail transport.**

Flat   **40'**

- Especially for heavy loads and overwidth cargo.

- Higher loadings possible if required (please see footnote 2).

- Strong bottom construction with fixed endwalls (which allow bracing and lashing of cargo as well as stacking).

- Gooseneck tunnel on both ends of all 40' flats.

- Numerous very strong lashing devices on the corner posts, longitudinal rails and on the floor. Lashing devices on the longitudinal rails and on the floor of 40' containers have a permissible load of 4 000 kg (8 820 lbs) each.

- Lashing winches with strong, 9 m (29' 6¹/₂") long synthetic lashing straps on some 40' Flats (please see footnote 1).
  Straps have a permissible load of up to 2 000 kg (4 410 lbs) each.

- **Maximum payload can only be used if distributed over the total floor area of the flat.**

If concentration of heavy load on a small part of floor area is required please contact your Hapag-Lloyd partner office for stowage advice.

- Flats are delivered without stanchions. If stanchions are required please inform us upon booking.

- Note permissible weight limits for road and rail transport.

Flat   **20'**

- Especially for heavy loads and overwidth cargo.

- Strong bottom construction with fixed endwalls (which allow bracing and lashing of cargo as well as stacking).

- Forklift pockets on a number of 20' flats (please see footnote 1).

- Numerous very strong lashing devices on the corner posts, longitudinal rails

and on the floor. Lashing devices on the longitudinal rails of 20' containers have a permissible load of 2 000 kg or 4 000 kg respectively (4 410 lbs or 8 820 lbs respectively) each.

- **Maximum payload can only be used if distributed over the total floor area of flatrack.**
  If concentration of heavy load on a

small part of floor area is required please contact your Hapag-Lloyd partner office for stowage advice.

- Flats are delivered without stanchions. If stanchions are required please inform us upon booking.

- Note permissible weight limits for road and rail transport.

Platform

40' / 20'

- Especially for heavy loads and over-sized cargo.
- Strong bottom construction.
- Gooseneck tunnel on both ends of all 40' Platforms.

- Numerous very strong lashing devices on the longitudinal rails. Lashing devices have a permissible load of 3 000 kg (6 615 lbs) each.

- **Transport of heavy loads concentrated on a small load transfer area is possible. Your Hapag-Lloyd partner will be pleased to advise you.**

Ventilated Container

20'

- Especially for cargo which needs ventilation.
- Natural ventilation is provided by openings in top and bottom longitudinal rails. The labyrinth construction of

these ventilation openings ensures weatherproofness.
- Numerous lashing devices on the top and bottom longitudinal rails and the corner posts. Lashing devices have

a permissible load of 1 000 kg (2 205 lbs) each.

- **Note permissible weight limits for road and rail transport.**

Insulated Container (Temperature Controlled Container)   40' / 20'

- Especially for cargo which needs constant temperatures above or below freezing point.
- Walls in "sandwich-construction", with Polyurethane foam in or to provide maximum insulation.
- Temperature is controlled by ship's/ terminal's cooling plant or "clip-on-unit".
- The air, delivered at the correct temperature, is circulated in the container through two apertures in the front wall (supply air via the lower aperture, return air via the upper aperture).

- Possible temperatures inside the 20' containers, depending on specification of respective cooling device, from about + 12 °C to − 25 °C (+ 54 °F to − 14 °F).
- Please note maximum stowage height in below table and as indicated by red line inside container in order to ensure proper ventilation.

- Possible temperatures inside the 40' containers, depending on specification of respective cooling device, from about + 13 °C to − 22 °C (+ 57 °F to − 8 °F).
- All 40' containers suitable for Gooseneck chassis.
- **Note permissible weight limits for road and rail transport.**

Refrigerated Container (Temperature Controlled Container)   40' / 20'

- Especially for cargo which needs constant temperatures above or below freezing point.
- Controlled fresh-air supply is possible. Containers are ATO-approved (formerly SPRENGER).
- Walls in "sandwich-construction", with Polyurethane foam in order to provide maximum insulation.

- The reefer unit is a compact-design compressor unit with aircooled condenser. It switches automatically from cooling to heating operation (and vice versa), if a change of the outside temperatures makes it necessary.
- Please note maximum stowage height in below table and as indicated by red line inside container in order to ensure proper ventilation.

- Possible voltages:
  - 380 V/50 Hz to 460 V/60 Hz (all refrigerated containers),
  - 200 V/50 Hz to 220 V/60 Hz **(exceptions footnote 2, see page 37-39).**
- Technical specification and illustration of electric plugs see page 46.
- **Note permissible weight limits for road and rail transport.**

Refrigerated High Cube Container   40′

(Temperature Controlled Container)

9′6″
2.9 m

- Particularly suitable for voluminous, light-weight cargoes (e.g. fruit, flowers, ferns).

- Mainly made of aluminium in order to allow high payload.

- Especially for cargo which needs constant temperatures above or below freezing point.

- Controlled fresh-air supply is possible. Containers are ATO-approved (formerly SPRENGER)

- Walls in "sandwich-construction", with Polyurethane foam in oder to provide maximum insulation.

- The reefer unit is a compact-design compressor unit with aircooled condenser. It switches automatically from cooling to heating-operation (and vice versa), if a change of the outside temperatures makes it necessary.

- Possible voltages:
  – 380 V/50 Hz to 460 V/60 Hz

- Technical specification and illustration of electric plugs see page 46.

- **Note permissible weight limits for road and rail transport.**

Bulk Container   20′

- Especially for dry bulk cargoes, e.g. malt.
- Three manholes for top loading of each container. Distance centerline to centerline manhole 1,83 m (6′).
- One discharge opening in each door wing. On demand short discharge

tubes can be installed to move the cargo in desired directions.
- Fastening of linerbag possible.
- Fork-lift pockets on a number of the containers (please see footnote 1).
- Lashing devices on the top longitudinal rails.

- Roof openings ∅ 455 mm (1 3/4″), discharge door openings ∅ 340 x 380 mm (1 3/8″ x 1 1/2″).

- **Note permissible weight limits for road and rail transport.**

Tank Container   **20'**

- Especially for liquid chemicals or potable liquids (e.g. spirits).

- All tank containers satisfy the requirements of the IMDG-Code for portable tanks of type 1 as well as the US-DOT specification for IM 101-tanks.

- All Tank Containers are designed for a working pressure of 3 bar (43.5 p.s.i.) (gauge pressure) the test pressure is 4.5 bar (65.3 p.s.i.) (gauge pressure).

- **For foodstuffs only certain containers are suitable (please see footnote 1). They are labeled "Potable Liquids only".**

- **Tank containers must be filled to at least 80 % to avoid dangerous surging-swell during transport (please see table).**

- **Generally tank containers must not be filled to more than 95 % to allow for possible heat expansion (please see table).**

- **Tank containers equipped for top discharge have no openings at bottom, therefore can only be** used for pressure discharge (please see subheadings).

- **Containers must be redelivered in clean condition.**

- **Note permissible weight limits for road and rail transport.**

Electric Plugs on Refrigerated Containers

- Depending on power sources refrigerated containers are equipped with 1 or 2 plugs
380V/50 Hz to 460V/60 Hz (32A),
200V/50 Hz to 220V/60 Hz (60A).

- There are fixed cables with a length of 15 m (49 ft).

- Couplings for adapters are available.

- **Adapters are subject to corresponding safety regulations.**

380/460 V plugs:
- 4poles according to CEE.
- According to ISO 1496/II annex O.
- **Earth contact in 3hr position according to socket.**

Earth Contact

all series

200/220 V plugs:
- 4poles
- According to ISO 1496/II annex M.
- **Position of earth contact according to illustration.**

Earth Contact

some series

Marine Insurance

Notes and comments on ocean cargo insurance

Material for this section has been provided by the Insurance Company of North America (INA), a CIGNA Worldwide Company. World Trade Press gratefully acknowledges INA and CIGNA for this contribution.

Introduction

The Ever Present Need for Marine Insurance

In spite of all our modern developments in marine transportation, marine disasters are an ever present hazard for those engaged in the foreign trade and commerce of the world.

Here are only a few dispatches from various ports of the world, selected at random during a period of a few weeks.

M/T Bridgewater
(Cia. Atlantica Pacifica, S.A.)

Sydney, January 30: Rescue vessels are heading for the *Bridgewater*, reported to have broken in two off Australia. The two sections have drifted about 12 miles apart. The stern is still afloat but the bow is reported to be sinking. Some of her crew were seen aboard both sections.

SS President Fillmore
(American President Lines, Inc.)

Jacksonville, March 3: From Gulf ports for Mediterranean ports via New York, encountered severe weather on March 1 and/or 2 and put into Jacksonville at 2130 today in distress. Bulwarks on starboard side forecastle head carried away and two of four steel pontoons on number 1 hatch as well as the three tarpaulins were carried overboard. The remaining two pontoons are adrift on deck Number 1 hold filled with seas to the height of number 1 LTP. Number 2 hold, by soundings, is dry. Number 1 LH is stowed with 300 tons flour, cement and steel anchors, corn meal, steel buoys, electronic apparatus and radio equipment. Foredeck cargo consists of large cases of structural steel which externally appear sound.

SS Green Island
(Central Gulf S.S. Corp.)

Charleston, March 4: From Corpus Christi, Orange and Houston for Alexandria, Egypt and Middle East ports via Charleston, S.C. (for bunkers), encountered severe weather during the evening of March 2, and put into Charleston at 0140 this morning in distress. The anchor windlass was immobilized and the cement plugs in the chain pipe carried away. The chain locker and the forepeak flooded and soundings of number 1 hold indicated 25 inches of water in the bilges. The after steering station was also KO'ed.

M/T Gem
(Urania Transportation Co., Inc.)

New York, March 8: *Gem*, from Rio Haina for Baltimore, in Lat 33.33 North, Long 75.18 West at 0530 March 8, broken amidships. *Jytte Skou* was alongside but due to state of weather was unable to stand by, navy vessels proceeding to assist.

Portsmouth, Virginia: The Lib. *M/V Victoria* today rescued seven men from the bow section of the Gem, several hours after the tanker broke in two.

SS La Parnpa
(Buries Markes, Ltd.)

London, April 5: *Clan Buchanan*, Glasgow for Chittagong, and *La Parnpa*, Glasgow and Newport for Vancouver, have been in collision at Newport, England on April 4. The *La Pampa* is holed below the water line and the propeller of the *Clan Buchanan* is being examined.

MV Lys-Point
(Simonsen & Slang)

Boston, July 18: Ro-ro *MV Rolf-Buck*, outwards, and *MV Lys-Point*, inwards in collision. Rolf-Buck slightly damaged at bow, proceeding to Felixstowe as planned. *Lys-Point* sustained damage to upper bow railings on starboard side and one container on deck.

Marijeannie
(D.J. Chandris)

Rosario, July 18: M bulk carrier/container vessel *Marijeannie* left Rosario July 14 for Paranagua. Enroute, when heaving anchor, leakage was discovered in number 6 double bottom tank. Presently berthed at San Nicolas port and being inspected.

Rosario, July 21: Agents at Rosario advise damage located in number 6 double bottom hopper tank, consisting of two perforations in way of shell plating close to bildge keel. Divers installing cement box as temporary repair.

MV Kirsten Wesch
(Jonny Wesch)

London, July 19: *MV Kirsten Wesch* en route from Rotterdam to Warri sustained damage to auxiliary engine July 10. Called Las Palmas as port of refuge for temporary repairs.

MV Tolga
(Government of Algeria)

Bizerta, July 21: Ro-ro *MV Tolga* on fire early morning of July 20 off Les Fratelli Islands. Crew rescued. Vessel taken in tow by Tunisian and Algerian tugs and brought to Bizerta Roads. Extinguishing operations still underway as vessel continues to burn due to strong winds and bad weather.

Sumber Agang

Jakarta, July 24: Freighter *Sumber Agang* sank off an island in eastern Indonesia earlier this month and at least 80 passengers were reported missing. The vessel, carrying more than 90 passengers and crew, was traveling from port of Ambori to Kisar Island when she sank July 14. Ten survivors including seven crew members were rescued. The port authorities said the vessel was authorized to carry only 20 passengers and had been swamped by heavy seas near Buru Island.

Each of these marine disasters resulted in financial loss. If the owners of the ships and cargoes had insurance, those losses were covered to the extent of the insurance.

Marine insurance plays a vital part in international trade and economic progress. Through marine insurance, the financial losses resulting from perils of and on the sea are transferred to professional risk-takers known as underwriters, the marine insurance companies. They can absorb those losses because of their financial strength and their application of underwriting experience and principles.

Marine insurance has sometimes been regarded as mysterious and strange, as beyond the understanding of the uninitiated. Perhaps this feelings arises from the fact that marine insurance well antecedes the Middle Ages. Perhaps it arises from the fact that marine insurance touches so many different countries, languages, currencies and forms of commercial practice. Perhaps it arises from the flavor of the sea itself.

But marine insurance is not strange, not mysterious. It is as easily understood as any other type of insurance coverage. The growing importance of foreign trade increasingly focuses attention on marine insurance and requires a better understanding of it. The questionable stability and remittability of certain foreign currencies emphasizes the security and hence the advantage of marine insurance in United States dollars.

This article is designed to present, in a simple and non-technical manner, some of the basic facts of marine insurance practice and marine insurance coverage as they apply to cargo insurance.

It is intended to help the exporter, the importer, the freight forwarder and others in the broad field of foreign trade in their consideration of cargo insurance. Moreover, we hope that the insurance agent and the insurance broker will find it helpful in their service to their clients.

For simplicity we are taking up the subject of cargo insurance, from the standpoint of the insurance buyer, under six headings:

- When to Insure
- How to Insure
- How Much to Insure
- Terms and Conditions of Coverage
- Cost of Insurance
- Adjustment of Claims

This article is not an extended treatise. In the interest of brevity it treats only with simple fundamental considerations. For those who wish to go into the subject more deeply, refer to "Selected References" on page 411.

However, if this article gives you a better understanding of marine insurance as it applies to cargo insurance, it will have accomplished its purpose.

When to Insure

One of the most basic and fundamental principles of insurance is that of insurable interest. Insurable interest is a deciding factor in the question of when to insure.

Generally speaking, a person has an interest in a marine adventure when he will benefit from the safe arrival of the vessel or cargo, or when he will be prejudiced by its loss, damage or detention. It is immediately apparent that this covers a broad field. Not only do the owners of the vessel and cargo benefit from their safe arrival, or suffer from their loss or damage but so do a number of other people, who, in the operation of trade, will have an ultimate benefit or loss.

Insurable interest, then, falls into two broad categories, the insurable interest of owners and the insurable interest of non-owners.

Ownership Situations: Terms of Sale

At what point does the title to property actually pass from seller to buyer? Determination of the ownership of goods moving in foreign or domestic trade is not always a simple matter.

The terms of sale govern this relationship of property to owner. An understanding of the different types of terms of sale is essential if we are to know when insurance should be placed.

The most widely accepted terms of sale definitions may be referenced in "Incoterms" available from the International Chamber of Commerce in New York, New York (212) 206-1150. However, the National Foreign Trade Council's "Revised American Foreign Trade Definitions—1941" are also considered an acceptable guide to the six groups of terms of sale.

1. Ex Point of Origin

(as "Ex Factory, "Ex Warehouse," etc.)

These terms require the seller to place the goods at the disposal of the buyer at the specified point of origin on the date, and within the period fixed. The buyer must then take delivery at the agreed place and must bear all future costs and risks.

It should be emphasized that the goods are at the risk of the buyer from the time he is obligated to take delivery, even though he may not actually take delivery at that time. He acquires an insurable interest as of that time and should protect his interest accordingly, since he can no longer look to the seller to do so.

2. FOB

(Free on Board)

Here the seller is required to bear costs and charges and to assume risks until the good are loaded on board a named carrier at a named point. This might be on board a railroad car at an inland point of departure or on board an ocean vessel at a port of shipment.

Loss or damage to the shipment is borne by the seller until loaded at the point named and by the buyer after loading at that point, and insurance protection should be arranged accordingly. Actual transfer of interest is evidenced by the carrier furnishing a clean bill of lading or other transportation receipt.

It should be noted that FOB sales terms, specifying named points beyond the seller's premises (for example, FOB vessel), place upon the seller the risks of transit until the title passes to the buyer at the point specified. In actual practice, however, FOB terms are often so loosely specified that it is not easily resolved whether the seller or the buyer should bear the risk of physical loss or damage.

The seller is better advised in this case to provide his own insurance protection through the use of an FOB Sales Endorsement to his policy, rather than rely on the warehouse-to-warehouse coverage contained in the buyer's insurance policy. The suggested coverage protects the seller from transit risks from the point of origin to the point at which title passes to the buyer. (Refer also second half of "Non-Ownership Situations" on page 397.)

When sales are made under letters of credit, the letters of credit normally cannot be used until an on-board bill of lading has been issued. If a loss or damage occurs before goods are loaded on board the ocean vessel, a clean on-board bill of lading will not be available and letters of credit cannot be used. This places a financial risk on the seller since he may not then be able to get the benefit of any insurance that the buyer may have arranged. Here again the seller should arrange for insurance to give him full protection.

At times, and particularly in certain trades, the seller on FOB terms may provide marine insurance on behalf of the buyer. However, this involves a non-ownership situation and is discussed on page 397.

3. FAS

(Free Along Side) as "FAS Vessel, named port of shipment"

These sales terms require the seller to place goods along side the vessel or on the dock designated by the buyer and to be responsible for loss or damage up to that point. Insurance under these terms is ordinarily placed by the buyer, but the seller should protect himself with an FOB Sales Endorsement, as described above, for risks prior to the transfer of title. As in the FOB discussion the non-ownership situation is discussed in "Non-Ownership Situations" which follows.

4. C & F

(Cost & Freight) Named Point of Destination

Under these terms, the seller's price includes the cost of transportation to the named point but does not include the cost of insurance. Insurance under these terms is the responsibility of the buyer. The seller is responsible for loss or damage until the goods enter the custody of the ocean carrier or, if an on-board bill of lading is required, when the good are actually delivered on board. Here again the seller needs insurance protection to that point at which his responsibility for loss or damage ceases.

5. CIF

(Cost, Insurance and Freight) Named Point of Destination

Under these terms the selling price includes the cost of the goods, marine insurance and transportation charges to the named point of destination. The seller is responsible for loss or damage until the goods have been delivered

into the custody of the ocean carrier or, when an "on board" bill of lading is required, until the goods have been delivered on board the vessel.

In CIF sales, the seller is obligated to provide and pay for marine insurance, and to provide war risk insurance as obtainable in his market at the time of shipment. War risk insurance is at the buyer's expense. The seller and buyer should be in clear agreement on this point since in time of war or crisis the cost of war risk insurance may change rapidly.

It is desirable that the goods be insured against both marine and war risk with the same underwriter so that there can be the least possibility of dispute arising as to the cause of loss, as in the case of missing vessels and, to a lesser degree, wartime collisions.

The character of the marine insurance should be agreed upon insofar as being WA (With Average) or FPA (Free of Particular Average), as well as any other special risks that are covered in specified trades, or against which the buyer may wish individual protection. Among the special risks that should be considered and agreed upon between seller and buyer, are theft, pilferage, leakage, breakage, sweat, contact with other cargoes and others peculiar to any particular trade. It is important that contingent or collect freight and customs duty should be insured to cover Free of Particular Average losses, as well as total loss after arrival and entry but before delivery.

In all cases, there should be a clear understanding as to the value for which the goods are to be insured. This may be of importance in case of assessment in general average (explained on page 409). Full insurance to value will avoid difficulty should a general average situation arise.

In CIF sales the seller must use ordinary care in selecting a financially sound underwriter. Should claims arise from a shipment, it is the buyer's responsibility to secure settlement. With the good will of the customer in mind, the exporter should select an underwriter providing fair, prompt and convenient loss service.

6. Ex Dock, Named Port of Importation

This term is more common to U.S. import than to export practice where it is seldom used. Under these terms the seller's price includes the cost of the goods and all additional charges necessary to put them on the dock at the named port of importation with import duty paid. The seller is then obligated to provide and pay for marine insurance and, in the absence of a specific agreement otherwise, war risk insurance.

The seller is responsible for any loss or damage, or both, until the expiration of the free time allowed on the dock at the named port of importation. Otherwise the comments under CIF terms above apply here as well.

Non-Ownership Situations

In many situations the seller has an insurable interest, even though title has passed to the buyer and he is therefore a non-owner. In these situations the seller should see that his interest is protected.

When the seller sells on terms FOB inland point, he transfers the title to the buyer before the commencement of the ocean voyage. In this case the obligation to place marine and war risk insurance rests, strictly speaking, with the buyer.

However, it is customary in many trades for the seller on FOB terms (or similar terms), by arrangement, to obtain insurance, as well as ocean freight space, for account of the buyer.

This is, in effect, an agency relationship. It can be provided for by a policy clause reading:

> "to cover all shipments made by or to the assured for their own account as principals, or as agents for others and in which they have an insurable interest, or for the account of others from which written instructions to insure them have been received prior to any known or reported loss, damage or accident or prior to sailing of vessel."

Moreover, the seller on FOB or other terms, under which the title passes to the buyer at some inland point of departure, will have a *financial* interest in the goods until payment has been received. This situation arises when the terms of payment call for sight draft against documents, or for acceptance at 30-60-90 days sight, or for open book account.

Under such circumstances, the seller will be well advised to place his own insurance to protect himself in the event that the loss or damage to the shipment impairs the buyer's desire to make payment as originally contemplated. For example, the buyer may be uninsured, or the buyer's coverage may be inadequate because of under-insurance or restricted conditions. The buyer's insurance company may be less liberal in loss adjustments than would the insurer of the seller or, because of currency restrictions, a foreign company may be hampered in its ability to transmit funds.

When claims are paid by a foreign insurance company, devaluation of foreign currencies may cause loss in exchange when the insurance is not expressed in United States dollars.

Insolvency of the foreign insurance carrier, while unlikely, could also occur to the embarrassment of the buyer.

In the event of the buyer's own insolvency, any claims collected under his own open policy might be recoverable in favor of his insolvent estate and not, in the first instance at least, in favor of the seller in this country.

At times the total loss of a shipment has prevented the payment for the goods. This has occurred in countries which would not allocate foreign exchange unless the goods are actually landed and cleared through customs.

While some of these contingencies may seem remote, others are not so remote. Certainly they all point up the fact that a seller does bear a financial risk until such time as payment from the foreign buyer is actually in hand.

The safe and simple way for the exporter to avoid these pitfalls is to merely stipulate in the sales terms that he will be responsible for providing the insurance as FOB Philadelphia, including Marine and War Risk insurance. This will enable him to place his own primary insurance coverage and deal throughout with his own insurance company in this country through his own agent or broker.

Whenever world currency dislocations exist this is a distinct advantage. In the event of a loss, the seller who has placed insurance in this country may be able to make replacement shipments without becoming involved in foreign exchange or import control difficulties. At the buyer's request, the seller can credit him with the insurance proceeds following the loss or damage to the original shipment and apply such credit to future shipments.

There are several countries whose laws require that marine insurance on shipments to those countries must be placed with local insurance companies. This has the effect of requiring the importer to furnish the insurance. However, the exporter can still protect himself by the purchase of "Contingency" or "Difference in Conditions" insurance which protects his own interests in the event the importer's insurance fails or falls short. While the cost of this is naturally less than the cost of primary insurance, it must be borne by the exporter.

In the situation facing the American importer the problems outlined above are reversed to some extent.

The American buyer on CIF terms must rely upon foreign underwriters, since the insurance will have been placed by the seller in the country of origin. Many of the insurance disadvantages already mentioned as applying to FOB export sales will apply to CIF purchases.

By purchasing on FOB, C & F or similar terms, the American importer can control his own insurance. He will then be able to deal with his own underwriters in case of loss or in case of demand for general average security.

In coastwise or intercoastal domestic shipments, sales are frequently made on an FOB dock basis, with or without instructions from the buyer as to the placing of marine insurance. However, a number of trade associations have adopted terms of sale under which the seller is required to effect insurance in the absence of instructions from the buyer to the contrary.

The terms of sale and terms of payment are all-important in the placing of marine insurance. The subject is a complex one, and needs will vary by trade and by commodity.

Both the foreign trader and the domestic trader will need to consult their insurance agents or brokers freely in working out the insurance protection best suited to his own requirements.

How to Insure

Formerly it was the practice to arrange specific marine insurance policies only when they were needed. This method is still used by those not regularly engaged in foreign trade—for example, by individuals shipping household goods or personal effects.

However, by far the greater volume of ocean marine insurance is now written under what is known as open policies. These are insurance contracts which remain in force until cancelled and under which individual successive shipments are reported or declared. The open policy saves time and expense for all concerned, whether underwriter, agent or assured.

The Open Policy

The shipper gains many advantages from the use of an open policy.

In the first place, he has automatic protection (up to the maximum limits stated in the policy) from the time shipments leave the warehouse at the place named in the policy for the commencement of transit. The policyholder warrants that shipments will be declared as soon as practicable, but unintentional failure to report will not void the insurance, since the goods are "held covered," subject to policy conditions. In effect, this is errors and omissions coverage, and it forestalls the possibility that, because of the press of business, goods may commence transit without being insured.

Second, the open policy provides a *convenient* way to report shipments. It also relieves the shipper from the necessity of arranging individual placings of insurance for each shipment.

Third, under an open policy the shipper has prior knowledge of the rate of premium that will be charged and thus can be *certain* of the cost. This in turn facilitates his quoting a landed sales price.

Finally, the use of the open policy creates a business relationship that may exist over a long period of time (CIGNA companies have more than one insured holding an open policy for over 100 years). This permits the insurer to learn the special requirements of its assureds and so to provide them with *individualized* protection, tailor-made to fit the specific situation. This may be an important factor in the case of loss adjustments at out-of-the-way ports around the world, or in overcoming problems peculiar to a given commodity.

From the underwriter's operating standpoint, the use of open policies represents a more *efficient* way of doing business. The ultimate benefits of this efficiency accrue to the policyholder through the reduction of the insurance company's expense.

Declarations, Bordereaus, Special Policies, and Certificates

There are two methods of reporting shipments under open policies.

In the case of imports, a short form of declaration will usually be sufficient, since there is no need to furnish evidence of insurance to third parties. This form calls for the name of the vessel and sailing date, points of shipment and destination, nature of commodity, description of units comprising the shipment, the amount of insurance desired and the number of the open policy under which the declaration is made. The declaration forms are prepared by the assured and are forwarded daily, weekly, or as shipments are made. The forms are forwarded to the insurance agent or broker for transmission to the company. When full information is not available at the time a declaration is made, a *provisional* report may be sent in. The "provisional" is closed when value is finally known. The premium is billed monthly in accordance with the schedule of rates provided by the policy. The bordereau is similar to the declaration in that it is simple to complete and is non-negotiable. It provides for multiple shipments within a prescribed monthly reporting period.

The same short form of declaration may be used at times for exports, if claims are to be returned by foreign consignees for adjustment in this country, in which case no special marine policy is issued.

However, in most cases the exporter must furnish evidence of insurance to his customer, to banks or to other third parties in order to permit the collection of claims abroad. This calls for a special marine policy, occasionally referred to as a certificate.

The special marine policy contains information similar to that shown on the declaration. In addition, it calls for the marks and numbers of the shipment, the name of the party to whom loss shall be payable (usually the assured "or orders" thus making the instrument negotiable upon endorsement by the assured), and the applicable policy provisions. Some of these provisions are standard clauses and are incorporated by reference only, while others are specific and apply to the individual shipment in question.

The special marine policy is generally prepared in four or more copies. The original (and duplicate if necessary) is negotiable and is forwarded with the shipping documents to the consignee. The remaining documents serve as office copies for the assured and for the company.

A special marine policy may be prepared by the assured, by the freight forwarder, by the insurance agent or broker or by the company. It is important that it be made out with care. The shipment should be described in sufficient detail to make identification clear, especially if more than one shipment is going forward by the same vessel. The voyage should be explicitly stated, as "New Castle, Pa., by rail to Philadelphia, *SS John Doe* to Santiago, Chile." If the ultimate destination is an inland city, this should be made clear.

The terms "special marine policy" and "certificate" are both used. The practical effect of the two is the same, but a word as to their difference will be of interest.

In former years the use of "certificate" was customary. This, as the name implies, certifies that a shipment has been insured under a given open policy, and that the certificate represents and takes the place of such open policy, the provisions of which are controlling.

Because of the objections that an instrument of this kind did not constitute a "policy" within the requirements of letters of credit, it has become the practice to use a special marine policy. This makes no reference to the open policy and stands on its own feet as an obligation of the underwriting company.

In some cases, exporters insure through freight forwarders when arranging for forwarding, warehousing, documentation, ocean freight space and the other requirements of overseas trade. While this method may have the merit of simplicity, it should be emphasized that there are definite advantages in having one's own policy and that this need not entail burdensome clerical detail. These advantages are cited below.

In the first place, the exporter gets conditions of insurance suited to his own requirements, rather than coverage designed for general application over a wide diversity of commodities and trades.

Second, rates will be based upon the known hazards and experience of the exporter's business, rather than upon an average of which his business is only a part. There will thus be control of insurance costs rather than the reverse.

Third, the exporter will be able to call upon the services of his local insurance agent or brother, and through him upon the services of the company, in such matters as loss prevention service and packing advice, and in the adjustment of claims.

Fourth, in certain circumstances where the shipper desires coverage even after the goods reach the consignee, the open policy is able to provide extended coverage.

Fifth, the open policy attaches automatically and remains continuous until cancelled thus allowing the exporter freedom to ship.

The use of his own policy need not necessarily require the exporter to prepare special policies. Arrangements can be made allowing the freight forwarder to provide these special policies through the facilities of the exporter's insurance company.

How Much to Insure

Valuation Clauses

The question of how much to insure is closely related to the question of how to insure.

Unlike the fire insurance policy, and many others, the marine insurance policy is a "valued" one. That is, when the insurance is placed, a value is agreed upon. In the case of total loss, this amount is paid. In the case of partial loss, a percentage of the total insured value is recoverable. This will be discussed more fully in considering adjustment of claims (refer to "Particular Average" on page 407).

The purpose in taking out insurance on goods moving in foreign trade is to be made whole in case of loss. This "whole" clearly includes a number of factors. There are the basic invoice costs, additional charges in the invoice for export packing, inland freight, consular and other fees, ocean freight, insurance premiums and anticipated profit.

The amount of insurance must be governed accordingly, if the "whole" is to be restored in case of loss. The profit item is customarily provided for by a percentage increase applied to the specific items. This increase is also useful in the event of assessment for general average contribution, which is based on the "sound arrival value" of the shipment. (Refer to "General Average" on page 408.) This value can well be larger than that contemplated at the time of shipment, because of an increase in market values while the shipment was in transit.

A valuation clause in common use reads:

> "valued premium included at amount of invoice, including all charges in the invoice and including prepaid and/or advanced and/or guaranteed freight, if any, plus _____%." (This is usually 10% on exports.)

This clause does not require the use of a formula to calculate the total premium, as is the case when the premium itself is included in the valuation as a specific item to which the increase also applies.

The "premium included" method is suitable when premium rates are low, as in normal times. However, when rates become higher, as for war risk in time of war, the premium should be calculated by separate item.

A clause may sometimes be used which provides that if insurance is declared prior to shipment or prior to known or reported loss, the valuation shall be in the amount of the declaration. This clause secures maximum flexibility, thus meeting the needs of letters of credit or other financial requirements. Shipments not so declared are valued as provided by the formula contained in the valuation clause.

At times of fluctuating values, importers dealing in such raw commodities as cotton, rubber, sugar, coffee, burlap, etc., may wish to be protected for an increase in value during the voyage. This can be accomplished by the use of an increased value clause. Under this, the premium is paid and losses are adjusted on the basis of the peak value reached while the shipment is in transit.

In certain trades special valuation classes may have become standardized by long usage and may be incorporated in the open policy accordingly.

Terms and Conditions of Coverage

More than a superficial knowledge of policy coverage is essential to a proper understanding of marine insurance. The study of an authoritative text is desirable, but it is hoped that this section will simplify an understanding of the more basic fundamentals of coverage.

Perils Insured Against

A current form of perils clause retains many quaint terms and may read as follows:

> "touching the adventures and perils which this company is contented to bear, and takes upon itself, they are of the seas, fires, assailing thieves, jettisons, barratry of the master and mariners and all other like perils, losses and misfortunes (illicit or contraband trade excepted in all cases) that have or shall come to the hurt, detriment or damage of the said goods and merchandise or any part thereof."

The terms in this clause might be explained.

"Perils of the sea" includes unusual action of wind and waves (often described as "stress of weather" or "heavy weather"), stranding, lightning, collision and damage by sea water when caused by insured perils such as opening of the seams of the vessel by stranding or collision.

"Fire" includes both direct fire damage and also consequential damage, as by smoke or steam, and loss resulting from efforts to extinguish a fire.

"Assailing thieves" refers to a forcible taking rather than clandestine theft or mere pilferage.

"Jettison" is the throwing of articles overboard, usually to lighten the ship in time of emergency.

"Barratry" is the willful misconduct of master or crew and would include theft, wrongful conversion, intentional casting away of vessel or any breach of trust with dishonest intent.

"All other perils" means perils like those already enumerated, i.e. perils of the sea. It does not mean "all risks" in the sense of today's use of that term.

Still other perils are included and represent extensions of coverage added from time to time to the basic protection of the sea perils.

Specific mention of explosion broadens the coverage to include explosion however caused, except by war perils. Explosion resulting from fire is covered under "fires."

The Inchmaree Clause (so-called for a celebrated legal decision involving a vessel of that name) extends the policy to cover loss resulting from a latent defect of the carrying vessel's hull or machinery. Defined as a defect that is not discoverable by due diligence, latent defect is not, by law, recoverable from the vessel owner, and the Inchmaree Clause thus plugs a gap that would otherwise exist in complete protection.

Loss resulting from errors of navigation or management of the vessel by the master or the crew, and for which the vessel owner is likewise relieved of liability by law, is also covered by the Inchmaree Clause.

A number of coverages refer to hazards to which goods are susceptible while on land. The shore clause extends the basic perils to include risks of collision, derailment, overturn, sprinkler leakage, windstorm, earthquake, flood and collapse of docks or wharves.

A third group of hazards may be specifically provided for and additional premium paid. The more common perils in this category are theft, pilferage, nondelivery, fresh water damage, oil damage, sweat damage (caused by condensation dripping from the skin or bulkheads of the vessel or forming on the cargo itself), contact with other cargo, breakage, leakage, hook hole damage and damage to refrigerated cargo resulting from the breakdown of refrigerating machinery.

Coverage is often provided upon an "all risks" basis. (*See* "Average Terms" which follows.)

"Average" Terms

The perils specified by the policy govern the *nature* of loss and damage recoverable under the insurance. The "average" terms govern the *extent* of coverage.

The word "average," in its insurance connotation, means "loss less than total." It comes from the French word *avarie*, which means "damage to ship or cargo," (and ultimately from the Arabic word *awarijah*, which means "merchandise damaged by sea water").

A "particular average" loss is one that affects specific interests only. A "general average" loss is one that affects all cargo interests on board the vessel as well as the ship herself. Particular average and general average losses will be discussed in the consideration of claims. (Refer to "Total Loss" on page 407, "Particular Average" on page 407, "General Average" on page 408, and "General Average: Illustration" on page 409.)

"Free of Particular Average" (FPA) coverage is the narrowest in common use. This clause provides that in addition to total losses, partial losses resulting from perils of the sea are recoverable, but only in the event that the carrying vessel has stranded, sunk, burnt, been on fire or been in collision.

Two forms of FPA coverage must be understood.

In the case of cargoes shipped underdeck, it is customary to use a modification of the English conditions form of FPA Clause (FPA-EC) reading:

> "Free of particular average (unless general) or *unless* the vessel or craft be stranded, sunk, burnt, on fire or in collision with another vessel..."

In the case of cargoes stowed on deck, it is more usual to find the American conditions form of FPA Clause (FPA-AC) reading:

> "Free of particular average (unless general) or *unless caused* by stranding, sinking, burning or collision with another vessel...."

It should be noted that under the English conditions, partial losses resulting from sea perils are recoverable, provided one of the enumerated disasters has taken place, without requiring that the damage actually be caused by such disaster. Under both the English and American forms of FPA Clause, both general average and salvage charges are recoverable.

"With Average" (WA) coverage is a more inclusive form of protection. In its standard form a typical clause may read:

> "Subject to particular average if amounting to 3%, unless general or the vessel and/or craft is stranded, sunk, burnt, on fire and/or in collision, each package separately insured or on the whole."

This coverage gives the assured protection for partial damage by sea perils, if the partial damage amounts to 3% (or other percentage as specified) or more of the value of the whole shipment or of a shipping package. If the vessel has stranded, sunk, been on fire or in collision, the percentage requirement is waived and losses from sea perils are recoverable in full.

Additional *named perils* may be added to the WA Clause. Theft, pilferage, nondelivery, fresh water damage, sweat damage, breakage and leakage are often covered. The combination of perils needed by a particular assured will naturally depend upon the commodity being shipped and the trade involved.

The "all risk" clause is a logical extension of the broader forms of "With Average" coverage. This clause reads:

> "To cover against all risks of physical loss or damage from any external cause irrespective of percentage, but excluding, nevertheless, the risk of war, strikes, riots, seizure, detention and other risks excluded by the F.C.&S. (Free of Capture and Seizure) Warranty and the S.R.&C.C. (Strikes, Riots and Civil Commotion) Warranty in this policy, excepting to the extent that such risk are specifically covered by endorsement."

Some types of loss are commonly excluded and others not recoverable, even under the "all risks" clauses.

Types of Loss Excluded

A careful reading of the so-called "all risk" clause will show that this coverage is not quite so all-inclusive as the name would indicate since it covers only physical loss or damage from external cause(s) and specifically affirms the exclusion of war risks and strikes and riots unless covered by endorsement. These losses are excluded, either by expressed exclusions, conditions or warranties written into the policy or by implied conditions or warranties that are read into every marine policy by legal interpretation.

An "all risks" policy may, of course, *expressly exclude* certain types of damage such as marring and scratching of unboxed automobiles or bending and twisting entirely or unless amounting to a specified percentage or amount.

Also, certain perils such as War and Strikes, Riots and Civil Commotions are commonly excluded, but these perils can be and usually are reinstated, at least in part, by special endorsement or by a separate policy for an additional premium. These perils are dealt with in this way to permit ready revision of terms, conditions and rates which may be required at short notice as world conditions change.

Another common exclusion is the "Delay Clause" which excludes claims for loss of market and for loss, damage or deterioration arising from delay. This exclusion appears in almost every cargo policy.

An underwriter is exceedingly reluctant, however, to assume any liability for loss of market, which is generally considered a "trade loss" and uninsurable. A market loss, furthermore, is an indirect or consequential damage. It is not a "physical loss or damage."

Legal decisions have established two important implied warranties in the marine policies, that of legality of the venture and that of seaworthiness. The latter is of little concern today since policies commonly waive the warranty of seaworthiness by stating that seaworthiness is admitted as between the assured and the insurer.

The insurer is not at liberty, however, to waive the implied warranty of legality. Such a waiver would be against public policy and the law of the land.

Certain implied conditions are not written into the policy but they are so basic to understanding between underwriter and assured that the law gives them much the same effect as if written. Thus, it is implied: (a) that the assured will exercise the utmost good faith in disclosing to his underwriter all facts material to the risk when applying for insurance; (b) that the generally established usages of trade applicable to the insured subject matter are followed; and (c) that the assured shall not contribute to loss through willful fault or negligence.

Furthermore, there is a rather broad class of losses, often described as arising from "inherent vice" whose exclusion is implied in every policy. This type of exclusion is reinforced by the words "from any external cause" in the "all risks" coverage. The word "risk" itself implies that only *fortuitous* losses are intended to be covered. Insurance protects against hazards, not certainties.

It is unreasonable to expect indemnity for damage which one can foresee is bound to occur during any normal transit, and which arises solely because of the nature or condition of the goods shipped. Such damage is said to arise from "inherent vice" which may be defined as an *internal* cause rather than an *external* cause of damage. An example of damage from inherent vice is deterioration of imperfectly cured skins.

Packing is an integral part of the thing shipped and damage caused by the original packing, or lack thereof, does not arise from an externality. It is excluded no matter when the damage itself may occur. For instance, nails may be driven by a careless packer into the contents of a package. Such damage occurring prior to attachment of the insurance is obviously not covered.

On the other hand, an underwriter may inspect a shipment and find that it is packed in an unusual and inferior manner, but may nevertheless accept the risk at a rate of premium which takes into account the hazard represented by the packing. In such a negotiation, the implied condition of utmost good faith, which is never waived, requires that the assured disclose fully all the facts bearing upon the special risk which he asks his insurer to assume.

Similarly, the underwriter is not liable for that ordinary and unavoidable loss of weight caused by evaporation as in ore shipments. Such loss of weight is a "trade loss," allowed for in the price quoted between traders and, from an insurance viewpoint, should not be regarded as a loss at all. In the United States it is not unusual to recognize this kind of exclusion, which would otherwise be implied, by stipulating the normal and expected shortage for which the underwriters will not respond.

When shortage, breakage or leakage is specifically insured "irrespective of percentage," the intent to so cover is clear.

Underwriters also have the ability to deal with small nuisance claims by introducing deductible averages and franchises into the policy. The deductible average is an amount that is subtracted from each loss whereby the assured always bears part of the loss. The franchise on the other hand rules out small claims. Franchises are usually stated as percentages, although occasionally a dollar amount is used. Claims equal to or in excess of the franchise will be paid in full.

It is thus seen that some exclusions can be modified by endorsement as a result of negotiation between assured and underwriter. Others such as the implied warranty of legality of the venture cannot be waived.

As the broadest form of coverage in common use, "all risks" insurance is also the most expensive, and it is not necessarily required by all types of cargo. A shipper whose goods are susceptible to many kinds of damage may need "all risks" insurance. But a shipper whose goods are not subject to various kinds of partial loss should not incur the expense of insurance protection that is broader than necessary.

Most exporters will wish to secure the most complete protection available to avoid controversy with customers, but a concern shipping to its own foreign branch may consider it unnecessary and uneconomical to insure against small losses as from breakage or pilferage. Similarly a large importer knowing by experience the range of losses from leakage or other causes may wish to treat this as a trade loss and insure only against those perils that entail the possibility of a large loss.

FPA coverage is ordinarily suitable for bulk cargoes such as oil, coal and ore.

In general, most manufactured goods will qualify for "all risks" protection. The policyholder's insurance agent or broker will be of help in arranging the coverage best suited to his needs. Letter of credit terms or other specific insurance instructions may determine the extent of coverage required by an exporter.

Damage resulting from negligence on the part of the vessel operators in loading, handling on board, stowing or discharging cargo is recoverable from the carrier under the provisions of the various "Carriage of Goods by Sea" Acts. However, prudent shippers will not rely on this to restrict their insurance coverage. By collecting such claims from underwriters, shippers need not concern themselves with seeking recovery from the carrier. They can leave this to the insurance company, confident that it will make every effort to secure all recoveries that may be due and to credit the assured's loss record with every possible deduction that will help him to merit lower rates.

Extensions of Coverage

Three specialized types of coverage are also provided by the open cargo policy.

The first covers *shipments by aircraft* on "all risks" conditions, irrespective of percentage, but excluding loss due to cold or changes in atmospheric pressure. While it is true that insurance on air express and air freight shipments can be obtained from the airlines, this has disadvantages over controlling the insurance of such shipments by declaring them under an open policy. The insurance purchased from the airlines may merely cover the shipment while it is in the possession of the carrier, without providing full warehouse-to-warehouse coverage. Moreover, the insurance perils may not be as broad as under the shipper's own policy. In addition, when insuring with the airlines, the shipper will be unable to deal with his own underwriters at the time of loss adjustment.

The second covers *mail shipments*, also upon "all risks" conditions, the insured warranting that all packages will be mailed in conformity with parcel post or foreign mail regulations in force at the time of shipment in the country of exportation. While mail insurance can be purchased through the post office, it has the same disadvantages as those given above for insurance purchased from airlines.

The third covers *U.S. import duties* in the case of shipments sustaining partial damage. A separate amount is declared on import shipments to cover the duty that will be due, and the assured agrees to make all reasonable efforts to secure refunds of duty on shipments arriving in damaged condition.

Currency (Term) of Insurance

Formerly, the marine policy covered only from the time the goods were actually loaded on board the ocean vessel at the port of shipment until they were "discharged and safely landed" at the port of destination. This was later extended by adding the words "including transit by craft, raft and/or lighter to and from the vessel."

More recently, warehouse-to-warehouse coverage was provided. Under this, the risks covered by the policy attach from the time goods leave the warehouse for commencement of transit and continue during ordinary course of transit until delivered to final warehouse at destination, or until the expiration of 15 days (30 if destination is outside the limits of the port), whichever shall first occur. In the case of delay in excess of the time limit specified, if it arises from circumstances beyond his control, the assured is "held covered" if he gives prompt notice and pays additional premium.

A growing demand for extension of coverage during World War II led underwriters to adopt the Marine Extension Clause 1943. This extension which supersedes the aforementioned Warehouse-to-Warehouse Clause, is found in practically all open cargo policies. The function of this clause is to broaden warehouse-to-warehouse coverage by eliminating the requirement that ordinary course of transit be maintained and the 15- or 30-day time limit at destination. Moreover, continuation of coverage is provided when certain conditions necessitate discharge of goods from vessel at a port other than the original destination. The most recent form of Marine Extension Clause was developed in 1952. It too provides for extensions as the 1943 version, and adds that the assured will act with reasonable dispatch.

The currency of insurance has thus been broadened from "waterborne" only to full warehouse-to-warehouse protection as extended. Underwriters must be notified and additional coverage secured only if interruption of transit under the assured's control is contemplated. Such situations will occur at times, and assureds should fully inform their insurance agents or brokers of their needs in this respect in order that coverage may be extended as necessary.

Strikes and War Risks

Strikes, riots and civil commotion coverage can be added to the open policy by endorsement. Usually referred to as the S.R.&C.C. Endorsement, it extends the policy to cover damage, theft, pilferage, breakage or destruction of the insured property directly caused by strikers, locked-out workmen or persons taking part in labor disturbances, riots or civil commotions.

Destruction of and damage to property caused by vandalism, sabotage and malicious acts of person(s) regardless of (political/ideological/terroristic) intent be it accidental or otherwise is also held covered under S.R.&C.C. unless so excluded in the F.C.&S. (free of capture and seizure) warranty in the policy.

The S.R.&C.C. Endorsement excludes coverage for any case damage or deterioration as a result of delay or loss of market, change in temperature/humidity, loss resulting from hostilities or warlike operations, absence/shortage/withholding power, fuel, labor during a strike (riot or civil commotion) weapons of war that employ atomic or nuclear fusion/fission.

The current form provides limited coverage within the United States, Commonwealth of Puerto Rico, Canal Zone, Virgin Islands and Canada for damage caused by any agent of any faction engaged in warlike hostilities/operations provided the agent is working secretly and is not in cohesion with the military forces where the described property is situated.

War coverage is customarily furnished in conjunction with marine insurance, even though it is written under a separate policy.

The older form of marine policies, in addition to insuring against the perils of the seas, insured against

> "men of war...enemies...letters of mart and countermart, arrests, restraint and detainments of all kings, princes and people of what nation, condition or quality soever..."

This ancient language granted war risks protection.

In order to eliminate the war cover from the marine policy it became customary to add a "free of capture and seizure" clause, stating that the policy did not cover warlike

operations or its consequences, whether before or after the actual declaration of war. The current open policy omits war perils from its insuring conditions and in all cases will include a F.C.&S. clause. War coverage is customarily furnished in conjunction with an open cargo policy and is written under a separate, distinct policy—the War Risk Only Policy.

Not unlike its marine counterpart as respects the basic policy conditions, the war policy covers only against war risks as outlined in detail in some dozen rather specific paragraphs. The policy conditions must be read for complete understanding. In general, they cover risks of capture and seizure, destruction or damage by warlike operations in prosecution of hostilities, civil wars and insurrections or in the application of sanctions under international agreements. Delay or loss of market is excluded. Loss or expense arising from detainments, nationalization of the government to or from which the goods are insured or seizure under quarantine or customs regulations is also excluded.

War risk insurance attaches as goods are first loaded on board an overseas vessel at the port of shipment, and it ceases to attach as goods are landed at the intended port of discharge or on expiry of 15 days from arrival of the overseas vessel whichever first occurs. It includes transshipment and intermediate overland transit to an on-carrying overseas vessel, if any, but in no case for more than 15 days counting from midnight of the day of arrival of the overseas vessel at the intended port of discharge. If in transshipment, the 15-day period is exceeded, the insurance re-attaches as the interest is loaded on the on-carrying vessel. In case the voyage is terminated and the goods are discharged at a port or place other than the original port of discharge, such port or place shall be deemed the intended port of discharge.

The war risk policy is subject to 48 hours cancellation by either party. However, it cannot be cancelled on shipments upon which insurance has already attached. Since the cancellation provision is used at times for changing the conditions of insurance the current coverage should be studied for exact understanding of the war risk policy.

Is war risk insurance needed in ordinary times? Or should it be bought only when international relations become strained to the breaking point?

Loss from floating mines are still deemed to be war risks. More than five hundred mine casualties have been reported since the close of World War II. It is unhappily true that civil strife or other warlike operations have rarely been entirely absent from one quarter of the world or another during the past several decades. The possibility of full scale warfare can seldom be dismissed from our thinking.

It would seem that the prudent assured must continue, for many years to come, to carry war risks insurance for the protection of his overseas shipments.

Cost of Insurance

Considerations in Rating

Unlike most other types of insurance rates, the rates for marine insurance are not standardized. Rather, they are generally determined by the cargo, experience of the risk and the judgment of the underwriter.

In a broad sense, underwriters consider certain basic factors of experience. One is the *cost of loss from major casualties* in specific *voyage* classifications. This factor may be modified for certain commodities indicating variation in major casualty experience because of peculiarities of the trade. A second is *particular average* experience by *commodity*. A third factor is *particular average* experience by *individual accounts*, which differ from each other in varying degree and for innumerable reasons.

Underwriters usually give specific consideration to these factors:

1. Type of coverage

2. Characteristics of commodities involved

3. Origin, destination and routing

4. Carriers used

5. Storage or transshipment en route, if any

6. Effect of trade losses, such as shrinkage, normal loss in weight, etc.

7. Seasonal character of shipments

8. Packing

9. Value—as it affects packing, susceptibility to pilferage, etc.

10. Assured's experience as a foreign trader

11. Shipping and delivery practices

12. Attitude toward claims by assured or his consignees

13. Attitude toward third party recoveries

14. Salvage possibilities under the individual account

Any number of these factors may affect the experience

As experience under an open cargo policy develops, the premium and loss record will be reviewed at intervals, and rate adjustments will be made, if the record and existing circumstances justify such action in the opinion of the underwriter.

Loss Prevention

The primary function of insurance is to redistribute loss and so to manage risk. An equally important function of insurance, and one which is economically more creative, is the actual prevention of loss.

Loss and damage to overseas shipments may be attacked at point of origin through improved packing and marking. They may also be attacked by supervision of loading and discharge to minimize pilferage or by study of storage and handling in course of transit to limit breakage, leakage and other causes of loss. Knowledge of port conditions, both here and in foreign countries, and many other kinds of in-

formation of interest made available to the foreign trader are of assistance in preventing or reducing marine losses.

Underwriters have not been unmindful of the assistance that they can render in this connection. The extent and quality of the service which an insurance company is prepared to render in helping with loss prevention problems is one factor that a shipper should bear in mind in selecting his underwriter.

The theoretical goal of packaging engineers is to devise export packing that will be just strong enough to enable the shipment to reach destination in a sound condition. Too weak a package will fail in its purpose; too strong a package will add unnecessarily to the ultimate cost of the product. The marine loss control department of an insurance company makes available its long accumulated experience in this highly specialized and technical field to the overseas shipper.

There are many types of packing: the solid and corrugated fiber cartons; the nailed wood box; the wire bound or strapped box; the cleated fibre board or plywood box; the open wooden or sheathed crates; the drums of metal, fibre or plywood; textile and multiple-ply bags and bales; barrels of many types. The physical properties of the commodity being shipped, its value and the voyage it must undergo will all have a bearing on the optimum packaging that must be provided. Domestic packing is seldom suitable for export purposes, where increased handling, stowage pressures and a wide range of other hazards are likely to be encountered. The "loss prevention" representative of the insurance company will frequently be able to suggest improvements that will result in reduced costs and improved outturns.

Breakage will be reduced by packaging of sufficient strength and proper construction. Water damage and corrosion can be controlled by the use of liners, by the coating of metal parts with special preservatives and in other ways.

Pilferage, one of the most serous forms of marine loss, may be reduced through the use of clips and seals, the use of corrugated fasteners and the marking of packages in such a way as not to disclose the nature of the contents. By making theft physically more difficult, packing designed to prevent pilferage increases the likelihood that a thief will be caught in the act. At the same time, it makes pilferage activity more evident, and thus places greater responsibility on the carrier in whose custody the loss has occurred. This, in turn, facilitates the collection of recoveries and encourages greater care in handling future shipments of a similar nature.

Proper marking will indicate the requirement for any special handling or stowage. It will also make for easier identification at destination.

The use of intermodal containers and air freight carriers for the transport of a great variety of cargo has become increasingly popular in recent years. When loaded and sealed at assured's plant, carried overland to the port, stowed under deck aboard ship and discharged with care, the containers can be an efficient and protective means of shipping cargo. Equally, adequate packing and marking air cargo can effectively influence the sound arrival of goods. Loss prevention experts give important advice on how to load the container or air freight carrier to prevent damage and assist in routing to prevent hijack.

Also new and growing is the shipment of cargo by air freight.

Technical assistance in the loss control field should be available to all holders of open policies. However, attention must necessarily be concentrated where the volume of shipment, and the nature of the commodity, permits worthwhile savings to be effected.

Prevention and reduction of losses through better packing and handling will have these positive results: a more satisfied consignee; lower insurance costs; an economic saving to the commercial community.

Adjustment of Claims

In the adjustment of claims, exporters and their consignees will tend to rely largely upon foreign claims and settling agents. Importers and domestic shippers will avail themselves of the services of their insurance agents and brokers.

However, some knowledge of loss procedure is valuable to those engaged in foreign and domestic trade. It is helpful both in facilitating claim recoveries and in maintaining a closer control over loss experience.

Duties of the Assured

When loss or damage occurs, it is the responsibility of the insurance company to indemnify the assured in accordance with the policy terms and conditions. Nevertheless, the policyholder must meet certain obligations, and these should be clearly understood.

First, the assured must make every reasonable effort to minimize the loss, to "*sue and labor*," in the language of marine insurance. Second he must *immediately notify* the nearest agent of his underwriters, arrange for a survey of the damage and supply the necessary commercial documents. Third, he must make *timely written claim* upon the carrier.

The *sue and labor* clause of the open cargo policy will read essentially as follows:

> "In case of any loss or misfortune it shall be lawful and necessary to and for the assured, his or their factors, servants and assigns to sue, labor, and travel, for, in and about the defense, safeguard and recovery of the goods and merchandise or any part thereof...to the charges whereof this company will contribute according to the rate and quantity of the sum herein insured."

In other words, the assured—shipper or consignee as the case may be—must act as a prudent uninsured owner would act in keeping his insured loss at a minimum. Reasonable charges incurred for this purpose are collectible under the policy.

Such steps should be taken promptly in order to prevent additional damage. For example, when a shipment of canned goods arrives with some leaking cans in each of several cartons, the leaking cans must be taken out if rusting and label damage are to be minimized. The expense insured in this operation may be recovered under the insurance.

Prompt notice of loss must be given to the nearest representative of the insurance company. In the United States and Canada, this will usually be given through the agent or broker to a claim and loss office of the insurance company. Abroad, underwriters are represented by claims or settling agents or, in some areas, by their own offices. Each special policy lists such loss representatives in the world's principal seaports. Representation at other ports will consist of the local correspondent of the Board of American Institute of Marine Underwriters, or, if none, the nearest Lloyd's Agent.

The claims agent or other representative should be asked to arrange survey and issue a certificate stating the cause and extent of loss or damage. Carrier's representative should be requested to attend the survey. Container and contents should be preserved in the condition in which received until survey has been completed, unless further damage would result by so doing. The survey fee is customarily paid by the consignee, but it is properly included in a valid claim under the insurance.

Claim upon the carrier (ocean or inland) should be made in writing in every instance, preferably before or at the time of taking delivery of the goods. In the case of concealed damage, claim should be made as soon as the damage is known. The form of claim is not important. It should identify the shipment by vessel and bill of lading and state that the carrier will be held responsible for damage thereto. A copy of this letter is necessary to support a claim on underwriters, who have a right to be subrogated to the assured's claim against the carrier.

If a shipment appears damaged or short weight at the time of taking delivery, the consignee or his agent should request an immediate survey by the carrier, and in receipting for the goods he should note the exact condition of the shipment as received. In the event that the carrier will not make delivery unless a clean receipt is given, he should immediately file written notice, describing the condition of the shipment as received and holding the carrier liable for any loss or damage that a subsequent survey may disclose.

Any reply from the carrier should be submitted with the other documents to the insurance company representative. However, the submission of the claim papers to the insurance company representative should not be held up for the carrier's acknowledgment.

The Adjustment

Should the survey confirm that loss or damage has occurred, the following documents will usually be needed in order that prompt adjustment may be carried out and payment secured.

1. Original and duplicate copies of the special marine policy or certificate of insurance.
2. Ocean bill of lading—also transshipment bill of lading and railway freight note when applicable.
3. Original shipper's invoice.
4. Packing list, weight certificates or other evidence of the nature and condition of the goods at the time of shipment.
5. Survey report of the underwriter's representative.
6. Copy of claim on ocean carrier and (if available) the reply thereto.
7. In special cases, other documents may be requested.

Total Loss

An *actual* total loss occurs when the goods are destroyed, when the assured is irretrievably deprived of their possession or when they arrive so damaged as to cease to be a thing of the kind insured. Examples of this last, which is spoken of as a "loss of Specie," are cement arriving as rock or textiles as rags.

Adjustment of actual total losses usually involves little difficulty. The policy being a valued one, payment for total loss is in the full amount of the policy. Disasters likely to give rise to total loss include fire, sinking or stranding of the vessel, collision and loss overboard in the course of loading or discharge.

A *constructive* total loss occurs when the expense of recovering or repairing the goods would exceed their value after this expenditure had been incurred.

In the adjustment of constructive total losses, the value of any remaining salvage abandoned to underwriters may at time, by agreement, be taken into consideration, with payment to the assured upon a net basis. Otherwise, underwriters pay full insured value and may then dispose of the salvage for their own account, provided they have elected to accept abandonment.

A survey report may not be practicable when a total loss has taken place, but the documents should include evidence that the shipment was actually loaded on board the ocean vessel in the full quantity claimed. If the loss was due to sea peril, a "master's protest" will usually be required. This certifies the fact that unusually heavy weather or other exceptional circumstance was encountered during the voyage and is extended to confirm the loss of the shipment in question. In claims for total loss, it is especially necessary that a full set of insurance certificates and bills of lading be submitted to the insurance company representative.

Particular Average

There are two kinds of particular average losses: the total loss of a part of the goods, and the arrival of goods at destination in a damaged condition.

In the first situation, it is necessary to determine how much of the total amount insured is applicable to the missing item. In homogeneous or fungible cargo that is, cargo which is capable of mutual substitution, like oil or coal—it is frequently a matter of simple arithmetic. The value of the unit of measurement of the cargo is found by dividing the amount of insurance by the total number of units in the shipment. This value multiplied by the number of missing units gives the value of the loss.

Where a normal or trade loss is to be expected, as in cargo subject to leakage, slackage or loss of moisture during the voyage, the method of calculation is slightly different. The value of the insurance is divided by the number of units in the "expected outturn," that is, the expected arrived quantity rather than the shipped quantity. This can be determined either by the normal percentage of trade loss for similar shipments or by examinations of sound arrived cargo forming part of the shipment in question. While this method will produce a somewhat higher insured value per unit, it naturally requires the normal or trade loss to be deducted in calculating the actual shortage sustained.

In the case of general cargo with the policy covering diverse articles as invoiced to the purchaser and insured in a lump sum, it will be necessary to apportion the total insurance over the specific item for which a claim is being made. The following example shows the usual method of doing this:

Total invoice	$1,000
Insured for	$1,100
Insurance ratio	110%
Invoice value of items lost	$50
Insured in proportion (110%)	$55

Adjustment of claims on goods arriving in a damaged condition requires a different method of approach. Here the consignee and the surveyor attempt to reach an agreed percentage of depreciation, and this is applied to the insured value of the damaged articles. At times the depreciation agreed upon may be in terms of units of goods (as yards of cloth, for example), and in such cases the insured value of such quantity is the loss recoverable. On the other hand, a flat dollar amount of depreciation may be assessed.

When the percentage of depreciation cannot be mutually agreed upon, the damaged goods must be sold in order to arrive at the extent of loss. When this method is used, the calculation is a comparison of the sound wholesale value of the goods with the damaged values at the time and place of sale. This percentage is then applied to the insured value of the damaged articles. Auction charges and other costs of sale are added to determine the total amount recoverable. The element of market fluctuation is thus eliminated.

It is sometimes incorrectly assumed that when damaged goods are sold to determine the extent of loss, the underwriter is obligated to pay the difference between the amount of insurance and the net proceeds of the sale. This method of adjustment, known as "salvage loss" is regularly used only if goods are justifiably sold short of destination.

If damaged goods can be advantageously repaired at destination, the underwriter will pay the actual cost of such repairs, not exceeding the insured value of the article. A specialized situation arises in the case of damage to *machinery*. Here the policy provides that either the company will be liable for the proportion of the insured value of the lost or damaged part, or it will be liable, at the assured's option, for the cost and expense (including labor and forwarding charges) of replacing or repairing the lost or damaged part. In no event, however, will the company's liability be greater than the insured value of the complete machine.

A somewhat similar situation arises in the case of damage to *labels or wrappers*. Here the policy ordinarily provides that the underwriter shall not be liable for more than an amount sufficient to pay the cost of new labels, together with the cost of reconditioning the goods, but in no event for more than the insured value of the damaged merchandise.

General Average

A general average loss may occur whether goods are insured or not. It is one that results from an intentional sacrifice (or expenditure) incurred by the master of a vessel in time of danger for the benefit of both ship and cargo. The classic example of this is jettison to lighten a stranded vessel. From the most ancient times, the maritime laws of all trading nations have held that such a sacrifice shall be borne by all for whose benefit the sacrifice was made, and not alone by the owner of the cargo thrown overboard.

The principles of general average have been refined over the years, and they have inevitably come to reflect the increasing complexity of present day commerce. A vessel owner may and does declare his vessel under general average whenever, *for the common good in time of danger* an intentional sacrifice of ship or cargo has been made, or an extraordinary expenditure has been incurred. In actual practice, general averages result mainly from strandings,

fires, collisions and from engaging salvage assistance or putting into a port of refuge following a machinery breakdown or other peril.

The preparation of a general average adjustment is a complex accounting operation. It is entrusted to professionally trained *average adjusters* (not the insurance company) and frequently requires two or three years for completion.

While the shipper need not concern himself with the adjustment itself, he or his consignee must take action at three points. First, he must post *security* in order to obtain release of cargo at port of destination. Second, he must furnish certain *information* relating to the value of the shipment. Third, he must pay the general average *contribution* at such time as the assessment is finally levied.

Security is required by vessel agents before they release cargo under general average. Until this security has been provided, the ship owner has a lien on the goods and has the right to retain them in his possession.

The security is in two parts. First is the general average bond or agreement *signed by the cargo owner* himself (not the underwriter) by which he agrees to pay such general average contribution as may become due. This document should be signed and returned directly to the adjusters, to save valuable time. Second is a cash deposit or an underwriter's guarantee, which is held by the ship owner as security for the ultimate general average contribution.

An insured cargo owner will usually ask his underwriters or their agents to furnish the guarantee. The uninsured cargo owner will have to make a cash deposit or furnish equivalent security.

The general average deposit receipt is a negotiable instrument and should be carefully preserved. It must be tendered to the average adjusters upon completion of the adjustment for refund of any excess payment over and above the general average contribution as finally determined. (In practice, the required cash deposit or guarantee will slightly exceed the anticipated contribution in order to provide a margin of safety.) An assured who has not waited for an underwriter's guarantee and has posted a cash deposit should surrender his general average deposit receipt to his underwriters at the first opportunity. If fully insured, he will then be reimbursed in full.

The general average adjusters will also require of the cargo owner certain *information*, in order that they may calculate the landed value on which the contribution is to be based. This information will include a certified copy of the original shipper's invoice and a "statement of value" showing the gross wholesale market value at the port of discharge. It is desirable that these documents, together with copies of the bills of lading, be routed through the underwriter to the general average adjusters.

If the cargo owner is insured to value, his eventual payment of the general average *contribution* will be made by the underwriter who furnished the guarantee. If but partially insured, contributions and credits are shared *pro rata* by the assured and underwriter. In the case of the uninsured cargo owner, the contribution will be offset against his cash deposit plus any credit for sacrifices (*see* "General Average: Illustration" below), and the balance refunded to him.

	Pays contribution of	Receives	Balance
Cargo	$35,000	$20,000	$15,000 to pay
	(35% of $100,000)		
Vessel	$140,000	$155,000	$15,000 to receive
	(35% of $400,000)		

If the cargo owner was fully insured, he will have had his underwriters furnish a general average guarantee in order to secure possession of the balance of his ore at destination. He will have been reimbursed for the insured value of the ore jettisoned. He will then be relieved of any further participation in the general average.

If the cargo owner was uninsured, he will have had to give security in the amount of about $30,000 in order to gain custody of the balance of his shipment of ore. Eventually he will be credited with the allowance for the jettisoned ore, and this will reduce his balance to pay to $15,000, which will represent an out-of-pocket expense. In addition, of course, he will have had to stand the $20,000 loss of the ore jettisoned.

The example given above has assumed a single cargo owner. The same principle applies equally to general cargo vessels, and each individual shipper must personally sign a general average bond, and he or his underwriter must furnish further security and pay any balance due after receiving credit for allowances.

It is clear that liability for contribution in general average is far from an academic matter to the ocean shipper or consignee. His ownership of cargo entails certain personal obligations (such as signing the bond and furnishing information) which he cannot avoid. But by fully insuring his goods, the financial obligation can be transferred to his underwriters.

Subrogation: Recoveries from Carriers

It might be thought that the assured has no further interest in a claim, once it has been settled. This is not the case. It is basic in the law of insurance that the insurer, upon payment of a loss, is entitled to the benefit of any rights against third parties that may be held by the assured himself.

Recoveries from vessel owners and others play an important part in reducing the loss experience under an open policy. It is thus of very real value to the shipper to be insured by a company that vigorously pursues its rights of subrogation against inland and ocean carriers and other parties that may be held responsible for losses covered by the policy.

When goods arrive at destination in a damaged condition, the question arises as to the extent of the carrier's liability for such damage. Liability will depend in part upon the provisions of the bill of lading as the contract of carriage, in part upon common law modifications of the freedom of contract in this field, and in part upon statutory enactments, notably the Harter Act of 1893 and the Carriage of Goods by Sea Act of 1936 (known as COGSA).

The degree to which a steamship company can be held responsible for damaged sustained by a specific shipment is frequently difficult to determine. COGSA applies to import and export shipments and, by agreement, to much of our coastwise and intercoastal business a well. Where COGSA applies, general speaking, the vessel *is* responsible for damage resulting from negligence in the loading,

General Average: Illustration

A simplified illustration based upon an actual case, will help to make the application of general average more understandable.

A vessel carrying a bulk cargo of ore was stranded. In attempts to get free, part of the cargo was jettisoned, both the engines and the ship were damaged, and a salvage vessel was employed. The ship was refloated after 10 days and put into a port of refuge for repairs.

Adjustment of the general average will work out as follows:

Sound market value at destination of jettisoned cargo (less duty and handling charges)		$20,000
Cost of hull and engine repairs chargeable to general average, i.e., resulting from "intentional" damage in efforts to refloat	$50,000	
Services of salvage vessel	$70,000	
Disbursements at port of refuge and other charges	$35,000	
Total "vessel" sacrifice	$155,000	$155,000
Total to be allowed or "made good" in general average		$175,000
Value of cargo (including sacrifice)		$100,000
Value of vessel (including sacrifice)		$400,000
Total contributory values		$500,000
Rate of general average contribution $\left(\dfrac{\$175,000}{\$500,000}\right)$		35%

The cargo and the vessel will each *contribute 35%* of their respective values, and they will *receive* their sacrifices and expenditures. The final reckoning will then be as follows:

The underwriters may not be liable for the full general average contribution of an assured unless the amount of insurance equals the landed value of the goods. The valuation clause in the open policy (which provides for declaring insurance in the amount of invoice, plus insurance, plus freight, plus 10%) provides a measure of leeway for just such a situation.

An insured cargo owner will collect his physical damage loss from his underwriters as in a particular average claim. Cargo interests that have had part or all of their goods sacrificed for the common safety will be entitled to receive an allowance in the general average. This appears as a credit entry in the adjustment and is offset against the contribution to determine the net amount to be paid or to receive. It is a fundamental principle of general average that contributions are assessed against credits allowed or "made good" for general average sacrifices. Otherwise the interests receiving allowances would be better off than those whose goods had not been sacrificed.

stowing and discharge of cargo. It *is not* responsible for damage resulting from errors of navigation or management of the ship, from unseaworthiness of the vessel (unless caused by lack of due diligence to make it seaworthy), or from perils of the sea, fire, and a number of other listed causes. The burden of proof in establishing fault will rest at times upon the shipper and at times upon the carrier.

The intricacies of these situations cannot be dealt with at length here. The subject is complex and one that calls for expert handling, if maximum recoveries from carriers are to be secured. For many years, certain underwriters have found it expedient to utilize the service of a recovery agency devoted entirely to their own claims work. The results have amply justified this specialized attention.

In selecting a marine insurance company, shippers should not fail to satisfy themselves as to the competence of its recovery facilities. The subrogation efforts of insurance companies benefit the individual account by keeping down the insurance cost. They are also an important factor in securing improved cargo handling by ocean carriers.

The overall loss policy of his insurance company is important to the assured. The purpose of an insurance company is to pay losses. Loses covered by the policy should be adjusted fairly and paid without delay. In fairness to others, losses not covered by the policy cannot be accepted.

Borderline situations are bound to occur from time to time. For one reason or another, full information as to the cause and extent of damage cannot always be secured. At these times, the assured has a right to expect that his claim will be sympathetically considered and that he will be given every reasonable benefit of doubt that the circumstances permit.

Regardless of the type of claim, the assured is entitled to prompt, courteous and competent loss adjustment. Those marine underwriters who have a long established record of honorable dealing to maintain will make every effort to meet these exacting standards and to justify the continued confidence of policyholders in the trading community throughout the world.

Conclusion

The Agent or Broker

What is the function of the insurance agent and the insurance broker in marine insurance?

The insurance agent or broker will render valuable assistance in selecting reliable marine underwriters.

He will arrange the amount and kind of protection that the shipper's operations and the nature of the commodity require. If FPA only, or limited conditions is needed, the shipper should not pay for more. If "all risk" insurance is needed, he should not be provided with less.

He will be of help, moreover, in the presentation of losses, and he can facilitate the release of goods in general average situations. By keeping a watchful eye on the premium and loss record of an account, he should make certain that justifiable rate reductions are not overlooked by the underwriter. At times, he can make suggestions for loss prevention studies that will lead to improved experience and so justify reduced rates of premium.

In short, the insurance agent or broker is the policyholder's representative in all that concerns his ocean marine coverage.

The Insurance Company

What should the foreign and domestic trader look for in his insurance company?

Financial strength is the first consideration. Financial strength represented by the policyholder's surplus should be adequate to withstand the sudden shock of catastrophic loss or the slow attrition of business depression. This is the ultimate safeguard that an insurance company will meet its obligations.

Know-how is the second consideration. There is no substitute for judgment based upon experience, in underwriting, in loss prevention, in loss adjustment and in loss recovery. Know-how at the head office is of little value unless it can be brought to bear upon the needs of the policyholder in his office, in his shipping room and in the warehouses of his consignees throughout the world. A network of trained branch office personnel throughout the United States will insure that this know-how is available when it is needed in this country. A network of foreign underwriting and claims agents, supplemented by company branch offices, will insure that this know-how is available to shippers and consignees abroad.

Obligation is the third consideration. Just as the cash and securities behind the policyholder's surplus are the most tangible evidence of an insurance company's strength, so the sense of obligation underlying its operation is the most intangible, but nonetheless important, evidence of its strength. The obligation of an insurance company to fulfill both the letter and spirit of its contracts is basic. Beyond this, there is its further obligation to pioneer in new areas of usefulness to the insuring public and to be a leader, not a follower, in the insurance industry and in the larger business world.

The efforts of the insurance organization by which this booklet has been prepared have been directed toward these objectives every since its founding in 1792.

Selected References

Arnould, Sir Joseph
Arnould on the law of marine insurance and average. 16th ed. Sir Michael J. Mustill & Jonathan C.B. Giltman. Stevens & Sons, Ltd., 1981.

Dover, Victor
A handbook to marine insurance. London, 1962.

Gow, William
Marine insurance; a handbook. London, Macmillan, 1931.

Institute of London Underwriters.
Institute handbook on marine contracts. Rev. ed. London, Witherby & Co., 1964.

Lowndes, R. & Rudolf, G. R.
The law of general average and the York-Antwerp rules. 10th Edition. John Donaldson/C.S. Slaughton. London, Stevens & Sons, Ltd., 1975

Poole, Fred W.S.
The marine insurance of goods. 5th ed. London, Macdonald & Crans, 1981.

Turner, Harold A.
The principles of marine insurance, a primer. 6th ed. London, Stone & Co., Ltd., 1971.

Winter, William D.
Marine insurance, its principles and practice. 3rd ed. New York, McGraw Hill Book Co., Inc., 1952.

Marine Lines
Written by the Marine and Aviation Department of the CIGNA Property and Casualty companies.

Your Ocean Cargo Policy Guide

Material for this section has been provided by the Insurance Company of North America (INA), a CIGNA Worldwide Company. World Trade Press gratefully acknowledges INA and CIGNA for this contribution.

Introduction

Your Policy is called an "open" policy because it has no expiration date and automatically covers all shipments made on and after the inception date shown in Clause 6 which come within its scope. For your protection, it is important to report promptly each and every shipment which is to be insured. We call your attention to Clause 43 which deals with declaration requirements.

The purpose of this Guide is to provide you with a handy reference to be kept with your Open Policy which contains the information necessary to insure your overseas shipments properly. It is not a part of your Open Policy and in no way extends or restricts the coverage provided therein. Determining the value to be insured and completing the insurance document are two of the most difficult tasks for an Insured. It is our aim in the pages that follow to assist you in both these endeavors and to call your attention specifically to certain other clauses in your policy which are important to the proper functioning of our mutual contract.

Determining the Value to Be Insured

Because it is frequently impossible to determine at what point in an overseas transit loss or damage occurred, or if it can be determined, how much the merchandise was worth at the time, marine cargo insurance is always written on a **valued** basis. This means that in the event of an insured total loss, you are paid the face amount of insurance without quibbling, whether it occurred just after the truck pulled away from your warehouse or just prior to delivery to the customer overseas. If only a portion of the shipment is involved, the percentage of the total shipment lost or damaged is determined and this percentage is then applied to the sum insured to compute the amount of the claim (less any applicable deductible). Thus depreciation and/or fluctuations in the market value of the merchandise during the course of transit are not a factor in any settlement.

To be fully insured, it is necessary that **all costs** incurred in effecting the sale and transfer of the merchandise from the seller to be buyer be included. In addition it is customary to apply a percentage loading on top of the sum of the invoice cost and all other known expenses to allow for appreciation in the value of the property at destination. (See the Valuation Clause, No. 5, in your Open Policy.) In most instances this optional percentage is 10%.

The premium for cargo insurance is an element to be included in the cost of the goods, but which must be computed on the value of the goods to be insured after application of the percentage increase. To assist you in determining the proper amount of insurance if your policy provides for the usual 10% increase, we have developed a table of factors which will take the cost of the goods excluding the insurance premium and project it to include both the increase and insurance charge.

The following example illustrates how the insured Value should be computed, assuming a voyage for which the Marine and War risk rates are 0.55% and 0.0375% respectively:

Step 1.

Determine the Cost of the Merchandise except for the insurance charge.

Invoice Value of Merchandise	$10,000.
Inland Freight	100.
Ocean Freight	260.
Cost of Packaging	65.
Freight Forwarding Charges	100.
Consular & Other Fees	25.
Total Cost	$10,550.

Step 2.

Add Marine and War Risk rates, round off sum to nearest cent (even half cent takes next highest cent) and determine factor from Table of Factors on facing page for the applicable rate.

.55 + .0375 = .5875 which becomes .59. Factor is 1.1065.

Step 3.

Multiply Cost from Step 1 by factor from Step 2 to compute value to be insured. $10,550 x 1.1065 = $11,674.

Notes:

a. To compute the factor for a combined rate in excess of 2.00%, do the following:

1. Round off rate to nearest cent as in Step 1 and deduct 2.00 (Ex: 2.37 - 2.00 = .37)

2. Multiply difference by .011 (.37 x .011 = .0041)

3. Add result to factor for 2.00 and round off to four decimal places (1.1220 + .0041 = 1.1261)

b. A table of factors for other than a 10% increase will be provided upon request to the Company.

Table of factors for 10% increase in valuation clause

Rate	Factor	Rate	Factor	Rate	Factor	Rate	Factor	Rate	Factor
.01	1.1001	.41	1.1045	.81	1.1089	1.21	1.1133	1.61	1.1177
.02	1.1002	.42	1.1046	.82	1.1090	1.22	1.1134	1.62	1.1178
.03	1.1003	.43	1.1047	.83	1.1091	1.23	1.1135	1.63	1.1179
.04	1.1004	.44	1.1048	.84	1.1092	1.24	1.1136	1.64	1.1180
.05	1.1006	.45	1.1050	.85	1.1094	1.25	1.1138	1.65	1.1182
.06	1.1007	.46	1.1051	.86	1.1095	1.26	1.1139	1.66	1.1183
.07	1.1008	.47	1.1052	.87	1.1096	1.27	1.1140	1.67	1.1184
.08	1.1009	.48	1.1053	.88	1.1097	1.28	1.1141	1.68	1.1185
.09	1.1010	.49	1.1054	.89	1.1098	1.29	1.1142	1.69	1.1186
.10	1.1011	.50	1.1055	.90	1.1099	1.30	1.1143	1.70	1.1187
.11	1.1012	.51	1.1056	.91	1.1100	1.31	1.1144	1.71	1.1188
.12	1.1013	.52	1.1057	.92	1.1101	1.32	1.1145	1.72	1.1189
.13	1.1014	.53	1.1058	.93	1.1102	1.33	1.1146	1.73	1.1190
.14	1.1015	.54	1.1059	.94	1.1103	1.34	1.1147	1.74	1.1191
.15	1.1017	.55	1.1061	.95	1.1105	1.35	1.1149	1.75	1.1193
.16	1.1018	.56	1.1062	.96	1.1106	1.36	1.1150	1.76	1.1194
.17	1.1019	.57	1.1063	.97	1.1107	1.37	1.1151	1.77	1.1195
.18	1.1020	.58	1.1064	.98	1.1108	1.38	1.1152	1.78	1.1196
.19	1.1021	.59	1.1065	.99	1.1109	1.39	1.1153	1.79	1.1197
.20	1.1022	.60	1.1066	1.00	1.1110	1.40	1.1154	1.80	1.1198
.21	1.1023	.61	1.1067	1.01	1.1111	1.41	1.1155	1.81	1.1199
.22	1.1024	.62	1.1068	1.02	1.1112	1.42	1.1156	1.82	1.1200
.23	1.1025	.63	1.1069	1.03	1.1113	1.43	1.1157	1.83	1.1201
.24	1.1026	.64	1.1070	1.04	1.1114	1.44	1.1158	1.84	1.1202
.25	1.1028	.65	1.1072	1.05	1.1116	1.45	1.1160	1.85	1.1204
.26	1.1029	.66	1.1073	1.06	1.1117	1.46	1.1161	1.86	1.1205
.27	1.1030	.67	1.1074	1.07	1.1118	1.47	1.1162	1.87	1.1206
.28	1.1031	.68	1.1075	1.08	1.1119	1.48	1.1163	1.88	1.1207
.29	1.1032	.69	1.1076	1.09	1.1120	1.49	1.1164	1.89	1.1208
.30	1.1033	.70	1.1077	1.10	1.1121	1.50	1.1165	1.90	1.1209
.31	1.1034	.71	1.1078	1.11	1.1122	1.51	1.1166	1.91	1.1210
.32	1.1035	.72	1.1079	1.12	1.1123	1.52	1.1167	1.92	1.1211
.33	1.1036	.73	1.1080	1.13	1.1124	1.53	1.1168	1.93	1.1212
.34	1.1037	.74	1.1081	1.14	1.1125	1.54	1.1169	1.94	1.1213
.35	1.1039	.75	1.1083	1.15	1.1127	1.55	1.1171	1.95	1.1215
.36	1.1040	.76	1.1084	1.16	1.1128	1.56	1.1172	1.96	1.1216
.37	1.1041	.77	1.1085	1.17	1.1129	1.57	1.1173	1.97	1.1217
.38	1.1042	.78	1.1086	1.18	1.1130	1.58	1.1174	1.98	1.1218
.39	1.1043	.79	1.1087	1.19	1.1131	1.59	1.1175	1.99	1.1219
.40	1.1044	.80	1.1088	1.20	1.1132	1.60	1.1176	2.00	1.1220

Declaring Shipments to Be Insured

There are three methods by which shipments, either export or import, can be declared by the policyholder.

1. **The Special Marine Policy** is a negotiable document issued to cover a single shipment and a complete policy unto itself. This is usually utilized on export shipments when the sale is financed through a bank by letter of credit or otherwise and evidence of insurance is a part of the required documentation. (Sometimes a Special Marine Policy is erroneously called a "Certificate." This latter is more correctly applied to evidence of insurance in a non-negotiable form).

2. **The Declaration** is a simple form used for reporting a single shipment to the Insurer when there is no requirement for a Special Marine Policy. It is quite generally used to declare import shipments or for intracompany movements of goods.

3. **The Bordereau** is similar to the Declaration in that it is quite simple to complete and is not negotiable. It provides for the reporting of multiple shipments within a prescribed reporting period, usually a month.

Instructions for completion of these forms will be found in the pages that follow.

The Special Marine Policy (SMP)

Upon request, a supply of these forms will be provided you in quintuplicate in pads (with more copies if you need them). The "Original" and "Duplicate" copies are negotiable and will be transmitted with the rest of the shipping papers to the consignee. It is only upon presentation of one of these two documents as evidence of ownership that the Company will pay a claim to a third party.

The "Memorandum" copy is sent to this Company through your agent or broker. There are also two "Office Copies." One of these is for your records, and the other is for the agent or broker.

Following the numbers in the blank spaces on the specimen Special Marine Policy on the facing page, instructions for its completion are as follows:

1. Establish the insured value as determined in the previous section and insert in figures.

2. Enter your Open Policy number if it hasn't been pre-printed.

3. Enter the place of issuance (your city) and today's date.

4. Enter the name of your Company, if it hasn't been pre-printed.

5. Enter the name of the overseas vessel (or airline). If the shipment is strictly overland such as to Mexico, indicate whether by truck and/or rail.

6. Enter the name of the place where inland transportation commences. If it is not obvious by which route the shipment will move, please show the name of the

seaport or coastal area. This is needed to determine the proper premium rate.

    Examples: Chicago via New York

                 Chicago via Pacific Ports

7. Enter the name of the place of ultimate destination where the consignee takes delivery. As above, if it isn't obvious, please show name of port or area of arrival.

8. Enter the marks that appear on the outside of the package and if each is separately numbered, what they are. In the event of a potential claim, this enables the marine surveyor to identify the insured shipment and verify whether all packages have been delivered.

9. Enter a description of the merchandise and the total number of packages.

10. Show in script the amount that appears in figures in Step 1.

11. This is almost without exception the same as the insured amount, so enter "sum insured." If for some reason the merchandise is to be insured for an amount different from its value, enter this latter amount in script. Bear in mind that in such cases loss settlement will be in proportion to the percentage that the sum insured bears to this value.

12. Enter "Assured" if any part of transit is at your risk. Policy can be endorsed when ownership transfers. Only if terms of sale call for "FOB, point of shipment" would you name the consignee. Endorsements are made on the revere side of the negotiable copies in the same manner as you would endorse a personal check.

13. Unless pre-printed, enter the applicable Average Terms as shown in Clause 12.

14. Enter your firm name and have a responsible official sign the original and duplicate.

SPECIAL MARINE POLICY

Insurance Company of North America
a CIGNA company

CIGNA No. **MA- 100000**

Open Policy No. 999999 **2**   of   SERVICE OFFICE: Pittsburg (512)   **ORIGINAL** (ORIGINAL AND DUPLICATE ISSUED) ONE OF WHICH BEING ACCOMPLISHED, THE OTHER TO BE NULL AND VOID)

$ 11,674. **1**   (PLACE AND DATE) Philadelphia, Pa., September 4, 1988 **3**

This Company, in consideration of a premium as agreed, and subject to the Terms and Conditions printed or stamped hereon and/or attached hereto, does insure, lost or not lost THE CLUTCH CO. **4**

For account of whom it may concern; to be shipped by the vessel SS "MARIA COSTA" **5**, and connecting conveyances.

MARKS AND NUMBERS

From   Woodwards Corner, Pa., via Philadelphia **6**
To   San Remo, Italy, via Levorno **7**
Interest Industrial Clutches **9**

C-CL-C
Livorno
#1 - 4

Number of Packages

Insured for **10** Eleven Thousand Six Hundred Seventy Four and no/100 Dollars
Valued at **Sum hereby insured**   Sum Insured **11**
Loss, if any, payable to **Assured** **12**   or order.

8 VOID

TERMS AND CONDITIONS — SEE ALSO BACK HEREOF

WAREHOUSE TO WAREHOUSE: This insurance attaches from the time the goods leave the Warehouse and/or Store at the place named in the Policy for the commencement of the transit and continues during the ordinary course of transit, including customary transhipment if any, until the goods are discharged overside from the overseas vessel at the final port. Thereafter the insurance continues whilst the goods are in transit and/or awaiting transit until delivered to final warehouse at the destination named in the Policy or until the expiry of 15 days (or 30 days if the destination to which the goods are insured is outside the limits of the port) whichever shall first occur. The time limits referred to above to be reckoned from midnight of the day on which the discharge overside of the goods hereby insured from the overseas vessel is completed. Held covered at a premium to be arranged in the event of transhipment, if any, other than as above and/or in the event of delay in excess of the above time limits arising from circumstances beyond the control of the Assured.

NOTE—IT IS NECESSARY FOR THE ASSURED TO GIVE PROMPT NOTICE TO THESE ASSURERS WHEN THEY BECOME AWARE OF AN EVENT FOR WHICH THEY ARE "HELD COVERED" UNDER THIS POLICY AND THE RIGHT TO SUCH COVER IS DEPENDENT ON COMPLIANCE WITH THIS OBLIGATION.

SHORE CLAUSE: Where this insurance by its terms covers while on docks, wharves or elsewhere on shore, and/or during land transportation, it shall include the risks of collision, derailment, overturning or other accident to the conveyance, fire, lightning, sprinkler leakage, cyclones, hurricanes, earthquakes, floods (meaning the rising of navigable waters), and/or collapse or subsidence of docks or wharves, even though the insurance be otherwise F. P. A.

BOTH TO BLAME CLAUSE: Where goods are shipped under a Bill of Lading containing the so-called "Both to Blame Collision" Clause, these Assurers agree as to all losses covered by this insurance, to indemnify the Assured for this Policy's proportion of any amount (not exceeding the amount insured) which the Assured may be legally bound to pay to the shipowners under such clause. In the event that such liability is asserted the Assured agrees to notify these Assurers who shall have the right at their own cost and expense to defend the Assured against such claim.

MACHINERY CLAUSE: When the property insured under this Policy includes a machine consisting when complete for sale or use of several parts, then in case of loss or damage covered by this insurance to any part of such machine, these Assurers shall be liable only for the proportion of the insured value of the part lost or damaged, or at the Assured's option, for the cost and expense, including labor and forwarding charges, of replacing and repairing the lost or damaged part; but in no event shall these Assurers be liable for more than the insured value of the complete machine.

LABELS CLAUSE: In case of damage affecting labels, capsules or wrappers, these Assurers, if liable therefor under the terms of this policy, shall not be liable for more than an amount sufficient to pay the cost of new labels, capsules or wrappers, and the cost of reconditioning the goods, but in no event shall these Assurers be liable for more than the insured value of the damaged merchandise.

DELAY CLAUSE: Warranted free of claim for loss of market or for loss, damage or deterioration arising from delay, whether caused by a peril insured against or otherwise, unless expressly assumed in writing hereon.

AMERICAN INSTITUTE CLAUSES: This insurance, in addition to the foregoing, is also subject to the following **American Institute Cargo Clauses**, current forms:

1. CRAFT, ETC.   4. GENERAL AVERAGE   7. INCHMAREE
2. DEVIATION   5. EXPLOSION   8. CONSTRUCTIVE TOTAL LOSS
3. WAREHOUSE & FORWARDING CHARGES, 6. BILL OF LADING, ETC.   9. CARRIER
   PACKAGES TOTALLY LOST LOADING, ETC.

PERILS CLAUSE: Touching the adventures and perils which this Company is contented to bear, and takes upon itself, they are of the seas, fires, assailing thieves, jettisons, barratry of the master and mariners, and all other like perils, losses and misfortunes (illicit or contraband trade excepted in all cases), that have or shall come to the hurt, detriment or damage of the said goods and merchandise, or any part hereof.

AVERAGE TERMS: ON DECK AND SUBJECT TO AN "ON DECK" BILL OF LADING—(which must be so declared by the Assured): Free of Particular Average unless caused by the vessel being stranded, sunk, burnt, on fire or in collision, but including jettison and/or washing overboard irrespective of percentage.

EXCEPT WHILE SUBJECT TO AN "ON DECK" BILL OF LADING:

To cover against all risks of physical loss or damage from any external cause irrespective of percentage, but excluding, nevertheless, the risks of war, strikes, riots, seizure, detention and other risks excluded by the F. C. & S. (Free of Capture & Seizure) Warranty and the S. R. & C. C. (Strikes, Riots and Civil Commotions) Warranty in this policy, excepting to the extent that such risks are specifically covered by endorsement., but also excluding rust and oxidation.

13

This Policy is extended to include the provisions of the following clauses as if the current form of each were endorsed hereon:

American Institute Clauses—   Where Appropriate—
  F. C. & S. Warranty
  Marine Extension Clauses
  S. R. & C. C. Endorsement
  War Risk Insurance   South America
                                            60-Day Clause

SPECIMEN

PARAMOUNT WARRANTIES: THE FOLLOWING WARRANTIES SHALL BE PARAMOUNT AND SHALL NOT BE MODIFIED OR SUPERSEDED BY ANY OTHER PROVISION INCLUDED HEREIN OR STAMPED OR ENDORSED HEREON UNLESS SUCH OTHER PROVISION REFERS SPECIFICALLY TO THE RISKS EXCLUDED BY THESE WARRANTIES AND EXPRESSLY ASSUMES THE SAID RISKS: F.C.&S. (a) NOTWITHSTANDING ANYTHING HEREIN CONTAINED TO THE CONTRARY THIS INSURANCE IS WARRANTED FREE FROM: (a) capture, seizure, arrest, restraint, detainment, confiscation, preemption, requisition or nationalization, and the consequences thereof or any attempt thereat, whether in time of peace or war and whether lawful or otherwise; (b) all loss, damage or expense, whether in time of peace or war, caused by (i) any weapon of war employing atomic or nuclear fission and/or fusion or other reaction or radioactive force or matter or (ii) any mine or torpedo; (c) all consequences of hostilities or warlike operations (whether there be a declaration of war or not), but this warranty shall not exclude collision or contact with aircraft, or with rockets or similar missiles (other than weapons of war) or with any fixed or floating object (other than a mine or torpedo), stranding, heavy weather, fire or explosion unless caused directly (and independently of the nature of the voyage or service which the vessel concerned or, in the case of a collision, any other vessel involved therein, is performing) by a hostile act by or against a belligerent power; and for the purposes of this warranty "power" includes any authority maintaining naval, military or air forces in association with a power; (d) the consequences of civil war, revolution, rebellion, insurrection, or civil strife arising therefrom; or from the consequences of the imposition of martial law, military or usurped power; or piracy. S.R.&C.C. (b) Notwithstanding anything herein contained to the contrary, this insurance is warranted free from loss, damage or expense caused by or resulting from: (1) strikes, lockouts, labor disturbances, riots, civil commotions, or the acts of any person or persons taking part in any such occurrences or disorders, (2) vandalism, sabotage or malicious act, which shall be deemed also to encompass the act or acts of one or more persons, whether or not agents of a sovereign power, carried out for political, terroristic or ideological purposes and whether any loss, damage or expense resulting therefrom is accidental or intentional.

Not transferable unless countersigned

Countersigned

14

INSTRUCTIONS TO CLAIMANTS ON REVERSE SIDE
MA-2098g Ptd in U S A

In Witness Whereof, this Company has caused these presents to be signed by its President and attested by its Secretary, in the City of Philadelphia.

Harry E. Hoyt
HARRY E. HOYT, Secretary

Caleb L. Fowler
CALEB L. FOWLER, President

The Declaration

This form is provided in pad form and can be made up in whatever number is required to meet your needs. Two copies are to be sent to your agent/broker.

Following the numbers in the blank spaces on the sample form on the facing page, instructions for completion are as follows:

1. Enter the name of your company.

2. Enter the number you have assigned to this declaration. This is for identification purposes only and is established to suit your needs. It can be from either a straight numerical sequence or with some identifying letter combination or year of issue prefix.

3. Enter today's date.

4. Enter the name of the overseas vessel (or airline). If the shipment is strictly overland, such as to Mexico, indicate whether by rail or truck.

5. Enter the number of your Open Policy.

6. Enter the name of the place where inland transportation commences. (*See* Step 6 of instructions for SMP for further clarification.)

7. Enter either the date of sailing or the date on the bill of lading and show which it is. In the event you ship merchandise on the same vessel on different sailings, this would enable us to identify the voyage in the event of a claim.

8. Enter a short description of the merchandise and how it is packed. (Example: Leaf Tobacco in bales.)

9. Enter the name of the ultimate destination. (*See* Step 7 of instructions for SMP for further clarification.)

10. Enter the number of packages.

11. Enter the name and address of your agent or broker.

12. Enter the amount of marine insurance computed as described in the previous section utilizing the blank for the invoice value, the sum of all other charges and their total. The applicable factor taken from the table is inserted in the blank "plus % advance."

13. If this is an import shipment and you wish to insure the U.S. duty separately, enter the amount of such duty here.

14. Computation of the premium by you is optional, using the rate schedule at the back of your Open Policy. It is not necessary since the Company will perform the same operation and send you an invoice for the premium due.

Insurance Company of North America
a CIGNA company

CIGNA

THE ACCEPTANCE OF THIS APPLICATION SHALL NOT COMMIT THE COMPANY IN THE EVENT OF CANCELLATION OF THE MARINE OR WAR RISK OPEN POLICIES, OR OF ANY ENDORSEMENT THEREON. IF SUCH CANCELLATION NOTICE BECOMES EFFECTIVE PRIOR TO ATTACHMENT OF THIS RISK UNDER THE INSURANCE SO CANCELLED.

ASSURED THE CLUTCH CO. **1**

NAME OF VESSEL OR CONVEYANCE SS "MARIA COSTA" **4**

VOYAGE: FROM Woodwards Corner, Pa., via Philadelphia **6**
(INITIAL POINT OF SHIPMENT)

KIND OF MERCHANDISE Industrial Clutches in wooden cases **8**
(DESCRIBE FULLY — STATE WHETHER CASES, CRATES, CARTONS, ETC.)
AMOUNT INSURED (SEE POLICY VALUATION CLAUSE)

DECLARATION NO. 74-95 **2**

DATE SEPTEMBER 4, 1988 **3**

OPEN POLICY NO. 999999 **5**

SAILING OR B.L. DATE September 4, 1988 **7** NAME WHICH

TO San Remo, Italy via Levorno **9**
(FINAL DESTINATION)

NO. OF PACKAGES 4 **10**

		AGENT OR BROKER		
INVOICE VALUE	10,000.	Marine Ins. Agency **11**		
FREIGHT & ALL OTHER CHARGES	550.	ADDRESS 2410 Creek Road, Embreeville, Pa.		
TOTAL	10,500.	BROKER OR AGENT CODE		
PLUS % ADVANCE	1,1065		RATE OF PREMIUM	PREMIUM
AMOUNT OF MARINE INSURANCE **12**	11,674.	MARINE	.55	$64.21 **14**
		WAR & OR S & R	.0375	4.38
ACTUAL AMOUNT OF U.S. DUTY **13**		DUTY		
		WAR & OR S & R		
		TOTAL PREMIUM		$68.59

MA-455a Printed in U.S.A.

The Bordereau

The form also comes in pads and the number of copies completed is up to you. Two copies are to be sent to your agent/broker. These should be sent to the Company at regular intervals, but at least monthly. Although there is no specific provision therefor, we ask that you indicate in the upper right hand corner either a consecutive numbering of this bordereaux or the month and year that it covers. This enables the Company to make certain all bordereaux are received and to identify it on the premium invoice.

Following the numbers in the blank spaces on the sample form on the facing page, instructions for completion are as follows:

1. Enter the number of your open policy.

2. Enter the name of your company.

3. Enter today's date.

4. Enter the name of the overseas vessel (or airline). If the shipment is strictly overland, such as to Mexico, indicate whether by rail or truck.

5. Enter either the date of sailing or the date on the bill of lading and show which it is. In the event you ship merchandise on the same vessel on different sailings, this would enable us to identify the voyage in the event of a claim.

6. Enter the name of the place where inland transportation commences. (*See* Step 6 of instructions for SMP for further clarification.)

7. Enter the name of the ultimate destination. (*See* Step 7 of instructions for SMP for further clarification.)

8. Enter a short description of the merchandise and how it is packed. (Example: Leaf Tobacco in bales.)

9. Enter the amount of marine insurance computed as described in the previous section utilizing the blank for the invoice value, the sum of all other charges and their total. When there is more than one coverage provided for a single shipment such as marine and war, please allow two lines per shipment. It will be understood that the first line will be for the marine coverage and the insertion of the word "War" in the "Amount Insured" column on the next line will provide for covering war risks without repeating all the information to the left. If duty or some other coverage is desired in a different amount of insurance, insert this in the "Amount Insured" column and identify it in the column to the left.

10. Computation of the premium by you is optional, using the rate schedule at the back of your open policy. It is not necessary since the Company will perform the same operation and send you an invoice for the premium due.

11. Enter the name and address of your agent or broker.

To the INSURANCE COMPANY OF NORTH AMERICA

Please enter the following shipments under Open Policy No. 999999 **1**   issued to THE CLUTCH CO. **2**

DATE **3**	VESSEL **4**	SAILING OR DATE B/L **5**	FROM **6**	TO **7**	MDSE **8**	AMOUNT INSURED **9**		RATE	PREMIUM **10**		REMARKS
Sept. 4	"MARIA COSTA"	Sept. 4	Woodward Corner, Pa.	San Remo, Italy	Industrial Clutches	11,674.	00	.55	64	21	
						War		.0375	4	38	

TAX

THIS SPACE RESERVED FOR THE COMPANY

The acceptance of this application shall not commit the company in the event of cancellation of the marine or war risk open policies, or of any endorsement thereon, if such cancellation notice becomes effective prior to attachment of this risk under the insurance so cancelled **11**

Broker _____

Approved for
the Company _____

(If within the terms and conditions of the policy)

MA-7/9 Ptd in U S A

Other Important Policy Provisions

While all the clauses in your open policy have a purpose, and we urge you to familiarize yourself with them, there are certain ones that requires special amplification if your policy is to provide you with the full protection intended from the outset.

9. **Limit of Liability**—We have endeavored to set these amounts in excess of your maximum needs. However, should you have shipment in excess of the limits shown, please notify the Company immediately through your agent or broker. In most cases the additional coverage required can be arranged without difficulty. However, failure to do so could leave you underinsured, particularly on shipments reported on Declarations or Bordereaux where the terms of your Open Policy prevail.

12. **Average Terms**—If your policy provides for an option in average terms such as FPA or All Risks, make certain that the coverage applying to each shipment is clearly shown on the reporting document.

28. **Import Duty**—When goods imported into the United States are subject to Customs duty, you must pay this in order to take delivery. If you then find the merchandise has been damaged and is useless, you are either out of pocket for the amount of the duty or faced with much red tape to effect a recovery.

    You can insure this potential loss by indicating the amount of duty on the reporting document and identifying it as such. Because there is no duty payable if the goods are lost before reaching the U.S. port of discharge, you are charged a reduced rate for this coverage, usually a percentage of the marine rates. See the rate schedule at the back of your policy.

29. **General Average**—This clause provides coverage for a type of claim which is unique to marine insurance, even though your policy may be written on very limited terms otherwise. Moreover, it is the result of a fortuitous action completely beyond your control.

    As the name implies, general average claims affect all the interests which stand to suffer a financial loss if a particular voyage is not successfully completed. These include the owner of the hull and the owners of all the cargoes aboard for their respective values plus the owner or charterer who stands to earn a specific income from freight charges for the voyage.

    A General Average is usually incurred when in the face of an impending disaster, some sacrifice is made on the part of one of the interests described above which is successful and the venture is brought to safety. This can be in the form of the deliberate destruction of some physical property such as the tossing overboard of a part of the cargo to lighten ship in a storm or the flooding of a cargo hold to prevent the spread of fire. It can also include the expenditure of funds by the vessel own to hire tugs in the event of a lost propeller at sea or a stranding on the shore. In such circumstances, the owner or master will declare a General Average and eventually all those with a financial interest are asked to share the reimbursement for the values which have been sacrificed for the good of all. This can be compared to a boy hitting a baseball through a window in a backyard game. It is basically his financial loss to replace the glass, but all the players, including said batter, chip in to share the cost with him.

How does this affect you? If a General Average is declared, delivery of cargo by the vessel is predicated on the cargo owner posting some form of security as evidence that they will pay their share of the ultimate G.A. assessment. The amount of the deposit is based on an estimate. While this can be met by a cash deposit or bond, the simplest and least expensive solution is for CIGNA to file a General Average Guarantee on your behalf with the G.A. adjusters, and your cargo will be released. Thus if you are informed that your merchandise is involved in a General Average, contact the Company or the nearest claim or settling agent listed on the reverse side of the Special Marine Policy.

As a rule of thumb, cargo is valued at the invoice cost plus 10% for General Average estimating purposes. If you have not insured your cargo in accordance with the Valuation Clause No. 5, you could find yourself sharing in the General Average settlement.

The Rate Schedule—The rates shown for the various voyages are predicated on the assumption that shipments will be made on approved vessels as described at the top of the endorsement. Otherwise you may be charged an additional premium computed at a rate which varies with the age and net tonnage of the ship and the voyage involved. It is in your interest to ship by steamer lines offering regular service to your destinations whenever possible.

Note the other provisions at the bottom of your rate schedule, particularly the fact that there is a minimum premium per shipment, rates to or from places or for commodities not listed in the rate schedule can be obtained upon request, and that the Company may charge an additional rate for transshipment if your cargo is off-loaded from one vessel and re-loaded onto another at some intermediate port of call. This latter does not apply to lighterage or where a transshipment is a natural part of the voyage to the destination listed.

The rates shown on the schedule are for the marine risk only, and do not include war perils. Rates for this coverage are in addition, and the war premium is computed separately. Generally, these rates stay pretty constant to most parts of the World, but if hostilities break out somewhere, the War Risk Policy does provide for a shorter time period before a rate can be changed than does the Open Marine Policy. Such changes as may become necessary would apply only to voyages commencing on and after the date they become effective.

When Loss or Damage Occurs

If you are an exporter insuring your shipments under special marine policies, it is most likely that your overseas customer will first become aware of a potential claim. There is a listing on the reverse side of the special marine policy of the steps he should take including the names and addresses of CIGNA's claims and settling agents in major ports of the world. If there is none nearby, the claimant is directed to contact the nearest correspondent of the American Institute of Marine Underwriters or Lloyd's agent.

If you are an importer, there are certain instructions to be given those in your organization who receive or take delivery of your merchandise. It is most important that all packages be examined and counted before signing for the shipment. If there are any signs of potential loss or damage such as breakage or wetting of the shipping package or the number delivered does not match that shown on the bill of lading, an exception should be taken by noting the damage and/or shortage on the bill of lading or freight bill before accepting delivery.

Once damage is discovered, there are three things you must do without delay:

1. Make every effort to reduce the loss and/or prevent further loss as provided under the sue and labor clause (no. 19) of your Open Policy. This could include rebagging, recoopering barrels, separating wet cargo from dry, etc. Reasonable expenses incurred in taking such steps are reimbursable by the Company in addition to any payment of the claim itself. In short, we expect the Insured to do exactly what he would do if the shipment were uninsured.

2. Notify your agent or broker (or the nearest CIGNA office) so that a survey of the damage can be arranged as promptly as possible. The carrier or his agent should be notified of the time and place of the survey, so he can be represented. Insofar as possible, the damaged property and the containers in which it was delivered should be retained in the condition received until after the survey unless further damage will result by so doing.

3. It is essential that a claim be made in writing against the carrier (inland or ocean) as soon as the loss is known or upon taking delivery. This can be in any form, but must include the bill of lading number, the name of the carrying vessel, a description of the loss or damage, and should state that the carrier will be held responsible for the loss or damage.

The rates you are charged for your cargo insurance are influenced in the ultimate by the experience (premiums versus losses) of your account, so it is in your best interest to see that losses are reduced by putting the Company in a good position to take action against the carrier to recover all or at least a portion of the claims the Company pays you. This is called subrogation and amounts recovered are credited to your account. The bills of lading include a time limit following delivery in which a claim on the carrier will be accepted, so it is necessary to put them on notice immediately.

If your merchandise is of a fragile or delicate nature subject to breakage, etc., it is important that you unpack and check its condition as soon as possible even though there is no evidence of damage to or on the packing. You may have what is known as concealed damage.

Once the survey has confirmed that loss or damage has occurred which was caused by one of the insured perils, the following documents will be needed to substantiate your claim:

1. Whatever document was issued to substantiate the amount of insurance placed and the coverage provided. On an export shipment this would be the original and duplicate of the special marine policy. For imports, it would probably be a copy of the declaration or bordereau if this has been issued prior to your learning of a possible claim.

2. Ocean (or Air) bill of lading—also transshipment bill of lading and railway freight note when applicable.

3. Original shipper's invoice.

4. Packing list, weight certificates, or other evidence of the nature and condition of the goods at time of shipment.

5. The survey report if an outside surveyor was called in to represent your interest.

6. Copy of claim on carrier and (if available) the reply thereto.

7. In special cases, other documents may be requested.

If all the above papers are included in the submission of your claim, it will certainly speed up the adjustment and the payment thereof.

Commodity Index
Contents

Introduction

This Commodity Index serves as a guide to the regulatory requirements relevant to imports into the U.S. It is organized according to the 99 chapters of the Harmonized Tariff Schedule of the United States (HTSUS). Each index chapter contains a broad range of information designed to assist you in being an educated importer. Listings are arranged according to the HTSUS. With a few exceptions, each chapter is designed to be a complete, stand-alone discussion, containing all the supplemental regulatory information of which you need to be aware when importing products assigned to the specific HTSUS chapter. Some chapters refer you to other pertinent material, either in the Commodity Index or elsewhere in this book. Be sure to read any such additional material, even if there is some duplication of information.

Each Commodity Index chapter is intended to give you an overview of the regulatory issues involved in importing a product. The purpose of this index is not to be an ultimate authority. Each chapter lists the government agencies with regulatory responsibility for the commodity. We strongly advise you to follow up on all references that direct you either to a U.S. government agency, a specific regulation, or other publications.

The section covering the commodity you wish to import may contain extensive and formidable details regarding restrictions, required forms, governmental agencies, procedures, etc. Don't be intimidated. Such details are a reflection of our conviction that knowledge is power: the more you know about importing a commodity, the less likely you are to experience problems. In practice, what looks complicated or even impossible may be as simple as having a customs broker fill out an extra form to go with your entry. On the other hand, some products are subject to stringent restrictions and are extremely difficult to import. Drugs and firearms are examples of such products.

Using the Commodity Index as a base, we recommend that you consult with your customs broker, U.S. Customs, and any relevant government agencies for clarification of your responsibilities before you make any financial commitments. In any activity as fast-paced as international trade, there are bound to be subtleties and changes relating to specific products and even whole classes of products. This index is not a substitute for the legwork necessary to confirm and clarify the material presented, but it will streamline that research and make it more effective.

Customs Brokers

Customs brokers are licensed by the U.S. Department of the Treasury to conduct business with U.S. Customs on behalf of importers. The primary function of a customs broker is to assist in clearing imports through Customs. Such individuals deal with Customs on a daily basis and are in a position to know both the theory and the practice of entering goods. Besides facilitating actual entry, customs brokers can often provide additional services to the importer. They can advise you in almost every aspect of the import process, including shipping, insurance, payment through draft or letter of credit, and delivery of cargo in the U.S.

We recommend the use of a licensed customs broker, especially if you are new to importing. A customs broker won't do everything for you—you still need to be closely involved with your own operation—but you won't need to reinvent the wheel. Brokers' fees are modest in comparison to the time and money you can save. Consult the yellow pages of a U.S. port city, under "Customs Brokers," for names and telephone numbers. You can also review the website of the National Customs Brokers & Forwarders Association of America, Inc. (www.ncbfaa.org) for a list of members in good standing. Refer also to "Selecting and Working with a Customs Broker" on page 73, and "Customs Brokers, Freight Forwarders, and Professional Associations" on page 72.

How to Use the Commodity Index

The Commodity Index is organized according to the HTSUS. To find the discussion relevant to your product, scan the Table of Contents of this Index for the 22 section headings of the HTSUS. These section headings represent broad classifications of goods. Refer to the specific chapters within the sections for more specific product types. If you still cannot find an appropriate listing for the product itself, look for a listing for the material the product is made of, such as Chapter 73, "Articles of Iron or Steel." The introductory part of each Commodity Index chapter explains the specific type of products it covers and also gives references to other chapters where some related products can be found. If no listing seems to cover the product you are interested in importing, consult the original HTSUS (with its more detailed index), a customs broker, or your nearest U.S. Customs office.

Commodity Index chapters are further divided into subsections containing the information you need to know to import the commodity. Some of these subsections are supplemental to general chapters in other parts of this manual dealing with the same topics. Each details the ways in which the general requirements apply to the specific commodity and lists special requirements. Requirements listed in these subsections should always be considered as being in addition to general import requirements. Each Commodity Index chapter is divided into the following subsections

Key Factors

The "Key Factors" subsection is designed to alert the importer to any complicating factors associated with importing a product. While for many products importation is straightforward, requiring nothing more than standard Customs entry, many "straightforward" products have important exceptions, and some categories represent a regulatory minefield. In the Commodity Index, we have focused on the exceptions—not to scare you away, but to alert you to important issues that could present major problems. For example, importing jewelry is straightforward, with the important exception of jewelry made in whole or in part of any endangered species (such as elephant ivory, which is banned).

"Key Factors," found near the beginning of each chapter, is a highly abbreviated, selective version of this information. It is intended to provide an at-a-glance overview of what is to follow. If you stop reading after "Key Factors," you will have a schematic list of issues to be aware of, but you won't have much specific information. However, once you have read the chapter, a review of "Key Factors" should serve to help you remember the details. ("Key Factors" is omitted from Commodity Index chapters pertaining to commodities that have no special requirements.)

General Considerations

"General Considerations" provides a broad stroke background of information to give you an introduction to major issues associated with your commodity. It will tell you briefly whether importation of the commodity is complex or straightforward, which agencies regulate importations of the product, and what the regulations are. For example, if your product is regulated by an agency requiring port-of-entry documentation or inspection, that will be mentioned in "General Considerations." (More details follow, under "Prohibitions and Restrictions," "Marking and Labeling Requirements," etc., where relevant. As with "Key Factors," when a product is so straightforward that no special circumstances or regulations apply, you will not see a "General Considerations" segment in the Commodity Index chapter.)

Customs Classification

The "Customs Classification" of a commodity determines its duty rate. Products that appear to be similar can, for Customs purposes, have very different classifications, and thus be assessed radically different duties. Therefore, it is crucial that you understand how Customs classifies your product. It is also helpful to consult a customs broker with experience in your product area and who knows how things are actually done. Currently, a difference of opinion with Customs over how your product should be classified leads to little more than a delay, but under the "reasonable care" provisions of the 1993 Customs Modernization Act (Mod Act)—unfounded, frivolous, or fraudulent misclassifications can lead to substantial fines and penalties. Therefore, you need to know precisely how Customs classifies your product, not just how you think it should be classified. Review "Classification—Liquidation" on page 229 for additional information.

Import Duties

Import duties vary (often dramatically) depending upon the Harmonized Tariff Schedule (HTSUS) classification of the goods or products imported. Since some products that look alike have different HTSUS classifications and different rates of duty, proper classification is vital. Note that "differences of opinion" between importers and the Bureau of Customs and Border Protection regarding classification keeps customs attorneys very busy.

Import duties can be assessed on the imported value of the goods ("ad valorem" rates of duty such as 2%, 4.4%, 50%, etc.), total units or weight of the goods ("specific" rates of duty such as 2 cents each or 1.5 cents/pound, etc.) or on a combination basis ("compound" rates of duty such as 5 cents each plus 6%).

Listed below is a sampling of several Column 1 import duty rates for Chapter 52 products:

For specific information on US import duties refer to the Harmonized Tariff Schedule of the US. The print version is available from the US Government Printing Office as well as third party suppliers who often add special features. Online versions are available in both static PDF pages as well as in formats with excellent search functionality. Search the Web with the term "Harmonized Tariff Schedule" to find sources.

Entry and Documentation

An overview of the general U.S. Customs entry and documentation process appears in each Commodity Index chapter, with specific mention of any additional documentation required by U.S. Customs and Border Protection for that commodity. We recommend that you review "Entry Process" on page 199.

Prohibitions and Restrictions

This subsection details prohibitions and restrictions associated with the importation of a commodity into the U.S. In some cases, the restrictions and prohibitions are so detailed that they cannot be explained completely in this index. For example, the limitations on the importation and sale in the U.S. of Food and Drug Administration (FDA)-regulated drugs would itself require several volumes. In such cases, we give an overview of the scope of the restrictions and prohibitions, a sampling of pertinent rules, and references to more complete sources of information. For highly regulated commodities, we recommend that you obtain copies of the actual laws and regulations governing the commodity. Refer to "Laws and Regulations" below.

Country-Specific Import Restrictions

Product-specific country-of-origin restrictions are outlined in "Country-Specific Import Restrictions" in each Commodity Index chapter when relevant.

Quotas

"Quotas" only appears when there are quotas on a commodity or commodity group. You should read the general entry on . as background for understanding the information you will find in the quota section for your commodity. If your commodity is subject to quota, the "Quota" subsection will give you information about the annual import limit, countries from which the product may be imported, and annual quantities allowed. The information is usually broken down by HTSUS classification number. Quotas are subject to change, and at any given point in time, the quota for your commodity may already be filled for the year. Some quota commodities require licensing and other forms of documentation. Never attempt to import a quota item without first consulting U.S. Customs and Border Protection or a customs broker regarding the product's current quota status.

Marking and Labeling Requirements

General U.S. Customs and Border Protection marking and labeling requirements pertain to most import commodities. These are covered in "Country of Origin Marking" on page 236, "Special Marking Requirements" on page 238 and "Marking—False Impression" on page 239. The "Marking and Labeling Requirements" portion of each Commodity Index chapter provides supplemental information specific to the product. You may also

Heading/ Subheading	Stat. Suf- fix	Article Description	Units of Quantity	Rates of Duty		
				1		2
				General	Special	
5212		Other woven fabrics of cotton: Weighing not more than 200 g/m²:				
5212.11		Unbleached:				
5212.11.10		Containing 36 percent or more by weight of wool or fine animal hair.	. . . . .	33%	3.3% (IL) 13.2% (CA) 20% (MX)	68.5%
	10	Not combed. . . . . . (410)	m² v kg			
	20	Combed. . . . . . . (410)	m² v kg			
5212.11.60		Other.	. . . . .	7.8%	Free (IL) 3.1% (CA) 7.1% (MX)	40%
	10	Mixed mainly or solely with wool or fine animal hair. . (220)	m² v kg			

want to refer to the U.S. Customs Service publication, "Marking of Country of Origin on U.S. Imports."

Relevant Government Agencies

Some commodities are regulated by many U.S. government agencies. For example, both the FDA and the U.S. Department of Agriculture (USDA) regulate the importation of dairy products. Each agency has its own area of regulatory responsibility. If you have a question about a commodity that is regulated by more than one agency, be sure to direct it to the appropriate agency. A USDA official will not be able to give you authoritative information on requirements for FDA permits for importing milk, and an FDA official will not be able to give you information about USDA-administered quotas on imported cheeses.

Each index section lists the headquarters, department, address, and phone number of the regulating agencies for the commodity covered. We recommend that you call these agencies for information. Many of these agencies have district offices in major U.S. cities. Such offices appear in the phone book under the "U.S. Government" listing. The headquarters can also direct you to the nearest district office or to the specific centralized office dealing with your issue. Note that it sometimes requires patience and several calls before you reach the person who can help you with your specific question. Persevere.

Laws and Regulations

This subsection lists the U.S. Government laws and regulations that are relevant to the importation of the commodity covered. Please note that this subsection does not cover state and local laws and regulations that may affect your commodity, although where such regulations exist for a general class of product, the Commodity Index section will alert you to this. You should always check with local authorities in the venue where you plan to do business.

Federal laws are contained in the United States Code (USC), which is generally available at larger public libraries and at law libraries. These laws form the basis of the regulatory actions that government agencies take with regard to the commodity. Specific regulations are published in the Code of Federal Regulations (CFR) to implement the laws. For example, The Federal Food, Drug, and Cosmetic Act (FDCA) is the foundation for regulatory activity for the listed product categories. It is found in Title 21 of the USC, and the supporting regulations are in 21 CFR. If you are dealing in a highly regulated commodity, obtain a copy of the relevant laws and regulations and study them. Copies of specific federal laws and regulations may be purchased from:

U.S. Government Printing Office
Superintendent of Documents
710 North Capital Street NW
Washington, DC 20401
Tel: (202) 512-1800
Fax: (202) 512-1657
Website: www.access.gpo.gov

Principal Exporting Countries

This subsection lists the major suppliers of products to the U.S. as compiled from Bureau of the Census statistics for customs value of entries for 2002. Countries are listed in descending rank order, beginning with the largest sources. The actual values are not given, and there can be huge differences between products and countries. The listing is organized by the major headings of the HTSUS chapters. Refer to the "Customs Classification" subsection for the key to the code numbers used.

The Harmonized Tariff Schedule of the United States (HTSUS)

This Commodity Index is organized according to the HTSUS, the document that Customs uses to classify and assign duty rates to all products imported into the U.S. It categorizes everything from ice and snow, to broccoli (*Brassica oleracea* var. *italica*), to 3-(N-Ethylanilino) propionic acid, to zippers, to skeet targets. As with any attempt at universal classification, it is complicated, and there are some idiosyncratic and questionable assignments, as well as some apparent contradictions, overlaps, and omissions. Omissions are often handled by "not elsewhere specified or included" (NESOI). The HTSUS can be obtained from the U.S. Government Printing Office (address listed earlier).

HTSUS Organization and Classification

The HTSUS consists of 22 sections, which contain 99 consecutively numbered chapters. Some sections contain a single chapter, while others have a dozen or more. The sections and the chapters they cover are as follows:

Section I —Live Animals and Animal Products (Chapters 1-5);

Section II—Vegetable Products (Chapters 6-14);

Section III—Animal and Vegetable Oils and Related Products (Chapter 15);

Section IV—Prepared Foods, Beverages, and Tobacco (Chapters 16-24);

Section V—Mineral Products (Chapters 25-27);

Section VI—Chemical and Allied Products (Chapters 28-38);

Section VII—Plastics and Rubber (Chapter 39-40);

Section VIII—Hides, Fur, Leather, and Leather Goods (Chapters 41-43);

Section IX—Wood, Cork, and Basketry (Chapters 44-46);

Section X—Pulp, Paper, and Paper Products (Chapters 47-49);

Section XI—Textiles (Chapters 50-63);

Section XII—Footwear, Headgear, Umbrellas, Prepared Feathers, and Artificial Flowers (Chapters 64-67);

Section XIII—Stone, Plaster, Cement, Ceramics, and Glassware (Chapters 68-70);

Section XIV—Gems and Jewelry (Chapter 71);

Section XV—Base Metals (Chapters 72-83);

Section XVI—Machinery and Electronics (Chapters 84-85);

Section XVII—Vehicles, Aircraft, Vessels, and Other Transportation Equipment (Chapter 86-89);

Section XVIII—Optical, Photographic, Scientific, Medical, Timekeeping, and Musical Instruments (Chapters 90-92);

Section XIX—Arms and Ammunition (Chapter 93);

Section XX—Miscellaneous Manufactures (Chapters 94-96);

Section XXI—Art and Antiques (Chapter 97);

Section XXII—Special and Temporary Classifications (Chapters 98-99).

There is no chapter 77—it is reserved for future use. Chapters 1 through 97 (77 excepted) represent the heart of the HTSUS, covering specific categories of products.

Below the chapter level, HTSUS is organized into nested categories beginning with major headings, such as the example "Other woven fabrics of cotton: Weighing not more than 200 g/m²," which is major heading 12 of chapter 52. In the HTSUS this is referred to as major heading 5212. If the fabric is unbleached, it falls into subheading 5212.11 (bleached fabrics of this type fall within subheading 5212.12). If unbleached and "containing 36% or more by weight of wool or of fine animal hair," it falls into the next more specific level of classification, sub-subheading 5212.11.10. This eight-digit level of classification is the one on which duties are assigned. There are even finer classifications for many products, although some are not divided beyond the major heading level (such as 0509.00.00—"Natural sponges of animal origin"). For the unbleached cotton woven fabrics noted above, if the cotton is "not combed," the 10-digit classification would be 5212.11.1010. Even though the 10-digit classification is used only for statistical reporting rather than for calculating tariffs owed, importers are nevertheless responsible for correctly classifying products to the 10-digit level of identification. Filing statistical data is part of the entry process.

Calculating Duty by the HTSUS

There are three subcolumns in the HTSUS which are all parts of the major column heading, "Rates of Duty." The first subcolumn—"General"—contains the base duty payable on goods of the corresponding category. For imports of product category 5212.11.10, the duty charged—an ad valorem duty based on a percentage of the value of the entry—is 21.4%. This tariff applies to imports from all Normal Trade Relations (NTR), and represents the base level of duty payable.

The next duty subcolumn—"Special"—lists the duty charged in special circumstances, usually constituting lower duties for entries of the product from specific places under certain conditions established by trade agreements. These are labeled with letters: A, A*or A+, B, C, CA, MX, D, E or E*, IL, J or J*, K, L, and R. "A", "A*", and "A+" designate those countries and commodities eligible for special reduced duty rates or duty-free entry under the terms of the Generalized System of Preferences (GSP) for less developed countries. "B" refers to the Automotive Products Trade Act, which covers eligible vehicle parts imported from Canada. "C" denotes the Agreement on Trade in Civil Aircraft, which covers eligible imports of aircraft and parts from countries certified by the Federal Aviation Administration.

"CA" refers to Canada and "MX" refers to Mexico, both of which are individually eligible to import certain products into the U.S. on favorable terms under the provisions of the North American Free Trade Agreement (NAFTA). "D" refers to the African Growth and Opportunity Act and gives favorable tariff rates to certain countries in sub-Saharan Africa. "E" and "E*" denote the Caribbean Basin Initiative (CBI)—technically, the Caribbean Basin Economic Recovery Act (CBERA)—which allows favorable or duty free treatment of certain products imported from member entities of the CBI. "IL" refers to the United States-Israel Free Trade Area, which allows duty free entry for eligible products imported from Israel. "J" and "J*" refer to the Andean Trade Preference Act (ATPA), which covers eligible imports of duty free or reduced rate merchandise from the signatory nations of the ATPA. "K" denotes products covered by the Agreement on Trade in Pharmaceutical Products. "L" refers to the treatment of products addressed by the Uruquay Round Concessions on Intermediate Chemicals for Dyes. Finally, "R" is in reference to the United States-Caribbean Basin Trade Partnership Act. For additional information on these programs see "Trade Agreements and Preferential Treatment Agreements" on page 226 or see the HTSUS General Notes 3-12.

The third and final subcolumn of "Rates of Duty" is labeled "2" for Column 2, which applies to countries that are assessed heavier duties than other countries on their imports into the U.S. In the past, most of the Column 2 countries have been Communist or former Communist states or other nations with which the U.S. allows trade to occur on restricted or unfavorable terms. The current edition of the HTSUS lists Afghanistan, Cuba, Laos, North Korea, and Vietnam as Column 2 countries. Those interested in trading with these countries should check with Customs regarding current Column 2 status, as diplomatic and trade initiatives can lead to alterations in this status.

Footnotes to the main HTSUS chapter headings usually refer the reader to an HTSUS chapter or section headnote, or to Chapter 99, which lists current quota and temporary tariff provisions. You should be sure to follow up on all such references, as they can contain significant information regarding your product.

Using the General Notes to the HTSUS

Time spent exploring the notes to the HTSUS can pay dividends to the importer. The introductory notes to the HTSUS—Supplement 1—which precede Section I, contain the latest information on trade issues covered in the HTSUS, as well as the basic rules for its use.

For example, the "General Rules of Interpretation" of these notes establish that the wording of the specific headings governs the assignments that can be made. If there is a disagreement over an assignment to a category based on apparent overlap or duplication, the category with the most specific description will prevail. Products consisting of mixtures of items will be classified under the category that gives the final product its essential character. Items—such as camera cases included with the camera (but not those imported separately)—and packing materials of a type customarily used with a product and not designed for reuse are classified with the primary product. In deciding between variant classifications, comparisons can be made only between subheadings of the same level of specificity (i.e., between subheadings, not between major headings and subheadings). The initial HTSUS notes set out general rules and procedures for making decisions on the these issues.

The "General Notes" provide information on basic definitions (Notes 1, 2, and 16), abbreviations used (Note 20), exemptions (Note 18), treatment of commingled goods (Note 19), and duty classifications and special provisions, primarily those established by treaty (Notes 3–12). "General Statistical Notes" (Notes 1–5) outline data required and procedures to be used in statistical reporting.

HTSUS Section and Chapter Notes

Some HTSUS sections and all individual HTSUS chapters have introductory notes, which give the ground rules for using those sections and chapters and often provide considerable additional information that can be of great use in navigating through HTSUS classifications. The amount of data varies by section and by chapter, but you should pay close attention to the information that can be gleaned from these often somewhat cryptic notes.

The introductory notes may include as many as four segments: "Notes," "Subheading Notes," "Additional U.S. Notes," and "Statistical Notes." The general notes usually outline the specific products and types of products that are not included in the section or chapter, and may redirect you to the appropriate chapter. "Subheading Notes" give specific information on definitions of products to be included in a particular subheading. The "Additional U.S. Notes" often give definitions or qualifications useful in classifying specific products. The "Statistical Notes" provide information for classifying products at the 10-digit level used for compiling import statistics.

Chapter 1:
Live Animals

This chapter relates to the importation of live animals, which are classified under Chapter 1 of the Harmonized Tariff Schedule of the United States (HTSUS). Specifically, it includes horses and related animals, cattle, pigs, sheep and goats, poultry, other birds, and virtually all other live animals, including pets and wildlife.

If you are interested in importing fish, crustaceans, molluscs, other aquatic animals, or cultures of microorganisms, refer to Commodity Index Chapter 3. Importation of live animals associated with traveling circuses, menageries, or similar exhibits is covered within Chapter 95.

Other special provisions affecting live animal imports include domesticated animals that stray or are driven across international boundaries for grazing purposes and are returned—along with their offspring—within eight months (HTSUS 9801.00.90); wild animals that are imported for use or for sale for scientific or educational purposes (HTSUS 9810.00.70); live animals, including poultry, that are imported for purposes of breeding, exhibition, or prize competition (HTSUS 9813.00.60); and live game animals that are imported for the purpose of stocking ranges (HTSUS 9817.00.70). No animals intended for use in fighting are allowed into the U.S.

Note: To understand key issues that will enable you to make best use of the information in this section we recommend that you see "Introduction" on page 425.

Key Factors

The key factors in the importation of live animals are:

- Compliance with U.S. Department of Agriculture (USDA) Animal and Plant Health Inspection Service (APHIS) and U.S. Fish and Wildlife Service (FWS) import regulations, restrictions, and quarantine requirements

- Entry at USDA designated ports (at FWS designated ports for imports of wildlife)

- USDA, FWS, and Customs port of entry inspections—prior notification required

- Acquisition of appropriate permits—required for most importations

- Acquisition of required veterinary certificates

- Compliance with importer's declaration requirements

- Compliance with Centers for Disease Control (CDC) regulations, restrictions, and quarantine requirements for potential vectors of human disease

- Compliance with APHIS Plant Protection and Quarantine (PPQ) branch requirements for living organisms which affect plants or with APHIS Veterinary Service (VS) requirements for living organisms which affect animals

- Compliance with endangered species restrictions on living animals

- Compliance with FWS licenses and recordkeeping requirements for persons in the business of importing wildlife (licenses required with certain exceptions)

- Compliance with U.S. Food and Drug Administration (FDA) regulations, restrictions, and entry notification, which may be required under certain circumstances

Although most importers utilize the services of a licensed customs broker in making their entries, and we recommend this practice, you should be aware of the regulatory, entry, and documentation issues involved in importing your product. You, as importer, are ultimately responsible for the fulfillment of any legal requirements applicable to your shipment.

General Considerations

Regulatory Agencies. Importation of many live animals is highly restricted under several laws administered by Federal agencies. Any of a number of agencies may have a regulatory interest in your importation. USDA APHIS, PPQ branch regulates the importation and interstate movement of live plant pests and vectors—such as insects that potentially carry disease-producing viruses—and articles that may harbor them, under applicable provisions of the Plant Quarantine Act of 1912 (PQA) and the Federal Plant Pest Act of 1957 (FPPA). Imports of live animals are regulated by the USDA, and in some instances by the FDA. The FWS may impose restrictions on imports of live wildlife, pets, or endangered species. The U.S National Marine Fisheries Service enforces regulations pertinent to imports of marine mammals in conjunction with FWS. Imports of live organisms that may be vectors of human disease are controlled by the U.S. Department of Health and Human Services through its Centers for Disease Control (CDC).

If you wish to import any kind of live animal, you should contact the government agencies listed for complete details. See "Relevant Government Agencies" below. Customs plays a monitoring and enforcement role for the voluminous import provisions of the various agencies. If you are at all unsure as to the regulatory status of your intended import, contact Customs for a referral to the appropriate regulating agency.

Most individual states also have import requirements for live animals in addition to those of Federal agencies. When planning your importation, you should always contact not only the pertinent federal agencies, but also the appropriate state regulatory agencies at your shipment's U.S. destination. You should also check on any state regulations in jurisdictions through which your shipment is to pass en route to its final destination. Do this before you attempt to enter the animals into the U.S.

Health Certificates. All live animal imports must be accompanied by a health certificate. Entry procedures for live animals coming from Mexico or Canada are somewhat less rigorous than for those entering from other countries.

Quarantine Regulations. The importation of live animals is subject to quarantine regulations under 9 CFR Part 92, administered and enforced by the USDA APHIS. APHIS restricts the import of live animals primarily to safeguard U.S. animals from communicable disease. The following categories of livestock are subject to USDA regulation: 1) ruminants, that is all cloven-hoofed animals, such as cattle, sheep, deer, antelope, camels, and giraffes;

2) swine; 3) horses, asses, mules, and zebras; and 4) live poultry. The USDA also regulates the import of birds and dogs. Also subject to separate regulation are animal byproducts, such as untanned hides, wool, hair, bones, bone meal, blood meal, animal casings, glands, organs, extracts or secretions of ruminants and swine, as well as hay and straw and other articles accompanying livestock imports.

This entry provides an overview of rather than an exhaustive treatment of APHIS and other agency requirements. Most live animal shipments must comply with the general requirements outlined here, although there are exceptions, as well as more stringent requirements which may apply in specific cases. Importation of certain live animals from listed countries in which certain communicable diseases are considered to be endemic is prohibited entirely. If you are interested in importing live animals, you should contact the APHIS for full information (see addresses at end of this chapter).

Endangered Species. The U.S. Department of the Interior's Fish and Wildlife Service (FWS) regulates importation of live animals covered under the Endangered Species Act (ESA) and the Convention on International Trade in Endangered Species (CITES). Importation of wildlife and pets is highly regulated and restricted. This category includes—but is not limited to—game animals, wild animals, game and wild birds and their eggs, and extends to any parts or products of the above. Importation of marine wildlife is also restricted.

The FWS enforces regulations pursuant to a number of wildlife protection laws, which are listed in 50 CFR. FWS licensing, permits, import declarations, and port inspections are generally required for imports of the species covered under these regulations. Shipments of FWS-regulated species must enter at designated ports (see below) listed in 50 CFR 10. If you are interested in importing any exotic live animal, you should contact FWS with the scientific name of the species to ascertain whether or not it is protected. If it is, you will need a FWS permit to import it. You may also need country of origin export permits and documentation.

Animal or Insect Pests and Vectors. If you wish to import living organisms classified as plant pests, you will need an APHIS PPQ import permit. USDA APHIS VS regulates importation and movement of live animal pests and vectors, under provisions of 9 CFR 122. If you wish to import such an organism, you will need an APHIS VS import permit. The CDC of the Department of Health and Human Services regulates the import of vectors of human disease. If your shipment contains any etiological agent or insect, animal or plant vector of human disease or any exotic living insect, animal, or plant capable of serving as a vector of human disease, you will need a CDC import permit.

Customs Classification

For customs purposes, live animals are classified under Chapter 1 of the HTSUS. This chapter is broken into major headings, which are further divided into subheadings, and often into sub-subheadings, each of which has its own HTSUS classification number. For example, the 2001 HTSUS number for cattle imported other than for dairy purposes is 0102.90.40, indicating that it is a subcategory of live cattle other than purebred breeding animals (0102.90), which is a subcategory of the major heading live bovine animals (0102). There are six major headings under Chapter 1.

0101—Live horses, asses, mules, and hinnies

0102—Live bovine animals

0103—Live swine

0104—Live sheep and goats

0105—Live poultry of the following kinds: chickens, ducks, geese, turkeys, and guineas

0106—Other live animals

For more details regarding classification of the specific animal you are interested in importing, consult a customs broker, the appropriate commodity specialist at your nearest customs port, or see the HTSUS. The 2001 HTSUS is available online from the Customs Service (www.customs.gov/impoexpo/impoexpo.htm) or for purchase from the U.S. Government Printing Office (see resources at the end of this chapter), and may be found in larger public libraries. For a general discussion of customs classification, see "Classification—Liquidation" on page 244.

Dutiable Status of Goods

For more information about duty rates and binding decisions see "Dutiable Status of Goods" on page 203; for a discussion of temporary importation of goods see "Temporary Free Importations" on page 220.

Valuation

Importers have a responsibility to use what U.S. Customs and Border Protection deems, "reasonable care," when determining the value of their goods. They must also provide any additional information that U.S. Customs and Border Protection needs for setting a final value on the goods. This process involves a number of factors and can be somewhat complicated; importers must be aware of applicable issues and details. Valuation information applies to all types of commodities, for further discussion on the subject see "Customs Valuation" on page 284.

Import Duties

Import duties vary (often dramatically) depending upon the Harmonized Tariff Schedule (HTSUS) classification of the product imported. Since some products that look alike have different HTSUS classifications and different rates of duty, proper classification is vital. Note that "differences of opinion" between importers and the Bureau of Customs and Border Protection regarding classification keeps customs attorneys very busy.

Import duties can be assessed on the imported value of the goods ("ad valorem" rates of duty such as 2%, 4.4%, 50%, etc.), total units or weight of the goods ("specific" rates of duty such as 2 cents each or 1.5 cents/pound, etc.) or on a combination basis ("compound" rates of duty such as 5 cents each plus 6%).

Listed below is a sampling of several Column 1 import duty rates for Chapter 01 products:
Mules and hinnies imported for immediate slaughter (0101.90.30.00): free
to
Asses (0101.90.20.00): 6.8%

For specific information on US import duties refer to the Harmonized Tariff Schedule of the US. The print version is available from the US Government Printing Office as well as third party suppliers who often add special features. Online versions are available in both static PDF pages as well as in formats with excellent search functionality. Search the Web with the term "Harmonized Tariff Schedule" to find sources.

Entry and Documentation

The entry of merchandise is a two-part process consisting of 1) filing the documents necessary to determine whether merchandise may be released from Customs custody and 2) filing the documents which contain information for duty assessment and statistical purposes. In certain instances all documents must be filed and accepted by Customs prior to the release of the goods. Unless you have been granted an extension, you must file entry documents at a location specified by the port or area director within five working days of your shipment's date of arrival at a U.S. port of entry. These include a number of standard documents required by Customs for any entry, and, where applicable:

- USDA permits as required
- Veterinary certificate(s) from the country of origin
- Importer's declaration, two copies
- Valid APHIS PPQ Import Permit for living plant pests Form PPQ 526
- Valid APHIS VS Import Permit for living animal pests Form VS 17-129
- Valid CDC Import Permit for living organisms that may carry human disease
- FWS import permits required under CITES, ESA, and any other regulations applicable to the particular shipment; and any export certification from country of origin required under the specific laws governing endangered or threatened species
- FWS Wildlife Declaration Form 3-177—an original plus 3 copies—a copy of air waybill or bill of lading, and a copy of invoice (proforma invoice if shipment is noncommercial)

After you present the entry, Customs may examine your shipment, or may waive examination. The shipment is then released provided no legal or regulatory violations have been noted. You must then file entry summary documentation and deposit estimated duties at a designated customhouse within 10 working days of your shipment's release. For a detailed description of entry procedures, standard documentation, and informal entry, see "Entry Process" on page 199.

Informed Compliance. Informed compliance was introduced with the Customs Modernization Act of 1993 (Mod Act) and defines the relationship between importers and U.S. Customs and Border Protection. It sets out the responsibilities of both parties. Providing the correct documentation and information for entry is a key factor that will make your importing operation run smoothly. We recommend that importers become familiar with the concept of informed comliance and the responsibilities that they have under the Mod Act. For further discussion about informed

Note: The Entry and Documentation section has been carefully designed to supply you, the importer, with sample documents and directions on how to satisfy Customs requirements. Be aware that you should consult the applicable authorities to ensure that you are correctly following the most current procedures.

Prohibitions and Restrictions

Absolute Prohibitions. Animals to be used in fighting may not be imported.

USDA APHIS Entry and Permit Requirements. In general, all live animals must 1) enter at APHIS-designated quarantine ports (see listing below); 2) undergo APHIS port of entry inspection; 3) after passing entry must be immediately confined in an APHIS-operated or APHIS-approved privately-owned quarantine facility for a period of time which varies according to species. During quarantine, certain tests may be required to ascertain the health of the animals.

Import Permit. With a few exceptions, all live animals must be covered by an APHIS import permit, which must be presented to Customs at the first port of arrival. These permits must be obtained prior to the export of the animals from their country of origin. At the time you apply for a permit to import animals subject to quarantine requirements, you will need to make reservations for space in an appropriate quarantine facility. Fees for quarantine reservations vary according to species, and are due and payable at the time the reservation is requested.

Each shipment entering under an APHIS permit must comply with the permit's specifications in every particular. If your shipment is found not to conform in any way (such as entering at a port of entry other than the one specified in the permit), it will be refused entry.

Veterinary Certificate. A veterinary certificate, issued by a salaried veterinarian of the country of origin, stating that the animals are free of applicable livestock diseases must accompany each shipment. The specific information required on the certificate varies depending upon the species you are importing, as well as its country of origin. You must also present an importer's declaration that states: 1) port of entry; 2) importer's name and address; 3) broker's name and address; 4) origin of the animal(s); 5) number, breed, species, and purpose of importation; and 6) consignee's name and location of intended delivery.

APHIS-designated Quarantine Ports. The following APHIS-designated ports generally have adequate quarantine facilities available for the import of live animals. With few exceptions, all shipments of live animals must enter at a designated port. Additional ports and any exceptions are listed under the heading pertaining to the particular type of livestock (such as ruminant, horse, etc.).

Air and ocean ports: Los Angeles, CA; Miami, FL; and Newburgh, NY.

Land border ports with Canada: Eastport, ID; Houlton and Jackman, MI; Detroit, Port Huron, and Sault Ste. Marie, MI; Baudette, MN; Opheim, Raymond, and Sweetgrass, MT; Alexandria Bay, Buffalo, and Champlain, NY; Dunseith, Pembina, and Portal, ND; Derby Line and Highgate Springs, VT; Lynden, Oroville, and Sumas, WA.

Land border ports with Mexico: Brownsville, Hidalgo, Laredo, Eagle Pass, Del Rio, and Presidio, TX; Douglas, Naco, Nogales, and San Luis, AZ; Calexico and San Ysidro, CA; Antelope Wells, Columbus, and Santa Teresa, NM.

Limited ports (ports with facilities for entry of live animals that do not appear to require restraint and holding inspection facilities): Anchorage and Fairbanks, AK; San Diego and San Francisco, CA; Denver, CO; Jacksonville, St. Petersburg-Clearwater, and Tampa, FL; Atlanta, GA; Honolulu, HI; Chicago, IL; New Orleans, LA; Portland, ME; Baltimore, MD; Boston, MA; Minneapolis, MN; Great Falls, MT; Dayton, OH; Portland, OR; San Juan, PR; Memphis, TN; El Paso, Galveston and Houston, TX; Seattle, Spokane, and Tacoma, WA.

These listed ports have been designated as quarantine stations. The USDA Administrator has authority to designate other ports as quarantine stations as needed.

USDA Requirements for Poultry. Except for live poultry and products entering through land ports from Canada, APHIS permits are required for all entries of live poultry. Permits covering multiple poultry shipments transiting the port of Anchorage, AK are available, and if issued, are valid for the duration of the calendar year of issue. For more information on these permits, contact APHIS (see addresses at end of this chapter).

Poultry includes chickens, doves, ducks, geese, grouse, guinea fowl, partridges, pea fowl, pheasant, pigeons, quail, swans, and turkeys, and the fertilized eggs of these species. Import and quarantine restrictions on these birds are designed to prevent the introduction into the U.S. of communicable poultry diseases, such as European fowl pest (fowl plague) or Exotic Newcastle disease (END).

Veterinary Certificate. The veterinary certificate must show, among other things, that the flock was inspected and found to be free of disease immediately prior to export, and that the poultry was not exposed to disease common to poultry during the 90 days immediately preceding export.

Quarantine Requirements. Most poultry (exception is made for poultry from Canada) is quarantined for not less than 30 days, beginning with the date of arrival at the port of entry. During quarantine, poultry is subject to whatever inspections, disinfections, and tests that may be required by the USDA to determine the health of the animals. Most fertile eggs are quarantined until hatched, and the poultry must remain in quarantine not less than 30 days after hatching. The reservation fee for APHIS quarantine space is 100% of the cost of providing care, feed, and handling during quarantine, as estimated by the quarantine facility's veterinarian in charge.

USDA Requirements for Horses. Quarantine regulations governing the import of horses are extensive and complex. The ones mentioned here represent only a partial summary. If you are interested in importing horses, you should contact APHIS for specifics.

Horses (except those originating in or transited through countries where African horsesickness is known to exist) destined for quarantine facilities provided by the importer may be imported at any international customs port, provided all applicable provisions of the regulation have been met. If you wish to provide your own quarantine facilities, you must obtain prior APHIS approval. Reservation fees for APHIS quarantine facilities are 100% of the cost of providing care, feed, and handling during quarantine, and may be satisfied by a letter of credit. Quarantine requirements for horses vary depending upon country of origin, and generally last until negative results to tests conducted at the port of entry are obtained and the horses are certified by the port veterinarian to be free from clinical evidence of disease.

CEM Restrictions. With a few limited exceptions, the importation of all horses from any of the following listed countries and the importation of all horses that have been in any listed country within the 12 months immediately preceding their being offered for entry into the United States is prohibited, either because contagious equine metritis (CEM) exists in the listed country or because the listed country trades horses freely with a country in which CEM exists without testing for CEM: Austria, Belgium, Bosnia and Herzegovina, Croatia, the Czech Republic, Denmark, Finland, France, Germany, Guinea-Bissau, Ireland, Italy, Japan, the Member States of the European Union, The Netherlands, Norway, Slovakia, Slovenia, Sweden, Switzerland, The Former Yugoslav Republic of Macedonia, the United Kingdom (England, Northern Ireland, Scotland, Wales, and the Isle of Man), Serbia and Montenegro.

Exceptions to this blanket prohibition may be made for specific animals under APHIS permit. Such special case imports require stringent preexport veterinary examinations, which must be documented on the veterinary certificate necessary for entry. The following horses meeting these conditions and originating in CEM countries may be imported: 1) horses imported under special provisions initiated by the USDA Administrator under 9 CFR 92.301(a); 2) geldings, weanlings, or yearlings whose age is certified on the import health certificate; 3) thoroughbred horses imported for permanent entry from Germany, the United Kingdom, Ireland, and France; 4) stallions over 731 days in age; 5) mares over 731 days in age; 5) horses over 731 days in age imported into the U.S. for no more than 90 days to compete in specified events; 6) horses temporarily exported from the U.S. to any listed country for a period not to exceed 60 days, not bred to any animal during that 60 days, and returned to the U.S. Each of these permissible importations are contingent on specific conditions as outlined in 9 CFR 92.301. For details, see that document, or contact APHIS (see addresses at end of this chapter).

You may import stallions over 731 days old originating in countries listed as affected with CEM only if destined for the following states: Alabama, California, Colorado, Florida, Kentucky, Louisiana, Maryland, Montana, New Hampshire, New Jersey, New York, North Carolina, Ohio, South Carolina, Tennessee, Texas, Virginia, and Wisconsin. Mares meeting the above specifications may be imported only if destined for: Alabama, California, Colorado, Kentucky, Louisiana, Maryland, Montana, New

Hampshire, New Jersey, New York, Ohio, South Carolina, Tennessee, Texas, Virginia, and Wisconsin. Horses destined for these states must undergo state quarantine pursuant to regulations in 9 CFR 92 Subpart C.

The regulations regarding the importation of horses from countries affected with CEM were amended in 1996 by incorporating new testing and treatment protocols for mares and stallions, providing for the use of accredited veterinarians to monitor horses temporarily imported into the U.S. for competition purposes, incorporating a new testing protocol for thoroughbred horses in training in their country of origin, and removing the requirements for endometrial cultures and clitoral sinusectomies in mares. These changes update, clarify, and streamline existing regulations and simplify the requirements for importing horses from countries affected with CEM without increasing the risk of the disease being introduced into the U.S.

African Horsesickness Restrictions. Horses imported from countries considered to be affected with African horsesickness—Portugal, Spain, Yemen, and all countries on the continent of Africa—must enter the U.S. through the port of New York. Such horses will have to be quarantined at the New York Animal Import Center in Newburgh, New York, for at least 60 days. This restriction also applies to horses that have stopped in or transited a country considered affected with African horsesickness.

USDA Requirements for Ruminants. Permits are required for all ruminants. Veterinary certificates are also required for all ruminants offered for import, with extra information required for sheep and goats. APHIS is particularly concerned with brucellosis and tuberculosis in cattle and goats. In most cases, you will have to include test results concerning these diseases on the veterinary certificate. Quarantine reservation fees are 100% of the cost of providing care, feed, and handling during quarantine, and may be satisfied by a letter of credit.

The port of Los Angeles, CA is not approved for importation of ruminants.

Country-Specific Exceptions. Import permits are not required for ruminants imported from Canada through designated U.S.-Canadian border ports, as long as the animals are of either Canadian or U.S. origin, and have not been in any other country, or, if imported to Canada from a foreign country, have been unconditionally released in Canada for 60 days or longer. Cattle originating in Canada must be accompanied by specified health documentation (consult 9 CFR 92.418 for details). Special provisions and requirements also apply to ruminants from Central America, the West Indies, and Mexico (9 CFR 92.422-429). Special restrictions apply to cattle imported from the Republic of Ireland (9 CFR 92.432) and to sheep imported from New Zealand. For specific details, see 9 CFR 92 or contact APHIS.

USDA Requirements for Swine. Permits are required for all swine. APHIS is particularly concerned with rinderpest and foot-and-mouth disease in swine. Quarantine reservation fees are 100% of the cost of providing care, feed, and handling during quarantine, and may be satisfied by a letter of credit. You will not need an import permit for swine imported from Canada through designated U.S.-Canadian border ports, as long as your animals are of either Canadian or U.S. origin, and have not been in any other country, or, if imported to Canada from a foreign country, have been unconditionally released in Canada for 60 days or longer.

Harry S. Truman Animal Import Center (HSTAIC). It may be possible to import ruminants and swine originating in countries from which imports are otherwise prohibited because of the presence of disease. Such importations enter through HSTAIC, under cooperative agreement between APHIS and the importer Application, accompanied by a $50,000 deposit, for this type of special import approval are made to APHIS. APHIS holds one lottery in October and another in April to choose which application will be approved. The applicant is responsible for all costs incurred in the HSTAIC quarantine process, as well as for fulfilling all of the requirements, such as providing a preexport quarantine site for the animals in the country of origin. For details, see 9 CFR 522 or contact APHIS.

USDA Requirements for Insects. It is impossible to list standard import requirements for all insects. Basically, insects that are in a live state and that are injurious to cultivated crops (including vegetables, field crops, bush fruit, and orchard, forest, or shade trees), and the eggs, pupae, or larvae of such insects, are prohibited entry. Exceptions are made for scientific purposes under regulations prescribed by the Secretary of Agriculture. Live insects—or their eggs, pupae, or larvae—that are not injurious to crops or trees, are permitted entry into the U.S. only if covered by an APHIS permit, which can be obtained only if the insects are not prohibited by the FWS.

The importation of certain species of insects does not require a permit. However, you must be very sure of such exemption before attempting unauthorized importation. We strongly advise that you provide all concerned federal agencies with specific biological information regarding any insect you intend to ship to the U.S., to be sure your bases are covered. Never assume that no permit is required. Let the agencies make that determination.

CDC Requirements for Insects. If you wish to import an insect that may be capable of being a vector of human disease, you will need a Centers for Disease Control (CDC) permit. You should complete and submit to CDC's Office of Biosafety (see addresses at end of this chapter), an original signed copy of CDC Application for Permit to Import or Transport Agents or Vectors of Human Disease. To qualify for a permit, you must reside in the U.S. You should only sign the application if you are actually the proposed permit holder. Permit applications signed by persons other than the proposed permit holder are invalid.

On the application, you will be expected to provide such information as: 1) person requesting permit, 2) source and description of material; 3) number of shipments; 4) method of transport; 5) quantity, i.e. volume and type of individual containers; 6) proposed use, including objectives, proposed plan of work, completion date, final disposition of materials; 7) description of available isolation and containment facilities; 8) qualifications and experience of technical personnel. If your approved permit stipulates additional restrictions and precautions, you must adhere to them.

FWS Regulations for Wild Animals and Pets.

If you import goods into a non-designated port a port exception permit is required, or if you import outside of normal business hours, additional fees will apply. For a full description of licensing and recordkeeping requirements, contact the FWS or see 50 CFR 14.

FWS Designated Wildlife Ports. All wildlife shipments must enter and leave the U.S. through FWS designated ports, as listed in 50 CFR 14.12. Currently there are 10 such designated ports: New York, NY; Miami, FL; New Orleans, LA; Dallas/Ft. Worth, TX; Los Angeles, CA; San Francisco, CA; Chicago, IL; Seattle, WA; Honolulu, HI; and Portland, OR. If special circumstances prevent you from making your entry at a designated port, an Exception to Designated Port Permit is required and must be obtained from FWS (see addresses at end of this chapter).

FWS Entry Requirements. At least 72 hours before your shipment is due to arrive at the designated port, you should notify both U.S. Customs and FWS inspectors there of its expected arrival. The FWS and Customs will inspect your shipment to verify compliance with all of the legal requirements for entry. Importations may also be subject to the quarantine requirements of the USDA and the U.S. Public Health Service (see below). Questions on these requirements should be directed to those agencies.

You will need to furnish the officials with any documentation required by the laws under which your import is protected. Documents required by FWS at port of entry vary depending upon the nature of the shipment, but in general include: 1) all permits or certificates required under CITES, ESA, and any other regulations applicable to the particular shipment; 2) Wildlife Declaration **Form 3-177**, available at the port of entry (an original plus 3 copies); 3) copy of air waybill or bill of lading; 4) copy of invoice (proforma invoice if shipment is noncommercial). Invoices for wildlife shipments must specify the species covered and the quantity of each species.

In addition to this paperwork, importers of fish and wildlife must also present any appropriate foreign export permits and other acceptable foreign documentary evidence of the lawful taking, transportation, or sale of the wildlife. Appropriate U.S. consular certificates must be presented for importation of species subject to such documentation requirements in 50 CFR 17.4. A Mexican export permit is required for any game animals (e.g., antelope, mountain sheep, deer, bears, peccaries, squirrels, rabbits, and hares), including their parts or products, imported from Mexico.

Can shipments be combined to avoid payment of fees? No. Individual shipments cannot be combined on one Declaration for Importation or Exportation (Form 3-177) to avoid payment of fees.

Detention of Shipment. If Customs has any doubt about compliance of your FWS-regulated wildlife shipment, such as the endangered status of the wildlife, fulfillment of permit requirement particulars, or accurate identification of species, your importation will not be released. If your shipment is detained, you will be responsible for making arrangements acceptable to the FWS for proper handling, custody, and care of the specimens. All such arrangements are at the expense and risk of the importer. Customs will not dispose of the importation until FWS determines the true nature of the species. If you refuse to have the identity established, the FWS will determine final disposition of the importation.

Designated Injurious Species. Species listed as "injurious" in 50 CFR 13 are prohibited importation because they pose a threat of injury to human beings, or to U.S. agriculture, horticulture, forestry, wildlife, or wildlife resources. You may import certain injurious species as exceptions under FWS permit. If you attempt to enter a shipment of injurious species without appropriate FWS authorization, however, it will be immediately exported or destroyed. Keep abreast of listing changes in prohibited and restricted injurious species by consulting 50 CFR 13.

Currently listed are: 1) any species of the so-called "flying fox" or fruit bat of the genus *Pteropus*; 2) any species of mongoose or meerkat of the genera *Atilax, Cynictis, Helogale, Herpestes, Ichneumia, Mungos,* and *Suricata*; 3) any species of European rabbit of the genus *Oryctolagus*; 4) any species of Indian wild dog, red dog, or dhole of the genus *Cuon*; 5) any species of the multimammate rat or mouse of the genus *Mastomys*; 6) any live specimens or fertile eggs of the species of so-called "pink starling" or "rosy pastor," *Sturnus roseus*; 7) the species of dioch (including the subspecies black-fronted, red-billed, or Sudan dioch) *Quelea quelea*; 8) any species of Java sparrow, *Padda oryzivora*; 9) the species of red-whiskered bulbul, *Pycnonotus jocosus*; 10) any live fish or viable eggs of the family *Clariidae*.

Designated Endangered and Threatened Species. The FWS enforces a variety of laws protecting endangered species of animals and birds. Protected species are listed in 50 CFR 17. Listed species are generally prohibited entry into the U.S. However, specimens of some species may be imported under FWS permit. Under CITES, certain animals, mammals, birds, reptiles, amphibians, fish, snails, and clams may be prohibited or may require FWS permits or certification. You may import antique articles otherwise prohibited under the ESA, provided certain conditions are met. These articles must be entered at designated antique ports.

Marine Mammals. The taking and importation of marine mammals and their products are subject to the requirements of the Marine Mammal Protection Act of 1972 (MMPA). Importation is prohibited except under permit from the National Marine Fisheries Service or from FWS. For more information, contact either of those agencies (addresses below).

Birds. Live wild birds protected under the Migratory Bird Treaty Act (MBTA) may be imported into the U.S. from foreign countries for scientific or propagating purposes under FWS permit. State game departments, municipal game farms or parks; public museums, zoological parks, or societies; and scientific or educational institutions may import migratory birds without a permit. Mexican export permits are required for all such migratory birds, including their parts or products, imported from Mexico.

USDA Regulations for Wild Animals and Pets. Wild ruminants (all animals that chew their cud, such as cattle, buffaloes, sheep, goats, deer, antelopes, camels, llamas, and giraffes) and swine (various varieties of wild hogs), and ducks, geese, swans, turkeys, pigeons, doves, pheasant, grouse, partridges, quail, guinea fowl, and pea fowl may be imported only under USDA APHIS VS permit (see addresses at end of this chapter). You must obtain your APHIS permit before the animals are shipped from the country of exportation. All wild ruminants and swine are inspected at designated ports of entry by USDA veterinarians. USDA also regulates importation of hedgehogs, opossums, elephants, rhinoceros, hippopotamus, and tapirs, under 9 CFR. Permits are required.

CDC Regulations for Wild Animals and Pets. Importation of birds, cats, dogs, nonhuman primates, and turtles is subject to the requirements of the CDC, Quarantine Division (see addresses at end of this chapter).

Psittacine Birds. Psittacine birds include all birds commonly known as parrots: Amazons, African grays, cockatoos, macaws, parrotlets, beebees, parakeets, lovebirds, lories, lorikeets, and all other birds of the order *Psittaciformes*. If you wish to import birds destined for a zoological park or medical research institution, which have not had prior confinement and treatment abroad at an approved treatment center, you must obtain a CDC permit. Permits are also required for birds previously exported from the U.S. and returned under 19 CFR 12.26(b)(4)(c) without having been confined in the foreign country.

Psittacine Birds as Pets. Psittacine birds may be imported under prescribed conditions (42 CFR 71.164(e)) without permit and without prior confinement and treatment, to be kept as pets by the owner. Such importations may not exceed two such birds by members of a family comprising a single household in any 12-month period. If your import falls into this category, you must be sure to comply with all applicable CDC Foreign Quarantine Regulations. Birds taken out of the U.S. and returned may be admitted without permit, provided there is full compliance with prescribed conditions. If your import fits this category, you should be aware that your birds will not be released from Customs custody until you have complied with all applicable Public Health Service requirements. For more information, contact the CDC (see addresses at end of this chapter).

Nonhuman primates. Nonhuman primates include but are not limited to such animals commonly known as monkeys, chimpanzees, orangutans, gorillas, gibbons, apes, baboons, marmosets, tamarins, lemurs, lorises, and galagos. Importation of nonhuman primates as pets is prohibited. Nonhuman primates may only be imported for permitted purposes, i.e. bona fide research, education, or exhibition, and only by importers registered with CDC. Bona fide exhibition purposes include 1) display in an organized zoological exhibit regularly open to the general public, and 2) full-time use in a trained animal act open to the public. Display in a pet store or private home, or maintenance and training of a nonhuman primate primarily as a hobby, with occasional display to groups such as school children, does not constitute a bona fide exhibition.

If you import nonhuman primates, you must not sell, resell, or otherwise distribute the animals for exhibition purposes without clear evidence that they will be used as a bona fide exhibit. The intended recipient's possession of a USDA Animal Exhibitor's License is not sufficient documentation. Importation of nonhuman primates for use in breeding colonies is permitted, provided that all descendants of these animals will be solely used for the permitted purposes.

If you wish to register as an importer of nonhuman primates, you must comply with specific CDC transport and quarantine requirements. Guidelines are published in CDC's Morbidity and Mortality Weekly Report (MMWR) Vol. 39, No. 2, January 19, 1990: "Interim Guidelines for Handling Nonhuman Primates During Transit and Quarantine." A special CDC permit is required, in addition to registration, if you wish to import cynomolgus, African green, or rhesus monkeys. Special permit requirements were published in the Federal Register, April 20, 1990. For more information, see that publication or contact the CDC (see addresses at end of this chapter).

Nonhuman primates not meeting the import requirements of the current quarantine regulation will be refused entry. If your shipment is refused, you have the option to export, destroy, or give the animals to a scientific, educational, or exhibition facility under CDC-approved arrangements. Any such disposition will be at the importer's expense. Pending exportation or other disposition, the animals will be detained in Customs custody at the port of arrival, also at the importer's expense. Nonhuman primates must also meet FWS import requirements.

Dogs and Cats. Dogs and cats are subject to quarantine requirements under 42 CFR 71.51. All dogs and cats must be inspected by a CDC officer at port of entry. Only those animals which show no signs of communicable disease will be admitted entry. If your animals show signs of disease, or have been exposed to disease during transit, you must provide for confinement quarters, and must arrange for all necessary veterinary examinations and tests to ensure the animal's health prior to importation. Such confinement is at your expense. A valid rabies vaccination certificate is required for each dog unless the dog meets specific exemption qualifications (see 42 CFR 71.51). The carrier responsible for transit of dogs and cats must submit at port of entry a record of all diseases and/or deaths occurring during transit. Any dog or cat refused entry will be detained in Customs custody pending reexportation, at your expense.

Live Turtles and Viable Turtle Eggs. Live turtles with a carapace length of less than four inches, and viable turtle eggs are prohibited importation into the U.S. unless such importation is not in connection with a business, and the lot is limited to fewer than seven live turtles, seven viable turtle eggs, or any combination thereof totaling no more than seven. You may import shipments of more than seven, for bona fide scientific, educational, or exhibition purposes, but only under CDC permit. A CDC permit does not preclude the necessity for any other authorization from other governmental agency, as in the case of a turtle also protected under the Endangered Species Act, etc. For more information, contact CDC (see addresses at end of this chapter).

USDA Animal and Plant Health Inspection Service Veterinary Services also has a regulatory interest in these shipments. Contact that agency for more information.

FDA Regulations for Wild Animals and Pets. Importation of turtles with a carapace length of less than four inches, and of psittacine birds, is also subject to the requirements of the FDA.

For a discussion about importing food see "Appendix: Foods" on page 924. For further information, contact FDA (see addresses at end of this chapter).

Country-Specific Import Restrictions

The USDA restricts the importation of domesticated animals based on country of origin and type of animal based on endemic disease among the types of animals in that geographic area. See the discussion above, or contact USDA APHIS (see addresses at end of this chapter) for more information. Endangered species restrictions under CITES are country-specific. Consult the FWS (see addresses at end of this chapter) for more information.

Regulatory Changes. APHIS has amended the animal and animal product importation regulations to allow for regionalization of countries—that is, disease classification of parts of a country, an entire country, or groups of countries. The rule change was made to recognize levels of disease risk in regions. Details about the criteria that APHIS considers when evaluating the regions that wish to export animals or animal products to the United States can be found at the APHIS Veterinary Service National Center for Import and Export (NCIE) website (www.aphis.usda.gov/ncie).

Live Animals from Canada, Mexico, Central America, and West Indies. There are special provisions for live animals originating in Canada, Mexico, Central America, and the West Indies. These provisions vary according to species, and include such elements as permit or quarantine waiver, special quarantine restrictions, and specific ports of entry for specific types of animals, as well as special provisions for animals imported for immediate slaughter or for transit across the U.S. only. For entries from these countries, only one copy of the import declaration must be presented to Customs. For more details, see the appropriate headings in 9 CFR 92, or contact APHIS.

Poultry from Canada, Virgin Islands, and Mexico. Poultry from Canada entering the U.S. at designated Canadian-U.S. land border ports do not require an APHIS permit, and are not subject to quarantine, provided all other requirements are met. APHIS may waive the permit requirement for poultry intended for immediate slaughter imported into the U.S. Virgin Islands from the British Virgin Islands. For poultry from Mexico, the importer must make application for inspection in writing, and submit it to the veterinary inspector at the port of entry. All poultry from Mexico must be imported through designated U.S.-Mexican land border ports. APHIS is particularly concerned with fever tick infestation in Mexican poultry. Any shipment of Mexican origin found to contain fever ticks will be refused entry and will be destroyed unless immediately removed.

Marking and Labeling Requirements

USDA APHIS Approved Imports. When APHIS PPQ issues a permit for a given shipment of insect, it also supplies a mailing label, which you must use on the package. The label provides specific instructions for packaging, marking, and labeling, which you must follow when preparing your package for transport.

Wildlife and Endangered Species. All wildlife shipments must be marked on the outside of the container with the names and addresses of the exporter and importer, an accurate identification of the species, and the numbers of each species in the container.

For a general discussion of U.S. Customs marking and labeling requirements, see "Country of Origin Marking" on page 251, "Special Marking Requirements" on page 253 and "Marking—False Impression" on page 239.

Shipping Considerations

You will need to ensure that animal imports are quartered and shipped with care so that they arrive in good condition and pass smoothly through Customs. You are responsible for ensuring that the shipment is in compliance with all applicable government regulations for shipping. In most instances, you should not leave these arrangements solely to the discretion of your supplier. Careful preparation of the shipment and selection of the mode of transport can be essential to a cost-effective, timely delivery of undamaged goods. We strongly advise you to consult your shipping representative, insurance agent, or freight broker for advice on packing and shipping. Refer also to the major tab section "Packing/Shipping/Insurance" for a general discussion of packing and shipping.

Publications and WWW Resources

The following publication gives brief, general guidelines on USDA regulated products. Although designed primarily for tourists, it contains a list of approved products that you may find helpful. It is available online from the USDA APHIS website (www.aphis.usda.gov).

Travelers Tips On Bringing Food, Plant, and Animal Products into the United States

The *Harmonized Tariff Schedule of the United States (2001)* (HTSUS) is available to view on the U.S Customs and Border Protection website (www.customs.treas.gov), or you may purchase a printed version from:

U.S. Government Printing Office
Superintendent of Documents
710 North Capital Street NW
Washington DC 20401
Tel: (202) 512-1800
Fax: (202) 512-1657
Website: www.access.gpo.gov

The USGPO also has copies of specific laws available for purchase. The USGPO accepts orders made by fax, phone or placed over the Internet, as well as mail orders paid by credit card. All orders must be accompanied by payment. Credit cards, checks drawn on a U.S. bank, or an international money order are all acceptable.

Address your questions regarding wildlife treaties and endangered plants and animals to:

Convention on International Trade in Endangered Species of Wild Fauna and Flora (CITES)
CITES Secretariat
15 chemin des Anemones
1219 Chatelaine-Geneva
Switzerland
Tel: [41] (22) 917-8139/40
Fax: [41] (22) 797-3417
Website: www.cites.org
Email: cites@unep.ch

Address your questions regarding USDA requirements for the importation of live animals to:

Animal and Plant Health Inspection Service (APHIS)
Veterinary Services (VS)
National Center for Import and Export
4700 River Rd., Unit 40
Riverdale, MD 20737
Tel: (301) 734-3277
Website: www.aphis.usda.gov/vs

Animal and Plant Health Inspection Service (APHIS)
International Services, Import/Export
4700 River Rd.
Riverdale, MD 20737
Tel: (301) 734-3277
Website: www.aphis.usda.gov

Address your questions regarding the importation of wildlife, pets, or endangered species to:

U.S. Fish and Wildlife Service (FWS)
Division of Management Authority
4401 N. Fairfax Dr., Rm. 700
Arlington, VA 22203-0700
Tel: (703) 358-2104
Website: www.fws.gov

National Marine Fisheries Service (NMFS)
1315 East West Highway
SSMC3
Silver Spring, MD 20910
Tel: (301) 713-2239
Office of Protected Resources: (301) 713-2332
Inspection Services Division: (301) 713-2355
Website: www.nmfs.noaa.gov

Address your questions regarding FDA requirements for the importation of live animals to:

Food and Drug Administration (FDA)
Center for Food Safety and Applied Nutrition (CFSAN)
Office of Compliance
Division of Enforcement, Imports Branch
5100 Paint Branch Parkway
College Park, MD 20740-3835
Tel: (301) 436-2080
Website: http://vm.cfsan.fda.gov/list.html

Address your questions or requests for permit applications for import of live organisms that may be vectors of human disease to:

Centers for Disease Control (CDC)
1600 Clifton Rd.
Atlanta, GA 30333
Tel: (404) 639-3311
Public Inquiries:
Tel: (404) 639-3534
Office of Health and Safety: (404) 639-2453
Quarantine Division: (404) 498-1670
Website: www.cdc.gov

Address your questions regarding the importation of live animals to the your local Customs port director. For addresses see "Ports of Entry and Customs Service Ports" on page 196" or contact:

U.S. Customs and Border Protection
Customs Headquarters
1300 Pennsylvania Avenue NW
Washington DC 20229
Tel: (202) 354-1000
Website: www.customs.treas.gov

Laws and Regulations

The following laws and regulations may be relevant to the importation of live animals. The laws are contained in the U.S. Code (USC) and the regulations are published in the code of Federal Regulations (CFR), both of which may be available at larger public and law libraries. Copies of specific laws are also available from the United States Government Printing Office (address above).

7 USC 2156
Animal Fighting Venture Prohibition
This Act prohibits the transport in foreign commerce of animals to be used in an animal fighting venture and authorizes U.S. Customs to enforce the prohibition.

7 USC 4801 et seq.
Pork Promotion, Research, and Consumer Information Act of 1985
This Act provides that each importer of porcine animal, pork, or pork product shall remit an assessment to Customs at the time the product is imported. See 7 CFR 1230.71 and 1230.110.

18 USC 42 et seq.

Importation of Injurious Animals, Birds, Fish, and Plants
This Act governs the importation of mammals, birds, fish, amphibia, and reptiles into the U.S. which, may be hazadous to humans or harmful to U.S. agriculture and it authorizes U.S. Customs to enforce the import requirements.

21 USC 101 et seq.
Importation of Cattle and Quarantine
This Act provides for suspension of importation of animals to prevent the spread of disease, and for the quarantine of prohibited classes of animals. Importation of all animals described by the Act is prohibited except at certain designated ports. All animals are to be inspected on import or export.

21 USC 113a
Foot-and-Mouth Memorandum of Understanding; Disease Research Act
This Act authorizes the study of animal disease and prohibits introduction of live foot-and-mouth disease virus into the United States except under certain defined circumstances. Customs enforces Agriculture restrictions and regulations.

42 USC 264 et seq.
Quarantine, Inspection, and Licensing
This Act restricts importations of dogs, cats, monkeys, psittacine birds, turtles, tortoises, and terrapins that do not comply with health standards. Customs enforces these restrictions. See 42 CFR 71.51 et seq.

19 CFR 12.24 and 12.26
Regulations for Animal and Animal Product Entry
These regulations provide for U.S. Customs entry declarations, documentation, and procedures for the animals and animal products subject to FWS and USDA regulations.

9 CFR Parts 92-96
Regulations on Animal Byproduct Quarantine Control
These regulations promulgated by the USDA prohibit the importation of animal products for use in industry unless the products meet certain processing standards and are not infected with certain diseases.

21 USC 135, 135a and 135b
Establishment of International Animal Quarantine Stations
This Act authorizes the establishment of international quarantine stations by the Secretary of Agriculture and describes possible means of funding them. These sections also describe civil and criminal penalties for smuggling animals into or out of Quarantine Stations.

7 USC 151 et seq.
The Plant Quarantine Act
This Act gives the Plant Protection and Quarantine (PPQ) branch of USDA authority to restrict/prohibit import of plants or seeds found to carry specific plant pests and pathogens.

7 USC 150aa et seq.
Federal Plant Pest Act (FPPA)
This Act prohibits the importation into or movement through the U.S. of plant pests as defined in the Act, and provides for the inspection of any letter, box, parcel, or container that may carry a plant pest. Inspection is to be performed by U.S. Department of Agriculture in conjunction with Customs.

7 CFR Part 351
Regulations for Entry and Inspection of Plants by Mail
These regulations set forth the plant imports that are prohibited, the requirements for entering restricted plants by mail, and the inspection procedures followed by the USDA's Animal and Plant Health Inspection Service (APHIS).

19 CFR 12.10 et seq.
Regulations for Entry and Release of Restricted Plants
These regulations prescribe procedures followed by U.S. Customs to enforce USDA requirements for importation of plants.

Convention on International Trade in Endangered Spe-

cies of Wild Fauna and Flora (CITES)
This comprehensive wildlife treaty signed by over 100 countries, including the United States, regulates and in many cases prohibits commercial imports and exports of wild animal and plant species threatened by trade.

16 USC 1531
Endangered Species Act of 1973
This Act prohibits the import and export of species listed as endangered and most species listed as threatened. It is the U.S. law that implements CITES.

16 USC 2401 et seq.
Antarctic Conservation Act of 1978
This Act prohibits the importation, absent a special permit, of any flora or fauna native to Antarctica into the U.S. pursuant to the Antarctic Treaty and the Protocol

16 USC 3371 et seq.
Control of Illegally Taken Fish and Wildlife
This Act prohibits the import of species taken, possessed, transported, or sold in violation of the law of a foreign country.

16 USC 1361 et seq.
The Marine Mammal Protection Act of 1972
This Act prohibits the import of certain marine mammals and their parts and products. These species include whales, walruses, narwhals, seals, sea lions, sea otters, and polar bears. It also defines parameters for importation of commercial fish or products that have been caught using methods, which involve incidental death or serious injury to protected marine mammals.

16 USC 703 et seq.
The Migratory Bird Treaty Act
This Act protects designated wild migratory game birds and prohibits importation of them for commercial purposes.

16 USC 4201 et seq.
The African Elephant Conservation Act
This Act prohibits imports of carved ivory products from any country and only permits imports of whole tusks from elephants legally hunted in certain African countries. It establishes U.S. adherence to the CITES Ivory Control System.

50 CFR Parts 10, 13, and 16
Regulations of FWS for Importing Wildlife and Fish
These regulations specify the animals and animal products subject to import prohibitions and restrictions.

16 USC 4901
Wild Bird Conservation Act of 1992
This act eliminated most commercial imports of CITES-regulated birds, except for limited imports of pet birds.

Principal Exporting Countries

The following listing includes samples of the main supplier nations of the products of this chapter. It is organized by HTSUS major heading. (Refer to "Customs Classification" above for the product codes.) Countries are listed in rank order of the value of products imported to the U.S. Statistics represent customs value of entries for 2002 from the Bureau of Census, U.S. Department of Commerce.

0101—Netherlands, Canada, Federal Republic of Germany, United Kingdom, France, United Arab Emirates, New Zealand, Belgium, Australia, Japan

0102—Canada, Mexico, Australia, Guatemala

0103—Canada, Norway

0104—Canada, Australia, New Zealand

0105—Canada

0106—Canada, China, Vietnam, Netherlands, Indonesia, Mauritius, Federal Republic of Germany, Taiwan, United Kingdom

Chapter 2:
Meat

Full title: Meat and Edible Meat Offal

This chapter relates to the importation of meat and edible meat offal, which are classified under Chapter 2 of the Harmonized Tariff Schedule of the United States (HTSUS). Specifically, it includes fresh, chilled, or frozen carcasses or processed cuts of meat of beef, pork, sheep, goat, horses, poultry, and miscellaneous animals (such as frogs' legs, rabbit, etc.), as well as the edible internal parts of such animals (tongue, liver, etc.), and cured portions of such animals (such as hams), ground meat, edible meat flours and meals, and unrendered food grade pork and poultry fats. For a general overview on importing food see "Appendix: Foods" on page 825.

If you are interested in importing certain prepared meats and meat products, such as sausage or canned meats, you should refer to Commodity Index Chapter 16. Meat byproducts such as guts, bladders, and blood which are not fit for human consumption fall within Chapter 5 (some animal blood products for pharmaceutical uses are covered in Chapter 30). If you are interested in importing eggs or dairy products, you should refer to Chapter 4. Partially or fully processed animal fats are covered within Chapter 15. Fresh and frozen fish and related products are covered in Chapter 3. Non-edible flours and meals made of meat and intended primarily as animal feed or for industrial uses are covered in Chapter 23. The importation of live animals is covered in Chapter 1.

Note: To understand key issues that will enable you to make best use of the information in this section we recommend that you see "Introduction" on page 425.

Key Factors

The key factors in the importation of meat and edible meat offal are:

- Compliance with U.S. Department of Agriculture (USDA) Food Safety and Inspection Service (FSIS) import restrictions, port inspections, and product certification

- Compliance with USDA Animal and Plant Health Inspection Service (APHIS) import restrictions, port inspections, and product certification

- APHIS permits are required for certain imports

- Compliance with U.S. Food and Drug Agency (FDA) requirements for certain imports

Although most importers utilize the services of a licensed customs broker in making their entries, and we recommend this practice, you should be aware of the regulatory, entry, and documentation issues involved in importing your product. You, as importer, are ultimately responsible for the fulfillment of any legal requirements applicable to your shipment.

General Considerations

Regulatory Agencies. Two agencies of the USDA, each having its own set of priorities, administer regulations regarding importation of meat and meat products. The APHIS Veterinary Service (VS) enforces the restrictions on importations of animals found in 9 CFR Chapter 1. The FSIS enforces the Federal Meat Inspection Act (FMIA) and the Poultry Products Inspection Act (PPIA) through regulations adopted as 9 CFR Chapter 3. These laws cover meat, poultry, and products derived from cattle, sheep, swine, goats, horses, and poultry.

Certain meat product imports are also controlled by the FDA under the Federal Food, Drug, and Cosmetic Act (FDCA). The FWS administers the provisions of the Endangered Species Act (ESA), the Convention on International Trade in Endangered Species of Wild Fauna and Flora (CITES), and the Marine Mammal Protection Act.

Entry Requirements. Meat and meat products are heavily regulated commodities. Relevant import regulation is extremely complex and specific. This discussion is in no way exhaustive. You should obtain further information from the USDA, the FDA, and U.S. Customs before attempting the importation of any meat or meat products into the U.S.

USDA Requirements. Import shipments of meat products must meet the inspection and certification requirements of both USDA departments. You must present foreign veterinary certification to the APHIS inspector at the port of entry for all shipments of meat and meat products. APHIS inspects every shipment to verify compliance with import regulations. Once APHIS passes a shipment, it then goes to FSIS personnel for further inspection prior to release. Your shipment will not be released until all USDA inspections have taken place, and Customs has received release clearances.

FDA Requirements. Although meat and meat products are primarily regulated by the USDA, imports of foods are also subject to the provisions of the FDCA, administered by the FDA. FDA regulations covering importation of foods of any kind are extensive and stringent. Meat products under USDA jurisdiction are not usually required to be entered using FDA personnel and procedures, but some products fall into a gray area and may be regulated by both agencies. Although the meats and meat products included in HTSUS Chapter 2 are usually handled by the USDA, certain food products containing meat—such as ravioli and other prepared food products containing meat, such as canned soups or stews—may be subject to primary FDA rather than USDA jurisdiction. If you have any doubt regarding your product, contact the FDA as well as the USDA for a determination.

Meats from wild game or domesticated varieties of wild game—such as rabbit—also fall within FDA jurisdiction. Imported products regulated by the FDA are subject to FDA port of entry inspection, and must comply with all FDCA requirements for those produced domestically. FDA Importer's Entry Notice. For information concerning FDA import procedures refer to "Appendix: Foods" on page 825.

Wildlife and Endangered Species. If you are interested in importing meat from exotic animals, including that of marine mammals, you should consult the U.S. Fish and Wildlife Service (FWS), which administers the provisions of the ESA, CITES, and the MMPA to be sure that your intended import is not covered by these regulations. No animals or products derived from animals on any of these lists may be imported. There are many restrictions on the importation and sale of meat from wild animals. However, meat from animals grown in captivity is unlikely to fall within the purview of endangered species legislation.

Detention of Shipment. If your shipment is found to be noncomplying, it may be detained at the port of entry. In the case of products subject to FDA jurisdiction, the FDA may allow you to bring the shipment into compliance before making a final decision regarding admittance. However, any sorting, reprocessing, or relabeling must be supervised by FDA personnel and is done at the

importer's expense. Such conditional release to allow the importer to bring a shipment into compliance is a privilege, not a right. The FDA may consider subsequent noncomplying shipments of the same type of product to constitute abuse of the privilege and require the importer to destroy or reexport the products. To ascertain what your legal responsibilities are, you should contact these agencies regarding the specific items to be imported.

Customs Classification

For customs purposes, meat and edible meat offal are classified under Chapter 2 of the HTSUS. This chapter is divided into major headings, which are further divided into subheadings, and often into sub-subheadings, each of which has its own HTSUS classification number. For example, the 2001 HTSUS number for other cuts of lamb with the bone in is 0204.42.20, indicating that it is a subcategory of other cuts with bone in (0204.42), which in turn is a subcategory of the major heading meat of sheep or goats, fresh, chilled, or frozen (0204). There are 10 major headings in Chapter 2.

0201—Meat of bovine animals, fresh or chilled

0202—Meat of bovine animals, frozen

0203—Meat of swine, fresh, chilled, or frozen

0204—Meat of sheep or goats, fresh, chilled, or frozen

0205—Meat of horses, asses, mules, or hinnies, fresh, chilled, or frozen

0206—Edible offal of bovine animals, swine, sheep, goats, horses, asses, mules, or hinnies, fresh, chilled, or frozen

0207—Meat and edible offal, of the poultry of heading 0105, fresh, chilled, or frozen

0208—Other meat and edible meat offal, fresh, chilled, or frozen

0209—Pig fat free of lean meat and poultry fat, not rendered or otherwise extracted, fresh, chilled, frozen, salted, in brine, dried, or smoked

0210—Meat and edible meat offal, salted, in brine, dried, or smoked; edible flours and meals of meat or meat offal

For more details regarding classification of the specific product you are interested in importing, consult a customs broker, the appropriate commodity specialist at your nearest Customs port, or see HTSUS. The 2001 HTSUS is available online from the Customs Service (www.customs.gov/impoexpo/impoexpo.htm) or for purchase from the U.S. Government Printing Office (see resources at the end of this chapter), and may be found in larger public libraries. For a general discussion of customs classification, see "Classification—Liquidation" on page 229.

Dutiable Status of Goods

For more information about duty rates and binding decisions see "Dutiable Status of Goods" on page 218; for a discussion of temporary importation of goods see "Temporary Free Importations" on page 205.

Valuation

Importers have a responsibility to use what U.S. Customs and Border Protection deems, "reasonable care," when determining the value of their goods. They must also provide any additional information that U.S. Customs and Border Protection needs for setting a final value on the goods. This process involves a number of factors and can be somewhat complicated; importers must be aware of applicable issues and details. Valuation information applies to all types of commodities, for further discussion on the subject see "Customs Valuation" on page 267.

Import Duties

Import duties vary (often dramatically) depending upon the Harmonized Tariff Schedule (HTSUS) classification of the goods or products imported. Since some products that look alike have different HTSUS classifications and different rates of duty, proper classification is vital. Note that "differences of opinion" between importers and the Bureau of Customs and Border Protection regarding classification keeps customs attorneys very busy.

Import duties can be assessed on the imported value of the goods ("ad valorem" rates of duty such as 2%, 4.4%, 50%, etc.), total units or weight of the goods ("specific" rates of duty such as 2 cents each or 1.5 cents/pound, etc.) or on a combination basis ("compound" rates of duty such as 5 cents each plus 6%).

Listed below is a sampling of several Column 1 import duty rates for Chapter 02 products:
Edible offal of swine, fresh or chilled (0206.30.00.00): free
to
Pig fat, free of lean meat, and poultry fat, not rendered or otherwise extracted, fresh, chilled, frozen, salted, in brine, dried or smoked (0209.00.00.00): 3.2%

For specific information on US import duties refer to the Harmonized Tariff Schedule of the US. The print version is available from the US Government Printing Office as well as third party suppliers who often add special features. Online versions are available in both static PDF pages as well as in formats with excellent search functionality. Search the Web with the term "Harmonized Tariff Schedule" to find sources.

Entry and Documentation

The entry of merchandise is a two-part process consisting of 1) filing the documents necessary to determine whether merchandise may be released from Customs custody and 2) filing the documents which contain information for duty assessment and statistical purposes. In certain instances all documents must be filed and accepted by Customs prior to release of the goods. Unless you have been granted an extension, you must file entry documents at a location specified by the port or area director within five working days of your shipment's date of arrival at a U.S. port of entry. These include a number of standard documents required by Customs for any entry, and:

- Foreign veterinary certification when required
- APHIS Import Permit when required

After you present the entry, Customs may examine your shipment, or may waive examination. The shipment is then released provided no legal or regulatory violations have been noted. You must then file entry summary documentation and deposit estimated duties at a designated customhouse within 10 working days of your shipment's release. For a detailed description of entry procedures, standard documentation, and informal entry, see "Entry Process" on page 185.

Informed Compliance. Informed compliance was introduced with the Customs Modernization Act of 1993 (Mod Act) and defines the relationship between importers and U.S. Customs and Border Protection. It sets out the responsibilities of both parties. Providing the correct documentation and information for entry is a key factor that will make your importing operation run smoothly. We recommend that importers become familiar with the concept of informed comliance and the responsibilities that they have under the Mod Act. For further discussion about informed compliance see "Informed Compliance" on page 211.

Entry Document Certification for Beef. For imports of fresh, chilled, or frozen beef, entry documents must include a certification from an appropriate foreign official stating that: "I hereby certify to the best of my knowledge and belief that the herein described fresh, chilled, or frozen beef meets the specifications prescribed in regulations issued by the U.S. Department of Agriculture (7 CFR 2853.106 (a) and (b)."

Note: The Entry and Documentation section has been carefully designed to supply you, the importer, with sample documents and directions on how to satisfy Customs requirements. Be aware that you should consult the applicable authorities to ensure that you are correctly following the most current procedures.

Prohibitions and Restrictions

USDA APHIS Restrictions. APHIS regulates imports of meat, poultry, and their products to prevent the introduction of certain infectious animal diseases into the U.S. APHIS operates primarily under the authority of Subpart 94,which establishes import restrictions and procedures. It restricts imports from countries known to have incidence of a variety of listed diseases. For ruminants and swine: rinderpest and foot-and-mouth disease; for swine: African swine fever, swine vesicular disease, and hog cholera; for poultry: fowl pest, Exotic Newcastle disease (END), and *Salmonella enteritis* (phage-type 4). See "Country-Specific Import Restrictions" below.

Not only does APHIS restrict imports from countries known to have a specific disease, it also restricts imports from countries that do not have the disease, but that 1) are known to import and use animal products from countries that do; 2) have less stringent regulations regarding entry of such products or of potentially-infected live animals into their borders than those of the U.S.; or 3) border on countries known to have the disease. APHIS also restricts imports that originate from disease-free countries but that, in the course of transport, enter the territory of countries known to have the disease.

The importation of meat and meat products involves a very complicated set of qualifying factors. APHIS administers these restrictions primarily through product certification by qualified veterinarians of the country of origin. In some cases, permits are required. There are stringent cooking, processing, marking, packing, and shipping requirements for certain imports. The variables are too complex to cover exhaustively in this discussion, but the following examples will give you an idea of the issues that need to be addressed when importing these products.

Example 1. Importation of fresh, chilled, or frozen meat of ruminants or swine raised and slaughtered in a disease-free country but passing through a restricted country during transport. Sometimes a product originating in a noninfected country must pass through an infected country, or a port in an infected country, in the course of transport to the U.S. If this is the case for your shipment, you must see that a qualified country of origin official seals the product in a hold or compartment of the transport vessel prior to export. The seal must be APHIS-approved and serially-numbered. The sealed compartment must not be opened until the vessel reaches the U.S. port of entry. The seal's serial number must appear on the foreign inspection certificate accompanying the meat. At the U.S. port of entry, an APHIS official will inspect not only the product, but also the seal and the certificate, to ensure that your product was in no way exposed to any infectious disease while passing through the infected port or country.

Example 2. Importation of the cured or cooked meat of ruminants or swine originating in a country where rinderpest or foot-and-mouth disease exist. (This does not include meat that has been sterilized by heat in hermetically sealed containers.) If you are importing cured meats of HTSUS Chapter 2 (e.g. jerked, dried, or corned beef, Westphalia hams, etc.), the following conditions apply: 1) all bones must have been removed in the country of origin; 2) the meat must have been held in an unfrozen, fresh condition for at least 3 days immediately following slaughter of the animals from which it was derived; and 3) the meat must have been thoroughly cured and fully dried in such a manner that it may be stored and handled without refrigeration. If your product is deemed by the port of entry inspector to be in violation of the prescribed water-protein ratio for cured meat, it will be tested by APHIS, and the shipment will be held at the port of entry pending test results. Finally, the requisite country-of-origin foreign meat inspection certificate must be presented to the USDA inspector at the port of entry.

Example 3. Importations of fresh, chilled, or frozen (uncooked) meat of ruminants or swine from countries free of rinderpest and foot-and-mouth disease but which are under special restriction. Certain countries that are deemed to be free of rinderpest and foot-and-mouth disease nevertheless have less stringent regulations regarding import and use of products from infected countries than the U.S. Because of the danger of infection slipping into the U.S. through products imported from such countries, special restrictions apply. All uncooked meat and meat products from these restricted countries must have been prepared only in an inspected establishment eligible under the FMIA to export products to the U.S. Such product must be accompanied by a USDA-approved meat inspection certificate. (See FSIS requirements, below, for more details.) Note that these requirements apply whether you are importing the product for personal use or in commercial lots.

For shipments that fall into this category you must also provide additional certification by a full-time salaried veterinary official of the country-of-origin's national animal health agency. This veterinary certification must state the name and official establishment number of the slaughterhouse certifying that: 1) the slaughterhouse is not permitted to receive animals that have ever been in, or in a port of, a country listed as infected with rinderpest or foot-and-mouth disease; 2) the slaughterhouse is not permitted to receive meat originating in, or which has been transported through, infected countries. (The only exception to these rules covers meat in containers sealed with serially numbered seals of the noninfected country of origin's national government—see above); 3) the product covered by the certificate comes from animals born and raised in a country listed as free of rinderpest and foot-and-mouth disease and that have never been in any infected country; and 4) the product has been processed, stored, and transported in such a manner as to preclude its being commingled with any noncomplying products.

Pork Import Restrictions for African Swine Fever, Hog Cholera, or Swine Vesicular Disease. Imports of fresh, chilled, or frozen pork and edible pork offal are usually prohibited from countries in which these diseases exist, or from countries bordering countries in which they exist. Pork from such sources must usually be thoroughly heat-processed in an approved manner in an approved packing plant to render harmless any disease organisms before it is allowed to be imported into the U.S. (such importations fall within HTSUS Chapter 16). If you import from listed infected countries pork products that do not comply with requirements of Subpart 94, your shipment will be seized, quarantined, and disposed of as the USDA determines necessary to prevent introduction of such diseases into the U.S.

Small amounts of pork or pork products from countries where swine vesicular disease exists that are restricted under Subpart 94.12, may be imported in specific cases for examination, testing, or analysis. You must apply for and receive written APHIS approval for such importation.

Hams. APHIS enforces Subpart 94 covering the importation of ham. Ham—a cured meat covered under heading 0210—is allowed entry under the following conditions: 1) it came from a swine that was never out of the country in which the ham was processed; 2) it came from a country determined by the USDA to have and to enforce laws requiring the immediate reporting to the country's national veterinary services any premises found to have any animal infected with foot-and-mouth disease, rinderpest, African Swine fever, hog cholera, or swine vesicular disease; 3) it came from a swine that was not on any premises where the diseases mentioned above exist or had existed within 60 days prior to slaughter; 4) the ham was accompanied from the slaughterhouse to the processing establishment by a numbered certificate issued by a person authorized by the national government of the country of origin stating that the above provisions were met; and 5) the ham must have been processed according to regulations in 9 CFR Subpart 94.17 in a single establishment.

If you are interested in importing hams, you should be aware of the restrictions on foreign establishments eligible to export hams to the U.S. Be sure to purchase your product from a meatpacker that complies with all relevant regulations for the processing of hams, and which employs someone authorized by national veterinary officials to oversee and attest to that compliance. Hams from establishments which do not meet these criteria may not be imported. The only foreign hams eligible for import into the U.S. are those processed in APHIS-inspected establishments whose proprietor has signed a written agreement with the APHIS to the effect that all hams for import to the U.S. will be processed in accordance with standards established in Subpart 94. Foreign meatpackers must also meet APHIS recordkeeping and inspection access requirements. Foreign hams imported into the U.S. must bear certain markings (see "Marking and Labeling Requirements" below), and must be accompanied by a certificate issued by an authorized person stating that the ham was processed for at least 400 days and that all relevant provisions of Subpart 94 have been fulfilled.

Poultry. The law defines poultry as chickens, turkeys, swans, partridges, guinea fowl, pea fowl, nonmigratory ducks, geese, pigeons, and doves as well as commercial, domestic, or pen-raised grouse, pheasants, and quail. It restricts import of these products from countries known to have incidences of fowl pest, Exotic Newcastle disease (END), and *Salmonella enteritis* (phage-type 4).

Restrictions for END. You may import poultry, game birds, or other birds raised and slaughtered in any country where END is considered to exist only if they meet at least one of the conditions listed below. These restrictions also apply to products imported from, or moved into or through, any country where the disease is considered to exist, at any time before arrival in the U.S. In other words, if your product originates in a noninfected country, but passes through an infected country en route to the U.S., it becomes a restricted product and must meet the requirements for products originating in infected countries. Similarly, if your product is imported from an infected country into a noninfected country for processing prior to export to the U.S, it must meet the requirements for products originating in infected countries.

Poultry products in these categories may be entered into U.S. Customs territory only if:1) Game bird carcasses are eviscerated, with heads and feet removed. Viscera, heads, and feet removed from game birds are ineligible for entry into the U.S.; or 2) products are intended for consignment to a USDA-approved museum, educational institution, or other establishment. Such establishment must have provided the USDA with evidence that it has the equipment, facilities, and capabilities to store, handle, process, or disinfect such articles so as to prevent the introduction or dissemination of END into the U.S. (Names and addresses of approved establishments may be obtained from, and requests for approval may be made to, the USDA Administrator, c/o the Import-Export Products Staff—see addresses at end of this chapter.) Otherwise, poultry products must be fully heat-treated and prepared before they will be allowed to enter the U.S.

Regulations regarding Exotic Newcastle disease in birds and poultry were revised in 1996; the final rule was published November 5, 1996 in the Federal Register, pages 56877–56891.

APHIS VS Permit Application. Requests for USDA APHIS VS permits authorizing importation of restricted products must be submitted on VS Form 16-3. You may obtain these forms from APHIS headquarters (see addresses at end of this chapter) or from any USDA port office. Application on a signed facsimile (copy) is acceptable, provided you send an original signed document as follow-up. If you need a supply of the forms on hand, you may photocopy the original Form 16-3.

Requested information on processing or production data and sources of meat products may often require more space than is provided on the application form. In such cases, you may attach extra sheets as necessary. You should include as much background information as possible in order for APHIS to properly evaluate the disease risk of the product you wish to import. Research papers intended as supporting information should not be sent by fax. It takes about two weeks for the APHIS to process an application and prepare a permit for return mail. If the application information is deemed insufficient, APHIS will contact you for clarification. The permit process can take longer in such cases. You should submit your requests for permit renewal or amendment in writing (fax is acceptable) to the USDA (see addresses at end of this chapter). You should note any changes from the original application and permit issued, such as addresses or production method, when making permit renewal requests.

Any importation for which a permit is issued must comply in all particulars with the permit's stipulations. You will facilitate the entry of your import shipments by making sure the permit number appears on the shipping documents—or simply include a copy of the permit with your entry documents. Meat products requiring permits will be subject to delay or refusal at the port of entry if an importation permit is not obtained before shipment to the U.S.

FSIS Requirements. The FMIA and the PPIA require countries exporting meat, poultry, and their products to the U.S. to impose domestic inspection requirements at least as stringent as those of the U.S. The FSIS reviews foreign inspection systems to ensure that they are equivalent to the U.S. system. Only those countries to which FSIS grants meat export eligibility may export these products to the U.S. See Country-Specific Import Restrictions below for list of currently eligible countries (by definition, imports from unlisted countries are prohibited).

An inspection certificate issued by the responsible official of the exporting country must accompany each shipment of meat or poultry products offered for entry into the U.S. Certificates identify products by country and packing plant of origin, destination, shipping marks, and amounts. They certify that the products have received ante-mortem and post-mortem inspection; that they are wholesome, unadulterated, and properly branded; and that they otherwise comply with U.S. requirements.

For imports of fresh, chilled, and frozen beef, entered under 0201.20.20, 0201.30.20, 0202.20.20, or 0202.30.20, 19 CFR 10.180 requires that the foreign official must attach an affidavit executed prior to export and to be filed with the entry documentation attesting that the beef in the shipment meets USDA specifications in 7 CFR 2853.106. Importers are urged to consult with the USDA prior to exportation of beef to be sure that their shipment will satisfy certification requirements.

In addition, the Pork Promotion, Research, and Consumer Information Act of 1985 (PPRCIA) requires that each importer of porcine animals, pork, or pork products shall remit an assessment to U.S. Customs at the time the product is imported.

Port-of-entry Inspection. The FSIS reinspects meat and meat products by sampling shipments as they enter the U.S. Your products may be checked for transportation damage, labeling compliance and accuracy, general condition, and proper certification. FSIS may also examine the product for accuracy of net weight, labeling requirements, and condition of the container, and make laboratory analyses of food chemistry (for example, fat, water, and nitrite levels) and test for drug and chemical residues. It may also test to confirm species. The actual inspection tasks and the scope of inspection are based on the nature of the product and on the performance history of the packing plant and country of origin.

If your shipment passes reinspection, FSIS will stamp the products "U.S. Inspected and Passed," and the shipment will be allowed entry. If the products fail this reinspection, they will be stamped "U.S. Refused Entry," in which case you must reexport or destroy the refused products. In some cases, such products may be converted to animal food. Once a shipment has been condemned, inspection is intensified for future shipments of that product from the same plant, and in some cases, for all meat shipments from the same country.

Residue Control. Chemical and drug residue control is one of the major features of an exporting country's inspection system that must be judged equal to the U.S. system. Exporting countries must be certified annually by FSIS as continuing to operate an equivalent residue control program. FSIS experts make sure that the country's residue program uses approved analytical methods, that officials are knowledgeable about the use of chemical compounds in their country, and that the country tests for those compounds which could potentially contaminate the food supply. Meat or meat products may not be imported from a country that fails to receive a FSIS annual residue certification.

As a further residue check, FSIS randomly samples products at the port of entry and analyzes them for drug and chemical residues. The FSIS annual import residue plan sets the initial sampling rate for each country based on the volume of product imported from that country. The plan includes the same chemical compounds as the domestic residue-monitoring program. Compounds are selected based on their likelihood of contaminating the food supply and their potential harm to the consuming public. The list can include chemical compounds not legal for use in the U.S. if they have the potential to contaminate a foreign country's meat supply.

If your shipment contains residues above the U.S. tolerance or action level, it will be considered adulterated and will be refused entry into the U.S. Shipments are not usually held pending laboratory test results unless FSIS has some reason to suspect contamination. If a laboratory reports a residue violation on a sample which has otherwise passed reinspection, as much as possible of the product must be recalled. Products so recovered may not be used for human food.

The occurrence of a residue violation at a port of entry raises concerns about the exporting country's ability to control residues. Port of entry sampling is then automatically increased for related products from the entire country, as well as on subsequent shipments from the specific plant where the noncomplying sample originated. From time to time, the FSIS will increase sampling for a specific country or for a specific compound. This can occur when there is an indication that a problem may exist or when there is a pattern of failed port of entry reinspections.

Country-Specific Import Restrictions

Regulatory Changes. APHIS has amended the animal and animal product importation regulations to allow for regionalization of countries—that is, disease classification of parts of a country, an entire country, or groups of countries. The rule change was made to recognize levels of disease risk in regions. Details about the criteria that APHIS considers when evaluating the regions that wish to export animals or animal products to the United States can be found at the APHIS Veterinary Service National Center for Import and Export (NCIE) website (www.aphis.usda.gov/ncie).

U.S.-Canada Free Trade Agreement. Canada has an inspection system that is virtually the same as that of the U.S. Under the U.S.-Canada Free Trade Agreement, FSIS has modified border reinspection requirements for Canadian products. Canadian plants may choose to follow the revised procedures or undergo traditional reinspection. Under the revised procedures, Agriculture Canada inspection officials provide information to be entered into the FSIS automated computer system before product destined for the U.S. leaves the Canadian plant. Unless the computer flags the shipment for reinspection at the border, the shipment automatically passes through U.S. Customs.

North American Free Trade Agreement (NAFTA). NAFTA reduces tariff and nontariff barriers to trade in meat and meat products between Mexico and the U.S. However, it does not specifically alter existing entry procedures for such trade. The existing provisions of the U.S.-Canada Free Trade Agreement continue in force to govern trade between those two countries.

Other FSIS-Certified Countries. The following countries are currently FSIS-certified for exportation of meat and poultry to the U.S.: Argentina, Australia, Belgium, Belize, Brazil, Canada, Costa Rica, the Czech Republic, Denmark, Dominican Republic, El Salvador, Finland, France, Guatemala, Honduras, Hong Kong, Hungary, Ireland, Israel, Italy, Mexico, Netherlands, New Zealand, Norway, Poland, Romania, the Slovak Republic, Sweden, Switzerland, United Kingdom, Uruguay, and the republics of the former Yugoslavia. Meat may not be imported from countries not on the list. The list is subject to change. For the most up-to-date information, contact FSIS (see addresses at end of this chapter).

APHIS-listed Countries. Countries certified free of rinderpest and foot-and-mouth disease from which ruminant and swine products may be imported: Australia, the Bahamas, Barbados, Belize, Bermuda, Canada, Channel Islands, Chile, Costa Rica, the Czech Republic, Denmark, Dominican Republic, El Salvador, Fiji, Finland, France, Great Britain (England, Scotland, Wales, and Isle of Man), Greenland, Guatemala, Haiti, Honduras, Iceland, Ireland, Italy, Jamaica, Japan, Mexico, Netherlands, New Caledonia, New Zealand, Nicaragua, Northern Ireland, Norway, Panama, Papua New Guinea, Poland, Spain, Sweden, Territory of St. Pierre and Miquelon, Trinidad and Tobago, and Trust Territory of the Pacific Islands.

African Swine Fever Prohibitions. African swine fever is believed to exist in the following countries, and pork imports are banned from them: Africa (all countries), Brazil, Cuba, Haiti, Italy, Malta, Portugal, and Spain.

Hog Cholera-free Countries. Countries deemed free of hog cholera and from which pork may be imported: Australia, Canada, Denmark, Dominican Republic, Fiji, Finland, Great Britain (England, Scotland, Wales, and Isle of Man), Iceland, the Netherlands, New Zealand, Northern Ireland, Norway, the Republic of Ireland, Spain, Sweden, and Trust Territory of the Pacific Islands.

Swine Vesicular Disease Prohibitions: The following countries are deemed free of swine vesicular disease, and pork may be imported from them: Australia, the Bahamas, Bulgaria, Canada, Central American countries, Chile, Denmark, Dominican Republic, Fiji, Finland, Great Britain (England, Scotland, Wales, and the Isle of Man), Greenland, Haiti, Hungary, Iceland, Luxembourg, Mexico, the Netherlands, New Zealand, Northern Ireland, Norway, Panama, Republic of Ireland, Rumania, Sweden, Switzerland, the Trust Territories of the Pacific Islands, and the republics of the former Yugoslavia.

Pork Import Restrictions. Imports from the following countries are subject to specific restrictions on the importation of pork products: the Bahamas, Bulgaria, Chile, Denmark, Great Britain (England, Scotland, Wales, and the Isle of Man), Hungary, Luxembourg, Northern Ireland, Republic of Ireland, Switzerland, and the republics of the former Yugoslavia.

Ruminant and Swine Import Restrictions. Countries subject to specific restrictions on the importation of ruminant and swine products: the Bahamas, Channel Islands, Denmark, Finland, Great Britain (England, Scotland, Wales, and Isle of Man), Japan, Northern Ireland, Norway, Papua New Guinea, and Sweden.

END-Free Countries. The following countries are certified free of Exotic Newcastle disease (END): Australia, Canada, Chile, Denmark, Fiji, Finland, Great Britain (England, Scotland, Wales, and the Isle of Man), Iceland, New Zealand, Northern Ireland, Norway, Republic of Ireland, Sweden.

***Salmonella enteritis* Free Countries.** The only country deemed free of *Salmonella enteritis* is Canada.

***Bovine Spongiform Encephalopathy* Prohibitions.** Imports of meat and meat products are banned or heavily restricted from the following countries where *bovine spongiform encephalopathy* is believed to exist: France, Great Britain, Northern Ireland, Republic of Ireland, Oman, Portugal, and Switzerland.

Quotas

Total meat imports are controlled by the Federal Meat Import Act (FMIA), which was designed to permit larger imports when the U.S. production is trending downward and to cut back on imports when U.S. production is rising. There is no licensing or absolute quota system in effect. However, P.L. 88-482, as amended, allows that certain meats may be made subject to absolute quota restriction by presidential proclamation.

The FMIA covers imports of fresh, chilled, or frozen beef, veal, mutton, and goat meat. It does not apply to beef that is prepared or preserved, nor does it cover pork, lamb, or poultry meat, or live animal imports. At the beginning of each year, the USDA announces the "trigger" import level at which quotas or restrictions may be applied. The law requires the USDA to estimate potential U.S. meat imports. If projected imports equal or exceed the trigger level, the U.S. Secretary of Agriculture is required to consider imposing import restrictions. The law specifies the actions that may be taken if the import estimate exceeds the trigger level. In addition to the option of imposing import quotas, the USDA may suspend potential import limitations or set them above the trigger level if it appears there will not be enough meat to supply U.S. demand at reasonable prices.

Quotas have been imposed only once since the FMIA became law. Generally, when it appears that meat imports will exceed the trigger level, the U.S. government negotiates agreements with exporting countries to voluntarily limit their exports to the U.S. in order to maintain imports slightly below the trigger level, while guaranteeing the supplier countries fair shares of the imports allowed under the law. As a result of the U.S.-Canada Free Trade Implementation Act of 1988, imports from Canada are excluded from the restrictions of the FMIA.

Marking and Labeling Requirements

FSIS Requirements. When meat and meat products are imported, the name of the country of origin must appear on the label. However, only imported products that reach consumers without further processing retain such labeling. For example, a can of ham or corned beef that goes directly to a retail outlet will name the country of origin on the label. However, if imported boneless beef is combined with U.S. beef and other ingredients in a U.S. plant to produce a can of beef stew, the label is not required to indicate the presence of imported beef.

The Farm Bill Amendments require foreign countries exporting products to the U.S. to impose controls equivalent to those administered by the FSIS to prevent species substitution. A product labeled "beef," for example, must be beef and cannot contain a less expensive or more readily available species. Exporting countries must maintain effective testing programs for species verification and adequate security measures to prevent species substitution.

APHIS Requirements. Imported hams must comply with all marking requirements of Subpart 94.17. Ham must bear a hot iron brand or an ink seal with the identifying number of the slaughterhouse. It must bear a button seal, approved by USDA to be tamper-proof, on the hock, stating the month and year the ham entered the processing establishment. It must bear a hot iron brand (with the identifying number of the processing establishment and the date salting began) executed at the processing establishment immediately prior to salting. All required branding must be performed under the direct supervision of a person authorized by the veterinary services of the country of origin's national government to supervise such activity.

FDA requirements. For basic FDA marking and labeling requirements, refer to "Appendix: Foods" on page 825.

For a general discussion of U.S. Customs marking and labeling requirements, refer to "Country of Origin Marking" on page 236, "Special Marking Requirements" on page 238 and "Marking—False Impression" on page 239.

Shipping Considerations

You will need to ensure that your goods are packaged and shipped with care so that they arrive in good condition and pass smoothly through Customs. You are responsible for ensuring that the shipment is in compliance with all applicable government regulations for packaging and shipping. In most instances, you should not leave these arrangements solely to the discretion of your supplier. Careful preparation of the cargo and selection of the mode of transport can be essential to a cost-effective, timely delivery of undamaged goods. We strongly advise you to consult your shipping representative, insurance agent, or freight broker for advice on packing and shipping.

Meat and meat products require expeditious and careful handling to avoid contamination and decomposition. They should always be moved under adequate refrigeration to ensure that they do not deteriorate into an unsalable condition during transit.

Publications and WWW Resources

The following publication may be relevant to the importation of meat and edible offal:

> Report of the Secretary of Agriculture to the U.S. Congress - Foreign Countries and Plants Certified to Export Meat and Poultry to the United States

This is a comprehensive listing of export-certified countries and plants, including previously certified plants that have been de-certified. It is available from the FSIS (see addresses at end of this chapter).

The following publication explains the FDA requirements for importing meat and poultry. It is published by the FDA and available online from their website (www.fda.gov/opacom/7pubs.html).

> Requirements of Laws and Regulations Enforced by the U.S. Food and Drug Administration

The following publication gives brief, general guidelines on USDA regulated products. Although designed primarily for tourists, it contains a list of approved products that you may find helpful. It is available online from the USDA APHIS website (www.aphis.usda.gov).

> Travelers Tips On Bringing Food, Plant, and Animal Products into the United States

The Harmonized Tariff Schedule of the United States (2001) (HTSUS) is available to view on the U.S. Customs and Border Protection website (www.customs.treas.gov), or you may purchase a printed version from:

U.S. Government Printing Office
Superintendent of Documents
710 North Capital Street NW
Washington DC 20401
Tel: (202) 512-1800
Fax: (202) 512-1657
Website: www.access.gpo.gov

The USGPO also has copies of specific laws available for purchase. The USGPO accepts orders made by fax, phone or placed over the Internet, as well as mail orders paid by credit card. All orders must be accompanied by payment. Credit cards, checks drawn on a U.S. bank, or an international money order are all acceptable.

Relevant Government Agencies

Address your questions regarding APHIS import requirements, port of entry inspections, permits, and approved establishments for the import of meat to:

Animal and Plant Health Inspection Service (APHIS)
Veterinary Services (VS)
National Center for Import and Export

4700 River Rd., Unit 40
Riverdale, MD 20737
Tel: (301) 734-3277
Website: www.aphis.usda.gov/vs

Address your questions regarding FSIS port of entry inspection or pre-import certification of meat, and meat products and establishments to:

U.S. Department of Agriculture (USDA)
Food Safety and Inspection Service (FSIS)
Import Inspection Division
1400 Independence Avenue SW
Room 2137, South Building
Washington DC 20250
Tel: (202) 720-6400
Fax:(202) 720-7990
Website: www.fsis.usda.gov

U.S. Department of Agriculture (USDA)
Food Safey and Inspection Service (FSIS)
International Policy Staff
1400 Independence Avenue SW
Room 2137, South Building
Washington DC 20250
Tel: (202) 720-6400
Fax: (202) 720-7990
Website: www.fsis.usda.gov

Address your questions regarding FDA requirements for meat products to:

Food and Drug Administration (FDA)
Center for Food Safety and Applied Nutrition (CFSAN)
Office of Compliance
Division of Enforcement, Imports Branch
5100 Paint Branch Parkway
College Park, MD 20740-3835
Tel: (301) 436-2080
Website: http://vm.cfsan.fda.gov/list.html

Address questions regarding any quota issues to:

U.S. Customs and Border Protection
Office of Field Operations, Quota Branch
1300 Pennsylvania Avenue NW
Washington DC 20229
Tel: (202) 927-5850
Website: www.customs.treas.gov

Address your questions regarding importation of meats and edible offal to your local Customs port director. For addresses see "Ports of Entry and Customs Service Ports" on page 196 or contact:

U.S. Customs and Border Protection
Customs Headquarters
1300 Pennsylvania Avenue NW
Washington DC 20229
Tel: (202) 354-1000
Website: www.customs.treas.gov

Laws and Regulations

The following laws and regulations may be relevant to the importation of meat and edible offal. The laws are contained in the U.S. Code (USC) and the regulations in the Code of Federal Regulations (CFR), both of which may be available at larger public and law libraries. Copies of specific laws are also available from the United States Government Printing Office (address above).

7 USC 1854
Delegations of Authority Concerning Certain Meats
EO 11539, as amended by EO 12188
These Executive Orders authorize Customs to enforce limitations on the importation and entry and withdrawal of meats from warehouses for consumption in the U.S.

19 CFR 12.1 et seq.

Regulations on Customs Inspection and Release of Meat and Meat Products

These regulations set forth the conditions and bond under which U.S. Customs will release meat and meat products for entry into the U.S. and the penalties for breach of the bond.

7 USC 4801 et seq.
Pork Promotion, Research, and Consumer Information Act of 1985

This Act provides that each importer of porcine animal, pork, or pork product shall remit an assessment to Customs at the time the product is imported. See 7 CFR 1230.71 and 1230.110.

21 USC 601 et seq.
Federal Meat Inspection Act

This Act provides standards for inspection, packaging, and sale of meat and meat products and prohibits the importation of adulterated, misbranded, or improperly slaughtered meat.

19 USC 1306
Prohibited Meat Imports

This law prohibits the importation of cattle, sheep, swine, and meats from countries with rinderpest and foot-and-mouth disease, as determined in regulations adopted by the Secretary of Agriculture, and provides for enforcement by Customs.

9 CFR 327 et seq.
Regulations of USDA on Entry of Animal Food Products

These regulations prescribe certification and inspection procedures and marking and labeling requirements for products derived from cattle, sheep, swine, goats, horses, mules, and other equines.

19 CFR 4.71
Regulation on U.S. Customs Clearance of Vessels Carrying Cattle and Other Animals

This regulation requires submission of a USDA inspector's certificate to U.S. Customs before a vessel carrying cattle and other animals is cleared for entry.

21 USC 451 et seq.
Poultry Products Inspection Act

This Act provides standards for inspection, packaging, and sale of poultry and poultry products and prohibits the importation of slaughtered poultry not in compliance with prescribed standards and regulations.

9 CFR Part 381
Regulations for Inspection of Poultry Products

These regulations prescribe standards for sanitation and composition, inspection procedures, marking and labeling—including nutrition—requirements, exporting and importing certification procedures, and requirements.

21 USC 111 et seq.
Prevention of Introduction and Spread of Contagion

This statute authorizes the Secretary of Agriculture to prevent the introduction, and the Secretary of the Treasury to prevent the exportation, of diseased livestock and poultry.

9 CFR Part 50 et seq.
Regulations on Animal Byproduct Quarantine Control

These regulations promulgated by the USDA prohibit the importation of animal products for use in industry unless the products meet certain processing standards and are not infected with certain diseases.

21 USC 301 et seq.
Federal Food, Drug, and Cosmetic Act

This Act prohibits deceptive practices and regulates the manufacture, sale and importation or exportation of food, drugs, cosmetics, and related products. See 21 USC 301, 301, 302.

19 CFR 12.1 et seq.; 21 CFR 1.83 et seq.
Regulations on Food, Drugs, and Cosmetics

These regulations of the Secretary of Health and Human Services and the Secretary of the Treasury govern the standards, labeling, marking, and importing of products used with food, drugs, and cosmetics.

Convention on International Trade in Endangered Species of Wild Fauna and Flora (CITES)

This comprehensive wildlife treaty signed by over 100 countries, including the United States, regulates and in many cases prohibits commercial imports and exports of wild animal and plant species threatened by trade.

16 USC 1531
Endangered Species Act of 1973

This Act prohibits the import and export of species listed as endangered and most species listed as threatened. It is the U.S. law that implements CITES.

16 USC 1361 et seq.
The Marine Mammal Protection Act of 1972

This Act prohibits the import of certain marine mammals and their parts and products. These species include whales, walruses, narwhals, seals, sea lions, sea otters, and polar bears. It also defines parameters for importation of commercial fish or products that have been caught using methods, which involve incidental death or serious injury to protected marine mammals.

19 CFR 12.26 et seq.
Regulations on Importation of Wild Animals

These regulations list the wild animals that are prohibited from importation or that require import permits.

50 CFR Parts 10, 13, and 16
Regulations of FWS for Importing Wildlife and Fish

These regulations specify the animals and animal products subject to import prohibitions and restrictions.

16 USC 4901
Wild Bird Conservation Act of 1992

This act eliminated most commercial imports of CITES-regulated birds, except for limited imports of pet birds.

Principal Exporting Countries

The following listing includes samples of the main supplier nations of the products of this chapter. It is organized by HTSUS major heading. (Refer to "Customs Classification" above for the product codes.) Countries are listed in rank order of the value of products imported to the U.S. Statistics represent customs value of entries for 2002 from the Bureau of Census, U.S. Department of Commerce.

0201—Canada, Australia, New Zealand, Mexico, Nicaragua, Costa Rica

0202—Australia, New Zealand, Canada, Nicaragua, Costa Rica, Mexico, Honduras, Netherlands, Argentina, Uruguay

0203—Canada, Denmark, Ireland, Finland, United Kingdom, Germany, Australia, Chile, Netherlands, China

0204—Australia, New Zealand, Canada, Iceland, Denmark

0205—Australia, Canada

0206—Canada, Australia, New Zealand, Denmark, Costa Rica, Nicaragua, Mexico, Iceland, Chile, Brazil, Finland, Turkey

0207—Canada, Israel, France, Peru, Ecuador, Vietnam

0208—New Zealand, China, Canada, Vietnam, Taiwan, Indonesia, Australia, Spain, Turkey, United Kingdom, France, Hong Kong, El Salvador

0209—Canada, Denmark

0210—Canada, Italy, Brazil, New Zealand, Spain, Germany, Uruguay, France, Belgium, Ireland, Denmark, Mexico, Austria

Chapter 3: Fish

Full title: Fish and Crustaceans, Molluscs, and Other Aquatic Invertebrates

This chapter relates to the importation of fish, crustaceans, molluscs, and other aquatic invertebrates, which are classified under Chapter 3 of the Harmonized Tariff Schedule of the United States (HTSUS). Specifically, it includes live fish, whole harvested fresh or chilled fish, frozen fish, fish fillets and other meat, fish preserved other than by freezing and its edible products, all crustaceans, and all molluscs and related aquatic invertebrates, such as squid, octopus, and sea urchins. For a general overview on importing food see "Appendix: Foods" on page 825.

If you are interested in importing preparations of fish, including canned fish or caviar, refer to Commodity Index Chapter 16. The importation of live marine mammals is covered in Chapter 1 (importation in connection with traveling circuses, menageries, or similar exhibits comes under Chapter 95), while the heavily restricted importation of meat of marine mammals is included in Chapter 2. Fish, crustaceans, molluscs, and other aquatic animals considered unfit for human consumption by reason of their species or condition are covered in Chapter 5. Fish oils are included in chapter 15. Edible products which contain a small portion of fish or seafood, such as seafood-filled pasta, are covered in Chapter 19, while soups with a fish or seafood base are included in Chapter 21. Inedible flours, meals, or pellets of fish and other aquatic species—largely imported for the preparation of animal feeds—are covered in Chapter 23.

Other special provisions that potentially affect fish and related aquatic species include those for wild, live specimens imported for use or sale for scientific or educational purposes (HTSUS 9801.00.00); live specimens imported for breeding, exhibition, or prize competition (HTSUS 9813.00.60); and live game specimens imported for the purpose of stocking ranges (HTSUS 9817.00.70).

Subchapter XV of Chapter 98 (major heading 9815) pertains explicitly to products of U.S. fisheries, which are defined as fishing enterprises conducted legally under treaty provisions or by international law under U.S. flag by U.S. vessels on the high seas or in foreign waters, whether or not they include operation of a shore station as part of the same enterprise. The heading excludes any marine products produced in a foreign country or its territorial waters involving the use of non-U.S. labor. Eligible marine products of such fisheries include those which have never been landed in a foreign country or which have been landed solely for transshipment without change in condition of the products; fish—except cod, cusk, haddock, hake, mackerel, pollock, and swordfish—which have been so landed for partial pro-

cessing, such as evisceration, chilling, or freezing; and those which have been landed for processing on the treaty coasts of Labrador, the Magdalen Islands, or Newfoundland as per the 1818 convention between Great Britain and the U.S. All such eligible products are admitted duty free.

Note: To understand key issues that will enable you to make best use of the information in this section we recommend that you see "Introduction" on page 425.

Key Factors

The key factors in the importation of fish, crustaceans, molluscs, and other aquatic species are:

- Compliance with Food and Drug Administration (FDA) purity, identity, manufacturing, and other standards

- Compliance with FDA entry notification and procedures

- Special duty status for products of U.S. fisheries

- Compliance with U.S. Department of Agriculture (USDA) Animal and Plant Health Inspection Service (APHIS) and U.S. Fish and Wildlife Service (FWS) import regulations and quarantine requirements for live specimens

Although most importers utilize the services of a licensed customs broker in making their entries, and we recommend this practice, you should be aware of the regulatory, entry, and documentation issues involved in importing your product. You, as importer, are ultimately responsible for the fulfillment of any legal requirements applicable to your shipment.

General Considerations

Regulatory Agencies. Importation of fish and seafood products falls primarily under the jurisdiction of the FDA, which enforces the requirements of the Federal Food, Drug, and Cosmetic Act (FDCA). The importation of live specimens is subject to quarantine regulations under 9 CFR Part 92, administered and enforced by the USDA APHIS. The U.S. Department of the Interior's FWS regulates importation of animals and animal parts and products covered under the Endangered Species Act (ESA), the Convention on International Trade in Endangered Species (CITES), and the Marine Mammal Protection Act (MMPA). Seafoods are also subject to the requirements of the U.S. Department of Commerce's c (NMFS) (see addresses at end of this chapter).

Foods Subject to FDCA. The FDA regulations on the importation of foods of any kind are extensive and stringent. Seafoods and fishery products imported into the U.S. must comply with all FDCA requirements for those produced domestically. Imported products regulated by FDA are subject to FDA port of entry inspection. For a general discussion of FDA import procedures refer to "Appendix: Foods" on page 825.

Live Animals. APHIS restricts the import of live animals primarily in order to safeguard U.S. animals from communicable diseases. This entry provides an overview of rather than an exhaustive treatment of APHIS and other agency requirements. Actual requirements vary depending on the circumstances and the species involved. If you are interested in importing live aquatic animals, you should contact APHIS for full information (see addresses at end of this chapter).

Wildlife and Endangered Species. If you are interested in importing any exotic live animal, you should contact FWS with the scientific name of the species to ascertain whether it is protected. If it is, you will need a FWS permit to import it. You may also need country of origin export permits and documentation.

Detention of Shipment. If your shipment is found to be noncomplying, it may be detained at the port of entry. For products subject to FDA jurisdiction, the FDA may allow you to bring such a shipment into compliance before making a final decision regarding admittance. However, any sorting, reprocessing, or relabeling must be supervised by FDA personnel and is done at the importer's expense. Such conditional release to allow the importer to bring a shipment into compliance is a privilege, not a right. The FDA may consider subsequent noncomplying shipments of the same type of product to constitute abuse of the privilege and require the importer to destroy or reexport the products. To ascertain what your legal responsibilities are, you should contact these agencies regarding the specific items to be imported.

Customs Classification

For customs purposes, fish, crustaceans, molluscs, and related aquatic species are classified under Chapter 3 of the HTSUS. This chapter is divided into major headings, which are further divided into subheadings, and often into sub-subheadings, each of which has its own HTSUS classification number. For example, the 2001 HTSUS number for smelts, cusk, pollock, shad, sturgeon, swordfish, and freshwater fish is 0303.79.20, indicating that it is a subcategory of fish other than cod (0303.71), which is a subcategory of the major heading fish, frozen, excluding fish fillets and other fish meat of heading 0304 (0303). There are seven major headings in Chapter 3.

0301—Live fish

0302—Fish, fresh or chilled, excluding fish fillets and other fish meat of heading 0304

0303—Fish, frozen, excluding fish fillets and other fish meat of heading 0304

0304—Fish fillets and other fish meat (whether or not minced), fresh, chilled, or frozen

0305—Fish, dried, salted, or in brine; smoked fish, whether or not cooked before or during the smoking process; flours, meals, and pellets of fish, fit for human consumption

0306—Crustaceans, whether in shell or not, live, fresh, chilled, frozen, dried, salted, or in brine; crustaceans, in shell, cooked by steaming or by boiling in water, whether or not chilled, frozen, dried, salted, or in brine; flours, meals, and pellets of crustaceans, fit for human consumption

0307—Molluscs, whether in shell or not, live, fresh, chilled, frozen, dried, salted, or in brine; aquatic invertebrates other than crustaceans and molluscs, live, fresh, chilled, frozen, dried, salted, or in brine; flours, meals, andpellets of aquatic invertebrates other than crustaceans, fit for human consumption

For more details regarding classification of the specific product you are interested in importing, consult a customs broker, the appropriate commodity specialist at your nearest customs port, or see the HTSUS. The 2001 HTSUS is available online from the Customs Service (www.customs.gov/impoexpo/impoexpo.htm) or for purchase from the U.S. Government Printing Office (see resources at the end of this chapter), and may be found in larger public libraries. For a general discussion of customs classification, see "Classification—Liquidation" on page 229.

Dutiable Status of Goods

For more information about duty rates and binding decissions see "Dutiable Status of Goods" on page 203; for a discussion of temporary importation of goods see "Temporary Free Importations" on page 205.

Valuation

Importers have a responsibility to use what the U.S. Customs Service deems, "reasonable care," when determining the value of their goods. They must also provide any additional information that U.S. Customs and Border Protection needs for setting a final value on the goods. This process involves a number of factors and can be somewhat complicated; importers must be aware of applicable issues and details. Valuation information applies to all types of commodities, for further discussion on the subject see "Customs Valuation" on page 267.

Import Duties

Import duties vary (often dramatically) depending upon the Harmonized Tariff Schedule (HTSUS) classification of the goods or products imported. Since some products that look alike have different HTSUS classifications and different rates of duty, proper classification is vital. Note that "differences of opinion" between importers and the Bureau of Customs and Border Protection regarding classification keeps customs attorneys very busy.

Import duties can be assessed on the imported value of the goods ("ad valorem" rates of duty such as 2%, 4.4%, 50%, etc.), total units or weight of the goods ("specific" rates of duty such as 2 cents each or 1.5 cents/pound, etc.) or on a combination basis ("compound" rates of duty such as 5 cents each plus 6%).

Listed below is a sampling of several Column 1 import duty rates for Chapter 03 products:
Live ornamental fish (0301.10.00.00): free
to
Sturgeon roe (0302.70.20.00): 15%

For specific information on US import duties refer to the Harmonized Tariff Schedule of the US. The print version is available from the US Government Printing Office as well as third party suppliers who often add special features. Online versions are available in both static PDF pages as well as in formats with excellent search functionality. Search the Web with the term "Harmonized Tariff Schedule" to find sources.

Entry and Documentation

The entry of merchandise is a two-part process consisting of 1) filing the documents necessary to determine whether merchandise may be released from Customs custody and 2) filing the documents which contain information for duty assessment and statistical purposes. In certain instances all documents must be filed and accepted by Customs prior to release of the goods. Unless you have been granted an extension, you must file entry documents at a location specified by the port or area director within five working days of your shipment's date of arrival at a U.S. port of entry. These include a number of standard documents required by Customs for any entry, and:

- USDA quarantine requirements
- Importer's declaration, two copies
- FWS import permits required under CITES, ESA, and any other regulations applicable to then particular shipment; and any export certification from country of origin required under the specific laws governing endangered or threatened species
- FWS Wildlife Declaration Form 3-177—an original plus 3 copies—a copy of air waybill or bill of lading, and a copy of invoice (proforma invoice if shipment is noncommercial)

After you present the entry, Customs may examine your shipment, or may waive examination. The shipment is then released provided no legal or regulatory violations have been noted. You must then file entry summary documentation and deposit estimated duties at a designated customhouse within 10 working days of your shipment's release. For a detailed description of entry procedures, standard documentation, and informal entry, see "Entry Process" on page 185.

Informed Compliance. Informed compliance was introduced with the Customs Modernization Act of 1993 (Mod Act) and defines the relationship between importers and U.S. Customs and Border Protection. It sets out the responsibilities of both parties. Providing the correct documentation and information for entry is a key factor that will make your importing operation run smoothly. We recommend that importers become familiar with the concept of informed comliance and the responsibilities that they have under the Mod Act. For further discussion about informed compliance see "Informed Compliance" on page 211.

Entry Invoice. Invoices for fish or fish livers imported in airtight containers classifiable under HTSUS Chapter 3 must include the following information: 1) statement of whether the articles contain any oil, fat, or grease; and 2) the name and quantity of any such oil, fat, or grease. For more general information about invoices see "Invoices" on page 277.

Note: The Entry and Documentation section has been carefully designed to supply you, the importer, with sample documents and directions on how to satisfy Customs requirements. Be aware that you should consult the applicable authorities to ensure that you are correctly following the most current procedures.

Prohibitions and Restrictions

Fresh and Prepared Fish and Seafood. The FDA regulates importation of fresh, frozen, pickled, canned, salted, dried, and smoked fish and seafood under the Food, Drug, and Cosmetic Act (FDCA) (21 CFR 161). Raw seafood is extremely perishable. You must take care that your product is handled expeditiously and carefully and that it is kept under adequate refrigeration to avoid contamination and decomposition. You may use only FDA-approved preservatives to prevent or retard spoilage. The use of artificial coloring to conceal damage or to improve the appearance of an inferior product is prohibited by provisions of the FDCA. For a more detailed discussion of FDCA food additive regulations and labeling requirements, refer to "Appendix: Foods" on page 825.

Species-specific Restrictions. Regulations covering fish and seafood products are extensive, complex, and specific, and the current discussion is far from exhaustive. Identity standards are particularly stringent. For example, regulations limit products represented as anchovies to fish of the family *Engraulidae*. Other small fish which may superficially resemble anchovies—such as small herring and herring-like fish—may not be labeled or sold as anchovies. The use of the term "sardines" is permitted for small clupeoid fish. Sea herring (*Clupea harengus*), European pilchards (*Sardina pilchardus* or *Clupea pilchardus*), and brisling or sprat (*Clupea sprattus*) are commonly called sardines, especially when packed. Large herring may not be labeled sardines. Only species listed as tuna in the FDCA standards of identity may be imported as such. Species resembling tuna, such as bonito (*Sarda chilenis*) and yellowtail (*Seriola dorsalis*), may not be imported or sold as tuna. Standards of identity have been set for shrimp and oysters, as have standards for size, and prescribed methods of washing and draining to prevent adulteration by excess water. The sea crayfish, *Palinurus vulgaris*, is frequently imported into the U.S. in the form of frozen tails. Common trade names used for these products include "rock lobster" and "spiny lobster." If you are importing this product, be sure that your labeling includes the modifying words "rock" or "spiny" in direct connection with the word "lobster," in type of equal size and prominence.

Contaminated and Decomposed Fish. Chapter 3 products are highly perishable and require extraordinary care if decomposition is to be avoided. You should exercise extreme care in selecting raw materials to remove any unfit, decomposed material,

and to maintain the product in a sound, wholesome condition. A common cause of detention at the port of entry is the presence of "feedy, belly-blown" fish in a shipment. "Feedy fish" are those with stomachs full of feed when caught. They deteriorate rapidly, and the viscera and thin belly walls disintegrate, producing a characteristic ragged appearance called "belly-blown." If your shipment contains such fish, it is in violation of the FDCA and is subject to detention at the port of entry.

You should be aware that certain species of fish are likely to contain chemical contamination from lakes, rivers, and oceans or excessive residues of pesticides, mercury, and other heavy metals. Presence of such substances in food violates the FDCA, and such products are subject to detention at the U.S. port of entry.

Shellfish. If you are interested in importing raw shellfish (clams, mussels, and oysters), be sure they are obtained from unpolluted waters and produced, handled, and distributed in a rapid, sanitary manner. Because they may transmit intestinal diseases such as typhoid fever, or may be carriers of natural or chemical toxins, shellfish are subject to special FDA controls and licensing. Foreign shellfish intended for sale in the U.S. are subject to controls equivalent to those applied to domestic products.

All shellfish must comply with the general requirements of the FDCA as well as those of state health agencies cooperating in both the FDA-administered National Shellfish Sanitation Program (NSSP) and Interstate Shellfish Sanitation Conference (ISSC). Shellfish harvesting is prohibited in areas contaminated by sewage or industrial wastes. State inspectors issue approval certificates to facilities that pass inspection. These certificates are equivalent to a state license to operate. The state-approved plant's certification number must appear on each container or package of shellfish shipped. In addition, shippers are required to keep records showing the origin and disposition of all shellfish handled and to make these records available to the control authorities.

Imported fresh and fresh frozen oysters, clams, and mussels are similarly certified under the auspices of the NSSP through bilateral agreements with the country of origin. Canada, Japan, Korea, Iceland, Mexico, the United Kingdom, Australia, and New Zealand have such joint agreements with the U.S. For further information on NSSP requirements, contact FDA's Sanitation Branch.

Salmon. Fish and eggs of salmonids of the fish family *Salmonidae* are prohibited entry into the U.S. for any purpose, unless such importations are by direct shipment and accompanied by the signed certification of a qualified fish pathologist in substantially the form as prescribed in 50 CFR 13.7. The following are exempted from certification requirements: 1) salmon landed in North America and brought into the U.S. for processing or sale; 2) any salmonid caught in the wild in North America under a valid sport or a commercial fishing license; and 3) fish or eggs of the family *Salmonidae* when processed or prepared in accordance with 50 CFR 13.7(c) or otherwise exempted from certification requirement.

Marking and Labeling Requirements

Substitution of one kind of seafood for another is prohibited. Whether or not identity standards apply, your seafood labels must identify the product by its common or usual U.S. name (i.e. pollock, cod, shrimp). You may not replace the common U.S. name of a seafood either with a name common in the country of origin but unfamiliar in the U.S., or with a coined name. If you are importing a seafood product not previously marketed in the U.S., its name must reflect proper biological classification and must not duplicate, or risk being confused with, the common or usual U.S. name of any other species. In addition, any seafood product for which standards of identity have been promulgated must conform precisely to the applicable standards. It is illegal to use the name of a standardized seafood on the label of a product which deviates from that standard. Refer to "Appendix: Foods" on page 825 for other labeling requirements pertinent to foods in general.

For a general discussion of U.S. Customs marking and labeling requirements, see "Country of Origin Marking" on page 236, "Special Marking Requirements" on page 238 and "Marking—False Impression" on page 239.

Shipping Considerations

You will need to ensure that fish and seafood product imports are packed and shipped with care so that they arrive in good condition and pass smoothly through Customs. You are responsible for ensuring that the shipment is in compliance with all applicable government regulations for shipping. In most instances, you should not leave these arrangements solely to the discretion of your supplier. Careful preparation of the shipment and selection of the mode of transport can be essential to a cost-effective, timely delivery of undamaged goods. We strongly advise you to consult your shipping representatives, insurance agent, or freight broker for advice on packing and shipping.

Publications and WWW Resources

The following publication explains the FDA requirements for importing meat and poultry. It is published by FDA and available online from their website ((www.fda.gov/opacom/7pubs.html)).

> *Requirements of Laws and Regulations Enforced by the U.S. Food and Drug Administration*

The *Harmonized Tariff Schedule of the United States (2001)* (HTSUS) is available to view on the U.S. Customs and Border Protection website (www.customs.treas.gov), or you may purchase a printed version from:

U.S. Government Printing Office
Superintendent of Documents
710 North Capital Street NW
Washington DC 20401
Tel: (202) 512-1800
Fax: (202) 512-1657
Website: www.access.gpo.gov

The USGPO also has copies of specific laws available for purchase. The USGPO accepts orders made by fax, phone or placed over the Internet, as well as mail orders paid by credit card. All orders must be accompanied by payment. Credit cards, checks drawn on a U.S. bank, or an international money order are all acceptable.

Relevant Government Agencies

Address your questions regarding FDA requirements for the importation of fish and seafood products and regarding the National Shellfish Sanitation Program to:

Food and Drug Administration (FDA)
Center for Food Safety and Applied Nutrition (CFSAN)
Office of Compliance
Division of Enforcement, Imports Branch
5100 Paint Branch Parkway
College Park, MD 20740-3835
Tel: (301) 436-2080
Website: http://vm.cfsan.fda.gov/list.html

Food and Drug Administration (FDA)
Center for Food Safety and Applied Nutrition (CFSAN)
Office of Seafood
5100 Paint Branch Parkway
College Park, MD 20740-3835
Tel: (301) 436-2300
Website: vm.cfsan.fda.gov/list.html

Address your questions regarding National Marine Fisheries Service requirements to:

National Marine Fisheries Service (NMFS)
1315 East West Highway
SSMC3
Silver Spring, MD 20910
Tel: (301) 713-2239
Office of Protected Resources: (301) 713-2332
Inspection Services Division: (301) 713-2355
Website: www.nmfs.noaa.gov

Address your questions regarding endangered species issues to:

U.S. Fish and Wildlife Service (FWS)
Division of Management Authority
4401 N. Fairfax Dr.
Arlington, VA 22203-0700
Tel: (703) 358-2104
Website: www.fws.gov

Address your questions regarding importation of fish and seafood products to your local Customs port director. For addresses refer to "U.S. Customs and Border Protection Offices" on page 65 or contact:

U.S. Customs and Border Protection
Customs Headquarters
1300 Pennsylvania Avenue NW
Washington DC 20229
Tel: (202) 354-1000
Website: www.customs.treas.gov

Laws and Regulations

The following laws and regulations may be relevant to the importation of fish and seafood products. The laws are contained in the U.S. Code (USC) and the regulations are found in the Code of Federal Regulations (CFR), both of which may be available at larger public and law libraries. Copies of specific laws are also available from the United States Government Printing Office (address above).

21 USC 301 et seq.
Federal Food, Drug, and Cosmetic Act
This Act prohibits deceptive practices and regulates the manufacture, sale and importation or exportation of food, drugs, cosmetics, and related products. It covers examination and refusal of imports and exports of unapproved products. See 21 USC 331, 381, 382.

19 CFR 12.1 et seq.; 21 CFR 1.83 et seq.
Regulations on Food, Drugs, and Cosmetics
These regulations of the Secretary of Health and Human Services and the Secretary of the Treasury govern the standards, labeling, marking, and importing of products used with food, drugs, and cosmetics.

18 USC 42 et seq.
mportation of Injurious Animals, Birds, Fish, and Plants
This Act governs the importation of mammals, birds, fish, amphibia, and reptiles into the U.S. which, may be hazadous to humans or harmful to U.S. agriculture and it authorizes U.S. Customs to enforce the import requirements.

19 CFR 10.78
Regulations on Entry of American Fishery Products
This regulation allows for the free entry of fish and fish products taken on the high seas by U.S. vessels.

Convention on International Trade in Endangered Species of Wild Fauna and Flora (CITES)
This comprehensive wildlife treaty signed by over 100 countries, including the United States, regulates and in many cases prohibits commercial imports and exports of wild animal and plant species threatened by trade.

16 USC 1531
Endangered Species Act of 1973
This Act prohibits the import and export of species listed as endangered and most species listed as threatened. It is the U.S. law that implements CITES.

16 USC 742a et seq.
Fish and Wildlife Act of 1956
This Act regulates and bars the import of certain wild animals or birds and authorizes U.S. Customs to enforce the restrictions.

16 USC 2401 et seq.
Antarctic Conservation Act of 1978
This Act prohibits the importation, absent a special permit, of any flora or fauna native to Antarctica into the U.S. pursuant to the Antarctic Treaty and the Protocol

16 USC 1361 et seq.
The Marine Mammal Protection Act of 1972
This Act prohibits the import of certain marine mammals and their parts and products. These species include whales, walruses, narwhals, seals, sea lions, sea otters, and polar bears. It also defines parameters for importation of commercial fish or products that have been caught using methods, which involve incidental death or serious injury to protected marine mammals.

50 CFR Parts 10, 13, and 16
Regulations of FWS for Importing Wildlife and Fish
These regulations specify the animals and animal products subject to import prohibitions and restrictions.

19 CFR 12.26, 12.28, 12.30
Regulations of Customs on Importation of Fish
These regulations list the fish that are prohibited from importation into the U.S., require licenses for certain imports, and set forth procedures for entry.

Principal Exporting Countries

The following listing includes samples of the main supplier nations of the products of this chapter. It is organized by HTSUS major heading. (Refer to "Customs Classification" above for the product codes.) Countries are listed in rank order of the value of products imported to the U.S. Statistics represent customs value of entries for 2002 from the Bureau of Census.

0301—Thailand, Singapore, Indonesia, Philippines, Canada, Hong Kong, Japan, Malaysia, Colombia, Sri Lanka

0302—Canada, Costa Rica, Panama, Chile, Mexico, Ecuador, Brazil, Vietnam, Trinidad and Tobago, United Kingdom, Philippines, Australia

0303—Taiwan, China, Canada, Indonesia, Norway, Philippines, Argentina, India, Chile, Singapore, Uruguay, Japan

0304—Chile, China, Canada, Iceland, New Zealand, Vietnam, Norway, Indonesia, Ecuador, Russia, Argentina, Thailand, Japan, Costa Rica

0305—Canada, Norway, China, Chile, Iceland, Philippines, Japan, South Korea, Indonesia, United Kingdom, New Zealand

0306—Canada, Thailand, Vietnam, India, Mexico, China, Russia, Ecuador, Brazil, Indonesia, Honduras

0307—Canada, China, New Zealand, Japan, Philippines, Taiwan, India, Thailand, Mexico, Argentina, South Korea

Chapter 4:
Dairy Products

Full title: Dairy Products; Birds' Eggs; Natural Honey; Edible Products of Animal Origin, Not Elsewhere Specified or Included

This chapter relates to the importation of dairy products, eggs, honey, and other edible products of animal origin not specified elsewhere, which are classified under Chapter 4 of the Harmonized Tariff Schedule of the United States (HTSUS). Specifically, it includes milk and cream, with or without sweetening; buttermilk, yogurt, and sour cream; whey; butter; cheese and curd; birds' eggs in the shell, shelled, and yolks; natural honey; and other edible products of animal origin. The key to the other products mentioned is that they must be edible. You should read this section in conjunction with the general information about importing foods at "Appendix: Foods" on page 825.

If you are interested in importing live dairy animals or poultry (or viable, fertile eggs), you should refer to Commodity Index Chapter 1. Meat of cattle and poultry is covered in Chapter 2. Other inedible animal products and byproducts, such as feathers, are covered in Chapter 5. If you are interested in importing animal fats other than butter, refer to Chapter 15. Food preparations containing dairy products are included in Chapters 17, 18, and 19. Albumins and globulins derived from eggs are covered in Chapter 35.

Note: To understand key issues that will enable you to make best use of the information in this section we recommend that you see "Introduction" on page 425.

Key Factors

The key factors in the importation of these products are:

- Compliance with the U.S. Food and Drug Administration (FDA) purity, identity, manufacturing, and other standards

- Compliance with FDA entry notifications and procedures

- For milk and cream, FDA dairy import permit required

- Compliance with the U.S. Department of Agriculture (USDA) Animal and Plant Health Inspection Service (APHIS) Veterinary Service (VS) livestock disease-prevention requirements and restrictions; permits required in some cases

- Compliance with USDA Food Safety and Inspection Service (FSIS) import restrictions, port inspections, and product certification

- Compliance with quotas and licensing for certain products

Although most importers utilize the services of a licensed customs broker in making their entries, and we recommend this practice, you should be aware of the regulatory, entry and documentation issues involved in importing your product. You, as importer, are ultimately responsible for the fulfillment of any legal requirements applicable to your shipment.

General Considerations

Regulatory Agencies. Importation of dairy products into the U.S. is regulated by the USDA and the FDA. The following discussion will be divided into sections that deal with the requirements of each separate agency. In reality, these requirements, restrictions, permits, licenses, quotas, and other requirements are not so neatly divided. If, for example, under the USDA heading we say you may import a product that meets certain criteria, in no sense should you construe that statement to mean that the product thereby automatically meets criteria of all the other agencies, or that only the USDA is concerned in that product's import. Agency requirements for dairy imports overlap in ways that are not always evident. For example, a product that is permitted under APHIS country-of-origin disease prevention restrictions may be restricted under the Import Milk Act (IMA), as well as be subject to Section 22 dairy quotas. You may meet all those criteria, but if your product does not also meet an applicable FDA standard under the Food, Drug, and Cosmetic Act (FDCA)—such as standards of quality, identity, and manufacturing practices—you do not yet have an admissible product. It is the importer's responsibility to satisfy all of the U.S agencies with a regulatory interest in dairy products.

FDA Requirements. The FDA enforces applicable provisions of the FDCA. The FDA regulations regarding foods of any kind are extensive and stringent, and dairy products imported into the U.S. must comply with all FDCA requirements for those produced domestically.

Port of Entry Requirements. Imported products regulated by the FDA are subject to port of entry inspection. FDA also enforces the IMA. Under IMA, an FDA import permit is required in order to import milk, cream, or products containing significant amounts of milk and cream. For a further discussion regarding FDA import procedures see "Appendix: Foods" on page 825.

Detention of Shipment. If your shipment is found to be noncomplying, it may be detained at the port of entry. In the case of products subject to FDA jurisdiction, the FDA may allow you to bring such a shipment into compliance before making a final decision regarding admittance. However, any sorting, reprocessing, or relabeling must be supervised by FDA personnel and is done at the importer's expense. Such conditional release to allow the importer to bring a shipment into compliance is a privilege, not a right. The FDA may consider subsequent noncomplying shipments of the same type of product to constitute abuse of the privilege and require the importer to destroy or reexport the products. To ascertain what your legal responsibilities are, you should contact these agencies regarding the specific items to be imported.

USDA Requirements. USDA APHIS VS enforces restrictions on importation of certain milk and milk products found in 9 CFR Chapter 1 Subpart 94. Importation of some of these products requires a USDA APHIS VS import permit. The USDA only grants dairy import permits when the Administrator is satisfied that the product will not introduce or disseminate contagious livestock diseases into the U.S. Under Section 22 of the Agricultural Adjustment Act (AAA), USDA assigns annual import quotas to many dairy products, mainly cheeses. You must have a USDA import license in order to import these items. The importation of poultry products and eggs is also regulated by the USDA FSIS, which enforces the Wholesome Poultry Act (WPA) and Federal Poultry Inspection Act (FPIA).

Import Advisory

Importing dairy products is complicated. You will have to satisfy more than one branch of more than one U.S. government agency, and there are a wide variety of factors to stay on top of at every phase. Each agency is a very good source of information about what you need to do, and the standards and procedures your product needs to comply with. However, do not expect an employee or official of one agency to be an accurate source of information about the requirements of another agency. Do not expect a government expert in a department regulating one aspect of dairy imports to be equally expert on the regulatory issues governed by a different department. This is true even though you are asking for information pertaining to a single commodity that is subject to regulation by both. For the most part, they simply do not know, and for good reason. Dairy regulations are complicated. Ask all relevant agencies about their requirements and only about their requirements.

Customs Classification

For customs purposes, dairy products are classified under Chapter 4 of the HTSUS. This chapter is divided into major headings, which are further divided into subheadings, and often into subsubheadings, each of which has its own HTSUS classification number. For example, the 2001 HTSUS number for milk or cream of a fat content by weight not exceeding 45% is 0401.30.05, indicating that it is a subcategory of milk and cream of a fat content by weight exceeding 6% (0401.30), which is a subcategory of milk and cream not concentrated nor containing added sugar or other sweetening matter (0401). There are 10 major headings in Chapter 4.

0401—Milk and cream, not concentrated nor containing added sugar or other sweetening matter

0402—Milk and cream, concentrated or containing added sugar or other sweetening matter

0403—Buttermilk, curdled milk and cream, yogurt, kephir, and other fermented or acidified milk and cream, whether or not concentrated or containing added sugar or other sweetening matter or flavored or containing added fruit, nuts, or cocoa

0404—Whey, whether or not concentrated or containing added sugar or other sweetening matter; products consisting of natural milk constituents, whether or not containing added sugar or other sweetening matter, not elsewhere specified or included

0405—Butter and other fats and oils derived from milk; dairy spreads

0406—Cheese and curd

0407—Birds' eggs, in shell, fresh, preserved, or cooked

0408—Birds' eggs, not in shell, and egg yolks, fresh, dried, cooked by steaming or by boiling in water, molded, frozen, or otherwise preserved, whether or not containing added sugar or sweetening matter

0409—Natural honey

0410—Edible products of animal origin, not elsewhere specified or included

For more details regarding classification of the specific product you are interested in importing, consult a customs broker, the appropriate commodity specialist at your nearest customs port, or see the HTSUS. The 2001 HTSUS is available online from the Customs Service (www.customs.gov/impoexpo/impoexpo.htm) or for purchase from the U.S. Government Printing Office (see resources at the end of this chapter), and may be found in larger public libraries. For a general discussion of customs classification, see "Classification—Liquidation" on page 229.

Dutiable Status of Goods

For more information about duty rates and binding decissions see "Dutiable Status of Goods" on page 203; for a discussion of temporary importation of goods see "Temporary Free Importations" on page 205.

Valuation

Importers have a responsibility to use what U.S. Customs and Border Protection deems, "reasonable care," when determining the value of their goods. They must also provide any additional information that U.S. Customs and Border Protection needs for setting a final value on the goods. This process involves a number of factors and can be somewhat complicated; importers must be aware of applicable issues and details. Valuation information applies to all types of commodities, for further discussion on the subject see "Customs Valuation" on page 267.

Import Duties

Import duties vary (often dramatically) depending upon the Harmonized Tariff Schedule (HTSUS) classification of the goods or products imported. Since some products that look alike have different HTSUS classifications and different rates of duty, proper classification is vital. Note that "differences of opinion" between importers and the Bureau of Customs and Border Protection regarding classification keeps customs attorneys very busy.

Import duties can be assessed on the imported value of the goods ("ad valorem" rates of duty such as 2%, 4.4%, 50%, etc.), total units or weight of the goods ("specific" rates of duty such as 2 cents each or 1.5 cents/pound, etc.) or on a combination basis ("compound" rates of duty such as 5 cents each plus 6%).

Listed below is a sampling of several Column 1 import duty rates for Chapter 04 products:
Edible products of animal origin, not elsewhere specified or included (0410.00.00.00): 1.1%
to
Colby cheese described in general note 15 of the tariff schedule and entered pursuant to its provisions (0406.90.51.00): 20%

For specific information on US import duties refer to the Harmonized Tariff Schedule of the US. The print version is available from the US Government Printing Office as well as third party suppliers who often add special features. Online versions are available in both static PDF pages as well as in formats with excellent search functionality. Search the Web with the term "Harmonized Tariff Schedule" to find sources.

Entry and Documentation

The entry of merchandise is a two-part process consisting of 1) filing the documents necessary to determine whether merchandise may be released from Customs custody and 2) filing the documents that contain information for duty assessment and statistical purposes. In certain instances, such as the entry of merchandise subject to quotas, all documents must be filed and accepted by Customs prior to the release of the goods. Unless you have been granted an extension, you must file entry documents at a location specified by the port or area director within five working days of your shipment's date of arrival at a U.S. port of entry. These include a number of standard documents required by Customs for any entry, and:

- When required to establish yourself as the importer of record Customs Form CF 7501 (page 342)

- For milk and cream and certain products containing large amounts of milk and cream: FDA Dairy Import Permit

- For certain products restricted by USDA: USDA APHIS Import Permit

- For cheeses imported from the European Community, an affidavit stating that the cheeses will not receive any restitution payments as per EO 11851 of April 5, 1975 and, if imported into Puerto Rico, will not be reexported into the U.S.; affidavits are not required on direct shipments to the U.S. on a through bill of lading

After you present the entry, Customs may examine your shipment, or may waive examination. The shipment is then released provided no legal or regulatory violations have been noted. You must then file entry summary documentation and deposit estimated duties at a designated customhouse within 10 working days of your shipment's release. For a detailed description of entry procedures, standard documentation, and informal entry, see "Entry Process" on page 185.

Informed Compliance. Informed compliance was introduced with the Customs Modernization Act of 1993 (Mod Act) and defines the relationship between importers and U.S. Customs and Border Protection. It sets out the responsibilities of both parties. Providing the correct documentation and information for entry is a key factor that will make your importing operation run smoothly. We recommend that importers become familiar with the concept of informed comliance and the responsibilities that they have under the Mod Act. For further discussion about informed compliance see "Informed Compliance" on page 211.

FDA Requirements—*Milk Safety.* Milk, cream, and the dairy products made from them offer ideal conditions for the propagation of microorganisms. Therefore, you should be sure that any milk and cream in the products you wish to import are obtained from disease-free animals. You should be sure that all materials used in manufactured dairy products have been handled at all times under sanitary conditions to prevent contamination with organisms that produce disease or cause spoilage. Pasteurization offers a considerable safeguard against disease transmission. Nevertheless, contamination by workers suffering from disease, by rodents, by unclean equipment, or by the addition of unpasteurized ingredients after pasteurization, can create a serious health hazard. Unsanitary handling can introduce spoilage organisms, such as undesirable bacteria, yeasts, and molds, into otherwise pure raw materials or finished products, causing decomposition. If your imported dairy products were prepared from decomposed raw materials, are undergoing active spoilage, or are contaminated with disease-producing organisms, the FDA considers them adulterated. Not only will they not be admitted, but you may also be subject to legal action.

Mandatory pasteurization for all milk and milk products in final packaged form intended for direct human consumption after distribution in interstate commerce became a Federal requirement as of August 10, 1987. The regulation (21 CFR 1240) defines pasteurization as heating and holding every particle of milk or milk product in properly designed and operated equipment at times and temperatures specified in the regulation. Exemptions are provided for acceptable alternative methods, such as aging procedures for certain cheeses.

Nonfat Dry Milk. Imported nonfat dry milk and nonfat dry milk fortified with vitamins A and D must comply with FDCA identity standards for these products. Nonfat dry milk is defined in a standard provided by Act of Congress on July 2, 1956, as follows: "nonfat dry milk is the product resulting from the removal of fat and water from milk and contains the lactose, milk proteins, and milk minerals in the same relative proportions as in the fresh milk from which it is made. It contains not over 5 per centum by weight of moisture. The fat content is not over 1 1/2 per centum by weight unless otherwise indicated. The term 'milk,' when used herein, means sweetmilk of cows."

Butter. Butter is defined in the standard provided by Act of Congress of March 4, 1923, as follows: "butter shall be understood to mean the food product usually known as butter, and which is made exclusively from milk or cream or both, with or without common salt, and with or without additional coloring matter, and containing not less than 80 per centum by weight of milk fat, all tolerances having been allowed for." The FDA examines butter shipments for evidence of the use of dirty cream or milk, and for mold indicating the use of decomposed cream. You may not import butter containing chemical additives or artificial flavor.

Cheese. Imports of cheese are highly regulated. Standards of identity have been promulgated for most natural cheeses, process cheeses, cheese foods, and cheese spreads (21 CFR 133). If you are importing a particular variety of cheese for which a standard has been adopted, you should be aware that all cheeses belonging to that variety must comply with that standard. Cheeses must be labeled with the name prescribed in the applicable standard. Most of the standards prescribe limits for moisture and for fat. A few natural cheeses are required to be made from pasteurized milk. However, most may be made from either raw or pasteurized milk. To ensure that the cheese is safe to eat, those made from raw milk must be aged for 60 days or longer. Requirements for longer aging apply to cheeses that need additional aging to develop the characteristics of the variety. If you are considering importing cheese and foods made of cheese, you should consult the FDA standards before making your purchase. The FDA will not permit entry of cheese that does not comply with applicable standards.

Basically, a narrow range of problems accounts for the majority of FDA detentions of cheese at the port of entry. By avoiding these problems—through exercising care in your foreign purchases and in subsequent handling of cheeses—you are likely to assure your shipment's entry into the U.S. Be sure that your cheese has not been contaminated with insect and rodent filth during the handling of the milk, manufacture of the cheese, or during transport or storage. Pesticides are also an issue. If you buy cheese from a foreign producer whose cows are exposed to pesticides, either from careless use in barns, or in feed, you may find that yours is among the large number of shipments that FDA detains for that particular violation.

Evaporated Milk, Sweetened Condensed Milk. There are standards of identity for both evaporated milk and sweetened condensed milk (21 CFR 131). Evaporated milk must contain not less than 7.5% milk fat and not less than 25.5% total milk solids. Sweetened condensed milk must contain not less than 28% total milk solids, and not less than 8.5% milk fat. If you are considering importing sweetened condensed milk, you will need a FDA Dairy Import Permit under IMA. Evaporated milk is not subject to IMA because it has been sterilized by heat.

FDA Import Permits. Under IMA, you must hold an FDA Dairy Import Permit in order to import milk, cream, or products containing significant amounts of milk or cream. Cheese and heat-sterilized, hermetically sealed products are exempt from this requirement. The application for an FDA dairy permit is not a simple matter. You will have to provide many types of health and sanitation verifications as part of the application process. The description that follows is not at all exhaustive, but is intended to convey a rough sense of what is involved.

Each cow from which an import shipment of milk or cream is to be derived must be physically examined and tested for tuberculosis by a government veterinarian of the country of origin. The dairy farm must be inspected for compliance with FDA sanitary and processing requirements. The plant where the milk is processed must be inspected and receive an FDA sanitary rating. The state and country in which the processing plant and dairy are located must certify that all requisite inspections have been carried out, within one year of your permit application, by a reg-

ulatory official of the country of origin. Your permit application must include documentation for each aspect of this process. You will need as many as twenty or thirty different FDA forms to apply for a permit for a single shipment of milk or cream. If you are interested in obtaining a Dairy Import Permit, you should contact FDA's Center for Food Safety for detailed instructions (see addresses at end of this chapter).

USDA Requirements—*APHIS VS Restrictions.* Under 9 CFR Subpart 94, APHIS restricts the importation of milk and milk products from countries that are known to be infected with rinderpest or foot-and-mouth disease (see Country-Specific Import Restrictions below). The following products are exempt from these restrictions: 1) cheese that does not contain liquid or other articles restricted under Subpart 94; 2) butter; and 3) butter oil.

Milk or Milk Products. For USDA purposes, you may import other milk or a milk product originating in countries known to be infected with rinderpest or foot-and-mouth disease, provided the product meets one of the following criteria:

1) It has been heat-processed and hermetically sealed. You may import products in a concentrated liquid form which have been processed by heat by a commercial method in a container hermetically sealed promptly after such heating, so as to be shelf-stable without refrigeration.

2) It is dry milk or a dry milk product. This includes dry whole milk, nonfat dry milk, dried whey, dried buttermilk, and formulations that contain any such dry milk products. You may import these products, but you must consign them directly to a USDA—approved establishment for further processing. With prior USDA permission, you may temporarily store your products in an approved warehouse under the supervision of an APHIS inspector, pending movement to an approved establishment. In any case, you must transport your product from the U.S. port of first arrival to either its destination (and, if temporarily stored, from the warehouse to the establishment) only under USDA or U.S. Customs and Border Protection seals. These seals may only be broken by an APHIS inspector or other USDA-authorized person. If you wish to remove your products from the warehouse or establishment, you must obtain special permission from the USDA Administrator, and comply with all the conditions and requirements specified for the move.

3) It is a milk product brought in under permit. If you wish to import milk products that are not covered by either of the two conditions listed above, you will need prior written permission from the USDA Administrator. Products requiring USDA import permits include—but are not limited to—condensed milk, long-life milks such as sterilized milk, casein and caseinates, lactose, and lactalbumin. For permit application procedures, see APHIS VS Permit Application below.

4) It is a milk product brought in under permit for testing. In specific cases USDA allows importation of small amounts of restricted milk products for examination, testing, or analysis. If your intended importation fits this description, you will need to obtain an APHIS VS permit prior to shipping the product to the U.S. For permit application procedures, see APHIS VS Permit Application below.

If your milk and milk products originate in and are shipped from countries listed as free of rinderpest and foot-and-mouth disease, but have entered a port or otherwise transited a country where the infection is present, they must meet the following conditions for import into the U.S. The product must be transported under serially numbered official seals, applied at the shipment's point of origin by an authorized representative of the country of origin. The numbers of the seals must be either listed directly on or attached to, the bill of lading or similar document accompanying the shipment. Upon arrival of the carrier at the U.S. port of entry, an APHIS inspector must determine that the seals on your shipment are intact and that the numbers match the numbers appearing on the accompanying document.

Poultry and Eggs. Subpart 94 details poultry and egg import restrictions and the procedures necessary to qualify a product for import. APHIS administers these restrictions primarily through import permits and product certification by qualified government veterinarians of the country of origin. (In the following information, "government veterinarian" always means full-time veterinary officer salaried by the national government of the country of origin.) The law defines poultry as chickens, turkeys, swans, partridges, guinea fowl, pea fowl; nonmigratory ducks, geese, pigeons, and doves; and commercial, domestic, or penraised grouse, pheasants, and quail. It restricts import of these products from countries known to have incidence of the following diseases: fowl pest, Exotic Newcastle Disease (END), and *Salmonella enteritidis*, phage-type 4. (See below, Country-Specific Import Restrictions, APHIS, for a list of countries currently under restriction because of the presence of these diseases.)

Subpart 94 restricts importation of eggs laid by poultry, game birds, or other birds raised in, imported from, or moved into or through any country where END or *S. enteritidis* is considered to exist at any time prior to importation to, or during shipment to, the U.S. *S. enteritidis* is considered to exist in all countries of the world except for Canada, and END in all but a few. For all practical purposes, the following restrictions apply to all importation of eggs into the U.S. You have four options for importing such eggs.

Option 1: Eggs brought in under certificate. If you bring eggs into the U.S. under this option, they must be imported in cases marked with the flock of origin's identity and sealed with the seal of the country of origin's national government. A certificate signed by a government veterinarian must accompany each shipment, which you must present to a USDA official at the U.S. port of entry. The certificate must identify: 1) flock of origin, 2) country of origin, 3) port of embarkation, 4) port of arrival, 5) names and addresses of exporter and importer, 6) total number of eggs and cases of eggs shipped with the certificate, 7) date the certificate was signed. In addition, the certificate must state that the eggs qualify for importation in accordance with all applicable requirements of Subpart 94.6.

No more than 90 days before the certificate is signed, a government veterinarian must inspect the flock of origin, finding no evidence of communicable poultry disease. Prior to export, the following processing must take place, all on the premises of origin: eggs must be 1) washed to remove foreign material from the shell surface; 2) sanitized with a hypochlorate solution of from 100 ppm to 200 ppm available chlorine; 3) packed in previously unused cases; and 4) the same government veterinarian who signs the certificate must seal the cases with a seal of the country of origin's national government.

If the eggs were laid in any country where END is considered to exist, the following restrictions also apply. There must be no evidence that the flock of origin was exposed to END during the 90 days before the certificate was signed, and no END occurred on the premises of origin during that time. The eggs must be from a flock of origin found free of END according to the specific veterinary testing and observation procedures outlined in 94.6 (ix)(C)(1,2). These procedures involve the use of "sentinel birds." These are chickens that 1) have been raised in an environment free of the pathogens that cause communicable poultry diseases, and 2) have not been infected with, exposed to, or immunized with any strain of virus that causes END. For information on sources of sentinel birds, contact APHIS VS (see addresses at end of this chapter).

If the eggs were laid in any country where *S. enteritidis*, phage type 4 is considered to exist, the flock of origin must similarly be found free of the disease by a government veterinarian, according to specific veterinary observation and testing procedures outlined in 94.6 (x)(C)(1-3).

Option 2: Eggs imported and moved to a USDA approved establishment for breaking and pasteurization. If you import eggs under this option, the shipment must be immediately moved under USDA seal from the U.S. port of arrival to an approved establishment for breaking and pasteurization. The USDA approves only those establishments it determines to have pasteurization and sanitation procedures for handling the eggs and for disposing of egg shells, cases, and packing materials adequate to prevent the introduction of communicable poultry disease into the U.S. The names and addresses of approved establishments may be obtained from USDA Import-Export Products staff (see addresses at end of this chapter). If you wish to request approval for an establishment, contact the USDA Administrator at the same address.

Option 3: Eggs entered under permit: those imported for scientific, educational, or research purposes. Eggs may be imported if they are imported for scientific, educational, or research purposes, and USDA has determined that the importation can be made under conditions that will prevent the introduction of END or *S. enteritidis* into the U.S. If your import fits this category, you will need to obtain an APHIS permit prior to importation. Your eggs must be moved and handled as specified on your permit. See APHIS VS Permit Application below for an outline of procedures and requirements for obtaining an APHIS permit.

Option 4: Eggs entered under permit: *those determined by USDA to have been cooked or processed or otherwise handled in a manner that will prevent introduction of disease into the U.S.* You may bring eggs in under APHIS permit when the Administrator determines that they have been cooked or processed or will be handled in a manner that will prevent the introduction of END or *S. enteritidis* into the U.S. You must obtain your permit prior to importation. Your eggs must be moved and handled as specified on the permit. See APHIS VS Permit Application below for an outline of procedures and requirements for obtaining an APHIS permit.

APHIS VS Permit Application Procedures. Requests for USDA APHIS VS permits authorizing importation of restricted products must be submitted on **VS Form 16-3**. You may obtain forms from APHIS headquarters (see addresses at end of this chapter) or any USDA port office. You may submit signed facsimiles, provided you send an original signed document as follow-up. If you intend multiple imports and need a supply of forms on hand, you may photocopy the original **Form 16-3**. Processing or production information and sources of milk products may often require more space than is allowed on the application form. In such cases, attach extra sheets as necessary. You should include as much background information as possible to allow APHIS to properly evaluate the disease risk associated with your import. You can send research papers as supporting evidence, but do not send them by fax.

It takes about two weeks for APHIS to process an application and prepare a permit for return mail. If your application information is insufficient, APHIS will contact you for clarification, and the permit process may take longer. Submit your requests for renewal or amendment of permits, in writing—submission by fax is acceptable—to USDA headquarters (see addresses at end of this chapter). Your renewal request should note any changes in particulars from the original application and permit issued. Once a permit has been issued, imports under that permit must comply in every detail with all of the permit's stipulations. Entry will be facilitated if your permit number appears on the shipping documents, or if a copy of the permit is attached. If you attempt to import products requiring permits without obtaining a permit prior to shipment, your import will be subject to delay or refusal at the port of entry.

FSIS Requirements. The Poultry Products Inspection Act (PPIA) requires countries exporting poultry to the U.S. to impose domestic inspection requirements at least equal to inspection requirements in the U.S. The FSIS reviews foreign inspection systems to ensure that they are equal to the U.S. system. Only those countries to which FSIS grants poultry export eligibility may export these products to the U.S. See Country-Specific Import Restrictions below for list of eligible countries.

An inspection certificate issued by the responsible official of the exporting country must accompany each import shipment of poultry and poultry products. Certificates identify products by country and plant of origin, destination, shipping marks, and amounts. They certify that the products have received ante-mortem and post-mortem inspection; that they are wholesome, not adulterated or misbranded, and that they otherwise comply with U.S. requirements.

Port of Entry Inspection. The FSIS reinspects poultry and poultry products on a sample basis as they enter the U.S. Your product will be checked for transportation damage, labeling, general condition, and proper certification. Additional inspection tasks that may be scheduled include: product examination; accuracy of net weight; condition of the container; laboratory analyses for food chemistry (such as fat, water, and nitrite levels) and drug and chemical residues; species testing; and monitoring of product labels. The actual inspection tasks and the scope of inspection are based on the nature of the product and on the performance history of the plant and country.

If your poultry or poultry products pass reinspection, FSIS will stamp them U.S. Inspected and Passed, and they will be allowed to enter U.S. commerce. If the products do not pass reinspection, they will be stamped U.S. Refused Entry. You must export, or destroy refused products. In some cases they may be converted to animal food. When condemnation occurs, inspection is intensified for future shipments of that product from the same plant, and in some cases, for all poultry shipments from the same country.

Residue Control. Chemical and drug residue control is one of the major features of an exporting country's inspection system that must be judged equal to the U.S. system. Each year, countries must be certified by the FSIS as continuing to operate an equivalent residue control program. FSIS experts make sure that the country's residue program uses approved analytical methods, that officials are knowledgeable about the use of chemical compounds in their country, and that the country tests for those compounds that could potentially contaminate the food supply. You cannot import poultry or eggs from a country that fails to receive an FSIS annual residue certification.

As a further residue check, the FSIS randomly samples products at the port of entry and analyzes them for drug and chemical residues. The FSIS annual import residue plan sets the initial sampling rate for each country based on the volume of product imported from that country. The plan includes the same chemical compounds as the domestic residue-monitoring program. Compounds are selected based on their likelihood of contaminating the food supply and their potential harm to the consuming public. The list can include chemical compounds not legal in the U.S. if they have the potential to contaminate a foreign country's poultry supply.

If your shipment contains residues above the U.S. tolerance or action level, it will be considered adulterated and will be refused entry into the U.S. Your shipment will not be held pending laboratory test results, however, unless FSIS has some reason to suspect contamination. If a laboratory reports a residue violation on a sample that has otherwise passed reinspection, as much as possible of the product must be recalled. Products so recovered may not be used for human food.

The occurrence of a residue violation at a port of entry raises concerns about the exporting country's ability to control residues. Port of entry sampling is then automatically increased for related products from the entire country, as well as on subsequent shipments from the specific plant where the violative sample originated.

From time to time, the FSIS will increase sampling for a specific country or for a specific compound. This can occur when there is an indication that a problem may exist or when a pattern develops of failed port-of-entry reinspections.

U.S.-Canada Free Trade Agreement. Canada has an inspection system that is virtually the same as that found in the US. Under the U.S.-Canada Free Trade Agreement, FSIS has modified border reinspection requirements for Canadian products. Canadian plants may choose to follow the revised procedures or go through traditional reinspection. Under the revised procedures, before a product destined for the U.S. leaves the Canadian plant, Agriculture Canada inspection officials provide information to be entered into the FSIS automated computer system. If the computer does not generate an assignment for reinspection at the border, the shipment automatically proceeds through U.S. Customs.

Entry of specific products can be difficult because many product categories affected by quota restrictions overlap, especially where milk and sugar products are concerned. Even when a product is not the target of a quota itself, it may be restricted because of other policy driven limitations. It is important to consult with the Quota Branch of U.S. Customs and Border Protection (see addresses at end of this chapter) to determine whether quota restrictions apply to your specific product.

Section 22 Dairy Quotas and Import Licensing System

Recent Changes. The program described here is currently operating on the basis of an interim rule which has applied the provisions of Revision 7 to the tariff-rate quotas (TRQs) that resulted from the Uruguay Round. The USDA is in the process of reviewing the entire dairy Import Regulation. An Advanced Notice of Proposed Rulemaking was published in the Federal Register on June 2, 1994, followed by the publication of the interim rule on January 6, 1995. This was followed by another interim rule to implement TRQ increments for countries implementing their Uruguay Round schedules. The USDA review is expected to result in a proposed rule to streamline and bring up-to-date the whole licensing system. During this process it is especially important that anyone interested in becoming a licensee contact the Dairy Import Group at (202) 720-9439 to ascertain the requirements in effect.

The Uruguay Round Agreement changed the dairy import regime by converting all of the absolute quotas which were implemented under the authority of Section 22 of the Agricultural Adjustment Act of 1933, as amended, to tariff-rate quotas. The in-quota amounts under these TRQ's for many dairy products were increased. The in-quota amount for all tariffed cheese will be increased by 30,992 metric tons by the year 2000, 5,550 of which are reserved for Mexico and not subject to license. The remainder are subject to license and will increase incrementally over the next five years.

Presidential Proclamation 4708 of December 11, 1979, limited imports of quota cheese entering the U.S. during any calendar year to an aggregate 111,000 metric tons. Any increase in the 111,000-ton limit for dairy products subject to quota restrictions involves hearings and investigations by the International Trade Commission (ITC).

Import Regulation. Under Import Regulation 7 CFR 6.20-6.34, importers of certain dairy products must be licensed by the USDA. The Import Regulation licensing system is designed to allocate quotas in a fair and equitable manner among importers and users. Since the beginning of the import system, the major portion of each quota has been allocated to historical licensees (persons who were actually in the business of importing during the representative period chosen for the particular quota in question). A small portion of each quota was allocated among eligible nonhistorical licensees. This system continues to apply to quota quantities in effect prior to January 1, 1980.

Beginning January 1, 1980, as a result of the Trade Agreements Act of 1979 and Presidential Proclamation 4708, new cheese import allocations increased the total quota and extended coverage to most cheese types that were not previously included in the quota, primarily those free of quota by virtue of their high price. These new quota shares are allocated so that no more than 50% goes to new historical licenses and at least 50% is allocated in the form of supplementary licenses to eligible applicants on a first-come, first-served basis.

The conversion of absolute quotas to TRQs pursuant to the Uruguay Round Agreement has, so far, not affected the actual allocation of licenses for the amounts previously under absolute quota. The interim rule published January 6, 1995 in the Federal Register maintained the licensing system under new authority. Further, it provided for the application of the provisions for "supplementary license" allocation to the TRQ increments for cheese. For the increments in non-cheese items, a new "rank order" lottery was introduced. All of these provisions are currently under review prior to an intended publication of a proposed rule which will supersede the current Revision 7.

Eligibility Standards for Historical Licenses. For continued eligibility for historical licenses, importers must submit a certification each year at least 60 days prior to the beginning of the quota year for which application is made. Licensees must certify that they have not used any other firm's license or permitted another firm to use their license.

Nonhistorical Licenses. Nonhistorical license eligibility criteria limit eligibility to those persons or firms operating viable businesses importing or manufacturing cheese or cheese products. To be considered as being in the cheese importing business, you must show evidence of importation of at least 10,000 pounds during the 12-month period ending August 1 of each year. You can also gain eligibility by showing proof of the manufacture of at least 100,000 pounds of cheese or cheese products in your own certified plant during the same 12-month period. Your plant must be listed in the most current issue of "Dairy Plants Surveyed and Approved for USDA Grading Services." To qualify for a nonhistorical license, you must also complete **Customs Forms 7501** and **7505,** showing yourself as the importer of record or importer of account.

Supplementary Licenses. Supplementary licenses are granted for items listed in Appendix 2 of the Import Regulation. In order to be eligible for one of these licenses you must: 1) meet the same eligibility criteria as those for nonhistorical licenses; or 2) have historical eligibility under Appendix 2 for articles from the same country of origin for which you are seeking a supplementary license; or, 3) be endorsed in writing by the government of the supplying country as a "preferred" importer, in addition to and meeting one or both of requirements (1) and (2) above.

Application Period. The application period begins August 1 each year and is open for 90 days. Your application must be made in writing to the Head, Import Licensing Group (see addresses at end of this chapter), and must be canceled by the U.S. Postal Service, certifying the date. Licenses are issued during the last week of December for use during the coming year and are valid for the 12-month period beginning January 1 and ending December 31.

Issuance of Licenses. If you have an established record of importing cheese (quota or nonquota), or are actively engaged in the cheese manufacturing business, you should have no difficulty in meeting the qualifications for license eligibility. However, because quotas are often fully subscribed, eligibility alone will

not guarantee that you will receive a license. Even if you do receive a license, there is no guarantee that it will be for the full allotment you have requested. Because of the limited shares available for each quota and the strong demand for certain quota products, it is quite possible that in any given year the nonhistorical quota shares for a specific quota will be fully subscribed by applicants who held shares for such quotas in the previous year. While supplementary licenses are granted on a first-come, first-served basis, established minima for such licenses may mean that some eligible applicants will not receive licenses despite having been granted licenses in previous years.

Cost of Licenses. The USDA charges an annual fee for licenses actually issued to cover the administrative costs of the licensing program. The fee is calculated each quota year for that year's license, and is announced in the Federal Register. License fees have consisted of relatively nominal amounts, primarily to cover processing costs.

Penalties. Licenses carry with them certain conditions and responsibilities. You may incur penalties if the Licensing Authority has reasonable cause to believe that you have 1) violated the provisions of the Import Regulation, or 2) furnished false or incomplete information in connection with your applications for or use of your license. In such cases the Authority may, after official notification, 1) revoke your historical eligibility and 2) bar you or your firm from receiving supplementary or nonhistorical licenses for a period of as long as three years. If your eligibility is revoked, you may appeal the determination to the Director of the Dairy, Livestock, and Poultry Division, Foreign Agricultural Service, Import Licensing Group (see addresses at end of this chapter), within 30 days from the date of notification.

Cancellation of Licenses. Licenses may also be canceled for the following reasons:

1) Historical licensees: If you fail to enter the article for which you hold the license during either a) two consecutive quota years or b) three nonconsecutive quota years within any five-year period, your eligibility for a historical license for that article will be suspended for the following quota year. Suspension may be lifted if you provide the Licensing Authority with documentary evidence that you did in fact enter the article during at least one of those years. If the you can provide an acceptable reason for failure to enter the article, the Licensing Authority may lift the suspension at its discretion. However, you will have to submit an application to the Licensing Authority, and that application will have to be approved three months after the beginning of the quota year for which your eligibility was suspended. 2) There is an 85% quota usage requirement per year. Failure to meet this requirement may result in the cancellation or reduction of your license. 3) Failure to pay the annual license fee is also cause for cancellation.

Licenses

Appendix 1: Old Historical. Old historical licenses (issued prior to 1979) and nonhistorical licenses are derived from Appendix 1 of the Import Regulation. Historical licenses were granted to firms that were in the business of importing certain articles that subsequently became subject to quota and licensing requirements. A representative period was used to determine the firm's quota base, which was used to calculate the basic annual allocations and license amount. For most Appendix 1 quotas, approximately 90% of the original quota was set aside for historical licenses. All old historical licenses have been applied for and issued, and no new licenses can be issued in this category.

Nonhistorical. These licenses are issued from Appendix 1 of the Import Regulation. Approximately 10% of the quotas were set aside so that new importers would have access to the licensing system. The amount available for nonhistorical licenses has subsequently been increased due to the cancellation of some historical licenses.

Appendix 2: New Historical. New historical licenses were issued as a result of the MTN of 1979. The MTN established several new quotas and expanded others. The basis for the establishment of these licenses was similar to the old historical licenses, with a representative period being used to calculate the firm's base quota. Some 50% of these quotas were set aside for new historical licenses. These licenses are listed together with supplementary licenses under Appendix 2 quotas of the Import Regulation. It should be noted that when a historical license is canceled, the license amount is moved to the portion of the quotas issued to either nonhistorical or supplementary licenses, whichever is appropriate. All new historical licenses have been applied for and issued, and none are available.

Supplementary. The provisions cited above apply to the Uruguay Round increments to the cheese TRQs. Licenses are issued either to preferred importers designated by the country of origin or on a first-come, first-served basis. The only change is that the EC will be permitted to designate preferred importers for these increments. For certain Uruguay Round increments to the non-cheese TRQs (non-fat dried milk, whole milk powder, butter and butteroil), a modified system was established by the interim rule of January 6, 1995. Eligibility may be based on a record of imports, exports or manufacture of dairy products. The import/export threshold is, however, considerably higher than that for cheese. Further, the lottery is not first-come, first-served, but based on rankings provided by the applicants which are subject to random selection if the TRQ is oversubscribed.

For more information on quota cheese import licensing, or for information on conditions under which limited quantities of quota cheeses may be imported without licenses, contact USDA's Import Licensing Group (see addresses at end of this chapter). See Quotas below for a listing of products that currently fall under import licensing regulations.

Quotas

The dairy products listed below are subject to annual import quotas assigned by the USDA and may be imported only under import licenses issued by that department (See USDA Requirements above). These quotas are administered through U.S. Customs and Border Protection.

Butter; dried cream; malted milk and compounds or mixtures of or substitutes for milk or cream; dried whole milk, dried skimmed milk, dried buttermilk and whey; cheddar cheese, and cheese and substitutes for cheese containing or processed from Cheddar cheese curd, and granular cheese and cheese substitutes for cheese containing or processed from such American-type cheese; cheese and substitutes for cheese containing, or processed from Edam and Gouda cheese; Swiss or Emmenthaler cheese with eye formation; Gruyere-process cheese, and cheese and substitutes for cheese containing, or processed from, such cheese; Edam and Gouda cheese; blue mold (except Stilton) cheese, and cheese and substitutes for cheese containing, or processed from, blue-mold cheese; Italian-type cheeses, made from cow's milk, in original loaves (Romano made from cow's milk, Reggiano, Parmesano, Provolone, Provoletti and Sbrinz); Italian-type cheese, not in original loaves; American-type cheese, including Colby, washed curd and granular cheese and cheese substitutes for cheese containing, or processed from such American-type cheese; cheese and substitutes for cheese; cheese and substitutes for cheese, containing 0.5% or less by weight of butterfat.

In addition, there are tariff-rate quotas on milk and cream, not concentrated nor containing added sugar or other sweetening matter, of a fat content that exceeds 1% but not 6%, as measured by weight.

Absolute Quotas. The Uruguay Round converted all of the absolute quotas which were implemented under the authority of

Section 22 of the Agricultural Adjustment Act of 1933, as amended, to tariff-rate quotas. The in-quota amounts under these TRQs for many dairy products were increased. The in-quota amount for all tariffied cheese will be increased by 30,992 metric tons by the year 2000, 5,550 of which are reserved for Mexico and not subject to license. The remainder are subject to license and will increase incrementally over a five-year period.

Country-specific Quotas. HTSUS Chapter 99, Subchapter IV contains safeguard measures established pursuant to Article 5 of the Agreement on Agriculture (as approved by section 101 of the Uruguay Round Agreements Act), which allows the imposition of additional duties based upon either the value or the quantity of goods imported into the United States for certain agricultural products. In addition, the subchapter contains provisions which may be proclaimed pursuant to section 22 of the Agricultural Adjustment Act, as amended (7 U.S.C. 624). All of the duties provided for in this subchapter are cumulative duties which apply in addition to the duties, if any, otherwise imposed in the tariff schedule on the goods described. Unless otherwise stated, the duties or limitations provided for in this subchapter apply until suspended or terminated. Goods of Canada or Mexico imported into the United States are not be subject to any of the provisions, duties or limitations of this subchapter.

For a general discussion of quotas see "Quotas Administered by Customs" on page 274.

Country-Specific Import Restrictions

Regulatory Changes. APHIS has amended the animal and animal product importation regulations to allow for regionalization of countries—that is, disease classification of parts of a country, an entire country, or groups of countries. The rule change was made to recognize levels of disease risk in regions. Details about the criteria that APHIS considers when evaluating the regions that wish to export animals or animal products to the United States can be found at the APHIS Veterinary Service National Center for Import and Export (NCIE) website (www.aphis.usda.gov/ncie).

Countries Free of Rinderpest and Foot-and-mouth Disease. The following countries are listed by APHIS as free of rinderpest and foot-and-mouth disease, meaning that dairy products are eligible to be imported from them: Australia, the Bahamas, Barbados, Bermuda, Belize, Canada, Channel Islands, Denmark, Finland, Great Britain (England, Scotland, Wales, and Isle of Man), Greenland, Guatemala, Haiti, Honduras, Iceland, Ireland, Jamaica, Japan, Costa Rica, Dominican Republic, El Salvador, Fiji, Mexico, New Zealand, Nicaragua, Northern Ireland, Norway, Panama, Panama Canal Zone, Papua New Guinea, Territory of St. Pierre and Miquelon, Sweden, Trinidad and Tobago, and Trust Territory of the Pacific Islands.

Countries Free of Exotic Newcastle Disease (END). The following countries are listed by APHIS as being free of Exotic Newcastle disease (END), meaning that egg products can be imported from them: Australia, Canada, Denmark, Fiji, Finland, Great Britain (England, Scotland, Wales, and the Isle of Man), Iceland, Ireland, New Zealand, Northern Ireland, Norway, and Sweden.

FSIS-certified Countries. The following are the countries that are currently FSIS-certified for exportation of poultry to the U.S.: Argentina, Australia, Belgium, Belize, Brazil, Canada, Costa Rica, the Czech Republic, Denmark, Dominican Republic, El Salvador, Finland, France, Guatemala, Honduras, Hong Kong, Hungary, Ireland, Israel, Italy, Mexico, Netherlands, New Zealand, Norway, Poland, Romania, the Slovak Republic, Sweden, Switzerland, United Kingdom, Uruguay, the republics of the former Yugoslavia. This list is subject to change. For the most up to date information, contact FSIS (see addresses at end of this chapter).

Countries Free of *Salmonella Enteritis.* The only country listed as free of *Salmonella enteritis* is Canada.

Marking and Labeling Requirements

Milk and cream. The Import Milk Act requires that a tag be firmly attached to each container of permit milk or cream imported into the U.S. This tag must show, in clear and legible type, the following information: the product (raw milk, pasteurized milk, raw cream, or pasteurized cream), the permit number, and the name and address of the shipper. For unit shipments consisting of milk only or cream only, under one permit number, each container need not be tagged if the vehicle of transportation is sealed, and tagged as described above. In that case the tag must show, in addition to the other required information, the number of containers and the contents of each. Customs officers will not permit the importation of any milk or cream that is not tagged in accordance with the regulations.

FSIS Requirements. The name of the country of origin of all poultry and egg products must appear on the label. However, only imported products that reach consumers without further processing retain such labeling. The Farm Bill Amendments also require foreign countries exporting products to the U.S. to impose controls equivalent to those of FSIS to prevent species substitution. Exporting countries must have effective testing programs for species verification and adequate security measures to prevent species substitution.

APHIS Requirements. Cases of eggs imported under certificate (see above) must be marked with the identity of the flock of origin and sealed with the seal of the national government of the country of origin.

For a general discussion of U.S. Customs marking and labeling requirements, see "Country of Origin Marking" on page 236, "Special Marking Requirements" on page 238 and "Marking— False Impression" on page 239.

Shipping Considerations

You will need to ensure that your goods are packaged and shipped with care so that they arrive in good condition and pass smoothly through Customs. You are responsible for ensuring that the shipment is in compliance with all applicable government regulations for packaging and shipping. In most instances, you should not leave these arrangements solely to the discretion of your supplier. Careful preparation of the cargo and selection of the mode of transport can be essential to a cost-effective, timely delivery of undamaged gods. We strongly advise you to consult your shipping representative, insurance agent, or freight broker for advice on packing and shipping.

Rapidity of transport and protection from contamination and spoilage are of critical importance when packing and shipping dairy products, many of which have a short shelf life.

Publications and WWW Resources

The following publication explains the FDA requirements for importing dairy products. It is published by the FDA and available online from their website ((www.fda.gov/opacom/7pubs.html)).

> *Requirements of Laws and Regulations Enforced by the U.S. Food and Drug Administration*

The following publication may be relevant to the importation of dairy products:

> *Report of the Secretary of Agriculture to the U.S. Congress - Foreign Countries and Plants Certified to Export Meat and Poultry to the United States*

This is a comprehensive listing of export-certified countries and plants, including previously certified plants that have been decertified. It is available from the FSIS (see addresses at end of this chapter).

The following publication gives brief, general guidelines on USDA regulated products. Although designed primarily for tourists, it contains a list of approved products that you may find helpful. It is available online from the USDA APHIS website (www.aphis.usda.gov).

> *Travelers Tips On Bringing Food, Plant, and Animal Products into the United States*

The *Harmonized Tariff Schedule of the United States (2001)* (HTSUS) is available to view on the U.S. Customs and Border Protection website (www.customs.treas.gov), or you may purchase a printed version from:

U.S. Government Printing Office
Superintendent of Documents
710 North Capital Street NW
Washington DC 20401
Tel: (202) 512-1800
Fax: (202) 512-1657
Website: www.access.gpo.gov

The USGPO also has copies of specific laws available for purchase. The USGPO accepts orders made by fax, phone or placed over the Internet, as well as mail orders paid by credit card. All orders must be accompanied by payment. Credit cards, checks drawn on a U.S. bank, or an international money order are all acceptable.

Relevant Government Agencies

Address your questions regarding FDA requirements for importation of dairy products to:

Food and Drug Administration (FDA)
Center for Food Safety and Applied Nutrition (CFSAN)
Office of Compliance
Division of Enforcement, Imports Branch
5100 Paint Branch Parkway
College Park, MD 20740-3835
Tel: (301) 436-2080
Website: http://vm.cfsan.fda.gov/list.html

Food and Drug Administration (FDA)
Center for Food Safety and Applied Nutrition (CFSAN)
Office of Plant and Dairy Foods and Beverages
5100 Paint Branch Parkway
College Park, MD 20740-3835
Tel: (301) 436-1700
Website: http://vm.cfsan.fda.gov/list.html

Address your questions regarding APHIS requirements and requests for APHIS import permit applications to:

Animal and Plant Health Inspection Service (APHIS)
Veterinary Services (VS)
National Center for Import and Export
4700 River Rd., Unit 40
Riverdale, MD 20737
Tel: (301) 734-3277
Animal products: (301) 734-4401
Website: www.aphis.usda.gov/vs

Animal and Plant Health Inspection Service (APHIS)
Plant Protection and Quarantine (PPQ)
Director's Office
4700 River Rd., Unit 131
Riverdale, MD 20737
Tel: (301) 734-8261
Tel (PPQ permits): (301) 734-8758
Website: www.aphis.usda.gov/ppq

Address your questions regarding FSIS port of entry inspection or pre-import certification of poultry and poultry products and establishments to:

U.S. Department of Agriculture (USDA)
Food Safety and Inspection Service (FSIS)
Technical Service Center - Imports
Suite 300 Landmark Center
1299 Farnam St.
Omaha, NE 68102
Tel: 800-233-3935
Fax: (402) 221-7438
Website: www.fsis.usda.gov

Address your questions regarding safe pesticide residue tolerances to:

Environmental Protection Agency (EPA)
Office of Pesticide Programs
Ariel Rios Building
1200 Pennsylvania Avenue NW
Mail Code: 3213A
Washington DC 20460
Tel: (703) 305-7090
Website: www.epa.gov

Address your questions regarding dairy quotas and licensing to:
USDA Agricultural Marketing Service (AMS)
USDA - AMS - Dairy Programs
1400 Independence Avenue SW
Washington DC 20250
Tel: (202) 720-4392
Dairy Import Group: (202) 720-2916
Website: www.usda.gov/ams

U.S. Customs and Border Protection
Office of Field Operations, Quota Branch
1300 Pennsylvania Avenue NW
Washington DC 20229
Tel: (202) 927-5850
Website: www.customs.treas.gov

Address your questions regarding importation of dairy products to your local Customs port director. For addresses refer to "U.S. Customs and Border Protection Offices" on page 65 or contact:
U.S. Customs and Border Protection
Customs Headquarters
1300 Pennsylvania Avenue NW
Washington DC 20229
Tel: (202) 354-1000
Website: www.customs.treas.gov

Laws and Regulations

The following laws and regulations may be relevant to the importation of dairy products. The laws are contained in the U.S. Code (USC) and the regulations are published in the Code of Federal Regulations (CFR), both of which may be available at larger public and law libraries. Copies of specific laws are also available from the United States Government Printing Office (address above).

21 USC 301 et seq.
Federal Food, Drug, and Cosmetic Act
This Act prohibits deceptive practices and regulates the manufacture, sale and importation or exportation of food, drugs, cosmetics, and related products. It covers examination and refusal of imports and exports of unapproved products. See 21 USC 331, 381, 382.

19 CFR 12.1 et seq.; 21 CFR 1.83 et seq.
Regulations on Food, Drugs, and Cosmetics
These regulations of the Secretary of Health and Human Services and the Secretary of the Treasury govern the standards, labeling, marking, bonding, and importing of products used with food, drugs, and cosmetics.

21 USC 141 et seq.
Import Milk Act

This Act sets purity, sanitary, inspection, and permit requirements on milk imported into the U.S.

7 USC 601 et seq.
Agricultural Adjustment Act (AAA)
This Act authorizes the Secretary of Agriculture to establish and maintain orderly market conditions for agricultural products, including cotton.

19 CFR Part 132
Regulations for Enforcement of AAA Quotas
These regulations provide for Customs enforcement of AAA quotas and higher duty rates imposed on imported agricultural products, whenever investigation reveals that orderly market conditions require such action.

9 CFR Part 94
Regulations on Country-Specific Import Restrictions
These regulations prescribe health inspection requirements and procedures in order to prevent the introduction of livestock diseases into the U.S.

9 CFR 95.13 et seq.
Regulations on Animal Byproduct Quarantine Control
These regulations prohibit the importation of animal products for use in industry unless the products meet certain processing standards and are not infected with certain diseases.

21 USC 1031 et seq.
Egg Product Inspection Act
This Act requires the inspection of edible and nonconsumable egg products, including imports, and sets labeling and processing standards.

7 CFR 56.1 et seq.
Regulations for U.S. Egg Shell Standards
These regulations control the processing of domestic or imported eggs and egg products to ensure that they meet certain standards for sale to consumers.

Principal Exporting Countries

The following listing includes samples of the main supplier nations of the products of this chapter. It is organized by HTSUS major heading. (Refer to "Customs Classification" above for the product codes.) Countries are listed in rank order of the value of products imported to the U.S. Statistics represent customs value of entries for 2002 from the Bureau of Census, U.S. Department of Commerce.

0401—New Zealand, Canada, France, Mexico, United Kingdom, Denmark, Australia, Germany

0402—Canada, Mexico, New Zealand, Chile, Israel, Australia, Netherlands, Panama, Ireland, Brazil

0403—Spain, Greece, Canada, Switzerland, Mexico, New Zealand, India, Israel, Brazil, France, Poland, Jordan

0404—New Zealand, Ireland, Australia, Canada, Germany, Netherlands, Denmark, Hungary, Poland, India

0405—New Zealand, Canada, France, Australia, Israel, Denmark, Ireland

0406—Italy, New Zealand, France, Denmark, Netherlands, Switzerland, Germany

0407—Canada, China, France, Netherlands, United Kingdom, Australia, New Zealand, Taiwan, Thailand, Denmark

0408—Canada, Thailand, Japan, Taiwan, China, South Africa

0409—Canada, Mexico, Vietnam, Argentina, Brazil, Uruguay, China, Thailand, Chile, Turkey, India, Australia, Romania, Malaysia, Germany, Ukraine

0410—Indonesia, China, Germany, New Zealand, Hong Kong, Taiwan, Australia, Canada, Japan, Thailand, Italy, South Korea, Iceland.

Chapter 5:
Other Animal Products

Full title: Products of Animal Origin, Not Elsewhere Specified or Included

This chapter relates to the importation of miscellaneous animal products not included elsewhere, which are classified under Chapter 5 of the Harmonized Tariff Schedule of the United States (HTSUS). Specifically, it includes human hair, horsehair, boar bristles, and other animal hair; birdskins with attached feathers, feathers and down (for stuffing), and feather meal; bone, horn, ivory, and tortoise-shell; coral and marine shell; natural sponges; guts, bladders, and stomachs; glands, organs, and animal secretions; dead animals not fit for human consumption; and miscellaneous animal products not otherwise classified.

Edible animal products are not covered within Commodity Index Chapter 5; if you are interested in importing edible animal products, refer to Chapter 2 for meat and meat products, Chapter 3 for fish and seafood products, and Chapter 16 for prepared animal food products. Live animal imports are covered in Chapter 1. Imports of hides, skins, furskins, and leather are covered in Chapters 41 through 43 (however, hide wastes are included in Chapter 5). Textile products made of animal hair are covered in Chapter 51, and intermediate products of animal bristles are found in Chapter 96. Although most imports of animal glands and substances for pharmaceutical manufacture are covered in Chapter 5, some imports of animal blood are reserved for Chapter 30—Pharmaceutical Products. If you are interested in importing prepared down or feathers, refer to Chapter 67; if you are interested in importing feather—or down—filled articles or apparel, refer to Chapter 62. Although Chapter 5 includes some raw and intermediate products used as animal feed and in the manufacture of animal feed, those interested in importing animal feeds as such should refer to Chapter 23.

Note: To understand key issues that will enable you to make best use of the information in this section we recommend that you see "Introduction" on page 425.

Key Factors

The key factors in the importation of animal products of HTSUS Chapter 5 are:

- Compliance with U.S. Food and Drug Administration (FDA) purity, identity, manufacturing, and other standards
- Compliance with FDA notification and entry procedures
- Compliance with U.S. Department of Agriculture (USDA) and U.S. Fish and Wildlife Service (FWS)

import regulations

- Feathers derived from wild migratory birds are subject to FWS restrictions and permit requirements; certain feathers are subject to quota restriction, FWS licenses and permits required; entry at FWS-designated ports for wildlife feathers; endangered species regulations may apply to certain feathers
- For raw down, down-feather ratio rating certification; if raw down is not derived from domesticated birds, compliance with any relevant wildlife and endangered species restrictions

Although most importers utilize the services of a licensed customs broker in making their entries, and we recommend this practice, you should be aware of the regulatory, entry, and documentation issues involved in importing your product. You, as importer, are ultimately responsible for the fulfillment of any legal requirements applicable to your shipment.

General Considerations

Regulatory Agencies. The FDA enforces the requirements of the Federal Food, Drug, and Cosmetic Act (FDCA), which governs all imports of goods intended for use as or in the manufacture of food, drugs, or cosmetics. The USDA regulates and inspects animal and animal—derived products presented for entry into the U.S. The Animal and Plant Health Inspection Service (APHIS) of the USDA is generally responsible for passing products derived from domesticated animals. The FWS controls the importation of products of animals classified as exotic wildlife or endangered species. U.S. Customs enforces USDA, FDA, and FWS requirements through entry documentation and restrictions. Because of the wide range of products covered within HTSUS Chapter 5 and the potentially complex regulations and overlapping jurisdictions covering them, you should contact these agencies to verify the specific requirements for your product. The following discussion covers only some of the major points involved in importing some of the prominent miscellaneous animal products of Chapter 5.

Feathers. Importation of certain feathers is highly restricted. Feathers taken from domesticated birds are not subject to FWS regulation and may be entered without authorization. The skins and feathers of certain game birds are subject to quota restrictions (see below), for which permits are required. Feathers or skins of the following species are permitted entry: chickens, turkeys, guinea fowl, geese, ducks, pigeons, ostriches, rheas, English ring-necked pheasants, and pea fowl not taken from the wild. Other feathers are usually prohibited. However, you may bring in fully manufactured fishing flies and personally taken, noncommercial game birds.

Feathers of certain species of birds as well as other animal products are restricted or prohibited importation because of status under the Endangered Species Act (ESA), or the Convention on International Trade in Endangered Species of Wild Fauna and Flora (CITES). If you are unsure whether the products you wish to import are derived from listed species, contact FWS with detailed species information.

If you are interested in importing feathers, you should become familiar with 50 CFR Parts 10, 13, 14, 15, and 21. Contact the regional FWS office nearest your intended port of entry for clarification of regulations, instructions, and import authorizations required.

Wildlife Products. Certain animal raw materials and products made of them, including ivory, coral, and sea turtle products, are banned from import into the U.S. under most circumstances. Many foreign countries have also established strict permit requirements for the export of such materials and articles. Most affected African countries have prohibited the export of elephant ivory, and many countries in the Pacific, Southeast Asia, and the Caribbean have banned the harvest and export of coral, making the import of such items into the U.S.—which requires compliance with country of origin export permits and documentation when applicable—even more difficult and problematical.

If you are importing wildlife products, you must enter them only at FWS-designated U.S. ports of entry (see Designated Ports below). You must present a FWS Wildlife Import Declaration Form 3-177 to the FWS agent at the U.S. port of entry for each shipment. The FWS conducts port of entry inspections on a case-by-case basis, as determined by the inspection agent after examining the entry paperwork. Your shipment will not be released from Customs custody until your FWS import declaration has been signed off by an FWS agent.

Down. Importation of raw down is also regulated by FWS. The exporter is required to test the down for percentage of feathers to down, with the down being given a rating based on that percentage. A certification of rating must accompany all import shipments of raw down. If your raw down is derived from domesticated raised birds, you need only fulfill normal customs entry requirements. However, the entry of down from wild migratory game birds is highly restricted and subject to FWS permit procedures under the Migratory Bird Treaty Act. If you are considering importing such products, you should contact the regional office of FWS closest to the intended port of entry for authorization. Do not attempt to import such products without FWS authorization.

Customs Classification

For customs purposes, miscellaneous animal products not elsewhere specified are classified under Chapter 5 of the HTSUS. This chapter is divided into major headings, which are further divided into subheadings, and often into sub-subheadings, each of which has its own HTSUS classification number. For example, the 2001 HTSUS number for other feathers is 0505.90.00, indicating that it is a subcategory of the major heading of skins and other parts of birds with their feathers or down, feathers and parts of feathers, not further worked; powder and waste of feathers or parts of feathers (0505). There are 11 major headings in Chapter 5.

0501—Human hair, unworked, whether or not washed or scoured; waste of human hair

0502—Pigs', hogs', or boars' bristles and hair; badger hair and other brushmaking hair; waste of such bristles or hair

0503—Horsehair and horsehair waste, whether or not put up as a layer with or without supporting material

0504—Guts, bladders, and stomach of animals (other than fish), whole and pieces thereof, fresh, chilled, frozen, salted, in brine, dried or smoked

0505—Skins and other parts of birds, with their feathers or down, feathers and parts of feathers (whether or not with trimmed edges) and down, not further worked than cleaned, disinfected or treated for preservation; powder and waste of feathers or parts of feathers

0506—Bones and horn-cores, unworked, defatted, simply prepared (but not cut to shape), treated with acid or degeletanized; powder and waste of these products

0507—Ivory, tortoise-shell, whalebone, and whalebone hair, horns, antlers, hooves, nails, claws, and beaks, unworked or simply prepared but not cut to shape; powder and waste of these products

0508—Coral and similar materials, unworked or simply prepared but not otherwise worked; shells of molluscs, crustaceans, or echinoderms and cuttlebone, unworked or simply prepared but not cut to shape, powder and waste thereof

0509—Natural sponges of animal origin

0510—Ambergris, castoreum, civet, and musk; cantharides; bile, whether or not dried; glands and other animal products used in the preparation of pharmaceutical products, fresh, chilled, frozen, or otherwise provisionally preserved

0511—Animal products not elsewhere specified or included; dead animals of chapter 1 or 3, unfit for human consumption

For more details regarding classification of the specific product you are interested in importing, consult a customs broker, the appropriate commodity specialist at your nearest Customs port, or see HTSUS. The 2001 HTSUS is available online from the Customs Service (www.customs.gov/impoexpo/impoexpo.htm) or for purchase from the U.S. Government Printing Office (see resources at the end of this chapter), and may be found in larger public libraries. For a general discussion of customs classification, see "Classification—Liquidation" on page 229.

Dutiable Status of Goods

For more information about duty rates and binding decissions see "Dutiable Status of Goods" on page 203; for a discussion of temporary importation of goods see "Temporary Free Importations" on page 205.

Valuation

Importers have a responsibility to use what U.S. Customs and Border Protection deems, "reasonable care," when determining the value of their goods. They must also provide any additional information that U.S. Customs and Border Protection needs for setting a final value on the goods. This process involves a number of factors and can be somewhat complicated; importers must be aware of applicable issues and details. Valuation information applies to all types of commodities, for further discussion on the subject see "Customs Valuation" on page 267.

Import Duties

Import duties vary (often dramatically) depending upon the Harmonized Tariff Schedule (HTSUS) classification of the goods or products imported. Since some products that look alike have different HTSUS classifications and different rates of duty, proper classification is vital. Note that "differences of opinion" between importers and the Bureau of Customs and Border Protection regarding classification keeps customs attorneys very busy.

Import duties can be assessed on the imported value of the goods ("ad valorem" rates of duty such as 2%, 4.4%, 50%, etc.), total units or weight of the goods ("specific" rates of duty such as 2 cents each or 1.5 cents/pound, etc.) or on a combination basis ("compound" rates of duty such as 5 cents each plus 6%).

Listed below is a sampling of several Column 1 import duty rates for Chapter 05 products:
Horsehair and horsehair waste, whether or not put up as a layer with or without supporting material (0503.00.00.00): free
to
Ambergris, castoreum, civet and musk (0510.00.20.00): 5.1%

For specific information on US import duties refer to the Harmonized Tariff Schedule of the US. The print version is available from the US Government Printing Office as well as third party suppliers who often add special features. Online versions are available in both static PDF pages as well as in formats with excellent search functionality. Search the Web with the term "Harmonized Tariff Schedule" to find sources.

Entry and Documentation

The entry of merchandise is a two-part process consisting of 1) filing the documents necessary to determine whether merchandise may be released from Customs custody and 2) filing the documents that contain information for duty assessment and statistical purposes. In certain instances all documents must be filed and accepted by Customs prior to release of the goods. Unless you have been granted an extension, you must file entry documents at a location specified by the port or area director within five working days of your shipment's date of arrival at a U.S. port of entry. These include a number of standard documents required by Customs for any entry, and:

- FWS Wildlife Declaration Form 3-177 for feathers derived from wild birds

- FWS Permit Form 3-200 when required

- If raw down: exporter's down-feather ratio rating certification of exporter

- If down is derived from wild migratory birds or other protected species, FWS authorization and any documentation required under relevant endangered species legislation

After you present the entry, Customs may examine your shipment, or may waive examination. The shipment is then released provided no legal or regulatory violations have been noted. You must then file entry summary documentation and deposit estimated duties at a designated customhouse within 10 working days of your shipment's release. For a detailed description of entry procedures, standard documentation, and informal entry, see "Entry Process" on page 185.

Informed Compliance. Informed compliance was introduced with the Customs Modernization Act of 1993 (Mod Act) and defines the relationship between importers and U.S. Customs and Border Protection. It sets out the responsibilities of both parties. Providing the correct documentation and information for entry is a key factor that will make your importing operation run smoothly. We recommend that importers become familiar with the concept of informed comliance and the responsibilities that they have under the Mod Act. For further discussion about informed compliance see "Informed Compliance" on page 211.

Note: The Entry and Documentation section has been carefully designed to supply you, the importer, with sample documents and directions on how to satisfy Customs requirements. Be aware that you should consult the applicable authorities to ensure that you are correctly following the most current procedures.

Prohibitions and Restrictions

Skins and feathers taken from wild migratory game birds listed in the Migratory Bird Treaty Act (16 USC 703) cannot be imported for commercial purposes. Plumage may be imported for scientific or educational purposes, as may fully manufactured artificial flies used for fishing made of such plumage. Plumage on game birds killed in foreign countries by hunters who are U.S. residents may also be imported as long as the plumage is not imported for sale or other commercial purposes.

Designated Ports. All wildlife shipments must enter and leave the U.S. through FWS designated ports, as listed in 50 CFR 14.12. Currently there are ten designated ports: New York, NY; Miami, FL; New Orleans, LA; Dallas/Ft. Worth, TX; Los Angeles, CA; San Francisco, CA; Chicago, IL; Seattle, WA; Honolulu, HI; and Portland, OR. If special circumstances preclude making entry at a designated port, an Exception to Designated Port Permit is required from FWS (see addresses at end of this chapter).

Quotas. Feathers of certain birds may be imported for use in the manufacture of artificial flies used for fishing, or for millinery purposes. These imports are restricted by annual quota allotments. You must have a permit and quota allotment issued by the FWS in order to import feathers subject to such quotas. Quota feathers are as follows: Mandarin ducks for use in manufacture of artificial flies used for fishing: 1,000 skins; Lady Amherst Pheasant, Golden Pheasant, Silver Pheasant, Reeves Pheasant,

Blue-eared Pheasant, and Brown-eared Pheasant for use in manufacturing of artificial flies used for fishing, or for use in millinery products: aggregate 45,000. Quotas for these products can be reduced or eliminated at the discretion of the U.S. Secretary of the Interior upon a finding of serious reduction in the wild of the affected species.

Permit Application. If you wish to import quota feathers, you must submit your application for feather quota allocations and permits to FWS on the standard Federal Fish and Wildlife License/Permit Application **Form 3-200.** The annual quota period begins on January 1 of each year, and runs through December 31. Your application for initial allocations must reach FWS between September 1 and September 30 of the calendar year preceding the quota year for which you are requesting allotment. Any portions of established annual quotas not used by July 1 become available for reallocation. Applications for reallocations must be received by FWS between July 1 and July 31 of the current quota year.

Permit/quota allocation requests must include not only the standard information required for any permit, but also 1) species quantity; 2) port of entry, or port of entry and amount in storage (see exceptions, below); 3) statement of intended use; 4) nature of request, i.e. initial allocation or reallocation. After making the initial allocations, the FWS will furnish you with a tabulation of quantities of each species you requested, plus quantities FWS proposes to allocate to you. You must then report your acceptance, by a letter addressed to the FWS Director and postmarked not later than 30 days after the date you receive your notice. Your letter must contain satisfactory proof (e.g. a copy of a currently confirmed order) that you have already placed your feather orders. FWS will interpret your failure to respond as withdrawal of your application. You should respond by certified mail.

Permits. Permits for feather quota imports are issued in two segments. Permits authorizing calendar year initial allocations are issued as of January 1 of that quota year, and remain in effect through June 30 of the year of issue. You must import all feathers and/or skins authorized under this permit no later than June 30. Once your initial permit has expired, any portion of your allotment that you have not used will be subject to reallocation. No exceptions or extensions are granted. Permits authorizing reallocations are issued as promptly as possible after July 31 of the current quota year, and remain in effect through December 31. Once your reallocation permit expires, any unused portion of the quota is forfeited. Again, no exceptions or extensions are granted.

Exceptions to Requirements. There are certain exceptions to the permit requirements for quota feathers. However, even when a permit is not necessary, you must still file an FWS Wildlife Declaration at the port of entry. Permit exceptions are as follows: 1) you may import quota skins/feathers for storage in a warehouse under customs bond without permit. (This exception only applies to birds that are subject to quota. In such cases you must obtain a valid FWS permit before you remove the articles from the warehouse for use in the U.S.); 2) articles imported for scientific or educational purposes; 3) fully manufactured artificial flies for fishing; 4) game birds killed by U.S. hunters abroad and imported by such person for noncommercial purposes; 5) live birds (there are other stringent FWS requirements for live birds—refer to HTSUS Chapter 1); 6) import of any of the following birds, whether or not such bird was raised in captivity: chickens (including hens and roosters), turkeys, guinea fowl, geese, ducks, pigeons, ostriches, rheas, English ring-necked pheasants, and pea fowl.

Marking and Labeling Requirements

Marking and labeling requirements will vary depending upon the nature of your product. All wildlife shipments must be marked on the outside of the container with the names and addresses of the exporter and importer, an accurate identification of the species, and the numbers of each species in the container.

For a general discussion of U.S. Customs marking and labeling requirements, see "Country of Origin Marking" on page 236, "Special Marking Requirements" on page 238 and "Marking—False Impression" on page 239.

Shipping Considerations

You will need to ensure that your goods are packaged and shipped with care so that they arrive in good condition and pass smoothly through Customs. You are responsible for ensuring that the shipment is in compliance with all applicable government regulations for packaging and shipping. In most instances, you should not leave these arrangements solely to the discretion of your supplier. Careful preparation of the cargo and selection of the mode of transport can be essential to a cost-effective, timely delivery of undamaged goods. We strongly advise you to consult your shipping representative, insurance agent, or freight broker for advice on packing and shipping.

Many of the products covered in HTSUS Chapter 5 must be packed so as to prevent contamination or decomposition. Some—such as shells—may require careful packing to avoid breakage.

Publications and WWW Resources

For questions regarding the Convention on Interantional Trade in Endangered Species of Wild Fauna and Flora (CITES) refer to:

CITES Secretariat
15 chemin des Anemones
1219 Chatelaine-Geneva
Switzerland
Tel: [41] (22) 917-8139/40
Fax: [41] (22) 797-3417
Website: www.cites.org
Email: cites@unep.ch

The following publication explains the FDA requirements for importing miscellaneous animal products. It is published by the FDA and is available online at their website (www.fda.gov/opacom/7pubs.html).

Requirements of Laws and Regulations Enforced by the U.S. Food and Drug Administration

The following publication gives brief, general guidelines on USDA regulated products. Although designed primarily for tourists, it contains a list of approved products that you may find helpful. It is available online from the USDA APHIS website (www.aphis.usda.gov).

Travelers Tips On Bringing Food, Plant, and Animal Products into the United States

Buyer Beware is a pamphlet published by the World Wildlife Fund. The pamphlet discusses the products that may not be imported into the U.S. because of endangered species considerations. To order *Buyer Beware*, or to request a catalog of related publications, contact:

World Wildlife Fund
1250 24th Street NW
Washington DC 20037
Tel: (202) 293-4800
Website: www.wwf.org

The *Harmonized Tariff Schedule of the United States (2001)* (HTSUS) is available to view on the U.S. Customs and Border Protection website (www.customs.treas.gov), or you may purchase a printed version from:

U.S. Government Printing Office
Superintendent of Documents
710 North Capital Street NW
Washington DC 20401
Tel: (202) 512-1800
Fax: (202) 512-1657
Website: www.access.gpo.gov

The USGPO also has copies of specific laws available for purchase. The USGPO accepts orders made by fax, phone or placed over the Internet, as well as mail orders paid by credit card. All orders must be accompanied by payment. Credit cards, checks drawn on a U.S. bank, or an international money order are all acceptable.

Relevant Government Agencies

Address your questions regarding FDA requirements for the importation of miscellaneous animal products covered in HTSUS Chapter 5 to:

Food and Drug Administration (FDA)
Center for Food Safety and Applied Nutrition (CFSAN)
Office of Compliance
Division of Enforcement, Imports Branch
5100 Paint Branch Parkway
College Park, MD 20740-3835
Tel: (301) 436-2080
Website: http://vm.cfsan.fda.gov/list.html

Address your questions regarding the importation of miscellaneous animal products of domesticated species to:

Animal and Plant Health Inspection Service (APHIS)
Veterinary Services (VS)
National Center for Import and Export
4700 River Rd., Unit 40
Riverdale, MD 20737
Tel: (301) 734-3277
Animal products: (301) 734-4401
Website: www.aphis.usda.gov/vs

Address your questions regarding the importation of raw feathers and down of wild animals and products of endangered or threatened species to:

U.S. Fish and Wildlife Service (FWS)
Division of Management Authority
4401 N. Fairfax Dr.
Arlington, VA 22203-0700
Tel: (703) 358-2104
Website: www.fws.gov

Address your questions regarding importation of miscellaneous animal products of Chapter 5 to your local Customs port director. For addresses refer to "U.S. Customs and Border Protection Offices" on page 65 or contact:

U.S. Customs and Border Protection
Customs Headquarters
1300 Pennsylvania Avenue NW
Washington DC 20229
Tel: (202) 354-1000
Website: www.customs.treas.gov

Laws and Regulations

The following laws and regulations may be relevant to the importation of miscellaneous animal products of Chapter 5. The laws are contained in the U.S. Code (USC) and the regulations are published in the Code of Federal Regulations (CFR), both of which may be available at larger public and law libraries. Copies of specific laws are also available from the United States Government Printing Office (address above).

21 USC 301 et seq.
Federal Food, Drug, and Cosmetic Act (FDCA)
This Act prohibits deceptive practices and regulates the manufacture, sale and importation or exportation of food, drugs, cosmetics, and related products. See 21 USC 331, 381, 382.

19 CFR 12.1 et seq.; 21 CFR 1.83 et seq.
Regulations on Food, Drugs, and Cosmetics
These regulations of the Secretary of Health and Human Services and the Secretary of the Treasury govern the

standards, labeling, marking, bonding, and importing of products used with food, drugs, and cosmetics.

Convention on International Trade in Endangered Species of Wild Fauna and Flora (CITES)

This comprehensive wildlife treaty signed by over 100 countries, including the United States, regulates and in many cases prohibits commercial imports and exports of wild animal and plant species threatened by trade.

16 USC 1531
Endangered Species Act of 1973

This Act prohibits the import and export of species listed as endangered and most species listed as threatened. It is the U.S. law that implements CITES.

16 USC 742a et seq.
Fish and Wildlife Act of 1956

This Act regulates and bars the import of certain wild animals or birds and authorizes U.S. Customs to enforce the restrictions.

16 USC 2401 et seq.
Antarctic Conservation Act of 1978

This Act prohibits the importation, absent a special permit, of any flora or fauna native to Antarctica into the U.S. pursuant to the Antarctic Treaty and the Protocol

16 USC 3371 et seq.
Control of Illegally Taken Fish and Wildlife

This Act prohibits the import of species taken, possessed, transported, or sold in violation of the law of a foreign country.

16 USC 1361 et seq.
The Marine Mammal Protection Act of 1972

This Act prohibits the import of certain marine mammals and their parts and products. These species include whales, walruses, narwhals, seals, sea lions, sea otters, and polar bears. It also defines parameters for importation of commercial fish or products that have been caught using methods, which involve incidental death or serious injury to protected marine mammals.

16 USC 4201 et seq.
The African Elephant Conservation Act

This Act prohibits imports of carved ivory products from any country and only permits imports of whole tusks from elephants legally hunted in certain African countries. It establishes U.S. adherence to the CITES Ivory Control System.

16 USC 703
The Migratory Bird Treaty Act

This Act protects designated wild migratory game birds and prohibits importation of them for commercial purposes.

18 USC 42 et seq.
Importation of Animals, Birds, Fish, and Plants

This Act governs the importation of mammals, birds, fish, amphibia, and reptiles into the U.S. which, may be hazadous to humans or harmful to U.S. agriculture and it authorizes U.S. Customs to enforce the import requirements.

50 CFR Parts 10, 13, and 16
Regulations of FWS for Importing Wildlife and Fish

These regulations specify the animals and animal products subject to import prohibitions and restrictions.

19 CFR 12.26 et seq.
Regulations of Customs on Importing Wild Animals

These regulations list the wild animals that are prohibited from importation or that require import permits.

16 USC 4901
Wild Bird Conservation Act of 1992

This act eliminated most commercial imports of CITES-regulated birds, except for limited imports of pet birds.

Principal Exporting Countries

The following listing includes samples of the main supplier nations of the products of this chapter. It is organized by HTSUS major heading. (Refer to "Customs Classification" above for the product codes.) Countries are listed in rank order of the value of products imported to the U.S. Statistics represent customs value of entries for 2002 from the Bureau of Census, U.S. Department of Commerce.

0501—China, India, Hong Kong, Austria, Italy, Israel, United Kingdom, Indonesia, Singapore

0502—China, United Kingdom, Germany, Brazil, Thailand, Dominican Republic, Belgium, South Korea

0503—China, Paraguay, Netherlands, Argentina, Australia, Ecuador

0504—China, Denmark, Canada, Australia, New Zealand, Netherlands, Mexico, Brazil, Portugal, Uruguay, Egypt, Argentina, Paraguay

0505—China, Taiwan, France, Hungary, Poland, Germany, Canada, South Africa

0506—Canada, Australia, Brazil, New Zealand, Russia, United Kingdom, Nigeria

0507—Canada, New Zealand, Russia, Brazil, Hungary, China, Taiwan, Mexico, Germany, Zimbabwe, Tajikistan, France, Hong Kong, India, Uruguay, Dominican Republic

0508—Indonesia, Fiji, Philippines, Tonga, China, Haiti, India, United Kingdom, Thailand, Italy, Solomon Islands, Bahamas, Federated States of Micronesia, Mexico, Japan, Tunisia

0509—Bahamas, Philippines, China, Greece

0510—Canada, New Zealand, Australia, Italy, Uruguay, Denmark, Mexico, China, Argentina, United Kingdom, Brazil, Germany, Netherlands

0511—Brazil, Canada, China, Thailand, New Zealand, Mexico, Colombia, Spain, Australia, Denmark, Paraguay, Ecuador, Germany, Argentina, Taiwan, Belgium, Japan, Iceland, India

Chapter 6:
Live Plants

Full title: Live Trees and Other Plants; Bulbs, Roots, and the Like; Cut Flowers and Ornamental Foliage

This chapter relates to the importation of live plants, bulbs and roots, and cut flowers and ornamental foliage, which are classified under Chapter 6 of the Harmonized Tariff Schedule of the United States (HTSUS). Specifically, it includes most live plants and plant parts designed for propagation—including live seedlings, bulbs, rhizomes, germ, shoots, and other similar products—and specimens plants and related items, as well as cut flowers and other plant parts intended for decorative uses, including finished floral arrangements.

If you are interested in importing sets or seedlings of edible plants such as onions, garlic, or shallots, you should refer to Commodity Index Chapter 7. Seeds of most agricultural products are covered under Chapter 12, while those of cereal grains are included in Chapter 10. Although baskets and other containers and materials incidental to decorative arrangements of plant materials are included in Chapter 6, those interested in importing baskets for such arrangements or for other uses should refer to Chapter 46. Some collages and decorative plaques incorporating plant materials may be classified as works of art in Chapter 97.

Note: To understand key issues that will enable you to make best use of the information in this section we recommend that you see "Introduction" on page 425.

Key Factors

The key factors in the importation of live plants, roots, and cut flowers are:

- Compliance with U.S. Department of Agriculture (USDA) restrictions and requirements (permits may be required)
- Compliance with any restrictions under endangered species legislation

Although most importers utilize the services of a licensed customs broker in making their entries, and we recommend this practice, you should be aware of the regulatory, entry, and documentation issues involved in importing your product. You, as importer, are ultimately responsible for the fulfillment of any legal requirements applicable to your shipment.

General Considerations

Regulatory Agencies. Importation of live plants, roots, and cut flowers is regulated by the USDA Animal and Plant Health Inspection Service (APHIS) Plant Protection and Quarantine (PPQ)

branch, primarily under provisions of the Plant Quarantine Act (PQA).

Inspection. All live plants and flowers imported into the United States are routinely inspected by APHIS. Preclearance inspection is available for some commodities in some countries through APHIS International Services (IS) foreign operations. In addition to seasonal commodities that require inspectors on a short-term basis, IS Regions II and IV operate permanent preclearance programs for fruits, vegetables, and flower bulbs destined for the United States from Chile, Argentina, and The Netherlands. All of the costs for operating preclearance programs are paid for by exporters through trust fund agreements that IS sets up in each participating country.

Flowers. The entry of cut flowers from all foreign countries except Canada is regulated under 7 CFR 319.74. No restrictions are imposed on cut flowers of Canadian origin, although these imports must be accompanied by a phytosanitary document stating that they originated in Canada. PPQ import permits are required for certain flowers (see Prohibitions and Restrictions below). You must submit duplicate copies of a PPQ Notice of Arrival to Customs at the U.S. port of entry for each commercial shipment of cut flowers entering under permit. When small quantities of flowers normally requiring formal permit are offered for entry without such permit, the APHIS port inspector may give oral entry authorization.

All admissible cut flowers, whether entering under permit or not, are subject to inspection at the first U.S. port of entry. If pests of quarantine significance are found in your shipment, the APHIS inspector will prescribe treatment in accordance with administratively authorized procedures known to be effective under similar conditions. Required treatments are at the importer's risk and expense and must be performed under the supervision of an APHIS inspector. If your products are found upon inspection to be infested with injurious insects, or infected with plant diseases that cannot be eliminated by treatment, they will be denied entry. In such cases, you have the option of abandoning the rejected shipment for destruction, or immediately shipping it to a point outside the U.S.

Certain flowers from specific countries are subject to antidumping actions and countervailing duties. These items are entered at additional rates of duty. For a general discussion of these extra duties, see "Drawback—Refunds of Duties" on page 224.

Customs Classification

For customs purposes, live plants, roots, and cut flowers are classified under Chapter 6 of the HTSUS. This chapter is broken down into major headings, which are further divided into subheadings, and often sub-subheadings, each with its own HTSUS classification number. For example, the 2001 HTSUS number for Narcissus bulbs is 0601.10.60, indicating that it is a subcategory of bulbs, tubers, tuberous roots, corms, crowns, and rhizomes, dormant (0601.10), which is a subcategory of the major heading, bulbs, tubers, tuberous roots, corms, crowns, and rhizomes, dormant, in growth, or in flower (0601). There are four major headings within Chapter 6:

0601—Bulbs, tubers, tuberous roots, corms, crowns, and rhizomes, dormant, in growth, or in flower; chickory plants and roots other than roots of heading 1212

0602—Other live plants (including their roots), cuttings, and slips; mushroom spawn

0603—Cut flowers and flower buds of a kind suitable for bouquets or for ornamental purposes, fresh, dried, dyed, bleached, impregnated, or otherwise prepared

0604—Foliage, branches, and other parts of plants, without flowers or flower buds, and grasses, mosses, and lichens, being goods of a kind suitable for bouquets or for ornamental purposes, fresh, dried, dyed, bleached, impregnated, or otherwise prepared

For more details regarding classification of the specific product you are interested in importing, consult a customs broker, the appropriate commodity specialist at your nearest Customs port, or see HTSUS. TThe 2001 HTSUS is available online from the Customs Service (www.customs.gov/impoexpo/impoexpo.htm) or for purchase from the U.S. Government Printing Office (see resources at the end of this chapter), and may be found in larger public libraries. For a general discussion of customs classification, see "Classification—Liquidation" on page 229.

Dutiable Status of Goods

For more information about duty rates and binding decissions see "Dutiable Status of Goods" on page 203; for a discussion of temporary importation of goods see "Temporary Free Importations" on page 205.

Valuation

Importers have a responsibility to use what U.S. Customs and Border Protection deems, "reasonable care," when determining the value of their goods. They must also provide any additional information that U.S. Customs and Border Protection needs for setting a final value on the goods. This process involves a number of factors and can be somewhat complicated; importers must be aware of applicable issues and details. Valuation information applies to all types of commodities, for further discussion on the subject see "Customs Valuation" on page 267.

Import Advisory! U.S. Customs and Border Protection has greatly increased its scrutiny of the agriculture industry, one of eight primary focus industries identified in its recent Trade Enforcement Plans. Imported products from these industries will attract significant attention from Customs in the areas of compliance measurement, compliance assessment, informed compliance, and interventions.

Import Duties

Import duties vary (often dramatically) depending upon the Harmonized Tariff Schedule (HTSUS) classification of the goods or products imported. Since some products that look alike have different HTSUS classifications and different rates of duty, proper classification is vital. Note that "differences of opinion" between importers and the Bureau of Customs and Border Protection regarding classification keeps customs attorneys very busy.

Import duties can be assessed on the imported value of the goods ("ad valorem" rates of duty such as 2%, 4.4%, 50%, etc.), total units or weight of the goods ("specific" rates of duty such as 2 cents each or 1.5 cents/pound, etc.) or on a combination basis ("compound" rates of duty such as 5 cents each plus 6%).

Listed below is a sampling of several Column 1 import duty rates for Chapter 06 products:
Trees, shrubs and bushes, grafted or not, of kinds which bear edible fruit or nuts (0602.20.00.00): free
to
Roses (0603.10.60): 6.8%

For specific information on US import duties refer to the Harmonized Tariff Schedule of the US. The print version is available from the US Government Printing Office as well as third party suppliers who often add special features. Online versions are available in both static PDF pages as well as in formats with excellent search functionality. Search the Web with the term "Harmonized Tariff Schedule" to find sources.

Entry and Documentation

The entry of merchandise is a two-part process consisting of 1) filing the documents necessary to determine whether merchandise may be released from Customs custody and 2) filing the documents that contain information for duty assessment and statistical purposes. In certain instances all documents must be filed and accepted by Customs prior to release of the goods. Unless you have been granted an extension, you must file entry documents at a location specified by the port or area director within five working days of your shipment's date of arrival at a U.S. port of entry. These include a number of standard documents required by Customs for any entry, and:

- PPQ Notice of Arrival
- PPQ permit Form 587, when required
- Phyto-sanitary certificate of origin (for Canadian cut flowers).

After you present the entry, Customs may examine your shipment, or may waive examination. The shipment is then released provided no legal or regulatory violations have been noted. You must then file entry summary documentation and deposit estimated duties at a designated customhouse within 10 working days of your shipment's release. For a detailed description of entry procedures, standard documentation, and informal entry, see "Entry Process" on page 185.

Informed Compliance. Informed compliance was introduced with the Customs Modernization Act of 1993 (Mod Act) and defines the relationship between importers and U.S. Customs and Border Protection. It sets out the responsibilities of both parties. Providing the correct documentation and information for entry is a key factor that will make your importing operation run smoothly. We recommend that importers become familiar with the concept of informed comliance and the responsibilities that they have under the Mod Act. For further discussion about informed compliance see "Informed Compliance" on page 211.

Note: The Entry and Documentation section has been carefully designed to supply you, the importer, with sample documents and directions on how to satisfy Customs requirements. Be aware that you should consult the applicable authorities to ensure that you are correctly following the most current procedures.

Prohibitions and Restrictions

Written APHIS PPQ permits are required for importation of cut flowers of the genus *Azalea, Camellia, Gardenia, Rhododendron, Rosa* (rose), and *Syringa* (lilac). No other admissible cut flowers require formal permits for entry. Permits are granted only to U.S. importers, upon receipt in the PPQ permit unit office (see addresses at end of this chapter) of a completed PPQ Form 587. APHIS will accept a letter or telegram stating the required information in lieu of an application on PPQ Form 587. You should submit your application for a permit in advance of your proposed importation. Your permit will be issued when PPQ approves your application. Permits authorize the specific importation, specify the port of entry, and prescribe any conditions necessary to safeguard against the entry of pests. You are responsible for fulfilling all permit conditions.

Your applications for a permit should name the cut flower you wish to import, using its botanical or scientific name. You will also need to supply the following information: your shipment's country of origin; means of shipment; first U.S. port of arrival; and your name, address (both street and P.O. box, if any), and telephone number (during regular business hours).

Proposed Changes. Under a 1996 proposal, cut flowers regulations may be amended by eliminating the import permit and notice of arrival requirements for imported cut flowers of camellia, gardenia, rhododendron, rose, and lilac.

Imports from Drug-producing Countries. There have been instances of narcotic substances being concealed in importations of fresh flowers from certain drug-producing countries and, consequently, Customs' examination of shipments of fresh flowers is quite thorough and delays may be encountered in obtaining release of fresh flowers shipped from certain drug-producing countries.

Camellias and Gardenias. Cut camellias and gardenias are prohibited entry when consigned to destinations in Florida. Shipments of cut camellias and gardenias may enter through Florida ports for transit to points outside the state, provided they are securely wrapped in polyethylene or an equivalent material. Cut gardenias must be given a precautionary fumigation when entering at California ports, regardless of destination.

Other Plants. Cut branches of *Chaenomeles* (flowering quince), *Cydonia* (quince), *Malus* (apple), *Prunus* (plums, peach, cherry, etc.), *Pyrus* (pear), *Eucalyptus,* and *Salix* (willow) are prohibited unless they meet the entry conditions established in 7 CFR 319.37, including post-entry growing conditions.

All botanical fruits, such as the fresh fruits of *Capsicum spp.* or *Ananas spp.* on dry stems intended for decorative purposes that fail to meet standards regarding the country of origin or other requirements established in 7 CFR 319.56, will be refused entry.

Flowers for Propagation. A cut flower permit does not authorize the importation of cut flowers for propagation. All cut flowers imported for the purpose of propagation must enter the U.S. under the requirements of the Nursery Stock Regulations, and other appropriate regulations in 7 CFR 319.37.

Endangered Species Restrictions. Certain plants and their products are protected under a variety of endangered species laws and regulations. The U.S. Fish and Wildlife Service (FWS) is the agency with general responsibility for administering these laws, although the USDA enforces those relevant to plant materials. You must also generally have documentation from the country of origin allowing export from that country before such materials can become eligible for admission into the U.S. If you are unsure of the protected status of a plant or plant product that you wish to import, contact USDA APHIS (see addresses at end of this chapter).

Country-Specific Import Restrictions

No cut flowers of the plant family *Proteaceae* may be imported from South Africa and Swaziland because port-of-entry inspections of these articles have revealed a high rate of significant agricultural pests requiring treatment, destruction, or reexportation of the cut flowers.

Chrysanthemum spp., including cut flowers, from Venezuela are prohibited entry because of white rust disease of chrysanthemums, *Puccinia horiana P. Henn.*

Marking and Labeling

For a general discussion of U.S. Customs marking and labeling requirements, see "Country of Origin Marking" on page 236, "Special Marking Requirements" on page 238 and "Marking—False Impression" on page 239.

Shipping Considerations

You will need to ensure that your goods are packaged and shipped with care so that they arrive in good condition and pass smoothly through Customs. You are responsible for ensuring that the shipment is in compliance with all applicable government regulations for packaging and shipping. In most instances, you should not leave these arrangements solely to the discretion of your supplier. Careful preparation of the cargo and selection of the mode of transport can be essential to a cost-effective, timely delivery of undamaged goods. We strongly advise you to consult your shipping representative, insurance agent, or freight broker for advice on packing and shipping.

Shipping live plants and such perishable commodities as cut flowers requires great care, special handling, and a short throughput period to ensure that the products arrive in a timely fashion and in marketable condition. Speed and ambient conditions are less critical for dormant live plant products—such as

cuttings or bulbs—and for partially processed plant parts for arrangements. Nevertheless, packing, maintenance of environmental conditions (often of refrigeration for perishable cut flowers), and time are of the essence in transporting live or even no longer living but somewhat fragile plant materials.

Publications and WWW Resources

The following publication gives brief, general guidelines on USDA regulated products. Although designed primarily for tourists, it contains a list of approved products that you may find helpful. It is available online from the USDA APHIS website (www.aphis.usda.gov).

> *Travelers Tips On Bringing Food, Plant, and Animal Products into the United States*

The *Harmonized Tariff Schedule of the United States (2001)* (HTSUS) is available to view on the U.S. Customs and Border Protection website (www.customs.treas.gov), or you may purchase a printed version from:

U.S. Government Printing Office
Superintendent of Documents
710 North Capital Street NW
Washington DC 20401
Tel: (202) 512-1800
Fax: (202) 512-1657
Website: www.access.gpo.gov

The USGPO also has copies of specific laws available for purchase. The USGPO accepts orders made by fax, phone or placed over the Internet, as well as mail orders paid by credit card. All orders must be accompanied by payment. Credit cards, checks drawn on a U.S. bank, or an international money order are all acceptable.

Relevant Government Agencies

Address questions regarding the importation of live plants, roots, and cut flowers, or requests for permit applications, to:

Animal and Plant Health Inspection Service (APHIS)
Plant Protection and Quarantine (PPQ)
Director's Office
4700 River Rd., Unit 131
Riverdale, MD 20737
Tel: (301) 734-8261
Tel (PPQ permits): (301) 734-8758
Website: www.aphis.usda.gov/ppq

Address your questions regarding endangered species restrictions to:

U.S. Fish and Wildlife Service (FWS)
Division of Management Authority
4401 N. Fairfax Dr.
Arlington, VA 22203-0700
Tel: (703) 358-2104
Website: www.fws.gov

Address questions regarding the importation of live plants, roots, and cut flowers, especially those regarding antidumping and countervailing duty rates on cut flowers to your local Customs port director. For addresses refer to "U.S. Customs and Border Protection Offices" on page 65 or contact:

U.S. Customs and Border Protection
Customs Headquarters
1300 Pennsylvania Avenue NW
Washington DC 20229
Tel: (202) 354-1000
Website: www.customs.treas.gov

Laws and Regulations

The following laws and regulations may be relevant to the importation of live plants, roots, and cut flowers. The laws are contained in the U.S. Code (USC) and the regulations are published in the Code of Federal Regulations (CFR), both of which may be available at larger public and law libraries. Copies of specific laws are also available from the United States Government Printing Office (address above).

7 USC 151 et seq.
The Plant Quarantine Act
This Act gives the Plant Protection and Quarantine branch of the USDA authority to restrict or prohibit importation of plants or their seeds found to carry specific plant pests and pathogens.

7 USC 150aa et seq.
Federal Plant Pest Act (FPPA)
This Act prohibits the importation into or movement through the U.S. of plant pests as defined in the Act, and provides for the inspection of any letter, box, parcel, or container that may carry a plant pest. Inspection is to be performed by U.S. Department of Agriculture in conjunction with Customs.

7 CFR Part 351
Regulations for Entry and Inspection of Plants by Mail
These regulations set forth the plant imports that are prohibited, the requirements for entering restricted plants by mail, and the inspection procedures followed by the USDA's Animal and Plant Health Inspection Service (APHIS).

19 CFR 12.10 et seq.
Regulations for Entry and Release of Restricted Plants
These regulations prescribe the procedures followed by U.S. Customs to enforce the USDA requirements for importation of plants.

Convention on International Trade in Endangered Species of Wild Fauna and Flora (CITES)
This comprehensive wildlife treaty signed by over 100 countries, including the United States, regulates and in many cases prohibits commercial imports and exports of wild animal and plant species threatened by trade.

16 USC 1531
Endangered Species Act of 1973
This Act prohibits the import and export of species listed as endangered and most species listed as threatened. It is the U.S. law that implements CITES.

Principal Exporting Countries

The following listing includes samples of the main supplier nations of the products of this chapter. It is organized by HTSUS major heading. (Refer to "Customs Classification" above for the product codes.) Countries are listed in rank order of the value of products imported to the U.S. Statistics represent customs value of entries for 2002 from the Bureau of Census, U.S. Department of Commerce.

0601—Netherlands, Canada, Israel, United Kingdom, Chile, South Africa, New Zealand, France, China, Belgium, Costa Rica, Brazil, Taiwan, India, Australia, Japan, Thailand

0602—Canada, Costa Rica, Guatemala, Taiwan, Netherlands, Mexico, China, Thailand, Israel, Belgium, New Zealand, South Korea, Japan

0603—Colombia, Ecuador, Netherland, Mexico, Canada, Costa Rica,

0604—Canada, Italy, Mexico, India, Colombia, China, Costa Rica, Philippines, Guatemala, Netherlands, Israel, Chile, France, South Africa

Chapter 7:
Vegetables and Related Products

Full title: Edible Vegetables and Certain Roots and Tubers

This chapter relates to the importation of edible vegetables and certain edible roots and tubers, which are classified under Chapter 7 of the Harmonized Tariff Schedule of the United States (HTSUS). Specifically, it includes fresh, dried, chilled, steamed or boiled, frozen, or otherwise provisionally preserved, whole, cut, or otherwise processed—but not prepared—vegetables as well as seeds and other means of propagating them. The category of vegetables includes not only those products understood in the standard sense of a herbaceous plant product grown for food use, but also such products as potatoes, tomatoes, mushrooms, olives, capers, pumpkins, eggplants, sweet corn, peppers, legumes, and herbs, which may be distinguished botanically as roots, tubers, fruits, or other forms distinct from vegetables. This section is supplemental to the discussion about importing foods. If you are interested in importing vegetable products, see "Appendix: Foods" on page 825 and read that section in conjunction with this one.

If you are interested in importing fruit or nuts, you should refer to Commodity Index Chapter 8. Prepared foods made from the vegetable products included in Chapter 7 are classified within Chapter 20. If you are interested in importing cereal grains, consult Chapter 10. Juices or extracts of products covered in Chapter 7 for use in beverages are found in Chapter 22. If you are interested in importing vegetable oils, refer to Chapter 15. Seeds of vegetables as well as related plant products, such as fodder, as covered in Chapter 12. Flour, meal, flakes, granules, or pellets of potatoes or dried leguminous vegetables are covered in Chapter 11, while dried crushed peppers and allspice—which when fresh are classified as vegetables within Chapter 7—are covered in chapter 9.

Note: To understand key issues that will enable you to make best use of the information in this section we recommend that you see "Introduction" on page 425.

Key Factors

The key factors in the importation of vegetables and roots are:

- Compliance with U.S. Food and Drug Administration (FDA) purity, identity, manufacturing, and other standards

- Compliance with FDA entry notification requirements and procedures

- Compliance with U.S. Department of Agriculture (USDA) plant quarantine restrictions—permits may be required

- Compliance with U.S. Department of Agriculture (USDA) Food Safety and Inspection Service (FSIS) import restrictions, port inspections, and product certification for grade, size, quality, etc.

- Observance of quotas on certain Chapter 7 agricultural products

- Compliance with U.S. Environmental Protection Agency (EPA) regulations on pesticide residues on imported agricultural products

Although most importers utilize the services of a licensed customs broker in making their entries, and we recommend this practice, you should be aware of the regulatory, entry, and documentation issues involved in importing your product. You, as importer, are ultimately responsible for the fulfillment of any legal requirements applicable to your shipment.

General Considerations

Regulatory Agencies. Importation into the U.S. of vegetables and edible roots is subject to regulation under several laws enforced by a number of U.S. governmental agencies. The USDA enforces provisions of the Agricultural Marketing Agreement Act (AMAA) and the Plant Quarantine Act (PQA). Plant standards under the Agricultural Adjustment Act are enforced by the FSIS of the USDA. The FDA enforces the Food, Drug, and Cosmetic Act (FDCA). The U.S. Environmental Protection Agency (EPA) enforces the Federal Insecticide, Fungicide, and Rodenticide Act (FIFRA) and the Food Quality Protection Act of 1996.

USDA Regulations on Vegetables and Roots. Vegetables and roots may require USDA Animal and Plant Health Inspection Service (APHIS) Plant Protection and Quarantine (PPQ) branch import permits, depending on the nature of the product, its point of origin, and its destination. You should contact APHIS PPQ (see addresses at end of this chapter) to find out if a permit is required for the specific product you wish to import. APHIS inspects all fruits and vegetables at the U.S. port of entry.

Preclearance inspection is available for some commodities in some countries through APHIS International Services (IS) foreign operations. In addition to seasonal commodities that require inspectors on a short-term basis, IS Regions II and IV operate permanent preclearance programs for fruits, vegetables, and flower bulbs destined for the United States from Chile, Argentina, and The Netherlands. All of the costs for operating preclearance programs are paid for by exporters through trust fund agreements that IS sets up in each participating country.

FDA Requirements on Foods. The FDA regulations regarding importation of foods of any kind are extensive and stringent. For example, 21 CFR 158 establishes extensive regulations governing frozen vegetables. Vegetables and roots imported into the U.S. must comply with all FDCA requirements for those produced domestically. Imported products regulated by the FDA are subject to port-of-entry inspection. For a general discussion regarding FDA import procedures see "Appendix: Foods" on page 825.

EPA Requirements on Pesticide Residues. The EPA, under authority of the FIFRA, establishes and enforces regulatory limits on pesticide residues on edible plant products. For more information, contact the EPA (see addresses at end of this chapter).

The Food Quality Protection Act (FQPA) of 1996. The new law establishes a strong, health-based safety standard for pesticide residues in all foods. It uses "a reasonable certainty of no harm" as the general safety standard. The FDA may impose civil penalties for tolerance level violations. Under the "right to know" provisions, it specifically recognizes a state's right to require warnings or labeling of food that has been treated with pesticides. The FQPA affects the two major federal statutes under which the EPA regulates pesticides, the Federal Insecticide, Fungicide, and Rodenticide Act (FIFRA) and the Federal Food, Drug, and Cosmetic Act (FFDCA).

Mexican and Canadian Vegetables. Fresh vegetables for human consumption arriving from Mexico or Canada are eligible for immediate release. Importers must apply for a Special Permit for Immediate Delivery (**Customs Form 3461**). Shipments must be removed from the area immediately contiguous to the border to the importer's premises within the port of importation.

Detention of Shipment. If your shipment is found to be non-complying, it may be detained at the port of entry. The inspecting agency may permit you to bring such a shipment into compliance before making a final decision regarding admittance. However, any sorting, reprocessing, or relabeling must usually be supervised by the agency's personnel and is done at the importer's expense. A conditional release to allow the importer to bring a shipment into compliance is a privilege, not a right. The inspecting agency may consider subsequent noncomplying shipments of the same type of product to constitute abuse of the privilege and may require the importer to destroy or reexport the products. To ascertain what your legal responsibilities are, you should contact these agencies regarding the specific items to be imported.

Mushrooms. In March, 1993, the Agricultural Marketing Service (AMS) entered into an agreement whereby U.S. Customs and Border Protection is required to collect a mushroom fee of $0.0045 per pound for fresh mushrooms entered or withdrawn from warehouse on or after February 1, 1996.

Customs Classification

For customs purposes, vegetables and roots are classified under Chapter 7 of the HTSUS. This chapter is broken into major headings, which are further divided into subheadings, and often sub-subheadings, each of which has its own HTSUS classification number. For example, the 2001 HTSUS number for head lettuce entered in the period from June 1 to October 31, inclusive, is 0705.11.20, indicating that it is a sub-subcategory of head lettuce (0705.11), which is a subcategory of the major heading, lettuce (*Lactuca sativa*) and chickory (*Cichorium spp.*), fresh or chilled (0705). There are 14 major headings within Chapter 7.

0701—Potatoes, fresh or chilled

0702—Tomatoes, fresh or chilled

0703—Onions, shallots, garlic, leeks, and other alliaceous vegetables, fresh or chilled

0704—Cabbages, cauliflower, kohlrabi, kale, and similar edible brassicas, fresh or chilled

0705—Lettuce (*Lactuca sativa*) and chickory (*Cichorium spp.*), fresh or chilled

0706—Carrots, turnips, salad beets (salad beetroot), salsify, celeriac, radishes, and similar edible roots, fresh or chilled

0707—Cucumbers, including gherkins, fresh or chilled

0708—Leguminous vegetables, shelled or unshelled, fresh or chilled

0709—Other vegetables, fresh or chilled

0710—Vegetables (uncooked or cooked by steaming or boiling in water), frozen

0711—Vegetables provisionally preserved (for example, by sulfur dioxide gas, in brine, in sulfur water, or in other preservative solutions), but unsuitable in that state for immediate consumption

0712—Dried vegetables, whole, cut, sliced, broken, or in powder, but not further prepared

0713—Dried leguminous vegetables, shelled, whether or not skinned or split

0714—Cassava (manioc), arrowroot, salep, Jerusalem artichokes, sweet potatoes, and similar roots and tubers with high starch or inulin content, fresh , chilled, frozen or dried, whether or not sliced, or in the form of pellets; sago pith

For more details regarding classification of the specific product you are interested in importing, consult a customs broker, the appropriate commodity specialist at your nearest Customs port, or see HTSUS. The 2001 HTSUS is available online from the Customs Service (www.customs.gov/impoexpo/impoexpo.htm) or for purchase from the U.S. Government Printing Office (see resources at the end of this chapter), and may be found in larger public libraries. For a general discussion of customs classification, see "Classification— Liquidation" on page 229.

Dutiable Status of Goods

For more information about duty rates and binding decissions see "Dutiable Status of Goods" on page 203; for a discussion of temporary importation of goods see "Temporary Free Importations" on page 205.

Valuation

Importers have a responsibility to use what U.S. Customs and Border Protection deems, "reasonable care," when determining the value of their goods. They must also provide any additional information that U.S. Customs and Border Protection needs for setting a final value on the goods. This process involves a number of factors and can be somewhat complicated; importers must be aware of applicable issues and details. Valuation information applies to all types of commodities, for further discussion on the subject see "Customs Valuation" on page 267.

Import Duties

Import duties vary (often dramatically) depending upon the Harmonized Tariff Schedule (HTSUS) classification of the goods or products imported. Since some products that look alike have different HTSUS classifications and different rates of duty, proper classification is vital. Note that "differences of opinion" between importers and the Bureau of Customs and Border Protection regarding classification keeps customs attorneys very busy.

Import duties can be assessed on the imported value of the goods ("ad valorem" rates of duty such as 2%, 4.4%, 50%, etc.), total units or weight of the goods ("specific" rates of duty such as 2 cents each or 1.5 cents/pound, etc.) or on a combination basis ("compound" rates of duty such as 5 cents each plus 6%).

Listed below is a sampling of several Column 1 import duty rates for Chapter 07 products:
Turnips (0706.10.40.00): free
to
Leeks and other alliaceous vegetables (0703.90.00.00): 20%

For specific information on US import duties refer to the Harmonized Tariff Schedule of the US. The print version is available from the US Government Printing Office as well as third party suppliers who often add special features. Online versions are available in both static PDF pages as well as in formats with excellent search functionality. Search the Web with the term "Harmonized Tariff Schedule" to find sources.

Entry and Documentation

The entry of merchandise is a two-part process consisting of 1) filing the documents necessary to determine whether merchandise may be released from Customs custody and 2) filing the documents that contain information for duty assessment and statistical purposes. In certain instances, such as entry of products under quota, all documents must be filed and accepted by Customs prior to the release of the goods. Unless you have been granted an extension, you must file entry documents at a location specified by the port or area director within five working days of your shipment's date of arrival at a U.S. port of entry. These include a number of standard documents required by Customs for any entry, and:

- USDA Import Permit Form PPQ 587 or Form PPQ 588 (when required)
- Special Permit for Immediate Delivery, Customs Form CF 3461 (for immediate release of Mexican or Canadian vegetables)

After you present the entry, Customs may examine your shipment, or may waive examination (food items are almost always inspected). The shipment is then released provided no legal or regulatory violations have been noted. You must then file entry summary documentation and deposit estimated duties at a designated customhouse within 10 working days of your shipment's release. For a detailed description of entry procedures, standard documentation, and informal entry, see "Entry Process" on page 185.

Informed Compliance. Informed compliance was introduced with the Customs Modernization Act of 1993 (Mod Act) and defines the relationship between importers and U.S. Customs and Border Protection. It sets out the responsibilities of both parties. Providing the correct documentation and information for entry is a key factor that will make your importing operation run smoothly. We recommend that importers become familiar with the concept of informed comliance and the responsibilities that they have under the Mod Act. For further discussion about informed compliance see "Informed Compliance" on page 211.

Note: The Entry and Documentation section has been carefully designed to supply you, the importer, with sample documents and directions on how to satisfy Customs requirements. Be aware that you should consult the applicable authorities to ensure that you are correctly following the most current procedures.

Prohibitions and Restrictions

USDA FSIS Product Standards. Section 8e of the AMAA requires that whenever the U.S. Secretary of Agriculture issues grade, size, quality, or maturity regulations for commodities produced domestically, the same or comparable regulations must apply to imports of those commodities. Such import regulations apply only during periods when domestic marketing order regulations are in effect. Vegetables that may be subject to these import regulations include olives in tins (other than Spanish-style olives), dry onions, Irish potatoes, avocados, fresh tomatoes, green peppers, cucumbers, and eggplants.

If you import products subject to marketing orders, USDA's FSIS will inspect your shipment at the U.S. port of entry for compliance. If your shipment meets with the applicable standards, the USDA officer will issue an inspection certificate. If your shipment is found to be noncomplying, it will be refused entry. For additional information regarding requirements for regulated commodities contact USDA's Agricultural Marketing Service (see addresses at end of this chapter).

USDA Permit Requirements. USDA plant quarantine regulations under the PQA are divided into two classes: prohibitory and restrictive. Prohibitory orders forbid entirely the entry of designated plants and plant products subject to attack by plant pests for which no treatment is available that would insure complete freedom from such pests (special arrangements may be made for importation for research purposes, although commercial imports are banned). Restrictive orders allow the entry of plants or plant products with either a treatment or an inspection requirement. To import vegetables under restrictive orders, you must obtain an APHIS import permit. To qualify for a permit, you must be a U.S. resident. You will be held responsible for carrying out all conditions of entry specified in your permit. Address your questions regarding entry requirements for your product to USDA APHIS PPQ branch (see addresses at end of this chapter).

EPA Restrictions. If you are importing fresh vegetables, you should beware of products bearing excessive residues from insecticide sprays or dusts These items are considered to be adulterated under Federal law, as established by the EPA. If your shipment falls into this category, it will be refused entry.

FDA Restrictions. The FDA issues specific product alerts. In particular, importers should be aware of the following problems. For other products, the importer should check with the FDA for the most current tips and restrictions.

Dried Vegetables. You should take extreme care to prevent contamination of dried vegetables you intend to import. These products are particularly vulnerable to attack by insects or animals, or to deterioration resulting in moldiness or other forms of decomposition.

Dried Mushrooms. If you are offering dried mushrooms for import, you must be certain that they are edible species. Inedible species of dried mushrooms are prohibited imports. The most common bar to entry, however, is insect infestation, usually by flies or maggots. You can prevent mushroom contamination by insects, rodent, and bird filth, or other objectionable material by taking protective measures during drying and storage. Don't buy mushrooms from heavily insect-infested areas to import into the U.S. They will be refused entry.

Olives. Pitted and stuffed olives containing more than an unavoidable minimum of pits or pit fragments are in violation of the FDCA. While it may not be possible to completely eliminate this problem, dealers have been put on notice that they must take steps to reduce it to the extent that is reasonable.

Country-Specific Import Restrictions

APHIS PPQ may restrict importation of plant products from certain countries. The variables are often so complex that determinations must be made effectively on a case-by-case basis. As an example, PPQ may restrict the import of a specific product from a specific country that is known to carry a specific pest for a specific period of time. However, the restriction may only apply to areas in the U.S. with a climate in which the particular pest can thrive. A product that is refused import into California may be allowed in if its destination is New York State, or vice versa. The importer of agricultural products should ascertain from APHIS PPQ whether or not a product is subject to any such restrictions.

Quotas

Olives of subheadings 0711.20.15 and 2005.70.13, green and not pitted, in saline solution, in containers each holding more than 8 kg drained weight, certified by the importer to be used for repacking or sale as green olives as subject to tariff-rate quotas (that is, unlimited quantities may be imported, but tariff rates rise once a baseline level has been imported). A duty rate of 3.7 cents/kg on drained weight applies to the first 4,400 metric tons imported under both subheadings combined in any calendar year. After the first 4,400 metric tons, the duty rises to 7.4 cents/kg.

Quotas—both the commodities affected and rates charged—can change on short notice. For up-to-the minute information, or further details on quotas, contact the port director of Customs nearest you, or the U.S. Customs Quota Branch (address below.) For a general discussion of quotas refer to "Quotas Administered by Customs" on page 274.

Marking and Labeling Requirements

For a general discussion of U.S. Customs marking and labeling requirements, see "Country of Origin Marking" on page 236, "Special Marking Requirements" on page 238 and "Marking—False Impression" on page 239.

Shipping Considerations

You will need to ensure that your goods are packaged and shipped with care so that they arrive in good condition and pass smoothly through Customs. You are responsible for ensuring that the shipment is in compliance with all applicable government regulations for packaging and shipping. In most instances, you should not leave these arrangements solely to the discretion of your supplier. Careful preparation of the cargo and selection of the mode of transport can be essential to a cost-effective, timely delivery of undamaged goods. We strongly advise you to consult your shipping representative, insurance agent, or freight broker for advice on packing and shipping.

Vegetables and edible root crops often require special handling to ensure that they reach their destination in marketable condition. It is also of critical importance that infestation by insects and other forms of contamination are avoided, or the shipment will be denied admission.

Publications and WWW Resources

The following publication explains the FDA requirements for importing vegetables and edible roots. It is published by the FDA and is available online from the FDA website (www.fda.gov/opacom/7pubs.html).

> *Requirements of Laws and Regulations Enforced by the U.S. Food and Drug Administration*

The following publication gives brief, general guidelines on USDA regulated products. Although designed primarily for tourists, it contains a list of approved products that you may find helpful. It is available online from the USDA APHIS (www.aphis.usda.gov/oa/pubs/brochures.html).

> *Travelers Tips On Bringing Food, Plant, and Animal Products into the United States*

The U.S. Customs Service publishes a series of "Informed Compliance" documents, which are available from the Customs Service website. Of particular interest:

> *What Every Member of the Trade Community Should Know About Mushrooms*

The *Harmonized Tariff Schedule of the United States (2001)* (HTSUS) is available to view on the Customs Service website (www.customs.gov), or you may purchase a printed version from:

U.S. Government Printing Office
Superintendent of Documents
710 North Capital Street NW
Washington DC 20401
Tel: (202) 512-1800
Fax: (202) 512-1657
Website: www.access.gpo.gov

The USGPO also has copies of specific laws available for purchase. The USGPO accepts orders made by fax, phone or placed over the Internet, as well as mail orders paid by credit card. All orders must be accompanied by payment. Credit cards, checks drawn on a U.S. bank, or an international money order are all acceptable.

Relevant Government Agencies

Address your questions regarding FDA requirements for the importation of vegetables and edible roots to:

Food and Drug Administration (FDA)
Center for Food Safety and Applied Nutrition (CFSAN)

Office of Compliance
Division of Enforcement, Imports Branch
5100 Paint Branch Parkway
College Park, MD 20740-3835
Tel: (301) 436-2080
Website: http://vm.cfsan.fda.gov/list.html

Food and Drug Administration (FDA)
Center for Food Safety and Applied Nutrition (CFSAN)
Office of Plant and Dairy Foods and Beverages
5100 Paint Branch Parkway
College Park, MD 20740-3835
Tel: (301) 436-1700
Website: http://vm.cfsan.fda.gov/list.html

Address your questions regarding USDA domestic marketing orders (AMAA) to:

USDA Agricultural Marketing Service (AMS)
Fruit and Vegetable Division
1400 Independence Avenue SW
Washington DC 20250
Tel: (202) 720-4722
Fax: (202) 720-0016
Website: www.usda.gov/ams

Address your questions regarding USDA prohibitory and restrictive orders and permits to import restricted plant products to:

Animal and Plant Health Inspection Service (APHIS)
Plant Protection and Quarantine (PPQ)
Director's Office
4700 River Rd., Unit 131
Riverdale, MD 20737
Tel: (301) 734-8261
Tel (PPQ permits): (301) 734-8758
Website: www.aphis.usda.gov/ppq

Address questions regarding allowable pesticide residues on vegetables and root crops to:

Environmental Protection Agency (EPA)
Office of Pesticide Programs
Ariel Rios Building
1200 Pennsylvania Avenue NW
Mail Code 3213A
Washington DC 20460
Tel: (703) 305-7090
Website: www.epa.gov

Address your questions regarding quotas to:

U.S. Customs and Border Protection
Office of Field Operations, Quota Branch
1300 Pennsylvania Avenue NW
Washington DC 20229
Tel: (202) 927-5850
Website: www.customs.treas.gov

Address your questions regarding the importation of vegetables and root crops to your local Customs port director. For addresses refer to "U.S. Customs and Border Protection Offices" on page 65 or contact:

U.S. Customs and Border Protection
Customs Headquarters
1300 Pennsylvania Avenue NW
Washington DC 20229
Tel: (202) 354-1000
Website: www.customs.treas.gov

Laws and Regulations

The following laws and regulations may be relevant to the importation of vegetables and root crops. The laws are contained in the U.S. Code (USC) and the regulations are published in the Code of Federal Regulations (CFR), both of which may be available at larger public and law libraries. Copies of specific laws are

also available from the United States Government Printing Office (address above).

21 USC 301 et seq.
Federal Food, Drug, and Cosmetic Act
This Act prohibits deceptive practices and regulates the manufacture, sale and importation or exportation of food, drugs, cosmetics, and related products. See 21 USC 331, 381, 382.

19 CFR 12.1 et seq.; 21 CFR 1.83 et seq.
Regulations on Food, Drugs, and Cosmetics
These regulations of the Secretary of Health and Human Services and the Secretary of the Treasury govern the standards, labeling, marking, and importing of products used with food, drugs, and cosmetics.

7 USC 601 et seq.
Agricultural Adjustment Act (AAA)
This Act authorizes the Secretary of Agriculture to establish and maintain orderly market conditions for agricultural products—including tomatoes, olives, green peppers, Irish potatoes, cucumbers, onions, or eggplant—and to impose quotas or higher duty rates on imported agricultural products whenever investigation reveals that orderly market conditions require such action.

19 CFR Part 132
Regulations for Enforcement of AAA Quotas
These regulations provide for Customs enforcement of AAA quotas and higher duty rates imposed on imported agricultural products.

7 USC 136 et seq.
Federal Insecticide, Fungicide, and Rodenticide Act (FIFRA)
This Act prohibits the importation of pesticides or devices that are adulterated, misbranded, or otherwise violative of the Act, provides for registration of pesticides and devices, and establishes standards for labeling and classifying pesticides. It was amended by the Food Quality Protection Act of 1996.

19 CFR 12; 40 CFR 162
Regulations on Pesticides
These regulations set forth the procedures and guidelines for importing products exposed to pesticides.

7 USC 150aa et seq.
Federal Plant Pest Act (FPPA)
This Act prohibits the importation into or movement through the U.S. of plant pests as defined in the Act, and provides for the inspection of any letter, box, parcel, or container that may carry a plant pest. Inspection is to be performed by U.S. Department of Agriculture in conjunction with Customs.

7 CFR Part 351
Regulations of USDA for Entry of Plants
These regulations set forth the plant imports that are prohibited, the requirements for entering restricted plants by mail, and the inspection procedures followed by the USDA's Animal and Plant Health Inspection Service.

19 CFR 12.10 et seq.
Regulations of Customs for Entry of Restricted Plants
These regulations prescribe the procedures followed by U.S. Customs to enforce the USDA requirements for importation of plants.

Principal Exporting Countries

The following listing includes samples of the main supplier nations of the products of this chapter. It is organized by HTSUS major heading. (Refer to "Customs Classification" above for the product codes.) Countries are listed in rank order of the value of products imported to the U.S. Statistics represent customs value of entries for 2002 from the Bureau of Census.

0701—Canada, Japan, Costa Rica, Brazil, Colombia

0702—Mexico, Canada, Netherlands, Spain, Israel, Belgium, Chile, Poland, Italy

0703—Mexico, Canada, China, Peru, Argentina, Chile, Spain, Thailand

0704—Mexico, Canada, Costa Rica, Guatemala, Belgium, China, Dominican Republic, Ecuador, Taiwan, Poland, Germany, Spain, Honduras, Nicaragua, Japan

0705—Mexico, Canada, Belgium, Chile, Netherlands, Peru, Guatemala, Italy, Dominican Republic

0706—Mexico, Canada, China, Costa Rica, Fiji, Japan, Belgium, Dominican Republic, Ecuador, Guatemala, Netherlands, Taiwan, Jamaica

0707—Mexico, Canada, Honduras, Spain, Dominican Republic, Netherlands, Costa Rica, Guatemala

0708—Mexico, Guatemala, Peru, Canada, Ecuador, Dominican Republic, Turkey, Colombia, India

0709—Mexico, Canada, Netherlands, Peru, Israel, Spain, Costa Rica, Trinidad and Tobago, Dominican Republic, Panama, China, Honduras, Chile

0710—Mexico, Canada, Guatemala, China, Peru, Ecuador, Belgium, Chile, France, El Salvador, Israel, Poland, Spain, Egypt, Italy, India

0711—India, Greece, Mexico, Spain, Turkey, Denmark, Israel, China, Colombia, Thailand, Guatemala, Canada, Costa Rica, Peru, Italy

0712—China, Spain, Israel, Morocco, Mexico, Chile, Turkey, Japan, Germany, Peru, Italy, France, Switzerland, Hungary, Poland, United Kingdom, India, Taiwan, Egypt

0713—Canada, India, China, Mexico, New Zealand, Argentina, Peru, El Salvador, Thailand, Australia, Chile, Brazil, Turkey, Ecuador, Netherlands, France

0714—Costa Rica, Dominican Republic, Jamaica, China, Ecuador, Nicaragua, Brazil, Ghana, Panama, Fiji, Japan, Colombia

Chapter 8:
Fruit and Nuts

Full title: Edible Fruit and Nuts; Peel of Citrus Fruit or Melons

This chapter relates to the importation of edible fruit and nuts and of the peel of citrus fruit or melons, which are classified under Chapter 8 of the Harmonized Tariff Schedule of the United States (HTSUS). Specifically, it includes fresh, dried, chilled, steamed or boiled, frozen, or otherwise provisionally preserved, shelled or in the shell nuts and whole or otherwise processed—but not prepared—fruits. The category includes all tree fruits, including citrus fruits, and vine or bush fruits—such as grapes, berries, and melons—as well as tree nuts and fruit peels. Products may be processed or provisionally preserved, but not prepared into other forms. This section is supplemental to the discussion about importing foods. If you are interested in importing fruit or nuts, you should see "Appendix: Foods" on page 825 and read that section in conjunction with this one.

If you are interested in importing vegetables or edible root crops, you should refer to Commodity Index Chapter 7. Peanuts are covered in Chapter 12. Prepared foods made from the products included in Chapter 8 are classified within Chapter 20. Juices or extracts of products covered in Chapter 8 for use in beverages are found in Chapters 20 and 22. If you are interested in importing fruit and nut oils, refer to Chapter 15. Imports of fruit and nut trees falls within Chapter 6, while imports of seed for fruit and nuts as well as imports of oleaginous fruits come within Chapter 12. Inedible fruit and nuts intended for industrial uses are also classified elsewhere.

Note: To understand key issues that will enable you to make best use of the information in this section we recommend that you see "Introduction" on page 425.

Key Factors

The key factors in the importation of fruit and nuts are:

- Compliance with U.S. Food and Drug Administration (FDA) purity, identity, manufacturing, and other standards

- Compliance with FDA entry notification requirements and procedures

- Compliance with U.S. Department of Agriculture (USDA) plant quarantine restrictions—permits may be required

- Compliance where applicable with USDA marketing orders for grade, size, quality, etc.

- Observation of quotas on certain Chapter 8 agricultural products

- Compliance with U.S. Environmental Protection Agency (EPA) regulations on pesticide residues on imported agricultural products

Although most importers utilize the services of a licensed customs broker in making their entries, and we recommend this practice, you should be aware of the regulatory, entry, and documentation issues involved in importing your product. You, as importer, are ultimately responsible for the fulfillment of any legal requirements applicable to your shipment.

General Considerations

Regulatory Agencies. Importation into the U.S. of fruit and nuts is subject to regulation under several laws enforced by a number of U.S. governmental agencies. The USDA enforces provisions of the Agricultural Marketing Agreement Act (AMAA) and the Plant Quarantine Act (PQA). The FDA enforces the Food, Drug, and Cosmetic Act (FDCA), and the EPA enforces the Federal Insecticide, Fungicide, and Rodenticide Act (FIFRA).

USDA Import and Quarantine Requirements. Fruit and nut products may require USDA Animal and Plant Health Inspection Service (APHIS) Plant Protection and Quarantine (PPQ) import permits, depending on the nature of the product, its point of origin, and its destination. You should contact APHIS PPQ (see addresses at end of this chapter) to find out if a permit is required for the specific product you wish to import.

APHIS inspects all fruit and nuts at the U.S. port of entry. Preclearance inspection is available for some commodities in some countries through APHIS International Services (IS) foreign operations. In addition to seasonal commodities that require inspectors on a short-term basis, IS Regions II and IV operate permanent preclearance programs for fruits, vegetables, and flower bulbs destined for the United States from Chile, Argentina, and The Netherlands. All of the costs for operating preclearance programs are paid for by exporters through trust fund agreements that IS sets up in each participating country.

FDA Food Regulations. FDA regulations on the importation of foods of any kind are extensive and stringent. For example, 21 CFR 164 establishes detailed regulations governing tree nut and peanut products. Fruit and nuts imported into the U.S. must comply with all FDCA requirements for those produced domestically. Imported products regulated by the FDA are subject to port-of-entry inspection. For a general discussion of required FDA import procedures see "Appendix: Foods" on page 825.

EPA Pesticide Requirements. The EPA, under authority of FIFRA, establishes regulatory limits on pesticide residues on edible plant products. For more information, contact the EPA (see addresses at end of this chapter).

The Food Quality Protection Act (FQPA) of 1996. The new law establishes a strong, health-based safety standard for pesticide residues in all foods. It uses "a reasonable certainty of no harm" as the general safety standard. The FDA may impose civil penalties for tolerance level violations. Under the "right to know" provisions, it specifically recognizes a state's right to require warnings or labelin of food that has been treated with pesticides. The FQPA affects the two major federal statutes under which the EPA regulates pesticides, the Federal Insecticide, Fungicide, and Rodenticide Act (FIFRA) and the Federal Food, Drug, and Cosmetic Act (FFDCA).

Mexican and Canadian Fruit. Fresh fruit for human consumption arriving from Mexico or Canada are eligible for immediate release. Importers must apply for a Special Permit for Immediate Delivery (Customs **Form 3461**). Shipments must be removed from the area immediately contiguous to the border to the importer's premises within the port of importation.

Detention of Shipment. If your shipment is found to be noncomplying, it may be detained at the port of entry. The inspecting agency may permit you to bring such a shipment into compliance before making a final decision regarding admittance. However, any sorting, reprocessing, or relabeling must usually be supervised by agency personnel and is done at the importer's expense. A conditional release to allow the importer to bring a shipment into compliance is a privilege, not a right. The inspecting agency may consider subsequent noncomplying shipments of the same type of product to constitute abuse of the privilege and may require the importer to destroy or reexport the products. To ascertain what your legal responsibilities are, you should contact these agencies regarding the specific items to be imported.

Customs Classification

For customs purposes, fruit and nuts are classified under Chapter 8 of the HTSUS. This chapter is broken into major headings, which are further divided into subheadings, and often sub-subheadings, each of which has its own HTSUS classification number. For example, the 2001 HTSUS number for pineapples not reduced in size in crates or other packages is 0804.30.40, indicating that it is a sub-subcategory of pineapples (0804.30), which is a subcategory of the major heading, Dates, figs, pineapples, avocados, guavas, mangoes, and mangosteens, fresh and dried (0804). There are 14 major headings within Chapter 8.

0801—Coconuts, Brazil nuts, and cashew nuts, fresh or dried, whether or not shelled or peeled

0802—Other nuts, fresh or dried, whether or not shelled or peeled

0803—Bananas and plantains, fresh or dried

0804—Dates, figs, pineapples, avocados, guavas, mangoes, and mangosteens, fresh or dried

0805—Citrus fruit, fresh or dried

0806—Grapes, fresh or dried

0807—Melons (including watermelons) and papayas (papaws), fresh

0808—Apples, pears, and quinces, fresh

0809—Apricots, cherries, peaches, (including nectarines), plums (including prune plums), and sloes, fresh

0810—Other fruit, fresh

0811—Fruit and nuts, uncooked or cooked by steaming or boiling in water, frozen, whether or not containing added sugar or other sweetening matter

0812—Fruit and nuts, provisionally preserved (for example, by sulfur dioxide gas, in brine, in sulfur water, or in other preservative solutions), but unsuitable in that state for immediate consumption

0813—Fruit, dried, other than that of heading 0801 to 0806; mixtures of nuts or dried fruits of this chapter

0814—Peel of citrus fruit or melons (including watermelons), fresh, frozen, dried, or provisionally preserved in brine, sulfur water, or in other preservative solutions

For more details regarding classification of the specific product you are interested in importing, consult a customs broker, the appropriate commodity specialist at your nearest Customs port, or see HTSUS. The 2001 HTSUS is available online from the Customs Service (www.customs.gov/impoexpo/impoexpo.htm) or for purchase from the U.S. Government Printing Office (see resources at the end of this chapter), and may be found in larger public libraries. For a general discussion of customs classification, see "Classification—Liquidation" on page 229.

Dutiable Status of Goods

For more information about duty rates and binding decissions see "Dutiable Status of Goods" on page 203; for a discussion of temporary importation of goods see "Temporary Free Importations" on page 205.

Valuation

Importers have a responsibility to use what the U.S. Customs Service deems, "reasonable care," when determining the value of their goods. They must also provide any additional information that the Customs Service needs for setting a final value on the goods. This process involves a number of factors and can be somewhat complicated; importers must be aware of applicable issues and details. Valuation information applies to all types of commodities, for further discussion on the subject see "Customs Valuation" on page 267.

Import Duties

Import duties vary (often dramatically) depending upon the Harmonized Tariff Schedule (HTSUS) classification of the goods or products imported. Since some products that look alike have different HTSUS classifications and different rates of duty, proper classification is vital. Note that "differences of opinion" between importers and the Bureau of Customs and Border Protection regarding classification keeps customs attorneys very busy.

Import duties can be assessed on the imported value of the goods ("ad valorem" rates of duty such as 2%, 4.4%, 50%, etc.), total units or weight of the goods ("specific" rates of duty such as 2 cents each or 1.5 cents/pound, etc.) or on a combination basis ("compound" rates of duty such as 5 cents each plus 6%).

Listed below is a sampling of several Column 1 import duty rates for Chapter 08 products:
Cashew nuts shelled (0801.32.00.00): free
to
Cantaloupes if entered any other time than August 1 to September 15 of any year (0807.19.20.00): 29.8%

For specific information on US import duties refer to the Harmonized Tariff Schedule of the US. The print version is available from the US Government Printing Office as well as third party suppliers who often add special features. Online versions are available in both static PDF pages as well as in formats with excellent search functionality. Search the Web with the term "Harmonized Tariff Schedule" to find sources.

Entry and Documentation

The entry of merchandise is a two-part process consisting of 1) filing the documents necessary to determine whether merchandise may be released from Customs custody and 2) filing the documents that contain information for duty assessment and statistical purposes. In certain instances, such as entry of products under quota, all documents must be filed and accepted by Customs prior to the release of the goods. Unless you have been granted an extension, you must file entry documents at a location specified by the port or area director within five working days of your shipment's date of arrival at a U.S. port of entry. These include a number of standard documents required by Customs for any entry, and:

- USDA Import Permit (when required)
- Special Permit for Immediate Delivery, Customs Form CF 3461 (for immediate release of Mexican or Canadian vegetables)

After you present the entry, Customs may examine your shipment, or may waive examination (food items are almost always inspected). The shipment is then released provided no legal or regulatory violations have been noted. You must then file entry summary documentation and deposit estimated duties at a designated customhouse within 10 working days of your shipment's release. For a detailed description of entry procedures, standard documentation, and informal entry, see "Entry Process" on page 185.

Informed Compliance. Informed compliance was introduced with the Customs Modernization Act of 1993 (Mod Act) and defines the relationship between importers and the Customs Service. It sets out the responsibilities of both parties. Providing the correct documentation and information for entry is a key factor that will make your importing operation run smoothly. We recommend that importers become familiar with the concept of informed comliance and the responsibilities that they have under the Mod Act. For further discussion about informed compliance see "Informed Compliance" on page 211.

Note: The Entry and Documentation section has been carefully designed to supply you, the importer, with sample documents and directions on how to satisfy Customs requirements. Be aware that you should consult the applicable authorities to ensure that you are correctly following the most current procedures.

Prohibitions and Restrictions

USDA Restrictions. Section 8e of AMAA requires that whenever the U.S. Secretary of Agriculture issues grade, size, quality, or maturity regulations for commodities produced domestically, the same or comparable regulations must apply to imports of those commodities. Such import regulations apply only during periods when domestic marketing order regulations are in effect. Fruit and nuts that may be subject to import regulations include raisins, mangoes, prunes, limes, avocados, grapefruit, oranges, walnuts, processed dates, and filberts.

If you import products subject to marketing orders, USDA's Food Safety and Quality Service Department will inspect your shipment at the U.S. port of entry for compliance. If your shipment meets with the applicable standards, the USDA officer will issue an inspection certificate. If your shipment is found to be noncomplying, it will be refused entry. For additional information regarding requirements for regulated commodities contact USDA's Agricultural Marketing Service (see addresses at end of this chapter).

USDA Permit Requirements. USDA plant quarantine regulations under the PQA are divided into two classes: prohibitory and restrictive. Prohibitory orders forbid entirely the entry of designated plants and plant products subject to attack by plant pests for which no treatment is available that would insure complete freedom from such pests (special arrangements may be made for importation for research purposes, although commercial imports are banned). Restrictive orders allow the entry of plants or plant products with either a treatment or an inspection requirement. To import fruit or nuts under restrictive orders, you must obtain an APHIS import permit. To qualify for a permit, you must be a U.S. resident. You will be held responsible for carrying out all conditions of entry specified in your permit. Address your questions regarding entry requirements for your product to USDA APHIS PPQ branch (see addresses at end of this chapter).

EPA Restrictions. If you are importing fresh fruit or nuts, you should beware of products bearing excessive residues from insecticide sprays or dusts These items are considered to be adulterated under federal law, as established by the EPA. If your shipment falls into this category, it will be refused entry.

FDA Restrictions. You should take extreme care to prevent contamination of dried fruit and nuts you intend for import. These products are particularly vulnerable to attack by insects or animals, or to deterioration resulting in moldiness or other forms of decomposition. The FDA issues specific product alerts. For other products, the importer should check with the FDA for the most current tips and restrictions.

Fresh Fruit. If you are importing fresh fruits, you should be aware of the following potential problems. If you are importing pineapples, be sure they are not showing or likely to show the internal condition known as "brown heart," or "black heart." Such pineapples will be refused entry. Blueberries and huckleberries sometimes contain small larvae, which render them unfit for consumption. Take care to avoid importing these berries from infested areas. If you are importing fresh blueberries, you should make sure they are held and transported under conditions that will prevent mold or other types of spoilage.

Dried Fruit. You should take extreme care to prevent contamination of dried fruit you intend for import. These products are particularly vulnerable to attack by insects or animals, or to deterioration resulting in moldiness or other forms of decomposition. Dried figs are susceptible to insect infestation both during growth and when improperly stored, and may become moldy if not properly stored and handled. The FDA refuses entry to dried figs and fig paste because of insect or rodent contamination, mold, sourness, or fermentation. Dried dates have been refused entry for insect infestation, presence of filth, mold, decomposition, and the presence of broken pieces of pits. You may avoid these problems by taking the necessary precautions during storage and transit.

Nuts and Nut Products. If you wish to import nut products, you should be aware of the FDA standards for mixed tree nuts, shelled nuts, and peanut butter (21 CFR 164). The standards establish such factors as proportions of various kinds of nuts and label designations for "mixed nuts," fill of container for shelled nuts, and ingredients and labeling for peanut butter. Nuts and nut meats must be prepared and stored under sanitary conditions to prevent contamination by insects, rodents, or other animals. Nuts imported for pressing for edible oil must be just as clean and sound as nuts intended to be eaten as such or to be used in manufactured foods.

If you wish to import nuts and nut products into the U.S., you should take care to prevent the following adulterating conditions: 1) Insect infestation. Nuts are insect-infected if they contain live or dead insects—larvae, pupae, or adults; if they show definite evidence of insect feeding or cutting; or if insect excreta pellets are present. 2) Dirt. Nut meats may become dirty because of lack of cleanliness in cracking, sorting, and packaging. 3) Mold. Nut meats are occasionally moldy in the shell and bear fruiting mold or mold hyphae. 4) Rancidity. Rancid nuts are frequently soft. They have a yellow, dark, or oily appearance and an abnormal flavor characterized by rancidity. 5) Extraneous material. Stems, shells, stones, or excreta should not be present.

FDA defect action levels have been established for tree nuts. You may not deliberately mix good and bad lots to result in defects below these levels, even though the percentage of defects in the mixed lots is thus rendered lower than the defect action level.

Aflatoxins. Aflatoxins are a group of chemically related substances produced naturally as the byproduct of the growth of certain common molds. Aflatoxins, especially aflatoxin B1, are highly toxic, causing acute liver damage in exposed animals. Aflatoxin B1 also exhibits highly potent carcinogenic properties in certain species of experimental animals. Studies of certain population groups reveal that the consumption of aflatoxin-containing foods is associated with liver cancer in humans. Excess aflatoxin levels in nuts and other products is a significant public health problem and is a basis for seizing or refusing imports of products containing it.

Bitter Almonds. Because of their toxicity, bitter almonds may not be marketed in the U.S. for unrestricted use. Shipments of sweet almonds may not contain more than 5% of bitter almonds. Almond paste and pastes made from other kernels should contain less than 25 parts per million of hydrocyanic acid (HCN), a compound that occurs naturally in the kernels.

Country-Specific Import Restrictions

APHIS PPQ may restrict importation of plant products from certain countries. The variables are often so complex that determinations must be made effectively on a case-by-case basis. As an example, PPQ may restrict the import of a specific product from a specific country that is known to carry a specific pest for a specific period of time. However, the restriction may only apply to areas in the U.S. in whose climate that particular pest can thrive. A product that is refused entry into California may be allowed in if its destination is New York State, or vice versa. The importer of agricultural products should ascertain from APHIS PPQ whether or not a product is subject to any such restrictions.

Quotas

Quotas—both the commodities affected and the rates charged—can change on short notice. For up-to-the minute information, or further details on quotas, contact the port director of Customs nearest you, or U.S. Customs Quota Branch (see addresses at end of this chapter). For a general discussion of quotas refer to "Quotas Administered by Customs" on page 274.

Mandarins (satsumas) in airtight containers are subject to tariff rate quotas (that is, any quantity may be imported, although tariff rates are higher once the base-level quantity has been entered). Apple or pear juices, not mixed and not containing over 1.0% of ethyl alcohol by volume are subject to an annual absolute quota limit of 531,240 liters, after which no more of these products may be admitted during the calendar year.

Marking and Labeling Requirements

For a general discussion of U.S. Customs marking and labeling requirements, see "Country of Origin Marking" on page 236, "Special Marking Requirements" on page 238 and "Marking—False Impression" on page 239.

Shipping Considerations

You will need to ensure that your goods are packaged and shipped with care so that they arrive in good condition and pass smoothly through Customs. You are responsible for ensuring that the shipment is in compliance with all applicable government regulations for packaging and shipping. In most instances, you should not leave these arrangements solely to the discretion of your supplier. Careful preparation of the cargo and selection of the mode of transport can be essential to a cost-effective, timely delivery of undamaged goods. We strongly advise you to consult your shipping representative, insurance agent, or freight broker for advice on packing and shipping.

Nuts and in particular fresh fruit often require special handling to ensure that they reach their destination in marketable condition. It is also of critical importance that infestation by insects and other forms of contamination are avoided, or the shipment will be denied admission.

Publications and WWW Resources

The following publication explains the FDA requirements for importing fruit and nuts. It is published by the FDA and is available online from the FDA website (www.fda.gov/opacom/7pubs.html).

> *Requirements of Laws and Regulations Enforced by the U.S. Food and Drug Administration*

The following publication gives brief, general guidelines on USDA regulated products. Although designed primarily for tourists, it contains a list of approved products that you may find helpful. It is available online from the USDA APHIS (www.aphis.usda.gov/oa/pubs/brochures.html).

> *Travelers Tips On Bringing Food, Plant, and Animal Products into the United States*

The *Harmonized Tariff Schedule of the United States (2001)* (HTSUS) is available to view on the Customs Service website (www.customs.gov), or you may purchase a printed version from:

U.S. Government Printing Office
Superintendent of Documents
710 North Capital Street NW
Washington DC 20401
Tel: (202) 512-1800
Fax: (202) 512-1657
Website: www.access.gpo.gov

The USGPO also has copies of specific laws available for purchase. The USGPO accepts orders made by fax, phone or placed over the Internet, as well as mail orders paid by credit card. All orders must be accompanied by payment. Credit cards, checks drawn on a U.S. bank, or an international money order are all acceptable.

Relevant Government Agencies

Address your questions regarding FDA requirements for the importation of fruit and nuts to:

Food and Drug Administration (FDA)
Center for Food Safety and Applied Nutrition (CFSAN)
Office of Compliance
Division of Enforcement, Imports Branch
5100 Paint Branch Parkway
College Park, MD 20740-3835
Tel: (301) 436-2080
Website: http://vm.cfsan.fda.gov/list.html

Food and Drug Administration (FDA)
Center for Food Safety and Applied Nutrition (CFSAN)
Office of Plant and Dairy Foods and Beverages
5100 Paint Branch Parkway
College Park, MD 20740-3835
Tel: (301) 436-1700
Website: http://vm.cfsan.fda.gov/list.html

Address your questions regarding USDA domestic marketing orders (AMAA) to:

USDA Agricultural Marketing Service (AMS)
Fruit and Vegetable Division
1400 Independence Avenue SW
Washington DC 20250
Tel: (202) 720-4722
Fax: (202) 720-0016
Website: www.usda.gov/ams

Address your questions regarding USDA prohibitory and restrictive orders and permits to import restricted plant products to:

Animal and Plant Health Inspection Service (APHIS)
Plant Protection and Quarantine (PPQ)
Director's Office
4700 River Rd., Unit 131
Riverdale, MD 20737
Tel: (301) 734-8261
Tel (PPQ permits): (301) 734-8758
Website: www.aphis.usda.gov/ppq

Address questions regarding allowable pesticide residues on fruit and nuts to:

Environmental Protection Agency (EPA)
Office of Pesticide Programs
Ariel Rios Building
1200 Pennsylvania Avenue NW
Mail Code 3213A
Washington DC 20460
Tel: (703) 305-7090
Website: www.epa.gov

Address your questions regarding quotas to:

U.S. Customs and Border Protection
Office of Field Operations, Quota Branch
1300 Pennsylvania Avenue NW
Washington DC 20229
Tel: (202) 927-5850
Website: www.customs.treas.gov

Address your questions regarding the importation of fruit and nuts to your local Customs port director. For addresses refer to "U.S. Customs and Border Protection Offices" on page 65 or contact:

U.S. Customs and Border Protection
Customs Headquarters
1300 Pennsylvania Avenue NW
Washington DC 20229
Tel: (202) 354-1000
Website: www.customs.treas.gov

Laws and Regulations

The following laws and regulations may be relevant to the importation of fruit and nuts. The laws are contained in the U.S. Code (USC) and the regulations are published in the Code of Federal Regulations (CFR), both of which may be available at larger public and law libraries. Copies of specific laws are also available from the United States Government Printing Office (address above).

21 USC 301 et seq.
Federal Food, Drug, and Cosmetic Act
This Act prohibits deceptive practices and regulates the manufacture, sale and importation or exportation of food, drugs, cosmetics, and related products. It was amended by the Food Quality Protection Act of 1996. See 21 USC 331, 381, 382.

19 CFR 12.1 et seq.; 21 CFR 1.83 et seq.
Regulations on Food, Drugs, and Cosmetics
These regulations of the Secretary of Health and Human Services and the Secretary of the Treasury govern the standards, labeling, marking, and importing of products used with food, drugs, and cosmetics.

7 USC 601 et seq.
Agricultural Adjustment Act (AAA)
This Act authorizes the Secretary of Agriculture to establish and maintain orderly market conditions for agricultural products—including raisins, prunes, avocados, mangoes, limes, grapefruit, oranges, walnuts, processed dates, and filberts—and to impose quotas or higher duty rates on imported agricultural products, whenever investigation reveals that orderly market conditions require such action.

19 CFR Part 132
Regulations for Enforcement of AAA Quotas
These regulations provide for Customs enforcement of AAA quotas and higher duty rates imposed on imported agricultural products, whenever investigation reveals that orderly market conditions require such action.

7 USC 150aa et seq.
Federal Plant Pest Act (FPPA)
This Act prohibits the importation into or movement through the U.S. of plant pests as defined in the Act, and provides for the inspection of any letter, box, parcel, or container that may carry a plant pest. Inspection is to be performed by U.S. Department of Agriculture in conjunction with Customs.

7 CFR Part 351
Regulations for Entry and Inspection of Plants by Mail
These regulations set forth the plant imports that are prohibited, the requirements for entering restricted plants by mail, and the inspection procedures followed by the USDA's Animal and Plant Health Inspection Service (APHIS).

19 CFR 12.10 et seq.
Regulations for Entry and Release of Restricted Plants
These regulations prescribe the procedures followed by U.S. Customs to enforce the USDA requirements for importation of plants.

7 USC 136 et seq.
Federal Insecticide, Fungicide, and Rodenticide Act (FIFRA)
This Act prohibits the importation of pesticides or devices that are adulterated, misbranded, or otherwise violative of the Act, provides for registration of pesticides and devices, and establishes standards for labeling and classifying pesticides. It was amended by the Food Quality Protection Act of 1996.

19 CFR 12; 40 CFR Part 162
Regulations on Pesticides
These regulations set forth the procedures and guidelines for importing products exposed to pesticides.

Principal Exporting Countries

The following listing includes samples of the main supplier nations of the products of this chapter. It is organized by HTSUS major heading. (Refer to "Customs Classification" above for the product codes.) Countries are listed in rank order of the value of products imported to the U.S. Statistics represent customs value of entries for 2002 from the Bureau of Census, U.S. Department of Commerce.

0801—India, Brazil, Vietnam, Philippines, Bolivia, Dominican Republic, Mexico, Thailand, Peru, Indonesia

0802—Mexico, China, Turkey, South Africa, Australia, Italy, Guatemala, Spain, Brazil, South Korea, Ivory Coast, Costa Rica, Kenya

0803—Ecuador, Guatemala, Costa Rica, Colombia, Honduras, Mexico, Nicaragua, Peru, Venezuela, Dominican Republic, Philippines, Panama, Jamaica, India

0804—Costa Rica, Mexico, Chile, Brazil, Peru, Ecuador, Dominican Republic, Thailand, Honduras, Haiti, Philippines, Guatemala, New Zealand, Spain, Turkey, Nicaragua, Pakistan, Greece, Iran

0805—Spain, Mexico, Australia, South Africa, Morocco, Chile, Bahamas, Jamaica, Israel, South Korea, Dominican Republic

0806—Chile, Mexico, South Africa, Argentina, Peru, Italy, Canada, Brazil, Iran, Pakistan

0807—Mexico, Guatemala, Costa Rica, Honduras, Dominican Republic, Belize, Panama, Brazil

0808—Chile, New Zealand, Argentina, Canada, South Korea, China, South Africa, Japan, Australia, Trinidad and Tobago, Bolivia

0809—Chile, New Zealand, Canada, Argentina, Poland, Guatemala, Mexico, Pakistan, Italy, Netherlands, China, Ecuador, Peru

0810—Mexico, Canada, Chile, New Zealand, Italy, Taiwan, Argentina, Israel, Thailand, Guatemala, Greece, Costa Rica, Australia, China

0811—Canada, Mexico, Poland, Chile, Costa Rica, Thailand, Ecuador, Guatemala

0812—Italy, Mexico, Bulgaria, Turkey, Taiwan, Jamaica, South Korea, China, Thailand, Hungary, India

0813—Turkey, Poland, China, Chile, France, Thailand, Argentina, Mexico, Canada, Germany

0814—Israel, Spain, China, Haiti, Mexico, Germany, France, Morocco, Honduras, Guatemala

Chapter 9:
Coffee, Tea, and Spices

Full title: Coffee, Tea, Maté, and Spices

This chapter relates to the importation of coffee, tea, maté, and spices, which are classified under Chapter 9 of the Harmonized Tariff Schedule of the United States (HTSUS). Specifically, it includes all forms of coffee or products containing coffee; green, black, and flavored teas; maté; pepper; vanilla, cinnamon, cloves, nutmegs, various spice seeds, ginger, various aromatic leaves, and mixtures or blends of spices, such as curry powder. This section is supplemental to the discussion about importing foods. If you are interested in importing coffee, tea, or spices, see "Appendix: Foods" on page 825 and read that section in conjunction with this one.

If you are interested in importing seasoning and flavoring preparations or condiments—such as prepared mustard—or edible extracts of coffee or tea as beverages, you should refer to Commodity Index Chapter 21; for citrus peel for use in infusions or flavorings, see Chapter 8. For the importation of vegetables and vegetable products used for flavoring—such as onions, garlic, and capers—or herbs—such as tarragon, fennel, marjoram, and savory—and for fresh peppers, see Chapter 7. Those interested in importing herb teas, cubeb pepper, or aromatic or other leaves from which infusions or preparations having medicinal properties can be made should refer to Chapter 12. If products are represented as having therapeutic properties or are listed in the U.S. Pharmacopoeia or the National Formulary, you should refer to Chapter 30.

Note: To understand key issues that will enable you to make best use of the information in this section we recommend that you see "Introduction" on page 425.

Key Factors

The key factors in the importation of coffee, tea, maté, and spices are:

- Compliance with U.S. Food and Drug Administration (FDA) purity, identity, manufacturing, and other standards

- Compliance with FDA entry notification and procedures

- If therapeutic claims are made for the product, compliance with the drug provisions of the Food, Drug, and Cosmetic Act (FDCA)

Although most importers utilize the services of a licensed customs broker in making their entries, and we recommend this practice, you should be aware of the regulatory, entry, and documentation issues involved in importing your product. You, as importer, are ultimately responsible for the fulfillment of any legal requirements applicable to your shipment.

General Considerations

Regulatory Agencies. Importation of coffee, tea, maté, and spices is regulated by the FDA, which enforces the Federal Food, Drug, and Cosmetic Act (FDCA). All products derived from plants may also be subject to U.S. Department of Agriculture (USDA) regulations and inspection.

USDA Regulations. In general, USDA does not restrict coffee, tea, maté, or spices, although products derived from plants are often subject to USDA-enforced quarantines, standards, and quotas. If you are in any doubt as to the regulatory status of your product, you should check with the USDA Animal and Plant Health Inspection Service (APHIS) (see addresses at end of this chapter). Information regarding USDA restrictions on edible plant products can be found in "Appendix: Foods" on page 825.

FDA Inspections. FDA regulations regarding importation of foods of any kind are extensive and stringent. All imported food products must meet all FDCA standards for food produced domestically. An exception is made for tea, which is not produced anywhere in the U.S., but which is subject to the standards of the Tea Importation Act (TIA). Imported products regulated by the FDA are subject to port-of-entry inspection. For a general discussion of required FDA import procedures see "Appendix: Foods" on page 825.

If your shipment is found to be noncomplying, it may be detained at the port of entry. The FDA may permit you to bring such a shipment into compliance before making a final decision regarding admittance. However, any sorting, reprocessing, or relabeling must be supervised by FDA personnel, and is done at the importer's expense. A conditional release to allow the importer to bring a shipment into compliance is a privilege, not a right. The FDA may consider subsequent noncomplying shipments of the same type of product to constitute abuse of the privilege and require the importer to destroy or reexport the products. To ascertain what your legal responsibilities are, you should contact the FDA about the specific items to be imported.

Customs Classification

For customs purposes, coffee, tea, maté, and spices are classified under Chapter 9 of the HTSUS. This chapter is broken into major headings, which are further divided into subheadings, each of which has its own HTSUS classification number. For example, the 2001 HTSUS number for flavored green tea is 0902.20.10, indicating that it is a sub-subcategory of other green tea (0902.20), which is a subcategory of the major heading tea, whether or not flavored (0902). There are 10 major headings within Chapter 9.

0901—Coffee, whether or not roasted or decaffeinated; coffee husks and skins; coffee substitutes containing coffee in any proportion

0902—Tea, whether or not flavored

0903—Maté

0904—Pepper of the genus *Piper*; dried or crushed or ground fruits of the genus *Capsicum* or of the genus *Pimenta*

0905—Vanilla beans

0906—Cinnamon and cinnamon tree flowers

0907—Cloves(whole fruit, cloves and stems)

0908—Nutmeg, mace, and cardamoms

0909—Seeds of anise, badian, fennel, coriander, cumin or caraway; juniper berries

0910—Ginger, saffron, turmeric (curcuma), thyme, bay leaves, curry, and other spices

For more details regarding classification of the specific product you are interested in importing, consult a customs broker, the appropriate commodity specialist at your nearest customs port, or see HTSUS. The 2001 HTSUS is available online from the Customs

Service (www.customs.gov/impoexpo/impoexpo.htm) or for purchase from the U.S. Government Printing Office (see resources at the end of this chapter), and may be found in larger public libraries. For a general discussion of customs classification, see "Classification—Liquidation" on page 229.

Dutiable Status of Goods

For more information about duty rates and binding decissions see "Dutiable Status of Goods" on page 203; for a discussion of temporary importation of goods see "Temporary Free Importations" on page 205.

Valuation

Importers have a responsibility to use what the U.S. Customs Service deems, "reasonable care," when determining the value of their goods. They must also provide any additional information that the Customs Service needs for setting a final value on the goods. This process involves a number of factors and can be somewhat complicated; importers must be aware of applicable issues and details. Valuation information applies to all types of commodities, for further discussion on the subject see "Customs Valuation" on page 267.

Import Duties

Import duties vary (often dramatically) depending upon the Harmonized Tariff Schedule (HTSUS) classification of the goods or products imported. Since some products that look alike have different HTSUS classifications and different rates of duty, proper classification is vital. Note that "differences of opinion" between importers and the Bureau of Customs and Border Protection regarding classification keeps customs attorneys very busy.

Import duties can be assessed on the imported value of the goods ("ad valorem" rates of duty such as 2%, 4.4%, 50%, etc.), total units or weight of the goods ("specific" rates of duty such as 2 cents each or 1.5 cents/pound, etc.) or on a combination basis ("compound" rates of duty such as 5 cents each plus 6%).

Listed below is a sampling of several Column 1 import duty rates for Chapter 09 products:

Decaffeinated coffee, not roasted (0901.12.00.00): free

to

Flavored green tea (not fermented) (0902.20.10.00): 6.4%

For specific information on US import duties refer to the Harmonized Tariff Schedule of the US. The print version is available from the US Government Printing Office as well as third party suppliers who often add special features. Online versions are available in both static PDF pages as well as in formats with excellent search functionality. Search the Web with the term "Harmonized Tariff Schedule" to find sources.

Entry and Documentation

The entry of merchandise is a two-part process consisting of 1) filing the documents necessary to determine whether merchandise may be released from Customs custody and 2) filing the documents that contain information for duty assessment and statistical purposes. In certain instances all documents must be filed and accepted by Customs prior to release of the goods. Unless you have been granted an extension, you must file entry documents at a location specified by the port or area director within five working days of your shipment's date of arrival at a U.S. port of entry. These include a number of standard documents required by Customs for any entry.

After you present the entry, Customs may examine your shipment, or may waive examination (food items are almost always inspected). The shipment is then released provided no legal or regulatory violations have been noted. You must then file entry summary documentation and deposit estimated duties at a designated customhouse within 10 working days of your shipment's release. For a detailed description of entry procedures, standard documentation, and informal entry, see "Entry Process" on page 185.

Informed Compliance. Informed compliance was introduced with the Customs Modernization Act of 1993 (Mod Act) and defines the relationship between importers and the Customs Service. It sets out the responsibilities of both parties. Providing the correct documentation and information for entry is a key factor that will make your importing operation run smoothly. We recommend that importers become familiar with the concept of informed comliance and the responsibilities that they have under the Mod Act. For further discussion about informed compliance see "Informed Compliance" on page 211.

Note: The Entry and Documentation section has been carefully designed to supply you, the importer, with sample documents and directions on how to satisfy Customs requirements. Be aware that you should consult the applicable authorities to ensure that you are correctly following the most current procedures.

Prohibitions and Restrictions

Coffee. If you are importing green coffee of the genus *Coffea*, you should be sure that your product is held at all times under sanitary conditions to prevent contamination by insects, rats, and mice. If you are aware of conditions the FDA sees as grounds for detention of a coffee berry shipment, you will not be able to do much to avoid having your shipment turned away at the U.S. port of entry. The following conditions class coffee berries as objectionable and subject to detention: 1) any black coloration; 2) moldy; 3) water-damaged; 4) evidence of insect infestation; 5) any brown coloration ("sour"); 6) immature berries ("Quakers"); 7) shriveled berries; 8) presence of foreign material e.g. pods, sticks, or stones; 9) "sweepings" of spilled coffee recovered from ships' holds or docks; 10) contamination by ores and other poisonous materials in the vessel's cargo.

Tea and Maté. Tea offered for entry must meet all requirements of the FDCA as well as those of purity, quality, and fitness for consumption established by the Tea Importation Act (TIA). Teas of other than the species *Thea sinensis* must be so labelled to avoid confusing them with the standard, regulated product.

Spices. Spices and spice seeds are particularly vulnerable to contamination by insects, rodents, birds, and mold or decomposition. You should take every precaution to be sure that your product has been harvested, stored, handled, packed, and shipped under sanitary conditions. Insect control is particularly difficult for these items. Once a spice lot becomes insect-infested it is beyond hope of compliance with FDCA requirements. The FDA will not permit entry of spices or spice seeds containing either live or dead insects. Fumigation of an insect-infested lot of herbs or spices does not constitute bringing the product into compliance, since no consumer would willingly season food with dead insects and pesticides.

Thorough pre-storage cleaning and fumigation of premises in which herbs are to be stored is a good preventive measure. However, there are stringent EPA regulations regarding pesticide residues on products intended for human ingestion. You should be cognizant of any pesticide or fumigant that has been used on the product or its premises before purchase. Presence of illegal pesticide residues is grounds for refusal of entry. See "Appendix: Foods" on page 825 for a discussion of pesticide residues on agricultural products.

Many spices once thought to have medicinal value continue to be marketed for various other purposes. If no therapeutic claims are made or implied in their labeling or promotional material, such products are regarded as foods and subject only to the food provisions of the law. FDA regulations are intended to prevent the marketing and use of such products for medicinal purposes unless they have been determined safe and effective for their intended uses. Spices that are presented as having therapeutic qualities, or that may be used for drug purposes, are subject to the drug provisions of the FDCA. In addition, any spices or spice oils that are listed in the U.S. Pharmacopoeia or the National Formulary are subject to the standards set forth in these compendia when sold for drug purposes. If the herbs or spices you intend to import fall into either of these categories, you should become familiar with the regulatory requirements for drugs under FDCA.

Standards of identity have been established for spices and herbs, based on botanical name. Common spice names on container labels must accurately reflect what is in the container according to this system. You may not, for example, label a product "dried thyme" if it is not entirely made up of the dried leaves and flowering tops of *Thymus vulgaris*. Under FDCA spices obtained from—or mixed with—material from other plants are both adulterated and misbranded. Such products will not be permitted into U.S., and if they slip by Customs and enter domestic trade, will be subject to seizure or—at minimum—recall. The FDA uses the following definitions for common spices:

Aromatic vegetable substances used for the seasoning of food. They are true to name, and from them no portion of any volatile oil or other flavoring principle has been removed. Onions, garlic, and celery are regarded as foods, not spices, even if dried.

Allspice. The dried nearly ripe fruit of *Pimentia officinalis*, Lind.

Anise. The dried fruit of *Pimpinella anisum* L.

Bay leaves. The dried leaves of *Laurus nobilis* L.

Caraway seed. The dried fruit of *Carum carvi* L.

Cardamom. The dried, nearly ripe fruit of *Elettaria cardamomum* Maton.

Cinnamon. The dried bark of cultivated varieties of *Cinnamomum zeylanicum* Nees (Ceylon cinnamon) or of *C. cassia* (L.) Blume (Saigon cinnamon or cassia), from which the outer layers may or may not have been removed.

Cloves. The dried flower buds of *Caryophyllus aromaticus* L.

Coriander. The dried fruit of *Coriandrum sativum* L.

Cumin Seed. The dried fruit of *Cuminum cyminum* L.

Ginger. The washed and dried, or decorticated and dried, rhizome of *Zingiber officinale* Roscoe.

Mace. The dried arillus of *Myristica fragrans* Houtt.

Macassar Mace, Papua Mace. The dried arillus of *Myristica argentea* Warb.

Nutmeg. The dried seed of *Myristica fragrans* Houtt, deprived of its testa, with or without a thin coating of lime (CaO).

Macassar Nutmeg, Papua Nutmeg, Male Nutmeg, Long Nutmeg. The dried seed of *Myristica argentea* Jarb, deprived of its testa.

Paprika. The dried, ripe fruit of *Capsicum annuum* L.

Black Pepper. The dried, immature berry of *Piper nigrum* L.

White Pepper. The dried mature berry of *Piper nigrum* L. from which the outer coating or the outer and inner coatings have been removed.

Saffron. The dried stigma of *Crocus sativus* L.

Thyme. The dried leaves and flowering tops of *Thymus vulgaris*.

As with any agricultural commodity, no product may contain either residues of pesticides illegal for use in the U.S., or illegal levels of legal pesticides. Nor may any products of Chapter 9 be represented directly or indirectly as being capable of producing health, energy, endurance, or other physiological side effects. For a full discussion of pesticide residue on agricultural products, see "Appendix: Foods" on page 825.

Marking and Labeling Requirements

Products must be clearly labeled to avoid misrepresentation of contents. Nor may products of Chapter 9 be marked to state or imply that they possess medicinal properties. For a general discussion of U.S. Customs marking and labeling requirements, see "Country of Origin Marking" on page 236, "Special Marking Requirements" on page 238 and "Marking—False Impression" on page 239.

Shipping Considerations

You will need to ensure that your goods are packaged and shipped with care so that they arrive in good condition and pass smoothly through Customs. You are responsible for ensuring that the shipment is in compliance with all applicable government regulations for packaging and shipping. In most instances, you should not leave these arrangements to the discretion of your supplier. Careful preparation of the cargo and selection of the mode of transport can be essential to a cost-effective, timely delivery of undamaged goods. We strongly advise you to consult your shipping representative, insurance agent, or freight broker for advice on packing and shipping.

Publications and WWW Resources

The following publication explains the FDA requirements for importing coffee. It is published by the FDA and is available on request from FDA headquarters, it can also be accessed online at the FDA website under FDA Manuals and Publications (www.fda.gov).

> *Requirements of Laws and Regulations Enforced by the U.S. Food and Drug Administration*

The following publication gives brief, general guidelines on USDA regulated products. Although designed primarily for tourists, it contains a list of approved products that you may find helpful. It is available online from the USDA APHIS (www.aphis.usda.gov/oa/pubs/brochures.html).

> *Travelers Tips On Bringing Food, Plant, and Animal Products into the United States*

The *Harmonized Tariff Schedule of the United States (2001)* (HTSUS) is available to view on the Customs Service website (www.customs.gov), or you may purchase a printed version from:

U.S. Government Printing Office
Superintendent of Documents
710 North Capital Street NW
Washington DC 20401
Tel: (202) 512-1800
Fax: (202) 512-1657
Website: www.access.gpo.gov

The USGPO also has copies of specific laws available for purchase. The USGPO accepts orders made by fax, phone or placed over the Internet, as well as mail orders paid by credit card. All orders must be accompanied by payment. Credit cards, checks drawn on a U.S. bank, or an international money order are all acceptable.

Relevant Government Agencies

Address your questions regarding FDA import requirements for coffee to:

Food and Drug Administration (FDA)
Center for Food Safety and Applied Nutrition (CFSAN)
Office of Compliance
Division of Enforcement, Imports Branch
5100 Paint Branch Parkway
College Park, MD 20740-3835
Tel: (301) 436-2080
Website: http://vm.cfsan.fda.gov/list.html

Food and Drug Administration (FDA)
Center for Food Safety and Applied Nutrition (CFSAN)
Office of Plant and Dairy Foods and Beverages
5100 Paint Branch Parkway
College Park, MD 20740-3835
Tel: (301) 436-1700
Website: http://vm.cfsan.fda.gov/list.html

Address your questions regarding USDA import requirements for coffee to:

Animal and Plant Health Inspection Service (APHIS)
Plant Protection and Quarantine (PPQ)
Director's Office
4700 River Rd., Unit 131
Riverdale, MD 20737
Tel: (301) 734-8261
Tel (PPQ permits): (301) 734-8758
Website: www.aphis.usda.gov/ppq

Address questions regarding allowable pesticide residues on coffee, tea, maté, and spices to:

Environmental Protection Agency (EPA)
Office of Pesticide Programs
Ariel Rios Building
1200 Pennsylvania Avenue NW
Mail Code 3213A
Washington DC 20460
Tel: (703) 305-7090
Website: www.epa.gov

Address your questions regarding importation of coffee to your local Customs port director. For addresses refer to "U.S. Customs and Border Protection Offices" on page 65 or contact:

U.S. Customs and Border Protection
Customs Headquarters
1300 Pennsylvania Avenue NW
Washington DC 20229
Tel: (202) 354-1000
Website: www.customs.treas.gov

Laws and Regulations

The following laws and regulations may be relevant to the importation of coffee, tea, maté, and spices. The laws are contained in the U. S. Code (USC) and the regulations are found in the Code of Federal Regulations (CFR), both of which may be available at larger public and law libraries. Copies of specific laws are also available from the United States Government Printing Office (address above).

21 USC 301 et seq.
Federal Food, Drug, and Cosmetic Act
This Act prohibits deceptive practices and regulates the manufacture, sale and importation or exportation of food, drugs, cosmetics, and related products. It was amended by the Food Quality Protection Act of 1996. See 21 USC 331, 381, 382.

19 CFR 12.1 et seq.; 21 CFR 1.83 et seq.
Regulations on Food, Drugs, and Cosmetics
These regulations of the Secretary of Health and Human Services and the Secretary of the Treasury govern the standards, labeling, marking, and importing of products used with food, drugs, and cosmetics.

19 CFR 12.33
Regulations on Importing Tea
These regulations set the standards for imported tea and govern the entry and inspection procedures.

7 USC 136 et seq.
Federal Insecticide, Fungicide, and Rodenticide Act (FIFRA)
This Act prohibits the importation of pesticides or devic-

es that are adulterated, misbranded, or otherwise violative of the Act, provides for registration of pesticides and devices, and establishes standards for labeling and classifying pesticides. It was amended by the Food Quality Protection Act of 1996.

19 CFR 12; 40 CFR 162
Regulations on Pesticides
These regulations set forth the procedures and guidelines for importing products exposed to pesticides.

7 CFR Part 351
Regulations for Entry and Inspection of Plants by Mail
These regulations set forth the plant imports that are prohibited, the requirements for entering restricted plants by mail, and the inspection procedures followed by the USDA's Animal and Plant Health Inspection Service (APHIS).

19 CFR 12.10 et seq.
Regulations for Entry and Release of Restricted Plants
These regulations prescribe the procedures followed by U.S. Customs to enforce the USDA requirements for importation of plants.

Principal Exporting Countries

The following listing includes samples of the main supplier nations of the products of this chapter. It is organized by HTSUS major heading. (Refer to "Customs Classification" above for the product codes.) Countries are listed in rank order of the value of products imported to the U.S. Statistics represent customs value of entries for 2002 from the Bureau of Census, U.S. Department of Commerce.

0901—Colombia, Brazil, Guatemala, Mexico, Costa Rica, Canada, Indonesia, Peru, Vietnam, Germany, El Salvador, Nicaragua, Honduras, Sweden, Italy

0902—Argentina, China, India, Germany, Sri Lanka, Malawi, Kenya, United Kingdom

0903—Argentina, Brazil, Paraguay, Antigua and Barbuda, Uruguay, Peru, Lebanon

0904—Indonesia, India, Mexico, China, Brazil, Vietnam, Chile, Spain, Peru, Malaysia

0905—Madagascar, Indonesia, Uganda, India, Comoros, Tonga, Mexico, French Polynesia, France

0906—Indonesia, Sri Lanka, Brazil, Vietnam, China, Italy, Germany, Thailand, France

0907—Brazil, Indonesia, Comoros, Madagascar, Singapore, Tanzania, Sri Lanka, Netherlands, France, South Africa, Malaysia

0908—Indonesia, Guatemala, Grenada, India, Singapore, Italy, Netherlands, Argentina, Sri Lanka, China Ethiopia, Albania

0909—Syria, India, Turkey, Canada, Egypt, China, Netherlands, Bulgaria, Brazil, Poland, Singapore, Greece, Vietnam

0910—Turkey, India, Spain, China, Mexico, Israel, Brazil, Thailand, Pakistan, Canada

Chapter 10:
Cereals

This chapter relates to the importation of cereals as raw agricultural products, either as grain or seed, which are classified under Chapter 10 of the Harmonized Tariff Schedule of the United States (HTSUS). Specifically, it includes wheat, corn, sorghum, rye, barley, oats, rice, and other grains—such as millet and buckwheat—as well as their seed (with the exception of rice). For a general overview on importing food see "Appendix: Foods" on page 825.

If you are interested in importing intermediate processed products such as flour, worked grain, starches, gluten, and similar products, you should refer to Commodity Index Chapter 11, while cereal preparations that are either finished or at an advanced stage of processing and baked goods are covered in Chapter 19. The importation of sweet corn—which is considered a vegetable rather than a cereal—is covered in Chapter 7. If you are interested in importing oil seeds—such as soybeans or flax seed—or fodder crops, refer to Chapter 12.

Note: To understand key issues that will enable you to make best use of the information in this section we recommend that you see "Introduction" on page 425.

Key Factors

The key factors in the importation of cereals are:

- Compliance with U.S. Food and Drug Administration (FDA) purity, identity, manufacturing, and other standards

- Compliance with FDA entry notification requirements and procedures

- Compliance with United States Department of Agriculture (USDA) plant quarantine restrictions—permits may be required

- Compliance with USDA import restrictions—permits may be required in some cases

- Compliance with USDA country-specific prohibitions on corn, wheat, and rice grain or seed

- Compliance with U.S. Environmental Protection Agency (EPA) regulations on pesticide residues on imported agricultural products

Although most importers use the services of a licensed customs broker in making their entries, and we recommend this practice, you should be aware of the regulatory, entry, and documentation issues involved in importing your product. You, as importer, are ultimately responsible for the fulfillment of any legal requirements applicable to your shipment.

General Considerations

Regulatory Agencies. The importation of cereal grains and seeds is regulated by a variety of U.S. government agencies. The USDA Animal and Plant Health Inspection Service (APHIS) Plant Protection and Quarantine Branch (PPQ) enforces the Plant Quarantine Act (PQA), while the FDA administers the provisions of the Food, Drug, and Cosmetic Act (FDCA). Other relevant regulations include the Federal Seed Act (FSA) and the Federal Noxious Weed Act (FNWA), also enforced by the USDA. The EPA enforces the Federal Insecticide, Fungicide, and Rodenticide Act (FIFRA), which establishes regulatory limits on pesticide residues on edible plant products, and the Food Quality Protection Act of 1996. For more information contact the EPA (see addresses at end of this chapter).

FDA Inspection Requirements. Cereals imported into the U.S. must comply with all requirements for those produced domestically. Imported products regulated by FDA regulations are subject to port of entry inspection. For information concerning import procedures, refer to "Appendix: Foods" on page 825.

Sampling. U.S. Customs is responsible for sampling cereal shipments imported from Canada. At all other border crossings, the Plant Protection and Quarantine unit of APHIS performs this sampling. The Federal Seed Act prescribes methods to be used in sampling. Quantities of cereals may be designated as a single lot for sampling purposes only if the shipment is uniform within established tolerances with respect to pure grain (that is, of a single kind, not of mixed varieties), percentage of weeds, and occurrence of noxious weed seed. When a shipment consists of more than a single lot, each lot is sampled separately. When importation is across the Canadian border, Customs will notify you that sampling has occurred and that the shipment is being held pending APHIS determination. Sampling done by APHIS PPQ officers is carried out at the port of entry. Shipments are usually released unless a suspected noxious weed is found.

Detention of Shipment. If your shipment is found to be noncomplying, it may be detained at the port of entry. The inspecting agency may allow you to bring such a shipment into compliance before making a final decision regarding admittance. However, any sorting, reprocessing, or relabeling must usually be supervised by agency personnel and is done at the importer's expense. A conditional release to allow the importer to bring a shipment into compliance is a privilege, not a right. The inspecting agency may consider subsequent noncomplying shipments of the same type of product to constitute abuse of the privilege and require the importer to destroy or reexport the products. To ascertain what your legal responsibilities are, you should contact these agencies regarding the specific items to be imported.

Customs Classification

For customs purposes, cereals are classified under Chapter 10 of the HTSUS. This chapter is broken into major headings, which are further divided into subheadings, and often sub-subheadings, each of which has its own HTSUS classification number. For example, the 2001 HTSUS number for red spring wheat is 1001.90.20, indicating it is a sub-subcategory of wheat other than durum wheat (1001.90), which is a subcategory of the major heading, wheat and meslin (1001). There are eight major headings within Chapter 10.

1001—Wheat and meslin

1002—Rye

1003—Barley

1004—Oats

1005—Corn (maize)

1006—Rice

1007—Grain sorghum

1008—Buckwheat, millet, and canary seed; other cereals

For more details regarding classification of the specific product you are interested in importing, consult a customs broker, the appropriate commodity specialist at your nearest Customs port, or see HTSUS. The 2001 HTSUS is available online from the Customs Service (www.customs.gov/impoexpo/impoexpo.htm) or for purchase from the U.S. Government Printing Office (see resources at the end of this chapter), and may be found in larger public libraries. For a general discussion of customs classification, see "Classification—Liquidation" on page 229.

Dutiable Status of Goods

For more information about duty rates and binding decisions see "Dutiable Status of Goods" on page 203; for a discussion of temporary importation of goods see "Temporary Free Importations" on page 205.

Valuation

Importers have a responsibility to use what the U.S. Customs Service deems, "reasonable care," when determining the value of their goods. They must also provide any additional information that the Customs Service needs for setting a final value on the goods. This process involves a number of factors and can be somewhat complicated; importers must be aware of applicable issues and details. Valuation information applies to all types of commodities, for further discussion on the subject see "Customs Valuation" on page 267.

Import Duties

Import duties vary (often dramatically) depending upon the Harmonized Tariff Schedule (HTSUS) classification of the goods or products imported. Since some products that look alike have different HTSUS classifications and different rates of duty, proper classification is vital. Note that "differences of opinion" between importers and the Bureau of Customs and Border Protection regarding classification keeps customs attorneys very busy.

Import duties can be assessed on the imported value of the goods ("ad valorem" rates of duty such as 2%, 4.4%, 50%, etc.), total units or weight of the goods ("specific" rates of duty such as 2 cents each or 1.5 cents/pound, etc.) or on a combination basis ("compound" rates of duty such as 5 cents each plus 6%).

Listed below is a sampling of several Column 1 import duty rates for Chapter 10 products:
Buckwheat (1008.10.00.00): free
to
Parboiled rice (1006.30.10): 11.2%

For specific information on US import duties refer to the Harmonized Tariff Schedule of the US. The print version is available from the US Government Printing Office as well as third party suppliers who often add special features. Online versions are available in both static PDF pages as well as in formats with excellent search functionality. Search the Web with the term "Harmonized Tariff Schedule" to find sources.

Entry and Documentation

The entry of merchandise is a two-part process consisting of 1) filing the documentation necessary to determine whether merchandise may be released from Customs custody and 2) filing the documents that contain information for duty assessment and statistical purposes. In certain instances all documents must be filed and accepted by Customs prior to release of the goods. Unless you have been granted an extension, you must file entry documents at a location specified by the port or area director within five working days of your shipment's date of arrival at a US port of entry. These include a number of standard documents required by Customs for any entry, and:

- USDA APHIS Import Permit when required

After you present the entry, Customs may examine your shipment, or may waive examination. The shipment is then released provided no legal or regulatory violations have been noted. You must then file entry summary documentation and deposit estimated duties at a designated customhouse within 10 working days of your shipment's release. For a detailed description of entry procedures, standard documentation, and informal entry, see "Entry Process" on page 185.

Informed Compliance. Informed compliance was introduced with the Customs Modernization Act of 1993 (Mod Act) and defines the relationship between importers and the Customs Service. It sets out the responsibilities of both parties. Providing the correct documentation and information for entry is a key factor that will make your importing operation run smoothly. We recommend that importers become familiar with the concept of informed comliance and the responsibilities that they have under the Mod Act. For further discussion about informed compliance see "Informed Compliance" on page 211.

Entry Invoice—Grain or Grain and Screenings. Customs requires the following specific information on invoices for cultivated grain or grain and screenings: 1) a statement that no screenings are included with the grain; or 2) if screenings are included, the percentage of the shipment that consists of screenings commingled with the principal grain.

Entry Invoice—Screenings or Scalpings. Customs requires special information on the entry invoice for grain screenings or scalpings of grain or cereal seeds: 1) whether the commodity is the product of a screening process; 2) if so, whether any cultivated grains have been added to such commodity; and 3) if any such grains have been added, the kind and percentage of each. For more general information about invoices see "Invoices" on page 277.

Note: The Entry and Documentation section has been carefully designed to supply you, the importer, with sample documents and directions on how to satisfy Customs requirements. Be aware that you should consult the applicable authorities to ensure that you are correctly following the most current procedures.

Prohibitions and Restrictions

The USDA establishes "temporary" restrictions on the importation of specific cereal grains and seeds originating in specific countries to protect U.S. agriculture or public health from the proliferation of pests or weeds. Importation of the grain or seed of wheat and of corn and plants considered to be closely related (such as millet and sorghum) is currently subject to country-specific prohibitions. Wheat from countries not on the prohibited list is eligible for import without advance authorization. However, imports of corn, even from countries not on the prohibited list, require import permits from the USDA. Other grains generally may be imported with advance permission. No rice seed may be imported into the U.S. from any country in the world. All rice imports must be processed so that propagation cannot occur.

Inspection. All shipments of cereals are subject to USDA inspection and sampling at the port of entry, although imports of cereal grain for uses other than as seed may be treated somewhat more leniently. If you are importing cereals for use as seed in small lots (that is, up to 100 lbs.), your shipment is unlikely to be sampled. For a more complete discussion of lot and sampling levels, see the Federal Seed Act, Regulation Parts 201-202 and Table 6.

Detention of Shipment. If your shipment is sampled and found to contain evidence of noxious weeds, insect infestation, disease, or other contamination, it will be detained pending a USDA ruling on whether to allow entry. If the contaminant is one which is rare or nonexistent in the U.S., the shipment will be refused admission. If your shipment is found to be adulterated or unfit for seeding purposes according to FSA requirements, you may be allowed to have it cleaned or processed under USDA supervision, at your expense. Once grain has been cleaned or processed, any portion of it shown by test, analysis, or examination to meet FSA requirements can be admitted. The USDA APHIS makes the decision to allow such cleaning or processing on a case-by-case basis.

In most instances, cereal grain imports that fail to meet the more stringent requirements for importation as seed may be admitted for use as animal feed or for industrial purposes. This practice does not apply to grain found to contain weeds prohibited under the Federal Noxious Weed Act (FNWA), which allows zero tolerance for the presence of such harmful plants. Seeds of plants listed in the FNWA which may be present in lots of cereal grains, are subject to the restrictions defined in the act. You can get up-to-date-information on current FNWA restrictions from USDA APHIS (see addresses at end of this chapter).

Screenings. Screenings of most seeds are banned from importation, although screenings of cereal grains including wheat, oats, rye, barley, buckwheat, field corn, sorghum, broomcorn, and proso millet may be imported as long as they are not from prohibited sources and are not intended for use as seed. The words "screenings for processing, not for seeding" must appear on the invoice or other paperwork for such imports.

Imports for Research Purposes. The USDA may permit small amounts of cereal seed of prohibited varieties or from prohibited countries into the U.S. under permit for research purposes on a case-by-case basis. Such research imports are closely monitored by APHIS, and are subject to stringent quarantine and handling requirements. If you are interested in importing small amounts of cereal seed for research purposes, contact the USDA APHIS Permit Unit for further information. Commercial lot amounts of prohibited seed will not be permitted to enter the U.S. For a listing of current prohibitions, refer to "Country-Specific Import Restrictions" below.

Country-Specific Import Restrictions

The following cereal grains and their seeds are banned from importation into the U.S. by the USDA if they originate from the countries listed.

Corn and closely related plants and their parts (including those of the genus *Chionachne, Coix, Echinochloa, Eleusina, Euchleana, Miscanthus, Panicum, Pennisetum, Polytoca, Sclerachne, Setaria, Sorghum, Trilobachne,* and *Tripsicum*) [Note: these restrictions are under review, but no changes are anticipated in the near term]: Africa (all countries), Australia, Bangladesh, Bhutan, Brunei, Bulgaria, Burma (Myanmar), Cambodia (Kampuchea), Hong Kong, India, Indonesia, Japan and adjacent islands, Laos, Malaysia, Nepal, New Zealand [shelled corn may be imported from New Zealand under permit], North Korea, Oceania, Pakistan, Papua New Guinea, People's Republic of China, Philippines, Russia and the other republics of the former Soviet Union, Singapore, South Korea, Sri Lanka, Taiwan, Thailand, and Vietnam.

Wheat—Prohibited because of flag smut: Algeria, Australia, Bangladesh, Bulgaria, Chile, China, Cyprus, Egypt, Falkland Islands/Malvinas, Greece, Guatemala, Hungary, Iran, Israel, Italy, Japan, Korea, Libya, Morocco, Oman, Portugal, Romania, Russia and the other republics of the former Soviet Union, South Africa, Spain, Tanzania, Tunisia, Turkey, and Venezuela.

Wheat—Prohibited because of Karnal bunt: Mexico.

Wheat—Prohibited because of flag smut and Karnal bunt: Afghanistan, India, Iraq, Nepal, and Pakistan.

Rice from Thailand. As of mid-1994, a countervailing duties case had been filed regarding imports of rice from Thailand and imports of such products were being held up at Customs pending resolution. Those interested in importing this item may experience delays in clearing Customs or be subject to additional duties and should check with U.S. Customs to verify the current status of imports of this product from Thailand.

Marking and Labeling Requirements

All food imports must be labeled with the country of origin of the product. Imports of cereal grains must bear a statement by the importer as to the intended use of the product. If the shipment is denied admission for use as seed but subsequently allowed in for other purposes, the importer may withdraw the original statement and submit an amended declaration stating that the shipment is intended for feed or industrial purposes and that no part is intended to be used as seed.

Seed imports are required to be packaged in separate containers and labeled with the certification of the appropriate official agency of the exporting country to the effect that the product was grown in that country and has been approved for use as seed. Containers must also bear a record number demonstrating inspection of the lot by agricultural officials in the exporting country.

The invoice and any other labeling shall bear the lot identification, the kind of product present, and note any treatment given to the product.

For a general discussion of U.S. Customs marking and labeling requirements, see "Country of Origin Marking" on page 236, "Special Marking Requirements" on page 238 and "Marking—False Impression" on page 239.

Shipping Considerations

You will need to ensure that your goods are packaged and shipped with care so that they arrive in good condition and pass smoothly through Customs. You are responsible for ensuring that the shipment is in compliance with all applicable government regulations for packaging and shipping. In most instances, you should not leave these arrangements solely to the discretion of your supplier. Careful preparation of the cargo and selection of the mode of transport can be essential to a cost-effective, timely delivery of undamaged goods. We strongly advise you to consult your shipping representative, insurance agent, or freight broker for advice on packing and shipping.

Cereal grains are usually transported in bulk, although in some instances they may be shipped in bags or other types of containers (seeds must be packaged separately). General considerations include protection from contamination by dirt, pests, or other foreign matter, as well as the effects of heat and dampness on the goods shipped.

Publications and WWW Resources

The following publication explains the FDA requirements for importing cereal grains. It is published by the FDA and is available online from the FDA website (www.fda.gov/opacom/7pubs.html).

Requirements of Laws and Regulations Enforced by the U.S. Food and Drug Administration

The *Harmonized Tariff Schedule of the United States (2001)* (HTSUS) is available to view on the Customs Service website (www.customs.gov), or you may purchase a printed version from:

U.S. Government Printing Office
Superintendent of Documents
710 North Capital Street NW
Washington DC 20401
Tel: (202) 512-1800
Fax: (202) 512-1657
Website: www.access.gpo.gov

The USGPO also has copies of specific laws available for purchase. The USGPO accepts orders made by fax, phone or placed over the Internet, as well as mail orders paid by credit card. All orders must be accompanied by payment. Credit cards, checks drawn on a U.S. bank, or an international money order are all acceptable.

Relevant Government Agencies

Address your inquiries regarding requirements for importation of cereal grains and any necessary permits to:

Food and Drug Administration (FDA)
Center for Food Safety and Applied Nutrition (CFSAN)
Office of Compliance
Division of Enforcement, Imports Branch
5100 Paint Branch Parkway
College Park, MD 20740-3835
Tel: (301) 436-2080
Website: http://vm.cfsan.fda.gov/list.html

Food and Drug Administration (FDA)
Center for Food Safety and Applied Nutrition (CFSAN)
Office of Plant and Dairy Foods and Beverages
5100 Paint Branch Parkway
College Park, MD 20740-3835
Tel: (301) 436-1700
Website: http://vm.cfsan.fda.gov/list.html

Animal and Plant Health Inspection Service (APHIS)
Plant Protection and Quarantine (PPQ)
Director's Office
4700 River Rd., Unit 131
Riverdale, MD 20737
Tel: (301) 734-8261
Tel (PPQ permits): (301) 734-8758
Website: www.aphis.usda.gov/ppq

Address questions regarding allowable pesticide residues on grain to:
Environmental Protection Agency (EPA)
Office of Pesticide Programs
Ariel Rios Building
1200 Pennsylvania Avenue NW
Washington DC 20460
Tel: (703) 305-7090
Website: www.epa.gov

Address your questions regarding importation of cereal grains to your local Customs port director. For addresses refer to "U.S. Customs and Border Protection Offices" on page 65 or contact:
U.S. Customs and Border Protection
Customs Headquarters
1300 Pennsylvania Avenue NW
Washington DC 20229
Tel: (202) 354-1000
Website: www.customs.treas.gov

Laws and Regulations

The following laws and regulations may be relevant to the importation of cereals. The laws are contained in the U.S. Code (USC) and the regulations are published in the Code of Federal Regulations (CFR), both of which may be available at larger public and law libraries. Copies of specific laws are also available from the United States Government Printing Office (address above).

21 USC 301 et seq.
Federal Food, Drug, and Cosmetic Act
This Act prohibits deceptive practices and regulates the manufacture, sale and importation or exportation of food, drugs, cosmetics, and related products. It was amended by the Food Quality Protection Act of 1996. See 21 USC 331, 381, 382.

19 CFR 12.1 et seq.; 21 CFR 1.83 et seq.
Regulations on Food, Drugs, and Cosmetics
These regulations of the Secretary of Health and Human Services and the Secretary of the Treasury govern the standards, labeling, marking, and importing of products used with food, drugs, and cosmetics.

7 USC 136 et seq.
Federal Insecticide, Fungicide, and Rodenticide Act (FIFRA)
This Act prohibits the importation of pesticides or devices that are adulterated, misbranded, or otherwise in vio-

lation of the Act, provides for registration of pesticides and devices, and establishes standards for labeling and classifying pesticides.

19 CFR 12; 40 CFR 162
Regulations on Pesticides
These regulations set forth the procedures and guidelines for importing products exposed to pesticides.

7 USC 1551 et seq.
Federal Seed Act
This Act restricts the entry of seed to ensure that it is as labeled and is free from any noxious weed as identified in the Federal Seed Act (not the same as the noxious weeds listed in the Federal Noxious Weed Act). Purity and germination standards are no longer covered by this act. Weeds specifically restricted under the act include: quack grass, Canada thistle, perennial sow thistle, dodder, whitetop, Johnsongrass, Russian knapweed, bindweed, and leafy spurge. A tolerance of two of these is allowed per given amount of seed.

7 USC 150aa et seq.
Federal Plant Pest Act (FPPA)
This Act prohibits the importation into or movement through the U.S. of plant pests as defined in the Act, and provides for the inspection of any letter, box, parcel, or container that may carry a plant pest. Inspection is to be performed by U.S. Department of Agriculture in conjunction with Customs.

7 CFR Part 351
Regulations for Entry and Inspection of Plants by Mail
These regulations set forth the plant imports that are prohibited, the requirements for entering restricted plants by mail, and the inspection procedures followed by the USDA's Animal and Plant Health Inspection Service (APHIS).

19 CFR 12.10 et seq.
Regulations for Entry and Release of Restricted Plants
These regulations prescribe the procedures followed by U.S. Customs to enforce the USDA requirements for importation of plants.

7 USC 2801
Federal Noxious Weed Act of 1974
This Act defines, delineates, and restricts weeds and their seeds found to be harmful to agricultural crops, livestock, irrigation, navigation, fish and wildlife resources, or public health. No tolerances are allowed.

Principal Exporting Countries

The following listing includes samples of the main supplier nations of the products of this chapter. It is organized by HTSUS major heading. (Refer to "Customs Classification" above for the product codes.) Countries are listed in rank order of the value of products imported to the U.S. Statistics represent customs value of entries for 2002 from the Bureau of Census, U.S. Department of Commerce.

1001—Canada, United Kingdom, France, Mexico, Germany, Turkey, Jordan, Egypt, Thailand, Peru

1002—Canada, Sweden, Denmark

1003—Canada, United Kingdom, China, El Salvador, Poland, South Korea, Thailand, Peru, Japan, Italy, Russia

1004—Canada, Sweden, Finland, Denmark, Ukraine, Jamaica, Australia, Mexico, United Kingdom, Japan, Ecuador

1005—Chile, Canada, Argentina, Mexico, Brazil, Hungary, France, Peru

1006—Thailand, India, Australia, Pakistan, Italy, United Arab Emirates, Mexico, China, Canada, South Korea, Hong Kong, United Kingdom, Japan, Spain

1007—South Korea, Chile

1008—Canada, France, Peru, China, Netherlands, Russia, Ethiopia, South Korea, Hungary

Chapter 11:
Milling Products

Full title: Products of the Milling Industry; Malt; Starches; Inulin; Wheat Gluten

This chapter relates to the importation of milled cereals and related intermediate processed products, which are classified under Chapter 11 of the Harmonized Tariff Schedule of the United States (HTSUS). Specifically it includes such products as flour, worked grains, starches, and gluten. This section is supplemental to the discussion regarding the importation of food. If you are interested in importing milled products, you should see "Appendix: Foods" on page 825 and read that section in conjunction with this one.

If you are interested in importing cereal grains as a raw agricultural product, you should refer to Commodity Index Chapter 10. If you are interested in importing finished products, more highly processed cereal-based preparations, or baked goods you should consult Chapter 19. Flours and meals of oil seeds or oleaginous fruits are classified under Chapter 12. Cereal products are classified within Chapter 11 if they have been partially processed and—specifically—if they have a starch content generally greater than 45 percent and an ash content of less than from 1.6 to 5 percent of dry weight, depending on the particular type of grain. Products are intended primarily to be further prepared for human or animal consumption and for industrial uses.

Note: To understand key issues that will enable you to make best use of the information in this section we recommend that you see "Introduction" on page 425.

Key Factors

The key factors in the importation of milled products are:

- Compliance with U.S. Food and Drug Administration (FDA) purity, identity, manufacturing, and other standards

- Compliance with FDA entry notification requirements and procedures

- Compliance with U.S. Department of Agriculture (USDA) plant quarantine restrictions—permits may be required

- Compliance with USDA import restrictions—permits may be required in some cases

- Compliance with USDA country-specific prohibitions on certain wheat and corn and related products

- Compliance with U.S. Environmental Protection Agency (EPA) restrictions on pesticide residues on agricultural products

Although most importers use the services of a licensed customs broker in making their entries, and we recommend this practice, you should be aware of the regulatory, entry, and documentation issues involved in importing your product. You, as the importer, are ultimately responsible for the fulfillment of any legal requirements applicable to your shipment.

General Considerations

Regulatory Agencies. The importation of milled products is regulated by a variety of U.S. government agencies. The USDA Animal and Plant Health Inspection Service (APHIS), Plant Protection and Quarantine Branch (PPQ) enforces the Plant Quarantine Act (PQA), while the FDA administers the provisions of the Food, Drug, and Cosmetic Act (FDCA). The EPA enforces the Federal Insecticide, Fungicide, and Rodenticide Act (FIFRA), and the Food Quality Protection Act of 1996, which establishe regulatory limits on pesticide residues in edible plant products. Note also that any chemicals that leave detectable traces must be approved for use in the U.S. For more information, contact the EPA (see addresses at end of this chapter).

FDA Inspections. Milled products imported into the U.S. must comply with all requirements for those produced domestically. These include standards for nomenclature, levels of nutritional elements, and allowable additives as prescribed in detail in 21 CFR 137. Imported products regulated by FDA regulations are subject to port of entry inspection. For a discussion of FDA import procedures, see "Appendix: Foods" on page 825.

Detention of Shipment. If your shipment is found to be noncomplying, it may be detained at the port of entry. The FDA may permit you to bring such a shipment into compliance before a final decision is made regarding admittance. However, any sorting, reprocessing, or relabeling must be supervised by FDA personnel and is done at the importer's expense. Such conditional release to allow the importer to bring a shipment into compliance is a privilege, not a right. The FDA may consider any subsequent noncomplying shipments of the same type of product to constitute abuse of the privilege and require the importer to destroy or reexport the products. To ascertain what your legal responsibilities are, you should contact this agency regarding the specific items to be imported.

USDA APHIS Sampling. U.S. Customs is responsible for sampling milled product shipments imported from Canada. At other border crossings, the Plant Protection and Quarantine (PPQ) Branch of APHIS performs this sampling directly. Quantities of milled products may be designated as a single lot for sampling purposes only if the shipment is uniform within established tolerances with respect to the variety of product involved, percentage of weeds and other foreign matter, and size uniformity within the shipment. When a shipment consists of more than a single lot, each lot is sampled separately. When importation is across the Canadian border, Customs will notify you that sampling has occurred and that the shipment is being held pending APHIS determination. Sampling done by PPQ officers is carried out at the port of entry.

Customs Classification

For customs purposes, milled products are classified under Chapter 11 of the HTSUS. This chapter is broken into major headings, which are further divided into subheadings, and often sub-subheadings, each of which has its own HTSUS classification number. For example, the 2001 HTSUS number for cornmeal is 1103.13.00.20, indicating that it is a sub-subcategory of corn (maize) (1103.13), which is a subcategory of the major heading cereal groats, meal, and pellets (1103). There are nine major headings within Chapter 11.

1101—Wheat or meslin flour

1102—Cereal flours other than of wheat or meslin

1103—Cereal groats, meal, and pellets

1104—Cereal grains otherwise worked (for example hulled, rolled, flaked, pearled, sliced or kibbled), except rice of 1006; germ of cereals, whole, rolled, flaked or ground

1105—Flour, meal, powder, flakes, granules, and pellets of potatoes

1106—Flour meal and powder of dried leguminous vegetables of heading 0713, of sagoor of roots or tubers of heading 0714 or of the products of Chapter 8

1107—Malt, whether or not roasted

1108—Starches and inulin

1109—Wheat gluten, whether or not dried

For more details regarding classification of the specific product you are interested in importing, consult a customs broker, the appropriate commodity specialist at your nearest customs port, or see HTSUS. The 2001 HTSUS is available online from the Customs Service (www.customs.gov/impoexpo/impoexpo.htm) or for purchase from the U.S. Government Printing Office (see resources at the end of this chapter), and may be found in larger public libraries. For a general discussion of customs classification, see "Classification—Liquidation" on page 229.

Dutiable Status of Goods

For more information about duty rates and binding decisions see "Dutiable Status of Goods" on page 203; for a discussion of temporary importation of goods see "Temporary Free Importations" on page 205.

Valuation

Importers have a responsibility to use what the U.S. Customs Service deems, "reasonable care," when determining the value of their goods. They must also provide any additional information that the Customs Service needs for setting a final value on the goods. This process involves a number of factors and can be somewhat complicated; importers must be aware of applicable issues and details. Valuation information applies to all types of commodities, for further discussion on the subject see "Customs Valuation" on page 267.

Import Duties

Import duties vary (often dramatically) depending upon the Harmonized Tariff Schedule (HTSUS) classification of the goods or products imported. Since some products that look alike have different HTSUS classifications and different rates of duty, proper classification is vital. Note that "differences of opinion" between importers and the Bureau of Customs and Border Protection regarding classification keeps customs attorneys very busy.

Import duties can be assessed on the imported value of the goods ("ad valorem" rates of duty such as 2%, 4.4%, 50%, etc.), total units or weight of the goods ("specific" rates of duty such as 2 cents each or 1.5 cents/pound, etc.) or on a combination basis ("compound" rates of duty such as 5 cents each plus 6%).

Listed below is a sampling of several Column 1 import duty rates for Chapter 11 products:
Buckwheat flour (1102.90.20.00): free
to
Germ of cereals, whole, rolled, flaked or ground (1104.30.00.00): 4.5%

For specific information on US import duties refer to the Harmonized Tariff Schedule of the US. The print version is available from the US Government Printing Office as well as third party suppliers who often add special features. Online versions are available in both static PDF pages as well as in formats with excellent search functionality. Search the Web with the term "Harmonized Tariff Schedule" to find sources.

Entry and Documentation

The entry of merchandise is a two-part process consisting of 1) filing the documentation necessary to determine whether merchandise may be released from Customs custody and 2) filing the documents that contain information for duty assessment and statistical purposes. In certain instances all documents must be filed and accepted by Customs prior to release of the goods. Unless you have been granted an extension, you must file entry documents at a location specified by the port or area director within five working days of your shipment's date of arrival at a U.S. port of entry. These include a number of standard documents required by Customs for any entry, and:

- USDA APHIS Import Permit when required (contact USDA APHIS regarding permit requirements)

After you present the entry, Customs may examine your shipment, or may waive examination (food items are almost always inspected). The shipment is then released provided no legal or regulatory violations have been noted. You must then file entry summary documentation and deposit estimated duties at a designated customhouse within 10 working days of your shipment's release. For a detailed description of entry procedures, standard documentation, and informal entry, see "Entry Process" on page 185.

Informed Compliance. Informed compliance was introduced with the Customs Modernization Act of 1993 (Mod Act) and defines the relationship between importers and the Customs Service. It sets out the responsibilities of both parties. Providing the correct documentation and information for entry is a key factor that will make your importing operation run smoothly. We recommend that importers become familiar with the concept of informed comliance and the responsibilities that they have under the Mod Act. For further discussion about informed compliance see "Informed Compliance" on page 211.

Note: The Entry and Documentation section has been carefully designed to supply you, the importer, with sample documents and directions on how to satisfy Customs requirements. Be aware that you should consult the applicable authorities to ensure that you are correctly following the most current procedures.

Prohibitions and Restrictions

The USDA establishes "temporary" restrictions on the importation of specific cereal grains and some intermediate products originating in specific countries to protect U.S. agriculture or public health from the proliferation of pests or weeds. Importation of wheat as well as of corn and closely related plants (such as millet and sorghum) is currently subject to country-specific prohibitions. For a listing of current prohibitions, see Country-Specific Import Restrictions below.

Imports of products made from corn and related plants (including millet and sorghum) require USDA permits. Intermediate milled products, such as meals (but not flours), made from wheat that originates in countries from which wheat imports are prohibited from entering the U.S. Milled products of wheat from other countries and those made from other grains require no special entry permits. All shipments of cereal products are subject to USDA quarantine, inspection, and sampling at the port of entry.

Country-Specific Import Restrictions

The following cereal grains are banned by the USDA from importation into the U.S. if they originate from the countries listed.

Corn and closely related plants, their parts, and intermediate products (including plants of the genus *Chionachne, Coix, Echinochloa, Eleusina, Euchleana, Miscanthus, Panicum, Pennisetum, Polytoca, Sclerachne, Setaria, Sorghum, Trilobachne,* and *Tripsicum*) [Note: regulations governing corn are under review, but no changes are anticipated in the near term]: Africa (all countries), Australia, Bangladesh, Bhutan, Brunei, Bulgaria, Burma (Myanmar), Cambodia (Kampuchea), Hong Kong, India, Indonesia, Japan and adjacent islands, Laos, Malaysia, Nepal, New Zealand [raw shelled corn may be imported from New

Zealand], North Korea, Oceania, Pakistan, Papua New Guinea, People's Republic of China, Philippines, Russia and the other republics of the former Soviet Union, Singapore, South Korea, Sri Lanka, Taiwan, Thailand, and Vietnam.

Wheat—Prohibited because of flag smut: Algeria, Australia, Bangladesh, Bulgaria, Chile, China, Cyprus, Egypt, Falkland Islands/Malvinas, Greece, Guatemala, Hungary, Iran, Israel, Italy, Japan, Korea, Libya, Morocco, Oman, Portugal, Romania, Russia and the other republics of the former Soviet Union, South Africa, Spain, Tanzania, Tunisia, Turkey, and Venezuela.

Wheat—Prohibited because of Karnal bunt: Mexico.

Wheat—Prohibited because of flag smut and Karnal bunt: Afghanistan, India, Iraq, Nepal, and Pakistan.

Marking and Labeling Requirements

Imports of milled products must declare the country of origin for all imported products. The invoice and any other labeling shall bear the lot identification, the kind of product present, and note any treatment given to the product.

For a general discussion of U.S. Customs marking and labeling requirements, see "Country of Origin Marking" on page 236, "Special Marking Requirements" on page 238 and "Marking—False Impression" on page 239.

Shipping Considerations

You will need to ensure that your goods are packaged and shipped with care so that they arrive in good condition and pass smoothly through Customs. You are responsible for ensuring that the shipment is in compliance with all applicable government regulations for packaging and shipping. In most instances, you should not leave these arrangements solely to the discretion of your supplier. Careful preparation of the cargo and selection of the mode of transport can be essential to a cost-effective, timely delivery of undamaged goods. We strongly advise you to consult your shipping representative, insurance agent, or freight broker for advice on packing and shipping.

Milled products are usually transported in bulk, although in some instances they are shipped in bags or other types of containers. General considerations include protection from contamination by dirt, pests, or other foreign matter, as well as the effects of heat and dampness on the goods shipped.

Publications and WWW Resources

The following publication explains the FDA requirements for importing milled cereal. It is published by the FDA and is available online from the FDA website (www.fda.gov/opacom/7pubs.html).

Requirements of Laws and Regulations Enforced by the U.S. Food and Drug Administration

The *Harmonized Tariff Schedule of the United States (2001)* (HTSUS) is available to view on the Customs Service website (www.customs.gov), or you may purchase a printed version from:

U.S. Government Printing Office
Superintendent of Documents
710 North Capital Street NW
Washington DC 20401
Tel: (202) 512-1800
Fax: (202) 512-1657
Website: www.access.gpo.gov

The USGPO also has copies of specific laws available for purchase. The USGPO accepts orders made by fax, phone or placed over the Internet, as well as mail orders paid by credit card. All orders must be accompanied by payment. Credit cards, checks drawn on a U.S. bank, or an international money order are all acceptable.

Relevant Government Agencies

Address your inquiries regarding requirements for importation of milled cereal products and requests for permits to:

Food and Drug Administration (FDA)
Center for Food Safety and Applied Nutrition (CFSAN)
Office of Compliance
Division of Enforcement, Imports Branch
5100 Paint Branch Parkway
College Park, MD 20740-3835
Tel: (301) 436-2080
Website: http://vm.cfsan.fda.gov/list.html

Food and Drug Administration (FDA)
Center for Food Safety and Applied Nutrition (CFSAN)
Office of Plant and Dairy Foods and Beverages
5100 Paint Branch Parkway
College Park, MD 20740-3835
Tel: (301) 436-1700
Website: http://vm.cfsan.fda.gov/list.html

Animal and Plant Health Inspection Service (APHIS)
Plant Protection and Quarantine (PPQ)
Director's Office
4700 River Rd., Unit 131
Riverdale, MD 20737
Tel: (301) 734-8261
Tel (PPQ permits): (301) 734-8758
Website: www.aphis.usda.gov/ppq

Address questions regarding allowable pesticide residues on milled products to:

Environmental Protection Agency (EPA)
Office of Pesticide Programs
Ariel Rios Building
1200 Pennsylvania Avenue NW
Mail Code 3213A
Washington DC 20460
Tel: (703) 305-7090
Website: www.epa.gov

Address your questions regarding importation of cereal grains to your local Customs port director or contact:

U.S. Customs and Border Protection
Customs Headquarters
1300 Pennsylvania Avenue NW
Washington DC 20229
Tel: (202) 354-1000
Website: www.customs.treas.gov

Laws and Regulations

The following laws and regulations may be relevant to the importation of milled products. The laws are contained in the U.S. Code (USC) and the regulations are published in the Code of Federal Regulations (CFR), both of which may be available at larger public and law libraries. Copies of specific laws are also available from the United States Government Printing Office (address above).

21 USC 301 et seq.
Federal Food, Drug, and Cosmetic Act
This Act prohibits deceptive practices and regulates the manufacture, sale and importation or exportation of food, drugs, cosmetics, and related products. It was amended by the Food Quality Protection Act of 1996. See 21 USC 331, 381, 382.

19 CFR 12.1 et seq.; 21 CFR 1.83 et seq.
Regulations on Food, Drugs, and Cosmetics
These regulations of the Secretary of Health and Human Services and the Secretary of the Treasury govern the standards, labeling, marking, and importing of products used with food, drugs, and cosmetics. See Part 137,

which establishes nomenclature and technical standards for cereal flours and related products.

7 USC 136 et seq.
Federal Insecticide, Fungicide, and Rodenticide Act (FIFRA)
This Act prohibits the importation of pesticides or devices that are adulterated, misbranded, or otherwise in violation of the Act, provides for registration of pesticides and devices, and establishes standards for labeling and classifying pesticides.

19 CFR 12; 40 CFR 162
Regulations on Pesticides
These regulations set forth the procedures and guidelines for importing products—including grains and other raw agricultural products—exposed to pesticides.

7 USC 150aa et seq.
Federal Plant Pest Act (FPPA)
This Act prohibits the importation into or movement through the U.S. of plant pests as defined in the Act, and provides for the inspection of any letter, box, parcel, or container that may carry a plant pest. Inspection is to be performed by U.S. Department of Agriculture in conjunction with Customs.

7 CFR Part 351
Regulations for Entry and Inspection of Plants by Mail
These regulations set forth the plant imports that are prohibited, the requirements for entering restricted plants by mail, and the inspection procedures followed by the USDA's Animal and Plant Health Inspection Service (APHIS).

19 CFR 12.10 et seq.
Regulations for Entry and Release of Restricted Plants
These regulations prescribe the procedures followed by U.S. Customs to enforce the USDA requirements for importation of plants.

Principal Exporting Countries

The following listing includes samples of the main supplier nations of the products of this chapter. It is organized by HTSUS major heading. (Refer to "Customs Classification" above for the product codes.) Countries are listed in rank order of the value of products imported to the U.S. Statistics represent customs value of entries for 2002 from the Bureau of Census, U.S. Department of Commerce.

1101—Canada, Mexico, South Korea, Japan, Hong Kong, China, Australia, India, Germany, Italy, Spain, Brazil, Belgium, Argentina, Singapore

1102—Canada, Mexico, Thailand, Venezuela, Colombia, El Salvador, India, South Korea, China, Belgium, Italy, United Kingdom, Japan, Peru, Pakistan

1103—Canada, Mexico, Colombia, Venezuela, South Africa, Russia, Argentina, Italy

1104—Canada, Colombia, Ireland, Peru, Ecuador, South Korea, Venezuela, Ethiopia, El Salvador, United Kingdom, Thailand

1105—Canada, Spain, Italy, Germany, Mexico

1106—Canada, China, Mexico, Ghana, Thailand, United Kingdom, India, Nigeria, Ecuador, Taiwan, Switzerland, Saint Vincent and the Grenadines, Japan

1107—Canada, France, United Kingdom, Germany, Belgium, Mexico, Denmark, Czech Republic

1108—Canada, Netherlands, Germany, Belgium, Thailand, Mexico, Denmark, China, Hong Kong, Taiwan, Japan, Brazil, Austria

1109—Australia, Netherlands, Canada, France, Poland, Germany, Belgium, China, Czech Republic

Chapter 12:
Oil Seeds and Related Products

Full title: Oil Seeds and Oleaginous Fruits; Miscellaneous Grains, Seeds, and Fruit; Industrial or Medicinal Plants; Straw and Fodder

This chapter relates to the importation of oil seeds and oily fruits; miscellaneous grains, seeds, and fruits; industrial and medicinal plants; and fodder crops, which are classified under Chapter 12 of the Harmonized Tariff Schedule of the United States (HTSUS). This chapter is somewhat of a catch-all, including such varied plant products as soybeans, peanuts, copra, linseed, rapeseed, sunflower seed, and sesame seed; seed for cultivation of fodder crops, vegetables, trees, shrubs, and fruits; straw and fodder crops, including those consisting of roots, grasses, or herbs; plants used for perfume or pharmaceuticals, and as insecticides or fungicides, including herb teas; as well as plant products not elsewhere specified, such as locust beans, sugar cane, algae, fruit pits, etc. Note that coca leaves—the source of cocaine and a controlled substance—are included in Chapter 12. Most agricultural and horticultural seeds are classified within this chapter, although coverage is not universal, and those interested in importing seed should verify whether their product is included. If you are interested in importing products of Chapter 12 for use in food preparations, you should read this section in conjunction with the general discussion about importing food at "Appendix: Foods" on page 825.

If you are interested in importing leguminous vegetable seeds, seed potatoes, or sweet corn seeds, refer to Commodity Index Chapter 7. The importation of spice seeds is covered under Chapter 9, while importation of cereal grains and their seeds are covered in Chapter 10. If you are interested in importing olives for the extraction of oil, refer to Chapters 7 and 20. If you are interested in importing prepared animal feeds or residues of other products used as animal feed, refer to Chapter 23. Although herb teas are covered under Chapter 12, if you are interested in importing regular tea products, you need to refer to Chapter 9. If products are represented as having therapeutic value or are listed in the U.S. Pharmacopoeia or the National Formulary, you should refer to Chapter 30. For products imported specifically for cosmetic purposes, refer to Chapter 33; insecticides, fungicides, herbicides, and disinfectants are covered under Chapter 38.

Note: To understand key issues that will enable you to make best use of the information in this section we recommend that you see "Introduction" on page 425.

Key Factors

The key factors in the importation of oil seeds, miscellaneous plant products, and fodder crops are:

- Compliance with U.S. Department of Agriculture (USDA) plant quarantine restrictions—permits may be required
- Compliance with USDA import restrictions—permits may be required
- Compliance with U.S. Food and Drug Administration (FDA) purity, identity, manufacturing, and other standards for products imported for human consumption
- Compliance with FDA entry notification requirements and procedures for products imported for use as food or drugs
- Compliance with U.S. Environmental Protection Agency (EPA) on pesticide residues on imported agricultural products
- Compliance with restrictions under endangered species regulation
- Compliance with Drug Enforcement Administration (DEA) requirements for permitting, importer registration, recordkeeping, and distribution (for importation of controlled substances)

Although most importers utilize the services of a licensed customs broker in making their entries, and we recommend this practice, you should be aware of the regulatory, entry, and documentation issues involved in importing your product. You, as importer, are ultimately responsible for the fulfillment of any legal requirements applicable to your shipment.

General Considerations

Regulatory Agencies. The importation of plant products of Chapter 12 is regulated primarily by the USDA Animal and Plant Health Inspection Service (APHIS), Plant Protection and Quarantine branch (PPQ). This agency acts primarily under the authorization of the Plant Quarantine Act (PQA). It specifically monitors the importation of seed under provisions of the Federal Seed Act of 1939 and the Federal Noxious Weed Act (FNWA). The USDA also enforces the provisions of the Agricultural Marketing Agreement Act of 1937 (AMAA), which limits the importation of certain commodities. The FDA enforces the Food, Drug, and Cosmetic Act (FDCA).

The U.S. Environmental Protection Agency (EPA) enforces the Federal Insecticide, Fungicide, and Rodenticide Act (FIFRA) and the Food Quality Protection Act of 1996, which establish regulatory limits on pesticide residues on edible plant products. Restrictions under the Endangered Species Act (ESA) and the Convention on International Trade in Endangered Species (CITES) apply to seeds of listed plant species, and are enforced by the U.S. Fish and Wildlife Service (FWS), usually in consultation with and often through the USDA.

FDA Inspection Requirements. The FDA regulations regarding importation of foods and drugs of any kind are extensive and stringent. Plant products intended for human consumption or as medicaments must comply with all the FDCA requirements for those produced domestically. Imported products regulated by the FDA are subject to port of entry inspection. For a discussion about importing food see "Appendix: Foods" on page 924.

Detention of Shipment. If your shipment is found to be noncomplying, it may be detained at the port of entry. In the case of products subject to FDA jurisdiction, the FDA may allow you to bring such a shipment into compliance before making a final decision regarding admittance. However, any sorting, reprocessing, or relabeling must be supervised by FDA personnel and is done at the importer's expense. Such conditional release to allow the importer to bring a shipment into compliance is a privilege, not a right. The FDA may consider subsequent noncomplying shipments of the same type of product to constitute abuse of the privilege and require the importer to destroy or reexport the products. To ascertain what your legal responsibilities are, you should contact this agency regarding the specific items to be imported.

Coca Leaves. The DEA, a unit of the U.S. Department of Justice, licenses and controls the importation of coca leaves—which are considered Schedule II items with high potential for abuse—under the provisions of the Controlled Substances Act (CSA). If you are interested in importing this product, contact the DEA (see addresses at end of this chapter).

Peanuts. A new rule promulgated in 1996 establishes minimum quality, identification,certification and safeguard requirements for imported farmers stock, shelled, and cleaned-inshell peanuts. The rule establishes the same quality requirements and handling procedures for imported peanuts as those which are in effect for domestically produced peanuts. The regulations are contained in a new CFR subsection, 7 CFR 999.600, "Regulation governing imports of peanuts," and was first published in the June 19, 1996 Federal Register, pages 31305–31322.

USDA Quarantines and Sampling. All shipments of plant materials, especially of seed, are subject to USDA inspection and sampling at the port of entry. If you are importing seed in small lots (that is, lots of between 25 and as much as 100 lbs., depending on the type of plant), your shipment is unlikely to be sampled. For a more complete listing of seed lot and sampling levels, see the Federal Seed Act, Regulation Parts 201-202, Table 6.

U.S. Customs is responsible for sampling grain and seed shipments imported from Canada. At all other border crossings, the USDA's PPQ branch performs this sampling. The FSA prescribes methods to be used in sampling. Quantities of products may be designated as a single lot for sampling purposes only if the shipment is uniform within established tolerances with respect to pure product (that is, of a single kind, not of mixed varieties), percentage of weeds, and occurrence of noxious weed seed. When a shipment consists of more than a single lot, each lot is sampled separately. When importation is across the Canadian border, Customs will notify you that sampling has occurred and that the shipment is being held pending APHIS determination. Sampling done by APHIS PPQ officers is carried out at the port of entry. Shipments are usually released unless a specific problem—such as a suspected noxious weed—is found.

Detention of Shipment. If your seed shipment is sampled and found to contain contaminants of any kind—noxious weed, insect, disease, or other contaminant—it will be detained pending USDA decision whether to allow entry. If the contaminant is one which is rare or nonexistent in the U.S., it will be refused admission. If a shipment of seed is found to be adulterated or unfit for seeding purposes according to FSA requirements, you may have it cleaned or processed under USDA supervision, at your expense. Once the seed has been cleaned or processed, any portion of it that is shown by analysis, test, or examination to meet FSA requirements will be admitted. Although this practice is allowed for seed contaminated under Federal Seed Act standards, it is not allowed for seed containing weeds prohibited under the Federal Noxious Weed Act. In those cases, the decision to allow cleaning or processing is made by USDA APHIS on a case-by-case basis.

Import Advisory

Regulations governing the importation of plant products, especially seed, are complex, and can change rapidly. APHIS permits are required for certain plant product imports, and FWS permits or CITES documentation may also be required. To ascertain what your legal responsibilities are, you should contact these agencies with specific identification of the materials you wish to import.

The Customs Service has greatly increased its scrutiny of the agriculture industry, one of eight primary focus industries identified in recent Trade Enforcement Plans. Imported products from these industries will attract significant attention from Customs in the ar-

eas of compliance measurement, compliance assessment, informed compliance, and interventions.

Customs Classification

For customs purposes, oil seeds and fruits; miscellaneous grains, seeds, and fruits; industrial and medicinal plants; and fodder crops are classified under Chapter 12 of the HTSUS. This chapter is broken into major headings, which are further divided into subheadings, and often into sub-subheadings, each of which has its own HTSUS classification number. For example, the 2001 HTSUS number for red double cut clover seed is 1209.22.40.41, indicating that it is a subcategory of clover seed other than white or ladino clover (1209.22.20), which is a subcategory of the major heading, seeds, fruits, and spores of a kind used for sowing (1209). There are 14 major headings in Chapter 12.

1201—Soybeans, whether or not broken

1202—Peanuts (ground nuts), not roasted or otherwise cooked, whether or not shelled or broken

1203—Copra

1204—Flaxseed (linseed), whether or not broken

1205—Rape or colza seeds, whether or not broken

1206—Sunflower seeds, whether or not broken

1207—Other oil seeds and oleaginous fruits, whether or not broken

1208—Flours and meals of oil seeds or oleaginous fruits, other than those of mustard

1209—Seeds, fruits, and spores, of a kind for sowing

1210—Hop cones, fresh or dried, whether or not ground, powdered, or in the form of pellets; lupulin

1211—Plants and parts of plants (including seeds and fruits), of a kind used primarily in perfumery, in pharmacy, or for insecticidal, fungicidal, or similar purposes, fresh or dried, whether or not cut, crushed, or powdered

1212—Locust beans, seaweeds and other algae, sugar beet and sugar cane, fresh chilled, frozen or dried, whether or not ground; fruit stones and kernels and other vegetable products (including unroasted chicory roots of the variety *Cichorium intybus sativum*) of a kind used primarily for human consumption, not elsewhere specified or included

1213—Cereal straw and husks, unprepared, whether or not chopped, ground, pressed, or in the form of pellets

1214—Rutabagas (swedes), mangolds, fodder roots, hay, alfalfa (lucerne), clover, sainfoin, forage kale, lupines, vetches, and similar forage products, whether or not in the form of pellets

For more details regarding classification of the specific product you are interested in importing, consult a customs broker, the appropriate commodity specialist at your nearest customs port, or see HTSUS. The 2001 HTSUS is available online from the Customs Service (www.customs.gov/impoexpo/impoexpo.htm) or for purchase from the U.S. Government Printing Office (see resources at the end of this chapter), and may be found in larger public libraries. For a general discussion of customs classification, see "Classification—Liquidation" on page 229.

Dutiable Status of Goods

For more information about duty rates and binding decisions see "Dutiable Status of Goods" on page 203; for a discussion of temporary importation of goods see "Temporary Free Importations" on page 205.

Valuation

Importers have a responsibility to use what the U.S. Customs Service deems, "reasonable care," when determining the value of their goods. They must also provide any additional information that the Customs Service needs for setting a final value on the goods. This process involves a number of factors and can be somewhat complicated; importers must be aware of applicable issues and details. Valuation information applies to all types of commodities, for further discussion on the subject see "Customs Valuation" on page 267.

Import Duties

Import duties vary (often dramatically) depending upon the Harmonized Tariff Schedule (HTSUS) classification of the goods or products imported. Since some products that look alike have different HTSUS classifications and different rates of duty, proper classification is vital. Note that "differences of opinion" between importers and the Bureau of Customs and Border Protection regarding classification keeps customs attorneys very busy.

Import duties can be assessed on the imported value of the goods ("ad valorem" rates of duty such as 2%, 4.4%, 50%, etc.), total units or weight of the goods ("specific" rates of duty such as 2 cents each or 1.5 cents/pound, etc.) or on a combination basis ("compound" rates of duty such as 5 cents each plus 6%).

Listed below is a sampling of several Column 1 import duty rates for Chapter 12 products:
Copra (1203.00.00.00): free
to
Peanuts (other) (1202.10.80): 163.8%

For specific information on US import duties refer to the Harmonized Tariff Schedule of the US. The print version is available from the US Government Printing Office as well as third party suppliers who often add special features. Online versions are available in both static PDF pages as well as in formats with excellent search functionality. Search the Web with the term "Harmonized Tariff Schedule" to find sources.

Entry and Documentation

The entry of merchandise is a two-part process consisting of 1) filing the documents necessary to determine whether merchandise may be released from Customs custody and 2) filing the documents that contain information for duty assessment and statistical purposes. In certain instances all documents must be filed and accepted by Customs prior to release of the goods. Unless you have been granted an extension, you must file entry documents at a location specified by the port or area director within five working days of your shipment's date of arrival at a U.S. port of entry. These include a number of standard documents required by Customs for any entry, and:

- USDA APHIS Import Permit when required (contact USDA, APHIS regarding permit requirements)

- DEA permits when required (contact DEA regarding permit requirements for importation of controlled substances) DEA Form 357

- DEA declaration of imports when required DEA Form 236

After you present the entry, Customs may examine your shipment, or may waive examination. The shipment is then released provided no legal or regulatory violations have been noted. You must then file entry summary documentation and deposit estimated duties at a designated customhouse within 10 working days of your shipment's release. For a detailed description of entry procedures, standard documentation, and informal entry, see "Entry Process" on page 185.

Informed Compliance. Informed compliance was introduced with the Customs Modernization Act of 1993 (Mod Act) and defines the relationship between importers and the Customs Service. It sets out the responsibilities of both parties. Providing the correct documentation and information for entry is a key factor that will make your importing operation run smoothly. We recommend that importers become familiar with the concept of informed comliance and the responsibilities that they have under the Mod Act. For further discussion about informed compliance see "Informed Compliance" on page 211.

Entry Invoice. Customs requires special information on the entry invoice for screenings or scalpings of grains or seeds: 1) whether the commodity is the product of a screening process; 2) if so, whether any cultivated grains have been added to such commodity; and 3) if any such grains have been added, the kind and percentage of each. For more general information about invoices see "Invoices" on page 277.

Note: The Entry and Documentation section has been carefully designed to supply you, the importer, with sample documents and directions on how to satisfy Customs requirements. Be aware that you should consult the applicable authorities to ensure that you are correctly following the most current procedures.

Prohibitions and Restrictions

The USDA establishes temporary restrictions on specific types of seeds originating in specific countries, as necessary to protect U.S. agriculture or public health from the proliferation of pests or weeds, although there are currently no prohibitions in effect with respect to plants or seeds of plants covered within Chapter 12. All seed imports must comply with the provisions of the Federal Noxious Weed Act (FNWA), which bans the importation of a variety of such weed seeds or plant parts directly or indirectly as contaminants within shipments of other plant materials. Seeds of plants listed in the FNWA, the Endangered Species Act, and in the Convention on International Trade in Endangered Species of Fauna and Flora (CITES) are subject to the restrictions defined in those acts. You can get up-to-date information on current FNWA restrictions from USDA APHIS (see addresses at end of this chapter). For information on seed restricted under CITES or other endangered species regulation, contact the Fish and Wildlife Service (see addresses at end of this chapter).

Screenings. With the following exceptions, screenings of all seed subject to the FSA are prohibited entry into the U.S. Screenings consisting of most edible grains as well as those of flax, soybeans, cowpeas, field peas, and field beans may be imported, as long as they are not imported for seeding purposes. The words "screening for processing, not for seeding" must appear on the invoice or other entry paperwork for these types of imports.

Certificate or Declaration of Origin. Customs requires documentation as to the origin of alfalfa and red clover seed, or any mixture of either or both. A certificate of origin from a properly authorized official of the foreign country in which the seed was grown, or a declaration of origin by the shipper can serve as documentation of the country of origin. In the absence of such documentation, Customs may accept other evidence as to the shipment's origin, or the seed may be permitted entry after being stained. Such seed, when its origin is other than Canada or South America, must be stained 10% red. When the seed's origin is South America, it must be stained 10% red or 10% orange.

Exemptions. Imported seed may be exempt from FSA import requirements under certain conditions:

1) Seed grown in the United States, exported, and returned from a foreign country is not subject to the prohibition against the importation of seed that is adulterated or unfit for seeding purposes. If your import falls in this category, you will have to provide statements or other documents with entry papers, establishing that the seed was grown in the U.S. and exported, that it was not admitted into the commerce of a foreign country, and that it was not commingled with other seed after being exported. You will have to include the quantity of seed, number of containers, date of exportation from the U.S., distinguishing marks on the containers at the time of exportation, and the name and address of the U.S. exporter in this documentation. The documentation verifying that the seed was not admitted into foreign commerce or commingled with other seed after being exported from the U.S. must come from a Customs officer or other appropriate govern-

ment official of the country from which the seed is being reimported into the U.S.

2) Seed shipped in bond through the U.S. is not subject to the import requirements of the FSA.

3) Seed imported for sowing for seed production only, by or for the importer or consignee, and not to be sold within the U.S., is not subject to the prohibition against the importation of seed that is adulterated, nor is it required to be stained. If your import falls into this category, you will be required to present a declaration with entry papers, identifying the port of entry, and stating the noncommercial purpose of the importation.

For information on country-specific restrictions under endangered species regulations, contact FWS (see addresses at end of this chapter).

Quotas

9904.20.00 Whenever in any 12-month period beginning August 1 in any year, the aggregate quantity specified below of peanuts (ground nuts), shelled or not shelled, blanched or otherwise prepared or preserved (except as peanut butter) of headings 1202.10, 1202.20, or 2008.11, has been entered, no such products may be entered during the remainder of such period: 775,189 kg, provided that peanuts in the shell shall be charged against this quota on the basis of 75 kg for each 100 kg of peanuts in the shell.

Quotas—both the commodities affected and the rates charged—can change on short notice. For up-to-the minute information, or further details on quotas, contact the Port Director of Customs nearest you, or the U.S. Customs Quota Branch (see addresses at end of this chapter). For a general discussion of quotas refer to "Quotas Administered by Customs" on page 274.

Marking and Labeling Requirements

Seed Labeling Requirements. For seed lots containing alfalfa or red clover, a declaration of origin is required. Imports of seeds or other plant material protected under endangered species regulations must be accompanied by any appropriate permits or export documentation established by the country from which the material originates.

All shipments of seed must be accompanied by a declaration of labeling, which must include the following information: 1) kind and variety of seed (if agricultural seed, just kind; if vegetable, variety); 2) lot numbers and weight of each lot; 3) country of origin; 4) for treated seed: chemical name of treatment substance and warning statement. The sales invoice and labeling tags on the seed container usually suffice for this declaration. In addition, each shipping container should be stenciled or otherwise labeled to show the lot designation and the name of the kind, or kind and variety appearing on the invoice and other entry papers. For information on specific labeling requirements for the type of seed you are interested in importing, contact APHIS (see addresses at end of this chapter).

For a general discussion of U.S. Customs marking and labeling requirements, see "Country of Origin Marking" on page 236, "Special Marking Requirements" on page 238 and "Marking—False Impression" on page 239.

Shipping Considerations

You will need to ensure that your goods are packaged and shipped with care so that they arrive in good condition and pass smoothly through Customs. You are responsible for ensuring that the shipment is in compliance with all applicable government regulations for packaging and shipping. In most instances, you should not leave these arrangements solely to the discretion of your supplier. Careful preparation of the cargo and selection of the mode of transport can be essential to a cost-effective, time-

ly delivery of undamaged goods. We strongly advise you to consult your shipping representative, insurance agent, or freight broker for advice on packing and shipping.

Products of Chapter 12 vary widely in their mode of shipping and specific considerations. Some are transported in bulk, while others are packaged in much smaller lots. Seeds in particular must be packaged separately. General considerations include protection from contamination by dirt, pests, or other foreign matter, as well as the effects of heat and dampness on the goods shipped. Timeliness is an additional consideration for some products that require relatively quick transit time in order to arrive in good and marketable condition.

Publications and WWW Resources

The *Harmonized Tariff Schedule of the United States (2001)* (HTSUS) is available to view on the Customs Service website (www.customs.gov), or you may purchase a printed version from:

U.S. Government Printing Office
Superintendent of Documents
710 North Capital Street NW
Washington DC 20401
Tel: (202) 512-1800
Fax: (202) 512-1657
Website: www.access.gpo.gov

The USGPO also has copies of specific laws available for purchase. The USGPO accepts orders made by fax, phone or placed over the Internet, as well as mail orders paid by credit card. All orders must be accompanied by payment. Credit cards, checks drawn on a U.S. bank, or an international money order are all acceptable.

Relevant Government Agencies

Address your questions regarding USDA requirements for importation of seeds and other Chapter 12 products as well as your requests for permits to:

Animal and Plant Health Inspection Service (APHIS)
Plant Protection and Quarantine (PPQ)
Director's Office
4700 River Rd., Unit 131
Riverdale, MD 20737
Tel: (301) 734-8261
Tel (PPQ permits): (301) 734-8758

Seeds and noxious weeds: (301) 734-5708
Website: www.aphis.usda.gov/ppq

You may also address questions on importation of agricultural and vegetable seed to:

USDA Agricultural Marketing Service (AMS)
Seed Regulatory and Testing Branch
801 Summit Crossing Place, Suite C
Gastonia, NC 28054-2193
Tel: (704) 810-8870
Fax: (704) 852-4189
Website: www.usda.gov

Address questions regarding FDA requirements for the importation of plant products intended for human consumption or as medicaments to:

Food and Drug Administration (FDA)
Center for Food Safety and Applied Nutrition (CFSAN)
Office of Compliance
Division of Enforcement, Imports Branch
5100 Paint Branch Parkway
College Park, MD 20740-3835
Tel: (301) 436-2080
Website: http://vm.cfsan.fda.gov/list.html

Food and Drug Administration (FDA)
Center for Food Safety and Applied Nutrition (CFSAN)
Office of Plant and Dairy Foods and Beverages
5100 Paint Branch Parkway
College Park, MD 20740-3835
Tel: (301) 436-1700
Website: http://vm.cfsan.fda.gov/list.html

Food and Drug Administration (FDA)
Center for Drug Evaluation and Research
Office of Compliance
11919 Rockville Pike
Rockville, MD 20852
Tel: (301) 827-8910
Website: www.fda.gov/cder

Address your questions regarding endangered species restrictions for seed to:

U.S. Fish and Wildlife Service (FWS)
Office of Management Authority
4401 N. Fairfax Dr.
Arlington, VA 22203-0700
Tel: (703) 358-2104
Website: www.fws.gov

Address questions regarding allowable pesticide residues on plant products to:

Environmental Protection Agency (EPA)
Office of Pesticide Programs
Ariel Rios Building
1200 Pennsylvania Avenue NW
Mail Code 3213A
Washington DC 20460
Tel: (703) 305-7090
Website: www.epa.gov

Address questions regarding the importation of controlled substances (coca leaves) to:

Drug Enforcement Administration (DEA)
Office of Public Affairs
700 Army-Navy Drive
Arlington, VA 22202
Tel: (202) 307-1000
Website: www.dea.gov

Address your questions regarding quotas to:

U.S. Customs and Border Protection
Office of Field Operations, Quota Branch
1300 Pennsylvania Avenue NW
Washington DC 20229
Tel: (202) 927-5850
Website: www.customs.treas.gov

Address your questions regarding importation of seed to your local Customs port director or contact:

U.S. Customs and Border Protection
Customs Headquarters
1300 Pennsylvania Avenue NW
Washington DC 20229
Tel: (202) 354-1000
Website: www.customs.treas.gov

Laws and Regulations

The following laws and regulations may be relevant to the importation of plant products of Chapter 12. The laws are contained in the U.S. Code (USC) and the regulations are published in the Cope of Federal Regulations (CFR), both of which may be available at larger public and law libraries. Copies of specific laws are also available from the United States Government Printing Office (address above).

7 USC 1551 et seq.
Federal Seed Act
This Act restricts the entry of agricultural seed to ensure

that the seed is what its label says it is and is free from any noxious weed as identified in the Federal Seed Act (not the same as the noxious weeds listed in the Federal Noxious Weed Act). Purity and germination standards are no longer covered by this Act. Weeds specifically restricted under the act include: quack grass, Canada thistle, perennial sow thistle, dodder, whitetop, Johnsongrass, Russian knapweed, bindweed, and leafy spurge. A tolerance of two of these is allowed per given amount of seed.

7 USC 150aa et seq.
Federal Plant Pest Act (FPPA)
This Act defines, and prohibits the import of, seeds of parasitic plants as defined in the Act, and provides for the inspection of any letter, box, parcel, or container that may carry a plant pest. Inspection is to be performed by U.S. Department of Agriculture in conjunction with Customs.

7 CFR Part 351
Regulations for Entry and Inspection of Plants by Mail

These regulations set forth the plant imports that are prohibited, the requirements for entering restricted plants by mail, and the inspection procedures followed by the USDA's Animal and Plant Health Inspection Service (APHIS).

19 CFR 12.10 et seq.
Regulations for Entry and Release of Restricted Plants
These regulations prescribe the procedures followed by U.S. Customs to enforce the USDA requirements for importation of plants.

7 USC 2801
Federal Noxious Weed Act of 1974
This Act defines, delineates, and restricts weeds and their seeds found to be harmful to agricultural crops, livestock, irrigation, navigation, fish and wildlife resources, or public health. No tolerances are allowed.

7 USC 601 et seq.
Agricultural Adjustment Act (AAA)
This Act authorizes the Secretary of Agriculture to establish and maintain orderly market conditions for agricultural products, including cotton.

19 CFR Part 132
Regulations for Enforcement of AAA Quotas
These regulations provide for Customs enforcement of AAA quotas and higher duty rates imposed on imported agricultural products, whenever investigation reveals that orderly market conditions require such action.

7 CFR Part 34
Regulations of USDA on Tobacco Products Permits
These regulations describe the permitting process and the tobacco products requiring permits for exportation.

21 USC 801 et seq.
Controlled Substances Act
This Act gives the Drug Enforcement Administration of the Justice Department authority to restrict or prohibit importation of products defined as controlled substances under the Act and authorizes stringent controls on permitting, registration, recordkeeping, and distribution of such substances.

Convention on International Trade in Endangered Species of Wild Fauna and Flora (CITES)
This comprehensive wildlife treaty signed by over 100 countries, including the United States, regulates and in many cases prohibits commercial imports and exports of wild animal and plant species threatened by trade.

16 USC 1531
Endangered Species Act of 1973
This Act prohibits the import and export of plant and seed species listed as endangered and most species listed

as threatened. Seeds labeled as "of cultivated origin" may be traded. It is the U.S. law that implements CITES.

21 USC 301 et seq.
Federal Food, Drug, and Cosmetic Act
This Act prohibits deceptive practices and regulates the manufacture, sale and importation or exportation of food, drugs, cosmetics, and related products. It was amended by the Food Quality Protection Act of 1996. See 21 USC 331, 381, 382.

19 CFR 12.1 et seq.; 21 CFR 1.83 et seq.
Regulations on Food, Drugs, and Cosmetics
These regulations of the Secretary of Health and Human Services and the Secretary of the Treasury govern the standards, labeling, marking, and importing of products used with food, drugs, and cosmetics.

7 USC 136 et seq.
Federal Insecticide, Fungicide, and Rodenticide Act (FIFRA)
This Act prohibits the importation of pesticides or devices that are adulterated, misbranded, or otherwise violative of the Act, provides for registration of pesticides and devices, and establishes standards for labeling and classifying pesticides. It was amended by the Food Quality Protection Act of 1996.

19 CFR 12; 40 CFR 162
Regulations on Pesticides
These regulations set forth the procedures and guidelines for importing products exposed to pesticides.

Principal Exporting Countries

The following listing includes samples of the main supplier nations of the products of this chapter. It is organized by HTSUS major heading. (Refer to "Customs Classification" above for the product codes.) Countries are listed in rank order of the value of products imported to the U.S. Statistics represent customs value of entries for 2002 from the Bureau of Census, U.S. Department of Commerce.

1201—Canada, Argentina, China, Taiwan, Brazil, Chile, Japan, Uruguay, Nicaragua, Switzerland, Costa Rica, South Korea

1202—Argentina, Nicaragua, Mexico, South Africa, Brazil, South Korea,

1203—Malaysia, Vietnam

1204—Canada, Argentina, China, Netherlands, United Kingdom, Belgium, Mexico

1205—Canada, New Zealand, Belgium, United Kingdom

1206—Canada, China, Chile, Israel, Argentina, Netherlands, Egypt, Denmark, South Africa, Bulgaria, France

1207—Australia, India, Canada, Guatemala, Mexico, Ethiopia, Venezuela, China, El Salvador, Netherlands

1208—Canada, Argentina, Belgium, Taiwan, Netherlands, China, South Africa, Mexico

1209—Canada, Netherlands, Chile, Japan, China, France, Mexico, Denmark, Israel, Guatemala, Germany, Thailand, India, Australia

1210—Germany, France, United Kingdom, Australia, Czech Republic, New Zealand, Hong Kong, Slovenia

1211—China, India, Italy, Germany, Hong Kong, Mexico, Egypt

1212—China, Japan, South Korea, Canada, Chile, Philippines, Taiwan, United Kingdom, Tanzania

1213—Canada, Mexico, United Kingdom, India, China, Austria

1214—Canada, Denmark, Mexico, Germany, France, Australia, China, Cyprus

Chapter 13: Gums and Resins

Full title: Lac; Gums; Resins and Other Vegetable Saps and Extracts

This chapter relates to the importation of naturally occurring substances that are gelatinous when moist but harden when dry and are classified under Chapter 13 of the Harmonized Tariff Schedule of the United States (HTSUS). These products are usually imported to be used in producing a variety of other items, from varnishes to plastics to medicines to food additives, primarily as thickeners. They may be derived from insects (lac), plants (gums, resins, and saps), algae (agar-agar), or other organic sources. Note that opium and its derivatives such as morphine—controlled substances obtained from the sap of the opium poppy—are included in Chapter 13. If you are interested in importing products of Chapter 13 for use in food preparations, you should read this section in conjunction with the discussion about importing food at "Appendix: Foods" on page 825.

Commodity Index Chapter 13 does not cover a variety of related specific products such as organic extracts of licorice for confectionery (heading 1704); inulin (1108); malt extract (1901); extracts of coffee or tea (2101); extracts for the preparation of alcoholic beverages (Chapter 22); camphor and related products (2914 and 2938); medicaments (3003 and 3004); blood grouping reagents (3006); tanning and dyeing extracts (3201 and 3203); essential oils (Chapter 33); or natural rubber, chicle, and related gum products (4001).

Note: To understand key issues that will enable you to make best use of the information in this section we recommend that you see "Introduction" on page 425.

Key Factors

The key factors in the importation of lac, gums, resins, and related products are:

- Compliance with U.S. Food and Drug Administration (FDA) purity, identity, manufacturing, and other standards

- Compliance with FDA entry and notification requirements and procedures

- Compliance with the requirements of the Toxic Substances Control Act (TSCA) for products not covered by FDA entry notifications

- Compliance with Drug Enforcement Administration (DEA) requirements for permitting, importer registration, recordkeeping, and distribution (for importation of controlled substances)

Although most importers use the services of a licensed customs broker in making their entries, and we recommend this practice, you should be aware of the regulatory, entry, and documentation issues involved in importing your product. You, as importer, are ultimately responsible for the fulfillment of any legal requirements applicable to your shipment.

General Considerations

The importation of lacs, gums, resins, and related products is regulated by a variety of U.S. government agencies, the primary one being the FDA, which administers the provisions of the Food, Drug, and Cosmetic Act (FDCA). All plant and animal products entering the U.S. are subject to port of entry inspection by the Animal and Plant Health Inspection Service (APHIS) of the U.S. Department of Agriculture (USDA). Products that are imported for uses other than those covered in the FDCA must comply with the requirements of the TSCA, administered through the U.S. Customs Service by the U.S. Environmental Protection Agency (EPA). The DEA, a unit of the U.S. Department of Justice, licenses and controls the importation of opium and opium products—which are considered Schedule II items with a high potential for abuse—under the provisions of the Controlled Substances Act (CSA). If you are interested in importing opium products, contact the DEA (see addresses at end of this chapter).

Customs Classification

For customs purposes, lac, gums, resins, and other vegetable extracts are classified under Chapter 13 of the HTSUS. This chapter is broken into major headings, which are further divided into subheadings, and often sub-subheadings, each of which has its own HTSUS classification number. For example, the 2001 HTSUS number for balsam is 1301.90.90.10, indicating that it is a subcategory of other gum-resins and oleoresins, which is a subcategory of the major heading lac; natural gums, resins, gum-resins, and oleoresins (for example, balsams) (1301). There are two major headings within Chapter 13.

1301—Lac; natural gums, resins, gum-resins, and oleoresins (for example, balsams)

1302—Vegetable saps and extracts; pectic substances, pectinates, and pectates; agar-agar and other mucilages and thickeners derived from vegetable products

For more details regarding classification of the specific product you are interested in importing, consult a customs broker, the appropriate commodity specialist at your nearest customs port, or see HTSUS. The 2001 HTSUS is available online from the Customs Service (www.customs.gov/impoexpo/impoexpo.htm) or for purchase from the U.S. Government Printing Office (see resources at the end of this chapter), and may be found in larger public libraries. For a general discussion of customs classification, see "Classification—Liquidation" on page 229.

Dutiable Status of Goods

For more information about duty rates and binding decisions see "Dutiable Status of Goods" on page 203; for a discussion of temporary importation of goods see "Temporary Free Importations" on page 205.

Valuation

Importers have a responsibility to use what the U.S. Customs Service deems, "reasonable care," when determining the value of their goods. They must also provide any additional information that the Customs Service needs for setting a final value on the goods. This process involves a number of factors and can be somewhat complicated; importers must be aware of applicable issues and details. Valuation information applies to all types of commodities, for further discussion on the subject see "Customs Valuation" on page 267.

Import Duties

Import duties vary (often dramatically) depending upon the Harmonized Tariff Schedule (HTSUS) classification of the goods or products imported. Since some products that look alike have different HTSUS classifications and different rates of duty, proper classification is vital. Note that "differences of opinion" between importers and the Bureau of Customs and Border Protection regarding classification keeps customs attorneys very busy.

Import duties can be assessed on the imported value of the goods ("ad valorem" rates of duty such as 2%, 4.4%, 50%, etc.), total units or weight of the goods ("specific" rates of duty such as 2 cents each or 1.5 cents/pound, etc.) or on a combination basis ("compound" rates of duty such as 5 cents each plus 6%).

Listed below is a sampling of several Column 1 import duty rates for Chapter 13 products:
Gum arabic (1301.20.00.00): free
or
Vegetable saps and extracts of licorice (1302.12.00.00): 3.8%

For specific information on US import duties refer to the Harmonized Tariff Schedule of the US. The print version is available from the US Government Printing Office as well as third party suppliers who often add special features. Online versions are available in both static PDF pages as well as in formats with excellent search functionality. Search the Web with the term "Harmonized Tariff Schedule" to find sources.

Entry and Documentation

The entry of merchandise is a two-part process consisting of 1) filing the documentation necessary to determine whether merchandise may be released from Customs custody and 2) filing the documents that contain information for duty assessment and statistical purposes. In certain instances all documents must be filed and accepted by Customs prior to release of the goods. Unless you have been granted an extension, you must file entry documents at a location specified by the port or area director within five working days of your shipment's date of arrival at a U.S. port of entry. These include a number of standard documents required by Customs for any entry, and:

- TSCA certification

- DEA permits Form DEA 357 when required (contact DEA regarding permit requirements for importation of controlled substances)

After you present the entry, Customs may examine your shipment, or may waive examination. The shipment is then released provided no legal or regulatory violations have been noted. You must then file entry summary documentation and deposit estimated duties at a designated customhouse within 10 working days of your shipment's release. For a detailed description of entry procedures, standard documentation, and informal entry, see "Entry Process" on page 185.

Informed Compliance. Informed compliance was introduced with the Customs Modernization Act of 1993 (Mod Act) and defines the relationship between importers and the Customs Service. It sets out the responsibilities of both parties. Providing the correct documentation and information for entry is a key factor that will make your importing operation run smoothly. We recommend that importers become familiar with the concept of informed comliance and the responsibilities that they have under the Mod Act. For further discussion about informed compliance see "Informed Compliance" on page 211.

Note: The Entry and Documentation section has been carefully designed to supply you, the importer, with sample documents and directions on how to satisfy Customs requirements. Be aware that you should consult the applicable authorities to ensure that you are correctly following the most current procedures.

Prohibitions and Restrictions

Specific requirements for importation of products covered under Chapter 13 generally depend on their intended use, and some products that may be allowed entry for a particular use may be subject to controls if imported for an alternative use.

Marking and Labeling Requirements

Specific labeling requirements depend on the use for which a particular product is intended. For a general discussion of U.S. Customs marking and labeling requirements, see "Country of Origin Marking" on page 236, "Special Marking Requirements" on page 238 and "Marking—False Impression" on page 239.

Shipping Considerations

You will need to ensure that your goods are packaged and shipped with care so that they arrive in good condition and pass smoothly through Customs. You are responsible for ensuring that the shipment is in compliance with all applicable government regulations for packaging and shipping. In most instances, you should not leave these arrangements solely to the discretion of your supplier. Careful preparation of the cargo and selection of the mode of transport can be essential to a cost-effective, timely delivery of undamaged goods. We strongly advise you to consult your shipping representative, insurance agent, or freight broker for advice on packing and shipping.

Because lac, gums, resins, and related products are soluble in water or other solvents, care should be taken to protect shipments from moisture. Also because of the intended use of many of these products as food additives or in medicinal preparations, and the fact that many can serve as a growth media for microorganisms, care must be taken that the products are packaged and handled so as to avoid contamination.

Publications and WWW Resources

The following publication explains the FDA requirements for importing lacs, gums, resins, and related products. It is published by the FDA and is available online from the FDA website (www.fda.gov/opacom/7pubs.html).

> *Requirements of Laws and Regulations Enforced by the U.S. Food and Drug Administration*

The *Harmonized Tariff Schedule of the United States (2001)* (HTSUS) is available to view on the Customs Service website (www.customs.gov), or you may purchase a printed version from:

U.S. Government Printing Office
Superintendent of Documents
710 North Capital Street NW
Washington DC 20401
Tel: (202) 512-1800
Fax: (202) 512-1657
Website: www.access.gpo.gov

The USGPO also has copies of specific laws available for purchase. The USGPO accepts orders made by fax, phone or placed over the Internet, as well as mail orders paid by credit card. All orders must be accompanied by payment. Credit cards, checks drawn on a U.S. bank, or an international money order are all acceptable.

Relevant Government Agencies

Address your inquiries regarding FDA requirements for importation of lacs, gums, resins, and related products for uses covered by the Food, Drug, and Cosmetic Act (FDCA) to:

Food and Drug Administration (FDA)
Center for Food Safety and Applied Nutrition (CFSAN)

Office of Compliance
Division of Enforcement, Imports Branch
5100 Paint Branch Parkway
College Park, MD 20740-3835
Tel: (301) 436-2080
Website: http://vm.cfsan.fda.gov/list.html

Food and Drug Administration (FDA)
Center for Food Safety and Applied Nutrition (CFSAN)
Office of Plant and Dairy Foods and Beverages
5100 Paint Branch Parkway
College Park, MD 20740-3835
Tel: (301) 436-1700
Website: http://vm.cfsan.fda.gov/list.html

Address your inquiries regarding USDA requirements for importation of lacs, gums, resins, and related products to:

Animal and Plant Health Inspection Service (APHIS)
Plant Protection and Quarantine (PPQ)
Director's Office
4700 River Rd., Unit 131
Riverdale, MD 20737
Tel: (301) 734-8261
Tel (PPQ permits): (301) 734-8758
Website: www.aphis.usda.gov/ppq

Address your inquiries regarding EPA requirements with respect to the TSCA for the importation of lac, gums, resins, and related products not intended for FDCA-approved uses to:

Environmental Protection Agency (EPA)
Office of Pollution Prevention and Toxics
TSCA System Information
1200 Pennsylvania Avenue NW
Washington DC 20460
Tel: (202) 564-3810
Tel: (202) 554-1404 (TSCA Information Hotline)
Email: oppt.homepage@epa.gov
Website: www.epa.gov/opptintr/contact.htm

Address questions regarding the importation of controlled substances (opium and its derivatives) to:

Drug Enforcement Administration (DEA)
Office of Public Affairs
700 Army-Navy Drive
Arlington, VA 22202
Tel: (202) 307-1000
Website: www.dea.gov

Address your questions regarding importation of lacs, gums, resins, and related products to your local Customs port director or contact:

U.S. Customs and Border Protection
Customs Headquarters
1300 Pennsylvania Avenue NW
Washington DC 20229
Tel: (202) 354-1000
Website: www.customs.treas.gov

Laws and Regulations

The following laws and regulations may be relevant to the importation of lacs, gums, resins, and related products. The laws are contained in the U.S. Code (USC) and the regulations are published in the Code of Federal Regulations (CFR), both of which may be available at larger public and law libraries. Copies of specific laws are also available from the United States Government Printing Office (address above).

21 USC 301 et seq.
Federal Food, Drug, and Cosmetic Act
This Act prohibits deceptive practices and regulates the manufacture, sale and importation or exportation of food, drugs, cosmetics, and related products. It was

amended by the Food Quality Protection Act of 1996. See 21 USC 331, 381, 382.

19 CFR 12.1 et seq.; 21 CFR 1.83 et seq.
Regulations on Food, Drugs, and Cosmetics
These regulations of the Secretary of Health and Human Services and the Secretary of the Treasury govern the standards, labeling, marking, and importing of products used with food, drugs, and cosmetics.

7 CFR Part 351
Regulations for Entry and Inspection of Plants by Mail
These regulations set forth the plant imports that are prohibited, the requirements for entering restricted plants by mail, and the inspection procedures followed by the US-DA's Animal and Plant Health Inspection Service (APHIS).

19 CFR 12.10 et seq.
Regulations for Entry and Release of Restricted Plants
These regulations prescribe the procedures followed by U.S. Customs to enforce the USDA requirements for importation of plants.

15 USC 2601 et seq.
Toxic Substances Control Act
This Act authorizes the EPA to determine whether a substance is harmful and to restrict importation, sale, and use of such substances.

19 CFR 12.118 et seq.
Regulations of Customs on Toxic Substances Control
These regulations require importers of chemical substances imported in bulk or as part of a mixture to certify to Customs that the shipment complies with the TSCA or is not subject to that Act.

21 USC 801 et seq.
Controlled Substances Act
This Act gives the Drug Enforcement Administration of the Justice Department authority to restrict or prohibit importation of products defined as controlled substances under the Act and authorizes stringent controls on permitting, registration, recordkeeping, and distribution of such substances.

Principal Exporting Countries

The following listing includes samples of the main supplier nations of the products of this chapter. It is organized by HTSUS major heading. (Refer to "Customs Classification" above for the product codes.) Countries are listed in rank order of the value of products imported to the U.S. Statistics represent customs value of entries for 2002 from the Bureau of Census, U.S. Department of Commerce.

1301—France, Chad, India, China, United Kingdom, Thailand, Germany, Sudan, Canada

1302—India, China, France, Denmark, Mexico, Australia, Spain, Germany, Italy

Chapter 14:
Vegetable Plaiting Materials

Full title: Vegetable Plaiting Materials; Vegetable Products Not Elsewhere Specified or Included

This section pertains to the importation of plaiting materials; vegetable materials used primarily as stuffing; vegetable materials used primarily for the manufacture of brushes and brooms; and miscellaneous vegetable materials, which are classified within Chapter 14 of the Harmonized Tariff Schedule of the United States (HTSUS). Specifically, it includes materials such as bamboo, rattan, reed, rush, osier, raffia, and prepared cereal straw; kapok; broomcorn and istle; and vegetable materials used primarily in dyeing and tanning.

If you are interested in importing finished products made of these materials, such as baskets, you should refer to Commodity Index Chapter 46. If you are interested in importing brooms and brushes—or intermediate products, such as prepared knots and tufts for the manufacture of these products—refer to Chapter 96. If you are interested in importing miscellaneous vegetable materials for use in the manufacture of textiles, refer to Chapter 53. Wood wool and chipwood made from plaiting materials are covered in Chapter 44. If you are interested in importing unprocessed cereal straw, refer to Chapter 12.

Note: To understand key issues that will enable you to make best use of the information in this section we recommend that you see "Introduction" on page 425.

Key Factors

The key factors in the importation of vegetable plaiting and related miscellaneous materials are:

- Random U.S. Department of Agriculture (USDA) port-of-entry inspections
- Import restrictions on certain plant materials
- Endangered species restrictions on certain plant materials

Although most importers utilize the services of a licensed customs broker in making their entries, and we recommend this practice, you should be aware of the regulatory, entry and documentation issues involved in importing your product. You, as importer, are ultimately responsible for the fulfillment of any legal requirements applicable to your shipment.

General Considerations

Importation of vegetable plaiting material and related miscellaneous plant products is regulated by the USDA under the Plant Quarantine Act (PQA). The USDA Animal Plant Health Inspection Service

(APHIS) Plant Protection and Quarantine (PPQ) branch inspects shipments of plaiting and related materials on a random basis, depending upon the port of entry, the risk factor involved in the type of material being offered for entry, etc. You do not generally need permits or licenses to import these products, but the type of plant material is pertinent (see Prohibitions and Restrictions, below). For most shipments of plaiting materials entering under Chapter 14, importation is straightforward. If you are importing related articles classified under different HTSUS chapters, there may be additional requirements administered by other governmental agencies. This depends entirely upon the specific article you are importing.

Restrictions under the Endangered Species Act (ESA) and the Convention on International Trade in Endangered Species (CITES) apply to plant materials of listed plants species, and are enforced by the U.S. Fish and Wildlife Service (FWS), usually in consultation with and often through the USDA. Regulations governing the importation of plant products are complex, and FWS permits or CITES documentation may be required. To ascertain what your legal responsibilities are, you should contact these agencies with specific identification of the materials you wish to import.

Customs Classification

For customs purposes, vegetable plaiting and related materials are classified under Chapter 14 of the HTSUS. This chapter is broken into major headings, which are further divided into subheadings, and often into sub-subheadings, each of which has its own HTSUS classification number. For example, the 2001 HTSUS number for willow (osier) is 1401.90.20, indicating that it is a subcategory of other vegetable materials (1401.90), which is a subcategory of the major heading, vegetable materials of a kind used primarily for plaiting (1401). There are four major headings in Chapter 14.

1401—Vegetable materials of a kind used primarily for plaiting (for example, bamboos, rattans, reeds, rushes, osier, raffia, cleaned, bleached, or dyed cereal straw, and lime bark)

1402—Vegetable materials of a kind used primarily as stuffing or as padding (for example, kapok, vegetable hair, and eelgrass), whether or not put up as a layer with or without supporting material

1403—Vegetable materials of a kind used primarily in brooms or in brushes (for example, broomcorn, piassava, couch grass, and istle), whether or not in hanks or bundles

1404—Vegetable products not elsewhere specified or included

For more details regarding classification of the specific product you are interested in importing, consult a customs broker, the appropriate commodity specialist at your nearest Customs port, or see HTSUS. The 2001 HTSUS is available online from the Customs Service (www.customs.gov/impoexpo/impoexpo.htm) or for purchase from the U.S. Government Printing Office (see resources at the end of this chapter), and may be found in larger public libraries. For a general discussion of customs classification, see "Classification—Liquidation" on page 229.

Dutiable Status of Goods

For more information about duty rates and binding decisions see "Dutiable Status of Goods" on page 203; for a discussion of temporary importation of goods see "Temporary Free Importations" on page 205.

Valuation

Importers have a responsibility to use what the U.S. Customs Service deems, "reasonable care," when determining the value of their goods. They must also provide any additional information that the Customs Service needs for setting a final value on the goods. This process involves a number of factors and can be somewhat complicated; importers must be aware of applicable issues and details. Valuation information applies to all types of commodities, for further discussion on the subject see "Customs Valuation" on page 267.

Import Duties

Import duties vary (often dramatically) depending upon the Harmonized Tariff Schedule (HTSUS) classification of the goods or products imported. Since some products that look alike have different HTSUS classifications and different rates of duty, proper classification is vital. Note that "differences of opinion" between importers and the Bureau of Customs and Border Protection regarding classification keeps customs attorneys very busy.

Import duties can be assessed on the imported value of the goods ("ad valorem" rates of duty such as 2%, 4.4%, 50%, etc.), total units or weight of the goods ("specific" rates of duty such as 2 cents each or 1.5 cents/pound, etc.) or on a combination basis ("compound" rates of duty such as 5 cents each plus 6%).

Listed below is a sampling of several Column 1 import duty rates for Chapter 14 products:
Bamboos (1401.10.00.00): free
to
Willow (osier) (1401.90.20.00): 4.4%

For specific information on US import duties refer to the Harmonized Tariff Schedule of the US. The print version is available from the US Government Printing Office as well as third party suppliers who often add special features. Online versions are available in both static PDF pages as well as in formats with excellent search functionality. Search the Web with the term "Harmonized Tariff Schedule" to find sources.

Entry and Documentation

The entry of merchandise is a two-part process consisting of 1) filing the documents necessary to determine whether merchandise may be released from Customs custody and 2) filing the documents that contain information for duty assessment and statistical purposes. In certain instances all documents must be filed and accepted by Customs prior to the release of the goods. Unless you have been granted an extension, you must file entry documents at a location specified by the port or area director within five working days of your shipment's date of arrival at a U.S. port of entry. These include a number of standard documents required by Customs for any entry, and:

- If applicable, USDA permits
- If applicable, FWS permits and/or export certification from the country of origin required under endangered species regulations

After you present the entry, Customs may examine your shipment, or may waive examination. The shipment is then released provided no legal or regulatory violations have been noted. You must then file entry summary documentation and deposit estimated duties at a designated customhouse within 10 working days of your shipment's release. For a detailed description of entry procedures, standard documentation, and informal entry, see "Entry Process" on page 185.

Informed Compliance. Informed compliance was introduced with the Customs Modernization Act of 1993 (Mod Act) and defines the relationship between importers and the Customs Service. It sets out the responsibilities of both parties. Providing the correct documentation and information for entry is a key factor that will make your importing operation run smoothly. We recommend that importers become familiar with the concept of informed comliance and the responsibilities that they have under the Mod Act. For further discussion about informed compliance see "Informed Compliance" on page 211.

Note: The Entry and Documentation section has been carefully designed to supply you, the importer, with sample documents and directions on how to satisfy Customs requirements. Be aware that you should consult the applicable authorities to ensure that you are correctly following the most current procedures.

Prohibitions and Restrictions

USDA Restrictions. In general, any shipment of vegetable plaiting material is subject to random port-of-entry inspection by USDA. If the inspector finds evidence of the presence of insects, you may be required to submit your shipment to USDA-prescribed fumigation procedures. If the insect is of a kind for which there is no viable U.S. treatment, your shipment will be refused. Our source at USDA assured us that most shipments that are found to be infested can be treated to allow entry.

The following USDA restrictions apply to the importation of vegetable plaiting and related materials. Shipments of the following plant materials will be inspected at the port of entry.

Grapevines. Shipments of grapevines must be accompanied by a Phytosanitary Certificate issued by the Plant Protection Service of the exporting country, attesting that the grapevines have been heat-treated to 135 degrees Fahrenheit (or the equivalent Celsius) for 2 hours. If your grapevines are dry (not green or fresh) and you have no certification to present to USDA at the port of entry, your shipment will be detained and samples will be taken and forwarded to the nearest USDA inspection station, where they will be examined under a microscope for viable or live buds. If the procedure reveals live buds, your shipment will be refused entry.

Rice straw. Rice straw must be accompanied by a Phytosanitary Certificate issued by the Plant Protection Service of the country of origin, attesting that the material has been fumigated with methyl bromide. The USDA may still refuse entry. Check with the USDA for conditions for admission of rice straw.

Tree Ferns. The importation of tree ferns is restricted under the Convention on International Trade in Endangered Species (CITES). Any such materials must meet applicable CITES requirements. The FWS is the regulatory agency generally responsible for monitoring compliance under endangered species regulation, but USDA enforces regulations applicable to plants and plant materials. If you are interested in importing this type of material, you should contact USDA PPQ branch (see addresses at end of this chapter) for instructions.

Willow. Green or fresh willow imported from Europe will be refused entry. Dry willow material from Europe is admissible, as are green or fresh willow from non-European countries.

Country-Specific Import Restrictions

Willows from Europe. Fresh or green willow materials from European countries are banned. Dry willow materials may be admitted. Fresh or green willow from other countries will be admitted.

Corn and Related Plants. Corn and closely related plants and their parts (including those of the genus *Chionachne, Coix, Echinochloa, Eleusina, Euchleana, Miscanthus, Panicum, Pennisetum, Polytoca, Sclerachne, Setaria, Sorghum, Trilobachne,* and *Tripsicum*), including materials used in plaiting and the manufacture of brooms and brushes—specifically broomcorn—are banned form importation into the U.S. if they originate from the following countries: Africa (all countries), Australia, Bangladesh, Bhutan, Brunei, Bulgaria, Burma (Myanmar), Cambodia (Kampuchea), Hong Kong, India, Nepal, New Zealand, North Korea, Oceania, Pakistan, Papua New Guinea, People's Republic of China, Philippines, Russia, and the other republics of the former Soviet Union, Singapore, South Korea, Sri Lanka, Taiwan, Thailand, and Vietnam. The import of corn-related products from other countries requires prior USDA approval.

Marking and Labeling Requirements

For a general discussion of U.S. Customs marking and labeling requirements, see "Country of Origin Marking" on page 236, "Special Marking Requirements" on page 238 and "Marking—False Impression" on page 239.

Shipping Considerations

You will need to ensure that your goods are packaged and shipped with care so that they arrive in good condition and pass smoothly through Customs. You are responsible for ensuring that the shipment is in compliance with all applicable government regulations for packaging and shipping. In most instances, you should not leave these arrangements solely to the discretion of your supplier. Careful preparation of the cargo and selection of the mode of transport can be essential to a cost-effective, timely delivery of undamaged goods. We strongly advise you to consult your shipping representative, insurance agent, or freight broker for advice on packing and shipping.

Vegetable plaiting and related materials may be transported in bulk or in other forms, such as in bales or bundles. General considerations include protection from infestation by insects or contamination by dirt or other foreign matter, as well as the effects of dampness on the materials.

Publications and WWW Resources

For questions regarding the Convention on Interantional Trade in Endangered Species of Wild Fauna and Flora (CITES) refer to:

CITES Secretariat
International Environment House
15 chemin des Anemones
1219 Chatelaine-Geneva
Switzerland
Tel: [41] (22) 917-8139/40
Fax: [41] (22) 797-3417
Website: www.cites.org
Email: cites@unep.ch

The *Harmonized Tariff Schedule of the United States (2001)* (HTSUS) is available to view on the Customs Service website (www.customs.gov), or you may purchase a printed version from:

U.S. Government Printing Office
Superintendent of Documents
710 North Capital Street NW
Washington DC 20401
Tel: (202) 512-1800
Fax: (202) 512-1657
Website: www.access.gpo.gov

The USGPO also has copies of specific laws available for purchase. The USGPO accepts orders made by fax, phone or placed over the Internet, as well as mail orders paid by credit card. All orders must be accompanied by payment. Credit cards, checks drawn on a U.S. bank, or an international money order are all acceptable.

Relevant Government Agencies

Address your questions regarding USDA requirements for imported basketry to:

Animal and Plant Health Inspection Service (APHIS)
Plant Protection and Quarantine (PPQ)
Director's Office
4700 River Rd., Unit 131
Riverdale, MD 20737
Tel: (301) 734-8261
Tel (PPQ permits): (301) 734-8758
Website: www.aphis.usda.gov/ppq

Address your questions regarding endangered species restrictions to:
U.S. Fish and Wildlife Service (FWS)
Office of Management Authority
4401 N. Fairfax Dr.
Arlington, VA 22203-0700
Tel: (703) 358-2104
Website: www.fws.gov

Address your questions regarding the importation of vegetable plaiting and related materials to your local Customs port director. For addresses refer to "U.S. Customs and Border Protection Offices" on page 65 or contact:

U.S. Customs and Border Protection
Customs Headquarters
1300 Pennsylvania Avenue NW
Washington DC 20229
Tel: (202) 354-1000
Website: www.customs.treas.gov

Laws and Regulations

The following laws and regulations may be relevant to the importation of vegetable plaiting and related materials. The laws are contained in the U.S. Code (USC) and the regulations are published in the code of Federal Regulations (CFR), both of which may be available at larger public and law libraries. Copies of specific laws are also available from the United States Government Printing Office (address above).

7 CFR Part 351
Regulations for Entry and Inspection of Plants by Mail
These regulations set forth the plant imports that are prohibited, the requirements for entering restricted plants by mail, and the inspection procedures followed by the USDA's Animal and Plant Health Inspection Service (APHIS).

19 CFR 12.10 et seq.
Regulations for Entry and Release of Restricted Plants
These regulations prescribe the procedures followed by U.S. Customs to enforce the USDA requirements for importation of plants.

Convention on International Trade in Endangered Species of Wild Fauna and Flora (CITES)
This comprehensive wildlife treaty signed by over 100 countries, including the United States, regulates and in many cases prohibits commercial imports and exports of wild animal and plant species threatened by trade.

16 USC 1531
Endangered Species Act of 1973
This Act prohibits the import and export of plant and seed species listed as endangered and most species listed as threatened. It is the U.S. law that implements CITES.

21 USC 301 et seq.
Federal Food, Drug, and Cosmetic Act
This Act prohibits deceptive practices and regulates the manufacture, sale and importation or exportation of food, drugs, cosmetics, and related products. It was amended by the Food Quality Protection Act of 1996. See 21 USC 331, 381, 382.

19 CFR 12.1 et seq.; 21 CFR 1.83 et seq.
Regulations on Food, Drugs, and Cosmetics
These regulations of the Secretary of Health and Human Services and the Secretary of the Treasury govern the standards, labeling, marking, and importing of products used with food, drugs, and cosmetics.

Principal Exporting Countries

The following listing includes samples of the main supplier nations of the products of this chapter. It is organized by HTSUS major heading. (Refer to "Customs Classification" above for the product codes.) Countries are listed in rank order of the value of products imported to the U.S. Statistics represent customs value of entries for 2002 from the Bureau of Census, U.S. Department of Commerce.

1401—China, Madagascar, Singapore, Hong Kong, Philippines, Taiwan, Mexico

1402—Indonesia, Thailand, Lithuania, China, India, South Korea

1403—Mexico, Hungary, India, China, Ethiopia, Germany

1404—Mexico, Argentina, Canada, Brazil, China, India, Peru, Syria, Germany, Taiwan

Chapter 15: Animal or Vegetable Fats and Oils

Full title: Animal or Vegetable Fats and Oils and their Cleavage Products; Prepared Edible Fats; Animal or Vegetable Waxes

This chapter relates to the importation of animal or vegetable fats or oils and related products; prepared edible oils; and organic waxes, which are classified under Chapter 15 of the Harmonized Tariff Schedule of the United States (HTSUS). Specifically, it includes rendered lard; tallow; stearins and related products; fish and other marine oils; wool grease and lanolin; other animal fats; soybean, peanut, olive oil, and related blends; palm oil; sunflower, cottonseed, and safflower oils; coconut oil; rapeseed and related oils; linseed oil, corn oil, and other vegetable oils; hydrogenated and partially hydrogenated animal and vegetable fats and oils; margarine and other cooking and edible oils; chemically-modified industrial animal or vegetable oils; industrial fatty acids; glycerol; vegetable and animal waxes; and degras and related products. If you are interested in importing products of Chapter 15 for use as foods or in food preparations, you should refer to "Appendix: Foods" on page 825 and read this section in conjunction with that section.

If you are interested in importing raw, unrendered pig or poultry fat, refer to Commodity Index Chapter 2. Importation of butter and products with butterfat content of up to 45 percent as well as related dairy products is covered under Chapter 4. If you are interested in importing cocoa butter, fat, or oil, refer to Chapter 18. Edible products containing more than 45 percent by weight of dairy fats and oils are classified under Chapter 21. Oilcake destined for processing into animal feed is classified within Chapter 23. Cod liver oil and related products are covered within Chapter 30 when put up as medicaments. In general, fatty acids and related products intended for use in the manufacture of other products, including waxes, medicaments, paints, varnishes, perfumes, or soaps and toilet articles are classified and treated under the specific headings for those products.

Note: To understand key issues that will enable you to make best use of the information in this section we recommend that you see "Introduction" on page 425.

Key Factors

The key factors in the importation of animal or vegetable fats or oils and related products are:

- Compliance with U.S. Food and Drug Administration (FDA) purity, identity, manufacturing, and other standards

- Compliance with FDA entry notification requirements and other procedures

- Compliance with U.S. Environmental Protection Agency (EPA) regulations on pesticide residues in imported agriculture products

Although most importers utilize the services of a licensed customs broker in making their entries, and we recommend this practice, you should be aware of the regulatory, entry, and documentation issues involved in importing your product. You, as importer, are ultimately responsible for the fulfillment of any legal requirements applicable to your shipment.

General Considerations

The importation of animal or vegetable fats or oils and related products falls primarily under the jurisdiction of the FDA, which enforces the provisions of the Federal Food, Drug, and Cosmetic Act (FDCA). FDA regulations regarding importation of food items of any kind are extensive and stringent. Such products imported into the U.S. must comply with all requirements for those produced domestically.

Imported products regulated by the FDA are subject to FDA port of entry inspection. For a general discussion of required FDA import procedures, see "Appendix: Foods" on page 825.

The EPA enforces the Federal Insecticide, Fungicide, and Rodenticide Act (FIFRA) and the Food Quality Protection Act of 1996, which establish regulatory limits on pesticide residues in edible plant products. For more information, contact EPA (see addresses at end of this chapter).

Detention of Shipment. If your shipment is found to be noncomplying, it may be detained at the port of entry. In the case of products subject to FDA jurisdiction, the FDA may allow you to bring such a shipment into compliance before making a final decision regarding admittance. However, any sorting, reprocessing, or relabeling must be supervised by FDA personnel and is done at the importer's expense. Such conditional release to allow the importer to bring a shipment into compliance is a privilege, not a right. The FDA may consider subsequent noncomplying shipments of the same type of product to constitute abuse of the privilege and require the importer to destroy or reexport the products. To ascertain what your legal responsibilities are, you should contact these agencies regarding the specific items to be imported.

Customs Classification

For customs purposes, animal and vegetable fats and oils and related products are classified under Chapter 15 of the HTSUS. This chapter is broken into major headings, which are further divided into subheadings, and often into sub-subheadings, each of which has its own HTSUS classification number. For example, the 2001 HTSUS number for denatured rape or colza seed oil is 1514.90.50.10, indicating that it is a subcategory of other oil (1514.90), which is a subcategory of the major heading Rapeseed, colza, or mustard oil, and fractions thereof, whether or not refined, but not chemically modified (1514). There are 22 major headings in Chapter 15.

1501—Pig fat (including lard) and poultry fat, other than that of heading 0209 or 1503

1502—Fats of bovine animals, sheep, or goats, other than those of heading 1503

1503—Lard stearin, lard oil, oleostearin, oleo-oil, and tallow oil, not emulsified or mixed or otherwise prepared

1504—Fats and oils and their fractions, of fish or marine mammals, whether or not refined, but not chemically modified

1505—Wool grease and fatty substances derived therefrom (including lanolin)

1506—Other animal fats and oils and their fractions, whether or not refined, but not chemically modified

1507—Soybean oil and its fractions, whether or not refined, but not chemically processed

1508—Peanut (ground-nut) oil and its fractions, whether or not refined, but not chemically modified

1509—Olive oil and its fractions, whether or not refined, but not chemically modified

1510—Other oils and their fractions, obtained solely from olives, whether or not refined, but not chemically modified, including blends of these oils and fractions with oils or fractions of heading 1509

1511—Palm oil and its fractions, whether or not refined, but nor chemically modified

1512—Sun-flower seed, safflower, or cottonseed oil, and fractions thereof, whether or not refined, but not chemically modified

1513—Coconut (copra), palm kernel, or babassu oil, and fractions thereof, whether or not refined, but not chemically modified

1514—Rapeseed, colza, or mustard oil, and fractions thereof, whether or not refined, but not chemically modified

1515—Other fixed vegetable fats and oils (including jojoba oil) and their fractions, whether or not refined, but not chemically modified

1516—Animal or vegetable fats and oils and their fractions, partly or wholly hydrogenated, inter-esterified, re-esterified or elaidinized, whether or not refined, but not further prepared

1517—Margarine; edible mixtures or preparations of animal or vegetable fats or oils or of fractions of different fats or oils of this chapter, other than edible fats or oils or their fractions of heading 1516

1518—Animal or vegetable fats or oils and their fractions, boiled, oxidized, dehydrated, sulfurized, blown, polymerized by heat in vacuum or in inert gas or otherwise chemically modified, excluding those of heading 1516; inedible mixtures or preparations of animal or vegetable fats or oils or of fractions of different fats or oils of this chapter not elsewhere specified or included

1519—Industrial monocarboxylic fatty acids; acid oils from refining; industrial fatty alcohols

1520—Glycerol, crude; glycerol waters and glycer lyes

1521—Vegetable waxes (other than triglycerides), beeswax, other insect waxes and spermaceti, whether or not refined or colored

1522—Degras; residues resulting from the treatment of fatty substances or animal or vegetable waxes

For more details regarding classification of the specific product you are interested in importing, consult a customs broker, the appropriate commodity specialist at your nearest customs port, or see HTSUS. The 2001 HTSUS is available online from the Customs Service (www.customs.gov/impoexpo/impoexpo.htm) or for purchase from the U.S. Government Printing Office (see resources at the end of this chapter), and may be found in larger public libraries. For a general discussion of customs classification, see "Classification—Liquidation" on page 229.

Dutiable Status of Goods

For more information about duty rates and binding decisions see "Dutiable Status of Goods" on page 203; for a discussion of temporary importation of goods see "Temporary Free Importations" on page 205.

Valuation

Importers have a responsibility to use what the U.S. Customs Service deems, "reasonable care," when determining the value of their goods. They must also provide any additional information that the Customs Service needs for setting a final value on the goods. This process involves a number of factors and can be somewhat complicated; importers must be aware of applicable issues and details. Valuation information applies to all types of commodities, for further discussion on the subject see "Customs Valuation" on page 267.

Import Duties

Import duties vary (often dramatically) depending upon the Harmonized Tariff Schedule (HTSUS) classification of the goods or products imported. Since some products that look alike have different HTSUS classifications and different rates of duty, proper classification is vital. Note that "differences of opinion" between importers and the Bureau of Customs and Border Protection regarding classification keeps customs attorneys very busy.

Import duties can be assessed on the imported value of the goods ("ad valorem" rates of duty such as 2%, 4.4%, 50%, etc.), total units or weight of the goods ("specific" rates of duty such as 2 cents each or 1.5 cents/pound, etc.) or on a combination basis ("compound" rates of duty such as 5 cents each plus 6%).

Listed below is a sampling of several Column 1 import duty rates for Chapter 15 products:
Palm oil's fraction, crude oil (1511.10.00.00): free
to
Vegetable fat and oil fraction, rapeseed oil (1516.20.10.00) 7.7%

For specific information on US import duties refer to the Harmonized Tariff Schedule of the US. The print version is available from the US Government Printing Office as well as third party suppliers who often add special features. Online versions are available in both static PDF pages as well as in formats with excellent search functionality. Search the Web with the term "Harmonized Tariff Schedule" to find sources.

Entry and Documentation

The entry of merchandise is a two-part process consisting of 1) filing the documents necessary to determine whether merchandise may be released from Customs custody and 2) filing the documents that contain information for duty assessment and statistical purposes. In certain instances all documents must be filed and accepted by Customs prior to release of the goods. Unless you have been granted an extension, you must file entry documents at a location specified by the port or area director within five working days of your shipment's date of arrival at a U.S. port of entry. These include a number of standard documents required by Customs for any entry.

After you present the entry, Customs may examine your shipment, or may waive examination. The shipment is then released provided no legal or regulatory violations have been noted. You must then file entry summary documentation and deposit estimated duties at a designated customhouse within 10 working days of your shipment's release. For a detailed description of entry procedures, standard documentation, and informal entry, see "Entry Process" on page 185.

Informed Compliance. Informed compliance was introduced with the Customs Modernization Act of 1993 (Mod Act) and defines the relationship between importers and the Customs Service. It sets out the responsibilities of both parties. Providing the correct documentation and information for entry is a key factor that will make your importing operation run smoothly. We recommend that importers become familiar with the concept of informed compliance and the responsibilities that they have under the Mod Act. For further discussion about informed compliance see "Informed Compliance" on page 211.

Note: The Entry and Documentation section has been carefully designed to supply you, the importer, with sample documents and directions on how to satisfy Customs requirements. Be aware that you should consult the applicable authorities to ensure that you are correctly following the most current procedures.

Prohibitions and Restrictions

Edible Oils. Margarine is subject to extensive regulation and standards found in 21 CFR 166, to which all imported products must conform. If you are importing olive oil, you must be sure your product complies with the established standard: olive oil is the edible oil expressed from the sound, mature fruit of the olive tree. Refined or extracted oil is not entitled to the unqualified name "olive oil." Other vegetable oils should be labeled by their common or usual name, such as cottonseed, sunflower, peanut, and sesame. If you import mixtures of edible oils, be sure they are labeled to show all the oils present, with names listed in descending order of prominence in the product. If the terms "vegetable oil" or "shortening" are used in food labeling, the plant and animal source of each oil or fat used in the product must be identified on the label (31 CFR 101).

Inedible Oils. Olive, palm kernel, rapeseed, sunflower, and sesame oils may be imported outside FDCA regulations and duty free for industrial or mechanical use, provided that they have been denatured and rendered unfit for food use. To qualify for this provision, such oils must bear certification from their country of origin that their method of production has rendered them unfit for consumption, or they must undergo prescribed processes under Customs supervision prior to release at the expense of the importer rendering them unfit. Customs will sample all lots of oils for which denatured status is claimed (19 CFR 10.56).

Cod Liver Oil. Cod liver oil is recognized as a drug in the U.S. Pharmacopoeia (USP). It is therefore both a food and a drug, and subject to both the food and drug provisions of the FDCA. If you are interested in importing cod liver oil, you should refer to Commodities Index Chapter 30. Any shipment you import into the U.S. as cod liver oil must conform to the USP identity standard for cod liver oil, as well as any other USP specifications for the product.

Quotas

Artificial mixtures of two or more of the products provided for in headings 1501 to 1515, inclusive (1517.90.40) are subject to the following quotas: 1) entry of products enumerated in 9904.10.75 is prohibited; 2) entry of products enumerated in 9904.10.81 is limited to 1,016,046 kg from Australia, 154,221 kg from Belgium and Denmark (aggregate), and none from other countries.

Quotas—both the commodities affected and rates charged—can change on short notice. For up-to-the-minute information, or further details on quotas, contact the U.S. Customs Service Quota Branch (see addresses at end of this chapter). For a general discussion of quotas, refer to "Quotas Administered by Customs" on page 274.

Marking and Labeling

For information about marking and labeling of foods for import see "Appendix: Foods" on page 825. For a general discussion of U.S. Customs marking and labeling requirements, see "Country of Origin Marking" on page 236, "Special Marking Requirements" on page 238 and "Marking—False Impression" on page 239.

Shipping Considerations

You will need to ensure that your goods are packaged and shipped with care so that they arrive in good condition and pass smoothly through Customs. You are responsible for ensuring that the shipment is in compliance with all applicable government regulations for packaging and shipping. In most instances, you should not leave these arrangements solely to the discretion of your supplier. Careful preparation of the cargo and selection of the mode of transport can be essential to a cost-effective, timely delivery of undamaged goods. We strongly advise you to consult your shipping representative, insurance agent, or freight broker for advice on packing and shipping.

Products of Chapter 15 vary in their mode of shipping, packaging, and special considerations. Some are transported in bulk, while others are packaged in much smaller lots. General considerations include protection from contamination by dirt, insects, or other foreign matter, as well as the effects of heat and dampness on the goods shipped. Timeliness is an additional consideration for some products that require relatively quick transit time in order to arrive in good and marketable condition.

Publications and WWW Resources

The following publication explains the FDA requirements for importing fats and oils. It is published by the FDA and is available online from the FDA website (www.fda.gov/opacom/7pubs.html).

Requirements of Laws and Regulations Enforced by the U.S. Food and Drug Administration

*T*The *Harmonized Tariff Schedule of the United States (2001)* (HTSUS) is available to view on the Customs Service website (www.customs.gov), or you may purchase a printed version from:

U.S. Government Printing Office
Superintendent of Documents
710 North Capital Street NW
Washington DC 20401
Tel: (202) 512-1800
Fax: (202) 512-1657
Website: www.access.gpo.gov

The USGPO also has copies of specific laws available for purchase. The USGPO accepts orders made by fax, phone or placed over the Internet, as well as mail orders paid by credit card. All orders must be accompanied by payment. Credit cards, checks drawn on a U.S. bank, or an international money order are all acceptable.

Relevant Government Agencies

Address your questions regarding FDA requirements for the importation of fats and oils of Chapter 15 to:

Food and Drug Administration (FDA)
Center for Food Safety and Applied Nutrition (CFSAN)
5100 Paint Branch Parkway
College Park, MD 20740-3835
Website: http://vm.cfsan.fda.gov/list.html

Office of Field Programs, Div. of Enforcement, Imports Br.:
Tel: (202) 205-4606
Office of Plant and Dairy Foods and Beverages:
Tel: (301) 436-1700
Website: http://vm.cfsan.fda.gov/list.html

Address your questions regarding allowable pesticide residues in fats and oils to:

Environmental Protection Agency (EPA)
Office of Pesticide Programs
Ariel Rios Building
1200 Pennsylvania Avenue NW
Mail Code 3213A

Washington DC 20460
Tel: (703) 305-7090
Website: www.epa.gov

Address your questions regarding quotas to:
U.S. Customs and Border Protection
Office of Field Operations, Quota Branch
1300 Pennsylvania Avenue NW
Washington DC 20229
Tel: (202) 927-5850
Website: www.customs.treas.gov

Address your questions regarding importation of fats and oils of Chapter 15 to your local Customs port director. For addresses refer to "U.S. Customs and Border Protection Offices" on page 65 or contact:

U.S. Customs and Border Protection
Customs Headquarters
1300 Pennsylvania Avenue NW
Washington DC 20229
Tel: (202) 354-1000
Website: www.customs.treas.gov

Laws and Regulations

The following laws and regulations may be relevant to the importation of fats and oils of Chapter 15. The laws are contained in the U.S. Code (USC) and the regulations are published in the Code of Federal Regulations (CFR), both of which may be available at larger public and law libraries. Copies of specific laws are also available from the United States Government Printing Office (address above).

21 USC 301 et seq.
Federal Food, Drug, and Cosmetic Act
This Act prohibits deceptive practices and regulates the manufacture, sale and importation or exportation of food, drugs, cosmetics, and related products. It was amended by the Food Quality Protection Act of 1996. See 21 USC 331, 381, 382.

19 CFR 12.1 et seq.; 21 CFR 1.83 et seq.
Regulations on Food, Drugs, and Cosmetics
These regulations of the Secretary of Health and Human Services and the Secretary of the Treasury govern the standards, labeling, marking, and importing of products used with food, drugs, and cosmetics.

7 USC 136 et seq.
Federal Insecticide, Fungicide, and Rodenticide Act (FIFRA)
This Act prohibits the importation of pesticides or devices that are adulterated, misbranded, or otherwise violative of the Act, provides for registration of pesticides and devices, and establishes standards for labeling and classifying pesticides. It was amended by the Food Quality Protection Act of 1996.

19 CFR 12; 40 CFR 162
Regulations on Pesticides
These regulations set forth the procedures and guidelines for importing products exposed to pesticides.

Principal Exporting Countries

The following listing includes samples of the main supplier nations of the products of this chapter. It is organized by HTSUS major heading. (Refer to "Customs Classification" above for the product codes.) Countries are listed in rank order of the value of products imported to the U.S. Statistics represent customs value entries for 1993 from the Bureau of Census, U.S. Department of Commerce.

1501—Canada, Bahamas, Haiti, France, Poland

1502—Canada, Mexico

1503—Canada

1504—Norway, Canada, United Kingdom, Mexico, Japan, Colombia, Germany, Netherlands, Australia, South Korea, Venezuela, China, Sweden, Iceland

1505—United Kingdom, Japan, Singapore, Australia, Belgium, Germany, Switzerland, France, Mexico

1506—Australia, Canada, Netherlands, United Kingdom

1507—Canada, Sweden, France, Mexico, Argentina, Taiwan, Belgium, Japan, United Arab Emirates, Brazil

1508—Argentina, Nicaragua, Canada, Germany, Hong Kong, China, Guinea, United Kingdom

1509—Italy, Spain, Turkey, Greece, Portugal, Tunisia, Argentina, France, Morocco, Lebanon, Switzerland, United Kingdom, Egypt, Mexico

1510—Italy, Spain, Greece, Portugal, Morocco, Turkey, Taiwan, Syria, France, Poland

1511—Malaysia, Belgium, Indonesia, Colombia, Philippines, Ghana, Guinea, Singapore, Ivory Coast, Jordan, Dominican Republic, Liberia, Sierra Leone, Netherlands, United Kingdom

1512—Mexico, Argentina, France, Japan, Australia, Switzerland, Spain, Germany, Canada

1513—Philippines, Malaysia, Indonesia, India, Ghana, Sri Lanka

1514—Canada, United Kingdom, China, Switzerland, Australia, Germany, Netherlands, France

1515—Canada, India, France, Japan

1516—Canada, Brazil, India, Germany, Italy, Norway

1517—Canada, United Kingdom, Netherlands, Denmark, Argentina

1518—Canada, South Korea, United Kingdom, Switzerland, Netherlands, Brazil, India, Indonesia, Mexico, Germany, France

1520—Malaysia, Germany, Ecuador, Canada, Mexico, Indonesia, Spain, Japan, United Kingdom, Peru, Guatemala, Honduras, China, France

1521—Brazil, Mexico, Japan, Germany, China, Canada, Argentina, Australia, France, Ethiopia, Central African Republic

1522—Canada, Germany, Brazil, France

Chapter 16:
Meat and Fish Preparations

Full title: Preparations of Meat, of Fish, or of Crustaceans, Molluscs, or Other Aquatic Invertebrates

This chapter relates to the importation of edible preparations of meat and fish and related animals, which are classified under Chapter 16 of the Harmonized Tariff Schedule of the United States (HTSUS). Specifically, it includes meat sausage, homogenized preparations of meat or poultry (primarily baby foods), prepared and canned meats (such as canned hams and corned beef), extracts and juices of fish, prepared or preserved fish (including caviar and canned tuna and salmon), fish sticks, fish paste, packed crabmeat, shrimp, lobster, and oysters, and other similar products. In general, any product that by weight includes 20% prepared meat, poultry, fish, or other seafood is included in Chapter 16. You should refer to "Appendix: Foods" on page 825 in conjunction with this section.

If you are interested in importing fresh or provisionally preserved meat, including smoked and cured meats such as some hams, refer to Commodity Index Chapter 2. Fresh or provisionally preserved fish, crustaceans, molluscs, and similar aquatic invertebrates are covered in Chapter 3. Live animals—meat on the hoof—are dealt with in Chapter 1. If you are interested in importing prepared foods made predominately of flour that have an incidental component of prepared meat, poultry, or fish—such as filled pasta products—refer to Chapter 19. Prepared foods that do not contain meat or fish—those made primarily of fruit, vegetables, and nuts—are covered in Chapter 20. Products of animal origin not fit or intended for human consumption are classified in Chapters 5 and 23.

Note: To understand key issues that will enable you to make best use of the information in this section we recommend that you see "Introduction" on page 425.

Key Factors

The key factors in the importation of these products are:

- Compliance with U.S. Food and Drug Administration (FDA) purity, identity, manufacturing, and other standards

- Compliance with FDA entry notification and other procedures

- Compliance with U.S. Department of Agriculture (USDA) Animal and Plant Health Inspection Services (APHIS) and the Food Safety and Inspection Service (FSIS) requirements; permits may be required

Although most importers utilize the services of a licensed customs broker in making their entries, and we recommend this practice, you should be aware of the regulatory, entry, and documentary issues involved in importing your product. You, as importer, are ultimately responsible for the fulfillment of any legal requirements applicable to your shipment.

General Considerations

Regulatory Agencies. Importation of prepared meat and fish products falls primarily under the jurisdiction of the FDA, which enforces the requirements of the Federal Food, Drug, and Cosmetic Act (FDCA). The USDA controls imports of meat, poultry, fish, and seafood products to prevent contamination of U.S. food sources. The FWS regulates importation of products prepared from endangered species and wildlife.

FDA Requirements. FDA regulations regarding importation of foods of any kind are extensive and stringent. Meat and fish products prepared from wild game and domesticated varieties of wild animals also fall within the FDA's purview. Prepared foods imported into the U.S. must comply with all requirements for those produced domestically.

FDA Inspections. Imported products regulated by the FDA are subject to port of entry inspection. For a general discussion of required FDA importing procedures see "Appendix: Foods" on page 825.

Detention of Shipment. If your shipment is found to be noncomplying, the FDA inspector may detain it at the port of entry. The FDA may allow you to bring the shipment into compliance before making a final decision regarding admittance. However, any sorting, reprocessing, or relabeling must be supervised by FDA personnel and is done at the importer's expense. Such conditional release to allow the importer to bring a shipment into compliance is a privilege, not a right. The FDA may consider subsequent noncomplying shipments of the same type of product to constitute abuse of the privilege and require the importer to destroy or reexport the products. To ascertain what your legal responsibilities are, you should contact the FDA regarding the specific items to be imported.

USDA Requirements. APHIS and FSIS are the main USDA agencies responsible for enforcement of the regulations on the import of meat, poultry, fish, and seafood. You should check with these agencies to ascertain what your USDA responsibilities are with respect to imports of HTSUS Chapter 16 products.

Wildlife Products. If you are interested in importing products prepared from exotic animals, you should consult the U.S. Fish and Wildlife Service (FWS), which administers the provisions of the Endangered Species Act (ESA) and the Convention on International Trade in Endangered Species of Wild Fauna and Flora (CITES), to be sure that your intended import is not covered by these regulations. No animal products derived from animals on these lists may be imported. There are many restrictions on the importation and sale of any products derived from wild animals. However, products made from the meat of animals raised in captivity is unlikely to fall within the jurisdiction of endangered species legislation.

Customs Classification

For customs purposes, preparations of meat and fish are classified under Chapter 16 of the HTSUS. This chapter is divided into major headings, which are further divided into subheadings, and often into sub-subheadings, each of which has its own HTSUS classification number. For example, the 2001 HTSUS number for beef sausages and similar products, of offal or blood or of food preparations based on these products other than in airtight containers is 1601.00.60.20, indicating that it is a subcategory of meat preparations other than pork or beef in airtight containers

(1601.00.60), which is a subcategory of sausages and similar products of meat, meat offal, or blood; food preparations based on these products (1601). There are five major headings in HTSUS Chapter 16.

1601—Sausages and similar products, of meat, meat offal, or blood; food preparations based on these products

1602—Other prepared or preserved meat, meat offal, or blood

1603—Extracts and juices of meat, fish, or crustaceans, molluscs, or other aquatic invertebrates

1604—Prepared or preserved fish; caviar and caviar substitutes prepared from fish eggs

1605—Crustaceans, molluscs, and other aquatic invertebrates, prepared or preserved

For more details regarding classification of then specific product you are interested in importing, consult a customs broker, the appropriate commodity specialist at your nearest customs port, or se HTSUS. The 2001 HTSUS is available online from the Customs Service (www.customs.gov/impoexpo/impoexpo.htm) or for purchase from the U.S. Government Printing Office (see resources at the end of this chapter), and may be found in larger public libraries. For a general discussion of customs classification, see "Classification—Liquidation" on page 229.

Dutiable Status of Goods

For more information about duty rates and binding decisions see "Dutiable Status of Goods" on page 203; for a discussion of temporary importation of goods see "Temporary Free Importations" on page 205.

Valuation

Importers have a responsibility to use what the U.S. Customs Service deems, "reasonable care," when determining the value of their goods. They must also provide any additional information that the Customs Service needs for setting a final value on the goods. This process involves a number of factors and can be somewhat complicated; importers must be aware of applicable issues and details. Valuation information applies to all types of commodities, for further discussion on the subject see "Customs Valuation" on page 267.

Import Duties

Import duties vary (often dramatically) depending upon the Harmonized Tariff Schedule (HTSUS) classification of the goods or products imported. Since some products that look alike have different HTSUS classifications and different rates of duty, proper classification is vital. Note that "differences of opinion" between importers and the Bureau of Customs and Border Protection regarding classification keeps customs attorneys very busy.

Import duties can be assessed on the imported value of the goods ("ad valorem" rates of duty such as 2%, 4.4%, 50%, etc.), total units or weight of the goods ("specific" rates of duty such as 2 cents each or 1.5 cents/pound, etc.) or on a combination basis ("compound" rates of duty such as 5 cents each plus 6%).

Listed below is a sampling of several Column 1 import duty rates for Chapter 16 products:
Corned beef in airtight containers (1602.50.10): free
to
Clam juice (1603.00.10.00): 8.5%

For specific information on US import duties refer to the Harmonized Tariff Schedule of the US. The print version is available from the US Government Printing Office as well as third party suppliers who often add special features. Online versions are available in both static PDF pages as well as in formats with excellent search functionality. Search the Web with the term "Harmonized Tariff Schedule" to find sources.

Entry and Documentation

The entry of merchandise is a two-part process consisting of 1) filing the documents necessary to determine whether merchandise may be released from Customs custody and 2) filing the documents that contain information for duty assessment and statistical purposes. In certain instances all documents must be filed and accepted by Customs prior to release of the goods. Unless you have been granted an extension, you must file entry documents at a location specified by the port or area director within five working days of your shipment's date of arrival at a U.S. port of entry. These include a number of standard documents required by Customs for any entry, and:

- APHIS Import Permit Form VS 16-3 where required
- Foreign veterinary certification where required

After you present the entry, Customs may examine your shipment, or may waive examination. The shipment is then released provided no legal or regulatory violations have been noted. You must then file entry summary documentation and deposit estimated duties at a designated customhouse within 10 working days of your shipment's release. For a detailed description of entry procedures, standard documentation, and informal entry, see "Entry Process" on page 185.

Informed Compliance. Informed compliance was introduced with the Customs Modernization Act of 1993 (Mod Act) and defines the relationship between importers and the Customs Service. It sets out the responsibilities of both parties. Providing the correct documentation and information for entry is a key factor that will make your importing operation run smoothly. We recommend that importers become familiar with the concept of informed comliance and the responsibilities that they have under the Mod Act. For further discussion about informed compliance see "Informed Compliance" on page 211.

Note: The Entry and Documentation section has been carefully designed to supply you, the importer, with sample documents and directions on how to satisfy Customs requirements. Be aware that you should consult the applicable authorities to ensure that you are correctly following the most current procedures.

Prohibitions and Restrictions

FSIS Requirements. The FSIS enforces the provisions of the Federal Meat Inspection Act (FMIA) and the Poultry Products Inspection Act (PPIA), which require countries exporting meat, poultry, and their products to the U.S. to impose domestic inspection requirements at least as stringent as those of the U.S. The FSIS reviews foreign inspection systems to ensure that they are equivalent to the U.S. system. Only those countries to which FSIS grants meat export eligibility may export these products to the U.S. See Country-Specific Import Restrictions below for list of currently eligible countries (by definition, imports from unlisted countries are prohibited).

An inspection certificate issued by the responsible official of the exporting country must accompany each shipment of meat or poultry products offered for entry into the U.S. Certificates identify products by country and packing plant of origin, destination, shipping marks, and amounts. They certify that the products have received ante-mortem and post-mortem inspection; that they are wholesome, unadulterated, and properly branded; and that they otherwise comply with U.S. requirements.

In addition, the Pork Promotion, Research, and Consumer Information Act of 1985 (PPRCIA) requires that each importer of porcine animals, pork, or pork products shall remit an assessment to U.S. Customs at the time the product is imported

Port of Entry Inspection. The FSIS reinspects meat and meat products by sampling shipments as they enter the U.S. Your products may be checked for transportation damage, labeling compliance

and accuracy, general condition, and proper certification. FSIS may also examine the product for accuracy of net weight, labeling requirements, and condition of the container, and make laboratory analyses of food chemistry (for example, fat, water, and nitrite levels) and test for drug and chemical residues. It may also test to confirm species. The actual inspection tasks and the scope of inspection are based on the nature of the product and on the performance history of the packing plant and country of origination.

If your shipment passes reinspection, FSIS will stamp the products "U.S. Inspected and Passed," and they will be allowed entry. If the products fail this reinspection, they will be stamped "U.S. Refused Entry," in which case you must reexport or destroy the refused products. In some cases, such products may be converted to animal food. Once a shipment has been condemned, inspection is intensified for future shipments of that product from the same plant, and in some cases, for all meat shipments from the same country.

Residue Control. Chemical and drug residue control is one of the major features of an exporting country's inspection system that must be judged equal to the U.S. system. Exporting countries must be certified annually by FSIS as continuing to operate an equivalent residue control program. FSIS experts make sure that the country's residue program uses approved analytical methods, that officials are knowledgeable about the use of chemical compounds in their country, and that the country tests for those compounds that could potentially contaminate the food supply. Meat or meat products may not be imported from a country that fails to receive a FSIS annual residue certification.

As a further residue check, FSIS randomly samples products at the port of entry and analyzes them for drug and chemical residues. The FSIS annual import residue plan sets the initial sampling rate for each country based on the volume of product imported from that country. The plan includes the same chemical compounds as the domestic residue-monitoring program. Compounds are selected based on their likelihood of contaminating the food supply and their potential harm to the consuming public. The list can include chemical compounds not legal for use in the U.S. if they have the potential to contaminate a foreign country's meat supply.

If your shipment contains residues above the U.S. tolerance or action level, it will be considered adulterated and will be refused entry into the U.S. Shipments are not usually held pending laboratory test results unless FSIS has some reason to suspect contamination. If a laboratory reports a residue violation on a sample that has otherwise passed reinspection, as much as possible of the product must be recalled. Products so recovered may not be used for human food.

The occurrence of a residue violation at a port of entry raises concerns about the exporting country's ability to control residues. Port of entry sampling is then automatically increased for related products from the entire country, as well as on subsequent shipments from the specific plant where the noncomplying sample originated. From time to time, the FSIS will increase sampling for a specific country or for a specific compound. This can occur when there is an indication that a problem may exist or when there is a pattern of failed port of entry reinspections.

USDA APHIS Requirements. APHIS regulates meat and meat product imports in order to prevent the introduction of certain infectious diseases into the U.S., operating primarily under the authority of Subpart 94 which establishes import restrictions and procedures. APHIS restricts imports from countries known to have incidence of a variety of listed diseases. For ruminants and swine: rinderpest and foot-and-mouth disease; for swine: African swine fever, swine vesicular disease, and hog cholera; for poultry: fowl pest, Exotic Newcastle disease (END), and *Salmo-*

nella enteritis (phage-type 4).(see "Country-Specific Import Restrictions" below).

Not only does APHIS restrict imports from countries known to have a specific disease, it also restricts imports from countries that do not have the disease, but that 1) are known to import and use animal products from countries that do; 2) whose regulations regarding entry of such products or of potentially-infected live animals into their borders are less stringent than those of the U.S.; or 3) that border on countries known to have the disease. APHIS also restricts imports originating from disease-free countries but which, in the course of transport, enter the territory of countries known to have the disease. Meat products may be allowed entry provided they are processed in such a fashion as to kill the disease organisms and prevent the transmission of the diseases in question.

The importation of prepared meat and fish products involves a very complicated set of qualifying factors. APHIS administers these restrictions primarily through product certification by qualified veterinarians of the country of origin. In some cases, permits are required. There are stringent cooking, processing, marking, packing, and shipping requirements for certain imports. The variables are too complex to cover exhaustively in this discussion, but the following examples will give you an idea of the issues that need to be addressed in importing these products.

Importation of Cured or Cooked Meat of Ruminants or Swine Originating in Country Where Rinderpest or Foot-and-Mouth Disease Exist. If you are importing cured meats—such as jerked or dried beef, corned beef, or Westphalia hams, but not including meat that has been sterilized by heat in hermetically sealed containers—of HTSUS Chapter 2, the following conditions apply: 1) all bones must have been removed in the country of origin; 2) the meat must have been held in an unfrozen, fresh condition for at least 3 days immediately following slaughter of the animals from which it was derived; and 3) the meat must have been thoroughly cured and fully dried in such a manner that it may be stored and handled without refrigeration. If your product is deemed by the port of entry inspector to be in violation of the prescribed water-protein ratio for cured meat, it will be tested by APHIS, and the shipment will be held at port of entry pending test results. Finally, the requisite country-of-origin foreign meat inspection certificate must be presented to the USDA inspector at port of entry.

Pork Products From Countries Where African Swine Fever Exists. If you are importing pork products that either originate in or were processed in a country identified as one in which African swine fever exists, you must be sure your products comply with the following requirements: 1) be a fully sterilized product that is shelf-stable without refrigeration because it was fully cooked by commercial method and packaged in a container hermetically sealed promptly after filling but prior to such cooking; or 2) is not otherwise prohibited and is consigned directly to a USDA-approved, federally inspected meat-processing establishment for further heat processing. You must convey the product under U.S. Customs or APHIS seals, which may not be broken except by USDA-authorized officials; and 3) if your product originated in a disease-free country, but was processed in an infected country, or transported through one, you must provide certification that it was sealed and inspected in accordance with the regulations governing such cases. Furthermore, all processing must have been accomplished in a single establishment in the infected country, which must meet both FSIS certification requirements and APHIS requirements for pork-processing plants (9 CFR 1 Subpart 94.8). After having all bones removed, the product must have been thoroughly heated according to regulations. Certification must be presented to the FDA inspector at U.S. port of entry.

If you would like the names and address of approved establishments, or if you wish to request approval to use an establishment, contact APHIS Import-Export Products Staff (see

addresses at end of this chapter). If you import pork products from listed infected countries, which do not comply with requirements of Subpart 94, your shipment will be seized, quarantined, and disposed of as the USDA determines necessary to prevent introduction of African swine fever into the U.S.

Hog Cholera and Swine Vesicular Disease. Regulations covering importation of pork from countries where hog cholera and vesicular swine fever exist are similar in nature (but not in specifics) to those covering African swine fever. Regulations similar to those covering products from countries that either border on or allow entry of products from infected countries also apply to hog cholera and vesicular swine fever countries. These regulations vary depending upon what is necessary to ensure that the product does not carry contaminating disease organisms into the U.S. Pork products originating in countries infected with these diseases must comply with specific processing and preparation provisions of Subpart 94. They must be offered for entry under government veterinary certification additional to that normally required by FMIA. The additional certification may be placed on the foreign meat inspection certificate or may be contained in a separate document. What must appear on the additional certificate varies depending upon the nature of the import.

Hams. APHIS enforces Subpart 94 covering the importation of ham and similar cured pork products. Ham products are allowed entry under the following conditions: 1) they came from a swine that was never out of the country in which the ham was processed; 2) they came from a country determined by the USDA to have and to enforce laws requiring the immediate reporting to the country's national veterinary services any premises found to have any animal infected with foot-and-mouth disease, rinderpest, African Swine fever, hog cholera, or swine vesicular disease; 3) they came from a swine that was not on any premises where the diseases mentioned above exist or had existed within 60 days prior to slaughter; 4) the hams were accompanied from the slaughterhouse to the processing establishment by a numbered certificate issued by a person authorized by the national government of the country of origin stating that the above provisions were met; and 5) the hams must have been processed according to regulations in 9 CFR 1 Subpart 94.17 in a single establishment.

If you are interested in importing hams, you should be aware of the restrictions on foreign establishments eligible to export hams to the U.S. Be sure to purchase your product from an meatpacker that complies with all relevant regulations for the processing of hams, and that employs someone authorized by national veterinary officials to oversee and attest to that compliance. Hams from establishments that do not meet these criteria may not be imported. The only foreign hams eligible for import into the U.S. are those processed in APHIS-inspected establishments whose proprietor has signed a written agreement with the APHIS to the effect that all hams for import to the U.S. will be processed in accordance with standards established in Subpart 94. Foreign meatpackers must also meet APHIS recordkeeping and inspection access requirements. Foreign hams imported into the U.S. must bear certain markings (see "Marking and Labeling Requirements" below), and must be accompanied by a certificate issued by an authorized person stating that the ham was processed for at least 400 days and that all relevant provisions of Subpart 94 have been fulfilled.

Poultry Products. The law defines poultry as chickens, turkeys, swans, partridges, guinea fowl, pea fowl, nonmigratory ducks, geese, pigeons, and doves as well as commercial, domestic, or pen-raised grouse, pheasants, and quail. It restricts import of these products from countries known to have incidences of fowl pest, Exotic Newcastle disease (END), and *Salmonella enteritis* (phage-type 4). Poultry products that have been fully processed into food preparations by methods that serve to kill the disease organisms are allowed entry, provided that compliance can be demonstrated. For example, poultry products originating, or passing through a country where END is considered endemic may be imported into the U.S. if 1) they are packed in hermetically sealed containers and cooked by a commercial method after such packing to produce articles that are shelf-stable without refrigeration; or 2) they are determined by a USDA inspector at the port of entry to have a thoroughly cooked appearance throughout (Subpart 94 defines "thoroughly cooked" as heated so that the flesh and juices have lost all red or pink color).

APHIS VS Permit Application. Requests for USDA APHIS VS permits authorizing importation of restricted products must be submitted on a completed VS Form 16-3. You may obtain these forms from APHIS headquarters (see addresses at end of this chapter) or from any USDA port office. Application on a signed facsimile (copy) is acceptable, provided you send an original signed document as follow-up. If you need a supply of the forms on hand, you may photocopy the original Form 16-3.

Requested information on processing or production data and sources of meat products may often require more space than is provided on the application form. In such cases, you may attach extra sheets as necessary. You should include as much background information as possible in order for APHIS to properly evaluate the disease risk of the product you wish to import. Research papers intended as supporting information should not be sent by fax. It takes about two weeks for the APHIS to process an application and prepare a permit for return mail. If the application information is deemed insufficient, APHIS will contact you for clarification. The permit process can take longer in such cases. You should submit your requests for permit renewal or amendment in writing (fax is acceptable) to the USDA (see addresses at end of this chapter). You should note any changes from the original application and permit issued, such as addresses or production method, when making permit renewal requests.

Any importation for which a permit is issued must comply in all particulars with the permit's stipulations. You will facilitate the entry of your import shipments by making sure the permit number appears on the shipping documents—or simply include a copy of the permit with your entry documents. Meat products requiring permits will be subject to delay or refusal at the port of entry if an importation permit is not obtained before shipment to the U.S.

FDA Requirements. The FDA regulates importation of all food products, including fresh, frozen, pickled, canned, salted, dried, and smoked meat, poultry, fish, and shellfish and preparations thereof under the Food, Drug, and Cosmetic Act (21 CFR 161). You may use only FDA-approved preservatives to prevent or retard spoilage. Artificial coloring that conceals damage or inferiority, or makes the product appear better or of greater value than it really is, is prohibited under FDCA. For more detailed discussion of FDCA food additive regulations and labeling requirements, see "Appendix: Foods" on page 825.

You should be aware that certain species of animals, especially of fish and seafood, may contain chemical contamination from lakes, rivers, and oceans, and/or excessive residues of pesticides, mercury, and other heavy metals. Presence of such substances in food is a violation of the FDCA, and renders the product subject to detention at the U.S. port of entry.

Canned Meat, Poultry, Fish, and Seafood. Many canned animal products are low-acid canned foods and as such must comply with applicable FDCA regulations. Packers are subject to registration requirements for low-acid canned food manufacturers. Low acid canned foods are heat-processed foods other than alcoholic beverages that have an acidity greater than pH 4.6, a water activity greater than 0.85, and that are packaged in hermetically sealed containers. "Water activity" is a measure of the water available for microbial growth. "Hermetically sealed containers"

include any package, regardless of composition, capable of maintaining the commercial sterility of contents after processing. Acidified foods are those to which acid(s) or acid food(s) are added to reduce the pH to 4.6 or lower (increase the acidity), and with a water activity greater than 0.85. If you are unsure whether your canned product fits one of these categories, contact the FDA's Industry Guidelines Branch for clarification (see addresses at end of this chapter).

You should be sure that your canned products are properly and adequately labeled. If they are not, they will not be permitted entry into U.S. Customs territory. The FDA has denied entry of canned products because labeling did not accurately declare: 1) presence of added salt; 2) nature of packing medium, e.g. type of oil; or 3) presence of artificial colors or chemical preservatives. Other violations for which shipments of canned products have been detained are: 1) excessive amounts of packing medium (e.g. oil), or 2) excessive headspace (the space between the lid of the can and the surface of the food). Canned foods must meet certain FDA standards of fill, including minimum drained weight and minimum total volume of product relative to that of the container. If you are importing a product for which no formal fill-of-container standards have been promulgated, you should be sure that containers are well filled with only enough packing medium to fill the interstitial spaces. There may also be regulations covering whether or not water may be added to a product and how it must be labeled if water is added.

Identity standards are relatively straightforward for meat products. They are somewhat more elaborate for fish and seafood products involving a variety of species. For example, there are standards of identity and fill-of-container for canned pacific salmon. The standards establish species, names required on labels, and permitted styles of pack. If you are importing these products, you should be sure they comply with any established standards in every respect.

Anchovies. Regulations limit products represented as anchovies to fish of the family *Engraulidae.* If you are importing anchovies, they must be of that family. You may not label other small fish that may superficially resemble anchovies, such as small herring and herring-like fish, as anchovies.

Sardines. The term "sardines" is permitted in the labeling of the canned products prepared from small clupeoid fish. Sea herring (*Clupea harengus*), European pilchards (*Sardina pilchardus* or *Clupea pilchardus*), and brisling or sprat (*Clupea sprattus*) are commonly packed in small cans and labeled as sardines. The terms "brisling sardines" and "sild sardines" are permissible in the labeling of canned small brisling and herring, respectively. Large herring may not be labeled sardines. If you are importing canned sardines, be sure they are adequately processed to prevent active spoilage by microorganisms. They must be free from all forms of decomposition. A common cause of detention is the presence of "feedy, belly-blown" fish in a shipment. "Feedy fish" are those whose stomachs are full of feed when they are caught. They deteriorate rapidly. Viscera and thin belly wall disintegrate, producing a characteristic ragged appearance called "belly-blown." If your shipment contains such fish it is in violation of FDCA and subject to detention at port of entry.

Tuna. If you are importing canned tuna, you should be aware of FDCA standards of identity and standards of fill, and make sure that your product complies. The standards provide for various styles of pack, including solid, chunk or chunk style, flakes, and grated. Provision is also made for various types of packing media, certain specified seasonings and flavorings, color designations, and methods for determining proper fill of containers. Fill-of-container standards for canned tuna specify minimum values for pressed cake weight, depending on tuna ingredient style (chunk, flake, etc.) and can size. Species of fish that resemble tuna, such as bonito (*Sarda chilensis*) and yellowtail (*Seriola dorsalis*) are sometimes canned and labeled as tuna. This is misbranding, and is cause for legal action if you attempt to import such products into the U.S. You may label as tuna only those species listed in FDCA tuna standards of identity.

Shellfish Certification and Imports. Standards of identity have been set for canned oysters. The standards define sizes of oysters, and prescribe methods of washing and draining to prevent adulteration with excess water. Fill-of-container standard for canned oysters fixes the drained weight at not less than 59% of the container's water capacity.

If you are interested in importing shellfish (clams, mussels, and oysters), be sure they are obtained from unpolluted waters and produced, handled, and distributed in a sanitary manner. Because they may transmit intestinal diseases such as typhoid fever, or be carriers of natural or chemical toxins, shellfish are subject to special FDA controls and licensing. Foreign shellfish products intended for sale in the U.S. are subject to controls equivalent to those applied to domestic products. All shellfish must comply with the general requirements of the FDCA plus those of state health agencies cooperating in both the FDA-administered National Shellfish Sanitation Program (NSSP) and Interstate Shellfish Sanitation Conference (ISSC). Shellfish harvesting is prohibited in areas contaminated by sewage or industrial wastes. State inspectors issue approval certificates to facilities that pass inspection. These certificates are equivalent to a state license to operate. The state-approved plant's certification number must appear on each container or package of shellfish shipped. In addition, shippers are required to keep records showing the origin and disposition of all shellfish handled and to make these records available to the control authorities.

Rock Lobster, Spiny Lobster, Sea Crayfish. The sea crayfish, *Palinurus vulgaris,* is frequently imported into the U.S. in the form of frozen tails, frozen cooked meat, or canned meat. Common or usual names for these products are "rock lobster" and "spiny lobster." If you are importing this product, be sure that your labeling shows the modifying words "rock" or "spiny" in direct connection with the word "lobster," in type of equal size and prominence.

Shrimp. There are standards of identity for shrimp in the following forms: 1) canned wet-and dry-pack, 2) frozen raw breaded, and 3) frozen raw lightly breaded.

Caviar and Fish Roe. The unqualified name "caviar" may be applied only to sturgeon eggs prepared by a process unique to caviar. If roe is prepared by caviar process, but from eggs of fish other than sturgeon, the label name must include the identity of that fish, e.g. "whitefish caviar."

The following violations are common reasons for detention of these products at port of entry: 1) decomposition of canned product due to the packing of decomposed raw material; 2) decomposition of canned product due to active bacterial spoilage; 3) presence in frozen cooked product of microorganisms indicative of contamination with human or animal filth; 4) decomposition of frozen cooked product.

Country-Specific Import Restrictions

Regulatory Changes. APHIS has amended the animal and animal product importation regulations to allow for regionalization of countries—that is, disease classification of parts of a country, an entire country, or groups of countries. The rule change was made to recognize levels of disease risk in regions. Details about the criteria that APHIS considers when evaluating the regions that wish to export animals or animal products to the United States can be found at the APHIS Veterinary Service National Center for Import and Export (NCIE) website (www.aphis.usda.gov/ncie).

Countries currently FSIS-certified for exportation of meat and poultry to the U.S.: Argentina, Australia, Belgium, Belize, Brazil, Canada, Costa Rica, the Czech Republic, Denmark, Dominican Republic, El Salvador, Finland, France, Guatemala, Honduras, Hong Kong, Hungary, Ireland, Israel, Italy, Mexico, Netherlands, New Zealand, Norway, Poland, Romania, the Slovak Republic, Sweden, Switzerland, United Kingdom, Uruguay, and the republics of the former Yugoslavia. Meat may not be imported from countries not on the list. The list is subject to change. For the most up-to-date information, contact FSIS (see addresses at end of this chapter).

APHIS-listed Countries. The following countries are listed by APHIS as being free of, or as having, the diseases indicated below. Imports of certain meat products are banned from countries where animal diseases are deemed to exist.

Countries certified free of rinderpest and foot-and-mouth disease, from which ruminant and swine products may be imported: Australia, the Bahamas, Barbados, Belize, Bermuda, Canada, Channel Islands, Costa Rica, Czech Republic, Denmark, Dominican Republic, El Salvador, Fiji, Finland, Great Britain (England, Scotland, Wales, and Isle of Man), Greenland, Guatemala, Haiti, Honduras, Iceland, Ireland, Italy, Jamaica, Japan, Mexico, New Zealand, Nicaragua, Northern Ireland, Norway, Panama, Panama Canal Zone, Papua New Guinea, Territory of St. Pierre and Miquelon, Sweden, Trinidad and Tobago, and Trust Territory of the Pacific Islands.

Countries where African swine fever is believed to exist and from which pork imports are banned: Africa (all countries), Brazil, Cuba, Haiti, Italy, Malta, Portugal, and Spain.

Countries deemed free of hog cholera and from which pork may be imported: Australia, Canada, Denmark, Dominican Republic, Fiji, Finland, Great Britain (England, Scotland, Wales, and Isle of Man), Iceland, New Zealand, Northern Ireland, Norway, the Republic of Ireland, Sweden, Trust Territory of the Pacific Islands.

Countries deemed free of swine vesicular disease and from which pork may be imported: Australia, the Bahamas, Bulgaria, Canada, Central American countries, Denmark, Dominican Republic, Fiji, Finland, Great Britain (England, Scotland, Wales, and the Isle of Man), Greenland, Haiti, Hungary, Iceland, Luxembourg, Mexico, New Zealand, Northern Ireland, Norway, Panama, Republic of Ireland, Rumania, Sweden, Switzerland, Trust Territories of the Pacific Islands, and the republics of the former Yugoslavia.

Countries subject to specific restrictions on the importation of pork products: the Bahamas, Bulgaria, Great Britain (England, Scotland, Wales, and the Isle of Man), Hungary, Luxembourg, Switzerland, and the republics of the former Yugoslavia.

Countries subject to specific restrictions on the importation of ruminant and swine products: the Bahamas, Channel Islands, Denmark, Finland, Great Britain (England, Scotland, Wales, and Isle of Man), Japan, Northern Ireland, Norway, Papua New Guinea, and Sweden.

Countries certified free of Exotic Newcastle disease (END): Australia, Canada, Denmark, Fiji, Finland, Great Britain (England, Scotland, Wales, and the Isle of Man), Iceland, New Zealand, Northern Ireland, Norway, Republic of Ireland, Sweden.

*Countries free of **Salmonella enteritis:*** Canada.

Marking and Labeling Requirements

FSIS Requirements. When meat and meat products are imported, the name of the country of origin must appear on the label. However, only imported products that reach consumers without further processing retain such labeling. For example, a can of ham or corned beef that goes directly to a retail outlet will name the country of origin on the label. However, if imported boneless beef is combined with U.S. beef and other ingredients in a U.S. plant to produce a can of beef stew, the label is not required to indicate the presence of imported beef.

The Farm Bill Amendments require foreign countries exporting products to the U.S. to impose controls, equivalent to those administered by the FSIS, to prevent species substitution. A product labeled "beef," for example, must be beef and cannot contain a less expensive or more readily available species. Exporting countries must maintain effective testing programs for species verification, and adequate security measures to prevent species substitution.

APHIS Requirements. Imported hams must comply with all marking requirements of Subpart 94.17. Ham must bear a hot iron brand or an ink seal with the identifying number of the slaughterhouse. It must bear a button seal, approved by USDA to be tamper-proof, on the hock, stating the month and year the ham entered the processing establishment. It must bear a hot iron brand (with the identifying number of the processing establishment and the date salting began) executed at the processing establishment immediately prior to salting. All required branding must be performed under the direct supervision of a person authorized by the veterinary services of the country of origin's national government to supervise such activity.

FDA Requirements. Substitution of one kind of species for another is prohibited. Whether or not identity standards apply, labels must identify the product by its common or usual U.S. name. You may not replace the common U.S. name of a product either with a name common in the country of origin but unfamiliar in the U.S. or with a coined name. If you are importing a product not previously marketed in the U.S., its name must reflect proper biological classification and must not duplicate, or risk being confused with, the common or usual U.S. name of any other species or product. Any product for which identity standards exist must conform precisely to those standards. It is illegal to use the name of a standard product on a product that deviates from that standard. For basic FDA marking and labeling requirements, see "Appendix: Foods" on page 825.

For a general discussion of U.S. Customs marking and labeling requirements, see "Country of Origin Marking" on page 236, "Special Marking Requirements" on page 238 and "Marking—False Impression" on page 239.

Shipping Considerations

You will need to ensure that your goods are packaged and shipped with care so that they arrive in good condition and pass smoothly through Customs. You are responsible for ensuring that the shipment is in compliance with all applicable government regulations for packaging and shipping. In most instances, you should not leave these arrangements solely to the discretion of your supplier. Careful preparation of the cargo and selection of the mode of transport can be essential to a cost-effective, timely delivery of undamaged goods. We strongly advise you to consult your shipping representative, insurance agent, or freight broker for advice on packing and shipping.

Publications and WWW Resources

The following publications may be relevant to the importation of meat:

Report of the Secretary of Agriculture to the U.S. Congress - Foreign Countries and Plants Certified to Export Meat and Poultry to the United States

This is a comprehensive listing of export-certified countries and plants, including previously certified plants that have been de-certified. It is available from the FSIS (see addresses at end of this chapter).

The following publication explains the FDA requirements for importing meat and fish. It is published by the FDA and is available online from the FDA website (www.fda.gov/opacom/7pubs.html).

Requirements of Laws and Regulations Enforced by the U.S. Food and Drug Administration

The following publication gives brief, general guidelines on USDA regulated products. Although designed primarily for tourists, it contains a list of approved products that you may find helpful. It is available online from the USDA APHIS website (www.aphis.usda.gov).

Travelers Tips On Bringing Food, Plant, and Animal Products into the United States

The *Harmonized Tariff Schedule of the United States (2001)* (HTSUS) is available to view on the Customs Service website (www.customs.gov), or you may purchase a printed version from:

U.S. Government Printing Office
Superintendent of Documents
710 North Capital Street NW
Washington DC 20401
Tel: (202) 512-1800
Fax: (202) 512-1657
Website: www.access.gpo.gov

The USGPO also has copies of specific laws available for purchase. The USGPO accepts orders made by fax, phone or placed over the Internet, as well as mail orders paid by credit card. All orders must be accompanied by payment. Credit cards, checks drawn on a U.S. bank, or an international money order are all acceptable.

Relevant Government Agencies

Address your questions regarding APHIS import requirements, port of entry inspections, permits, and approved establishments for the import of meat to:

Animal and Plant Health Inspection Service (APHIS)
Veterinary Services (VS)
National Center for Import and Export
4700 River Rd., Unit 40
Riverdale, MD 20737
Tel: (301) 734-3277
Meat and poultry products: (301) 734-3277
Animal products: (301) 734-4401
Website: www.aphis.usda.gov/vs

Address your questions regarding FSIS port of entry inspection or pre-import certification of meat, fish, and related products and establishments to:

U.S. Department of Agriculture (USDA)
Food Safety and Inspection Service (FSIS)
Technical Service Center-Imports
Suite 300 Landmark Center
1299 Farnam St.
Omaha, NE 68102
Tel: (402) 221-7400
Fax: (402) 221-7479
Website: www.fsis.usda.gov

Address your questions regarding FDA requirements for meat products and canned products to:

Food and Drug Administration (FDA)
Center for Food Safety and Applied Nutrition (CFSAN)
Office of Compliance
Division of Enforcement, Imports Branch
5100 Paint Branch Parkway
College Park, MD 20740-3835
Tel: (301) 436-2080
Website: http://vm.cfsan.fda.gov/list.html

Address your questions regarding importation of meats and edible offal to your local Customs port director. For addresses refer to "U.S. Customs and Border Protection Offices" on page 65 or contact:

U.S. Customs and Border Protection
Customs Headquarters
1300 Pennsylvania Avenue NW
Washington DC 20229
Tel: (202) 354-1000
Website: www.customs.treas.gov

Laws and Regulations

The following laws and regulations may be relevant to the importation of meat and edible offal. The laws are contained in the U.S. Code (USC) and the regulations in the Code of Federal Regulations (CFR), both of which may be available at larger public and law libraries. Copies of specific laws are also available from the United States Government Printing Office (address above).

19 CFR 12.1 et seq.
Regulations on Customs Inspection and Release of Meat and Meat Products
These regulations set forth the conditions and bond under which U.S. Customs will release meat and meat products for entry into the U.S. and the penalties for breach of the bond.

7 USC 1854
Delegations of Authority Concerning Certain Meats EO 11539, as amended by EO 12188
These Executive Orders authorize Customs to enforce limitations on the importation and entry and withdrawal of meats from warehouses for consumption in the U.S.

7 USC 4801 et seq.
Pork Promotion, Research, and Consumer Information Act of 1985
This Act provides that each importer of porcine animal, pork, or pork product shall remit an assessment to Customs at the time the product is imported. See 7 CFR 1230.71 and 1230.110.

21 USC 601 et seq.
Federal Meat Inspection Act
This act provides standards for inspection, packaging, and sale of meat and meat products and prohibits the importation of adulterated, misbranded, or improperly slaughtered meat.

21 USC 451 et seq.
Poultry Products Inspection Act
This Act provides standards for inspection, packaging, and sale of poultry and poultry products and prohibits the importation of slaughtered poultry not in compliance with prescribed standards and regulations.

9 CFR Part 381
Regulations for Inspection of Poultry Products
These regulations prescribe standards for sanitation and composition, inspection procedures, marking and labeling—including nutrition—requirements, exporting and importing certification procedures, and requirements.

9 CFR Part 50 et seq.
Regulations on Animal Byproduct Quarantine Control
These regulations promulgated by the USDA prohibit the importation of animal products for use in industry unless the products meet certain processing standards and are not infected with certain diseases.

21 USC 301 et seq.
Federal Food, Drug, and Cosmetic Act
This Act prohibits deceptive practices and regulates the manufacture, sale and importation or exportation of food, drugs, cosmetics, and related products. It was amended by the Food Quality Protection Act of 1996. See 21 USC 331, 381, 382.

19 CFR 12.1 et seq.; 21 CFR 1.83 et seq.
Regulations on Food, Drugs, and Cosmetics
These regulations of the Secretary of Health and Human Services and the Secretary of the Treasury govern the standards, labeling, marking, and importing of products used with food, drugs, and cosmetics.

Convention on International Trade in Endangered Species of Wild Fauna and Flora (CITES)
This comprehensive wildlife treaty signed by over 100 countries, including the United States, regulates and in many cases prohibits commercial imports and exports of wild animal and plant species threatened by trade.

16 USC 1531
Endangered Species Act of 1973
This Act prohibits the import and export of species listed as endangered and most species listed as threatened. It is the U.S. law that implements CITES.

19 CFR 12.26 et seq.
Regulations on Importation of Wild Animals
These regulations list the wild animals that are prohibited from importation or that require import permits.

50 CFR Parts 10, 13, and 16
Regulations of FWS for Importing Wildlife and Fish
These regulations specify the animals and animal products subject to import prohibitions and restrictions.

Principal Exporting Countries

The following listing includes samples of the main supplier nations of the products of this chapter. It is organized by HTSUS major heading. (Refer to "Customs Classification" above for the product codes.) Countries are listed in rank order of the value of products imported to the U.S. Statistics represent customs value of entries for 2002 from the Bureau of Census, U.S. Department of Commerce.

1601—Canada, Denmark, Mexico, Poland, Spain, Italy, Ireland, Germany, France, Hungary, Netherlands, Argentina, Brazil, Austria

1602—Canada, Brazil, Argentina, Denmark, Poland, Netherlands, Mexico, Uruguay, Belgium, Hungary, Australia, Israel, New Zealand, Italy

1603—Brazil, Japan, Uruguay, Netherlands, Iceland, Mexico, France, Australia, Thailand, Argentina

1604—Thailand, Ecuador, Canada, Philippines, Fiji, Indonesia

1605—Thailand, Canada, China, Vietnam, Indonesia

Chapter 17: Sugars and Sugar Confectionery

This chapter relates to the importation of sugars and sugar confectionery, which are classified within Chapter 17 of the Harmonized Tariff Schedule of the United States (HTSUS). Specifically, it includes cane and beet sugar; lactose, maltose, glucose, and fructose; maple sugar; molasses; candies not including chocolate; and chemically pure sugars for food and beverage uses. If you are interested in importing sugars for food purposes or candy, should read this section in conjunction with "Appendix: Foods" on page 825.

If you are interested in importing candies containing cocoa, you should refer to Commodity Index Chapter 18. Chemically pure sugars other than lactose, maltose, sucrose, glucose, and fructose destined for industrial uses are included in Chapter 29, while sugars for medical or pharmaceutical purposes or used in the manufacture of such products are covered in Chapter 30.

Note: To understand key issues that will enable you to make best use of the information in this section we recommend that you see "Introduction" on page 425.

Key Factors

The key factors in the importation of sugars and candy are:

- Compliance with U.S. Food and Drug Administration (FDA) purity, identity, manufacturing, and other standards

- Compliance with FDA entry notifications and procedures

- Quotas on certain sugar products derived from sugar beets and sugar cane as well as on confectionery

For dutiable sugars imported in bulk, U.S. Customs requires a description of the unloading facilities in advance of the shipment.

Although most importers utilize the services of a licensed customs broker in making their entries, and we recommend this practice, you should be aware of the regulatory, entry, and documentation issues involved in importing your product. You, as importer, are ultimately responsible for the fulfillment of any legal requirements applicable to your shipment.

General Considerations

Certain sugars and sugar products derived from sugar cane or sugar beets are subject to quotas or additional duties levied pursuant to Section 22 of the Agricultural Adjustment Act (AAA). For specifics regarding the nature and extent of these quotas and fees, refer to HTSUS Chapter 99, Subchapter V. Sugars subject to additional duties under HTSUS headings 9904.40.20 through .60 and intended for use in the production (other than distillation) of polyhydric alcohols (except for polyhydric alcohols intended as a substitute for sugar in human food products) may be entered free of the extra fees under a license issued by the Secretary of Agriculture. For more information concerning such licensing contact the USDA International Trade Policy Staff (see addresses at end of this chapter).

Chapter 17 products are subject to regulation under the Federal Food, Drug, and Cosmetic Act (FDCA), administered by the FDA. For a more detailed discussion of FDA requirements, and an annotated diagram of FDA entry procedures see "Appendix: Foods" on page 825. For more information concerning FDA requirements for imported sugar, contact the nearest regional FDA import operations office, or FDA headquarters (see addresses at end of this chapter).

Under 19 CFR 151, Subpart B, importers of dutiable sugar in bulk must submit a full description of the unloading facilities to the Commissioner of Customs as far in advance of the dates of importation as possible. Customs will then issue special weighing and sampling instructions to you. Any weighing or sampling required for your shipment must be done when the shipment is unloaded. When both weighing and sampling are required, you must have these operations performed simultaneously.

When importing molasses in tank cars, you must file a certificate with the Port Director of the port of entry showing whether there is any substantial difference either in the total sugars or the character of the molasses in the different cars. When you import syrup or molasses that is to be pumped or discharged into storage tanks in bulk in tank vessels, you must file a certified copy of the plans of the storage tanks and the gauge table with the port Port Director before discharging. The plans must accurately state tank capacity and show all inlets and outlets. After discharge and prior to gauging, all tank inlets must be carefully sealed and the syrup or molasses left undisturbed for a period not to exceed 20 days to allow for settling. Immediate gauging will be allowed if you so request in writing. No expense incidental to the unloading, transporting, or handling of sugar, syrup, or molasses for convenient weighing, gauging, measuring, sampling, or marking will be borne by the U.S. Government.

The U.S. Environmental Protection Agency (EPA) enforces the Federal Insecticide, Fungicide, and Rodenticide Act (FIFRA), which establishes regulatory limits on pesticide and other chemical residues found in edible plant products. For more information, contact EPA (see addresses at end of this chapter).

Compliance. If your shipment is found to be noncomplying, it may be detained at the port of entry. In the case of products subject to FDA jurisdiction, the FDA may allow you to bring such a shipment into compliance before making a final decision regarding admittance. However, any sorting, reprocessing, or relabeling must be supervised by FDA personnel and is done at the importer's expense. Such conditional release to allow the importer to bring a shipment into compliance is a privilege, not a right. The FDA may consider subsequent noncomplying shipments of the same type of product to constitute abuse of the privilege and require the importer to destroy or reexport the products. To ascertain what your legal responsibilities are, you should contact these agencies regarding the specific items to be imported.

Customs Classification

For customs purposes, sugars and candy are classified under Chapter 17 of the HTSUS. This chapter is divided into major headings, which are further divided into subheadings, and often into subheadings, each of which has its own HTSUS classification number. For example, the 2001 HTSUS number for invert molasses is 1702.90.35, indicating that it is a subcategory of invert sugars derived from sugar cane or sugar beets (1702.90), which is a subcategory of other sugars (1702). There are four major headings in HTSUS Chapter 17.

1701—Cane or beet sugar and chemically pure sucrose, in solid form

1702—Other sugars, including chemically pure lactose, maltose, glucose, and fructose, in solid form; sugar syrups not containing added flavoring or coloring matter; artificial honey, whether or not mixed with natural honey; caramel

1703—Molasses, resulting from the extraction or refining of sugar

1704—Sugar confectionery (including white chocolate) not containing cocoa

For more details regarding classification of the specific product you are interested in importing, consult a customs broker, the appropriate commodity specialist at your nearest customs port, or see HTSUS. The 2001 HTSUS is available online from the Customs Service (www.customs.gov/impoexpo/impoexpo.htm) or for purchase from the U.S. Government Printing Office (see resources at the end of this chapter), and may be found in larger public libraries. For a general discussion of customs classification, see "Classification—Liquidation" on page 229.

Dutiable Status of Goods

For more information about duty rates and binding decisions see "Dutiable Status of Goods" on page 203; for a discussion of temporary importation of goods see "Temporary Free Importations" on page 205.

Valuation

Importers have a responsibility to use what the U.S. Customs Service deems, "reasonable care," when determining the value of their goods. They must also provide any additional information that the Customs Service needs for setting a final value on the goods. This process involves a number of factors and can be somewhat complicated; importers must be aware of applicable issues and details. Valuation information applies to all types of commodities, for further discussion on the subject see "Customs Valuation" on page 267.

Import Duties

Import duties vary (often dramatically) depending upon the Harmonized Tariff Schedule (HTSUS) classification of the goods or products imported. Since some products that look alike have different HTSUS classifications and different rates of duty, proper classification is vital. Note that "differences of opinion" between importers and the Bureau of Customs and Border Protection regarding classification keeps customs attorneys very busy.

Import duties can be assessed on the imported value of the goods ("ad valorem" rates of duty such as 2%, 4.4%, 50%, etc.), total units or weight of the goods ("specific" rates of duty such as 2 cents each or 1.5 cents/pound, etc.) or on a combination basis ("compound" rates of duty such as 5 cents each plus 6%).

Listed below is a sampling of several Column 1 import duty rates for Chapter 17 products:
Cough drops (1704.90.25.00): free
to
Chemically pure fructose (1702.50.00.00): 9.6%

For specific information on US import duties refer to the Harmonized Tariff Schedule of the US. The print version is available from the US Government Printing Office as well as third party suppliers who often add special features. Online versions are available in both static PDF pages as well as in formats with excellent search functionality. Search the Web with the term "Harmonized Tariff Schedule" to find sources.

Entry and Documentation

The entry of merchandise is a two-part process consisting of 1) filing the documents necessary to determine whether merchandise may be released from Customs custody and 2) filing the documents that contain information for duty assessment and statistical purposes. In certain instances all documents must be filed and accepted by Customs prior to release of the goods. Unless you have been granted an extension, you must file entry documents at a location specified by the port or area director within five working days of your shipment's date of arrival at a U.S. port of entry. These include a number of standard documents required by Customs for any entry, and:

- For molasses imported in tank cars, certificates showing any substantial difference in total sugars or character of the molasses from car to car

After you present the entry, Customs may examine your shipment, or may waive examination. The shipment is then released provided no legal or regulatory violations have been noted. You must then file entry summary documentation and deposit estimated duties at a designated customhouse within 10 working days of your shipment's release. For a detailed description of entry procedures, standard documentation, and informal entry, see "Entry Process" on page 185.

Informed Compliance. Informed compliance was introduced with the Customs Modernization Act of 1993 (Mod Act) and defines the relationship between importers and the Customs Service. It sets out the responsibilities of both parties. Providing the correct documentation and information for entry is a key factor that will make your importing operation run smoothly. We recommend that importers become familiar with the concept of informed comliance and the responsibilities that they have under the Mod Act. For further discussion about informed compliance see "Informed Compliance" on page 211.

Note: The Entry and Documentation section has been carefully designed to supply you, the importer, with sample documents and directions on how to satisfy Customs requirements. Be aware that you should consult the applicable authorities to ensure that you are correctly following the most current procedures.

Prohibitions and Restrictions

If you are considering importing confectionery, you should ascertain before making your purchase that the utmost in cleanliness and sanitation have governed the product's manufacture. Both the raw materials and finished products tend to attract rodents and insects. Your stored materials should be inspected frequently and carefully. Any equipment you use in relation to your product, or that the manufacturer uses, should be washed thoroughly and kept free from accumulation of materials that would attract vermin.

The following FDA requirements pertain to confectionery products. The only non-nutritive substances allowed in confectionery are those that are: 1) not harmful to health, and 2) of practical functional value to the product. Only such alcohol as is contained in flavoring extracts may be present in confectionery, with a ceiling of 0.5 percent by weight. Color additives must fulfill all pertinent requirements of the FDCA. Only colors authorized for use in the U.S. are permitted in imported confectionery. Some colors require FDA certification. If these are used in your products, you should be sure that they are from a certified batch and are identified on the product labeling (see "Appendix: Foods" on page 825 for details). If your shipment is in violation of these requirements (21 CFR 101), it may be detained at the U.S. port of entry.

Other common causes of confectionery shipment detention at U.S. ports of entry are: 1) incorrect label listing of ingredients (misbranding); 2) evidence of vermin or insect contamination; or 3) improper labeling of fruit-type candies using artificial flavorings (these must be identified on the label).

Quotas

The importation of sugars is strictly controlled to protect the domestic industry. This is accomplished through the use and administration of extremely complex quota mechanisms, including quotas and duties on finished products containing sugars that could potentially be processed to extract their sugar content for other uses in order to get around the primary controls. Entry of specific products can be difficult because many product categories affected by quota restrictions overlap, especially where sugar and dairy products are concerned. A wide variety of products containing sugar may be restricted because of policy-driven limitations. It is important to consult the Quota Branch of the U.S. Customs Service (see addresses at end of this chapter) to determine whether quota restrictions apply to your specific product.

A number of quotas in Chapter 99 of the HTSUS apply to certain types of sugars and confectionary products.

Tariff-Rate Quota for Imported Sugars and Syrups. Almost continuously since 1934, the United States has restricted the quantity of sugar which may be imported. Currently, additional U.S. note 5 to chapter 17 of the HTSUS provides that a specified quantity of sugar, determined and announced by the Secretary of Agriculture, may be imported duty free or at a nominal tariff rate; any additional quantity may be imported at a higher tariff rate (i.e., 17 cents per pound, raw basis) but such importations generally are not commercially feasible. The tariff-rate quota amount is currently subject to a country-by-country allocation by the United States Trade Representative (USTR) according to a specified table of percentage shares corresponding to shares during a representative period. The tariff-rate quota, which replaced an absolute quota that was in place since 1982, is allocated to some 39 supplying countries.

The Secretary of Agriculture establishes the tariff-rate quota amount, and is authorized to increase the total quota amount (above the GATT minimum) if domestic supplies of sugars may be inadequate to meet domestic demand at reasonable prices. In general, the Secretary determines the import quota amount by determining the quantity of total supply on the domestic market that will trade at prices sufficient to avoid forfeitures of sugar under loan to the CCC. The Uruguay Round minimum tariff-rate quota amount is 1.139 million metric tons, of which 22,000 tons are reserved for other (refined) sugars. Also, the domestic sugar marketing allotment provisions are widely viewed as guaranteeing an annual minimum import level of 1.25 million short tons, raw value.

Specialty Sugar Import Quota. A small portion of the TRQ quota quantity for sugars and syrups may be reserved each year by the Secretary of Agriculture for the importation of specialty sugars as defined by the USTR. The authority to operate and administer the program is delegated under the regulations to the USDA.

U.S. importers interested in importing specialty sugars can apply each quota period for an import certificate issued by the USDA. Application information along with the descriptions of what specialty sugars are and the eligible source countries for specialty sugars are provided in the interim rules provided by the USTR as described in 15 CFR Part 2011 Subpart B.

Post Uruguay Round and NAFTA. As a result of the Uruguay Round there are no longer any measures taken under Section 22 of the Agricultural Adjustment Act with respect to sugar, including quotas on certain products containing sugar and an import fee of one cent per pound for refined sugar. There are also no import restrictions currently in effect under Section 22 with respect to raw sugar. In the Uruguay Round of the GATT, the U.S. committed to tariffy its Section 22 quotas at the current levels of access, and reduce the over-quota tariff by 15 percent over the six-year transition period.

Beginning in 1995, the U.S. replaced the Section 22 import quotas for sugar-containing articles with tariff-rate quotas at their historical levels. However, the quantity historically imported as mixed condiments and seasonings was separated from the other quotas and increased to a total quantity of 700 tons. The over-quota tariff rates for these products are based on the tariff equivalent for refined sugar, and will be reduced by the minimum required 15% in equal annual installments over 6 years. Modifications to the definitions of these quotas will be made to maintain the product coverage intended when they were first introduced.

Quota allocations for certain sugar-containing articles were also reduced and redistributed from their historical levels with the implementation of the North American Free Trade Agreement (NAFTA). The cocoa and cocoa preparations sugar-containing article quota described in Additional U.S. Note 1 in chapter 18 of the HTSUS provides for imports other than from Mexico of 2,313 metric tons during the each 12 month period beginning October 1, 1995. The preparations of cereals, flour, starch or milk; bakers' wares identified under the sugar containing article quota described in Additonal U.S. Note 3 in chapter 19 of the HTSUS provides for imports other than from Mexico of 5,398 metric tons during each 12 month period beginning October 1, 1995. The sugar and sugar and containing article quota described in additional U.S. note 8 in chapter 17 of the Harmonized Tariff Schedule provides for imports other than from Mexico of 64,709 metric tons during each 12 month period beginning October 1, 1995.

Annual schedules (beginning October 1) during the 1994 through 2002 period of quantitative limitations for imports of sugar containing articles from Mexico pursuant to NAFTA are provided in the following sections of the HTSUS:

- For sugar and sugar and containing article described in U.S. note 18 in chapter 99 and subchapter VI of the Harmonized Tariff Schedule;

- For sugar and sugar and containing article described in U.S. note 19 in chapter 99 and subchapter VI of the Harmonized Tariff Schedule;

- For sugar and sugar and containing article described in U.S. note 20 in chapter 99 and subchapter VI of the Harmonized Tariff Schedule.

Beginning in calendar year 2003 all above quantitive limitations shall cease to apply on the qualifying sugar containing goods from Mexico pursuant to NAFTA.

NAFTA Sugar Provisions. As with all other agricultural trade between Mexico and the United States, the general approach to bilateral trade in sugar in NAFTA was comprehensive free trade. In the case of trade in sugar, one of the most sensitive sectors on both sides of the Rio Grande, the transition period negotiated was the longest available—15 years. However, based on the concerns of the U.S. domestic industry, several unique provisions were negotiated with respect to trade in sugar.

Although bilateral trade is sugar will be free of tariffs and nontariff barriers at the end of 15 years, the shape of trade in sugar during this transition period is governed by the concept of "net production surplus." In essence, this is a means-tested approach to trade, with the decision parameter being the surplus of production over consumption. The level of duty free access to the market for sugar in the importing country is determined by calculating whether the exporting country is a "net surplus producer." This duty-free access is capped at a maximum of 25,000 metric tons in years one through six, and 250,000 metric tons in years 7 through 15. The caps cease at the end of the 15- year transition period. In addition, bilateral tariffs on sugar entering above the duty-free amount (the second tier duties) will be reduced by 15% in the first six years, and will be linearly reduced to zero at the end of year 15.

The aggregate quantity of sugars, syrups, and molasses entered under subheadings 9906.17.01, 9906.17.16, 9906.18.11, and 906.21.29 that are qualifying goods is the quantity determined by the Secretary of Agriculture in accordance with paragraphs 13 through 15 of Section A, Annex 703.2, Chapter Seven of NAFTA. The Secretary of Agriculture shall inform the Secretary of the Treasury of any determination made under such provisions and shall publish a notice of such determination in the Federal Register. Beginning October 1, 2008, quantitative limitations shall cease to apply to such qualifying goods.

Raw and Refined Sugar. Notwithstanding the quota provided for in this note, effective on or about October 1, 1994, raw sugar that is a qualifying good and that is entered for refining in the U.S. and reexported to Mexico, and refined sugar that is a qualifying good and that is entered after refining in Mexico from raw sugar produced in and exported from the U.S., in accordance with paragraph 22 of the Section A, Annex 703.2, Chapter Seven of NAFTA shall not be subject to duty. Such sugar shall be entered only under such terms, conditions, bonds, or other requirements as the Secretary of Agriculture may determine are necessary to ensure compliance with the provisions of paragraph 22.

Sugars from Cane or Beets and Not Prepared for Retail. The aggregate quantity of articles containing over 65% by dry weight of sugars derived from sugar cane or sugar beets, whether or not mixed with other ingredients, capable of being further processed or mixed with similar or other ingredients, and not prepared for marketing to retail consumers in the identical form and package in which imported, that are qualifying goods entered under subheadings 9906.17.03, 906.17.32, 9906.18.04, 9906.18.17, 9906.18.41, 906.19.08, 9906.19.31, 9906.21.01, 906.21.11, and 9906.21.44 in any calendar year shall not exceed the quantity specified below for that year: 1994: 1,500,000 kg; 1995: 1,545,000 kg; 1996: 1,591,000 kg; 1997: 1.639,000 kg; 1998: 1,688,000 kg; 1999: 1,739,000 kg; 2000: 1,791,000 kg; 2001: 1,845,000 kg; 2002: 1,900,000 kg Beginning in calendar year 2003, quantitative limitations shall cease to apply on such qualifying goods.

Blended Syrups of Sugars from Cane or Beets and Not Prepared for Retail. The aggregate quantity of blended syrups containing sugars derived from sugar cane and sugar beets capable of being further processed or mixed with similar or other ingredients and not prepared for marketing to retail consumers in the identical form and package in which imported that are qualifying goods entered under subheadings 9906.17.07, 9906.17.12, 9906.17.21, 9906.18.27, 9906.18.44, 9906.21.04, and 9906.21.47 in any calendar year shall not exceed the quantity specified below for that year: 1994: 1,500,000 kg; 1995: 1,545,000 kg; 1996: 1,591,000 kg; 1997: 1,639,000 kg; 1998: 1,688,000 kg; 1999: 1,739,000 kg; 2000: 1,791,000 kg; 2001: 1,845,000 kg; 2002: 1,900,000 kg. Beginning in calendar year 2003, quantitative limitations shall cease to apply to such qualifying goods.

Other Articles of Sugars from Cane or Beets. The aggregate quantity of articles containing over 10% by dry weight of sugars derived from sugar cane or sugar beets whether or not mixed with other ingredients except (a) articles not principally of crystalline structure or not in dry amorphous form that are prepared for marketing to retail consumers in the identical form and package in which imported, (b) blended syrups containing sugars derived from sugar cane or sugar beets capable of being further processed or mixed with similar or other ingredients and not prepared for marketing to retail consumers in the identical form and package in which imported, (c) articles containing over 65% by dry weight of sugars derived from sugar cane or sugar beets whether or not mixed with other ingredients capable of being further processed or mixed with similar or other ingredients and not prepared for marketing to retail consumers in the identical form or package in which imported, or (d) cake decorations and similar products to be used in the same condition as imported without any further processing other than the direct application to individual pastries or confections; finely ground or masticated coconut meat or juice thereof mixed with those sugars; and sauces and preparations thereof that are qualifying goods entered under subheadings 9906.17.35, 9906.18.01, 9906.18.07, 9906.18.20, 9906.18.30, 9906.18.47, 9906.19.11, 9906.19.34, 9906.21.07, 9906.21.14, and 9906.21.50 in any calendar year shall not exceed the quantity specified below for that year: 1994: 12,791,000 kg; 1995: 13,175,000 kg; 1995: 13,570,000 kg; 1997: 13,977,000 kg; 1998: 14,396,000 kg; 1999: 14,828,000 kg; 2000: 15,273,000 kg; 2001: 15,731,000 kg; 2002: 16,203,000 kg; beginning in calendar year 2003 quantitative limitations shall cease to apply on such qualifying goods.

Uruguay Round Provisions for Sugar. The major features of the Uruguay Round provisions for sugar and sugar-containing products include commitments to reduce subsidized exports by the European Union (EU) and South Africa (340,000 and 200,000 metric ton reductions, respectively, by the end of the implementation period), reductions in tariffs for sugar-containing products for a number of countries, and U.S. commitments to bind a current access level for sugar under the tariff-rate quota of 1,139,195 metric tons. In addition, the U.S. is replacing the current tariff-rate quota for sugar with a tariff equivalent of 17 cents per pound, to be reduced by 15 percent (to 14.45 cents per pound) by the end of the implementation period. The U.S. has also committed to replace the current Section 22 quotas for sugar-containing products with tariff-rate quotas at the current levels of access. These tariffs will reduced by 15% over the implementation period. Modifications to the definitions of these quotas will be made to maintain the product coverage intended when they were first introduced.

Sugar. The United States has replaced tariff- rate quotas for sugar with a tariff equivalent equal to 17 cents/lb., raw value, which will be reduced the minimum required 15% to 14.45 cents/lb. by the year 2000. The Section 22 fee of 1 cent/lb. for refined sugar and syrups will also be reduced by the minimum required 15% over six years. The U.S. is establishing a tariff-rate quota of 1,117,195 tons for raw sugar and 22,000 tons for other sugar and syrups effective in the first year of the agreement.

Sugar-Containing Products. For sugar-containing products the United States is replacing the current Section 22 quotas with tariff-rate quotas at their current levels. However, the quantity historically imported as mixed condiments and seasonings will be separated from the other quotas and increased to a total quantity of 700 tons. The over-quota tariff rates for these products are based on the tariff equivalent for refined sugar, and will be reduced by the minimum required 15% in equal annual installments over six years. Modifications to the definitions of these quotas will be made to maintain the product coverage intended when they were first introduced.

Administration of Programs for Importation of Sugar Exempt from the Tariff-Rate Quota. Additional U.S. Note 6 to chapter 17 of the HTSUS authorizes the Secretary of Agriculture to allow the entry of imported raw cane sugar exempt from the higher tier duties and quota limitations of the tariff-rate quota provided that the sugar is refined and re-exported in refined form or in sugar-containing products or is used for the production of polyhydric alcohols (except polyhydric alcohols for use as a substitute for sugar in human food consumption). Such sugar must be entered under licenses issued pursuant to regulations promulgated by the Secretary of Agriculture. See 7 CFR 1530.

There are three quota-exempt programs for sugar administered by Import Policies and Trade Analysis. These are the Refined Sugar Re-Export Program, the Sugar-Containing Products Re-Export Program, and the Polyhydric Alcohol Program. The first two programs provide for access to quota-exempt sugar (at world price) provided that the sugar refined or the product manufactured is subsequently exported. The Polyhydric Alcohol

Program allows for access to world-priced sugar to use in the manufacture of polyhydric alcohol which is used for non-food industrial processes.

On June 1, 1994 an advance notice of proposed rulemaking; extension of comment period was published in the Federal Register. The notice announced that FAS is considering revising the regulations and other program provisions for the sugar import licensing programs in order to improve program efficiency and compliance as well as to carry out relevant provisions of NAFTA. The comment period ended on July 8, 1994.

For a general discussion of quotas, refer to "Quotas Administered by Customs" on page 274.

Marking and Labeling Requirements

For a general discussion of U.S. Customs marking and labeling requirements, see "Country of Origin Marking" on page 236, "Special Marking Requirements" on page 238 and "Marking—False Impression" on page 239.

Shipping Considerations

You will need to ensure that your goods are packaged and shipped with care so that they arrive in good condition and pass smoothly through Customs. You are responsible for ensuring that the shipment is in compliance with all applicable government regulations for packaging and shipping. In most instances, you should not leave these arrangements solely to the discretion of your supplier. Careful preparation of the cargo and selection of the mode of transport can be essential to a cost-effective, timely delivery of undamaged goods. We strongly advise you to consult your shipping representative, insurance agent, or freight broker for advice on packing and shipping.

Sugar and sugar products require careful handling during transit. Although most sugars are not subject to spoilage, care must be taken to prevent contamination during storage, packing, and transport. Sugar confectionery products are often considerably more fragile and perishable, and require greater care to protect them from damage, spoilage, or contamination en route.

Publications and WWW Resources

The following publication explains the FDA requirements for importing sugars and sugar confectionery. It is published by the FDA and is available online from the FDA website (www.fda.gov/opacom/7pubs.html).

> *Requirements of Laws and Regulations Enforced by the U.S. Food and Drug Administration*

The *Harmonized Tariff Schedule of the United States (2001)* (HTSUS) is available to view on the Customs Service website (www.customs.gov), or you may purchase a printed version from:

U.S. Government Printing Office
Superintendent of Documents
710 North Capital Street NW
Washington DC 20401
Tel: (202) 512-1800
Fax: (202) 512-1657
Website: www.access.gpo.gov

The USGPO also has copies of specific laws available for purchase. The USGPO accepts orders made by fax, phone or placed over the Internet, as well as mail orders paid by credit card. All orders must be accompanied by payment. Credit cards, checks drawn on a U.S. bank, or an international money order are all acceptable.

Relevant Government Agencies

Address your questions regarding USDA licensing to:
U.S. Department of Agriculture (USDA)
Foreign Agricultural Service

Public Affairs
Ag Stop 1004
FAF-USDA
1400 Independence Avenue SW
Washington DC 20250-1004
Tel: (202) 720-7115
Fax: (202) 720-1727
Import License Information: (202) 720-1342
Website: www.fas.usda.gov

Address your questions regarding requirements for FDA-regulated products to:
Food and Drug Administration (FDA)
Center for Food Safety and Applied Nutrition (CFSAN)
Office of Compliance
Division of Enforcement, Imports Branch
5100 Paint Branch Parkway
College Park, MD 20740-3835
Tel: (301) 436-2080
Website: http://vm.cfsan.fda.gov/list.html

Food and Drug Administration (FDA)
Center for Food Safety and Applied Nutrition (CFSAN)
Office of Plant and Dairy Foods and Beverages
5100 Paint Branch Parkway
College Park, MD 20740-3835
Tel: (301) 436-1700
Website: http://vm.cfsan.fda.gov/list.html

Address questions regarding allowable chemical residues in sugar and confectionery products to:
Environmental Protection Agency (EPA)
Office of Pesticide Programs
Ariel Rios Building
1200 Pennsylvania Avenue NW
Mail Code 3213A
Washington DC 20460
Tel: (703) 305-7090
Website: www.epa.gov

Address questions regarding quotas to:
U.S. Customs and Border Protection
Office of Field Operations, Quota Branch
1300 Pennsylvania Avenue NW
Washington DC 20229
Tel: (202) 927-5850
Website: www.customs.treas.gov

Address your questions regarding Customs requirements, quotas and duties for sugars and candies to your local Customs port director. For addresses refer to "U.S. Customs and Border Protection Offices" on page 81 or contact:
U.S. Customs and Border Protection
Customs Headquarters
1300 Pennsylvania Avenue NW
Washington DC 20229
Tel: (202) 354-1000
Website: www.customs.treas.gov

Laws and Regulations

The following laws and regulations may be relevant to the importation of sugars and sugar confectionery. The laws are contained in the U.S. Code (USC) and the regulations are published in the Code of Federal Regulations (CFR), both of which may be available at larger public and law libraries. Copies of specific laws are also available from the United States Government Printing Office (address above).

7 USC 3601 et seq.
Implementation of International Sugar Agreement of 1977
This Agreement authorizes Customs to regulate the en-

try of sugar into the U.S.

15 CFR 2011.1
Regulations Allocating Tariff-Rate Quotas on Imported Sugars, Syrups, and Molasses
These regulations specify the terms and conditions under which certificates of quota eligibility will be issued to foreign countries that have been allocated shares of the US sugar tariff-rate quota.

7 USC 601 et seq.
Agricultural Adjustment Act (AAA)
This Act authorizes the Secretary of Agriculture to establish and maintain orderly market conditions for agricultural products and to impose quotas or higher duty rates on imported agricultural products whenever investigation reveals that orderly market conditions require such action.

19 CFR Part 132
Regulations for Enforcement of AAA Quotas
These regulations provide for Customs enforcement of AAA quotas and higher duty rates imposed on imported agricultural products.

21 USC 301 et seq.
Federal Food, Drug, and Cosmetic Act
This Act prohibits deceptive practices and regulates the manufacture, sale and importation or exportation of food, drugs, cosmetics, and related products. It was amended by the Food Quality Protection Act of 1996. See 21 USC 331, 381, 382.

19 CFR 12.1 et seq.; 21 CFR 1.83 et seq.
Regulations on Food, Drugs, and Cosmetics
These regulations of the Secretary of Health and Human Services and the Secretary of the Treasury govern the standards, labeling, marking, and importing of products used with food, drugs, and cosmetics.

7 USC 136 et seq.
Federal Insecticide, Fungicide, and Rodenticide Act (FIFRA)
This Act prohibits the importation of pesticides or devices that are adulterated, misbranded, or otherwise violative of the Act, provides for registration of pesticides and devices, and establishes standards for labeling and classifying pesticides. It was amended by the Food Quality Protection Act of 1996.

19 CFR 12; 40 CFR 162
Regulations on Pesticides
These regulations set forth the procedures and guidelines for importing products exposed to pesticides.

Principal Exporting Countries

The following listing includes samples of the main supplier nations of the products of this chapter. It is organized by HTSUS major heading. (Refer to "Customs Classification" above for the product codes.) Countries are listed in rank order of the value of products imported to the U.S. Statistics represent customs value of entries for 2002 from the Bureau of Census, U.S. Department of Commerce.

1701—Mexico, Dominican Republic, Brazil, Guatemala, Australia, Philippines, Colombia, Argentina, South Africa, El Salvador, Peru, Canada, Panama, Zimbabwe

1702—Canada, Netherlands, Mexico, Brazil, Thailand, Guatemala, Belgium, Pakistan, China

1703—Mexico, Guatemala, Dominican Republic, Colombia, Pakistan, El Salvador, Brazil, Australia, Honduras, Poland, Mauritius

1704—Canada, Mexico, United Kingdom, China, Argentina, Brazil, Spain, Netherlands, Germany

Chapter 18: Cocoa and Cocoa Preparations

This chapter relates to the importation of cocoa (cacao), chocolate, and other products derived primarily from the cacao plant, which are classified within Chapter 18 of the Harmonized Tariff Schedule of the United States (HTSUS). Specifically, it includes cocoa beans and parts of cocoa beans; cocoa paste, butter, fat, and oil; unsweetened cocoa powder; and chocolate in whatever form and products containing chocolate as a major constituent. This section is supplemental to the "Appendix: Foods" on page 825 and should be read in conjunction with it.

If you are interested in importing confectionery that does not contain chocolate (including white chocolate), refer to Commodity Index Chapter 17 (heading 1704). Dairy products, such as yogurt, that contain chocolate flavoring are covered in heading 0403 of Chapter 4. Products containing cocoa or chocolate that are covered in Chapter 19 include malt extract (heading 1901), breakfast cereals and related products (heading 1904), and baked goods, such as cakes (heading 1905). If you are interested in importing ice cream containing chocolate flavoring, refer to Chapter 21 (heading 2105). Beverages containing chocolate, such as chocolate milk, are covered in Chapter 22 (heading 2202), while alcoholic beverages containing chocolate, such as liqueurs, are found in heading 2208 of that chapter. Pharmaceuticals that contain cocoa are covered in Chapter 30 (headings 3003 and 3004).

Note: To understand key issues that will enable you to make best use of the information in this section we recommend that you see "Introduction" on page 425.

Key Factors

The key factors in the importation of cocoa and cocoa products are:

- Compliance with U.S. Food and Drug Administration (FDA) purity, identity, manufacturing, and other standards

- Compliance with FDA entry notifications and procedures

- Import quotas on certain types of chocolate

Although most importers utilize the services of a licensed customs broker in making their entries, and we recommend this practice, you should be aware of the regulatory, entry, and documentation issues involved in importing your product. You, as importer, are ultimately responsible for the fulfillment of any legal requirements applicable to your shipment.

General Considerations

Regulatory Agencies. Importation of cocoa and products containing chocolate falls primarily under the jurisdiction of the FDA, which enforces the requirements of the Federal Food, Drug, and Cosmetic Act (FDCA). The USDA controls imports of plant products to prevent contamination of U.S. food sources. The EPA inspects imported edible plant products for pesticide residues.

FDA Requirements. FDA regulations regarding importation of foods of any kind are extensive and stringent. Cocoa products imported into the U.S. must comply with all FDCA requirements for those produced domestically.

Entry Requirements. Imported products regulated by the FDA are subject to FDA port-of-entry inspection. For a general discussion of required FDA import procedures see "Appendix: Foods" on page 825.

Detention of Shipment. If your shipment is found to be noncomplying, it may be detained at the port of entry. The FDA may allow you to bring such a shipment into compliance before making a final decision regarding admittance. However, any sorting, reprocessing, or relabeling must be supervised by FDA personnel, and is done at the importer's expense. Such conditional release to allow an importer to bring a shipment into compliance is a privilege, not a right. The FDA may consider subsequent noncomplying shipments of the same type of product to constitute abuse of the privilege and require the importer to destroy or reexport the products. To ascertain what your legal responsibilities are, you should contact this agencies regarding the specific items to be imported.

USDA Requirements. All products derived from plants are also subject to U.S. Department of Agriculture (USDA) regulations. In general, USDA does not restrict processed cacao products. If you are in any doubt as to the regulatory status of your product, you should check with USDA Animal and Plant Health Inspection Service (APHIS) (see addresses at end of this chapter).

EPA Requirements. The U.S. Environmental Protection Agency (EPA) enforces the Federal Insecticide, Fungicide, and Rodenticide Act (FIFRA), which establishes regulatory limits on pesticide and other chemical residues found in edible plant products. For more information, contact EPA (see addresses at end of this chapter).

Quotas. Some cocoa products from certain countries are subject to quotas under Section 22 of the Agricultural Adjustment Act (AAA) as amended.

Customs Classification

For customs purposes, cocoa and cocoa products are classified under Chapter 18 of the HTSUS. This chapter is broken into major headings, which are further divided into subheadings, and often sub-subheadings, each of which has its own HTSUS classification number. For example, the 2001 HTSUS number for cocoa powder containing less than 65% by weight of sugar is 1806.10.22, indicating that it is a sub-subcategory of cocoa powder containing added sugar or other sweetening matter (1806.10), which is a subcategory of the major heading Chocolate and other food preparations containing cocoa (1806). There are six major headings in HTSUS Chapter 18.

1801—Cocoa beans, whole or broken, raw or roasted

1802—Cocoa shells, husks, skins, and other cocoa waste

1803—Cocoa paste, whether or not defatted

1804—Cocoa butter, fat, or oil

1805—Cocoa powder, not containing added sugar or other sweetening matter

1806—Chocolate and other food preparations containing cocoa

For more details regarding classification of the specific product you are interested in importing, consult a customs broker, the appropriate commodity specialist at your nearest customs port, or see HTSUS. The 2001 HTSUS is available online from the Customs Service (www.customs.gov/impoexpo/impoexpo.htm) or for purchase from the U.S. Government Printing Office (see resources at the end of this chapter), and may be found in larger public libraries. For a general discussion of customs classification, see "Classification—Liquidation" on page 229.

Dutiable Status of Goods

For more information about duty rates and binding decisions see "Dutiable Status of Goods" on page 203; for a discussion of temporary importation of goods see "Temporary Free Importations" on page 205.

Valuation

Importers have a responsibility to use what the U.S. Customs Service deems, "reasonable care," when determining the value of their goods. They must also provide any additional information that the Customs Service needs for setting a final value on the goods. This process involves a number of factors and can be somewhat complicated; importers must be aware of applicable issues and details. Valuation information applies to all types of commodities, for further discussion on the subject see "Customs Valuation" on page 267.

Import Duties

Import duties vary (often dramatically) depending upon the Harmonized Tariff Schedule (HTSUS) classification of the goods or products imported. Since some products that look alike have different HTSUS classifications and different rates of duty, proper classification is vital. Note that "differences of opinion" between importers and the Bureau of Customs and Border Protection regarding classification keeps customs attorneys very busy.

Import duties can be assessed on the imported value of the goods ("ad valorem" rates of duty such as 2%, 4.4%, 50%, etc.), total units or weight of the goods ("specific" rates of duty such as 2 cents each or 1.5 cents/pound, etc.) or on a combination basis ("compound" rates of duty such as 5 cents each plus 6%).

Listed below is a sampling of several Column 1 import duty rates for Chapter 18 products:
Cocoa beans, whole or broken, raw or roasted (1801.00.00.00):: free
to
Articles containing 65 percent or more but less than 90 percent by dry weight of sugar described in general note 15 of the tariff schedule and entered pursuant to its provisions (1806.10.24.00): 10%

For specific information on US import duties refer to the Harmonized Tariff Schedule of the US. The print version is available from the US Government Printing Office as well as third party suppliers who often add special features. Online versions are available in both static PDF pages as well as in formats with excellent search functionality. Search the Web with the term "Harmonized Tariff Schedule" to find sources.

Entry and Documentation

The entry of merchandise is a two-part process consisting of 1) filing the documents necessary to determine whether merchandise may be released from Customs custody and 2) filing the documents that contain information for duty assessment and statistical purposes. In certain instances, such as the entry of merchandise subject to quotas, all documents must be filed and accepted by Customs prior to the release of the goods. Unless you have been granted an extension, you must file entry documents at a location specified by the port or area director within five working days of your shipment's date of arrival at a U.S. port of entry. These include a number of standard documents required by Customs for any entry.

After you present the entry, Customs may examine your shipment, or may waive examination. The shipment is then released provided no legal or regulatory violations have been noted. You must then file entry summary documentation and deposit estimated duties at a designated customhouse within 10 working days of your shipment's release. For a detailed description of entry procedures, standard documentation, and informal entry, see "Entry Process" on page 185.

Informed Compliance. Informed compliance was introduced with the Customs Modernization Act of 1993 (Mod Act) and defines the relationship between importers and the Customs Service. It sets out the responsibilities of both parties. Providing the correct documentation and information for entry is a key factor that will make your importing operation run smoothly. We recommend that importers become familiar with the concept of informed comliance and the responsibilities that they have under the Mod Act. For further discussion about informed compliance see "Informed Compliance" on page 211.

Note: The Entry and Documentation section has been carefully designed to supply you, the importer, with sample documents and directions on how to satisfy Customs requirements. Be aware that you should consult the applicable authorities to ensure that you are correctly following the most current procedures.

Prohibitions and Restrictions

Standards of identity have been promulgated under the FDCA for approximately 40 cocoa products. If your cocoa product is labeled as one of the standardized products listed in the regulations, it must conform to the standard for that product (21 CFR 163). There are some frequent problems with cocoa shipments that you would be wise to guard against.

Excess shell is a frequent cause for port of entry detention of various standardized cocoa products. The presence of the following types of contamination often form the basis for detention of cocoa bean imports: 1) mold, 2) worms, 3) live or dead insects, their excreta, or webbing, 4) animal excreta. Precautions taken prior to shipping cocoa beans can eliminate many of these problems. Remove any moldy and insect-infested beans before and during shipping, and store the good beans in such a way as to prevent contamination. Such actions will materially lessen the chance of having a shipment detained at the U.S. port of entry.

Quotas

Entry of specific products can be difficult because many product categories affected by quota restrictions overlap, especially if the product contains sugar or milk—both of which are major components of prepared cocoa products. Even if cocoa itself is not the target of a quota, products containing cocoa, whether listed within Chapter 18 or elsewhere in the HTSUS, may be restricted because of other policy driven limitations. It is important to consult with the Quota Branch of the U.S. Customs Service (see addresses at end of this chapter) to determine whether quota restrictions apply to your specific product.

Quotas on chocolate and other food preparations containing cocoa include the following.

Subheadings 1806.10.10, 1806.10.34 and 1806.10.65. The aggregate quantity of cocoa powder containing over 10% by dry weight of sugars derived from sugar cane or sugar beets, whether or not mixed with other ingredients (except certain exceptions noted in Chapter 19, Additional U.S. Note 1), the foregoing goods entered under subheadings 1806.10.10, 1806.10.34 and 1806.10.65 during the 12-month period from October 1 in any year to the following September 30, inclusive, shall not exceed

2,313 metric tons. Imports from Mexico are not be permitted or included under this quantitative limitation and no such articles shall be classifiable therein.

Subheadings 1806.20.24, 1806.32.04 and 1806.90.15. The aggregate quantity of chocolate containing over 5.5% by weight of butterfat (excluding articles for consumption at retail as candy or confection), the foregoing entered under subheadings 1806.20.24, 1806.32.04 and 1806.90.15 in any calendar year shall not exceed 17,607,700 kilograms. Imports from Mexico shall not be permitted or included under the aforementioned quantitative limitation and no such articles shall be classifiable therein. Of the quantitative limitations provided for in this note, the countries listed here will have access to not less than the quantities specified here: Ireland, 4,286,491 kg; United Kingdom, 3,379,297 kg; Netherlands, 45,359; Australia, 2,000,000 kg; New Zealand, 1 kg.

Subheadings 1806.20.34, 1806.20.85, 1806.32.14 and 1806.90.25. The aggregate quantity of chocolate and low fat chocolate crumb containing 5.5% or less by weight of butterfat (excluding articles for consumption at retail as candy or confection), the foregoing entered under subheadings 1806.20.34, 1806.20.85, 1806.32.14 and 1806.90.25 in any calendar year shall not exceed 2,122,834 kilograms. Imports from Mexico shall not be permitted or included under the aforementioned quantitative limitation and no such articles shall be classifiable therein. Of the quantitative limitations provided for in this note, the countries listed here will have access to not less than the quantities specified here: Ireland, 1,700,988 kg; United Kingdom, 421,845 kg; New Zealand, 1 kg.

Other Quotas. Goods classified at the following may be subject to quotas under Chapter 99, Subchapter IV: 1806.10.15, 1806.10.28, 1806.10.38, 1806.10.55, 1806.20.73, 1806.10.75, 1806.20.26, 1806.20.28, 1806.20.36, 1806.20.38, 1806.20.77, 1806.20.82, 1806.20.83, 1806.20.87, 1806.20.89, 1806.20.94, 1806.20.98, 1806.32.06, 1806.32.08, 1806.32.16, 1806.32.18, 1806.32.70, 1806.32.80, 1806.90.08, 1806.90.10, 1806.90.18, 1806.90.20, 1806.90.28, 1806.90.30, 1806.90.39, 1806.90.49, or 1806.90.59.

For a general discussion of quotas, refer to "Quotas Administered by Customs" on page 274.

Marking and Labeling Requirements

For basic FDA marking and labeling requirements, see "Appendix: Foods" on page 825. For a general discussion of U.S. Customs marking and labeling requirements, see "Country of Origin Marking" on page 236, "Special Marking Requirements" on page 238 and "Marking—False Impression" on page 239.

Shipping Considerations

You will need to ensure that your goods are packaged and shipped with care so that they arrive in good condition and pass smoothly through Customs. You are responsible for ensuring that the shipment is in compliance with all applicable government regulations for packaging and shipping. In most instances, you should not leave these arrangements solely to the discretion of your supplier. Careful preparation of the cargo and selection of the mode of transport can be essential to a cost-effective, timely delivery of undamaged goods. We strongly advise you to consult your shipping representative, insurance agent, or freight broker for advice on packing and shipping.

As with any edible product, careful packing is necessary to prevent contamination and spoilage en route. Protection from insect and animal contamination is especially important for cocoa and cocoa products. Heat and moisture control are also important. Because cocoa contains oils that can become rancid and is subject to the growth of mold if kept in a hot, moist environment, packing and the avoidance of delays in transit are important to ensuring the delivery of a salable product.

Publications and WWW Resources

The following publication explains the FDA requirements for importing cocoa and cocoa products. It is published by the FDA and is available online from the FDA website (www.fda.gov/opacom/7pubs.html).

Requirements of Laws and Regulations Enforced by the U.S. Food and Drug Administration

The following publication gives brief, general guidelines on USDA regulated products. Although designed primarily for tourists, it contains a list of approved products that you may find helpful. It is available online from the USDA APHIS website (www.aphis.usda.gov).

Travelers Tips On Bringing Food, Plant, and Animal Products into the United States

The *Harmonized Tariff Schedule of the United States (2001)* (HTSUS) is available to view on the Customs Service website (www.customs.gov), or you may purchase a printed version from:

U.S. Government Printing Office
Superintendent of Documents
710 North Capital Street NW
Washington DC 20401
Tel: (202) 512-1800
Fax: (202) 512-1657
Website: www.access.gpo.gov

The USGPO also has copies of specific laws available for purchase. The USGPO accepts orders made by fax, phone or placed over the Internet, as well as mail orders paid by credit card. All orders must be accompanied by payment. Credit cards, checks drawn on a U.S. bank, or an international money order are all acceptable.

Relevant Government Agencies

Address your questions regarding FDA requirements for the importation of cocoa and cocoa products to:

Food and Drug Administration (FDA)
Center for Food Safety and Applied Nutrition (CFSAN)
Office of Compliance
Division of Enforcement, Imports Branch
5100 Paint Branch Parkway
College Park, MD 20740-3835
Tel: (301) 436-2080
Website: http://vm.cfsan.fda.gov/list.html

Food and Drug Administration (FDA)
Center for Food Safety and Applied Nutrition (CFSAN)
Office of Plant and Dairy Foods and Beverages
5100 Paint Branch Parkway
College Park, MD 20740-3835
Tel: (301) 436-1700
Website: http://vm.cfsan.fda.gov/list.html

Address your questions regarding USDA requirements for the importation of cocoa and cocoa products to:

Animal and Plant Health Inspection Service (APHIS)
Plant Protection and Quarantine (PPQ)
Director's Office
4700 River Rd., Unit 131
Riverdale, MD 20737
Tel: (301) 734-8261
Tel (PPQ permits): (301) 734-8758
Website: www.aphis.usda.gov/ppq

Address questions regarding allowable chemical residues in cocoa and cocoa products to:

Environmental Protection Agency (EPA)
Office of Pesticide Programs
Ariel Rios Building
1200 Pennsylvania Avenue NW
Mail Code 3213A
Washington DC 20460

Tel: (703) 305-7090
Website: www.epa.gov

Address your questions regarding quotas to:

U.S. Customs and Border Protection
Office of Field Operations, Quota Branch
1300 Pennsylvania Avenue NW
Washington DC 20229
Tel: (202) 927-5850
Website: www.customs.treas.gov

Address your questions regarding importation of cocoa and cocoa products to your local Customs port director. For addresses refer to ""U.S. Customs and Border Protection Offices" on page 81 or contact:

U.S. Customs and Border Protection
Customs Headquarters
1300 Pennsylvania Avenue NW
Washington DC 20229
Tel: (202) 354-1000
Website: www.customs.treas.gov

Laws and Regulations

The following laws and regulations may be relevant to the importation of cocoa and cocoa products. The laws are contained in the U.S. Code (USC) and the regulations are published in the Code of Federal Regulations (CFR), both of which may be available at larger public and law libraries. Copies of specific laws are also available from the United States Government Printing Office (address above).

7 USC 601 et seq.
Agricultural Adjustment Act (AAA)
This Act authorizes the Secretary of Agriculture to establish and maintain orderly market conditions for agricultural products and to impose quotas or higher duty rates on imported agricultural products whenever investigation reveals that orderly market conditions require such action.

19 CFR Part 132
Regulations for Enforcement of AAA Quotas
These regulations provide for Customs enforcement of AAA quotas and higher duty rates imposed on imported agricultural products.

21 USC 301 et seq.
Federal Food, Drug, and Cosmetic Act
This Act prohibits deceptive practices and regulates the manufacture, sale and importation or exportation of food, drugs, cosmetics, and related products. It was amended by the Food Quality Protection Act of 1996. See 21 USC 331, 381, 382.

19 CFR 12.1 et seq.; 21 CFR 1.83 et seq.
Regulations on Food, Drugs, and Cosmetics
These regulations of the Secretary of Health and Human Services and the Secretary of the Treasury govern the standards, labeling, marking, and importing of products used with food, drugs, and cosmetics.

7 USC 136 et seq.
Federal Insecticide, Fungicide, and Rodenticide Act (FIFRA)
This Act prohibits the importation of pesticides or devices that are adulterated, misbranded, or otherwise violative of the Act, provides for registration of pesticides and devices, and establishes standards for labeling and classifying pesticides. It was amended by the Food Quality Protection Act of 1996.

19 CFR 12; 40 CFR 162
Regulations on Pesticides
These regulations set forth the procedures and guidelines for importing products exposed to pesticides.

Principal Exporting Countries

The following listing includes samples of the main supplier nations of the products of this chapter. It is organized by HTSUS major heading. (Refer to "Customs Classification" above for the product codes.) Countries are listed in rank order of the value of products imported to the U.S. Statistics represent customs value of entries for 2002 from the Bureau of Census, U.S. Department of Commerce.

1801—Ivory Coast, Indonesia, Dominican Republic, Ecuador, Papua New Guinea, Ghana, Nigeria, Haiti, Mexico

1802—Ghana, Canada, India, Germany

1803—Ivory Coast, Cameroon, Indonesia, Canada, Malaysia, United Kingdom, Ghana, Brazil, Ecuador, Switzerland, Netherlands

1804—Indonesia, Malaysia, Brazil, China, Mexico, Singapore, Thailand, Ghana, Netherlands, Peru, Dominican Republic, Philippines, Colombia, Ecuador, Ivory Coast, Spain

1805—Netherlands, Ivory Coast, Singapore, France, Brazil, United Kingdom, Spain, Indonesia

1806—Canada, Germany, Belgium, Mexico, United Kingdom

Chapter 19:
Baked Goods

Full title: Preparations of Cereals, Flour, Starch, or Milk; Bakers' Wares

This chapter relates to the importation of processed foods consisting primarily of cereals essentially as finished products, which are classified under Chapter 19 of the Harmonized Tariff Schedule of the United States (HTSUS). Specifically, it includes preparations of flour, such as dough, mixes, and finished baked goods—bread, pasta, cakes, pastries, puddings, prepared pizzas, breakfast foods, and corn chips—as well as tapioca and related products, some products containing milk—such as malted milk and some infant formulas—some products containing cocoa—other than confections—and some products with meat fillings, such as ravioli. This section is supplemental to the "Appendix: Foods" on page 825. If you are interested in importing cereal preparations, bakers' wares, or related products, you should read that section in conjunction with this one.

If you are interested in importing intermediate, partially processed cereal products—such as flour, worked grains, starches, and gluten—you should refer to Commodity Index Chapter 11. Those interested in importing fabricated cereal-based products intended for use as animal feed should refer to Chapter 23. For importation of any cereal-based medicated products for which the preparation is intended either primarily as a vehicle to deliver the medication or to have some inherent medicinal property, refer to Chapter 30. Those interested in importing prepared foods with a meat content of more than 20% by weight should refer to Chapter 16, while those interested in importing prepared foods with a cocoa content greater than 8% should refer to Chapter 18. Chapter 19 uses the same definitions—such as for "flour" and "meal"—as Chapter 11, but pertains to products that have been processed to an extent beyond that provided for in Chapter 11.

Note: To understand key issues that will enable you to make best use of the information in this section we recommend that you see "Introduction" on page 425.

Key Factors

The key factors in the importation of cereal preparations and related products are:

- Compliance with U.S. Food and Drug Administration (FDA) purity, identity, manufacturing, and other standards

- Compliance with FDA entry notification procedures

- Compliance with Environmental Protection Agency (EPA) pesticide residue requirements

Although most importers use the services of a licensed customs broker in making their entries, and we recommend this practice, you should be aware of the regulatory, entry, and documentation issues involved in importing your product. You, as importer, are ultimately responsible for the fulfillment of any legal requirements applicable to your shipment.

General Considerations

The importation of cereal preparations is regulated primarily by the FDA, which administers the provisions of the Food, Drug, and Cosmetic Act (FDCA). The EPA also exercises jurisdiction over pesticide residues in foodstuffs through the Federal Insecticide, Fungicide, and Rodenticide Act (FIFRA) and the Food Quality Protection Act of 1996, which establish allowable levels for the presence of such residues. Not only must any chemical residues found on foodstuffs fall within the designated levels, but residues must also be from approved chemicals—the presence of chemicals not approved for use on U.S. food crops is grounds for refusing entry regardless of the status of the chemical in its country of origin.

Cereal preparations imported into the U.S. must comply with all requirements for those produced domestically. These include standards of nomenclature, levels of nutritional elements, and allowable additives as prescribed in detail in 21 CFR, particularly Parts 107 (Infant Formula), 136 (Bakery Products), and 139 (Macaroni and Noodle Products). Imported products regulated by the FDA are subject to port of entry inspection. For a general discussion of required FDA import procedures, see "Appendix: Foods" on page 825.

Detention of Shipment. If your shipment is found to be noncomplying, it may be detained at the port of entry. The FDA may permit you to bring such a shipment into compliance before making a final decision regarding admittance. However, any sorting, reprocessing, or relabeling must be supervised by FDA personnel and is done at the importer's expense. Such conditional release to allow the importer to bring a shipment into compliance is a privilege, not a right. The FDA may consider subsequent noncomplying shipments of the same type of product to constitute abuse of the privilege and require the importer to destroy or reexport the products. To ascertain what your legal responsibilities are, you should contact these agencies regarding the specific items to be imported.

Customs Classifications

For customs purposes, cereal preparations are classified under Chapter 19 of the HTSUS. This chapter is broken into major headings, which are further divided into subheadings, and often sub-subheadings, each of which has its own HTSUS classification number. For example, the 2001 HTSUS number for pasta packaged with sauce preparations is 1902.11.40, indicating that it is a sub-subcategory of uncooked pasta containing eggs (1902.11), which is a subcategory of the major heading pasta whether or not cooked or stuffed or otherwise prepared (1902). There are five major headings within Chapter 19.

1901—Malt extract; food preparations of flour, meal, starch or malt extract, not containing cocoa or containing less than 40 percent by weight of cocoa calculated on a totally defatted basis, not elsewhere specified or included; food preparations of goods of headings 0401 to 0404, not containing cocoa or containing less than 5% by weight of cocoa calculated on a totally defatted basis, not elsewhere specified or included

1902—Pasta, whether or not cooked or stuffed (with meat or other substances) or otherwise prepared, such as spaghetti, macaroni, noodles, lasagna, gnocchi, ravioli, canneloni; couscous, whether or not prepared

1903—Tapioca and substitutes therefor prepared from starch, in the form of flakes, grains, pearls, siftings, or in similar forms

1904—Prepared foods obtained by the swelling or roasting of cereals or cereal products (for example, cornflakes); cereals (other than corn (maize) in grain form or in the form of flakes or other worked grains (except flour and meal), precooked or otherwise prepared, not elsewhere specified or included

1905—Bread, pastry, cakes, biscuits, and other bakers' wares, whether or not containing cocoa; communion wafers, empty capsules of a kind suitable for pharmaceutical use, sealing wafers, rice paper, and similar products

For more details regarding classification of the specific product you are interested in importing, consult a customs broker, the appropriate commodity specialist at your nearest customs port, or see HTSUS. The 2001 HTSUS is available online from the Customs Service (www.customs.gov/impoexpo/impoexpo.htm) or for purchase from the U.S. Government Printing Office (see resources at the end of this chapter), and may be found in larger public libraries. For a general discussion of customs classification, see "Classification—Liquidation" on page 229.

Dutiable Status of Goods

For more information about duty rates and binding decisions see "Dutiable Status of Goods" on page 203; for a discussion of temporary importation of goods see "Temporary Free Importations" on page 205.

Valuation

Importers have a responsibility to use what the U.S. Customs Service deems, "reasonable care," when determining the value of their goods. They must also provide any additional information that the Customs Service needs for setting a final value on the goods. This process involves a number of factors and can be somewhat complicated; importers must be aware of applicable issues and details. Valuation information applies to all types of commodities, for further discussion on the subject see "Customs Valuation" on page 267.

Import Duties

Import duties vary (often dramatically) depending upon the Harmonized Tariff Schedule (HTSUS) classification of the goods or products imported. Since some products that look alike have different HTSUS classifications and different rates of duty, proper classification is vital. Note that "differences of opinion" between importers and the Bureau of Customs and Border Protection regarding classification keeps customs attorneys very busy.

Import duties can be assessed on the imported value of the goods ("ad valorem" rates of duty such as 2%, 4.4%, 50%, etc.), total units or weight of the goods ("specific" rates of duty such as 2 cents each or 1.5 cents/pound, etc.) or on a combination basis ("compound" rates of duty such as 5 cents each plus 6%).

Listed below is a sampling of several Column 1 import duty rates for Chapter 19 products:

Puddings ready for immediate consumption without further preparation (1901.90.25.00): free

to

Infant formula containing oligosaccharides described in additional U.S. note 2 to this chapter and entered pursuant to its provisions (1901.10.15.00): 17.5%

For specific information on US import duties refer to the Harmonized Tariff Schedule of the US. The print version is available from the US Government Printing Office as well as third party suppliers who often add special features. Online versions are available in both static PDF pages as well as in formats with excellent search functionality. Search the Web with the term "Harmonized Tariff Schedule" to find sources.

Entry and Documentation

The entry of merchandise is a two-part process consisting of 1) filing the documentation necessary to determine whether merchandise may be released from Customs custody and 2) filing the documents that contain the information for duty assessment and statistical purposes. In certain instances all documents must be filed and accepted by Customs prior to release of the goods. Unless you have been granted an extension, you must file entry documents at a location specified by the port or area director within five working days of your shipment's arrival at a U.S. port of entry. These include a number of standard documents required by Customs for entry.

After you present the entry, Customs may examine your shipment, or may waive examination (food items are almost always inspected). The shipment is then released provided no legal or regulatory violations have been noted. You must then file entry summary documentation and deposit estimated duties at a designated customhouse within 10 working days of your shipment's release. For a detailed description of entry procedures, standard documentation, and informal entry, see "Entry Process" on page 185.

Informed Compliance. Informed compliance was introduced with the Customs Modernization Act of 1993 (Mod Act) and defines the relationship between importers and the Customs Service. It sets out the responsibilities of both parties. Providing the correct documentation and information for entry is a key factor that will make your importing operation run smoothly. We recommend that importers become familiar with the concept of informed comliance and the responsibilities that they have under the Mod Act. For further discussion about informed compliance see "Informed Compliance" on page 211.

Note: The Entry and Documentation section has been carefully designed to supply you, the importer, with sample documents and directions on how to satisfy Customs requirements. Be aware that you should consult the applicable authorities to ensure that you are correctly following the most current procedures.

Prohibitions and Restrictions

Prepared cereal products falling within Chapter 19 are generally allowed into the U.S. without the need for prior authorization regardless of country of origin, provided they meet all domestic standards set for such products (some intermediate and raw cereal products are prohibited under USDA restrictions). Note that passage of a shipment by Customs does not relieve the importer from future responsibility should a discrepancy or violation come to light at a later time.

Quotas

Entry of specific products can be difficult because many product categories affected by quota restrictions overlap, especially where sugar, milk, and cocoa products—all of which are major components in many baked goods—are concerned. Although baked goods themselves are not the target of a quota, they contain products that may be restricted because of other policy driven limitations. It is important to consult with the Quota Branch of the U.S. Customs Service (see addresses at end of this chapter) to determine whether quota restrictions apply to your specific product.

The aggregate quantity of infant formula containing oligosaccharides, approved by the FDA, the foregoing goods entered under subheadings 1901.10.15 and 1901.10.60 in any calendar year may not exceed 100 metric tons (imports from Mexico shall not be permitted or included under the aforementioned quantitative limitation and no such articles shall be classifiable therein).

The aggregate quantity of mixes and doughs, the foregoing goods entered under subheadings 1901.20.30 and 1901.20.65 during the 12-month period from October 1 in any year to the following September 30, inclusive, may not exceed 5,398 metric tons. Imports from Mexico shall not be permitted or included under this quantitative limitation and no such articles shall be classifiable therein. (For the purposes of this chapter, the term "mixes and doughs" means articles containing over 10 percent by dry weight of sugars derived from sugar cane or sugar beets, whether or not mixed with other ingredients (with some exceptions, as noted in Chapter 19, Additional U.S. Note 1).

In addition, goods classified under the following may be subject to quotas specified in Chapter 99, Subchapter IV: 1901.10.40, 1901.10.85, 1901.20.15, 1901.20.25, 1901.20.50, 1901.20.60, 1901.90.36, 1901.90.43, 1901.90.47, 1901.90.54, 1901.90.58, 1901.90.58.

For a general discussion of quotas, refer to "Quotas Administered by Customs" on page 274.

Marking and Labeling Requirements

Imports of cereal preparations must declare the country of origin for all imported products. The invoice and any other labeling shall bear the lot identification, the kind of product present, note any treatment given to the product, and comply with all nutritional labeling requirements.

For a general discussion of U.S. Customs marking and labeling requirements, see "Country of Origin Marking" on page 236, "Special Marking Requirements" on page 238 and "Marking—False Impression" on page 239.

Shipping Considerations

You will ned to ensure that your goods are packaged and shipped with care so that they arrive in good condition and pass smoothly through Customs. You are responsible for ensuring that the shipment is in compliance with all applicable government regulations for packaging and shipping. In most instances, you should not leave these arrangements solely to the discretion of your supplier. Careful preparation of the cargo and selection of the mode of transport can be essential to a cost-effective, timely delivery of undamaged goods. We strongly advise you to consult your shipping representative, insurance agent, or freight broker for advice on packing and shipping. Refer to the section "Packing/Shipping/Insurance" for a general discussion of packing and shipping.

Cereal preparations may be transported in bulk, although in most instances they are shipped in various types of containers designed to prevent damage during transit, and may be packaged by units for retail sale. General considerations include protection from contamination by dirt, pests, or other foreign matter, as well as the effects of heat and dampness on the goods shipped. Many cereal preparations—especially bakers' wares—have a limited shelf life and care must be taken that they arrive at their destination in a timely fashion as well as in marketable condition.

Publications and WWW Resources

The following publication explains the FDA requirements for importing cereal preparations. It is published by the FDA and is available online from the FDA website (www.fda.gov/opacom/7pubs.html).

> *Requirements of Laws and Regulations Enforced by the U.S. Food and Drug Administration*

The *Harmonized Tariff Schedule of the United States (2001)* (HTSUS) is available to view on the Customs Service website (www.customs.gov), or you may purchase a printed version from:

U.S. Government Printing Office
Superintendent of Documents
710 North Capital Street NW
Washington DC 20401
Tel: (202) 512-1800

Fax: (202) 512-1657
Website: www.access.gpo.gov

The USGPO also has copies of specific laws available for purchase. The USGPO accepts orders made by fax, phone or placed over the Internet, as well as mail orders paid by credit card. All orders must be accompanied by payment. Credit cards, checks drawn on a U.S. bank, or an international money order are all acceptable.

Relevant Government Agencies

Address your inquiries regarding USDA requirements for importation of cereal preparations to:

Food and Drug Administration (FDA)
Center for Food Safety and Applied Nutrition (CFSAN)
Office of Compliance
Division of Enforcement, Imports Branch
5100 Paint Branch Parkway
College Park, MD 20740-3835
Tel: (301) 436-2080
Website: http://vm.cfsan.fda.gov/list.html

Food and Drug Administration (FDA)
Center for Food Safety and Applied Nutrition (CFSAN)
Office of Plant and Dairy Foods and Beverages
5100 Paint Branch Parkway
College Park, MD 20740-3835
Tel: (301) 436-1700
Website: http://vm.cfsan.fda.gov/list.html

Address questions regarding allowable pesticide residues on cereal preparations to:

Environmental Protection Agency (EPA)
Office of Pesticide Programs
Ariel Rios Building
1200 Pennsylvania Avenue NW
Washington DC 20460
Tel: (703) 305-7090
Website: www.epa.gov

Address your questions regarding importation of cereal preparations to your local Customs port director. For addresses refer to "U.S. Customs and Border Protection Offices" on page 65 or contact:

U.S. Customs and Border Protection
Customs Headquarters
1300 Pennsylvania Avenue NW
Washington DC 20229
Tel: (202) 354-1000
Website: www.customs.treas.gov

Laws and Regulations

The following laws and regulations may be relevant to the importation of cereal preparations. The laws are contained in the U.S. Code (USC) and the regulations are published in the Code of Federal Regulations (CFR), both of which may be available at larger public and law libraries. Copies of specific laws are also available from the United States Government Printing Office (address above).

21 USC 301 et seq.
Federal Food, Drug, and Cosmetic Act
This Act prohibits deceptive practices and regulates the manufacture, sale and importation or exportation of food, drugs, cosmetics, and related products. It was amended by the Food Quality Protection Act of 1996. See 21 USC 331, 381, 382.

19 CFR 12.1 et seq.; 21 CFR 1.83 et seq.
Regulations on Food, Drugs, and Cosmetics
These regulations of the Secretary of Health and Human Services and the Secretary of the Treasury govern the standards, labeling, marking, and importing of products

used with food, drugs, and cosmetics.

21 CFR Parts 107, 136, and 139
Regulations of FDA on Infant Formula (Part 107), Bakery Products (Part 136), Macaroni and Noodle Products (Part 139)
These regulations establish nomenclatural and technical standards and requirements for many of the major products covered in Chapter 19.

7 USC 136 et seq.
Federal Insecticide, Fungicide, and Rodenticide Act (FIFRA)
This Act prohibits the importation of pesticides or devices that are adulterated, misbranded, or otherwise violative of the Act, provides for registration of pesticides and devices, and establishes standards for labeling and classifying pesticides. It was amended by the Food Quality Protection Act of 1996.

19 CFR 12; 40 CFR 162
Regulations on Pesticides
These regulations set forth the procedures and guidelines for importing products exposed to pesticides.

Principal Exporting Countries

The following listing includes samples of the main supplier nations of the products of this chapter. It is organized by HTSUS major heading. (Refer to "Customs Classification" above for the product codes.) Countries are listed in rank order of the value of products imported to the U.S. Statistics represent customs value of entries for 2002 from the Bureau of Census, U.S. Department of Commerce.

1901—Canada, Mexico, China, United Kingdom, Denmark, Japan, France, Taiwan, Thailand

1902—Italy, Canada, South Korea, Thailand, Mexico, Japan, China

1903—Thailand, Brazil, Taiwan

1904—Canada, Mexico, Guatemala, Colombia, United Kingdom, Taiwan, Switzerland, Thailand, India

1905—Canada, Mexico, Italy, Denmark, United Kingdom, Germany, France

Chapter 20:
Vegetable, Fruit, and Nut Preparations

Full title: Preparations of Vegetables, Fruit, Nuts, and Other Parts of Plants

This section pertains to the importation of edible preparations of vegetables, fruit, nuts, and other plant products, which are classified under Chapter 20 of the Harmonized Tariff Schedule of the United States (HTSUS). Specifically, it includes pickled and canned vegetables; fruit and nuts prepared and preserved using sugar; jams, jellies, and pastes; fruit and nut preparations, including canned and otherwise preserved; and natural (that is, unfortified) fruit and vegetable juices. You should read this section in conjunction with "Appendix: Foods" on page 825.

If you are interested in importing fresh or provisionally preserved but not prepared, fruit, vegetables, or nuts, refer to Commodity Index Chapters 7 and 8. Seeds and live plants are included in Chapter 6. Edible vegetable fats and oils are covered in Chapter 15. Confectionery of fruit and nuts without chocolate is covered in Chapter 17 (with chocolate in Chapter 18). Preparations of flour and baked goods with an incidental component of vegetables, fruit, or nuts are covered in Chapter 19. Miscellaneous food preparations—such as extracts, sauces, condiments, soups, and various other preparations—are included in Chapter 21. Foods in which meat or fish make up a significant portion—greater than 20% by weight—are classified in Chapter 16, no matter what their other contents. Fortified fruit and vegetable juices are treated as beverages in Chapter 22.

Note: To understand key issues that will enable you to make best use of the information in this section we recommend that you see "Introduction" on page 425.

Key Factors

The key factors in the importation of prepared vegetables, fruit, and nuts are:

- Compliance with U.S. Food and Drug Administration (FDA) purity, identity, manufacturing, and other standards
- Compliance with FDA entry notifications and procedures

Although most importers utilize the services of a licensed customs broker in making their entries, and we recommend this practice, you should be aware of the regulatory, entry, and documentation issues involved in importing your product. You, as importer, are ultimately responsible for the fulfillment of any legal requirements applicable to your shipment.

General Considerations

Importation of prepared vegetable, fruit, and nut products falls primarily under the jurisdiction of the FDA, which enforces the requirements of the Federal Food, Drug, and Cosmetic Act (FDCA). FDA regulations regarding importation of foods of any kind are extensive and stringent. Prepared vegetable, fruit, and nut food products imported into the U.S. must comply with all FDCA requirements for those produced domestically.

Imported products regulated by the FDA are subject to FDA port of entry inspection. For a general discussion of required FDA importing procedures see "Appendix: Foods" on page 825.

Food products imported into the U.S. must also comply with established tolerances for pesticide and other chemical residues. The U.S. Environmental Protection Agency (EPA) enforces the provisions of the Federal Insecticide, Fungicide, and Rodenticide Act (FIFRA) and the Food Quality Protection Act of 1996, which establish regulatory limits on pesticide residues on edible plant products. For more information, contact EPA (see addresses at end of this chapter).

Detention of Shipment. If your shipment is found to be noncomplying, it may be detained at the port of entry. In the case of products subject to FDA jurisdiction, the FDA may allow you to bring such a shipment into compliance before making a final decision regarding admittance. However, any sorting, reprocessing, or relabeling must be supervised by FDA personnel, and is done at the importer's expense. Such conditional release to allow the importer to bring a shipment into compliance is a privilege, not a right. The FDA may consider subsequent noncomplying shipments of the same type of product to constitute abuse of the privilege and require the importer to destroy or reexport the products. To ascertain what your legal responsibilities are, you should contact the agencies involved in advance regarding the specific items to be imported.

Customs Classification

For customs purposes, prepared vegetable, fruit, or nut products are classified within Chapter 20 of the HTSUS. This chapter is divided into major headings, which are further divided into subheadings, and often into sub-subheadings, each of which has its own HTSUS classification number. For example, the 2001 HTSUS number for artichokes is 2001.90.25, which is a subcategory of other vegetables (2001.90.20), indicating that it is a subcategory of vegetables other than cucumbers and onions (2001.90), which is a subcategory of the major heading vegetables, fruit, and nuts and other edible parts of plants, prepared or preserved by vinegar or acetic acid (2001). There are nine major headings in HTSUS Chapter 20.

2001—Vegetables, fruit, nuts, and other edible parts of plants, prepared or preserved by vinegar or acetic acid

2002—Tomatoes prepared or preserved otherwise than by vinegar or acetic acid

2003—Mushrooms and truffles, prepared or preserved otherwise than by vinegar or acetic acid

2004—Other vegetables prepared or preserved otherwise than by vinegar or acetic acid, frozen, other than products of heading 2006

2005—Other vegetables prepared or preserved otherwise than by vinegar or acetic acid, not frozen, other than products of heading 2006

2006—Vegetables, fruit, nuts, fruit peel, and other parts of plants, preserved by sugar (drained, glacé, or crystallized)

2007—Jams, fruit jellies, marmalades, fruit or nut puree, and fruit or nut pastes, being cooked preparations, whether or not containing added sugar or other sweetening matter

2008—Fruit, nuts, and other edible parts of plants, otherwise prepared or preserved, whether or not containing added sugar or other sweetening matter or spirit, not elsewhere specified or included

2009—Fruit juices (including grape must) and vegetable juices, not fortified with vitamins or minerals, unfermented and not containing added spirit, whether or not containing added sugar or other sweetening matter

For more details regarding classification of the specific product you are interested in importing, consult a customs broker, the appropriate commodity specialist at your nearest customs port, or see HTSUS. The 2001 HTSUS is available online from the Customs Service (www.customs.gov/impoexpo/impoexpo.htm) or for purchase from the U.S. Government Printing Office (see resources at the end of this chapter), and may be found in larger public libraries. For a general discussion of customs classification, see "Classification—Liquidation" on page 229.

Dutiable Status of Goods

For more information about duty rates and binding decisions see "Dutiable Status of Goods" on page 203; for a discussion of temporary importation of goods see "Temporary Free Importations" on page 205.

Valuation

Importers have a responsibility to use what the U.S. Customs Service deems, "reasonable care," when determining the value of their goods. They must also provide any additional information that the Customs Service needs for setting a final value on the goods. This process involves a number of factors and can be somewhat complicated; importers must be aware of applicable issues and details. Valuation information applies to all types of commodities, for further discussion on the subject see "Customs Valuation" on page 267.

Import Duties

Import duties vary (often dramatically) depending upon the Harmonized Tariff Schedule (HTSUS) classification of the goods or products imported. Since some products that look alike have different HTSUS classifications and different rates of duty, proper classification is vital. Note that "differences of opinion" between importers and the Bureau of Customs and Border Protection regarding classification keeps customs attorneys very busy.

Import duties can be assessed on the imported value of the goods ("ad valorem" rates of duty such as 2%, 4.4%, 50%, etc.), total units or weight of the goods ("specific" rates of duty such as 2 cents each or 1.5 cents/pound, etc.) or on a combination basis ("compound" rates of duty such as 5 cents each plus 6%).

Listed below is a sampling of several Column 1 import duty rates for Chapter 20 products:
Truffles (2003.20.00.00): free
to
Yellow (Solano) potatoes (2004.10.40.00): 6.4%

For specific information on US import duties refer to the Harmonized Tariff Schedule of the US. The print version is available from the US Government Printing Office as well as third party suppliers who often add special features. Online versions are available in both static PDF pages as well as in formats with excellent search functionality. Search the Web with the term "Harmonized Tariff Schedule" to find sources.

Entry and Documentation

The entry of merchandise is a two-part process consisting of 1) filing the documents necessary to determine whether merchandise may be released from Customs custody and 2) filing the documents that contain information for duty assessment and

statistical purposes. In certain instances all documents must be filed and accepted by Customs prior to the release of the goods. Unless you have been granted an extension, you must file entry documents at a location specified by the port or area director within five working days of your shipment's date of arrival at a U.S. port of entry. These include a number of standard documents required by Customs for any entry and:

- USDA permit Form PPQ 587 to import plant or plant products, when necessary

After you present the entry, Customs may examine your shipment, or may waive examination. The shipment is then released provided no legal or regulatory violations have been noted. You must then file entry summary documentation and deposit estimated duties at a designated customhouse within 10 working days of your shipment's release. For a detailed description of entry procedures, standard documentation, and informal entry, see "Entry Process" on page 185.

Informed Compliance. Informed compliance was introduced with the Customs Modernization Act of 1993 (Mod Act) and defines the relationship between importers and the Customs Service. It sets out the responsibilities of both parties. Providing the correct documentation and information for entry is a key factor that will make your importing operation run smoothly. We recommend that importers become familiar with the concept of informed comliance and the responsibilities that they have under the Mod Act. For further discussion about informed compliance see "Informed Compliance" on page 211.

Note: The Entry and Documentation section has been carefully designed to supply you, the importer, with sample documents and directions on how to satisfy Customs requirements. Be aware that you should consult the applicable authorities to ensure that you are correctly following the most current procedures.

Restrictions and Prohibitions

All food products whether produced domestically or imported must comply with a variety of established standards, guidelines, and procedures. These include specific for premarket testing and approval of products, testing and certification on food additives and colors, regulations for interstate transport, and nutritional and other product labeling. For a discussion of these aspects, see "Appendix: Foods" on page 825.

Low-Acid Canned Foods and Acidified Foods. Low-acid canned foods are heat-processed foods other than alcoholic beverages that have an acidity greater than pH 4.6 and a water activity greater than 0.85 and that are packaged in hermetically sealed containers. "Water activity" is a measure of the water available for microbial growth. Hermetically sealed containers are any packages, regardless of composition, that are capable of maintaining the commercial sterility of their contents after processing. Acidified foods are low-acid foods to which acid(s) or acid food(s) have been added to reduce the pH to 4.6 or below (increase the acidity), and with a water activity greater than 0.85. Pimientos, artichokes, some puddings, and some sauces are examples of acidified foods. If you are unsure whether your food product falls within these categories, contact FDA's Industry Guidance Branch for clarification (see addresses at end of this chapter).

Registration Requirements. The FDA requires all commercial processors of low-acid canned foods and acidified foods intended for sale in the U.S. to register their establishments and file processing information for each product. This applies both to U.S. and foreign firms. If you are purchasing canned foods for import, you should be sure that the company from which you buy is FDA-registered. For more information, or for registration and processing forms, contact FDA's Industry Guidance Branch (see addresses at end of this chapter).

Canned Fruits and Fruit Juices. If you are importing canned fruit and fruit juices, you are responsible for seeing that your product meets all FDA standards of identity, quality, and fill-of-container. You can find these standards detailed in 21 CFR 145 and 146. What follows is a brief overview of the standards for such products; it is not intended to be exhaustive and importers should consult the agencies involved and the governing regulations.

Fill-of-Container Standards for Fruit. The standards of fill for canned peaches, pears, apricots, and cherries require that the fill of the solid food component be the maximum practicable quantity that can be sealed in the container and processed by heat without crushing or breaking the individual fruit. Standards for canned fruit cocktail, grapefruit, and plums specify minimum drained weights for the solid food component, expressed as a percentage of the water capacity of the container. The drained weight requirements are as follows: fruit cocktail 65%; grapefruit and whole plums 50%; plum halves 55%. Plums and applesauce in metal containers, crushed pineapple, and pineapple in juice have an additional 90% fill requirement, based on total container capacity for both the solid and liquid components. A similar 85% fill applies to applesauce in glass containers. Crushed pineapple may be labeled as "heavy pack" or "solid pack," as long as the fruit component has a minimum drained weight of 63% of the net weight.

If you are importing canned fruit for which no standards have been officially set, you must be sure that the containers are well filled with fruit. Only as much packing medium as is needed to fill the interstitial spaces may be added. If your products deviate from this guideline, they may be considered deceptive, and prohibited by FDCA. Deceptive fill is grounds for shipment refusal at the U.S. port of entry.

Canned Vegetables. There are FDA standards of identity, quality, and fill-of-container for many canned vegetables. FDA identity standards require that "the food is processed by heat, in an appropriate manner, before or after being sealed in a container so as to prevent spoilage." The special regulations for low-acid canned foods emphasize the importance of adequate heat-processing for canned vegetables, particularly the nonacid types that are more prone to the growth of bacteria if inadequately processed. If you are importing canned vegetables, you should be sure that your product complies with all applicable standards and guidelines.

Standards of Quality. Quality standards provide for special labeling of any product that is not up to the usual expectations of the consumer but is nevertheless a wholesome food. FDA standards of quality for canned vegetables establish minimum specifications for tenderness, color, freedom from defects, etc. The fact that your food does not measure up to these standards does not necessarily mean that you may not import it. However, if this is the case you must make sure your cans are labeled in bold type "Below Standard in Quality" followed by the statement "Good Food-Not High Grade," or a clear statement explaining in what respect the product fails to meet the standard, such as "excessively broken," or "excessive peel" (21 CFR 130).

Fill-of-Container Standards for Vegetables. Your canned vegetables must meet certain FDA standards of fill. Canned tomatoes and canned corn must be in the container such that solid and liquid together occupy not less than 90% of total container capacity. Minimum drained weight of the actual corn in canned corn must be no less than 61% of the container's water capacity. Minimum drained weight for solid tomatoes in canned tomatoes is 50% of the container's water capacity. Canned mushrooms must meet minimum drained weight requirements, stated in ounces, for various can sizes. Under volumetric fill requirements for canned green and field peas, the peas must completely fill the container before the addition of liquid packing medium.

If you are importing a canned vegetable for which no fill-of-container standard has been promulgated, you should be sure that the container is well filled with the vegetable, with only enough packing medium to fill the interstitial spaces. You are not permitted to add water to canned tomatoes.

Tomato Products. If you are importing tomato products (canned tomatoes, tomato juice, paste, puree, and catsup), you should consult the standards of identity for these items in 21 CFR 155. No artificial colors or preservatives are permitted in tomato products. Tomato juice may not be concentrated. Tomato puree must contain not less than 8%, and tomato paste not less than 24%, of salt free tomato solids.

Canned tomato products are occasionally contaminated with rot, flies, and worms resulting from improper processing. You should be very careful about the conditions under which your product was processed. If your shipment contains contaminated product, it is adulterated under FDCA rules and will be refused entry. The FDA uses the Howard mold-count test to determine whether tomato products have been properly prepared. If your shipment contains mold filaments in excess of amounts stated in the Food Defect Action Levels, it will be refused entry, as will any food products in which the cans have become swollen or otherwise abnormal.

Fruit Jams (Preserves), Jellies, Fruit Butters, and Marmalade. If you are importing fruit jams, jellies, butters, or marmalades, you need to be aware of the following FDA standards of identity for these products. Jams and jellies must be prepared by mixing not less than 45 parts by weight of certain specified fruits (or fruit juice in the case of jelly), and 47 parts by weight of other designated fruits, to each 55 parts by weight of sugar or other optional nutritive carbohydrate sweetening ingredient. Pectin may be added to jams and jellies only in quantities sufficient to compensate for a deficiency, if any, of the particular fruit's natural pectin content. As finished product, both jams (preserves) and jellies must be concentrated to not less than 65% soluble solids. Standards of identity for artificially sweetened jams and jellies require the fruit ingredient to be not less than 55% by weight of the finished food product.

Fruit butters must be smooth, semisolid foods made from not less than five parts by weight of fruit ingredient to each two parts by weight of sweetening ingredient. Only enough pectin may be added to compensate for a deficiency, if any, of the particular fruit's natural pectin content. Your finished fruit butter must be concentrated to not less than 43% soluble solids.

There is no formal standard of identity for citrus marmalade. However, the FDA expects a product labeled "sweet orange marmalade" to be prepared by mixing at least 30 pounds of fruit (peel and juice) to each 70 pounds of sweetening ingredients. Sour or bitter (Seville) orange marmalade, lemon marmalade, and lime marmalade would be prepared by mixing at least 25 pounds of fruit (peel and juice) to each 75 pounds of sweetening ingredient. Peel should not exceed amounts normally associated with the raw fruit. The product should be concentrated to not less than 65% soluble solids. If your imported citrus marmalade product follows these guidelines, FDA would not regard it as misbranded.

Mushrooms. If you are offering mushrooms for import, you must be sure that they are edible species. Inedible species may not be imported. However, the most common bar to entry is insect infestation, usually by flies or maggots. You can prevent mushroom contamination with insects, rodent and bird filth, or other objectionable material by taking protective measures during processing. Don't buy mushrooms from heavily insect-infested areas to import into the U.S. They will be refused entry.

Nuts and Nut Products. Nuts and nut meats must be prepared and stored under sanitary conditions to prevent contamination by insects, rodents, or other animals. If you wish to import nuts and nut products into the U.S., you should take care to prevent the following adulterating conditions: 1) Insect infestation. Nuts are insect-infected if they contain live or dead insects, whether larvae, pupae, or adults, or if they show definite evidence of insect feeding or cutting, or if insect excreta pellets are present. 2) Dirt. Nut meats may become dirty because of lack of cleanliness in cracking, sorting, and packaging. 3) Mold. Nut meats are occasionally moldy in the shell and bear fruiting mold or mold hyphae. 4) Rancidity. Rancid nuts are frequently soft. They have a yellow, dark, or oily appearance and an abnormal flavor characterized by rancidity. 5) Extraneous material. Stems, shells, stones, excreta or other foreign material should not be present.

FDA defect action levels have been established for tree nuts. You may not deliberately mix good and bad lots to result in defects below these levels, even though the percentage of defects in the mixed lots is thus rendered lower than the defect action level.

Aflatoxins. Aflatoxins are a group of chemically related substances produced naturally by the growth of certain common molds. Aflatoxins, especially aflatoxin B1, are highly toxic, primarily causing acute liver damage in exposed animals. Alfatoxin B1 also exhibits cancer-producing properties in certain species of experimental animals. Studies of certain population groups reveal that the consumption of aflatoxin-containing foods is associated with liver cancer in humans. Excess aflatoxin levels in nuts and other products is a significant public health problem and is a basis for seizing or refusing imports of products containing it.

Bitter Almonds. Because of their toxicity, bitter almonds may not be marketed in the U.S. for unrestricted use. Shipments of sweet almonds may not contain more than 5% of bitter almonds. Almond paste and pastes made from other kernels should contain less than 25 parts per million of hydrocyanic acid (HCN) naturally occurring in the kernels.

Standards for Nut Products. If you wish to import nut products, you should be aware of the FDA standards for mixed tree nuts, shelled nuts, and peanut butter (21 CFR 164). The standards establish such factors as proportions of various kinds of nuts and label designations for "mixed nuts," fill of container for shelled nuts, and ingredients and labeling for peanut butter.

Olives. Pitted and stuffed olives containing more than an unavoidable minimum of pits or pit fragments are in violation of FDCA provisions. While it may not be possible to completely eliminate this problem, dealers have been put on notice that they must take steps to reduce it to the extent that is reasonably feasible.

Quotas

Peanut Butter. The aggregate quantity of peanut butter and paste entered under subheading 2008.11.05 in any calendar year shall not exceed the quantities specified below. Imports from Mexico shall not be permitted or included under the aforementioned quantitative limitation and no such articles shall be classifiable therein. Canada, 14,500 metric tons; Argentina, 3,650 metric tons; Countries or territories identified in Chapter 20, Additional U.S. Note 6 combined (aggregate), 920 metric tons; Other countries or areas, 250 metric tons. Imports of peanut butter and paste under this note are subject to regulations as may be issued by the United States Trade Representative or other designated agency.

Olives. Most imported olives are under complex quotas; refer to HTSUS Chapter 20 for details.

For current information, or further details on quotas, contact the Port Director of Customs nearest you, or U.S. Customs Quota Branch (see addresses at end of this chapter). For a general discussion of quotas see

Marking and Labeling Requirements

Refer to "Appendix: Foods" on page 825 for nutritional labeling requirements. For a general discussion of U.S. Customs marking and labeling requirements, see "Country of Origin Marking" on page 236, "Special Marking Requirements" on page 238 and "Marking—False Impression" on page 239.

Shipping Considerations

You will need to ensure that your goods are packaged and shipped with care to ensure that they arrive in good condition and pass smoothly through Customs. You are responsible for ensuring that the shipment is in compliance with all applicable government regulations for packaging and shipping. In most instances, you should not leave these arrangements solely to the discretion of your supplier. Careful preparation of the cargo and selection of the mode of transport can be essential to a cost-effective, timely delivery of undamaged goods. We strongly advise you to consult your shipping representative, insurance agent, or freight broker for advice on packing and shipping.

As with all edible products, careful attention to packing and shipping conditions are necessary to prevent contamination and spoilage en route. Although prepared foods of Chapter 20 are generally required to be shelf-stable and not require refrigeration—some products may be dated and require both expeditious and refrigerated transport—they nevertheless must be properly handled to maintain their integrity and salability. Protection from insect or animal contamination is especially important, as contamination from filth is a major cause of the rejection of entry of food products.

Publications and WWW Resources

The following publication explains the FDA requirements for importing prepared vegetable, fruit, or nut products. It is published by the FDA and is available online from the FDA website (www.fda.gov/opacom/7pubs.html).

> *Requirements of Laws and Regulations Enforced by the U.S. Food and Drug Administration*

The following publication gives brief, general guidelines on USDA regulated products. Although designed primarily for tourists, it contains a list of approved products that you may find helpful. It is published by USDA APHIS (www.aphis.usda.gov/oa/travel.html).

> *Travelers Tips On Bringing Food, Plant, and Animal Products into the United States*

The U.S. Customs Service launched a series of "Informed Compliance" publications in 1996, which are available from the Customs Service website (www.customs.gov/impoexpo/impoexpo.htm). Of particular interest:

> *What Every Member of the Trade Community Should Know About Mushrooms*

The *Harmonized Tariff Schedule of the United States (2001)* (HTSUS) is available to view on the Customs Service website (www.customs.gov), or you may purchase a printed version from:

U.S. Government Printing Office
Superintendent of Documents
710 North Capital Street NW
Washington DC 20401
Tel: (202) 512-1800
Fax: (202) 512-1657
Website: www.access.gpo.gov

The USGPO also has copies of specific laws available for purchase. The USGPO accepts orders made by fax, phone or placed over the Internet, as well as mail orders paid by credit card. All orders must be accompanied by payment. Credit cards, checks drawn on a U.S. bank, or an international money order are all acceptable.

Relevant Government Agencies

Address general inquiries regarding importation of foods to:

Food and Drug Administration (FDA)
Center for Food Safety and Applied Nutrition (CFSAN)
Office of Compliance
Division of Enforcement, Imports Branch
5100 Paint Branch Parkway
College Park, MD 20740-3835
Tel: (301) 436-2080
Website: http://vm.cfsan.fda.gov/list.html

Food and Drug Administration (FDA)
Center for Food Safety and Applied Nutrition (CFSAN)
Office of Plant and Dairy Foods and Beverages
5100 Paint Branch Parkway
College Park, MD 20740-3835
Tel: (301) 436-1700
Website: http://vm.cfsan.fda.gov/list.html

Address your questions regarding safe pesticide residue tolerances to:

Environmental Protection Agency (EPA)
Office of Pesticide Programs
Ariel Rios Building
1200 Pennsylvania Avenue NW
Mail Code 3213A
Washington DC 20460
Tel: (703) 305-7090
Website: www.epa.gov

Address your questions regarding quotas to:

U.S. Customs and Border Protection
Office of Field Operations, Quota Branch
1300 Pennsylvania Avenue NW
Washington DC 20229
Tel: (202) 927-5850
Website: www.customs.treas.gov

Address questions regarding the importation of prepared vegetable, fruit, and nut products to your local Customs port director. For addresses refer to "U.S. Customs and Border Protection Offices" on page 65 or contact:

U.S. Customs and Border Protection
Customs Headquarters
1300 Pennsylvania Avenue NW
Washington DC 20229
Tel: (202) 354-1000
Website: www.customs.treas.gov

Laws and Regulations

The following laws and regulations may be relevant to the importation of prepared vegetable, fruit, or nut products. The laws are contained in the U.S. Code (USC) and the regulations are published in the Code of Federal Regulations (CFR), both of which may be available at larger public and law libraries. Copies of specific laws are also available from the United States Government Printing Office (address above).

21 USC 301 et seq.
Federal Food, Drug, and Cosmetic Act
This Act prohibits deceptive practices and regulates the manufacture, sale and importation or exportation of food, drugs, cosmetics, and related products. It was amended by the Food Quality Protection Act of 1996. See 21 USC 331, 381, 382.

19 CFR 12.1 et seq.; 21 CFR 1.83 et seq.
Regulations on Food, Drugs, and Cosmetics
These regulations of the Secretary of Health and Human Services and the Secretary of the Treasury govern the standards, labeling, marking, and importing of products used with food, drugs, and cosmetics.

7 USC 136 et seq.
Federal Insecticide, Fungicide, and Rodenticide Act (FIFRA)
This Act prohibits the importation of pesticides or devices that are adulterated, misbranded, or otherwise violative of the Act, provides for registration of pesticides and devices, and establishes standards for labeling and classifying pesticides. It was amended by the Food Quality Protection Act of 1996.

19 CFR 12; 40 CFR 162
Regulations on Pesticides
These regulations set forth the procedures and guidelines for importing products exposed to pesticides.

Principal Exporting Countries

The following listing includes samples of the main supplier nations of the products of this chapter. It is organized by HTSUS major heading. (Refer to "Customs Classification" above for the product codes.) Countries are listed in rank order of the value of products imported to the U.S. Statistics represent customs value of entries for 2002 from the Bureau of Census, U.S. Department of Commerce.

2001—Mexico, Spain, Canada, Greece, Honduras, Turkey, Poland, India, China, Italy, Morocco

2002—Canada, Mexico, Italy, Israel, China

2003—Indonesia, India, China, Netherlands, Taiwan, France, Mexico, Spain, Canada, Malaysia, Colombia, Italy

2004—Canada, Mexico, France, Dominican Republic, Netherlands, Guatemala, Belgium

2005—Spain, Canada, Greece, China, Mexico, Morocco, Peru, Italy, Japan

2006—Thailand, Australia, Canada, China

2007—Canada, France, Mexico, Switzerland, Denmark, United Kingdom, Costa Rica, Poland, Germany, Dominican Republic

2008—Thailand, China, Philippines, Mexico, Canada, Indonesia, Greece, Spain, Japan, Costa Rica, South Africa

2009—Brazil, Argentina, Mexico, Chile, China, Philippines, Costa Rica, Germany, Canada, Thailand

Chapter 21:
Miscellaneous Edible
Preparations

This section pertains to the importation of miscellaneous edible preparations, which are classified within Chapter 21 of the Harmonized Tariff Schedule of the United States (HTSUS). Specifically, it includes extracts and essences of tea or coffee; yeast and other similar baking products; sauces and condiments; soups; ice cream; and miscellaneous protein and dairy substitutes, juices, and related products. This section is supplemental to "Appendix: Foods" on page 825. If you are interested in importing products of Chapter 21, you should read that section as well.

If you are interested in importing prepared products of vegetables, fruit, or nuts for which identity standards exist or that are recognizable as identifiable products, refer to Commodity Index Chapter 20. Prepared products of meat, fish, and other aquatic products containing more than 20% of such ingredients are covered in Chapter 16, with the exception of some sauces, condiments, and soups covered in subheadings 2103 and 2104. Coffee and tea, including flavored teas and coffee substitutes, and spices, are covered in Chapter 9 (although essences and extracts are covered in Chapter 21). With the exception of ice cream and some condiments that contain or are based on milk products, dairy products are covered in Chapter 4. Many Chapter 21 products contain oils and fats, however these products are primarily covered as such in Chapter 15, while sugars are covered in Chapter 17 and preparations of flour and baked goods in Chapter 19. Ethyl alcohol may be a component of products in Chapter 21, but alcoholic beverages and beverage components are covered in Chapter 22, as are other products designed specifically as beverages. Yeasts for medicinal use or as part of a medicament are classified within Chapter 30. Prepared enzyme products are covered by Chapter 35.

Note: To understand key issues that will enable you to make best use of the information in this section we recommend that you see "Introduction" on page 425.

Key Factors

The key factors in the importation of miscellaneous edible preparations are:

- Compliance with U.S. Food and Drug Administration (FDA) purity, identity, manufacturing, and other standards
- Compliance with FDA entry notifications and procedures

Although most importers utilize the services of a licensed customs broker in making their entries, and we recommend this practice, you should be aware of the regulatory, entry, and documentation issues involved in importing your product. You, as importer, are ultimately responsible for the fulfillment of any legal requirements applicable to your shipment.

General Considerations

Importation of miscellaneous edible products falls primarily under the jurisdiction of the FDA, which enforces requirements of the Federal Food, Drug, and Cosmetic Act (FDCA). FDA regulations regarding importation of foods of any kind are extensive and stringent. All Chapter 21 food products imported into the U.S. must comply with all FDCA requirements for those produced domestically. Imported products regulated by the FDA are subject to FDA port of entry inspection. For a discussion of required FDA import procedures see "Appendix: Foods" on page 825.

The U.S. Environmental Protection Agency (EPA) enforces the Federal Insecticide, Fungicide, and Rodenticide Act (FIFRA) and the Food Quality Protection Act of 1996, which establish regulatory limits on pesticide residues on edible plant products. For more information, contact the EPA (see addresses at end of this chapter).

Compliance. If your shipment is found to be noncomplying, it may be detained at the port of entry. In the case of products subject to FDA jurisdiction, the FDA may allow you to bring such a shipment into compliance before making a final decision regarding admittance. However, any sorting, reprocessing, or relabeling must be supervised by FDA personnel, and is done at the importer's expense. Such conditional release to allow the importer to bring a shipment into compliance is a privilege, not a right. The FDA may consider subsequent noncomplying shipments of the same type of product to constitute an abuse of the privilege and require you to destroy or reexport the products. To ascertain what your legal responsibilities are, you should contact the agencies involved in advance regarding the specific items to be imported.

Customs Classification

For customs purpose, miscellaneous edible preparations are classified within Chapter 21 of the HTSUS. This chapter is divided into major headings, which are further divided into subheadings, and often into sub-subheadings, each of which has its own HTSUS classification number. For example, the 2001 HTSUS number for tomato ketchup is 2103.20.20, indicating that it is a subcategory of tomato ketchup and other tomato sauces (2103.20), which is a subcategory of the major heading sauces and preparations therefor; mixed condiments and mixed seasonings; mustard flour and meal and prepared mustard (2103). There are six major headings in HTSUS Chapter 21.

2101—Extracts, essences, and concentrates of coffee, tea, or maté and preparations with a base of these products or with a basis of coffee, tea, or maté; roasted chicory and other roasted coffee substitutes, and extracts, essences, and concentrates thereof

2102—Yeasts (active and inactive); other single-celled microorganisms, dead (but not including vaccines of heading 3002); prepared baking powders

2103—Sauces and preparations therefor; mixed condiments and mixed seasonings; mustard flour and meal and prepared mustard

2104—Soups and broths and preparations therefor; homogenized composite food preparations

2105—Ice cream and other edible ice, whether or not containing cocoa

2106—Food preparations not elsewhere specified or included

For more details regarding classification of the specific product you are interested in importing, consult a customs broker, the appropriate commodity specialist at your nearest customs port, or see HTSUS. The 2001 HTSUS is available online from the Customs Service (www.customs.gov/impoexpo/impoexpo.htm) or for purchase from the U.S. Government Printing Office (see resources at the end of this chapter), and may be found in larger public libraries. For a general discussion of customs classification, see "Classification—Liquidation" on page 229.

Dutiable Status of Goods

For more information about duty rates and binding decisions see "Dutiable Status of Goods" on page 203; for a discussion of temporary importation of goods see "Temporary Free Importations" on page 205.

Valuation

Importers have a responsibility to use what the U.S. Customs Service deems, "reasonable care," when determining the value of their goods. They must also provide any additional information that the Customs Service needs for setting a final value on the goods. This process involves a number of factors and can be somewhat complicated; importers must be aware of applicable issues and details. Valuation information applies to all types of commodities, for further discussion on the subject see "Customs Valuation" on page 267.

Import Duties

Import duties vary (often dramatically) depending upon the Harmonized Tariff Schedule (HTSUS) classification of the goods or products imported. Since some products that look alike have different HTSUS classifications and different rates of duty, proper classification is vital. Note that "differences of opinion" between importers and the Bureau of Customs and Border Protection regarding classification keeps customs attorneys very busy.

Import duties can be assessed on the imported value of the goods ("ad valorem" rates of duty such as 2%, 4.4%, 50%, etc.), total units or weight of the goods ("specific" rates of duty such as 2 cents each or 1.5 cents/pound, etc.) or on a combination basis ("compound" rates of duty such as 5 cents each plus 6%).

Listed below is a sampling of several Column 1 import duty rates for Chapter 21 products:
Prepared baking powders (2102.30.00.00): free
to
Extracts, essences and concentrates described in general note 15 of the tariff schedule and entered pursuant to its provisions (2101.20.32.00): 10%

For specific information on US import duties refer to the Harmonized Tariff Schedule of the US. The print version is available from the US Government Printing Office as well as third party suppliers who often add special features. Online versions are available in both static PDF pages as well as in formats with excellent search functionality. Search the Web with the term "Harmonized Tariff Schedule" to find sources.

Entry and Documentation

The entry of merchandise is a two-part process consisting of 1) filing the documents necessary to determine whether merchandise may be released from Customs custody and 2) filing the documents that contain information for duty assessment and statistical purposes. In certain instances all documents must be filed and accepted by Customs prior to the release of the goods. Unless you have been granted an extension, you must file entry documents at a location specified by the port or area director within five working days of your shipment's date of arrival at a U.S. port of entry. These include a number of standard documents required by Customs for any entry.

After you present the entry, Customs may examine your shipment, or may waive examination. The shipment is then released, provided no legal or regulatory violations have been noted. You must then file entry summary documentation and deposit estimated duties at a designated customhouse within 10 working days of your shipment's release. For a detailed description of entry procedures, standard documentation, and informal entry, see "Entry Process" on page 185.

Informed Compliance. Informed compliance was introduced with the Customs Modernization Act of 1993 (Mod Act) and defines the relationship between importers and the Customs Service. It sets out the responsibilities of both parties. Providing the correct documentation and information for entry is a key factor that will make your importing operation run smoothly. We recommend that importers become familiar with the concept of informed comliance and the responsibilities that they have under the Mod Act. For further discussion about informed compliance see "Informed Compliance" on page 211.

Note: The Entry and Documentation section has been carefully designed to supply you, the importer, with sample documents and directions on how to satisfy Customs requirements. Be aware that you should consult the applicable authorities to ensure that you are correctly following the most current procedures.

Prohibitions and Restrictions

Dressings. Standards of identity have been established for mayonnaise, French dressing, and salad dressing (21 CFR 169). If you intend to import these products, you should be sure that they comply in every way with those standards. Dressings for which no standards have been established should be labeled according to general FDCA food labeling requirements. Mineral oil is not a permitted ingredient in any of these foods (21 CFR 169).

Low-Acid Canned Foods and Acidified Foods. Low-acid canned foods are heat-processed foods other than alcoholic beverages that have an acidity greater than pH 4.6 and a water activity greater than 0.85 and that are packaged in hermetically sealed containers. "Water activity" is a measure of the water available for microbial growth. Hermetically sealed containers are any packages, regardless of composition, that are capable of maintaining the commercial sterility of their contents after processing. Acidified foods are low-acid foods to which acid(s) or acid food(s) are added to reduce the pH to 4.6 or below (increase the acidity), and with a water activity greater than 0.85. Some sauces are classified as acidified foods. If you are unsure whether your canned food fits one of these categories, you may contact FDA's Industry Guidance Branch for clarification (see addresses at end of this chapter).

Registration Requirements. The FDA requires all commercial processors of low-acid canned foods and acidified foods intended for sale in the U.S. to register their establishments and file processing information for each product. This applies both to U.S. and foreign firms. If you are purchasing canned foods for import, you should be sure that the company from which you buy is FDA-registered. For more information, or for registration and processing forms, contact FDA's Industry Guidance Branch (see addresses at end of this chapter).

Canned Fruit and/or Vegetable Juices and Other Products. If you are importing canned fruit or vegetable juices or other fruit-or vegetable-based preparations, you are responsible for seeing that your product meets FDA standards of identity, quality, and fill-of-container. You can find these standards detailed in 21 CFR 145, 146.

Fill-of-container. Your canned food preparations must meet certain FDA standards of fill. If you are importing products for which no fill-of-container standard has been promulgated, you should be sure that the container is well filled with the product, with only enough packing medium to fill the interstitial spaces.

Tomato Products. If you are importing tomato products (including ketchup), you should consult the standards of identity for these items in 21 CFR 155. Neither artificial color nor preservatives are permitted in tomato products. Tomato juice is unconcentrated. Tomato products are occasionally contaminated with rot, flies. and worms resulting from improper processing. You should be very careful about the conditions under which your product was processed. If your shipment contains contaminated product, it is adulterated under the FDCA and will be refused entry. The FDA uses the Howard mold-count test to determine whether tomato products have been properly prepared. If your shipment contains mold filaments in excess of amounts stated in the Food Defect Action Levels, it will be refused entry, as will cans of food that have become swollen or otherwise abnormal.

Quotas

Entry of specific products can be difficult because many product categories affected by quota restrictions overlap, especially where dairy products and sugars are concerned. It is important to consult the U.S. Customs Service Quota Branch (see addresses at end of this chapter) to determine whether quota restrictions apply to your specific product. For a general discussion of quotas, refer to "Quotas Administered by Customs" on page 274. Quotas affecting miscellaneous edible products of HTSUS Chapter 21 include the following:

Mixed Condiments and Seasonings. The aggregate quantity of mixed condiments and mixed seasonings described below and entered under subheading 2103.90.74 during the 12-month period from October 1 in any year to the following September 30, inclusive, shall not exceed 689 metric tons. Imports from Mexico shall not be permitted or included in the aforementioned quantitative limitation and no such articles shall be classifiable therein. "Mixed condiments and mixed seasonings" means articles containing over 10% by dry weight of sugars derived from sugar cane or sugar beets, whether or not mixed with other ingredients, except (a) articles not principally of crystalline structure or not in dry amorphous form that are prepared for marketing to the ultimate consumer in the identical form and package in which imported; or (b) cake decorations and similar products to be used in the same condition as imported without any further processing other than the direct application to individual pastries or confections, finely ground or masticated coconut meat or juice thereof mixed with those sugars, and sauces and preparations therefor.

Ice Cream. The aggregate quantity of ice cream entered under subheading 2105.00.10 in any calendar year shall not exceed 3,760,587 liters. Imports from Mexico shall not be permitted or included in the aforementioned quantitative limitation and no such articles shall be classifiable therein. Of the quantitative limitations provided for here, the countries listed below shall have access to not less than the quantities specified below: Belgium, 922,315 liters; Denmark, 13,059 liters; Jamaica, 3,596 liters; Netherlands, 104,477 liters; New Zealand, 589,312 liters.

Other Quotas. A variety of other quotas may be applied to Chapter 21 goods under Chapter 99, Subchapter IV.

Marking and Labeling Requirements

Refer to "Appendix: Foods" on page 825 for information regarding the marking and labeling of food for importation. For a general discussion of U.S. Customs marking and labeling requirements, see "Country of Origin Marking" on page 236, "Special Marking Requirements" on page 238 and "Marking—False Impression" on page 239.

Shipping Considerations

You will need to ensure that your goods are packaged and shipped with care to ensure that they arrive in good condition and pass smoothly through Customs. You are responsible for ensuring that the shipment is in compliance with all applicable government regulations for packaging and shipping. In most instances, you should not leave these arrangements solely to the discretion of your supplier. Careful preparation of the cargo and selection of the mode of transport can be essential to a cost-effective, timely delivery of undamaged goods. We strongly advise you to consult your shipping representative, insurance broker, or freight broker for advice on packing and shipping.

As with all edible products, careful attention to packing and shipping conditions are necessary to prevent contamination and spoilage en route. Although many miscellaneous edible preparations are required to be shelf-stable, some products—especially ice cream—may be dated and require expeditious and climate controlled transport. All products must be handled properly to maintain their integrity and salability. Protection from insect or animal contamination is especially important, as contamination from filth is a major cause of the rejection of entry of food products.

Publications and WWW Resources

The following publication explains the FDA requirements for importing miscellaneous edible preparations. It is published by the FDA and is available online from the FDA website (www.fda.gov/opacom/7pubs.html).

Requirements of Laws and Regulations Enforced by the U.S. Food and Drug Administration

The *Harmonized Tariff Schedule of the United States (2001)* (HTSUS) is available to view on the Customs Service website (www.customs.gov), or you may purchase a printed version from:

U.S. Government Printing Office
Superintendent of Documents
710 North Capital Street NW
Washington DC 20401
Tel: (202) 512-1800
Fax: (202) 512-1657
Website: www.access.gpo.gov

The USGPO also has copies of specific laws available for purchase. The USGPO accepts orders made by fax, phone or placed over the Internet, as well as mail orders paid by credit card. All orders must be accompanied by payment. Credit cards, checks drawn on a U.S. bank, or an international money order are all acceptable.

Relevant Government Agencies

Address questions regarding FDA requirements for the importation of miscellaneous edible preparations to:

Food and Drug Administration (FDA)
Center for Food Safety and Applied Nutrition (CFSAN)
Office of Compliance
Division of Enforcement, Imports Branch
5100 Paint Branch Parkway
College Park, MD 20740-3835
Tel: (301) 436-2080
Website: http://vm.cfsan.fda.gov/list.html

Food and Drug Administration (FDA)
Center for Food Safety and Applied Nutrition (CFSAN)
Office of Plant and Dairy Foods and Beverages
5100 Paint Branch Parkway
College Park, MD 20740-3835
Tel: (301) 436-1700
Website: http://vm.cfsan.fda.gov/list.html

Address your questions regarding safe pesticide residue tolerances to:

Environmental Protection Agency (EPA)
Office of Pesticide Programs
Ariel Rios Building
1200 Pennsylvania Avenue NW
Mail Code 3213A
Washington DC 20460
Tel: (703) 305-7090
Website: www.epa.gov

Address questions regarding quotas to:
U.S. Customs and Border Protection
Office of Field Operations, Quota Branch
1300 Pennsylvania Avenue NW
Washington DC 20229
Tel: (202) 927-5850
Website: www.customs.treas.gov

Address questions regarding importation of miscellaneous edible preparations to your local Customs port director. For addresses refer to "U.S. Customs and Border Protection Offices" on page 65 or contact:

U.S. Customs and Border Protection
Customs Headquarters
1300 Pennsylvania Avenue NW
Washington DC 20229
Tel: (202) 354-1000
Website: www.customs.treas.gov

Laws and Regulations

The following laws may be relevant to the importation of miscellaneous edible preparations. The laws are contained in the U.S. Code (USC) and the regulations are published in the Code of Federal Regulations (CFR), both of which may be available at larger public and law libraries. Copies of specific laws are also available from the United States Government Printing Office (address above).

21 USC 301 et seq.
Federal Food, Drug, and Cosmetic Act
This Act prohibits deceptive practices and regulates the manufacture, sale and importation or exportation of food, drugs, cosmetics, and related products. It was amended by the Food Quality Protection Act of 1996. See 21 USC 331, 381, 382.

19 CFR 12.1 et seq.; 21 CFR 1.83 et seq.
Regulations on Food, Drugs, and Cosmetics
These regulations of the Secretary of Health and Human Services and the Secretary of the Treasury govern the standards, labeling, marking, and importing of products used with food, drugs, and cosmetics.

7 USC 136 et seq.
Federal Insecticide, Fungicide, and Rodenticide Act (FIFRA)
This Act prohibits the importation of pesticides or devices that are adulterated, misbranded, or otherwise violative of the Act, provides for registration of pesticides and devices, and establishes standards for labeling and classifying pesticides. It was amended by the Food Quality Protection Act of 1996.

19 CFR 12; 40 CFR 162
Regulations on Pesticides
These regulations set forth the procedures and guidelines for importing products exposed to pesticides.

Principal Exporting Countries

The following listing includes samples of the main supplier nations of the products of this chapter. It is organized by HTSUS major heading. (Refer to "Customs Classification" above for the product codes.) Countries are listed in rank order of the value of products imported to the U.S. Statistics represent customs value of entries for 2002 from the Bureau of Census, U.S. Department of Commerce.

2101—Canada, Mexico, Netherlands, Brazil, Switzerland, India, Colombia, China, Chile, Germany, Singapore, Madagascar, Kenya, Japan, Hong Kong, France

2102—Canada, Mexico, Japan, Portugal, Switzerland, United Kingdom, Germany, France, Chile, Denmark, Yugoslavia, Netherlands

2103—Canada, Mexico, Italy, New Zealand, Hong Kong, Japan, Thailand, Taiwan, China

2104—Canada, Mexico, Japan, Guatemala, South Korea, Argentina, Switzerland, Thailand, Venezuela, Philippines, Dominican Republic, Israel, Croatia, China, Germany

2105—Canada, South Korea, France, Italy, Philippines, Spain, South Africa, Taiwan, Lithuania, Israel, Indonesia, Russia, Japan

2106—Canada, Thailand, France, New Zealand, Italy, Mexico, Denmark, Japan, Switzerland, China, United Kingdom, Australia, Germany

Chapter 22: Beverages, Spirits, and Vinegar

This section pertains to the importation of beverages, spirits, and vinegar, which are classified within Chapter 22 of the Harmonized Tariff Schedule of the United States (HTSUS). Specifically, it covers all beverages, including bottled water, fruit and vegetable juices prepared and fortified with vitamins, carbonated or uncarbonated soft drinks, milk-based drinks, beer, wine, other fermented beverages, ethyl alcohol suitable for both beverage and industrial uses, liquors, liqueurs, and vinegar for culinary purposes. Generally, it includes all preparations designed to be drunk.

If you are interested in importing food preparations containing beverages or alcohol but not designed to be drunk, refer to Commodity Index Chapter 21. Plain fruit and vegetable juices—that is, natural juices unfortified with vitamins or minerals—and tomato juice with a tomato content of greater than 7% are classified within Chapter 20. Dairy beverages—milk other than prepared milk-based drinks such as chocolate milk—are found in Chapter 4. Other liquid products covered elsewhere include sea water (Chapter 25); distilled, conductivity, or other pure water for industrial uses (Chapter 28); acetic acid of a concentration of greater than 10% by weight for industrial purposes (Chapter 29); medicaments in beverage form or containing beverage products, including alcohol (Chapter 30); and perfumes or toilet articles (Chapter 33). Some commercial samples of beverages that may be imported duty free are covered in Chapter 98, under heading 9811.00.20.

Note: To understand key issues that will enable you to make best use of the information in this section we recommend that you see "Introduction" on page 425.

Key Factors

The key factors in the importation of nonalcoholic beverages are:

- Compliance with U.S. Food and Drug Administration (FDA) purity, identity, manufacturing, and other standards
- Compliance with FDA entry notifications and procedures

The key factors in the importation of alcoholic beverages are:

- U.S. Treasury Bureau of Alcohol, Tobacco, and Firearms (ATF) permits for importation of alcoholic beverages
- Compliance with federal, state, and municipal alcohol regulations

- Federal excise taxes payable at entry; red strip stamps required for distilled spirits
- Standards of fill and standards of identity
- Certificates of various standards required at entry
- Extensive labeling requirements, including ATF pre-approval of all labels

Although most importers utilize the services of a licensed customs broker in making their entries, and we recommend this practice, you should be aware of the regulatory, entry, and documentation issues involved in importing your product. You, as importer, are ultimately responsible for the fulfillment of any legal requirements applicable to your shipment.

General Considerations

Nonalcoholic Beverages. The importation of nonalcoholic beverages falls primarily under the jurisdiction of the FDA, which enforces requirements of the Federal Food, Drug, and Cosmetic Act (FDCA). FDA regulations regarding the importation of products of any kind designed to be ingested are extensive and stringent. Nonalcoholic beverages imported into the U.S. must comply with all FDCA requirements for those produced domestically.

Alcoholic Beverages. The importation of alcoholic beverages is a complex business, requiring lots of specialized knowledge, not only of federal, state, and municipal regulations, but of the products themselves. It is an enterprise not to be entered into without extensive preparation.

The term "alcoholic beverage" includes any beverage in liquid form intended for human consumption that contains not less than one-half of one percent (0.5%) of alcohol by volume. For customs purposes, any beverage that contains more than 0.5% alcohol is an alcoholic beverage. However, for Internal Revenue Service (IRS) or Treasury Department ATF purposes, such products may not be considered alcoholic beverages unless they contain more than 7% alcohol. In addition, there may be separate FDA standards that apply to products, such as cooking wines, hard ciders, wine coolers, or similar products, that contain between 0.5% and 7% alcohol. U.S. Customs does not consider cooking wine a beverage, but a preparation that falls within HTSUS Chapter 20.

Alcoholic beverages are divided into three major categories: distilled spirits, wines, and malt beverages. Importation of alcoholic beverages is strictly regulated by U.S. Customs and by the ATF, primarily under the provisions of the Federal Alcohol Administration Act (FAAA). If you wish to engage in the business of importing distilled spirits, wines, or malt beverages into the U.S., you must first obtain an Importer's Basic Permit from the ATF (see addresses at end of this chapter). You must also comply with the separate licensing requirements of any state in which you expect to sell your product. Individual cities or other local jurisdictions sometimes have specific regulations as well. You will have to fulfill stringent federal and state requirements for recordkeeping and reporting. Distilled spirits imported in bulk containers of a capacity of more than one gallon may be withdrawn from customs custody only by persons to whom it is lawful to sell or otherwise dispose of distilled spirits in bulk. Customs will not release alcoholic beverages destined to any U.S. state for use in violation of that state's laws. Importation of alcoholic beverages by mail is prohibited.

Although most alcoholic beverages fall under ATF jurisdiction, there are certain exceptions. Beverages and other products containing less than 7% alcohol by volume are solely within the jurisdiction of the FDA, under the FDCA. The FDA also regulates the presence of deleterious substances in any alcoholic beverage (including those covered primarily by the ATF), such as excess fusel oil and excess aldehydes in whisky; the presence of methyl alcohol in brandy; glass splinters from defective bottles; and toxic ingredients, such as arsenic, lead, or fluorine, resulting from spraying of fruit used to make wine or of the manufacturing process, as well as residues of toxic clarifying substances. "Appendix: Foods" on page 825 is an overview of general FDA import requirements. If you are interested in importing alcoholic beverages that fall under FDA regulation, you should read that section in conjunction with this one. For further information on applicable FDA standards, contact the regional FDA Import Operations office nearest you, or FDA headquarters (see addresses at end of this chapter).

FDA Requirements. Imported products regulated by the FDA are subject to FDA port of entry inspection.

Detention of Shipment. If your shipment is found to be noncomplying, it may be detained at the port of entry. The FDA may permit you to bring such a shipment into compliance before making a final decision regarding admittance. However, any sorting, reprocessing, or relabeling must be supervised by FDA personnel, and is done at the importer's expense. Such conditional release to allow an importer to bring a shipment into compliance is a privilege, not a right. The FDA may consider subsequent noncomplying shipments of the same type of product to constitute abuse of the privilege and require the importer to destroy or reexport the products. To ascertain what your legal responsibilities are, you should contact the FDA regarding the specific items to be imported.

Bottle Jackets of Plant Materials. Certain plant materials used for bottle jackets—such as the raffia covers of traditional bottles of Chianti wine—are subject to special restrictions under the plant quarantine regulations of the U.S. Department of Agriculture's (USDA) Animal and Plant Health Inspection Service (APHIS). All bottle jackets made of dried or unmanufactured plant materials are subject to APHIS port of entry inspection.

Customs Classification

For customs purposes, beverages, spirits, and vinegar products are classified under Chapter 22 of the HTSUS. This chapter is broken into major headings, which are further divided into subheadings, and often sub-subheadings, each of which has its own HTSUS classification number. For example, the 2001 HTSUS number for tequila in containers which hold more than 4 liters is 2208.90.55.00, which is a subcategory of other spirits (2208.90), itself a subcategory of the major heading undenatured ethyl alcohol of an alcoholic strength by volume of less than 80%; spirits, liqueurs, and other spirituous beverages (2208). There are nine major headings in Chapter 22.

2201—Waters, including natural or artificial mineral waters and aerated waters, not containing added sugar or other sweetening matter not flavored; ice and snow

2202—Waters, including mineral waters and aerated waters, containing added sugar or other sweetening matter or flavored, and other nonalcoholic beverages, not including fruit or vegetable juices of heading 2009

2203—Beer made from malt

2204—Wine of fresh grapes, including fortified wines; grape must other than that of heading 2009

2205—Vermouth and other wine of fresh grapes flavored with plants or aromatic substances

2206—Other fermented beverages (for example, cider, perry, mead); mixtures of fermented beverages and mixtures of fermented beverages and nonalcoholic beverages not elsewhere specified or included

2207—Undenatured ethyl alcohol of an alcoholic strength by volume of 80% or higher; ethyl alcohol and other spirits, denatured, of any strength

2208—Undenatured ethyl alcohol of an alcoholic strength by volume of less than 80% vol.; spirits, liqueurs, and other spirituous beverages

2209—Vinegar and substitutes for vinegar obtained from acetic acid

For more details regarding classification of the specific product you are interested in importing, consult a customs broker, the appropriate commodity specialist at your nearest customs port, or see HTSUS. The 2001 HTSUS is available online from the Customs Service (www.customs.gov/impoexpo/impoexpo.htm) or for purchase from the U.S. Government Printing Office (see resources at the end of this chapter), and may be found in larger public libraries. For a general discussion of customs classification, see "Classification—Liquidation" on page 229.

Dutiable Status of Goods

For more information about duty rates and binding decisions see "Dutiable Status of Goods" on page 203; for a discussion of temporary importation of goods see "Temporary Free Importations" on page 205.

Valuation

Importers have a responsibility to use what the U.S. Customs Service deems, "reasonable care," when determining the value of their goods. They must also provide any additional information that the Customs Service needs for setting a final value on the goods. This process involves a number of factors and can be somewhat complicated; importers must be aware of applicable issues and details. Valuation information applies to all types of commodities, for further discussion on the subject see "Customs Valuation" on page 267.

Import Duties

Import duties vary (often dramatically) depending upon the Harmonized Tariff Schedule (HTSUS) classification of the goods or products imported. Since some products that look alike have different HTSUS classifications and different rates of duty, proper classification is vital. Note that "differences of opinion" between importers and the Bureau of Customs and Border Protection regarding classification keeps customs attorneys very busy.

Import duties can be assessed on the imported value of the goods ("ad valorem" rates of duty such as 2%, 4.4%, 50%, etc.), total units or weight of the goods ("specific" rates of duty such as 2 cents each or 1.5 cents/pound, etc.) or on a combination basis ("compound" rates of duty such as 5 cents each plus 6%).

Listed below is a sampling of several Column 1 import duty rates for Chapter 22 products:
Other waters (2201.90.00.00): free
to
Chocolate milk drink (2202.90.10.00): 17%

For specific information on US import duties refer to the Harmonized Tariff Schedule of the US. The print version is available from the US Government Printing Office as well as third party suppliers who often add special features. Online versions are available in both static PDF pages as well as in formats with excellent search functionality. Search the Web with the term "Harmonized Tariff Schedule" to find sources.

Entry and Documentation

The entry of merchandise is a two-part process consisting of 1) filing the documents necessary to determine whether merchandise may be released from Customs custody and 2) filing the documents that contain information for duty assessment and statistical purposes. In certain instances all documents must be filed and accepted by Customs prior to the release of the goods. Unless you have been granted an extension, you must file entry documents at a location specified by the port or area director within five working days of your shipment's date of arrival at a U.S. port of entry. These include a number of standard documents required by Customs for any entry, and:

- U.S. Treasury Bureau of Alcohol, Tobacco, and Firearms (ATF) permits for importation of alcoholic beverages Form ATF 5100.24
- Certificate of Label Approval Form ATF 5100.31
- For wines: Certificate of Origin
- For distilled spirits: Certificates of Age and Origin
- For certain non-standard fill items: Certificates of Non-Standard Fill

After you present the entry, Customs may examine your shipment, or may waive examination. The shipment is then released provided no legal or regulatory violations have been noted. You must then file entry summary documentation and deposit estimated duties at a designated customhouse within 10 working days of your shipment's release. For a detailed description of entry procedures, standard documentation, and informal entry, see "Entry Process" on page 185.

Informed Compliance. Informed compliance was introduced with the Customs Modernization Act of 1993 (Mod Act) and defines the relationship between importers and the Customs Service. It sets out the responsibilities of both parties. Providing the correct documentation and information for entry is a key factor that will make your importing operation run smoothly. We recommend that importers become familiar with the concept of informed comliance and the responsibilities that they have under the Mod Act. For further discussion about informed compliance see "Informed Compliance" on page 211.

Note: The Entry and Documentation section has been carefully designed to supply you, the importer, with sample documents and directions on how to satisfy Customs requirements. Be aware that you should consult the applicable authorities to ensure that you are correctly following the most current procedures.

Prohibitions and Restrictions

Fruit Juices. Products sold as fruit juices may be sweetened provided the label states the presence of the added sugar or some other approved wholesome, nutritive sweetening agent. If you add water, the product is no longer considered "fruit juice." Added water is prohibited for products presented as fruit juice. Fruit juice beverages containing added water are subject to all the requirements for nonstandard foods, particularly the use of a common or usual name. If your product fits this category, you should be sure that its labeling includes a declaration of the percent of any characterizing ingredient that has a material bearing on the price, or on consumer acceptance of the product. Labels on diluted orange juice beverages, for example, are specifically required to show the percentage of juice, expressed in increments of 5% (21 CFR 102).

Noncarbonated Beverages. Noncarbonated beverages containing no fruit or vegetable juice must be named as required by the regulation (21 CFR 102). If your label in any way suggests that fruit or vegetable juice is present in your product, you must be sure the label includes an added statement such as "contains no juice." You should include the name of the fruit or vegetable indicated by the flavor, color, or labeling of the product.

Carbonated Beverages. Nonalcoholic carbonated beverages are subject to the standards established for "soda water" (21 CFR 165). Caffeine from kola nut extract or other natural caffeine-containing extracts may be used in any soda water but may not exceed 0.02% by weight of the finished food. All optional ingredients must be declared on the label.

Bottled Waters. The FDA has established standards of quality for bottled drinking water (21 CFR 103). All bottled waters other than mineral waters must comply with these standards. The FDA assumes that natural mineral waters, by their very nature, would exceed physical and chemical limits prescribed in the Bottled Drinking Water Standard. Therefore mineral waters are exempt from the standard. However, in no case will the FDA permit the presence of any substance in bottled mineral water at any level deemed toxic. The FDA has also established Current Good Manufacturing Practice Regulations for processing and bottling waters (21 CFR 129), with which your product must comply.

It is misleading to list on the label of mineral water products minerals that are only present in the product in insignificant amounts. Such a listing may be deemed an attempt to imply that your product has nutritional and/or therapeutic benefit that it cannot actually be shown to possess. Furthermore, if you make any nutritional or health claims in your product's labeling, then you must comply in full with all nutritional labeling requirements. You should be sure that all bottled waters you offer for import are: 1) obtained from sources free from pollution; 2) bottled or otherwise prepared for the market under sanitary conditions, with special reference to the condition of the bottles or other containers and of their stoppers; 3) free from microorganisms of the coliform group; 4) of good sanitary quality when judged by the result of a bacteriological examination to determine the numbers of bacteria growing on gelatin at 20°C and on agar at 37°C; and 5) of good sanitary quality when judged by the results of a sanitary chemical analysis.

Customs will refuse misbranded shipments of mineral waters. Furthermore, if you offer misbranded shipments for import, you are subject to legal action. The following are some frequently assessed examples of misbranding on mineral water labels: 1) objectionable therapeutic claims; 2) false and misleading statements other than therapeutic claims; 3) inaccurate or otherwise misleading label statement of analysis; 4) undeclared addition of salts, carbon dioxide, etc.; and 5) labeling of artificially prepared waters as "mineral water."

Alcoholic Beverages. Regulations governing the importation of alcoholic beverages are complex and vary depending upon the category of alcohol in question. They cover such issues as documentation, storage, labeling, content, and bottling. This section is in no way exhaustive. If you are interested in importing alcoholic beverages, you should contact the ATF for an importer's information packet, and consult with any pertinent state regulatory agencies for details regarding their requirements.

Classification and standards of identity (distilled spirits, wine, and malt beverages). Wines and distilled spirits are divided into separate classifications under which customs duties are calculated. Malt liquors are divided into separate classifications for labeling purposes only.

Distilled Spirits. Distilled spirits classifications are as follows: 1) neutral spirits of alcohol; 2) whisky; 3) gin; 4) brandy; 5) blended applejack; 6) rum; 7) tequila; 8) cordials and liqueurs; 9) flavored brandy, gin, rum, vodka, and whiskey; 10) imitations; 11) distinctive types known by geographical designation; and 12) types distinctive of a particular place but without geographical designation.

Wines. Wines are classified as follows: 1) grape wine; 2) sparkling grape wine; 3) carbonated grape wine; 4) citrus wine; 5) fruit wine; 6) wine from other agricultural products; 7) aperitif wine; 8) imitation and substandard wine; and 9) retsina wine. These classifications are further complicated by three factors: 1) alteration: if a wine is altered by a process such as blending or carbonation, it must be reclassified. If there is no known trade classification for such a wine, its label must give a truthful and adequate description of the wine's composition; 2) varietal des-

ignation: if the wine derives its predominant taste, aroma, characteristics, and at least 51% of its volume from a particular variety of grape, the variety can be used in its type designation; e.g. Cabernet Sauvignon or Chenin Blanc; 3) geographical or place of origin designations: the ATF has a number of rules regarding the naming of wines, mainly to ensure that consumers get the product from the location specified on the label. In some cases these rules are not specifically defined in the law except by example; the final decision as to the proper identity of the wine is up to the ATF specialist.

Wines named with a geographic term that relates to a whole group of wines, such as vermouth, are called "generic" wines. Those named with a geographic term specific to a region of origin and distinguishable from all others are called "nongeneric" wines. Nongeneric names cannot be said to be the distinctive name of a specific wine from a particular place or region distinguishable from all others, unless the ATF director finds that it is known to consumers and to the trade as such. Examples of nongeneric wines are Bordeaux Rouge and Liebfraumilch. Examples of distinctive nongeneric wines are St. Emilion and Chateauneuf-du-Pape.

Malt Beverages. The system of classification and standards of identity for malt beverages is used only to label the product correctly, there being no elaborate classification for determining duty as there is for wine and distilled spirits. Several types of malt beverages are mentioned in the ATF regulations, although they are not precisely defined. Categories include: 1) beer; 2) lager beer; 3) lager; 4) ale; 5) porter; 6) stout; 7) half and half; and 8) types distinguished by geographical name, such as Pilsner and Dortmunder.

Customs will inspect your shipment to ensure proper classification for duty and federal excise tax purposes.

Standards of Fill and Bottles Per Case (Distilled Liquor and Wine Only). Standards of fill are specifications established by the law standardizing bottle size and headroom. Size of liquor and wine bottle, the amount of liquid allowed in a bottle of a given size, and the number of bottles that may be shipped in a case are strictly regulated, varying with the category of alcohol. If you are importing distilled spirits bottled or packed on or after January 1, 1980, and imported wines bottled or packed on or after January 1, 1979, your product must comply with metric standards of fill. If the products were packed or bottled prior to these respective dates, you must include with your entry a Certificate of Non-Standard Fill, signed by a duly authorized country-of-origin government official, stating that such is the case. This statement may be a separate document or may be included on the invoice. If you wish to import wines or distilled liquors that were bottled or packed after the respective dates and that do not comply with the standards, you may petition the ATF on a case-by-case basis for an exemption. Your petition must show cause for the noncompliance. For details on standards of fill, contact the ATF or see 27 CFR.

Red Strip Stamps (Distilled Liquors Only). All distilled liquors are subject to federal excise taxes, which must be paid at entry. ATF Red Strip Stamps, which show that IRS excise taxes have been paid, are affixed to all individual bottles of distilled liquor of one-gallon size or less. Red strip stamps are not required on bulk containers. You may obtain red strip stamps in quantity from the ATF at no charge. They must be imprinted with your basic permit number, and affixed to each individual bottle so that when the bottle is opened the number is still identifiable on the remaining stamp. Stamps may be affixed 1) by the foreign bottler; 2) while the shipment is being stored in a foreign trade zone or Customs bonded warehouse; 3) at the U.S. bottler's warehouse (for liquor imported in bulk); or 4) in some cases, if you can document prior payment of the IRS excise tax, Customs will release the shipment to your custody, allowing you to apply the stamps at any time before the bottles enter the commercial market.

Certificate of Age and Origin (Distilled Spirits Only). Scotch, Irish, and Canadian whiskies, brandy, cognac, rum, tequila, and all Class 2 whiskies and blends require special documentation of age and origin. Many specific rules apply to these Certificates of Age and Origin, which are issued by a duly authorized country of origin official. Because these certificates are issued by foreign governments, their form and content varies. However, they must at least state that the products are what they purport to be, have been manufactured in compliance with the applicable laws of that government, and are of the specified age. You must present the certificate to Customs before your shipment will be released. For complete details regarding Certificates of Age and Origin, see ATF Industry Circular #89-1 available from ATF (see addresses at end of this chapter).

Certificate of Origin (Wine Only). A Certificate of Origin signed by an authorized country of origin government official must confirm the identity of the wine, and its production in compliance with that government's laws regulating the production of wines manufactured for home consumption. You must present the certificate to Customs before your shipment will be released. For complete details regarding Certificates of Origin, see ATF Industry Circular #89-1 available from ATF (see addresses at end of this chapter).

Original certificates of origin are required for wines and distilled spirits from Bulgaria, Canada, Chile, France, Germany, Ireland, Jamaica, Mexico, Portugal, Romania, Spain, and the United Kingdom.

Invoices (Distilled Spirits, Wines, and Malt Beverages). You must present a copy of the shipping invoice or bill of lading for each shipment of alcoholic beverages in order to obtain release from Customs. This documentation must show the nature and quantity of the contents and the name of the consignee.

Excise Taxes and Duty Payments (Distilled Spirits, Wines, and Malt Beverages). Federal excise tax on wine and distilled spirits is a set fee per gallon (by category) levied by the IRS but collected by U.S. Customs. For malt beverages it is levied on a per barrel basis. The customs duty per gallon varies according to type of alcohol. All federal excise taxes and all customs duties are payable at the time of entry.

Customs Bonded Warehouses. Since payment of duties and taxes is not required until goods are withdrawn from Customs custody, you may wish to store shipments in a Customs bonded warehouse until you are ready to deliver the goods to your buyers. Goods may be stored for a period of up to three years, after which time extensions are possible. You can either pay a fee to store products in a bonded warehouse operated by someone else, or you can apply to the ATF to establish your own bonded warehouse. For more information on Customs bonded warehouse options, consult your local Port Director of Customs.

Quotas

Milk-Based Beverage Products Some milk-based beverage products classified under heading 2202.90.28 may be under quotas noted in Chapter 99, Subchapter IV.

For a general discussion of quotas, refer to "Quotas Administered by Customs" on page 274.

Marking and Labeling Requirements

Certificate of Label Approval. The following discussion of labeling requirements is meant to serve only as a general guidelines. The ATF regulations regarding labeling of alcoholic beverage containers are specific and extensive. For complete details, see 27 CFR or contact the ATF (see addresses at end of this chapter).

Approval Procedures. The ATF has specific regulations governing labeling of all final packaging of alcoholic beverages. The label requirements vary depending on the category of alcohol, i.e. distilled spirits, wines, or malt beverages. You must submit samples of your printed labels for pre-approval, using Form ATF-F-1649. If the label is approved, the ATF director will endorse the form and return it to you as a Certificate of Label Approval. You must present the certificate to Customs before your shipment will be released. ATF recommends that importers submit mock-ups of proposed labels for informal feedback prior to printing. You should send these with a letter, not with Form 1649.

Distilled Spirit Labels. In general, labels for distilled spirits must contain the following information: brand name, class and type, alcoholic contents, net contents, name and address of the importer, country of origin, coloring or flavoring where applicable, percentage of neutral spirits where applicable, and statement of age, if required.

Wine Labels. In general, labels for wines must show: brand name; class, type, or other lawful designation; statement of the exact percentage of foreign wine if the bottle contains a blend of foreign and domestic; net contents; alcoholic content—or the term "table" or "light" wine if the alcoholic content is less than 14%—name and business address of the importer. As discussed in the paragraph on classification, wine designation and classification is strictly regulated and must be accurately reflected on the label.

Malt Beverage Labels. In general, labels for malt beverages must show: brand name, class and type, net contents, name and address of importer, name of bottler or packer—if required by state or foreign law—and alcoholic content—when required by state law.

Warning and Content Labels. All alcoholic beverages containing 10 parts per million or more of sulfites must bear warning labels to that effect. The presence of FD&C Yellow #5—tartrazine—in any alcoholic beverage, must be stated on the label.

The use of the word "light" or "lite" on alcoholic beverage labels must be accompanied by statement of calorie, carbohydrate, fat, and protein content. The statement will not be required when "light" is used as authorized in other regulations (e.g. "light sherry") or when the term is used to describe a characteristic of the product ("light taste"), versus an imputation regarding caloric content.

All alcoholic beverages bottled on or after November 18, 1989 must include, in a conspicuous place on the label, the following warning statement: "GOVERNMENT WARNING: (1) According to the Surgeon General, women should not drink alcoholic beverages during pregnancy because of the risks of birth defects. (2) Consumption of alcoholic beverages impairs your ability to drive a car or operate machinery and may cause health problems." The ATF strictly regulates wording, type size, number of words per inch, and other variables relating to the presentation of the warning. Noncompliance with this labeling regulation can result in huge fines, levied on a daily basis during the period of noncompliance, and the revocation of your import permit. For complete information regarding warning statements on alcohol labels see ATF Industry Circular #90-1, available from the ATF (see addresses at end of this chapter).

Prohibited Labels. The ATF not only regulates what must appear on bottle labels, but also what must not appear on bottle labels. For example, labels of alcoholic beverages may not contain any statements that are false or misleading, disparaging to a competitor's product, obscene or indecent, that relate to scientific tests or standards that may be misleading, or specific reference other than permit number to the product's compliance with state or government regulations. For complete details regarding label requirements, contact the ATF or see 27 CFR.

Bottle and Container Labels. If distilled spirits are bottled abroad in containers having a capacity of 200 milliliters or more, these containers must be legibly and permanently marked with

1) the words "Liquor Bottle" and 2) the city or country address of the manufacturer of the spirits or of the exporter abroad, or the city of address of the U.S. importer. Empty liquor bottles imported to be filled in the U.S. shall be marked with the words "Liquor Bottle" and the location of the bottle manufacturer. You may import empty or filled distinctive liquor bottles not bearing such indicia only with prior ATF approval.

Each bottle, cask, or other immediate container of imported distilled spirits, wines, or malt beverages must be marked for customs purposes to indicate the country of origin of the alcoholic beverage contained therein.

For a general discussion of U.S. Customs marking and labeling requirements, see "Country of Origin Marking" on page 236, "Special Marking Requirements" on page 238 and "Marking— False Impression" on page 239.

Shipping Considerations

You will need to ensure that your goods are packaged and shipped with care so that they arrive in good condition and pass smoothly through Customs. You are responsible for ensuring that the shipment is in compliance with all applicable government regulations for packing and shipping. In most instances, you should not leave these arrangements solely to the discretion of your supplier. Careful preparation of the cargo and selection of the mode of transport can be essential to a cost-effective, timely delivery of undamaged goods. We strongly advise you to consult your shipping representative, insurance agent, or freight broker for advice on packing and shipping.

Shipping procedures are an important factor in the importation of malt beverages and of fine wines, since both products can be ruined by too much movement and sharp shifts in temperature. It is best to pack them in container sizes which reduce the amount of individual handling, and to store them below decks and as close to the ship's center of gravity as possible. You should be familiar with your particular product's requirements before arranging for shipping. Security against pilferage is also a concern.

Publications and WWW Resources

The following publication explains the FDA requirements for importing beverages. It is published by the FDA and is available online from the FDA website (www.fda.gov/opacom/7pubs.html).

> *Requirements of Laws and Regulations Enforced by the U.S. Food and Drug Administration*

The *Harmonized Tariff Schedule of the United States (2001)* (HTSUS) is available to view on the Customs Service website (www.customs.gov), or you may purchase a printed version from:

U.S. Government Printing Office
Superintendent of Documents
710 North Capital Street NW
Washington DC 20401
Tel: (202) 512-1800
Fax: (202) 512-1657
Website: www.access.gpo.gov

The USGPO also has copies of specific laws available for purchase. The USGPO accepts orders made by fax, phone or placed over the Internet, as well as mail orders paid by credit card. All orders must be accompanied by payment. Credit cards, checks drawn on a U.S. bank, or an international money order are all acceptable.

Relevant Government Agencies

Address your questions regarding ATF requirements for importation of alcoholic beverages to:

Bureau of Alcohol, Tobacco, Firearms and Explosives
Firearms and Explosives Import Branch
650 Massachusetts Avenue NW
Washington DC 20226
Tel: (202) 927-8320
Website: www.atf.treas.gov

Address your questions regarding FDA import requirements for all beverages containing less than 7% alcohol by volume to:

Food and Drug Administration (FDA)
Center for Food Safety and Applied Nutrition (CFSAN)
Office of Compliance
Division of Enforcement, Imports Branch
5100 Paint Branch Parkway
College Park, MD 20740-3835
Tel: (301) 436-2080
Website: http://vm.cfsan.fda.gov/list.html

Food and Drug Administration (FDA)
Center for Food Safety and Applied Nutrition (CFSAN)
Office of Plant and Dairy Foods and Beverages
5100 Paint Branch Parkway
College Park, MD 20740-3835
Tel: (301) 436-1700
Website: http://vm.cfsan.fda.gov/list.html

Address your questions regarding importation of beverages to your local Customs port director. For addresses refer to "U.S. Customs and Border Protection Offices" on page 65 or contact:

U.S. Customs and Border Protection
Customs Headquarters
1300 Pennsylvania Avenue NW
Washington DC 20229
Tel: (202) 354-1000
Website: www.customs.treas.gov

Laws and Regulations

The following laws and regulations may be relevant to the importation of beverages. The laws are contained in the U.S. Code (USC) and the regulations in the Code of Federal Regulations (CFR), both of which may be available at larger public and law libraries. Copies of specific laws are also available from the United States Government Printing Office (address above).

21 USC 301 et seq.
Federal Food, Drug, and Cosmetic Act
This Act prohibits deceptive practices and regulates the manufacture, sale and importation or exportation of food, drugs, cosmetics, and related products. It was amended by the Food Quality Protection Act of 1996. See 21 USC 331, 381, 382.

19 CFR 12.1 et seq.; 21 CFR 1.83 et seq.
Regulations on Food, Drugs, and Cosmetics
These regulations of the Secretary of Health and Human Services and the Secretary of the Treasury govern the standards, labeling, marking, and importing of products used with food, drugs, and cosmetics.

18 USC 960 et seq.
Exportation of Armed Vessels, Arms, Liquor, and Narcotics
Customs enforces the provisions of law regulating the prerequisites to a vessel's departure and the prohibitions against exportation of armed vessels, arms, liquor, and narcotics.

18 USC 1263
Marks and Labels on Packages of Liquor
This Act provides for imposition of a fine or imprisonment on persons who knowingly ship into the U.S. any unmarked or unlabeled package of liquor, and the seizure and forfeiture of any such liquor. See also 18 USC 3615; 21 USC 342(d); 27 USC 201 et seq.

19 CFR 12.37, 12.38; 27 CFR 251, Part 1
Regulations on Labeling Alcoholic Beverages
These regulations describe the required labeling for alcoholic beverages and set forth the procedures for approval of labels and enforcement of the label requirements.

26 USC 5001 et seq.
Excise Tax on Alcohol
This law imposes a tax on distilled spirits, wines, and beers.

27 CFR 251.48, 251.173
Regulations on Collection of Alcohol Excise Taxes
These regulations authorize Customs to collect excise taxes imposed on distilled spirits, wines, and beer, including taxes paid by electronic funds transfer (EFT). Customs further assists in the enforcement of the tax laws through its inspection powers. A Customs officer must not release distilled spirits until he or she inspects them, with particular emphasis on losses in transit, and makes certain that various documentary requirements are met.

27 USC 122
Transportation in Interstate Commerce of Intoxicating Liquor
This Act authorizes Customs to enforce prohibitions against the importation of alcoholic beverages contrary to the laws of individual states.

27 USC 201 et seq.
Federal Alcohol Administration Act (FAAA)
This Act prohibits the importation of distilled spirits, wine, or malt beverages into the U.S. without a permit issued by the Secretary of the Treasury and authorizes Customs to enforce this prohibition and any labeling requirements.

19 CFR 12.37
Regulations of Customs for Entry of Alcohol
This regulation sets forth the procedures by which Customs will enforce compliance with the FAAA.

Principal Exporting Countries

The following listing includes samples of the main supplier nations of the products of this chapter. It is organized by HTSUS major heading. (Refer to "Customs Classification" above for the product codes.) Countries are listed in rank order of the value of products imported to the U.S. Statistics represent customs value of entries for 2002 from the Bureau of Census, U.S. Department of Commerce.

2201—Canada, France, Italy, Fiji, Mexico, Germany, Norway, United Kingdom, Portugal, Poland, New Zealand

2202—Mexico, Canada, Austria, Thailand, South Korea, France, Germany, Taiwan, Spain, Japan, Netherlands, Italy, Hong Kong

2203—Mexico, Netherlands, Canada, Germany, United Kindom, Ireland, Japan, Dominican Republic, Belgium, Czech Republic, Jamaica

2204—France, Italy, Australia, Chile, Spain, Portugal, Germany, Argentina, New Zealand, South Africa, Greece, Belgium, Israel, Canada. Austria, United Kingdom

2205—Italy, France, Japan, Germany, Spain, United Kingdom, Denmark, Bulgaria, Brazil, Argentina, China

2206—Canada, Japan, Ireland, Italy, Spain, South Korea, United Kingdom, China, Mexico, Taiwan, France, Denmark, Argentina

2207—Saudi Arabia, Jamaica, Costa Rica, Canada, Mexico, United Kingdom, South Africa, Brazil, Argentina, El Salvador, Barbados, Ireland, Germany

2208—United Kingdom, France, Mexico, Sweden, Canada, Ireland, Netherlands, Russia, Italy, Germany, Poland, Finland, Jamaica, Denmark, Spain

2209—Italy, China, Spain, France, Japan, Canada, Philippines, Taiwan, Hong Kong, Germany, Mexico, Austria, United Kingdom

Chapter 23:
Prepared Animal Feed

Full title: Residues and Waste from the Food Industry; Animal Feeds

This section pertains to the importation of prepared animal feeds and byproducts of the food industry generally unfit for human consumption and used for industrial purposes, which are classified within Chapter 23 of the Harmonized Tariff Schedule of the United States (HTSUS). Specifically, it includes meat and fish meals, cereal and starch residues, oilcake residues from oil seed extraction, other vegetable processing residues, and prepared pet and animal feeds. This section is supplemental to "Appendix: Foods" on page 825. If you are interested in importing products of Chapter 23, you should read that section in conjunction with this one.

If you are interested in importing medicated feeds or medicated feed premixes, refer to Commodity Index Chapter 30. Primary products producing the residues covered in Chapter 23 are covered in Chapter 2, 3, 7, 8, 10, and 12.

Note: To understand key issues that will enable you to make best use of the information in this section we recommend that you see "Introduction" on page 425.

Key Factors

The key factors in the importation of animal feeds are:

- Compliance with U.S. Food and Drug Administration (FDA) purity, safety, manufacturing, and other standards

- FDA import entry notification

- Compliance with U.S. Environmental Protection Agency (EPA) pesticide regulations, including pesticide residue monitoring for feeds that could affect U.S. food supplies

- Import quotas on animal feeds containing milk or milk derivatives, licensing required

Although most importers utilize the services of a licensed customs broker in making their entries, and we recommend this practice, you should be aware of the regulatory, entry, and documentation issues involved in importing your product. You, as importer, are ultimately responsible for the fulfillment of any legal requirements applicable to your shipment.

General Considerations

Regulations governing certain products intended for animal use are stringent and complex. Importation of these products is regulated by the FDA under applicable provisions of the Federal Food, Drug, and Cosmetic Act (FDCA). Products designed for use by animals imported into the U.S. must comply with all FDCA requirements for those produced domestically. Animal feeds and pet foods, including color and food additives, are generally subject to the same FDCA requirements for similar products intended for human use.

Imported products regulated by the FDA are subject to FDA port of entry inspection. For a discussion of required FDA import procedures see "Appendix: Foods" on page 825.

Detention of Shipment. If your shipment is found to be noncomplying, it may be detained at the port of entry. The FDA may permit you to bring such a shipment into compliance before making a final decision regarding admittance. However, any sorting, reprocessing, or relabeling must be supervised by FDA personnel, and will be done at the importer's expense. Such conditional release to allow an importer to bring a shipment into compliance is a privilege, not a right. The FDA may consider subsequent noncomplying shipments of the same type of product to constitute abuse of the privilege and require the importer to destroy or reexport the products. To ascertain what your legal responsibilities are, you should contact the FDA regarding the specific items to be imported.

Customs Classification

For customs purposes, animal feeds and food residues are classified under Chapter 23 of the HTSUS. This chapter is broken into major headings, which are further divided into subheadings, and often sub-subheadings, each of which has its own HTSUS classification number. For example, the 2001 HTSUS number for animal feeds containing egg is 2309.90.60, indicating that it is a subcategory of feeds other than prepared dog and cat food put up for retail sale (2309.90), itself a subcategory of the major heading preparations of a kind used in animal feeding (2309). There are nine major headings in HTSUS Chapter 23.

2301—Flour, meals, and pellets, of meat or meat offal, of fish or of crustaceans, molluscs, or other aquatic invertebrates; unfit for human consumption; greaves (cracklings)

2302—Bran, sharps (middlings), and other residues, whether or not in the form of pellets, derived from the sifting, milling, or other working of cereals or of leguminous plants

2303—Residues of starch manufacture and similar residues, beet-pulp, bagasse, and other waste of sugar manufacture, brewing, or distillation of dregs and waste, whether or not in the form of pellets

2304—Oilcake and other solid residues, whether or not ground or in the form of pellets, resulting from the extraction of soybean oil

2305—Oilcake and other solid residues, whether or not ground or in the form of pellets, resulting from the extraction of peanut (ground-nut) oil

2306—Oilcake and other solid residues, whether or not ground or in the form of pellets, resulting from the extraction of vegetable fats or oils, other than those of heading 2304 or 2305

2307—Wine lees; argol

2308—Vegetable materials and vegetable waste, vegetable residues and byproducts, whether or not in the form of pellets, of a kind used in animal feeding, not elsewhere specified or included

2309—Preparations of a kind used in animal feeding

For more details regarding classification of the specific product you are interested in importing, consult a customs broker, the appropriate commodity specialist at your nearest Customs port, or see HTSUS. The 2001 HTSUS is available online from the Customs Service (www.customs.gov/impoexpo/impoexpo.htm) or for purchase from the US Government Printing Office (see resources at the end of this chapter), and may be found in larger public libraries. For a general discussion of customs classification, see "Classification—Liquidation" on page 229.

Dutiable Status of Goods

For more information about duty rates and binding decisions see "Dutiable Status of Goods" on page 203; for a discussion of temporary importation of goods see "Temporary Free Importations" on page 205.

Valuation

Importers have a responsibility to use what the U.S. Customs Service deems, "reasonable care," when determining the value of their goods. They must also provide any additional information that the Customs Service needs for setting a final value on the goods. This process involves a number of factors and can be somewhat complicated; importers must be aware of applicable issues and details. Valuation information applies to all types of commodities, for further discussion on the subject see "Customs Valuation" on page 267.

Import Duties

Import duties vary (often dramatically) depending upon the Harmonized Tariff Schedule (HTSUS) classification of the goods or products imported. Since some products that look alike have different HTSUS classifications and different rates of duty, proper classification is vital. Note that "differences of opinion" between importers and the Bureau of Customs and Border Protection regarding classification keeps customs attorneys very busy.

Import duties can be assessed on the imported value of the goods ("ad valorem" rates of duty such as 2%, 4.4%, 50%, etc.), total units or weight of the goods ("specific" rates of duty such as 2 cents each or 1.5 cents/pound, etc.) or on a combination basis ("compound" rates of duty such as 5 cents each plus 6%).

Listed below is a sampling of several Column 1 import duty rates for Chapter 23 products:
Flours, meals and pellets, of fish or of crustaceans, molluscs or other aquatic invertebrates (2301.20.00): free
to
Animal feeds containing milk or milk derivatives containing over ten percent by weight of milk solids described in general note 15 of the tariff schedule and entered pursuant to its provisions (2309.90.22): 7.5%

For specific information on US import duties refer to the Harmonized Tariff Schedule of the US. The print version is available from the US Government Printing Office as well as third party suppliers who often add special features. Online versions are available in both static PDF pages as well as in formats with excellent search functionality. Search the Web with the term "Harmonized Tariff Schedule" to find sources.

Entry and Documentation

The entry of merchandise is a two-part process consisting of 1) filing the documents necessary to determine whether merchandise may be released from Customs custody and 2) filing the documents that contain information for duty assessment and statistical purposes. In certain instances all documents must be filed and accepted by Customs prior to the release of the goods. Unless you have been granted an extension, you must file entry documents at a location specified by the port or area director within five working days of your shipment's date of arrival at a U.S. port of entry. These include a number of standard documents required by Customs for any entry.

After you present the entry, Customs may examine your shipment, or may waive examination. The shipment is then released provided no legal or regulatory violations have been noted. You must then file entry summary documentation and deposit estimated duties at a designated customhouse within 10 working days of your shipment's release. For a detailed description of entry procedures, standard documentation, and informal entry, see "Entry Process" on page 185.

Informed Compliance. Informed compliance was introduced with the Customs Modernization Act of 1993 (Mod Act) and defines the relationship between importers and the Customs Service. It sets out the responsibilities of both parties. Providing the correct documentation and information for entry is a key factor that will make your importing operation run smoothly. We recommend that importers become familiar with the concept of informed comliance and the responsibilities that they have under the Mod Act. For further discussion about informed compliance see "Informed Compliance" on page 211.

Note: The Entry and Documentation section has been carefully designed to supply you, the importer, with sample documents and directions on how to satisfy Customs requirements. Be aware that you should consult the applicable authorities to ensure that you are correctly following the most current procedures.

Prohibitions and Restrictions

Although the FDCA defines food and drugs as articles intended "for man and other animals," you should be aware of some important distinctions between the law's provisions for products intended for human use and those intended for animal use. For example, drugs, food additives, and color additives for use in food-producing animals are evaluated for safety in meat, milk, and eggs, as well as safety and effectiveness for the animal itself. The FDCA requires approval of applications for use of new animal drugs in the manufacture of animal feed.

Animal Feeds and Pet Foods. Commercial animal feeds are commonly sold in bags or in bulk through feed stores and mills, while pet foods are commonly sold through the same distribution channels as human food. Both commercial feed and pet food must meet the requirements of the FDCA and those of individual state's laws (see "Marking and Labeling Requirements" below). As with human food, animal feeds and pet food may not be adulterated or misbranded. For example, animal feeds may not contain any 1) poisonous or deleterious substances; 2) residues of pesticides in excess of established tolerances; 3) unsafe food or color additives; or 4) filthy, putrid, or decomposed material.

You may not import or sell animal feed or pet food in which damage or inferiority has been concealed in any manner; under the name of any other food; or that has any valuable constituents omitted or extracted. You should be sure that canned pet food is manufactured and registered in accordance with the regulations for low-acid canned foods (21 CFR 507, 508).

Food Additives. Substances that by their intended use may become components of animal feed or pet food either directly or indirectly, or that may otherwise affect the characteristics of the animal feed or pet food are defined as "food additives" (21 CFR 570, 571, 573). Food additives are illegal in the absence of prior FDA approval (sanction) or regulation for their safe use. The FDA promulgates food additive regulations based on data submitted in a formal Food Additive Petition. If you wish to initiate the FDA approval process for an additive for animal feed ingredient, submit a Food Additive Petition to FDA's Center for Veterinary Medicine, Division of Animal Feeds (see addresses at end of this chapter).

Food additives that have been found to induce cancer, or whose metabolites have been found to induce cancer, may be used in feed for food-producing animals if no harm comes to the animal and there is no residue of the substance or its metabolites in edible tissues or other products reaching the consumer (21 CFR Sec. 409). However, such substances may not be added to other animal or pet foods.

Quotas

Entry of specific products can be difficult because many product categories affected by quota restrictions overlap, especially where dairy products—which may be components of animal feeds—are concerned. It is important to consult the USDA Import Licensing Group or the U.S. Customs Service Quota Branch (addresses below) to determine whether quota restrictions apply to your specific product.

Quotas do exist for animal feeds containing milk or milk derivatives. These quotas are administered by the Department of Agriculture under license and may not be imported unless the importer holds a license issued by the Department of Agriculture.

For a general discussion of quotas, refer to "Quotas Administered by Customs" on page 274.

Marking and Labeling Requirements

Animal feed and pet food labeling may not be false or misleading in any particular. U.S. state laws require that animal feed labels bear, in addition to the information required by federal law, a label statement of "Guaranteed Analysis" for minimum protein and fat content, maximum fiber content, and, in some instances, maximum moisture content. You may obtain additional information concerning state registration and labeling requirements from the U.S. state(s) in which you intend to sell your products, or from the Official Publication of the Association of American Feed Control Officials, Inc. (see addresses at end of this chapter).

In addition to the labeling requirements specified by the FDCA and the individual states, pet foods are subject to labeling requirements of the Fair Packaging and Labeling Act (FPLA). Commercial feeds are not. For further details regarding labeling requirements contact FDA (see addresses at end of this chapter).

For a general discussion of U.S. Customs marking and labeling requirements, see "Country of Origin Marking" on page 236, "Special Marking Requirements" on page 238 and "Marking—False Impression" on page 239.

Shipping Considerations

You will need to ensure that your goods are packaged and shipped with care to ensure that they arrive in good condition and pass smoothly through Customs. You are responsible for ensuring that the shipment is in compliance with all applicable government regulations for packaging and shipping. In most instances, you should not leave these arrangements solely to the discretion of your supplier. Careful preparation of the cargo and selection of the mode of transport can be essential to a cost-effective, timely delivery of undamaged goods. We strongly advise you to consult your shipping representative, insurance agent, or freight broker for advice on packing and shipping.

As with any edible product, careful packing is necessary to prevent contamination and spoilage en route. Protection from insect and animal contamination is especially important for such products, as contamination with filth is cause for a shipment to be rejected by Customs. Heat and moisture control is also important. Because many food residues contain oils that can become rancid and are subject to the growth of mold if kept in a hot, moist environment, packing and avoidance of delays in transit are important to ensuring the delivery of a salable product.

Publications and WWW Resources

The following publication explains the FDA requirements for importing animal feed products. It is published by the FDA and is available online from the FDA website (www.fda.gov/opacom/7pubs.html).

Requirements of Laws and Regulations Enforced by the U.S. Food and Drug Administration

The *Harmonized Tariff Schedule of the United States (2001)* (HTSUS) is available to view on the Customs Service website (www.customs.gov), or you may purchase a printed version from:

U.S. Government Printing Office
Superintendent of Documents
710 North Capital Street NW
Washington DC 20401
Tel: (202) 512-1800
Fax: (202) 512-1657
Website: www.access.gpo.gov

The USGPO also has copies of specific laws available for purchase. The USGPO accepts orders made by fax, phone or placed over the Internet, as well as mail orders paid by credit card. All orders must be accompanied by payment. Credit cards, checks drawn on a U.S. bank, or an international money order are all acceptable.

Relevant Government Agencies

Address general questions regarding FDA import requirements for products intended for animal use and questions regarding registration and compliance status of animal products to:

Food and Drug Administration (FDA)
Center for Veterinary Medicine
Center for Veterinary Medicine
Office of Surveillance and Compliance
7500 Standish Place
Rockville, MD 20855
Tel: (301) 827-6647
Website: www.fda.gov/cvm/default.html

Food and Drug Administration (FDA)
Center for Food Safety and Applied Nutrition (CFSAN)
Office of Compliance
Division of Enforcement, Imports Branch
5100 Paint Branch Parkway
College Park, MD 20740-3835
Tel: (301) 436-2080
Website: http://vm.cfsan.fda.gov/list.html

Address questions regarding import licensing of quota animal feeds to:

USDA Agricultural Marketing Service (AMS)
Livestock and Seed Division
1400 Independence Avenue SW
Washington DC 20250
Tel: (202) 720-5705
Website: www.ams.usda.gov/lsg

Address questions regarding regulation of pesticide residues to:

Environmental Protection Agency (EPA)
Office of Pesticide Programs
Ariel Rios Building
1200 Pennsylvania Avenue NW
Mail Code 3213A
Washington DC 20460
Tel: (703) 305-7090
Website: www.epa.gov

Address questions regarding quotas to:

U.S. Customs and Border Protection
Office of Field Operations, Quota Branch
1300 Pennsylvania Avenue NW
Washington DC 20229
Tel: (202) 927-5850
Website: www.customs.treas.gov

Address general questions regarding importation of animal feeds to your local Customs port director. For addresses refer to "U.S. Customs and Border Protection Offices" on page 65 or contact:

U.S. Customs and Border Protection
Customs Headquarters
1300 Pennsylvania Avenue NW
Washington DC 20229
Tel: (202) 354-1000
Website: www.customs.treas.gov

Laws and Regulations

The following laws and regulations may be relevant to the importation of animal feeds and pet foods of HTSUS Chapter 23. The laws are contained in the U.S. Code (USC) and the regulations are published in the Code of Federal Regulations (CFR), both of which may be available at larger public and law libraries. Copies of specific laws are also available from the United States Government Printing Office (address above).

21 USC 301 et seq.
Federal Food, Drug, and Cosmetic Act
This Act prohibits deceptive practices and regulates the manufacture, sale and importation or exportation of food, drugs, cosmetics, and related products. It was amended by the Food Quality Protection Act of 1996. See 21 USC 331, 381, 382.

19 CFR 12.1 et seq.; 21 CFR 1.83 et seq.
Regulations on Food, Drugs, and Cosmetics
These regulations of the Secretary of Health and Human Services and the Secretary of the Treasury govern the standards, labeling, marking, and importing of products used with food, drugs, and cosmetics.

7 USC 136 et seq.
Federal Insecticide, Fungicide, and Rodenticide Act (FIFRA)
This Act prohibits the importation of pesticides or devices that are adulterated, misbranded, or otherwise violative of the Act, provides for registration of pesticides and devices, and establishes standards for labeling and classifying pesticides. It was amended by the Food Quality Protection Act of 1996.

19 CFR 12; 40 CFR 162
Regulations on Pesticides
These regulations set forth the procedures and guidelines for importing products exposed to pesticides.

Sources of Additional Information

You may obtain state registration and labeling requirements for animal feeds and pet foods from the Official Publication of the:

Association of American Feed Control Officials, Inc.
Capitol Complex
Guthrie Center
Charleston, WV 25305.

Principal Exporting Countries

The following listing includes samples of the main supplier nations of the products of this chapter. It is organized by HTSUS major heading. (Refer to "Customs Classification" above for the product codes.) Countries are listed in rank order of the value of products imported to the U.S. Statistics represent customs value of entries for 2002 from the Bureau of Census, U.S. Department of Commerce.

2301—Iceland, Canada, Mexico, Australia, New Zealand, Peru, Panama, Chile

2302—Canada, Nigeria, Argentina, Japan

2303—Canada, France, Netherlands, Belgium, Pakistan, Sweden, Thailand, Italy, United Kingdom

2304—Brazil, Canada, China, Japan

2305—Argentina

2306—Canada, China, Argentina, Spain, Greece, India, Taiwan, Guatemala

2307—Italy, Japan

2308—Canada, Brazil, Argentina, Chile, Denmark, United Kingdom, Mexico, Thailand, China, Belgium, Germany, Japan

2309—Canada, Germany, Thailand, China, Japan

Chapter 24:
Tobacco Products

Full title: Tobacco and Manufactured Tobacco Substitutes

This section pertains to the importation of tobacco and tobacco products, which are classified within Chapter 24 of the Harmonized Tariff Schedule of the United States (HTSUS). Specifically, it includes all recognized varieties of unmanufactured tobacco for wrappers and filler as well as tobacco waste; cigars, cheroots, cigarillos, and cigarettes of tobacco or of tobacco substitutes; other tobacco products, including pipe tobacco and snuff; and reconstituted tobacco products. All tobacco products are included in this chapter with the exception of some medicinal cigarettes, which are covered in Commodity Index Chapter 30. Certain tobacco products brought in as samples may be entered duty free (refer to Chapter 98).

Note: To understand key issues that will enable you to make best use of the information in this section we recommend that you see "Introduction" on page 425.

Key Factors

The key factors in the importation of tobacco products are:

- U.S. Treasury Department Bureau of Alcohol, Tobacco, and Firearms (ATF) excise tax, collected by Customs

- ATF labeling requirements

- Federal Trade Commission (FTC) labeling and ingredient-reporting requirements

Although most importers utilize the services of a licensed customs broker in making their entries, and we recommend this practice, you should be aware of the regulatory, entry, and documentation issues involved in importing your product. You, as importer, are ultimately responsible for the fulfillment of any legal requirements applicable to your shipment.

General Considerations

Importation of processed tobacco products into the U.S. is straightforward. No permits, prior licensing, or special entry paperwork are required. However, there are several regulatory issues you should be aware of if you are considering importing these commodities.

ATF Requirements. The U.S. Treasury Bureau of Alcohol, Tobacco, and Firearms (ATF) administers certain marking and labeling requirements under 27 CFR 270. ATF also levies excise taxes on tobacco products. Customs collects the ATF tax on each shipment at port of entry. Tobacco imported from beneficiary countries under the Caribbean Basin Initiative (CBI) enters duty-free.

USDA Requirements. As with any plant product, tobacco falls under the jurisdiction of the U.S. Department of Agriculture (USDA) as authorized by the Plant Quarantine Act of 1912 (PQA). Because no raw or fresh tobacco enters the U.S.—only cured or processed tobacco is allowed into the country—there are no prohibitions or restrictions under PQA. USDA's Animal and Plant Health Inspection Service (APHIS) may inspect your tobacco shipment at the port of entry, but most shipments of tobacco enter without such inspection.

FTC Requirements. The Federal Trade Commission (FTC) administers the Federal Cigarette Labeling and Advertising Act (FCLAA) as amended by the Public Health Cigarette Smoking Act of 1969 (PHCSA) and the Comprehensive Smoking Education Act (CSEA). FCLAA as amended requires that specific health warnings appear on cigarette and small cigar packages. These requirements apply equally to domestic and imported products. The importer is responsible for complying with any applicable labeling regulations for any tobacco products. For more details, see "Marking and Labeling Requirements" below.

Although the importation of tobacco products is straightforward in the sense that there are no licensing or permit requirements, and no out-of-the-ordinary entry paperwork, you should take the requirements of FCLAA seriously. The law specifically states that importers are responsible for making sure that any foreign-made cigarettes they offer for entry into the U.S. comply with all of its provisions. Noncompliance is a federal offense and may result in a misdemeanor conviction, with fines of up to $10,000.

If you are importing cigarettes for commercial purposes, you must provide the FTC annually with a list of ingredients added to the tobacco during the manufacture of the cigarettes. Your list should not identify the company that uses the ingredients, or the brand of cigarettes in which they are contained. The purpose of the annual listing is not to restrict added ingredients, but to provide FTC with information to conduct ongoing research into the health hazards of cigarettes, and to enable the FTC to make periodic reports to Congress based on the information provided. The FTC considers these ingredient lists to be confidential trade secrets, to be provided only to authorized Congressional committee or subcommittee. Recent leaks of such information resulted in the unattributed release of some such data.

Customs Classification

For customs purposes, tobacco and tobacco products are classified under Chapter 24 of the HTSUS. This chapter is broken into major headings, which are further divided into subheadings, and often sub-subheadings, each of which has its own HTSUS classification number. For example, the 2001 HTSUS number for cigarette leaf, not containing wrapper tobacco, or not containing over 35% wrapper tobacco is 2401.20.23, indicating that it is a subcategory of tobacco, partly or wholly stemmed / stripped (2401.20), which is a subcategory of the major heading unmanufactured tobacco (whether or not threshed or similarly processed) (2401). There are three major headings in HTSUS Chapter 24.

2401—Unmanufactured tobacco (whether or not threshed or similarly processed); tobacco refuse

2402—Cigars, cheroots, cigarillos, and cigarettes, of tobacco or of tobacco substitutes

2403—Other manufactured tobacco and manufactured tobacco substitutes; "homogenized" or "reconstituted" tobacco; tobacco extracts and essences

For more details regarding classification of the specific product you are interested in importing, consult a customs broker, the appropriate commodity specialist at your nearest Customs port, or see HTSUS. The 2001 HTSUS is available online from the Customs

Service (www.customs.gov/impoexpo/impoexpo.htm) or for purchase from the U.S. Government Printing Office (see resources at the end of this chapter), and may be found in larger public libraries. For a general discussion of customs classification, see "Classification—Liquidation" on page 229.

Dutiable Status of Goods

For more information about duty rates and binding decisions see "Dutiable Status of Goods" on page 203; for a discussion of temporary importation of goods see "Temporary Free Importations" on page 205.

Valuation

Importers have a responsibility to use what the U.S. Customs Service deems, "reasonable care," when determining the value of their goods. They must also provide any additional information that the Customs Service needs for setting a final value on the goods. This process involves a number of factors and can be somewhat complicated; importers must be aware of applicable issues and details. Valuation information applies to all types of commodities, for further discussion on the subject see "Customs Valuation" on page 267.

Import Duties

Import duties vary (often dramatically) depending upon the Harmonized Tariff Schedule (HTSUS) classification of the goods or products imported. Since some products that look alike have different HTSUS classifications and different rates of duty, proper classification is vital. Note that "differences of opinion" between importers and the Bureau of Customs and Border Protection regarding classification keeps customs attorneys very busy.

Import duties can be assessed on the imported value of the goods ("ad valorem" rates of duty such as 2%, 4.4%, 50%, etc.), total units or weight of the goods ("specific" rates of duty such as 2 cents each or 1.5 cents/pound, etc.) or on a combination basis ("compound" rates of duty such as 5 cents each plus 6%).

Listed below is a sampling of several Column 1 import duty rates for Chapter 24 products:
Cigarette leaf (2401.10.44.00): free
to
Other tobacco (flue-cured, burley, fire-cured Kentucky and Tenessee, dark air-cured Kentucky and Tennessee, Virginia fire-cured, and Virginia sun-cured) (2401.30.70): 350%

For specific information on US import duties refer to the Harmonized Tariff Schedule of the US. The print version is available from the US Government Printing Office as well as third party suppliers who often add special features. Online versions are available in both static PDF pages as well as in formats with excellent search functionality. Search the Web with the term "Harmonized Tariff Schedule" to find sources.

Entry and Documentation

The entry of merchandise is a two-part process consisting of 1) filing the documents necessary to determine whether merchandise may be released from Customs custody and 2) filing the documents that contain information for duty assessment and statistical purposes. In certain instances all documents must be filed and accepted by Customs prior to the release of the goods. Unless you have been granted an extension, you must file entry documents at a location specified by the port or area director within five working days of your shipment's date of arrival at a U.S. port of entry. These include a number of standard documents required by Customs for any entry and:

- U.S. Treasury Department Bureau of Alcohol, Tobacco, and Firearms (ATF) permit to import tobacco Form ATF 5230.4

After you present the entry, Customs may examine your shipment, or may waive examination. The shipment is then released provided no legal or regulatory violations have been noted. You must then file entry summary documentation and deposit estimated duties at a designated customhouse within 10 working days of your shipment's release. For a detailed description of entry procedures, standard documentation, and informal entry, see "Entry Process" on page 185.

Informed Compliance. Informed compliance was introduced with the Customs Modernization Act of 1993 (Mod Act) and defines the relationship between importers and the Customs Service. It sets out the responsibilities of both parties. Providing the correct documentation and information for entry is a key factor that will make your importing operation run smoothly. We recommend that importers become familiar with the concept of informed comliance and the responsibilities that they have under the Mod Act. For further discussion about informed compliance see "Informed Compliance" on page 211.

Entry Invoice. You must provide the following information for all shipments of unmanufactured tobacco on the entry invoice: 1) Specify in detail the character of the tobacco in each bale by giving a) country and province of origin, b) year of production, c) grade or grades in each bale, d) number of carrots or pounds of each grade if more than one grade is packed in a bale, e) the time when, place where, and person from whom purchased, f) price paid or to be paid for each bale or package, or price for the vega or lot if purchased in bulk—if obtained otherwise than by purchase, state the actual market value per bale; 2) if an invoice covers or includes bales of tobacco that are part of a vega or lot purchased in bulk, the invoice must contain or be accompanied by a full description of the complete vega or lot purchased; or if such description has been furnished with a previous importation, the reference to such entry, including date and identity of such shipment; 3) packages or bales containing only filler leaf must be invoiced as filler; when containing filler and wrapper but not more than 35% wrapper, they must be invoiced as mixed; and when containing more than 35% wrapper, they must be invoiced as wrapper. For more general information about invoices see "Invoices" on page 277.

Note: The Entry and Documentation section has been carefully designed to supply you, the importer, with sample documents and directions on how to satisfy Customs requirements. Be aware that you should consult the applicable authorities to ensure that you are correctly following the most current procedures.

Country-Specific Import Restrictions

Cuban Tobacco Products. An embargo exists on all products, including cigars and unmanufactured tobacco, from Cuba.

Marking and Labeling Requirements

ATF Requirements. The ATF enforces specific requirements for tobacco product package labeling. The manufacturer's name or Tobacco Products Permit number must appear on the package label. (Note: Tobacco Products Permits are not required. They simply offer the manufacturer an alternative method of company identification on the label.) The product's tax class must be stated (i.e. cigar, cigarette, chewing tobacco, snuff, etc.). If there are subclasses within a given class, e.g. large and small cigarettes, the subclass must also be identified. The words "Class A" may be substituted for "large" and the words "Class B" may be substituted for "small." The labeling must show the number of individual product units contained in the package, e.g. "20 cigarettes," or "5 cigars." Bulk products such as loose pipe tobacco must show content in terms of net weight, using the U.S. (English) system of avoirdupois pounds and ounces. No statement that U.S. tax has been paid may be made on tobacco product labeling. Labeling may contain no depiction or display that is deemed immoral. Tobacco products may not be associated in any way with lottery material. For more information, contact ATF (see addresses at end of this chapter).

FTC Requirements. The Federal Cigarette Labeling and Advertising Act, as amended, is designed to inform the public about the health risks associated with smoking in a consistent and clear manner. To that end, a specifically worded warning must appear on each package, print advertisement, and outdoor billboard advertisement. The Act specifies such aspects of the warning statement as: 1) placement on package; 2) type size and style; 3) size of the border rectangle enclosing the statement; 4) width of the rule bordering the rectangle; and 5) distance of statement from outer edge of the advertisement or package, among other specific requirements.

Four separate health warnings required by law:

SURGEON GENERAL'S WARNING: Smoking Causes Lung Cancer, Heart Disease, and Emphysema.

SURGEON GENERAL'S WARNING: Quitting Smoking Now Greatly Reduces Serious Health Risks.

SURGEON GENERAL'S WARNING: Pregnant Women Who Smoke Risk Fetal Injury and Premature Birth.

SURGEON GENERAL'S WARNING: Cigarette Smoke Contains Carbon Monoxide.

All four warnings must appear on cigarette packaging, advertisements, and outdoor billboards during any one-year period. Companies must rotate the warnings quarterly, in alternating sequence, for each brand or brand style of cigarettes. If you are importing these products, you must submit a rotation plan for FTC approval. The proposed rotation plan must be such that the printed warning will be the same on packaging, advertising, and billboards during a given quarter. The FTC-approved rotation plan becomes effective for the one-year period beginning on the date of application approval. During this period each warning statement must appear an equal number of times. For more information, contact the FTC (see addresses at end of this chapter).

For a general discussion of U.S. Customs marking and labeling requirements, see "Country of Origin Marking" on page 236, "Special Marking Requirements" on page 238 and "Marking—False Impression" on page 239.

Shipping Considerations

You will need to ensure that your goods are packaged and shipped with care so that they arrive in good condition and pass smoothly through Customs. You are responsible for ensuring that the shipment is in compliance with all applicable government regulations for packaging and shipping. In most instances, you should not leave these arrangements solely to the discretion of your supplier. Careful preparation of the cargo and selection of the mode of transport can be essential to a cost-effective, timely delivery of undamaged goods. We strongly advise you to consult your shipping representative, insurance agent, or freight broker for advice on packing and shipping. Refer to the section "Packing/Shipping/Insurance" for a general discussion of packing and shipping.

Heat, humidity, and moisture can affect the quality of tobacco and tobacco products. Shipments must be packed and transported so as to minimize any damage from these sources. Care must also be taken to avoid contamination by insects, animals, or other sources.

Publications and WWW Resources

The *Harmonized Tariff Schedule of the United States (2001)* (HTSUS) is available to view on the Customs Service website (www.customs.gov), or you may purchase a printed version from:

U.S. Government Printing Office
Superintendent of Documents
710 North Capital Street NW
Washington DC 20401
Tel: (202) 512-1800
Fax: (202) 512-1657
Website: www.access.gpo.gov

The USGPO also has copies of specific laws available for purchase. The USGPO accepts orders made by fax, phone or placed over the Internet, as well as mail orders paid by credit card. All orders must be accompanied by payment. Credit cards, checks drawn on a U.S. bank, or an international money order are all acceptable.

Relevant Government Agencies

Address questions regarding the importation of partially processed and cured unmanufactured tobacco to:

Animal and Plant Health Inspection Service (APHIS)
Plant Protection and Quarantine (PPQ)
Director's Office
4700 River Rd., Unit 131
Riverdale, MD 20737
Tel: (301) 734-8261
Tel (PPQ permits): (301) 734-8758
Website: www.aphis.usda.gov/ppq

Address your questions regarding labeling requirements for imported tobacco products to:

Federal Trade Commission (FTC)
Division of Advertising Practices
600 Pennsylvania Avenue NW
Washington DC 20580
Tel: (202) 326-3076
Website: www.ftc.gov

Address your questions regarding importation of tobacco products to:

Tax and Trade Bureau
National Revenue Center
650 Massachusettes Avenue NW
Washington DC 20226
Tel: (513) 684-3337
Website: www.ttb.gov

USDA Agricultural Marketing Service (AMS)
USDA, AMS, Tobacco Programs STOP 0280
1400 Independence Avenue SW
Washington DC 20250-0280
Tel: (202) 205-0567
Tobacco Specialist: (202) 927-8210
Website: www.ams.usda.gov/tob

USDA Foreign Agricultural Service (FAS)
Cotton, Oil Seeds, Tobacco and Seeds Division (COTS)
1400 Independence Avenue SW, Room 5646
Washington DC 20250-1051
Tel: (202) 720-9516
Fax: (202) 690-1171
Website: www.fas.usda.gov

Address your questions regarding importation of tobacco products to your local Customs port director. For addresses refer to "U.S. Customs and Border Protection Offices" on page 65 or contact:

U.S. Customs and Border Protection
Customs Headquarters
1300 Pennsylvania Avenue NW
Washington DC 20229
Tel: (202) 354-1000
Website: www.customs.treas.gov

Laws and Regulations

The following laws and regulations may be relevant to the importation of tobacco and tobacco products. The laws are contained in the U.S. Code (USC) and the regulations are published in the Code of Federal Regulations (CFR), both of which may be available at larger public and law libraries. Copies of specific laws are also available from the United States Government Printing Office (address above).

7 USC 511 et seq.

Tobacco Inspection Act

This Act prohibits the importation of tobacco unless the shipment is accompanied by a certificate as prescribed by the Secretary of Agriculture.

7 CFR Part 29

Regulations on Tobacco Certificates

These regulations prescribe the form of the certificate required by the USDA for importation of tobacco and the procedure for obtaining a certificate.

15 USC 1331 et seq.

Federal Cigarette Labeling and Advertising Act

This Act prohibits the manufacture, importation, or packaging for sale within the U.S. of any cigarettes that fail to bear the Surgeon General's warning label. Cigarettes for export are exempt from the labeling requirement.

15 USC 4401 et seq.

Comprehensive Smokeless Tobacco Health Education Act of 1986

This Act prohibits the manufacture, importation, or package for sale within the U.S. of any smokeless tobacco product that fails to bear the Surgeon General's warning label.

16 CFR 307 et seq.

Regulations on Tobacco Warning Labels

These regulations set forth the labels required for tobacco products sold within the U.S.

26 USC 5701 et seq.

Tax on Tobacco

This law imposes an excise tax on tobacco products and cigarette papers and tubes imported or brought into the U.S. The taxes are to be collected, accounted for, and deposited as internal revenue collections by the Port Director of Customs.

27 CFR 275.62, 275.63

Regulations on Collection of Tobacco Excise Tax

These regulations provide for the collection of the tobacco excise tax by Customs, including by means of electronic funds transfer (EFT).

Principal Exporting Countries

The following listing includes samples of the main supplier nations of the products of this chapter. It is organized by HTSUS major heading. (Refer to "Customs Classification" above for the product codes.) Countries are listed in rank order of the value of products imported to the U.S. Statistics represent customs value of entries for 2002 from the Bureau of Census, U.S. Department of Commerce.

2401—Brazil, Turkey, Argentina, Malawi, Greece, Canada, Zimbabwe, Mexico, Macedonia, Bulgaria

2402—Dominican Republic, Honduras, Canada, Colombia, Japan, Latvia, China, South Korea, Nicaragua

2403—Sweden, Denmark, Spain, Italy, Germany, Canada, United Kingdom, Philippines

Chapter 25:
Quarry Products

Full title: Salt; Sulfur; Earths and Stone; Plastering Materials, Lime, and Cement

This chapter relates to the importation of minerals and mineral products, which are classified under Chapter 25 of the Harmonized Tariff Schedule of the United States (HTSUS). Specifically, it includes salt and salt solutions; unroasted iron pyrites; sulfur; natural graphite, sand, barium, calcium, magnesium, steatite, cryolite, chiolite, and borate substances, quartz, feldspar, and mica; kaolin, other clays, and earth substances, chalk; pumice, emery, and other natural abrasive; slate; granite, marble, and calcareous stones for monuments or buildings; pebbles, gravel, and crushed stones; dolomite; gypsum, limestone, and lime products; cements; asbestos; and a few miscellaneous minerals.

If you are interested in importing sublimed, precipitated, or colloidal sulfur, you should refer to Commodity Index Chapter 28, which also covers separately defined organic chemicals, including certain earth colors. Products that are intended for use as medicaments should be imported in accordance with the requirements discussed in Chapter 30. If you are interested in importing perfumery, cosmetics, or toilet preparations, refer to Chapter 33. Prepared stones, such as setts, curbstones, flagstones, mosaic cubes, and roofing, facing, or damp course slates are found in Chapter 68. For precious or semiprecious stones, refer to Chapter 71. The importation of cultured crystals and optical elements is covered in Chapter 90, billiard chalks in Chapter 95, and writing, drawing, and tailors' chalks in Chapter 96. You should also consult the related chapters on ores (Chapter 26) and mineral fuels (Chapter 27).

Note: To understand key issues that will enable you to make best use of the information in this section we recommend that you see "Introduction" on page 425.

Key Factors

The key factors in the importation of minerals and mineral products are:

- Compliance with U.S. Food and Drug Administration (FDA) regulations and entry notification (if the product can be used in foods, pharmaceuticals, or cosmetics)
- Compliance with U.S. Environmental Protection Agency (EPA) requirements under Toxic Substances Control Act (TSCA) (if the product contains asbestos or other hazardous substances)
- Compliance with U.S. Department of Transportation (DOT) regulations for transport of hazardous cargo (if the product is a hazardous substance)

Although most importers use the services of a licensed customs broker in making their entries, and we recommend this practice, you should be aware of the regulatory, entry, and documentation issues involved in importing your product. You, as importer, are ultimately responsible for the fulfillment of any legal requirements applicable to your shipment.

General Considerations

Regulatory Agencies. As a general category, minerals are straightforward importations. The FDA regulates the importation of minerals used in foodstuffs, cosmetics, and pharmaceuticals. The EPA, under authority of the TSCA, imposes certain controls on the importation of asbestos and any other minerals that contain toxic substances. The TSCA defines a toxic substance as any substance determined to present the possibility of an unreasonable risk of injury to health and the environment. The DOT enforces regulations for transporting hazardous cargo. Materials are deemed hazardous if listed in DOT transport regulations (49 CFR 172 appendix).

FDA-Regulated Minerals. The products of HTSUS Chapter 25 that are subject to regulation by the FDA are as follows: salt and pure sodium chloride, sea water; kaolin and other kaolinic clays; bentonite; pumice; calcined dolomite; plasters consisting of calcined gypsum or calcium sulfate; and epsom salts. For a discussion of FDA import procedures see "Appendix: Foods" on page 825. If you are interested in importing one of these products, you should ascertain its regulatory status by contacting FDA (see addresses at end of this chapter).

Toxic or Hazardous Substances. Products containing asbestos and other mineral products listed as hazardous or toxic substances and imported in bulk, as articles, or as part of a mixture must be in compliance with toxic and hazardous substance regulations of the EPA and DOT. These include packaging, shipping, marking, and labeling requirements. Refer to listing of laws and regulations below. For more information on Environmental Protection Agency requirements and TSCA certification as it pertains to asbestos, contact EPA's Office of Toxic Substances (see addresses at end of this chapter).

You must file a TSCA certification of compliance or exemption at the time you make the entry at Customs. The certification may be in the form of a typed or stamped statement on an appropriate entry document or commercial invoice or a preprinted attachment to such entry document or invoice. You may sign the certificate by means of an authorized facsimile signature. If your entry is electronically processed, the certification will be in the form of a Certification Code, which is part of the Automated Broker Interface (ABI) transmission. Customs will not release your shipment without proper certification.

If you will be importing several or regular shipments, you should ask the appropriate Customs Port Director to authorize your use of a blanket certification. If you receive such authorization, you must include on the commercial invoice or entry document for each shipment a statement that the blanket certification is on file and that it is incorporated by reference. This statement need not be signed. The blanket certification is valid for one calendar year, is subject to renewal, and may be revoked at any time for cause.

Articles Exclusion. If you are importing products that are classified as hazardous substances but are part of articles, you are subject to TSCA certification requirements only if certification for your product is specifically required by a rule or order promulgated under the TSCA. No specific rules have been adopted at this time. An "article" is a manufactured item 1) that is formed into a specific shape or design during manufacture, 2) that has end-use functions dependent on the shape or design during end use, and 3) that during the end use, does not change in its chemical composition or that changes only for a noncommercial pur-

pose separate from the article and only as allowed by law (19 CFR 12.120(2)). Fluids and particles are not articles, regardless of shape or design.

Shipment Detention. A shipment containing inorganic chemicals will be detained at the U.S. port of arrival (or entry if same), at your risk and expense, if: 1) it contains banned substances (15 USC 2604, 2605); or 2) it contains substances ordered seized because of imminent hazards (15 USC 2606). Further detention will occur at the port of entry, again at your risk and expense, if: 1) the EPA administrator or Customs Port Director has reasonable grounds to believe the shipment is not in compliance with the TSCA; or 2) you do not provide proper TSCA certification.

If your shipment is detained, it will be held by Customs for no more than 48 hours. It will then be turned over to the EPA administrator, unless you have arranged to release it in bond. You must either bring it into TSCA compliance or reexport it within the earlier of 90 days after notice of detention or 30 days of demand for redelivery. Customs may grant an extension if failure to comply or reexport is the result of delays in EPA or Customs procedures. If you fail to comply or reexport within the time allowed, the EPA administrator is authorized to have the shipment stored or disposed of at your expense.

Customs Classification

For customs purposes, minerals and mineral products are classified under Chapter 25 of the HTSUS. This chapter is broken into major headings, which are further divided into subheadings, and often sub-subheadings, each of which has its own HTSUS classification number. For example, the 2001 HTSUS number for cut blocks of marble is 2515.12.10, indicating it is a sub-subcategory of cut marble and travertine (2515.12), which is a subcategory of the major heading, marble, travertine, and other calcareous monumental or building stone, etc. (2515). There are 28 major headings within Chapter 25.

2501—Salt (including table salt and denatured salt) and pure sodium chloride, whether or not in aqueous solution or containing added anticaking or free-flowing agents; sea water

2502—Unroasted iron pyrites

2503—Sulfur of all kinds, other than sublimed sulfur, precipitated sulfur, and colloidal sulfur

2504—Natural graphite

2505—Natural sands of all kinds, whether or not colored, other than metal-bearing sands of Chapter 26

2506—Quartz (other than natural sands); quartzite, whether or not roughly trimmed or merely cut, by sawing or otherwise, into blocks or slabs of a rectangular (including square) shape

2507—Kaolin and other kaolinic clays, whether or not calcined

2508—Other clays (not including expanded clays of heading 6806) andalusite, kyanite, and sillimanite, whether or not calcined; mullite; chamotte or dinas earths

2509—Chalk

2510—Natural calcium phosphates, natural aluminum calcium phosphates and phosphatic chalk

2511—Natural barium sulfate (barytes); natural barium carbonate (witherite), whether or not calcined, other than barium oxide of heading 2816

2512—Siliceous fossil meals (for example, kieselguhr, tripolite, and diatomite) and similar siliceous earths, whether or not calcined, of an apparent specific gravity of 1 or less

2513—Pumice; emery; natural corundum, natural garnet, and other natural abrasives, whether or not heat-treated

2514—Slate, whether or not roughly trimmed or merely cut, by sawing or otherwise, into blocks or slabs of a rectangular (including square) shape

2515—Marble, travertine, and other calcareous monumental or building stone of an apparent specific gravity of 2.5 or more, and alabaster, whether or not roughly trimmed or merely cut, by sawing or otherwise, into blocks or slabs of a rectangular (including square) shape

2516—Granite, porphyry, basalt, sandstone, and other monumental or building stone, whether or not roughly trimmed or merely cut, by sawing or otherwise, into blocks or slabs of a rectangular (including square) shape

2517—Pebbles, gravel, broken, or crushed stone, of a kind commonly used for concrete aggregates, for road metalling, or for railway or other ballast; shingle and flint, whether or not heat-treated; macadam of slag, dross, or similar industrial waste, whether or not incorporating the materials cited in the first part of the heading; tarred macadam; granules, chippings, and powder, of stones of heading 2515 or 2516, whether or not heat-treated

2518—Dolomite, whether or not calcined; dolomite roughly trimmed or merely cut, by sawing or otherwise, into blocks or slabs of a rectangular (including square) shape; agglomerated dolomite (including tarred dolomite)

2519—Natural magnesium carbonate (magnesite); fused magnesia; dead-burned (sintered) magnesia, whether or not containing small quantities of other oxides added before sintering; other magnesium oxide, whether or not pure

2520—Gypsum; anhydrite; plasters (consisting of calcined gypsum or calcium sulfate) whether or not colored, with or without small quantities of accelerators or retarders

2521—Limestone flux; limestone and other calcareous stone, of a kind used for the manufacture of lime or cement

2522—Quicklime, slaked lime, and hydraulic lime, other than calcium oxide and hydroxide of heading 2825

2523—Portland cement, aluminous cement, slag cement, supersulfate cement, and similar hydraulic cements, whether or not colored or in the form of clinkers

2524—Asbestos

2525—Mica, including splittings; mica waste

2526—Natural steatite, roughly trimmed or merely cut, by sawing or otherwise into blocks or slabs of a rectangular (including square) shape; talc

2527—Natural cryolite; natural chiolite

2528—Natural borates and concentrates thereof (calcined or not), but not including borates separated from natural brine; natural boric acid containing not more than 85 % of H_3Bo_3 calculated on the dry weight

2529—Feldspar; leucite; nepheline and nepheline syenite; fluorspar

2530—Mineral substances not elsewhere specified or included

For more details regarding classifications of the specific product you are interested in importing, consult a customs broker, the appropriate commodity specialist at your nearest customs port, or the HTSUS. The 2001 HTSUS is available online from the Customs Service (www.customs.gov/impoexpo/impoexpo.htm) or for purchase from the U.S. Government Printing Office (see resources at the end of this chapter), and may be found in larger public libraries. For a general discussion of customs classification, see "Classification—Liquidation" on page 229.

Dutiable Status of Goods

For more information about duty rates and binding decisions see "Dutiable Status of Goods" on page 203; for a discussion of temporary importation of goods see "Temporary Free Importations" on page 205.

Valuation

Importers have a responsibility to use what the U.S. Customs Service deems, "reasonable care," when determining the value of their goods. They must also provide any additional information that the Customs Service needs for setting a final value on the goods. This process involves a number of factors and can be somewhat complicated; importers must be aware of applicable issues and details. Valuation information applies to all types of commodities, for further discussion on the subject see "Customs Valuation" on page 267.

Import Duties

Import duties vary (often dramatically) depending upon the Harmonized Tariff Schedule (HTSUS) classification of the goods or products imported. Since some products that look alike have different HTSUS classifications and different rates of duty, proper classification is vital. Note that "differences of opinion" between importers and the Bureau of Customs and Border Protection regarding classification keeps customs attorneys very busy.

Import duties can be assessed on the imported value of the goods ("ad valorem" rates of duty such as 2%, 4.4%, 50%, etc.), total units or weight of the goods ("specific" rates of duty such as 2 cents each or 1.5 cents/pound, etc.) or on a combination basis ("compound" rates of duty such as 5 cents each plus 6%).

Listed below is a sampling of several Column 1 import duty rates for Chapter 25 products:
Salt (2501.00.00.00): free
to
Other calcareous monumental or building stone; alabaster (2515.20.00.00): 3%

For specific information on US import duties refer to the Harmonized Tariff Schedule of the US. The print version is available from the US Government Printing Office as well as third party suppliers who often add special features. Online versions are available in both static PDF pages as well as in formats with excellent search functionality. Search the Web with the term "Harmonized Tariff Schedule" to find sources.

Entry and Documentation

The entry of merchandise is a two-part process consisting of 1) filing the documentation necessary to determine whether merchandise may be released from Customs custody, and 2) filing the documents that contain information for duty assessment and statistical purposes. In certain instances, all documents must be filed and accepted by Customs prior to release of the goods. Unless you have been granted an extension, you must file entry documents at a location specified by the port or area director within five working days of your shipment's date of arrival at a U.S. port of entry. These include a number of standard documents required by Customs for any entry, and:

- U.S. Customs TSCA Certification (hazardous materials)

After you present the entry, Customs may examine your shipment or may waive examination. The shipment is then released provided no legal or regulatory violations have been noted. You must then file entry summary documentation and deposit estimated duties at a designated customhouse within 10 working days of your shipment's release. For a detailed description of entry procedures, standard documentation, and informal entry, see "Entry Process" on page 185.

Informed Compliance. Informed compliance was introduced with the Customs Modernization Act of 1993 (Mod Act) and defines the relationship between importers and the Customs Service. It sets out the responsibilities of both parties. Providing the correct documentation and information for entry is a key factor that will make your importing operation run smoothly. We recommend that importers become familiar with the concept of informed comliance and the responsibilities that they have under the Mod Act. For further discussion about informed compliance see "Informed Compliance" on page 211.

Note: The Entry and Documentation section has been carefully designed to supply you, the importer, with sample documents and directions on how to satisfy Customs requirements. Be aware that you should consult the applicable authorities to ensure that you are correctly following the most current procedures.

Marking and Labeling Requirements

A shipment of any products containing substances that are classified as hazardous (49 CFR 172) must comply with the marking and labeling regulations adopted by the EPA (46 CFR 147.30) and the DOT (49 CFR 171 et seq.).

For a general discussion of U.S. Customs marking and labeling requirements, see "Country of Origin Marking" on page 236, "Special Marking Requirements" on page 238 and "Marking—False Impression" on page 239.

Shipping Considerations

You will need to ensure that your goods are packaged and shipped with care so that they pass smoothly through Customs and arrive in good condition. You are responsible for ensuring that the shipment is in compliance with all applicable government regulations for packaging and shipping. In most instances, you should not leave these arrangements solely to the discretion of your supplier. Careful preparation of the cargo and selection of the mode of transport can be essential to a cost-effective, timely delivery of undamaged goods. We strongly advise you to consult your shipping representative, insurance agent, or freight broker for advice on packing and shipping.

Minerals and mineral products may be shipped in bulk, bags, crates, or other types of containers, depending on the type of product and whether it is prepackaged. General considerations include protection from contamination, weather, and pests. If a product must be kept in a sanitary environment, all tables, utensils, platforms, and devices used for moving or handling the product, the compartments in which it is stowed while being transported will need to be maintained in a sanitary condition. For liquid shipments, venting and vapor collection systems may be required. Safety precautions should also be implemented as required to protect against breakage, spillage, corrosion of containers, and combustion. Containers should be constructed so as to be safe for handling during transport.

Mineral products. Mineral products in particular may have to be shipped in pressurized, ventilated, and temperature-and vapor-controlled enclosures. Solid products that are listed as hazardous substances (49 CFR 172 appendix) may be transported in bulk only on compliance with Coast Guard notification procedures, shipping permit requirements, and complex transportation regulations (46 CFR 148). All hazardous substances must be packaged and transported in accordance with DOT regulations (49 CFR 171 et seq.).

Publications and WWW Resources

The following publication explains the FDA requirements for importing minerals and mineral products. It is published by the FDA and is available online from the FDA website (www.fda.gov).

Requirements of Laws and Regulations Enforced by the U.S. FDA

The following publications may be relevant to the importation of toxic or hazardous minerals and mineral products:

Toxic Substances Control Act: A Guide for Chemical Importers/ Exporters (published by EPA)

This document is available from the TSCA Assistance Information Service (see Relevant Government Agencies)

The following publication provides a listing of existing chemical substances in the United States. It can be purchased in electronic format or a search of the document can be requested via telephone. Contact the Chemical Abstract Service (CAS) at (800)631-1884 or at (614) 447-3600 ext 2308.

TSCA Chemical Substance Inventory

In order to check whether or not a chemical is subject to any rules or regulations under Sections 5, 6, or 7 of TSCA, search the following document (www.epa.gov/opptintr/CORR)

Chemical on Reporting Rules List (CORR)

The U.S. Customs Service launched a series of "Informed Compliance" publications in 1996, available from the Customs Service website. Of particular interest:

What Every Member of the Trade Community Should Know About Marble

The *Harmonized Tariff Schedule of the United States (2001)* (HTSUS) is available to view on the Customs Service website (www.customs.gov), or you may purchase a printed version from:

U.S. Government Printing Office
Superintendent of Documents
710 North Capital Street NW
Washington DC 20401
Tel: (202) 512-1800; Fax: (202) 512-1657
Website: www.access.gpo.gov

The USGPO also has copies of specific laws available for purchase. The USGPO accepts orders made by fax, phone or placed over the Internet, as well as mail orders paid by credit card. All orders must be accompanied by payment. Credit cards, checks drawn on a U.S. bank, or an international money order are all acceptable.

Relevant Government Agencies

Address your questions regarding TSCA requirements for asbestos products to:

Environmental Protection Agency (EPA)
Office of Pollution Prevention and Toxics
TSCA System Information
1200 Pennsylvania Avenue NW
Washington DC 20460
Tel: (202) 564-3810
Tel: (202) 554-1404 (TSCA Information Hotline)
Email: oppt.homepage@epa.gov
Website: www.epa.gov/opptintr/contact.htm

Address your questions regarding FDA requirements to:

Food and Drug Administration (FDA)
Center for Drug Evaluation and Research
Office of Compliance
11919 Rockville Pike
Rockville, MD 20852
Tel: (301) 827-8910
Website: www.fda.gov/cder

Food and Drug Administration (FDA)
Center for Food Safety and Applied Nutrition (CFSAN)
Office of Field Compliance
Division of Enforcement, Imports Branch
5100 Paint Branch Parkway
College Park, MD 20740-3835
Tel: (301) 436-2080
Website: http://vm.cfsan.fda.gov/list.html

Address your questions regarding transportation of hazardous substances to:

U.S. Department of Transportation (DOT)
Research and Special Programs Administration
Hazardous Materials Information Center
400 7th St. SW
Washington DC 20590
Tel: (202) 366-4488
Website: http://hazmat.dot.gov

Address your questions regarding the importation of minerals and mineral products to your local Customs port director. For addresses refer to "U.S. Customs and Border Protection Offices" on page 65 or contact:

U.S. Customs and Border Protection
Customs Headquarters
1300 Pennsylvania Avenue NW
Washington DC 20229
Tel: (202) 354-1000
Website: www.customs.treas.gov

Laws and Regulations

The following laws and regulations may be relevant to the importation of minerals and mineral products. The laws are contained in the United States Code (USC), and the regulations are published in the Code of Federal Regulations (CFR), both of which are available at larger public and law libraries. Copies of specific laws and regulations may be purchased from the USGPO.

21 USC 301 et seq.
Federal Food, Drug, and Cosmetic Act
This Act prohibits deceptive practices and regulates the manufacture, sale and importation or exportation of food, drugs, cosmetics, and related products. It was amended by the Food Quality Protection Act of 1996. See 21 USC 331, 381, 382.

19 CFR 12.1 et seq.; 21 CFR 1.83 et seq.
Regulations on Food, Drugs, and Cosmetics
These regulations of the Secretary of Health and Human Services and the Secretary of the Treasury govern the standards, labeling, marking, and importing of products used with food, drugs, and cosmetics.

15 USC 2601 et seq.
Toxic Substances Control Act
This Act authorizes the EPA to determine whether a substance is harmful and to restrict importation, sale, and use of such substances.

19 CFR 12.118 et seq.
Regulations on Toxic Substances Control
These regulations require importers of chemical substances imported in bulk or as part of a mixture to certify to Customs that the shipment complies with the TSCA or is not subject to that Act.

15 USC 1261 et seq.
Federal Hazardous Substances Act
This Act controls the importation of hazardous substances, sets forth prohibited imports, and authorizes various agencies to promulgate labeling, marking, and transport requirements.

49 CFR 171 et seq.
Regulations on Hazardous Materials
These regulations list all substances deemed hazardous and provide transport, marking, labeling, safety, and emergency response rules.

46 CFR 147.30
Regulations on Labeling of Hazardous Materials
This regulation requires the labeling of containers of hazardous substances and specifies the label contents.

46 CFR 148 et seq.
Regulations on Carriage of Solid Hazardous Materials in Bulk

These regulations govern the transport of solid hazardous substances in bulk, including reporting, permitting, loading, stowing, and shipping requirements.

Principal Exporting Countries

The following listing includes samples of the main supplier nations of the products of this chapter. It is organized by HTSUS major heading. (Refer to "Customs Classification" above for the product codes.) Countries are listed in rank order of the value of products imported to the U.S. Statistics represent customs value of entries for 2002 from the Bureau of Census.

2501—Canada, Chile, Mexico, Bahamas, Netherlands, France, Peru, Netherlands Antilles, Jordan, Brazil, Australia

2502—Italy, France, Austria, Peru

2503—Mexico, Canada, Venezuela, France, South Korea, Germany, Chile, Italy, Brazil, India, Martinique, Australia

2504—China, Canada, Brazil, Switzerland, Japan, Mexico, Madagascar, United Kingdom, Sri Lanka

2505—Canada, China, Japan, Mexico, Australia, United Kingdom, Bahamas, Chile

2506—Japan, Canada, Turkey, Germany, Brazil, China, united Kingdom, Switzerland

2507—Brazil, United Kingdom, Germany, France, Japan, Canada, Peru, Mexico, China, Australia

2508—Canada, Germany, South Africa, Turkey, Greece, Spain, United Kingdom, China, Mexico, Japan, Taiwan, Brazil

2509—China, Netherlands, Taiwan, United Kingdom, Belgium, Canada, Australia, Germany, Mexico, France

2510—Morocco, South Korea, United KIngdom, Canada, Chile, Japan

2511—China, India, Morocco, Canada, Germany, Japan, Russia, Mexico, France, Italy

2512—France, Italy, Mexico, Australia, Spain, Canada

2513—China, India, Greece, Turkey, Australia, Italy

2514—China, Italy, India, Brazil, South Africa, United Kingdom, Canada, Spain, Mexico, Ireland, Israel, Germany, Indonesia

2515—Italy, Turkey, Spain, Peru, China, Israel, Mexico, India, Brazil, France, Portugal, Argentina, Egypt, Taiwan

2516—Canada, South Africa, India, Italy, Brazil, China, Spain, Zimbabwe, United Kingdom, Mexico, Norway, France, Colombia

2517—Canada, Mexico, Bahamas, Dominican Republic, China, France, Spain, New Zealand, Norway, Colombia, Italy, Japan

2518—Canada, United Kingdom, Mexico, Japan, Spain, Italy, China, Austria, Argentina, Germany

2519—China, Australia, Israel, Canada, Japan, Austria, Greece, Mexico, Hong Kong, Slovakia

2520—Canada, Mexico, Spain, United Kingdom, Thailand, Italy, Germany, Japan, Israel, France, South Korea, China

2521—Canada, Bahamas, Jamaica, China, Israel, France, Mexico, Turkey, Egypt, Italy, Portugal, Colombia, Dominican Republic

2522—Canada, Mexico, France, Brazil, Germany, Japan, China, Australia, Italy, United Kingdom, Switzerland, Belgium, Netherlands

2523—Canada, Thailand, China, Greece, Colombia, Mexico, Venezuela, South Korea, Sweden, Turkey, Norway

2524—Canada, South Africa, Zimbabwe, Germany

2525—Canada, India, Japan, Argentina, China, Finland, Germany, Brazil, Malaysia

2526—Canada, China, France, Japan, Italy, Austria, Brazil, Monaco, Germany, India

2527—

2528—Turkey, Chile, China, Argentina, Spain, Russia, Peru, Finland, Israel

2529—China, Canada, South Africa, Mexico, Japan, United Kingdom, France, Germany, Netherlands, Austria

2530—Morocco, Canada, Turkey, Mexico, South Africa, Greece, Germany, China, Norway, United Kingdom, Cyprus

Chapter 26:
Ores, Slag, and Ash

This chapter relates to the importation of ores, slag, and ash, which are classified under Chapter 26 of the Harmonized Tariff Schedule of the United States (HTSUS). Specifically, it includes ores of iron, manganese, nickel, cobalt, aluminum, lead, zinc, tin, chromium, tungsten, uranium, molybdenum, titanium, niobium, tantalum, vanadium, zirconium, precious metals, antimony, beryllium, and others. It also covers slag, dross, other waste from manufacture of iron or steel, and ash and ash residues.

If you are interested in importing minerals, you should read Commodity Index Chapter 25, which covers such related products as slag prepared as macadam and natural magnesium carbonate. Slag wool, rock wool, and other mineral wools are found in Chapter 68, and basic slag is in Chapter 31. For importing precious metal waste or scrap or metal clad with precious metal, refer to Chapter 71. The importation of base metal products is covered in Chapters 72 through 81.

Note: To understand key issues that will enable you to make best use of the information in this section we recommend that you see "Introduction" on page 425.

Key Factors

The key factors in the importation of ores, slag, and ash are:

- Port-of-entry sampling (if product is a copper-bearing or metal-bearing ore)

Although most importers use the services of a licensed customs broker in making their entries, and we recommend this practice, you should be aware of the regulatory, entry, and documentation issues involved in importing your product. You, as importer, are ultimately responsible for the fulfillment of any legal requirements applicable to your shipment.

General Considerations

The importation of ores, slag, and ash is generally straightforward. The primary regulation of these products is by U.S. Customs, which requires sampling of copper-bearing and metal-bearing ores at the time of entry.

Copper-Bearing Fluxing Material. If you are importing ores that contain copper (2603.00.00) and that are usable as flux or sulphur reagent, you must submit a declaration to U.S. Customs stating that the material is to be used for fluxing purposes only. If the entry is for consumption, you must deposit the estimated tax at the time of the entry. Entry will be delayed until you provide this declaration or other proof of use for fluxing purposes.

There is a sampling requirement for this type of ore. Customs will take samples of the ore in a shipment to be tested for copper content by a government chemist.

If you are importing this type of ore for a smelting or converting plant, the plant management must file with Customs at all appropriate ports of entry a detailed statement about plant operations for each quarter. This statement must be based on the plant's records of operation, showing for each furnace or converter the quantities of material charged, materials used for fluxing, and imported materials used for fluxing and claimed for free entry. It must also specify the copper content of the imported ores, as computed by the government assay. If at any time during the quarterly period, the quantity of ores used for fluxing in any furnace or converter exceeds 25% of the charge, the quarterly statement must also explain the reason for the excess usage.

Metal-bearing Ores: Sampling Requirements. When metal-bearing ores and other metal-bearing materials are offered for entry, they must be sampled for assay and moisture purposes (19 CFR 151.51). If proper weighing or sampling facilities are not available at the port of entry, your merchandise will have to be transported under bond to an appropriate facility. If your products are sampled at any place other than the port of entry, you will be required to bear the expense.

The Port Director of the port of entry may allow exceptions to the sampling requirement for low-metal-content ores if the director is satisfied, based on invoice information, the nature of available samples, knowledge of prior importations of similar materials, and other data, that the ores have been accurately classified. Sampling procedures are described in 19 CFR 151.52. If you have questions regarding metal-ore sampling, contact your nearest U.S. Customs port office.

Customs Classification

For customs purposes, ores, slag, and ash are classified under Chapter 26 of the HTSUS. This chapter is broken into major headings, which are further divided into subheadings, and often sub-subheadings, each of which has its own HTSUS classification number. For example, the 2001 HTSUS number for zinc dross is 2620.19.30, indicating it is a sub-subcategory of other zinc-containing ash and residues (2620.19), which is a subcategory of the major heading ash and residues containing metals or metal compounds (2620). There are 21 major headings within Chapter 26.

2601—Iron ores and concentrates, including roasted iron pyrites

2602—Manganese ores and concentrates including ferruginous manganiferous ores and concentrates with a manganese content of 20%or more, calculated on the dry weight

2603—Copper ores and concentrates

2604—Nickel ores and concentrates

2605—Cobalt ores and concentrates

2606—Aluminum ores and concentrates

2607—Lead ores and concentrates

2608—Zinc ores and concentrates

2609—Tin ores and concentrates

2610—Chromium ores and concentrates

2611—Tungsten ores and concentrates

2612—Uranium or thorium ores and concentrates

2613—Molybdenum ores and concentrates

2614—Titanium ores and concentrates

2615—Niobium (columbium), tantalum, vanadium, or zirconium ores and concentrates

2616—Precious metal ores and concentrates

2617—Other ores and concentrates

2618—Granulated slag (slag sand) from the manufacture of iron or steel

2619—Slag, dross (other than granulated slag), scalings, and other waste from the manufacture of iron or steel

2620—Ash and residues (other than from the manufacture of iron or steel) containing metals or metal compounds

2621—Other slag and ash, including seaweed ash (kelp)

For more details regarding classifications of the specific product you are interested in importing, consult a customs broker, the appropriate commodity specialist at your nearest customs port, or the HTSUS. The 2001 HTSUS is available online from the Customs Service (www.customs.gov/impoexpo/impoexpo.htm) or for purchase from the U.S. Government Printing Office (see resources at the end of this chapter), and may be found in larger public libraries. For a general discussion of customs classification, see "Classification—Liquidation" on page 229.

Dutiable Status of Goods

For more information about duty rates and binding decisions see "Dutiable Status of Goods" on page 203; for a discussion of temporary importation of goods see "Temporary Free Importations" on page 205.

Valuation

Importers have a responsibility to use what the U.S. Customs Service deems, "reasonable care," when determining the value of their goods. They must also provide any additional information that the Customs Service needs for setting a final value on the goods. This process involves a number of factors and can be somewhat complicated; importers must be aware of applicable issues and details. Valuation information applies to all types of commodities, for further discussion on the subject see "Customs Valuation" on page 267.

Import Duties

Import duties vary (often dramatically) depending upon the Harmonized Tariff Schedule (HTSUS) classification of the goods or products imported. Since some products that look alike have different HTSUS classifications and different rates of duty, proper classification is vital. Note that "differences of opinion" between importers and the Bureau of Customs and Border Protection regarding classification keeps customs attorneys very busy.

Import duties can be assessed on the imported value of the goods ("ad valorem" rates of duty such as 2%, 4.4%, 50%, etc.), total units or weight of the goods ("specific" rates of duty such as 2 cents each or 1.5 cents/pound, etc.) or on a combination basis ("compound" rates of duty such as 5 cents each plus 6%).

Listed below is a sampling of several Column 1 import duty rates for Chapter 26 products:

Cobalt ores and concentrates (2605.00.00.00): free

to

Of a kind used only for the extraction of arsenic or the manufacture of its chemical compounds (2620.60.10.00): 5%

For specific information on US import duties refer to the Harmonized Tariff Schedule of the US. The print version is available from the US Government Printing Office as well as third party suppliers who often add special features. Online versions are available in both static PDF pages as well as in formats with excellent search functionality. Search the Web with the term "Harmonized Tariff Schedule" to find sources.

Entry and Documentation

The entry of merchandise is a two-part process consisting of 1) filing the documentation necessary to determine whether merchandise may be released from Customs custody, and 2) filing the documents that contain information for duty assessment and statistical purposes. In certain instances, all documents must be filed and accepted by Customs prior to release of the goods. Unless you have been granted an extension, you must file entry documents at a location specified by the port or area director within five working days of your shipment's date of arrival at a U.S. port of entry. These include a number of standard documents required by Customs for any entry, and:

- Customs declaration on usage of copper-bearing fluxing materials (if product is copper ore or concentrate)

After you present the entry, Customs may examine your shipment or may waive examination. The shipment is then released provided no legal or regulatory violations have been noted. You must then file entry summary documentation and deposit estimated duties at a designated customhouse within 10 working days of your shipment's release. For a detailed description of entry procedures, standard documentation, and informal entry, see "Entry Process" on page 185.

Informed Compliance. Informed compliance was introduced with the Customs Modernization Act of 1993 (Mod Act) and defines the relationship between importers and the Customs Service. It sets out the responsibilities of both parties. Providing the correct documentation and information for entry is a key factor that will make your importing operation run smoothly. We recommend that importers become familiar with the concept of informed comliance and the responsibilities that they have under the Mod Act. For further discussion about informed compliance see "Informed Compliance" on page 211.

Entry Invoice. For copper ores and concentrates classifiable under heading 2603 and subheadings 2620.19.60, 2620.20.00, 2620.30.00, and heading 7401, the invoice must include a statement of the percentage by weight of copper content and any other metallic element. For more general information about invoices see "Invoices" on page 277.

Note: The Entry and Documentation section has been carefully designed to supply you, the importer, with sample documents and directions on how to satisfy Customs requirements. Be aware that you should consult the applicable authorities to ensure that you are correctly following the most current procedures.

Marking and Labeling Requirements

For a general discussion of U.S. Customs marking and labeling requirements, see "Country of Origin Marking" on page 236, "Special Marking Requirements" on page 238 and "Marking—False Impression" on page 239.

Shipping Considerations

You will need to ensure that your goods are packaged and shipped with care so that they pass smoothly through Customs and arrive in good condition. You are responsible for ensuring that the shipment is in compliance with all applicable government regulations for packaging and shipping. In most instances, you should not leave these arrangements solely to the discretion of your supplier. Careful preparation of the cargo and selection of the mode of transport can be essential to a cost-effective, timely delivery of undamaged goods. We strongly advise you to consult your shipping representative, insurance agent, or freight broker for advice on packing and shipping.

Ores, slag, and ash may be shipped in bulk, bags, crates, or other types of containers, depending on the type of product and whether it is prepackaged. General considerations include protection from contamination, weather, and pests. If a product must be kept in a sanitary environment, all tables, utensils, platforms, and devices used for moving or handling the product, the compartments in which it is stowed while being transported will need to be maintained in a sanitary condition. Safety precautions should also be implemented as required to protect against breakage, spillage, corrosion of containers, and combustion. Containers should be constructed so as to be safe for handling during transport.

Publications and WWW Resources

The *Harmonized Tariff Schedule of the United States (2001)* (HTSUS) is available to view on the Customs Service website (www.customs.gov), or you may purchase a printed version from:

U.S. Government Printing Office
Superintendent of Documents
710 North Capital Street NW
Washington DC 20401
Tel: (202) 512-1800
Fax: (202) 512-1657
Website: www.access.gpo.gov

The USGPO also has copies of specific laws available for purchase. The USGPO accepts orders made by fax, phone or placed over the Internet, as well as mail orders paid by credit card. All orders must be accompanied by payment. Credit cards, checks drawn on a U.S. bank, or an international money order are all acceptable.

Relevant Government Agencies

Address your questions regarding the importation of minerals and mineral products to your local Customs port director. For addresses refer to "U.S. Customs and Border Protection Offices" on page 65 or contact:

U.S. Customs and Border Protection
Customs Headquarters
1300 Pennsylvania Avenue NW
Washington DC 20229
Tel: (202) 354-1000
Website: www.customs.treas.gov

Laws and Regulations

The following laws and regulations may be relevant to the importation of ores, slag, and ash. The laws are contained in the United States Code (USC), and the regulations are published in the Code of Federal Regulations (CFR), both of which are available at larger public and law libraries. Copies of specific laws are also available from the United States Government Printing Office (address above).

26 USC 4611 et seq.
Environmental Taxes
This law imposes an excise tax on a number of imported petroleum products, chemicals, and "taxable substances" if the Secretary of the Treasury determines, after consulting with Customs and the EPA, that taxable chemicals constitute more than 50% of the weight. Customs is authorized to collect this excise tax.

19 CFR 10.98
Regulations on Sampling of Copper-Bearing Flux Materials
These regulations set forth the procedures for Customs entry declarations and sampling of copper-bearing flux materials.

19 CFR 151.51 et seq.
Regulations on Sampling of Metal-Bearing Ores
These regulations set forth the procedures for Customs entry declarations and sampling of copper-bearing flux materials.

Principal Exporting Countries

The following listing includes samples of the main supplier nations of the products of this chapter. It is organized by HTSUS major heading. (Refer to "Customs Classification" above for the product codes.) Countries are listed in rank order of the value of products imported to the U.S. Statistics represent customs value of entries for 2002 from the Bureau of Census, U.S. Department of Commerce.

2601—Canada, Brazil, Chile, Australia, Venezuela, Mexico, Peru, Sweden

2602—Gabon, South Africa, Australia, Brazil, Mexico, Belgium, France, China, Morocco

2603—Chile, Canada, Peru, Indonesia, Turkey, Taiwan, Austria

2604—Indonesia, Canada

2605—Finland, Germany

2606—Jamaica, Guinea, Guyana, Brazil, China, Australia, Greece, United Kingdom, France, Netherlands

2607—United Kingdom, China

2608—Peru, Australia, Mexico, Ireland, Canada

2609—

2610—South Africa, Philippines, Canada, Germany

2611—Canada, Portugal, Bolivia, China, Peru, Hong Kong, Uganda, Rwanda, Mongolia, India, Israel

2612—Australia, Uzbekistan, Russia

2613—Canada, Mexico, China, Chile, Belgium, Italy, Netherlands

2614—Australia, South Africa, Ukraine, Malaysia, Canada, Vietnam, India, South Korea, Netherlands, Japan, United Kingdom

2615—Australia, Canada, South Africa, China, Zimbabwe, Brazil, Mozambique, Rwanda, Russia, Nigeria, Italy

2616—Canada, Australia, Ghana, Colombia, Mexico, Taiwan

2617—Turkey, Austria, China, Mexico, Australia, Yugoslavia, Brazil, Germany

2618—South Africa, Italy, France, Japan, Canada, Brazil, Spain, Turkey, Sweden, China, Belgium

2619—Canada, Chile, Germany, France

2620—South Africa, Canada, United Kingdom, Germany, Japan, Mexico, Argentina, Brazil, Dominican Republic, Taiwan

2621—Canada, Netherlands, Spain, Germany, South Africa, Thailand, United Kingdom, China

Chapter 27:
Mineral Fuels, Oils, and Waxes

Full title: Mineral Fuels, Mineral Oils and Products of Their Distillation; Bituminous Substances; Mineral Waxes

This chapter relates to the importation of mineral fuels, oils, and waxes and bituminous substances, which are classified under Chapter 27 of the Harmonized Tariff Schedule of the United States (HTSUS). Specifically, it includes coal; lignite; peat; coke; coal, water, and producer gases; mineral tars; mineral oils; pitch and pitch coke; petroleum oils and gases; hydrocarbon gases; petroleum jelly, paraffin and other mineral waxes; petroleum oil residues; bitumen, asphalt, and derivatives; bituminous mixtures; and electrical energy.

If you are interested in importing separately defined organic compounds, you should refer to Commodity Index Chapter 29. Products that are intended as medicaments will probably be classified under Chapter 30. For the importation requirements related to essential oils and perfume oils, refer to Chapter 33. Terpenic oils are covered in Chapter 38. Review of the related Chapter 25, "Minerals and Mineral Products," may also be useful.

Note: To understand key issues that will enable you to make best use of the information in this section we recommend that you see "Introduction" on page 425.

Key Factors

The key factors in the importation of mineral fuels, oils, and waxes and bituminous substances, are:

- Compliance with U.S. Federal Trade Commission (FTC) and Consumer Product Safety Commission (CPSC) standards (if a consumer product)

- Compliance with U.S. Food and Drug Administration (FDA) entry notification and standards requirements (petroleum jelly, white mineral oil, and paraffin wax)

- Compliance with U.S. Customs port-of-entry sampling and metering requirements (petroleum products)

- Compliance with U.S. Environmental Protection Agency (EPA) requirements under Toxic Substances Control Act (TSCA) (if the product is a hazardous material)

- Compliance with U.S. Department of Transportation (DOT) regulations for transport of hazardous cargo (if the product is a hazardous material)

- Authorization of U.S. Department of Energy (DOE) (natural gas) and compliance with regulations of Federal Energy Regulatory Commission (FERC)

Although most importers use the services of a licensed customs broker in making their entries, and we recommend this practice, you should be aware of the regulatory, entry, and documentation issues involved in importing your product. You, as importer, are ultimately responsible for the fulfillment of any legal requirements applicable to your shipment.

General Considerations

Regulatory Agencies. The EPA, under authority of the TSCA, imposes certain controls on the importation of mineral fuels, oils, waxes, and bituminous materials that contain toxic substances. The TSCA defines a toxic substance as any substance determined to present the possibility of an unreasonable risk of injury to health and the environment. The DOT enforces regulations for transporting hazardous cargo. Materials are deemed hazardous if listed in DOT transport regulations (49 CFR 172 appendix). Import of natural gas requires DOE authorization and compliance with the FERC requirements. The FDA, under the Federal Food, Drug, and Cosmetic Act (FDCA) and the Public Health Service Act (PHSA), regulates the importation of petroleum jelly, white mineral oil, and paraffin wax. The FTC sets standards for processing and labeling products that are sold to consumers.

Natural Gas. Importation of natural gas is subject to regulation by both the DOE and the FERC. Depending on the nature of the import, authorization is required from one or both of these agencies. The DOE enforces regulations in 10 CFR 590 for importing natural gas through existing facilities. If you wish to import natural gas through existing facilities, you should contact the DOE Office of Fossil Energy, FE-14GTN (see addresses at end of this chapter) for Section 3 Authorization. The FERC administers regulations in 18 CFR 153 regarding importation of natural gas through newly constructed facilities. If you are intending this type of import, you should contact the FERC Office of Pipeline and Producer Regulation (see addresses at end of this chapter). In addition to federal requirements, you have the responsibility for obtaining any licenses required by the country of export. For more information, contact the relevant agency.

Petroleum Products. Customs regulations regarding import of petroleum and petroleum products are found in 19 CFR 151, Subpart C. This subpart details the information required on each petroleum entry summary, Customs controls on unloading and measuring bulk petroleum shipments, requirements for storage tanks, and options for using storage tanks bonded as warehouses for bulk shipments. The U.S. Department of Energy (DOE) also regulates petroleum importation and may require an oil import license fee. In general, import licensing is no longer required for these commodities, except for Canadian crude oils entered under a bilateral trade agreement (see Canadian crude oil below). For more information, contact DOE (see addresses at end of this chapter).

Entry Summary. On the entry summary for petroleum or petroleum products in bulk, you must show the API gravity at 600F, in accordance with the current edition of the ASTM-IP Petroleum Measurement Tables (American Edition), approved by the American Society for Testing and Materials. The appropriate unabridged table must be used in the reduction of volume to 600F. If the exact volumetric quantity cannot be determined in advance, the entry summary may be made for "___ barrels, more or less," but in no case may the estimate vary by more than 3% from the gross quantity unladen. The term "barrels" is defined in Chapter 27, Additional U.S. Note 7, HTSUS. You must also show the required information on your entry summary permit if the entry summary is filed at the time of entry, and on each entry summary continuation sheet regardless of when your entry summary is filed.

Sampling and Metering. Each Port Director of Customs establishes checks and controls on the unlading and measurement of petroleum and petroleum products imported in bulk by any means. One of the following methods will be used: 1) Customs-approved metering and sampling installations provided by the importer; 2) shore tank gauging; or 3) weighing for trucks and railroad cars. Importer-provided metering and sampling installations are approved by Customs on a case-by-case basis. If you wish to seek approval for a metering and sampling installation, you must send a complete description of the installation to the port director of the intended port of entry. Approved installations are subject to periodic verification by Customs. Once Customs has approved your installation, you may not modify it without first obtaining Customs approval.

Canadian Crude Oil. Crude petroleum oils, crude bituminous mineral oils, and reconstituted crude petroleum produced in Canada may be admitted free of duty. For duty-free treatment of Canadian crude oils, you must submit with your entry a certificate establishing that 1) the oil is imported pursuant to a commercial exchange agreement between U.S. and Canadian refiners that has been approved by the U.S. Secretary of Energy; 2) the oil is imported under import license issued by the Secretary of Energy; 3) an equivalent amount of domestic or duty-paid foreign crude oil, on which you have executed a written waiver of drawback, has been exported to Canada under an export license and previously has not been used to effect the duty-free entry of like Canadian products; and 4) an export license has been issued by the Secretary of Commerce for the oil exported to Canada.

The provisions above may be applied to: 1) liquidated or reliquidated entries if the required certification is filed with the port director at the port where the original entry was made on or before the 180th day after the date of entry; and 2) articles entered or withdrawn from storage for consumption pursuant to a commercial exchange agreement. Verification of the quantities of crude oil exported to or imported from Canada under such a commercial exchange agreement must be made in accordance with import verification provided in 19 CFR 151, Subpart C. Details are in 19 CFR 10.179. For more information on importation of Canadian crude, contact U.S. Customs or the DOE.

Coal. Customs distinguishes between two types of coal: anthracite and bituminous. Anthracite (HTSUS 2701.11) is coal having a volatile matter limit on a dry mineral-matter-free basis not exceeding 14%. Bituminous coal (HTSUS 2701.12) is coal having a volatile matter limit on a dry mineral-matter-free basis exceeding 14% and a calorific value limit on a moist, mineral-matter-free basis equal to or greater than 5,833 kcal/kg.

Electrical Energy. Electrical energy is subject to regulations prescribed by the Secretary of the Treasury, instead of the entry requirements for imported merchandise under the Tariff Act (19 USC 1484). An exclusion is made for electrical energy transmitted as a medium of communication.

FDA-Regulated Products. Imports of petroleum jelly, white mineral oil, and paraffin wax are regulated by the FDA. For a discussion of FDA import procedures see "Appendix: Foods" on page 825. If you are interested in importing one of these products, you should ascertain its regulatory status by contacting the FDA (see addresses at end of this chapter).

Toxic or Hazardous Substances. Mineral fuels, oils, and waxes and bituminous substances listed as hazardous or toxic substances and imported in bulk, as articles, or as part of a mixture must be in compliance with toxic and hazardous substance regulations of the EPA and DOT. These include packaging, shipping, marking, and labeling requirements.

You must file a TSCA certification of compliance or exemption at the time you make the entry at Customs. The certification may be in the form of a typed or stamped statement on an appropriate entry document or commercial invoice or a preprinted attachment to such entry document or invoice. You may sign the certificate by means of an authorized facsimile signature. If your entry is electronically processed, the certification will be in the form of

a Certification Code, which is part of the Automated Broker Interface (ABI) transmission. Customs will not release your shipment without proper certification.

If you will be importing several or regular shipments, you should ask the appropriate Customs port director to authorize your use of a blanket certification. If you receive such authorization, you must include on the commercial invoice or entry document for each shipment a statement that the blanket certification is on file and that it is incorporated by reference. This statement need not be signed. The blanket certification is valid for one calendar year, is subject to renewal, and may be revoked at any time for cause.

Articles Exclusion. If you are importing products that are classified as hazardous substances but are part of articles, you are subject to TSCA certification requirements only if certification for your product is specifically required by a rule or order promulgated under the TSCA. No specific rules have been adopted at this time. An "article" is a manufactured item 1) that is formed into a specific shape or design during manufacture, 2) that has end-use functions dependent on the shape or design during end use, and 3) that during the end use, does not change in its chemical composition or that changes only for a noncommercial purpose separate from the article and only as allowed by law (19 CFR 12.120(2)). Fluids and particles are not articles, regardless of shape or design.

Shipment Detention. A shipment containing inorganic chemicals will be detained at the U.S. port of arrival (or entry if same), at your risk and expense, if: 1) it contains banned substances (15 USC 2604, 2605); or 2) it contains substances ordered seized because of imminent hazard (15 USC 2606). Further detention will occur at the port of entry, again at your risk and expense, if: 1) the EPA administrator or Customs port director has reasonable grounds to believe the shipment is not in compliance with the TSCA; or 2) you do not provide proper TSCA certification.

If your shipment is detained, it will be held by Customs for no more than 48 hours. It will then be turned over to the EPA administrator, unless you have arranged to release it in bond. You must either bring it into TSCA compliance or reexport it within the earlier of 90 days after notice of detention or 30 days of demand for redelivery. Customs may grant an extension if failure to comply or reexport is the result of delays in EPA or Customs procedures. If you fail to comply or reexport within the time allowed, the EPA administrator is authorized to have the shipment stored or disposed of at your expense.

Hazardous Consumer Products. Under the FHSA, a mineral fuel, oil, wax, or bituminous substance intended for the consumer market is a hazardous substance if it is flammable, combustible, or has the potential to cause substantial personal injury during, or as a proximate result of, any customary or reasonably foreseeable handling or use. The CPSC does not require permits, special invoicing, limited entry, licenses, or any special approval process for importing hazardous consumer products into the U.S. However, if you are importing these types of products, you are responsible for ensuring that they meet all applicable FHSA and CPSA requirements. There are detailed regulations regarding testing and labeling of hazardous products. The Commission's enforcement posture regarding compliance with labeling and product safety standards changes as new facts become available. Contact the CPSC (see addresses at end of this chapter) for specific requirements on the consumer product you are considering importing.

Substantial Product Hazard Reports. Defect-reporting is required for products covered under the CPSA. The law requires every manufacturer, distributor, or retailer of such products, who obtains information that reasonably supports the conclusion that such products fail to comply with an applicable consumer product safety rule, or contain a defect that could create a substantial product hazard, to immediately inform the CPSC of the potential violation or defect. A firm's willful failure to make a Substantial Product Hazard Report can result in litigation by the CPSC.

Customs Classification

For customs purposes, mineral fuels, oils, and waxes and bituminous substances, are classified under Chapter 27 of the HTSUS. This chapter is broken into major headings, which are further divided into subheadings, and often sub-subheadings, each of which has its own HTSUS classification number. For example, the 2001 HTSUS number for montan wax is 2712.90.10, indicating it is a sub-subcategory of other mineral waxes (2712.90), which is a subcategory of the major heading, petroleum jelly, paraffin wax, etc. (2712). There are 16 major headings within Chapter 27.

2701—Coal; briquettes, ovoids, and similar solid fuels manufactured from coal

2702—Lignite, whether or not agglomerated, excluding jet

2703—Peat (including peat litter), whether or not agglomerated

2704—Coke and semicoke of coal, of lignite or of peat, whether or not agglomerated; retort carbon

2705—Coal gas, water gas, producer gas, and similar gases, other than petroleum gases and other gaseous hydrocarbons

2706—Tars distilled from coal, from lignite, or from peat, and other mineral tars, whether or not dehydrated or partially distilled, including reconstituted tars

2707—Oils and other products of the distillation of high temperature coal tar; similar products in which the weight of the aromatic constituents exceeds that of the nonaromatic constituents

2708—Pitch and pitch coke, obtained from coal tar or other mineral tars

2709—Petroleum oils and oils obtained from bituminous minerals, crude

2710—Petroleum oils and oils obtained from bituminous minerals, other than crude; preparations not otherwise specified or included, containing by weight 70% or more of petroleum oils or of oils obtained from bituminous minerals, these oils being the basic constituents of the preparations

2711—Petroleum gases and other gaseous hydrocarbons

2712—Petroleum jelly; paraffin wax, microcrystalline petroleum wax, slack wax, ozokerite, lignite wax, peat wax, other mineral waxes, and similar products obtained by synthesis or by other processes, whether or not colored

2713—Petroleum coke, petroleum bitumen, and other residues of petroleum oils or of oils obtained from bituminous minerals

2714—Bitumen and asphalt, natural; bituminous or oil shale and tar sands; asphaltites and asphaltic rocks

2715—Bituminous mixtures based on natural asphalt, on natural bitumen, on petroleum bitumen, on mineral tar, or on mineral tar pitch (for example, bituminous mastics, cutbacks)

2716—Electrical energy

For more details regarding classifications of the specific product you are interested in importing, consult a customs broker, the appropriate commodity specialist at your nearest customs port, or the HTSUS. The 2001 HTSUS is available online from the Customs Service (www.customs.gov/impoexpo/impoexpo.htm) or for purchase from the U.S. Government Printing Office (see resources at the end of this chapter), and may be found in larger public libraries. For a general discussion of customs classification, see "Classification—Liquidation" on page 229.

Dutiable Status of Goods

For more information about duty rates and binding decisions see "Dutiable Status of Goods" on page 203; for a discussion of temporary importation of goods see "Temporary Free Importations" on page 205.

Valuation

Importers have a responsibility to use what the U.S. Customs Service deems, "reasonable care," when determining the value of their goods. They must also provide any additional information that the Customs Service needs for setting a final value on the goods. This process involves a number of factors and can be somewhat complicated; importers must be aware of applicable issues and details. Valuation information applies to all types of commodities, for further discussion on the subject see "Customs Valuation" on page 267.

Import Duties

Import duties vary (often dramatically) depending upon the Harmonized Tariff Schedule (HTSUS) classification of the goods or products imported. Since some products that look alike have different HTSUS classifications and different rates of duty, proper classification is vital. Note that "differences of opinion" between importers and the Bureau of Customs and Border Protection regarding classification keeps customs attorneys very busy.

Import duties can be assessed on the imported value of the goods ("ad valorem" rates of duty such as 2%, 4.4%, 50%, etc.), total units or weight of the goods ("specific" rates of duty such as 2 cents each or 1.5 cents/pound, etc.) or on a combination basis ("compound" rates of duty such as 5 cents each plus 6%).

Listed below is a sampling of several Column 1 import duty rates for Chapter 27 products:
Electrical energy (2716.00.00.00): free
to
Greases containing not over 10 percent by weight of salts of fatty acids of animal (including marine animal) or vegetable origin: 5.8%

For specific information on US import duties refer to the Harmonized Tariff Schedule of the US. The print version is available from the US Government Printing Office as well as third party suppliers who often add special features. Online versions are available in both static PDF pages as well as in formats with excellent search functionality. Search the Web with the term "Harmonized Tariff Schedule" to find sources.

Entry and Documentation

The entry of merchandise is a two-part process consisting of 1) filing the documentation necessary to determine whether merchandise may be released from Customs custody, and 2) filing the documents that contain information for duty assessment and statistical purposes. In certain instances, all documents must be filed and accepted by Customs prior to release of the goods. Unless you have been granted an extension, you must file entry documents at a location specified by the port or area director within five working days of your shipment's date of arrival at a U.S. port of entry. These include a number of standard documents required by Customs for any entry, and:

- Import certificate (duty-free classification of Canadian crude oils)
- U.S. Customs TSCA Certification (hazardous materials) document
- DOE or FERC authorization (natural gas)

After you present the entry, Customs may examine your shipment or may waive examination. The shipment is then released provided no legal or regulatory violations have been noted. You must then file entry summary documentation and deposit estimated duties at a designated customhouse within 10 working days of your shipment's release. For a detailed description of entry procedures, standard documentation, and informal entry, see "Entry Process" on page 185.

Informed Compliance. Informed compliance was introduced with the Customs Modernization Act of 1993 (Mod Act) and defines the relationship between importers and the Customs Service. It sets out the responsibilities of both parties. Providing the correct documentation and information for entry is a key factor that will make your importing operation run smoothly. We recommend that importers become familiar with the concept of informed comliance and the responsibilities that they have under the Mod Act. For further discussion about informed compliance see "Informed Compliance" on page 211.

Entry Invoice. The entry invoice should specify the use and the Chemical Abstracts Service (CAS) number of the chemical compounds in your shipment. For more general information about invoices see "Invoices" on page 277.

Note: The Entry and Documentation section has been carefully designed to supply you, the importer, with sample documents and directions on how to satisfy Customs requirements. Be aware that you should consult the applicable authorities to ensure that you are correctly following the most current procedures.

Prohibitions and Restrictions

Hazardous Consumer Products. Importation of any consumer product that has been declared a banned hazardous substance by a rule under the CPSA is prohibited. Any product considered hazardous and not labeled according to provisions of the FHSA is a misbranded hazardous substance and is an illegal import. Certain hazardous substances listed in the FHSA and in regulations promulgated by the CPSC are completely banned from importation. A shipment of consumer products cannot be imported if it poses an imminent hazard. See 15 USC 1261, 2604-2606; 16 CFR 1500.265-1500.272.

The CPSC may detain your shipment of hazardous substances and take samples for testing to determine compliance with the FHSA. If your shipment is found to contain banned hazardous substances, it will be refused admission and will be destroyed if not exported within 90 days of the date of refusal notice. If it is found to contain misbranded hazardous substances, you may make arrangements to bring it into conformance through relabeling. For complete details regarding testing, labeling, and safety regulations for hazardous products, contact the CPSC (see addresses at end of this chapter).

Marking and Labeling Requirements

Hazardous Substances. A shipment of products containing substances classified as hazardous (49 CFR 172) must comply with the marking and labeling regulations adopted by the EPA (46 CFR 147.30) and the DOT (49 CFR 171 et seq.).

Flammable Products. Any flammable product must be conspicuously and appropriately labeled according to regulations under FHSA. The labeling must distinguish between "extremely flammable," "flammable," and "combustible," and must accurately reflect the form of the product (liquid, solid, or other) or the contents of a self-pressurized container. The label must appear on the immediate container intended for the end user. If the product is being shipped in bulk, the labeling must be affixed to the bulk container in a conspicuous place. Any accompanying printed material that has instructions for use must also bear the same warning in a conspicuous place.

Labeling for a flammable product must contain the following information: 1) name and place of business of the manufacturer, packer, distributor, or seller; 2) common or usual name (or chemical name if there is no common name) of the hazardous substance, or of each component that contributes substantially to its hazard; 3) the word "DANGER" on extremely flammable substances; 4) the word "CAUTION" or "WARNING" on flammable or combustible substances; 5) an affirmative statement of the principle hazard or hazards (i.e. "flammable," "extremely flammable," or "combustible"); 6) precautionary measures describing the action to be followed or avoided; 7) instruction, if necessary, for first-aid treatment; 8) instructions for handling and storage of packages that require special care in handling and storage; 9) the statement "Keep Out of Reach of Children" or its practical equivalent. For more information, contact the CPSC (see addresses at end of this chapter).

For a general discussion of U.S. Customs marking and labeling requirements, see "Country of Origin Marking" on page 236, "Special Marking Requirements" on page 238 and "Marking—False Impression" on page 239.

Shipping Considerations

You will need to ensure that your goods are packaged and shipped with care so that they pass smoothly through Customs and arrive in good condition. You are responsible for ensuring that the shipment is in compliance with all applicable government regulations for packaging and shipping. In most instances, you should not leave these arrangements solely to the discretion of your supplier. Careful preparation of the cargo and selection of the mode of transport can be essential to a cost-effective, timely delivery of undamaged goods. We strongly advise you to consult your shipping representative, insurance agent, or freight broker for advice on packing and shipping.

Mineral fuels, oils, and waxes and bituminous substances, may be shipped in bulk, bags, tanks, bottles, or other types of containers, depending on the type of product and whether it is prepackaged. General considerations include protection from contamination, weather, and pests. If a product must be kept in a sanitary environment, all tables, utensils, platforms, and devices used for moving or handling the product, the compartments in which it is stowed while being transported will need to be maintained in a sanitary condition. For liquid shipments, venting and vapor collection systems may be required. Safety precautions should also be implemented as required to protect against breakage, spillage, corrosion of containers, and combustion. Containers should be constructed so as to be safe for handling during transport.

Mineral and chemical products. Mineral products in particular may have to be shipped in pressurized, ventilated, and temperature-and vapor-controlled enclosures. Solid mineral and chemical products that are listed as hazardous substances (49 CFR 172 appendix) may be transported in bulk only on compliance with Coast Guard notification procedures, shipping permit requirements, and complex transportation regulations (46 CFR 148). All hazardous substances must be packaged and transported in accordance with DOT regulations (49 CFR 171 et seq.).

Publications and WWW Resources

The following publication explains the FDA requirements for importing mineral fuels, oils, and waxes. It is published by the FDA and is available online from the FDA website (www.fda.gov/opacom/7pubs.html).

Requirements of Laws and Regulations Enforced by the U.S. Food and Drug Administration

The following publications may be relevant to the importation of toxic or hazardous mineral fuels, oils, and waxes:

Toxic Substances Control Act: A Guide for Chemical Importers/Exporters (published by EPA)

This document is available from the TSCA Assistance Information Service (see Relevant Government Agencies)

The following publication provides a listing of existing chemical substances in the United States. It can be purchased in electronic format or a search of the document can be requested via telephone. Contact the Chemical Abstract Service (CAS) at (800)631-1884 or at (614) 447-3600 ext 2308.

TSCA Chemical Substance Inventory

In order to check whether or not a chemical is subject to any rules or regulations under Sections 5, 6, or 7 of TSCA, search the following document (www.epa.gov/opptintr/CORR)

Chemical on Reporting Rules List (CORR)

The *Harmonized Tariff Schedule of the United States (2001)* (HTSUS) is available to view on the Customs Service website (www.customs.gov), or you may purchase a printed version from:

U.S. Government Printing Office
Superintendent of Documents
710 North Capital Street NW
Washington DC 20401
Tel: (202) 512-1800
Fax: (202) 512-1657
Website: www.access.gpo.gov

The USGPO also has copies of specific laws available for purchase. The USGPO accepts orders made by fax, phone or placed over the Internet, as well as mail orders paid by credit card. All orders must be accompanied by payment. Credit cards, checks drawn on a U.S. bank, or an international money order are all acceptable.

Relevant Government Agencies

Address your questions regarding CPSC requirements for mineral fuels, oils, and waxes and bituminous substances to:

Consumer Product Safety Commission (CPSC)
Office of Compliance
Washington DC 20207-0001
Tel: 800-638-2772 or (301) 504-7912
Fax: (301) 504-0359
Website: www.cpsc.gov

Address your inquiries regarding TSCA and EPA requirements for importation of mineral fuels, oils, and waxes and bituminous substances to:

Environmental Protection Agency (EPA)
Office of Pollution Prevention and Toxics
TSCA System Information
1200 Pennsylvania Avenue NW
Washington DC 20460
Tel: (202) 564-3810
Tel: (202) 554-1404 (TSCA Information Hotline)
Email: oppt.homepage@epa.gov
Website: www.epa.gov/opptintr/contact.htm

Address your questions regarding transportation of hazardous substances to:

U.S. Department of Transportation (DOT)
Research and Special Programs Administration
Hazardous Materials Information Center
400 7th St. SW
Washington DC 20590
Tel: (202) 366-4488
Website: http://hazmat.dot.gov

Address your questions regarding importation of natural gas through existing facilities to:

Department of Energy
Office of Natural Gas and Petroleum, Import and Export Activities
1000 Independence Avenue SW, Room 3E-042
Washington DC 20585

Tel: (202) 586-9484
Website: www.fe.doe.gov

Address your questions regarding importation of natural gas involving the construction of new facilities to:

Federal Energy Regulatory Commission (FERC)
Office of Energy Projects, Division of Pipeline Certificates
888 First Street NE
Washington DC 20426
Tel: (202) 208-2245
Website: www.ferc.gov

Address your questions regarding the importation of mineral fuels, oils, and waxes and bituminous substances to your local Customs port director. For addresses refer to "U.S. Customs and Border Protection Offices" on page 65 or contact:

U.S. Customs and Border Protection
Customs Headquarters
1300 Pennsylvania Avenue NW
Washington DC 20229
Tel: (202) 354-1000
Website: www.customs.treas.gov

Laws and Regulations

The following laws and regulations may be relevant to the importation of mineral fuels, oils, and waxes and bituminous substances. The laws are contained in the United States Code (USC), and the regulations are published in the Code of Federal Regulations (CFR), both of which are available at larger public and law libraries. Copies of specific laws and regulations may be purchased from the U.S. Government Printing Office (address above).

15 USC 717 et seq.
The Natural Gas Act
This Act regulates the transport and sale of natural gas in interstate and foreign commerce. Section 717b prohibits the exportation or importation of natural gas without authorization from the Federal Energy Regulatory Commission (FERC).

18 CFR 152, 153
Regulations of FERC on Natural Gas
These regulations specify the requirements and procedures for obtaining authorization for the import or export of natural gas. Customs enforces these provisions.

15 USC 761
Federal Energy Administration Act of 1974
Customs ensures that petroleum imports comply with licensing requirements.

33 USC 1321, 1901 et seq.
Act to Prevent Pollution From Ships
This Act prohibits the discharge of oil or hazardous substances into or on the navigable waters of the U.S. and authorizes Customs to withhold clearance of any vessel not in compliance.

19 CFR 4.66b, 4.66c, 33 CFR 153.105
Regulations on Vessel Clearance
These regulations require vessels to be in compliance with the oil and hazardous substance discharge laws before Customs will grant clearance from the port.

15 USC 2051 et seq.
Consumer Product Safety Act (CPSA)
This Act sets standards for the manufacturing, processing, and labeling of products sold to U.S. consumers.

15 USC 2601 et seq.
Toxic Substances Control Act (TSCA)
This Act authorizes the EPA to determine whether a substance is harmful and to restrict importation, sale, and use of such substances.

19 CFR 12.118 et seq.
Regulations on Toxic Substances Control
These regulations require importers of chemical substances imported in bulk or as part of a mixture to certify to Customs that the shipment complies with the TSCA or is not subject to that Act.

15 USC 1261 et seq.
Federal Hazardous Substances Act (FHSA)
This Act controls the importation of hazardous substances, sets forth prohibited imports, and authorizes various agencies to promulgate labeling, marking, and transport requirements.

49 CFR 171 et seq.
Regulations on Hazardous Materials
These regulations list all substances deemed hazardous and provide transport, marking, labeling, safety, and emergency response rules.

46 CFR 147.30
Regulations on Labeling of Hazardous Materials
This regulation requires the labeling of containers of hazardous substances and specifies the label contents.

46 CFR 148 et seq.
Regulations on Carriage of Solid Hazardous Materials in Bulk
These regulations govern the transport of solid hazardous substances in bulk, including reporting, permitting, loading, stowing, and shipping requirements.

16 CFR 1500 et seq.
Regulations on Hazardous Substances Safety Standards
These regulations set standards for processing, manufacturing, importing, and labeling all substances classified as hazardous that are to be sold to U.S. consumers.

Principal Exporting Countries

The following listing includes samples of the main supplier nations of the products of this chapter. It is organized by HTSUS major heading. (Refer to "Customs Classification" above for the product codes.) Countries are listed in rank order of the value of products imported to the U.S. Statistics represent customs value of entries for 2002 from the Bureau of Census, U.S. Department of Commerce.

2701—Colombia, Venezuela, Canada, Indonesia, Australia, Trinidad and Tobago, Poland, China, Russia, South Africa

2702—Canada, India, Trinidad and Tobago

2703—Canada, Latvia, Ireland, New Zealand, Denmark, Finland, China, Netherlands, Germany

2704—Japan, China, Canada, Egypt, Netherlands, Poland, Spain, Germany

2705—

2706—Mexico, Canada, United Kingdom, Netherlands, Ukraine, Denmark, Germany, Japan

2707—Canada, United Kingdom, Brazil, Saudi Arabia, Netherlands, Spain, South Korea, Venezuela, Germany, Belgium

2708—Japan, South Korea, Canada, South Africa, France, Mexico

2709—Saudi Arabia, Mexico, Canada, Venezuela, Nigeria, United Kingdom, Norway, Iraq, Angola, Colombia

2710—Canada, Venezuela, Russia, Algeria, United Kingdom, Belgium, Aruba, Netherlands, Mexico, Brazil

2711—Canada, Trinidad and Tobago, Algeria, Qatar, Norway

2712—China, Canada, Japan, Malaysia, South Africa, Germany

2713—Canada, Venezuela, Mexico, Argentina, Kuwait, Spain

2714—Venezuela, Canada, Netherlands Antilles, Mexico

2715—Canada, India, United Kingdom, Mexico, Germany, China

2716—Canada

Chapter 28:
Inorganic Chemicals

Full title: Inorganic Chemicals; Organic or Inorganic Compounds of Precious Metals, of Rare-Earth Metals, of Radioactive Elements, or of Isotopes

This chapter relates to the importation of separate inorganic chemical elements and chemically defined compounds, which are classified under Chapter 28 of the Harmonized Tariff Schedule of the United States (HTSUS). Specifically, it includes inorganic chemical elements; inorganic acids; nonmetal oxygen, halogen, and sulfur compounds; metal oxides, hydroxides, and peroxides; colloidal and other compounds of precious metal; certain radioactive chemicals; and phosphides, carbides, hydrides, nitrides, azides, silicides, and borides.

The importation of organic chemical substances is covered in related Commodity Index Chapter 29. If you are interested in importing a product that is not in the form of a bulk chemical, you should read the chapters that pertain to the specific type of product. For importing requirements related to mineral products, see Chapters 25 through 27. The importation of chemical fertilizers is covered in Chapter 31, and inorganic products used as luminophores are in Chapter 32. Chapter 38 discusses artificial graphite, fire-extinguishing grenades and charges, ink removers, and nonoptical cultured crystals of halides of alkali or alkaline-earth metals. Chapter 71 covers the importation of precious and semiprecious stones, metals, and metal alloys. Refer to Chapters 72 through 83 if you are importing base metals and related products. Nuclear reactors and related equipment are classified within Chapter 84. Requirements for importing optical elements are in Chapter 90.

Note: To understand key issues that will enable you to make best use of the information in this section we recommend that you see "Introduction" on page 425.

Key Factors

The key factors in the importation of inorganic chemical substances are:

- Compliance with U.S. Environmental Protection Agency (EPA) requirements under the Toxic Substances Control Act (TSCA) (if the product is a hazardous substance)

- Compliance with U.S. Department of Transportation (DOT) regulations for transport of hazardous cargo (if the product is a hazardous substance)

- Compliance with Nuclear Regulatory Commission (NRC) requirements, including NRC import authorization (if the product is radioactive)

Although most importers use the services of a licensed customs broker in making their entries, and we recommend this practice, you should be aware of the regulatory, entry, and documentation issues involved in importing your product. You, as importer, are ultimately responsible for the fulfillment of any legal requirements applicable to your shipment.

General Considerations

Regulatory Agencies. The EPA, under authority of the TSCA, imposes certain controls on the importation of inorganic chemicals that contain toxic substances. The TSCA defines a toxic substance as any substance determined to present the possibility of an unreasonable risk of injury to health and the environment. The DOT enforces regulations for transporting hazardous cargo. Substances are deemed hazardous if listed in DOT transport regulations (49 CFR 172 appendix).

Toxic and Hazardous Substances. Inorganic chemicals imported in bulk, as articles, or as part of a mixture must be in compliance with toxic and hazardous substance regulations of the EPA and DOT. These include packaging, shipping, marking, and labeling requirements. Refer to "Laws and Regulations" below.

In addition, all inorganic chemical products are subject to the U.S. Customs Service TSCA Import Certification Rule (19 CFR 12.118 et seq.). If you import these products, you must sign one of the following statements: "I certify that all chemical substances in this shipment comply with all applicable rules or orders under TSCA and that I am not offering a chemical substance for entry in violation of TSCA or any applicable rule or order thereunder" or "I certify that all chemicals in this shipment are not subject to TSCA."

You must file this TSCA certification of compliance or exemption at the time you make the entry at Customs. The certification may be in the form of a typed or stamped statement on an appropriate entry document or commercial invoice or a preprinted attachment to such entry document or invoice. You may sign the certificate by means of an authorized facsimile signature. If your entry is electronically processed, the certification will be in the form of a Certification Code, which is part of the Automated Broker Interface (ABI) transmission. Customs will not release your shipment without proper certification.

If you will be importing several or regular shipments, you should ask the appropriate Customs port director to authorize your use of a blanket certification. If you receive such authorization, you must include on the commercial invoice or entry document for each shipment a statement that the blanket certification is on file and that it is incorporated by reference. This statement need not be signed. The blanket certification is valid for one calendar year, is subject to renewal, and may be revoked at any time for cause.

In filling out TSCA forms and Customs entry documents, you should provide the Chemical Abstracts Service (CAS) number for each chemical in the shipment. These CAS numbers are given in the appendix to the HTSUS. You are not required to include the CAS number, but Customs will be able to process your shipment more quickly if you give this number.

Articles Exclusion. If you are importing products that are classified as hazardous substances but are part of articles, you are subject to TSCA certification requirements only if certification for your product is specifically required by a rule or order promulgated under the TSCA. No specific rules have been adopted at this time. An "article" is a manufactured item 1) that is formed into a specific shape or design during manufacture, 2) that has end-use functions dependent on the shape or design during end use, and 3) that during the end use, does not change in its chemical composition or that changes only for a noncommercial purpose separate from the article and only as allowed by law (19 CFR 12.120(a)). Fluids and particles are not articles, regardless of shape or design.

Shipment Detention. A shipment containing inorganic chemicals will be detained at the U.S. port of arrival (or entry if same), at your risk and expense, if: 1) it contains banned chemical substances (15 USC 2604, 2605); or 2) it contains chemical substances ordered seized because of imminent hazard (15 USC 2606). Further detention will occur at the port of entry, again at your risk and expense, if: 1) the EPA administrator or Customs port director has reasonable grounds to believe the shipment is not in compliance with the TSCA; or 2) you do not provide proper TSCA certification.

If your shipment is detained, it will be held by Customs for no more than 48 hours. It will then be turned over to the EPA administrator, unless you have arranged to release it in bond. You must either bring it into TSCA compliance or reexport it within the earlier of 90 days after notice of detention or 30 days of demand for redelivery. Customs may grant an extension if failure to comply or reexport is the result of delays in EPA or Customs procedures. If you fail to comply or reexport within the time allowed, the EPA administrator is authorized to have the shipment stored or disposed of at your expense.

Radioactive Compounds. Many radioisotopes and all forms of uranium, thorium, and plutonium imported into the U.S. are subject to the regulations of the NRC in addition to import regulations imposed by any other U.S. agency. Authority to import these commodities, or articles containing these commodities, is granted by the NRC.

To comply with NRC requirements, the importer must be aware of the identity and amount of all NRC-controlled radioisotopes or uranium, thorium, and plutonium being imported into the U.S. To assure passage through Customs, the importer must demonstrate to U.S. Customs that the NRC has authorized import of the controlled commodity. The authority cited may be the number of a specific or general license, or the specific section of an NRC regulation that allows a general license or an exemption to the regulations. A foreign exporter may save time for a prospective importer by furnishing complete information about the presence of NRC-controlled commodities in the imported shipment.

Customs Classification

For customs purposes, inorganic chemical substances are classified under Chapter 28 of the HTSUS. This chapter is broken into major headings, which are further divided into subheadings, and often sub-subheadings, each of which has its own HTSUS classification number. For example, the 2001 HTSUS number for fluorine is 2801.30.10, indicating it is a sub-subcategory of fluorine and bromine (2801.30), which is a subcategory of the major heading, fluorine, chlorine, bromine, and iodine (2801). There are 51 major headings within Chapter 28.

2801—Fluorine, chlorine, bromine, and iodine

2802—Sulfur, sublimed or precipitated; colloidal sulfur

2803—Carbon (carbon blacks and other forms of carbon not elsewhere specified or included)

2804—Hydrogen, rare gases, and other nonmetals

2805—Alkali or alkaline-earth metals; rare-earth metals, scandium, and yttrium, whether or not intermixed or interalloyed; mercury

2806—Hydrogen chloride (Hydrochloric acid); chlorosulfuric acid

2807—Sulfuric acid; oleum

2808—Nitric acid; sulfonitric acids

2809—Diphosphorus pentaoxide; phosphoric acid and polyphosphoric acids

2810—Oxides of boron; boric acids

2811—Other inorganic acids and other inorganic oxygen compounds of nonmetals

2812—Halides and halide oxides of nonmetals

2813—Sulfides of nonmetals; commercial phosphorus trisulfide

2814—Ammonia, anhydrous or in aqueous solution

2815—Sodium hydroxide (Caustic soda); potassium hydroxide (Caustic potash); peroxides of sodium or potassium

2816—Hydroxide and peroxide of magnesium; oxides, hydroxides, and peroxides of strontium and barium

2817—Zinc oxide; zinc peroxide

2818—Artificial corundum, whether or not chemically defined; aluminum oxide; aluminum hydroxide

2819—Chromium oxides and hydroxides

2820—Manganese oxides

2821—Iron oxides and hydroxides; earth colors containing 70% or more by weight of combined iron evaluated as Fe_2O_3

2822—Cobalt oxides and hydroxides; commercial cobalt oxides

2823—Titanium oxides

2824—Lead oxides; red lead and orange lead

2825—Hydrazine and hydroxylamine and their inorganic salts; other inorganic bases; other metal oxides, hydroxides and peroxides

2826—Fluorides; fluorosilicates, fluoroaluminates, and other complex fluorine salts

2827—Chlorides, chloride oxides, and chloride hydroxides; bromides and bromide oxides; iodides and iodide oxides

2828—Hypochlorites; commercial calcium hypochlorite; chlorites; hypobromites

2829—Chlorates and perchlorates; bromates and perbromates; iodates and periodates

2830—Sulfides; polysulfides

2831—Dithionites and sulfoxylates

2832—Sulfites; thiosulfates

2833—Sulfates; alums; peroxosulfates (persulfates)

2834—Nitrites; nitrates

2835—Phosphinates (hypophosphites), phosphonates (phosphites), phosphates, and polyphosphates

2836—Carbonates; peroxocarbonates (percarbonates); commercial ammonium carbonate containing ammonium carbamate

2837—Cyanides, cyanide oxides, and complex cyanides

2838—Fulminates, cyanates, and thiocyanates

2839—Silicates; commercial alkali metal silicates

2840—Borates; peroxoborates (perborates)

2841—Salts of oxometallic or peroxometallic acids

2842—Other salts of inorganic acids or peroxoacids, excluding azides

2843—Colloidal precious metals; inorganic or organic compounds of precious metals, whether or not chemically defined; amalgams of precious metals

2844—Radioactive chemical elements and radioactive isotopes (including the fissile or fertile chemical elements and isotopes) and their compounds; mixtures and residues containing these products

2845—Isotopes other than those of heading 2844; compounds, inorganic or organic, of such isotopes, whether or not chemically defined

2846—Compounds, inorganic or organic, of rare-earth metals, of yttrium or of scandium, or of mixtures of these metals

2847—Hydrogen peroxide, whether or not solidified with urea

2848—Phosphides, whether or not chemically defined, excluding ferrophosphorus

2849—Carbides, whether or not chemically defined

2850—Hydrides, nitrides, azides, silicides, and borides, whether or not chemically defined, other than compounds which are also carbides of heading 2849

2851—Other inorganic compounds (including distilled or conductivity water and water of similar purity); liquid air (whether or not rare gases have been removed); compressed air; amalgams, other than amalgams of precious metals

For more details regarding classifications of the specific product you are interested in importing, consult a customs broker, the appropriate commodity specialist at your nearest customs port, or the HTSUS. The 2001 HTSUS is available online from the Customs Service (www.customs.gov/impoexpo/impoexpo.htm) or for purchase from the U.S. Government Printing Office (see resources at the end of this chapter), and may be found in larger public libraries. For a general discussion of customs classification, see "Classification—Liquidation" on page 229.

Dutiable Status of Goods

For more information about duty rates and binding decisions see "Dutiable Status of Goods" on page 203; for a discussion of temporary importation of goods see "Temporary Free Importations" on page 205.

Valuation

Importers have a responsibility to use what the U.S. Customs Service deems, "reasonable care," when determining the value of their goods. They must also provide any additional information that the Customs Service needs for setting a final value on the goods. This process involves a number of factors and can be somewhat complicated; importers must be aware of applicable issues and details. Valuation information applies to all types of commodities, for further discussion on the subject see "Customs Valuation" on page 267.

Import Duties

Import duties vary (often dramatically) depending upon the Harmonized Tariff Schedule (HTSUS) classification of the goods or products imported. Since some products that look alike have different HTSUS classifications and different rates of duty, proper classification is vital. Note that "differences of opinion" between importers and the Bureau of Customs and Border Protection regarding classification keeps customs attorneys very busy.

Import duties can be assessed on the imported value of the goods ("ad valorem" rates of duty such as 2%, 4.4%, 50%, etc.), total units or weight of the goods ("specific" rates of duty such as 2 cents each or 1.5 cents/pound, etc.) or on a combination basis ("compound" rates of duty such as 5 cents each plus 6%).

Listed below is a sampling of several Column 1 import duty rates for Chapter 28 products:
Chlorine (2801.10.00.00): free
to
Rare-earth metals, scandium and yttrium, whether or not intermixed or interalloyed (2805.30.00.00): 5%

For specific information on US import duties refer to the Harmonized Tariff Schedule of the US. The print version is available from the US Government Printing Office as well as third party suppliers who often add special features. Online versions are available in both static PDF pages as well as in formats with excellent search functionality. Search the Web with the term "Harmonized Tariff Schedule" to find sources.

Entry and Documentation

The entry of merchandise is a two-part process consisting of 1) filing the documents necessary to determine whether merchandise may be released from Customs custody and 2) filing the documents that contain information for duty assessment and statistical purposes. In certain instances, all documents must be filed and accepted by Customs prior to release of the goods. Unless you have been granted an extension, you must file entry documents at a location specified by the port or area director within five working days of your shipment's date of arrival at a U.S. port of entry. These include a number of standard documents required by Customs for any entry, and:

- U.S. Customs TSCA Certification when required
- Documentation of NRC import authorization, if required

After you present the entry, Customs may examine your shipment, or may waive examination. The shipment is then released, provided no legal or regulatory violations have been noted. You must then file entry summary documentation and deposit estimated duties at a designated customhouse within 10 working days of your shipment's release. For a detailed description of entry procedures, standard documentation, and informal entry, see "Entry Process" on page 185.

Informed Compliance. Informed compliance was introduced with the Customs Modernization Act of 1993 (Mod Act) and defines the relationship between importers and the Customs Service. It sets out the responsibilities of both parties. Providing the correct documentation and information for entry is a key factor that will make your importing operation run smoothly. We recommend that importers become familiar with the concept of informed comliance and the responsibilities that they have under the Mod Act. For further discussion about informed compliance see "Informed Compliance" on page 211.

Entry Invoice. Specify the use and Chemical Abstracts Service (CAS) number of the inorganic chemical compounds included in the shipment. For more general information about invoices see "Invoices" on page 277.

Note: The Entry and Documentation section has been carefully designed to supply you, the importer, with sample documents and directions on how to satisfy Customs requirements. Be aware that you should consult the applicable authorities to ensure that you are correctly following the most current procedures.

Prohibitions and Restrictions

Importation of inorganic chemicals that are considered hazardous substances is prohibited if the chemicals are misbranded. Certain hazardous substances listed in the FHSA and in regulations promulgated by the Consumer Product Safety Commission (CPSC) are completely banned from importation. A shipment of an inorganic chemical cannot be imported if it poses an imminent hazard. See 15 USC 1261, 2604-2606; 16 CFR 1500.265-1500.272.

Marking and Labeling Requirements

A shipment of any products containing inorganic chemicals that are classified as hazardous substances (49 CFR 172) must comply with the marking and labeling regulations adopted by the EPA (46 CFR 147.30) and the DOT (49 CFR 171 et seq.).

For a general discussion of U.S. Customs marking and labeling requirements, see "Country of Origin Marking" on page 236, "Special Marking Requirements" on page 238 and "Marking—False Impression" on page 239.

Shipping Considerations

You will need to ensure that your goods are packaged and shipped with care so that they pass smoothly through Customs and arrive in good condition. You are responsible for ensuring that the shipment is in compliance with all applicable government regulations for packaging and shipping. In most instances, you should not leave these arrangements solely to the discretion of your supplier. Careful preparation of the cargo and selection of the mode of transport can be essential to a cost-effective, timely delivery of undamaged goods. We strongly advise you to consult your shipping representative, insurance agent, or freight broker for advice on packing and shipping.

Inorganic chemicals may be shipped in bulk, bags, bottles, crates, or other types of containers, depending on the type of product and whether it is prepackaged. General considerations include protection from contamination, weather, and pests. For liquid shipments, venting and vapor collection systems may be required. Safety precautions should also be implemented as required to protect against breakage, spillage, corrosion of containers, combustion, and explosion. Containers should be constructed so as to be safe for handling during transport.

Chemical products in particular may have to be shipped in pressurized, ventilated, and temperature-and vapor-controlled enclosures. Solid chemical products that are listed as hazardous substances (49 CFR 172 appendix) may be transported in bulk only on compliance with Coast Guard notification procedures, shipping permit requirements, and complex transportation regulations (46 CFR 148). All hazardous substances must be packaged and transported in accordance with DOT regulations (49 CFR 171 et seq.).

Publications and WWW Resources

The following publications may be relevant to the importation of toxic or hazardous inorganic chemicals:

Toxic Substances Control Act: A Guide for Chemical Importers/Exporters (published by EPA)

This document is available from the TSCA Assistance Information Service (see Relevant Government Agencies)

The following publication provides a listing of existing chemical substances in the United States. It can be purchased in electronic format or a search of the document can be requested via telephone. Contact the Chemical Abstract Service (CAS) at (800)631-1884 or at (614) 447-3600 ext 2308.

TSCA Chemical Substance Inventory

In order to check whether or not a chemical is subject to any rules or regulations under Sections 5, 6, or 7 of TSCA, search the following document (www.epa.gov/opptintr/CORR)

Chemical on Reporting Rules List (CORR)

The *Harmonized Tariff Schedule of the United States (2001)* (HTSUS) is available to view on the Customs Service website (www.customs.gov), or you may purchase a printed version from:

U.S. Government Printing Office
Superintendent of Documents
710 North Capital Street NW
Washington DC 20401
Tel: (202) 512-1800
Fax: (202) 512-1657
Website: www.access.gpo.gov

The USGPO also has copies of specific laws available for purchase. The USGPO accepts orders made by fax, phone or placed over the Internet, as well as mail orders paid by credit card. All orders must be accompanied by payment. Credit cards, checks drawn on a U.S. bank, or an international money order are all acceptable.

Relevant Government Agencies

Address your inquiries regarding TSCA and EPA requirements for importation of inorganic chemical substances to:

Environmental Protection Agency (EPA)
Office of Pollution Prevention and Toxics
TSCA System Information
1200 Pennsylvania Avenue NW
Washington DC 20460
Tel: (202) 564-3810
Tel: (202) 554-1404 (TSCA Information Hotline)
Email: oppt.homepage@epa.gov
Website: www.epa.gov/opptintr/contact.htm

Address your questions regarding transportation of hazardous substances to:

U.S. Department of Transportation (DOT)
Research and Special Programs Administration
Hazardous Materials Information Center
400 7th St. SW
Washington DC 20590
Tel: (202) 366-4488
Website: http://hazmat.dot.gov

Address your questions regarding importation of inorganic chemical substances generally to your local Customs port director. For addresses, refer to "U.S. Customs and Border Protection Offices" on page 65 or contact:

U.S. Customs and Border Protection
Customs Headquarters
1300 Pennsylvania Avenue NW
Washington DC 20229
Tel: (202) 354-1000
Website: www.customs.treas.gov

Laws and Regulations

The following laws and regulations may be relevant to the importation of inorganic chemical substances. The laws are contained in the United States Code (USC), and the regulations are published in the Code of Federal Regulations (CFR), both of which are available at larger public and law libraries. Specific laws and regulations may also be purchased from the U.S. Government Printing Office (address above).

18 USC 831 et seq.
Explosives and Other Dangerous Articles
This Act restricts the import of nuclear substances into the U.S. and authorizes Customs to enforce the restrictions.

42 USC 2077, 2111, 2122, 2131, 2155
Atomic Energy Act of 1954
This Act restricts the importation of certain nuclear substance, atomic weapons, and byproduct material into the U.S.

10 CFR 30, 40, 50, 70, 110
Regulations on Nuclear Materials, Weapons, and Byproducts
These regulations implement the laws restricting importation of special nuclear substance, atomic weapons, and byproduct material and authorize enforcement by Customs.

15 USC 2601 et seq.
Toxic Substances Control Act
This Act authorizes the EPA to determine whether a substance is harmful and to restrict importation, sale, and use of such substances.

19 CFR 12.118 et seq.
Regulations on Toxic Substances Control
These regulations require importers of chemical substances imported in bulk or as part of a mixture to certify to Customs that the shipment complies with the TSCA or is not subject to that Act.

15 USC 1261 et seq.
Federal Hazardous Substances Act
This Act controls the importation of hazardous substances, sets forth prohibited imports, and authorizes various agencies to promulgate labeling, marking, and transport requirements.

49 CFR 17149 CFR 171 35 seq. et seq.
Regulations on Hazardous Materials
These regulations list all substances deemed hazardous and provide transport, marking, labeling, safety, and emergency response rules.

46 CFR 147.30
Regulations on Labeling of Hazardous Materials
This regulation requires the labeling of containers of hazardous substances and specifies the label contents.

46 CFR 148 et seq.
Regulations on Carriage of Solid Hazardous Materials in Bulk
These regulations govern the transport of solid hazardous substances in bulk, including reporting, permitting, loading, stowing, and shipping requirements.

Sources of Additional Information

The TSCA Chemical Substance Inventory is available through various commercial online databases and from:

National Technical Information Service (NTIS)
U.S. Department of Commerce
5285 Port Royal Road
Springfield, VA 22161
(703) 605-6000; FAX (703) 605-6900
Web site: www.ntis.gov

Principal Exporting Countries

The following listing includes samples of the main supplier nations of the products of this chapter. It is organized by HTSUS major heading. (Refer to "Customs Classification" above for the product codes.) Countries are listed in rank order of the value of products imported to the U.S. Statistics represent customs value of entries for 2002 from the Bureau of Census, U.S. Department of Commerce.

2801—Chile, Canada, Japan, Mexico, Israel, France, Germany, Belgium, Netherlands, India, South Africa, United Kingdom, China

2802—Japan, France, Israel

2803—Canada, Venezuela, Egypt, Germany, Norway, Japan, Mexico, China, Russia, Colombia, Czech Republic, United Kingdom, Netherlands, Spain

2804—Canada, Germany, Brazil, China, Russia, South Africa, Japan, Italy

2805—China, Japan, France, Russia, Germany, Austria

2806—Canada, Japan, Germany

2807—Canada, Mexico, Germany, Sweden

2808—Canada, Japan, Norway, Germany, Egypt

2809—Belgium, Israel, Morocco, China, Japan, France, Germany, Netherlands

2810—Chile, Turkey, Russia, Italy, Peru, Bolivia, Argentina, China

2811—Mexico, Canada, Germany, Japan, China, United Kingdom, Austria

2812—Germany, Japan, South Africa, France, Russia, Switzerland, Italy, India, United Kingdom

2813—Canada, United Kingdom, India, Germany, Italy, Japan, Poland, Belgium, France

2814—Trinidad and Tobago, Canada, Ukraine, Venezuela, Russia, Brazil, Mexico, Colombia, Argentina, Latvia, Indonesia, Japan

2815—Canada, Venezuela, Taiwan, Sweden, South Korea, Germany, Japan, France, United Kingdom, Belgium, Italy

2816—Germany, Netherlands, Austria, Italy, Japan, China, Israel, Mexico

2817—Canada, Mexico, Netherlands, Japan, Germany, China, United Kingdom, Russia, Belgium

2818—Australia, Suriname, Germany, Canada, Jamaica, China, France, Japan, Brazil

2819—Turkey, Kazakhstan, China, Germany, Japan, United Kingdom, Brazil

2820—Australia, Ireland, South Africa, Japan, Greece, China, Belgium

2821—China, Germany, Japan, Italy, Brazil, India, United Kingdom, Mexico, Canada, Hong Kong

2822—Belgium, Finland, United Kingdom, France, South Africa, Germany, Japan, China, Switzerland, Netherlands

2823—France, Germany, China, Brazil, Czech Republic, Japan, South Korea, Poland

2824—Mexico, Canada, Portugal, Japan, Germany, Argentina, Switzerland, United Kingdom

2825—China, Germany, Japan, Mexico, United Kingdom, Belgium, Canada, Brazil, Australia, France, South Africa

2826—Germany, Thailand, China, Japan, Italy, Mexico, Canada, South Africa

2827—Canada, Israel, China, Argentina, Germany, Mexico

2828—Canada, Mexico, Japan, Italy, France, China, South Africa

2829—Canada, Israel, China, Spain, United Kingdom

2830—Germany, Japan, Sweden, Mexico, Canada

2831—Germany, Canada, China, India, Taiwan, Italy, Belgium, Switzerland, South Korea

2832—Germany, South Africa, Canada, Thailand, Chile, United Kingdom, Italy, India, China

2833—Mexico, Germany, China, Canada, Finland, Japan, Belgium, Turkey, Taiwan, Italy

2834—Chile, Israel, Norway, China, Germany, Denmark, Japan

2835—Canada, Germany, Israel, China, Mexico, United Kingdom

2836—China, Mexico, Sweden, Chile, Germany, Finland, Japan

2837—Germany, China, Czech Republic, South Korea, United Kingdom, Japan, Canada, India, Chile

2838—China, Japan, Germany, United Kingdom, Taiwan, South Korea, Switzerland, Italy

2839—Canada, Japan, Germany, Netherlands, France, United Kingdom

2840—Belgium, Germany, Turkey, United Kingdom, Italy

2841—Japan, China, United Kingdom, Germany, Chile

2842—Germany, Japan, Netherlands, United Kingdom, Canada

2843—Canada, South Africa, United Kingdom, Japan, Germany

2844—Russia, Canada, France, United Kingdom, Germany

2845—Russia, Israel, Netherlands, Canada, China, France

2846—China, France, Japan, United Kingdom, Norway, Austria

2847—Canada, France, Germany, Japan

2848—Canada, Germany, India, Japan, Brazil, Mexico

2849—China, Germany, Norway, South Africa, Japan, Canada

2850—United Kingdom, Brazil, Germany, Japan, India, China

2851—Canada, Germany, Japan, United Kingdom, France, Taiwan, South Korea, Israel, Belgium

Chapter 29:
Organic Chemicals

This chapter pertains to the importation of separate organic chemical elements and chemically defined compounds, which are classified under Chapter 29 of the Harmonized Tariff Schedule of the United States (HTSUS). Specifically, it includes hydrocarbons; alcohols, phenols, and phenol-alcohols; ethers; peroxides and epoxides; acetals; aldehyde-, ketone-, quinone-, and nitrogen-function compounds; organo-inorganic compounds; carboxylic acids; heterocyclic compounds; nucleic acids; sulfonamides; provitamins, vitamins, and hormones; glycosides, vegetable alkaloids, and certain sugars; and antibiotics.

The importation of inorganic chemical substances is covered in related Commodity Index Chapter 28, which includes certain forms of carbon. If you are interested in importing a product that is not in the form of a bulk chemical, you should read the chapters that pertain to the specific type of product. Fat and oil substances are covered in Chapter 15. For ethyl alcohol products, refer to Chapter 22. The importation requirements for methane and propane are found in Chapter 27, for urea in Chapter 31, and for enzymes in Chapter 35. If you are interested in importing dyes, tannins, and other coloring agents, refer to Chapter 32. Chemicals put up in forms for use as fuels are covered in Chapter 36, for fertilizers are in Chapter 31, for ink removers and fire extinguishers in Chapter 38. Optical elements are classified in Chapter 90.

Note: To understand key issues that will enable you to make best use of the information in this section we recommend that you see "Introduction" on page 425.

Key Factors

The key factors in the importation of organic chemical substances are:

- Compliance with U.S. Environmental Protection Agency (EPA) requirements under the Toxic Substances Control Act (TSCA) (if the product is a hazardous substance)

- Compliance with U.S. Department of Transportation (DOT) regulations for transport of hazardous cargo (if the product is a hazardous substance)

Although most importers use the services of a licensed customs broker in making their entries, and we recommend this practice, you should be aware of the regulatory, entry, and documentation issues involved in importing your product. You, as importer, are ultimately responsible for the fulfillment of any legal requirements applicable to your shipment.

General Considerations

Regulatory Agencies. The EPA, under authority of the TSCA, imposes certain controls on the importation of organic chemicals that contain toxic substances. The TSCA defines a toxic substance as any substance determined to present the possibility of an unreasonable risk of injury to health and the environment. The DOT enforces regulations for transporting hazardous cargo. Substances are deemed hazardous if listed in DOT transport regulations (49 CFR 172 appendix).

Toxic and Hazardous Substances. Organic chemicals imported in bulk, as articles, or as part of a mixture must be in compliance with toxic and hazardous substance regulations of the EPA and DOT. These include packaging, shipping, marking, and labeling requirements. In addition, all organic chemical products are subject to the U.S. Customs Service TSCA Import Certification Rule (19 CFR 12.118 et seq.). If you import these products, you must sign one of the following statements: "I certify that all chemical substances in this shipment comply with all applicable rules or orders under TSCA and that I am not offering a chemical substance for entry in violation of TSCA or any applicable rule or order thereunder" or "I certify that all chemicals in this shipment are not subject to TSCA."

You must file this TSCA certification of compliance or exemption at the time you make the entry at Customs. The certification may be in the form of a typed or stamped statement on an appropriate entry document or commercial invoice or a preprinted attachment to such entry document or invoice. You may sign the certificate by means of an authorized facsimile signature. If your entry is electronically processed, the certification will be in the form of a Certification Code, which is part of the Automated Broker Interface (ABI) transmission. Customs will not release your shipment without proper certification.

If you will be importing several or regular shipments, you should ask the appropriate Customs port director to authorize your use of a blanket certification. If you receive such authorization, you must include on the commercial invoice or entry document for each shipment a statement that the blanket certification is on file and that it is incorporated by reference. This statement need not be signed. The blanket certification is valid for one calendar year, is subject to renewal, and is may be revoked at any time for cause.

In filling out TSCA forms and Customs entry documents, you should provide the Chemical Abstracts Service (CAS) number for each chemical in the shipment. These CAS numbers are given in the appendix to the HTSUS. You are not required to include the CAS number, but Customs will be able to process your shipment more quickly if you give this number.

Articles Exclusion. If you are importing organic chemicals that are classified as hazardous substances but are part of articles, you are subject to TSCA certification requirements only if certification for your product is specifically required by a rule or order promulgated under the TSCA. No specific rules have been adopted at this time. An "article" is a manufactured item 1) that is formed into a specific shape or design during manufacture, 2) that has end-use functions dependent on the shape or design during end use, and 3) that during the end use, does not change in its chemical composition or that changes only for a noncommercial purpose separate from the article and only as allowed by law (19 CFR 12.120(2)). Fluids and particles are not articles, regardless of shape or design.

Shipment Detention. A shipment containing organic chemicals will be detained at the U.S. port of arrival (or entry if same), at your risk and expense, if: 1) it contains banned chemical substances (15 USC 2604, 2605); or 2) it contains chemical substances ordered seized because of imminent hazards (15 USC 2606). Further detention will occur at the port of entry, again at your risk and expense, if: 1) the EPA administrator or Customs port director has reasonable grounds to believe the shipment is not in compliance with the TSCA; or 2) you do not provide proper TSCA certification.

If your shipment is detained, it will be held by Customs for no more than 48 hours. It will then be turned over to the EPA administrator, unless you have arranged to release it in bond. You must either bring it into TSCA compliance or reexport it within the earlier of 90 days after notice of detention or 30 days of demand for redelivery. Customs may grant an extension if failure to comply or reexport is the result of delays in EPA or Customs procedures. If you fail to comply or reexport within the time allowed, the EPA administrator is authorized to have the shipment stored or disposed of at your expense.

Customs Classification

For customs purposes, organic chemical substances are classified under Chapter 29 of the HTSUS. This chapter is broken into major headings, which are further divided into subheadings, and often sub-subheadings, each of which has its own HTSUS classification number. For example, the 2001 HTSUS number for nitrated benzene is 2904.20.35, indicating it is a sub-subcategory of derivatives containing only nitro or nitroso groups (2904.20), which is a subcategory of the major heading, sulfonated, nitrated, or nitrosated derivatives of hydrocarbons (2904). There are 41 major headings within Chapter 29.

2901—Acyclic hydrocarbons

2902—Cyclic hydrocarbons

2903—Halogenated derivatives of hydrocarbons

2904—Sulfonated, nitrated, or nitrosated derivatives of hydrocarbons, whether or not halogenated

2905—Acyclic alcohols and their halogenated, sulfonated, nitrated, or nitrosated derivatives

2906—Cyclic alcohols and their halogenated, sulfonated, nitrated, or nitrosated derivatives

2907—Phenol, phenol-alcohols

2908—Halogenated, sulfonated, nitrated, or nitrosated derivatives of phenols or phenol-alcohols

2909—Ethers, ether-alcohols, ether-phenols, ether-alcohol-phenols, alcohol peroxides, ether peroxides, ketone peroxides (whether or not chemically defined), and their halogenated, sulfonated, nitrated, or nitrosated derivatives

2910—Epoxides, epoxyalcohols, epoxyphenols, and epoxyethers, with a three-membered ring, and their halogenated, sulfonated, nitrated, or nitrosated derivatives

2911—Acetals and hemiacetals, whether or not with other oxygen function, and their halogenated, sulfonated, nitrated, or nitrosated derivatives

2912—Aldehydes, whether or not with other oxygen function; cyclic polymers of aldehydes; paraformaldehyde

2913—Halogenated, sulfonated, nitrated, or nitrosated derivatives of products of heading 2912

2914—Ketones and quinones, whether or not with other oxygen function, and their halogenated, sulfonated, nitrated, or nitrosated derivatives

2915—Saturated acyclic monocarboxylic acids and their anhydrides, halides, peroxides, and peroxyacids; their halogenated, sulfonated, nitrated, or nitrosated derivatives

2916—Unsaturated acyclic monocarboxylic acids, cyclic monocarboxylic acids, their anhydrides, halides, peroxides, and peroxyacids; their halogenated, sulfonated, nitrated, or nitrosated derivatives

2917—Polycarboxylic acids, their anhydrides, halides, peroxides, and peroxyacids; their halogenated, sulfonated, nitrated, or nitrosated derivatives

2918—Carboxylic acid with additional oxygen function and their anhydrides, halides, peroxides, and peroxyacids; their halogenated, sulfonated, nitrated, or nitrosated derivatives

2919—Phosphoric esters and their salts, including lactophosphates; their halogenated, sulfonated, nitrated, or nitrosated derivatives

2920—Esters of other inorganic acids (excluding esters of hydrogen halides) and their salts; their halogenated, sulfonated, nitrated, or nitrosated derivatives

2921—Amine-function compounds

2922—Oxygen-function amino-compounds

2923—Quaternary ammonium salts and hydroxides; lecithins and other phosphoaminolipids

2924—Carboxyamide-function compounds; amide-function compounds of carbonic acid

2925—Carboxyimide-function compounds (including saccharin and its salts) and imine-function compounds

2926—Nitrile-function compounds

2927—Diazo-, azo-, or azoxy-compounds

2928—Organic derivatives of hydrazine or of hydroxylamine

2930—Organo-sulfur compounds

2932—Heterocyclic compounds with oxygen hetero-atom(s) only

2933—Heterocyclic compounds with nitrogen hetero-atom(s) only

2934---Nucleic acids and their salts; other heterocyclic compounds

2935—Sulfonamides

2936—Provitamins and vitamins, natural or reproduced by synthesis (including natural concentrates), derivatives thereof used primarily as vitamins, and intermixtures of the foregoing, whether or not in any solvent

2937—Hormones, natural or reproduced by synthesis; derivatives thereof, used primarily as hormones; other steroids used primarily as hormones

2938—Glycosides, natural or reproduced by synthesis, and their salts, ethers, esters, and other derivatives

2939—Vegetable alkaloids, natural or reproduced by synthesis, and their salts, ethers, esters, and other derivatives

2940—Sugars, chemically pure, other than sucrose, lactose, maltose, glucose, and fructose; sugar ethers and sugar esters, and their salts, other than products of heading 2937, 2938 or 2939

2941—Antibiotics

For more details regarding classifications of the specific product you are interested in importing, consult a customs broker, the appropriate commodity specialist at your nearest customs port, or the HTSUS. The 2001 HTSUS is available online from the U. S. Customs Service (www.customs.gov/impoexpo/impoexpo.htm) or can be purchased from the U.S. Government Printing Office (see resources at the end of this chapter), and may be found in larger public libraries. For a general discussion of customs classification, see "Classification—Liquidation" on page 229.

Dutiable Status of Goods

For more information about duty rates and binding decisions see "Dutiable Status of Goods" on page 203; for a discussion of temporary importation of goods see "Temporary Free Importations" on page 205.

Valuation

Importers have a responsibility to use what the U.S. Customs Service deems, "reasonable care," when determining the value of their goods. They must also provide any additional information that the Customs Service needs for setting a final value on the goods. This process involves a number of factors and can be somewhat complicated; importers must be aware of applicable issues and details. Valuation information applies to all types of commodities, for further discussion on the subject see "Customs Valuation" on page 267.

Import Duties

Import duties vary (often dramatically) depending upon the Harmonized Tariff Schedule (HTSUS) classification of the goods or products imported. Since some products that look alike have different HTSUS classifications and different rates of duty, proper classification is vital. Note that "differences of opinion" between importers and the Bureau of Customs and Border Protection regarding classification keeps customs attorneys very busy.

Import duties can be assessed on the imported value of the goods ("ad valorem" rates of duty such as 2%, 4.4%, 50%, etc.), total units or weight of the goods ("specific" rates of duty such as 2 cents each or 1.5 cents/pound, etc.) or on a combination basis ("compound" rates of duty such as 5 cents each plus 6%).

Listed below is a sampling of several Column 1 import duty rates for Chapter 29 products:
Ethane and butane (2901.10.10.00): free
to
hrdrocarbons (chloromethane and chloroethane) (2903.11.00): 7%

For specific information on US import duties refer to the Harmonized Tariff Schedule of the US. The print version is available from the US Government Printing Office as well as third party suppliers who often add special features. Online versions are available in both static PDF pages as well as in formats with excellent search functionality. Search the Web with the term "Harmonized Tariff Schedule" to find sources.

Entry and Documentation

The entry of merchandise is a two-part process consisting of 1) filing the documents necessary to determine whether merchandise may be released from Customs custody and 2) filing the documents that contain information for duty assessment and statistical purposes. In certain instances, all documents must be filed and accepted by Customs prior to release of the goods. Unless you have been granted an extension, you must file entry documents at a location specified by the port or area director within five working days of your shipment's date of arrival at a U.S. port of entry. These include a number of standard documents required by Customs for any entry, and:

- U.S. Customs TSCA Certification when required

After you present the entry, Customs may examine your shipment, or may waive examination. The shipment is then released, provided no legal or regulatory violations have been noted. You must then file entry summary documentation and deposit estimated duties at a designated customhouse within 10 working days of your shipment's release. For a detailed description of entry procedures, standard documentation, and informal entry, see "Entry Process" on page 185.

Informed Compliance. Informed compliance was introduced with the Customs Modernization Act of 1993 (Mod Act) and defines the relationship between importers and the Customs Service. It sets out the responsibilities of both parties. Providing the correct documentation and information for entry is a key factor that will make your importing operation run smoothly. We recommend that importers become familiar with the concept of informed comliance and the responsibilities that they have under the Mod Act. For further discussion about informed compliance see "Informed Compliance" on page 211.

Entry Invoice. Specify the use and Chemical Abstracts Service (CAS) number of the organic chemical compounds included in the shipment. For more general information about invoices see "Invoices" on page 277.

Note: The Entry and Documentation section has been carefully designed to supply you, the importer, with sample documents and directions on how to satisfy Customs requirements. Be aware that you should consult the applicable authorities to ensure that you are correctly following the most current procedures.

Prohibitions and Restrictions

Importation of organic chemicals that are considered hazardous substances is prohibited if the chemicals are misbranded. Certain hazardous substances listed in the FHSA and in regulations promulgated by the Consumer Product Safety Commission (CPSC) are completely banned from importation. A shipment of an organic chemical cannot be imported if it poses an imminent hazard. See 15 USC 1261, 2604-2606; 16 CFR 1500.265-1500.272.

Marking and Labeling Requirements

A shipment of any products containing organic chemicals that are classified as hazardous substance (49 CFR 172) must comply with the marking and labeling regulations adopted by the EPA (46 CFR 147.30) and the DOT (49 CFR 171 et seq.).

For a general discussion of U.S. Customs marking and labeling requirements, see "Country of Origin Marking" on page 236, "Special Marking Requirements" on page 238 and "Marking— False Impression" on page 239.

Shipping Considerations

You will need to ensure that your goods are packaged and shipped with care so that they pass smoothly through Customs and arrive in good condition. You are responsible for ensuring that the shipment is in compliance with all applicable government regulations for packaging and shipping. In most instances, you should not leave these arrangements solely to the discretion of your supplier. Careful preparation of the cargo and selection of the mode of transport can be essential to a cost-effective, timely delivery of undamaged goods. We strongly advise you to consult your shipping representative, insurance agent, or freight broker for advice on packing and shipping.

Organic chemicals may be shipped in bulk, bags, bottles, crates, or other types of containers, depending on the type of product and whether it is prepackaged. General considerations include protection from contamination, weather, and pests. For liquid shipments, venting and vapor collection systems may be required. Safety precautions should also be implemented as required to protect against breakage, spillage, corrosion of containers, combustion, and explosion. Containers should be constructed so as to be safe for handling during transport.

Organic chemical products in particular may have to be shipped in pressurized, ventilated, and temperature-and vapor-controlled enclosures. Solid organic chemical products that are listed as hazardous substances (49 CFR 172 appendix) may be transported in bulk only on compliance with Coast Guard notification procedures, shipping permit requirements, and complex transportation regulations (46 CFR 148). All hazardous substances must be packaged and transported in accordance with DOT regulations (49 CFR 171 et seq.).

Publications and WWW Resources

The following publications may be relevant to the importation of toxic or hazardous organic chemicals:

Toxic Substances Control Act: A Guide for Chemical Importers/ Exporters (published by EPA)

This document is available from the TSCA Assistance Information Service (see Relevant Government Agencies)

The following publication provides a listing of existing chemical substances in the United States. It can be purchased in electronic format or a search of the document can be requested via telephone. Contact the Chemical Abstract Service (CAS) at (800)631-1884 or at (614) 447-3600 ext 2308.

TSCA Chemical Substance Inventory

In order to check whether or not a chemical is subject to any rules or regulations under Sections 5, 6, or 7 of TSCA, search the following document (www.epa.gov/opptintr/CORR)

Chemical on Reporting Rules List (CORR)

The *Harmonized Tariff Schedule of the United States (2001)* (HTSUS) is available to view on the Customs Service website (www.customs.gov), or you may purchase a printed version from:

U.S. Government Printing Office
Superintendent of Documents
710 North Capital Street NW
Washington DC 20401
Tel: (202) 512-1800
Fax: (202) 512-1657
Website: www.access.gpo.gov

The USGPO also has copies of specific laws available for purchase. The USGPO accepts orders made by fax, phone or placed over the Internet, as well as mail orders paid by credit card. All orders must be accompanied by payment. Credit cards, checks drawn on a U.S. bank, or an international money order are all acceptable.

Relevant Government Agencies

Address your inquiries regarding TSCA and EPA requirements for importation of inorganic chemical substances to:

Environmental Protection Agency (EPA)
Office of Pollution Prevention and Toxics
TSCA System Information
1200 Pennsylvania Avenue NW
Washington DC 20460
Tel: (202) 564-3810
Tel: (202) 554-1404 (TSCA Information Hotline)
Email: oppt.homepage@epa.gov
Website: www.epa.gov/opptintr/contact.htm

Address your questions regarding transportation of hazardous substances to:

U.S. Department of Transportation (DOT)
Research and Special Programs Administration
Hazardous Materials Information Center
400 7th St. SW
Washington DC 20590
Tel: (202) 366-4488
Website: http://hazmat.dot.gov

Address your questions regarding importation of organic chemical substances generally to your local Customs port director. For addresses, refer to "U.S. Customs and Border Protection Offices" on page 65 or contact:

U.S. Customs and Border Protection
Customs Headquarters
1300 Pennsylvania Avenue NW
Washington DC 20229
Tel: (202) 354-1000
Website: www.customs.treas.gov

Laws and Regulations

The following laws and regulations may be relevant to the importation of organic chemicals. The laws are contained in the United States Code (USC), and the regulations are published in the Code of Federal Regulations (CFR), both of which are available at larger public and law libraries. Specific laws and regulations may also be purchased from the U.S. Government Printing Office (address above).

15 USC 2601 et seq.
Toxic Substances Control Act
This Act authorizes the EPA to determine whether a substance is harmful and to restrict importation, sale, and use of such substances.

19 CFR 12.118 et seq.
Regulations on Toxic Substances Control
These regulations require importers of chemical substances imported in bulk or as part of a mixture to certify to Customs that the shipment complies with the TSCA or is not subject to that Act.

15 USC 1261 et seq.
Federal Hazardous Substances Act
This Act controls the importation of hazardous substances, sets forth prohibited imports, and authorizes various agencies to promulgate labeling, marking, and transport requirements.

49 CFR 171 35 seq.
Regulations on Hazardous Materials
These regulations list all substances deemed hazardous and provide transport, marking, labeling, safety, and emergency response rules.

46 CFR 147.30
Regulations on Labeling of Hazardous Materials
This regulation requires the labeling of containers of hazardous substances and specifies the label contents.

46 CFR 148 et seq.
Regulations on Carriage of Solid Hazardous Materials in Bulk
These regulations govern the transport of solid hazardous substances in bulk, including reporting, permitting, loading, stowing, and shipping requirements.

Sources of Additional Information

The TSCA Chemical Substance Inventory is available through various commercial online databases and from:

National Technical Information Service (NTIS)
U.S. Department of Commerce
5285 Port Royal Road
Springfield, VA 22161
(703) 605-6000; FAX (703) 605-6900
Web site: www.ntis.gov

Principal Exporting Countries

The following listing includes samples of the main supplier nations of the products of this chapter. It is organized by HTSUS major heading. (Refer to "Customs Classification" above for the product codes.) Countries are listed in rank order of the value of products imported to the U.S. Statistics represent customs value of entries for 2002 from the Bureau of Census, U.S. Department of Commerce.

2901—Canada, South Africa, Norway, United Kingdom, Portugal, Japan, Aruba, Brazil, France

2902—Canada, Netherlands, Brazil, South Korea, Japan, Germany

2903—Canada, Germany, France, United Kingdom, China, Netherlands, Japan, Israel

2904—United Kingdom, Belgium, China, Japan, Germany, Canada, France, India

2905—Trinidad and Tobago, Canada, Chile, Venezuela, Germany, Equatorial Guinea

2906—China, India, Germany, Netherlands, Japan, Mexico, United Kingdom, Spain, Italy, Switzerland, Singapore, France, Brazil

2907—Japan, Germany, United Kingdom, Belgium, France, China

2908—Japan, China, Brazil, Mexico, Germany, United Kingdom

2909—Saudi Arabia, Canada, Venezuela, United Arab Emireates, Brazil, Qatar, Japan, Malaysia

2910—Japan, Canada, Belgium, South Korea, Poland, Germany, Netherlands

2911—Japan, Germany, Netherlands, Switzerland, Spain, Israel

2912—Japan, Switzerland, Germany, China, Mexico, United Kingdom, Spain

2913—Germany, China, France, Japan, Switzerland, United Kingdom, India

2914—Japan, Germany, Switzerland, China, France, Italy, Netherlands, United Kingdom, Mexico, Taiwan, South Africa

2915—United Kingdom, Mexico, Germany, Netherlands, Malaysia, France, Japan, Denmark, Belgium

2916—Japan, United Kingdom, Germany, China, France, Mexico, India, Netherlands

2917—Canada, Japan, Germany, China, Italy, South Korea

2918—Japan, Hungary, Mexico, China, United KIngdom, France

2919—Germany, United Kingdom, Japan, China, Russia, Netherlands, Switzerland, France, India, Belgium

2920—Israel, Canada, France, Germany, Italy, Denmark, Japan, Mexico, India, Taiwan, China, South Korea

2921—United Kingdom, Canada, Japan, Germany, Italy, China, South Korea, Belgium, India, Netherlands, Switzerland

2922—United Kingdom, Germany, Ireland, Japan, Switzerland, France, China, Italy

2923—Japan, Canada, Czech Republic, Italy, Sweden, Germany, Switzerland, South Korea, China, Finland, France, Israel

2924—Switzerland, Japan, Norway, Germany, Italy, Ireland, United Kingdom, France, Netherlands

2925—France, Japan, Germany, Spain, China, India, United Kingdom, South Korea, Austria, Switzerland, Taiwan

2926—United Kingdom, Japan, Germany, Italy, India, Switzerland, China

2927—Japan, Belgium, Germany, Indonesia, South Korea, Mexico, India, United Kingdom, France

2928—Italy, Spain, Netherlands, Japan, Germany, Israel, China, Ireland, Czech Republic, Hungary

2929—Germany, Switzerland, Japan, France, United Kingdom, Canada

2930—France, Japan, Denmark, Germany, India, China, United Kingdom, Mexico, Italy, Belgium

2931—Ireland, Germany, United Kingdom, Japan, Italy, China, France, Netherlands, India, Canada

2932—Ireland, Singapore, Germany, Switzerland, Italy, Hungary, United Kingdom, China, Japan, France, India

2933—Ireland, Germany, United Kingdom, Singapore, Japan, France, Switzerland, Italy, Spain, Netherlands

2934—Ireland, United Kingdom, Belgium, Japan, Germany, Italy, France, Switzerland, Netherlands, China, Israel, Austria, Finland, Czech Republic, Spain, India

2935—Singapore, United Kingdom, Germany, Ireland, Japan, Italy, China, Switzerland

2936—China, Germany, Switzerland, Japan, France, United Kingdom, Denmark, India

2937—Hungary, United Kingdom, Denmark, Netherlands, Switzerland, France, Ireland

2938—Japan, China, United Kingdom, Switzerland, Germany, France, Brazil, India

2939—Germany, China, India, Belgium, Canada, Switzerland, Slovenia

2940—Japan, Germany, Italy, China, France, Canada, Switzerland, South Korea, Belgium, Denmark, South Africa, United Kingdom

2941—United Kingdom, Japan, Italy, France, China, Croatia

2942—United Kingdom, Germany, Japan, Canada, India, Italy, China, Israel, France, Thailand, Belgium

Chapter 30: Pharmaceutical Products

Drugs. Although it is not a requirement for foreign drug firms to register their establishments, their products must be listed with the FDA. Forms required to obtain a labeler code (FD 2656) and drug list their product (FD 2657) should be requested from the Center for Drug Evaluation and Research, Product Information Management Branch (HFD-058), 5600 Fishers Lane, Rockville, MD 20857.

This chapter relates to the importation of pharmaceutical products, which are classified under Chapter 30 of the Harmonized Tariff Schedule of the United States (HTSUS). Specifically, it includes human and animal substances prepared for therapeutic or prophylactic uses; medicaments; wadding, gauze, and bandages; and miscellaneous related items. It includes pharmaceuticals for both human and animal use.

If you are interested in importing food or beverage products for special diets—such as dietetic foods or mineral waters—refer to Commodity Index Chapters 16 through 24. For plasters used in dentistry, refer to Chapter 25. The importing requirements for cosmetics, perfume, and essential oil products are covered in Chapter 33. Soap and similar products that contain medicaments are classified under Chapter 34, which also covers the importation of dental preparations with a plaster base. Refer to Chapter 35 for importing requirements related to blood albumin not prepared for therapeutic or prophylactic uses. For importing separately defined chemicals, refer to Chapters 28 (inorganic) and 29 (organic).

Note: To understand key issues that will enable you to make best use of the information in this section we recommend that you see "Introduction" on page 425.

Key Factors

The key factors in the importation of pharmaceuticals are:

- Compliance with Food and Drug Administration (FDA) safety, purity, identity, manufacturing, labeling, packaging, recordkeeping, reporting, and other standards

- Compliance with FDA pharmaceutical registration, testing, approval, and listing procedures

- Compliance with FDA import entry notification and procedures

- Compliance with U.S. Federal Trade Commission (FTC) and Consumer Product Safety Commission (CPSC) standards

- Compliance with U.S. Department of Agriculture (USDA) permit requirements (if the product is biological derivative intended for veterinary use)

- Compliance with Environmental Protection Agency (EPA) pesticide regulations, including pesticide residue monitoring for animal feeds that could affect U.S. food supplies

- Compliance with EPA requirements under Toxic Substances Control Act (TSCA) (if the product is a hazardous substance)

- Compliance with U.S. Department of Transportation (DOT) regulations for transport of hazardous cargo (if the product contains a hazardous substance)

- Compliance with U.S. Public Health Service Centers for Disease Control (CDC) permit requirements (if the product is a vector of human disease)

Although most importers use the services of a licensed customs broker in making their entries, and we recommend this practice, you should be aware of the regulatory, entry, and documentation issues involved in importing your product. You, as importer, are ultimately responsible for the fulfillment of any legal requirements applicable to your shipment.

General Considerations

Regulatory Agencies. Regulations governing pharmaceutical products are stringent and complex. The FDA, under the Federal Food, Drug, and Cosmetic Act (FDCA) and the Public Health Service Act (PHSA), regulates the importation of pharmaceuticals for human and animal use. The USDA, pursuant to the Virus Serum Toxin Act (VSTA), licenses importers who ship veterinary biologic drugs. The EPA, under authority of the TSCA, imposes certain controls on the importation of toxic substances. The TSCA defines a toxic substance as any substance determined to present possibility of an unreasonable risk of injury to health and the environment. The FTC, CPSC, and DOT enforce regulations for transporting hazardous cargo. Materials are deemed hazardous if listed in DOT transport regulations (49 CFR 172 appendix). Pharmaceutical products consisting of vectors of human disease may be shipped only under permit issued by the CDC. This discussion is in no way exhaustive. If you are interested in importing pharmaceuticals, you should contact relevant federal agencies at the addresses below.

The intended use of a pharmaceutical determines whether an item is a drug. Foods and cosmetics may be subject to the drug provisions of the FDCA if therapeutic claims are made for them. To arrange for entry of a pharmaceutical preparation or component, you must determine which regulatory category applies to your product and make sure that all requirements for that category have been met. The general discussion of pharmaceutical regulation that follows is not exhaustive. You should be sure to contact FDA with your specific questions.

FDA Regulations. All drugs imported into the U.S. must comply with the FDCA requirements that apply to domestically produced pharmaceuticals. Manufacturing firms must be registered, and the drugs those firms produce must be listed with the FDA. The FDCA defines drugs as "articles intended for use in the diagnosis, cure, mitigation, treatment, or prevention of disease in man or other animals" and "articles (other than food) intended to affect the structure or any function of the body of man or other animals" (for example, articles intended for weight reduction). This definition encompasses homeopathic substances and biological derivatives.

Biological Products. A biological product is any virus, therapeutic serum, toxin, antitoxin, vaccine, blood, blood component or derivative, allergenic product, or analogous product applicable to the prevention, treatment, or cure of diseases or injuries of man. Biologics include such products as polio and measles vaccines, diphtheria and tetanus toxoids, skin test substances, whole blood, and blood components for transfusion. Samples of the licensed product must accompany each importation for forwarding by the port-of-entry Customs port director to the Director, National Center for Biologics Evaluation and Research (see addresses at end of this chapter).

Homeopathic Pharmaceuticals. The Homeopathic Pharmacopoeia of the United States (HP) is designated as the official compendium for homeopathic medicines. All medicines named in HP are required by law to meet the standards of strength, quality, or purity set forth therein, and to conform to all packaging and labeling requirements. If your medicine differs in strength, quality, or purity under or above the limits specified in HP, you should be sure that the nature and extent of that difference is plainly stated on the label.

Animal Pharmaceuticals. For importing purposes, the law makes several significant distinctions between products and pharmaceuticals intended for human use and those intended for animal use. For example, drugs for use in food-producing animals are evaluated for safety in products derived from those animals—meat, milk, and eggs—as well as safety and effectiveness for the animal. The FDCA requires approval of applications for use of new animal drugs in the manufacture of animal feed. Animal biological products are subject to the provisions of the VSTA administered by USDA's Veterinary Biologics staff (see addresses at end of this chapter).

To import viruses, serums, toxins and analogous products, and organisms and vectors for use in the treatment of domestic animals, you must hold a USDA import permit covering the specific product. These importations are subject to special labeling requirements. If you wish to import any etiological agent or insect, animal, or plant vector of human disease or any exotic living insect, animal, or plant capable of serving as a vector of human disease, you must first obtain a permit from the CDC (see addresses at end of this chapter).

Medical devices for animals, while subject to the same prohibitions against misbranding and adulteration as human medical devices, are not subject to premarket approval. FDCA regulates cosmetics for human use only. Similar products for animal use are termed "grooming aids" and are not subject to FDCA, provided no therapeutic claims are made.

Inspection. Imported products regulated by the FDA are subject to port-of-entry inspection. For a general discussion of required FDA import procedures, see "Appendix: Foods" on page 825.

Shipment Detention. If your shipment is found to be noncomplying, it may be detained at the port of entry. FDA may permit you to bring an illegal importation into compliance with the law before a final decision is made regarding admittance. However, any sorting, reprocessing, or relabeling must be supervised by an FDA investigator, and will be done at your expense. Conditional release of an illegal importation to allow an importer to bring it into compliance is not a right but a privilege. If you repeat noncomplying shipments of the same article, the FDA may interpret this as abuse of the privilege and may require you to destroy or reexport subsequent shipments.

Hazardous or Toxic Substances. Shipments of products containing chemicals must be in compliance with toxic and hazardous substance regulations of the EPA and DOT. These include packaging, shipping, marking, and labeling requirements. In addition, all products containing chemicals are subject to the U.S. Customs Service TSCA Import Certification Rule (19 CFR 12.118 et seq.). If you import these products, you must sign one of the following statements: "I certify that all chemical substances in this shipment comply with all applicable rules or orders under TSCA and that I am not offering a chemical substance for entry in violation of TSCA or any applicable rule or order thereunder" or "I certify that all chemicals in this shipment are not subject to TSCA."

You must file this TSCA certification of compliance or exemption at the time you make the entry at Customs. The certification may be in the form of a typed or stamped statement on an appropriate entry document or commercial invoice or a preprinted attachment to such entry document or invoice. You may sign the certificate by means of an authorized facsimile signature. If your entry is electronically processed, the certification will be in the form of a Certification Code, which is part of the Automated Broker Interface (ABI) transmission. Customs will not release your shipment without proper certification.

If you will be importing several or regular shipments, you should ask the appropriate Customs port director to authorize your use of a blanket certification. If you receive such authorization, you must include on the commercial invoice or entry document for each shipment a statement that the blanket certification is on file and that it is incorporated by reference. This statement need not be signed. The blanket certification is valid for one calendar year, is subject to renewal, and may be revoked at any time for cause.

In filling out TSCA forms and Customs entry documents, you should provide the Chemical Abstracts Service (CAS) number for each chemical in the shipment. These CAS numbers are given in the appendix to the HTSUS. You are not required to include the CAS number, but Customs will be able to process your shipment more quickly if you include this number.

Articles Exclusion. If you are importing items that are classified as hazardous substances but are part of articles, you are subject to TSCA certification requirements only if certification for your product is specifically required by a rule or order promulgated under the TSCA. No specific rules have been adopted at this time. An "article" is a manufactured item 1) that is formed into a specific shape or design during manufacture, 2) that has end-use functions dependent on the shape or design during end use, and 3) that during the end use, does not change in its chemical composition or that changes only for a noncommercial purpose separate from the article and only as allowed by law (19 CFR 12.120(2)). Fluids and particles are not articles, regardless of shape or design.

Shipment Detention. A shipment containing chemicals will be detained at the U.S. port of arrival (or entry if same), at your risk and expense, if: 1) it contains banned chemical substances (15 USC 2604, 2605); or 2) it contains chemical substances ordered seized because of imminent hazards (15 USC 2606). Further detention will occur at the port of entry, again at your risk and expense, if: 1) the EPA administrator or Customs port director has reasonable grounds to believe the shipment is not in compliance with the TSCA; or 2) you do not provide proper TSCA certification.

If your shipment is detained, it will be held by Customs for no more than 48 hours. It will then be turned over to the EPA administrator, unless you have arranged to release it in bond. You must either bring it into TSCA compliance or reexport it within the earlier of 90 days after notice of detention or 30 days of demand for redelivery. Customs may grant an extension if failure to comply or reexport is the result of delays in EPA or Customs procedures. If you fail to comply or reexport within the time allowed, the EPA administrator is authorized to have the shipment stored or disposed of at your expense.

Customs Classification

For customs purposes, pharmaceuticals are classified under Chapter 30 of the HTSUS. This chapter is broken into major headings, which are further divided into subheadings, and often sub-subheadings, each of which has its own HTSUS classification number. For example, the 2001 HTSUS number for cough drops is 3004.90.30, indicating it is a sub-subcategory of other medicants (3004.90), which is a subcategory of the major heading medicaments put up for retail (3004). There are six major headings within Chapter 30.

3001—Glands and other organs for organotherapeutic uses, dried, whether or not powdered; extracts of glands or other organs or of their secretions for organotherapeutic uses; heparin and its salts; other human or animal substances prepared for therapeutic or prophylactic uses, not elsewhere specified or included

3002—Human blood; animal blood prepared for therapeutic, prophylactic or diagnostic uses; anti-sera and other blood fractions and modified immunological products whether or not obtained by means of biotechnological processes; vaccines, toxins, cultures of micro-organisms (excluding yeasts), and similar products

3003—Medicaments (excluding goods of heading 3002, 3005, or 3006) consisting of two or more constituents which have been mixed together for therapeutic or prophylactic uses, not put up in measured doses or in forms or packings for retail sale

3004—Medicaments (excluding goods of heading 3002, 3005, or 3006) consisting of mixed or unmixed products for therapeutic or prophylactic uses, put up in measured doses or in forms or packings for retail sale

3005—Wadding, gauze, bandages, and similar articles (for example, dressings, adhesive plasters, poultices), impregnated or coated with pharmaceutical substances or put up in forms or packings for retail sale for medical, surgical, dental, or veterinary purposes

3006—Pharmaceutical goods specified in HTSUS note 4 to Chapter 30

For more details regarding classifications of the specific product you are interested in importing, consult a customs broker, the appropriate commodity specialist at your nearest customs port, or the HTSUS. The 2001 HTSUS is available online from the Customs Service (www.customs.gov/impoexpo/impoexpo.htm) or for purchase from the U.S. Government Printing Office (see resources at the end of this chapter), and may be found in larger public libraries. For a general discussion of customs classification, see "Classification—Liquidation" on page 229.

Dutiable Status of Goods

For more information about duty rates and binding decisions see "Dutiable Status of Goods" on page 203; for a discussion of temporary importation of goods see "Temporary Free Importations" on page 205.

Valuation

Importers have a responsibility to use what the U.S. Customs Service deems, "reasonable care," when determining the value of their goods. They must also provide any additional information that the Customs Service needs for setting a final value on the goods. This process involves a number of factors and can be somewhat complicated; importers must be aware of applicable issues and details. Valuation information applies to all types of commodities, for further discussion on the subject see "Customs Valuation" on page 267.

Import Duties

Import duties vary (often dramatically) depending upon the Harmonized Tariff Schedule (HTSUS) classification of the goods or products imported. Since some products that look alike have different HTSUS classifications and different rates of duty, proper classification is vital. Note that "differences of opinion" between importers and the Bureau of Customs and Border Protection regarding classification keeps customs attorneys very busy.

Import duties can be assessed on the imported value of the goods ("ad valorem" rates of duty such as 2%, 4.4%, 50%, etc.), total units or weight of the goods ("specific" rates of duty such as 2 cents each or 1.5 cents/pound, etc.) or on a combination basis ("compound" rates of duty such as 5 cents each plus 6%).

Listed below is a sampling of several Column 1 import duty rates for Chapter 30 products:

Glands and other organs, dried, whether or not powdered (3001.10.00): free

to

Gel preparations designed to be used in human or veterinary medicine as a lubricant for parts of the body for surgical operations or physical examinations or as a coupling agent between the body and medical instruments (3006.70.00.00): 5%

For specific information on US import duties refer to the Harmonized Tariff Schedule of the US. The print version is available from the US Government Printing Office as well as third party suppliers who often add special features. Online versions are available in both static PDF pages as well as in formats with excellent search functionality. Search the Web with the term "Harmonized Tariff Schedule" to find sources.

Entry and Documentation

The entry of merchandise is a two-part process consisting of 1) filing the documentation necessary to determine whether merchandise may be released from Customs custody, and 2) filing the documents that contain information for duty assessment and statistical purposes. In certain instances, all documents must be filed and accepted by Customs prior to release of the goods. Unless you have been granted an extension, you must file entry documents at a location specified by the port or area director within five working days of your shipment's date of arrival at a U.S. port of entry. These include a number of standard documents required by Customs for any entry, and:

- U.S. Customs TSCA Certification (hazardous substances) document
- USDA permit (veterinary biologics)
- CDC permit (agents or vectors of human disease) document

After you present the entry, Customs may examine your shipment or may waive examination. The shipment is then released provided no legal or regulatory violations have occurred. You must then file entry summary documentation and deposit estimated duties at a designated customhouse within 10 working days of your shipment's release. For a detailed description of entry procedures, standard documentation, and informal entry, see "Entry Process" on page 185.

Informed Compliance. Informed compliance was introduced with the Customs Modernization Act of 1993 (Mod Act) and defines the relationship between importers and the Customs Service. It sets out the responsibilities of both parties. Providing the correct documentation and information for entry is a key factor that will make your importing operation run smoothly. We recommend that importers become familiar with the concept of informed comliance and the responsibilities that they have under the Mod Act. For further discussion about informed compliance see "Informed Compliance" on page 211.

Note: The Entry and Documentation section has been carefully designed to supply you, the importer, with sample documents and directions on how to satisfy Customs requirements. Be aware that you should consult the applicable authorities to ensure that you are correctly following the most current procedures.

Prohibitions and Restrictions

FDCA prohibits the misbranding or adulteration of any drug and requires that "new drugs" be reviewed and approved by the FDA before they go on the market. A drug that has been used outside the U.S. and that may be regarded as safe and effective by experts in other countries, but that has not been marketed in the U.S., is likely to be regarded as a new drug under U.S. law. The Prescription Drug Marketing Act (PDMA) generally prohibits the reimportation of U.S.-made drugs by anyone other than the original manufacturer.

For purposes of regulation, drugs are divided into several major categories, each subject to particular requirements as follows:

New Drugs. This is the largest regulatory category of drugs. A drug may be categorized as new for many reasons. For example, a drug is new if: 1) it contains a newly developed chemical; 2) it contains a chemical or substance not previously used in medicine; 3) it has previously been used in medicine but not in the dosages or conditions for which the sponsor now recommends its use; or 4) as a result of investigational studies it has become recognized by qualified experts as safe and effective for its intended uses, but it has not otherwise been used to a material extent or for a material time.

A new drug may not be imported into, commercially marketed in, or exported from the U.S., unless it has been approved as safe and effective by the FDA. Such approval is based on a New Drug Application (NDA) (21 CFR 314) submitted to FDA by the sponsor of the drug (usually, but not always, its manufacturer). An NDA must contain acceptable scientific data, results of specific tests to evaluate safety, and substantial evidence of effectiveness for the conditions for which the drug is to be offered.

Once a drug is approved, its formula, manufacturing process, labeling, packaging, dosage, methods of testing, etc., generally may not be changed from those stated in its approved NDA. Supplemental application may be filed by sponsors wishing to make such change. A change may be made only with FDA approval (21 CFR 314). However, changes to increase assurance of safety and effectiveness should be put into effect at the earliest possible time, without waiting for approval. Detailed instructions are given in the regulations. Antibiotics are treated as new drugs and must have the equivalent of an approved NDA before being offered on the U.S. market.

Drugs that are not "new" are not subject to the new drug procedure, but must comply with all other drug requirements, including registration, labeling, and manufacturing practices. Obviously, you should ascertain the status of any drug you intend to import, and be sure that the product complies with applicable regulation. For further information regarding NDAs, contact the FDA (see addresses at end of this chapter).

Investigational Drugs. These are new drugs intended solely for investigational use by qualified scientific experts. If your import falls into this category, you may bring it into the U.S. and distribute it without an approved NDA. However, the drug and the plans for research must comply with FDA's Investigational New Drug (IND) regulations (21 CFR 312). Investigational drugs may not be distributed or imported for trial on humans unless the sponsor has filed a Notice of Claimed Investigational Exemption for a New Drug and has received FDA approval. Information on regulations covering INDs and application forms should be requested from CDER Executive Secretariat (HFD-8), Center for Drug Evaluation and Research, 5600 Fishers Lane, Rockville, MD 20857.

Insulin. Section 506 requires FDA batch-testing and certification for both insulin crystal and finished dosage forms. An NDA for the product must be approved before FDA will accept samples for certification. FDA tests samples for conformance to standards published in the insulin regulations, and charges testing fees to defray costs of the insulin certification program.

Biological Products. Since most biological products are derived from living organisms, they are by their nature potentially dangerous if improperly prepared or tested. FDA's Center for Biologics Evaluation and Research (CBER) monitors biologics production closely, does batch testing, and conducts research toward improving the quality of biologics. CBER's research provides standards for these products, as well as proper control procedures.

In addition to the traditional biological products described in the Public Health Service Act, the Federal Food, Drug, and Cosmetic Act gives CBER jurisdiction over selected medical devices and drug products. The devices are primarily articles used in blood banks or plasmapheresis centers, such as containers for collect-

ing and processing blood components, blood storage refrigeration, and blood bank supplies.

Licensing. Under PHSA, a manufacturer wishing to ship a biological product for sale in U.S. commerce or for import or export must obtain a U.S. license for both the manufacturing establishment and the product intended for shipment. These licenses are granted if the manufacturer shows that the establishment and product meet specific standards that insure continued safety, purity, potency, and effectiveness (21 CFR 600-680,211). To apply for licensing, the manufacturer must submit protocols detailing affirmative proof that the manufactured product meets PHSA standards. The manufacturer must pass a prelicensing inspection by FDA inspectors. Once licensed, most establishments are inspected annually by FDA.

Lot-release Procedures: Samples and Protocols. Certain licensed products are subject to special pre-release procedures. The manufacturer must submit specified materials to the CBER for clearance. These materials include: 1) a sample of the product in the size specified in the regulations; 2) detailed records (protocols) of the manufacture of each lot; and 3) all results of each test required by CBER for that particular product. CBER reviews the protocols and may conduct its own safety, purity, and potency tests on the samples before issuing a release for that product lot. A product subject to these lot-release procedures cannot be issued by the manufacturer until notification of official release is received from the FDA.

Standard Preparations. CBER supplies standard reference preparations for potency tests of certain licensed products, including antitoxins, bacterial and viral vaccines, and skin tests. Manufacturers are required to obtain and use these preparations in their testing of licensed products.

Blood Banks. Interstate shipment of blood and blood components requires the issuance of U.S. product and establishment licenses in accordance with PHSA. A licensed blood bank must comply with appropriate federal standards in preparing and testing the products being shipped. In accordance with FDA regulations (21 CFR 607), every blood bank collecting units of blood must register with the FDA within five days after commencing operations and submit a list of blood products prepared. All blood banks must operate in compliance with FDA current Good Manufacturing Practice Regulations for Blood and Blood Components (21 CFR 606), and are by law subject to FDA inspection every two years.

Blood bank establishment registration and product listing must be submitted on Form FD 2830. Only those blood banks that have complied with the necessary establishment registration and product listing and also hold valid U.S. establishment and product licenses may ship blood or blood components in U.S. interstate commerce.

Investigational New Drugs (INDs). The requirements for filing an IND application for a biological product are essentially the same as for drugs, except that it should be sent to the Director, Office of Biological Product Review (see addresses at end of this chapter).

Veterinary Biologics (USDA-regulated). Biologics intended for use with animals are subject to licensing provisions of the VSTA enforced by the USDA Animal and Plant Health Inspection Service's (APHIS) Veterinary Biologics Staff. Technically, biologics are also drugs under FDCA, but are not subject to the new animal drug provisions of the Act when in full compliance with the VSTA.

You must have a USDA permit for each shipment and each separate product of any veterinary biologic you wish to import. Only persons residing in the U.S., or operating a business establishment in the U.S., who hold a valid USDA Veterinary Services (VS) permit, may import a veterinary biologic. USDA VS issues three types of permits for import of biological products: Permit for Research and Evaluation; Permit for Distribution and Sale; Permit for Transit Shipment Only. Each type of permit has its own general requirements and conditions, to which specific conditions may be added for any given shipment at the discretion of the USDA Biologics Staff.

The USDA will not issue permits for products originating from any country known to have exotic diseases of livestock, if such products may endanger U.S. livestock or poultry. For a complete listing of countries listed by USDA as having such diseases, refer to Chapter 2 and Chapter 1. USDA inspection of producer and applicant equipment and facilities is a prerequisite to permit approval. Permits will not be issued for biologic products prepared in the U.S., exported, and presented for re-entry, except in cases where a small quantity of product is required for in vitro research and evaluation. In these cases, your product will be admitted only if USDA has determined that it poses no threat to U.S. livestock or poultry.

If you wish to import a veterinary biological product, you should contact Veterinary Services (see addresses at end of this chapter) for application forms. Your application should specify the type of permit you need, the intended port of entry, the estimated quantity of product, and the anticipated date of your importation. In addition, certain specific requirements apply, depending upon the type of permit requested.

Permit for Research and Evaluation. On your application for this type of permit, VS requires a brief description of your product, methods of propagating antigens (including composition of the medium), species of animals or cell cultures involved, degree of inactivation or attenuation, recommendations for use, and the proposed plan of evaluation in addition to general permit application information. The USDA may also ask you to supply information necessary to assess your product's impact on the environment. Special restrictions or tests may be specified as part of the permit when deemed necessary or advisable by USDA. The product under permit must comply with all applicable provisions of the law, and must be packaged and labeled in accordance with 9 CFR 112.

Permit for Distribution and Sale. In addition to general information required on the permit application, you must provide the USDA with supporting materials necessary to satisfy the following requirements: 1) The product must be prepared in such a way as to insure its purity, safety, potency, and effectiveness. Three copies of blueprints of the producing foreign establishment must accompany the application, unless satisfactory plans are already on file with Veterinary Services. Production facilities to be used for each product prepared at the establishment must be designated. The manufacturer must submit written authorization for USDA inspectors to inspect the premises without previous notification. You must provide written assurance that the product under permit will be prepared under supervision of a person with requisite education and experience and in accordance with any applicable regulation. Methods of production must be written into an approved Outline of Production, four copies of which must be submitted to USDA and approved before the permit will be issued. You will also have to furnish data that establishes that the product complies with the law. In some cases, VS may require product testing under field conditions before issuing a permit.

As a permit holder, you will be required to provide the following: 1) adequate facilities for storing biologics; 2) information regarding all claims to be made on labels and advertising matter relating to the product; 3) mounted copies of final container and carton labels and enclosures to be used with the product; and 4) samples of each serial from each shipment of biological product. The product being sampled may not be distributed until released by Veterinary Services.

Permit for Transit Shipment Only. This type of permit is only required when a biological product is being shipped from one foreign country to another by way of the U.S. Such a shipment may only move under permit, subject to the following restrictions: 1)

When the shipment is to transit the U.S. on the same carrier on which it arrived, it must be confined to that carrier at all times. If it is to transit the U.S. on a carrier other than that on which it arrived, a schedule of arrival and departure of each shipment must be furnished by the permit holder to Veterinary Services prior to arrival in the U.S. 2) The permit holder is responsible to VS for handling, storing, and forwarding of the biological product. VS must be notified of all shipments received and forwarded by the permit holder, and an accurate accounting must be made.

Illegal Shipments. If you present veterinary biologics for importation without a permit, your products will be returned to the country of origin at your own expense, or else destroyed by USDA personnel. If you present biological products for importation under permit for distribution and sale, and they are found to be worthless, contaminated, dangerous, or harmful, either you will have to return them to the country of origin at your own expense, or they will be destroyed by USDA personnel. This remedial action must be accomplished within 30 days after such finding. If your product is returned to the country of origin, it must not bear a U.S. permit number on the label. For more information, or to request permit application, contact APHIS VS (see addresses at end of this chapter).

APHIS VS Permits for Controlled Material, Organisms, and Vectors. The USDA APHIS's VS regulates the importation of all animal-origin materials that could represent a disease risk to U.S. livestock. This includes not only animal products and byproducts, but also biological materials that contain or have been in contact with animal material (including all cell cultures). You should submit your request for USDA APHIS VS permit authorizing the importation of such controlled materials on a completed VS Form 16-3. Cell cultures and their products need a VS Form 16-7 in addition. You may obtain forms from the Veterinary Services Import-Export office (see addresses at end of this chapter) or from any USDA port office.

When applying for an import permit, you should include as much background information on the material as you feel might be necessary for the VS to evaluate the disease risk. You may include research papers if you think they will be helpful in the evaluation process, but don't send them by fax.

For shipments of cell lines, including human cell lines and cell culture deriviates such as monoclonal antibodies, you should complete both the basic permit application and the supplemental Form 16-7. This form requests such information as cell line history, country of origin, and source of nutrient supplement used in the media. If you do not provide the information in full, APHIS will not issue you a permit.

It takes about two weeks for APHIS to process the application and have a permit ready for return mail. If the information on your application is incomplete, there will be a delay while VS contacts you for the missing information. You can make your application on a signed facsimile, as long as you send an original signed document as a follow-up. If you will need more than one application form, you are free to make copies. Once your permit is issued, you are responsible to comply with all of its stipulations. For more information, or to request a permit application, contact APHIS VS (see addresses at end of this chapter).

CDC Permit Requirements. An original signed copy of the Centers for Disease Control Application for Permit to Import or Transport Agents or Vectors of Human Disease must be completed and submitted to CDC's Office of Biosafety (see addresses at end of this chapter). The person signing the permit application must reside in the U.S. and must be the proposed permit holder. The application requires such information as: 1) person requesting permit; 2) source and description of material; 3) number of shipments; 4) method of transport; 5) quantity, i.e. volume and type of individual containers; 6) proposed use, including objectives, proposed plan of work, completion date, and final disposition of materials; 7) description of available isolation and containment facilities; and 8) qualifications and experience of technical personnel. Your approved permit may stipulate additional restrictions and precautions that you must strictly adhere to. There are specific packaging and labeling requirements for etiologic agents and biomedical materials specified in 42 CFR Part 72. (See "Marking and Labeling Requirements" and "Shipping Considerations" below.)

Dispensing Requirements. Prescription drugs may be dispensed only by or on the prescription of a licensed practitioner, such as a physician, dentist, or veterinarian. They must be labeled: "Caution: Federal law prohibits dispensing without prescription." In general, a drug is restricted to the prescription class if it is not safe for use except under professional supervision. Under the law, this includes habit-forming drugs and any drug that is unsafe because of its toxicity or other potential for harmful effect, or the method of its use, or the collateral measures necessary to its use. Most prescription drugs are new drugs under the FDCA.

You may legally ship prescription drugs only to persons and firms who are regularly and lawfully engaged in the wholesale or retail distribution of prescription drugs, and to hospitals, clinics, physicians, and others licensed to prescribe such drugs.

Nonprescription drugs are those generally regarded as safe for the consumer to use when following the required label directions and warnings. These are commonly called "over-the-counter" (OTC) drugs because they may be purchased without a prescription. Nonprescription OTC drugs must comply with the requirements of the Fair Packaging and Labeling Act (FPLA) (21 CFR 201).

Registration Requirements. Owners or operators of all establishments that manufacture or process drugs and devices in the U.S. must register their establishments and list their products with the FDA. All drugs marketed within the U.S., including imported drugs, must be listed with the FDA. Establishments required to register include facilities to repackage or otherwise change the container, wrapper, or labeling of any drug or device package for distribution from the original place of manufacture to the person who makes final delivery or sale to the ultimate consumer. The law applies to both bulk and finished-dosage-form drugs, finished devices, products exported to the U.S. by foreign firms, and products exported by domestic firms.

Foreign establishments offering drugs or devices for import into the U.S. must comply with the listing requirements. Bulk drug substances being brought in by a domestic firm, even when imported from a foreign subsidiary, must also be listed. Drug and device distributors not required to register their establishments may submit listing information directly to FDA for products they distribute under their own label or trade name.

All registration and product listing submissions must be in English, except for labeling in a foreign language, which should be the actual labeling on the product and accompanied by an English translation.

Establishment registration must be updated annually. Product listing submissions must be updated each June and December if certain material changes have occurred. Changes requiring updated listings include: 1) newly introduced drugs; 2) discontinued drugs; 3) changes in information previously submitted (i.e. change in product name, quantity or identity of active ingredients, etc.); or 4) significant change in labeling.

No registration or listing fees are required. Failure to register and list is a violation of the FDCA.

The National Drug Code (NDC) provides index numbers to specifically identify drug products. The labeler code portion of the number is assigned by the FDA, and product and package portions are assigned by the vendor. The NDC number may be printed on the label, but such printing is not required at the present time.

Wholesale Drug Distributors. FDCA requires wholesale drug distributors to be licensed by the state where they do business. State licensing laws must meet minimum federally prescribed standards, including requirements for storage, handling, and recordkeeping. Wholesale drug distributors who are not authorized distributors-of-record for a particular drug are required to provide wholesale purchasers with a statement identifying each prior sale.

Reporting Requirements. The FDCA requires drug sponsors to keep the FDA apprised of developments that may affect the safety and effectiveness of their products. This applies both to drugs under clinical study and those that have received FDA approval for marketing. 21 CFR 310, 312, 314, 343 and 431 detail required records and reports. The most significant of these are **adverse reaction reports**. These notify the FDA of "any adverse experience associated with the use of a drug, whether or not considered drug-related, and includes any side effect, injury, toxicity, or sensitivity reaction, or significant failure of expected pharmacological action." Such reports originate largely as voluntary communications from physicians, pharmacists, or other health professionals to the manufacturer. The drug firm must transmit such information to FDA within 15 working days from its receipt, or in the periodic reports required on approved new drugs. Forms, instructions, and additional information regarding reporting may be obtained from FDA's Division of Epidemiology and Surveillance (see addresses at end of this chapter).

Sales Restrictions. The FDCA prohibits selling, purchasing, or trading of drug samples and drug coupons. Resale of drugs purchased by hospitals or health care entities is prohibited, with exceptions for group purchasing organizations, nonprofit affiliates, and entities under common control.

Drug Samples. Manufacturers or distributors are permitted to distribute samples to a licensed practitioner or health care entity by common carrier or through marketing representatives, upon written request. Certain drug sample records must be maintained and made available to government officials on request. Manufacturers and distributors must maintain their products in a manner that will prevent contamination, deterioration, or adulteration of their samples; they must provide the FDA with the name and phone number of an employee or agent in charge of drug samples; and they must maintain lists of representatives and drug sample storage sites. Manufacturers and distributors must notify the FDA of losses, thefts, and in the event that representatives are convicted for illegal trafficking in drug samples.

Drug Manufacturing Controls. The FDCA requires that drug manufacturers operate in conformity with current Good Manufacturing Practice regulations (21 CFR 210, 211). These include adequately equipped manufacturing facilities, adequately trained personnel, stringent controls over the manufacturing processes, reliable and secure computerized operations, and appropriate finished product examination and testing. Each manufacturing plant must have a quality assurance unit or person with responsibility and authority to accept or reject all drugs and raw materials. The FDA also publishes guidelines for acceptable methods and procedures for compliance. For more information, contact the FDA's Center for Biologics Evaluation and Research (see addresses at end of this chapter).

Sanitary Safeguards. A drug must not consist in whole or in part of any filthy, putrid, or decomposed substance. A drug must not be prepared, packed, or held under insanitary conditions whereby it may be contaminated with filth, or whereby it may be rendered injurious to health.

Containers. Drug containers must not be composed, in whole or in part, of any poisonous or deleterious substance that may render the contents injurious to health. They must not be made, formed, or filled so as to be misleading as to content amount. Containers and their components, such as caps, cap liners, etc.

must not be reactive, additive, or absorptive so as to alter the safety, identity, strength, quality, or purity of the contents beyond official or established requirements. They must provide adequate protection against external factors that can cause deterioration or contamination of the product (21 CFR 211).

Tamper-resistant packaging is required for certain drugs, cosmetics, and medical devices sold through retail outlets. Tamper-resistant packaging is defined as packaging in such a manner that any product tampering will be visibly evident to the consumer-purchaser. Oral OTC drug products (except dentifrices, dermatologics, and insulin); nasal, optic, ophthalmic, rectal, and vaginal drugs; cosmetics used orally, such as mouth washes, gargles, breath fresheners, etc.; and vaginal cosmetics all requires this type of packaging. Address questions regarding compliance of a particular package to the FDA's Division of Manufacturing and Product Quality. Contact FDA headquarters for address.

Imitations. A drug must not imitate another drug or be offered for sale under the name of another drug. A drug or its container or labeling must not bear the trademark, tradename, or other identifying mark, imprint, device, or any likeness thereof, of another drug manufacturer, processor, packer, or distributor.

Germicides and Antiseptics. A product represented as a germicide should be capable, in the dilutions mentioned in its labeling, of meeting the criteria and standards set in official references for killing microorganisms. A product represented as an antiseptic should be germicidal when used as its labeling directs. However, if the recommended conditions of use provide for prolonged contact with the body (wet dressing, ointment, dusting powder, etc.), capability of inhibiting bacterial growth is sufficient.

Official Drugs. The law designates the United States Pharmacopoeia (USP), the Homeopathic Pharmacopoeia of the United States (HP), and the National Formulary (NF) as official compendia. All drugs named therein are required by law to meet the standards of strength, quality, or purity set forth in such compendia. They must be packaged and labeled in the manner prescribed therein. If a drug differs in strength, quality, or purity under or above the limits specified in an official compendium, the nature and extent of that difference must be plainly stated on the label.

A drug not recognized in an official compendium is adulterated if its strength differs from, or its purity or quality falls below, that which it purports to have or is represented to posses. For example, any drug intended for use by injection, and any ophthalmic ointment or solution, must be sterile.

A drug is adulterated under the law if any substance has been mixed or packed therewith so as to reduce the quality or strength of the article or to constitute a substitute. For example, the addition of exhausted belladonna leaves to unexhausted leaves not only reduces quality and strength, but also constitutes substitution.

Danger to Health. A drug must not be dangerous to health when used in the dosage or with the frequency or duration prescribed, recommended, or suggested in its labeling.

Drugs of Abuse. There are severe criminal penalties for the distribution of anabolic steroids and human growth hormones without a doctor's prescription. Butylnitrate and its isomers are banned from sale except for commercial purposes that may not result in its misuse for euphoric effects, and uses approved by the FDA. At this time, there are no FDA-approved uses for this drug.

Animal Dosage-Form Drugs. Veterinary drugs are divided into the same major classes as other drugs, each being subject to additional requirements.

Animal prescription drugs may be dispensed only by a licensed veterinarian, or on the prescription or other order of a licensed veterinarian. In general, a drug is restricted to the prescription class if it is only safe for use under professional supervision (21 CFR 201). The label must state: "Caution: Federal law restricts this drug to use by or on the order of a licensed veterinarian."

Animal nonprescription drugs are those for which adequate directions for safe and effective lay use can be written.

New Animal Drugs (NADs) are drugs not generally recognized as safe and effective for use in the animal species for which they are intended (21 CFR. 201). You may not import an NAD for commercial marketing unless it has been FDA-approved as safe and effective for use in the United States. To request approval, you should file a New Animal Drug Application with FDA's Center for Veterinary Medicine (see addresses at end of this chapter). Form FDA 356V must contain substantial evidence supporting the drug's effectiveness, including results of adequate tests to establish safety (21 CFR Sec. 512). The data you provide must be specific for each species of animal for which your drug is intended. For food-producing animals, the data must include evidence of safety from residues of both the drug and its metabolites. This includes acceptable methods for recovery, and measurement of such residues from edible tissues of any food-producing animal for which the drug is intended. The FDA may approve an NAD or metabolites thereof found to induce cancer, if no harm comes to the animal and if there is no residue of drug or metabolites in any edible product reaching the consumer. Such a drug, however, may not be approved for pets. You must also submit technical data regarding manufacturing methods and controls, and the environmental impact of the manufacture and use of the drug.

Investigational New Animal Drugs (INADs) may only be distributed for investigational use by qualified scientific experts, for a particular purpose (21 CFR Sec. 512). If you fit this category, you may import an INAD for distribution in the U.S. without an approved New Animal Drug Application. However, your INAD and plans for research must comply with the INAD regulations (21 CFR 511). Before shipping an INAD for clinical tests in animals, you must submit a Notice of Claimed Investigational Exemption for New Animal Drug to the Center for Veterinary Medicine (see addresses at end of this chapter) (21 CFR 511).

Antibiotic Drugs. The law provides for FDA testing and certification of each batch of animal drugs composed in whole or in part of any kind of penicillin, streptomycin, chlortetracycline, chloramphenicol, or bacitracin, or any derivative thereof except where exempted by regulation. These antibiotic drugs for animal use are also NAD's under the law (Sec. 201) The regulations now exempt all antibiotic drugs from the requirements of batch certification, though not from meeting specified quality characteristics.

Pesticidal Drugs. Animal products that are pesticidal preparations such as rodenticides, fungicides, and insecticides, are subject to the Federal Insecticide, Fungicide, and Rodenticide Act (FIFRA) administered by the Pesticide Registration Division of the Environmental Protection Agency (EPA) (see addresses at end of this chapter). Depending upon the claims made, such products may be subject both to FIFRA and the FDCA. A Memorandum of Understanding between the two agencies specifies which agency will process petitions for products under dual jurisdiction. Petitions may be submitted to either agency and will be referred if necessary.

Medicated Feeds. If you are importing medicated feeds and medicated feed premixes (Type A articles), you should be sure that they are manufactured, processed, packaged, or held under methods, facilities, and controls that conform to the requirements of FDA Good Manufacturing Practice Regulations (21 CFR 225-6). In order to import NADs for commercial distribution, you must submit a Medicated Feed Mill License Application, unless you have been granted a waiver by the regulations (21 CFR 558). You should submit Form FDA-3448 to the Center for Veterinary Medicine (see addresses at end of this chapter).

The information you submit with the application must include the NAD approval regulation on which you base your expectation of FDA's approval.

Animal Grooming Aids. Products intended for cleansing or promoting attractiveness of animals are not subject to FDA control. However, if you represent your products as having any therapeutic purpose or as containing an active drug ingredient, they are subject to FDCA as animal drugs or possibly as animal devices. In this case, you must comply with any applicable part of the regulation.

Animal Devices. Veterinary medical devices and diagnostic aids are subject to general FDCA misbranding and adulteration provisions (21 CFR Secs. 501 and 502). Though FDA approval of devices intended for animal use is not required, you should be sure that your device's labeling is not false or misleading in any particular, and that the device is not otherwise misbranded or adulterated. If your device is dangerous to animal health when used in the manner prescribed, recommended, or suggested in its labeling, it is a prohibited import.

Animal prescription devices may be dispensed only by a licensed veterinarian or on the prescription or other order of a licensed veterinarian. In general, a device is restricted to the prescription class if it is not safe for use except under professional supervision (21 CFR 801). The label must state: "Caution: Federal law restricts this device to sale by or on the order of a veterinarian."

Animal Drug Registration and Listing. The FDCA requires all U.S. manufacturers of animal drugs and certain medicated feeds to register annually. This includes manufacturers of 1) dosage form drugs; 2) type A medicated articles (premixes); 3) medicated feeds that require approved **Form FDA-1900.** Foreign manufacturers are permitted to register (21 CFR Sec. 510). All registered establishments, except medicated feed manufacturers, must file a listing of all drugs manufactured, prepared, propagated, compounded, or processed for commercial distribution. Dosage-form drugs and medicated feed premixes must be listed. Foreign products imported into the U.S. must be listed. Listing is not required for medicated feeds.

You may obtain additional information concerning registration and status of animal products under FDCA from FDA's Division of Compliance, Center for Veterinary Medicine (see addresses at end of this chapter). When making inquiries, you should provide full information concerning the product identity, including, insofar as possible, a quantitative formula and a draft label.

Marking and Labeling Requirements

How your drug must be labeled is determined by its regulatory category; i.e., whether it is an investigational drug, a new drug, a prescription-only drug, or an OTC drug. The law defines "label" to mean the written, printed, or graphic matter on the immediate container. Any information required in the label must also appear on the outer carton or wrapper of the package. "Labeling" includes all labels and other written, printed, or graphic matter accompanying the product. The word "accompanying" is interpreted very broadly, so that "labeling" may include material that does not physically accompany the product if it serves to identify the article, tell its uses, give directions, etc.

The following discussion is an overview of drug labeling requirements. You should contact FDA for specific details pertinent to the product you wish to import. For a general discussion of U.S. Customs marking and labeling requirements, see "Country of Origin Marking" on page 236, "Special Marking Requirements" on page 238 and "Marking—False Impression" on page 239.

Chemical Products. A shipment of any products containing chemicals that are classified as hazardous substance (49 CFR 172) must comply with the marking and labeling regulations adopted by the EPA (46 CFR 147.30) and the DOT (49 CFR 171 et seq.).

All Drugs. All labeling information required by the FDCA must be in English and must appear conspicuously on the label and in the labeling so that such information will be read and understood by the ordinary individual under customary conditions of purchase and use. Labeling information may also be given in a foreign language, but if any statement is made in a foreign language, all of the labeling information required by FDCA must appear in the foreign language as well as in English.

The label must bear: 1) name and address of manufacturer, packer, or distributor; 2) accurate statement of dosage strength; 3) quantity of contents in terms of weight, measure, or numerical count (prescription drugs may show quantity either in "English" or metric units. OTC drugs must show quantity in the "English" system of measure, but may also have a separate metric declaration); 4) list of active ingredients, using the established name for each such active ingredient; 5) an expiration date (applies to all prescription drugs and most OTC drugs); 6) name and quantity or proportions of any habit-forming substance or derivative, with the statement "Warning—May be habit-forming"; 7) established name and quantity or proportion of the following, if present (or if any derivative or preparation of such is present) in the drug: alcohol, bromides, ether, chloroform, acetanilide, acetophenetidin, amidopyrine, antipyrine atropine, hyoscine, hyoscyamine, arsenic, digitalis, digitalis glucosides, mercury, ouabain, strophanthin, strychnine, or thyroid; 8) If the drug has an established name, it must be displayed with the trade name. For prescription drugs, the established name must appear in type that is at least half as large as the type used for the trade name.

Prescription Drugs. The label must bear: 1) the legend "Caution: Federal law prohibits dispensing without prescription"; 2) quantity or portion of each active ingredient, and, if the drug is intended for any use other than oral, the names of all other ingredients; 3) if the drug is intended for injection, the label must state the names and quantities of all ingredients; 4) a statement of recommended or usual dosage; 5) package labeling (such as booklet or circular) should ordinarily contain information in substantially the following format and order and with section headings as follows: Descriptions, Actions, Indications, Warnings, Precautions, Adverse Reactions, Dosage and Administration, Overdosage (where applicable), and How Supplied.

OTC Drugs. The principal display panel must bear: 1) an identity statement followed by general pharmacological category or principal intended actions, and 2) quantity of contents declaration. The requirements for the latter are the same as those for foods except that in the case of a drug that is in tablet, capsule, ampule or other unit form, the quantity must be expressed in terms of numerical count, augmented, when necessary, with the strength, e.g. "100 tablets, 5 grains each."

Outer Wrapper or Carton. If the immediate container has an outer wrapper or carton, it must also bear all required label information, unless such wording is legible through the outer wrapper or carton.

Adequate Directions for Use. The package labeling must bear adequate directions for use. Omission (in whole or in part) of the following information on products distributed to the public, constitute inadequate directions. 1) Statements of all conditions, purposes, or uses for which the drug is intended, including conditions, purposes, or uses for which it is prescribed, recommended, or suggested in its oral, written, printed, or graphic advertising and conditions, purposes, or uses for which the drug is commonly used. Such statements shall not refer to conditions, uses, or purposes for which the drug can be safely used only under the supervision of a practitioner licensed by law and for which it is advertised solely to such practitioners; 2) quantity of dose, including usual quantities for each of the uses for which it is intended and usual quantities for persons of different ages and different physical conditions; 3) frequency, duration, route or method, and time (in relation to time of meals, time of onset of symptoms, or other time factors) of administration or application; 4) preparation for use (shaking, dilution, adjustment of temperature, or other manipulation or process).

Adequate Warnings. The package labeling must bear adequate warnings, when necessary, for the protection of users. Label warnings may be needed because of the nature of the ingredients. For example, antacids are required to be labeled with specific warnings, depending upon product composition. For example: "GENERAL WARNING--Do not take more than maximum recommended daily dosage"; for aluminum-containing antacids: "Drug interaction precaution—do not take this product if you are taking a prescription antibiotic drug containing any form of tetracycline."

A warning may be needed because of the nature of the intended use. For example, one type of cough syrup should bear a warning such as: "WARNING—Keep out of the reach of children. Do not administer to children under 2 years of age unless directed by physician. Persistent cough may indicate the presence of a serious condition. Persons with a high fever or persistent cough should not use this preparation unless directed by physician."

False and Misleading Statements. Labeling must not contain any statement that is false or misleading in any particular. A drug should be recommended for use only for those conditions for which it has been shown by scientific tests to be effective treatment. Serious disease conditions that cannot be diagnosed or successfully treated by consumers should not be referred to in labeling of OTC drugs. User testimonials that imply that a preparation is effective for a certain condition for which it is in fact ineffective or has not been demonstrated to be effective, constitutes misbranding.

Biologics for Human Use. The Public Health Service Act specifies that biologics be plainly labeled with the proper name of the article, the name, address, and license number of the manufacturer, and the appropriate expiration date of the product. The Center for Biologics Evaluation and Research reviews and approves all labeling for biologics prior to their licensing. In addition, all important changes in approved labeling must be submitted for approval. For prescription biological drugs, the manufacturer must also comply with FDA regulations pertaining to the package insert (21 CFR 201).

Biologics for Animal Use. The USDA requires each separate container in a shipment of biologics for animal use to bear the true name of the product, the permit number assigned by the USDA, the serial number affixed by the manufacturer to identify the product with the records of its preparation, and the return date of the product.

CDC-regulated Biomedical Materials. Any etiologic agent regulated by the Centers for Disease Control must be labeled precisely as illustrated and described in 42 CFR 72.

Shipping Considerations

You will need to ensure that your goods are packaged and shipped with care so that they pass smoothly through Customs and arrive in good condition. You are responsible for ensuring that the shipment is in compliance with all applicable government regulations for packaging and shipping. In most instances, you should not leave these arrangements solely to the discretion of your supplier. Careful preparation of the cargo and selection of the mode of transport can be essential to a cost-effective, timely delivery of undamaged goods. We strongly advise you to consult your shipping representative, insurance agent, or freight broker for advice on packing and shipping.

Pharmaceutical products may be shipped in bulk, bags, bottles, or other types of containers, depending on the type of product and whether it is prepackaged. General considerations include protection from contamination, weather, and pests. If a product must be kept in a sanitary environment, all tables, utensils, platforms, and devices used for moving or handling the product, the compartments in which it is stowed while being transported will need to be maintained in a sanitary condition. For liquid shipments, venting and vapor collection systems may be required. Safety precautions should also be implemented as required to protect against breakage, spillage, corrosion of containers, and combustion. Containers should be constructed so as to be safe for handling during transport.

Chemical Products. Chemical products in particular may have to be shipped in pressurized, ventilated, and temperature-and vapor-controlled enclosures. Solid chemical products that are listed as hazardous substances (49 CFR 172 appendix) may be transported in bulk only on compliance with Coast Guard notification procedures, shipping permit requirements, and complex transportation regulations (46 CFR 148). All hazardous substances must also be packaged and transported in accordance with DOT regulations (49 CFR 171 et seq.).

CDC-regulated Etiologic and Biologic Agents. If you are importing diagnostic specimens and biological products that may contain an etiologic agent you should see that they are packaged to withstand leakage of contents, shocks, pressure changes, and other conditions incident to ordinary handling in transportation. 45 CFR 72 lists specific bacterial and fungal agents and details minimum packaging requirements for these substances. Your biological materials must be placed in a securely closed, watertight container (primary container) such as test tube or vial. You should then enclose this primary container in a second, durable watertight container (secondary container). You may enclose more than one primary container in the secondary container. The space surrounding the primary container must be filled with enough absorbent material to absorb its entire contents in case of breakage or leakage. Paper towel will suffice. You should enclose the secondary container in an outer shipping container constructed of corrugated fiberboard, cardboard, wood, or other material of equivalent strength.

When the volume of the substance to be transported exceeds 50 ml., a shock-absorbent material in volume at least equal to that of the absorbent material between the primary and secondary containers must surround the secondary container, filling the space between it and the outer shipping container. The maximum amount of etiologic agent enclosed within a single outer shipping container must not exceed 4,000 ml. If you use dry ice as a refrigerant, you must place it outside the secondary container(s). In such cases, the shock absorbent material between secondary and outer containers must be placed so that the secondary container does not become loose inside the outer shipping container as the dry ice sublimates.

Certain etiologic agents may only be shipped by registered mail or by an equivalent system that requires or provides for sending notification of receipt to the sender immediately upon delivery. In such cases, if notice of delivery is not received by the sender within 5 days following anticipated delivery, CDC must be notified.

Publications and WWW Resources

The following publication explains the FDA requirements for importing pharmaceuticals. It is published by the FDA and is available online from the FDA website (www.fda.gov/opacom/7pubs.html).

> *Requirements of Laws and Regulations Enforced by the U.S. Food and Drug Administration*

The following publications may be relevant to the importation of toxic or hazardous pharmaceutical substances:

> *Toxic Substances Control Act: A Guide for Chemical Importers/ Exporters* (published by EPA)

This document is available from the TSCA Assistance Information Service (see Relevant Government Agencies)

The following publication provides a listing of existing chemical substances in the United States. It can be purchased in electronic format or a search of the document can be requested via telephone. Contact the Chemical Abstract Service (CAS) at (800)631-1884 or at (614) 447-3600 ext 2308.

TSCA Chemical Substance Inventory

In order to check whether or not a chemical is subject to any rules or regulations under Sections 5, 6, or 7 of TSCA, search the following document (www.epa.gov/opptintr/CORR)

Chemical on Reporting Rules List (CORR)

The *Harmonized Tariff Schedule of the United States (2001)* (HTSUS) is available to view on the Customs Service website (www.customs.gov), or you may purchase a printed version from:

U.S. Government Printing Office
Superintendent of Documents
710 North Capital Street NW
Washington DC 20401
Tel: (202) 512-1800
Fax: (202) 512-1657
Website: www.access.gpo.gov

The USGPO also has copies of specific laws available for purchase. The USGPO accepts orders made by fax, phone or placed over the Internet, as well as mail orders paid by credit card. All orders must be accompanied by payment. Credit cards, checks drawn on a U.S. bank, or an international money order are all acceptable.

Relevant Government Agencies

Note: It is not a simple matter to import biological products and vectors. Never assume that a material you wish to import is regulated only by one of the federal agencies mentioned in this chapter. Contact each agency with specific details regarding your product, and let agency personnel determine your need for a permit.

Address your questions regarding FDA requirements for the importation of pharmaceuticals to:

Food and Drug Administration (FDA)
Center for Drug Evaluation and Research
Office of Compliance
11919 Rockville Pike
Rockville, MD 20852
Tel: (301) 827-8910
Website: www.fda.gov/cder

Food and Drug Administration (FDA)
Center for Food Safety and Applied Nutrition (CFSAN)
Office of Compliance
Division of Enforcement, Imports Branch
5100 Paint Branch Parkway
College Park, MD 20740-3835
Tel: (301) 436-2080
Website: http://vm.cfsan.fda.gov/list.html

Address your questions for information regarding compliance with Good Manufacturing Practice as well as requests for license applications, or registration forms regarding biologics for human consumption to:

U.S. Food and Drug Administration (FDA)
Center for Biologics Evaluation and Research
Office of Compliance
1401 Rockville Pike
Rockville, MD 20852-1448
Tel: (301) 827-1800
Website: www.fda.gov/cber

Address your requests for permit applications or information regarding importation of veterinary biologics, organisms, and vectors to:

Animal and Plant Health Inspection Service (APHIS)
Veterinary Services (VS)
National Center for Import and Export
4700 River Rd., Unit 40
Riverdale, MD 20737
Tel: (301) 734-3277
Veterinary biologics: (515) 663-7599
Website: www.aphis.usda.gov/vs

Animal and Plant Health Inspection Service (APHIS)
International Services, Import/Export
4700 River Rd.
Riverdale, MD 20737
Tel: (301) 734-3277
Website: www.aphis.usda.gov

Address your requests for information or permit applications for importation of etiologic agents or insects to:

Centers for Disease Control (CDC)
1600 Clifton Rd.
Atlanta, GA 30333
Tel: (404) 639-3311
Public Inquiries:
Tel: (404) 639-3534
Office of Health and Safety: (404) 639-2453
Quarantine Division: (404) 498-1670
Website: www.cdc.gov

Address your questions regarding registration and compliance status of animal products to:

U.S. Food and Drug Administration (FDA)
Center for Veterinary Medicine
Office of Surveillance and Compliance
7500 Standish Place
Rockville, MD 20855
Tel: (301) 827-6647
Website: www.fda.gov/cvm/default.html

Address your questions regarding regulation of pesticide residues to:

Environmental Protection Agency (EPA)
Office of Pesticide Programs
Ariel Rios Building
1200 Pennsylvania Avenue NW
Mail Code 3213A
Washington DC 20460
Tel: (703) 305-7090
Website: www.epa.gov

Address your inquiries regarding TSCA and EPA requirements for importation of inorganic chemical substances to:

Environmental Protection Agency (EPA)
Office of Pollution Prevention and Toxics
TSCA System Information
1200 Pennsylvania Avenue NW
Washington DC 20460
Tel: (202) 564-3810
Tel: (202) 554-1404 (TSCA Information Hotline)
Email: oppt.homepage@epa.gov
Website: www.epa.gov/opptintr/contact.htm

Address your questions regarding transportation of hazardous substances to:

U.S. Department of Transportation (DOT)
Research and Special Programs Administration
Hazardous Materials Information Center
400 7th St. SW
Washington DC 20590
Tel: (202) 366-4488
Website: http://hazmat.dot.gov

Address your questions regarding importation of pharmaceutical products generally to your local Customs port director. For addresses, refer to "U.S. Customs and Border Protection Offices" on page 65 or contact:

U.S. Customs and Border Protection
Customs Headquarters
1300 Pennsylvania Avenue NW
Washington DC 20229
Tel: (202) 354-1000
Website: www.customs.treas.gov

Laws and Regulations

The following laws and regulations may be relevant to the importation of pharmaceuticals. The laws are contained in the United States Code (USC), and the regulations are published in the Code of Federal Regulations (CFR), both of which are available at larger public and law libraries. Specific laws and regulations may also be purchased from the U.S. Government Printing Office (address above).

15 USC 1261 et seq.
Federal Hazardous Substances Act
This Act controls the importation of hazardous substances, sets forth prohibited imports, and authorizes various agencies to promulgate labeling, marking, and transport requirements.

49 CFR 171 et seq.
Hazardous Materials Regulations
These regulations list all substances deemed hazardous and provide transport, marking, labeling, safety, and emergency response rules.

46 CFR 147.30
Labeling of Hazardous Materials
This regulation requires the labeling of containers of hazardous substances and specifies the label contents.

46 CFR 148 et seq.
Carriage of Solid Hazardous Materials in Bulk
These regulations govern the transport of solid hazardous substances in bulk, including reporting, permitting, loading, stowing, and shipping requirements.

15 USC 2601 et seq.
Toxic Substances Control Act
This Act authorizes the EPA to determine whether a substance is harmful and to restrict importation, sale, and use of such substances.

19 CFR 12.118 et seq.
Toxic Substances Control Regulations
These regulations require importers of chemical substances imported in bulk or as part of a mixture to certify to Customs that the shipment complies with the TSCA or is not subject to that Act.

21 USC 301 et seq.
Federal Food, Drug, and Cosmetic Act
This Act prohibits deceptive practices and regulates the manufacture, sale and importation or exportation of food, drugs, cosmetics, and related products. It was amended by the Food Quality Protection Act of 1996. See 21 USC 331, 381, 382.

19 CFR 12.1 et seq.; 21 CFR 1.83 et seq.
Regulations on Food, Drugs, and Cosmetics
These regulations of the Secretary of Health and Human Services and the Secretary of the Treasury govern the standards, labeling, marking, and importing of pharmaceutical products.

21 USC 151 et seq.
Virus Serum Toxin Act
This Act prohibits the preparation, sale and importation of any worthless or harmful virus, serum, toxin, or analogous product for use in the treatment of domestic animals without a permit. Special rules apply to such importations from Canada. See 21 USC 152.

42 USC 262
Licensing of Biological Products
This Act requires persons dealing in biological products, including importers and exporters, to adhere to specific standards and to be licensed.

9 CFR 101 et seq.; 19 CFR 12.17 et seq.; 21 CFR 5, 7, 25, 50, 58 and 510
Regulations on Biological Products
These regulations include procedures and requirements for importing, exporting, labeling, and transporting biological products.

42 USC 201 et seq.
Public Health Service Act
This Act provides regulatory mechanism for premarket controls of biological products to protect the U.S. consumer from health dangers associated with improperly prepared or tested substances.

7 USC 136 et seq.
Federal Insecticide, Fungicide, and Rodenticide Act (FIFRA)
This Act prohibits the importation of products exposed to certain pesticides or devices that are adulterated, misbranded, or otherwise in violation of the Act, provides for registration of pesticides and devices, and establishes standards for labeling and classifying pesticides.

19 CFR 12; 40 CFR 162
Regulations on Pesticides
These regulations set forth the procedures and guidelines for importing products exposed to pesticides.

Sources of Additional Information

The TSCA Chemical Substance Inventory is available through various commercial online databases and from:

National Technical Information Service (NTIS)
U.S. Department of Commerce
5285 Port Royal Road
Springfield, VA 22161
(703) 605-6000; FAX (703) 605-6900
Web site: www.ntis.gov

Principal Exporting Countries

The following listing includes samples of the main supplier nations of the products of this chapter. It is organized by HTSUS major heading. (Refer to "Customs Classification" above for the product codes.) Countries are listed in rank order of the value of products imported to the U.S. Statistics represent customs value of entries for 2002 from the Bureau of Census, U.S. Department of Commerce.

3001—Canada, Germany, China, Belgium, Netherlands, Brazil, France, Denmark, Switzerland, Argentina

3002—France, Belgium, Denmark, Germany, United Kingdom, Ireland, Switzerland, Austria, Netherlands

3003—United Kingdom, Israel, Japan, Switzerland, France, Canada, Germany, Belgium, Italy

3004—Ireland, United Kingdom, Germany, France, Japan, Canada, Switzerland, Sweden

3005—United Kingdom, China, Japan, Canada, Mexico, Germany, South Korea

3006—Germany, United Kingdom, Austria, Ireland, Norway, Canada, Japan

Chapter 31: Fertilizers

This chapter relates to the importation of fertilizers, which are classified under Chapter 31 of the Harmonized Tariff Schedule of the United States (HTSUS). Specifically, it includes solid and liquid forms of fertilizers derived from animal, vegetable, mineral, and chemical substances.

If you are interested in importing separate chemical compounds that are not intended for use as fertilizer, you should refer to Commodity Index Chapters 28 (inorganic) and 29 (organic). This chapter includes animal blood products imported as components of fertilizer, but not animal blood products covered in Chapter 5. Refer to Chapter 90 for importation requirements related to optical elements of potassium chloride. Cultured potassium chloride crystals, other than optical elements, that weigh no less than 2.5 grams each are covered in Chapter 38.

Note: To understand key issues that will enable you to make best use of the information in this section we recommend that you see "Introduction" on page 425.

Key Factors

The key factors in the importation of fertilizers are:

- Compliance with U.S. Department of Agriculture (USDA) requirements (if the product is derived from an animal or vegetable substance)

- Compliance with Federal Plant Pest Act (if the product is derived from a vegetable, soil, or quarry substance)

- Compliance with Plant Quarantine Act (if the product is derived from a vegetable, soil, or quarry substance)

- Compliance with U.S. Federal Trade Commission (FTC) and Consumer Product Safety Commission (CPSC) standards (if the product will be marketed to consumers)

- Compliance with U.S. Environmental Protection Agency (EPA) requirements under Toxic Substances Control Act (TSCA) (if the product contains a hazardous substance)

- Compliance with U.S. Department of Transportation (DOT) regulations for transport of hazardous cargo

Although most importers use the services of a licensed customs broker in making their entries, and we recommend this practice, you should be aware of the regulatory, entry, and documentation issues involved in importing your product. You, as importer, are ultimately responsible for the fulfillment of any legal requirements applicable to your shipment.

General Considerations

Regulatory Agencies. The USDA regulates animal and vegetable fertilizers and fertilizers containing soil or quarry products. The EPA, under authority of the TSCA., imposes certain controls on the importation of chemical fertilizers. The TSCA defines a toxic substance as any substance determined to present the possibility of an unreasonable risk of injury to health and the environment. The DOT enforces regulations for transporting hazardous cargo. Materials are deemed hazardous if listed in DOT transport regulations (49 CFR 172 appendix).

Animal Byproduct Fertilizers. Byproducts of animals intended for use as fertilizer, including blood meal, bone meal, hoof meal, and animal organs, secretions, or similar items, are subject to quarantine regulations, marking requirements, and processing standards. Shipments of these products are inspected at the port of arrival by the Animal and Plant Health Inspection Service (APHIS) of the USDA. Unless the shipment is in compliance with all applicable laws and regulations, it will be denied entry into the U.S. Some shipments may be restricted or prohibited completely.

Vegetable, Soil, and Quarry Fertilizers. Shipments of fertilizers containing vegetable, soil, or quarry products will be inspected at the port of arrival by APHIS. Entry may be denied for noncompliance with the regulations, and the shipment could be seized, quarantined, destroyed, treated, or otherwise dealt with at the discretion of the inspector. Some shipments may be restricted or prohibited completely.

Chemical fertilizers. All chemical fertilizers are subject to the U.S. Customs Service TSCA Import Certification Rule (19 CFR 12.118 et seq.). If you import these products, you must sign one of the following statements: "I certify that all chemical substances in this shipment comply with all applicable rules or orders under TSCA and that I am not offering a chemical substance for entry in violation of TSCA or any applicable rule or order thereunder" or "I certify that all chemicals in this shipment are not subject to TSCA."

You must file this TSCA certification of compliance or exemption at the time you make the entry at Customs. The certification may be in the form of a typed or stamped statement on an appropriate entry document or commercial invoice or a preprinted attachment to such entry document or invoice. You may sign the certificate by means of an authorized facsimile signature. If your entry is electronically processed, the certification will be in the form of a Certification Code, which is part of the Automated Broker Interface (ABI) transmission. Customs will not release your shipment of chemical fertilizer without proper certification.

If you will be importing several or regular shipments of chemical fertilizer, you should ask the appropriate Customs port director to authorize your use of a blanket certification. If you receive such authorization, you must include on the commercial invoice or entry document for each shipment a statement that the blanket certification is on file and that it is incorporated by reference. This statement need not be signed. The blanket certification is valid for one calendar year, is subject to renewal, and may be revoked at any time for cause.

In filling out TSCA forms and Customs entry documents, you should provide the Chemical Abstracts Service (CAS) number for each chemical in the shipment. These CAS numbers are given in the appendix to the HTSUS. You are not required to include the CAS number, but Customs will be able to process your shipment more quickly if you include this number.

Shipments of chemical fertilizers must additionally be in compliance with toxic and hazardous substance regulations of the EPA and DOT. These include packaging, shipping, marking, and labeling requirements.

Articles Exclusion. If you are importing products that are classified as hazardous substances but are part of articles, you are subject to TSCA certification requirements only if certification for your product is specifically required by a rule or order promulgated under the TSCA. No specific rules have been adopted at this time. An "article" is a manufactured item 1) that is formed into a specific shape or design during manufacture, 2) that has end-use functions dependent on the shape or design during end use, and 3) that during the end use, does not change in its chemical composition or that changes only for a noncommercial purpose separate from the article and only as allowed by law (19 CFR 12.120(2)). Fluids and particles are not articles, regardless of shape or design.

Shipment Detention. A shipment of chemical fertilizer will be detained at the U.S. port of arrival (or entry if same), at your risk and expense, if: 1) it contains banned chemical substances (15 USC 2604, 2605); or 2) it contains chemical substances ordered seized because of imminent hazards (15 USC 2606). Further detention will occur at the port of entry, again at your risk and expense, if: 1) the EPA administrator or Customs port director has reasonable grounds to believe the shipment is not in compliance with the TSCA; or 2) you do not provide proper TSCA certification.

If your shipment is detained, it will be held by Customs for no more than 48 hours. It will then be turned over to the EPA administrator, unless you have arranged to release it in bond. You must either bring it into TSCA compliance or reexport it within the earlier of 90 days after notice of detention or 30 days of demand for redelivery. Customs may grant an extension if failure to comply or reexport is the result of delays in EPA or Customs procedures. If you fail to comply or reexport within the time allowed, the EPA administrator is authorized to have the shipment stored or disposed of at your expense.

Hazardous Consumer Products. Under the Federal Hazardous Substances Act (FHSA), a fertilizer intended for the consumer market is a hazardous substance if it is flammable, combustible, or has the potential to cause substantial personal injury during, or as a proximate result of, any customary or reasonably foreseeable handling or use. The CPSC does not require permits, special invoicing, limited entry, licenses, or any special approval process for importing hazardous consumer products into the U.S. However, if you are importing these types of products, you are responsible for ensuring that they meet all applicable FHSA and Consumer Product Safety Act (CPSA) requirements. There are detailed regulations regarding testing and labeling of hazardous products. The Commission's enforcement posture regarding compliance with labeling and product safety standards changes as new facts become available. Contact the CPSC (see addresses at end of this chapter) for specific requirements on the consumer product you are considering importing.

Substantial Product Hazard Reports. Defect-reporting is required for products covered under the CPSA. The law requires every manufacturer, distributor, or retailer of such products, who obtains information that reasonably supports the conclusion that such products fail to comply with an applicable consumer product safety rule, or contain a defect that could create a substantial product hazard, to immediately inform the CPSC of the potential violation or defect. A firm's willful failure to make a Substantial Product Hazard Report can result in litigation by the CPSC.

Customs Classification

For customs purposes, fertilizers are classified under Chapter 31 of the HTSUS. This chapter is broken into major headings, which are further divided into subheadings, and often sub-subheadings, each of which has its own HTSUS classification number. For example, the 2001 HTSUS number for potassium chloride fertilizer is 3104.20, indicating it is a subcategory of potassic mineral

or chemical fertilizers (3104). There are five major headings within Chapter 31.

3101—Animal or vegetable fertilizers, whether or not mixed together or chemically treated; fertilizers produced by the mixing or chemical treatment of animal or vegetable products

3102—Mineral or chemical fertilizers, nitrogenous

3103—Mineral or chemical fertilizers, phosphatic

3104—Mineral or chemical fertilizers, potassic

3105—Mineral or chemical fertilizers containing two or three of the fertilizing elements nitrogen, phosphorus, and potassium; other fertilizers; goods of this chapter in tablets or similar forms or in packages of a gross weight not exceeding 10 kg

For more details regarding classifications of the specific product you are interested in importing, consult a customs broker, the appropriate commodity specialist at your nearest customs port, or the HTSUS. The 2001 HTSUS is available online from the Customs Service (www.customs.gov/impoexpo/impoexpo.htm) or for purchase from the U.S. Government Printing Office (see resources at the end of this chapter), and may be found in larger public libraries. For a general discussion of customs classification, see "Classification—Liquidation" on page 229.

Dutiable Status of Goods

For more information about duty rates and binding decisions see "Dutiable Status of Goods" on page 203; for a discussion of temporary importation of goods see "Temporary Free Importations" on page 205.

Valuation

Importers have a responsibility to use what the U.S. Customs Service deems, "reasonable care," when determining the value of their goods. They must also provide any additional information that the Customs Service needs for setting a final value on the goods. This process involves a number of factors and can be somewhat complicated; importers must be aware of applicable issues and details. Valuation information applies to all types of commodities, for further discussion on the subject see "Customs Valuation" on page 267.

Import Duties

Import duties vary (often dramatically) depending upon the Harmonized Tariff Schedule (HTSUS) classification of the goods or products imported. Since some products that look alike have different HTSUS classifications and different rates of duty, proper classification is vital. Note that "differences of opinion" between importers and the Bureau of Customs and Border Protection regarding classification keeps customs attorneys very busy.

Import duties can be assessed on the imported value of the goods ("ad valorem" rates of duty such as 2%, 4.4%, 50%, etc.), total units or weight of the goods ("specific" rates of duty such as 2 cents each or 1.5 cents/pound, etc.) or on a combination basis ("compound" rates of duty such as 5 cents each plus 6%).

Listed below is a sampling of several Column 1 import duty rates for Chapter 31 products:
Basic slag (3103.20.00.00): free
and
Mineral or chemical fertilizers containing the three fertilizing elements nitrogen, phosphorus and potassium (3105.20.00.00): free

For specific information on US import duties refer to the Harmonized Tariff Schedule of the US. The print version is available from the US Government Printing Office as well as third party suppliers who often add special features. Online versions are available in both static PDF pages as well as in formats with excellent search functionality. Search the Web with the term "Harmonized Tariff Schedule" to find sources.

Entry and Documentation

The entry of merchandise is a two-part process consisting of 1) filing the documentation necessary to determine whether merchandise may be released from Customs custody, and 2) filing the documents that contain information for duty assessment and statistical purposes. In certain instances, all documents must be filed and accepted by Customs prior to release of the goods. Unless you have been granted an extension, you must file entry documents at a location specified by the port or area director within five working days of your shipment's date of arrival at a U.S. port of entry. These include a number of standard documents required by Customs for any entry, and:

- U.S. Customs TSCA Certification (for chemical fertilizers) document

After you present the entry, Customs may examine your shipment or may waive examination. The shipment is then released provided no legal or regulatory violations have been noted. You must then file entry summary documentation and deposit estimated duties at a designated customhouse within 10 working days of your shipment's release. For a detailed description of entry procedures, standard documentation, and informal entry, see "Entry Process" on page 185.

Informed Compliance. Informed compliance was introduced with the Customs Modernization Act of 1993 (Mod Act) and defines the relationship between importers and the Customs Service. It sets out the responsibilities of both parties. Providing the correct documentation and information for entry is a key factor that will make your importing operation run smoothly. We recommend that importers become familiar with the concept of informed comliance and the responsibilities that they have under the Mod Act. For further discussion about informed compliance see "Informed Compliance" on page 211.

Note: The Entry and Documentation section has been carefully designed to supply you, the importer, with sample documents and directions on how to satisfy Customs requirements. Be aware that you should consult the applicable authorities to ensure that you are correctly following the most current procedures.

Prohibitions and Restrictions

Animal Byproduct Fertilizers. Animal byproduct fertilizers are subject to quarantine if they arrive from certain countries that are known to have specific infectious diseases. These countries are listed in 9 CFR 94. If a USDA inspector determines that a shipment is infected with anthrax, foot-and-mouth disease, rinderpest, or bovine spongiform encephalopathy, entry will be denied.

Bone meal may be imported without restriction, provided it has been processed in compliance with USDA regulations; is free of pieces of bone, hide, flesh, and sinew; and contains no more than traces of hair or wool (9 CFR 95.13). Entry is denied for shipments that are not in compliance.

Dried blood, blood meal, animal organs, tankage, meat meal, wool waste, wool manure, and similar animal byproducts for use as fertilizer cannot be imported unless: 1) the product originated in and was shipped from a country that is not on the quarantine list for foot-and-mouth disease or rinderpest; 2) the USDA inspector finds that the product has been fully processed by tanking under live steam or by dry rendering; or 3) the products are handled through quarantine procedures at the port of arrival and are found to be in compliance with USDA conditions (9 CFR 95.14, 95.16).

Manure of horses, cattle, sheep, other ruminants, and swine cannot be imported without permission of the Deputy Administrator, Veterinary Services.

Vegetable, Soil, or Quarry Fertilizers. At the port of entry, the USDA inspector will examine fertilizers with plant, soil, or quarry components for pest infestation. If an infestation is found or reasonably suspected, the inspector has authority to deny entry and to dispose of the shipment by the least drastic means available that will protect against spread of the infestation. Disposal will be at the expense of the owner of the shipment.

Hazardous Substances. Importation of fertilizers that contain chemicals considered hazardous is prohibited if the chemicals are misbranded. Certain hazardous substances listed in the FHSA and in regulations promulgated by the Consumer Product Safety Commission (CPSC) are completely banned from importation. A shipment of chemical fertilizer cannot be imported if it poses an imminent hazard. See 15 USC 1261, 2604-2606; 16 CFR 1500.265-1500.272.

Marking and Labeling Requirements

Animal Byproduct Fertilizers. Containers of fertilizers composed of animal byproducts must be marked with the country of origin—that is, the country where the animal was located. If fertilizers are quarantined at the port of arrival, marks and signs are required on shipping documents and any mode of transport used to move the product while under restrictions (9 CFR 95.25).

Chemical Fertilizers. A shipment of any chemical fertilizer that contains a hazardous substance must comply with the marking and labeling regulations adopted by the EPA (46 CFR 147.30) and the DOT (49 CFR 171 et seq.)

For a general discussion of U.S. Customs marking and labeling requirements, see "Country of Origin Marking" on page 236, "Special Marking Requirements" on page 238 and "Marking—False Impression" on page 239.

Shipping Considerations

You will need to ensure that your goods are packaged and shipped with care so that they pass smoothly through Customs and arrive in good condition. You are responsible for ensuring that the shipment is in compliance with all applicable government regulations for packaging and shipping. In most instances, you should not leave these arrangements solely to the discretion of your supplier. Careful preparation of the cargo and selection of the mode of transport can be essential to a cost-effective, timely delivery of undamaged goods. We strongly advise you to consult your shipping representative, insurance agent, or freight broker for advice on packing and shipping.

Fertilizers may be shipped in bulk, bags, bottles, or other types of containers, depending on the type of fertilizer and whether it is prepackaged. General considerations include protection from contamination, weather, and pests. Venting and vapor collection systems may be required. Safety precautions should also be implemented as required to protect against spillage, air pollution, corrosion of containers, and combustion. Containers should be constructed so as to be safe for handling during transport.

Chemical Fertilizers. Chemical fertilizers in particular may have to be shipped in pressurized, ventilated, and temperature-and vapor-controlled enclosures. Solid chemical fertilizers that are listed as hazardous substances (49 CFR 172 appendix) may be transported in bulk only on compliance with Coast Guard notification procedures, shipping permit requirements, and complex transportation regulations (46 CFR 148). All hazardous substances must also be packaged and transported in accordance with DOT regulations (49 CFR 171 et seq.).

Publications and WWW Resources

The following publications may be relevant to the importation of toxic or hazardous fertilizers:

Toxic Substances Control Act: A Guide for Chemical Importers/ Exporters (published by EPA)

This document is available from the TSCA Assistance Information Service (see Relevant Government Agencies)

The following publication provides a listing of existing chemical substances in the United States. It can be purchased in electronic format or a search of the document can be requested via telephone. Contact the Chemical Abstract Service (CAS) at (800)631-1884 or at (614) 447-3600 ext 2308.

TSCA Chemical Substance Inventory

In order to check whether or not a chemical is subject to any rules or regulations under Sections 5, 6, or 7 of TSCA, search the following document (www.epa.gov/opptintr/CORR)

Chemical on Reporting Rules List (CORR)

The *Harmonized Tariff Schedule of the United States (2001)* (HTSUS) is available to view on the Customs Service website (www.customs.gov), or you may purchase a printed version from:

U.S. Government Printing Office
Superintendent of Documents
710 North Capital Street NW
Washington DC 20401
Tel: (202) 512-1800
Fax: (202) 512-1657
Website: www.access.gpo.gov

The USGPO also has copies of specific laws available for purchase. The USGPO accepts orders made by fax, phone or placed over the Internet, as well as mail orders paid by credit card. All orders must be accompanied by payment. Credit cards, checks drawn on a U.S. bank, or an international money order are all acceptable.

Relevant Government Agencies

Address your inquiries regarding USDA requirements for importation of animal or vegetable byproduct fertilizers to:

Animal and Plant Health Inspection Service (APHIS)
Veterinary Services (VS)
National Center for Import and Export
4700 River Rd., Unit 40
Riverdale, MD 20737
Tel: (301) 734-3277
Animal products: (301) 734-4401
Website: www.aphis.usda.gov/vs

Animal and Plant Health Inspection Service (APHIS)
International Services, Import/Export
4700 River Rd.
Riverdale, MD 20737
Tel: (301) 734-3277
Website: www.aphis.usda.gov

Animal and Plant Health Inspection Service (APHIS)
Plant Protection and Quarantine (PPQ)
Director's Office
4700 River Rd., Unit 131
Riverdale, MD 20737
Tel: (301) 734-8261
Tel (PPQ permits): (301) 734-8758
Website: www.aphis.usda.gov/ppq

Address your inquiries regarding TSCA and EPA requirements for importation of inorganic chemical substances to:

Environmental Protection Agency (EPA)
Office of Pollution Prevention and Toxics
TSCA System Information
1200 Pennsylvania Avenue, NW
Washington DC 20460
Tel: (202) 564-3810
Tel: (202) 554-1404 (TSCA Information Hotline)
Email: oppt.homepage@epa.gov
Website: www.epa.gov/opptintr/contact.htm

Address your questions regarding transportation of hazardous substances to:

U.S. Department of Transportation (DOT)
Research and Special Programs Administration
Hazardous Materials Information Center
400 7th St. SW
Washington, DC 20590
Tel: (202) 366-4488
Website: http://hazmat.dot.gov

Address your questions regarding CPSC requirements for fertilizers marketed to consumers to:

Consumer Product Safety Commission (CPSC)
Office of Compliance
Washington, DC 20207-0001
Tel: 800-638-2772 or (301) 504-7912
Fax: (301) 504-0359
Website: www.cpsc.gov

Address your questions regarding importation of fertilizers generally to your local Customs port director. For addresses, refer to "U.S. Customs and Border Protection Offices" on page 65 or contact:

U.S. Customs and Border Protection
Customs Headquarters
1300 Pennsylvania Avenue NW
Washington DC 20229
Tel: (202) 354-1000
Website: www.customs.treas.gov

Laws and Regulations

The following laws and regulations may be relevant to the importation of fertilizers. The laws are contained in the United States Code (USC), and the regulations are published in the Code of Federal Regulations (CFR), both of which are available at larger public and law libraries. Specific laws and regulations may also be purchased from the U.S. Government Printing Office (address above).

15 USC 2601 et seq.
Toxic Substances Control Act
This Act authorizes the EPA to determine whether a substance is harmful and to restrict importation, sale, and use of such substances.

19 CFR 12.118 et seq.
Regulations on Toxic Substances Control
These regulations require importers of chemical substances imported in bulk or as part of a mixture to certify to Customs that the shipment complies with the TSCA or is not subject to that Act.

15 USC 1261 et seq.
Federal Hazardous Substances Act
This Act controls the importation of hazardous substances, sets forth prohibited imports, and authorizes various agencies to promulgate labeling, marking, and transport requirements.

49 CFR 171 et seq.
Regulations of Hazardous Materials
These regulations list all substances deemed hazardous and provide transport, marking, labeling, safety, and emergency response rules.

46 CFR 147.30
Regulations on Labeling on Hazardous Materials
This regulation requires the labeling of containers of hazardous substances and specifies the label contents.

46 CFR 148 et seq.
Regulations of Carriage of Solid Hazardous Materials in Bulk
These regulations govern the transport of solid hazardous substances in bulk, including reporting, permitting, loading, stowing, and shipping requirements.

15 USC 2051 et seq.
Consumer Product Safety Act (CPSA)
This Act gives the Consumer Product Safety Commission authority to set safety standards, testing procedures, and reporting requirements to ensure that consumer products not already covered under other regulations are not harmful.

9 CFR 95.13 et seq.
Regulations on Animal Byproduct Quarantine Control
These regulations prohibit the importation of animal byproducts for use in fertilizer unless the byproducts meet certain processing standards and are not infected with certain diseases.

Sources of Additional Information

The TSCA Chemical Substance Inventory is available through various commercial online databases and from:

National Technical Information Service (NTIS)
U.S. Department of Commerce
5285 Port Royal Road
Springfield, VA 22161
(703) 605-6000; FAX (703) 605-6900
Web site: www.ntis.gov

Principal Exporting Countries

The following listing includes samples of the main supplier nations of the products of this chapter. It is organized by HTSUS major heading. (Refer to "Customs Classification" above for the product codes.) Countries are listed in rank order of the value of products imported to the U.S. Statistics represent customs value of entries for 2002 from the Bureau of Census, U.S. Department of Commerce.

3101—Canada, Mexico, France, Peru, Spain

3102—Canada, Saudi Arabia, Trinidad and Tobago, Qatar, Russia, Norway, Bahrain, Netherlands, Venezuela

3103—Morocco, Tunisia, Mexico, Canada, China, France, New Zealand, Australia, Germany, Japan, Dominican Republic

3104—Canada, Belarus, Germany, Russia, Chile, Israel, Belgium

3105—Russia, Canada, Japan, Norway, Mexico

Chapter 32:
Paints and Related Products

Full title: Tanning or Dyeing Extracts; Tannins and Their Derivatives; Dyes, Pigments, and Other Coloring Matter; Paints and Varnishes; Putty and Other Mastics; Inks

This chapter relates to the importation of dyes, tannins, paints, mastics, and inks, which are classified under Chapter 32 of the Harmonized Tariff Schedule of the United States (HTSUS). Specifically, it includes vegetable and synthetic tannins and tanning extracts; vegetable, animal, and synthetic coloring extracts; color lakes, prepared pigments, opacifiers, enamels, glazes, paints, varnishes, prepared driers, putties, resin cements, mastics, and inks.

If you are interested in importing separate chemical compounds, you should refer to Commodity Index Chapters 28 (inorganic) or 29 (organic). The importing requirements for specific types of dyed fabrics are covered in Chapters 50 through 63. Leather products are found in Chapters 41 (raw leather) and 42 (leather goods). If you are interested in importing separately defined organic chemicals or tannates or tannin derivatives, you should refer to Chapters 29 or 35, respectively. Mastics of asphalt and other bituminous mastics are covered in Chapter 27. You should also refer to Chapter 38 for a number of related products, including ink removers, turpentines, graphite, animal black and activated carbons, and various rosin and resin products. Importation of glues and other adhesives is discussed in Chapter 35.

Note: To understand key issues that will enable you to make best use of the information in this section we recommend that you see "Introduction" on page 425.

Key Factors

The key factors in the importation of flammable household products are:

- Compliance with U.S. Federal Trade Commission (FTC) and Consumer Product Safety Commission (CPSC) standards (if the product will be marketed to consumers)

- Compliance with U.S. Environmental Protection Agency (EPA) requirements under Toxic Substances Control Act (TSCA) (if the product is a hazardous substance)

- Compliance with U.S. Department of Transportation (DOT) regulations for transport of hazardous cargo (if the product is a hazardous substance)

Although most importers use the services of a licensed customs broker in making their entries, and we recommend this practice, you should be aware of the regulatory, entry, and documentation issues involved in importing your product. You, as importer, are ultimately responsible for the fulfillment of any legal requirements applicable to your shipment.

General Considerations

Regulatory Agencies. The CPSC, under the Federal Hazardous Substances Act (FHSA) and the Consumer Product Safety Act (CPSA) regulates the importation of products considered hazardous. The EPA, under authority of the TSCA, regulates the importation of combustible materials that contain toxic substances The TSCA defines a toxic substance as any substance determined to present the possibility of an unreasonable risk of injury to health and the environment. The DOT enforces regulations for transporting hazardous cargo. Materials are deemed hazardous if listed in DOT transport regulations (49 CFR 172 appendix).

Hazardous Consumer Products. Under the FHSA, a product intended for the consumer market is a hazardous substance if it is flammable, combustible, or could potentially cause substantial personal injury during, or as a proximate result of, any customary or reasonably foreseeable handling or use. The CPSC does not require permits, special invoicing, limited entry, licenses, or any special approval process for importing hazardous consumer products into the U.S. However, if you are importing these types of products, you are responsible for ensuring that they meet all applicable FHSA and CPSA requirements. There are detailed regulations regarding testing and labeling of hazardous products. The Commission's enforcement posture regarding compliance with labeling and product safety standards changes as new facts become available. Contact the CPSC (see addresses at end of this chapter) for specific requirements on the consumer product you are considering importing.

Substantial Product Hazard Reports. Defect-reporting is required for products covered under the CPSA. The law requires every manufacturer, distributor, or retailer of such products, who obtains information that reasonably supports the conclusion that such products fail to comply with an applicable consumer product safety rule, or contain a defect that could create a substantial product hazard, to immediately inform the CPSC of the potential violation or defect. A firm's willful failure to make a Substantial Product Hazard Report can result in litigation by the CPSC.

Toxic and Hazardous Substances. Shipments of products containing chemical substances must be in compliance with toxic and hazardous substance regulations of the EPA and DOT. These include packaging, shipping, marking, and labeling requirements. In addition, all products containing chemicals are subject to the U.S. Customs Service TSCA Import Certification Rule (19 CFR 12.118 et seq.). If you import these products, you must sign one of the following statements: "I certify that all chemical substances in this shipment comply with all applicable rules or orders under TSCA and that I am not offering a chemical substance for entry in violation of TSCA or any applicable rule or order thereunder" or "I certify that all chemicals in this shipment are not subject to TSCA."

You must file this TSCA certification of compliance or exemption at the time you make the entry at Customs. The certification may be in the form of a typed or stamped statement on an appropriate entry document or commercial invoice or a preprinted attachment to such entry document or invoice. You may sign the certificate by means of an authorized facsimile signature. If your entry is electronically processed, the certification will be in the form of a Certification Code, which is part of the Automated Broker Interface (ABI) transmission. Customs will not release your shipment without proper certification.

If you will be importing several or regular shipments, you should ask the appropriate Customs port director to authorize your use of a blanket certification. If you receive such authorization, you must include on the commercial invoice or entry document for each shipment a statement that the blanket certification is on file and that it is incorporated by reference. This statement need not be signed. The blanket certification is valid for one calendar year, is subject to renewal, and may be revoked at any time for cause.

In filling out TSCA forms and Customs entry documents, you should provide the Chemical Abstracts Service (CAS) number for each chemical in the shipment. These CAS numbers are given in the appendix to the HTSUS. You are not required to include the CAS number, but Customs will be able to process your shipment more quickly if you include this number.

Articles Exclusion. If you are importing items that are classified as hazardous substances but are part of articles, you are subject to TSCA certification requirements only if certification for your product is specifically required by a rule or order promulgated under the TSCA. No specific rules have been adopted at this time. An "article" is a manufactured item 1) that is formed into a specific shape or design during manufacture, 2) that has end-use functions dependent on the shape or design during end use, and 3) that during the end use, does not change in its chemical composition or that changes only for a noncommercial purpose separate from the article and only as allowed by law (19 CFR 12.120(2)). Fluids and particles are not articles, regardless of shape or design.

Shipment Detention. A shipment containing chemicals will be detained at the U.S. port of arrival (or entry if same), at your risk and expense, if: 1) it contains banned chemical substances (15 USC 2604, 2605); or 2) it contains chemical substances ordered seized because of imminent hazards (15 USC 2606). Further detention will occur at the port of entry, again at your risk and expense, if: 1) the EPA administrator or Customs port director has reasonable grounds to believe the shipment is not in compliance with the TSCA; or 2) you do not provide proper TSCA certification.

If your shipment is detained, it will be held by Customs for no more than 48 hours. It will then be turned over to the EPA administrator, unless you have arranged to release it in bond. You must either bring it into TSCA compliance or reexport it within the earlier of 90 days after notice of detention or 30 days of demand for redelivery. Customs may grant an extension if failure to comply or reexport is the result of delays in EPA or Customs procedures. If you fail to comply or reexport within the time allowed, the EPA administrator is authorized to have the shipment stored or disposed of at your expense.

Customs Classification

For customs purposes, dyes, tannins, paints, mastics, and inks are classified under Chapter 32 of the HTSUS. This chapter is broken into major headings, which are further divided into subheadings, and often sub-subheadings, each of which has its own HTSUS classification number. For example, the 2001 HTSUS number for drawing ink is 3215.90.10, indicating it is a sub-subcategory of non-printing inks (3215.90), which is a subcategory of the major heading printing, writing, drawing, and other inks (3215). There are 15 major headings within Chapter 32.

3201—Tanning extracts of vegetable origin; tannins and their salts, ethers, esters, and other derivatives

3202—Synthetic organic tanning substances; inorganic tanning substances; tanning preparations, whether or not containing natural tanning substances; enzymatic preparations for pre-tanning

3203—Coloring matter of vegetable or animal origin (including dyeing extracts but excluding animal black), whether or not chemically defined; preparations as specified in note 3 to this chapter based on coloring matter of vegetable or animal origin

3204—Synthetic organic coloring matter, whether or not chemically defined; preparations as specified in note 3 to this chapter based on synthetic organic coloring matter; synthetic organic products of a kind used as fluorescent brightening agents or as luminophores, whether or not chemically defined

3205—Color lakes; preparations as specified in note 3 to this chapter based on color lakes

3206—Other coloring matter; preparations as specified in note 3 to this chapter, other than those of heading 3203, 3204 or 3205; inorganic products of a kind used as luminophores, whether or not chemically defined

3207—Prepared pigments, prepared opacifiers, and prepared colors, vitrifiable enamels and glazes, engobes (slips), liquid lustres, and similar preparations, of a kind used in the ceramic, enamelling, or glass industry; glass frit and other glass, in the form of powder, granules, or flakes

3208—Paints and varnishes (including enamels and lacquers) based on synthetic polymers or chemically modified natural polymers, dispersed or dissolved in a nonaqueous medium; solutions as defined in note 4 to this chapter

3209—Paints and varnishes (including enamels and lacquers) based on synthetic polymers or chemically modified natural polymers, dispersed or dissolved in an aqueous medium

3210—Other paints and varnishes (including enamels, lacquers, and distempers); prepared water pigments of a kind used for finishing leather

3211—Prepared driers

3212—Pigments (including metallic powders and flakes) dispersed in nonaqueous media, in liquid or paste form, of a kind used in the manufacture of paints (including enamels); stamping foils; dyes and other coloring matter put up in forms or packings for retail sale

3213—Artists', students', or signboard painters' colors, modifying tints, amusement colors, and the like, in tablets, tubes, jars, bottles, pans, or in similar forms or packings

3214—Glaziers' putty, grafting putty, resin cements, caulking compounds, and other mastics; painters' fillings; nonrefractory surfacing preparations for facades, indoor walls, floors, ceilings, or the like

3215—Printing ink, writing or drawing ink, and other inks, whether or not concentrated or solid

For more details regarding classifications of the specific product you are interested in importing, consult a customs broker, the appropriate commodity specialist at your nearest customs port, or the HTSUS. The 2001 HTSUS is available online from the Customs Service (www.customs.gov/impoexpo/impoexpo.htm) or for purchase from the U.S. Government Printing Office (see resources at the end of this chapter), and may be found in larger public libraries. For a general discussion of customs classification, see "Classification—Liquidation" on page 229.

Dutiable Status of Goods

For more information about duty rates and binding decisions see "Dutiable Status of Goods" on page 203; for a discussion of temporary importation of goods see "Temporary Free Importations" on page 205.

Valuation

Importers have a responsibility to use what the U.S. Customs Service deems, "reasonable care," when determining the value of their goods. They must also provide any additional information that the Customs Service needs for setting a final value on the goods. This process involves a number of factors and can be somewhat complicated; importers must be aware of applicable issues and details. Valuation information applies to all types of commodities, for further discussion on the subject see "Customs Valuation" on page 267.

Import Duties

Import duties vary (often dramatically) depending upon the Harmonized Tariff Schedule (HTSUS) classification of the goods or products imported. Since some products that look alike have different HTSUS classifications and different rates of duty, proper classification is vital. Note that "differences of opinion" between importers and the Bureau of Customs and Border Protection regarding classification keeps customs attorneys very busy.

Import duties can be assessed on the imported value of the goods ("ad valorem" rates of duty such as 2%, 4.4%, 50%, etc.), total units or weight of the goods ("specific" rates of duty such as 2 cents each or 1.5 cents/pound, etc.) or on a combination basis ("compound" rates of duty such as 5 cents each plus 6%).

Listed below is a sampling of several Column 1 import duty rates for Chapter 32 products:
Wattle extract (3201.20.00.00): free
or
Synthetic organic tanning substances (aromatic or modified aromatic): 7.3%

For specific information on US import duties refer to the Harmonized Tariff Schedule of the US. The print version is available from the US Government Printing Office as well as third party suppliers who often add special features. Online versions are available in both static PDF pages as well as in formats with excellent search functionality. Search the Web with the term "Harmonized Tariff Schedule" to find sources.

Entry and Documentation

The entry of merchandise is a two-part process consisting of 1) filing the documentation necessary to determine whether merchandise may be released from Customs custody, and 2) filing the documents that contain information for duty assessment and statistical purposes. In certain instances, all documents must be filed and accepted by Customs prior to release of the goods. Unless you have been granted an extension, you must file entry documents at a location specified by the port or area director within five working days of your shipment's date of arrival at a U.S. port of entry. These include a number of standard documents required by Customs for any entry, and:

- U.S. Customs TSCA Certification (for hazardous substances) document

After you present the entry, Customs may examine your shipment or may waive examination. The shipment is then released provided no legal or regulatory violations have been noted. You must then file entry summary documentation and deposit estimated duties at a designated customhouse within 10 working days of your shipment's release. For a detailed description of entry procedures, standard documentation, and informal entry, see "Entry Process" on page 185.

Informed Compliance. Informed compliance was introduced with the Customs Modernization Act of 1993 (Mod Act) and defines the relationship between importers and the Customs Service. It sets out the responsibilities of both parties. Providing the correct documentation and information for entry is a key factor that will make your importing operation run smoothly. We recommend that importers become familiar with the concept of informed comliance and the responsibilities that they have under the Mod Act. For further discussion about informed compliance see "Informed Compliance" on page 211.

Invoices—Colors, Dyes, Stains, and Related Products. Invoices for colors, dyes, stains, and related products provided for under HTSUS heading 3204 must show the following information: 1) invoice name of products; 2) trade name of products; 3) identity and percent by weight of each component; 4) color index number or a statement that there is none; 5) color index generic name or a statement that there is none; 6) Chemical Abstracts Service (CAS) number of the active ingredient; 7) class of merchandise as acid type dye, basic dye, disperse dye, fluorescent brightener, soluble dye, vat dye, toner, or other described substance; 8) material to which the color dye or toner is primarily designed to be applied.

Note: The Entry and Documentation section has been carefully designed to supply you, the importer, with sample documents and direc-

tions on how to satisfy Customs requirements. Be aware that you should consult the applicable authorities to ensure that you are correctly following the most current procedures.

Prohibitions and Restrictions

Importation of any consumer product that has been declared a banned hazardous substance by a rule under the CPSA is prohibited. Any product considered hazardous and not labeled according to provisions of the FHSA is a misbranded hazardous substance and is an illegal import. Certain hazardous substances listed in the FHSA and in regulations promulgated by the CPSC are completely banned from importation. A shipment of consumer products cannot be imported if it poses an imminent hazard. See 15 USC 1261, 2604-2606; 16 CFR 1500.265-1500.272.

The CPSC may detain your shipment of hazardous substances and take samples for testing to determine compliance with the FHSA. If your shipment is found to contain banned hazardous substances, it will be refused admission and will be destroyed if not exported within 90 days of the date of refusal notice. If it is found to contain misbranded hazardous substances, you may make arrangements to bring it into conformance through relabeling. For complete details regarding testing, labeling, and safety regulations for hazardous products, contact the CPSC (see addresses at end of this chapter).

Marking and Labeling Requirements

Chemical Products. A shipment of any products containing chemicals that are classified as hazardous substance (49 CFR 172) must comply with the marking and labeling regulations adopted by the EPA (46 CFR 147.30) and the DOT (49 CFR 171 et seq.).

Flammable Products. Any flammable product must be conspicuously and appropriately labeled according to regulations under FHSA. The labeling must distinguish between "extremely flammable," "flammable," and "combustible," and must accurately reflect the form of the product (liquid, solid, or other) or the contents of a self-pressurized container. The label must appear on the immediate container intended for the end user. If the product is being shipped in bulk, the labeling must be affixed to the bulk container in a conspicuous place. Any accompanying printed material that has instructions for use must also bear the same warning in a conspicuous place. Labeling for a flammable product must contain the following information: 1) name and place of business of the manufacturer, packer, distributor, or seller; 2) common or usual name (or chemical name if there is no common name) of the hazardous substance, or of each component that contributes substantially to its hazard; 3) the word "DANGER" on extremely flammable substances; 4) the word "CAUTION" or "WARNING" on flammable or combustible substances; 5) an affirmative statement of the principle hazard or hazards (i.e. "flammable," "extremely flammable," or "combustible"); 6) precautionary measures describing the action to be followed or avoided; 7) instruction, if necessary, for first-aid treatment; 8) instructions for handling and storage of packages that require special care in handling and storage; 9) the statement "Keep Out of Reach of Children" or its practical equivalent. For more information, contact the CPSC (see addresses at end of this chapter).

For a general discussion of U.S. Customs marking and labeling requirements, see "Country of Origin Marking" on page 236, "Special Marking Requirements" on page 238 and "Marking—False Impression" on page 239.

Shipping Considerations

You will need to ensure that your goods are packaged and shipped with care so that they pass smoothly through Customs and arrive in good condition. You are responsible for ensuring that the shipment is in compliance with all applicable government regulations for packaging and shipping. In most instances, you should not leave these arrangements solely to the discretion of your supplier. Careful preparation of the cargo and selection of the mode of transport can be essential to a cost-effective, timely delivery of undamaged goods. We strongly advise you to consult your shipping representative, insurance agent, or freight broker for advice on packing and shipping.

Dyes, tannins, paints, mastics, and inks may be shipped in bulk, bags, bottles, crates, or other types of containers, depending on the type of product and whether it is prepackaged. General considerations include protection from contamination, weather, and pests. For liquid shipments, venting and vapor collection systems may be required. Safety precautions should also be implemented as required to protect against breakage, spillage, corrosion of containers, combustion, and explosion. Containers should be constructed so as to be safe for handling during transport.

Chemical Products. Chemical products in particular may have to be shipped in pressurized, ventilated, and temperature-and vapor-controlled enclosures. Solid chemical products that are listed as hazardous substances (49 CFR 172 appendix) may be transported in bulk only on compliance with Coast Guard notification procedures, shipping permit requirements, and complex transportation regulations (46 CFR 148). All hazardous substances must also be packaged and transported in accordance with DOT regulations (49 CFR 171 et seq.).

Publications and WWW Resources

The following publications may be relevant to the importation of toxic or hazardous dyes, tannins, paints, mastics, and inks:

Toxic Substances Control Act: A Guide for Chemical Importers/ Exporters (published by EPA)

This document is available from the TSCA Assistance Information Service (see Relevant Government Agencies)

The following publication provides a listing of existing chemical substances in the United States. It can be purchased in electronic format or a search of the document can be requested via telephone. Contact the Chemical Abstract Service (CAS) at (800)631-1884 or at (614) 447-3600 ext 2308.

TSCA Chemical Substance Inventory

In order to check whether or not a chemical is subject to any rules or regulations under Sections 5, 6, or 7 of TSCA, search the following document (www.epa.gov/opptintr/CORR)

Chemical on Reporting Rules List (CORR)

The *Harmonized Tariff Schedule of the United States (2001)* (HTSUS) is available to view on the Customs Service website (www.customs.gov), or you may purchase a printed version from:

U.S. Government Printing Office
Superintendent of Documents
710 North Capital Street NW
Washington DC 20401
Tel: (202) 512-1800
Fax: (202) 512-1657
Website: www.access.gpo.gov

The USGPO also has copies of specific laws available for purchase. The USGPO accepts orders made by fax, phone or placed over the Internet, as well as mail orders paid by credit card. All orders must be accompanied by payment. Credit cards, checks drawn on a U.S. bank, or an international money order are all acceptable.

Relevant Government Agencies

Address your questions regarding CPSC requirements for dyes, tannins, paints, mastics, and inks to:

Consumer Product Safety Commission (CPSC)
Office of Compliance
Washington DC 20207-0001
Tel: 800-638-2772 or (301) 504-7912
Fax: (301) 504-0359
Website: www.cpsc.gov

Address your inquiries regarding TSCA and EPA requirements for importation of inorganic chemical substances to:

Environmental Protection Agency (EPA)
Office of Pollution Prevention and Toxics
TSCA System Information
1200 Pennsylvania Avenue, NW
Washington DC 20460
Tel: (202) 564-3810
Tel: (202) 554-1404 (TSCA Information Hotline)
Email: oppt.homepage@epa.gov
Website: www.epa.gov/opptintr/contact.htm

Address your questions regarding transportation of hazardous substances to:

U.S. Department of Transportation (DOT)
Research and Special Programs Administration
Hazardous Materials Information Center
400 7th St. SW
Washington DC 20590
Tel: (202) 366-4488
Website: http://hazmat.dot.gov

Address your questions regarding importation of dyes, tannins, paints, mastics, and inks to your local Customs port director. For addresses refer to "U.S. Customs and Border Protection Offices" on page 65 or contact:

U.S. Customs and Border Protection
Customs Headquarters
1300 Pennsylvania Avenue NW
Washington DC 20229
Tel: (202) 354-1000
Website: www.customs.treas.gov

Laws and Regulations

The following laws and regulations may be relevant to the importation of dyes, tannins, paints, mastics, and inks. The laws are contained in the United States Code (USC), and the regulations are published in the Code of Federal Regulations (CFR), both of which are available at larger public and law libraries. Specific laws and regulations may also be purchased from the U.S. Government Printing Office (address above).

15 USC 2051 et seq.
Consumer Product Safety Act (CPSA)
This Act gives the Consumer Product Safety Commission authority to set safety standards, testing procedures, and reporting requirements to ensure that consumer products not already covered under other regulations are not harmful.

16 CFR 1500 et seq.
Regulations on Hazardous Substances Safety Standards
These regulations set standards for processing, manufacturing, importing, and labeling all substances classified as hazardous that are to be sold to U.S. consumers.

15 USC 2601 et seq.
Toxic Substances Control Act
This Act authorizes the EPA to determine whether a substance is harmful and to restrict importation, sale, and use of such substances.

19 CFR 12.118 et seq.
Regulations on Toxic Substances Control
These regulations require importers of chemical substances imported in bulk or as part of a mixture to certify to Customs that the shipment complies with the TSCA or is not subject to that Act.

15 USC 1261 et seq.
Federal Hazardous Substances Act
This Act controls the importation of hazardous substances, sets forth prohibited imports, and authorizes various agencies

to promulgate labeling, marking, and transport requirements.

49 CFR 171 et seq.
Regulations on Hazardous Materials
These regulations list all substances deemed hazardous and provide transport, marking, labeling, safety, and emergency response rules.

46 CFR 147.30
Regulations on Labeling of Hazardous Materials
This regulation requires the labeling of containers of hazardous substances and specifies the label contents.

46 CFR 148 et seq.
Regulations on Carriage of Solid Hazardous Materials in Bulk
These regulations govern the transport of solid hazardous substances in bulk, including reporting, permitting, loading, stowing, and shipping requirements.

Sources of Additional Information

The TSCA Chemical Substance Inventory is available through various commercial online databases and from:

National Technical Information Service (NTIS)
U.S. Department of Commerce
5285 Port Royal Road
Springfield, VA 22161
(703) 605-6000; FAX (703) 605-6900
Web site: www.ntis.gov

Principal Exporting Countries

The following listing includes samples of the main supplier nations of the products of this chapter. It is organized by HTSUS major heading. (Refer to "Customs Classification" above for the product codes.) Countries are listed in rank order of the value of products imported to the U.S. Statistics represent customs value of entries for 2002 from the Bureau of Census, U.S. Department of Commerce.

3201—Argentina, South Africa, Belgium, Peru, Italy, Brazil

3202—Germany, Canada, France, Turkey, United Kingdom, Mexico, South Africa, Brazil

3203—Japan, Israel, Mexico, Netherlands, Peru, Australia, Spain

3204—Germany, Switzerland, China, India, United Kingdom, Japan, Mexico, South Korea, France, Canada

3205—Peru, Spain, Japan, Canada, India, United Kingdom

3206—Canada, Germany, Japan, United Kingdom, Italy, France, South Korea, Mexico, China, Spain, South Africa, Netherlands, Thailand

3207—Spain, Germany, Mexico, Japan, Italy, Switzerland, United Kingdom, Canada, Netherlands

3208—Canada, Germany, Japan, Mexico, United Kingdom, Netherlands

3209—Canada, Sweden, Germany, Japan, Mexico, Costa Rica, United Kingdom, France, Italy, Belgium, Dominican Republic, Netherlands

3210—Japan, United Kingdom, Germany, Canada, France, Italy, Switzerland, Austria, China

3211—Canada, Thailand, Spain, India, Germany, Colombia, United Kingdom, South Korea, Netherlands, Sweden

3212—Canada, Thailand, Spain, India, Germany, Colombia, United Kingdom, South Korea, Netherlands, Sweden

3213—Canada, Thailand, Spain, India, Germany

3214—Canada, Germany, United Kingdom, France, Japan, Belgium, Switzerland, Italy, Netherlands

3215—Japan, Canada, United Kingdom, Germany, Switzerland, India, Mexico

Chapter 33:
Perfumes and Cosmetics

Full title: Essential Oils and Resinoids; Perfumery, Cosmetic, or Toilet Preparations

This chapter relates to the importation of essential oils, perfumes, and cosmetics, which are classified under Chapter 33 of the Harmonized Tariff Schedule of the United States (HTSUS). Specifically, it includes essential oils in various solid and liquid forms, resinoids, perfumes, toilet waters, mixtures of such substances used as raw materials, animal toilet products, make-up, sun lotions, deodorants and antiperspirants, room deodorizers, and hair, dental hygiene, shaving, and bath products.

If you are importing cosmetics that have therapeutic or medicinal value, you should also read Commodity Index Chapter 30, "Pharmaceuticals." For the importation of separately defined chemicals, refer to Chapters 28 (inorganic) and 29 (organic). If you are importing soap products, refer to Chapter 34. Alcohol preparations used for the manufacture of beverages are covered in Chapter 22.

Note: To understand key issues that will enable you to make best use of the information in this section we recommend that you see "Introduction" on page 425.

Key Factors

The key factors in the importation of essential oils, perfumes, and cosmetics are:

- Compliance with U.S. Food and Drug Administration (FDA) purity, identity, manufacturing, and other standards

- Compliance with FDA entry notification and procedures

- Compliance with U.S. Environmental Protection Agency (EPA) requirements under Toxic Substances Control Act (TSCA) (if the product is a hazardous substance)

- Compliance with U.S. Department of Transportation (DOT) regulations for transport of hazardous cargo (if the product is a hazardous substance)

Although most importers use the services of a licensed customs broker in making their entries, and we recommend this practice, you should be aware of the regulatory, entry, and documentation issues involved in importing your product. You, as importer, are ultimately responsible for the fulfillment of any legal requirements applicable to your shipment.

General Considerations

Regulatory Agencies. The FDA, under the Federal Food, Drug, and Cosmetic Act (FDCA), regulates the importation of essential oils, perfumes, and cosmetics. Cosmetics imported into the United States must comply with all FDCA requirements for those produced domestically. Cosmetics are also subject to the Fair Packaging and Labeling Act (FPLA). The EPA, under authority of the TSCA, imposes certain controls on the importation of any of these products that contain toxic substances. The TSCA defines a toxic substance as any substance determined to present the possibility of an unreasonable risk of injury to health and the environment. The DOT enforces regulations for transporting hazardous cargo. Materials are deemed hazardous if listed in DOT transport regulations (49 CFR 172 appendix).

Essential Oils, Perfumes, and Cosmetics. Imported cosmetics regulated by the FDA are subject to port-of-entry inspection. The FDCA defines cosmetics as articles intended to be applied to the human body for cleansing, beautifying, promoting attractiveness, or altering the appearance, without affecting the body's structure or functions. Included in this definition are products such as skin creams, lotions, perfumes, lipsticks, fingernail polishes, eye and facial make-up preparations, shampoos, permanent waves, hair colors, toothpastes, deodorants, and any ingredient intended for use as a component of a cosmetic product. Soap products consisting primarily of an alkali salt of fatty acid and making no label claim other than cleansing of the human body are not considered cosmetics under the law.

For a general discussion of required FDA import procedures see "Appendix: Foods" on page 825.

Shipment Detention. If your shipment fails to comply with applicable laws and regulations, it may be detained at the port of entry. The FDA may permit you to bring an illegal importation into compliance with the law before a final decision is made regarding admittance. However, any sorting, reprocessing, or relabeling must be supervised by an FDA investigator, and will be done at your expense. Conditional release of an illegal importation to allow an importer to bring it into compliance is not a right but a privilege. If you repeat noncomplying shipments of the same article, the FDA may interpret this as abuse of the privilege and require you to destroy or reexport subsequent shipments.

Hazardous Chemicals. All products containing hazardous chemicals are subject to the U.S. Customs Service TSCA Import Certification Rule (19 CFR 12.118 et seq.). If you import these products, you must sign one of the following statements: "I certify that all chemical substances in this shipment comply with all applicable rules or orders under TSCA and that I am not offering a chemical substance for entry in violation of TSCA or any applicable rule or order thereunder" or "I certify that all chemicals in this shipment are not subject to TSCA."

You must file this TSCA certification of compliance or exemption at the time you make the entry at Customs. The certification may be in the form of a typed or stamped statement on an appropriate entry document or commercial invoice or a preprinted attachment to such entry document or invoice. You may sign the certificate by means of an authorized facsimile signature. If your entry is electronically processed, the certification will be in the form of a Certification Code, which is part of the Automated Broker Interface (ABI) transmission. Customs will not release your shipment without proper certification.

If you will be importing several or regular shipments of the same product, you should ask the appropriate Customs port director to authorize your use of a blanket certification. If you receive such authorization, you must include on the commercial invoice or entry document for each shipment a statement that the blanket certification is on file and that it is incorporated by reference. This statement need not be signed. The blanket certification is valid for one calendar year, is subject to renewal, and may be revoked at any time for cause.

In filling out TSCA forms and Customs entry documents, you should provide the Chemical Abstracts Service (CAS) number for each chemical in the shipment. These CAS numbers are given in the appendix to the HTSUS. You are not required to include the CAS number, but Customs will be able to process your shipment more quickly if you include this number.

Shipments of products containing hazardous chemicals must additionally be in compliance with toxic and hazardous substance regulations of the EPA and DOT. These include packaging, shipping, marking, and labeling requirements.

Articles Exclusion. If you are importing products that are classified as hazardous substances but are part of articles, you are subject to TSCA certification requirements only if certification for your product is specifically required by a rule or order promulgated under the TSCA. No specific rules have been adopted at this time. An "article" is a manufactured item 1) that is formed into a specific shape or design during manufacture, 2) that has end-use functions dependent on the shape or design during end use, and 3) that during the end use, does not change in its chemical composition or that changes only for a noncommercial purpose separate from the article and only as allowed by law (19 CFR 12.120(2)). Fluids and particles are not articles, regardless of shape or design.

Shipment Detention. A shipment of a chemical product will be detained at the U.S. port of arrival (or entry if same), at your risk and expense, if: 1) it contains banned chemical substances (15 USC 2604, 2605); or 2) it contains chemical substances ordered seized because of imminent hazards (15 USC 2606). Further detention will occur at the port of entry, again at your risk and expense, if: 1) the EPA administrator or Customs port director has reasonable grounds to believe the shipment is not in compliance with the TSCA; or 2) you do not provide proper TSCA certification.

If your shipment is detained, it will be held by Customs for no more than 48 hours. It will then be turned over to the EPA administrator, unless you have arranged to release it in bond. You must either bring it into TSCA compliance or reexport it within the earlier of 90 days after notice of detention or 30 days of demand for redelivery. Customs may grant an extension if failure to comply or reexport is the result of delays in EPA or Customs procedures. If you fail to comply or reexport within the time allowed, the EPA administrator is authorized to have the shipment stored or disposed of at your expense.

Customs Classification

For customs purposes, essential oils, perfumes, and cosmetics are classified under Chapter 33 of the HTSUS. This chapter is broken into major headings, which are further divided into sub-headings, and often sub-subheadings, each of which has its own HTSUS classification number. For example, the 2001 HTSUS number for bath salts is 3307.30.10, indicating it is a sub-subcategory of perfumed bath salts and other bath preparations (3307.30), which is a subcategory of the major heading, shaving, deodorant, and bath preparations, etc. (3307). There are seven major headings within Chapter 33.

3301—Essential oils (terpeneless or not), including concretes and absolutes; resinoids; extracted oleoresins; concentrates of essential oils in fats, in fixed oils, in waxes, or the like, obtained by enfleurage or maceration; terpenic byproducts of the deterpenation of essential oils; aqueous distillates and aqueous solutions of essential oils

3302—Mixtures of odoriferous substances and mixtures (including alcoholic solutions) with a basis of one or more of these substances, of a kind used as raw materials in industry; other preparations based on odoriferous substances, of a kind used for the manufacture of beverages

3303—Perfumes and toilet waters

3304—Beauty or make-up preparations and preparations for the care of the skin (other than medicaments), including sunscreen or suntan preparations; manicure or pedicure preparations

3305—Preparations for use on the hair

3306—Preparations for oral or dental hygiene, including denture fixative pastes and powders; yarn used to clean between the teeth (dental floss), in individual retail packages

3307—Pre-shave, shaving, or after-shave preparations, personal deodorants, bath preparations, depilatories and other perfumery, cosmetic, or toilet preparations, not elsewhere specified or included; prepared room deodorizers, whether or not perfumed or having disinfectant properties

For more details regarding classifications of the specific product you are interested in importing, consult a customs broker, the appropriate commodity specialist at your nearest customs port, or the HTSUS. The 2001 HTSUS is available online from the Customs Service (www.customs.gov/impoexpo/impoexpo.htm) or for purchase from the U.S. Government Printing Office (see resources at the end of this chapter), and may be found in larger public libraries. For a general discussion of customs classification, see "Classification—Liquidation" on page 229.

Dutiable Status of Goods

For more information about duty rates and binding decisions see "Dutiable Status of Goods" on page 203; for a discussion of temporary importation of goods see "Temporary Free Importations" on page 205.

Valuation

Importers have a responsibility to use what the U.S. Customs Service deems, "reasonable care," when determining the value of their goods. They must also provide any additional information that the Customs Service needs for setting a final value on the goods. This process involves a number of factors and can be somewhat complicated; importers must be aware of applicable issues and details. Valuation information applies to all types of commodities, for further discussion on the subject see "Customs Valuation" on page 267.

Import Duties

Import duties vary (often dramatically) depending upon the Harmonized Tariff Schedule (HTSUS) classification of the goods or products imported. Since some products that look alike have different HTSUS classifications and different rates of duty, proper classification is vital. Note that "differences of opinion" between importers and the Bureau of Customs and Border Protection regarding classification keeps customs attorneys very busy.

Import duties can be assessed on the imported value of the goods ("ad valorem" rates of duty such as 2%, 4.4%, 50%, etc.), total units or weight of the goods ("specific" rates of duty such as 2 cents each or 1.5 cents/pound, etc.) or on a combination basis ("compound" rates of duty such as 5 cents each plus 6%).

Listed below is a sampling of several Column 1 import duty rates for Chapter 33 products:

Essential oils of citrus fruit (of bergamot) (3301.11.00): free to

Bath salts (whether or not perfumed) (3307.30.10.00): 5.8%

For specific information on US import duties refer to the Harmonized Tariff Schedule of the US. The print version is available from the US Government Printing Office as well as third party suppliers who often add special features. Online versions are available in both static PDF pages as well as in formats with excellent search functionality. Search the Web with the term "Harmonized Tariff Schedule" to find sources.

Entry and Documentation

The entry of merchandise is a two-part process consisting of 1) filing the documentation necessary to determine whether merchandise may be released from Customs custody, and 2) filing the documents that contain information for duty assessment and statistical purposes. In certain instances, all documents must be filed and accepted by Customs prior to release of the goods. Unless you have been granted an extension, you must file entry documents at a location specified by the port or area director within five working days of your shipment's date of arrival at a U.S. port of entry. These include a number of standard documents required by Customs for any entry, and:

- U.S. Customs TSCA Certification (for hazardous substances) document

After you present the entry, Customs may examine your shipment or may waive examination. The shipment is then released provided no legal or regulatory violations have been noted. You must then file entry summary documentation and deposit estimated duties at a designated customhouse within 10 working days of your shipment's release. For a detailed description of entry procedures, standard documentation, and informal entry, see "Entry Process" on page 185.

Informed Compliance. Informed compliance was introduced with the Customs Modernization Act of 1993 (Mod Act) and defines the relationship between importers and the Customs Service. It sets out the responsibilities of both parties. Providing the correct documentation and information for entry is a key factor that will make your importing operation run smoothly. We recommend that importers become familiar with the concept of informed comliance and the responsibilities that they have under the Mod Act. For further discussion about informed compliance see "Informed Compliance" on page 211.

Note: The Entry and Documentation section has been carefully designed to supply you, the importer, with sample documents and directions on how to satisfy Customs requirements. Be aware that you should consult the applicable authorities to ensure that you are correctly following the most current procedures.

Prohibitions and Restrictions

Cosmetics Containing Drugs. Cosmetic products that contain elements for treating or preventing disease, or affecting the structure or functions of a human body, must comply with the drug, as well as the cosmetic, provisions of the law. Examples include "fluoride" toothpaste, hormone creams, suntan preparations with skin protective components, antiperspirants mixed with deodorants, and anti-dandruff shampoos. Most of these cosmetics contain over-the-counter drugs. The regulations for importing and retailing drugs are more extensive than those for cosmetics. If you are interested in importing cosmetics that may fall under this category, you should also review the information in Chapter 30 regarding the importation of pharmaceuticals.

Adulterated or Misbranded Cosmetics. The FDCA prohibits the importation and distribution of cosmetics that are adulterated. Your cosmetic product is considered adulterated if it meets any of the following conditions: 1) it contains a substance that may make it harmful to consumers under customary conditions of use; 2) it contains a filthy, putrid, or decomposed substance; 3) its container is composed of a harmful substance; 4) it is manufactured or held in insanitary conditions under which it may have become contaminated with filth or harmful to consumers; or 5) it contains an impermissible color and is not a hair dye. Coal-tar hair dyes labeled with the caution statement prescribed by law (21 CFR Sec. 601) and "patch-test" instructions are exempt from the adulteration provision, even if they are irritating to the skin or otherwise harmful. This exemption does not apply to eyelash and eyebrow dyes, which must be approved by the FDA for such use.

The FDCA also prohibits the importation and distribution of cosmetics that are misbranded. If your cosmetic meets any of the following conditions, it is misbranded: 1) its labeling is false or misleading; 2) it does not bear the required labeling information; or 3) the container is made or filled in a deceptive manner (21 CFR Sec. 602).

Cosmetic Safety. The FDCA does not require cosmetic manufacturers or marketers to test their products for safety. However, the FDA strongly urges cosmetic manufacturers to conduct all toxicological or other tests appropriate to substantiate the safety of the cosmetics. A product whose safety is not adequately substantiated may be considered misbranded and may be subject to regulatory action unless the label bears the following statement: "Warning: The safety of this product has not been determined" (21 CFR 740).

With the exception of color additives and a few prohibited ingredients, a cosmetic manufacturer may, at his or her own risk, use any raw material as a cosmetic ingredient and market the product without FDA approval. The law requires that every color additives used in food, drugs, and cosmetics be tested for safety and approved by the FDA for its intended use. A cosmetic containing an unlisted color additive (i.e., one not approved by the FDA) is considered adulterated and its use is subject to regulatory action. The colors approved for use in cosmetics are listed in 21 CFR 73, 74, 81 and 82.

Restricted Ingredients. The use of the following ingredients in cosmetics is restricted or prohibited: bithionol, mercury compounds, vinyl chloride, halogenated salicylanilides, zirconium complexes in aerosol cosmetics, chloroform, chlorofluorocarbon propellants, and hexachlorophene (21 CFR 700, 250). Cosmetic nail products containing methyl methacrylate monomer or those containing more than 5% formaldehyde are considered adulterated under the FDCA.

Voluntary Registration. The FDCA does not require cosmetic firms to register their establishments or formulas with the FDA, or to make available safety data or other information before a product is marketed in the U.S. However, manufacturers or distributors may submit their information voluntarily. Voluntary registration and assignment of a registration number by the FDA does not denote approval of a firm, raw material, or product. If you are registered with the FDA and you use your registration number in labeling, you must include on the label a conspicuous disclaimer phrase as prescribed by regulation (21 CFR 710, 720, and 730).

Tamper-resistant Packaging. Liquid oral hygiene products (e.g., mouthwashes, fresheners) and all cosmetic vaginal products (e.g., douches, tablets) must be packaged in tamper-resistant packages when sold at retail. A package is considered tamper-resistant if it has an indicator or barrier to entry (e.g., shrink or tape seal, sealed carton, tube, or pouch, or aerosol container) that, if breached or missing, alerts a consumer that tampering has occurred. The indicator must be distinctive by design (breakable cap or blister) or appearance (logo, vignette, or other illustration) to preclude substitution. The tamper-resistant feature may involve the immediate or outer container, or both. The package must also bear a prominently placed statement alerting the consumer to the tamper-resistant feature. This statement must remain unaffected if the tamper-resistant feature is breached or missing (21 CFR 700).

Enforcement Authority. For enforcement of the law, the FDA may conduct examinations and investigations of products, inspect establishments where products are manufactured or held, and seize adulterated or misbranded cosmetics. If you attempt to import adulterated or misbranded foreign products, your shipment may be refused entry into the U.S. To prevent further shipment of an adulterated or misbranded product, the FDA may request a Federal port court to issue a restraining order against the U.S. manufacturer or distributor of the cosmetic in question. The FDA may also initiate criminal action against you for violating the law. Examples of products seized in recent years are nail preparations containing methyl methacrylate and formaldehyde, various eyebrow and eyelash dye products containing prohibited coal-tar dyes, and products contaminated with harmful microorganisms.

If you have questions regarding regulatory requirements for cosmetics, contact FDA's Division of Colors and Cosmetics (see addresses at end of this chapter). If you have questions regarding requirements for products that are also drugs, contact FDA's Division of Drug Labeling Compliance (see addresses at end of this chapter).

Marking and Labeling Requirements

Cosmetic Labeling. Cosmetics distributed in the U.S. must comply with the labeling regulations published by the FDA under the FDCA and the Fair Packaging and Labeling Act (FPLA). "Labeling" means all labels and other written, printed, or graphic matter on or accompanying a product. The label statements required by FDCA must appear on the inside as well as any outside container or wrapper. FPLA requirements (e.g., ingredient labeling) only apply to the label of the outer container. The labeling requirements are detailed at 21 CFR 701 and 740. Cosmetics bearing false or misleading label statements, or otherwise not labeled in accordance with these requirements, may be considered misbranded and may be subject to regulatory action. All label statements required by regulation must be in the English language and must be placed conspicuously on the label or labeling with such prominence that they are readily noticed and understood by consumers under customary conditions of purchase (21 CFR 701).

Display and Informational Panels. The principal display panel must state the product name, identify by descriptive name or illustration the product's nature or use, and bear an accurate statement of the net quantity of contents in terms of weight, measure, numerical count, or a combination of numerical count and weight or measure. The declaration must be distinct. It must be placed in the bottom area of the panel, in a line generally parallel to the base on which the package rests, and in a type size commensurate with the size of the container as prescribed by regulation. The net quantity of contents of a solid, semisolid, or viscous cosmetic must be stated in terms of the avoirdupois pound and ounce. A statement of liquid measure must be in terms of the U.S. gallon of 321 cubic inches and the quart, pint, and fluid ounce subdivisions thereof. If the net quantity of contents is one pound or one pint or more, it must be expressed in ounces, followed in parenthesis by a declaration of the largest whole units (i.e., pounds and ounces or quarts and pints and ounces). The net quantity of contents may also be stated in terms of the U.S. system and the metric system of weights or measures.

The name and place of business of the firm marketing the product must be stated on an information panel of the label (21 CFR 701). The address must state the street address, city, state, and zip code. If a domestic firm is listed in a current city or telephone directory, the street address may be omitted. If the distributor is not the manufacturer or packer, this fact must be stated on the label by the qualifying phrase "Manufactured for ___" or "Distributed by ___" or similar, appropriate wording. A firm located outside the U.S. may omit the zip code.

Declaration of Ingredients. Cosmetics produced or distributed for retail sale to consumers for their personal care are required to bear an ingredient declaration (21 CFR 701). Cosmetics not customarily distributed for retail sale, e.g. hair preparations or make-up products used by professionals on customers at their establishments and skin cleansing or emollient creams used by persons at their places of work, are exempt from the requirement. However, if professional establishments or workplaces sell these products to consumers for home use, the requirements apply.

The ingredient declaration must be conspicuous so that it is likely to be read at the time of purchase. It may appear on any information panel of the package including a firmly affixed tag, tape, or card. The letters must not be less than 1/16 of an inch in height. If the total package surface available to bear labeling is less than 12 square inches, the letters must not be less than half an inch in height. Off-package ingredient labeling is permitted if the cosmetic is held in tightly compartmented trays or racks, is not enclosed in a folding carton, and the package surface area is less than 12 square inches.

The ingredients must be declared in descending order of predominance. Color additives and ingredients present at 1% or less may be declared without regard for predominance. The ingredients must be identified by the names established or adopted by regulation; those accepted by the FDA as exempt from public disclosure may be stated as "and other ingredients."

Label Warnings. Cosmetics that may be hazardous to consumers when misused must bear appropriate label warnings and adequate directions for safe use. The statements must be prominent and conspicuous. Some cosmetics (e.g. aerosol products, feminine deodorant sprays, children's bubble bath products) must bear label warnings or cautions prescribed by regulation (21 CFR 740).

Hazardous Chemicals. A shipment of any products containing chemicals that are classified as hazardous substance (49 CFR 172) must comply with the marking and labeling regulations adopted by the EPA (46 CFR 147.30) and the DOT (49 CFR 171 et seq.).

For a general discussion of U.S. Customs marking and labeling requirements, see "Country of Origin Marking" on page 236, "Special Marking Requirements" on page 238 and "Marking—False Impression" on page 239.

Shipping Considerations

You will need to ensure that your goods are packaged and shipped with care so that they pass smoothly through Customs and arrive in good condition. You are responsible for ensuring that the shipment is in compliance with all applicable government regulations for packaging and shipping. In most instances, you should not leave these arrangements solely to the discretion of your supplier. Careful preparation of the cargo and selection of the mode of transport can be essential to a cost-effective, timely delivery of undamaged goods. We strongly advise you to consult your shipping representative, insurance agent, or freight broker for advice on packing and shipping.

Cosmetic products may be shipped in bulk, bags, bottles, or other types of containers, depending on the type of product and whether it is prepackaged. General considerations include protection from contamination, weather, and pests. If a product must be kept in a sanitary environment, all tables, utensils, platforms, and devices used for moving or handling the product, the compartments in which it is stowed while being transported will need to be maintained in a sanitary condition. For liquid shipments, venting and vapor collection systems may be required. Safety precautions should also be implemented as required to protect against breakage, spillage, corrosion of containers, and combustion. Containers should be constructed so as to be safe for handling during transport.

Chemical Products. Chemical products in particular may have to be shipped in pressurized, ventilated, and temperature-and vapor-controlled enclosures. Solid chemical products that are listed as hazardous substances (49 CFR 172 appendix) may be transported in bulk only on compliance with Coast Guard notification procedures, shipping permit requirements, and complex transportation regulations (46 CFR 148). All hazardous substances must also be packaged and transported in accordance with DOT regulations (49 CFR 171 et seq.).

Publications and WWW Resources

The following publication explains the FDA requirements for importing cosmetics. It is published by the FDA and is available online from the FDA website (www.fda.gov).

Requirements of Laws and Regulations Enforced by the U.S. Food and Drug Administration

The following publications may be relevant to the importation of toxic or hazardous cosmetic ingredients:

Toxic Substances Control Act: A Guide for Chemical Importers/ Exporters (published by EPA)

This document is available from the TSCA Assistance Information Service (see Relevant Government Agencies)

The following publication provides a listing of existing chemical substances in the United States. It can be purchased in electronic format or a search of the document can be requested via telephone. Contact the Chemical Abstract Service (CAS) at (800)631-1884 or at (614) 447-3600 ext 2308.

TSCA Chemical Substance Inventory

In order to check whether or not a chemical is subject to any rules or regulations under Sections 5, 6, or 7 of TSCA, search the following document (www.epa.gov/opptintr/CORR)

Chemical on Reporting Rules List (CORR)

The *Harmonized Tariff Schedule of the United States (2001)* (HTSUS) is available to view on the Customs Service website (www.customs.gov), or you may purchase a printed version from:

U.S. Government Printing Office
Superintendent of Documents
710 North Capital Street NW
Washington DC 20401
Tel: (202) 512-1800
Fax: (202) 512-1657
Website: www.access.gpo.gov

The USGPO also has copies of specific laws available for purchase. The USGPO accepts orders made by fax, phone or placed over the Internet, as well as mail orders paid by credit card. All orders must be accompanied by payment. Credit cards, checks drawn on a U.S. bank, or an international money order are all acceptable.

Relevant Government Agencies

Address your questions regarding FDA requirements for cosmetics to:

Food and Drug Administration (FDA)
Center for Food Safety and Applied Nutrition
Office of Cosmetics and Colors
5100 Paint Branch Parkway
College Park, MD 20740-3835
Tel: (301) 436-2600
Website: http://vm.cfsan.fda.gov/~dms/cos-toc.html

Food and Drug Administration (FDA)
Center for Food Safety and Applied Nutrition (CFSAN)
Office of Compliance
Division of Enforcement, Imports Branch
5100 Paint Branch Parkway
College Park, MD 20740-3835
Tel: (301) 436-2080
Website: http://vm.cfsan.fda.gov/list.html

Address your questions regarding FDA requirements for products that are also drugs to:

Food and Drug Administration (FDA)
Center for Drug Evaluation and Research
Office of Compliance
11919 Rockville Pike
Rockville, MD 20852

Tel: (301) 827-8910
Website: www.fda.gov/cder

Address your questions regarding CPSC requirements for cosmetics and other products under chapter 33 to:

Consumer Product Safety Commission (CPSC)
Office of Compliance
Washington DC 20207-0001
Tel: 800-638-2772 or (301) 504-7912
Fax: (301) 504-0359
Website: www.cpsc.gov

Address your inquiries regarding TSCA and EPA requirements for importation of inorganic chemical substances to:

Environmental Protection Agency (EPA)
Office of Pollution Prevention and Toxics
TSCA System Information
1200 Pennsylvania Avenue, NW
Washington DC 20460
Tel: (202) 564-3810
Tel: (202) 554-1404 (TSCA Information Hotline)
Email: oppt.homepage@epa.gov
Website: www.epa.gov/opptintr/contact.htm

Address your questions regarding transportation of hazardous substances to:

U.S. Department of Transportation (DOT)
Research and Special Programs Administration
Hazardous Materials Information Center
400 7th St. SW
Washington DC 20590
Tel: (202) 366-4488
Website: http://hazmat.dot.gov

Address your questions regarding importation of cosmetics to your local Customs port director. For addresses refer to "U.S. Customs and Border Protection Offices" on page 65 or contact:

U.S. Customs and Border Protection
Customs Headquarters
1300 Pennsylvania Avenue NW
Washington DC 20229
Tel: (202) 354-1000
Website: www.customs.treas.gov

Laws and Regulations

The following laws and regulations may be relevant to the importation of cosmetics. The laws are contained in the United States Code (USC), and the regulations are published in the Code of Federal Regulations (CFR), both of which are available at larger public and law libraries. Specific laws and regulations may also be purchased from the U.S. Government Printing Office (address above).

21 USC 301 et seq.
Federal Food, Drug, and Cosmetic Act
This Act prohibits deceptive practices and regulates the manufacture, sale and importation or exportation of food, drugs, cosmetics, and related products. It was amended by the Food Quality Protection Act of 1996. See 21 USC 331, 381, 382.

19 CFR 12.1 et seq.; 21 CFR 1.83 et seq.
Regulations on Food, Drugs, and Cosmetics
These regulations of the Secretary of Health and Human Services and the Secretary of the Treasury govern the standards, labeling, marking, and importing of products used with food, drugs, and cosmetics.

15 USC 2601 et seq.
Toxic Substances Control Act
This Act authorizes the EPA to determine whether a substance is harmful and to restrict importation, sale, and use of such substances.

19 CFR 12.118 et seq.
Regulations on Toxic Substances Control
These regulations require importers of chemical substances imported in bulk or as part of a mixture to certify to Customs that the shipment complies with the TSCA or is not subject to that Act.

15 USC 1261 et seq.
Federal Hazardous Substances Act
This Act controls the importation of hazardous substances, sets forth prohibited imports, and authorizes various agencies to promulgate labeling, marking, and transport requirements.

49 CFR 171 et seq.
Regulations on Hazardous Materials
These regulations list all substances deemed hazardous and provide transport, marking, labeling, safety, and emergency response rules.

46 CFR 147.30
Regulations on Labeling of Hazardous Materials
This regulation requires the labeling of containers of hazardous substances and specifies the label contents.

46 CFR 148 et seq.
Regulations on Carriage of Solid Hazardous Materials in Bulk
These regulations govern the transport of solid hazardous substances in bulk, including reporting, permitting, loading, stowing, and shipping requirements.

Sources of Additional Information

The TSCA Chemical Substance Inventory is available through various commercial online databases and from:

National Technical Information Service (NTIS)
U.S. Department of Commerce
5285 Port Royal Road
Springfield, VA 22161
(703) 605-6000; FAX (703) 605-6900
Web site: www.ntis.gov

Principal Exporting Countries

The following listing includes samples of the main supplier nations of the products of this chapter. It is organized by HTSUS major heading. (Refer to "Customs Classification" above for the product codes.) Countries are listed in rank order of the value of products imported to the U.S. Statistics represent customs value of entries for 2002 from the Bureau of Census, U.S. Department of Commerce.

3301—France, Argentina, India, China, Brazil, Indonesia, Mexico, United Kingdom, Canada, Spain

3302—Switzerland, France, Germany, United Kingdom, Ireland, Japan, Brazil, Canada, Mexico, Spain, India, Netherlands, Israel

3303—France, United Kingdom, Italy, Switzerland, Spain, Canada, Germany, United Arab Emirates

3304—Canada, France, China, Germany, United Kingdom, Japan, Belgium, Italy

3305—Canada, Italy, Mexico, United Kingdom, Germany, France, Japan, Spain

3306—Canada, Ireland, United Kingdom, Dominican Republic, China, South Africa, India

3307—Canada, China, France, United Kingdom, India, Japan, Germany, Thailand, Mexico, Spain, Australia, Italy

Chapter 34:
Soaps and Waxes

Full title: Soap, Organic Surface-active Agents, Washing Preparations, Lubricating Preparations, Artificial Waxes, Prepared Waxes, Polishing or Scouring Preparations, Candles and Similar Articles, Modeling Pastes, "Dental Waxes" and Dental Preparations With a Basis of Plaster

This chapter relates to the importation of soaps, washing and lubricating products, and wax articles, which are classified under Chapter 34 of the Harmonized Tariff Schedule of the United States (HTSUS). Specifically, it includes soap, organic products used as soap, items impregnated, coated, or covered with soap or detergent, and washing and cleaning products. It also covers lubricating preparations, preparations for oiling or greasing textiles, leather, furskins, or other materials, and polishes and creams. This chapter additionally contains artificial and prepared waxes, candles, tapers, modeling pastes, dental wax and impression compounds, and dentistry preparations with a plaster base.

If you are interested in importing edible mixtures or preparations of animal or vegetable fats or oils used as mold release preparations, you should refer to Commodity Index Chapter 15. Separate chemically defined compounds are found in Chapters 28 (inorganic) or 29 (organic). Refer to Chapter 33 for the importation requirements for shampoos, dentifrices, shaving creams and foams, or bath preparations that contain soap or other organic surface-active agents.

Note: To understand key issues that will enable you to make best use of the information in this section we recommend that you see "Introduction" on page 425.

Key Factors

The key factors in the importation of soaps, washing and lubricating products, and wax articles are:

- Compliance with U.S. Federal Trade Commission (FTC) and Consumer Product Safety Commission (CPSC) standards (if the product will be marketed to consumers)

- Compliance with U.S. Environmental Protection Agency (EPA) requirements under Toxic Substances Control Act (TSCA) (if the product is a hazardous substance)

- Compliance with U.S. Department of Transportation (DOT) regulations for transport of hazardous cargo (if the product is a hazardous substance)

Although most importers use the services of a licensed customs broker in making their entries, and we recommend this practice, you should be aware of the regulatory, entry, and documentation issues involved in importing your product. You, as importer, are ultimately responsible for the fulfillment of any legal requirements applicable to your shipment.

General Considerations

Regulatory Agencies. The EPA, under authority of the TSCA, regulates the importation of soap, washing, lubricating, or wax products that contain toxic substances. The TSCA defines a toxic substance as any substance determined to present the possibility of an unreasonable risk of injury to health and the environment. The DOT enforces regulations for transporting hazardous cargo. Materials are deemed hazardous if listed in DOT transport regulations (49 CFR 172 appendix).

Hazardous Consumer Products. Under the Federal Hazardous Substances Act (FHSA), soap, washing, lubricating, or wax products intended for the consumer market are hazardous substances if they are flammable, combustible, or have the potential to cause substantial personal injury during, or as a proximate result of, any customary or reasonably foreseeable handling or use. The CPSC does not require permits, special invoicing, limited entry, licenses, or any special approval process for importing hazardous consumer products into the U.S. However, if you are importing these types of products, you are responsible for ensuring that they meet all applicable FHSA and Consumer Product Safety Act (CPSA) requirements. There are detailed regulations regarding testing and labeling of hazardous products. The Commission's enforcement posture regarding compliance with labeling and product safety standards changes as new facts become available. Contact the CPSC (see addresses at end of this chapter) for specific requirements on the consumer product you are considering importing.

Substantial Product Hazard Reports. Defect-reporting is required for products covered under the CPSA. The law requires every manufacturer, distributor, or retailer of such products, who obtains information that reasonably supports the conclusion that such products fail to comply with an applicable consumer product safety rule, or contain a defect that could create a substantial product hazard, to immediately inform the CPSC of the potential violation or defect. A firm's willful failure to make a Substantial Product Hazard Report can result in litigation by the CPSC.

Hazardous Substances. Shipments of products containing toxic or hazardous chemicals must be in compliance with regulations of the EPA and DOT. These include packaging, shipping, marking, and labeling requirements. In addition, all products containing chemicals are subject to the U.S. Customs Service TSCA Import Certification Rule (19 CFR 12.118 et seq.). If you import these products, you must sign one of the following statements: "I certify that all chemical substances in this shipment comply with all applicable rules or orders under TSCA and that I am not offering a chemical substance for entry in violation of TSCA or any applicable rule or order thereunder" or "I certify that all chemicals in this shipment are not subject to TSCA."

You must file this TSCA certification of compliance or exemption at the time you make the entry at Customs. The certification may be in the form of a typed or stamped statement on an appropriate entry document or commercial invoice or a preprinted attachment to such entry document or invoice. You may sign the certificate by means of an authorized facsimile signature. If your entry is electronically processed, the certification will be in the form of a Certification Code, which is part of the Automated Broker Interface (ABI) transmission. Customs will not release your shipment without proper certification.

If you will be importing several or regular shipments, you should ask the appropriate Customs port director to authorize your use of a blanket certification. If you receive such authorization, you must include on the commercial invoice or entry document for each shipment a statement that the blanket certification is on file and that it is incorporated by reference. This statement need not be signed. The blanket certification is valid for one calendar year, is subject to renewal, and may be revoked at any time for cause.

In filling out TSCA forms and Customs entry documents, you should provide the Chemical Abstracts Service (CAS) number for each chemical in the shipment. These CAS numbers are given in the appendix to the HTSUS. You are not required to include the CAS number, but Customs will be able to process your shipment more quickly if you include this number.

Articles Exclusion. If you are importing items that are classified as hazardous substances but are part of articles, you are subject to TSCA certification requirements only if certification for your product is specifically required by a rule or order promulgated under the TSCA. No specific rules have been adopted at this time. An "article" is a manufactured item 1) that is formed into a specific shape or design during manufacture, 2) that has end-use functions dependent on the shape or design during end use, and 3) that during the end use, does not change in its chemical composition or that changes only for a noncommercial purpose separate from the article and only as allowed by law (19 CFR 12.120(2)). Fluids and particles are not articles, regardless of shape or design.

Shipment Detention. A shipment containing chemicals will be detained at the U.S. port of arrival (or entry if same), at your risk and expense, if: 1) it contains banned chemical substances (15 USC 2604, 2605); or 2) it contains chemical substances ordered seized because of imminent hazards (15 USC 2606). Further detention will occur at the port of entry, again at your risk and expense, if: 1) the EPA administrator or Customs port director has reasonable grounds to believe the shipment is not in compliance with the TSCA; or 2) you do not provide proper TSCA certification.

If your shipment is detained, it will be held by Customs for no more than 48 hours. It will then be turned over to the EPA administrator, unless you have arranged to release it in bond. You must either bring it into TSCA compliance or reexport it within the earlier of 90 days after notice of detention or 30 days of demand for redelivery. Customs may grant an extension if failure to comply or reexport is the result of delays in EPA or Customs procedures. If you fail to comply or reexport within the time allowed, the EPA administrator is authorized to have the shipment stored or disposed of at your expense.

Customs Classification

For customs purposes, soaps, washing and lubricating products, and wax articles are classified under Chapter 34 of the HTSUS. This chapter is broken into major headings, which are further divided into subheadings, and often sub-subheadings, each of which has its own HTSUS classification number. For example, the HTSUS number for castile soap is 3401.11.10, indicating it is a sub-subcategory of soap for toilet use (3401.11), which is a subcategory of the major heading, soap and other soap products (3401). There are seven major headings within Chapter 34.

3401—Soap; organic surface-active products and preparations for use as soap, in the form of bars, cakes, molded pieces, or shapes, whether or not containing soap; paper, wadding, felt, and nonwovens impregnated, coated, or covered with soap or detergent

3402—Organic surface-active agents (other than soap); surface-active preparations, washing preparations (including auxiliary washing preparations) and cleaning preparations, whether or not containing soap, other than those of heading 3401

3403—Lubricating preparations (including cutting-oil preparations, bolt or nut release preparations, antirust or anticorrosion preparations, and mold release preparations, based on lubricants) and preparations of a kind used for the oil or grease treatment of textile materials, leather, furskins, or other materials, but excluding preparations containing, as basic constituents, 70% or more, by weight, of petroleum oils or oils obtained from bituminous minerals

3404—Artificial waxes and prepared waxes

3405—Polishes and creams, for footwear, furniture, floors, coachwork, glass or metal, scouring pastes and powders, and similar preparations (whether or not in the form of paper, wadding, felt, nonwovens, cellular plastics, or cellular rubber, impregnated, coated, or covered with such preparations), excluding waxes of heading 3404

3406—Candles, tapers, and the like

3407—Modeling pastes, including those put up for children's amusement; preparations known as "dental wax" or as "dental impression compounds", put up in sets, in packings for retail sale, or in plates, horseshoe shapes, sticks, or similar forms; other preparations for use in dentistry, with a basis of plaster (of calcined gypsum or calcium sulfate)

For more details regarding classifications of the specific product you are interested in importing, consult a customs broker, the appropriate commodity specialist at your nearest customs port, or the HTSUS. The 2001 HTSUS is available online from the Customs Service (www.customs.gov/impoexpo/impoexpo.htm) or for purchase from the U.S. Government Printing Office (see resources at the end of this chapter), and may be found in larger public libraries. For a general discussion of customs classification, see "Classification—Liquidation" on page 229.

Dutiable Status of Goods

For more information about duty rates and binding decisions see "Dutiable Status of Goods" on page 203; for a discussion of temporary importation of goods see "Temporary Free Importations" on page 205.

Valuation

Importers have a responsibility to use what the U.S. Customs Service deems, "reasonable care," when determining the value of their goods. They must also provide any additional information that the Customs Service needs for setting a final value on the goods. This process involves a number of factors and can be somewhat complicated; importers must be aware of applicable issues and details. Valuation information applies to all types of commodities, for further discussion on the subject see "Customs Valuation" on page 267.

Import Duties

Import duties vary (often dramatically) depending upon the Harmonized Tariff Schedule (HTSUS) classification of the goods or products imported. Since some products that look alike have different HTSUS classifications and different rates of duty, proper classification is vital. Note that "differences of opinion" between importers and the Bureau of Customs and Border Protection regarding classification keeps customs attorneys very busy.

Import duties can be assessed on the imported value of the goods ("ad valorem" rates of duty such as 2%, 4.4%, 50%, etc.), total units or weight of the goods ("specific" rates of duty such as 2 cents each or 1.5 cents/pound, etc.) or on a combination basis ("compound" rates of duty such as 5 cents each plus 6%).

Listed below is a sampling of several Column 1 import duty rates for Chapter 34 products:

Castile soap (3401.11.10.00): free
to Aromatic or modified aromatic (linear alkylbenzene sulfonic acid and linear alkylbenzene sulfonates) (3402.11.20.00): 6.5%

For specific information on US import duties refer to the Harmonized Tariff Schedule of the US. The print version is available from the US Government Printing Office as well as third party suppliers who often add special features. Online versions are available in both static PDF pages as well as in formats with excellent search functionality. Search the Web with the term "Harmonized Tariff Schedule" to find sources.

Entry and Documentation

The entry of merchandise is a two-part process consisting of 1) filing the documentation necessary to determine whether merchandise may be released from Customs custody, and 2) filing the documents that contain information for duty assessment and statistical purposes. In certain instances, all documents must be filed and accepted by customs prior to release of the goods. Unless you have been granted an extension, you must file entry documents at a location specified by the port or area director within five working days of your shipment's date of arrival at a U.S. port of entry. These include a number of standard documents required by Customs for any entry, and:

- U.S. Customs TSCA Certification (for hazardous substances) document

After you present the entry, Customs may examine your shipment or may waive examination. The shipment is then released provided no legal or regulatory violations have been noted. You must then file entry summary documentation and deposit estimated duties at a designated customhouse within 10 working days of your shipment's release. For a detailed description of entry procedures, standard documentation, and informal entry, see "Entry Process" on page 185.

Informed Compliance. Informed compliance was introduced with the Customs Modernization Act of 1993 (Mod Act) and defines the relationship between importers and the Customs Service. It sets out the responsibilities of both parties. Providing the correct documentation and information for entry is a key factor that will make your importing operation run smoothly. We recommend that importers become familiar with the concept of informed comliance and the responsibilities that they have under the Mod Act. For further discussion about informed compliance see "Informed Compliance" on page 211.

Note: The Entry and Documentation section has been carefully designed to supply you, the importer, with sample documents and directions on how to satisfy Customs requirements. Be aware that you should consult the applicable authorities to ensure that you are correctly following the most current procedures.

Prohibitions and Restrictions

Importation of any consumer product that has been declared a banned hazardous substance by a rule under the CPSA is prohibited. Any product considered hazardous and not labeled according to provisions of the FHSA is a misbranded hazardous substance and is an illegal import. Certain hazardous substances listed in the FHSA and in regulations promulgated by the CPSC are completely banned from importation. A shipment of consumer products cannot be imported if it poses an imminent hazard. See 15 USC 1261, 2604-2606; 16 CFR 1500.265-1500.272.

The CPSC may detain your shipment of hazardous substances and take samples for testing to determine compliance with the FHSA. If your shipment is found to contain banned hazardous substances, it will be refused admission and will be destroyed if not exported within 90 days of the date of refusal notice. If it is found to contain misbranded hazardous substances, you may make arrangements to bring it into conformance through relabeling. For complete details regarding testing, labeling, and safety regulations for hazardous products, contact the CPSC (see addresses at end of this chapter).

Marking and Labeling Requirements

Chemical Products. A shipment of any products containing chemicals that are classified as hazardous substance (49 CFR 172) must comply with the marking and labeling regulations adopted by the EPA (46 CFR 147.30) and the DOT (49 CFR 171 et seq.).

For a general discussion of U.S. Customs marking and labeling requirements, see "Country of Origin Marking" on page 236, "Special Marking Requirements" on page 238 and "Marking—False Impression" on page 239.

Shipping Considerations

You will need to ensure that your goods are packaged and shipped with care so that they pass smoothly through Customs and arrive in good condition. You are responsible for ensuring that the shipment is in compliance with all applicable government regulations for packaging and shipping. In most instances, you should not leave these arrangements solely to the discretion of your supplier. Careful preparation of the cargo and selection of the mode of transport can be essential to a cost-effective, timely delivery of undamaged goods. We strongly advise you to consult your shipping representative, insurance agent, or freight broker for advice on packing and shipping.

Soaps, washing and lubricating products, and wax articles may be shipped in bulk, bags, bottles, crates, or other types of containers, depending on the type of product and whether it is prepackaged. General considerations include protection from contamination, weather, and pests. For liquid shipments, venting and vapor collection systems may be required. Safety precautions should also be implemented as required to protect against breakage, spillage, corrosion of containers, and combustion. Containers should be constructed so as to be safe for handling during transport.

Chemical Products. Chemical products in particular may have to be shipped in pressurized, ventilated, and temperature-and vapor-controlled enclosures. Solid chemical products that are listed as hazardous substances (49 CFR 172 appendix) may be transported in bulk only on compliance with Coast Guard notification procedures, shipping permit requirements, and complex transportation regulations (46 CFR 148). All hazardous substances must also be packaged and transported in accordance with DOT regulations (49 CFR 171 et seq.).

Publications and WWW Resources

The following publications may be relevant to the importation of toxic or hazardous ingredients for soaps, washing and lubricating products, and wax articles:

Toxic Substances Control Act: A Guide for Chemical Importers/ Exporters (published by EPA)

This document is available from the TSCA Assistance Information Service (see Relevant Government Agencies)

The following publication provides a listing of existing chemical substances in the United States. It can be purchased in electronic format or a search of the document can be requested via telephone. Contact the Chemical Abstract Service (CAS) at (800)631-1884 or at (614) 447-3600 ext 2308.

TSCA Chemical Substance Inventory

In order to check whether or not a chemical is subject to any rules or regulations under Sections 5, 6, or 7 of TSCA, search the following document (www.epa.gov/opptintr/CORR)

Chemical on Reporting Rules List (CORR)

The *Harmonized Tariff Schedule of the United States (2001)* (HTSUS) is available to view on the Customs Service website (www.customs.gov), or you may purchase a printed version from:

U.S. Government Printing Office
Superintendent of Documents
710 North Capital Street NW
Washington DC 20401
Tel: (202) 512-1800
Fax: (202) 512-1657
Website: www.access.gpo.gov

The USGPO also has copies of specific laws available for purchase. The USGPO accepts orders made by fax, phone or placed over the Internet, as well as mail orders paid by credit card. All orders must be accompanied by payment. Credit cards, checks drawn on a U.S. bank, or an international money order are all acceptable.

Relevant Government Agencies

Address your questions regarding CPSC requirements for soaps, washing and lubricating products, and wax articles to:

Consumer Product Safety Commission (CPSC)
Office of Compliance
Washington DC 20207-0001
Tel: 800-638-2772 or (301) 504-7912
Fax: (301) 504-0359
Website: www.cpsc.gov

Address your inquiries regarding TSCA and EPA requirements for importation of inorganic chemical substances to:

Environmental Protection Agency (EPA)
Office of Pollution Prevention and Toxics
TSCA System Information
1200 Pennsylvania Avenue NW
Washington DC 20460
Tel: (202) 564-3810
Tel: (202) 554-1404 (TSCA Information Hotline)
Email: oppt.homepage@epa.gov
Website: www.epa.gov/opptintr/contact.htm

Address your questions regarding transportation of hazardous substances to:

U.S. Department of Transportation (DOT)
Research and Special Programs Administration
Hazardous Materials Information Center
400 7th St. SW
Washington DC 20590
Tel: (202) 366-4488
Website: http://hazmat.dot.gov

Address your questions regarding importation of soaps, washing and lubricating products, and wax articles generally to your local Customs port director. For addresses, refer to "U.S. Customs and Border Protection Offices" on page 65 or contact:

U.S. Customs and Border Protection
Customs Headquarters
1300 Pennsylvania Avenue NW
Washington DC 20229
Tel: (202) 354-1000
Website: www.customs.treas.gov

Laws and Regulations

The following laws and regulations may be relevant to the importation of soaps, washing and lubricating products, and wax articles. The laws are contained in the United States Code (USC), and the regulations are published in the Code of Federal Regulations (CFR), both of which are available at larger public and law libraries. Specific laws and regulations may also be purchased from the U.S. Government Printing Office (address above).

21 USC 301 et seq.
Federal Food, Drug, and Cosmetic Act
This Act prohibits deceptive practices and regulates the manufacture, sale and importation or exportation of

food, drugs, cosmetics, and related products. It was amended by the Food Quality Protection Act of 1996. See 21 USC 331, 381, 382.

19 CFR 12.1 et seq.; 21 CFR 1.83 et seq.
Regulations on Food, Drugs, and Cosmetics
These regulations of the Secretary of Health and Human Services and the Secretary of the Treasury govern the standards, labeling, marking, and importing of products used with food, drugs, and cosmetics.

15 USC 2051 et seq.
Consumer Product Safety Act (CPSA)
This Act gives the Consumer Product Safety Commission authority to set safety standards, testing procedures, and reporting requirements to ensure that consumer products not already covered under other regulations are not harmful.

16 CFR 1500 et seq.
Regulations on Hazardous Substances Safety Standards
These regulations set standards for processing, manufacturing, importing, and labeling all substances classified as hazardous that are to be sold to U.S. consumers.

15 USC 2601 et seq.
Toxic Substances Control Act
This Act authorizes the EPA to determine whether a substance is harmful and to restrict importation, sale, and use of such substances.

19 CFR 12.118 et seq.
Regulations on Toxic Substances Control
These regulations require importers of chemical substances imported in bulk or as part of a mixture to certify to Customs that the shipment complies with the TSCA or is not subject to that Act.

15 USC 1261 et seq.
Federal Hazardous Substances Act
This Act controls the importation of hazardous substances, sets forth prohibited imports, and authorizes various agencies to promulgate labeling, marking, and transport requirements.

49 CFR 171 et seq.
Regulations on Hazardous Materials
These regulations list all substances deemed hazardous and provide transport, marking, labeling, safety, and emergency response rules.

46 CFR 147.30
Regulations on Labeling of Hazardous Materials
This regulation requires the labeling of containers of hazardous substances and specifies the label contents.

46 CFR 148 et seq.
Regulations on Carriage of Solid Hazardous Materials in Bulk
These regulations govern the transport of solid hazardous substances in bulk, including reporting, permitting, loading, stowing, and shipping requirements.

Sources of Additional Information
The TSCA Chemical Substance Inventory is available through various commercial online databases and from:

National Technical Information Service (NTIS)
U.S. Department of Commerce
5285 Port Royal Road
Springfield, VA 22161
(703) 605-6000; FAX (703) 605-6900
Web site: www.ntis.gov

Principal Exporting Countries
The following listing includes samples of the main supplier nations of the products of this chapter. It is organized by HTSUS major heading. (Refer to "Customs Classification" above for the product codes.) Countries are listed in rank order of the value of products imported to the U.S. Statistics represent customs value of entries for 2002 from the Bureau of Census, U.S. Department of Commerce.

3401—Canada, United Kingdom, Mexico, France, China, Israel, Guatemala, Italy

3402—Canada, Mexico, Germany, United Kingdom, Japan, Spain, France, Belgium, China, Italy, Russia

3403—Germany, Canada, France, Japan, Malaysia, United Kingdom, Italy, Belgium, Spain, Austria, Switzerland

3404—Germany, United Kingdom, Malaysia, Canada, Japan, France, Mexico, South Korea

3405—Japan, Canada, United Kingdom, Germany, Spain, France, Denmark, Mexico

3406—China, Canada, Mexico, Israel, Guatemala, Hong Kong, Thailand, Taiwan, Italy, El Salvador, France

3407—China, Germany, Switzerland, Italy, Israel

Chapter 35:
Albumins, Glues, and Enzymes

Full title: Albuminoidal Substances; Modified Starches; Glues; Enzymes

This chapter relates to the importation of albuminoidal substances, modified starches, glues, and enzymes, which are classified under Chapter 35 of the Harmonized Tariff Schedule of the United States (HTSUS). Specifically, it includes caseins, albumins, gelatins, peptones, other protein substances, hide powder, dextrins, other modified starches, and animal, fish, and synthetic glues and adhesives.

If you are interested in importing yeasts, you should refer to Commodity Index Chapter 21. Blood fractions (except blood albumin not for therapeutic or prophylactic uses), medicaments, or other products are classified under Chapter 30. Enzymatic preparations for pretanning are found in Chapter 32, and other enzymatic preparations, such as for soaking or washing, are in Chapter 34. This chapter also does not apply to hardened proteins, which are in Chapter 39. Gelatin products of the printing industry fall under Chapter 49.

Note: To understand key issues that will enable you to make best use of the information in this section we recommend that you see "Introduction" on page 425.

Key Factors

The key factors in the importation of albuminoidal substances, modified starches, glues, and enzymes are:

- Compliance with U.S. Department of Agriculture (USDA) requirements (if an animal or fish product)

- Compliance with U.S. Federal Trade Commission (FTC) and Consumer Product Safety Commission (CPSC) standards (if a consumer product)

- Compliance with U.S. Environmental Protection Agency (EPA) requirements under Toxic Substances Control Act (TSCA) (if the product is a hazardous substance)

- Compliance with U.S. Department of Transportation (DOT) regulations for transport of hazardous cargo (if the product is a hazardous substance)

Although most importers use the services of a licensed customs broker in making their entries, and we recommend this practice, you should be aware of the regulatory, entry, and documentation issues involved in importing your product. You, as importer, are ultimately responsible for the fulfillment of any legal requirements applicable to your shipment.

General Considerations

Regulatory Agencies. The USDA regulates the importation of products derived from animals. The FTC sets standards for processing and labeling products that are sold to consumers. The EPA, under authority of the TSCA, imposes certain controls on the importation of albuminoidal substances, modified starches, glues, and enzymes that contain toxic substances. The TSCA defines a toxic substance as any substance determined to present the possibility of an unreasonable risk of injury to health and the environment. The DOT enforces regulations for transporting hazardous cargo. Materials are deemed hazardous if listed in DOT transport regulations (49 CFR 172 appendix).

Animal Products. Products derived from animals are subject to quarantine regulations, marking requirements, and processing standards. Shipments of these products are inspected at the port of arrival by the Animal and Plant Health Inspection Service (APHIS) of the USDA. Unless the shipment is in compliance with all applicable laws and regulations, it will be denied entry into the U.S. Some shipments may be restricted or prohibited completely.

The USDA heavily regulates eggs and egg products, including dried egg substances. An importer of egg products must apply for inspection on PY **Form 222**-Import Request, Eggs and Egg Products. The application should be made as far in advance before arrival at a U.S. port as possible. It may be submitted to the Poultry Division of the Poultry Grading Branch office at the port of importation (7 CFR 59.920). Each shipment of egg products must also be accompanied by a foreign egg products inspection certificate (7 CFR 59.915) and a warning sign or special import seal must be affixed to the packages or means of conveyance for the products. Before admittance into the U.S., the shipment will be inspected at the port of arrival for compliance with product and labeling standards. For small shipments, an importer may be required to transport the product to the inspector's location. Importers may also be required to supply an inspector with a sample. Egg products may be released in bond prior to inspection. Exemptions from these requirements are allowed for small importations (up to 30 pounds of liquid or frozen, or 50 pounds of dried, egg products) for laboratory analysis or personal use.

To be sold in the U.S., dried and frozen egg albumin and other products must be processed and labeled in compliance with FTC regulations.

Hazardous Consumer Products. Under the Federal Hazardous Substances Act (FHSA), albuminoidal substances, modified starches, glues, and enzymes intended for the consumer market are hazardous substances if they are flammable, combustible, or have the potential to cause substantial personal injury during, or as a proximate result of, any customary or reasonably foreseeable handling or use. The CPSC does not require permits, special invoicing, limited entry, licenses, or any special approval process for importing hazardous consumer products into the U.S. However, if you are importing these types of products, you are responsible for ensuring that they meet all applicable FHSA and CPSA requirements. There are detailed regulations regarding testing and labeling of hazardous products. The Commission's enforcement posture regarding compliance with labeling and product safety standards changes as new facts become available. Contact the CPSC (see addresses at end of this chapter) for specific requirements on the consumer product you are considering importing.

Substantial Product Hazard Reports. Defect-reporting is required for products covered under the Consumer Product Safety Act (CPSA). The law requires every manufacturer, distributor, or retailer of such products, who obtains information that reasonably supports the conclusion that such products fail to comply with an applicable consumer product safety rule, or contain a defect that could create a substantial product hazard, to immediately inform the CPSC of the potential violation or defect. A firm's willful failure to make a Substantial Product Hazard Report can result in litigation by the CPSC.

Chemical Products. Shipments of products containing chemicals must be in compliance with toxic and hazardous substance regulations of the EPA and DOT. These include packaging, shipping, marking, and labeling requirements. In addition, all products containing chemicals are subject to the U.S. Customs Service TSCA Import Certification Rule (19 CFR 12.118 et seq.). If you import these products, you must sign one of the following statements: "I certify that all chemical substances in this shipment comply with all applicable rules or orders under TSCA and that I am not offering a chemical substance for entry in violation of TSCA or any applicable rule or order thereunder" or "I certify that all chemicals in this shipment are not subject to TSCA."

You must file this TSCA certification of compliance or exemption at the time you make the entry at Customs. The certification may be in the form of a typed or stamped statement on an appropriate entry document or commercial invoice or a preprinted attachment to such entry document or invoice. You may sign the certificate by means of an authorized facsimile signature. If your entry is electronically processed, the certification will be in the form of a Certification Code, which is part of the Automated Broker Interface (ABI) transmission. Customs will not release your shipment without proper certification.

If you will be importing several or regular shipments, you should ask the appropriate Customs port director to authorize your use of a blanket certification. If you receive such authorization, you must include on the commercial invoice or entry document for each shipment a statement that the blanket certification is on file and that it is incorporated by reference. This statement need not be signed. The blanket certification is valid for one calendar year, is subject to renewal, and may be revoked at any time for cause.

In filling out TSCA forms and Customs entry documents, you should provide the Chemical Abstracts Service (CAS) number for each chemical in the shipment. These CAS numbers are given in the appendix to the HTSUS. You are not required to include the CAS number, but Customs will be able to process your shipment more quickly if you include this number.

Articles Exclusion. If you are importing items that are classified as hazardous substances but are part of articles, you are subject to TSCA certification requirements only if certification for your product is specifically required by a rule or order promulgated under the TSCA. No specific rules have been adopted at this time. An "article" is a manufactured item 1) that is formed into a specific shape or design during manufacture, 2) that has end-use functions dependent on the shape or design during end use, and 3) that during the end use, does not change in its chemical composition or that changes only for a noncommercial purpose separate from the article and only as allowed by law (19 CFR 12.120(2)). Fluids and particles are not articles, regardless of shape or design.

Shipment Detention. A shipment containing chemicals will be detained at the U.S. port of arrival (or entry if same), at your risk and expense, if: 1) it contains banned chemical substances (15 USC 2604, 2605); or 2) it contains chemical substances ordered seized because of imminent hazards (15 USC 2606). Further detention will occur at the port of entry, again at your risk and expense, if: 1) the EPA administrator or Customs port director has reasonable grounds to believe the shipment is not in compliance with the TSCA; or 2) you do not provide proper TSCA certification.

If your shipment is detained, it will be held by Customs for no more than 48 hours. It will then be turned over to the EPA administrator, unless you have arranged to release it in bond. You must

either bring it into TSCA compliance or reexport it within the earlier of 90 days after notice of detention or 30 days of demand for redelivery. Customs may grant an extension if failure to comply or reexport is the result of delays in EPA or Customs procedures. If you fail to comply or reexport within the time allowed, the EPA administrator is authorized to have the shipment stored or disposed of at your expense.

Customs Classification

For customs purposes, albuminoidal substances, modified starches, glues, and enzymes are classified under Chapter 35 of the HT-SUS. This chapter is broken into major headings, which are further divided into subheadings, and often sub-subheadings, each of which has its own HTSUS classification number. For example, the 2001 HTSUS number for milk protein concentrate is 3501.10.10, indicating it is a sub-subcategory of casein (3501.10), which is a subcategory of the major heading, casein and related products (3501). There are seven major headings within Chapter 35.

3501—Casein, caseinates, and other casein derivatives; casein glues

3502—Albumins (including concentrates of two or more whey proteins, containing by weight more than 80% whey proteins, calculated on the dry matter), albuminates, and other albumin derivatives

3503—Gelatin (including gelatin in rectangular (including square) sheets, whether or not surface-worked or colored) and gelatin derivatives; isinglass; other glues of animal origin, excluding casein glues of heading 3501

3504—Peptones and their derivatives; other protein substances and their derivatives, not elsewhere specified or included; hide powder, whether or not chromed

3505—Dextrins and other modified starches (for example, pregelatinized or esterified starches); glues based on starches, or on dextrins or other modified starches

3506—Prepared glues and other prepared adhesives, not elsewhere specified or included; products suitable for use as glues or adhesives, put up for retail sale as glues or adhesives, not exceeding a net weight of 1 kg

3507—Enzymes; prepared enzymes not elsewhere specified or included

For more details regarding classifications of the specific product you are interested in importing, consult a customs broker, the appropriate commodity specialist at your nearest customs port, or the HTSUS. The 2001 HTSUS is available online from the Customs Service (www.customs.gov/impoexpo/impoexpo.htm) or for purchase from the U.S. Government Printing Office (see resources at the end of this chapter), and may be found in larger public libraries. For a general discussion of customs classification, see "Classification—Liquidation" on page 229.

Dutiable Status of Goods

For more information about duty rates and binding decisions see "Dutiable Status of Goods" on page 203; for a discussion of temporary importation of goods see "Temporary Free Importations" on page 205.

Valuation

Importers have a responsibility to use what the U.S. Customs Service deems, "reasonable care," when determining the value of their goods. They must also provide any additional information that the Customs Service needs for setting a final value on the goods. This process involves a number of factors and can be somewhat complicated; importers must be aware of applicable issues and details. Valuation information applies to all types of commodities, for further discussion on the subject see "Customs Valuation" on page 267.

Import Duties

Import duties vary (often dramatically) depending upon the Harmonized Tariff Schedule (HTSUS) classification of the goods or products imported. Since some products that look alike have different HTSUS classifications and different rates of duty, proper classification is vital. Note that "differences of opinion" between importers and the Bureau of Customs and Border Protection regarding classification keeps customs attorneys very busy.

Import duties can be assessed on the imported value of the goods ("ad valorem" rates of duty such as 2%, 4.4%, 50%, etc.), total units or weight of the goods ("specific" rates of duty such as 2 cents each or 1.5 cents/pound, etc.) or on a combination basis ("compound" rates of duty such as 5 cents each plus 6%).

Listed below is a sampling of several Column 1 import duty rates for Chapter 35 products:
Milk albumin, including concentrates of two or more whey proteins (3502.20.00.00): free
to
Casein glues (3501.90.20.00): 6%

For specific information on US import duties refer to the Harmonized Tariff Schedule of the US. The print version is available from the US Government Printing Office as well as third party suppliers who often add special features. Online versions are available in both static PDF pages as well as in formats with excellent search functionality. Search the Web with the term "Harmonized Tariff Schedule" to find sources.

Entry and Documentation

The entry of merchandise is a two-part process consisting of 1) filing the documentation necessary to determine whether merchandise may be released from Customs custody, and 2) filing the documents that contain information for duty assessment and statistical purposes. In certain instances, all documents must be filed and accepted by Customs prior to release of the goods. Unless you have been granted an extension, you must file entry documents at a location specified by the port or area director within five working days of your shipment's date of arrival at a U.S. port of entry. These include a number of standard documents required by Customs for any entry, and:

- PY Form 222-Import Request (for egg products)
- Foreign inspection certificate (for egg products)
- U.S. Customs TSCA Certification (for hazardous substances) document

After you present the entry, Customs may examine your shipment or may waive examination. The shipment is then released provided no legal or regulatory violations have been noted. You must then file entry summary documentation and deposit estimated duties at a designated customhouse within 10 working days of your shipment's release. For a detailed description of entry procedures, standard documentation, and informal entry, see "Entry Process" on page 185.

Informed Compliance. Informed compliance was introduced with the Customs Modernization Act of 1993 (Mod Act) and defines the relationship between importers and the Customs Service. It sets out the responsibilities of both parties. Providing the correct documentation and information for entry is a key factor that will make your importing operation run smoothly. We recommend that importers become familiar with the concept of informed comliance and the responsibilities that they have under the Mod Act. For further discussion about informed compliance see "Informed Compliance" on page 211.

Note: The Entry and Documentation section has been carefully designed to supply you, the importer, with sample documents and directions on how to satisfy Customs requirements. Be aware that you should consult the applicable authorities to ensure that you are correctly following the most current procedures.

Prohibitions and Restrictions

Animal Products. Animal products are subject to quarantine if they arrive from certain countries that are known to have specific infectious diseases. These countries are listed in 9 CFR 94. If a USDA inspector determines that a shipment is infected with anthrax, foot-and-mouth disease, rinderpest, or bovine spongiform encephalopathy, entry will be denied.

Bone meal may be imported without restriction, provided it has been processed in compliance with USDA regulations; is free of pieces of bone, hide, flesh, and sinew; and contains no more than traces of hair or wool (9 CFR 95.13). Entry is denied for shipments that are not in compliance.

Dried blood, blood meal, animal organs, tankage, meat meal, wool waste, wool manure, and similar animal byproducts for industrial use cannot be imported unless 1) the product originated in and was shipped from a country that is not on the quarantine list for foot-and-mouth disease or rinderpest; or 2) the products are handled through quarantine procedures at the port of arrival and are found to be in compliance with USDA conditions (9 CFR 95.15, 95.16).

Hazardous Consumer Products. Importation of any consumer product that has been declared a banned hazardous substance by a rule under the CPSA is prohibited. Any product considered hazardous and not labeled according to provisions of the FHSA is a misbranded hazardous substance and is an illegal import. Certain hazardous substances listed in the FHSA and in regulations promulgated by the CPSC are completely banned from importation. A shipment of consumer products cannot be imported if it poses an imminent hazard. See 15 USC 1261, 2604-2606; 16 CFR 1500.265-1500.272.

The CPSC may detain your shipment of hazardous substances and take samples for testing to determine compliance with the FHSA. If your shipment is found to contain banned hazardous substances, it will be refused admission and will be destroyed if not exported within 90 days of the date of refusal notice. If it is found to contain misbranded hazardous substances, you may make arrangements to bring it into conformance through relabeling. For complete details regarding testing, labeling, and safety regulations for hazardous products, contact the CPSC (see addresses at end of this chapter).

Country-Specific Restrictions

Egg products can be imported only from Canada and the Netherlands. Importation from all other countries is prohibited except for small importations (up to 30 pounds of liquid or frozen, or 50 pounds of dried egg products) for laboratory analysis or personal use.

Regulatory Changes. APHIS has amended the animal and animal product importation regulations to allow for regionalization of countries—that is, disease classification of parts of a country, an entire country, or groups of countries. The rule change was made to recognize levels of disease risk in regions. Details about the criteria that APHIS considers when evaluating the regions that wish to export animals or animal products to the United States can be found at the APHIS Veterinary Service National Center for Import and Export (NCIE) website (www.aphis.usda.gov/ncie).

Marking and Labeling Requirements

Animal Products. Containers in which animal products are packaged and shipped must be marked with the country of origin—that is, the country where the animal was located. If the products are quarantined at the port of arrival, marks and signs are required on shipping documents and any mode of transport used to move the product while under restrictions (9 CFR 95.25).

Special labeling requirements are required for immediate containers of egg products and for the containers in which they are shipped (7 CFR 59.950, 59.955). A USDA inspector can deny these products entry if the labeling is false or misleading.

Chemical Products. A shipment of any products containing chemicals that are classified as hazardous substance (49 CFR 172) must comply with the marking and labeling regulations adopted by the EPA (46 CFR 147.30) and the DOT (49 CFR 171 et seq.).

For a general discussion of U.S. Customs marking and labeling requirements, see "Country of Origin Marking" on page 236, "Special Marking Requirements" on page 238 and "Marking—False Impression" on page 239.

Shipping Considerations

You will need to ensure that your goods are packaged and shipped with care so that they pass smoothly through Customs and arrive in good condition. You are responsible for ensuring that the shipment is in compliance with all applicable government regulations for packaging and shipping. In most instances, you should not leave these arrangements solely to the discretion of your supplier. Careful preparation of the cargo and selection of the mode of transport can be essential to a cost-effective, timely delivery of undamaged goods. We strongly advise you to consult your shipping representative, insurance agent, or freight broker for advice on packing and shipping.

Albuminoidal substances, modified starches, glues, and enzymes may be shipped in bulk, bags, bottles, or other types of containers, depending on the type of product and whether it is prepackaged. General considerations include protection from contamination, weather, and pests. If a product must be kept in a sanitary environment, all tables, utensils, platforms, and devices used for moving or handling the product, the compartments in which it is stowed while being transported will need to be maintained in a sanitary condition. For liquid shipments, venting and vapor collection systems may be required. Safety precautions should also be implemented as required to protect against breakage, spillage, corrosion of containers, and combustion. Containers should be constructed so as to be safe for handling during transport.

Chemical Products. Chemical products in particular may have to be shipped in pressurized, ventilated, and temperature-and vapor-controlled enclosures. Solid chemical products that are listed as hazardous substances (49 CFR 172 appendix) may be transported in bulk only on compliance with Coast Guard notification procedures, shipping permit requirements, and complex transportation regulations (46 CFR 148). All hazardous substances must also be packaged and transported in accordance with DOT regulations (49 CFR 171 et seq.).

Publications and WWW Resources

The following publication explains the FDA requirements for importing albuminoidal substances, modified starches, glues, and enzymes. It is published by the FDA and is available online from the FDA website (www.fda.gov).

> *Requirements of Laws and Regulations Enforced by the U.S. Food and Drug Administration*

The following publications may be relevant to the importation of toxic or hazardous albuminoidal substances, modified starches, glues, and enzymes:

> *Toxic Substances Control Act: A Guide for Chemical Importers/ Exporters* (published by EPA)

This document is available from the TSCA Assistance Information Service (see Relevant Government Agencies)

The following publication provides a listing of existing chemical substances in the United States. It can be purchased in electronic format or a search of the document can be requested via telephone. Contact the Chemical Abstract Service (CAS) at (800)631-1884 or at (614) 447-3600 ext 2308.

TSCA Chemical Substance Inventory

In order to check whether or not a chemical is subject to any rules or regulations under Sections 5, 6, or 7 of TSCA, search the following document (www.epa.gov/opptintr/CORR)

Chemical on Reporting Rules List (CORR)

The above publications and the *Harmonized Tariff Schedule of the United States (2001)* (HTSUS) is available to view on the Customs Service website (www.customs.gov), or you may purchase a printed version from:

U.S. Government Printing Office
Superintendent of Documents
710 North Capital Street NW
Washington DC 20401
Tel: (202) 512-1800
Fax: (202) 512-1657
Website: www.access.gpo.gov

The USGPO also has copies of specific laws available for purchase. The USGPO accepts orders made by fax, phone or placed over the Internet, as well as mail orders paid by credit card. All orders must be accompanied by payment. Credit cards, checks drawn on a U.S. bank, or an international money order are all acceptable.

Relevant Government Agencies

Address your inquiries regarding USDA requirements for importation of animal products to:

Animal and Plant Health Inspection Service (APHIS)
Veterinary Services (VS)
National Center for Import and Export
4700 River Road, Unit 40
Riverdale, MD 20737
Tel: (301) 734-3277
Animal products: (301) 734-4401
Biological materials and vectors: (301) 734-3277
Website: www.aphis.usda.gov/vs

Address your inquiries regarding importation of egg products to:

USDA Agricultural Marketing Service (AMS)
Poultry Division
USDA - AMS - Dairy Programs
1400 Independence Avenue SW
Washington DC 20250
Tel: (202) 720-4392
Dairy Import Group: (202) 720-2916
Website: www.usda.gov/ams

Address your questions regarding CPSC requirements for albuminoidal substances, modified starches, glues, and enzymes to:

Consumer Product Safety Commission (CPSC)
Office of Compliance
Washington DC 20207-0001
Tel: 800-638-2772 or (301) 504-7912
Fax: (301) 504-0359
Website: www.cpsc.gov

Address your inquiries regarding TSCA and EPA requirements for importation of inorganic chemical substances to:

Environmental Protection Agency (EPA)
Office of Pollution Prevention and Toxics
TSCA System Information
1200 Pennsylvania Avenue NW
Washington DC 20460
Tel: (202) 564-3810
Tel: (202) 554-1404 (TSCA Information Hotline)
Email: oppt.homepage@epa.gov
Website: www.epa.gov/opptintr/contact.htm

Address your questions regarding transportation of hazardous substances to:

U.S. Department of Transportation (DOT)
Research and Special Programs Administration
Hazardous Materials Information Center
400 7th St. SW
Washington DC 20590
Tel: (202) 366-4488
Website: http://hazmat.dot.gov

Address your questions regarding importation of albuminoidal substances, modified starches, glues, and enzymes generally to your local Customs port director. For addresses, refer to "U.S. Customs and Border Protection Offices" on page 65 or contact:

U.S. Customs and Border Protection
Customs Headquarters
1300 Pennsylvania Avenue NW
Washington DC 20229
Tel: (202) 354-1000
Website: www.customs.treas.gov

Laws and Regulations

The following laws and regulations may be relevant to the importation of albuminoidal substances, modified starches, glues, and enzymes. The laws are contained in the United States Code (USC), and the regulations are published in the Code of Federal Regulations (CFR), both of which are available at larger public and law libraries. Specific laws and regulations may also be purchased from the U.S. Government Printing Office (address above).

21 USC 301 et seq.
Federal Food, Drug, and Cosmetic Act
This Act prohibits deceptive practices and regulates the manufacture, sale and importation or exportation of food, drugs, cosmetics, and related products. It was amended by the Food Quality Protection Act of 1996. See 21 USC 331, 381, 382.

19 CFR 12.1 et seq.; 21 CFR 1.83 et seq.
Regulations on Food, Drugs, and Cosmetics
These regulations of the Secretary of Health and Human Services and the Secretary of the Treasury govern the standards, labeling, marking, and importing of products used with food, drugs, and cosmetics.

15 USC 2051 et seq.
Consumer Product Safety Act (CPSA)
This Act gives the Consumer Product Safety Commission authority to set safety standards, testing procedures, and reporting requirements to ensure that consumer products not already covered under other regulations are not harmful.

16 CFR 1500 et seq.
Regulations on Hazardous Substances Safety Standards
These regulations set standards for processing, manufacturing, importing, and labeling all substances classified as hazardous that are to be sold to U.S. consumers.

21 USC 1031 et seq.
Egg Product Inspection Act
This Act requires the inspection of edible and nonconsumable egg products, including imports, and sets labeling and processing standards.

9 CFR 95.13 et seq.
Regulations for Animals Destroyed Because of Tuberculosis
These regulations prohibit the importation of animal products for use in industry unless the products meet certain processing standards and are not infected with certain diseases.

15 USC 2601 et seq.
Toxic Substances Control Act
This Act authorizes the EPA to determine whether a substance is harmful and to restrict importation, sale, and use of such substances.

19 CFR 12.118 et seq.
Regulations on Toxic Substances Control
These regulations require importers of chemical substances imported in bulk or as part of a mixture to certify to Customs that the shipment complies with the TSCA or is not subject to that Act.

15 USC 1261 et seq.
Federal Hazardous Substances Act
This Act controls the importation of hazardous substances, sets forth prohibited imports, and authorizes various agencies to promulgate labeling, marking, and transport requirements.

49 CFR 171 et seq.
Regulations on Hazardous Materials
These regulations list all substances deemed hazardous and provide transport, marking, labeling, safety, and emergency response rules.

46 CFR 147.30
Regulations on Labeling of Hazardous Materials
This regulation requires the labeling of containers of hazardous substances and specifies the label contents.

46 CFR 148 et seq.
Regulations on Carriage of Solid Hazardous Materials in Bulk
These regulations govern the transport of solid hazardous substances in bulk, including reporting, permitting, loading, stowing, and shipping requirements.

Sources of Additional Information

The TSCA Chemical Substance Inventory is available through various commercial online databases and from:

National Technical Information Service (NTIS)
U.S. Department of Commerce
5285 Port Royal Road
Springfield, VA 22161
(703) 605-6000; FAX (703) 605-6900
Web site: www.ntis.gov

Principal Exporting Countries

The following listing includes samples of the main supplier nations of the products of this chapter. It is organized by HTSUS major heading. (Refer to "Customs Classification" above for the product codes.) Countries are listed in rank order of the value of products imported to the U.S. Statistics represent customs value of entries for 2002 from the Bureau of Census, U.S. Department of Commerce.

3501—New Zealand, Ireland, France, Netherlands, Australia, Germany, India

3502—New Zealand, Canada, United Kingdom, Australia, Spain, Denmark, Germany, Ireland, Norway

3503—France, Brazil, United Kingdom, Japan, Argentina, Germany, India, Belgium

3504—United Kingdom, Germany, Canada, France, Denmark, Brazil, Japan, Netherlands, Austria, Mexico

3505—Canada, Netherlands, France, Czech Republic, Germany, Thailand, Sweden, Japan, Mexico

3506—Canada, Germany, Japan, South Korea, China, United Kingdom, Switzerland, Mexico, Netherlands, Taiwan

3507—Denmark, Japan, Germany, France, United Kingdom, Finland, Belgium, Canada

Chapter 36:
Explosives, Fireworks, and Other Combustibles

Full title: Explosives; Pyrotechnic Products; Matches; Pyrophoric Alloys; Certain Combustible Preparations

This chapter relates to the importation of explosives, fireworks, and other combustible materials, which are classified under Chapter 36 of the Harmonized Tariff Schedule of the United States (HTSUS). Specifically, it includes propellant powders, other prepared explosives, fuses, detonators, igniters, fireworks, flares, rain rockets, matches, ferrocerium, other pyrophoric alloys, and lighter fuels.

If you are interested in importing separate chemical compounds, you should refer to Commodity Index Chapters 28 (inorganic) or 29 (organic). Refer to Chapter 22 for a discussion of the importation of ethyl alcohol for fuel or other purposes. The importation of arms and ammunition is covered in Chapter 93.

Note: To understand key issues that will enable you to make best use of the information in this section we recommend that you see "Introduction" on page 425.

Key Factors

The key factors in the importation of explosives, fireworks, and other combustible materials are:

- Compliance with U.S. Federal Trade Commission (FTC) and Consumer Product Safety Commission (CPSC) standards (for matches, lighter fluids, and hazardous substances)

- Compliance with U.S. Mine Safety and Health Administration (MSHA) standards (for explosives and detonators for use in underground mines)

- Compliance with U.S. Bureau of Alcohol, Tobacco, and Firearms (ATF) regulations, including license and permit requirements

- Compliance with U.S. Environmental Protection Agency (EPA) requirements under Toxic Substances Control Act (TSCA) (if the product is a hazardous substance)

- Compliance with U.S. Department of Transportation (DOT) regulations for transport of hazardous cargo (if the product is a hazardous substance)

Although most importers use the services of a licensed customs broker in making their entries, and we recommend this practice, you should be aware of the regulatory, entry, and documentation issues involved in importing your product. You, as importer, are ultimately responsible for the fulfillment of any legal requirements applicable to your shipment.

General Considerations

Regulatory Agencies. The ATF controls commerce in all explosives, including those listed in the regulations (27 CFR 55.23). The MSHA approves explosives and detonators used in underground mines. The FTC and CPSC enforce standards for consumer products that contain hazardous substances, as well as specific requirements for matchbooks and lighter fluids. The EPA, under authority of the TSCA, regulates the importation of explosives, fireworks, and other combustible materials that contain toxic substances The TSCA defines a toxic substance as any substance determined to present the possibility of an unreasonable risk of injury to health and the environment. The DOT enforces regulations for transporting hazardous cargo. Materials are deemed hazardous if listed in DOT transport regulations (49 CFR 172 appendix).

Explosives. If you intend to engage in business as an importer of explosives you must first obtain a license from the ATF. The term "explosives" includes any chemical compound, mixture, or device that has a primary or common purpose to function by an explosion. With few exceptions, you must have a license for each business premises at which you import or distribute these substances. The application for a license is Form ATF F 5400.13. If you want to acquire for use explosive materials from a foreign supplier, you must obtain a permit from the ATF. You will also need a permit to transport explosives in interstate or foreign commerce. The application for a permit is Form ATF F 5400.16. These application forms are available from the ATF. Most original licenses and permits are valid for one year and may then be renewed for three-year periods.

There are a number of exemptions from the ATF explosive regulations, such as for small arms ammunition, common fireworks regulated by the DOT, products delivered to a government agency or military installation, products used as medicines and medicinal agents, gasoline, fertilizers, propellant-actuated devices or industrial tools, and industrial or laboratory chemicals intended for use as reagents. The ATF regulations also exclude commercially manufactured black powder in quantities not exceeding 50 pounds or contained in percussion caps, safety and pyrotechnic fuses, quills, quick and slow matches, and friction primers, provided it intended use is for sporting, recreational, or cultural purposes in antique firearms or devices.

Matches. At the time of filing an entry for imported matches, the importer must make a declaration that to the best of the importer's knowledge and belief no matches included in the invoice and entry are white phosphorus matches.

With two exceptions, the invoice covering a shipment of matches imported to the U.S. must be accompanied by a certificate of official inspection from the government of the country of manufacture. That certificate must be signed by a person who conducts a chemical analysis of the matches, stating that the analysis shows no white or yellow phosphorus in the matches. It must also list the cases of matches tested and, for each case, a description of the matches, the manufacturer, the consignee, and information on shipping. Customs will detain any shipment of matches until this certificate is produced.

The certificate need not be produced if the importer submits other satisfactory evidence that the matches were not manufactured with the use of poisonous white or yellow phosphorus or if the matches were manufactured in a country that prohibits the use of such phosphorus in the manufacture of matches.

Hazardous Consumer Products. The Federal Hazardous Substances Act (FHSA) imposes special controls on hazardous consumer products, which are defined as substances that are flammable, combustible, or have the potential to cause substantial personal injury during, or as a proximate result of, any customary or reasonably foreseeable handling or use. The CPSC does not require permits, special invoicing, limited entry, licenses, or any special approval process for importing hazardous consumer products into the U.S. However, if you are importing these types of products, you are responsible for ensuring that they meet all applicable FHSA and Consumer Product Safety Act (CPSA) requirements. There are detailed regulations regarding testing and labeling of hazardous products. The Commission's enforcement posture regarding compliance with labeling and product safety standards changes as new facts become available. Contact the CPSC (see addresses at end of this chapter) for specific requirements on the consumer product you are considering importing.

Substantial Product Hazard Reports. Defect-reporting is required for products covered under the CPSA. The law requires every manufacturer, distributor, or retailer of such products, who obtains information that reasonably supports the conclusion that such products fail to comply with an applicable consumer product safety rule, or contain a defect that could create a substantial product hazard, to immediately inform the CPSC of the potential violation or defect. A firm's willful failure to make a Substantial Product Hazard Report can result in litigation by the CPSC.

Toxic and Hazardous Substances. Shipments of products containing chemicals must be in compliance with toxic and hazardous substance regulations of the EPA and DOT. These include packaging, shipping, marking, and labeling requirements. In addition, all products containing chemicals are subject to the U.S. Customs Service TSCA Import Certification Rule (19 CFR 12.118 et seq.). If you import these products, you must sign one of the following statements: "I certify that all chemical substances in this shipment comply with all applicable rules or orders under TSCA and that I am not offering a chemical substance for entry in violation of TSCA or any applicable rule or order thereunder" or "I certify that all chemicals in this shipment are not subject to TSCA."

You must file this TSCA certification of compliance or exemption at the time you make the entry at Customs. The certification may be in the form of a typed or stamped statement on an appropriate entry document or commercial invoice or a preprinted attachment to such entry document or invoice. You may sign the certificate by means of an authorized facsimile signature. If your entry is electronically processed, the certification will be in the form of a Certification Code, which is part of the Automated Broker Interface (ABI) transmission. Customs will not release your shipment without proper certification.

If you will be importing several or regular shipments, you should ask the appropriate Customs port director to authorize your use of a blanket certification. If you receive such authorization, you must include on the commercial invoice or entry document for each shipment a statement that the blanket certification is on file and that it is incorporated by reference. This statement need not be signed. The blanket certification is valid for one calendar year, is subject to renewal, and may be revoked at any time for cause.

In filling out TSCA forms and Customs entry documents, you should provide the Chemical Abstracts Service (CAS) number for each chemical in the shipment. These CAS numbers are given in the appendix to the HTSUS. You are not required to include the CAS number, but Customs will be able to process your shipment more quickly if you include this number.

Articles Exclusion. If you are importing items that are classified as hazardous substances but are part of articles, you are subject to TSCA certification requirements only if certification for your product is specifically required by a rule or order promulgated under the TSCA. No specific rules have been adopted at this time. An "article" is a manufactured item 1) that is formed into a specific shape or design during manufacture, 2) that has end-use functions dependent on the shape or design during end use, and 3) that during the end use, does not change in its chemical composition or that changes only for a noncommercial purpose separate from the article and only as allowed by law (19 CFR 12.120(2)). Fluids and particles are not articles, regardless of shape or design.

Shipment Detention. A shipment containing chemicals will be detained at the U.S. port of arrival (or entry if same), at your risk and expense, if: 1) it contains banned chemical substances (15 USC 2604, 2605); or 2) it contains chemical substances ordered seized because of imminent hazards (15 USC 2606). Further detention will occur at the port of entry, again at your risk and expense, if: 1) the EPA administrator or Customs port director has reasonable grounds to believe the shipment is not in compliance with the TSCA; or 2) you do not provide proper TSCA certification.

If your shipment is detained, it will be held by Customs for no more than 48 hours. It will then be turned over to the EPA administrator, unless you have arranged to release it in bond. You must either bring it into TSCA compliance or reexport it within the earlier of 90 days after notice of detention or 30 days of demand for redelivery. Customs may grant an extension if failure to comply or reexport is the result of delays in EPA or Customs procedures. If you fail to comply or reexport within the time allowed, the EPA administrator is authorized to have the shipment stored or disposed of at your expense.

Customs Classification

For customs purposes, explosives, fireworks, and other combustible materials are classified under Chapter 36 of the HTSUS. This chapter is broken into major headings, which are further divided into subheadings, and often sub-subheadings, each of which has its own HTSUS classification number. For example, the 2001 HTSUS number for ferrocerium is 3606.90.30, indicating it is a sub-subcategory of other liquid fuels (3606.90), which is a subcategory of the major heading, ferrocerium, other pyrophoric alloys, and lighter fuels (3606). There are six major headings within Chapter 36.

3601—Propellant powders

3602—Prepared explosives, other than propellant powders

3603—Safety fuses, detonating fuses; percussion or detonating caps; igniters; electric detonators

3604—Fireworks, signaling flares, rain rockets, fog signals, and other pyrotechnic articles

3605—Matches, other than pyrotechnic articles of heading 3604

3606—Ferrocerium and other pyrophoric alloys in all forms; articles of combustible materials as specified in note 2 to this chapter

For more details regarding classifications of the specific product you are interested in importing, consult a customs broker, the appropriate commodity specialist at your nearest customs port, or the HTSUS. The 2001 HTSUS is available online from the Customs Service (www.customs.gov/impoexpo/impoexpo.htm) or for purchase from the U.S. Government Printing Office (see resources at the end of this chapter), and may be found in larger public libraries. For a general discussion of customs classification, see "Classification—Liquidation" on page 229.

Dutiable Status of Goods

For more information about duty rates and binding decisions see "Dutiable Status of Goods" on page 203; for a discussion of temporary importation of goods see "Temporary Free Importations" on page 205.

Valuation

Importers have a responsibility to use what the U.S. Customs Service deems, "reasonable care," when determining the value of their goods. They must also provide any additional information that the Customs Service needs for setting a final value on the goods. This process involves a number of factors and can be somewhat complicated; importers must be aware of applicable issues and details. Valuation information applies to all types of commodities, for further discussion on the subject see "Customs Valuation" on page 267.

Import Duties

Import duties vary (often dramatically) depending upon the Harmonized Tariff Schedule (HTSUS) classification of the goods or products imported. Since some products that look alike have different HTSUS classifications and different rates of duty, proper classification is vital. Note that "differences of opinion" between importers and the Bureau of Customs and Border Protection regarding classification keeps customs attorneys very busy.

Import duties can be assessed on the imported value of the goods ("ad valorem" rates of duty such as 2%, 4.4%, 50%, etc.), total units or weight of the goods ("specific" rates of duty such as 2 cents each or 1.5 cents/pound, etc.) or on a combination basis ("compound" rates of duty such as 5 cents each plus 6%).

Listed below is a sampling of several Column 1 import duty rates for Chapter 36 products:
Matches, other than pyrotechnic articles of heading 3604 (3605.00.00): free
to
Propellant powders (3601.00.00.00): 6.5%

For specific information on US import duties refer to the Harmonized Tariff Schedule of the US. The print version is available from the US Government Printing Office as well as third party suppliers who often add special features. Online versions are available in both static PDF pages as well as in formats with excellent search functionality. Search the Web with the term "Harmonized Tariff Schedule" to find sources.

Entry and Documentation

The entry of merchandise is a two-part process consisting of 1) filing the documentation necessary to determine whether merchandise may be released from Customs custody, and 2) filing the documents that contain information for duty assessment and statistical purposes. In certain instances, all documents must be filed and accepted by Customs prior to release of the goods. Unless you have been granted an extension, you must file entry documents at a location specified by the port or area director within five working days of your shipment's date of arrival at a U.S. port of entry. These include a number of standard documents required by Customs for any entry, and:

- Importer's license or permit from the ATF (for explosives) Form 5400.13
- U.S. Customs TSCA Certification (for hazardous substances) document

After you present the entry, Customs may examine your shipment or may waive examination. The shipment is then released provided no legal or regulatory violations have been noted. You must then file entry summary documentation and deposit estimated duties at a designated customhouse within 10 working days of your shipment's release. For a detailed description of entry procedures, standard documentation, and informal entry, see "Entry Process" on page 185.

Informed Compliance. Informed compliance was introduced with the Customs Modernization Act of 1993 (Mod Act) and defines the relationship between importers and the Customs Service. It sets out the responsibilities of both parties. Providing the correct documentation and information for entry is a key factor that will make your importing operation run smoothly. We recommend that importers become familiar with the concept of informed comliance and the responsibilities that they have under the Mod Act. For further discussion about informed compliance see "Informed Compliance" on page 211.

Note: The Entry and Documentation section has been carefully designed to supply you, the importer, with sample documents and directions on how to satisfy Customs requirements. Be aware that you should consult the applicable authorities to ensure that you are correctly following the most current procedures.

Prohibitions and Restrictions

Matches. The importation of white phosphorus matches is prohibited.

Hazardous Consumer Products. Importation of any consumer product that has been declared a banned hazardous substance by a rule under the CPSA is prohibited. Any product considered hazardous and not labeled according to provisions of the FHSA is a misbranded hazardous substance and is an illegal import. Certain hazardous substances listed in the FHSA and in regulations promulgated by the CPSC are completely banned from importation. A shipment of consumer products cannot be imported if it poses an imminent hazard. See 15 USC 1261, 2604-2606; 16 CFR 1500.265-1500.272.

The CPSC may detain your shipment of hazardous substances and take samples for testing to determine compliance with the FHSA. If your shipment is found to contain banned hazardous substances, it will be refused admission and will be destroyed if not exported within 90 days of the date of refusal notice. If it is found to contain misbranded hazardous substances, you may make arrangements to bring it into conformance through relabeling. For complete details regarding testing, labeling, and safety regulations for hazardous products, contact the CPSC (see addresses at end of this chapter).

Marking and Labeling Requirements

Chemical Products. A shipment of any products containing chemicals that are classified as hazardous substance (49 CFR 172) must comply with the marking and labeling regulations adopted by the EPA (46 CFR 147.30) and the DOT (49 CFR 171 et seq.).

Explosives. A shipment of explosive substances must comply with marking and labeling regulations adopted by the ATF (46 CFR 55) and the DOT (49 CFR 171 et seq.).

For a general discussion of U.S. Customs marking and labeling requirements, see "Country of Origin Marking" on page 236, "Special Marking Requirements" on page 238 and "Marking—False Impression" on page 239.

Shipping Considerations

You will need to ensure that your goods are packaged and shipped with care so that they pass smoothly through Customs and arrive in good condition. You are responsible for ensuring that the shipment is in compliance with all applicable government regulations for packaging and shipping. In most instances, you should not leave these arrangements solely to the discretion of your supplier. Careful preparation of the cargo and selection of the mode of transport can be essential to a cost-effective, timely delivery of undamaged goods. We strongly advise you to consult your shipping representative, insurance agent, or freight broker for advice on packing and shipping.

Explosives, fireworks, and other combustible materials may be shipped in bulk, bags, bottles, crates, or other types of containers, depending on the type of product and whether it is prepackaged. General considerations include protection from contamination, weather, and pests. For liquid shipments, venting and vapor collection systems may be required. Safety precautions should also be implemented as required to protect against breakage, spillage, corrosion of containers, combustion, and explosion. Containers should be constructed so as to be safe for handling during transport.

Chemical Products. Chemical products in particular may have to be shipped in pressurized, ventilated, and temperature-and-vapor-controlled enclosures. Solid chemical products that are listed as hazardous substances (49 CFR 172 appendix) may be transported in bulk only on compliance with Coast Guard notification procedures, shipping permit requirements, and complex transportation regulations (46 CFR 148). All hazardous substances must also be packaged and transported in accordance with DOT regulations (49 CFR 171 et seq.).

Publications and WWW Resources

The following publications may be relevant to the importation of toxic or hazardous explosives, fireworks, and other combustible materials:

Toxic Substances Control Act: A Guide for Chemical Importers/ Exporters (published by EPA)

This document is available from the TSCA Assistance Information Service (see Relevant Government Agencies)

The following publication provides a listing of existing chemical substances in the United States. It can be purchased in electronic format or a search of the document can be requested via telephone. Contact the Chemical Abstract Service (CAS) at (800)631-1884 or at (614) 447-3600 ext 2308.

TSCA Chemical Substance Inventory

In order to check whether or not a chemical is subject to any rules or regulations under Sections 5, 6, or 7 of TSCA, search the following document (www.epa.gov/opptintr/CORR)

Chemical on Reporting Rules List (CORR)

The *Harmonized Tariff Schedule of the United States (2001)* (HTSUS) is available to view on the Customs Service website (www.customs.gov), or you may purchase a printed version from:

U.S. Government Printing Office
Superintendent of Documents
710 North Capital Street NW
Washington DC 20401
Tel: (202) 512-1800
Fax: (202) 512-1657
Website: www.access.gpo.gov

The USGPO also has copies of specific laws available for purchase. The USGPO accepts orders made by fax, phone or placed over the Internet, as well as mail orders paid by credit card. All orders must be accompanied by payment. Credit cards, checks drawn on a U.S. bank, or an international money order are all acceptable.

Relevant Government Agencies

Address your inquiries regarding TSCA and EPA requirements for importation of chemical products to:

Environmental Protection Agency (EPA)
Office of Pollution Prevention and Toxics
TSCA System Information
1200 Pennsylvania Avenue NW
Washington DC 20460
Tel: (202) 564-3810
Tel: (202) 554-1404 (TSCA Information Hotline)
Email: oppt.homepage@epa.gov
Website: www.epa.gov/opptintr/contact.htm

Address your questions regarding import licenses and permits for explosives to a local ATF office or to:

Bureau of Alcohol, Tobacco, Firearms and Explosives
Firearms and Explosives Import Branch
650 Massachusetts Avenue NW
Washington DC 20226
Tel: (202) 927-8320
Website: www.atf.treas.gov

Address your questions regarding standards for mining explosives to:

Mine Safety and Health Administration (MSHA)
Approval and Certification Center
RR #1, Box 251
Triadelphia, WV 26059

Tel: (304) 547-0400
Website: http://msha.gov

Address your questions regarding CPSC requirements for explosives, fireworks, and consumer combustible materials to:

Consumer Product Safety Commission (CPSC)
Office of Compliance
Washington DC 20207-0001
Tel: 800-638-2772 or (301) 504-7912
Fax: (301) 504-0359
Website: www.cpsc.gov

Address your questions regarding transportation of hazardous substances to:

U.S. Department of Transportation (DOT)
Research and Special Programs Administration
Hazardous Materials Information Center
400 7th St. SW
Washington DC 20590
Tel: (202) 366-4488
Website: http://hazmat.dot.gov

Address your questions regarding importation of explosives, fireworks, and other combustible materials generally to your local Customs port director. For addresses, refer to "U.S. Customs and Border Protection Offices" on page 65 or contact:

U.S. Customs and Border Protection
Customs Headquarters
1300 Pennsylvania Avenue NW
Washington DC 20229
Tel: (202) 354-1000
Website: www.customs.treas.gov

Laws and Regulations

The following laws may be relevant to the importation of explosives, fireworks, and other combustible materials. They are contained in the United States Code (USC), which is available at larger public and law libraries. Specific laws and regulations may also be purchased from the U.S. Government Printing Office (address above).

27 CFR 55
Regulations on Explosives in Interstate and Foreign Commerce
These regulations require licenses and permits for importing and transporting explosives, set forth standards for recordkeeping, business operations, storage, labeling, and transport, and establish procedures for inspection and seizure of noncomplying goods.

15 USC 2051 et seq.
Consumer Product Safety Act (CPSA)
This Act gives the Consumer Product Safety Commission authority to set safety standards, testing procedures, and reporting requirements to ensure that consumer products not already covered under other regulations are not harmful.

16 CFR 1202
Matchbook Safety Standards
These regulations set standards for processing, manufacturing, importing, and labeling matchbooks to be sold to U.S. consumers.

16 CFR 1210 et seq.
Cigarette Lighter Safety Standards
These regulations set standards for processing, manufacturing, and labeling cigarette lighters to be sold in the U.S. and require importers to certify that their products meet these standards.

16 CFR 1500 et seq.
Regulations on Hazardous Substances Safety Standards
These regulations set standards for processing, manufacturing, importing, and labeling all substances classified as hazardous that are to be sold to U.S. consumers.

15 USC 2601 et seq.
Toxic Substances Control Act
This Act authorizes the EPA to determine whether a substance is harmful and to restrict importation, sale, and use of such substances.

19 CFR 12.118 et seq.
Regulations on Toxic Substances Control
These regulations require importers of chemical substances imported in bulk or as part of a mixture to certify to Customs that the shipment complies with the TSCA or is not subject to that Act.

15 USC 1261 et seq.
Federal Hazardous Substances Act
This Act controls the importation of hazardous substances, sets forth prohibited imports, and authorizes various agencies to promulgate labeling, marking, and transport requirements.

49 CFR 171 et seq.
Regulations on Hazardous Materials
These regulations list all substances deemed hazardous and provide transport, marking, labeling, safety, and emergency response rules.

46 CFR 147.30
Regulations on Labeling of Hazardous Materials
This regulation requires the labeling of containers of hazardous substances and specifies the label contents.

46 CFR 148 et seq.
Regulations on Carriage of Solid Hazardous Materials in Bulk
These regulations govern the transport of solid hazardous substances in bulk, including reporting, permitting, loading, stowing, and shipping requirements.

Sources of Additional Information

The TSCA Chemical Substance Inventory is available through various commercial online databases and from:

National Technical Information Service (NTIS)
U.S. Department of Commerce
5285 Port Royal Road
Springfield, VA 22161
(703) 605-6000; FAX (703) 605-6900
Web site: www.ntis.gov

Principal Exporting Countries

The following listing includes samples of the main supplier nations of the products of this chapter. It is organized by HTSUS major heading. (Refer to "Customs Classification" above for the product codes.) Countries are listed in rank order of the value of products imported to the U.S. Statistics represent customs value of entries for 2002 from the Bureau of Census, U.S. Department of Commerce.

3601—Canada, Australia, Germany, Sweden, Switzerland, Finland, Belgium

3602—Canada, China, Sweden, Mexico, Germany, United Kingdom, Switzerland, Spain

3603—Canada, China, Sweden, Mexico, Germany, United Kingdom, Switzerland, Spain

3604—China, Hong Kong, United Kingdom, Italy, Germany, Thailand

3605—China, Japan, Mexico, Sweden, Taiwan, Czech Republic

3606—Mexico, South Korea, France, Philippines, United Kingdom, China, Austria, Brazil

Chapter 37: Photographic or Cinematographic Goods

This chapter relates to the importation of photographic and cinematographic goods, which are classified under Chapter 37 of the Harmonized Tariff Schedule of the United States (HTSUS). Specifically, it includes photographic film, paper, plates, and other media, motion picture film, and chemical preparations for photographic uses.

If you are interested in importing separately defined chemicals, you should refer to Commodity Index Chapters 28 (inorganic) and 29 (organic). Cameras and photographic equipment are covered in Chapter 90. Import requirements for works of art are covered in Chapter 97.

Note: To understand key issues that will enable you to make best use of the information in this section we recommend that you see "Introduction" on page 425.

Key Factors

The key factors in the importation of photographic or cinematographic goods are:

- Compliance with U.S. Environmental Protection Agency (EPA) requirements under Toxic Substances Control Act (TSCA) (if the product is a hazardous substance)
- Compliance with U.S. Department of Transportation (DOT) regulations for transport of hazardous cargo (if the product is a hazardous substance)
- Compliance with U.S. Federal Trade Commission (FTC) and Consumer Product Safety Commission (CPSC) standards (if a consumer product)

Although most importers use the services of a licensed customs broker in making their entries, and we recommend this practice, you should be aware of the regulatory, entry, and documentation issues involved in importing your product. You, as importer, are ultimately responsible for the fulfillment of any legal requirements applicable to your shipment.

General Considerations

Regulatory Agencies. Importation of photographic and cinematographic goods, other than chemicals, is straightforward. For many products, no permits, licenses, or special entry paperwork are required. The FTC sets standards for processing and labeling products that are sold to consumers. The EPA, under authority of the TSCA, imposes certain controls on the importation of photographic or cinematographic supplies that contain toxic substances. The TSCA defines a toxic substance as any substance determined to present the possibility of an unreasonable risk of injury to health and the environment. The DOT enforces regulations for transporting hazardous cargo. Materials are deemed hazardous if listed in DOT transport regulations (49 CFR 172 appendix).

Hazardous Consumer Products. The Federal Hazardous Substances Act (FHSA) imposes special controls on hazardous consumer products, which are defined as substances that are flammable, combustible, or have the potential to cause substantial personal injury during, or as a proximate result of, any customary or reasonably foreseeable handling or use. The CPSC does not require permits, special invoicing, limited entry, licenses, or any special approval process for importing hazardous consumer products into the U.S. However, if you are importing these types of products, you are responsible for ensuring that they meet all applicable FHSA and Consumer Product Safety Act (CPSA) requirements. There are detailed regulations regarding testing and labeling of hazardous products. The Commission's enforcement posture regarding compliance with labeling and product safety standards changes as new facts become available. Contact the CPSC (see addresses at end of this chapter) for specific requirements on the consumer product you are considering importing.

Substantial Product Hazard Reports. Defect-reporting is required for products covered under the CPSA. The law requires every manufacturer, distributor, or retailer of such products, who obtains information that reasonably supports the conclusion that such products fail to comply with an applicable consumer product safety rule, or contain a defect that could create a substantial product hazard, to immediately inform the CPSC of the potential violation or defect. A firm's willful failure to make a Substantial Product Hazard Report can result in litigation by the CPSC.

Toxic and Hazardous Substances. Shipments of photochemical products—such as developer, fixer, and toner—must be in compliance with toxic and hazardous substance regulations of the EPA and DOT. These include packaging, shipping, marking, and labeling requirements. In addition, all products containing chemicals are subject to the U.S. Customs Service TSCA Import Certification Rule (19 CFR 12.118 et seq.). If you import these products, you must sign one of the following statements: "I certify that all chemical substances in this shipment comply with all applicable rules or orders under TSCA and that I am not offering a chemical substance for entry in violation of TSCA or any applicable rule or order thereunder" or "I certify that all chemicals in this shipment are not subject to TSCA."

You must file this TSCA certification of compliance or exemption at the time you make the entry at Customs. The certification may be in the form of a typed or stamped statement on an appropriate entry document or commercial invoice or a preprinted attachment to such entry document or invoice. You may sign the certificate by means of an authorized facsimile signature. If your entry is electronically processed, the certification will be in the form of a Certification Code, which is part of the Automated Broker Interface (ABI) transmission. Customs will not release your shipment without proper certification.

If you will be importing several or regular shipments, you should ask the appropriate Customs port director to authorize your use of a blanket certification. If you receive such authorization, you must include on the commercial invoice or entry document for each shipment a statement that the blanket certification is on file and that it is incorporated by reference. This statement need not be signed. The blanket certification is valid for one calendar year, is subject to renewal, and may be revoked at any time for cause.

In filling out TSCA forms and Customs entry documents, you should provide the Chemical Abstracts Service (CAS) number for each chemical in the shipment. These CAS numbers are given in the appendix to the HTSUS. You are not required to include the CAS number, but Customs will be able to process your shipment more quickly if you include this number.

Articles Exclusion. If you are importing items that are classified as hazardous substances but are part of articles, you are subject to TSCA certification requirements only if certification for your product is specifically required by a rule or order promulgated under the TSCA. No specific rules have been adopted at this time. An "article" is a manufactured item 1) that is formed into a specific shape or design during manufacture, 2) that has end-use functions dependent on the shape or design during end use, and 3) that during the end use, does not change in its chemical composition or that changes only for a noncommercial purpose separate from the article and only as allowed by law (19 CFR 12.120(2)). Fluids and particles are not articles, regardless of shape or design.

Shipment Detention. A shipment containing chemicals will be detained at the U.S. port of arrival (or entry if same), at your risk and expense, if: 1) it contains banned chemical substances (15 USC 2604, 2605); or 2) it contains chemical substances ordered seized because of imminent hazards (15 USC 2606). Further detention will occur at the port of entry, again at your risk and expense, if: 1) the EPA administrator or Customs port director has reasonable grounds to believe the shipment is not in compliance with the TSCA; or 2) you do not provide proper TSCA certification.

If your shipment is detained, it will be held by Customs for no more than 48 hours. It will then be turned over to the EPA administrator, unless you have arranged to release it in bond. You must either bring it into TSCA compliance or reexport it within the earlier of 90 days after notice of detention or 30 days of demand for redelivery. Customs may grant an extension if failure to comply or reexport is the result of delays in EPA or Customs procedures. If you fail to comply or reexport within the time allowed, the EPA administrator is authorized to have the shipment stored or disposed of at your expense.

Customs Classification

For customs purposes, photographic and cinematographic goods are classified under Chapter 37 of the HTSUS. This chapter is broken into major headings, which are further divided into subheadings, and often sub-subheadings, each of which has its own HTSUS classification number. For example, the 2001 HTSUS number for sound recordings on motion picture film suitable for exhibits is 3706.10.30, indicating it is a sub-subcategory of film that is 35 mm or wider (3706.10), which is a subcategory of the major heading, motion picture film (3706). There are seven major headings within Chapter 37.

3701—Photographic plates and film in the flat, sensitized, unexposed, of any material other than paper, paperboard, or textiles; instant print film in the flat, sensitized, unexposed, whether or not in packs

3702—Photographic film in rolls, sensitized, unexposed, of any material other than paper, paperboard, or textiles; instant print film in rolls, sensitized, unexposed

3703—Photographic paper, paperboard, and textiles, sensitized, unexposed

3704—Photographic plates, film, paper, paperboard, and textiles, exposed but not developed

3705—Photographic plates and film, exposed and developed, other than motion picture film

3706—Motion picture film, exposed and developed, whether or not incorporating sound track or consisting only of sound track

3707—Chemical preparations for photographic uses (other than varnishes, glues, adhesives, and similar preparations); unmixed products for photographic uses, put up in measured portions or put up for retail sale in a form ready for use

For more details regarding classifications of the specific product you are interested in importing, consult a customs broker, the appropriate commodity specialist at your nearest customs port, or the HTSUS. The 2001 HTSUS is available online from the Customs Service (www.customs.gov/impoexpo/impoexpo.htm) or for purchase from the U.S. Government Printing Office (see resources at the end of this chapter), and may be found in larger public libraries. For a general discussion of customs classification, see "Classification—Liquidation" on page 229.

Dutiable Status of Goods

For more information about duty rates and binding decisions see "Dutiable Status of Goods" on page 203; for a discussion of temporary importation of goods see "Temporary Free Importations" on page 205.

Valuation

Importers have a responsibility to use what the U.S. Customs Service deems, "reasonable care," when determining the value of their goods. They must also provide any additional information that the Customs Service needs for setting a final value on the goods. This process involves a number of factors and can be somewhat complicated; importers must be aware of applicable issues and details. Valuation information applies to all types of commodities, for further discussion on the subject see "Customs Valuation" on page 267.

Import Duties

Import duties vary (often dramatically) depending upon the Harmonized Tariff Schedule (HTSUS) classification of the goods or products imported. Since some products that look alike have different HTSUS classifications and different rates of duty, proper classification is vital. Note that "differences of opinion" between importers and the Bureau of Customs and Border Protection regarding classification keeps customs attorneys very busy.

Import duties can be assessed on the imported value of the goods ("ad valorem" rates of duty such as 2%, 4.4%, 50%, etc.), total units or weight of the goods ("specific" rates of duty such as 2 cents each or 1.5 cents/pound, etc.) or on a combination basis ("compound" rates of duty such as 5 cents each plus 6%).

Listed below is a sampling of several Column 1 import duty rates for Chapter 37 products:
Photographic plates, film, paper, paperboard and textiles,exposed but not developed (3704.00.00.00): Free
to
Dry plates (3701.99.30 00): 4.9%

For specific information on US import duties refer to the Harmonized Tariff Schedule of the US. The print version is available from the US Government Printing Office as well as third party suppliers who often add special features. Online versions are available in both static PDF pages as well as in formats with excellent search functionality. Search the Web with the term "Harmonized Tariff Schedule" to find sources.

Entry and Documentation

The entry of merchandise is a two-part process consisting of 1) filing the documentation necessary to determine whether merchandise may be released from Customs custody, and 2) filing the documents that contain information for duty assessment and statistical purposes. In certain instances, all documents must be filed and accepted by Customs prior to release of the goods. Unless you have been granted an extension, you must file entry documents at a location specified by the port or area director within five working days of your shipment's date of arrival at a U.S. port of entry. These include a number of standard documents required by Customs for any entry, and:

- U.S. Customs TSCA Certification (for hazardous substances) document

After you present the entry, Customs may examine your shipment or may waive examination. The shipment is then released provided no legal or regulatory violations have been noted. You must then file entry summary documentation and deposit estimated duties at a designated customhouse within 10 working days of your shipment's release. For a detailed description of entry procedures, standard documentation, and informal entry, see "Entry Process" on page 185.

Informed Compliance. Informed compliance was introduced with the Customs Modernization Act of 1993 (Mod Act) and defines the relationship between importers and the Customs Service. It sets out the responsibilities of both parties. Providing the correct documentation and information for entry is a key factor that will make your importing operation run smoothly. We recommend that importers become familiar with the concept of informed comliance and the responsibilities that they have under the Mod Act. For further discussion about informed compliance see "Informed Compliance" on page 211.

Entry Invoice. An invoice for a shipment of motion picture film must include the following: 1) a statement of the footage, title, and subject matter of each film; 2) a declaration of the shipper, cameraman, or other person with knowledge of the facts identifying the films with the invoice and stating that the basic films were to the best of that person's knowledge and belief exposed abroad and returned for use as newsreel; and 3) a declaration of the importer that the importer believes the films entered are the ones covered by the preceding declaration and that the films are intended for use as newsreel. For more general information about invoices see "Invoices" on page 277.

Prohibitions and Restrictions

Hazardous Consumer Products. Importation of any consumer product that has been declared a banned hazardous substance by a rule under the CPSA is prohibited. Any product considered hazardous and not labeled according to provisions of the FHSA is a misbranded hazardous substance and is an illegal import. Certain hazardous substances listed in the FHSA and in regulations promulgated by the CPSC are completely banned from importation. A shipment of consumer products cannot be imported if it poses an imminent hazard. See 15 USC 1261, 2604-2606; 16 CFR 1500.265-1500.272.

The CPSC may detain your shipment of hazardous substances and take samples for testing to determine compliance with the FHSA. If your shipment is found to contain banned hazardous substances, it will be refused admission and will be destroyed if not exported within 90 days of the date of refusal notice. If it is found to contain misbranded hazardous substances, you may make arrangements to bring it into conformance through relabeling. For complete details regarding testing, labeling, and safety regulations for hazardous products, contact the CPSC (see addresses at end of this chapter).

Marking and Labeling Requirements

Chemical Products. A shipment of any chemical product that contains a hazardous substance must comply with the marking and labeling regulations adopted by the EPA (46 CFR 147.30) and the DOT (49 CFR 171 et seq.)

For a general discussion of U.S. Customs marking and labeling requirements, see "Country of Origin Marking" on page 236, "Special Marking Requirements" on page 238 and "Marking—False Impression" on page 239.

Shipping Considerations

You will need to ensure that your goods are packaged and shipped with care so that they pass smoothly through Customs and arrive in good condition. You are responsible for ensuring that the shipment is in compliance with all applicable government regulations for packaging and shipping. In most instances, you should not leave these arrangements solely to the discretion of your supplier. Careful preparation of the cargo and selection of the mode of transport can be essential to a cost-effective, timely delivery of undamaged goods. We strongly advise you to consult your shipping representative, insurance agent, or freight broker for advice on packing and shipping.

Photographic and cinematographic goods may be shipped in bulk, bags, bottles, or other types of containers, depending on the type of product and whether it is prepackaged. General considerations include protection from contamination, weather, and pests. For liquid shipments, venting and vapor collection systems may be required. Safety precautions should also be implemented as required to protect against breakage, spillage, corrosion of containers, and combustion. Containers should be constructed so as to be safe for handling during transport.

Chemical Products. Chemical products in particular may have to be shipped in pressurized, ventilated, and temperature-and vapor-controlled enclosures. Solid chemical products that are listed as hazardous substances (49 CFR 172 appendix) may be transported in bulk only on compliance with Coast Guard notification procedures, shipping permit requirements, and complex transportation regulations (46 CFR 148). All hazardous substances must also be packaged and transported in accordance with DOT regulations (49 CFR 171 et seq.).

Publications and WWW Resources

The following publications may be relevant to the importation of toxic or hazardous photographic and cinematographic goods:

Toxic Substances Control Act: A Guide for Chemical Importers/ Exporters (published by EPA)

This document is available from the TSCA Assistance Information Service (see Relevant Government Agencies)

The following publication provides a listing of existing chemical substances in the United States. It can be purchased in electronic format or a search of the document can be requested via telephone. Contact the Chemical Abstract Service (CAS) at (800)631-1884 or at (614) 447-3600 ext 2308.

TSCA Chemical Substance Inventory

In order to check whether or not a chemical is subject to any rules or regulations under Sections 5, 6, or 7 of TSCA, search the following document (www.epa.gov/opptintr/CORR)

Chemical on Reporting Rules List (CORR)

The *Harmonized Tariff Schedule of the United States (2001)* (HTSUS) is available to view on the Customs Service website (www.customs.gov), or you may purchase a printed version from:

U.S. Government Printing Office
Superintendent of Documents
710 North Capital Street NW
Washington DC 20401
Tel: (202) 512-1800
Fax: (202) 512-1657
Website: www.access.gpo.gov

The USGPO also has copies of specific laws available for purchase. The USGPO accepts orders made by fax, phone or placed over the Internet, as well as mail orders paid by credit card. All orders must be accompanied by payment. Credit cards, checks drawn on a U.S. bank, or an international money order are all acceptable.

Relevant Government Agencies

Address your inquiries regarding EPA regulation of imported photochemicals to:

Environmental Protection Agency (EPA)
Office of Pollution Prevention and Toxics
TSCA System Information
1200 Pennsylvania Avenue NW
Washington DC 20460
Tel: (202) 564-3810
Tel: (202) 554-1404 (TSCA Information Hotline)
Email: oppt.homepage@epa.gov
Website: www.epa.gov/opptintr/contact.htm

Address your questions regarding transportation of hazardous substances to:

U.S. Department of Transportation (DOT)
Research and Special Programs Administration
Hazardous Materials Information Center
400 7th St. SW
Washington DC 20590
Tel: (202) 366-4488
Website: http://hazmat.dot.gov

Address your questions regarding CPSC requirements for photographic and cinematographic goods to:

Consumer Product Safety Commission (CPSC)
Office of Compliance
Washington DC 20207-0001
Tel: 800-638-2772 or (301) 504-7912
Fax: (301) 504-0359
Website: www.cpsc.gov

Address questions regarding the importation of photographic and cinematographic goods to your local Customs port director. For addresses refer to "U.S. Customs and Border Protection Offices" on page 65 or contact:

U.S. Customs and Border Protection
Customs Headquarters
1300 Pennsylvania Avenue NW
Washington DC 20229
Tel: (202) 354-1000
Website: www.customs.treas.gov

Laws and Regulations

The following laws and regulations may be relevant to the importation of photographic and cinematographic goods. The laws are contained in the United States Code (USC), and the regulations are published in the Code of Federal Regulations (CFR), both of which are available at larger public and law libraries. Specific laws and regulations may also be purchased from the U.S. Government Printing Office (address above).

15 USC 2051 et seq.
Consumer Product Safety Act (CPSA)
This Act gives the Consumer Product Safety Commission authority to set safety standards, testing procedures, and reporting requirements to ensure that consumer products not already covered under other regulations are not harmful.

15 USC 2601 et seq.
Toxic Substances Control Act
This Act authorizes the EPA to determine whether a substance is harmful and to restrict importation, sale, and use of such substances.

19 CFR 12.118 et seq.
Regulations on Toxic Substances Control
These regulations require importers of chemical substances imported in bulk or as part of a mixture to certify to Customs that the shipment complies with the TSCA or is not subject to that Act.

15 USC 1261 et seq.
Federal Hazardous Substances Act
This Act controls the importation of hazardous substances, sets forth prohibited imports, and authorizes various agencies to promulgate labeling, marking, and transport requirements.

49 CFR 171 et seq.
Regulations on Hazardous Materials
These regulations list all substances deemed hazardous and provide transport, marking, labeling, safety, and emergency response rules.

46 CFR 147.30
Regulations on Labeling of Hazardous Materials
This regulation requires the labeling of containers of hazardous substances and specifies the label contents.

46 CFR 148 et seq.
Regulations on Carriage of Solid Hazardous Materials in Bulk
These regulations govern the transport of solid hazardous substances in bulk, including reporting, permitting, loading, stowing, and shipping requirements.

Sources of Additional Information

The TSCA Chemical Substance Inventory is available through various commercial online databases and from:

National Technical Information Service (NTIS)
U.S. Department of Commerce
5285 Port Royal Road
Springfield, VA 22161
(703) 605-6000; FAX (703) 605-6900
Web site: www.ntis.gov

Principal Exporting Countries

The following listing includes samples of the main supplier nations of the products of this chapter. It is organized by HTSUS major heading. (Refer to "Customs Classification" above for the product codes.) Countries are listed in rank order of the value of products imported to the U.S. Statistics represent customs value of entries for 2002 from the Bureau of Census, U.S. Department of Commerce.

3701—Japan, Netherlands, Mexico, United Kingdom, Germany, France, Belgium

3702—Japan, Belgium, Mexico, Canada, Germany, Italy, United Kingdom

3703—Canada, Japan, Germany, United Kingdom, France, Netherlands

3704—Japan, Germany, Italy, Canada, Mexico

3705—Japan, South Korea, Germany, Taiwan, Italy

3706—Canada, Italy, Australia, United Kingdom, France

3707—Japan, Netherlands, South Korea, Belgium, China, Germany, Switzerland

Chapter 38:
Miscellaneous Chemical Products

This chapter relates to the importation of miscellaneous chemical substances, which are classified under Chapter 38 of the Harmonized Tariff Schedule of the United States (HTSUS). Specifically, it includes organic and inorganic chemical products and preparations that are not otherwise specified or included in any other chapter of the HTSUS. A few of these items are artificial graphite, activated carbon, mineral, and animal products; tall oil, residual lyes from wood pulp, turpentines, wood tars, creosote, and naptha; insecticides, pesticides, disinfectants, finishing agents, metal pickling preparations, antiknock and other additives for lubricating oils, rubber or plastics additives, fire-extinguisher preparations and charges, hydraulic fluids, and anitfreezing preparations and fluids. For a more detailed listing, refer to "Customs Classification" in this chapter.

If you are interested in importing a separate chemically defined chemical substance, you should read this chapter in conjunction with Commodity Index Chapter 28 (inorganic) or 29 (organic) to determine which of these chapters covers that particular chemical substance. Chapter 21 covers mixtures of chemicals with foodstuffs and other substances having nutritive value and used in preparation of human foodstuffs. For products that are medicaments, refer to Chapter 30.

Note: To understand key issues that will enable you to make best use of the information in this section we recommend that you see "Introduction" on page 425.

Key Factors

The key factors in the importation of chemical substances are:

- Compliance with U.S. Federal Trade Commission (FTC) and Consumer Product Safety Commission (CPSC) standards (if a consumer product)

- Compliance with U.S. Environmental Protection Agency (EPA) registration, safety, import, and recordkeeping requirements for the import of poisons (if the product is insecticide, pesticide, or other poisonous substance)

- Compliance with EPA requirements under Toxic Substances Control Act (TSCA) (if the product is a hazardous substance)

- Compliance with U.S. Department of Transportation (DOT) regulations for transport of hazardous cargo (if the product is a hazardous substance)

Although most importers use the services of a licensed customs broker in making their entries, and we recommend this practice, you should be aware of the regulatory, entry, and documentation issues involved in importing your product. You, as importer, are ultimately responsible for the fulfillment of any legal requirements applicable to your shipment.

General Considerations

Regulatory Agencies. The FTC sets standards for processing and labeling products that are sold to consumers. The EPA, under authority of the Federal Insecticide, Fungicide, and Rodenticide Act of 1947 (FIFRA), regulates the import of poisons, including insecticides, Paris greens, lead arsenates, fungicides, herbicides, and rodenticides. Under authority of the TSCA, the EPA also imposes certain controls on the importation of chemicals that contain toxic substances. The TSCA defines a toxic substance as any substance determined to present the possibility of an unreasonable risk of injury to health and the environment. The DOT enforces regulations for transporting hazardous cargo. Materials are deemed hazardous if listed in DOT transport regulations (49 CFR 172 appendix).

Toxic and Hazardous Substances. Chemicals imported in bulk, as articles, or as part of a mixture must be in compliance with toxic and hazardous substance regulations of the EPA and DOT. These include packaging, shipping, marking, and labeling requirements. In addition, all chemical products are subject to the U.S. Customs Service TSCA Import Certification Rule (19 CFR 12.118 et seq.). If you import these products, you must sign one of the following statements: "I certify that all chemical substances in this shipment comply with all applicable rules or orders under TSCA and that I am not offering a chemical substance for entry in violation of TSCA or any applicable rule or order thereunder" or "I certify that all chemicals in this shipment are not subject to TSCA."

You must file this TSCA certification of compliance or exemption at the time you make the entry at Customs. The certification may be in the form of a typed or stamped statement on an appropriate entry document or commercial invoice or a preprinted attachment to such entry document or invoice. You may sign the certificate by means of an authorized facsimile signature. If your entry is electronically processed, the certification will be in the form of a Certification Code, which is part of the Automated Broker Interface (ABI) transmission. Customs will not release your shipment without proper certification.

If you will be importing several or regular shipments, you should ask the appropriate Customs port director to authorize your use of a blanket certification. If you receive such authorization, you must include on the commercial invoice or entry document for each shipment a statement that the blanket certification is on file and that it is incorporated by reference. This statement need not be signed. The blanket certification is valid for one calendar year, is subject to renewal, and may be revoked at any time for cause.

In filling out TSCA forms and Customs entry documents, you should provide the Chemical Abstracts Service (CAS) number for each chemical in the shipment. These CAS numbers are given in the appendix to the HTSUS. You are not required to include the CAS number, but Customs will be able to process your shipment more quickly if you include this number.

Articles Exclusion. If you are importing products that are classified as hazardous substances but are part of articles, you are subject to TSCA certification requirements only if certification for your product is specifically required by a rule or order promulgated under the TSCA. No specific rules have been adopted at this time. An "article" is a manufactured item 1) that is formed into a specific shape or design during manufacture, 2) that has end-use functions dependent on the shape or design during end

use, and 3) that during the end use, does not change in its chemical composition or that changes only for a noncommercial purpose separate from the article and only as allowed by law (19 CFR 12.120(2)). Fluids and particles are not articles, regardless of shape or design.

Shipment Detention. A shipment containing chemicals will be detained at the U.S. port of arrival (or entry if same), at your risk and expense, if: 1) it contains banned chemical substances (15 USC 2604, 2605); or 2) it contains chemical substances ordered seized because of imminent hazards (15 USC 2606). Further detention will occur at the port of entry, again at your risk and expense, if: 1) the EPA administrator or Customs port director has reasonable grounds to believe the shipment is not in compliance with the TSCA; or 2) you do not provide proper TSCA certification.

If your shipment is detained, it will be held by Customs for no more than 48 hours. It will then be turned over to the EPA administrator, unless you have arranged to release it in bond. You must either bring it into TSCA compliance or reexport it within the earlier of 90 days after notice of detention or 30 days of demand for redelivery. Customs may grant an extension if failure to comply or reexport is the result of delays in EPA or Customs procedures. If you fail to comply or reexport within the time allowed, the EPA administrator is authorized to have the shipment stored or disposed of at your expense.

Hazardous Consumer Products. The Federal Hazardous Substances Act (FHSA) imposes special controls on hazardous consumer products, which are defined as substances that are flammable, combustible, or have the potential to cause substantial personal injury during, or as a proximate result of, any customary or reasonably foreseeable handling or use. The CPSC does not require permits, special invoicing, limited entry, licenses, or any special approval process for importing hazardous consumer products into the U.S. However, if you are importing these types of products, you are responsible for ensuring that they meet all applicable FHSA and Consumer Product Safety Act (CPSA) requirements. There are detailed regulations regarding testing and labeling of hazardous products. The Commission's enforcement posture regarding compliance with labeling and product safety standards changes as new facts become available. Contact the CPSC (see addresses at end of this chapter) for specific requirements on the consumer product you are considering importing.

Substantial Product Hazard Reports. Defect-reporting is required for products covered under the CPSA. The law requires every manufacturer, distributor, or retailer of such products, who obtains information that reasonably supports the conclusion that such products fail to comply with an applicable consumer product safety rule, or contain a defect that could create a substantial product hazard, to immediately inform the CPSC of the potential violation or defect. A firm's willful failure to make a Substantial Product Hazard Report can result in litigation by the CPSC.

Insecticides and Pesticides. Before importation, all insecticides and pesticides must be registered in accordance with the criteria established by the EPA's Office of Pesticides Programs (OPP) (see addresses at end of this chapter). For each import shipment, an EPA Notice of Arrival of Pesticides or Devices **Form 3540-1** must be presented to Customs at the U.S. port of entry. You should obtain this form from either an EPA regional office or the EPA's Office of Compliance Monitoring. You need to fill out the applicable part of the form and submit it to the appropriate EPA office for completion. The EPA regional office completes the form, indicating how the shipment is to be handled when it arrives at the U.S. port, and returns it to you. When your shipment arrives at the port, it may be released immediately if the product and all the papers are in order.

Shipment Detention. Your shipment may be detained at the port of entry if: 1) the Notice of Arrival is incomplete; 2) the Notice refuses entry of the shipment; 3) the Notice orders that the shipment be examined or analyzed to determine if it is in compliance with FIFRA. If your shipment is detained, you can avoid storage charges at the port by posting a delivery bond approximately equal to the shipment's value. You may not sell or distribute your insecticide or pesticide without EPA release. If you do, your delivery bond may be forfeited.

Customs Classification

For customs purposes, miscellaneous chemical substances are classified under Chapter 38 of the HTSUS. This chapter is broken into major headings, which are further divided into subheadings, and often sub-subheadings, each of which has its own HTSUS classification number. For example, the 2001 HTSUS number for ribbon fly catchers is 3808.10.10, indicating it is a sub-subcategory of insecticides (3808.10), which is a subcategory of the major heading, insecticides, rodenticides, fungicides, etc. (3808). There are 23 major headings within Chapter 38.

3801—Artificial graphite; colloidal or semi-colloidal graphite; preparations based on graphite or other carbon in the form of pastes, blocks, plates, or other semimanufactures

3802—Activated carbon; activated natural mineral products; animal black, including spent animal black

3803—Tall oil, whether or not refined

3804—Residual lyes from the manufacture of wood pulp, whether or not concentrated, desugared or chemically treated, including lignin sulfonates, but excluding tall oil of heading 3803

3805—Gum, wood, or sulfate turpentine and other terpenic oils produced by the distillation or other treatment of coniferous woods; crude dipentene; sulfite turpentine and other crude para-cymene; pine oil containing alpha-terpineol as the main constituent

3806—Rosin and resin acids, and derivatives thereof; rosin spirit and rosin oils; run gums

3807—Wood tar; wood tar oils; wood creosote; wood naphtha; vegetable pitch; brewers' pitch and similar preparations based on rosin, resin acids, or on vegetable pitch

3808—Insecticides, rodenticides, fungicides, herbicides, anti-sprouting products, and plant-growth regulators, disinfectants, and similar products, put up in forms or packages for retail sale or as preparations or articles (for example, sulfur-treated bands, wicks and candles, and flypapers)

3809—Finishing agents, dye carriers to accelerate the dyeing or fixing of dyestuffs, and other products and preparations (for example, dressings and mordants), of a kind used in the textile, paper, leather, or like industries, not elsewhere specified or included

3810—Pickling preparations for metal surfaces; fluxes and other auxiliary preparations for soldering, brazing, or welding; soldering, brazing, or welding powders and pastes consisting of metal and other materials; preparations of a kind used as cores or coatings for welding electrodes or rods

3811—Antiknock preparations, oxidation inhibitors, gum inhibitors, viscosity improvers, anti-corrosive preparations, and other prepared additives, for mineral oils (including gasoline) or for other liquids used for the same purposes as mineral oils

3812—Prepared rubber accelerators; compound plasticizers for rubber or plastics, not elsewhere specified or included; antioxidizing preparations and other compound stabilizers for rubber or plastics

3813—Preparations and charges for fire extinguishers; charged fire-extinguishing grenades

3814—Organic composite solvents and thinners, not elsewhere specified or included; prepared paint or varnish removers

3815—Reaction initiators, reaction accelerators, and catalytic preparations, not elsewhere specified or included

3816—Refractory cements, mortars, concretes, and similar compositions, other than products of heading 3801

3817—Mixed alkylbenzenes & mixed alkylnaphthalenes, other than those of heading 2707 or 2902

3818—Chemical elements doped for use in electronics, in the form of discs, wafers, or similar forms; chemical compounds doped for use in electronics

3819—Hydraulic brake fluids and other prepared liquids for hydraulic transmission, not containing or containing less than 70% by weight of petroleum oils or oils obtained from bituminous minerals

3820—Antifreezing preparations and prepared de-icing fluids

3821—Prepared culture media for development of microorganisms

3822—Diagnostic or laboratory reagents on a backing and prepared diagnostic or laboratory reagents whether or not on a backing, other than those of heading 3002 or 3006

3823—Industrial monocarboxylic fatty acids; acid oils from refining; industrial fatty alcohols:

3824—Prepared binders for foundry molds or cores; chemical products and preparations of the chemical or allied industries (including those consisting of mixtures of natural products), not elsewhere specified or included; residual products of the chemical or allied industries, not elsewhere specified or included

For more details regarding classifications of the specific product you are interested in importing, consult a customs broker, the appropriate commodity specialist at your nearest customs port, or the HTSUS. The 2001 HTSUS is available online from the Customs Service (www.customs.gov/impoexpo/impoexpo.htm) or for purchase from the U.S. Government Printing Office (see resources at the end of this chapter), and may be found in larger public libraries. For a general discussion of customs classification, see "Classification—Liquidation" on page 229.

Dutiable Status of Goods

For more information about duty rates and binding decisions see "Dutiable Status of Goods" on page 203; for a discussion of temporary importation of goods see "Temporary Free Importations" on page 205.

Valuation

Importers have a responsibility to use what the U.S. Customs Service deems, "reasonable care," when determining the value of their goods. They must also provide any additional information that the Customs Service needs for setting a final value on the goods. This process involves a number of factors and can be somewhat complicated; importers must be aware of applicable issues and details. Valuation information applies to all types of commodities, for further discussion on the subject see "Customs Valuation" on page 267.

Import Duties

Import duties vary (often dramatically) depending upon the Harmonized Tariff Schedule (HTSUS) classification of the goods or products imported. Since some products that look alike have different HTSUS classifications and different rates of duty, proper classification is vital. Note that "differences of opinion" between importers and the Bureau of Customs and Border Protection regarding classification keeps customs attorneys very busy.

Import duties can be assessed on the imported value of the goods ("ad valorem" rates of duty such as 2%, 4.4%, 50%, etc.), total units or weight of the goods ("specific" rates of duty such as 2 cents each or 1.5 cents/pound, etc.) or on a combination basis ("compound" rates of duty such as 5 cents each plus 6%).

Listed below is a sampling of several Column 1 import duty rates for Chapter 38 products:
Colloidal or semi-colloidal graphite (3801.20.00 00): Free
or
Bone black (3802.90.10 00): 5.8%

For specific information on US import duties refer to the Harmonized Tariff Schedule of the US. The print version is available from the US Government Printing Office as well as third party suppliers who often add special features. Online versions are available in both static PDF pages as well as in formats with excellent search functionality. Search the Web with the term "Harmonized Tariff Schedule" to find sources.

Entry and Documentation

The entry of merchandise is a two-part process consisting of 1) filing the documentation necessary to determine whether merchandise may be released from Customs custody, and 2) filing the documents that contain information for duty assessment and statistical purposes. In certain instances, all documents must be filed and accepted by Customs prior to release of the goods. Unless you have been granted an extension, you must file entry documents at a location specified by the port or area director within five working days of your shipment's date of arrival at a U.S. port of entry. These include a number of standard documents required by Customs for any entry, and:

- U.S. Customs TSCA Certification (hazardous substances) document

- EPA Notice of Arrival of Pesticides or Devices Form EPA 3540-1

After you present the entry, Customs may examine your shipment or may waive examination. The shipment is then released provided no legal or regulatory violations have been noted. You must then file entry summary documentation and deposit estimated duties at a designated customhouse within 10 working days of your shipment's release. For a detailed description of entry procedures, standard documentation, and informal entry, see "Entry Process" on page 185.

Informed Compliance. Informed compliance was introduced with the Customs Modernization Act of 1993 (Mod Act) and defines the relationship between importers and the Customs Service. It sets out the responsibilities of both parties. Providing the correct documentation and information for entry is a key factor that will make your importing operation run smoothly. We recommend that importers become familiar with the concept of informed comliance and the responsibilities that they have under the Mod Act. For further discussion about informed compliance see "Informed Compliance" on page 211.

Note: The Entry and Documentation section has been carefully designed to supply you, the importer, with sample documents and directions on how to satisfy Customs requirements. Be aware that you should consult the applicable authorities to ensure that you are correctly following the most current procedures.

Prohibitions and Restrictions

Hazardous Consumer Products. Importation of any consumer product that has been declared a banned hazardous substance by a rule under the CPSA is prohibited. Any product considered hazardous and not labeled according to provisions of the FHSA

is a misbranded hazardous substance and is an illegal import. Certain hazardous substances listed in the FHSA and in regulations promulgated by the CPSC are completely banned from importation. A shipment of consumer products cannot be imported if it poses an imminent hazard. See 15 USC 1261, 2604-2606; 16 CFR 1500.265-1500.272.

The CPSC may detain your shipment of hazardous substances and take samples for testing to determine compliance with the FHSA. If your shipment is found to contain banned hazardous substances, it will be refused admission and will be destroyed if not exported within 90 days of the date of refusal notice. If it is found to contain misbranded hazardous substances, you may make arrangements to bring it into conformance through relabeling. For complete details regarding testing, labeling, and safety regulations for hazardous products, contact the CPSC (see addresses at end of this chapter).

Insecticides and Pesticides. Insecticides or pesticides not cleared through the EPA's stringent product-and establishment-registration procedures cannot be imported into the U.S. EPA registration is designed to ensure, among other things, that an insecticide or pesticide entering the U.S., when used as directed: 1) is effective against the pests listed on the label; 2) is neither injurious to human, animals, and crops, nor damaging to the environment; and 3) will not result in illegal residues on food or feed. All imported insecticides and pesticides must meet FIFRA requirements before they can enter the U.S.

A single exception is made for chemicals imported in small amounts to test for pesticidal value. If your importation fits this category, and you have no intention of receiving any direct pest control benefits from your chemicals, the only requirement you must fulfill for importation is to be sure that the products carry instructions for proper handling during transport.

Inspections. All other shipments must comply with EPA import procedures, and are subject to port-of-entry inspections. EPA may examine your incoming shipment at the port of entry to determine if it is properly labeled. If you are importing products never previously sampled, or products of firms with histories of violations, the EPA may take samples of your shipment for testing. If your products were previously in violation of FIFRA, they will be inspected, and samples will be analyzed to determine current compliance. After the inspection, the EPA may: 1) release the shipment if it is in compliance; 2) order changes to bring the shipment into compliance; or 3) refuse entry, in which case you must return it to the country of origin or destroy it.

Product Registration. All insecticides and pesticides intended for sale in the U.S.—including imported products—must be registered with the EPA. Application for registration is a complex procedure requiring specific types of product data and documentation. Registration must be completed for each type of pesticide being imported. If you need to seek registration for the product you wish to import, contact the EPA (see addresses at end of this chapter). The agency publishes an information manual designed to help importers and producers complete the application process.

Establishment Registration. The Federal Insecticide, Fungicide, and Rodenticide Act requires both domestic and foreign producers of pesticides and devices to register the establishments in which they these products are produced. Producers should obtain EPA **Form 3540-8,** Application for the Registration of Pesticide-Producing Establishments from the EPA's Office of Compliance Monitoring (EN-342) (see addresses at end of this chapter) or from any regional EPA office. Completed forms should be submitted to the EPA headquarters office.

If the application is approved, the establishment will be assigned an EPA Establishment Number (EPA Est.). This number must appear on the label or container of each pesticide product. The foreign producer must submit annual reports to the EPA on all types and amounts of pesticides shipped to the U.S.

Recordkeeping Requirements. All registered establishments must maintain detailed books and records of production and distribution of insecticides and pesticides. For any materials shipped to the U.S., a foreign producer must keep the following records: 1) brand names, registration numbers, batch numbers, and amounts per batch; 2) brand names and quantities of devices; 3) brand names and quantities of receipts and shipments, as well as the name of the originating or delivering carrier, the name and address of the shipper, name and address of the consignee, and the dates of receipt or shipment. Such records are required even for transfers between plants of the same company; 4) inventories covering the brand names and quantities in stock; 5) all tests conducted on human beings and any adverse effects on the environment.

Production and shipment records must be retained for two years. Other records must be retained for various periods as specified by federal regulations. All records are subject to inspection and reproduction by authorized EPA representatives.

Marking and Labeling Requirements

Chemicals. A shipment of any products containing chemicals that are classified as hazardous substance (49 CFR 172) must comply with the marking and labeling regulations adopted by the EPA (46 CFR 147.30) and the DOT (49 CFR 171 et seq.).

Insecticides and Pesticides. Registered insecticide and pesticide products must meet all FIFRA labeling requirements. Your product's label must include the EPA product registration number, EPA Establishment Number, an ingredient statement, the name and address of the producer or the registrant, the necessary cautionary statements, and directions for use. Required label information must also be included on any printed materials that accompany the product to the end user. Statements or graphic representations on the label may not be false or misleading. If the product is to be used on a food or feed crop, a tolerance level for residues must be established by the EPA. Products failing to comply with registration or labeling requirements will be denied entry into the U.S. For more details on marking and labeling requirements, see FIFRA and implementing regulations, and contact the EPA (see addresses at end of this chapter).

For a general discussion of U.S. Customs marking and labeling requirements, see "Country of Origin Marking" on page 236, "Special Marking Requirements" on page 238 and "Marking—False Impression" on page 239.

Shipping Considerations

You will need to ensure that your goods are packaged and shipped with care so that they pass smoothly through Customs and arrive in good condition. You are responsible for ensuring that the shipment is in compliance with all applicable government regulations for packaging and shipping. In most instances, you should not leave these arrangements solely to the discretion of your supplier. Careful preparation of the cargo and selection of the mode of transport can be essential to a cost-effective, timely delivery of undamaged goods. We strongly advise you to consult your shipping representative, insurance agent, or freight broker for advice on packing and shipping.

Chemical products may be shipped in bulk, bags, bottles, or other types of containers, depending on the type of product and whether it is prepackaged. General considerations include protection from contamination, weather, and pests. If a product must be kept in a sanitary environment, all tables, utensils, platforms, and devices used for moving or handling the product, the compartments in which it is stowed while being transported will need to be maintained in a sanitary condition. For liquid ship-

ments, venting and vapor collection systems may be required. Safety precautions should also be implemented as required to protect against breakage, spillage, corrosion of containers, and combustion. Containers should be constructed so as to be safe for handling during transport.

Chemical products in particular may have to be shipped in pressurized, ventilated, and temperature-and vapor-controlled enclosures. Solid chemical products that are listed as hazardous substances (49 CFR 172 appendix) may be transported in bulk only on compliance with Coast Guard notification procedures, shipping permit requirements, and complex transportation regulations (46 CFR 148). All hazardous substances must be packaged and transported in accordance with DOT regulations (49 CFR 171 et seq.).

Publications and WWW Resources

The following publications may be relevant to the importation of toxic or hazardous chemicals:

Toxic Substances Control Act: A Guide for Chemical Importers/ Exporters (published by EPA)

This document is available from the TSCA Assistance Information Service (see Relevant Government Agencies)

The following publication provides a listing of existing chemical substances in the United States. It can be purchased in electronic format or a search of the document can be requested via telephone. Contact the Chemical Abstract Service (CAS) at (800)631-1884 or at (614) 447-3600 ext 2308.

TSCA Chemical Substance Inventory

In order to check whether or not a chemical is subject to any rules or regulations under Sections 5, 6, or 7 of TSCA, search the following document (www.epa.gov/opptintr/CORR)

Chemical on Reporting Rules List (CORR)

The *Harmonized Tariff Schedule of the United States (2001)* (HTSUS) is available to view on the Customs Service website (www.customs.gov), or you may purchase a printed version from:

U.S. Government Printing Office
Superintendent of Documents
710 North Capital Street NW
Washington DC 20401
Tel: (202) 512-1800
Fax: (202) 512-1657
Website: www.access.gpo.gov

The USGPO also has copies of specific laws available for purchase. The USGPO accepts orders made by fax, phone or placed over the Internet, as well as mail orders paid by credit card. All orders must be accompanied by payment. Credit cards, checks drawn on a U.S. bank, or an international money order are all acceptable.

The following publication is relevant to the importation of pesticides:

General Information on Applying for Registration of Pesticides in the United States - Second Edition (this document will become available in the Fall of 2001).

Check the follwoing website for current resources (www.epa.gov/opprd001/PestApp).

Relevant Government Agencies

Address your inquiries regarding TSCA and EPA requirements for importation of chemical substances to:

Environmental Protection Agency (EPA)
Office of Pollution Prevention and Toxics
TSCA System Information
1200 Pennsylvania Avenue NW
Washington DC 20460
Tel: (202) 564-3810

Tel: (202) 554-1404 (TSCA Information Hotline)
Email: oppt.homepage@epa.gov
Website: www.epa.gov/opptintr/contact.htm

Address your questions regarding EPA requirements for the importation of insecticides and pesticides to:

Environmental Protection Agency (EPA)
Office of Pesticide Programs
Ariel Rios Building
1200 Pennsylvania Avenue NW
Mail Code 3213A
Washington DC 20460
Tel: (703) 305-7090
Website: www.epa.gov

To obtain Environmental Protection Agency forms relating to the registration of products, call (703) 305-5447 or add to the main address: Registration Support Branch, Registration Division (H5704C).

Address your questions regarding transportation of hazardous substances to:

U.S. Department of Transportation (DOT)
Research and Special Programs Administration
Hazardous Materials Information Center
400 7th St. SW
Washington DC 20590
Tel: (202) 366-4488
Website: http://hazmat.dot.gov

Address your questions regarding CPSC requirements for photographic and cinematographic goods to:

Consumer Product Safety Commission (CPSC)
Office of Compliance
Washington DC 20207-0001
Tel: 800-638-2772 or (301) 504-7912
Fax: (301) 504-0359
Website: www.cpsc.gov

Address your questions regarding importation of chemical substances generally to your local Customs port director. For addresses, refer to "U.S. Customs and Border Protection Offices" on page 65 or contact:

U.S. Customs and Border Protection
Customs Headquarters
1300 Pennsylvania Avenue NW
Washington DC 20229
Tel: (202) 354-1000
Website: www.customs.treas.gov

Laws and Regulations

The following laws and regulations may be relevant to the importation of chemical substances. The laws are contained in the United States Code (USC), and the regulations are published in the Code of Federal Regulations (CFR), both of which are available at larger public and law libraries. Specific laws and regulations may also be purchased from the U.S. Government Printing Office (address above).

15 USC 2051 et seq.
Consumer Product Safety Act (CPSA)
This Act gives the Consumer Product Safety Commission authority to set safety standards, testing procedures, and reporting requirements to ensure that consumer products not already covered under other regulations are not harmful.

7 USC 136 et seq.
Federal Insecticide, Fungicide, and Rodenticide Act (FIFRA)
This Act prohibits the importation of pesticides or devices that are adulterated, misbranded, or otherwise in violation of the Act, provides for registration of pesticides

and devices, and establishes standards for labeling and classifying pesticides.

19 CFR 12; 40 CFR 162
Regulations on Pesticides
These regulations set forth the procedures and guidelines for importing products exposed to pesticides.

15 USC 2601 et seq.
Toxic Substances Control Act
This Act authorizes the EPA to determine whether a substance is harmful and to restrict importation, sale, and use of such substances.

19 CFR 12.118 et seq.
Regulations on Toxic Substances Control
These regulations require importers of chemical substances imported in bulk or as part of a mixture to certify to Customs that the shipment complies with the TSCA or is not subject to that Act.

15 USC 1261 et seq.
Federal Hazardous Substances Act
This Act controls the importation of hazardous substances, sets forth prohibited imports, and authorizes various agencies to promulgate labeling, marking, and transport requirements.

49 CFR 171 et seq.
Regulations on Hazardous Materials
These regulations list all substances deemed hazardous and provide transport, marking, labeling, safety, and emergency response rules.

46 CFR 147.30
Regulations on Labeling of Hazardous Materials
This regulation requires the labeling of containers of hazardous substances and specifies the label contents.

46 CFR 148 et seq.
Regulations on Carriage of Solid Hazardous Materials in Bulk
These regulations govern the transport of solid hazardous substances in bulk, including reporting, permitting, loading, stowing, and shipping requirements.

Sources of Additional Information

The TSCA Chemical Substance Inventory is available through various commercial online databases and from:

National Technical Information Service (NTIS)
U.S. Department of Commerce
5285 Port Royal Road
Springfield, VA 22161
(703) 605-6000; FAX (703) 605-6900
Web site: www.ntis.gov

Principal Exporting Countries

The following listing includes samples of the main supplier nations of the products of this chapter. It is organized by HTSUS major heading. (Refer to "Customs Classification" above for the product codes.) Countries are listed in rank order of the value of products imported to the U.S. Statistics represent customs value of entries for 2002 from the Bureau of Census, U.S. Department of Commerce.

3801—Japan, Switzerland, France, Germany, China, Canada, Inda

3802—China, Philippines, Sri Lanka, France, Mexico, United Kingdom, Japan, Germany, Canada

3803—Canada, Brazil

3804—Norway, Canada, Finland, China, Sweden, Germany

3805—Canada, China, Brazil, Mexico, Argentina, Chile, Japan

3806—Canada, China, Mexico, Brazil, Argentina, Indonesia, Turkey

3807—India, Canada, Sweden, Malaysia, China, Brazil, Germany

3808—United Kingdom, Germany, Canada, France, Mexico, China, Italy, Japan

3809—Mexico, Canada, Germany, Switzerland, United Kingdom, Japan

3810—Japan, France, Germany, United Kingdom, Canada, Brazil, Czech Republic, Sweden, Belgium

3811—Canada, United Kingdom, Germany, Mexico, France, Italy

3812—Germany, Canada, Italy, Japan, United Kingdom, Mexico, Switzerland, Taiwan, Belgium, France

3813—Mexico, France, Canada, Germany, United Kingdom

3814—Canada, Germany, Japan, Brazil, United Kingdom

3815—Canada, Germany, Japan, Netherlands, United Kingdom, Denmark

3816—Canada, Austria, Brazil, Germany, United Kingdom

3817—Canada, France, Venezuela, Indonesia, Singapore

3818—Japan, Germany, South Korea, France, Finland, Taiwan, Malaysia

3819—Germany, Canada, United Kingdom, Netherlands, Japan, Mexico, France

3820—Canada, United Kingdom, Belgium, Japan, Germany

3821—Italy, Germany, United Kingdom, Canada, Finland, France, Belgium

3822—United Kingdom, Japan, Germany, Canada, France, Ireland, Sweden

3823—Malaysia, Germany, Philippines, Indonesia, Netherlands, Norway, Canada

3824—Canada, Japan, Germany, France, United Kingdon, China, Netherlands

3825—Canada, Mexico, Japan, Poland, China, Germany, United Kingdom, Malaysia

Chapter 39:
Plastics and Articles Thereof

This chapter relates to the importation of plastics and plastic products, which are classified under Chapter 39 of the Harmonized Tariff Schedule of the United States (HTSUS). Specifically, it includes 1) primary forms of plastics—such as polymers of ethylene, olefins, styrene, halogenated olefins, vinyl esters, and acrylic; polyethers, polyesters, and polyamides; amino-resins, phenolic resins, and polyurethanes; silicones; petroleum resin; cellulose and its derivatives; natural polymers; and ion-exchangers; 2) plastic articles—such as tubes, piping, adhesives, bath and sanitary ware, containers, housewares, gloves, and statutes; and 3) semimanufactures, waste, parings, and scrap of plastics.

If you are interested in importing separate chemically defined organic compounds, refer to Commodity Index Chapter 29. If you are interested in importing a specific plastic product, such as toys or lighting fixtures, you should also look for a relevant chapter in this index pertaining to that particular product. For example, importing requirements for textiles with plastic fibers are found in Chapters 50 through 63, plastic footwear in Chapter 64, umbrellas in Chapter 66, headgear in Chapter 65, imitation jewelry in Chapter 71, and wall coverings in Chapter 48. Mineral waxes are covered in Chapter 27 and prepared waxes are in Chapter 34. For importing plastics and plastic products printed with motifs, characters, or pictures not merely incidental to the use of the product, refer to Chapter 49 on printed articles.

Note: To understand key issues that will enable you to make best use of the information in this section we recommend that you see "Introduction" on page 425.

Key Factors

The key factors in the importation of plastics and plastic products are:

- Compliance with U.S. Federal Trade Commission (FTC) and Consumer Product Safety Commission (CPSC) standards (if a consumer product)

- Compliance with U.S. Food and Drug Administration (FDA) entry notification and standards requirements (for products used with food, for sanitation, and for medical or similar purposes)

- Compliance with U.S. Environmental Protection Agency (EPA) requirements under Toxic Substances Control Act (TSCA) (if the product is a hazardous material)

- Compliance with U.S. Department of Transportation (DOT) regulations for transport of hazardous cargo (if the product is a hazardous material)

Although most importers use the services of a licensed customs broker in making their entries, and we recommend this practice, you should be aware of the regulatory, entry, and documentation issues involved in importing your product. You, as importer, are ultimately responsible for the fulfillment of any legal requirements applicable to your shipment.

General Considerations

Regulatory Agencies. The agency that regulates your imported shipment of plastics depends on whether the products are in primary form or in the form of articles, semimanufactures, waste, parings, or scrap. The EPA, under authority of the TSCA, imposes certain controls on the importation of plastics, mainly in primary form, that contain toxic substances. The TSCA defines a toxic substance as any substance determined to present the possibility of an unreasonable risk of injury to health and the environment. The DOT enforces regulations for transporting hazardous cargo. Materials are deemed hazardous if listed in DOT transport regulations (49 CFR 172 appendix). Articles of plastic that are intended for use with food, for sanitation, and for medicinal or similar purposes are regulated by the FDA, under the Federal Food, Drug, and Cosmetic Act (FDCA) and the Public Health Service Act (PHSA). The FTC sets standards for processing and labeling products sold to consumers.

Hazardous or Toxic Substances. Plastics in primary form are chemical mixtures. If listed as hazardous or toxic substances and imported in bulk, as articles, or as part of a mixture, these plastics must be in compliance with toxic and hazardous substance regulations of the EPA and DOT. These include packaging, shipping, marking, and labeling requirements.

In addition, all chemical products are subject to the U.S. Customs Service TSCA Import Certification Rule (19 CFR 12.118 et seq.). If you import these products, you must sign one of the following statements: "I certify that all chemical substances in this shipment comply with all applicable rules or orders under TSCA and that I am not offering a chemical substance for entry in violation of TSCA or any applicable rule or order thereunder" or "I certify that all chemicals in this shipment are not subject to TSCA."

You must file a TSCA certification of compliance or exemption at the time you make the entry at Customs. The certification may be in the form of a typed or stamped statement on an appropriate entry document or commercial invoice or a preprinted attachment to such entry document or invoice. You may sign the certificate by means of an authorized facsimile signature. If your entry is electronically processed, the certification will be in the form of a Certification Code, which is part of the Automated Broker Interface (ABI) transmission. Customs will not release your shipment without proper certification.

If you will be importing several or regular shipments, you should ask the appropriate Customs port director to authorize your use of a blanket certification. If you receive such authorization, you must include on the commercial invoice or entry document for each shipment a statement that the blanket certification is on file and that it is incorporated by reference. This statement need not be signed. The blanket certification is valid for one calendar year, is subject to renewal, and may be revoked at any time for cause.

Articles Exclusion. If you are importing products that are classified as hazardous substances but are part of articles, you are subject to TSCA certification requirements only if certification for your product is specifically required by a rule or order promulgated under the TSCA. No specific rules have been adopted at this time. An "article" is a manufactured item 1) that is formed into a specific shape or design during manufacture, 2) that has end-use functions dependent on the shape or design during end use, and 3) that during the end use, does not change in its chemical composition or that changes only for a noncommercial purpose separate from the article and only as allowed by law (19 CFR 12.120(2)). Fluids and particles are not articles, regardless of shape or design.

Shipment Detention. A shipment containing chemicals will be detained at the U.S. port of arrival (or entry if same), at your risk and expense, if: 1) it contains banned substances (15 USC 2604, 2605); or 2) it contains substances ordered seized because of imminent hazards (15 USC 2606). Further detention will occur at the port of entry, again at your risk and expense, if: 1) the EPA administrator or Customs port director has reasonable grounds to believe the shipment is not in compliance with the TSCA; or 2) you do not provide proper TSCA certification.

If your shipment is detained, it will be held by Customs for no more than 48 hours. It will then be turned over to the EPA administrator, unless you have arranged to release it in bond. You must either bring it into TSCA compliance or reexport it within the earlier of 90 days after notice of detention or 30 days of demand for redelivery. Customs may grant an extension if failure to comply or reexport is the result of delays in EPA or Customs procedures. If you fail to comply or reexport within the time allowed, the EPA administrator is authorized to have the shipment stored or disposed of at your expense.

FDA-Regulated Products. Imports of plastic products intended for use with food, for sanitation, or for medicinal or similar purposes are regulated by the FDA. Selectivity criteria and entry notification may be reinstituted at any time, at the discretion of the FDA. If you are interested in importing plastic articles intended for these purposes, you should be familiar with FDA import entry procedures and the requirements of the governing laws, the FDCA and the PHSA. For a general discussion of FDA import procedures see "Appendix: Foods" on page 825. If you are interested in importing one of these products, you should ascertain its regulatory status by contacting the FDA (see addresses at end of this chapter).

Hazardous Consumer Products. Under the Federal Hazardous Substances Act (FHSA), a plastic product intended for the consumer market is a hazardous substance if it is flammable, combustible, or has the potential to cause substantial personal injury during, or as a proximate result of, any customary or reasonably foreseeable handling or use. The CPSC does not require permits, special invoicing, limited entry, licenses, or any special approval process for importing hazardous consumer products into the U.S. However, if you are importing these types of products, you are responsible to ensure that they meet all applicable FHSA and CPSA requirements. There are detailed regulations regarding testing and labeling of hazardous products. The Commission's enforcement posture regarding compliance with labeling and product safety standards changes as new facts become available. Contact the CPSC (see addresses at end of this chapter) for specific requirements on the consumer product you are considering importing.

Substantial Product Hazard Reports. Defect-reporting is required for products covered under the CPSA. The law requires every manufacturer, distributor, or retailer of such products, who obtains information that reasonably supports the conclusion that such products fail to comply with an applicable consumer product safety rule, or contain a defect that could create a substantial product hazard, to immediately inform the CPSC of the potential violation or defect. A firm's willful failure to make a Substantial Product Hazard Report can result in litigation by the CPSC.

Customs Classification

For customs purposes, plastics and plastic products are classified under Chapter 39 of the HTSUS. This chapter is broken into major headings, which are further divided into subheadings, and often sub-subheadings, each of which has its own HTSUS classification number. For example, the 2001 HTSUS number for plastic trays is 3924.10.30, indicating it is a sub-subcategory of tableware and kitchenware (3924.10), which is a subcategory of the major heading, tableware, kitchenware, other household articles and toilet articles of plastics (3924). There are 26 major headings within Chapter 39.

3901—Polymers of ethylene, in primary forms

3902—Polymers of propylene or of other olefins, in primary forms

3903—Polymers of styrene, in primary forms

3904—Polymers of vinyl chloride or of other halogenated olefins, in primary forms

3905—Polymers of vinyl acetate or of other vinyl esters, in primary forms; other vinyl polymers in primary forms

3906—Acrylic polymers in primary forms

3907—Polyacetals, other polyethers and expoxide resins, in primary forms; polycarbonates, alkyd resins, polyallyl esters, and other polyesters, in primary forms

3908—Polyamides in primary forms

3909—Amino-resins, phenolic resins, and polyurethanes, in primary forms

3910—Silicones in primary forms

3911—Petroleum resins, coumarone-indene resins, polyterpenes, polysulfides, polysulfones, and other products specified in note 3 to this chapter, not elsewhere specified or included, in primary forms

3912—Cellulose and its chemical derivatives, not elsewhere specified or included, in primary forms

3913—Natural polymers (for example, alginic acid) and modified natural polymers (for example, hardened proteins, chemical derivatives of natural rubber), not elsewhere specified or included, in primary forms

3914—Ion-exchangers based on polymers of headings 3901 to 3913, in primary forms

3915—Waste, parings, and scrap of plastics

3916—Monofilament of which any cross-sectional dimension exceeds 1 mm, rods, sticks, and profile shapes, whether or not surface-worked but not otherwise worked, of plastics

3917—Tubes, pipes, and hoses and fittings therefor (for example, joints, elbows, flanges), of plastics

3918—Floor coverings of plastics, whether or not self-adhesive, in rolls or in the form of tiles; wall or ceiling coverings of plastics, as defined in note 9 to this chapter

3919—Self-adhesive plates, sheets, film, foil, tape, strip, and other flat shapes, of plastics, whether or not in rolls

3920—Other plates, sheets, film, foil, and strip, of plastics, noncellular and not reinforced, laminated, supported, or similarly combined with other materials

3921—Other plates, sheets, film, foil, and strip, of plastics

3922—Baths, shower baths, washbasins, bidets, lavatory pans, seats and covers, flushing cisterns, and similar sanitary ware, of plastics

3923—Articles for the conveyance or packing of goods of plastics; stoppers, lids, caps, and other closures, of plastics

3924—Tableware, kitchenware, other household articles, and toilet articles, of plastics

3925—Builders' ware of plastics, not elsewhere specified or included

3926—Other articles of plastics and articles of other materials of headings 3901 to 3914

For more details regarding classifications of the specific product you are interested in importing, consult a customs broker, the appropriate commodity specialist at your nearest customs port, or the HTSUS. The 2001 HTSUS is available online from the Customs Service (www.customs.gov/impoexpo/impoexpo.htm) or for purchase from the U.S. Government Printing Office (see resources at the end of this chapter), and may be found in larger public libraries. For a general discussion of customs classification, see "Classification—Liquidation" on page 229.

Dutiable Status of Goods

For more information about duty rates and binding decisions see "Dutiable Status of Goods" on page 203; for a discussion of temporary importation of goods see "Temporary Free Importations" on page 205.

Valuation

Importers have a responsibility to use what the U.S. Customs Service deems, "reasonable care," when determining the value of their goods. They must also provide any additional information that the Customs Service needs for setting a final value on the goods. This process involves a number of factors and can be somewhat complicated; importers must be aware of applicable issues and details. Valuation information applies to all types of commodities, for further discussion on the subject see "Customs Valuation" on page 267.

Import Duties

Import duties vary (often dramatically) depending upon the Harmonized Tariff Schedule (HTSUS) classification of the goods or products imported. Since some products that look alike have different HTSUS classifications and different rates of duty, proper classification is vital. Note that "differences of opinion" between importers and the Bureau of Customs and Border Protection regarding classification keeps customs attorneys very busy.

Import duties can be assessed on the imported value of the goods ("ad valorem" rates of duty such as 2%, 4.4%, 50%, etc.), total units or weight of the goods ("specific" rates of duty such as 2 cents each or 1.5 cents/pound, etc.) or on a combination basis ("compound" rates of duty such as 5 cents each plus 6%).

Listed below is a sampling of several Column 1 import duty rates for Chapter 39 products:
Vinyl acetate-vinyl chloride-ethylene terpolymers, containing by weight less than 50 percent derivatives of vinyl acetate, except those polymerized from aromatic or modified aromatic monomers (3904.30.20 00): Free
to
Poly(vinyl chloride), not mixed with any other substances (3904.10.00 00): 6.9%

For specific information on US import duties refer to the Harmonized Tariff Schedule of the US. The print version is available from the US Government Printing Office as well as third party suppliers who often add special features. Online versions are available in both static PDF pages as well as in formats with excellent search functionality. Search the Web with the term "Harmonized Tariff Schedule" to find sources.

Entry and Documentation

The entry of merchandise is a two-part process consisting of 1) filing the documentation necessary to determine whether merchandise may be released from Customs custody, and 2) filing the documents that contain information for duty assessment and statistical purposes. In certain instances, all documents must be filed and accepted by Customs prior to release of the goods. Unless you have been granted an extension, you must file entry documents at a location specified by the port or area director within five working days of your shipment's date of arrival at a U.S. port of entry. These include a number of standard documents required by Customs for any entry, and:

- U.S. Customs TSCA Certification (for plastics in primary form that are toxic or hazardous substances)

After you present the entry, Customs may examine your shipment or may waive examination. The shipment is then released provided no legal or regulatory violations have been noted. You must then file entry summary documentation and deposit estimated duties at a designated customhouse within 10 working days of your shipment's release. For a detailed description of entry procedures, standard documentation, and informal entry, see "Entry Process" on page 185.

Informed Compliance. Informed compliance was introduced with the Customs Modernization Act of 1993 (Mod Act) and defines the relationship between importers and the Customs Service. It sets out the responsibilities of both parties. Providing the correct documentation and information for entry is a key factor that will make your importing operation run smoothly. We recommend that importers become familiar with the concept of informed comliance and the responsibilities that they have under the Mod Act. For further discussion about informed compliance see "Informed Compliance" on page 211.

Note: The Entry and Documentation section has been carefully designed to supply you, the importer, with sample documents and directions on how to satisfy Customs requirements. Be aware that you should consult the applicable authorities to ensure that you are correctly following the most current procedures.

Entry Invoice for Plates, Sheets, Film, Foil, and Strip. The following additional information is required on entry invoices for plastic plates, sheets, film, foil, and strip of HTSUS headings 3920 and 3921: 1) statement as to whether the plastic is cellular or noncellular; 2) specification of the type of plastic; 3) indication of whether the plastic is flexible or inflexible and whether it is combined with a textile or other material.

Entry Invoice for Plastic-Coated or -Laminated Textiles. For articles manufactured of textile materials and coated or laminated with plastics, include a description indicating whether the fabric is coated or laminated on both sides, on the exterior surface, or on the interior surface.

Entry Invoice for Bags. The entry invoice for bags manufactured of plastic sheeting and not of a reinforced or laminated construction must indicate the gauge of the plastic sheeting.

Entry Invoice for Plastic Beads. For beads of plastic, specify: 1) the length of the string, if strung; 2) the size of the beads in mm; and 3) the material of which the beads are composed. For more general information about invoices see "Invoices" on page 277.

Prohibitions and Restrictions

Hazardous Consumer Products. Importation of any consumer product that has been declared a banned hazardous substance by a rule under the CPSA is prohibited. Any product considered hazardous and not labeled according to provisions of the FHSA is a misbranded hazardous substance and is an illegal import. Certain hazardous substances listed in the FHSA and in regulations promulgated by the CPSC are completely banned from importation. A shipment of consumer products cannot be imported if it poses an imminent hazard. See 15 USC 1261, 2604-2606; 16 CFR 1500.265-1500.272.

The CPSC may detain your shipment of hazardous substances and take samples for testing to determine compliance with the FHSA. If your shipment is found to contain banned hazardous substances, it will be refused admission and will be destroyed if not exported within 90 days of the date of refusal notice. If it is found to contain misbranded hazardous substances, you may arrange to bring it into conformance through relabeling. For complete details on testing, labeling, and safety regulations for hazardous products, contact the CPSC (see addresses at end of this chapter).

Marking and Labeling Requirements

Hazardous or Toxic Substances. A shipment of products containing substances classified as toxic or hazardous (49 CFR 172) must comply with the marking and labeling regulations adopted by the EPA (46 CFR 147.30) and the DOT (49 CFR 171 et seq.).

Consumer Products. A specific type of consumer product may have marking or labeling requirements, such as children's articles or electronic musical instruments. For further details, refer to the Commodity Index chapter applicable to the specific product in question. For a general discussion of U.S. Customs marking and labeling requirements, see "Country of Origin Marking" on page 236, "Special Marking Requirements" on page 238 and "Marking—False Impression" on page 239.

Shipping Considerations

You will need to ensure that your goods are packaged and shipped with care so that they pass smoothly through Customs and arrive in good condition. You are responsible for ensuring that the shipment is in compliance with all applicable government regulations for packaging and shipping. In most instances, you should not leave these arrangements solely to the discretion of your supplier. Careful preparation of the cargo and selection of the mode of transport can be essential to a cost-effective, timely delivery of undamaged goods. We strongly advise you to consult your shipping representative, insurance agent, or freight broker for advice on packing and shipping.

Plastics and plastic products may be shipped in bulk, bags, tanks, bottles, or other types of containers, depending on the type of product and whether it is prepackaged. General considerations include protection from contamination, weather, and pests. If a product must be kept in a sanitary environment, all tables, utensils, platforms, and devices used for moving or handling the product, the compartments in which it is stowed while being transported will need to be maintained in a sanitary condition. For liquid shipments, venting and vapor collection systems may be required. Safety precautions should also be implemented as required to protect against breakage, spillage, corrosion of containers, and combustion. Containers should be constructed so as to be safe for handling during transport.

Plastics in Primary Form. A plastic that is shipped in its primary liquid form may have to be enclosed in pressurized, ventilated, and temperature-and vapor-controlled containers. Solid plastics in primary form that are listed as hazardous substances (49 CFR 172 appendix) may be transported in bulk only on compliance with Coast Guard notification procedures, shipping permit requirements, and complex transportation regulations (46 CFR 148). All hazardous substances must be packaged and transported in accordance with DOT regulations (49 CFR 171 et seq.).

Publications and WWW Resources

The following publication explains the FDA requirements related to importing plastics and plastic products for sanitary use. It is published by the FDA and is available online from the FDA website (www.fda.gov).

Requirements of Laws and Regulations Enforced by the U.S. Food and Drug Administration

The following publications may be relevant to the importation of toxic or hazardous chemicals:

Toxic Substances Control Act: A Guide for Chemical Importers/ Exporters (published by EPA)

This document is available from the TSCA Assistance Information Service (see Relevant Government Agencies)

The following publication provides a listing of existing chemical substances in the United States. It can be purchased in electronic format or a search of the document can be requested via telephone. Contact the Chemical Abstract Service (CAS) at (800)631-1884 or at (614) 447-3600 ext 2308.

TSCA Chemical Substance Inventory

In order to check whether or not a chemical is subject to any rules or regulations under Sections 5, 6, or 7 of TSCA, search the following document (www.epa.gov/opptintr/CORR)

Chemical on Reporting Rules List (CORR)

The above publications and the *Harmonized Tariff Schedule of the United States (2001)* (HTSUS) is available to view on the Customs Service website (www.customs.gov), or you may purchase a printed version from:

U.S. Government Printing Office
Superintendent of Documents
710 North Capital Street NW
Washington DC 20401
Tel: (202) 512-1800
Fax: (202) 512-1657
Website: www.access.gpo.gov

The USGPO also has copies of specific laws available for purchase. The USGPO accepts orders made by fax, phone or placed over the Internet, as well as mail orders paid by credit card. All orders must be accompanied by payment. Credit cards, checks drawn on a U.S. bank, or an international money order are all acceptable.

Relevant Government Agencies

Address your questions regarding CPSC requirements for plastic products to:

Consumer Product Safety Commission (CPSC)
Office of Compliance
Washington DC 20207-0001
Tel: 800-638-2772 or (301) 504-7912
Fax: (301) 504-0359
Website: www.cpsc.gov

Address your questions regarding FDA regulation or requirements for plastic products to:

Food and Drug Administration (FDA)
Center for Food Safety and Applied Nutrition (CFSAN)
Office of Compliance
Division of Enforcement, Imports Branch
5100 Paint Branch Parkway
College Park, MD 20740-3835
Tel: (301) 436-2080
Website: http://vm.cfsan.fda.gov/list.html

Address your questions regarding TSCA and EPA requirements for importation of plastic products in primary form to:

Environmental Protection Agency (EPA)
Office of Pollution Prevention and Toxics
TSCA System Information
1200 Pennsylvania Avenue, NW
Washington, DC 20460
Tel: (202) 564-3810
Tel: (202) 554-1404 (TSCA Information Hotline)
Email: oppt.homepage@epa.gov
Website: www.epa.gov/opptintr/contact.htm

Address your questions regarding transportation of hazardous substances to:

U.S. Department of Transportation (DOT)
Research and Special Programs Administration
Hazardous Materials Information Center
400 7th St. SW
Washington DC 20590
Tel: (202) 366-4488
Website: http://hazmat.dot.gov

Address your questions regarding the importation of plastics and plastic products to your local Customs port director. For addresses refer to "U.S. Customs and Border Protection Offices" on page 65 or contact:

U.S. Customs and Border Protection
Customs Headquarters
1300 Pennsylvania Avenue NW
Washington DC 20229

Tel: (202) 354-1000
Website: www.customs.treas.gov

Laws and Regulations

The following laws and regulations may be relevant to the importation of plastics and plastic products. The laws are contained in the United States Code (USC), and the regulations are published in the Code of Federal Regulations (CFR), both of which are available at larger public and law libraries. Copies of specific laws and regulations may be purchased from the U.S. Government Printing Office (address above).

15 USC 2051 et seq.
Consumer Product Safety Act (CPSA)
This Act gives the Consumer Product Safety Commission authority to set safety standards, testing procedures, and reporting requirements to ensure that consumer products not already covered under other regulations are not harmful.

21 USC 301 et seq.
Federal Food, Drug, and Cosmetic Act
This Act prohibits deceptive practices and regulates the manufacture, sale and importation or exportation of food, drugs, cosmetics, and related products. It was amended by the Food Quality Protection Act of 1996. See 21 USC 331, 381, 382.

19 CFR 12.1 et seq.; 21 CFR 1.83 et seq.
Regulations on Food, Drugs, and Cosmetics
These regulations of the Secretary of Health and Human Services and the Secretary of the Treasury govern the standards, labeling, marking, and importing of products used with food, drugs, and cosmetics.

15 USC 2601 et seq.
Toxic Substances Control Act
This Act authorizes the EPA to determine whether a substance is harmful and to restrict importation, sale, and use of such substances.

19 CFR 12.118 et seq.
Regulations on Toxic Substances Control
These regulations require importers of chemical substances imported in bulk or as part of a mixture to certify to Customs that the shipment complies with the TSCA or is not subject to that Act.

15 USC 1261 et seq.
Federal Hazardous Substances Act
This Act controls the importation of hazardous substances, sets forth prohibited imports, and authorizes various agencies to promulgate labeling, marking, and transport requirements.

49 CFR 171 et seq.
Regulations on Hazardous Materials
These regulations list all substances deemed hazardous and provide transport, marking, labeling, safety, and emergency response rules.

46 CFR 147.30
Regulations on Labeling of Hazardous Materials
This regulation requires the labeling of containers of hazardous substances and specifies the label contents.

46 CFR 148 et seq.
Regulations on Carriage of Solid Hazardous Materials in Bulk
These regulations govern the transport of solid hazardous substances in bulk, including reporting, permitting, loading, stowing, and shipping requirements.

Principal Exporting Countries

The following listing includes samples of the main supplier nations of the products of this chapter. It is organized by HTSUS major heading. (Refer to "Customs Classification" above for the product codes.) Countries are listed in rank order of the value of products imported to the U.S. Statistics represent customs value of entries for 2002 from the Bureau of Census, U.S. Department of Commerce.

3901—Canada, Japan, France, Germany, Brazil, Thailand

3902—Canada, Japan, Germany, Netherlands, Mexico, Belgium

3903—Mexico, Canada, Bahamas, South Korea, Taiwan, Japan

3904—Canada, Japan, Germany, Italy, Netherlands, Mexico, France

3905—Germany, Japan, Canada, Taiwan, China, Italy, United Kingdom

3906—Canada, Japan, United Kingdom, Germany, France, South Korea, Mexico

3907—Canada, Japan, South Korea, Thailand, Mexico, Indonesia, Germany

3908—Canada, Germany, Japan, France, Mexico, Switzerland, Israel, Netherlands, Italy

3909—Canada, Germany, Japan, United Kingdom, Mexico, France, Italy

3910—Germany, Japan, Canada, United Kingdom, France, Mexico, Belgium, Spain, China, Italy, Netherlands, Russia

3911—United Kingdom, Japan, Germany, Belgium, Canada, France

3912—Japan, Germany, Finland, Netherlands, Sweden, Ireland, United Kingdom, Taiwan, Belgium

3913—China, France, Austria, Ireland, Japan, United Kingdom

3914—Sweden, France, Austria, Germany, Mexico, China, Japan, United Kingdom

3915—Mexico, Germany, Canada, Italy, China

3916—Canada, Taiwan, China, Japan, France, Germany, Italy, Israel

3917—Canada, Japan, Germany, United Kingdom, Mexico, Taiwan, China

3918—Canada, China, Taiwan, Germany, United Kingdom

3919—Canada, Taiwan, Japan, Germany, China, United Kingdom

3920—Canada, Japan, Germany, South Korea, Mexico, Taiwan

3921—Canada, Germany, South Korea, Japan, Mexico, Taiwan

3922—Canada, Mexico, China, Germany, Taiwan, United Kingdom

3923—Canada, China, Mexico, Taiwan, Japan, Germany, France, Hong Kong, South Korea, Thailand

3924—China, Taiwan, Mexico, Canada, Hong Kong, Thailand, Israel, Italy, South Korea, United Kingdom

3925—Canada, China, Taiwan, Mexico, Hong Kong, United Kingdom, Italy, Dominican Republic

3926—China, Canada, Mexico, Taiwan, Japan, Germany, United Kingdom

Chapter 40:
Rubber and Articles Thereof

This chapter relates to the importation of rubber and rubber articles, which are classified under Chapter 40 of the Harmonized Tariff Schedule of the United States (HTSUS). Specifically, it includes natural rubber and other gums, synthetic rubber and similar products derived from oils; reclaimed rubber; rubber waste, parings, and scrap; vulcanized and unvulcanized rubber in various forms; conveyor or transmission belts; new, retreaded, or used tires; inner tubes; hygienic or pharmaceutical rubber articles; rubber apparel and accessories; and a variety of soft vulcanized rubber articles.

If you are interested in importing specific rubber products, you should check this index for the chapter that relates to that particular item. For example, footwear is covered in Commodity Index Chapter 64, headgear in Chapter 65, mechanical and electrical appliances in Chapters 84 and 85, watches in Chapter 91, furniture in Chapter 94, and toys in Chapter 95. If you are interested in importing separate chemically defined organic substances, you should refer to Chapter 29. For textiles that may contain rubber substances, refer to Chapters 50 through 63.

Note: To understand key issues that will enable you to make best use of the information in this section we recommend that you see "Introduction" on page 425.

Key Factors

The key factors in the importation of rubber and rubber products are:

- Compliance with U.S. Food and Drug Administration (FDA) regulations and entry notification (if the product is chicle, hygienic or pharmaceutical articles, or gloves)

- Compliance with U.S. Federal Trade Commission (FTC) and Consumer Product Safety Commission (CPSC) labeling and safety standards (for consumer products, such as bicycle tires)

- Compliance with U.S. Environmental Protection Agency (EPA) requirements under Toxic Substances Control Act (TSCA) (if the product is a hazardous material)

- Compliance with U.S. Department of Transportation (DOT) regulations for transport of hazardous cargo (if the product is a hazardous material)

- Compliance with DOT, National Highway Traffic Safety Administration (NHTSA), safety standards and regulations (for motor vehicle tires)

Although most importers use the services of a licensed customs broker in making their entries, and we recommend this practice, you should be aware of the regulatory, entry, and documentation issues involved in importing your product. You, as importer, are ultimately responsible for the fulfillment of any legal requirements applicable to your shipment.

General Considerations

Regulatory Agencies. The agency that regulates your imported shipment of rubber depends on whether the products are in primary form or in a manufactured form. The EPA, under authority of the TSCA, imposes certain controls on the importation of rubber products, mainly in primary form, classified as toxic substances. The TSCA defines a toxic substance as any substance determined to present the possibility of an unreasonable risk of injury to health and the environment. The DOT enforces regulations for transporting hazardous cargo. Materials are deemed hazardous if listed in DOT transport regulations (49 CFR 172 appendix). The import of chicle, hygienic articles, pharmaceuticals, and gloves made of rubber are regulated by the FDA, under the Federal Food, Drug, and Cosmetic Act (FDCA) and the Public Health Service Act (PHSA). The FTC sets standards for processing and labeling products sold to consumers.

Primary Forms of Rubber. Importation of rubber in its premanufactured state is straightforward. Unless the product is listed as hazardous or toxic, there are no restrictions or prohibitions. No permits or licenses are required. You must provide additional information on the entry invoice for your shipments of rubber and rubber products (see "Entry and Documentation," below).

Hazardous or Toxic Substances. Rubber substances in primary form are chemical mixtures. If listed as hazardous or toxic substances and imported in bulk, as articles, or as part of a mixture, rubber products must be in compliance with toxic and hazardous substance regulations of the EPA and DOT. These include packaging, shipping, marking, and labeling requirements.

In addition, all chemical products are subject to the U.S. Customs Service TSCA Import Certification Rule (19 CFR 12.118 et seq.). If you import these products, you must sign one of the following statements: "I certify that all chemical substances in this shipment comply with all applicable rules or orders under TSCA and that I am not offering a chemical substance for entry in violation of TSCA or any applicable rule or order thereunder" or "I certify that all chemicals in this shipment are not subject to TSCA."

You must file a TSCA certification of compliance or exemption at the time you make the entry at Customs. The certification may be in the form of a typed or stamped statement on an appropriate entry document or commercial invoice or a preprinted attachment to such entry document or invoice. You may sign the certificate by means of an authorized facsimile signature. If your entry is electronically processed, the certification will be in the form of a Certification Code, which is part of the Automated Broker Interface (ABI) transmission. Customs will not release your shipment without proper certification.

If you will be importing several or regular shipments, you should ask the appropriate Customs port director to authorize your use of a blanket certification. If you receive such authorization, you must include on the commercial invoice or entry document for each shipment a statement that the blanket certification is on file and that it is incorporated by reference. This statement need not be signed. The blanket certification is valid for one calendar year, is subject to renewal, and may be revoked at any time for cause.

Articles Exclusion. If you are importing products that are classified as hazardous substances but are part of articles, you are subject to TSCA certification requirements only if certification for your product is specifically required by a rule or order promul-

gated under the TSCA. No specific rules have been adopted at this time. An "article" is a manufactured item 1) that is formed into a specific shape or design during manufacture, 2) that has end-use functions dependent on the shape or design during end use, and 3) that during the end use, does not change in its chemical composition or that changes only for a noncommercial purpose separate from the article and only as allowed by law (19 CFR 12.120(2)). Fluids and particles are not articles, regardless of shape or design.

Shipment Detention. A shipment containing chemicals will be detained at the U.S. port of arrival (or entry if same), at your risk and expense, if: 1) it contains banned substances (15 USC 2604, 2605); or 2) it contains substances ordered seized because of imminent hazards (15 USC 2606). Further detention will occur at the port of entry, again at your risk and expense, if: 1) the EPA administrator or Customs port director has reasonable grounds to believe the shipment is not in compliance with the TSCA; or 2) you do not provide proper TSCA certification.

If your shipment is detained, it will be held by Customs for no more than 48 hours. It will then be turned over to the EPA administrator, unless you have arranged to release it in bond. You must either bring it into TSCA compliance or reexport it within the earlier of 90 days after notice of detention or 30 days of demand for redelivery. Customs may grant an extension if failure to comply or reexport is the result of delays in EPA or Customs procedures. If you fail to comply or reexport within the time allowed, the EPA administrator is authorized to have the shipment stored or disposed of at your expense.

FDA-Regulated Products. The following Chapter 40 products are subject to regulation under the Federal Food, Drug, and Cosmetic Act (FDCA), enforced by the FDA: 1) chicle (natural gum); 2) hygienic or pharmaceutical articles, including sheath contraceptives and nursing nipples; and 3) surgical, medical, and other rubber gloves. If you are interested in importing these articles, you should be familiar with the FDA import entry procedures and requirements under the FDCA. For an a general discussion of FDA entry regulations see "Appendix: Foods" on page 825. For more information on FDA requirements, contact the regional FDA office nearest you, or FDA headquarters (see addresses at end of this chapter).

Motor Vehicle Tires. Importation of motor vehicle tires for resale is highly regulated. The DOT, through the NHTSA administers the National Traffic and Motor Vehicle Safety Act (NTMVSA). Regulations pertaining to motor vehicle equipment are found in 49 CFR 591. For regulatory purposes under this law, importers of motor vehicle tires for resale are considered manufacturers. As such, the importer is responsible for compliance with all pertinent regulations.

As a general rule, all tires manufactured on or after the date on which any applicable Federal Motor Vehicle Safety Standard (FMVSS) takes effect must conform to that standard to be imported into the U.S. When you import tires, you must provide the original manufacturer's certification of compliance with the applicable standard. Unless otherwise specified in the applicable standard, this certification must be in the form of a label or tag directly on the tire or on the outside of the container in which the tire is delivered. If you attempt to import tires for which there is an applicable standard without certification by the original manufacturer, your shipment will be refused entry. In addition, before offering tires for importation into the U.S., a foreign manufacturer is required to register as an "Agent-for-Service" of process, as set forth in 49 CFR 551.45.

In addition to the manufacturer's certification, the importer must submit DOT Declaration **HS-7** in duplicate to U.S. Customs at the time of the entry of the shipment. In this declaration, the importer must affirm 1) whether the imported tires are subject to a FMVSS;

2) whether the tires are in compliance or will be brought into compliance within the period allowed by the regulations; and 3) whether the tires are within one of the exceptions to compliance. The contents of the declaration are detailed in 19 CFR 12.80.

If you are interested in importing motor vehicle tires, you should contact the DOT (see addresses at end of this chapter). On request, a DOT compliance specialist will send you a packet of instructional and informational materials enumerating the responsibilities you will incur on bringing tires into the U.S. for resale. For a list of the materials, refer to "Publications and WWW Resources" below.

Bicycle Tires. If you are interested in importing bicycle tires, no special permits, licenses, or entry paperwork is required. However, the tires must be in compliance with stringent bicycle safety standards promulgated under the Consumer Product Safety Act (CPSA), and enforced by the CPSC (16 CFR 1512). To ascertain compliance, the CPSC randomly inspects shipments of bicycles at the port of entry. Contact CPSC (see addresses at end of this chapter) with your questions.

Customs Classification

For customs purposes, rubber and rubber products are classified under Chapter 40 of the HTSUS. This chapter is broken into major headings, which are further divided into subheadings, and often sub-subheadings, each of which has its own HTSUS classification number. For example, the 2001 HTSUS number for retreaded tractor tires is 4012.10.20, indicating it is a sub-subcategory of retreaded tires (4012.10), which is a subcategory of the major heading, retreaded or used pneumatic rubber tires, etc. (4012). There are 17 major headings within Chapter 40.

4001—Natural rubber, balata, gutta-percha, guayule, chicle, and similar natural gums, in primary forms or in plates, sheets, or strip

4002—Synthetic rubber and factice derived from oils, in primary forms or in plates, sheets, or strip; mixtures of any product of heading 4001 with any product of this heading, in primary forms or in plates, sheets, or strip

4003—Reclaimed rubber in primary forms or in plates, sheets, or strips

4004—Waste, parings, and scrap of rubber (other than hard rubber) and powders and granules obtained therefrom

4005—Compounded rubber, unvulcanized, in primary forms or in plates, sheets, or strip

4006—Other forms (for example, rods, tubes, and profile shapes) and articles (for example, discs and rings), of unvulcanized rubber

4007—Vulcanized rubber thread and cord

4008—Plates, sheets, strip, rods, and profile shapes, of vulcanized rubber other than hard rubber

4009—Tubes, pipes, and hoses, of vulcanized rubber other than hard rubber, with or without their fittings (for example, joints, elbows, flanges)

4010—Conveyor or transmission belts or belting, of vulcanized rubber

4011—New pneumatic tires, of rubber

4012—Retreaded or used pneumatic tires of rubber; solid or cushion tires, interchangeable tire treads and tire flaps, of rubber

4013—Inner tubes, of rubber

4014—Hygienic or pharmaceutical articles (including nursing nipples), of vulcanized rubber other than hard rubber, with or without fittings of hard rubber

4015—Articles of apparel and clothing accessories (including gloves), for all purposes, of vulcanized rubber other than hard rubber

4016—Other articles of vulcanized rubber other than hard rubber

4017—Hard rubber (for example, ebonite) in all forms, including waste and scrap; articles of hard rubber

For more details regarding classifications of the specific product you are interested in importing, consult a customs broker, the appropriate commodity specialist at your nearest customs port, or the HTSUS. The 2001 HTSUS is available online from the Customs Service (www.customs.gov/impoexpo/impoexpo.htm) or for purchase from the U.S. Government Printing Office (see resources at the end of this chapter), and may be found in larger public libraries. For a general discussion of customs classification, see "Classification—Liquidation" on page 229.

Dutiable Status of Goods

For more information about duty rates and binding decisions see "Dutiable Status of Goods" on page 203; for a discussion of temporary importation of goods see "Temporary Free Importations" on page 205.

Valuation

Importers have a responsibility to use what the U.S. Customs Service deems, "reasonable care," when determining the value of their goods. They must also provide any additional information that the Customs Service needs for setting a final value on the goods. This process involves a number of factors and can be somewhat complicated; importers must be aware of applicable issues and details. Valuation information applies to all types of commodities, for further discussion on the subject see "Customs Valuation" on page 267.

Import Duties

Import duties vary (often dramatically) depending upon the Harmonized Tariff Schedule (HTSUS) classification of the goods or products imported. Since some products that look alike have different HTSUS classifications and different rates of duty, proper classification is vital. Note that "differences of opinion" between importers and the Bureau of Customs and Border Protection regarding classification keeps customs attorneys very busy.

Import duties can be assessed on the imported value of the goods ("ad valorem" rates of duty such as 2%, 4.4%, 50%, etc.), total units or weight of the goods ("specific" rates of duty such as 2 cents each or 1.5 cents/pound, etc.) or on a combination basis ("compound" rates of duty such as 5 cents each plus 6%).

Listed below is a sampling of several Column 1 import duty rates for Chapter 40 products:
Balata, gutta-percha, guayule, chicle and similar natural gums (4001.30.00): Free
to
With textile components in which man-made fibers predominate by weight over any other single textile fiber of a width exceeding 20 cm (4010.36.41.00): 8%

For specific information on US import duties refer to the Harmonized Tariff Schedule of the US. The print version is available from the US Government Printing Office as well as third party suppliers who often add special features. Online versions are available in both static PDF pages as well as in formats with excellent search functionality. Search the Web with the term "Harmonized Tariff Schedule" to find sources.

Entry and Documentation

The entry of merchandise is a two-part process consisting of 1) filing the documentation necessary to determine whether merchandise may be released from Customs custody, and 2) filing the documents that contain information for duty assessment and statistical purposes. In certain instances, all documents must be filed and accepted by Customs prior to release of the goods. Unless you have been granted an extension, you must file entry documents at a location specified by the port or area director within five working days of your shipment's date of arrival at a U.S. port of entry. These include a number of standard documents required by Customs for any entry, and:

- DOT Declaration HS-7, in duplicate (for motor vehicle tires)
- U.S. Customs TSCA Certification (for rubber in primary form classified as a hazardous or toxic substance)

After you present the entry, Customs may examine your shipment or may waive examination. The shipment is then released provided no legal or regulatory violations have been noted. You must then file entry summary documentation and deposit estimated duties at a designated customhouse within 10 working days of your shipment's release. For a detailed description of entry procedures, standard documentation, and informal entry, see "Entry Process" on page 185.

Informed Compliance. Informed compliance was introduced with the Customs Modernization Act of 1993 (Mod Act) and defines the relationship between importers and the Customs Service. It sets out the responsibilities of both parties. Providing the correct documentation and information for entry is a key factor that will make your importing operation run smoothly. We recommend that importers become familiar with the concept of informed comliance and the responsibilities that they have under the Mod Act. For further discussion about informed compliance see "Informed Compliance" on page 211.

Note: The Entry and Documentation section has been carefully designed to supply you, the importer, with sample documents and directions on how to satisfy Customs requirements. Be aware that you should consult the applicable authorities to ensure that you are correctly following the most current procedures.

Entry Invoice for Rubber and Rubber Products. Entry invoices for Chapter 40 rubber and rubber products must state the following: 1) whether the rubber is combined with textile or other material; 2) whether the rubber is cellular or noncellular, vulcanized or unvulcanized; and 3) if vulcanized, whether the rubber is or is not hard.

Entry Invoice for Tires and Inner Tubes. When you import tires or inner tubes for tires, you must include the following information on your entry invoice: 1) specify the kind of vehicle for which the tire is intended—i.e., airplane, bicycle, passenger car, on-the-highway light or heavy truck or bus, motorcycle; 2) if designed for tractors (HTSUS 8601.90.10), or for agricultural or horticultural machinery or implements (HTSUS Chapter 84 or 8716.80.10), designate whether the tire is new, recapped, or used and whether it is pneumatic or solid; and 3) indicate whether the tube is designed for tires classified in HTSUS 4011.91.10, 4011.99.10, 4012.10.20, or 4012.20.20.

Entry Invoice for Rubber-Coated or -Laminated Textiles. For articles manufactured of textile materials and coated or laminated with rubber, include a description indicating whether the fabric is coated or laminated on both sides, on the exterior surface, or on the interior surface. For more general information about invoices see "Invoices" on page 277.

Prohibitions and Restrictions

Tires. Motor vehicle tires covered by a Federal Motor Vehicle Safety Standards (FMVSS) must conform to that standard to be imported into the U.S. If you attempt to import tires covered by an applicable standard without the vehicle equipment DOT Declaration **HS-7** or a certification of compliance by the original manufacturer, your shipment will be refused entry.

Bicycle tires must be in compliance with the CPSC safety and labeling regulations. The CPSC enforces these restrictions through random border inspections, and if your tires are found to be noncomplying, the shipment will be refused entry. If your shipment passes through Customs without inspection, but is later found to be noncomplying, you are liable for a product recall. The CPSC has authority to take legal action for noncompliance as part of its responsibility to protect consumers.

Substantial Product Hazard Reports. Defect-reporting is required for products covered under the CPSA. The law requires every manufacturer, distributor, or retailer of such products, who obtains information that reasonably supports the conclusion that such products fail to comply with an applicable consumer product safety rule, or contain a defect that could create a substantial product hazard, to immediately inform the CPSC of the potential violation or defect. A firm's willful failure to make a Substantial Product Hazard Report can result in litigation by the CPSC.

Marking and Labeling Requirements

Motor Vehicle Tires. There are specific DOT marking requirements for motor vehicle tires. You can obtain a copy of these requirements by contacting the DOT Office of Vehicle Safety Compliance (see addresses at end of this chapter) and requesting the importers' information packet.

Hazardous or Toxic Substances. A shipment of products containing substances classified as toxic or hazardous (49 CFR 172) must comply with the marking and labeling regulations adopted by the EPA (46 CFR 147.30) and the DOT (49 CFR 171 et seq.).

Consumer Products. A specific type of consumer product may have marking or labeling requirements, such as pharmaceuticals and rubber inflatable articles. For further details, refer to the Commodity Index chapter applicable to the specific product in question.

For a general discussion of U.S. Customs marking and labeling requirements, see "Country of Origin Marking" on page 236, "Special Marking Requirements" on page 238 and "Marking—False Impression" on page 239.

Shipping Considerations

You will need to ensure that your goods are packaged and shipped with care so that they pass smoothly through Customs and arrive in good condition. You are responsible for ensuring that the shipment is in compliance with all applicable government regulations for packaging and shipping. In most instances, you should not leave these arrangements solely to the discretion of your supplier. Careful preparation of the cargo and selection of the mode of transport can be essential to a cost-effective, timely delivery of undamaged goods. We strongly advise you to consult your shipping representative, insurance agent, or freight broker for advice on packing and shipping.

Rubber and rubber products may be shipped in bulk, bags, bales, tanks, or other types of containers, depending on the type of product and whether it is prepackaged. General considerations include protection from contamination, weather, and pests. If a product must be kept in a sanitary environment, all tables, utensils, platforms, and devices used for moving or handling the product, the compartments in which it is stowed while being transported will need to be maintained in a sanitary condition. For liquid shipments, venting and vapor collection systems may be required. Safety precautions should also be implemented as required to protect against breakage, spillage, corrosion of containers, and combustion. Containers should be constructed so as to be safe for handling during transport.

Rubber in Primary Form. Rubber that is shipped in its primary form may have to be enclosed in pressurized, ventilated, and temperature-and vapor-controlled containers. Solid rubber in primary form that is listed as a hazardous substance (49 CFR 172 appendix) may be transported in bulk only on compliance with Coast Guard notification procedures, shipping permit requirements, and complex transportation regulations (46 CFR 148). All hazardous substances must be packaged and transported in accordance with DOT regulations (49 CFR 171 et seq.).

Publications and WWW Resources

The following informational materials are available from the DOT website (www.nhtsa.dot.gov/cars/rules/maninfo).

How to Become a Registered Importer

Registered Importers Procedures and Requirements

Newsletters

The following publication explains the FDA requirements for importing rubber and rubber products for sanitary use. It is published by the FDA and is available online at the FDA website (www.fda.gov).

Requirements of Laws and Regulations Enforced by the U.S. Food and Drug Administration

The following publications may be relevant to the importation of toxic or hazardous chemicals:

Toxic Substances Control Act: A Guide for Chemical Importers/ Exporters (published by EPA)

This document is available from the TSCA Assistance Information Service (see Relevant Government Agencies)

The following publication provides a listing of existing chemical substances in the United States. It can be purchased in electronic format or a search of the document can be requested via telephone. Contact the Chemical Abstract Service (CAS) at (800)631-1884 or at (614) 447-3600 ext 2308.

TSCA Chemical Substance Inventory

In order to check whether or not a chemical is subject to any rules or regulations under Sections 5, 6, or 7 of TSCA, search the following document (www.epa.gov/opptintr/CORR)

Chemical on Reporting Rules List (CORR)

The above publications and the *Harmonized Tariff Schedule of the United States (2001)* (HTSUS) is available to view on the Customs Service website (www.customs.gov), or you may purchase a printed version from:

U.S. Government Printing Office
Superintendent of Documents
710 North Capital Street NW
Washington DC 20401
Tel: (202) 512-1800
Fax: (202) 512-1657
Website: www.access.gpo.gov

The USGPO also has copies of specific laws available for purchase. The USGPO accepts orders made by fax, phone or placed over the Internet, as well as mail orders paid by credit card. All orders must be accompanied by payment. Credit cards, checks drawn on a U.S. bank, or an international money order are all acceptable.

Relevant Government Agencies

Address your questions regarding requirements for FDA-regulated rubber products to:

Food and Drug Administration (FDA)
Center for Food Safety and Applied Nutrition (CFSAN)
Office of Compliance
Division of Enforcement, Imports Branch
5100 Paint Branch Parkway
College Park, MD 20740-3835

Tel: (301) 436-2080
Website: http://vm.cfsan.fda.gov/list.html

Address your questions regarding the importation of motor vehicle tires to:

National Highway Traffic Safety Administration
Office of Vehicle Safety Compliance
Equipment & Import Division
400 7th St. SW
Washington DC 20590
Tel: (202) 366-2832
Website: www.nhtsa.dot.gov

Address your questions regarding CPSC requirements for bicycle tires and other consumer products to:

Consumer Product Safety Commission (CPSC)
Office of Compliance
Washington DC 20207-0001
Tel: 800-638-2772 or (301) 504-7912
Fax: (301) 504-0359
Website: www.cpsc.gov

Address your inquiries regarding TSCA and EPA requirements for importation of rubber products in primary form to:

Environmental Protection Agency (EPA)
Office of Pollution Prevention and Toxics
TSCA System Information
1200 Pennsylvania Avenue NW
Washington DC 20460
Tel: (202) 564-3810
Tel: (202) 554-1404 (TSCA Information Hotline)
Email: oppt.homepage@epa.gov
Website: www.epa.gov/opptintr/contact.htm

Address your questions regarding transportation of hazardous substances to:

U.S. Department of Transportation (DOT)
Research and Special Programs Administration
Hazardous Materials Information Center
400 7th St. SW
Washington DC 20590
Tel: (202) 366-4488
Website: http://hazmat.dot.gov

Address your questions regarding the importation of rubber and rubber products to your local Customs port director. For addresses refer to "U.S. Customs and Border Protection Offices" on page 65 or contact:

U.S. Customs and Border Protection
Customs Headquarters
1300 Pennsylvania Avenue NW
Washington DC 20229
Tel: (202) 354-1000
Website: www.customs.treas.gov

Laws and Regulations

The following laws and regulations may be relevant to the importation of rubber and rubber products. The laws are contained in the United States Code (USC), and the regulations are published in the Code of Federal Regulations (CFR), both of which are available at larger public and law libraries. Copies of specific laws and regulations may be purchased from the U.S. Government Printing Office (address above).

21 USC 301 et seq.
Federal Food, Drug, and Cosmetic Act
This Act prohibits deceptive practices and regulates the manufacture, sale and importation or exportation of food, drugs, cosmetics, and related products. It was amended by the Food Quality Protection Act of 1996. See 21 USC 331, 381, 382.

19 CFR 12.1 et seq.; 21 CFR 1.83 et seq.

Regulations on Food, Drugs, and Cosmetics
These regulations of the Secretary of Health and Human Services and the Secretary of the Treasury govern the standards, labeling, marking, and importing of products used with food, drugs, and cosmetics.

15 USC 2051 et seq.
Consumer Product Safety Act (CPSA)
This Act gives the Consumer Product Safety Commission authority to set safety standards, testing procedures, and reporting requirements to ensure that consumer products not already covered under other regulations are not harmful.

49 CFR 571
Regulations on Motor Vehicle Safety Standards
These regulations are safety standards prescribed by the Secretary of Transportation pursuant to the NTMVSA to regulate the quality of motor vehicles and motor vehicle equipment imported into the U.S., as well as offered for sale in, introduced into, or delivered for introduction into interstate commerce.

19 CFR 12.80
Regulations on Motor Vehicle Entry Declaration
These regulations govern the import of motor vehicles and motor vehicle equipment through U.S. Customs, require the importer to submit a specific detailed declaration, and authorize Customs to deny entry in the absence of a declaration.

15 USC 2601 et seq.
Toxic Substances Control Act
This Act authorizes the EPA to determine whether a substance is harmful and to restrict importation, sale, and use of such substances.

19 CFR 12.118 et seq.
Regulations on Toxic Substances Control
These regulations require importers of chemical substances imported in bulk or as part of a mixture to certify to Customs that the shipment complies with the TSCA or is not subject to that Act.

15 USC 1261 et seq.
Federal Hazardous Substances Act
This Act controls the importation of hazardous substances, sets forth prohibited imports, and authorizes various agencies to promulgate labeling, marking, and transport requirements.

49 CFR 171 et seq.
Regulations on Hazardous Materials
These regulations list all substances deemed hazardous and provide transport, marking, labeling, safety, and emergency response rules.

16 CFR 1500 et seq.
Regulations on Hazardous Substances Safety Standards
These regulations set standards for processing, manufacturing, importing, and labeling all substances classified as hazardous that are to be sold to U.S. consumers.

46 CFR 147.30
Regulations on Labeling of Hazardous Materials
This regulation requires the labeling of containers of hazardous substances and specifies the label contents.

46 CFR 148 et seq.
Regulations on Carriage of Solid Hazardous Materials in Bulk
These regulations govern the transport of solid hazardous substances in bulk, including reporting, permitting, loading, stowing, and shipping requirements.

Principal Exporting Countries

The following listing includes samples of the main supplier nations of the products of this chapter. It is organized by HTSUS major heading. (Refer to "Customs Classification" above for the product codes.) Countries are listed in rank order of the value of products imported to the U.S. Statistics represent customs value of entries for 2002 from the Bureau of Census, U.S. Department of Commerce.

4001—Indonesia, Thailand, Malaysia, Liberia, Vietnam

4002—Canada, Japan, Mexico, Germany, France, South Korea, Brazil, Belgium, Italy, Russia, Taiwan, Netherlands

4003—Canada, Netherlands, Germany, India, United Kingdom, Bulgaria

4004—Canada, United Kingdom, Mexico, Netherlands

4005—Canada, France, Japan, Mexico, Germany, Switzerland, United Kingdom, Belgium

4006—Canada, Italy, South Korea, Brazil, Germany, France

4007—Malaysia, Indonesia, Thailand, Canada, India, China, Japan

4008—Germany, Canada, Japan, South Korea, United Kingdom, Taiwan, Malaysia, Mexico

4009—Mexico, Japan, Canada, Italy, Germany, United Kingdom, Brazil

4010—Canada, Japan, Mexico, Germany, Taiwan, Switzerland, France

4011—Canada, Japan, China, South Korea, Taiwan, Germany, Brazil, France, United Kingdom

4012—Canada, Sri Lanka, Mexico, Japan, China, Taiwan, United Kingdom, Germany, South Korea, France, Netherlands

4013—South Korea, China, Taiwan, Canada, Japan, Thailand, Venezuela

4014—Thailand, India, Japan, Spain, Singapore, Malaysia, United Kingdom, Germany, China

4015—Malaysia, Thailand, China, Indonesia, Sri Lanka, Mexico

4016—Canada, Japan, Mexico, China, Germany, Taiwan

4017—Canada, China, India, Taiwan, United Kingdom, Germany

Chapter 41:
Raw Hides, Skins, and Leather

Full title: Raw Hides and Skins (Other than Furskins) and Leather.

This chapter relates to the importation of raw hides, skins, and leather, which are classified under Chapter 41 of the Harmonized Tariff Schedule of the United States (HTSUS). Specifically, it includes raw and prepared animal and reptile hides and skins; chamois leather; patent leather; leather parings and waste not suitable for making articles; leather dust, powder, and flour; and composition leather.

If you are interested in importing leather articles, you should read Commodity Index Chapter 41. Furskins are covered in Chapter 43. Import requirements for bird skins, feathers, and down are found in Chapters 5 and 67. The importation of live animals is covered in Chapter 1.

Note: To understand key issues that will enable you to make best use of the information in this section we recommend that you see "Introduction" on page 425.

Key Factors

The key factors in the importation of raw hides, skins, and leather are:

- Compliance with Fish and Wildlife Service (FWS) license, permit, country-of-origin permit, import documentation, and recordkeeping requirements (if the products are derived from exotic wildlife or endangered species)

- Entry at FWS-designated ports, and compliance with FWS and Customs advance notification and port-of-entry inspection requirements (if the products are derived from exotic wildlife or endangered species)

- Compliance with U.S. Department of Agriculture (USDA) APHIS import, quarantine, permit, and certification requirements (if the products are derived from domesticated animals)

- Entry at USDA-designated ports (if the products are derived from domesticated animals)

Although most importers use the services of a licensed customs broker in making their entries, and we recommend this practice, you should be aware of the regulatory, entry, and documentation issues involved in importing your product. You, as importer, are ultimately responsible for the fulfillment of any legal requirements applicable to your shipment.

General Considerations

Regulatory Agencies. The USDA regulates and inspects the importation of all products derived from animals. The FWS, primarily under provisions of the U.S. Endangered Species Act (ESA) and the Convention on International Trade in Endangered Species of Wild Fauna and Flora (CITES), controls the importation of products derived from animals that are classified as exotic wildlife or endangered or threatened species. U.S. Customs enforces USDA and FWS requirements through entry documentation and restrictions.

Domesticated Animal Hides, Skins, and Leathers. Importation of hides, skins, and leathers of domesticated animals—such as cattle, pigs, sheep, and goats—is generally straightforward. Products derived from such animals are subject to quarantine regulations, marking requirements, and processing standards. Shipments of these products are inspected at the port of arrival by USDA'S Animal and Plant Health Inspection Service (APHIS). Unless the shipment is in compliance with all applicable laws and regulations, it will be denied entry into the U.S. Some shipments may be restricted or prohibited completely.

Quarantine and Inspection. At the time of applying for a permit to import animal products subject to quarantine requirements, you will have to make reservations for space in an appropriate quarantine facility. Fees for quarantine reservations vary according to species, and are due and payable when the reservation is requested. Each shipment entering under APHIS permit must comply in every detail with the permit's specifications. If your shipment is found to be aberrant in any way (such as entering at a port of entry other than the one specified in the permit), it will be refused entry.

Veterinary Certificates. A veterinary certificate, issued by a salaried veterinarian of the country of origin, stating that the animal products are free of applicable livestock diseases, must accompany each shipment. The specific information required on the certificate varies depending on the species you are importing, and its country of origin. You must also present an importer's declaration, which states: 1) port of entry; 2) importer's name and address; 3) broker's name and address; 4) livestock origin; 5) number, breed, species, and purpose of importation; 6) consignee's name, and location of intended delivery.

APHIS-designated Quarantine Ports. The following listings are APHIS-designated ports with adequate quarantine facilities available for the import of livestock and livestock products. With very few exceptions, all shipments of livestock and livestock products must enter at one of these designated ports:

Air and Ocean Ports: Los Angeles, CA; Miami, FL; and Newburgh, NY.

Land border ports with Canada: Eastport, ID; Houlton and Jackman, MI; Detroit, Port Huron, and Sault Ste. Marie, MI; Baudette, MN; Opheim, Raymond, and Sweetgrass, MT; Alexandria Bay, Buffalo, and Champlain, NY; Dunseith, Pembina, and Portal, ND; Derby Line and Highgate Springs, VT; Lynden, Oroville, and Sumas, WA.

Land border ports with Mexico: Brownsville, Hidalgo, Laredo, Eagle Pass, Del Rio, and Presidio, TX; Douglas, Naco, Nogales, and San Luis, AZ; Calexico and San Ysidro, CA; Antelope Wells, Columbus, and Santa Teresa, NM.

Limited ports (ports with facilities for entry of live animals that do not appear to require restraint and holding inspection facilities): Anchorage and Fairbanks, AK; San Diego and San Francisco, CA; Denver, CO; Jacksonville, St. Petersburg-Clearwater, and Tampa, FL; Atlanta, GA; Honolulu, HI; Chicago, IL; New Orleans, LA; Portland, ME; Baltimore, MD; Boston, MA; Minneapolis, MN; Great Falls, MT; Dayton, OH; Portland, OR; San

Juan, PR; Memphis, TN; El Paso, Galveston and Houston, TX; Seattle, Spokane, and Tacoma, WA.

The ports listed above have been designated as quarantine stations. The USDA Administrator has authority to designate other ports as quarantine stations as needed.

Exotic and Endangered Species. The FWS enforces a complex set of laws and regulations (see 50 CFR 1 et seq.) pertaining to wildlife and wildlife product importation. These laws include the international Convention on International Trade in Endangered Species of Wild Fauna and Flora (CITES), the Endangered Species Act (ESA), and a number of other U.S. laws, such as the African Elephant Conservation Act (AECA), Marine Mammal Protection Act (MMPA), Migratory Bird Treaty Act (MBTA), Eagle Protection Act (EPA), and the Lacey Act (LA). Most foreign countries also have their own domestic measures, and you will need to meet the requirements of the country of export in addition to U.S. requirements. For more information, contact the FWS Office of Management Authority (OMA) (see addresses at end of this chapter).

Certain types of hides, skins, and leathers are entirely prohibited, others are allowed entry only under permit and/or license, and still others are allowed entry only for specific noncommercial purposes. When applying for a permit, you must satisfy the requirements of all laws under which the species is protected. The following briefly describes the two major laws governing importation of protected wildlife products into the U.S. This discussion is not comprehensive or exhaustive. If you wish to import hides, skins, or leathers of exotic or endangered animals, you should always contact the FWS (see addresses at end of this chapter) with species information before making any transactions.

CITES. Over 100 nations participate in the Convention on International Trade in Endangered Species of Wild Fauna and Flora (CITES) treaty, which took effect in May 1977. The degree of protection afforded to a species depends on which of the three CITES appendices contains the name of that species. Documentation required for import varies depending on the species, and the CITES section where it is listed. The CITES export documentation from the country of origin is always required. If you are importing a CITES-listed species from a country that does not participate in the treaty, you must still obtain from that nation documents that contain all the information normally required in CITES export permits.

Appendix I. This appendix lists species deemed presently threatened with extinction (e.g., orangutan, chinchilla, gray whale). Importation of Appendix I species for commercial purposes is prohibited. You must have two permits to import these species: one from the U.S., which must be obtained first, and one from the exporting country. If you are importing Appendix I species taken in the marine environment and outside the jurisdiction of any country or state, you must have an Introduction from the Sea Permit.

Appendix II. This appendix lists species that are not presently threatened with extinction but may become threatened if their trade is not regulated (e.g., brown bear, musk deer, elephant seal). There are no restrictions on the purpose of import, provided it is not detrimental to the survival of the species. You will need an export permit or reexport certificate from the exporting country. If you are importing Appendix II species taken in the marine environment and outside the jurisdiction of any country or state, you will need an Introduction from the Sea Permit.

Appendix III. This appendix lists species for which any CITES member country has domestic regulations "for the purpose of preventing or restricting exploitation, and as needing the cooperation of other Parties in control of trade." For example, Canada lists the walrus, and Nepal lists the blackbuck antelope. Three different types of documents are issued for Appendix III species:

1) Export Permit: Issued for specimens that originated in a country that listed the species on Appendix III; 2) Certificate of Origin: Issued by any country other than the listing country if the wildlife in question originated in that country; 3) Reexport Certificate: Issued for the export of Appendix III specimens that were previously imported into the U.S.

Exemptions. Under certain conditions, Certificates of Exemption may be issued for the importation of wildlife products listed under CITES. Exceptions are allowed for shipments of wildlife transiting a country under Customs bond, shipments between U.S. states or territories, and certain personal or household effects. For information, contact FWS (see addresses at end of this chapter).

Permit Applications. Applications for CITES permits and certificates are available from the FWS Office of Management Authority (see addresses at end of this chapter). You will need to fill out the FWS Standard Permit Application **(Form 3-200)** and provide certain information specifically required under CITES. You should submit your application at least 60 days before the date you wish the permit to take effect. FWS charges processing fees for CITES applications.

ESA. The U.S. Endangered Species Act (ESA) was passed on December 28, 1973, to prevent the extinction of many species of animals and plants and to protect their habitats. By definition, an "endangered species" is any animal or plant listed by regulation as being in danger of extinction. A "threatened species" is any animal or plant likely to become endangered within the foreseeable future. The U.S. List of Endangered and Threatened Wildlife and Plants includes native and foreign species.

Permits. ESA's import provisions prohibit the import or export of any endangered or threatened species or products derived from them without one of the following permits from the FWS Federal Wildlife Permit Office (FWPO):

> *Endangered Species Permits:* This permit is issued for importation for purposes of 1) scientific research; 2) enhancement of propagation or survival of the species; or 3) incidental taking.

> *Threatened Species Permits:* This permit is issued for importation for purposes of 1) scientific research; 2) enhancement of propagation or survival of the species; 3) zoological, horticultural, or botanical exhibition; 4) education purposes; 5) special purposes consistent with ESA purposes and policy; or 6) incidental taking.

Permit Exemptions. A few imports of endangered species products are exempt from the ESA permit requirements. For example, if a species is listed as threatened or as an experimental population, special rules may allow otherwise prohibited activities. Some species covered by special rules include certain kangaroos, several primates, the grizzly bear, gray wolf, African elephant, American alligator, and leopard. If you are unsure as to the exemption status of your import, contact FWS (see addresses at end of this chapter).

FWS Import Licenses. With some exceptions, persons engaged in the business of importing wildlife products valued in excess of $25,000 per year must be licensed by the FWS. If your annual importations are valued at less than $25,000, or if you qualify for another exemption from licensing, you are still responsible for keeping thorough records of all wildlife transactions and of making these records available to FWS officers if necessary. For a full description of exemptions from licensing, and of recordkeeping requirements, contact the Fish and Wildlife Service (see addresses at end of this chapter) or see 50 CFR 14.

Procedures at Port of Entry. At least 72 hours before your shipment is due to arrive at a designated port, you should notify U.S. Customs and the FWS inspectors of its expected arrival. The

FWS conducts port-of-entry shipment inspections on a case-by-case basis, as determined by the inspection agent after looking at the entry paperwork. Both FWS and Customs may inspect your shipment to verify compliance with all of the legal requirements for entry. Any documentation required by the laws governing your import must be submitted by the time of entry. You must present an FWS Wildlife Declaration **Form 3-177**, available at the port of entry, with every shipment, regardless of any other paperwork required. Customs will not release your shipment until the import declaration has been signed off by an FWS agent.

Designated Ports. Shipments of wildlife products are restricted to designated U.S. ports of entry. All wildlife shipments must enter and leave through one of the ports listed in 50 CFR 14.12. Currently, 10 ports are designated: New York, NY; Miami, FL; New Orleans, LA; Dallas/Ft. Worth, TX; Los Angeles, CA; San Francisco, CA; Chicago, IL; Seattle, WA; Honolulu, HI; and Portland, OR. If special circumstances prevent you from making your entry at a designated port, you will need to obtain an Exception to Designated Port Permit from the FWS Divisions of Law Enforcement (see addresses at end of this chapter).

Country-Specific Import Regulations

There are special provisions for livestock products originating in Canada, Mexico, Central America, and the West Indies. These provisions vary according to species, and include such things as permit or quarantine waivers, special quarantine restrictions, specific ports of entry for specific types of livestock products, and provisions for transit across the U.S. only. One general requirement applicable across the board is that two import declarations (see above) must be presented, instead of only one. For more details see appropriate headings in 9 CFR 92, or contact the Animal and Plant Health Inspection Service.

Regulatory Changes. APHIS has amended the animal and animal product importation regulations to allow for regionalization of countries—that is, disease classification of parts of a country, an entire country, or groups of countries. The rule change was made to recognize levels of disease risk in regions. Details about the criteria that APHIS considers when evaluating the regions that wish to export animals or animal products to the United States can be found at the APHIS Veterinary Service National Center for Import and Export (NCIE) website (www.aphis.usda.gov/ncie).

Import Advisory

Always be prepared to provide the Fish and Wildlife Service or U.S. Customs with both common and scientific names of any species you have questions about or are planning to import. When you are unsure of the regulations governing the export or import of a wildlife product, check with the FWS or TRAFFIC (USA) World Wildlife Fund (see addresses at end of this chapter) well in advance of going abroad, or once there, with the local authorities or the U.S. Embassy before making a purchase. When in doubt, don't buy! Products made from parts of endangered species will be seized and in some cases an importer may be subject to substantial fines.

Wildlife Products [reprinted with permission by World Wildlife Fund from its brochure: "Buyer Beware"]:

Ensuring that your wildlife product is legal to import is not simple. Wildlife may be "laundered" to conceal its true country of origin. It is often illegally killed or collected in one country, smuggled into another, and then exported with false permits to a third, making its origins hard to trace. If you are considering the purchase of any wildlife or wildlife product while abroad, you should first try to determine its origin and any U.S. restrictions on its import.

Customs Classification

For customs purposes, raw hides, skins, and leather are classified under Chapter 41 of the HTSUS. This chapter is broken into major headings, which are further divided into subheadings, and often sub-subheadings, each of which has its own HTSUS classification number. For example, the 2001 HTSUS number for lining leather is 4104.10.40, indicating it is a sub-subcategory of whole bovine skin leather not exceeding 28 square feet. (4104.10), which is a subcategory of the major heading, leather of bovine or equine animals, without hair, etc. (4104). There are 11 major headings within Chapter 41.

4101—Raw hides and skins of bovine or equine animals (fresh, or salted, dried, limed, pickled, or otherwise preserved, but not tanned, parchment-dressed, or further prepared), whether or not dehaired or split

4102—Raw skins of sheep or lambs (fresh, salted, dried, limed, pickled, or otherwise preserved, but not tanned, parchment-dressed, or further prepared), whether or not with wool on or split, other than those excluded by note 1(c) to this chapter

4103—Other raw hides and skins (fresh, salted, dried, limed, pickled, or otherwise preserved, but not tanned, parchment-dressed, or further prepared), whether or not dehaired or split, other than those excluded by note 1(b) or 1(c) to this chapter

4104—Leather of bovine or equine animals, without hair on, other than leather of heading 4108 or 4109

4105—Sheep or lamb skin leather, without wool on, other than leather of heading 4108 or 4109

4106—Goat or kidskin leather, without hair on, other than leather of heading 4108 or 4109

4107—Leather of other animals, without hair on, other than leather of heading 4108 or 4109

4108—Chamois (including combination chamois) leather

4109—Patent leather and patent laminated leather; metallized leather

4110—Parings and other waste of leather or of composition leather, not suitable for the manufacture of leather articles; leather dust, powder, and flour

4111—Composition leather with a basis of leather or leather fiber, in slabs, sheets, or strip, whether or not in rolls

For more details regarding classifications of the specific product you are interested in importing, consult a customs broker, the appropriate commodity specialist at your nearest customs port, or the HTSUS. The 2001 HTSUS is available online from the Customs Service (www.customs.gov/impoexpo/impoexpo.htm) or for purchase from the U.S. Government Printing Office (see resources at the end of this chapter), and may be found in larger public libraries. For a general discussion of customs classification, see "Classification—Liquidation" on page 229.

Dutiable Status of Goods

For more information about duty rates and binding decisions see "Dutiable Status of Goods" on page 203; for a discussion of temporary importation of goods see "Temporary Free Importations" on page 205.

Valuation

Importers have a responsibility to use what the U.S. Customs Service deems, "reasonable care," when determining the value of their goods. They must also provide any additional information that the Customs Service needs for setting a final value on the goods. This process involves a number of factors and can be somewhat complicated; importers must be aware of applicable issues and details. Valuation information applies to all types of commodities, for further discussion on the subject see "Customs Valuation" on page 267.

Import Duties

Import duties vary (often dramatically) depending upon the Harmonized Tariff Schedule (HTSUS) classification of the goods or products imported. Since some products that look alike have different HTSUS classifications and different rates of duty, proper classification is vital. Note that "differences of opinion" between importers and the Bureau of Customs and Border Protection regarding classification keeps customs attorneys very busy.

Import duties can be assessed on the imported value of the goods ("ad valorem" rates of duty such as 2%, 4.4%, 50%, etc.), total units or weight of the goods ("specific" rates of duty such as 2 cents each or 1.5 cents/pound, etc.) or on a combination basis ("compound" rates of duty such as 5 cents each plus 6%).

Listed below is a sampling of several Column 1 import duty rates for Chapter 41 products:
Whole hides and skins, of a weight exceeding 16 kg (not pretanned) (4101.50.10): Free
to
Upper leather; sole leather (4104.11.40): 5%

For specific information on US import duties refer to the Harmonized Tariff Schedule of the US. The print version is available from the US Government Printing Office as well as third party suppliers who often add special features. Online versions are available in both static PDF pages as well as in formats with excellent search functionality. Search the Web with the term "Harmonized Tariff Schedule" to find sources.

Entry and Documentation

The entry of merchandise is a two-part process consisting of 1) filing the documentation necessary to determine whether merchandise may be released from Customs custody, and 2) filing the documents that contain information for duty assessment and statistical purposes. In certain instances, all documents must be filed and accepted by Customs prior to release of the goods. Unless you have been granted an extension, you must file entry documents at a location specified by the port or area director within five working days of your shipment's date of arrival at a U.S. port of entry. These include a number of standard documents required by Customs for any entry, and:

- FWS Import Declaration Form 3-177, original and 3 copies (if the products are derived from exotic wildlife or endangered species)
- FWS permit or import documentation (if the products are derived from exotic wildlife or endangered species)
- Permits or certificates required under CITES, ESA, and any other regulations applicable to the particular shipment (if the products are derived from exotic wildlife or endangered species)
- Certificates of export, origin, sanitation, veterinary inspection, and other conditions from the country of origin or export, as required by Customs, FWS, or USDA
- Copy of air waybill or bill of lading
- Copy of invoice (pro forma invoice if the shipment is noncommercial)

After you present the entry, Customs may examine your shipment or may waive examination. The shipment is then released provided no legal or regulatory violations have been noted. You must then file entry summary documentation and deposit estimated duties at a designated customhouse within 10 working days of your shipment's release. For a detailed description of entry procedures, standard documentation, and informal entry, see "Entry Process" on page 185.

Informed Compliance. Informed compliance was introduced with the Customs Modernization Act of 1993 (Mod Act) and defines the relationship between importers and the Customs Service. It sets out the responsibilities of both parties. Providing the correct documentation and information for entry is a key factor that will make your importing operation run smoothly. We recommend that importers become familiar with the concept of informed comliance and the responsibilities that they have under the Mod Act. For further discussion about informed compliance see "Informed Compliance" on page 211.

Note: The Entry and Documentation section has been carefully designed to supply you, the importer, with sample documents and directions on how to satisfy Customs requirements. Be aware that you should consult the applicable authorities to ensure that you are correctly following the most current procedures.

Prohibitions and Restrictions

Animal Products. Animal products are subject to quarantine if they arrive from certain countries that are known to have specific infectious diseases. These countries are listed in 9 CFR 94. If a USDA inspector determines that a shipment is infected with anthrax, foot-and-mouth disease, rinderpest, or bovine spongiform encephalopathy, entry will be denied.

Exotic and Endangered Species. Hides of certain animals are restricted or prohibited from importation because of species status under the CITES, ESA, or another U.S. law. For example, importation of species listed in CITES Appendix I for commercial purposes is prohibited. Prohibitions and restrictions may additionally be imposed by the law of the exporting country. You are legally responsible for fulfilling the requirements of all of them, as well as any laws of the country of export. If you import, or attempt to import, a product in violation of a wildlife or endangered species law, even if you are not aware of the violation, your product may be seized, you may be charged substantial fines, and you could be imprisoned.

Importers should be particularly cautious in importing the following wildlife products, which are prohibited from import into the U.S. [reprinted with permission by World Wildlife Fund from its brochure: "Buyer Beware"]:

Reptile Skins and Leathers. Products made from most crocodile skins, including black caiman, American crocodile, Orinoco crocodile, and, in many cases, the common caiman from Latin America and the Caribbean; Philippine crocodile, Chinese alligator, and Nile crocodile. Most lizard skin products originating in Brazil, Colombia, Costa Rica, Ecuador, Paraguay, Peru, Venezuela, and a number of Asian countries, including India, Nepal, and Pakistan. Many snakeskin products originating in Latin America— Argentina, Brazil, Colombia, Costa Rica, Ecuador, Guatemala, Mexico, Paraguay, and Venezuela, for example— and certain Asian countries, such as India. All sea turtle products, including [leather].

Other Leather Products. Made from pangolin (sometimes labeled "anteater") skin originating in Thailand, Malaysia, and Indonesia.

Country-Specific Restrictions

Duty on certain leathers from Japan is temporarily increased. Refer to "Import Duties" above.

Marking and Labeling Requirements

Animal Products. Containers of animal hides, skins, and leathers must be marked with the country of origin—that is, the country where the animal was located. If hides, skins, or leathers are quarantined at the port of arrival, marks and signs are required on shipping documents and any mode of transport used to move the product while under restrictions (9 CFR 95.25).

Wildlife Hides, Skins, and Leather. All wildlife shipments must be marked on the outside of the container with the names and addresses of the exporter and importer, an accurate identification of the species, and the numbers of each species in the container.

For a general discussion of U.S. Customs marking and labeling requirements, see "Country of Origin Marking" on page 236, "Special Marking Requirements" on page 238 and "Marking—False Impression" on page 239.

Shipping Considerations

You will need to ensure that your goods are packaged and shipped with care so that they pass smoothly through Customs and arrive in good condition. You are responsible for ensuring that the shipment is in compliance with all applicable government regulations for packaging and shipping. In most instances, you should not leave these arrangements solely to the discretion of your supplier. Careful preparation of the cargo and selection of the mode of transport can be essential to a cost-effective, timely delivery of undamaged goods. We strongly advise you to consult your shipping representative, insurance agent, or freight broker for advice on packing and shipping.

Hides, skins, and leathers may be shipped in bulk, sacks, crates, or other types of containers, depending on the type of product. General considerations include protection from contamination, weather, and pests. Containers should be constructed so as to be safe for handling during transport.

Publications and WWW Resources

For questions regarding the Convention on Interational Trade in Endangered Species of Wild Fauna and Flora (CITES) refer to:

CITES Secretariat
15 chemin des Anemones
1219 Chatelaine-Geneva
Switzerland
Tel: [41] (22) 917-8139/40
Fax: [41] (22) 797-3417
Website: www.cites.org
Email: cites@unep.ch

The *Harmonized Tariff Schedule of the United States (2001)* (HTSUS) is available to view on the Customs Service website (www.customs.gov), or you may purchase a printed version from:

U.S. Government Printing Office
Superintendent of Documents
710 North Capital Street NW
Washington DC 20401
Tel: (202) 512-1800
Fax: (202) 512-1657
Website: www.access.gpo.gov

The USGPO also has copies of specific laws available for purchase. The USGPO accepts orders made by fax, phone or placed over the Internet, as well as mail orders paid by credit card. All orders must be accompanied by payment. Credit cards, checks drawn on a U.S. bank, or an international money order are all acceptable.

Relevant Government Agencies

Address your questions regarding USDA requirements for the importation of domesticated animal products to:

Animal and Plant Health Inspection Service (APHIS)
Veterinary Services (VS)
National Center for Import and Export
4700 River Rd., Unit 40
Riverdale, MD 20737
Tel: (301) 734-3277
Animal products: (301) 734-4401
Website: www.aphis.usda.gov/vs

Address your questions regarding the importation of exotic or endangered animal hides, skins, and leathers to:

U.S. Fish and Wildlife Service (FWS)
Office of Management Authority
4401 N. Fairfax Dr.
Arlington, VA 22203-0700
Tel: (703) 358-2104
Website: www.fws.gov

National Marine Fisheries Service (NMFS)
1315 East West Highway
SSMC3
Silver Spring, MD 20910
Tel: (301) 713-2239
Office of Protected Resources: (301) 713-2332
Inspection Services Division: (301) 713-2355
Website: www.nmfs.noaa.gov

Address your questions regarding importation of hides, skins and leathers to your local Customs port director. For addresses refer to "U.S. Customs and Border Protection Offices" on page 65 or contact:

U.S. Customs and Border Protection
Customs Headquarters
1300 Pennsylvania Avenue NW
Washington DC 20229
Tel: (202) 354-1000
Website: www.customs.treas.gov

Laws and Regulations

The following laws and regulations may be relevant to the importation of hides, skins, and leathers. The laws are contained in the United States Code (USC), and the regulations are published in the Code of Federal Regulations (CFR), both of which are available at larger public and law libraries. Copies of specific laws and regulations are also available from the USGPO (address above.

7 USC 4801 et seq.
Pork Promotion, Research, and Consumer Information Act of 1985
This Act provides that each importer of porcine animal, pork, or pork product shall remit an assessment to Customs at the time the product is imported. See 7 CFR 1230.71 and 1230.110.

18 USC 42 et seq.
Importation of Animals, Birds, Fish, and Plants
This Act governs the importation of mammals, birds, fish, amphibia, and reptiles into the U.S. and authorizes U.S. Customs to enforce the import requirements.

21 USC 101 et seq.
Importation of Cattle and Quarantine
This Act provides for suspension of importation of animals to prevent the spread of disease, and for the quarantine of prohibited classes of animals. Importation of all animals described by the Act is prohibited except at certain designated ports. All animals are to be inspected on import or export.

21 USC 113a
Foot-and-Mouth Disease Memorandum of Understanding; Disease Research Act
This Act authorizes the study of animal disease and prohibits introduction of live foot-and-mouth disease virus into the U.S. except under certain defined circumstances. Customs enforces Agriculture restrictions and regulations.

21 USC 135
Establishment of International Animal Quarantine Stations
This Act authorizes the establishment of international quarantine stations. Customs enforces laws regarding importation of livestock.

42 USC 264 et seq.
Quarantine, Inspection, and Licensing
This Act restricts importations of dogs, cats, monkeys, psittacine birds, turtles, tortoises, and terrapins that do not comply with health standards. Customs enforces these restrictions. See 42 CFR 71.51 et seq.

19 CFR 12.24 and 12.26
Regulations for Animal and Animal Product Entry
These regulations provide for U.S. Customs entry declarations, documentation, and procedures for the animals and animal products subject to FWS and USDA regulations.

9 CFR Parts 91-96
Regulations on Animal Byproduct Quarantine Control
These regulations promulgated by the USDA prohibit the importation of animal products for use in industry unless the products meet certain processing standards and are not infected with certain diseases.

Convention on International Trade in Endangered Species of Wild Fauna and Flora (CITES)
This comprehensive wildlife treaty signed by over 100 countries, including the United States, regulates and in many cases prohibits commercial imports and exports of wild animal and plant species threatened by trade.

16 USC 1531
Endangered Species Act of 1973
This Act prohibits the import and export of species listed as endangered and most species listed as threatened. It is the U.S. law that implements CITES.

16 USC 742a et seq.
Fish and Wildlife Act of 1956
This Act regulates and bars the import of certain wild animals or birds and authorizes U.S. Customs to enforce the restrictions.

50 CFR Parts 10, 13, and 16
Regulations of FWS for Importing Wildlife and Fish
These regulations specify the animals and animal products subject to import prohibitions and restrictions.

16 USC 2401
Antarctic Conservation Act of 1978
This Act prohibits the importation, absent a special permit, of any flora or fauna native to Antarctica into the U.S. pursuant to the Antarctic Treaty and the Protocol

16 USC 3371 et seq.
Control of Illegally Taken Fish and Wildlife
This Act prohibits the import of species taken, possessed, transported, or sold in violation of the law of a foreign country.

16 USC 1361 et seq.
The Marine Mammal Protection Act of 1972
This Act prohibits the import of certain marine mammals and their parts and products. These species include whales, walruses, narwhals, seals, sea lions, sea otters and polar bears. It also defines parameters for importa-tion of commercial fish or products that have been caught using methods, which involve incidental death or serious injury to protected marine mammals.

16 USC 4201 et seq.
The African Elephant Conservation Act
This Act prohibits imports of carved ivory products from any country and only permits imports of whole tusks from elephants legally hunted in certain African countries. It establishes U.S. adherence to the CITES Ivory Control System.

16 USC 4901
Wild Bird Conservation Act of 1992
This act eliminated most commercial imports of CITES-regulated birds, except for limited imports of pet birds.

Principal Exporting Countries
The following listing includes samples of the main supplier nations of the products of this chapter. It is organized by HTSUS major heading. (Refer to "Customs Classification" above for the product codes.) Countries are listed in rank order of the value of products imported to the U.S. Statistics represent customs value of entries for 2002 from the Bureau of Census, U.S. Department of Commerce.

4101—Canada, Mexico, Belgium, Thailand, Taiwan, Brazil, Argentina, Spain, United Kingdom

4102—New Zealand, Canada, Saudi Arabia, France, Spain

4103—Canada, New Zealand, Czech Republic, Australia, Pakistan

4104—Italy, Argentina, Mexico, Brazil, Germany, Spain, France

4105—Italy, Nigeria, United Kingdom, France, Spain, Haiti

4106—India, Slovenia, Haiti, Pakistan, Taiwan, Italy, United Kingdom, Colombia, Mexico, South Korea

4107—Italy, Argentina, Brazil, Uruguay, Mexico, Germany, Slovakia, China, Thailand, Australia

4112—Italy, New Zealand, Spain, France, Canada, United Kingdom, China

4113—South Africa, Colombia, Zimbabwe, Taiwan, Singapore, Finland, Mexico, Italy, India, South Korea, Australia

4114—Mexico, United Kingdom, Italy, Turkey, New Zealand, China, Spain, Canada, Belgium

4115—Mexico, Spain, Germany, Italy.

Chapter 42:
Leather Articles

Full title: Articles of Leather; Saddlery, and Harness; Travel Goods, Handbags, and Similar Containers; Articles of Animal Gut (Other Than Silkworm Gut)

This chapter relates to the importation of articles of leather and animal gut, which are classified under Chapter 42 of the Harmonized Tariff Schedule of the United States (HTSUS). Specifically, it includes leather and composition leather saddlery, harness equipment, cases, bags, other containers, apparel, clothing accessories; leather and composition leather articles for machinery, mechanical applications, and technical uses; shoelaces, straps, and other leather articles; and articles made from animal gut, bladders, or tendons.

If you are interested in importing raw hides, skins, or leathers, you should refer to Commodity Index Chapter 41. The importation requirements for articles of apparel or clothing accessories, except gloves, lined or covered with furskins, are covered in Chapter 43. The requirements for importing fittings or trimmings for harnesses are covered in Chapters 72 through 83. For importing specific products that contain leather or composition leather, you should refer to the Commodity Index chapters that cover the particular item of interest. For example, footwear is covered in Chapter 64, headgear in Chapter 65, plaiting materials in Chapter 46, whips and riding crops in Chapter 66, imitation jewelry in Chapter 71, and furniture in Chapter 94. If you are interested in importing articles of netting, refer to Chapter 56. The importation of sterile surgical catgut or other suture materials is discussed in Chapter 30; strings, drum skins, and other parts of musical instruments in Chapter 92; and toys, games, and sports equipment in Chapter 95.

Note: To understand key issues that will enable you to make best use of the information in this section we recommend that you see "Introduction" on page 425.

Key Factors

The key factors in the importation of articles of leather and animal gut goods:

- Compliance with U.S. Fish and Wildlife Service (FWS) requirements (if the product is derived from endangered species or wildlife)
- Entry at FWS-designated ports, and compliance with FWS and Customs advance notification and port-of-entry inspection requirements (if the products are derived from exotic wildlife or endangered species)

- Compliance with U.S. Department of Agriculture (USDA) APHIS import, quarantine, permit, and certification requirements (if the products are derived from domesticated animals)
- Entry at USDA-designated ports (if the products are derived from domesticated animals)
- Compliance with U.S. Customs and U.S. Department of Commerce (DOC) textile import regulations and procedures (if the product includes textiles)
- Compliance with U.S. Federal Trade Commission (FTC) and Consumer Product Safety Commission (CPSC) standards (if the product includes textiles)

Although most importers use the services of a licensed customs broker in making their entries, and we recommend this practice, you should be aware of the regulatory, entry, and documentation issues involved in importing your product. You, as importer, are ultimately responsible for the fulfillment of any legal requirements applicable to your shipment.

General Considerations

Regulatory Agencies. The USDA regulates the importation of products derived from animals. The FWS, primarily under provisions of the U.S. Endangered Species Act (ESA) and the Convention on International Trade in Endangered Species of Wild Fauna and Flora (CITES), controls the importation of products derived from animals that are classified as exotic wildlife or endangered or threatened species. U.S. Customs enforces USDA and FWS requirements through entry documentation and restrictions. Customs also administers the import of textile luggage under the U.S. Customs Textile Import Program.

Domesticated Animal Products. Importation of articles made of leather or animal gut derived from domesticated animals—such as cattle, pigs, sheep, and goats—is generally straightforward. Products derived from such animals are subject to quarantine regulations, marking requirements, and processing standards. Shipments of these products are inspected at the port of arrival by the Animal and Plant Health Inspection Service (APHIS) of the USDA. Unless the shipment is in compliance with all applicable laws and regulations, it will be denied entry into the U.S. Some shipments may be restricted or prohibited completely.

Quarantine and Inspection. At the time of applying for a permit to import animal products subject to quarantine requirements, you will have to make reservations for space in an appropriate quarantine facility. Fees for quarantine reservations vary according to species, and are due and payable when the reservation is requested. Each shipment entering under USDA APHIS permit must comply in every detail with the permit's specifications. If your shipment is found to be aberrant in any way (such as entering at a port of entry other than the one specified in the permit), it will be refused entry.

Veterinary Certificates. A veterinary certificate, issued by a salaried veterinarian of the country of origin, stating that the animal products are free of applicable livestock diseases, must accompany each shipment. The specific information required on the certificate varies depending on the species you are importing and its country of origin. You must also present an importer's declaration, which states: 1) port of entry; 2) importer's name and address; 3) broker's name and address; 4) livestock origin; 5) number, breed, species, and purpose of importation; 6) consignee's name and location of intended delivery.

APHIS-designated Quarantine Ports. The following listings are APHIS-designated ports with adequate quarantine facilities available for the import of livestock and livestock products. With very few exceptions, all shipments of livestock and livestock products must enter at one of these designated ports:

Air and Ocean Ports: Los Angeles, CA; Miami, FL; and Newburgh, NY.

Land border ports with Canada: Eastport, ID; Houlton and Jackman, MI; Detroit, Port Huron, and Sault Ste. Marie, MI; Baudette, MN; Opheim, Raymond, and Sweetgrass, MT; Alexandria Bay, Buffalo, and Champlain, NY; Dunseith, Pembina, and Portal, ND; Derby Line and Highgate Springs, VT; Lynden, Oroville, and Sumas, WA.

Land border ports with Mexico: Brownsville, Hidalgo, Laredo, Eagle Pass, Del Rio, and Presidio, TX; Douglas, Naco, Nogales, and San Luis, AZ; Calexico and San Ysidro, CA; Antelope Wells, Columbus, and Santa Teresa, NM.

Limited ports (ports with facilities for entry of live animals that do not appear to require restraint and holding inspection facilities): Anchorage and Fairbanks, AK; San Diego and San Francisco, CA; Denver, CO; Jacksonville, St. Petersburg-Clearwater, and Tampa, FL; Atlanta, GA; Honolulu, HI; Chicago, IL; New Orleans, LA; Portland, ME; Baltimore, MD; Boston, MA; Minneapolis, MN; Great Falls, MT; Dayton, OH; Portland, OR; San Juan, PR; Memphis, TN; El Paso, Galveston and Houston, TX; Seattle, Spokane, and Tacoma, WA.

The ports listed above have been designated as quarantine stations. The USDA Administrator has authority to designate other ports as quarantine stations as needed.

Exotic and Endangered Species. The FWS enforces a complex set of laws and regulations (see 50 CFR 1 et seq.) pertaining to wildlife and wildlife product importation. These laws include the international Convention on International Trade in Endangered Species of Wild Fauna and Flora (CITES), the Endangered Species Act (ESA), and a number of other U.S. laws, such as the African Elephant Conservation Act (AECA), Marine Mammal Protection Act (MMPA), Migratory Bird Treaty Act (MBTA), Eagle Protection Act (EPA), and the Lacey Act (LA). Most foreign countries also have their own domestic measures, and you will need to meet the requirements of the country of export in addition to U.S. requirements. For more information, contact the FWS Office of Management Authority (OMA) (see addresses at end of this chapter).

Certain articles of leather and animal gut are entirely prohibited, others are allowed entry only under permit and/or license, and still others are allowed entry only for specific noncommercial purposes. When applying for a permit, you must satisfy the requirements of all laws under which the species is protected. The following briefly describes the two major laws governing importation of protected wildlife products into the U.S. This discussion is not comprehensive or exhaustive. If you wish to import hides, skins, or leathers of exotic or endangered animals, you should always contact the FWS (see addresses at end of this chapter) with species information before making any transactions.

CITES. Over 100 nations participate in the Convention on International Trade in Endangered Species of Wild Fauna and Flora (CITES) treaty, which took effect in May 1977. The degree of protection afforded to a species depends on which of the three CITES appendices contains the name of that species. Documentation required for import varies depending on the species, and the CITES section where it is listed. The CITES export documentation from the country of origin is always required. If you are importing a CITES-listed species from a country that does not participate in the treaty, you must still obtain from that nation documents that contain all the information normally required in CITES export permits.

Appendix I. This appendix lists species deemed presently threatened with extinction (e.g., orangutan, chinchilla, gray whale). Importation of Appendix I species for commercial purposes is prohibited. You must have two permits to import these species: one from the U.S., which must be obtained first, and one from the exporting country. If you are importing Appendix I species taken in the marine environment and outside the jurisdiction of any country or state, you must have an Introduction from the Sea Permit.

Appendix II. This appendix lists species that are not presently threatened with extinction but may become threatened if their trade is not regulated (e.g., brown bear, musk deer, elephant seal). There are no restrictions on the purpose of import, provided it is not detrimental to the survival of the species. You will need an export permit or reexport certificate from the exporting country. If you are importing Appendix II species taken in the marine environment and outside the jurisdiction of any country or state, you will need an Introduction from the Sea Permit.

Appendix III. This appendix lists species for which any CITES member country has domestic regulations "for the purpose of preventing or restricting exploitation, and as needing the cooperation of other Parties in control of trade." For example, Canada lists the walrus, and Nepal lists the blackbuck antelope. Three different types of documents are issued for Appendix III species: 1) Export Permit: Issued for specimens that originated in a country that listed the species on Appendix III; 2) Certificate of Origin: Issued by any country other than the listing country if the wildlife in question originated in that country; 3) Reexport Certificate: Issued for the export of Appendix III specimens that were previously imported into the U.S.

Exemptions. Under certain conditions, Certificates of Exemption may be issued for the importation of wildlife products listed under CITES. Exceptions are allowed for shipments of wildlife transiting a country under Customs bond, shipments between U.S. states or territories, and certain personal or household effects. For information, contact FWS (see addresses at end of this chapter).

Permit Applications. Applications for CITES permits and certificates are available from the FWS Office of Management Authority (see addresses at end of this chapter). You will need to fill out the FWS Standard Permit Application **(Form 3-200)** and provide certain information specifically required under CITES. You should submit your application at least 60 days before the date you wish the permit to take effect. FWS charges processing fees for CITES applications.

ESA. The U.S. Endangered Species Act (ESA) was passed on December 28, 1973, to prevent the extinction of many species of animals and plants and to protect their habitats. By definition, an "endangered species" is any animal or plant listed by regulation as being in danger of extinction. A "threatened species" is any animal or plant likely to become endangered within the foreseeable future. The U.S. List of Endangered and Threatened Wildlife and Plants includes native and foreign species.

Permits. ESA's import provisions prohibit the import or export of any endangered or threatened species or products derived from them without one of the following permits from the FWS Federal Wildlife Permit Office (FWPO):

> *Endangered Species Permits:* This permit is issued for importation for purposes of 1) scientific research; 2) enhancement of propagation or survival of the species; or 3) incidental taking.

> *Threatened Species Permits:* This permit is issued for importation for purposes of 1) scientific research; 2) enhancement of propagation or survival of the species; 3) zoological, horticultural, or botanical exhibition; 4) education purposes; 5) special purposes consistent with ESA purposes and policy; or 6) incidental taking.

Permit Exemptions. A few imports of endangered species products are exempt from the ESA permit requirements. For example, if a species is listed as threatened or as an experimental population, special rules may allow otherwise prohibited activities. Some species covered by special rules include certain kangaroos, several primates, the grizzly bear, gray wolf, African elephant, American alligator, and leopard. If you are unsure as to the exemption status of your import, contact FWS (see addresses at end of this chapter).

FWS Import Licenses. With some exceptions, persons engaged in the business of importing wildlife products valued in excess of $25,000 per year must be licensed by the FWS. If your annual importations are valued at less than $25,000, or if you qualify for another exemption from licensing, you are still responsible for keeping thorough records of all wildlife transactions and of making these records available to FWS officers if necessary. For a full description of exemptions from licensing, and of recordkeeping requirements, contact the Fish and Wildlife Service (see addresses at end of this chapter) or see 50 CFR 14.

Procedures at Port of Entry. At least 72 hours before your shipment is due to arrive at a designated port, you should notify U.S. Customs and the FWS inspectors of its expected arrival. The FWS conducts port-of-entry shipment inspections on a case-by-case basis, as determined by the inspection agent after looking at the entry paperwork. Both FWS and Customs may inspect your shipment to verify compliance with all of the legal requirements for entry. Any documentation required by the laws governing your import must be submitted by the time of entry. You must present an FWS Wildlife Declaration **Form 3-177**, available at the port of entry, with every shipment, regardless of any other paperwork required. Customs will not release your shipment until the import declaration has been signed off by an FWS agent.

Designated Ports. Shipments of wildlife products are restricted to designated U.S. ports of entry. All wildlife shipments must enter and leave through one of the ports listed in 50 CFR 14.12. Currently, 10 ports are designated: New York, NY; Miami, FL; New Orleans, LA; Dallas/Ft. Worth, TX; Los Angeles, CA; San Francisco, CA; Chicago, IL; Seattle, WA; Honolulu, HI; and Portland, OR. If special circumstances prevent you from making your entry at a designated port, you will need to obtain an Exception to Designated Port Permit from the FWS Divisions of Law Enforcement (see addresses at end of this chapter).

Textile Luggage. Regulation of textile product imports is complex, and luggage that includes textiles is subject to stringent textile import regulations. If your luggage imports contain textile fibers, you should read the Commodity Index chapter (Chapters 50 through 63) that pertains to that particular textile. The following discussion outlines the basic requirements.

U.S. Customs administers import controls on certain cotton, wool, man-made fiber, silk blend, and other vegetable fiber articles manufactured or produced in designated countries. When considering importation of textile luggage, you should first ascertain if the product is subject to textile restrictions or quotas. The DOC Office of Textile and Apparel should be able to advise you on the regulatory status of specific products. Textile luggage must be entered under regulations of the U.S. Customs Textile Import Program. Customs requires a U.S. Customs Country-of-Origin Declaration to be submitted at the port of entry with each shipment of any textile or textile product. You are also responsible for your textile luggage's compliance with the Textile Fiber Products Identification Act (TFPIA), administered by the FTC. Entry invoices for articles subject to TFPIA must show certain additional information.

Specific Country Import Regulations

There are special provisions for livestock products originating in Canada, Mexico, Central America, and the West Indies. These provisions vary according to species, and include such things as permit or quarantine waivers, special quarantine restrictions, specific ports of entry for specific types of livestock products, and provisions for transit across the U.S. only. One general requirement applicable across the board is that two import declarations (see above) must be presented, instead of only one. For more details see appropriate headings in 9 CFR 92, or contact the Animal and Plant Health Inspection Service.

Import Advisory

Always be prepared to provide the Fish and Wildlife Service or U.S. Customs with both common and scientific names of any species you have questions about or are planning to import. When you are unsure of the regulations governing the export or import of a wildlife product, check with the FWS or TRAFFIC (USA) World Wildlife Fund (see addresses at end of this chapter) well in advance of going abroad, or once there, with the local authorities or the U.S. Embassy before making a purchase. When in doubt, don't buy! Products made from parts of endangered species will be seized and in some cases the importer will be subject to substantial fines.

Wildlife Products [reprinted with permission by World Wildlife Fund from its brochure: "Buyer Beware"]:

> Ensuring that your wildlife product is legal to import is not simple. Wildlife may be "laundered" to conceal its true country of origin. It is often illegally killed or collected in one country, smuggled into another, and then exported with false permits to a third, making its origins hard to trace. If you are considering the purchase of any wildlife or wildlife product while abroad, you should first try to determine its origin and any U.S. restrictions on its import.

Customs Classification

For customs purposes, articles of leather and animal gut are classified under Chapter 42 of the HTSUS. This chapter is broken into major headings, which are further divided into subheadings, and often sub-subheadings, each of which has its own HTSUS classification number. For example, the 2001 HTSUS number for reptile leather handbags is 4202.21.30, indicating it is a sub-subcategory of handbags with outer surface of leather, of composition leather or of patent leather (4202.21), which is a subcategory of the major heading, trunks, suitcases, etc. (4202). There are six major headings within Chapter 42.

4201—Saddlery and harness for any animal (including traces, leads, knee pads, muzzles, saddle cloths, saddle bags, dog coats, and the like), of any material

4202—Trunks, suitcases, vanity cases, attache cases, briefcases, school satchels, spectacle cases, binocular cases, camera cases, musical instrument cases, gun cases, holsters, and similar containers; traveling bags, toiletry bags, knapsacks and backpacks, handbags, shopping bags, wallets, purses, map cases, cigarette cases, tobacco pouches, tool bags, sports bags, bottle cases, jewelry boxes, powder cases, cutlery cases, and similar containers, of leather or of composition leather, of sheeting of plastics, of textile materials, of vulcanized fiber, or of paperboard, or wholly or mainly covered with such materials or with paper

4203—Articles of apparel and clothing accessories, of leather or of composition leather

4204—Articles of leather or of composition leather of a kind used in machinery or mechanical appliances of for other technical uses

4205—Other articles of leather or of composition leather

4206—Articles of gut (other than silkworm gut), of goldbeater's skin, of bladders, or of tendons

For more details regarding classifications of the specific product you are interested in importing, consult a customs broker, the appropriate commodity specialist at your nearest customs port, or the HTSUS. The 2001 HTSUS is available online from the Customs Service (www.customs.gov/impoexpo/impoexpo.htm) or for purchase from the U.S. Government Printing Office (see resources at the end of this chapter), and may be found in larger public libraries. For a general discussion of customs classification, see "Classification—Liquidation" on page 229.

Dutiable Status of Goods

For more information about duty rates and binding decisions see "Dutiable Status of Goods" on page 203; for a discussion of temporary importation of goods see "Temporary Free Importations" on page 205.

Valuation

Importers have a responsibility to use what the U.S. Customs Service deems, "reasonable care," when determining the value of their goods. They must also provide any additional information that the Customs Service needs for setting a final value on the goods. This process involves a number of factors and can be somewhat complicated; importers must be aware of applicable issues and details. Valuation information applies to all types of commodities, for further discussion on the subject see "Customs Valuation" on page 267.

Import Duties

Import duties vary (often dramatically) depending upon the Harmonized Tariff Schedule (HTSUS) classification of the goods or products imported. Since some products that look alike have different HTSUS classifications and different rates of duty, proper classification is vital. Note that "differences of opinion" between importers and the Bureau of Customs and Border Protection regarding classification keeps customs attorneys very busy.

Import duties can be assessed on the imported value of the goods ("ad valorem" rates of duty such as 2%, 4.4%, 50%, etc.), total units or weight of the goods ("specific" rates of duty such as 2 cents each or 1.5 cents/pound, etc.) or on a combination basis ("compound" rates of duty such as 5 cents each plus 6%).

Listed below is a sampling of several Column 1 import duty rates for Chapter 42 products:
Trunks, suitcases, vanity cases, attache cases, briefcases, school satchels, spectacle cases, binocular cases, camera cases, musical instrument cases, gun cases, holsters and similar containers; traveling bags, insulated food or beverage bags, toiletry bags, knapsacks and backpacks, handbags, shopping bags, wallets, purses, map cases, cigarette cases, tobacco pouches, tool bags, sports bags, bottle cases, jewelry boxes, powder cases, cutlery cases and similar containers, of leather or of composition leather, of sheeting of plastics, of textile materials, of vulcanized fiber or of paperboard, or wholly or mainly covered with such materials or with paper (con.) (Lined with textile fabrics) (4202.99.30.00): Free
to
With outer surface of plastics (4202.12.20): 20%

For specific information on US import duties refer to the Harmonized Tariff Schedule of the US. The print version is available from the US Government Printing Office as well as third party suppliers who often add special features. Online versions are available in both static PDF pages as well as in formats with excellent search functionality. Search the Web with the term "Harmonized Tariff Schedule" to find sources.

Entry and Documentation

The entry of merchandise is a two-part process consisting of 1) filing the documentation necessary to determine whether merchandise may be released from Customs custody, and 2) filing

the documents that contain information for duty assessment and statistical purposes. In certain instances, all documents must be filed and accepted by Customs prior to release of the goods. Unless you have been granted an extension, you must file entry documents at a location specified by the port or area director within five working days of your shipment's date of arrival at a U.S. port of entry. These include a number of standard documents required by Customs for any entry, and:

- FWS Import Declaration Form 3-177, original and 3 copies (if the products are derived from exotic wildlife or endangered species)
- FWS permit or import documentation Form 3-200, (if the products are derived from exotic wildlife or endangered species)
- Permits or certificates required under CITES, ESA, and any other regulations applicable to the particular shipment (if the products are derived from exotic wildlife or endangered species)
- Certificates of export, origin, sanitation, veterinary inspection, and other conditions from the country of origin or export, as required by Customs, FWS, or USDA
- USDA importer's declaration (if the products are derived from domesticated animals).
- U.S. Customs Textile Entry Declaration (if textile luggage is imported)
- Export visa or other documentation (textile luggage subject to Multi-Fiber Arrangement)
- Copy of air waybill or bill of lading
- Copy of invoice (pro forma invoice if shipment is noncommercial)

After you present the entry, Customs may examine your shipment or may waive examination. The shipment is then released provided no legal or regulatory violations have been noted. You must then file entry summary documentation and deposit estimated duties at a designated customhouse within 10 working days of your shipment's release. For a detailed description of entry procedures, standard documentation, and informal entry, see "Entry Process" on page 185.

Informed Compliance. Informed compliance was introduced with the Customs Modernization Act of 1993 (Mod Act) and defines the relationship between importers and the Customs Service. It sets out the responsibilities of both parties. Providing the correct documentation and information for entry is a key factor that will make your importing operation run smoothly. We recommend that importers become familiar with the concept of informed comliance and the responsibilities that they have under the Mod Act. For further discussion about informed compliance see "Informed Compliance" on page 211.

Entry Invoice for Textile Luggage. The invoice presented at the port of entry for luggage composed of textiles must be in compliance with the requirements of the Textile Fiber Products Identification Act (TFPIA), as enforced by U.S. Customs (19 CFR 11.12b). For more general information about invoices see "Invoices" on page 277.

Note: The Entry and Documentation section has been carefully designed to supply you, the importer, with sample documents and directions on how to satisfy Customs requirements. Be aware that you should consult the applicable authorities to ensure that you are correctly following the most current procedures.

Prohibitions and Restrictions

Animal Products. Animal products are subject to quarantine if they arrive from certain countries that are known to have specific infectious diseases. These countries are listed in 9 CFR 94. If a USDA inspector determines that a shipment is infected with anthrax, foot-and-mouth disease, rinderpest, or bovine spongiform encephalopathy, entry will be denied.

Exotic and Endangered Species. Products derived from certain animals are restricted or prohibited from importation because of species status under the CITES, ESA, or another U.S. law. For example, importation of species listed in CITES Appendix I for commercial purposes is prohibited. Prohibitions and restrictions may additionally be imposed by the law of the exporting country. You are legally responsible for fulfilling the requirements of all of them, as well as any laws of the country of export. If you import, or attempt to import, a product in violation of a wildlife or endangered species law, even if you are not aware of the violation, your product may be seized, you may be charged substantial fines, and you could be imprisoned.

Importers should be particularly cautious in importing the following wildlife products, which are prohibited from import into the U.S. [reprinted with permission by World Wildlife Fund from its brochure: "Buyer Beware"]:

> *Reptile Skins and Leathers.* Products made from most crocodile skins, including black caiman, American crocodile, Orinoco crocodile, and, in many cases, the common caiman from Latin America and the Caribbean; Philippine crocodile, Chinese alligator, and Nile crocodile. Most lizard skin products originating in Brazil, Colombia, Costa Rica, Ecuador, Paraguay, Peru, Venezuela, and a number of Asian countries, including India, Nepal, and Pakistan. Many snakeskin products originating in Latin America— Argentina, Brazil, Colombia, Costa Rica, Ecuador, Guatemala, Mexico, Paraguay, and Venezuela, for example— and certain Asian countries, such as India. All sea turtle products, including [leather].

> *Other Leather Products.* Made from pangolin (sometimes labeled "anteater") skin originating in Thailand, Malaysia, and Indonesia.

Textile Luggage. The import of certain textiles is restricted under the U.S. Department of Commerce Multi-Fiber Arrangements. The Department of Commerce Office of Textile and Apparel (see addresses at end of this chapter) can advise you on the regulatory status of specific products originating in certain countries.

Quotas

Textile Luggage. Textile product import quotas are issued on a per country basis. A product may be under quota if it originates from one country but not from another. To find out if a particular type of luggage from a particular country is subject to textile quota, contact the Department of Commerce textile team (see addresses at end of this chapter). For details regarding quotas on luggage made from textile products, see the Commodity Index chapter (Chapters 50 through 63) that covers the particular type of fabric used in the luggage you are interested in importing

Marking and Labeling Requirements

Animal Products. Containers of animal products must be marked with the country of origin—that is, the country where the animal was located. If leather or animal gut products are quarantined at the port of arrival, marks and signs are required on shipping documents and any mode of transport used to move the product while under restrictions (9 CFR 95.25).

Wildlife Hides, Skins, and Leather. All wildlife shipments must be marked on the outside of the container with the names and addresses of the exporter and importer, an accurate identification of the species, and the numbers of each species in the container.

Textile Luggage. With certain exceptions, textile products must be labeled in accordance with the Textile Fiber Products Identification Act (TFPIA). For details on marking and labeling requirements, refer to the Commodity Index chapter (Chapters 50 through 63) that covers the particular type of fabric used in the luggage you are interested in importing.

For a general discussion of U.S. Customs marking and labeling requirements, see "Country of Origin Marking" on page 236, "Special Marking Requirements" on page 238 and "Marking— False Impression" on page 239.

Shipping Considerations

You will need to ensure that your goods are packaged and shipped with care so that they pass smoothly through Customs and arrive in good condition. You are responsible for ensuring that the shipment is in compliance with all applicable government regulations for packaging and shipping. In most instances, you should not leave these arrangements solely to the discretion of your supplier. Careful preparation of the cargo and selection of the mode of transport can be essential to a cost-effective, timely delivery of undamaged goods. We strongly advise you to consult your shipping representative, insurance agent, or freight broker for advice on packing and shipping.

Articles of leather or animal gut may be shipped in bulk, sacks, crates, packages, or other types of containers, depending on the type of product and whether it is prepackaged for consumers. General considerations include protection from contamination, weather, and pests. Containers should be constructed so as to be safe for handling during transport.

Publications and WWW Resources

For questions regarding the Convention on Interational Trade in Endangered Species of Wild Fauna and Flora (CITES) refer to:

CITES Secretariat
15 chemin des Anemones
1219 Chatelaine-Geneva
Switzerland
Tel: [41] (22) 917-8139/40
Fax: [41] (22) 797-3417
Website: www.cites.org
Email: cites@unep.ch

The *Harmonized Tariff Schedule of the United States (2001)* (HTSUS) is available to view on the Customs Service website (www.customs.gov), or you may purchase a printed version from:

U.S. Government Printing Office
Superintendent of Documents
710 North Capital Street NW
Washington DC 20401
Tel: (202) 512-1800
Fax: (202) 512-1657
Website: www.access.gpo.gov

The USGPO also has copies of specific laws available for purchase. The USGPO accepts orders made by fax, phone or placed over the Internet, as well as mail orders paid by credit card. All orders must be accompanied by payment. Credit cards, checks drawn on a U.S. bank, or an international money order are all acceptable.

Relevant Government Agencies

Address your questions regarding USDA requirements for the importation of domesticated animal products to:

Animal and Plant Health Inspection Service (APHIS)
Veterinary Services (VS)
National Center for Import and Export
4700 River Rd., Unit 40
Riverdale, MD 20737

Tel: (301) 734-3277
Animal products: (301) 734-4401
Website: www.aphis.usda.gov/vs

Address your questions regarding the importation of products of exotic or endangered animals to:

U.S. Fish and Wildlife Service (FWS)
Office of Management Authority
4401 N. Fairfax Dr.
Arlington, VA 22203-0700
Tel: (703) 358-2104
Website: www.fws.gov

National Marine Fisheries Service (NMFS)
1315 East West Highway
SSMC3
Silver Spring, MD 20910
Tel: (301) 713-2239
Office of Protected Resources: (301) 713-2332
Inspection Services Division: (301) 713-2355
Website: www.nmfs.noaa.gov

Address your questions regarding textile import regulations to:

U.S. Department of Commerce
International Trade Administration
Office of Textiles and Apparel
Director's Office
14th and Constitution Avenue NW, Rm. H3100
Washington DC 20230
Tel: (202) 482-5078
Fax: (202) 482-2331
Agreements Division: (202) 482-4212
Website: http://otexa.ita.doc.gov

Address your questions regarding TFPIA to:

Federal Trade Commission (FTC)
Division of Enforcement
600 Pennsylvania Avenue NW
Washington DC 20580
Tel: (202) 326-2996
Web site: www.ftc.gov

Address your questions regarding textile quotas to:

U.S. Customs and Border Protection
Office of Field Operations, Quota Branch
1300 Pennsylvania Avenue NW
Washington DC 20229
Tel: (202) 927-5850
Website: www.customs.treas.gov

The U.S. Customs Service provices updated status reports on textile quota on their web site (see address above). If the country you need information on is not listed, call the Quota Branch office at (202) 927-5850.

Address your questions regarding importation of leather or animal gut products generally to your local Customs port director. For addresses refer to "U.S. Customs and Border Protection Offices" on page 65 or contact:

U.S. Customs and Border Protection
Customs Headquarters
1300 Pennsylvania Avenue NW
Washington DC 20229
Tel: (202) 354-1000
Website: www.customs.treas.gov

Laws and Regulations

The following laws and regulations may be relevant to the importation of articles of leather or animal gut. The laws are contained in the United States Code (USC), and the regulations are published in the Code of Federal Regulations (CFR), both of which are available at larger public and law libraries. Copies of specific laws are also available from the United States Government Printing Office (address above).

7 USC 4801 et seq.
Pork Promotion, Research, and Consumer Information Act of 1985
This Act provides that each importer of porcine animal, pork, or pork product shall remit an assessment to Customs at the time the product is imported. See 7 CFR 1230.71 and 1230.110.

18 USC 42 et seq.
Importation of Animals, Birds, Fish, and Plants
This Act governs the importation of mammals, birds, fish, amphibia, and reptiles into the U.S. and authorizes U.S. Customs to enforce the import requirements.

21 USC 101 et seq.
Importation of Cattle and Quarantine
This Act provides for suspension of importation of animals to prevent the spread of disease, and for the quarantine of prohibited classes of animals. Importation of all animals described by the Act is prohibited except at certain designated ports. All animals are to be inspected on import or export.

21 USC 113a
Foot-and-Mouth Disease Memorandum of Understanding; Disease Research Act
This Act authorizes the study of animal disease and prohibits introduction of live foot-and-mouth disease virus into the U.S. except under certain defined circumstances. Customs enforces Agriculture restrictions and regulations.

21 USC 135
Establishment of International Animal Quarantine Stations
This Act authorizes the establishment of international quarantine stations. Customs enforces laws regarding importation of livestock.

42 USC 264 et seq.
Quarantine, Inspection, and Licensing
This Act restricts importations of dogs, cats, monkeys, psittacine birds, turtles, tortoises, and terrapins that do not comply with health standards. Customs enforces these restrictions. See 42 CFR 71.51 et seq.

19 CFR 12.24 and 12.26
Regulations for Animal and Animal Product Entry
These regulations provide for U.S. Customs entry declarations, documentation, and procedures for the animals and animal products subject to FWS and USDA regulations.

9 CFR Parts 91-96
Regulations on Animal Byproduct Quarantine Control
These regulations promulgated by the USDA prohibit the importation of animal products for use in industry unless the products meet certain processing standards and are not infected with certain diseases.

Convention on International Trade in Endangered Species of Wild Fauna and Flora (CITES)
This comprehensive wildlife treaty signed by over 100 countries, including the United States, regulates and in many cases prohibits commercial imports and exports of wild animal and plant species threatened by trade.

16 USC 1531
Endangered Species Act of 1973
This Act prohibits the import and export of species listed as endangered and most species listed as threatened. It is the U.S. law that implements CITES.

16 USC 742a et seq.
Fish and Wildlife Act of 1956

This Act regulates and bars the import of certain wild animals or birds and authorizes U.S. Customs to enforce the restrictions.

50 CFR Parts 10, 13, and 16
Regulations of FWS for Importing Wildlife and Fish
These regulations specify the animals and animal products subject to import prohibitions and restrictions.

16 USC 2401
Antarctic Conservation Act of 1978
This Act prohibits the importation, absent a special permit, of any flora or fauna native to Antarctica into the U.S. pursuant to the Antarctic Treaty and the Protocol.

16 USC 3371 et seq.
Control of Illegally Taken Fish and Wildlife
This Act prohibits the import of species taken, possessed, transported, or sold in violation of the law of a foreign country.

16 USC 1361 et seq.
The Marine Mammal Protection Act of 1972
This Act prohibits the import of certain marine mammals and their parts and products. These species include whales, walruses, narwhals, seals, sea lions, sea otters, and polar bears. It also defines parameters for importation of commercial fish or products that have been caught using methods, which involve incidental death or serious injury to protected marine mammals.

16 USC 4201 et seq.
The African Elephant Conservation Act
This Act prohibits imports of carved ivory products from any country and only permits imports of whole tusks from elephants legally hunted in certain African countries. It establishes U.S. adherence to the CITES Ivory Control System.

7 USC 1854
Textile Trade Agreements and Import Program Implementation
This Act limits the importation of textiles and textile products to the U.S. and their introduction to U.S. consumer.

19 CFR 12.134 et seq.
Regulations of Customs on Country of Origin and Import Entry
These Regulations define the country of origin to be specified on import documents and set forth the mandatory declarations to be submitted at the port of entry for each shipment of textile products.

15 USC 70 et seq.
Textile Fiber Products Identification Act
This Act prohibits false or deceptive labeling and advertising of textile products, requires the labeling of these products, and authorizes enforcement of labeling standards by Customs.

19 CFR 11.12b
Regulations of Customs on TFPIA Entry Labeling
These regulations set forth procedures, including invoice requirements, that U.S. Customs follows to enforce the Textile Fiber Products Identification Act with regard to the labeling of imported textile products.

16 CFR 303
Regulations of FTC on Textile Marking and Labeling
These regulations are promulgated and enforced by the FTC to ensure compliance with the Textile Fiber Products Identification Act.

15 USC 1191-1204
Flammable Fabrics Act
This Act authorizes the Consumer Product Safety Commission (CPSC) to set flammability standards for fabric

sold to U.S. consumers.

16 CFR 1610 et seq.
Regulations and Standards for Flammable Fabrics
These regulations fix the textile flammability standards and allow for Customs to prohibit the importation of any products that fail to conform to the standards.

16 USC 4901
Wild Bird Conservation Act of 1992
This act eliminated most commercial imports of CITES-regulated birds, except for limited imports of pet birds.

Principal Exporting Countries

The following listing includes samples of the main supplier nations of the products of this chapter. It is organized by HTSUS major heading. (Refer to "Customs Classification" above for the product codes.) Countries are listed in rank order of the value of products imported to the U.S. Statistics represent customs value of entries for 2002 from the Bureau of Census, U.S. Department of Commerce.

4201—China, Mexico, Taiwan, Germany, India, United Kingdom

4202—China, Italy, Thailand, France, Philippines, Indonesia, India

4203—China, Italy, India, Pakistan, Indonesia, Philippines, Canada, South Korea, Hong Kong, Thailand

4204—Switzerland, Italy, Slovenia, India, United Kingdom, China, Germany

4205—China, Mexico, India, Argentina, Italy, Canada, Thailand

4206—Mexico, Dominican Republic, Brazil, United Kingdom, Germany, France

Chapter 43:
Fur and Fur Products

Full title: Furskins and Artificial Fur; Manufactures Thereof

This chapter relates to the importation of animal furs, artificial furs, and fur products, which are classified within Chapter 43 of the Harmonized Tariff Schedule of the United States (HTSUS). Specifically, it includes raw, tanned, and dressed furskins, articles made of furskins, artificial fur, and articles of artificial fur.

If you are interested in importing bird skins with feathers or down, refer to Commodity Index Chapters 5 or 67. The import requirements for most raw hides or skins covered with hair are discussed in Chapter 41. If you are interested in importing gloves of leather and furskin or artificial fur, you should read Chapter 42, which also covers leather articles. If you want to import wool or shorn animal hair, refer to Chapter 51. Requirements for importing fur footwear are in Chapter 64, fur headgear in Chapter 65, and parts for toys, games, and sports equipment in Chapter 95. Imitation furskins that are derived from weaving or knitting, instead of wool, hair, or other fibers attached to leather, are covered under Chapters 58 or 60.

Note: To understand key issues that will enable you to make best use of the information in this section we recommend that you see "Introduction" on page 425.

Key Factors

The key factors in the importation of furskins and fur products are:

- Compliance with U.S. Fish and Wildlife Service (FWS) requirements (if the product is derived from endangered species or wildlife

- Entry at FWS-designated ports, and compliance with FWS and Customs advance notification and port-of-entry inspection requirements (if the products are derived from exotic wildlife or endangered species)

- Compliance with Federal Trade Commission (FTC) labeling requirements under the Fur Products Labeling Act (FPLA)

- Compliance with U.S. Department of Agriculture (USDA) APHIS import, quarantine, permit, and certification requirements (if the products are derived from domesticated animals)

- Entry at USDA designated ports (if the products are derived from domesticated animals)

Although most importers use the services of a licensed customs broker in making their entries, and we recommend this practice, you should be aware of the regulatory, entry, and documentation issues involved in importing your product. You, as importer, are ultimately responsible for the fulfillment of any legal requirements applicable to your shipment.

General Considerations

Regulatory Agencies. The USDA regulates and inspects the importation of all products derived from animals, including furskins. The FWS, primarily under provisions of the U.S. Endangered Species Act (ESA) and the Convention on International Trade in Endangered Species of Wild Fauna and Flora (CITES), controls the importation of products derived from animals that are classified as exotic wildlife or endangered species. U.S. Customs enforces USDA and FWS requirements through entry documentation and restrictions.

Domesticated Animal Furskins and Fur Products. Importation of furskins and fur products of domesticated animals—such as sheep and lambs—and of animals bred in captivity for the purpose of providing furskins for commercial uses is generally straightforward. Products derived from such animals are subject to quarantine regulations, marking requirements, and processing standards. Shipments of these products are inspected at the port of arrival by the Animal and Plant Health Inspection Service (APHIS) of the USDA. Unless the shipment is in compliance with all applicable laws and regulations, it will be denied entry into the U.S. Some shipments may be restricted or prohibited completely.

Quarantine and Inspection. At the time of applying for a permit to import animals products subject to quarantine requirements, you will have to make reservations for space in an appropriate quarantine facility. Fees for quarantine reservations vary according to species, and are due and payable when the reservation is requested. Each shipment entering under USDA APHIS permit must comply in every detail with the permit's specifications. If your shipment is found to be aberrant in any way (such as entering at a port of entry other than the one specified in the permit), it will be refused entry.

Veterinary Certificates. A veterinary certificate, issued by a salaried veterinarian of the country of origin, stating that the animal products are free of applicable livestock diseases, must accompany each shipment. The specific information required on the certificate varies depending on the species you are importing and its country of origin. You must also present an importer's declaration, which states: 1) port of entry; 2) importer's name and address; 3) broker's name and address; 4) livestock origin; 5) number, breed, species, and purpose of importation; 6) consignee's name and location of intended delivery.

APHIS-designated Quarantine Ports. The following listings are APHIS-designated ports with adequate quarantine facilities available for the import of livestock and livestock products. With very few exceptions, all shipments of livestock and livestock products must enter at one of these designated ports:

Air and Ocean Ports: Los Angeles, CA; Miami, FL; and Newburgh, NY.

Land border ports with Canada: Eastport, ID; Houlton and Jackman, MI; Detroit, Port Huron, and Sault Ste. Marie, MI; Baudette, MN; Opheim, Raymond, and Sweetgrass, MT; Alexandria Bay, Buffalo, and Champlain, NY; Dunseith, Pembina, and Portal, ND; Derby Line and Highgate Springs, VT; Lynden, Oroville, and Sumas, WA.

Land border ports with Mexico: Brownsville, Hidalgo, Laredo, Eagle Pass, Del Rio, and Presidio, TX; Douglas, Naco, Nogales, and San Luis, AZ; Calexico and San Ysidro, CA; Antelope Wells, Columbus, and Santa Teresa, NM.

Limited ports (ports with facilities for entry of live animals that do not appear to require restraint and holding inspection facilities): Anchorage and Fairbanks, AK; San Diego and San Francisco, CA; Denver, CO; Jacksonville, St. Petersburg-Clearwater, and Tampa, FL; Atlanta, GA; Honolulu, HI; Chicago, IL; New Orleans, LA; Portland, ME; Baltimore, MD; Boston, MA; Minneapolis, MN; Great Falls, MT; Dayton, OH; Portland, OR; San Juan, PR; Memphis, TN; El Paso, Galveston and Houston, TX; Seattle, Spokane, and Tacoma, WA.

The ports listed above have been designated as quarantine stations. The USDA Administrator has authority to designate other ports as quarantine stations as needed.

Exotic and Endangered Species. The FWS enforces a complex set of laws and regulations (see 50 CFR 1 et seq.) pertaining to wildlife and wildlife product importation. These laws include the international Convention on International Trade in Endangered Species of Wild Fauna and Flora (CITES), the Endangered Species Act (ESA), and a number of other U.S. laws, such as the African Elephant Conservation Act (AECA), Marine Mammal Protection Act (MMPA), Migratory Bird Treaty Act (MBTA), Eagle Protection Act (EPA), and the Lacey Act (LA). Most foreign countries also have their own domestic measures, and you will need to meet the requirements of the country of export in addition to U.S. requirements. For more information, contact the FWS Office of Management Authority (OMA) (see addresses at end of this chapter).

Certain types of furskins and fur products are entirely prohibited, others are allowed entry only under permit and/or license, and still others are allowed entry only for specific noncommercial purposes. When applying for a permit, you must satisfy the requirements of all laws under which the species is protected. The following briefly describes the two major laws governing importation of protected wildlife products into the U.S. This discussion is not comprehensive or exhaustive. If you wish to import furskins or fur products of exotic or endangered animals, you should always contact the FWS (see addresses at end of this chapter) with species information before making any transactions.

CITES. Over 100 nations participate in the Convention on International Trade in Endangered Species of Wild Fauna and Flora (CITES) treaty, which took effect in May 1977. The degree of protection afforded to a species depends on which of the three CITES appendices contains the name of that species. Documentation required for import varies depending on the species, and the CITES section where it is listed. The CITES export documentation from the country of origin is always required. If you are importing a CITES-listed species from a country that does not participate in the treaty, you must still obtain from that nation documents that contain all the information normally required in CITES export permits.

Appendix I. This appendix lists species deemed presently threatened with extinction (e.g., orangutan, chinchilla, gray whale). Importation of Appendix I species for commercial purposes is prohibited. You must have two permits to import these species: one from the U.S., which must be obtained first, and one from the exporting country. If you are importing Appendix I species taken in the marine environment and outside the jurisdiction of any country or state, you must have an Introduction from the Sea Permit.

Appendix II. This appendix lists species that are not presently threatened with extinction but may become threatened if their trade is not regulated (e.g., brown bear, musk deer, elephant seal). There are no restrictions on the purpose of import, provided it is not detrimental to the survival of the species. You will need an export permit or reexport certificate from the exporting country. If you are importing Appendix II species taken in the marine environment and outside the jurisdiction of any country or state, you will need an Introduction from the Sea Permit.

Appendix III. This appendix lists species for which any CITES member country has domestic regulations "for the purpose of preventing or restricting exploitation, and as needing the cooperation of other Parties in control of trade." For example, Canada lists the walrus, and Nepal lists the blackbuck antelope. Three different types of documents are issued for Appendix III species: 1) Export Permit: Issued for specimens that originated in a country that listed the species on Appendix III; 2) Certificate of Origin: Issued by any country other than the listing country if the wildlife in question originated in that country; 3) Reexport Certificate: Issued for the export of Appendix III specimens that were previously imported into the U.S.

Exemptions. Under certain conditions, Certificates of Exemption may be issued for the importation of wildlife products listed under CITES. Exceptions are allowed for shipments of wildlife transiting a country under Customs bond, shipments between U.S. states or territories, and certain personal or household effects. For information, contact FWS (see addresses at end of this chapter).

Permit Applications. Applications for CITES permits and certificates are available from the FWS Office of Management Authority (see addresses at end of this chapter). You will need to fill out the FWS Standard Permit Application **(Form 3-200)** and provide certain information specifically required under CITES. You should submit your application at least 60 days before the date you wish the permit to take effect. FWS charges processing fees for CITES applications.

ESA. The U.S. Endangered Species Act (ESA) was passed on December 28, 1973, to prevent the extinction of many species of animals and plants and to protect their habitats. By definition, an "endangered species" is any animal or plant listed by regulation as being in danger of extinction. A "threatened species" is any animal or plant likely to become endangered within the foreseeable future. The U.S. List of Endangered and Threatened Wildlife and Plants includes native and foreign species.

Permits. ESA's import provisions prohibit the import or export of any endangered or threatened species or products derived from them without one of the following permits from the FWS Federal Wildlife Permit Office (FWPO):

> *Endangered Species Permits:* This permit is issued for importation for purposes of 1) scientific research; 2) enhancement of propagation or survival of the species; or 3) incidental taking.

> *Threatened Species Permits:* This permit is issued for importation for purposes of 1) scientific research; 2) enhancement of propagation or survival of the species; 3) zoological, horticultural, or botanical exhibition; 4) education purposes; 5) special purposes consistent with ESA purposes and policy; or 6) incidental taking.

Permit Exemptions. A few imports of endangered species products are exempt from the ESA permit requirements. For example, if a species is listed as threatened or as an experimental population, special rules may allow otherwise prohibited activities. Some species covered by special rules include certain kangaroos, several primates, the grizzly bear, gray wolf, and leopard. If you are unsure as to the exemption status of your import, contact FWS (see addresses at end of this chapter).

FWS Import Licenses. With some exceptions, persons engaged in the business of importing wildlife products valued in excess of $25,000 per year must be licensed by the FWS. If your annual importations are valued at less than $25,000, or if you qualify for another exemption from licensing, you are still responsible for keeping thorough records of all wildlife transactions and of making these records available to FWS officers if necessary. For a full description of exemptions from licensing, and of recordkeeping requirements, contact the Fish and Wildlife Service (see addresses at end of this chapter) or see 50 CFR 14.

Procedures at Port of Entry. At least 72 hours before your shipment is due to arrive at a designated port, you should notify U.S. Customs and the FWS inspectors of its expected arrival. The FWS conducts port-of-entry shipment inspections on a case-by-case basis, as determined by the inspection agent after looking at the entry paperwork. Both FWS and Customs may inspect your shipment to verify compliance with all of the legal requirements for entry. Any documentation required by the laws governing your import must be submitted by the time of entry. You must present an FWS Wildlife Declaration Form 3-177, available at the port of entry, with every shipment, regardless of any other paperwork required. Customs will not release your shipment until the import declaration has been signed off by an FWS agent.

Designated Ports. Shipments of wildlife products are restricted to designated U.S. ports of entry. All wildlife shipments must enter and leave through one of the ports listed in 50 CFR 14.12. Currently, ten ports are designated: New York, NY; Miami, FL; New Orleans, LA; Dallas/Ft. Worth, TX; Los Angeles, CA; San Francisco, CA; Chicago, IL; Seattle, WA; Honolulu, HI; and Portland, OR. If special circumstances prevent you from making your entry at a designated port, you will need to obtain an Exception to Designated Port Permit from the FWS Divisions of Law Enforcement (see addresses at end of this chapter).

You may import fur and fur products derived from animals bred in captivity for the purpose of providing furskins for commercial uses, without permit or special paperwork. These products are not restricted to FWS-designated ports. Certain fur products are subject to the requirements of the Fur Products Labeling Act (FPLA), administered by the Federal Trade Commission (FTC), and enforced by U.S. Customs at the port of entry. It is your responsibility as importer to make sure that your shipment complies in every detail with FPLA requirements. Customs entry is contingent upon proper labeling.

If Customs finds your import shipment to be mislabeled, you will be allowed to relabel the products under Customs supervision, as long as the port director is satisfied that your labeling error or omission did not involve fraud or willful neglect. If your shipment is discovered after entry to have been mislabeled, it will be recalled to Customs custody at your expense, unless you can satisfy the port director that your products have since been brought into compliance. You will be held responsible for all expenses incurred in bringing your shipment into compliance, including compensation and expenses related to Customs supervision.

Fraudulent violations of FPLA will result in seizure of the shipment. Shipments already released from Customs custody and later found to be in fraudulent violation of FPLA will be ordered to be redelivered to Customs. Customs reports all cases of fraudulent violation to the FTC in Washington, DC.

Specific-Country Import Regulations

There are special provisions for livestock products originating in Canada, Mexico, Central America, and the West Indies. These provisions vary according to species, and include such things as permit or quarantine waivers, special quarantine restrictions, specific ports of entry for specific types of livestock products, and provisions for transit across the U.S. only. One general requirement applicable across the board is that two import declarations (see above) must be presented, instead of only one. For more details see appropriate headings in 9 CFR 92, or contact the Animal and Plant Health Inspection Service.

Customs Classification

For customs purposes, animal furs, artificial furs, and fur products are classified under Chapter 43 of the HTSUS. This chapter is broken into major headings, which are further divided into subheadings, and often sub-subheadings, each of which has its own HTSUS classification number. For example, the 2001 HTSUS number for whole silver, black, or platinum fox skins is 4301.60.30, indicating it is a sub-subcategory of fox, whole, with or without head, tail, or paws (4301.60), which is a subcategory of the major heading, raw furskins (4301). There are 43 major headings within Chapter 43.

4301—Raw furskins (including heads, tails, paws, and other pieces or cuttings, suitable for furriers' use), other than raw hides and skins of heading 4101, 4102, or 4103

4302—Tanned or dressed furskins (including heads, tails, paws, and other pieces or cuttings), unassembled, or assembled (without the addition of other materials) other than those of heading 4303

4303—Articles of apparel, clothing accessories, and other articles of furskin

4304—Artificial fur and articles thereof

For more details regarding classifications of the specific product you are interested in importing, consult a customs broker, the appropriate commodity specialist at your nearest customs port, or the HTSUS. The 2001 HTSUS is available online from the Customs Service (www.customs.gov/impoexpo/impoexpo.htm) or for purchase from the U.S. Government Printing Office (see resources at the end of this chapter), and may be found in larger public libraries. For a general discussion of customs classification, see "Classification—Liquidation" on page 229.

Dutiable Status of Goods

For more information about duty rates and binding decisions see "Dutiable Status of Goods" on page 203; for a discussion of temporary importation of goods see "Temporary Free Importations" on page 205.

Valuation

Importers have a responsibility to use what the U.S. Customs Service deems, "reasonable care," when determining the value of their goods. They must also provide any additional information that the Customs Service needs for setting a final value on the goods. This process involves a number of factors and can be somewhat complicated; importers must be aware of applicable issues and details. Valuation information applies to all types of commodities, for further discussion on the subject see "Customs Valuation" on page 267.

Import Duties

Import duties vary (often dramatically) depending upon the Harmonized Tariff Schedule (HTSUS) classification of the goods or products imported. Since some products that look alike have different HTSUS classifications and different rates of duty, proper classification is vital. Note that "differences of opinion" between importers and the Bureau of Customs and Border Protection regarding classification keeps customs attorneys very busy.

Import duties can be assessed on the imported value of the goods ("ad valorem" rates of duty such as 2%, 4.4%, 50%, etc.), total units or weight of the goods ("specific" rates of duty such as 2 cents each or 1.5 cents/pound, etc.) or on a combination basis ("compound" rates of duty such as 5 cents each plus 6%).

Listed below is a sampling of several Column 1 import duty rates for Chapter 43 products:
Of lamb, the following: Astrakhan, Broadtail, Caracul, Persian and similar lamb, Indian, Chinese, Mongolian or Tibetan lamb, whole, with or without head, tail or paws (4301.30.00.00): Free to
Of silver, black or platinum fox (including those of any fox which is a mutation, or type developed, from silver, black or platinum foxes) (4301.60.30.00): 5.1%

For specific information on US import duties refer to the Harmonized Tariff Schedule of the US. The print version is available from the US Government Printing Office as well as third party suppliers who often add special features. Online versions are available in both static PDF pages as well as in formats with excellent search functionality. Search the Web with the term "Harmonized Tariff Schedule" to find sources.

Entry and Documentation

The entry of merchandise is a two-part process consisting of 1) filing the documentation necessary to determine whether merchandise may be released from Customs custody, and 2) filing the documents that contain information for duty assessment and statistical purposes. In certain instances, all documents must be filed and accepted by Customs prior to release of the goods. Unless you have been granted an extension, you must file entry documents at a location specified by the port or area director within five working days of your shipment's date of arrival at a U.S. port of entry. These include a number of standard documents required by Customs for any entry, and:

- FWS Import Declaration Form 3-177, original and 3 copies (if the products are derived from exotic wildlife or endangered species)

- FWS permit or import documentation Form 3-200 (if the products are derived from exotic wildlife or endangered species)

- Permits or certificates required under ESA, and any other regulations applicable to the particular shipment (if the products are derived from exotic wildlife or endangered species)

- Certificates of export, origin, sanitation, veterinary inspection, and other conditions from the country of origin or export, as required by Customs, FWS, or USDA

- USDA importer's declaration (if the products are derived from domesticated animals)

- Copy of air waybill or bill of lading

- Copy of invoice (pro forma invoice if shipment is noncommercial)

After you present the entry, Customs may examine your shipment or may waive examination. The shipment is then released provided no legal or regulatory violations have been noted. You must then file entry summary documentation and deposit estimated duties at a designated customhouse within 10 working days of your shipment's release. For a detailed description of entry procedures, standard documentation, and informal entry, see "Entry Process" on page 185.

Informed Compliance. Informed compliance was introduced with the Customs Modernization Act of 1993 (Mod Act) and defines the relationship between importers and the Customs Service. It sets out the responsibilities of both parties. Providing the correct documentation and information for entry is a key factor that will make your importing operation run smoothly. We recommend that importers become familiar with the concept of informed comliance and the responsibilities that they have under the Mod Act. For further discussion about informed compliance see "Informed Compliance" on page 211.

Entry Invoice. The entry invoice for a shipment of fur or fur products must specify the following: 1) name or names (as set forth in the Fur Products Name Guide (16 CFR 301.0)) of the animal or animals that produced the fur, and such qualifying statements as may be required pursuant to section 7(c) of the Fur Products Labeling Act (15 USC 69e(c)); 2) a statement that the fur product contains or is composed of used fur, when such is the fact; 3) a statement that the fur product contains or is composed

of bleached, dyed, or otherwise artificially colored fur, when such is the fact; 4) a statement that the fur product is composed in whole or in substantial part of paws, tails, bellies, or waste fur, when such is the fact; 5) name and address of the manufacturer of the fur product; 6) name of the country of origin of the furs or those contained in the fur product.

If a fur product shipment valued at over $500 and subject to the FPLA is offered for entry, special information must appear on the entry invoice. This information is intended to facilitate Customs monitoring and enforcement of the FPLA. It is identical to that required by the FPLA on labeling (see "Marking and Labeling Requirements" below). For more general information about invoices see "Invoices" on page 277.

Note: The Entry and Documentation section has been carefully designed to supply you, the importer, with sample documents and directions on how to satisfy Customs requirements. Be aware that you should consult the applicable authorities to ensure that you are correctly following the most current procedures.

Prohibitions and Restrictions

Animal Products. Animal products are subject to quarantine if they arrive from certain countries that are known to have specific infectious diseases. These countries are listed in 9 CFR 94. If a USDA inspector determines that a shipment is infected with anthrax, foot-and-mouth disease, rinderpest, or bovine spongiform encephalopathy, entry will be denied.

Exotic and Endangered Species. Hides of certain animals are restricted or prohibited from importation because of species status under the CITES, ESA, or another U.S. law. For example, importation of species listed in CITES Appendix I for commercial purposes is prohibited. Prohibitions and restrictions may additionally be imposed by the law of the exporting country. You are legally responsible for fulfilling the requirements of all of them, as well as any laws of the country of export. If you import, or attempt to import, a product in violation of a wildlife or endangered species law, even if you are not aware of the violation, your product may be seized, you may be charged substantial fines, and you could be imprisoned.

Importers should be particularly cautious in importing the following wildlife products, which are prohibited from import into the U.S. [reprinted with permission by World Wildlife Fund from its brochure: "Buyer Beware"]:

Furs from the larger spotted cats, such as jaguar, leopard, snow leopard, and tiger, and from most smaller cats, such as ocelot, margay, and tiger cat, cannot enter the United States legally, nor can furs of marine mammals like seals and polar bears.

Marking and Labeling Requirements

Animal Products. Containers of animal furskins and fur products must be marked with the country of origin—that is, the country where the animal was located. If these items are quarantined at the port of arrival, marks and signs are required on shipping documents and any mode of transport used to move the product while under restrictions (9 CFR 95.25).

Wildlife Furskins and Fur Products. All wildlife shipments must be marked on the outside of the container with the names and addresses of the exporter and importer, an accurate identification of the species, and the numbers of each species in the container.

Fur Products Labeling Act (FPLA). You should be sure that any article of wearing apparel made in whole or in part of fur that you are importing into the U.S. is tagged, labeled, or otherwise clearly marked to show the following FPLA-required information: 1) name of the manufacturer or importer. If you have an FTC-issued registered identification number, you may use that number instead of your name.; 2) the name or names of the animal or animals that produced the fur, as set forth in the Fur Products Name

Guide, and as permitted under the rules and regulations; 3) that the fur product contains used or damaged fur when such is the fact; 4) that the fur product is bleached, dyed, or otherwise artificially colored when such is the fact; 5) that the fur product is composed in whole or in substantial part of paws, tails, bellies, or waste fur when such is the fact; 6) the name of the country of origin of any imported furs contained in a fur product.

This discussion does not include all FPLA requirements. The regulations are extensive and detailed. They specify such things as arrangement of required information; allowable wording and punctuation on required labels; size; means of attachment and position of labeling; requirements for labeling articles made of more than one type of fur, or of fur and other materials; labeling of multi-unit garments; labeling of samples; invoicing; record-keeping, etc. If you are interested in importing fur garments, you should contact the Federal Trade Commission (address above) for the booklet entitled *Rules and Regulations under the Fur Products Labeling Act*, available from that agency free of charge.

If Customs finds your import shipment to be mislabeled, you will be allowed to relabel the products under Customs supervision, as long as the port director is satisfied that your labeling error or omission did not involve fraud or willful neglect. If your shipment is discovered after entry to have been mislabeled, it will be recalled to Customs custody at your expense, unless you can satisfy the port director that your products have since been brought into compliance. You will be held responsible for all expenses incurred in bringing your shipment into compliance, including compensation and expenses related to Customs supervision.

Fraudulent violations of FPLA will result in seizure of the shipment. Shipments already released from Customs custody and later found to be in fraudulent violation of FPLA will be ordered to be redelivered to Customs. Customs reports all cases of fraudulent violation to the FTC in Washington, DC.

Exemptions. Articles made of new fur of which the cost or manufacturer's selling price does not exceed $7 are not subject to FPLA.

For a general discussion of U.S. Customs marking and labeling requirements, see "Country of Origin Marking" on page 236, "Special Marking Requirements" on page 238 and "Marking—False Impression" on page 239.

Shipping Considerations

You will need to ensure that your goods are packaged and shipped with care so that they pass smoothly through Customs and arrive in good condition. You are responsible for ensuring that the shipment is in compliance with all applicable government regulations for packaging and shipping. In most instances, you should not leave these arrangements solely to the discretion of your supplier. Careful preparation of the cargo and selection of the mode of transport can be essential to a cost-effective, timely delivery of undamaged goods. We strongly advise you to consult your shipping representative, insurance agent, or freight broker for advice on packing and shipping.

Animal furs, artificial furs, and fur products may be shipped in bulk, bags, cartons, or other types of containers, depending on the type of product. General considerations include protection from contamination, weather, and pests. Containers should be constructed so as to be safe for handling during transport.

Publications and WWW Resources

For questions regarding the Convention on Interational Trade in Endangered Species of Wild Fauna and Flora (CITES) refer to:

CITES Secretariat
15 chemin des Anemones
1219 Chatelaine-Geneva
Switzerland

Tel: [41] (22) 917-8139/40
Fax: [41] (22) 797-3417
Website: www.cites.org
Email: cites@unep.ch

The *Harmonized Tariff Schedule of the United States (2001)* (HTSUS) is available to view on the Customs Service website (www.customs.gov), or you may purchase a printed version from:

U.S. Government Printing Office
Superintendent of Documents
710 North Capital Street NW
Washington DC 20401
Tel: (202) 512-1800
Fax: (202) 512-1657
Website: www.access.gpo.gov

The USGPO also has copies of specific laws available for purchase. The USGPO accepts orders made by fax, phone or placed over the Internet, as well as mail orders paid by credit card. All orders must be accompanied by payment. Credit cards, checks drawn on a U.S. bank, or an international money order are all acceptable.

Relevant Government Agencies

Address your questions regarding USDA requirements for the importation of domesticated animal products to:

Animal and Plant Health Inspection Service (APHIS)
Veterinary Services (VS)
National Center for Import and Export
4700 River Rd., Unit 40
Riverdale, MD 20737
Tel: (301) 734-3277
Animal products: (301) 734-4401
Website: www.aphis.usda.gov/vs

Address your questions regarding the importation of products of exotic or endangered animals to:

U.S. Fish and Wildlife Service (FWS)
Office of Management Authority
4401 N. Fairfax Dr.
Arlington, VA 22203-0700
Tel: (703) 358-2104
Website: www.fws.gov

National Marine Fisheries Service (NMFS)
1315 East West Highway
SSMC3
Silver Spring, MD 20910
Tel: (301) 713-2239
Office of Protected Resources: (301) 713-2332
Inspection Services Division: (301) 713-2355
Website: www.nmfs.noaa.gov

Address your questions regarding FPLA requirements to:

Federal Trade Commission (FTC)
Division of Enforcement
600 Pennsylvania Avenue NW
Washington DC 20580
Tel: (202) 326-2996
Website: www.ftc.gov

Address your questions regarding importation of furskins, artificial furs, and fur products generally to your local Customs port director. For addresses refer to "U.S. Customs and Border Protection Offices" on page 65 or contact:

U.S. Customs and Border Protection
Customs Headquarters
1300 Pennsylvania Avenue NW
Washington DC 20229
Tel: (202) 354-1000
Website: www.customs.treas.gov

Laws and Regulations

The following laws and regulations may be relevant to the importation of furskins, artificial furs, and fur products. The laws are contained in the United States Code (USC), and the regulations are published in the Code of Federal Regulations (CFR), both of which are available at larger public and law libraries. Copies of specific laws are also available from the United States Government Printing Office (address above).

15 USC 69-69j
Fur Products Labeling Act
This Act prohibits false or deceptive labeling (misbranding) and false advertising of fur products. It also requires the labeling of fur products to indicate composition and specific information that must be included on the invoices provided at the time of importation.

16 CFR 301 et seq.; 19 CFR 11.12.a
Labeling of Fur Products Regulations
These regulations contain the FTC rules and procedures for labeling fur products and the procedures for Customs to enforce the labeling requirements.

18 USC 42 et seq.
Importation of Animals, Birds, Fish, and Plants
This Act governs the importation of mammals, birds, fish, amphibia, and reptiles into the U.S. and authorizes U.S. Customs to enforce the import requirements.

21 USC 135
Establishment of International Animal Quarantine Stations
This Act authorizes the establishment of international quarantine stations. Customs enforces laws regarding importation of livestock.

42 USC 264 et seq.
Quarantine, Inspection, and Licensing
This Act restricts importations of dogs, cats, monkeys, psittacine birds, turtles, tortoises, and terrapins that do not comply with health standards. Customs enforces these restrictions. See 42 CFR 71.51 et seq.

19 CFR 12.24 and 12.26
Regulations for Animal and Animal Product Entry
These regulations provide for U.S. Customs entry declarations, documentation, and procedures for the animals and animal products subject to FWS and USDA regulations.

9 CFR Parts 91-96
Regulations on Animal Byproduct Quarantine Control
These regulations promulgated by the USDA prohibit the importation of animal products for use in industry unless the products meet certain processing standards and are not infected with certain diseases.

Convention on International Trade in Endangered Species of Wild Fauna and Flora (CITES)
This comprehensive wildlife treaty signed by over 100 countries, including the United States, regulates and in many cases prohibits commercial imports and exports of wild animal and plant species threatened by trade.

16 USC 1531
Endangered Species Act of 1973
This Act prohibits the import and export of species listed as endangered and most species listed as threatened. It is the U.S. law that implements CITES.

16 USC 742a et seq.
Fish and Wildlife Act of 1956
This Act regulates and bars the import of certain wild animals or birds and authorizes U.S. Customs to enforce the restrictions.

50 CFR Parts 10, 13, and 16
Regulations of FWS for Importing Wildlife and Fish

These regulations specify the animals and animal products subject to import prohibitions and restrictions.

16 USC 2401
Antarctic Conservation Act of 1978
This Act prohibits the importation, absent a special permit, of any flora or fauna native to Antarctica into the U.S. pursuant to the Antarctic Treaty and the Protocol.

16 USC 3371 et seq.
Control of Illegally Taken Fish and Wildlife
This Act prohibits the import of species taken, possessed, transported, or sold in violation of the law of a foreign country.

16 USC 1361 et seq.
The Marine Mammal Protection Act of 1972
This Act prohibits the import of certain marine mammals and their parts and products. These species include whales, walruses, narwhals, seals, sea lions, sea otters, and polar bears. It also defines parameters for importation of commercial fish or products that have been caught using methods, which involve incidental death or serious injury to protected marine mammals.

16 USC 4901
Wild Bird Conservation Act of 1992
This act eliminated most commercial imports of CITES-regulated birds, except for limited imports of pet birds.

Principal Exporting Countries

The following listing includes samples of the main supplier nations of the products of this chapter. It is organized by HTSUS major heading. (Refer to "Customs Classification" above for the product codes.) Countries are listed in rank order of the value of products imported to the U.S. Statistics represent customs value of entries for 2002 from the Bureau of Census, U.S. Department of Commerce.

4301—Canada, Netherlands, Sweden, Finland, Denmark, Russia

4302—Spain, Canada, China, Brazil, New Zealand, Italy, Portugal

4303—China, Canada, Italy, New Zealand, Greece, Turkey

4304—China, United Kingdom, Turkey, France

Chapter 44:
Wood and Wood Products

Full tile: Wood and Articles of Wood; Wood Charcoal

This chapter relates to the importation of wood and wood products, which are classified under Chapter 44 of the Harmonized Tariff Schedule of the United States (HTSUS). Specifically, it includes fuel wood; wood charcoal; rough wood; hoopwood; poles and stakes; wood wool and flour; railway and tramway ties; wood sawn, chipped, sliced, and peeled; veneers, plywoods, particle boards, fiberboards, and laminates; densified wood; wooden frames; wooden packing materials; coopers' products; tool and tool parts; carpentry and builders' joinery items; tableware and kitchenware; wood marquetry and inlaid articles; and small wooden articles (e.g., clothes hangers, clothespins, canoe paddles, wooden blind slats, and toothpicks).

If you are interested in importing wood pieces for perfumery, pharmaceutical, insecticidal, fungicidal, or similar purposes, you should refer to Commodity Index Chapter 12. The importing of bamboo and plaiting materials is covered in Chapter 14, which also includes chipped, shaved, ground, or powdered wood used for dyeing or tanning. For import requirements related to activated charcoal, refer to Chapter 38. If you are interested in importing a particular manufactured wood product, you should refer to the Commodity Index chapter that covers that product. For example, import requirements for baskets and wickerware are in Chapter 46, footwear parts are in Chapter 64, umbrellas and walking canes are in Chapter 66, imitation jewelry is in Chapter 71, wood cases, covers, and other parts used in machinery are in Chapters 84 through 89, clock cases are in Chapter 91, musical instruments are in Chapter 92, firearm parts are in Chapter 93, furniture is in Chapter 94, toys, games, and sports equipment are in Chapter 95, and works of art are in Chapter 97.

Note: To understand key issues that will enable you to make best use of the information in this section we recommend that you see "Introduction" on page 425.

Key Factors

The key factors in the importation of wood and wood products are:

- Compliance with U.S. Department of Agriculture (USDA) port-of-entry inspections and other requirements
- Compliance with Federal Plant Pest Act
- Compliance with Plant Quarantine Act
- Compliance with U.S. Federal Trade Commission (FTC) and Consumer Product Safety Commission (CPSC) standards (if the product will be marketed to consumers)
- Submission of Canadian Government Export Notice (if importing softwood lumber from Canada)

- Compliance with invoice requirements (if importing certain types of lumber)
- Compliance with Fish and Wildlife Service (FWS) license, permit, country-of-origin permit, import documentation, and recordkeeping requirements (if the products are derived from endangered species)
- Entry at FWS-designated ports, and compliance with FWS and Customs advance notification and port-of-entry inspection requirements (if the products are derived from endangered species)

Although most importers use the services of a licensed customs broker in making their entries, and we recommend this practice, you should be aware of the regulatory, entry, and documentation issues involved in importing your product. You, as importer, are ultimately responsible for the fulfillment of any legal requirements applicable to your shipment.

General Considerations

Regulatory Agencies. The USDA administers applicable provisions of the Plant Quarantine Act (PQA), which are designed to prevent the introduction into the U.S. of any plant pest or disease potentially harmful to U.S. agriculture. The FWS, primarily under provisions of the U.S. Endangered Species Act (ESA) and the Convention on International Trade in Endangered Species of Wild Fauna and Flora (CITES), controls the importation of products derived from plants that are classified as endangered species. The FTC and CPSC sets standards for products being sold to U.S. consumers. U.S. Customs enforces USDA and FWS requirements through entry documentation and restrictions.

Lumber and Other Raw Wood. Shipments of lumber and raw wood are inspected at the port of arrival by the USDA's Animal and Plant Health Inspection Service (APHIS). Entry may be denied for noncompliance with the regulations, and the shipment could be seized, quarantined, destroyed, treated, or otherwise dealt with at the discretion of the inspector. Some shipments may be restricted or prohibited completely. APHIS inspectors also enforce FWS requirements under the ESA and the CITES. Lumber derived from an endangered species may be prohibited, or may require export and/or import permits (see below). You are responsible for ensuring that your shipment is either not derived from listed species, or if it is, that you have the appropriate import authorization.

Elm Logs and Lumber. The import of elm logs and elm lumber with bark attached requires a permit from AHPIS.

Wood Products. If you wish to import wood products, for the most part you will not need permits or other special paperwork. However, goods classified as hazardous consumer products must comply with consumer standards to be sold in the U.S. (see below) and goods derived from endangered tree species are subject to complex import restrictions (see below).

Hazardous Consumer Products. Under the Federal Hazardous Substances Act (FHSA) and the Consumer Products Safety Act (CPSA), a wood product that is flammable or combustible and that is intended for the consumer market is a hazardous substance. To be sold in the U.S., the product must be in compliance with FTC and CPSC standards. The CPSC does not require permits, special invoicing, limited entry, licenses, or any special approval process for importing hazardous consumer products into the U.S. However, if you are importing these types of products, you are responsible for making sure that they meet all applicable FHSA and CPSA requirements. There are detailed regulations regarding testing and labeling of hazardous products. The Commission's enforcement posture regarding compliance with labeling and product safety standards changes as new facts become available. Contact the CPSC (see addresses at end of this chapter) for specific requirements on the consumer product you are considering importing.

Substantial Product Hazard Reports. Defect-reporting is required for products covered under the CPSA. The law requires every manufacturer, distributor, or retailer of such products, who obtains information that reasonably supports the conclusion that such products fail to comply with an applicable consumer product safety rule, or contain a defect that could create a substantial product hazard, to immediately inform the CPSC of the potential violation or defect. A firm's willful failure to make a Substantial Product Hazard Report can result in litigation by the CPSC.

Exotic and Endangered Species. The FWS enforces a complex set of laws and regulations (see 50 CFR 1 et seq.) pertaining to endangered species product importation. These laws include the CITES, ESA, and a number of other U.S. laws, such as the Lacey Act (LA). Most foreign countries also have their own domestic measures, and you will need to meet the requirements of the country of export in addition to U.S. requirements. For more information, contact the FWS Office of Management Authority (OMA) (see addresses at end of this chapter).

Certain types of woods are entirely prohibited, others are allowed entry only under permit and/or license, and still others are allowed entry only for specific noncommercial purposes. When applying for a permit, you must satisfy the requirements of all laws under which the species is protected. The following briefly describes the two major laws governing importation of protected products into the U.S. This discussion is not comprehensive or exhaustive. If you wish to import endangered species, you should always contact the FWS (see addresses at end of this chapter) with species information before making any transactions.

CITES. Over 100 nations participate in CITES, which took effect in May 1977. The degree of protection afforded to a species depends on which of the three CITES appendices contains the name of that species. Documentation required for import varies depending on the species, and the CITES section where it is listed. The CITES export documentation from the country of origin is always required. If you are importing a CITES-listed species from a country that does not participate in the treaty, you must still obtain from that nation documents that contain all the information normally required in CITES export permits.

Appendix I. This appendix lists species deemed presently threatened with extinction. Importation of Appendix I species for commercial purposes is prohibited. You must have two permits to import these species: one from the U.S., which must be obtained first, and one from the exporting country.

Appendix II. This appendix lists species that are not presently threatened with extinction but may become threatened if their trade is not regulated (e.g., boojum tree). There are no restrictions on the purpose of import, provided it is not detrimental to the survival of the species. You will need an export permit or reexport certificate from the exporting country.

Appendix III. This appendix lists species for which any CITES member country has domestic regulations "for the purpose of preventing or restricting exploitation, and as needing the cooperation of other Parties in control of trade." For example, Nepal lists several varieties of magnolia. Three different types of documents are issued for Appendix III species: 1) Export Permit: Issued for specimens that originated in a country that listed the species on Appendix III; 2) Certificate of Origin: Issued by any country other than the listing country if the species in question originated in that country; 3) Reexport Certificate: Issued for the export of Appendix III specimens that were previously imported into the U.S.

Exemptions. Under certain conditions, Certificates of Exemption may be issued for the importation of endangered species products listed under CITES. Exceptions are allowed for shipments of products transiting a country under Customs bond, shipments between U.S. states or territories, and certain personal or household effects. For information, contact FWS (see addresses at end of this chapter).

Permit Applications. Applications for CITES permits and certificates are available from the FWS Office of Management Authority (see addresses at end of this chapter). You will need to fill out the FWS Standard Permit Application **(Form 3-200)** and provide certain information specifically required under CITES. You should submit your application at least 60 days before the date you wish the permit to take effect. FWS charges processing fees for CITES applications.

ESA. The U.S. Endangered Species Act (ESA) was passed on December 28, 1973, to prevent the extinction of many species of animals and plants and to protect their habitats. By definition, an "endangered species" is any animal or plant listed by regulation as being in danger of extinction. A "threatened species" is any animal or plant likely to become endangered within the foreseeable future. The U.S. List of Endangered and Threatened Wildlife and Plants includes native and foreign species.

Permits. ESA's import provisions prohibit the import or export of any endangered or threatened species or products derived from them without one of the following permits from the FWS Federal Wildlife Permit Office (FWPO):

> *Endangered Species Permits:* This permit is issued for importation for purposes of 1) scientific research; 2) enhancement of propagation or survival of the species; or 3) incidental taking.

> *Threatened Species Permits:* This permit is issued for importation for purposes of 1) scientific research; 2) enhancement of propagation or survival of the species; 3) zoological, horticultural, or botanical exhibition; 4) education purposes; 5) special purposes consistent with ESA purposes and policy; or 6) incidental taking.

Permit Exemptions. A few imports of endangered species products are exempt from the ESA permit requirements. For example, if a species is listed as threatened or as an experimental population, special rules may allow otherwise prohibited activities. If you are unsure as to the exemption status of your import, contact FWS (see addresses at end of this chapter).

FWS Import Licenses. With some exceptions, persons engaged in the business of importing endangered species products valued in excess of $25,000 per year must be licensed by the FWS. If your annual importations are valued at less than $25,000, or if you qualify for another exemption from licensing, you are still responsible for keeping thorough records of all transactions and of making these records available to FWS officers if necessary. For a full description of exemptions from licensing, and of recordkeeping requirements, contact the FWS (see addresses at end of this chapter) or see 50 CFR 14.

Procedures at Port of Entry. At least 72 hours before your shipment is due to arrive at a designated port, you should notify U.S. Customs and the FWS inspectors of its expected arrival. The FWS conducts port-of-entry shipment inspections on a case-by-case basis, as determined by the inspection agent after looking at the entry paperwork. Both FWS and Customs may inspect your shipment to verify compliance with all of the legal requirements for entry. Any documentation required by the laws governing your import must be submitted by the time of entry. You must present an FWS Wildlife Declaration **Form 3-177**, available at the port of entry, with every shipment, regardless of any other paperwork required. Customs will not release your shipment until the import declaration has been signed off by an FWS agent.

Designated Ports. Shipments of endangered species products are restricted to designated U.S. ports of entry. All shipments must enter and leave through one of the ports listed in 50 CFR 14.12. Currently, 10 ports are designated: New York, NY; Miami, FL; New Orleans, LA; Dallas/Ft. Worth, TX; Los Angeles, CA; San Francisco, CA; Chicago, IL; Seattle, WA; Honolulu, HI; and Portland, OR. If special circumstances prevent you from making your entry at a designated port, you will need to obtain an Exception to Designated Port Permit from the FWS Divisions of Law Enforcement (see addresses at end of this chapter).

Import Advisory

The endangered species issue is particularly important. As the list of endangered trees expands, the likelihood that your lumber or timber is of a protected species increases. It is your responsibility as importer to be aware of the regulatory status of your commodity. If you have any doubts as to the compliance status of your product under the PQA, CITES, or the ESA, you should check with APHIS, the FWS, or U.S. Customs. Always be prepared to provide the common and scientific names of any species you have questions about or are planning to import. When you are unsure of the regulations governing the export or import of a product, check with the FWS before making a purchase. When in doubt, don't buy! The importation of products made from endangered species can be seized and in some cases the importer can be subject to substantial fines.

Customs Classification

For customs purposes, wood and wood products are classified under Chapter 44 of the HTSUS. This chapter is broken into major headings, which are further divided into subheadings, and often sub-subheadings, each of which has its own HTSUS classification number. For example, the 2001 HTSUS number for pine wood molding is 4409.10.40, indicating it is a sub-subcategory of coniferous (4409.10), which is a subcategory of the major heading, wood continuously shaped along any of its edges or faces (4409). There are 21 major headings within Chapter 44.

4401—Fuel wood, in logs, in billets, in twigs, in faggots, or in similar forms; wood in chips or particles; sawdust and wood waste and scrap, whether or not agglomerated in logs, briquettes, pellets, or similar forms

4402—Wood charcoal (including shell or nut charcoal), whether or not agglomerated

4403—Wood in the rough, whether or not stripped of bark or sapwood, or roughly squared

4404—Hoopwood; split poles; piles, pickets, and stakes of wood, pointed but not sawn lengthwise; wooden sticks, roughly trimmed but not turned, bent, or otherwise worked, suitable for the manufacture of walking-sticks, umbrellas, tool handles, or the like; chipwood and the like

4405—Wood wool (excelsior); wood flour

4406—Railway or tramway sleepers (cross-ties) of wood

4407—Wood sawn or chipped lengthwise, sliced or peeled, whether or not planed, sanded, or finger-jointed, of a thickness exceeding 6 mm

4408—Veneer sheets and sheets for plywood (whether or not spliced) and other wood sawn lengthwise, sliced or peeled, whether or not planed, sanded, or finger-jointed, of a thickness not exceeding 6 mm

4409—Wood (including strips and friezes for parquet flooring, not assembled) continuously shaped (tongued, grooved, rebated, chamfered, V-jointed, beaded, molded, rounded, or the like) along any of its edges or faces, whether or not planed, sanded, or finger-jointed

4410—Particle board and similar board of wood or other ligneous materials, whether or not agglomerated with resins or other organic binding substances.

4411—Fiberboard of wood or other ligneous materials, whether or not bonded with resins or other organic substances

4412—Plywood, veneered panels, and similar laminated wood

4413—Densified wood, in blocks, plates, strips, or profile shapes

4414—Wooden frames for paintings, photographs, mirrors, or similar objects

4415—Packing cases, boxes, crates, drums, and similar packings, of wood; cable-drums, of wood; pallets, box-pallets, and other load boards, of wood; pallet collars of wood

4416—Casks, barrels, vats, tubs, and other coopers' products and parts thereof, of wood, including staves

4417—Tools, tool bodies, tool handles, broom or brush bodies, and handles, of wood; boot or shoe lasts and trees, of wood

4418—Builders' joinery and carpentry of wood, including cellular wood panels and assembled parquet panels; shingles and shakes

4419—Tableware and kitchenware, of wood

4420—Wood marquetry and inlaid wood; caskets and cases for jewelry or cutlery and similar articles, of wood; statuettes and other ornaments, of wood; wooden articles of furniture not falling within chapter 94

4421—Other articles of wood

For more details regarding classifications of the specific product you are interested in importing, consult a customs broker, the appropriate commodity specialist at your nearest customs port, or the HTSUS. The 2001 HTSUS is available online from the Customs Service (www.customs.gov/impoexpo/impoexpo.htm) or for purchase from the U.S. Government Printing Office (see resources at the end of this chapter), and may be found in larger public libraries. For a general discussion of customs classification, see "Classification—Liquidation" on page 229.

Dutiable Status of Goods

For more information about duty rates and binding decisions see "Dutiable Status of Goods" on page 203; for a discussion of temporary importation of goods see "Temporary Free Importations" on page 205.

Valuation

Importers have a responsibility to use what the U.S. Customs Service deems, "reasonable care," when determining the value of their goods. They must also provide any additional information that the Customs Service needs for setting a final value on the goods. This process involves a number of factors and can be somewhat complicated; importers must be aware of applicable issues and details. Valuation information applies to all types of commodities, for further discussion on the subject see "Customs Valuation" on page 267.

Import Duties

Import duties vary (often dramatically) depending upon the Harmonized Tariff Schedule (HTSUS) classification of the goods or products imported. Since some products that look alike have different HTSUS classifications and different rates of duty, proper classification is vital. Note that "differences of opinion" between importers and the Bureau of Customs and Border Protection regarding classification keeps customs attorneys very busy.

Import duties can be assessed on the imported value of the goods ("ad valorem" rates of duty such as 2%, 4.4%, 50%, etc.), total units or weight of the goods ("specific" rates of duty such as 2 cents each or 1.5 cents/pound, etc.) or on a combination basis ("compound" rates of duty such as 5 cents each plus 6%).

Listed below is a sampling of several Column 1 import duty rates for Chapter 44 products:
Fuel wood, in logs, in billets, in twigs, in faggots or in similar forms (4401.10.00 00): Free
to
Sanded, grooved, or otherwise advanced in condition (4409.10.65 00): 4.9%

For specific information on US import duties refer to the Harmonized Tariff Schedule of the US. The print version is available from the US Government Printing Office as well as third party suppliers who often add special features. Online versions are available in both static PDF pages as well as in formats with excellent search functionality. Search the Web with the term "Harmonized Tariff Schedule" to find sources.

Entry and Documentation

The entry of merchandise is a two-part process consisting of 1) filing the documentation necessary to determine whether merchandise may be released from Customs custody, and 2) filing the documents that contain information for duty assessment and statistical purposes. In certain instances, all documents must be filed and accepted by Customs prior to release of the goods. Unless you have been granted an extension, you must file entry documents at a location specified by the port or area director within five working days of your shipment's date of arrival at a U.S. port of entry. These include a number of standard documents required by Customs for any entry, and:

- FWS Import Declaration Form 3-177, original and 3 copies (if the products are derived from endangered species)

- FWS permit or import documentation Form 3-200 (if the products are derived from endangered species)

- Permits or certificates required under CITES, ESA, and any other regulations applicable to the particular shipment (if the products are derived from endangered species)

- Certificates of export, origin, sanitation, inspection, and other conditions from the country of origin or export, as required by Customs, FWS, or USDA

- USDA importer's declaration (if importing lumber or raw wood)

- USDA APHIS permit for import of logs or lumber with bark attached Form PPQ 585 (if required by USDA, such as for importing elm logs or lumber)

- Canadian Government Export Notice (if importing softwood originating in Canada)

- Copy of air waybill or bill of lading

- Copy of invoice (pro forma invoice if shipment is noncommercial)

After you present the entry, Customs may examine your shipment or may waive examination. The shipment is then released provided no legal or regulatory violations have been noted. You must then file entry summary documentation and deposit estimated duties at a designated customhouse within 10 working days of your shipment's release. For a detailed description of entry procedures, standard documentation, and informal entry, see "Entry Process" on page 185.

Informed Compliance. Informed compliance was introduced with the Customs Modernization Act of 1993 (Mod Act) and defines the relationship between importers and the Customs Service. It sets out the responsibilities of both parties. Providing the correct documentation and information for entry is a key factor that will make your importing operation run smoothly. We recommend that importers become familiar with the concept of informed comliance and the responsibilities that they have under the Mod Act. For further discussion about informed compliance see "Informed Compliance" on page 211.

Entry Invoice. If you are importing wood classified under the following headings, the entry invoice must additionally include the information noted below:

1) The quantity of the wood in cubic meters (m^3) before dressing, if importing the following: Wood sawed or chipped lengthwise, sliced or peeled, whether or not planed, sanded, or finger-jointed, of a thickness exceeding 6 mm (lumber) (HTSUS heading 4407), and wood continuously shaped along any of its edges or faces, whether or not planed, sanded, or fingerjointed—coniferous (HTSUS subheading 4409.10.90) and nonconiferous (HTSUS subheading 4409.20.90)—and dutiable on the basis of cubic meters.

2) The density in grams per cubic cm (cm^3) if importing the following: Fiberboard of wood or other ligneous materials whether or not bonded with resins or other organic substances (HTSUS

subheadings 4412.11, 4412.12, and 4412.19) and classifiable according to its density.

3) The thickness of each ply in mm, if importing the following: Plywood consisting solely of sheets of wood (HTSUS subheading 4412.11, 4412.12, and 4412.19) and classifiable according to the thickness of the wood sheets. For more general information about invoices see "Invoices" on page 277.

Note: The Entry and Documentation section has been carefully designed to supply you, the importer, with sample documents and directions on how to satisfy Customs requirements. Be aware that you should consult the applicable authorities to ensure that you are correctly following the most current procedures.

Prohibitions and Restrictions

Lumber and Raw Wood. At the port of entry, the USDA inspector will examine lumber and raw wood for pest infestation. If an infestation is found or reasonably suspected, the inspector has authority to deny entry and to dispose of the shipment by the least drastic means available that will protect against spread of the infestation. Disposition will be at the expense of the owner of the shipment.

Elm Logs and Lumber. The import of elm logs and elm lumber with bark attached requires a permit from AHPIS.

Plants and Plant Products. When plants and plant products are particularly vulnerable to plant pests for which the U.S. has no reliable method of extermination, USDA designates those items as being subject to prohibitory orders. Prohibitory orders forbid completely the entry of designated plants and plant products. Restrictive orders allow the entry of plants or plant products either under a treatment or an inspection requirement. If the plant product you wish to import is under restrictive orders, you will need an APHIS import permit, issued only to resident importers in the U.S. Once a permit has been issued to you, you will be held responsible for carrying out any conditions of entry specified in the permit. Questions on entry requirements for plants and plant products should be addressed to USDA APHIS PPQ (see addresses at end of this chapter).

Endangered Species. If you are importing exotic woods or articles derived from exotic woods, you should ascertain whether the tree from which the wood is derived is a protected species. The import of certain woods is restricted or prohibited because of species status under the CITES, ESA, or another U.S. law. For example, importation of species listed in CITES Appendix I for commercial purposes is prohibited. Prohibitions and restrictions may additionally be imposed by the law of the exporting country. You are legally responsible for fulfilling the requirements of all of them, as well as any laws of your country of export. If you import, or attempt to import, a product in violation of a wildlife or endangered species law, even if you are not aware of the violation, your product may be seized, you may be charged substantial fines, and you could be imprisoned.

Country-Specific Import Restrictions

Canadian Softwood Lumber. If you are importing softwood lumber from Canada, you must obtain an Export Notice from the Canadian Government. This requirement is enforced and administered on the U.S. side by the U.S. Department of Commerce (DOC). The notice requires much the same information found on the normal invoice, but also includes the Canadian province of origination and the amount of Canadian tax levied before entry into the U.S. Your Export Notice must be filled out in full, and you must present it to U.S. Customs officials at the U.S. port of entry. For more information, contact the DOC (see addresses at end of this chapter).

Siberian Logs. APHIS has issued PQA-authorized administrative quarantines on raw lumber from Siberia. These products are considered to constitute a substantial risk to U.S. agriculture. The agency is in process of developing new regulations that will specify conditions of entry for these products. Until such regulations are promulgated, all raw logs from Siberia are prohibited. Any such shipment will be refused entry.

Marking and Labeling Requirements

Endangered Tree Species. All shipments of wood and wood products derived from endangered tree species must be marked on the outside of the container with the names and addresses of the exporter and importer, an accurate identification of the species, and the numbers of each species in the container.

For a general discussion of U.S. Customs marking and labeling requirements, see "Country of Origin Marking" on page 236, "Special Marking Requirements" on page 238 and "Marking—False Impression" on page 239.

Shipping Considerations

You will need to ensure that your goods are packaged and shipped with care so that they pass smoothly through Customs and arrive in good condition. You are responsible for ensuring that the shipment is in compliance with all applicable government regulations for packaging and shipping. In most instances, you should not leave these arrangements solely to the discretion of your supplier. Careful preparation of the cargo and selection of the mode of transport can be essential to a cost-effective, timely delivery of undamaged goods. We strongly advise you to consult your shipping representative, insurance agent, or freight broker for advice on packing and shipping.

Wood and wood products may be shipped in bulk, bags, crates, or other types of containers, depending on the type of product and whether it is prepackaged. General considerations include protection from contamination, weather, and pests. Containers should be constructed so as to be safe for handling during transport. If a product must be kept in a sanitary environment, all tables, utensils, platforms, and devices used for moving or handling the product, the compartments in which it is stowed while being transported will need to be maintained in a sanitary condition. Safety precautions should also be implemented as required to protect against breakage and combustion. Containers should be constructed so as to be safe for handling during transport.

Publications and WWW Resources

For questions regarding the Convention on Interantional Trade in Endangered Species of Wild Fauna and Flora (CITES) refer to:

>CITES Secretariat
>15 chemin des Anemones
>1219 Chatelaine-Geneva
>Switzerland
>Tel: [41] (22) 917-8139/40
>Fax: [41] (22) 797-3417
>Website: www.cites.org
>Email: cites@unep.ch

The *Harmonized Tariff Schedule of the United States (2001)* (HTSUS) is available to view on the Customs Service website (www.customs.gov), or you may purchase a printed version from:

>U.S. Government Printing Office
>Superintendent of Documents
>710 North Capital Street NW
>Washington DC 20401
>Tel: (202) 512-1800
>Fax: (202) 512-1657
>Website: www.access.gpo.gov

The USGPO also has copies of specific laws available for purchase. The USGPO accepts orders made by fax, phone or placed over the Internet, as well as mail orders paid by credit card. All orders must be accompanied by payment. Credit cards, checks drawn on a U.S. bank, or an international money order are all acceptable.

Relevant Government Agencies

Address your inquiries regarding USDA requirements for importation of lumber or raw wood to:

>**Animal and Plant Health Inspection Service (APHIS)**
>**Plant Protection and Quarantine (PPQ)**
>**Director's Office**
>4700 River Rd., Unit 131
>Riverdale, MD 20737
>Tel: (301) 734-8261
>Tel (PPQ permits): (301) 734-8758
>Website: www.aphis.usda.gov/ppq

Address your questions regarding endangered species regulation to:

>**U.S. Fish and Wildlife Service (FWS)**
>**Office of Management Authority**
>4401 N. Fairfax Dr.
>Arlington, VA 22203-0700
>Tel: (703) 358-2104
>Website: www.fws.gov

Address your questions regarding importation of wood and wood products to your local Customs port director. For addresses refer to "U.S. Customs and Border Protection Offices" on page 65 or contact:

>**U.S. Customs and Border Protection**
>**Customs Headquarters**
>1300 Pennsylvania Avenue NW
>Washington DC 20229
>Tel: (202) 354-1000
>Website: www.customs.treas.gov

Laws and Regulations

The following laws and regulations may be relevant to the importation of woods and wood products. The laws are contained in the United States Code (USC), and the regulations are published in the Code of Federal Regulations (CFR), both of which are available at larger public and law libraries. Copies of specific laws are also available from the United States Government Printing Office (address above).

15 USC 2051 et seq.
Consumer Product Safety Act
This Act gives the Consumer Product Safety Commission authority to set safety standards, testing procedures, and reporting requirements to ensure that consumer products not already covered under other regulations are not harmful.

18 USC 42 et seq.
Importation of Animals, Birds, Fish, and Plants
This Act governs the importation of plants, mammals, birds, fish, amphibia, and reptiles into the U.S. and authorizes U.S. Customs to enforce the import requirements.

7 CFR Part 351
Regulations of USDA on Plant Inspection
These regulations set forth the plant imports that are prohibited, the requirements for entering restricted plants by mail, and the inspection procedures followed by the USDA's Animal and Plant Health Inspection Service (APHIS).

19 CFR 12.10 et seq.
Regulations of Customs on Plant Inspection and Entry
These regulations specify the procedure for importing plants and plant products into the U.S. including USDA inspection requirements, submission of notices of arrival for products requiring quarantine permits, release under bond, disposition of unclaimed or detained shipments.

Convention on International Trade in Endangered Species of Wild Fauna and Flora (CITES)
This comprehensive wildlife treaty signed by over 100 countries, including the United States, regulates and in many cases prohibits commercial imports and exports of wild animal and plant species threatened by trade.

16 USC 1531
Endangered Species Act of 1973
This Act prohibits the import and export of species listed as endangered and most species listed as threatened. It is the U.S. law that implements CITES.

16 USC 3371 et seq.
Control of Illegally Taken Fish and Wildlife
This Act prohibits the import of species taken, possessed, transported, or sold in violation of the law of a foreign country.

Principal Exporting Countries

The following listing includes samples of the main supplier nations of the products of this chapter. It is organized by HTSUS major heading. (Refer to "Customs Classification" above for the product codes.) Countries are listed in rank order of the value of products imported to the U.S. Statistics represent customs value of entries for 2002 from the Bureau of Census, U.S. Department of Commerce.

4401—Canada, Argentina, Honduras, Mexico, France, China

4402—Mexico, Canada, China, Netherlands, Argentina, South Korea, Brazil, Japan, Germany, Indonesia

4403—Canada, Mexico, Brazil, New Zealand, Austria, Chile, Finland, Australia, France, Germany

4404—Canada, Indonesia, China, Chile, Singapore, Malaysia, Honduras, Brazil

4405—Germany, Canada, Belgium, China

4406—Canada, Guyana, Cameroon, South Africa, Ivory Coast, Russia, Belgium

4407—Canada, Brazil, Chile, New Zealand, Germany, Sweden

4408—Canada, Brazil, Germany, Ghana, Italy

4409—Canada, Chile, Brazil, China, Mexico, New Zealand

4410—Canada, Ireland, Mexico, France, Germany, Colombia, Spain, Lithuania, South Africa

4411—Canada, Germany, Belgium, Chile, Spain, Brazil, Austria, New Zealand, Sweden

4412—Canada, Indonesia, Brazil, Malaysia, Russia, China, Chile, Germany, Finland

4413—Germany, Italy, Russia, Estonia, China, Ecuador, Canada, Mexico

4414—China, Thailand, Mexico, Indonesia, Canada, Taiwan, India, Malaysia, Italy, Hong Kong

4415—Canada, Mexico, China, Brazil, Chile, Germany, Argentina, Honduras, Malaysia, Netherlands

4416—France, Hungary, Canada, Italy, Bulgaria, Chile, China, Netherlands, Australia

4417—Canada, Indonesia, Italy, Brazil, Chile, Honduras, China, Germany

4418—Canada, Brazil, Chile, China, Indonesia, Mexico, Malaysia

4419—China, Thailand, Taiwan, United Kingdom, Philippines, Canada, Japan, India, Malaysia, Italy, Latvia

4420—China, Thailand, Indonesia, India, Taiwan, Philippines, Italy, Canada, Mexico, Hong Kong, Ghana

Chapter 45:
Cork and Articles of Cork

This chapter relates to the importation of cork and cork articles, which are classified under Chapter 45 of the Harmonized Tariff Schedule of the United States (HTSUS). Specifically, it includes natural raw cork, waste cork, and crushed, granulated or ground cork; debacked or squared cork pieces; cork stoppers, disks, wafers, washers, wall coverings, and other cork articles; and items made of agglomerated cork, such as vulcanized sheets, insulation, floor and wall coverings, and stoppers, disks, wafers, washers, gaskets, and other cork seals.

If you are interested in importing cork parts for footwear, you should refer to Commodity Index Chapter 64. Requirements for importing headgear and headgear parts made of cork are covered in chapter 65. If you are interested in importing toys, games, or sports equipment that contain cork pieces, refer to Chapter 95.

Note: To understand key issues that will enable you to make best use of the information in this section we recommend that you see "Introduction" on page 425.

Key Factors

Although most importers use the services of a licensed customs broker in making their entries, and we recommend this practice, you should be aware of the regulatory, entry, and documentation issues involved in importing your product. You, as importer, are ultimately responsible for the fulfillment of any legal requirements applicable to your shipment.

General Considerations

Importation of cork is straightforward. There are no restrictions or prohibitions. You need no permits or licenses, nor is special entry paperwork required.

Customs Classification

For customs purposes, cork and cork articles are classified under Chapter 45 of the HTSUS. This chapter is broken into major headings, which are further divided into subheadings, and often sub-subheadings, each of which has its own HTSUS classification number. For example, the 2001 HTSUS number for compressed cork insulation is 4504.10.20, indicating it is a sub-subcategory of blocks, plates, sheets, and strip, etc. (4504.10), which is a subcategory of the major heading, agglomerated cork (4504). There are four major headings within Chapter 45.

4501—Natural cork, raw or simply prepared; waste cork; crushed, granulated, or ground cork

4502—Natural cork, debacked or roughly squared, or in rectangular (including square) blocks, plates, sheets, or strip (including sharp-edged blanks for corks or stoppers)

4503—Articles of natural cork

4504—Agglomerated cork (with or without a binding substance) and articles of agglomerated cork

For more details regarding classifications of the specific product you are interested in importing, consult a customs broker, the appropriate commodity specialist at your nearest customs port, or the HTSUS. The 2001 HTSUS is available online from the Customs Service (www.customs.gov/impoexpo/impoexpo.htm) or for purchase from the U.S. Government Printing Office (see resources at the end of this chapter), and may be found in larger public libraries. For a general discussion of customs classification, see "Classification—Liquidation" on page 229.

Dutiable Status of Goods

For more information about duty rates and binding decisions see "Dutiable Status of Goods" on page 203; for a discussion of temporary importation of goods see "Temporary Free Importations" on page 205.

Valuation

Importers have a responsibility to use what the U.S. Customs Service deems, "reasonable care," when determining the value of their goods. They must also provide any additional information that the Customs Service needs for setting a final value on the goods. This process involves a number of factors and can be somewhat complicated; importers must be aware of applicable issues and details. Valuation information applies to all types of commodities, for further discussion on the subject see "Customs Valuation" on page 267.

Import Duties

Import duties vary (often dramatically) depending upon the Harmonized Tariff Schedule (HTSUS) classification of the goods or products imported. Since some products that look alike have different HTSUS classifications and different rates of duty, proper classification is vital. Note that "differences of opinion" between importers and the Bureau of Customs and Border Protection regarding classification keeps customs attorneys very busy.

Import duties can be assessed on the imported value of the goods ("ad valorem" rates of duty such as 2%, 4.4%, 50%, etc.), total units or weight of the goods ("specific" rates of duty such as 2 cents each or 1.5 cents/pound, etc.) or on a combination basis ("compound" rates of duty such as 5 cents each plus 6%).

Listed below is a sampling of several Column 1 import duty rates for Chapter 45 products:

Natural cork, debacked or roughly squared, or inrectangular (including square) blocks, plates, sheets or strip (including sharp-edged blanks for corks or stoppers) (4502.00.00.00): Free

to

Other articles of natural cork (4503.90.60.00): 14%

For specific information on US import duties refer to the Harmonized Tariff Schedule of the US. The print version is available from the US Government Printing Office as well as third party suppliers who often add special features. Online versions are available in both static PDF pages as well as in formats with excellent search functionality. Search the Web with the term "Harmonized Tariff Schedule" to find sources.

Entry and Documentation

The entry of merchandise is a two-part process consisting of 1) filing the documentation necessary to determine whether merchandise may be released from Customs custody, and 2) filing the documents that contain information for duty assessment and statistical purposes. In certain instances, all documents must be filed and accepted by Customs prior to release of the goods. Unless you have been granted an extension, you must file entry documents at a location specified by the port or area director within five working days of your shipment's date of arrival at a U.S. port of entry. These include a number of standard documents required by Customs for any entry.

After you present the entry, Customs may examine your shipment or may waive examination. The shipment is then released provided no legal or regulatory violations have been noted. You must then file entry summary documentation and deposit estimated duties at a designated customhouse within 10 working days of your shipment's release. For a detailed description of entry procedures, standard documentation, and informal entry, see "Entry Process" on page 185.

Informed Compliance. Informed compliance was introduced with the Customs Modernization Act of 1993 (Mod Act) and defines the relationship between importers and the Customs Service. It sets out the responsibilities of both parties. Providing the correct documentation and information for entry is a key factor that will make your importing operation run smoothly. We recommend that importers become familiar with the concept of informed comliance and the responsibilities that they have under the Mod Act. For further discussion about informed compliance see "Informed Compliance" on page 211.

Note: The Entry and Documentation section has been carefully designed to supply you, the importer, with sample documents and directions on how to satisfy Customs requirements. Be aware that you should consult the applicable authorities to ensure that you are correctly following the most current procedures.

Marking and Labeling Requirements

For a general discussion of U.S. Customs marking and labeling requirements, see "Country of Origin Marking" on page 236, "Special Marking Requirements" on page 238 and "Marking—False Impression" on page 239.

Shipping Considerations

You will need to ensure that your goods are packaged and shipped with care so that they pass smoothly through Customs and arrive in good condition. You are responsible for ensuring that the shipment is in compliance with all applicable government regulations for packaging and shipping. In most instances, you should not leave these arrangements solely to the discretion of your supplier. Careful preparation of the cargo and selection of the mode of transport can be essential to a cost-effective, timely delivery of undamaged goods. We strongly advise you to consult your shipping representative, insurance agent, or freight broker for advice on packing and shipping.

Cork and cork articles may be shipped in bulk, bags, crates, or other types of containers, depending on the type of product and whether it is prepackaged. General considerations include protection from contamination, weather, and pests. If a product must be kept in a sanitary environment, all tables, utensils, platforms, and devices used for moving or handling the product, the compartments in which it is stowed while being transported will need to be maintained in a sanitary condition. Containers should be constructed so as to be safe for handling during transport.

Publications and WWW Resources

The *Harmonized Tariff Schedule of the United States (2001)* (HTSUS) is available to view on the Customs Service website (www.customs.gov), or you may purchase a printed version from:

U.S. Government Printing Office
Superintendent of Documents
710 North Capital Street NW
Washington DC 20401
Tel: (202) 512-1800
Fax: (202) 512-1657
Website: www.access.gpo.gov

The USGPO also has copies of specific laws available for purchase. The USGPO accepts orders made by fax, phone or placed over the Internet, as well as mail orders paid by credit card. All orders must be accompanied by payment. Credit cards, checks drawn on a U.S. bank, or an international money order are all acceptable.

Relevant Government Agencies

Address your questions regarding importation of cork to your local Customs port director. For addresses refer to "U.S. Customs and Border Protection Offices" on page 65 or contact:

U.S. Customs and Border Protection
Customs Headquarters
1300 Pennsylvania Avenue NW
Washington DC 20229
Tel: (202) 354-1000
Website: www.customs.treas.gov

Principal Exporting Countries

The following listing includes samples of the main supplier nations of the products of this chapter. It is organized by HTSUS major heading. (Refer to "Customs Classification" above for the product codes.) Countries are listed in rank order of the value of products imported to the U.S. Statistics represent customs value of entries for 2002 from the Bureau of Census, U.S. Department of Commerce.

4501—Portugal, China, Netherlands, France

4502—Portugal, Spain, India

4503—Portugal, Spain, France, Italy, Germany, Argentina, China, Australia, Taiwan, India

4504—Portugal, Spain, China, Italy, Canada, France, Mexico, Germany

Chapter 46:
Baskets and Wickerware

Full title: Manufactures of Straw, of Esparto, or of Other Plaiting Materials; Basketware and Wickerwork

This chapter relates to the importation of baskets and wickerware, which are classified under Chapter 46 of the Harmonized Tariff Schedule of the United States (HTSUS). Specifically, it includes plaited articles in sheets—such as mats, matting, and screens; and basketwork, wickerwork, and other shaped plaited articles—such as bags, handbags, and luggage. Articles covered in this chapter are those plaited from straw, osier, willow, bamboos, rushes, reeds, strips of wood, raffia, strips of other vegetable matter, bark, unspun natural textile fibers, and monofilament, strip, and similar forms of plastics and paper strips.

The importing of plaiting materials in unfinished form is covered in Commodity Index Chapter 14. If you are interested in importing articles plaited from strips of leather, composition leather, felt or other nonwoven fabrics, human hair, horsehair, textile rovings, yarn, or monofilament, strip, and the like, refer to Chapter 54. For the importing requirements related to twine, ropes, cables, and cordage, regardless of whether plaited, refer to Chapter 56. If you are interested in importing furniture, lamps, and lighting fixtures, you should read Chapter 94. Basketware for vehicles and bodies of vehicles is covered in Chapter 87, footwear in Chapter 64, headgear in Chapter 65, and wall coverings in Chapter 48.

Note: To understand key issues that will enable you to make best use of the information in this section we recommend that you see "Introduction" on page 425.

Key Factors

The key factors in the importation of baskets and wickerware are:

- Compliance with U.S. Department of Agriculture (USDA) random port-of-entry inspections, import restrictions and quarantines, and other entry requirements

- Compliance with Federal Plant Pest Act

- Compliance with Plant Quarantine Act

- Compliance with Fish and Wildlife Service (FWS) license, permit, country-of-origin permit, import documentation, and recordkeeping requirements (if the products are derived from endangered species)

- Entry at FWS-designated ports, and compliance with FWS and Customs advance notification and port-of-entry inspection requirements (if the products are derived from endangered species)

Although most importers use the services of a licensed customs broker in making their entries, and we recommend this practice, you should be aware of the regulatory, entry, and documentation issues involved in importing your product. You, as importer, are ultimately responsible for the fulfillment of any legal requirements applicable to your shipment.

General Considerations

Regulatory Agencies. The USDA administers applicable provisions of the Plant Quarantine Act (PQA), which are designed to prevent the introduction into the U.S. of any plant pest or disease potentially harmful to U.S. agriculture. The FWS, primarily under provisions of the U.S. Endangered Species Act (ESA) and the Convention on International Trade in Endangered Species of Wild Fauna and Flora (CITES), controls the importation of products derived from plants that are classified as endangered species. U.S. Customs enforces USDA and FWS requirements through entry documentation and restrictions.

Baskets and Wickerware. For most shipments of baskets and wickerware, importation is straightforward. With some exceptions, you do not need permits or licenses to import these products (see "Prohibitions and Restrictions" below). The USDA's Animal and Plant Health Inspection Service (APHIS) inspects shipments of baskets and wickerware on a random basis, depending on such factors as the port of entry, the country of origin, and the risk of contamination involved in the type of material being imported.

Entry may be denied for noncompliance with the regulations, and the shipment could be seized, quarantined, destroyed, treated, or otherwise dealt with at the discretion of the inspector. APHIS inspectors also enforce FWS requirements for plaited products derived from endangered plant species, the import of which may be prohibited or may require export and/or import permits (see below). You are responsible to be sure that your shipment is either not derived from listed species, or if it is, that you have the appropriate import authorization.

Exotic and Endangered Species. The FWS enforces a complex set of laws and regulations (see 50 CFR 1 et seq.) pertaining to endangered species product importation. These laws include CITES, the ESA, and a number of other U.S. laws, such as the Lacey Act (LA). Most foreign countries also have their own domestic measures, and you will need to meet the requirements of the country of export in addition to U.S. requirements. For more information, contact the FWS Office of Management Authority (OMA) (see addresses at end of this chapter).

Certain types of vegetable plaiting materials and products made from them are entirely prohibited, others are allowed entry only under permit and/or license, and still others are allowed entry only for specific noncommercial purposes. When applying for a permit, you must satisfy the requirements of all laws under which the species is protected. The following briefly describes the two major laws governing importation of protected products into the U.S. This discussion is not comprehensive or exhaustive. If you wish to import endangered species, you should always contact the FWS (see addresses at end of this chapter) with specific species information before making any transactions.

CITES. Over 100 nations participate in CITES, which took effect in May 1977. The degree of protection afforded to a species depends on which of the three CITES appendices contains the name of that species. Documentation required for import varies depending on the species, and the CITES section where it is listed. The CITES export documentation from the country of origin is always required. If you are importing a CITES-listed species from a country that does not participate in the treaty, you must still obtain from that nation documents that contain all the information normally required in CITES import permits.

Appendix I. This appendix lists species deemed presently threatened with extinction. Importation of Appendix I species for commercial purposes is prohibited. You must have two permits to import these species: one from the U.S., which must be obtained first, and one from the exporting country.

Appendix II. This appendix lists species that are not presently threatened with extinction but may become threatened if their trade is not regulated (e.g., boojum tree). There are no restrictions on the purpose of import, provided it is not detrimental to the survival of the species. You will need an export permit or reexport certificate from the exporting country.

Appendix III. This appendix lists species for which any CITES member country has domestic regulations "for the purpose of preventing or restricting exploitation, and as needing the cooperation of other Parties in control of trade." For example, Nepal lists several varieties of magnolia. Three different types of documents are issued for Appendix III species: 1) Export Permit: Issued for specimens that originated in a country that listed the species on Appendix III; 2) Certificate of Origin: Issued by any country other than the listing country if the species in question originated in that country; 3) Reexport Certificate: Issued for the export of Appendix III specimens that were previously imported into the U.S.

Exemptions. Under certain conditions, Certificates of Exemption may be issued for the importation of endangered species products listed under CITES. Exceptions are allowed for shipments of products transiting a country under Customs bond, shipments between U.S. states or territories, and certain personal or household effects. For information, contact FWS (see addresses at end of this chapter).

Permit Applications. Applications for CITES permits and certificates are available from the FWS Office of Management Authority (see addresses at end of this chapter). You will need to fill out the FWS Standard Permit Application **(Form 3-200)** and provide certain information specifically required under CITES. You should submit your application at least 60 days before the date you wish the permit to take effect. FWS charges processing fees for CITES applications.

ESA. The U.S. Endangered Species Act (ESA) was passed on December 28, 1973, to prevent the extinction of many species of animals and plants and to protect their habitats. By definition, an "endangered species" is any animal or plant listed by regulation as being in danger of extinction. A "threatened species" is any animal or plant likely to become endangered within the foreseeable future. The U.S. List of Endangered and Threatened Wildlife and Plants includes native and foreign species.

Permits. ESA's import provisions prohibit the import or export of any endangered or threatened species or products derived from them without one of the following permits from the FWS Federal Wildlife Permit Office (FWPO):

Endangered Species Permits: This permit is issued for importation for purposes of 1) scientific research; 2) enhancement of propagation or survival of the species; or 3) incidental taking.

Threatened Species Permits: This permit is issued for importation for purposes of 1) scientific research; 2) enhancement of propagation or survival of the species; 3) zoological, horticultural, or botanical exhibition; 4) education purposes; 5) special purposes consistent with ESA purposes and policy; or 6) incidental taking.

Permit Exemptions. A few imports of endangered species products are exempt from the ESA permit requirements. For example, if a species is listed as threatened or as an experimental population, special rules may allow otherwise prohibited activities. If you are unsure as to the exemption status of your import, contact FWS (see addresses at end of this chapter).

FWS Import Licenses. With some exceptions, persons engaged in the business of importing endangered species products valued in excess of $25,000 per year must be licensed by the FWS. If your annual importations are valued at less than $25,000, or if you qualify for another exemption from licensing, you are still responsible for keeping thorough records of all transactions and of making these records available to FWS officers if necessary. For a full description of exemptions from licensing, and of recordkeeping requirements, contact the FWS (see addresses at end of this chapter) or see 50 CFR 14.

Procedures at Port of Entry. At least 72 hours before your shipment is due to arrive at a designated port, you should notify U.S. Customs and the FWS inspectors of its expected arrival. The FWS conducts port-of-entry shipment inspections on a case-by-case basis, as determined by the inspection agent after looking at the entry paperwork. Both FWS and Customs may inspect your shipment to verify compliance with all of the legal requirements for entry. Any documentation required by the laws governing your import must be submitted by the time of entry. You must present an FWS Wildlife Declaration **Form 3-177**, available at the port of entry, with every shipment, regardless of any other paperwork required. Customs will not release your shipment until the import declaration has been signed off by an FWS agent.

Designated Ports. Shipments of endangered species products are restricted to designated U.S. ports of entry. All shipments must enter and leave through one of the ports listed in 50 CFR 14.12. If special circumstances prevent you from making your entry at a designated port, you will need to obtain an Exception to Designated Port Permit from the FWS Divisions of Law Enforcement (see addresses at end of this chapter).

Import Advisory

The endangered species issue is particularly important. As the list of endangered plants expands, the likelihood that your plaited article import is derived from a protected plant species increases. It is your responsibility as importer to be aware of the regulatory status of your commodity. If you have any doubts as to the compliance status of your product under the PQA, CITES, or the ESA, you should check with APHIS, the FWS, or U.S. Customs. Always be prepared to provide the common and scientific names of any species you have questions about or are planning to import. When you are unsure of the regulations governing the export or import of a product, check with the FWS before making a purchase. When in doubt, don't buy! The importation of products made from endangered species can be seized and in some cases the importer can be subject to substantial fines.

Customs Classification

For customs purposes, baskets and wickerware are classified under Chapter 46 of the HTSUS. This chapter is broken into major headings, which are further divided into subheadings, and often sub-subheadings, each of which has its own HTSUS classification number. For example, the 2001 HTSUS number for rattan webbing is 4601.20.20, indicating it is a sub-subcategory of mats, matting and screens of vegetable materials (4601.20), which is a subcategory of the major heading, plaits and similar products of plaiting materials, etc. (4601). There are two major headings within Chapter 46.

4601—Plaits and similar products of plaiting materials, whether or not assembled into strips; plaiting materials, plaits, and similar products of plaiting materials, bound together in parallel strands or woven, in sheet form, whether or not being finished articles (for example, mats, matting, screens)

4602—Basketwork, wickerwork, and other articles, made directly to shape from plaiting materials or made up from articles of heading 4601; articles of loofah

For more details regarding classifications of the specific product you are interested in importing, consult a customs broker, the appropriate commodity specialist at your nearest customs port, or the HTSUS. The 2001 HTSUS is available online from the Customs Service (www.customs.gov/impoexpo/impoexpo.htm) or for purchase from the U.S. Government Printing Office (see resources at the end of this chapter), and may be found in larger public libraries. For a general discussion of customs classification, see "Classification—Liquidation" on page 229.

Dutiable Status of Goods

For more information about duty rates and binding decisions see "Dutiable Status of Goods" on page 203; for a discussion of temporary importation of goods see "Temporary Free Importations" on page 205.

Valuation

Importers have a responsibility to use what the U.S. Customs Service deems, "reasonable care," when determining the value of their goods. They must also provide any additional information that the Customs Service needs for setting a final value on the goods. This process involves a number of factors and can be somewhat complicated; importers must be aware of applicable issues and details. Valuation information applies to all types of commodities, for further discussion on the subject see "Customs Valuation" on page 267.

Import Duties

Import duties vary (often dramatically) depending upon the Harmonized Tariff Schedule (HTSUS) classification of the goods or products imported. Since some products that look alike have different HTSUS classifications and different rates of duty, proper classification is vital. Note that "differences of opinion" between importers and the Bureau of Customs and Border Protection regarding classification keeps customs attorneys very busy.

Import duties can be assessed on the imported value of the goods ("ad valorem" rates of duty such as 2%, 4.4%, 50%, etc.), total units or weight of the goods ("specific" rates of duty such as 2 cents each or 1.5 cents/pound, etc.) or on a combination basis ("compound" rates of duty such as 5 cents each plus 6%).

Listed below is a sampling of several Column 1 import duty rates for Chapter 46 products:

Mats, matting and screens of vegetable materials (rattan webbing) (4601.20.20.00): Free

to

Luggage, handbags and flatgoods, whether or not lined (of bamboo) (4602.10.21.00): 6.2%

For specific information on US import duties refer to the Harmonized Tariff Schedule of the US. The print version is available from the US Government Printing Office as well as third party suppliers who often add special features. Online versions are available in both static PDF pages as well as in formats with excellent search functionality. Search the Web with the term "Harmonized Tariff Schedule" to find sources.

Entry and Documentation

The entry of merchandise is a two-part process consisting of 1) filing the documents necessary to determine whether merchandise may be released from Customs custody and 2) filing the documents that contain information for duty assessment and statistical purposes. In certain instances all documents must be filed and accepted by Customs prior to the release of the goods. Unless you have been granted an extension, you must file entry documents at a location specified by the port or area director within five working days of your shipment's date of arrival at a

U.S. port of entry. These include a number of standard documents required by Customs for any entry, and

- Phytosanitary certificate (if importing rice straw baskets originating in North Korea or grapevine baskets)
- FWS Import Declaration Form 3-177 original and 3 copies (if the products are derived from endangered species)
- FWS permit or import documentation (if the products are derived from endangered species)
- Permits or certificates required under ESA, and any other regulations applicable to the particular shipment (if the products are derived from endangered species CITES permits and certificates
- Certificates of export, origin, sanitation, inspection, and other conditions from the country of origin or export, as required by Customs, FWS, or USDA
- Copy of air waybill or bill of lading
- Copy of invoice (pro forma invoice if shipment is noncommercial)

After you present the entry, Customs may examine your shipment or may waive examination. The shipment is then released provided no legal or regulatory violations have been noted. You must then file entry summary documentation and deposit estimated duties at a designated customhouse within 10 working days of your shipment's release. For a detailed description of entry procedures, standard documentation, and informal entry, see "Entry Process" on page 185.

Informed Compliance. Informed compliance was introduced with the Customs Modernization Act of 1993 (Mod Act) and defines the relationship between importers and the Customs Service. It sets out the responsibilities of both parties. Providing the correct documentation and information for entry is a key factor that will make your importing operation run smoothly. We recommend that importers become familiar with the concept of informed comliance and the responsibilities that they have under the Mod Act. For further discussion about informed compliance see "Informed Compliance" on page 211.

Note: The Entry and Documentation section has been carefully designed to supply you, the importer, with sample documents and directions on how to satisfy Customs requirements. Be aware that you should consult the applicable authorities to ensure that you are correctly following the most current procedures.

Prohibitions and Restrictions

In general, any shipment of basketry is subject to random port-of-entry inspection by the USDA. If the inspector finds evidence of the presence of insects in your basketry, you may be required to submit your shipment to USDA-prescribed fumigation procedures. If the insect is of a kind for which there is no viable U.S. treatment, your shipment will be refused. Our source at USDA assured us that most shipments that are found to have insects in them can be treated to afford entry.

Baskets of Grapevines. Baskets made from grapevines must be accompanied by a Phytosanitary Certificate issued by the Plant Protection Service of the exporting country. The certificate must show evidence that the grapevines have been heat-treated to 135 degrees Fahrenheit (or the equivalent Celsius) for 2 hours. If your grapevine baskets are dry (not green or fresh) and you have no certification to present to the USDA at the port of entry, your shipment will be detained and samples will be taken and forwarded to the nearest USDA inspection station. If the examination procedure reveals live buds, your shipment will be refused entry.

Baskets of Rice Straw. Baskets made of rice straw that are intended for outdoor use will be refused entry. Those intended for indoor use

will be permitted. If your baskets could be construed as being both for indoor and outdoor use, the USDA is likely to refuse entry.

Baskets of Endangered Plant Species. The import of baskets made from endangered plant species—such as tree ferns—are restricted under CITES. Any such baskets offered for import must meet applicable CITES requirements, as enforced by the FWS and the USDA. If you are interested in importing this type of basketry, you should contact USDA's APHIS PPQ office (see addresses at end of this chapter).

Country-Specific Import Restrictions

Korean Rice Straw Baskets. Baskets made of rice straw and originating in North Korea must be accompanied by a Phytosanitary Certificate issued by the North Korean Plant Protection Service. The certificate must show that the shipment has been fumigated with methyl bromide. A shipment without certification will be denied entry into the U.S.

European Willow Baskets. If willow baskets imported from Europe are found, on inspection at the port of entry, to be green or fresh will be refused entry. Baskets of dry willow from Europe are admissible, as are baskets of green or fresh willow from non-European countries.

Corn Baskets and Wickerware. Corn and closely related plants and their parts (including those of the genus *Chionachne, Coix, Echinochloa, Eleusina, Euchleana, Miscanthus, Panicum, Pennisetum, Polytoca, Sclerachne, Setaria, Sorghum, Trilobachne,* and *Tripsicum*), including materials used in plaited articles, are banned from importation into the U.S. if they originate from the countries listed: Africa (all countries), Australia, Bangladesh, Bhutan, Brunei, Bulgaria, Burma (Myanmar), Cambodia (Kampuchea), Hong Kong, India, Nepal, New Zealand, North Korea, Oceania, Pakistan, Papua New Guinea, People's Republic of China, Philippines, Russia, and the other republics of the former Soviet Union, Singapore, South Korea, Sri Lanka, Taiwan, Thailand, and Vietnam. Corn-related products from other countries require prior USDA approval.

Marking and Labeling Requirements

Endangered Plant Species. All shipments of baskets and wickerware derived from endangered plant species must be marked on the outside of the container with the names and addresses of the exporter and importer, an accurate identification of the species, and the numbers of each species in the container.

For a general discussion of U.S. Customs marking and labeling requirements, see "Country of Origin Marking" on page 236, "Special Marking Requirements" on page 238 and "Marking—False Impression" on page 239.

Shipping Considerations

You will need to ensure that your goods are packaged and shipped with care so that they arrive in good condition and pass smoothly through Customs. You are responsible for ensuring that the shipment is in compliance with all applicable government regulations for packaging and shipping. In most instances, you should not leave these arrangements solely to the discretion of your supplier. Careful preparation of the cargo and selection of the mode of transport can be essential to a cost-effective, timely delivery of undamaged goods. We strongly advise you to consult your shipping representative, insurance agent, or freight broker for advice on packing and shipping.

Baskets and wickerware may be transported in bulk, boxes, crates, or other forms of packaging. General considerations include protection from infestation by insects, contamination by dirt or other foreign matter, and damage from exposure to dampness or other weather conditions.

Publications and WWW Resources

For questions regarding the Convention on Interantional Trade in Endangered Species of Wild Fauna and Flora (CITES) refer to:

CITES Secretariat
15 chemin des Anemones
1219 Chatelaine-Geneva
Switzerland
Tel: [41] (22) 917-8139/40
Fax: [41] (22) 797-3417
Website: www.cites.org
Email: cites@unep.ch

The *Harmonized Tariff Schedule of the United States (2001)* (HTSUS) is available to view on the Customs Service website (www.customs.gov), or you may purchase a printed version from:

U.S. Government Printing Office
Superintendent of Documents
710 North Capital Street NW
Washington DC 20401
Tel: (202) 512-1800
Fax: (202) 512-1657
Website: www.access.gpo.gov

The USGPO also has copies of specific laws available for purchase. The USGPO accepts orders made by fax, phone or placed over the Internet, as well as mail orders paid by credit card. All orders must be accompanied by payment. Credit cards, checks drawn on a U.S. bank, or an international money order are all acceptable.

Relevant Government Agencies

Address your questions regarding USDA requirements for imported baskets and wickerware to:

Animal and Plant Health Inspection Service (APHIS)
Plant Protection and Quarantine (PPQ)
Director's Office
4700 River Rd., Unit 131
Riverdale, MD 20737
Tel: (301) 734-8261
Tel (PPQ permits): (301) 734-8758
Website: www.aphis.usda.gov/ppq

Address your questions regarding endangered species regulation to:

U.S. Fish and Wildlife Service (FWS)
Office of Management Authority
4401 N. Fairfax Dr.
Arlington, VA 22203-0700
Tel: (703) 358-2104
Website: www.fws.gov

Address your questions regarding the importation of baskets and wickerware to your local Customs port director. For addresses refer to "U.S. Customs and Border Protection Offices" on page 65 or contact:

U.S. Customs and Border Protection
Customs Headquarters
1300 Pennsylvania Avenue NW
Washington DC 20229
Tel: (202) 354-1000
Website: www.customs.treas.gov

Laws and Regulations

The following laws and regulations may be relevant to the importation of woods and wood products. The laws are contained in the United States Code (USC), and the regulations are published in the Code of Federal Regulations (CFR), both of which are available at larger public and law libraries. Copies of specific laws are also available from the United States Government Printing Office (address above).

18 USC 42 et seq.
Importation of Animals, Birds, Fish, and Plants
This Act governs the importation of plants, mammals, birds, fish, amphibia, and reptiles into the U.S. and authorizes U.S. Customs to enforce the import requirements.

7 CFR Part 351
Regulations of USDA on Plant Inspection
These regulations set forth the plant imports that are prohibited, the requirements for entering restricted plants by mail, and the inspection procedures followed by the USDA's Animal and Plant Health Inspection Service (APHIS).

19 CFR 12.10 et seq.
Regulations of Customs on Plant Inspection and Entry
These regulations specify the procedure for importing plants and plant products into the U.S, including USDA inspection requirements, submission of notices of arrival for products requiring quarantine permits, release under bond, disposition of unclaimed or detained shipments.

Convention on International Trade in Endangered Species of Wild Fauna and Flora (CITES)
This comprehensive wildlife treaty signed by over 100 countries, including the United States, regulates and in many cases prohibits commercial imports and exports of wild animal and plant species threatened by trade.

16 USC 1531
Endangered Species Act of 1973
This Act prohibits the import and export of species listed as endangered and most species listed as threatened. It is the U.S. law that implements CITES.

16 USC 3371 et seq.
Control of Illegally Taken Fish and Wildlife
This Act prohibits the import of species taken, possessed, transported, or sold in violation of the law of a foreign country.

Principal Exporting Countries

The following listing includes samples of the main supplier nations of the products of this chapter. It is organized by HTSUS major heading. (Refer to "Customs Classification" above for the product codes.) Countries are listed in rank order of the value of products imported to the U.S. Statistics represent customs value of entries for 2002 from the Bureau of Census, U.S. Department of Commerce.

4601—China, India, South Korea, Taiwan, Philippines, Indonesia

4602—China, Philippines, Indonesia, Hong Kong, Canada, Taiwan, Vietnam, India, Thailand, El Salvador

Chapter 47:
Wood Pulp and Paper Waste

Full title: Pulp of Wood or of Other Fibrous Cellulosic Material; Waste and Scrap of Paper or Paperboard

This chapter relates to the importation of wood pulp and paper waste, which are classified under Chapter 47 of the Harmonized Tariff Schedule of the United States (HTSUS). Specifically, it includes mechanical, chemical, and semichemical wood pulps; fibrous cellulosic pulps; and waste and scrap.

If you are interested in importing paper and paperboard products, you should refer to Commodity Index Chapter 48. The import requirements for wood and wood products are covered in Chapter 44.

Note: To understand key issues that will enable you to make best use of the information in this section we recommend that you see "Introduction" on page 425.

Key Factors

The key factors in the importation of wood pulp and paper waste are:

- Compliance with U.S. Customs documentation
- Compliance with invoice requirements (if importing chemical wood pulp, dissolving grades)

Although most importers use the services of a licensed customs broker in making their entries, and we recommend this practice, you should be aware of the regulatory, entry, and documentation issues involved in importing your product. You, as importer, are ultimately responsible for the fulfillment of any legal requirements applicable to your shipment.

General Considerations

Importation of wood pulp and paper waste is straightforward. There are no restrictions or prohibitions. You do not need permits or licenses, nor is special entry paperwork required. If you are importing chemical wood pulp of dissolving grades (HTSUS heading 4702), your entry invoice must show certain additional information.

Customs Classification

For customs purposes, wood pulp and paper waste are classified under Chapter 47 of the HTSUS. This chapter is broken into major headings, which are further divided into subheadings, and often sub-subheadings, each of which has its own HTSUS classification number. For example, the 2001 HTSUS number for cotton linters pulp is 4706.10.00, indicating it is a subcategory of the major heading, pulps of fibers derived from recovered paper or paperboard or of other fibrous cellulosic material (4706). There are seven major headings within Chapter 47.

4701—Mechanical wood pulp

4702—Chemical wood pulp, dissolving grades

4703—Chemical wood pulp, soda or sulfate, other than dissolving grades

4704—Chemical wood pulp, sulfite, other than dissolving grades

4705—Semichemical wood pulp

4706—Pulps of fibers derived from recovered (waste and scrap) paper or paperboard or of other fibrous cellulosic material

4707—Recovered (waste and scrap) paper and paperboard

For more details regarding classifications of the specific product you are interested in importing, consult a customs broker, the appropriate commodity specialist at your nearest customs port, or the HTSUS. The 2001 HTSUS is available online from the Customs Service (www.customs.gov/impoexpo/impoexpo.htm) or for purchase from the U.S. Government Printing Office (see resources at the end of this chapter), and may be found in larger public libraries. For a general discussion of customs classification, see "Classification—Liquidation" on page 229.

Dutiable Status of Goods

For more information about duty rates and binding decisions see "Dutiable Status of Goods" on page 203; for a discussion of temporary importation of goods see "Temporary Free Importations" on page 205.

Valuation

Importers have a responsibility to use what the U.S. Customs Service deems, "reasonable care," when determining the value of their goods. They must also provide any additional information that the Customs Service needs for setting a final value on the goods. This process involves a number of factors and can be somewhat complicated; importers must be aware of applicable issues and details. Valuation information applies to all types of commodities, for further discussion on the subject see "Customs Valuation" on page 267.

Import Duties

Import duties vary (often dramatically) depending upon the Harmonized Tariff Schedule (HTSUS) classification of the goods or products imported. Since some products that look alike have different HTSUS classifications and different rates of duty, proper classification is vital. Note that "differences of opinion" between importers and the Bureau of Customs and Border Protection regarding classification keeps customs attorneys very busy.

Import duties can be assessed on the imported value of the goods ("ad valorem" rates of duty such as 2%, 4.4%, 50%, etc.), total units or weight of the goods ("specific" rates of duty such as 2 cents each or 1.5 cents/pound, etc.) or on a combination basis ("compound" rates of duty such as 5 cents each plus 6%).

Listed below is a sampling of several Column 1 import duty rates for Chapter 47 products:
Mechanical woodpulp (4701.00.00.00): Free
and
Wood pulp obtained by a combination of mechanical and chemical pulping processes (4705.00.00.00): Free

For specific information on US import duties refer to the Harmonized Tariff Schedule of the US. The print version is available from the US Government Printing Office as well as third party suppliers who often add special features. Online versions are available in both static PDF pages as well as in formats with excellent search functionality. Search the Web with the term "Harmonized Tariff Schedule" to find sources.

Entry and Documentation

The entry of merchandise is a two-part process consisting of 1) filing the documentation necessary to determine whether merchandise may be released from Customs custody, and 2) filing the documents that contain information for duty assessment and statistical purposes. In certain instances, all documents must be filed and accepted by Customs prior to release of the goods. Unless you have been granted an extension, you must file entry documents at a location specified by the port or area director within five working days of your shipment's date of arrival at a U.S. port of entry. These include a number of standard documents required by Customs for any entry.

After you present the entry, Customs may examine your shipment or may waive examination. The shipment is then released provided no legal or regulatory violations have been noted. You must then file entry summary documentation and deposit estimated duties at a designated customhouse within 10 working days of your shipment's release. For a detailed description of entry procedures, standard documentation, and informal entry, see "Entry Process" on page 185.

Informed Compliance. Informed compliance was introduced with the Customs Modernization Act of 1993 (Mod Act) and defines the relationship between importers and the Customs Service. It sets out the responsibilities of both parties. Providing the correct documentation and information for entry is a key factor that will make your importing operation run smoothly. We recommend that importers become familiar with the concept of informed comliance and the responsibilities that they have under the Mod Act. For further discussion about informed compliance see "Informed Compliance" on page 211.

Entry Invoice. Invoices covering chemical wood pulp, dissolving grades, (HTSUS heading 4702) must state the insoluble fraction (as a percentage) after 1 hour in a caustic soda solution containing 18% sodium hydroxide at 20 degrees Centigrade. Invoices for sulfate or soda chemical wood pulp, dissolving grades (HTSUS subheading 4702.00.00.40) must additionally contain, on or with the invoice, a notation of the ash content as a percentage by weight. For more general information about invoices see "Invoices" on page 277.

Note: The Entry and Documentation section has been carefully designed to supply you, the importer, with sample documents and directions on how to satisfy Customs requirements. Be aware that you should consult the applicable authorities to ensure that you are correctly following the most current procedures.

Marking and Labeling Requirements

For a general discussion of U.S. Customs marking and labeling requirements, see "Country of Origin Marking" on page 236, "Special Marking Requirements" on page 238 and "Marking—False Impression" on page 239.

Shipping Considerations

You will need to ensure that your goods are packaged and shipped with care so that they pass smoothly through Customs and arrive in good condition. You are responsible for ensuring that the shipment is in compliance with all applicable government regulations for packaging and shipping. In most instances, you should not leave these arrangements solely to the discretion of your supplier. Careful preparation of the cargo and selection of the mode of transport can be essential to a cost-effective, timely delivery of undamaged goods. We strongly advise you to consult your shipping representative, insurance agent, or freight broker for advice on packing and shipping.

Wood pulp and paper waste may be shipped in bulk, bags, barrels, or other types of containers, depending on the type of product. General considerations include protection from contamination, weather, and pests. For liquid shipments, venting and vapor collection systems may be required. Safety precautions should also be implemented as required to protect against spillage and corrosion of containers. Containers should be constructed so as to be safe for handling during transport.

Publications and WWW Resources

The *Harmonized Tariff Schedule of the United States (2001)* (HTSUS) is available to view on the Customs Service website (www.customs.gov), or you may purchase a printed version from:

U.S. Government Printing Office
Superintendent of Documents
710 North Capital Street NW
Washington DC 20401
Tel: (202) 512-1800
Fax: (202) 512-1657
Website: www.access.gpo.gov

The USGPO also has copies of specific laws available for purchase. The USGPO accepts orders made by fax, phone or placed over the Internet, as well as mail orders paid by credit card. All orders must be accompanied by payment. Credit cards, checks drawn on a U.S. bank, or an international money order are all acceptable.

Relevant Government Agencies

Address your questions regarding importation of wood pulp and paper waste to your local Customs port director. For addresses refer to "U.S. Customs and Border Protection Offices" on page 65 or contact:

U.S. Customs and Border Protection
Customs Headquarters
1300 Pennsylvania Avenue NW
Washington DC 20229
Tel: (202) 354-1000
Website: www.customs.treas.gov

Principal Exporting Countries

The following listing includes samples of the main supplier nations of the products of this chapter. It is organized by HTSUS major heading. (Refer to "Customs Classification" above for the product codes.) Countries are listed in rank order of the value of products imported to the U.S. Statistics represent customs value of entries for 2002 from the Bureau of Census, U.S. Department of Commerce.

4701—Canada, Sweden, Japan, Italy, Spain

4702—Canada, South Africa, Norway, France, Brazil, Ireland

4703—Canada, Brazil, Finland, Sweden, Spain, Chile, New Zealand, Swaziland, South Africa, Russia

4704—Canada, New Zealand, Norway, Germany, Japan

4705—Canada, Finland, Italy

4706—United Kingdom, Spain, Germany, Canada, Philippines

4707—Canada, Mexico, Venezuela, Sweden, Japan, Netherlands

Chapter 48:
Paper and Paperboard

Full title: Paper and Paperboard; Articles of Paper Pulp, of Paper, or of Paperboard

This chapter relates to the importation of paper and paperboard products, which are classified under Chapter 48 of the Harmonized Tariff Schedule of the United States (HTSUS). Specifically, it includes newsprint; writing and drawing papers; personal hygiene paper products; paper articles for household use and food service; ledgers, notebooks, and paper pads; composite, corrugated, creped, crinkled, embossed, or perforated papers and paperboards; parchment, transparent, and translucent papers; carbon and other transfer papers; filters composed of paper pulp; cigarette paper; paper wallcoverings and floor coverings; paper packaging materials; paper and paperboard labels; and paper or paperboard bobbins, spools, and similar supports.

If you are interested in importing printed paper materials, you should refer to Commodity Index Chapter 49. For articles made of paper or paperboard products, refer to the Chapter that covers the particular article. For example, papers used with pharmaceutical products are in Chapter 30, papers for photographic purposes in Chapter 37, plaited articles in Chapter 46, footwear in Chapter 64, and headgear in Chapter 65. For papers that have been impregnated, coated, or covered for a particular use, you should refer to the Commodity Index Chapter that deals with products for that intended use. For example, papers treated with perfume or cosmetics are classified in Chapter 33, soap, detergent, polishes, or creams in Chapter 34, plastics in Chapter 39. Stamping foils are covered in Chapter 32, paper-backed metal foils are in Chapters 72 through 83, and abrasive papers are in Chapter 68. If you are interested in importing wood pulp or paper waste, you should refer to Chapter 47. The importing requirements for articles made from a combination of textiles and paper are covered in Chapters 50 through 63. Vinyl wallcoverings must be imported in accordance with the requirements explained in Chapter 39, and textile wallcoverings in compliance with the requirements noted in Chapters 50 through 63.

Note: To understand key issues that will enable you to make best use of the information in this section we recommend that you see "Introduction" on page 425.

Key Factors

The key factors in the importation of paper and paperboard products are:

- Compliance with U.S. Food and Drug Administration (FDA) inspection and entry requirements (if the products are intended for use with food or for medical or sanitary purposes)

- Compliance with U.S. Customs regulations on invoicing (for imports of paper stock)

Although most importers use the services of a licensed customs broker in making their entries, and we recommend this practice, you should be aware of the regulatory, entry, and documentation issues involved in importing your product. You, as importer, are ultimately responsible for the fulfillment of any legal requirements applicable to your shipment.

General Considerations

Regulatory Agencies. The FDA, under authority of the Federal Food, Drug, and Cosmetic Act (FDCA), regulates the importation of products intended for use with food or for medical or sanitary purposes. U.S. Customs enforces entry requirements for the importation of paper stock and inspects products subject to FDCA requirements for compliance.

Paper and Paperboard Products. In general, importation of paper and paper products is straightforward. There are no restrictions or prohibitions. You do not need permits or licenses. For most products, no special entry paperwork is required. However, if you are importing paper stock, you will need to provide extra information on the entry invoice (see below).

Paper Products Used With Food. The importation of paper products intended for use with food—such as food and beverage containers, dishes, trays, and coffee filters—is regulated by the FDA. Usually, if you import FDA-regulated articles, you must follow certain import procedures prescribed by that agency. If you are importing these articles at present, however, you are not required to follow normal FDA entry procedures because these articles are exempt. If routine Customs examinations of applicable shipments reveal problems that could have adverse effects on public health, the FDA will reconsider this exempt status. Selectivity criteria and entry notification may be reinstituted at any time, at the discretion of FDA. Therefore, if your products fall into this category, you should be familiar with FDA import entry procedures and requirements under FDCA. For a general discussion of FDA import procedures see "Appendix: Foods" on page 825. If you are interested in importing a food-related paper product, you should ascertain its regulatory status by contacting the FDA (see addresses at end of this chapter).

Customs Classification

For customs purposes, paper and paperboard products are classified under Chapter 48 of the HTSUS. This chapter is broken into major headings, which are further divided into subheadings, and often sub-subheadings, each of which has its own HTSUS classification number. For example, the 2001 HTSUS number for record sleeves is 4819.50.30, indicating it is a sub-subcategory of other packing containers (4819.50), which is a subcategory of the major heading, cartons, boxes, cases, bags, and other packing containers, etc. (4819). There are 23 major headings within Chapter 48.

4801—Newsprint, in rolls or sheets

4802—Uncoated paper and paperboard, of a kind used for writing, printing or other graphic purposes, and punch card stock and punch tape paper, in rolls or sheets, other than paper of heading 4801 or 4803; handmade paper and paperboard

4803—Toilet or facial tissue stock, towel or napkin stock, and similar paper of a kind used for household or sanitary purposes, cellulose wadding and webs of cellulose fibers, whether or not creped, crinkled, embossed, perforated, surface-colored, surface-decorated, or printed, in rolls or sheets

4804—Uncoated kraft paper and paperboard, in rolls or sheets, other than that of heading 4802 or 4803

4805—Other uncoated paper and paperboard, in rolls or sheets, not further worked or processed than as specified in note 2 to this chapter

4806—Vegetable parchment, greaseproof papers, tracing papers, and glassine and other glazed transparent or translucent papers, in rolls or sheets

4807—Composite paper and paperboard (made by sticking flat layers of paper or paperboard together with an adhesive), not surface-coated or impregnated, whether or not internally reinforced, in rolls or sheets

4808—Paper and paperboard, corrugated (with or without glued flat surface sheets), creped, crinkled, embossed, or perforated, in rolls or sheets, other than paper of the kind described in heading 4803

4809—Carbon paper, self-copy paper, and other copying or transfer papers (including coated or impregnated paper for duplicator stencils or offset plates). whether or not printed, in rolls or sheets

4810—Paper and paperboard, coated on one or both sides with kaolin (China clay) or other inorganic substances, with or without a binder, and with no other coating, whether or not surface-colored, surface-decorated, or printed, in rolls or sheets

4811—Paper, paperboard, cellulose wadding, and webs of cellulose fibers, coated, impregnated, covered, surface-colored, surface-decorated, or printed, in rolls or sheets, other than goods of heading 4803, 4809 or 4810

4812—Filter blocks, slabs, and plates, of paper pulp

4813—Cigarette paper, whether or not cut to size or in the form of booklets or tubes

4814—Wallpaper and similar wallcoverings; window transparencies of paper

4815—Floor coverings on a base of paper or of paperboard, whether or not cut to size

4816—Carbon paper, self-copy paper, and other copying or transfer papers (other than those of heading 4809), duplicator stencils and offset plates, of paper, whether or not put up in boxes

4817—Envelopes, letter cards, plain postcards, and correspondence cards, of paper or paperboard; boxes, pouches, wallets, and writing compendiums, of paper or paperboard, containing an assortment of paper stationery;

4818—Toilet paper and similar paper, cellulose wadding or webs of cellulose fibers, of a kind used for household or sanitary purposes, in rolls of a width not exceeding 36 cm, or cut to size or shape; handkerchiefs, cleansing tissues, towels, tablecloths, table napkins, diapers, tampons, bed sheets and similar household, sanitary or hospital articles, articles of apparel and clothing accessories, of paper pulp, paper, cellulose wadding or webs of cellulose fibers

4819—Cartons, boxes, cases, bags, and other packing containers, of paper, paperboard, cellulose, wadding or webs of cellulose fibers; box files, letter trays, and similar articles, of paper or paperboard of a kind used in offices, shops, or the like

4820—Registers, account books, notebooks, order books, receipt books, letter pads, memorandum pads, diaries, and similar articles, exercise books, blotting pads, binders (looseleaf or other), folders, file covers, manifold business forms, interleaved carbon sets, and other articles of stationery, of paper or paperboard; albums for samples or for collections and book covers (including cover boards and book jackets) of paper or paperboard

4821—Paper and paperboard labels of all kinds, whether or not printed

4822—Bobbins, spools, cops, and similar supports of paper pulp, paper, or paperboard (whether or not perforated or hardened)

4823—Other paper, paperboard, cellulose wadding and webs of cellulose fibers, cut to size or shape; other articles of paper pulp, paper, paperboard, cellulose wadding or webs of cellulose fibers

For more details regarding classifications of the specific product you are interested in importing, consult a customs broker, the appropriate commodity specialist at your nearest customs port, or the HTSUS. The 2001 HTSUS is available online from the Customs Service (www.customs.gov/impoexpo/impoexpo.htm) or for purchase from the U.S. Government Printing Office (see resources at the end of this chapter), and may be found in larger public libraries. For a general discussion of customs classification, see "Classification—Liquidation" on page 229.

Dutiable Status of Goods

For more information about duty rates and binding decisions see "Dutiable Status of Goods" on page 203; for a discussion of temporary importation of goods see "Temporary Free Importations" on page 205.

Valuation

Importers have a responsibility to use what the U.S. Customs Service deems, "reasonable care," when determining the value of their goods. They must also provide any additional information that the Customs Service needs for setting a final value on the goods. This process involves a number of factors and can be somewhat complicated; importers must be aware of applicable issues and details. Valuation information applies to all types of commodities, for further discussion on the subject see "Customs Valuation" on page 267.

Import Duties

Import duties vary (often dramatically) depending upon the Harmonized Tariff Schedule (HTSUS) classification of the goods or products imported. Since some products that look alike have different HTSUS classifications and different rates of duty, proper classification is vital. Note that "differences of opinion" between importers and the Bureau of Customs and Border Protection regarding classification keeps customs attorneys very busy.

Import duties can be assessed on the imported value of the goods ("ad valorem" rates of duty such as 2%, 4.4%, 50%, etc.), total units or weight of the goods ("specific" rates of duty such as 2 cents each or 1.5 cents/pound, etc.) or on a combination basis ("compound" rates of duty such as 5 cents each plus 6%).

Listed below is a sampling of several Column 1 import duty rates for Chapter 48 products:
Newsprint, in rolls or sheets (4801.00.00): Free
to
Pressboard (4805.93.20.00): 0.5%

For specific information on US import duties refer to the Harmonized Tariff Schedule of the US. The print version is available from the US Government Printing Office as well as third party suppliers who often add special features. Online versions are available in both static PDF pages as well as in formats with excellent search functionality. Search the Web with the term "Harmonized Tariff Schedule" to find sources.

Entry and Documentation

The entry of merchandise is a two-part process consisting of 1) filing the documentation necessary to determine whether merchandise may be released from Customs custody, and 2) filing the documents that contain information for duty assessment and statistical purposes. In certain instances, all documents must be filed and accepted by Customs prior to release of the goods. Unless you have been granted an extension, you must file entry documents at a location specified by the port or area director within five working days of your shipment's date of arrival at a U.S. port of entry. These include a number of standard documents required by Customs for any entry.

After you present the entry, Customs may examine your shipment or may waive examination. The shipment is then released provided no legal or regulatory violations have been noted. You must then file entry summary documentation and deposit estimated duties at a designated customhouse within 10 working days of your shipment's release. For a detailed description of entry procedures, standard documentation, and informal entry, see "Entry Process" on page 185.

Informed Compliance. Informed compliance was introduced with the Customs Modernization Act of 1993 (Mod Act) and defines the relationship between importers and the Customs Service. It sets out the responsibilities of both parties. Providing the correct documentation and information for entry is a key factor that will make your importing operation run smoothly. We recommend that importers become familiar with the concept of informed comliance and the responsibilities that they have under the Mod Act. For further discussion about informed compliance see "Informed Compliance" on page 211.

Entry Invoice. To facilitate classification of your paper shipment, Customs requires certain additional information on the invoice. You should be sure the information is either included on the invoice or on additional specification sheets submitted with it. Your invoice must show: 1) weight of paper in grams per square meter; 2) thickness, in micrometers (microns); 3) if imported in rectangular sheets, length and width sheets, in cm; 4) if imported in strips or rolls, the width in cm. In the case of rolls, the diameter of rolls in cm; 5) whether the paper is coated or impregnated, and with what materials; 6) weight of coating, in grams per square meter; 7) percentage by weight of the total fiber content consisting of wood fibers contained by a mechanical process, chemical sulfate or soda process, chemical sulfite process, or semichemical process, as appropriate; 8) commercial designation, as "writing," "cover," "drawing," "Bristol," "newsprint," etc.; 9) ash content; 10) color; 11) glaze or finish; 12) Mullen bursting strength, and Mullen index; 13) stretch factor, in machine direction and in cross direction; 14) tear and tensile readings; in machine direction, in cross direction, and in machine direction plus cross direction; 15) identification of fibers as "hardwood" where appropriate; 16) crush resistance; 17) brightness; 18) smoothness; 19) if bleached, whether bleached uniformly throughout the mass; and 20) whether embossed, perforated, creped, or crinkled. For more general information about invoices see "Invoices" on page 277.

Note: The Entry and Documentation section has been carefully designed to supply you, the importer, with sample documents and directions on how to satisfy Customs requirements. Be aware that you should consult the applicable authorities to ensure that you are correctly following the most current procedures.

Marking and Labeling Requirements

For a general discussion of U.S. Customs marking and labeling requirements, see "Country of Origin Marking" on page 236, "Special Marking Requirements" on page 238 and "Marking—False Impression" on page 239.

Shipping Considerations

You will need to ensure that your goods are packaged and shipped with care so that they pass smoothly through Customs and arrive in good condition. You are responsible for ensuring that the shipment is in compliance with all applicable government regulations for packaging and shipping. In most instances, you should not leave these arrangements solely to the discretion of your supplier. Careful preparation of the cargo and selection of the mode of transport can be essential to a cost-effective, timely delivery of undamaged goods. We strongly advise you to consult your shipping representative, insurance agent, or freight broker for advice on packing and shipping.

Paper and paperboard products may be shipped in bulk, bags, crates, or other types of containers, depending on the type of prod-

uct and whether it is prepackaged. General considerations include protection from contamination, weather, and pests. If a product must be kept in a sanitary environment, all tables, utensils, platforms, and devices used for moving or handling the product, and the compartments in which it is stowed while being transported will need to be maintained in a sanitary condition. Containers should be constructed so as to be safe for handling during transport.

Publications and WWW Resources

The following publication explains the FDA requirements for importing paper and paperboard products for sanitary use. It is published by the FDA and is available online from the FDA website (www.fda.gov).

Requirements of Laws and Regulations Enforced by the U.S. Food and Drug Administration

The *Harmonized Tariff Schedule of the United States (2001)* (HTSUS) is available to view on the Customs Service website (www.customs.gov), or you may purchase a printed version from:

U.S. Government Printing Office
Superintendent of Documents
710 North Capital Street NW
Washington DC 20401
Tel: (202) 512-1800
Fax: (202) 512-1657
Website: www.access.gpo.gov

The USGPO also has copies of specific laws available for purchase. The USGPO accepts orders made by fax, phone or placed over the Internet, as well as mail orders paid by credit card. All orders must be accompanied by payment. Credit cards, checks drawn on a U.S. bank, or an international money order are all acceptable.

Relevant Government Agencies

Address your questions regarding FDA regulation or requirements for paper products intended for use with food to:

Food and Drug Administration (FDA)
Center for Food Safety and Applied Nutrition (CFSAN)
Office of Compliance
Division of Enforcement, Imports Branch
5100 Paint Branch Parkway
College Park, MD 20740-3835
Tel: (301) 436-2080
Website: http://vm.cfsan.fda.gov/list.html

Address your questions regarding the importation of paper and paperboard products to your local Customs port director. For addresses, refer to "U.S. Customs and Border Protection Offices" on page 65 or contact:

U.S. Customs and Border Protection
Customs Headquarters
1300 Pennsylvania Avenue NW
Washington DC 20229
Tel: (202) 354-1000
Website: www.customs.treas.gov

Laws and Regulations

The following laws and regulations may be relevant to the importation of paper and paperboard products. The laws are contained in the United States Code (USC), and the regulations are published in the Code of Federal Regulations (CFR), both of which are available at larger public and law libraries. Copies of specific laws are also available from the United States Government Printing Office (address above).

21 USC 301 et seq.
Federal Food, Drug, and Cosmetic Act
This Act prohibits deceptive practices and regulates the manufacture, sale and importation or exportation of

food, drugs, cosmetics, and related products. It was amended by the Food Quality Protection Act of 1996. See 21 USC 331, 381, 382.

19 CFR 12.1 et seq.; 21 CFR 1.83 et seq.
Regulations on Food, Drugs, and Cosmetics
These regulations of the Secretary of Health and Human Services and the Secretary of the Treasury govern the standards, labeling, marking, and importing of pharmaceutical products.

Principal Exporting Countries

The following listing includes samples of the main supplier nations of the products of this chapter. It is organized by HTSUS major heading. (Refer to "Customs Classification" above for the product codes.) Countries are listed in rank order of the value of products imported to the U.S. Statistics represent customs value of entries for 2002 from the Bureau of Census, U.S. Department of Commerce.

4801—Canada, South Korea, Sweden, Russia, Finland, Chile, United Kingdom

4802—Canada, Finland, Norway, Germany, Brazil, Sweden, Portugal, Netherlands, France

4803—Canada, Mexico, Brazil, Spain, China, Sweden, Germany, New Zealand, France, Indonesia, Colombia, Venezuela

4804—Canada, Germany, Sweden, Australia, Japan, Mexico, China, France

4805—Canada, Germany, Netherlands, United Kingdom, Finland, Australia

4806—France, Norway, Sweden, Germany, United Kingdom, Canada, Switzerland, Mexico

4807—Canada, United Kingdom, Mexico, Australia, Netherlands, Germany, Sweden, France

4808—Canada, Germany, China, United Kingdom, Indonesia, Mexico, Venezuela

4809—Germany, Japan, Indonesia, United Kingdom, Belgium, France, Sweden

4810—Canada, Finland, South Korea, Germany, Japan, Austria, Italy

4811—Canada, Japan, Germany, United Kingdom, Finland, France, Switzerland, China

4812—Germany, Switzerland, United Kingdom, Neherlands, Japan, Sweden

4813—France, Canada, Finland, Austria, Spain, Germany, United Kingdom, Brazil

4814—Canada, United Kingdom, Italy, France, Japan, Germany, New Zealand, China

4815—United Kingdom, South Korea

4816—Indonesia, Japan, South Korea, United Kingdom, Finland, Belgium

4817—China, Canada, Mexico, Hong Kong, Thailand, France, United Kingdom, Germany, Indonesia, South Korea

4818—Canada, Mexico, Germany, El Salvador, United Kingdom, Netherlands, China, Japan

4819—Canada, China, Mexico, Germany, Hong Kong, Indonesia, France, South Korea, Taiwan, Italy, Denmark, Thailand

4820—China, Mexico, Canada, Indonesia, Brazil, Hong Kong, India, South Korea, Italy

4821—Canada, Mexico, United Kingdom, China, Australia, Hong Kong, Taiwan, France

4822—Canada, Germany, Italy, Japan, Mexico, South Korea

4823—Canada, China, Mexico, Brazil, Japan, Germany, United Kingdom, Finland, Indonesia

Chapter 49: Printed Materials

Full title: Printed Books, Newspapers, Pictures, and Other Products of the Printing Industry; Manuscripts, Typescripts, and Plans

This chapter relates to the importation of printed materials, which are classified under Chapter 49 of the Harmonized Tariff Schedule of the United States (HTSUS). Specifically, it includes printed books, brochures, leaflets, newspapers, periodicals, children's books, printed and manuscript music, maps, charts, plans, drawings, unused stamps, banknotes and other financial instruments, printed or illustrated postcards, greeting cards, calendars, trade and commercial advertising materials, tourist and similar literature, and printed forms.

If you are interested in importing photographic negatives or positives on transparent bases, refer to Commodity Index Chapter 37. The import requirements for maps, plans, or globes in relief are explained in Chapter 90. Playing cards and printed materials for toys, games, and sports equipment are imported in accordance with the requirements in Chapter 95. If you are interested in importing original engravings, prints, lithographs, postage or revenue stamps, stamp-postmarks, first-day covers, postal stationery, or antique printed materials, refer to Chapter 97.

Note: To understand key issues that will enable you to make best use of the information in this section we recommend that you see "Introduction" on page 425.

Key Factors

The key factors in the importation of printed materials are:

- Compliance with copyright laws and regulations
- Compliance with trademark laws and regulations
- Compliance with counterfeit laws and regulations
- Compliance with restrictions pertaining to seditious, obscene, or threatening subject matter
- Compliance with restrictions on the importation of facsimiles (if importing postage stamps)
- Submission of Customs **Form 4790** (if importing currencies or negotiable instruments valued at more than $10,000)

Although most importers use the services of a licensed customs broker in making their entries, and we recommend this practice, you should be aware of the regulatory, entry, and documentation issues involved in importing your product. You, as importer, are ultimately responsible for the fulfillment of any legal requirements applicable to your shipment.

General Considerations

Regulatory Agencies. The U.S. Customs Intellectual Property Rights branch enforces pertinent copyright laws and regulations to ensure that pirated versions of copyrighted materials do not enter the U.S. The principle laws include Section 305 of the Tariff Act of 1930, as amended, Section 602(a) of the Copyright Revision Act of 1976 (CRA), and Section 42 of the Trademark Act (TMA). These laws and regulations are designed to protect the general consumer, the holders of copyrights, and the national security of the U.S.

Books, Newspapers, and Periodicals. The importation of books, magazines, newspapers, and periodicals into the U.S. is relatively straightforward. There are no quotas, no duties, and no special licensing or permit requirements. However, you need to be concerned about three major issues pertinent to these printed materials: marking, copyrights, and content. If your shipments of books, newspapers, or periodicals are found to violate any of the U.S. copyright or trademark laws, they are subject to seizure by Customs. Such shipments may be destroyed, auctioned, or reexported, depending on the nature of the item and the nature of the violation (see "Prohibitions and Restrictions" below).

Currency and Negotiable Instruments. All imports of currency and negotiable instruments are subject to the Currency and Foreign Transactions Reporting Act, 31 U.S. 1101 et seq. (CFTR). Under CFTR, you must file a transaction report, Customs **Form 4790**, with U.S. Customs when you transport more than $10,000 in monetary instruments, by any means, on any occasion, into or out of the U.S. Monetary instruments include U.S. or foreign currency, traveler's checks, money orders, and negotiable instruments or investment securities in bearer form. Bank checks, travelers checks, or money orders made payable to the order of a named person but that have not been endorsed, or that bear restrictive endorsement, are not considered monetary instruments.

Postage Stamps. Importation of foreign postage stamps into the U.S. is straightforward. You do not need permits or licenses, nor is special paperwork required. Importation of facsimiles of U.S. postage stamps is regulated by the U.S. Secret Service (see "Prohibitions and Restrictions" below).

Articles Exempt from Formal Customs Entry. The following articles pass Customs without issuing an entry: 1) Articles imported by mail, marked for copyright, and addressed to the Library of Congress, to the Copyright Office, or to the Register of Copyrights, Washington, DC; 2) negotiable instruments in current circulation in any country and imported into the U.S. for monetary purposes; and 3) postage stamps in current use.

Customs Classification

For customs purposes, printed materials are classified under Chapter 49 of the HTSUS. This chapter is broken into major headings, which are further divided into subheadings, and often sub-subheadings, each of which has its own HTSUS classification number. For example, the 2001 HTSUS number for newspaper supplements printed by a gravure process is 4902.90.10, indicating it is a sub-subcategory of other materials (4902.90), which is a subcategory of the major heading, newspapers, journals, and periodicals, etc. (4902). There are 11 major headings within Chapter 49.

4901—Printed books, brochures, leaflets, and similar printed matter, whether or not in single sheets

4902—Newspapers, journals, and periodicals, whether or not illustrated or containing advertising material

4903—Children's picture, drawing or coloring books

4904—Music, printed or in manuscript, whether or not bound or illustrated

4905—Maps and hydrographic or similar charts of all kinds, including atlases, wall maps, topographical plans, and globes, printed

4906—Plans and drawings for architectural, engineering, industrial, commercial, topographical, or similar purposes, being originals drawn by hand; handwritten texts; photographic reproductions on sensitized paper and carbon copies of the foregoing

4907—Unused postage, revenue or similar stamps of current or new issue in the country to which they are destined; stamp-impressed paper; banknotes; check forms; stock, share, or bond certificates and similar documents of title

4908—Transfers (decalcomanias)

4909—Printed or illustrated post cards; printed cards bearing personal greetings, messages or announcements, whether or not illustrated, with or without envelopes or trimmings

4910—Calendars of any kind, printed, including calendar blocks

4911—Other printed matter, including printed pictures and photographs

For more details regarding classifications of the specific product you are interested in importing, consult a customs broker, the appropriate commodity specialist at your nearest customs port, or the HTSUS. The 2001 HTSUS is available online from the Customs Service (www.customs.gov/impoexpo/impoexpo.htm) or for purchase from the U.S. Government Printing Office (see resources at the end of this chapter), and may be found in larger public libraries. For a general discussion of customs classification, see "Classification—Liquidation" on page 229.

Dutiable Status of Goods

For more information about duty rates and binding decisions see "Dutiable Status of Goods" on page 203; for a discussion of temporary importation of goods see "Temporary Free Importations" on page 205.

Valuation

Importers have a responsibility to use what the U.S. Customs Service deems, "reasonable care," when determining the value of their goods. They must also provide any additional information that the Customs Service needs for setting a final value on the goods. This process involves a number of factors and can be somewhat complicated; importers must be aware of applicable issues and details. Valuation information applies to all types of commodities, for further discussion on the subject see "Customs Valuation" on page 267.

Import Duties

Import duties vary (often dramatically) depending upon the Harmonized Tariff Schedule (HTSUS) classification of the goods or products imported. Since some products that look alike have different HTSUS classifications and different rates of duty, proper classification is vital. Note that "differences of opinion" between importers and the Bureau of Customs and Border Protection regarding classification keeps customs attorneys very busy.

Import duties can be assessed on the imported value of the goods ("ad valorem" rates of duty such as 2%, 4.4%, 50%, etc.), total units or weight of the goods ("specific" rates of duty such as 2 cents each or 1.5 cents/pound, etc.) or on a combination basis ("compound" rates of duty such as 5 cents each plus 6%).

Listed below is a sampling of several Column 1 import duty rates for Chapter 49 products:

Children's picture, drawing or coloring books (4903.00.00.00): Free

to

Globes (4905.10.00.00): 0.5%

For specific information on US import duties refer to the Harmonized Tariff Schedule of the US. The print version is available from the US Government Printing Office as well as third party suppliers who often add special features. Online versions are available in both static PDF pages as well as in formats with excellent search functionality. Search the Web with the term "Harmonized Tariff Schedule" to find sources.

Entry and Documentation

The entry of merchandise is a two-part process consisting of 1) filing the documentation necessary to determine whether merchandise may be released from Customs custody, and 2) filing the documents that contain information for duty assessment and statistical purposes. In certain instances, all documents must be filed and accepted by Customs prior to release of the goods. Unless you have been granted an extension, you must file entry documents at a location specified by the port or area director within five working days of your shipment's date of arrival at a U.S. port of entry. These include a number of standard documents required by Customs for any entry, and:

- Customs Form CF 4790 (if importing currencies or negotiable instruments valued at more than $10,000)

After you present the entry, Customs may examine your shipment or may waive examination. The shipment is then released provided no legal or regulatory violations have been noted. You must then file entry summary documentation and deposit estimated duties at a designated customhouse within 10 working days of your shipment's release. For a detailed description of entry procedures, standard documentation, and informal entry, see "Entry Process" on page 185.

Informed Compliance. Informed compliance was introduced with the Customs Modernization Act of 1993 (Mod Act) and defines the relationship between importers and the Customs Service. It sets out the responsibilities of both parties. Providing the correct documentation and information for entry is a key factor that will make your importing operation run smoothly. We recommend that importers become familiar with the concept of informed comliance and the responsibilities that they have under the Mod Act. For further discussion about informed compliance see "Informed Compliance" on page 211.

Entry Invoice. If you seek entry for printed matter in the following headings, you must include on the invoice, or on a separate sheet submitted with the invoice, the following information:

HTSUS Heading 4901: 1) whether the books are dictionaries; encyclopedias; textbooks; bound newspapers, journals, or periodicals; directories; bibles or other prayer books; technical, scientific, or professional books; art or pictorial books; or "other" books; 2) if "other" books, whether hardbound or paperbound; 3) if "other" books and paperbound but not "rack size," number of pages (excluding covers).

HTSUS Heading 4902: 1) Whether they appear at least four times a week; 2) if they appear other than at least four times a week, whether they are newspaper supplements printed by a gravure process, newspapers, business or professional journals or periodicals, or other than these.

HTSUS Heading 4904: Whether the printed or manuscript music is sheet music, not bound (except by stapling or folding).

HTSUS Heading 4905: 1) Whether globes or not; 2) if not globes, whether in book form or not; and 3) in any case, whether or not in relief;

HTSUS Heading 4908: Whether or not vitrifiable.

HTSUS Heading 4909: Whether post cards, greeting cards, or other.

HTSUS Heading 4910: 1) Whether or not printed on paper by a lithographic process; 2) if printed on paper by a lithographic process, the thickness of the paper, in mm.

HTSUS Subheading 4911.91: 1) Whether or not printed over 20 years at time of importation; 2) if not printed over 20 years at time of importation, whether suitable for use in the production of articles of heading 4901; 3) if not printed over 20 years at time of importation, and not suitable for use in the production of articles of heading 4901, whether the merchandise is lithographs on paper or paperboard; 4) if lithographs on paper or paperboard, under the terms of the immediately preceding description, thickness of the paper or paperboard, and whether or not posters; 5) in any case, whether or not posters; and 6) in any case, whether or not photographic negatives or positives on transparent bases.

HTSUS Subheading 4911.99: If not carnets, or parts thereof, in English or French, whether or not printed on paper in whole or in part by a lithographic process. For more general information about invoices see "Invoices" on page 277.

Note: The Entry and Documentation section has been carefully designed to supply you, the importer, with sample documents and directions on how to satisfy Customs requirements. Be aware that you should consult the applicable authorities to ensure that you are correctly following the most current procedures.

Prohibitions and Restrictions

Content. Under Section 305 of the Tariff Act of 1930, as amended, you may not import any book, writing, advertisement, circular, or picture containing any matter advocating or urging the following unlawful acts: 1) treason or insurrection against the U.S.; or 2) forcible resistance to any U.S. law. You may not import any book, writing, advertisement, circular, or picture containing any threat to take the life of, or inflict bodily harm on, any person in the U.S. Importation of any obscene book, writing, advertisement, circular, picture or other representation, figure, or image on or of paper is also prohibited.

Copyright. Section 602(a) of the CRA makes it an infringement of copyright to import copies of a work acquired outside the U.S. without the copyright owner's authorization. If you import articles in violation of Section 602(a), your shipment will be subject to seizure and forfeiture. Customs destroys forfeited articles. If Customs is satisfied, however, that your violation was unintentional, you may have the option of returning the articles to the country of export. Customs employs the substantial similarity test to determine if a design has been copied. Copyright owners seeking import protection from U.S. Customs must register their claim to copyright with the U.S. Copyright Office and record their registration with Customs in accordance with applicable regulations (19 CFR Part 133, Subpart D).

Counterfeit Articles. Articles bearing facsimiles or replicas of U.S. or foreign securities are prohibited from importation. Also prohibited are counterfeited, forged, or altered obligations or other securities of the U.S. or of any foreign government.

Exceptions. Black and white illustrations of U.S. postage stamps are permitted entry under the following conditions. The illustrations must be for philatelic, numismatic, educational, historical or newsworthy purposes. They must be published in articles, books, journals, newspapers, or albums. If the illustrations are intended for advertising purposes, the advertising must be limited to legitimate philatelic or numismatic purposes.

Motion-picture films, microfilms, or slides of postage and revenue stamps and other obligations and securities of the U.S. and or foreign countries are permitted, provided they are intended for projection on a screen or for use in telecasting. Reproductions in printed matter that adheres to the requirements of 18 USC 504 are permitted entry. However, printed matter containing illustrations or reproductions not executed in accordance with Section 504 will be considered counterfeit and are subject to forfeiture.

Forfeiture. If no application for exportation or assent to forfeiture is received by the port director of Customs within 30 days from the date of notification to the importer that articles are prohibited, the articles will be reported to the U.S. attorney for forfeiture.

For more information regarding distinctions under the law between counterfeit and noncounterfeit representations, see 18 USC 504 and 19 CFR 12.48, or contact U.S. Customs.

Postage Stamps. Facsimiles of postage stamps are prohibited entry except those for philatelic, educational, historical, or newsworthy purposes. You may obtain further information from the U.S. Secret Service (see addresses at end of this chapter).

Country-Specific Import Restrictions

If you wish to import books, magazines, newspapers, or periodicals into the U.S. from countries that fall under Foreign Assets Control import bans, you may apply for a waiver from the U.S. Department of Treasury's Office of Foreign Assets Control (see addresses at end of this chapter).

The importation of monetary instruments from countries that are under economic sanctions by the U.S.—such as Iran, North Korea, Libya, and Cuba—is severely restricted. In some instances, importation is prohibited altogether. For more information, contact the Office of Foreign Assets Control (see addresses at end of this chapter).

Marking and Labeling Requirements

Foreign Books. Section 42 of the TMA specifies marking requirements for foreign books imported into the U.S. The Section deems the words "United States," the letters "U.S.A.," or the name of any city or locality in the U.S. appearing on an item of foreign origin, as calculated to induce the public to believe that the item was manufactured in the U.S. In such cases, for your item to be considered properly marked, the name of the foreign country of origin must appear in close proximity to the name that implies a U.S. origin.

This regulation applies to imported, foreign-printed (bound or unbound) books that bear on the title page either 1) the name and address of the U.S. importer, consignee, or publisher; or 2) the name of any country or locality other than the one in which the book was actually printed. The ultimate purchaser could construe these names to mean that the book is a product of the U.S. Customs will accept the usual practice in the printing and publishing trade for meeting the requirements of TMA, which is to have the following wording in close proximity to the potentially misleading information: 1) the words "Printed in," followed by the name of the country of origin; or 2) the words "Printed by," followed by the name and address of the foreign printer and the name of the country of origin, or 3) words of similar significance. This wording must appear either 1) on the front or back of the title page, or 2) on the inside or outside of the cover (provided the marking is not covered by a dust cover or jacket), or 3) on a page near the front or back of your book.

Seizure and Forfeiture. An imported article bearing a name or mark prohibited by Section 42 of TMA is subject to seizure and forfeiture. A shipment that violates the Trademark Act may be reexported or destroyed at the importer's cost. If your shipment is seized by Customs for a TMA violation, you may file a petition prior to the final disposition, requesting the port director to release it on the condition that the prohibited marking will be removed or obliterated or that the article will be properly marked. The final decision regarding disposition of a mismarked shipment rests with Customs.

For a general discussion of U.S. Customs marking and labeling requirements, see "Country of Origin Marking" on page 236, "Special Marking Requirements" on page 238 and "Marking—False Impression" on page 239.

Shipping Considerations

You will need to ensure that your goods are packaged and shipped with care so that they pass smoothly through Customs and arrive in good condition. You are responsible for ensuring that the shipment is in compliance with all applicable government regulations for packaging and shipping. In most instances, you should not leave these arrangements solely to the discretion of your supplier. Careful preparation of the cargo and selection of the mode of transport can be essential to a cost-effective, timely delivery of undamaged goods. We strongly advise you to consult your shipping representative, insurance agent, or freight broker for advice on packing and shipping.

Printed materials may be shipped in bulk, boxes, crates, or other types of containers, depending on the type of product and whether it is prepackaged. General considerations include protection from contamination, weather, and pests. Containers should be constructed so as to be safe for handling during transport.

Publications and WWW Resources

The *Harmonized Tariff Schedule of the United States (2001)* (HTSUS) is available to view on the Customs Service website (www.customs.gov), or you may purchase a printed version from:

> **U.S. Government Printing Office**
> **Superintendent of Documents**
> 710 North Capital Street NW
> Washington DC 20401
> Tel: (202) 512-1800
> Fax: (202) 512-1657
> Website: www.access.gpo.gov

The USGPO also has copies of specific laws available for purchase. The USGPO accepts orders made by fax, phone or placed over the Internet, as well as mail orders paid by credit card. All orders must be accompanied by payment. Credit cards, checks drawn on a U.S. bank, or an international money order are all acceptable.

Relevant Government Agencies

Address your questions regarding waiver of country-specific import restrictions under Foreign Assets Control to:

> **U.S. Treasury Department**
> **Office of Foreign Assets Control**
> 1500 Pennsylvania Avenue NW
> Washington DC 20220
> Tel: (202) 622-2500
> Compliance: (202) 622-2490
> OFAC Fax-on-Demand: (202) 622-0077
> Web site: www.treas.gov/ofac

Address your questions regarding Customs-enforced copyright regulations to:

> **U.S. Customs and Border Protection**
> **Office of Regulations & Rulings**
> **Intellectual Property Rights Branch**
> 1300 Pennsylvania Avenue NW
> Washington DC 20229
> Tel: (202) 572-8710
> Website: www.customs.treas.gov

Address other copyright-related questions to:

> **U.S. Copyright Office**
> LM 455, Library of Congress
> Washington D.C. 20559-6000
> Tel: (202) 707-3000
> Website: http://lcweb.loc.gov/copyright

Address your questions regarding importation of facsimiles of U.S. postage stamps to:

U.S. Secret Service
Department of Public Affairs
950 H St. NW, Suite 8400
Washington DC 20223
Tel: (202) 406-5708
Website: www.treas.gov/usss

Address your questions regarding importation of printed materials to your local Customs port director. For addresses, refer to "U.S. Customs and Border Protection Offices" on page 65 or contact:

U.S. Customs and Border Protection
Customs Headquarters
1300 Pennsylvania Avenue NW
Washington DC 20229
Tel: (202) 354-1000
Website: www.customs.treas.gov

Laws and Regulations

The following laws and regulations may be relevant to the importation of printed materials. The laws are contained in the United States Code (USC), and the regulations are published in the Code of Federal Regulations (CFR), both of which are available at larger public and law libraries. Copies of specific laws are also available from the USGPO(address above).

15 USC 1124
Importation of Goods Bearing Infringing Marks or Names Forbidden
This Act provides, among other things, that no imported article of foreign origin that bears a name or mark calculated to induce the public to believe that it was manufactured in the U.S., or in any foreign country or locality other than the country or locality where it was in fact manufactured, shall be admitted entry at any customhouse in the U.S.

17 USC 101 et seq.
Copyrights
Provides that the importation into the U.S. of copies of a work acquired outside the U.S. without authorization of the copyright owner is an infringement of the copyright.

19 CFR 133.31 et seq.
Regulations of Customs on Recordation of Copyrights, Trademarks, and Trade Names
These regulations provide procedures and requirements for registering a copyright, trademark, or trade name with U.S. Customs, as well as procedures for enforcement, forfeiture of merchandise, and assessment of monetary penalties.

31 USC 5311 et seq.
Records and Reports on Monetary Instruments Transactions
This Act controls the import of currency and negotiable instruments and requires the filing of a transaction report, Customs **Form 4790**, with U.S. Customs when you transport more than $10,000 in monetary instruments into or out of the U.S.

18 USC 471 et seq.
Counterfeiting and Forgery
This law prohibits the import of counterfeit obligations, securities, coins, currency, Customs forms, ships' papers, and the plates or stones for counterfeiting the same.

18 USC 955
Financial Transactions with Foreign Governments
This law restricts transactions involving securities, bonds and similar items. It prohibits dealings with certain countries based on their status in regard to their payment of existing obligations to the United States.

18 USC 2318
Trafficking in Counterfeit Labels
This law forbids the importation of counterfeit phon-

orecord labels, copies of motion pictures, and other audiovisual works.

18 USC 2320
Trafficking in Counterfeit Goods or Services
This law prohibits trafficking of counterfeit goods or services.

19 CFR 12.48
Regulations of Customs on Enforcement of Counterfeit Laws
These regulations describe the printed material prohibited from importation under counterfeit restrictions and the exceptions allowed.

31 CFR Part 401
Seizure and Forfeiture of Vessels, Vehicles, and Aircraft Used to Transport Counterfeit Coins, Obligations, and Paraphernalia
These regulations authorize the Port Director of Customs to hold in custody vessels, vehicles, and aircraft used to violate 49 USC 781 and seized by the U.S. Secret Service officers while enforcing counterfeit laws.

46 USC App. 98
Conveyance of Bullion, Coin, Notes, or Bonds for U.S.
This law governs the carriage and conveyance of U.S. securities on vessels between U.S. ports and between U.S. ports and foreign ports.

Principal Exporting Countries

The following listing includes samples of the main supplier nations of the products of this chapter. It is organized by HTSUS major heading. (Refer to "Customs Classification" above for the product codes.) Countries are listed in rank order of the value of products imported to the U.S. Statistics represent customs value of entries for 2002 from the Bureau of Census, U.S. Department of Commerce.

4901—China, Canada, United Kingdom, Hong Kong, Singapore, Italy, Germany, Spain

4902—Canada, United Kingdom, Mexico, Spain, Japan, Italy, Germany, France

4903—China, Hong Kong, Mexico, Canada, Singapore

4904—United Kingdom, Germany, France, Netherlands, China, Italy, Canada, Singapore, Australia

4905—Canada, China, United Kingdom, Italy, Germany, Spain, France

4906—Canada, Singapore, Japan, France, Germany, Mexico, China, United Kingdom

4907—United Kingdom, Germany, Canada, France, Norway, Lithuania, Russia, Japan, Latvia, Netherlands, Israel

4908—France, Germany, Italy, United Kingdom, China, South Korea, Japan

4909—China, Canada, Mexico, United Kingdom, Hong Kong

4910—Canada, China, South Korea, Hong Kong, Mexico

4911—Canada, China, Mexico, Netherlands, United Kingdom, Germany

Chapter 50:
Silk

This chapter relates to the importation of silk products, which are classified under Chapter 50 of the Harmonized Tariff Schedule of the United States (HTSUS). Specifically, it includes silkworm cocoons for reeling, raw silk, silk waste, silk yarns, and fabrics woven of silk or silk waste.

If you are interested in importing silk apparel, you should refer to Commodity Index Chapter 62. If you are interested in importing footwear or leggings made of silk, you should refer to Chapter 64. For import requirements related to headgear made of silk, refer to Chapter 65.

Note: To understand key issues that will enable you to make best use of the information in this section we recommend that you see "Introduction" on page 425.

Key Factors

The key factors in the importation of silk products are:

- Compliance with quota restraints and visa requirements
- Submission of U.S. Customs Country-of-Origin Declaration(s)
- Compliance with entry invoice requirements
- Compliance with labeling requirements under Textile Fiber Products Identification Act (TFPIA) and/ or the Wool Products Labeling Act (WPLA) and the Care Labeling Rule
- Compliance with flammability standards adopted and enforced by the Consumer Product Safety Commission (CPSC) under the Flammable Fabrics Act (FFA)

Although most importers use the services of a licensed customs broker in making their entries, and we recommend this practice, you should be aware of the regulatory, entry, and documentation issues involved in importing your product. The importer is ultimately responsible for the fulfillment of any legal requirements applicable to a shipment.

General Considerations

Regulatory Agencies. The Committee for Implementation of Textile Agreements (CITA) regulates certain textile imports under Section 204 of the Agricultural Adjustment Act. U.S. Customs enforces CITA textile and textile product entry quotas. Customs also enforces compliance with labeling and invoice requirements of the TFPIA and flammability standards under the FFA. The CPSC monitors imports and from time to time inspects textile shipments for compliance with FFA standards. If you are importing wool textiles, importation is subject to complex textile import regulations. The Federal Trade Commission (FTC) administers the WPLA requirements.

Quotas. If you are interested in importing silk products, the most important issue you need to be aware of is quotas. Under the Multi-Fiber Arrangement provisions of Section 204 of the Agricultural Adjustment Act, CITA initiates specific agreements with individual exporting countries. Section 204 of the Agricultural Adjustment Act covers textiles that: 1) are in chief value of cotton, wool, or man-made fibers, any textile fibers subject to the terms of any textile trade agreement, or any combination of such fibers; 2) contain 50% or more by weight of cotton or man-made fibers, or any textile fibers subject to the terms of any textile trade agreement; 3) contain 17% or more by weight of wool; or 4) if in chief value of textile fibers or textile materials, contain a blend of cotton, wool, or man-made fibers, any textile fibers subject to the terms of any textile trade agreement, or any combination of such fibers that, in total, amount to 50% or more by weight of all component fibers. For silk textile products, quotas currently apply to blends of silk and other fibers.

The U.S. has bilateral agreements with over 40 countries. Each agreement with each country is unique, and may specify quotas for a type of textile or a specific article. Visas or export licenses may be required. Currently, certain silk blends are subject to some quota restraints, but these agreements often change. Therefore, if you are interested in importing any silk products, you should contact the International Trade Administration's Office of Textile and Apparel (see addresses at end of this chapter). Refer to "Prohibitions and Restrictions" below for further details.

Country-of-Origin Declarations. U.S. Customs enforces CITA textile and textile product entry quotas (see Prohibitions and Restrictions below). Requirements for entry include submission of Country-of-Origin Declarations with every silk textile shipment, regardless of whether it is subject to a specific multi-fiber arrangement (19 CFR 12.130, 12.131).

Country of Origin. Quota restrictions are country-specific and therefore are applied based on the country of origin for the textiles shipped. The last country from which a textile shipment was exported to the U.S. is not necessarily its country of origin. A textile or textile product imported into the U.S. is considered a product of the particular foreign territory or country, or a U.S. insular possession, where it is wholly grown, produced, or manufactured. For the following discussion, "country" means a foreign territory or country, or a U.S. insular possession.

In 1996, the U.S. Customs Service made major changes to country of origin rules for textile imports. The regulations at 19 CFR 102.21, "Textile and apparel products" were added to the 1996 Customs Regulations and became effective July 1, 1996. The new rules do not provide for cutting components or cutting and hemming to confer country of origin as in the past. The basis of the new law is processing operations or assembly. Some of the most important changes for importers to be aware of are:

- Cutting does not determine the country of origin (previously cutting determined country of origin for 90 percent of wearing apparel imports). The new rules are based on processing or assembly operations.
- A subjective determination under the provisions of 19 CFR 12.130 is replaced by objective processing operations expressed in terms of tariff shifts. Dyeing, printing, and other finishing processes applied to fabrics no longer confer or change country of origin.
- Country of origin for textile and apparel products processed, assembled or manufactured in two or more countries is determined by where the most important processing occurs, and, if that cannot be ascertained, the last country in which an important processing operation occurs

The country of origin is the country in which a product is wholly produced when a textile or apparel product is completely produced or manufactured (except for minor parts) in one country. For fabric, the country of origin is the country in which the fabric is woven, knitted, needled, tufted, felted, entangled or created by any other fabric-making process. The country of origin for staple yarn is the country in which yarn is spun; for filament yarn, the country in which filament is extruded; and for plied, gimped and cabled yarns, the country in which the fibers or filaments used in the yarn are spun or extruded. The country of origin of all other textile and apparel products is the country in which the components of a textile or apparel product are wholly assembled (except for minor attachments) except for knit-to-shape products. Knit-to-shape products are those composed of panels or parts ,which, are knitted or crocheted directly into the shape that will be used in construction of the final product. Minor cutting or sewing does not influence whether the product is considered knit-to-shape. The country of origin for knit-to-shape products is that country in which the major parts are knitted into the shape that will constitute the finished product. Once again, note that assembly, not cutting, now confers country of origin.

Declarations. All importations of textiles and textile products must be accompanied by one of the following three declarations. Goods subject to Section 204, Agricultural Act of 1956, as amended, must be accompanied by either a single-country or a multiple-country declaration. Goods not subject to Section 204 must be accompanied by a negative declaration.

- **Single-country declarations** are used for entries of textiles or textile products which are wholly the growth, product, or manufacture of a single foreign country, territory, or U.S. insular possession. Information required includes: marks of identification and numbers; description of article and quantity; country of origin; and date of exportation.

- **Multiple-country declarations** are used for entries of textiles or textile products which were subjected to manufacturing or processing operations in, and/or incorporate materials originating in more than one foreign country or territory. Information required includes: marks of identification and numbers; for articles, description, quantity, identification of manufacturing and/or processing operations, country, and date of exportation; for materials used to make articles, description of materials, country of production, and date of exportation.

- **Negative declarations** must accompany all textile imports that are not subject to AAA Section 204 restrictions. Information required includes: marks of identification and numbers; descriptions of article and quantity; and country of origin.

The date of exportation to be indicated on the above declarations is the date on which the carrier leaves the last port in the country of origin, as determined by Customs. Diversion to another country during transit does not affect the export date.

Procedure for Declarations. The manufacturer, producer, exporter, or importer may prepare the declaration. If more than one of these parties is involved in the importation, each party may prepare a separate declaration. You may file a separate declaration for each invoice presented with your entry. The declaration must be dated and signed by the responsible party, and must include the person's title and the company name and address. Your shipment's entry will be denied unless it is accompanied by a properly executed declaration. Customs will not treat a textile declaration as a missing document for which a bond may be filed.

Customs will base its country-of-origin determination on the information contained in each declaration, unless the information is insufficient. If the information on the declaration is insufficient, Customs will require that you submit such additional information as will enable the determination to be made. The shipment will not be released until the determination is made. Thus, if you want to clear Customs with minimal delay, be sure that the information on the declarations is as complete as possible for each shipment.

Textile Labeling and Invoice Requirements. You are responsible for your imported silk textile product's compliance with applicable provisions of the TFPIA. Silk textile products that require labeling under TFPIA must already be labeled at entry, or the shipment will be refused. (See "Marking and Labeling Requirements" below.) If you import shipments of silk textiles subject to TFPIA and valued at over $500, you must provide special information on the entry invoice (see "Entry and Documentation" below).

Flammability Standards. Silk textile products imported into the U.S. for use in consumer products must be in compliance with the FFA, a federal law that gives the CPSC the authority and responsibility for protecting the public from the hazards of dangerously flammable items of wearing apparel and interior furnishings. Under the FFA, standards have been established for flammability. You cannot import any article of wearing apparel or interior furnishing, or any fabric or related material that is intended for use or that may be used in such items, if it fails to conform to an applicable flammability standard (FFA Section 4). Certain products may be imported into the U.S. (FFA Section 11c) for finishing or processing to render them less flammable so as to meet the standards. For these products, the exporter must state on the invoice or other paper relating to the shipment that the shipment is being made for that purpose.

The CPSC monitors imports of textiles under its Import Surveillance Program. From time to time, your textile shipments may be inspected to ascertain compliance with mandatory safety standards. Shipments may also be subject to testing by the CPSC to determine compliance. If the CPSC believes a product, fabric, or related material does not comply with a flammability standard, it is authorized to pursue a variety of legal sanctions (see "Prohibitions and Restrictions" below).

Substantial Product Hazard Reports. Any firm that obtains information that reasonably supports the conclusion that one of its products presents an unreasonable risk of serious injury or death must report that information to the CPSC's Division of Corrective Actions (CPSC address below). Importers must also report to the CPSC if 1) a type of product is the subject of at least three civil actions filed in U.S. federal or state courts, 2) each suit alleges the involvement of that product type in death or grievous bodily injury (as defined in FFA Section 37(3)1), and 3) at least three of the actions result in a final settlement with the manufacturer or in a judgment for the plaintiff within any one of the two-year periods specified in FFA Section 37(b).

Wool Product Entry Requirements. Depending on the nature of your wool fiber imports, as many as three different types of special entry documents may be required. First, for all imported textile fibers and yarns covered by the Agricultural Adjustment Act (AAA), including wool, you must file a U.S. Customs Textile Entry Declaration (see "Country-of-Origin Declarations" below). Second, for all wool products subject to the WPLA, special information is required on the entry invoices (see "Entry and Documentation" below). Finally, certain wool articles manufactured or produced in certain countries may be subject to quotas under U.S. Department of Commerce Multi-Fiber Arrangements. Such products require export certificates or visas issued by the appropriate country of origin, in addition to other requisite entry paperwork (see "Quotas" above).

Wool Products Labeling Act. The term "wool product" means any product or any portion of a product that contains, purports to contain, or in any way is represented as containing wool, reprocessed wool, or reused wool. All wool products imported into the U.S., except those made more than 20 years before importation, and except carpets, rugs, mats, and upholsteries, must have affixed a stamp, tag, label, or other means of identification as required by the WPLA. If you are importing wool products exempt from labeling under the WPLA, do not assume they are also exempt from labeling under the TFPIA. These are two distinct laws, with some overlapping requirements (see "Marking and Labeling Requirements" below).

Import Advisory

Importation of textiles is trade-sensitive and highly regulated. Shipments of textiles and textile products not complying with all government regulations, including quotas and visas, are subject to seizure and could result in the imposition of penalties as well as possible forfeiture of the goods. You should always verify the available quota for any textile product you plan to import before your shipment leaves the country of manufacture. Furthermore, Customs textile classification rulings change frequently, and prior administrative rulings are often modified and sometimes reversed. You should be particularly careful to comply with country of origin determination regulations, which were changed in 1996, and affect quotas and visas, marking and labeling, and other important aspects of tariff classification. See "Publications and WWW Resources" for information on important Customs Service informed compliance publications.

Customs Classification

For customs purposes, silk products are classified under Chapter 50 of the HTSUS. This chapter is broken into major headings, which are further divided into subheadings, and often sub-sub-headings, each of which has its own HTSUS classification number. For example, the 2001 HTSUS number for noil silk fabric with 85% or more by weight of silk or silk waste is 5007.10.30, indicating it is a sub-subcategory of noil silk fabric (5007.10), which is a subcategory of the major heading, woven fabrics of silk or silk waste (5007). There are seven major headings within Chapter 50.

5001—Silkworm cocoons suitable for reeling

5002—Raw silk (not thrown)

5003—Silk waste (including cocoons unsuitable for reeling, yarn waste, and garnetted stock)

5004—Silk yarn (other than yarn spun from silk waste) not put up for retail sale

5005—Yarn spun from silk waste, not put up for retail sale

5006—Silk yarn and yarn spun from silk waste, put up for retail sale; silkworm gut

5007—Woven fabrics of silk or silk waste

For more details regarding classifications of the specific product you are interested in importing, consult a customs broker, the appropriate commodity specialist at your nearest customs port, or the HTSUS. The 2001 HTSUS is available online from the Customs Service (www.customs.gov/impoexpo/impoexpo.htm) or for purchase from the U.S. Government Printing Office (see resources at the end of this chapter), and may be found in larger public libraries. For a general discussion of customs classification, see "Classification—Liquidation" on page 229.

Dutiable Status of Goods

For more information about duty rates and binding decisions see "Dutiable Status of Goods" on page 203; for a discussion of temporary importation of goods see "Temporary Free Importations" on page 205.

Valuation

Importers have a responsibility to use what the U.S. Customs Service deems, "reasonable care," when determining the value of their goods. They must also provide any additional information that the Customs Service needs for setting a final value on the goods. This process involves a number of factors and can be somewhat complicated; importers must be aware of applicable issues and details. Valuation information applies to all types of commodities, for further discussion on the subject see "Customs Valuation" on page 267.

Import Duties

Import duties vary (often dramatically) depending upon the Harmonized Tariff Schedule (HTSUS) classification of the goods or products imported. Since some products that look alike have different HTSUS classifications and different rates of duty, proper classification is vital. Note that "differences of opinion" between importers and the Bureau of Customs and Border Protection regarding classification keeps customs attorneys very busy.

Import duties can be assessed on the imported value of the goods ("ad valorem" rates of duty such as 2%, 4.4%, 50%, etc.), total units or weight of the goods ("specific" rates of duty such as 2 cents each or 1.5 cents/pound, etc.) or on a combination basis ("compound" rates of duty such as 5 cents each plus 6%).

Listed below is a sampling of several Column 1 import duty rates for Chapter 50 products:

Silkworm cocoons suitable for reeling (5001.00.00.00): Free

to

Other silk waste (including cocoons unsuitable for reeling, yarn waste and garnetted stock) (5003.90.00.00): 2.5%

For specific information on US import duties refer to the Harmonized Tariff Schedule of the US. The print version is available from the US Government Printing Office as well as third party suppliers who often add special features. Online versions are available in both static PDF pages as well as in formats with excellent search functionality. Search the Web with the term "Harmonized Tariff Schedule" to find sources.

Entry and Documentation

The entry of merchandise is a two-part process consisting of 1) filing the documentation necessary to determine whether merchandise may be released from Customs custody, and 2) filing the documents that contain information for duty assessment and statistical purposes. In certain instances, all documents must be filed and accepted by Customs prior to release of the goods. Unless you have been granted an extension, you must file entry documents at a location specified by the port or area director within five working days of your shipment's date of arrival at a U.S. port of entry. These include a number of standard documents required by Customs for any entry, and:

- U.S. Customs Country-of-Origin Declaration Form CF 3229

- Export documentation and/or visa for textiles subject to bilateral agreement

After you present the entry, Customs may examine your shipment or may waive examination. The shipment is then released provided no legal or regulatory violations have been noted. If not already completed you must then file entry summary documentation and deposit estimated duties at a designated customhouse within 10 working days of your shipment's release. For a detailed description of entry procedures, standard documentation, and informal entry, see "Entry Process" on page 185.

Informed Compliance. Informed compliance was introduced with the Customs Modernization Act of 1993 (Mod Act) and defines the relationship between importers and the Customs Service. It sets out the responsibilities of both parties. Providing the correct documentation and information for entry is a key factor that will make your importing operation run smoothly. We recommend that importers become familiar with the concept of informed comliance and the responsibilities that they have under the Mod Act. For further discussion about informed compliance see "Informed Compliance" on page 211.

NAFTA Certificates of Origin. An importer of textiles for which NAFTA treatment is sought need not file a separate NAFTA Certificate of Origin in addition to the Customs Country-of-Origin Declaration. The declaration is sufficient. However, the importer must take care to submit a declaration from each U.S., Canadian, or Mexican producer or manufacturer. Thus, for multiple producers or manufacturers, a separate declaration must be filed for each. If a Customs port director cannot determine the country of origin because the declaration is absent or incomplete, the shipment is not entitled to preferential NAFTA tariff treatment or other NAFTA benefits. See 19 CFR 12.132.

Entry Invoices. You must provide certain additional information on the entry invoice for silk and silk products. The specific information varies depending on the nature of your product, as noted below.

TFPIA Requirements. For the purpose of TFPIA enforcement, a commercial shipment of textile products exceeding $500 in value and subject to TFPIA labeling requirements must show the following information: 1) The constituent fiber or combination of fibers, designating with equal prominence each natural or manufactured fiber by its generic name, in order of predominance by weight if the weight of such fiber is 5% or more of the total fiber weight of the product; 2) percentage of each fiber present, by weight, in the total fiber content; 3) the name or other identification issued and registered by the FTC of the manufacturer of the product or one or more persons subject to Section 3 of the TFPIA with respect to such product; 4) the name of the country where processed or manufactured.

Wool Products Subject to WPLA. When you offer for entry a wool product shipment valued at over $500 and subject to the WPLA, you must include certain information intended to facilitate Customs monitoring and enforcement of that Act. This extra information is identical to that required by WPLA on labeling (see "Marking and Labeling Requirements" below), with the addition of the manufacturer's name. If your product consists of mixed waste, residues, and similar merchandise obtained from several suppliers or unknown sources, you may omit the manufacturer's name from the entry invoice.

Yarn. All entry invoices for yarn should show: 1) Fiber content by weight; 2) whether the yarn is single or plied; 3) whether or not the yarn is put up for retail sale (as defined in HTSUS Section XI, Note 4); and 4) whether or not the yarn is intended for use as sewing thread.

In addition, if the yarn's chief weight is of silk, the entry invoice must show whether the silk is spun or filament. For more general information about invoices see "Invoices" on page 277.

Note: The Entry and Documentation section has been carefully designed to supply you, the importer, with sample documents and directions on how to satisfy Customs requirements. Be aware that you should consult the applicable authorities to ensure that you are correctly following the most current procedures.

Prohibitions and Restrictions

Quotas. Textile import restrictions are primarily a matter of quotas and the way in which these quotas are administered and monitored. Under the Multi-Fiber Arrangement provisions of Section 204 of the Agricultural Adjustment Act, CITA has negotiated bilateral agreements with over 40 countries. These Agreements may impose quotas for a type of textile or a specific article, and they are country-specific. Currently, certain silk blends are subject to some quota restraints, but these agreements often change. Therefore, if you are interested in importing any silk products, you should contact the International Trade Administration's Office of Textile and Apparel (see addresses at end of this chapter). The Office of Textile and Apparel has a team of country specialists who can inform you of the latest developments and inform you about a product's quota or restriction status.

U.S. Customs enforces CITA textile and textile product entry quotas. If formal entry procedures are not followed, Customs will usually refuse entry for textiles that are subject to Section 204. Formal entry requires submission of a Country-of-Origin Declaration (see "General Considerations" above). U.S. Customs maintains a current textile quota status report. In addition, U.S.

Customs in Washington, DC, provides quota status reports online, which are regularly updated (www.customs.gov/impoexpo/impoexpo.htm).

Flammable Fabrics. U.S. Customs may refuse entry for any article of wearing apparel or interior furnishing, or any fabric or related material that is intended for use or that may be used in wearing apparel or interior furnishings, if it fails to conform to an applicable flammability standard issued under Section 4 of the FFA. An exception is allowed for certain products (FFA Section 11c) that are imported for finishing or processing to bring them within the legal standard. For these products, the exporter must state on the invoice or other paper relating to the shipment that the shipment is being made for that purpose.

The CPSC, as the primary enforcement agency of flammability standards, inspects products for compliance with the FFA. If the CPSC believes a product, fabric, or related material does not comply with a flammability standard, it is authorized to pursue a variety of legal sanctions, including: 1) seizure, condemnation, and forfeiture of the noncomplying products; 2) administrative cease-and-desist order requiring an individual or firm to stop sale and distribution of the noncomplying products or; 3) temporary injunction requiring the individual or firm to stop sale and distribution of the noncomplying products, pending final disposition of an administrative cease-and-desist proceeding. The CPSC also has authority to seek civil penalties against any person who knowingly violates a regulation or standard issued under Section 4 of the FFA.

Country-Specific Restrictions

Restrictions under bilateral agreements are country-specific. A product originating in one country may be subject to quota and to export license or visa requirements, while the same product originating in a different country may not. At present, the U.S. has Multi-Fiber Arrangements with 40 countries. Many different categories of products are covered under these Arrangements; it is beyond the scope of this book to list each country and its restricted commodities. If you are interested in importing textiles and textile products, you should contact the International Trade Administration's Office of Textile and Apparel (see addresses at end of this chapter) or U.S. Customs to ascertain your product's restraint status.

The U.S. Customs service provides quota reports on their website (www.customs.gov/impoexpo/impoexpo.htm). These reports are constantly updated and have an effective date noted. The most recent quota information can be accessed by clicking on the country name that interests you. This location holds information regarding quotas, transshipments, and visa requirements.

Marking and Labeling Requirements

TFPIA Requirements. All textile fiber products imported into the U.S. must be stamped, tagged, labeled, or otherwise marked with the following information as required by the TFPIA, unless exempt from marking (see TFPIA, Section 12): 1) the generic names and percentages by weight of the constituent fibers present in the textile fiber product, exclusive of permissible ornamentation, in amounts of more than 5% in order of predominance by weight, with any percentage of fiber or fibers required to be designated as "other fiber" or "other fibers" (including those present in amounts of 5% or less) appearing last; and 2) the name of the manufacturer or the name or registered identification number issued by the FTC of one or more persons marketing or handling the textile fiber product; and 3) the name of the country where processed. A word trademark, used as a house mark and registered with the U.S. Patent Office, may appear on labels instead of the name otherwise required, provided the owner of the trademark furnishes a copy of the registration to the FTC prior to use (see "Registered Identification Numbers" below).

The information listed above is not exhaustive. TFPIA requirements are extensive. The Act specifies such details as types of labels, means of attachment, label position on the article, package labeling, unit labeling for two-piece garments, and arrangement of information on the label; allowable fiber designations; country-of-origin indications; requirements for trim and ornamentation, linings and interlinings, and pile fabrics; sectional disclosure; use of trade names and trademarks; and requirements for swatches and samples. The FTC publishes a document intended to clarify TFPIA requirements to facilitate voluntary compliance in the industry It is available on request, at no charge, from the FTC (see "Publications and WWW Resources" below).

Wool Products Labeling Act (WPLA). Wool product labeling requirements for foreign products are the responsibility of the importer. The WPLA requires the following information to appear on wool products subject to the Act: 1) percentage of the wool product's total fiber weight (exclusive of ornamentation) not exceeding 5% of the total fiber weight of a) wool, b) recycled wool, c) each fiber other than wool if the percent by weight of such fiber is 5% or more, and d) the aggregate of all other fibers; 2) the maximum percent of the wool product's total weight, of any nonfibrous loading, filling, or adulterating matter; and 3) the importer's name. If you, as importer, have a registered identification number issued by the FTC, that number may be used instead of your name (see "Registered Identification Numbers" below).

Customs entry is contingent on proper labeling. If your shipment is found to be mislabeled at entry, you will be given the option of relabelling the products under Customs supervision, as long as the port director is satisfied that your labeling error or omission did not involve fraud or willful neglect. If your shipment is discovered after entry to have been noncomplying with WPLA, it will be recalled to Customs custody at your expense, unless you can satisfy the port director that the products have since been brought into compliance. You will be held responsible for all expenses incurred in bringing a shipment into compliance, including compensation of personnel and other expenses related to Customs supervision.

Fraudulent violations of WPLA will result in seizure of the shipment. Shipments already released from Customs custody will be ordered to be redelivered to Customs. Customs reports all cases of fraudulent violation to the FTC in Washington, DC.

The information listed above is not intended to be exhaustive. WPLA requirements are extensive. The Act specifies such details as types of labels, means of attachment, label position on the article, package labeling, unit labeling (as in the case of a two-piece garment), arrangement of information on the label, allowable fiber designations, country-of-origin indications, trim and ornamentation, pile fabrics, sectional disclosure, use of trade names and trademarks, requirements for swatches and samples, etc. The FTC publishes a booklet intended to clarify WPLA requirements in order to facilitate voluntary compliance within the industry (see "Publications and WWW Resources" below). It is available on request, at no charge, from the FTC (see addresses at end of this chapter).

The Care Labeling Rule. Regulations under this rule require manufacturers and importers of textile clothing and fabrics to attach specific care instructions for washing or dry cleaning, as well as information on the fiber composition of the article. They are enforced by the FTC Division of Enforcement. The Care Labeling Rule was amended September 2000, detailed information is available on the FTC website (www.ftc.gov/os/statutes/textilejump.htm).

Registered Identification Numbers. Any domestic firm or person residing in the U.S. and engaged in the manufacture or marketing of textile products covered under the TTPIA may obtain an FTC-registered identification number for use on required tags and labels instead of the name of a firm or person. For applications, contact the FTC (address below.)

For a general discussion of U.S. Customs marking and labeling requirements, see "Country of Origin Marking" on page 236, "Special Marking Requirements" on page 238 and "Marking—False Impression" on page 239.

Shipping Considerations

You will need to ensure that your goods are packaged and shipped with care so that they pass smoothly through Customs and arrive in good condition. You are responsible for ensuring that the shipment is in compliance with all applicable government regulations for packaging and shipping. In most instances, you should not leave these arrangements solely to the discretion of your supplier. Careful preparation of the cargo and selection of the mode of transport can be essential to a cost-effective, timely delivery of undamaged goods. We strongly advise you to consult your shipping representative, insurance agent, or freight broker for advice on packing and shipping.

Silk products may be shipped in bulk, bolts, cartons, or other types of containers, depending on the type of product and whether it is prepackaged. General considerations include protection from contamination, weather, and pests. Containers should be constructed so as to be safe for handling during transport.

Publications and WWW Resources

The following publications may be relevant to the importation of silk textiles, silk articles, and silk-wool blends:

> *Threading Your Way Through the Labeling Requirements Under the Textile and Wool Acts*

> *Writing a Care Label : How to Comply with Care Labeling Rule*

Available free of charge on request from the Federal Trade Commission website (www.ftc.gov/os/statutes/textilejump.htm), these publications are excellent sources of information written in clear lay language. We recommend that anyone interested in importing textile fiber products but unfamiliar with the regulations obtain a copy of each of these booklets.

The U.S. Customs Service launched a series of "Informed Compliance" publications in 1996, which are available on the Customs Service website (www.customs.gov/impoexpo/impoexpo.htm). Of particular interest:

> *What Every Member of the Trade Community Should Know About Textile & Apparel Rules of Origin*

> *What Every Member of the Trade community Should Know About NAFTA for Textiles and Textile Articles*

> *Fibers & Yarns Construction and Classification Under the HTSUS*

The *Harmonized Tariff Schedule of the United States (2001)* (HTSUS) is available to view on the Customs Service website (www.customs.gov), or you may purchase a printed version from:

U.S. Government Printing Office
Superintendent of Documents
710 North Capital Street NW
Washington DC 20401
Tel: (202) 512-1800
Fax: (202) 512-1657
Website: www.access.gpo.gov

The USGPO also has copies of specific laws available for purchase. The USGPO accepts orders made by fax, phone or placed over the Internet, as well as mail orders paid by credit card. All orders must be accompanied by payment. Credit cards, checks drawn on a U.S. bank, or an international money order are all acceptable.

Relevant Government Agencies

Address your questions regarding textile Multi-Fiber Arrangements to:

U.S. Department of Commerce
International Trade Administration
Office of Textiles and Apparel
Director's Office
14th and Constitution Ave. NW, Rm. H3100
Washington DC 20230
Tel: (202) 482-5078
Fax: (202) 482-2331
Agreements Division: (202) 482-4212
Website: http://otexa.ita.doc.gov

Address your questions regarding the Flammable Fabrics Act (FFA) to:

Consumer Product Safety Commission (CPSC)
Office of Compliance
Washington DC 20207-0001
Tel: 800-638-2772 or (301) 504-7912
Fax: (301) 504-0359
Website: www.cpsc.gov

Address your questions regarding requirements under the Textile Fiber Products Identification Act (TFPIA) or the Wool Products Labeling Act (WPLA) to:

Federal Trade Commission (FTC)
Division of Enforcement
600 Pennsylvania Avenue NW
Washington DC 20580
Tel: (202) 326-2996
Website: www.ftc.gov

Address your questions regarding textile quotas to:

U.S. Customs and Border Protection
Office of Field Operations, Quota Branch
1300 Pennsylvania Avenue NW
Washington DC 20229
Tel: (202) 927-5850
Website: www.customs.treas.gov

The U.S. Customs Service provices updated status reports on textile quota on their web site (see address above). If the country you need information on is not listed, call the Quota Branch office at (202) 927-5850.

Address your questions regarding silk textile imports to your local Customs port director. For addresses, refer to "U.S. Customs and Border Protection Offices" on page 65 or contact:

U.S. Customs and Border Protection
Customs Headquarters
1300 Pennsylvania Avenue NW
Washington DC 20229
Tel: (202) 354-1000
Website: www.customs.treas.gov

Laws and Regulations

The following laws and regulations may be relevant to the importation of silk products. The laws are contained in the United States Code (USC), and the regulations are published in the Code of Federal Regulations (CFR), both of which are available at larger public and law libraries. Copies of specific laws are also available from the United States Government Printing Office (address above).

7 USC 1854
Textile Trade Agreements
(EO 11651, as amended by EO 11951 and 12188, and supplemented by EO 12475)
This Act authorizes the CITA of the DOC to enter into Multi-Fiber Agreements with other countries to control trade in textiles and establishes the Textile Import Program, which is enforced by U.S. Customs.

19 CFR 12.130 et seq.
Regulations on Entry of Textiles
These regulations provide the requirements and proce-

dures followed by Customs in enforcing limitations on the importation and entry and withdrawal of textiles and textile products from warehouses for consumption in the U.S.

19 CFR 141.89
Regulation on Additional Invoice Requirements
This regulation specifies the additional information for certain classes of merchandise, including footwear and textile products, being imported into the U.S.

15 USC 70-77
Textile Fiber Products Identification Act (TFPIA)
This Act prohibits false or deceptive labeling (misbranding) and false advertising of any textile fiber products and requires all textile fiber products imported into the U.S. to be labeled in accordance with the requirements set forth in the law.

19 CFR 11.12b; 16 CFR 303 et seq.
Regulations on Labeling and Marking
These regulations detail the labeling and marking requirements for textiles as specified by the CPSC and the invoice contents required by U.S. Customs for purpose of enforcing the labeling and marking rules.

15 USC 68-68j
Wool Products Labeling Act (WPLA) of 1939
This Act prohibits the false or deceptive labeling (misbranding) of wool products and requires all wool products imported into the U.S. to be labeled in accordance with requirements set forth in the law.

19 CFR 11.12; 16 CFR 300 et seq.
Regulations on WPLA Labeling and Marking
These regulations set forth the wool labeling and marking requirements adopted by the FTC to administer the requirements of the WPLA and provide the procedures followed by U.S. Customs in enforcing the WPLA and the FTC regulations, including entry invoice requirements.

15 USC 1191-1204
Flammable Fabrics Act (FFA)
This Act provides for the setting of flammability standards for fabric by the Consumer Product Safety Commission (CPSC) and for enforcement by U.S. Customs.

16 CFR 1610, 1611, 1615, 1616, 1630-1632
Regulations on Flammable Fabric Standards
These regulations specify the flammability standards adopted by the CPSC under the FFA for various types of textiles.

16 CFR 423
Care Labeling Rule
Requires fiber composition and washing or dry cleaning instructions for textile apparel and certain piece goods.

Principal Exporting Countries

The following listing includes samples of the main supplier nations of the products of this chapter. It is organized by HTSUS major heading. (Refer to "Customs Classification" above for the product codes.) Countries are listed in rank order of the value of products imported to the U.S. Statistics represent customs value of entries for 2002 from the Bureau of Census.

5001—China

5002—Malaysia, China, India, Brazil, Thailand, United Kingdom, Italy, Philippines

5003—India, China, Italy, Germany, United Kingdom, Canada, Nepal, Thailand

5004—China, Italy, Brazil, Switzerland, France, Japan

5005—Italy, China, Switzerland, France, United Kingdom, Spain, Nepal, India, Hong Kong, South Korea, Japan

5006—China, United Kingdom, France, Italy, Japan, Germany

5007—India, Italy, China, South Korea, United Kingdom

Chapter 51:
Wool and Animal Hair

Full title: Wool, Fine or Coarse Animal Hair; Horsehair Yarn and Woven Fabric

This chapter relates to the importation of wool and animal hair products, which are classified under Chapter 51 of the Harmonized Tariff Schedule of the United States (HTSUS). Specifically, it includes uncarded and uncombed wool, uncarded and uncombed fine or coarse animal hair, yarn waste and other waste of wool or animal hair, wool or animal hair yarns, and woven fabrics of wool or animal hair. Animal hair includes the hair of alpaca, llama, vicuna, camel, yak, goat, rabbit, beaver, nutria, muskrat, and horse.

If you are interested in importing horsehair, human hair, brush-making hair, and bristles, you should refer to Commodity Index Chapter 5. If you are interested in importing hides and skins with hair or wool attached, read Chapters 41 and 43. For importing a particular product made of wool or animal hair, you should refer to the Commodity Index chapter for that product. For example, wigs are covered in Chapter 67, footwear and leggings in Chapter 64, headgear in Chapter 65, carpets in Chapter 57, needlework sets and other textile art products in Chapter 63, and apparel in Chapters 60 through 62.

Note: To understand key issues that will enable you to make best use of the information in this section we recommend that you see "Introduction" on page 425.

Key Factors

The key factors in the importation of wool and animal hair products are:

- Compliance with quota restraints and visa requirements
- Determination of grade and/or purpose of wool products being imported to ascertain dutiable status.
- Submission of U.S. Customs Country-of-Origin Declaration(s)
- Compliance with entry invoice requirements.
- Compliance with Wool Products Labeling Act (WPLA) or the Textile Fiber Products Identification Act (TFPIA)
- Compliance with flammability standards adopted and enforced by the Consumer Product Safety Commission (CPSC) under the Flammable Fabrics Act (FFA) (if importing fabrics and other textile products)

Although most importers use the services of a licensed customs broker in making their entries, and we recommend this practice, you should be aware of the regulatory, entry, and documentation issues involved in importing your product. You, as importer, are ultimately responsible for the fulfillment of any legal requirements applicable to your shipment.

General Considerations

Regulatory Agencies. Importation of wool and wool products is subject to complex textile import regulations. The Federal Trade Commission (FTC) administers the WPLA requirements. The Committee for Implementation of Textile Agreements (CITA) regulates certain textile imports under Section 204 of the Agricultural Adjustment Act. U.S. Customs enforces CITA textile and textile product entry quotas. Customs also enforces compliance with labeling and invoice requirements of the WPLA and the TFPIA, as well as flammability standards under the FFA. The CPSC monitors imports and from time to time inspects textile shipments for compliance with FFA standards.

Entry Requirements. Depending on the nature of your wool product imports, as many as three different types of special entry documents may be required. First, for all imported textile fibers, yarns, and fabrics covered by the Agricultural Adjustment Act (AAA), including wool, you must file a U.S. Customs Textile Entry Declaration (see "Country-of-Origin Declarations" below). Second, for all wool products subject to the WPLA and all raw wool dutiable at a rate per clean kilogram, special information is required on the entry invoices (see "Entry and Documentation" below). Third, for shipments of wool dutiable at a rate per clean kilogram, you must also file one extra copy of the standard entry summary in addition to the copies otherwise required. Finally, certain wool articles manufactured or produced in certain countries may be subject to quotas under bilateral agreements. Such products require export certificates or visas issued by the appropriate country of origin, in addition to other requisite entry paperwork (see "Quotas" below). The DOC's Office of Textiles and Apparel (OTEXA) provides detailed information about specific trade agreements on the OTEXA website (http://otexa.ita.doc.gov).

Wool Products Labeling Act. The term "wool product" means any product or any portion of a product that contains, purports to contain, or in any way is represented as containing wool, reprocessed wool, or reused wool. All wool products imported into the U.S., except those made more than 20 years before importation, and except carpets, rugs, mats, and upholsteries, must have affixed a stamp, tag, label, or other means of identification as required by the WPLA. If you are importing wool products exempt from labeling under the WPLA, do not assume they are also exempt from labeling under the TFPIA. These are two distinct laws, with some overlapping requirements (see "Marking and Labeling Requirements" below).

Quotas. If you are interested in importing wool and animal hair products, the most important issue you need to be aware of is quotas. Under the Multi-Fiber Arrangement provisions of Section 204 of the Agricultural Adjustment Act, CITA initiates specific agreements with individual exporting countries. Section 204 of the Agricultural Adjustment Act covers textiles that: 1) are in chief value of cotton, wool, or man-made fibers, any textile fibers subject to the terms of any textile trade agreement, or any combination of such fibers; 2) contain 50% or more by weight of cotton or man-made fibers, or any textile fibers subject to the terms of any textile trade agreement; 3) contain 17% or more by weight of wool; or 4) if in chief value of textile fibers or textile materials, contain a blend of cotton, wool, or man-made fibers, any textile fibers subject to the terms of any textile trade agreement, or any combination of such fibers that, in total, amount to 50% or more by weight of all component fibers.

The U.S. has bilateral agreements with over 40 countries. Each agreement with each country is unique, and may specify quotas for a type of textile or a specific article. Visas or export licenses may be required. These agreements, however, often change. Therefore, if you are interested in importing any wool or animal hair products, you should contact the International Trade Administration's Office of Textile and Apparel (see addresses at end of this chapter). Refer to "Prohibitions and Restrictions" below for further details.

Country-of-Origin Declarations. U.S. Customs enforces CITA textile and textile product entry quotas (see "Prohibitions and Restrictions" below). Requirements for entry include submission of Country-of-Origin Declarations with every wool or animal hair textile shipment, regardless of whether it is subject to a specific multi-fiber arrangement (19 CFR 12.130, 12.131).

In 1996, the U.S. Customs Service made major changes to country of origin rules for textile imports. The regulations at 19 CFR 102.21, "Textile and apparel products" were added to the 1996 Customs Regulations and became effective July 1, 1996. The new rules do not provide for cutting components or cutting and hemming to confer country of origin as in the past. The basis of the new law is processing operations or assembly. Some of the most important changes for importers to be aware of are:

- Cutting does not determine the country of origin (previously cutting determined country of origin for 90 percent of wearing apparel imports). The new rules are based on processing or assembly operations.

- A subjective determination under the provisions of 19 CFR 12.130 is replaced by objective processing operations expressed in terms of tariff shifts. Dyeing, printing, and other finishing processes applied to fabrics no longer confer or change country of origin.

- Country of origin for textile and apparel products processed, assembled or manufactured in two or more countries is determined by where the most important processing occurs, and, if that cannot be ascertained, the last country in which an important processing operation occurs.

The country of origin is the country in which a product is wholly produced when a textile or apparel product is completely produced or manufactured (except for minor parts) in one country. For fabric, the country of origin is the country in which the fabric is woven, knitted, needled, tufted, felted, entangled or created by any other fabric-making process. The country of origin for staple yarn is the country in which yarn is spun; for filament yarn, the country in which filament is extruded; and for plied, gimped and cabled yarns, the country in which the fibers or filaments used in the yarn are spun or extruded. The country of origin of all other textile and apparel products is the country in which the components of a textile or apparel product are wholly assembled (except for minor attachments) except for knit-to-shape products. Knit-to-shape products are those composed of panels or parts ,which, are knitted or crocheted directly into the shape that will be used in construction of the final product. Minor cutting or sewing does not influence whether the product is considered knit-to-shape. The country of origin for knit-to-shape products is that country in which the major parts are knitted into the shape that will constitute the finished product. Once again, note that assembly, not cutting, now confers country of origin.

Declarations. All importations of textiles and textile products must be accompanied by one of the following three declarations. Goods subject to Section 204, Agricultural Act of 1956, as amended, must be accompanied by either a single-country or a multi-ple-country declaration. Goods not subject to Section 204 must be accompanied by a negative declaration.

- **Single-country declarations** are used for entries of textiles or textile products which are wholly the growth, product, or manufacture of a single foreign country, territory, or U.S. insular possession. Information required includes: marks of identification and numbers; description of article and quantity; country of origin; and date of exportation.

- **Multiple-country declarations** are used for entries of textiles or textile products which were subjected to manufacturing or processing operations in, and/or incorporate materials originating in more than one foreign country or territory. Information required includes: marks of identification and numbers; for articles, description, quantity, identification of manufacturing and/or processing operations, country, and date of exportation; for materials used to make articles, description of materials, country of production, and date of exportation.

- **Negative declarations** must accompany all textile imports that are not subject to AAA Section 204 restrictions. Information required includes: marks of identification and numbers; descriptions of article and quantity; and country of origin.

The date of exportation to be indicated on the above declarations is the date on which the carrier leaves the last port in the country of origin, as determined by Customs. Diversion to another country during transit does not affect the export date.

Procedure for Declarations. The manufacturer, producer, exporter, or importer may prepare the declaration. If more than one of these parties is involved in the importation, each party may prepare a separate declaration. You may file a separate declaration for each invoice presented with your entry. The declaration must be dated and signed by the responsible party, and must include the person's title and the company name and address. Your shipment's entry will be denied unless it is accompanied by a properly executed declaration. Customs will not treat a textile declaration as a missing document for which a bond may be filed.

Customs will base its country-of-origin determination on the information contained in each declaration, unless the information is insufficient. If the information on the declaration is insufficient, Customs will require that you submit such additional information as will enable the determination to be made. The shipment will not be released until the determination is made. Thus, if you want to clear Customs with minimal delay, be sure that the information on the declarations is as complete as possible for each shipment.

Flammability Standards. Wool and animal hair textile products imported into the U.S. for use in consumer products must be in compliance with the FFA, a federal law that gives the CPSC the authority and responsibility for protecting the public from the hazards of dangerously flammable items of wearing apparel and interior furnishings. Under the FFA, standards have been established for flammability. You cannot import any article of wearing apparel or interior furnishing, or any fabric or related material that is intended for use or that may be used in such items, if it fails to conform to an applicable flammability standard (FFA Section 4). Certain products may be imported into the U.S. (FFA Section 11c) for finishing or processing to render them less flammable so as to meet the standards. For these products, the exporter must state on the invoice or other paper relating to the shipment that the shipment is being made for that purpose.

The CPSC monitors imports of textiles under its Import Surveillance Program. From time to time, your textile shipments may be inspected to ascertain compliance with mandatory safety standards. Shipments may also be subject to testing by the CPSC to determine compliance. If the CPSC believes a product, fabric, or related material does not comply with a flammability standard, it is authorized to pursue a variety of legal sanctions (see "Prohibitions and Restrictions" below).

Substantial Product Hazard Reports. Any firm that obtains information that reasonably supports the conclusion that one of its products presents an unreasonable risk of serious injury or death must report that information to the CPSC's Division of Corrective Actions (CPSC address below). Importers must also report to the CPSC if 1) a type of product is the subject of at least three civil actions filed in U.S. federal or state courts, 2) each suit alleges the involvement of that product type in death or grievous bodily injury (as defined in FFA Section 37(3)1), and 3) at least three of the actions result in a final settlement with the manufacturer or in a judgment for the plaintiff within any one of the two-year periods specified in FFA Section 37(b).

Import Advisory

Importation of textiles is trade-sensitive and highly regulated. Shipments of textiles and textile products not complying with all government regulations, including quotas and visas, are subject to seizure and could result in the imposition of penalties as well as possible forfeiture of the goods. You should always verify the available quota for any textile product you plan to import before your shipment leaves the country of manufacture. Furthermore, Customs textile classification rulings change frequently, and prior administrative rulings are often modified and sometimes reversed. You should be particularly careful to comply with country of origin determination regulations, which were changed in 1996, and affect quotas and visas, marking and labeling, and other important aspects of tariff classification. See "Publications and WWW Resources" for information on important Customs Service informed compliance publications.

The Customs Service has greatly increased its scrutiny of the textile industry, one of eight primary focus industries identified in the most recent Trade Compliance & Enforcement Plan. Imported products from these industries will likely attract significant attention from Customs in the areas of compliance measurement, compliance assessment, informed compliance, and interventions.

Customs Classification

For customs purposes, wool and animal hair products are classified under Chapter 51 of the HTSUS. This chapter is broken into major headings, which are further divided into subheadings, and often sub-subheadings, each of which has its own HTSUS classification number. For example, the 2001 HTSUS number for carded Angora rabbit hair yarn is 5108.10.30, indicating it is a sub-subcategory of carded yarn (5108.10), which is a subcategory of the major heading, yarn of fine animal hair, etc., not for retail sale (5108). There are 13 major headings within Chapter 51.

5101—Wool, not carded or combed

5102—Fine or coarse animal hair, not carded or combed

5103—Waste of wool or of fine or coarse animal hair, including yarn waste but excluding garnetted stock

5104—Garnetted stock of wool or of fine or coarse animal hair

5105—Wool and fine or coarse animal hair, carded or combed (including combed wool in fragments)

5106—Yarn of carded wool, not put up for retail sale

5107—Yarn of combed wool, not put up for retail sale

5108—Yarn of fine animal hair (carded or combed), not put up for retail sale

5109—Yarn of wool or fine animal hair, put up for retail sale

5110—Yarn of coarse animal hair or of horsehair (including gimped horsehair yarn), whether or not put up for retail sale

5111—Woven fabrics of carded wool or of carded fine animal hair

5112—Woven fabrics of combed wool or of combed fine animal hair

5113—Woven fabrics of coarse animal hair or of horsehair

Classification of Wool. Customs makes several basic distinctions among wools for duty classification purposes. Duty rates vary depending on the degree to which the wool is processed (i.e. sheared and degreased only versus in finished fabric form), whether the wool is rated as unimproved, and whether the wool is brought in "for special uses."

Processed and Unprocessed Wool. In general, wool not carded or combed and not processed other than degreased enters free under bond. Most other "raw" wool is dutiable per clean kilogram, with rates rising as the grade of wool becomes finer. All shipments of wool are examined to determine grade based on the standards established by the Secretary of Agriculture and in effect on the date of importation. Roughly defined, clean yield means absolute clean content (i.e. all that portion of the merchandise that consists exclusively of wool and is free from all vegetable and other foreign material). There are allowances for moisture content and other factors. If you need more technical details, see Additional U.S. Note 2 to HTSUS Chapter 51. For information on duty determination procedures, see 19 CFR 151.65 et seq.

Unimproved and Improved Wool. Unimproved wool includes Aleppo, Arabian, Bagdad, Black Spanish, Chinese, Cordova, Cyprus, Donskoi, East Indian, Ecuadorian, Egyptian, Georgian, Haslock, Iceland, Karakul, Kerry, Manchurian, Mongolian, Oporto, Persian, Pyrenean, Sardinian, Scotch Blackface, Sistan, Smyrna, Sudan, Syrian, Tibetan Turkestan, Valparaiso, or Welsh Mountain wool, and similar wool not improved by an admixture of merino or English blood.

Wool for Special Uses. Unimproved wool and other wool of any blood or origin not finer than 46s may be entered duty-free under the category "for special uses" by a dealer, manufacturer, or processor. It must be certified for use only in the manufacture of the following: 1) felt or knit boots; 2) floor coverings; 3) heavy filled lumbermen's socks; 3) press cloth; 4) papermakers' felts; or 5) pressed felt for polishing plate and mirror glass.

If you enter wool for special purposes, you must file a bond with the Customs port of entry which insures that the wool will be used only for the allowed purposes. Your shipment will be released when the bond is filed. As original importer, you are liable for the use limitations of the bond, until or unless you transfer the shipment under similar bond to a different dealer, manufacturer, or processor.

If the wool is used, or transferred for use, outside permitted uses under the bond, the current bondholder will be liable for any duties applicable because of tariff reclassification. Furthermore, every bondholder is required to report any such transfer or use of merchandise within 30 days to the port director of Customs in whose district the bond is filed. Failure to report will result in a penalty—in addition to duties—equal to the value of the merchandise in question.

Sampling for Classification. Customs determines clean yield for classification purposes by testing samples taken from all raw wool shipments. Testing is done in a Customs laboratory, pursuant to regulations in 19 CFR 151.71. If sampling is not feasible for your shipment, Customs will estimate the percentage clean yield of each lot by examination. For either means of clean-yield determination, Customs will report the percentage clean yield of each lot to you by mail.

If, as a result of Customs examination, the wool is classified at a higher grade than the grade you stated at entry, thus incurring a higher rate of duty, the port director will notify you by mail. You have the option to contest the assessment by filing within 14 days of the date on which Customs mails your clean-yield notification a request, in duplicate, for redetermination of grade. You will have to state reasons for requesting this reexamination, and you will need to make a second general sample available for such re-testing, or an adequate number of the packages represented by the general sample must be available in their original imported condition. All costs of this retesting or re-examination, except for compensation of Customs employees, will be charged to you. Customs will mail a notice of reexamination results to you.

If you are not satisfied with the results of the second test or examination, you may request testing in a commercial lab. Again, this request must be filed with the appropriate port director within 14 days of the date on which Customs mails you the second test results. The port director chooses the commercial lab. All costs associated with such testing, including any travel-related expenses for Customs officers, are your responsibility.

Preliminary duties may be estimated when you file the entry summary, on the basis of the clean yield shown on it. However, liquidated duties are based on the port director's final determination of clean yield. If more than one examination or test has been performed on your shipment, the port director will take the findings from all applicable tests or examinations into consideration in making the final duty determination. For more details regarding sampling, testing, and contesting procedures, see 19 CFR 151.68-75.

For more details regarding classifications of the specific product you are interested in importing, consult a customs broker, the appropriate commodity specialist at your nearest customs port, or the HTSUS. The 2001 HTSUS is available online from the Customs Service (www.customs.gov/impoexpo/impoexpo.htm) or for purchase from the U.S. Government Printing Office (see resources at the end of this chapter), and may be found in larger public libraries. For a general discussion of customs classification, see "Classification—Liquidation" on page 229.

Dutiable Status of Goods

For more information about duty rates and binding decisions see "Dutiable Status of Goods" on page 203; for a discussion of temporary importation of goods see "Temporary Free Importations" on page 205.

Valuation

Importers have a responsibility to use what the U.S. Customs Service deems, "reasonable care," when determining the value of their goods. They must also provide any additional information that the Customs Service needs for setting a final value on the goods. This process involves a number of factors and can be somewhat complicated; importers must be aware of applicable issues and details. Valuation information applies to all types of commodities, for further discussion on the subject see "Customs Valuation" on page 267.

Import Duties

Import duties vary (often dramatically) depending upon the Harmonized Tariff Schedule (HTSUS) classification of the goods or products imported. Since some products that look alike have different HTSUS classifications and different rates of duty, proper classification is vital. Note that "differences of opinion" between importers and the Bureau of Customs and Border Protection regarding classification keeps customs attorneys very busy.

Import duties can be assessed on the imported value of the goods ("ad valorem" rates of duty such as 2%, 4.4%, 50%, etc.), to-

tal units or weight of the goods ("specific" rates of duty such as 2 cents each or 1.5 cents/pound, etc.) or on a combination basis ("compound" rates of duty such as 5 cents each plus 6%).

Listed below is a sampling of several Column 1 import duty rates for Chapter 51 products:
Wool for special uses (5101.11.10.00): Free
to
Other hair (not processed in any manner beyond the degreased or carbonized condition) (5102.11.10 00): 5.1¢/clea kg

For specific information on US import duties refer to the Harmonized Tariff Schedule of the US. The print version is available from the US Government Printing Office as well as third party suppliers who often add special features. Online versions are available in both static PDF pages as well as in formats with excellent search functionality. Search the Web with the term "Harmonized Tariff Schedule" to find sources.

Entry and Documentation

The entry of merchandise is a two-part process consisting of 1) filing the documentation necessary to determine whether merchandise may be released from Customs custody, and 2) filing the documents that contain information for duty assessment and statistical purposes. In certain instances, all documents must be filed and accepted by Customs prior to release of the goods. Unless you have been granted an extension, you must file entry documents at a location specified by the port or area director within five working days of your shipment's date of arrival at a U.S. port of entry. These include a number of standard documents required by Customs for any entry, and:

- U.S. Customs Country-of-Origin Declaration Form CF 3229

- Export documentation and/or visa for textiles subject to bilateral agreement

- One extra copy of the standard entry summary (for shipments of wool dutiable at a rate per clean kg)

After you present the entry, Customs may examine your shipment or may waive examination. The shipment is then released provided no legal or regulatory violations have been noted. If not already completed you must then file entry summary documentation and deposit estimated duties at a designated customhouse within 10 working days of your shipment's release. For a detailed description of entry procedures, standard documentation, and informal entry, see "Entry Process" on page 185.

Informed Compliance. Informed compliance was introduced with the Customs Modernization Act of 1993 (Mod Act) and defines the relationship between importers and the Customs Service. It sets out the responsibilities of both parties. Providing the correct documentation and information for entry is a key factor that will make your importing operation run smoothly. We recommend that importers become familiar with the concept of informed comliance and the responsibilities that they have under the Mod Act. For further discussion about informed compliance see "Informed Compliance" on page 211.

NAFTA Certificates of Origin. An importer of textiles for which NAFTA treatment is sought need not file a separate NAFTA Certificate of Origin in addition to the Customs Country-of-Origin Declaration. The declaration is sufficient. However, the importer must take care to submit a declaration from each U.S., Canadian, or Mexican producer or manufacturer. Thus, for multiple producers or manufacturers, a separate declaration must be filed for each. If a Customs port director cannot determine the country of origin because the declaration is absent or incomplete, the shipment is not entitled to preferential NAFTA tariff treatment or other NAFTA benefits. See 19 CFR 12.132.

Entry Invoices. You must provide certain additional information on the entry invoice for wool and wool products. The specific information varies depending on the nature of your product, as noted below.

Wool Products Subject to WPLA. When you offer for entry a wool product shipment valued at over $500 and subject to the WPLA, you must include certain information intended to facilitate Customs monitoring and enforcement of that Act. This extra information is identical to that required by WPLA on labeling (see "Marking and Labeling Requirements" below), with the addition of the manufacturer's name. If your product consists of mixed waste, residues, and similar merchandise obtained from several suppliers or unknown sources, you may omit the manufacturer's name from the entry invoice.

Raw Wool. Invoices of wool subject to duty at a rate per clean kilogram under HTSUS Chapter 51 must show the following detailed information in addition to other information required: 1) Condition—that is, whether greasy, washed, pulled, on the skin, scoured, carbonized, burrpicked, willowed, handshaken, or beaten; 2) whether free of vegetable matter, practically free, slightly burry, medium burry, or heavy burry; 3) whether in fleece, skirted, matchings, or sorted; 4) length—that is, whether super combing, ordinary combing, clothing, or filling; 5) country of origin, and, if possible, the province, section, or locality of production; 6) the type symbol by which the wool is bought and sold in the country of origin, and the grade of each lot, specifying the standard or basis used—that is, U.S. Official Standards or the country of shipment's commercial grade designation terms; and 7) net weight of each lot covered by the invoice in the condition in which it is shipped, and the shipper's estimate of the clean yield of each lot by weight or by percentage.

Wool Products Subject to TFPIA. For the purpose of TFPIA enforcement, a commercial shipment of textile products exceeding $500 in value and subject to TFPIA labeling requirements must show the following information: 1) the constituent fiber or combination of fibers, designating with equal prominence each natural or manufactured fiber by its generic name, in order of predominance by weight if the weight of such fiber is 5% or more of the total fiber weight of the product; 2) percentage of each fiber present, by weight, in the total fiber content; 3) the name or other identification issued and registered by the FTC of the manufacturer of the product or one or more persons subject to Section 3 of the TFPIA with respect to such product; and 4) the name of the country where processed or manufactured.

Yarn. All entry invoices for yarn should show: 1) fiber content by weight; 2) whether the yarn is single or plied; 3) whether or not the yarn is put up for retail sale (as defined in HTSUS Section XI, Note 4); and 4) whether or not the yarn is intended for use as sewing thread. For more general information about invoices see "Invoices" on page 277.

Note: The Entry and Documentation section has been carefully designed to supply you, the importer, with sample documents and directions on how to satisfy Customs requirements. Be aware that you should consult the applicable authorities to ensure that you are correctly following the most current procedures.

Prohibitions and Restrictions

Quotas. Textile import restrictions are primarily a matter of quotas and the way in which these quotas are administered and monitored. Under the Multi-Fiber Arrangement provisions of Section 204 of the Agricultural Adjustment Act, CITA has negotiated bilateral agreements with over 40 countries. These Agreements may impose quotas for a type of textile or a specific article, and they are country-specific. These agreements, however, often change. Therefore, if you are interested in importing any wool products, you should contact the International Trade Administration's Office of Textile and Apparel (see addresses at end of this chapter). The Office of Textile and Apparel has a team of country specialists who can inform you of the latest developments and inform you about a product's quota or restriction status.

U.S. Customs enforces CITA textile and textile product entry quotas. If formal entry procedures are not followed, Customs will usually refuse entry for textiles. Formal entry requires submission of a Country-of-Origin Declaration (see "General Considerations" above). U.S. Customs maintains a current textile quota status report. In addition, U.S. Customs in , DC, provides quota status reports online, which are updated regularly (see "Relevant Government Agencies" below).

Flammable Fabrics. U.S. Customs may refuse entry for any article of wearing apparel or interior furnishing, or any fabric or related material that is intended for use or that may be used in wearing apparel or interior furnishings, if it fails to conform to an applicable flammability standard issued under Section 4 of the FFA. An exception is allowed for certain products (FFA Section 11c) that are imported for finishing or processing to bring them within the legal standard. For these products, the exporter must state on the invoice or other paper relating to the shipment that the shipment is being made for that purpose.

The CPSC, as the primary enforcement agency of flammability standards, inspects products for compliance with the FFA. If the CPSC believes a product, fabric, or related material does not comply with a flammability standard, it is authorized to pursue a variety of legal sanctions, including: 1) seizure, condemnation, and forfeiture of the noncomplying products; 2) administrative cease-and-desist order requiring an individual or firm to stop sale and distribution of the noncomplying products or; 3) temporary injunction requiring the individual or firm to stop sale and distribution of the noncomplying products, pending final disposition of an administrative cease-and-desist proceeding. The CPSC also has authority to seek civil penalties against any person who knowingly violates a regulation or standard issued under Section 4 of the FFA.

Country-Specific Restrictions

Restrictions under bilateral agreements are country-specific. A product originating in one country may be subject to quota and to export license or visa requirements, while the same product originating in a different country may not. At present, the U.S. has Multi-Fiber Arrangements with 40 countries. Many different categories of products are covered under these Arrangements; it is beyond the scope of this book to list each country and its restricted commodities. If you are interested in importing textiles and textile products, you should contact the International Trade Administration's Office of Textile and Apparel (see addresses at end of this chapter) or U.S. Customs to ascertain your product's restraint status.

The U.S. Customs service provides quota reports on their website (www.customs.gov/impoexpo/impoexpo.htm). These reports are constantly updated and have an effective date noted. The most recent quota information can be accessed by clicking on the country name that interests you. This location holds information regarding quotas, transshipments, and visa requirements.

Marking and Labeling Requirements

Wool Products Labeling Act (WPLA). Wool product labeling requirements for foreign products are the responsibility of the importer. The WPLA requires the following information to appear on wool products subject to the Act: 1) percentage of the wool product's total fiber weight (exclusive of ornamentation) not exceeding 5% of the total fiber weight of a) wool, b) reprocessed wool, c) reused wool, d) each fiber other than wool if the percentage by weight of such fiber is 5% or more, and e) the aggregate of all other fibers; 2) the maximum percentage of the wool product's total weight, of any nonfibrous loading, filling, or adulterating matter; and 3) the importer's name. If you, as importer, have a registered identification number issued by the FTC, that number may be used instead of your name (see Registered Identification Numbers below).

Customs entry is contingent on proper labeling. If your shipment is found to be mislabeled at entry, you will be given the option of relabelling the products under Customs supervision, as long as the port director is satisfied that your labeling error or omission did not involve fraud or willful neglect. If your shipment is discovered after entry to have been noncomplying with WPLA, it will be recalled to Customs custody at your expense, unless you can satisfy the port director that the products have since been brought into compliance. You will be held responsible for all expenses incurred in bringing a shipment into compliance, including compensation of personnel and other expenses related to Customs supervision.

Fraudulent violations of WPLA will result in seizure of the shipment. Shipments already released from Customs custody will be ordered to be redelivered to Customs. Customs reports all cases of fraudulent violation to the FTC in Washington, DC.

The information listed above is not intended to be exhaustive. WPLA requirements are extensive. The Act specifies such details as types of labels, means of attachment, label position on the article, package labeling, unit labeling (as in the case of a two-piece garment), arrangement of information on the label, allowable fiber designations, country-of-origin indications, trim and ornamentation, pile fabrics, sectional disclosure, use of trade names and trademarks, requirements for swatches and samples, etc. The FTC publishes a booklet intended to clarify WPLA requirements in order to facilitate voluntary compliance within the industry (see "Publications and WWW Resources" below). It is available on request, at no charge, from the FTC website (see addresses at end of this chapter).

Wool Products Subject to TFPIA. All textile fiber products imported into the U.S. must be stamped, tagged, labeled, or otherwise marked with the following information as required by the TFPIA, unless exempt from marking (see TFPIA, Section 12): 1) the generic names and percentages by weight of the constituent fibers present in the textile fiber product, exclusive of permissible ornamentation, in amounts of more than 5% in order of predominance by weight, with any percentage of fiber or fibers required to be designated as "other fiber" or "other fibers" (including those present in amounts of 5% or less) appearing last; and 2) the name of the manufacturer or the name or registered identification number issued by the FTC of one or more persons marketing or handling the textile fiber product; and 3) the name of the country where processed. A word trademark, used as a house mark and registered with the U.S. Patent Office, may appear on labels instead of the name otherwise required, provided the owner of the trademark furnishes a copy of the registration to the FTC prior to use (see "Registered Identification Numbers" below).

The information listed above is not exhaustive. TFPIA requirements are extensive. The Act specifies such details as types of labels, means of attachment, label position on the article, package labeling, unit labeling for two-piece garments, and arrangement of information on the label; allowable fiber designations; country-of-origin indications; requirements for trim and ornamentation, linings and interlinings, and pile fabrics; sectional disclosure; use of trade names and trademarks; and requirements for swatches and samples. The FTC publishes a booklet intended to clarify TFPIA requirements to facilitate voluntary compliance in the industry (see "Publications and WWW Resources" below). It is available on request, at no charge, from the FTC (see addresses at end of this chapter).

The Care Labeling Rule. Regulations under this rule require manufacturers and importers of textile clothing and fabrics to attach specific care instructions for washing or dry cleaning, as well as information on the fiber composition of the article. They are enforced by the FTC Division of Enforcement. The Care Labeling Rule was amended September 2000, detailed information is available on the FTC website (www.ftc.gov/os/statutes/textilejump.htm).

Registered Identification Numbers. Any domestic firm or person residing in the U.S. and engaged in the manufacture or marketing of textile products covered under the WPLA or the TFPIA may obtain an FTC-registered identification number for use on required tags and labels instead of the name of a firm or person. For applications, contact the FTC (address below.)

For a general discussion of U.S. Customs marking and labeling requirements, see "Country of Origin Marking" on page 236, "Special Marking Requirements" on page 238 and "Marking—False Impression" on page 239.

Shipping Considerations

You will need to ensure that your goods are packaged and shipped with care so that they pass smoothly through Customs and arrive in good condition. You are responsible for ensuring that the shipment is in compliance with all applicable government regulations for packaging and shipping. In most instances, you should not leave these arrangements solely to the discretion of your supplier. Careful preparation of the cargo and selection of the mode of transport can be essential to a cost-effective, timely delivery of undamaged goods. We strongly advise you to consult your shipping representative, insurance agent, or freight broker for advice on packing and shipping.

Wool products may be shipped in bulk, bolts, cartons, or other types of containers, depending on the type of product and whether it is prepackaged. General considerations include protection from contamination, weather, and pests. Containers should be constructed so as to be safe for handling during transport.

Publications and WWW Resources

The following publications may be relevant to the importation of wool products.

Threading Your Way Through the Labeling Requirements of the Textile and Wool Acts

Available free of charge from the Federal Trade Commission, as well as online (www.ftc.gov/bcp/conline/pubs/buspubs/thread.htm) this publication is an excellent source of information written in clear lay language. We recommend that anyone interested in importing wool products but unfamiliar with the regulations obtain a copy.

The U.S. Customs Service launched a series of "Informed Compliance" publications in 1996, which are available on the Customs Service website (www.customs.gov/impoexpo/impoexpo.htm). Of particular interest:

What Every Member of the Trade Community Should Know About Textile & Apparel Rules of Origin

What Every Member of the Trade community Should Know About NAFTA for Textiles and Textile Articles

Fibers & Yarns Construction and Classification Under the HTSUS

The *Harmonized Tariff Schedule of the United States (2001)* (HTSUS) is available to view on the Customs Service website (www.customs.gov), or you may purchase a printed version from:

U.S. Government Printing Office
Superintendent of Documents
710 North Capital Street NW
Washington DC 20401

Tel: (202) 512-1800
Fax: (202) 512-1657
Website: www.access.gpo.gov

The USGPO also has copies of specific laws available for purchase. The USGPO accepts orders made by fax, phone or placed over the Internet, as well as mail orders paid by credit card. All orders must be accompanied by payment. Credit cards, checks drawn on a U.S. bank, or an international money order are all acceptable.

Relevant Government Agencies

Address your questions regarding FTC wool labeling requirements and requirements under the Textile Fiber Products Identification Act (TFPIA) to:

Federal Trade Commission (FTC)
Division of Enforcement
600 Pennsylvania Ave. NW
Washington, DC 20580
Tel: (202) 326-2996
Website: www.ftc.gov

Address your questions regarding textile Multi-Fiber Arrangements to:

U.S. Department of Commerce
International Trade Administration
Office of Textiles and Apparel
Director's Office
14th and Constitution Ave. NW, Rm. H3100
Washington, DC 20230
Tel: (202) 482-5078
Fax: (202) 482-2331
Agreements Division: (202) 482-4212
Website: http://otexa.ita.doc.gov

Address your questions regarding the Flammable Fabrics Act (FFA) to:

Consumer Product Safety Commission (CPSC)
Office of Compliance
Washington DC 20207-0001
Tel: 800-638-2772 or (301) 504-7912
Fax: (301) 504-0359
Website: www.cpsc.gov

Address your questions regarding textile quotas to:
U.S. Customs and Border Protection
Office of Field Operations, Quota Branch
1300 Pennsylvania Avenue NW
Washington DC 20229
Tel: (202) 927-5850
Website: www.customs.treas.gov

The U.S. Customs Service provices updated status reports on textile quota on their web site (see address above). If the country you need information on is not listed, call the Quota Branch office at (202) 927-5850.

Address your questions regarding wool product imports to your local Customs port director. For addresses, refer to "U.S. Customs and Border Protection Offices" on page 65 or contact:

U.S. Customs and Border Protection
Customs Headquarters
1300 Pennsylvania Avenue NW
Washington DC 20229
Tel: (202) 354-1000
Website: www.customs.treas.gov

Laws and Regulations

The following laws and regulations may be relevant to the importation of wool products. The laws are contained in the United States Code (USC), and the regulations are published in the Code of Federal Regulations (CFR), both of which are available at larger public

and law libraries. Copies of specific laws are also available from the United States Government Printing Office (address above).

15 USC 68-68j
Wool Products Labeling Act (WPLA) of 1939
This Act prohibits the false or deceptive labeling (misbranding) of wool products and requires all wool products imported into the U.S. to be labeled in accordance with requirements set forth in the law.

19 CFR 11.12; 16 CFR 300 et seq.
Regulations on WPLA Labeling and Marking
These regulations set forth the wool labeling and marking requirements adopted by the FTC to administer the requirements of the WPLA and provide the procedures followed by U.S. Customs in enforcing the WPLA and the FTC regulations, including entry invoice requirements.

7 USC 1854
Textile Trade Agreements
(EO 11651, as amended by EO 11951 and 12188, and supplemented by EO 12475)
This Act authorizes the CITA of the DOC to enter into Multi-Fiber Agreements with other countries to control trade in textiles and establishes the Textile Import Program, which is enforced by U.S. Customs.

19 CFR 12.130 et seq.
Regulations on Entry of Textiles
These regulations provide the requirements and procedures followed by Customs in enforcing limitations on the importation and entry and withdrawal of textiles and textile products from warehouses for consumption in the U.S.

19 CFR 141.89
Regulation on Additional Invoice Requirements
This regulation specifies the additional information for certain classes of merchandise, including footwear and textile products, being imported into the U.S.

15 USC 70-77
Textile Fiber Products Identification Act
This Act prohibits false or deceptive labeling (misbranding) and false advertising of any textile fiber products and requires all textile fiber products imported into the U.S. to be labeled in accordance with the requirements set forth in the law.

19 CFR 11.12b; 16 CFR 303 et seq.
Regulations on TFPIA Labeling and Marking
These regulations detail the labeling and marking requirements for textiles as specified by the CPSC and the invoice contents required by U.S. Customs for purpose of enforcing the labeling and marking rules.

15 USC 1191-1204
Flammable Fabrics Act (FFA)
This Act provides for the setting of flammability standards for fabric by the Consumer Product Safety Commission (CPSC) and for enforcement by U.S. Customs.

16 CFR 1610, 1611, 1615, 1616, 1630-1632
Regulations on Flammable Fabric Standards
These regulations specify the flammability standards adopted by the CPSC under the FFA for various types of textiles.

16 CFR 423
Care Labeling Rule
Requires fiber composition and washing or dry cleaning instructions for textile apparel and certain piece goods.

Principal Exporting Countries

The following listing includes samples of the main supplier nations of the products of this chapter. It is organized by HTSUS major heading. (Refer to "Customs Classification" above for the product codes.) Countries are listed in rank order of the value of products imported to the U.S. Statistics represent customs value of entries for 2002 from the Bureau of Census, U.S. Department of Commerce.

5101—Australia, New Zealand, United Kingdom, South Africa, Canada, Uruguay, Argentina, Mexico

5102—China, Mongolia, Portugal, Belgium, Netherlands

5103—United Kingdom, Australia, China, Mongolia, Uruguay, South Africa, Canada, Mexico, France, New Zealand

5104—Canada, China, United Kingdom, Australia, Italy

5105—Australia, Germany, United Kingdom, New Zealand, Italy

5106—United Kingdom, New Zealand, Italy, Canada, Germany

5107—Italy, Canada, New Zealand, Germany, India

5108—Italy, United Kingdom, Japan, Peru, France

5109—Italy, United Kingdom, Peru, Canada, France, New Zealand, Japan, Germany

5110—United Kingdom, Italy, France, Switzerland, Ireland, Norway

5111—Mexico, Canada, Italy, United Kingdom, France, Denmark, South Korea, Switzerland

5112—Italy, Mexico, Canada, United Kingdom, South Korea, Israel, Belgium, Germany, China, India

5113—Italy, France, United Kingdom, Austria, China, Germany, Belgium, Canada, Ecuador

Chapter 52: Cotton

This chapter relates to the importation of cotton products, which are classified under Chapter 52 of the Harmonized Tariff Schedule of the United States (HTSUS). Specifically, it includes unprocessed cotton, cotton waste, carded and combed cotton, cotton sewing thread and yarn, and cotton fabrics.

If you are interested in importing cotton apparel, you should refer to Commodity Index Chapters 61 through 63. For importation of cotton-blend fibers and fabrics, you should consider whether your product might be classified under the Commodity Index chapter that covers the specific blended fiber. For example, silk blends are covered in Chapter 50, blends with man-made filaments are in Chapter 54, and those with man-made staple fibers are in Chapter 55. If you are interested in importing footwear or leggings made of cotton, you should refer to Chapter 64. For import requirements related to headgear made of cotton, refer to Chapter 65. Cotton linters are covered in Chapter 14, cotton rugs and carpets are in Chapter 57, and cotton wadding and cordage may be under Chapter 56.

Note: To understand key issues that will enable you to make best use of the information in this section we recommend that you see "Introduction" on page 425.

Key Factors

The key factors in the importation of cotton products are:

- Compliance with absolute quota restraints.

- Compliance with quota restraints and visa requirements

- Compliance with import quotas on certain raw and semi-processed cottons

- Submission of U.S. Customs Country-of-Origin Declaration(s)

- Compliance with entry invoice requirements

- Compliance with labeling requirements under Textile Fiber Products Identification Act (TFPIA) and/or the Wool Products Labeling Act (WPLA) and the Care Labeling Rule

- Compliance with flammability standards adopted and enforced by the Consumer Product Safety Commission (CPSC) under the Flammable Fabrics Act (FFA) (if importing fabrics and other textile products)

Although most importers use the services of a licensed customs broker in making their entries, and we recommend this practice, you should be aware of the regulatory, entry, and documentation issues involved in importing your product. You, as importer, are ultimately responsible for the fulfillment of any legal requirements applicable to your shipment.

General Considerations

Regulatory Agencies. The Committee for Implementation of Textile Agreements (CITA) regulates certain textile imports under Section 204 of the Agricultural Adjustment Act. U.S. Customs enforces CITA textile and textile product entry quotas. Customs also enforces compliance with labeling and invoice requirements of the TFPIA and flammability standards under the FFA. The CPSC monitors imports and from time to time inspects textile shipments for compliance with FFA standards. If you are importing textiles containing wool, importation is subject to complex textile import regulations. The Federal Trade Commission (FTC) administers the WPLA requirements.

Entry of Cotton. Cotton enters the U.S. in various conditions, including raw uncombed and uncarded, raw combed and carded, waste, yarn, thread, and woven fabric of various types. Different types of special entry documents may be required, depending on which type of cotton you are importing. You must provide additional information on the entry invoice for certain cotton imports (see "Entry and Documentation" below). If you are importing textiles, you must file a U.S. Customs Textile Entry Declaration at the U.S port of entry. This declaration is required for all textiles (see "Textile Country-of-Origin Declarations" below). Some cotton products are subject to absolute quotas (see "Absolute Quotas" below). In addition, certain cotton and cotton articles manufactured or produced in certain countries are subject to quota and other restraints under U.S. bilateral agreements pursuant to Section 204 of the Agricultural Adjustment Act (AAA) (see "Quotas" below). Such products may require export certificates or visas issued by the appropriate country of origin, in addition to other entry documents for cotton. Cotton-wool blends may be subject to further requirements and restrictions placed on the import of wool (see "Wool Product Entry Requirements" below).

Absolute Quotas. The Agricultural Adjustment Act, Section 22, establishes absolute quotas on raw cotton from certain countries. Do not confuse these quotas with bilateral agreement quotas for textiles and manufactured textile products. They are different. For details, see "Country-Specific Prohibitions" below.

Bilateral Agreement Quotas. If you are interested in importing cotton products, the most important issue you need to be aware of is quotas. Under the Multi-Fiber Arrangement provisions of Section 204 of the Agricultural Adjustment Act, CITA initiates specific agreements with individual exporting countries. Section 204 of the Agricultural Adjustment Act covers textiles that: 1) are in chief value of cotton, wool, or man-made fibers, any textile fibers subject to the terms of any textile trade agreement, or any combination of such fibers; 2) contain 50% or more by weight of cotton or man-made fibers, or any textile fibers subject to the terms of any textile trade agreement; 3) contain 17% or more by weight of wool; or 4) if in chief value of textile fibers or textile materials, contain a blend of cotton, wool, or man-made fibers, any textile fibers subject to the terms of any textile trade agreement, or any combination of such fibers that, in total, amount to 50% or more by weight of all component fibers.

The U.S. has bilateral agreements with over 40 countries. Each agreement with each country is unique, and may specify quotas for a type of textile or a specific article. Visas or export licenses may be required. These agreements, however, often change. Therefore, if you are interested in importing any cotton products, you should contact the International Trade Administration's Office of Textile and Apparel (see addresses at end of this chapter). Refer to "Prohibitions and Restrictions" below for further details.

Textile Country-of-Origin Declarations. U.S. Customs enforces CITA textile and textile product entry quotas (see "Prohibitions and Restrictions" below). Requirements for entry include submission of Country-of-Origin Declarations with every cotton shipment, regardless of whether it is subject to a specific multifiber arrangement (19 CFR 12.130, 12.131).

Country of Origin. Quota restrictions are country-specific and therefore are applied based on the country of origin for the textiles shipped. The last country from which a textile shipment was exported to the U.S. is not necessarily its country of origin. A textile or textile product imported into the U.S. is considered a product of the particular foreign territory or country, or a U.S. insular possession, where it is wholly grown, produced, or manufactured. For the following discussion, "country" means a foreign territory or country, or a U.S. insular possession.

In 1996, the U.S. Customs Service made major changes to country of origin rules for textile imports. The regulations at 19 CFR 102.21, "Textile and apparel products" were added to the 1996 Customs Regulations and became effective July 1, 1996. The new rules do not provide for cutting components or cutting and hemming to confer country of origin as in the past. The basis of the new law is processing operations or assembly. Some of the most important changes for importers to be aware of are:

- Cutting does not determine the country of origin (previously cutting determined country of origin for 90 percent of wearing apparel imports). The new rules are based on processing or assembly operations.

- A subjective determination under the provisions of 19 CFR 12.130 is replaced by objective processing operations expressed in terms of tariff shifts. Dyeing, printing, and other finishing processes applied to fabrics no longer confer or change country of origin.

- Country of origin for textile and apparel products processed, assembled or manufactured in two or more countries is determined by where the most important processing occurs, and, if that cannot be ascertained, the last country in which an important processing operation occurs.

The country of origin is the country in which a product is wholly produced when a textile or apparel product is completely produced or manufactured (except for minor parts) in one country. For fabric, the country of origin is the country in which the fabric is woven, knitted, needled, tufted, felted, entangled or created by any other fabric-making process. The country of origin for staple yarn is the country in which yarn is spun; for filament yarn, the country in which filament is extruded; and for plied, gimped and cabled yarns, the country in which the fibers or filaments used in the yarn are spun or extruded. The country of origin of all other textile and apparel products is the country in which the components of a textile or apparel product are wholly assembled (except for minor attachments) except for knit-to-shape products. Knit-to-shape products are those composed of panels or parts ,which, are knitted or crocheted directly into the shape that will be used in construction of the final product. Minor cutting or sewing does not influence whether the product is considered knit-to-shape. The country of origin for knit-to-shape products is that country in which the major parts are knitted into the shape that will constitute the finished product. Once again, note that assembly, not cutting, now confers country of origin.

Declarations. All importations of textiles and textile products must be accompanied by one of the following three declarations. Goods subject to Section 204, Agricultural Act of 1956, as amended, must be accompanied by either a single-country or a multiple-country declaration. Goods not subject to Section 204 must be accompanied by a negative declaration.

- **Single-country declarations** are used for entries of textiles or textile products which are wholly the growth, product, or manufacture of a single foreign country, territory, or U.S. insular possession. Information required includes: marks of identification and numbers; description of article and quantity; country of origin; and date of exportation.

- **Multiple-country declarations** are used for entries of textiles or textile products which were subjected to manufacturing or processing operations in, and/or incorporate materials originating in more than one foreign country or territory. Information required includes: marks of identification and numbers; for articles, description, quantity, identification of manufacturing and/or processing operations, country, and date of exportation; for materials used to make articles, description of materials, country of production, and date of exportation.

- **Negative declarations** must accompany all textile imports that are not subject to AAA Section 204 restrictions. Information required includes: marks of identification and numbers; descriptions of article and quantity; and country of origin.

The date of exportation to be indicated on the above declarations is the date on which the carrier leaves the last port in the country of origin, as determined by Customs. Diversion to another country during transit does not affect the export date.

Procedure for Declarations. The manufacturer, producer, exporter, or importer may prepare the declaration. If more than one of these parties is involved in the importation, each party may prepare a separate declaration. You may file a separate declaration for each invoice presented with your entry. The declaration must be dated and signed by the responsible party, and must include the person's title and the company name and address. Your shipment's entry will be denied unless it is accompanied by a properly executed declaration. Customs will not treat a textile declaration as a missing document for which a bond may be filed.

Customs will base its country-of-origin determination on the information contained in each declaration, unless the information is insufficient. If the information on the declaration is insufficient, Customs will require that you submit such additional information as will enable the determination to be made. The shipment will not be released until the determination is made. Thus, if you want to clear Customs with minimal delay, be sure that the information on the declarations is as complete as possible for each shipment.

Textile Labeling and Invoice Requirements. You are responsible for your imported cotton fabric's compliance with applicable provisions of the TFPIA. Cotton fabrics that require labeling under TFPIA must already be labeled at entry, or the shipment will be refused. (See "Marking and Labeling Requirements" below.) If you import shipments of cotton fabrics subject to TFPIA and valued at over $500, you must provide special information on the entry invoice (see "Entry and Documentation" below).

Flammability Standards. Cotton fabrics imported into the U.S. for use in consumer products must be in compliance with the FFA, a federal law that gives the CPSC the authority and responsibility for protecting the public from the hazards of dangerously flammable items of wearing apparel and interior furnishings. Under the FFA, standards have been established for flammability of clothing textiles. You cannot import any article of wearing apparel or interior furnishing, or any fabric or related material that is intended for use or that may be used in such items, if it fails to conform to an applicable flammability standard (FFA Section 4). Certain products may be imported into the U.S. (FFA Section 11c) for finishing or processing to render them less

flammable so as to meet the standards. For these products, the exporter must state on the invoice or other paper relating to the shipment that the shipment is being made for that purpose.

The CPSC monitors imports of textiles under its Import Surveillance Program. From time to time, your textile shipments may be inspected to ascertain compliance with mandatory safety standards. Shipments may also be subject to testing by the CPSC to determine compliance. If the CPSC believes a product, fabric, or related material does not comply with a flammability standard, it is authorized to pursue a variety of legal sanctions (see "Prohibitions and Restrictions" below).

Substantial Product Hazard Reports. Any firm that obtains information that reasonably supports the conclusion that one of its products presents an unreasonable risk of serious injury or death must report that information to the CPSC's Division of Corrective Actions (CPSC address below). Importers must also report to the CPSC if 1) a type of product is the subject of at least three civil actions filed in U.S. federal or state courts, 2) each suit alleges the involvement of that product type in death or grievous bodily injury (as defined in FFA Section 37(3)1), and 3) at least three of the actions result in a final settlement with the manufacturer or in a judgment for the plaintiff within any one of the two-year periods specified in FFA Section 37(b).

Wool Product Entry Requirements. If you are importing cotton-wool blends, depending on the nature of your wool fiber imports, as many as three different types of special entry documents may be required. First, for all imported textile fibers and yarns covered by the Agricultural Adjustment Act (AAA), including wool, you must file a U.S. Customs Textile Entry Declaration (see "Textile Country-of-Origin Declarations" above). Second, for all wool products subject to the WPLA, special information is required on the entry invoices (see "Entry and Documentation" below). Finally, certain wool articles manufactured or produced in certain countries may be subject to quotas under U.S. bilateral agreements. Such products require export certificates or visas issued by the appropriate country of origin, in addition to other requisite entry paperwork (see "Quotas" above).

Certified Hand-Loomed Fabric. Foreign fabrics made on a hand loom—that is, a nonpower-driven loom—by cottage industry producers may be entered under a special tariff category. Textile restraints may not apply to such products when exported from developing countries. If you import a shipment of these fabrics, you must have them certified by a government official of the country-of-origin before exporting them to the U.S. To enter a cotton fabric as a certified hand-loomed fabric, you must present the appropriate certification to Customs at the port of entry. You should mark your entry summary or withdrawal forms with the symbol "F" as a prefix to the appropriate 10-digit statistical reporting number.

Wool Products Labeling Act. The term "wool product" means any product or any portion of a product that contains, purports to contain, or in any way is represented as containing wool, reprocessed wool, or reused wool. All wool products imported into the U.S., except those made more than 20 years before importation, and except carpets, rugs, mats, and upholsteries, must have affixed a stamp, tag, label, or other means of identification as required by the WPLA. If you are importing wool products exempt from labeling under the WPLA, do not assume they are also exempt from labeling under the TFPIA. These are two distinct laws, with some overlapping requirements (see "Marking and Labeling Requirements" below).

Import Advisory

Importation of textiles is trade-sensitive and highly regulated. Shipments of textiles and textile products not complying with all government regulations, including quotas and visas, are subject to seizure and could result in the imposition of penalties as well as possible forfeiture of the goods. You should always verify the available quota for any textile product you plan to import before your shipment leaves the country of manufacture. Furthermore, Customs textile classification rulings change frequently, and prior administrative rulings are often modified and sometimes reversed. You should be particularly careful to comply with country of origin determination regulations, which were changed in 1996, and affect quotas and visas, marking and labeling, and other important aspects of tariff classification. See "Publications and WWW Resources" for information on important Customs Service informed compliance publications.

The Customs Service has greatly increased its scrutiny of the textile industry, one of eight primary focus industries identified in the most recent Trade Compliance & Enforcement Plan. Imported products from these industries will likely attract significant attention from Customs in the areas of compliance measurement, compliance assessment, informed compliance, and interventions.

Customs Classification

For customs purposes, cotton products are classified under Chapter 52 of the HTSUS. This chapter is broken into major headings, which are further divided into subheadings, and often sub-subheadings, each of which has its own HTSUS classification number. For example, the 2001 HTSUS number for satin weave or twill weave of cotton is 5208.19.20, indicating it is a sub-subcategory of other fabrics (5208.19), which is a subcategory of the major heading, unbleached woven fabrics of cotton, with 85% or more by weight of cotton, etc. (5208). There are 12 major headings within Chapter 52.

5201—Cotton, not carded or combed

5202—Cotton waste (including yarn waste and garnetted stock)

5203—Cotton, carded or combed

5204—Cotton sewing thread, whether or not put up for retail sale

5205—Cotton yarn (other than sewing thread), containing 85% or more by weight of cotton, not put up for retail sale

5206—Cotton yarn (other than sewing thread), containing less than 85% by weight of cotton, not put up for retail sale

5207—Cotton yarn (other than sewing thread) put up for retail sale

5208—Woven fabrics of cotton, containing 85% or more by weight of cotton, weighing not more than 200 g/m2

5209—Woven fabrics of cotton, containing 85% or more by weight of cotton, weighing more than 200 g/m2

5210—Woven fabrics of cotton, containing less than 85% by weight of cotton, mixed mainly or solely with man-made fibers, weighing not more than 200 g/m2

5211—Woven fabrics of cotton, containing less than 85% by weight of cotton, mixed mainly or solely with man-made fibers, weighing more than 200 g/m2

5212—Other woven fabrics of cotton

For more details regarding classifications of the specific product you are interested in importing, consult a customs broker, the appropriate commodity specialist at your nearest customs port, or the HTSUS. The 2001 HTSUS is available online from the Customs Service (www.customs.gov/impoexpo/impoexpo.htm) or for purchase from the U.S. Government Printing Office (see resources at the end of this chapter), and may be found in larger public libraries. For a general discussion of customs classification, see "Classification—Liquidation" on page 229.

Dutiable Status of Goods

For more information about duty rates and binding decisions see "Dutiable Status of Goods" on page 203; for a discussion of temporary importation of goods see "Temporary Free Importations" on page 205.

Valuation

Importers have a responsibility to use what the U.S. Customs Service deems, "reasonable care," when determining the value of their goods. They must also provide any additional information that the Customs Service needs for setting a final value on the goods. This process involves a number of factors and can be somewhat complicated; importers must be aware of applicable issues and details. Valuation information applies to all types of commodities, for further discussion on the subject see "Customs Valuation" on page 267.

Import Duties

Import duties vary (often dramatically) depending upon the Harmonized Tariff Schedule (HTSUS) classification of the goods or products imported. Since some products that look alike have different HTSUS classifications and different rates of duty, proper classification is vital. Note that "differences of opinion" between importers and the Bureau of Customs and Border Protection regarding classification keeps customs attorneys very busy.

Import duties can be assessed on the imported value of the goods ("ad valorem" rates of duty such as 2%, 4.4%, 50%, etc.), total units or weight of the goods ("specific" rates of duty such as 2 cents each or 1.5 cents/pound, etc.) or on a combination basis ("compound" rates of duty such as 5 cents each plus 6%).

Listed below is a sampling of several Column 1 import duty rates for Chapter 52 products:

Card strips made from cotton having a staple length under 30.1625 mm (1-3/16 inches) and lap waste, sliver waste and roving waste (described in general note 15 of the tariff schedule and entered pursuant to its provisions) (5202.99.05 00): Free to

Cotton yarn exceeding 80 nm per single yarn (300) (5205.35.00. 00): 12%

For specific information on US import duties refer to the Harmonized Tariff Schedule of the US. The print version is available from the US Government Printing Office as well as third party suppliers who often add special features. Online versions are available in both static PDF pages as well as in formats with excellent search functionality. Search the Web with the term "Harmonized Tariff Schedule" to find sources.

Entry and Documentation

The entry of merchandise is a two-part process consisting of 1) filing the documentation necessary to determine whether merchandise may be released from Customs custody, and 2) filing the documents that contain information for duty assessment and statistical purposes. In certain instances, all documents must be filed and accepted by Customs prior to release of the goods. Unless you have been granted an extension, you must file entry documents at a location specified by the port or area director within five working days of your shipment's date of arrival at a U.S. port of entry. These include a number of standard documents required by Customs for any entry, and:

- U.S. Customs Country-of-Origin Declaration Form 3229

- Export documentation and/or visa for textiles subject to bilateral agreement

After you present the entry, Customs may examine your shipment or may waive examination. The shipment is then released provided no legal or regulatory violations have been noted. If not already done, you must then file entry summary documentation and deposit estimated duties at a designated customhouse within 10 working days of your shipment's release. For a detailed description of entry procedures, standard documentation, and informal entry, see "Entry Process" on page 185.

Informed Compliance. Informed compliance was introduced with the Customs Modernization Act of 1993 (Mod Act) and defines the relationship between importers and the Customs Service. It sets out the responsibilities of both parties. Providing the correct documentation and information for entry is a key factor that will make your importing operation run smoothly. We recommend that importers become familiar with the concept of informed comliance and the responsibilities that they have under the Mod Act. For further discussion about informed compliance see "Informed Compliance" on page 211.

NAFTA Certificates of Origin. An importer of textiles for which NAFTA treatment is sought need not file a separate NAFTA Certificate of Origin in addition to the Customs Country-of-Origin Declaration. The declaration is sufficient. However, the importer must take care to submit a declaration from each U.S., Canadian, or Mexican producer or manufacturer. Thus, for multiple producers or manufacturers, a separate declaration must be filed for each. If a Customs port director cannot determine the country of origin because the declaration is absent or incomplete, the shipment is not entitled to preferential NAFTA tariff treatment or other NAFTA benefits. See 19 CFR 12.132.

Entry Invoices. You must provide certain additional information on the entry invoice for cotton and cotton products. The specific information varies depending on the nature of your product, as noted below.

TFPIA Requirements. For the purpose of TFPIA enforcement, a commercial shipment of textile products exceeding $500 in value and subject to TFPIA labeling requirements must show the following information: 1) the constituent fiber or combination of fibers, designating with equal prominence each natural or manufactured fiber by its generic name, in order of predominance by weight if the weight of such fiber is 5% or more of the total fiber weight of the product; 2) percentage of each fiber present, by weight, in the total fiber content; 3) the name or other identification issued and registered by the FTC of the manufacturer of the product or one or more persons subject to Section 3 of the TFPIA with respect to such product; 4) the name of the country where processed or manufactured.

Cotton Products. The following headings describe the invoice information required for different types of cotton shipments. If your shipment fits one or more of these categories, you will need to supply this information on your entry invoice, in addition to what is normally expected.

Raw Cotton. If you are importing raw cotton, your invoice must identify: 1) quota category, in terms of staple length and type of cotton; 2) country of origin, and, if practicable, province or other country subdivision where grown; 3) cotton variety, e.g. Karnak, Gisha, Pima, Tanguis, etc.

Cotton Waste. If you are importing cotton waste, your invoice must state: 1) name by which the cotton waste is known (e.g. cotton card strips; cotton comber waste; cotton lap waste; cotton sliver waste; cotton roving waste; cotton fly waste; etc.; 2) cotton staple length, identified in the following terms: either a) less than 3.016 cm (1 3/16 inches), or b) 3.016 cm or more.

Cotton Fabrics. If you are importing cotton fabrics (HTSUS headings 5208, 5209, 5210, 5211, and 5212), your invoice must show the following information: 1) marks on shipping packages; 2) numbers on shipping packages; 3) customer's call number, if any; 4) exact width of your merchandise; 5) detailed description of your merchandise: trade name, if any; whether bleached, unbleached, printed, composed of yarns of different color, or dyed; if com-

posed of cotton plus other materials, percentage of each component material by weight; 6) number of single threads per cm^2 (ply yarns must be counted in terms of single threads comprising the yarn); 7) exact weight per m^2, in grams; 8) average yarn number; 9) warp yarn size or sizes; 10) filling yarn size or sizes; 11) statement of whether the yarns are combed or carded; 12) number of colors or kinds (different yarn sizes or materials) in the filling; 13) statement of whether the fabric is napped or not; 14) type of weave; and 15) type of machine on which your fabric was woven.

Yarn. All entry invoices for yarn should show: 1) fiber content by weight; 2) whether the yarn is single or plied; 3) whether or not the yarn is put up for retail sale (as defined in HTSUS Section XI, Note 4); and 4) whether or not the yarn is intended for use as sewing thread.

In addition, if the yarn's chief weight is of cotton, the entry invoice must show: 1) Whether the cotton is combed or uncombed; 2) the metric number (mn); and 3) whether it is bleached and or mercerized.

Wool Products Subject to WPLA. When you offer for entry a shipment of cotton-wool blend fibers or fabrics valued at over $500 and subject to WPLA, you must include certain information intended to facilitate Customs monitoring and enforcement of that Act. This extra information is identical to that required by WPLA on labeling (see "Marking and Labeling Requirements" below), with the addition of the manufacturer's name. If your product consists of mixed waste, residues, and similar merchandise obtained from several suppliers or unknown sources, you may omit the manufacturer's name from the entry invoice. For more general information about invoices see "Invoices" on page 277.

Note: *The Entry and Documentation section has been carefully designed to supply you, the importer, with sample documents and directions on how to satisfy Customs requirements. Be aware that you should consult the applicable authorities to ensure that you are correctly following the most current procedures.*

Prohibitions and Restrictions

Textile Quotas. Textile import restrictions are primarily a matter of quotas and the way in which these quotas are administered and monitored. Under the Multi-Fiber Arrangement provisions of Section 204 of the Agricultural Adjustment Act, CITA has negotiated bilateral agreements with over 40 countries. These Agreements may impose quotas for a type of textile or a specific article, and they are country-specific. The agreements, however, often change. Therefore, if you are interested in importing any special woven fabric products, you should contact the International Trade Administration's Office of Textile and Apparel (see addresses at end of this chapter). The Office of Textile and Apparel has a team of country specialists who can inform you of the latest developments and inform you about a product's quota or restriction status.

U.S. Customs enforces CITA textile and textile product entry quotas. If formal entry procedures are not followed, Customs will usually refuse entry for textiles. Formal entry requires submission of a Country-of-Origin Declaration (see "General Considerations" above). U.S. Customs maintains a current textile quota status report, available for perusal at any Customs port. In addition, U.S. Customs in Washington, DC, provides quota status reports online, which are regularly updated (www.customs.gov/impoexpo/impoexpo.htm).

Flammable Fabrics. U.S. Customs may refuse entry for any article of wearing apparel or interior furnishing, or any fabric or related material that is intended for use or that may be used in wearing apparel or interior furnishings, if it fails to conform to an applicable flammability standard issued under Section 4 of the FFA. An exception is allowed for certain products (FFA Section 11c) that are imported for finishing or processing to bring them within the legal standard. For these products, the exporter must state on the invoice or other paper relating to the shipment that the shipment is being made for that purpose.

The CPSC, as the primary enforcement agency of flammability standards, inspects products for compliance with the FFA. If the CPSC believes a product, fabric, or related material does not comply with a flammability standard, it is authorized to pursue a variety of legal sanctions, including: 1) seizure, condemnation, and forfeiture of the noncomplying products; 2) administrative cease-and-desist order requiring an individual or firm to stop sale and distribution of the noncomplying products or; 3) temporary injunction requiring the individual or firm to stop sale and distribution of the noncomplying products, pending final disposition of an administrative cease-and-desist proceeding. The CPSC also has authority to seek civil penalties against any person who knowingly violates a regulation or standard issued under Section 4 of the FFA.

Quotas

There are a number of complex quotas applied to imported cotton under the Agricultural Adjustment Act, Section 22. Refer to HTSUS Chapter 52, Additional U.S. Notes, and to Chapter 99, Subheading IV for specifics.

Global Import Quota on *Gossypium hirsutum*. Notwithstanding any other quantitative limits on upland cotton imports, varieties of *Gossypium hirsutum* cotton certified by agents of the country of origin may be entered according to established procedures and in the amounts specified in the Secretary of Agriculture's Special Limited Global Import Quota Announcements and Special Cotton Quota Announcements.

Bilateral Agreement Quotas. Restrictions under bilateral agreements are country-specific. A product originating in one country may be subject to quota and to export license or visa requirements, while the same product originating in a different country may not. At present, the U.S. has bilateral agreements with over 40 countries. Many different categories of products are covered under these Arrangements; it is beyond the scope of this book to list each country and its restricted commodities. If you are interested in importing textiles and textile products, you should contact the International Trade Administration's Office of Textile and Apparel (see addresses at end of this chapter) or U.S. Customs to ascertain your product's restraint status.

Marking and Labeling Requirements

TFPIA Requirements. All textile fiber products imported into the U.S. must be stamped, tagged, labeled, or otherwise marked with the following information as required by the TFPIA, unless exempt from marking (see TFPIA, Section 12): 1) the generic names and percentages by weight of the constituent fibers present in the textile fiber product, exclusive of permissible ornamentation, in amounts of more than 5% in order of predominance by weight, with any percentage of fiber or fibers required to be designated as "other fiber" or "other fibers" (including those present in amounts of 5% or less) appearing last; and 2) the name of the manufacturer or the name or registered identification number issued by the FTC of one or more persons marketing or handling the textile fiber product; and 3) the name of the country where processed. A word trademark, used as a house mark and registered with the U.S. Patent Office, may appear on labels instead of the name otherwise required, provided the owner of the trademark furnishes a copy of the registration to the FTC prior to use (see "Registered Identification Numbers" below).

The information listed above is not exhaustive. TFPIA requirements are extensive. The Act specifies such details as types of labels, means of attachment, label position on the article, package labeling, unit labeling for two-piece garments, and arrangement of information on the label; allowable fiber designations; country-of-origin indications; requirements for trim and ornamentation, linings and interlinings, and pile fabrics; sectional disclosure; use of trade names and trademarks; and requirements for swatches and samples. The FTC publishes a booklet intended to clarify TFPIA requirements to facilitate voluntary compliance in the industry (see "Publications and WWW Resources" below). It is available on request, at no charge, from the FTC (see addresses at end of this chapter).

Wool Products Labeling Act (WPLA). Wool product labeling requirements for foreign products are the responsibility of the importer. The WPLA requires the following information to appear on wool products subject to the Act: 1) percentage of the wool product's total fiber weight (exclusive of ornamentation) not exceeding 5% of the total fiber weight of a) wool, b) recycled wool, c) each fiber other than wool if the percent by weight of such fiber is 5% or more, and d) the aggregate of all other fibers; 2) the maximum percent of the wool product's total weight, of any nonfibrous loading, filling, or adulterating matter; and 3) the importer's name. If you, as importer, have a registered identification number issued by the FTC, that number may be used instead of your name (see "Registered Identification Numbers" below).

Customs entry is contingent on proper labeling. If your shipment is found to be mislabeled at entry, you will be given the option of relabeling the products under Customs supervision, as long as the port director is satisfied that your labeling error or omission did not involve fraud or willful neglect. If your shipment is discovered after entry to have been noncomplying with WPLA, it will be recalled to Customs custody at your expense, unless you can satisfy the port director that the products have since been brought into compliance. You will be held responsible for all expenses incurred in bringing a shipment into compliance, including compensation of personnel and other expenses related to Customs supervision.

Fraudulent violations of WPLA will result in seizure of the shipment. Shipments already released from Customs custody will be ordered to be redelivered to Customs. Customs reports all cases of fraudulent violation to the FTC in Washington, DC.

The information listed above is not intended to be exhaustive. WPLA requirements are extensive. The Act specifies such details as types of labels, means of attachment, label position on the article, package labeling, unit labeling (as in the case of a two-piece garment), arrangement of information on the label, allowable fiber designations, country-of-origin indications, trim and ornamentation, pile fabrics, sectional disclosure, use of trade names and trademarks, requirements for swatches and samples, etc. The FTC publishes a booklet intended to clarify WPLA requirements in order to facilitate voluntary compliance within the industry (see "Publications and WWW Resources" below). It is available on request, at no charge, from the FTC (see addresses at end of this chapter).

The Care Labeling Rule. Regulations under this rule require manufacturers and importers of textile clothing and fabrics to attach specific care instructions for washing or dry cleaning, as well as information on the fiber composition of the article. They are enforced by the FTC Division of Enforcement. The Care Labeling Rule was amended September 2000 detailed information is available on the FTC website (www.ftc.gov/os/statutes/textilejump.htm).

Registered Identification Numbers. Any domestic firm or person residing in the U.S. and engaged in the manufacture or marketing of textile products covered under the TFPIA may obtain an FTC-registered identification number for use on required tags and labels instead of the name of a firm or person. For applications, contact the FTC (see addresses at end of this chapter).

For a general discussion of U.S. Customs marking and labeling requirements, see "Country of Origin Marking" on page 236, "Special Marking Requirements" on page 238 and "Marking—False Impression" on page 239.

Shipping Considerations

You will need to ensure that your goods are packaged and shipped with care so that they pass smoothly through Customs and arrive in good condition. You are responsible for ensuring that the shipment is in compliance with all applicable government regulations for packaging and shipping. In most instances, you should not leave these arrangements solely to the discretion of your supplier. Careful preparation of the cargo and selection of the mode of transport can be essential to a cost-effective, timely delivery of undamaged goods. We strongly advise you to consult your shipping representative, insurance agent, or freight broker for advice on packing and shipping.

Cotton fabrics may be shipped in bulk, bolts, rolls, or other types of containers, depending on the type of product and whether it is prepackaged. General considerations include protection from contamination, weather, and pests. Containers should be constructed so as to be safe for handling during transport.

Publications and WWW Resources

The following publication is from the Federal Trade Commission and may be relevant to the importation of cotton fabrics and cotton-wool blend fabrics. It is available free of charge online from the FTC (www.ftc.gov/bcp/conline/pubs/buspubs/thread.htm). We recommend that anyone interested in importing textile fiber products but unfamiliar with the regulations obtain a copy.

> *Threading Your Way Through the Labeling Requirements of the Textile and Wool Acts*

The U.S. Customs Service launched a series of "Informed Compliance" publications in 1996, which are available on the Customs Service website (www.customs.gov/impoexpo/impoexpo.htm). Of particular interest:

> *What Every Member of the Trade Community Should Know About Textile & Apparel Rules of Origin*

> *What Every Member of the Trade community Should Know About NAFTA for Textiles and Textile Articles*

> *Fibers & Yarns Construction and Classification Under the HTSUS*

> *What Every Member of the Trade community Should Know About Raw Cotton: Tariff Classification and Import Quotas*

The *Harmonized Tariff Schedule of the United States (2001)* (HTSUS) is available to view on the Customs Service website (www.customs.gov), or you may purchase a printed version from:

U.S. Government Printing Office
Superintendent of Documents
710 North Capital Street NW
Washington DC 20401
Tel: (202) 512-1800
Fax: (202) 512-1657
Website: www.access.gpo.gov

The USGPO also has copies of specific laws available for purchase. The USGPO accepts orders made by fax, phone or placed over the Internet, as well as mail orders paid by credit card. All orders must be accompanied by payment. Credit cards, checks drawn on a U.S. bank, or an international money order are all acceptable.

Relevant Government Agencies

Address your questions regarding absolute raw cotton quotas to:

USDA Foreign Agricultural Service (FAS)
Cotton, Oil Seeds, Tobacco and Seeds Division (COTS)
1400 Independence Avenue SW, Room 5646
Washington DC 20250-1051
Tel: (202) 720-9516
Fax: (202) 690-1171
Website: www.fas.usda.gov

USDA Agricultural Marketing Service (AMS)
Cotton Program
1400 Independence Avenue SW, Room 2641-S
Washington DC 20050
Tel: (202) 720-3193
Website: www.ams.usda.gov/cotton

Address your questions regarding textile Multi-Fiber Arrangements to:

U.S. Department of Commerce
International Trade Administration
Office of Textiles and Apparel
Director's Office
14th and Constitution Avenue NW, Rm. H3100
Washington DC 20230
Tel: (202) 482-5078
Fax: (202) 482-2331
Agreements Division: (202) 482-4212
Website: http://otexa.ita.doc.gov

Address your questions regarding the Flammable Fabrics Act (FFA) to:

Consumer Product Safety Commission (CPSC)
Office of Compliance
Washington DC 20207-0001
Tel: 800-638-2772 or (301) 504-7912
Fax: (301) 504-0359
Website: www.cpsc.gov

Address your questions regarding labeling requirements under the Textile Fiber Products Identification Act (TFPIA) or the Wool Products Labeling Act (WPLA) to:

Federal Trade Commission (FTC)
Division of Enforcement
600 Pennsylvania Avenue NW
Washington DC 20580
Tel: (202) 326-2996
Website: www.ftc.gov

Address your questions regarding textile quotas to:

U.S. Customs and Border Protection
Office of Field Operations, Quota Branch
1300 Pennsylvania Avenue NW
Washington DC 20229
Tel: (202) 927-5850
Website: www.customs.treas.gov

The U.S. Customs Service provices updated status reports on textile quota on their web site (see address above). If the country you need information on is not listed, call the Quota Branch office at (202) 927-5850.

Address your questions regarding cotton product imports to your local Customs port director. For addresses, refer to "U.S. Customs and Border Protection Offices" on page 65 or contact:

U.S. Customs and Border Protection
Customs Headquarters
1300 Pennsylvania Avenue NW
Washington DC 20229
Tel: (202) 354-1000
Website: www.customs.treas.gov

Laws and Regulations

The following laws and regulations may be relevant to the importation of special woven fabrics. The laws are contained in the

United States Code (USC), and the regulations are published in the Code of Federal Regulations (CFR), both of which are available at larger public and law libraries. Copies of specific laws are also available from the United States Government Printing Office (address above).

7 USC 601 et seq.
Agricultural Adjustment Act (AAA)
This Act authorizes the Secretary of Agriculture to establish and maintain orderly market conditions for agricultural products, including cotton.

19 CFR Part 132
Regulations for Enforcement of AAA Quotas
These regulations provide for Customs enforcement of AAA quotas and higher duty rates imposed on imported agricultural products, whenever investigation reveals that orderly market conditions require such action.

7 USC 1854
Textile Trade Agreements
(EO 11651, as amended by EO 11951 and 12188, and supplemented by EO 12475)
This Act authorizes the CITA of the DOC to enter into Multi-Fiber Agreements with other countries to control trade in textiles and establishes the Textile Import Program, which is enforced by U.S. Customs.

19 CFR 12.130 et seq.
Regulations on Entry of Textiles
These regulations provide the requirements and procedures followed by Customs in enforcing limitations on the importation and entry and withdrawal of textiles and textile products from warehouses for consumption in the U.S.

15 USC 70-77
Textile Fiber Products Identification Act (TFPIA)
This Act prohibits false or deceptive labeling (misbranding) and false advertising of any textile fiber products and requires all textile fiber products imported into the U.S. to be labeled in accordance with the requirements set forth in the law.

19 CFR 11.12b; 16 CFR 303 et seq.
Regulations on Labeling and Marking
These regulations detail the labeling and marking requirements for textiles as specified by the CPSC and the invoice contents required by U.S. Customs for purpose of enforcing the labeling and marking rules.

15 USC 68-68j
Wool Products Labeling Act (WPLA) of 1939
This Act prohibits the false or deceptive labeling (misbranding) of wool products and requires all wool products imported into the U.S. to be labeled in accordance with requirements set forth in the law.

19 CFR 11.12; 16 CFR 300 et seq.
Regulations on WPLA Labeling and Marking
These regulations set forth the wool labeling and marking requirements adopted by the FTC to administer the requirements of the WPLA and provide the procedures followed by U.S. Customs in enforcing the WPLA and the FTC regulations, including entry invoice requirements.

15 USC 1191-1204
Flammable Fabrics Act (FFA)
This Act provides for the setting of flammability standards for fabric by the Consumer Product Safety Commission (CPSC) and for enforcement by U.S. Customs.

16 CFR 1610, 1611, 1615, 1616, 1630-1632
Regulations on Flammable Fabric Standards
These regulations specify the flammability standards adopted by the CPSC under the FFA for various types of textiles.

16 CFR 423
Care Labeling Rule
Requires fiber composition and washing or dry cleaning instructions for textile apparel and certain piece goods.

Principal Exporting Countries

The following listing includes samples of the main supplier nations of the products of this chapter. It is organized by HTSUS major heading. (Refer to "Customs Classification" above for the product codes.) Countries are listed in rank order of the value of products imported to the U.S. Statistics represent customs value of entries for 2002 from the Bureau of Census, U.S. Department of Commerce.

5201—Egypt, Australia, Mexico, India, Italy, Japan, Germany, South Korea, Ireland

5202—Mexico, France, Pakistan, Italy, Turkey, Spain

5203—Canada, Pakistan, Indonesia, Dominican Republic, Italy, Spain, China, United Kingdom, India

5204—Germany, Egypt, India, China, Peru, Thailand, Greece

5205—Pakistan, Mexico, Canada, Egypt, Malaysia, Brazil, Uzbekistan, Italy

5206—Canada, Pakistan, Italy, Spain, Thailand

5207—France, Canada, Mexico, Netherlands, Belgium, Italy

5208—Pakistan, China, South Korea, Thailand, Japan, Italy

5209—Mexico, Hong Kong, Taiwan, Pakistan, India, Turkey

5210—Pakistan, Indonesia, Thailand, China, United Arab Emirates

5211—Taiwan, Italy, Mexico, China, Belgium, Pakistan, France

5212—Italy, Pakistan, France, United Kingdom, India

Chapter 53:
Other Vegetable Textile Fibers

Full title: Other Vegetable Textile Fibers; Paper Yarn and Woven Fabrics of Paper Yarn

This chapter relates to the importation of vegetable textile fibers, yarns, and fabrics, which are classified under Chapter 53 of the Harmonized Tariff Schedule of the United States (HTSUS). Specifically, it includes raw or processed unspun flax, true hemp, jute, sisal, coconut, abaca, and ramie; flax, jute, paper, and other vegetable textile fiber yarns; and woven fabrics of flax, jute, paper, and other vegetable yarns.

If you are interested in importing cotton textiles and products, you should refer to Commodity Index Chapter 52. The import requirements for vegetable plaiting materials are covered in Chapter 14. For importing paper products, including cellulose wadding, you should read Chapter 48. If you are interested in importing apparel, refer to Chapters 60 through 63.

Note: To understand key issues that will enable you to make best use of the information in this section we recommend that you see "Introduction" on page 425.

Key Factors

The key factors in the importation of other vegetable textile fibers, yarns, and fabrics are:

- Compliance with quota restraints and visa requirements

- Submission of U.S. Customs Country-of-Origin Declaration(s)

- Compliance with entry invoice requirements

- Compliance with labeling requirements under Textile Fiber Products Identification Act (TFPIA) and/or the Wool Products Labeling Act (WPLA) and the Care Labeling Rule

- Compliance with flammability standards adopted and enforced by the Consumer Product Safety Commission (CPSC) under the Flammable Fabrics Act (FFA)

Although most importers use the services of a licensed customs broker in making their entries, and we recommend this practice, you should be aware of the regulatory, entry, and documentation issues involved in importing your product. You, as importer, are ultimately responsible for the fulfillment of any legal requirements applicable to your shipment.

General Considerations

Regulatory Agencies. The Committee for Implementation of Textile Agreements (CITA) regulates certain textile imports under Section 204 of the Agricultural Adjustment Act. U.S. Customs enforces CITA textile and textile product entry quotas. Customs also enforces compliance with labeling and invoice requirements of the TFPIA and flammability standards under the FFA. The CPSC monitors imports and from time to time inspects textile shipments for compliance with FFA standards. If you are importing products that contain wool fibers, importation is subject to complex textile import regulations. The Federal Trade Commission (FTC) administers the WPLA requirements.

Textile Quotas. If you are interested in importing vegetable textile products, the most important issue you need to be aware of is quotas. Under the Multi-Fiber Arrangement provisions of Section 204 of the Agricultural Adjustment Act, CITA initiates specific agreements with individual exporting countries. Section 204 of the Agricultural Adjustment Act covers textiles that: 1) are in chief value of cotton, wool, or man-made fibers, any textile fibers subject to the terms of any textile trade agreement, or any combination of such fibers; 2) contain 50% or more by weight of cotton or man-made fibers, or any textile fibers subject to the terms of any textile trade agreement; 3) contain 17% or more by weight of wool; or 4) if in chief value of textile fibers or textile materials, contain a blend of cotton, wool, or man-made fibers, any textile fibers subject to the terms of any textile trade agreement, or any combination of such fibers that, in total, amount to 50% or more by weight of all component fibers. For vegetable textile products, quotas currently apply to blends with other fibers.

The U.S. has bilateral agreements with over 40 countries. Each agreement with each country is unique, and may specify quotas for a type of textile or a specific article. Visas or export licenses may be required. The DOC's Office of Textiles and Apparel (OTEXA) provides detailed information about specific trade agreements on the OTEXA website (http://otexa.ita.doc.gov). Currently, certain vegetable textile blends are subject to some quota restraints, but these agreements often change. Therefore, if you are interested in importing any vegetable textile products, you should contact the International Trade Administration's Office of Textile and Apparel (see addresses at end of this chapter). Refer to "Prohibitions and Restrictions" below for further details.

Country-of-Origin Declarations. U.S. Customs enforces CITA textile and textile product entry quotas (see "Prohibitions and Restrictions" below). Requirements for entry include submission of Country-of-Origin Declarations with every textile shipment, regardless of whether it is subject to a specific multi-fiber arrangement (19 CFR 12.130, 12.131).

Country of Origin. Quota restrictions are country-specific and therefore are applied based on the country of origin for the textiles shipped. The last country from which a textile shipment was exported to the U.S. is not necessarily its country of origin. A textile or textile product imported into the U.S. is considered a product of the particular foreign territory or country, or a U.S. insular possession, where it is wholly grown, produced, or manufactured. For the following discussion, "country" means a foreign territory or country, or a U.S. insular possession.

In 1996, the U.S. Customs Service made major changes to country of origin rules for textile imports. The regulations at 19 CFR 102.21, "Textile and apparel products" were added to the 1996 Customs Regulations and became effective July 1, 1996. The new rules do not provide for cutting components or cutting and hemming to confer country of origin as in the past. The basis of the new law is processing operations or assembly. Some of the most important changes for importers to be aware of are:

- Cutting does not determine the country of origin

(previously cutting determined country of origin for 90 percent of wearing apparel imports). The new rules are based on processing or assembly operations.

- A subjective determination under the provisions of 19 CFR 12.130 is replaced by objective processing operations expressed in terms of tariff shifts. Dying, printing, and other finishing processes applied to fabrics no longer confer or change country of origin.

- Country of origin for textile and apparel products processed, assembled or manufactured in two or more countries is determined by where the most important processing occurs, and, if that cannot be ascertained, the last country in which an important processing operation occurs.

The country of origin is the country in which a product is wholly produced when a textile or apparel product is completely produced or manufactured (except for minor parts) in one country. For fabric, the country of origin is the country in which the fabric is woven, knitted, needled, tufted, felted, entangled or created by any other fabric-making process. The country of origin for staple yarn is the country in which yarn is spun; for filament yarn, the country in which filament is extruded; and for plied, gimped and cabled yarns, the country in which the fibers or filaments used in the yarn are spun or extruded. The country of origin of all other textile and apparel products is the country in which the components of a textile or apparel product are wholly assembled (except for minor attachments) except for knit-to-shape products. Knit-to-shape products are those composed of panels or parts ,which, are knitted or crocheted directly into the shape that will be used in construction of the final product. Minor cutting or sewing does not influence whether the product is considered knit-to-shape. The country of origin for knit-to-shape products is that country in which the major parts are knitted into the shape that will constitute the finished product. Once again, note that assembly, not cutting, now confers country of origin.

Declarations. All importations of textiles and textile products must be accompanied by one of the following three declarations. Goods subject to Section 204, Agricultural Act of 1956, as amended, must be accompanied by either a single-country or a multiple-country declaration. Goods not subject to Section 204 must be accompanied by a negative declaration.

- **Single-country declarations** are used for entries of textiles or textile products which are wholly the growth, product, or manufacture of a single foreign country, territory, or U.S. insular possession. Information required includes: marks of identification and numbers; description of article and quantity; country of origin; and date of exportation.

- **Multiple-country declarations** are used for entries of textiles or textile products which were subjected to manufacturing or processing operations in, and/or incorporate materials originating in more than one foreign country or territory. Information required includes: marks of identification and numbers; for articles, description, quantity, identification of manufacturing and/or processing operations, country, and date of exportation; for materials used to make articles, description of materials, country of production, and date of exportation.

- **Negative declarations** must accompany all textile imports that are not subject to AAA Section 204 restrictions. Information required includes: marks of identification and numbers; descriptions of article and quantity; and country of origin.

The date of exportation to be indicated on the above declarations is the date on which the carrier leaves the last port in the country of origin, as determined by Customs. Diversion to another country during transit does not affect the export date.

Procedure for Declarations. The manufacturer, producer, exporter, or importer may prepare the declaration. If more than one of these parties is involved in the importation, each party may prepare a separate declaration. You may file a separate declaration for each invoice presented with your entry. The declaration must be dated and signed by the responsible party, and must include the person's title and the company name and address. Your shipment's entry will be denied unless it is accompanied by a properly executed declaration. Customs will not treat a textile declaration as a missing document for which a bond may be filed.

Customs will base its country-of-origin determination on the information contained in each declaration, unless the information is insufficient. If the information on the declaration is insufficient, Customs will require that you submit such additional information as will enable the determination to be made. The shipment will not be released until the determination is made. Thus, if you want to clear Customs with minimal delay, be sure that the information on the declarations is as complete as possible for each shipment.

Textile Labeling and Invoice Requirements. You are responsible for your imported vegetable textile product's compliance with applicable provisions of the TFPIA. Vegetable textile products that require labeling under TFPIA must already be labeled at entry, or the shipment will be refused. (See "Marking and Labeling Requirements" below.) If you import shipments of vegetable textiles subject to TFPIA and valued at over $500, you must provide special information on the entry invoice (see "Entry and Documentation" below).

Flammability Standards. Vegetable textile products imported into the U.S. for use in consumer products must be in compliance with the FFA, a federal law that gives the CPSC the authority and responsibility for protecting the public from the hazards of dangerously flammable items of wearing apparel and interior furnishings. Under the FFA, standards have been established for flammability of clothing textiles. You cannot import any article of wearing apparel or interior furnishing, or any fabric or related material that is intended for use or that may be used in such items, if it fails to conform to an applicable flammability standard (FFA Section 4). Certain products may be imported into the U.S. (FFA Section 11c) for finishing or processing to render them less flammable so as to meet the standards. For these products, the exporter must state on the invoice or other paper relating to the shipment that the shipment is being made for that purpose.

The CPSC monitors imports of textiles under its Import Surveillance Program. From time to time, your textile shipments may be inspected to ascertain compliance with mandatory safety standards. Shipments may also be subject to testing by the CPSC to determine compliance. If the CPSC believes a product, fabric, or related material does not comply with a flammability standard, it is authorized to pursue a variety of legal sanctions (see "Prohibitions and Restrictions" below).

Substantial Product Hazard Reports. Any firm that obtains information that reasonably supports the conclusion that one of its products presents an unreasonable risk of serious injury or death must report that information to the CPSC's Division of Corrective Actions (CPSC address below). Importers must also report to the CPSC if 1) a type of product is the subject of at least three civil actions filed in U.S. federal or state courts, 2) each suit alleges the involvement of that product type in death or grievous bodily injury (as defined in FFA Section 07(3)1, and 3) at least three of the actions result in a final settlement with the manufacturer or in a judgment for the plaintiff within any one of the two-year periods specified in FFA Section 37(b).

Wool Product Entry Requirements. Depending on the nature of your wool fiber imports, as many as four different types of special entry documents may be required. First, for all imported textile fibers and yarns covered by the Agricultural Adjustment Act (AAA), including wool, you must file a U.S. Customs Textile Entry Declaration (see "Country-of-Origin Declarations" above). Second, for all wool products subject to the WPLA, special information is required on the entry invoices (see "Entry and Documentation" below). Finally, certain wool articles manufactured or produced in certain countries may be subject to quotas under U.S. bilateral agreements. Such products require export certificates or visas issued by the appropriate country of origin, in addition to other requisite entry paperwork (see "Quotas" above).

Wool Products Labeling Act. The term "wool product" means any product or any portion of a product that contains, purports to contain, or in any way is represented as containing wool, reprocessed wool, or reused wool. All wool products imported into the U.S., except those made more than 20 years before importation, and except carpets, rugs, mats, and upholsteries, must have affixed a stamp, tag, label, or other means of identification as required by the WPLA. If you are importing wool products exempt from labeling under the WPLA, do not assume they are also exempt from labeling under the TFPIA. These are two distinct laws, with some overlapping requirements (see "Marking and Labeling Requirements" below).

Import Advisory

Importation of textiles is trade-sensitive and highly regulated. Shipments of textiles and textile products not complying with all government regulations, including quotas and visas, are subject to seizure and could result in the imposition of penalties as well as possible forfeiture of the goods. You should always verify the available quota for any textile product you plan to import before your shipment leaves the country of manufacture. Furthermore, Customs textile classification rulings change frequently, and prior administrative rulings are often modified and sometimes reversed. You should be particularly careful to comply with country of origin determination regulations, which were changed in 1996, and affect quotas and visas, marking and labeling, and other important aspects of tariff classification. See "Publications and WWW Resources" for information on important Customs Service informed compliance publications.

The Customs Service has increased its scrutiny of the textile industry, it is one of eight primary focus industries identified in the most recent Trade Compliance & Enforcement Plan. Imported products from these industries will likely attract significant attention from Customs in the areas of compliance measurement, compliance assessment, informed compliance, and interventions.

Customs Classification

For customs purposes, other vegetable textile fibers, yarns, and fabrics are classified under Chapter 53 of the HTSUS. This chapter is broken into major headings, which are further divided into subheadings, and often sub-subheadings, each of which has its own HTSUS classification number. For example, the 2001 HTSUS number for woven fabrics of flax, bleached or unbleached, containing less than 85% by weight of flax and more than 17 percent by weight of wool or fine animal hair is 5309.21.20, indicating it is a sub-subcategory of unbleached or bleached with less than 85% by weight of flax (5309.21), which is a subcategory of the major heading, woven fabrics of flax (5309). There are 11 major headings within Chapter 53.

5301—Flax, raw or processed but not spun; flax tow and waste (including yarn waste and garnetted stock)

5302—True hemp (*Cannabis sativa* L.), raw or processed but not spun; tow and waste of true hemp (including yarn waste and garnetted stock)

5303—Jute and other textile bast fibers (excluding flax, true hemp, and ramie), raw or processed but not spun; tow and waste of these fibers (including yarn waste and garnetted stock)

5304—Sisal and other textile fibers of the genus *Agave*, raw or processed but not spun; tow and waste of these fibers (including yarn waste and garnetted stock)

5305—Coconut, abaca (Manila hemp or *Musa textiles Nee*), ramie, and other vegetable textile fibers, not elsewhere specified or included, raw or processed but not spun; tow, noils, and waste of these fibers (including yarn waste and garnetted stock)

5306—Flax yarn

5307—Yarn of jute or of other textile bast fibers of heading 5303

5308—Yarn of other vegetable textile fibers; paper yarn

5309—Woven fabrics of flax

5310—Woven fabrics of jute or of other textile bast fibers of heading 5303

5311—Woven fabrics of other vegetable textile fibers; woven fabrics of paper yarn

For more details regarding classifications of the specific product you are interested in importing, consult a customs broker, the appropriate commodity specialist at your nearest customs port, or the HTSUS. The 2001 HTSUS is available online from the Customs Service (www.customs.gov/impoexpo/impoexpo.htm) or for purchase from the U.S. Government Printing Office (see resources at the end of this chapter), and may be found in larger public libraries. For a general discussion of customs classification, see "Classification—Liquidation" on page 229.

Dutiable Status of Goods

For more information about duty rates and binding decisions see "Dutiable Status of Goods" on page 203; for a discussion of temporary importation of goods see "Temporary Free Importations" on page 205.

Valuation

Importers have a responsibility to use what the U.S. Customs Service deems, "reasonable care," when determining the value of their goods. They must also provide any additional information that the Customs Service needs for setting a final value on the goods. This process involves a number of factors and can be somewhat complicated; importers must be aware of applicable issues and details. Valuation information applies to all types of commodities, for further discussion on the subject see "Customs Valuation" on page 267.

Import Duties

Import duties vary (often dramatically) depending upon the Harmonized Tariff Schedule (HTSUS) classification of the goods or products imported. Since some products that look alike have different HTSUS classifications and different rates of duty, proper classification is vital. Note that "differences of opinion" between importers and the Bureau of Customs and Border Protection regarding classification keeps customs attorneys very busy.

Import duties can be assessed on the imported value of the goods ("ad valorem" rates of duty such as 2%, 4.4%, 50%, etc.), total units or weight of the goods ("specific" rates of duty such as 2 cents each or 1.5 cents/pound, etc.) or on a combination basis ("compound" rates of duty such as 5 cents each plus 6%).

Listed below is a sampling of several Column 1 import duty rates for Chapter 53 products:
Flax, raw or retted (5301.10.00.00): Free
to
Containing more than 17 percent by weight of wool or fine animal hair (410) (5309.21.20.00): 15.6%

For specific information on US import duties refer to the Harmonized Tariff Schedule of the US. The print version is available from the US Government Printing Office as well as third party suppliers who often add special features. Online versions are available in both static PDF pages as well as in formats with excellent search functionality. Search the Web with the term "Harmonized Tariff Schedule" to find sources.

Entry and Documentation

The entry of merchandise is a two-part process consisting of 1) filing the documentation necessary to determine whether merchandise may be released from Customs custody, and 2) filing the documents that contain information for duty assessment and statistical purposes. In certain instances, all documents must be filed and accepted by Customs prior to release of the goods. Unless you have been granted an extension, you must file entry documents at a location specified by the port or area director within five working days of your shipment's date of arrival at a U.S. port of entry. These include a number of standard documents required by Customs for any entry, and:

- U.S. Customs Country-of-Origin Declaration Form CF 3229
- Export documentation and/or visa for textiles subject to bilateral agreement

After you present the entry, Customs may examine your shipment or may waive examination. The shipment is then released provided no legal or regulatory violations have been noted. If not already done you must then file entry summary documentation and deposit estimated duties at a designated customhouse within 10 working days of your shipment's release. For a detailed description of entry procedures, standard documentation, and informal entry, see "Entry Process" on page 185.

Informed Compliance. Informed compliance was introduced with the Customs Modernization Act of 1993 (Mod Act) and defines the relationship between importers and the Customs Service. It sets out the responsibilities of both parties. Providing the correct documentation and information for entry is a key factor that will make your importing operation run smoothly. We recommend that importers become familiar with the concept of informed comliance and the responsibilities that they have under the Mod Act. For further discussion about informed compliance see "Informed Compliance" on page 211.

NAFTA Certificates of Origin. An importer of textiles for which NAFTA treatment is sought need not file a separate NAFTA Certificate of Origin in addition to the Customs Country-of-Origin Declaration. The declaration is sufficient. However, the importer must take care to submit a declaration from each U.S., Canadian, or Mexican producer or manufacturer. Thus, for multiple producers or manufacturers, a separate declaration must be filed for each. If a Customs port director cannot determine the country of origin because the declaration is absent or incomplete, the shipment is not entitled to preferential NAFTA tariff treatment or other NAFTA benefits. See 19 CFR 12.132.

Entry Invoices. You must provide certain additional information on the entry invoice for vegetable textile products. The specific information varies depending on the nature of your product, as noted below.

TFPIA Requirements. For the purpose of TFPIA enforcement, a commercial shipment of textile products exceeding $500 in value

and subject to TFPIA labeling requirements must show the following information: 1) the constituent fiber or combination of fibers, designating with equal prominence each natural or manufactured fiber by its generic name, in order of predominance by weight if the weight of such fiber is 5% or more of the total fiber weight of the product; 2) percentage of each fiber present, by weight, in the total fiber content; 3) the name or other identification issued and registered by the FTC of the manufacturer of the product or one or more persons subject to Section 3 of the TFPIA with respect to such product; 4) the name of the country where processed or manufactured.

Wool Products Subject to WPLA. When you offer for entry a wool product shipment valued at over $500 and subject to WPLA, you must include certain information intended to facilitate Customs monitoring and enforcement of that Act. This extra information is identical to that required by WPLA on labeling (see "Marking and Labeling Requirements" below), with the addition of the manufacturer's name. If your product consists of mixed waste, residues, and similar merchandise obtained from several suppliers or unknown sources, you may omit the manufacturer's name from the entry invoice.

Yarn. All entry invoices for yarn should show: 1) fiber content by weight; 2) whether the yarn is single or plied; 3) whether or not the yarn is put up for retail sale (as defined in HTSUS Section XI, Note 4); and 4) whether or not the yarn is intended for use as sewing thread. For more general information about invoices see "Invoices" on page 277.

Prohibitions and Restrictions

Quotas. Textile import restrictions are primarily a matter of quotas and the way in which these quotas are administered and monitored. Under the Multi-Fiber Arrangement provisions of Section 204 of the Agricultural Adjustment Act, CITA has negotiated bilateral agreements with over 40 countries. These Agreements may impose quotas for a type of textile or a specific article, and they are country-specific. Currently, certain vegetable textiles blended with other fibers are subject to quota restraints, but these agreements often change. Therefore, if you are interested in importing any vegetable textiles fiber, yarns, or fabrics, you should contact the International Trade Administration's Office of Textile and Apparel (see addresses at end of this chapter). The Office of Textile and Apparel has a team of country specialists who can inform you of the latest developments and inform you about a product's quota or restriction status.

U.S. Customs enforces CITA textile and textile product entry quotas. If formal entry procedures are not followed, Customs will usually refuse entry for textiles that are subject to Section 204. Formal entry requires submission of a Country-of-Origin Declaration (see "General Considerations" above). U.S. Customs maintains a current textile quota status report, available for perusal at any Customs port. In addition, U.S. Customs in Washington, DC, provides quota status reports online, which are updated on a regular basis (www.customs.gov/impoexpo/impoexpo.htm).

Flammable Fabrics. U.S. Customs may refuse entry for any article of wearing apparel or interior furnishing, or any fabric or related material that is intended for use or that may be used in wearing apparel or interior furnishings, if it fails to conform to an applicable flammability standard issued under Section 4 of the FFA. An exception is allowed for certain products (FFA Section 11c) that are imported for finishing or processing to bring them within the legal standard. For these products, the exporter must state on the invoice or other paper relating to the shipment that the shipment is being made for that purpose.

The CPSC, as the primary enforcement agency of flammability standards, inspects products for compliance with the FFA. If the CPSC believes a product, fabric, or related material does not comply with a flammability standard, it is authorized to pursue a variety of legal sanctions, including: 1) seizure, condemnation, and forfeiture of the noncomplying products; 2) administrative cease-and-desist order requiring an individual or firm to stop sale and distribution of the noncomplying products or; 3) temporary injunction requiring the individual or firm to stop sale and distribution of the noncomplying products, pending final disposition of an administrative cease-and-desist proceeding. The CPSC also has authority to seek civil penalties against any person who knowingly violates a regulation or standard issued under Section 4 of the FFA.

Note: The Entry and Documentation section has been carefully designed to supply you, the importer, with sample documents and directions on how to satisfy Customs requirements. Be aware that you should consult the applicable authorities to ensure that you are correctly following the most current procedures.

Country-Specific Restrictions

Restrictions under bilateral agreements are country-specific. A product originating in one country may be subject to quota and to export license or visa requirements, while the same product originating in a different country may not. At present, the U.S. has bilateral agreements with over 40 countries. Many different categories of products are covered under these Arrangements; it is beyond the scope of this book to list each country and its restricted commodities. If you are interested in importing textiles and textile products, you should contact the International Trade Administration's Office of Textile and Apparel (see addresses at end of this chapter) or U.S. Customs to ascertain your product's restraint status.

The U.S. Customs service provides quota reports on their website (www.customs.gov/impoexpo/impoexpo.htm). These reports are constantly updated and have an effective date noted. The most recent quota information can be accessed by clicking on the country name that interests you. This location holds information regarding quotas, transshipments, and visa requirements.

Marking and Labeling Requirements

TFPIA Requirements. All textile fiber products imported into the U.S. must be stamped, tagged, labeled, or otherwise marked with the following information as required by the TFPIA, unless exempt from marking (see TFPIA, Section 12): 1) the generic names and percentages by weight of the constituent fibers present in the textile fiber product, exclusive of permissible ornamentation, in amounts of more than 5% in order of predominance by weight, with any percentage of fiber or fibers required to be designated as "other fiber" or "other fibers" (including those present in amounts of 5% or less) appearing last; and 2) the name of the manufacturer or the name or registered identification number issued by the FTC of one or more persons marketing or handling the textile fiber product; and 3) the name of the country where processed. A word trademark, used as a house mark and registered with the U.S. Patent Office, may appear on labels instead of the name otherwise required, provided the owner of the trademark furnishes a copy of the registration to the FTC prior to use (see "Registered Identification Numbers" below).

The information listed above is not exhaustive. TFPIA requirements are extensive. The Act specifies such details as types of labels, means of attachment, label position on the article, package labeling, unit labeling for two-piece garments, and arrangement of information on the label; allowable fiber designations; country-of-origin indications; requirements for trim and ornamentation, linings and interlinings, and pile fabrics; sectional disclosure; use of trade names and trademarks; and requirements for swatches and samples. The FTC publishes a booklet intended to clarify TFPIA requirements to facilitate voluntary

compliance in the industry (see "Publications and WWW Resources" below). It is available on request, at no charge, from the FTC (see addresses at end of this chapter).

Wool Products Labeling Act (WPLA). Wool product labeling requirements for foreign products are the responsibility of the importer. The WPLA requires the following information to appear on wool products subject to the Act: 1) percentage of the wool product's total fiber weight (exclusive of ornamentation) not exceeding 5% of the total fiber weight of a) wool, b) recycled wool, c) each fiber other than wool if the percent by weight of such fiber is 5% or more, and d) the aggregate of all other fibers; 2) the maximum percent of the wool product's total weight, of any nonfibrous loading, filling, or adulterating matter; and 3) the importer's name. If you, as importer, have a registered identification number issued by the FTC, that number may be used instead of your name (see "Registered Identification Numbers" below).

Customs entry is contingent on proper labeling. If your shipment is found to be mislabeled at entry, you will be given the option of relabeling the products under Customs supervision, as long as the port director is satisfied that your labeling error or omission did not involve fraud or willful neglect. If your shipment is discovered after entry to have been noncomplying with WPLA, it will be recalled to Customs custody at your expense, unless you can satisfy the port director that the products have since been brought into compliance. You will be held responsible for all expenses incurred in bringing a shipment into compliance, including compensation of personnel and other expenses related to Customs supervision.

Fraudulent violations of WPLA will result in seizure of the shipment. Shipments already released from Customs custody will be ordered to be redelivered to Customs. Customs reports all cases of fraudulent violation to the FTC in Washington, DC.

The information listed above is not intended to be exhaustive. WPLA requirements are extensive. The Act specifies such details as types of labels, means of attachment, label position on the article, package labeling, unit labeling (as in the case of a two-piece garment), arrangement of information on the label, allowable fiber designations, country-of-origin indications, trim and ornamentation, pile fabrics, sectional disclosure, use of trade names and trademarks, requirements for swatches and samples, etc. The FTC publishes a booklet intended to clarify WPLA requirements in order to facilitate voluntary compliance within the industry (see "Publications and WWW Resources" below). It is available on request, at no charge, from the FTC (see addresses at end of this chapter).

The Care Labeling Rule. Regulations under this rule require manufacturers and importers of textile clothing and fabrics to attach specific care instructions for washing or dry cleaning, as well as information on the fiber composition of the article. They are enforced by the FTC Division of Enforcement. The Care Labeling Rule was amended September 2000, detailed information is available on the FTC website (www.ftc.gov/os/statutes/textilejump.htm).

Registered Identification Numbers. Any domestic firm or person residing in the U.S. and engaged in the manufacture or marketing of textile products covered under the TFPIA may obtain an FTC-registered identification number for use on required tags and labels instead of the name of a firm or person. For applications, contact the FTC (address below.)

For a general discussion of U.S. Customs marking and labeling requirements, see "Country of Origin Marking" on page 236, "Special Marking Requirements" on page 238 and "Marking—False Impression" on page 239.

Shipping Considerations

You will need to ensure that your goods are packaged and shipped with care so that they pass smoothly through Customs and arrive in good condition. You are responsible for ensuring that the shipment is in compliance with all applicable government regulations for packaging and shipping. In most instances, you should not leave these arrangements solely to the discretion of your supplier. Careful preparation of the cargo and selection of the mode of transport can be essential to a cost-effective, timely delivery of undamaged goods. We strongly advise you to consult your shipping representative, insurance agent, or freight broker for advice on packing and shipping.

Vegetable textile fibers, yarns, and fabrics may be shipped in bulk, bolts, cartons, or other types of containers, depending on the type of product and whether it is prepackaged. General considerations include protection from contamination, weather, and pests. Containers should be constructed so as to be safe for handling during transport.

Publications and WWW Resources

The following publications may be relevant to the importation of vegetable textile fiber, yarn, and fabric:

> *Threading Your Way Through the Labeling Requirements of the Textile and Wool Acts*

Available free of charge on request from the Federal Trade Commission and online from the FTC website (www.ftc.gov/bcp/conline/pubs/buspubs/thread.htm). This publication is an excellent source of information written in clear lay language. We recommend that anyone interested in importing textile fiber products but unfamiliar with the regulations obtain a copy of each of this booklet.

The U.S. Customs Service launched a series of "Informed Compliance" publications in 1996, which are available on the Customs Service website (www.customs.gov/impoexpo/impoexpo.htm). Of particular interest:

> *What Every Member of the Trade Community Should Know About Textile & Apparel Rules of Origin*
>
> *What Every Member of the Trade community Should Know About NAFTA for Textiles and Textile Articles*
>
> *Fibers & Yarns Construction and Classification Under the HTSUS*

The *Harmonized Tariff Schedule of the United States (2001)* (HTSUS) is available to view on the Customs Service website (www.customs.gov), or you may purchase a printed version from:

U.S. Government Printing Office
Superintendent of Documents
710 North Capital Street NW
Washington DC 20401
Tel: (202) 512-1800
Fax: (202) 512-1657
Website: www.access.gpo.gov

The USGPO also has copies of specific laws available for purchase. The USGPO accepts orders made by fax, phone or placed over the Internet, as well as mail orders paid by credit card. All orders must be accompanied by payment. Credit cards, checks drawn on a U.S. bank, or an international money order are all acceptable.

Relevant Government Agencies

Address your questions regarding textile Multi-Fiber Arrangements to:

U.S. Department of Commerce
International Trade Administration
Office of Textiles and Apparel
Director's Office
14th and Constitution Ave. NW, Rm. H3100
Washington DC 20230
Tel: (202) 482-5078
Fax: (202) 482-2331

Agreements Division: (202) 482-4212
Website: http://otexa.ita.doc.gov

Address your questions regarding the Flammable Fabrics Act (FFA) to:

Consumer Product Safety Commission (CPSC)
Office of Compliance
Washington DC 20207-0001
Tel: 800-638-2772 or (301) 504-7912
Fax: (301) 504-0359
Website: www.cpsc.gov

Address your questions regarding requirements under the Textile Fiber Products Identification Act (TFPIA) or the Wool Products Labeling Act (WPLA) to:

Federal Trade Commission (FTC)
Division of Enforcement
600 Pennsylvania Avenue NW
Washington DC 20580
Tel: (202) 326-2996
Website: www.ftc.gov

Address your questions regarding textile quotas to:

U.S. Customs and Border Protection
Office of Field Operations, Quota Branch
1300 Pennsylvania Avenue NW
Washington DC 20229
Tel: (202) 927-5850
Website: www.customs.treas.gov

The U.S. Customs Service provices updated status reports on textile quota on their web site (see address above). If the country you need information on is not listed, call the Quota Branch office at (202) 927-5850.

Address your questions regarding vegetable textile fiber, yarn, and fabric imports to your local Customs port director. For addresses, refer to "U.S. Customs and Border Protection Offices" on page 65 or contact:

U.S. Customs and Border Protection
Customs Headquarters
1300 Pennsylvania Avenue NW
Washington DC 20229
Tel: (202) 354-1000
Website: www.customs.treas.gov

Laws and Regulations

The following laws and regulations may be relevant to the importation of vegetable textile fiber, yarn, and fabric products. The laws are contained in the United States Code (USC), and the regulations are published in the Code of Federal Regulations (CFR), both of which are available at larger public and law libraries. Copies of specific laws are also available from the United States Government Printing Office (address above).

7 USC 1854
Textile Trade Agreements
(EO 11651, as amended by EO 11951 and 12188, and supplemented by EO 12475)
This Act authorizes the CITA of the DOC to enter into Multi-Fiber Agreements with other countries to control trade in textiles and establishes the Textile Import Program, which is enforced by U.S. Customs.

19 CFR 12.130 et seq.
Regulations on Entry of Textiles
These regulations provide the requirements and procedures followed by Customs in enforcing limitations on the importation and entry and withdrawal of textiles and textile products from warehouses for consumption in the U.S.

15 USC 70-77
Textile Fiber Products Identification Act (TFPIA)
This Act prohibits false or deceptive labeling (misbrand-

ing) and false advertising of any textile fiber products and requires all textile fiber products imported into the U.S. to be labeled in accordance with the requirements set forth in the law.

19 CFR 11.12b; 16 CFR 303 et seq.
Regulations on Labeling and Marking
These regulations detail the labeling and marking requirements for textiles as specified by the CPSC and the invoice contents required by U.S. Customs for purpose of enforcing the labeling and marking rules.

15 USC 68-68j
Wool Products Labeling Act (WPLA) of 1939
This Act prohibits the false or deceptive labeling (misbranding) of wool products and requires all wool products imported into the U.S. to be labeled in accordance with requirements set forth in the law.

19 CFR 11.12; 16 CFR 300 et seq.
Regulations on WPLA Labeling and Marking
These regulations set forth the wool labeling and marking requirements adopted by the FTC to administer the requirements of the WPLA and provide the procedures followed by U.S. Customs in enforcing the WPLA and the FTC regulations, including entry invoice requirements.

15 USC 1191-1204
Flammable Fabrics Act (FFA)
This Act provides for the setting of flammability standards for fabric by the Consumer Product Safety Commission (CPSC) and for enforcement by U.S. Customs.

16 CFR 1610, 1611, 1615, 1616, 1630-1632
Regulations on Flammable Fabric Standards
These regulations specify the flammability standards adopted by the CPSC under the FFA for various types of textiles.

16 CFR 423
Care Labeling Rule
Requires fiber composition and washing or dry cleaning instructions for textile apparel and certain piece goods.

Principal Exporting Countries

The following listing includes samples of the main supplier nations of the products of this chapter. It is organized by HTSUS major heading. (Refer to "Customs Classification" above for the product codes.) Countries are listed in rank order of the value of products imported to the U.S. Statistics represent customs value of entries for 2002 from the Bureau of Census, U.S. Department of Commerce.

5301—Canada, France, Belgium, Lithuania, Egypt, Ukraine, Latvia

5302—Canada, France, Hungary, Netherlands, China, Italy, United Kingdom

5303—Germany, Balgladesh, India, Thailand, United Kingdom, Canada, Italy, Hungary, Belgium, Indonesia

5304—Brazil, Mexico, United Kingdom, Philippines, China, Belgium, South Korea, Canada, India, Italy, Kenya

5305—Sri Lanka, Philippines, Ecuador, India, Mexico, Netherlands, China, Pakistan, Ghana

5306—France, United Kingdom, Belgium, Canada, Italy, Austria, China, Spain, Slovenia, Hungary, Latvia, Sweden, Switzerland

5307—Bangladesh, India, Belgium, Thailand, China, United Kingdom, Turkey

5308—India, Italy, Romania, Sri Lanka, Germany

5309—China, United Kingdom, Italy, Belgium, Belarus, Poland, France, Czech Republic

5310—India, Bangladesh, China, United Kingdom, Indonesia, Italy, Netherlands, Taiwan, Belgium, Germany

5311—China, Italy, Mexico, Brazil, India, South Korea, Switzerland, United Kingdom, Philippines

Chapter 54: Man-made Filaments

This chapter relates to the importation of man-made filament products, which are classified under Chapter 54 of the Harmonized Tariff Schedule of the United States (HTSUS). Specifically, it includes sewing threads of synthetic—such as nylon or polyester—or artificial—such as viscose rayon or cellulose acetate—filaments, synthetic and artificial filament yarns, and woven fabrics of synthetic or artificial filament yarns.

If you are interested in importing cotton textiles and products, you should refer to Commodity Index Chapter 52. The import requirements for wool textile products are covered in Chapter 53. For importing monofilaments of plastics, you should also read Chapter 39. If you are interested in importing apparel, refer to Chapters 60 through 63. Hairnets and headgear of man-made filaments are covered in Chapter 65.

Note: To understand key issues that will enable you to make best use of the information in this section we recommend that you see "Introduction" on page 425.

Key Factors

The key factors in the importation of man-made filament products are:

- Compliance with quota restraints and visa requirements

- Submission of U.S. Customs Country-of-Origin Declaration(s)

- Compliance with entry invoice requirements

- Compliance with labeling requirements under Textile Fiber Products Identification Act (TFPIA) and/ or the Wool Products Labeling Act (WPLA) and the Care Labeling Rule

- Compliance with flammability standards adopted and enforced by the Consumer Product Safety Commission (CPSC) under the Flammable Fabrics Act (FFA)

Although most importers use the services of a licensed customs broker in making their entries, and we recommend this practice, you should be aware of the regulatory, entry, and documentation issues involved in importing your product. You, as importer, are ultimately responsible for the fulfillment of any legal requirements applicable to your shipment.

General Considerations

Regulatory Agencies. The Committee for Implementation of Textile Agreements (CITA) regulates certain textile imports under Section 204 of the Agricultural Adjustment Act. U.S. Customs enforces CITA textile and textile product entry quotas. Customs also enforces compliance with labeling and invoice requirements of the TFPIA and flammability standards under the FFA. The CPSC monitors imports and from time to time inspects textile shipments for compliance with FFA standards. If you are importing products that contain wool fibers, importation is subject to complex textile import regulations. The Federal Trade Commission (FTC) administers the WPLA requirements.

Quotas. If you are interested in importing man-made filament products, the most important issue you need to be aware of is quotas. Under the Multi-Fiber Arrangement provisions of Section 204 of the Agricultural Adjustment Act, CITA initiates specific agreements with individual exporting countries. Section 204 of the Agricultural Adjustment Act covers textiles that: 1) are in chief value of cotton, wool, or man-made fibers, any textile fibers subject to the terms of any textile trade agreement, or any combination of such fibers; 2) contain 50% or more by weight of cotton or man-made fibers, or any textile fibers subject to the terms of any textile trade agreement; 3) contain 17% or more by weight of wool; or 4) if in chief value of textile fibers or textile materials, contain a blend of cotton, wool, or man-made fibers, any textile fibers subject to the terms of any textile trade agreement, or any combination of such fibers that, in total, amount to 50% or more by weight of all component fibers.

The U.S. has bilateral agreements with over 40 countries. Each agreement with each country is unique, and may specify quotas for a type of textile or a specific article. Visas or export licenses may be required. These agreements, however, often change. Therefore, if you are interested in importing any man-made filament products, you should contact the International Trade Administration's Office of Textile and Apparel (see addresses at end of this chapter) or visit the website (www.otexa.ita.doc.gov). Refer to "Prohibitions and Restrictions" below for further details.

Country-of-Origin Declarations. U.S. Customs enforces CITA textile and textile product entry quotas (see "Prohibitions and Restrictions" below). Requirements for entry include submission of Country-of-Origin Declarations with every textile shipment, regardless of whether it is subject to a specific multi-fiber arrangement (19 CFR 12.130, 12.131).

Country of Origin. Quota restrictions are country-specific and therefore are applied based on the country of origin for the textiles shipped. The last country from which a textile shipment was exported to the U.S. is not necessarily its country of origin. A textile or textile product imported into the U.S. is considered a product of the particular foreign territory or country, or a U.S. insular possession, where it is wholly grown, produced, or manufactured. For the following discussion, "country" means a foreign territory or country, or a U.S. insular possession.

In 1996, the U.S. Customs Service made major changes to country of origin rules for textile imports. The regulations at 19 CFR 102.21, "Textile and apparel products" were added to the 1996 Customs Regulations and became effective July 1, 1996. The new rules do not provide for cutting components or cutting and hemming to confer country of origin as in the past. The basis of the new law is processing operations or assembly. Some of the most important changes for importers to be aware of are:

- Cutting does not determine the country of origin (previously cutting determined country of origin for 90 percent of wearing apparel imports). The new rules are based on processing or assembly operations.

- A subjective determination under the provisions of 19 CFR 12.130 is replaced by objective processing operations expressed in terms of tariff shifts. Dying, printing, and other finishing processes applied to fabrics no longer confer or change country of origin.

- Country of origin for textile and apparel products processed, assembled or manufactured in two or more countries is determined by where the most important processing occurs, and, if that cannot be ascertained, the last country in which an important processing operation occurs.

The country of origin is the country in which a product is wholly produced when a textile or apparel product is completely produced or manufactured (except for minor parts) in one country. For fabric, the country of origin is the country in which the fabric is woven, knitted, needled, tufted, felted, entangled or created by any other fabric-making process. The country of origin for staple yarn is the country in which yarn is spun; for filament yarn, the country in which filament is extruded; and for plied, gimped and cabled yarns, the country in which the fibers or filaments used in the yarn are spun or extruded. The country of origin of all other textile and apparel products is the country in which the components of a textile or apparel product are wholly assembled (except for minor attachments) except for knit-to-shape products. Knit-to-shape products are those composed of panels or parts ,which, are knitted or crocheted directly into the shape that will be used in construction of the final product. Minor cutting or sewing does not influence whether the product is considered knit-to-shape. The country of origin for knit-to-shape products is that country in which the major parts are knitted into the shape that will constitute the finished product. Once again, note that assembly, not cutting, now confers country of origin.

Declarations. All importations of textiles and textile products must be accompanied by one of the following three declarations. Goods subject to Section 204, Agricultural Act of 1956, as amended, must be accompanied by either a single-country or a multiple-country declaration. Goods not subject to Section 204 must be accompanied by a negative declaration.

- **Single-country declarations** are used for entries of textiles or textile products which are wholly the growth, product, or manufacture of a single foreign country, territory, or U.S. insular possession. Information required includes: marks of identification and numbers; description of article and quantity; country of origin; and date of exportation.

- **Multiple-country declarations** are used for entries of textiles or textile products which were subjected to manufacturing or processing operations in, and/or incorporate materials originating in more than one foreign country or territory. Information required includes: marks of identification and numbers; for articles, description, quantity, identification of manufacturing and/or processing operations, country, and date of exportation; for materials used to make articles, description of materials, country of production, and date of exportation.

- **Negative declarations** must accompany all textile imports that are not subject to AAA Section 204 restrictions. Information required includes: marks of identification and numbers; descriptions of article and quantity; and country of origin.

The date of exportation to be indicated on the above declarations is the date on which the carrier leaves the last port in the country of origin, as determined by Customs. Diversion to another country during transit does not affect the export date.

Procedure for Declarations. The manufacturer, producer, exporter, or importer may prepare the declaration. If more than one of these parties is involved in the importation, each party may prepare a separate declaration. You may file a separate declaration for each invoice presented with your entry. The declaration must be dated and signed by the responsible party, and must include the person's title and the company name and address. Your shipment's entry will be denied unless it is accompanied by a properly executed declaration. Customs will not treat a textile declaration as a missing document for which a bond may be filed.

Customs will base its country-of-origin determination on the information contained in each declaration, unless the information is insufficient. If the information on the declaration is insufficient, Customs will require that you submit such additional information as will enable the determination to be made. The shipment will not be released until the determination is made. Thus, if you want to clear Customs with minimal delay, be sure that the information on the declarations is as complete as possible for each shipment.

Textile Labeling and Invoice Requirements. You are responsible for your imported man-made filament product's compliance with applicable provisions of the TFPIA. Man-made filament products that require labeling under TFPIA must already be labeled at entry, or the shipment will be refused. (See "Marking and Labeling Requirements" below.) If you import shipments of man-made filaments subject to TFPIA and valued at over $500, you must provide special information on the entry invoice (see "Entry and Documentation" below).

Flammability Standards. Man-made filament products imported into the U.S. for use in consumer products must be in compliance with the FFA, a federal law that gives the CPSC the authority and responsibility for protecting the public from the hazards of dangerously flammable items of wearing apparel and interior furnishings. Under the FFA, standards have been established for flammability of clothing textiles. You cannot import any article of wearing apparel or interior furnishing, or any fabric or related material that is intended for use or that may be used in such items, if it fails to conform to an applicable flammability standard (FFA Section 4). Certain products may be imported into the U.S. (FFA Section 11c) for finishing or processing to render them less flammable so as to meet the standards. For these products, the exporter must state on the invoice or other paper relating to the shipment that the shipment is being made for that purpose.

The CPSC monitors imports of textiles under its Import Surveillance Program. From time to time, your textile shipments may be inspected to ascertain compliance with mandatory safety standards. Shipments may also be subject to testing by the CPSC to determine compliance. If the CPSC believes a product, fabric, or related material does not comply with a flammability standard, it is authorized to pursue a variety of legal sanctions (see "Prohibitions and Restrictions" below).

Substantial Product Hazard Reports. Any firm that obtains information that reasonably supports the conclusion that one of its products presents an unreasonable risk of serious injury or death must report that information to the CPSC's Division of Corrective Actions (CPSC address below). Importers must also report to the CPSC if 1) a type of product is the subject of at least three civil actions filed in U.S. federal or state courts, 2) each suit alleges the involvement of that product type in death or grievous bodily injury (as defined in FFA Section 37(3)1), and 3) at least three of the actions result in a final settlement with the manufacturer or in a judgment for the plaintiff within any one of the two-year periods specified in FFA Section 37(b).

Wool Product Entry Requirements. Depending on the nature of your wool fiber imports, as many as three different types of special entry documents may be required. First, for all imported textile fibers and yarns covered by the Agricultural Adjustment Act (AAA), including wool, you must file a U.S. Customs Textile En-try Declaration (see "Country-of-Origin Declarations" above). Second, for all wool products subject to the WPLA, special information is required on the entry invoices (see "Entry and Documentation" below). Finally, certain wool articles manufactured or produced in certain countries may be subject to quotas under U.S. Department of Commerce Multi-Fiber Arrangements. Such products require export certificates or visas issued by the appropriate country of origin, in addition to other requisite entry paperwork (see "Quotas" above).

Wool Products Labeling Act. The term "wool product" means any product or any portion of a product that contains, purports to contain, or in any way is represented as containing wool, reprocessed wool, or reused wool. All wool products imported into the U.S., except those made more than 20 years before importation, and except carpets, rugs, mats, and upholsteries, must have affixed a stamp, tag, label, or other means of identification as required by the WPLA. If you are importing wool products exempt from labeling under the WPLA, do not assume they are also exempt from labeling under the TFPIA. These are two distinct laws, with some overlapping requirements (see "Marking and Labeling Requirements" below).

Import Advisory

Importation of textiles is trade-sensitive and highly regulated. Shipments of textiles and textile products not complying with all government regulations, including quotas and visas, are subject to seizure and could result in the imposition of penalties as well as possible forfeiture of the goods. You should always verify the available quota for any textile product you plan to import before your shipment leaves the country of manufacture. Furthermore, Customs textile classification rulings change frequently, and prior administrative rulings are often modified and sometimes reversed. You should be particularly careful to comply with country of origin determination regulations, which were changed in 1996, and affect quotas and visas, marking and labeling, and other important aspects of tariff classification. See "Publications and WWW Resources" for information on important Customs Service informed compliance publications.

The Customs Service has greatly increased its scrutiny of the textile industry, one of eight primary focus industries identified in the most recent Trade Compliance & Enforcement Plan. Imported products from these industries will likely attract significant attention from Customs in the areas of compliance measurement, compliance assessment, informed compliance, and interventions.

Customs Classification

For customs purposes, man-made filament product's are classified under Chapter 54 of the HTSUS. This chapter is broken into major headings, which are further divided into subheadings, and often sub-subheadings, each of which has its own HTSUS classification number. For example, the 2001 HTSUS number for single high tenacity polyester yarns is 5402.20.30, indicating it is a sub-subcategory of high tenacity yarn of polyesters (5402.20.00), which is a subcategory of the major heading, synthetic filament yarn, etc. (5402.00.00). There are eight major headings within Chapter 54.

5401—Sewing thread of man-made filaments, whether or not put up for retail sale

5402—Synthetic filament yarn (other than sewing thread), not put up for retail sale, including synthetic monofilament of less than 67 decitex

5403—Artificial filament yarn (other than sewing thread), not put up for retail sale, including artificial monofilament of less than 67 decitex

5404—Synthetic monofilament of 67 decitex or more and of which no cross-sectional dimension exceeds 1 mm; strip and the like (for example, artificial straw) of synthetic textile materials of an apparent width not exceeding 5 mm

5405—Artificial monofilament of 67 decitex or more and of which no cross-sectional dimension exceeds 1 mm; strip and the like (for example, artificial straw) of artificial textile materials of an apparent width not exceeding 5 mm

5406—Man-made filament yarn (other than sewing thread), put up for retail sale

5407—Woven fabrics of synthetic filament yarn, including woven fabrics obtained from materials of heading 5404

5408—Woven fabrics of artificial filament yarn, including woven fabrics obtained from materials of heading 5405

For more details regarding classifications of the specific product you are interested in importing, consult a customs broker, the appropriate commodity specialist at your nearest customs port, or the HTSUS. The 2001 HTSUS is available online from the Customs Service (www.customs.gov/impoexpo/impoexpo.htm) or for purchase from the U.S. Government Printing Office (see resources at the end of this chapter), and may be found in larger public libraries. For a general discussion of customs classification, see "Classification—Liquidation" on page 229.

Dutiable Status of Goods

For more information about duty rates and binding decisions see "Dutiable Status of Goods" on page 203; for a discussion of temporary importation of goods see "Temporary Free Importations" on page 205.

Valuation

Importers have a responsibility to use what the U.S. Customs Service deems, "reasonable care," when determining the value of their goods. They must also provide any additional information that the Customs Service needs for setting a final value on the goods. This process involves a number of factors and can be somewhat complicated; importers must be aware of applicable issues and details. Valuation information applies to all types of commodities, for further discussion on the subject see "Customs Valuation" on page 267.

Import Duties

Import duties vary (often dramatically) depending upon the Harmonized Tariff Schedule (HTSUS) classification of the goods or products imported. Since some products that look alike have different HTSUS classifications and different rates of duty, proper classification is vital. Note that "differences of opinion" between importers and the Bureau of Customs and Border Protection regarding classification keeps customs attorneys very busy.

Import duties can be assessed on the imported value of the goods ("ad valorem" rates of duty such as 2%, 4.4%, 50%, etc.), total units or weight of the goods ("specific" rates of duty such as 2 cents each or 1.5 cents/pound, etc.) or on a combination basis ("compound" rates of duty such as 5 cents each plus 6%).

Listed below is a sampling of several Column 1 import duty rates for Chapter 54 products:
Colored multifilament, untwisted or with a twist of less than 5 turns per meter, measuring not less than 22 decitex per filament, certified by the importer to be used in the manufacture of wigs for dolls (5402.41.10.00): Free
to
Single yarn (5403.10.30): 10%

For specific information on US import duties refer to the Harmonized Tariff Schedule of the US. The print version is available from the US Government Printing Office as well as third party suppliers who often add special features. Online versions are available in both static PDF pages as well as in formats with excellent search functionality. Search the Web with the term "Harmonized Tariff Schedule" to find sources.

Entry and Documentation

The entry of merchandise is a two-part process consisting of 1) filing the documentation necessary to determine whether merchandise may be released from Customs custody, and 2) filing the documents that contain information for duty assessment and statistical purposes. In certain instances, all documents must be filed and accepted by Customs prior to release of the goods. Unless you have been granted an extension, you must file entry documents at a location specified by the port or area director within five working days of your shipment's date of arrival at a U.S. port of entry. These include a number of standard documents required by Customs for any entry, and:

- U.S. Customs Country-of-Origin Declaration Form CF 3229

- Export documentation and/or visa for textiles subject to bilateral agreement

After you present the entry, Customs may examine your shipment or may waive examination. The shipment is then released provided no legal or regulatory violations have been noted. If not already done you must then file entry summary documentation and deposit estimated duties at a designated customhouse within 10 working days of your shipment's release. For a detailed description of entry procedures, standard documentation, and informal entry, see "Entry Process" on page 185.

Informed Compliance. Informed compliance was introduced with the Customs Modernization Act of 1993 (Mod Act) and defines the relationship between importers and the Customs Service. It sets out the responsibilities of both parties. Providing the correct documentation and information for entry is a key factor that will make your importing operation run smoothly. We recommend that importers become familiar with the concept of informed comliance and the responsibilities that they have under the Mod Act. For further discussion about informed compliance see "Informed Compliance" on page 211.

NAFTA Certificates of Origin. An importer of textiles for which NAFTA treatment is sought need not file a separate NAFTA Certificate of Origin in addition to the Customs Country-of-Origin Declaration. The declaration is sufficient. However, the importer must take care to submit a declaration from each U.S., Canadian, or Mexican producer or manufacturer. Thus, for multiple producers or manufacturers, a separate declaration must be filed for each. If a Customs port director cannot determine the country of origin because the declaration is absent or incomplete, the shipment is not entitled to preferential NAFTA tariff treatment or other NAFTA benefits. See 19 CFR 12.132.

Entry Invoices. You must provide certain additional information on the entry invoice for man-made filament products. The specific information varies depending on the nature of your product, as noted below.

TFPIA Requirements. For the purpose of TFPIA enforcement, a commercial shipment of textile products exceeding $500 in value and subject to TFPIA labeling requirements must show the following information: 1) the constituent fiber or combination of fibers, designating with equal prominence each natural or manufactured fiber by its generic name, in order of predominance by weight if the weight of such fiber is 5% or more of the total fiber weight of the product; 2) percentage of each fiber present, by weight, in the total fiber content; 3) the name or other identification issued and registered by the Federal Trade Commission of the manufacturer of the product or one or more persons subject to Section 3 of the TFPIA with respect to such product; 4) the name of the country where processed or manufactured.

Woven Fabrics. The invoice for woven fabric of man-made fibers in HTSUS headings 5407 and 5408 must include the following information: 1) exact width of fabric; 2) detailed description of the merchandise; 3) any trade name; 4) indication of whether bleached, unbleached, dyed, of yarns of different colors, and/or printed; 5) if composed of more than one material, percentage by weight of each; 6) identification of the man-made fibers as artificial or synthetic, filament or staple, and high tenacity or other; 7) number of turns per meter in each yarn; 8) yarn sizes in warp and filling; 9) type of weave—such as plain weave, twill, sateen, dobby, jacquard, swivel, lappet; 10) number of single threads per cm^2 in both warp and filling; 11) weight per m^2 in grams; 12) average yarn number; 13) for spun or filament yarns, indication of whether textured.

Yarn. All entry invoices for yarn should show: 1) fiber content by weight; 2) whether the yarn is single or plied; 3) whether or not the yarn is put up for retail sale (as defined in HTSUS Section XI, Note 4); and 4) whether or not the yarn is intended for use as sewing thread.

In addition, if the yarn's chief weight is of filament man-made fiber, the entry invoice must show: 1) whether the filament is high tenacity (as defined in HTSUS Section XI, Note 6); 2) whether it is monofilament, multifilament, or strip; 3) whether it is texturized; 4) the yarn number in decitex; 5) the number of turns per meter; 5) for monofilaments, the cross-sectional dimension in millimeters; and 6) for strips, the width of the strip in mm (measure in folded or twisted condition if so imported).

Wool Products Subject to WPLA. When you offer for entry a wool product shipment valued at over $500 and subject to WPLA, you must include certain information intended to facilitate Customs monitoring and enforcement of that Act. This extra information is identical to that required by WPLA on labeling (see "Marking and Labeling Requirements" below), with the addition of the manufacturer's name. If your product consists of mixed waste, residues, and similar merchandise obtained from several suppliers or unknown sources, you may omit the manufacturer's name from the entry invoice. For more general information about invoices see "Invoices" on page 277.

Note: The Entry and Documentation section has been carefully designed to supply you, the importer, with sample documents and directions on how to satisfy Customs requirements. Be aware that you should consult the applicable authorities to ensure that you are correctly following the most current procedures.

Prohibitions and Restrictions

Quotas. Textile import restrictions are primarily a matter of quotas and the way in which these quotas are administered and monitored. Under the Multi-Fiber Arrangement provisions of Section 204 of the Agricultural Adjustment Act, CITA has negotiated bilateral agreements with over 40 countries. These Agreements may impose quotas for a type of textile or a specific article, and they are country-specific. The agreements, however, often change. Therefore, if you are interested in importing any man-made filament products, you should contact the International Trade Administration's Office of Textile and Apparel (see addresses at end of this chapter). The Office of Textile and Apparel has a team of country specialists who can inform you of the latest developments and inform you about a product's quota or restriction status.

U.S. Customs enforces CITA textile and textile product entry quotas. If formal entry procedures are not followed, Customs will usually refuse entry for textiles that are subject to Section 204. Formal entry requires submission of a Country-of-Origin Declaration (see "General Considerations" above). U.S. Customs maintains a current textile quota status report, available for perusal at any Customs port. In addition, U.S. Customs in Washington, DC, provides quota status reports online, which are updated on a regular basis (www.customs.gov/impoexpo/impoexpo.htm).

Flammable Fabrics. U.S. Customs may refuse entry for any article of wearing apparel or interior furnishing, or any fabric or related material that is intended for use or that may be used in wearing apparel or interior furnishings, if it fails to conform to an applicable flammability standard issued under Section 4 of the FFA. An exception is allowed for certain products (FFA Section 11c) that are imported for finishing or processing to bring them within the legal standard. For these products, the exporter must state on the invoice or other paper relating to the shipment that the shipment is being made for that purpose.

The CPSC, as the primary enforcement agency of flammability standards, inspects products for compliance with the FFA. If the CPSC believes a product, fabric, or related material does not comply with a flammability standard, it is authorized to pursue a variety of legal sanctions, including: 1) seizure, condemnation, and forfeiture of the noncomplying products; 2) administrative cease-and-desist order requiring an individual or firm to stop sale and distribution of the noncomplying products or; 3) temporary injunction requiring the individual or firm to stop sale and distribution of the noncomplying products, pending final disposition of an administrative cease-and-desist proceeding. The CPSC also has authority to seek civil penalties against any person who knowingly violates a regulation or standard issued under Section 4 of the FFA.

Country-Specific Restrictions

Restrictions under bilateral agreements are country-specific. A product originating in one country may be subject to quota and to export license or visa requirements, while the same product originating in a different country may not. At present, the U.S. has Multi-Fiber Arrangements with 40 countries. Many different categories of products are covered under these Arrangements; it is beyond the scope of this book to list each country and its restricted commodities. If you are interested in importing textiles and textile products, you should contact the International Trade Administration's Office of Textile and Apparel (see addresses at end of this chapter) or U.S. Customs to ascertain your product's restraint status.

The U.S. Customs service provides quota reports on their website (www.customs.gov/impoexpo/impoexpo.htm). These reports are constantly updated and have an effective date noted. The most recent quota information can be accessed by clicking on the country name that interests you. This location holds information regarding quotas, transshipments, and visa requirements.

Marking and Labeling Requirements

TFPIA Requirements. All textile fiber products imported into the U.S. must be stamped, tagged, labeled, or otherwise marked with the following information as required by the TFPIA, unless exempt from marking (see TFPIA, Section 12): 1) the generic names and percentages by weight of the constituent fibers present in the textile fiber product, exclusive of permissible ornamentation, in amounts of more than 5% in order of predominance by weight, with any percentage of fiber or fibers required to be designated as "other fiber" or "other fibers" (including those present in amounts of 5% or less) appearing last; and 2) the name of the manufacturer or the name or registered identification number issued by the FTC of one or more persons marketing or handling the textile fiber product; and 3) the name of the country where processed. A word trademark, used as a house mark and registered with the U.S. Patent Office, may appear on labels instead of the name otherwise required, provided the owner of the trademark furnishes a copy of the registration to the FTC prior to use (see "Registered Identification Numbers" below).

The information listed above is not exhaustive. TFPIA requirements are extensive. The Act specifies such details as types of labels, means of attachment, label position on the article, package labeling, unit labeling for two-piece garments, and arrangement of information on the label; allowable fiber designations; country-of-origin indications; requirements for trim and ornamentation, linings and interlinings, and pile fabrics; sectional disclosure; use of trade names and trademarks; and requirements for swatches and samples. The FTC publishes a booklet intended to clarify TFPIA requirements to facilitate voluntary compliance in the industry (see "Publications and WWW Resources" below). It is available on request, at no charge, from the FTC (see addresses at end of this chapter).

Wool Products Labeling Act (WPLA). Wool product labeling requirements for foreign products are the responsibility of the importer. The WPLA requires the following information to appear on wool products subject to the Act: 1) percentage of the wool product's total fiber weight (exclusive of ornamentation) not exceeding 5% of the total fiber weight of a) wool, b) recycled wool, c) each fiber other than wool if the percent by weight of such fiber is 5% or more, and d) the aggregate of all other fibers; 2) the maximum percent of the wool product's total weight, of any nonfibrous loading, filling, or adulterating matter; and 3) the importer's name. If you, as importer, have a registered identification number issued by the FTC, that number may be used instead of your name (see "Registered Identification Numbers" below).

Customs entry is contingent on proper labeling. If your shipment is found to be mislabeled at entry, you will be given the option of relabeling the products under Customs supervision, as long as the port director is satisfied that your labeling error or omission did not involve fraud or willful neglect. If your shipment is discovered after entry to have been noncomplying with WPLA, it will be recalled to Customs custody at your expense, unless you can satisfy the port director that the products have since been brought into compliance. You will be held responsible for all expenses incurred in bringing a shipment into compliance, including compensation of personnel and other expenses related to Customs supervision.

Fraudulent violations of WPLA will result in seizure of the shipment. Shipments already released from Customs custody will be ordered to be redelivered to Customs. Customs reports all cases of fraudulent violation to the FTC in Washington, DC.

The information listed above is not intended to be exhaustive. WPLA requirements are extensive. The Act specifies such details as types of labels, means of attachment, label position on the article, package labeling, unit labeling (as in the case of a two-piece garment), arrangement of information on the label, allowable fiber designations, country-of-origin indications, trim and ornamentation, pile fabrics, sectional disclosure, use of trade names and trademarks, requirements for swatches and samples, etc. The FTC publishes a booklet intended to clarify WPLA requirements in order to facilitate voluntary compliance within the industry (see "Publications and WWW Resources" below). It is available on request, at no charge, from the FTC (see addresses at end of this chapter).

The Care Labeling Rule. Regulations under this rule require manufacturers and importers of textile clothing and fabrics to attach specific care instructions for washing or dry cleaning, as well as information on the fiber composition of the article. They are enforced by the FTC Division of Enforcement. The Care Labeling Rule was amended September 2000, detailed information is available on the FTC website (www.ftc.gov/os/statutes/textilejump.htm).

Registered Identification Numbers. Any domestic firm or person residing in the U.S. and engaged in the manufacture or marketing of textile products covered under the TFPIA may obtain an FTC-registered identification number for use on required tags and labels instead of the name of a firm or person. For applications, contact the FTC (address below.)

For a general discussion of U.S. Customs marking and labeling requirements, see "Country of Origin Marking" on page 236, "Special Marking Requirements" on page 238 and "Marking—False Impression" on page 239.

Shipping Considerations

You will need to ensure that your goods are packaged and shipped with care so that they pass smoothly through Customs and arrive in good condition. You are responsible for ensuring that the shipment is in compliance with all applicable government regulations for packaging and shipping. In most instances, you should not leave these arrangements solely to the discretion of your supplier. Careful preparation of the cargo and selection of the mode of transport can be essential to a cost-effective, timely delivery of undamaged goods. We strongly advise you to consult your shipping representative, insurance agent, or freight broker for advice on packing and shipping.

Man-made filament products may be shipped in bulk, spools, cartons, or other types of containers, depending on the type of product and whether it is prepackaged. General considerations include protection from contamination, weather, and pests. Containers should be constructed so as to be safe for handling during transport.

Publications and WWW Resources

The following publications may be relevant to the importation of man-made fibers:

> *Threading Your Way Through the Labeling Requirements Under the Textile and Wool Acts*

Available free of charge on request from the Federal Trade Commission and online from the FTC website (www.ftc.gov/bcp/conline/pubs/buspubs/thread.htm). This publication is an excellent source of information written in clear lay language. We recommend that anyone interested in importing textile fiber products but unfamiliar with the regulations obtain a copy of each of this booklet.

The U.S. Customs Service launched a series of "Informed Compliance" publications in 1996, which are available on the Customs Service website (www.customs.gov/impoexpo/impoexpo.htm). Of particular interest:

> *What Every Member of the Trade Community Should Know About Textile & Apparel Rules of Origin*

> *What Every Member of the Trade community Should Know About NAFTA for Textiles and Textile Articles*

> *Fibers & Yarns Construction and Classification Under the HTSUS*

The *Harmonized Tariff Schedule of the United States (2001)* (HTSUS) is available to view on the Customs Service website (www.customs.gov), or you may purchase a printed version from:

U.S. Government Printing Office
Superintendent of Documents
710 North Capital Street NW
Washington DC 20401
Tel: (202) 512-1800
Fax: (202) 512-1657
Website: www.access.gpo.gov

The USGPO also has copies of specific laws available for purchase. The USGPO accepts orders made by fax, phone or placed over the Internet, as well as mail orders paid by credit card. All orders must be accompanied by payment. Credit cards, checks drawn on a U.S. bank, or an international money order are all acceptable.

Relevant Government Agencies

Address your questions regarding textile Multi-Fiber Arrangements to:

U.S. Department of Commerce
International Trade Administration
Office of Textiles and Apparel
Director's Office
14th and Constitution Avenue NW, Rm. H3100
Washington DC 20230
Tel: (202) 482-5078

Fax: (202) 482-2331
Agreements Division: (202) 482-4212
Website: http://otexa.ita.doc.gov

Address your questions regarding the Flammable Fabrics Act (FFA) to:

Consumer Product Safety Commission (CPSC)
Office of Compliance
Washington DC 20207-0001
Tel: 800-638-2772 or (301) 504-7912
Fax: (301) 504-0359
Website: www.cpsc.gov

Address your questions regarding requirements under the Textile Fiber Products Identification Act (TFPIA) or the Wool Products Labeling Act (WPLA) to:

Federal Trade Commission (FTC)
Division of Enforcement
600 Pennsylvania Avenue NW
Washington DC 20580
Tel: (202) 326-2996
Website: www.ftc.gov

Address your questions regarding textile quotas to:

U.S. Customs and Border Protection
Office of Field Operations, Quota Branch
1300 Pennsylvania Avenue NW
Washington DC 20229
Tel: (202) 927-5850
Website: www.customs.treas.gov

The U.S. Customs Service provices updated status reports on textile quota on their web site (see address above). If the country you need information on is not listed, call the Quota Branch office at (202) 927-5850.

Address your questions regarding man-made filament imports to your local Customs port director. For addresses, refer to "U.S. Customs and Border Protection Offices" on page 65 or contact:

U.S. Customs and Border Protection
Customs Headquarters
1300 Pennsylvania Avenue NW
Washington DC 20229
Tel: (202) 354-1000
Website: www.customs.treas.gov

Laws and Regulations

The following laws and regulations may be relevant to the importation of man-made filament products. The laws are contained in the United States Code (USC), and the regulations are published in the Code of Federal Regulations (CFR), both of which are available at larger public and law libraries. Copies of specific laws are also available from the United States Government Printing Office (address above).

7 USC 1854
Textile Trade Agreements
(EO 11651, as amended by EO 11951 and 12188, and supplemented by EO 12475)
This Act authorizes the CITA of the DOC to enter into Multi-Fiber Agreements with other countries to control trade in textiles and establishes the Textile Import Program, which is enforced by U.S. Customs.

19 CFR 12.130 et seq.
Regulations on Entry of Textiles
These regulations provide the requirements and procedures followed by Customs in enforcing limitations on the importation and entry and withdrawal of textiles and textile products from warehouses for consumption in the U.S.

15 USC 70-77
Textile Fiber Products Identification Act (TFPIA)

This Act prohibits false or deceptive labeling (misbranding) and false advertising of any textile fiber products and requires all textile fiber products imported into the U.S. to be labeled in accordance with the requirements set forth in the law.

19 CFR 11.12b; 16 CFR 303 et seq.
Regulations on Labeling and Marking
These regulations detail the labeling and marking requirements for textiles as specified by the CPSC and the invoice contents required by U.S. Customs for purpose of enforcing the labeling and marking rules.

15 USC 68-68j
Wool Products Labeling Act (WPLA) of 1939
This Act prohibits the false or deceptive labeling (misbranding) of wool products and requires all wool products imported into the U.S. to be labeled in accordance with requirements set forth in the law.

19 CFR 11.12; 16 CFR 300 et seq.
Regulations on WPLA Labeling and Marking
These regulations set forth the wool labeling and marking requirements adopted by the FTC to administer the requirements of the WPLA and provide the procedures followed by U.S. Customs in enforcing the WPLA and the FTC regulations, including entry invoice requirements.

15 USC 1191-1204
Flammable Fabrics Act (FFA)
This Act provides for the setting of flammability standards for fabric by the Consumer Product Safety Commission (CPSC) and for enforcement by U.S. Customs.

16 CFR 1610, 1611, 1615, 1616, 1630-1632
Regulations on Flammable Fabric Standards
These regulations specify the flammability standards adopted by the CPSC under the FFA for various types of textiles.

16 CFR 423
Care Labeling Rule
Requires fiber composition and washing or dry cleaning instructions for textile apparel and certain piece goods.

Principal Exporting Countries

The following listing includes samples of the main supplier nations of the products of this chapter. It is organized by HTSUS major heading. (Refer to "Customs Classification" above for the product codes.) Countries are listed in rank order of the value of products imported to the U.S. Statistics represent customs value of entries for 2002 from the Bureau of Census, U.S. Department of Commerce.

5401—Mexico, Germany, Canada, Switzerland, Philippines, Japan, Turkey, Taiwan, China

5402—Canada, Mexico, South Korea, Japan, Israel, Netherlands, Germany

5403—Germany, Italy, Belgium, Japan, Netherlands, India, Brazil, Spain, France

5404—Canada, Germany, United Kingdom, Japan, Mexico, Taiwan, China, Guatemala, France

5405—Japan, Italy, Switzerland, South Korea, France, Belgium, South Africa, Hong Kong, United Kingdom, India, Brazil

5406—Israel, Germany, Mexico, Italy, Japan, China, United Kingdom

5407—South Korea, Canada, Japan, Turkey, Italy, Taiwan, Philippines, Mexico, Pakistan

5408—Italy, Japan, South Korea, China, Turkey, France, Germany, Canada, India, United Kingdom

Chapter 55:
Man-made Staple Fibers

This chapter relates to the importation of man-made staple fiber products, which are classified under Chapter 55 of the Harmonized Tariff Schedule of the United States (HTSUS). Specifically, it includes synthetic (such as nylon or polyester) or artificial (such as viscose rayon or cellulose acetate) stable fibers combed, carded, otherwise processed, or not processed; filament tow; waste from such fibers; and sewing thread, yarn, and woven fabrics made of such fibers.

If you are interested in importing products derived from man-made filaments, you should read Commodity Index Chapter 54. The import requirements for cotton textiles and products are covered in Chapter 52, and for wool textile products in Chapter 53. For importing monofilaments of plastics, you should also read Chapter 39. If you are interested in importing apparel, refer to Chapters 60 through 63. Hairnets and headgear of man-made filaments are covered in Chapter 65, and footwear in Chapter 64. Import requirements for specific types of fibers are found in related chapters, such as glass fibers in Chapter 70.

Note: To understand key issues that will enable you to make best use of the information in this section we recommend that you see "Introduction" on page 425.

Key Factors

The key factors in the importation of man-made staple fiber products are:

- Compliance with quota restraints and visa requirements
- Submission of U.S. Customs Country-of-Origin Declaration(s)
- Compliance with entry invoice requirements
- Compliance with labeling requirements under Textile Fiber Products Identification Act (TFPIA) and/or the Wool Products Labeling Act (WPLA) and the Care Labeling Rule
- Compliance with flammability standards adopted and enforced by the Consumer Product Safety Commission (CPSC) under the Flammable Fabrics Act (FFA).

Although most importers use the services of a licensed customs broker in making their entries, and we recommend this practice, you should be aware of the regulatory, entry, and documentation issues involved in importing your product. You, as importer, are ultimately responsible for the fulfillment of any legal requirements applicable to your shipment.

General Considerations

Regulatory Agencies. The Committee for Implementation of Textile Agreements (CITA) regulates certain textile imports under Section 204 of the Agricultural Adjustment Act. U.S. Customs enforces CITA textile and textile product entry quotas. Customs also enforces compliance with labeling and invoice requirements of the TFPIA and flammability standards under the FFA. The CPSC monitors imports and from time to time inspects textile shipments for compliance with FFA standards. If you are importing products that contain wool fibers, importation is subject to complex textile import regulations. The Federal Trade Commission (FTC) administers the WPLA requirements.

Textile Quotas. If you are interested in importing man-made staple fiber products, the most important issue you need to be aware of is quotas. Under the Multi-Fiber Arrangement provisions of Section 204 of the Agricultural Adjustment Act, CITA initiates specific agreements with individual exporting countries. Section 204 of the Agricultural Adjustment Act covers textiles that: 1) Are in chief value of cotton, wool, or man-made fibers, any textile fibers subject to the terms of any textile trade agreement, or any combination of such fibers; 2) contain 50% or more by weight of cotton or man-made fibers, or any textile fibers subject to the terms of any textile trade agreement; 3) contain 17% or more by weight of wool; or 4) if in chief value of textile fibers or textile materials, contain a blend of cotton, wool, or man-made fibers, any textile fibers subject to the terms of any textile trade agreement, or any combination of such fibers that, in total, amount to 50% or more by weight of all component fibers.

The U.S. has bilateral agreements with over 40 countries. Each agreement with each country is unique, and may specify quotas for a type of textile or a specific article. Visas or export licenses may be required. These agreements, however, often change. Therefore, if you are interested in importing any man-made staple fiber products, you should contact the International Trade Administration's Office of Textile and Apparel (see addresses at end of this chapter). Refer to "Prohibitions and Restrictions" below for further details.

Country-of-Origin Declarations. U.S. Customs enforces CITA textile and textile product entry quotas (see "Prohibitions and Restrictions" below). Requirements for entry include submission of Country-of-Origin Declarations with every textile shipment, regardless of whether it is subject to a specific multi-fiber arrangement (19 CFR 12.130, 12.131).

Country of Origin. Quota restrictions are country-specific and therefore are applied based on the country of origin for the textiles shipped. The last country from which a textile shipment was exported to the U.S. is not necessarily its country of origin. A textile or textile product imported into the U.S. is considered a product of the particular foreign territory or country, or a U.S. insular possession, where it is wholly grown, produced, or manufactured. For the following discussion, "country" means a foreign territory or country, or a U.S. insular possession.

In 1996, the U.S. Customs Service made major changes to country of origin rules for textile imports. The regulations at 19 CFR 102.21, "Textile and apparel products" were added to the 1996 Customs Regulations and became effective July 1, 1996. The new rules do not provide for cutting components or cutting and hemming to confer country of origin as in the past. The basis of the new law is processing operations or assembly. Some of the most important changes for importers to be aware of are:

- Cutting does not determine the country of origin (previously cutting determined country of origin for 90 percent of wearing apparel imports). The new rules are based on processing or assembly operations.

- A subjective determination under the provisions of 19 CFR 12.130 is replaced by objective processing operations expressed in terms of tariff shifts. Dying, printing, and other finishing processes applied to fabrics no longer confer or change country of origin.

- Country of origin for textile and apparel products processed, assembled or manufactured in two or more countries is determined by where the most important processing occurs, and, if that cannot be ascertained, the last country in which an important processing operation occurs.

The country of origin is the country in which a product is wholly produced when a textile or apparel product is completely produced or manufactured (except for minor parts) in one country. For fabric, the country of origin is the country in which the fabric is woven, knitted, needled, tufted, felted, entangled or created by any other fabric-making process. The country of origin for staple yarn is the country in which yarn is spun; for filament yarn, the country in which filament is extruded; and for plied, gimped and cabled yarns, the country in which the fibers or filaments used in the yarn are spun or extruded. The country of origin of all other textile and apparel products is the country in which the components of a textile or apparel product are wholly assembled (except for minor attachments) except for knit-to-shape products. Knit-to-shape products are those composed of panels or parts ,which, are knitted or crocheted directly into the shape that will be used in construction of the final product. Minor cutting or sewing does not influence whether the product is considered knit-to-shape. The country of origin for knit-to-shape products is that country in which the major parts are knitted into the shape that will constitute the finished product. Once again, note that assembly, not cutting, now confers country of origin.

Declarations. All importations of textiles and textile products must be accompanied by one of the following three declarations. Goods subject to Section 204, Agricultural Act of 1956, as amended, must be accompanied by either a single-country or a multiple-country declaration. Goods not subject to Section 204 must be accompanied by a negative declaration.

- **Single-country declarations** are used for entries of textiles or textile products which are wholly the growth, product, or manufacture of a single foreign country, territory, or U.S. insular possession. Information required includes: marks of identification and numbers; description of article and quantity; country of origin; and date of exportation.

- **Multiple-country declarations** are used for entries of textiles or textile products which were subjected to manufacturing or processing operations in, and/or incorporate materials originating in more than one foreign country or territory. Information required includes: marks of identification and numbers; for articles, description, quantity, identification of manufacturing and/or processing operations, country, and date of exportation; for materials used to make articles, description of materials, country of production, and date of exportation.

- **Negative declarations** must accompany all textile imports that are not subject to AAA Section 204 restrictions. Information required includes: marks of identification and numbers; descriptions of article and quantity; and country of origin.

The date of exportation to be indicated on the above declarations is the date on which the carrier leaves the last port in the country of origin, as determined by Customs. Diversion to another country during transit does not affect the export date.

Procedure for Declarations. The manufacturer, producer, exporter, or importer may prepare the declaration. If more than one of these parties is involved in the importation, each party may prepare a separate declaration. You may file a separate declaration for each invoice presented with your entry. The declaration must be dated and signed by the responsible party, and must include the person's title and the company name and address. Your shipment's entry will be denied unless it is accompanied by a properly executed declaration. Customs will not treat a textile declaration as a missing document for which a bond may be filed.

Customs will base its country-of-origin determination on the information contained in each declaration, unless the information is insufficient. If the information on the declaration is insufficient, Customs will require that you submit such additional information as will enable the determination to be made. The shipment will not be released until the determination is made. Thus, if you want to clear Customs with minimal delay, be sure that the information on the declarations is as complete as possible for each shipment.

Textile Labeling and Invoice Requirements. You are responsible for your imported man-made staple fiber product's compliance with applicable provisions of the TFPIA. Man-made staple fiber products that require labeling under TFPIA must already be labeled at entry, or the shipment will be refused. (See "Marking and Labeling Requirements" below.) If you import shipments of man-made staple fiber textiles subject to TFPIA and valued at over $500, you must provide special information on the entry invoice (see "Entry and Documentation" below).

Flammability Standards. Man-made staple fiber products imported into the U.S. for use in consumer products must be in compliance with the FFA, a federal law that gives the CPSC the authority and responsibility for protecting the public from the hazards of dangerously flammable items of wearing apparel and interior furnishings. Under the FFA, standards have been established for flammability of clothing textiles. You cannot import any article of wearing apparel or interior furnishing, or any fabric or related material that is intended for use or that may be used in such items, if it fails to conform to an applicable flammability standard (FFA Section 4). Certain products may be imported into the U.S. (FFA Section 11c) for finishing or processing to render them less flammable so as to meet the standards. For these products, the exporter must state on the invoice or other paper relating to the shipment that the shipment is being made for that purpose.

The CPSC monitors imports of textiles under its Import Surveillance Program. From time to time, your textile shipments may be inspected to ascertain compliance with mandatory safety standards. Shipments may also be subject to testing by the CPSC to determine compliance. If the CPSC believes a product, fabric, or related material does not comply with a flammability standard, it is authorized to pursue a variety of legal sanctions (see "Prohibitions and Restrictions" below).

Substantial Product Hazard Reports. Any firm that obtains information that reasonably supports the conclusion that one of its products presents an unreasonable risk of serious injury or death must report that information to the CPSC's Division of Corrective Actions (CPSC address below). Importers must also report to the CPSC if 1) a type of product is the subject of at least three civil actions filed in U.S. federal or state courts, 2) each suit alleges the involvement of that product type in death or grievous bodily injury (as defined in FFA Section 37(3)1), and 3) at least three of the actions result in a final settlement with the manufacturer or in a judgment for the plaintiff within any one of the two-year periods specified in FFA Section 37(b).

Wool Product Entry Requirements. Depending on the nature of your wool fiber imports, as many as three different types of special entry documents may be required. First, for all imported textile fibers and yarns covered by the Agricultural Adjustment Act (AAA), including wool, you must file a U.S. Customs Textile Entry Declaration (see "Country-of-Origin Declarations" above). Second, for all wool products subject to the WPLA, special information is required on the entry invoices (see "Entry and Documentation" below). Finally, certain wool articles manufactured or produced in certain countries may be subject to quotas under U.S. Department of Commerce Multi-Fiber Arrangements. Such products require export certificates or visas issued by the appropriate country of origin, in addition to other requisite entry paperwork (see "Quotas" above).

Wool Products Labeling Act. The term "wool product" means any product or any portion of a product that contains, purports to contain, or in any way is represented as containing wool, reprocessed wool, or reused wool. All wool products imported into the U.S., except those made more than 20 years before importation, and except carpets, rugs, mats, and upholsteries, must have affixed a stamp, tag, label, or other means of identification as required by the WPLA. If you are importing wool products exempt from labeling under the WPLA, do not assume they are also exempt from labeling under the TFPIA. These are two distinct laws, with some overlapping requirements (see "Marking and Labeling Requirements" below).

Import Advisory

Importation of textiles is trade-sensitive and highly regulated. Shipments of textiles and textile products not complying with all government regulations, including quotas and visas, are subject to seizure and could result in the imposition of penalties as well as possible forfeiture of the goods. You should always verify the available quota for any textile product you plan to import before your shipment leaves the country of manufacture. Furthermore, Customs textile classification rulings change frequently, and prior administrative rulings are often modified and sometimes reversed. You should be particularly careful to comply with country of origin determination regulations, which were changed in 1996, and affect quotas and visas, marking and labeling, and other important aspects of tariff classification. See "Publications and WWW Resources" for information on important Customs Service informed compliance publications.

The Customs Service has greatly increased its scrutiny of the textile industry, one of eight primary focus industries identified in the most recent Trade Compliance & Enforcement Plan. Imported products from these industries will likely attract significant attention from Customs in the areas of compliance measurement, compliance assessment, informed compliance, and interventions.

For customs purposes, man-made staple fiber product's are classified under Chapter 55 of the HTSUS. This chapter is broken into major headings, which are further divided into subheadings, and often sub-subheadings, each of which has its own HTSUS classification number. For example, the 2001 HTSUS number for dyed woven fabrics with 85% by weight of artificial staple fibers mixed with 36% or more by weight of wool or fine animal hair is 5516.32.05, indicating it is a sub-subcategory of dyed woven fabrics with less than 85% by weight of artificial staple fibers mixed wool or fine animal hair (5516.32), which is a subcategory of the major heading, woven fabrics of artificial staple fibers (5516). There are 16 major headings within Chapter 55.

5501—Synthetic filament tow

5502—Artificial filament tow

5503—Synthetic staple fibers, not carded, combed, or otherwise processed for spinning

5504—Artificial staple fibers, not carded, combed, or otherwise processed for spinning

5505—Waste (including noils, yarn waste, and garnetted stock) of man-made fibers

5506—Synthetic staple fibers, carded, combed, or otherwise processed for spinning

5507—Artificial staple fibers, carded, combed, or otherwise processed for spinning

5508—Sewing thread of man-made staple fibers, whether or not put up for retail sale

5509—Yarn (other than sewing thread) of synthetic staple fibers, not put up for retail sale

5510—Yarn (other than sewing thread) of artificial staple fibers, not put up for retail sale

5511—Yarn (other than sewing thread) of man-made staple fibers, put up for retail sale

5512—Woven fabrics of synthetic staple fibers, containing 85% or more by weight of synthetic staple fibers

5513—Woven fabrics of synthetic staple fibers, containing less than 85% by weight of such fibers, mixed mainly or solely with cotton, of a weight not exceeding 170 g/m^2

5514—Woven fabrics of synthetic staple fibers, containing less than 85% by weight of such fibers, mixed mainly or solely with cotton, of a weight exceeding 170 g/m^2

5515—Other woven fabrics of synthetic staple fibers

5516—Woven fabrics of artificial staple fibers

For more details regarding classifications of the specific product you are interested in importing, consult a customs broker, the appropriate commodity specialist at your nearest customs port, or the HTSUS. The 2001 HTSUS is available online from the Customs Service (www.customs.gov/impoexpo/impoexpo.htm) or for purchase from the U.S. Government Printing Office (see resources at the end of this chapter), and may be found in larger public libraries. For a general discussion of customs classification, see "Classification—Liquidation" on page 229.

Dutiable Status of Goods

For more information about duty rates and binding decisions see "Dutiable Status of Goods" on page 203; for a discussion of temporary importation of goods see "Temporary Free Importations" on page 205.

Valuation

Importers have a responsibility to use what the U.S. Customs Service deems, "reasonable care," when determining the value of their goods. They must also provide any additional information that the Customs Service needs for setting a final value on the goods. This process involves a number of factors and can be somewhat complicated; importers must be aware of applicable issues and details. Valuation information applies to all types of commodities, for further discussion on the subject see "Customs Valuation" on page 267.

Import Duties

Import duties vary (often dramatically) depending upon the Harmonized Tariff Schedule (HTSUS) classification of the goods or products imported. Since some products that look alike have different HTSUS classifications and different rates of duty, proper classification is vital. Note that "differences of opinion" between importers and the Bureau of Customs and Border Protection regarding classification keeps customs attorneys very busy.

Import duties can be assessed on the imported value of the goods ("ad valorem" rates of duty such as 2%, 4.4%, 50%, etc.), total units or weight of the goods ("specific" rates of duty such as 2 cents each or 1.5 cents/pound, etc.) or on a combination basis ("compound" rates of duty such as 5 cents each plus 6%).

Listed below is a sampling of several Column 1 import duty rates for Chapter 55 products:

Containing 10 percent or more by weight of nylon 12 (5503.10.10.00): Free

to

Sewing thread of man-made staple fibers, whether or not put up for retail sale (of synthetic staple fibers) (200) (5508.10.00.00): 11.6%

For specific information on US import duties refer to the Harmonized Tariff Schedule of the US. The print version is available from the US Government Printing Office as well as third party suppliers who often add special features. Online versions are available in both static PDF pages as well as in formats with excellent search functionality. Search the Web with the term "Harmonized Tariff Schedule" to find sources.

Entry and Documentation

The entry of merchandise is a two-part process consisting of 1) filing the documentation necessary to determine whether merchandise may be released from Customs custody, and 2) filing the documents that contain information for duty assessment and statistical purposes. In certain instances, all documents must be filed and accepted by Customs prior to release of the goods. Unless you have been granted an extension, you must file entry documents at a location specified by the port or area director within five working days of your shipment's date of arrival at a U.S. port of entry. These include a number of standard documents required by Customs for any entry, and:

- U.S. Customs Country-of-Origin Declaration Form CF 3229
- Export documentation and/or visa for textiles subject to bilateral agreement

After you present the entry, Customs may examine your shipment or may waive examination. The shipment is then released provided no legal or regulatory violations have been noted. If not already done you must then file entry summary documentation and deposit estimated duties at a designated customhouse within 10 working days of your shipment's release. For a detailed description of entry procedures, standard documentation, and informal entry, see "Entry Process" on page 185.

Informed Compliance. Informed compliance was introduced with the Customs Modernization Act of 1993 (Mod Act) and defines the relationship between importers and the Customs Service. It sets out the responsibilities of both parties. Providing the correct documentation and information for entry is a key factor that will make your importing operation run smoothly. We recommend that importers become familiar with the concept of informed comliance and the responsibilities that they have under the Mod Act. For further discussion about informed compliance see "Informed Compliance" on page 211.

NAFTA Certificates of Origin. An importer of textiles for which NAFTA treatment is sought need not file a separate NAFTA Certificate of Origin in addition to the Customs Country-of-Origin Declaration. The declaration is sufficient. However, the importer must take care to submit a declaration from each U.S., Canadian, or Mexican producer or manufacturer. Thus, for multiple producers or manufacturers, a separate declaration must be filed for each. If a Customs port director cannot determine the country of origin because the declaration is absent or incomplete, the shipment is not entitled to preferential NAFTA tariff treatment or other NAFTA benefits. See 19 CFR 12.132.

Entry Invoices. You must provide certain additional information on the entry invoice for man-made stable fiber products. The specific information varies depending on the nature of your product, as noted below.

TFPIA Requirements. For the purpose of TFPIA enforcement, a commercial shipment of textile products exceeding $500 in value and subject to TFPIA labeling requirements must show the following information: 1) the constituent fiber or combination of fibers, designating with equal prominence each natural or manufactured fiber by its generic name, in order of predominance by weight if the weight of such fiber is 5% or more of the total fiber weight of the product; 2) percentage of each fiber present, by weight, in the total fiber content; 3) the name or other identification issued and registered by the Federal Trade Commission of the manufacturer of the product or one or more persons subject to Section 3 of the TFPIA with respect to such product; 4) the name of the country where processed or manufactured.

Woven Fabrics. The invoice for woven fabric of man-made fibers in HTSUS headings 5512 through 5516 must include the following information: 1) exact width of fabric; 2) detailed description of the merchandise; 3) any trade name; 4) indication of whether bleached, unbleached, dyed, of yarns of different colors, and/or printed; 5) if composed of more than one material, percentage by weight of each; 6) identification of the man-made fibers as artificial or synthetic, filament or staple, and high tenacity or other; 7) number of turns per meter in each yarn; 8) yarn sizes in warp and filling; 9) type of weave—such as plain weave, twill, sateen, dobby, jacquard, swivel, lappet; 10) number of single threads per cm^2 in both warp and filling; 11) weight per m^2 in grams; 12) average yarn number; 13) for spun or filament yarns, indication of whether textured.

Yarn. All entry invoices for yarn should show: 1) fiber content by weight; 2) whether the yarn is single or plied; 3) whether or not the yarn is put up for retail sale (as defined in HTSUS Section XI, Note 4); and 4) whether or not the yarn is intended for use as sewing thread.

In addition, if the yarn's chief weight is of man-made fibers, the entry invoice must show:1) whether the fibers are filament, spun, or a combination of filament and spun; and 2) if a combination, the percentage of filament and spun by weight.

Wool Products Subject to WPLA. When you offer for entry a wool product shipment valued at over $500 and subject to WPLA, you must include certain information intended to facilitate Customs monitoring and enforcement of that Act. This extra information is identical to that required by WPLA on labeling (see "Marking and Labeling Requirements" below), with the addition of the manufacturer's name. If your product consists of mixed waste, residues, and similar merchandise obtained from several suppliers or unknown sources, you may omit the manufacturer's name from the entry invoice. For more general information about invoices see "Invoices" on page 277.

Note: The Entry and Documentation section has been carefully designed to supply you, the importer, with sample documents and directions on how to satisfy Customs requirements. Be aware that you should consult the applicable authorities to ensure that you are correctly following the most current procedures.

Prohibitions and Restrictions

Quotas. Textile import restrictions are primarily a matter of quotas and the way in which these quotas are administered and monitored. Under the Multi-Fiber Arrangement provisions of Section 204 of the Agricultural Adjustment Act, CITA has negotiated bilateral agreements with over 40 countries. These Agreements may impose quotas for a type of textile or a specific article, and they are country-specific. The agreements, however, often change. Therefore, if you are interested in importing any man-made staple fiber products, you should contact the International Trade Administration's Office of Textile and Apparel (see addresses at end of this chapter). The Office of Textile and Apparel has a team of country specialists who can inform you of the latest developments and inform you about a product's quota or restriction status.

U.S. Customs enforces CITA textile and textile product entry quotas. If formal entry procedures are not followed, Customs will usually refuse entry for textiles that are subject to Section 204. Formal entry requires submission of a Country-of-Origin Declaration (see "General Considerations" above). U.S. Customs maintains a current textile quota status report. In addition, U.S. Customs in Washington, DC, provides quota status reports on-line, which are updated on a regular basis (www.customs.gov/impoexpo/impoexpo.htm).

Flammable Fabrics. U.S. Customs may refuse entry for any article of wearing apparel or interior furnishing, or any fabric or related material that is intended for use or that may be used in wearing apparel or interior furnishings, if it fails to conform to an applicable flammability standard issued under Section 4 of the FFA. An exception is allowed for certain products (FFA Section 11c) that are imported for finishing or processing to bring them within the legal standard. For these products, the exporter must state on the invoice or other paper relating to the shipment that the shipment is being made for that purpose.

The CPSC, as the primary enforcement agency of flammability standards, inspects products for compliance with the FFA. If the CPSC believes a product, fabric, or related material does not comply with a flammability standard, it is authorized to pursue a variety of legal sanctions, including: 1) seizure, condemnation, and forfeiture of the noncomplying products; 2) administrative cease-and-desist order requiring an individual or firm to stop sale and distribution of the noncomplying products or; 3) temporary injunction requiring the individual or firm to stop sale and distribution of the noncomplying products, pending final disposition of an administrative cease-and-desist proceeding. The CPSC also has authority to seek civil penalties against any person who knowingly violates a regulation or standard issued under Section 4 of the FFA.

Country-Specific Restrictions

Restrictions under bilateral agreements are country-specific. A product originating in one country may be subject to quota and to export license or visa requirements, while the same product originating in a different country may not. At present, the U.S. has bilateral agreements with over 40 countries. Many different categories of products are covered under these Arrangements; it is beyond the scope of this book to list each country and its restricted commodities. If you are interested in importing textiles and textile products, you should contact the International Trade Administration's Office of Textile and Apparel (see addresses at end of this chapter) or U.S. Customs to ascertain your product's restraint status.

The U.S. Customs service provides quota reports on their website (www.customs.gov/impoexpo/impoexpo.htm). These reports are constantly updated and have an effective date noted. The most recent quota information can be accessed by clicking on the country name that interests you. This location holds information regarding quotas, transshipments, and visa requirements.

Marking and Labeling Requirements

TFPIA Requirements. All textile fiber products imported into the U.S. must be stamped, tagged, labeled, or otherwise marked with the following information as required by the TFPIA, unless exempt from marking (see TFPIA, Section 12): 1) the generic names and percentages by weight of the constituent fibers present in the textile fiber product, exclusive of permissible ornamentation, in amounts of more than 5% in order of predominance by weight,

with any percentage of fiber or fibers required to be designated as "other fiber" or "other fibers" (including those present in amounts of 5% or less) appearing last; and 2) the name of the manufacturer or the name or registered identification number issued by the FTC of one or more persons marketing or handling the textile fiber product; and 3) the name of the country where processed. A word trademark, used as a house mark and registered with the U.S. Patent Office, may appear on labels instead of the name otherwise required, provided the owner of the trademark furnishes a copy of the registration to the FTC prior to use (see "Registered Identification Numbers" below).

The information listed above is not exhaustive. TFPIA requirements are extensive. The Act specifies such details as types of labels, means of attachment, label position on the article, package labeling, unit labeling for two-piece garments, and arrangement of information on the label; allowable fiber designations; country-of-origin indications; requirements for trim and ornamentation, linings and interlinings, and pile fabrics; sectional disclosure; use of trade names and trademarks; and requirements for swatches and samples. The FTC publishes a booklet intended to clarify TFPIA requirements to facilitate voluntary compliance in the industry (see "Publications and WWW ResourcesPublications and WWW Resources" below). It is available on request, at no charge, from the FTC (see addresses at end of this chapter).

Wool Products Labeling Act (WPLA). Wool product labeling requirements for foreign products are the responsibility of the importer. The WPLA requires the following information to appear on wool products subject to the Act: 1) percentage of the wool product's total fiber weight (exclusive of ornamentation) not exceeding 5% of the total fiber weight of a) wool, b) recycled wool, c) each fiber other than wool if the percent by weight of such fiber is 5% or more, and d) the aggregate of all other fibers; 2) the maximum percent of the wool product's total weight, of any nonfibrous loading, filling, or adulterating matter; and 3) the importer's name. If you, as importer, have a registered identification number issued by the FTC, that number may be used instead of your name (see "Registered Identification Numbers" below).

Customs entry is contingent on proper labeling. If your shipment is found to be mislabeled at entry, you will be given the option of relabeling the products under Customs supervision, as long as the port director is satisfied that your labeling error or omission did not involve fraud or willful neglect. If your shipment is discovered after entry to have been noncomplying with WPLA, it will be recalled to Customs custody at your expense, unless you can satisfy the port director that the products have since been brought into compliance. You will be held responsible for all expenses incurred in bringing a shipment into compliance, including compensation of personnel and other expenses related to Customs supervision.

Fraudulent violations of WPLA will result in seizure of the shipment. Shipments already released from Customs custody will be ordered to be redelivered to Customs. Customs reports all cases of fraudulent violation to the FTC in Washington, DC.

The information listed above is not intended to be exhaustive. WPLA requirements are extensive. The Act specifies such details as types of labels, means of attachment, label position on the article, package labeling, unit labeling (as in the case of a two-piece garment), arrangement of information on the label, allowable fiber designations, country-of-origin indications, trim and ornamentation, pile fabrics, sectional disclosure, use of trade names and trademarks, requirements for swatches and samples, etc. The FTC publishes a booklet intended to clarify WPLA requirements in order to facilitate voluntary compliance within the industry (see "Publications and WWW Resources" below). It is available on request, at no charge, from the FTC (see addresses at end of this chapter).

The Care Labeling Rule. Regulations under this rule require manufacturers and importers of textile clothing and fabrics to attach specific care instructions for washing or dry cleaning, as well as information on the fiber composition of the article. They are enforced by the FTC Division of Enforcement. The Care Labeling Rule was amended September 2000, detailed information is available on the FTC website (www.ftc.gov/os/statutes/textilejump.htm).

Registered Identification Numbers. Any domestic firm or person residing in the U.S. and engaged in the manufacture or marketing of textile products covered under the TFPIA may obtain an FTC-registered identification number for use on required tags and labels instead of the name of a firm or person. For applications, contact the FTC (address below.)

For a general discussion of U.S. Customs marking and labeling requirements, see "Country of Origin Marking" on page 236, "Special Marking Requirements" on page 238 and "Marking—False Impression" on page 239.

Shipping Considerations

You will need to ensure that your goods are packaged and shipped with care so that they pass smoothly through Customs and arrive in good condition. You are responsible for ensuring that the shipment is in compliance with all applicable government regulations for packaging and shipping. In most instances, you should not leave these arrangements solely to the discretion of your supplier. Careful preparation of the cargo and selection of the mode of transport can be essential to a cost-effective, timely delivery of undamaged goods. We strongly advise you to consult your shipping representative, insurance agent, or freight broker for advice on packing and shipping.

Man-made staple fiber products may be shipped in bulk, spools, cartons, or other types of containers, depending on the type of product and whether it is prepackaged. General considerations include protection from contamination, weather, and pests. Containers should be constructed so as to be safe for handling during transport.

Publications and WWW Resources

The following publications may be relevant to the importation of man-made staple fibers:

Threading Your Way Through the Labeling Requirements Under the Textile and Wool Acts

Available free of charge on request from the Federal Trade Commission and online from the FTC website (www.ftc.gov/bcp/conline/pubs/buspubs/thread.htm). This publication is an excellent source of information written in clear lay language. We recommend that anyone interested in importing textile fiber products but unfamiliar with the regulations obtain a copy of each of this booklet.

The U.S. Customs Service launched a series of "Informed Compliance" publications in 1996, which are available on the Customs Service website (www.customs.gov/impoexpo/impoexpo.htm). Of particular interest:

What Every Member of the Trade Community Should Know About Textile & Apparel Rules of Origin

What Every Member of the Trade community Should Know About NAFTA for Textiles and Textile Articles

Fibers & Yarns Construction and Classification Under the HTSUS

The *Harmonized Tariff Schedule of the United States (2001)* (HTSUS) is available to view on the Customs Service website (www.customs.gov), or you may purchase a printed version from:

U.S. Government Printing Office
Superintendent of Documents
710 North Capital Street NW
Washington DC 20401
Tel: (202) 512-1800
Fax: (202) 512-1657
Website: www.access.gpo.gov

The USGPO also has copies of specific laws available for purchase. The USGPO accepts orders made by fax, phone or placed over the Internet, as well as mail orders paid by credit card. All orders must be accompanied by payment. Credit cards, checks drawn on a U.S. bank, or an international money order are all acceptable.

Relevant Government Agencies

Address your questions regarding textile Multi-Fiber Arrangements to:

U.S. Department of Commerce
International Trade Administration
Office of Textiles and Apparel
Director's Office
14th and Constitution Avenue NW, Rm. H3100
Washington DC 20230
(202) 482-5078
Fax: (202) 482-2331
Agreements Division: (202) 482-4212
Website: http://otexa.ita.doc.gov

Address your questions regarding the Flammable Fabrics Act (FFA) to:

Consumer Product Safety Commission (CPSC)
Office of Compliance
Washington DC 20207-0001
Tel: 800-638-2772 or (301) 504-7912
Fax: (301) 504-0359
Website: www.cpsc.gov

Address your questions regarding requirements under the Textile Fiber Products Identification Act (TFPIA) or the Wool Products Labeling Act (WPLA) to:

Federal Trade Commission (FTC)
Division of Enforcement
600 Pennsylvania Ave. NW
Washington DC 20580
Tel: (202) 326-2996
Website: www.ftc.gov

Address your questions regarding textile quotas to:

U.S. Customs and Border Protection
Office of Field Operations, Quota Branch
1300 Pennsylvania Avenue NW
Washington DC 20229
Tel: (202) 927-5850
Website: www.customs.treas.gov

The U.S. Customs Service provices updated status reports on textile quota on their web site (see address above). If the country you need information on is not listed, call the Quota Branch office at (202) 927-5850.

Address your questions regarding man-made staple fiber imports to your local Customs port director. For addresses, refer to "U.S. Customs and Border Protection Offices" on page 65 or contact:

U.S. Customs and Border Protection
Customs Headquarters
1300 Pennsylvania Avenue NW
Washington DC 20229
Tel: (202) 354-1000
Website: www.customs.treas.gov

Laws and Regulations

The following laws and regulations may be relevant to the importation of man-made staple fiber products. The laws are contained in the United States Code (USC), and the regulations are published in the Code of Federal Regulations (CFR), both of which are available at larger public and law libraries. Copies of specific laws are also available from the United States Government Printing Office (address above).

7 USC 1854
Textile Trade Agreements
(EO 11651, as amended by EO 11951 and 12188, and supplemented by EO 12475)
This Act authorizes the CITA of the DOC to enter into Multi-Fiber Agreements with other countries to control trade in textiles and establishes the Textile Import Program, which is enforced by U.S. Customs.

19 CFR 12.130 et seq.
Regulations on Entry of Textiles
These regulations provide the requirements and procedures followed by Customs in enforcing limitations on the importation and entry and withdrawal of textiles and textile products from warehouses for consumption in the U.S.

15 USC 70-77
Textile Fiber Products Identification Act (TFPIA)
This Act prohibits false or deceptive labeling (misbranding) and false advertising of any textile fiber products and requires all textile fiber products imported into the U.S. to be labeled in accordance with the requirements set forth in the law.

19 CFR 11.12b; 16 CFR 303 et seq.
Regulations on Labeling and Marking
These regulations detail the labeling and marking requirements for textiles as specified by the CPSC and the invoice contents required by U.S. Customs for purpose of enforcing the labeling and marking rules.

15 USC 68-68j
Wool Products Labeling Act (WPLA) of 1939
This Act prohibits the false or deceptive labeling (misbranding) of wool products and requires all wool products imported into the U.S. to be labeled in accordance with requirements set forth in the law.

19 CFR 11.12; 16 CFR 300 et seq.
Regulations on WPLA Labeling and Marking
These regulations set forth the wool labeling and marking requirements adopted by the FTC to administer the requirements of the WPLA and provide the procedures followed by U.S. Customs in enforcing the WPLA and the FTC regulations, including entry invoice requirements.

15 USC 1191-1204
Flammable Fabrics Act (FFA)
This Act provides for the setting of flammability standards for fabric by the Consumer Product Safety Commission (CPSC) and for enforcement by U.S. Customs.

16 CFR 1610, 1611, 1615, 1616, 1630-1632
Regulations on Flammable Fabric Standards
These regulations specify the flammability standards adopted by the CPSC under the FFA for various types of textiles.

16 CFR 423
Care Labeling Rule
Requires fiber composition and washing or dry cleaning instructions for textile apparel and certain piece goods.

Principal Exporting Countries

The following listing includes samples of the main supplier nations of the products of this chapter. It is organized by HTSUS major heading. (Refer to "Customs Classification" above for the product codes.) Countries are listed in rank order of the value of products imported to the U.S. Statistics represent customs value of entries for 2002 from the Bureau of Census, U.S. Department of Commerce.

5501—United Kingdom, Germany, Japan, France, Turkey

5502—Mexico, Germany, Sweden, Canada, France, United Kingdom, Switzerland

5503—South Korea, Mexico, Taiwan, Japan, Germany, Thailand, China

5504—Germany, Sweden, United Kingdom, Austria, Finland, Spain

5505—Mexico, Canada, United Kingdom, Taiwan, Germany, Pakistan

5506—South Korea, Italy, Mexico, Turkey, United Kingdom, Canada, France, Japan, Germany

5507—Italy, Japan, Canada, China, Germany, Australia, United Kingdom, France, Spain

5508—Thailand, China, South Korea, Mexico, Canada, Indonesia, Taiwan, Malaysia, Germany, Philippines, Japan

5509—Canada, Mexico, Turkey, Philippines, Indonesia, Germany, Romania, Thailand, Italy, Spain, United Kingdom

5510—Thailand, Sri Lanka, Austria, Philippines, Indonesia, Spain

5511—Canada, Turkey, Italy, United Kingdom, France, Spain, Mexico, Norway, Germany

5512—Canada, Italy, Mexico, Germany, Turkey, France, Cambodia, Pakistan

5513—Pakistan, China, Thailand, Indonesia, Canada, Malaysia, Mexico, Brazil, Sri Lanka

5514—Canada, China, Thailand, Mexico, Pakistan, India, Indonesia, Italy

5515—China, Mexico, Canada, Taiwan, Italy, Turkey, India, Israel, Philippines, France, Thailand, South Korea

5516—Italy, Belgium, Canada, South Korea, China, Mexico, Taiwan, France, Japan

Chapter 56:
Nonwovens and Cordage

Full title: Wadding, Felt, and Nonwovens; Special Yarns; Twine, Cordage, Ropes, and Cables and Articles Thereof

This chapter relates to the importation of nonwoven fabrics and cordage, which are classified under Chapter 56 of the Harmonized Tariff Schedule of the United States (HTSUS). Specifically, it includes sanitary articles of wadding; felt, nonwoven fabrics, textile-covered rubber thread and cord, textile yarn with rubber or plastic components, metalized and gimped yarn, twine, cordage, ropes, cables, and netting.

If you are interested in importing sewing thread, yarns, and other fibers or filaments, you should refer to Commodity Index Chapters 50 through 55. For importing nonwoven fabrics that are impregnated, coated, or covered with substances or preparations, you should read the Commodity Index chapter that covers that particular substance or preparation. For example, articles containing perfumes and cosmetics are in Chapter 33, soaps, detergents, polishes, and creams are in Chapter 34, and fabric softeners are in Chapter 38. If your product has plastic or rubber components, it may be classified under Chapter 39 or 40, respectively. If you are interested in importing metal foil on a backing of felt or nonwovens, refer to Chapters 72 through 81. Import requirements for articles consisting of mica or abrasive powder or grain on felt or nonwoven backing are covered in Chapter 68

Imports of cellulose and other paper wadding products are covered in Chapter 48. If you are interested in importing wadding, gauze, bandages, suture materials, and other articles for medical or surgical purposes, read Chapter 30. The import requirements for asbestos products are covered in Chapters 25 and 68. Hairnets are classified as headgear under Chapter 65. For importing nonwovens or cordage incorporated into toys, games, or sports equipment, refer to Chapter 95. If your product could be used as plaiting material, you should read Chapters 14 and 46. You should also review Chapter 58 to determine whether your import is classified as a special woven product.

Note: To understand key issues that will enable you to make best use of the information in this section we recommend that you see "Introduction" on page 425.

Key Factors

The key factors in the importation of nonwoven fabrics and cordage are:

- Compliance with quota restraints and visa requirements (if importing fabrics and other textile products)

- Submission of U.S. Customs Country-of-Origin Declaration(s)
- Compliance with entry invoice requirements
- Compliance with labeling requirements under Textile Fiber Products Identification Act (TFPIA) and/or the Wool Products Labeling Act (WPLA) and the Care Labeling Rule
- Compliance with flammability standards adopted and enforced by the Consumer Product Safety Commission (CPSC) under the Flammable Fabrics Act (FFA) (if importing fabrics and other textile products)
- Compliance with U.S. Food and Drug Administration (FDA) inspection and entry requirements (if importing products intended for sanitary purposes for which there is no exemption)
- Compliance with Federal Plant Pest Act (FPPA) and Plant Quarantine Act (PQA) requirements, and with U.S. Department of Agriculture (USDA) random port-of-entry inspections, import restrictions and quarantines, and other entry requirements (if importing cordage composed of vegetable materials)

Although most importers use the services of a licensed customs broker in making their entries, and we recommend this practice, you should be aware of the regulatory, entry, and documentation issues involved in importing your product. You, as importer, are ultimately responsible for the fulfillment of any legal requirements applicable to your shipment.

General Considerations

Regulatory Agencies. The DOC's Committee for Implementation of Textile Agreements (CITA) regulates certain textile imports under Section 204 of the Agricultural Adjustment Act. U.S. Customs enforces CITA textile and textile product entry quotas. Customs also enforces compliance with labeling and invoice requirements of the TFPIA and flammability standards under the FFA. The CPSC monitors imports and from time to time inspects textile shipments for compliance with FFA standards. If you are importing products that contain wool fibers, importation is subject to complex textile import regulations. The Federal Trade Commission (FTC) administers the WPLA requirements.

The USDA administers applicable provisions of the Plant Quarantine Act (PQA) and the Federal Plant Pest Act (FPPA), which are designed to prevent introduction into the U.S. of any plant pest or disease potentially harmful to U.S. agriculture. Shipments of cordage made of vegetable materials—e.g., jute or sisal—must be in compliance with PQA, FPPA, and USDA requirements. The FDA, under authority of the Federal Food, Drug, and Cosmetic Act (FDCA), regulates the importation of products intended for medical or sanitary purposes. U.S. Customs enforces entry requirements for products subject to FDCA requirements for compliance.

Cordage of Vegetable Materials. For most shipments of cordage made of vegetable materials, importation is straightforward. With some exceptions, you do not need permits or licenses to import these products (see "Prohibitions and Restrictions" below). The USDA's Animal and Plant Health Inspection Service (APHIS) inspects shipments of cordage made of vegetable materials on a random basis, depending on such factors as the port of entry, the country of origin, and the risk of contamination involved in the type of material being imported. Entry may be denied for noncompliance with the regulations, and the shipment could be seized, quarantined, destroyed, treated, or otherwise dealt with at the discretion of the inspector.

Wadding and Nonwoven Products for Sanitary Purposes. The importation of wadding and nonwoven products intended for sanitary uses—diapers, sanitary napkins, and similar items—is regulated by the FDA. Usually, if you import FDA-regulated articles, you must follow certain import procedures prescribed by that agency. If you are importing these articles at present, however, you are not required to follow normal FDA entry procedures because these articles are exempt. If routine Customs examinations of applicable shipments reveal problems that could have adverse effects on public health, the FDA will reconsider this exempt status. Selectivity criteria and entry notification may be reinstituted at any time at the discretion of FDA. Therefore, if your products fall into this category, you should be familiar with FDA import entry procedures and requirements under the FDCA. For a discussion of FDA import procedures see "Appendix: Foods" on page 825. If you are interested in importing a food-related product, you should ascertain its regulatory status by contacting the FDA (see addresses at end of this chapter).

Textile Quotas. If you are interested in importing nonwoven fabrics, the most important issue you need to be aware of is quotas. Under the Multi-Fiber Arrangement provisions of Section 204 of the Agricultural Adjustment Act, CITA initiates specific agreements with individual exporting countries. Section 204 of the Agricultural Adjustment Act covers textiles that: 1) are in chief value of cotton, wool, or man-made fibers, any textile fibers subject to the terms of any textile trade agreement, or any combination of such fibers; 2) contain 50% or more by weight of cotton or man-made fibers, or any textile fibers subject to the terms of any textile trade agreement; 3) contain 17% or more by weight of wool; or 4) if in chief value of textile fibers or textile materials, contain a blend of cotton, wool, or man-made fibers, any textile fibers subject to the terms of any textile trade agreement, or any combination of such fibers that, in total, amount to 50% or more by weight of all component fibers.

The U.S. has Multi-Fiber Arrangements with 40 countries. Each agreement with each country is unique, and may specify quotas for a type of textile or a specific article. Visas or export licenses may be required. These agreements, however, often change. Therefore, if you are interested in importing any nonwoven fabrics, you should contact the International Trade Administration's Office of Textile and Apparel (see addresses at end of this chapter). Refer to "Prohibitions and Restrictions" below for further details.

Textile Country-of-Origin Declarations. U.S. Customs enforces CITA textile and textile product entry quotas (see "Prohibitions and Restrictions" below). Requirements for entry include submission of Country-of-Origin Declarations with every nonwoven fabric shipment, regardless of whether it is subject to a specific multi-fiber arrangement (19 CFR 12.130, 12.131).

Country of Origin. Quota restrictions are country-specific and therefore are applied based on the country of origin for the textiles shipped. The last country from which a textile shipment was exported to the U.S. is not necessarily its country of origin. A textile or textile product imported into the U.S. is considered a product of the particular foreign territory or country, or a U.S. insular possession, where it is wholly grown, produced, or manufactured. For the following discussion, "country" means a foreign territory or country, or a U.S. insular possession.

In 1996, the U.S. Customs Service made major changes to country of origin rules for textile imports. The regulations at 19 CFR 102.21, "Textile and apparel products" were added to the 1996 Customs Regulations and became effective July 1, 1996. The new rules do not provide for cutting components or cutting and hemming to confer country of origin as in the past. The basis of the new law is processing operations or assembly. Some of the most important changes for importers to be aware of are:

- Cutting does not determine the country of origin (previously cutting determined country of origin for 90 percent of wearing apparel imports). The new rules are based on processing or assembly operations.

- Essential character does not determine country of origin because the new rules are based on processing.

- A subjective determination under the provisions of 19 CFR 12.130 is replaced by objective processing operations expressed in terms of tariff shifts. Dying, printing, and other finishing processes applied to fabrics no longer confer or change country of origin.

- Country of origin for textile and apparel products processed, assembled or manufactured in two or more countries is determined by where the most important processing occurs, and, if that cannot be ascertained, the last country in which an important processing operation occurs.

The country of origin is the country in which a product is wholly produced when a textile or apparel product is completely produced or manufactured (except for minor parts) in one country. For fabric, the country of origin is the country in which the fabric is woven, knitted, needled, tufted, felted, entangled or created by any other fabric-making process. The country of origin for staple yarn is the country in which yarn is spun; for filament yarn, the country in which filament is extruded; and for plied, gimped and cabled yarns, the country in which the fibers or filaments used in the yarn are spun or extruded. The country of origin of all other textile and apparel products is the country in which the components of a textile or apparel product are wholly assembled (except for minor attachments). Once again, note that assembly, not cutting, now confers country of origin.

Declarations. All importations of textiles and textile products must be accompanied by one of the following three declarations. Goods subject to Section 204, Agricultural Act of 1956, as amended, must be accompanied by either a single-country or a multiple-country declaration. Goods not subject to Section 204 must be accompanied by a negative declaration.

- **Single-country declarations** are used for entries of textiles or textile products which are wholly the growth, product, or manufacture of a single foreign country, territory, or U.S. insular possession. Information required includes: marks of identification and numbers; description of article and quantity; country of origin; and date of exportation.

- **Multiple-country declarations** are used for entries of textiles or textile products which were subjected to manufacturing or processing operations in, and/or incorporate materials originating in more than one foreign country or territory. Information required includes: marks of identification and numbers; for articles, description, quantity, identification of manufacturing and/or processing operations, country, and date of exportation; for materials used to make articles, description of materials, country of production, and date of exportation.

- **Negative declarations** must accompany all textile imports that are not subject to FFA Section 204 restrictions. Information required includes: marks of identification and numbers; descriptions of article and quantity; and country of origin.

The date of exportation to be indicated on the above declarations is the date on which the carrier leaves the last port in the country of origin, as determined by Customs. Diversion to another country during transit does not affect the export date.

Procedure for Declarations. The manufacturer, producer, exporter, or importer may prepare the declaration. If more than one of these parties is involved in the importation, each party may prepare a separate declaration. You may file a separate declaration for each invoice presented with your entry. The declaration must be dated and signed by the responsible party, and must include the person's title and the company name and address. Your shipment's entry will be denied unless it is accompanied by a properly executed declaration. Customs will not treat a textile declaration as a missing document for which a bond may be filed.

Customs will base its country-of-origin determination on the information contained in each declaration, unless the information is insufficient. If the information on the declaration is insufficient, Customs will require that you submit such additional information as will enable the determination to be made. The shipment will not be released until the determination is made. Thus, if you want to clear Customs with minimal delay, be sure that the information on the declarations is as complete as possible for each shipment.

Textile Labeling and Invoice Requirements. You are responsible for your imported nonwoven fabric product's compliance with applicable provisions of the TFPIA. Nonwoven fabric products that require labeling under TFPIA must already be labeled at entry, or the shipment will be refused. (See "Marking and Labeling Requirements" below.) If you import shipments of nonwoven fabrics subject to TFPIA and valued at over $500, you must provide special information on the entry invoice (see "Entry and Documentation" below).

Flammability Standards. Nonwoven fabric products imported into the U.S. for use in consumer products must be in compliance with the FFA, a federal law that gives the CPSC the authority and responsibility for protecting the public from the hazards of dangerously flammable items of wearing apparel and interior furnishings. Under the FFA, standards have been established for flammability of clothing textiles. You cannot import any article of wearing apparel or interior furnishing, or any fabric or related material that is intended for use or that may be used in such items, if it fails to conform to an applicable flammability standard (FFA Section 4). Certain products may be imported into the U.S. (FFA Section 11c) for finishing or processing to render them less flammable so as to meet the standards. For these products, the exporter must state on the invoice or other paper relating to the shipment that the shipment is being made for that purpose.

The CPSC monitors imports of textiles under its Import Surveillance Program. From time to time, your textile shipments may be inspected to ascertain compliance with mandatory safety standards. Shipments may also be subject to testing by the CPSC to determine compliance. If the CPSC believes a product, fabric, or related material does not comply with a flammability standard, it is authorized to pursue a variety of legal sanctions (see "Prohibitions and Restrictions" below).

Substantial Product Hazard Reports. Any firm that obtains information that reasonably supports the conclusion that one of its products presents an unreasonable risk of serious injury or death must report that information to the CPSC's Division of Corrective Actions (CPSC address below). Importers must also report to the CPSC if 1) a type of product is the subject of at least three civil actions filed in U.S. federal or state courts, 2) each suit alleges the involvement of that product type in death or grievous bodily injury (as defined in FFA Section 37(3)1), and 3) at least three of the actions result in a final settlement with the manufacturer or in a judgment for the plaintiff within any one of the two-year periods specified in FFA Section 37(b).

Wool Product Entry Requirements. Depending on the nature of your wool fiber imports, as many as three different types of special entry documents may be required. First, for all imported textile fibers and yarns covered by the Agricultural Adjustment Act (AAA), including wool, you must file a U.S. Customs Textile Entry Declaration (see "Textile Country-of-Origin Declarations" above). Second, for all wool products subject to the WPLA, special information is required on the entry invoices (see "Entry and Documentation" below). Finally, certain wool articles manufactured or produced in certain countries may be subject to quotas under U.S. Department of Commerce Multi-Fiber Arrangements. Such products require export certificates or visas issued by the appropriate country of origin, in addition to other requisite entry paperwork (see "Quotas" above).

Wool Products Labeling Act. The term "wool product" means any product or any portion of a product that contains, purports to contain, or in any way is represented as containing wool, reprocessed wool, or reused wool. All wool products imported into the U.S., except those made more than 20 years before importation, and except carpets, rugs, mats, and upholsteries, must have affixed a stamp, tag, label, or other means of identification as required by the WPLA. If you are importing wool products exempt from labeling under the WPLA, do not assume they are also exempt from labeling under the TFPIA. These are two distinct laws, with some overlapping requirements (see "Marking and Labeling Requirements" below).

Import Advisory

Importation of textiles is trade-sensitive and highly regulated. Shipments of textiles and textile products not complying with all government regulations, including quotas and visas, are subject to seizure and could result in the imposition of penalties as well as possible forfeiture of the goods. You should always verify the available quota for any textile product you plan to import before your shipment leaves the country of manufacture. Furthermore, Customs textile classification rulings change frequently, and prior administrative rulings are often modified and sometimes reversed. You should be particularly careful to comply with country of origin determination regulations, which were changed in 1996, and affect quotas and visas, marking and labeling, and other important aspects of tariff classification. See "Publications and WWW Resources" for information on important Customs Service informed compliance publications.

The Customs Service has greatly increased its scrutiny of the textile industry, one of eight primary focus industries identified in the most recent Trade Compliance & Enforcement Plan. Imported products from these industries will likely attract significant attention from Customs in the areas of compliance measurement, compliance assessment, informed compliance, and interventions.

Customs Classification

For customs purposes, nonwoven fabrics and cordage are classified under Chapter 56 of the HTSUS. This chapter is broken into major headings, which are further divided into subheadings, and often sub-subheadings, each of which has its own HTSUS classification number. For example, the 2001 HTSUS number for laminated needleloom felt fabrics is 5602.10.10, indicating it is a sub-subcategory of needleloom felt and stitch-bonded fiber fabrics (5602.10.00), which is a subcategory of the major heading, felt, whether or not impregnated, coated, covered, or laminated (5602.00.00). There are nine major headings within Chapter 56.

5601—Wadding of textile materials and articles thereof; textile fibers, not exceeding 5 mm in length (flock), textile dust, and mill neps

5602—Felt, whether or not impregnated, coated, covered, or laminated

5603—Nonwovens, whether or not impregnated, coated, covered, or laminated

5604—Rubber thread and cord, textile covered; textile yarn, strip, and the like of heading 5404 or 5405, impregnated, coated, covered, or sheathed with rubber or plastics

5605—Metalized yarn, whether or not gimped, being textile yarn, or strip or the like of heading 5404 or 5405, combined with metal in the form of thread, strip, or powder or covered with metal

5606—Gimped yarn, strip, and the like of heading 5404 or 5405, gimped (other than those of heading 5605 and gimped horsehair yarn); chenille yarn (including flock chenille yarn); loop wale-yarn

5607—Twine, cordage, rope, and cables, whether or not plaited or braided and whether or not impregnated, coated, covered, or sheathed with rubber or plastics

5608—Knotted netting of twine, cordage, or rope; made up fishing nets and other made up nets, of textile materials

5609—Articles of yarn, strip, or the like of heading 5404 or 5405, twine, cordage, rope, or cables, not elsewhere specified or included

For more details regarding classifications of the specific product you are interested in importing, consult a customs broker, the appropriate commodity specialist at your nearest customs port, or the HTSUS. The 2001 HTSUS is available online from the Customs Service (www.customs.gov/impoexpo/impoexpo.htm) or for purchase from the U.S. Government Printing Office (see resources at the end of this chapter), and may be found in larger public libraries. For a general discussion of customs classification, see "Classification—Liquidation" on page 229.

Dutiable Status of Goods

For more information about duty rates and binding decisions see "Dutiable Status of Goods" on page 203; for a discussion of temporary importation of goods see "Temporary Free Importations" on page 205.

Valuation

Importers have a responsibility to use what the U.S. Customs Service deems, "reasonable care," when determining the value of their goods. They must also provide any additional information that the Customs Service needs for setting a final value on the goods. This process involves a number of factors and can be somewhat complicated; importers must be aware of applicable issues and details. Valuation information applies to all types of commodities, for further discussion on the subject see "Customs Valuation" on page 267.

Import Duties

Import duties vary (often dramatically) depending upon the Harmonized Tariff Schedule (HTSUS) classification of the goods or products imported. Since some products that look alike have different HTSUS classifications and different rates of duty, proper classification is vital. Note that "differences of opinion" between importers and the Bureau of Customs and Border Protection regarding classification keeps customs attorneys very busy.

Import duties can be assessed on the imported value of the goods ("ad valorem" rates of duty such as 2%, 4.4%, 50%, etc.), total units or weight of the goods ("specific" rates of duty such as 2 cents each or 1.5 cents/pound, etc.) or on a combination basis ("compound" rates of duty such as 5 cents each plus 6%).

Listed below is a sampling of several Column 1 import duty rates for Chapter 56 products:

Nonwovens weighing more than 70 g/m2 but not more than 150 g/m2 (5603.93.00): Free

to

High tenacity yarn of polyesters, of nylon or other polyamides or of viscose rayon, impregnated or coated (201) (5604.20.00.00): 8.9%

For specific information on US import duties refer to the Harmonized Tariff Schedule of the US. The print version is available from the US Government Printing Office as well as third party suppliers who often add special features. Online versions are available in both static PDF pages as well as in formats with excellent search functionality. Search the Web with the term "Harmonized Tariff Schedule" to find sources.

Entry and Documentation

The entry of merchandise is a two-part process consisting of 1) filing the documentation necessary to determine whether merchandise may be released from Customs custody, and 2) filing the documents that contain information for duty assessment and statistical purposes. In certain instances, all documents must be filed and accepted by Customs prior to release of the goods. Unless you have been granted an extension, you must file entry documents at a location specified by the port or area director within five working days of your shipment's date of arrival at a U.S. port of entry. These include a number of standard documents required by Customs for any entry, and:

- U.S. Customs Country-of-Origin Declaration Form CF 3229

- Export documentation and/or visa for textiles subject to Multi-Fiber Arrangement

- Phytosanitary certificate (if importing cordage made of vegetable material)

After you present the entry, Customs may examine your shipment or may waive examination. The shipment is then released provided no legal or regulatory violations have been noted. You must then file entry summary documentation and deposit estimated duties at a designated customhouse within 10 working days of your shipment's release. For a detailed description of entry procedures, standard documentation, and informal entry, see "Entry Process" on page 185.

Informed Compliance. Informed compliance was introduced with the Customs Modernization Act of 1993 (Mod Act) and defines the relationship between importers and the Customs Service. It sets out the responsibilities of both parties. Providing the correct documentation and information for entry is a key factor that will make your importing operation run smoothly. We recommend that importers become familiar with the concept of informed comliance and the responsibilities that they have under the Mod Act. For further discussion about informed compliance see "Informed Compliance" on page 211.

NAFTA Certificates of Origin. An importer of textiles for which NAFTA treatment is sought need not file a separate NAFTA Certificate of Origin in addition to the Customs Country-of-Origin Declaration. The declaration is sufficient. However, the importer must take care to submit a declaration from each U.S., Canadian, or Mexican producer or manufacturer. Thus, for multiple producers or manufacturers, a separate declaration must be filed for each. If a Customs port director cannot determine the country of origin because the declaration is absent or incomplete, the shipment is not entitled to preferential NAFTA tariff treatment or other NAFTA benefits. See 19 CFR 12.132.

Entry Invoices. You must provide certain additional information on the entry invoice for nonwoven and cordage products. The specific information varies depending on the nature of your product, as noted below.

TFPIA Requirements. For the purpose of TFPIA enforcement, a commercial shipment of textile products exceeding $500 in value and subject to TFPIA labeling requirements must show the following information: 1) the constituent fiber or combination of fibers, designating with equal prominence each natural or manufactured fiber by its generic name, in order of predominance by weight if the weight of such fiber is 5% or more of the total fiber weight of the product; 2) percentage of each fiber present, by weight, in the total fiber content; 3) the name or other identification issued and registered by the Federal Trade Commission of the manufacturer of the product or one or more persons subject to Section 3 of the TFPIA with respect to such product; 4) the name of the country where processed or manufactured.

Wool Products Subject to WPLA. When you offer for entry a wool product shipment valued at over $500 and subject to WPLA, you must include certain information intended to facilitate Customs monitoring and enforcement of that Act. This extra information is identical to that required by WPLA on labeling (see "Marking and Labeling Requirements" below), with the addition of the manufacturer's name. If your product consists of mixed waste, residues, and similar merchandise obtained from several suppliers or unknown sources, you may omit the manufacturer's name from the entry invoice.

Yarn. All entry invoices for yarn should show: 1) fiber content by weight; 2) whether the yarn is single or plied; 3) whether or not the yarn is put up for retail sale (as defined in HTSUS Section XI, Note 4); and 4) whether or not the yarn is intended for use as sewing thread. For more general information about invoices see "Invoices" on page 277.

Note: The Entry and Documentation section has been carefully designed to supply you, the importer, with sample documents and directions on how to satisfy Customs requirements. Be aware that you should consult the applicable authorities to ensure that you are correctly following the most current procedures.

Prohibitions and Restrictions

Cordage of Vegetable Materials. In general, any shipment of cordage made of vegetable materials is subject to random port-of-entry inspection by the USDA. If the inspector finds evidence of the presence of insects in your shipment, you may be required to submit your shipment to USDA-prescribed fumigation procedures. If the insect is of a kind for which there is no viable U.S. treatment, your shipment will be refused. Our source at USDA assured us that most shipments that are found to have insects in them can be treated to afford entry.

Textile Quotas. Textile import restrictions are primarily a matter of quotas and the way in which these quotas are administered and monitored. Under the Multi-Fiber Arrangement provisions of Section 204 of the Agricultural Adjustment Act, CITA has negotiated Multi-Fiber Arrangements with 40 countries. These Agreements may impose quotas for a type of textile or a specific article, and they are country-specific. The agreements, however, often change. Therefore, if you are interested in importing any nonwoven fabric products, you should contact the International Trade Administration's Office of Textile and Apparel (see addresses at end of this chapter). The Office of Textile and Apparel has a team of country specialists who can inform you of the latest developments and inform you about a product's quota or restriction status.

U.S. Customs enforces CITA textile and textile product entry quotas. If formal entry procedures are not followed, Customs will usually refuse entry for textiles that are subject to Section 204. Formal entry requires submission of a Country-of-Origin Declaration (see General Considerations above). U.S. Customs maintains a current textile quota status report, available for perusal at any Customs port. In addition, U.S. Customs in Washington, DC, provides quota status reports online, which are updated on a regular basis (www.customs.gov/impoexpo/impoexpo.htm).

Flammable Fabrics. U.S. Customs may refuse entry for any article of wearing apparel or interior furnishing, or any fabric or related material that is intended for use or that may be used in wearing apparel or interior furnishings, if it fails to conform to an applicable flammability standard issued under Section 4 of the FFA. An exception is allowed for certain products (FFA Section 11c) that are imported for finishing or processing to bring them within the legal standard. For these products, the exporter must state on the invoice or other paper relating to the shipment that the shipment is being made for that purpose.

The CPSC, as the primary enforcement agency of flammability standards, inspects products for compliance with the FFA. If the CPSC believes a product, fabric, or related material does not comply with a flammability standard, it is authorized to pursue a variety of legal sanctions, including: 1) seizure, condemnation, and forfeiture of the noncomplying products; 2) administrative cease-and-desist order requiring an individual or firm to stop sale and distribution of the noncomplying products or; 3) temporary injunction requiring the individual or firm to stop sale and distribution of the noncomplying products, pending final disposition of an administrative cease-and-desist proceeding. The CPSC also has authority to seek civil penalties against any person who knowingly violates a regulation or standard issued under Section 4 of the FFA.

Country-Specific Restrictions

Restrictions under Multi-Fiber Arrangements are country-specific. A product originating in one country may be subject to quota and to export license or visa requirements, while the same product originating in a different country may not. At present, the U.S. has Multi-Fiber Arrangements with 40 countries. Many different categories of products are covered under these Arrangements; it is beyond the scope of this book to list each country and its restricted commodities. If you are interested in importing textiles and textile products, you should contact the International Trade Administration's Office of Textile and Apparel (see addresses at end of this chapter) or U.S. Customs to ascertain your product's restraint status.

The U.S. Customs service provides quota reports on their website (www.customs.gov/impoexpo/impoexpo.htm). These reports are constantly updated and have an effective date noted. The most recent quota information can be accessed by clicking on the country name that interests you. This location holds information regarding quotas, transshipments, and visa requirements.

Marking and Labeling Requirements

TFPIA Requirements. All textile fiber products imported into the U.S. must be stamped, tagged, labeled, or otherwise marked with the following information as required by the TFPIA, unless exempt from marking (see TFPIA, Section 12): 1) the generic names and percentages by weight of the constituent fibers present in the textile fiber product, exclusive of permissible ornamentation, in amounts of more than 5% in order of predominance by weight, with any percentage of fiber or fibers required to be designated as "other fiber" or "other fibers" (including those present in amounts of 5% or less) appearing last; and 2) the name of the manufacturer or the name or registered identification number issued by the FTC of one or more persons marketing or handling the textile fiber product; and 3) the name of the country where processed. A word trademark, used as a house mark and registered with the U.S. Patent Office, may appear on labels instead of the name otherwise required, provided the owner of the trademark furnishes a copy of the registration to the

FTC prior to use (see "Registered Identification Numbers" below).

The information listed above is not exhaustive. TFPIA requirements are extensive. The Act specifies such details as types of labels, means of attachment, label position on the article, package labeling, unit labeling for two-piece garments, and arrangement of information on the label; allowable fiber designations; country-of-origin indications; requirements for trim and ornamentation, linings and interlinings, and pile fabrics; sectional disclosure; use of trade names and trademarks; and requirements for swatches and samples. The FTC publishes a booklet intended to clarify TFPIA requirements to facilitate voluntary compliance in the industry (see "Publications and WWW Resources" below). It is available on request, at no charge, from the FTC (see addresses at end of this chapter).

Wool Products Labeling Act (WPLA). Wool product labeling requirements for foreign products are the responsibility of the importer. The WPLA requires the following information to appear on wool products subject to the Act: 1) percentage of the wool product's total fiber weight (exclusive of ornamentation) not exceeding 5% of the total fiber weight of a) wool, b) recycled wool, c) each fiber other than wool if the percent by weight of such fiber is 5% or more, and d) the aggregate of all other fibers; 2) the maximum percent of the wool product's total weight, of any nonfibrous loading, filling, or adulterating matter; and 3) the importer's name. If you, as importer, have a registered identification number issued by the FTC, that number may be used instead of your name (see "Registered Identification Numbers" below).

Customs entry is contingent on proper labeling. If your shipment is found to be mislabeled at entry, you will be given the option of relabeling the products under Customs supervision, as long as the port director is satisfied that your labeling error or omission did not involve fraud or willful neglect. If your shipment is discovered after entry to have been noncomplying with WPLA, it will be recalled to Customs custody at your expense, unless you can satisfy the port director that the products have since been brought into compliance. You will be held responsible for all expenses incurred in bringing a shipment into compliance, including compensation of personnel and other expenses related to Customs supervision.

Fraudulent violations of WPLA will result in seizure of the shipment. Shipments already released from Customs custody will be ordered to be redelivered to Customs. Customs reports all cases of fraudulent violation to the FTC in Washington, DC.

The information listed above is not intended to be exhaustive. WPLA requirements are extensive. The Act specifies such details as types of labels, means of attachment, label position on the article, package labeling, unit labeling (as in the case of a two-piece garment), arrangement of information on the label, allowable fiber designations, country-of-origin indications, trim and ornamentation, pile fabrics, sectional disclosure, use of trade names and trademarks, requirements for swatches and samples, etc. The FTC publishes a booklet intended to clarify WPLA requirements in order to facilitate voluntary compliance within the industry (see "Publications and WWW Resources" below). It is available on request, at no charge, from the FTC (see addresses at end of this chapter).

The Care Labeling Rule. Regulations under this rule require manufacturers and importers of textile clothing and fabrics to attach specific care instructions for washing or dry cleaning, as well as information on the fiber composition of the article. They are enforced by the FTC Division of Enforcement. The Care Labeling Rule was amended September 2000, detailed information is available on the FTC website (www.ftc.gov/os/statutes/textilejump.htm).

Registered Identification Numbers. Any domestic firm or person residing in the U.S. and engaged in the manufacture or marketing of textile products covered under the TFPIA may obtain an FTC-registered identification number for use on required tags and labels instead of the name of a firm or person. For applications, contact the FTC (address below.)

For a general discussion of U.S. Customs marking and labeling requirements, see "Country of Origin Marking" on page 236, "Special Marking Requirements" on page 238 and "Marking—False Impression" on page 239.

Shipping Considerations

You will need to ensure that your goods are packaged and shipped with care so that they pass smoothly through Customs and arrive in good condition. You are responsible for ensuring that the shipment is in compliance with all applicable government regulations for packaging and shipping. In most instances, you should not leave these arrangements solely to the discretion of your supplier. Careful preparation of the cargo and selection of the mode of transport can be essential to a cost-effective, timely delivery of undamaged goods. We strongly advise you to consult your shipping representative, insurance agent, or freight broker for advice on packing and shipping.

Nonwoven fabrics and cordage may be shipped in bulk, bolts, rolls, or other types of containers, depending on the type of product and whether it is prepackaged. General considerations include protection from contamination, weather, and pests. If a product must be kept in a sanitary environment, all tables, utensils, platforms, and devices used for moving or handling the product, the compartments in which it is stowed while being transported will need to be maintained in a sanitary condition. Safety precautions should also be implemented as required to protect against breakage, spillage, corrosion of containers, and combustion. Containers should be constructed so as to be safe for handling during transport.

Publications and WWW Resources

The following publication explains the FDA requirements for importing textile wadding products for sanitary use. It is published by the FDA and is available online from the FDA website (www.fda.gov/opacom/7pubs.html).

> *Requirements of Laws and Regulations Enforced by the U.S. Food and Drug Administration*

The following publication may be relevant to the importation of nonwoven fabric products:

> *Threading Your Way Through the Labeling Requirements Under the Textile and Wool Acts*

Available free of charge on request from the Federal Trade Commission and online from the FTC website (www.ftc.gov/bcp/conline/pubs/buspubs/thread.htm). This publication is an excellent source of information written in clear lay language. We recommend that anyone interested in importing textile fiber products but unfamiliar with the regulations obtain a copy of each of this booklet.

The U.S. Customs Service launched a series of "Informed Compliance" publications in 1996, which are available on the Customs Service website (www.customs.gov/impoexpo/impoexpo.htm). Of particular interest:

> *What Every Member of the Trade Community Should Know About Textile & Apparel Rules of Origin*

> *What Every Member of the Trade community Should Know About NAFTA for Textiles and Textile Articles*

> *Fibers & Yarns Construction and Classification Under the HTSUS*

The *Harmonized Tariff Schedule of the United States (2001)* (HTSUS) is available to view on the Customs Service website (www.customs.gov), or you may purchase a printed version from:

U.S. Government Printing Office
Superintendent of Documents
710 North Capital Street NW
Washington DC 20401
Tel: (202) 512-1800
Fax: (202) 512-1657
Website: www.access.gpo.gov

The USGPO also has copies of specific laws available for purchase. The USGPO accepts orders made by fax, phone or placed over the Internet, as well as mail orders paid by credit card. All orders must be accompanied by payment. Credit cards, checks drawn on a U.S. bank, or an international money order are all acceptable.

Relevant Government Agencies

Address your questions regarding FDA regulation or requirements for textile wadding products intended for sanitary uses to:

U.S. Food and Drug Administration (FDA)
5600 Fishers Lane
Rockville, MD 20857-0001
Tel: 888-463-6332
Website: www.fda.gov

Address your questions regarding USDA requirements for imported cordage made of vegetable materials to:

Animal and Plant Health Inspection Service (APHIS)
Plant Protection and Quarantine (PPQ)
Director's Office
4700 River Rd., Unit 131
Riverdale, MD 20737
Tel: (301) 734-8261
Tel (PPQ permits): (301) 734-8758
Website: www.aphis.usda.gov/ppq

Address your questions regarding textile Multi-Fiber Arrangements to:

U.S. Department of Commerce
International Trade Administration
Office of Textiles and Apparel
Director's Office
14th and Constitution Avenue NW, Rm. H3100
Washington DC 20230
Tel: (202) 482-5078
Agreements Division: (202) 482-4212
Website: http://otexa.ita.doc.gov

Address your questions regarding the Flammable Fabrics Act (FFA) to:

Consumer Product Safety Commission (CPSC)
Office of Compliance
Washington DC 20207-0001
Tel: 800-638-2772 or (301) 504-7912
Fax: (301) 504-0359
Website: www.cpsc.gov

Address your questions regarding requirements under the Textile Fiber Products Identification Act (TFPIA) or the Wool Products Labeling Act (WPLA) to:

Federal Trade Commission (FTC)
Division of Enforcement
600 Pennsylvania Avenue NW
Washington DC 20580
Tel: (202) 326-2996
Website: www.ftc.gov

Address your questions regarding textile quotas to:

U.S. Customs and Border Protection
Office of Field Operations, Quota Branch
1300 Pennsylvania Avenue NW
Washington DC 20229
Tel: (202) 927-5850
Website: www.customs.treas.gov

The U.S. Customs Service provices updated status reports on textile quota on their web site (see address above). If the country you need information on is not listed, call the Quota Branch office at (202) 927-5850.

Address your questions regarding cordage and nonwoven fabric imports to your local Customs port director. For addresses, refer to "U.S. Customs and Border Protection Offices" on page 65 or contact:

U.S. Customs and Border Protection
Customs Headquarters
1300 Pennsylvania Avenue NW
Washington DC 20229
Tel: (202) 354-1000
Website: www.customs.treas.gov

Laws and Regulations

The following laws and regulations may be relevant to the importation of cordage and nonwoven fabrics. The laws are contained in the United States Code (USC), and the regulations are published in the Code of Federal Regulations (CFR), both of which are available at larger public and law libraries. Copies of specific laws are also available from the United States Government Printing Office (address above).

7 USC 1854
Textile Trade Agreements
(EO 11651, as amended by EO 11951 and 12188, and supplemented by EO 12475)
This Act authorizes the CITA of the DOC to enter into Multi-Fiber Agreements with other countries to control trade in textiles and establishes the Textile Import Program, which is enforced by U.S. Customs.

19 CFR 12.130 et seq.
Regulations on Entry of Textiles
These regulations provide the requirements and procedures followed by Customs in enforcing limitations on the importation and entry and withdrawal of textiles and textile products from warehouses for consumption in the U.S.

15 USC 70-77
Textile Fiber Products Identification Act (TFPIA)
This Act prohibits false or deceptive labeling (misbranding) and false advertising of any textile fiber products and requires all textile fiber products imported into the U.S. to be labeled in accordance with the requirements set forth in the law.

19 CFR 11.12b; 16 CFR 303 et seq.
Regulations on Labeling and Marking
These regulations detail the labeling and marking requirements for textiles as specified by the CPSC and the invoice contents required by U.S. Customs for purpose of enforcing the labeling and marking rules.

15 USC 68-68j
Wool Products Labeling Act (WPLA) of 1939
This Act prohibits the false or deceptive labeling (misbranding) of wool products and requires all wool products imported into the U.S. to be labeled in accordance with requirements set forth in the law.

19 CFR 11.12; 16 CFR 300 et seq.
Regulations on WPLA Labeling and Marking
These regulations set forth the wool labeling and marking requirements adopted by the FTC to administer the re-

quirements of the WPLA and provide the procedures followed by U.S. Customs in enforcing the WPLA and the FTC regulations, including entry invoice requirements.

15 USC 1191-1204
Flammable Fabrics Act (FFA)
This Act provides for the setting of flammability standards for fabric by the Consumer Product Safety Commission (CPSC) and for enforcement by U.S. Customs.

16 CFR 1610, 1611, 1615, 1616, 1630-1632
Regulations on Flammable Fabric Standards
These regulations specify the flammability standards adopted by the CPSC under the FFA for various types of textiles.

21 USC 301 et seq.
Federal Food, Drug, and Cosmetic Act
This Act prohibits deceptive practices and regulates the manufacture, sale and importation or exportation of food, drugs, cosmetics, and related products. It was amended by the Food Quality Protection Act of 1996. See 21 USC 331, 381, 382.

19 CFR 12.1 et seq.; 21 CFR 1.83 et seq.
Regulations on Food, Drugs, and Cosmetics
These regulations of the Secretary of Health and Human Services and the Secretary of the Treasury govern the standards, labeling, marking, and importing of products used with food, drugs, and cosmetics.

16 CFR 423
Care Labeling Rule
Requires fiber composition and washing or dry cleaning instructions for textile apparel and certain piece goods.

Principal Exporting Countries

The following listing includes samples of the main supplier nations of the products of this chapter. It is organized by HTSUS major heading. (Refer to "Customs Classification" above for the product codes.) Countries are listed in rank order of the value of products imported to the U.S. Statistics represent customs value of entries for 2002 from the Bureau of Census, U.S. Department of Commerce.

5601—Canada, Mexico, Netherlands, United Kingdom, Switzerland, China, Germany, France, Japan, South Korea, Italy, Ukraine

5602—Canada, United Kingdom, Mexico, Italy, Germany, Spain, Slovenia, Japan, France, Brazil, China, Netherlands, India

5603—Japan, Germany, Israel, Canada, Italy, United Kingdom, Mexico, Luxembourg, France, Netherlands

5604—France, Japan, Mexico, Taiwan, China, Germany, United Kingdom, Canada, Sri Lanka, Malaysia

5605—Japan, Italy, Taiwan, India, Germany, Belgium, South Korea, China

5606—Mexico, Italy, Colombia, Romania, Germany, Thailand, Japan, Taiwan

5607—Mexico, Brazil, Canada, Philippines, Portugal, South Korea, Costa Rica, Taiwan, United Kingdom, Japan, Austria

5608—China, Mexico, Taiwan, Canada, Japan, Portugal

5609—China, Dominican Republic, Malaysia, Taiwan, India, Mexico, Indonesia, Canada, Turkey

Chapter 57:
Carpets and Other Textile Floor Coverings

This chapter relates to the importation of carpets and other textile floor coverings, which are classified under Chapter 57 of the Harmonized Tariff Schedule of the United States (HTSUS). Specifically, it includes knotted, hand-woven, and machine-woven textile floor coverings. Articles are classified in this chapter only if the textile materials are exposed on the surface when the item is in use. This chapter also includes articles with characteristics of textile floor coverings but intended for other uses.

If you are interested in importing floor covering underlays, you should refer to Commodity Index Chapter 56. The import requirements for vinyl and other plastic floor coverings are in Chapter 39. If you are interested in importing rubber floor coverings and mats, read Chapter 40. Textile floor coverings that are more than 100 years old are classified under Chapter 97.

Note: To understand key issues that will enable you to make best use of the information in this section we recommend that you see "Introduction" on page 425.

Key Factors

The key factors in the importation of carpets and other textile floor coverings are:

- Compliance with quota restraints and visa requirements
- Submission of U.S. Customs Country-of-Origin Declaration(s)
- Compliance with entry invoice requirements
- Compliance with labeling requirements under Textile Fiber Products Identification Act (TFPIA) and the Care Labeling Rule
- Compliance with flammability standards adopted and enforced by the Consumer Product Safety Commission (CPSC) under the Flammable Fabrics Act (FFA)
- Prohibition and license requirements for Iranian carpets and rugs

Although most importers use the services of a licensed customs broker in making their entries, and we recommend this practice, you should be aware of the regulatory, entry, and documentation issues involved in importing your product. The importer is ultimately responsible for the fulfillment of any legal requirements applicable to a shipment.

General Considerations

Regulatory Agencies. The DOC's Committee for Implementation of Textile Agreements (CITA) regulates certain textile imports under Section 204 of the Agricultural Adjustment Act. U.S. Customs enforces CITA textile and textile product entry quotas. Customs also enforces compliance with labeling and invoice requirements of the TFPIA and flammability standards under the FFA. The CPSC monitors imports and from time to time inspects textile shipments for compliance with FFA standards.

Wool Carpets and Flooring Coverings. Carpets, rugs, and mats made of wool are specifically exempted from the requirements of the Wool Products Labeling Act (WPLA). These articles must, however, be labeled in accordance with the TFPIA.

Textile Quotas. If you are interested in importing carpets, rugs, and other textile floor coverings, the most important issue you need to be aware of is quotas. Under the Multi-Fiber Arrangement provisions of Section 204 of the Agricultural Adjustment Act, CITA initiates specific agreements with individual exporting countries. Section 204 of the Agricultural Adjustment Act covers textiles that: 1) are in chief value of cotton, wool, or man-made fibers, any textile fibers subject to the terms of any textile trade agreement, or any combination of such fibers; 2) contain 50% or more by weight of cotton or man-made fibers, or any textile fibers subject to the terms of any textile trade agreement; 3) contain 17% or more by weight of wool; or 4) if in chief value of textile fibers or textile materials, contain a blend of cotton, wool, or man-made fibers, any textile fibers subject to the terms of any textile trade agreement, or any combination of such fibers that, in total, amount to 50% or more by weight of all component fibers.

The U.S. has Multi-Fiber Arrangements with 40 countries. Each agreement with each country is unique, and may specify quotas for a type of textile or a specific article. Visas or export licenses may be required. These agreements, however, often change. Therefore, if you are interested in importing any carpets, rugs, or other textile floor coverings, you should contact the International Trade Administration's Office of Textile and Apparel (see addresses at end of this chapter). Refer to "Prohibitions and Restrictions" below for further details.

Textile Country-of-Origin Declarations. U.S. Customs enforces CITA textile and textile product entry quotas (see "Prohibitions and Restrictions" below). Requirements for entry include submission of Country-of-Origin Declarations with every carpet, rug, and other textile floor covering shipment, regardless of whether it is subject to a specific multi-fiber arrangement (19 CFR 12.130, 12.131).

Country of Origin. Quota restrictions are country-specific and therefore are applied based on the country of origin for the textiles shipped. The last country from which a textile shipment was exported to the U.S. is not necessarily its country of origin. A textile or textile product imported into the U.S. is considered a product of the particular foreign territory or country, or a U.S. insular possession, where it is wholly grown, produced, or manufactured. For the following discussion, "country" means a foreign territory or country, or a U.S. insular possession.

In 1996, the U.S. Customs Service made major changes to country of origin rules for textile imports. The regulations at 19 CFR 102.21, "Textile and apparel products" were added to the 1996 Customs Regulations and became effective July 1, 1996. The new rules do not provide for cutting components or cutting and hemming to confer country of origin as in the past. The basis of the new law is processing operations or assembly. Some of the most important changes for importers to be aware of are:

- Cutting does not determine the country of origin (previously cutting determined country of origin for 90 percent of wearing apparel imports). The new rules are based on processing or assembly operations.

- Essential character does not determine country of origin because the new rules are based on processing.

- A subjective determination under the provisions of 19 CFR 12.130 is replaced by objective processing operations expressed in terms of tariff shifts. Dying, printing, and other finishing processes applied to fabrics no longer confer or change country of origin.

- Country of origin for textile and apparel products processed, assembled or manufactured in two or more countries is determined by where the most important processing occurs, and, if that cannot be ascertained, the last country in which an important processing operation occurs.

The country of origin is the country in which a product is wholly produced when a textile or apparel product is completely produced or manufactured (except for minor parts) in one country. For fabric, the country of origin is the country in which the fabric is woven, knitted, needled, tufted, felted, entangled or created by any other fabric-making process. The country of origin for staple yarn is the country in which yarn is spun; for filament yarn, the country in which filament is extruded; and for plied, gimped and cabled yarns, the country in which the fibers or filaments used in the yarn are spun or extruded. The country of origin of all other textile and apparel products is the country in which the components of a textile or apparel product are wholly assembled (except for minor attachments). Once again, note that assembly, not cutting, now confers country of origin.

Declarations. All importations of textiles and textile products must be accompanied by one of the following three declarations. Goods subject to Section 204, Agricultural Act of 1956, as amended, must be accompanied by either a single-country or a multiple-country declaration. Goods not subject to Section 204 must be accompanied by a negative declaration.

- **Single-country declarations** are used for entries of textiles or textile products which are wholly the growth, product, or manufacture of a single foreign country, territory, or U.S. insular possession. Information required includes: marks of identification and numbers; description of article and quantity; country of origin; and date of exportation.

- **Multiple-country declarations** are used for entries of textiles or textile products which were subjected to manufacturing or processing operations in, and/or incorporate materials originating in more than one foreign country or territory. Information required includes: marks of identification and numbers; for articles, description, quantity, identification of manufacturing and/or processing operations, country, and date of exportation; for materials used to make articles, description of materials, country of production, and date of exportation.

- **Negative declarations** must accompany all textile imports that are not subject to FFA Section 204 restrictions. Information required includes: marks of identification and numbers; descriptions of article and quantity; and country of origin.

The date of exportation to be indicated on the above declarations is the date on which the carrier leaves the last port in the country of origin, as determined by Customs. Diversion to another country during transit does not affect the export date.

Procedure for Declarations. The manufacturer, producer, exporter, or importer may prepare the declaration. If more than one of these parties is involved in the importation, each party may prepare a separate declaration. You may file a separate declaration for each invoice presented with your entry. The declaration must be dated and signed by the responsible party, and must include the person's title and the company name and address. Your shipment's entry will be denied unless it is accompanied by a properly executed declaration. Customs will not treat a textile declaration as a missing document for which a bond may be filed.

Customs will base its country-of-origin determination on the information contained in each declaration, unless the information is insufficient. If the information on the declaration is insufficient, Customs will require that you submit such additional information as will enable the determination to be made. The shipment will not be released until the determination is made. Thus, if you want to clear Customs with minimal delay, be sure that the information on the declarations is as complete as possible for each shipment.

Textile Labeling and Invoice Requirements. You are responsible for your imported textile floor covering product's compliance with applicable provisions of the TFPIA. Textile floor coverings that require labeling under TFPIA must already be labeled at entry, or the shipment will be refused. (See "Marking and Labeling Requirements" below.) If you import shipments of textile floor coverings subject to TFPIA and valued at over $500, you must provide special information on the entry invoice (see "Entry and Documentation" below).

Flammability Standards. Textile floor coverings imported into the U.S. for use in consumer products must be in compliance with the FFA, a federal law that gives the CPSC the authority and responsibility for protecting the public from the hazards of dangerously flammable items of wearing apparel and interior furnishings. Under the FFA, standards have been established for flammability of such textiles. You cannot import any textile floor covering if it fails to conform to an applicable flammability standard (FFA Section 4). Certain products may be imported into the U.S. (FFA Section 11c) for finishing or processing to render them less flammable so as to meet the standards. For these products, the exporter must state on the invoice or other paper relating to the shipment that the shipment is being made for that purpose.

The CPSC monitors imports of textiles under its Import Surveillance Program. From time to time, your textile shipments may be inspected to ascertain compliance with mandatory safety standards. Shipments may also be subject to testing by the CPSC to determine compliance. If the CPSC believes a product, fabric, or related material does not comply with a flammability standard, it is authorized to pursue a variety of legal sanctions (see "Prohibitions and Restrictions" below)

Substantial Product Hazard Reports. Any firm that obtains information that reasonably supports the conclusion that one of its products presents an unreasonable risk of serious injury or death must report that information to the CPSC's Division of Corrective Actions (CPSC address below). Importers must also report to the CPSC if 1) a type of product is the subject of at least three civil actions filed in U.S. federal or state courts, 2) each suit alleges the involvement of that product type in death or grievous bodily injury (as defined in FFA Section 37(3)1), and 3) at least three of the actions result in a final settlement with the manufacturer or in a judgment for the plaintiff within any one of the two-year periods specified in FFA Section 37(b).

Certified Hand-loomed Products. Foreign rugs made on a hand loom—that is, a nonpower-driven loom—by cottage industry producers may be entered under a special tariff category. Textile restraints may not apply to such products when exported from developing countries. A country-of-origin government official must certify your products before exportation. To enter a rug as a certified hand-loomed product, you must present the certification at the port of entry. You should mark your entry summary or withdrawal forms with the symbol "F" as a prefix to the appropriate 10-digit statistical reporting number.

Import Advisory

Importation of textiles is trade-sensitive and highly regulated. Shipments of textiles and textile products not complying with all government regulations, including quotas and visas, are subject to seizure and could result in the imposition of penalties as well as possible forfeiture of the goods. You should always verify the available quota for any textile product you plan to import before your shipment leaves the country of manufacture. Furthermore, Customs textile classification rulings change frequently, and prior administrative rulings are often modified and sometimes reversed. You should be particularly careful to comply with country of origin determination regulations, which were changed in 1996, and affect quotas and visas, marking and labeling, and other important aspects of tariff classification. See "Publications and WWW Resources" for information on important Customs Service informed compliance publications.

The Customs Service has greatly increased its scrutiny of the textile industry, one of eight primary focus industries identified in the most recent Trade Compliance & Enforcement Plan. Imported products from these industries will likely attract significant attention from Customs in the areas of compliance measurement, compliance assessment, informed compliance, and interventions.

Customs Classification

For customs purposes, carpets and other textile flooring coverings are classified under Chapter 57 of the HTSUS. This chapter is broken into major headings, which are further divided into subheadings, and often sub-subheadings, each of which has its own HTSUS classification number. For example, the 2001 HTSUS number for woven, certified hand-loomed and folklore rugs is 5702.10.10, indicating it is a sub-subcategory of "Kelem", "Schumacks", "Karamanie" and similar hand-woven rugs (5702.10.00), which is a subcategory of the major heading, carpets and other textile floor coverings, woven, etc. (5702.00.00). There are five major headings within Chapter 57.

5701—Carpets and other textile floor coverings, knotted, whether or not made up

5702—Carpets and other textile floor coverings, woven, not tufted or flocked, whether or not made up, including "Kelem", "Schumacks", "Karamanie," and similar hand-woven rugs

5703—Carpets and other textile floor coverings, tufted, whether or not made up

5704—Carpets and other textile floor coverings, of felt, not tufted or flocked, whether or not made up

5705—Other carpets and other textile floor coverings, whether or not made up

For more details regarding classifications of the specific product you are interested in importing, consult a customs broker, the appropriate commodity specialist at your nearest customs port, or the HTSUS. The 2001 HTSUS is available online from the Customs Service (www.customs.gov/impoexpo/impoexpo.htm) or for purchase from the U.S. Government Printing Office (see resources at the end of this chapter), and may be found in larger public libraries. For a general discussion of customs classification, see "Classification—Liquidation" on page 229.

Dutiable Status of Goods

For more information about duty rates and binding decisions see "Dutiable Status of Goods" on page 203; for a discussion of temporary importation of goods see "Temporary Free Importations" on page 205.

Valuation

Importers have a responsibility to use what the U.S. Customs Service deems, "reasonable care," when determining the value of their goods. They must also provide any additional information that the Customs Service needs for setting a final value on the goods. This process involves a number of factors and can be somewhat complicated; importers must be aware of applicable issues and details. Valuation information applies to all types of commodities, for further discussion on the subject see "Customs Valuation" on page 267.

Import Duties

Import duties vary (often dramatically) depending upon the Harmonized Tariff Schedule (HTSUS) classification of the goods or products imported. Since some products that look alike have different HTSUS classifications and different rates of duty, proper classification is vital. Note that "differences of opinion" between importers and the Bureau of Customs and Border Protection regarding classification keeps customs attorneys very busy.

Import duties can be assessed on the imported value of the goods ("ad valorem" rates of duty such as 2%, 4.4%, 50%, etc.), total units or weight of the goods ("specific" rates of duty such as 2 cents each or 1.5 cents/pound, etc.) or on a combination basis ("compound" rates of duty such as 5 cents each plus 6%).

Listed below is a sampling of several Column 1 import duty rates for Chapter 57 products:
Other carpets and other textile floor coverings, whether or not made up of coir (5705.00.10.00): Free
to
Of other textile materials of cotton (5702.99.10): 6.9%

For specific information on US import duties refer to the Harmonized Tariff Schedule of the US. The print version is available from the US Government Printing Office as well as third party suppliers who often add special features. Online versions are available in both static PDF pages as well as in formats with excellent search functionality. Search the Web with the term "Harmonized Tariff Schedule" to find sources.

Entry and Documentation

The entry of merchandise is a two-part process consisting of 1) filing the documentation necessary to determine whether merchandise may be released from Customs custody, and 2) filing the documents that contain information for duty assessment and statistical purposes. In certain instances, all documents must be filed and accepted by Customs prior to release of the goods. Unless you have been granted an extension, you must file entry documents at a location specified by the port or area director within five working days of your shipment's date of arrival at a U.S. port of entry. These include a number of standard documents required by Customs for any entry, and:

- U.S. Customs Country-of-Origin Declaration Form CF 3229
- Export documentation and/or visa for textiles subject to Multi-Fiber Arrangement
- Certification for products entered as Certified Hand-loomed Products

After you present the entry, Customs may examine your shipment or may waive examination. The shipment is then released provided no legal or regulatory violations have been noted. You must then file entry summary documentation and deposit estimated duties at a designated customhouse within 10 working days of your shipment's release. For a detailed description of entry procedures, standard documentation, and informal entry, see "Entry Process" on page 185.

Informed Compliance. Informed compliance was introduced with the Customs Modernization Act of 1993 (Mod Act) and defines the relationship between importers and the Customs Service. It sets out the responsibilities of both parties. Providing the correct documentation and information for entry is a key factor that will make your importing operation run smoothly. We recommend that importers become familiar with the concept of informed comliance and the responsibilities that they have under the Mod Act. For further discussion about informed compliance see "Informed Compliance" on page 211.

NAFTA Certificates of Origin. An importer of textiles for which NAFTA treatment is sought need not file a separate NAFTA Certificate of Origin in addition to the Customs Country-of-Origin Declaration. The declaration is sufficient. However, the importer must take care to submit a declaration from each U.S., Canadian, or Mexican producer or manufacturer. Thus, for multiple producers or manufacturers, a separate declaration must be filed for each. If a Customs port director cannot determine the country of origin because the declaration is absent or incomplete, the shipment is not entitled to preferential NAFTA tariff treatment or other NAFTA benefits. See 19 CFR 12.132.

Entry Invoice TFPIA Requirements. For the purpose of TFPIA enforcement, a commercial shipment of textile products exceeding $500 in value and subject to TFPIA labeling requirements must show the following information: 1) The constituent fiber or combination of fibers, designating with equal prominence each natural or manufactured fiber by its generic name, in order of predominance by weight if the weight of such fiber is 5% or more of the total fiber weight of the product; 2) percentage of each fiber present, by weight, in the total fiber content; 3) the name or other identification issued and registered by the FTC of the manufacturer of the product or one or more persons subject to Section 3 of the TFPIA with respect to such product; and 4) the name of the country where processed or manufactured. For more general information about invoices see "Invoices" on page 277.

Note: The Entry and Documentation section has been carefully designed to supply you, the importer, with sample documents and directions on how to satisfy Customs requirements. Be aware that you should consult the applicable authorities to ensure that you are correctly following the most current procedures.

Prohibitions and Restrictions

Textile Quotas. Textile import restrictions are primarily a matter of quotas and the way in which these quotas are administered and monitored. Under the Multi-Fiber Arrangement provisions of Section 204 of the Agricultural Adjustment Act, CITA has negotiated Multi-Fiber Arrangements with 40 countries. These Agreements may impose quotas for a type of textile or a specific article, and they are country-specific. The agreements, however, often change. Therefore, if you are interested in importing any textile floor coverings, you should contact the International Trade Administration's Office of Textile and Apparel (see addresses at end of this chapter). The Office of Textile and Apparel has a team of country specialists who can inform you of the latest developments and inform you about a product's quota or restriction status.

U.S. Customs enforces CITA textile and textile product entry quotas. If formal entry procedures are not followed, Customs will usually refuse entry for textiles that are subject to Section 204. Formal entry requires submission of a Country-of-Origin Declaration (see General Considerations above). U.S. Customs maintains a current textile quota status report, available for perusal at any Customs port. In addition, U.S. Customs in Washington, DC, provides quota status reports online, which are updated on a regular basis (www.customs.gov/impoexpo/impoexpo.htm).

Flammable Fabrics. U.S. Customs may refuse entry for any article of wearing apparel or interior furnishing, or any fabric or related material that is intended for use or that may be used in wearing apparel or interior furnishings, if it fails to conform to an applicable flammability standard issued under Section 4 of the FFA. An exception is allowed for certain products (FFA Section 11c) that are imported for finishing or processing to bring them within the legal standard. For these products, the exporter must state on the invoice or other paper relating to the shipment that the shipment is being made for that purpose.

The CPSC, as the primary enforcement agency of flammability standards, inspects products for compliance with the FFA. If the CPSC believes a product, fabric, or related material does not comply with a flammability standard, it is authorized to pursue a variety of legal sanctions, including: 1) seizure, condemnation, and forfeiture of the noncomplying products; 2) administrative cease-and-desist order requiring an individual or firm to stop sale and distribution of the noncomplying products or; 3) temporary injunction requiring the individual or firm to stop sale and distribution of the noncomplying products, pending final disposition of an administrative cease-and-desist proceeding. The CPSC also has authority to seek civil penalties against any person who knowingly violates a regulation or standard issued under Section 4 of the FFA.

Country-Specific Restrictions

Multi-Fiber Arrangements. Restrictions under Multi-Fiber Arrangements are country-specific. A product originating in one country may be subject to quota and to export license or visa requirements, while the same product originating in a different country may not. At present, the U.S. has Multi-Fiber Arrangements with 40 countries. Many different categories of products are covered under these Arrangements; it is beyond the scope of this book to list each country and its restricted commodities. If you are interested in importing textiles and textile products, you should contact the International Trade Administration's Office of Textile and Apparel (see addresses at end of this chapter) or U.S. Customs to ascertain your product's restraint status.

The U.S. Customs service provides quota reports on their website (www.customs.gov/impoexpo/impoexpo.htm). These reports are constantly updated and have an effective date noted. The most recent quota information can be accessed by clicking on the country name that interests you. This location holds information regarding quotas, transshipments, and visa requirements.

Iranian Carpets. Iranian carpets and rugs that were still in Iran as of October 29, 1987, may not be imported into the United States. There are some exceptions for carpets imported together with household goods by the owner. If it can be established that they left Iran before that date, they may then be commercially imported, but only after a license has been obtained from the Office of Foreign Assets Control (see addresses at end of this chapter).

Marking and Labeling Requirements

TFPIA Requirements. All textile fiber products imported into the U.S. must be stamped, tagged, labeled, or otherwise marked with the following information as required by the TFPIA, unless exempt from marking (see TFPIA, Section 12): 1) the generic names and percentages by weight of the constituent fibers present in the textile fiber product, exclusive of permissible ornamentation, in amounts of more than 5% in order of predominance by weight, with any percentage of fiber or fibers required to be designated as "other fiber" or "other fibers" (including those present in amounts of 5% or less) appearing last; and 2) the name of the manufacturer or the name or registered identification number issued by the FTC of one or more persons marketing or handling the textile fiber product; and 3) the name of the country where processed. A word

trademark, used as a house mark and registered with the U.S. Patent Office, may appear on labels instead of the name otherwise required, provided the owner of the trademark furnishes a copy of the registration to the FTC prior to use. (See "Registered Identification Numbers" below.)

The information listed above is not exhaustive. TFPIA requirements are extensive. The Act specifies such details as types of labels, means of attachment, label position on the article, package labeling, unit labeling for two-piece garments, and arrangement of information on the label; allowable fiber designations; country-of-origin indications; requirements for trim and ornamentation, linings and interlinings, and pile fabrics; sectional disclosure; use of trade names and trademarks; and requirements for swatches and samples. The FTC publishes a booklet intended to clarify TFPIA requirements to facilitate voluntary compliance in the industry (see "Publications and WWW Resources" below). It is available on request, at no charge, from the FTC (see addresses at end of this chapter).

The Care Labeling Rule. Regulations under this rule require manufacturers and importers of textile clothing and fabrics to attach specific care instructions for washing or dry cleaning, as well as information on the fiber composition of the article. They are enforced by the FTC Division of Enforcement. The Care Labeling Rule was amended September 2000, detailed information is available on the FTC website (www.ftc.gov/os/statutes/textilejump.htm).

Registered Identification Numbers. Any domestic firm or person residing in the U.S. and engaged in the manufacture or marketing of textile products covered under the TFPIA may obtain an FTC-registered identification number for use on required tags and labels instead of the name of a firm or person. For applications, contact the FTC (address below.)

For a general discussion of U.S. Customs marking and labeling requirements, see "Country of Origin Marking" on page 236, "Special Marking Requirements" on page 238 and "Marking—False Impression" on page 239.

Shipping Considerations

You will need to ensure that your goods are packaged and shipped with care so that they pass smoothly through Customs and arrive in good condition. You are responsible for ensuring that the shipment is in compliance with all applicable government regulations for packaging and shipping. In most instances, you should not leave these arrangements solely to the discretion of your supplier. Careful preparation of the cargo and selection of the mode of transport can be essential to a cost-effective, timely delivery of undamaged goods. We strongly advise you to consult your shipping representative, insurance agent, or freight broker for advice on packing and shipping.

Textile floor coverings may be shipped in bulk, bolts, rolls, or other types of containers, depending on the type of product and whether it is prepackaged. General considerations include protection from contamination, weather, and pests. Safety precautions should also be implemented as required to protect against breakage, spillage, corrosion of containers, and combustion. Containers should be constructed so as to be safe for handling during transport.

Publications and WWW Resources

The following publication may be relevant to the importation of textile floor coverings:

> *Threading Your Way Through the Labeling Requirements Under the Textile and Wool Acts*

Available free of charge on request from the Federal Trade Commission and online from the FTC website (www.ftc.gov/bcp/conline/pubs/buspubs/thread.htm). This publication is an excellent source of information written in clear lay language. We recommend that anyone interested in importing textile fiber products but unfamiliar with the regulations obtain a copy of each of this booklet.

The U.S. Customs Service launched a series of "Informed Compliance" publications in 1996, which are available from the Customs Service website (www.customs.gov/impoexpo/impoexpo.htm). Of particular interest:

What Every Member of the Trade Community Should Know About Textile & Apparel Rules of Origin

What Every Member of the Trade community Should Know About NAFTA for Textiles and Textile Articles

Fibers & Yarns Construction and Classification Under the HTSUS

The *Harmonized Tariff Schedule of the United States (2001)* (HTSUS) is available to view on the Customs Service website (www.customs.gov), or you may purchase a printed version from:

U.S. Government Printing Office
Superintendent of Documents
710 North Capital Street NW
Washington DC 20401
Tel: (202) 512-1800
Fax: (202) 512-1657
Website: www.access.gpo.gov

The USGPO also has copies of specific laws available for purchase. The USGPO accepts orders made by fax, phone or placed over the Internet, as well as mail orders paid by credit card. All orders must be accompanied by payment. Credit cards, checks drawn on a U.S. bank, or an international money order are all acceptable.

Relevant Government Agencies

Address your questions regarding textile Multi-Fiber Arrangements to:

U.S. Department of Commerce
International Trade Administration
Office of Textiles and Apparel
Director's Office
14th and Constitution Ave. NW, Rm. H3100
Washington, DC 20230
Tel: (202) 482-5078
Fax: (202) 482-2331
Agreements Division: (202) 482-4212
Website: http://otexa.ita.doc.gov

Address your questions regarding the Flammable Fabrics Act (FFA) to:

Consumer Product Safety Commission (CPSC)
Office of Compliance
Washington DC 20207-0001
Tel: 800-638-2772 or (301) 504-7912
Fax: (301) 504-0359
Website: www.cpsc.gov

Address your questions regarding requirements under the Textile Fiber Products Identification Act (TFPIA) to:

Federal Trade Commission (FTC)
Division of Enforcement
600 Pennsylvania Avenue NW
Washington DC 20580
Tel: (202) 326-2996
Website: www.ftc.gov

Address your questions regarding licenses for Iranian carpets and rugs to:

U.S. Treasury Department
Office of Foreign Assets Control
1500 Pennsylvania Avenue NW
Washington DC 20220

Tel: (202) 622-2500
Compliance: 622-2490
OFAC Fax-on-Demand: (202) 622-0077
Website: www.treas.gov/ofac

Address your questions regarding textile quotas to:

U.S. Customs and Border Protection
Office of Field Operations, Quota Branch
1300 Pennsylvania Avenue NW
Washington DC 20229
Tel: (202) 927-5850
Website: www.customs.treas.gov

The U.S. Customs Service provices updated status reports on textile quota on their web site (see address above). If the country you need information on is not listed, call the Quota Branch office at (202) 927-5850.

Address your questions regarding textile floor covering imports to your local Customs port director. For addresses, refer to "U.S. Customs and Border Protection Offices" on page 65 or contact:

U.S. Customs and Border Protection
Customs Headquarters
1300 Pennsylvania Avenue NW
Washington DC 20229
Tel: (202) 354-1000
Website: www.customs.treas.gov

Laws and Regulations

The following laws and regulations may be relevant to the importation of textile floor coverings. The laws are contained in the United States Code (USC), and the regulations are published in the Code of Federal Regulations (CFR), both of which are available at larger public and law libraries. Copies of specific laws are also available from the United States Government Printing Office (address above).

7 USC 1854
Textile Trade Agreements
(EO 11651, as amended by EO 11951 and 12188, and supplemented by EO 12475)
This Act authorizes the CITA of the DOC to enter into Multi-Fiber Agreements with other countries to control trade in textiles and establishes the Textile Import Program, which is enforced by U.S. Customs.

19 CFR 12.130 et seq.
Regulations on Entry of Textiles
These regulations provide the requirements and procedures followed by Customs in enforcing limitations on the importation and entry and withdrawal of textiles and textile products from warehouses for consumption in the U.S.

15 USC 70-77
Textile Fiber Products Identification Act (TFPIA)
This Act prohibits false or deceptive labeling (misbranding) and false advertising of any textile fiber products and requires all textile fiber products imported into the U.S. to be labeled in accordance with the requirements set forth in the law.

19 CFR 11.12b; 16 CFR 303 et seq.
Regulations on Labeling and Marking
These regulations detail the labeling and marking requirements for textiles as specified by the CPSC and the invoice contents required by U.S. Customs for purpose of enforcing the labeling and marking rules.

15 USC 1191-1204
Flammable Fabrics Act (FFA)
This Act provides for the setting of flammability standards for fabric by the Consumer Product Safety Commission (CPSC) and for enforcement by U.S. Customs.

16 CFR 1610, 1611, 1615, 1616, 1630-1632

Regulations on Flammable Fabric Standards
These regulations specify the flammability standards adopted by the CPSC under the FFA for various types of textiles.

16 CFR 423
Care Labeling Rule
Requires fiber composition and washing or dry cleaning instructions for textile apparel and certain piece goods.

Principal Exporting Countries

The following listing includes samples of the main supplier nations of the products of this chapter. It is organized by HTSUS major heading. (Refer to "Customs Classification" above for the product codes.) Countries are listed in rank order of the value of products imported to the U.S. Statistics represent customs value of entries for 2002 from the Bureau of Census.

5701—India, Iran, Pakistan, China, Nepal, Turkey, Romania, Egypt

5702—India, Belgium, Egypt, United Kingdom, China, Ireland, Spain, Canada

5703—Canada, China, India, Egypt, Belgium, Germany, South Korea, Thailand

5704—Netherlands, Canada, United Kingdom, Belgium, China, Germany, South Korea

5705—China, India, Mexico, United Kingdom, Canada, Bulgaria, Turkey, Netherlands

Chapter 58:
Special Woven Fabrics

Full title: Special Woven Fabrics; Tufted Textile Fabrics; Lace; Tapestries; Trimmings; Embroidery

This chapter relates to the importation of special woven fabrics, which are classified under Chapter 58 of the Harmonized Tariff Schedule of the United States (HTSUS). Specifically, it includes woven pile and chenille fabrics, terry cloth and tufted textile fabrics, gauze, tulles and other net fabric, lace, hand-woven and needle-work tapestries, labels and similar articles of textile materials, braids, pompons, tassels, and other ornamental trimmings, woven fabrics of metal thread and metalized yarn, embroidery articles, and quilted textile products.

If you are interested in importing sewing thread, yarns, and other fibers or filaments, you should refer to Commodity Index Chapters 50 through 55. Articles of cordage are covered in Chapter 56, hair-nets are classified as headgear under Chapter 65, and special woven fabrics incorporated into footwear are covered under Chapter 64. If you are interested in importing articles created from glass fibers, read Chapter 58. For importing special woven fabrics as part of toys, games, or sports equipment, refer to Chapter 95. The import requirements for impregnated, coated, covered, or laminated textile fabrics and textile articles suitable for industrial use are found in Chapter 59.

Note: To understand key issues that will enable you to make best use of the information in this section we recommend that you see "Introduction" on page 425.

Key Factors

The key factors in the importation of special woven fabrics are:

- Compliance with quota restraints and visa requirements
- Submission of U.S. Customs Country-of-Origin Declaration(s)
- Compliance with entry invoice requirements
- Compliance with labeling requirements under Textile Fiber Products Identification Act (TFPIA) and/or the Wool Products Labeling Act (WPLA) and the Care Labeling Rule
- Compliance with flammability standards adopted and enforced by the Consumer Product Safety Commission (CPSC) under the Flammable Fabrics Act (FFA)

Although most importers use the services of a licensed customs broker in making their entries, and we recommend this practice, you should be aware of the regulatory, entry, and documentation issues involved in importing your product. You, as importer, are ultimately responsible for the fulfillment of any legal requirements applicable to your shipment.

General Considerations

Regulatory Agencies. The DOC's Committee for Implementation of Textile Agreements (CITA) regulates certain textile imports under Section 204 of the Agricultural Adjustment Act. U.S. Customs enforces CITA textile and textile product entry quotas. Customs also enforces compliance with labeling and invoice requirements of the TFPIA and flammability standards under the FFA. The CPSC monitors imports and from time to time inspects textile shipments for compliance with FFA standards. If you are importing wool textiles, importation is subject to complex textile import regulations. The Federal Trade Commission (FTC) administers the WPLA requirements.

Wool Product Entry Requirements. Depending on the nature of your wool fabric imports, as many as three different types of special entry documents may be required. First, for all imported textile fibers, yarns, and fabrics covered by the Agricultural Adjustment Act (AAA), including wool, you must file a U.S. Customs Textile Entry Declaration (see "Textile Country-of-Origin Declarations" below). Second, for all wool products subject to the WPLA, special information is required on the entry invoices (see "Entry and Documentation" below). Finally, certain wool articles manufactured or produced in certain countries may be subject to quotas under U.S. Department of Commerce Multi-Fiber Arrangements. Such products require export certificates or visas issued by the appropriate country of origin, in addition to other requisite entry paperwork (see "Quotas" below).

Wool Products Labeling Act. The term "wool product" means any product or any portion of a product that contains, purports to contain, or in any way is represented as containing wool, reprocessed wool, or reused wool. All wool products imported into the U.S., except those made more than 20 years before importation, and except carpets, rugs, mats, and upholsteries, must have affixed a stamp, tag, label, or other means of identification as required by the WPLA. If you are importing wool products exempt from labeling under the WPLA, do not assume they are also exempt from labeling under the TFPIA. These are two distinct laws, with some overlapping requirements (see "Marking and Labeling Requirements" below).

Textile Quotas. If you are interested in importing special woven fabrics, the most important issue you need to be aware of is quotas. Under the Multi-Fiber Arrangement provisions of Section 204 of the Agricultural Adjustment Act, CITA initiates specific agreements with individual exporting countries. Section 204 of the Agricultural Adjustment Act covers textiles that: 1) are in chief value of cotton, wool, or man-made fibers, any textile fibers subject to the terms of any textile trade agreement, or any combination of such fibers; 2) contain 50% or more by weight of cotton or man-made fibers, or any textile fibers subject to the terms of any textile trade agreement; 3) contain 17% or more by weight of wool; or 4) if in chief value of textile fibers or textile materials, contain a blend of cotton, wool, or man-made fibers, any textile fibers subject to the terms of any textile trade agreement, or any combination of such fibers that, in total, amount to 50% or more by weight of all component fibers.

The U.S. has Multi-Fiber Arrangements with 40 countries. Each agreement with each country is unique, and may specify quotas for a type of textile or a specific article. Visas or export licenses may be required. These agreements, however, often change. Therefore, if you are interested in importing any special woven fabrics, you should contact the International Trade Administration's Office of Textile and Apparel (see addresses at end of this chapter). Refer to "Prohibitions and Restrictions" below for further details.

Textile Country-of-Origin Declarations. U.S. Customs enforces CITA textile and textile product entry quotas (see "Prohibitions

and Restrictions" below). Requirements for entry include submission of Country-of-Origin Declarations with every special woven fabric shipment, regardless of whether it is subject to a specific multi-fiber arrangement (19 CFR 12.130, 12.131).

Country of Origin. Quota restrictions are country-specific and therefore are applied based on the country of origin for the textiles shipped. The last country from which a textile shipment was exported to the U.S. is not necessarily its country of origin. A textile or textile product imported into the U.S. is considered a product of the particular foreign territory or country, or a U.S. insular possession, where it is wholly grown, produced, or manufactured. For the following discussion, "country" means a foreign territory or country, or a U.S. insular possession.

In 1996, the U.S. Customs Service made major changes to country of origin rules for textile imports. The regulations at 19 CFR 102.21, "Textile and apparel products" were added to the 1996 Customs Regulations and became effective July 1, 1996. The new rules do not provide for cutting components or cutting and hemming to confer country of origin as in the past. The basis of the new law is processing operations or assembly. Some of the most important changes for importers to be aware of are:

- Cutting does not determine the country of origin (previously cutting determined country of origin for 90 percent of wearing apparel imports). The new rules are based on processing or assembly operations.

- Essential character does not determine country of origin because the new rules are based on processing.

- A subjective determination under the provisions of 19 CFR 12.130 is replaced by objective processing operations expressed in terms of tariff shifts. Dying, printing, and other finishing processes applied to fabrics no longer confer or change country of origin.

- Country of origin for textile and apparel products processed, assembled or manufactured in two or more countries is determined by where the most important processing occurs, and, if that cannot be ascertained, the last country in which an important processing operation occurs.

The country of origin is the country in which a product is wholly produced when a textile or apparel product is completely produced or manufactured (except for minor parts) in one country. For fabric, the country of origin is the country in which the fabric is woven, knitted, needled, tufted, felted, entangled or created by any other fabric-making process. The country of origin for staple yarn is the country in which yarn is spun; for filament yarn, the country in which filament is extruded; and for plied, gimped and cabled yarns, the country in which the fibers or filaments used in the yarn are spun or extruded. The country of origin of all other textile and apparel products is the country in which the components of a textile or apparel product are wholly assembled (except for minor attachments). Once again, note that assembly, not cutting, now confers country of origin.

Declarations. All importations of textiles and textile products must be accompanied by one of the following three declarations. Goods subject to Section 204, Agricultural Act of 1956, as amended, must be accompanied by either a single-country or a multiple-country declaration. Goods not subject to Section 204 must be accompanied by a negative declaration.

- **Single-country declarations** are used for entries of textiles or textile products which are wholly the growth, product, or manufacture of a single foreign country, territory, or U.S. insular possession. Information required includes: marks of identification and numbers; description of article and quantity; country of origin; and date of exportation.

- **Multiple-country declarations** are used for entries of textiles or textile products which were subjected to manufacturing or processing operations in, and/or incorporate materials originating in more than one foreign country or territory. Information required includes: marks of identification and numbers; for articles, description, quantity, identification of manufacturing and/or processing operations, country, and date of exportation; for materials used to make articles, description of materials, country of production, and date of exportation.

- **Negative declarations** must accompany all textile imports that are not subject to FFA Section 204 restrictions. Information required includes: marks of identification and numbers; descriptions of article and quantity; and country of origin.

The date of exportation to be indicated on the above declarations is the date on which the carrier leaves the last port in the country of origin, as determined by Customs. Diversion to another country during transit does not affect the export date.

Procedure for Declarations. The manufacturer, producer, exporter, or importer may prepare the declaration. If more than one of these parties is involved in the importation, each party may prepare a separate declaration. You may file a separate declaration for each invoice presented with your entry. The declaration must be dated and signed by the responsible party, and must include the person's title and the company name and address. Your shipment's entry will be denied unless it is accompanied by a properly executed declaration. Customs will not treat a textile declaration as a missing document for which a bond may be filed.

Customs will base its country-of-origin determination on the information contained in each declaration, unless the information is insufficient. If the information on the declaration is insufficient, Customs will require that you submit such additional information as will enable the determination to be made. The shipment will not be released until the determination is made. Thus, if you want to clear Customs with minimal delay, be sure that the information on the declarations is as complete as possible for each shipment.

Textile Labeling and Invoice Requirements. You are responsible for your imported special woven fabric product's compliance with applicable provisions of the TFPIA. Special woven fabrics that require labeling under TFPIA must already be labeled at entry, or the shipment will be refused. (See "Marking and Labeling Requirements" below.) If you import shipments of special woven fabrics subject to TFPIA and valued at over $500, you must provide special information on the entry invoice (see "Entry and Documentation" below).

Flammability Standards. Special woven fabric products imported into the U.S. for use in consumer products must be in compliance with the FFA, a federal law that gives the CPSC the authority and responsibility for protecting the public from the hazards of dangerously flammable items of wearing apparel and interior furnishings. Under the FFA, standards have been established for flammability of clothing textiles. You cannot import any article of wearing apparel or interior furnishing, or any fabric or related material that is intended for use or that may be used in such items, if it fails to conform to an applicable flammability standard (FFA Section 4). Certain products may be imported into the U.S. (FFA Section 11c) for finishing or processing to render them less flammable so as to meet the standards. For these products, the exporter must state on the invoice or other paper relating to the shipment that the shipment is being made for that purpose.

The CPSC monitors imports of textiles under its Import Surveillance Program. From time to time, your textile shipments may be inspected to ascertain compliance with mandatory safety standards. Shipments may also be subject to testing by the CPSC to determine compliance. If the CPSC believes a product, fabric, or related material does not comply with a flammability standard, it is authorized to pursue a variety of legal sanctions (see "Prohibitions and Restrictions" below).

Substantial Product Hazard Reports. Any firm that obtains information that reasonably supports the conclusion that one of its products presents an unreasonable risk of serious injury or death must report that information to the CPSC's Division of Corrective Actions (CPSC address below). Importers must also report to the CPSC if 1) a type of product is the subject of at least three civil actions filed in U.S. federal or state courts, 2) each suit alleges the involvement of that product type in death or grievous bodily injury (as defined in FFA Section 37(3)1), and 3) at least three of the actions result in a final settlement with the manufacturer or in a judgment for the plaintiff within any one of the two-year periods specified in FFA Section 37(b).

Import Advisory

Importation of textiles is trade-sensitive and highly regulated. Shipments of textiles and textile products not complying with all government regulations, including quotas and visas, are subject to seizure and could result in the imposition of penalties as well as possible forfeiture of the goods. You should always verify the available quota for any textile product you plan to import before your shipment leaves the country of manufacture. Furthermore, Customs textile classification rulings change frequently, and prior administrative rulings are often modified and sometimes reversed. You should be particularly careful to comply with country of origin determination regulations, which were changed in 1996, and affect quotas and visas, marking and labeling, and other important aspects of tariff classification. See "Publications and WWW Resources" for information on important Customs Service informed compliance publications.

The Customs Service has greatly increased its scrutiny of the textile industry, one of eight primary focus industries identified in the most recent Trade Compliance & Enforcement Plan. Imported products from these industries will likely attract significant attention from Customs in the areas of compliance measurement, compliance assessment, informed compliance, and interventions.

Customs Classification

For customs purposes, special woven fabrics are classified under Chapter 58 of the HTSUS. This chapter is broken into major headings, which are further divided into subheadings, and often sub-subheadings, each of which has its own HTSUS classification number. For example, the 2001 HTSUS number for gauze made of man-made fibers is 5803.90.30, indicating it is a sub-subcategory of gauze of other textile materials (5803.90.00), which is a subcategory of the major heading gauze, other than narrow fabrics of heading 5806 (5803.00.00). There are 11 major headings within Chapter 56.

5801—Woven pile fabrics and chenille fabrics, other than fabrics of heading 5802 or 5806

5802—Terry toweling and similar woven terry fabrics, other than narrow fabrics of heading 5806; tufted textile fabrics, other than products of heading 5703

5803—Gauze, other than narrow fabrics of heading 5806

5804—Tulles and other net fabrics, not including woven, knitted or crocheted fabrics; lace in the piece, in strips, or in motifs, other than fabrics of heading 6002

5805—Hand-woven tapestries of the type Gobelins, Flanders, Aubusson, Beauvais, and the like, and needle-worked tapestries (for example, petit point, cross stitch), whether or not made up

5806—Narrow woven fabrics, other than goods of heading 5807; narrow fabrics consisting of warp without weft assembled by means of an adhesive (bolducs)

5807—Labels, badges, and similar articles of textile materials, in the piece, in strips or cut to shape or size, not embroidered

5808—Braids in the piece; ornamental trimmings in the piece, without embroidery, other than knitted or crocheted; tassels, pompons, and similar articles

5809—Woven fabrics of metal thread and woven fabrics of metalized yarn of heading 5605, of a kind used in apparel, as furnishing fabrics, or for similar purposes, not elsewhere specified or included

5810—Embroidery in the piece, in strips or in motifs

5811—Quilted textile products in the piece, composed of one or more layers of textile materials assembled with padding by stitching or otherwise, other than embroidery of heading 5810

For more details regarding classifications of the specific product you are interested in importing, consult a customs broker, the appropriate commodity specialist at your nearest customs port, or the HTSUS. The 2001 HTSUS is available online from the Customs Service (www.customs.gov/impoexpo/impoexpo.htm) or for purchase from the U.S. Government Printing Office (see resources at the end of this chapter), and may be found in larger public libraries. For a general discussion of customs classification, see "Classification—Liquidation" on page 229.

Dutiable Status of Goods

For more information about duty rates and binding decisions see "Dutiable Status of Goods" on page 203; for a discussion of temporary importation of goods see "Temporary Free Importations" on page 205.

Valuation

Importers have a responsibility to use what the U.S. Customs Service deems, "reasonable care," when determining the value of their goods. They must also provide any additional information that the Customs Service needs for setting a final value on the goods. This process involves a number of factors and can be somewhat complicated; importers must be aware of applicable issues and details. Valuation information applies to all types of commodities, for further discussion on the subject see "Customs Valuation" on page 267.

Import Duties

Import duties vary (often dramatically) depending upon the Harmonized Tariff Schedule (HTSUS) classification of the goods or products imported. Since some products that look alike have different HTSUS classifications and different rates of duty, proper classification is vital. Note that "differences of opinion" between importers and the Bureau of Customs and Border Protection regarding classification keeps customs attorneys very busy.

Import duties can be assessed on the imported value of the goods ("ad valorem" rates of duty such as 2%, 4.4%, 50%, etc.), total units or weight of the goods ("specific" rates of duty such as 2 cents each or 1.5 cents/pound, etc.) or on a combination basis ("compound" rates of duty such as 5 cents each plus 6%).

Listed below is a sampling of several Column 1 import duty rates for Chapter 58 products:
Hand-woven tapestries fit only for use as wall hangings and valued over $215 per square meter (5805.00.10.00): Free

to

Fabrics consisting of warp without weft assembled by means of an adhesive (bolducs) (5806.40.00.00): 8.8%
For specific information on US import duties refer to the Harmonized Tariff Schedule of the US. The print version is available from the US Government Printing Office as well as third party suppliers who often add special features. Online versions are available in both static PDF pages as well as in formats with ex-cellent search functionality. Search the Web with the term "Harmonized Tariff Schedule" to find sources.

Entry and Documentation

The entry of merchandise is a two-part process consisting of 1) filing the documentation necessary to determine whether merchandise may be released from Customs custody, and 2) filing the documents that contain information for duty assessment and statistical purposes. In certain instances, all documents must be filed and accepted by Customs prior to release of the goods. Unless you have been granted an extension, you must file entry documents at a location specified by the port or area director within five working days of your shipment's date of arrival at a U.S. port of entry. These include a number of standard documents required by Customs for any entry, and:

- U.S. Customs Country-of-Origin Declaration Form CF 3229

- Export documentation and/or visa for textiles subject to Multi-Fiber Arrangement

After you present the entry, Customs may examine your shipment or may waive examination. The shipment is then released provided no legal or regulatory violations have been noted. You must then file entry summary documentation and deposit estimated duties at a designated customhouse within 10 working days of your shipment's release. For a detailed description of entry procedures, standard documentation, and informal entry, see "Entry Process" on page 185.

Informed Compliance. Informed compliance was introduced with the Customs Modernization Act of 1993 (Mod Act) and defines the relationship between importers and the Customs Service. It sets out the responsibilities of both parties. Providing the correct documentation and information for entry is a key factor that will make your importing operation run smoothly. We recommend that importers become familiar with the concept of informed comliance and the responsibilities that they have under the Mod Act. For further discussion about informed compliance see "Informed Compliance" on page 211.

NAFTA Certificates of Origin. An importer of textiles for which NAFTA treatment is sought need not file a separate NAFTA Certificate of Origin in addition to the Customs Country-of-Origin Declaration. The declaration is sufficient. However, the importer must take care to submit a declaration from each U.S., Canadian, or Mexican producer or manufacturer. Thus, for multiple producers or manufacturers, a separate declaration must be filed for each. If a Customs port director cannot determine the country of origin because the declaration is absent or incomplete, the shipment is not entitled to preferential NAFTA tariff treatment or other NAFTA benefits. See 19 CFR 12.132.

Entry Invoices. You must provide certain additional information on the entry invoice for special woven fabric products. The specific information varies depending on the nature of your product, as noted below.

TFPIA Requirements. For the purpose of TFPIA enforcement, a commercial shipment of textile products exceeding $500 in value and subject to TFPIA labeling requirements must show the following information: 1) the constituent fiber or combination of fibers, designating with equal prominence each natural or manufactured fiber by its generic name, in order of predominance by weight if the weight of such fiber is 5% or more of the total fiber weight of the product; 2) percentage of each fiber present, by weight, in the total fiber content; 3) the name or other identification issued and registered by the Federal Trade Commission of the manufacturer of the product or one or more persons subject to Section 3 of the TFPIA with respect to such product; 4) the name of the country where processed or manufactured.

Wool Products Subject to WPLA. When you offer for entry a wool product shipment valued at over $500 and subject to WP-LA, you must include certain information intended to facilitate Customs monitoring and enforcement of that Act. This extra information is identical to that required by WPLA on labeling (see "Marking and Labeling Requirements" below), with the addition of the manufacturer's name. If your product consists of mixed waste, residues, and similar merchandise obtained from several suppliers or unknown sources, you may omit the manufacturer's name from the entry invoice.

Invoice for Madeira Embroideries. The entry invoice for Madeira embroideries must show the following information: 1) about the materials used: a) country of production; b) width of the material in the piece; c) name of the manufacturer; d) kind of material (indicating manufacturer's quality number); e) landed cost of the material used in each item; f) date of the order; g) date of the invoice; h) invoice unit value in the currency of the purchase; i) discount from purchase price allowed, if any; 2) about the finished embroidered articles: a) manufacturer's name, design number, and quality number; b) importer's design number, if any; c) finished size; d) number of embroidery points per unit of quantity; and e) total for overhead and profit added in arriving at the price or value of the merchandise covered by the invoice. For more general information about invoices see "Invoices" on page 277.

Note: The Entry and Documentation section has been carefully designed to supply you, the importer, with sample documents and directions on how to satisfy Customs requirements. Be aware that you should consult the applicable authorities to ensure that you are correctly following the most current procedures.

Prohibitions and Restrictions

Textile Quotas. Textile import restrictions are primarily a matter of quotas and the way in which these quotas are administered and monitored. Under the Multi-Fiber Arrangement provisions of Section 204 of the Agricultural Adjustment Act, CITA has negotiated Multi-Fiber Arrangements with 40 countries. These Agreements may impose quotas for a type of textile or a specific article, and they are country-specific. The agreements, however, often change. Therefore, if you are interested in importing any special woven fabric products, you should contact the International Trade Administration's Office of Textile and Apparel (see addresses at end of this chapter). The Office of Textile and Apparel has a team of country specialists who can inform you of the latest developments and inform you about a product's quota or restriction status.

U.S. Customs enforces CITA textile and textile product entry quotas. If formal entry procedures are not followed, Customs will usually refuse entry for textiles that are subject to Section 204. Formal entry requires submission of a Country-of-Origin Declaration (see "General Considerations" above). U.S. Customs maintains a current textile quota status report, available for perusal at any Customs port. In addition, U.S. Customs in Washington, DC, provides quota status reports online, which are updated on a regular basis (www.customs.gov/impoexpo/impoexpo.htm).

Flammable Fabrics. U.S. Customs may refuse entry for any article of wearing apparel or interior furnishing, or any fabric or related material that is intended for use or that may be used in wearing apparel or interior furnishings, if it fails to conform to an applicable flammability standard issued under Section 4 of the FFA. An exception is allowed for certain products (FFA Section 11c) that are imported for finishing or processing to bring them within the legal standard. For these products, the exporter must state on the invoice or other paper relating to the shipment that the shipment is being made for that purpose.

The CPSC, as the primary enforcement agency of flammability Standards, inspects products for compliance with the FFA. If the CPSC believes a product, fabric, or related material does not comply with a flammability standard, it is authorized to pursue a variety of legal sanctions, including: 1) seizure, condemnation, and forfeiture of the noncomplying products; 2) administrative cease-and-desist order requiring an individual or firm to stop sale and distribution of the noncomplying products or; 3) temporary injunction requiring the individual or firm to stop sale and distribution of the noncomplying products, pending final disposition of an administrative cease-and-desist proceeding. The CPSC also has authority to seek civil penalties against any person who knowingly violates a regulation or standard issued under Section 4 of the FFA.

Country-Specific Restrictions

Restrictions under Multi-Fiber Arrangements are country-specific. A product originating in one country may be subject to quota and to export license or visa requirements, while the same product originating in a different country may not. At present, the U.S. has Multi-Fiber Arrangements with 40 countries. Many different categories of products are covered under these Arrangements; it is beyond the scope of this book to list each country and its restricted commodities. If you are interested in importing textiles and textile products, you should contact the International Trade Administration's Office of Textile and Apparel (see addresses at end of this chapter) or U.S. Customs to ascertain your product's restraint status.

The U.S. Customs service provides quota reports on their website (www.customs.gov/impoexpo/impoexpo.htm). These reports are constantly updated and have an effective date noted. The most recent quota information can be accessed by clicking on the country name that interests you. This location holds information regarding quotas, transshipments, and visa requirements.

Marking and Labeling Requirements

TFPIA Requirements. All textile fiber products imported into the U.S. must be stamped, tagged, labeled, or otherwise marked with the following information as required by the TFPIA, unless exempt from marking (see TFPIA, Section 12): 1) the generic names and percentages by weight of the constituent fibers present in the textile fiber product, exclusive of permissible ornamentation, in amounts of more than 5% in order of predominance by weight, with any percentage of fiber or fibers required to be designated as "other fiber" or "other fibers" (including those present in amounts of 5% or less) appearing last; and 2) the name of the manufacturer or the name or registered identification number issued by the FTC of one or more persons marketing or handling the textile fiber product; and 3) the name of the country where processed. A word trademark, used as a house mark and registered with the U.S. Patent Office, may appear on labels instead of the name otherwise required, provided the owner of the trademark furnishes a copy of the registration to the FTC prior to use (see "Registered Identification Numbers" below).

The information listed above is not exhaustive. TFPIA requirements are extensive. The Act specifies such details as types of labels, means of attachment, label position on the article, package labeling, unit labeling for two-piece garments, and arrangement of information on the label; allowable fiber designations; country-of-origin indications; requirements for trim and ornamentation, linings and interlinings, and pile fabrics; sectional disclosure; use of trade names and trademarks; and requirements for swatches and samples. The FTC publishes a booklet intended to clarify TFPIA requirements to facilitate voluntary compliance in the industry (see "Publications and WWW Resources" below). It is available on request, at no charge, from the FTC (see addresses at end of this chapter).

Wool Products Labeling Act (WPLA). Wool product labeling requirements for foreign products are the responsibility of the importer. The WPLA requires the following information to appear on wool products subject to the Act: 1) percentage of the wool product's total fiber weight (exclusive of ornamentation) not exceeding 5% of the total fiber weight of a) wool, b) recycled wool, c) each fiber other than wool if the percent by weight of such fiber is 5% or more, and d) the aggregate of all other fibers; 2) the maximum percent of the wool product's total weight, of any nonfibrous loading, filling, or adulterating matter; and 3) the importer's name. If you, as importer, have a registered identification number issued by the FTC, that number may be used instead of your name (see "Registered Identification Numbers" below).

Customs entry is contingent on proper labeling. If your shipment is found to be mislabeled at entry, you will be given the option of relabeling the products under Customs supervision, as long as the port director is satisfied that your labeling error or omission did not involve fraud or willful neglect. If your shipment is discovered after entry to have been noncomplying with WPLA, it will be recalled to Customs custody at your expense, unless you can satisfy the port director that the products have since been brought into compliance. You will be held responsible for all expenses incurred in bringing a shipment into compliance, including compensation of personnel and other expenses related to Customs supervision.

Fraudulent violations of WPLA will result in seizure of the shipment. Shipments already released from Customs custody will be ordered to be redelivered to Customs. Customs reports all cases of fraudulent violation to the FTC in Washington, DC.

The information listed above is not intended to be exhaustive. WPLA requirements are extensive. The Act specifies such details as types of labels, means of attachment, label position on the article, package labeling, unit labeling (as in the case of a two-piece garment), arrangement of information on the label, allowable fiber designations, country-of-origin indications, trim and ornamentation, pile fabrics, sectional disclosure, use of trade names and trademarks, requirements for swatches and samples, etc. The FTC publishes a booklet intended to clarify WPLA requirements in order to facilitate voluntary compliance within the industry (see "Publications and WWW Resources" below). It is available on request, at no charge, from the FTC (see addresses at end of this chapter).

The Care Labeling Rule. Regulations under this rule require manufacturers and importers of textile clothing and fabrics to attach specific care instructions for washing or dry cleaning, as well as information on the fiber composition of the article. They are enforced by the FTC Division of Enforcement. The Care Labeling Rule was amended September 2000, detailed information is available on the FTC website (www.ftc.gov/os/statutes/textilejump.htm).

Registered Identification Numbers. Any domestic firm or person residing in the U.S. and engaged in the manufacture or marketing of textile products covered under the TFPIA may obtain an FTC-registered identification number for use on required tags and labels instead of the name of a firm or person. For applications, contact the FTC (see addresses at end of this chapter).

For a general discussion of U.S. Customs marking and labeling requirements, see "Country of Origin Marking" on page 236, "Special Marking Requirements" on page 238 and "Marking—False Impression" on page 239.

Shipping Considerations

You will need to ensure that your goods are packaged and shipped with care so that they pass smoothly through Customs and arrive in good condition. You are responsible for ensuring that the shipment is in compliance with all applicable government regulations for packaging and shipping. In most instances, you should not leave these arrangements solely to the discretion of your supplier. Careful preparation of the cargo and selection of the mode of transport can be essential to a cost-effective, timely delivery of undamaged goods. We strongly advise you to consult your shipping representative, insurance agent, or freight broker for advice on packing and shipping.

Special woven fabrics may be shipped in bulk, bolts, rolls, or other types of containers, depending on the type of product and whether it is prepackaged. General considerations include protection from contamination, weather, and pests. Safety precautions should also be implemented as required to protect against breakage, spillage, corrosion of containers, and combustion. Containers should be constructed so as to be safe for handling during transport.

Publications and WWW Resources

The following publications may be relevant to the importation of special woven fabrics and wool fabrics:

Threading Your Way Through the Labeling Requirements Under the Textile and Wool Acts

Available free of charge on request from the Federal Trade Commission and online from the FTC website (www.ftc.gov/bcp/conline/pubs/buspubs/thread.htm). This publication is an excellent source of information written in clear lay language. We recommend that anyone interested in importing textile fiber products but unfamiliar with the regulations obtain a copy of each of this booklet.

The U.S. Customs Service launched a series of "Informed Compliance" publications in 1996, which are available on the Customs Service website (www.customs.gov/impoexpo/impoexpo.htm). Of particular interest:

What Every Member of the Trade Community Should Know About Textile & Apparel Rules of Origin

What Every Member of the Trade community Should Know About NAFTA for Textiles and Textile Articles

Fibers & Yarns Construction and Classification Under the HTSUS

The *Harmonized Tariff Schedule of the United States (2001)* (HTSUS) is available to view on the Customs Service website (www.customs.gov), or you may purchase a printed version from:

U.S. Government Printing Office
Superintendent of Documents
710 North Capital Street NW
Washington DC 20401
Tel: (202) 512-1800
Fax: (202) 512-1657
Website: www.access.gpo.gov

The USGPO also has copies of specific laws available for purchase. The USGPO accepts orders made by fax, phone or placed over the Internet, as well as mail orders paid by credit card. All orders must be accompanied by payment. Credit cards, checks drawn on a U.S. bank, or an international money order are all acceptable.

Relevant Government Agencies

Address your questions regarding textile Multi-Fiber Arrangements to:

U.S. Department of Commerce
International Trade Administration
Office of Textiles and Apparel
Director's Office
14th and Constitution Avenue NW, Rm. H3100
Washington DC 20230
Tel: (202) 482-5078

Fax: (202) 482-2331
Agreements Division: (202) 482-4212
Website: http://otexa.ita.doc.gov

Address your questions regarding the Flammable Fabrics Act (FFA) to:

Consumer Product Safety Commission (CPSC)
Office of Compliance
Washington DC 20207-0001
Tel: 800-638-2772 or (301) 504-7912
Fax: (301) 504-0359
Website: www.cpsc.gov

Address your questions regarding labeling requirements under the Textile Fiber Products Identification Act (TFPIA) or the Wool Products Labeling Act (WPLA) to:

Federal Trade Commission (FTC)
Division of Enforcement
600 Pennsylvania Avenue NW
Washington DC 20580
Tel: (202) 326-2996
Website: www.ftc.gov

Address your questions regarding textile quotas to:

U.S. Customs and Border Protection
Office of Field Operations, Quota Branch
1300 Pennsylvania Avenue NW
Washington DC 20229
Tel: (202) 927-5850
Website: www.customs.treas.gov

The U.S. Customs Service provices updated status reports on textile quota on their web site (see address above). If the country you need information on is not listed, call the Quota Branch office at (202) 927-5850.

Address your questions regarding special woven fabric imports to your local Customs port director. For addresses, refer to "U.S. Customs and Border Protection Offices" on page 65 or contact:

U.S. Customs and Border Protection
Customs Headquarters
1300 Pennsylvania Avenue NW
Washington DC 20229
Tel: (202) 354-1000
Website: www.customs.treas.gov

Laws and Regulations

The following laws and regulations may be relevant to the importation of special woven fabrics. The laws are contained in the United States Code (USC), and the regulations are published in the Code of Federal Regulations (CFR), both of which are available at larger public and law libraries. Copies of specific laws are also available from the United States Government Printing Office (address above).

7 USC 1854
Textile Trade Agreements
(EO 11651, as amended by EO 11951 and 12188, and supplemented by EO 12475)
This Act authorizes the CITA of the DOC to enter into Multi-Fiber Agreements with other countries to control trade in textiles and establishes the Textile Import Program, which is enforced by U.S. Customs.

19 CFR 12.130 et seq.
Regulations on Entry of Textiles
These regulations provide the requirements and procedures followed by Customs in enforcing limitations on the importation and entry and withdrawal of textiles and textile products from warehouses for consumption in the US.

15 USC 70-77
Textile Fiber Products Identification Act (TFPIA)
This Act prohibits false or deceptive labeling (misbrand-

ing) and false advertising of any textile fiber products and requires all textile fiber products imported into the U.S. to be labeled in accordance with the requirements set forth in the law.

19 CFR 11.12b; 16 CFR 303 et seq.
Regulations on Labeling and Marking
These regulations detail the labeling and marking requirements for textiles as specified by the CPSC and the invoice contents required by U.S. Customs for purpose of enforcing the labeling and marking rules.

15 USC 1191-1204
Flammable Fabrics Act (FFA)
This Act provides for the setting of flammability standards for fabric by the Consumer Product Safety Commission (CPSC) and for enforcement by U.S. Customs.

16 CFR 1610, 1611, 1615, 1616, 1630-1632
Regulations on Flammable Fabric Standards
These regulations specify the flammability standards adopted by the CPSC under the FFA for various types of textiles.

15 USC 68-68j
Wool Products Labeling Act (WPLA) of 1939
This Act prohibits the false or deceptive labeling (misbranding) of wool products and requires all wool products imported into the U.S. to be labeled in accordance with requirements set forth in the law.

19 CFR 11.12; 16 CFR 300 et seq.
Regulations on WPLA Labeling and Marking
These regulations set forth the wool labeling and marking requirements adopted by the FTC to administer the requirements of the WPLA and provide the procedures followed by U.S. Customs in enforcing the WPLA and the FTC regulations, including entry invoice requirements.

16 CFR 423
Care Labeling Rule
Requires fiber composition and washing or dry cleaning instructions for textile apparel and certain piece goods.

Principal Exporting Countries

The following listing includes samples of the main supplier nations of the products of this chapter. It is organized by HTSUS major heading. (Refer to "Customs Classification" above for the product codes.) Countries are listed in rank order of the value of products imported to the U.S. Statistics represent customs value of entries for 2002 from the Bureau of Census.

5801—Italy, China, Canada, Belgium, Mexico, United Kingdom

5802—Turkey, Israel, Pakistan, Mexico, Canada, Brazil, China

5803—United Kingdom, Mexico, Spain, Germany, Switzerland

5804—Mexico, France, South Korea, United Kingdom, Taiwan, China

5805—France, United Kingdom, Belgium, Italy, China, India

5806—Taiwan, Canada, China, South Korea, Mexico, France, Germany, Japan, Italy

5807—Canada, South Korea, Taiwan, Hong Kong, China, Dominican Republic, Italy, Colombia, United Kingdom

5808—Mexico, China, France, India, South Africa, Taiwan

5809—Japan, India, South Korea, France, Turkey

5810—China, Taiwan, India, Thailand, South Korea, Mexico, Austria, Switzerland, Costa Rica, Canada

5811—Canada, Italy, China, Taiwan, Mexico, Belgium, Germany, Ireland

Chapter 59:
Coated Textiles

Full title: Impregnated, Coated, Covered, or Laminated Textile Fabrics; Textile Articles of a Kind Suitable for Industrial Use

This chapter relates to the importation of coated textiles, which are classified under Chapter 59 of the Harmonized Tariff Schedule of the United States (HTSUS). Specifically, it includes textile fabrics stiffened with a coating of gum, amylaceous substances, or other coatings for book covers, tracing cloth, painting canvas, hat foundations, theatrical scenery, and studio back-cloths; tire cord fabric and other rubberized textile fabrics; textile fabrics coated with plastics; linoleum or other floor coverings on textile backing; textile wall coverings; textile wicks, textile hosepiping and tubing; textile transmission or conveyor belts or belting; and textile products for technical uses.

The term "textile fabrics" refers to woven fabrics of Commodity Index Chapters 50 through 55, gauze (HTSUS heading 5803), narrow woven fabrics (HTSUS heading 5806), braids and ornamental trimmings (HTSUS heading 5808), and knitted or crocheted fabrics (HTSUS heading 6002).

If you are interested in importing textile products that are combined with plastic or rubber substances, you should also read Commodity Index Chapters 39 (plastics) or 40 (rubber). Fabrics that are partially covered with plastics, that bear designs resulting from such treatments, or that are combined with rubber are also covered in Chapters 50 through 55, 58, and 60. For importing sensitized textiles, refer to Chapter 37. The import requirements for abrasive-coated textile material are covered in Chapter 68. Wall coverings consisting of textile flock or dust fixed on paper backing are classified under Chapter 48. If you are interested in importing wood veneer on a textile fabric backing, refer to Chapter 44. Metal foils with a textile fabric backing is covered in Chapter 72 through 81. The import requirements for certain types of transmission and conveyor belts are dealt with in Chapter 40.

Note: To understand key issues that will enable you to make best use of the information in this section we recommend that you see "Introduction" on page 425.

Key Factors

The key factors in the importation of coated textiles are:

- Compliance with quota restraints and visa requirements
- Submission of U.S. Customs Country-of-Origin Declaration(s)
- Compliance with entry invoice requirements

- Compliance with labeling requirements under Textile Fiber Products Identification Act (TFPIA) and/or the Wool Products Labeling Act (WPLA) and the Care Labeling Rule
- Compliance with flammability standards adopted and enforced by the Consumer Product Safety Commission (CPSC) under the Flammable Fabrics Act (FFA)

Although most importers use the services of a licensed customs broker in making their entries, and we recommend this practice, you should be aware of the regulatory, entry, and documentation issues involved in importing your product. You, as importer, are ultimately responsible for the fulfillment of any legal requirements applicable to your shipment.

General Considerations

Regulatory Agencies. The DOC's Committee for Implementation of Textile Agreements (CITA) regulates certain textile imports under Section 204 of the Agricultural Adjustment Act. U.S. Customs enforces CITA textile and textile product entry quotas. Customs also enforces compliance with labeling and invoice requirements of the TFPIA and flammability standards under the FFA. The CPSC monitors imports and from time to time inspects textile shipments for compliance with FFA standards. If you are importing products that contain wool fibers, importation is subject to complex textile import regulations. The Federal Trade Commission (FTC) administers the WPLA requirements.

Textile Quotas. If you are interested in importing coated textiles, the most important issue you need to be aware of is quotas. Under the Multi-Fiber Arrangement provisions of Section 204 of the Agricultural Adjustment Act, CITA initiates specific agreements with individual exporting countries. Section 204 of the Agricultural Adjustment Act covers textiles that: 1) are in chief value of cotton, wool, or man-made fibers, any textile fibers subject to the terms of any textile trade agreement, or any combination of such fibers; 2) contain 50% or more by weight of cotton or man-made fibers, or any textile fibers subject to the terms of any textile trade agreement; 3) contain 17% or more by weight of wool; or 4) if in chief value of textile fibers or textile materials, contain a blend of cotton, wool, or man-made fibers, any textile fibers subject to the terms of any textile trade agreement, or any combination of such fibers that, in total, amount to 50% or more by weight of all component fibers.

The U.S. has Multi-Fiber Arrangements with 40 countries. Each agreement with each country is unique, and may specify quotas for a type of textile or a specific article. Visas or export licenses may be required. These agreements, however, often change. Therefore, if you are interested in importing any coated textiles, you should contact the International Trade Administration's Office of Textile and Apparel (see addresses at end of this chapter). Refer to "Prohibitions and Restrictions" below for further details.

Textile Country-of-Origin Declarations. U.S. Customs enforces CITA textile and textile product entry quotas (see "Prohibitions and Restrictions" below). Requirements for entry include submission of Country-of-Origin Declarations with every coated textile shipment, regardless of whether it is subject to a specific multi-fiber arrangement (19 CFR 12.130, 12.131).

Country of Origin. Quota restrictions are country-specific and therefore are applied based on the country of origin for the textiles shipped. The last country from which a textile shipment was exported to the U.S. is not necessarily its country of origin. A textile or textile product imported into the U.S. is considered a product of the particular foreign territory or country, or a U.S. insular possession, where it is wholly grown, produced, or manufactured. For the following discussion, "country" means a foreign territory or country, or a U.S. insular possession.

In 1996, the U.S. Customs Service made major changes to country of origin rules for textile imports. The regulations at 19 CFR 102.21, "Textile and apparel products" were added to the 1996 Customs Regulations and became effective July 1, 1996. The new rules do not provide for cutting components or cutting and hemming to confer country of origin as in the past. The basis of the new law is processing operations or assembly. Some of the most important changes for importers to be aware of are:

- Cutting does not determine the country of origin (previously cutting determined country of origin for 90 percent of wearing apparel imports). The new rules are based on processing or assembly operations.

- Essential character does not determine country of origin because the new rules are based on processing.

- A subjective determination under the provisions of 19 CFR 12.130 is replaced by objective processing operations expressed in terms of tariff shifts. Dying, printing, and other finishing processes applied to fabrics no longer confer or change country of origin.

- Country of origin for textile and apparel products processed, assembled or manufactured in two or more countries is determined by where the most important processing occurs, and, if that cannot be ascertained, the last country in which an important processing operation occurs.

The country of origin is the country in which a product is wholly produced when a textile or apparel product is completely produced or manufactured (except for minor parts) in one country. For fabric, the country of origin is the country in which the fabric is woven, knitted, needled, tufted, felted, entangled or created by any other fabric-making process. The country of origin for staple yarn is the country in which yarn is spun; for filament yarn, the country in which filament is extruded; and for plied, gimped and cabled yarns, the country in which the fibers or filaments used in the yarn are spun or extruded. The country of origin of all other textile and apparel products is the country in which the components of a textile or apparel product are wholly assembled (except for minor attachments). Once again, note that assembly, not cutting, now confers country of origin.

Declarations. All importations of textiles and textile products must be accompanied by one of the following three declarations. Goods subject to Section 204, Agricultural Act of 1956, as amended, must be accompanied by either a single-country or a multiple-country declaration. Goods not subject to Section 204 must be accompanied by a negative declaration.

- **Single-country declarations** are used for entries of textiles or textile products which are wholly the growth, product, or manufacture of a single foreign country, territory, or U.S. insular possession. Information required includes: marks of identification and numbers; description of article and quantity; country of origin; and date of exportation.

- **Multiple-country declarations** are used for entries of textiles or textile products which were subjected to manufacturing or processing operations in, and/or incorporate materials originating in more than one foreign country or territory. Information required includes: marks of identification and numbers; for articles, description, quantity, identification of manufacturing and/or processing operations, country, and date of exportation; for materials used to make articles, description of materials, country of production, and date of exportation.

- **Negative declarations** must accompany all textile imports that are not subject to FFA Section 204 restrictions. Information required includes: marks of identification and numbers; descriptions of article and quantity; and country of origin.

The date of exportation to be indicated on the above declarations is the date on which the carrier leaves the last port in the country of origin, as determined by Customs. Diversion to another country during transit does not affect the export date.

Procedure for Declarations. The manufacturer, producer, exporter, or importer may prepare the declaration. If more than one of these parties is involved in the importation, each party may prepare a separate declaration. You may file a separate declaration for each invoice presented with your entry. The declaration must be dated and signed by the responsible party, and must include the person's title and the company name and address. Your shipment's entry will be denied unless it is accompanied by a properly executed declaration. Customs will not treat a textile declaration as a missing document for which a bond may be filed.

Customs will base its country-of-origin determination on the information contained in each declaration, unless the information is insufficient. If the information on the declaration is insufficient, Customs will require that you submit such additional information as will enable the determination to be made. The shipment will not be released until the determination is made. Thus, if you want to clear Customs with minimal delay, be sure that the information on the declarations is as complete as possible for each shipment.

Textile Labeling and Invoice Requirements. You are responsible for your imported coated textile product's compliance with applicable provisions of the TFPIA. Coated textile products that require labeling under TFPIA must already be labeled at entry, or the shipment will be refused. (See "Marking and Labeling Requirements" below.) If you import shipments of coated textiles subject to TFPIA and valued at over $500, you must provide special information on the entry invoice (see "Entry and Documentation" below).

Flammability Standards. Coated textile products imported into the U.S. for use in consumer products must be in compliance with the FFA, a federal law that gives the CPSC the authority and responsibility for protecting the public from the hazards of dangerously flammable items of wearing apparel and interior furnishings. Under the FFA, standards have been established for flammability of clothing textiles. You cannot import any article of wearing apparel or interior furnishing, or any fabric or related material that is intended for use or that may be used in such items, if it fails to conform to an applicable flammability standard (FFA Section 4). Certain products may be imported into the U.S. (FFA Section 11c) for finishing or processing to render them less flammable so as to meet the standards. For these products, the exporter must state on the invoice or other paper relating to the shipment that the shipment is being made for that purpose.

The CPSC monitors imports of textiles under its Import Surveillance Program. From time to time, your textile shipments may be inspected to ascertain compliance with mandatory safety standards. Shipments may also be subject to testing by the CPSC to determine compliance. If the CPSC believes a product, fabric, or related material does not comply with a flammability standard, it is authorized to pursue a variety of legal sanctions (see "Prohibitions and Restrictions" below).

Substantial Product Hazard Reports. Any firm that obtains information that reasonably supports the conclusion that one of its products presents an unreasonable risk of serious injury or death must report that information to the CPSC's Division of Corrective Actions (CPSC address below). Importers must also report to the CPSC if 1) a type of product is the subject of at least three civil actions filed in U.S. federal or state courts, 2) each suit alleges the involvement of that product type in death or grievous bodily injury (as defined in FFA Section 37(3)1), and 3) at least three of the actions result in a final settlement with the manufacturer or in a judgment for the plaintiff within any one of the two-year periods specified in FFA Section 37(b).

Wool Product Entry Requirements. Depending on the nature of your wool fiber imports, as many as three different types of special entry documents may be required. First, for all imported textile fibers and yarns covered by the Agricultural Adjustment Act (AAA), including wool, you must file a U.S. Customs Textile Entry Declaration (see "Textile Country-of-Origin Declarations" above). Second, for all wool products subject to the WPLA, special information is required on the entry invoices (see "Entry and Documentation" below). Finally, certain wool articles manufactured or produced in certain countries may be subject to quotas under U.S. Department of Commerce Multi-Fiber Arrangements. Such products require export certificates or visas issued by the appropriate country of origin, in addition to other requisite entry paperwork (see "Quotas" above).

Wool Products Labeling Act. The term "wool product" means any product or any portion of a product that contains, purports to contain, or in any way is represented as containing wool, reprocessed wool, or reused wool. All wool products imported into the U.S., except those made more than 20 years before importation, and except carpets, rugs, mats, and upholsteries, must have affixed a stamp, tag, label, or other means of identification as required by the WPLA. If you are importing wool products exempt from labeling under the WPLA, do not assume they are also exempt from labeling under the TFPIA. These are two distinct laws, with some overlapping requirements (see "Marking and Labeling Requirements" below).

Import Advisory

Importation of textiles is trade-sensitive and highly regulated. Shipments of textiles and textile products not complying with all government regulations, including quotas and visas, are subject to seizure and could result in the imposition of penalties as well as possible forfeiture of the goods. You should always verify the available quota for any textile product you plan to import before your shipment leaves the country of manufacture. Furthermore, Customs textile classification rulings change frequently, and prior administrative rulings are often modified and sometimes reversed. You should be particularly careful to comply with country of origin determination regulations, which were changed in 1996, and affect quotas and visas, marking and labeling, and other important aspects of tariff classification. See "Publications and WWW Resources" for information on important Customs Service informed compliance publications.

The Customs Service has greatly increased its scrutiny of the textile industry, one of eight primary focus industries identified in the most recent Trade Compliance & Enforcement Plan. Imported products from these industries will likely attract significant attention from Customs in the areas of compliance measurement, compliance assessment, informed compliance, and interventions.

Customs Classification

For customs purposes, coated textiles are classified under Chapter 59 of the HTSUS. This chapter is broken into major headings, which are further divided into subheadings, and often sub-subheadings, each of which has its own HTSUS classification number. For example, the 2001 HTSUS number for textile fabrics of man-made fibers is 5901.10.10, indicating it is a sub-subcategory of textile fabrics coated with gum or amylaceous substances for

book covers (5901.10.00), which is a subcategory of the major heading, textile fabrics coated with coated with gum or amylaceous substances, etc. (5901.00.00). There are 11 major headings within Chapter 59.

5901—Textile fabrics coated with gum or amylaceous substances, of a kind used for the outer covers of books or the like; tracing cloth; prepared painting canvas; buckram and similar stiffened textile fabrics of a kind used for hat foundations

5902—Tire cord fabric of high tenacity yarn of nylon or other polyamides, polyesters, or viscose rayon

5903—Textile fabrics impregnated, coated, covered, or laminated with plastics, other than those of heading 5902

5904—Linoleum, whether or not cut to shape; floor coverings consisting of a coating or covering applied on a textile backing, whether or not cut to shape

5905—Textile wall coverings

5906—Rubberized textile fabrics, other than those of heading 5902

5907—Textile fabrics otherwise impregnated, coated, or covered; painted canvas being theatrical scenery, studio backcloths, or the like

5908—Textile wicks, woven, plaited, or knitted for lamps, stoves, lighters, candles or the like; incandescent gas mantles and tubular knitted gas mantle fabric therefor, whether or not impregnated

5909—Textile hosepiping and similar textile tubing, with or without lining, armor or accessories of other materials

5910—Transmission or conveyor belts or belting, of textile material, whether or not impregnated, coated, covered or laminated with plastics, or reinforced with metal or other material

5911—Textile products and articles, for technical uses, specified in note 7 to this chapter

For more details regarding classifications of the specific product you are interested in importing, consult a customs broker, the appropriate commodity specialist at your nearest customs port, or the HTSUS. The 2001 HTSUS is available online from the Customs Service (www.customs.gov/impoexpo/impoexpo.htm) or for purchase from the U.S. Government Printing Office (see resources at the end of this chapter), and may be found in larger public libraries. For a general discussion of customs classification, see "Classification—Liquidation" on page 229.

Dutiable Status of Goods

For more information about duty rates and binding decisions see "Dutiable Status of Goods" on page 203; for a discussion of temporary importation of goods see "Temporary Free Importations" on page 205.

Valuation

Importers have a responsibility to use what the U.S. Customs Service deems, "reasonable care," when determining the value of their goods. They must also provide any additional information that the Customs Service needs for setting a final value on the goods. This process involves a number of factors and can be somewhat complicated; importers must be aware of applicable issues and details. Valuation information applies to all types of commodities, for further discussion on the subject see "Customs Valuation" on page 267.

Import Duties

Import duties vary (often dramatically) depending upon the Harmonized Tariff Schedule (HTSUS) classification of the goods or products imported. Since some products that look alike have different HTSUS classifications and different rates of duty, proper classification is vital. Note that "differences of opinion" between importers and the Bureau of Customs and Border Protection regarding classification keeps customs attorneys very busy.

Import duties can be assessed on the imported value of the goods ("ad valorem" rates of duty such as 2%, 4.4%, 50%, etc.), total units or weight of the goods ("specific" rates of duty such as 2 cents each or 1.5 cents/pound, etc.) or on a combination basis ("compound" rates of duty such as 5 cents each plus 6%).

Listed below is a sampling of several Column 1 import duty rates for Chapter 59 products:
Backed with permanently affixed paper (5905.00.10 00): Free
to
Straining cloth of a kind used in oil presses or the like, including that of human hair (5911.40.00.00): 8.5%

For specific information on US import duties refer to the Harmonized Tariff Schedule of the US. The print version is available from the US Government Printing Office as well as third party suppliers who often add special features. Online versions are available in both static PDF pages as well as in formats with excellent search functionality. Search the Web with the term "Harmonized Tariff Schedule" to find sources.

Entry and Documentation

The entry of merchandise is a two-part process consisting of 1) filing the documentation necessary to determine whether merchandise may be released from Customs custody, and 2) filing the documents that contain information for duty assessment and statistical purposes. In certain instances, all documents must be filed and accepted by Customs prior to release of the goods. Unless you have been granted an extension, you must file entry documents at a location specified by the port or area director within five working days of your shipment's date of arrival at a U.S. port of entry. These include a number of standard documents required by Customs for any entry, and:

- U.S. Customs Country-of-Origin Declaration Form CF 3229

- Export documentation and/or visa for textiles subject to Multi-Fiber Arrangement

After you present the entry, Customs may examine your shipment or may waive examination. The shipment is then released provided no legal or regulatory violations have been noted. You must then file entry summary documentation and deposit estimated duties at a designated customhouse within 10 working days of your shipment's release. For a detailed description of entry procedures, standard documentation, and informal entry, see "Entry Process" on page 185.

Informed Compliance. Informed compliance was introduced with the Customs Modernization Act of 1993 (Mod Act) and defines the relationship between importers and the Customs Service. It sets out the responsibilities of both parties. Providing the correct documentation and information for entry is a key factor that will make your importing operation run smoothly. We recommend that importers become familiar with the concept of informed comliance and the responsibilities that they have under the Mod Act. For further discussion about informed compliance see "Informed Compliance" on page 211.

NAFTA Certificates of Origin. An importer of textiles for which NAFTA treatment is sought need not file a separate NAFTA Certificate of Origin in addition to the Customs Country-of-Origin Declaration. The declaration is sufficient. However, the importer must take care to submit a declaration from each U.S., Canadian, or Mexican producer or manufacturer. Thus, for multiple producers or manufacturers, a separate declaration must be filed for each. If a Customs port director cannot determine the country of

origin because the declaration is absent or incomplete, the shipment is not entitled to preferential NAFTA tariff treatment or other NAFTA benefits. See 19 CFR 12.132.

Entry Invoices. You must provide additional information on the entry invoice for certain coated textiles. The specific information varies with the nature of your product, as noted below.

TFPIA Requirements. For the purpose of TFPIA enforcement, a commercial shipment of textile products exceeding $500 in value and subject to TFPIA labeling requirements must show the following information: 1) the constituent fiber or combination of fibers, designating with equal prominence each natural or manufactured fiber by its generic name, in order of predominance by weight if the weight of such fiber is 5% or more of the total fiber weight of the product; 2) percentage of each fiber present, by weight, in the total fiber content; 3) the name or other identification issued and registered by the Federal Trade Commission of the manufacturer of the product or one or more persons subject to Section 3 of the TFPIA with respect to such product; 4) the name of the country where processed or manufactured.

Wool Products Subject to WPLA. When you offer for entry a wool product shipment valued at over $500 and subject to WPLA, you must include certain information intended to facilitate Customs monitoring and enforcement of that Act. This extra information is identical to that required by WPLA on labeling (see "Marking and Labeling Requirements" below), with the addition of the manufacturer's name. If your product consists of mixed waste, residues, and similar merchandise obtained from several suppliers or unknown sources, you may omit the manufacturer's name from the entry invoice. For more general information about invoices see "Invoices" on page 277.

Note: The Entry and Documentation section has been carefully designed to supply you, the importer, with sample documents and directions on how to satisfy Customs requirements. Be aware that you should consult the applicable authorities to ensure that you are correctly following the most current procedures.

Prohibitions and Restrictions

Textile Quotas. Textile import restrictions are primarily a matter of quotas and the way in which these quotas are administered and monitored. Under the Multi-Fiber Arrangement provisions of Section 204 of the Agricultural Adjustment Act, CITA has negotiated Multi-Fiber Arrangements with 40 countries. These Agreements may impose quotas for a type of textile or a specific article, and they are country-specific. The agreements, however, often change. Therefore, if you are interested in importing any coated textile products, you should contact the International Trade Administration's Office of Textile and Apparel (see addresses at end of this chapter). The Office of Textile and Apparel has a team of country specialists who can inform you of the latest developments and inform you about a product's quota or restriction status.

U.S. Customs enforces CITA textile and textile product entry quotas. If formal entry procedures are not followed, Customs will usually refuse entry for textiles that are subject to Section 204. Formal entry requires submission of a Country-of-Origin Declaration (see "General Considerations" above). U.S. Customs maintains a current textile quota status report, available for perusal at any Customs port. In addition, U.S. Customs in Washington, DC, provides quota status reports online, which are updated on a regular basis (www.customs.gov/impoexpo/impoexpo.htm).

Flammable Fabrics. U.S. Customs may refuse entry for any article of wearing apparel or interior furnishing, or any fabric or related material that is intended for use or that may be used in wearing apparel or interior furnishings, if it fails to conform to an applicable flammability standard issued under Section 4 of the FFA. An exception is allowed for certain products (FFA Sec tion 11c) that are imported for finishing or processing to bring them within the legal standard. For these products, the exporter must state on the invoice or other paper relating to the shipment that the shipment is being made for that purpose.

The CPSC, as the primary enforcement agency of flammability standards, inspects products for compliance with the FFA. If the CPSC believes a product, fabric, or related material does not comply with a flammability standard, it is authorized to pursue a variety of legal sanctions, including: 1) seizure, condemnation, and forfeiture of the noncomplying products; 2) administrative cease-and-desist order requiring an individual or firm to stop sale and distribution of the noncomplying products or; 3) temporary injunction requiring the individual or firm to stop sale and distribution of the noncomplying products, pending final disposition of an administrative cease-and-desist proceeding. The CPSC also has authority to seek civil penalties against any person who knowingly violates a regulation or standard issued under Section 4 of the FFA.

Country-Specific Restrictions

Restrictions under Multi-Fiber Arrangements are country-specific. A product originating in one country may be subject to quota and to export license or visa requirements, while the same product originating in a different country may not. At present, the U.S. has Multi-Fiber Arrangements with 40 countries. Many different categories of products are covered under these Arrangements; it is beyond the scope of this book to list each country and its restricted commodities. If you are interested in importing textiles and textile products, you should contact the International Trade Administration's Office of Textile and Apparel (see addresses at end of this chapter) or U.S. Customs to ascertain your product's restraint status.

The U.S. Customs service provides quota reports on their website (www.customs.gov/impoexpo/impoexpo.htm). These reports are constantly updated and have an effective date noted. The most recent quota information can be accessed by clicking on the country name that interests you. This location holds information regarding quotas, transshipments, and visa requirements.

Marking and Labeling Requirements

TFPIA Requirements. All textile fiber products imported into the U.S. must be stamped, tagged, labeled, or otherwise marked with the following information as required by the TFPIA, unless exempt from marking (see TFPIA, Section 12): 1) the generic names and percentages by weight of the constituent fibers present in the textile fiber product, exclusive of permissible ornamentation, in amounts of more than 5% in order of predominance by weight, with any percentage of fiber or fibers required to be designated as "other fiber" or "other fibers" (including those present in amounts of 5% or less) appearing last; and 2) the name of the manufacturer or the name or registered identification number issued by the FTC of one or more persons marketing or handling the textile fiber product; and 3) the name of the country where processed. A word trademark, used as a house mark and registered with the U.S. Patent Office, may appear on labels instead of the name otherwise required, provided the owner of the trademark furnishes a copy of the registration to the FTC prior to use (see "Registered Identification Numbers" below).

The information listed above is not exhaustive. TFPIA requirements are extensive. The Act specifies such details as types of labels, means of attachment, label position on the article, package labeling, unit labeling for two-piece garments, and arrangement of information on the label; allowable fiber designations; country-of-origin indications; requirements for trim and ornamentation, linings and interlinings, and pile fabrics; sectional disclosure; use of trade names and trademarks; and requirements for swatches and samples. The FTC publishes a booklet intended to clarify TFPIA requirements to facilitate voluntary compliance in the industry (see "Publications and WWW Resources" below). It is available on request, at no charge, from the FTC (see addresses at end of this chapter).

Wool Products Labeling Act (WPLA). Wool product labeling requirements for foreign products are the responsibility of the importer. The WPLA requires the following information to appear on wool products subject to the Act: 1) percentage of the wool product's total fiber weight (exclusive of ornamentation) not exceeding 5% of the total fiber weight of a) wool, b) recycled wool, c) each fiber other than wool if the percent by weight of such fiber is 5% or more, and d) the aggregate of all other fibers; 2) the maximum percent of the wool product's total weight, of any nonfibrous loading, filling, or adulterating matter; and 3) the importer's name. If you, as importer, have a registered identification number issued by the FTC, that number may be used instead of your name (see "Registered Identification Numbers" below).

Customs entry is contingent on proper labeling. If your shipment is found to be mislabeled at entry, you will be given the option of relabeling the products under Customs supervision, as long as the port director is satisfied that your labeling error or omission did not involve fraud or willful neglect. If your shipment is discovered after entry to have been noncomplying with WPLA, it will be recalled to Customs custody at your expense, unless you can satisfy the port director that the products have since been brought into compliance. You will be held responsible for all expenses incurred in bringing a shipment into compliance, including compensation of personnel and other expenses related to Customs supervision.

Fraudulent violations of WPLA will result in seizure of the shipment. Shipments already released from Customs custody will be ordered to be redelivered to Customs. Customs reports all cases of fraudulent violation to the FTC in Washington, DC.

The information listed above is not intended to be exhaustive. WPLA requirements are extensive. The Act specifies such details as types of labels, means of attachment, label position on the article, package labeling, unit labeling (as in the case of a two-piece garment), arrangement of information on the label, allowable fiber designations, country-of-origin indications, trim and ornamentation, pile fabrics, sectional disclosure, use of trade names and trademarks, requirements for swatches and samples, etc. The FTC publishes a booklet intended to clarify WPLA requirements in order to facilitate voluntary compliance within the industry (see "Publications and WWW Resources" below). It is available on request, at no charge, from the FTC (see addresses at end of this chapter).

The Care Labeling Rule. Regulations under this rule require manufacturers and importers of textile clothing and fabrics to attach specific care instructions for washing or dry cleaning, as well as information on the fiber composition of the article. They are enforced by the FTC Division of Enforcement. The Care Labeling Rule was amended September 2000, detailed information is available on the FTC website (www.ftc.gov/os/statutes/textilejump.htm).

Registered Identification Numbers. Any domestic firm or person residing in the U.S. and engaged in the manufacture or marketing of textile products covered under the TFPIA may obtain an FTC-registered identification number for use on required tags and labels instead of the name of a firm or person. For applications, contact the FTC (address below.)

For a general discussion of U.S. Customs marking and labeling requirements, see "Country of Origin Marking" on page 236, "Special Marking Requirements" on page 238 and "Marking—False Impression" on page 239.

Shipping Considerations

You will need to ensure that your goods are packaged and shipped with care so that they pass smoothly through Customs and arrive in good condition. You are responsible for ensuring that the shipment is in compliance with all applicable government regulations for packaging and shipping. In most instances, you should not leave these arrangements solely to the discretion of your supplier. Careful preparation of the cargo and selection of the mode of transport can be essential to a cost-effective, timely delivery of undamaged goods. We strongly advise you to consult your shipping representative, insurance agent, or freight broker for advice on packing and shipping.

Coated textiles may be shipped in bulk, bolts, rolls, or other types of containers, depending on the type of product and whether it is prepackaged. General considerations include protection from contamination, weather, and pests. For textiles coated or impregnated with combustible substances, safety precautions should be taken to allow for ventilation and to prevent combustion. Containers should be constructed so as to be safe for handling during transport.

Publications and WWW Resources

The following publications may be relevant to the importation of coated textiles:

> *Threading Your Way Through the Labeling Requirements Under the Textile and Wool Acts*

Available free of charge on request from the Federal Trade Commission and online from the FTC website (www.ftc.gov/bcp/conline/pubs/buspubs/thread.htm). This publication is an excellent source of information written in clear lay language. We recommend that anyone interested in importing textile fiber products but unfamiliar with the regulations obtain a copy of each of this booklet.

The U.S. Customs Service launched a series of "Informed Compliance" publications in 1996, which are available on the Customs Service website (www.customs.gov/impoexpo/impoexpo.htm). Of particular interest:

> *What Every Member of the Trade Community Should Know About Textile & Apparel Rules of Origin*

> *What Every Member of the Trade community Should Know About NAFTA for Textiles and Textile Articles*

> *Fibers & Yarns Construction and Classification Under the HTSUS*

The *Harmonized Tariff Schedule of the United States (2001)* (HTSUS) is available to view on the Customs Service website (www.customs.gov), or you may purchase a printed version from:

U.S. Government Printing Office
Superintendent of Documents
710 North Capital Street NW
Washington DC 20401
Tel: (202) 512-1800
Fax: (202) 512-1657
Website: www.access.gpo.gov

The USGPO also has copies of specific laws available for purchase. The USGPO accepts orders made by fax, phone or placed over the Internet, as well as mail orders paid by credit card. All orders must be accompanied by payment. Credit cards, checks drawn on a U.S. bank, or an international money order are all acceptable.

Relevant Government Agencies

Address your questions regarding textile Multi-Fiber Arrangements to:

U.S. Department of Commerce
International Trade Administration
Office of Textiles and Apparel
Director's Office
14th and Constitution Avenue NW, Rm. H3100
Washington DC 20230

Tel: (202) 482-5078
Fax: (202) 482-2331
Agreements Division: (202) 482-4212
Website: http://otexa.ita.doc.gov

Address your questions regarding requirements under the Textile Fiber Products Identification Act (TFPIA) or the Wool Products Labeling Act (WPLA)to:

Federal Trade Commission (FTC)
Division of Enforcement
600 Pennsylvania Avenue NW
Washington DC 20580
Tel: (202) 326-2996
Website: www.ftc.gov

Address your questions regarding the Flammable Fabrics Act (FFA) to:

Consumer Product Safety Commission (CPSC)
Office of Compliance
Washington DC 20207-0001
Tel: 800-638-2772 or (301) 504-7912
Fax: (301) 504-0359
Website: www.cpsc.gov

Address your questions regarding textile quotas to:

U.S. Customs and Border Protection
Office of Field Operations, Quota Branch
1300 Pennsylvania Avenue NW
Washington DC 20229
Tel: (202) 927-5850
Website: www.customs.treas.gov

The U.S. Customs Service provices updated status reports on textile quota on their web site (see address above). If the country you need information on is not listed, call the Quota Branch office at (202) 927-5850.

Address your questions regarding cordage and nonwoven fabric imports to your local Customs port director. For addresses, refer to "U.S. Customs and Border Protection Offices" on page 65 or contact:

U.S. Customs and Border Protection
Customs Headquarters
1300 Pennsylvania Avenue NW
Washington DC 20229
Tel: (202) 354-1000
Website: www.customs.treas.gov

Laws and Regulations

The following laws and regulations may be relevant to the importation of cordage and nonwoven fabrics. The laws are contained in the United States Code (USC), and the regulations are published in the Code of Federal Regulations (CFR), both of which are available at larger public and law libraries. Copies of specific laws are also available from the United States Government Printing Office (address above).

7 USC 1854
Textile Trade Agreements
(EO 11651, as amended by EO 11951 and 12188, and supplemented by EO 12475)
This Act authorizes the CITA of the DOC to enter into Multi-Fiber Agreements with other countries to control trade in textiles and establishes the Textile Import Program, which is enforced by U.S. Customs.

19 CFR 12.130 et seq.
Regulations on Entry of Textiles
These regulations provide the requirements and procedures followed by Customs in enforcing limitations on the importation and entry and withdrawal of textiles and textile products from warehouses for consumption in the U.S.

15 USC 70-77

Textile Fiber Products Identification Act (TFPIA)
This Act prohibits false or deceptive labeling (misbranding) and false advertising of any textile fiber products and requires all textile fiber products imported into the U.S. to be labeled in accordance with the requirements set forth in the law.

19 CFR 11.12b; 16 CFR 303 et seq.
Regulations on Labeling and Marking
These regulations detail the labeling and marking requirements for textiles as specified by the CPSC and the invoice contents required by U.S. Customs for purpose of enforcing the labeling and marking rules.

15 USC 68-68j
Wool Products Labeling Act (WPLA) of 1939
This Act prohibits the false or deceptive labeling (misbranding) of wool products and requires all wool products imported into the U.S. to be labeled in accordance with requirements set forth in the law.

19 CFR 11.12; 16 CFR 300 et seq.
Regulations on WPLA Labeling and Marking
These regulations set forth the wool labeling and marking requirements adopted by the FTC to administer the requirements of the WPLA and provide the procedures followed by U.S. Customs in enforcing the WPLA and the FTC regulations, including entry invoice requirements.

15 USC 1191-1204
Flammable Fabrics Act (FFA)
This Act provides for the setting of flammability standards for fabric by the Consumer Product Safety Commission (CPSC) and for enforcement by U.S. Customs.

16 CFR 1610, 1611, 1615, 1616, 1630-1632
Regulations on Flammable Fabric Standards
These regulations specify the flammability standards adopted by the CPSC under the FFA for various types of textiles.

16 CFR 423
Care Labeling Rule
Requires fiber composition and washing or dry cleaning instructions for textile apparel and certain piece goods.

Principal Exporting Countries

The following listing includes samples of the main supplier nations of the products of this chapter. It is organized by HTSUS major heading. (Refer to "Customs Classification" above for the product codes.) Countries are listed in rank order of the value of products imported to the U.S. Statistics represent customs value of entries for 2002 from the Bureau of Census, U.S. Department of Commerce.

5901—Mexico, United Kingdom, China, Italy, Belgium, Canada

5902—Canada, South Korea, Mexico, Taiwan, Poland, Indonesia, France, Italy

5903—Canada, South Korea, Germany, Taiwan, Japan, Mexico, Italy

5904—Netherlands, United Kingdom, Germany, Sweden, Italy

5905—Netherlands, Japan, Germany, Belgium, Czech Republic, Denmark

5906—Taiwan, Canada, China, Japan, Portugal, Germany

5907—Canada, South Korea, Italy, Taiwan, China, India

5908—Germany, India, Mexico, United Kingdom, Malta, China, Brazil, Taiwan

5909—Canada, Taiwan, China, United Kingdom, Ireland, Germany, Norway

5910—Germany, Spain, Italy, United Kingdom, Sweden, France

5911—Canada, Japan, Mexico, Germany, Switzerland, Italy, United Kingdom

Chapter 60:
Knitted or Crocheted Fabrics

This chapter relates to the importation of knitted or crocheted fabrics, which are classified under Chapter 60 of the Harmonized Tariff Schedule of the United States (HTSUS). Specifically, it includes knitted or crocheted pile and terry fabrics, fabrics containing elastomeric yarn or rubber thread, and warp knit fabrics—such as open-work, circular, and double or interlock knitted fabrics. The term "knitted goods" includes stitch-bonded goods in which the chain stitches are formed of textile yarns.

If you are interested in importing sewing thread, yarns, and other fibers or filaments, you should refer to Commodity Index Chapters 50 through 55. For importing knitted apparel, review Chapter 61. The import requirements for particular articles made of knitted or crocheted fabrics are covered in the Commodity Index chapters related to that article. For example, knitted or crocheted headgear is in Chapter 65 and footwear is in Chapter 64. Fabrics that are impregnated, coated, or covered with substances or preparations—with the exception of knitted or crocheted pile fabrics—are classified in Chapter 59 or in the Commodity Index chapter that covers the particular substance or preparation. For example, items impregnated with perfumes and cosmetics are in Chapter 33, soaps, detergents, polishes, and creams are in Chapter 34, and fabric softeners are in Chapter 38. If your product has plastic or rubber components, it may come under Chapter 39 or 40, respectively. If you are interested in importing knitted or crocheted lace, labels, badges, and similar items, you should refer to Chapter 58.

Note: To understand key issues that will enable you to make best use of the information in this section we recommend that you see "Introduction" on page 425.

Key Factors

The key factors in the importation of knitted or crocheted fabrics are:

- Compliance with quota restraints and visa requirements (if importing fabrics and other textile products)

- Submission of U.S. Customs Country-of-Origin Declaration(s)

- Compliance with entry invoice requirements

- Compliance with labeling requirements under Textile Fiber Products Identification Act (TFPIA) and/or the Wool Products Labeling Act (WPLA) and the Care Labeling Rule

- Compliance with flammability standards adopted and enforced by the Consumer Product Safety Commission (CPSC) under the Flammable Fabrics Act (FFA)

Although most importers use the services of a licensed customs broker in making their entries, and we recommend this practice, you should be aware of the regulatory, entry, and documentation issues involved in importing your product. You, as importer, are ultimately responsible for the fulfillment of any legal requirements applicable to your shipment.

General Considerations

Regulatory Agencies. The DOC's Committee for Implementation of Textile Agreements (CITA) regulates certain textile imports under Section 204 of the Agricultural Adjustment Act. U.S. Customs enforces CITA textile and textile product entry quotas. Customs also enforces compliance with labeling and invoice requirements of the TFPIA and flammability standards under the FFA. The CPSC monitors imports and from time to time inspects textile shipments for compliance with FFA standards. If you are importing wool textiles, importation is subject to complex textile import regulations. The Federal Trade Commission (FTC) administers the WPLA requirements.

Wool Product Entry Requirements. Depending on the nature of your wool fabric imports, as many as three different types of special entry documents may be required. First, for all imported textile fibers, yarns, and fabrics covered by the Agricultural Adjustment Act (AAA), including wool, you must file a U.S. Customs Textile Entry Declaration (see "Textile Country-of-Origin Declarations" below). Second, for all wool products subject to the WPLA, special information is required on the entry invoices (see "Entry and Documentation" below). Finally, certain wool articles manufactured or produced in certain countries may be subject to quotas under U.S. Department of Commerce Multi-Fiber Arrangements. Such products require export certificates or visas issued by the appropriate country of origin, in addition to other requisite entry paperwork (see "Quotas" below).

Wool Products Labeling Act. The term "wool product" means any product or any portion of a product that contains, purports to contain, or in any way is represented as containing wool, reprocessed wool, or reused wool. All wool products imported into the U.S., except those made more than 20 years before importation, and except carpets, rugs, mats, and upholsteries, must have affixed a stamp, tag, label, or other means of identification as required by the WPLA. If you are importing wool products exempt from labeling under the WPLA, do not assume they are also exempt from labeling under the TFPIA. These are two distinct laws, with some overlapping requirements (see "Marking and Labeling Requirements" below).

Textile Quotas. If you are interested in importing knitted or crocheted fabrics, the most important issue you need to be aware of is quotas. Under the Multi-Fiber Arrangement provisions of Section 204 of the Agricultural Adjustment Act, CITA initiates specific agreements with individual exporting countries. Section 204 of the Agricultural Adjustment Act covers textiles that: 1) are in chief value of cotton, wool, or man-made fibers, any textile fibers subject to the terms of any textile trade agreement, or any combination of such fibers; 2) contain 50% or more by weight of cotton or man-made fibers, or any textile fibers subject to the terms of any textile trade agreement; 3) contain 17% or more by weight of wool; or 4) if in chief value of textile fibers or textile materials, contain a blend of cotton, wool, or man-made fibers, any textile fibers subject to the terms of any textile trade agreement, or any combination of such fibers that, in total, amount to 50% or more by weight of all component fibers.

The U.S. has Multi-Fiber Arrangements with 40 countries. Each agreement with each country is unique, and may specify quotas for a type of textile or a specific article. Visas or export licenses may be required. These agreements, however, often change. Therefore, if you are interested in importing any knitted or crocheted fabrics, you should contact the International Trade Ad-ministration's Office of Textile and Apparel (see addresses at end of this chapter). Refer to "Prohibitions and Restrictions" below for further details.

Textile Country-of-Origin Declarations. U.S. Customs enforces CITA textile and textile product entry quotas (see "Prohibitions and Restrictions" below). Requirements for entry include submission of Country-of-Origin Declarations with every knitted or crocheted fabric shipment, regardless of whether it is subject to a specific multi-fiber arrangement (19 CFR 12.130, 12.131).

Country of Origin. Quota restrictions are country-specific and therefore are applied based on the country of origin for the textiles shipped. The last country from which a textile shipment was exported to the U.S. is not necessarily its country of origin. A textile or textile product imported into the U.S. is considered a product of the particular foreign territory or country, or a U.S. insular possession, where it is wholly grown, produced, or manufactured. For the following discussion, "country" means a foreign territory or country, or a U.S. insular possession.

In 1996, the U.S. Customs Service made major changes to country of origin rules for textile imports. The regulations at 19 CFR 102.21, "Textile and apparel products" were added to the 1996 Customs Regulations and became effective July 1, 1996. The new rules do not provide for cutting components or cutting and hemming to confer country of origin as in the past. The basis of the new law is processing operations or assembly. Some of the most important changes for importers to be aware of are:

- Cutting does not determine the country of origin (previously cutting determined country of origin for 90 percent of wearing apparel imports). The new rules are based on processing or assembly operations.

- Essential character does not determine country of origin because the new rules are based on processing.

- A subjective determination under the provisions of 19 CFR 12.130 is replaced by objective processing operations expressed in terms of tariff shifts. Dying, printing, and other finishing processes applied to fabrics no longer confer or change country of origin.

- Country of origin for textile and apparel products processed, assembled or manufactured in two or more countries is determined by where the most important processing occurs, and, if that cannot be ascertained, the last country in which an important processing operation occurs.

The country of origin is the country in which a product is wholly produced when a textile or apparel product is completely produced or manufactured (except for minor parts) in one country. For fabric, the country of origin is the country in which the fabric is woven, knitted, needled, tufted, felted, entangled or created by any other fabric-making process. The country of origin for staple yarn is the country in which yarn is spun; for filament yarn, the country in which filament is extruded; and for plied, gimped and cabled yarns, the country in which the fibers or filaments used in the yarn are spun or extruded. The country of origin of all other textile and apparel products is the country in which the components of a textile or apparel product are wholly assembled (except for minor attachments). Once again, note that assembly, not cutting, now confers country of origin.

Declarations. All importations of textiles and textile products must be accompanied by one of the following three declarations. Goods subject to Section 204, Agricultural Act of 1956, as amended, must be accompanied by either a single-country or a multiple-country declaration. Goods not subject to Section 204 must be accompanied by a negative declaration.

- **Single-country declarations** are used for entries of textiles or textile products which are wholly the growth, product, or manufacture of a single foreign country, territory, or U.S. insular possession. Information required includes: marks of identification and numbers; description of article and quantity; country of origin; and date of exportation.

- **Multiple-country declarations** are used for entries of textiles or textile products which were subjected to manufacturing or processing operations in, and/or incorporate materials originating in more than one foreign country or territory. Information required includes: marks of identification and numbers; for articles, description, quantity, identification of manufacturing and/or processing operations, country, and date of exportation; for materials used to make articles, description of materials, country of production, and date of exportation.

- **Negative declarations** must accompany all textile imports that are not subject to FFA Section 204 restrictions. Information required includes: marks of identification and numbers; descriptions of article and quantity; and country of origin.

The date of exportation to be indicated on the above declarations is the date on which the carrier leaves the last port in the country of origin, as determined by Customs. Diversion to another country during transit does not affect the export date.

Procedure for Declarations. The manufacturer, producer, exporter, or importer may prepare the declaration. If more than one of these parties is involved in the importation, each party may prepare a separate declaration. You may file a separate declaration for each invoice presented with your entry. The declaration must be dated and signed by the responsible party, and must include the person's title and the company name and address. Your shipment's entry will be denied unless it is accompanied by a properly executed declaration. Customs will not treat a textile declaration as a missing document for which a bond may be filed.

Customs will base its country-of-origin determination on the information contained in each declaration, unless the information is insufficient. If the information on the declaration is insufficient, Customs will require that you submit such additional information as will enable the determination to be made. The shipment will not be released until the determination is made. Thus, if you want to clear Customs with minimal delay, be sure that the information on the declarations is as complete as possible for each shipment.

Textile Labeling and Invoice Requirements. You are responsible for your imported knitted or crocheted fabric's compliance with applicable provisions of the TFPIA. Knitted or crocheted fabrics that require labeling under TFPIA must already be labeled at entry, or the shipment will be refused. (See "Marking and Labeling Requirements" below.) If you import shipments of special woven fabrics subject to TFPIA and valued at over $500, you must provide special information on the entry invoice (see "Entry and Documentation" below).

Flammability Standards. Knitted or crocheted fabrics imported into the U.S. for use in consumer products must be in compliance with the FFA, a federal law that gives the CPSC the authority and responsibility for protecting the public from the hazards of dangerously flammable items of wearing apparel and interior furnishings. Under the FFA, standards have been established for flammability of clothing textiles. You cannot import any article of wearing apparel or interior furnishing, or any fabric or related material that is intended for use or that may be used in such items, if it fails to conform to an applicable flammability standard (FFA Section 4). Certain products may be imported into the

U.S. (FFA Section 11c) for finishing or processing to render them less flammable so as to meet the standards. For these products, the exporter must state on the invoice or other paper relating to the shipment that the shipment is being made for that purpose.

The CPSC monitors imports of textiles under its Import Surveillance Program. From time to time, your textile shipments may be inspected to ascertain compliance with mandatory safety standards. Shipments may also be subject to testing by the CPSC to determine compliance. If the CPSC believes a product, fabric, or related material does not comply with a flammability standard, it is authorized to pursue a variety of legal sanctions (see "Prohibitions and Restrictions" below).

Substantial Product Hazard Reports. Any firm that obtains information that reasonably supports the conclusion that one of its products presents an unreasonable risk of serious injury or death must report that information to the CPSC's Division of Corrective Actions (CPSC address below). Importers must also report to the CPSC if 1) a type of product is the subject of at least three civil actions filed in U.S. federal or state courts, 2) each suit alleges the involvement of that product type in death or grievous bodily injury (as defined in FFA Section 37(3)1), and 3) at least three of the actions result in a final settlement with the manufacturer or in a judgment for the plaintiff within any one of the two-year periods specified in FFA Section 37(b).

Import Advisory

Importation of textiles is trade-sensitive and highly regulated. Shipments of textiles and textile products not complying with all government regulations, including quotas and visas, are subject to seizure and could result in the imposition of penalties as well as possible forfeiture of the goods. You should always verify the available quota for any textile product you plan to import before your shipment leaves the country of manufacture. Furthermore, Customs textile classification rulings change frequently, and prior administrative rulings are often modified and sometimes reversed. You should be particularly careful to comply with country of origin determination regulations, which were changed in 1996, and affect quotas and visas, marking and labeling, and other important aspects of tariff classification. See "Publications and WWW Resources" for information on important Customs Service informed compliance publications.

The Customs Service has greatly increased its scrutiny of the textile industry, one of eight primary focus industries identified in the most recent Trade Compliance & Enforcement Plan. Imported products from these industries will likely attract significant attention from Customs in the areas of compliance measurement, compliance assessment, informed compliance, and interventions.

Customs Classification

For customs purposes, knitted or crocheted fabrics are classified under Chapter 60 of the HTSUS. This chapter is broken into major headings, which are further divided into subheadings, and often sub-subheadings, each of which has its own HTSUS classification number. For example, the 2001 HTSUS number for long pile fabrics of man-made fibers is 6001.10.20, indicating it is a sub-subcategory of long-pile fabrics (6001.10), which is a subcategory of the major heading pile fabrics, etc. (6001). There are two major headings within Chapter 60.

6001—Pile fabrics, including "long pile" fabrics and terry fabrics, knitted or crocheted

6002—Other knitted or crocheted fabrics

For more details regarding classifications of the specific product you are interested in importing, consult a customs broker, the appropriate commodity specialist at your nearest customs port, or the HTSUS. The 2001 HTSUS is available online from the Customs

Service (www.customs.gov/impoexpo/impoexpo.htm) or for purchase from the U.S. Government Printing Office (see resources at the end of this chapter), and may be found in larger public libraries. For a general discussion of customs classification, see "Classification—Liquidation" on page 229.

Dutiable Status of Goods

For more information about duty rates and binding decisions see "Dutiable Status of Goods" on page 203; for a discussion of temporary importation of goods see "Temporary Free Importations" on page 205.

Valuation

Importers have a responsibility to use what the U.S. Customs Service deems, "reasonable care," when determining the value of their goods. They must also provide any additional information that the Customs Service needs for setting a final value on the goods. This process involves a number of factors and can be somewhat complicated; importers must be aware of applicable issues and details. Valuation information applies to all types of commodities, for further discussion on the subject see "Customs Valuation" on page 267.

Import Duties

Import duties vary (often dramatically) depending upon the Harmonized Tariff Schedule (HTSUS) classification of the goods or products imported. Since some products that look alike have different HTSUS classifications and different rates of duty, proper classification is vital. Note that "differences of opinion" between importers and the Bureau of Customs and Border Protection regarding classification keeps customs attorneys very busy.

Import duties can be assessed on the imported value of the goods ("ad valorem" rates of duty such as 2%, 4.4%, 50%, etc.), total units or weight of the goods ("specific" rates of duty such as 2 cents each or 1.5 cents/pound, etc.) or on a combination basis ("compound" rates of duty such as 5 cents each plus 6%).

Listed below is a sampling of several Column 1 import duty rates for Chapter 60 products:
Containing 85 percent or more by weight of silk or silk waste (6001.99.10.00): 4.4%
and
Open-work fabrics, warp knit (229) (6003.40.10.00): 14.3%

For specific information on US import duties refer to the Harmonized Tariff Schedule of the US. The print version is available from the US Government Printing Office as well as third party suppliers who often add special features. Online versions are available in both static PDF pages as well as in formats with excellent search functionality. Search the Web with the term "Harmonized Tariff Schedule" to find sources.

Entry and Documentation

The entry of merchandise is a two-part process consisting of 1) filing the documentation necessary to determine whether merchandise may be released from Customs custody, and 2) filing the documents that contain information for duty assessment and statistical purposes. In certain instances, all documents must be filed and accepted by Customs prior to release of the goods. Unless you have been granted an extension, you must file entry documents at a location specified by the port or area director within five working days of your shipment's date of arrival at a U.S. port of entry. These include a number of standard documents required by Customs for any entry, and:

- U.S. Customs Country-of-Origin Declaration Form CF 3229

- Export documentation and/or visa for textiles subject to Multi-Fiber Arrangement

After you present the entry, Customs may examine your shipment or may waive examination. The shipment is then released provided no legal or regulatory violations have been noted. You must then file entry summary documentation and deposit estimated duties at a designated customhouse within 10 working days of your shipment's release. For a detailed description of entry procedures, standard documentation, and informal entry, see "Entry Process" on page 185.

Informed Compliance. Informed compliance was introduced with the Customs Modernization Act of 1993 (Mod Act) and defines the relationship between importers and the Customs Service. It sets out the responsibilities of both parties. Providing the correct documentation and information for entry is a key factor that will make your importing operation run smoothly. We recommend that importers become familiar with the concept of informed comliance and the responsibilities that they have under the Mod Act. For further discussion about informed compliance see "Informed Compliance" on page 211.

NAFTA Certificates of Origin. An importer of textiles for which NAFTA treatment is sought need not file a separate NAFTA Certificate of Origin in addition to the Customs Country-of-Origin Declaration. The declaration is sufficient. However, the importer must take care to submit a declaration from each U.S., Canadian, or Mexican producer or manufacturer. Thus, for multiple producers or manufacturers, a separate declaration must be filed for each. If a Customs port director cannot determine the country of origin because the declaration is absent or incomplete, the shipment is not entitled to preferential NAFTA tariff treatment or other NAFTA benefits. See 19 CFR 12.132.

Entry Invoice TFPIA Requirements. For the purpose of TFPIA enforcement, a commercial shipment of textile products exceeding $500 in value and subject to TFPIA labeling requirements must show the following information: 1) the constituent fiber or combination of fibers, designating with equal prominence each natural or manufactured fiber by its generic name, in order of predominance by weight if the weight of such fiber is 5% or more of the total fiber weight of the product; 2) percentage of each fiber present, by weight, in the total fiber content; 3) the name or other identification issued and registered by the Federal Trade Commission of the manufacturer of the product or one or more persons subject to Section 3 of the TFPIA with respect to such product; 4) the name of the country where processed or manufactured.

Wool Products Subject to WPLA. When you offer for entry a wool product shipment valued at over $500 and subject to WPLA, you must include certain information intended to facilitate Customs monitoring and enforcement of that Act. This extra information is identical to that required by WPLA on labeling (see "Marking and Labeling Requirements" below), with the addition of the manufacturer's name. If your product consists of mixed waste, residues, and similar merchandise obtained from several suppliers or unknown sources, you may omit the manufacturer's name from the entry invoice.

Note: The Entry and Documentation section has been carefully designed to supply you, the importer, with sample documents and directions on how to satisfy Customs requirements. Be aware that you should consult the applicable authorities to ensure that you are correctly following the most current procedures.

Prohibitions and Restrictions

Textile Quotas. Textile import restrictions are primarily a matter of quotas and the way in which these quotas are administered and monitored. Under the Multi-Fiber Arrangement provisions of Section 204 of the Agricultural Adjustment Act, CITA has negotiated Multi-Fiber Arrangements with 40 countries. These Agreements may impose quotas for a type of textile or a specific article, and they are country-specific. The agreements, however, often change. Therefore, if you are interested in importing any knitted or crocheted fabrics, you should contact the International Trade Administration's Office of Textile and Apparel (see addresses at end of this chapter). The Office of Textile and Apparel has a team of country specialists who can inform you of the latest developments and inform you about a product's quota or restriction status.

U.S. Customs enforces CITA textile and textile product entry quotas. If formal entry procedures are not followed, Customs will usually refuse entry for textiles that are subject to Section 204. Formal entry requires submission of a Country-of-Origin Declaration (see General Considerations above). U.S. Customs maintains a current textile quota status report, available for perusal at any Customs port. In addition, U.S. Customs in Washington, DC, provides quota status reports online, which are updated on a regular basis (www.customs.gov/impoexpo/impoexpo.htm).

Flammable Fabrics. U.S. Customs may refuse entry for any article of wearing apparel or interior furnishing, or any fabric or related material that is intended for use or that may be used in wearing apparel or interior furnishings, if it fails to conform to an applicable flammability standard issued under Section 4 of the FFA. An exception is allowed for certain products (FFA Section 11c) that are imported for finishing or processing to bring them within the legal standard. For these products, the exporter must state on the invoice or other paper relating to the shipment that the shipment is being made for that purpose.

The CPSC, as the primary enforcement agency of flammability standards, inspects products for compliance with the FFA. If the CPSC believes a product, fabric, or related material does not comply with a flammability standard, it is authorized to pursue a variety of legal sanctions, including: 1) seizure, condemnation, and forfeiture of the noncomplying products; 2) administrative cease-and-desist order requiring an individual or firm to stop sale and distribution of the noncomplying products or; 3) temporary injunction requiring the individual or firm to stop sale and distribution of the noncomplying products, pending final disposition of an administrative cease-and-desist proceeding. The CPSC also has authority to seek civil penalties against any person who knowingly violates a regulation or standard issued under Section 4 of the FFA.

Country-Specific Restrictions

Restrictions under Multi-Fiber Arrangements are country-specific. A product originating in one country may be subject to quota and to export license or visa requirements, while the same product originating in a different country may not. At present, the U.S. has Multi-Fiber Arrangements with 40 countries. Many different categories of products are covered under these Arrangements; it is beyond the scope of this book to list each country and its restricted commodities. If you are interested in importing textiles and textile products, you should contact the International Trade Administration's Office of Textile and Apparel (see addresses at end of this chapter) or U.S. Customs to ascertain your product's restraint status.

The U.S. Customs service provides quota reports on their website (www.customs.gov/impoexpo/impoexpo.htm). These reports are constantly updated and have an effective date noted. The most recent quota information can be accessed by clicking on the country name that interests you. This location holds information regarding quotas, transshipments, and visa requirements.

Marking and Labeling Requirements

TFPIA Requirements. All textile fiber products imported into the U.S. must be stamped, tagged, labeled, or otherwise marked with the following information as required by the TFPIA, unless exempt from marking (see TFPIA, Section 12): 1) the generic names and percentages by weight of the constituent fibers present in the textile fiber product, exclusive of permissible ornamentation, in amounts of more than 5% in order of predominance by weight, with any percentage of fiber or fibers required to be designated as "other fiber" or "other fibers" (including those present in amounts of 5% or less) appearing last; and 2) the name of the manufacturer or the name or registered identification number issued by the FTC of one or more persons marketing or handling the textile fiber product; and 3) the name of the country where processed. A word trademark, used as a house mark and registered with the U.S. Patent Office, may appear on labels instead of the name otherwise required, provided the owner of the trademark furnishes a copy of the registration to the FTC prior to use (see "Registered Identification Numbers" below).

The information listed above is not exhaustive. TFPIA requirements are extensive. The Act specifies such details as types of labels, means of attachment, label position on the article, package labeling, unit labeling for two-piece garments, and arrangement of information on the label; allowable fiber designations; country-of-origin indications; requirements for trim and ornamentation, linings and interlinings, and pile fabrics; sectional disclosure; use of trade names and trademarks; and requirements for swatches and samples. The Federal Trade Commission publishes a booklet intended to clarify TFPIA requirements to facilitate voluntary compliance in the industry (see "Publications and WWW Resources" below). It is available on request, at no charge, from the FTC (see addresses at end of this chapter).

Wool Products Labeling Act (WPLA). Wool product labeling requirements for foreign products are the responsibility of the importer. The WPLA requires the following information to appear on wool products subject to the Act: 1) percentage of the wool product's total fiber weight (exclusive of ornamentation) not exceeding 5% of the total fiber weight of a) wool, b) recycled wool, c) each fiber other than wool if the percent by weight of such fiber is 5% or more, and d) the aggregate of all other fibers; 2) the maximum percent of the wool product's total weight, of any nonfibrous loading, filling, or adulterating matter; and 3) the importer's name. If you, as importer, have a registered identification number issued by the FTC, that number may be used instead of your name (see "Registered Identification Numbers" below).

Customs entry is contingent on proper labeling. If your shipment is found to be mislabeled at entry, you will be given the option of relabeling the products under Customs supervision, as long as the port director is satisfied that your labeling error or omission did not involve fraud or willful neglect. If your shipment is discovered after entry to have been noncomplying with WPLA, it will be recalled to Customs custody at your expense, unless you can satisfy the port director that the products have since been brought into compliance. You will be held responsible for all expenses incurred in bringing a shipment into compliance, including compensation of personnel and other expenses related to Customs supervision.

Fraudulent violations of WPLA will result in seizure of the shipment. Shipments already released from Customs custody will be ordered to be redelivered to Customs. Customs reports all cases of fraudulent violation to the FTC in Washington, DC.

The information listed above is not intended to be exhaustive. WPLA requirements are extensive. The Act specifies such details as types of labels, means of attachment, label position on the article, package labeling, unit labeling (as in the case of a two-piece garment), arrangement of information on the label, allowable fiber designations, country-of-origin indications, trim and ornamentation, pile fabrics, sectional disclosure, use of trade names and trademarks, requirements for swatches and samples, etc. The FTC publishes a booklet intended to clarify WPLA requirements in order to facilitate voluntary compliance within the industry (see "Publications and WWW Resources" below). It is available on request, at no charge, from the FTC (see addresses at end of this chapter).

The Care Labeling Rule. Regulations under this rule require manufacturers and importers of textile clothing and fabrics to attach specific care instructions for washing or dry cleaning, as well as information on the fiber composition of the article. They are enforced by the FTC Division of Enforcement. The Care Labeling Rule was amended September 2000, detailed information is available on the FTC website (www.ftc.gov/os/statutes/textilejump.htm).

Registered Identification Numbers. Any domestic firm or person residing in the U.S. and engaged in the manufacture or marketing of textile products covered under the TFPIA may obtain an FTC-registered identification number for use on required tags and labels instead of the name of a firm or person. For applications, contact the FTC (see addresses at end of this chapter).

For a general discussion of U.S. Customs marking and labeling requirements, see "Country of Origin Marking" on page 236, "Special Marking Requirements" on page 238 and "Marking—False Impression" on page 239.

Shipping Considerations

You will need to ensure that your goods are packaged and shipped with care so that they pass smoothly through Customs and arrive in good condition. You are responsible for ensuring that the shipment is in compliance with all applicable government regulations for packaging and shipping. In most instances, you should not leave these arrangements solely to the discretion of your supplier. Careful preparation of the cargo and selection of the mode of transport can be essential to a cost-effective, timely delivery of undamaged goods. We strongly advise you to consult your shipping representative, insurance agent, or freight broker for advice on packing and shipping.

Knitted or crocheted fabrics may be shipped in bulk, bolts, rolls, or other types of containers, depending on the type of product and whether it is prepackaged. General considerations include protection from contamination, weather, and pests. Safety precautions should also be implemented as required to protect against breakage, spillage, corrosion of containers, and combustion. Containers should be constructed so as to be safe for handling during transport.

Publications and WWW Resources

The following publications may be relevant to the importation of knitted or crocheted fabrics and wool fabrics:

Threading Your Way Through the Labeling Requirements Under the Textile and Wool Acts

Available free of charge on request from the Federal Trade Commission and online from the FTC website (www.ftc.gov/bcp/conline/pubs/buspubs/thread.htm). This publication is an excellent source of information written in clear lay language. We recommend that anyone interested in importing textile fiber products but unfamiliar with the regulations obtain a copy of each of this booklet.

The *Harmonized Tariff Schedule of the United States (2001)* (HTSUS) is available to view on the Customs Service website (www.customs.gov), or you may purchase a printed version from:

U.S. Government Printing Office
Superintendent of Documents
710 North Capital Street NW
Washington DC 20401
Tel: (202) 512-1800
Fax: (202) 512-1657
Website: www.access.gpo.gov

The USGPO also has copies of specific laws available for purchase. The USGPO accepts orders made by fax, phone or placed over the Internet, as well as mail orders paid by credit card. All orders must be accompanied by payment. Credit cards, checks drawn on a U.S. bank, or an international money order are all acceptable.

Relevant Government Agencies

Address your questions regarding textile Multi-Fiber Arrangements to:

U.S. Department of Commerce
International Trade Administration
Office of Textiles and Apparel
Director's Office
14th and Constitution Ave. NW, Rm. H3100
Washington, DC 20230
Tel: (202) 482-5078
Fax: (202) 482-2331
Agreements Division: (202) 482-4212
Website: http://otexa.ita.doc.gov

Address your questions regarding the Flammable Fabrics Act (FFA) to:

Consumer Product Safety Commission (CPSC)
Office of Compliance
Washington DC 20207-0001
Tel: 800-638-2772 or (301) 504-7912
Fax: (301) 504-0359
Website: www.cpsc.gov

Address your questions regarding labeling requirements under the Textile Fiber Products Identification Act (TFPIA) or the Wool Products Labeling Act (WPLA) to:

Federal Trade Commission (FTC)
Division of Enforcement
600 Pennsylvania Avenue NW
Washington DC 20580
Tel: (202) 326-2996
Website: www.ftc.gov

Address your questions regarding textile quotas to:

U.S. Customs Service
Office of Field Operations, Quota Branch
1300 Pennsylvania Avenue NW
Washington DC 20229
Tel: (202) 927-5850
Website: www.customs.treas.gov

The U.S. Customs Service provices updated status reports on textile quota on their web site (see address above). If the country you need information on is not listed, call the Quota Branch office at (202) 927-5850.

Address your questions regarding knitted or crocheted fabric imports to your local Customs port director. For addresses, refer to "U.S. Customs and Border Protection Offices" on page 65 or contact:

U.S. Customs Service
Customs Headquarters
1300 Pennsylvania Avenue NW
Washington DC 20229
Tel: (202) 354-1000
Website: www.customs.gov

Laws and Regulations

The following laws and regulations may be relevant to the importation of knitted or crocheted fabrics. The laws are contained in the United States Code (USC), and the regulations are published in the Code of Federal Regulations (CFR), both of which are available at larger public and law libraries. Copies of specific laws are also available from the United States Government Printing Office (address above).

7 USC 1854
Textile Trade Agreements
(EO 11651, as amended by EO 11951 and 12188, and supplemented by EO 12475)

This Act authorizes the CITA of the DOC to enter into Multi-Fiber Agreements with other countries to control trade in textiles and establishes the Textile Import Program, which is enforced by U.S. Customs.

19 CFR 12.130 et seq.
Regulations on Entry of Textiles
These regulations provide the requirements and procedures followed by Customs in enforcing limitations on the importation and entry and withdrawal of textiles and textile products from warehouses for consumption in the U.S.

15 USC 70-77
Textile Fiber Products Identification Act (TFPIA)
This Act prohibits false or deceptive labeling (misbranding) and false advertising of any textile fiber products and requires all textile fiber products imported into the U.S. to be labeled in accordance with the requirements set forth in the law.

19 CFR 11.12b; 16 CFR 303 et seq.
Regulations on Labeling and Marking
These regulations detail the labeling and marking requirements for textiles as specified by the CPSC and the invoice contents required by U.S. Customs for purpose of enforcing the labeling and marking rules.

15 USC 68-68j
Wool Products Labeling Act (WPLA) of 1939
This Act prohibits the false or deceptive labeling (misbranding) of wool products and requires all wool products imported into the U.S. to be labeled in accordance with requirements set forth in the law.

19 CFR 11.12; 16 CFR 300 et seq.
Regulations on WPLA Labeling and Marking
These regulations set forth the wool labeling and marking requirements adopted by the FTC to administer the requirements of the WPLA and provide the procedures followed by U.S. Customs in enforcing the WPLA and the FTC regulations, including entry invoice requirements.

15 USC 1191-1204
Flammable Fabrics Act (FFA)
This Act provides for the setting of flammability standards for fabric by the Consumer Product Safety Commission (CPSC) and for enforcement by U.S. Customs.

16 CFR 1610, 1611, 1615, 1616, 1630-1632
Regulations on Flammable Fabric Standards
These regulations specify the flammability standards adopted by the CPSC under the FFA for various types of textiles.

16 CFR 423
Care Labeling Rule
Requires fiber composition and washing or dry cleaning instructions for textile apparel and certain piece goods.

Principal Exporting Countries

The following listing includes samples of the main supplier nations of the products of this chapter. It is organized by HTSUS major heading. (Refer to "Customs Classification" above for the product codes.) Countries are listed in rank order of the value of products imported to the U.S. Statistics represent customs value of entries for 2002 from the Bureau of Census, U.S. Department of Commerce.

6001—Taiwan, South Korea, Canada, Japan, France, China, Germany, Italy, Netherlands, Belgium, Mexico, United Kingdom

6002—Israel, Mexico, Italy, Canada, France, Hong Kong, China, Germany, Taiwan, South Korea, Pakistan, South Africa

6003—Mexico, Canada, Taiwan, Spain, China, United Kingdom

6004—South Korea, Canada, Taiwan, Mexico, Italy, China

6005—South Korea, Canada, Taiwan, Mexico, Italy, China

6006—Canada, South Korea, Taiwan, Mexico, China, Italy

Chapter 61:
Knitted or Crocheted Articles of Apparel

Full title: Articles of Apparel and Clothing Accessories, Knitted or Crocheted

This chapter relates to the importation of knitted or crocheted apparel, which is classified under Chapter 61 of the Harmonized Tariff Schedule of the United States (HTSUS). Specifically, it covers knitted or crocheted garments for adults and children, including coats and jackets; suits, blazers, trousers, overalls, shorts, dresses, skirts, shirts, and blouses; undergarments and night clothes; t-shirts, tank tops, and singlets; sweaters, sweatshirts, and vests; track suits, ski suits, and swimwear; stockings and hosiery; footwear without applied soles; gloves, mittens, and mitts; and shawls, scarves, and similar clothing accessories.

If you are interested in importing articles of apparel that are not knitted or crocheted, you should read Commodity Index Chapter 62. Worn articles of apparel are covered in Chapter 63, and surgical belts and orthopedic items are classified in Chapter 90. If you are interested in importing footwear or headgear, you should refer to Chapter 64 or 65, respectively. Textiles, garment parts, thread, yarns, and other similar materials are covered in Chapters 50 through 58. Articles of apparel that contain leather parts may be imported in accordance with the requirements explained in Chapter 42.

Note: To understand key issues that will enable you to make best use of the information in this section we recommend that you see "Introduction" on page 425.

Key Factors

The key factors in the importation of knitted or crocheted apparel are:

- Compliance with quota restraints and visa requirements

- Submission of U.S. Customs Country-of-Origin Declaration(s)

- Compliance with entry invoice requirements

- Compliance with labeling requirements under Textile Fiber Products Identification Act (TFPIA) and/or the Wool Products Labeling Act (WPLA) and the Care Labeling Rule

- Compliance with flammability standards adopted and enforced by the Consumer Product Safety Commission (CPSC) under the Flammable Fabrics Act (FFA)

- Compliance with export licence requirements (if importing made-to-measure suits from Hong Kong)

Although most importers use the services of a licensed customs broker in making their entries, and we recommend this practice, you should be aware of the regulatory, entry, and documentation issues involved in importing your product. You, as importer, are ultimately responsible for the fulfillment of any legal requirements applicable to your shipment.

General Considerations

Regulatory Agencies. The Committee for Implementation of Textile Agreements (CITA) regulates certain textile imports under Section 204 of the Agricultural Adjustment Act. U.S. Customs enforces CITA textile and textile product entry quotas. Customs also enforces compliance with labeling and invoice requirements of the TFPIA and flammability standards under the FFA. The CPSC monitors imports and from time to time inspects textile shipments for compliance with FFA standards. If you are importing wool textiles, importation is subject to complex textile import regulations. The Federal Trade Commission (FTC) administers the WPLA requirements.

Wool Product Entry Requirements. Depending on the nature of your wool article imports, as many as three different types of special entry documents may be required. First, for all imported articles that contain textile fibers, yarns, and fabrics covered by the Agricultural Adjustment Act (AAA), including wool, you must file a U.S. Customs Textile Entry Declaration (see "Textile Country-of-Origin Declarations" below). Second, for all wool products subject to the WPLA, special information is required on the entry invoices (see "Wool Products Labeling Act" below). Third, certain articles of apparel manufactured or produced in certain countries may be subject to quotas and other restraints under U.S. Bilateral Agreements. Such products require export licenses, certificates, or visas issued by the appropriate country of origin, in addition to other requisite entry paperwork (see "Textile Quotas" below).

Wool Products Labeling Act. The term "wool product" means any product or any portion of a product that contains, purports to contain, or in any way is represented as containing wool, reprocessed wool, or reused wool. All wool products imported into the U.S., except those made more than 20 years before importation, and except carpets, rugs, mats, and upholsteries, must have affixed a stamp, tag, label, or other means of identification as required by the WPLA. If you are importing wool products exempt from labeling under the WPLA, do not assume they are also exempt from labeling under the TFPIA. These are two distinct laws, with some overlapping requirements (see "Marking and Labeling Requirements" below).

Textile Quotas. If you are interested in importing knitted or crocheted articles, the most important issue you need to be aware of is quotas. Under the Multi-Fiber Arrangement provisions of Section 204 of the Agricultural Adjustment Act, CITA initiates specific agreements with individual exporting countries. Section 204 of the Agricultural Adjustment Act covers textiles articles that: 1) are in chief value of cotton, wool, or man-made fibers, any textile fibers subject to the terms of any textile trade agreement, or any combination of such fibers; 2) contain 50% or more by weight of cotton or man-made fibers, or any textile fibers subject to the terms of any textile trade agreement; 3) contain 17% or more by weight of wool; or 4) if in chief value of textile fibers or textile materials, contain a blend of cotton, wool, or man-made fibers, any textile fibers subject to the terms of any textile trade agreement, or any combination of such fibers that, in total, amount to 50% or more by weight of all component fibers.

The U.S. has Bilateral Agreements with over 40 countries. Each agreement with each country is unique, and may specify quotas for a type of textile or a specific article. Visas or export licenses may be required. These agreements, however, often change. Therefore, if you are interested in importing any knitted or cro-

cheted articles of apparel, you should contact the International Trade Administration's Office of Textile and Apparel (see addresses at end of this chapter). Refer to "Prohibitions and Restrictions" below for further details.

Textile Country-of-Origin Declarations. U.S. Customs enforces CITA textile and textile product entry quotas (see "Prohibitions and Restrictions" below). Requirements for entry include submission of Country-of-Origin Declarations with every shipment of knitted or crocheted apparel articles, regardless of whether it is subject to a specific bilateral agreement (19 CFR 12.130, 12.131).

Country of Origin. Quota restrictions are country-specific and therefore are applied based on the country of origin for the textiles shipped. The last country from which a textile shipment was exported to the U.S. is not necessarily its country of origin. A textile or textile product imported into the U.S. is considered a product of the particular foreign territory or country, or a U.S. insular possession, where it is wholly grown, produced, or manufactured. For the following discussion, "country" means a foreign territory or country, or a U.S. insular possession.

In 1996, the U.S. Customs Service made major changes to country of origin rules for textile imports. The regulations at 19 CFR 102.21, "Textile and apparel products" were added to the 1996 Customs Regulations and became effective July 1, 1996. The new rules do not provide for cutting components or cutting and hemming to confer country of origin as in the past. The basis of the new law is processing operations or assembly. Some of the most important changes for importers to be aware of are:

- Cutting does not determine the country of origin (previously cutting determined country of origin for 90 percent of wearing apparel imports). The rules are now based on processing or assembly operations.

- A subjective determination under the provisions of 19 CFR 12.130 is replaced by objective processing operations expressed in terms of tariff shifts. Dyeing, printing, and other finishing processes applied to fabrics no longer confer or change country of origin.

- Country of origin for textile and apparel products processed, assembled or manufactured in two or more countries is determined by where the most important processing occurs, and, if that cannot be ascertained, the last country in which an important processing operation occurs.

The country of origin is the country in which a product is wholly produced when a textile or apparel product is completely produced or manufactured (except for minor parts) in one country. For fabric, the country of origin is the country in which the fabric is woven, knitted, needled, tufted, felted, entangled or created by any other fabric-making process. The country of origin for staple yarn is the country in which yarn is spun; for filament yarn, the country in which filament is extruded; and for plied, gimped and cabled yarns, the country in which the fibers or filaments used in the yarn are spun or extruded. The country of origin of all other textile and apparel products is the country in which the components of a textile or apparel product are wholly assembled (except for minor attachments) except for knit-to-shape products. Knit-to-shape products are those composed of panels or parts ,which, are knitted or crocheted directly into the shape that will be used in construction of the final product. Minor cutting or sewing does not influence whether the product is considered knit-to-shape. The country of origin for knit-to-shape products is that country in which the major parts are knitted into the shape that will constitute the finished product. Once again, note that assembly, not cutting, now confers country of origin.

Declarations. All importations of textiles and textile products must be accompanied by one of the following three declarations. Goods subject to Section 204, Agricultural Act of 1956, as amended, must be accompanied by either a single-country or a multiple-country declaration. Goods not subject to Section 204 must be accompanied by a negative declaration.

- **Single-country declarations** are used for entries of textiles or textile products which are wholly the growth, product, or manufacture of a single foreign country, territory, or U.S. insular possession. Information required includes: marks of identification and numbers; description of article and quantity; country of origin; and date of exportation.

- **Multiple-country declarations** are used for entries of textiles or textile products which were subjected to manufacturing or processing operations in, and/or incorporate materials originating in more than one foreign country or territory. Information required includes: marks of identification and numbers; for articles, description, quantity, identification of manufacturing and/or processing operations, country, and date of exportation; for materials used to make articles, description of materials, country of production, and date of exportation.

- **Negative declarations** must accompany all textile imports that are not subject to AAA Section 204 restrictions. Information required includes: marks of identification and numbers; descriptions of article and quantity; and country of origin.

The date of exportation to be indicated on the above declarations is the date on which the carrier leaves the last port in the country of origin, as determined by Customs. Diversion to another country during transit does not affect the export date.

Procedure for Declarations. The manufacturer, producer, exporter, or importer may prepare the declaration. If more than one of these parties is involved in the importation, each party may prepare a separate declaration. You may file a separate declaration for each invoice presented with your entry. The declaration must be dated and signed by the responsible party, and must include the person's title and the company name and address. Your shipment's entry will be denied unless it is accompanied by a properly executed declaration. Customs will not treat a textile declaration as a missing document for which a bond may be filed.

Customs will base its country-of-origin determination on the information contained in each declaration, unless the information is insufficient. If the information on the declaration is insufficient, Customs will require that you submit such additional information as will enable the determination to be made. The shipment will not be released until the determination is made. Thus, if you want to clear Customs with minimal delay, be sure that the information on the declarations is as complete as possible for each shipment.

Textile Labeling and Invoice Requirements. You are responsible for your imported product's compliance with applicable provisions of the TFPIA. Knitted or crocheted apparel articles that require labeling under TFPIA must already be labeled at entry, or the shipment will be refused. (See "Marking and Labeling Requirements" below.) If you import shipments of knitted or crocheted articles subject to TFPIA and valued at over $500, you must provide special information on the entry invoice (see "Entry and Documentation" below).

Flammability Standards. Knitted or crocheted apparel articles imported into the U.S. for use in consumer products must be in compliance with the FFA, a federal law that gives the CPSC the authority and responsibility for protecting the public from the hazards of dangerously flammable items of wearing apparel and interior furnishings. Under the FFA, standards have been established for flammability of clothing textiles. You cannot import any article of wearing apparel or interior furnishing, or any fabric or related material that is intended for use or that may be used in such items, if it fails to conform to an applicable flammability standard (FFA Section 4). Certain products may be imported into the U.S. (FFA Section 11c) for finishing or processing to render them less flammable so as to meet the standards. For these products, the exporter must state on the invoice or other paper relating to the shipment that the shipment is being made for that purpose.

The CPSC monitors imports of textiles under its Import Surveillance Program. From time to time, your textile shipments may be inspected to ascertain compliance with mandatory safety standards. Shipments may also be subject to testing by the CPSC to determine compliance. If the CPSC believes a product, fabric, or related material does not comply with a flammability standard, it is authorized to pursue a variety of legal sanctions (see "Prohibitions and Restrictions" below).

Substantial Product Hazard Reports. Any firm that obtains information that reasonably supports the conclusion that one of its products presents an unreasonable risk of serious injury or death must report that information to the CPSC's Division of Corrective Actions (CPSC address below). Importers must also report to the CPSC if 1) a type of product is the subject of at least three civil actions filed in U.S. federal or state courts, 2) each suit alleges the involvement of that product type in death or grievous bodily injury (as defined in FFA Section 37(3)1), and 3) at least three of the actions result in a final settlement with the manufacturer or in a judgment for the plaintiff within any one of the two-year periods specified in FFA Section 37(b).

Import Advisory

Importation of textile products is trade-sensitive and highly regulated. Shipments of textile products not complying with all government regulations, including quotas and visas, are subject to seizure and could result in the imposition of penalties as well as possible forfeiture of the goods. You should always verify the available quota for any textile product you plan to import before your shipment leaves the country of manufacture. Furthermore, Customs textile classification rulings change frequently, and prior administrative rulings are often modified and sometimes reversed. You should be particularly careful to comply with country of origin determination regulations, which were changed in 1996, and affect quotas and visas, marking and labeling, and other important aspects of tariff classification. See "Publications and WWW Resources" for information on important Customs Service informed compliance publications.

The Customs Service has greatly increased its scrutiny of the textile industry, one of eight primary focus industries identified in the most recent Trade Compliance & Enforcement Plan. Imported products from these industries will likely attract significant attention from Customs in the areas of compliance measurement, compliance assessment, informed compliance, and interventions.

Customs Classification

For customs purposes, knitted or crocheted articles of apparel are classified under Chapter 61 of the HTSUS. This chapter is broken into major headings, which are further divided into subheadings, and often sub-subheadings, each of which has its own HTSUS classification number. For example, the 2001 HTSUS number for men's wool trousers, breeches, and shorts is 6103.41.10, indicating it is a sub-subcategory of trousers, etc., of wool or fine animal hair (6103.41), which is a subcategory of the major heading men's and boys' suits, ensembles, etc. (6103). There are 17 major headings within Chapter 61.

6101—Men's or boys' overcoats, carcoats, capes, cloaks, anoraks (including ski-jackets), windbreakers, and similar articles, knitted or crocheted, other than those of heading 6103

6102—Women's or girls' overcoats, carcoats, capes, cloaks, anoraks (including ski-jackets), windbreakers, and similar articles, knitted or crocheted, other than those of heading 6104

6103—Men's or boys' suits, ensembles, suit-type jackets, blazers, trousers, bib and brace overalls, breeches and shorts (other than swimwear), knitted or crocheted

6104—Women's or girl's suits, ensembles, suit-type jackets, blazers, dresses, skirts, divided skirts, trousers, bib and brace overalls, breeches and shorts (other than swimwear), knitted or crocheted

6105—Men's or boys' shirts, knitted or crocheted

6106—Women's or girls' blouses and shirts, knitted or crocheted

6107—Men's or boys' underpants, briefs, nightshirts, pajamas, bathrobes, dressing gowns, and similar articles, knitted or crocheted

6108—Women's or girls' slips, petticoats, briefs, panties, nightdresses, pajamas, negligees, bathrobes, dressing gowns, and similar articles, knitted or crocheted

6109—T-shirts, singlets, tank tops, and similar garments, knitted or crocheted

6110—Sweaters, pullovers, sweatshirts, waistcoats (vests), and similar articles, knitted or crocheted

6111—Babies' garments and clothing accessories, knitted or crocheted

6112—Track suits, ski suits, and swimwear, knitted or crocheted

6113—Garments, made up of knitted or crocheted fabrics of heading 5903, 5906, or 5907

6114—Other garments, knitted or crocheted

6115—Panty hose, tights, stockings, socks, and other hosiery, including stockings for varicose veins, and footwear without applied soles, knitted or crocheted

6116—Gloves, mittens and mitts, knitted or crocheted

6117—Other made up clothing accessories, knitted or crocheted; knitted or crocheted parts of garments or of clothing accessories

Definitions. For duty purposes, Customs defines suits, ensembles, and ski suits as follows.

Suits. The term "suit" means a set of garments composed of two or three pieces made up in identical fabric and comprising: 1) one garment designed to cover the lower part of the body and consisting of trousers, breeches, or shorts, (other than swimwear), or a skirt or a divided skirt, having neither braces nor bibs; and 2) one suit coat or jacket, with the outer shell, exclusive of sleeves, made of four or more panels, designed to cover the upper part of the body, possibly with a tailored waistcoat in addition. if several separate components to cover the lower part of the body are entered together—such as trousers and shorts—the trousers, or for women's or girl's suits, the skirt or divided skirt will be considered part of the suit, and the other garments will be considered separately. All components of a suit must be of the same fabric construction, style, color, and composition. They must also be of corresponding or compatible size.

The following sets of garments are considered suits, whether or not they fulfill all the above conditions: l) morning dress, comprising a plain jacket (cutaway) with rounded tails hanging well down at the back and striped trousers; 2) evening dress (tailcoat), generally made of black fabric, the jacket of which is relatively short at the front, does not close and has narrow skirts cut in at the hips and hanging down behind; or 3) dinner jacket suits, in which the jacket is similar in style to an ordinary jacket (though

perhaps revealing more of the shirt front), but has shiny silk or imitation silk lapels.

Ensembles. The term "ensemble" means a set of garments (other than suits and articles of HTSUS heading 6107, 6108, or 6109) composed of several pieces made up in identical fabric, put up for retail sale, and comprising: 1) one garment designed to cover the upper part of the body, (with the exception of pullovers, which may form a second upper garment in the sole context of twin sets, and of waistcoats, which may also form a second upper garment), and 2) one or two different garments, designed to cover the lower part of the body and consisting of trousers, bib and brace overalls, breeches, shorts (other than swimwear), a skirt, or a divided skirt. All of the components must be of the same fabric construction, style, color, and composition and must be of corresponding or compatible sizes. Track suits and ski suits are not classified as ensembles.

Ski Suits. The term "ski suit" means garments or sets of garments that, by their general appearance and texture, are identifiable as intended to be worn principally for skiing (cross-country or alpine). They consist either of: 1) a ski overall—that is, a one-piece garment that is designed to cover the upper and the lower parts of the body and that may have sleeves, a collar, pockets, and/or footstraps; or 2) a ski ensemble—that is a set of garments composed of two or three pieces, put up for retail sale and comprising: a) one garment, such as an anorak, windbreaker, or similar article, closed by a slide fastener (zipper), possibly with a waistcoat in addition; and b) one pair of trousers whether or not extending above waist level, one pair of breeches, or one bib and brace overall. A ski ensemble may also consist of an overall similar to the one mentioned in paragraph (a) above and a type of padded, sleeveless jacket worn over the overall. All components of a ski ensemble must be made up in a fabric of the same texture, style, and composition, whether or not of the same color. They also must be of corresponding or compatible size.

For more details regarding classifications of the specific product you are interested in importing, consult a customs broker, the appropriate commodity specialist at your nearest customs port, or the HTSUS. The 2001 HTSUS is available online from the Customs Service (www.customs.gov/impoexpo/impoexpo.htm) or for purchase from the U.S. Government Printing Office (see resources at the end of this chapter), and may be found in larger public libraries. For a general discussion of customs classification, see "Classification—Liquidation" on page 229.

Dutiable Status of Goods

For more information about duty rates and binding decisions see "Dutiable Status of Goods" on page 203; for a discussion of temporary importation of goods see "Temporary Free Importations" on page 205.

Valuation

Importers have a responsibility to use what the U.S. Customs Service deems, "reasonable care," when determining the value of their goods. They must also provide any additional information that the Customs Service needs for setting a final value on the goods. This process involves a number of factors and can be somewhat complicated; importers must be aware of applicable issues and details. Valuation information applies to all types of commodities, for further discussion on the subject see "Customs Valuation" on page 267.

Import Duties

Import duties vary (often dramatically) depending upon the Harmonized Tariff Schedule (HTSUS) classification of the goods or products imported. Since some products that look alike have different HTSUS classifications and different rates of duty, proper classification is vital. Note that "differences of opinion" between importers and the Bureau of Customs and Border Protection regarding classification keeps customs attorneys very busy.

Import duties can be assessed on the imported value of the goods ("ad valorem" rates of duty such as 2%, 4.4%, 50%, etc.), total units or weight of the goods ("specific" rates of duty such as 2 cents each or 1.5 cents/pound, etc.) or on a combination basis ("compound" rates of duty such as 5 cents each plus 6%).

Listed below is a sampling of several Column 1 import duty rates for Chapter 61 products:
Containing 70 percent or more by weight of silk or silk waste (735) (6102.90.10 00): 1.4%
to
Of other textile materials of artificial fibers (633) (6103.39.10.00): 16.4%

For specific information on US import duties refer to the Harmonized Tariff Schedule of the US. The print version is available from the US Government Printing Office as well as third party suppliers who often add special features. Online versions are available in both static PDF pages as well as in formats with excellent search functionality. Search the Web with the term "Harmonized Tariff Schedule" to find sources.

Entry and Documentation

The entry of merchandise is a two-part process consisting of 1) filing the documentation necessary to determine whether merchandise may be released from Customs custody, and 2) filing the documents that contain information for duty assessment and statistical purposes. In certain instances, all documents must be filed and accepted by Customs prior to release of the goods. Unless you have been granted an extension, you must file entry documents at a location specified by the port or area director within five working days of your shipment's date of arrival at a U.S. port of entry. These include a number of standard documents required by Customs for any entry, and:

- U.S. Customs Country-of-Origin Declaration Form CF 3229

- Export documentation and/or visa for textiles subject to Bilateral Agreements

- Hong Kong government export license (if importing made-to-measure suits from Hong Kong)

After you present the entry, Customs may examine your shipment or may waive examination. The shipment is then released provided no legal or regulatory violations have been noted. If not already completed you must then file entry summary documentation and deposit estimated duties at a designated customhouse within 10 working days of your shipment's release. For a detailed description of entry procedures, standard documentation, and informal entry, see "Entry Process" on page 185.

Informed Compliance. Informed compliance was introduced with the Customs Modernization Act of 1993 (Mod Act) and defines the relationship between importers and the Customs Service. It sets out the responsibilities of both parties. Providing the correct documentation and information for entry is a key factor that will make your importing operation run smoothly. We recommend that importers become familiar with the concept of informed comliance and the responsibilities that they have under the Mod Act. For further discussion about informed compliance see "Informed Compliance" on page 211.

NAFTA Certificates of Origin. An importer of textiles for which NAFTA treatment is sought need not file a separate NAFTA Certificate of Origin in addition to the Customs Country-of-Origin Declaration. The declaration is sufficient. However, the importer must take care to submit a declaration from each U.S., Canadian, or Mexican producer or manufacturer. Thus, for multiple producers or manufacturers, a separate declaration must be filed for each. If a Customs port director cannot determine the country of origin because the declaration is absent or incomplete, the shipment is not entitled to preferential NAFTA tariff treatment or other NAFTA benefits. See 19 CFR 12.132.

Entry Invoices. You must provide certain additional information on the entry invoice for knitted or crocheted articles of apparel. The specific information varies depending on the nature of your product, as noted below.

TFPIA Requirements. All invoices for textile wearing apparel should indicate: 1) a component material breakdown in percentages by weight for all component fibers present in the entire garment, as well as separate breakdowns of the fibers in the (outer) shell (exclusive of linings, cuffs, waistbands, collars and other trimmings) and in the lining; 2) for garments that are constructed of more than one component or material (combination of knit and not-knit fabric or combinations of knit and/or not-knit fabric with leather, fur, plastic—including vinyl, etc.) the invoice must show a fiber breakdown in percentages by weight for each separate textile material in the garment and a breakdown in percentages by weight for each nontextile material of the entire garment; 3) for woven garments: indicate whether the fabric is yarn-dyed and whether there are "two or more colors in the warp and/or filling;" 4) for all-white T-shirts and singlets: indicate whether or not the garment contains pockets, trim, or embroidery; 5) for mufflers: state the exact dimensions, length, and width of the merchandise.

Wool Products Subject to WPLA. When you offer for entry a wool product shipment valued at over $500 and subject to WPLA, you must include certain information intended to facilitate Customs monitoring and enforcement of that Act. This extra information is identical to that required by WPLA on labeling (see "Marking and Labeling Requirements" below), with the addition of the manufacturer's name. If your product consists of mixed waste, residues, and similar merchandise obtained from several suppliers or unknown sources, you may omit the manufacturer's name from the entry invoice. For more general information about invoices see "Invoices" on page 277.

Invoices for Gloves. For any gloves classifiable under HTSUS subheading 6116.10.20, the entry invoice must state whether the gloves have been covered with plastics on both sides.

Invoices for Hosiery. The entry invoice for items of hosiery must indicate 1) whether a single yarn measures less than 67 decitex; 2) whether the hosiery is full length, knee length, or less than knee length; and 3) whether it contains lace or net.

Invoices for Hong Kong Made-to-Measure Suits. Imports from Hong Kong of "made-to-measure" suits that do not accompany a returning traveler are subject to a special agreement. Suits made to the specific measurements of a particular person require a "made-to-measure" export license from the Hong Kong government. You must identify "made-to-measure" suits of Hong Kong origin on your entry summary by placing the symbol "G" as a prefix to the appropriate tariff number. The importer is responsible for the payment of any Customs duties at the time of importation, even if the suits are made to measure for an individual person. For more information, contact your nearest U.S. Customs port office.

Special Access or Regime Entries. Certain garments assembled abroad from components formed and cut in the U.S. that, after assembly have been subject to bleaching, garment dyeing, or perma-pressing abroad, may be eligible for entry under the Special Access Program. Eligibility must be established under a bilateral agreement, and entry must be in compliance with procedures established by the Committee for the Implementation of Textile Agreements. You must identify such garments on the entry summary or withdrawal forms by placing the symbol "H" as a prefix to the appropriate tariff number.

Note: The Entry and Documentation section has been carefully designed to supply you, the importer, with sample documents and directions on how to satisfy Customs requirements. Be aware that you should consult the applicable authorities to ensure that you are correctly following the most current procedures.

Prohibitions and Restrictions

Textile Quotas. Textile import restrictions are primarily a matter of quotas and the way in which these quotas are administered and monitored. Under the Multi-Fiber Arrangement provisions of Section 204 of the Agricultural Adjustment Act, CITA has negotiated bilateral agreements with over 40 countries. These Agreements may impose quotas for a type of textile or a specific article, and they are country-specific. The agreements, however, often change. Therefore, if you are interested in importing any knitted or crocheted apparel articles, you should contact the International Trade Administration's Office of Textile and Apparel (see addresses at end of this chapter). The Office of Textile and Apparel has a team of country specialists who can inform you of the latest developments and inform you about a product's quota or restriction status.

U.S. Customs enforces CITA textile and textile product entry quotas. If formal entry procedures are not followed, Customs will usually refuse entry. Formal entry requires submission of a Country-of-Origin Declaration (see "General Considerations" above). U.S. Customs maintains a current textile quota status report, available for perusal online, which is updated on a regular basis (www.customs.gov/impoexpo/impoexpo.htm).

Flammable Fabrics. U.S. Customs may refuse entry for any article of wearing apparel or interior furnishing, or any fabric or related material that is intended for use or that may be used in wearing apparel or interior furnishings, if it fails to conform to an applicable flammability standard issued under Section 4 of the FFA. An exception is allowed for certain products (FFA Section 11c) that are imported for finishing or processing to bring them within the legal standard. For these products, the exporter must state on the invoice or other paper relating to the shipment that the shipment is being made for that purpose.

The CPSC, as the primary enforcement agency of flammability standards, inspects products for compliance with the FFA. If the CPSC believes a product, fabric, or related material does not comply with a flammability standard, it is authorized to pursue a variety of legal sanctions, including: 1) seizure, condemnation, and forfeiture of the noncomplying products; 2) administrative cease-and-desist order requiring an individual or firm to stop sale and distribution of the noncomplying products or; 3) temporary injunction requiring the individual or firm to stop sale and distribution of the noncomplying products, pending final disposition of an administrative cease-and-desist proceeding. The CPSC also has authority to seek civil penalties against any person who knowingly violates a regulation or standard issued under Section 4 of the FFA.

Country-Specific Restrictions

Restrictions under Bilateral Agreements are country-specific. A product originating in one country may be subject to quota and to export license or visa requirements, while the same product originating in a different country may not. At present, the U.S. has Multi-Fiber Arrangements with 40 countries. Many different categories of products are covered under these Arrangements; it is beyond the scope of this book to list each country and its restricted commodities. If you are interested in importing textiles and textile products, you should contact the International Trade Administration's Office of Textile and Apparel (see addresses at end of this chapter) or U.S. Customs to ascertain your product's restraint status.

The U.S. Customs service provides quota reports on their website (www.customs.gov/impoexpo/impoexpo.htm). These reports are constantly updated and have an effective date noted. The most recent quota information can be accessed by clicking on the country name that interests you. This location holds information regarding quotas, transshipments, and visa requirements.

Marking and Labeling Requirements

TFPIA Requirements. All textile products imported into the U.S. must be stamped, tagged, labeled, or otherwise marked with the following information as required by the TFPIA, unless exempt from marking (see TFPIA, Section 12): 1) the generic names and percentages by weight of the constituent fibers present in the textile fiber product, exclusive of permissible ornamentation, in amounts of more than 5% in order of predominance by weight, with any percentage of fiber or fibers required to be designated as "other fiber" or "other fibers" (including those present in amounts of 5% or less) appearing last; and 2) the name of the manufacturer or the name or registered identification number issued by the FTC of one or more persons marketing or handling the textile fiber product; and 3) the name of the country where processed. A word trademark, used as a house mark and registered with the U.S. Patent Office, may appear on labels instead of the name otherwise required, provided the owner of the trademark furnishes a copy of the registration to the FTC prior to use (see "Registered Identification Numbers" below).

The information listed above is not exhaustive. TFPIA requirements are extensive. The Act specifies such details as types of labels, means of attachment, label position on the article, package labeling, unit labeling for two-piece garments, and arrangement of information on the label; allowable fiber designations; country-of-origin indications; requirements for trim and ornamentation, linings and interlinings, and pile fabrics; sectional disclosure; use of trade names and trademarks; and requirements for swatches and samples. The FTC publishes a booklet intended to clarify TFPIA requirements to facilitate voluntary compliance in the industry (see "Publications and WWW Resources" below). It is available online from the FTC.

Wool Products Labeling Act (WPLA). Wool product labeling requirements for foreign products are the responsibility of the importer. The WPLA requires the following information to appear on wool products subject to the Act: 1) percentage of the wool product's total fiber weight (exclusive of ornamentation) not exceeding 5% of the total fiber weight of a) wool, b) recycled wool, c) each fiber other than wool if the percent by weight of such fiber is 5% or more, and d) the aggregate of all other fibers; 2) the maximum percent of the wool product's total weight, of any nonfibrous loading, filling, or adulterating matter; and 3) the importer's name. If you, as importer, have a registered identification number issued by the FTC, that number may be used instead of your name (see "Registered Identification Numbers" below).

Customs entry is contingent on proper labeling. If your shipment is found to be mislabeled at entry, you will be given the option of relabeling the products under Customs supervision, as long as the port director is satisfied that your labeling error or omission did not involve fraud or willful neglect. If your shipment is discovered after entry to have been noncomplying with WPLA, it will be recalled to Customs custody at your expense, unless you can satisfy the port director that the products have since been brought into compliance. You will be held responsible for all expenses incurred in bringing a shipment into compliance, including compensation of personnel and other expenses related to Customs supervision.

Fraudulent violations of WPLA will result in seizure of the shipment. Shipments already released from Customs custody will be ordered to be redelivered to Customs. Customs reports all cases of fraudulent violation to the FTC in Washington, DC.

The information listed above is not intended to be exhaustive. WPLA requirements are extensive. The Act specifies such details as types of labels, means of attachment, label position on the article, package labeling, unit labeling (as in the case of a two-piece garment), arrangement of information on the label, allowable fiber designations, country-of-origin indications, trim and ornamentation, pile fabrics, sectional disclosure, use of trade names and trademarks, requirements for swatches and samples, etc. The FTC publishes a booklet intended to clarify WPLA requirements in order to facilitate voluntary compliance within the industry (see "Publications and WWW Resources" below). It is available online, from the FTC.

The Care Labeling Rule. Regulations under this rule require manufacturers and importers of textile clothing and fabrics to attach specific care instructions for washing or dry cleaning, as well as information on the fiber composition of the article. They are enforced by the FTC Division of Enforcement. The Care Labeling Rule was amended September 2000, detailed information is available on the FTC website (www.ftc.gov/os/statutes/textilejump.htm).

Registered Identification Numbers. Any domestic firm or person residing in the U.S. and engaged in the manufacture or marketing of textile products covered under the TFPIA may obtain an FTC-registered identification number for use on required tags and labels instead of the name of a firm or person. For applications, contact the FTC (see addresses at end of this chapter).

For a general discussion of U.S. Customs marking and labeling requirements, see "Country of Origin Marking" on page 236, "Special Marking Requirements" on page 238 and "Marking—False Impression" on page 239.

Shipping Considerations

You will need to ensure that your goods are packaged and shipped with care so that they pass smoothly through Customs and arrive in good condition. You are responsible for ensuring that the shipment is in compliance with all applicable government regulations for packaging and shipping. In most instances, you should not leave these arrangements solely to the discretion of your supplier. Careful preparation of the cargo and selection of the mode of transport can be essential to a cost-effective, timely delivery of undamaged goods. We strongly advise you to consult your shipping representative, insurance agent, or freight broker for advice on packing and shipping.

Knitted or crocheted apparel articles may be shipped in bulk, cartons, or other types of containers, depending on the type of product and whether it is prepackaged. General considerations include protection from contamination, weather, and pests. Containers should be constructed so as to be safe for handling during transport.

Publications and WWW Resources

The following publications may be relevant to the importation of knitted or crocheted apparel articles:

Threading Your Way Through the Labeling Requirements Under the Textile and Wool Acts

Available from the Federal Trade Commission wesite (www.ftc.gov/bcp/conline/pubs/buspubs/thread.htm), this publication is an excellent source of information written in clear lay language. We recommend that anyone interested in importing textile products but unfamiliar with the regulations refer to this document.

The U.S. Customs Service launched a series of "Informed Compliance" publications in 1996, which are available on the Customs Service website (www.customs.gov/impoexpo/impoexpo.htm). Of particular interest:

What Every Member of the Trade Community Should Know About Textile & Apparel Rules of Origin

What Every Member of the Trade community Should Know About NAFTA for Textiles and Textile Articles

Fibers & Yarns Construction and Classification Under the HTSUS

The *Harmonized Tariff Schedule of the United States (2001)* (HTSUS) is available to view on the Customs Service website (www.customs.gov), or you may purchase a printed version from:

U.S. Government Printing Office
Superintendent of Documents
710 North Capital Street NW
Washington DC 20401
Tel: (202) 512-1800
Fax: (202) 512-1657
Website: www.access.gpo.gov

The USGPO also has copies of specific laws available for purchase. The USGPO accepts orders made by fax, phone or placed over the Internet, as well as mail orders paid by credit card. All orders must be accompanied by payment. Credit cards, checks drawn on a U.S. bank, or an international money order are all acceptable.

Relevant Government Agencies

Address your questions regarding textile Multi-Fiber Arrangements to:

U.S. Department of Commerce
International Trade Administration
Office of Textiles and Apparel
Director's Office
14th and Constitution Avenue NW, Rm. H3100
Washington DC 20230
Tel: (202) 482-5078
Fax: (202) 482-2331
Agreements Division: (202) 482-4212
Website: http://otexa.ita.doc.gov

Address your questions regarding the Flammable Fabrics Act (FFA) to:

Consumer Product Safety Commission (CPSC)
Office of Compliance
Washington DC 20207-0001
Tel: 800-638-2772 or (301) 504-7912
Fax: (301) 504-0359
Website: www.cpsc.gov

Address your questions regarding labeling requirements under the Textile Fiber Products Identification Act (TFPIA) or the Wool Products Labeling Act (WPLA) to:

Federal Trade Commission (FTC)
Division of Enforcement
600 Pennsylvania Avenue NW
Washington DC 20580
Tel: (202) 326-2996
Website: www.ftc.gov

Address your questions regarding textile quotas to:

U.S. Customs and Border Protection
Office of Field Operations, Quota Branch
1300 Pennsylvania Avenue NW
Washington DC 20229
Tel: (202) 927-5850
Website: www.customs.treas.gov

The U.S. Customs Service provices updated status reports on textile quota on their web site (see address above). If the country you need information on is not listed, call the Quota Branch office at (202) 927-5850.

Address your questions regarding knitted or crocheted apparel article imports to your local Customs port director. For addresses, refer to "U.S. Customs and Border Protection Offices" on page 65 or contact:

U.S. Customs and Border Protection
Customs Headquarters
1300 Pennsylvania Avenue NW
Washington DC 20229
Tel: (202) 354-1000
Website: www.customs.treas.gov

Laws and Regulations

The following laws and regulations may be relevant to the importation of knitted or crocheted apparel articles. The laws are contained in the United States Code (USC), and the regulations are published in the Code of Federal Regulations (CFR), both of which are available at larger public and law libraries. Copies of specific laws are also available from the United States Government Printing Office (address above).

7 USC 1854
Textile Trade Agreements
(EO 11651, as amended by EO 11951 and 12188, and supplemented by EO 12475)
This Act authorizes the CITA of the DOC to enter into Multi-Fiber Agreements with other countries to control trade in textiles and establishes the Textile Import Program, which is enforced by U.S. Customs.

19 CFR 12.130 et seq.
Regulations on Entry of Textiles
These regulations provide the requirements and procedures followed by Customs in enforcing limitations on the importation and entry and withdrawal of textiles and textile products from warehouses for consumption in the U.S.

15 USC 70-77
Textile Fiber Products Identification Act (TFPIA)
This Act prohibits false or deceptive labeling (misbranding) and false advertising of any textile fiber products and requires all textile fiber products imported into the U.S. to be labeled in accordance with the requirements set forth in the law.

19 CFR 11.12b; 16 CFR 303 et seq.
Regulations on Labeling and Marking
These regulations detail the labeling and marking requirements for textiles as specified by the CPSC and the invoice contents required by U.S. Customs for purpose of enforcing the labeling and marking rules.

15 USC 68-68j
Wool Products Labeling Act (WPLA) of 1939
This Act prohibits the false or deceptive labeling (misbranding) of wool products and requires all wool products imported into the U.S. to be labeled in accordance with requirements set forth in the law.

19 CFR 11.12; 16 CFR 300 et seq.
Regulations on WPLA Labeling and Marking
These regulations set forth the wool labeling and marking requirements adopted by the FTC to administer the requirements of the WPLA and provide the procedures followed by U.S. Customs in enforcing the WPLA and the FTC regulations, including entry invoice requirements.

15 USC 1191-1204
Flammable Fabrics Act (FFA)
This Act provides for the setting of flammability standards for fabric by the Consumer Product Safety Commission (CPSC) and for enforcement by U.S. Customs.

16 CFR 1610, 1611, 1615, 1616, 1630-1632
Regulations on Flammable Fabric Standards

These regulations specify the flammability standards adopted by the CPSC under the FFA for various types of textiles.

16 CFR 423
Care Labeling Rule
Requires fiber composition and washing or dry cleaning instructions for textile apparel and certain piece goods.

Principal Exporting Countries

The following listing includes samples of the main supplier nations of the products of this chapter. It is organized by HTSUS major heading. (Refer to "Customs Classification" above for the product codes.) Countries are listed in rank order of the value of products imported to the U.S. Statistics represent customs value of entries for 2002 from the Bureau of Census, U.S. Department of Commerce.

6101—Mexico, Pakistan, China, South Korea, Vietnam, Thailand, Macao, Philippines, Jordan, Hong Kong

6102—Taiwan, China, Philippines, Mexico, Canada, South Korea, Hong Kong, Malaysia

6103—Mexico, Thailand, South Korea, Taiwan, Indonesia, Guatemala, China, Philippines, El Salvador, Bangladesh, Honduras, Malaysia, Vietnam

6104—Mexico, Taiwan, El Salvador, Hong Kong, Guatemala, South Korea

6105—India, Pakistan, Honduras, El Salvador, Thailand, South Korea, Philippines

6106—Mexico, China, Guatemala, Macao, Hong Kong, Taiwan, Philippines

6107—Dominican Republic, Honduras, El Salvador, Thailand, Costa Rica, Canada, Cambodia

6108—Mexico, Hong Kong, China, Costa Rica, El Salvador, Israel, Honduras, Turkey

6109—Mexico, Honduras, El Salvador, Dominican Republic, Canada

6110—China, Hong Kong, Mexico, South Korea, Honduras, Guatemala, Taiwan, Macao, Thailand

6111—China, Thailand, Malaysia, Philippines, Indonesia, South Korea, Hong Kong

6112—Mexico, Canada, Dominican Republic, Taiwan, China, Indonesia

6113—China, Thailand, Taiwan, Philippines, Sri Lanka, Bangladesh

6114—Mexico, Hong Kong, China, Guatemala, Taiwan, South Korea, Canada, Sri Lanka, Macao

6115—Mexico, South Korea, El Salvador, Canada, Costa Rica, Taiwan

6116—China, Mexico, Taiwan, Sri Lanka, Malaysia, South Korea, Indonesia, Philippines

6117—China, Mexico, Taiwan, Canada, Italy, South Korea, Thailand, Philippines

Chapter 62:
Apparel Not Knitted or Crocheted

Full title: Articles of Apparel and Clothing Accessories, Not Knitted or Crocheted

This chapter relates to the importation of textile apparel articles and clothing accessories other than knitted or crocheted items, which are classified under Chapter 62 of the Harmonized Tariff Schedule of the United States (HTSUS). Specifically, it covers textile garments, not knitted or crocheted, for adults and children, including coats and jackets; suits, blazers, trousers, overalls, shorts, dresses, skirts, shirts, and blouses; undergarments and night clothes; track suits, ski suits, and swimwear; handkerchiefs; shawls, scarves, and similar clothing accessories; ties, bows, and cravats; and gloves, mittens, and mitts.

If you are interested in importing articles of apparel that are knitted or crocheted, you should read Commodity Index Chapter 61. Articles made of textile wadding are covered in Chapter 56, worn articles of apparel are covered in Chapter 63, and surgical belts and orthopedic items are classified in Chapter 90. If you are interested in importing footwear or headgear, you should refer to Chapter 64 or 65, respectively. Textiles, garment parts, thread, yarns, and other similar materials are covered in Chapters 50 through 58. Articles of apparel that contain leather parts may be imported in accordance with the requirements explained in Chapter 42.

Note: To understand key issues that will enable you to make best use of the information in this section we recommend that you see "Introduction" on page 425.

Key Factors

The key factors in the importation of articles not knitted or crocheted are:

- Compliance with quota restraints and visa requirements

- Submission of U.S. Customs Country-of-Origin Declaration(s)

- Compliance with entry invoice requirements

- Compliance with labeling requirements under Textile Fiber Products Identification Act (TFPIA) and/or the Wool Products Labeling Act (WPLA) and the Care Labeling Rule

- Compliance with flammability standards adopted and enforced by the Consumer Product Safety Commission (CPSC) under the Flammable Fabrics Act (FFA)

- Compliance with export licence requirements (if importing made-to-measure suits from Hong Kong)

- Compliance with Special Access or Regime entry requirements (if importing garments assembled and bleached, dyed, stone-washed, acid-washed, or perma-pressed abroad from components formed and cut in the US)

Although most importers use the services of a licensed customs broker in making their entries, and we recommend this practice, you should be aware of the regulatory, entry, and documentation issues involved in importing your product. You, as importer, are ultimately responsible for the fulfillment of any legal requirements applicable to your shipment.

General Considerations

Regulatory Agencies. The DOC's Committee for Implementation of Textile Agreements (CITA) regulates certain textile imports under Section 204 of the Agricultural Adjustment Act. U.S. Customs enforces CITA textile and textile product entry quotas. Customs also enforces compliance with labeling and invoice requirements of the TFPIA and flammability standards under the FFA. The CPSC monitors imports and from time to time inspects textile shipments for compliance with FFA standards. If you are importing wool textiles, importation is subject to complex textile import regulations. The Federal Trade Commission (FTC) administers the WPLA requirements.

Wool Product Entry Requirements. Depending on the nature of your wool article imports, as many as three different types of special entry documents may be required. First, for all imported articles that contain textile fibers, yarns, and fabrics covered by the Agricultural Adjustment Act (AAA), including wool, you must file a U.S. Customs Textile Entry Declaration (see "Textile Country-of-Origin Declarations" below). Second, for all wool products subject to the WPLA, special information is required on the entry invoices (see "Wool Products Labeling Act" below). Finally, certain articles of apparel manufactured or produced in certain countries may be subject to quotas and other restraints under U.S. bilateral agreements. Such products require export licenses, certificates, or visas issued by the appropriate country of origin, in addition to other requisite entry paperwork (see "Textile Quotas" below).

Wool Products Labeling Act. The term "wool product" means any product or any portion of a product that contains, purports to contain, or in any way is represented as containing wool, reprocessed wool, or reused wool. All wool products imported into the U.S., except those made more than 20 years before importation, and except carpets, rugs, mats, and upholsteries, must have affixed a stamp, tag, label, or other means of identification as required by the WPLA. If you are importing wool products exempt from labeling under the WPLA, do not assume they are also exempt from labeling under the TFPIA. These are two distinct laws, with some overlapping requirements (see "Marking and Labeling Requirements" below).

Textile Quotas. If you are interested in importing textile apparel articles or clothing accessories, the most important issue you need to be aware of is quotas. Under the Multi-Fiber Arrangement provisions of Section 204 of the Agricultural Adjustment Act, CITA initiates specific agreements with individual exporting countries. Section 204 of the Agricultural Adjustment Act covers textiles articles that: 1) are in chief value of cotton, wool, or man-made fibers, any textile fibers subject to the terms of any textile trade agreement, or any combination of such fibers; 2) contain 50% or more by weight of cotton or man-made fibers, or any textile fibers subject to the terms of any textile trade agreement; 3) contain 17% or more by weight of wool; or 4) if in chief value of textile fibers or textile materials, contain a blend of cotton, wool, or man-made fibers, any textile fibers subject to the terms of any textile trade agreement, or any combination of such fibers that, in total, amount to 50% or more by weight of all component fibers.

The U.S. has bilateral agreements with over 40 countries. Each agreement with each country is unique, and may specify quotas for a type of textile or a specific article. Visas or export licenses may be required. These agreements, however, often change. Therefore, if you are interested in importing any textile apparel articles or clothing accessories, you should contact the International Trade Administration's Office of Textile and Apparel (see addresses at end of this chapter). Refer to "Prohibitions and Restrictions" below for further details.

Textile Country-of-Origin Declarations. U.S. Customs enforces CITA textile and textile product entry quotas (see "Prohibitions and Restrictions" below). Requirements for entry include submission of Country-of-Origin Declarations with every shipment of woven textile apparel articles or clothing accessories, regardless of whether it is subject to a specific multi-fiber arrangement (19 CFR 12.130, 12.131).

Country of Origin. Quota restrictions are country-specific and therefore are applied based on the country of origin for the textiles shipped. The last country from which a textile shipment was exported to the U.S. is not necessarily its country of origin. A textile or textile product imported into the U.S. is considered a product of the particular foreign territory or country, or a U.S. insular possession, where it is wholly grown, produced, or manufactured. For the following discussion, "country" means a foreign territory or country, or a U.S. insular possession.

In 1996, the U.S. Customs Service made major changes to country of origin rules for textile imports. The regulations at 19 CFR 102.21, "Textile and apparel products" were added to the 1996 Customs Regulations and became effective July 1, 1996. The new rules do not provide for cutting components or cutting and hemming to confer country of origin as in the past. The basis of the new law is processing operations or assembly. Some of the most important changes for importers to be aware of are:

- Cutting does not determine the country of origin (previously cutting determined country of origin for 90 percent of wearing apparel imports). The new rules are based on processing or assembly operations.

- A subjective determination under the provisions of 19 CFR 12.130 is replaced by objective processing operations expressed in terms of tariff shifts. Dying, printing, and other finishing processes applied to fabrics no longer confer or change country of origin.

- Country of origin for textile and apparel products processed, assembled or manufactured in two or more countries is determined by where the most important processing occurs, and, if that cannot be ascertained, the last country in which an important processing operation occurs.

The country of origin is the country in which a product is wholly produced when a textile or apparel product is completely produced or manufactured (except for minor parts) in one country. For fabric, the country of origin is the country in which the fabric is woven, knitted, needled, tufted, felted, entangled or created by any other fabric-making process. The country of origin for staple yarn is the country in which yarn is spun; for filament yarn, the country in which filament is extruded; and for plied, gimped and cabled yarns, the country in which the fibers or filaments used in the yarn are spun or extruded. The country of origin of all other textile and apparel products is the country in which the components of a textile or apparel product are wholly assembled (except for minor attachments) except for knit-to-shape products.

Knit-to-shape products are those composed of panels or parts ,which, are knitted or crocheted directly into the shape that will be used in construction of the final product. Minor cutting or sewing does not influence whether the product is considered knit-to-shape. The country of origin for knit-to-shape products is that country in which the major parts are knitted into the shape that will constitute the finished product. Once again, note that assembly, not cutting, now confers country of origin.

Declarations. All importations of textiles and textile products must be accompanied by one of the following three declarations. Goods subject to Section 204, Agricultural Act of 1956, as amended, must be accompanied by either a single-country or a multiple-country declaration. Goods not subject to Section 204 must be accompanied by a negative declaration.

- **Single-country declarations** are used for entries of textiles or textile products which are wholly the growth, product, or manufacture of a single foreign country, territory, or U.S. insular possession. Information required includes: marks of identification and numbers; description of article and quantity; country of origin; and date of exportation.

- **Multiple-country declarations** are used for entries of textiles or textile products which were subjected to manufacturing or processing operations in, and/or incorporate materials originating in more than one foreign country or territory. Information required includes: marks of identification and numbers; for articles, description, quantity, identification of manufacturing and/or processing operations, country, and date of exportation; for materials used to make articles, description of materials, country of production, and date of exportation.

- **Negative declarations** must accompany all textile imports that are not subject to AAA Section 204 restrictions. Information required includes: marks of identification and numbers; descriptions of article and quantity; and country of origin.

The date of exportation to be indicated on the above declarations is the date on which the carrier leaves the last port in the country of origin, as determined by Customs. Diversion to another country during transit does not affect the export date.

Procedure for Declarations. The manufacturer, producer, exporter, or importer may prepare the declaration. If more than one of these parties is involved in the importation, each party may prepare a separate declaration. You may file a separate declaration for each invoice presented with your entry. The declaration must be dated and signed by the responsible party, and must include the person's title and the company name and address. Your shipment's entry will be denied unless it is accompanied by a properly executed declaration. Customs will not treat a textile declaration as a missing document for which a bond may be filed.

Customs will base its country-of-origin determination on the information contained in each declaration, unless the information is insufficient. If the information on the declaration is insufficient, Customs will require that you submit such additional information as will enable the determination to be made. The shipment will not be released until the determination is made. Thus, if you want to clear Customs with minimal delay, be sure that the information on the declarations is as complete as possible for each shipment.

Textile Labeling and Invoice Requirements. You are responsible for your imported product's compliance with applicable provisions of the TFPIA. Textile apparel articles or clothing accessories that require labeling under TFPIA must already be labeled at entry, or the shipment will be refused. (See "Marking and Labeling Requirements" below.) If you import shipments of textile apparel articles or clothing accessories subject to TFPIA and valued at over $500, you must provide special information on the entry invoice (see "Entry and Documentation" below).

Flammability Standards. Textile apparel articles or clothing accessories imported into the U.S. for use in consumer products must be in compliance with the FFA, a federal law that gives the CPSC the authority and responsibility for protecting the public from the hazards of dangerously flammable items of wearing apparel and interior furnishings. Under the FFA, standards have been established for flammability of clothing textiles. You cannot import any article of wearing apparel or interior furnishing, or any fabric or related material that is intended for use or that may be used in such items, if it fails to conform to an applicable flammability standard (FFA Section 4). Certain products may be imported into the U.S. (FFA Section 11c) for finishing or processing to render them less flammable so as to meet the standards. For these products, the exporter must state on the invoice or other paper relating to the shipment that the shipment is being made for that purpose.

The CPSC monitors imports of textiles under its Import Surveillance Program. From time to time, your textile shipments may be inspected to ascertain compliance with mandatory safety standards. Shipments may also be subject to testing by the CPSC to determine compliance. If the CPSC believes a product, fabric, or related material does not comply with a flammability standard, it is authorized to pursue a variety of legal sanctions (see "Prohibitions and Restrictions" below).

Substantial Product Hazard Reports. Any firm that obtains information that reasonably supports the conclusion that one of its products presents an unreasonable risk of serious injury or death must report that information to the CPSC's Division of Corrective Actions (CPSC address below). Importers must also report to the CPSC if 1) a type of product is the subject of at least three civil actions filed in U.S. federal or state courts, 2) each suit alleges the involvement of that product type in death or grievous bodily injury (as defined in FFA Section 37(3)1), and 3) at least three of the actions result in a final settlement with the manufacturer or in a judgment for the plaintiff within any one of the two-year periods specified in FFA Section 37(b).

Import Advisory

Importation of textile products is trade-sensitive and highly regulated. Shipments of textile products not complying with all government regulations, including quotas and visas, are subject to seizure and could result in the imposition of penalties as well as possible forfeiture of the goods. You should always verify the available quota for any textile product you plan to import before your shipment leaves the country of manufacture. Furthermore, Customs textile classification rulings change frequently, and prior administrative rulings are often modified and sometimes reversed. You should be particularly careful to comply with country of origin determination regulations, which were changed in 1996, and affect quotas and visas, marking and labeling, and other important aspects of tariff classification. See "Publications and WWW Resources" for information on important Customs Service informed compliance publications.

The Customs Service has greatly increased its scrutiny of the textile industry, one of eight primary focus industries identified in the most recent Trade Compliance & Enforcement Plan. Imported products from these industries will likely attract significant attention from Customs in the areas of compliance measurement, compliance assessment, informed compliance, and interventions.

Customs Classification

For customs purposes, textile apparel articles or clothing accessories are classified under Chapter 62 of the HTSUS. This chapter is broken into major headings, which are further divided into subheadings, and often sub-subheadings, each of which has its own HTSUS classification number. For example, the 2001 HTSUS number for babies' cotton dresses is 6209.20.10, indicating it is a sub-subcategory of garments of cotton (6209.20), which is a sub-category of the major heading babies' garments and clothing accessories (6209). There are 17 major headings within Chapter 62.

6201—Men's or boys' overcoats, carcoats, capes, cloaks, anoraks (including ski-jackets), windbreakers, and similar articles (including padded, sleeveless jackets), other than those of heading 6203

6202—Women's or girls' overcoats, carcoats, capes cloaks, anoraks (including ski-jackets), windbreakers, and similar articles (including padded, sleeveless jackets), other than those of heading 6204

6203—Men's or boys' suits, ensembles, suit-type jackets, blazers, trousers, bib and brace overalls, breeches, and shorts (other than swimwear)

6204—Women's or girls' suits, ensembles, suit-type jackets, blazers, dresses, skirts, divided skirts, trousers, bib and brace overalls, breeches, and shorts (other than swimwear)

6205—Men's or boys' shirts

6206—Women's or girls' blouses, shirts, and shirt-blouses

6207—Men's or boys' singlets and other undershirts, underpants, briefs, nightshirts, pajamas, bathrobes, dressing gowns, and similar articles

6208—Women's or girls' singlets, and other undershirts, slips, petticoats, briefs, panties, nightdresses, pajamas, negligees, bathrobes, dressing gowns, and similar articles

6209—Babies' garments and clothing accessories

6210—Garments, made up of fabrics of heading 5602, 5603, 5903, 5906, or 5907

6211—Track suits, ski suits, and swimwear; other garments

6212—Brassieres, girdles, corsets, braces, suspenders, garters, and similar articles and parts thereof, whether or not knitted or crocheted

6213—Handkerchiefs

6214—Shawls, scarves, mufflers, mantillas, veils, and the like

6215—Ties, bow ties, and cravats

6216—Gloves, mittens, and mitts

6217—Other made up clothing accessories; parts of garments or of clothing accessories, other than those of heading 6212

Definitions. For classification for duty purposes, Customs defines suits, ensembles, and ski suits as follows.

Suits. The term "suit" means a set of garments composed of two or three pieces made up in identical fabric and comprising: 1) one garment designed to cover the lower part of the body and consisting of trousers, breeches, or shorts (other than swimwear), or a skirt or divided skirt, having neither braces nor bibs; and 2) one suit coat or jacket, with the outer shell, exclusive of sleeves, made of four or more panels, designed to cover the upper part of the body, possibly with a tailored waistcoat in addition. If several separate components to cover the lower part of the body are entered together—such as trousers and shorts—the trousers, or for women's or girl's suits, the skirt or divided skirt, will be considered part of the suit, and the other garments will be considered separately. All components of a suit must be of the same fabric construction, style, color, and composition. They must also be of corresponding or compatible size.

The following sets of garments are considered suits, whether or not they fulfill all the above conditions: 1) morning dress, comprising a plain jacket (cutaway) with rounded tails hanging well down at the back and striped trousers; 2) evening dress (tailcoat), generally made of black fabric, the jacket of which is relatively short at the front, does not close and has narrow skirts cut in at the hips and hanging down behind; or 3) dinner jacket suits, in which the jacket is similar in style to an ordinary jacket (though perhaps revealing more of the shirt front), but has shiny silk or imitation silk lapels.

Ensembles. The term "ensemble" means a set of garments (other than suits and articles of HTSUS heading 6207 or 6208) composed of several pieces made up in identical fabric, put up for retail sale, and comprising: 1) one garment designed to cover the upper part of the body, (with the exception of waistcoats, which may form a second upper garment), and 2) one or two different garments, designed to cover the lower part of the body, and consisting of trousers, bib and brace overalls, breeches, shorts (other than swimwear), a skirt, or a divided skirt. All of the components must be of the same fabric construction, style, color, and composition and must be of corresponding or compatible sizes. Track suits and ski suits are not classified as ensembles.

Ski Suits. The term "ski suit" means garments or sets of garments that, by their general appearance and texture, are identifiable as intended to be worn principally for skiing (cross-country or alpine). They consist either of: 1) a ski overall—that is, a one-piece garment that is designed to cover the upper and the lower parts of the body and that may have sleeves, a collar, pockets, and/or footstraps; or 2) a ski ensemble—that is a set of garments composed of two or three pieces, put up for retail sale and comprising: a) one garment, such as an anorak, windbreaker, or similar article, closed by a slide fastener (zipper), possibly with a waistcoat in addition; and b) one pair of trousers whether or not extending above waist level, one pair of breeches, or one bib and brace overall. A ski ensemble may also consist of an overall similar to the one mentioned in paragraph (a) above and a type of padded, sleeveless jacket worn over the overall. All components of a ski ensemble must be made up in a fabric of the same texture, style, and composition, whether or not of the same color. They also must be of corresponding or compatible size.

For more details regarding classifications of the specific product you are interested in importing, consult a customs broker, the appropriate commodity specialist at your nearest customs port, or the HTSUS. The 2001 HTSUS is available online from the Customs Service (www.customs.gov/impoexpo/impoexpo.htm) or for purchase from the U.S. Government Printing Office (see resources at the end of this chapter), and may be found in larger public libraries. For a general discussion of customs classification, see "Classification—Liquidation" on page 229.

Dutiable Status of Goods

For more information about duty rates and binding decisions see "Dutiable Status of Goods" on page 203; for a discussion of temporary importation of goods see "Temporary Free Importations" on page 205.

Valuation

Importers have a responsibility to use what the U.S. Customs Service deems, "reasonable care," when determining the value of their goods. They must also provide any additional information that the Customs Service needs for setting a final value on the goods. This process involves a number of factors and can be somewhat complicated; importers must be aware of applicable issues and details. Valuation information applies to all types of commodities, for further discussion on the subject see "Customs Valuation" on page 267.

Import Duties

Import duties vary (often dramatically) depending upon the Harmonized Tariff Schedule (HTSUS) classification of the goods or products imported. Since some products that look alike have different HTSUS classifications and different rates of duty, proper

classification is vital. Note that "differences of opinion" between importers and the Bureau of Customs and Border Protection regarding classification keeps customs attorneys very busy.

Import duties can be assessed on the imported value of the goods ("ad valorem" rates of duty such as 2%, 4.4%, 50%, etc.), total units or weight of the goods ("specific" rates of duty such as 2 cents each or 1.5 cents/pound, etc.) or on a combination basis ("compound" rates of duty such as 5 cents each plus 6%).

Listed below is a sampling of several Column 1 import duty rates for Chapter 62 products:
Containing 15 percent or more by weight of down and waterfowl plumage and of which down comprises 35 percent or more by weight; containing 10 percent or more by weight of down (6203.42.10.00): 0.5%
to
Containing 36 percent or more by weight of wool or fine animal hair (6204.69.20): 13.9%

For specific information on US import duties refer to the Harmonized Tariff Schedule of the US. The print version is available from the US Government Printing Office as well as third party suppliers who often add special features. Online versions are available in both static PDF pages as well as in formats with excellent search functionality. Search the Web with the term "Harmonized Tariff Schedule" to find sources.

Entry and Documentation

The entry of merchandise is a two-part process consisting of 1) filing the documentation necessary to determine whether merchandise may be released from Customs custody, and 2) filing the documents that contain information for duty assessment and statistical purposes. In certain instances, all documents must be filed and accepted by Customs prior to release of the goods. Unless you have been granted an extension, you must file entry documents at a location specified by the port or area director within five working days of your shipment's date of arrival at a U.S. port of entry. These include a number of standard documents required by Customs for any entry, and:

- U.S. Customs Country-of-Origin Declaration Form CF 3229
- Export documentation and/or visa for textiles subject to bilateral agreement
- Hong Kong government export license (if importing made-to-measure suits from Hong Kong)

After you present the entry, Customs may examine your shipment or may waive examination. The shipment is then released provided no legal or regulatory violations have been noted. If not already done you must then file entry summary documentation and deposit estimated duties at a designated customhouse within 10 working days of your shipment's release. For a detailed description of entry procedures, standard documentation, and informal entry, see "Entry Process" on page 185.

Informed Compliance. Informed compliance was introduced with the Customs Modernization Act of 1993 (Mod Act) and defines the relationship between importers and the Customs Service. It sets out the responsibilities of both parties. Providing the correct documentation and information for entry is a key factor that will make your importing operation run smoothly. We recommend that importers become familiar with the concept of informed comliance and the responsibilities that they have under the Mod Act. For further discussion about informed compliance see "Informed Compliance" on page 211.

NAFTA Certificates of Origin. An importer of textiles for which NAFTA treatment is sought need not file a separate NAFTA Certificate of Origin in addition to the Customs Country-of-Origin Declaration. The declaration is sufficient. However, the importer must take care to submit a declaration from each U.S., Canadian, or Mexican producer or manufacturer. Thus, for multiple producers or manufacturers, a separate declaration must be filed for each. If a Customs port director cannot determine the country of origin because the declaration is absent or incomplete, the shipment is not entitled to preferential NAFTA tariff treatment or other NAFTA benefits. See 19 CFR 12.132.

Entry Invoices. You must provide certain additional information on the entry invoice for apparel which is neither knitted nor crocheted. The specific information varies depending on the nature of your product, as noted below.

TFPIA Requirements. All invoices for textile wearing apparel should indicate: 1) a component material breakdown in percentages by weight for all component fibers present in the entire garment, as well as separate breakdowns of the fibers in the (outer) shell (exclusive of linings, cuffs, waistbands, collars and other trimmings) and in the lining; 2) for garments that are constructed of more than one component or material (combination of knit and not-knit fabric or combinations of knit and/or not-knit fabric with leather, fur, plastic—including vinyl, etc.) the invoice must show a fiber breakdown in percentages by weight for each separate textile material in the garment and a breakdown in percentages by weight for each nontextile material of the entire garment; 3) for woven garments: indicate whether the fabric is yarn-dyed and whether there are "two or more colors in the warp and/or filling;" 4) for all-white T-shirts and singlets: indicate whether or not the garment contains pockets, trim, or embroidery; 5) for mufflers: state the exact dimensions, length, and width of the merchandise.

Wool Products Subject to WPLA. When you offer for entry a wool product shipment valued at over $500 and subject to WPLA, you must include certain information intended to facilitate Customs monitoring and enforcement of that Act. This extra information is identical to that required by WPLA on labeling (see "Marking and Labeling Requirements" below), with the addition of the manufacturer's name. If your product consists of mixed waste, residues, and similar merchandise obtained from several suppliers or unknown sources, you may omit the manufacturer's name from the entry invoice.

Handkerchiefs. The entry invoice for a shipment of handkerchiefs must show: 1) the exact dimensions (length and width) of the merchandise, and 2) if made of cotton, whether hemmed and whether containing lace or embroidery.

Made-to-Measure Suits. Imports from Hong Kong of "made-to-measure" suits that do not accompany a returning traveler are subject to a special agreement. Suits made to the specific measurements of a particular person require a "made-to-measure" export license from the Hong Kong government. You must identify "made-to-measure" suits of Hong Kong origin on your entry summary by placing the symbol "G" as a prefix to the appropriate tariff number. The importer is responsible for the payment of any Customs duties at the time of importation, even if the suits are made to measure for an individual person. For more information, contact your nearest U.S. Customs port office. For more general information about invoices see "Invoices" on page 277.

Special Access or Regime Entries. Certain garments assembled abroad from components formed and cut in the U.S. that, after assembly have been subject to bleaching, garment dyeing, or perma-pressing abroad, may be eligible for entry under the Special Access Program. Eligibility must be established under a bilateral agreement, and entry must be in compliance with procedures established by the Committee for the Implementation of Textile Agreements. You must identify such garments on the entry summary or withdrawal forms by placing the symbol "H" as a prefix to the appropriate tariff number.

Note: The Entry and Documentation section has been carefully designed to supply you, the importer, with sample documents and directions on how to satisfy Customs requirements. Be aware that you should consult the applicable authorities to ensure that you are correctly following the most current procedures.

Prohibitions and Restrictions

Textile Quotas. Textile import restrictions are primarily a matter of quotas and the way in which these quotas are administered and monitored. Under the Multi-Fiber Arrangement provisions of Section 204 of the Agricultural Adjustment Act, CITA has negotiated bilateral agreements with over 40 countries. These Agreements may impose quotas for a type of textile or a specific article, and they are country-specific. The agreements, however, often change. Therefore, if you are interested in importing any textile apparel articles or clothing accessories, you should contact the International Trade Administration's Office of Textile and Apparel (see addresses at end of this chapter). The Office of Textile and Apparel has a team of country specialists who can inform you of the latest developments and inform you about a product's quota or restriction status.

U.S. Customs enforces CITA textile and textile product entry quotas. If formal entry procedures are not followed, Customs will usually refuse entry for textiles. Formal entry requires submission of a Country-of-Origin Declaration (see General Considerations above). U.S. Customs maintains a current textile quota status report, available for perusal at any Customs port. In addition, U.S. Customs in Washington, DC, provides quota status reports online, which are updated on a regular basis (www.customs.gov/impoexpo/impoexpo.htm).

Flammable Fabrics. U.S. Customs may refuse entry for any article of wearing apparel or interior furnishing, or any fabric or related material that is intended for use or that may be used in wearing apparel or interior furnishings, if it fails to conform to an applicable flammability standard issued under Section 4 of the FFA. An exception is allowed for certain products (FFA Section 11c) that are imported for finishing or processing to bring them within the legal standard. For these products, the exporter must state on the invoice or other paper relating to the shipment that the shipment is being made for that purpose.

The CPSC, as the primary enforcement agency of flammability standards, inspects products for compliance with the FFA. If the CPSC believes a product, fabric, or related material does not comply with a flammability standard, it is authorized to pursue a variety of legal sanctions, including: 1) seizure, condemnation, and forfeiture of the noncomplying products; 2) administrative cease-and-desist order requiring an individual or firm to stop sale and distribution of the noncomplying products or; 3) temporary injunction requiring the individual or firm to stop sale and distribution of the noncomplying products, pending final disposition of an administrative cease-and-desist proceeding. The CPSC also has authority to seek civil penalties against any person who knowingly violates a regulation or standard issued under Section 4 of the FFA.

Country-Specific Restrictions

Restrictions under bilateral agreements are country-specific. A product originating in one country may be subject to quota and to export license or visa requirements, while the same product originating in a different country may not. At present, the U.S. has Bilateral Agreements with 40 countries. Many different categories of products are covered under these Arrangements; it is beyond the scope of this book to list each country and its restricted commodities. If you are interested in importing textiles and textile products, you should contact the International Trade Administration's Office of Textile and Apparel (see addresses at end of this chapter) or U.S. Customs to ascertain your product's restraint status.

The U.S. Customs service provides quota reports on their website (www.customs.gov/impoexpo/impoexpo.htm). These reports are constantly updated and have an effective date noted. The most recent quota information can be accessed by clicking on the country name that interests you. This location holds information regarding quotas, transshipments, and visa requirements.

Marking and Labeling Requirements

TFPIA Requirements. All textile products imported into the U.S. must be stamped, tagged, labeled, or otherwise marked with the following information as required by the TFPIA, unless exempt from marking (see TFPIA, Section 12): 1) the generic names and percentages by weight of the constituent fibers present in the textile fiber product, exclusive of permissible ornamentation, in amounts of more than 5% in order of predominance by weight, with any percentage of fiber or fibers required to be designated as "other fiber" or "other fibers" (including those present in amounts of 5% or less) appearing last; and 2) the name of the manufacturer or the name or registered identification number issued by the FTC of one or more persons marketing or handling the textile fiber product; and 3) the name of the country where processed. A word trademark, used as a house mark and registered with the U.S. Patent Office, may appear on labels instead of the name otherwise required, provided the owner of the trademark furnishes a copy of the registration to the FTC prior to use (see "Registered Identification Numbers" below).

The information listed above is not exhaustive. TFPIA requirements are extensive. The Act specifies such details as types of labels, means of attachment, label position on the article, package labeling, unit labeling for two-piece garments, and arrangement of information on the label; allowable fiber designations; country-of-origin indications; requirements for trim and ornamentation, linings and interlinings, and pile fabrics; sectional disclosure; use of trade names and trademarks; and requirements for swatches and samples. The FTC publishes a booklet intended to clarify TFPIA requirements to facilitate voluntary compliance in the industry (see "Publications and WWW Resources" below). It is available on request, at no charge, from the FTC (see addresses at end of this chapter).

Wool Products Labeling Act (WPLA). Wool product labeling requirements for foreign products are the responsibility of the importer. The WPLA requires the following information to appear on wool products subject to the Act: 1) percentage of the wool product's total fiber weight (exclusive of ornamentation) not exceeding 5% of the total fiber weight of a) wool, b) recycled wool, c) each fiber other than wool if the percent by weight of such fiber is 5% or more, and d) the aggregate of all other fibers; 2) the maximum percent of the wool product's total weight, of any nonfibrous loading, filling, or adulterating matter; and 3) the importer's name. If you, as importer, have a registered identification number issued by the FTC, that number may be used instead of your name (see "Registered Identification Numbers" below).

Customs entry is contingent on proper labeling. If your shipment is found to be mislabeled at entry, you will be given the option of relabeling the products under Customs supervision, as long as the port director is satisfied that your labeling error or omission did not involve fraud or willful neglect. If your shipment is discovered after entry to have been noncomplying with WPLA, it will be recalled to Customs custody at your expense, unless you can satisfy the port director that the products have since been brought into compliance. You will be held responsible for all expenses incurred in bringing a shipment into compliance, including compensation of personnel and other expenses related to Customs supervision.

Fraudulent violations of WPLA will result in seizure of the shipment. Shipments already released from Customs custody will be ordered to be redelivered to Customs. Customs reports all cases of fraudulent violation to the FTC in Washington, DC.

The information listed above is not intended to be exhaustive. WPLA requirements are extensive. The Act specifies such details as types of labels, means of attachment, label position on the article, package labeling, unit labeling (as in the case of a two-piece garment), arrangement of information on the label, allowable fiber designations, country-of-origin indications, trim and ornamentation, pile fabrics, sectional disclosure, use of trade names and trademarks, requirements for swatches and samples, etc. The FTC publishes a booklet intended to clarify WPLA requirements in order to facilitate voluntary compliance within the industry (see "Publications and WWW Resources" below). It is available on line from the FTC.

The Care Labeling Rule. Regulations under this rule require manufacturers and importers of textile clothing and fabrics to attach specific care instructions for washing or dry cleaning, as well as information on the fiber composition of the article. They are enforced by the FTC Division of Enforcement. The Care Labeling Rule was amended September 2000 detailed information is available on the FTC website (www.ftc.gov/os/statutes/textilejump.htm).

Registered Identification Numbers. Any domestic firm or person residing in the U.S. and engaged in the manufacture or marketing of textile products covered under the TFPIA may obtain an FTC-registered identification number for use on required tags and labels instead of the name of a firm or person. For applications, contact the FTC (see addresses at end of this chapter).

For a general discussion of U.S. Customs marking and labeling requirements, see "Country of Origin Marking" on page 236, "Special Marking Requirements" on page 238 and "Marking—False Impression" on page 239.

Shipping Considerations

You will need to ensure that your goods are packaged and shipped with care so that they pass smoothly through Customs and arrive in good condition. You are responsible for ensuring that the shipment is in compliance with all applicable government regulations for packaging and shipping. In most instances, you should not leave these arrangements solely to the discretion of your supplier. Careful preparation of the cargo and selection of the mode of transport can be essential to a cost-effective, timely delivery of undamaged goods. We strongly advise you to consult your shipping representative, insurance agent, or freight broker for advice on packing and shipping.

Textile apparel articles or clothing accessories may be shipped in bulk, cartons, or other types of containers, depending on the type of product and whether it is prepackaged. General considerations include protection from contamination, weather, and pests. Containers should be constructed so as to be safe for handling during transport.

Publications and WWW Resources

The following publications may be relevant to the importation of textile apparel articles or clothing accessories:

Threading Your Way Through the Labeling Requirements of the Textile and Wool Acts

Available from the Federal Trade Commission wesite (www.ftc.gov/bcp/conline/pubs/buspubs/thread.htm), this publication is an excellent source of information written in clear lay language. We recommend that anyone interested in importing textile products but unfamiliar with the regulations obtain a copy.

The U.S. Customs Service launched a series of "Informed Compliance" publications in 1996, which are available on the Customs Service website (www.customs.gov/impoexpo/impoexpo.htm). Of particular interest:

What Every Member of the Trade Community Should Know About Textile & Apparel Rules of Origin

What Every Member of the Trade community Should Know About NAFTA for Textiles and Textile Articles

Fibers & Yarns Construction and Classification Under the HTSUS

The *Harmonized Tariff Schedule of the United States (2001)* (HTSUS) is available to view on the Customs Service website (www.customs.gov), or you may purchase a printed version from:

U.S. Government Printing Office
Superintendent of Documents
710 North Capital Street NW
Washington DC 20401
Tel: (202) 512-1800
Fax: (202) 512-1657
Website: www.access.gpo.gov

The USGPO also has copies of specific laws available for purchase. The USGPO accepts orders made by fax, phone or placed over the Internet, as well as mail orders paid by credit card. All orders must be accompanied by payment. Credit cards, checks drawn on a U.S. bank, or an international money order are all acceptable.

Relevant Government Agencies

Address your questions regarding textile Multi-Fiber Arrangements to:

U.S. Department of Commerce
International Trade Administration
Office of Textiles and Apparel
Director's Office
14th and Constitution Avenue NW, Rm. H3100
Washington DC 20230
Tel: (202) 482-5078
Fax: (202) 482-2331
Agreements Division: (202) 482-4212
Website: http://otexa.ita.doc.gov

Address your questions regarding the Flammable Fabrics Act (FFA) to:

Consumer Product Safety Commission (CPSC)
Office of Compliance
Washington DC 20207-0001
Tel: 800-638-2772 or (301) 504-7912
Fax: (301) 504-0359
Website: www.cpsc.gov

Address your questions regarding labeling requirements under the Textile Fiber Products Identification Act (TFPIA) or the Wool Products Labeling Act (WPLA) to:

Federal Trade Commission (FTC)
Division of Enforcement
600 Pennsylvania Avenue NW
Washington DC 20580
Tel: (202) 326-2996
Website: www.ftc.gov

Address your questions regarding textile quotas to:

U.S. Customs and Border Protection
Office of Field Operations, Quota Branch
1300 Pennsylvania Avenue NW
Washington DC 20229
Tel: (202) 927-5850
Website: www.customs.treas.gov

The U.S. Customs Service provices updated status reports on textile quota on their website (see address above). If the country you need information on is not listed, call the Quota Branch office at (202) 927-5850.

Address your questions regarding imports of textile apparel articles or clothing accessories to your local Customs port director. For addresses, refer to "U.S. Customs and Border Protection Offices" on page 65 or contact:

U.S. Customs and Border Protection
Customs Headquarters
1300 Pennsylvania Avenue NW
Washington DC 20229
Tel: (202) 354-1000
Website: www.customs.treas.gov

Laws and Regulations

The following laws and regulations may be relevant to the importation of textile apparel articles or clothing accessories. The laws are contained in the United States Code (USC), and the regulations are published in the Code of Federal Regulations (CFR), both of which are available at larger public and law libraries. Copies of specific laws are also available from the United States Government Printing Office (address above).

7 USC 1854
Textile Trade Agreements
(EO 11651, as amended by EO 11951 and 12188, and supplemented by EO 12475)
This Act authorizes the CITA of the DOC to enter into Multi-Fiber Agreements with other countries to control trade in textiles and establishes the Textile Import Program, which is enforced by U.S. Customs.

19 CFR 12.130 et seq.
Regulations on Entry of Textiles
These regulations provide the requirements and procedures followed by Customs in enforcing limitations on the importation and entry and withdrawal of textiles and textile products from warehouses for consumption in the U.S.

15 USC 70-77
Textile Fiber Products Identification Act (TFPIA)
This Act prohibits false or deceptive labeling (misbranding) and false advertising of any textile fiber products and requires all textile fiber products imported into the U.S. to be labeled in accordance with the requirements set forth in the law.

19 CFR 11.12b; 16 CFR 303 et seq.
Regulations on Labeling and Marking
These regulations detail the labeling and marking requirements for textiles as specified by the CPSC and the invoice contents required by U.S. Customs for purpose of enforcing the labeling and marking rules.

15 USC 68-68j
Wool Products Labeling Act (WPLA) of 1939
This Act prohibits the false or deceptive labeling (misbranding) of wool products and requires all wool products imported into the U.S. to be labeled in accordance with requirements set forth in the law.

19 CFR 11.12; 16 CFR 300 et seq.
Regulations on WPLA Labeling and Marking
These regulations set forth the wool labeling and marking requirements adopted by the FTC to administer the requirements of the WPLA and provide the procedures followed by U.S. Customs in enforcing the WPLA and the FTC regulations, including entry invoice requirements.

15 USC 1191-1204
Flammable Fabrics Act (FFA)
This Act provides for the setting of flammability stan-

dards for fabric by the Consumer Product Safety Commission (CPSC) and for enforcement by U.S. Customs.

16 CFR 1610, 1611, 1615, 1616, 1630-1632
Regulations on Flammable Fabric Standards
These regulations specify the flammability standards adopted by the CPSC under the FFA for various types of textiles.

16 CFR 423
Care Labeling Rule
Requires fiber composition and washing or dry cleaning instructions for textile apparel and certain piece goods.

Principal Exporting Countries

The following listing includes samples of the main supplier nations of the products of this chapter. It is organized by HTSUS major heading. (Refer to "Customs Classification" above for the product codes.) Countries are listed in rank order of the value of products imported to the U.S. Statistics represent customs value of entries for 2002 from the Bureau of Census, U.S. Department of Commerce.

6201—China, South Korea, Sri Lanka, Bangladesh, Hong Kong, Thailand, Vietnam, Mexico

6202—China, Hong Kong, Bangladesh, Italy, Thailand, Philippines, Sri Lanka, Indonesia, Vietnam, India, Dominican Republic

6203—Mexico, Dominican Republic, China, Italy, Canada, Hong Kong, Indonesia, Guatemala, Bangladesh, Honduras

6204—Mexico, China, Hong Kong, Philippines, Indonesia, India, Italy, Guatemala

6205—Hong Kong, China, South Korea, Bangladesh, India, Indonesia, Mexico, Honduras, Sri Lanka

6206—China, India, Hong Kong, Indonesia, Bangladesh, Sri Lanka, Philippines, Thailand, Mexico, South Korea

6207—China, El Salvador, Indonesia, Cambodia, Costa Rica, Thailand, Philippines, Honduras, Turkey

6208—China, Turkey, Cambodia, Sri Lanka, Hong Kong, Philippines, Bangladesh, Pakistan, India, Indonesia

6209—China, Philippines, Bangladesh, Indonesia, Thailand, India, Sri Lanka, Mexico

6210—China, Mexico, Honduras, Thailand, South Korea, Canada, Vietnam, Bangladesh, Taiwan

6211—Mexico, China, India, Bangladesh, Indonesia, Canada, Sri Lanka, Hong Kong, Taiwan, Thailand, Pakistan

6212—China, Honduras, Mexico, Dominican Republic, Indonesia, Thailand

6213—China, South Korea, India, Italy, Czech Republic, Pakistan, United Kingdom

6214—Italy, China, India, South Korea, United Kingdom, France, Germany

6215—Italy, South Korea, China, France, Dominican Republic, Costa Rica, United Kingdom, Canada

6216—China, Pakistan, Sri Lanka, Mexico, Hong Kong, Indonesia, Canada, Vietnam

6217—Mexico, China, Taiwan, Italy, Canada, South Korea, Thailand.

Chapter 63:
Other Textile Articles

Full title: Other Made-up Articles; Needlecraft Sets; Worn Clothing and Worn Textile Articles; Rags

This chapter relates to the importation of textile articles not covered elsewhere, which are classified under Chapter 63 of the Harmonized Tariff Schedule of the United States (HTSUS). Specifically, it covers blankets and traveling rugs; bed, table, bath, and kitchen linen; curtains, interior blinds, and valances; bedspreads not classified under HTSUS 9404, sacks and bags; tarpaulins, awning, sunblinds, tents, and camping goods; sails for boats, sailboards, or landcraft; cleaning cloths; lifejackets and life belts; dress patterns; footwear and other lacings; textile pet toys; wall banners; surgical towels; needlecraft sets; worn clothing and other articles; rags, scrap cordage, and worn out cordage. Articles are classified as worn only if the show signs of appreciable wear and are entered in bulk or in bales, sacks, or similar packings.

If you are interested in importing articles of apparel that are not worn, you should read Commodity Index Chapter 61 (knitted or crocheted) or Chapter 62 (not knitted or crocheted). Quilts and textile furnishings are found in Chapter 94, and surgical belts and orthopedic items are classified in Chapter 90. If you are interested in importing footwear or headgear, you should refer to Chapter 64 or 65, respectively. Textiles, garment parts, thread, yarns, and other similar materials are covered in Chapters 50 through 58. Articles of apparel that contain leather parts may be imported in accordance with the requirements explained in Chapter 42. Cordage that is not scrap or worn out must be imported in accordance with Chapter 56.

Note: To understand key issues that will enable you to make best use of the information in this section we recommend that you see "Introduction" on page 425.

Key Factors

The key factors in the importation of other textile articles are:

- Compliance with quota restraints and visa requirements

- Submission of U.S. Customs Country-of-Origin Declaration(s)

- Compliance with entry invoice requirements

- Compliance with labeling requirements under Textile Fiber Products Identification Act (TFPIA) and/or the Wool Products Labeling Act (WPLA) and the Care Labeling Rule

- Compliance with flammability standards adopted and enforced by the Consumer Product Safety Commission (CPSC) under the Flammable Fabrics Act (FFA) (if importing fabrics and other textile products)

- Compliance with U.S. Food and Drug Administration (FDA) inspection and entry requirements (if importing products intended for sanitary purposes and no exemption applies)

- Compliance with Federal Plant Pest Act (FPPA) and Plant Quarantine Act (PQA) requirements, and with U.S. Department of Agriculture (USDA) random port-of-entry inspections, import restrictions and quarantines, and other entry requirements (if importing cordage of vegetable materials)

Although most importers use the services of a licensed customs broker in making their entries, and we recommend this practice, you should be aware of the regulatory, entry, and documentation issues involved in importing your product. You, as importer, are ultimately responsible for the fulfillment of any legal requirements applicable to your shipment.

General Considerations

Regulatory Agencies. The DOC's Committee for Implementation of Textile Agreements (CITA) regulates certain textile imports under Section 204 of the Agricultural Adjustment Act. U.S. Customs enforces CITA textile and textile product entry quotas. Customs also enforces compliance with labeling and invoice requirements of the TFPIA and flammability standards under the FFA. The CPSC monitors imports and from time to time inspects textile shipments for compliance with FFA standards. If you are importing wool articles, importation is subject to complex textile import regulations. The Federal Trade Commission (FTC) administers the WPLA requirements.

The USDA administers applicable provisions of the Plant Quarantine Act (PQA) and the Federal Plant Pest Act (FPPA), which are designed to prevent introduction into the U.S. of any plant pest or disease potentially harmful to U.S. agriculture. Shipments of cordage made of vegetable materials—e.g., jute—must be in compliance with PQA, FPPA, and USDA requirements. The FDA, under authority of the Federal Food, Drug, and Cosmetic Act (FDCA), regulates the importation of products intended for medical or sanitary purposes. U.S. Customs enforces compliance with entry requirements for products subject to the FDCA.

Wool Product Entry Requirements. Depending on the nature of your wool article imports, as many as three different types of special entry documents may be required. First, for all imported articles that contain textile fibers, yarns, and fabrics covered by the Agricultural Adjustment Act (AAA), including wool, you must file a U.S. Customs Textile Entry Declaration (see "Textile Country-of-Origin Declarations" below). Second, for all wool products subject to the WPLA, special information is required on the entry invoices (see "Wool Products Labeling Act" below). Finally, certain articles of apparel manufactured or produced in certain countries may be subject to quotas and other restraints under U.S. DOC Multi-Fiber Arrangements. Such products require export licenses, certificates, or visas issued by the appropriate country of origin, in addition to other requisite entry paperwork (see "Textile Quotas" below).

Wool Products Labeling Act. The term "wool product" means any product or any portion of a product that contains, purports to contain, or in any way is represented as containing wool, reprocessed wool, or reused wool. All wool products imported into the U.S., except those made more than 20 years before importation, and except carpets, rugs, mats, and upholsteries, must have affixed a stamp, tag, label, or other means of identification as required by the WPLA. If you are importing wool products exempt from labeling under the WPLA, do not assume they are also exempt from labeling under the TFPIA. These are two dis-

tinct laws, with some overlapping requirements (see "Marking and Labeling Requirements" below).

Cordage of Vegetable Materials. For most shipments of worn out cordage made of vegetable materials, importation is straightforward. With some exceptions, you do not need permits or licenses to import these products (see "Prohibitions and Restrictions", below). The USDA's Animal and Plant Health Inspection Service (APHIS) inspects shipments of cordage made of vegetable materials on a random basis, depending on such factors as the port of entry, the country of origin, and the risk of contamination involved in the type of material being imported. Entry may be denied for noncompliance with the regulations, and the shipment could be seized, quarantined, destroyed, treated, or otherwise dealt with at the discretion of the inspector.

Products for Sanitary Purposes. The importation of products intended for surgical, medical, or other sanitary uses are regulated by the FDA. Usually, if you import FDA-regulated articles, you must follow certain import procedures prescribed by that agency. For a general discussion of FDA import procedures, see "Appendix: Foods" on page 825. If you are interested in importing such a product, you should ascertain its regulatory status by contacting the FDA (see addresses at end of this chapter).

Textile Quotas. If you are interested in importing other textile articles, the most important issue you need to be aware of is quotas. Under the Multi-Fiber Arrangement provisions of Section 204 of the Agricultural Adjustment Act, CITA initiates specific agreements with individual exporting countries. Section 204 of the Agricultural Adjustment Act covers textiles articles that: 1) are in chief value of cotton, wool, or man-made fibers, any textile fibers subject to the terms of any textile trade agreement, or any combination of such fibers; 2) contain 50% or more by weight of cotton or man-made fibers, or any textile fibers subject to the terms of any textile trade agreement; 3) contain 17% or more by weight of wool; or 4) if in chief value of textile fibers or textile materials, contain a blend of cotton, wool, or man-made fibers, any textile fibers subject to the terms of any textile trade agreement, or any combination of such fibers that, in total, amount to 50% or more by weight of all component fibers.

The U.S. has Multi-Fiber Arrangements with 40 countries. Each agreement with each country is unique, and may specify quotas for a type of textile or a specific article. Visas or export licenses may be required. These agreements, however, often change. Therefore, if you are interested in importing any other textile articles, you should contact the International Trade Administration's Office of Textile and Apparel (see addresses at end of this chapter). Refer to "Prohibitions and Restrictions" below for further details.

Textile Country-of-Origin Declarations. U.S. Customs enforces CITA textile and textile product entry quotas (see "Prohibitions and Restrictions" below). Requirements for entry include submission of Country-of-Origin Declarations with every shipment of other textile articles, regardless of whether it is subject to a specific multi-fiber arrangement (19 CFR 12.130, 12.131).

Country of Origin. Quota restrictions are country-specific and therefore are applied based on the country of origin for the textiles shipped. The last country from which a textile shipment was exported to the U.S. is not necessarily its country of origin. A textile or textile product imported into the U.S. is considered a product of the particular foreign territory or country, or a U.S. insular possession, where it is wholly grown, produced, or manufactured. For the following discussion, "country" means a foreign territory or country, or a U.S. insular possession.

In 1996, the U.S. Customs Service made major changes to country of origin rules for textile imports. The regulations at 19 CFR 102.21, "Textile and apparel products" were added to the 1996 Customs Regulations and became effective July 1, 1996. The new rules do not provide for cutting components or cutting and hemming to confer country of origin as in the past. The basis of the new law is processing operations or assembly. Some of the most important changes for importers to be aware of are:

- Cutting does not determine the country of origin (previously cutting determined country of origin for 90 percent of wearing apparel imports). The new rules are based on processing or assembly operations.

- Essential character does not determine country of origin because the new rules are based on processing.

- A subjective determination under the provisions of 19 CFR 12.130 is replaced by objective processing operations expressed in terms of tariff shifts. Dying, printing, and other finishing processes applied to fabrics no longer confer or change country of origin.

- Country of origin for textile and apparel products processed, assembled or manufactured in two or more countries is determined by where the most important processing occurs, and, if that cannot be ascertained, the last country in which an important processing operation occurs.

The country of origin is the country in which a product is wholly produced when a textile or apparel product is completely produced or manufactured (except for minor parts) in one country. For fabric, the country of origin is the country in which the fabric is woven, knitted, needled, tufted, felted, entangled or created by any other fabric-making process. The country of origin for staple yarn is the country in which yarn is spun; for filament yarn, the country in which filament is extruded; and for plied, gimped and cabled yarns, the country in which the fibers or filaments used in the yarn are spun or extruded. The country of origin of all other textile and apparel products is the country in which the components of a textile or apparel product are wholly assembled (except for minor attachments). Once again, note that assembly, not cutting, now confers country of origin.

Declarations. All importations of textiles and textile products must be accompanied by one of the following three declarations. Goods subject to Section 204, Agricultural Act of 1956, as amended, must be accompanied by either a single-country or a multiple-country declaration. Goods not subject to Section 204 must be accompanied by a negative declaration.

- **Single-country declarations** are used for entries of textiles or textile products which are wholly the growth, product, or manufacture of a single foreign country, territory, or U.S. insular possession. Information required includes: marks of identification and numbers; description of article and quantity; country of origin; and date of exportation.

- **Multiple-country declarations** are used for entries of textiles or textile products which were subjected to manufacturing or processing operations in, and/or incorporate materials originating in more than one foreign country or territory. Information required includes: marks of identification and numbers; for articles, description, quantity, identification of manufacturing and/or processing operations, country, and date of exportation; for materials used to make articles, description of materials, country of production, and date of exportation.

- **Negative declarations** must accompany all textile imports that are not subject to FFA Section 204 restrictions. Information required includes: marks of identification and numbers; descriptions of article and quantity; and country of origin.

The date of exportation to be indicated on the above declarations is the date on which the carrier leaves the last port in the country of origin, as determined by Customs. Diversion to another country during transit does not affect the export date.

Procedure for Declarations. The manufacturer, producer, exporter, or importer may prepare the declaration. If more than one of these parties is involved in the importation, each party may prepare a separate declaration. You may file a separate declaration for each invoice presented with your entry. The declaration must be dated and signed by the responsible party, and must include the person's title and the company name and address. Your shipment's entry will be denied unless it is accompanied by a properly executed declaration. Customs will not treat a textile declaration as a missing document for which a bond may be filed.

Customs will base its country-of-origin determination on the information contained in each declaration, unless the information is insufficient. If the information on the declaration is insufficient, Customs will require that you submit such additional information as will enable the determination to be made. The shipment will not be released until the determination is made. Thus, if you want to clear Customs with minimal delay, be sure that the information on the declarations is as complete as possible for each shipment.

Textile Labeling and Invoice Requirements. You are responsible for your imported product's compliance with applicable provisions of the TFPIA. Other textile articles that require labeling under TFPIA must already be labeled at entry, or the shipment will be refused. (See "Marking and Labeling Requirements" below.) If you import shipments of other textile articles subject to TFPIA and valued at over $500, you must provide special information on the entry invoice (see "Entry and Documentation" below).

Flammability Standards. Other textile articles imported into the U.S. for use in consumer products must be in compliance with the FFA, a federal law that gives the CPSC the authority and responsibility for protecting the public from the hazards of dangerously flammable items of wearing apparel and interior furnishings. Under the FFA, standards have been established for flammability of clothing textiles. You cannot import any article of wearing apparel or interior furnishing, or any fabric or related material that is intended for use or that may be used in such items, if it fails to conform to an applicable flammability standard (FFA Section 4). Certain products may be imported into the U.S. (FFA Section 11c) for finishing or processing to render them less flammable so as to meet the standards. For these products, the exporter must state on the invoice or other paper relating to the shipment that the shipment is being made for that purpose.

The CPSC monitors imports of textiles under its Import Surveillance Program. From time to time, your textile shipments may be inspected to ascertain compliance with mandatory safety standards. Shipments may also be subject to testing by the CPSC to determine compliance. If the CPSC believes a product, fabric, or related material does not comply with a flammability standard, it is authorized to pursue a variety of legal sanctions (see "Prohibitions and Restrictions" below).

Substantial Product Hazard Reports. Any firm that obtains information that reasonably supports the conclusion that one of its products presents an unreasonable risk of serious injury or death must report that information to the CPSC's Division of Corrective Actions (CPSC address below). Importers must also report to the CPSC if 1) a type of product is the subject of at least three civil actions filed in U.S. federal or state courts, 2) each suit alleges the involvement of that product type in death or grievous bodily injury (as defined in FFA Section 37(3)1), and 3) at least three of the actions result in a final settlement with the manufacturer or in a judgment for the plaintiff within any one of the two-year periods specified in FFA Section 37(b).

Import Advisory

Importation of textile products is trade-sensitive and highly regulated. Shipments of textile products not complying with all government regulations, including quotas and visas, are subject to seizure and could result in the imposition of penalties as well as possible forfeiture of the goods. You should always verify the available quota for any textile product you plan to import before your shipment leaves the country of manufacture. Furthermore, Customs textile classification rulings change frequently, and prior administrative rulings are often modified and sometimes reversed. You should be particularly careful to comply with country of origin determination regulations, which were changed in 1996, and affect quotas and visas, marking and labeling, and other important aspects of tariff classification. See "Publications and WWW Resources" for information on important Customs Service informed compliance publications.

The Customs Service has greatly increased its scrutiny of the textile industry, one of eight primary focus industries identified in the most recent Trade Compliance & Enforcement Plan. Imported products from these industries will likely attract significant attention from Customs in the areas of compliance measurement, compliance assessment, informed compliance, and interventions.

Customs Classification

For customs purposes, other textile articles are classified under Chapter 63 of the HTSUS. This chapter is broken into major headings, which are further divided into subheadings, and often sub-subheadings, each of which has its own HTSUS classification number. For example, the 2001 HTSUS number for table linen, knitted or crocheted, of vegetable fiber other than cotton, is 6302.40.10, indicating it is a sub-subcategory of table linen, knitted or crocheted (6302.40), which is a subcategory of the major heading bed linen, table linen, etc. (6302). There are 10 major headings within Chapter 63.

6301—Blankets and traveling rugs

6302—Bed linen, table linen, toilet linen, and kitchen linen

6303—Curtains (including drapes) and interior blinds; curtain or bed valances

6304—Other furnishing articles, excluding those of heading 9404

6305—Sacks and bags, of a kind used for the packing of goods

6306—Tarpaulins, awnings, and sunblinds; tents; sails for boats, sailboards, or landcraft; camping goods

6307—Other made up articles, including dress patterns

6308—Needlecraft sets consisting of woven fabric and yarn, whether or not with accessories, for making up into rugs, tapestries, embroidered tablecloths or napkins, or similar textile articles, put up in packings for retail sale

6309—Worn clothing and other worn articles

6310—Used or new rags, scrap twine, cordage, rope, and cables, and worn out articles of twine, cordage, rope, or cables, of textile materials

For more details regarding classifications of the specific product you are interested in importing, consult a customs broker, the appropriate commodity specialist at your nearest customs port, or the HTSUS. The 2001 HTSUS is available online from the Customs Service (www.customs.gov/impoexpo/impoexpo.htm) or for purchase from the U.S. Government Printing Office (see resources at the end of this chapter), and may be found in larger public libraries. For a general discussion of customs classification, see "Classification—Liquidation" on page 229.

Dutiable Status of Goods

For more information about duty rates and binding decisions see "Dutiable Status of Goods" on page 203; for a discussion of temporary importation of goods see "Temporary Free Importations" on page 205.

Valuation

Importers have a responsibility to use what the U.S. Customs Service deems, "reasonable care," when determining the value of their goods. They must also provide any additional information that the Customs Service needs for setting a final value on the goods. This process involves a number of factors and can be somewhat complicated; importers must be aware of applicable issues and details. Valuation information applies to all types of commodities, for further discussion on the subject see "Customs Valuation" on page 267.

Import Duties

Import duties vary (often dramatically) depending upon the Harmonized Tariff Schedule (HTSUS) classification of the goods or products imported. Since some products that look alike have different HTSUS classifications and different rates of duty, proper classification is vital. Note that "differences of opinion" between importers and the Bureau of Customs and Border Protection regarding classification keeps customs attorneys very busy.

Import duties can be assessed on the imported value of the goods ("ad valorem" rates of duty such as 2%, 4.4%, 50%, etc.), total units or weight of the goods ("specific" rates of duty such as 2 cents each or 1.5 cents/pound, etc.) or on a combination basis ("compound" rates of duty such as 5 cents each plus 6%).

Listed below is a sampling of several Column 1 import duty rates for Chapter 63 products:
Containing 85 percent or more by weight of silk or silk waste (6302.99.10 00): 3%
to
Synthetic fibers of other textile materials (6303.99.00): 11.4%

For specific information on US import duties refer to the Harmonized Tariff Schedule of the US. The print version is available from the US Government Printing Office as well as third party suppliers who often add special features. Online versions are available in both static PDF pages as well as in formats with excellent search functionality. Search the Web with the term "Harmonized Tariff Schedule" to find sources.

Entry and Documentation

The entry of merchandise is a two-part process consisting of 1) filing the documentation necessary to determine whether merchandise may be released from Customs custody, and 2) filing the documents that contain information for duty assessment and statistical purposes. In certain instances, all documents must be filed and accepted by Customs prior to release of the goods. Unless you have been granted an extension, you must file entry documents at a location specified by the port or area director within five working days of your shipment's date of arrival at a U.S. port of entry. These include a number of standard documents required by Customs for any entry, and:

- U.S. Customs Country-of-Origin Declaration Form CF 3229

- Export documentation and/or visa for textiles subject to Multi-Fiber Arrangement

- Phytosanitary certificate (if importing cordage made of vegetable material)

After you present the entry, Customs may examine your shipment or may waive examination. The shipment is then released provided no legal or regulatory violations have been noted. You must then file entry summary documentation and deposit estimated duties at a designated customhouse within 10 working days of your shipment's release. For a detailed description of entry procedures, standard documentation, and informal entry, see "Entry Process" on page 185.

Informed Compliance. Informed compliance was introduced with the Customs Modernization Act of 1993 (Mod Act) and defines the relationship between importers and the Customs Service. It sets out the responsibilities of both parties. Providing the correct documentation and information for entry is a key factor that will make your importing operation run smoothly. We recommend that importers become familiar with the concept of informed comliance and the responsibilities that they have under the Mod Act. For further discussion about informed compliance see "Informed Compliance" on page 211.

NAFTA Certificates of Origin. An importer of textiles for which NAFTA treatment is sought need not file a separate NAFTA Certificate of Origin in addition to the Customs Country-of-Origin Declaration. The declaration is sufficient. However, the importer must take care to submit a declaration from each U.S., Canadian, or Mexican producer or manufacturer. Thus, for multiple producers or manufacturers, a separate declaration must be filed for each. If a Customs port director cannot determine the country of origin because the declaration is absent or incomplete, the shipment is not entitled to preferential NAFTA tariff treatment or other NAFTA benefits. See 19 CFR 12.132.

Entry Invoices. You must provide certain additional information on the entry invoice for other textile articles. The specific information varies depending on the nature of your product, as noted below.

TFPIA Requirements. All invoices for textile wearing apparel should indicate a component material breakdown in percentages by weight for all component fibers present in the entire garment, as well as separate breakdowns of the fibers in the (outer) shell (exclusive of linings, cuffs, waistbands, collars and other trimmings) and in the lining; 2) for garments that are constructed of more than one component or material (combination of knit and not-knit fabric or combinations of knit and/or not-knit fabric with leather, fur, plastic—including vinyl, etc.) the invoice must show a fiber breakdown in percentages by weight for each separate textile material in the garment and a breakdown in percentages by weight for each non-textile material of the entire garment; 3) for woven garments: indicate whether the fabric is yarn-dyed and whether there are "two or more colors in the warp and/or filling;" 4) for all-white T-shirts and singlets: indicate whether or not the garment contains pockets, trim, or embroidery; 5) for mufflers: state the exact dimensions, length, and width of the merchandise. For more general information about invoices see "Invoices" on page 277.

Wool Products Subject to WPLA. When you offer for entry a wool product shipment valued at over $500 and subject to WPLA, you must include certain information intended to facilitate Customs monitoring and enforcement of that Act. This extra information is identical to that required by WPLA on labeling (see "Marking and Labeling Requirements" below), with the addition of the manufacturer's name. If your product consists of mixed waste, residues, and similar merchandise obtained from several suppliers or unknown sources, you may omit the manufacturer's name from the entry invoice.

Bed Linens and Bedspreads. The entry invoice for a shipment of bed linens or bedspreads must state whether the article contains any embroidery, lace, braid, edging, trimming, piping, or applique work.

Note: The Entry and Documentation section has been carefully designed to supply you, the importer, with sample documents and directions on how to satisfy Customs requirements. Be aware that you should consult the applicable authorities to ensure that you are correctly following the most current procedures.

Prohibitions and Restrictions

Textile Quotas. Textile import restrictions are primarily a matter of quotas and the way in which these quotas are administered and monitored. Under the Multi-Fiber Arrangement provisions of Section 204 of the Agricultural Adjustment Act, CITA has negotiated Multi-Fiber Arrangements with 40 countries. These Agreements

may impose quotas for a type of textile or a specific article, and they are country-specific. The agreements, however, often change. Therefore, if you are interested in importing other textile articles, you should contact the International Trade Administration's Office of Textile and Apparel (see addresses at end of this chapter). The Office of Textile and Apparel has a team of country specialists who can inform you of the latest developments and inform you about a product's quota or restriction status.

U.S. Customs enforces CITA textile and textile product entry quotas. If formal entry procedures are not followed, Customs will usually refuse entry for textiles that are subject to Section 204. Formal entry requires submission of a Country-of-Origin Declaration (see "General Considerations" above). U.S. Customs maintains a current textile quota status report, available for perusal at any Customs port. In addition, U.S. Customs in , DC, provides quota status reports online, which are updated on a regular basis (www.customs.gov/impoexpo/impoexpo.htm).

Flammable Fabrics. U.S. Customs may refuse entry for any article of wearing apparel or interior furnishing, or any fabric or related material that is intended for use or that may be used in wearing apparel or interior furnishings, if it fails to conform to an applicable flammability standard issued under Section 4 of the FFA. An exception is allowed for certain products (FFA Section 11c) that are imported for finishing or processing to bring them within the legal standard. For these products, the exporter must state on the invoice or other paper relating to the shipment that the shipment is being made for that purpose.

The CPSC, as the primary enforcement agency of flammability standards, inspects products for compliance with the FFA. If the CPSC believes a product, fabric, or related material does not comply with a flammability standard, it is authorized to pursue a variety of legal sanctions, including: 1) seizure, condemnation, and forfeiture of the noncomplying products; 2) administrative cease-and-desist order requiring an individual or firm to stop sale and distribution of the noncomplying products or; 3) temporary injunction requiring the individual or firm to stop sale and distribution of the noncomplying products, pending final disposition of an administrative cease-and-desist proceeding. The CPSC also has authority to seek civil penalties against any person who knowingly violates a regulation or standard issued under Section 4 of the FFA.

Cordage of Vegetable Materials. In general, any shipment of cordage made of vegetable materials is subject to random port-of-entry inspection by the USDA. If the inspector finds evidence of the presence of insects in your shipment, you may be required to submit your shipment to USDA-prescribed fumigation procedures. If the insect is of a kind for which there is no viable U.S. treatment, your shipment will be refused. Our source at USDA assured us that most shipments that are found to have insects in them can be treated to afford entry.

Country-Specific Restrictions

Restrictions under Multi-Fiber Arrangements are country-specific. A product originating in one country may be subject to quota and to export license or visa requirements, while the same product originating in a different country may not. At present, the U.S. has Multi-Fiber Arrangements with 40 countries. Many different categories of products are covered under these Arrangements; it is beyond the scope of this book to list each country and its restricted commodities. If you are interested in importing textiles and textile products, you should contact the International Trade Administration's Office of Textile and Apparel (see addresses at end of this chapter) or U.S. Customs to ascertain your product's restraint status.

The U.S. Customs service provides quota reports on their website (www.customs.gov/impoexpo/impoexpo.htm). These reports are constantly updated and have an effective date noted. The most recent quota information can be accessed by clicking on the country name that interests you. This location holds information regarding quotas, transshipments, and visa requirements.

Marking and Labeling Requirements

TFPIA Requirements. All textile products imported into the U.S. must be stamped, tagged, labeled, or otherwise marked with the following information as required by the TFPIA, unless exempt from marking (see TFPIA, Section 12): 1) the generic names and percentages by weight of the constituent fibers present in the textile fiber product, exclusive of permissible ornamentation, in amounts of more than 5% in order of predominance by weight, with any percentage of fiber or fibers required to be designated as "other fiber" or "other fibers" (including those present in amounts of 5% or less) appearing last; and 2) the name of the manufacturer or the name or registered identification number issued by the FTC of one or more persons marketing or handling the textile fiber product; and 3) the name of the country where processed. A word trademark, used as a house mark and registered with the U.S. Patent Office, may appear on labels instead of the name otherwise required, provided the owner of the trademark furnishes a copy of the registration to the FTC prior to use (see "Registered Identification Numbers" below).

The information listed above is not exhaustive. TFPIA requirements are extensive. The Act specifies such details as types of labels, means of attachment, label position on the article, package labeling, unit labeling for two-piece garments, and arrangement of information on the label; allowable fiber designations; country-of-origin indications; requirements for trim and ornamentation, linings and interlinings, and pile fabrics; sectional disclosure; use of trade names and trademarks; and requirements for swatches and samples. The FTC n publishes a booklet intended to clarify TFPIA requirements to facilitate voluntary compliance in the industry (see "Publications and WWW Resources" below). It is available on request, at no charge, from the FTC (see addresses at end of this chapter).

Wool Products Labeling Act (WPLA). Wool product labeling requirements for foreign products are the responsibility of the importer. The WPLA requires the following information to appear on wool products subject to the Act: 1) percentage of the wool product's total fiber weight (exclusive of ornamentation) not exceeding 5% of the total fiber weight of a) wool, b) recycled wool, c) each fiber other than wool if the percent by weight of such fiber is 5% or more, and d) the aggregate of all other fibers; 2) the maximum percent of the wool product's total weight, of any nonfibrous loading, filling, or adulterating matter; and 3) the importer's name. If you, as importer, have a registered identification number issued by the FTC, that number may be used instead of your name (see "Registered Identification Numbers" below).

Customs entry is contingent on proper labeling. If your shipment is found to be mislabeled at entry, you will be given the option of relabeling the products under Customs supervision, as long as the port director is satisfied that your labeling error or omission did not involve fraud or willful neglect. If your shipment is discovered after entry to have been noncomplying with WPLA, it will be recalled to Customs custody at your expense, unless you can satisfy the port director that the products have since been brought into compliance. You will be held responsible for all expenses incurred in bringing a shipment into compliance, including compensation of personnel and other expenses related to Customs supervision.

Fraudulent violations of WPLA will result in seizure of the shipment. Shipments already released from Customs custody will be ordered to be redelivered to Customs. Customs reports all cases of fraudulent violation to the FTC in , DC.

The information listed above is not intended to be exhaustive. WPLA requirements are extensive. The Act specifies such details as types of labels, means of attachment, label position on the article, package labeling, unit labeling (as in the case of a two-piece garment), arrangement of information on the label, allowable fiber designations, country-of-origin indications, trim and ornamentation, pile fabrics, sectional disclosure, use of trade names and trademarks, requirements for swatches and samples, etc. The FTC publishes a booklet intended to clarify WPLA requirements in order to facilitate voluntary compliance within the industry (see "Publications and WWW Resources" below). It is available on request, at no charge, from the FTC (see addresses at end of this chapter).

The Care Labeling Rule. Regulations under this rule require manufacturers and importers of textile clothing and fabrics to attach specific care instructions for washing or dry cleaning, as well as information on the fiber composition of the article. They are enforced by the FTC Division of Enforcement. The Care Labeling Rule was amended September 2000, detailed information is available on the FTC website (www.ftc.gov/os/statutes/textilejump.htm).

Registered Identification Numbers. Any domestic firm or person residing in the U.S. and engaged in the manufacture or marketing of textile products covered under the TFPIA may obtain an FTC-registered identification number for use on required tags and labels instead of the name of a firm or person. For applications, contact the FTC (see addresses at end of this chapter).

For a general discussion of U.S. Customs marking and labeling requirements, see "Country of Origin Marking" on page 236, "Special Marking Requirements" on page 238 and "Marking—False Impression" on page 239.

Shipping Considerations

You will need to ensure that your goods are packaged and shipped with care so that they pass smoothly through Customs and arrive in good condition. You are responsible for ensuring that the shipment is in compliance with all applicable government regulations for packaging and shipping. In most instances, you should not leave these arrangements solely to the discretion of your supplier. Careful preparation of the cargo and selection of the mode of transport can be essential to a cost-effective, timely delivery of undamaged goods. We strongly advise you to consult your shipping representative, insurance agent, or freight broker for advice on packing and shipping.

Other textile articles may be shipped in bulk, cartons, sacks, bales, or other types of containers, depending on the type of product and whether it is prepackaged. General considerations include protection from contamination, weather, and pests. Containers should be constructed so as to be safe for handling during transport.

Publications and WWW Resources

The following publications may be relevant to the importation of other textile articles:

> *Threading Your Way Through the Labeling Requirements Under the Textile and Wool Acts*

Available free of charge on request from the Federal Trade Commission (see addresses at end of this chapter), these publications are excellent sources of information written in clear lay language. We recommend that anyone interested in importing textile products but unfamiliar with the regulations obtain a copy of each of these booklets.

The U.S. Customs Service launched a series of "Informed Compliance" publications in 1996, which are available on the Customs Service website (www.customs.gov/impoexpo/impoexpo.htm). Of particular interest:

> *What Every Member of the Trade Community Should Know About Textile & Apparel Rules of Origin*

What Every Member of the Trade community Should Know About NAFTA for Textiles and Textile Articles

Fibers & Yarns Construction and Classification Under the HTSUS

The following publication explains the FDA requirements for importing textile wadding products for sanitary use. It is published by the FDA and is available online from the FDA website (www.fda.gov/opacom/7pubs.html).

Requirements of Laws and Regulations Enforced by the U.S. Food and Drug Administration

The *Harmonized Tariff Schedule of the United States (2001)* (HTSUS) is available to view on the Customs Service website (www.customs.gov), or you may purchase a printed version from:

U.S. Government Printing Office
Superintendent of Documents
710 North Capital Street NW
Washington DC 20401
Tel: (202) 512-1800
Fax: (202) 512-1657
Website: www.access.gpo.gov

The USGPO also has copies of specific laws available for purchase. The USGPO accepts orders made by fax, phone or placed over the Internet, as well as mail orders paid by credit card. All orders must be accompanied by payment. Credit cards, checks drawn on a U.S. bank, or an international money order are all acceptable.

Relevant Government Agencies

Address your questions regarding textile Multi-Fiber Arrangements to:

U.S. Department of Commerce
International Trade Administration
Office of Textiles and Apparel
Director's Office
14th and Constitution Avenue NW, Rm. H3100
Washington DC 20230
Tel: (202) 482-5078
Fax: (202) 482-2331
Agreements Division: (202) 482-4212
Website: http://otexa.ita.doc.gov

Address your questions regarding the Flammable Fabrics Act (FFA) to:

Consumer Product Safety Commission (CPSC)
Office of Compliance
Washington DC 20207-0001
Tel: 800-638-2772 or (301) 504-7912
Fax: (301) 504-0359
Website: www.cpsc.gov

Address your questions regarding labeling requirements under the Textile Fiber Products Identification Act (TFPIA) or the Wool Products Labeling Act (WPLA) to:

Federal Trade Commission (FTC)
Division of Enforcement
600 Pennsylvania Avenue NW
Washington DC 20580
Tel: (202) 326-2996
Website: www.ftc.gov

Address your questions regarding FDA regulation or requirements for textile wadding products intended for sanitary uses to:

U.S. Food and Drug Administration (FDA)
5600 Fishers Lane
Rockville, MD 20857-0001
Tel: 888-463-6332
Website: www.fda.gov

Address your questions regarding USDA requirements for imported cordage made of vegetable materials to:

Animal and Plant Health Inspection Service (APHIS)
Plant Protection and Quarantine (PPQ)
Director's Office
4700 River Rd., Unit 131
Riverdale, MD 20737
Tel: (301) 734-8261
Tel (PPQ permits): (301) 734-8758
Website: www.aphis.usda.gov/ppq

Address your questions regarding textile quotas to:

U.S. Customs and Border Protection
Office of Field Operations, Quota Branch
1300 Pennsylvania Avenue NW
Washington DC 20229
Tel: (202) 927-5850
Website: www.customs.treas.gov

The U.S. Customs Service provices updated status reports on textile quota on their web site (see address above). If the country you need information on is not listed, call the Quota Branch office at (202) 927-5850.

Address your questions regarding other textile article imports to your local Customs port director. For addresses, refer to "U.S. Customs and Border Protection Offices" on page 65 or contact:

U.S. Customs and Border Protection
Customs Headquarters
1300 Pennsylvania Avenue NW
Washington DC 20229
Tel: (202) 354-1000
Website: www.customs.treas.gov

Laws and Regulations

The following laws and regulations may be relevant to the importation of other textile articles. The laws are contained in the United States Code (USC), and the regulations are published in the Code of Federal Regulations (CFR), both of which are available at larger public and law libraries. Copies of specific laws are also available from the United States Government Printing Office (address above).

7 USC 1854
Textile Trade Agreements
(EO 11651, as amended by EO 11951 and 12188, and supplemented by EO 12475)
This Act authorizes the CITA of the DOC to enter into Multi-Fiber Agreements with other countries to control trade in textiles and establishes the Textile Import Program, which is enforced by U.S. Customs.

19 CFR 12.130 et seq.
Regulations on Entry of Textiles
These regulations provide the requirements and procedures followed by Customs in enforcing limitations on the importation and entry and withdrawal of textiles and textile products from warehouses for consumption in the U.S.

15 USC 70-77
Textile Fiber Products Identification Act (TFPIA)
This Act prohibits false or deceptive labeling (misbranding) and false advertising of any textile fiber products and requires all textile fiber products imported into the U.S. to be labeled in accordance with the requirements set forth in the law.

19 CFR 11.12b; 16 CFR 303 et seq.
Regulations on Labeling and Marking
These regulations detail the labeling and marking requirements for textiles as specified by the CPSC and the invoice contents required by U.S. Customs for purpose of enforcing the labeling and marking rules.

15 USC 68-68j
Wool Products Labeling Act (WPLA) of 1939

This Act prohibits the false or deceptive labeling (misbranding) of wool products and requires all wool products imported into the U.S. to be labeled in accordance with requirements set forth in the law.

19 CFR 11.12; 16 CFR 300 et seq.
Regulations on WPLA Labeling and Marking
These regulations set forth the wool labeling and marking requirements adopted by the FTC to administer the requirements of the WPLA and provide the procedures followed by U.S. Customs in enforcing the WPLA and the FTC regulations, including entry invoice requirements.

15 USC 1191-1204
Flammable Fabrics Act (FFA)
This Act provides for the setting of flammability standards for fabric by the Consumer Product Safety Commission (CPSC) and for enforcement by U.S. Customs.

16 CFR 1610, 1611, 1615, 1616, 1630-1632
Regulations on Flammable Fabric Standards
These regulations specify the flammability standards adopted by the CPSC under the FFA for various types of textiles.

21 USC 301 et seq.
Federal Food, Drug, and Cosmetic Act
This Act prohibits deceptive practices and regulates the manufacture, sale and importation or exportation of food, drugs, cosmetics, and related products. It was amended by the Food Quality Protection Act of 1996. See 21 USC 331, 381, 382.

19 CFR 12.1 et seq.; 21 CFR 1.83 et seq.
Regulations on Food, Drugs, and Cosmetics
These regulations of the Secretary of Health and Human Services and the Secretary of the Treasury govern the standards, labeling, marking, and importing of products used with food, drugs, and cosmetics.

16 CFR 423
Care Labeling Rule
Requires fiber composition and washing or dry cleaning instructions for textile apparel and certain piece goods.

Principal Exporting Countries

The following listing includes samples of the main supplier nations of the products of this chapter. It is organized by HTSUS major heading. (Refer to "Customs Classification" above for the product codes.) Countries are listed in rank order of the value of products imported to the U.S. Statistics represent customs value of entries for 2002 from the Bureau of Census.

6301—China, South Korea, Mexico, Pakistan, India, Thailand, Taiwan

6302—India, Pakistan, China, Brazil, Portugal, Turkey, Mexico

6303—China, Turkey, Mexico, India, Pakistan, Taiwan, Canada

6304—China, India, Portugal, Pakistan, Mexico

6305—Mexico, Turkey, Indonesia, Canada, India, Thailand, China

6306—China, Bangladesh, South Korea, Sri Lanka, Thailand

6307—China, Mexico, Pakistan, India, Canada, Taiwan, Dominican Republic

6308—United Kingdom, Canada, Denmark, China, Netherlands, France, New Zealand

6309—Canada, Dominican Republic, United Kingdom, Germany, France, Italy, Belgium, Netherlands

6310—Canada, Mexico, Pakistan, Turkey, Honduras, El Salvador, Dominican Republic, Netherlands, Russia

Chapter 64: Footwear

Full title: Footwear, Gaiters, and the Like; Parts of Such Articles

This chapter relates to the importation of footwear, which are classified under Chapter 64 of the Harmonized Tariff Schedule of the United States (HTSUS). Specifically, it covers footwear for adults and children and made of rubber, plastic, leather, composition leather, pigskin, wood, cork, and textiles. Articles covered include footwear with metal toe-caps, ski boots, work boots and shoes, sandals, thongs, rain boots, house slippers, tennis shoes, sports shoes, and disposable footwear. This chapter also covers parts of footwear, gaiters, and leggings.

If you are interested in importing footwear without applied soles and made of textile material, you should read Commodity Index Chapter 61 (knitted or crocheted) or Chapter 62 (not knitted or crocheted). Worn footwear is covered in Chapter 63, and footwear containing asbestos is classified in Chapter 68. For importing orthopedic appliances and footwear, refer to Chapter 90. Toy footwear, ice or roller skating boots, shin-guards, and other protective sportswear are covered in Chapter 95. If you are interested in importing parts of footwear not covered in this chapter, you should read the Commodity Index chapter in which those parts are classified. For example, eyelets and buckles are covered in Chapter 96, and braid, lace, pompoms, and other textile trimmings are covered in Chapter 58.

Note: To understand key issues that will enable you to make best use of the information in this section we recommend that you see "Introduction" on page 425.

Key Factors

The key factors in the importation of footwear are:

- Compliance with entry invoice requirements for footwear and component materials
- Compliance with textile quota restraints and visa requirements (if importing footwear with textile components)
- Submission of U.S. Customs Country-of-Origin Declaration(s) (if importing footwear with textile components)
- Compliance with labeling requirements under the Textile Fiber Products Identification Act (TFPIA) and the Wool Products Labeling Act (WPLA) (if importing footwear with textile components)
- Compliance with flammability standards adopted and enforced by the Consumer Product Safety Com-

mission (CPSC) under the Flammable Fabrics Act (FFA) (if importing footwear with textile components)

Although most importers use the services of a licensed customs broker in making their entries, and we recommend this practice, you should be aware of the regulatory, entry, and documentation issues involved in importing your product. You, as importer, are ultimately responsible for the fulfillment of any legal requirements applicable to your shipment.

General Considerations

Regulatory Agencies. U.S. Customs determines the classification of footwear for purposes of import duties. The DOC's Committee for Implementation of Textile Agreements (CITA) regulates certain textile imports under Section 204 of the Agricultural Adjustment Act. U.S. Customs enforces CITA textile and textile product entry quotas. Customs also enforces compliance with labeling and invoice requirements of the TFPIA and flammability standards under the FFA. The CPSC monitors imports and from time to time inspects textile shipments for compliance with FFA standards. If you are importing wool textiles, importation is subject to complex textile import regulations. The Federal Trade Commission (FTC) administers the WPLA requirements.

Import Duties on Footwear. The main issue associated with the importation of footwear is determination of duty. Duty rates vary widely depending first on the material of the upper and outer sole, and then on construction and/or intended use of the footwear. The value of the footwear also affects the duty status. Because there are so many variables in determining duty status, extensive extra information is required on each invoice for an import shipment entering under HTSUS headings 6401 through 6405. You may furnish this information on Customs **Form 5523** or in another appropriate format. There are numerous definitions regarding footwear found in HTSUS Chapter 64 that are essential to the classification of imported footwear as well as providing the information called for on Customs **Form 5523**.

Footwear with Textile Components. A few articles of footwear are subject to textile restraints under Multi-Fiber Arrangements and to wool product entry requirements. These articles are generally within HTSUS headings 6405 and 6406, and include removable insoles, heel cushions, gaiters, and leggings of cotton, wool, fine animal hair, man-made, and other fibers. Footwear with uppers and soles made of wool felt are also subject to these requirements. The following is an overview of the textile importing requirements.

Wool Product Entry Requirements. Depending on the nature of your wool footwear imports, as many as three different types of special entry documents may be required. First, for all imported articles that contain textile fibers, yarns, and fabrics covered by the Agricultural Adjustment Act of 1924 (1956) (AAA), including wool, you must file a U.S. Customs Textile Entry Declaration (see "Textile Country-of-Origin Declarations" below). Second, for all wool products subject to the WPLA, special information is required on the entry invoices (see "Wool Products Labeling Act" below). Finally, certain articles of apparel manufactured or produced in certain countries may be subject to quotas and other restraints under U.S. DOC Multi-Fiber Arrangements. Such products require export licenses, certificates, or visas issued by the appropriate country of origin, in addition to other requisite entry paperwork (see "Textile Quotas" below).

Wool Products Labeling Act. The term "wool product" means any product or any portion of a product that contains, purports to contain, or in any way is represented as containing wool, reprocessed wool, or reused wool. All wool products imported into the U.S., except those made more than 20 years before importation, and except carpets, rugs, mats, and upholsteries, must have affixed a stamp, tag, label, or other means of identification

as required by the WPLA. If you are importing wool products exempt from labeling under the WPLA, do not assume they are also exempt from labeling under the TFPIA. These are two distinct laws, with some overlapping requirements (see "Marking and Labeling Requirements" below).

Textile Quotas. If you are interested in importing footwear with textile components, the most important issue you need to be aware of is quotas. Under the Multi-Fiber Arrangement provisions of Section 204 of the Agricultural Adjustment Act, CITA initiates specific agreements with individual exporting countries. Section 204 of the Agricultural Adjustment Act covers textiles articles that: 1) are in chief value of cotton, wool, or man-made fibers, any textile fibers subject to the terms of any textile trade agreement, or any combination of such fibers; 2) contain 50% or more by weight of cotton or man-made fibers, or any textile fibers subject to the terms of any textile trade agreement; 3) contain 17% or more by weight of wool; or 4) if in chief value of textile fibers or textile materials, contain a blend of cotton, wool, or man-made fibers, any textile fibers subject to the terms of any textile trade agreement, or any combination of such fibers that, in total, amount to 50% or more by weight of all component fibers.

The U.S. has Multi-Fiber Arrangements with 40 countries. Each agreement with each country is unique, and may specify quotas for a type of textile or a specific article. Visas or export licenses may be required. These agreements, however, often change. Therefore, if you are interested in importing any footwear with textile components, you should contact the International Trade Administration's Office of Textile and Apparel (see addresses at end of this chapter). Refer to "Prohibitions and Restrictions" below for further details.

Textile Country-of-Origin Declarations. U.S. Customs enforces CITA textile and textile product entry quotas (see "Prohibitions and Restrictions" below). Requirements for entry include submission of Country-of-Origin Declarations with every shipment of footwear with textile components, regardless of whether it is subject to a specific multi-fiber arrangement (19 CFR 12.130, 12.131).

Country of Origin. Quota restrictions are country-specific and therefore are applied based on the country of origin for the textiles shipped. The last country from which a textile shipment was exported to the U.S. is not necessarily its country of origin. A textile or textile product imported into the U.S. is considered a product of the particular foreign territory or country, or a U.S. insular possession, where it is wholly grown, produced, or manufactured. For the following discussion, "country" means a foreign territory or country, or a U.S. insular possession.

In 1996, the U.S. Customs Service made major changes to country of origin rules for textile imports. The regulations at 19 CFR 102.21, "Textile and apparel products" were added to the 1996 Customs Regulations and became effective July 1, 1996. The new rules do not provide for cutting components or cutting and hemming to confer country of origin as in the past. The basis of the new law is processing operations or assembly. Some of the most important changes for importers to be aware of are:

- Cutting does not determine the country of origin (previously cutting determined country of origin for 90 percent of wearing apparel imports). The new rules are based on processing or assembly operations.

- Essential character does not determine country of origin because the new rules are based on processing.

- A subjective determination under the provisions of 19 CFR 12.130 is replaced by objective processing operations expressed in terms of tariff shifts. Dyeing, printing, and other finishing processes applied to fabrics no longer confer or change country of origin.

- Country of origin for textile and apparel products processed, assembled or manufactured in two or more countries is determined by where the most important processing occurs, and, if that cannot be ascertained, the last country in which an important processing operation occurs.

The country of origin is the country in which a product is wholly produced when a textile or apparel product is completely produced or manufactured (except for minor parts) in one country. For fabric, the country of origin is the country in which the fabric is woven, knitted, needled, tufted, felted, entangled or created by any other fabric-making process. The country of origin for staple yarn is the country in which yarn is spun; for filament yarn, the country in which filament is extruded; and for plied, gimped and cabled yarns, the country in which the fibers or filaments used in the yarn are spun or extruded. The country of origin of all other textile and apparel products is the country in which the components of a textile or apparel product are wholly assembled (except for minor attachments). Once again, note that assembly, not cutting, now confers country of origin.

Declarations. All importations of textiles and textile products must be accompanied by one of the following three declarations. Goods subject to Section 204, Agricultural Act of 1956, as amended, must be accompanied by either a single-country or a multiple-country declaration. Goods not subject to Section 204 must be accompanied by a negative declaration.

- **Single-country declarations** are used for entries of textiles or textile products which are wholly the growth, product, or manufacture of a single foreign country, territory, or U.S. insular possession. Information required includes: marks of identification and numbers; description of article and quantity; country of origin; and date of exportation.

- **Multiple-country declarations** are used for entries of textiles or textile products which were subjected to manufacturing or processing operations in, and/or incorporate materials originating in more than one foreign country or territory. Information required includes: marks of identification and numbers; for articles, description, quantity, identification of manufacturing and/or processing operations, country, and date of exportation; for materials used to make articles, description of materials, country of production, and date of exportation.

- **Negative declarations** must accompany all textile imports that are not subject to FFA Section 204 restrictions. Information required includes: marks of identification and numbers; descriptions of article and quantity; and country of origin.

The date of exportation to be indicated on the above declarations is the date on which the carrier leaves the last port in the country of origin, as determined by Customs. Diversion to another country during transit does not affect the export date.

Procedure for Declarations. The manufacturer, producer, exporter, or importer may prepare the declaration. If more than one of these parties is involved in the importation, each party may prepare a separate declaration. You may file a separate declaration for each invoice presented with your entry. The declaration must be dated and signed by the responsible party, and must include the person's title and the company name and address. Your shipment's entry will be denied unless it is accompanied by a properly executed declaration. Customs will not treat a textile declaration as a missing document for which a bond may be filed.

Customs will base its country-of-origin determination on the information contained in each declaration, unless the information is insufficient. If the information on the declaration is insuffi-

cient, Customs will require that you submit such additional information as will enable the determination to be made. The shipment will not be released until the determination is made. Thus, if you want to clear Customs with minimal delay, be sure that the information on the declarations is as complete as possible for each shipment.

Textile Labeling and Invoice Requirements. You are responsible for your imported product's compliance with applicable provisions of the TFPIA. Footwear with textile components that require labeling under TFPIA must already be labeled at entry, or the shipment will be refused. (See "Marking and Labeling Requirements" below.) If you import shipments of footwear with textile components subject to TFPIA and valued at over $500, you must provide special information on the entry invoice (see "Entry and Documentation" below).

Flammability Standards. Footwear with textile components imported into the U.S. for use in consumer products must be in compliance with the FFA, a federal law that gives the CPSC the authority and responsibility for protecting the public from the hazards of dangerously flammable items of wearing apparel and interior furnishings. Under the FFA, standards have been established for flammability of clothing textiles. You cannot import any article of wearing apparel or interior furnishing, or any fabric or related material that is intended for use or that may be used in such items, if it fails to conform to an applicable flammability standard (FFA Section 4). Certain products may be imported into the U.S. (FFA Section 11c) for finishing or processing to render them less flammable so as to meet the standards. For these products, the exporter must state on the invoice or other paper relating to the shipment that the shipment is being made for that purpose.

The CPSC monitors imports of textiles under its Import Surveillance Program. From time to time, your textile shipments may be inspected to ascertain compliance with mandatory safety standards. Shipments may also be subject to testing by the CPSC to determine compliance. If the CPSC believes a product, fabric, or related material does not comply with a flammability standard, it is authorized to pursue a variety of legal sanctions (see "Prohibitions and Restrictions" below).

Substantial Product Hazard Reports. Any firm that obtains information that reasonably supports the conclusion that one of its products presents an unreasonable risk of serious injury or death must report that information to the CPSC's Division of Corrective Actions (CPSC address below). Importers must also report to the CPSC if 1) a type of product is the subject of at least three civil actions filed in U.S. federal or state courts, 2) each suit alleges the involvement of that product type in death or grievous bodily injury (as defined in FFA Section 37(3)1), and 3) at least three of the actions result in a final settlement with the manufacturer or in a judgment for the plaintiff within any one of the two-year periods specified in FFA Section 37(b).

Import Advisory

Importation of textile products is trade-sensitive and highly regulated. Shipments of textile products not complying with all government regulations, including quotas and visas, are subject to seizure and could result in the imposition of penalties as well as possible forfeiture of the goods. You should always verify the available quota for any textile product you plan to import before your shipment leaves the country of manufacture. Furthermore, Customs textile classification rulings change frequently, and prior administrative rulings are often modified and sometimes reversed. You should be particularly careful to comply with country of origin determination regulations, which were changed in 1996, and affect quotas and visas, marking and labeling, and other important aspects of tariff classification. See "Publications and WWW Resources" for information on important Customs Service informed compliance publications.

The Customs Service has greatly increased its scrutiny of the textile industry, one of eight primary focus industries identified in the most recent Trade Compliance & Enforcement Plan. Imported products from these industries will likely attract significant attention from Customs in the areas of compliance measurement, compliance assessment, informed compliance, and interventions.

Customs Classification

For customs purposes, footwear with textile components are classified under Chapter 64 of the HTSUS. This chapter is broken into major headings, which are further divided into subheadings, and often sub-subheadings, each of which has its own HTSUS classification number. For example, the 2001 HTSUS number for plastic ski-boots is 6401.92.30, indicating it is a sub-subcategory of other footwear covering the ankle but not the knee (6401.92), which is a subcategory of the major heading waterproof footwear with outer soles and uppers of rubber or plastics, etc. (6401). There are six major headings within Chapter 64.

6401—Waterproof footwear with outer soles and uppers of rubber or plastics, the uppers of which are neither fixed to the sole nor assembled by stitching, riveting, nailing, screwing, plugging, or similar processes

6402—Other footwear with outer soles and uppers of rubber or plastics

6403—Footwear with outer soles of rubber, plastics, leather, or composition leather and uppers of leather

6404—Footwear with outer soles of rubber, plastics, leather, or composition leather and uppers of textile materials

6405—Other footwear

6406—Parts of footwear (including uppers whether or not attached to soles other than outer soles); removable insoles, heel cushions, and similar articles; gaiters, leggings, and similar articles, and parts thereof

For more details regarding classifications of the specific product you are interested in importing, consult a customs broker, the appropriate commodity specialist at your nearest customs port, or the HTSUS. The 2001 HTSUS is available online from the Customs Service (www.customs.gov/impoexpo/impoexpo.htm) or for purchase from the U.S. Government Printing Office (see resources at the end of this chapter), and may be found in larger public libraries. For a general discussion of customs classification, see "Classification—Liquidation" on page 229.

Dutiable Status of Goods

For more information about duty rates and binding decisions see "Dutiable Status of Goods" on page 203; for a discussion of temporary importation of goods see "Temporary Free Importations" on page 205.

Valuation

Importers have a responsibility to use what the U.S. Customs Service deems, "reasonable care," when determining the value of their goods. They must also provide any additional information that the Customs Service needs for setting a final value on the goods. This process involves a number of factors and can be somewhat complicated; importers must be aware of applicable issues and details. Valuation information applies to all types of commodities, for further discussion on the subject see "Customs Valuation" on page 267.

Import Duties

Import duties vary (often dramatically) depending upon the Harmonized Tariff Schedule (HTSUS) classification of the goods or products imported. Since some products that look alike have different HTSUS classifications and different rates of duty, proper classification is vital. Note that "differences of opinion" between importers and the Bureau of Customs and Border Protection regarding classification keeps customs attorneys very busy.

Import duties can be assessed on the imported value of the goods ("ad valorem" rates of duty such as 2%, 4.4%, 50%, etc.), total units or weight of the goods ("specific" rates of duty such as 2 cents each or 1.5 cents/pound, etc.) or on a combination basis ("compound" rates of duty such as 5 cents each plus 6%).

Listed below is a sampling of several Column 1 import duty rates for Chapter 64 products:

Ski-boots and snowboard boots (6401.92.30.00): Free
to
Footwear designed to be worn over, or in lieu of, other footwear as a protection against water, oil, grease or chemicals or cold or inclement weather (6402.30.50.00): 37.5%

For specific information on US import duties refer to the Harmonized Tariff Schedule of the US. The print version is available from the US Government Printing Office as well as third party suppliers who often add special features. Online versions are available in both static PDF pages as well as in formats with excellent search functionality. Search the Web with the term "Harmonized Tariff Schedule" to find sources.

Entry and Documentation

The entry of merchandise is a two-part process consisting of 1) filing the documentation necessary to determine whether merchandise may be released from Customs custody, and 2) filing the documents that contain information for duty assessment and statistical purposes. In certain instances, all documents must be filed and accepted by Customs prior to release of the goods. Unless you have been granted an extension, you must file entry documents at a location specified by the port or area director within five working days of your shipment's date of arrival at a U.S. port of entry. These include a number of standard documents required by Customs for any entry, and:

- Customs Form CF 5523, footwear entry invoice

- U.S. Customs Country-of-Origin Declaration Form CF 3229, general form, NAFTA certificate Form CF 434, and the Caribbean Basin (CBTPA) certificate (if importing textile products) Form CF 450

- Export documentation and/or visa (if importing textiles products subject to Multi-Fiber Arrangements

After you present the entry, Customs may examine your shipment or may waive examination. The shipment is then released provided no legal or regulatory violations have been noted. You must then file entry summary documentation and deposit estimated duties at a designated customhouse within 10 working days of your shipment's release. For a detailed description of entry procedures, standard documentation, and informal entry, see "Entry Process" on page 185.

Informed Compliance. Informed compliance was introduced with the Customs Modernization Act of 1993 (Mod Act) and defines the relationship between importers and the Customs Service. It sets out the responsibilities of both parties. Providing the correct documentation and information for entry is a key factor that will make your importing operation run smoothly. We recommend that importers become familiar with the concept of informed comliance and the responsibilities that they have under the Mod Act. For further discussion about informed compliance see "Informed Compliance" on page 211.

Entry Invoice for Footwear—Definitions. Customs will employ the following terms and definitions in assessing the duty status of your shipment of footwear:

1)   Exclusively adhesive construction: all pieces of the bottom would separate from the upper or from each other if all adhe-

sives, cements, and glues were dissolved. It includes shoes with pieces of the upper stitched to each other, but not to any part of the bottom. Examples include: a) vulcanized construction footwear; b) simultaneous molded construction footwear; c) molded footwear with the upper and the bottom made as one piece of molded rubber or plastic; and d) footwear in which staples, rivets, stitching, or any of the methods above are either primary or even just extra or auxiliary, even though adhesive is a major part of the reason the bottom will not separate from the upper.

2)   Composition leather: made by binding together leather fibers or small pieces of natural leather. This does not include imitation leathers not based on natural leather.

3)   Leather: the tanned skin of any animal from which the fur or hair has been removed. Tanned skins coated or laminated with rubber and/or plastics are "leather" only if leather gives the material its essential character.

4)   Line of demarcation: exists if one can indicate where the sole ends and the upper begins. For example, knit booties do not normally have a line of demarcation.

5)   Men's, boy's, and youth's sizes cover footwear of American youths size 11 1/2 and larger for males, and does not include footwear commonly worn by both sexes. If more than 4% of the shoes sold in a given size will be worn by females, that size is "commonly worn by both sexes."

6)   Protective footwear: footwear is designed to protect against water, oil, or cold or inclement weather only if it is substantially more of a protection against those conditions than the usual shoes of that type. For example, though wearing leather oxfords will clearly keep your feet warmer and drier than going barefoot, they afford only a normal degree of protection. On the other hand, the snow-jogger is the protective version of the nonprotective jogging shoe.

7)   Rubber and/or plastics includes any textile material visibly coated (or covered) externally with one or both of those materials.

8)   Slip-on includes: a) a boot that must be pulled on; b) footwear with elastic cores that must be stretched to get it on, but not a separate piece of elasticized fabric that forms a full circle around the foot or ankle.

9)   Sports footwear includes only a) footwear designed for a sporting activity and having, or having provision for, the attachment of spikes, sprigs, cleats, stops, clips, bars, or the like; b) skating boots (without skates attached), ski boots, and cross-country ski footwear, wrestling boots, boxing boots, and cycling shoes.

10) Tennis shoes, basketball shoes, gym shoes, training shoes, and the like cover athletic footwear other than sports footwear, whether or not principally used for such athletic games or purposes.

11) Textile materials are made from cotton, other vegetable fibers, wool, hair, silk, or man-made fibers. Note: cork, wood, cardboard, and leather are not textile materials.

12) Turned construction: the upper is stitched to the leather sole wrong side out, and the shoe is then turned right side out.

13) Vegetable fibers include cotton, flax, and ramie, but not rayon or plaiting materials, such as rattan or wood strips.

14) Waterproof footwear includes footwear designed to protect against penetration by water or other liquids, whether or not such footwear is primarily designed for such purposes.

15) Welt footwear means footwear construction with a welt, which extends around the edge of the outer sole, and in which the welt and shoe upper are sewed to a lip on the surface of the insole, and the outer sole of which is sewed or cemented to the welt.

16) A zori has an upper consisting only of straps or thongs of molded rubber or plastic. This upper is assembled to a formed rubber or plastic sole by means of plugs.

Entry Invoice for Footwear—Contents. The invoice or other entry documentation for footwear must show:

1) manufacturer's style number; 2) importer's style and/or stock number; 3) for the upper, the percent by area of external surface area (excluding reinforcements and accessories), that is a) leather, b) composition leather, c) rubber and/or plastics, d) textile materials, e) other, by percentage; and 4) for the outersole, the same percentage breakdown as required for uppers.

Depending on the percentages of component materials cited in items 3) and 4) above, a combination of additional questions must be answered. You may choose to answer all the questions, or only those required by your answers to items 3) and 4) above. The questions are as follows: a) What percent of external surface area of upper (including leather reinforcements and accessories) is leather? b) What percent by area of external surface area of upper (including all reinforcements and accessories) is rubber and/or plastics? c) What percent by weight is of rubber and/or plastics? d) What percent by weight is textile materials plus rubber and/or plastics? e) Is it waterproof? f) Does it have a protective metal toe cap? g) Will it cover the wearer's ankle bone? h) Will it cover the wearer's knee cap? i) [Reserved]; j) Is it designed to be a protection against water, oil, grease, or chemicals, or cold or inclement weather? k) Is it a slip-on? l) Is it a downhill or cross-country ski boot? m) Is it serious sports footwear other than ski boots? n) Is it a tennis, basketball, gym, or training shoe or the like? o) Is it made on a base or platform of wood? p) Does it have open toes or open heels? q) Is it made by the (lipped insole) welt construction? r) Is it made by the turned construction? s) Is it worn exclusively by men, boys, or youths? t) Is it made by an exclusively adhesive construction? u) Are the fibers of the upper, by weight, predominantly vegetable fibers? v) Is it disposable, i.e. intended for one-time use? w) Is it a "Zori"? x) Is the leather in the upper pigskin? y) Are the sole and upper made of wool felt? z) Is there a line of demarcation between the outer sole and upper?

If you claim duty classification under subheading 6401.99.80, 6402.19.10, 6402.30.30, 6402.91.40, 6402.99.15, 6402.99.30, 6404.11.40, 6404.11.60, 6404.19.35, 6404.19.40, or 6404.19.60, you must also provide the following information: Does the shoe have a foxing or foxing-like band? If so, state its material(s). Does the sole overlap the upper other than just at the front of the toe and/or at the back of the heel?

Entry Invoice—TFPIA Requirements. All invoices for textile wearing apparel should indicate: 1) a component material breakdown in percentages by weight for all component fibers present in the entire garment, as well as separate breakdowns of the fibers in the (outer) shell (exclusive of linings, cuffs, waistbands, collars and other trimmings) and in the lining; 2) for garments that are constructed of more than one component or material (combination of knit and not-knit fabric or combinations of knit and/or not-knit fabric with leather, fur, plastic—including vinyl, etc.) the invoice must show a fiber breakdown in percentages by weight for each separate textile material in the garment and a breakdown in percentages by weight for each nontextile material of the entire garment; 3) for woven garments: indicate whether the fabric is yarn-dyed and whether there are "two or more colors in the warp and/or filling;" 4) for all-white T-shirts and singlets: indicate whether or not the garment contains pockets, trim, or embroidery; 5) for mufflers: state the exact dimensions, length, and width of the merchandise.

Entry Invoice—Wool Products Subject to WPLA. When you offer for entry a wool product shipment valued at over $500 and subject to WPLA, you must include certain information intended to facilitate Customs monitoring and enforcement of that Act. This extra information is identical to that required by WPLA on labeling (see "Marking and Labeling Requirements" below), with the addition of the manufacturer's name. If your product consists of mixed waste, residues, and similar merchandise obtained from several suppliers or unknown sources, you may omit the manufacturer's name from the entry invoice. For more general information about invoices see "Invoices" on page 277.

Note: The Entry and Documentation section has been carefully designed to supply you, the importer, with sample documents and directions on how to satisfy Customs requirements. Be aware that you should consult the applicable authorities to ensure that you are correctly following the most current procedures.

Prohibitions and Restrictions

Textile Quotas. Textile import restrictions are primarily a matter of quotas and the way in which these quotas are administered and monitored. Under the Multi-Fiber Arrangement provisions of Section 204 of the Agricultural Adjustment Act, CITA has negotiated Multi-Fiber Arrangements with 40 countries. These Agreements may impose quotas for a type of textile or a specific article, and they are country-specific. The agreements, however, often change. Therefore, if you are interested in importing any knitted or crocheted apparel articles, you should contact the International Trade Administration's Office of Textile and Apparel (see addresses at end of this chapter). The Office of Textile and Apparel has a team of country specialists who can inform you of the latest developments and inform you about a product's quota or restriction status.

U.S. Customs enforces CITA textile and textile product entry quotas. If formal entry procedures are not followed, Customs will usually refuse entry for textiles that are subject to Section 204. Formal entry requires submission of a Country-of-Origin Declaration (see "General Considerations" above). U.S. Customs maintains a current textile quota status report, available for perusal at any Customs port. In addition, U.S. Customs in , DC, provides quota status reports online, which are updated on a regular basis (www.customs.gov/impoexpo/impoexpo.htm).

Flammable Fabrics. U.S. Customs may refuse entry for any article of wearing apparel or interior furnishing, or any fabric or related material that is intended for use or that may be used in wearing apparel or interior furnishings, if it fails to conform to an applicable flammability standard issued under Section 4 of the FFA. An exception is allowed for certain products (FFA Section 11c) that are imported for finishing or processing to bring them within the legal standard. For these products, the exporter must state on the invoice or other paper relating to the shipment that the shipment is being made for that purpose.

The CPSC, as the primary enforcement agency of flammability standards, inspects products for compliance with the FFA. If the CPSC believes a product, fabric, or related material does not comply with a flammability standard, it is authorized to pursue a variety of legal sanctions, including: 1) seizure, condemnation, and forfeiture of the noncomplying products; 2) administrative cease-and-desist order requiring an individual or firm to stop sale and distribution of the noncomplying products or; 3) temporary injunction requiring the individual or firm to stop sale and distribution of the noncomplying products, pending final disposition of an administrative cease-and-desist proceeding. The CPSC also has authority to seek civil penalties against any person who knowingly violates a regulation or standard issued under Section 4 of the FFA.

Country-Specific Restrictions

Restrictions under Multi-Fiber Arrangements are country-specific. A product originating in one country may be subject to quota and to export license or visa requirements, while the same product originating in a different country may not. At present, the U.S. has Multi-Fiber Arrangements with 40 countries. Many different categories of products are covered under these Arrangements; it is beyond the scope of this book to list each country and its restricted commodities. If you are interested in

importing textiles and textile products, you should contact the International Trade Administration's Office of Textile and Apparel (see addresses at end of this chapter) or U.S. Customs to ascertain your product's restraint status.

The U.S. Customs service provides quota reports on their website (www.customs.gov/impoexpo/impoexpo.htm). These reports are constantly updated and have an effective date noted. The most recent quota information can be accessed by clicking on the country name that interests you. This location holds information regarding quotas, transshipments, and visa requirements.

Marking and Labeling Requirements

TFPIA Requirements. All textile products imported into the U.S. must be stamped, tagged, labeled, or otherwise marked with the following information as required by the TFPIA, unless exempt from marking (see TFPIA, Section 12): 1) the generic names and percentages by weight of the constituent fibers present in the textile fiber product, exclusive of permissible ornamentation, in amounts of more than 5% in order of predominance by weight, with any percentage of fiber or fibers required to be designated as "other fiber" or "other fibers" (including those present in amounts of 5% or less) appearing last; and 2) the name of the manufacturer or the name or registered identification number issued by the FTC of one or more persons marketing or handling the textile fiber product; and 3) the name of the country where processed. A word trademark, used as a house mark and registered with the U.S. Patent Office, may appear on labels instead of the name otherwise required, provided the owner of the trademark furnishes a copy of the registration to the FTC prior to use (see "Registered Identification Numbers" below).

The information listed above is not exhaustive. TFPIA requirements are extensive. The Act specifies such details as types of labels, means of attachment, label position on the article, package labeling, unit labeling for two-piece garments, and arrangement of information on the label; allowable fiber designations; country-of-origin indications; requirements for trim and ornamentation, linings and interlinings, and pile fabrics; sectional disclosure; use of trade names and trademarks; and requirements for swatches and samples. The FTC publishes a booklet intended to clarify TFPIA requirements to facilitate voluntary compliance in the industry (see "Publications and WWW Resources" below). It is available on request, at no charge, from the FTC (see addresses at end of this chapter).

Wool Products Labeling Act (WPLA). Wool product labeling requirements for foreign products are the responsibility of the importer. The WPLA requires the following information to appear on wool products subject to the Act: 1) percentage of the wool product's total fiber weight (exclusive of ornamentation) not exceeding 5% of the total fiber weight of a) wool, b) recycled wool, c) each fiber other than wool if the percent by weight of such fiber is 5% or more, and d) the aggregate of all other fibers; 2) the maximum percent of the wool product's total weight, of any nonfibrous loading, filling, or adulterating matter; and 3) the importer's name. If you, as importer, have a registered identification number issued by the FTC, that number may be used instead of your name (see "Registered Identification Numbers" below).

Customs entry is contingent on proper labeling. If your shipment is found to be mislabeled at entry, you will be given the option of relabeling the products under Customs supervision, as long as the port director is satisfied that your labeling error or omission did not involve fraud or willful neglect. If your shipment is discovered after entry to have been noncomplying with WPLA, it will be recalled to Customs custody at your expense, unless you can satisfy the port director that the products have since been brought into compliance. You will be held responsible for all expenses incurred in bringing a shipment into compliance, including compensation of personnel and other expenses related to Customs supervision.

Fraudulent violations of WPLA will result in seizure of the shipment. Shipments already released from Customs custody will be ordered to be redelivered to Customs. Customs reports all cases of fraudulent violation to the FTC in , DC.

The information listed above is not intended to be exhaustive. WPLA requirements are extensive. The Act specifies such details as types of labels, means of attachment, label position on the article, package labeling, unit labeling (as in the case of a two-piece garment), arrangement of information on the label, allowable fiber designations, country-of-origin indications, trim and ornamentation, pile fabrics, sectional disclosure, use of trade names and trademarks, requirements for swatches and samples, etc. The FTC publishes a booklet intended to clarify WPLA requirements in order to facilitate voluntary compliance within the industry (see "Publications and WWW Resources" below). It is available on request, at no charge, from the FTC (see addresses at end of this chapter).

The Care Labeling Rule. Regulations under this rule require manufacturers and importers of textile clothing and fabrics to attach specific care instructions for washing or dry cleaning, as well as information on the fiber composition of the article. They are enforced by the FTC Division of Enforcement. The Care Labeling Rule was amended September 2000, detailed information is available on the FTC website (www.ftc.gov/os/statutes/textilejump.htm).

Registered Identification Numbers. Any domestic firm or person residing in the U.S. and engaged in the manufacture or marketing of textile products covered under the TFPIA or WPLA may obtain an FTC-registered identification number for use on required tags and labels instead of the name of a firm or person. For applications, contact the FTC (see addresses at end of this chapter).

For a general discussion of U.S. Customs marking and labeling requirements, see "Country of Origin Marking" on page 236, "Special Marking Requirements" on page 238 and "Marking—False Impression" on page 239.

Shipping Considerations

You will need to ensure that your goods are packaged and shipped with care so that they pass smoothly through Customs and arrive in good condition. You are responsible for ensuring that the shipment is in compliance with all applicable government regulations for packaging and shipping. In most instances, you should not leave these arrangements solely to the discretion of your supplier. Careful preparation of the cargo and selection of the mode of transport can be essential to a cost-effective, timely delivery of undamaged goods. We strongly advise you to consult your shipping representative, insurance agent, or freight broker for advice on packing and shipping.

Footwear may be shipped in bulk, crates, boxes, or other types of containers, depending on the type of product and whether it is prepackaged. General considerations include protection from contamination, weather, and pests. Containers should be constructed so as to be safe for handling during transport.

Publications and WWW Resources

The following publications may be relevant to the importation of footwear:

> *Threading Your Way Through the Labeling Requirements Under the Textile and Wool Acts*

Available free of charge on request from the Federal Trade Commission and online from the FTC website (www.ftc.gov/bcp/

conline/pubs/buspubs/thread.htm). This publication is an excellent source of information written in clear lay language. We recommend that anyone interested in importing textile fiber products but unfamiliar with the regulations obtain a copy of each of this booklet.

The U.S. Customs Service launched a series of "Informed Compliance" publications in 1996, which are available on the Customs Service website (www.customs.gov/impoexpo/impoexpo.htm). Of particular interest:

> *What Every Member of the Trade Community Should Know About Textile & Apparel Rules of Origin*
>
> *What Every Member of the Trade community Should Know About NAFTA for Textiles and Textile Articles*
>
> *Fibers & Yarns Construction and Classification Under the HTSUS*

The *Harmonized Tariff Schedule of the United States (2001)* (HTSUS) is available to view on the Customs Service website (www.customs.gov), or you may purchase a printed version from:

U.S. Government Printing Office
Superintendent of Documents
710 North Capital Street NW
Washington DC 20401
Tel: (202) 512-1800
Fax: (202) 512-1657
Website: www.access.gpo.gov

The USGPO also has copies of specific laws available for purchase. The USGPO accepts orders made by fax, phone or placed over the Internet, as well as mail orders paid by credit card. All orders must be accompanied by payment. Credit cards, checks drawn on a U.S. bank, or an international money order are all acceptable.

Relevant Government Agencies

Address your questions regarding textile Multi-Fiber Arrangements to:

U.S. Department of Commerce
International Trade Administration
Office of Textiles and Apparel
Director's Office
14th and Constitution Avenue NW, Rm. H3100
Washington DC 20230
Tel: (202) 482-5078
Fax: (202) 482-2331
Agreements Division: (202) 482-4212
Website: http://otexa.ita.doc.gov

Address your questions regarding the Flammable Fabrics Act (FFA) to:

Consumer Product Safety Commission (CPSC)
Office of Compliance
Washington DC 20207-0001
Tel: 800-638-2772 or (301) 504-7912
Fax: (301) 504-0359
Website: www.cpsc.gov

Address your questions regarding labeling requirements under the Textile Fiber Products Identification Act (TFPIA) or the Wool Products Labeling Act (WPLA) to:

Federal Trade Commission (FTC)
Division of Enforcement
600 Pennsylvania Avenue NW
Washington DC 20580
Tel: (202) 326-2996
Website: www.ftc.gov

Address your questions regarding textile quotas to:

U.S. Customs and Border Protection
Office of Field Operations, Quota Branch
1300 Pennsylvania Avenue NW
Washington DC 20229
Tel: (202) 927-5850
Website: www.customs.treas.gov

The U.S. Customs Service provides updated status reports on textile quota on their web site (see address above). If the country you need information on is not listed, call the Quota Branch office at (202) 927-5850.

Address your questions regarding footwear imports to your local Customs port director. For addresses, refer to "U.S. Customs and Border Protection Offices" on page 65 or contact:

U.S. Customs and Border Protection
Customs Headquarters
1300 Pennsylvania Avenue NW
Washington DC 20229
Tel: (202) 354-1000
Website: www.customs.treas.gov

Laws and Regulations

The following laws and regulations may be relevant to the importation of footwear. The laws are contained in the United States Code (USC), and the regulations are published in the Code of Federal Regulations (CFR), both of which are available at larger public and law libraries. Copies of specific laws are also available from the United States Government Printing Office (address above).

7 USC 1854
Textile Trade Agreements
(EO 11651, as amended by EO 11951 and 12188, and supplemented by EO 12475 below)
This Act authorizes the CITA of the DOC to enter into Multi-Fiber Agreements with other countries to control trade in textiles and establishes the Textile Import Program, which is enforced by U.S. Customs.

19 CFR 12.130 et seq.
Regulations on Entry of Textiles
These regulations provide the requirements and procedures followed by Customs in enforcing limitations on the importation and entry and withdrawal of textiles and textile products from warehouses for consumption in the U.S.

19 CFR 141.89
Regulation on Additional Invoice Requirements
This regulation specifies the additional information for certain classes of merchandise, including footwear and textile products, being imported into the U.S.

15 USC 70-77
Textile Fiber Products Identification Act (TFPIA)
This Act prohibits false or deceptive labeling (misbranding) and false advertising of any textile fiber products and requires all textile fiber products imported into the U.S. to be labeled in accordance with the requirements set forth in the law.

19 CFR 11.12b; 16 CFR 303 et seq.
Regulations on Labeling and Marking
These regulations detail the labeling and marking requirements for textiles as specified by the CPSC and the invoice contents required by U.S. Customs for purpose of enforcing the labeling and marking rules.

15 USC 68-68j
Wool Products Labeling Act (WPLA) of 1939
This Act prohibits the false or deceptive labeling (misbranding) of wool products and requires all wool products imported into the U.S. to be labeled in accordance with requirements set forth in the law.

19 CFR 11.12; 16 CFR 300 et seq.

Regulations on WPLA Labeling and Marking
These regulations set forth the wool labeling and marking requirements adopted by the FTC to administer the requirements of the WPLA and provide the procedures followed by U.S. Customs in enforcing the WPLA and the FTC regulations, including entry invoice requirements.

15 USC 1191-1204
Flammable Fabrics Act (FFA)
This Act provides for the setting of flammability standards for fabric by the Consumer Product Safety Commission (CPSC) and for enforcement by U.S. Customs.

16 CFR 1610, 1611, 1615, 1616, 1630-1632
Regulations on Flammable Fabric Standards
These regulations specify the flammability standards adopted by the CPSC under the FFA for various types of textiles.

Principal Exporting Countries

The following listing includes samples of the main supplier nations of the products of this chapter. It is organized by HTSUS major heading. (Refer to "Customs Classification" above for the product codes.) Countries are listed in rank order of the value of products imported to the U.S. Statistics represent customs value of entries for 2002 from the Bureau of Census, U.S. Department of Commerce.

6401—China, Canada, Mexico, Italy, Germany, South Korea, Malaysia, Netherlands

6402—China, Indonesia, Italy, Thailand, Vietnam, Brazil, Taiwan

6403—China, Italy, Brazil, Indonesia, Spain, Thailand, Mexico, Vietnam

6404—China, Italy, Mexico, Vietnam, Indonesia, Thailand, Spain, Brazil, Dominican Republic

6405—China, Brazil, Italy, Spain, Thailand, Hong Kong, Germany

6406—China, Dominican Republic, Mexico, Canada, Italy, Taiwan, Germany, South Korea, India

- Import restrictions on certain plant materials
- Endangered species restrictions on certain plan materials

Although most importers use the services of a licensed customs broker in making their entries, and we recommend this practice, you should be aware of the regulatory, entry, and documentation issues involved in importing your product. You, as importer, are ultimately responsible for the fulfillment of any legal requirements applicable to your shipment.

General Considerations

Regulatory Agencies. U.S. Customs determines the classification of headgear for purposes of import duties. The DOC's Committee for Implementation of Textile Agreements (CITA) regulates certain textile imports under Section 204 of the Agricultural Adjustment Act. U.S. Customs enforces CITA textile and textile product entry quotas. Customs also enforces compliance with labeling and invoice requirements of the TFPIA and flammability standards under the FFA. The CPSC monitors imports and from time to time inspects textile shipments for compliance with FFA standards. If you are importing wool textiles, importation is subject to complex textile import regulations. The Federal Trade Commission (FTC) administers the WPLA requirements.

Wool Product Entry Requirements. Depending on the nature of your wool headgear imports, as many as three different types of special entry documents may be required. First, for all imported articles that contain textile fibers, yarns, and fabrics covered by the Agricultural Adjustment Act (AAA), including wool, you must file a U.S. Customs Textile Entry Declaration (see Textile Country-of-Origin Declarations below). Second, for all wool products subject to the WPLA, special information is required on the entry invoices (see "Wool Products Labeling Act" below). Finally, certain articles of headgear manufactured or produced in certain countries may be subject to quotas and other restraints under U.S. DOC Multi-Fiber Arrangements. Such products require export licenses, certificates, or visas issued by the appropriate country of origin, in addition to other requisite entry paperwork (see "Textile Quotas" below).

Wool Products Labeling Act. The term "wool product" means any product or any portion of a product that contains, purports to contain, or in any way is represented as containing wool, reprocessed wool, or reused wool. All wool products imported into the U.S., except those made more than 20 years before importation, and except carpets, rugs, mats, and upholsteries, must have affixed a stamp, tag, label, or other means of identification as required by the WPLA. If you are importing wool products exempt from labeling under the WPLA, do not assume they are also exempt from labeling under the TFPIA. These are two distinct laws, with some overlapping requirements (see "Marking and Labeling Requirements" below).

Textile Quotas. If you are interested in importing headgear with textile components, the most important issue you need to be aware of is quotas. Under the Multi-Fiber Arrangement provisions of Section 204 of the Agricultural Adjustment Act, CITA initiates specific agreements with individual exporting countries. Section 204 of the Agricultural Adjustment Act covers textiles articles that: 1) are in chief value of cotton, wool, or man-made fibers, any textile fibers subject to the terms of any textile trade agreement, or any combination of such fibers; 2) contain 50% or more by weight of cotton or man-made fibers, or any textile fibers subject to the terms of any textile trade agreement; 3) contain 17% or more by weight of wool; or 4) if in chief value of textile fibers or textile materials, contain a blend of cotton, wool, or man-made fibers, any textile fibers subject to the terms of any textile trade agreement, or any combination of such fibers that, in total, amount to 50% or more by weight of all component fibers.

Chapter 65:
Headgear

Full title: Headgear and Parts Thereof

This chapter relates to the importation of headgear, which are classified under Chapter 65 of the Harmonized Tariff Schedule of the United States (HTSUS). Specifically, it covers hats and parts of hats of felt, and plaited, woven, and knitted materials; helmets and other headgear; and articles such as headbands, linings, covers, foundations, visors, chinstraps, and similar parts of headgear.

Materials for weaving straw hats are covered in Commodity Index Chapter 14. If you are interested in importing worn headgear, refer to Chapter 63. Headgear made from asbestos is covered in Chapter 68. Dolls' hats, party hats, and similar articles are found in Chapter 95. If you are interested in importing scarves, shawls, veils, and similar products, refer to Chapters 61 or 62.

Note: To understand key issues that will enable you to make best use of the information in this section we recommend that you see "Introduction" on page 425.

Key Factors

The key factors in the importation of headgear are:

- Compliance with entry invoice requirements for headgear and component materials
- Compliance with textile quota restraints and visa requirements (if importing headgear with textile components)
- Submission of U.S. Customs Country-of-Origin Declaration(s) (if importing headgear with textile components)
- Compliance with labeling requirements under Textile Fiber Products Identification Act (TFPIA) and/or the Wool Products Labeling Act (WPLA) and the Care Labeling Rule (if importing headgear with textile components)
- Compliance with flammability standards adopted and enforced by the Consumer Product Safety Commission (CPSC) under the Flammable Fabrics Act (FFA) (if importing headgear with textile components)
- Motor vehicle helmets must meet U.S. Department of Transportation (DOT) safety, labeling, and entry documentation requirements
- Bicycle helmets must meet voluntary safety standards enforced by the CPSC
- Random U.S. Department of Agriculture (USDA) port-of-entry inspections on certain plant materials

The U.S. has Multi-Fiber Arrangements with 40 countries. Each agreement with each country is unique, and may specify quotas for a type of textile or a specific article. Visas or export licenses may be required. These agreements, however, often change. Therefore, if you are interested in importing any headgear with textile components, you should contact the International Trade Administration's Office of Textile and Apparel (see addresses at end of this chapter). Refer to "Prohibitions and Restrictions" below for further details.

Textile Country-of-Origin Declarations. U.S. Customs enforces CITA textile and textile product entry quotas (see "Prohibitions and Restrictions" below). Requirements for entry include submission of Country-of-Origin Declarations with every shipment of headgear with textile components, regardless of whether it is subject to a specific multi-fiber arrangement (19 CFR 12.130, 12.131).

Country of Origin. Quota restrictions are country-specific and therefore are applied based on the country of origin for the textiles shipped. The last country from which a textile shipment was exported to the U.S. is not necessarily its country of origin. A textile or textile product imported into the U.S. is considered a product of the particular foreign territory or country, or a U.S. insular possession, where it is wholly grown, produced, or manufactured. For the following discussion, "country" means a foreign territory or country, or a U.S. insular possession.

In 1996, the U.S. Customs Service made major changes to country of origin rules for textile imports. The regulations at 19 CFR 102.21, "Textile and apparel products" were added to the 1996 Customs Regulations and became effective July 1, 1996. The new rules do not provide for cutting components or cutting and hemming to confer country of origin as in the past. The basis of the new law is processing operations or assembly. Some of the most important changes for importers to be aware of are:

- Cutting does not determine the country of origin (previously cutting determined country of origin for 90 percent of wearing apparel imports). The new rules are based on processing or assembly operations.

- Essential character does not determine country of origin because the new rules are based on processing.

- A subjective determination under the provisions of 19 CFR 12.130 is replaced by objective processing operations expressed in terms of tariff shifts. Dying, printing, and other finishing processes applied to fabrics no longer confer or change country of origin.

- Country of origin for textile and apparel products processed, assembled or manufactured in two or more countries is determined by where the most important processing occurs, and, if that cannot be ascertained, the last country in which an important processing operation occurs.

The country of origin is the country in which a product is wholly produced when a textile or apparel product is completely produced or manufactured (except for minor parts) in one country. For fabric, the country of origin is the country in which the fabric is woven, knitted, needled, tufted, felted, entangled or created by any other fabric-making process. The country of origin for staple yarn is the country in which yarn is spun; for filament yarn, the country in which filament is extruded; and for plied, gimped and cabled yarns, the country in which the fibers or filaments used in the yarn are spun or extruded. The country of origin of all other textile and apparel products is the country in which the components of a textile or apparel product are wholly assembled (except for minor attachments). Once again, note that assembly, not cutting, now confers country of origin.

Declarations. All importations of textiles and textile products must be accompanied by one of the following three declarations. Goods subject to Section 204, Agricultural Act of 1956, as amended, must be accompanied by either a single-country or a multiple-country declaration. Goods not subject to Section 204 must be accompanied by a negative declaration.

- **Single-country declarations** are used for entries of textiles or textile products which are wholly the growth, product, or manufacture of a single foreign country, territory, or U.S. insular possession. Information required includes: marks of identification and numbers; description of article and quantity; country of origin; and date of exportation.

- **Multiple-country declarations** are used for entries of textiles or textile products which were subjected to manufacturing or processing operations in, and/or incorporate materials originating in more than one foreign country or territory. Information required includes: marks of identification and numbers; for articles, description, quantity, identification of manufacturing and/or processing operations, country, and date of exportation; for materials used to make articles, description of materials, country of production, and date of exportation.

- **Negative declarations** must accompany all textile imports that are not subject to FFA Section 204 restrictions. Information required includes: marks of identification and numbers; descriptions of article and quantity; and country of origin.

The date of exportation to be indicated on the above declarations is the date on which the carrier leaves the last port in the country of origin, as determined by Customs. Diversion to another country during transit does not affect the export date.

Procedure for Declarations. The manufacturer, producer, exporter, or importer may prepare the declaration. If more than one of these parties is involved in the importation, each party may prepare a separate declaration. You may file a separate declaration for each invoice presented with your entry. The declaration must be dated and signed by the responsible party, and must include the person's title and the company name and address. Your shipment's entry will be denied unless it is accompanied by a properly executed declaration. Customs will not treat a textile declaration as a missing document for which a bond may be filed.

Customs bases its country-of-origin determination on the information contained in each declaration, unless the information is insufficient. If the information on the declaration is insufficient, Customs will require that you submit such additional information as will enable the determination to be made. The shipment will not be released until the determination is made. Thus, if you want to clear Customs with minimal delay, be sure that the information on the declarations is as complete as possible for each shipment.

Textile Labeling and Invoice Requirements. You are responsible for your imported product's compliance with applicable provisions of the TFPIA. Headgear with textile components that require labeling under TFPIA must already be labeled at entry, or the shipment will be refused. (See "Marking and Labeling Requirements" below.) If you import shipments of headgear with textile components subject to TFPIA and valued at over $500, you must provide special information on the entry invoice (see "Entry and Documentation" below).

Flammability Standards. Headgear with textile components imported into the U.S. for use in consumer products must be in compliance with the FFA, a federal law that gives the CPSC the authority and responsibility for protecting the public from the hazards of dangerously flammable items of wearing apparel and interior furnishings. Under the FFA, standards have been established for flammability of clothing textiles. You cannot import any article of wearing apparel or interior furnishing, or any fabric or related material that is intended for use or that may be used in such items, if it fails to conform to an applicable flammability standard (FFA Section 4). Certain products may be imported into the U.S. (FFA Section 11c) for finishing or processing to render them less flammable so as to meet the standards. For these products, the exporter must state on the invoice or other paper relating to the shipment that the shipment is being made for that purpose.

The CPSC monitors imports of textiles under its Import Surveillance Program. From time to time, your textile shipments may be inspected to ascertain compliance with mandatory safety standards. Shipments may also be subject to testing by the CPSC to determine compliance. If the CPSC believes a product, fabric, or related material does not comply with a flammability standard, it is authorized to pursue a variety of legal sanctions (see "Prohibitions and Restrictions" below).

Substantial Product Hazard Reports. Any firm that obtains information that reasonably supports the conclusion that one of its products presents an unreasonable risk of serious injury or death must report that information to the CPSC's Division of Corrective Actions (CPSC address below). Importers must also report to the CPSC if 1) a type of product is the subject of at least three civil actions filed in U.S. federal or state courts, 2) each suit alleges the involvement of that product type in death or grievous bodily injury (as defined in FFA Section 37(3)1), and 3) at least three of the actions result in a final settlement with the manufacturer or in a judgment for the plaintiff within any one of the two-year periods specified in FFA Section 37(b).

Motor Vehicle Helmets. Helmets for use with motor vehicles are considered motor vehicle equipment, and are regulated by U.S. Department of Transportation (DOT), National Highway Traffic Safety Administration (NHTSA), Office of Vehicle Safety Compliance (OVSC). Motor vehicle helmets must bear labeling certifying that they comply with provisions of Federal Motor Vehicle Safety Standard (FMVSS) Number 218 (see "Marking and Labeling Requirements" below). You must present a completed DOT **Declaration HS-7**, in duplicate, with each shipment at the U.S. port of entry. You can get Declaration HS-7 forms at any Customs port office or from your customs broker. No permits or licenses are required.

Bicycle Helmets. Helmets for use with bicycles are subject to voluntary standards published by the American National Standards Institute, Inc. (ANSI) (see addresses at end of this chapter). ANSI is a U.S. society whose members develop and coordinate both domestic and international voluntary consensus standards for more than 10,000 products. For the most part, the helmet industry itself is responsible for compliance enforcement. However, if you are importing foreign-made bicycle helmets, you should be cognizant of applicable ANSI standards. You are responsible for your shipment's compliance with these standards. Since compliance is voluntary, the CPSC will not inspect your shipments at the port of entry to ascertain compliance. But if, for example, your product is noncomplying, and is later found to be a causative factor in a head injury, CPSC would assume an enforcement role. CPSC is authorized to initiate various administrative and legal enforcement proceedings to prevent imports that pose a hazard to the ultimate consumer. So although standards for bicycle helmets are voluntary, compliance with those standards is nevertheless important. For further information, see "Publications and WWW Resources" below.

Hats Woven from Vegetable Materials. Importation of vegetable plaiting material and related miscellaneous plant products is regulated by the USDA under the Plant Quarantine Act (PQA). The USDA Animal Plant Health Inspection Service (APHIS) Plant Protection and Quarantine (PPQ) branch inspects shipments of plaiting and related materials on a random basis, depending upon the port of entry, the risk factor involved in the type of material being offered for entry, etc. You do not generally need permits or licenses to import these products, but the type of plant material is pertinent (see "Prohibitions and Restrictions", below). For most shipments of plaiting materials, importation is straightforward. If you are importing related articles classified under different Commodity Index chapters, there may be additional requirements administered by other governmental agencies. This depends entirely upon the specific article you are importing.

Restrictions under the Endangered Species Act (ESA) and the Convention on International Trade in Endangered Species (CITES) apply to plant materials of listed plants species, and are enforced by the U.S. Fish and Wildlife Service (FWS), usually in consultation with and often through the USDA. Regulations governing the importation of plant products are complex, and FWS permits or CITES documentation may be required. To ascertain what your legal responsibilities are, you should contact these agencies with specific identification of the materials you wish to import.

Import Advisory

Importation of textile products is trade-sensitive and highly regulated. Shipments of textile products not complying with all government regulations, including quotas and visas, are subject to seizure and could result in the imposition of penalties as well as possible forfeiture of the goods. You should always verify the available quota for any textile product you plan to import before your shipment leaves the country of manufacture. Furthermore, Customs textile classification rulings change frequently, and prior administrative rulings are often modified and sometimes reversed. You should be particularly careful to comply with country of origin determination regulations, which were changed in 1996, and affect quotas and visas, marking and labeling, and other important aspects of tariff classification. See "Publications and WWW Resources" for information on important Customs Service informed compliance publications.

The Customs Service has greatly increased its scrutiny of the textile industry, one of eight primary focus industries identified in the most recent Trade Compliance & Enforcement Plan. Imported products from these industries will likely attract significant attention from Customs in the areas of compliance measurement, compliance assessment, informed compliance, and interventions.

Customs Classification

For customs purposes, headgear with textile components are classified under Chapter 65 of the HTSUS. This chapter is broken into major headings, which are further divided into subheadings, and often sub-subheadings, each of which has its own HTSUS classification number. For example, the 2001 HTSUS number for knitted hats of cotton for babies is 6505.90.15, indicating it is a sub-subcategory of other knitted headgear of cotton or flax other than hairnets (6505.90), which is a subcategory of the major heading hats and other headgear knitted or crocheted (6505). There are seven major headings in HTSUS chapter 65.

6501—Hat forms, hat bodies, and hoods of felt, neither blocked to shape nor with made brims; plateaux and manchons (including slit manchons), of felt

6502—Hat shapes, plaited or made by assembling strips of any material, neither blocked to shape, nor with made brims, not lined nor trimmed

6503—Felt hats and other felt headgear, made from the hat bodies or hoods or plateaux of heading 6501, whether or not lined or trimmed

6504—Hats and other headgear, plaited or made by assembling strips of any material, whether or not lined or trimmed

6505—Hats and other headgear, knitted or crocheted, or made up from lace, felt, or other textile fabric, in the piece (but not in strips), whether or not lined or trimmed; hair-nets of any material, whether or not lined or trimmed

6506—Other headgear, whether or not lined or trimmed

6507—Headbands, linings, covers, hat foundations, hat frames, peaks (visors), and chinstraps, for headgear

For more details regarding classifications of the specific product you are interested in importing, consult a customs broker, the appropriate commodity specialist at your nearest customs port, or the HTSUS. The 2001 HTSUS is available online from the Customs Service (www.customs.gov/impoexpo/impoexpo.htm) or for purchase from the U.S. Government Printing Office (see resources at the end of this chapter), and may be found in larger public libraries. For a general discussion of customs classification, see "Classification—Liquidation" on page 229.

Dutiable Status of Goods

For more information about duty rates and binding decisions see "Dutiable Status of Goods" on page 203; for a discussion of temporary importation of goods see "Temporary Free Importations" on page 205.

Valuation

Importers have a responsibility to use what the U.S. Customs Service deems, "reasonable care," when determining the value of their goods. They must also provide any additional information that the Customs Service needs for setting a final value on the goods. This process involves a number of factors and can be somewhat complicated; importers must be aware of applicable issues and details. Valuation information applies to all types of commodities, for further discussion on the subject see "Customs Valuation" on page 267.

Import Duties

Import duties vary (often dramatically) depending upon the Harmonized Tariff Schedule (HTSUS) classification of the goods or products imported. Since some products that look alike have different HTSUS classifications and different rates of duty, proper classification is vital. Note that "differences of opinion" between importers and the Bureau of Customs and Border Protection regarding classification keeps customs attorneys very busy.

Import duties can be assessed on the imported value of the goods ("ad valorem" rates of duty such as 2%, 4.4%, 50%, etc.), total units or weight of the goods ("specific" rates of duty such as 2 cents each or 1.5 cents/pound, etc.) or on a combination basis ("compound" rates of duty such as 5 cents each plus 6%).

Listed below is a sampling of several Column 1 import duty rates for Chapter 65 products:
Headbands, linings, covers, hat foundations, hat frames, peaks (visors) and chinstraps, for headgear (6507.00.00 00): Free
to
Hair-nets (6505.10.00.00): 9.5%

For specific information on US import duties refer to the Harmonized Tariff Schedule of the US. The print version is available from the US Government Printing Office as well as third party suppliers who often add special features. Online versions are available in both static PDF pages as well as in formats with excellent search functionality. Search the Web with the term "Harmonized Tariff Schedule" to find sources.

Entry and Documentation

The entry of merchandise is a two-part process consisting of 1) filing the documentation necessary to determine whether merchandise may be released from Customs custody, and 2) filing the documents that contain information for duty assessment and statistical purposes. In certain instances, all documents must be filed and accepted by Customs prior to release of the goods. Unless you have been granted an extension, you must file entry documents at a location specified by the port or area director within five working days of your shipment's date of arrival at a U.S. port of entry. These include a number of standard documents required by Customs for any entry, and:

- U.S. Customs Country-of-Origin Declaration Form CF 3229, (if importing textile products)
- Export documentation and/or visa (if importing textiles products subject to Multi-Fiber Arrangements
- For motor vehicle helmets: DOT Declaration HS-7 , in duplicate
- Where applicable for hats of woven vegetable materials, USDA permits
- Where applicable for hats of woven vegetable materials, FWS permits and/or export certification from the country of origin required under endangered species regulations

After you present the entry, Customs may examine your shipment or may waive examination. The shipment is then released provided no legal or regulatory violations have been noted. You must then file entry summary documentation and deposit estimated duties at a designated customhouse within 10 working days of your shipment's release. For a detailed description of entry procedures, standard documentation, and informal entry, see "Entry Process" on page 185.

Informed Compliance. Informed compliance was introduced with the Customs Modernization Act of 1993 (Mod Act) and defines the relationship between importers and the Customs Service. It sets out the responsibilities of both parties. Providing the correct documentation and information for entry is a key factor that will make your importing operation run smoothly. We recommend that importers become familiar with the concept of informed comliance and the responsibilities that they have under the Mod Act. For further discussion about informed compliance see "Informed Compliance" on page 211.

Special Entry Invoices. Hats and headgear classified under subheading 6502.00.40 or 6502.00.60 require a statement as to whether or not the article has been bleached or colored. Articles classified subheading 6502.00.20 through 6502.00.60 or 6504.00.30 through 6504.00.90 require a statement as to whether or not the article is sewed or not, exclusive of any ornamentation or trimming.

Entry Invoice—TFPIA Requirements. All invoices for textile wearing apparel should indicate: 1) a component material breakdown in percentages by weight for all component fibers present in the entire garment, as well as separate breakdowns of the fibers in the (outer) shell (exclusive of linings, cuffs, waistbands, collars and other trimmings) and in the lining; 2) for garments which are constructed of more than one component or material (combination of knit and not-knit fabric or combinations of knit and/or not-knit fabric with leather, fur, plastic—including vinyl, etc.) the invoice must show a fiber breakdown in percentages by weight for each separate textile material in the garment and a breakdown in percentages by weight for each nontextile material of the entire garment; 3) for woven garments: indicate whether the fabric is yarn-dyed and whether there are "two or more colors in the warp and/or filling."

Entry Invoice—Wool Products Subject to WPLA. When you offer for entry a wool product shipment valued at more than $500 and subject to WPLA, you must include certain information intended to facilitate Customs monitoring and enforcement of that act. This extra information is identical to that required by WPLA on labeling (see "Marking and Labeling Requirements" below), with the addition of the manufacturer's name. If your product consists of mixed waste, residues, and similar merchandise obtained from several suppliers or unknown sources, you may omit the manufacturer's name from the entry invoice. For more general information about invoices see "Invoices" on page 277.

Note: The Entry and Documentation section has been carefully designed to supply you, the importer, with sample documents and directions on how to satisfy Customs requirements. Be aware that you should consult the applicable authorities to ensure that you are correctly following the most current procedures.

Prohibitions and Restrictions

Textile Quotas. Textile import restrictions are primarily a matter of quotas and the way in which these quotas are administered and monitored. Under the Multi-Fiber Arrangement provisions of Section 204 of the Agricultural Adjustment Act, CITA has negotiated Multi-Fiber Arrangements with 40 countries. These agreements may impose quotas for a type of textile or a specific article, and they are country-specific. However, the agreements often change. Therefore, if you are interested in importing any knitted or crocheted apparel articles, you should contact the International Trade Administration's Office of Textile and Apparel (see addresses at end of this chapter). The Office of Textile and Apparel has a team of country specialists who can inform you of the latest developments and inform you about a product's quota or restriction status.

U.S. Customs enforces CITA textile and textile product entry quotas. If formal entry procedures are not followed, Customs will usually refuse entry for textiles that are subject to Section 204. Formal entry requires submission of a Country-of-Origin Declaration (see "General Considerations" above). U.S. Customs maintains a current textile quota status report, available for perusal at any customs port. In addition, U.S. Customs in Washington, D.C., operates a telephone service to provide quota status reports, which are updated weekly (see "Relevant Government Agencies" below).

Flammable Fabrics. U.S. Customs may refuse entry for any article of wearing apparel or interior furnishing, or any fabric or related material that is intended for use or that may be used in wearing apparel or interior furnishings, if it fails to conform to an applicable flammability standard issued under Section 4 of the FFA. An exception is allowed for certain products (FFA Section 11c) that are imported for finishing or processing to bring them within the legal standard. For these products, the exporter must state on the invoice or other document relating to the shipment that the shipment is being made for that purpose.

The CPSC, as the primary enforcement agency of flammability standards, inspects products for compliance with the FFA. If the CPSC believes a product, fabric, or related material does not comply with a flammability standard, it is authorized to pursue a variety of legal sanctions, including: 1) seizure, condemnation, and forfeiture of the noncomplying products; 2) administrative cease-and-desist order requiring an individual or firm to stop sale and distribution of the noncomplying products or; 3) temporary injunction requiring the individual or firm to stop sale and distribution of the noncomplying products, pending final disposition of an administrative cease-and-desist proceeding. The CPSC also has authority to seek civil penalties against any person who knowingly violates a regulation or standard issued under Section 4 of the FFA.

Helmets. Motor vehicle helmets that do not comply with provisions of FMVSS Number 218 are prohibited. Unlike the voluntary standards for bicycle helmets, these standards are compulsory. You, as importer, are responsible for your product's compliance. The standard has been developed in order to reduce deaths and injuries to motorcyclists and other motor vehicle users resulting from head impacts. Each helmet must meet specific requirements when subjected to certain conditioning and testing procedures contained within the regulation. Components of the testing procedures include impact attenuation, penetration, and testing of retention systems (i.e. straps and assemblies that keep the helmet on the head). In addition to meeting testing requirements, helmets must meet configuration requirements that determine such things as peripheral vision clearance, brow opening, and continuous contour of the protective surface. Helmets may not have any rigid projections inside the shell, and those outside the shell must be limited to those required for operation of essential accessories. The regulation limits the size of such projections to 0.20 inch. Manufacturers must establish a positioning index for each helmet manufactured. If you make inquiry regarding that index for a helmet specified by manufacturer, model designation and size, the manufacturer is required by law to provide the information. For more details, contact DOT (see addresses at end of this chapter).

Hats and Components of Woven Vegetable Materials. In general, any shipment of vegetable plaiting material is subject to random port-of-entry inspection by USDA. If the inspector finds evidence of the presence of insects, you may be required to submit your shipment to USDA-prescribed fumigation procedures. If the insect is of a kind for which there is no viable U.S. treatment, your shipment will be refused. Our source at USDA assured us that most shipments that are found to be infested can be treated to afford entry.

Country-Specific Restrictions

Restrictions under Multi-Fiber Arrangements are country-specific. A product originating in one country may be subject to quota and to export license or visa requirements, while the same product originating in a different country may not. At present, the U.S. has Multi-Fiber Arrangements with 40 countries. Many different categories of products are covered under these arrangements; it is beyond the scope of this discussion to list each country and its restricted commodities. If you are interested in importing textiles and textile products, you should contact the International Trade Administration's Office of Textile and Apparel (see addresses at end of this chapter) or U.S. Customs to ascertain your product's restraint status.

The U.S. Customs service provides quota reports on their website (www.customs.gov/impoexpo/impoexpo.htm). These reports are constantly updated and have an effective date noted. The most recent quota information can be accessed by clicking on the country name that interests you. This location holds information regarding quotas, transshipments, and visa requirements.

Marking and Labeling Requirements

TFPIA Requirements. All textile products imported into the U.S. must be stamped, tagged, labeled, or otherwise marked with the following information as required by the TFPIA, unless exempt from marking—such as sweatbands for the head—(see TFPIA, Section 12): 1) the generic names and percentages by weight of the constituent fibers present in the textile fiber product, exclusive of permissible ornamentation, in amounts of more than 5% in order of predominance by weight, with any percentage of fiber or fibers required to be designated as "other fiber" or "other fibers" (including those present in amounts of 5% or less) appearing last; and 2) the name of the manufacturer or the name or registered identification number issued by the FTC of one or more persons marketing or handling the textile fiber product; and 3) the name of the country where processed. A word trademark, used as a house mark and registered with the U.S. Patent Office, may appear on labels instead of the name otherwise required, provided the owner of the trademark furnishes a copy of the registration to FTC prior to use (see "Registered Identification Numbers" below).

The information listed above is not exhaustive. TFPIA requirements are extensive. The Act specifies such details as types of labels, means of attachment, label position on the article, package labeling, unit labeling for two-piece garments, and arrangement of information on the label; allowable fiber designations; country-of-origin indications; requirements for trim and ornamentation, linings and interlinings, and pile fabrics; sectional disclosure; use of trade names and trademarks; and requirements for swatches and samples. The FTC publishes a booklet intended to clarify TFPIA requirements to facilitate voluntary compliance in the industry (see "Publications and WWW Resources" below). It is available on request, at no charge, from the FTC (see addresses at end of this chapter).

Wool Products Labeling Act (WPLA). Wool product labeling requirements for foreign products are the responsibility of the importer. The WPLA requires the following information to appear on wool products subject to the act: 1) percentage of the wool product's total fiber weight (exclusive of ornamentation) not exceeding 5% of the total fiber weight of a) wool, b) recycled wool, c) each fiber other than wool if the percent by weight of such fiber is 5% or more, and d) the aggregate of all other fibers; 2) the maximum percent of the wool product's total weight, of any nonfibrous loading, filling, or adulterating matter; and 3) the importer's name. If you, as importer, have a registered identification number issued by the FTC, that number may be used instead of your name (see "Registered Identification Numbers" below).

Customs entry is contingent on proper labeling. If your shipment is found to be mislabeled at entry, you will be given the option of relabeling the products under Customs supervision, as long as the port director is satisfied that your labeling error or omission did not involve fraud or willful neglect. If your shipment is discovered after entry to have been noncomplying with WPLA, it will be recalled to Customs custody at your expense, unless you can satisfy the port director that the products have since been brought into compliance. You will be held responsible for all expenses incurred in bringing a shipment into compliance, including compensation of personnel and other expenses related to Customs supervision.

Fraudulent violations of WPLA will result in seizure of the shipment. Shipments already released from Customs custody will be ordered to be redelivered to Customs. Customs reports all cases of fraudulent violation to the FTC in , D.C.

The information listed above is not intended to be exhaustive. WPLA requirements are extensive. The act specifies such details as types of labels, means of attachment, label position on the article, package labeling, unit labeling (as in the case of a two-piece garment), arrangement of information on the label, allowable fiber designations, country-of-origin indications, trim and ornamentation, pile fabrics, sectional disclosure, use of trade names and trademarks, requirements for swatches and samples, etc. The FTC publishes a booklet intended to clarify WPLA requirements in order to facilitate voluntary compliance within the industry (see "Publications and WWW Resources" below). It is available on request, at no charge, from the FTC (see addresses at end of this chapter).

The Care Labeling Rule. Regulations under this rule require manufacturers and importers of textile clothing and fabrics to attach specific care instructions for washing or dry cleaning, as well as information on the fiber composition of the article. They are enforced by the FTC Division of Enforcement. The Care Labeling Rule was amended September 2000, detailed information is available on the FTC website (www.ftc.gov/os/statutes/textilejump.htm).

Registered Identification Numbers. Any domestic firm or person residing in the U.S. and engaged in the manufacture or marketing of textile products covered under the TFPIA or WPLA may obtain an FTC-registered identification number for use on required tags and labels instead of the name of a firm or person. For applications, contact the FTC (see addresses at end of this chapter).

Helmets. Motor vehicle helmets must be labeled permanently and legibly, in such a manner that labels can be read easily without removing padding or any other permanent helmet part. Labeling must include the following information: 1) manufacturer's name or identification; 2) precise model designation; 3) size; 4) month and year of manufacture, either spelled out (e.g. June 1988) or expressed in numerals (e.g. 6/88); 5) the symbol "DOT," constituting the manufacturer's certification that the helmet conforms to the applicable FMVSS. This symbol must appear on the outer surface of the helmet, in a color that contrasts with the background, in letters at least 3/8 inch high, centered laterally with the horizontal center line of the symbol located a minimum of 1-1/8 inches and a maximum of 1-3/8 inches from the bottom edge of the posterior portion of the helmet. In addition, labeling must include the following instructions to purchasers: 1) "Shell and liner constructed of (identify types of materials);" 2) "Helmet can be seriously damaged by some common substances without damage being visible to the user. Apply only the following: (recommended cleaning agents, paints, adhesives, etc., as appropriate);" 3) "Make no modifications. Fasten helmet securely. If helmet experiences a severe blow, return it to the manufacturer for inspection, or destroy it and replace it." Any additional relevant safety information should be supplied at the time of purchase, by means of an attached tag, brochure, or other suitable means.

For a general discussion of U.S. Customs marking and labeling requirements, see "Country of Origin Marking" on page 236, "Special Marking Requirements" on page 238 and "Marking—False Impression" on page 239.

Shipping Considerations

You will need to ensure that your goods are packaged and shipped with care so that they pass smoothly through Customs and arrive in good condition. You are responsible for ensuring that the shipment is in compliance with all applicable government regulations for packaging and shipping. In most instances, you should not leave these arrangements solely to the discretion of your supplier. Careful preparation of the cargo and selection of the mode of transport can be essential to a cost-effective, timely delivery of undamaged goods. We strongly advise you to consult your shipping representative, insurance agent, or freight broker for advice on packing and shipping.

Headgear may be shipped in bulk, crates, boxes, or other types of containers, depending on the type of product and whether it is prepackaged. General considerations include protection from contamination, weather, and pests. Containers should be constructed so as to be safe for handling during transport.

Publications and WWW Resources

The following publications may be relevant to the importation of headgear:

Threading Your Way Through the Labeling Requirements Under the Textile and Wool Acts

Available from the Federal Trade Commission wesite (www.ftc.gov/bcp/conline/pubs/buspubs/thread.htm), this publication is an excellent source of information written in clear lay language. We recommend that anyone interested in importing textile products but unfamiliar with the regulations obtain a copy The U.S. Customs Service launched a series of "Informed Compliance" publications in 1996, which are available on the Customs Service website (www.customs.gov/impoexpo/impoexpo.htm). Of particular interest:

What Every Member of the Trade Community Should Know About Textile & Apparel Rules of Origin

What Every Member of the Trade community Should Know About NAFTA for Textiles and Textile Articles

Fibers & Yarn Construction and Classification Under the HTSUS

The American National Standards Institute, Inc. (ANSI) publishes domestic and international voluntary consensus standards for more than 10,000 commodities. Electronic products are available directly from ANSI. However, Global Engineering Documents (Global) as been appointed by ANSI as their primary distributor of hardcopy documents. Contact information for both are given below. For ANSI standards applicable to bicycle helmets, request: Document ANSI Z-90.4, 1984 Edition: *Protective Headgear for Bicyclists*; $25.00. Address your inquiries to:

American National Standards Institute, Inc. (ANSI)
25 West 43rd Street, 4th Floor
New York, NY 10036
Tel: (212) 642-4900
Website: htp://www.ansi.org

Global Engineering Documents
15 Inverness Way East
Englewood, CO 80112
Tel: 800-854-7179 or (303) 397-7956
Fax: (303) 397-2740
Website: www.global.ihs.com

The *Harmonized Tariff Schedule of the United States (2001)* (HTSUS) is available to view on the Customs Service website (www.customs.gov), or you may purchase a printed version from:

U.S. Government Printing Office
Superintendent of Documents
710 North Capital Street NW
Washington DC 20401
Tel: (202) 512-1800
Fax: (202) 512-1657
Website: www.access.gpo.gov

The USGPO also has copies of specific laws available for purchase. The USGPO accepts orders made by fax, phone or placed over the Internet, as well as mail orders paid by credit card. All orders must be accompanied by payment. Credit cards, checks drawn on a U.S. bank, or an international money order are all acceptable.

Relevant Government Agencies

Address questions regarding textile Multi-Fiber Arrangements to:

U.S. Department of Commerce
International Trade Administration
Office of Textiles and Apparel
Director's Office
14th and Constitution Avenue NW, Rm. H3100
Washington DC 20230
Tel: (202) 482-5078
Fax: (202) 482-2331
Agreements Division: (202) 482-4212
Website: http://otexa.ita.doc.gov

Address questions regarding the Flammable Fabrics Act (FFA) to:

Consumer Product Safety Commission (CPSC)
Office of Compliance
Washington DC 20207-0001
Tel: 800-638-2772 or (301) 504-7912
Fax: (301) 504-0359
Website: www.cpsc.gov

Address questions regarding labeling requirements under the Textile Fiber Products Identification Act (TFPIA) or the Wool Products Labeling Act (WPLA) to:

Federal Trade Commission (FTC)
Division of Enforcement
600 Pennsylvania Avenue NW
Washington DC 20580
Tel: (202) 326-2996
Website: www.ftc.gov

Address questions regarding DOT requirements for motor vehicle helmets to:

National Highway Traffic Safety Administration
Office of Vehicle Safety Compliance
Equipment & Import Division
400 7th St. SW
Washington DC 20590
Tel: (202) 366-2832
Website: www.nhtsa.dot.gov

Address questions regarding USDA requirements for importation of vegetable woven materials to:

Animal and Plant Health Inspection Service (APHIS)
Plant Protection and Quarantine (PPQ)
Director's Office
4700 River Rd., Unit 133
Riverdale, MD 20737
Tel: (301) 734-8896
PPQ Permit Unit: (301) 734-8645
Website: www.aphis.usda.gov/ppq

Address questions regarding endangered species restrictions to:

U.S. Fish and Wildlife Service (FWS)
Office of Management Authority
4401 N. Fairfax Dr.
Arlington, VA 22203-0700
Tel: (703) 358-2104
Website: www.fws.gov

Address your questions regarding textile quotas to:

U.S. Customs and Border Protection
Office of Field Operations, Quota Branch
1300 Pennsylvania Avenue NW
Washington DC 20229
Tel: (202) 927-5850
Website: www.customs.treas.gov

The U.S. Customs Service provices updated status reports on textile quota on their web site (see address above). If the country you need information on is not listed, call the Quota Branch office at (202) 927-5850.

Address your questions regarding headgear imports to your local Customs port director. For addresses, refer to "U.S. Customs and Border Protection Offices" on page 65 or contact:

U.S. Customs and Border Protection
Customs Headquarters
1300 Pennsylvania Avenue NW
Washington DC 20229
Tel: (202) 354-1000
Website: www.customs.treas.gov

Laws and Regulations

The following laws and regulations may be relevant to the importation of footwear. The laws are contained in the United States Code (USC), and the regulations are published in the Code of Federal Regulations (CFR), both of which are available at larger public and law libraries. Copies of specific laws are also available from the United States Government Printing Office (address above).

19 CFR 141.89
Regulation on Additional Invoice Requirements
This regulation specifies the additional information for certain classes of merchandise, including footwear and textile products, being imported into the U.S.

7 USC 1854
Textile Trade Agreements
(EO 11651, as amended by EO 11951 and 12188, and supplemented by EO 12475 below)
This Act authorizes the CITA of the DOC to enter into Multi-Fiber Agreements with other countries to control trade in textiles and establishes the Textile Import Program, which is enforced by U.S. Customs.

19 CFR 12.130 et seq.
Regulations on Entry of Textiles
These regulations provide the requirements and procedures followed by Customs in enforcing limitations on the importation and entry and withdrawal of textiles and textile products from warehouses for consumption in the U.S.

15 USC 70-77
Textile Fiber Products Identification Act (TFPIA)
This Act prohibits false or deceptive labeling (misbranding) and false advertising of any textile fiber products and requires all textile fiber products imported into the U.S. to be labeled in accordance with the requirements set forth in the law.

19 CFR 11.12b; 16 CFR 303 et seq.
Regulations on Labeling and Marking
These regulations detail the labeling and marking requirements for textiles as specified by the CPSC and the invoice contents required by U.S. Customs for purpose of enforcing the labeling and marking rules.

15 USC 68-68j
Wool Products Labeling Act (WPLA) of 1939
This Act prohibits the false or deceptive labeling (misbranding) of wool products and requires all wool products imported into the U.S. to be labeled in accordance with requirements set forth in the law.

19 CFR 11.12; 16 CFR 300 et seq.
Regulations on WPLA Labeling and Marking
These regulations set forth the wool labeling and marking requirements adopted by the FTC to administer the requirements of the WPLA and provide the procedures followed by U.S. Customs in enforcing the WPLA and the FTC regulations, including entry invoice requirements.

15 USC 1191-1204
Flammable Fabrics Act (FFA)
This Act provides for the setting of flammability standards for fabric by the Consumer Product Safety Commission (CPSC) and for enforcement by U.S. Customs.

16 CFR 1610, 1611, 1615, 1616, 1630-1632
Regulations on Flammable Fabric Standards
These regulations specify the flammability standards adopted by the CPSC under the FFA for various types of textiles.

Convention on International Trade in Endangered Species of Wild Fauna and Flora (CITES)
This comprehensive wildlife treaty signed by over 100 countries, including the United States, regulates and in many cases prohibits commercial imports and exports of wild animal and plant species threatened by trade.

16 USC 1531

Endangered Species Act of 1973
This Act prohibits the import and export of plant and seed species listed as endangered and most species listed as threatened. Seeds labeled as "of cultivated origin" may be traded. It is the U.S. law that implements CITES.

16 CFR 423
Care Labeling Rule
Requires fiber composition and washing or dry cleaning instructions for textile apparel and certain piece goods.

Principal Exporting Countries

The following listing includes samples of the main supplier nations of the products of this chapter. It is organized by HTSUS major heading. (Refer to "Customs Classification" above for the product codes.) Countries are listed in rank order of the value of products imported to the U.S. Statistics represent customs value of entries for 2002 from the Bureau of Census, U.S. Department of Commerce.

6501—Portugal, Czech Republic, Brazil, Colombia, Ecuador, Italy

6502—China, Ecuador, Mexico, Taiwan, Hong Kong, Philippines, Czech Republic

6503—Italy, China, Canada, Mexico, Czech Republic, Spain

6504—China, Mexico, Taiwan, Italy, Canada, Philippines, Sri Lanka

6505—China, Bangladesh, Taiwan, South Korea, Dominican Republic, Canada, Mexico

6506—China, South Korea, Taiwan, Japan, Canada, Italy

6507—China, Canada, Taiwan, Trinidad and Tobago, Mexico, South Korea, United Kingdom, Sweden, Japan, Hong Kong

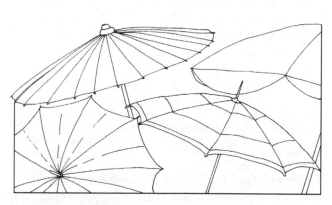

Chapter 66:
Umbrellas and Related Items

Full title: Umbrellas, Sun Umbrellas, Walking-Sticks, Seat-Sticks, Whips, Riding Crops, and Parts Thereof

This chapter relates to the importation of umbrellas, walking-sticks, whips, and related items, which are classified under Chapter 66 of the Harmonized Tariff Schedule of the United States (HTSUS). Specifically, it covers sun, garden, rain, walking-stick, and other umbrellas, walking-sticks, seat-sticks, whips, riding crops, and parts of these articles—such as handles, knobs, and umbrella frames and shafts.

If you are interested in importing measure walking-sticks and similar items, you should read Commodity Index Chapter 90. Toy umbrellas, sticks, and whips are covered in Chapter 95. The import requirements for sticks designed for use as weapons, such as firearm-sticks, sword-sticks, and loaded walking-sticks, are explained in Chapter 93. Trimmings or accessories of textile material, covers, tassels, thongs, cases, and similar items entered with but not fitted to articles imported under Chapter 66 are classified separately under the chapter applicable to the specific item.

Note: To understand key issues that will enable you to make best use of the information in this section we recommend that you see "Introduction" on page 425.

Key Factors

Although most importers use the services of a licensed customs broker in making their entries, and we recommend this practice, you should be aware of the regulatory, entry, and documentation issues involved in importing your product. You, as importer, are ultimately responsible for the fulfillment of any legal requirements applicable to your shipment.

General Considerations

Importation of umbrellas, walking-sticks, whips, and related items is straightforward. There are no restrictions or prohibitions. You do not need permits or licenses, nor is special entry documentation required.

Customs Classification

For customs purposes, umbrellas, walking-sticks, whips, and related items are classified under Chapter 66 of the HTSUS. This chapter is broken into major headings, which are further divided into subheadings, and often sub-subheadings, each of which has its own HTSUS classification number. For example, the 2001 HTSUS number for frames for hand-held rain umbrellas is 6603.20.30, indicating it is a sub-subcategory of umbrella frames, etc. (6603.20), which is a subcategory of the major heading parts,

trimmings, and accessories, etc. (6603). There are three major headings within Chapter 64.

6601—Umbrellas and sun umbrellas (including walking-sticks, umbrellas, garden umbrellas, and similar umbrellas)

6602—Walking-sticks, seat-sticks, whips, riding-crops, and the like

6603—Parts, trimmings, and accessories of articles of heading 6601 or 6602

For more details regarding classifications of the specific product you are interested in importing, consult a customs broker, the appropriate commodity specialist at your nearest customs port, or the HTSUS. The 2001 HTSUS is available online from the Customs Service (www.customs.gov/impoexpo/impoexpo.htm) or for purchase from the U.S. Government Printing Office (see resources at the end of this chapter), and may be found in larger public libraries. For a general discussion of customs classification, see "Classification—Liquidation" on page 229.

Dutiable Status of Goods

For more information about duty rates and binding decisions see "Dutiable Status of Goods" on page 203; for a discussion of temporary importation of goods see "Temporary Free Importations" on page 205.

Valuation

Importers have a responsibility to use what the U.S. Customs Service deems, "reasonable care," when determining the value of their goods. They must also provide any additional information that the Customs Service needs for setting a final value on the goods. This process involves a number of factors and can be somewhat complicated; importers must be aware of applicable issues and details. Valuation information applies to all types of commodities, for further discussion on the subject see "Customs Valuation" on page 267.

Import Duties

Import duties vary (often dramatically) depending upon the Harmonized Tariff Schedule (HTSUS) classification of the goods or products imported. Since some products that look alike have different HTSUS classifications and different rates of duty, proper classification is vital. Note that "differences of opinion" between importers and the Bureau of Customs and Border Protection regarding classification keeps customs attorneys very busy.

Import duties can be assessed on the imported value of the goods ("ad valorem" rates of duty such as 2%, 4.4%, 50%, etc.), total units or weight of the goods ("specific" rates of duty such as 2 cents each or 1.5 cents/pound, etc.) or on a combination basis ("compound" rates of duty such as 5 cents each plus 6%).

Listed below is a sampling of several Column 1 import duty rates for Chapter 66 products:
Umbrella handles and knobs (6603.10.40.00): Free
to
Other umbrella frames, including frames mounted on shafts (sticks) (6603.20.90.00): 12%

For specific information on US import duties refer to the Harmonized Tariff Schedule of the US. The print version is available from the US Government Printing Office as well as third party suppliers who often add special features. Online versions are available in both static PDF pages as well as in formats with excellent search functionality. Search the Web with the term "Harmonized Tariff Schedule" to find sources.

Entry and Documentation

The entry of merchandise is a two-part process consisting of 1) filing the documentation necessary to determine whether merchandise may be released from Customs custody, and 2) filing the documents that contain information for duty assessment and statistical purposes. In certain instances, all documents must be filed and accepted by Customs prior to release of the goods. Unless you have been granted an extension, you must file the standard entry documents at a location specified by the port or area director within five working days of your shipment's date of arrival at a U.S. port of entry.

After you present the entry, Customs may examine your shipment or may waive examination. The shipment is then released provided no legal or regulatory violations have been noted. You must then file entry summary documentation and deposit estimated duties at a designated customhouse within 10 working days of your shipment's release. For a detailed description of entry procedures, standard documentation, and informal entry, see "Entry Process" on page 185.

Informed Compliance. Informed compliance was introduced with the Customs Modernization Act of 1993 (Mod Act) and defines the relationship between importers and the Customs Service. It sets out the responsibilities of both parties. Providing the correct documentation and information for entry is a key factor that will make your importing operation run smoothly. We recommend that importers become familiar with the concept of informed comliance and the responsibilities that they have under the Mod Act. For further discussion about informed compliance see "Informed Compliance" on page 211.

Marking and Labeling Requirements

For a general discussion of U.S. Customs marking and labeling requirements, see "Country of Origin Marking" on page 236, "Special Marking Requirements" on page 238 and "Marking—False Impression" on page 239.

Shipping Considerations

You will need to ensure that your goods are packaged and shipped with care so that they pass smoothly through Customs and arrive in good condition. You are responsible for ensuring that the shipment is in compliance with all applicable government regulations for packaging and shipping. In most instances, you should not leave these arrangements solely to the discretion of your supplier. Careful preparation of the cargo and selection of the mode of transport can be essential to a cost-effective, timely delivery of undamaged goods. We strongly advise you to consult your shipping representative, insurance agent, or freight broker for advice on packing and shipping.

Umbrellas, walking-sticks, whips, and related items may be shipped in bulk, crates, boxes, bags, or other types of containers, depending on the type of product and whether it is prepackaged. General considerations include protection from contamination, weather, and pests. Containers should be constructed so as to be safe for handling during transport.

Publications and WWW Resources

The U.S. Customs Service launched a series of "Informed Compliance" publications in 1996, which are available on the Customs Service website (www.customs.gov/impoexpo/impoexpo.htm). Of particular interest:

What Every Member of the Trade Community Should Know About Textile & Apparel Rules of Origin

What Every Member of the Trade community Should Know About NAFTA for Textiles and Textile Articles

The *Harmonized Tariff Schedule of the United States (2001)* (HTSUS) is available to view on the Customs Service website (www.customs.gov), or you may purchase a printed version from:

U.S. Government Printing Office
Superintendent of Documents
710 North Capital Street NW
Washington DC 20401
Tel: (202) 512-1800
Fax: (202) 512-1657
Website: www.access.gpo.gov

The USGPO also has copies of specific laws available for purchase. The USGPO accepts orders made by fax, phone or placed over the Internet, as well as mail orders paid by credit card. All orders must be accompanied by payment. Credit cards, checks drawn on a U.S. bank, or an international money order are all acceptable.

Relevant Government Agencies

Address your questions regarding umbrellas and related items to your local Customs port director. For addresses, refer to "U.S. Customs and Border Protection Offices" on page 65 or contact:

U.S. Customs and Border Protection
Customs Headquarters
1300 Pennsylvania Avenue NW
Washington DC 20229
Tel: (202) 354-1000
Website: www.customs.treas.gov

Principal Exporting Countries

The following listing includes samples of the main supplier nations of the products of this chapter. It is organized by HTSUS major heading. (Refer to "Customs Classification" above for the product codes.) Countries are listed in rank order of the value of products imported to the U.S. Statistics represent customs value of entries for 2002 from the Bureau of Census, U.S. Department of Commerce.

6601—China, Indonesia, Taiwan, Hong Kong, Thailand, Poland, Costa Rica

6602—Taiwan, Mexico, Austria, China, Czech Republic

6603—China, Canada, Taiwan, South Africa, Mexico, Indonesia, Hong Kong, Germany

Chapter 67:
Feathers, Down, Artificial Flowers, and Wigs

Full title: Prepared Feathers and Down and Articles Made of Feathers or of Down; Artificial Flowers; Articles of Human Hair

This chapter relates to the importation of feathers, down, artificial flowers, and wigs and related items, which are classified under Chapter 67 of the Harmonized Tariff Schedule of the United States (HTSUS). Specifically, it covers feathers, down, articles of feathers or down, bird skins with feathers or down; artificial flowers, foliage, and fruit made of plastics, feathers, man-made fibers, or other materials; human or animal hair or other textile materials prepared for use in wigs; and wigs, false beards, eyebrows, eyelashes, and similar articles made of human or animal hair or textile materials.

If you are interested in importing straining cloth of human hair, you should read Commodity Index Chapter 59. Footwear and parts of footwear are covered in Chapter 63, and headgear and hair-nets are in Chapter 65. For importing worked quills and scapes, refer to Chapter 5. Toys, sports equipment, and carnival articles are covered in Chapter 95. If you are interested in importing feather dusters, powder-puffs, or hair sieves, you should read Chapter 96. Articles in which feathers or down are used only as filling or padding are covered in the specific Commodity Index chapters related to the particular article. For example, down or feather quilts are in Chapter 94, and down or feather jackets are in Chapter 62. Flowers made of glass are imported in accordance with Chapter 70.

Note: To understand key issues that will enable you to make best use of the information in this section we recommend that you see "Introduction" on page 425.

Key Factors

The key factors in the importation of feathers, down, artificial flowers, and wigs and related items are:

- Compliance with down-feather ratio rating certification (if importing raw down)
- Compliance with Fish and Wildlife Service (FWS) license, permit, country-of-origin permit, import documentation, and recordkeeping requirements (if feathers or down are derived from exotic wildlife or endangered species)
- Entry at FWS-designated ports, and compliance with FWS and Customs advance notification and port-of-entry inspection requirements (if feathers or

down are derived from exotic wildlife or endangered species)
- Compliance with U.S. Department of Agriculture (USDA) APHIS import, quarantine, permit, and certification requirements (if products are derived from domesticated animals)
- Entry at USDA-designated ports (if products are derived from domesticated animals)
- Compliance with textile quota restraints and visa requirements under U.S. Department of Commerce (DOC) Multi-Fiber Arrangements (if importing articles with textile components)
- Submission of U.S. Customs Country-of-Origin Declaration(s) (if importing articles with textile components)
- Compliance with labeling requirements under the Wool Products Labeling Act (WPLA) (if importing articles containing wool)
- Compliance with flammability standards adopted and enforced by the Consumer Product Safety Commission (CPSC) under the Flammable Fabrics Act (FFA) (if importing articles with textile components)

Although most importers use the services of a licensed customs broker in making their entries, and we recommend this practice, you should be aware of the regulatory, entry, and documentation issues involved in importing your product. You, as importer, are ultimately responsible for the fulfillment of any legal requirements applicable to your shipment.

General Considerations

Regulatory Agencies. The USDA regulates and inspects the importation of all products derived from animals, including down and feathers. The FWS, primarily under provisions of the U.S. Endangered Species Act (ESA) and the Convention on International Trade in Endangered Species of Wild Fauna and Flora (CITES), controls the importation of products derived from animals that are classified as exotic wildlife, endangered species, or threatened species. U.S. Customs enforces USDA and FWS requirements through entry documentation and restrictions.

If you are importing articles with textile components, you must be aware of the standards adopted by the CPSC under authority of the Flammable Fabrics Act (FFA). U.S. Customs enforces compliance with labeling requirements related to the flammability standards under the FFA. The CPSC monitors imports and from time to time inspects textile shipments for compliance with FFA standards. If you are importing articles containing wool, importation is subject to complex textile import regulations. The Federal Trade Commission (FTC) administers the WPLA requirements. Wigs and artificial flowers made of textiles are exempt from the labeling requirements of Textile Fiber Products Identification Act (TFPIA). However, these products may be subject to regulation by the DOC's Committee for Implementation of Textile Agreements (CITA) under Section 204 of the Agricultural Adjustment Act.

Down Products. Down products may or may not be regulated, depending on the nature of the product. For example, a down-filled sleeping bag might be a straightforward entry, requiring no special entry paperwork or labeling, etc. But a down-filled article of wearing apparel, depending on the textile used and the origin of the article, might be subject to textile quota regulations, and would probably be subject to labeling requirements under the TFPIA. This is a grey area. You need to be aware of any regulations pertinent to the specific product you are importing, and should read the Commodity Index chapter pertaining to the particular textile used in the product. If you are unsure as to the regulatory status of your product, contact the nearest U.S Customs port office or your customs broker.

Importation of raw down is regulated by the FWS. The exporter is required to test the down for percentage of feathers to down. The down is given a rating based on that percentage. A certification of rating must accompany all import shipments of raw down. If your raw down is derived from domesticated raised birds, there are no FWS regulatory issues. However, down from wild migratory game birds is highly restricted and subject to FWS permit procedures under the Migratory Bird Treaty Act. If you are considering such products, you should contact the regional office of FWS closest to the intended port of entry, for authorization. Do not attempt such importation without FWS authorization (see "Exotic and Endangered Species" below).

Domesticated Bird Skins. Products derived from skins and other parts of domesticated animals are subject to quarantine regulations, marking requirements, and processing standards. Shipments of these products are inspected at the port of arrival by the Animal and Plant Health Inspection Service (APHIS) of the USDA. Unless the shipment is in compliance with all applicable laws and regulations, it will be denied entry into the U.S. Some shipments may be restricted or prohibited completely.

Quarantine and Inspection. At the time of applying for a permit to import animals products subject to quarantine requirements, you will have to make reservations for space in an appropriate quarantine facility. Fees for quarantine reservations vary according to species, and are due and payable when the reservation is requested. Each shipment entering under APHIS permit must comply in every detail with the permit's specifications. If your shipment is found to be aberrant in any way (such as entering at a port of entry other than the one specified in the permit), it will be refused entry.

Veterinary Certificates. A veterinary certificate, issued by a salaried veterinarian of the country of origin, stating that the animal products are free of applicable livestock diseases, must accompany each shipment. The specific information required on the certificate varies depending on the species you are importing, and its country of origin. You must also present an importer's declaration, which states: 1) port of entry; 2) importer's name and address; 3) broker's name and address; 4) livestock origin; 5) number, breed, species, and purpose of importation; AND 6) consignee's name and location of intended delivery.

Specific Country Import Regulations. There are special provisions for livestock products originating in Canada, Mexico, Central America, and the West Indies. These provisions vary according to species, and include such things as permit or quarantine waivers, special quarantine restrictions, specific ports of entry for specific types of products, and provisions for transit across the U.S. only. One general requirement applicable across the board is that two import declarations (see above) must be presented, instead of only one. For more details see appropriate headings in 9 CFR 92, or contact the APHIS.

APHIS-designated Quarantine Ports. Certain ports are designated by APHIS to have adequate quarantine facilities available for the import of animal products. With very few exceptions, all shipments of animal products must enter at one of these designated ports. Check with APHIS for a current list of ports.

Exotic and Endangered Species. The FWS enforces a complex set of laws and regulations (see 50 CFR 1 et seq.) pertaining to wildlife and wildlife product importation. These laws include the international Convention on International Trade in Endangered Species of Wild Fauna and Flora (CITES), the Endangered Species Act (ESA), and a number of other U.S. laws, such as the Migratory Bird Treaty Act (MBTA), Eagle Protection Act (EPA), and the Lacey Act (LA). Most foreign countries also have their own domestic measures, and you will need to meet the requirements of the country of export in addition to U.S. requirements. For more information, contact the FWS Office of Management Authority (OMA) (see addresses at end of this chapter).

Certain types of bird skins are entirely prohibited; others are allowed entry only under permit and/or license; and still others are allowed entry only for specific noncommercial purposes. When applying for a permit, you must satisfy the requirements of all laws under which the species is protected. The following briefly describes the two major laws governing importation of protected wildlife products into the U.S. This discussion is not comprehensive or exhaustive. If you wish to import bird skins of exotic or endangered animals, you should always contact the FWS (see addresses at end of this chapter) with specific species information before making any transactions.

CITES. More than 100 nations participate in the CITES treaty, which took effect in May 1977. The degree of protection afforded to a species depends on which of the three CITES appendices contains the name of that species. Documentation required for import varies depending on the species, and the CITES section where it is listed. The CITES export documentation from the country of origin is always required. If you are importing a CITES-listed species from a country that does not participate in the treaty, you must still obtain from that nation documents that contain all the information normally required in CITES export permits.

Appendix I. This appendix lists species deemed presently threatened with extinction. Importation of Appendix I species for commercial purposes is prohibited. You must have two permits to import these species: one from the U.S., which must be obtained first, and one from the exporting country. If you are importing Appendix I species taken in the marine environment and outside the jurisdiction of any country or state, you must have an Introduction from the Sea Permit.

Appendix II. This appendix lists species that are not presently threatened with extinction but may become threatened if their trade is not regulated. There are no restrictions on the purpose of import, provided it is not detrimental to the survival of the species. You will need an export permit or reexport certificate from the exporting country. If you are importing Appendix II species taken in the marine environment and outside the jurisdiction of any country or state, you will need an Introduction from the Sea Permit.

Appendix III. This appendix lists species for which any CITES member country has domestic regulations "for the purpose of preventing or restricting exploitation, and as needing the cooperation of other Parties in control of trade." Three different types of documents are issued for Appendix III species: 1) Export Permit: Issued for specimens that originated in a country that listed the species on Appendix III; 2) Certificate of Origin: Issued by any country other than the listing country if the wildlife in question originated in that country; 3) Reexport Certificate: Issued for the export of Appendix III specimens that were previously imported into the U.S.

Exemptions. Under certain conditions, Certificates of Exemption may be issued for the importation of wildlife products listed under CITES. Exceptions are allowed for shipment of wildlife transiting a country under Customs bond, shipments between U.S. states or territories, and certain personal or household effects. For information, contact FWS (see addresses at end of this chapter).

Permit Applications. Applications for CITES permits and certificates are available from the FWS Office of Management Authority (see addresses at end of this chapter). You will need to fill out the FWS Standard Permit Application (**Form 3-200**) and provide certain information specifically required under CITES. You should submit your application at least 60 days before the date you wish the permit to take effect. FWS charges processing fees for CITES applications.

ESA. The U.S. Endangered Species Act (ESA) was passed on December 28, 1973, to prevent the extinction of many species of animals and plants and to protect their habitats. By definition, an endangered species is any animal or plant listed by regulation as being in danger of extinction. A "threatened species" is any animal or plant likely to become endangered within the foreseeable future. The U.S. List of Endangered and Threatened Wildlife and Plants includes native and foreign species.

Permits. ESA's import provisions prohibit the import or export of any endangered or threatened species or products derived from them without one of the following permits from the FWS Federal Wildlife Permit Office (FWPO):

> *Endangered Species Permits:* This permit is issued for importation for purposes of 1) scientific research; 2) enhancement of propagation or survival of the species; or 3) incidental taking.

> *Threatened Species Permits:* This permit is issued for importation for purposes of 1) scientific research; 2) enhancement of propagation or survival of the species; 3) zoological, horticultural, or botanical exhibition; 4) education purposes; 5) special purposes consistent with ESA purposes and policy; or 6) incidental taking.

Permit Exemptions. A few imports of endangered species products are exempt from the ESA permit requirements. For example, if a species is listed as threatened or as an experimental population, special rules may allow otherwise prohibited activities. If you are unsure as to the exemption status of your import, contact FWS (see addresses at end of this chapter).

FWS Import Licenses. With some exceptions, persons engaged in the business of importing wildlife products valued in excess of $25,000 per year must be licensed by the FWS. If your annual importations are valued at less than $25,000, or if you qualify for another exemption from licensing, you are still responsible for keeping thorough records of all wildlife transactions and of making these records available to FWS officers if necessary. For a full description of exemptions from licensing, and of recordkeeping requirements, contact the Fish and Wildlife Service (see addresses at end of this chapter) or see 50 CFR 14.

Procedures at Port of Entry. At least 72 hours before your shipment is due to arrive at a designated port, you should notify U.S. Customs and the FWS inspectors of its expected arrival. The FWS conducts port-of-entry shipment inspections on a case-by-case basis, as determined by the inspection agent after looking at the entry paperwork. Both FWS and Customs may inspect your shipment to verify compliance with all of the legal requirements for entry. Any documentation required by the laws governing your import must be submitted by the time of entry. You must present an FWS Wildlife Declaration Form 3-177, available at the port of entry, with every shipment, regardless of any other paperwork required. Customs will not release your shipment until the import declaration has been signed off by an FWS agent.

Designated Ports. Shipments of wildlife products are restricted to designated U.S. ports of entry. All wildlife shipments must enter and leave through one of the ports listed in 50 CFR 14.12. Currently, 10 ports are designated: New York, NY; Miami, FL; New Orleans, LA; Dallas/Ft. Worth, TX; Los Angeles, CA; San Francisco, CA; Chicago, IL; Seattle, WA; Honolulu, HI; and Portland, OR. If special circumstances prevent you from making your entry at a designated port, you will need to obtain an Exception to Designated Port Permit from the FWS Divisions of Law Enforcement (see addresses at end of this chapter).

Articles with Textile Components. Articles with textile components may be subject to absolute quotas, textile restraints under Multi-Fiber Arrangements, or wool product entry requirements. The following is an overview of the textile importing requirements.

Wool Product Entry Requirements. Depending on the nature of your wool imports, as many as three different types of special entry documents may be required. First, for all imported articles that contain textile fibers, yarns, and fabrics covered by the Agricultural Adjustment Act (AAA), including wool, you must file

a U.S. Customs Textile Entry Declaration (see "Textile Country-of-Origin Declarations" below). Second, for all wool products subject to the WPLA, special information is required on the entry invoices (see "Wool Products Labeling Act" below). Finally, certain articles of apparel manufactured or produced in certain countries may be subject to quotas and other restraints under U.S. DOC Multi-Fiber Arrangements. Such products require export licenses, certificates, or visas issued by the appropriate country of origin, in addition to other requisite entry paperwork (see "Textile Quotas" below).

Wool Products Labeling Act. The term "wool product" means any product or any portion of a product that contains, purports to contain, or in any way is represented as containing wool, reprocessed wool, or reused wool. All wool products imported into the U.S., except those made more than 20 years before importation, and except carpets, rugs, mats, and upholsteries, must have affixed a stamp, tag, label, or other means of identification as required by the WPLA. If you are importing wool products exempt from labeling under the WPLA, do not assume they are also exempt from labeling under the TFPIA. These are two distinct laws, with some overlapping requirements (see "Marking and Labeling Requirements" below).

Textile Quotas. If you are interested in importing articles with textile components, the most important issue you need to be aware of is quotas. Under the Multi-Fiber Arrangement provisions of Section 204 of the Agricultural Adjustment Act, CITA initiates specific agreements with individual exporting countries. Section 204 of the Agricultural Adjustment Act covers textiles articles that: 1) are in chief value of cotton, wool, or man-made fibers, any textile fibers subject to the terms of any textile trade agreement, or any combination of such fibers; 2) contain 50% or more by weight of cotton or man-made fibers, or any textile fibers subject to the terms of any textile trade agreement; 3) contain 17% or more by weight of wool; or 4) if in chief value of textile fibers or textile materials, contain a blend of cotton, wool, or man-made fibers, any textile fibers subject to the terms of any textile trade agreement, or any combination of such fibers that, in total, amount to 50% or more by weight of all component fibers.

The U.S. has Multi-Fiber Arrangements with 40 countries. Each agreement with each country is unique, and may specify quotas for a type of textile or a specific article. Visas or export licenses may be required. These agreements, however, often change. Therefore, if you are interested in importing any articles with textile components, you should contact the International Trade Administration's Office of Textile and Apparel (see addresses at end of this chapter). Refer to "Prohibitions and Restrictions" below for further details.

Textile Country-of-Origin Declarations. U.S. Customs enforces CITA textile and textile product entry quotas (see "Prohibitions and Restrictions" below). Requirements for entry include submission of Country-of-Origin Declarations with every shipment of articles with textile components, regardless of whether it is subject to a specific multi-fiber arrangement (19 CFR 12.130, 12.131).

Country of Origin. Quota restrictions are country-specific and therefore are applied based on the country of origin for the textiles shipped. The last country from which a textile shipment was exported to the U.S. is not necessarily its country of origin. A textile or textile product imported into the U.S. is considered a product of the particular foreign territory or country, or a U.S. insular possession, where it is wholly grown, produced, or manufactured. For the following discussion, "country" means a foreign territory or country, or a U.S. insular possession.

In 1996, the U.S. Customs Service made major changes to country of origin rules for textile imports. The regulations at 19 CFR 102.21, "Textile and apparel products" were added to the 1996 Customs Regulations and became effective July 1, 1996. The new rules do not provide for cutting components or cutting and hemming to confer country of origin as in the past. The basis of the new law is processing operations or assembly. Some of the most important changes for importers to be aware of are:

- Cutting does not determine the country of origin (previously, cutting determined country of origin for 90 percent of wearing apparel imports). The new rules are based on processing or assembly operations.

- Essential character does not determine country of origin because the new rules are based on processing.

- A subjective determination under the provisions of 19 CFR 12.130 is replaced by objective processing operations expressed in terms of tariff shifts. Dying, printing, and other finishing processes applied to fabrics no longer confer or change country of origin.

- Country of origin for textile and apparel products processed, assembled or manufactured in two or more countries is determined by where the most important processing occurs, and, if that cannot be ascertained, the last country in which an important processing operation occurs.

The country of origin is the country in which a product is wholly produced when a textile or apparel product is completely produced or manufactured (except for minor parts) in one country. For fabric, the country of origin is the country in which the fabric is woven, knitted, needled, tufted, felted, entangled or created by any other fabric-making process. The country of origin for staple yarn is the country in which yarn is spun; for filament yarn, the country in which filament is extruded; and for plied, gimped and cabled yarns, the country in which the fibers or filaments used in the yarn are spun or extruded. The country of origin of all other textile and apparel products is the country in which the components of a textile or apparel product are wholly assembled (except for minor attachments). Once again, note that assembly, not cutting, now confers country of origin.

Declarations. All importations of textiles and textile products must be accompanied by one of the following three declarations. Goods subject to Section 204, Agricultural Act of 1956, as amended, must be accompanied by either a single-country or a multiple-country declaration. Goods not subject to Section 204 must be accompanied by a negative declaration.

- **Single-country declarations** are used for entries of textiles or textile products which are wholly the growth, product, or manufacture of a single foreign country, territory, or U.S. insular possession. Information required includes: marks of identification and numbers; description of article and quantity; country of origin; and date of exportation.

- **Multiple-country declarations** are used for entries of textiles or textile products which were subjected to manufacturing or processing operations in, and/or incorporate materials originating in more than one foreign country or territory. Information required includes: marks of identification and numbers; for articles, description, quantity, identification of manufacturing and/or processing operations, country, and date of exportation; for materials used to make articles, description of materials, country of production, and date of exportation.

- **Negative declarations** must accompany all textile imports that are not subject to FFA Section 204 restrictions. Information required includes: marks of identification and numbers; descriptions of article and quantity; and country of origin.

The date of exportation to be indicated on the above declarations is the date on which the carrier leaves the last port in the country of origin, as determined by Customs. Diversion to another country during transit does not affect the export date.

Procedure for Declarations. The manufacturer, producer, exporter, or importer may prepare the declaration. If more than one of these parties is involved in the importation, each party may prepare a separate declaration. You may file a separate declaration for each invoice presented with your entry. The declaration must be dated and signed by the responsible party, and must include the person's title and the company name and address. Your shipment's entry will be denied unless it is accompanied by a properly executed declaration. Customs will not treat a textile declaration as a missing document for which a bond may be filed.

Customs will base its country-of-origin determination on the information contained in each declaration, unless the information is insufficient. If the information on the declaration is insufficient, Customs will require that you submit such additional information as will enable the determination to be made. The shipment will not be released until the determination is made. Thus, if you want to clear Customs with minimal delay, be sure that the information on the declarations is as complete as possible for each shipment.

Flammability Standards. Articles with textile components imported into the U.S. for use in consumer products must be in compliance with the FFA, a federal law that gives the CPSC the authority and responsibility for protecting the public from the hazards of dangerously flammable items of wearing apparel and interior furnishings. Under the FFA, standards have been established for flammability of clothing textiles. You cannot import any article of wearing apparel or interior furnishing, or any fabric or related material that is intended for use or that may be used in such items, if it fails to conform to an applicable flammability standard (FFA Section 4). Certain products may be imported into the U.S. (FFA Section 11c) for finishing or processing to render them less flammable so as to meet the standards. For these products, the exporter must state on the invoice or other paper relating to the shipment that the shipment is being made for that purpose.

The CPSC monitors imports of textiles under its Import Surveillance Program. From time to time, your textile shipments may be inspected to ascertain compliance with mandatory safety standards. Shipments may also be subject to testing by the CPSC to determine compliance. If the CPSC believes a product, fabric, or related material does not comply with a flammability standard, it is authorized to pursue a variety of legal sanctions (see "Prohibitions and Restrictions" below).

Substantial Product Hazard Reports. Any firm that obtains information that reasonably supports the conclusion that one of its products presents an unreasonable risk of serious injury or death must report that information to the CPSC's Division of Corrective Actions (CPSC address below). Importers must also report to the CPSC if 1) a type of product is the subject of at least three civil actions filed in U.S. federal or state courts, 2) each suit alleges the involvement of that product type in death or grievous bodily injury (as defined in FFA Section 37(3)1), and 3) at least three of the actions result in a final settlement with the manufacturer or in a judgment for the plaintiff within any one of the two-year periods specified in FFA Section 37(b).

Import Advisory

Feathers and Down. Always be prepared to provide the FWS or U.S. Customs with both common and scientific names of any species of bird skins that you have questions about or are planning to import. When you are unsure of the regulations governing the export or import of a wildlife product, check with the FWS or TRAF-

FIC (USA) World Wildlife Fund (see addresses at end of this chapter) well in advance of going abroad, or once there, with the local authorities or the U.S. Embassy before making a purchase. When in doubt, don't buy! Products made from parts of endangered species incur seizure and in some cases substantial fines.

Wildlife Products [reprinted with permission by World Wildlife Fund from its brochure: "Buyer Beware"].

It's difficult to be sure what wildlife products may be brought into the United States. Regulations are complex, and wildlife may be "laundered" to conceal its true country of origin. Wildlife is often illegally killed or collected in one country, smuggled into another, and then exported with false permits to a third, making its origins hard to trace. If you're considering the purchase of any wildlife or wildlife product while abroad, you should first try to determine its origin and any U.S. restrictions on its import.

Articles with Textile Components. Importation of textile products is trade-sensitive and highly regulated. Shipments of textile products not complying with all government regulations, including quotas and visas, are subject to seizure and could result in the imposition of penalties as well as possible forfeiture of the goods. You should always verify the available quota for any textile product you plan to import before your shipment leaves the country of manufacture. Furthermore, Customs textile classification rulings change frequently, and prior administrative rulings are often modified and sometimes reversed.

Customs Classification

For customs purposes, feathers, down, artificial flowers, and wigs and related items are classified under Chapter 67 of the HTSUS. This chapter is broken into major headings, which are further divided into subheadings, and often sub-subheadings, each of which has its own HTSUS classification number. For example, the 2001 HTSUS number for artificial flowers made of feathers is 6702.90.10, indicating it is a sub-subcategory of artificial flowers, etc., of other materials (6702.90), which is a subcategory of the major heading artificial flowers, foliage, and fruit, etc. (6702). There are four major headings within Chapter 67.

6701—Skins and other parts of birds with their feathers or down, feathers, parts of feathers, down, and articles thereof (other than goods of heading 0505 and worked quills and scapes)

6702—Artificial flowers, foliage and fruit, and parts thereof; articles made of artificial flowers, foliage, or fruit

6703—Human hair, dressed, thinned, bleached, or otherwise worked; wool or other animal hair or other textile materials, prepared for use in making wigs or the like

6704—Wigs, false beards, eyebrows and eyelashes, switches, and the like, of human or animal hair or of textile materials; articles of human hair not elsewhere specified or included

For more details regarding classifications of the specific product you are interested in importing, consult a customs broker, the appropriate commodity specialist at your nearest customs port, or the HTSUS. The 2001 HTSUS is available online from the Customs Service (www.customs.gov/impoexpo/impoexpo.htm) or for purchase from the U.S. Government Printing Office (see resources at the end of this chapter), and may be found in larger public libraries. For a general discussion of customs classification, see "Classification—Liquidation" on page 229.

Dutiable Status of Goods

For more information about duty rates and binding decisions see "Dutiable Status of Goods" on page 203; for a discussion of temporary importation of goods see "Temporary Free Importations" on page 205.

Valuation

Importers have a responsibility to use what the U.S. Customs Service deems, "reasonable care," when determining the value of their goods. They must also provide any additional information that the Customs Service needs for setting a final value on the goods. This process involves a number of factors and can be somewhat complicated; importers must be aware of applicable issues and details. Valuation information applies to all types of commodities, for further discussion on the subject see "Customs Valuation" on page 267.

Import Duties

Import duties vary (often dramatically) depending upon the Harmonized Tariff Schedule (HTSUS) classification of the goods or products imported. Since some products that look alike have different HTSUS classifications and different rates of duty, proper classification is vital. Note that "differences of opinion" between importers and the Bureau of Customs and Border Protection regarding classification keeps customs attorneys very busy.

Import duties can be assessed on the imported value of the goods ("ad valorem" rates of duty such as 2%, 4.4%, 50%, etc.), total units or weight of the goods ("specific" rates of duty such as 2 cents each or 1.5 cents/pound, etc.) or on a combination basis ("compound" rates of duty such as 5 cents each plus 6%).

Listed below is a sampling of several Column 1 import duty rates for Chapter 67 products:
Human hair (6703.00.30.00): Free
to
Assembled by binding with flexible materials such as wire, paper, textile materials, or foil, or by gluing or by similar methods (6702.10.20.00): 8.4%

For specific information on US import duties refer to the Harmonized Tariff Schedule of the US. The print version is available from the US Government Printing Office as well as third party suppliers who often add special features. Online versions are available in both static PDF pages as well as in formats with excellent search functionality. Search the Web with the term "Harmonized Tariff Schedule" to find sources.

Entry and Documentation

The entry of merchandise is a two-part process consisting of 1) filing the documentation necessary to determine whether merchandise may be released from Customs custody, and 2) filing the documents that contain information for duty assessment and statistical purposes. In certain instances, all documents must be filed and accepted by Customs prior to release of the goods. Unless you have been granted an extension, you must file entry documents at a location specified by the port or area director within five working days of your shipment's date of arrival at a U.S. port of entry. These include a number of standard documents required by Customs for any entry, and:

- Exporter's down-feather ratio rating certification (if importing raw down)

- FWS Import Declaration Form 3-177, original and 3 copies (if products are derived from exotic wildlife or endangered species)

- FWS permit or import documentation Form 3-200 (if products are derived from exotic wildlife or endangered species)

- Permits or certificates required under CITES, ESA, and any other regulations applicable to the particular shipment (if products are derived from exotic wildlife or endangered species), CITES permits and certificates

- Certificates of export, origin, sanitation, veterinary inspection, and other conditions from the country of origin or export, as required by Customs, FWS, or USDA (if importing feathers, down, bird skins, or parts thereof)

- USDA importer's declaration (if products are derived from domesticated birds)

- U.S. Customs Country-of-Origin Declaration Form CF 3229, (if importing textile products)

- Export documentation and/or visa (if importing textiles products subject to Multi-Fiber Arrangements

After you present the entry, Customs may examine your shipment or may waive examination. The shipment is then released provided no legal or regulatory violations have been noted. You must then file entry summary documentation and deposit estimated duties at a designated customhouse within 10 working days of your shipment's release. For a detailed description of entry procedures, standard documentation, and informal entry, see "Entry Process" on page 185.

Informed Compliance. Informed compliance was introduced with the Customs Modernization Act of 1993 (Mod Act) and defines the relationship between importers and the Customs Service. It sets out the responsibilities of both parties. Providing the correct documentation and information for entry is a key factor that will make your importing operation run smoothly. We recommend that importers become familiar with the concept of informed comliance and the responsibilities that they have under the Mod Act. For further discussion about informed compliance see "Informed Compliance" on page 211.

Wool Products Subject to WPLA. When you offer for entry a wool product shipment valued at over $500 and subject to WPLA, you must include certain information intended to facilitate Customs monitoring and enforcement of that Act. This extra information is identical to that required by WPLA on labeling (see "Marking and Labeling Requirements" below), with the addition of the manufacturer's name. If your product consists of mixed waste, residues, and similar merchandise obtained from several suppliers or unknown sources, you may omit the manufacturer's name from the entry invoice. For more general information about invoices see "Invoices" on page 277.

Note: The Entry and Documentation section has been carefully designed to supply you, the importer, with sample documents and directions on how to satisfy Customs requirements. Be aware that you should consult the applicable authorities to ensure that you are correctly following the most current procedures.

Prohibitions and Restrictions

Bird Products. Feathers and skins of the following species are permitted entry: chickens, turkeys, guinea fowl, geese, ducks, pigeons, ostriches, rheas, English ring-necked pheasants, and pea fowl not taken from the wild. Other feathers are usually prohibited. Skins and feathers taken from wild migratory game birds listed in the Migratory Bird Treaty Act (50 CFR 10) are prohibited imports. Bird products that can be imported are subject to quarantine if they arrive from certain countries that are known to have specific infectious diseases.

There are a number of exceptions: plumage imported for scientific or educational purposes, fully manufactured artificial flies used for fishing, and plumage on game birds killed in foreign countries by hunters who are U.S. residents as long as the plumage is not imported for sale or other commercial purposes.

Quota Birds. Feathers of certain birds may be imported for use in the manufacture of artificial flies used for fishing, and/or for millinery purposes. These imports are restricted by annual quota allotments. You must have a permit and quota allotment issued by the FWS to import quota feathers. Quota feathers are as follows: Mandarin ducks for use in the manufacture of artificial

flies used for fishing: 1,000 skins; Lady Amherst Pheasant, Golden Pheasant, Silver Pheasant, Reeves Pheasant, and Blue-eared Pheasant, for use in the manufacture of artificial flies used for fishing, or for use in millinery products: aggregate 45,000.

Permit Application. If you wish to import quota feathers, submit your application for feather quota allocations and permits to FWS on the standard Federal Fish and Wildlife License/Permit Application **Form 3-200.** The annual quota begins on January 1 of each year, and runs through December 31. Your application for initial allocations must reach FWS between September 1 and September 30 of the calendar year preceding the quota year for which you are requesting allotment. Any portions of established annual quotas not used by July 1 become available for reallocation. Applications for reallocations must be received by FWS between July 1 and July 31 of the current quota year.

Your permit/quota allocation request must include not only the standard information required for any permit, but also 1) species quantity; 2) port of entry, or port of entry and amount in storage (see "Exceptions to Requirements" below); 3) statement of intended use; and 4) nature of request, i.e. initial allocation or reallocation.

After making the initial allocations, the FWS will furnish you with a tabulation of quantities of each species you requested, plus quantities FWS proposes to allocate to you. You must then report your acceptance, by a letter addressed to the FWS Director and postmarked not later than 30 days after the date you receive your notice. Your letter must contain satisfactory proof (e.g. a copy of a currently confirmed order) that you have already placed your feather orders. FWS will interpret your failure to respond as withdrawal of your application. You would be wise to make your response by certified mail.

Permits. Permits for feather quota imports are issued in two segments. Permits authorizing calendar year initial allocations are issued as of January 1 of that quota year, and remain in effect through June 30 of the year of issue. You must import all feathers and/or skins authorized under this permit no later than June 30. Once your initial permit has expired, any portion of your allotment that you have not used will be subject to reallocation. There are no exceptions, and no extensions are granted. Permits authorizing reallocations are issued as promptly as possible after July 31 of the current quota year, and remain in effect through December 31. Once your reallocation permit expires, any unused portion of the quota is forfeited. There are no exceptions, and no extensions are granted.

Exceptions to Requirements. There are certain exceptions to the permit requirements for quota feathers. However, even when a permit is not necessary, you must still file an FWS Wildlife Declaration at the port of entry. Permit exceptions are as follows: 1) you may import quota skins/feathers for storage in a warehouse under Customs bond without permit. This exception only applies to birds that are subject to quota. In such cases you must obtain a valid FWS permit before you remove the articles from the warehouse for use in the U.S.; 2) articles imported for scientific or educational purposes; 3) fully manufactured artificial flies for fishing; 4) game birds killed by U.S. hunters abroad and imported by such person for noncommercial purposes; 5) live birds (there are other FWS requirements for live birds); and 6) import of any of the following birds, whether or not such bird was raised in captivity: chickens (including hens and roosters), turkeys, guinea fowl, geese, ducks, pigeons, ostriches, rheas, English ring-necked pheasants, and pea fowl.

Exotic and Endangered Species. Hides of certain animals are restricted or prohibited from importation because of species status under the CITES, ESA, or another U.S. law. For example, importation of species listed in CITES Appendix I for commercial purposes is prohibited. Prohibitions and restrictions may additionally be imposed by the law of the exporting country. You are legally responsible to fulfill the requirements of all of them, as well as any laws of your country of export. If you import, or attempt to import, a product in violation of a wildlife or endangered species law, even if you are not aware of the violation, your product may be seized, you may be charged substantial fines, and you could be imprisoned.

Wildlife Products [reprinted with permission by World Wildlife Fund from its brochure: "Buyer Beware"].

> Birds and feathers may not be imported into the United States, except under certain conditions. The survival of many wild bird species is threatened by habitat destruction and trade. Alarming numbers of birds die during capture, transit, and the required 30-day quarantine period (for some species, as much as 70% of the shipment). Birds frequently are taken from countries that ban their export to neighboring countries where falsified documents can be obtained. Concerned consumers should be aware of the protected status of any wild bird before attempting to bring it into this country. Prohibited from import are: Most wild bird feathers, mounted birds, and skins.

Textile Quotas. Textile import restrictions are primarily a matter of quotas and the way in which these quotas are administered and monitored. Under the Multi-Fiber Arrangement provisions of Section 204 of the Agricultural Adjustment Act, CITA has developed Multi-Fiber Arrangements with 40 countries. These Agreements may impose quotas for a type of textile or a specific article, and they are country-specific. The agreements, however, often change. Therefore, if you are interested in importing any articles with textile components, you should contact the International Trade Administration's Office of Textile and Apparel (see addresses at end of this chapter). The Office of Textile and Apparel has a team of country specialists who can inform you of the latest developments and inform you about a product's quota or restriction status.

U.S. Customs enforces CITA textile and textile product entry quotas. If formal entry procedures are not followed, Customs will usually refuse entry for textiles that are subject to Section 204. Formal entry requires submission of a Country-of-Origin Declaration (see "General Considerations" above). U.S. Customs maintains a current textile quota status report, available for perusal at any Customs port. In addition, U.S. Customs in , DC, provides quota status reports online, which are updated on a regular basis (www.customs.gov/impoexpo/impoexpo.htm).

Flammable Fabrics. U.S. Customs may refuse entry for any article of wearing apparel or interior furnishing, or any fabric or related material that is intended for use or that may be used in wearing apparel or interior furnishings, if it fails to conform to an applicable flammability standard issued under Section 4 of the FFA. An exception is allowed for certain products (FFA Section 11c) that are imported for finishing or processing to bring them within the legal standard. For these products, the exporter must state on the invoice or other paper relating to the shipment that the shipment is being made for that purpose.

The CPSC, as the primary enforcement agency of flammability standards, inspects products for compliance with the FFA. If the CPSC believes a product, fabric, or related material does not comply with a flammability standard, it is authorized to pursue a variety of legal sanctions, including: 1) seizure, condemnation, and forfeiture of the noncomplying products; 2) administrative cease-and-desist order requiring an individual or firm to stop sale and distribution of the noncomplying products or; 3) temporary injunction requiring the individual or firm to stop sale and distribution of the noncomplying products, pending final disposition of an administrative cease-and-desist proceeding. The CPSC also has authority to seek civil penalties against any per-

son who knowingly violates a regulation or standard issued under Section 4 of the FFA.

Country-Specific Restrictions

Restrictions under Multi-Fiber Arrangements are country-specific. A product originating in one country may be subject to quota and to export license or visa requirements, while the same product originating in a different country may not. At present, the U.S. has Multi-Fiber Arrangements with 40 countries. Many different categories of products are covered under these Arrangements; it is beyond the scope of this book to list each country and its restricted commodities. If you are interested in importing textiles and textile products, you should contact the International Trade Administration's Office of Textile and Apparel (see addresses at end of this chapter) or U.S. Customs to ascertain your product's restraint status.

The U.S. Customs service provides quota reports on their website (www.customs.gov/impoexpo/impoexpo.htm). These reports are constantly updated and have an effective date noted. The most recent quota information can be accessed by clicking on the country name that interests you. This location holds information regarding quotas, transshipments, and visa requirements.

Marking and Labeling Requirements

Animal Products. Containers of animal skins must be marked with the country of origin—that is, the country where the animal was located. If skins are quarantined at the port of arrival, marks and signs are required on shipping documents and any mode of transport used to move the product while under restrictions (9 CFR 95.25).

Wildlife Skins. All wildlife shipments must be marked on the outside of the container with the names and addresses of the exporter and importer, an accurate identification of the species, and the numbers of each species in the container.

Wool Products Labeling Act (WPLA). Wool product labeling requirements for foreign products are the responsibility of the importer. The WPLA requires the following information to appear on wool products subject to the Act: 1) percentage of the wool product's total fiber weight (exclusive of ornamentation) not exceeding 5% of the total fiber weight of a) wool, b) recycled wool, c) each fiber other than wool if the percent by weight of such fiber is 5% or more, and d) the aggregate of all other fibers; 2) the maximum percent of the wool product's total weight, of any nonfibrous loading, filling, or adulterating matter; and 3) the importer's name. If you, as importer, have a registered identification number issued by the FTC, that number may be used instead of your name (see "Registered Identification Numbers" below).

Customs entry is contingent on proper labeling. If your shipment is found to be mislabeled at entry, you will be given the option to relabel the products under Customs supervision, as long as the port director is satisfied that your labeling error or omission did not involve fraud or willful neglect. If your shipment is discovered after entry to have been noncomplying with WPLA, it will be recalled to Customs custody at your expense, unless you can satisfy the port director that the products have since been brought into compliance. You will be held responsible for all expenses incurred in bringing a shipment into compliance, including compensation of personnel and other expenses related to Customs supervision.

Fraudulent violations of WPLA will result in seizure of the shipment. Shipments already released from Customs custody will be ordered to be redelivered to Customs. Customs reports all cases of fraudulent violation to the FTC in , DC.

The information listed above is not intended to be exhaustive. WPLA requirements are extensive. The Act specifies such details as types of labels, means of attachment, label position on the article, package labeling, unit labeling (as in the case of a two-piece garment), arrangement of information on the label, allowable fiber designations, country-of-origin indications, trim and ornamentation, pile fabrics, sectional disclosure, use of trade names and trademarks, requirements for swatches and samples, etc. The FTC publishes a booklet intended to clarify WPLA requirements in order to facilitate voluntary compliance within the industry (see "Publications and WWW Resources" below). It is available on request, at no charge, from the FTC (see addresses at end of this chapter).

The Care Labeling Rule. Regulations under this rule require manufacturers and importers of textile clothing and fabrics to attach specific care instructions for washing or dry cleaning, as well as information on the fiber composition of the article. They are enforced by the FTC Division of Enforcement. The Care Labeling Rule was amended September 2000, detailed information is available on the FTC website (www.ftc.gov/os/statutes/textilejump.htm).

Registered Identification Numbers. Any domestic firm or person residing in the U.S. and engaged in the manufacture or marketing of textile products covered under the WPLA may obtain an FTC-registered identification number for use on required tags and labels instead of the name of a firm or person. For applications, contact the FTC (see addresses at end of this chapter).

For a general discussion of U.S. Customs marking and labeling requirements, see "Country of Origin Marking" on page 236, "Special Marking Requirements" on page 238 and "Marking—False Impression" on page 239.

Shipping Considerations

You will need to ensure that your goods are packaged and shipped with care so that they pass smoothly through Customs and arrive in good condition. You are responsible for ensuring that the shipment is in compliance with all applicable government regulations for packaging and shipping. In most instances, you should not leave these arrangements solely to the discretion of your supplier. Careful preparation of the cargo and selection of the mode of transport can be essential to a cost-effective, timely delivery of undamaged goods. We strongly advise you to consult your shipping representative, insurance agent, or freight broker for advice on packing and shipping.

Feathers, down, artificial flowers, and wigs and related items may be shipped in bulk, crates, boxes, bags, or other types of containers, depending on the type of product and whether it is prepackaged. General considerations include protection from contamination, weather, and pests. Containers should be constructed so as to be safe for handling during transport.

Publications and WWW Resources

The U.S. Customs Service launched a series of "Informed Compliance" publications in 1996, which are available on the Customs Service website (www.customs.gov/impoexpo/impoexpo.htm). Of particular interest:

What Every Member of the Trade Community Should Know About Textile & Apparel Rules of Origin

What Every Member of the Trade community Should Know About NAFTA for Textiles and Textile Articles

Fibers & Yarns Construction and Classification Under the HTSUS

The *Harmonized Tariff Schedule of the United States (2001)* (HTSUS) is available to view on the Customs Service website (www.customs.gov) or you may purchase a printed version from:

U.S. Government Printing Office
Superintendent of Documents
710 North Capital Street NW
Washington DC 20401
Tel: (202) 512-1800
Fax: (202) 512-1657
Website: www.access.gpo.gov

The USGPO also has copies of specific laws available for purchase. The USGPO accepts orders made by fax, phone or placed over the Internet, as well as mail orders paid by credit card. All orders must be accompanied by payment. Credit cards, checks drawn on a U.S. bank, or an international money order are all acceptable.

Relevant Government Agencies

Address your questions regarding USDA requirements for the importation of domestic animal products to:

Animal and Plant Health Inspection Service (APHIS)
Veterinary Services (VS)
National Center for Import and Export
4700 River Rd., Unit 40
Riverdale, MD 20737
Tel: (301) 734-3277
Animal products: (301) 734-4401
Website: www.aphis.usda.gov/vs

Address your questions regarding the importation of raw down or exotic or endangered bird skins to:

U.S. Fish and Wildlife Service (FWS)
Division of Management Authority
4401 N. Fairfax Dr.
Arlington, VA 22203-0700
Tel: (703) 358-2104
Website: www.fws.gov

Address your questions regarding textile Multi-Fiber Arrangements to:

U.S. Department of Commerce
International Trade Administration
Office of Textiles and Apparel
Director's Office
14th and Constitution Ave. NW, Rm. H3100
Washington DC 20230
Tel: (202) 482-5078
Fax: (202) 482-2331
Agreements Division: (202) 482-4212
Website: http://otexa.ita.doc.gov

Address your questions regarding the Flammable Fabrics Act (FFA) to:

Consumer Product Safety Commission (CPSC)
Office of Compliance
Washington DC 20207-0001
Tel: 800-638-2772 or (301) 504-7912
Fax: (301) 504-0359
Website: www.cpsc.gov

Address your questions regarding labeling requirements under the Wool Products Labeling Act (WPLA) to:

Federal Trade Commission (FTC)
Division of Enforcement
600 Pennsylvania Avenue NW
Washington DC 20580
Tel: (202) 326-2996
Website: www.ftc.gov

Address your questions regarding textile quotas to:

U.S. Customs and Border Protection
Office of Field Operations, Quota Branch
1300 Pennsylvania Avenue NW
Washington DC 20229

Tel: (202) 927-5850
Website: www.customs.treas.gov

The U.S. Customs Service provices updated status reports on textile quota on their web site (see address above). If the country you need information on is not listed, call the Quota Branch office at (202) 927-5850.

Address your questions regarding imports of feathers, down, artificial flowers, and wigs and related items to your local Customs port director. For addresses, refer to "U.S. Customs and Border Protection Offices" on page 65 or contact:

U.S. Customs and Border Protection
Customs Headquarters
1300 Pennsylvania Avenue NW
Washington DC 20229
Tel: (202) 354-1000
Website: www.customs.treas.gov

Laws and Regulations

The following laws and regulations may be relevant to the importation of feathers, down, artificial flowers, and wigs and related items. The laws are contained in the United States Code (USC), and the regulations are published in the Code of Federal Regulations (CFR), both of which are available at larger public and law libraries. Copies of specific laws are also available from the United States Government Printing Office (address above).

18 USC 42 et seq.
Importation of Animals, Birds, Fish, and Plants
This Act governs the importation of animals, including birds, into the U.S.

50 CFR Parts 10, 13 and 16
Regulations of FWS for Importing Wildlife and Fish
These Regulations specify the animals and animal products subject to import prohibitions and restrictions.

21 USC 135
Establishment of International Animal Quarantine Stations
This Act authorizes the establishment of international quarantine stations. Customs enforces laws regarding importation of livestock.

42 USC 264-271
Regulations to Control Cummunicable Diseases
These regulations govern the importation of products which may carry communicable disease. It estblishes the authority of the Surgeon General and the role of the Customs Service. Customs enforces these restrictions. See 19 CFR 12.26 and 42 CFR 71.51 et seq.

19 CFR 12.24, 12.26
U.S. Customs Animal and Animal Product Entry Regulations
These regulations provide for entry declarations, documentation, and procedures for the animals and animal products subject to FWS and USDA regulations.

9 CFR 95.13 et seq.
Animal Byproduct Quarantine Control Regulations
These regulations prohibit the importation of animal products for use in industry unless the products meet certain processing standards and are not infected with certain diseases.

Convention on International Trade in Endangered Species of Wild Fauna and Flora (CITES)
This comprehensive wildlife treaty signed by over 100 countries, including the United States, regulates and in many cases prohibits commercial imports and exports of wild animal and plant species threatened by trade.

16 USC 1531
Endangered Species Act of 1973
This Act prohibits the import and export of plant and seed species listed as endangered and most species listed as threatened. Seeds labeled as "of cultivated origin" may be traded. It is the U.S. law that implements CITES.

16 USC 3371-3378
Lacey Act
This Act prohibits the import of species taken, possessed, transported, or sold in violation of foreign law.

7 USC 1854
Textile Trade Agreements
(EO 11651, as amended by EO 11951 and 12188, and supplemented by EO 12475 below)
This Act authorizes the CITA of the DOC to enter into Multi-Fiber Agreements with other countries to control trade in textiles and establishes the Textile Import Program, which is enforced by U.S. Customs.

19 CFR 12.130 et seq.
Regulations on Entry of Textiles
These regulations provide the requirements and procedures followed by Customs in enforcing limitations on the importation and entry and withdrawal of textiles and textile products from warehouses for consumption in the U.S.

15 USC 68-68j
Wool Products Labeling Act (WPLA) of 1939
This Act prohibits the false or deceptive labeling (misbranding) of wool products and requires all wool products imported into the U.S. to be labeled in accordance with requirements set forth in the law.

19 CFR 11.12; 16 CFR 300 et seq.
Regulations on WPLA Labeling and Marking
These regulations set forth the wool labeling and marking requirements adopted by the FTC to administer the requirements of the WPLA and provide the procedures followed by U.S. Customs in enforcing the WPLA and the FTC regulations, including entry invoice requirements.

15 USC 1191-1204
Flammable Fabrics Act (FFA)
This Act provides for the setting of flammability standards for fabric by the Consumer Product Safety Commission (CPSC) and for enforcement by U.S. Customs.

16 CFR 1610, 1611, 1615, 1616, 1630-1632
Regulations on Flammable Fabric Standards
These regulations specify the flammability standards adopted by the CPSC under the FFA for various types of textiles.

16 CFR 423
Care Labeling Rule
Requires fiber composition and washing or dry cleaning instructions for textile apparel and certain piece goods.

Principal Exporting Countries

The following listing includes samples of the main supplier nations of the products of this chapter. It is organized by HTSUS major heading. (Refer to "Customs Classification" above for the product codes.) Countries are listed in rank order of the value of products imported to the U.S. Statistics represent customs value of entries for 2002 from the Bureau of Census, U.S. Department of Commerce.

6701—China, Hong Kong, South Africa, Dominican Republic, Italy, Belgium, Taiwan

6702—China, Thailand, Hong Kong, Sri Lanka, Mexico

6703—China, South Korea, Indonesia, India, Italy, Hong Kong

6704—China, Indonesia, South Korea, Canada, Hong Kong, Thailand, Germany, Italy, Philippines

Chapter 68:
Articles of Stone and Related Products

Full title: Articles of Stone, Plaster, Cement, Asbestos, Mica, or Similar Materials

This section pertains to the importation of finished and semifinished stone and related items, which are classified within Chapter 68 of the Harmonized Tariff Schedule of the United States (HTSUS). Specifically, it includes such finished and semifinished products as stone flagstones; worked building stones, including marble, travertine, and granite; worked slate; grinding stones; abrasive powders and sandpapers; insulation materials; asphalt roofing; plasterboard and fabricated building materials; cement blocks, tiles, and pipes; and fabricated asbestos products, including brake liners and pads; worked mica; and various other products made of stone. Many building materials are included within this chapter.

If you are interested in importing raw stone or unfinished products of stone and related materials, refer to Commodity Index Chapter 25. Coated or impregnated papers are covered in Chapter 48, while coated or impregnated textiles are covered in Chapters 58 and 59. Gemstones related to the jewelry trade are included in Chapter 71. Tools for cutting and working stone and related products are found in Chapter 82. If you are interested in importing stones for lithographic printing, refer to Chapter 84. Stone products used as electrical insulators are covered in Chapter 85; dental grinding equipment is covered in Chapter 90; and works of art including worked stone—such as statuary—are found in Chapter 97. Stone and related materials which are incidental components of other products are covered in various other Commodity Index chapters: clocks (chapter 91), furniture (chapter 94), toys and games (chapter 95), and other items, such as drawing slates (chapter 96).

Note: To understand key issues that will enable you to make best use of the information in this section we recommend that you see "Introduction" on page 425.

Key Factors

The key factors in importing finished and semifinished stone and related products of Chapter 68 are:

- Compliance with U.S. Environmental Protection Agency (EPA) requirements under the Toxic Substances Control Act (TSCA) if the product contains asbestos or other hazardous substances
- Compliance with U.S. Department of Transportation (DOT) regulations for transport of hazardous cargo (if the product contains a hazardous substance)

Although most importers utilize the services of a licensed customs broker in making their entries, and we recommend this practice, you should be aware of the regulatory, entry, and documentation issues involved in importing your product. You, as importer, are ultimately responsible for the fulfillment of any legal requirements applicable to your shipment.

General Considerations

Regulatory Agencies. As a general rule, finished stone and related products are straightforward importations. The EPA, under the authority of the TSCA, imposes certain controls on the importation of asbestos and any other products containing toxic substances. The TSCA defines toxic substances as those determined to present the possibility of an unreasonable risk of injury to health or the environment. The DOT enforces regulations for transportation of hazardous cargo. Products are deemed hazardous if listed in DOT transport regulations (49 CFR 172, appendix). The relevant regulations include packaging, shipping, marking, and labeling requirements. Refer to "Laws and Regulations" below. For additional information on EPA requirements and TSCA certification as it pertains to asbestos products, contact EPA's Office of Toxic Substances (see addresses at end of this chapter).

Hazardous Substances. If importing a hazardous substance, you must file a TSCA certification of compliance or exemption at the time you make a regulated entry at customs. This certification may be in the form of a typed or stamped statement on an appropriate entry document or commercial invoice. You may endorse the statement by means of an authorized facsimile signature. If your entry is electronically processed, the certification will be in the form of a Certification Code, which is part of the Automated Broker Interface (ABI) transmission. Customs will not release a shipment until proper certification has been obtained.

If you are importing several or regular shipments, you should ask the appropriate customs port director to authorize the use of a blanket certification. If you receive such authorization, you must include on the commercial invoice or entry document for each shipment a statement that the blanket certification is on file and that it is incorporated by specific reference. This statement need not be signed. The blanket certification is valid for one calendar year, is renewable, and may be revoked at any time for cause.

Articles Excluded. If you are bringing in articles that contain materials classified as hazardous substances, you are subject to TSCA certification requirements only if certification is specifically required by a rule or order promulgated under the TSCA. No specific rules have been adopted at this time. An "article" is a manufactured item 1) that is formed into a specific shape or design during manufacture, 2) that has end-use functions dependent on the shape or design, and 3) that during its intended end use does not change its chemical composition or changes it only into noncommercial byproducts as allowed by law (19 CFR 12.120(2)). Fluids and particles are not articles.

Shipment Detention. Detention can occur at a port of entry if the EPA administrator or customs port director has reasonable grounds to believe that it is not in compliance with the TSCA or if the importer fails to provide proper TSCA certification. If your shipment is detained, it will be held by customs for no more than 48 hours before it is turned over to the EPA administrator unless arrangements have been made by the importer to release it under bond. The importer must then bring it into compliance or re-export it within 90 days after notice of detention or 30 days after demand for redelivery. Customs may grant an extension if the importer can show that delays were due to inaction by the EPA or by customs. Failure by the importer to comply within the time allotted allows the EPA to order storage or disposal of the shipment at the importer's expense.

Customs Classification

For customs purposes, finished and semifinished stone and related products are classified under Chapter 68 of the HTSUS. This chapter is broken down into major headings, which are further divided into subheadings, and often sub-subheadings, each with its own HTSUS classification number. For example, the 2001 HTSUS number for dressed or polished but otherwise unworked travertine is 6802.91.20, indicating that it is a subcategory of marble, travertine and alabaster (6802.91), which is a subcategory of the major heading worked monumental or building stone (except slate) and articles thereof (6802). There are 15 major headings in Chapter 68.

6801—Setts, curbstones, and flagstones, of natural stone (except slate)

6802—Worked monumental or building stone (except slate) and articles thereof, other than goods of heading 6801; mosaic cubes, and the like, of natural stone (including slate), whether or not on a backing; artificially colored granules, chippings, and powder, of natural stone (including slate)

6803—Worked slate and articles of slate or of agglomerated slate

6804—Millstones, grindstones, grinding wheels, and the like, without frameworks, for grinding, sharpening, polishing, trueing, or cutting; hand sharpening or polishing stones, and parts thereof, of natural stone, of agglomerated natural or artificial abrasives, or of ceramics, with or without parts of other materials

6805—Natural or artificial abrasive powder or grain, on a base of textile material, of paper, of paperboard, or of other materials, whether of not cut to shape or sewn or otherwise made up

6806—Slag wool, rock wool, and similar mineral wools; exfoliated vermiculite, expanded clays, foamed slag, and similar expanded mineral materials; mixtures and articles of heat-insulating, sound insulating, or sound-absorbing mineral materials, other than those of heading 6811 or 6812, or of chapter 69

6807—Articles of asphalt or of similar material (for example, petroleum bitumen or coal tar pitch)

6808—Panels, boards, tiles, blocks, and similar articles of vegetable fiber, of straw, or of shavings, chips, particles, sawdust, or other waste, of wood, agglomerated with cement, plaster or other mineral binders

6809—Articles of plaster or of compositions based on plaster

6810—Articles of cement, of concrete, or of artificial stone, whether or not reinforced

6811—Articles of asbestos-cement; of cellulose fiber cement, or the like

6812—Fabricated asbestos fibers; mixtures with a basis of asbestos or with a basis of asbestos and magnesium carbonate; articles of such mixtures or of asbestos (for example, thread, woven fabric, clothing, headgear, footwear, gaskets), whether or not reinforced, other than goods of heading 6811 or 6813

6813—Friction material and articles thereof (for example, sheets, rolls, strips, segments, discs, washers, pads), not mounted, for brakes, for clutches, or the like, with a basis of asbestos, of other mineral substances or of cellulose, whether or not combined with textile or other materials

6814—Worked mica and articles of mica, including agglomerated or reconstituted mica, whether or not on a support of paper, paperboard, or other materials

6815—Articles of stone or of other mineral substances (including carbon fibers, articles of carbon fibers and articles of peat), not elsewhere specified or included

For more details regarding classification of the specific product you are interested in importing, consult a customs broker, the appropriate commodity specialist at your nearest customs port, or see HTSUS. The 2001 HTSUS is available online from the Customs Service (www.customs.gov/impoexpo/impoexpo.htm) or for purchase from the U.S. Government Printing Office (see resources at the end of this chapter), and may be found in larger public libraries. For a general discussion of customs classification, see "Classification—Liquidation" on page 229.

Dutiable Status of Goods

For more information about duty rates and binding decisions see "Dutiable Status of Goods" on page 203; for a discussion of temporary importation of goods see "Temporary Free Importations" on page 205.

Valuation

Importers have a responsibility to use what the U.S. Customs Service deems, "reasonable care," when determining the value of their goods. They must also provide any additional information that the Customs Service needs for setting a final value on the goods. This process involves a number of factors and can be somewhat complicated; importers must be aware of applicable issues and details. Valuation information applies to all types of commodities, for further discussion on the subject see "Customs Valuation" on page 267.

Import Duties

Import duties vary (often dramatically) depending upon the Harmonized Tariff Schedule (HTSUS) classification of the goods or products imported. Since some products that look alike have different HTSUS classifications and different rates of duty, proper classification is vital. Note that "differences of opinion" between importers and the Bureau of Customs and Border Protection regarding classification keeps customs attorneys very busy.

Import duties can be assessed on the imported value of the goods ("ad valorem" rates of duty such as 2%, 4.4%, 50%, etc.), total units or weight of the goods ("specific" rates of duty such as 2 cents each or 1.5 cents/pound, etc.) or on a combination basis ("compound" rates of duty such as 5 cents each plus 6%).

Listed below is a sampling of several Column 1 import duty rates for Chapter 68 products:
Millstones and grindstones for milling, grinding or pulping (6804.10.00.00): Free
to
Footwear (6812.50.10.00): 8.3%

For specific information on US import duties refer to the Harmonized Tariff Schedule of the US. The print version is available from the US Government Printing Office as well as third party suppliers who often add special features. Online versions are available in both static PDF pages as well as in formats with excellent search functionality. Search the Web with the term "Harmonized Tariff Schedule" to find sources.

Entry and Documentation

The entry of merchandise is a two-part process consisting of 1) filing the documents necessary to determine whether merchandise may be released from Customs custody and 2) filing the documents that contain information for duty assessment and statistical purposes. In certain instances all documents must be filed and accepted by Customs prior to the release of the goods. Unless you have been granted an extension, you must file entry documents at a location specified by the port or area director within five working days of your shipment's date of arrival at a U.S. port of entry. These include a number of standard documents required by Customs for any entry and:

- TSCA certification for products containing asbestos or other hazardous substance, tsca certification

After you present the entry, Customs may examine your shipment, or may waive examination. The shipment is then released provided no legal or regulatory violations have been noted. You must then file entry summary documentation and deposit estimated duties at a designated customhouse within 10 working days of your shipment's release. For a detailed description of entry procedures, standard documentation, and informal entry, see "Entry Process" on page 185.

Informed Compliance. Informed compliance was introduced with the Customs Modernization Act of 1993 (Mod Act) and defines the relationship between importers and the Customs Service. It sets out the responsibilities of both parties. Providing the correct documentation and information for entry is a key factor that will make your importing operation run smoothly. We recommend that importers become familiar with the concept of informed comliance and the responsibilities that they have under the Mod Act. For further discussion about informed compliance see "Informed Compliance" on page 211.

Note: The Entry and Documentation section has been carefully designed to supply you, the importer, with sample documents and directions on how to satisfy Customs requirements. Be aware that you should consult the applicable authorities to ensure that you are correctly following the most current procedures.

Marking and Labeling Requirements

A shipment of any products containing substances that are classified as hazardous (49 CFR 172) must comply with the marking and labeling regulations adopted by the EPA (46 CFR 147.30) and the DOT (49 CFR 171 et seq.).

For a general discussion of U.S. Customs marking and labeling requirements, see "Country of Origin Marking" on page 236, "Special Marking Requirements" on page 238 and "Marking—False Impression" on page 239.

Shipping Considerations

You will need to ensure that your goods are packaged and shipped with care to ensure that they arrive in good condition and pass smoothly through Customs. You are responsible for ensuring that the shipment is in compliance with all applicable government regulations for packaging and shipping. In most instances, you should not leave these arrangements solely to the discretion of your supplier. Careful preparation of the cargo and selection of the mode of transport can be essential to a cost-effective, timely delivery of undamaged goods. We strongly advise you to consult your shipping representative, insurance agent, or freight broker for advice on packing and shipping.

Finished and semifinished stone and related products may be shipped in bulk, in crates, or in other types of containers and packages, depending on the nature of the products and whether or not they are prepackaged. General considerations include contamination, weather, and pests. Safety precautions should be taken to protect against breakage, spillage, corrosion, and combustion. Containers should be constructed to be safe during transport. Some products that are listed as hazardous substances (49 CFR 172 appendix) may be transported in bulk only in compliance with Coast Guard notification procedures, shipping permit requirements, and complex transportation regulations (46 CFR 148). All hazardous substances must be packaged and transported in accordance with DOT regulations (49 CFR 171 et seq.).

Publications and WWW Resources

The following publication may be relevant to the importation of finished and semifinished stone and related products. It is published by the EPA (see addresses at end of this chapter) and discusses the various categories of toxic substances and specific procedures required for dealing with them:

Toxic Substances Control Act: A Guide for Chemical Importers/ Exporters

The U.S. Customs Service launched a series of "Informed Compliance" publications in 1996, which are available on the Customs Service website (www.customs.gov/impoexpo/ impoexpo.htm). Of particular interest:

What Every Member of the Trade Community Should Know About Marble

The *Harmonized Tariff Schedule of the United States (2001)* (HTSUS) is available to view on the Customs Service website (www.customs.gov), or you may purchase a printed version from:

U.S. Government Printing Office
Superintendent of Documents
710 North Capital Street NW
Washington DC 20401
Tel: (202) 512-1800
Fax: (202) 512-1657
Website: www.access.gpo.gov

The USGPO also has copies of specific laws available for purchase. The USGPO accepts orders made by fax, phone or placed over the Internet, as well as mail orders paid by credit card. All orders must be accompanied by payment. Credit cards, checks drawn on a U.S. bank, or an international money order are all acceptable.

Relevant Government Agencies

Address questions regarding TSCA requirements for asbestos products to:

Environmental Protection Agency (EPA)
Office of Pollution Prevention and Toxics
TSCA System Information
1200 Pennsylvania Avenue NW
Washington DC 20460
Tel: (202) 564-3810
Tel: (202) 554-1404 (TSCA Information Hotline)
Email: oppt.homepage@epa.gov
Website: www.epa.gov/opptintr/contact.htm

Address questions regarding transportation of hazardous materials to:

U.S. Department of Transportation (DOT)
Research and Special Programs Administration
Hazardous Materials Information Center
400 7th St. SW
Washington DC 20590
Tel: (202) 366-4488
Website: http://hazmat.dot.gov

Address your questions regarding the importation of finished and semifinished stone and related products to your local Customs port director. For addresses refer to "U.S. Customs and Border Protection Offices" on page 65 or contact:

U.S. Customs and Border Protection
Customs Headquarters
1300 Pennsylvania Avenue NW
Washington DC 20229
Tel: (202) 354-1000
Website: www.customs.treas.gov

Laws and Regulations

The following laws and regulations may be relevant to the importation of finished and semifinished stone and related products. The laws are contained in the U.S. Code (USC), and the regulations are published in the Code of Federal Regulations (CFR), both of which may be available at larger public and law libraries. Copies of specific laws are also available from the United States Government Printing Office (address above).

15 USC 2601 et seq.
Toxic Substances Control Act
This Act authorizes the EPA to determine whether a substance is harmful and to restrict importation, sale, and use of such substances.

19 CFR 12.118 et seq.
Regulations on Toxic Substances Control
These regulations require importers of chemical substances imported in bulk or as part of a mixture to certify to Customs that the shipment complies with the TSCA or is not subject to that Act.

15 USC 1261 et seq.
Federal Hazardous Substances Act
This Act controls the importation of hazardous substances, sets forth prohibited imports, and authorizes various agencies to promulgate labeling, marking, and transport requirements.

49 CFR 171 et seq.
Regulations on Hazardous Materials
These regulations list all substances deemed hazardous and provide transport, marking, labeling, safety, and emergency response rules.

46 CFR 147.30
Regulations on Labeling of Hazardous Materials
This regulation requires the labeling of containers of hazardous substances and specifies the label contents.

46 CFR 148 et seq.
Regulations on Carriage of Solid Hazardous Materials in Bulk
These regulations govern the transport of solid hazardous substances in bulk, including reporting, permitting, loading, stowing, and shipping requirements.

Principal Exporting Countries

The following listing includes samples of the main supplier nations of the products of this chapter. It is organized by HTSUS major heading. (Refer to "Customs Classification" above for the product codes.) Countries are listed in rank order of the value of products imported to the U.S. Statistics represent customs value of entries for 2002 from the Bureau of Census, U.S. Department of Commerce.

6801—Canada, Italy, Mexico, United Kingdom, Portugal, Argentina, China, France

6802—Italy, Brazil, Turkey, India, Spain, Mexico, China, Canada

6803—India, China, Brazil, Italy, United Kingdom, Canada, Spain, South Africa

6804—Japan, Germany, Italy, Mexico, South Korea, Taiwan

6805—Canada, Germany, Mexico, United Kingdom, Finland, South Korea, Brazil, Italy, Japan

6806—Canada, Japan, Belgium, Mexico, United Kingdom, Germany, Italy, Denmark, Netherlands

6807—Canada, Mexico, Venezuela, Germany, Spain, Italy, France, Netherlands, Netherlands Antilles, United Kingdom, Colombia, Bahamas, Brazil

6808—Canada, United Kingdom, Malaysia, Spain, Portugal, Indonesia, South Africa, China, Italy, Mexico

6809—Canada, Mexico, China, Thailand, United Kingdom, Poland

6810—China, Canada, Mexico, Spain, Italy, Israel, Hong Kong, United Kingdom, Thailand, Philippines, Taiwan, Germany

6811—Canada, Mexico, Japan, Belgium, Malaysia, China, New Zealand, Finland, Germany, Colombia

6812—Canada, Brazil, Japan, Mexico, South Africa, United Kingdom, Germany, France

6813—Canada, Japan, Brazil, Mexico, United Kingdom, France, China, Colombia, Australia, Austria, Germany

6814—Belgium, Austria, India, Switzerland, China, United Kingdom, Japan, Canada

Chapter 69:
Ceramic Products

This section pertains to the importation of ceramic products, which are classified within Chapter 69 of the Harmonized Tariff Schedule of the United States (HTSUS). Specifically, it includes articles of siliceous fossil meals; refractory ceramic bricks and tiles; other refractory items, such as crucibles; ceramic architectural products, such as building blocks, roofing tiles, pipes, and glazed tiles; ceramic laboratory and agricultural fixtures; ceramic sinks, tubs, and bathroom fixtures; ceramic packaging; tableware, kitchenware, and other housewares of porcelain, china, earthenware, stoneware, and other types of ceramic materials; and ornamental and other ceramic items, all of which possess the characteristic of having been fired after shaping.

If you are interested in importing glass or glassware, refer to Commodity Index Chapter 70. Ceramic jewelry is covered under Chapter 71. Cermets—products of combined ceramics and metal, such as are used in turbine blades—are covered in Chapter 81. Tools with a ceramic component or used in working or making ceramics are found in Chapter 82. Ceramic electrical insulators and fittings are covered in Chapter 85. For dental ceramics, refer to Chapter 90. Articles for which ceramics are an incidental component are covered under other Commodity Index chapters: clocks (Chapter 91), furniture and lamps (Chapter 94), toys and games (Chapter 95), ceramic buttons or smoking pipes (Chapter 96), and works of art of ceramics or containing ceramic components (Chapter 97).

Note: To understand key issues that will enable you to make best use of the information in this section we recommend that you see "Introduction" on page 425.

Key Factors

The key factors in the importation of ceramics and ceramic products are:

- For U.S. Food and Drug Administration (FDA) regulated ceramics, compliance with FDA standards

- For FDA-regulated ceramics, compliance with FDA entry notifications and procedures

- For articles intended for use with food, compliance with FDA regulatory limits for extractable lead and cadmium content

- For decorative items not intended for use with food, compliance with FDA marking and labeling requirements

- Restrictions on china from People's Republic of China (certificates required), and on china from or transshipped through Hong Kong

- Automatic port of entry sampling of products originating in, or transshipped through, countries other than the People's Republic of China and Hong Kong

Although most importers utilize the services of a licensed customs broker in making their entries, and we recommend this practice, you should be aware of the regulatory, entry, and documentation issues involved in importing your product. You, as importer, are ultimately responsible for the fulfillment of any legal requirements applicable to your shipment.

General Considerations

Regulatory Agencies. In general, no permits or licenses are required to import ceramic articles. However, some governmental agencies may have requirements that must be met when importing specific products. For example, ceramic products intended for use with food, or products that could be construed as being used with food, such as decorative ceramicware, are subject to regulations under the Federal Food, Drug, and Cosmetic Act (FDCA), enforced by the FDA. For a general discussion of required FDA entry procedures and requirements see "Appendix: Foods" on page 825.

Articles Used with Food. We cannot stress highly enough the importance of complying with FDA limits on extractable lead or cadmium levels in articles intended for use with food. Toxic levels result in chronic, essentially irreversible lead or cadmium poisoning. The FDA is both vigilant and stringent in administering its procedures to protect the consumer. The fact that your product is manufactured by a well-known overseas producer is no guarantee that it is in compliance. When a specific item or group of items offered for entry into the U.S. is found to be in violation, the FDA issues an Import Alert to all regional FDA Import Operations offices ordering detention of all related shipments at U.S. ports of entry. If an imported product previously released for resale in the U.S. is later found to be in violation, for example through sampling of a subsequent shipment, all of that product will be recalled. Any expenses incurred in recalling, relabeling, or reexporting noncomplying products accrue to the importer and distributor.

Clearly, you stand to lose significant amounts of money if your shipment contains higher than permitted lead or cadmium levels. It is in your best interest as well as the best interest of your customers, to ascertain your product's compliance prior to purchase. In the same way, Customs is not lenient in dealing with decorative plates that are not labeled according to FDA requirements. If such items are detected at entry, you could incur considerable expense in modifying them. If you are importing ceramic items not intended for food use, be sure your products are properly marked.

Tableware and Kitchenware. U.S. Customs makes the following distinctions among certain ceramic products designated as tableware or kitchenware: 1) porcelain, china, and chinaware: ceramicware other than stoneware, whether or not glazed or decorated, having a fired white body (unless artificially colored) that will absorb no more than 0.5% of its weight in water, and is translucent in thicknesses of several millimeters; 2) stoneware: ceramicware with clay as an essential ingredient, not commonly white, which will absorb no more than 3% of its weight of water, and is naturally opaque (except in very thin pieces) even when absorption is less than 0.1%; 3) bone chinaware: chinaware or porcelain, the body of which contains 25% or more of calcined bone or tricalcium phosphate; 4) earthenware: ceramicware, whether or not glazed or decorated, having a fired body with clay as an essential ingredient, which will absorb more than 3% of its weight of water. Customs also maintains special technical definitions for refractory ceramics that reflect the properties of these items. Ceramic tiles are also generally defined as being no more than 3.2 cm in thickness.

These definitions are based on technical specifications, which for dinnerware have to do with factors such as the nature of the clay body, thickness, water absorption, and opacity. In addition, there are provisions for classification of articles available in specified sets. For example, dinnerware offered as a set must contain specified numbers of pieces of specified sizes. You should be familiar with these definitions when contracting for certain ceramic products for import. A product fitting the definition of stoneware cannot be entered as porcelain or vice versa, and a set of dishes that does not contain the requisite size and number of pieces may not be entered.

Detention of Shipment. If your shipment is found to be noncomplying, it may be detained at the port of entry. In the case of products subject to FDA jurisdiction, the FDA may permit you to bring such a shipment into compliance before making a final decision regarding admittance. However, any sorting, reprocessing, or relabeling must be supervised by FDA personnel, and is done at the importer's expense. Such conditional release to allow an importer to bring a shipment into compliance is a privilege, not a right. The FDA may consider subsequent noncomplying shipments of the same type of product to constitute an abuse of the privilege and require you to destroy or reexport the products. Note that the FDA is particularly strict with noncomplying ceramic dinnerware shipments. To ascertain what your legal responsibilities are, you should contact the agencies involved in advance regarding the specific items to be imported.

Customs Classification

For customs purposes, ceramic products are classified within Chapter 69 of the HTSUS. This chapter is divided into major headings, which are further divided into subheadings, and often into sub-subheadings, each of which has its own HTSUS classification number. For example, the 2001 HTSUS number for bone chinaware is 6911.10.20, indicating that it is a subcategory of tableware and kitchenware (6911.10), which is a subcategory of the major heading tableware, kitchenware, other household articles and toilet articles, of porcelain or china (6911). There are 14 major headings in Chapter 69.

6901—Bricks, blocks, tiles, and other ceramic goods of siliceous fossil meals (for example, kieselguhr, tripolite, or diatomite) or of similar siliceous earths

6902—Refractory bricks, blocks, tiles, and similar refractory ceramic constructional goods, other than those of siliceous fossil meals or similar siliceous earths

6903—Other refractory ceramic goods (for example, retorts, crucibles, muffles, nozzles, plugs, supports, cupels, tubes, pipes, sheaths, and rods), other than those of siliceous fossil meals or of similar siliceous earths

6904—Ceramic building bricks, flooring blocks, support or filler tiles, and the like

6905—Roofing tiles, chimney pots, cowls, chimney liners, architectural ornaments, and other ceramic constructional goods

6906—Ceramic pipes, conduits, guttering, and pipe fittings

6907—Unglazed ceramic flags and paving, hearth or wall tiles; unglazed ceramic mosaic cubes and the like, whether or not on a backing

6908—Glazed ceramic flags and paving, hearth or wall tiles; glazed ceramic mosaic cubes and the like, whether or not on a backing

6909—Ceramic wares for laboratory, chemical, or other technical uses; ceramic troughs, tubs, and similar receptacles of a kind used in agriculture; ceramic pots, jars, and similar articles of a kind used for the conveyance or packing of goods

6910—Ceramic sinks, washbasins, washbasin pedestals, baths, bidets, water closet bowls, flush tanks, urinals, and similar sanitary fixtures

6911—Tableware, kitchenware, other household articles and toilet articles, of porcelain or china

6912—Ceramic tableware, kitchenware, other household articles and toilet articles, other than of porcelain or china

6913—Statuettes and other ornamental ceramic articles

6914—Other ceramic articles

For more details regarding classification of the specific product you are interested in importing, consult a customs broker, the appropriate commodity specialist at your nearest customs port, or see HTSUS. The 2001 HTSUS is available online from the Customs Service (www.customs.gov/impoexpo/impoexpo.htm) or for purchase from the U.S. Government Printing Office (see resources at the end of this chapter), and may be found in larger public libraries. For a general discussion of customs classification, see "Classification—Liquidation" on page 229.

Dutiable Status of Goods

For more information about duty rates and binding decisions see "Dutiable Status of Goods" on page 203; for a discussion of temporary importation of goods see "Temporary Free Importations" on page 205.

Valuation

Importers have a responsibility to use what the U.S. Customs Service deems, "reasonable care," when determining the value of their goods. They must also provide any additional information that the Customs Service needs for setting a final value on the goods. This process involves a number of factors and can be somewhat complicated; importers must be aware of applicable issues and details. Valuation information applies to all types of commodities, for further discussion on the subject see "Customs Valuation" on page 267.

Import Duties

Import duties vary (often dramatically) depending upon the Harmonized Tariff Schedule (HTSUS) classification of the goods or products imported. Since some products that look alike have different HTSUS classifications and different rates of duty, proper classification is vital. Note that "differences of opinion" between importers and the Bureau of Customs and Border Protection regarding classification keeps customs attorneys very busy.

Import duties can be assessed on the imported value of the goods ("ad valorem" rates of duty such as 2%, 4.4%, 50%, etc.), total units or weight of the goods ("specific" rates of duty such as 2 cents each or 1.5 cents/pound, etc.) or on a combination basis ("compound" rates of duty such as 5 cents each plus 6%).

Listed below is a sampling of several Column 1 import duty rates for Chapter 69 products:
Ceramic pipes, conduits, guttering and pipe fittings (6906.00.00 .00): Free
to
Roofing tiles (6905.10.00.00): 13.5%

For specific information on US import duties refer to the Harmonized Tariff Schedule of the US. The print version is available from the US Government Printing Office as well as third party suppliers who often add special features. Online versions are available in both static PDF pages as well as in formats with excellent search functionality. Search the Web with the term "Harmonized Tariff Schedule" to find sources.

Entry and Documentation

The entry of merchandise is a two-part process consisting of 1) filing the documents necessary to determine whether merchandise may be released from Customs custody and 2) filing the documents that contain information for duty assessment and statistical purposes. In certain instances all documents must be filed and accepted by Customs prior to the release of the goods. Unless you have been granted an extension, you must file entry documents at a location specified by the port or area director within five working days of your shipment's date of arrival at a U.S. port of entry. These include a number of standard documents required by Customs for any entry, and:

- For shipments of restricted products from the People's Republic of China, valid CCIB certificate

After you present the entry, Customs may examine your shipment, or may waive examination. The shipment is then released provided no legal or regulatory violations have been noted. You must then file entry summary documentation and deposit estimated duties at a designated customhouse within 10 working days of your shipment's release. For a detailed description of entry procedures, standard documentation, and informal entry, see "Entry Process" on page 185.

Informed Compliance. Informed compliance was introduced with the Customs Modernization Act of 1993 (Mod Act) and defines the relationship between importers and the Customs Service. It sets out the responsibilities of both parties. Providing the correct documentation and information for entry is a key factor that will make your importing operation run smoothly. We recommend that importers become familiar with the concept of informed comliance and the responsibilities that they have under the Mod Act. For further discussion about informed compliance see "Informed Compliance" on page 211.

Entry Invoice for Ceramic Tile. Entry invoices for ceramic tile should state the shape and size of the individual tiles, quantity per case, and whether the tiles are glazed or unglazed.

Entry Invoice for Earthenware or Crockeryware. The entry invoice for articles composed of a nonvitrified absorbent body (including white granite and semiporcelain earthenware and cream-colored ware, stoneware, and terra cotta, but not including common brown, gray, red, or yellow earthenware), embossed or plain; common salt-glazed stoneware; stoneware or earthenware crucibles; Rockingham earthenware; china, porcelain, or other vitrified wares, composed of a vitrified nonabsorbent body that, when broken, shows a vitrified, vitreous, semivitrified, or semivitreous fracture; and bisque or parian ware (T.D. 53236) must show the following: 1) if in sets, the kinds of articles in each set in the shipment and the quantity of each kind of article in each set in the shipment; 2) the exact maximum diameter, expressed in cm, of each size of all plates in the shipment; and 3) the unit value for each style and size of plate, cup, saucer, or other separate piece in the shipment. For more general information about invoices see "Invoices" on page 277.

Note: The Entry and Documentation section has been carefully designed to supply you, the importer, with sample documents and directions on how to satisfy Customs requirements. Be aware that you should consult the applicable authorities to ensure that you are correctly following the most current procedures.

Prohibitions and Restrictions

Articles for Use with Food. FDA regulations regarding the importation of china, porcelain, and ceramic flatware and hollowware intended for use with food are designed to ensure that extractable lead and/or cadmium levels in the product are at a lower-than-toxic level, as defined by the FDCA. At time of entry, the FDA may 1) accept the documentation as proof of compliance and release the shipment; 2) take a sample for testing and release the shipment provisionally, pending test results; 3) take a sample for testing and hold the shipment in customs custody pending test results. If your shipment is sample-audited and provisionally released, and test results show higher-than-permissible extractable lead or cadmium content, the FDA will issue a recall order and you will have to comply immediately. Noncomplying shipments will be detained in customs custody and must be either modified to effect compliance, immediately reexported, or destroyed. In addition, a shipment of goods that passes customs as in compliance, and that is identical to a later shipment found to be in violation, will be recalled.

Release of a Detained Shipment. If your shipment is detained due to toxic levels of extractable lead or cadmium, you may qualify the shipment for release by rendering the articles unsuitable for use with food. Articles so rendered are not required to meet FDA safety guidelines for dinnerware. There are two ways to do this: 1) render the articles unsuitable for food use by some artifice such as holes bored through the potential food contact surface; or 2) permanently affix a label, incapable of obliteration, to the article's potential food contact surface. If you choose the second option, your label must identify the article as "Not for Food Use" and state the specific hazard associated with its use for food service. When your china violation is due to toxic cadmium levels, your label must include the words "Article May Poison Food." The FDA releases modified shipments on a lot-by-lot basis, with checks by the district laboratory to verify compliance.

Exemptions. Articles manufactured solely for ornamental display, and not intended for use with food, are not subject to the regulations for dinnerware. These include, but are not limited to: commemorative plates, souvenir plates, hand-painted plates, and other highly decorated plates. If your shipment of these types of items comes in place settings for the table, it qualifies by definition as a dinnerware shipment, and you are liable for any lead and cadmium content. Articles imported solely as ornaments must be permanently labeled on the back of the plate as follows: "Not for Food Use-Plate May Poison Food. For Decorative Purposes Only."

Country-Specific Import Restrictions

Chinese Ceramicware. An Import Alert is in force for shipments of ceramicware coming directly from the People's Republic of China (PRC), or originating in the PRC but coming through Hong Kong. If your import fits this description, you must present for each shipment—along with the shipping manifest and packing list supplied by the manufacturer—a validated certificate issued by the Chinese government's Import and Export Commodity Inspection Bureau (CCIB). Your CCIB certificate must show production lot identification, name and address of the manufacturer, test methodology and results for lead and cadmium, number and types of ceramicware pieces in the production lot and those tested, date of certification, name of the authorizing official, and seal of the office. In addition, shipments of ceramicware originating in the Peoples Republic of China and shipped via Hong Kong must be sealed by the CCIB in such a way as to prevent opening during transit. Even if your shipment complies with these procedures, the FDA may choose to audit-sample it when it arrives at the U.S. port of entry. Any shipment of ceramicware from the PRC that is not accompanied by a valid CCIB certificate will be automatically detained in customs custody while you arrange for a private lab test of a sample of the product. Testing is done at your expense.

Shipments of ceramicware originating (manufactured) in Hong Kong, or transshipped through Hong Kong from countries other than the People's Republic of China, will be automatically detained at the U.S. port of entry for audit-sampling. Certain Hong Kong firms have been exempted from automatic detention. For

details, contact the nearest regional FDA Import Operations office, or FDA headquarters (see addresses at end of this chapter).

Marking and Labeling Requirements

Articles Used with Food. FDA-regulated ceramic articles are subject to specific labeling requirements under the FDCA. There are marking and/or labeling requirements for noncomplying articles rendered unsuitable for use with food in order to qualify for entry, and for articles intended solely for decorative purposes. See "Prohibitions and Restrictions" above.

For a general discussion of U.S. Customs marking and labeling requirements, see "Country of Origin Marking" on page 236, "Special Marking Requirements" on page 238 and "Marking—False Impression" on page 239.

Shipping Considerations

You will need to ensure that your goods are packaged and shipped with care to ensure that they arrive in good condition and pass smoothly through Customs. You are responsible for ensuring that the shipment is in compliance with all applicable government regulations for packaging and shipping. In most instances, you should not leave these arrangements solely to the discretion of your supplier. Careful preparation of the cargo and selection of the mode of transport can be essential to a cost-effective, timely delivery of undamaged goods. We strongly advise you to consult your shipping representative, insurance agent, or freight broker for advice on packing and shipping.

As with all fragile products, packing and shipping must take breakage into account. All shipments of ceramic products must be packaged to withstand the rigors of transport.

Publications and WWW Resources

The *Harmonized Tariff Schedule of the United States (2001)* (HTSUS) is available to view on the Customs Service website (www.customs.gov), or you may purchase a printed version from:

> **U.S. Government Printing Office**
> **Superintendent of Documents**
> 710 North Capital Street NW
> Washington DC 20401
> Tel: (202) 512-1800
> Fax: (202) 512-1657
> Website: www.access.gpo.gov

The USGPO also has copies of specific laws available for purchase. The USGPO accepts orders made by fax, phone or placed over the Internet, as well as mail orders paid by credit card. All orders must be accompanied by payment. Credit cards, checks drawn on a U.S. bank, or an international money order are all acceptable.

Relevant Government Agencies

Address questions regarding requirements for FDA-regulated products to:

> **Food and Drug Administration (FDA)**
> **Center for Food Safety and Applied Nutrition (CFSAN)**
> **Office of Compliance**
> **Division of Enforcement, Imports Branch**
> 5100 Paint Branch Parkway
> College Park, MD 20740-3835
> Tel: (301) 436-2080
> Website: http://vm.cfsan.fda.gov/list.html

Address questions regarding the importation of ceramics and ceramic products to your local Customs port director. For addresses refer to "U.S. Customs and Border Protection Offices" on page 65 or contact:

U.S. Customs and Border Protection
Customs Headquarters
1300 Pennsylvania Avenue NW
Washington DC 20229
Tel: (202) 354-1000
Website: www.customs.treas.gov

Laws and Regulations

The following laws and regulations may be relevant to the importation of ceramics and ceramic products. The laws are contained in the U.S. Code (USC) and the regulations are published in the Code of Federal Regulations (CFR), both of which may be available at larger public and law libraries. Copies of specific laws are also available from the United States Government Printing Office (address above).

21 USC 301 et seq.
Federal Food, Drug, and Cosmetic Act
This Act prohibits deceptive practices and regulates the manufacture, sale and importation or exportation of food, drugs, cosmetics, and related products. It was amended by the Food Quality Protection Act of 1996. See 21 USC 331, 381, 382.

19 CFR 12.1 et seq.; 21 CFR 1.83 et seq.
Regulations on Food, Drugs, and Cosmetics
These regulations of the Secretary of Health and Human Services and the Secretary of the Treasury govern the standards, labeling, marking, and importing of products used with food, drugs, and cosmetics.

Principal Exporting Countries

The following listing includes samples of the main supplier nations of the products of this chapter. It is organized by HTSUS major heading. (Refer to "Customs Classification" above for the product codes.) Countries are listed in rank order of the value of products imported to the U.S. Statistics represent customs value of entries for 2002 from the Bureau of Census, U.S. Department of Commerce.

6901—Turkey, France, United Kingdom, Ecuador, Australia

6902—Canada, China, Germany, United Kingdom, Brazil, France, Japan, Mexico, Poland, Austria, Italy

6903—Japan, Mexico, Canada, United Kingdom, Germany

6904—Canada, Germany, Italy, United Kingdom, France, Austria

6905—Mexico, Venezuela, Colombia, Spain, Denmark, France, Germany

6906—Germany, Vietnam, China, Japan, Italy, United Kingdom

6907—Italy, Mexico, Argentina, Spain, Colombia, Germany, Indonesia, Netherlands, United Kingdom

6908—Italy, Spain, Mexico, Brazil, Turkey, Indonesia, Thailand, Argentina, Venezuela

6909—Japan, Germany, France, Sweden, China, Canada, Mexico, South Korea, United Kingdom, Australia

6910—Mexico, China, Thailand, Colombia, Brazil, Chile, Ecuador, Venezuela, Guatemala, Turkey

6911—China, United Kingdom, Japan, Germany, France, Thailand, Indonesia, Sri Lanka

6912—China, Italy, United Kingdom, Thailand, Indonesia, Portugal, Japan, Mexico, Malaysia, France, Taiwan

6913—China, Spain, Mexico, Italy, Thailand, Germany, Malaysia, Indonesia, Philippines

6914—Japan, China, Mexico, Italy, Germany, Hungary, France, Taiwan, United Kingdom, Vietnam, Canada, Thailand, South Koreal

Chapter 70:
Glass and Glassware

This section pertains to the importation of glass and glassware, which are classified within Chapter 70 of the Harmonized Tariff Schedule of the United States (HTSUS). Specifically, it includes glass waste; balls, rods, or tubes for further manufacture; cast or rolled glass; drawn or blown glass; float or ground glass; edgeworked or similar intermediate glass products; safety glass; multilayered insulating glass; mirrors; carboys, bottles, jars, and similar products; glass envelopes, such as bulbs and tubes; glass liners for vacuum flasks; glass tableware, kitchenware, and items for toilet, office, or home use; optical glass; watch crystals; architectural elements of glass; laboratory or pharmaceutical glassware; glass fibers and fabrics; and other miscellaneous articles of glass.

Although Chapter 70 is generally comprehensive with respect to products made of or containing glass, certain specific glass products may be classified within other Commodity Index chapters. If you are interested in importing glazes and vitrifiable enamels, refer to Commodity Index Chapter 32. Jewelry made from glass is classified in Chapter 71, although some related products are found in heading 7018. Glass fiber optic cables, electrical insulators, and fittings are covered in Chapter 85.

Specific products, including optical fibers, worked optical elements, hypodermic syringes, artificial eyes, thermometers, barometers, hydrometers, and similar devices and scientific instruments are found in Chapter 90. Lamps, lighting fixtures, illuminated signs, and similar products having a fixed light source are covered in Chapter 94. Toys, games, and related products, including glass Christmas tree ornaments, are classified within Chapter 95. Such miscellaneous manufactured glass products as buttons, vacuum flasks, and scent and similar spray bottles are found in Chapter 96.

Note: To understand key issues that will enable you to make best use of the information in this section we recommend that you see "Introduction" on page 425.

Key Factors

The key factors in the importation of glass and glass products are:

- For glass products intended for use with food, compliance with U.S. Food and Drug Administration (FDA) requirements

- For some FDA-regulated products subject to entry notification, compliance with FDA entry procedures and notification, as needed

- Compliance with FDA regulations regarding leachable lead and cadmium

- Special invoice information required
- Invoice documentation required for lead crystal

Although most importers utilize the services of a licensed customs broker in making their entries, and we recommend this practice, you should be aware of the regulatory, entry, and documentation issues involved in importing your product. You, as importer, are ultimately responsible for the fulfillment of any legal requirements applicable to your shipment.

General Considerations

Regulatory Agencies. Glass is for the most part a straightforward import commodity. No licenses or permits are required; nor, with certain exceptions, is any special entry documentation necessary. U.S. Customs does require certain specific information on the entry invoice for certain glass and glassware products. Special packing requirements apply to glass entering under HTSUS headings 7003 and 7004 (see "Packing Requirements" below). However, depending on the nature of your product, you may have to meet the requirements of other governmental agencies, particularly the U.S. Food and Drug Administration (FDA).

Articles Used with Food. All glass products intended for table or kitchen purposes, such as drinking glasses, bowls, and other containers, are subject to regulations under the Federal Food Drug, and Cosmetic Act (FDCA), enforced by the FDA. The following glass items are also subject to FDA regulation: 1) HTSUS heading 7010: carboys, bottles, flasks, jars, pots, vials, ampoules, and related products; 2) HTSUS heading 7012.00.00: glass liners for vacuum flasks or for other vacuum vessels; 3) HTSUS heading 7015.10.00: glasses for corrective spectacles; 4) HTSUS heading 7015.90.50: clock or watch crystals; and 5) HTSUS heading 7017: laboratory, hygienic, or pharmaceutical glassware.

Entry Procedures. If you are interested in importing any FDA-regulated glass product, you should be familiar with FDA import entry procedures and requirements under the FDCA, and be prepared to comply with all requirements. For more details regarding FDA import requirements, see "Appendix: Foods" on page 825.

Lead and Cadmium Restrictions. Although FDA entry notification is not currently required for glassware, all the FDA lead and cadmium restrictions pertinent to ceramic tableware also apply to glassware. Regulations are designed to ensure that extractable lead and/or cadmium levels in the product are at a-lower-than toxic level, as defined by the FDCA. At the time of entry, the FDA and/or U.S. Customs, acting on behalf of the FDA, may accept implicit compliance; retain a sample for testing while provisionally releasing the shipment pending test results; or detain the shipment pending test results. If your shipment is sampled-audited and provisionally released, and test results show higher-than-permissible levels of extractable lead or cadmium, the FDA will issue a recall order and you will have to comply immediately. Noncomplying shipments will be detained in customs, and must be modified, reexported, or destroyed. In addition, a shipment of goods that passes customs as in compliance, and that is identical to a later shipment found to be in violation, will be recalled. Toxic levels of these elements are rare in glassware, but they do occur occasionally. If your shipment is in violation of admissible levels, you will be held financially responsible for any necessary detention, modification, or product recall. Contact your regional FDA Import Operations office, or FDA headquarters (see addresses at end of this chapter) with specific questions.

Customs distinguishes between lead crystal glassware and that which is not lead crystal. Glassware entered as lead crystal is subject to a lower duty rate than other types. When you enter a shipment, you should be prepared to present documentation at the port of entry stating that the glassware contains not less than 24% lead monoxide by content to qualify as lead crystal. No special

form or certificate is necessary: a statement of lead content on the invoice will suffice. However, if the customs official suspects that your glassware is not true lead crystal, a sample will be taken and tested for lead content. If your glassware is found to contain less than 24% lead, you will be charged the higher rate of duty.

Customs Classification

For customs purposes, glass and glassware products are classified within Chapter 70 of the HTSUS. This chapter is divided into major headings, which are further divided into subheadings, and often into sub-subheadings, each of which has its own HTSUS classification number. For example, the 2001 HTSUS number for glass measuring more than 2 mm but less than 3.5 mm in thickness is 7004.90.25, indicating that it is a subcategory of other glass, rectangular in shape (7004.90), which is a subcategory of drawn glass and blown glass, in sheets, whether of not having an absorbent or reflecting layer, but not otherwise worked (7004). There are 20 major headings within HTSUS Chapter 70.

7001—Cullet and other waste and scrap of glass; glass in the mass

7002—Glass in balls (other than microspheres of heading 7018), rods or tubes, unworked

7003—Cast glass and rolled glass, in sheets or profiles, whether or not having an absorbent, reflecting or non-reflecting layer, but not otherwise worked

7004—Drawn glass and blown glass, in sheets, whether or not having an absorbent, reflecting or non-reflecting layer, but not otherwise worked

7005—Float glass and surface ground or polished glass, in sheets, whether or not having an absorbent, reflecting or non-reflecting layer, but not otherwise worked

7006—Glass of heading 7003, 7004, or 7005, bent, edge-worked, engraved, drilled, enameled, or otherwise worked, but not framed or fitted with other materials

7007—Safety glass, consisting of toughened (tempered) or laminated glass

7008—Multiple-walled insulating units of glass

7009—Glass mirrors, whether or not framed, including rear-view mirrors

7010—Carboys, bottles, flasks, jars, pots, vials, ampoules, and other containers, of glass, of a kind used for the conveyance or packing of goods; preserving jars of glass; stoppers, lids, and other closures, of glass

7011—Glass envelopes (including bulbs and tubes), open, and glass parts thereof, without fittings, for electric lamps, cathode-ray tubes, or the like

7012—Glass liners for vacuum flasks or for other vacuum vessels

7013—Glassware of a kind used for table, kitchen, toilet, office, indoor decoration, or similar purposes (other than that of heading 7010 or 7018)

7014—Signaling glassware and optical elements of glass (other than those of heading 7015), not optically worked

7015—Clock and watch glasses and similar glasses, glasses for noncorrective or corrective spectacles, curved, bent, hollowed, or the like, not optically worked; hollow glass spheres and their segments, for the manufacture of such glasses

7016—Paving blocks, slabs, bricks, squares, tiles, and other articles of pressed or molded glass, whether or not wired, of a kind used for building or construction purposes; glass cubes and other glass smallwares, whether or not on a backing, for mosaics or similar decorative purposes; leaded glass windows, and the like, multicellular or foam glass in blocks, panels, plates, shells, or similar forms

7017—Laboratory, hygienic, or pharmaceutical glassware, whether or not graduated or calibrated

7018—Glass beads, imitation pearls, imitation precious or semi-precious stones, and similar glass smallwares and articles thereof other than imitation jewelry; glass eyes other than prosthetic articles; statuettes and other ornaments of lamp-worked glass, other than imitation jewelry; glass microspheres not exceeding 1 mm in diameter

7019—Glass fibers (including glass wool) and articles thereof (for example, yarn, woven fabrics)

7020—Other articles of glass

For more details regarding classification of the specific product you are interested in importing, consult a customs broker, the appropriate commodity specialist at your nearest customs port, or see HTSUS. The 2001 HTSUS is available online from the Customs Service (www.customs.gov/impoexpo/impoexpo.htm) or for purchase from the U.S. Government Printing Office (see resources at the end of this chapter), and may be found in larger public libraries. For a general discussion of customs classification, see "Classification—Liquidation" on page 229.

Dutiable Status of Goods

For more information about duty rates and binding decisions see "Dutiable Status of Goods" on page 203; for a discussion of temporary importation of goods see "Temporary Free Importations" on page 205.

Valuation

Importers have a responsibility to use what the U.S. Customs Service deems, "reasonable care," when determining the value of their goods. They must also provide any additional information that the Customs Service needs for setting a final value on the goods. This process involves a number of factors and can be somewhat complicated; importers must be aware of applicable issues and details. Valuation information applies to all types of commodities, for further discussion on the subject see "Customs Valuation" on page 267.

Import Duties

Import duties vary (often dramatically) depending upon the Harmonized Tariff Schedule (HTSUS) classification of the goods or products imported. Since some products that look alike have different HTSUS classifications and different rates of duty, proper classification is vital. Note that "differences of opinion" between importers and the Bureau of Customs and Border Protection regarding classification keeps customs attorneys very busy.

Import duties can be assessed on the imported value of the goods ("ad valorem" rates of duty such as 2%, 4.4%, 50%, etc.), total units or weight of the goods ("specific" rates of duty such as 2 cents each or 1.5 cents/pound, etc.) or on a combination basis ("compound" rates of duty such as 5 cents each plus 6%).

Listed below is a sampling of several Column 1 import duty rates for Chapter 70 products:
Tubes of fused quartz or other fused silica (7002.31.00.00): Free to
Tubes of other glass having a linear coefficient of expansion not exceeding 5 x 10-6 per Kelvin within a temperature range of 0EC to 300EC (7002.32.00.00): 6%

For specific information on US import duties refer to the Harmonized Tariff Schedule of the US. The print version is available from the US Government Printing Office as well as third party suppliers who often add special features. Online versions are available in both static PDF pages as well as in formats with excellent search functionality. Search the Web with the term "Harmonized Tariff Schedule" to find sources.

Entry and Documentation

The entry of merchandise is a two-part process consisting of 1) filing the documents necessary to determine whether merchandise may be released from Customs custody and 2) filing the documents that contain information for duty assessment and statistical purposes. In certain instances all documents must be filed and accepted by Customs prior to the release of the goods. Unless you have been granted an extension, you must file entry documents at a location specified by the port or area director within five working days of your shipment's date of arrival at a U.S. port of entry. These include a number of standard documents required by Customs for any entry.

After you present the entry, customs may examine your shipment, or may waive examination. The shipment is then released provided no legal or regulatory violations have been noted. You must then file entry summary documentation and deposit estimated duties at a designated customhouse within 10 working days of your shipment's release. For a detailed description of entry procedures, standard documentation, and informal entry, see "Entry Process" on page 185.

Informed Compliance. Informed compliance was introduced with the Customs Modernization Act of 1993 (Mod Act) and defines the relationship between importers and the Customs Service. It sets out the responsibilities of both parties. Providing the correct documentation and information for entry is a key factor that will make your importing operation run smoothly. We recommend that importers become familiar with the concept of informed comliance and the responsibilities that they have under the Mod Act. For further discussion about informed compliance see "Informed Compliance" on page 211.

Entry Invoice for Glassware. Invoices for glassware and other glass products must show a statement of the separate value of each component article in the set.

Entry Invoice For Lead Crystal. Entry invoices for shipments entered as lead crystal must bear a verification statement that the glassware contains not less than 24% lead monoxide by content.

Entry Invoice for Beads. An entry invoice for glass beads must state: 1) The length of the string, if strung; 2) the size of the beads in mm; and 3) the material of which the beads are composed. For more general information about invoices see "Invoices" on page 277.

Note: The Entry and Documentation section has been carefully designed to supply you, the importer, with sample documents and directions on how to satisfy Customs requirements. Be aware that you should consult the applicable authorities to ensure that you are correctly following the most current procedures.

Restrictions and Prohibitions

Lead or Cadmium Content. Most shipments of glass products pass customs easily. However, once the FDA has identified a shipment of glassware as containing unlawful quantities of leachable lead or cadmium, it issues an Import Alert regarding either products of the responsible foreign manufacturer, or those brought in by the specific importer. In some instances, all glassware from a certain country will be named in an Import Alert. If you propose to enter a shipment covered by an FDA Import Alert, customs will certainly inspect and possibly detain it for testing. If it is found to be noncomplying, you will be required either to modify the product so that it does comply, or to destroy or reexport the shipment.

Release of Shipment. If your shipment is detained due to toxic levels of extractable lead or cadmium, you may be able to obtain its release by rendering the articles unsuitable for food or beverage uses. There are two ways to do this: 1) render the articles unsuitable for food use by a modification such as drilling holes through the potential food contact surface; or 2) permanently affix a label—incapable of obliteration or removal—to the article's potential food contact surface. If you choose the second option, your label must identify the article as "Not for Food Use" and state the specific hazard associated with its use for food or beverage service. When your product has toxic levels of cadmium, your label must include the words "Article May Poison Food." The FDA releases modified shipments on a lot-by-lot basis, with checks by the district laboratory to verify compliance. These procedures will be undertaken at the importer's expense.

Exemptions. Articles manufactured solely for ornamental display and not intended for food or beverage service are exempt from these requirements. Such articles must be permanently labeled as follows: "Not for Food Use-May Poison Food. For Decorative Purposes Only."

Import Advisory

Before purchasing foreign glassware for importation into the United States, check with the FDA or U.S. Customs to make sure that the manufacturer or pattern of glassware is not the subject of an FDA Import Alert. Although noncomplying glassware is much less common than noncomplying ceramicware, if your shipment is found to be toxic, you stand to lose large sums of money as a result of detention, testing, modifying, or even destruction of the products.

Marking and Labeling Requirements

Ceramic with Cadmium or Lead. The FDA requires noncomplying glassware containing toxic levels of cadmium or lead to be either 1) marked indelibly with the words "Not for Food Use" and a statement of the potential hazard, or 2) rendered unsuitable for food use by some artifice such as a hole bored through the potential food contact surface. Articles intended for decorative purposes must be so marked. Contact FDA's Import Operations office (see addresses at end of this chapter) for answers to specific questions.

For a general discussion of U.S. Customs marking and labeling requirements, see "Country of Origin Marking" on page 236, "Special Marking Requirements" on page 238 and "Marking—False Impression" on page 239.

Shipping Considerations

You will need to ensure that your goods are packaged and shipped with care to ensure that they arrive in good condition and pass smoothly through Customs. You are responsible for ensuring that the shipment is in compliance with all applicable government regulations for packaging and shipping. In most instances, you should not leave these arrangements solely to the discretion of your supplier. Careful preparation of the cargo and selection of the mode of transport can be essential to a cost-effective, timely delivery of undamaged goods. We strongly advise you to consult your shipping representative, insurance agent, or freight broker for advice on packing and shipping.

Specific Packing Requirements. For the purposes of headings 7003 and 7004, glass of the same size and thickness imported in any shipment in quantities over 4.6 m^2 shall be denied entry unless it is: 1) packed in units containing, as nearly as the particular size permits, 4.6 m^2, or multiples thereof; or 2) packed in units containing multiples of the number of sheets of the same size and thickness that would be contained in a unit if packed to contain, as nearly as such size permits, 4.6 or 9.3 m^2; or 3) otherwise packed in a manner that conforms to the packing practices of the domestic glass industry as determined and published from time to time by the Secretary of the Treasury.

As with all fragile products, packing and shipping must take breakage into account. All shipments of glass products must be packaged to withstand the rigors of transport.

Publications and WWW Resources

The *Harmonized Tariff Schedule of the United States (2001)* (HTSUS) is available to view on the Customs Service website (www.customs.gov), or you may purchase a printed version from:

U.S. Government Printing Office
Superintendent of Documents
710 North Capital Street NW
Washington DC 20401
Tel: (202) 512-1800
Fax: (202) 512-1657
Website: www.access.gpo.gov

The USGPO also has copies of specific laws available for purchase. The USGPO accepts orders made by fax, phone or placed over the Internet, as well as mail orders paid by credit card. All orders must be accompanied by payment. Credit cards, checks drawn on a U.S. bank, or an international money order are all acceptable.

Relevant Government Agencies

Address questions regarding requirements for FDA-regulated products to:

Food and Drug Administration (FDA)
Center for Food Safety and Applied Nutrition (CFSAN)
Office of Compliance
Division of Enforcement, Imports Branch
5100 Paint Branch Parkway
College Park, MD 20740-3835
Tel: (301) 436-2080
Website: http://vm.cfsan.fda.gov/list.html

Address questions regarding the importation of glass and glass products to your local Customs port director. For addresses refer to "U.S. Customs and Border Protection Offices" on page 65 or contact:

U.S. Customs and Border Protection
Customs Headquarters
1300 Pennsylvania Avenue NW
Washington DC 20229
Tel: (202) 354-1000
Website: www.customs.treas.gov

Laws and Regulations

The following laws and regulations may be relevant to the importation of glass and glass products. The laws are contained in the U.S. Code (USC) and the regulations are published in the Code of Federal Regulations (CFR), both of which may be available at larger public and law libraries. Copies of specific laws are also available from the United States Government Printing Office (address above).

21 USC 301 et seq.
Federal Food, Drug, and Cosmetic Act
This Act prohibits deceptive practices and regulates the manufacture, sale and importation or exportation of food, drugs, cosmetics, and related products. It was amended by the Food Quality Protection Act of 1996. See 21 USC 331, 381, 382.

19 CFR 12.1 et seq.; 21 CFR 1.83 et seq.
Regulations on Food, Drugs, and Cosmetics
These regulations of the Secretary of Health and Human Services and the Secretary of the Treasury govern the standards, labeling, marking, and importing of products used with food, drugs, and cosmetics.

Principal Exporting Countries

The following listing includes samples of the main supplier nations of the products of this chapter. It is organized by HTSUS major heading. (Refer to "Customs Classification" above for the product codes.) Countries are listed in rank order of the value of products imported to the U.S. Statistics represent customs value of entries for 2002 from the Bureau of Census, U.S. Department of Commerce.

7001—United Kingdom, Japan, Canada, Mexico, Taiwan, Germany

7002—Germany, United Kingdom, Netherlands, Brazil, China, Japan, Czech Republic, France

7003—Germany, France, United Kingdom, Japan, Mexico, Belgium, China, Russia, Spain, Netherlands, South Africa

7004—Germany, United Kingdom, China, Switzerland, India, Mexico, France, Italy

7005—Canada, Mexico, Japan, Germany, United Kingdom, China, Belgium, Switzerland, Indonesia, Thailand

7006—Philippines, Thailand, Japan, Mexico, China, Canada, Germany, Belgium, Indonesia, Romania, Italy

7007—Mexico, Canada, China, Germany, Japan, United Kingdom, Finland, South Africa

7008—Canada, Mexico, China, Germany, Thailand, United Kingdom

7009—China, Mexico, Canada, Taiwan, Japan, Germany

7010—Mexico, France, Canada, Italy, Germany, Taiwan, Colombia, China

7011—Japan, China, Malaysia, Germany, Thailand, Spain, Mexico

7012—Japan, China, Taiwan, United Kingdom, Brazil, India

7013—China, France, Ireland, Germany, Austria, Italy, Poland, Mexico

7014—Germany, Japan, United Kingdom, Liechtenstein, France

7015—France, China, Switzerland, Japan, Hong Kong, Belgium, Germany

7016—China, Italy, Germany, Canada, Indonesia, Mexico, Czech Republic

7017—Germany, United Kingdom, Mexico, Switzerland, Italy, China, South Korea, Japan, Czech Republic, France

7018—Austria, China, Czech Republic, India, Canada, Japan, Germany, Taiwan, Mexico, Hong Kong

7019—Canada, Mexico, China, Japan, Italy, Germany, United Kingdom, France

7020—Japan, Germany, China, Canada, Taiwan, France, United Kingdom, Italy, South Korea, India, Mexico

Chapter 71: Gems, Jewelry, and Related Products

Full title: Natural or Cultured Pearls, Precious or Semiprecious Stones, Precious Metals, Metals Clad With Precious Metals, and Articles Thereof; Imitation Jewelry; Coin

This section pertains to the importation of pearls, precious and semiprecious stones, precious metals, jewelry, and coins, which are classified within Chapter 71 of the Harmonized Tariff Schedule of the United States (HTSUS). In general, articles or parts that are wholly made of or derive their primary value from precious stones, precious metals, or other products of this chapter are classified within Chapter 71.

Specifically, this chapter includes worked or unworked, but not strung or set natural or cultured pearls; worked or unworked industrial and gemstone diamonds, unmounted and not set; other precious and semiprecious stones, worked or unworked, but not mounted or set; synthetic or reconstructed stones; dust and powder of precious, semiprecious, or synthetic stones; silver, whether as powder, bullion, semimanufactured, or plated; base metals plated with silver; gold, whether as powder, bullion, semimanufactured, or as coins; base metals or silver plated with gold; platinum and related metals; base metals, silver, or gold plated with platinum; precious metal scrap; jewelry made of precious metals; other articles of goldsmiths' or silversmiths' wares; industrial products that include precious metals; articles of pearls or stones; imitation jewelry; and coins and medallions valued primarily for their precious metal content.

Although the tariff classification for precious metals includes certain products made from these metals, many products made from or containing precious metals are entered under different Commodity Index chapters. In general, articles containing precious metals but in which the precious metal component is minor and incidental to the nature and value of the article are entered under the classification of the primary article. For example, a gold-handled umbrella would be entered under Commodity Index Chapter 66, while a piece of original statuary made from a precious metal, would be entered under Chapter 97. Watch and clock cases are covered in Chapter 91.

If you are interested in importing amalgams of precious metal or colloidal precious metal, refer to Chapter 28. Precious metals used for medical purposes—such as sutures and dental fillings—are covered in Chapter 30. Precious metal components of paints and dyes, such as lustres, are found in Chapter 32. Leather goods with precious metal fittings are found in Chapter 42, while ornamented fur products are covered in Chapter 43. Decorated textiles and textile products are covered in Commodity Index Chapters 50 through 63. Industrial abrasives containing precious or semiprecious stones or material from them are covered in Chapter 68, while such items contained as incidental parts of other apparatus are classified within Chapters 82, 84, or 85 (the latter includes precious stones used in record styli). Products of Chapter 71 may be found as components in the products of Chapters 90 through 97. Chapter 96 in particular includes items, such as hair ornaments, that may include precious stones, metals, or pearls, but that are classified there rather than as jewelry in Chapter 71.

Note: To understand key issues that will enable you to make best use of the information in this section we recommend that you see "Introduction" on page 425.

Key Factors

The key factors in the importation of gems and jewelry and related products are:

- Requirements for accurate fineness marking on sterling silver and gold items

- Marking requirements and restrictions for certain articles

- Alloy classifications

- Compliance with marking requirements under the National Stamping Act

- Compliance with marking requirements under the Hobby Protection Act

- Compliance with endangered species prohibitions and restrictions on any wildlife components of jewelry

- Submission of Customs Form 4790 for entries of monetary instruments valued at more than $10,000

Although most importers utilize the services of a licensed customs broker in making their entries, and we recommend this practice, you should be aware of the regulatory, entry, and documentation issues involved in importing your product. You, as importer, are ultimately responsible for the fulfillment of any legal requirements applicable to your shipment.

General Considerations

Gems, Jewelry, and Related Articles. Jewelry is defined as any small object of personal adornment or any article of personal use normally carried about the person. Examples of the category include rings, bracelets, necklaces, brooches, earrings, watch chains, tie pins, cufflinks, religious or other medals or insignia, cigarette cases, compacts, and pill boxes. Articles of the goldsmiths' or silversmiths' arts generally refer to items such as ornaments, silverware, toilet articles, smokers' articles, and other items used in the home or office, or for religious purposes.

The importation of gems, jewelry, and related products is relatively straightforward. No permits, licenses, or special entry paperwork are required. However, there are certain restrictions of which you should be aware. These are explained below.

Wildlife Products. If your jewelry contains components derived from wildlife, it is subject to extensive regulation, including laws that protect endangered and threatened species. The U.S. Fish and Wildlife Service (FWS) enforces, among many other laws, the U.S. Endangered Species Act (ESA) and the Convention on International Trade in Endangered Species of Wild Fauna and Flora (CITES). Jewelry containing items such as feathers, shell, horn, or ivory may be entirely prohibited, prohibited when originating from certain countries, or restricted in other ways. See "Prohibitions and Restrictions" below.

Pearls. Importation of pearls is straightforward. There are no restrictions or prohibitions. You do not need permits or licenses, nor is special entry paperwork required. Customs distinguishes

between natural and cultured pearls for duty purposes, and all commercially grown pearls are considered cultured pearls. A truly "natural" pearl is rarely seen, and Customs considers all shipments of pearls to be de facto cultured pearls. If you attempt to enter a shipment of pearls as "natural," you must be prepared to show documentation that your pearls were not commercially grown, but were found in the wild.

Coins. Gold and silver coins must comply with provisions of the National Stamping Act (NSA) as amended, which is enforced by the Department of the Treasury (see "Prohibitions and Restrictions" below). If you are importing imitation numismatic items, you should be sure that they meet provisions of the Hobby Protection Act (HPA). You should be prepared to present documentation of government authorization for any coins, especially any nonstandard coins or medallions (see "Marking and Labeling Requirements" below). Coins currently in circulation in any country and imported as monetary instruments enter duty free. However, any entries made on a single occasion and valued at $10,000 or more must be declared.

Precious Metals. Importation of precious metals is relatively straightforward, with few prohibitions or restrictions, most of which have to do with accurate marking to identify the fineness of the metal. Marking requirements are found primarily in provisions of the NSA. No permits, licenses, or special entry paperwork are required. The term "precious metals" as defined in Chapter 71 of the Harmonized Tariff Schedule (HTSUS) means silver, gold, and platinum. "Platinum" is also defined to include platinum, iridium, omnium, palladium, rhodium, and ruthenium.

Alloys. Any alloy containing a precious metal is considered an alloy of precious metal if any one precious metal constitutes as much as 2% by weight of the alloy. Specifically, an alloy containing 2% or more by weight of platinum is considered an alloy of platinum. An alloy containing 2% or more by weight of gold but no platinum or with less than 2% by weight of platinum, is considered an alloy of gold. Other alloys containing 2% or more by weight of silver are considered alloys of silver. There are special requirements for accurate fineness marking on sterling silver and gold items. See "Marking and Labeling Requirements" below.

Form of Metal. For precious metals, "unwrought" refers to refined or unrefined metal in the form of ingots, pigs, sponge, pellets, or similar manufactured primary forms. "Semimanufactured" refers to processed, or wrought, products in the form of bars, plates, sheets, wires, tubes, and similar intermediate forms. "Scrap" refers to leftovers suited only for recovery of the metal content.

Customs Classification

For customs purposes, gems, jewelry, and related products are classified within Chapter 71 of the HTSUS. This chapter is divided into major headings, which are further divided into subheadings, and often into sub-subheadings, each of which has its own HTSUS classification number. For example, the 2001 HTSUS number for unwrought gold other than powder is 7108.12.50, indicating that it is a sub-subcategory of other unwrought forms of nonmonetary gold (7108.12), which itself is a subcategory of the major heading gold, unwrought or in semimanufactured forms (7108). There are 18 major headings in HTSUS Chapter 71.

7101—Pearls, natural or cultured, whether or not worked or graded but not strung, mounted, or set; pearls, natural or cultured, temporarily strung for convenience of transport

7102—Diamonds, whether or not worked, but not mounted or set

7103—Precious stones (other than diamonds) and semiprecious stones, whether or not worked or graded but not strung, mounted, or set; ungraded precious stones (other than diamonds) and semiprecious stones, temporarily strung for convenience of transport

7104—Synthetic or reconstructed precious or semiprecious stones, whether or not worked or graded but not strung, mounted, or set; ungraded synthetic or reconstructed precious or semiprecious stones, temporarily strung for convenience of transport

7105—Dust and powder of natural or synthetic precious or semiprecious stones

7106—Silver (including silver plated with gold or platinum), unwrought or in semimanufactured forms, or in powder form

7107—Base metals clad with silver, not further worked than semimanufactured

7108—Gold (including gold plated with platinum) unwrought or in semimanufactured forms, or in powder form

7109—Base metals or silver, clad with gold, not further worked than semimanufactured

7110—Platinum, unwrought or in semimanufactured forms, or in powder form

7111—Base metals, silver or gold, clad with platinum, not further worked than semimanufactured

7112—Waste and scrap of precious metal or of metal clad with precious metal; other waste and scrap containing precious metal or precious metal compunds, of a kind used principally for the recovery of precious metal:

7113—Articles of jewelry and parts thereof, of precious metal or of metal clad with precious metal

7114—Articles of goldsmiths' or silversmiths' wares and parts thereof, of precious metal or of metal clad with precious metal

7115—Other articles of precious metal or of metal clad with precious metal

7116—Articles of natural or cultured pearls, precious or semiprecious stones (natural, synthetic, or reconstructed)

7117—Imitation jewelry

7118—Coin

For more details regarding classification of the specific product you are interested in importing, consult a customs broker, the appropriate commodity specialist at your nearest customs port, or see HTSUS. The 2001 HTSUS is available online from the Customs Service (www.customs.gov/impoexpo/impoexpo.htm) or for purchase from the U.S. Government Printing Office (see resources at the end of this chapter), and may be found in larger public libraries. For a general discussion of customs classification, see "Classification—Liquidation" on page 229.

Dutiable Status of Goods

For more information about duty rates and binding decisions see "Dutiable Status of Goods" on page 203; for a discussion of temporary importation of goods see "Temporary Free Importations" on page 205.

Valuation

Importers have a responsibility to use what the U.S. Customs Service deems, "reasonable care," when determining the value of their goods. They must also provide any additional information that the Customs Service needs for setting a final value on the goods. This process involves a number of factors and can be somewhat complicated; importers must be aware of applicable issues and details. Valuation information applies to all types of commodities, for further discussion on the subject see "Customs Valuation" on page 267.

Import Duties

Import duties vary (often dramatically) depending upon the Harmonized Tariff Schedule (HTSUS) classification of the goods or

products imported. Since some products that look alike have different HTSUS classifications and different rates of duty, proper classification is vital. Note that "differences of opinion" between importers and the Bureau of Customs and Border Protection regarding classification keeps customs attorneys very busy.

Import duties can be assessed on the imported value of the goods ("ad valorem" rates of duty such as 2%, 4.4%, 50%, etc.), total units or weight of the goods ("specific" rates of duty such as 2 cents each or 1.5 cents/pound, etc.) or on a combination basis ("compound" rates of duty such as 5 cents each plus 6%).

Listed below is a sampling of several Column 1 import duty rates for Chapter 71 products:
Rubies, sapphires and emeralds (7103.91.00): Free
to
Base metals, silver or gold, clad with platinum, not further worked than semimanufactured (7111.00.00.00): 10%

For specific information on US import duties refer to the Harmonized Tariff Schedule of the US. The print version is available from the US Government Printing Office as well as third party suppliers who often add special features. Online versions are available in both static PDF pages as well as in formats with excellent search functionality. Search the Web with the term "Harmonized Tariff Schedule" to find sources.

Entry and Documentation

The entry of merchandise is a two-part process consisting of 1) filing the documents necessary to determine whether merchandise may be released from Customs custody and 2) filing the documents that contain information for duty assessment and statistical purposes. In certain instances all documents must be filed and accepted by Customs prior to the release of the goods. Unless you have been granted an extension, you must file entry documents at a location specified by the port or area director within five working days of your shipment's date of arrival at a U.S. port of entry. These include a number of standard documents required by Customs for any entry, and

- For unofficial gold coin restrikes: a copy of the legal proclamation under which the coin was issued, or official bank affidavit

- For jewelry that is admissible but comprised of components from protected species, any documentation required under applicable endangered species regulations

After you present the entry, Customs may examine your shipment, or may waive examination. The shipment is then released provided no legal or regulatory violations have been noted. You must then file entry summary documentation and deposit estimated duties at a designated customhouse within 10 working days of your shipment's release. For a detailed description of entry procedures, standard documentation, and informal entry, see "Entry Process" on page 185.

Informed Compliance. Informed compliance was introduced with the Customs Modernization Act of 1993 (Mod Act) and defines the relationship between importers and the Customs Service. It sets out the responsibilities of both parties. Providing the correct documentation and information for entry is a key factor that will make your importing operation run smoothly. We recommend that importers become familiar with the concept of informed comliance and the responsibilities that they have under the Mod Act. For further discussion about informed compliance see "Informed Compliance" on page 211.

Note: The Entry and Documentation section has been carefully designed to supply you, the importer, with sample documents and directions on how to satisfy Customs requirements. Be aware that you should consult the applicable authorities to ensure that you are correctly following the most current procedures.

Prohibitions and Restrictions

Coins. Counterfeit coins or the means of counterfeiting them may not be imported into the U.S., nor may representations of such articles be imported. Penalties for such actions can be extreme, including criminal penalties (under the Importation of Counterfeit or Forged Obligations or Securities Act), seizure of the goods (under the Contraband Seizure Act), and even forfeiture of the means of transport involved in an attempt to import such items (under regulations governing the Seizure and Forfeiture of Vessels, Vehicles, and Aircraft).

Gold and Silver. Additional prohibitions and restrictions on importation of coins have to do with the composition of the coin. All restrictions on the purchase, holding, selling, or otherwise dealing with gold by U.S. citizens were removed effective December 31, 1974. However, legislation exists providing a framework for revoking or controlling the export or import of gold or silver coins or bullion in times of war or national emergency. Nevertheless, you may freely import gold—or other precious metals—subject to the usual customs declaration and entry requirements.

Marking and Labeling Requirements. Articles or containers of articles that bear false designations of origin, or false descriptions or representations, are prohibited importation under 15 USC. This is especially pertinent to the importation of precious metals intended for commercial sale, because such articles are often marked with degree of fineness indicating value. Particular fineness marking requirements are detailed in "Marking and Labeling Requirements" below. If you import articles intended for resale in the U.S. that fail to meet these requirements, your shipment is subject to detention by U.S. Customs at the port of entry.

Detention of Shipments. Customs notifies the U.S. attorney when noncomplying shipments are discovered and detained. The U.S. attorney may or may not initiate litigation against the importer. If the U.S. attorney chooses not to prosecute, the mismarked shipment will be subject to normal Customs seizure and forfeiture. If your shipment is seized because of mismarking, you may petition the port director of the customs port of entry for release of the shipment on condition the noncompliance is redressed. If the port director releases your shipment you will be required either to remove or obliterate the prohibited marking, or to see that the articles and containers are properly marked to indicate their origin, contents, or condition. As an alternative to remarking, customs may permit you to export the articles or to destroy them under customs supervision. All remedial procedures resulting from mismarking will be undertaken at your expense.

Wildlife Products. Endangered species regulation is complex. The number of protected species grows every year. If you are considering importing jewelry that could contain wildlife components of any kind, you should be familiar with the various laws. Ivory, for example, is a prohibited import unless the importer presents documentary proof that the ivory is antique (more than 100 years old) and that it meets certain other requirements. Entry of wildlife products is restricted to FWS-designated ports. Contact FWS (see addresses at end of this chapter) with your specific questions.

It is difficult to overstress the importance of endangered species regulation. Ignorance of these laws can result in the loss of your shipment, and therefore your investment. In some cases a prohibited shipment can incur sizable additional fines. If you are importing items constructed using parts from protected species, such as ivory, certain types of shell, horn, feathers, etc., it is essential that you ascertain the status of those components before making your purchase. Country of origin is a tricky issue here, and it is crucial. Under CITES, some species are prohibited export for commercial purposes from certain countries, but not from others. Wildlife pirating is a common practice, and the country of origin of a jewelry component may not be the same as the country from which you purchased the final product. Many items are categorically prohibited, regardless of country of origin. Items only mildly restricted under CITES may be entirely prohibited under the ESA or one of the other more stringent regulations. If you inadvertently import products made from protected species, the fact that you were not aware of your shipment's violation will not protect you from the consequences.

Marking and Labeling Requirements

Goods that bear markings denoting value, such as carat markings for gold, or the designation "sterling" on silver, must be accurately marked. Gold or silver articles marked or labeled in a manner indicating a greater-than-actual degree of metal fineness, and imported for sale by manufacturers or dealers, are prohibited entry. This prohibition applies regardless of the actual amount of precious metal in the article, and also applies to alloys. Under the National Stamping Act (NSA), articles made of gold or gold alloys may not be imported into the U.S. if the gold content is one-half carat below the indicated fineness. In the case of articles made of gold or gold alloys that include solder and alloy of inferior fineness, a one-carat divergence below the indicated fineness is permitted. Articles marked "sterling" or "sterling silver" must assay at least 0.925 of pure silver, with a 0.004 allowable divergence. Other articles of silver or silver alloys must assay not less than 0.004 part below the indicated fineness. Articles marked "coin" or "coin silver" must contain at least 0.900 part pure silver with an allowable divergence of 0.004 part.

It is unlawful to enter for import into the U.S. items of jewelry bearing inaccurate or misleading valuation markings. If your shipment is found to be inaccurately marked, it is subject to seizure by customs.

Articles bearing the words "United States Assay" are prohibited. Articles made wholly or in part of inferior metal and plated or filled with gold or silver or alloys thereof, and that are marked with the degree of fineness, must also be marked to indicate the plated or filled content. In such cases, the use of the words "sterling" or "coin" is prohibited.

If you deal via mail or operate in interstate commerce in articles of gold or silver that bear a fineness or quality mark such as 14K, sterling, or other mark, you must place your name or registered trademark next to the fineness mark, in letters the same size as the fineness mark. This trademark or name is not required at the time of importation; therefore, customs has no direct responsibility for enforcement of this law and shipments are not held up on this count. Address your questions regarding this requirement to the U.S. Department of Justice (see addresses at end of this chapter).

Under the Hobby Protection Act, any imitation numismatic item must be plainly and permanently marked "copy." Those that do not comply are subject to seizure and forfeiture. Unofficial gold coin restrikes must be marked with the country of origin. If you are importing these types of coins, you should obtain a copy of the legal proclamation under which the coins are issued. If you are unable to procure the proclamation, you should get an affidavit of government sanction of the coins from a responsible banking official.

For marking or labeling requirements applicable to specific products or types of products made from precious metals (e.g. watches), see the pertinent Commodity Index chapter.

For a general discussion of U.S. Customs marking and labeling requirements, see "Country of Origin Marking" on page 236, "Special Marking Requirements" on page 238 and "Marking—False Impression" on page 239.

Shipping Considerations

You will need to ensure that your goods are packaged and shipped with care to ensure that they arrive in good condition and pass smoothly through Customs. You are responsible for ensuring that the shipment is in compliance with all applicable government regulations for packaging and shipping. In most instances, you should not leave these arrangements solely to the discretion of your supplier. Careful preparation of the cargo and selection of the mode of transport can be essential to a cost-effective, timely delivery of undamaged goods. We strongly advise you to consult your shipping representative, insurance agent, or freight broker for advice on packaging and shipping.

Although goods of Chapter 71 may be subject to damage during transport if improperly packaged, the major concern lies in ensuring adequate security en route for these high-value, often highly portable products. The weight factor relative to the bulk of many of these goods is also a consideration.

Publications and WWW Resources

The *Harmonized Tariff Schedule of the United States (2001)* (HTSUS) is available to view on the Customs Service website (www.customs.gov), or you may purchase a printed version from:

U.S. Government Printing Office
Superintendent of Documents
710 North Capital Street NW
Washington DC 20401
Tel: (202) 512-1800
Fax: (202) 512-1657
Website: www.access.gpo.gov

The USGPO also has copies of specific laws available for purchase. The USGPO accepts orders made by fax, phone or placed over the Internet, as well as mail orders paid by credit card. All orders must be accompanied by payment. Credit cards, checks drawn on a U.S. bank, or an international money order are all acceptable.

Relevant Government Agencies

Address questions regarding the importation of jewelry involving protected species to:

U.S. Fish and Wildlife Service (FWS)
Division of Management Authority
4401 N. Fairfax Dr.
Arlington, VA 22203-0700
Tel: (703) 358-2104
Website: www.fws.gov

Address questions regarding the importation of gems, jewelry, and related products to your local Customs port director. For addresses refer to "U.S. Customs and Border Protection Offices" on page 65 or contact:

U.S. Customs and Border Protection
Customs Headquarters
1300 Pennsylvania Avenue NW
Washington DC 20229
Tel: (202) 354-1000
Website: www.customs.treas.gov

Laws and Regulations

The following laws and regulations may be relevant to the importation of gems, jewelry, and related products. The laws are contained in the U.S. Code (USC) and the regulations are published in the code of Federal Regulations (CFR), both of which may be available at larger public and law libraries. Copies of specific laws are also available from the United States Government Printing Office (address above).

15 USC 2101
Hobby Protection Act (HPA)
This act prescribes marking requirements for imitation numismatic items and for unofficial gold coin restrikes.

15 USC 291-300

Jewelers' Liability Act (Gold and Silver Articles)
This Act provides requirements for accurate fineness marking on articles of gold or gold alloy.

Convention on International Trade in Endangered Species of Wild Fauna and Flora (CITES)
This comprehensive wildlife treaty signed by over 100 countries, including the United States, regulates and in many cases prohibits commercial imports and exports of wild animal and plant species threatened by trade.

16 USC 1531
Endangered Species Act of 1973
This Act prohibits the import and export of plant and seed species listed as endangered and most species listed as threatened. Seeds labeled as "of cultivated origin" may be traded. It is the U.S. law that implements CITES.

12 USC 95a
Importation and Exportation of Gold and Silver
Customs enforces laws relating to the importation or exportation of gold and silver coins or bullion during times of war or national emergency.

15 USC 294 et seq/
Gold Labeling Act of 1976
Customs enforces restrictions on the importation of gold or silver stamped with the words "United States Assay" or any words calculated to convey the impression that an official U.S. agency has certified the quality of such gold or silver. Section 294 prohibits the importation of falsely marked gold or silver See 19 CFR 11.12.

18 USC 471 et seq.
Counterfeiting and Forgery
Customs enforces the law prohibiting the importation of counterfeit obligations, securities, coins, currency, customs forms, ships' papers, and the plates or other means for counterfeiting the same.

31 CFR Part 401
Seizure and Forfeiture of Vessels, Vehicles, and Aircraft used to transport Counterfeit Coins, Obligations, and Paraphernalia
These regulations authorize the port director of customs to hold in custody the means of transport used to violate 49 USC 781 and seized by the Secret Service in enforcing laws against counterfeiting.

Principal Exporting Countries

The following listing includes samples of the main supplier nations of the products of this chapter. It is organized by HTSUS major heading. (Refer to "Customs Classification" above for the product codes.) Countries are listed in rank order of the value of products imported to the U.S. Statistics represent customs value of entries for 2002 from the Bureau of Census in Commerce.

7101—Japan, Australia, Hong Kong, China, French Polynesia, United Kingdom, France, Switzerland, Indonesia, Philippines, Singapore, Germany

7102—Israel, India, Belgium, South Africa, Hong Kong, United Kingdom, Switzerland, Russia

7103—Thailand, India, Colombia, Hong Kong, Switzerland, Sri Lanka, Israel, China, Brazil, Germany

7104—China, Germany, Switzerland, Austria, Hong Kong, Thailand, Canada, France, Japan

7105—Ireland, China, South Korea, Japan, Belgium, Russia, Czech Republic, Ukraine, Switzerland, United Kingdom

7106—Mexico, Canada, Peru, Brazil, China, Chile, Germany, Japan, Poland

7107—Mexico, Canada, Israel, Germany, South Africa, India, Thailand

7108—Canada, Brazil, Colombia, Peru, Honduras, Mexico, Chile, United Kingdom

7109—Japan, Italy, United Arab Emirates, China, Germany, Thailand

7110—South Africa, Russia, United Kingdom, Belgium, Germany, Norway, Switzerland

7111—Switzerland, Japan, Canada, Italy, Germany, South Korea, India

7112—Canada, Mexico, Dominican Republic, Germany, United Kingdom

7113—Italy, India, Thailand, China, Hong Kong, Israel, Canada

7114—Italy, United Kingdom, Israel, France, China, India

7115—Japan, Switzerland, United Kingdom, Italy, Germany, Brazil, India

7116—China, Hong Kong, Ireland, India, Italy, Thailand

7117—China, South Korea, Thailand, India, Hong Kong, Taiwan, Mexico

7118—Canada, United Kingdom, Austria, Switzerland, South Africa

Chapter 72:
Iron and Steel

This chapter relates to the importation of iron and steel, which are classified within Chapter 72 of the Harmonized Tariff Schedule of the United States (HTSUS). Specifically, it includes primary materials, such as pig iron, ferroalloys, and waste and scrap; iron and nonalloy steel, including flat-rolled, bars, rods, and wire in rolls, coils, and basic intermediate shapes; stainless steel in the same forms as iron and nonalloy steel; and other alloy steel in the same forms as stainless steel, but including hollow drill bars and rods. Basically, Chapter 72 includes all primary and intermediate products of iron and steel.

If you are interested in importing finished goods of iron or steel, refer to Commodity Index Chapter 73. Goods of base metals in which metals other than iron or steel predominate are covered in other Commodity Index chapters, including copper and its alloys, such as brass, bronze, nickel-silver, and cupro-nickel (Chapter 74), nickel (Chapter 75), aluminum (Chapter 76), lead (Chapter 78), zinc (Chapter 79), tin (Chapter 80), and other base metals (Chapter 81). Tools, other implements, and cutlery are found in Chapter 82, while miscellaneous articles of base metals are contained in Chapter 83. Precious metals, alloys of precious metals, and articles containing the same are covered specifically in Chapter 71.

Other products for which metals are incidental—even if critical and major—components are found within a variety of Commodity Index chapters and headings. For example, if you are interested in importing metallic paints, refer to Chapter 36. For headgear with metal elements, see Chapter 65; for umbrella frames and related items, see Chapter 66. Finished and semifinished products classified as machinery, mechanical appliances, and electrical goods are found in Chapters 84 and 85. Assembled railway track and related equipment is covered in chapter 86, vehicles in Chapter 87, aircraft in Chapter 88, and boats in Chapter 89. Instruments and apparatus are covered in other Commodity Index chapters on the particular items, including optical, medical, and precision instruments (Chapter 90), clocks and watches (Chapter 91), and musical instruments (Chapter 92). Metal articles as parts of firearms, including ammunition, are found in Chapter 93. The Commodity Index chapters that cover miscellaneous manufactures include furniture (Chapter 94), toys, games, and sporting goods (Chapter 95), and miscellaneous manufactured articles (Chapter 96). Works of art in which iron and steel are components, even dominant components, are covered in Chapter 97 if the primary value derives from the artistry rather than from the metal content.

Note: To understand key issues that will enable you to make best use of the information in this section we recommend that you see "Introduction" on page 425.

Note: To understand key issues that will enable you to make best use of the information in this section we recommend that you see "Introduction" on page 425.

Key Factors

The key factors in the importation of iron and steel are:

- Compliance with U.S. Environmental Protection Agency (EPA) requirements under the Toxic Substances Control Act (TSCA) (if the product is classified as a hazardous substance)

- Compliance with U.S. Department of Transportation (DOT) regulations for transport of hazardous cargo (if the product is a hazardous substance)

Although most importers utilize the services of a licensed customs broker in making their entries, and we recommend this practice, you should be aware of the regulatory, entry, and documentation issues involved in importing your product. You, as importer, are ultimately responsible for the fulfillment of any legal requirements applicable to your shipment.

General Considerations

Regulatory Agencies. Importation of iron and steel is relatively straightforward, with few restrictions or special requirements. The Environmental Protection Agency (EPA), under authority of the Toxic Substances Control Act (TSCA), imposes certain controls on the importation of products that contain toxic substances. The Department of Transportation (DOT) enforces regulations for transporting hazardous cargo.

Definitions. Unlike alloys of precious metals, in which any alloy having as much as 2% of a precious metal is considered an alloy of that metal, alloys of base metals are classified according to the metal that predominates by weight over every other individual metal in the alloy. For customs purposes, alloys of a metal are included with the metal that they are an alloy of. Similarly, for customs purposes, iron and steel—which is processed iron—are considered to be the same metal.

Pig iron is defined for customs purposes as an iron-carbon alloy not usefully malleable that contains more than 2% by weight of carbon and less than the listed percentages of the any of the following materials: chromium, 10%; manganese, 6%; phosphorus, 3%; silicon, 8%; and other elements, 10%. Spiegeleisen is an iron-carbon alloy containing by weight between 6% and 30% of manganese but otherwise conforming to the definition of pig iron. Ferroalloys contain by weight more than 4% iron and more than the listed percentages of the following materials: chromium, 10%; manganese, 30%; phosphorus, 3%; silicon, 8%; and a total of more than 10% of other elements excluding carbon and with a maximum of 10% for copper. Steel is defined as a ferrous material that is usefully malleable and contains by weight no more than 2% of carbon (chromium steels may have a higher carbon content). Stainless steel consists of alloy steels containing by weight no more than 1.2% carbon and at least 10.5% chromium. Other alloy steels include specified varying percentages of elements such as aluminum, boron, chromium, cobalt, copper, lead, manganese, molybdenum, nickel, niobium, silicon, titanium, tungsten, vanadium, zirconium, and other elements—except sulfur, phosphorus, carbon, and nitrogen. HTSUS also gives specific definitions and ranges for such products as tool steel, chipper knife steel, heat-resisting steel, and ball-bearing steel. For details, see the notes to HTSUS Chapter 72.

Hazardous Substances Regulations. The EPA imposes certain controls on the importation of toxic substances. The TSCA defines a toxic substance as any substance determined to present the possibility of an unreasonable risk of injury to health and the environment. The DOT enforces regulations for transporting hazardous cargo. Substances are deemed hazardous if listed in DOT trans-port regulations (49 CFR 172 appendix). Unwrought primary metals, such as pigs, ingots, billets, blooms, and similar materials, are generally categorized as toxic substances within the definitions of the TSCA and thus are required to be in compliance with its provisions. These include packaging, shipping, marking, and labeling requirements. Refer to "Laws and Regulations" below.

Products defined as articles—that is, any manufactured item 1) that is formed into a specific shape or design during manufacture, 2) that has end-use functions dependent on the shape or design during end use, and 3) that during the end use, does not change in its chemical composition or that changes only for a noncommercial purpose separate from the article and only as allowed by law (19 CFR 12.120(2))—are not subject to the provisions of the TSCA. Metal products other than primary metals are generally considered to be articles even if they are to be further processed. For example, rolled steel is an article even if it is to be subsequently processed.

Certification. All products covered by the TSCA are subject to the U.S. Customs Service TSCA Import Certification Rule (19 CFR 12.118 et seq.). If you import these products, you must sign one of the following statements: "I certify that all materials in this shipment comply with all applicable rules or orders under TSCA and that I am not offering a chemical substance for entry in violation of TSCA or any applicable rule or order thereunder" or "I certify that all materials in this shipment are not subject to TSCA." You must file this TSCA certification of compliance or exemption at the time you make the entry at customs. Customs will not release your shipment without proper certification.

If you will be importing several or regular shipments, you should ask the appropriate Customs port director to authorize your use of a blanket certification. A blanket certification is valid for one calendar year, is renewable, and may be revoked at any time for cause.

Dumping or Countervailing Duty Actions. Actions to restrict importation of or impose punitive duties on imports of iron and steel products from countries that are alleged to be involved in selling these products in the U.S. at below cost or the prices charged in their home countries (dumping) are occasionally brought to protect the domestic steel industry. Although no such actions are currently in force, restrictions can be imposed on short notice. You should contact customs to verify the status of your proposed imports.

Customs Classification

For customs purposes, iron and steel are classified within Chapter 72 of the HTSUS. This chapter is divided into major headings, which are further divided into subheadings, and often into sub-subheadings, each of which has its own HTSUS classification number. For example, the 2001 HTSUS number for iron or non-alloy steel not coated or plated with metal and not clad is 7210.70.30, indicating that it is a subcategory of iron and nonalloy steel, painted, varnished, or coated with plastics (7210.70), which is a subcategory of the major heading flat-rolled products of iron or steel, of a width of 600 mm or more, clad, plated, or coated (7210). There are 29 major headings in HTSUS Chapter 72.

7201—Pig iron and spiegeleisen in pigs, blocks, or other primary forms

7202—Ferroalloys

7203—Ferrous products obtained by direct reduction of iron ore and other spongy ferrous products, in lumps, pellets or similar forms; iron having a minimum purity by weight of 99.94%, in lumps, pellets, or similar forms

7204—Ferrous waste and scrap; remelting scrap ingots of iron or steel

7205—Granules and powders, of pig iron, spiegeleisen, iron, and steel

7206—Iron and nonalloy steel in ingots or other primary forms (excluding iron of heading 7203)

7207—Semifinished products of iron or nonalloy steel

7208—Flat-rolled products of iron or nonalloy steel, of a width of 600 mm or more, hot-rolled, not clad, plated, or coated

7209—Flat-rolled products of iron or nonalloy steel, of a width of 600 mm or more, cold-rolled (cold-reduced), not clad, plated, or coated

7210—Flat-rolled products of iron or nonalloy steel, of a width of 600 mm or more, clad, plated, or coated

7211—Flat-rolled products of iron or nonalloy steel, of a width of less than 600 mm, not clad, plated, or coated

7212—Flat-rolled products of iron or nonalloy steel, of a width of less than 600 mm, clad, plated, or coated

7213—Bars and rods, hot-rolled, in irregularly wound coils, of iron or nonalloy steel

7214—Other bars and rods of iron or nonalloy steel, not further worked than forged, hot-rolled, hot-drawn, or hot-extruded, but including those twisted after rolling

7215—Other bars and rods of iron or nonalloy steel

7216—Angles, shapes, and sections of iron or nonalloy steel

7217—Wire of iron or nonalloy steel

7218—Stainless steel in ingots or other primary forms; semifinished products of stainless steel

7219—Flat-rolled products of stainless steel, of a width of 600 mm or more

7220—Flat-rolled products of stainless steel, of a width of less than 600 mm

7221—Bars and rods, hot-rolled, in irregularly wound coils, of stainless steel

7222—Other bars and rods of stainless steel; angles, shapes, and sections of stainless steel

7223—Wire of stainless steel

7224—Other alloy steel in ingots or other primary forms; semifinished products of other alloy steel

7225—Flat-rolled products of other alloy steel, of a width of 600 mm or more

7226—Flat-rolled products of other alloy steel, of a width of less than 600 mm

7227—Bars and rods, hot-rolled, in irregularly wound coils, of other alloy steel

7228—Other bars and rods of other alloy steel; angles, shapes, and sections, of other alloy steel; hollow drill bars and rods, of alloy or nonalloy steel

7229—Wire of other alloy steel

For more details regarding classification of the specific product you are interested in importing, consult a customs broker, the appropriate commodity specialist at your nearest customs port, or see HTSUS. The 2001 HTSUS is available online from the Customs Service (www.customs.gov/impoexpo/impoexpo.htm) or for purchase from the U.S. Government Printing Office (see resources at the end of this chapter), and may be found in larger public libraries. For a general discussion of customs classification, see "Classification—Liquidation" on page 229.

Dutiable Status of Goods

For more information about duty rates and binding decisions see "Dutiable Status of Goods" on page 203; for a discussion of temporary importation of goods see "Temporary Free Importations" on page 205.

Valuation

Importers have a responsibility to use what the U.S. Customs Service deems, "reasonable care," when determining the value of their goods. They must also provide any additional information that the Customs Service needs for setting a final value on the goods. This process involves a number of factors and can be somewhat complicated; importers must be aware of applicable issues and details. Valuation information applies to all types of commodities, for further discussion on the subject see "Customs Valuation" on page 267.

Import Duties

Import duties vary (often dramatically) depending upon the Harmonized Tariff Schedule (HTSUS) classification of the goods or products imported. Since some products that look alike have different HTSUS classifications and different rates of duty, proper classification is vital. Note that "differences of opinion" between importers and the Bureau of Customs and Border Protection regarding classification keeps customs attorneys very busy.

Import duties can be assessed on the imported value of the goods ("ad valorem" rates of duty such as 2%, 4.4%, 50%, etc.), total units or weight of the goods ("specific" rates of duty such as 2 cents each or 1.5 cents/pound, etc.) or on a combination basis ("compound" rates of duty such as 5 cents each plus 6%).

Listed below is a sampling of several Column 1 import duty rates for Chapter 72 products:

Nonalloy pig iron containing by weight 0.5 percent or less of phosphorus (7201.10.00.00): Free

to

Ferromanganese containing by weight not more than 1 percent of carbon (7202.19.10.00): 2.3%

For specific information on US import duties refer to the Harmonized Tariff Schedule of the US. The print version is available from the US Government Printing Office as well as third party suppliers who often add special features. Online versions are available in both static PDF pages as well as in formats with excellent search functionality. Search the Web with the term "Harmonized Tariff Schedule" to find sources.

Entry and Documentation

The entry of merchandise is a two-part process consisting of 1) filing the documents necessary to determine whether merchandise may be released from Customs custody and 2) filing the documents that contain information for duty assessment and statistical purposes. In certain instances all documents must be filed and accepted by Customs prior to the release of the goods. Unless you have been granted an extension, you must file entry documents at a location specified by the port or area director within five working days of your shipment's date of arrival at a U.S. port of entry. These include a number of standard documents required by Customs for any entry, and:

- U.S. Customs TSCA Certification when required

After you present the entry, Customs may examine your shipment, or may waive examination. The shipment is then released provided no legal or regulatory violations have been noted. You must then file entry summary documentation and deposit estimated duties at a designated customhouse within 10 working days of your shipment's release. For a detailed description of entry procedures, standard documentation, and informal entry, see "Entry Process" on page 185.

Informed Compliance. Informed compliance was introduced with the Customs Modernization Act of 1993 (Mod Act) and defines the relationship between importers and the Customs Service. It sets out the responsibilities of both parties. Providing the correct documentation and information for entry is a key factor that will make your importing operation run smoothly. We recommend that importers become familiar with the concept of informed comliance and the responsibilities that they have under the Mod Act. For further discussion about informed compliance see "Informed Compliance" on page 211.

Entry Invoice. For all products entered under HTSUS Chapter 72, a statement is required giving the percentages by weight of carbon and any other metallic elements contained in the articles. The statement must be in the form of a mill analysis or mill test certificate.

Summary Steel Invoice. The requirement that an importer submit a Special Summary Steel Invoice (**Customs Form 5520**) was removed effective April 26, 1993. No such invoice is needed. For more general information about invoices see "Invoices" on page 277.

Piping, Manhole Fittings, and Gas Cylinders. Special country of origin markings are required for iron and steel pipe and pipe fittings; manhole rings, frames, and covers; and compressed gas cylinders. These articles must be marked by die-stamping, cast-in-mold lettering, acid or electrolytic etching, or engraving.

Hazardous Substances. Shipments including any products that are classified as hazardous substances (49 CFR 172) must comply with the marking and labeling regulations adopted by the EPA (46 CFR 147.30) and the DOT (49 CFR 171 et seq.).

For a general discussion of U.S. Customs marking and labeling requirements, see "Country of Origin Marking" on page 236, "Special Marking Requirements" on page 238 and "Marking—False Impression" on page 239.

Note: The Entry and Documentation section has been carefully designed to supply you, the importer, with sample documents and directions on how to satisfy Customs requirements. Be aware that you should consult the applicable authorities to ensure that you are correctly following the most current procedures.

Shipping Considerations

You will need to ensure that your goods are packaged and shipped with care to ensure that they arrive in good condition and pass smoothly through Customs. You are responsible for ensuring that the shipment is in compliance with all applicable government regulations for packaging and shipping. In most instances, you should not leave these arrangements solely to the discretion of your supplier. Careful preparation of the cargo and selection of the mode of transport can be essential to a cost-effective, timely delivery of undamaged goods. We strongly advise you to consult your shipping representative, insurance agent, or freight broker for advice on packing and shipping.

Solid chemical products that are listed as hazardous substances (49 CFR 172 appendix) may be transported in bulk only on compliance with Coast Guard notification procedures, shipping permit requirements, and complex transportation regulations (46 CFR 148). All hazardous substances must be packaged and transported in accordance with DOT regulations (49 CFR 171 et seq.).

Iron and steel products are often heavy and bulky, and should be securely stowed to avoid damage due to shifting en route. Ferrous products are subject to corrosion, which should be guarded against, especially as no allowance is made by customs for partial damage or loss due to discoloration or rusting.

Publications and WWW Resources

The *Harmonized Tariff Schedule of the United States (2001)* (HTSUS) is available to view on the Customs Service website (www.customs.gov), or you may purchase a printed version from:

U.S. Government Printing Office
Superintendent of Documents
710 North Capital Street NW
Washington DC 20401
Tel: (202) 512-1800
Fax: (202) 512-1657
Website: www.access.gpo.gov

The USGPO also has copies of specific laws available for purchase. The USGPO accepts orders made by fax, phone or placed over the Internet, as well as mail orders paid by credit card. All orders must be accompanied by payment. Credit cards, checks drawn on a U.S. bank, or an international money order are all acceptable.

Relevant Government Agencies

Address inquiries regarding TSCA and EPA requirements for importation of hazardous or toxic substances to:

Environmental Protection Agency (EPA)
Office of Pollution Prevention and Toxics
TSCA System Information
1200 Pennsylvania Avenue NW
Washington DC 20460
Tel: (202) 564-3810
Tel: (202) 554-1404 (TSCA Information Hotline)
Email: oppt.homepage@epa.gov
Website: www.epa.gov/opptintr/contact.htm

Address questions regarding transportation of hazardous substances to:

U.S. Department of Transportation (DOT)
Research and Special Programs Administration
Hazardous Materials Information Center
400 7th St. SW
Washington DC 20590
Tel: (202) 366-4488
Website: http://hazmat.dot.gov

Address questions regarding the importation of iron and steel to your local Customs port director. For addresses refer to "U.S. Customs and Border Protection Offices" on page 65 or contact:

U.S. Customs and Border Protection
Customs Headquarters
1300 Pennsylvania Avenue NW
Washington DC 20229
Tel: (202) 354-1000
Website: www.customs.treas.gov

Laws and Regulations

The following laws and regulations may be relevant to the importation of iron and steel products. The laws are contained in the U.S. Code (USC) and the regulations are published in the code of federal Regulations (CFR), both of which may be available at larger public and law libraries. Copies of specific laws are also available from the United States Government Printing Office (address above).

15 USC 2601 et seq.
Toxic Substances Control Act
This Act authorizes the EPA to determine whether a substance is harmful and to restrict importation, sale, and use of such substances.

19 CFR 12.118 et seq.
Regulations on Toxic Substances Control
These regulations require importers of chemical substances imported in bulk or as part of a mixture to certify to Customs that the shipment complies with the TSCA or is not subject to that Act.

15 USC 1261 et seq.
Federal Hazardous Substances Act

This Act controls the importation of hazardous substances, sets forth prohibited imports, and authorizes various agencies to promulgate labeling, marking, and transport requirements.

49 CFR 171 et seq.
Regulations on Hazardous Materials
These regulations list all substances deemed hazardous and provide transport, marking, labeling, safety, and emergency response rules.

46 CFR 147.30
Regulations on Labeling of Hazardous Materials
This regulation requires the labeling of containers of hazardous substances and specifies the label contents.

46 CFR 148 et seq.
Regulations of Carriage of Solid Hazardous Materials in Bulk
These regulations govern the transport of solid hazardous substances in bulk, including reporting, permitting, loading, stowing, and shipping requirements.

Principal Exporting Countries

The following listing includes samples of the main supplier nations of the products of this chapter. It is organized by HTSUS major heading. (Refer to "Customs Classification" above for the product codes.) Countries are listed in rank order of the value of products imported to the U.S. Statistics represent customs value of entries for 2002 from the Bureau of Census, U.S. Department of Commerce.

7201—Brazil, Russia, Ukraine, Canada, South Africa, Bahamas, Hungary, Venezuela

7202—South Africa, Kazakhstan, Brazil, China, Dominican Republic, Venezuela, Norway, Canada, France, Russia

7203—Venezuela, Trinidad and Tobago, Canada, Ukraine, Mexico

7204—Canada, United Kingdom, Mexico, Sweden, Russia

7205—Canada, Sweden, Germany, Japan, China, United Kingdom, South Africa, Belgium

7206—Venezuela, Canada, Germany, China, United Kingdom, Japan, Italy, Belgium, Denmark

7207—Brazil, Mexico, Russia, Germany, Australia, Ukraine, China, Canada, Belgium

7208—Canada, South Korea, Mexico, Netherlands, Turkey, France, Australia

7209—Canada, Mexico, Japan, South Korea, Russia, Belgium, France, Netherlands, Chile, Indonesia, Turkey, El Salvador

7210—Canada, India, Mexico, South Korea, Taiwan, Germany, Brazil, Netherlands

7211—Canada, Germany, United Kingdom, Sweden, Mexico, Austria, Japan, France

7212—Canada, Mexico, Germany, Japan, Belgium, South Korea, Sweden, United Kingdom

7213—Canada, Turkey, China, Trinidad and Tobago, United Kingdom, Brazil, Japan

7214—Canada, Japan, Turkey, Mexico, Germany, Brazil, United Kingdom, Dominican Republic, Egypt

7215—Canada, United Kingdom, Spain, Germany, Russia, Ukraine, India, Japan

7216—Canada, Mexico, Poland, South Korea, United Kingdom, Luxembourg, Germany

7217—Canada, China, Japan, France, Mexico, Belgium, South Korea, South Africa

7218—Canada, Spain, India, United Kingdom, Sweden

7219—Mexico, Belgium, Canada, Taiwan, Germany, South Africa, France, Italy, Sweden, Brazil, Japan

7220—Japan, Sweden, Canada, Taiwan, Mexico, Germany, France, South Korea, Finland, Austria

7221—Taiwan, France, Italy, United Kingdom, Sweden, Spain, India, South Korea, Germany, China, Japan

7222—Italy, India, Canada, Taiwan, France, Germany

7223—South Korea, Sweden, India, Taiwan, France, Japan, China, Germany, Italy, United Kingdom, Switzerland

7224—Brazil, Mexico, Germany, Canada, Finland, France, Italy, Belgium

7225—Canada, Germany, Japan, France, Sweden, Netherlands, South Korea, Russia

7226—Germany, Canada, Sweden, France, Japan, United Kingdom, Switzerland, Austria

7227—Canada, Japan, Trinidad and Tobago, France, Sweden, Austria

7228—Canada, United Kingdom, Germany, Japan, France, Sweden, Mexico

7229—Japan, Italy, South Korea, Mexico, Canada, Germany, United Kingdom, Sweden, Taiwan, Austria

Chapter 73:
Articles of Iron and Steel

This chapter relates to the importation of articles of iron and steel, which are classified within Chapter 73 of the Harmonized Tariff Schedule of the United States (HTSUS). Specifically, it includes sheet pilings, welded angles, and similar products; railway track materials; cast iron and other steel pipes and casings, including drilling and pipeline sections; fittings; parts of architectural structures; tanks and reservoirs; containers, including those for compressed or liquefied gases; stranded wire, rope, and cable; barbed wire and other fencing wire; woven metal fabrics, including chain-link fencing and netting; chains; anchors and related items; nails, screws, nuts and bolts, and similar fasteners; needles; wound and leaf springs; stoves, ranges, and ovens—other than electric appliances; radiators and furnaces; table, kitchen, and household articles; sanitary wares, such as bathtubs and basins; and other miscellaneous articles—such as horseshoes—of iron and steel.

If you are interested in importing primary or intermediate products of iron or steel, refer to Commodity Index Chapter 72. Goods of base metals and their alloys in which metals other than iron or steel predominate in related chapters, including copper (Chapter 74), nickel (Chapter 75), aluminum (Chapter 76), lead (Chapter 78), zinc (Chapter 79), tin (Chapter 80), and other base metals (Chapter 81). Tools, other implements, and cutlery are found in Chapter 82, while miscellaneous articles of base metals—including hinges, fittings, and similar articles—are contained in Chapter 83. Precious metals, alloys of precious metals, and articles containing the same are covered specifically in Chapter 71.

Other products for which metals are incidental to use—even if critical and major components—are found within a variety of Commodity Index chapters and headings. For example, if you are interested in importing metallic paints, refer to Chapter 36. Under haberdashery, see Chapter 65 for headgear with metal elements, and Chapter 66 for umbrella frames and related items. Finished and semifinished products classified as machinery, mechanical appliances, and electrical goods are found in Chapters 84 and 85. Assembled railway track and related equipment is covered in chapter 86, vehicles in Chapter 87, aircraft in Chapter 88, and boats in Chapter 89. Instruments and apparatus are covered in Commodity Index chapters that cover the particular type of article, including optical, medical, and precision instruments (Chapter 90), clocks and watches (Chapter 91), and musical instruments (Chapter 92). Metal articles used as parts of firearms, including ammunition, are found in Chapter 93. Other chapters cover miscellaneous manufactures, including furniture and prefabricated structures (Chapter 94), toys, games, and sporting

goods (Chapter 95), and miscellaneous manufactured articles (Chapter 96). Works of art in which iron and steel are components, even dominant components, are covered in Chapter 97 if the primary value derives from the artistry rather than from the metal content.

Note: To understand key issues that will enable you to make best use of the information in this section we recommend that you see "Introduction" on page 425.

Key Factors

The key factors in the importation of articles of iron and steel are:

- For items to be used with food, compliance with U.S. Food and Drug Administration (FDA) requirements for entry notification

Although most importers utilize the services of a licensed customs broker in making their entries, and we recommend this practice, you should be aware of the regulatory, entry, and documentation issues involved in importing your product. You, as importer, are ultimately responsible for the fulfillment of any legal requirements applicable to your shipment.

General Considerations

Regulatory Agencies. Importation of articles of iron and steel products is straightforward. There are no restrictions or prohibitions. You do not need a permit or license, nor is special entry paperwork required in most cases (see "Entry and Documentation" below). The Food and Drug Administration (FDA) controls the importation of items for use with food.

Definitions. Unlike alloys of precious metals, in which any alloy having as much as 2% of a precious metal is considered an alloy of that metal, alloys of base metals are classified according to the metal that predominates by weight over every other individual metal in the alloy. For customs purposes, alloys of a metal are included with the metal that they are an alloy of. Similarly, for customs purposes, articles of iron and steel—which is processed iron—are considered to be the same metal.

Cast iron refers to products obtained by casting in which iron predominates by weight over each of the remaining elements, and that does not qualify as steel. Steel is defined as a ferrous material that is usefully malleable and contains by weight no more than 2% of carbon (chromium steels may have a higher carbon content). Stainless steel consists of alloy steels containing by weight no more than 1.2% carbon and at least 10.5% chromium. Other alloy steels include specified varying percentages of elements such as aluminum, boron, chromium, cobalt, copper, lead, manganese, molybdenum, nickel, niobium, silicon, titanium, tungsten, vanadium, zirconium, and other elements—except sulfur, phosphorus, carbon, and nitrogen. HTSUS also gives specific definitions and ranges for such products as tool steel, chipper knife steel, heat-resisting steel, and ball-bearing steel. For details, see the notes to Chapter 72 in HTSUS.

HTSUS Chapter 73 covers a wide variety of products. Many articles included in the chapter, such as bolts, nuts, and screws, are frequently utilized as parts of machines or other products. To avoid the difficulties inherent in determining whether a particular piece is a part of a particular machine or not, there is a legal definition in the HTSUS (Note 2, Section XV), which provides that parts of general use—such as nuts, bolts, screws, and springs—are always classified in their own heading rather than as a part of a particular machine or other product.

Articles Used with Food. Kitchenware and tableware of iron and steel intended for use with food are subject to the provisions of the Federal Food, Drug, and Cosmetic Act (FDCA) enforced by the FDA. Shipments of FDA-regulated products are subject to FDA port of entry inspection. For more information on FDA import procedures see "Appendix: Foods" on page 825. Contact your nearest regional FDA office or FDA headquarters with questions regarding the importation of food-related iron and steel products (see addresses at end of this chapter).

Dumping and Countervailing Duties Actions. Actions to restrict importation of or impose punitive duties on imports of certain iron and steel products from countries that are alleged to be involved in selling these products in the U.S. at below cost or the prices charged in their home country (dumping) are occasionally brought to protect the domestic steel industry. Although no such actions are currently pending, restrictions can be imposed on short notice. You should contact customs to verify the status of your proposed imports.

Customs Classification

For customs purposes, articles of iron and steel are classified within Chapter 73 of the HTSUS. This chapter is divided into major headings, which are further divided into subheadings, and often into sub-subheadings, each of which has its own HTSUS classification number. For example, the 2001 HTSUS number for iron or nonalloy steel drill pipe used to drill for oil or gas is 7314.21.30, indicating that it is a subcategory of casing, tubing, or drill pipe of a kind used in drilling for oil or gas (7304.21), which is a subcategory of the major heading tubes, pipes, and hollow profiles, seamless, of iron (other than cast iron) or steel (7304). There are 26 major headings in HTSUS Chapter 73.

7301—Sheet piling of iron or steel, whether or not drilled, punched, or made from assembled elements; welded angles, shapes, and sections of iron or steel

7302—Railway or tramway track construction material of iron or steel, including the following: rails, check-rails, and rack rails, switch blades, crossing frogs, point rods, and other crossing pieces, sleepers (cross-ties), fish-plates, chairs, chair wedges, sole plates (base plates), rail clips, bedplates, ties, and other material specialized for jointing or fixing rails

7303—Tubes, pipes, and hollow profiles of cast iron

7304—Tubes, pipes, and hollow profiles, seamless, of iron (other than cast iron) or steel

7305—Other tubes and pipes (for example, welded, riveted or similarly closed), having circular cross sections, the external diameter of which exceeds 406.4 mm, of iron or steel

7306—Other tubes, pipes, and hollow profiles (for example, open seamed or welded, riveted, or similarly closed), of iron or steel

7307—Tube or pipe fittings (for example, couplings, elbows, sleeves), of iron or steel

7308—Structures (excluding prefabricated buildings of heading 9406) and parts of structures (for example, bridges and bridge sections, lock gates, towers, lattice masts, roofs, roofing, frameworks, doors and windows and their frames and thresholds for doors, shutters, balustrades, pillars, and columns) of iron or steel; plates, rods, angles, shapes, sections, tubes, and the like, prepared for use in structures, of iron or steel

7309—Reservoirs, tanks, vats, and similar containers for any material (other than compressed or liquefied gas), of iron or steel, of a capacity exceeding 300 liters, whether or not lined or heat insulated, but not fitted with mechanical or thermal equipment

7310—Tanks, casks, drums, cans, boxes, and similar containers, for any material (other than compressed or liquefied gas), of iron or steel, of a capacity not exceeding 300 liters, whether or not lined or heat insulated, but not fitted with mechanical or thermal equipment

7311—Containers for compressed or liquefied gas, of iron or steel

7312—Stranded wire, ropes, cables, plaited bands, slings, and the like, of iron or steel, not electrically insulated

7313—Barbed wire of iron or steel; twisted hoop or single flat wire, barbed or not, and loosely twisted double wire, of a kind used for fencing, of iron or steel

7314—Cloth (including endless bands), grill, netting, and fencing, of iron or steel wire; expanded metal of iron or steel

7315—Chain and parts thereof, of iron or steel

7316—Anchors, grapnels, and parts thereof, of iron or steel

7317—Nails, tacks, drawing pins, corrugated nails, staples (other than those of heading 8305), and similar articles, of iron or steel, whether or not with heads of other material, but excluding such articles with heads of copper

7318—Screws, bolts, nuts, coach screws, screw hooks, rivets, cotters, cotter pins, washers, (including spring washers), and similar articles, of iron or steel

7319—Sewing needles, knitting needles, bodkins, crochet hooks, embroidery stilettos, and similar articles for use in the hand, of iron or steel; safety pins and other pins of iron or steel, not elsewhere specified or included

7320—Springs and leaves for springs, of iron or steel

7321—Stoves, ranges, grates, cookers (including those with subsidiary boilers for central heating), barbecues, braziers, gas rings, plate warmers, and similar nonelectric domestic appliances, and parts thereof, of iron or steel

7322—Radiators for central heating, not electrically heated, and parts thereof, of iron or steel; air heaters and hot air distributors (including distributors which can also distribute fresh or conditioned air), not electrically heated, incorporating a motor-driven fan or blower, and parts thereof, of iron or steel

7323—Table, kitchen, or other household articles and parts thereof, of iron or steel; iron or steel wool; pot scourers, and scouring or polishing pads, gloves, and the like, of iron or steel

7324—Sanitary ware and parts thereof, of iron or steel

7325—Other cast articles of iron or steel

7326—Others articles of iron or steel

For more details regarding classification of the specific product you are interested in importing, consult a customs broker, the appropriate commodity specialist at your nearest customs port, or see HTSUS. The 2001 HTSUS is available online from the Customs Service (www.customs.gov/impoexpo/impoexpo.htm) or for purchase from the U.S. Government Printing Office (see resources at the end of this chapter), and may be found in larger public libraries. For a general discussion of customs classification, see "Classification—Liquidation" on page 229.

Dutiable Status of Goods

For more information about duty rates and binding decisions see "Dutiable Status of Goods" on page 203; for a discussion of temporary importation of goods see "Temporary Free Importations" on page 205.

Valuation

Importers have a responsibility to use what the U.S. Customs Service deems, "reasonable care," when determining the value of their goods. They must also provide any additional information that the Customs Service needs for setting a final value on the goods. This process involves a number of factors and can be somewhat complicated; importers must be aware of applicable issues and details. Valuation information applies to all types of commodities, for further discussion on the subject see "Customs Valuation" on page 267.

Import Duties

Import duties vary (often dramatically) depending upon the Harmonized Tariff Schedule (HTSUS) classification of the goods or products imported. Since some products that look alike have different HTSUS classifications and different rates of duty, proper classification is vital. Note that "differences of opinion" between importers and the Bureau of Customs and Border Protection regarding classification keeps customs attorneys very busy.

Import duties can be assessed on the imported value of the goods ("ad valorem" rates of duty such as 2%, 4.4%, 50%, etc.), total units or weight of the goods ("specific" rates of duty such as 2 cents each or 1.5 cents/pound, etc.) or on a combination basis ("compound" rates of duty such as 5 cents each plus 6%).

Listed below is a sampling of several Column 1 import duty rates for Chapter 73 products:
Rails of iron or nonalloy steel (7302.10.10): Free
to
Having a wall thickness of less than 1.65 mm (7306.50.10.00): 0.8%

For specific information on US import duties refer to the Harmonized Tariff Schedule of the US. The print version is available from the US Government Printing Office as well as third party suppliers who often add special features. Online versions are available in both static PDF pages as well as in formats with excellent search functionality. Search the Web with the term "Harmonized Tariff Schedule" to find sources.

Entry and Documentation

The entry of merchandise is a two-part process consisting of 1) filing the documents necessary to determine whether merchandise may be released from Customs custody and 2) filing the documents that contain information for duty assessment and statistical purposes. In certain instances all documents must be filed and accepted by Customs prior to the release of the goods. Unless you have been granted an extension, you must file entry documents at a location specified by the port or area director within five working days of your shipment's date of arrival at a U.S. port of entry. These include a number of standard documents required by Customs for any entry.

After you present the entry, Customs may examine your shipment, or may waive examination. The shipment is then released provided no legal or regulatory violations have been noted. You must then file entry summary documentation and deposit estimated duties at a designated customhouse within 10 working days of your shipment's release. For a detailed description of entry procedures, standard documentation, and informal entry, see "Entry Process" on page 185.

Informed Compliance. Informed compliance was introduced with the Customs Modernization Act of 1993 (Mod Act) and defines the relationship between importers and the Customs Service. It sets out the responsibilities of both parties. Providing the correct documentation and information for entry is a key factor that will make your importing operation run smoothly. We recommend that importers become familiar with the concept of informed comliance and the responsibilities that they have under the Mod Act. For further discussion about informed compliance see "Informed Compliance" on page 211.

Entry Invoice for Articles of Iron or Steel. For articles entered under HTSUS headings 7301 through 7307, a statement is required giving the percentages by weight of carbon and any metallic elements contained in the articles. This must be in the form of a mill analysis or mill test certificate.

Summary Steel Invoice. The requirement that an importer submit a Special Summary Steel Invoice (**Customs Form 5520**) was removed effective April 26, 1993. No such invoice is needed. For more general information about invoices see "Invoices" on page 277.

Note: The Entry and Documentation section has been carefully designed to supply you, the importer, with sample documents and directions on how to satisfy Customs requirements. Be aware that you should consult the applicable authorities to ensure that you are correctly following the most current procedures.

Marking and Labeling Requirements

Piping, Manhole Fittings, and Gas Cylinders. Special country-of-origin marking requirements apply to certain iron and steel items covered under HTSUS Chapter 73. Iron and steel pipe and pipe fittings, manhole rings, frames or covers, and compressed gas cylinders must generally be marked by one of four methods: die-stamped, cast-in-mold lettering, etching (acid or electrolytic), or engraving. In general, the exemptions from required country-of-origin marking do not apply to iron and steel pipe and pipe fittings.

For a general discussion of U.S. Customs marking and labeling requirements, see "Country of Origin Marking" on page 236, "Special Marking Requirements" on page 238 and "Marking—False Impression" on page 239.

Shipping Considerations

You will need to ensure that your goods are packaged and shipped with care to ensure that they arrive in good condition and pass smoothly through Customs. You are responsible for ensuring that the shipment is in compliance with all applicable government regulations for packaging and shipping. In most instances, you should not leave these arrangements solely to the discretion of your supplier. Careful preparation of the cargo and selection of the mode of transport can be essential to a cost-effective, timely delivery of undamaged goods. We strongly advise you to consult your shipping representative, insurance agent, or freight broker for advice on packing and shipping.

Articles of iron and steel are often bulky and heavy, and should be securely stowed to avoid damage due to shifting en route. Articles of iron and steel are also subject to corrosion, which should be guarded against, especially as no allowance is made by customs for partial loss due to discoloration or rusting or to damage during shipping.

Publications and WWW Resources

The *Harmonized Tariff Schedule of the United States (2001)* (HTSUS) is available to view on the Customs Service website (www.customs.gov), or you may purchase a printed version from:

> **U.S. Government Printing Office**
> **Superintendent of Documents**
> 710 North Capital Street NW
> Washington DC 20401
> Tel: (202) 512-1800
> Fax: (202) 512-1657
> Website: www.access.gpo.gov

The USGPO also has copies of specific laws available for purchase. The USGPO accepts orders made by fax, phone or placed over the Internet, as well as mail orders paid by credit card. All orders must be accompanied by payment. Credit cards, checks drawn on a U.S. bank, or an international money order are all acceptable.

Relevant Government Agencies

Address questions regarding FDA requirements for iron and steel products intended for use with foods to:

> **Food and Drug Administration (FDA)**
> **Center for Food Safety and Applied Nutrition (CFSAN)**

Office of Compliance
Division of Enforcement, Imports Branch
5100 Paint Branch Parkway
College Park, MD 20740-3835
Tel: (301) 436-2080
Website: http://vm.cfsan.fda.gov/list.html

Address questions regarding the importation of articles of iron and steel to your local Customs port director. For addresses refer to "U.S. Customs and Border Protection Offices" on page 65 or contact:

U.S. Customs and Border Protection
Customs Headquarters
1300 Pennsylvania Avenue NW
Washington DC 20229
Tel: (202) 354-1000
Website: www.customs.treas.gov

Laws and Regulations

Various laws and regulations may be relevant to importing. Laws are contained in the U.S. Code (USC) and regulations are published in the Code of Federal Regulations (CFR), both of which may be available in larger public and law libraries. Copies of specific laws are also available from the United States Government Printing Office (address above).

21 USC 301 et seq.
Federal Food, Drug, and Cosmetic Act
This Act prohibits deceptive practices and regulates the manufacture, sale and importation or exportation of food, drugs, cosmetics, and related products. It was amended by the Food Quality Protection Act of 1996. See 21 USC 331, 381, 382.

19 CFR 12.1 et seq.; 21 CFR 1.83 et seq.
Regulations on Food, Drugs, and Cosmetics
These regulations of the Secretary of Health and Human Services and the Secretary of the Treasury govern the standards, labeling, marking, and importing of products used with food, drugs, and cosmetics.

Principal Exporting Countries

The following listing includes samples of the main supplier nations of the products of this chapter. It is organized by HTSUS major heading. (Refer to "Customs Classification" above for the product codes.) Countries are listed in rank order of the value of products imported to the U.S. Statistics represent customs value of entries for 2002 from the Bureau of Census, U.S. Department of Commerce.

7301—Luxembourg, Canada, Germany, United Kingdom, Japan, Italy

7302—Japan, Canada, Russia, France, Australia, Ukraine, United Kingdom, Germany

7303—China, Canada, Venezuela, Switzerland, India, Spain

7304—Japan, Germany, France, China, Canada, Austria, Spain

7305—Japan, Canada, United Kingdom, Germany, South Korea, Brazil

7306—Canada, Mexico, South Korea, Japan, Taiwan, Turkey, India, Thailand, Venezuela, Germany

7307—China, Mexico, Canada, Italy, India, Taiwan, South Korea, Japan, Germany

7308—Canada, Mexico, China, United Kingdom, Germany, South Korea

7309—Canada, Japan, South Korea, Italy, Mexico, Germany, United Kingdom

7310—Canada, Mexico, China, Germany, United Kingdom, Japan, Denmark, Italy

7311—Canada, Mexico, Portugal, China, Thailand, Italy, Israel, South Korea

7312—South Korea, Japan, Canada, Mexico, United Kingdom, China, France, Italy, Germany

7313—Mexico, Brazil, New Zealand, Canada, Australia, China, South Africa, Spain, India, Germany

7314—Mexico, China, Canada, Germany, Switzerland, South Korea, Japan, Taiwan

7315—Japan, China, Germany, Taiwan, Canada, Italy, United Kingdom, France

7316—China, Germany, Taiwan, Mexico, United Kingdom, Argentina, Denmark, Canada, Sweden, Hong Kong, Netherlands, Norway

7317—South Korea, China, Taiwan, Canada, Mexico, United Arab Emirates, Liechtenstein, Austria

7318—Taiwan, Japan, Canada, China, Germany, United Kingdom, Italy, South Korea

7319—China, Malaysia, Japan, Taiwan, United Kingdom, Germany, India, Czech Republic, South Korea, Canada

7320—China, Malaysia, Japan, Taiwan, United Kingdom, Germany, India, Czech Republic

7321—China, Mexico, Canada, Taiwan, South Korea, Japan, Australia, Hong Kong, Netherlands, Germany, Spain, Norway

7322—Canada, Mexico, South Korea, Japan, Germany, China, United Kingdom

7323—China, Taiwan, India, Thailand, South Korea, Indonesia, Italy, Mexico, France, Hong Kong, Germany

7324—China, Taiwan, Canada, Germany, Switzerland, South Korea, Italy, Portugal, Mexico, Spain, Sweden

7325—China, India, Canada, Mexico, Brazil, United Kingdom, Taiwan

7326—China, Canada, Mexico, Taiwan, Germany, Japan, Italy

Chapter 74:
Copper and Articles Thereof

This section pertains to the importation of copper, copper alloys, and articles made from these products, which are classified within Chapter 74 of the Harmonized Tariff Schedule of the United States (HTSUS). Specifically, it includes copper mattes and other forms of unrefined copper; refined copper and copper alloys—including brass, bronze, cupro-nickel, and nickel-silver, among others; copper waste and scrap; master alloys of copper—including those of phosphorus and beryllium; powder and flakes; bars, rods, wire, plates, sheets, strips, and foil; copper tubes, pipes, and fittings; stranded wire cables; woven copper fabrics; nails and other fasteners; springs; heating apparatus; pots and other kitchen, table, and housewares; and miscellaneous articles of copper, such as chain, brass plumbing goods, and containers.

Goods of base metals in which metals other than copper predominate are covered in the Commodity Index chapters on the particular metal, including iron and steel (Chapter 72), nickel (Chapter 75), aluminum (Chapter 76), lead (Chapter 78), zinc (Chapter 79), tin (Chapter 80), and other base metals (Chapter 81). Tools, other implements, and cutlery are found in Chapter 82, while miscellaneous articles of base metals are contained in Chapter 83. Precious metals, alloys of precious metals, and articles containing the same are covered specifically in Chapter 71.

Other products for which metals are incidental—even if critical and major—components are found within a variety of Commodity Index chapters. For example, if you are interested in importing metallic paints, refer to Chapter 36. For headgear with metal elements, see Chapter 65; for umbrella frames and related items, see Chapter 66. Finished and semifinished products classified as machinery, mechanical appliances, and electrical goods are found in Chapters 84 and 85. Assembled railway track and related equipment is covered in Chapter 86, vehicles in Chapter 87, aircraft in Chapter 88, and boats in Chapter 89. Instruments and apparatus are covered in Commodity Index chapters specific to the type of article, including optical, medical, and precision instruments (Chapter 90), clocks and watches (Chapter 91), and musical instruments (Chapter 92). Metal articles as parts of firearms, including ammunition, are found in Chapter 93. Commodity Index chapters that cover miscellaneous manufactures include furniture (Chapter 94), toys, games, and sporting goods (Chapter 95), and miscellaneous manufactured articles (Chapter 96). Works of art in which copper or its alloys are components, even dominant components, are covered in Chapter 97 if the primary value derives from the artistry rather than from the metal content.

Note: To understand key issues that will enable you to make best use of the information in this section we recommend that you see "Introduction" on page 425.

Key Factors

The key factors in importing copper and copper alloy products are:

- Compliance with U.S. Environmental Protection Agency (EPA) requirements under the Toxic Substances Control Act (TSCA) (if the product is classified as a hazardous substance)

- Compliance with U.S. Department of Transportation (DOT) regulations for transport of hazardous cargo (if the product is a hazardous substance)

- For items to be used with food, compliance with U.S. Food and Drug Administration (FDA) requirements and entry notification

Although most importers utilize the services of a licensed customs broker in making their entries, and we recommend this practice, you should be aware of the regulatory, entry, and documentation issues involved in importing your product. You, as importer, are ultimately responsible for the fulfillment of any legal requirements applicable to your shipment.

General Considerations

Regulatory Agencies. The importation of copper, copper alloys, and products made of them is relatively straightforward, with few restrictions or special requirements. The Food and Drug Administration (FDA) controls the importation of items for use with food. The Environmental Protection Agency (EPA), under authority of the Toxic Substances Control Act (TSCA), imposes certain controls on the importation of copper and copper articles that contain toxic substances. The Department of Transportation (DOT) enforces regulations for transporting hazardous cargo.

Definitions. Unlike alloys of precious metals, in which any alloy having as much as 2% of a precious metal is considered an alloy of that metal, alloys of base metals are classified according to the metal that predominates by weight over every other individual metal in the alloy. For customs purposes, alloys of a metal are included with the metal that they are an alloy of.

Chapter 74 of HTSUS covers copper and copper alloys. Refined copper is defined as metal containing at least 99.85% by weight of copper or metal containing at least 97.5% by weight of copper, provided that the content by weight of any other element does not exceed specified limits as set out in the notes to the chapter. Copper alloys are defined as being metallic substances other than unrefined copper in which copper predominates by weight over each of the other elements, provided that the content by weight of at least one of the other elements is greater than the limit specified in the notes to HTSUS Chapter 74 or the total content by weight of such other elements exceeds 2.5%. There are also specific definitions for copper-zinc base alloys (brass), copper-tin base alloys (bronze), copper-nickel-zinc base alloys (nickel silver) and copper-nickel (cupro-nickel) base alloys.

FDA Regulations. Kitchenware and tableware of copper and its alloys intended for use with food are subject to the provisions of the Federal Food, Drug, and Cosmetic Act (FDCA) enforced by the FDA. FDA entry notification is required for applicable items. Shipments of FDA-regulated products are subject to FDA port of entry inspection. For more information regarding FDA entry procedures and requirements see "Appendix: Foods" on page 825. Contact your nearest regional FDA office or FDA headquarters with questions regarding the importation of food-related copper products (see addresses at end of this chapter).

Hazardous Substances Regulations. The EPA imposes certain controls on the importation of toxic substances. The TSCA defines a toxic substance as any substance determined to present the possibility of an unreasonable risk of injury to health and the environment. The DOT enforces regulations for transporting hazardous cargo. Substances are deemed hazardous if listed in DOT transport regulations (49 CFR 172 appendix). Unwrought primary metals, such as pigs, ingots, billets, blooms, and similar materials, are generally categorized as toxic substances within the definitions of the TSCA and thus are required to be in compliance with its provisions. These include packaging, shipping, marking, and labeling requirements. Refer to "Laws and Regulations" below.

Products defined as articles—that is, any manufactured item 1) that is formed into a specific shape or design during manufacture, 2) that has end-use functions dependent on the shape or design during end use, and 3) that during the end use, does not change in its chemical composition or that changes only for a noncommercial purpose separate from the article and only as allowed by law (19 CFR 12.120(2))—are not subject to the provisions of the TSCA. Metal products other than primary metals are generally considered to be articles even if they are to be further processed. For example, copper in sheets is an article even if it is to be subsequently fabricated into other products.

Certification. All products covered by the TSCA are subject to the U.S. Customs Service TSCA Import Certification Rule (19 CFR 12.118 et seq.). If you import these products, you must sign one of the following statements: "I certify that all materials in this shipment comply with all applicable rules or orders under TSCA and that I am not offering a chemical substance for entry in violation of TSCA or any applicable rule or order thereunder" or "I certify that all materials in this shipment are not subject to TSCA." You must file this TSCA certification of compliance or exemption at the time you make the entry at customs. Customs will not release your shipment without proper certification.

If you will be importing several or regular shipments, you should ask the appropriate Customs port director to authorize your use of a blanket certification. A blanket certification is valid for one calendar year, may be renewed, and may be revoked at any time for cause.

Customs Classification

For customs purposes, copper, copper alloys, and their products are classified within Chapter 74 of the HTSUS. This chapter is divided into headings, which are further divided into subheadings, and often into sub-subheadings, each of which has its own HTSUS classification number. For example, the 2001 HTSUS number for low fuming brazing rods of copper is 7407.21.50, indicating that it is a subcategory of rods of copper-zinc base alloys (brass) (7407.21), which is a subsubcategory of the major heading copper bars, rods, and profiles (7407). There are 19 major headings in HTSUS Chapter 74.

7401—Copper mattes; cement copper (precipitated copper)

7402—Unrefined copper; copper anodes for electrolytic refining

7403—Refined copper and copper alloys, unwrought (other than master alloys of heading 7405)

7404—Copper waste and scrap

7405—Master alloys of copper

7406—Copper powders and flakes

7407—Copper bars, rods, and profiles

7408—Copper wire

7409—Copper plates, sheets, and strip, of a thickness exceeding 0.15 mm.

7410—Copper foil (whether or not printed or backed with paper, paperboard, plastics, or similar backing materials) of a thickness (excluding any backing) not exceeding 0.15 mm.

7411—Copper tubes and pipes

7412—Copper tube or pipe fittings (for example couplings, elbows, sleeves)

7413—Stranded wire, cables, plaited bands, and the like, including slings and similar articles, of copper, not electrically insulated

7414—Cloth (including endless bands), grill, and netting, of copper wire; expanded metal of copper

7415—Nails, tacks, drawing pins, staples (other than those of heading 8305), and similar articles of copper or of iron or steel with heads of copper; screws, bolts, nuts, screw hooks, rivets, cotters, cotter pins, washers (including spring washers), and similar articles of copper

7416—Copper springs

7417—Cooking or heating apparatus of a kind used for domestic purposes, non-electric, and parts thereof, of copper

7418—Table, kitchen, or other household articles and parts thereof, of copper; pot scourers and scouring or polishing pads, gloves, and the like, of copper; sanitary ware and parts thereof, of copper

7419—Other articles of copper

For more details regarding classification of the specific product you are interested in importing, consult a customs broker, the appropriate commodity specialist at your nearest customs port, or see HTSUS. The 2001 HTSUS is available online from the Customs Service (www.customs.gov/impoexpo/impoexpo.htm) or for purchase from the U.S. Government Printing Office (see resources at the end of this chapter), and may be found in larger public libraries. For a general discussion of customs classification, see "Classification—Liquidation" on page 229.

Dutiable Status of Goods

For more information about duty rates and binding decisions see "Dutiable Status of Goods" on page 203; for a discussion of temporary importation of goods see "Temporary Free Importations" on page 205.

Valuation

Importers have a responsibility to use what the U.S. Customs Service deems, "reasonable care," when determining the value of their goods. They must also provide any additional information that the Customs Service needs for setting a final value on the goods. This process involves a number of factors and can be somewhat complicated; importers must be aware of applicable issues and details. Valuation information applies to all types of commodities, for further discussion on the subject see "Customs Valuation" on page 267.

Import Duties

Import duties vary (often dramatically) depending upon the Harmonized Tariff Schedule (HTSUS) classification of the goods or products imported. Since some products that look alike have different HTSUS classifications and different rates of duty, proper classification is vital. Note that "differences of opinion" between importers and the Bureau of Customs and Border Protection regarding classification keeps customs attorneys very busy.

Import duties can be assessed on the imported value of the goods ("ad valorem" rates of duty such as 2%, 4.4%, 50%, etc.), total units or weight of the goods ("specific" rates of duty such as 2 cents each or 1.5 cents/pound, etc.) or on a combination basis ("compound" rates of duty such as 5 cents each plus 6%).

Listed below is a sampling of several Column 1 import duty rates for Chapter 74 products:

Fourdrinier wires, seamed or not seamed, suitable for use in papermaking machines with 94 or more wires to the lineal centimeter (7414.20.30.00): Free

to

Not fitted with fittings and not made up into articles: Stranded wire (7413.00.10.00): 3%

For specific information on US import duties refer to the Harmonized Tariff Schedule of the US. The print version is available from the US Government Printing Office as well as third party suppliers who often add special features. Online versions are available in both static PDF pages as well as in formats with excellent search functionality. Search the Web with the term "Harmonized Tariff Schedule" to find sources.

Entry and Documentation

The entry of merchandise is a two-part process consisting of 1) filing the documents necessary to determine whether merchandise may be released from Customs custody and 2) filing the documents that contain information for duty assessment and statistical purposes. In certain instances all documents must be filed and accepted by Customs prior to the release of the goods. Unless you have been granted an extension, you must file entry documents at a location specified by the port or area director within five working days of your shipment's date of arrival at a U.S. port of entry. These include a number of standard documents required by Customs for any entry, and

- U.S. Customs TSCA Certification when required

After you present the entry, Customs may examine your shipment, or may waive examination. The shipment is then released provided no legal or regulatory violations have been noted. You must then file entry summary documentation and deposit estimated duties at a designated customhouse within 10 working days of your shipment's release. For a detailed description of entry procedures, standard documentation, and informal entry, see "Entry Process" on page 185.

Informed Compliance. Informed compliance was introduced with the Customs Modernization Act of 1993 (Mod Act) and defines the relationship between importers and the Customs Service. It sets out the responsibilities of both parties. Providing the correct documentation and information for entry is a key factor that will make your importing operation run smoothly. We recommend that importers become familiar with the concept of informed comliance and the responsibilities that they have under the Mod Act. For further discussion about informed compliance see "Informed Compliance" on page 211.

Entry Invoice. For articles of copper entered under HTSUS Heading 7401, the entry invoice must state the percentage—by weight—of copper content and of any other metallic elements. For more general information about invoices see "Invoices" on page 277.

Note: The Entry and Documentation section has been carefully designed to supply you, the importer, with sample documents and directions on how to satisfy Customs requirements. Be aware that you should consult the applicable authorities to ensure that you are correctly following the most current procedures.

Marking and Labeling Requirements

For a general discussion of U.S. Customs marking and labeling requirements, see "Country of Origin Marking" on page 236, "Special Marking Requirements" on page 238 and "Marking— False Impression" on page 239.

Shipping Considerations

You will need to ensure that your goods are packaged and shipped with care to ensure that they arrive in good condition and pass smoothly through Customs. You are responsible for ensuring that the shipment is in compliance with all applicable government regulations for packaging and shipping. In most instances, you should not leave these arrangements solely to the discretion of your supplier. Careful preparation of the cargo and selection of the mode of transport can be essential to a cost-effective, timely delivery of undamaged goods. We strongly advise you to consult your shipping representative, insurance agent, or freight broker for advice on packing and shipping.

Products that are listed as hazardous substances (49 CFR 172 appendix) may be transported in bulk only on compliance with Coast Guard notification procedures, shipping permit requirements, and complex transportation regulations (46 CFR 148). All hazardous substances must be packaged and transported in accordance with DOT regulations (49 CFR 171 et seq.).

Copper, copper alloys, and products made of them are often bulky and heavy, and should be securely stowed to avoid damage due to shifting en route. Copper and its products are also subject to tarnish and corrosion, which should be guarded against, especially as no allowance is made by customs for partial damage or loss due to such.

Publications and WWW Resources

The *Harmonized Tariff Schedule of the United States (2001)* (HTSUS) is available to view on the Customs Service website (www.customs.gov), or you may purchase a printed version from:

U.S. Government Printing Office
Superintendent of Documents
710 North Capital Street NW
Washington DC 20401
Tel: (202) 512-1800
Fax: (202) 512-1657
Website: www.access.gpo.gov

The USGPO also has copies of specific laws available for purchase. The USGPO accepts orders made by fax, phone or placed over the Internet, as well as mail orders paid by credit card. All orders must be accompanied by payment. Credit cards, checks drawn on a U.S. bank, or an international money order are all acceptable.

Relevant Government Agencies

Address inquiries regarding TSCA and EPA requirements for importation of hazardous or toxic substances to:

Environmental Protection Agency (EPA)
Office of Pollution Prevention and Toxics
TSCA System Information
1200 Pennsylvania Avenue NW
Washington DC 20460
Tel: (202) 564-3810
Tel: (202) 554-1404 (TSCA Information Hotline)
Email: oppt.homepage@epa.gov
Website: www.epa.gov/opptintr/contact.htm

Address questions regarding transportation of hazardous substances to:

U.S. Department of Transportation (DOT)
Research and Special Programs Administration
Hazardous Materials Information Center
400 7th St. SW
Washington DC 20590
Tel: (202) 366-4488
Website: http://hazmat.dot.gov

Address your questions regarding FDA requirements for copper products intended for use with food to:

Food and Drug Administration (FDA)
Center for Food Safety and Applied Nutrition (CFSAN)
Office of Compliance
Division of Enforcement, Imports Branch
5100 Paint Branch Parkway
College Park, MD 20740-3835
Tel: (301) 436-2080
Website: http://vm.cfsan.fda.gov/list.html

Address questions regarding the importation of copper and copper products to your local Customs port director. For addresses refer to "U.S. Customs and Border Protection Offices" on page 65 or contact:

U.S. Customs and Border Protection
Customs Headquarters
1300 Pennsylvania Avenue NW
Washington DC 20229
Tel: (202) 354-1000
Website: www.customs.treas.gov

Laws and Regulations

The following laws and regulations may be relevant to the importation of copper and copper products. The laws are contained in the U.S. Code (USC) and the regulations are published in the Code of Federal Regulations (CFR), both of which may be available at larger public and law libraries. Copies of specific laws are also available from the United States Government Printing Office (address above).

15 USC 2601 et seq.
Toxic Substances Control Act
This Act authorizes the EPA to determine whether a substance is harmful and to restrict importation, sale, and use of such substances.

19 CFR 12.118 et seq.
Regulations on Toxic Substances Control
These regulations require importers of chemical substances imported in bulk or as part of a mixture to certify to Customs that the shipment complies with the TSCA or is not subject to that Act.

15 USC 1261 et seq.
Federal Hazardous Substances Act
This Act controls the importation of hazardous substances, sets forth prohibited imports, and authorizes various agencies to promulgate labeling, marking, and transport requirements.

49 CFR 171 et seq.
Regulations on Hazardous Materials
These regulations list all substances deemed hazardous and provide transport, marking, labeling, safety, and emergency response rules.

46 CFR 147.30
Regulations on Labeling of Hazardous Materials
This regulation requires the labeling of containers of hazardous substances and specifies the label contents.

46 CFR 148 et seq.
Regulations of Carriage of Solid Hazardous Materials in Bulk
These regulations govern the transport of solid hazardous substances in bulk, including reporting, permitting, loading, stowing, and shipping requirements.

21 USC 301 et seq.
Federal Food, Drug, and Cosmetic Act
This Act prohibits deceptive practices and regulates the manufacture, sale and importation or exportation of food, drugs, cosmetics, and related products. It was amended by the Food Quality Protection Act of 1996. See 21 USC 331, 381, 382.

19 CFR 12.1 et seq.; 21 CFR 1.83 et seq.
Regulations on Food, Drugs, and Cosmetics
These regulations of the Secretary of Health and Human Services and the Secretary of the Treasury govern the standards, labeling, marking, and importing of products used with food, drugs, and cosmetics.

Principal Exporting Countries

The following listing includes samples of the main supplier nations of the products of this chapter. It is organized by HTSUS major heading. (Refer to "Customs Classification" above for the product codes.) Countries are listed in rank order of the value of products imported to the U.S. Statistics represent customs value

of entries for 2002 from the Bureau of Census, U.S. Department of Commerce.

7401—Chile, Mexico, Japan, China, Canada

7402—Canada, Chile, Mexico, Namibia, Peru

7403—Chile, Peru, Canada, Mexico, Brazil, Russia, Japan

7404—Canada, Mexico, United Kingdom, Germany, Guatemala, Dominican Republic, Venezuela, Honduras, Costa Rica, Philippines

7405—Kazakhstan, Japan, Belgium, Germany, China, Italy

7406—United Kingdom, Germany, Japan, Italy, France, China, Canada, Belgium

7407—Russia, Canada, Germany, France, United Kingdom, Peru, South Korea, Poland, Australia

7408—Canada, Mexico, Brazil, Russia, Germany, Japan, Turkey

7409—Germany, Japan, Netherlands, Mexico, Italy, Poland, Canada, Chile, Spain, Switzerland

7410—Japan, Sweden, Taiwan, China, Luxembourg, Netherlands, Germany, United Kingdom, Canada

7411—Mexico, Canada, Germany, Japan, Malaysia, China, South Korea, Greece, France, United Kingdom

7412—Canada, Mexico, China, Taiwan, Italy, Thailand, United Kingdom, Germany

7413—Israel, Canada, Germany, Turkey

7414—Germany, China, United Kingdom, Japan, France, Switzerland, Netherlands

7415—Taiwan, China, Germany, Canada, Switzerland, Japan, India

7416—Taiwan, China, Germany, Canada, Switzerland, Japan, India

7417—Taiwan, China, Germany, Canada, Switzerland, Japan, India

7418—China, India, Taiwan, United Kingdom, Italy, South Korea, France, Thailand, Germany

7419—China, Taiwan, Canada, India, Thailand, Italy, Germany

Chapter 75:
Nickel and Articles Thereof

This section pertains to the importation of nickel, nickel alloys, and articles made from these products, which are classified within Chapter 75 of the Harmonized Tariff Schedule of the United States (HTSUS). Specifically, it includes nickel mattes and other intermediate forms of nickel; unwrought nickel and nickel alloys; nickel waste and scrap; powder and flakes; bars, rods, profiles, wire, plates, sheets, strips, and foil; nickel tubes, pipes, and fittings; and other miscellaneous articles of nickel.

Goods of base metals and their alloys in which metals other than nickel predominate are covered in Commodity Index chapters on the specific metals, including iron and steel (Chapter 72), copper (Chapter 74), aluminum (Chapter 76), lead (Chapter 78), zinc (Chapter 79), tin (Chapter 80), and other base metals (Chapter 81). Tools, other implements, and cutlery are found in Chapter 82, while miscellaneous articles of base metals are contained in Chapter 83. Precious metals, alloys of precious metals, and articles containing the same are covered specifically in Chapter 71.

Other products for which metals are incidental—even if critical and major—components are found within a variety of Commodity Index chapters. For example, if you are interested in importing metallic paints, refer to Chapter 36. For headgear with metal elements, see Chapter 65; for umbrella frames and related items, see Chapter 66. Finished and semifinished products classified as machinery, mechanical appliances, and electrical goods are found in Chapters 84 and 85. Assembled railway track and related equipment is covered in chapter 86, vehicles in Chapter 87, aircraft in Chapter 88, and boats in Chapter 89. Instruments and apparatus are covered in Commodity Index chapters related to the specific articles, including optical, medical, and precision instruments (Chapter 90), clocks and watches (Chapter 91), and musical instruments (Chapter 92). Metal articles as parts of firearms, including ammunition, are found in Chapter 93. Commodity Index chapters that cover miscellaneous manufactures include furniture (Chapter 94), toys, games, and sporting goods (Chapter 95), and miscellaneous manufactured articles (Chapter 96). Works of art in which nickel or its alloys are components, even dominant components, are covered in Chapter 97 if the primary value derives from the artistry rather than from the metal content.

Note: To understand key issues that will enable you to make best use of the information in this section we recommend that you see "Introduction" on page 425.

Key Factors
The key factors in importing nickel and nickel alloy products are:
- Compliance with U.S. Environmental Protection

Agency (EPA) requirements under the Toxic Substances Control Act (TSCA) (if the product is classified as a hazardous substance)
- Compliance with U.S. Department of Transportation (DOT) regulations for transport of hazardous cargo (if the product is a hazardous substance)

Although most importers utilize the services of a licensed customs broker in making their entries, and we recommend this practice, you should be aware of the regulatory, entry, and documentation issues involved in importing your product. You, as importer, are ultimately responsible for the fulfillment of any legal requirements applicable to your shipment.

General Considerations
Regulatory Agencies. The importation of nickel, nickel alloys, and products made of them is relatively straightforward, with few restrictions or special requirements. The Environmental Protection Agency (EPA), under authority of the Toxic Substances Control Act (TSCA), imposes certain controls on the importation of nickel and nickel articles that contain toxic substances. The Department of Transportation (DOT) enforces regulations for transporting hazardous cargo.

Definitions. Unlike alloys of precious metals, in which any alloy containing as much as 2% by weight of a precious metal is considered an alloy of that metal, alloys of base metals are classified according to the metal that predominates by weight over every other individual metal in the alloy. For customs purposes, alloys of a metal are included with the metal that they are an alloy of.

Chapter 75 of HTSUS covers nickel and nickel alloys. Nickel is defined as metal containing at least 99% by weight of nickel plus cobalt, provided the cobalt content does not exceed 1.5% by weight and the content by weight is less than 0.5% for iron, 0.4% for oxygen, and 0.3% individually for any other elements. Nickel alloys are defined as being metallic substances in which nickel predominates by weight, provided that the content by weight of cobalt exceeds 1.5%, the content of at least one of the other elements is greater than the limit specified above, or the total content by weight of such other elements other than nickel and cobalt exceeds 1%.

Hazardous Substances Regulations. The EPA imposes certain controls on the importation of toxic substances. The TSCA defines a toxic substance as any substance determined to present the possibility of an unreasonable risk of injury to health and the environment. The DOT enforces regulations for transporting hazardous cargo. Substances are deemed hazardous if listed in DOT transport regulations (49 CFR 172 appendix). Unwrought primary metals, such as pigs, ingots, billets, blooms, and similar materials, are generally categorized as toxic substances within the definitions of the TSCA and thus are required to be in compliance with its provisions. These include packaging, shipping, marking, and labeling requirements. Refer to "Laws and Regulations" below.

Products defined as articles—that is, any manufactured item 1) that is formed into a specific shape or design during manufacture, 2) that has end-use functions dependent on the shape or design during end use, and 3) that during the end use, does not change in its chemical composition or that changes only for a noncommercial purpose separate from the article and only as allowed by law (19 CFR 12.120(2))—are not subject to the provisions of the TSCA. Metal products other than primary metals are generally considered to be articles even if they are to be further processed. For example, nickel in bars is an article even if it is to be subsequently fabricated into other products.

Certification. All products covered by the TSCA are subject to the U.S. Customs Service TSCA Import Certification Rule (19 CFR 12.118 et seq.). If you import these products, you must sign one of the following statements: "I certify that all materials in this shipment comply with all applicable rules or orders under TSCA and that I am not offering a chemical substance for entry in violation of TSCA or any applicable rule or order thereunder" or "I certify that all materials in this shipment are not subject to TSCA." You must file this TSCA certification of compliance or exemption at the time you make the entry at customs. Customs will not release your shipment without proper certification.

If you will be importing several or regular shipments, you should ask the appropriate customs port director to authorize your use of a blanket certification. A blanket certification is valid for one calendar year, may be renewed, and may be revoked at any time for cause.

Customs Classification

For customs purposes, nickel, nickel alloys, and their products are classified within Chapter 75 of the HTSUS. This chapter is divided into headings, which are further divided into subheadings, and often into sub-subheadings, each of which has its own HTSUS classification number. For example, the 2001 HTSUS number for cold-formed bars is 7505.12.10, indicating that it is a subcategory of bars and rods of nickel alloy (7405.12), which is a subsubcategory of the major heading nickel bars, rods, profiles, and wire (7405). There are eight major headings in HTSUS Chapter 75.

7501—Nickel mattes, nickel oxide sinters, and other intermediate products of nickel metallurgy

7502—Unwrought nickel

7503—Nickel waste and scrap

7504—Nickel powders and flakes

7505—Nickel bars, rods, profiles, and wire

7506—Nickel plates, sheets, strip, and foil

7507—Nickel tubes, pipes, and tube or pipe fittings (for example, couplings, elbows, sleeves)

7508—Other articles of nickel

For more details regarding classification of the specific product you are interested in importing, consult a customs broker, the appropriate commodity specialist at your nearest customs port, or see HTSUS. The 2001 HTSUS is available online from the Customs Service (www.customs.gov/impoexpo/impoexpo.htm) or for purchase from the U.S. Government Printing Office (see resources at the end of this chapter), and may be found in larger public libraries. For a general discussion of customs classification, see "Classification—Liquidation" on page 229.

Dutiable Status of Goods

For more information about duty rates and binding decisions see "Dutiable Status of Goods" on page 203; for a discussion of temporary importation of goods see "Temporary Free Importations" on page 205.

Valuation

Importers have a responsibility to use what the U.S. Customs Service deems, "reasonable care," when determining the value of their goods. They must also provide any additional information that the Customs Service needs for setting a final value on the goods. This process involves a number of factors and can be somewhat complicated; importers must be aware of applicable issues and details. Valuation information applies to all types of commodities, for further discussion on the subject see "Customs Valuation" on page 267.

Import Duties

Import duties vary (often dramatically) depending upon the Harmonized Tariff Schedule (HTSUS) classification of the goods or products imported. Since some products that look alike have different HTSUS classifications and different rates of duty, proper classification is vital. Note that "differences of opinion" between importers and the Bureau of Customs and Border Protection regarding classification keeps customs attorneys very busy.

Import duties can be assessed on the imported value of the goods ("ad valorem" rates of duty such as 2%, 4.4%, 50%, etc.), to-tal units or weight of the goods ("specific" rates of duty such as 2 cents each or 1.5 cents/pound, etc.) or on a combination basis ("compound" rates of duty such as 5 cents each plus 6%).

Listed below is a sampling of several Column 1 import duty rates for Chapter 75 products:
Nickel oxide sinters and other intermediate products of nickel metallurgy (7501.20.00.00): Free
to
Other articles of nickel; Cloth, grill and netting, of nickel wire (7508.10.00.00): 3%

For specific information on US import duties refer to the Harmonized Tariff Schedule of the US. The print version is available from the US Government Printing Office as well as third party suppliers who often add special features. Online versions are available in both static PDF pages as well as in formats with excellent search functionality. Search the Web with the term "Harmonized Tariff Schedule" to find sources.

Entry and Documentation

The entry of merchandise is a two-part process consisting of 1) filing the documents necessary to determine whether merchandise may be released from Customs custody and 2) filing the documents that contain information for duty assessment and statistical purposes. In certain instances all documents must be filed and accepted by Customs prior to the release of the goods. Unless you have been granted an extension, you must file entry documents at a location specified by the district/area director within five working days of your shipment's date of arrival at a U.S. port of entry. These include a number of standard documents required by Customs for any entry, and

- U.S. Customs TSCA Certification, if required

After you present the entry, Customs may examine your shipment, or may waive examination. The shipment is then released provided no legal or regulatory violations have been noted. You must then file entry summary documentation and deposit estimated duties at a designated customhouse within 10 working days of your shipment's release. For a detailed description of entry procedures, standard documentation, and informal entry, see "Entry Process" on page 185.

Informed Compliance. Informed compliance was introduced with the Customs Modernization Act of 1993 (Mod Act) and defines the relationship between importers and the Customs Service. It sets out the responsibilities of both parties. Providing the correct documentation and information for entry is a key factor that will make your importing operation run smoothly. We recommend that importers become familiar with the concept of informed comliance and the responsibilities that they have under the Mod Act. For further discussion about informed compliance see "Informed Compliance" on page 211.

Note: The Entry and Documentation section has been carefully designed to supply you, the importer, with sample documents and directions on how to satisfy Customs requirements. Be aware that you should consult the applicable authorities to ensure that you are correctly following the most current procedures.

Marking and Labeling Requirements

For a general discussion of U.S. Customs marking and labeling requirements, see "Country of Origin Marking" on page 236, "Special Marking Requirements" on page 238 and "Marking—False Impression" on page 239.

Shipping Considerations

You will need to ensure that your goods are packaged and shipped with care to ensure that they arrive in good condition and pass smoothly through Customs. You are responsible for ensuring that the shipment is in compliance with all applicable government regulations for packaging and shipping. In most instances, you should not leave these arrangements solely to the discretion of your supplier. Careful preparation of the cargo and selection of the mode of transport can be essential to a cost-effective, timely delivery of undamaged goods. We strongly advise you to consult your shipping representative, insurance agent, or freight broker for advice on packing and shipping.

Products that are listed as hazardous substances (49 CFR 172 appendix) may be transported in bulk only on compliance with Coast Guard notification procedures, shipping permit requirements, and complex transportation regulations (46 CFR 148). All hazardous substances must be packaged and transported in accordance with DOT regulations (49 CFR 171 et seq.).

Nickel, nickel alloy, and products made of them are often bulky and heavy, and should be securely stowed to avoid damage due to shifting en route. Nickel and its products are also subject to tarnish and corrosion, which should be guarded against, especially as no allowance is made by customs for partial damage or loss due to such.

Publications and WWW Resources

The *Harmonized Tariff Schedule of the United States (2001)* (HTSUS) is available to view on the Customs Service website (www.customs.gov), or you may purchase a printed version from:

U.S. Government Printing Office
Superintendent of Documents
710 North Capital Street NW
Washington DC 20401
Tel: (202) 512-1800
Fax: (202) 512-1657
Website: www.access.gpo.gov

The USGPO also has copies of specific laws available for purchase. The USGPO accepts orders made by fax, phone or placed over the Internet, as well as mail orders paid by credit card. All orders must be accompanied by payment. Credit cards, checks drawn on a U.S. bank, or an international money order are all acceptable.

Relevant Government Agencies

Address inquiries regarding TSCA and EPA requirements for importation of hazardous or toxic substances to:

Environmental Protection Agency (EPA)
Office of Pollution Prevention and Toxics
TSCA System Information
1200 Pennsylvania Avenue NW
Washington DC 20460
Tel: (202) 564-3810
Tel: (202) 554-1404 (TSCA Information Hotline)
Email: oppt.homepage@epa.gov
Website: www.epa.gov/opptintr/contact.htm

Address questions regarding transportation of hazardous substances to:

U.S. Department of Transportation (DOT)
Research and Special Programs Administration
Hazardous Materials Information Center
400 7th St. SW
Washington DC 20590
Tel: (202) 366-4488
Website: http://hazmat.dot.gov

Address questions regarding the importation of nickel and nickel products to your local Customs port director. For addresses refer to "U.S. Customs and Border Protection Offices" on page 65 or contact:

U.S. Customs and Border Protection
Customs Headquarters
1300 Pennsylvania Avenue NW
Washington DC 20229
Tel: (202) 354-1000
Website: www.customs.treas.gov

Laws and Regulations

The following laws and regulations may be relevant to the importation of nickel and nickel products. The laws are contained in the U.S. Code (USC) and the regulations are published in the Code of Federal Regulations (CFR), both of which may be available at larger public and law libraries. Copies of specific laws are also available from the United States Government Printing Office (address above).

15 USC 2601 et seq.
Toxic Substances Control Act
This Act authorizes the EPA to determine whether a substance is harmful and to restrict importation, sale, and use of such substances.

19 CFR 12.118 et seq.
Regulations on Toxic Substances Control
These regulations require importers of chemical substances imported in bulk or as part of a mixture to certify to Customs that the shipment complies with the TSCA or is not subject to that Act.

15 USC 1261 et seq.
Federal Hazardous Substances Act
This Act controls the importation of hazardous substances, sets forth prohibited imports, and authorizes various agencies to promulgate labeling, marking, and transport requirements.

49 CFR 171 et seq.
Regulations on Hazardous Materials
These regulations list all substances deemed hazardous and provide transport, marking, labeling, safety, and emergency response rules.

46 CFR 147.30
Regulations on Labeling of Hazardous Materials
This regulation requires the labeling of containers of hazardous substances and specifies the label contents.

46 CFR 148 et seq.
Regulations of Carriage of Solid Hazardous Materials in Bulk
These regulations govern the transport of solid hazardous substances in bulk, including reporting, permitting, loading, stowing, and shipping requirements.

Principal Exporting Countries

The following listing includes samples of the main supplier nations of the products of this chapter. It is organized by HTSUS major heading. (Refer to "Customs Classification" above for the product codes.) Countries are listed in rank order of the value of products imported to the U.S. Statistics represent customs value of entries for 2002 from the Bureau of Census, U.S. Department of Commerce.

7501—Canada, Australia, Japan, United Kingdom

7502—Canada, Russia, Australia, Norway, Finland

7503—France, United Kingdom, Canada, Germany, Israel, Argentina, Turkey, Belgium

7504—Canada, Australia, Japan, Finland, Russia, Germany, United Kingdom, Sweden

7505—Germany, Sweden, France, United Kingdom, Italy, Austria, Japan

7506—Germany, Japan, United Kingdom, Sweden, France, Canada, South Korea, India

7507—Japan, Germany, France, United Kingdom, Sweden, Canada, Italy

7508—Mexico, Canada, Netherlands, Switzerland, Taiwan, United Kingdom, China, Japan

Chapter 76:
Aluminium and Articles Thereof

This section pertains to the importation of aluminum, aluminum alloys, and articles made from these products, which are classified within Chapter 76 of the Harmonized Tariff Schedule of the United States (HTSUS). Specifically, it includes unwrought aluminum; aluminum waste and scrap; powder and flakes; bars, rods, wire, plates, sheets, strips, and foil; aluminum tubes, pipes, and fittings; aluminum structural elements, reservoirs, and tanks; aluminum containers, including those for pressurized gases; stranded wire cables; tableware, kitchenware, and other household articles; aluminum hardware; and miscellaneous articles of aluminum, such as ladders, venetian blinds, pipe hangars, and castings.

Goods of base metals in which metals other than aluminum predominate are covered in Commodity Index chapters specific to the type of metal, including iron and steel (Chapter 72), copper (Chapter 74), nickel (Chapter 75), lead (Chapter 78), zinc (Chapter 79), tin (Chapter 80), and other base metals (Chapter 81). Tools, other implements, and cutlery are found in Chapter 82, while miscellaneous articles of base metals are contained in Chapter 83. Precious metals, alloys of precious metals, and articles containing the same are covered specifically in Chapter 71.

Other products for which metals are incidental—even if critical and major—components are found within a variety of Commodity Index chapters. For example, if you are interested in importing metallic paints, refer to Chapter 36. For headgear with metal elements, see Chapter 65; for umbrella frames and related items, see Chapter 66. Finished and semifinished products classified as machinery, mechanical appliances, and electrical goods are found in Chapters 84 and 85. Assembled railway track and related equipment is covered in Chapter 86, vehicles in Chapter 87, aircraft in Chapter 88, and boats in Chapter 89. Instruments and apparatus are covered in Commodity Index chapters covering specific items, including optical, medical, and precision instruments (Chapter 90), clocks and watches (Chapter 91), and musical instruments (Chapter 92). Metal articles as parts of firearms, including ammunition, are found in Chapter 93. Chapters that cover miscellaneous manufactures include furniture (Chapter 94), toys, games, and sporting goods (Chapter 95), and miscellaneous manufactured articles (Chapter 96). Works of art in which aluminum or its alloys are components, even dominant components, are covered in Chapter 97 if the primary value derives from the artistry rather than from the metal content.

Note: To understand key issues that will enable you to make best use of the information in this section we recommend that you see "Introduction" on page 425.

Key Factors

The key factors in importing aluminum and aluminum alloy products are:

- Compliance with U.S. Environmental Protection Agency (EPA) requirements under the Toxic Substances Control Act (TSCA) (if the product is classified as a hazardous substance)

- Compliance with U.S. Department of Transportation (DOT) regulations for transport of hazardous cargo (if the product is a hazardous substance)

- Classification of alloy

- For items to be used with food, compliance with U.S. Food and Drug Administration (FDA) requirements and entry notification

Although most importers utilize the services of a licensed customs broker in making their entries, and we recommend this practice, you should be aware of the regulatory, entry, and documentation issues involved in importing your product. You, as importer, are ultimately responsible for the fulfillment of any legal requirements applicable to your shipment.

General Considerations

Regulatory Agencies. The importation of aluminum, aluminum alloys, and products made of them is relatively straightforward, with few restrictions or special requirements. The Food and Drug Administration (FDA) controls the importation of items for use with food. The Environmental Protection Agency (EPA), under authority of the Toxic Substances Control Act (TSCA), imposes certain controls on the importation of aluminum and aluminum articles that contain toxic substances. The Department of Transportation (DOT) enforces regulations for transporting hazardous cargo.

Definitions. Unlike alloys of precious metals, in which any alloy having as much as 2% of a precious metal is considered an alloy of that metal, alloys of base metals are classified according to the metal that predominates by weight over every other individual metal in the alloy. For customs purposes, alloys of a metal are included with the metal that they are an alloy of.

Chapter 76 of HTSUS covers aluminum and aluminum alloys. Aluminum is defined as metal containing at least 99% by weight of aluminum provided that the content by weight of iron plus silicon does not exceed 1%, and that the content of other elements is limited to no more than 0.1% for any given element. Copper is permitted at levels of between 0.1% and 0.2%, provided that neither the chromium nor the manganese content exceeds 0.05%. Aluminum alloys are defined as being metallic substances in which aluminum predominates by weight over each of the other elements, provided that the content by weight of at least one of the other elements is greater than the limit specified in the notes to HTSUS Chapter 76 or the total content by weight of such other elements exceeds 1%. Aluminum vanadium master alloy is also defined as an aluminum alloy that contains more than 20% vanadium by weight.

FDA Regulation. Kitchenware and tableware of aluminum and its alloys intended for use with food are subject to the provisions of the Federal Food, Drug, and Cosmetic Act (FDCA) enforced by the FDA. FDA entry notification is required for applicable items. Shipments of FDA-regulated products are subject to FDA port of entry inspection. For more information about FDA entry procedures and requirements see "Appendix: Foods" on page 825. Contact your nearest regional FDA office or FDA headquarters with questions regarding the importation of aluminum products (see addresses at end of this chapter).

Hazardous Substances Regulations. The EPA imposes certain controls on the importation of toxic substances. The TSCA defines a toxic substance as any substance determined to present the possibility of an unreasonable risk of injury to health and the environment. The DOT enforces regulations for transporting hazardous cargo. Substances are deemed hazardous if listed in DOT transport regulations (49 CFR 172 appendix). Unwrought primary metals, such as pigs, ingots, billets, blooms, and similar materials, are generally categorized as toxic substances within the definitions of the TSCA and thus are required to be in compliance with its provisions. These include packaging, shipping, marking, and labeling requirements. Refer to "Laws and Regulations" below.

Products defined as articles—that is, any manufactured item 1) that is formed into a specific shape or design during manufacture, 2) that has end-use functions dependent on the shape or design during end use, and 3) that during the end use, does not change in its chemical composition or that changes only for a noncommercial purpose separate from the article and only as allowed by law (19 CFR 12.120(2))—are not subject to the provisions of the TSCA. Metal products other than primary metals are generally considered to be articles even if they are to be further processed. For example, copper in sheets is an article even if it is to be subsequently fabricated into other products.

Certification. All products covered by the TSCA are subject to the U.S. Customs Service TSCA Import Certification Rule (19 CFR 12.118 et seq.). If you import these products, you must sign one of the following statements: "I certify that all materials in this shipment comply with all applicable rules or orders under TSCA and that I am not offering a chemical substance for entry in violation of TSCA or any applicable rule or order thereunder" or "I certify that all materials in this shipment are not subject to TSCA." You must file this TSCA certification of compliance or exemption at the time you make the entry at customs. Customs will not release your shipment without proper certification.

If you will be importing several or regular shipments, you should ask the appropriate Customs port director to authorize your use of a blanket certification. A blanket certification is valid for one calendar year, may be renewed, and may be revoked at any time for cause.

Customs Classification

For customs purposes, aluminum and aluminum products are classified within Chapter 76 of the HTSUS. This chapter is divided into headings, which are further divided into subheadings, and often into sub-subheadings, each of which has its own HTSUS classification number. For example, the 2001 HTSUS number for aluminum alloy bars and rods other than with a round cross-section is 7604.29.50, indicating that it is a subcategory of aluminum alloys other than hollow profiles (7604.29), which is a subsubcategory of the major heading aluminum bars, rods, and profiles (7604). There are 16 major headings in HTSUS Chapter 76.

7601—Unwrought aluminum

7602—Aluminum waste and scrap

7603—Aluminum powders and flakes

7604—Aluminum bars, rods, and profiles

7605—Aluminum wire

7606—Aluminum plates, sheets, and strip, of a thickness exceeding 0.2 mm.

7607—Aluminum foil (whether or not printed or backed with paper, paperboard, plastics, or similar backing materials) of a thickness (excluding any backing) not exceeding 0.2 mm.

7608—Aluminum tubes and pipes

7609—Aluminum tube or pipe fittings (for example, couplings, elbows, sleeves)

7610—Aluminum structures (excluding prefabricated buildings of heading 9406) and parts of structures (for example, bridges and bridge sections, towers, lattice masts, roofs, roofing frameworks, doors and windows and their frames and thresholds for doors, balustrades, pillars, and columns); aluminum plates, rods, profiles, tubes, and the like, prepared for use in structures

7611—Aluminum reservoirs, tanks, vats, and similar containers, for any material (other than compressed or liquefied gas), of a capacity exceeding 300 liters, whether or not lined or heat insulated, but not fitted with mechanical or thermal equipment

7612—Aluminum casks, drums, cans, boxes, and similar containers (including rigid or collapsible tubular containers) for any material (other than compressed or liquefied gas), of a capacity not exceeding 300 liters, whether or not lined or heat insulated, but not fitted with mechanical or thermal equipment

7613—Aluminum containers for compressed or liquefied gas

7614—Stranded wire, cables, plaited bands, and the like, including slings and similar articles, of aluminum, not electrically insulated

7615—Table, kitchen, or other household articles and parts thereof, of aluminum; pot scourers and scouring or polishing pads, gloves, and the like, of aluminum,; sanitary ware and parts thereof, of aluminum

7616—Other articles of aluminum

For more details regarding classification of the specific product you are interested in importing, consult a customs broker, the appropriate commodity specialist at your nearest customs port, or see HTSUS. The 2001 HTSUS is available online from the Customs Service (www.customs.gov/impoexpo/impoexpo.htm) or for purchase from the U.S. Government Printing Office (see resources at the end of this chapter), and may be found in larger public libraries. For a general discussion of customs classification, see "Classification—Liquidation" on page 229.

Dutiable Status of Goods

For more information about duty rates and binding decisions see "Dutiable Status of Goods" on page 203; for a discussion of temporary importation of goods see "Temporary Free Importations" on page 205.

Valuation

Importers have a responsibility to use what the U.S. Customs Service deems, "reasonable care," when determining the value of their goods. They must also provide any additional information that the Customs Service needs for setting a final value on the goods. This process involves a number of factors and can be somewhat complicated; importers must be aware of applicable issues and details. Valuation information applies to all types of commodities, for further discussion on the subject see "Customs Valuation" on page 267.

Import Duties

Import duties vary (often dramatically) depending upon the Harmonized Tariff Schedule (HTSUS) classification of the goods or products imported. Since some products that look alike have different HTSUS classifications and different rates of duty, proper classification is vital. Note that "differences of opinion" between importers and the Bureau of Customs and Border Protection regarding classification keeps customs attorneys very busy.

Import duties can be assessed on the imported value of the goods ("ad valorem" rates of duty such as 2%, 4.4%, 50%, etc.), total units or weight of the goods ("specific" rates of duty such as 2 cents each or 1.5 cents/pound, etc.) or on a combination basis ("compound" rates of duty such as 5 cents each plus 6%).

Listed below is a sampling of several Column 1 import duty rates for Chapter 76 products:

Luggage frames (7616.99.10.00): Free

to

Fitted with fittings or made up into articles (7614.90.50.00): 5.7%

For specific information on US import duties refer to the Harmonized Tariff Schedule of the US. The print version is available from the US Government Printing Office as well as third party suppliers who often add special features. Online versions are available in both static PDF pages as well as in formats with excellent search functionality. Search the Web with the term "Harmonized Tariff Schedule" to find sources.

Entry and Documentation

The entry of merchandise is a two-part process consisting of 1) filing the documents necessary to determine whether merchandise may be released from Customs custody and 2) filing the documents that contain information for duty assessment and statistical purposes. In certain instances all documents must be filed and accepted by Customs prior to the release of the goods. Unless you have been granted an extension, you must file entry documents at a location specified by the district/area director within five working days of your shipment's date of arrival at a U.S. port of entry. These include a number of standard documents required by Customs for any entry, and

- U.S. Customs TSCA Certification when required

After you present the entry, Customs may examine your shipment, or may waive examination. The shipment is then released provided no legal or regulatory violations have been noted. You must then file entry summary documentation and deposit estimated duties at a designated customhouse within 10 working days of your shipment's release. For a detailed description of entry procedures, standard documentation, and informal entry, see "Entry Process" on page 185.

Informed Compliance. Informed compliance was introduced with the Customs Modernization Act of 1993 (Mod Act) and defines the relationship between importers and the Customs Service. It sets out the responsibilities of both parties. Providing the correct documentation and information for entry is a key factor that will make your importing operation run smoothly. We recommend that importers become familiar with the concept of informed comliance and the responsibilities that they have under the Mod Act. For further discussion about informed compliance see "Informed Compliance" on page 211.

Entry Invoice. If you are importing aluminum and alloys of aluminum classifiable under subheadings 7601.10.60, 7601.20.60, 7601.20.90, or 7602.00.00, your invoice must include a statement of the percentages by weight of any metallic element contained in the article. For more general information about invoices see "Invoices" on page 277.

Note: The Entry and Documentation section has been carefully designed to supply you, the importer, with sample documents and directions on how to satisfy Customs requirements. Be aware that you should consult the applicable authorities to ensure that you are correctly following the most current procedures.

Marking and Labeling Requirements

For a general discussion of U.S. Customs marking and labeling requirements, see "Country of Origin Marking" on page 236, "Special Marking Requirements" on page 238 and "Marking—False Impression" on page 239.

Shipping Considerations

You will need to ensure that your goods are packaged and shipped with care to ensure that they arrive in good condition and pass smoothly through Customs. You are responsible for ensuring that the shipment is in compliance with all applicable government regulations for packaging and shipping. In most instances, you should not leave these arrangements solely to the discretion of your supplier. Careful preparation of the cargo and selection of the mode of transport can be essential to a cost-effective, timely delivery of undamaged goods. We strongly advise you to consult your shipping representative, insurance agent, or freight broker for advice on packing and shipping.

Products that are listed as hazardous substances (49 CFR 172 appendix) may be transported in bulk only on compliance with Coast Guard notification procedures, shipping permit requirements, and complex transportation regulations (46 CFR 148). All hazardous substances must be packaged and transported in accordance with DOT regulations (49 CFR 171 et seq.).

Aluminum, aluminum alloy, and products made of them are often bulky, and should be securely stowed to avoid damage due to shifting en route. Aluminum and its products are also subject to tarnish and corrosion, which should be guarded against, especially as no allowance is made by customs for partial damage or loss due to such.

Publications and WWW Resources

The *Harmonized Tariff Schedule of the United States (2001)* (HTSUS) is available to view on the Customs Service website (www.customs.gov), or you may purchase a printed version from:

U.S. Government Printing Office
Superintendent of Documents
710 North Capital Street NW
Washington DC 20401
Tel: (202) 512-1800
Fax: (202) 512-1657
Website: www.access.gpo.gov

The USGPO also has copies of specific laws available for purchase. The USGPO accepts orders made by fax, phone or placed over the Internet, as well as mail orders paid by credit card. All orders must be accompanied by payment. Credit cards, checks drawn on a U.S. bank, or an international money order are all acceptable.

Relevant Government Agencies

Address inquiries regarding TSCA and EPA requirements for importation of hazardous or toxic substances to:

Environmental Protection Agency (EPA)
Office of Pollution Prevention and Toxics
TSCA System Information
1200 Pennsylvania Avenue NW
Washington DC 20460
Tel: (202) 564-3810
Tel: (202) 554-1404 (TSCA Information Hotline)
Email: oppt.homepage@epa.gov
Website: www.epa.gov/opptintr/contact.htm

Address questions regarding transportation of hazardous substances to:

U.S. Department of Transportation (DOT)
Research and Special Programs Administration
Hazardous Materials Information Center
400 7th St. SW
Washington DC 20590
Tel: (202) 366 4488
Website: http://hazmat.dot.gov

Address your questions regarding FDA requirements for aluminum products intended for use with food to:

Food and Drug Administration (FDA)
Center for Food Safety and Applied Nutrition (CFSAN)
Office of Compliance
Division of Enforcement, Imports Branch
5100 Paint Branch Parkway
College Park, MD 20740-3835
Tel: (301) 436-2080
Website: http://vm.cfsan.fda.gov/list.html

Address questions regarding the importation of aluminum and aluminum products to your local Customs port director. For addresses refer to "U.S. Customs and Border Protection Offices" on page 65 or contact:

U.S. Customs and Border Protection
Customs Headquarters
1300 Pennsylvania Avenue NW
Washington DC 20229
Tel: (202) 354-1000
Website: www.customs.treas.gov

Laws and Regulations

The following laws and regulations may be relevant to the importation of aluminum and aluminum products. The laws are contained in the U.S. Code (USC) and the regulations are published in the Code of Federal Regulations (CFR), both of which may be available at larger public and law libraries. Copies of specific laws are also available from the United States Government Printing Office (address above).

15 USC 2601 et seq.
Toxic Substances Control Act
This Act authorizes the EPA to determine whether a substance is harmful and to restrict importation, sale, and use of such substances.

19 CFR 12.118 et seq.
Regulations on Toxic Substances Control
These regulations require importers of chemical substances imported in bulk or as part of a mixture to certify to Customs that the shipment complies with the TSCA or is not subject to that Act.

15 USC 1261 et seq.
Federal Hazardous Substances Act
This Act controls the importation of hazardous substances, sets forth prohibited imports, and authorizes various agencies to promulgate labeling, marking, and transport requirements.

49 CFR 171 et seq.
Regulations on Hazardous Materials
These regulations list all substances deemed hazardous and provide transport, marking, labeling, safety, and emergency response rules.

46 CFR 147.30
Regulations on Labeling of Hazardous Materials
This regulation requires the labeling of containers of hazardous substances and specifies the label contents.

46 CFR 148 et seq.
Regulations of Carriage of Solid Hazardous Materials in Bulk
These regulations govern the transport of solid hazardous substances in bulk, including reporting, permitting, loading, stowing, and shipping requirements.

21 USC 301 et seq.
Federal Food, Drug, and Cosmetic Act
This Act prohibits deceptive practices and regulates the manufacture, sale and importation or exportation of food, drugs, cosmetics, and related products. It was amended by the Food Quality Protection Act of 1996. See 21 USC 331, 381, 382.

19 CFR 12.1 et seq.; 21 CFR 1.83 et seq.
Regulations on Food, Drugs, and Cosmetics
These regulations of the Secretary of Health and Human Services and the Secretary of the Treasury govern the standards, labeling, marking, and importing of products used with food, drugs, and cosmetics.

Principal Exporting Countries

The following listing includes samples of the main supplier nations of the products of this chapter. It is organized by HTSUS major heading. (Refer to "Customs Classification" above for the product codes.) Countries are listed in rank order of the value of products imported to the U.S. Statistics represent customs value of entries for 2002 from the Bureau of Census, U.S. Department of Commerce.

7601—Canada, Russia, Venezuela, Australia, Argentina, United Arab Emirates, Brazil, Bahrain, South Africa

7602—Canada, Mexico, Russia, Guatemala, Venezuela, Germany, Dominican Republic, United Kingdom, Panama, Brazil, Saudi Arabia, France

7603—Brazil, Germany, United Kingdom, Austria, France, South Korea

7604—Canada, Russia, China, Mexico, Germany, Hong Kong

7605—Canada, United Kingdom, France, Norway, Germany, Japan, Spain, Switzerland, Italy, Brazil, China, Singapore

7606—Canada, Germany, South Africa, Russia, Bahrain, Venezuela, Greece, Austria, United Kingdom, Japan

7607—Canada, Germany, Japan, France, Russia, Italy, Sweden, United Kingdom, Switzerland

7608—Canada, Japan, Mexico, Germany, United Kingdom, France, Russia, Taiwan, China, Switzerland

7609—India, Canada, Japan, Germany, China, Mexico, Taiwan, United Kingdom

7610—Canada, Mexico, Germany, Italy, South Korea, Colombia, China

7611—Canada, Netherlands, Italy, Spain, Switzerland, Japan, United Kingdom

7612—Canada, Germany, Venezuela, Mexico, France, United Kingdom, Japan

7613—Venezuela, Canada, Russia, Germany, Japan, Israel, Czech Republic, Australia, Finland, France, Argentina

7614—Canada, Mexico, Colombia, Turkey, Ecuador, Bahrain, China, Indonesia

7615—China, Thailand, Italy, France, Canada, South Korea, Indonesia

7616—Mexico, China, Canada, Japan, Taiwan, Germany, South Korea, United Kingdom

RESERVED FOR FUTURE USE

Chapter 77: Reserved

Chapter 77 is reserved for future use by the U.S. Customs Service.

Chapter 78: Lead and Articles Thereof

This section pertains to the importation of lead, lead alloys, and articles made from these products, which are classified within Chapter 78 of the Harmonized Tariff Schedule of the United States (HTSUS). Specifically, it includes unwrought lead and lead alloys; lead waste and scrap; powders and flakes; lead bars, rods, profiles, wire, plates, sheets, strips, and foil; lead tubes, pipes, and fittings; and other miscellaneous articles of lead.

Goods of base metals and their alloys in which metals other than lead predominate are covered in Commodity Index chapters related to the specific metals, including iron and steel (Chapter 72), copper (Chapter 74), nickel (Chapter 75), aluminum (Chapter 76), zinc (Chapter 79), tin (Chapter 80), and other base metals (Chapter 81). Tools, other implements, and cutlery are found in Chapter 82, while miscellaneous articles of base metals are contained in Chapter 83. Precious metals, alloys of precious metals, and articles containing the same are covered specifically in Chapter 71.

Other products for which metals are incidental components are found within a variety of Commodity Index chapters and headings. For example, if you are interested in importing metallic paints, refer to Chapter 36. For headgear with metal elements, see Chapter 65; for umbrella frames and related items, see Chapter 66. Finished and semifinished products classified as machinery, mechanical appliances, and electrical goods are found in Chapters 84 and 85. Assembled railway track and related equipment is covered in Chapter 86, vehicles in Chapter 87, aircraft in Chapter 88, and boats in Chapter 89. Instruments and apparatus are covered in Commodity Index chapters related to the particular articles, including optical, medical, and precision instruments (Chapter 90), clocks and watches (Chapter 91), and musical instruments (Chapter 92). Metal articles as parts of firearms, including ammunition, are found in Chapter 93. Commodity Index chapters that cover miscellaneous manufactures include furniture (Chapter 94), toys, games, and sporting goods (Chapter 95), and miscellaneous manufactured articles (Chapter 96). Works of art in which lead or its alloys are components, even dominant components, are covered in chapter 97 if the primary value derives from the artistry rather than from the metal content.

Note: To understand key issues that will enable you to make best use of the information in this section we recommend that you see "Introduction" on page 425.

Key Factors

The key factors in importing lead and lead alloy products are:

- Compliance with U.S. Environmental Protection Agency (EPA) requirements under the Toxic Substances Control Act (TSCA) (if the product is classified as a hazardous substance)

- Compliance with U.S. Department of Transportation (DOT) regulations for transport of hazardous cargo (if the product is a hazardous substance)

Although most importers utilize the services of a licensed customs broker in making their entries, and we recommend this practice, you should be aware of the regulatory, entry, and documentation issues involved in importing your product. You, as importer, are ultimately responsible for the fulfillment of any legal requirements applicable to your shipment.

General Considerations

Regulatory Agencies. The importation of lead, lead alloys, and products made of them is relatively straightforward, with few restrictions or special requirements. The Environmental Protection Agency (EPA), under authority of the Toxic Substances Control Act (TSCA), imposes certain controls on the importation of lead and lead articles that constitute toxic substances. The Department of Transportation (DOT) enforces regulations for transporting hazardous cargo.

Definitions. Unlike alloys of precious metals, in which any alloy containing as much as 2% by weight of a precious metal is considered an alloy of that metal, alloys of base metals are classified according to the metal that predominates by weight over every other individual metal in the alloy. For customs purposes, alloys of a metal are included with the metal that they are an alloy of.

Chapter 78 of HTSUS covers lead and lead alloys. Refined lead is defined as metal containing at least 99.9% by weight provided that the content of any other element does not exceed, by weight, that noted in the table found in the notes to HTSUS Chapter 78, which ranges from a low of 0.001% for other elements and a high of 0.05% bismuth. Lead alloys are defined as being metallic substances in which lead is less than 99% by weight, but not less than any other metallic element.

Toxic Substances Regulations. The EPA imposes certain controls on the importation of toxic substances. The TSCA defines a toxic substance as any substance determined to present the possibility of an unreasonable risk of injury to health and the environment. Because of long-term deleterious effects on health caused by lead, regulators pay special heed to it. The DOT enforces regulations for transporting hazardous cargo. Substances are deemed hazardous if listed in DOT transport regulations (49 CFR 172 appendix). Unwrought primary metals, such as pigs, ingots, billets, blooms, and similar materials, are generally categorized as toxic substances within the definitions of the TSCA and thus are required to be in compliance with its provisions. These include packaging, shipping, marking, and labeling requirements. Refer to listing of laws and regulations below.

Products defined as articles—that is, any manufactured item 1) that is formed into a specific shape or design during manufacture, 2) that has end-use functions dependent on the shape or design during end use, and 3) that during the end use, does not change in its chemical composition or that changes only for a noncommercial purpose separate from the article and only as allowed by law (19 CFR 12.120(2))—are not subject to the provisions of the TSCA. Metal products other than primary metals are generally considered to be articles even if they are to be further processed. For example, lead in bars is an article even if it is to be subsequently fabricated into other products.

Certification. All products covered by the TSCA are subject to the U.S. Customs Service TSCA Import Certification Rule (19 CFR 12.118 et seq.). If you import these products, you must sign one of the following statements: "I certify that all materials in this shipment comply with all applicable rules or orders under TSCA and that I am not offering a chemical substance for entry in violation of TSCA or any applicable rule or order thereunder" or "I certify that all materials in this shipment are not subject to

TSCA." You must file this TSCA certification of compliance or exemption at the time you make the entry at customs. Customs will not release your shipment without proper certification.

If you will be importing several or regular shipments, you should ask the appropriate Customs port director to authorize your use of a blanket certification. A blanket certification is valid for one calendar year, may be renewed, and may be revoked at any time for cause.

Customs Classification

For customs purposes, lead, lead alloys, and their products are classified within Chapter 78 of the HTSUS. This chapter is divided into headings, which are further divided into subheadings, and often into sub-subheadings, each of which has its own HTSUS classification number. For example, the 2001 HTSUS number for unwrought alloys of lead other than lead bullion is 7801.99.90, indicating that it is a subcategory of lead other than refined lead that does not contain by weight antimony as the principal other element (7801.99), which is a subsubcategory of the major heading unwrought lead (7801). There are six major headings in HTSUS Chapter 75.

7801—Unwrought lead

7802—Lead waste and scrap

7803—Lead bars, rods, profiles, and wire

7804—Lead plates, sheets, strip, and foil; lead powders and flakes

7805—Leads tubes, pipes, and tube or pipe fittings (for example, couplings, elbows, sleeves)

7806—Other articles of lead

For more details regarding classification of the specific product you are interested in importing, consult a customs broker, the appropriate coThe 2001 HTSUS is available online from the Customs Service (www.customs.gov/impoexpo/impoexpo.htm) or for purchase from the U.S. Government Printing Office (see resources at the end of this chapter), and may be found in larger public libraries. For a general discussion of customs classification, see "Classification—Liquidation" on page 229.

Dutiable Status of Goods

For more information about duty rates and binding decisions see "Dutiable Status of Goods" on page 203; for a discussion of temporary importation of goods see "Temporary Free Importations" on page 205.

Valuation

Importers have a responsibility to use what the U.S. Customs Service deems, "reasonable care," when determining the value of their goods. They must also provide any additional information that the Customs Service needs for setting a final value on the goods. This process involves a number of factors and can be somewhat complicated; importers must be aware of applicable issues and details. Valuation information applies to all types of commodities, for further discussion on the subject see "Customs Valuation" on page 267.

Import Duties

Import duties vary (often dramatically) depending upon the Harmonized Tariff Schedule (HTSUS) classification of the goods or products imported. Since some products that look alike have different HTSUS classifications and different rates of duty, proper classification is vital. Note that "differences of opinion" between importers and the Bureau of Customs and Border Protection regarding classification keeps customs attorneys very busy.

Import duties can be assessed on the imported value of the goods ("ad valorem" rates of duty such as 2%, 4.4%, 50%, etc.), total units or weight of the goods ("specific" rates of duty such as 2 cents each or 1.5 cents/pound, etc.) or on a combination basis ("compound" rates of duty such as 5 cents each plus 6%).

Listed below is a sampling of several Column 1 import duty rates for Chapter 78 products:
Powders and flakes (7804.20.00.00): Free
to
Lead bars, rods, profiles and wire (7803.00.00.00): 1.2%

For specific information on US import duties refer to the Harmonized Tariff Schedule of the US. The print version is available from the US Government Printing Office as well as third party suppliers who often add special features. Online versions are available in both static PDF pages as well as in formats with excellent search functionality. Search the Web with the term "Harmonized Tariff Schedule" to find sources.

Entry and Documentation

The entry of merchandise is a two-part process consisting of 1) filing the documents necessary to determine whether merchandise may be released from Customs custody and 2) filing the documents that contain information for duty assessment and statistical purposes. In certain instances all documents must be filed and accepted by Customs prior to the release of the goods. Unless you have been granted an extension, you must file entry documents at a location specified by the district/area director within five working days of your shipment's date of arrival at a U.S. port of entry. These include a number of standard documents required by Customs for any entry, and

- U.S. Customs TSCA Certification when required

After you present the entry, Customs may examine your shipment, or may waive examination. The shipment is then released provided no legal or regulatory violations have been noted. You must then file entry summary documentation and deposit estimated duties at a designated customhouse within 10 working days of your shipment's release. For a detailed description of entry procedures, standard documentation, and informal entry, see "Entry Process" on page 185.

Informed Compliance. Informed compliance was introduced with the Customs Modernization Act of 1993 (Mod Act) and defines the relationship between importers and the Customs Service. It sets out the responsibilities of both parties. Providing the correct documentation and information for entry is a key factor that will make your importing operation run smoothly. We recommend that importers become familiar with the concept of informed comliance and the responsibilities that they have under the Mod Act. For further discussion about informed compliance see "Informed Compliance" on page 211.

Note: The Entry and Documentation section has been carefully designed to supply you, the importer, with sample documents and directions on how to satisfy Customs requirements. Be aware that you should consult the applicable authorities to ensure that you are correctly following the most current procedures.

Marking and Labeling Requirements

For a general discussion of U.S. Customs marking and labeling requirements, see "Country of Origin Marking" on page 236, "Special Marking Requirements" on page 238 and "Marking—False Impression" on page 239.

Shipping Considerations

You will need to ensure that your goods are packaged and shipped with care to ensure that they arrive in good condition and pass smoothly through Customs. You are responsible for ensuring that the shipment is in compliance with all applicable government regulations for packaging and shipping. In most instances, you should not leave these arrangements solely to the

discretion of your supplier. Careful preparation of the cargo and selection of the mode of transport can be essential to a cost-effective, timely delivery of undamaged goods. We strongly advise you to consult your shipping representative, insurance agent, or freight broker for advice on packing and shipping.

Products that are listed as hazardous substances (49 CFR 172 appendix) may be transported in bulk only on compliance with Coast Guard notification procedures, shipping permit requirements, and complex transportation regulations (46 CFR 148). All hazardous substances must be packaged and transported in accordance with DOT regulations (49 CFR 171 et seq.).

Lead, lead alloy, and products made of them are often bulky and heavy, and should be securely stowed to avoid damage due to shifting en route. Lead and its products are also subject to oxidation and corrosion, which should be guarded against, especially as no allowance is made by customs for partial damage or loss due to such.

Publications and WWW Resources

The *Harmonized Tariff Schedule of the United States (2001)* (HTSUS) is available to view on the Customs Service website (www.customs.gov), or you may purchase a printed version from:

U.S. Government Printing Office
Superintendent of Documents
710 North Capital Street NW
Washington DC 20401
Tel: (202) 512-1800
Fax: (202) 512-1657
Website: www.access.gpo.gov

The USGPO also has copies of specific laws available for purchase. The USGPO accepts orders made by fax, phone or placed over the Internet, as well as mail orders paid by credit card. All orders must be accompanied by payment. Credit cards, checks drawn on a U.S. bank, or an international money order are all acceptable.

Relevant Government Agencies

Address inquiries regarding TSCA and EPA requirements for importation of hazardous or toxic substances to:

Environmental Protection Agency (EPA)
Office of Pollution Prevention and Toxics
TSCA System Information
1200 Pennsylvania Avenue NW
Washington DC 20460
Tel: (202) 564-3810
Tel: (202) 554-1404 (TSCA Information Hotline)
Email: oppt.homepage@epa.gov
Website: www.epa.gov/opptintr/contact.htm

Address questions regarding transportation of hazardous substances to:

U.S. Department of Transportation (DOT)
Research and Special Programs Administration
Hazardous Materials Information Center
400 7th St. SW
Washington DC 20590
Tel: (202) 366-4488
Website: http://hazmat.dot.gov

Address questions regarding the importation of lead and lead products to your local Customs port director. For addresses refer to "U.S. Customs and Border Protection Offices" on page 65 or contact:

U.S. Customs and Border Protection
Customs Headquarters
1300 Pennsylvania Avenue NW
Washington DC 20229
Tel: (202) 354-1000
Website: www.customs.treas.gov

Laws and Regulations

The following laws and regulations may be relevant to the importation of lead, lead alloys, and products made of them. The laws are contained in the U.S. Code (USC) and the regulations are published in the Code of Federal Regulations (CFR), both of which may be available at larger public and law libraries. Copies of specific laws are also available from the United States Government Printing Office (address above).

15 USC 2601 et seq.
Toxic Substances Control Act
This Act authorizes the EPA to determine whether a substance is harmful and to restrict importation, sale, and use of such substances.

19 CFR 12.118 et seq.
Regulations on Toxic Substances Control
These regulations require importers of chemical substances imported in bulk or as part of a mixture to certify to Customs that the shipment complies with the TSCA or is not subject to that Act.

15 USC 1261 et seq.
Federal Hazardous Substances Act
This Act controls the importation of hazardous substances, sets forth prohibited imports, and authorizes various agencies to promulgate labeling, marking, and transport requirements.

49 CFR 171 et seq.
Regulations on Hazardous Materials
These regulations list all substances deemed hazardous and provide transport, marking, labeling, safety, and emergency response rules.

46 CFR 147.30
Regulations on Labeling of Hazardous Materials
This regulation requires the labeling of containers of hazardous substances and specifies the label contents.

46 CFR 148 et seq.
Regulations of Carriage of Solid Hazardous Materials in Bulk
These regulations govern the transport of solid hazardous substances in bulk, including reporting, permitting, loading, stowing, and shipping requirements.

Principal Exporting Countries

The following listing includes samples of the main supplier nations of the products of this chapter. It is organized by HTSUS major heading. (Refer to "Customs Classification" above for the product codes.) Countries are listed in rank order of the value of products imported to the U.S. Statistics represent customs value of entries for 2002 from the Bureau of Census, U.S. Department of Commerce.

7801—Canada, Australia, China, Mexico, Poland, Germany, Belgium, United Kingdom, Argentina

7802—Mexico, Colombia, Canada, Brazil, Jamaica, Russia, Ecuador, Venezuela, Italy, Sweden

7803—Canada, Germany, Italy, China, United Kingdom, Japan, South Korea

7804—Germany, Canada, Russia, United Kingdom, New Zealand, Netherlands

7805—China, Taiwan, Spain, Canada, United Kingdom, Germany, Mexico

7806—Canada, China, Netherlands, United Kingdom, Taiwan, Japan, Germany

Chapter 79:
Zinc and Articles Thereof

This section pertains to the importation of zinc, zinc alloys, and articles made from these products, which are classified within Chapter 79 of the Harmonized Tariff Schedule of the United States (HTSUS). Specifically, it includes unwrought zinc; zinc waste and scrap; zinc dust, powders, and flakes; bars, rods, wire, plates, sheets, strips, and foil; zinc tubes, pipes, and fittings; and miscellaneous articles of zinc, such as gutters, skylight frames, and household articles.

Goods of base metals and their alloys in which metals other than zinc predominate are covered in Commodity Index chapters that relate to the specific metals, including iron and steel (Chapter 72), copper (Chapter 74), nickel (Chapter 75), aluminum (Chapter 76), lead (Chapter 78), tin (Chapter 80), and other base metals (Chapter 81). Tools, other implements, and cutlery are found in Chapter 82, while miscellaneous articles of base metals are contained in Chapter 83. Precious metals, alloys of precious metals, and articles containing the same are covered specifically in Chapter 71.

Other products for which metals are incidental—even if critical and major—components are found within a variety of Commodity Index chapters. For example, if you are interested in importing metallic paints, refer to Chapter 36. For headgear with metal elements, see Chapter 65; for umbrella frames and related items, see Chapter 66. Finished and semifinished products classified as machinery, mechanical appliances, and electrical goods are found in Chapters 84 and 85. Assembled railway track and related equipment is covered in Chapter 86, vehicles in Chapter 87, aircraft in Chapter 88, and boats in Chapter 89. Instruments and apparatus are covered in Commodity Index chapters that relate to the specific article, including optical, medical, and precision instruments (Chapter 90), clocks and watches (Chapter 91), and musical instruments (Chapter 92). Metal articles as parts of firearms, including ammunition, are found in Chapter 93. Commodity Index chapters that cover miscellaneous manufactures include furniture (Chapter 94), toys, games, and sporting goods (Chapter 95), and miscellaneous manufactured articles (Chapter 96). Works of art in which zinc or its alloys are components, even dominant components, are covered in Chapter 97 if the primary value derives from the artistry rather than from the metal content.

Note: To understand key issues that will enable you to make best use of the information in this section we recommend that you see "Introduction" on page 425.

Key Factors

The key factors in importing zinc and zinc alloy products are:

- Compliance with U.S. Environmental Protection Agency (EPA) requirements under the Toxic Substances Control Act (TSCA) (if the product is classified as a hazardous substance)

- Compliance with U.S. Department of Transportation (DOT) regulations for transport of hazardous cargo (if the product is a hazardous substance)

- For items to be used with food, compliance with U.S. Food and Drug Administration (FDA) requirements and entry notification

Although most importers utilize the services of a licensed customs broker in making their entries, and we recommend this practice, you should be aware of the regulatory, entry, and documentation issues involved in importing your product. You, as importer, are ultimately responsible for the fulfillment of any legal requirements applicable to your shipment.

General Considerations

Regulatory Agencies. The importation of zinc, zinc alloys, and products made of them is relatively straightforward, with few restrictions or special requirements. The Food and Drug Administration (FDA) controls the importation of items for use with food. The Environmental Protection Agency (EPA), under authority of the Toxic Substances Control Act (TSCA), imposes certain controls on the importation of zinc and zinc articles that contain toxic substances. The Department of Transportation (DOT) enforces regulations for transporting hazardous cargo.

Definitions. Unlike alloys of precious metals, in which any alloy having as much as 2% of a precious metal is considered an alloy of that metal, alloys of base metals are classified according to the metal that predominates by weight over every other individual metal in the alloy. For customs purposes, alloys of a metal are included with the metal that they are an alloy of.

Chapter 79 of HTSUS covers zinc and zinc alloys. Zinc is defined as metal containing by weight at least 97.5% by weight of zinc. Zinc alloys are defined as being metallic substances in which zinc predominates by weight over each of the other elements, provided that the content by weight of at least one of the other elements exceeds 2.5%. Zinc dust is defined as the product obtained from condensation of vapor that is finer than zinc powder (generally finer than 63 micrometers and composed of at least 85% by weight of metallic zinc). Casting-grade zinc is defined as containing specified components of various other metals, such as 1.8% of cadmium, etc., as specified in the notes to HTSUS Chapter 79.

FDA Regulation. Kitchenware and tableware of zinc and its alloys intended for use with food are subject to the provisions of the Federal Food, Drug, and Cosmetic Act (FDCA) enforced by the FDA. FDA entry notification is required for applicable items. Shipments of FDA-regulated products are subject to FDA port of entry inspection. For more information about FDA entry procedures and requirements see "Appendix: Foods" on page 825. Contact your nearest regional FDA office or FDA headquarters with questions regarding the importation of zinc products (see addresses at end of this chapter).

Toxic Substances Regulations. The EPA imposes certain controls on the importation of toxic substances. The TSCA defines a toxic substance as any substance determined to present the possibility of an unreasonable risk of injury to health and the environment. The DOT enforces regulations for transporting hazardous cargo. Substances are deemed hazardous if listed in DOT transport regulations (49 CFR 172 appendix). Unwrought primary metals, such as pigs, ingots, billets, blooms, and similar materials, are generally categorized as toxic substances within the definitions of the TSCA and thus are required to be in compliance with its provisions. These include packaging, shipping, marking, and labeling requirements. Refer to "Laws and Regulations" below.

Products defined as articles—that is, any manufactured item 1) that is formed into a specific shape or design during manufacture, 2) that has end-use functions dependent on the shape or design during end use, and 3) that during the end use, does not change in its chemical composition or that changes only for a noncommercial purpose separate from the article and only as allowed by law (19 CFR 12.120(2))—are not subject to the provisions of the TSCA. Metal products other than primary metals are generally considered to be articles even if they are to be further processed. For example, zinc in sheets is an article even if it is to be subsequently fabricated into other products.

Certification. All products covered by the TSCA are subject to the U.S. Customs Service TSCA Import Certification Rule (19 CFR 12.118 et seq.). If you import these products, you must sign one of the following statements: "I certify that all materials in this shipment comply with all applicable rules or orders under TSCA and that I am not offering a chemical substance for entry in violation of TSCA or any applicable rule or order thereunder" or "I certify that all materials in this shipment are not subject to TSCA." You must file this TSCA certification of compliance or exemption at the time you make the entry at customs.

If you will be importing several or regular shipments, you should ask the appropriate Customs port director to authorize your use of a blanket certification. A blanket certification is valid for one calendar year, may be renewed, and may be revoked at any time for cause.

Customs Classification

For customs purposes, zinc and zinc products are classified within Chapter 79 of the HTSUS. This chapter is divided into headings, which are further divided into subheadings, and often into sub-subheadings, each of which has its own HTSUS classification number. For example, the 2001 HTSUS number for zinc powders is 7903.90.30, indicating that it is a sub-subcategory of zinc powders, dust, and flakes other than zinc dust (7903.90), which is a subcategory of the major heading zinc dust, powders, and flakes (7903). There are seven major headings in HTSUS Chapter 79.

7901—Unwrought zinc

7902—Zinc waste and scrap

7903—Zinc dust, powders, and flakes

7904—Zinc bars, rods, profiles and wire

7905—Zinc plates, sheets, strip, and foil

7906—Zinc tubes, pipes, and tube or pipe fittings (for example, couplings, elbows, sleeves)

7907—Other articles of zinc

For more details regarding classification of the specific product you are interested in importing, consult a customs broker, the appropriate commodity specialist at your nearest customs port, or see HTSUS. The 2001 HTSUS is available online from the Customs Service (www.customs.gov/impoexpo/impoexpo.htm) or for purchase from the U.S. Government Printing Office (see resources at the end of this chapter), and may be found in larger public libraries. For a general discussion of customs classification, see "Classification—Liquidation" on page 229.

Dutiable Status of Goods

For more information about duty rates and binding decisions see "Dutiable Status of Goods" on page 203; for a discussion of temporary importation of goods see "Temporary Free Importations" on page 205.

Valuation

Importers have a responsibility to use what the U.S. Customs Service deems, "reasonable care," when determining the value of their goods. They must also provide any additional information that the Customs Service needs for setting a final value on the goods. This process involves a number of factors and can be somewhat complicated; importers must be aware of applicable issues and details. Valuation information applies to all types of commodities, for further discussion on the subject see "Customs Valuation" on page 267.

Import Duties

Import duties vary (often dramatically) depending upon the Harmonized Tariff Schedule (HTSUS) classification of the goods or products imported. Since some products that look alike have different HTSUS classifications and different rates of duty, proper classification is vital. Note that "differences of opinion" between importers and the Bureau of Customs and Border Protection regarding classification keeps customs attorneys very busy.

Import duties can be assessed on the imported value of the goods ("ad valorem" rates of duty such as 2%, 4.4%, 50%, etc.), total units or weight of the goods ("specific" rates of duty such as 2 cents each or 1.5 cents/pound, etc.) or on a combination basis ("compound" rates of duty such as 5 cents each plus 6%).

Listed below is a sampling of several Column 1 import duty rates for Chapter 79 products:
Zinc waste and scrap (7902.00.00.00): Free
to
Zinc bars, rods, profiles and wire (7904.00.00.00): 4.2%

For specific information on US import duties refer to the Harmonized Tariff Schedule of the US. The print version is available from the US Government Printing Office as well as third party suppliers who often add special features. Online versions are available in both static PDF pages as well as in formats with excellent search functionality. Search the Web with the term "Harmonized Tariff Schedule" to find sources.

Entry and Documentation

The entry of merchandise is a two-part process consisting of 1) filing the documents necessary to determine whether merchandise may be released from Customs custody and 2) filing the documents that contain information for duty assessment and statistical purposes. In certain instances all documents must be filed and accepted by Customs prior to the release of the goods. Unless you have been granted an extension, you must file entry documents at a location specified by the port or area director within five working days of your shipment's date of arrival at a U.S. port of entry. These include a number of standard documents required by Customs for any entry, and

- U.S. Customs TSCA Certification when required

After you present the entry, Customs may examine your shipment, or may waive examination. The shipment is then released provided no legal or regulatory violations have been noted. You must then file entry summary documentation and deposit estimated duties at a designated customhouse within 10 working days of your shipment's release. For a detailed description of entry procedures, standard documentation, and informal entry, see "Entry Process" on page 185.

Informed Compliance. Informed compliance was introduced with the Customs Modernization Act of 1993 (Mod Act) and defines the relationship between importers and the Customs Service. It sets out the responsibilities of both parties. Providing the correct documentation and information for entry is a key factor that will make your importing operation run smoothly. We recommend that importers become familiar with the concept of informed comliance and the responsibilities that they have under the Mod Act. For further discussion about informed compliance see "Informed Compliance" on page 211.

Note: The Entry and Documentation section has been carefully designed to supply you, the importer, with sample documents and directions on how to satisfy Customs requirements. Be aware that you should consult the applicable authorities to ensure that you are correctly following the most current procedures.

Marking and Labeling Requirements

For a general discussion of U.S. Customs marking and labeling requirements, see "Country of Origin Marking" on page 236, "Special Marking Requirements" on page 238 and "Marking—False Impression" on page 239.

Shipping Considerations

You will need to ensure that your goods are packaged and shipped with care to ensure that they arrive in good condition and pass smoothly through Customs. You are responsible for ensuring that the shipment is in compliance with all applicable government regulations for packaging and shipping. In most instances, you should not leave these arrangements solely to the discretion of your supplier. Careful preparation of the cargo and selection of the mode of transport can be essential to a cost-effective, timely delivery of undamaged goods. We strongly advise you to consult your shipping representative, insurance agent, or freight broker for advice on packing and shipping.

Products that are listed as hazardous substances (49 CFR 172 appendix) may be transported in bulk only on compliance with Coast Guard notification procedures, shipping permit requirements, and complex transportation regulations (46 CFR 148). All hazardous substances must be packaged and transported in accordance with DOT regulations (49 CFR 171 et seq.).

Zinc, zinc alloy, and products made of them are often bulky, and should be securely stowed to avoid damage due to shifting en route. Zinc and its products are also subject to tarnish and corrosion, which should be guarded against, especially as no allowance is made by customs for partial damage or loss due to such.

Publications and WWW Resources

The *Harmonized Tariff Schedule of the United States (2001)* (HTSUS) is available to view on the Customs Service website (www.customs.gov), or you may purchase a printed version from:

U.S. Government Printing Office
Superintendent of Documents
710 North Capital Street NW
Washington DC 20401
Tel: (202) 512-1800
Fax: (202) 512-1657
Website: www.access.gpo.gov

The USGPO also has copies of specific laws available for purchase. The USGPO accepts orders made by fax, phone or placed over the Internet, as well as mail orders paid by credit card. All orders must be accompanied by payment. Credit cards, checks drawn on a U.S. bank, or an international money order are all acceptable.

Relevant Government Agencies

Address inquiries regarding TSCA and EPA requirements for importation of hazardous or toxic substances to:

Environmental Protection Agency (EPA)
Office of Pollution Prevention and Toxics
TSCA System Information
1200 Pennsylvania Avenue NW
Washington DC 20460
Tel: (202) 564-3810

Tel: (202) 554-1404 (TSCA Information Hotline)
Email: oppt.homepage@epa.gov
Website: www.epa.gov/opptintr/contact.htm

Address questions regarding transportation of hazardous substances to:

U.S. Department of Transportation (DOT)
Research and Special Programs Administration
Hazardous Materials Information Center
400 7th St. SW
Washington DC 20590
Tel: (202) 366-4488
Website: http://hazmat.dot.gov

Address your questions regarding FDA requirements for zinc products intended for use with food to:

Food and Drug Administration (FDA)
Center for Food Safety and Applied Nutrition (CFSAN)
Office of Compliance
Division of Enforcement, Imports Branch
5100 Paint Branch Parkway
College Park, MD 20740-3835
Tel: (301) 436-2080
Website: http://vm.cfsan.fda.gov/list.html

Address questions regarding the importation of zinc and zinc products to your local Customs port director. For addresses refer to "U.S. Customs and Border Protection Offices" on page 65 or contact:

U.S. Customs and Border Protection
Customs Headquarters
1300 Pennsylvania Avenue NW
Washington DC 20229
Tel: (202) 354-1000
Website: www.customs.treas.gov

Laws and Regulations

The following laws and regulations may be relevant to the importation of zinc and zinc products. The laws are contained in the U.S. Code (USC) and the regulations are published in the Code of Federal Regulations (CFR), both of which may be available at larger public and law libraries. Copies of specific laws are also available from the United States Government Printing Office (address above).

15 USC 2601 et seq.
Toxic Substances Control Act
This Act authorizes the EPA to determine whether a substance is harmful and to restrict importation, sale, and use of such substances.

19 CFR 12.118 et seq.
Regulations on Toxic Substances Control
These regulations require importers of chemical substances imported in bulk or as part of a mixture to certify to Customs that the shipment complies with the TSCA or is not subject to that Act.

15 USC 1261 et seq.
Federal Hazardous Substances Act
This Act controls the importation of hazardous substances, sets forth prohibited imports, and authorizes various agencies to promulgate labeling, marking, and transport requirements.

49 CFR 171 et seq.
Regulations on Hazardous Materials
These regulations list all substances deemed hazardous and provide transport, marking, labeling, safety, and emergency response rules.

46 CFR 147.30
Regulations on Labeling of Hazardous Materials
This regulation requires the labeling of containers of haz-

ardous substances and specifies the label contents.

46 CFR 148 et seq.
Regulations of Carriage of Solid Hazardous Materials in Bulk
These regulations govern the transport of solid hazardous substances in bulk, including reporting, permitting, loading, stowing, and shipping requirements.

21 USC 301 et seq.
Federal Food, Drug, and Cosmetic Act
This Act prohibits deceptive practices and regulates the manufacture, sale and importation or exportation of food, drugs, cosmetics, and related products. It was amended by the Food Quality Protection Act of 1996. See 21 USC 331, 381, 382.

19 CFR 12.1 et seq.; 21 CFR 1.83 et seq.
Regulations on Food, Drugs, and Cosmetics
These regulations of the Secretary of Health and Human Services and the Secretary of the Treasury govern the standards, labeling, marking, and importing of products used with food, drugs, and cosmetics.

Principal Exporting Countries

The following listing includes samples of the main supplier nations of the products of this chapter. It is organized by HTSUS major heading. (Refer to "Customs Classification" above for the product codes.) Countries are listed in rank order of the value of products imported to the U.S. Statistics represent customs value of entries for 2002 from the Bureau of Census, U.S. Department of Commerce.

7901—Canada, Mexico, Kazakhstan, South Korea, China, Peru, Australia, Brazil

7902—Canada, Mexico, Guatemala, Taiwan, Belgium, Nicaragua

7903—Canada, Belgium, Germany, Austria, Mexico, United Kingdom, Guatemala, Japan, Switzerland, South Korea, China

7904—Finland, Germany, Canada, South Africa, United Kingdom, Japan, China, Belgium, Turkey

7905—France, Germany, Japan, China, Canada, Belgium

7906—India, Mexico, Canada, China, Taiwan, United Kingdom, Germany, Netherlands, South Korea, Ireland

7907—China, Mexico, Taiwan, Canada, United Kingdom, Hong Kong, South Korea, Malaysia

Chapter 80:
Tin and Articles Thereof

This section pertains to the importation of tin, tin alloys, and articles made from these products, which are classified within Chapter 80 of the Harmonized Tariff Schedule of the United States (HTSUS). Specifically, it includes unwrought tin; tin waste and scrap; tin bars, rods, wire, plates, sheets, strips, and foil; tin tubes, pipes, and fittings; and miscellaneous articles of tin, including household articles suitable for food and beverage service.

Goods of base metals and their alloys in which metals other than tin predominate are covered in Commodity Index chapters on the specific metals, including iron and steel (Chapter 72), copper (Chapter 74), nickel (Chapter 75), aluminum (Chapter 76), lead (Chapter 78), zinc (Chapter 79), and other base metals (Chapter 81). Tools, other implements, and cutlery are found in Chapter 82, while miscellaneous articles of base metals are contained in Chapter 83. Precious metals, alloys of precious metals, and articles containing the same are covered specifically in Chapter 71.

Other products for which metals are incidental—even if critical and major—components are found within a variety of Commodity Index chapters. For example, if you are interested in importing metallic paints, refer to Chapter 36. For headgear with metal elements, see Chapter 65; for umbrella frames and related items, see Chapter 66. Finished and semifinished products classified as machinery, mechanical appliances, and electrical goods are found in Chapters 84 and 85. Assembled railway track and related equipment is covered in Chapter 86, vehicles in Chapter 87, aircraft in Chapter 88, and boats in Chapter 89. Instruments and apparatus are covered in Commodity Index chapters that relate to the particular article, including optical, medical, and precision instruments (Chapter 90), clocks and watches (Chapter 91), and musical instruments (Chapter 92). Metal articles as parts of firearms, including ammunition, are found in Chapter 93. Commodity Index chapters that cover miscellaneous manufactures include furniture (Chapter 94), toys, games, and sporting goods (Chapter 95), and miscellaneous manufactured articles (Chapter 96). Works of art in which tin or its alloys are components, even dominant components, are covered in Chapter 97 if the primary value derives from the artistry rather than from the metal content.

Note: To understand key issues that will enable you to make best use of the information in this section we recommend that you see "Introduction" on page 425.

Key Factors

The key factors in importing tin and tin alloy products are:

- Compliance with U.S. Environmental Protection Agency (EPA) requirements under the Toxic Sub-

stances Control Act (TSCA) (if the product is classified as a hazardous substance)

- Compliance with U.S. Department of Transportation (DOT) regulations for transport of hazardous cargo (if the product is a hazardous substance)

- For items to be used with food, compliance with U.S. Food and Drug Administration (FDA) requirements and entry notification

Although most importers utilize the services of a licensed customs broker in making their entries, and we recommend this practice, you should be aware of the regulatory, entry, and documentation issues involved in importing your product. You, as importer, are ultimately responsible for the fulfillment of any legal requirements applicable to your shipment.

General Considerations

Regulatory Agencies. The importation of tin, tin alloys, and products made of them is relatively straightforward, with few restrictions or special requirements. The Food and Drug Administration (FDA) controls the importation of items for use with food. The Environmental Protection Agency (EPA), under authority of the Toxic Substances Control Act (TSCA), imposes certain controls on the importation of tin and tin articles that contain toxic substances. The Department of Transportation (DOT) enforces regulations for transporting hazardous cargo.

Definitions. Unlike alloys of precious metals, in which any alloy having as much as 2% of a precious metal is considered an alloy of that metal, alloys of base metals are classified according to the metal that predominates by weight over every other individual metal in the alloy. For customs purposes, alloys of a metal are included with the metal that they are an alloy of.

Chapter 80 of HTSUS covers tin and tin alloys. Tin is defined as metal containing by weight at least 99% by weight of tin with no more than 0.1% of bismuth or 0.4% of copper. Tin alloys are defined as being metallic substances in which tin predominates by weight over each of the other elements, provided that the total content by weight of the other elements exceeds 1%, with the total content of bismuth or copper being greater than that defined for unalloyed tin.

FDA Regulation. Kitchenware and tableware of tin and its alloys intended for use with food are subject to the provisions of the Federal Food, Drug, and Cosmetic Act (FDCA) enforced by the FDA. FDA entry notification is required for applicable items. Shipments of FDA-regulated products are subject to FDA port of entry inspection. For more information about FDA entry procedures and requirements see "Appendix: Foods" on page 825. Contact your nearest regional FDA office or FDA headquarters with questions regarding the importation of tin products (see addresses at end of this chapter).

Toxic Substances Regulations. The EPA imposes certain controls on the importation of toxic substances. The TSCA defines a toxic substance as any substance determined to present the possibility of an unreasonable risk of injury to health and the environment. The DOT enforces regulations for transporting hazardous cargo. Substances are deemed hazardous if listed in DOT transport regulations (49 CFR 172 appendix). Unwrought primary metals, such as pigs, ingots, billets, blooms, and similar materials, are generally categorized as toxic substances within the definitions of the TSCA and thus are required to be in compliance with its provisions. These include packaging, shipping, marking, and labeling requirements. Refer to "Laws and Regulations" below.

Products defined as articles—that is, any manufactured item 1) that is formed into a specific shape or design during manufacture, 2) that has end-use functions dependent on the shape or design during end use, and 3) that during the end use, does not change in its chemical composition or that changes only for a noncommercial purpose separate from the article and only as allowed by law (19 CFR 12.120(2))—are not subject to the provisions of the TSCA. Metal products other than primary metals are generally considered to be articles even if they are to be further processed. For example, tin in sheets is an article even if it is to be subsequently fabricated into other products.

Certification. All products covered by the TSCA are subject to the U.S. Customs Service TSCA Import Certification Rule (19 CFR 12.118 et seq.). If you import these products, you must sign one of the following statements: "I certify that all materials in this shipment comply with all applicable rules or orders under TSCA and that I am not offering a chemical substance for entry in violation of TSCA or any applicable rule or order thereunder" or "I certify that all materials in this shipment are not subject to TSCA." You must file this TSCA certification of compliance or exemption at the time you make the entry at customs. Customs will not release your shipment without proper certification.

If you will be importing several or regular shipments, you should ask the appropriate Customs port director to authorize your use of a blanket certification. A blanket certification is valid for one calendar year, may be renewed, and may be revoked at any time for cause.

Customs Classification

For customs purposes, tin and tin products are classified within Chapter 80 of the HTSUS. This chapter is divided into headings, which are further divided into subheadings, and often into sub-subheadings, each of which has its own HTSUS classification number. For example, the 2001 HTSUS number for tin alloys is 8001.20, indicating that it is a subcategory of the major heading unwrought tin (8001). There are seven major headings in HTSUS Chapter 80.

8001—Unwrought tin

8002—Tin waste and scrap

8003—Tin bars, rods, profiles, and wire

8004—Tin plates, sheets, and strip, of a thickness exceeding 0.2 mm.

8005—Tin foil (whether or not printed of backed with paper, paperboard, plastics, or similar backing materials), of a thickness (excluding any backing) not exceeding 0.2 mm; tin powders and flakes

8006—Tin tubes, pipes, and tube or pipe fittings (for examples, couplings, elbows, sleeves)

8007—Other articles of tin

For more details regarding classification of the specific product you are interested in importing, consult a customs broker, the appropriate commodity specialist at your nearest customs port, or see HTSUS. The 2001 HTSUS is available online from the Customs Service (www.customs.gov/impoexpo/impoexpo.htm) or for purchase from the U.S. Government Printing Office (see resources at the end of this chapter), and may be found in larger public libraries. For a general discussion of customs classification, see "Classification—Liquidation" on page 229.

Dutiable Status of Goods

For more information about duty rates and binding decisions see "Dutiable Status of Goods" on page 203; for a discussion of temporary importation of goods see "Temporary Free Importations" on page 205.

Valuation

Importers have a responsibility to use what the U.S. Customs Service deems, "reasonable care," when determining the value of their goods. They must also provide any additional information that the Customs Service needs for setting a final value on the goods. This process involves a number of factors and can be somewhat complicated; importers must be aware of applicable issues and details. Valuation information applies to all types of commodities, for further discussion on the subject see "Customs Valuation" on page 267.

Import Duties

Import duties vary (often dramatically) depending upon the Harmonized Tariff Schedule (HTSUS) classification of the goods or products imported. Since some products that look alike have different HTSUS classifications and different rates of duty, proper classification is vital. Note that "differences of opinion" between importers and the Bureau of Customs and Border Protection regarding classification keeps customs attorneys very busy.

Import duties can be assessed on the imported value of the goods ("ad valorem" rates of duty such as 2%, 4.4%, 50%, etc.), total units or weight of the goods ("specific" rates of duty such as 2 cents each or 1.5 cents/pound, etc.) or on a combination basis ("compound" rates of duty such as 5 cents each plus 6%).

Listed below is a sampling of several Column 1 import duty rates for Chapter 80 products:
Tin waste and scrap (8002.00.00.00): Free
to
Powders and flakes (8005.00.20.00): 2.8%

For specific information on US import duties refer to the Harmonized Tariff Schedule of the US. The print version is available from the US Government Printing Office as well as third party suppliers who often add special features. Online versions are available in both static PDF pages as well as in formats with excellent search functionality. Search the Web with the term "Harmonized Tariff Schedule" to find sources.

Entry and Documentation

The entry of merchandise is a two-part process consisting of 1) filing the documents necessary to determine whether merchandise may be released from Customs custody and 2) filing the documents that contain information for duty assessment and statistical purposes. In certain instances all documents must be filed and accepted by Customs prior to the release of the goods. Unless you have been granted an extension, you must file entry documents at a location specified by the port or area director within five working days of your shipment's date of arrival at a U.S. port of entry. These include a number of standard documents required by Customs for any entry, and

- U.S. Customs TSCA Certification when required

After you present the entry, Customs may examine your shipment, or may waive examination. The shipment is then released provided no legal or regulatory violations have been noted. You must then file entry summary documentation and deposit estimated duties at a designated customhouse within 10 working days of your shipment's release. For a detailed description of entry procedures, standard documentation, and informal entry, see "Entry Process" on page 185.

Informed Compliance. Informed compliance was introduced with the Customs Modernization Act of 1993 (Mod Act) and defines the relationship between importers and the Customs Service. It sets out the responsibilities of both parties. Providing the correct documentation and information for entry is a key factor that will make your importing operation run smoothly. We recommend that importers become familiar with the concept of informed comliance and the responsibilities that they have under the Mod Act. For further discussion about informed compliance see "Informed Compliance" on page 211.

Note: The Entry and Documentation section has been carefully designed to supply you, the importer, with sample documents and directions on how to satisfy Customs requirements. Be aware that you should consult the applicable authorities to ensure that you are correctly following the most current procedures.

Marking and Labeling Requirements

For a general discussion of U.S. Customs marking and labeling requirements, see "Country of Origin Marking" on page 236, "Special Marking Requirements" on page 238 and "Marking—False Impression" on page 239.

Shipping Considerations

You will need to ensure that your goods are packaged and shipped with care to ensure that they arrive in good condition and pass smoothly through Customs. You are responsible for ensuring that the shipment is in compliance with all applicable government regulations for packaging and shipping. In most instances, you should not leave these arrangements solely to the discretion of your supplier. Careful preparation of the cargo and selection of the mode of transport can be essential to a cost-effective, timely delivery of undamaged goods. We strongly advise you to consult your shipping representative, insurance agent, or freight broker for advice on packing and shipping.

Products that are listed as hazardous substances (49 CFR 172 appendix) may be transported in bulk only on compliance with Coast Guard notification procedures, shipping permit requirements, and complex transportation regulations (46 CFR 148). All hazardous substances must be packaged and transported in accordance with DOT regulations (49 CFR 171 et seq.).

Tin, tin alloys, and products made of them are often bulky, and should be securely stowed to avoid damage due to shifting en route. Tin and its products are also subject to tarnish and corrosion, which should be guarded against, especially as no allowance is made by customs for partial damage or loss due to such.

Publications and WWW Resources

The *Harmonized Tariff Schedule of the United States (2001)* (HTSUS) is available to view on the Customs Service website (www.customs.gov), or you may purchase a printed version from:

U.S. Government Printing Office
Superintendent of Documents
710 North Capital Street NW
Washington DC 20401
Tel: (202) 512-1800
Fax: (202) 512-1657
Website: www.access.gpo.gov

The USGPO also has copies of specific laws available for purchase. The USGPO accepts orders made by fax, phone or placed over the Internet, as well as mail orders paid by credit card. All orders must be accompanied by payment. Credit cards, checks drawn on a U.S. bank, or an international money order are all acceptable.

Relevant Government Agencies

Address inquiries regarding TSCA and EPA requirements for importation of hazardous or toxic substances to:

Environmental Protection Agency (EPA)
Office of Pollution Prevention and Toxics
TSCA System Information
1200 Pennsylvania Avenue NW
Washington DC 20460
Tel: (202) 564-3810
Tel: (202) 554-1404 (TSCA Information Hotline)
Email: oppt.homepage@epa.gov
Website: www.epa.gov/opptintr/contact.htm

Address questions regarding transportation of hazardous substances to:

U.S. Department of Transportation (DOT)
Research and Special Programs Administration
Hazardous Materials Information Center
400 7th St. SW
Washington DC 20590
Tel: (202) 366-4488
Website: http://hazmat.dot.gov

Address your questions regarding FDA requirements for tin products intended for use with food to:

Food and Drug Administration (FDA)
Center for Food Safety and Applied Nutrition (CFSAN)
Office of Compliance
Division of Enforcement, Imports Branch
5100 Paint Branch Parkway
College Park, MD 20740-3835
Tel: (301) 436-2080
Website: http://vm.cfsan.fda.gov/list.html

Address questions regarding the importation of tin and tin products to your local Customs port director. For addresses refer to "U.S. Customs and Border Protection Offices" on page 65 or contact:

U.S. Customs and Border Protection
Customs Headquarters
1300 Pennsylvania Avenue NW
Washington DC 20229
Tel: (202) 354-1000
Website: www.customs.treas.gov

Laws and Regulations

The following laws and regulations may be relevant to the importation of tin and tin products. The laws are contained in the U.S. Code (USC) and the regulations are published in the Code of Federal Regulations (CFR), both of which may be available at larger public and law libraries. Copies of specific laws are also available from the United States Government Printing Office (address above).

15 USC 2601 et seq.
Toxic Substances Control Act
This Act authorizes the EPA to determine whether a substance is harmful and to restrict importation, sale, and use of such substances.

19 CFR 12.118 et seq.
Regulations on Toxic Substances Control
These regulations require importers of chemical substances imported in bulk or as part of a mixture to certify to Customs that the shipment complies with the TSCA or is not subject to that Act.

15 USC 1261 et seq.
Federal Hazardous Substances Act
This Act controls the importation of hazardous substances, sets forth prohibited imports, and authorizes various agencies to promulgate labeling, marking, and transport requirements.

49 CFR 171 et seq.
Regulations on Hazardous Materials
These regulations list all substances deemed hazardous and provide transport, marking, labeling, safety, and emergency response rules.

46 CFR 147.30
Regulations of Labeling of Hazardous Materials
This regulation requires the labeling of containers of hazardous substances and specifies the label contents.

46 CFR 148 et seq.
Regulations of Carriage of Solid Hazardous Materials in Bulk

These regulations govern the transport of solid hazardous substances in bulk, including reporting, permitting, loading, stowing, and shipping requirements.**21 USC 301 et seq.**

Federal Food, Drug, and Cosmetic Act

This Act prohibits deceptive practices and regulates the manufacture, sale and importation or exportation of food, drugs, cosmetics, and related products. It was amended by the Food Quality Protection Act of 1996. See 21 USC 331, 381, 382.

19 CFR 12.1 et seq.; 21 CFR 1.83 et seq.

Regulations on Food, Drugs, and Cosmetics

These regulations of the Secretary of Health and Human Services and the Secretary of the Treasury govern the standards, labeling, marking, and importing of products used with food, drugs, and cosmetics.

Principal Exporting Countries

The following listing includes samples of the main supplier nations of the products of this chapter. It is organized by HTSUS major heading. (Refer to "Customs Classification" above for the product codes.) Countries are listed in rank order of the value of products imported to the U.S. Statistics represent customs value of entries for 2002 from the Bureau of Census, U.S. Department of Commerce.

8001—Peru, Bolivia, China, Brazil, Indonesia, Malaysia, Canada

8002—Mexico, Canada, Singapore, Japan, France

8003—Canada, Japan, Germany, Netherlands, Mexico, South Korea, Russia

8004—Canada, China, Venezuela, Germany, Belgium, Australia, United Kingdom, Taiwan

8005—France, United Kingdom, Germany, Canada, Netherlands, Singapore, Malaysia

8006—Germany, United Kingdom, Japan

8007—China, Italy, Taiwan, Spain, Hong Kong, United Kingdom, Philippines, Germany, Mexico, France, Canada

Chapter 81: Other Base Metals; Cermets; and Articles Thereof

This section pertains to the importation of base metals not specified elsewhere, their alloys, materials of combined ceramics and metals (cermets), and articles made from these products, which are classified within Chapter 81 of the Harmonized Tariff Schedule of the United States (HTSUS). Specifically, it includes tungsten (wolfram), molybdenum, tantalum, magnesium, cobalt, bismuth, cadmium, titanium, zirconium, antimony, manganese, beryllium, chromium, germanium, vanadium, gallium, hafnium, indium, niobium, rhenium, and thallium and articles of these metals, as well as cermets and articles made of them. Chapter 81 represents a catch-all designation for relatively minor but highly specialized base metals.

Goods of base metals and their alloys in which metals other than those listed in Chapter 81 predominate are covered in Commodity Index chapters that relate to the specific metals, including iron and steel (Chapter 72), copper (Chapter 74), nickel (Chapter 75), aluminum (Chapter 76), lead (Chapter 78), zinc (Chapter 79), and tin (Chapter 80). Tools, other implements, and cutlery are found in Chapter 82, while miscellaneous articles of base metals are contained in Chapter 83. Precious metals, alloys of precious metals, and articles containing the same are covered specifically in Chapter 71.

Other products for which metals are incidental components are found within a variety of Commodity Index chapters. For example, if you are interested in importing metallic paints, refer to Chapter 36. For headgear with metal elements, see Chapter 65; for umbrella frames and related items, see Chapter 66. Finished and semifinished products classified as machinery, mechanical appliances, and electrical goods are found in Chapters 84 and 85. Assembled railway track and related equipment is covered in Chapter 86, vehicles in Chapter 87, aircraft in Chapter 88, and boats in Chapter 89. Instruments and apparatus are covered in Commodity Index chapters that relate to the specific articles, including optical, medical, and precision instruments (Chapter 90), clocks and watches (Chapter 91), and musical instruments (Chapter 92). Metal articles as parts of firearms, including ammunition, are found in Chapter 93. Commodity Index chapters that cover miscellaneous manufactures include furniture (Chapter 94), toys, games, and sporting goods (Chapter 95), and miscellaneous manufactured articles (Chapter 96). Works of art in which lead or its alloys are components, even dominant components, are covered in Chapter 97 if the primary value derives from the artistry rather than from the metal content.

Note: To understand key issues that will enable you to make best use of the information in this section we recommend that you see "Introduction" on page 425.

Key Factors

The key factors in importing products of miscellaneous base metals are:

- Compliance with U.S. Environmental Protection Agency (EPA) requirements under the Toxic Substances Control Act (TSCA) (if the product is classified as a hazardous substance)

- Compliance with U.S. Department of Transportation (DOT) regulations for transport of hazardous cargo (if the product is a hazardous substance)

Although most importers utilize the services of a licensed customs broker in making their entries, and we recommend this practice, you should be aware of the regulatory, entry, and documentation issues involved in importing your product. You, as importer, are ultimately responsible for the fulfillment of any legal requirements applicable to your shipment.

General Considerations

Regulatory Agencies. The importation of specialized base metals, their alloys, and products made of them is relatively straightforward, with few restrictions or special requirements. The Environmental Protection Agency (EPA), under authority of the Toxic Substances Control Act (TSCA), imposes certain controls on the importation of base metals and articles that contain toxic substances. The Department of Transportation (DOT) enforces regulations for transporting hazardous cargo.

Definitions. Unlike alloys of precious metals, in which any alloy containing as much as 2% by weight of a precious metal is considered an alloy of that metal, alloys of base metals are classified according to the metal that predominates by weight over every other individual metal in the alloy. For customs purposes, alloys of a metal are included with the metal that they are an alloy of.

Chapter 81 of HTSUS covers other base metals and their alloys. The metals covered are defined as containing at least 99% by weight of the specified metal. Alloys are defined as being metallic substances in which the specified metal is less than 99% by weight, but not less than any other metallic element.

Toxic Substances Regulations. The EPA imposes certain controls on the importation of toxic substances. The TSCA defines a toxic substance as any substance determined to present the possibility of an unreasonable risk of injury to health and the environment. The DOT enforces regulations for transporting hazardous cargo. Substances are deemed hazardous if listed in DOT transport regulations (49 CFR 172 appendix). Unwrought primary metals, such as pigs, ingots, billets, blooms, and similar materials, are generally categorized as toxic substances within the definitions of the TSCA and thus are required to be in compliance with its provisions. These include packaging, shipping, marking, and labeling requirements. Refer to "Laws and Regulations" below.

Products defined as articles—that is, any manufactured item 1) that is formed into a specific shape or design during manufacture, 2) that has end-use functions dependent on the shape or design during end use, and 3) that during the end use, does not change in its chemical composition or that changes only for a noncommercial purpose separate from the article and only as allowed by law (19 CFR 12.120(2))—are not subject to the provisions of the TSCA. Metal products other than primary metals are generally considered to be articles even if they are to be further processed. For example, base metal products are articles even if they are to be subsequently fabricated into other products.

Certification. All products covered by the TSCA are subject to the U.S. Customs Service TSCA Import Certification Rule (19 CFR 12.118 et seq.). If you import these products, you must sign one of the following statements: "I certify that all materials in this shipment comply with all applicable rules or orders under TSCA and that I am not offering a chemical substance for entry in violation of TSCA or any applicable rule or order thereunder" or "I certify that all materials in this shipment are not subject to TSCA." You must file this TSCA certification of compliance or exemption at the time you make the entry at customs. Customs will not release your shipment without proper certification.

If you will be importing several or regular shipments, you should ask the appropriate customs port director to authorize your use of a blanket certification. A blanket certification is valid for one calendar year, may be renewed, and may be revoked at any time for cause.

Customs Classification

For customs purposes, specialized base metals, their alloys, and their products are classified within Chapter 81 of the HTSUS. This chapter is divided into headings, which are further divided into subheadings, and often into sub-subheadings, each of which has its own HTSUS classification number. For example, the 2001 HTSUS number for unwrought molybdenum is 8102.91.10, indicating that it is a subcategory of molybdenum other than powders (8102.91), which is a subsubcategory of the major heading molybdenum and articles thereof, including waste and scrap (8102). There are 13 major headings in HTSUS Chapter 81.

8101—Tungsten (wolfram) and articles thereof, including waste and scrap

8102—Molybdenum and articles thereof, including waste and scrap

8103—Tantalum and articles thereof, including waste and scrap

8104—Magnesium and articles thereof, including waste and scrap

8105—Cobalt mattes and other intermediate products of cobalt metallurgy; cobalt and articles thereof, including waste and scrap

8106—Bismuth and articles thereof, including waste and scrap

8107—Cadmium and articles thereof, including waste and scrap

8108—Titanium and articles thereof, including waste and scrap

8109—Zirconium and articles thereof, including waste and scrap

8110—Antimony and articles thereof, including waste and scrap

8111—Manganese and articles thereof, including waste and scrap

8112—Beryllium, chromium, germanium, vanadium, gallium, hafnium, indium, niobium (colombium), rhenium, and thallium, and articles of these metals, including waste and scrap

8113—Cermets and articles thereof, including waste and scrap

For more details regarding classification of the specific product you are interested in importing, consult a customs broker, the appropriate commodity specialist at your nearest customs port, or see HTSUS. The 2001 HTSUS is available online from the Customs Service (www.customs.gov/impoexpo/impoexpo.htm) or for purchase from the U.S. Government Printing Office (see resources at the end of this chapter), and may be found in larger public libraries. For a general discussion of customs classification, see "Classification—Liquidation" on page 229.

Dutiable Status of Goods

For more information about duty rates and binding decisions see "Dutiable Status of Goods" on page 203; for a discussion of temporary importation of goods see "Temporary Free Importations" on page 205.

Valuation

Importers have a responsibility to use what the U.S. Customs Service deems, "reasonable care," when determining the value of their goods. They must also provide any additional information that the Customs Service needs for setting a final value on the goods. This process involves a number of factors and can be somewhat complicated; importers must be aware of applicable issues and details. Valuation information applies to all types of commodities, for further discussion on the subject see "Customs Valuation" on page 267.

Import Duties

Import duties vary (often dramatically) depending upon the Harmonized Tariff Schedule (HTSUS) classification of the goods or products imported. Since some products that look alike have different HTSUS classifications and different rates of duty, proper classification is vital. Note that "differences of opinion" between importers and the Bureau of Customs and Border Protection regarding classification keeps customs attorneys very busy.

Import duties can be assessed on the imported value of the goods ("ad valorem" rates of duty such as 2%, 4.4%, 50%, etc.), total units or weight of the goods ("specific" rates of duty such as 2 cents each or 1.5 cents/pound, etc.) or on a combination basis ("compound" rates of duty such as 5 cents each plus 6%).

Listed below is a sampling of several Column 1 import duty rates for Chapter 81 products:
Waste and scrap (8103.30.00.00): Free
to
Bars and rods (8102.95.30.00): 6.6%

For specific information on US import duties refer to the Harmonized Tariff Schedule of the US. The print version is available from the US Government Printing Office as well as third party suppliers who often add special features. Online versions are available in both static PDF pages as well as in formats with excellent search functionality. Search the Web with the term "Harmonized Tariff Schedule" to find sources.

Entry and Documentation

The entry of merchandise is a two-part process consisting of 1) filing the documents necessary to determine whether merchandise may be released from Customs custody and 2) filing the documents that contain information for duty assessment and statistical purposes. In certain instances all documents must be filed and accepted by Customs prior to the release of the goods. Unless you have been granted an extension, you must file entry documents at a location specified by the district/area director within five working days of your shipment's date of arrival at a U.S. port of entry. These include a number of standard documents required by Customs for any entry, and

- U.S. Customs TSCA Certification when required

After you present the entry, Customs may examine your shipment, or may waive examination. The shipment is then released provided no legal or regulatory violations have been noted. You must then file entry summary documentation and deposit estimated duties at a designated customhouse within 10 working days of your shipment's release. For a detailed description of entry procedures, standard documentation, and informal entry, see "Entry Process" on page 185.

Informed Compliance. Informed compliance was introduced with the Customs Modernization Act of 1993 (Mod Act) and defines the relationship between importers and the Customs Service. It sets out the responsibilities of both parties. Providing the correct documentation and information for entry is a key factor that will make your importing operation run smoothly. We recommend that importers become familiar with the concept of in-

formed comliance and the responsibilities that they have under the Mod Act. For further discussion about informed compliance see "Informed Compliance" on page 211.

Note: The Entry and Documentation section has been carefully designed to supply you, the importer, with sample documents and directions on how to satisfy Customs requirements. Be aware that you should consult the applicable authorities to ensure that you are correctly following the most current procedures.

Marking and Labeling Requirements

For a general discussion of U.S. Customs marking and labeling requirements, see "Country of Origin Marking" on page 236, "Special Marking Requirements" on page 238 and "Marking—False Impression" on page 239.

Shipping Considerations

You will need to ensure that your goods are packaged and shipped with care to ensure that they arrive in good condition and pass smoothly through Customs. You are responsible for ensuring that the shipment is in compliance with all applicable government regulations for packaging and shipping. In most instances, you should not leave these arrangements solely to the discretion of your supplier. Careful preparation of the cargo and selection of the mode of transport can be essential to a cost-effective, timely delivery of undamaged goods. We strongly advise you to consult your shipping representative, insurance agent, or freight broker for advice on packing and shipping.

Products that are listed as hazardous substances (49 CFR 172 appendix) may be transported in bulk only on compliance with Coast Guard notification procedures, shipping permit requirements, and complex transportation regulations (46 CFR 148). All hazardous substances must be packaged and transported in accordance with DOT regulations (49 CFR 171 et seq.).

Specialized base metals, their alloy, and products made of them are often bulky and heavy, and should be securely stowed to avoid damage due to shifting en route. Products made of these metals are also subject to oxidation and corrosion, which should be guarded against, especially as no allowance is made by customs for partial damage or loss due to such.

Publications and WWW Resources

The *Harmonized Tariff Schedule of the United States (2001)* (HTSUS) is available to view on the Customs Service website (www.customs.gov), or you may purchase a printed version from:

U.S. Government Printing Office
Superintendent of Documents
710 North Capital Street NW
Washington DC 20401
Tel: (202) 512-1800
Fax: (202) 512-1657
Website: www.access.gpo.gov

The USGPO also has copies of specific laws available for purchase. The USGPO accepts orders made by fax, phone or placed over the Internet, as well as mail orders paid by credit card. All orders must be accompanied by payment. Credit cards, checks drawn on a U.S. bank, or an international money order are all acceptable.

Relevant Government Agencies

Address inquiries regarding TSCA and EPA requirements for importation of hazardous or toxic substances to:

Environmental Protection Agency (EPA)
Office of Pollution Prevention and Toxics
TSCA System Information
1200 Pennsylvania Avenue, NW
Washington DC 20460

Tel: (202) 564-3810
Tel: (202) 554-1404 (TSCA Information Hotline)
Email: oppt.homepage@epa.gov
Website: www.epa.gov/opptintr/contact.htm

Address questions regarding transportation of hazardous substances to:

U.S. Department of Transportation (DOT)
Research and Special Programs Administration
Hazardous Materials Information Center
400 7th St. SW
Washington DC 20590
Tel: (202) 366-4488
Website: http://hazmat.dot.gov

Address questions regarding the importation of specialized base metals and their products to your local Customs port director. For addresses refer to "U.S. Customs and Border Protection Offices" on page 65 or contact:

U.S. Customs and Border Protection
Customs Headquarters
1300 Pennsylvania Avenue NW
Washington DC 20229
Tel: (202) 354-1000
Website: www.customs.treas.gov

Laws and Regulations

The following laws and regulations may be relevant to the importation of specialized base metals, their alloys, and products made of them. The laws are contained in the U.S. Code (USC) and the regulations are published in the Code of Federal Regulations (CFR), both of which may be available at larger public and law libraries. Copies of specific laws are also available from the United States Government Printing Office (address above).

15 USC 2601 et seq.
Toxic Substances Control Act
This Act authorizes the EPA to determine whether a substance is harmful and to restrict importation, sale, and use of such substances.

19 CFR 12.118 et seq.
Regulations on Toxic Substances Control
These regulations require importers of chemical substances imported in bulk or as part of a mixture to certify to Customs that the shipment complies with the TSCA or is not subject to that Act.

15 USC 1261 et seq.
Federal Hazardous Substances Act
This Act controls the importation of hazardous substances, sets forth prohibited imports, and authorizes various agencies to promulgate labeling, marking, and transport requirements.

49 CFR 171 et seq.
Regulations on Hazardous Materials
These regulations list all substances deemed hazardous and provide transport, marking, labeling, safety, and emergency response rules.

46 CFR 147.30
Regulations on Labeling of Hazardous Materials
This regulation requires the labeling of containers of hazardous substances and specifies the label contents.

46 CFR 148 et seq.
Regulations of Carriage of Solid Hazardous Materials in Bulk
These regulations govern the transport of solid hazardous substances in bulk, including reporting, permitting, loading, stowing, and shipping requirements.

Principal Exporting Countries

The following listing includes samples of the main supplier nations of the products of this chapter. It is organized by HTSUS major heading. (Refer to "Customs Classification" above for the product codes.) Countries are listed in rank order of the value of products imported to the U.S. Statistics represent customs value of entries for 2002 from the Bureau of Census, U.S. Department of Commerce.

8101—China, Germany, Japan, Austria, Israel, United Kingdom, South Korea

8102—Austria, China, Germany, Russia, Japan, Hong Kong, Switzerland, United Kingdom

8103—Japan, Kazakhstan, China, Thailand, Germany, United Kingdom, Austria, Israel

8104—Canada, Russia, Israel, China, United Kingdom, Italy, Brazil, Mexico, Kazakhstan, Germany

8105—Norway, Canada, Finland, Russia, Belgium, United Kingdom, Brazil, Zambia, Congo, Japan, South Africa

8106—Belgium, Mexico, China, United Kingdom, Hong Kong, Canada, Japan, Peru

8107—Canada, Belgium, Australia, China, France, Japan, Mexico, United Kingdom

8108—Japan, Russia, Kazakhstan, United Kingdom, Canada, Germany

8109—France, Germany, Canada, Belgium, Sweden, Austria, Japan, China, Russia

8110—China, Peru, Mexico, Canada, Hong Kong, Bolivia, United Kingdom, Japan

8111—South Africa, China, Germany, France, Canada, Spain, Netherlands

8112—France, Chile, China, Russia, United Kingdom, Estonia, Germany, Brazil, Kazakhstan, Japan, Belgium, Canada

8113—Germany, United Kingdom, South Africa, Japan, Netherlands, China, Belgium, Australia, Sweden, Czech Republic, Luxembourg

Chapter 82:
Metal Tools and Implements

Full title: Implements, Cutlery, Spoons, and Forks, of Base Metal; Parts Thereof of Base Metal

This section pertains to the importation of metal tools and implements, which are classified within Chapter 82 of the Harmonized Tariff Schedule of the United States (HTSUS). Specifically, it includes hand tools of a type involved primarily in gardening and agriculture; handsaws and blades; files, rasps, and cutting tools designed primarily to cut or work metal; wrenches; other hand tools, including torches, hammers, woodworking tools, screwdrivers, and other household tools, including sets of tools for retail sale; interchangeable parts and bits for hand tools—including pieces for power or machine tools but not the tools themselves; industrial knives; kitchen and table knives; razors and blades; scissors; other cutlery; and kitchen and table utensils. With the exception of blowtorches, portable forges, grinding wheels, and goods of heading 8209, articles covered in Chapter 82 basically represent implements with a blade, working edge or surface, or other similar part. Cutting tools of cermets (materials of ceramic and metal), and of precious and semiprecious stones, natural or synthetic, are also covered.

If you are interested in importing power tools, refer to Commodity Index Chapter 84. Other electrical machinery, including parts and working edges—such as blades or cutting plates for electric shavers or electric hair clippers—are covered in Chapter 85. Medical instruments are covered in Chapter 90. Intermediate products of base metals and their alloys are covered in various other Commodity Index chapters, including iron and steel (Chapter 73), copper (Chapter 74), nickel (Chapter 75), aluminum (Chapter 76), lead (Chapter 78), zinc (Chapter 79), tin (Chapter 80), and other base metals (Chapter 81). Articles of precious metals are found in Chapter 71.

Note: To understand key issues that will enable you to make best use of the information in this section we recommend that you see "Introduction" on page 425.

Key Factors

The key factors in the importation of metal tools and implements are:

- Compliance with U.S. Federal Trade Commission (FTC) and Consumer Product Safety Commission (CPSC) standards for consumer products

- Compliance with U.S. Food and Drug Administration (FDA) regulations (for items to be used with food)

- For many edged tools, compliance with special marking requirements

Although most importers utilize the services of a licensed customs broker in making their entries, and we recommend this practice, you should be aware of the regulatory, entry, and documentation issues involved in importing your product. You, as importer, are ultimately responsible for the fulfillment of any legal requirements applicable to your shipment.

General Considerations

Regulatory Agencies. The importation of metal tools and implements is generally straightforward. There are few Customs restrictions or prohibitions. No permits, licenses, or special entry paperwork are required. However, regulations of other agencies may apply. For example, the Consumer Product Safety Commission (CPSC) regulates the import and sale of hazardous consumer products. The Food and Drug Administration (FDA) may control the import of products used with food.

Consumer Products. Many of the products found in this section are covered by the provisions of the Consumer Product Safety Act (CPSA), which establishes standards for the manufacturing and labeling of potentially hazardous consumer products. Imported consumer products for which such standards exist must comply with the full range of requirements prescribed for domestic products. In addition, the CPSA requires all manufacturers, distributors, retailers, and others involved in the commercial handling of such products to report immediately any potentially hazardous defects or failures to conform to established standards to the CPSC for investigation and potential action. Failure to submit such a Substantial Product Hazard Report can result in action by the CPSC. Contact the CPSC (see addresses at end of this chapter) with questions regarding specific products.

Articles Used with Foods. The importation of some metal tools and implements designed for use with food is regulated by the FDA under the provisions of the Federal Food, Drug, and Cosmetic Act (FDCA). The FDA's regulatory focus is on items that pose immediate and long-term public health hazards, such as lead-glaze dinnerware. Historically, imported implements of base metals have not posed threats of this nature. The FDA is authorized to institute entry notice requirements at any time should it rule that a problem exists. Therefore, if you are interested in importing these products, you should be familiar with FDA import entry procedures and requirements. For a general discussion of FDA entry procedures see "Appendix: Foods" on page 825.

Cutting Tools. Importers should be aware of the special country of origin marking requirements for knives and some other cutting tools. For details, see "Marking and Labeling Requirements" below. If your shipment is ruled not to be in compliance with these requirements, it will be refused entry.

Tool Sets. If you are importing hand tools or other implements in sets—including sets of silverware—keep in mind that duties are levied on the basis of the highest rate applicable to any given piece contained in the set. To keep your duty rates as low as possible, choose the components of your sets carefully.

Customs Classification

For customs purposes, metal tools and implements are classified within Chapter 82 of the HTSUS. This chapter is divided into headings, which are further divided into subheadings, and often into sub-subheadings, each of which has its own HTSUS classification number. For example, the 2001 HTSUS number for slip joint pliers is 8203.20.40, indicating that it is a subcategory of pliers, pincers, tweezers, and similar tools (8203.20), which is a subcategory of the major heading files, rasps, pliers, pincers, tweezers, metal cutting shears, pipe-cutters, bolt cutters, perforating punches, and similar hand tools and base metal parts thereof (8203). There are 15 major headings in HTSUS chapter 82.

8201—Hand tools of the following kinds and base metal parts thereof: spades, shovels, mattocks, picks, hoes, forks, and rakes; axes, bill hooks, and similar hewing tools; secateurs and pruners of any kind; scythes, sickles, hay knives, hedge shears, timber wedges, and other tools of a kind used in agriculture, horticulture, or forestry

8202—Handsaws and metal parts thereof; blades for saws of all kinds (including slitting, slotting, or toothless saw blades), and base metal parts thereof

8203—Files, rasps, pliers (including cutting pliers), pincers, tweezers, metal cutting shears, pipe-cutters, bolt cutters, perforating punches, and similar hand tools, and base metal parts thereof

8204—Hand-operated spanners and wrenches (including torque meter wrenches but not including tap wrenches); socket wrenches, with or without handles, drives, or extensions; base metal parts thereof

8205—Hand tools (including glass cutters) not elsewhere specified or included; blow torches and similar self-contained torches; vises, clamps, and the like, other than accessories for and parts of machine tools; anvils; portable forges; hand-or pedal-operated grinding wheels with frameworks; base metal parts thereof

8206—Tools of two or more headings 8202 to 8205, put up in sets for retail sale

8207—Interchangeable tools for hand tools, whether or not power-operated, or for machine tools (for example, for pressing, stamping, punching, tapping, threading, drilling, boring, broaching, milling, turning, or screwdriving), including dies for drawing or extruding metal, and rock drilling or earth boring tools; base metal parts thereof

8208—Knives and cutting blades, for machines or for mechanical appliances, and base metal parts thereof

8209—Plates, sticks, tips, and the like for tools, unmounted, of cermets

8210—Hand-operated mechanical appliances, weighing 10 kg or less, used in the preparation, conditioning, or serving of food or drink, and base metal parts thereof

8211—Knives with cutting blades, serrated or not (including pruning knives), other than knives of heading 8208, and blades and other base metal parts thereof

8212—Razors and razor blades (including razor blade blanks and strips), and base metal parts thereof

8213—Scissors, tailors' shears, and similar shears, and blades and other base metal parts thereof

8214—Other articles of cutlery (for example hair clippers, butchers' or kitchen cleavers, chopping or mincing knives, paper knives); manicure or pedicure sets and instruments (including nail files); base metal parts thereof

8215—Spoons, forks, ladles, skimmers, cake-servers, fish-knives, butter-knives, sugar tongs, and similar kitchen or tableware; base metal parts thereof

For more details regarding classification of the specific product you are interested in importing, consult a customs broker, the appropriate commodity specialist at your nearest Customs port, or see HTSUS. The 2001 HTSUS is available online from the Customs Service (www.customs.gov/impoexpo/impoexpo.htm) or for purchase from the U.S. Government Printing Office (see resources at the end of this chapter), and may be found in larger public libraries. For a general discussion of customs classification, see "Classification—Liquidation" on page 229.

Dutiable Status of Goods

For more information about duty rates and binding decisions see "Dutiable Status of Goods" on page 203; for a discussion of temporary importation of goods see "Temporary Free Importations" on page 205.

Valuation

Importers have a responsibility to use what the U.S. Customs Service deems, "reasonable care," when determining the value of their goods. They must also provide any additional information that the Customs Service needs for setting a final value on the goods. This process involves a number of factors and can be somewhat complicated; importers must be aware of applicable issues and details. Valuation information applies to all types of commodities, for further discussion on the subject see "Customs Valuation" on page 267.

Import Duties

Import duties vary (often dramatically) depending upon the Harmonized Tariff Schedule (HTSUS) classification of the goods or products imported. Since some products that look alike have different HTSUS classifications and different rates of duty, proper classification is vital. Note that "differences of opinion" between importers and the Bureau of Customs and Border Protection regarding classification keeps customs attorneys very busy.

Import duties can be assessed on the imported value of the goods ("ad valorem" rates of duty such as 2%, 4.4%, 50%, etc.), total units or weight of the goods ("specific" rates of duty such as 2 cents each or 1.5 cents/pound, etc.) or on a combination basis ("compound" rates of duty such as 5 cents each plus 6%).

Listed below is a sampling of several Column 1 import duty rates for Chapter 82 products:
Spades and shovels, and parts thereof (8201.10.00 00): Free to
Chain saw blades and parts thereof with cutting parts containing by weight over 0.2 percent of chromium, molybdenum, or tungsten or over 0.1 percent of vanadium (8202.40.30 00): 7.2%

For specific information on US import duties refer to the Harmonized Tariff Schedule of the US. The print version is available from the US Government Printing Office as well as third party suppliers who often add special features. Online versions are available in both static PDF pages as well as in formats with excellent search functionality. Search the Web with the term "Harmonized Tariff Schedule" to find sources.

Entry and Documentation

The entry of merchandise is a two-part process consisting of 1) filing the documents necessary to determine whether merchandise may be released from Customs custody and 2) filing the documents that contain information for duty assessment and statistical purposes. In certain instances all documents must be filed and accepted by Customs prior to the release of the goods. Unless you have been granted an extension, you must file entry documents at a location specified by the port or area director within five working days of your shipment's date of arrival at a U.S. port of entry. These include a number of standard documents required by Customs for any entry.

After you present the entry, Customs may examine your shipment, or may waive examination. The shipment is then released provided no legal or regulatory violations have been noted. You must then file entry summary documentation and deposit estimated duties at a designated customhouse within 10 working days of your shipment's release. For a detailed description of entry procedures, standard documentation, and informal entry, see "Entry Process" on page 185.

Informed Compliance. Informed compliance was introduced with the Customs Modernization Act of 1993 (Mod Act) and defines the relationship between importers and the Customs Service. It sets out the responsibilities of both parties. Providing the correct documentation and information for entry is a key factor that will make your importing operation run smoothly. We recommend that importers become familiar with the concept of informed comliance and the responsibilities that they have under the Mod Act. For further discussion about informed compliance see "Informed Compliance" on page 211.

Note: The Entry and Documentation section has been carefully designed to supply you, the importer, with sample documents and directions on how to satisfy Customs requirements. Be aware that you should consult the applicable authorities to ensure that you are correctly following the most current procedures.

Prohibitions and Restrictions

The importation of switchblade knives is prohibited, with two exceptions: 1) the military may officially import switchblade knives, although individual military personnel may not; and 2) an individual who has only one arm may import, on his or her person, a switchblade knife the blade of which may not exceed three inches in length.

Marking and Labeling Requirements

Clippers, shears, safety razors, surgical instruments, scientific and laboratory instruments, pliers, pincers, knives, and other similar cutting tools must be marked legibly and conspicuously to indicate country of origin by one of the following methods: 1) die-stamping; 2) cast-in-the-mold lettering; 3) etching (acid or electrolytic); 4) engraving; 5) metal plates that bear the prescribed marking and that are securely attached to the article in a conspicuous place by welding, screws, or rivets.

For a general discussion of U.S. Customs marking and labeling requirements, see "Country of Origin Marking" on page 236, "Special Marking Requirements" on page 238 and "Marking—False Impression" on page 239.

Shipping Considerations

You will need to ensure that your goods are packaged and shipped with care to ensure that they arrive in good condition and pass smoothly through Customs. You are responsible for ensuring that the shipment is in compliance with all applicable government regulations for packaging and shipping. In most instances, you should not leave these arrangements solely to the discretion of your supplier. Careful preparation of the cargo and selection of the mode of transport can be essential to a cost-effective, timely delivery of undamaged goods. We strongly advise you to consult your shipping representative, insurance agent, or freight broker for advice on packing and shipping.

Although most products of HTSUS Chapter 82 are neither perishable nor particularly fragile in nature, they must still be properly packaged and stowed to avoid damage during transit.

Publications and WWW Resources

The *Harmonized Tariff Schedule of the United States (2001)* (HTSUS) is available to view on the Customs Service website (www.customs.gov), or you may purchase a printed version from:
U.S. Government Printing Office
Superintendent of Documents
710 North Capital Street NW
Washington DC 20401
Tel: (202) 512-1800
Fax: (202) 512-1657
Website: www.access.gpo.gov

The USGPO also has copies of specific laws available for purchase. The USGPO accepts orders made by fax, phone or placed over the Internet, as well as mail orders paid by credit card. All orders must be accompanied by payment. Credit cards, checks drawn on a U.S. bank, or an international money order are all acceptable.

Relevant Government Agencies

Address questions regarding consumer product safety standards for hand tools and other implements to:
Consumer Product Safety Commission (CPSC)
Office of Compliance
Washington DC 20207-0001
Tel: 800-638-2772 or (301) 504-7912
Fax: (301) 504-0359
Website: www.cpsc.gov

Address your questions regarding FDA's involvement in importation of tools, utensils, cutlery, and silverware to:
Food and Drug Administration (FDA)
Center for Food Safety and Applied Nutrition (CFSAN)
Office of Compliance
Division of Enforcement, Imports Branch
5100 Paint Branch Parkway
College Park, MD 20740-3835
Tel: (301) 436-2080
Website: http://vm.cfsan.fda.gov/list.html

Address your other questions regarding the importation of tools, utensils, cutlery, and silverware to your local Customs port director. For addresses refer to "U.S. Customs and Border Protection Offices" on page 65 or contact:
U.S. Customs and Border Protection
Customs Headquarters
1300 Pennsylvania Avenue NW
Washington DC 20229
Tel: (202) 354-1000
Website: www.customs.treas.gov

Laws and Regulations

The following laws and regulations may be relevant to the importation of metal tools and implements. The laws are contained in the U.S. Code (USC) and the regulations are published in the Code of federal Regulations (CFR), both of which may be available at larger public and law libraries. Copies of specific laws are also available from the United States Government Printing Office (address above).

15 USC 2051 et seq.
Consumer Product Safety Act
This Act sets standards for the manufacture, processing, and labeling of products sold to U.S. consumers.

21 USC 301 et seq.
Federal Food, Drug, and Cosmetic Act
This Act prohibits deceptive practices and regulates the manufacture, sale and importation or exportation of food, drugs, cosmetics, and related products. It was amended by the Food Quality Protection Act of 1996. See 21 USC 331, 381, 382.

19 CFR 12.1 et seq.; 21 CFR 1.83 et seq.
Regulations on Food, Drugs, and Cosmetics
These regulations of the Secretary of Health and Human Services and the Secretary of the Treasury govern the standards, labeling, marking, and importing of products used with food, drugs, and cosmetics.

Principal Exporting Countries

The following listing includes samples of the main supplier nations of the products of this chapter. It is organized by HTSUS major heading. (Refer to "Customs Classification" above for the product codes.) Countries are listed in rank order of the value of products imported to the U.S. Statistics represent customs value of entries for 2002 from the Bureau of Census, U.S. Department of Commerce.

8201—China, Taiwan, Mexico, South Korea, Finland, Canada, Switzerland, India, Austria, Japan, Germany, Brazil

8202—Switzerland, Japan, China, South Korea, Italy, Canada, Germany, New Zealand, United Kingdom, Taiwan, Sweden

8203—China, Taiwan, Switzerland, Japan, Germany, Mexico, India, Pakistan, Sweden, United Kingdom, South Korea, Portugal, Ireland

8204—Taiwan, China, India, Canada, Japan, Germany, Spain, Mexico, Malaysia, United Kingdom, Barbados

8205—China, Taiwan, Mexico, Germany, United Kingdom, Japan, Austria, Italy, Canada, France

8206—China, Taiwan, Japan, Malaysia, Germany, France, India

8207—Japan, Canada, Germany, China, United Kingdom, Taiwan, Italy, Mexico, South Korea, Israel, Sweden, Switzerland, Ireland

8208—Germany, Japan, Canada, United Kingdom, South Korea, Itlay, China

8209—Sweden, Israel, Japan, Germany, Canada, Mexico, Luxembourg, United Kingdom, Austria, South Korea

8210—China, Germany, Taiwan, France, Italy, Switzerland, Portugal, Thailand, Denmark

8211—China, Germany, Taiwan, Japan, Switzerland, Spain

8212—Mexico, China, Canada, Germany, Greece, France, Japan, India, South Korea, United Kingdom, Egypt

8213—China, Taiwan, Germany, Italy, Japan, Pakistan, South Korea, Mexico, Finland, Brazil

8214—China, South Korea, Germany, Pakistan, Mexico, Taiwan, Italy, Hong Kong, Canada

8215—China, South Korea, Taiwan, Indonesia, Japan, Mexico, France, India, Italy, Hong Kong, Thailand

Chapter 83: Miscellaneous Articles of Base Metal

This chapter relates to the importation of miscellaneous articles of base metals, which are classified within Chapter 83 of the Harmonized Tariff Schedule of the United States (HTSUS). Specifically, it includes locks, padlocks, keys, and lock hardware; mountings and fittings used for furniture, vehicles, architectural accents, leather goods, and window coverings, such as hinges, castors, harness fittings, drapery hardware, and hatracks; safes and strong-boxes; metal desk equipment; office accessories, such as ring binder hardware and paper clips; ornaments, picture frames, and mirrors of metal; flexible metal tubing; clasps, buckles, eyelets, grommets, and other metal fasteners; stoppers, caps, and lids; name plates and signs; and rods, such as for soldering. Chapter 83 represents something of a catch-all classification for a variety of products that are only tenuously related, often simply by the fact that they are made of metal and have not been classified elsewhere.

If you are interested in importing primary or intermediate products of iron or steel, refer to Commodity Index Chapter 72. Many other intermediate and finished goods of iron and steel are covered in Chapter 73. Other base metals, their alloys, and many products made from them in which specified base metals predominate are covered in Commodity Index chapters on the specific metal, including copper (Chapter 74), nickel (Chapter 75), aluminum (Chapter 76), lead (Chapter 78), zinc (Chapter 79), tin (Chapter 80), and other base metals (Chapter 81). Basic hardware items, such as nails and screws, are found in the chapter that covers the specific metal from which the articles are made. Hand tools, other implements, and cutlery are found in Chapter 82. Precious metals, alloys of precious metals, and articles containing the same are covered specifically in Chapter 71.

Other products for which metals are incidental—even if critical and major—components are found within a variety of Commodity Index chapters. For example, if you are interested in importing metallic paints, refer to Chapter 36. For haberdashery, see Chapter 65 for headgear with metal elements, and Chapter 66 for umbrella frames and related items. Finished and semifinished products classified as machinery, mechanical appliances, and electrical goods are found in Chapters 84 and 85. Assembled railway track and other equipment related to railways is covered in chapter 86; vehicles are covered in Chapter 87, aircraft in Chapter 88, and boats in Chapter 89. Instruments and apparatus are covered in Commodity Index chapters that relate to the specific articles, including optical, medical, and precision instruments (Chapter 90), clocks and watches (Chapter 91), and musical instruments (Chapter 92). Metal articles as parts of firearms, including ammunition, are found in Chapter 93. Commodity Index chapters that cover miscellaneous manufactures include furniture and prefabricated structures (Chapter 94), toys, games, and sporting goods (Chapter 95), and miscellaneous manufactured articles (Chapter 96), all of which may contain metal components. Works of art that include metals, even as dominant components, are covered in Chapter 97 if the primary interest derives from the artistry rather than from the value of the metal content.

Although most importers utilize the services of a licensed customs broker in making their entries, and we recommend this practice, you should be aware of the regulatory, entry, and documentation issues involved in importing your product. You, as importer, are ultimately responsible for the fulfillment of any legal requirements applicable to your shipment.

General Considerations

Importation of articles of base metals of Chapter 83 is straightforward. There are no restrictions or prohibitions. You do not need permits or licenses, nor is special entry paperwork required.

HTSUS Chapter 83 covers a wide variety of products. Many articles included in this chapter are frequently utilized as parts of machines or other products. To avoid the difficulties inherent in determining whether a specific piece is a part of a particular machine or not, Note 2 of the introduction to HTSUS Section XV provides that parts of general use are always classified in their own heading rather than as a part of a particular machine or other product.

Consumer Products. Some of the products found in this section may be covered by the provisions of the Consumer Product Safety Act (CPSA), which establishes standards for the manufacturing and labeling of potentially hazardous consumer products. Imported consumer products for which such standards exist must comply with the full range of requirements prescribed for domestic products. In addition, the CPSA requires all manufacturers, distributors, retailers, and others involved in the commercial handling of such products to report immediately any potentially hazardous defects or failures to conform to established standards to the CPSC for investigation and potential action. Failure to submit such a Substantial Product Hazard Report can result in action by the CPSC. Contact the CPSC (see addresses at end of this chapter) with questions regarding specific products.

Dumping and Countervailing Duties Actions. Actions to restrict importation of or impose equalizing or punitive duties on imports of certain metal products from countries that are alleged to be involved in selling these products in the U.S. at below cost or their home country sale price (dumping) are occasionally brought, primarily to protect the domestic steel industry or other metalworking operations. Although no such actions are currently in force, restrictions can be imposed on short notice. You should contact U.S. Customs to verify the status of your proposed imports.

Customs Classification

For customs purposes, miscellaneous articles of base metals are classified within Chapter 83 of the HTSUS. This chapter is divided into major headings, which are further divided into subheadings, and often into sub-subheadings, each of which has its own HTSUS classification number. For example, the 2001 HTSUS number for hat-racks, hat pegs, brackets and similar fixtures is 8302.50, which is a subcategory of the major heading base metal mountings, fittings, and similar articles (8302). There are 11 major headings in HTSUS Chapter 83.

8301—Padlocks and locks (key, combination, or electronically operated), of base metal; clasps and frames with clasps, incorporating locks, of base metal; keys and parts of any of the foregoing articles of base metal

8302—Base metal mountings, fittings, and similar articles suitable for furniture, doors, staircases, windows, blinds, coachwork, saddlery, trunks, chests, caskets, or the like; base metal hat racks, hatpegs, brackets, and similar fix-

tures; castors with mountings of base metal; automatic door closers of base metal; and base metal parts thereof

8303—Armored or reinforced safes, strong-boxes, and doors and safe deposit lockers for strong-rooms, cash, or deed boxes and the like, and parts thereof, of base metal

8304—Desk-top filing or card-index cabinets, paper trays, paper rests, pen trays, office-stamp stands, and similar office or desk equipment and parts thereof, of base metal, other than office furniture of heading 9403

8305—Fittings for looseleaf binders or files, letter clips, letter corners, paper clips, indexing tags, and similar office articles, and parts thereof, of base metal; staples in strips (for example, for office, upholstery, packing), of base metal

8306—Bells, gongs, and the like, nonelectric, of base metal; statuettes and other ornaments, of base metal; photograph, picture or similar frames, of base metal; mirrors of base metal; and base metal parts thereof

8307—Flexible tubing of base metal, with or without fittings

8308—Clasps, frames with clasps, buckles, buckle clasps, hooks, eyes, eyelets, and the like and parts thereof, of base metal, of a kind used for clothing, footwear, awnings, handbags, travel goods or other madeup articles; tubular or bifurcated rivets of base metal; beads and spangles of base metal

8309—Stoppers, caps, and lids (including crown corks, screw caps, and pouring stoppers), capsules for bottles, threaded bungs, bung covers, seals, and other packing accessories, and parts thereof, of base metal

8310—Sign plates, name plates, address plates, and similar plates, numbers, letters, and other symbols, and parts thereof, of base metal, excluding those of heading 9405

8311—Wire, rods, tubes, plates, electrodes, and similar products of base metal or of metal carbides, coated or cored with flux material, of a kind used for soldering, brazing, welding, or deposition of metal or of metal carbides; wire and rods, of agglomerated base metal powder, used for metal spraying; base metal parts thereof

For more details regarding classification of the specific product you are interested in importing, consult a customs broker, the appropriate commodity specialist at your nearest customs port, or see HTSUS. The 2001 HTSUS is available online from the Customs Service (www.customs.gov/impoexpo/impoexpo.htm) or for purchase from the U.S. Government Printing Office (see resources at the end of this chapter), and may be found in larger public libraries. For a general discussion of customs classification, see "Classification—Liquidation" on page 229.

Dutiable Status of Goods

For more information about duty rates and binding decisions see "Dutiable Status of Goods" on page 203; for a discussion of temporary importation of goods see "Temporary Free Importations" on page 205.

Valuation

Importers have a responsibility to use what the U.S. Customs Service deems, "reasonable care," when determining the value of their goods. They must also provide any additional information that the Customs Service needs for setting a final value on the goods. This process involves a number of factors and can be somewhat complicated; importers must be aware of applicable issues and details. Valuation information applies to all types of commodities, for further discussion on the subject see "Customs Valuation" on page 267.

Import Duties

Import duties vary (often dramatically) depending upon the Harmonized Tariff Schedule (HTSUS) classification of the goods or products imported. Since some products that look alike have different HTSUS classifications and different rates of duty, proper classification is vital. Note that "differences of opinion" between importers and the Bureau of Customs and Border Protection regarding classification keeps customs attorneys very busy.

Import duties can be assessed on the imported value of the goods ("ad valorem" rates of duty such as 2%, 4.4%, 50%, etc.), total units or weight of the goods ("specific" rates of duty such as 2 cents each or 1.5 cents/pound, etc.) or on a combination basis ("compound" rates of duty such as 5 cents each plus 6%).

Listed below is a sampling of several Column 1 import duty rates for Chapter 83 products:
Hat-racks, hat pegs, brackets and similar fixtures, and parts thereof (8302.50.00.00): Free
to
Desk-top filing or card-index cabinets, paper trays, paper rests, pen trays, office-stamp stands and similar office or desk equipment and parts thereof, of base metal, other than office furniture of heading 9403 (8304.00.00.00): 3.9%

For specific information on US import duties refer to the Harmonized Tariff Schedule of the US. The print version is available from the US Government Printing Office as well as third party suppliers who often add special features. Online versions are available in both static PDF pages as well as in formats with excellent search functionality. Search the Web with the term "Harmonized Tariff Schedule" to find sources.

Entry and Documentation

The entry of merchandise is a two-part process consisting of 1) filing the documents necessary to determine whether merchandise may be released from Customs custody and 2) filing the documents that contain information for duty assessment and statistical purposes. In certain instances all documents must be filed and accepted by Customs prior to the release of the goods. Unless you have been granted an extension, you must file entry documents at a location specified by the port or area director within five working days of your shipment's date of arrival at a U.S. port of entry. These include a number of standard documents required by Customs for any entry.

After you present the entry, Customs may examine your shipment, or may waive examination. The shipment is then released provided no legal or regulatory violations have been noted. You must then file entry summary documentation and deposit estimated duties at a designated customhouse within 10 working days of your shipment's release. For a detailed description of entry procedures, standard documentation, and informal entry, see "Entry Process" on page 185.

Informed Compliance. Informed compliance was introduced with the Customs Modernization Act of 1993 (Mod Act) and defines the relationship between importers and the Customs Service. It sets out the responsibilities of both parties. Providing the correct documentation and information for entry is a key factor that will make your importing operation run smoothly. We recommend that importers become familiar with the concept of informed comliance and the responsibilities that they have under the Mod Act. For further discussion about informed compliance see "Informed Compliance" on page 211.

Entry Invoice for Metal Beads. If importing beads made of a base metal, the entry invoice must show: 1) the length of the string, if strung; 2) the size of the beads expressed in millimeters; and 3) the material of which the beads are composed. For more general information about invoices see "Invoices" on page 277.

Note: The Entry and Documentation section has been carefully designed to supply you, the importer, with sample documents and directions on how to satisfy Customs requirements. Be aware that you

should consult the applicable authorities to ensure that you are correctly following the most current procedures.

Marking and Labeling Requirements

For a general discussion of U.S. Customs marking and labeling requirements, see "Country of Origin Marking" on page 236, "Special Marking Requirements" on page 238 and "Marking—False Impression" on page 239.

Shipping Considerations

You will need to ensure that your goods are packaged and shipped with care to ensure that they arrive in good condition and pass smoothly through Customs. You are responsible for ensuring that the shipment is in compliance with all applicable government regulations for packaging and shipping. In most instances, you should not leave these arrangements solely to the discretion of your supplier. Careful preparation of the cargo and selection of the mode of transport can be essential to a cost-effective, timely delivery of undamaged goods. We strongly advise you to consult your shipping representative, insurance agent, or freight broker for advice on packing and shipping.

Articles of base metals are often bulky and heavy, and should be well packed and securely stowed to avoid damage due to shifting en route. Articles of base metals are also subject to oxidation and corrosion, which should be guarded against, especially as no allowance is made by customs for partial loss due to discoloration or rusting or to damage during shipping.

Publications and WWW Resources

The *Harmonized Tariff Schedule of the United States (2001)* (HTSUS) is available to view on the Customs Service website (www.customs.gov), or you may purchase a printed version from:

U.S. Government Printing Office
Superintendent of Documents
710 North Capital Street NW
Washington DC 20401
Tel: (202) 512-1800
Fax: (202) 512 1657
Website: www.access.gpo.gov

The USGPO also has copies of specific laws available for purchase. The USGPO accepts orders made by fax, phone or placed over the Internet, as well as mail orders paid by credit card. All orders must be accompanied by payment. Credit cards, checks drawn on a U.S. bank, or an international money order are all acceptable.

Relevant Government Agencies

Address questions regarding consumer product safety standards for articles of base metals to:

Consumer Product Safety Commission (CPSC)
Office of Compliance
Washington DC 20207-0001
Tel: 800-638-2772 or (301) 504-7912
Fax: (301) 504-0359
Website: www.cpsc.gov

Address questions regarding the importation of miscellaneous articles of base metals to your local Customs port director. For addresses refer to "U.S. Customs and Border Protection Offices" on page 65 or contact:

U.S. Customs and Border Protection
Customs Headquarters
1300 Pennsylvania Avenue NW
Washington DC 20229
Tel: (202) 354-1000
Website: www.customs.treas.gov

Laws and Regulations

Various laws and regulations may be relevant to importing miscellaneous articles of base metals. Laws are contained in the U.S. Code (USC) and regulations are published in the Code of Federal Regulations (CFR), both of which may be available in larger public and law libraries. Copies of specific laws are also available from the United States Government Printing Office (address above).

15 USC 2051 et seq.
Consumer Product Safety Act
This Act sets standards for the manufacture, processing, and labeling of products sold to U.S. consumers.

Principal Exporting Countries

The following listing includes samples of the main supplier nations of the products of this chapter. It is organized by HTSUS major heading. (Refer to "Customs Classification" above for the product codes.) Countries are listed in rank order of the value of products imported to the U.S. Statistics represent customs value of entries for 2002 from the Bureau of Census, U.S. Department of Commerce.

8301—Mexico, China, Taiwan, Germany, Japan, Canada, South Korea, Dominican Republic, Hong Kong

8302—Canada, China, Mexico, Taiwan, Japan, Germany, Austria, Italy, United Kingdom, South Korea, India

8303— China, South Korea, Canada, Israel, Norway, Spain, Thailand, Taiwan

8304—China, Taiwan, Thailand, India, Hong Kong, Canada, Japan

8305—China, Mexico, Taiwan, Japan, Germany, Sweden, South Korea, Italy

8306—China, India, Mexico, Taiwan, Thailand, Philippines, Hong Kong, France, South Korea

8307—United Kingdom, Japan, France, China, Canada, Spain, Germany, South Korea, Mexico

8308—Taiwan, China, United Kingdom, Mexico, Italy, Philippines, Hong Kong, Canada, South Korea, France, India

8309—Canada, Mexico, Spain, France, China, Italy, Denmark, Germany

8310—Canada, China, Japan, Taiwan, Denmark, Germany, Sweden, United Kingdom, Thailand, South Korea

8311—Canada, China, Japan, Taiwan, Denmark, Germany, Sweden, United Kingdom, Thailand, South Korea

Chapter 84:
Large Mechanical Appliances and Machines

Full title: Nuclear Reactors, Boilers, Machinery, and Mechanical Appliances; Parts Thereof.

This chapter relates to the importation of large mechanical appliances and machines, which are classified within Chapter 84 of the Harmonized Tariff Schedule of the United States (HTSUS). Chapter 84 covers an extremely broad range of often highly specialized, generally large machinery, equipment, parts, and assemblies. The items in the chapter are those that are mechanical rather than electrical in function and power, although the primary function of the product determines its inclusion more than the nature of the power source. In general, items classified in Chapter 84 are those used to produce or prepare other goods rather than end-user products themselves.

Specifically, Chapter 84 includes power generating equipment; internal combustion engines, turbines, turbojets, and other types of engines; pumps; air conditioners; furnaces and industrial and laboratory ovens, refrigerators, and freezers; machinery designed to process materials by changing their temperature; rolling machines; centrifuges; washing and packing machinery; weighing machines; dispensers; cranes, forklifts, and other loading/unloading machinery; self-propelled heavy equipment, including construction and farm equipment; food processing machinery; pulp and paper-making machinery; printing equipment; textile spinning, weaving, knitting, and sewing machinery; laundry machinery; leatherworking machinery; metallurgical machinery; machine tools for working wood, metal, and other materials; hand power tools; soldering and welding machinery; calculators, adding machines, cash registers, postage meters, and similar office machines; computers; machinery for working minerals, electronics and electrical goods, rubber, plastics, and tobacco; molding apparatus; valves, bearings, transmissions, and other vehicle apparatus; miscellaneous machinery; and parts for all of the above.

Some machines, assemblies, components, and parts are covered elsewhere in the Commodity Index. For example, grindstones and milling stones are found in Commodity Index Chapter 68; machinery and parts made of ceramic materials are covered in Chapter 69; while industrial glassware and associated articles are covered in Chapter 70. Although parts of the machines covered in Chapter 84 are generally included with those machines, parts of general use—such as nuts and bolts, screws, and other general hardware—are found in Chapters 72-83 if made of a base metal, in Chapter 39 if made of plastic, and in Chapter 40 if made of rubber.

If you are interested in importing electronics products, refer to Chapter 85, which includes electric motors; transformers; batteries; some hand power tools; furnaces and heaters; communications devices; audio, video, and related systems; tapes and records; radio and television receivers and transmitters; radars; signaling devices; resistors, circuits, switches, tubes, and semiconductors; lightbulbs; and insulated wire and cable. Small hand tools, implements, and utensils are covered in Chapter 82, while finished products are found in Chapters 86-89 (transportation equipment), Chapters 90-92 (optical, precision, medical, and musical instruments and clocks), Chapter 93 (arms and ammunition), and Chapters 94-96 (miscellaneous manufactured articles).

Note: To understand key issues that will enable you to make best use of the information in this section we recommend that you see "Introduction" on page 425.

Key Factors

The key factors in the importation of large appliances and machinery are:

- Compliance with Nuclear Regulatory Commission (NRC) requirements, including NRC import authorization, as needed for radioactive materials and equipment

- Compliance with U.S. Food and Drug Administration (FDA) requirements and FDA entry notification, as needed

- Compliance with U.S. Federal Communications Commission (FCC) requirements and FCC entry notification, as needed

- Compliance with U.S. Department of Energy (DOE) performance standards

- Compliance with Occupational Safety and Health Administration (OSHA) requirements for industrial products

- Compliance with Consumer Product Safety Commission (CPSC) and Federal Trade Commission (FTC) requirements for consumer products

Although most importers utilize the services of a licensed customs broker in making their entries, and we recommend this practice, you should be aware of the regulatory, entry, and documentation issues involved in importing your product. You, as importer, are ultimately responsible for the fulfillment of any legal requirements applicable to your shipment.

General Considerations

Regulatory Agencies. For the majority of items classified within HTSUS Chapter 84, no particular restrictions or prohibitions are imposed on importations into the U.S. and no permits, licenses, or special entry paperwork are required. For example, the importation of engines, machine tools, power tools, and most other forms of machinery included in the classification is straightforward.

However, some appliances or machines within Chapter 84 may be imported only on compliance with certain government regulations. For this reason, U.S. Customs requires special information on the entry invoice for machine tools (see below). All imports of industrial machinery and apparatus must comply with the appropriate regulations of the Occupational Safety and Health Administration (OSHA), while those intended for consumer use must comply with the appropriate regulations of the Consumer Product Safety Commission (CPSC) and Federal Trade Commission (FTC). Electronic products are subject to controls based on their compliance with standards for radioactive emissions, radio frequency limits, and performance standards, which are enforced, respectively, by the Food and Drug Administration (FDA), the Federal Communications Commission (FCC), and the

Department of Energy (DOE). Nuclear and radioactive products are licensed and controlled by the Nuclear Regulatory Commission (NRC). Because of the wide range of products and the variety of specialized requirements involved, it is necessary for importers to proceed with considerable care in ascertaining what agencies regulate the products they wish to import and what their legal responsibilities are early in the process.

FDA Regulations. Both domestic and imported electronic products are subject to federal radiation performance standards under the Radiation Control for Health and Safety Act of 1968 (RCHSA), enforced by the FDA. You will have to file an FDA forms with each import shipment of these products: an Electronic Product Declaration **Form FD2877**. If you are interested in importing any products regulated by the FDA, you should be familiar with that agency's import requirements and procedures. For a general discussion of FDA import entry procedures, see "Appendix: Foods" on page 825.

Radiation-producing devices are subject to relevant portions of the Federal Food, Drug, and Cosmetic Act (FDCA), enforced by the FDA. Radioisotopes and radioactive sources for medical use are also subject to provisions of the FDCA. Imported products regulated by the FDA are subject to port of entry inspection.

Form FD2877 identifies your product's compliance status as one of the following: 1) manufactured prior to the effective date of the applicable federal standard; 2) complies with the standard, with manufacturer's certification label affixed; 3) noncomplying, imported only for purposes of research investigation, study, demonstration, or training; or 4) noncomplying, to be brought into compliance. Certain products subject to FDA regulation are also subject to FCC regulation.

Detention of Shipment. If your shipment is found to be noncomplying, it may be detained at the port of entry. In the case of products subject to FDA jurisdiction, the FDA may allow you to bring such a shipment into compliance before making a final decision regarding admittance. However, any sorting, reprocessing, or relabeling must be supervised by FDA personnel, and is done at the importer's expense. Such conditional release to allow an importer to bring a shipment into compliance is a privilege, not a right. The FDA may consider subsequent noncomplying shipments of the same type of product to constitute abuse of the privilege and require the importer to destroy or reexport the products. To ascertain what your legal responsibilities are, you should contact these agencies regarding the specific items to be imported.

FCC Regulations. Most items of computer hardware, such as cathode ray tube (CRT) screens/monitors, keyboards, floppy and flexible disk drives, hard drives, printers, central processing units, and peripherals, as well as other electronic devices such as computer machine controls, are radio frequency (rf) devices. RF devices are subject to FCC regulation under 47 CFR 2 and 15. You will have to file an FCC entry notification—**Form 740**—for each shipment. If your shipment includes a number of different items of computer hardware, a separate **Form 740** must be submitted for each type of item. Subassemblies that are essentially complete devices requiring only minor attachment or assembly prior to marketing and use—such as circuit boards and disk drives—are also subject to FCC regulation.

Form 740 must be filed with both the FCC and U.S. Customs prior to entry. You must certify on the form that the devices or subassemblies being entered comply with FCC technical regulations and thus can legally be imported. This requirement is intended to keep noncomplying devices from reaching the general public, thereby reducing the potential for harmful interference with authorized communications channels.

If you have questions regarding the regulatory status of an item such as computer hardware, how to fill out **Form 740**, or other questions, contact the regional FCC office nearest you, FCC headquarters (see addresses at end of this chapter), or your customs broker.

DOE Regulations. Both domestic and imported household consumer appliances must comply with applicable energy efficiency standards and labeling requirements under the Energy Policy and Conservation Act (EPCA). The DOE Consumer Products Efficiency Branch is responsible for test procedures and energy performance standards. The FTC Division of Energy and Product Information regulates labeling of such appliances. Importers should contact these agencies (addresses below) to find out about any requirements that may be in effect at the time they anticipate making their shipments.

EPCA covers 1) refrigerators, 2) freezers, 3) dishwashers, 4) clothes dryers, 5) water heaters, 6) room air conditioners, 7) home heating equipment, 8) television sets, 9) kitchen ranges and ovens, 10) clothes washers, 11) humidifiers, 12) central air conditioning, 13) furnaces, and 14) certain other types of household appliances. Not all appliances are covered by both agencies.

NRC Regulations. Many radioisotopes, all forms of uranium, thorium, and plutonium, and all nuclear reactors imported into the U.S. are subject to the regulations of the NRC, which are in addition to the import regulations that may be imposed by other U.S. agencies. Authority to import these items, or articles containing these items, is granted solely by the NRC.

To comply with NRC requirements, the importer must be aware of the identity and amount of any NRC-controlled radioisotopes, or uranium, thorium, and plutonium, and of any nuclear reactor being imported into the U.S. It is up to the importer to present to U.S. Customs satisfactory proof of the NRC authorization under which the controlled commodity is being imported. The authority cited may be the number of a specific or general license, or the specific section of NRC regulations that establishes a general license or grants a standing exemption for the specific type of product being entered. The foreign exporter may save time for the prospective importer by furnishing him or her complete information concerning the presence of NRC-controlled commodities in the importation.

OSHA Regulations. OSHA establishes and enforces regulations designed to ensure safety in the workplace, including standards for equipment and its use. Although most OSHA regulations deal with installation and use procedures, some equipment is subject to OSHA-imposed specifications. Imported machinery must comply with all OSHA standards and procedures, which are often specific and voluminous. Consult OSHA (see addresses at end of this chapter) for more information regarding specific products.

CPSC and FTC Regulations. Some of the products found in this section are covered by the provisions of the Consumer Product Safety Act (CPSA), which establishes standards for the manufacturing and labeling of potentially hazardous consumer products. Imported consumer products for which such standards exist must comply with the full range of requirements prescribed for domestic products. In addition, the CPSA requires all manufacturers, distributors, retailers, and others involved in the commercial handling of such products to report immediately any potentially hazardous defects or failures to conform to established standards to the CPSC for investigation and potential action. Failure to submit such a Substantial Product Hazard Report can result in action by the CPSC. Contact the CPSC (see addresses at end of this chapter) with questions regarding specific products.

Customs Classification

For customs purposes, large appliances and machinery are classified within Chapter 84 of the HTSUS. This chapter is divided into major headings, which are further divided into subheadings, and often into sub-subheadings, each of which has its own HTSUS classification number. For example, the 2001 HTSUS number for other (screw-type) compressors is 8414.30.80, indicating that it is a subcategory of compressors of a kind used in refrigerating equipment (8414.30), which is a subcategory of the major heading air or vacuum pumps, air or other gas compressors and fans (8414). There are 85 major headings in HTSUS Chapter 84.

8401—Nuclear reactors; fuel elements (cartridges), non-irradiated, for nuclear reactors; machinery and apparatus for isotopic separation; parts thereof

8402—Steam and other vapor generating boilers (other than central heating hot water boilers capable also of producing low pressure steam); super-heated water boilers; parts thereof

8403—Central heating boilers (other than those of heading 8402) and parts thereof

8404—Auxiliary plant for use with boilers of heading 8402 or 8403 (for example, economizers, superheaters, soot removers, gas recoverers); condensers for steam or other vapor power units; parts thereof

8405—Producer gas or water gas generators, with or without their purifiers; acetylene gas generators and similar water process gas generators, with or without their purifiers; parts thereof

8406—Steam turbines and other vapor turbines, and parts thereof

8407—Spark-ignition reciprocating or rotary internal combustion piston engines

8408—Compression-ignition internal combustion piston engines (diesel or semi-diesel engines)

8409—Parts suitable for use solely or principally with the engines of heading 8407 or 8408

8410—Hydraulic turbines, water wheels, and regulators therefor; parts thereof

8411—Turbojets, turbopropellers, and other gas turbines, and parts thereof

8412—Other engines and motors, and parts thereof

8413—Pumps for liquids, whether or not fitted with a measuring device; liquid elevators; parts thereof

8414—Air or vacuum pumps, air or other gas compressors and fans; ventilating or recycling hoods incorporating a fan, whether or not fitted with filters; parts thereof

8415—Air conditioning machines, comprising a motor-driven fan and elements for changing the temperature and humidity, including those machines in which the humidity cannot be separately regulated; parts thereof

8416—Furnace burners for liquid fuel, for pulverized solid fuel or for gas; mechanical stokers, including their mechanical grates, mechanical ash dischargers and similar appliances; parts thereof

8417—Industrial or laboratory furnaces and ovens, including incinerators, nonelectric, and parts thereof

8418—Refrigerators, freezers, and other refrigerating or freezing equipment, electric or other; heat pumps, other than the air conditioning machines of heading 8415; parts thereof

8419—Machinery, plant, or laboratory equipment, whether or not electrically heated, for the treatment of materials by a process involving a change of temperature such as heating, cooking, roasting, distilling, rectifying, sterilizing, pasteurizing, steaming, drying, evaporating, vaporizing, condensing or cooling, other than machinery or plant of a kind used for domestic purposes; instantaneous or storage water heaters, nonelectric; parts thereof

8420—Calendering or other rolling machines, other than for metals or glass, and cylinders therefor; parts thereof

8421—Centrifuges, including centrifugal dryers; filtering or purifying machinery and apparatus, for liquids or gases; parts thereof

8422—Dishwashing machines; machinery for cleaning or drying bottles or other containers; machinery for filling, closing, sealing, or labeling bottles, cans, boxes, bags, or other containers; machinery for capsuling bottles, jars, tubes and similar containers; other packing or wrapping machinery; machinery (including heat-shrink wrapping machinery); machinery for aerating beverages; parts thereof

8423—Weighing machinery (excluding balances of a sensitivity of 5 cg or better), including weight-operated counting or checking machines; weighing machine weights of all kinds; parts of weighing machinery

8424—Mechanical appliances (whether or not hand operated) for projecting, dispersing, or spraying liquids or powders; fire extinguishers, whether or not charged; spray guns and similar appliances; steam or sand blasting machines and similar jet projecting machines; parts thereof

8425—Pulley tackle and hoists other than skip hoists; winches and capstans; jacks

8426—Ships derricks; cranes, including cable cranes; mobile lifting frames, straddle carriers and works trucks fitted with a crane

8427—Fork-lift trucks; other works trucks fitted with lifting or handling equipment

8428—Other lifting, handling, loading or unloading machinery (for example, elevators, escalators, conveyers, teleferics)

8429—Self-propelled bulldozers, angledozers, graders, levelers, scrapers, mechanical shovels, excavators, shovel loaders, tamping machines, and road rollers

8430—Other moving, grading, leveling, scraping, excavating, tamping, compacting, extracting or boring machinery, for earth, minerals or ores; pile-drivers and pile-extractors; snowplows and snowblowers

8431—Parts suitable for use solely or principally with the machinery of heading 8425 to 8430

8432—Agricultural, horticultural or forestry machinery for soil preparation or cultivation; lawn or sports ground rollers; parts thereof

8433—Harvesting or threshing machinery, including straw or fodder balers; grass or hay mowers; machines for cleaning, sorting, or grading eggs, fruit or other agricultural produce, other than machinery of heading 8437; parts thereof

8434—Milking machines and dairy machinery, and parts thereof

8435—Presses, crushers, and similar machinery, used in the manufacture of wine, cider, fruit juices or similar beverages; parts thereof

8436—Other agricultural, horticultural, forestry, poultry-keeping or bee-keeping machinery, including germination plant fitted with mechanical or thermal equipment; poultry incubators and brooders; parts thereof

8437—Machines for cleaning, sorting, or grading seed, grain, or dried leguminous vegetables, and parts thereof; machinery used in the milling industry or for the working of cereals or dried leguminous vegetables, other than farm-type machinery; parts thereof

8438—Machinery, not specified or included elsewhere in this chapter, for the industrial preparation or manufacture of food or drink, other than machinery for the extraction or preparation of animal or fixed vegetable fats or oils; parts thereof

8439—Machinery for making pulp of fibrous cellulosic material or for making or finishing paper or paperboard (other than the machinery of heading 8419); parts thereof

8440—Bookbinding machinery, including book-sewing machines, and parts thereof

8441—Other machinery for making up paper pulp, paper or paperboard, including cutting machines of all kinds, and parts thereof

8442—Machinery, apparatus, and equipment (other than the machine tools of heading 8456 to 8465), for type-founding or typesetting, for preparing or making printing blocks, plates, cylinders or other printing components; printing type, blocks, plates, cylinders, and other printing components; blocks, plates, cylinders and lithographic stones, prepared for printing purposes (for example, planed, grained, or polished); parts thereof

8443—Printing machinery, including ink-jet printing machines, other than those of heading 8471; machines for uses ancillary to printing; parts thereof

8444—Machines for extruding, drawing, texturing or cutting man-made textile materials

8445—Machines for preparing textile fibers; spinning, doubling or twisting machines, and other machinery for producing textile yarns; textile reeling or winding (including weft winding) machines and machines for preparing textile yarns for use on the machines of heading 8446 or 8447

8446—Weaving machines (looms)

8447—Knitting machines, stitch-bonding machines, and machines for making gimped yarn, tulle, lace, embroidery, trimmings, braid, or net and machines for tufting

8448—Auxiliary machinery for use with machines of heading 8444, 8445, 8446, or 8447 (for example, dobbies, Jacquards, automatic stop motions, and shuttle changing mechanisms); parts and accessories suitable for use solely or principally with the machines of this heading or of heading 8444, 8445, 8446 or 8447 (for example, spindles and spindle flyers, card clothing, combs, extruding nipples, shuttles, healds and heald-frames, hosiery needles)

8449—Machinery for the manufacture or finishing of felt or nonwovens in the piece or in shapes, including machinery for making felt hats; blocks for making hats; parts thereof

8450—Household-or laundry-type washing machines, including machines which both wash and dry; parts thereof

8451—Machinery (other than machines of heading 8450) for washing, cleaning, wringing, drying, ironing, pressing (including fusing presses), bleaching, dyeing, dressing, finishing, coating or impregnating textile yarns, fabrics or made up textile articles and machines for applying the paste to the base fabric or other support used in the manufacture of floor coverings such as linoleum; machines for reeling, unreeling, folding, cutting or pinking textile fabrics; parts thereof

8452—Sewing machines, other than book-sewing machines of heading 8440; furniture, bases and covers specially designed for sewing machines; sewing machine needles; parts thereof

8453—Machinery for preparing, tanning or working hides, skins, or leather or for making or repairing footwear or other articles of hides, skins or leather, other than sewing machines; parts thereof

8454—Converters, ladles, ingot molds, and casting machines, of a kind used in metallurgy or in metal foundries, and parts thereof

8455—Metal-rolling mills and rolls therefore; parts thereof

8456—Machine tools for working any material by removal of material, by laser or other light or photon beam, ultrasonic, electro-discharge, electro-chemical, electron-beam, ionic beam or plasma arc processes

8457—Machining centers, unit construction machines (single station) and multistation transfer machines, for working metal

8458—Lathes (including turning centers) for removing metal

8459—Machine tools (including way-type unit head machines) for drilling, boring, milling, threading or tapping by removing metal, other than lathes (including turning centers) of heading 8458

8460—Machine tools for deburring, sharpening, grinding, honing, lapping, polishing or otherwise finishing metal or cermets by means of grinding stones, abrasives, or polishing products, other than gear cutting, gear grinding or gear finishing machines of heading 8461

8461—Machine tools for planing, shaping, slotting, broaching, gear cutting, gear grinding or gear finishing, sawing, cutting-off, and other machine tools working by removing metal or cermets, not elsewhere specified or included

8462—Machine tools (including presses) for working metal by forging, hammering or die-stamping; machine tools (including presses) for working metal by bending, folding, straightening, flattening, shearing, punching or notching; presses for working metal or metal carbides, not specified above

8463—Other machine tools for working metal or cermets, without removing material

8464—Machine tools for working stone, ceramics, concrete, asbestos-cement or like mineral materials or for cold working glass

8465—Machine tools (including machines for nailing, stapling, gluing or otherwise assembling) for working wood, cork, bone, hard rubber, hard plastics or similar hard materials

8566—Parts and accessories suitable for use solely or principally with the machines of heading 8456 to 8465, including work or tool holders, self-opening dieheads, dividing heads, and other special attachments for machine tools; tool holders for any type of tool for working in the hand

8467—Tools for working in the hand, pneumatic or with self-contained nonelectric motor, and parts thereof

8468—Machinery and apparatus for soldering, brazing or welding, whether of not capable of cutting, other than those of heading 8515; gas-operated surface tempering machines and appliances; parts thereof

8469—Typewriters other than printers of heading 8471; word processing machines

8470—Calculating machines and pocket-size data recording, reproducing and displaying machines with calculating functions; accounting machines, postage-franking machines, ticket-issuing machines, and similar machines, incorporating a calculating device; cash registers

8471—Automatic data processing machines and units thereof; magnetic or optical readers, machines for transcribing data onto data media in coded form and machines for processing such data, not elsewhere specified or included

8472—Other office machines (for example, hectograph or stencil duplicating machines, addressing machines, automatic bank-note dispensers, coin-sorting machines, coin-counting or wrapping machines, pencil-sharpening machines, perforating or stapling machines)

8473—Parts and accessories (other than covers, carrying cases, and the like) suitable for use solely or principally with machines of headings 8469 to 8472

8474—Machinery for sorting, screening, separating, washing, crushing, grinding, mixing or kneading earth, stone, ores or other mineral substances, in solid (including powder or paste) form; machinery for agglomerating, shaping or molding solid mineral fuels, ceramic paste, unhardened

cements, plastering materials or other mineral products, in powder or paste form; machines for forming foundry molds of sand; parts thereof

8475—Machines for assembling electric or electronic lamps, tubes or flashbulbs, in glass envelopes; machines for manufacturing or hot-working glass or glassware; parts thereof

8476—Automatic goods-vending machines (for example, postage stamp, cigarette, food or beverage machines), including money-changing machines; parts thereof

8477—Machinery for working rubber or plastics or for the manufacture of products from these materials, not specified or included elsewhere in this chapter; parts thereof

8478—Machinery for preparing or making up tobacco, not specified or included elsewhere in this chapter; parts thereof

8479—Machines and mechanical appliances having individual functions, not specified or included elsewhere in this chapter; parts thereof

8480—Molding boxes for metal foundry; mold bases; molding patterns; molds for metal (other than ingot molds), metal carbides, glass, mineral materials, rubber or plastics

8481—Taps, cocks, valves, and similar appliances, for pipes, boiler shells, tanks, vats or the like, including pressure-reducing valves and thermostatically controlled valves; parts thereof

8482—Ball or roller bearings, and parts thereof

8483—Transmission shafts (including camshafts and crankshafts) and cranks; bearing housings, housed bearings, and plain shaft bearings; gears and gearing; ball or roller screws; gear boxes and other speed changers, including torque converters; flywheels and pulleys, including pulley blocks; clutches and shaft couplings (including universal joints); parts thereof

8484—Gaskets and similar joints of metal sheeting combined with other material or of two or more layers of metal; sets of assortments of gaskets and similar joints, dissimilar in composition, put up in pouches, envelopes or similar packings; mechanical seals

8485—Machinery parts, not containing electrical connectors, insulators, coils, contacts or other electrical features, and not specified or included elsewhere in this chapter

For more details regarding classification of the specific product you are interested in importing, consult a customs broker, the appropriate commodity specialist at your nearest customs port, or see HTSUS. The 2001 HTSUS is available online from the Customs Service (www.customs.gov/impoexpo/impoexpo.htm) or for purchase from the U.S. Government Printing Office (see resources at the end of this chapter), and may be found in larger public libraries. For a general discussion of customs classification, see "Classification—Liquidation" on page 229.

Dutiable Status of Goods

For more information about duty rates and binding decisions see "Dutiable Status of Goods" on page 203; for a discussion of temporary importation of goods see "Temporary Free Importations" on page 205.

Valuation

Importers have a responsibility to use what the U.S. Customs Service deems, "reasonable care," when determining the value of their goods. They must also provide any additional information that the Customs Service needs for setting a final value on the goods. This process involves a number of factors and can be somewhat complicated; importers must be aware of applicable issues and details. Valuation information applies to all types of commodities, for further discussion on the subject see "Customs Valuation" on page 267.

Import Duties

Import duties vary (often dramatically) depending upon the Harmonized Tariff Schedule (HTSUS) classification of the goods or products imported. Since some products that look alike have different HTSUS classifications and different rates of duty, proper classification is vital. Note that "differences of opinion" between importers and the Bureau of Customs and Border Protection regarding classification keeps customs attorneys very busy.

Import duties can be assessed on the imported value of the goods ("ad valorem" rates of duty such as 2%, 4.4%, 50%, etc.), total units or weight of the goods ("specific" rates of duty such as 2 cents each or 1.5 cents/pound, etc.) or on a combination basis ("compound" rates of duty such as 5 cents each plus 6%).

Listed below is a sampling of several Column 1 import duty rates for Chapter 84 products:
Boilers (8403.10.00.00): Free
to
Watertube boilers with a steam production exceeding 45 t per hour (8402.11.00.00): 5.2%

For specific information on US import duties refer to the Harmonized Tariff Schedule of the US. The print version is available from the US Government Printing Office as well as third party suppliers who often add special features. Online versions are available in both static PDF pages as well as in formats with excellent search functionality. Search the Web with the term "Harmonized Tariff Schedule" to find sources.

Entry and Documentation

The entry of merchandise is a two-part process consisting of 1) filing the documents necessary to determine whether merchandise may be released from Customs custody and 2) filing the documents that contain information for duty assessment and statistical purposes. In certain instances all documents must be filed and accepted by Customs prior to the release of the goods. Unless you have been granted an extension, you must file entry documents at a location specified by the port or area director within five working days of your shipment's date of arrival at a U.S. port of entry. These include a number of standard documents required by Customs for any entry, and:

- For radio frequency devices, FCC Entry Notification Form FCC 740
- FDA Electronic Product Declaration, Form FDA 2877
- Documentation of NRC import authorization

After you present the entry, Customs may examine your shipment, or may waive examination. The shipment is then released provided no legal or regulatory violations have been noted. You must then file entry summary documentation and deposit estimated duties at a designated customhouse within 10 working days of your shipment's release. For a detailed description of entry procedures, standard documentation, and informal entry, see "Entry Process" on page 185.

Informed Compliance. Informed compliance was introduced with the Customs Modernization Act of 1993 (Mod Act) and defines the relationship between importers and the Customs Service. It sets out the responsibilities of both parties. Providing the correct documentation and information for entry is a key factor that will make your importing operation run smoothly. We recommend that importers become familiar with the concept of informed comliance and the responsibilities that they have under the Mod Act. For further discussion about informed compliance see "Informed Compliance" on page 211.

Entry Invoice for Machinery, Equipment, and Apparatus. For all articles of machinery, equipment, and apparatus, a statement is required detailing the use or method of operation of each type of machine.

Entry Invoices for Machine Parts. For machine parts, a statement is required specifying the kind of machine for which the parts are intended, or—if it is not known to the shipper—the kinds of machines for which the parts are suitable.

Entry Invoices for Machine Tools. Special information is required on invoices of machine tools entered under the following HTSUS headings: 1) 8456—8462, if equipped with a Computer Numerical Control (CNC) or the facings (electrical interface) for a CNC, must so state; 2) 8458—8463, if rebuilt, must so state; 3) 8456.30.10 Electrical Discharge Machines (EDM), if a Traveling Wire (Wire Cut) type, must so state. Wire EDM's use a copper or brass wire for the electrode; 4) 8457.10.0010—8457.10.0050 Machining Centers: must state whether or not they have an Automatic Tool Changer (ATC); vertical spindle machine centers with an ATC must also indicate the Y-travel; 5) 8458.11.0030—8458.11.00.90, horizontal lathes, numerically controlled: must indicate the rated hp (or kw rating) of the main spindle motor. (Use the continuous rather than 30-minute rating.)

Entry Invoices for Refrigerator-Freezers. For refrigerator-freezers classifiable under subheading 8418.10.00 and refrigerators classifiable under subheading 8418.20.00, a statement is required as to 1) whether they are compression or absorption type; and 2) refrigerated volume in liters. For freezers classifiable under subheadings 8418.30.00 and 8418.40.00, a statement is required as to whether they are chest or upright type. Liquid chilling units classifiable under subheadings 8418.69.0045 through 8418.69.0060 must include a statement as to whether they are centrifugal open-type, centrifugal hermetic-type, absorption-type, or reciprocating-type.

Entry Invoices for Rolling Mills. For rolling mills classifiable under subheadings 8455.30.0005 through 8455.30.0085, a statement is required indicating the composition of the roll—gray iron, cast steel, or other—and the weight of each roll.

Entry Invoices for Bearings. For ball or roller bearings classified under headings 8482.10.50 through 8482.80.00, the invoice must state 1) the type of bearing (whether ball or roller); 2) if a roller bearing, whether spherical, tapered, cylindrical, needled, or other; 3) whether a combination bearing (one containing both ball and roller components); and 4) if a ball bearing (excluding bearings with integral shafts or parts of ball bearings) whether or not radial, the following additional information: a) outside diameter of each bearing; and b) whether or not a radial bearing (i.e., an antifriction bearing primarily designed to support a load perpendicular to the shaft axis). For more general information about invoices see "Invoices" on page 277.

Restrictions and Prohibitions

Radioactive Materials. Many radioisotopes, all forms of uranium, thorium, and plutonium, and all nuclear reactors imported into the U.S. are subject to the regulations of the NRC (see addresses at end of this chapter), in addition to any other regulations imposed by any other agency (for example, the FDA also exercises jurisdiction over radioactive materials imported for medical uses). Formal authority to import these commodities or articles containing these commodities must be granted by the NRC, which exercises very tight controls.

Machine Tools. Certain types of machine tools from Japan and Taiwan are subject to Voluntary Restraint Agreements (VRAs) negotiated by the U.S. Trade Representative with those countries. Under these agreements, the level of exports by these countries to the U.S. are kept below an agreed-upon level. These agreements are monitored by the Department of Commerce (DOC). Presentation of an export certificate or license issued by the country of origin is a condition of entry through Customs.

Note: The Entry and Documentation section has been carefully designed to supply you, the importer, with sample documents and directions on how to satisfy Customs requirements. Be aware that you should consult the applicable authorities to ensure that you are correctly following the most current procedures.

Marking and Labeling Requirements

Country of origin markings may not be required on certain whole engines or on engine parts that are imported in order to be further manufactured in the U.S. Customs makes this determination on a case-by-case basis. If you have questions, you should contact the nearest customs port office for more information.

All electronic devices subject to FCC regulation are required to bear special labeling. The FTC has specific labeling requirements for electrical appliances.

All radiation-producing products for which federal standards have been determined must be certified for compliance. The manufacturer must affix a certification label to each product stating that it conforms to the applicable standard. If you attempt to import products that require certification but that are not labeled, your shipment will be refused entry.

For a general discussion of U.S. Customs marking and labeling requirements, see "Country of Origin Marking" on page 236, "Special Marking Requirements" on page 238 and "Marking—False Impression" on page 239.

Shipping Considerations

You will need to ensure that your goods are packaged and shipped with care to ensure that they arrive in good condition and pass smoothly through Customs. You are responsible for ensuring that the shipment is in compliance with all applicable government regulations for packaging and shipping. In most instances, you should not leave these arrangements solely to the discretion of your supplier. Careful preparation of the cargo and selection of the mode of transport can be essential to a cost-effective, timely delivery of undamaged goods. We strongly advise you to consult your shipping representative, insurance agent, or freight broker for advice on packing and shipping.

Machinery and large appliances are often bulky and heavy, and should be securely stowed to avoid damage due to shifting en route. Many products of Chapter 84 are also subject to corrosion, which should be guarded against, especially as no allowance is made by customs for partial loss due to deterioration or to damage during shipping.

Publications and WWW Resources

The *Harmonized Tariff Schedule of the United States (2001)* (HTSUS) is available to view on the Customs Service website (www.customs.gov), or you may purchase a printed version from:

U.S. Government Printing Office
Superintendent of Documents
710 North Capital Street NW
Washington DC 20401
Tel: (202) 512-1800
Fax: (202) 512-1657
Website: www.access.gpo.gov

The USGPO also has copies of specific laws available for purchase. The USGPO accepts orders made by fax, phone or placed over the Internet, as well as mail orders paid by credit card. All orders must be accompanied by payment. Credit cards, checks drawn on a U.S. bank, or an international money order are all acceptable.

Relevant Government Agencies

Address questions concerning FCC requirements for the importation of radiation-producing devices and radio frequency devices to:

Federal Communications Commission (FCC)
Consumer and Governmental Affairs Bureau
445 12th Street SW
Washington DC 20554
(202) 418-1400
Website: www.fcc.gov

Address questions regarding FDA requirements for the importation of radiation-producing devices to:

Food and Drug Administration (FDA)
Center for Devices and Radiological Health
Division of Small Manufacturers Assistance
1350 Piccard Drive
Rockville, MD 20850-4307
Tel: 800-638-2041
Fax: (301) 443-8818
Email: dsmica@cdrh.fda.gov
Website: www.fda.gov/cdrh

To obtain addresses of regional FDA offices contact FDA headquarters at:

U.S. Food and Drug Administration (FDA)
5600 Fishers Lane
Rockville, MD 20857-0001
Tel: 888-463-6332
Website: www.fda.gov

Address questions regarding energy labeling and consumer product safety issues on household appliances to:

Federal Trade Commission (FTC)
Division of Enforcement
600 Pennsylvania Ave. NW
Washington DC 20580
Tel: (202) 326-2996
Website: www.ftc.gov

Address questions regarding energy performance and testing standards for household appliances to:

U.S. Department of Energy (DOE)
Office of Codes and Standards
1000 Independence Avenue
Washington DC 20585
EE2J
(202) 586-9127
Website: www.doe.gov

Address questions regarding the NRC regulations pertinent to importation of radioactive materials and nuclear reactors to:

Nuclear Regulatory Commission (NRC)
Office of International Programs
USNRC 04E21
Washington DC 20555
(301) 415-2344; FAX (301) 415-2395
Web site: www.nrc.gov

Address questions regarding consumer product safety standards for machinery and appliances to:

Consumer Product Safety Commission (CPSC)
Office of Compliance
Washington DC 20207-0001
Tel: 800-638-2772 or (301) 504-7912
Fax: (301) 504-0359
Website: www.cpsc.gov

Address questions regarding the importation of machinery and large appliances to your local Customs port director. For addresses refer to "U.S. Customs and Border Protection Offices" on page 65 or contact:

U.S. Customs and Border Protection
Customs Headquarters
1300 Pennsylvania Avenue NW
Washington DC 20229
Tel: (202) 354-1000
Website: www.customs.treas.gov

Laws and Regulations

The following laws and regulations may be relevant to the importation of computer hardware. The laws are contained in the U.S. Code (USC) and the regulations are published in the code of Federal Regulations (CFR), both of which may be available at larger public and law libraries. Copies of specific laws are also available from the United States Government Printing Office (address above).

42 USC 6201 et seq.
Energy Policy and Conservation Act (EPCA)
This Act authorizes adoption of standards for operating at maximum energy efficiency and prescribes labeling and testing requirements for compliance.

10 CFR Part 430
Regulations on EPCA
These regulations set test procedures and standards for measuring energy consumption of refrigerators, freezers, dishwashers, clothes washers and dryers, water heaters, air conditioners, heaters and furnaces, televisions, oven and cooking appliances, and fluorescent lamps.

29 USC 651 et seq.
Occupational Safety and Health Act of 1970
This Act authorizes the adoption of standards for safety of employees in the workplace, including safety requirements for machinery being operated, and provides incentives for compliance and penalties for noncompliance.

29 CFR Part 1926
Regulations of OSHA
These regulations specify safety and health standards and inspection procedures for certain equipment, including equipment used in shipbuilding and repairing, protective equipment, hand and power tools, welding tools, cranes, derricks, hoists, elevators, conveyors, mechanized equipment, and motor vehicles.

15 USC 2051 et seq.
Consumer Product Safety Act
This Act sets standards for the manufacture, processing, and labeling of products sold to U.S. consumers.

18 USC 831 et seq.
Explosives and Other Dangerous Articles
This Act restricts the import of fireworks and nuclear materials and authorizes enforcement by Customs. See 49 CFR Parts 170-171, 173, 177, 179, and 195; 46 USC 870.

21 USC 301 et seq.
Federal Food, Drug, and Cosmetic Act
This Act prohibits deceptive practices and regulates the manufacture, sale and importation or exportation of food, drugs, cosmetics, and related products. It was amended by the Food Quality Protection Act of 1996. See 21 USC 331, 381, 382.

19 CFR 12.1 et seq.; 21 CFR 1.83 et seq.
Regulations on Food, Drugs, and Cosmetics
These regulations of the Secretary of Health and Human Services and the Secretary of the Treasury govern the standards, labeling, marking, and importing of products used with food, drugs, and cosmetics.

42 USC 2077, 2111, 2122, 2131, 2155
Atomic Energy Act of 1954

These laws restrict importation and exportation of special nuclear material, atomic weapons, and byproduct material, and authorizes enforcement by Customs. See 10 CFR 30, 40, 50, 70 and 110.

21 USC 360 et seq.
Radiation Control for Health and Safety Act of 1968
This Act prohibits entry of electronic products found not to be in compliance with prescribed standards. See 21 CFR Part 1005. Customs enforces this prohibition. See 19 CFR 12.90 et seq.

47 USC 302a
Devices That Interfere with Radio Reception
This law prohibits the importation of devices or home electronic equipment that fail to comply with regulations promulgated by the FCC. See 47 CFR 2.1201 et seq. and 18.119. Customs enforces the prohibition.

47 USC 303(s) and 330
Importation of Certain Television Receivers
These laws prohibit importation of television receivers that are incapable of receiving all frequencies allocated to television broadcasting and authorizes enforcement by Customs. See 47 CFR 15.61-15.72. Such receivers are subject to seizure and forfeiture if a person willfully or knowingly violates this prohibition. See 47 USC 510.

Principal Exporting Countries

The following listing includes samples of the main supplier nations of the products of this chapter. It is organized by HTSUS major heading. (Refer to "Customs Classification" above for the product codes.) Countries are listed in rank order of the value of products imported to the U.S. Statistics represent customs value of entries for 2002 from the Bureau of Census, U.S. Department of Commerce.

8401—Germany, Sweden, France, Japan, Croatia, Czech Republic, Spain, Canada

8402—South Korea, Canada, Italy, Spain, Japan, Indonesia, Mexico, Thailand, Portugal, China, Sweden, Czech Republic

8403—Canada, Germany, South Korea, France, Netherlands, Italy

8404—South Korea, Canada, India, Japan, China, Portugal, Spain, Turkey, Israel, Thailand, Belgium, United Kingdom, Germany

8405—Turkey, Mexico, Japan, Germany, Canada, Unitd Kingdom

8406—Japan, Germany, United Kingdom, Mexico, South Korea, France, Poland

8407—Japan, Canada, Mexico, Germany, United Kingdom, Austria

8408—Japan, Germany, Mexico, Brazil, United Kingdom, Sweden, Italy

8409—Japan, Canada, Mexico, Germany, Brazil, United Kingdom, China, Italy, France

8410—Canada, Brazil, Austria, Bulgaria, Germany, Norway, Venezuela, Japan

8411—United Kingdom, France, Canada, Germany, Japan, Italy, South Korea, Mexico, Israel, Sweden

8412—Canada, Japan, Germany, United Kingdom, Italy, France, Sweden

8413—Germany, Canada, Mexico, Japan, United Kingdom, Italy, China

8414—China, Mexico, Japan, Canada, Taiwan, Brazil, Germany, Italy, United Kingdom

8415—Mexico, China, South Korea, Canada, Japan, Thailand

8416—France, Canada, Mexico, Germany, United Kingdom, China, Italy

8417—Canada, Japan, Italy, Germany, France, United Kingdom, Czech Republic, Mexico

8418—Mexico, China, Canada, South Korea, Sweden, Italy, Germany

8419—Canada, Mexico, Germany, Japan, Italy, South Korea, United Kingdom

8420—Germany, Japan, Italy, United Kingdom, Switzerland, South Korea, Finland

8421—Canada, Mexico, Germany, Japan, United Kingdom, South Africa

8422—Germany, Italy, Canada, Japan, Switzerland, France, United Kingdom

8423—China, Japan, Germany, United Kingdom, Canada

8424—Canada, Italy, Germany, China, Taiwan, Mexico, Japan, France

8425—China, Canada, Mexico, Japan, Taiwan, Germany, United Kingdom, Italy

8426—China, Germany, Japan, Italy, South Korea, Sweden, France, Austria, Finland

8427—Canada, United Kingdom, Germany, South Korea, Netherlands, Ireland, Japan, Italy, France

8428—Canada, Japan, Germany, Mexico, United Kingdom, Sweden, Italy, France

8429—Japan, France, United Kingdom, Germany, Canada, South Korea, Belgium, Brazil

8430—Germany, Canada, United Kingdom, Japan, Italy, Finland, China, France, Sweden

8431—Canada, Mexico, Japan, Germany, Italy, United Kingdom

8432—Canada, Italy, Mexico, South Korea, China, Netherlands

8433—Canada, Germany, Italy, France, Belgium, Japan, Mexico

8434—United Kingdom, New Zealand, Israel, Italy, Sweden, Germany, Denmark, Ireland, Mexico, Netherlands

8435—Italy, France, Germany, Switzerland, South Korea, Spain, Brazil, China, Hong Kong

8436—Canada, Germany, China, Netherlands, Finland, Sweden, Israel

8437—Switzerland, Germany, Canada, United Kingdom, Japan, Denmark, Netherlands, Italy

8438—Germany, Netherlands, Italy, Denmark, France, Switzerland, Canada

8439—Germany, Canada, Sweden, Finland, Italy, Switzerland

8440—Germany, Switzerland, Portugal, Belgium, Italy, Japan, Sweden, United Kingdom

8441—Germany, Switzerland, Canada, Italy, France, United Kingdom, Japan, Spain

8442—Canada, Israel, Germany, United Kingdom, Denmark, Japan, France

8443—Germany, Japan, United Kingdom, Italy, Israel, France

8444—Germany, Italy, United Kingdom, Austria, Switzerland, Canada, South Korea

8445—Germany, France, Italy, Switzerland, Japan, Belgium

8446—Switzerland, Germany, Belgium, Italy, Japan, Austria, Netherlands

8447—Japan, Italy, Germany, Taiwan, South Korea, Czech Republic

8448—Germany, Japan, Switzerland, France, Italy, United Kingdom, Belgium

8449—Germany, France, Japan, Portugal, Austria

8450—Germany, Sweden, Mexico, New Zealand, Italy

8451—Canada, Germany, Italy, Japan, Denmark, Switzerland, France

8452—Japan, Taiwan, China, Sweden, Switzerland, Germany, Brazil

8453—Italy, Germany, France, Canada, United Kingdom, Denmark, Taiwan, Spain

8454—Canada, Japan, Italy, Germany, United Kingdom, Switzerland, France, China, Brazil

8455—United Kingdom, Canada, Italy, Germany, Japan, Sweden

8456—Japan, Switzerland, United Kingdom, Germany, Canada, Thailand, Italy, Ireland

8457—Japan, Germany, Taiwan, Italy, South Korea, Switzerland, Canada

8458—Japan, Germany, South Korea, Taiwan, China, Italy, United Kingdom, Canada

8459—Japan, Germany, Taiwan, Italy, Canada, China, Switzerland, France, Spain, Austria

8460—Germany, Switzerland, Japan, China, Italy, Taiwan

8461—Germany, Japan, Taiwan, China, Canada, Italy

8462—Japan, Germany, Canada, Italy, Switzerland, United Kingdom, Finland, Taiwan, Sweden, China

8463—Germany, Japan, Italy, Switzerland, France, Netherlands, Sweden, Taiwan, Canada, Belgium, United Kingdom

8464—Japan, Italy, Germany, Switzerland, China, France

8465—Taiwan, Germany, China, Italy, Canada, Japan, Austria, United Kingdom

8466—Japan, Germany, Canada, Taiwan, Switzerland, United Kingdom, Italy, Sweden

8467—China, Mexico, Japan, Taiwan, Germany, Sweden, United Kingdom, Liechtenstein

8468—Mexico, Japan, Canada, Germany, Sweden, France, United Kingdom

8469—Malaysia, United Kingdom, China, Indonesia, Japan, India, Mexico

8470—China, Canada, Singapore, Taiwan, Israel, Japan, Malaysia

8471—China, Mexico, Malaysia, Taiwan, Singapore, Japan, South Korea, Philippines

8472—China, Japan, Germany, Canada, Mexico, South Korea, United Kingdom

8473—China, Japan, Singapore, Taiwan, Malaysia, South Korea, Mexico, Canada

8474—Canada, United Kingdom, Germany, Japan, Italy, Austria, South Africa

8475—Germany, Japan, France, United Kingdom, Finland, Belgium

8476—Mexico, Japan, China, Canada, Taiwan, United Kingdom, Italy, South Korea, Germany, Switzerland

8477—Canada, Germany, Japan, France, Italy, Austria, Switzerland, United Kingdom, Luxembourg, Taiwan

8478—Germany, United Kingdom, Netherlands, Italy, Brazil

8479—Japan, Germany, Canada, Italy, Switzerland, United Kingdom

8480—Canada, Japan, Germany, Italy, Taiwan, Portugal, France, South Korea, China

8481—Mexico, Japan, Germany, China, Canada, Taiwan, Italy, United Kingdom, South Korea, France

8482—Japan, Canada, China, Germany, France, Italy, Mexico, South Korea, Brazil

8483—Japan, Canada, Germany, Italy, United Kingdom, Mexico, Brazil, France

8484—Mexico, Japan, Germany, United Kingdom, Canada, Taiwan

8485—Germany, Japan, Canada, United Kingdom, Taiwan, Italy

Chapter 85:
Electronics and Components

Full title: Electrical Machinery and Equipment and Parts Thereof; Sound Recorders and Reproducers, Television Image and Sound Recorders and Reproducers and Parts and Accessories of Such Articles

This chapter relates to the importation of electrically-powered products, electronics, and their components, which are classified within Chapter 85 of the Harmonized Tariff Schedule of the United States (HTSUS). Chapter 85 covers a very broad range of often highly specialized equipment, assemblies, components, and parts. The items in this chapter are those that are powered by or involve the use of electricity. Specifically, it includes electric motors and generators; transformers; electromagnets; batteries; power hand tools; electrical appliances, such as vacuum cleaners, food processors, garbage disposals, electric toothbrushes, and electric shavers; electrical starters; lighting and signaling equipment, including automotive components; flashlights; electrical industrial furnaces; lasers; water heaters, hair dryers, irons, microwave ovens, and other electric cookers; telephones and related equipment; microphones, loudspeakers, and stereo equipment; audio and video recorders and players; blank and prerecorded tapes, records, and computer disks; radio and television broadcasting, receiving, and related equipment; television sets; radars; capacitors, resistors, printed circuits, switches, panels, diodes, transistors, semiconductors, tubes, circuits, and similar components; lightbulbs; integrated electrical industrial apparatus; insulated wire; electrodes and other carbon products; insulated fittings; other miscellaneous electrical machinery; and parts of the above.

Large machinery, equipment, and appliances, especially industrial equipment, are generally classified in Commodity Index Chapter 84. For example, while many electrically-powered household appliances are covered in Chapter 85, appliances weighing more than 20 kg and such specific types of appliances as fans, clothes washers and dryers, dishwashers, pressing machines, and sewing machines are covered in Chapter 84. If you are interested in importing electric blankets, refer to Chapter 63. Consult the Commodity Index chapter for the specific product category involved for other electrically warmed articles of clothing, such as jackets (Chapter 62), socks (Chapter 61), earmuffs (Chapter 65), and boots (Chapter 65). Although assembled lightbulbs are covered in Chapter 85, the glass envelopes for such articles are found in Chapter 70. Electrically heated furniture is covered in Chapter 94. Although the parts of the articles covered in Chapter 85 are generally included with those products, parts of general use—such as nuts and bolts, screws, and other general hardware—are classified in Chapters 72-83 by the particular material of which they are composed, if made of base metals, or in Chapter 39 if made of plastic or chapter 40 if made of rubber. Unpowered or mechanically powered hand tools are covered in Chapter 82, while specialized equipment—such as optical, scientific, medical, and other precision instruments; clocks and watches; and musical instruments—are covered respectively in Chapters 90, 91, and 92, regardless of their reliance on electrical power or components.

Note: To understand key issues that will enable you to make best use of the information in this section we recommend that you see "Introduction" on page 425.

Key Factors

The key factors in the importation of electronics and components are:

- Compliance with U.S. Food and Drug Administration (FDA) standards and entry notification for radiation-producing devices

- Compliance with U.S. Federal Communications Commission (FCC) standards and entry notification for radio frequency devices

- Compliance with U.S Department of Energy (DOE) performance standards

- Compliance with Consumer Product Safety Commission (CPSC) and Federal Trade Commission (FTC) requirements for consumer products

- Compliance with trademark, trade name, and copyright restrictions

Although most importers utilize the services of a licensed customs broker in making their entries, and we recommend this practice, you should be aware of the regulatory, entry, and documentation issues involved in importing your product. You, as importer, are ultimately responsible for the fulfillment of any legal requirements applicable to your shipment.

General Considerations

Many electronic products and components may be imported without restrictions, permits, prior approval, special requirements, or additional paperwork. However, many others are subject to a variety of requirements enforced by a wide range of agencies, and it is necessary for importers to carefully check with the major agencies well in advance to be sure that they are in compliance with all relevant requirements for their specific electronics and component products.

Categories. From a regulatory viewpoint, many electronic devices subject to regulation fall into two general categories: those that produce radio frequency energy, and those that produce radiation. Radiation-producing electronic devices are regulated by the FDA (see addresses at end of this chapter) under the provisions of the Federal Food, Drug, and Cosmetic Act (FDCA) and the Radiation Control for Health and Safety Act of 1968 (RCHSA). Both imported and domestically produced electronic products must comply with all relevant FDA regulations. Whether you are importing a single product for personal use, or a commercial shipment for resale in the U.S., you must file an Electronic Product Declaration, Form FD2877 for each product type for which official standards exist. You will not be permitted to enter a shipment unless you have filed these forms. You may obtain them from FDA, National Center for Devices and Radiological Health (see addresses at end of this chapter) or from your customs broker. For a general discussion of FDA import procedures, see "Appendix: Foods" on page 825.

Radio frequency (rf) devices are regulated by the FCC (see addresses at end of this chapter) under the provisions of 47 CFR Parts 2 and 15. You must file a copy of FCC Form 740 with each shipment of rf devices. If your shipment consists of more than one type of device, you must file a separate form for each type. The form certifies that the imported model or device is either in compliance with, or is exempt from, FCC requirements, and is so labeled. An FCC entry declaration form (FCC **Form 740**) is required for products covered under FCC regulations.

Some products, such as ultrasonic therapeutic devices and television receivers, fall under the jurisdiction of both the FCC and the FDA and must comply with both sets of regulations. Although for purposes of simplicity this section will discuss the two categories as if they do not overlap, they do, and you should ascertain exactly which regulations your product is required to meet for which agency. Do not rely on one agency for information concerning the requirements of another agency. If you are in doubt as to the status of your commodity, contact both the FCC and the FDA.

Energy Efficiency Requirements. Both domestic and imported household consumer appliances must comply with applicable energy efficiency standards and labeling requirements under the Energy Policy and Conservation Act (EPCA) as amended. The DOE Consumer Products Efficiency Branch is responsible for test procedures and energy performance standards. The FTC Division of Energy and Product Information regulates household appliance labeling. You should contact these agencies (addresses below) to find out about any requirements that may be in effect at the time you anticipate making your shipment.

EPCA covers the following types of consumer products: 1) refrigerators and refrigerator-freezers; 2) freezers; 3) dishwashers; 4) clothes dryers; 5) water heaters; 6) room air conditioners; 7) home heating equipment other than furnaces; 8) television sets; 9) kitchen ranges and ovens; 10) clothes washers; 11) humidifiers and dehumidifiers; 12) central air conditioners; 13) furnaces; and 14) certain other types of household consumer appliances, as appropriate. Not all appliances are covered by requirements of both agencies.

Intellectual Property Provisions. Products such as microchips and recorded media (prerecorded tapes, records, computer software, and similar products) are subject to patent and trademark restrictions. (See "Prohibitions and Restrictions" below.) The Intellectual Property Rights (IPR) branch of U.S. Customs enforces laws pertinent to entry of such products. Importers must be prepared to show valid authorization from trademark and copyright holders. Pirated products are subject to seizure.

CPSC and FTC Regulations. Some of the products found in this section are covered by the provisions of the Consumer Product Safety Act (CPSA), which establishes standards for the manufacturing and labeling of potentially hazardous consumer products. Imported consumer products for which such standards exist must comply with the full range of requirements prescribed for domestic products. In addition, the CPSA requires all manufacturers, distributors, retailers, and others involved in the commercial handling of such products to report immediately any potentially hazardous defects or failures to conform to established standards to the CPSC for investigation and potential action. Failure to submit such a Substantial Product Hazard Report can result in action by the CPSC. Contact the CPSC (see addresses at end of this chapter) with questions regarding specific products.

Customs Classification

For customs purposes, electronics and electrical products and components are classified within Chapter 85 of HTSUS. This chapter is divided into major headings, which are further divided into subheadings, and often into sub-subheadings, each of which has its own HTSUS classification number. For example, the 2001 HTSUS number for DC generators is 8501.31.80, indicating that it is a subcategory of other DC motors and generators

not exceeding 750 W (8501.31), which is a subcategory of the major heading electric motors and generators (excluding generating sets) (8501). There are 48 major headings in HTSUS chapter 85.

8501—Electric motors and generators (excluding generating sets)

8502—Electric generating sets and rotary converters

8503—Parts suitable for use solely or principally with the machines of heading 8501 or 8502

8504—Electrical transformers, static converters (for example, rectifiers), and inductors; parts thereof

8505—Electromagnets; permanent magnets and articles intended to become permanent magnets after magnetization; electromagnetic or permanent magnet chucks, clamps and similar holding devices; electromagnetic couplings, clutches, and brakes; electromagnetic lifting heads; parts thereof

8506—Primary cells and primary batteries; parts thereof

8507—Electric storage batteries, including separators thereof, whether or not rectangular (including square); parts thereof

8508—Electromechanical tools for working in the hand with self-contained electric motor; parts thereof

8509—Electromechanical domestic appliances, with self-contained electric motor; parts thereof

8510—Shavers, hair clippers, and hair-removing appliances, with self-contained electric motor; parts thereof

8511—Electrical ignition or starting equipment of a kind used for spark-ignition or compression-ignition internal combustion engines (for example, ignition magnetos, magneto-dynamos, ignition coils, spark plugs and glow plugs, starter motors); generators (for example, dynamos, alternators), and cut-outs of a kind used in conjunction with such engines; parts thereof

8512—Electrical lighting or signaling equipment (excluding articles of heading 8539), windshield wipers, defrosters, and demisters, of a kind used for cycles or motor vehicles; parts thereof

8513—Portable electric lamps designed to function by their own source of energy (for example, dry batteries, storage batteries, magnetos), other than lighting equipment of heading 8512; parts thereof

8514—Industrial or laboratory electric (including induction or dielectric) furnaces and ovens; other industrial or laboratory induction or dielectric heating equipment; parts thereof

8515—Electric (including electrically heated gas), laser or other light or photon beam, ultrasonic, electron beam, magnetic pulse or plasma arc, soldering, brazing, or welding machines and apparatus, whether or not capable of cutting; electric machines and apparatus for hot spraying of metals or cermets; parts thereof

8516—Electric instantaneous or storage water heaters and immersion heaters; electric space heating apparatus and soil heating apparatus; electrothermic hair-dressing apparatus (for example, hair dryers, hair curlers, curling tong heaters) and hand dryers; electric flatirons; other electrothermic appliances of a kind used for domestic purposes; electric heating resistors, other than those of heading 8545; parts thereof

8517—Electrical apparatus for line telephony or line telegraphy, including line telephone sets with cordless handsets and telecommunication apparatus for carrier-current line systems or for digital line systems; videophones; parts thereof

8518—Microphones and stands therefor; loudspeakers, whether or not mounted in their enclosures; headphones, earphones, and combined microphone/speaker sets; audio-frequency electric amplifiers; electric sound amplifier sets; parts thereof

8519—Turntables, record players, cassette players, and other sound reproducing apparatus, not incorporating a sound recording device

8520—Magnetic tape recorders and other sound recording apparatus, whether or not incorporating a sound reproducing device

8521—Video recording or reproducing apparatus, whether or not incorporating a video tuner

8522—Parts and accessories suitable for use solely or principally with the apparatus of heading 8519 to 8521

8523—Prepared unrecorded media for sound recording or similar recording of other phenomena, other than products of chapter 37

8524—Records, tapes, and other recorded media for sound or other similarly recorded phenomena, including matrices and masters for the production of records, but excluding products of chapter 37

8525—Transmission apparatus for radiotelephony, radiotelegraphy, radiobroadcasting or television, whether or not incorporating reception apparatus or sound recording or reproducing apparatus; television cameras

8526—Radar apparatus, radio navigational aid apparatus, and radio remote control apparatus

8527—Reception apparatus for radiotelephony, radiotelegraphy or radiobroadcasting, whether or not combined, in the same housing, with sound recording or reproducing apparatus or a clock

8528—Reception apparatus for television, whether or not incorporating radiobroadcast receivers or sound or video recording or reproducing apparatus; video monitors and video projectors

8529—Parts suitable for use solely or principally with the apparatus of heading 8525 to 8528

8530—Electrical signaling, safety or traffic control equipment for railways, streetcar lines, subways, roads, inland waterways, parking facilities, port installations, or airfields (other than those of heading 8608); parts thereof

8531—Electric sound or visual signaling apparatus (for example, bells, sirens, indicator panels, burglar or fire alarms), other than those of heading 8512 or 8530; parts thereof

8532—Electrical capacitors, fixed, variable, or adjustable (preset); parts thereof

8533—Electrical resistors (including rheostats and potentiometers), other than heating resistors; parts thereof

8534—Printed circuits

8535—Electrical apparatus for switching or protecting electrical circuits, or for making connections to or in electrical circuits (for example, switches, fuses, lightning arrestors, voltage limiters, surge suppressors, plugs, junction boxes), for a voltage exceeding 1,000 v

8536—Electrical apparatus for switching or protecting electrical circuits, or for making connections to or in electrical circuits (for example, switches, relays, fuses, surge suppressors, plugs sockets, lamp-holders, junction boxes), for a voltage not exceeding 1,000 v

8537—Boards, panels, consoles, desks, cabinets, and other bases, equipped with two or more apparatus of heading 8535 or 8536, for electric control or the distribution of electricity, including those incorporating instruments or apparatus of chapter 90, and numerical control apparatus, other than switching apparatus of heading 8517

8538—Parts suitable for use solely or principally with the apparatus of heading 8535, 8536 or 8537

8539—Electrical filament or discharge lamps, including sealed beam lamp units and ultraviolet or infrared lamps; arc lamps; parts thereof

8540—Thermionic, cold cathode or photocathode tubes (for example, vacuum or vapor or gas filled tubes, mercury arc rectifying tubes, cathode-ray tubes, television camera tubes); parts thereof

8541—Diodes, transistors, and similar semiconductor devices; photosensitive semiconductor devices, including photovoltaic cells whether or not assembled in modules or made up into panels; light-emitting diodes; mounted piezoelectric crystals; parts thereof

8542—Electronic integrated circuits and microassemblies; parts thereof

8543—Electrical machines and apparatus, having individual functions, not specified or included elsewhere in this chapter; parts thereof

8544—Insulated (including enameled or anodized) wire, cable (including coaxial cable) and other insulated electric conductors, whether or not fitted with connectors; optical fiber cables, made up of individually sheathed fibers, whether or not assembled with electric conductors or fitted with connectors

8545—Carbon electrodes, carbon brushes, lamp carbons, battery carbons, and other articles of graphite or other carbon, with or without metal, of a kind used for electrical purposes

8546—Electrical insulators of any materials

8547—Insulating fittings for electrical machines, appliances, or equipment, being fittings wholly of insulated material apart from any minor components (for example, threaded sockets) incorporated during molding solely for the purposes of assembly, other than insulators of heading 8546; electrical conduit tubing and joints therefor, of base metal lined with insulating material

8548—Waste and scrap of primary cells, primary batteries and electric storage batteries; spent primary cells, spent primary batteries and spent electric storage batteries; electrical parts of machinery or apparatus, not specified or included elsewhere in this chapter

For more details regarding classification of the specific product you are interested in importing, consult a customs broker, the appropriate commodity specialist at your nearest customs port, or see HTSUS. The 2001 HTSUS is available online from the Customs Service (www.customs.gov/impoexpo/impoexpo.htm) or for purchase from the U.S. Government Printing Office (see resources at the end of this chapter), and may be found in larger public libraries. For a general discussion of customs classification, see "Classification—Liquidation" on page 229.

Dutiable Status of Goods

For more information about duty rates and binding decisions see "Dutiable Status of Goods" on page 203; for a discussion of temporary importation of goods see "Temporary Free Importations" on page 205.

Valuation

Importers have a responsibility to use what the U.S. Customs Service deems, "reasonable care," when determining the value of their goods. They must also provide any additional information that the Customs Service needs for setting a final value on the goods. This process involves a number of factors and can be somewhat complicated; importers must be aware of applicable issues and details. Valuation information applies to all types of commodities, for further discussion on the subject see "Customs Valuation" on page 267.

Import Duties

Import duties vary (often dramatically) depending upon the Harmonized Tariff Schedule (HTSUS) classification of the goods or products imported. Since some products that look alike have different HTSUS classifications and different rates of duty, proper classification is vital. Note that "differences of opinion" between importers and the Bureau of Customs and Border Protection regarding classification keeps customs attorneys very busy.

Import duties can be assessed on the imported value of the goods ("ad valorem" rates of duty such as 2%, 4.4%, 50%, etc.), total units or weight of the goods ("specific" rates of duty such as 2 cents each or 1.5 cents/pound, etc.) or on a combination basis ("compound" rates of duty such as 5 cents each plus 6%).

Listed below is a sampling of several Column 1 import duty rates for Chapter 85 products:

Electric motors of a kind used as the primary source of mechanical power for electrically powered vehicles of subheading 8703.90 (8501.32.45.00): Free
and
Stators and rotors for the goods of heading 8501 for motors of under 18.65 W (8503.00.35.00): 6.5%

For specific information on US import duties refer to the Harmonized Tariff Schedule of the US. The print version is available from the US Government Printing Office as well as third party suppliers who often add special features. Online versions are available in both static PDF pages as well as in formats with excellent search functionality. Search the Web with the term "Harmonized Tariff Schedule" to find sources.

Entry and Documentation

The entry of merchandise is a two-part process consisting of 1) filing the documents necessary to determine whether merchandise may be released from Customs custody and 2) filing the documents that contain information for duty assessment and statistical purposes. In certain instances all documents must be filed and accepted by Customs prior to the release of the goods. Unless you have been granted an extension, you must file entry documents at a location specified by the port or area director within five working days of your shipment's date of arrival at a U.S. port of entry. These include a number of standard documents required by Customs for any entry, and:

- For radiation-producing devices, Electronic Product Declaration Form FD 2877
- For radio frequency devices, FCC Declaration Form FCC 740
- For products subject to regulation by both agencies, both forms mentioned above
- For products subject to copyright or trademark laws, authorization from the copyright or trademark holder

After you present the entry, Customs may examine your shipment, or may waive examination. The shipment is then released provided no legal or regulatory violations have been noted. You must then file entry summary documentation and deposit estimated duties at a designated customhouse within 10 working days of your shipment's release. For a detailed description of entry procedures, standard documentation, and informal entry, see "Entry Process" on page 185.

Informed Compliance. Informed compliance was introduced with the Customs Modernization Act of 1993 (Mod Act) and defines the relationship between importers and the Customs Service. It sets out the responsibilities of both parties. Providing the correct documentation and information for entry is a key factor that will make your importing operation run smoothly. We rec-

ommend that importers become familiar with the concept of informed comliance and the responsibilities that they have under the Mod Act. For further discussion about informed compliance see "Informed Compliance" on page 211.

Entry Invoice. For all articles of machinery, equipment, and apparatus, a statement is required detailing the use or method of operation of each type of machine. For machine parts, a statement is required specifying the kind of machine for which the parts are intended, or—if it is not known to the shipper—the kinds of machines for which the parts are suitable. For more general information about invoices see "Invoices" on page 277.

Note: The Entry and Documentation section has been carefully designed to supply you, the importer, with sample documents and directions on how to satisfy Customs requirements. Be aware that you should consult the applicable authorities to ensure that you are correctly following the most current procedures.

Prohibitions and Restrictions

Radio Frequency (rf) Devices. Under the Communications Act of 1934, as amended, all radio frequency (rf) devices are subject to FCC radio emission standards. You must file an FCC declaration FCC Form 740 certifying that your model or device is in conformity with, will be brought into conformity with, or is exempt from the FCC requirements, for each shipment of rf devices you import. FCC standards and procedures have been developed to limit potential sources of rf interference to authorized radio services in the U.S. The FCC defines a radio frequency device as a product that emits rf energy, either intentionally or as a design byproduct. Radio frequency devices must meet specific FCC equipment authorization standards. When rf devices are imported into the U.S., a declaration is required that states that the appropriate FCC authorization has been granted. This declaration is made on FCC Form 740.

Equipment Authorization. FCC equipment authorization is required for certain types of rf devices imported into the U.S. Although compliance with these procedures is the responsibility of the foreign manufacturer, you should be aware of them, since noncomplying shipments will not be permitted entry. Equipment authorization procedures include: 1) type approval (requires testing of equipment sample); 2) type acceptance (requires review and evaluation of written application and equipment test report); 3) certification (requires review and evaluation of written application and equipment test report); 4) notification (requires submission of brief application); 5) verification (manufacturer tests device for compliance with FCC regulations prior to marketing, and retains test data); and 6) registration (applies to subscriber-owned and common-carrier-owned telephone devices; requires review and evaluation of written application and test report). Except for verification and registration procedures, a separate FCC Form 731 should be filed with the FCC for each type of device for which equipment authorization is being requested. FCC Form 730 is used for registration of telephone equipment under Part 68 of FCC rules. No application is required for verification. Fees are required for equipment authorization filings. Fee information is available from any FCC office or by calling (202) 643-FEES. If you would like more complete details regarding authorization procedures, contact the nearest regional FCC office, or the FCC Office of Engineering and Technology in , D.C. (see addresses at end of this chapter).

Importation of Radio Frequency Devices. Each time you import a shipment of rf devices, you must file a separate FCC Form 740 for each type of rf device represented in your shipment. Send your original completed Form 740(s) to the FCC Field Operations Bureau in , D.C. (see addresses at end of this chapter). Attach a copy of your form(s) to the customs entry summary for your shipment, and present it to customs at the U.S. port of entry.

Some examples of rf devices requiring Form 740 are: digital electronic weighing machinery; automatic typewriters; electronic calculating machines (not handheld); hard magnetic disc drives; cartridge-type radio-tape player for motor vehicles; microwave ovens; television cameras, receivers, and monitors; video players; video game equipment; radio receivers; digital clock radios; cordless handset telephones; and music synthesizer keyboards. For more information, contact any FCC office, or the FCC headquarters (see addresses at end of this chapter).

Exclusions from Form 740 Filing Requirements. The following products do not require **Form 740**: digital watches/clocks; electronic (musical) greeting cards; battery-powered handheld calculators; and battery-powered handheld electronic games.

Radiation-producing Devices. The comprehensive Radiation Control for Health and Safety Act (RCHSA) was enacted in 1968 to protect the public from unnecessary exposure to radiation from electronic products. Administration of the law is carried out through the setting and enforcement of radiation performance standards to limit radiation emissions. The standards apply to products offered for sale or use in the U.S., whether manufactured in this country or elsewhere. Electronic products include all products or equipment capable of emitting ionizing or nonionizing radiation, or sonic, infrasonic, or ultrasonic waves. Television receivers, microwave ovens, X-ray equipment, lasers, ultraviolet lights, diathermy units, infrared heaters, ultrasonic cleaners, and particle accelerators are examples of products required to comply with RCHSA. Regulations for the enforcement of the act are published in 21 CFR Parts 1000-1050. The law is enforced by FDA's Center for Devices and Radiological Health (CDRH) (see addresses at end of this chapter).

Radiation Performance Standards and Product Certification. Performance standards are prescribed for electronic products when the FDA determines that federal regulations are necessary for the protection of the public health and safety. The standards (21 CFR Parts 1020-1050) prescribe maximum allowable radiation levels and other approaches to control of radiation emission, without specifying design features. If you are interested in importing a radiation-producing product, you should ascertain whether or not it is subject to a standard. The manufacturer of an electronic product for which there is an applicable federal performance standard must obtain certification for the product. Certification is based upon a test prescribed by the standard, or a testing program that is in accord with Good Manufacturing Practices as determined by CDRH. When considering an overseas purchase, you must determine that the product is in compliance. Certified products must bear a certification label stating that the product conforms to the applicable standard. Keep in mind that it is not as simple to identify a product that is eligible for certification but has not been certified. When in doubt, contact the FDA.

Noncomplying or Defective Products. RCHSA specifically provides that test samples may be taken from any import shipment to determine whether a product complies with an applicable standard. The FDA may—through authorization from the U.S. Customs Service—take a sample from your shipment for testing. Such samples are returned after testing is completed. If your product is discovered not to meet the provisions of an applicable standard, or if it contains any defect related to its safe use by reason of radiation emissions, the FDA will refuse entry. The manufacturer of a defective electronic product that has entered the commercial market is responsible for notifying the consumer, repairing the defect, and replacing the product or refunding the purchaser's money.

Recordkeeping. The FDA requires dealers and distributors of electronic products for which standards have been issued to maintain records. These records are intended to facilitate the location of purchasers for notification concerning defective or non-complying devices, or to facilitate the recall of such products. In addition, manufacturers of certain electronic products designated by the regulation are required to maintain relevant product testing records and to make reports necessary to demonstrate compliance with the act.

Entry Documentation. **Form FD2877**, Electronic Product Declaration, is required for each shipment of radiation-producing devices to which federal radiation performance standards apply. (For a discussion of FDA import entry procedures, see "Appendix: Foods" on page 825) **Form 2877** must describe the compliance status of the product. You will have to affirm that the product either was 1) manufactured prior to the effective date of the applicable federal standard; 2) complies with the standard and has a label affixed by the manufacturer certifying compliance; 3) does not comply with the standard but is being imported only for purposes of research, investigation, study, demonstration, or training; or 4) does not now comply with the standard but will be brought into compliance. The provisions of RCHSA apply equally to electronic products manufactured in the U.S. and to those that are imported.

Products Covered By Radiation Performance Standards. The following products are currently covered by federal radiation performance standards. If you are considering importation of any of these products, be sure that the foreign manufacturer has obtained U.S. certification and has so labeled the items before attempting to enter a shipment into U.S. Customs territory. Uncertified products—even those that are eligible for certification—are refused entry, and any disposal or modification is undertaken at the importer's expense. Further information may be obtained from any FDA office or by referring to 21 CFR Parts 1000-1050.

Many foreign manufacturers produce electronic devices for export that conform to applicable FDA and FCC regulations. If you limit your purchases to such products and verify that the appropriate labels are affixed, you should have no difficulty with U.S. Customs.

Television Receivers. Standard effective January 16, 1970. Applies to products designed to receive and display a television picture through broadcast, cable, or closed-circuit television. Includes home television receivers, electronic viewfinders on TV cameras, TV projectors, and video monitors used with X-ray and other medical systems.

Demonstration-type Cold Cathode Gas Discharge Tubes. Standard effective May 19, 1970. Applies to tubes in which an electron flow is produced and sustained for purposes of demonstrating electron flow or X-ray production.

Microwave Ovens. Standard effective October 7, 1971. Applies to home and commercial products designed to heat or cook food through the application of electromagnetic energy.

Cabinet X-ray Systems. Standard effective April 10, 1975, except for systems designed primarily for the inspection of carry-on baggage, which became effective April 25, 1974. In addition to baggage inspection system, applies to other X-ray machines in enclosed freestanding cabinets.

Laser Products. Standard effective August 2, 1976. Amendment effective August 20, 1985, applies to all laser products, as well as products containing lasers.

Mercury Vapor Lamps. Standard effective March 8, 1980. Applies to any high intensity mercury vapor discharge lamp that is designed, intended, or promoted for illumination purposes.

Sunlamps. Standard effective May 7, 1980, amendment effective September 8, 1986, applies to sunlamp products and ultraviolet lamps intended for use in sunlamp products and intended to induce skin tanning.

Trademarks and Trade Names. Articles bearing counterfeit trademarks, or marks that copy or simulate a registered trademark of a U.S. or foreign corporation are prohibited importation, provided a copy of the U.S. trademark registration is filed with the Commissioner of Customs and recorded in the manner provided by regulations (19 CFR 133). The U.S. Customs Service also affords similar protection against unauthorized shipments bearing trade names that are recorded with customs pursuant to regulations (19 CFR 133, Subpart B). If your article bears a genuine trademark that is 1) owned by a U.S. citizen or company, 2) registered with U.S. Customs, you may not import the article without written permission from the U.S. trademark holder.

It is unlawful to import articles bearing genuine trademarks owned by a U.S. citizen or corporation without permission of the U.S. trademark owner, if the foreign and domestic trademark owners are not parent and subsidiary companies or otherwise under common ownership and control, provided the trademark has been recorded with customs.

The Customs Reform and Simplification Act of 1978 strengthened the protection afforded trademark owners against the importation of articles bearing a counterfeit mark. A "counterfeit trademark" is defined as a spurious trademark that is identical with, or substantially indistinguishable from, a registered trademark. Articles bearing a counterfeit trademark that are seized by customs and forfeited to the government may be 1) given to any federal, state, or local government agency that has established a need for the article; 2) given to a charitable institution; or 3) sold at public auction if more than 1 year has passed since forfeiture and no eligible organization has established a need for the article. The counterfeit marks must be removed before the forfeited articles may be given away or sold. If this is not feasible, the articles are destroyed. The law also provides an exemption from all restrictions on trademarked articles (limited to one of each type) accompanying a person arriving in the U.S. when the articles are for personal use and not for sale.

Copyrights. Section 602(a) of the Copyright Revision Act of 1976 provides that the importation into the U.S. of copies of a work acquired outside the U.S. without authorization of the copyright owner is an infringement of the copyright. Articles imported in violation of the import prohibitions are subject to seizure and forfeiture. Forfeited articles shall be destroyed. However, the articles may be returned to the country of export whenever customs is satisfied that there was no intentional violation. Copyright owners seeking import protection from the U.S. Customs Service must register their claim to copyright with the U.S. Copyright Office and record their registration with customs in accordance with applicable regulations (19 CFR 133, Subpart D).

Note that enforcement of copyright law has a high priority at customs, and even someone who is discovered unwittingly trying to bring in even a single copy of pirated software, audio-or video-tape, or similar article is subject to the full penalties of the applicable laws.

Country-Specific Import Restrictions

Recently, 3.5 inch floppy disks from Japan have been the subject of an antidumping action and have been banned from import into the U.S. Such actions are subject to change on relatively short notice, and the situation should be verified prior to attempting to import such products.

Marking and Labeling Requirements

FCC Requirements. All rf devices subject to FCC authorization procedures, whether manufactured within the U.S. or outside it, must bear labeling to show compliance. Devices that are not so labeled will not be permitted entry into U.S. Customs territory. For details on label wording, contact FCC (see addresses at end of this chapter).

FDA Requirements. All radiation-emitting devices for which federal standards have been determined must be certified for compliance. The manufacturer must affix a certification label to each product stating that it conforms to the applicable standard. Products requiring certification that are not so labeled will not be permitted entry.

Other Requirements. Contact the FTC (see addresses at end of this chapter) for information regarding labeling requirements.

For a general discussion of U.S. Customs marking and labeling requirements, see "Country of Origin Marking" on page 236, "Special Marking Requirements" on page 238 and "Marking—False Impression" on page 239.

Shipping Considerations

You will need to ensure that your goods are packaged and shipped with care to ensure that they arrive in good condition and pass smoothly through Customs. You are responsible for ensuring that the shipment is in compliance with all applicable government regulations for packaging and shipping. In most instances, you should not leave these arrangements solely to the discretion of your supplier. Careful preparation of the cargo and selection of the mode of transport can be essential to a cost-effective, timely delivery of undamaged goods. We strongly advise you to consult your shipping representative, insurance agent, or freight broker for advice on packing and shipping.

Electronic products are subject to damage from excessive heat and moisture, and exposure must be guarded against. Electronic goods may be fragile, and should be carefully packed and securely stowed to avoid damage due to shifting en route.

Publications and WWW Resources

The following publications may be relevant to the importation of electronics and components of Chapter 85:

> *The FCC Equipment Authorization Program for Radio Frequency Devices* (Bulletin Number 61)

The bulletin is available from any regional FCC office and online (www.fcc.gov/oet/info/documents/bulletins/).

> *Requirements of Laws and Regulations Enforced by the U.S. Food and Drug Administration*

This document is published by FDA and available on their website (www.fda.gov/opacom/7pubs.html). Look under "Enforcement."

The *Harmonized Tariff Schedule of the United States (2001)* (HTSUS) is available to view on the Customs Service website (www.customs.gov), or you may purchase a printed version from:

U.S. Government Printing Office
Superintendent of Documents
710 North Capital Street NW
Washington DC 20401
Tel: (202) 512-1800
Fax: (202) 512-1657
Website: www.access.gpo.gov

The USGPO also has copies of specific laws available for purchase. The USGPO accepts orders made by fax, phone or placed over the Internet, as well as mail orders paid by credit card. All orders must be accompanied by payment. Credit cards, checks drawn on a U.S. bank, or an international money order are all acceptable.

Relevant Government Agencies

Address questions regarding energy labeling of household appliances to:

Federal Trade Commission (FTC)
Division of Enforcement
600 Pennsylvania Avenue NW
Washington DC 20580
Tel: (202) 326-2996
Website: www.ftc.gov

Address questions regarding FCC rules on rf devices or FCC equipment authorization to the nearest FCC regional office or to:

Federal Communications Commission (FCC)
Office of Engineering and Technology
445 12th Street SW
Washington DC 20554
Tel: (301) 418-2470

Address inquiries concerning FCC **Form 740** requirements to:

Federal Communications Commission (FCC)
Consumer and Governmental Affairs Bureau
445 12th Street SW
Washington DC 20554
(202) 418-1400
Website: www.fcc.gov

Address inquiries regarding importation of radiation-producing devices to either:

Food and Drug Administration (FDA)
Center for Devices and Radiological Health
Division of Small Manufacturers Assistance
1350 Piccard Drive
Rockville, MD 20850
Tel: 800-638-2041
Fax: (301) 443-8818
Email: dsmica@cdrh.fda.gov
Website: www.fda.gov/cdrh

Food and Drug Administration (FDA)
Center for Food Safety and Applied Nutrition (CFSAN)
Office of Compliance
Division of Enforcement, Imports Branch
5100 Paint Branch Parkway
College Park, MD 20740-3835
Tel: (301) 436-2080
Website: http://vm.cfsan.fda.gov/list.html

Address questions regarding energy performance testing and standards for household appliances to:

U.S. Department of Energy (DOE)
Office of Building Technologies
1000 Independence Avenue SW
Washington DC 20585
EE2J
Tel: (202) 586-9127
Website: www.doe.gov

Address questions regarding copyright and trademark laws to:

U.S. Customs and Border Protection
Office of Regulations & Rulings
Intellectual Property Rights Branch
1300 Pennsylvania Avenue NW
Washington DC 20229
Tel: (202) 572-8710
Website: www.customs.treas.gov

Address questions regarding importation of electronic products to your local Customs port director. For addresses refer to "U.S. Customs and Border Protection Offices" on page 65 or contact:

U.S. Customs and Border Protection
Customs Headquarters
1300 Pennsylvania Avenue NW
Washington DC 20229
Tel: (202) 354-1000
Website: www.customs.treas.gov

Laws and Regulations

The following laws and regulations may be relevant to the importation of electronics, electrical appliances, and components. They are contained in the U.S. Code (USC) and the regulations are published in the Code of Federal Regulations (CFR), both of which may be available at larger public and law libraries. Copies of specific laws are also available from the United States Government Printing Office (address above).

42 USC 6201 et seq.
Energy Policy and Conservation Act (EPCA)
This Act authorizes adoption of standards for operating at maximum energy efficiency and prescribes labeling and testing requirements for compliance.

10 CFR Part 430
Regulations on EPCA
These regulations set test procedures and standards for measuring energy consumption of refrigerators, freezers, dishwashers, clothes washers and dryers, water heaters, air conditioners, heaters and furnaces, televisions, oven and cooking appliances, and fluorescent lamps.

15 USC 2051 et seq.
Consumer Product Safety Act
This Act sets standards for the manufacture, processing, and labeling of products sold to U.S. consumers.

15 USC 1051 et seq.
Trademark Act of 1946
This Act provides, among other things, that no imported article of foreign origin that bears a name or mark calculated to induce the public to believe that it was manufactured in the United States, or in any foreign country or locality other than the country or locality where it was in fact manufactured, shall be admitted entry at any customhouse in the U.S.

17 USC 101 et seq.
Copyrights
This law provides that the importation into the U.S. of copies of a work acquired outside the U.S. without authorization of the copyright owner is an infringement of the copyright.

19 CFR 133.31 et seq.
Regulations of Customs on Recordation of Copyrights, Trademarks, and Trade Names
These regulations provide procedures and requirements for registering a copyright, trademark, or trade name with U.S. Customs, as well as procedures for enforcement, forfeiture of merchandise, and assessment of monetary penalties.

21 USC 301 et seq.
Federal Food, Drug, and Cosmetic Act
This Act prohibits deceptive practices and regulates the manufacture, sale and importation or exportation of food, drugs, cosmetics, and related products. It was amended by the Food Quality Protection Act of 1996. See 21 USC 331, 381, 382.

19 CFR 12.1 et seq.; 21 CFR 1.83 et seq.
Regulations on Food, Drugs, and Cosmetics
These regulations of the Secretary of Health and Human Services and the Secretary of the Treasury govern the standards, labeling, marking, and importing of products used with food, drugs, and cosmetics.

21 USC 360 et seq.
Radiation Control for Health and Safety Act of 1968
This Act prohibits entry of electronic products found not to be in compliance with prescribed standards. See 21 CFR Part 1005. Customs enforces this prohibition. See 19 CFR 12.90 et seq.

47 USC 302a
Devices That Interfere with Radio Reception
This law prohibits the importation of devices or home electronic equipment that fail to comply with regulations promulgated by the FCC. See 47 CFR 2.1201 et seq. and 18.119. Customs enforces the prohibition.

47 USC 303(s) and 330

Importation of Certain Television Receivers
These laws prohibit importation of television receivers that are incapable of receiving all frequencies allocated to television broadcasting and authorizes enforcement by Customs. See 47 CFR 15.61-15.72. Such receivers are subject to seizure and forfeiture if a person willfully or knowingly violates this prohibition. See 47 USC 510.

47 USC 605

Unauthorized Publication or Use of Communications
Customs enforces this provision which prohibits the importation or exportation of any device or equipment used primarily for the unauthorized decryption of satellite cable programming, or is intended for any other activity prohibited by 47 USC 605(a).

Principal Exporting Countries

The following listing includes samples of the main supplier nations of the products of this chapter. It is organized by HTSUS major heading. (Refer to "Customs Classification" above for the product codes.) Countries are listed in rank order of the value of products imported to the U.S. Statistics represent customs value of entries for 2002 from the Bureau of Census, U.S. Department of Commerce.

8501—Mexico, Japan, China, Germany, Canada, South Korea, United Kingdom, France

8502—Japan, Germany, Denmark, United Kingdom, Canada, Hungary, Norway, Italy

8503—Mexico, Canada, Japan, Germany, China, South Korea, France, Brazil

8504—Mexico, China, Canada, Japan, Taiwan, Thailand, Philippines, Germany, United Kingdom

8505—Japan, Mexico, China, United Kingdom, Canada, Germany, South Korea, Taiwan, France, Italy, Switzerland

8506—China, Japan, Indonesia, Taiwan, Malaysia, United Kingdom, South Korea, Singapore, Canada, Israel

8507—Japan, Mexico, China, Taiwan, South Korea, France, Canada, Malaysia

8508—

8509—China, Mexico, South Korea, Germany, Canada, Italy

8510—China, Netherlands, Germany, Japan, Austria

8511—Japan, Mexico, South Korea, Germany, Canada, China, Taiwan

8512—Mexico, Taiwan, Japan, Canada, Germany, China, United Kingdom

8513—China, Mexico, Thailand, France, Taiwan, Hong Kong

8514—Japan, Netherlands, Germany, Canada, United Kingdom, Italy, Austria

8515—Japan, Canada, Germany, Switzerland, Italy, Mexico, United Kingdom, France

8516—China, Mexico, South Korea, Canada, Italy, Thailand, Japan, Malaysia

8517—China, Mexico, Canada, Malaysia, Taiwan, Japan, Sweden, Israel, Ireland, Thailand, Singapore, France

8518—China, Mexico, South Korea, Taiwan, Malaysia, Japan, Canada

8519—China, Japan, Malaysia, Thailand, Mexico, Hungary

8520—China, Taiwan, Japan, Malaysia, South Korea, Singapore

8521—China, South Korea, Japan, Indonesia, Malaysia, Thailand, Mexico

8522—Japan, China, Hong Kong, Mexico, South Korea, United Kingdom

8523—Japan, Taiwan, China, Mexico, South Korea, Germany, France, Canada, Thailand, Singapore

8524—Canada, Taiwan, Hong Kong, United Kingdom, Mexico, Japan, Germany

8525—South Korea, Japan, Mexico, China, Malaysia, Brazil, Canada

8526—Mexico, Taiwan, Japan, Canada, China, Germany

8527—China, Mexico, Malaysia, Japan, Indonesia

8528—Mexico, Japan, Malaysia, China, Thailand, South Korea, Taiwan, Indonesia

8529—Mexico, Canada, China, Japan, Sweden, Malaysia, Taiwan, United Kingdom, South Korea

8530—Canada, Mexico, Germany, China, France, Finland, Belgium, Switzerland

8531—China, Taiwan, Mexico, Japan, Canada, United Kingdom, South Korea

8532—Japan, Mexico, Israel, Taiwan, Czech Republic, China, South Korea, Thailand, El Salvador

8533—Mexico, Japan, Taiwan, Costa Rica, Israel, China, United Kingdom, Malaysia, Canada

8534—Taiwan, Canada, China, Japan, South Korea, Mexico, Singapore, Germany, Hong Kong

8535—Mexico, Switzerland, Canada, Germany, Japan, Indonesia, France, China, South Korea

8536—Mexico, Japan, China, Germany, Canada, Taiwan, Dominican Republic

8537—Mexico, Canada, Japan, China, Germany, United Kingdom

8538—Germany, Mexico, Japan, Canada, France, China, Switzerland, United Kingdom, Taiwan

8539—China, Mexico, Japan, Canada, Germany, Hungary, South Korea

8540—Mexico, Japan, France, Germany, China, Taiwan, Brazil, United Kingdom, South Korea

8541—Japan, Malaysia, Mexico, China, Philippines, Germany, Taiwan

8542—Malaysia, South Korea, Philippines, Taiwan, Japan, Singapore, Canada

8543—China, Canada, Japan, Mexico, United Kingdom, Germany

8544—Mexico, China, Canada, Philippines, Japan, Thailand, Taiwan

8545—Mexico, Japan, France, Canada, Germany, China, Brazil

8546—Japan, Germany, Mexico, Switzerland, Czech Republic

8547—Germany, Japan, Mexico, China, Canada, United Kingdom, Taiwan, Switzerland

8548—Mexico, Canada, Japan, Costa Rica, Philippines, Thailand

Chapter 86:
Railway Equipment

Full title: Railway or Tramway Locomotives, Rolling Stock, and Parts Thereof; Railway or Tramway Track Fixtures and Fittings and Parts Thereof; Mechanical (Including Electro-Mechanical) Traffic Signaling Equipment of All Kinds

This chapter relates to the importation of railroad equipment, which is classified within HTSUS Chapter 86 of the Harmonized Tariff Schedule of the United States (HTSUS). Specifically, it includes locomotives; self-propelled coaches; rail maintenance vehicles; rolling stock, including passenger and freight cars; parts of locomotives and rolling stock; track fittings and fixtures; and containers designed for rail and intermodal transport.

If you are interested in importing rails for track construction, refer to Commodity Index Chapter 73. Cross-ties (sleepers) are classified by their material: of wood in Chapter 44, of concrete Chapter 68. Many specialized mechanical subassemblies are covered in Chapter 84 and electrical components are found in Chapter 85, as are electrical signaling, safety, and traffic control equipment. Although Chapter 86 covers most parts and accessories, it is generally restricted to components and subassemblies, with individual parts being included in the chapters covering the type of article or the material of which it is composed—of rubber, plastics, base metals, ceramics, or glass. Instrumentation is covered in Chapter 90. Seats for vehicles are found in Chapter 94.

Note: To understand key issues that will enable you to make best use of the information in this section we recommend that you see "Introduction" on page 425.

Key Factors

The key factors in the importation of railway equipment are:

- Compliance with all product and safety standards set by the Federal Railroad Administration (FRA)
- Compliance with all standards established by the U.S. Environmental Protection Agency (EPA) for noise and emissions

Although most importers use the services of a licensed customs broker in making their entries, and we recommend this practice, you should be aware of the regulatory, entry, and documentation issues involved in importing your product. The importer is ultimately responsible for the fulfillment of any legal requirements applicable to a shipment.

General Considerations

The importation of railway equipment is relatively straightforward. However, all imports of such equipment must conform to the product and safety standards for such articles established by the U.S. Department of Transportation's FRA. These are specific to the particular types of equipment in question, and are found in 42 CFR 200 et seq. Many of these regulations cover standards for specific types of equipment, such as the freight car safety standards, which define the types of rolling stock covered and detail standards for their components and bodies; locomotive safety standards, which do the same for locomotives; the safety appliance standard, which sets requirements for safety apparatus and features on cars; and safety glazing standards, which give particulars for windows on locomotives, passenger cars, and cabooses. Other standards are specific to certain components or categories of components, for example, covering specifications for brakes, and signal systems. Other standards are less direct, such as the track safety standards, which deal primarily with specifications for roadbed preparation and installation of track, but are specific enough that they affect the rails and auxiliary components that may be imported.

In addition, railway equipment must comply with standards established by the EPA for noise, emissions, and treatment of hazardous waste.

Customs Classification

For customs purposes railway equipment is classified within Chapter 86 of the HTSUS. The chapter is divided into major headings, which are further divided into subheadings and often into sub-subheadings, each with its own HTSUS classification number. For example, the 2001 HTSUS number for air brakes for rolling stock is 8607.21.10, indicating that it is a subcategory of brakes and parts thereof (8607.21), which is a subcategory of the major heading parts of railway or tramway locomotives or rolling stock (8607). There are nine major headings in HTSUS Chapter 86.

8601—Rail locomotives powered from an external source of electricity or by electric accumulators (batteries)

8602—Other rail locomotives; locomotives tenders

8603—Self-propelled railway or tramway coaches, vans, and trucks, other than those of heading 8604.

8604—Railway or tramway maintenance or service vehicles, whether or not self-propelled (for example, workshops, cranes, ballast tampers, trackliners, testing coaches, and track inspectors)

8605—Railway or tramway passenger coaches, not self-propelled; luggage vans, post office coaches, and other special purpose railway or tramway coaches, not self-propelled (excluding those of heading 8604)

8606—Railway or tramway freight cars, not self-propelled

8607—Parts of railway or tramway locomotives or rolling stock

8608—Railway or tramway track fixtures and fittings; mechanical (including electro-mechanical) signaling, safety or traffic control equipment for railways, tramways, roads, inland waterways, parking facilities, port installations or airfields; parts of the foregoing

8609—Containers (including containers for the transport of fluids) specially designed and equipped for carriage by one or more modes of transport

For more details regarding classification of the specific product you are interested in importing, consult a customs broker, the appropriate commodity specialist at your nearest customs port, or see HTSUS. The 2001 HTSUS is available online from the Customs Service (www.customs.gov/impoexpo/impoexpo.htm) or for purchase from the U.S. Government Printing Office (see resources at the end of this chapter), and may be found in larger public libraries. For a general discussion of customs classification, see "Classification—Liquidation" on page 229.

Dutiable Status of Goods

For more information about duty rates and binding decisions see "Dutiable Status of Goods" on page 203; for a discussion of temporary importation of goods see "Temporary Free Importations" on page 205.

Valuation

Importers have a responsibility to use what the U.S. Customs Service deems, "reasonable care," when determining the value of their goods. They must also provide any additional information that the Customs Service needs for setting a final value on the goods. This process involves a number of factors and can be somewhat complicated; importers must be aware of applicable issues and details. Valuation information applies to all types of commodities, for further discussion on the subject see "Customs Valuation" on page 267.

Import Duties

Import duties vary (often dramatically) depending upon the Harmonized Tariff Schedule (HTSUS) classification of the goods or products imported. Since some products that look alike have different HTSUS classifications and different rates of duty, proper classification is vital. Note that "differences of opinion" between importers and the Bureau of Customs and Border Protection regarding classification keeps customs attorneys very busy.

Import duties can be assessed on the imported value of the goods ("ad valorem" rates of duty such as 2%, 4.4%, 50%, etc.), total units or weight of the goods ("specific" rates of duty such as 2 cents each or 1.5 cents/pound, etc.) or on a combination basis ("compound" rates of duty such as 5 cents each plus 6%).

Listed below is a sampling of several Column 1 import duty rates for Chapter 86 products:
Powered from an external source of electricity (8601.10.00.00): Free
to
Railway or tramway passenger coaches, not selfpropelled; luggage vans, post office coaches and other special purpose railway or tramway coaches, not selfpropelled (excluding those of heading 8604) (8605.00.00.00): 14.8%

For specific information on US import duties refer to the Harmonized Tariff Schedule of the US. The print version is available from the US Government Printing Office as well as third party suppliers who often add special features. Online versions are available in both static PDF pages as well as in formats with excellent search functionality. Search the Web with the term "Harmonized Tariff Schedule" to find sources.

Entry and Documentation

The entry of merchandise is a two-part process consisting of 1) filing the documentation necessary to determine whether merchandise may be released from Customs custody and 2) filing the documents that contain information for duty assessment and statistical purposes. In certain instances all documents must be filed and accepted by Customs prior to the release of the goods. Unless you have been granted an extension, you must file entry documents at a location specified by the port or area director within five working days of your shipment's date of arrival at a U.S. port of entry. These include a number of standard documents required by Customs for entry, and:

- Certification of compliance with FRA safety standards

After you present the entry, Customs may examine your shipment, or may waive examination. The shipment is then released provided no legal or regulatory violations have been noted. You must then file entry summary documentation and deposit estimated duties at a designated customhouse within 10 working days of your shipment's release. For a detailed description of entry procedures, standard documentation, and informal entry, see "Entry Process" on page 185.

Informed Compliance. Informed compliance was introduced with the Customs Modernization Act of 1993 (Mod Act) and defines the relationship between importers and the Customs Service. It sets out the responsibilities of both parties. Providing the correct documentation and information for entry is a key factor

that will make your importing operation run smoothly. We recommend that importers become familiar with the concept of informed comliance and the responsibilities that they have under the Mod Act. For further discussion about informed compliance see "Informed Compliance" on page 211.

Note: The Entry and Documentation section has been carefully designed to supply you, the importer, with sample documents and directions on how to satisfy Customs requirements. Be aware that you should consult the applicable authorities to ensure that you are correctly following the most current procedures.

Prohibitions and Restrictions

Locomotives, rolling stock, and ancillary equipment that do not conform to the standards established by the FRA may not be imported for use in the U.S. For example, all locomotives constructed or rebuilt after December 31, 1979 must comply with the new locomotive standards found in 49 CFR 229, including specifications for brake, coupling, suspension, and electrical, internal combustion, and steam power systems, as well as cab and other equipment standards.

Marking and Labeling Requirements

For a general discussion of U.S. Customs marking and labeling requirements, see "Country of Origin Marking" on page 236, "Special Marking Requirements" on page 238 and "Marking—False Impression" on page 239.

Shipping Considerations

You will need to ensure that your goods are packaged and shipped with care to ensure that they arrive in good condition and pass smoothly through Customs. You are responsible for ensuring that the shipment is in compliance with all applicable government regulations for packaging and shipping. In most instances, you should not leave these arrangements solely to the discretion of your supplier. Careful preparation of the cargo and selection of the mode of transport can be essential to a cost-effective, timely delivery of undamaged goods. We strongly advise you to consult your shipping representative, insurance agent, or freight broker for advice on packing and shipping.

Railway equipment is often heavy and bulky. It must be packed and stowed carefully to ensure that it is not damaged due to shifting en route or due to exposure to heat, moisture, or other hazards.

Publications and WWW Resources

The *Harmonized Tariff Schedule of the United States (2001)* (HTSUS) is available to view on the Customs Service website (www.customs.gov), or you may purchase a printed version from:

U.S. Government Printing Office
Superintendent of Documents
710 North Capital Street NW
Washington DC 20401
Tel: (202) 512-1800
Fax: (202) 512-1657
Website: www.access.gpo.gov

The USGPO also has copies of specific laws available for purchase. The USGPO accepts orders made by fax, phone or placed over the Internet, as well as mail orders paid by credit card. All orders must be accompanied by payment. Credit cards, checks drawn on a U.S. bank, or an international money order are all acceptable.

Relevant Government Agencies

Address questions regarding DOT requirements for railway imports to:

U.S. Department of Transportation (DOT)
Federal Railroad Administration (FRA)
Office of Public Affairs
1120 Vermont Avenue NW
Washington DC 20590

Tel: (202) 493-6000
Website: www.fra.dot.gov/site

Address questions regarding EPA requirements for railway equipment imports to:

Environmental Protection Agency (EPA)
Office of Transportation and Air Quality (OTAQ)
Imports Section USEPA
1200 Pennsylvania Avenue NW
Washington DC 20460
MC6405J
(202) 564-9240
Website: www.epa.gov/otaq/imports

Address questions regarding importation of railway equipment to your local Customs port director. For addresses refer to "U.S. Customs and Border Protection Offices" on page 65 or contact:

U.S. Customs and Border Protection
Customs Headquarters
1300 Pennsylvania Avenue NW
Washington DC 20229
Tel: (202) 354-1000
Website: www.customs.treas.gov

Laws and Regulations

The following laws and regulations may be relevant to the importation of vehicles. They are contained in the U.S. Code (USC) and the regulations are published in the Code of Federal Regulations (CFR), both of which may be available at larger public and law libraries. Copies of specific laws are also available from the United States Government Printing Office (address above).

49 USC Subtitle B, Section II
Federal Railroad Administration Act
This Act establishes the FRA and authorizes that agency to govern railroads and set standards for their operations.

40 CFR 201
Regulation on Railroad Noise Standards
This regulation publishes the standards of the Railroad Noise Commission of the EPA.

49 CFR 200 et seq.
Regulation on Rail Equipment Safety
This regulation publishes the safety and design regulations for rail equipment used in the U.S.

Principal Exporting Countries

The following listing includes samples of the main supplier nations of the products of this chapter. It is organized by HTSUS major heading. (Refer to "Customs Classification" above for the product codes.) Countries are listed in rank order of the value of products imported to the U.S. Statistics represent customs value of entries for 2002 from the Bureau of Census, U.S. Department of Commerce.

8601—Germany, Canada

8602—Canada, Germany, Mexico

8603—Canada, Germany, Czech Republic, Spain, Austria

8604—Canada, Germany, Australia, Japan, Italy, France, United Kingdom, Mexico

8605—Canada, Japan, Mexico

8606—Canada, Mexico, Germany, China, France, Austria, Israel, Spain, Japan

8607—Canada, Japan, Italy, Spain, Mexico, Brazil, Germany

8608—Canada, Mexico, Italy, Germany, Spain, United Kingdom

8609—China, Mexico, France, Japan, South Africa, Netherlands, Germany

Chapter 87: Vehicles

Full title: Vehicles Other than Railway or Tramway Rolling-Stock and Parts and Accessories Thereof

This section pertains to the importation of vehicles, which are classified within Chapter 87 of the Harmonized Tariff Schedule of the United States (HTSUS). This chapter covers a broad range of products, including tractors; buses; automobiles; trucks; special purpose vehicles, such as firetrucks; chassis fitted with engines, bodies, and most subassemblies and components for motor vehicles; self-propelled work carts; military fighting vehicles; motorcycles; bicycles; wheelchairs; baby carriages; and trailers.

Only wheeled (and some tracked) vehicles are included in Commodity Index Chapter 87. Railroads and trams running on tracks are covered in Chapter 86; watercraft are found in Chapter 89; aircraft are classified in Chapter 88; while conveyances such as sleds are covered within Chapter 95. However, children's bicycles and tricycles are included in Chapter 87. If you are interested in importing construction equipment—such as bulldozers or backhoes—loading equipment—such as forklifts—or agricultural equipment—such as plows or combines—refer to Chapter 84. Tires are covered in Chapter 40. Although Chapter 87 covers most parts and accessories, it is generally restricted to components and subassemblies, with individual parts being included in the chapters covering the type of article or the material of which it is composed—of rubber, plastics, base metals, ceramics, or glass. Seats for vehicles are found in Chapter 94. Many specialized mechanical subassemblies are covered in Chapter 84 and electrical components are found in Chapter 85.

Note: To understand key issues that will enable you to make best use of the information in this section we recommend that you see "Introduction" on page 425.

Key Factors

The key factors in the importation of vehicles are:

* Compliance with U.S. Department of Transportation (DOT) safety standards and other regulations

* Compliance with U.S. Environmental Protection Agency (EPA) emission control standards

* Vehicles not complying with DOT standards must enter through a DOT Registered Importer (RI)

* Vehicles not complying with EPA standards must enter through an EPA Independent Commercial Importer (ICI)

* Compliance of bicycles with Consumer Product Safety Act (CPSA) safety standards and labeling requirements

Although most importers utilize the services of a licensed customs broker in making their entries, and we recommend this practice, you should be aware of the regulatory, entry, and documentation issues involved in importing your product. You, as importer, are ultimately responsible for the fulfillment of any legal requirements applicable to your shipment.

General Considerations

The DOT's National Highway Traffic Safety Administration (NHTSA) regulates importation of motor vehicles and motor vehicle equipment under the provisions of the National Traffic and Motor Vehicle Safety Act of 1966 (NTMVSA), the Motor Vehicle Information Cost Savings Act (MVICSA), and the Imported Vehicle Safety Compliance Act of 1988 (IVSCA). The Federal Motor Vehicle Safety Standards (FMVSS) are based on these three laws. The EPA regulates the importation of automobiles under the provisions of the Clean Air Act (CAA) as amended. All motor vehicles and motor vehicle equipment imported into the U.S. must meet the safety and emission-control requirements of these governmental agencies prior to entry. If you wish to import a new or used motor vehicle, you must make an appropriate declaration on DOT Declaration HS Form 7—in duplicate—at the port of entry whether or not it meets any or all U.S. market requirements. You can get HS Form 7 from your customs broker, or from any U.S. Customs port office.

If you are considering importing a foreign vehicle, you should obtain the very latest DOT and EPA requirements for that specific vehicle before purchasing it. The modifications necessary to bring a nonconforming vehicle into conformity with regulations governing such issues as safety, bumper, and emission standards may require extensive reengineering; the labor, materials, storage fees, and other costs involved may be unduly high; and it may effectively be impractical or impossible to refit specific vehicles to comply. Certain models are prohibited from importation altogether, and if imported will have to be destroyed or reexported.

Independent Commercial Importers. Authorized ICIs are allowed to import only certain vehicles, based on which certificates of conformity they have obtained. The fact that an ICI may hold a certificate of conformity for a particular vehicle does not guarantee that the ICI will choose to import it, nor is it required to. Before buying or shipping any noncomplying motor vehicle, make final arrangements with an ICI, or obtain written EPA prior approval or exemption. Otherwise, Customs may assess costly storage fees at the port of entry while you take the steps necessary to render your import legal, and/or the vehicles may not be eligible for importation at all.

Bicycles. Importation of bicycles is regulated by the Consumer Product Safety Commission (CPSC) under applicable provisions of the CPSA. You do not need any permits or licenses to import bicycles, nor is any special entry paperwork required. However, you should be sure that your bicycles comply with the extensive mandatory safety standards listed in 16 CFR 1512 (see "Prohibitions and Restrictions" below). To ascertain compliance, the CPSC randomly inspects shipments of bicycles at port of entry from time to time.

Customs Classification

For customs purposes vehicles are classified within Chapter 87 of the HTSUS. This chapter is divided into major headings, which are further divided into subheading, and often into sub-subheadings, each with its own HTSUS classification number. For example, the 2001 HTSUS number for mounted brake linings for agricultural tractors is 8708.31.10, indicating that it is a subcategory of brakes and servo-brakes and parts thereof (8708.31), which is a subcategory of the major heading parts and accessories of the motor vehicles of heading 8701 to 8705 (8708). There are 16 major headings in HTSUS Chapter 87.

8701—Tractors (other than tractors of heading 8709)

8702—Motor vehicles for the transport of 10 or more persons, including the driver

8703—Motor cars and other motor vehicles principally designed for the transport of persons (other than those of heading 8702), including station wagons and racing cars

8704—Motor vehicles for the transport of goods

8705—Special purpose motor vehicles, other than those principally designed for the transport of persons or goods (for example, wreckers, mobile cranes, firefighting vehicles, concrete mixers, road sweepers, spraying vehicles, mobile workshops, mobile radiological units)

8706—Chassis fitted with engines, for the motor vehicles of headings 8701 to 8705

8707—Bodies (including cabs) for the motor vehicles of headings 8701 to 8705

8708—Parts and accessories of the motor vehicles of headings 8701 to 8705

8709—Works trucks, self-propelled, not fitted with lifting or handling equipment, of the type used in factories, warehouses, dock areas or airports for short distance transport of goods; tractors of the type used on railway station platforms; parts of the foregoing vehicles

8710—Tanks and other armored fighting vehicles, motorized, whether or not fitted with weapons, and parts of such vehicles

8711—Motorcycles (including mopeds) and cycles fitted with an auxiliary motor, with or without sidecars; side-cars

8712—Bicycles and other cycles (including delivery tricycles), not motorized

8713—Invalid carriages, whether or not motorized or otherwise mechanically propelled

8714—Parts and accessories of vehicles of headings 8711 to 8713

8715—Baby carriages (including strollers) and parts thereof

8716—Trailers and semi-trailers; other vehicles, not mechanically propelled; and parts thereof

For more details regarding classification of the specific product you are interested in importing, consult a customs broker, the appropriate commodity specialist at your nearest customs port, or see HTSUS. The 2001 HTSUS is available online from the Customs Service (www.customs.gov/impoexpo/impoexpo.htm) or for purchase from the U.S. Government Printing Office (see resources at the end of this chapter), and may be found in larger public libraries. For a general discussion of customs classification, see "Classification—Liquidation" on page 229.

Dutiable Status of Goods

For more information about duty rates and binding decisions see "Dutiable Status of Goods" on page 203; for a discussion of temporary importation of goods see "Temporary Free Importations" on page 205.

Valuation

Importers have a responsibility to use what the U.S. Customs Service deems, "reasonable care," when determining the value of their goods. They must also provide any additional information that the Customs Service needs for setting a final value on the goods. This process involves a number of factors and can be somewhat complicated; importers must be aware of applicable issues and details. Valuation information applies to all types of commodities, for further discussion on the subject see "Customs Valuation" on page 267.

Import Duties

Import duties vary (often dramatically) depending upon the Harmonized Tariff Schedule (HTSUS) classification of the goods or products imported. Since some products that look alike have different HTSUS classifications and different rates of duty, proper classification is vital. Note that "differences of opinion" between importers and the Bureau of Customs and Border Protection regarding classification keeps customs attorneys very busy.

Import duties can be assessed on the imported value of the goods ("ad valorem" rates of duty such as 2%, 4.4%, 50%, etc.), total units or weight of the goods ("specific" rates of duty such as 2 cents each or 1.5 cents/pound, etc.) or on a combination basis ("compound" rates of duty such as 5 cents each plus 6%).

Listed below is a sampling of several Column 1 import duty rates for Chapter 87 products:
Cab chassis (8704.10.10.00): Free
to
G.V.W. not exceeding 5 metric tons (8704.21.00.00): 25%

For specific information on US import duties refer to the Harmonized Tariff Schedule of the US. The print version is available from the US Government Printing Office as well as third party suppliers who often add special features. Online versions are available in both static PDF pages as well as in formats with excellent search functionality. Search the Web with the term "Harmonized Tariff Schedule" to find sources.

Entry and Documentation

The entry of merchandise is a two-part process consisting of 1) filing the documents necessary to determine whether merchandise may be released from Customs custody and 2) filing the documents that contain information for duty assessment and statistical purposes. In certain instances all documents must be filed and accepted by Customs prior to the release of the goods. Unless you have been granted an extension, you must file entry documents at a location specified by the district/area director within five working days of your shipment's date of arrival at a U.S. port of entry. These include a number of standard documents required by Customs for any entry, and:

- DOT Entry Declaration HS Form 7
- For vehicles not complying with DOT requirements: DOT bond Form HS 474 (1-90)
- For certain vehicles: EPA bond Form 3520-1

After you present the entry, Customs may examine your shipment, or may waive examination. The shipment is then released, provided no legal or regulatory violations have occurred. You must then file entry summary documentation and deposit estimated duties at a designated customhouse within 10 working days of your shipment's release. For a detailed description of entry procedures, standard documentation, and informal entry, see "Entry Process" on page 185.

Informed Compliance. Informed compliance was introduced with the Customs Modernization Act of 1993 (Mod Act) and defines the relationship between importers and the Customs Service. It sets out the responsibilities of both parties. Providing the correct documentation and information for entry is a key factor that will make your importing operation run smoothly. We recommend that importers become familiar with the concept of informed comliance and the responsibilities that they have under the Mod Act. For further discussion about informed compliance see "Informed Compliance" on page 211.

Note: The Entry and Documentation section has been carefully designed to supply you, the importer, with sample documents and directions on how to satisfy Customs requirements. Be aware that you should consult the applicable authorities to ensure that you are correctly following the most current procedures.

Prohibitions and Restrictions

DOT Requirements—Safety, Bumper, and Theft Prevention Standards. The DOT requires that all imported motor vehicles and items of motor vehicle equipment comply with all applicable FMVSS standards in effect when these vehicles or items were manufactured. The best qualified source of safety conformance information is the vehicle's original manufacturer. Only the original manufacturer is capable of proving the date of manufacture and the state of FMVSS conformity on that date. Complying vehicles have the original manufacturer's certification permanently affixed to the vehicle or item of equipment. Customs will inspect your vehicle at the time of entry in order to determine compliance. Dealer statements and foreign registration documents are not acceptable verifications of compliance.

Temporary Importation of Noncomplying Vehicles. All temporary imports of noncomplying vehicles require advance written approval from the DOT. Various classes of vehicles and of importers are eligible for such waivers.

Motor vehicles and motor vehicle equipment that are imported solely with the intention of reexportation and that are so labeled are exempt (see 19 CFR 12.85).

Nonresidents of the U.S. may import a noncomplying foreign-registered motor vehicle for personal use for a period of time not to exceed one year. The passport number and country of issue of the nonresident importer must appear on the declaration form.

Vehicles not licensed for use on public roads that have been brought in for test, experimentation, training, demonstration, or competitive racing events are exempt. Such vehicles must be accompanied by documentation describing the purpose of importation, estimated use on public roads, and estimated time before reexport. There is a three-year maximum time limit for this kind of importation. You must obtain a special DOT waiver for periods beyond three years.

Members of the foreign military, diplomatic corps, or other official delegation temporarily stationed in the U.S. may import noncomplying vehicles for personal use. Such vehicles may be sold to another eligible individual at the end of the stay of the individual entitled to use it. Otherwise, the noncomplying vehicle must be exported when the authorized individual's tour of duty ends. Eligible members of foreign delegations must register all imported vehicles through the U.S. Department of State's Office of Foreign Missions (OFM), and must obtain an ownership title to the vehicle (good for export only) from the OFM before departing the U.S. and exporting the vehicle.

Noncomplying Vehicles Imported for Permanent Use. Unless specifically exempted, imports of noncertified or nonconforming vehicles for permanent use in the U.S., must be made under contract through a DOT-Registered Importer. Prior to the vehicle's entry, the RI will petition the NHTSA for a determination of the vehicle model and model year's eligibility for importation. (Refer to 49 CFR 593-594 for details on the eligibility process.) Once eligibility has been determined, the RI will contract to modify the vehicle to conform with all applicable safety and bumper standards. A copy of this contract must be furnished to U.S. Customs at the port of entry.

In addition, a DOT bond, **Form HS-474 (1-90)**, in the amount of 150% of the vehicle's dutiable value must be posted at the port of entry. This bond is intended to assure conformance of the vehicle within 120 days after entry. In some cases the DOT may extend the deadline to within 180 days after entry. Vehicle modification work may be performed either before or after the vehicle is imported. However, the steps for bonding and to substantiate that federal standards are being met are the same in either case.

When the vehicle has been brought up to standard, the RI certifies to the NHTSC that the modification(s) have been completed, and the bond is released. The vehicle may not be released for use or resale until 30 days after the RI has certified compliance to NHTSA, or until NHTSA has notified the importer that the vehicle and the bond may be released. In some cases NHTSA will require inspection of the vehicle to ascertain compliance.

Canadian Vehicles. The NHTSA has granted eligibility to certain Canadian-built automobiles that do not comply with applicable FMVSS but that comply with the analogous Canadian Motor Vehicle Safety Standards. These vehicles have already been cleared for importation and do not require specific authorization through NHTSA, but must still be imported as noncomplying vehicles under contract with an RI and under bond. Covered vehicles include 1) all passenger cars manufactured between January 1, 1988 and August 31, 1989 bearing a model year designation of 1988 or 1989; 2) all passenger cars manufactured on or after September 1, 1989 and equipped with an automatic restraint system by the original manufacturer that complies with FMVSS No. 208; 3) all other types of motor vehicles manufactured from January 1, 1988 on, that are certified by their original manufacturer as complying with all applicable Canadian motor vehicle safety standards, and that are of the same make, model, and model year of any vehicle originally manufactured for importation into and sale in the U.S., or originally manufactured in the U.S. for sale there, and that bear a certification of compliance with all applicable federal motor vehicle safety standards. For specific information, consult 19 CFR 10.84, or contact the DOT (see addresses at end of this chapter).

Registered Importers. If you wish to register with the DOT to import vehicles not originally manufactured to comply with applicable FMVSS, you must file a notarized Application for Registration as Importer with NHTSA. For details regarding requirements and fees, contact the NHTSA (see addresses at end of this chapter). The responsibilities of a Registered Importer are defined in 49 CFR 592.

EPA Requirements—Emission Standards. The Clean Air Act prohibits importation into the U.S. of any motor vehicle or motor vehicle engine that does not meet EPA emission standards. Requirements have been in effect for gasoline-powered cars since 1968 and for motorcycles since 1978. These standards apply to imported vehicles whether they are new or used, made domestically or abroad, and whether or not they have been previously altered. These requirements apply to all types of vehicles—passenger cars, trucks, and other vehicles, such as campers and all-terrain vehicles—that the EPA deems are capable of being used on a public road. There are basically two vehicle categories subject to import restrictions (which are found in 19 CFR 12.73):

Vehicles Manufactured in Conformity With U.S. Emission Requirements. Anyone may import U.S.-version vehicles dating from 1971 on. Vehicles originally equipped with a catalytic converter and/or oxygen sensor and 1) that have been driven less than 50 miles; 2) are diesel fueled; or 3) have been operated only within the U.S., Canada, Mexico, Japan, Australia, Taiwan, and Grand Bahama Island may be imported without having to post a bond. (Vehicles driven outside of these countries may have had their emissions systems contaminated by leaded gasoline.) Vehicles in these categories will have U.S. emissions compliance labels in the engine compartment that will identify them as complying. If this label is missing, the importer must secure a manufacturer's statement that the particular model complies (a dealer's statement will not suffice).

Unless the vehicle meets these requirements or other specific exceptions (see below), the EPA requires that the vehicle be imported by an ICI and that the importer post a bond to ensure that the vehicle will be brought into compliance. Customs determines the amount of the bond, which is generally the value of the vehicle. If you are importing such a vehicle, you must file an EPA **Form 3520-1** (obtainable either from Customs or your bonding compa-

ny) at the port of entry. The vehicle must be brought into compliance with EPA emissions standards within 120 days after entry. For specific details on options for compliance, see EPA's Automotive Imports Fact Sheet (available from EPA, address below).

Exceptions to the bond requirement include: 1) vehicles participating in Department of State, Department of Defense, or Panama Canal Commission programs approved by EPA; or 2) vehicles participating in one of the EPA-approved Manufacturers or Shippers Catalyst Control Programs. For further information contact the EPA (see addresses at end of this chapter).

Vehicles not equipped by the manufacturer with an emissions control system (model years 1968 and earlier) are not subject to import restrictions and may be imported without bond. However, you must provide proof that the vehicle was not equipped with a catalytic converter at the time of manufacture.

Vehicles Not Manufactured in Conformity With U.S. Emission Requirements. These vehicles will not be labeled as complying with U.S. emission requirements. If you wish to import such a vehicle, you must arrange for importation through an ICI holding a valid EPA Certificate of Conformity for the specific class of vehicle. ICI certificate holders are responsible for undertaking all modifications and testing required to bring the vehicle into conformance with EPA standards, and for assuring the vehicle's compliance for 5 years or 5,000 miles. For more details regarding ICIs operating in the U.S. or options for specific compliance requirements, contact the EPA (see addresses at end of this chapter) or see the Automotive Imports Fact Sheet.

Exclusions Based on Age of Vehicles or Engines. The following vehicles are excluded from EPA emission requirements and may be imported without a bond by any individual or business: 1) gasoline-fueled light-duty vehicles and light-duty trucks originally manufactured prior to January 1, 1968; 2) diesel-fueled light-duty vehicles originally manufactured prior to January 1, 1975; 3) diesel-fueled light-duty trucks originally manufactured prior to January 1, 1976; 4) motorcycles originally manufactured prior to January 1, 1978; 5) gasoline-fueled and diesel-fueled heavy-duty engines originally manufactured prior to January 1, 1970.

Racing Exclusions. Certain racing vehicles that are not capable of being operated on public roads and that are to be used only for racing events are excluded from EPA emission requirements, and may be imported by any individual or business. However, you must obtain the EPA's prior written approval prior to importation. For more information, see the Automotive Imports Fact Sheet or contact the EPA (see addresses at end of this chapter).

Miscellaneous Exemptions. Other exemptions from compliance but that require EPA's prior written permission include: 1) vehicles imported solely for repair or alteration; 2) vehicles imported for testing; 3) vehicles imported by an ICI for testing in order to obtain a certificate of conformity; 4) vehicles imported solely for display; 5) vehicles imported by individuals under circumstances of severe hardship; 6) vehicles imported by the manufacturer for national security reasons. Each of the above exemptions involves specific limitations, requirements, and documentation. For further information see the Automotive Imports Fact Sheet or contact the EPA (see addresses at end of this chapter).

Canadian Vehicles. Vehicles manufactured in Canada that are not labeled with an unconditional statement of conformity with U.S. emission standards are subject to restriction. The label may be located under the hood or in the door jamb of the vehicle. For further information see the Automotive Imports Fact Sheet or contact the EPA (see addresses at end of this chapter).

Bicycles. All bicycles and bicycle parts introduced into U.S. commerce must comply with safety regulations enumerated in 16 CFR 1512. These requirements can be divided into 1) general mechanical requirements, and 2) component-specific requirements.

The regulations also prescribe specific testing procedures for steering, wheel, pedal, crank, and brake systems.

General Bicycle Mechanical Requirements. Any mechanical skills required by the consumer for assembling your bicycle must not exceed those possessed by an adult of normal intelligence and ability. Your bicycles should have no unfinished sheared metal edges or other sharp parts that are, or may be, exposed to the hands or legs. Sheared metal edges that are not rolled must be finished so as to remove any feathering of edges, burrs, or spurs caused during the shearing process. Your bicycle frame or other component should show no visible fracture as a result of prescribed testing. Attachment hardware should also be free of damage as a result of such testing.

Component-specific Bicycle Requirements. The regulation provides specific standards for: the 1) braking system; 2) steering system; 3) pedals; 4) drive chain; 5) protective guards; 6) tires; 7) wheels; 8) wheel hubs; 9) front fork; 10) fork and frame assembly; 11) seat; and 12) reflectors. Although these requirements are highly technical, and enumerating them is beyond the scope of this entry, you should be aware that the CPSC tests for and enforces them. If you are ignorant of the standards and attempt to import a noncomplying shipment, you may find that your shipment is refused entry. If your product passes Customs without inspection, but is later found to be noncomplying, you are liable for product recall. The CPSA gives the CPSC both the authority and the responsibility to protect the U.S. consumer, and to take legal action in cases when noncompliance is determined.

Substantial Product Hazard Reports. There are defect-reporting requirements for any product covered under the CPSA, including bicycles. Section 15(b) of CPSA requires any manufacturer, distributor, or retailer of such products who obtains information that reasonably supports the conclusion that such products fail to comply with an applicable consumer product safety rule or contain a defect that could create a substantial product hazard to immediately inform the Commission of the potential violation or defect. A firm's willful failure to make a Substantial Product Hazard Report can result in litigation by the CPSC.

Marking and Labeling Requirements

The DOT and the EPA each have separate labeling requirements for motor vehicles and motor vehicle equipment. Vehicles imported into the U.S. must meet the requirements of both agencies.

DOT Labeling Requirements. The DOT requires vehicles in compliance with FMVSS to have the original manufacturer's certification label permanently affixed. The label must be in English. It usually appears near the driver's door pillar or door edge. Any vehicle without such labeling is considered to be noncomplying and must be imported following the procedures outlined in the section on DOT requirements (see above). Passenger cars subject to the Federal Motor Theft Prevention Standard must be brought into compliance and have a certification label affixed before importation. These are cars listed as most likely to be stolen in Appendix A, 49 CFR Part 541, with model years beginning in 1986. Such cars must have their major parts inscribed (not merely labeled) with their original Vehicle Identification Number (VIN) before they reach the U.S. Vehicles imported for export only must also be similarly labeled. For specific details, contact DOT (see addresses at end of this chapter).

EPA Labeling Requirements. Conforming vehicles manufactured in 1968-1970 will have a label on the doorpost indicating compliance with FMVSS; those manufactured in 1971 and later will have a label in the engine compartment entitled Vehicle Emission Control Information. This label will contain the name and trademark of the manufacturer and an unconditional statement of compliance with EPA emission regulations. Motorcycles

will have the label on the frame. Any vehicles manufactured from 1968 on not labeled are considered noncomplying and must be imported through procedures described in EPA Requirements section (see above). For specific details, contact the EPA (see addresses at end of this chapter).

Bicycles—Instruction Manual. If you are importing bicycles as a commercial venture, you need to be aware of the following requirements. A bicycle must have an instruction manual attached to its frame or included with the packaged unit. The manual must include at a minimum the following: 1) operations and safety instructions describing operation of the brakes and gears, cautions concerning wet-weather and night-time operation, and a guide for safe on-and off-road operation; 2) assembly instructions for accomplishing complete and proper assembly; and 3) instructions for proper maintenance of brakes, control cables, bearing adjustments, wheel adjustments, lubrication, reflectors, tires, and handlebar and seat adjustments. If such maintenance is beyond the average consumer's capability, the manual must specify locations where such maintenance service can be obtained. If the bicycle is not fully assembled and fully adjusted for the ultimate consumer, it must have the following information clearly displayed on any promotional display material and on the outside surface of the shipping carton: 1) a list of tools necessary to properly accomplish assembly and adjustment; 2) a drawing illustrating the minimum leg-length dimension of a rider, and a method of measurement of this dimension. The dimension must be readily understandable and must be based on allowing no less than one inch of clearance between the top tube of the bicycle and the ground plane, and the crotch measurement of the rider. A girl's-style frame must be specified in the same way, using a corresponding boy's model as a basis.

Mandatory Bicycle Label. Every bicycle subject to the requirements of 16 CFR 1512 must bear a marking or label securely affixed on, or to the frame of, the bicycle. The marking or label must be affixed in such a manner that it cannot be removed without being defaced or destroyed. It must identify the name of the manufacturer or private labeler. It must also bear some form of marking from which the manufacturer can identify the month and year of manufacture, or from which the private labeler can identify the manufacturer and the month and year of manufacture.

For a general discussion of U.S. Customs marking and labeling requirements, see "Country of Origin Marking" on page 236, "Special Marking Requirements" on page 238 and "Marking—False Impression" on page 239.

Shipping Considerations

You will need to ensure that your goods are packaged and shipped with care to ensure that they arrive in good condition and pass smoothly through Customs. You are responsible for ensuring that the shipment is in compliance with all applicable government regulations for packaging and shipping. In most instances, you should not leave these arrangements solely to the discretion of your supplier. Careful preparation of the cargo and selection of the mode of transport can be essential to a cost-effective, timely delivery of undamaged goods. We strongly advise you to consult your shipping representative, insurance agent, or freight broker for advice on packing and shipping.

Vehicles must be packed and stowed carefully to ensure that they are not damaged due to shifting en route or due to exposure to heat, moisture, or other hazards.

Publications and WWW Resources

The following publications may be relevant to importing vehicles.

Automotive Imports Fact Manual (Available from the EPA)

Vehicle , Parts and Accesories(Available from the Customs Service as an informed compliance document)

The *Harmonized Tariff Schedule of the United States (2001)* (HTSUS) is available to view on the Customs Service website (www.customs.gov), or you may purchase a printed version from:

U.S. Government Printing Office
Superintendent of Documents
710 North Capital Street NW
Washington DC 20401
Tel: (202) 512-1800
Fax: (202) 512-1657
Website: www.access.gpo.gov

The USGPO also has copies of specific laws available for purchase. The USGPO accepts orders made by fax, phone or placed over the Internet, as well as mail orders paid by credit card. All orders must be accompanied by payment. Credit cards, checks drawn on a U.S. bank, or an international money order are all acceptable.

Relevant Government Agencies

Address questions regarding DOT requirements for vehicle imports to:

National Highway Traffic Safety Administration
Office of Vehicle Safety Compliance
Equipment & Import Division
400 7th St. SW
Washington DC 20590
Tel: (202) 366-2832
Website: www.nhtsa.dot.gov

Address questions regarding EPA requirements for vehicle imports to:

Environmental Protection Abency (EPA)
Office of Transportation and Air Quality (OTAQ)
Imports Section USEPA
1200 Pennsylvania Avenue NW
Washington DC 20460
MC6405J
(202) 564-9240
Website: www.epa.gov/otaq/imports

Address questions regarding bicycle regulation to:

Consumer Product Safety Commission (CPSC)
Office of Compliance
Washington DC 20207-0001
Tel: 800-638-2772 or (301) 504-7912
Fax: (301) 504-0359
Website: www.cpsc.gov

Address questions regarding importation of vehicles to:

U.S. Department of Commerce
International Trade Administration
Office of Automotive Affairs
1401 Constitution Avenue NW
Washington DC 20230
Tel: (202) 482-0554
Website: www.ita.doc.gov/td/auto

Address questions regarding importation of vehicles to your local Customs port director. For addresses see "U.S. Customs and Border Protection Offices" on page 65 or contact:

U.S. Customs and Border Protection
Customs Headquarters
1300 Pennsylvania Avenue NW
Washington DC 20229
Tel: (202) 354-1000
Automotive imports: (202) 927-0639
Website: www.customs.treas.gov

Laws and Regulations

The following laws and regulations may be relevant to the importation of vehicles. They are contained in the U.S. Code (USC) and the regulations are published in the Code of Federal Regulations (CFR), both of which may be available at larger public and law libraries. Copies of specific laws are also available from the United States Government Printing Office (address above).

15 USC 1231 et seq.
Automobile Information Disclosure Act
This Act requires the labeling of automobiles and is enforced by Customs for imported vehicles.

15 USC 2021-2034
National Traffic and Motor Vehicle Safety Act (Theft Prevention)
This Act provides for the setting of motor vehicle theft prevention standards by the Secretary of Transportation concerning major automotive parts, and prohibits the manufacture, sale, delivery, or importation of vehicles that do not meet the standard. Customs will deny entry to vehicles in violation of this Act. Temporary importations may be permitted for the purpose of bringing substandard vehicles into conformity with the standards (Section 2027).

18 USC 511-512
Motor Vehicles
These laws prohibit the alteration or removal of motor vehicle identification numbers. Customs is authorized to inspect vehicles for purposes of enforcing this prohibition.

18 USC 553
Importation or Exportation of Stolen Motor Vehicles
This law prohibits the importation or exportation of stolen motor vehicles, vessels, aircraft, and other mobile equipment. Customs assists in enforcing this law.

18 USC 2312 and 2313
Transportation, Sale, or Receipt of Stolen Vehicles
These laws prohibit the transportation, sale, or receipt of stolen vehicles or aircraft.

19 USC 2001 et seq.
Automotive Products Trade Act of 1965
This Act allows duty-free importation of bona fide products of Canada that are actually used in the manufacture of original automotive equipment. Customs assists in enforcing this law.

49 CFR 591
Importation of Vehicles and Equipment Subject to Federal Safety, Bumper, and Theft Prevention Standards
Regulations defining the requirements for importing vehicles.

42 USC 7401 et seq.
Clean Air Act
This Act restricts importations of motor vehicle engines found not to be in compliance with federal motor vehicle emission standards. Customs will test and inspect engines for compliance with this Act. See 19 CFR 12.73; 40 CFR 80, 85, 86 and 600.

15 USC 2051 et seq.
Consumer Product Safety Act
This Act sets standards for the manufacture, processing, and labeling of products sold to U.S. consumers.

Principal Exporting Countries

The following listing includes samples of the main supplier nations of the products of this chapter. It is organized by HTSUS major heading. (Refer to "Customs Classification" above for the product codes.) Countries are listed in rank order of the value of products imported to the U.S. Statistics represent customs value of entries for 2002 from the Bureau of Census, U.S. Department of Commerce.

8701—Canada, Japan, Mexico, United Kingdom, Germany, Italy, France

8702—Canada, Mexico, Hungary, Belgium, United Kingdom, Germany, Austria, France

8703—Japan, Canada, Germany, Mexico, South Korea, United Kingdom, Sweden

8704—Canada, Mexico, Japan, United Kingdom, France, Sweden, South Africa, Norway, Italy

8705—Germany, Canada, United Kingdom, Norway, Italy, Japan, Ukraine

8706—Japan, Canada, United Kingdom, Italy, Spain, Mexico

8707—Canada, Germany, Mexico, Japan, South Africa, Sweden, United Kingdom, Ireland, Spain

8708—Canada, Japan, Mexico, Germany, France, China, Taiwan, South Korea, Italy, United Kingdom

8709—Canada, Japan, Germany, Australia, Taiwan, China, France, South Korea

8710—Canada, Germany, Norway, United Kingdom, Israel, Switzerland, Denmark

8711—Japan, Italy, Germany, Austria, Taiwan, China, Thailand, Brazil

8712—China, Taiwan, Canada, Italy, Hong Kong, South Korea, Germany, Spain, United Kingdom

8713—Taiwan, China, Mexico, Sweden, South Korea, Spain, Indonesia

8714—Japan, Taiwan, Italy, China, Canada, Australia, South Korea, Mexico, United Kingdom

8715—China, Italy, Taiwan, Hong Kong, South Korea, Sweden, Germany, United Kingdom

8716—Canada, China, Mexico, Taiwan, South Korea, Germany

Chapter 88:
Aircraft and Parts

Full title: Aircraft, Spacecraft, and Parts Thereof

This chapter relates to the importation of aircraft and related equipment, which are classified within HTSUS Chapter 88 of the Harmonized Tariff Schedule of the United States (HTSUS). Specifically, it includes balloons, dirigibles, gliders, and similar aircraft; all other aircraft and spacecraft, including helicopters, rockets, and airplanes—whether civilian or military, or jet, turbojet, rocket, or propeller driven; parts and assemblies of these craft; parachutes; launching and recovery gear; and flight simulators and trainers.

If you are interested in importing hovercraft, refer to Commodity Index Chapter 86 if the craft are rail guided, Chapter 87 if designed to travel over both land and water, and Chapter 89 if designed to travel exclusively over water or ice. Electrical signaling, safety, and traffic control equipment are found in Chapters 85 and 86. Although Chapter 88 covers most parts and accessories, it is generally restricted to components and subassemblies, with individual parts of general use being included in the chapters covering the type of article or the material of which it is composed—of rubber, plastics, base metals, ceramics, or glass. Instrumentation is found in Chapter 90, while seats for aircraft are found in Chapter 94. Many specialized mechanical subassemblies are covered in Chapter 84 and electrical components are found in Chapter 85.

Note: To understand key issues that will enable you to make best use of the information in this section we recommend that you see "Introduction" on page 425.

Key Factors

The key factors in the importation of aircraft are:

- Federal Aviation Administration (FAA) type certification for aircraft model to be imported

- FAA airworthiness certification for specific examples of aircraft equipment to be imported

- Compliance with quota restraints and visa requirements under U.S. Department of Commerce (DOC) Multi-Fiber Arrangements; submission of country of origin declaration; compliance with entry invoice requirements; and compliance with labeling requirements under the Textile Fiber Products Identification Act (TFPIA) for parachutes

- Compliance with U.S. Environmental Protection Agency (EPA) standards on equipment noise levels and fuel and exhaust emissions

Although most importers use the services of a licensed customs broker in making their entries, and we recommend this practice, you should be aware of the regulatory, entry, and documentation issues involved in importing your product. You, as importer, are ultimately responsible for the fulfillment of any legal requirements applicable to your shipment.

General Considerations

Product Certifications. All aircraft and related equipment used in the U.S., whether manufactured domestically or imported, must be approved by the U.S. Department of Transportation's FAA, which has established detailed and rigorous standards for such articles. Entry of aircraft or parts must include certification that the imports have received approval specifically by the FAA or from the analogous foreign authority in the country of origin—which must adhere to standards accepted by the FAA. This adherence is established through a series of bilateral agreements between the U.S. and foreign countries whereby each party agrees to comply with set rigorous standards for design, materials, manufacture, quality control procedures, and testing and oversight functions. In order to be imported into the U.S., a foreign-made aircraft model, significant component, or part must be type certified by the FAA, while specific examples of these articles must be certified (or certifiable) as airworthy. Everyone, from the manufacturer and importer to the end users, are also obligated to report any instances of specific failures, design flaws, or injuries resulting from the items imported.

An interested importer can petition the Administrator of the FAA for type certification of a product. However, it is difficult for a firm other than a major established concern to gain approval for the certification of a major new product. The materials incorporated by reference to 14 CFR I, 1-59 catalogues technical publications by major aircraft manufacturers. Not only do are these publications officially incorporated into the regulatory standards, but they provide a de facto listing of the major countries and manufacturers from which aircraft have been authorized for type certification and import.

To receive type certification, the product must first come from a country with which the U.S. has a bilateral export-import agreement covering aircraft (this is generally restricted to the larger, well-established countries that support their own active aerospace industries). The FAA must then satisfy itself that the certification procedures in the country from which the items come is adequate to allow the FAA to accept the authority of that country's inspectors, i.e., that they comply with all necessary standards (see below). In addition, the FAA requires the submission and revue of technical specifications and data, and reserves the right to independently test the equipment.

Once a type certification has been issued, it usually remains in effect indefinitely. The Administrator of the FAA can revoke a type certification at any time on the grounds that a particular article covered by such certification is defective or if the office finds that foreign oversight has slipped to an unacceptable standard.

Standards. Regulations covering these standards are found in 14 CFR 21 et seq. in sections called Special Federal Aviation Regulations (SFAR). For example, SFAR 26 establishes the procedures for type certification approvals, while SFAR 41 governs the standards for commuter aircraft—those designed to accommodate between 10 and 19 passengers. In general, the FAA classifies aircraft into normal, utility, acrobatic, commuter, transport, manned free balloon, and special categories, with specific standards being established for each category (refer to 14 CFR Parts 23-36). Standards include compliance with mandated acceptable levels for noise, fuel consumption, and exhaust emissions.

Once type certification has been established for the product in question, importers also require airworthiness certification for the specific articles to be imported. The FAA must pass the particular examples of products as airworthy and thus eligible to be registered and/or used in the U.S. Certification by the exporting country is generally considered to constitute adequate evidence of airworthiness provided the country of origin is in compliance with FAA standards. However, importers must be prepared to submit specific technical data and/or actual products for examination and testing.

All entries under HTSUS chapter 88 must be accompanied by all necessary technical data and instruction or user manuals translated into English.

Importer Certification. Importers must be certified by the FAA to import aircraft, components, and parts. The importing firm must satisfy the FAA that it has the requisite experience, knowledge, and financial stability to be able to interpret and administer FAA requirements for entering aircraft. Once approved, importers may make an entry by entry certification, or they may make a blanket certification good for one year. A blanket certification must be filed with the port director of customs for each customs district in which the importer enters products of HTSUS Chapter 88. Renewal is by application to each affected port director prior to the expiration of the existing certification. Customs may audit sample entries to verify compliance with FAA requirements. For details refer to 19 CFR 10.183.

Environmental Issues. The EPA sets and administers standards for the environmental impact—noise, fuel, exhaust, and hazardous materials—for aircraft. All aircraft, components, and parts, including imported ones, must meet established standards with respect to these issues. The Environment and Energy Section of the FAA (see addresses at end of this chapter) is directly responsible for monitoring and enforcing these rules, and should be contacted with questions concerning aircraft-related environmental standards.

Textile Products—Parachutes. HTSUS Chapter 88 covers the importation of parachutes and related equipment, which is subject to the regulations governing the textile products used in such articles, including silk and manmade fibers. The Department of Commerce (DOC) regulates certain textile imports under the Agricultural Adjustment Act. Customs enforces textile quotas, as well as the provisions of the TFPIA. Quotas apply to certain textiles under the Multi-Fiber Arrangements (MFA), including blends of silk and/or man-made fibers. For specific information, contact the International Trade Administration's Office of Textile and Apparel (see addresses at end of this chapter). All textile imports must be accompanied by a Country of Origin Declaration. The country of origin is the country in which the material was grown, produced, or manufactured. Textile imports remain subject to country-specific quota restrictions affecting this country of origin unless they have been substantially transformed—as defined by Customs—in another country before entering the U.S. The importation of textile products is sensitive and highly regulated. Shipments of such products that do not comply exactly with all regulations will not only be denied entry, but may be seized, forfeited, and result in penalties. Always verify all procedural information, quota status, and customs rulings immediately prior to trying to enter such textile products.

Customs Classification

For customs purposes aircraft classified within Chapter 88 of the HTSUS. The chapter is divided into major headings, which are further divided into subheadings and often into sub-subheadings, each with its a own HTSUS classification number. For example, the 2001 HTSUS number for other parts for use in civil aircraft is 8803.90.90, indicating that it is a subcategory of other parts (8803.90), which is a subcategory of the major heading parts of goods of powered and unpowered aircraft (8803). There are five major headings in HTSUS Chapter 88.

8801—Balloons and dirigibles; gliders, hang gliders, and other non-powered aircraft

8802—Other aircraft (for example, helicopters, airplanes); spacecraft (including satellites) and suborbital and spacecraft launch vehicles

8803—Parts of goods of heading 8801 and 8802

8804—Parachutes (including dirigible parachutes and paragliders) and rotochutes; parts thereof and accessories thereto

8805—Aircraft launching gear; deck-arrestor or similar gear; ground flying trainers; parts of the foregoing articles

For more details regarding classification of the specific product you are interested in importing, consult a customs broker, the appropriate commodity specialist at your nearest customs port, or see HTSUS. The 2001 HTSUS is available online from the Customs Service (www.customs.gov/impoexpo/impoexpo.htm) or for purchase from the U.S. Government Printing Office (see resources at the end of this chapter), and may be found in larger public libraries. For a general discussion of customs classification, see "Classification—Liquidation" on page 229.

Dutiable Status of Goods

For more information about duty rates and binding decisions see "Dutiable Status of Goods" on page 203; for a discussion of temporary importation of goods see "Temporary Free Importations" on page 205.

Valuation

Importers have a responsibility to use what the U.S. Customs Service deems, "reasonable care," when determining the value of their goods. They must also provide any additional information that the Customs Service needs for setting a final value on the goods. This process involves a number of factors and can be somewhat complicated; importers must be aware of applicable issues and details. Valuation information applies to all types of commodities, for further discussion on the subject see "Customs Valuation" on page 267.

Import Duties

Import duties vary (often dramatically) depending upon the Harmonized Tariff Schedule (HTSUS) classification of the goods or products imported. Since some products that look alike have different HTSUS classifications and different rates of duty, proper classification is vital. Note that "differences of opinion" between importers and the Bureau of Customs and Border Protection regarding classification keeps customs attorneys very busy.

Import duties can be assessed on the imported value of the goods ("ad valorem" rates of duty such as 2%, 4.4%, 50%, etc.), total units or weight of the goods ("specific" rates of duty such as 2 cents each or 1.5 cents/pound, etc.) or on a combination basis ("compound" rates of duty such as 5 cents each plus 6%).

Listed below is a sampling of several Column 1 import duty rates for Chapter 88 products:
Communications satellites (8802.60.30.00): Free
and
Parts of communications satellites (8803.90.30.00): Free

For specific information on US import duties refer to the Harmonized Tariff Schedule of the US. The print version is available from the US Government Printing Office as well as third party suppliers who often add special features. Online versions are available in both static PDF pages as well as in formats with excellent search functionality. Search the Web with the term "Harmonized Tariff Schedule" to find sources.

Entry and Documentation

The entry of merchandise is a two-part process consisting of 1) filing the documentation necessary to determine whether merchandise may be released from Customs custody and 2) filing the documents that contain information for duty assessment and statistical purposes. In certain instances all documents must be filed and accepted by Customs prior to the release of the goods. Unless you have been granted an extension, you must file entry documents at a location specified by the port or area director within five working days of your shipment's date of arrival at a U.S. port of entry. These include a number of standard documents required by Customs for entry, and:

- Federal Aviation Administration (FAA) type certification for aircraft model to be imported
- FAA airworthiness certification for aircraft equipment to be imported
- For parachutes, Country of Origin Declaration and export documentation and/or visa for textiles subject to MFA

After you present the entry, Customs may examine your shipment, or may waive examination. The shipment is then released provided no legal or regulatory violations have been noted. You must then file entry summary documentation and deposit estimated duties at a designated customhouse within 10 working days of your shipment's release. For a detailed description of entry procedures, standard documentation, and informal entry, see "Entry Process" on page 185.

Informed Compliance. Informed compliance was introduced with the Customs Modernization Act of 1993 (Mod Act) and defines the relationship between importers and the Customs Service. It sets out the responsibilities of both parties. Providing the correct documentation and information for entry is a key factor that will make your importing operation run smoothly. We recommend that importers become familiar with the concept of informed comliance and the responsibilities that they have under the Mod Act. For further discussion about informed compliance see "Informed Compliance" on page 211.

Note: The Entry and Documentation section has been carefully designed to supply you, the importer, with sample documents and directions on how to satisfy Customs requirements. Be aware that you should consult the applicable authorities to ensure that you are correctly following the most current procedures.

Prohibitions and Restrictions

All aircraft, components, and parts must comply with detailed product and airworthiness standards. These include performance, characteristics, controllability and maneuverability, trim, stability, stalls, spins, ground and water handling ability, and miscellaneous performance elements, such as vibration and high speed operation. Structural specifications establish parameters for loads, control system, surface loads, horizontal stability/balance surface, vertical stability, ground loads, water loads, emergency landing, and fatigue. Design and construction specifications include required standards for wings, controls, landing gear, floats and hulls, personnel and cargo accommodations, pressurization, and fire protection. In addition there exist further requirements for power plants, equipment, operational limits, and markings (see "Marking and Requirements" below). All aircraft, components, and parts imported into the U.S. must conform to these specifications in every detail. These regulations are found in 14 CFR Parts 23-36.

Quotas

Restrictions on quotas under the MFA for textile materials are country-specific. Contact the U.S. Customs Quota Branch for current information regarding quotas.

Marking and Labeling Requirements

All aircraft and airframes imported into the U.S. must be labeled indelibly and in a conspicuous place (as detailed in the regulations in 14 CFR 45.11) with an airframe number. All critical assemblies and parts must be labeled indelibly with identification that include the name and number of the manufacturer.

All textile products subject to TFPIA must be marked with 1) the name and percentage by weight of the constituent fibers present in the textile product in amounts greater than 5%, in order of their predominance; 2) the name of the manufacturer or the name of the registered identification number issued by the Federal Trade Commission (FTC); and 3) the name of the country where processed. Contact the FTC (see addresses at end of this chapter) for additional information.

For a general discussion of U.S. Customs marking and labeling requirements, see "Country of Origin Marking" on page 236, "Special Marking Requirements" on page 238 and "Marking—False Impression" on page 239.

Shipping Considerations

You will need to ensure that your goods are packaged and shipped with care to ensure that they arrive in good condition and pass smoothly through Customs. You are responsible for ensuring that the shipment is in compliance with all applicable government regulations for packaging and shipping. In most instances, you should not leave these arrangements solely to the discretion of your supplier. Careful preparation of the cargo and selection of the mode of transport can be essential to a cost-effective, timely delivery of undamaged goods. We strongly advise you to consult your shipping representative, insurance agent, or freight broker for advice on packing and shipping.

Aircraft are sometimes flown in rather than transported on other carriers. Aircraft and related equipment are often heavy and bulky. They must be packed and stowed carefully to ensure against not damage due to shifting en route or due to exposure to heat, moisture, or other hazards.

Publications and WWW Resources

The *Harmonized Tariff Schedule of the United States (2001)* (HTSUS) is available to view on the Customs Service website (www.customs.gov), or you may purchase a printed version from:

U.S. Government Printing Office
Superintendent of Documents
710 North Capital Street NW
Washington DC 20401
Tel: (202) 512-1800
Fax: (202) 512-1657
Website: www.access.gpo.gov

The USGPO also has copies of specific laws available for purchase. The USGPO accepts orders made by fax, phone or placed over the Internet, as well as mail orders paid by credit card. All orders must be accompanied by payment. Credit cards, checks drawn on a U.S. bank, or an international money order are all acceptable.

Relevant Government Agencies

Address questions regarding DOT/FAA requirements for aircraft to one of 12 local FAA Aircraft Certification Offices. If you are not sure where to find one or have further questions, contact:

U.S. Department of Transportation (DOT)
Federal Aviation Administration (FAA)
International Airworthiness Programs Office
800 Independence Avenue SW
Washington DC 20591
Tel: (202) 267-7000
Website: www.faa.gov

Address questions regarding environmental standards and regulation for aircraft to:

Federal Aviation Administration
Office of Environment and Energy
800 Independence Avenue SW
Washington DC 20591
Tel: (202) 267-3576
Website: www.aee.faa.gov

Address questions regarding textile requirements for aircraft-related imports to:

U.S. Department of Commerce
International Trade Administration
Office of Textiles and Apparel
Director's Office
14th and Constitution Avenue NW, Rm. H3100
Washington DC 20230
Tel: (202) 482-5078
Fax: (202) 482-2331
Agreements Division: (202) 482-4212
Website: http://otexa.ita.doc.gov

Address questions regarding requirements under the TFPIA to:

Federal Trade Commission (FTC)
Division of Enforcement
600 Pennsylvania Avenue NW
Washington DC 20580
Tel: (202) 326-2996
Website: www.ftc.gov

Address your questions regarding current textile quota information to:

U.S. Customs and Border Protection
Office of Field Operations, Quota Branch
1300 Pennsylvania Avenue NW
Washington DC 20229
Tel: (202) 927-5850
Website: www.customs.treas.gov

Address questions regarding importation of aircraft to:

U.S. Department of Commerce
International Trade Administration
Office of Aerospace
1400 Constitution Avenue NW
Washington DC 20230
Tel: (202) 482-1228
Website: www.ita.doc.gov/td/aerospace

Address questions regarding importation for aircraft to your local Customs port director. For addresses refer to "U.S. Customs and Border Protection Offices" on page 65 or contact:

U.S. Customs and Border Protection
Customs Headquarters
1300 Pennsylvania Avenue NW
Washington DC 20229
Tel: (202) 354-1000
Website: www.customs.treas.gov

Laws and Regulations

The following laws and regulations may be relevant to the importation of vehicles. They are contained in the U.S. Code (USC) and the regulations are published in the Code of Federal Regulations (CFR), both of which may be available at larger public and law libraries. Copies of specific laws are also available from the United States Government Printing Office (address above).

49 USC 106, 44501 et seq., 44701 et seq.
Federal Transportation Act
These laws establish the authority of the FAA to set procedures and specifications for aircraft, components, and parts to be used in U.S. aviation.

14 CFR 21 et seq.

Regulations of FAA on Aircraft Use

These regulations detail the procedures and specifications governing the use of aircraft, components, and parts in U.S. aviation.

7 USC 1854

Textile Trade Agreements

This act authorizes the DOC to enter into Multi-Fiber Agreements with other countries to control trade in textiles and establishes the Textile Import Program, enforced by Customs.

15 USC 70-77

Textile Fiber Products Identification Act

This act prohibits false or deceptive labeling (misbranding) and false advertising of any textile fiber products and requires all such products imported into the U.S. to be labeled in accordance with the requirements set forth in the law.

Principal Exporting Countries

The following listing includes samples of the main supplier nations of the products of this chapter. It is organized by HTSUS major heading. (Refer to "Customs Classification" above for the product codes.) Countries are listed in rank order of the value of products imported to the U.S. Statistics represent customs value of entries for 2002 from the Bureau of Census, U.S. Department of Commerce.

8801—United Kingdom, Czech Republic, Germany, Japan, Canada, Australia, Russia

8802—France, Canada, Brazil, Germany, Italy, Israel, Switzerland

8803—Japan, Canada, United Kingdom, France, Italy, Mexico

8804—Canada, France, United Kingdom, Honduras, South Africa, China, Spain, Germany, South Korea, Israel

8805—Canada, United Kingdom, France, Netherlands, Japan, Germany

Chapter 89:
Ships and Boats

Full title: Ships, Boats, and Floating Structures

This section pertains to the importation of ships and boats, which are classified within Chapter 89 of the Harmonized Tariff Schedule of the United States (HTSUS). Specifically, it covers whole vessels, including large ships; fishing vessels; yachts and other pleasure boats; tugs; light vessels, dredges, floating docks, and drilling platforms; other vessels, such as warships and lifeboats; other floating structures, such as inflatable rafts and buoys; and vessels for scrap.

If you are interested in importing parts of or for ships or boats, refer to the Commodity Index chapter for that category of product or the specific material of which it is composed.

Note: To understand key issues that will enable you to make best use of the information in this section we recommend that you see "Introduction" on page 425.

Key Factors

The key factors in importing ships and boats are:

- The type of boat and the purpose for which it is imported

- Compliance with U.S. Coast Guard (USCG) regulations, safety standards, and labeling requirements for boats and boat equipment

Although most importers utilize the services of a licensed customs broker in making their entries, and we recommend this practice, you should be aware of the regulatory, entry, and documentation issues involved in importing your product. You, as importer, are ultimately responsible for the fulfillment of any legal requirements applicable to your shipment.

General Considerations

U.S. Customs and USCG regulations distinguish between boats being imported permanently for commercial use or for resale, and those being imported either permanently or temporarily for personal recreational use or temporarily for purposes incidental to international trade. Customs regulations covering procedures, fees, rights, and responsibilities of vessels entering temporarily into U.S. jurisdiction are detailed in 19 CFR Part 4.

If you are importing a foreign-built pleasure boat you must notify Customs of the date the boat will arrive at the first U.S. port of entry, so that entry procedures can be completed. If you wish to import foreign-built vessels or parts thereof for resale in the U.S., you should contact the USCG Commandant (see addresses at end of this chapter) for details concerning your legal obligations.

Customs Classification

For customs purposes ships and boats are classified within Chapter 89 of HTSUS. This chapter is divided into major headings, which are further divided into subheadings, and often into sub-subheadings, each with its own HTSUS classification number. For example, the 2001 HTSUS number for canoes is 8903.99.05, indicating that it is a subcategory of other—rowboats and canoes which are not of a type designed to be principally used with motors or sails (8903.99), which is a subcategory of the major heading yachts and other vessels for pleasure or sport (8903). There are eight major headings in HTSUS Chapter 89.

8901—Cruise ships, excursion boats, ferry boats, cargo ships, barges, and similar vessels for the transport of persons or goods

8902—Fishing vessels; factory ships and other vessels for processing or preserving fishery products

8903—Yachts and other vessels for pleasure or sports; rowboats and canoes

8904—Tugs and pusher craft

8905—Light-vessels, fire-floats, dredges, floating cranes, and other vessels the navigability of which is subsidiary to their main function; floating docks; floating or submersible drilling or production platforms

8906—Other vessels, including warships and lifeboats other than rowboats

8907—Other floating structures (for example, rafts, tanks, cofferdams, landing-stages, buoys, and beacons)

8908—Vessels and other floating structures for breaking up (scrapping)

For more details regarding classification of the specific product you are interested in importing, consult a customs broker, the appropriate commodity specialist at your nearest Customs port, or see HTSUS. The 2001 HTSUS is available online from the Customs Service (www.customs.gov/impoexpo/impoexpo.htm) or for purchase from the U.S. Government Printing Office (see resources at the end of this chapter), and may be found in larger public libraries. For a general discussion of customs classification, see "Classification—Liquidation" on page 229.

Dutiable Status of Goods

For more information about duty rates and binding decisions see "Dutiable Status of Goods" on page 203; for a discussion of temporary importation of goods see "Temporary Free Importations" on page 205.

Valuation

Importers have a responsibility to use what the U.S. Customs Service deems, "reasonable care," when determining the value of their goods. They must also provide any additional information that the Customs Service needs for setting a final value on the goods. This process involves a number of factors and can be somewhat complicated; importers must be aware of applicable issues and details. Valuation information applies to all types of commodities, for further discussion on the subject see "Customs Valuation" on page 267.

Import Duties

Import duties vary (often dramatically) depending upon the Harmonized Tariff Schedule (HTSUS) classification of the goods or products imported. Since some products that look alike have different HTSUS classifications and different rates of duty, proper classification is vital. Note that "differences of opinion" between importers and the Bureau of Customs and Border Protection regarding classification keeps customs attorneys very busy.

Import duties can be assessed on the imported value of the goods ("ad valorem" rates of duty such as 2%, 4.4%, 50%, etc.), total units or weight of the goods ("specific" rates of duty such as 2 cents each or 1.5 cents/pound, etc.) or on a combination basis ("compound" rates of duty such as 5 cents each plus 6%).

Listed below is a sampling of several Column 1 import duty rates for Chapter 89 products:

Cruise ships, excursion boats and similar vessels principally designed for the transport of persons; ferry boats of all kinds (8901.10.00.00): Free

to

Motorboats, other than outboard motorboats (8903.92.00): 1.5%

For specific information on US import duties refer to the Harmonized Tariff Schedule of the US. The print version is available from the US Government Printing Office as well as third party suppliers who often add special features. Online versions are available in both static PDF pages as well as in formats with excellent search functionality. Search the Web with the term "Harmonized Tariff Schedule" to find sources.

Entry and Documentation

The entry of merchandise is a two-part process consisting of 1) filing the documents necessary to determine whether merchandise may be released from Customs custody and 2) filing the documents that contain information for duty assessment and statistical purposes. In certain instances all documents must be filed and accepted by Customs prior to the release of the goods. Unless you have been granted an extension, you must file entry documents at a location specified by the port or area director within five working days of your shipment's date of arrival at a U.S. port of entry. These include a number of standard documents required by Customs for any entry, and:

- For boats that do not comply with USCG safety standards, Form CG-5096
- Original bill of lading from the shipper or carrier
- Bill of sale
- Foreign registration, if any

After you present the entry, Customs may examine your shipment, or may waive examination. The shipment is then released provided no legal or regulatory violations have been noted. You must then file entry summary documentation and deposit estimated duties at a designated customhouse within 10 working days of your shipment's release. For a detailed description of entry procedures, standard documentation, and informal entry, see "Entry Process" on page 185.

Informed Compliance. Informed compliance was introduced with the Customs Modernization Act of 1993 (Mod Act) and defines the relationship between importers and the Customs Service. It sets out the responsibilities of both parties. Providing the correct documentation and information for entry is a key factor that will make your importing operation run smoothly. We recommend that importers become familiar with the concept of informed comliance and the responsibilities that they have under the Mod Act. For further discussion about informed compliance see "Informed Compliance" on page 211.

Note: The Entry and Documentation section has been carefully designed to supply you, the importer, with sample documents and directions on how to satisfy Customs requirements. Be aware that you should consult the applicable authorities to ensure that you are correctly following the most current procedures.

Prohibitions and Restrictions

Safety Standards. Imported boats and associated equipment are subject to USCG safety regulations or standards under the Federal Boat Safety Act of 1971. Any imported boat or boat-associated equipment must meet applicable USCG safety and marine sanitation regulations before it will be allowed final entry. Details regarding these safety standards are found in USCG Consumer Fact Sheet #14. Boats without toilets or marine heads are admitted into the U.S. without further restrictions. However, if a boat has a toilet or marine head, these must either be connected to a holding tank or equipped with an operable Marine Sanitation Device (MSD) in order to be admitted. Details are found in USCG Consumer Fact Sheet #13. You can obtain copies of these fact sheets from the USCG (see addresses at end of this chapter). Regulations governing Customs treatment of entering vessels are found in 19 CFR 12.85.

Customs usually inspects boats and items of associated equipment for compliance at the port of entry. If the boat is being sailed into the U.S.—rather than shipped in by carrier—the operator is responsible for reporting to U.S. Customs immediately upon arrival to arrange for inspection.

Vessels that are foreign-built or of foreign registry may be used in the U.S. for pleasure purposes and in foreign trade with or on behalf of the U.S. However, federal law prohibits the use of such vessels in the coastwise trade, i.e. the transportation of passengers or merchandise between points in the U.S., including the carrying of fishing parties or other excursions for hire. Address questions concerning the use of foreign-built or foreign-flag vessels to the U.S. Customs Service Carrier Rulings Branch (see addresses at end of this chapter).

Noncompliance. If your boat or piece of boat-related equipment does not comply with USCG requirements, you will have to post a bond and file a declaration, **Form CG 5096**. This declaration states that the boat is not in compliance but that you, the importer, will bring it into compliance. You may obtain **Form CG 5096** from any U.S. Customs port office. You are required to bring your boat into compliance within 180 days of filing the declaration. During this time, you may use or operate your boat or equipment only as is necessary to bring it into compliance. Once you have done all necessary work to bring it into compliance, notify the port director of Customs. You must be prepared to make available all supporting paperwork and receipts, as requested, to verify that the work has been done. The port director may also require you to deliver the boat or equipment to a specified site for a Customs inspection. When the port director is satisfied that compliance has been effected, Customs will release the bond and permit final entry. If you are unable to effect compliance within 180 days, you will have to redeliver your boat or equipment to Customs for export from the U.S. under Customs supervision.

Exemptions from Compliance. A noncomplying boat or item of related equipment is exempt from compliance under any one of the following conditions: 1) it has received a specific USCG Grant of Exemption from regulations that would otherwise apply; 2) it is entered temporarily for the purpose of exhibit, test, or participation in boat races; 3) it is owned by a member of a foreign military or government agency or public international organization on official assignment in the U.S.; or 4) it is being entered temporarily, for a period of up to one year, for repairs or alterations. The exact terms and conditions of entry will vary, but in any case you must file **Form CG 5096**.

Marking and Labeling Requirements

All boats manufactured on or after November 1, 1972 must be affixed with a Hull Identification Number (HIN) meeting USCG regulations. If your boat's foreign manufacturer has not affixed such an HIN you will have to have one assigned. You should contact the State Boating Law Administrator of the U.S. state in which your boat will be registered and used to request an HIN. To find out how to contact the appropriate Boating Law Administrator, call the Coast Guard Customer Info Line: 800-368-5647.

All recreational boats subject to a safety standard or standards must bear either a certification label or an exemption label. Standards vary depending upon the type of boat. Contact the USCG (see addresses at end of this chapter) or the nearest port director of Customs to find out what is required for the boat you wish to import.

For a general discussion of U.S. Customs marking and labeling requirements, see "Country of Origin Marking" on page 236, "Special Marking Requirements" on page 238 and "Marking—False Impression" on page 239.

Shipping Considerations

You will need to ensure that your goods are packaged and shipped with care to ensure that they arrive in good condition and pass smoothly through Customs. You are responsible for ensuring that the shipment is in compliance with all applicable government regulations for packaging and shipping. In most instances, you should not leave these arrangements solely to the discretion of your supplier. Careful preparation of the cargo and selection of the mode of transport can be essential to a cost-effective, timely delivery of undamaged goods. We strongly advise you to consult your shipping representative, insurance agent, or freight broker for advice on packing and shipping.

Most ships and larger boats will arrive at a U.S. port of entry under their own power. The exporter and importer must see that they are fully seaworthy prior to the transfer and voyage. Smaller vessels and other components may be packed aboard larger carriers. Care must be taken that these are stowed in such a manner as to avoid damage en route from shifting, moisture, or other hazard.

Publications and WWW Resources

The *Harmonized Tariff Schedule of the United States (2001)* (HTSUS) is available to view on the Customs Service website (www.customs.gov), or you may purchase a printed version from:

U.S. Government Printing Office
Superintendent of Documents
710 North Capital Street NW
Washington DC 20401
Tel: (202) 512-1800
Fax: (202) 512-1657
Website: www.access.gpo.gov

The USGPO also has copies of specific laws available for purchase. The USGPO accepts orders made by fax, phone or placed over the Internet, as well as mail orders paid by credit card. All orders must be accompanied by payment. Credit cards, checks drawn on a U.S. bank, or an international money order are all acceptable.

Relevant Government Agencies

Address questions regarding the importation of pleasure boats to:

U.S. Coast Guard (USCG)
Recreational Boating Product Assurance Division
2100 2nd St. SW
Washington DC 20593
Tel: (202) 267-0984
Website: www.uscgboating.org

Address questions regarding the use of foreign-built or foreign flag vessels to:

U.S. Customs and Border Protection
Office of Regulations and Rulings
Entry Procedures & Carrier Rulings Branch
1300 Pennsylvania Avenue NW
Washington DC 20229
Tel: (202) 572-8730
Website: www.customs.treas.gov

Address any other questions regarding the importation of ships or boats to your local Customs port director. For addresses refer to "U.S. Customs and Border Protection Offices" on page 65 or contact:

U.S. Customs and Border Protection
Customs Headquarters
1300 Pennsylvania Avenue NW
Washington DC 20229
Tel: (202) 354-1000
Website: www.customs.treas.gov

Principal Exporting Countries

The following listing includes samples of the main supplier nations of the products of this chapter. It is organized by HTSUS major heading. (Refer to "Customs Classification" above for the product codes.) Countries are listed in rank order of the value of products imported to the U.S. Statistics represent customs value of entries for 2002 from the Bureau of Census, U.S. Department of Commerce.

8901—Canada, United Kingdom, Philippines, Luxembourg, Germany, Japan, New Zealand

8902—Canada, Australia, Mexico

8903—Canada, Taiwan, Italy, United Kingdom, Japan, France, Australia

8904—Norway, New Zealand, Canada

8905—Romania, Canada, Singapore, United Kingdom, Netherlands, Australia, Mexico

8906—Canada, United Kingdom, Norway, China, Germany, Denmark, New Zealand, Australia, Russia

8907—Finland, Canada, China, Denmark, France, United Kingdom, Norway

8908—Finland, Italy

Chapter 90: Optical, Medical, and Precision Instruments

Full title: Optical, Photographic, Cinematographic, Measuring, Checking, Precision, Medical, or Surgical Instruments and Apparatus; Parts and Accessories Thereof

This section pertains to the importation of optical, medical, and precision instruments, which are classified within Chapter 90 of the Harmonized Tariff Schedule of the United States (HTSUS). Chapter 90 encompasses a broad range of equipment, including optical fibers; lenses, prisms, and mirrors; eyeglasses, sunglasses, and goggles; binoculars and telescopes; still and movie cameras and projectors; film developing equipment; photocopiers; microscopes; magnifiers; navigational instruments; surveying instruments; scales; drafting and measuring devices; medical apparatus, equipment, and supplies; X-ray machines; testing and analytic equipment; gauges and regulators; and parts and accessories of these items.

If you are interested in importing specific components of machines made of vulcanized rubber, refer to Commodity Index Chapter 40; of leather, Chapter 42; or of textile materials, Chapters 50-63. Elastic belts and wrappings are covered in Chapters 50-63 under the materials of which they are composed. Laboratory ceramics are found in Chapter 69 and glassware in Chapter 70. Components of precious metals are covered in Chapter 71. Some associated equipment is covered in Chapter 84, while electronics not specifically listed in Chapter 90 are found in Chapter 85 (including some fiber optic cables). Timepieces are covered in Chapter 91; some medical and auxiliary furniture and light fixtures are found in Chapter 94; and toy articles of optical, medical, precision instruments are covered in Chapter 95. Parts of general use—such as screws, nuts and bolts, and nails—are classified within the headings covering the materials of which they are composed (Chapters 72-83 or Chapter 39).

Note: To understand key issues that will enable you to make best use of the information in this section we recommend that you see "Introduction" on page 425.

Key Factors

The key factors in the importation of optical, medical, and precision instruments are:

- Compliance with U.S. Food and Drug Administration (FDA) requirements for medical devices and for radiation-producing devices
- Compliance with FDA entry notification and procedures
- Compliance with U.S. Federal Communications Commission (FCC) standards and entry notification for radio frequency devices

Although most importers utilize the services of a licensed customs broker in making their entries, and we recommend this practice, you should be aware of the regulatory, entry, and documentation issues involved in importing your product. You, as importer, are ultimately responsible for the fulfillment of any legal requirements applicable to your shipment.

General Considerations

Importation of optical products—such as cameras and binoculars—is straightforward. There are no restrictions or prohibitions. No permits, licenses, or special entry paperwork are required.

Categories. From a regulatory viewpoint, many electronic devices subject to regulation fall into two general categories: those that produce radio frequency energy, and those that produce radiation. Radiation-producing electronic devices are regulated by the FDA (see addresses at end of this chapter) under the provisions of the Federal Food, Drug, and Cosmetic Act (FDCA) and the Radiation Control for Health and Safety Act of 1968 (RCHSA). Both imported and domestically produced electronic products must comply with all relevant FDA regulations. Whether you are importing a single product for personal use, or a commercial shipment for resale in the U.S., you must file an Electronic Product Declaration, **Form FD2877** for each product type for which official standards exist. You will not be permitted to enter a shipment unless you have filed these forms. You may obtain them from FDA, National Center for Devices and Radiological Health (see addresses at end of this chapter) or from your customs broker. For a discussion of FDA import procedures, see "Appendix: Foods" on page 825.

Radio frequency (rf) devices are regulated by the FCC (see addresses at end of this chapter) under the provisions of 47 CFR Parts 2 and 15. You must file a copy of FCC **Form 740** with each shipment of rf devices. If your shipment consists of more than one type of device, you must file a separate form for each type. The form certifies that the imported model or device is either in compliance with, or is exempt from, FCC requirements, and is so labeled. An FCC entry declaration form (FCC **Form 740**) is required for products covered under FCC regulations.

Some products, such as ultrasonic therapeutic devices and television receivers, fall under the jurisdiction of both the FCC and the FDA and must comply with both sets of regulations. Although for purposes of simplicity this section will discuss the two categories as if they do not overlap, they do, and you should ascertain exactly which regulations your product is required to meet for which agency. Do not rely on one agency for information concerning the requirements of another agency. If you are in doubt as to the status of your commodity, contact both the FCC and the FDA.

Medical Devices. Importation of medical products, including radioisotopes and radioactive materials, is regulated by the FDA, under the Federal Food, Drug, and Cosmetic Act (FDCA), as amended by the Medical Device Amendments of 1976 (MDA). MDA defines a device as any health-care product that does not achieve any of its principal intended purposes by chemical action in or on the body, or by being metabolized. For example, eyeglasses (both prescription and nonprescription) are considered medical devices, as is the syringe that injects a vaccine (although the vaccine itself is not a device).

Entry Requirements. Imported products regulated by the FDA are subject to FDA port of entry inspection. . The FDA controls radiation-emitting electrical devices under the provisions of the Radiation Control for Health and Safety Act of 1968, as amended (RCHSA). An Electronic Product Declaration **Form FD2877** must be filed for every product type for which official standards exist. No medical devices (or other electronic instruments affected by the requirements) will be admitted unless these documents are filed and approved. For a general discussion of required FDA import procedures see "Appendix: Foods" on page 825.

Shipment Detention. If your shipment is found to be noncomplying, it may be detained at the port of entry. In the case of products subject to FDA jurisdiction, the FDA may permit you to bring such a shipment into compliance before making a final decision regarding admittance. However, any sorting, reprocessing, or relabeling must be supervised by FDA personnel, and will be done at the importer's expense. Such conditional release to allow an importer to bring a shipment into compliance is a privilege, not a right. The FDA may consider subsequent noncomplying shipments of the same type of product to constitute abuse of the privilege and require the importer to destroy or reexport the products. To ascertain what your legal responsibilities are, you should contact these agencies regarding the specific items to be imported.

Customs Classification

For customs purposes optical, medical, and precision instruments are classified within Chapter 90 of the HTSUS. This chapter is divided into major headings, which are further divided into subheadings, and often into sub-subheadings, each of which has its own HTSUS classification number. For example, the 2001 HTSUS number for parts and accessories of X-ray tubes is 9022.90.40, indicating that it is a subcategory of other apparatus, including parts and accessories (9022.90), which is a subcategory of the major heading apparatus based on the use of X-rays for medical uses (9022). There are 33 major headings in HTSUS Chapter 90.

9001—Optical fibers and optical fiber bundles; optical fiber cables other than those of heading 8544; sheets and plates of polarizing material; lenses (including contact lenses), prisms, mirrors, other optical elements, of any material, unmounted, other than such elements of glass not optically worked

9002—Lenses, prisms, mirrors, and other optical elements, of any material, mounted, being parts of or fittings for instruments or apparatus, other than such elements of glass not optically worked; parts and accessories thereof

9003—Frames and mountings for spectacles, goggles, or the like, and parts thereof

9004—Spectacles, goggles, and the like, corrective, protective, or other

9005—Binoculars, monoculars, other optical telescopes, and mountings thereof; other astronomical instruments and mountings therefor, but not including instruments for radio-astronomy; parts and accessories thereof

9006—Photographic (other than cinematographic) cameras; photographic flashlight apparatus and flashbulbs other than discharge lamps of heading 8539; parts and accessories thereof

9007—Cinematographic cameras and projectors, whether or not incorporating sound recording or reproducing apparatus; parts and accessories thereof

9008—Image projectors, other than cinematographic; photographic (other than cinematographic) enlargers and reducers; parts and accessories thereof

9009—Photocopying apparatus incorporating an optical system or of the contact type and thermocopying apparatus; parts and accessories thereof

9010—Apparatus and equipment for photographic (including cinematographic) laboratories (including apparatus for the projection or drawing of circuit patterns on sensitized semiconductor materials), not specified or included elsewhere in this chapter; negatoscopes; projection screens; parts and accessories thereof

9011—Compound optical microscopes, including those for photomicrography, cinemicrography or microprojection; parts and accessories

9012—Microscopes other than optical microscopes; diffraction apparatus; parts and accessories thereof.

9013—Liquid crystal devices not constituting articles provided for more specifically in other headings; lasers, other than laser diodes; other optical appliances and instruments, not specified or included elsewhere in this chapter; parts and accessories thereof

9014—Direction finding compasses; other navigational instruments and appliances; parts and accessories thereof

9015—Surveying (including photogrammetrical surveying), hydrographic, oceanographic, hydrological, meteorological, or geophysical instruments and appliances, excluding compasses; rangefinders; parts and accessories thereof

9016—Balances of a sensitivity of a 5 cg or better, with or without weights; parts and accessories thereof

9017—Drawing, marking-out, or mathematical calculating instruments (for example, drafting machines, pantographs, protractors, drawing sets, slide rules, disc calculators); instruments for measuring length, for use in the hand (for example, measuring rods and tapes, micrometers, calipers), not specified or included elsewhere in this chapter; parts and accessories thereof

9018—Instruments and appliances used in medical, surgical, dental, or veterinary sciences, including scintigraphic apparatus, other electro-medical apparatus, and sight-testing instruments; parts and accessories thereof

9019—Mechano-therapy appliances; massage apparatus; psychological aptitude-testing apparatus; ozone therapy, oxygen therapy, aerosol therapy, artificial respiration, or other therapeutic respiration apparatus; parts and accessories thereof

9020—Other breathing appliances and gas masks, excluding protective masks having neither mechanical parts nor replaceable filters; parts and accessories thereof

9021—Orthopedic appliances, including crutches, surgical belts, and trusses; splints and other fracture appliances; artificial parts of the body; hearing aids and other appliances which are worn or carried or implanted in the body, to compensate for a defect or disability; parts and accessories thereof

9022—Apparatus based on the use of X-rays or of alpha, beta, or gamma radiations, whether or not for medical, surgical, dental, or veterinary uses, including radiography or radiotherapy apparatus, X-ray tubes and other X-ray generators, high tension generators, control panels, and desks, screens, examination or treatment tables, chairs, and the like; parts and accessories thereof

9023—Instruments, apparatus, and models, designed for demonstrational purposes (for example, in education or exhibitions), unsuitable for other uses, and parts and accessories thereof

9024—Machines and appliances for testing the hardness, strength, compressibility, elasticity or other mechanical properties of materials (for example, metals, woods, textiles, paper, plastics), and parts and accessories thereof

9025—Hydrometers and similar floating instruments, thermometers, pyrometers, barometers, hygrometers, and psychrometers, recording or not, and any combination of these instruments; parts and accessories thereof

9026—Instruments and apparatus for measuring or checking the flow, level, pressure or other variables of liquids or gases (for example, flow meters, level gauges, manometers, heat meters), excluding instruments and apparatus of heading 9014, 9015, 9028, or 9032; parts and accessories thereof

9027—Instruments and apparatus for physical or chemical analysis (for example, polarimeters, refractometers, spectrometers, gas or smoke analysis apparatus); instruments and apparatus for measuring or checking viscosity, porosity, expansion, surface tension, or the like; instruments and apparatus for measuring or checking quantities of heat, sound or light (including exposure meters); microtomes; parts and accessories thereof

9028—Gas, liquid or electricity supply or production meters, including calibrating meters thereof; parts and accessories thereof

9029—Revolution counters, production counters, taximeters, odometers, pedometers, and the like; speedometers and tachometers; other than those of heading 9014 or 9015; stroboscopes; parts and accessories thereof

9030—Oscilloscopes, spectrum analyzers, and other instruments and apparatus for measuring or checking electrical quantities, excluding meters of heading 9028; instruments and apparatus for measuring or detecting alpha, beta, gamma, X-ray, cosmic or other ionizing radiations; parts and accessories thereof

9031—Measuring and checking instruments, appliances and machines, not specified or included elsewhere in this chapter; profile projectors; parts and accessories thereof

9032—Automatic regulating or controlling instruments and apparatus; parts and accessories thereof

9033—Parts and accessories (not specified or included elsewhere in this chapter) for machines and appliances, instruments, or apparatus of chapter 90

For more details regarding classification of the specific product you are interested in importing, consult a customs broker, the appropriate commodity specialist at your nearest customs port, or see HTSUS. The 2001 HTSUS is available online from the Customs Service (www.customs.gov/impoexpo/impoexpo.htm) or for purchase from the U.S. Government Printing Office (see resources at the end of this chapter), and may be found in larger public libraries. For a general discussion of customs classification, see "Classification—Liquidation" on page 229.

Dutiable Status of Goods

For more information about duty rates and binding decisions see "Dutiable Status of Goods" on page 203; for a discussion of temporary importation of goods see "Temporary Free Importations" on page 205.

Valuation

Importers have a responsibility to use what the U.S. Customs Service deems, "reasonable care," when determining the value of their goods. They must also provide any additional information that the Customs Service needs for setting a final value on the goods. This process involves a number of factors and can be somewhat complicated; importers must be aware of applicable issues and details. Valuation information applies to all types of commodities, for further discussion on the subject see "Customs Valuation" on page 267.

Import Duties

Import duties vary (often dramatically) depending upon the Harmonized Tariff Schedule (HTSUS) classification of the goods or products imported. Since some products that look alike have different HTSUS classifications and different rates of duty, proper classification is vital. Note that "differences of opinion" between importers and the Bureau of Customs and Border Protection regarding classification keeps customs attorneys very busy.

Import duties can be assessed on the imported value of the goods ("ad valorem" rates of duty such as 2%, 4.4%, 50%, etc.), total units or weight of the goods ("specific" rates of duty such as 2 cents each or 1.5 cents/pound, etc.) or on a combination basis ("compound" rates of duty such as 5 cents each plus 6%).

Listed below is a sampling of several Column 1 import duty rates for Chapter 90 products:

Mounted lenses suitable for use in, and entered separately from, closed-circuit television cameras, with or without attached electrical or non-electrical closed-circuit television camera connectors, and with or without attached motors (9002.11.60.00): Free

to ·
Prisms (9001.90.50.00): 2.8%

For specific information on US import duties refer to the Harmonized Tariff Schedule of the US. The print version is available from the US Government Printing Office as well as third party suppliers who often add special features. Online versions are available in both static PDF pages as well as in formats with excellent search functionality. Search the Web with the term "Harmonized Tariff Schedule" to find sources.

Entry and Documentation

The entry of merchandise is a two-part process consisting of 1) filing the documents necessary to determine whether merchandise may be released from Customs custody and 2) filing the documents that contain information for duty assessment and statistical purposes. In certain instances all documents must be filed and accepted by Customs prior to the release of the goods. Unless you have been granted an extension, you must file entry documents at a location specified by the port or area director within five working days of your shipment's date of arrival at a U.S. port of entry. These include a number of standard documents required by Customs for any entry, and:

- FDA Electronic Product Declaration Form FD 2877for radiation-emitting devices

- FCC Declaration Form 740 for radio frequency devices

After you present the entry, Customs may examine your shipment, or may waive examination. The shipment is then released provided no legal or regulatory violations have been noted. You must then file entry summary documentation and deposit estimated duties at a designated customhouse within 10 working days of your shipment's release. For a detailed description of entry procedures, standard documentation, and informal entry, see "Entry Process" on page 185.

Informed Compliance. Informed compliance was introduced with the Customs Modernization Act of 1993 (Mod Act) and defines the relationship between importers and the Customs Service. It sets out the responsibilities of both parties. Providing the correct documentation and information for entry is a key factor that will make your importing operation run smoothly. We recommend that importers become familiar with the concept of informed comliance and the responsibilities that they have under the Mod Act. For further discussion about informed compliance see "Informed Compliance" on page 211.

Note: The Entry and Documentation section has been carefully designed to supply you, the importer, with sample documents and directions on how to satisfy Customs requirements. Be aware that you should consult the applicable authorities to ensure that you are correctly following the most current procedures.

Prohibitions and Restrictions

If you wish to import medical devices into the U.S., you should bear in mind that your products are likely to be detained if they do not comply with all applicable requirements under the FDCA.Nonprescription devices must also comply with the Fair Packaging and Labeling Act (FPLA). Manufacturers of finished devices intended for importation into the U.S. must comply with the FDA's Good Manufacturing Practice regulations. If your shipment was produced by a manufacturer that does not comply with these regulations, it may be detained at the port of entry.

Medical devices include several thousand health products, from simple articles such as thermometers, tongue depressors, and heating pads, to intrauterine contraceptive devices, heart pacemakers, and kidney dialysis machines. The term "devices" also includes components, parts, or accessories of devices, diagnostic aids such as reagents, antibiotic sensitivity discs, and test kits for invitro diagnosis of disease (e.g., diabetes), and other conditions, (e.g., pregnancy).

Classification of Devices. The FDCA, as amended, requires that the FDA classify all devices intended for human use marketed in the U.S. prior to passage of the Medical Device Amendments of 1976 (MDA) ("pre-amendment devices") into one of three regulatory classes. This ensures that each device is subject to controls appropriate for it.

Class I: General Controls. Class I products are subject only to the general controls applicable to all devices. General controls include manufacturer registration, recordkeeping requirements, labeling requirements, and Good Manufacturing Practice regulations. (See "Requirements for all devices" below.)

Class II: Performance Standards. The FDA establishes performance standards for devices for which general controls are deemed insufficient in and of themselves to ensure safety and effectiveness, and for which adequate information exists to develop such a standard. Class II devices must meet applicable FDA performance standards. Performance standards may specify materials, construction, components, ingredients, labeling, and other properties of the device. A standard may also provide for device testing to ensure that different lots of individual products conform to requirements. Regulations establishing performance standards for Class II devices are found in 21 CFR Part 861.

Class III: Premarket Approval. Unless it determines that such approval is unnecessary, the FDA requires official approval for implants and life-supporting or life-sustaining devices prior to marketing. Premarket approval applications for pre-amendment Class III devices cannot be required until 30 months after they are classified or until 90 days after a regulation calling for the application, whichever comes later. Premarket approval can also be required for other devices if general controls are deemed insufficient to ensure safety and effectiveness and there is inadequate information to establish a performance standard.

Post-MDA Devices. For purposes of regulation, there are two types of devices marketed after the passage of the MDA: those that are and those that are not substantially the same as a pre-amendment device. New devices that are substantially equivalent to a pre-amendment device are classified the same as the equivalent pre-amendment product. Those not considered substantially equivalent are automatically placed in Class III, requiring premarket approval.

Pre-amendment and post-amendment devices regarded as new drugs (e.g., soft contact lenses) prior to MDA are automatically classified in Class III. Regulations on classification of devices are found in 21 CFR 860, 862-890.

Reclassification. Any interested person may petition the FDA to reclassify a device either to lower the classification from III to II or from II to I, or in some instances to raise the classification. For example, a manufacturer may decide to submit a petition when new product information becomes available on a device, or when the FDA finds that a new product is not substantially equivalent to a pre-amendment device and thus is automatically put in Class III. The FDA may also begin a reclassification action on its own initiative. Regulations on reclassification of devices are found in 21 CFR 860, Subpart C.

Premarket Notification for New Devices. A premarket notification or 510(k) submission is required when the following occurs: (a) a foreign manufacturer intends to export a medical device to the U.S. that the firm has never before shipped to the U.S.; (b) either the foreign manufacturer or initial distributor changes the intended uses of devices that are legally being marketed in the U.S.; or (c) changes or modifications to a legally marketed device that could significantly affect its safety or effectiveness. During the 90-day notification period, the FDA determines whether the device is or is not equivalent to a pre-amendment device. If the

FDA determines that the device is not equivalent, it is automatically placed in Class III, and the manufacturer must provide FDA with a premarket approval application containing evidence that the device is safe and effective. The device may not be commercially distributed to the public until the FDA approves the application. However, the manufacturer may try to convince the FDA to reclassify the device by filing a reclassification petition.

A premarket notification to the FDA must include the following information: 1) the device's trade and common name; 2) labeling and advertisements describing the device, its intended use, and directions for use; 3) the device's classification; and 4) a statement detailing the device's similarity to or difference from others on the market, accompanied by supporting data.

Premarket notification regulations are found in 21 CFR 807, Subpart E. Detailed information regarding the premarket notification process can be obtained from the publications: *Premarket Notification: 510(k), Regulatory Requirements for Marketing a Device,* and *510(k) Review Program.*

Requirements for All Devices. All medical devices are subject to general control requirements.

Adulteration. The FDA may initiate an enforcement action (seizure, injunction, or prosecution) to protect the public from adulterated or misbranded devices (Sec. 501). A device is considered adulterated under any of the following conditions: 1) it has been manufactured, packed, or held under insanitary conditions; 2) its container is composed of a dangerous substance; 3) it contains an unsafe color additive; 4) its quality or purity falls below that which it purports to possess; 5) it does not comply with an applicable performance standard; 6) it is a banned device; 8) it is not manufactured in accordance with Good Manufacturing Practice regulations; or 9) it is an investigational device that fails to comply with applicable requirements under investigational device regulations.

Misbranding. A device is considered misbranded under any of the following conditions (Sec. 502): 1) its labeling is false or misleading; 2) its label does not contain the name and address of manufacturer, packer, or distributor, and an accurate statement of quality of contents; 3) required information is not prominently and legibly placed on the label in English; 4) the device's established name does not appear in type at least half as large as the proprietary name used; 5) its labeling does not bear adequate directions for use and adequate warnings against unsafe use; 6) it is dangerous to health; 7) it is a restricted device and its advertisements are false or misleading or do not meet minimum requirements for disclosure of product information; 8) it is a restricted device and it is not sold, distributed, or used in compliance with regulations; 9) it does not comply with an applicable performance standard labeling requirement; 10) it was made in an establishment not registered under Section 510, or not listed under Section 510(j), or if a notice respecting a device was not provided as required by Section 510(h); or 11) there was a failure to comply with a requirement under Section 518 (notification and other remedies) or Section 519 (records and reports). General labeling requirements are found in 21 CFR 801; in vitro diagnostics labeling requirements are in 21 CFR 809.

Registration and Device Listing. Every person who owns or operates any domestic establishment engaged in manufacturing a medical device intended for human use must register that establishment and list its products with the FDA (Sec. 510). This requirement also applies to any repacker, relabeler, and initial distributor of imported devices. The following are exempted (21 CFR 807) from registration and listing: 1) manufacturers of raw materials or components used in manufacturing a finished device; 2) licensed practitioners manufacturing or altering devices solely for use in practice (physicians, dentists, optometrists, clinical laboratories, etc.); 3) pharmacies and retail outlets; 4) re-

searchers, teachers, or analysts; 5) wholesalers or common carriers whose function is to process a previously manufactured device in order to comply with the needs of the individual consumer.

You may register by submitting a completed Form FD 2891. To obtain this form, contact: FDA, HFZ-342 (see addresses at end of this chapter), or any FDA District Office. Regulations for registration and device listing are contained in 21 CFR 807.

Good Manufacturing Practice Regulations. Manufacturers of finished devices must comply with regulations prescribing current Good Manufacturing Practice for devices. Designed to prevent the production of defective products, these regulations include requirements for building maintenance, personnel training, recordkeeping, equipment design and maintenance, and packaging and labeling controls (21 CFR 820). The FDA revised the good manufacturing practice (CGMP) requirements for medical devices and incorporated them into a quality system regulation in 1996. The quality system regulation includes requirements related to the methods used in, and the facilities and controls used for, designing, manufacturing, packaging, labeling, storing, installing, and servicing of medical devices intended for human use. This was done in order to add preproduction design controls and to achieve consistency with quality system requirements worldwide. The regulation sets forth the framework for device manufacturers to follow and gives them greater flexibility in achieving quality requirements. For more information, refer to the *Federal Register,* October 6, 1996, Vol. 61, No. 195, p. 52601–52662.

Inspection, Administrative Detention, and Records and Reports. FDA investigators are authorized to enter and inspect any factory, warehouse, or establishment where devices are manufactured, processed, packed, or held. Upon approval of the FDA District Office Director, an investigator may order a firm to detain, for a period of up to 30 days, a device that the investigator suspects is adulterated or misbranded (21 CFR 800). Manufacturers of restricted devices must permit FDA investigators to inspect the premises and documents kept there—including all records, files, papers, processes, controls, and facilities with the exception of certain financial, sales, personnel, or research data (Secs. 704 and 304). Manufacturers of all devices must permit investigators to inspect records required by Good Manufacturing Practice regulations.

Should you receive information that one of your devices has been responsible for, or is associated with, a death or serious injury, you are required to notify the FDA's Center for Devices and Radiological Health and the local FDA field office as soon as possible. Such notification must be made within five calendar days. Any other problems with devices should be reported within 15 working days.

Notification, Repairs, Replacements, and Refunds. The FDA can order manufacturers to notify the public of any product defect that could constitute a health hazard, and can order manufacturers to repair, replace, or refund the cost of these defective devices. (Sec. 518).

Banned Devices. The FDA may issue a regulation banning any device that presents a substantial deception or substantial and unreasonable risk of causing injury or illness. When a change in labeling may suffice to bring a product into compliance, manufacturers are provided the opportunity to correct the device's labeling before a ban is initiated. Where a device presents an unreasonable, direct, or substantial danger, FDA may order the ban to take effect upon publication of the proposed banning regulation. Procedural regulations are found in 21 CFR 895.

Investigational Devices. Investigational devices (Sec. 520) are those used on human subjects by qualified experts, in order to conduct investigations of device safety and effectiveness. The

FDA may grant such sponsors exemptions from certain FDCA requirements that would otherwise impede their studies. If you wish to obtain such an exemption, you must file an Application for an Investigational Device Exemption with the FDA. FDA regulations designed to protect the subjects of research on investigational devices are found in 21 CFR 812 (general) and 813 (intraocular lenses).

Custom Devices. Custom devices are devices ordered by members of the health professions to conform to their own special needs or to those of their patients (e.g. certain dental devices and specially designed orthopedic footwear). These are exempt from registration and from otherwise applicable performance standards or premarket approval requirements (Sec. 520). The exemption applies only to devices not generally available to or used by other health professionals. Custom devices are not exempt from other provisions of the Act and regulations.

Procedures. The importer of medical devices into the U.S. is required to register with the FDA, just as is any domestic manufacturer of similar devices. In addition, if the shipment represents the initial importation of the device into the U.S., the manufacturer is required to file a premarket notification with the FDA. If the FDA determines that the device is in Class III and requires premarket approval prior to import, the agency will deny importation until 1) a premarket approval application is approved; or 2) the device is reclassified to Class I or Class II; or 3) an investigational device exemption is in effect. If the device is reclassified into Class I or Class II, and other applicable FDCA requirements are met, the FDA will allow importation. For more details contact the FDA (see addresses at end of this chapter).

Radiation-producing Devices. The comprehensive Radiation Control for Health and Safety Act (RCHSA) was enacted in 1968 to protect the public from unnecessary exposure to radiation from electronic products. FDA administration of the law is carried out through the setting and enforcement of radiation performance standards to limit radiation emissions. The standards apply to products offered for sale or use in the U.S., whether manufactured in this country or elsewhere. Electronic products include all products or equipment capable of emitting ionizing or nonionizing radiation, or sonic, infrasonic, or ultrasonic waves. Television receivers, microwave ovens, X-ray equipment, lasers, ultraviolet lights, diathermy units, infrared heaters, ultrasonic cleaners, and particle accelerators are examples of products required to comply with RCHSA. Regulations for the enforcement of the act are published in 21 CFR Parts 1000-1050. The law is enforced by FDA's Center for Devices and Radiological Health (CDRH) (see addresses at end of this chapter).

Radiation Performance Standards and Product Certification. Performance standards are prescribed for electronic products when the FDA determines that federal regulations are necessary for the protection of the public health and safety. The standards (21 CFR Parts 1020-1050) prescribe maximum allowable radiation levels and other approaches to control of radiation emission, without specifying design features. If you are interested in importing a radiation-producing product, you should ascertain whether or not it is subject to a standard. The manufacturer of an electronic product for which there is an applicable federal performance standard must obtain certification for the product. Certification is based upon a test prescribed by the standard, or a testing program that is in accord with Good Manufacturing Practices as determined by CDRH. When considering an overseas purchase, you must determine that the product is in compliance. Approved products must bear a certification label stating that the product conforms to the applicable standard. Keep in mind that it is not as simple to identify a product that is eligible for certification but has not been certified. When in doubt, contact the FDA.

Noncomplying or Defective Products. RCHSA specifically provides that test samples may be taken from any import shipment to determine whether a product complies with an applicable standard. The FDA may—through authorization from the U.S. Customs Service—take a sample from your shipment for testing. Such samples are returned after testing is completed. If your product is discovered not to meet the provisions of an applicable standard, or if it contains any defect related to its safe use by reason of radiation emissions, the FDA will refuse entry. The manufacturer of a defective electronic product that has entered the commercial market is responsible for notifying the consumer, repairing the defect, and replacing the product or refunding the purchaser's money.

Recordkeeping. The FDA requires dealers and distributors of electronic products for which standards have been issued to maintain records. These records are intended to facilitate the location of purchasers for notification concerning defective or noncomplying devices, or to facilitate the recall of such products. In addition, manufacturers of certain electronic products designated by the regulation are required to maintain relevant product testing records and to make reports necessary to demonstrate compliance with the act.

Products Covered by Radiation Performance Standards. The following products for medical use are currently covered by federal radiation performance standards. If you are considering importation of any of these products, be sure that the foreign manufacturer has obtained U.S. certification and has so labeled the items before attempting to enter a shipment into U.S. Customs territory. Uncertified products—even those that are eligible for certification—are refused entry, and any disposal or modification is undertaken at the importer's expense. Further information may be obtained from any FDA office or by referring to 21 CFR Parts 1000-1050.

Television Receivers. Standard effective January 15, 1970. Applies to television receivers designed to receive and display a television picture, and includes electronic viewfinders on TV cameras, TV projectors, and TV monitors used with X-ray and other medical systems.

Diagnostic X-ray Equipment. Standard effective August 1, 1974. Applies to complete diagnostic X-ray systems, as well as major components, including tube-housing assemblies, X-ray controls, high voltage X-ray generators, fluoroscopic imaging assemblies, X-ray tables, cradles, film changers, cassette holders, and beam limiting devices.

Cabinet X-ray Systems. Standard effective April 10, 1975. In addition to baggage inspection system, applies to other X-ray machines in enclosed freestanding cabinets.

Laser Products. Standard effective August 2, 1976. Amendment effective August 20, 1985, applies to all laser products, as well as products containing lasers.

Sunlamp Products and Ultraviolet Lamps for Use in Sunlamp Products. Standard May 7, 1980. Applies to all sunlamp products and ultraviolet lamps intended to induce sun-tanning.

Ultrasonic Therapy Products. Standard effective February 17, 1979. Applies to any device intended to generate and emit ultrasonic radiation for therapeutic purposes at frequencies above 16 kilohertz, or any generator or applicator designed or specifically designated for use in such a device.

Note: Many foreign manufacturers produce electronic devices for export that conform to applicable FDA and FCC regulations. If you limit your purchases to such products and verify that the appropriate labels are affixed, you should have no difficulty with U.S. Customs entry.

Radio Frequency Devices. Under the Communications Act of 1934, as amended, all radio frequency (rf) devices are subject to FCC radio emission standards. You must file an FCC declaration FCC Form 740 certifying that your model or device is in conformity with, will be brought into conformity with, or is exempt from the FCC requirements, for each shipment of rf devices you import. FCC standards and procedures have been developed to limit potential sources of rf interference to authorized radio services in the U.S. The FCC defines a radio frequency device as a product that emits rf energy, either intentionally or as a design byproduct. Radio frequency devices must meet specific FCC equipment authorization standards. When rf devices are imported into the U.S., a declaration is required that states that the appropriate FCC authorization has been granted. This declaration is made on FCC Form 740.

Equipment Authorization. FCC equipment authorization is required for certain types of rf devices imported into the U.S. Although compliance with these procedures is the responsibility of the foreign manufacturer, you should be aware of them, since non-complying shipments will not be permitted entry. Equipment authorization procedures include: 1) type approval (requires testing of equipment sample); 2) type acceptance (requires review and evaluation of written application and equipment test report); 3) certification (requires review and evaluation of written application and equipment test report); 4) notification (requires submission of brief application; 5) verification (manufacturer tests device for compliance with FCC regulations prior to marketing, and retains test data); 6) registration (applies to subscriber-owned and common-carrier-owned telephone devices; requires review and evaluation of written application and test report). Except for verification and registration procedures, a separate FCC **Form 731** should be filed with the FCC for each type of device for which equipment authorization is being requested. FCC **Form 730** is used for registration of telephone equipment under Part 68 of FCC rules. No application is required for verification. Fees are required for equipment authorization filings. Fee information is available from any FCC office or by calling the FCC Licensing Division at 800-322-1117. If you would like more complete details regarding authorization procedures, contact the nearest regional FCC office, or the FCC Office of Engineering and Technology in Washington, D.C. (see addresses at end of this chapter).

Importation of Radio Frequency Devices. Each time you import a shipment of rf devices, you must file a separate FCC **Form 740** for each type of rf device represented in your shipment. Send your original completed **Form 740(s)** to the FCC Field Operations Bureau in Washington, D.C. (see addresses at end of this chapter). Attach a copy of your form(s) to the customs entry summary for your shipment, and present it to customs at the U.S. port of entry. For more information, contact any FCC office, or the FCC Washington headquarters (see addresses at end of this chapter).

Marking and Labeling Requirements

FDA Requirements. Labeling requirements for devices vary depending upon the device's status under the FDCA. Address questions concerning the current status of your product to the FDA Center for Devices and Radiological Health, Division of Small Manufacturers Assistance (see addresses at end of this chapter). You should provide full information concerning the device and include a copy of the proposed labeling if you are considering shipping the device within the U.S. Proposed labeling may be submitted in draft form and need not be printed.

All radiation-emitting devices for which federal standards have been determined must be certified for compliance. The manufacturer must affix a certification label to each product stating that it conforms to the applicable standard. Products requiring certification that are not so labeled will not be permitted entry.

FCC Requirements. All rf devices subject to FCC authorization procedures, whether manufactured within the U.S. or outside it, must bear labeling to show compliance. Devices that are not so labeled will not be permitted entry into U.S. Customs territory. For details on label wording, contact FCC (see addresses at end of this chapter).

For a general discussion of U.S. Customs marking and labeling requirements, see "Country of Origin Marking" on page 236, "Special Marking Requirements" on page 238 and "Marking—False Impression" on page 239.

Shipping Considerations

You will need to ensure that your goods are packaged and shipped with care to ensure that they arrive in good condition and pass smoothly through Customs. You are responsible for ensuring that the shipment is in compliance with all applicable government regulations for packaging and shipping. In most instances, you should not leave these arrangements solely to the discretion of your supplier. Careful preparation of the cargo and selection of the mode of transport can be essential to a cost-effective, timely delivery of undamaged goods. We strongly advise you to consult your shipping representative, insurance agent, or freight broker for advice on packing and shipping.

Optical, medical, and precision instruments are usually fragile and should be securely packed and stowed to avoid damage due to shifting en route. Special care must be taken to ensure that they are adequately protected from excessive vibration, heat, humidity, or water damage.

Publications and WWW Resources

The following publication explains the FDA requirements for importing optical, medical and precision instruments. It is published by the FDA and is available online from the FDA website (www.fda.gov/opacom/7pubs.html).

> *Requirements of Laws and Regulations Enforced by the U.S. Food and Drug Administration*

The following bulletin is available from any regional FCC office and online (www.fcc.gov/oet/info/documents/bulletins/).

> *FCC Equipment Authorization Program for Radio Frequency Devices* (Bulletin Number 61)

The *Harmonized Tariff Schedule of the United States (2001)* (HTSUS) is available to view on the Customs Service website (www.customs.gov), or you may purchase a printed version from:

> **U.S. Government Printing Office**
> **Superintendent of Documents**
> 710 North Capital Street NW
> Washington DC 20401
> Tel: (202) 512-1800
> Fax: (202) 512-1657
> Website: www.access.gpo.gov

The USGPO also has copies of specific laws available for purchase. The USGPO accepts orders made by fax, phone or placed over the Internet, as well as mail orders paid by credit card. All orders must be accompanied by payment. Credit cards, checks drawn on a U.S. bank, or an international money order are all acceptable.

Relevant Government Agencies

Address requests for information, forms, instructions regarding establishment registration and product listing, the current status of a device, or required labeling to:

> **Food and Drug Administration (FDA)**
> **Center for Devices and Radiological Health**
> **Division of Small Manufacturers Assistance**
> 1350 Piccard Drive
> Rockville, MD 20850
> Tel: 800-638-2041
> Fax: (301) 443-8818
> Email: dsmica@cdrh.fda.gov
> Website: www.fda.gov/cdrh

Address inquiries concerning FCC Form 740 requirements to:

Federal Communications Commission (FCC)
Consumer and Governmental Affairs Bureau
445 12th Street SW
Washington DC 20554
(202) 418-1400
Website: www.fcc.gov

Address questions regarding importation of optical, medical, and precision instruments to your local Customs port director. For addresses refer to "U.S. Customs and Border Protection Offices" on page 65 or contact:

U.S. Customs and Border Protection
Customs Headquarters
1300 Pennsylvania Avenue NW
Washington DC 20229
Tel: (202) 354-1000
Website: www.customs.treas.gov

Laws and Regulations

The following laws and regulations may be relevant to the importation of optical, medical, and precision instruments. The laws are contained in the U.S. Code (USC) and the regulations are published in the code of Federal Regulations (CFR), both of which may be available at larger public and law libraries. Copies of specific laws are also available from the United States Government Printing Office (address above).

21 USC 301 et seq.
Federal Food, Drug, and Cosmetic Act
This Act prohibits deceptive practices and regulates the manufacture, sale and importation or exportation of food, drugs, cosmetics, and related products. It was amended by the Food Quality Protection Act of 1996. See 21 USC 331, 381, 382.

19 CFR 12.1 et seq.; 21 CFR 1.83 et seq.
Regulations on Food, Drugs, and Cosmetics
These regulations of the Secretary of Health and Human Services and the Secretary of the Treasury govern the standards, labeling, marking, and importing of products used with food, drugs, and cosmetics.

21 USC 360 et seq.
Radiation Control for Health and Safety Act of 1968
This Act prohibits entry of electronic products found not to be in compliance with prescribed standards. See 21 CFR Part 1005. Customs enforces this prohibition. See 19 CFR 12.90 et seq.

47 USC 302a
Devices That Interfere with Radio Reception
This law prohibits the importation of devices or home electronic equipment that fail to comply with regulations promulgated by the FCC. See 47 CFR 2.1201 et seq. and 18.119. Customs enforces the prohibition.

Principal Exporting Countries

The following listing includes samples of the main supplier nations of the products of this chapter. It is organized by HTSUS major heading. (Refer to "Customs Classification" above for the product codes.) Countries are listed in rank order of the value of products imported to the U.S. Statistics represent customs value of entries for 2002 from the Bureau of Census, U.S. Department of Commerce.

9001—Indonesia, Japan, United Kingdom, Ireland, Germany, Mexico

9002—Japan, Canada, Germany, Netherlands, China, Singapore, South Korea

9003—Italy, China, Japan, Hong Kong, South Korea, Austria, France

9004—China, Italy, Taiwan, Japan, France, Hong Kong, Canada

9005—China, Japan, Israel, Germany, Taiwan, Russia, Austria, Mexico

9006—China, Mexico, Japan, Taiwan, Malaysia, Thailand, Philippines, Hong Kong, Germany

9007—Germany, Japan, Canada, Italy, United Kingdom, South Korea

9008—Japan, China, Canada, United Kingdom, Slovenia, Singapore

9009—Japan, Thailand, China, Mexico, Netherlands, United Kingdom

9010—Japan, Netherlands, Germany, United Kingdom, Switzerland, Itlay, Mexico, Denmark

9011—Germany, Japan, China, United Kingdom, Switzerland

9012—Germany, Israel, Japan, Netherlands, United Kingdom, Czech Republic, China, Switzerland

9013—Japan, Canada, Germany, China, Taiwan, United Kingdom, South Korea

9014—United Kingdom, Mexico, France, Canada, Israel, Germany, Japan

9015—Canada, United Kingdom, Japan, China, Germany, France, Switzerland, Sweden, Norway, Australia, Finland

9016—Switzerland, Germany, China, Japan, United Kingdom, Israel, Philippines, Italy

9017—China, Japan, Taiwan, Sweden, South Korea, Germany, Mexico, Canada, Thailand, United Kingdom

9018—Mexico, Germany, Japan, Ireland, Dominican Republic, Costa Rica, Singapore, Israel, Netherlands, United Kingdom

9019—China, Mexico, Canada, Ireland, New Zealand, Taiwan, Germany, Sweden, South Korea

9020—France, United Kingdom, Germany, Mexico, Italy, Canada, Japan

9021—Ireland, Switzerland, Mexico, Singapore, Germany, France

9022—Germany, Japan, Netherlands, France, Mexico, United Kingdom, Israel, Switzerland

9023—Japan, Canada, Germany, United Kingdom, Netherlands, Sweden, China, Norway

9024—United Kingdom, Germany, Sweden, Japan, Canada, Ireland, Switzerland

9025—China, Mexico, Germany, Japan, Taiwan, Singapore, Finland, Canada, United Kingdom

9026—Mexico, Japan, Germany, United Kingdom, Canada, China, Singapore, Switzerland, France, Taiwan

9027—Japan, Germany, United Kingdom, Canada, China, Switzerland, Sweden, France

9028—Mexico, Canada, Malaysia, Israel, United Kingdom, Germany

9029—Mexico, Japan, Germany, China, Canada, Brazil, Taiwan, Switzerland, Thailand

9030—Japan, Germany, United Kingdom, Canada, Malaysia, France, China, Singapore

9031—Japan, Germany, Canada, United Kingdom, Israel, Mexico

9032—Mexico, Japan, Germany, Canada, United Kingdom, China

9033—Germany, Japan, United Kingdom, Italy, Switzerland, China, Canada

Chapter 91: Clocks and Watches

Full title: Clocks and Watches and Parts Thereof

This section pertains to the importation of watches and clocks, their movements, and parts, which are classified within Chapter 91 of the Harmonized Tariff Schedule of the United States (HTSUS). Specifically, it includes watches and clocks of whatever variety; watch and clock movements; instrument panel clocks; alarm and other types of clocks; time clocks, time and date stamping equipment, and parking meters; time switches; watch and clock cases; watch bands; and other watch and clock parts.

If you are interested in importing watch or clock crystals, refer to Commodity Index Chapter 70; for weights, see Chapters 73-81 for the specific type of material from which they are made. Watch chains and fobs are covered in Chapter 71. Bearings are found in Chapters 73 or 84. Articles that include a clock mechanism as a subsidiary feature—such as a clock-radio—are covered in Chapter 85. Parts of general use—such as screws—are classified within the chapters covering the specific materials of which they are composed. If accessories—such as watchbands and watch batteries—are entered as part of a watch or as part of the package for use with the watch, they are classified with the watch itself; if entered separately, they are covered in the Commodity Index chapter that relates to the materials of which they are made.

Note: To understand key issues that will enable you to make best use of the information in this section we recommend that you see "Introduction" on page 425.

Key Factors

The key factors in the importation of watches and clocks are:

- Compliance with U.S. Customs special marking requirements
- Special duty provisions for watch producers in U.S. insular possessions
- Extra information required on entry invoices

Although most importers utilize the services of a licensed customs broker in making their entries, and we recommend this practice, you should be aware of the regulatory, entry, and documentation issues involved in importing your product. You, as importer, are ultimately responsible for the fulfillment of any legal requirements applicable to your shipment.

General Considerations

Country of Origin. Watches, watch movements, clocks, and clock movements imported into the U.S. must be marked in compliance with both the usual country of origin marking required by customs, and with certain special marking requirements (see "Marking and Labeling Requirements" below) detailed in note 4 of HTSUS Chapter 91. These marking requirements are complex, stringent, and strictly monitored by customs. Customs can be expected to inspect watch and clock shipments to determine compliance. If your shipment does not comply in every respect with marking regulations, it will be denied entry.

Customs considers the origin of the watch or clock to be the origin of its movement, not the country in which it was assembled. If, for example, you wish to import a shipment of items assembled in Hong Kong whose movements were manufactured in Japan, Customs would require the items to be conspicuously labeled to indicate Japan as the country of origin. This is in addition to any requirements the country in which the item was manufactured might have regarding marking for export. The indelible special marking requirements must also be scrupulously followed. If your shipment is not in compliance with these requirements, it will be refused entry. It is virtually impossible for an importer to bring a noncomplying shipment into compliance at the port of entry. Be familiar with marking requirements and make sure the items you are considering comply before you buy them.

Insular Watch Assembly Program. The U.S. Department of Commerce's International Trade Administration (ITA) operates the Insular Watch Assembly Program. This program allows duty-free entry of watches and watch movements into the U.S. by eligible watch producers located in U.S. insular possessions—the U.S. Virgin Islands, Guam, and American Samoa—on an annual licensing basis. To import watches under this program, special documentation must be submitted to customs at the port of entry.

As detailed in note 5 of HTSUS Chapter 91, insular producers of watches may import annually-allocated quantities of product into the U.S. either duty-free or at reduced rates, depending on the percentage of foreign content. The ITA determines annual duty-free import allocations on a licensing basis. Insular watch producers wishing to receive an annual allocation must apply each year, using Form ITA-334P: Application for License to Enter Watches and Watch Movements into the Customs Territory of the United States. If you are issued an allocation, the ITA will send you Form ITA-333: License to Enter Watches and Watch Movements into the Customs Territory of the United States. This form serves as authorization to the territorial government to issue specific shipment permits to you, as well as to record the balance of your remaining duty-exemptions after each shipment permit is issued. If you hold a valid ITA license, the specific territorial government will issue you Form ITA-340: Permit to Enter Watches and Watch Movements into the Customs Territory of the United States. This form authorizes entry of a specified number of watches or watch movements, at a specified U.S. Customs port. It is only valid within the calendar year in which it is issued, and must be presented to Customs when you offer your shipment for entry.

If you participate in the program, you must submit Form ITA-321P: Mid-year Report on Watch Assembly Operations of Firms Granted a Duty-free Watch Allocation, to ITA on or before July 15 of each calendar year. In addition to duty-free allocations, you may be eligible for a Certificate of Entitlement, Form ITA-360 authorizing duty refunds on watches entered into U.S. Customs territory. These refunds are based on specified percentages of your verified creditable wages in the insular possession.

More information concerning rules and participation in the insular watch program see HTSUS or contact the ITA's Statutory Import Programs Staff (address below.)

Customs Classification

For customs purposes watches and clocks are classified within Chapter 91 of the HTSUS. This chapter is divided into major heads ings, which are further divided into subheadings, and often into sub-subheadings, each with its own HTSUS classification. For example, the 2001 HTSUS number for other watches with gold-or silver-plated case is 9102.11.70, indicating that it is a subcategory of watches with a mechanical display only (9102.11), which is a subcategory of the major heading wrist watches, pocket watches, and other watches, including stop watches, other than those of heading 9101 (9102). There are 14 major headings in HTSUS Chapter 91.

9101—Wrist watches, pocket watches, and other watches, including stop watches, with case of precious metal or of metal clad with precious metal

9102—Wrist watches, pocket watches, and other watches, including stop watches, other than those of heading 9101

9103—Clocks with watch movements, excluding clocks of heading 9104

9104—Instrument panel clocks and clocks of a similar type for vehicles, aircraft, spacecraft, or vessels

9105—Other clocks

9106—Time of day recording apparatus and apparatus for measuring, recording, or otherwise indicating intervals of time, with clock or watch movement or with synchronous motor (for example, time registers, time recorders)

9107—Time switches with clock or watch movement or with synchronous motor

9108—Watch movements, complete and assembled

9109—Clock movements, complete and assembled

9110—Complete watch or clock movements, unassembled or partly assembled (movement sets); incomplete watch or clock movements, assembled; rough watch or clock movements

9111—Watch cases and parts thereof

9112—Clock cases and cases of a similar type for other goods of this chapter, and parts thereof

9113—Watch straps, watch bands, and watch bracelets, and parts thereof

9114—Other clock or watch parts

For more details regarding classification of the specific product you are interested in importing, consult a customs broker, the appropriate commodity specialist at your nearest customs port, or see HTSUS. The 2001 HTSUS is available online from the Customs Service (www.customs.gov/impoexpo/impoexpo.htm) or for purchase from the U.S. Government Printing Office (see resources at the end of this chapter), and may be found in larger public libraries. For a general discussion of customs classification, see "Classification—Liquidation" on page 229.

Dutiable Status of Goods

For more information about duty rates and binding decisions see "Dutiable Status of Goods" on page 203; for a discussion of temporary importation of goods see "Temporary Free Importations" on page 205.

Valuation

Importers have a responsibility to use what the U.S. Customs Service deems, "reasonable care," when determining the value of their goods. They must also provide any additional information that the Customs Service needs for setting a final value on the goods. This process involves a number of factors and can be somewhat complicated; importers must be aware of applicable issues and details. Valuation information applies to all types of commodities, for further discussion on the subject see "Customs Valuation" on page 267.

Import Duties

Import duties vary (often dramatically) depending upon the Harmonized Tariff Schedule (HTSUS) classification of the goods or products imported. Since some products that look alike have different HTSUS classifications and different rates of duty, proper classification is vital. Note that "differences of opinion" between importers and the Bureau of Customs and Border Protection regarding classification keeps customs attorneys very busy.

Import duties can be assessed on the imported value of the goods ("ad valorem" rates of duty such as 2%, 4.4%, 50%, etc.), total units or weight of the goods ("specific" rates of duty such as 2 cents each or 1.5 cents/pound, etc.) or on a combination basis ("compound" rates of duty such as 5 cents each plus 6%).

Listed below is a sampling of several Column 1 import duty rates for Chapter 91 products:
Of textile material or of base metal, whether or not gold- or silver-plated (9101.12.20.00): Free
to
Of textile material or of base metal, whether or not gold- or silver-plated (9101.21.10.00): 3.1%

For specific information on US import duties refer to the Harmonized Tariff Schedule of the US. The print version is available from the US Government Printing Office as well as third party suppliers who often add special features. Online versions are available in both static PDF pages as well as in formats with excellent search functionality. Search the Web with the term "Harmonized Tariff Schedule" to find sources.

Entry and Documentation

The entry of merchandise is a two-part process consisting of 1) filing the documents necessary to determine whether merchandise may be released from Customs custody and 2) filing the documents that contain information for duty assessment and statistical purposes. In certain instances all documents must be filed and accepted by Customs prior to the release of the goods. Unless you have been granted an extension, you must file entry documents at a location specified by the port or area director within five working days of your shipment's date of arrival at a U.S. port of entry. These include a number of standard documents required by Customs for any entry, and:

- For insular producers importing watches under the Insular Watch Assembly Program: Form ITA-340

After you present the entry, Customs may examine your shipment, or may waive examination. The shipment is then released, provided no legal or regulatory violations have occurred. You must then file entry summary documentation and deposit estimated duties at a designated customhouse within 10 working days of your shipment's release. For a detailed description of entry procedures, standard documentation, and informal entry, see "Entry Process" on page 185.

Informed Compliance. Informed compliance was introduced with the Customs Modernization Act of 1993 (Mod Act) and defines the relationship between importers and the Customs Service. It sets out the responsibilities of both parties. Providing the correct documentation and information for entry is a key factor that will make your importing operation run smoothly. We recommend that importers become familiar with the concept of informed comliance and the responsibilities that they have under the Mod Act. For further discussion about informed compliance see "Informed Compliance" on page 211.

Entry Invoice. For all commercial shipments of watches and watch movements, the following information must appear on the invoice or on a separate sheet attached to and constituting a part of the invoice for each group, type, or model: 1) for watches: a thorough description of the composition of the watch cases, the bracelets, bands, or straps; the commercial description (ebauche caliber number, ligne size, and number of jewels) of the movements contained in the watches; and the type of battery (manufacturer's name and reference number), if the watch is battery-operated; 2) for watch movements: the commercial description (ebauche caliber number, ligne size, and number of jewels); if battery-operated, the type of battery (manufacturer's name and reference number); and 3) the name of the manufacturer of the exported watch movements and the name of the country in which the movements were manufactured. For more general information about invoices see "Invoices" on page 277.

Note: The Entry and Documentation section has been carefully designed to supply you, the importer, with sample documents and directions on how to satisfy Customs requirements. Be aware that you should consult the applicable authorities to ensure that you are correctly following the most current procedures.

Prohibitions and Restrictions

See "Country-Specific Import Restrictions" below.

Country-Specific Import Restrictions

Watches or watch movements containing any material that is the product of any country with respect to which HTSUS Column 2 rates of duty apply are not eligible for duty-free import under the Insular Watch Assembly Program.

Quotas

The U.S. Departments of Interior and Commerce administer import quotas on watches and watch movements from insular possessions admissible free of duty that are described in detail in note 5 to HTSUS Chapter 91 on a licensing basis. Information concerning licenses may be obtained from the Statutory Import Programs Staff of the International Trade Administration (see addresses at end of this chapter).

Marking and Labeling Requirements

All watches, watch movements, clocks, and clock movements imported into the U.S. must be marked in accordance with general customs country of origin markings and in accordance with regulations detailed in note 4 of HTSUS Chapter 91, specifically applicable to watch movements.

General Marking Requirements. Foreign made watches, watch movements, clocks, and clock movements must comply with the usual country of origin marking requirements. Customs considers the country of origin of watches and clocks to be the country of manufacture of the movement. The name of this country should appear either on the outside back cover or on the face of the dial and may be in the form of a sticker or label.

Special Marking Requirements. The terms "watch movement" and "clock movement" refer to devices regulated by a balance wheel and hairspring, quartz crystal, or any other system capable of determining intervals of time, with a display or system to which a mechanical display can be incorporated. "Watch movements" include those devices that do not exceed 12 mm. in thickness and 50 mm. in width, length, or diameter; "clock movements" include those devices that are larger than the watch movement dimensional specifications. The term "cases" embraces inner and outer cases, containers, and housings for movements, together with parts or pieces, such as—but not limited to—rings, feet, posts, bases, and outer frames, and any auxiliary or incidental features, that (with appropriate movements) serve to complete the watches, clocks, time switches, and other apparatus provided for in HTSUS Chapter 91. Chapter 91 requires items to be conspicuously and indelibly marked by cutting, die-sinking, engraving, or stamping. Articles required to be so marked shall be denied entry unless marked in exact conformity with these requirements.

Opto-Electronic Displays. Movements with opto-electronic display only and cases designed for use with them, whether entered as separate articles or components of assembled watches or clocks, are not subject to these special marking requirements.

Such items need only to be marked according to the requirements of 19 USC 1304.

Watch Movements. Watch movements must be marked on one or more of the bridges or top plates to show 1) the name of the country of manufacture, 2) the name of the manufacturer or purchaser, and 3) the number of jewels, if any.

Clock Movements. Clock movements must be marked on the most visible part of the front or back plate to show 1) the name of the country of manufacture, 2) the name of the manufacturer or purchaser, and 3) the number of jewels, if any.

Watch Cases. Watch cases must be marked on the inside or outside of the back cover to show 1) the name of the country of manufacture, and 2) the name of the manufacturer or purchaser.

Clock Cases. Clock cases and other cases must be marked on the inside or outside of the back cover to show 1) the name of the country of manufacture, and 2) the name of the manufacturer or purchaser.

For a general discussion of U.S. Customs marking and labeling requirements, see "Country of Origin Marking" on page 236, "Special Marking Requirements" on page 238 and "Marking—False Impression" on page 239.

Shipping Considerations

You will need to ensure that your goods are packaged and shipped with care to ensure that they arrive in good condition and pass smoothly through Customs. You are responsible for ensuring that the shipment is in compliance with all applicable government regulations for packaging and shipping. In most instances, you should not leave these arrangements solely to the discretion of your supplier. Careful preparation of the cargo and selection of the mode of transport can be essential to a cost-effective, timely delivery of undamaged goods. We strongly advise you to consult your shipping representative, insurance agent, or freight broker for advice on packing and shipping.

Clocks and watches are usually fragile and should be securely packed and stowed to avoid damage due to shifting en route. Special care must be taken to ensure that they are adequately protected from excessive heat, humidity, or water damage.

Publications and WWW Resources

The *Harmonized Tariff Schedule of the United States (2001)* (HTSUS) is available to view on the Customs Service website (www.customs.gov), or you may purchase a printed version from:

U.S. Government Printing Office
Superintendent of Documents
710 North Capital Street NW
Washington DC 20401
Tel: (202) 512-1800
Fax: (202) 512-1657
Website: www.access.gpo.gov

The USGPO also has copies of specific laws available for purchase. The USGPO accepts orders made by fax, phone or placed over the Internet, as well as mail orders paid by credit card. All orders must be accompanied by payment. Credit cards, checks drawn on a U.S. bank, or an international money order are all acceptable.

Relevant Government Agencies

Address questions regarding the Insular Watch Assembly Program to:
International Trade Administration
Import Administration
Statutory Import Programs Staff - FCB
1099 14th Street, Suite 4100W
Washington DC 20005
Tel: (202) 482-1660
Website: www.ita.doc.gov

Address general questions regarding the importation of watches, clocks, movements, and parts to your local Customs port director. For addresses refer to "U.S. Customs and Border Protection Offices" on page 65 or contact:

U.S. Customs and Border Protection
Customs Headquarters
1300 Pennsylvania Avenue NW
Washington DC 20229
Tel: (202) 354-1000
Website: www.customs.treas.gov

Laws and Regulations

The following laws and regulations may be relevant to the importation of watches and clocks. The laws are contained in the U.S. Code (USC) and the regulations are published in the Code of Federal Regulations (CFR), both of which may be available at larger public and law libraries. Copies of specific laws are also available from the United States Government Printing Office (address above).

19 CFR 10.181
Regulations on Refunded Duties for Watches and Movements Imported from US Insular Possessions
These regulations prescribe the process by which an importer of watches and watch movements can secure a refund of duties from Customs for imports from US insular possessions.

Principal Exporting Countries

The following listing includes samples of the main supplier nations of the products of this chapter. It is organized by HTSUS major heading. (Refer to "Customs Classification" above for the product codes.) Countries are listed in rank order of the value of products imported to the U.S. Statistics represent customs value of entries for 2002 from the Bureau of Census, U.S. Department of Commerce.

9101—Switzerland, United Kingdom, Italy, Germany, France, Hong Kong, Japan, China, Turkey, Mexico

9102—Switzerland, Japan, China, Philippines, Thailand, Hong Kong

9103—China, Japan, Hong Kong, Ireland, Taiwan, Switzerland, Singapore, Czech Republic, Germany, United Kingdom

9104—Japan, China, United Kingdom, Mexico, France, Germany, South Korea, Taiwan

9105—China, Taiwan, Germany, Hong Kong, Japan, Switzerland, Canada, India

9106—China, Canada, Japan, France, Switzerland, Thailand, United Kingdom

9107—Mexico, China, Taiwan, Japan, Germany, Israel, Tunisia, Malaysia

9108—Switzerland, Japan, Germany, China, Taiwan, Hong Kong, Thailand

9109—Germany, China, Switzerland, Taiwan, Hong Kong, Japan, Thailand, France

9110—Switzerland, China, Hong Kong, Singapore, Japan

9111—Switzerland, Hong Kong, China, Italy, Japan, Thailand, Germany

9112—Canada, China, Taiwan, Switzerland, Philippines, Germany, Hong Kong, India

9113—Switzerland, China, Hong Kong, Italy, France, Japan, Turkey, Austria, Thailand

9114—Switzerland, Germany, China, Japan, Hong Kong, France, Israel

Chapter 92:
Musical Instruments

Full title: Musical Instruments; Parts and Accessories of Such Articles

This section pertains to the importation of musical instruments, which are classified within Chapter 92 of the Harmonized Tariff Schedule of the United States (HTSUS). Specifically, it includes pianos and similar instruments; other stringed instruments; other keyboard instruments; accordions; brass and woodwind instruments; percussion instruments; electrified musical instruments; music boxes, mechanical, and other instruments, such as whistles; and parts and accessories of all of the above.

If you are interested in importing electrical accessories, such as microphones, loudspeakers, headphones, switches, or similar accessories, refer to Commodity Index Chapter 85. Some specialized instrumentation is also covered under Chapter 90. Toy instruments are found within Chapter 95; brushes for cleaning instruments are covered in Chapter 96; and antique or collectors' instruments are entered under Chapter 97.

Note: To understand key issues that will enable you to make best use of the information in this section we recommend that you see "Introduction" on page 425.

Key Factors

The key factors in the importation of musical instruments are:

- For electronic instruments, compliance with Federal Communications Commission (FCC) regulations and entry notification for radio frequency devices

Although most importers utilize the services of a licensed customs broker in making their entries, and we recommend this practice, you should be aware of the regulatory, entry, and documentation issues involved in importing your product. You, as importer, are ultimately responsible for the fulfillment of any legal requirements applicable to your shipment.

General Considerations

Importation of most musical instruments is straightforward. You do not need permits, licenses, or special entry paperwork. However, there is one important exception: importation of electronic keyboards is regulated by the FCC under the provisions of the Federal Communications Act as amended (47 USC). Other electronic instruments generally do not affect radio frequencies. However, you should consult with the FCC regional office nearest you, or contact FCC headquarters (see addresses at end of this chapter) if you have questions regarding the applicability of these regulations to your specific product.

FCC entry notification Form 740 is required for importation of any electronic device capable of interfering with established and assigned radio frequencies. FCC Form 740 certifies that the instruments to be entered have been tested by the manufacturer, comply with FCC radio frequency standards, and are so labeled. You must file a completed Form 740 with the FCC for each import shipment, as well as for each type of electronic device in the shipment. Mail your completed original form to the FCC Field Operations Bureau in Washington, D.C. Present a copy of the completed form to U.S. Customs when you enter your shipment. **Form 740** is available at any regional FCC office, from FCC headquarters, or from your customs broker

Customs Classification

For customs purposes musical instruments are classified within Chapter 92 of the HTSUS. This chapter is divided into major headings, which are further divided into subheadings, and often into sub-subheadings, each with its own HTSUS classification number. For example, the 2001 HTSUS number for bagpipes is 9205.90.20, indicating that it is a subcategory of woodwind instruments (9205.90.20), which is a subcategory of the major heading other wind instruments (9205). There are nine major headings in HTSUS Chapter 92.

9201—Pianos, including player pianos; harpsichords and other keyboard stringed instruments

9202—Other string musical instruments (for example, guitars, violins, harps)

9203—Keyboard pipe organs; harmoniums and similar keyboard instruments with free metal reeds

9204—Accordions and similar instruments; mouth organs

9205—Other wind musical instruments (for example, clarinets, trumpets, bagpipes)

9206—Percussion musical instruments (for example, drums, xylophones, cymbals, castanets, maracas)

9207—Musical instruments the sound of which is produced, or must be amplified, electrically (for example, organs, guitars, accordions)

9208—Music boxes, fairground organs, mechanical street organs, mechanical singing birds, musical saws, and other musical instruments not falling within any other heading of this chapter; decoy calls of all kinds; whistles, call horns, and other mouth-blown sound signaling instruments

9209—Parts (for example, mechanisms for music boxes) and accessories (for example, cards, discs, and rolls for mechanical instruments) of musical instruments; metronomes, tuning forks, and pitch pipes of all kinds

For more details regarding classification of the specific product you are interested in importing, consult a customs broker, the appropriate commodity specialist at your nearest customs port, or see HTSUS. The 2001 HTSUS is available online from the Customs Service (www.customs.gov/impoexpo/impoexpo.htm) or for purchase from the U.S. Government Printing Office (see resources at the end of this chapter), and may be found in larger public libraries. For a general discussion of customs classification, see "Classification—Liquidation" on page 229.

Dutiable Status of Goods

For more information about duty rates and binding decisions see "Dutiable Status of Goods" on page 203; for a discussion of temporary importation of goods see "Temporary Free Importations" on page 205

Valuation

Importers have a responsibility to use what the U.S. Customs Service deems, "reasonable care," when determining the value of their goods. They must also provide any additional information that the Customs Service needs for setting a final value on the goods. This process involves a number of factors and can be somewhat complicated; importers must be aware of applicable issues and details. Valuation information applies to all types of commodities, for further discussion on the subject see "Customs Valuation" on page 267.

Import Duties

Import duties vary (often dramatically) depending upon the Harmonized Tariff Schedule (HTSUS) classification of the goods or products imported. Since some products that look alike have different HTSUS classifications and different rates of duty, proper classification is vital. Note that "differences of opinion" between importers and the Bureau of Customs and Border Protection regarding classification keeps customs attorneys very busy.

Import duties can be assessed on the imported value of the goods ("ad valorem" rates of duty such as 2%, 4.4%, 50%, etc.), total units or weight of the goods ("specific" rates of duty such as 2 cents each or 1.5 cents/pound, etc.) or on a combination basis ("compound" rates of duty such as 5 cents each plus 6%).

Listed below is a sampling of several Column 1 import duty rates for Chapter 92 products:
Tuning pins (9209.91.40.00): Free
to
Collapsible musical instrument stands (9209.94.40.00): 5.7%

For specific information on US import duties refer to the Harmonized Tariff Schedule of the US. The print version is available from the US Government Printing Office as well as third party suppliers who often add special features. Online versions are available in both static PDF pages as well as in formats with excellent search functionality. Search the Web with the term "Harmonized Tariff Schedule" to find sources.

Entry and Documentation

The entry of merchandise is a two-part process consisting of 1) filing the documents necessary to determine whether merchandise may be released fromCustoms custody and 2) filing the documents that contain information for duty assessment and statistical purposes. In certain instances all documents must be filed and accepted by Customs prior to the release of the goods. Unless you have been granted an extension, you must file entry documents at a location specified by the district/area director within five working days of your shipment's date of arrival at a U.S. port of entry. These include a number of standard documents required by Customs for any entry, and:

- For electronic instruments, FCC Form 740

After you present the entry, Customs may examine your shipment, or may waive examination. The shipment is then released, provided no legal or regulatory violations have occurred. You must then file entry summary documentation and deposit estimated duties at a designated customhouse within 10 working days of your shipment's release. For a detailed description of entry procedures, standard documentation, and informal entry, see "Entry Process" on page 185.

Informed Compliance. Informed compliance was introduced with the Customs Modernization Act of 1993 (Mod Act) and defines the relationship between importers and the Customs Service. It sets out the responsibilities of both parties. Providing the correct documentation and information for entry is a key factor that will make your importing operation run smoothly. We recommend that importers become familiar with the concept of in formed comliance and the responsibilities that they have under the Mod Act. For further discussion about informed compliance see "Informed Compliance" on page 211.

Note: The Entry and Documentation section has been carefully designed to supply you, the importer, with sample documents and directions on how to satisfy Customs requirements. Be aware that you should consult the applicable authorities to ensure that you are correctly following the most current procedures.

Prohibitions and Restrictions

Electronic musical instruments not in compliance with FCC frequency regulations are not permitted into the U.S.

Marking and Labeling Requirements

Any electronic instrument of a type regulated by the FCC that is imported into the U.S. must bear a manufacturer's label certifying that it has been tested for compliance with FCC frequency standards, and is in compliance. For more details, contact the FCC.

For a general discussion of U.S. Customs marking and labeling requirements, see "Country of Origin Marking" on page 236, "Special Marking Requirements" on page 238 and "Marking—False Impression" on page 239.

Shipping Considerations

You will need to ensure that your goods are packaged and shipped with care to ensure that they arrive in good condition and pass smoothly through Customs. You are responsible for ensuring that the shipment is in compliance with all applicable government regulations for packaging and shipping. In most instances, you should not leave these arrangements solely to the discretion of your supplier. Careful preparation of the cargo and selection of the mode of transport can be essential to a cost-effective, timely delivery of undamaged goods. We strongly advise you to consult your shipping representative, insurance agent, or freight broker for advice on packing and shipping.

Musical instruments are usually fragile and should be securely packed and stowed to avoid damage due to shifting en route. Special care must be taken to ensure that they are adequately protected from excessive heat, humidity, or water damage.

Publications and WWW Resources

The *Harmonized Tariff Schedule of the United States (2001)* (HTSUS) is available to view on the Customs Service website (www.customs.gov), or you may purchase a printed version from:

U.S. Government Printing Office
Superintendent of Documents
710 North Capital Street NW
Washington DC 20401
Tel: (202) 512-1800
Fax: (202) 512-1657
Website: www.access.gpo.gov

The USGPO also has copies of specific laws available for purchase. The USGPO accepts orders made by fax, phone or placed over the Internet, as well as mail orders paid by credit card. All orders must be accompanied by payment. Credit cards, checks drawn on a U.S. bank, or an international money order are all acceptable.

Relevant Government Agencies

Address questions regarding FCC requirements for the importation of electronic musical instruments to:

Federal Communications Commission (FCC)
Consumer and Governmental Affairs Bureau
445 12th Street SW
Washington DC 20554
(202) 418-1400
Website: www.fcc.gov

Address questions regarding the importation of musical instruments to your local Customs port director. For addresses refer to "U.S. Customs and Border Protection Offices" on page 65 or contact:

U.S. Customs and Border Protection
Customs Headquarters
1300 Pennsylvania Avenue NW
Washington DC 20229
Tel: (202) 354-1000
Website: www.customs.treas.gov

Laws and Regulations

The following laws and regulations may be relevant to the importation of musical instruments. The laws are contained in the U.S. Code (USC) and the regulations are published in the Code of Federal Regulations (CFR), both of which may be available at larger public and law libraries. Copies of specific laws are also available from the United States Government Printing Office (address above).

47 USC 302a
Devices That Interfere with Radio Reception
This law prohibits the importation of devices or home electronic equipment that fail to comply with regulations promulgated by the FCC. See 47 CFR 2.1201 et seq. and 18.119. Customs enforces the prohibition.

Principal Exporting Countries

The following listing includes samples of the main supplier nations of the products of this chapter. It is organized by HTSUS major heading. (Refer to "Customs Classification" above for the product codes.) Countries are listed in rank order of the value of products imported to the U.S. Statistics represent customs value of entries for 2002 from the Bureau of Census, U.S. Department of Commerce.

9201—Japan, China, South Korea, Indonesia, Germany, Czech Republic, Austria, Estonia, Italy

9202—China, South Korea, Indonesia, Canada, Taiwan, Germany, Romania, Japan, Spain, Italy

9203—Canada, United Kingdom, China, Germany, Indonesia, Czech Republic, Italy, Netherlands, Slovenia

9204—Germany, China, Italy, Japan, Czech Republic, Slovenia, Austria, France, United Kingdom

9205—Japan, Taiwan, France, Germany, China, United Kingdom, Czech Republic, South Korea, Indonesia, Brazil

9206—Taiwan, China, Canada, Japan, Thailand, Indonesia, Germany, Netherlands, Switzerland, United Kingdom

9207—China, Japan, Indonesia, South Korea, Malaysia, Mexico, Italy, Taiwan, Germany, Netherlands, Canada, Sweden

9208—China, Taiwan, Canada, Thailand, Germany, United Kingdom

9209—Japan, Taiwan, China, Germany, Mexico, Canada, France

Chapter 93:
Arms and Ammunition

Full title: Arms and Ammunition; Parts and Accessories Thereof

This section pertains to the importation of arms and ammunition, which are classified within Chapter 93 of the Harmonized Tariff Schedule of the United States (HTSUS). Specifically, it includes military rifles and artillery; revolvers and pistols; sporting longarms; air, gas, and spring-fired guns; military munitions and other ammunition; military-type edged weapons, such as swords and bayonets; and miscellaneous articles fired by charges, such as ramsets, riveters, flare guns, and starters' pistols.

If you are interested in importing explosives or propellant powders not manufactured into ammunitions or munitions, refer to Commodity Index Chapter 36. Edged tools and cutlery not designed specifically for military use are covered in Chapter 82. Armored or other military vehicles are found in Chapter 87. Unless attached to firearms, telescopic sights or other optical devices are classified within and entered under Chapter 90. If you are interested in importing archery products, fencing foils, replica firearms, or related toy or novelty items, refer to Chapter 95. Collectors' pieces and antiques are covered in Chapter 97. Although the parts of articles covered in Chapter 93 are generally included with those products, other general hardware—such as nuts and bolts, screws, and other general hardware—are classified in Chapters 72-83 by the particular material of which they are composed, if made of base metals, or in Chapter 39 if made of plastic.

Note: To understand key issues that will enable you to make best use of the information in this section we recommend that you see "Introduction" on page 425.

Key Factors

The key factors in the importation of arms and ammunition are:

- U.S. Bureau of Alcohol, Tobacco, and Firearms (ATF) import license required
- ATF import permit required
- Compliance with ATF regulations pertinent to the specific type of weapon involved

Although most importers utilize the services of a licensed customs broker in making their entries, and we recommend this practice, you should be aware of the regulatory, entry, and documentation issues involved in importing your product. You, as importer, are ultimately responsible for the fulfillment of any legal requirements applicable to your shipment.

General Considerations

The importation of arms and ammunition into the U.S. is subject to very strict and complex regulation. The information in this listing is not exhaustive. Penalties for failure to comply with regulations are serious. Before you attempt to import these items into the country, be very sure you have fulfilled all legal requirements.

ATF Regulations. Importation of firearms is strictly regulated under the Gun Control Act of 1968 (GCA) and the import provisions of the Arms Export Control Act of 1976 (AECA), which are enforced by the ATF. You must be a ATF-licensed importer to import these articles, and, with certain exceptions, only those firearms generally recognized as particularly suitable for, or readily adaptable to, sporting purposes may be imported. Except for sporting shotguns, shotgun parts, or shotgun ammunition, all firearms, ammunition, and implements of war are listed on the U.S. Munitions Import List and are subject to AECA import controls (27 CFR 47). If you wish to import items on the Munitions Import List, you must register with the ATF (see addresses at end of this chapter). Even the temporary in-transit importation of arms and ammunition destined for a destination outside the U.S. is banned unless the importer has a license from the Office of Defense Trade Controls, U.S. State Department (see addresses at end of this chapter).

Firearms fall into four general categories: sporting, military, antique, and NFA (those that are regulated by the National Firearms Act, including firearms with a bore of greater than .50 caliber; machine-guns; destructive devices, such as mines and grenades; silencers; short-barreled rifles; and short-barreled shotguns). Licensing and permit requirements vary according to category. You must have an approved ATF Form 6 Import Permit for the importation of any firearms except for antiques (firearms actually manufactured in or before 1898 are classified as antiques and require no permit). Form 6 permits are valid for six months from the date of issue. Separate licenses are required to import explosives or munitions in bulk (ATF F 5400.13) or to transport them interstate (ATF F 5400.16). However, these licenses are not required for imports of small arms and related ammunition.

Toxic and Hazardous Substances. Shipments of products deemed toxic or hazardous must generally be in compliance with the requirements of the U.S. Environmental Protection Agency (EPA) and the U.S. Department of Transportation (DOT), including packaging, shipping, marking, and labeling requirements. Arms and ammunition are not considered chemical substances under the Toxic Substances Control Act (TSCA). However, importers are required to include a negative certification ("I certify that all chemical substances in this shipment are not subject to TSCA") with their documentation. This statement must be filed at the time of entry.

Consumer Products Regulation. The Federal Hazardous Substances Act (FHSA) imposes special controls on hazardous consumer products, which are defined as substances that are flammable, combustible, or have the potential to cause substantial personal injury during or as a proximate result of any customary or reasonably foreseeable handling or use. The Consumer Product Safety Commission (CPSC) does not require permits, special invoicing, limited entry, licenses, or any special approval process for importing hazardous consumer products into the U.S. However, if you are importing these types of products, you are responsible for ensuring that they meet all applicable FHSA and Consumer Product Safety Act (CPSA) requirements. There detailed regulations cover testing and labeling of such products. Contact the CPSC (see addresses at end of this chapter) for specific requirements on the product you are importing.

Customs Classification

For customs purposes, arms and ammunition are classified within Chapter 93 of the HTSUS. This chapter is divided into major headings, which are further divided into subheadings, and often into sub-subheadings, each of which has its own HTSUS classification number. For example, the 2001 HTSUS number for parts of rifles is 9305.90.10, indicating that it is a subcategory of parts of arms of articles of heading 9301 (9305.90), which is a subcategory of the major heading parts and accessories of articles of headings 9301 to 9304 (9305). There are seven major heading in HTSUS Chapter 93.

9301—Military weapons, other than revolvers, pistols, and the arms of heading 9307

9302—Revolvers and pistols, other than those of heading 9303 or 9304

9303—Other firearms and similar devices which operate by the firing of an explosive charge (for example, sporting shotguns and rifles, muzzle-loading firearms, Very pistols, and other devices designed to project only signal flares; pistols and revolvers for firing blank ammunition; captive-bolt humane killers; line-throwing guns)

9304—Other arms (for example, spring, air or gas guns and pistols, truncheons), excluding those of heading 9307

9305—Parts and accessories of articles of headings 9301 to 9304

9306—Bombs, grenades, torpedoes, mines, missiles, and similar munitions of war and parts thereof; cartridges and other ammunition and projectiles and parts thereof, including shot and cartridge wads

9307—Swords, cutlasses, bayonets, lances, and similar arms and parts thereof and scabbards and sheaths therefor

For more details regarding classification of the specific product you are interested in importing, consult a customs broker, the appropriate commodity specialist at your nearest customs port, or see HTSUS. The 2001 HTSUS is available online from the Customs Service (www.customs.gov/impoexpo/impoexpo.htm) or for purchase from the U.S. Government Printing Office (see resources at the end of this chapter), and may be found in larger public libraries. For a general discussion of customs classification, see "Classification—Liquidation" on page 229.

Dutiable Status of Goods

For more information about duty rates and binding decisions see "Dutiable Status of Goods" on page 203; for a discussion of temporary importation of goods see "Temporary Free Importations" on page 205.

Valuation

Importers have a responsibility to use what the U.S. Customs Service deems, "reasonable care," when determining the value of their goods. They must also provide any additional information that the Customs Service needs for setting a final value on the goods. This process involves a number of factors and can be somewhat complicated; importers must be aware of applicable issues and details. Valuation information applies to all types of commodities, for further discussion on the subject see "Customs Valuation" on page 267.

Import Duties

Import duties vary (often dramatically) depending upon the Harmonized Tariff Schedule (HTSUS) classification of the goods or products imported. Since some products that look alike have different HTSUS classifications and different rates of duty, proper classification is vital. Note that "differences of opinion" between importers and the Bureau of Customs and Border Protection regarding classification keeps customs attorneys very busy.

Import duties can be assessed on the imported value of the goods ("ad valorem" rates of duty such as 2%, 4.4%, 50%, etc.), total units or weight of the goods ("specific" rates of duty such as 2 cents each or 1.5 cents/pound, etc.) or on a combination basis ("compound" rates of duty such as 5 cents each plus 6%).

Listed below is a sampling of several Column 1 import duty rates for Chapter 93 products:
Self propelled (9301.11.00.00): Free
to
Shotguns (9301.90.60.00): 2.6%

For specific information on US import duties refer to the Harmonized Tariff Schedule of the US. The print version is available from the US Government Printing Office as well as third party suppliers who often add special features. Online versions are available in both static PDF pages as well as in formats with excellent search functionality. Search the Web with the term "Harmonized Tariff Schedule" to find sources.

Entry and Documentation

The entry of merchandise is a two-part process consisting of 1) filing the documents necessary to determine whether merchandise may be released from Customs custody and 2) filing the documents that contain information for duty assessment and statistical purposes. In certain instances all documents must be filed and accepted by Customs prior to the release of the goods. Unless you have been granted an extension, you must file entry documents at a location specified by the district/area director within five working days of your shipment's date of arrival at a U.S. port of entry. These include a number of standard documents required by Customs for any entry, and:

- ATF Form 6 Import Permit.

- If importing antique firearms, documentary verification of the article's age

- Any documentation required for surplus military curio and relic firearms

Note: Individuals who are members of the United States Armed Forces and wish to import firearms must obtain a special Armed Forces ATF Import Permit.

After you present the entry, Customs may examine your shipment, or may waive examination. The shipment is then released, provided no legal or regulatory violations have occurred. You must then file entry summary documentation and deposit estimated duties at a designated customhouse within 10 working days of your shipment's release. For a detailed description of entry procedures, standard documentation, and informal entry, see "Entry Process" on page 185.

Informed Compliance. Informed compliance was introduced with the Customs Modernization Act of 1993 (Mod Act) and defines the relationship between importers and the Customs Service. It sets out the responsibilities of both parties. Providing the correct documentation and information for entry is a key factor that will make your importing operation run smoothly. We recommend that importers become familiar with the concept of informed comliance and the responsibilities that they have under the Mod Act. For further discussion about informed compliance see "Informed Compliance" on page 211

Note: The Entry and Documentation section has been carefully designed to supply you, the importer, with sample documents and directions on how to satisfy Customs requirements. Be aware that you should consult the applicable authorities to ensure that you are correctly following the most current procedures.

Prohibitions and Restrictions

The importation of arms and ammunition is highly restricted. You may import firearms on the U.S. Munitions Imports List and NFA firearms only if you have satisfied the ATF that the items are 1) for U.S. government use; 2) for scientific or research purposes; 3) for testing or use as a model by a registered manufacturer; or 4) solely for use as a sample by a registered importer or registered dealer. You must include with your permit application a detailed explanation substantiating your claim that the importation meets one of the above criteria. NFA firearms are also subject to the restrictive conditions found in 26 USC 4844 and 27 CFR 179.111.

Assault Weapons. Automatic and semi-automatic "assault" weapons—rapid fire, large clip military style firearms—are prohibited imports, and restrictions on such arms have recently been tightened further. Surplus military firearms are also a prohibited import, except for those classified as curios or relics that also meet the sporting-purpose criterion. It is unlawful to own—and therefore to import—a machine-gun (i.e. a fully automatic firearm) that was registered prior to May 19, 1986.

Surplus Military Curio and Relic Firearms. If you wish to import surplus military weapons classified as curios or relics, you must first be a licensed importer, and must then make specific application to the ATF for this category of import. The ATF will consider your application if 1) the firearms were manufactured in a non-proscribed country or area; 2) the firearms were manufactured in a proscribed country or area prior to the date the country or area became proscribed; or 3) the firearms manufactured in a proscribed country or area have been stored in a non-proscribed country or area for at least five years immediately prior to importation. (See "Country-Specific Import Restrictions" below for a list of currently proscribed countries or areas.) You must provide a certification statement with your application explaining how your proposed shipment meets the above criteria. You must also provide documentary information on the country or area of storage for the five-year period immediately prior to importation. Such information may, for example, include 1) a verifiable statement in English by a government official or any other bona fide official, agent, or custodian having knowledge of the date and place of manufacture and/or the place of storage, and whose identity and position can be verified from the information provided; 2) a warehouse receipt or other document that provides the required storage history; or 3) any other document you believe substantiates the place and date of manufacture and the place of storage. The ATF may require you to furnish additional documentation to aid in its determination of whether your import permit application should be approved. All certification statements must be sworn and executed under penalties of perjury.

Country-Specific Import Restrictions

Firearms manufactured in certain countries after certain years may not be imported into the U.S. Importation of firearms manufactured in and after the year in parentheses originating in the following countries is prohibited: Albania (1944), Bulgaria (1944), Cuba (1959), the Czech and Slovak Republics (1948), Estonia (1939), Hungary (1947), Kampuchea (Cambodia) (1975), Latvia (1939), Lithuania (1939), North Korea (1948), Outer Mongolia (1921), Poland (1947), Rumania (1947), the republics of the former Soviet Union (1917), Vietnam (1954). Many of these restrictions may be under review. You should check with customs regarding specific proposed imports.

Certain types of military rifles manufactured in the People's Republic of China are currently banned from import into the U.S.

Shipping Considerations

You will need to ensure that your goods are packaged and shipped with care to ensure that they arrive in good condition and pass smoothly through Customs. You are responsible for ensuring that the shipment is in compliance with all applicable government regulations for packaging and shipping. In most instances, you should not leave these arrangements solely to the

discretion of your supplier. Careful preparation of the cargo and selection of the mode of transport can be essential to a cost-effective, timely delivery of undamaged goods. We strongly advise you to consult your shipping representative, insurance agent, or freight broker for advice on packaging and shipping.

The DOT, the U.S. Coast Guard (USCG), and the U.S. Customs Service all have regulations regarding the shipment of arms and ammunition. These regulations are designed to ensure the safety of any carrier transporting weaponry as well as that of other carriers and personnel, and vary depending on the type, nature, and quantity of the product being shipped. Contact the USCG Port Captain of the shipping district into which you plan to import your product with details about type of weapon, quantity, etc., for specific USCG requirements.

Arms and ammunition must be carefully packed and stowed to not only for safety but also to avoid damage during transit. Heat and sharp blows to cargoes of munitions must be avoided, as must excessive humidity or water damage. Security of the cargo is an added concern.

Publications and WWW Resources

The following publication may be relevant to the importation of arms and ammunition of Chapter 93:

Your Guide to Federal Firearms Regulation (published by ATF, address below).

The *Harmonized Tariff Schedule of the United States (2001)* (HTSUS) is available to view on the Customs Service website (www.customs.gov), or you may purchase a printed version from:

U.S. Government Printing Office
Superintendent of Documents
710 North Capital Street NW
Washington DC 20401
Tel: (202) 512-1800
Fax: (202) 512-1657
Website: www.access.gpo.gov

The USGPO also has copies of specific laws available for purchase. The USGPO accepts orders made by fax, phone or placed over the Internet, as well as mail orders paid by credit card. All orders must be accompanied by payment. Credit cards, checks drawn on a U.S. bank, or an international money order are all acceptable.

Relevant Government Agencies

Address questions regarding ATF requirements for importation of arms and ammunition to:

Bureau of Alcohol, Tobacco, Firearms and Explosives
Firearms and Explosives Import Branch
650 Massachusetts Avenue NW
Washington DC 20226
Tel: (202) 927-8320
Website: www.atf.treas.gov

Address questions concerning licensing for in-transit shipments of arms and ammunition to:

U.S. Department of State
Directorate of Defense Trade Controls
2401 E Street NW Suite 1200
Washington DC 20522-0112
Tel: (202) 663-2714 /2700
Fax: (202) 261-8199
Website: www.pmdtc.org

Address questions on the consumer product safety aspects of importing arms and ammunition to:

Consumer Product Safety Commission (CPSC)
Office of Compliance
Washington DC 20207-0001
Tel: 800-638-2772 or (301) 504-7912

Fax: (301) 504-0359
Website: www.cpsc.gov

Address questions regarding the importation of arms and ammunition to your local Customs port director. For addresses refer to "U.S. Customs and Border Protection Offices" on page 65 or contact:

U.S. Customs and Border Protection
Customs Headquarters
1300 Pennsylvania Avenue NW
Washington DC 20229
Tel: (202) 354-1000
Website: www.customs.treas.gov

Laws and Regulations

The following laws and regulations may be relevant to the importation of arms and ammunition. The laws are contained in the U.S. Code (USC) and the regulations are published in the Code of Federal Regulations (CFR), both of which may be available at larger public and law libraries. Copies of specific laws are also available from the United States Government Printing Office (address above).

22 USC 2751 et seq.
Arms Export Control Act
This Act restricts the sales of arms, authorizes Presidential control over the import and export of defense articles, and creates a U.S. Munitions List, where items subject to control appear. It also prescribes licensing and registration requirements for manufacturers, exporters, and importers.

15 USC 2051 et seq.
Consumer Product Safety Act
This Act sets standards for the manufacture, processing, and labeling of products sold to U.S. consumers.

18 USC 831 et seq.
Explosives and Other Dangerous Articles
This Act places import restrictions on fireworks and nuclear materials, and Customs enforces these laws. See 49 CFR Parts 170-171, 173, 177, 179, and 195; 46 USC 870

18 USC 841 et seq.
Importation of Explosive Materials
This law imposes criminal penalties for the unauthorized importation of explosive materials. Customs aids in the enforcement of this statute. See 26 CFR Part 181.

18 USC 921 et seq.
Firearms
This Act restricts the importation of firearms and is enforced by Customs. See 26 CFR Part 178 and 26 CFR 251.

18 USC 960 et seq.
Foreign Relations
These laws regulate the prerequisites to a vessel's departure and the prohibitions against exportation of armed vessels, arms, liquor, and narcotics. Customs will refuse clearance to vessels not in compliance with these laws.

26 USC 5801
National Firearms Act
This law requires all imported explosives, munitions of war, firearms, and ammunition be covered by a ATF permit. Customs will deny entry without such permit.

18 USC 2277
Explosives or Dangerous Weapons Aboard Vessels
This law prohibits the existence of explosives and dangerous weapons aboard vessels. Customs is authorized to enforce this law. See 46 USC 170.

22 USC 401 et seq.
Illegal Exportation of War Materials
This law authorizes customs seizure and forfeiture of arms, munitions of war, and other articles exported in vi-

olation of 22 CFR 127.

26 USC 5801 et seq.
Occupatonal Tax for Firearms Dealers
This law establishes taxes to apply to importers of firearms. Reduced rates are set out for small importers and businesses.

Principal Exporting Countries

The following listing includes samples of the main supplier nations of the products of this chapter. It is organized by HTSUS major heading. (Refer to "Customs Classification" above for the product codes.) Countries are listed in rank order of the value of products imported to the U.S. Statistics represent customs value of entries for 2002 from the Bureau of Census, U.S. Department of Commerce.

9301—Germany, Sweden, Yugoslavia, Ukraine, Switzerland, United Kingdom

9302—Austria, Brazil, Germany, Italy, Canada, Israel, Argentina, Croatia, Czech Republic

9303—Italy, Spain, Japan, Brazil, Turkey, Canada, United Kingdom

9304—Taiwan, China, Mexico, Spain, United Kingdom, Germany

9305—Germany, Japan, Italy, Belgium, Canada, Mexico, Netherlands, Taiwan, Austria, United Kingdom

9306—Canada, Israel, United Kingdom, Germany, Russia, Italy, Czech Republic, South Korea

9307—China, Pakistan, Taiwan, India, Spain, Germany, Philippines, Switzerland, Hong Kong, Greece

Chapter 94: Furnishings

Full title: Furniture; Bedding, Mattresses, Mattress Supports, Cushions, and Similar Stuffed Furnishings; Lamps and Lighting Fittings, Not Elsewhere Specified or Included; Illuminated Signs, Illuminated Nameplates, and the Like; Prefabricated Buildings

This section pertains to the importation of furnishings, which are classified within Chapter 94 of the Harmonized Tariff Schedule of the United States (HTSUS). Specifically, it includes chairs of all kinds; medical and related furniture; other furniture for home, office, or other use, of whatever materials; beds, mattresses, and bedding; lighting fixtures and lamps; parts of the above items, including furnishings for vehicles; and prefabricated buildings and structures.

Although this chapter is comprehensively broad and straightforward, some related products are classified in other Commodity Index chapters. If you are interested in importing pneumatic or water mattresses, pillows, or cushions, refer to the Commodities Index chapters covering the primary material of manufacture: plastic (Chapter 39), rubber (Chapter 40), or other textile materials (Chapter 63). Mirrors designed to rest on the floor are classified in Chapter 70. Any articles involving precious metals are found in Chapter 71, Parts of general usage—such as nuts and bolts, screws, and similar fittings—are covered in the chapters pertaining to the material of which they are composed: Chapters 72-83, if of base metals, or chapter 39 if of plastics. Specific hardware fittings for furniture are found in Chapter 83. Furniture designed as parts of refrigeration units or as parts of sewing machines are found in Chapter 84, while furniture designed as parts of apparatus of Chapter 85 is also classified with those articles. Flashlights, special purpose lighting, and related fixtures are also covered in Chapter 85. Although some components of vehicles are covered in Chapter 94, the bulk of automotive components are found in Chapter 87, pertaining specifically to vehicles. Dental chairs incorporating dental appliances or spittoons are classified within Chapter 90. Furnishings of which the primary component is a clock are included in Chapter 91. Toy furniture, billiard tables and similar game articles, special furniture for shows or exhibits, and decorative furnishings are covered in Chapter 95.

Note: To understand key issues that will enable you to make best use of the information in this section we recommend that you see "Introduction" on page 425.

Key Factors

The key factors in the importation of furnishings are:

- For cribs: compliance with Consumer Product Safety Commission (CPSC) safety standards
- For mattresses: compliance with Flammable Fabrics Act (FFA) flammability standards
- For lighting fixtures: compliance with voluntary Underwriters' Laboratory (UL) lighting standards, monitored by the Consumer Product Safety Commission (CPSC)

Although most importers utilize the services of a licensed customs broker in making their entries, and we recommend this practice, you should be aware of the regulatory, entry, and documentation issues involved in importing your product. You, as importer, are ultimately responsible for the fulfillment of any legal requirements applicable to your shipment.

General Considerations

Regulations. Chapter 94 covers a wide variety of articles within a very few headings and subheadings relative to other chapters of the HTSUS, and its classifications are generally broad and inclusive. With a few important exceptions, importation of furnishings is straightforward. No permits, licenses, or special entry paperwork are required. Infants' and children's furnishings are regulated by the CPSC, under the provisions of the Consumer Product Safety Act (CPSA). Specific restrictions, prohibitions, and requirements apply to full-size and non-full-size baby cribs under the law. (See "Prohibitions and Restrictions" below.)

Definitions. Under previous Customs regulations, furnishings had to fit on the floor or ground to be classified as furniture. However, under the HTSUS, certain furniture—including cupboards, bookcases, shelved furniture, unit furniture, seats, and beds are also considered to be furniture even if they are designed to be hung, fixed to a wall, or stand on another piece of furniture or some other architectural element.

Furniture with Textile Content. Furniture incorporating textile elements is not considered a textile quota commodity, and is not restricted by the terms of Multi-Fiber Arrangements (MFA). However, such furniture must be labeled according to provisions of the Textile Fiber Products Identification Act (TFPIA), which is administered by the Federal Trade Commission (FTC).

Textile Labeling and Invoice Requirements. You are responsible for your imported product's compliance with applicable provisions of the TFPIA. Furniture with textile components that require labeling under TFPIA must already be labeled at entry, or the shipment will be refused. (See "Marking and Labeling Requirements" below.) If you import shipments of furniture with textile components subject to TFPIA and valued at over $500, you must provide special information on the entry invoice (see "Entry and Documentation" below).

Flammability Standards. Furniture containing textile elements also falls under provisions of the Flammable Fabrics Act (FFA) administered by the CPSC. You should be aware that introduction into U.S. commerce of any item for which there is an applicable FFA standard, and that does not comply with that standard, is subject to legal action by the CPSC. If the commission believes a product does not comply with a flammability standard, it is authorized to pursue a variety of legal sanctions, including 1) seizure, condemnation, and forfeiture of the noncomplying product; 2) administrative cease-and-desist order requiring an individual or firm to stop sale and distribution of the noncomplying product; or 3) temporary injunction requiring the individual or firm to stop sale and distribution of the noncomplying product pending final disposition of the administrative cease-and-desist proceeding.

For most items of textile furniture there are at present no regulations or standards promulgated under FFA, and importation of these items is not actively monitored by CPSC. However, mattresses and mattress pads are subject to specific FFA standards, and are actively monitored by the CPSC. Importers are legally responsible for all aspects of compliance. (See "Prohibitions and Restrictions" below.)

Product Safety. The CPSC also has authority, under the Consumer Product Safety Improvement Act of 1990, to seek civil penalties against any person who knowingly violates a regulation or standard issued under section 4 of the FFA. The commission may seek a civil penalty of up to $5,000 per product involved, up to a maximum penalty of $1.25 million for any related series of violations.

The CPSC takes its responsibility for consumer protection seriously, and the wise importer will make sure that products are in compliance with applicable standards. Not only that, but persons who trade in articles covered under CPSA are responsible for making Substantial Product Hazard Reports to CPSC when they become aware that such product could have a defect that presents substantial risk of injury or death to the public.

In addition, importers of consumer products are responsible to report to the commission if: 1) a particular model of the product is the subject of at least three civil actions filed in federal or state court; 2) each suit alleges the involvement of that model in death or grievous bodily injury; and 3) at least three of the actions result in a final settlement involving the manufacturer in a judgment for the plaintiff within any one of the two-year periods specified in section 37 of CPSA.

Lighting. Importation of lighting and lighting fixtures is relatively straightforward. You do not need permits or licenses. U.S. Customs requires a breakdown, by weight, of materials composing each article (i.e. how much metal, how much glass, how much wood) for tariff classification purposes. The breakdown may appear on the invoice presented at entry, or may be attached as a separate sheet provided by the supplier.

Lighting and lighting fixtures fall under the jurisdiction of the CPSC, which administers the Consumer Product Safety Act (CPSA). CPSC does not require any special entry documentation or procedures. There are no restrictions or prohibitions under CPSA pertaining to lighting or lighting fixtures. However, voluntary UL standards have been established for indoor and outdoor lights, including Christmas lights. Manufacturers may list complying products with UL, and may mark or label those products as UL-listed, thus assuring the U.S. consumer that the products meet with voluntary compliance standards. Only products that are UL-listed may bear such labeling or marking. Though there is no federal requirement that an item be listed with UL, requirements vary by state. Certain states prohibit the sale and use of non-listed electrical products. Products that are not listed with are not necessarily noncomplying products, nor does unlisted status necessarily imply that the product is dangerous.

Consumer Product Import Surveillance Program. The CPSC monitors imports of many different types of commodities under its Import Surveillance Program. From time to time, CPSC inspects shipments to ascertain compliance with voluntary standards. In addition, Section 15 of the CPSA requires manufacturers, importers, distributors, or retailers to provide CPSC with Substantial Product Hazard Reports when a product defect is discovered that presents substantial risk of injury to the consumer. In such cases, CPSC must be notified, and remedial corrective action (i.e., a product recall) will be required. For more information regarding voluntary compliance standards for lighting and lighting fixtures, contact the CPSC (see addresses at end of this chapter).

Customs Classification

For customs purposes, furnishings are classified within Chapter 94 of the HTSUS. This chapter is divided into major headings, which are further divided into subheadings, and often into subsubheadings, each of which has its own HTSUS classification number. For example, the 2001 HTSUS number for chairs of teak is 9401.61.20, indicating that it is a subcategory of other upholstered seats with wooden frames (9401.61), which is a subcategory of the major heading seats, whether or not convertible into beds, and parts thereof (9401). There are six major headings in HTSUS Chapter 94.

9401—Seats (other than those of heading 9402), whether or not convertible into beds, and parts thereof

9402—Medical, surgical, dental or veterinary furniture (for example, operating tables, examination tables, hospital beds with mechanical fittings, dentists chairs); barbers' chairs and similar chairs, having rotating as well as both reclining and elevating movements; parts of the foregoing articles

9403—Other furniture and parts thereof

9404—Mattress supports; articles of bedding and similar furnishing (for example, mattresses, quilts, eiderdowns, cushions, pouffes, and pillows) fitted with springs or stuffed or internally fitted with any material or of cellular rubber or plastics, whether or not covered

9405—Lamps and lighting fittings including searchlights and spotlights and parts thereof, not elsewhere specified or included; illuminated signs, illuminated nameplates and the like, having a permanent fixed light source, and parts thereof not elsewhere specified or included

9406—Prefabricated buildings

For more details regarding classification of the specific product you are interested in importing, consult a customs broker, the appropriate commodity specialist at your nearest customs port, or see HTSUS. The 2001 HTSUS is available online from the Customs Service (www.customs.gov/impoexpo/impoexpo.htm) or for purchase from the U.S. Government Printing Office (see resources at the end of this chapter), and may be found in larger public libraries. For a general discussion of customs classification, see "Classification—Liquidation" on page 229.

Dutiable Status of Goods

For more information about duty rates and binding decisions see "Dutiable Status of Goods" on page 203; for a discussion of temporary importation of goods see "Temporary Free Importations" on page 205.

Valuation

Importers have a responsibility to use what the U.S. Customs Service deems, "reasonable care," when determining the value of their goods. They must also provide any additional information that the Customs Service needs for setting a final value on the goods. This process involves a number of factors and can be somewhat complicated; importers must be aware of applicable issues and details. Valuation information applies to all types of commodities, for further discussion on the subject see "Customs Valuation" on page 267.

Import Duties

Import duties vary (often dramatically) depending upon the Harmonized Tariff Schedule (HTSUS) classification of the goods or products imported. Since some products that look alike have different HTSUS classifications and different rates of duty, proper classification is vital. Note that "differences of opinion" between importers and the Bureau of Customs and Border Protection regarding classification keeps customs attorneys very busy.

Import duties can be assessed on the imported value of the goods ("ad valorem" rates of duty such as 2%, 4.4%, 50%, etc.), total units or weight of the goods ("specific" rates of duty such as 2 cents each or 1.5 cents/pound, etc.) or on a combination basis ("compound" rates of duty such as 5 cents each plus 6%).

Listed below is a sampling of several Column 1 import duty rates for Chapter 94 products:
Seats other than garden seats or camping equipment, convertible into beds (9401.40.00.00): Free
to
Mattresses of cellular rubber or plastics, whether or not covered (9404.21.00. 00): 3%

For specific information on US import duties refer to the Harmonized Tariff Schedule of the US. The print version is available from the US Government Printing Office as well as third party suppliers who often add special features. Online versions are available in both static PDF pages as well as in formats with excellent search functionality. Search the Web with the term "Harmonized Tariff Schedule" to find sources.

Entry and Documentation

The entry of merchandise is a two-part process consisting of 1) filing the documents necessary to determine whether merchandise may be released from Customs custody and 2) filing the documents that contain information for duty assessment and statistical purposes. In certain instances all documents must be filed and accepted by Customs prior to the release of the goods. Unless you have been granted an extension, you must file entry documents at a location specified by the district/area director within five working days of your shipment's date of arrival at a U.S. port of entry. These include a number of standard documents required by Customs for any entry.

After you present the entry, Customs may examine your shipment, or may waive examination. The shipment is then released, provided no legal or regulatory violations have occurred. You must then file entry summary documentation and deposit estimated duties at a designated customhouse within 10 working days of your shipment's release. For a detailed description of entry procedures, standard documentation, and informal entry, see "Entry Process" on page 185.

Informed Compliance. Informed compliance was introduced with the Customs Modernization Act of 1993 (Mod Act) and defines the relationship between importers and the Customs Service. It sets out the responsibilities of both parties. Providing the correct documentation and information for entry is a key factor that will make your importing operation run smoothly. We recommend that importers become familiar with the concept of informed comliance and the responsibilities that they have under the Mod Act. For further discussion about informed compliance see "Informed Compliance" on page 211.

Entry Invoice—TFPIA Requirements. All invoices for furnishings containing textiles should indicate: 1) the constituent fiber or combination of fibers in the textile fiber product, designating with equal prominence each natural or manufactured fiber in the textile fiber product by its generic name in the order of predominance by the weight thereof if the weight of such fiber is 5%or more of the total fiber weight of the product; 2) percentage of each fiber present, by weight, in the total fiber content of the textile fiber product; 3) the name, or other identification issued and registered by the FTC, of the manufacturer of the product or one or more persons subject to Section 3 of the TFPIA (15 USC 70a) with respect to such product; and 4) the name of the country where processed or manufactured. For more general information about invoices see "Invoices" on page 277.

*Note: The Entry and Documentation section has been carefully designed to supply you, the importer, with sample documents and direc-*tions on how to satisfy Customs requirements. Be aware that you should consult the applicable authorities to ensure that you are correctly following the most current procedures.

Prohibitions and Restrictions

Although furniture designers, manufacturers, and importers usually have considerable leeway in the products they may deal in, detailed regulations and specifications do exist for specific types of furnishings, including infant furniture and bedding.

Baby Cribs. Specific standards have been adopted for baby cribs, including rail height, spacing of crib components, interior dimensions, acceptable hardware, finishing details, and instructions to be included with items that require assembly, for both full-size and non-full-size cribs. These specifications are extremely detailed and must be strictly followed. See 16 CFR 1508 and 1509.

Such items as mesh/net/screen cribs, nonrigidly constructed baby cribs, cradles (both rocker and pendulum types), car beds, baby baskets, and bassinets (also known as junior cribs) are not subject to the requirements. However, these items are regulated by the CPSC under the CPSA. If you are interested in importing them, you should be familiar with basic applicable safety regulations for items intended for use by children. For more information, contact the CPSC (see addresses at end of this chapter).

Recordkeeping. If you import cribs, you must keep and maintain the following records, for three years after production or importation of each product lot: 1) sale, 2) distribution, and 3) results of all inspections and tests conducted in accordance with 16 CFR 1508. When any CPSC officer, employee, or agent asks to see your records, you must allow full access to them, as long as the request was made at a reasonable time. If he or she needs to make copies, conduct inventories, or in any other way verify the accuracy of the records you provide, you must allow him to do so.

Mattresses and Mattress Pads. Standards have been established under the FFA for the flammability of mattresses and mattress pads. These standards are found in 16 CFR 1632. The law defines "mattress" as a ticking filled with a resilient material, used alone or in combination with other products, intended or promoted for sleeping upon. This includes, but is not limited to: adult, youth, crib, and bunk bed mattresses; futons, water beds and air mattresses that contain upholstery material between the ticking and the mattress core; any detachable mattresses used in any item of upholstered furniture, e.g. convertible sofa bed, corner group, day bed, roll-away bed, high riser, and trundle bed mattresses.

Not subject to this regulation are such items as: sleeping bags; pillows; mattress foundations; liquid-and gaseous-filled tickings such as water beds and air mattresses that do not contain upholstery material between the ticking and mattress core; upholstered furniture that does not contain a detachable mattress such as chaise lounges; drop-arm loveseats; press-back lounges; push-back sofas; sleep lounges; sofa beds (including jackknife sofa beds); sofa lounges (including glide-outs); studio couches and divans (including twin studio divans and studio beds); juvenile product pads, e.g. such as car bed, carriage basket, infant carrier and lounge, dressing table, stroller, and playpen pads; or crib bumpers.

The terms "mattress and mattress pad" will be used to refer only to those mattresses and mattress pads that are subject to the regulatory standards of the FFA.

Prototype Testing Requirements. Each manufacturer of mattresses and mattress pads intended for sale in the U.S., and all other persons or firms initially introducing such articles into U.S. commerce, must meet all applicable requirements under the FFA. This includes importers. If you are interested in importing these products, you will benefit from an awareness of general testing requirements, since no mattress or mattress pad may be introduced into U.S. commerce unless it has been subjected to prototype testing and has been certified as being in compliance. It is not within the purview of this index to outline testing procedures. If you need more information on prototype testing than what is briefly outlined below, you should contact CPSC for pertinent details.

The specified tests are designed to determine an article's ignition resistance when exposed to a lighted cigarette. The necessary testing is a premarket procedure. Therefore, no mattress or mattress pad for which a prototype has not passed the required tests may be marketed in the U.S. No failed prototype may be marketed in the U.S. unless the prototype is reworked to rectify the problem, retested, and passed in a new test.

The test method measures the ignition resistance of a mattress or mattress pad by exposing the surface to lighted cigarettes in a draft-protected environment. The surfaces to be tested include smooth, tape edge, and any quilted or tufted locations. A two-sheet test is also conducted on similar surface locations. In the latter test, the burning cigarettes are placed between the sheets. The regulation provides specific technical requirements for specimen selection and test procedures.

It should be noted that a minimum of three, and in some cases six samples must be tested for clearance of a single prototype. If even one sample fails, the whole prototype will be disqualified unless and until it is reworked, retested, and passed. Failure to comply, and especially knowing failure to comply, may result in legal penalties.

Recordkeeping. The FFA requires that every manufacturer, importer, or other person initially introducing mattresses or mattress pads into U.S. commerce maintain certain records. You must maintain records for each prototype, for as long as the prototype is in production, and/or the ticking and/or the tape edge material is being used on it. All required records must be retained for three years thereafter. You must maintain the following records: 1) manufacturing specification and description of each mattress or mattress pad prototype with an assigned prototype identification number; 2) test results for all or any of the three separate testing procedures described in the standards, as follows: prototype test (16 CFR 1632.4, 1632.5), ticking classification test (16 CFR 1632.6), and tape edge materials test (16 CFR 1637.7).

Required records common to all three tests are: Test results and details of each test performed, including a) prototype identification number; b) ticking classification (A, B, or C) if known (this is a mandatory record for ticking classification test results); c) test room conditions; d) cigarette locations; e) number of relights for each location; f) whether each cigarette location passed or failed; g) name and signature of person conducting test; and h) date of test.

In addition to the above information, records for prototype and type of edge materials tests must include: a) test supervisor's certification of standard testing procedures and result accuracy; b) photograph of the bare surface of each mattress or mattress pad tested, with each prototype identification number and a clear designation as to which part of the article was sheeted and that part was bare during testing; 3) certification from the ticking supplier, stating the ticking's classification and that the test was performed in accordance with 16 CFR 1632.6 is a valid alternative to ticking classification test result records; 4) records to support any determination that a particular material used in a prototype (other than ticking or tape edge material) did not influence the prototype's ignition resistance during testing and therefore could be substituted by another material—such record should include photographs of physical specimens; 5) manufacturing specifications and description of any new ticking or tape edge material substituted, with the identification number of the prototype involved; 6) where mattress pad laundering is required during testing procedure, details of any approved alternate laundering procedure used; 7) identification, composition,

and details of the application of any flame retardant treatments employed relative to mattress pads or mattress pad components; and 8) disposition of all failing or rejected prototype mattress or mattress pads. Such records must either: a) demonstrate that the items were retested and reworked in accordance with the standard, and were in compliance prior to sale or distribution, or b) otherwise show the disposition of such items.

Exemptions. "One of a kind" mattresses are exempt from prototype testing. This is a mattress or mattress pad manufactured in accordance with either a physician's written prescription or other comparable written medical therapeutic specification, to be used in connection with the treatment or management of a named individual's physical illness or injury. Such an article must bear a warning label (see "Marking and Labeling Requirements" below). The manufacturer or importer of this type of mattress, in lieu of recordkeeping requirements named above, must keep a copy of the written prescription or other comparable written medical therapeutic specification for each mattress or mattress pad, during a period of three years, measured from the date of manufacture.

Marking and Labeling Requirements

Furniture with Textile Content. Furniture that includes a textile element must be labeled according to requirements of the Textile Fiber Products Identification Act (TFPIA). All textile products imported into the U.S. must be stamped, tagged, labeled, or otherwise marked with the following information as required by the TFPIA, unless exempt from marking (see TFPIA, Section 12): 1) the generic names and percentages by weight of the constituent fibers present in the textile fiber product, exclusive of permissible ornamentation, in amounts of more than 5% in order of predominance by weight, with any percentage of fiber or fibers required to be designated as "other fiber" or "other fibers" (including those present in amounts of 5% or less) appearing last; and 2) the name of the manufacturer or the name or registered identification number issued by the FTC of one or more persons marketing or handling the textile fiber product; and 3) the name of the country where processed. A word trademark, used as a house mark and registered with the U.S. Patent Office, may appear on labels instead of the name otherwise required, provided the owner of the trademark furnishes a copy of the registration to FTC prior to use.

The information listed above is not exhaustive. TFPIA requirements are extensive. The Act specifies such details as types of labels, means of attachment, label position on the article, package labeling, unit labeling for two-piece garments, and arrangement of information on the label; allowable fiber designations; country-of-origin indications; requirements for trim and ornamentation, linings and interlinings, and pile fabrics; sectional disclosure; use of trade names and trademarks; and requirements for swatches and samples. The FTC publishes a booklet intended to clarify TFPIA requirements to facilitate voluntary compliance in the industry (see "Publications and WWW Resources" below). It is available on request, at no charge, from the FTC (see addresses at end of this chapter).

Cribs and Their Retail Cartons. Each crib and retail carton must be clearly marked to indicate: 1) name and place of business (city and state) of manufacturer, importer, distributor and/or seller; and 2) model, stock, catalog, or item number, or other numerical symbol to identify articles of identical construction, composition, and dimensions.

A warning statement regarding mattress dimensions is required both for full-size and non-full-size cribs. For the statement required on non-full-size cribs, see below. The following is the required statement for full-size cribs. It must appear both on the retail carton and the inside of the head end-panel or the top surface of the mattress support. "CAUTION: Any mattress used in this crib must be at least 27 1/4 inches by 51 5/8 inches with a thickness not exceeding 6 inches" or "CAUTION: Any mattress used in this crib must be at least 69 cm by 131 cm with a thickness not exceeding 15 cm." The marking must appear in block letters at least one-fourth inch high, must contrast sharply with the background (by color, projection, and/or indentation), and must be clearly visible and legible. Mattress dimension must be taken from seam to seam, or edge to edge where appropriate.

Crib markings must be of a permanent nature. They may be paint-stenciled, die-stamped, molded, or indelibly stamped directly on the crib, or permanently affixed, fastened, or attached to it by means of a tag, token, or other suitable medium. Markings must not be readily removable or subject to obliteration either during normal crib use or as a result of reasonably foreseeable damage or abuse.

Non-Full-Size Cribs. In addition to marking and labeling requirements outlined above, which are applicable to all cribs regardless of type or size, the following mattress caution statements are required for non-full-size cribs. The inside surface of any rectangular crib must bear the warning: "CAUTION: Any mattress used in this crib must be at least X inches long by Y inches wide and not more than Z inches thick." The manufacturer should fill the blanks with applicable dimensions complying with mattress size requirements in 16 CFR 1509.9. The inside surface of any nonrectangular crib must bear the warning: "CAUTION: Check proper fit of mattress. Should be not more than X inches thick. The maximum gap between mattress and inside of crib border (or edge) should be no more than 1 inch." The specifications should state applicable dimension to effect compliance with 16 CFR 1509.9.

Mattress and Mattress Pad Labeling Under the FFA. All mattresses and mattress pads subject to the standard must bear a permanent accessible and legible label containing the month and year of manufacture and manufacturer's location. All FFA-required label information must be set forth separately from any other label information Other information, representations, or disclosures appearing on any required or other label may not interfere with, minimize, detract from, or conflict with required information. Only the ultimate consumer may remove or mutilate any required label.

All mattress pads that contain a chemical fire retardant must be labeled with precautionary instructions to protect the pads from agents or treatments known to cause deterioration of their flame resistance. Such labels must be permanent, prominent, conspicuous, and legible. If a mattress contains a chemical fire retardant, it must be prominently, conspicuously, and legibly labeled with the letter "T."

One-of-a-kind mattresses and mattress pads must bear a permanent, conspicuous and legible label with the following statement: "WARNING: This mattress or mattress pad may be subject to ignition and hazardous smoldering from cigarettes. It was manufactured in accordance with a physician's prescription and has not been tested under the Federal Standard for the Flammability of Mattresses (FF 4-72)." This labeling must be attached to the mattress or mattress pad so as to remain on or affixed to it for the useful life of the article. It must be at least 40 square inches (250 sq. cm.) with no linear dimension less than 5 inches (12.5 cm). The letters in the word "Warning" must be no less than 0.5 inch (1.27 cm) in height. All letters on the label must be in a color that contrasts with label background. The label warning statement must also be conspicuously displayed on the invoice or other sales papers that accompany the mattress in commerce from manufacturer to final point of sale to a consumer.

For a general discussion of U.S. Customs marking and labeling requirements, see "Country of Origin Marking" on page 236, "Special Marking Requirements" on page 238 and "Marking—False Impression" on page 239.

Shipping Considerations

You will need to ensure that your goods are packaged and shipped with care to ensure that they arrive in good condition and pass smoothly through Customs. You are responsible for ensuring that the shipment is in compliance with all applicable government regulations for packaging and shipping. In most instances, you should not leave these arrangements solely to the discretion of your supplier. Careful preparation of the cargo and selection of the mode of transport can be essential to a cost-effective, timely delivery of undamaged goods. We strongly advise you to consult your shipping representative, insurance agent, or freight broker for advice on packing and shipping.

Furnishings are goods that may be heavy, bulky, and fragile. They require careful packing and stowing to withstand the rigors of transport. Care must be taken to avoid damage due to shifting of the cargo, as well as to protect the goods from heat, humidity, or water, which can damage surfaces and components of some products.

Publications and WWW Resources

The following publication may be relevant to the importation of furnishings containing textiles:

> *Threading Your Way Through the Labeling Requirements Under the Textile & Wool Acts*

Available free of charge online from the Federal Trade Commission (www.ftc.gov/os/statutes/textilejump.htm), this publication is an excellent source of information written in clear lay language. We recommend that anyone interested in importing textile products but unfamiliar with the regulations obtain a copy of this document.

The *Harmonized Tariff Schedule of the United States (2001)* (HTSUS) is available to view on the Customs Service website (www.customs.gov), or you may purchase a printed version from:

U.S. Government Printing Office
Superintendent of Documents
710 North Capital Street NW
Washington DC 20401
Tel: (202) 512-1800
Fax: (202) 512-1657
Website: www.access.gpo.gov

The USGPO also has copies of specific laws available for purchase. The USGPO accepts orders made by fax, phone or placed over the Internet, as well as mail orders paid by credit card. All orders must be accompanied by payment. Credit cards, checks drawn on a U.S. bank, or an international money order are all acceptable.

Relevant Government Agencies

Address questions regarding labeling requirements under TFPIA to:

Federal Trade Commission (FTC)
Division of Enforcement
600 Pennsylvania Avenue NW
Washington DC 20580
Tel: (202) 326-2996
Website: www.ftc.gov

Address questions regarding FFA and/or CPSA requirements for imported furniture to:

Consumer Product Safety Commission (CPSC)
Office of Compliance
Washington DC 20207-0001
Tel: 800-638-2772 or (301) 504-7912
Fax: (301) 504 0359
Website: www.cpsc.gov

Address questions regarding the importation of furnishings to your local Customs port director. For addresses refer to "U.S. Customs and Border Protection Offices" on page 65 or contact:

U.S. Customs and Border Protection
Customs Headquarters
1300 Pennsylvania Avenue NW
Washington DC 20229
Tel: (202) 354-1000
Website: www.customs.treas.gov

Laws and Regulations

The following laws and regulations may be relevant to the importation of furnishings. The laws are contained in the U.S. Code (USC) and the regulations are published in the Code of Federal Regulations (CFR), both of which may be available at larger public and law libraries. Copies of specific laws are also available from the United States Government Printing Office (address above).

15 USC 2051 et seq.
Consumer Product Safety Act
This act gives the Consumer Product Safety Commission authority to set safety standards, testing procedures, and reporting requirements to ensure that consumer products not already covered under other regulations are not harmful.

15 USC 70-77
Textile Fiber Products Identification Act (TFPIA)
This Act prohibits false or deceptive labeling (misbranding) and false advertising of any textile fiber products and requires all textile fiber products imported into the U.S. to be labeled in accordance with the requirements set forth in the law.

19 CFR 11.12b; 16 CFR 303 et seq.
Regulations on Labeling and Marking
These regulations detail the labeling and marking requirements for textiles as specified by the CPSC and the invoice contents required by U.S. Customs for purpose of enforcing the labeling and marking rules.

15 USC 1191-1204
Flammable Fabrics Act (FFA)
This Act provides for the setting of flammability standards for fabric by the Consumer Product Safety Commission (CPSC) and for enforcement by U.S. Customs.

16 CFR 1610, 1611, 1615, 1616, 1630-1632
Regulations on Flammable Fabric Standards
These regulations specify the flammability standards adopted by the CPSC under the FFA for various types of textiles.

Principal Exporting Countries

The following listing includes samples of the main supplier nations of the products of this chapter. It is organized by HTSUS major heading. (Refer to "Customs Classification" above for the product codes.) Countries are listed in rank order of the value of products imported to the U.S. Statistics represent customs value of entries for 2002 from the Bureau of Census, U.S. Department of Commerce.

9401—Mexico, China, Canada, Italy, Taiwan, Argentina, Malaysia, Indonesia, Germany, Thailand

9402—Canada, Taiwan, Japan, China, United Kingdom, Germany, Sweden

9403—China, Canada, Mexico, Italy, Taiwan, Indonesia, Malaysia, Thailand

9404—China, Mexico, Canada, India, Pakistan, Thailand

9405—China, Mexico, Canada, Taiwan, Hong Kong, India, Italy, Germany

9406—Canada, Israel, United Kingdom, China, Germany, United Arab Emirates, Mexico, Sweden

Chapter 95:
Toys, Games, and Sports Equipment

Full title: Toys, Games, and Sports Equipment; Parts and Accessories Thereof

This section pertains to the importation of toys, games, sporting goods, and related items, which are classified within Chapter 95 of the Harmonized Tariff Schedule of the United States (HTSUS). Specifically, it includes wheeled children's riding toys, dolls and other figures, stuffed toys, models, mechanical and electrically-driven toys, puzzles, games, video games and game equipment, Christmas decorations, party goods, sports equipment, swimming pools, exercise equipment, fishing equipment, and carnival rides and equipment.

If you are interested in importing hunting equipment, including firearms and ammunition, refer to Commodity Index Chapter 93. Fireworks and similar articles are covered in Chapter 36. Line not made up into fishing line is found in Chapters 39 and 42, or in the Commodity Index chapters covering the various types of textile materials (Chapters 50-63). Sports bags are covered in Chapters 42 and 43, while sports clothes are included in Chapters 61 or 62, and flags, bunting, and similar articles are covered in Chapter 63. Sports footwear and headgear are found, respectively, in Chapters 64 and 65. Walking sticks, riding crops, and similar items are covered in Chapter 66. Unmounted glass eyes for dolls or other toys are classified in Chapter 70. Electric motors, transformers, and remote control devices are found in Chapter 85. Bicycles are covered in Chapter 87 and boats in Chapter 89. Goggles and other eyewear for sports use are classified in Chapter 90. Christmas tree candles are found in Chapter 34 and Christmas tree lights in Chapter 94. Sporting arms and ammunition are covered in Chapter 93. Parts of general use—screws, nails, nuts, bolts, and washers—are covered according to the material of which they are composed: of base metals in Chapters 72-83, of plastics in Chapter 39, and of rubber in Chapter 40.

Note: To understand key issues that will enable you to make best use of the information in this section we recommend that you see "Introduction" on page 425.

Key Factors

The key factors in the importation of games are:

- Compliance with any applicable Consumer Product Safety Commission (CPSC) safety requirements
- Compliance with U.S. Food and Drug Administration (FDA) standards and entry notification for radiation-producing electronic devices

- Compliance with U.S. Federal Communications Commission (FCC) standards and entry notification for electronic radio frequency devices

- Compliance with trademark, trade name, and copyright restrictions, where applicable

Although most importers utilize the services of a licensed customs broker in making their entries, and we recommend this practice, you should be aware of the regulatory, entry, and documentation issues involved in importing your product. You, as importer, are ultimately responsible for the fulfillment of any legal requirements applicable to your shipment.

General Considerations

CPSC Regulation. There are no permits and licenses required to import products of HTSUS chapter 95. However, toys, games, and sporting goods fall under the jurisdiction of the CPSC, which administers and enforces the Consumer Product Safety Act (CPSA), and these products must comply with CPSA's extensive safety standards. Although the CPSC does not require any special import entry documentation or procedures, there are extensive restrictions on the types of toys and related items that may be introduced into U.S. commerce. Certain types of toys are banned from import entirely; others are banned unless they meet applicable CPSA safety and testing requirements. (See "Prohibitions and Restrictions" below.) The CPSC monitors imports of many different types of commodities under its Import Surveillance Program. From time to time, shipments may be inspected at random or for cause to ascertain compliance with mandatory safety standards. Products may also be tested by CPSC in order to determine compliance.

Substantial Product Hazard Reports. Defect-reporting requirements exist for any product covered under the CPSA, including toys. Section 15(b) of CPSA requires every manufacturer, distributor, or retailer of such products, who obtains information that reasonably supports the conclusion that such products either 1) fail to comply with an applicable consumer product safety rule, or 2) contain a defect that could create a substantial product hazard, to immediately inform the CSPC of the potential violation or defect. Your willful failure to make a Substantial Product Hazard Report can result in civil litigation by the CPSC.

The Commission is rigorous in its enforcement of safety standards for toys and other articles intended for recreational use, especially by children. Seven major U.S. importers of foreign toys have recently been sued by the CPSC for infractions of safety standards, or for failing to comply with substantial product hazard reporting as required under the CPSA. U.S. Customs cooperates with CPSC by seizing shipments identified as hazardous.

Litigation is not the CPSC's first course of action in cases of noncompliance. The Commission first issues warnings, giving importers ample opportunity to correct problems. However, do not let the fact that port of entry inspections are not performed on each and every toy shipment lull you into believing that noncomplying toys may be entered into U.S. commerce if they can slip through customs. Products that do not comply can be recalled at any point. Repeated noncompliance may result in investigation by CPSC and in possible litigation. Be familiar with the regulations applicable to your product, and be sure your product is in compliance. If you have any doubts, contact the CPSC before making your purchase.

Electronic Devices. Many electronic devices subject to regulation fall into two general categories: those that produce radio frequency energy, and those that produce radiation. Radiation-producing electronic devices are regulated by the FDA (see addresses at end of this chapter) under the provisions of the Federal Food, Drug, and Cosmetic Act (FDCA) and the Radiation Control for Health and Safety Act of 1968 (RCHSA). Both imported and domestically produced electronic products must comply with all relevant FDA and FCC regulations. Whether you are importing a single product

for personal use, or a commercial shipment for resale in the U.S., you must file an Electronic Product Declaration (**Form FD2877**) for each product type for which official standards exist. You will not be permitted to enter a shipment unless you have filed these forms. You may obtain them from FDA, National Center for Devices and Radiological Health (see addresses at end of this chapter) or from your customs broker. For a general discussion of FDA import procedures, see "Appendix: Foods" on page 825.

Radio frequency (rf) devices are regulated by the FCC (see addresses at end of this chapter) under the provisions of 47 CFR Parts 2 and 15. You must file a copy of FCC **Form 740** with each shipment of rf devices. If your shipment consists of more than one type of device, you must file a separate form for each type. The form certifies that the imported model or device is either in compliance with, or is exempt from, FCC requirements, and is so labeled.

Products that fall under the jurisdiction of both the FCC and the FDA and must comply with both sets of regulations. Do not rely on one agency for information concerning the requirements of another agency. If you are in doubt as to the status of your product, contact both the FCC and the FDA.

Copyright and Trademark Provisions. Products such as some video games or branded toys may be subject to patent and trademark restrictions. (See "Prohibitions and Restrictions" below.) The Intellectual Property Rights (IPR) branch of U.S. Customs enforces laws pertinent to entry of such products. Importers must be prepared to show valid authorization from trademark and copyright holders. Pirated products are subject to seizure.

IRS Considerations. Certain types of fishing tackle have a 10% Internal Revenue Service (IRS) tax levied in addition to customs duty rates. Customs does not collect this tax at entry, and the tax is not part of the Customs entry procedures. If you are considering importation of fishing tackle, you should contact the IRS for relevant information.

Customs Classification

For customs purposes toys, games, and sporting goods are classified within Chapter 95 of the HTSUS. This chapter is divided into major headings, which are further divided into subheadings, and often into sub-subheadings, each of which has its own HTSUS classification number. For example, the 2001 HTSUS number for stuffed dolls is 9502.10.00.10, indicating that it is a subcategory of dolls, whether or not dressed (9502.10), which is a subcategory of the major heading dolls representing only human beings and parts and accessories thereof (9502). There are eight major headings in HTSUS Chapter 95.

9501—Wheeled toys designed to be ridden by children (for example, tricycles, scooters, pedal cars); dolls' carriages and dolls' strollers; parts and accessories thereof

9502—Dolls representing only human beings and parts and accessories thereof

9503—Other toys; reduced size ("scale") models and similar recreational models, working or not; puzzles of all kinds; parts and accessories thereof

9504—Articles for arcade, table, or parlor games, including pinball machines, bagatelle, billiards, and special tables for casino games; automatic bowling alley equipment; parts and accessories thereof

9505—Festive, carnival or other entertainment articles, including magic tricks and practical joke articles; parts and accessories thereof

9506—Articles and equipment for general physical exercises, gymnastics, athletics, other sports (including table-tennis) or outdoor games, not specified or included elsewhere in this chapter; swimming pools and wading pools; parts and accessories thereof

9507—Fishing rods, fish hooks, and other line fishing tackle; fish landing nets, butterfly nets, and similar nets; decoy "birds" (other than those of heading 9208 or 9705), and similar hunting or shooting equipment; parts and accessories thereof

9508—Merry-go-rounds, boat-swings, shooting galleries, and other fairground amusements; traveling circuses, traveling menageries, and traveling theaters; parts and accessories thereof

For more details regarding classification of the specific product you are interested in importing, consult a customs broker, the appropriate commodity specialist at your nearest Customs port, or see HTSUS. The 2001 HTSUS is available online from the Customs Service (www.customs.gov/impoexpo/impoexpo.htm) or for purchase from the U.S. Government Printing Office (see resources at the end of this chapter), and may be found in larger public libraries. For a general discussion of customs classification, see "Classification—Liquidation" on page 229.

Dutiable Status of Goods

For more information about duty rates and binding decisions see "Dutiable Status of Goods" on page 203; for a discussion of temporary importation of goods see "Temporary Free Importations" on page 205.

Valuation

Importers have a responsibility to use what the U.S. Customs Service deems, "reasonable care," when determining the value of their goods. They must also provide any additional information that the Customs Service needs for setting a final value on the goods. This process involves a number of factors and can be somewhat complicated; importers must be aware of applicable issues and details. Valuation information applies to all types of commodities, for further discussion on the subject see "Customs Valuation" on page 267.

Import Duties

Import duties vary (often dramatically) depending upon the Harmonized Tariff Schedule (HTSUS) classification of the goods or products imported. Since some products that look alike have different HTSUS classifications and different rates of duty, proper classification is vital. Note that "differences of opinion" between importers and the Bureau of Customs and Border Protection regarding classification keeps customs attorneys very busy.

Import duties can be assessed on the imported value of the goods ("ad valorem" rates of duty such as 2%, 4.4%, 50%, etc.), total units or weight of the goods ("specific" rates of duty such as 2 cents each or 1.5 cents/pound, etc.) or on a combination basis ("compound" rates of duty such as 5 cents each plus 6%).

Listed below is a sampling of several Column 1 import duty rates for Chapter 95 products:
Chain-driven wheeled toys (9501.00.20.00): Free
to
Articles and equipment for table-tennis, and parts and accessories thereof (9506.40.00.00): 5.1%

For specific information on US import duties refer to the Harmonized Tariff Schedule of the US. The print version is available from the US Government Printing Office as well as third party suppliers who often add special features. Online versions are available in both static PDF pages as well as in formats with excellent search functionality. Search the Web with the term "Harmonized Tariff Schedule" to find sources.

Entry and Documentation

The entry of merchandise is a two-part process consisting of 1) filing the documents necessary to determine whether merchandise may be released from Customs custody and 2) filing the documents that contain information for duty assessment and statistical purposes. In certain instances all documents must be filed and accepted by Customs prior to the release of the goods.

Unless you have been granted an extension, you must file entry documents at a location specified by the port or area director within five working days of your shipment's date of arrival at a U.S. port of entry. These include a number of standard documents required by Customs for any entry, and:

- Electronic Product Declaration Form FD 2877
- For electronic devices, FCC Declaration Form FCC 740
- For products subject to regulation by both agencies, both forms mentioned above
- For products subject to copyright or trademark laws, authorization from the copyright or trademark holder

After you present the entry, Customs may examine your shipment, or may waive examination. The shipment is then released provided no legal or regulatory violations have been noted. You must then file entry summary documentation and deposit estimated duties at a designated customhouse within 10 working days of your shipment's release. For a detailed description of entry procedures, standard documentation, and informal entry, see "Entry Process" on page 185.

Informed Compliance. Informed compliance was introduced with the Customs Modernization Act of 1993 (Mod Act) and defines the relationship between importers and the Customs Service. It sets out the responsibilities of both parties. Providing the correct documentation and information for entry is a key factor that will make your importing operation run smoothly. We recommend that importers become familiar with the concept of informed comliance and the responsibilities that they have under the Mod Act. For further discussion about informed compliance see "Informed Compliance" on page 211.

Note: The Entry and Documentation section has been carefully designed to supply you, the importer, with sample documents and directions on how to satisfy Customs requirements. Be aware that you should consult the applicable authorities to ensure that you are correctly following the most current procedures.

Prohibitions and Restrictions

Potential Hazards. In general, 16 CFR 1500 seeks to prevent articles intended for children's use from presenting potential hazards resulting either from normal use or from reasonably foreseeable damage, abuse, or unintended use. To this end, the regulation prescribes stringent safety tests for toys deemed to present even a potential hazard. The tests are designed to simulate use and abuse of toys in order to determine resultant potential hazards. Regulations and tests vary depending upon the nature of the toy and the age group for which the toy is targeted. Toys not specified by the manufacturer for any particular age range are subjected to the most stringent testing composed of the procedures for all age groups. The regulation makes the following age distinctions: toys intended for use by children 1) 18 months of age or less; 2) 18 months to 36 months of age; or 3) 36 months to 96 months of age.

Toys deemed to represent a hazard under normal use or under reasonably foreseeable damage or abuse fall within three categories: 1) those that present mechanical hazards; 2) electric toys or articles that present electrical, thermal, or certain other mechanical hazards; and 3) those that are not electrical toys, but that present an electrical or thermal hazard. In addition, certain toys may be prohibited under the Federal Hazardous Substances Act (FHSA).

Mechanical Hazards. For purposes of regulation, toys present mechanical hazards by virtue of the following:

1) Toys with sharp points, sharp glass or metal edges, or sharp wires or protrusions. Hazards include possible lacerations, puncture wound injuries. Types of toys: certain rattles and pacifiers, toys with noisemaking elements, stuffed toys with certain internal and external components, certain walkers or jumpers,

lawn darts. (Note: lawn darts are unconditionally banned articles; there are no exceptions and no exemptions.)

2) Toys with small parts that can become dislodged or be willfully removed by the child. Hazards: aspiration, ingestion, choking, etc. Types of toys: certain rattles and certain toys with noisemaking elements, etc.

3) Toys with exposed parts such as coil springs that may expand sufficiently to allow an infant's finger, toe, etc. to be caught between the coils and injured. Hazards: amputation, crushing, lacerations, fractures, hematomas, bruises, or other injuries to fingers, toes, or other parts of the anatomy of young children. Articles: such items as baby bouncers, walker-jumpers, baby-walkers, etc.

4) Toys with impulse-type sound at a peak pressure level at or above 138 decibels. Hazard: hearing damage; article: toy caps intended for use with toy guns (see "Caps" below).

5) Toys constructed and used as noisemakers, whereby the parts can fracture, fragment, or disassemble during use. Toys of this nature are called "clacker balls." Design and construction of these items is highly regulated (see "Clacker Balls" below).

For each mechanical hazard listed above there are provisions under the regulation by which an article which could present such hazard can be considered in compliance and safe for the child.

Baby Bouncers and Jumpers. Importers of baby bouncers, walker-jumpers, baby-walkers, or similar articles are responsible for ensuring that these products are designed and constructed in keeping with specific requirements outlined in 16 CFR 1500.86(a)(4). There are also labeling requirements for these items (see "Marking and Labeling Requirements" below). If you import these toys, you are responsible for recordkeeping identical to that required for electrical toys (see "Recordkeeping" below).

Sharp Objects. Sharp points, sharp glass, or metal edge restrictions. 16 CFR 1500 prescribes tests to determine the accessibility of any sharp points or edges, or of any sharp metal or glass edges, in toys intended for children eight years old and under. The regulation exempts from such testing toys that by reason of their function necessitate the inclusion of sharp points (e.g. sewing machines) or sharp metal or glass edges (e.g. toy scissors or toy tool kits) and that do not have any nonfunctional sharp points or glass or metal edges. Exempted toys must be conspicuously labeled (see "Marking and Labeling Requirements" below). The regulation also exempts any children's non-toy articles that meet the criteria for exempted toys (e.g. ballpoint pens, children's ice skates, and children's cutlery).

Small Parts Restrictions. The regulation bans toys or articles intended for children under the age of three years that because of small parts present a hazard of choking, aspiration, or ingestion. Articles banned if they do not comply with the CPSA's specific safety standards include, but are not limited to: squeeze toys; teethers; crib exercisers; crib gyms; crib mobiles; other toys or articles intended to be affixed to a crib, stroller, playpen, or baby carriage; pull and push toys; pounding toys; blocks and stacking sets; bathtub, wading pool, and sand toys; rocking spring and stick horses, and other figures; chimes, musical balls, and carousels; jack-in-the-box toys; stuffed plush and flocked animals and other figures; preschool toys, games, and puzzles intended for use by children under three; infant and juvenile furniture articles intended for use by children under three, such as cribs, playpens, baby bouncers, walkers, strollers, and carriages; dolls intended for use by children under three, such as baby dolls, rag dolls, and bean bag dolls; toy cars, trucks, and other vehicles intended for use by children under three. With certain exceptions, all toys or articles intended, marketed, or labeled to be entrusted to, or used by, children under three years of age are subject to this regulation.

Exemptions to Small Parts Restrictions. The following are exempt from small parts restrictions: 1) balloons; 2) books and other articles made of paper; 3) writing materials such as crayons, chalk, pencils, and pens; 4) children's clothing and accessories, such as shoelace

holders and buttons; 5) grooming, feeding, and hygiene products, such as diaper pins and clips, barrettes, toothbrushes, drinking glasses, dishes, and eating utensils; 6) phonograph records; 7) modeling clay and similar products; 8) fingerpaints, watercolors, and other paint sets; 9) rattles (when in compliance with 16 CFR 1510.2) and 10) pacifiers (when in compliance with 16 CFR 1511.2(a)).

Rattles. Rattles are banned articles unless they comply with applicable requirements under the CPSA. These requirements are intended to eliminate from U.S. commerce infant rattles that may cause choking and/or suffocation because their design or construction permits them to enter an infant's mouth and become lodged in the throat. 16 CFR 1510 describes the tests required to determine compliance.

Pacifiers. Pacifiers are banned articles unless they meet requirements laid out in 16 CFR 1511. The regulation provides specifications and tests for structural integrity, guard or shield requirements, and protrusions. The attachment of ribbons, strings, cords, or other attachments, is expressly prohibited. Warning labeling is required (see "Marking and Labeling Requirements" below). In addition, rubber pacifiers containing significant levels of nitrosamines are banned hazardous substances as defined in Section 2(g) of FHSA. If you import pacifiers containing more than 60 parts per billion of nitrosamines as measured by methylene chloride extraction, the CPSC will bring an enforcement case against you.

Caps. Both paper and plastic caps for use in toy guns must be such that they do not produce peak sound pressure levels greater than 158 decibels when tested in accordance with 16 CFR 1500.47. They must bear warning labeling (see "Marking and Labeling Requirements" below). If you wish to distribute toy caps, you must notify CPSC Bureau of Compliance (CPSC address below) of your intention. You must either conduct or participate in a program to develop caps that produce a sound pressure level of not more than 138 decibels when tested in accordance with 16 CFR 1500.47. After notifying the CPSC of your intention, you must submit a progress report to the Bureau of Compliance at least once every three months concerning program status. If you are interested in importing caps, you should be aware that the prescribed maximum decibel level is under investigation, and that the regulation may be changed, pending CPSC's findings. Check with the CPSC for an update.

Clacker Balls. Clacker balls are banned unless they comply with all provisions in 16 CFR 1500.86(5)(i-vi). Clacker balls must be designed, manufactured, assembled, labeled, and tested in ways specified by the regulation (see "Marking and Labeling Requirements" below). Such articles must be tested according to regulation at time of production. Tested shipments must not exceed the failure rate outlined in the table found in 16 CFR 1500.86. Toys must be fully assembled at the time of sale. Recordkeeping requirements applicable to clacker balls are identical to those applicable to children's electrical items (see "Recordkeeping" below).

Electric Toys and Articles. Electrical toys for children include any toy, game, or other article designed, labeled, advertised, or otherwise intended for use by children, and powered by electrical current from nominal 120 volt branch circuits. Such articles are banned articles if in normal use or when subjected to reasonably foreseeable damage or abuse, the design or manufacture may: 1) cause personal injury or illness by electric shock; and/or 2) present an unreasonable risk of personal injury or illness because of heat (as from heated parts, substances, or surfaces), or because of certain mechanical hazards. Extensive manufacturing requirements specify standards for such elements of the toy as: protective coatings, mechanical assembly, structural integrity, switch mountings, insulating material, electrical design and construction, and performance.

Each manufacturer of electrical toys and articles for children must establish and maintain quality assurance programs to ensure compliance with all 16 CFR 1500 requirements. Electrical toys must be produced in accordance with detailed material specifications, production specifications, and quality assurance programs. They must be 1) constructed out of materials safe and suitable for the particular use for which the toy is intended; and 2) finished with a high degree of uniformity and as fine a grade of workmanship as is practicable in a well-equipped manufacturing establishment. Each component of a toy must comply with all applicable requirements in 16 CFR 1505. Electric toys and other children's articles require extensive labeling (see "Marking and Labeling Requirements" below).

Recordkeeping. If you import foreign electrical toys and articles, you are responsible for the compliance of your shipment. You must keep and maintain for three years after importation of each lot of toys, the following: 1) material and production specifications and description of required quality assurance program; 2) results of all inspections and tests conducted; and 3) records of sale and distribution. You are required to make these records available, upon request at reasonable times, to any officer or employee of the CPSC. You must also permit the CPSC to inspect and copy records, to make such inventories of stock as are deemed necessary, and to otherwise verify the accuracy of the records you keep.

Electrical and Thermal Hazards—Nonelectrical Toys. Kites 10 inches or greater in any dimension and constructed of aluminized polyester film, or any kite having a tail or other component consisting of a piece of aluminized polyester film 10 inches or greater in any dimension present a risk of personal injury from electric shock. Such kites conduct electricity, and may become entangled in, or otherwise contact, high voltage electric power lines. These kites are unconditionally banned, and there are no exceptions and no exemptions.

Other Hazards. Toys composed in part of flammable solids are prohibited. The regulation specifies testing whereby a substance may be determined to be "flammable." Toys painted with any coating substance containing lead are prohibited under 16 CFR 1303. There are no exceptions or exemptions associated with these prohibitions.

Exemptions. Certain articles are exempted from classification as banned hazardous substances, on condition that they are adequately labeled, and that adequate instructions and warnings are provided for safe use. They are: 1) chemistry sets and other science education sets, and their replacement components, when labeled according to 16 CFR 1500.83; 2) firecrackers designed to produce audible effects, if such effect is produced by a charge of not more than 500 milligrams of pyrotechnic composition; 3) educational materials such as art materials, preserved biological specimens, laboratory chemicals, and other articles intended and used for educational purpose; 4) liquid fuels containing more than 4% by weight of methyl alcohol, and intended for operation of miniature engines for model boats, cars, etc.; 5) novelties consisting of a mixture of polyvinyl acetate, U.S. Certified Colors, and not more than 25% by weight of acetone, and intended for blowing plastic balloons; 6) games containing, as the sole hazardous component, a self-pressurized container of soap solution or similar foam-generating mixture that has no hazardous ingredient; 7) model rocket propellant devices designed for use in light-weight, recoverable, and reusable model rockets, provided certain technical conditions laid out in the regulation (16 CFR 1500.85) are met; 8) separate delay train/or recovery system activation devices intended for use with premanufactured model rocket engines wherein all of the chemical ingredients are preloaded so the user does not handle any chemical ingredient, and are so designed that the main casing or container does not rupture during operation; 9) solid fuel pellets intended for use in miniature jet engines for propelling model jet airplanes, speedboats, etc., provided such pellets meet technical specifications in 16 CFR 1500.85(a)(10); 10) fuses intended for igniting the fuel pellets named in 9) above; 11) kits intended for construction of model rockets and jet propelled model airplanes requiring the use of difluorodichloromethane as a propellant, provided the outer carton bears a specified warning statement (see "Marking and Labeling Requirements" below.); 12) flammable wire materials intended for electro-mechanical actuation and release devices for the model kits described above, provided each wire does not exceed 15 milligrams in weight.

Radio Frequency Devices. Under the Communications Act of 1934, as amended, all radio frequency (rf) devices are subject to FCC radio emission standards. Video game players—other than battery-operated, handheld electronic games, which are exempted from the standards—are classified as rf devices and must comply with the requirements and procedures for such products. You must file an FCC declaration certifying that your model or device is in conformity with, will be brought into conformity with, or is exempt from the FCC requirements, for each shipment of rf devices you import. FCC standards and procedures have been developed to limit potential sources of rf interference to authorized radio services in the U.S. The FCC defines a radio frequency device as a product that emits rf energy, either intentionally or as a design byproduct. Radio frequency devices must meet specific FCC equipment authorization standards. When rf devices are imported into the U.S., a declaration is required that states that the appropriate FCC authorization has been granted.

Radiation-Producing Devices. The comprehensive Radiation Control for Health and Safety Act (RCHSA) was enacted in 1968 to protect the public from unnecessary exposure to radiation from electronic products. Administration of the law is carried out through the setting and enforcement of radiation performance standards to limit radiation emissions. The standards apply to products offered for sale or use in the U.S., whether manufactured in this country or elsewhere. Electronic products include all products or equipment capable of emitting ionizing or nonionizing radiation, or sonic, infrasonic, or ultrasonic waves. Few items classified within Chapter 95 are likely to be directly affected by these regulations. However, if you have any doubts about the status of your product, contact the FDA's Center for Devices and Radiological Health (CDRH) (see addresses at end of this chapter).

Trademarks and Trade Names. Articles bearing counterfeit trademarks, or marks that copy or simulate the registered trademark of a U.S. or foreign corporation are prohibited importation, provided a copy of the U.S. trademark registration has been filed with the Commissioner of Customs and recorded in the manner provided by regulations (19 CFR 133). The U.S. Customs Service also affords similar protection against unauthorized shipments bearing trade names that are recorded with customs pursuant to regulations (19 CFR 133, Subpart B). If your article bears a genuine trademark that is 1) owned by a U.S. citizen or company, 2) registered with U.S. Customs, you may not import the article without written permission from the U.S. trademark holder.

It is unlawful to import articles bearing genuine trademarks owned by a U.S. citizen or corporation without permission of the U.S. trademark owner, if the foreign and domestic trademark owners are not parent and subsidiary companies or otherwise under common ownership and control, provided such trademark has been recorded with customs.

Copyrights. Section 602(a) of the Copyright Revision Act of 1976 provides that the importation into the U.S. of copies of a work acquired outside the U.S. without authorization of the copyright owner is an infringement of the copyright. Articles imported in violation of the import prohibitions are subject to seizure and forfeiture. Forfeited articles shall be destroyed. However, the articles may be returned to the country of export whenever customs is satisfied that there was no intentional violation. Copyright owners seeking import protection from the U.S. Customs Service must register their claim to copyright with the U.S. Copyright Office and record their registration with customs in accordance with applicable regulations (19 CFR 133, Subpart D).

Note that enforcement of copyright law has a high priority at customs, and even someone who is discovered unwittingly trying to bring in even a single copy of pirated software, audio-or video-tape, or similar article is subject to the full penalties of the applicable laws.

Marking and Labeling Requirements

Toys that by reason of their functional purpose necessarily present the hazard of sharp points, or of sharp metal or glass edges, and that do not have any nonfunctional sharp points, metal or glass edges, must be so identified by a conspicuous, legible, and visible label at the time of any sale.

Pacifiers. Pacifiers must bear the following label statement legibly and conspicuously on any retail display carton containing two or more pacifiers: "Warning—Do Not Tie Pacifier Around Child's Neck As It Presents a Strangulation Danger." This statement must also appear on each individually packaged pacifier.

Caps. Both paper and plastic caps intended for use in toy guns must bear the following statement on the carton and in the accompanying literature: "WARNING—Do not fire closer than 1 foot to the ear. Do not use indoors."

Clacker Balls. Clacker balls must be conspicuously labeled with: 1) name and address of manufacturer, packer, distributor, or seller; 2) code or mark that will permit the manufacturer to identify any given batch, lot, or shipment in the future. This mark must appear on one or all of the following: the toy itself, its package, its shipping container; it must also appear on all invoices and shipping documents; 3) warning statement on the main panel of the retail container and display carton, and on any accompanying literature, to the effect that if cracks develop in a ball, or if the cord becomes frayed or loose or unfastened, use of the toy should be discontinued. An additional statement is required if a ring or loop or other holding device is present: "In use, the ring or loop must be placed around the middle finger and the two cords positioned over the forefinger and held securely between the thumb and forefinger." Any wording is permissible, as long as it provides adequate instructions and warnings to prevent the holding device from accidentally slipping out of the hand during use. All warning statements must be printed in sharply contrasting color within a borderline, and in letters at least one-quarter inch high on the main panel of the container, and at least one-eighth inch high on all accompanying literature.

Construction Kits. Kits for model rockets and jet-propelled airplanes must bear a warning on the main panel on the outer carton, in conspicuous type. The warning should state: "WARNING—Carefully read instructions and cautions before use."

Baby Walkers, Baby Bouncers, Walker-Bouncers, etc. These articles must be conspicuously labeled with the following: 1) name and address of manufacturer, packer, distributor, or seller; and 2) code mark on the article itself, its package container, and any invoices or shipping documents, which will enable the manufacturer to identify the particular model at any future time. When the manufacturer makes significant structural or design changes to a particular model, the model number must also be changed.

Electrically Operated Toys. The extensive provisions of the CPSA labeling requirements for these toys include but are not limited to the following:

General Requirements. All labeling must be prominently and conspicuously displayed under customary conditions of purchase, storage, and use. All required information must be readily visible, noticeable, clear, and, except where coding is permitted, in legible English (other languages may also be included as appropriate). Such factors governing labeling and location, type size, and contrast against background may be based on necessary condensations to provide a reasonable display.

Specific Requirements. Both the toy and its packaging must be marked to indicate: 1) electrical ratings; 2) any required precautionary statements (see below); 3) the date (month and year) of manufacture (or appropriate codes). The date may appear on the instructions provided with the toy instead of on the toy itself if the manufacturer wishes.

Markings. Markings required to be placed on the toy itself must be of a permanent nature, such as paint-stenciled, die-stamped, molded, or indelibly stamped, and should not readily wash off for any reason. All required markings on the toy and package labeling must contrast sharply with the background (whether by color, projection, or indentation) and must be readily visible and legible. There are specific minimum size requirements for type.

Adequate instructions, easily understood by children of those ages for which the toy is intended, must accompany each toy. Instructions must describe applicable installation, assembly, use, cleaning, maintenance (including lubrication), and other functions as appropriate. Applicable precautions must be included, as well as information required on the labeling (except for date of manufacture if it is placed on the toy itself). Instructions must also contain a statement addressed to parents, recommending that the toy be periodically examined for potential hazards and that any parts thus found to be potentially hazardous be repaired or replaced.

If a toy is produced or assembled at more than one establishment, the toy and its shelf pack or package must have a distinctive mark (which may be in code) identifying the toy as the product of a particular establishment. A toy must be marked to indicate its rating in volts as well as in amperes and/or watts. If a toy utilizes a single motor as its only electric energy-consuming component, the electrical rating may be marked on a motor nameplate. In this case, the rating need not be marked elsewhere on the toy if the nameplate is readily visible after the motor has been installed. A toy must be rated for 1) alternating current only, 2) direct current only, or 3) both alternating and direct current. The alternating current rating must include frequency or frequency range requirement, if necessary because of a special component.

Precautionary Statements. Electrically operated toys must bear the statement: "CAUTION—ELECTRIC TOY." The following statement must appear both on accompanying instructional materials and on the upper right hand corner of the package and shelf pack display panel: "CAUTION—ELECTRIC TOY: Not recommended for children under (___) years of age. As with all electric products, precautions should be observed during handling and use to prevent electric shock." The blank in the preceding statement should be filled in by the manufacturer. In no instance may the manufacturer indicate that the article is recommended for children under eight years of age if it contains a heating element. The term "ELECTRICALLY OPERATED PRODUCT" may be substituted for the term "ELECTRIC TOY" in the case of other electrically operated products that may not be considered "toys" but are intended for use by children.

Thermal Hazards. Toys having surfaces defined in the regulation as Type C or Type D (16 CFR 1505.6(g)(2)), and that have temperatures greater than those shown in the table in 16 CFR 1505.7, are defined as "hot." Hot toys must be marked with the statement: "HOT—Do Not Touch," where readily noticeable when the hot surface is in view. When the marking is on other than the hot surface, the word "HOT" must be followed by appropriate descriptive words such as "Molten Material," "Sole Plate," or "Heating Element," and the statement "Do Not Touch." An alternative statement for a surface intended to be handheld as a functional part of the toy shall be "HOT (___) Handle Carefully." The blank should be filled in by the manufacturer with a description of the potential hazard (e.g. "Curler" or "Cooking Surface"). The regulation prescribes tests to determine temperature hazard.

Lamp Hazards. A toy with one or more replaceable incandescent lamps having a potential difference of more than 30 volts rms (42.4 volts peak) between any of its electrodes or lampholder contacts and any other part or ground, must be marked inside the lamp compartment where readily noticeable during lamp replacement with the statement: "WARNING—Do not use light bulbs larger than (___) watts." The manufacturer should fill in the blank with a number specifying the wattage rating of the lamp. Such toys must bear the statement: "WARNING—Shock Hazard. Pull plug before changing light bulb" on the outside of the lamp compartment, where the user will readily notice it before gaining access to the compartment. Toys that utilize one or more nonreplaceable incandescent lamps (other than pilot or indicator lamps) must be marked where clearly visible with the statement: "SEALED UNIT—Do not attempt to change light bulb" or an equivalent statement.

Water. If not suitable for immersion in water, a toy cooking appliance (such as a corn popper, skillet, or candy-maker) or other article that may conceivably be immersed in water, must be marked with the statement: "DANGER—To prevent electric shock, do not immerse in water; wipe clean with damp cloth," or an equivalent statement.

FCC Requirements. All rf devices subject to FCC authorization procedures, whether manufactured within the U.S. or outside it, must bear labeling to show compliance. Devices that are not so labeled will not be permitted entry into U.S. Customs territory. For details on label wording, contact FCC (see addresses at end of this chapter).

FDA Requirements. All radiation-emitting devices for which federal standards have been determined must be certified for compliance. The manufacturer must affix a certification label to each product stating that it conforms to the applicable standard. Products requiring certification that are not so labeled will not be permitted entry.

For a general discussion of U.S. Customs marking and labeling requirements, see "Country of Origin Marking" on page 236, "Special Marking Requirements" on page 238 and "Marking—False Impression" on page 239.

Shipping Considerations

You will need to ensure that your goods are packaged and shipped with care to ensure that they arrive in good condition and pass smoothly through Customs. You are responsible for ensuring that the shipment is in compliance with all applicable government regulations for packaging and shipping. In most instances, you should not leave these arrangements solely to the discretion of your supplier. Careful preparation of the cargo and selection of the mode of transport can be essential to a cost-effective, timely delivery of undamaged goods. We strongly advise you to consult your shipping representative, insurance agent, or freight broker for advice on packing and shipping.

Toys, games, and sporting goods must be carefully packed and stowed to avoid damage en route. In addition, some more fragile components may require special handling and additional attention to protect them from heat or water damage.

Publications and WWW Resources

The following publication explains the FDA requirements for importing radiation-producing products. It is published by the FDA and is available online from the FDA website (www.fda.gov/opacom/7pubs.html).
> *Requirements of Laws and Regulations Enforced by the U.S. Food and Drug Administration*

The following bulletin is available from any regional FCC office and online (www.fcc.gov/oet/info/documents/bulletins/).
> *FCC Equipment Authorization Program for Radio Frequency Devices* (Bulletin Number 61)

The *Harmonized Tariff Schedule of the United States (2001)* (HTSUS) is available to view on the Customs Service website (www.customs.gov), or you may purchase a printed version from:

U.S. Government Printing Office
Superintendent of Documents
710 North Capital Street NW
Washington DC 20401
Tel: (202) 512-1800
Fax: (202) 512-1657
Website: www.access.gpo.gov

The USGPO also has copies of specific laws available for purchase. The USGPO accepts orders made by fax, phone or placed over the Internet, as well as mail orders paid by credit card. All orders must be accompanied by payment. Credit cards, checks drawn on a U.S. bank, or an international money order are all acceptable.

Relevant Government Agencies

Address questions regarding CPSC requirements for toys, games, and sporting goods to:
Consumer Product Safety Commission (CPSC)
Office of Compliance
Washington DC 20207-0001
Tel: 800-638-2772 or (301) 504-7912
Fax: (301) 504-0359
Website: www.cpsc.gov

Address questions regarding FCC rules on rf devices to the nearest FCC regional office or to:
Federal Communications Commission (FCC)
Office of Engineering and Technology Laboratory
7435 Oakland Mills Rd.
Columbia, MD 21046
Tel: (301) 362-3000
Fax: (301) 344-2050
Website: www.fcc.gov/oet

Address inquiries regarding importation of radiation-producing devices to either:
Food and Drug Administration (FDA)
Center for Devices and Radiological Health
Division of Small Manufacturers Assistance
1350 Piccard Drive
Rockville, MD 20850
Tel: 800-638-2041
Fax: (301) 443-8818
Email: dsmica@cdrh.fda.gov
Website: www.fda.gov/cdrh

Food and Drug Administration (FDA)
Center for Food Safety and Applied Nutrition (CFSAN)
Office of Compliance
Division of Enforcement, Imports Branch
5100 Paint Branch Parkway
College Park, MD 20740-3835
Tel: (301) 436-2080
Website: http://vm.cfsan.fda.gov/list.html

Address questions regarding copyright and trademark laws to:
U.S. Customs and Border Protection
Office of Regulations & Rulings
Intellectual Property Rights Branch
1300 Pennsylvania Avenue NW
Washington DC 20229
Tel: (202) 572-8710
Website: www.customs.treas.gov

Address questions regarding the importation of toys, games, and sporting goods to your local Customs port director. For addresses refer to "U.S. Customs and Border Protection Offices" on page 65 or contact:
U.S. Customs and Border Protection
Customs Headquarters
1300 Pennsylvania Avenue NW
Washington DC 20229
Tel: (202) 354-1000
Website: www.customs.treas.gov

Laws and Regulations

The following laws and regulations may be relevant to the importation of toys, games, and sporting goods. The laws are contained in the U.S. Code (USC) and the regulations are published in the Code of Federal Regulations (CFR), both of which may be available at larger public and law libraries. Copies of specific laws are also available from the United States Government Printing Office (address above).

15 USC 2051 et seq.
Consumer Product Safety Act
This act gives the Consumer Product Safety Commission authority to set safety standards, testing procedures, and reporting requirements to ensure that consumer products not already covered under other regulations are not harmful.

16 CFR 1500.18
Regulation of CPSC on Banned Toys
This regulation lists the types of toys banned as creating an unreasonable risk of personal injury or illness when subjected to reasonably foreseeable damage or abuse.

16 CFR 1500.50-1500.53
Regulations on Testing Methods for Toys
These regulations prescribe testing methods by which CPSC will determine whether toys intended for use by children are substantially hazardous, and therefore fall within the proscriptions of 16 CFR 1500.18.

16 CFR Part 1501
Regulations on Testing Toys for Ingestion, Choking, or Aspiration Hazards
These regulations prescribe testing methods by which CPSC will determine whether toys intended for use by children under age 3 present an unreasonable risk of choking, aspiration, or ingestion, and therefore fall within the proscriptions of 16 CFR 1500.18.

16 CFR Parts 1115, 1116
Regulations on Substantial Product Hazard Reports
These regulations outline the requirements for filing substantial product hazard reports, including persons who must file, content of reports, confidentiality, and filing procedures.

15 USC 1051 et seq.
Trademark Act of 1946
This Act provides, among other things, that no imported article of foreign origin that bears a name or mark calculated to induce the public to believe that it was manufactured in the United States, or in any foreign country or locality other than the country or locality where it was in fact manufactured, shall be admitted entry at any customhouse in the U.S.

17 USC 101 et seq.
Copyrights
This law provides that the importation into the U.S. of copies of a work acquired outside the U.S. without authorization of the copyright owner is an infringement of the copyright.

19 CFR 133.31 et seq.
Regulations of Customs on Recordation of Copyrights, Trademarks, and Trade Names
These regulations provide procedures and requirements for registering a copyright, trademark, or trade name with U.S. Customs, as well as procedures for enforcement, forfeiture of merchandise, and assessment of monetary penalties.

15 USC 1261 et seq.
Federal Hazardous Substances Act
This Act controls the importation of hazardous substances, sets forth prohibited imports, and authorizes various agencies to promulgate labeling, marking, and transport requirements.

49 CFR 171 et seq.
Regulations on Hazardous Materials
These regulations list all substances deemed hazardous and provide transport, marking, labeling, safety, and emergency response rules.

21 USC 301 et seq.
Federal Food, Drug, and Cosmetic Act
This Act prohibits deceptive practices and regulates the manufacture, sale and importation or exportation of food, drugs, cosmetics, and related products. It was amended by the Food Quality Protection Act of 1996. See 21 USC 331, 381, 382.

19 CFR 12.1 et seq.; 21 CFR 1.83 et seq.
Regulations on Food, Drugs, and Cosmetics
These regulations of the Secretary of Health and Human Services and the Secretary of the Treasury govern the standards, labeling, marking, and importing of products used with food, drugs, and cosmetics.

21 USC 360 et seq.
Radiation Control for Health and Safety Act of 1968 as amended
Customs refuses entry to all electronic products found not to be in compliance with standards prescribed under this act. See 19 CFR 12.90 et seq.; 21 CFR Part 1005.

47 USC 302a
Devices That Interfere with Radio Reception
This law prohibits the importation of devices or home electronic equipment that fail to comply with regulations promulgated by the FCC. See 47 CFR 2.1201 et seq. and 18.119. Customs enforces the prohibition.

Principal Exporting Countries

The following listing includes samples of the main supplier nations of the products of this chapter. It is organized by HTSUS major heading. (Refer to "Customs Classification" above for the product codes.) Countries are listed in rank order of the value of products imported to the U.S. Statistics represent customs value of entries for 2002 from the Bureau of Census, U.S. Department of Commerce.

9501—Mexico, China, Taiwan, Germany, Canada, Italy, Vietnam, South Korea, Hong Kong

9502—China, Indonesia, Hong Kong, Germany, Philippines, Taiwan, Mexico, Spain

9503—China, Mexico, Taiwan, Denmark, Canada, Hong Kong, Thailand, Malaysia

9504—China, Japan, Mexico, Malaysia, Canada, Taiwan, South Korea, United Kingdom

9505—China, Poland, Thailand, India, Taiwan, Germany, Hong Kong, Mexico, Philippines, United Kingdom

9506—China, Taiwan, Canada, Mexico, Thailand, Japan, France, Austria, Italy, South Korea

9507—China, Japan, South Korea, Malaysia, Sweden, Taiwan, Mexico, Thailand, Ireland, Canada, Estonia, Norway

9508—Italy, Canada, Switzerland, Germany, United Kingdom, Slovakia, Netherlands, France, China

Chapter 96: Miscellaneous Manufactured Articles

This section pertains to the importation of miscellaneous manufactured articles, which are classified within Chapter 96 of the Harmonized Tariff Schedule of the United States (HTSUS). This chapter is largely a catch-all for a variety of products that don't fit in easily in other categories. Specifically, it includes such diverse and various items as worked animal products—such as ivory, bone, horn, and coral; worked vegetable or mineral products—such as gelatins and waxes; brooms and brushes; sieves; toilet sets; buttons, zippers, and other fasteners; pens and pencils; blackboards; typewriter ribbons, cigarette lighters; smoking pipes; combs, hairpins and other hair dressing articles; misters and sprayers; vacuum bottles; and mannequins.

Various fittings and ornaments are covered in Commodity Index Chapter 96, but products for specific uses or defined articles are usually classified elsewhere. For example, if you are interested in importing pencils for cosmetic use—such as eyebrow pencils—refer to Chapter 33. Items for umbrellas and walking sticks are found in Chapter 66, while real and imitation jewelry is covered in Chapter 71. (Nevertheless, hair ornaments, whether or not they include precious metals and/or precious or semi-precious stones or pearls, are classified in Chapter 96.) Assembled cutlery is included in Chapter 82, but knife handles imported separately enter under Chapter 96. Scientific instruments—such as drawing pens—or special brushes for medical uses would fall within Chapter 90. If you are interested in importing antiques or works of art consisting of carved animal products, refer to Chapter 97. Parts of general use—such as nuts, bolts, screws, and nails—are classified within the chapter that applies to the materials of which they are made, Chapters 72-81 for base metals, and 39 for plastics.

Note: To understand key issues that will enable you to make best use of the information in this section we recommend that you see "Introduction" on page 425.

Key Factors

The key factors in the importation of brushes are:

- For brushes intended for use on humans or animals: compliance with U.S. Food and Drug Administration (FDA) regulations, entry notification, and procedures
- For products made from endangered species: compliance with U.S. Fish and Wildlife Service (FWS) license, permit, country-of-origin permit, import documentation, and recordkeeping requirements
- For certain brooms and intermediate broom-making materials: restrictions and random U.S. Department of Agricultural (USDA) inspection for some species

Although most importers utilize the services of a licensed customs broker in making their entries, and we recommend this practice, you should be aware of the regulatory, entry, and documentation issues involved in importing your product. You, as importer, are ultimately responsible for the fulfillment of any legal requirements applicable to your shipment.

General Considerations

Importation of most miscellaneous manufactured products—such as hair products, buttons, and pens and pencils—is straightforward. You do not need permits or licenses, nor is special entry paperwork required.

Products Derived from Endangered Species. Importers interested in importing articles such as some hair products and other items of ivory, horn, bone, and coral should be aware of potential conflicts with endangered species regulations, which are extremely rigid. Pertinent laws and regulations include the Endangered Species Act (ESA) and the Convention on International Trade in Endangered Species of Wild Flora and Fauna (CITES), administered by the FWS (see "Prohibitions and Restrictions" below).

Brushes. Brushes fall into two categories for regulatory purposes. Those that are not used on the human body or on animals—such as scrub brushes and artists' brushes—are not regulated. If you are importing these types of brushes you need no licenses or permits, nor is any special paperwork required for entry.

Brushes or any other products intended for use on humans or animals are regulated under the Federal Food, Drug, and Cosmetic Act (FDCA), enforced by the FDA. All items, both domestic and foreign, that fall within these regulations must comply with the requirements established by the FDCA and its enforcers in every detail. Imported products regulated by the FDA are subject to FDA port of entry inspection. For a general discussion of required FDA import procedures see "Appendix: Foods" on page 825.

Some brush-making materials, particularly broom corn (*Sorghum vulgare* variety *technicum*), are restricted (see "Prohibitions and Restrictions" below), while others—such as some boar bristles—may be subject to endangered species regulation. Products made of broom corn are subject to random USDA port inspections. The USDA may require fumigation or other treatment to ensure that no harmful insects or plant species capable of reproducing are brought into the U.S.

Detention of Shipment. If your shipment is found to be noncomplying, it may be detained at the port of entry. In the case of products subject to FDA jurisdiction, the FDA may permit you to bring such a shipment into compliance before making a final decision regarding admittance. However, any sorting, reprocessing, or relabeling must be supervised by FDA personnel, and is done at the importer's expense. Such conditional release to allow an importer to bring a shipment into compliance is a privilege, not a right. The FDA may consider subsequent noncomplying shipments of the same type of product to constitute abuse of the privilege and require the importer to destroy or reexport the products. To ascertain what your legal responsibilities are, you should contact these agencies regarding the specific items to be imported.

Customs Classification

For customs purposes miscellaneous manufactured articles are classified within Chapter 96 of the HTSUS. This chapter is divided into major headings, which are further divided into subheadings, and often into sub-subheadings, each of which has its own HTSUS classification number. For example, the 2001 HTSUS number for hairbrushes valued over 40 cents apiece is 9603.29.80.10, indicating that it is a subcategory of other brushes (9603.29), which is a subcategory of the major heading brooms, brushes, hand operated mechanical sweepers, mops and feather dusters (9603). There are 18 major headings in HTSUS Chapter 96.

9601—Worked ivory, bone, tortoise-shell, horn, antlers, coral, mother-of-pearl, and other animal carving material, and articles of these materials (including articles obtained by molding)

9602—Worked vegetable or mineral carving material and articles of these materials; molded or carved articles of wax, of stearin, of natural gums, or natural resins, of modeling pastes, and other molded or carved articles, not elsewhere specified or included; worked, unhardened gelatin (except gelatin of heading 3503) and articles of unhardened gelatin

9603—Brooms, brushes (including brushes constituting parts of machines, appliances, or vehicles), hand-operated mechanical floor sweepers, not motorized, mops, and feather dusters; prepared knots and tufts for broom or brush making; paint pads and rollers; squeegees (other than roller squeegees)

9604—Hand sieves and hand riddles

9605—Travel sets for personal toilet, sewing or shoe or clothes cleaning (other than manicure and pedicure sets of heading 8214)

9606—Buttons, press-fasteners, snap-fasteners, and press studs, button molds, and other parts of these articles; button blanks

9607—Slide fasteners and parts thereof

9608—Ball point pens; felt-tipped and other porous-tipped pens and markers; fountain pens, stylograph pens, and other pens; duplicating styli; propelling or sliding pencils (for example, mechanical pencils); pen-holders, pencil-holders, and similar holders; parts (including caps and clips) of the foregoing articles, other than those of heading 9609

9609—Pencils (other than those pencils of heading 9608), crayons, pencil leads, pastels, drawing charcoals, writing or drawing chalks, and tailor's chalks

9610—Slates and boards, with writing or drawing surfaces, whether or not framed

9611—Date, sealing, or numbering stamps and the like (including devices for printing or embossing labels), designed for operating in the hand; hand-operated composing sticks and hand printing sets incorporating such composing sticks

9612—Typewriter or similar ribbons, inked or otherwise prepared for giving impressions, whether or not on spools or in cartridges; ink pads, whether or not inked, with or without boxes

9613—Cigarette lighters and other lighters, whether or not mechanical or electrical, and parts thereof other than flints or wicks

9614—Smoking pipes (including pipe bowls) and cigar or cigarette holders, and parts thereof

9615—Combs, hair-slides, and the like; hairpins, curling pins, curling grips, hair-curlers, and the like, other than those of heading 8516, and parts thereof

9616—Scent sprayers and similar toilet sprayers, and mounts and heads therefor; powder puffs and pads for the application of cosmetics or toilet preparations

9617—Vacuum flasks and other vacuum vessels, complete with cases; parts thereof other than glass liners

9618—Tailors' dummies and other mannequins; automatons and other animate displays used for shop window dressing

For more details regarding classification of the specific product you are interested in importing, consult a customs broker, the appropriate commodity specialist at your nearest customs port, or see HTSUS. The 2001 HTSUS is available online from the Customs Service (www.customs.gov/impoexpo/impoexpo.htm) or for purchase from the U.S. Government Printing Office (see resources at the end of this chapter), and may be found in larger public libraries. For a general discussion of customs classification, see "Classification—Liquidation" on page 229.

Dutiable Status of Goods

For more information about duty rates and binding decisions see "Dutiable Status of Goods" on page 203; for a discussion of temporary importation of goods see "Temporary Free Importations" on page 205.

Valuation

Importers have a responsibility to use what the U.S. Customs Service deems, "reasonable care," when determining the value of their goods. They must also provide any additional information that the Customs Service needs for setting a final value on the goods. This process involves a number of factors and can be somewhat complicated; importers must be aware of applicable issues and details. Valuation information applies to all types of commodities, for further discussion on the subject see "Customs Valuation" on page 267.

Import Duties

Import duties vary (often dramatically) depending upon the Harmonized Tariff Schedule (HTSUS) classification of the goods or products imported. Since some products that look alike have different HTSUS classifications and different rates of duty, proper classification is vital. Note that "differences of opinion" between importers and the Bureau of Customs and Border Protection regarding classification keeps customs attorneys very busy.

Import duties can be assessed on the imported value of the goods ("ad valorem" rates of duty such as 2%, 4.4%, 50%, etc.), total units or weight of the goods ("specific" rates of duty such as 2 cents each or 1.5 cents/pound, etc.) or on a combination basis ("compound" rates of duty such as 5 cents each plus 6%).

Listed below is a sampling of several Column 1 import duty rates for Chapter 96 products:
Worked ivory and articles of ivory (9601.10.00.00): Free
to
Travel sets for personal toilet, sewing or shoe or clothes cleaning (other than manicure and pedicure sets of heading 8214) (9605.00.00.00): 8.1%

For specific information on US import duties refer to the Harmonized Tariff Schedule of the US. The print version is available from the US Government Printing Office as well as third party suppliers who often add special features. Online versions are available in both static PDF pages as well as in formats with excellent search functionality. Search the Web with the term "Harmonized Tariff Schedule" to find sources.

Entry and Documentation

The entry of merchandise is a two-part process consisting of 1) filing the documents necessary to determine whether merchandise may be released from Customs custody and 2) filing the documents that contain information for duty assessment and statistical purposes. In certain instances all documents must be filed and accepted by Customs prior to the release of the goods. Unless you have been granted an extension, you must file entry documents at a location specified by the port or area director within five working days of your shipment's date of arrival at a U.S. port of entry. These include a number of standard documents required by Customs for any entry, and:

- For products made from endangered species, U.S. Fish and Wildlife Service (FWS) Import Declaration Form 3-177, original and 3 copies (if products are derived from exotic wildlife or endangered species)

- FWS permit or import documentation FWS 3200 (if products are derived from exotic wildlife or endangered species)

- Permits or certificates required under Convention on International Trade in Endangered Species (CITES), Endangered Species Act (ESA), and any other regulations applicable to the particular shipment, CITES permits and certificates

- Where applicable, USDA import permits for brooms and broom-making materials

After you present the entry, Customs may examine your shipment, or may waive examination. The shipment is then released provided no legal or regulatory violations have been noted. You must then file entry summary documentation and deposit estimated duties at a designated customhouse within 10 working days of your shipment's release. For a detailed description of entry procedures, standard documentation, and informal entry, see "Entry Process" on page 185.

Informed Compliance. Informed compliance was introduced with the Customs Modernization Act of 1993 (Mod Act) and defines the relationship between importers and the Customs Service. It sets out the responsibilities of both parties. Providing the correct documentation and information for entry is a key factor that will make your importing operation run smoothly. We recommend that importers become familiar with the concept of informed comliance and the responsibilities that they have under the Mod Act. For further discussion about informed compliance see "Informed Compliance" on page 211.

Note: The Entry and Documentation section has been carefully designed to supply you, the importer, with sample documents and directions on how to satisfy Customs requirements. Be aware that you should consult the applicable authorities to ensure that you are correctly following the most current procedures.

Prohibitions and Restrictions

Exotic and Endangered Species. Products of certain plants and animals are restricted or prohibited from importation because of their status under the CITES, ESA, or other U.S. laws. Additional prohibitions or restrictions may be imposed by the laws of the exporting country. You are legally responsible for fulfilling the requirements of all applicable rules and regulations. If you import or attempt to import a product in violation of such laws, whether or not you are aware of the violation, your product may be seized and you may be subject to stiff fines and/or imprisonment.

Virtually all articles made from exotic leathers or other parts of reptiles and amphibians; sea turtles; exotic tropical bird feathers or other parts; ivory from elephants or marine mammals; and coral from many Caribbean, Pacific Island, and Southeast Asian countries are prohibited entry under various endangered species laws.

Importers must provide the FWS with both the common and scientific species names for any products about which they have questions or are planning to import well in advance of the proposed importation. If you are unsure of the regulations or their applicability, check with the FWS or with the World Wildlife Fund (addresses below). Also be sure to check with the local authorities in the country you expect to import from; your embassy or consulate in that country should be able to direct you to the proper local authorities. You should be prepared to furnish full documentation to FWS or Customs personnel for any even potentially questionable product.

Country-Specific Import Restrictions

Corn and closely related plants and their parts (including those of the genus *Chionachne, Coix, Echinochloa, Eleusina, Euchleana, Miscanthus, Panicum, Pennisetum, Polytoca, Sclerachne, Setaria, Sorghum, Trilobachne,* and *Tripsicum*), including materials used in the manufacture of brooms and brushes—specifically broomcorn— are banned form importation into the U.S. if they originate from the countries listed: Africa (all countries), Australia, Bangladesh, Bhutan, Brunei, Bulgaria, Burma (Myanmar), Cambodia (Kampuchea), Hong Kong, India, Nepal, New Zealand, North Korea, Oceania, Pakistan, Papua New Guinea, People's Republic of China, Philippines, Russia and the other republics of the former Soviet Union, Singapore, South Korea, Sri Lanka, Taiwan, Thailand, and Vietnam. Corn-related products from other countries require prior USDA approval.

Quotas

The following items are subject to tariff-rate quotas:

9603.10.10–.30 Whiskbrooms wholly or in part of broom corn: in any calendar year prior to the entry, or withdrawal from the warehouse for consumption, of 61,655 dozen whiskbrooms classifiable under subheadings 9603.10.10 to 9603.10.30, inclusive.

9603.10.40–.60 Brooms, wholly or in part of broom corn: in any calendar year prior to the entry or withdrawal from warehouse for consumption, of 121,478 dozen brooms classifiable under subheadings 9603.10.40 to 9603.10.60, inclusive.

Marking and Labeling Requirements

For a general discussion of U.S. Customs marking and labeling requirements, see "Country of Origin Marking" on page 236, "Special Marking Requirements" on page 238 and "Marking— False Impression" on page 239.

Shipping Considerations

You will need to ensure that your goods are packaged and shipped with care to ensure that they arrive in good condition and pass smoothly through Customs. You are responsible for ensuring that the shipment is in compliance with all applicable government regulations for packaging and shipping. In most instances, you should not leave these arrangements solely to the discretion of your supplier. Careful preparation of the cargo and selection of the mode of transport can be essential to a cost-effective, timely delivery of undamaged goods. We strongly advise you to consult your shipping representative, insurance agent, or freight broker for advice on packing and shipping.

Miscellaneous manufactured articles include a wide range of goods, some of which are fragile. They require careful packing and stowing to withstand the rigors of transport. Care must be taken to avoid damage due to shifting of the cargo, as well as to protect the goods from heat, humidity, or water, which can damage some products.

Publications and WWW Resources

The following publication explains the FDA requirements for importing miscellaneous manufactured articles for sanitary use. It is published by the FDA and is available online from the FDA website (www.fda.gov/opacom/7pubs.html). The complete version can be found under the heading "Enforcement."
Requirements of Laws and Regulations Enforced by the FDA

The *Harmonized Tariff Schedule of the United States (2001)* (HTSUS) is available to view on the Customs Service website (www.customs.gov), or you may purchase a printed version from:
U.S. Government Printing Office
Superintendent of Documents
710 North Capital Street NW
Washington DC 20401
Tel: (202) 512-1800
Fax: (202) 512-1657
Website: www.access.gpo.gov

The USGPO also has copies of specific laws available for purchase. The USGPO accepts orders made by fax, phone or placed over the Internet, as well as mail orders paid by credit card. All orders must be accompanied by payment. Credit cards, checks drawn on a U.S. bank, or an international money order are all acceptable.

Relevant Government Agencies

Address questions regarding FDA requirements for importation of brushes for human or animal use to:
Food and Drug Administration (FDA)
Center for Food Safety and Applied Nutrition (CFSAN)

Office of Compliance
Division of Enforcement, Imports Branch
5100 Paint Branch Parkway
College Park, MD 20740-3835
Tel: (301) 436-2080
Website: http://vm.cfsan.fda.gov/list.html

Address questions regarding products derived from wildlife or endangered species to:

U.S. Fish and Wildlife Service (FWS)
Office of Management Authority
4401 N. Fairfax Dr.
Arlington, VA 22203-0700
Tel: (703) 358-2104
Website: www.fws.gov

Address questions regarding restrictions on brooms and broom-making materials to:

Animal and Plant Health Inspection Service (APHIS)
Plant Protection and Quarantine (PPQ)
Director's Office
4700 River Rd., Unit 133
Riverdale, MD 20737
Tel: (301) 734-8896
PPQ Permit Unit: (301) 734-8645
Plant pests: (301) 734-8758
Website: www.aphis.usda.gov/ppq

Address questions regarding importation of miscellaneous manufactured articles to your local Customs port director. Refer to "U.S. Customs and Border Protection Offices" on page 65 or contact:

U.S. Customs and Border Protection
Customs Headquarters
1300 Pennsylvania Avenue NW
Washington DC 20229
Tel: (202) 354-1000
Website: www.customs.treas.gov

Laws and Regulations

The following laws and regulations may be relevant to the importation of miscellaneous manufactured articles. The laws are contained in the U.S. Code (USC) and the regulations are published in the Code of Federal Regulations (CFR), both of which may be available at larger public and law libraries. Copies of specific laws are also available from the United States Government Printing Office (address above).

21 USC 301 et seq.
Federal Food, Drug, and Cosmetic Act
This Act prohibits deceptive practices and regulates the manufacture, sale and importation or exportation of food, drugs, cosmetics, and related products. It was amended by the Food Quality Protection Act of 1996. See 21 USC 331, 381, 382.

19 CFR 12.1 et seq.; 21 CFR 1.83 et seq.
Regulations on Food, Drugs, and Cosmetics
These regulations of the Secretary of Health and Human Services and the Secretary of the Treasury govern the standards, labeling, marking, and importing of products used with food, drugs, and cosmetics.

Convention on International Trade in Endangered Species of Wild Fauna and Flora (CITES)
This comprehensive wildlife treaty signed by over 100 countries, including the United States, regulates and in many cases prohibits commercial imports and exports of wild animal and plant species threatened by trade.

16 USC 1531
Endangered Species Act of 1973
This Act prohibits the import and export of species listed as endangered and most species listed as threatened. It is the U.S. law that implements CITES.

16 USC 1361 et seq.

The Marine Mammal Protection Act of 1972
This Act prohibits the import of marine mammals and their parts and products. These species include whales, walruses, narwhals, seals, sea lions, sea otters, and polar bears.

19 CFR 12.26 et seq.
Regulations on Importation of Wild Animals
These regulations list the wild animals that are prohibited from importation or that require import permits.

50 CFR Parts 10, 13, and 16
Regulations of FWS for Importing Wildlife and Fish
These regulations specify the animals and animal products subject to import prohibitions and restrictions.

16 USC 3371 et seq.
Control of Illegally Taken Fish and Wildlife
This Act prohibits the import of species taken, possessed, transported, or sold in violation of the law of a foreign country.

16 USC 4201 et seq.
The African Elephant Conservation Act
This Act prohibits imports of carved ivory products from any country and only permits imports of whole tusks from elephants legally hunted in certain African countries.

Principal Exporting Countries

The following listing includes samples of the main supplier nations of the products of this chapter. It is organized by HTSUS major heading. (Refer to "Customs Classification" above for the product codes.) Countries are listed in rank order of the value of products imported to the U.S. Statistics represent customs value of entries for 2002 from the Bureau of Census, U.S. Department of Commerce.

9601—Philippines, India, China, Taiwan, Italy, Hong Kong, Indonesia, South Korea, Thailand

9602—Mexico, Canada, South Korea, India, Colombia, China, France, Belgium, Venezuela

9603—China, Mexico, Germany, Taiwan, Italy, South Korea, Macao, Japan, Honduras, Hong Kong, Canada

9604—China, France, United Kingdom, Belgium, South Korea, Taiwan, Japan

9605—China, South Korea, Hong Kong, Taiwan, United Kingdom, Brazil, Mexico, Philippines

9606—China, Taiwan, Italy, Hong Kong, Japan, Mexico, Thailand, Germany, Canada, South Korea

9607—Japan, China, Taiwan, Indonesia, South Korea, Canada, Hong Kong, Switzerland

9608—Japan, China, Mexico, Taiwan, Germany, South Korea, France, Italy, Spain

9609—China, Brazil, Japan, Indonesia, Taiwan, Thailand, Mexico

9610—China, Mexico, Canada, Brazil, Thailand, Taiwan, Portugal

9611—China, Austria, Japan, Taiwan, Malaysia, Canada, Czech Republic, Germany

9612—Japan, Mexico, China, Belgium, Malaysia, Thailand, United Kingdom, Tunisia, Taiwan, Germany, Canada

9613—China, France, Mexico, Japan, Thailand, South Korea, Spain, Hong Kong, Italy, Philippines

9614—Italy, United Kingdom, Denmark, Turkey, France, Egypt, Ireland, Greece, Germany, China

9615—China, South Korea, Taiwan, France, Thailand, Hong Kong, Japan, United Kingdom, Colombia, Mexico

9616—France, China, Italy, Malaysia, Germany, South Korea, Japan, United Kingdom

9617—China, Japan, Taiwan, Malaysia, South Korea, Thailand, Canada, Germany

9618—China, Canada, Taiwan, Italy, Hong Kong, United Kingdom, France

Chapter 97: Works of Art, Collector's Pieces, and Antiques

This section pertains to the importation of works or art, collectors' pieces, and antiques, which are classified within Chapter 97 of the Harmonized Tariff Schedule of the United States (HTSUS). This rather broad category includes graphic arts—paintings, drawings, prints, and engravings—sculpture and other three dimensional art; philatelic, numismatic, and other collectible items of virtually any variety; and antique objects of at least 100 years of age.

Unused postage stamps and similar items with current use value are covered under Commodity Index Chapter 49. Theatrical scenery, backdrops, and similar articles are covered within Chapter 59 unless the artistry of the item or the reputation of the artist is such that it outweighs the value of the pieces if used in their intended manner, in which case they would be entered under Chapter 97. Unless the age or the artistry of the object is exceptional, such that it would clearly belong within Chapter 97, articles of pearls, precious or semi-precious stones, or other precious materials would be entered under Chapter 71. Articles produced in bulk for commercial purposes—including most handicrafts and many folk art objects—even if individually hand-made or finished, are entered under the category covering the materials of which they are made or the category of the article, as would be the case with any entry. This rule also applies to articles that are less than 100 years old and ineligible for entry as antiques. Neither will reproductions of existing artworks be entered as original art, except within narrowly defined limits (see "General Considerations" below).

Note: To understand key issues that will enable you to make best use of the information in this section we recommend that you see "Introduction" on page 425.

Key Factors

The key factors in importing works of art, collectors' pieces, and antiques are:

- For artworks, documentary proof that the work is original, unique, and handmade
- Special information on invoices for certain categories of art
- If entered for exhibition only, a customs bond and additional documentation required, sale prohibited
- For antiques, proof of age (must be more than 100 years old) in order to qualify for duty-free status
- Whether or not the item is intended for personal use or resale

- If repaired, the proportion of new materials used, and to what extent the item has been transformed (affects dutiability)
- Products derived from species listed under endangered or threatened species regulation require authorization and must enter at U.S. Fish and Wildlife Service (FWS) designated ports
- Restrictions under cultural property protection convention: certification required to ensure the export of such articles was legal
- Restrictions on pre-Columbian artifacts: certification required to ensure the export of such articles was legal
- Restrictions on the importation of facsimiles of postage stamps
- Restrictions or prohibitions from other U.S. governmental agencies as applicable

Although most importers utilize the services of a licensed customs broker in making their entries, and we recommend this practice, you should be aware of the regulatory, entry, and documentation issues involved in importing your product. You, as importer, are ultimately responsible for the fulfillment of any legal requirements applicable to your shipment.

General Considerations

Works of Art. Beauty may be in the eye of the beholder, but the U.S. Customs Service has somewhat narrower and more specific criteria in mind. Customs defines a work of art as one that is an original, unique, handmade item. For items such as engravings, prints, or lithographs, the definition hinges on the execution of the master plates and the actual imprinting of the examples from them by the artist or with the artist's authorization and supervision. This definition excludes reproduction by mechanical or photochemical processes, which may place art photographs in a somewhat anomalous position, requiring additional testimony regarding their artistic nature. Customs also defines original sculpture as including the first twelve castings, replicas, or reproductions made from a sculptor's original work, model, or mold by the sculptor or by another artist whether or not the sculptor is alive at the time the castings, replicas, or reproductions are completed.

Artwork enters the U.S. duty-free. Mass-produced manufactured items that happen to be hand-painted or hand-decorated are not considered works of art, and are dutiable according to the category into which they fall. Frames and similar mountings are included along with the art, provided they are of a kind and value normally associated with those articles; otherwise they will be entered and charged separately. If you wish to import original works of art you must provide two declarations at the time of customs entry that verify the originality of the work, its maker, the fact that it is handmade, and how it was made: 1) a declaration by the artist, (or, if that is impossible, a declaration by the seller or shipper), and 2) a declaration by the importer. If this documentation is provided, the piece will invariably be entered duty-free. In some cases customs may waive the artist's or shipper's declaration, but the importer's declaration is always required. In addition, extra information may be required on the entry invoice.

Authenticity. When importing artists' proof etchings, engravings, woodcuts, lithographs, or prints made by other hand-transfer processes, be sure that they bear the genuine signature or mark of the artist as evidence of their authenticity. If they do not, you should be prepared to present some kind of documentary evidence to establish authenticity. For some imports the port director of Customs may require proof of the character of the article, which might include certificates from curators or other recognized authorities on art, that the imported article represents some recognized school, kind, or medium of the free fine arts.

Antiques. Customs classification of an article as "antique" is primarily an issue of dutiability, because items classified as antiques under Chapter 97 enter duty free while others are subject to duty according to their category. If you wish to enter an item as an antique, you must present adequate documentation verifying the date of production of the article in question. Antique documentation for customs purposes can be a gray area. There is no official customs certificate of antiquity. However, a letter from you stating something like "this item is more than 100 years old," will not suffice. You must obtain specific documentary verification of the item's date of manufacture. On the other hand, a certified statement from an appraiser or trade association, or even a letter from the foreign supplier, is often adequate. Some countries certify antiques, usually as part of the process of controlling their export. Where exit permits are required because of the antiquity of the item, such documents may serve as an official determination by officials of the exporting country of the age of the article. Certain items may be regulated under laws administered by governmental agencies other than U.S. Customs, and may require special additional documentation (see "Entry and Documentation" below.)

If you are entering antiques for resale in the U.S., you are subject to duties. Resellers are also subject to penalties if it is determined after entry that the items are less than 100 years old. The base rate of such penalties is 6.6%, and can rise to as high as 25%, in addition to pertinent duties. (Entries made for personal use are generally somewhat easier, and penalties do not apply on any items subsequently assessed to be less than 100 years old.) Because Customs levies duty on antique items based on the percentage of any non-antique materials used in repairs, it is important to have a record of all recent repairs or reconstructions made using non-antique materials. In some cases, if the transformation of the article is significant due to such repairs, Customs will reclassify the item as recent rather than as an antique and levy duties accordingly. Customs regulations regarding antique imports are found in 19 CFR 10.53.

Cultural Property. The Convention on the Means of Prohibiting and Preventing the Illicit Import, Export, and Transfer of Ownership of Cultural Property ("the Convention"), to which the U.S. is a signatory, was adopted by the General Conference of the United Nations Education, Scientific, and Cultural Organization (UNESCO) to provide cultural property import protection for listed countries. The Convention is designed to prevent the illicit importation of archaeological or ethnologically significant property from the listed countries. At present, 68 countries are contracting parties to the Convention. (See "Country-Specific Import Restrictions" below.)

Customs enforces regulations governing the import of cultural property found in 19 CFR 12.104. Import of cultural property not otherwise prohibited under Convention restrictions is straightforward.

Postage Stamps. Importation of foreign postage stamps into the U.S. is straightforward. You do not need permits or licenses, nor is special paperwork required. If you are importing postage stamps in current use, you are not even required to make a formal customs entry. Importation of facsimiles of U.S. postage stamps is regulated by the U.S. Secret Service (see "Prohibitions and Restrictions" below).

Used, canceled, or postage stamps not in current use valued for their collectibility are found in Chapter 97.

Articles Intended for Exhibition. If you are acting under the authority of a museum or other recognized cultural institution to import works of art, antiques, collectors' pieces, or cultural property for temporary exhibition, under the terms specified in Commodity Index Chapter 98, you will need additional documentation for your import, and you will be required to make the entry under customs bond. See "Surety" on page 201. You should have an officer of your institution complete a declaration on **Customs Form 3325.** Customs may require that you produce at entry a copy of the charter of the institution you represent, or an original order from such institution authorizing you to act as its agent in making the import. You may file this extra documentation with the port director of the port of entry any time within six months of making entry. Chapter 98 entry rules specifically prohibit the sale of items entered under its provisions. If the works of art that you enter under Chapter 98 are sold or offered for sale, exposed for sale, or transferred or used in any manner contrary to regulations governing these imports, you will be required to pay duties immediately to the port director of the port of entry.

Endangered Species Items. Those interested in importing articles including materials derived from listed endangered or threatened species should be aware of potential conflicts with endangered species regulations, which are complex and extremely rigid. Pertinent laws and regulations include the Endangered Species Act (ESA) and the Convention on International Trade in Endangered Species of Wild Flora and Fauna (CITES), administered by the FWS (see "Prohibitions and Restrictions" below).

Although antiques made of or otherwise incorporating such materials are usually allowed entry if properly documented, works of art incorporating such materials are somewhat more problematical. Entries of any such materials are required to be made through designated FWS entry ports to ensure that trained personnel are available to rule on them.

Customs Classification

For customs purposes, works of art, collectors' pieces, and antiques are classified within Chapter 97 of the HTSUS. This chapter is divided into major headings, which are further divided into subheadings, and often into sub-subheadings, each of which has its own HTSUS classification number. For example, the 2001 HTSUS number for paintings, drawings, and pastels is 9701.10.00, indicating that it is a subcategory of the major heading paintings, drawings, and pastels, executed entirely by hand, other than drawings of heading 4906 and other than hand-painted or hand-decorated manufactured articles (9701.00.00). There are six major headings in HTSUS Chapter 97.

9701—Paintings, drawings, and pastels, executed entirely by hand, other than drawings of heading 4906 and other than hand-painted or hand-decorated manufactured articles; collages and similar decorative plaques; all the foregoing framed or unframed

9702—Original engravings, prints, and lithographs, framed or not framed

9703—Original sculptures and statuary, in any material

9704—Postage or revenue stamps, stamp-postmarks, first-day covers, postal stationery (stamped paper), and the like, or, if unused, not of current or new issue in the country to which they are destined

9705—Collections and collectors' pieces of zoological, botanical, mineralogical, anatomical, historical, archeological, paleontological, ethnographic, or numismatic interest

9706—Antiques of an age exceeding one hundred years

For more details regarding classification of the specific product you are interested in importing, consult a customs broker, the appropriate commodity specialist at your nearest Customs port, or see HTSUS. The 2001 HTSUS is available online from the Customs

Service (www.customs.gov/impoexpo/impoexpo.htm) or for purchase from the U.S. Government Printing Office (see resources at the end of this chapter), and may be found in larger public libraries. For a general discussion of customs classification, see "Classification—Liquidation" on page 229.

Dutiable Status of Goods

For more information about duty rates and binding decisions see "Dutiable Status of Goods" on page 203; for a discussion of temporary importation of goods see "Temporary Free Importations" on page 205.

Valuation

Importers have a responsibility to use what the U.S. Customs Service deems, "reasonable care," when determining the value of their goods. They must also provide any additional information that the Customs Service needs for setting a final value on the goods. This process involves a number of factors and can be somewhat complicated; importers must be aware of applicable issues and details. Valuation information applies to all types of commodities, for further discussion on the subject see "Customs Valuation" on page 267.

Import Duties

Import duties vary (often dramatically) depending upon the Harmonized Tariff Schedule (HTSUS) classification of the goods or products imported. Since some products that look alike have different HTSUS classifications and different rates of duty, proper classification is vital. Note that "differences of opinion" between importers and the Bureau of Customs and Border Protection regarding classification keeps customs attorneys very busy.

Import duties can be assessed on the imported value of the goods ("ad valorem" rates of duty such as 2%, 4.4%, 50%, etc.), total units or weight of the goods ("specific" rates of duty such as 2 cents each or 1.5 cents/pound, etc.) or on a combination basis ("compound" rates of duty such as 5 cents each plus 6%).

Listed below is a sampling of several Column 1 import duty rates for Chapter 97 products:
Paintings, drawings and pastels (9701.10.00.00): Free
and
Original engravings, prints and lithographs, framed or not framed (9702.00.00.00): Free

For specific information on US import duties refer to the Harmonized Tariff Schedule of the US. The print version is available from the US Government Printing Office as well as third party suppliers who often add special features. Online versions are available in both static PDF pages as well as in formats with excellent search functionality. Search the Web with the term "Harmonized Tariff Schedule" to find sources.

Entry and Documentation

The entry of merchandise is a two-part process consisting of 1) filing the documents necessary to determine whether merchandise may be released from Customs custody and 2) filing the documents that contain information for duty assessment and statistical purposes. In certain instances all documents must be filed and accepted by Customs prior to the release of the goods. Unless you have been granted an extension, you must file entry documents at a location specified by the port or area director within five working days of your shipment's date of arrival at a U.S. port of entry. These include a number of standard documents required by Customs for any entry, and:

- For works of art, artist's declaration, where possible; if artist's declaration is not possible, declaration from shipper or other authority

- Importer's declaration
- If the work is being imported by a museum or other recognized institution for exhibition only, Customs Form CF 3325, and Customs Form CF 301 " (entry under bond) and, occasionally a copy of the institutional charter of the importing institution, and/or original of the order from such institution to the importer or agent offering the artwork for entry
- For antiques, adequate documentation to certify that the item is more than 100 years old
- For antique firearms, Bureau of Alcohol, Tobacco, and Firearms (ATF) authorization
- If derived from endangered species, entry through FWS-designated port
- For restricted articles, country-of-export certification of legality

After you present the entry, Customs may examine your shipment, or may waive examination. The shipment is then released provided no legal or regulatory violations have been noted. You must then file entry summary documentation and deposit estimated duties at a designated customhouse within 10 working days of your shipment's release. For a detailed description of entry procedures, standard documentation, and informal entry, see "Entry Process" on page 185.

Informed Compliance. Informed compliance was introduced with the Customs Modernization Act of 1993 (Mod Act) and defines the relationship between importers and the Customs Service. It sets out the responsibilities of both parties. Providing the correct documentation and information for entry is a key factor that will make your importing operation run smoothly. We recommend that importers become familiar with the concept of informed comliance and the responsibilities that they have under the Mod Act. For further discussion about informed compliance see "Informed Compliance" on page 211.

Entry Invoices. Entry invoices for works of art entered duty-free under HTSUS headings 9701.90.00, 9702.00.00, and 9703.00.00 must show whether they are originals, replicas, reproductions, or copies, and also the name of the artist, or who produced them, unless upon examination the appraiser is satisfied that such statement is not necessary to a proper determination of the facts. For more general information about invoices see "Invoices" on page 277.

Note: The Entry and Documentation section has been carefully designed to supply you, the importer, with sample documents and directions on how to satisfy Customs requirements. Be aware that you should consult the applicable authorities to ensure that you are correctly following the most current procedures.

Prohibitions and Restrictions

Antiques. An item classified as antique by U.S. Customs may also be an item regulated by another governmental agency, requiring separate special documentation or even licensing. For example, antique firearms are strictly regulated by the ATF (see addresses at end of this chapter). You must be licensed by that agency to import these items into the U.S. ATF import documentation requirements are complex, stringent, and highly specific.

Products derived from species of wildlife listed under endangered species laws are subject to regulation by the FWS. If, for example, you intend to import antique scrimshaw (carvings in ivory), you must do so through one of the ports designated by FWS for that purpose.

Cultural Property. Articles of cultural property documented as appertaining to the inventory of a museum, public monument, or similar institution in any Contracting Party State, deemed to be removed after April 12, 1983, or after the Contracting Party State's date of entry into the Convention, whichever date is later, are prohibited importation into the U.S.

Classification. For Convention purposes, cultural property falls into eleven categories: 1) rare collections and specimens of fauna, flora, minerals, anatomy, and objects of paleontological interest; 2) property relating to a) history—including the history of science and technology—and military and social history; b) the lives of national leaders, thinkers, scientists, artists, and other like figures; and c) events of national importance; 3) products of archaeological excavations or of archaeological discoveries; 4) elements of artistic and historical monuments or archaeological sites that have been dismembered; 5) antiquities more than 100 years old, such as inscriptions, coins, and engraved seals; 6) objects of ethnological interest; 7) property of artistic interest, such as pictures, paintings, and drawings produced entirely by hand, or original works in any material, of statuary art, sculpture, engravings, prints, lithographs, artistic assemblages, and montages; 8) rare manuscripts and incunabula, old books, documents, and publications of special interest (historical, artistic, scientific, literary, etc.), singly or in collections; 9) postage, revenue, and similar stamps, singly or in collections; 10) archives, including sound, photographic, and cinematographic archives; and 11) articles of furniture and musical instruments older than 100 years.

Archaeological or Ethnological Designation. Articles originating in Contracting Party State countries and falling into any of these categories are subject to import protection, and may be listed by a U.S. Treasury Decision as designated archaeological or ethnological materials. Articles so designated are prohibited import under the Convention on Cultural Property Implementation Act (CCPIA). Unless you can provide extensive certification ensuring that the articles are authorized for export by officials of the country of origin, any shipment of designated articles you attempt to import will be subject to seizure and forfeiture. For details regarding import restriction, exemptions, and certification requirements, see 19 CFR 12.104c.

If you are importing cultural property from any listed country, you are responsible for knowing the artifact's status under the Convention. At present, there are four countries that have designated cultural property: 1) El Salvador (prehistoric archaeological objects from the Cara Sucia Archaeological Region); 2) Bolivia (antique ceremonial textiles from Coroma); 3) Guatemala (archaeological material from the Peten Archaeological Region forming part of the remains of the ancient Maya culture; and 4) Peru (archaeological materials from the Sipan Archaeological Region forming part of the remains of the Moche culture). Treasury Decisions are published in the Federal Register. CCPIA import restrictions are generally effective for five years from the date on which the party state requests the restriction, with optional three-year extensions if a need is determined.

For more details, see 19 CFR 12.104(a-i), or contact your nearest customs port.

Pre-Columbian Monumental and Architectural Sculpture and Murals. Import restrictions apply to any stone carving or wall art that is the product of a pre-Columbian Indian culture of Belize, Bolivia, Colombia, Costa Rica, the Dominican Republic, Ecuador, El Salvador, Guatemala, Honduras, Mexico, Panama, Peru, or Venezuela. 19 CFR 12.105 lists as restricted articles: 1) such stone monuments as altars and altar bases, archways, ball court markers, basins, calendars and calendrical markers, columns, monoliths, obelisks, statues, stelae, sarcophagi, thrones, and zoomorphs; 2) such architectural structures as aqueducts, ball courts, buildings, bridges, causeways, courts, doorways, (including lintels and jambs), forts, observatories, plazas, platforms, facades, reservoirs, retaining walls, roadways, shrines, temples, tombs, walls, walkways, and wells; 3) architectural masks, decorated capstones, decorative beams of wood, frescoes,

friezes, glyphs, graffiti, mosaics, moldings, or any other carving or decoration that had been part of or affixed to any monument or architectural structure, including cave paintings or designs; and 4) any fragment or part of any stone carving or wall art. The country of origin of these items is considered to be the country in which the item was initially discovered.

Pre-Columbian articles of the above categories exported from their country of origin after June 1, 1973 are prohibited import into the U.S.

You may import pre-Columbian articles provided you fulfill one of the following conditions of entry: 1) file with the port director of customs at the port of entry a certificate, issued by the government of the country of origin, certifying that the specific exportation was not made in violation of the laws of that country; 2) present satisfactory documentary or sworn testamentary evidence to the port director of customs that the article was exported from the country of origin on or before June 1, 1973; or 3) present satisfactory evidence that the article is not one covered by 19 CFR 12.105.

If you cannot produce the certificate or evidence required at the time of making entry, your shipment will be detained in Customs custody, at the risk and expense of the consignee, until the necessary documentation is presented to Customs. You must provide documentation within 90 days of shipment detention, unless other arrangements are explicitly authorized by the port director. Articles for which appropriate documentation is not presented within the required time limit are subject to forfeiture.

Philatelic Items. Facsimiles of postage stamps are prohibited entry except those for philatelic, educational, historical, or newsworthy purposes. You may obtain further information from the U.S. Secret Service (see addresses at end of this chapter).

If you are not sure whether your import is subject to restriction, check the Commodity Index under the specific item name. The port director of customs nearest you will also be able to give you information regarding possible restrictions, see"U.S. Customs and Border Protection Offices" on page 65.

Exotic and Endangered Species. Products of certain plants and animals are restricted or prohibited from importation because of their status under the CITES, ESA, or other U.S. laws. Additional prohibitions or restrictions may be imposed by the laws of the exporting country. You are legally responsible for fulfilling the requirements of all applicable rules and regulations. If you import or attempt to import a product in violation of such laws, whether or not you are aware of the violation, your product may be seized and you may be subject to stiff fines and/or imprisonment.

Virtually all articles made from exotic leathers or other parts of reptiles and amphibians; sea turtles; exotic tropical bird feathers or other parts; ivory from elephants or marine mammals; and coral from many Caribbean, Pacific Island, and Southeast Asian countries are prohibited entry under various endangered species laws.

Importers must provide the FWS with both the common and scientific species names for any products about which you have questions or are planning to import well in advance of the proposed importation. If you are unsure of the regulations or their applicability, check with the FWS or with the World Wildlife Fund (addresses below). Also be sure to check with the local authorities in the country you expect to import from; your embassy or consulate in that country should be able to direct you to the proper local authorities. You should be prepared to furnish full documentation to FWS or Customs personnel for any even potentially questionable product.

Country-Specific Import Restrictions

Country-specific import restrictions depend upon the item in question. Endangered species regulation is country-specific. The

ATF prohibits importation of firearms from certain countries. For details, see the index section pertinent to your import.

Cultural Property. More than 70 countries are currently State Parties in the Convention on Cultural Property. It is best to assume that the country you are importing from is a party to the Convention unless you are *sure* it is not. Additions to and deletions from the list of State Parties are accomplished by Federal Register notice, from time to time, as the necessity arises.

Marking Requirements

Works of Art. Original works of art are exempt from country of origin marking. However, the country of origin must be conspicuously marked on the outside of the crate or packing material in which the work of art is shipped.

Antiques. Individual antique items are exempt from country of origin marking, but the country of origin must be marked on the outside of their packing or shipping crate.

For a general discussion of U.S. Customs marking and labeling requirements, see "Country of Origin Marking" on page 236, "Special Marking Requirements" on page 238 and "Marking—False Impression" on page 239.

Shipping Considerations

You will need to ensure that your goods are packaged and shipped with care to ensure that they arrive in good condition and pass smoothly through Customs. You are responsible for ensuring that the shipment is in compliance with all applicable government regulations for packaging and shipping. In most instances, you should not leave these arrangements solely to the discretion of your supplier. Careful preparation of the cargo and selection of the mode of transport can be essential to a cost-effective, timely delivery of undamaged goods. We strongly advise you to consult your shipping representative, insurance agent, or freight broker for advice on packing and shipping.

Works of art, collectors' pieces, and antiques encompasses a wide range of items, many of which are exceedingly fragile. They require careful packing and stowing to withstand the rigors of transport. Care must be taken to avoid damage due to shifting of the cargo, as well as to protect the goods from heat, humidity, or water, which in many cases can ruin them.

Publications and WWW Resources

For questions regarding the Convention on Interantional Trade in Endangered Species of Wild Fauna and Flora (CITES) refer to:

CITES Secretariat
15 chemin des Anemones
1219 Chatelaine-Geneva
Switzerland
Tel: [41] (22) 917-8139/40
Fax: [41] (22) 797-3417
Website: www.cites.org
Email: cites@unep.ch

The *Harmonized Tariff Schedule of the United States (2001)* (HTSUS) is available to view on the Customs Service website (www.customs.gov), or you may purchase a printed version from:

U.S. Government Printing Office
Superintendent of Documents
710 North Capital Street NW
Washington DC 20401
Tel: (202) 512-1800
Fax: (202) 512-1657
Website: www.access.gpo.gov

The USGPO also has copies of specific laws available for purchase. The USGPO accepts orders made by fax, phone or placed over the Internet, as well as mail orders paid by credit card. All orders must be accompanied by payment. Credit cards, checks drawn on a U.S. bank, or an international money order are all acceptable.

Relevant Government Agencies

Address questions regarding ATF requirements for importation of antique firearms to:

Bureau of Alcohol, Tobacco, Firearms and Explosives
Firearms and Explosives Import Branch
650 Massachusetts Avenue NW
Washington DC 20226
Tel: (202) 927-8320
Website: www.atf.treas.gov

Address questions regarding FWS requirements for importation of antiques or artworks derived from endangered species to:

U.S. Fish and Wildlife Service (FWS)
Office of Management Authority
4401 N. Fairfax Dr.
Arlington, VA 22203-0700
Tel: (703) 358-2104
Website: www.fws.gov

Address questions regarding importation of facsimiles of U.S. postage stamps to:

U.S. Customs and Border Protection
Office of Regulations & Rulings
Intellectual Property Rights Branch
1300 Pennsylvania Avenue NW
Washington DC 20229
Tel: (202) 572-8710
Website: www.customs.treas.gov

Address questions regarding the importation of works of art, collectors' pieces, and antiques to your local Customs port director. For addresses refer to "U.S. Customs and Border Protection Offices" on page 65 or contact:

U.S. Customs and Border Protection
Customs Headuarters
1300 Pennsylvania Avenue NW
Washington DC 20229
Tel: (202) 354-1000
Website: www.customs.treas.gov

Laws and Regulations

The following laws and regulations may be relevant to the importation of works of art, collectors' pieces, and antiques. The laws are contained in the U.S. Code (USC) and the regulations are published in the Code of Federal Regulations (CFR), both of which may be available at larger public and law libraries. Copies of specific laws are also available from the United States Government Printing Office (address above).

19 CFR 10.48
Regulations of Customs for Entry as Works of Art
Customs enforces the provisions requiring documentary proof at time of entry that original works of sculpture and/or engraving are not mass produced.

19 CFR 2091 et seq.
Regulation on Importation of Pre-Columbian Art
These regulations require that all importations of Pre-Columbian art be accompanied by a certificate from the country of origin certifying that such exportation was lawful.

Convention on Cultural Property Implementation Act (CCPIA)
This act provides the implementing authority to enforce UNESCO's Convention on the Means of Prohibiting and Preventing the Illicit Import, Export, and Transfer of Ownership of Cultural Property. The U.S. Customs Ser-

vice is responsible for administering its provisions.

Convention on International Trade in Endangered Species of Wild Fauna and Flora (CITES)
This comprehensive wildlife treaty signed by over 100 countries, including the United States, regulates and in many cases prohibits commercial imports and exports of wild animal and plant species threatened by trade.

16 USC 1531
Endangered Species Act of 1973
This Act prohibits the import and export of species listed as endangered and most species listed as threatened. It is the U.S. law that implements CITES.

16 USC 1361 et seq.
The Marine Mammal Protection Act of 1972
This Act prohibits the import of marine mammals and their parts and products. These species include whales, walruses, narwhals, seals, sea lions, sea otters, and polar bears.

19 CFR 12.26 et seq.
Regulations on Importation of Wild Animals
These regulations list the wild animals that are prohibited from importation or that require import permits.

50 CFR Parts 10, 13, and 16
Regulations of FWS for Importing Wildlife and Fish
These regulations specify the animals and animal products subject to import prohibitions and restrictions.

16 USC 3371 et seq.
Control of Illegally Taken Fish and Wildlife
This Act prohibits the import of species taken, possessed, transported, or sold in violation of the law of a foreign country.

16 USC 4201 et seq.
The African Elephant Conservation Act
This Act prohibits imports of carved ivory products from any country and only permits imports of whole tusks from elephants legally hunted in certain African countries.

Principal Exporting Countries

The following listing includes samples of the main supplier nations of the products of this chapter. It is organized by HTSUS major heading. (Refer to "Customs Classification" above for the product codes.) Countries are listed in rank order of the value of products imported to the U.S. Statistics represent customs value of entries for 2002 from the Bureau of Census, U.S. Department of Commerce.

9701—France, United Kingdom, Spain, Italy, Germany, Switzerland, Netherlands

9702—United Kingdom, France, Germany, Switzerland, Japan, Netherlands, Canada, Spain, Italy, Israel

9703—France, United Kingdom, Italy, Switzerland, Germany, Spain, Canada

9704—United Kingdom, Switzerland, Russia, Germany, China, Denmark, Canada

9705—United Kingdom, Switzerland, France, Canada, Greece, Germany, Italy, Mexico, South Africa

9706—United Kingdom, France, China, Italy, Germany, Belgium, Switzerland, Japan, Netherlands, Iran

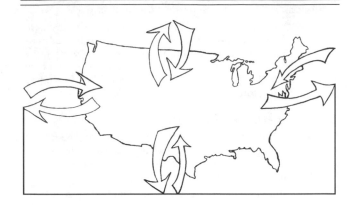

Chapter 98:
Special Classification Provisions

This chapter pertains to the importation of specific products or types of products under specified conditions and/or by specified classes of persons or other entities, which exceptions are classified within Chapter 98 of the Harmonized Tariff Schedule of the United States (HTSUS). The classification of any article that is described in any provision of this chapter will fall within the chapter—that is, this chapter takes precedence over any other potential classification of the article—as long as the article meets the conditions specified in the appropriate provisions of HTSUS Chapter 98. Any article failing to meet all of the conditions established for inclusion in HTSUS Chapter 98 will be entered under the provisions of the HTSUS chapter in which it would normally be classified absent the special conditions.

Although most importers utilize the services of a licensed customs broker in making their entries, and we recommend this practice, you should be aware of the regulatory, entry, and documentation issues involved in importing your product. You, as importer, are ultimately responsible for the fulfillment of any legal requirements applicable to your shipment.

General Considerations

HTSUS Chapter 98 is designed to cover exceptions and special circumstances as decreed by legal provisions, agency regulations, or diplomatic courtesies. Some of the provisions are highly specific, while others are broad in application. Many have extensive qualifying provisions, limits, and procedures that need to be carefully assessed to determine eligibility.

Many of the applications within HTSUS Chapter 98 represent personal or noncommercial entries that will be of little interest to importers. However, subchapters I and II cover items exported from and returned to the U.S.; III deals with containers used in international trade; VIII through X refer to imports of specifically defined official organizations for which importers may act as agents; XI through XIV cover importation of commercial samples and items under bond; XV refers to products of U.S. fisheries; and XVI includes various specific miscellaneous categories.

Any article exempted from duty under subchapters IV through VII—those pertaining to allowable personal exemptions—will also be exempted from any internal revenue taxes which would have been levied on such articles if imported under regular circumstances.

No specific authorizations are needed to import articles under the provisions of HTSUS Chapter 98. However, the importer must satisfy Customs that the entry qualifies under the terms of the specific provision of Chapter 98, which may require specific documentation. Importers should ascertain what documentation Customs will require in advance and be prepared to furnish it to facilitate their entries.

Customs Classification

For customs purposes, articles covered by special provisions are classified within Chapter 98 of the HTSUS. This chapter is divided into subchapters, which are the equivalents of the major headings of other HTSUS chapters, which are further divided into subheadings, each of which has its own HTSUS classification number. There are 17 subchapters in HTSUS Chapter 98.

9801—Articles exported and returned, not advanced or improved in condition; animal exported and returned

9802—Articles exported and returned, advanced or improved abroad

9803—Substantial containers or holders

9804—Personal exemptions extended to residents and nonresidents

9805—Personal exemptions extended to United States personnel and evacuees

9806—Personal exemptions extended to distinguished visitors and to personnel of foreign government or international organizations

9807—Other personal exemptions

9808—Importations of the United States government

9809—Importations of foreign governments and international organizations

9810—Importations of religious, educational, scientific, and other institutions

9811—Samples for soliciting orders

9812—Articles admitted free of duty under bond for permanent exhibition

9813—Articles admitted temporarily free of duty under bond

9814—Tea admitted free under bond

9815—Products of American fisheries

9816—Noncommercial importations of limited values

9817—Other special classification provisions

Import Duties

Import duties vary (often dramatically) depending upon the Harmonized Tariff Schedule (HTSUS) classification of the goods or products imported. Since some products that look alike have different HTSUS classifications and different rates of duty, proper classification is vital. Note that "differences of opinion" between importers and the Bureau of Customs and Border Protection regarding classification keeps customs attorneys very busy.

Import duties can be assessed on the imported value of the goods ("ad valorem" rates of duty such as 2%, 4.4%, 50%, etc.), total units or weight of the goods ("specific" rates of duty such as 2 cents each or 1.5 cents/pound, etc.) or on a combination basis ("compound" rates of duty such as 5 cents each plus 6%).

Listed below is a sampling of several Column 1 import duty rates for Chapter 98 products:
Professional books, implements, instruments, and tools of trade, occupation, or employment, when returned to the United States after having been exported for use temporarily abroad, if imported by or for the account of the person who exported such items (9801.00.85.00): Free
and
Articles, previously imported, with respect to which the duty was paid upon such previous importation or which were previ-

ously free of duty pursuant to the Caribbean Basin Economic Recovery Act or Title V of the Trade Act of 1974, if (1) reimported, without having been advanced in value or improved in condition by any process of manufacture or other means while abroad, after having been exported under lease or similar use agreements, and (2) reimported by or for the account of the person who imported it into, and exported it from, the United States (9801.00.20.00): Free

For specific information on US import duties refer to the Harmonized Tariff Schedule of the US. The print version is available from the US Government Printing Office as well as third party suppliers who often add special features. Online versions are available in both static PDF pages as well as in formats with excellent search functionality. Search the Web with the term "Harmonized Tariff Schedule" to find sources.

Entry and Documentation

The entry of merchandise is a two-part process consisting of 1) filing the documents necessary to determine whether merchandise may be released from Customs custody and 2) filing the documents that contain information for duty assessment and statistical purposes. In certain instances all documents must be filed and accepted by Customs prior to the release of the goods. Unless you have been granted an extension, you must file entry documents at a location specified by the port or area director within five working days of your shipment's date of arrival at a U.S. port of entry. These include a number of standard documents required by Customs for any entry, and:

- Such supporting documentation as Customs may specify for the given import

After you present the entry, Customs may examine your shipment, or may waive examination. The shipment is then released provided no legal or regulatory violations have been noted. You must then file entry summary documentation and deposit estimated duties at a designated customhouse within 10 working days of your shipment's release. For a detailed description of entry procedures, standard documentation, and informal entry, see "Entry Process" on page 185.

Informed Compliance. Informed compliance was introduced with the Customs Modernization Act of 1993 (Mod Act) and defines the relationship between importers and the Customs Service. It sets out the responsibilities of both parties. Providing the correct documentation and information for entry is a key factor that will make your importing operation run smoothly. We recommend that importers become familiar with the concept of informed comliance and the responsibilities that they have under the Mod Act. For further discussion about informed compliance see "Informed Compliance" on page 211.

Note: The Entry and Documentation section has been carefully designed to supply you, the importer, with sample documents and directions on how to satisfy Customs requirements. Be aware that you should consult the applicable authorities to ensure that you are correctly following the most current procedures.

Marking Requirements

For a general discussion of U.S. Customs marking and labeling requirements, see "Country of Origin Marking" on page 236, "Special Marking Requirements" on page 238 and "Marking—False Impression" on page 239.

Shipping Considerations

You will need to ensure that your goods are packaged and shipped with care to ensure that they arrive in good condition and pass smoothly through Customs. You are responsible for ensuring that the shipment is in compliance with all applicable government regulations for packaging and shipping. In most instances, you should not leave these arrangements solely to the discretion of your supplier. Careful preparation of the cargo and selection of the mode of transport can be essential to a cost-effective, timely delivery of undamaged goods. We strongly advise you to consult your shipping representative, insurance agent, or freight broker for advice on packing and shipping.

Publications and WWW Resources

The *Harmonized Tariff Schedule of the United States (2001)* (HTSUS) is available to view on the Customs Service website (www.customs.gov), or you may purchase a printed version from:

U.S. Government Printing Office
Superintendent of Documents
710 North Capital Street NW
Washington DC 20401
Tel: (202) 512-1800
Fax: (202) 512-1657
Website: www.access.gpo.gov

The USGPO also has copies of specific laws available for purchase. The USGPO accepts orders made by fax, phone or placed over the Internet, as well as mail orders paid by credit card. All orders must be accompanied by payment. Credit cards, checks drawn on a U.S. bank, or an international money order are all acceptable.

Relevant Government Agencies

Address questions regarding special provisions of HTSUS Chapter 98 to your local Customs port director. For addresses refer to "U.S. Customs and Border Protection Offices" on page 65 or contact:

U.S. Customs and Border Protection
Customs Headquarters
1300 Pennsylvania Avenue NW
Washington DC 20229
Tel: (202) 354-1000
Website: www.customs.treas.gov

Principal Exporting Countries

The following listing includes samples of the main supplier nations of some of the product categories of this chapter. It is organized by HTSUS major heading. (Refer to "Customs Classification" above for the product codes.) Countries are listed in rank order of the value of products imported to the U.S. Statistics represent customs value of entries for 2002 from the Bureau of Census, U.S. Department of Commerce.

9801—Canada, Mexico, United Kingdom, Japan, Germany, France, Singapore, Netherlands

9802—Canada, Mexico, Germany, United Kingdom, Italy, Israel, Japan, France, Sweden

9808—Canada, Germany, France, Italy, Japan, United Kingdom

9810—Germany, Japan, Netherlands, United Kingdom, Italy, Canada, Sweden

9812—Egypt, Russia, Mexico, United Kingdom, Austria, Australia, Canada, Germany

9814—Finland, Mexico

9817—Mexico, China, Netherlands, Spain, Italy, Germany, Taiwan, Canada

9818—Canada, Singapore, China, Japan, Portugal, Bulgaria, Italy, Panama, Romania, New Zealand, Spain

---

TEMPORARY AND ADDITIONAL CHANGES

Chapter 99:
Temporary and Additional Changes

Full title: Temporary Legislation; Temporary Modifications Established Pursuant to Trade Legislation; Additional Import Restrictions Established Pursuant to Section 22 of the Agricultural Adjustment Act

This chapter pertains to the importation of specific products or types of products that are subject to special and/or temporary alterations in duty rates or other customs treatment, which exceptions are classified within Chapter 99 of the Harmonized Tariff Schedule of the United States (HTSUS). The classification of any article that is described in any provision of this chapter will fall within the chapter—that is, this chapter takes precedence over any other potential classification of the article—as long as the article meets the conditions specified in the appropriate provisions of HTSUS Chapter 99. Any article failing to meet the conditions established for inclusion in HTSUS Chapter 99 will be entered under the provisions of the HTSUS chapter in which it would normally be classified absent the special conditions.

Although most importers utilize the services of a licensed customs broker in making their entries, and we recommend this practice, you should be aware of the regulatory, entry, and documentation issues involved in importing your product. You, as importer, are ultimately responsible for the fulfillment of any legal requirements applicable to your shipment.

General Considerations

Commodity Index Chapter 99 is designed to cover exceptions and special circumstances as decreed by legislative, executive, or other agency actions. All represent temporary modifications—usually a raising or lowering of applicable duty rates—to the customs treatment of products usually classified elsewhere in the HTSUS. Some of the provisions are highly specific, while others are broad in application. Many have extensive qualifying provisions, limits, and procedures that need to be carefully assessed to determine eligibility.

Products covered in **Subchapter I** are subject to cumulative duties, which are payable in addition to the normal duties levied on the items (this subchapter applies to a limited range of organic chemicals). **Subchapter II** covers temporary reductions in duty rates for the specified products. Note that the items listed in this subchapter are subject to provisions that have a specific period of applicability, the vast majority of which expired at the end of 1990 or 1992 (expired provisions are shaded).

Subchapter III pertains to import restrictions imposed by congressional action. These provisions, which primarily affect various agricultural, food, and textile products, as well as footwear and motor vehicles, are of indefinite applicability. Recent provisions that are no longer in force are shaded.

Subchapter IV covers additional restrictions on agricultural products. These restrictions are instituted by the Secretary of Agriculture in accord with the procedures established in Section 22 of the Agricultural Adjustment Act. These provisions primarily affect dairy products, such as milk and cheese, as well as peanuts, cotton, and sugar. Agricultural quotas for the products covered are also established in this subchapter.

Subchapter V covers the extensive special provisions of the U.S.-Canada Free Trade Agreement. Unless otherwise provided, the provisions and notes of this subchapter are effective through the close of December 31, 1998, on which date this subchapter shall be deleted from the tariff schedule and shall cease to apply to any goods entered after that date.

Subchapter VI covers the special provisions of the North American Free Trade Agreement (NAFTA) that apply to imports to the U.S. from Mexico. These provisions are extensive, detailed, and generally favorable.

Subchapter VII covers the special provisions of the Uruguay Round Tariff Protocol negotiated under the auspices of the General Agreement of Tariffs and Trade (GATT) or its successor entity, the World Trade Organization (WTO).

Some specific authorizations may be needed to import articles under the provisions of HTSUS Chapter 99. The importer must satisfy Customs that the entry qualifies under the terms of the specific provision of Chapter 99, which may require specific documentation. Importers should ascertain what documentation Customs will require in advance and be prepared to furnish it to facilitate their entries.

Customs Classification

For customs purposes, articles covered by temporary special provisions are classified within Chapter 99 of the HTSUS. This chapter is divided into subchapters, which are the equivalents of the major headings of other HTSUS chapters, which are further divided into subheadings, each of which has its own HTSUS classification number. There are seven subchapters in HTSUS Chapter 99.

9901—Temporary legislation providing for additional duties

9902—Temporary reductions in rates of duty

9903—Temporary modifications established pursuant to trade legislation

9904—Safeguard measures pursuant to the agreement on agriculture and additional import restrictions established pursuant to Section 2 of the Agricultural Adjustment Act

9905—Deleted

9906—Temporary modifications established pursuant to the North American Free Trade Agreement

9907—Temporary modifications established pursuant to the Uruguay Round Tariff Protocol.

Import Duties

Import duties vary (often dramatically) depending upon the Harmonized Tariff Schedule (HTSUS) classification of the goods or products imported. Since some products that look alike have different HTSUS classifications and different rates of duty, proper classification is vital. Note that "differences of opinion" between importers and the Bureau of Customs and Border Protection regarding classification keeps customs attorneys very busy.

Import duties can be assessed on the imported value of the goods ("ad valorem" rates of duty such as 2%, 4.4%, 50%, etc.), total units or weight of the goods ("specific" rates of duty such as 2 cents each or 1.5 cents/pound, etc.) or on a combination basis ("compound" rates of duty such as 5 cents each plus 6%).

Listed below is a sampling of several Column 1 import duty rates for Chapter 99 products:

Footwear with outer soles of leather and uppers wholly or in part of leather, and footwear with outer soles of rubber or plastics and uppers having an exterior surface area predominantly of leather, the foregoing provided for in chapter 64, except (a) slip-on footwear of a type not suitable for outdoor use, without backs or backstraps, having outer soles with a thickness of less than 5 mm and with less than 20 mm difference between the thickness of the bottom at the ball of the foot and at the heel, and (b) footwear which is designed for a sporting activity and has, or has provision for, attached spikes, sprigs, stops, clips, bars or the like, and skating boots, ski-boots and cross-country ski footwear, wrestling boots, boxing boots and cycling shoes (9903.41.10): 40%

and

Electropneumatic rotary and percussion hammers (provided for in subheading 8467.29) (9903.41.30): 100%

For specific information on US import duties refer to the Harmonized Tariff Schedule of the US. The print version is available from the US Government Printing Office as well as third party suppliers who often add special features. Online versions are available in both static PDF pages as well as in formats with excellent search functionality. Search the Web with the term "Harmonized Tariff Schedule" to find sources.

Entry and Documentation

The entry of merchandise is a two-part process consisting of 1) filing the documents necessary to determine whether merchandise may be released from Customs custody and 2) filing the documents that contain information for duty assessment and statistical purposes. In certain instances all documents must be filed and accepted by Customs prior to the release of the goods. Unless you have been granted an extension, you must file entry documents at a location specified by the port or area director within five working days of your shipment's date of arrival at a U.S. port of entry. These include a number of standard documents required by Customs for any entry, and:

- Such supporting documentation as Customs may specify for the given import

After you present the entry, Customs may examine your shipment, or may waive examination. The shipment is then released provided no legal or regulatory violations have been noted. You must then file entry summary documentation and deposit estimated duties at a designated customhouse within 10 working days of your shipment's release. For a detailed description of entry procedures, standard documentation, and informal entry, see "Entry Process" on page 185.

Informed Compliance. Informed compliance was introduced with the Customs Modernization Act of 1993 (Mod Act) and defines the relationship between importers and the Customs Service. It sets out the responsibilities of both parties. Providing the correct documentation and information for entry is a key factor that will make your importing operation run smoothly. We recommend that importers become familiar with the concept of informed comliance and the responsibilities that they have under the Mod Act. For further discussion about informed compliance see "Informed Compliance" on page 211.

Note: The Entry and Documentation section has been carefully designed to supply you, the importer, with sample documents and direc-

tions on how to satisfy Customs requirements. Be aware that you should consult the applicable authorities to ensure that you are correctly following the most current procedures.

Marking Requirements

For a general discussion of U.S. Customs marking and labeling requirements, see "Country of Origin Marking" on page 236, "Special Marking Requirements" on page 238 and "Marking—False Impression" on page 254.

Shipping Considerations

You will need to ensure that your goods are packaged and shipped with care to ensure that they arrive in good condition and pass smoothly through Customs. You are responsible for ensuring that the shipment is in compliance with all applicable government regulations for packaging and shipping. In most instances, you should not leave these arrangements solely to the discretion of your supplier. Careful preparation of the cargo and selection of the mode of transport can be essential to a cost-effective, timely delivery of undamaged goods. We strongly advise you to consult your shipping representative, insurance agent, or freight broker for advice on packing and shipping.

Publications and WWW Resources

The *Harmonized Tariff Schedule of the United States (2001)* (HTSUS) is available to view on the Customs Service website (www.customs.gov), or you may purchase a printed version from:

U.S. Government Printing Office
Superintendent of Documents
710 North Capital Street NW
Washington DC 20401
Tel: (202) 512-1800
Fax: (202) 512-1657
Website: www.access.gpo.gov

The USGPO also has copies of specific laws available for purchase. The USGPO accepts orders made by fax, phone or placed over the Internet, as well as mail orders paid by credit card. All orders must be accompanied by payment. Credit cards, checks drawn on a U.S. bank, or an international money order are all acceptable.

Relevant Government Agencies

Address questions regarding special provisions of HTSUS Chapter 99 to your local Customs port director. For addresses refer to "U.S. Customs and Border Protection Offices" on page 65 or contact:

U.S. Customs and Border Protection
Customs Headquarters
1300 Pennsylvania Avenue NW
Washington DC 20229
Tel: (202) 354-1000
Website: www.customs.treas.gov

Laws and Regulations

Various laws and regulations may be relevant to the importation of special provisions classifications. Laws are contained in the U.S. Code (USC) and regulations are published in the Code of Federal Regulations (CFR), both of which may be available at larger public and law libraries. Copies of specific laws are also available from the United States Government Printing Office (address above).

7 USC 624
Limitation on Imports, Authority of the President
This act, through Section 22, establishes the authority of the Secretary of Agriculture to institute quotas and other restrictions on various agricultural products.

Appendix: Foods

This index entry presents a broad overview of general U.S. Food and Drug Administration (FDA) requirements for the importation of foods into the United States. It is by no means exhaustive, and is intended to supplement the information in the commodity index chapters dealing specifically with food and with FDA entry procedures in general, including those for products such as drugs and cosmetics. If you are interested in importing FDA-regulated products, you should read this general section, as well as any pertinent specific chapter. You should also contact all regulating agencies applicable to your product for more details.

Although most importers utilize the services of a licensed customs broker in making their entries, and we recommend this practice, you should be aware of the regulatory, entry, and documentation issues involved in importing your product. You, as importer, are ultimately responsible for the fulfillment of any legal requirements applicable to your shipment.

Importation of food is regulated primarily by the FDA, under the Federal Food, Drug, and Cosmetic Act (FDCA), the Fair Packaging and Labeling Act (FPLA), and sections of the Public Health Service Act (PHSA). FDA regulations regarding importation of foods of any kind are extensive and stringent. In addition to FDA requirements there may be U.S. Department of Agriculture (USDA) and/or National Marine Fisheries Service (NMFS) regulations pertinent to specific products. USDA or NMFS requirements will be outlined under the commodity to which they pertain.

Imported products regulated by the FDA are subject to FDA port-of-entry inspection. If your shipment is found to be noncomplying with applicable laws and regulations, it may be detained at the port of entry. The FDA may permit you to bring a noncomplying shipment into compliance before a final decision is made regarding admittance. However, any sorting, reprocessing, or relabeling must be supervised by FDA personnel, and at the importer's expense. Conditional release of an illegal importation to allow an importer to bring it into compliance is not a right but a privilege. If you repeat noncomplying shipments of the same article, the FDA may interpret this as abuse of the privilege and require you to destroy or reexport subsequent shipments.

Both domestic and imported products are subject to the same legal requirements under the FDCA, FPLA, and PHSA. Since this is an importer's manual, we will consider primarily those aspects of the relevant laws which apply directly to importation. However, you should be aware that FDA requirements for interstate shipping, premarket testing, etc. directly affect your business. The fact that such information is only briefly touched on in this index is no indication of its scope, breadth, complexity, or of the potential fines, penalties, and loss of revenue which could result from ignorance of these laws. If you are interested in importing FDA-regulated products, you should become familiar with

FDA regulations not only on importation but also on interstate shipping, storage, handling, packaging, etc.

Note: To understand key issues that will enable you to make best use of the information in this section we recommend that you see "Introduction" on page 425.

Basic Requirements and Prohibitions. The FDCA prohibits importation of articles that are adulterated or misbranded. You will find detailed definitions of these terms in the text of the law. In brief, products that are defective, unsafe, filthy, or produced under insanitary conditions are considered to be adulterated. Products labeled with inadequate information or with false or misleading statements, designs, or pictures are considered misbranded. The law also prohibits distribution of any article requiring prior FDA approval if such approval has not been given. Depending upon the nature of your product, you may be required to provide required reports and to allow the FDA to inspect your facilities.

Premarket Testing and Approval. You should be aware that the FDCA and PHSA require manufacturers of certain consumer products to establish, prior to marketing, that such products meet the safety and effectiveness requirements of the law, and that they are properly labeled. Substances added to food must be "generally recognized as safe," "prior sanctioned," or approved by specific FDA regulations, based on scientific data. Samples of color additives must be tested and certified by FDA laboratories. Residues of pesticide chemicals in food commodities must not exceed safe tolerances set by the Environmental Protection Agency (EPA) and enforced by the FDA. Such premarketing clearances are based on scientific data provided by the manufacturer, subject to review and acceptance by U.S. Government scientists. For more information regarding your responsibilities as importer, contact FDA's Bioresearch Monitoring Staff (see addresses at end of this chapter).

Interstate Shipments. It is possible that an imported food product which violates one of the U.S. food laws may pass Customs without FDA sampling or detention. The fact that such a product slips through Customs undetected does not render it legal under U.S. law. You should be aware that introducing food products that violate applicable laws and regulations into U.S. commerce can have serious consequences. The FDA periodically inspects U.S. facilities and food products introduced into interstate commerce to ensure compliance with the FDCA. Penalties for violation of FDCA regulations range from fines to imprisonment. Products found to be in violation are subject to either immediate recall or to seizure by the court.

Recall may be voluntary, or may be ordered by the FDA. You may initiate voluntary recall of products by contacting the nearest FDA field office. Guidelines on industry responsibilities and FDA recall procedures can be found in 21 CFR 7. However, if you are responsible for introducing a product into U.S. commerce in violation of applicable laws and regulations, your voluntary cooperation in a recall does not relieve you of any liability for the violation.

Seizure is a civil court action taken in order to remove goods from commerce. If your goods are seized, you may 1) abandon them to the disposal of the court; 2) file a claim contesting the government's charges (thus initiating a trial); or 3) request permission to bring the goods into compliance. Seized goods may not be altered, moved, or used without permission of the court. You will also be held responsible for all expenses incurred as a result of seizure of your goods.

Carriers of food in interstate commerce are required to use only FDA-approved equipment and support facilities. Sanitation requirements protecting passengers and crew on interstate carriers are in the regulations for Control of Communicable Disease (21 CFR 1240) and Interstate Conveyance Sanitation (21 CFR 1250). These regulations specify requirements for equipment and operations for handling food, water, and waste both on conveyances and in support facilities. For further information, contact FDA's Division of Regulatory Guidance (see addresses at end of this chapter).

Color Additives. A color additive is a dye, pigment, or other substance, whether synthetic or derived from a vegetable, animal, mineral, or other source, which imparts a color when added or applied to a food. Foods containing color additives that have not been proved safe for the particular use to FDA's satisfaction are considered adulterated under the FDCA. You will find a list of approved color additives and the conditions under which they may be safely used, including the amounts that may be used when limitations are necessary, in 21 CFR 73,74, and 81. Unless specifically exempted by regulation, each batch of color must be tested and certified by the FDA before that batch can be used in food. FDA certification is not limited to colors made by U.S. manufacturers. The FDA will consider a request by a foreign manufacturer for certification, if the request is signed by both the foreign manufacturer and an agent residing in the U.S. Certification of a color by an official agency of a foreign country will not be accepted as a substitute for certification by the FDA. Send your requests for certification or for information regarding certification procedures and regulations, to FDA Division of Color Technology (see addresses at end of this chapter).

Canned Foods. Foreign firms must register and file processing information before shipping any low-acid canned food or acidified low-acid canned food to the United States. This information must be provided to FDA for each affected product at the time of importation in order to assure compliance with registration and process filing acceptance. Establishment registration (FDA 2541) and process filing forms (FDA 2541a: Food Process Filing For All Methods Except Low-Acid Aseptic; FDA 2541c: Food Process Filing for Low-Acid Aseptic Systems) can be obtained from the LACF Registration Coordinator, (HFS-618), Regulatory Food Processing and Technology Branch, Division of HACCP Programs, Center for Food Safety and Applied Nutrition, 200 C Street SW, Washington, DC 20204.

Additional Forms

In addition to required entry forms, certain products require specific information to be presented to FDA at time of importation:

Medical Devices. There are several forms required to be filed with FDA prior to the importation of medical devices into the United States.

A premarket notification or 510(k) submission is required when the following occurs: (a) a foreign manufacturer intends to export a medical device to the U.S. that the firm has never before shipped to the U.S.; (b) either the foreign manufacturer or initial distributor changes the intended uses of devices that are legally being marketed in the U.S.; or (c) changes or modifications to a legally marketed device that could significantly affect its safety or effectiveness. Detailed information regarding the premarket notification process can be obtained from the following documents: Premarket Notification: 510(k), Regulatory Requirements for Marketing a Device, and 510(k) Review Program.

Firms are required to submit a properly completed form FDA 2892 (Medical Device Listing) before their medical device can be imported into the United States. Although, it is not a requirement for foreign medical device firms to register their establishments, it is requested that they do so. This can be done by submitting a properly completed form FDA 2891 (Initial Registration of Medical Device Establishment). Form FDA 2877 (Declaration for Radiation Standard) is required for radiation-emitting electronic products entering the United States.

To obtain these above forms, or information concerning premarket notification, radiation control standards, or Drug and Device Listing and Establishment Registration contact the Center for Devices and Radiological Health, Division of Small Manufacturers Assistance, (HFZ-220), 5600 Fishers Lane, Rockville, MD 20857, telephone 800-638-2041).

The Federal Food, Drug, and Cosmetic Act

The FDCA is the most comprehensive food law of its kind. If you are interested in importing food products into the U.S., you should be familiar with its provisions. The following sections briefly cover principal FDCA requirements applicable to the importation of food items. These are not exhaustive, but rather are meant to give you a sense of the degree and nature of the regulation. You should address specific questions, or requests for further details to the FDA.

Health Safeguards. Adulterated food is illegal and will be refused entry. A food is considered adulterated under the following conditions: 1) it contains any added or naturally occurring poisonous or harmful substance; 2) it contains additives not determined safe by the FDA prior to use; 3) it contains residues of pesticides not authorized by, or in excess of tolerances established by EPA regulations; 4) it contains non-FDA-certified colors; 5) any part of it is filthy, putrid, or decomposed; 6) it is the product of a diseased animal or one that has died otherwise than by slaughter; 7) it has been prepared, packed, or held under insanitary conditions whereby it may have become contaminated with filth or have become harmful to health; or 8) it is in packaging material which contains a poisonous or harmful substance. Some packaging materials are considered food additives and are thus subject to regulation.

Economic Safeguards. You must not conceal damage or inferiority in foods in any manner. Food labels must not contain false or misleading statements or omit material facts required by regulation. A food must not be sold under the name of another food. A substance recognized as a valuable constituent of a food must not be omitted or abstracted in whole or in part, nor may any substance be substituted for the food. Food containers must not be so made, formed, or filled as to be misleading. If you import a food for which a standard has been established for fill-of-container, it must either comply with such requirements, or bear a label statement that it falls below such requirements.

Label Information. The law states that required label information must be conspicuously displayed and in terms that the ordinary consumer is likely to be able to read and understand under ordinary conditions of purchase and use. If the label bears representations in a foreign language it must also bear all of the required statements in English. All imported foods must be marked in English with the name of the country of origin. For details concerning type sizes and styles, location, etc. of required label information, see 21 CFR 101. What follows is a brief overview of labeling information required on packaged food.

1) The name, street address, city, state, and zip code of either the manufacturer, packer, or distributor. A foreign address may omit the zip code. Street address may be omitted if the firm is listed in a current city or telephone directory. If the food is not manufactured by the person or company whose name appears on the label, the name must be qualified by "Manufactured for," "Distributed by" or a similar expression.

2) An accurate statement of the amount of food in the package. The required units of measure are the avoirdupois pound and the U.S. gallon. Metric measurements may be used in addition to the required units of measure. The law provides specific, detailed regulations regarding position, type size, etc. of the net weight declaration. There are varieties of application, depending upon the size of package, the nature of the product, i.e., whether it is liquid or solid, etc.

3) The common or usual name of a food must appear on the principal display panel, as well as the form of the product (i.e. "chopped," "whole," "sliced," etc.)

4) Unless the food is standardized, its ingredients must be listed by their common names in order of their predominance by weight. Labeling of standardized foods need only include those ingredients which the standard makes optional. (Most ingredients in standardized foods are optional and therefore must be listed on the label.) For purposes of labeling, a food's ingredients are those individual food components which go into making a mixed food. If a certain ingredient is the characterizing one in a food, it may be required to appear as part of the name of the food (e.g., shrimp in shrimp cocktail). Food additives and colors must be listed as ingredients except in butter, cheese, and ice cream.

Nutrition Labeling. Labeling of food products must include specific nutritional information. Required information is described in 21 CFR Part 101 and is extremely complex and specific. Additional requirements for specific products and product categories may be found in other regulations as well. Nutrition labeling regulations were substantially overhauled in 1993; major new provisions and requirements went into effect May 8, 1994. The minimum requirements, found in 21 CFR 101.9, include the following (see sample): 1) serving size and number of servings per package; 2) total calories and calories from fat per serving; 3) total fat and saturated fat (in grams), total cholesterol and sodium (in milligrams), total carbohydrates, dietary fiber, sugars, and protein (in grams) per serving; 4) percent of all of the constituents listed in the preceding number as a percent of the daily values based on a recommended base 2,000 calorie daily diet; 5) U.S. Recommended Daily Allowances (U.S. RDA) in percentages of certain vitamins and minerals per serving; and 6) a display of the daily values with the recommended values in grams or milligrams—depending on the constituent—for fat, saturated fat, cholesterol, sodium, carbohydrates, and dietary fiber, plus the calories per gram for fats, carbohydrates, and protein. Other nutrients recognized as essential in the human diet may be listed if they contribute at least 2% of the U.S. RDA. The regulations provide highly specific instructions for such labels, and offer several display options based on the shape, size, and other variables of the particular type of package. For further information, consult 21 CFR Part 1 or contact the FDA (see addresses at end of this chapter).

Nutrition Facts

Serving Size 1 Cup (228g)
Servings Per Container 2

Amount Per Serving

Calories 260   Calories from Fat 120

	%Daily Value*
Total Fat 13g	**20%**
Saturated Fat 5g	**25%**
Cholesterol 30mg	**10%**
Sodium 660 mg	**28%**
Total Carbohydrate 31g	**10%**
Dietary Fiber 0g	**0%**
Sugars 5g	
Protein 5g	

Vitamin A 4%	•	Vitamin C 2%	
Calcium 15%	•	Iron 4%	

* Percent Daily Values are based on a 2,000 calorie diet. Your daily values may be higher or lower depending on your calorie needs:

	Calories:	2,000	2,500
Total Fat	Less than	65g	80g
Sat Fat	Less than	20g	25g
Cholesterol	Less than	300mg	300mg
Sodium	Less than	2,400mg	2,400mg
Total Carbohydrate		300g	375g
Dietary Fiber		25g	30g

Calories per gram:
Fat 9 • Carbohydrate 4 • Protein 4

Sample nutritional labeling.

Foods for Special Dietary Use. There are specific content labeling requirements for foods purporting to have special dietary use. Foods labeled with claims of disease prevention, treatment, mitigation, cure, or diagnosis must also comply with the drug provisions of FDCA. You should consult the detailed regulations under sections 403(j), 411, and 412 before importing foods purporting to have special dietary use.

Sanitation Requirements. FDCA regulations require that foods be produced in sanitary facilities, and be free of filth (e.g. rodent hairs and excreta, insect parts and excreta, parasitic worms). Foods containing filth are adulterated, whether or not harm to health can be shown, and whether or not such elements can be detected in the laboratory. The law requires action against illegal merchandise no matter where it may have become illegal. You should be sure that your products are packed and handled in the shipping vehicle in such a way as to prevent goods unadulterated at point of origin from spoilage or contamination en route. If your shipment is found to be contaminated at the port of entry, it will be detained. If it is contaminated after Customs entry and landing, it will be subject to the same seizure or recall proceedings used for domestic products.

Detailed description of the FDA's standard of sanitary conditions in food establishments are published in Current Good Manufacturing Practice Regulations. You may obtain a copy of these regulations from the FDA (see addresses at end of this chapter).

Food Defect Action Levels. There are no specific regulated tolerances for filth in food per se. The FDCA considers food adulterated if it consists in whole or in part of a filthy, putrid, or decomposed substance. However, your product will not be condemned because of the presence of foreign matter in amounts below the irreducible minimum after all possible precautions have been taken. The FDA's food defect action levels establish the amounts of contamination which render foods subject to enforcement action. These levels pose no hazard to health and are subject to change by the FDA. Any products which might be harmful to consumers, or which are produced in violation of FDA's Current Good Manufacturing Practice Regulations are subject to regulatory action, whether or not they exceed the defect levels. To obtain a copy of published food defect action levels, contact FDA headquarters (see addresses at end of this chapter)

Pesticide residues on raw agricultural commodities. "Raw agricultural commodity" means any food in its raw or natural state, including all unprocessed fruits, vegetables, nuts, and grains. Foods that have been washed, colored, waxed, or otherwise treated in their unpeeled natural form are considered to be unprocessed. Tolerances for pesticide residues on specific raw agricultural commodities are established, revoked, or changed, as the facts warrant such action, by EPA. Section 408 of the FDCA lists current tolerances in force. Raw products containing pesticide residues are in violation of FDCA unless: 1) the pesticide chemical has been exempted from the requirement of a residue tolerance; or 2) the residue does not exceed the tolerance established for that food.

Processed foods that contain any residue of a pesticide which is not exempted or for which no tolerance has been established are considered adulterated. If a tolerance has been established, a pesticide residue in the processed food does not adulterate the ready-to-eat food if the residue does not exceed the tolerance established for the raw agricultural commodity. If you are considering importation of foods which could contain pesticide residues, you should contact FDA's Division of Regulatory Guidance (see addresses at end of this chapter) for current information regarding tolerances.

The Food Quality Protection Act (FQPA) of 1996. The new law establishes a strong, health-based safety standard for pesticide residues in all foods. It uses "a reasonable certainty of no harm"

as the general safety standard. The FDA may impose civil penalties for tolerance level violations. Under the "right to know" provisions, it specifically recognizes a state's right to require warnings or labelin of food that has been treated with pesticides. The FQPA affects the two major federal statutes under which the EPA regulates pesticides, the Federal Insecticide, Fungicide, and Rodenticide Act (FIFRA) and the Federal Food, Drug, and Cosmetic Act (FFDCA).

Food additives. Any substance intended for use in producing, manufacturing, packing, processing, preparing, treating, packaging, transporting, or holding food may be considered a food additive under the FDCA. Excluded from this category are the following: 1) substances generally recognized as safe by qualified experts; 2) substances used in accordance with previous approval under FDCA, the Poultry Products Inspection Act (PPIA), or the Meat Inspection Act (MIA); 3) pesticide chemicals in or on raw agricultural products; 4) a color additive; or 5) new animal drugs. Items 3, 4, and 5 are subject to similar safety requirements of other sections of the law.

If you are not certain whether the chemicals or other ingredients used in your foods are subject to the safety clearance requirements of the Food Additives Amendment, you may seek an opinion from FDA. General principles for preparing a food additive petition are in 21 CFR 171. FDA premarket approval for food additives involves scientific studies and testing. When the FDA gives premarket approval for an additive, it issues a regulation permitting and circumscribing its use in foods. A substance cleared under the Food Additive Regulations is still subject to all the general requirements of FDCA.

The Food Additive Regulations (21 CFR 180) list foods allowed to be artificially sweetened, and permitted amounts of such sweetener. If your product is artificially sweetened, it must be labeled as a special dietary food. Products containing saccharine must bear a warning label which states: "Use of this product may be hazardous to your health. This product contains saccharin, which has been determined to cause cancer in laboratory animals." For further information regarding food additives, contact FDA (see addresses at end of this chapter).

Food standards. 21 CFR 103-169 contains full details on FDA food standards. Standards of identity define what a given food product is, its name, its ingredients, and required label information. Standards of quality are minimum standards which specify quality requirements over and above those generally established under the FDCA. Do not confuse FDA standards of quality with USDA grades for agricultural products, and U.S. Department of the Interior (USDI) grades for fishery products. Fill-of-container standards define how full the container must be and how this is measured.

If you import a food represented as one for which a standard of identity has been promulgated, it must comply with the specifications of that standard in every respect. If your foods fall below applicable standards of quality or fill of container, you must identify it as substandard on the label. The FDA does not require identification of USDA or USDI grades on food labels, but when the label contains this information, the product must comply with the specifications for the declared grade. The terms "Fancy" or "Grade A" may be used only on the labels of those products meeting the specifications established for such grades by USDA. For more information contact FDA (see addresses at end of this chapter).

IMPORTING FOODS INTO THE UNITED STATES

A Summary of the Procedures U.S. Importers Must Follow When Handling Food Products

(Shaded boxes are importer responsibilities)

1. Importer files Entry Notice with U.S. Customs.

2. FDA notified of entry.

3. FDA reviews importer's Entry Notice.

4A. FDA doesn't want sample. May Proceed Notice sent to U.S. Customs and importer.

4B. FDA wants sample. Notice of Sampling sent to U.S. Customs and importer.

5. U.S. Customs/FDA collects physical sample. Sample is analyzed by FDA.

6A. FDA finds sample in compliance. Release Notice sent to U.S. Customs and importer.

6B. FDA determines sample is violative. Notice of Detention and Hearing sent to U.S. Customs and importer.

7A. Importer responds to Notice of Hearing and Detention.

7B. Importer does not respond to Notice of Hearing & Detention.

8A. FDA holds hearing on detained product.

8B. FDA sends Notice of Refusal of Admission.

9A. Importer presents evidence indicating product is "in compliance."

9B. Importer submits application to recondition.

9C. FDA receives verification of exportation or destruction.

10A. FDA collects follow-up sample.

10B. FDA reviews importer's proposed reconditioning procedure.

11A. FDA finds sample in compliance. Release Notice sent to U.S. Customs and Importer.

11B. FDA finds sample not in compliance.

11C. FDA approves importer's reconditioning procedures.

11D. FDA disapproves importer's reconditioning proposal.

12. Importer completes all reconditioning procedures.

13. FDA conducts follow-up inspection/sample collection.

14A. FDA finds sample in compliance. Release Notice sent to U.S. Customs & importer.

14B. FDA sample not in compliance.

Food and Drug Administration, Center for Food Safety and Applied Nutrition, Industry Activities Section, Washington, DC 20204

FDA Import Procedures

1. Importer or agent files entry documents with U.S. Customs Service within five working days of the date of arrival of a shipment at a port of entry.

2. FDA is notified of an entry of a regulated food through:

   • Duplicate copy of Customs entry documents (Customs Form 3461, CF 3461 ALT, CF 7501 or alternative)

   • Copy of commercial invoice; and

   • Surety to cover potential duties, taxes, and penalties.

3. FDA reviews Importer's Entry Documents to determine if a physical examination, wharf examination, or sample examination should be made.

4A. Decision is made not to collect a sample. FDA issues a May Proceed Notice to U.S. Customs and the importer of record. The shipment is released as far as FDA is concerned.

4B. Decisions is made to collect a sample based on:

   • Nature of the product,

   • FDA priorities, and

   • Past history of the commodity.

   FDA issues a Notice of Sampling to U.S. Customs and the importer of record. The shipment must be held intact pending further notice. A sample will be collected from the shipment. The importer of record may move the shipment from the dock to another port or warehouse (contact U.S. Customs for details).

5. FDA obtains a physical sample. The sample is sent to an FDA District Laboratory for analysis.

6A. FDA analysis finds the sample to be in compliance with requirements. FDA sends a Release Notice to U.S. Customs and the importer of record.

6B. FDA analysis determines that the sample "appears to be in violation of the FDCA or other related Acts." FDA sends U.S. Customs and the importer of record a Notice of Detention and Hearing which:

   • Specifies the nature of the violation, and

   • Gives the importer of record 10 working days to introduce testimony as to the admissibility of the shipment.

   The hearing is the importer's only opportunity offer a defense of the importation and/or to present evidence as to how the shipment may be made eligible for entry.

7A. Consignee, true owner, importer of record, or a designated representative *responds* to the Notice of Detention and Hearing. The response permits the introduction of testimony, either orally or written, as to the admissibility of the shipment.

7B. Consignee, true owner, importer of record, or a designated representative *neither* responds to the Notice of Detention and Hearing *nor* requests an extension of the hearing period.

8A. FDA conducts a hearing concerning the admissibility of the product. The hearing is an opportunity to present relevant matters and is confined to the submission of pertinent evidence.

8B. FDA issues a Notice of Refusal of Admission to the importer of record. This is the same person or firm who was sent a Notice of Sampling. All recipients of the Notice of Sampling and the Notice of Detention and Hearing are sent a copy of the Notice of Refusal.

9A. Importer of record presents evidence indicating that the product is in compliance. Certified analytical results of samples, examined by a reliable laboratory and which are within the published guidelines for levels of contaminants and defects in food for human use, may be presented.

9B. Importer of record submits an Application for Authorization to Recondition or to Perform Other Action FDA Form FD 766. The form requests permission to try to bring a food that is adulterated or misbranded into compliance by relabeling or other action, or by converting to a non-food use. A detailed method to bring the food into compliance must be given.

9C. FDA receives verification of the exportation or destruction of the shipment from U.S. Customs. The exportation or destruction of the merchandise listed on the Notice of Refusal of Admission is carried out under the direction of U.S. Customs.

10A. FDA collects follow-up sample to determine compliance with guidelines.

10B. FDA evaluates the reconditioning procedure proposed by the importer. A bond is required for payment of liquidated damages.

11A. FDA finds that the sample is "in compliance." A Release Notice with the statement "Originally Detained and Now Released" is sent to U.S. Customs and the importer.

11B. FDA finds that the sample is not in compliance. The importer may either submit an Application for Authorization to Recondition or to Perform Other Action (see 9B), or FDA will issue a Notice of Refusal of Admission (see 8B).

11C. FDA approves importer's recondition procedures. The approved application contains the statement "Merchandise Should Be Held Intact Pending the Receipt of FDA's Release Notice."

11D. FDA disapproves applicant's reconditioning procedure if past experience shows that the proposed method will not succeed. A second and final request will not be considered unless it contains meaningful changes in the reconditioning operation to ensure a reasonable chance of success. The applicant is informed on FDA **Form FD 766**.

12. Importer completes all reconditioning procedures and advises FDA that the goods are ready for inspection/sample collection.

13. FDA conducts follow-up inspection/sample collection to determine compliance with the terms of the reconditioning authorization.

14A. FDA analysis finds that the sample is in compliance. A Release Notice is sent to the importer and to U.S. Customs. The charges for FDA supervision are assessed on FDA Form **FD 790**. Copies are sent to U.S. Customs which is responsible for obtaining total payment including any expenses incurred by their personnel.

14B. FDA analysis finds that the sample is still not in compliance. Charges for FDA supervision are assessed on FDA **Form FD 790**. Copies are sent to U.S. Customs which is responsible for obtaining total payment including expenses incurred by their personnel.

Importers Can Speed Food Entries

1. Determine before shipment that the product to be imported is legal.

2. Have private laboratories examine samples of foods to be imported and certify the analysis of the processor. While not conclusive, these analyses might serve as an indication of the processor's ability to produce acceptable, legal products.

3. Become acquainted with FDA's legal requirements, before contracting for a shipment.

4. Request assistance form the FDA District Office responsible for your port of entry.

5. Know the food importing procedures described here.

Import Alerts and Automatic Detention

The FDA has developed an Import Alert procedure to communicate possible problems. Import Alerts identify and disseminate import information (problems, violative trends, etc.) to FDA personnel to provide for more uniform and effective import coverage. In some instances products identified in Import Alerts may be automatically detained when they enter the U.S. For example, swordfish from all countries is automatically detained because it repeatedly is found to contain high levels of mercury. Canned and brined mushrooms from the People's Republic of China are automatically detained because they have caused several outbreaks of staphylococcal food poisoning.

This procedure is an administrative act of detaining a product without physical examination and is generally based on past history and/or other information indicating the product may be violative. Once a product is placed on automatic detention, normal entry may not resume until the shipper or importer proves that the product meets FDA standards.

Occasionally, FDA places products from an entire country or region of a country on automatic detention when the violative conditions appears to be geographically widespread. Automatic detentions of this breadth are rare, and are initiated only after other avenues for resolving the problem have been exhausted.

Import Alerts are available on the FDA's website (www.fda.gov). For more information or questions regarding automatic detention, Import Alerts or import bulletins policy contact Division of Import Operations and Policy (DIOP), HFC-170, 5600 Fisher Lane, Rockville, MD 20857.

Computerization of FDA Procedures

The FDA has automated its import operations to expidite handling of imported products. The agency has combined its Operational and Administrative System for Import Support (OASIS) with the Customs Service Automated Commercial System (ACS). The import filer transmits the required shipment-specific FDA data into the ACS. Within several minutes, that individual receives notification that either their shipment has been released or FDA wishes to review it. This system provides FDA with immediate data on products imported, information on potential problems, and maintains national historical data files to develop profiles on specific products, shippers, and manufacturers.

Publications and WWW Resources

All FDA regulations are updated and republished annually in *Title 21, Code of Federal Regulations*. The CFR is available at law libraries and some major public libraries, and may be purchased from the U.S. Government Printing Office (USGPO). The USGPO accepts credit card orders over the phone, as well as mail orders paid by credit card, a check drawn on a U.S. bank, or an international money order.

U.S. Government Printing Office
Superintendent of Documents
710 North Capital Street NW
Washington DC 20401
Tel: (202) 512-1800; Fax: (202) 512-1657
Website: www.access.gpo.gov

Many FDA publications explaining regulations are available upon request from the FDA at (202) 205-5241; others may be available from the USGPO (address above). One of particular interest is *A Food Labeling Guide*, a 65-page booklet produced by the Center for Food Safety and Applied Nutrition, summarizes the required statements that must appear on labels of foods imported into or produced in the U.S. It can be ordered from the USGPO for $7; the ordering number is 017-012-00399-1. This information is also available online through the FDA/CFSAN website (http://vm.cfsan.fda.gov/~dms/flg-toc.html.)

Relevant Government Agencies

Address general inquiries regarding importation of foods to:
Food and Drug Administration (FDA)
Center for Food Safety and Applied Nutrition (CFSAN)

Office of Compliance
Division of Enforcement, Imports Branch
5100 Paint Branch Parkway
College Park, MD 20740-3835
Tel: (301) 436-2080
Website: http://vm.cfsan.fda.gov/list.html

Food and Drug Administration (FDA)
Center for Food Safety and Applied Nutrition (CFSAN)
Office of Plant and Dairy Foods and Beverages
5100 Paint Branch Parkway
College Park, MD 20740-3835
Tel: (301) 436-1700
Website: http://vm.cfsan.fda.gov/list.html

Address your inquiries regarding premarket testing and approval to:
U.S. Food and Drug Administration (FDA)
Center for Food Safety and Applied Nutrition
Office of Food Additive Safety
5100 Paint Branch Parkway
College Park, MD 20740-3835
Tel: (202) 418-3087

Address your inquiries regarding testing and certification of color additives to:
Food and Drug Administration (FDA)
Center for Food Safety and Applied Nutrition
Office of Cosmetics and Colors
5100 Paint Branch Parkway
College Park, MD 20740-3835
Tel: (202) 418-3412

Address your inquiries regarding import permits for milk and cream, for interstate travel sanitation, and general regulatory questions to:
U.S. Food and Drug Administration (FDA)
Center for Food Safety and Applied Nutrition (CFSAN)
Office of Field Programs
Office of Plant and Dairy Foods and Beverages
5100 Paint Branch Parkway
College Park, MD 20740-3835
Tel: (301) 436-1700
Website: http://vm.cfsan.fda.gov/list.html

Address your inquiries regarding canned foods to:
U.S. Food and Drug Administration (FDA)
Center for Food Safety and Applied Nutrition (CFSAN)
Office of Constituant Operations
5100 Paint Branch Parkway
College Park, MD 20740-3835
Tel: (301) 436-2380
Website: http://vm.cfsan.fda.gov/list.html

Address your inquiries regarding the National Shellfish Sanitation Program to:
U.S. Food and Drug Administration (FDA)
Center for Food Safety and Applied Nutrition (CFSAN)
Office of Seafood
5100 Paint Branch Parkway
College Park, MD 20740-3835
Tel: (301) 436-2300
Website: http://vm.cfsan.fda.gov/list.html

Address your inquiries regarding food labeling to:
U.S. Food and Drug Administration (FDA)
Center for Food Safety and Applied Nutrition (CFSAN)
Office of Nutritional Products Labeling and Dietary Supplements
5100 Paint Branch Parkway
College Park, MD 20740-3835
Tel: (301) 436-2373
Website: http://vm.cfsan.fda.gov/list.html

INDEX

B

C

D

F

G

H

I

M

N

O

P

S

T

X

Y

Z